America at the Polls 1920-1956

Harding to Eisenhower

A Handbook of American Presidential Election Statistics

Alice V. McGillivray
Richard M. Scammon

Congressional Quarterly Inc.
1414 22nd Street, N.W., Washington, D.C. 20037

Printed and bound in the United States of America.

Library of Congress Cataloging-in-Publication Data

America at the polls : a handbook of American presidential election statistics / [compiled by] Alice V. McGillivray, Richard M. Scammon.
p. cm.
The election returns for the 1920 to 1964 presidential contests contained in v. 1 were originally published in 1965 by the University of Pittsburgh Press.
Contents: [v. 1] Harding to Eisenhower, 1920-1956 -- [v. 2] Kennedy to Clinton, 1960-1992.
ISBN 1-56802-058-9 (v. 1). -- ISBN 1-56802-059-7 -- [v. 2]
1. Presidents--United States--Election--Statistics. 2. Elections--United States--History--20th century--Statistics. I. McGillivray, Alice V., 1934- . II. Scammon, Richard M.
JK524.A73 1994
324.973'09'021--dc20 94-30937
CIP

CONTENTS

INTRODUCTION i

UNITED STATES SUMMARY 1
President 1920-1956
Electoral College 1920-1956
State-by-State, President 1920-1956

STATE CHAPTERS

Alabama	22
Arizona	45
Arkansas	53
California	76
Colorado	89
Connecticut	112
Delaware	120
Florida	127
Georgia	150
Idaho	183
Illinois	196
Indiana	219
Iowa	242
Kansas	265
Kentucky	288
Louisiana	311
Maine	334
Maryland	342
Massachusetts	355
Michigan	363
Minnesota	386
Mississippi	409
Missouri	432
Montana	455
Nebraska	468
Nevada	491
New Hampshire	499
New Jersey	507
New Mexico	520
New York	533
North Carolina	546
North Dakota	569
Ohio	582
Oklahoma	605
Oregon	628
Pennsylvania	641
Rhode Island	664
South Carolina	671
South Dakota	684
Tennessee	707
Texas	730
Utah	783
Vermont	796
Virginia	804
Washington	837
West Virginia	850
Wisconsin	863
Wyoming	886

PRESIDENTIAL PRIMARIES

1956	899
1952	904
1948	908
1944	911
1940	914
1936	917
1932	920
1928	924
1924	928
1920	933

INTRODUCTION

America at the Polls reports American electoral behavior in presidential elections beginning with the 1920 Republican landslide victory of Warren G. Harding and Calvin Coolidge over Democrats James M. Cox and Franklin D. Roosevelt, and ending with the most recent election. This reference work provides students of American politics and elections the state-by-state, county-by-county details of each presidential contest in an easy-to-read format.

This volume covers the ten presidential elections from the 1920 Harding victory to the 1956 landslide win of Dwight D. Eisenhower. Later elections beginning with the 1960 victory of Democrat John F. Kennedy over Republican Richard M. Nixon are reported in a second volume. All election material is presented with the same organization: a front section containing national summary tables of the state-by-state vote and electoral college vote for each of the elections; a chapter for each state beginning with a summary page that sets out the statewide vote and electoral college vote in the state; a county outline map; and the county-by-county details of each election. Each decennial census is carried with the appropriate voting data tables that include the Republican-Democratic-Other breakdown, pluralities, and percentages of total and major party votes for Republican and Democratic candidates.

In special cases, when a third party candidate received an appreciable vote, the statistics have been expanded to a four-column format and the plurality is calculated on a first-second party basis. In the volume covering 1920 to 1956, this four-column format will be found in the 1924 data in the eighteen states in the West and Midwest where the Progressive candidate, Robert M. La Follette, received over 17 percent of the statewide vote, and in the 1948 tables in the four southern states that were carried by States' Rights candidate Strom Thurmond. The four-column format also is used for the 1956 elections in South Carolina where an independent elector ticket ran second statewide and carried almost one-half of the counties, and in Mississippi where an independent ticket carried a number of counties and ran second in many others.

In using these volumes, special attention should be taken of the notes sections for each state. These notes give the composition of the "Other" vote and indicate any special circumstances of the state vote such as dual elector tickets, canvassing problems, and discrepancies or corrections in the canvassed returns. Creation of new counties also is noted and the county-by-county tables carry all counties that voted in any election year covered in the volume. Therefore, voting data for any unit of a state will be in the same order for each election. The exception is Virginia, where only the counties and independent cities that voted in each election are carried.

Population data are not available for counties created between decennial censuses. In earlier elections, it should be noted that some states required a vote for each individual elector and the data presented are for the "highest elector" except in Michigan and New Jersey as indicated in the Notes sections for these states.

The final section details the votes cast in the presidential preference primaries by state and candidate with a chronological state-by-state summary table for each election year covered in the volume. The presidential preference primary data from 1920 to 1952 are from Congressional Quarterly's publication *Presidential Elections Since 1789* with minor adjustments. The data for 1956 was taken from official state canvass reports.

Except where indicated in the state note sections, the data compiled in *America at the Polls* have been taken from the official state canvass reports. For a few of the early elections in the 1920-1956 volume, these reports have been supplemented and interpreted by reference to the reports of the Clerk of the House of Representatives, files in the National Archives, various state publications, contemporary almanacs, and press material. The most important sources for interpretation of data for the early elections have been the Edgar Eugene Robinson volumes: *The Presidential Vote, 1896-1932* and *They Voted for Roosevelt: The Presidential Vote: 1932-1944.* Although differences will be noted in the data published in *America at the Polls* and the figures used in these and other reference studies, the differences usually will be small and stem most often from varying interpretations of the available statistics.

The election returns for the 1920 to 1964 presidential contests contained in these volumes were originally published in 1965 in *America at the Polls.* That work, which is out of print, presented the returns in a more difficult-to-read format and did not include many enhancements that have been added to the new compilation. The current volumes include census data for each decade; additional columns of votes for prominent candidates outside the major parties, such as La Follette, Thurmond, Wallace, and Perot; county outline maps; and statewide summary vote tables. Perhaps most important for the user, all the tables for each of the elections are presented in the same format.

UNITED STATES

POPULAR VOTE FOR PRESIDENT 1920 TO 1956

Year	Total Vote	Republican Vote	Republican Candidate	Democratic Vote	Democratic Candidate	Other Vote	Plurality	Percentage Total Vote Rep.	Percentage Total Vote Dem.	Percentage Major Vote Rep.	Percentage Major Vote Dem.
1956	62,026,908	35,590,472	Eisenhower, Dwight D.	26,022,752	Stevenson, Adlai E.	413,684	9,567,720 R	57.4%	42.0%	57.8%	42.2%
1952	61,550,918	33,936,234	Eisenhower, Dwight D.	27,314,992	Stevenson, Adlai E.	299,692	6,621,242 R	55.1%	44.4%	55.4%	44.6%
1948	48,793,826	21,991,291	Dewey, Thomas E.	24,179,345	Truman, Harry S.	2,623,190	2,188,054 D	45.1%	49.6%	47.6%	52.4%
1944	47,976,670	22,017,617	Dewey, Thomas E.	25,612,610	Roosevelt, Franklin D.	346,443	3,594,993 D	45.9%	53.4%	46.2%	53.8%
1940	49,900,418	22,348,480	Willkie, Wendell	27,313,041	Roosevelt, Franklin D.	238,897	4,964,561 D	44.8%	54.7%	45.0%	55.0%
1936	45,654,763	16,684,231	Landon, Alfred M.	27,757,333	Roosevelt, Franklin D.	1,213,199	11,073,102 D	36.5%	60.8%	37.5%	62.5%
1932	39,758,759	15,760,684	Hoover, Herbert C.	22,829,501	Roosevelt, Franklin D.	1,168,574	7,068,817 D	39.6%	57.4%	40.8%	59.2%
1928	36,805,951	21,437,277	Hoover, Herbert C.	15,007,698	Smith, Alfred E.	360,976	6,429,579 R	58.2%	40.8%	58.8%	41.2%
1924	29,095,023	15,719,921	Coolidge, Calvin	8,386,704	Davis, John W.	4,988,398	7,333,217 R	54.0%	28.8%	65.2%	34.8%
1920	26,768,613	16,153,115	Harding, Warren G.	9,133,092	Cox, James M.	1,482,406	7,020,023 R	60.3%	34.1%	63.9%	36.1%

For detail of other vote, see note section included with each U.S. summary table that follows.

ELECTORAL COLLEGE VOTE 1920 TO 1956

Year	Total	Republican	Democratic	Other
1956	531	457	73	1 JONES
1952	531	442	89	—
1948	531	189	303	39 SR
1944	531	99	432	—
1940	531	82	449	—
1936	531	8	523	—
1932	531	59	472	—
1928	531	444	87	—
1924	531	382	136	13 PROGRESSIVE
1920	531	404	127	—

PRESIDENT 1956

In Alabama, one of the eleven Democratic electors voted in the Electoral College for Walter B. Jones and Herman Talmadge rather than for the natioanl Democratic candidates.

The Republican figures in Mississippi include votes cast for two elector tickets. In New York the Democratic figures include Liberal votes.

The candidates listed below include all those who appeared on the ballot in at least one state.

35,590,472	Dwight D. Eisenhower and Richard M. Nixon, *Republican.*
26,022,752	Adlai E. Stevenson and Estes Kefauver, *Democratic.*
111,178	T. Coleman Andrews and Thomas H. Werdel, *States Rights.*
44,450	Eric Hass and Georgia Cozzini, *Socialist Labor.*
41,937	Enoch A. Holtwick and Edwin M. Cooper, *Prohibition.*
7,797	Farrell Dobbs and Myra Tanner Weiss, *Socialist Workers.*
2,657	Harry Flood Byrd and William E. Jenner, *States Rights.*
2,126	Darlington Hoopes and Samuel H. Friedman, *Socialist.*
1,829	Hanry B. Krajewski and Anne Marie Yezo, *American Third Party.*

Votes were cast for Unpledged States Rights electors; in Mississippi 42,966 votes were cast for Independent electors and South Carolina 88,509 votes were cast for Independent electors. In addition, 5,384 scattered write-in votes were reported from various states.

UNITED STATES

PRESIDENT 1956

State	Electoral Vote Rep.	Electoral Vote Dem.	Electoral Vote Other	Total Vote	Republican	Democratic	Other	Plurality	Percentage Total Vote Rep.	Percentage Total Vote Dem.	Percentage Major Vote Rep.	Percentage Major Vote Dem.
Alabama		10	1	496,861	195,694	280,844	20,323	85,150 D	39.4%	56.5%	41.1%	58.9%
Arizona	4			290,173	176,990	112,880	303	64,110 R	61.0%	38.9%	61.1%	38.9%
Arkansas		8		406,572	186,287	213,277	7,008	26,990 D	45.8%	52.5%	46.6%	53.4%
California	32			5,466,355	3,027,668	2,420,135	18,552	607,533 R	55.4%	44.3%	55.6%	44.4%
Colorado	6			657,074	394,479	257,997	4,598	136,482 R	60.0%	39.3%	60.5%	39.5%
Connecticut	8			1,117,121	711,837	405,079	205	306,758 R	63.7%	36.3%	63.7%	36.3%
Delaware	3			177,988	98,057	79,421	510	18,636 R	55.1%	44.6%	55.3%	44.7%
Florida	10			1,125,762	643,849	480,371	1,542	163,478 R	57.2%	42.7%	57.3%	42.7%
Georgia		12		669,655	222,778	444,688	2,189	221,910 D	33.3%	66.4%	33.4%	66.6%
Idaho	4			272,989	166,979	105,868	142	61,111 R	61.2%	38.8%	61.2%	38.8%
Illinois	27			4,407,407	2,623,327	1,775,682	8,398	847,645 R	59.5%	40.3%	59.6%	40.4%
Indiana	13			1,974,607	1,182,811	783,908	7,888	398,903 R	59.9%	39.7%	60.1%	39.9%
Iowa	10			1,234,564	729,187	501,858	3,519	227,329 R	59.1%	40.7%	59.2%	40.8%
Kansas	8			866,243	566,878	296,317	3,048	270,561 R	65.4%	34.2%	65.7%	34.3%
Kentucky	10			1,053,805	572,192	476,453	5,160	95,739 R	54.3%	45.2%	54.6%	45.4%
Louisiana	10			617,544	329,047	243,977	44,520	85,070 R	53.3%	39.5%	57.4%	42.6%
Maine	5			351,706	249,238	102,468		146,770 R	70.9%	29.1%	70.9%	29.1%
Maryland	9			932,827	559,738	372,613	476	187,125 R	60.0%	39.9%	60.0%	40.0%
Massachusetts	16			2,348,506	1,393,197	948,190	7,119	445,007 R	59.3%	40.4%	59.5%	40.5%
Michigan	20			3,080,468	1,713,647	1,359,898	6,923	353,749 R	55.6%	44.1%	55.8%	44.2%
Minnesota	11			1,340,005	719,302	617,525	3,178	101,777 R	53.7%	46.1%	53.8%	46.2%
Mississippi		8		248,104	60,685	144,453	42,966	83,768 D	24.5%	58.2%	29.6%	70.4%
Missouri		13		1,832,562	914,289	918,273		3,984 D	49.9%	50.1%	49.9%	50.1%
Montana	4			271,171	154,933	116,238		38,695 R	57.1%	42.9%	57.1%	42.9%
Nebraska	6			577,137	378,108	199,029		179,079 R	65.5%	34.5%	65.5%	34.5%
Nevada	3			96,689	56,049	40,640		15,409 R	58.0%	42.0%	58.0%	42.0%
New Hampshire	4			266,994	176,519	90,364	111	86,155 R	66.1%	33.8%	66.1%	33.9%
New Jersey	16			2,484,312	1,606,942	850,337	27,033	756,605 R	64.7%	34.2%	65.4%	34.6%
New Mexico	4			253,926	146,788	106,098	1,040	40,690 R	57.8%	41.8%	58.0%	42.0%
New York	45			7,095,971	4,345,506	2,747,944	2,521	1,597,562 R	61.2%	38.7%	61.3%	38.7%
North Carolina		14		1,165,592	575,062	590,530		15,468 D	49.3%	50.7%	49.3%	50.7%
North Dakota	4			253,991	156,766	96,742	483	60,024 R	61.7%	38.1%	61.8%	38.2%
Ohio	25			3,702,265	2,262,610	1,439,655		822,955 R	61.1%	38.9%	61.1%	38.9%
Oklahoma	8			859,350	473,769	385,581		88,188 R	55.1%	44.9%	55.1%	44.9%
Oregon	6			736,132	406,393	329,204	535	77,189 R	55.2%	44.7%	55.2%	44.8%
Pennsylvania	32			4,576,503	2,585,252	1,981,769	9,482	603,483 R	56.5%	43.3%	56.6%	43.4%
Rhode Island	4			387,609	225,819	161,790		64,029 R	58.3%	41.7%	58.3%	41.7%
South Carolina		8		300,583	75,700	136,372	88,511	47,863 D	25.2%	45.4%	35.7%	64.3%
South Dakota	4			293,857	171,569	122,288		49,281 R	58.4%	41.6%	58.4%	41.6%
Tennessee	11			939,404	462,288	456,507	20,609	5,781 R	49.2%	48.6%	50.3%	49.7%
Texas	24			1,955,168	1,080,619	859,958	14,591	220,661 R	55.3%	44.0%	55.7%	44.3%
Utah	4			333,995	215,631	118,364		97,267 R	64.6%	35.4%	64.6%	35.4%
Vermont	3			152,978	110,390	42,549	39	67,841 R	72.2%	27.8%	72.2%	27.8%
Virginia	12			697,978	386,459	267,760	43,759	118,699 R	55.4%	38.4%	59.1%	40.9%
Washington	9			1,150,889	620,430	523,002	7,457	97,428 R	53.9%	45.4%	54.3%	45.7%
West Virginia	8			830,831	449,297	381,534		67,763 R	54.1%	45.9%	54.1%	45.9%
Wisconsin	12			1,550,558	954,844	586,768	8,946	368,076 R	61.6%	37.8%	61.9%	38.1%
Wyoming	3			124,127	74,573	49,554		25,019 R	60.1%	39.9%	60.1%	39.9%
United States	457	73	1	62,026,908	35,590,472	26,022,752	413,684	9,567,720 R	57.4%	42.0%	57.8%	42.2%

PRESIDENT 1952

Republican figures in South Carolina include votes cast for two elector tickets. In Mississippi the Republican total is the vote cast for an Independent elector ticket "pledged to vote for the nominees of the national Republican party." In New York the Democratic figures include Liberal votes.

Douglas MacArthur appeared on the ballot with various party designations and Vice-Presidential running mates.

The candidates listed below include all those who appeared on the ballot in at least one state.

33,936,234	Dwight D. Eisenhower and Richard M. Nixon, *Republican.*
27,314,992	Adlai E. Stevenson and John J. Sparkman, *Democratic.*
140,023	Vincent Hallinan and Charlotta Bass, *Progressive.*
72,949	Stuart Hamblen and Enoch A. Holtwick, *Prohibition.*
30,267	Eric Hass and Stephen Emery, *Socialist Labor.*
20,203	Darlington Hoopes and Samuel H. Friedman, *Socialist.*
17,205	Douglas MacArthur and Vivian Kellems, *Constitution.*
10,312	Farrell Dobbs and Myra Tanner Weiss, *Socialist Workers.*
4,203	Hanry B. Krajewski and Frank Jenkins, *Poor Man's Party.*

In addition, 4,530 scattered write-in votes were reported from various states.

UNITED STATES

PRESIDENT 1952

State	Electoral Vote Rep.	Electoral Vote Dem.	Electoral Vote Other	Total Vote	Republican	Democratic	Other	Plurality	Percentage Total Vote Rep.	Percentage Total Vote Dem.	Percentage Major Vote Rep.	Percentage Major Vote Dem.
Alabama		11		426,120	149,231	275,075	1,814	125,844 D	35.0%	64.6%	35.2%	64.8%
Arizona	4			260,570	152,042	108,528		43,514 R	58.3%	41.7%	58.3%	41.7%
Arkansas		8		404,800	177,155	226,300	1,345	49,145 D	43.8%	55.9%	43.9%	56.1%
California	32			5,141,849	2,897,310	2,197,548	46,991	699,762 R	56.3%	42.7%	56.9%	43.1%
Colorado	6			630,103	379,782	245,504	4,817	134,278 R	60.3%	39.0%	60.7%	39.3%
Connecticut	8			1,096,911	611,012	481,649	4,250	129,363 R	55.7%	43.9%	55.9%	44.1%
Delaware	3			174,025	90,059	83,315	651	6,744 R	51.8%	47.9%	51.9%	48.1%
Florida	10			989,337	544,036	444,950	351	99,086 R	55.0%	45.0%	55.0%	45.0%
Georgia		12		655,785	198,961	456,823	1	257,862 D	30.3%	69.7%	30.3%	69.7%
Idaho	4			276,254	180,707	95,081	466	85,626 R	65.4%	34.4%	65.5%	34.5%
Illinois	27			4,481,058	2,457,327	2,013,920	9,811	443,407 R	54.8%	44.9%	55.0%	45.0%
Indiana	13			1,955,049	1,136,259	801,530	17,260	334,729 R	58.1%	41.0%	58.6%	41.4%
Iowa	10			1,268,773	808,906	451,513	8,354	357,393 R	63.8%	35.6%	64.2%	35.8%
Kansas	8			896,166	616,302	273,296	6,568	343,006 R	68.8%	30.5%	69.3%	30.7%
Kentucky		10		993,148	495,029	495,729	2,390	700 D	49.8%	49.9%	50.0%	50.0%
Louisiana		10		651,952	306,925	345,027		38,102 D	47.1%	52.9%	47.1%	52.9%
Maine	5			351,786	232,353	118,806	627	113,547 R	66.0%	33.8%	66.2%	33.8%
Maryland	9			902,074	499,424	395,337	7,313	104,087 R	55.4%	43.8%	55.8%	44.2%
Massachusetts	16			2,383,398	1,292,325	1,083,525	7,548	208,800 R	54.2%	45.5%	54.4%	45.6%
Michigan	20			2,798,592	1,551,529	1,230,657	16,406	320,872 R	55.4%	44.0%	55.8%	44.2%
Minnesota	11			1,379,483	763,211	608,458	7,814	154,753 R	55.3%	44.1%	55.6%	44.4%
Mississippi		8		285,532	112,966	172,566		59,600 D	39.6%	60.4%	39.6%	60.4%
Missouri	13			1,892,062	959,429	929,830	2,803	29,599 R	50.7%	49.1%	50.8%	49.2%
Montana	4			265,037	157,394	106,213	1,430	51,181 R	59.4%	40.1%	59.7%	40.3%
Nebraska	6			609,660	421,603	188,057		233,546 R	69.2%	30.8%	69.2%	30.8%
Nevada	3			82,190	50,502	31,688		18,814 R	61.4%	38.6%	61.4%	38.6%
New Hampshire	4			272,950	166,287	106,663		59,624 R	60.9%	39.1%	60.9%	39.1%
New Jersey	16			2,418,554	1,373,613	1,015,902	29,039	357,711 R	56.8%	42.0%	57.5%	42.5%
New Mexico	4			238,608	132,170	105,661	777	26,509 R	55.4%	44.3%	55.6%	44.4%
New York	45			7,128,239	3,952,813	3,104,601	70,825	848,212 R	55.5%	43.6%	56.0%	44.0%
North Carolina		14		1,210,910	558,107	652,803		94,696 D	46.1%	53.9%	46.1%	53.9%
North Dakota	4			270,127	191,712	76,694	1,721	115,018 R	71.0%	28.4%	71.4%	28.6%
Ohio	25			3,700,758	2,100,391	1,600,367		500,024 R	56.8%	43.2%	56.8%	43.2%
Oklahoma	8			948,984	518,045	430,939		87,106 R	54.6%	45.4%	54.6%	45.4%
Oregon	6			695,059	420,815	270,579	3,665	150,236 R	60.5%	38.9%	60.9%	39.1%
Pennsylvania	32			4,580,969	2,415,789	2,146,269	18,911	269,520 R	52.7%	46.9%	53.0%	47.0%
Rhode Island	4			414,498	210,935	203,293	270	7,642 R	50.9%	49.0%	50.9%	49.1%
South Carolina		8		341,087	168,082	173,004	1	4,922 D	49.3%	50.7%	49.3%	50.7%
South Dakota	4			294,283	203,857	90,426		113,431 R	69.3%	30.7%	69.3%	30.7%
Tennessee	11			892,553	446,147	443,710	2,696	2,437 R	50.0%	49.7%	50.1%	49.9%
Texas	24			2,075,946	1,102,878	969,228	3,840	133,650 R	53.1%	46.7%	53.2%	46.8%
Utah	4			329,554	194,190	135,364		58,826 R	58.9%	41.1%	58.9%	41.1%
Vermont	3			153,557	109,717	43,355	485	66,362 R	71.5%	28.2%	71.7%	28.3%
Virginia	12			619,689	349,037	268,677	1,975	80,360 R	56.3%	43.4%	56.5%	43.5%
Washington	9			1,102,708	599,107	492,845	10,756	106,262 R	54.3%	44.7%	54.9%	45.1%
West Virginia		8		873,548	419,970	453,578		33,608 D	48.1%	51.9%	48.1%	51.9%
Wisconsin	12			1,607,370	979,744	622,175	5,451	357,569 R	61.0%	38.7%	61.2%	38.8%
Wyoming	3			129,253	81,049	47,934	270	33,115 R	62.7%	37.1%	62.8%	37.2%
United States	442	89	—	61,550,918	33,936,234	27,314,992	299,692	6,621,242 R	55.1%	44.4%	55.4%	44.6%

PRESIDENT 1948

One of the twelve Democratic electors chosen in Tennessee cast his Electoral College vote for the States Rights nominees rather than for the national Democratic candidates.

In Alabama the Democratic electors were pledged to the States Rights candidates and there were no national Democratic electors on the ballot. The Republican figures in Mississippi include votes cast for two elector tickets. In New York the Democratic figures include Liberal votes.

The candidates listed below include all those who appeared on the ballot in at least one state.

24,179,345	Harry S. Truman and Alben W. Barkely, *Democratic.*
21,991,291	Thomas E. Dewey and Earl Warren, *Republican.*
1,176,125	Strom Thurmond and Fielding L. Wright, *States Rights.*
1,157,326	Henry A. Wallace and Glen H. Taylor, *Progressive.*
139,572	Norman Thomas and Tucker P. Smith, *Socialist.*
103,900	Claude A. Watson and Dale H. Learn, *Prohibition.*
29,241	Edward A. Teicher and Stephen Emery, *Socialist Labor.*
13,614	Farrell Dobbs and Grace Carlson, *Socialist Workers.*

In addition, 3,412 scattered write-in votes were reported from various states.

UNITED STATES

PRESIDENT 1948

State	Electoral Vote Rep.	Electoral Vote Dem.	Electoral Vote Other	Total Vote	Republican	Democratic	Other	Plurality	Percentage Total Vote Rep.	Percentage Total Vote Dem.	Percentage Major Vote Rep.	Percentage Major Vote Dem.
Alabama			11	214,980	40,930		174,050	130,513 SR	19.0%		100.0%	
Arizona		4		177,065	77,597	95,251	4,217	17,654 D	43.8%	53.8%	44.9%	55.1%
Arkansas		9		242,475	50,959	149,659	41,857	98,700 D	21.0%	61.7%	25.4%	74.6%
California		25		4,021,538	1,895,269	1,913,134	213,135	17,865 D	47.1%	47.6%	49.8%	50.2%
Colorado		6		515,237	239,714	267,288	8,235	27,574 D	46.5%	51.9%	47.3%	52.7%
Connecticut	8			883,518	437,754	423,297	22,467	14,457 R	49.5%	47.9%	50.8%	49.2%
Delaware	3			139,073	69,588	67,813	1,672	1,775 R	50.0%	48.8%	50.6%	49.4%
Florida		8		577,643	194,280	281,988	101,375	87,708 D	33.6%	48.8%	40.8%	59.2%
Georgia		12		418,844	76,691	254,646	87,507	169,511 D	18.3%	60.8%	23.1%	76.9%
Idaho		4		214,816	101,514	107,370	5,932	5,856 D	47.3%	50.0%	48.6%	51.4%
Illinois		28		3,984,046	1,961,103	1,994,715	28,228	33,612 D	49.2%	50.1%	49.6%	50.4%
Indiana	13			1,656,212	821,079	807,831	27,302	13,248 R	49.6%	48.8%	50.4%	49.6%
Iowa		10		1,038,264	494,018	522,380	21,866	28,362 D	47.6%	50.3%	48.6%	51.4%
Kansas	8			788,819	423,039	351,902	13,878	71,137 R	53.6%	44.6%	54.6%	45.4%
Kentucky		11		822,658	341,210	466,756	14,692	125,546 D	41.5%	56.7%	42.2%	57.8%
Louisiana			10	416,336	72,657	136,344	207,335	67,946 SR	17.5%	32.7%	34.8%	65.2%
Maine	5			264,787	150,234	111,916	2,637	38,318 R	56.7%	42.3%	57.3%	42.7%
Maryland	8			596,748	294,814	286,521	15,413	8,293 R	49.4%	48.0%	50.7%	49.3%
Massachusetts		16		2,107,146	909,370	1,151,788	45,988	242,418 D	43.2%	54.7%	44.1%	55.9%
Michigan	19			2,109,609	1,038,595	1,003,448	67,566	35,147 R	49.2%	47.6%	50.9%	49.1%
Minnesota		11		1,212,226	483,617	692,966	35,643	209,349 D	39.9%	57.2%	41.1%	58.9%
Mississippi			9	192,190	5,043	19,384	167,763	148,154 SR	2.6%	10.1%	20.6%	79.4%
Missouri		15		1,578,628	655,039	917,315	6,274	262,276 D	41.5%	58.1%	41.7%	58.3%
Montana		4		224,278	96,770	119,071	8,437	22,301 D	43.1%	53.1%	44.8%	55.2%
Nebraska	6			488,940	264,774	224,165	1	40,609 R	54.2%	45.8%	54.2%	45.8%
Nevada		3		62,117	29,357	31,291	1,469	1,934 D	47.3%	50.4%	48.4%	51.6%
New Hampshire	4			231,440	121,299	107,995	2,146	13,304 R	52.4%	46.7%	52.9%	47.1%
New Jersey	16			1,949,555	981,124	895,455	72,976	85,669 R	50.3%	45.9%	52.3%	47.7%
New Mexico		4		187,063	80,303	105,464	1,296	25,161 D	42.9%	56.4%	43.2%	56.8%
New York	47			6,177,337	2,841,163	2,780,204	555,970	60,959 R	46.0%	45.0%	50.5%	49.5%
North Carolina		14		791,209	258,572	459,070	73,567	200,498 D	32.7%	58.0%	36.0%	64.0%
North Dakota	4			220,716	115,139	95,812	9,765	19,327 R	52.2%	43.4%	54.6%	45.4%
Ohio		25		2,936,071	1,445,684	1,452,791	37,596	7,107 D	49.2%	49.5%	49.9%	50.1%
Oklahoma		10		721,599	268,817	452,782		183,965 D	37.3%	62.7%	37.3%	62.7%
Oregon	6			524,080	260,904	243,147	20,029	17,757 R	49.8%	46.4%	51.8%	48.2%
Pennsylvania	35			3,735,348	1,902,197	1,752,426	80,725	149,771 R	50.9%	46.9%	52.0%	48.0%
Rhode Island		4		327,702	135,787	188,736	3,179	52,949 D	41.4%	57.6%	41.8%	58.2%
South Carolina			8	142,571	5,386	34,423	102,762	68,184 SR	3.8%	24.1%	13.5%	86.5%
South Dakota	4			250,105	129,651	117,653	2,801	11,998 R	51.8%	47.0%	52.4%	47.6%
Tennessee		11	1	550,283	202,914	270,402	76,967	67,488 D	36.9%	49.1%	42.9%	57.1%
Texas		23		1,249,577	303,467	824,235	121,875	520,768 D	24.3%	66.0%	26.9%	73.1%
Utah		4		276,306	124,402	149,151	2,753	24,749 D	45.0%	54.0%	45.5%	54.5%
Vermont	3			123,382	75,926	45,557	1,899	30,369 R	61.5%	36.9%	62.5%	37.5%
Virginia		11		419,256	172,070	200,786	46,400	28,716 D	41.0%	47.9%	46.1%	53.9%
Washington		8		905,058	386,314	476,165	42,579	89,851 D	42.7%	52.6%	44.8%	55.2%
West Virginia		8		748,750	316,251	429,188	3,311	112,937 D	42.2%	57.3%	42.4%	57.6%
Wisconsin		12		1,276,800	590,959	647,310	38,531	56,351 D	46.3%	50.7%	47.7%	52.3%
Wyoming		3		101,425	47,947	52,354	1,124	4,407 D	47.3%	51.6%	47.8%	52.2%
United States	189	303	39	48,793,826	21,991,291	24,179,345	2,623,190	2,188,054 D	45.1%	49.6%	47.6%	52.4%

PRESIDENT 1944

The Republican figures in Georgia, Mississippi and South Carolina include votes cast for two elector tickets. The Democratic figures in Mississippi include votes cast for two elector tickets and the Democratic figures in New York include American Labor and Liberal votes.

In South Carolina an uncommitted Southern Democratic elector ticket ran in second place ahead of the Republican candidates.

The candidates listed below include all those who appeared on the ballot in at least one state.

25,612,610	Franklin D. Roosevelt and Harry S. Truman, *Democratic.*
22,017,617	Thomas E. Dewey and John W. Bricker, *Republican.*
79,003	Norman Thomas and Darlington Hoopes, *Socialist.*
74,779	Claude A. Watson and Andrew Johnson, *Prohibition.*
45,191	Edward A. Teichert and Arla A. Albaugh, *Socialist Labor.*
1,780	Gerald L. K. Smith and Harry Romer, *America First.*

In Texas 135,444 votes were cast for a Texas Regulars elector ticket and 7,799 votes were cast in South Carolina for an uncommitted Southern Democratic elector ticket. In addition, 2,447 scattered write-in votes were reported from various states.

UNITED STATES

PRESIDENT 1944

State	Electoral Vote			Total Vote	Republican	Democratic	Other	Plurality	Percentage			
									Total Vote		Major Vote	
	Rep.	Dem.	Other						Rep.	Dem.	Rep.	Dem.
Alabama		11		244,743	44,540	198,918	1,285	154,378 D	18.2%	81.3%	18.3%	81.7%
Arizona		4		137,634	56,287	80,926	421	24,639 D	40.9%	58.8%	41.0%	59.0%
Arkansas		9		212,954	63,551	148,965	438	85,414 D	29.8%	70.0%	29.9%	70.1%
California		25		3,520,875	1,512,965	1,988,564	19,346	475,599 D	43.0%	56.5%	43.2%	56.8%
Colorado	6			505,039	268,731	234,331	1,977	34,400 R	53.2%	46.4%	53.4%	46.6%
Connecticut		8		831,990	390,527	435,146	6,317	44,619 D	46.9%	52.3%	47.3%	52.7%
Delaware		3		125,361	56,747	68,166	448	11,419 D	45.3%	54.4%	45.4%	54.6%
Florida		8		482,803	143,215	339,377	211	196,162 D	29.7%	70.3%	29.7%	70.3%
Georgia		12		328,129	59,900	268,187	42	208,287 D	18.3%	81.7%	18.3%	81.7%
Idaho		4		208,321	100,137	107,399	785	7,262 D	48.1%	51.6%	48.3%	51.7%
Illinois		28		4,036,061	1,939,314	2,079,479	17,268	140,165 D	48.0%	51.5%	48.3%	51.7%
Indiana	13			1,672,091	875,891	781,403	14,797	94,488 R	52.4%	46.7%	52.9%	47.1%
Iowa	10			1,052,599	547,267	499,876	5,456	47,391 R	52.0%	47.5%	52.3%	47.7%
Kansas	8			733,776	442,096	287,458	4,222	154,638 R	60.2%	39.2%	60.6%	39.4%
Kentucky		11		867,924	392,448	472,589	2,887	80,141 D	45.2%	54.5%	45.4%	54.6%
Louisiana		10		349,383	67,750	281,564	69	213,814 D	19.4%	80.6%	19.4%	80.6%
Maine	5			296,400	155,434	140,631	335	14,803 R	52.4%	47.4%	52.5%	47.5%
Maryland		8		608,439	292,949	315,490		22,541 D	48.1%	51.9%	48.1%	51.9%
Massachusetts		16		1,960,665	921,350	1,035,296	4,019	113,946 D	47.0%	52.8%	47.1%	52.9%
Michigan		19		2,205,223	1,084,423	1,106,899	13,901	22,476 D	49.2%	50.2%	49.5%	50.5%
Minnesota		11		1,125,504	527,416	589,864	8,224	62,448 D	46.9%	52.4%	47.2%	52.8%
Mississippi		9		180,234	11,613	168,621		157,008 D	6.4%	93.6%	6.4%	93.6%
Missouri		15		1,571,697	761,175	807,356	3,166	46,181 D	48.4%	51.4%	48.5%	51.5%
Montana		4		207,355	93,163	112,556	1,636	19,393 D	44.9%	54.3%	45.3%	54.7%
Nebraska	6			563,126	329,880	233,246		96,634 R	58.6%	41.4%	58.6%	41.4%
Nevada		3		54,234	24,611	29,623		5,012 D	45.4%	54.6%	45.4%	54.6%
New Hampshire		4		229,625	109,916	119,663	46	9,747 D	47.9%	52.1%	47.9%	52.1%
New Jersey		16		1,963,761	961,335	987,874	14,552	26,539 D	49.0%	50.3%	49.3%	50.7%
New Mexico		4		152,225	70,688	81,389	148	10,701 D	46.4%	53.5%	46.5%	53.5%
New York		47		6,316,790	2,987,647	3,304,238	24,905	316,591 D	47.3%	52.3%	47.5%	52.5%
North Carolina		14		790,554	263,155	527,399		264,244 D	33.3%	66.7%	33.3%	66.7%
North Dakota	4			220,182	118,535	100,144	1,503	18,391 R	53.8%	45.5%	54.2%	45.8%
Ohio	25			3,153,056	1,582,293	1,570,763		11,530 R	50.2%	49.8%	50.2%	49.8%
Oklahoma		10		722,636	319,424	401,549	1,663	82,125 D	44.2%	55.6%	44.3%	55.7%
Oregon		6		480,147	225,365	248,635	6,147	23,270 D	46.9%	51.8%	47.5%	52.5%
Pennsylvania		35		3,794,793	1,835,054	1,940,479	19,260	105,425 D	48.4%	51.1%	48.6%	51.4%
Rhode Island		4		299,276	123,487	175,356	433	51,869 D	41.3%	58.6%	41.3%	58.7%
South Carolina		8		103,382	4,617	90,601	8,164	82,802 D	4.5%	87.6%	4.8%	95.2%
South Dakota	4			232,076	135,365	96,711		38,654 R	58.3%	41.7%	58.3%	41.7%
Tennessee		12		510,692	200,311	308,707	1,674	108,396 D	39.2%	60.4%	39.4%	60.6%
Texas		23		1,150,334	191,423	821,605	137,306	630,182 D	16.6%	71.4%	18.9%	81.1%
Utah		4		248,319	97,891	150,088	340	52,197 D	39.4%	60.4%	39.5%	60.5%
Vermont	3			125,361	71,527	53,820	14	17,707 R	57.1%	42.9%	57.1%	42.9%
Virginia		11		388,485	145,243	242,276	966	97,033 D	37.4%	62.4%	37.5%	62.5%
Washington		8		856,328	361,689	486,774	7,865	125,085 D	42.2%	56.8%	42.6%	57.4%
West Virginia		8		715,596	322,819	392,777		69,958 D	45.1%	54.9%	45.1%	54.9%
Wisconsin	12			1,339,152	674,532	650,413	14,207	24,119 R	50.4%	48.6%	50.9%	49.1%
Wyoming	3			101,340	51,921	49,419		2,502 R	51.2%	48.8%	51.2%	48.8%
United States	99	432	—	47,976,670	22,017,617	25,612,610	346,443	3,594,993 D	45.9%	53.4%	46.2%	53.8%

PRESIDENT 1940

The Republican figures in Connecticut, Georgia, Mississippi and South Carolina include votes cast for more than one elector ticket. In New York the Democratic figures include American Labor votes.

The candidates listed below include all those who appeared on the ballot in at least one state.

27,313,041	Franklin D. Roosevelt and Henry A. Wallace, *Democratic.*
22,348,480	Wendell Willkie and Charles L. McNary, *Republican.*
116,410	Norman Thomas and Maynard C. Krueger, *Socialist.*
58,708	Roger Babson and Edgar V. Moorman, *Prohibition.*
46,259	Earl Browder and James W. Ford, *Communist.*
14,892	John W. Aiken and Aaron M. Orange, *Socialist Labor.*
545	Alfred Knutson with no Vice Presidential candidate, *Independent.*

In addition, 2,083 scattered write-in votes were reported from various states.

UNITED STATES

PRESIDENT 1940

	Electoral Vote								Percentage			
									Total Vote		Major Vote	
State	Rep.	Dem.	Other	Total Vote	Republican	Democratic	Other	Plurality	Rep.	Dem.	Rep.	Dem.
Alabama		11		294,219	42,184	250,726	1,309	208,542 D	14.3%	85.2%	14.4%	85.6%
Arizona		3		150,039	54,030	95,267	742	41,237 D	36.0%	63.5%	36.2%	63.8%
Arkansas		9		200,429	42,122	157,213	1,094	115,091 D	21.0%	78.4%	21.1%	78.9%
California		22		3,268,791	1,351,419	1,877,618	39,754	526,199 D	41.3%	57.4%	41.9%	58.1%
Colorado	6			549,004	279,576	265,554	3,874	14,022 R	50.9%	48.4%	51.3%	48.7%
Connecticut		8		781,502	361,819	417,621	2,062	55,802 D	46.3%	53.4%	46.4%	53.6%
Delaware		3		136,374	61,440	74,599	335	13,159 D	45.1%	54.7%	45.2%	54.8%
Florida		7		485,640	126,158	359,334	148	233,176 D	26.0%	74.0%	26.0%	74.0%
Georgia		12		312,686	46,495	265,194	997	218,699 D	14.9%	84.8%	14.9%	85.1%
Idaho		4		235,168	106,553	127,842	773	21,289 D	45.3%	54.4%	45.5%	54.5%
Illinois		29		4,217,935	2,047,240	2,149,934	20,761	102,694 D	48.5%	51.0%	48.8%	51.2%
Indiana	14			1,782,747	899,466	874,063	9,218	25,403 R	50.5%	49.0%	50.7%	49.3%
Iowa	11			1,215,432	632,370	578,802	4,260	53,568 R	52.0%	47.6%	52.2%	47.8%
Kansas	9			860,297	489,169	364,725	6,403	124,444 R	56.9%	42.4%	57.3%	42.7%
Kentucky		11		970,163	410,384	557,322	2,457	146,938 D	42.3%	57.4%	42.4%	57.6%
Louisiana		10		372,305	52,446	319,751	108	267,305 D	14.1%	85.9%	14.1%	85.9%
Maine	5			320,840	163,951	156,478	411	7,473 R	51.1%	48.8%	51.2%	48.8%
Maryland		8		660,104	269,534	384,546	6,024	115,012 D	40.8%	58.3%	41.2%	58.8%
Massachusetts		17		2,026,993	939,700	1,076,522	10,771	136,822 D	46.4%	53.1%	46.6%	53.4%
Michigan	19			2,085,929	1,039,917	1,032,991	13,021	6,926 R	49.9%	49.5%	50.2%	49.8%
Minnesota		11		1,251,188	596,274	644,196	10,718	47,922 D	47.7%	51.5%	48.1%	51.9%
Mississippi		9		175,824	7,364	168,267	193	160,903 D	4.2%	95.7%	4.2%	95.8%
Missouri		15		1,833,729	871,009	958,476	4,244	87,467 D	47.5%	52.3%	47.6%	52.4%
Montana		4		247,873	99,579	145,698	2,596	46,119 D	40.2%	58.8%	40.6%	59.4%
Nebraska	7			615,878	352,201	263,677		88,524 R	57.2%	42.8%	57.2%	42.8%
Nevada		3		53,174	21,229	31,945		10,716 D	39.9%	60.1%	39.9%	60.1%
New Hampshire		4		235,419	110,127	125,292		15,165 D	46.8%	53.2%	46.8%	53.2%
New Jersey		16		1,972,552	945,475	1,016,808	10,269	71,333 D	47.9%	51.5%	48.2%	51.8%
New Mexico		3		183,258	79,315	103,699	244	24,384 D	43.3%	56.6%	43.3%	56.7%
New York		47		6,301,596	3,027,478	3,251,918	22,200	224,440 D	48.0%	51.6%	48.2%	51.8%
North Carolina		13		822,648	213,633	609,015		395,382 D	26.0%	74.0%	26.0%	74.0%
North Dakota	4			280,775	154,590	124,036	2,149	30,554 R	55.1%	44.2%	55.5%	44.5%
Ohio		26		3,319,912	1,586,773	1,733,139		146,366 D	47.8%	52.2%	47.8%	52.2%
Oklahoma		11		826,212	348,872	474,313	3,027	125,441 D	42.2%	57.4%	42.4%	57.6%
Oregon		5		481,240	219,555	258,415	3,270	38,860 D	45.6%	53.7%	45.9%	54.1%
Pennsylvania		36		4,078,714	1,889,848	2,171,035	17,831	281,187 D	46.3%	53.2%	46.5%	53.5%
Rhode Island		4		321,152	138,654	182,181	317	43,527 D	43.2%	56.7%	43.2%	56.8%
South Carolina		8		99,830	4,360	95,470		91,110 D	4.4%	95.6%	4.4%	95.6%
South Dakota	4			308,427	177,065	131,362		45,703 R	57.4%	42.6%	57.4%	42.6%
Tennessee		11		522,823	169,153	351,601	2,069	182,448 D	32.4%	67.3%	32.5%	67.5%
Texas		23		1,124,437	212,692	909,974	1,771	697,282 D	18.9%	80.9%	18.9%	81.1%
Utah		4		247,819	93,151	154,277	391	61,126 D	37.6%	62.3%	37.6%	62.4%
Vermont	3			143,062	78,371	64,269	422	14,102 R	54.8%	44.9%	54.9%	45.1%
Virginia		11		346,608	109,363	235,961	1,284	126,598 D	31.6%	68.1%	31.7%	68.3%
Washington		8		793,833	322,123	462,145	9,565	140,022 D	40.6%	58.2%	41.1%	58.9%
West Virginia		8		868,076	372,414	495,662		123,248 D	42.9%	57.1%	42.9%	57.1%
Wisconsin		12		1,405,522	679,206	704,821	21,495	25,615 D	48.3%	50.1%	49.1%	50.9%
Wyoming		3		112,240	52,633	59,287	320	6,654 D	46.9%	52.8%	47.0%	53.0%
United States	82	449	—	49,900,418	22,348,480	27,313,041	238,897	4,964,561 D	44.8%	54.7%	45.0%	55.0%

PRESIDENT 1936

The Republican figures in Delaware, Mississippi, and South Carolina include votes cast for two elector tickets. In New York the Democratic figures include American Labor votes.

The candidates listed below include all those who appeared on the ballot in at least one state.

27,757,333	Franklin D. Roosevelt and John N. Garner, *Democratic.*
16,684,231	Alfred M. Landon and Frank Know, *Republican.*
892,267	William Lemke and Thomas C. O'Brien, *Union.*
187,833	Norman Thomas and George A. Nelson, *Socialist.*
80,171	Earl Browder and James W. Ford, *Communist.*
37,677	D. Leigh Colvin and Claude A. Watson, *Prohibition.*
12,829	John W. Aiken and Emil F. Teichert, *Socialist Labor.*
1,598	William Dudley Pelley and Willard W. Kemp, *Christian.*

In addition, 824 scattered write-in votes were reported from various states.

UNITED STATES

PRESIDENT 1936

State	Electoral Vote Rep.	Electoral Vote Dem.	Electoral Vote Other	Total Vote	Republican	Democratic	Other	Plurality	Percentage Total Vote Rep.	Percentage Total Vote Dem.	Percentage Major Vote Rep.	Percentage Major Vote Dem.
Alabama		11		275,744	35,358	238,196	2,190	202,838 D	12.8%	86.4%	12.9%	87.1%
Arizona		3		124,163	33,433	86,722	4,008	53,289 D	26.9%	69.8%	27.8%	72.2%
Arkansas		9		179,431	32,049	146,765	617	114,716 D	17.9%	81.8%	17.9%	82.1%
California		22		2,638,882	836,431	1,766,836	35,615	930,405 D	31.7%	67.0%	32.1%	67.9%
Colorado		6		488,685	181,267	295,021	12,397	113,754 D	37.1%	60.4%	38.1%	61.9%
Connecticut		8		690,723	278,685	382,129	29,909	103,444 D	40.3%	55.3%	42.2%	57.8%
Delaware		3		127,603	57,236	69,702	665	12,466 D	44.9%	54.6%	45.1%	54.9%
Florida		7		327,436	78,248	249,117	71	170,869 D	23.9%	76.1%	23.9%	76.1%
Georgia		12		293,170	36,943	255,363	864	218,420 D	12.6%	87.1%	12.6%	87.4%
Idaho		4		199,617	66,256	125,683	7,678	59,427 D	33.2%	63.0%	34.5%	65.5%
Illinois		29		3,956,522	1,570,393	2,282,999	103,130	712,606 D	39.7%	57.7%	40.8%	59.2%
Indiana		14		1,650,897	691,570	934,974	24,353	243,404 D	41.9%	56.6%	42.5%	57.5%
Iowa		11		1,142,737	487,977	621,756	33,004	133,779 D	42.7%	54.4%	44.0%	56.0%
Kansas		9		865,507	397,727	464,520	3,260	66,793 D	46.0%	53.7%	46.1%	53.9%
Kentucky		11		926,214	369,702	541,944	14,568	172,242 D	39.9%	58.5%	40.6%	59.4%
Louisiana		10		329,778	36,791	292,894	93	256,103 D	11.2%	88.8%	11.2%	88.8%
Maine	5			304,240	168,823	126,333	9,084	42,490 R	55.5%	41.5%	57.2%	42.8%
Maryland		8		624,896	231,435	389,612	3,849	158,177 D	37.0%	62.3%	37.3%	62.7%
Massachusetts		17		1,840,357	768,613	942,716	129,028	174,103 D	41.8%	51.2%	44.9%	55.1%
Michigan		19		1,805,098	699,733	1,016,794	88,571	317,061 D	38.8%	56.3%	40.8%	59.2%
Minnesota		11		1,129,975	350,461	698,811	80,703	348,350 D	31.0%	61.8%	33.4%	66.6%
Mississippi		9		162,142	4,467	157,333	342	152,866 D	2.8%	97.0%	2.8%	97.2%
Missouri		15		1,828,635	697,891	1,111,043	19,701	413,152 D	38.2%	60.8%	38.6%	61.4%
Montana		4		230,502	63,598	159,690	7,214	96,092 D	27.6%	69.3%	28.5%	71.5%
Nebraska		7		608,023	247,731	347,445	12,847	99,714 D	40.7%	57.1%	41.6%	58.4%
Nevada		3		43,848	11,923	31,925		20,002 D	27.2%	72.8%	27.2%	72.8%
New Hampshire		4		218,114	104,642	108,460	5,012	3,818 D	48.0%	49.7%	49.1%	50.9%
New Jersey		16		1,820,437	720,322	1,083,850	16,265	363,528 D	39.6%	59.5%	39.9%	60.1%
New Mexico		3		169,135	61,727	106,037	1,371	44,310 D	36.5%	62.7%	36.8%	63.2%
New York		47		5,596,398	2,180,670	3,293,222	122,506	1,112,552 D	39.0%	58.8%	39.8%	60.2%
North Carolina		13		839,475	223,294	616,141	40	392,847 D	26.6%	73.4%	26.6%	73.4%
North Dakota		4		273,716	72,751	163,148	37,817	90,397 D	26.6%	59.6%	30.8%	69.2%
Ohio		26		3,012,660	1,127,855	1,747,140	137,665	619,285 D	37.4%	58.0%	39.2%	60.8%
Oklahoma		11		749,740	245,122	501,069	3,549	255,947 D	32.7%	66.8%	32.8%	67.2%
Oregon		5		414,021	122,706	266,733	24,582	144,027 D	29.6%	64.4%	31.5%	68.5%
Pennsylvania		36		4,138,105	1,690,300	2,353,788	94,017	663,488 D	40.8%	56.9%	41.8%	58.2%
Rhode Island		4		310,278	125,031	164,338	20,909	39,307 D	40.3%	53.0%	43.2%	56.8%
South Carolina		8		115,437	1,646	113,791		112,145 D	1.4%	98.6%	1.4%	98.6%
South Dakota		4		296,452	125,977	160,137	10,338	34,160 D	42.5%	54.0%	44.0%	56.0%
Tennessee		11		477,086	147,055	328,083	1,948	181,028 D	30.8%	68.8%	30.9%	69.1%
Texas		23		849,701	104,661	739,952	5,088	635,291 D	12.3%	87.1%	12.4%	87.6%
Utah		4		216,679	64,555	150,248	1,876	85,693 D	29.8%	69.3%	30.1%	69.9%
Vermont	3			143,689	81,023	62,124	542	18,899 R	56.4%	43.2%	56.6%	43.4%
Virginia		11		334,590	98,336	234,980	1,274	136,644 D	29.4%	70.2%	29.5%	70.5%
Washington		8		692,338	206,892	459,579	25,867	252,687 D	29.9%	66.4%	31.0%	69.0%
West Virginia		8		829,945	325,358	502,582	2,005	177,224 D	39.2%	60.6%	39.3%	60.7%
Wisconsin		12		1,258,560	380,828	802,984	74,748	422,156 D	30.3%	63.8%	32.2%	67.8%
Wyoming		3		103,382	38,739	62,624	2,019	23,885 D	37.5%	60.6%	38.2%	61.8%
United States	8	523	—	45,654,763	16,684,231	27,757,333	1,213,199	11,073,102 D	36.5%	60.8%	37.5%	62.5%

PRESIDENT 1932

The Republican figures in Mississippi include votes cast for two elector tickets.

The candidates listed below include all those who appeared on the ballot in at least one state.

22,829,501	Franklin D. Roosevelt and John N. Garner, *Democratic.*
15,760,684	Herbert C. Hoover and Charles Curtis, *Republican.*
884,649	Norman Thomas and James H. Maurer, *Socialist.*
103,253	William Z. Foster and James W. Ford, *Communist.*
81,872	William D. Upshaw and Frank S. Regan, *Prohibition.*
53,247	William H. Harvey and Frank Hemenway, *Liberty.*
34,043	Verne L. Reynolds and John W. Aiken, *Socialist Labor.*
7,431	Jacob S. Coxey and Julius J. Reiter, *Farmer-Labor.*
1,645	John Zahnd and Florence Garvin, *National.*
740	James R. Cox and Victor C. Tisdal, *Jobless.*

In Texas, 157 votes were cast for a Jacksonian elector ticket; in Arizona 9 votes were cast for an Arizona Progressive Democratic elector ticket. In addition, 1,528 scattered write-in votes were reported from various states.

UNITED STATES

PRESIDENT 1932

State	Electoral Vote Rep.	Electoral Vote Dem.	Electoral Vote Other	Total Vote	Republican	Democratic	Other	Plurality	Percentage Total Vote Rep.	Percentage Total Vote Dem.	Percentage Major Vote Rep.	Percentage Major Vote Dem.
Alabama		11		245,303	34,675	207,910	2,718	173,235 D	14.1%	84.8%	14.3%	85.7%
Arizona		3		118,251	36,104	79,264	2,883	43,160 D	30.5%	67.0%	31.3%	68.7%
Arkansas		9		216,569	27,465	186,829	2,275	159,364 D	12.7%	86.3%	12.8%	87.2%
California		22		2,266,972	847,902	1,324,157	94,913	476,255 D	37.4%	58.4%	39.0%	61.0%
Colorado		6		457,696	189,617	250,877	17,202	61,260 D	41.4%	54.8%	43.0%	57.0%
Connecticut	8			594,183	288,420	281,632	24,131	6,788 R	48.5%	47.4%	50.6%	49.4%
Delaware	3			112,901	57,073	54,319	1,509	2,754 R	50.6%	48.1%	51.2%	48.8%
Florida		7		276,943	69,170	206,307	1,466	137,137 D	25.0%	74.5%	25.1%	74.9%
Georgia		12		255,590	19,863	234,118	1,609	214,255 D	7.8%	91.6%	7.8%	92.2%
Idaho		4		186,520	71,312	109,479	5,729	38,167 D	38.2%	58.7%	39.4%	60.6%
Illinois		29		3,407,926	1,432,756	1,882,304	92,866	449,548 D	42.0%	55.2%	43.2%	56.8%
Indiana		14		1,576,927	677,184	862,054	37,689	184,870 D	42.9%	54.7%	44.0%	56.0%
Iowa		11		1,036,687	414,433	598,019	24,235	183,586 D	40.0%	57.7%	40.9%	59.1%
Kansas		9		791,978	349,498	424,204	18,276	74,706 D	44.1%	53.6%	45.2%	54.8%
Kentucky		11		983,059	394,716	580,574	7,769	185,858 D	40.2%	59.1%	40.5%	59.5%
Louisiana		10		268,804	18,853	249,418	533	230,565 D	7.0%	92.8%	7.0%	93.0%
Maine	5			298,444	166,631	128,907	2,906	37,724 R	55.8%	43.2%	56.4%	43.6%
Maryland		8		511,054	184,184	314,314	12,556	130,130 D	36.0%	61.5%	36.9%	63.1%
Massachusetts		17		1,580,114	736,959	800,148	43,007	63,189 D	46.6%	50.6%	47.9%	52.1%
Michigan		19		1,664,765	739,894	871,700	53,171	131,806 D	44.4%	52.4%	45.9%	54.1%
Minnesota		11		1,002,843	363,959	600,806	38,078	236,847 D	36.3%	59.9%	37.7%	62.3%
Mississippi		9		146,034	5,180	140,168	686	134,988 D	3.5%	96.0%	3.6%	96.4%
Missouri		15		1,609,894	564,713	1,025,406	19,775	460,693 D	35.1%	63.7%	35.5%	64.5%
Montana		4		216,479	78,078	127,286	11,115	49,208 D	36.1%	58.8%	38.0%	62.0%
Nebraska		7		570,135	201,177	359,082	9,876	157,905 D	35.3%	63.0%	35.9%	64.1%
Nevada		3		41,430	12,674	28,756		16,082 D	30.6%	69.4%	30.6%	69.4%
New Hampshire	4			205,520	103,629	100,680	1,211	2,949 R	50.4%	49.0%	50.7%	49.3%
New Jersey		16		1,630,063	775,684	806,630	47,749	30,946 D	47.6%	49.5%	49.0%	51.0%
New Mexico		3		151,606	54,217	95,089	2,300	40,872 D	35.8%	62.7%	36.3%	63.7%
New York		47		4,688,614	1,937,963	2,534,959	215,692	596,996 D	41.3%	54.1%	43.3%	56.7%
North Carolina		13		711,498	208,344	497,566	5,588	289,222 D	29.3%	69.9%	29.5%	70.5%
North Dakota		4		256,290	71,772	178,350	6,168	106,578 D	28.0%	69.6%	28.7%	71.3%
Ohio		26		2,609,728	1,227,319	1,301,695	80,714	74,376 D	47.0%	49.9%	48.5%	51.5%
Oklahoma		11		704,633	188,165	516,468		328,303 D	26.7%	73.3%	26.7%	73.3%
Oregon		5		368,751	136,019	213,871	18,861	77,852 D	36.9%	58.0%	38.9%	61.1%
Pennsylvania	36			2,859,021	1,453,540	1,295,948	109,533	157,592 R	50.8%	45.3%	52.9%	47.1%
Rhode Island		4		266,170	115,266	146,604	4,300	31,338 D	43.3%	55.1%	44.0%	56.0%
South Carolina		8		104,407	1,978	102,347	82	100,369 D	1.9%	98.0%	1.9%	98.1%
South Dakota		4		288,438	99,212	183,515	5,711	84,303 D	34.4%	63.6%	35.1%	64.9%
Tennessee		11		390,273	126,752	259,473	4,048	132,721 D	32.5%	66.5%	32.8%	67.2%
Texas		23		874,382	98,218	771,109	5,055	672,891 D	11.2%	88.2%	11.3%	88.7%
Utah		4		206,578	84,795	116,750	5,033	31,955 D	41.0%	56.5%	42.1%	57.9%
Vermont	3			136,980	78,984	56,266	1,730	22,718 R	57.7%	41.1%	58.4%	41.6%
Virginia		11		297,942	89,637	203,979	4,326	114,342 D	30.1%	68.5%	30.5%	69.5%
Washington		8		614,814	208,645	353,260	52,909	144,615 D	33.9%	57.5%	37.1%	62.9%
West Virginia		8		743,774	330,731	405,124	7,919	74,393 D	44.5%	54.5%	44.9%	55.1%
Wisconsin		12		1,114,814	347,741	707,410	59,663	359,669 D	31.2%	63.5%	33.0%	67.0%
Wyoming		3		96,962	39,583	54,370	3,009	14,787 D	40.8%	56.1%	42.1%	57.9%
United States	59	472	—	39,758,759	15,760,684	22,829,501	1,168,574	7,068,817 D	39.6%	57.4%	40.8%	59.2%

PRESIDENT 1928

The Republican figures in Georgia, Mississippi, and South Carolina include votes cast for two or three elector tickets; in Pennsylvania the Communist total includes votes cast for two elector tickets.

The full list of candidates for President and Vice-President was:

21,437,277	Herbert C. Hoover and Charles Curtis, *Republican.*
15,007,698	Alfred E. Smith and Joseph T. Robinson, *Democratic.*
265,583	Norman Thomas and James H. Maurer, *Socialist.*
46,896	William Z. Foster and Benjamin Gitlow, *Communist*
21,586	Verne L. Reynolds and Jeremiah D. Crowley, *Socialist Labor.*
20,101	William F. Varney and James A. Edgerton, *Prohibition.*
6,390	Frank E. Webb and L. R. Tillman, *Farmer-Labor.*

In addition, 420 scattered write-in votes were reported from various states.

UNITED STATES

PRESIDENT 1928

State	Electoral Vote Rep.	Electoral Vote Dem.	Electoral Vote Other	Total Vote	Republican	Democratic	Other	Plurality	Percentage Total Vote Rep.	Percentage Total Vote Dem.	Percentage Major Vote Rep.	Percentage Major Vote Dem.
Alabama		12		248,981	120,725	127,796	460	7,071 D	48.5%	51.3%	48.6%	51.4%
Arizona	3			91,254	52,533	38,537	184	13,996 R	57.6%	42.2%	57.7%	42.3%
Arkansas		9		197,726	77,784	119,196	746	41,412 D	39.3%	60.3%	39.5%	60.5%
California	13			1,796,656	1,162,323	614,365	19,968	547,958 R	64.7%	34.2%	65.4%	34.6%
Colorado	6			392,242	253,872	133,131	5,239	120,741 R	64.7%	33.9%	65.6%	34.4%
Connecticut	7			553,118	296,641	252,085	4,392	44,556 R	53.6%	45.6%	54.1%	45.9%
Delaware	3			104,602	68,860	35,354	388	33,506 R	65.8%	33.8%	66.1%	33.9%
Florida	6			252,068	145,860	101,764	4,444	44,096 R	57.9%	40.4%	58.9%	41.1%
Georgia		14		231,592	101,800	129,604	188	27,804 D	44.0%	56.0%	44.0%	56.0%
Idaho	4			151,541	97,322	52,926	1,293	44,396 R	64.2%	34.9%	64.8%	35.2%
Illinois	29			3,107,489	1,769,141	1,313,817	24,531	455,324 R	56.9%	42.3%	57.4%	42.6%
Indiana	15			1,421,314	848,290	562,691	10,333	285,599 R	59.7%	39.6%	60.1%	39.9%
Iowa	13			1,009,189	623,570	379,011	6,608	244,559 R	61.8%	37.6%	62.2%	37.8%
Kansas	10			713,200	513,672	193,003	6,525	320,669 R	72.0%	27.1%	72.7%	27.3%
Kentucky	13			940,521	558,064	381,070	1,387	176,994 R	59.3%	40.5%	59.4%	40.6%
Louisiana		10		215,833	51,160	164,655	18	113,495 D	23.7%	76.3%	23.7%	76.3%
Maine	6			262,170	179,923	81,179	1,068	98,744 R	68.6%	31.0%	68.9%	31.1%
Maryland	8			528,348	301,479	223,626	3,243	77,853 R	57.1%	42.3%	57.4%	42.6%
Massachusetts		18		1,577,823	775,566	792,758	9,499	17,192 D	49.2%	50.2%	49.5%	50.5%
Michigan	15			1,372,082	965,396	396,762	9,924	568,634 R	70.4%	28.9%	70.9%	29.1%
Minnesota	12			970,976	560,977	396,451	13,548	164,526 R	57.8%	40.8%	58.6%	41.4%
Mississippi		10		151,568	27,030	124,538		97,508 D	17.8%	82.2%	17.8%	82.2%
Missouri	18			1,500,845	834,080	662,684	4,081	171,396 R	55.6%	44.2%	55.7%	44.3%
Montana	4			194,108	113,300	78,578	2,230	34,722 R	58.4%	40.5%	59.0%	41.0%
Nebraska	8			547,128	345,745	197,950	3,433	147,795 R	63.2%	36.2%	63.6%	36.4%
Nevada	3			32,417	18,327	14,090		4,237 R	56.5%	43.5%	56.5%	43.5%
New Hampshire	4			196,757	115,404	80,715	638	34,689 R	58.7%	41.0%	58.8%	41.2%
New Jersey	14			1,549,381	926,050	616,517	6,814	309,533 R	59.8%	39.8%	60.0%	40.0%
New Mexico	3			118,077	69,708	48,211	158	21,497 R	59.0%	40.8%	59.1%	40.9%
New York	45			4,405,626	2,193,344	2,089,863	122,419	103,481 R	49.8%	47.4%	51.2%	48.8%
North Carolina	12			635,150	348,923	286,227		62,696 R	54.9%	45.1%	54.9%	45.1%
North Dakota	5			239,845	131,419	106,648	1,778	24,771 R	54.8%	44.5%	55.2%	44.8%
Ohio	24			2,508,346	1,627,546	864,210	16,590	763,336 R	64.9%	34.5%	65.3%	34.7%
Oklahoma	10			618,427	394,046	219,174	5,207	174,872 R	63.7%	35.4%	64.3%	35.7%
Oregon	5			319,942	205,341	109,223	5,378	96,118 R	64.2%	34.1%	65.3%	34.7%
Pennsylvania	38			3,150,612	2,055,382	1,067,586	27,644	987,796 R	65.2%	33.9%	65.8%	34.2%
Rhode Island		5		237,194	117,522	118,973	699	1,451 D	49.5%	50.2%	49.7%	50.3%
South Carolina		9		68,605	5,858	62,700	47	56,842 D	8.5%	91.4%	8.5%	91.5%
South Dakota	5			261,857	157,603	102,660	1,594	54,943 R	60.2%	39.2%	60.6%	39.4%
Tennessee	12			353,192	195,388	157,143	661	38,245 R	55.3%	44.5%	55.4%	44.6%
Texas	20			717,733	372,324	344,542	867	27,782 R	51.9%	48.0%	51.9%	48.1%
Utah	4			176,603	94,618	80,985	1,000	13,633 R	53.6%	45.9%	53.9%	46.1%
Vermont	4			135,191	90,404	44,440	347	45,964 R	66.9%	32.9%	67.0%	33.0%
Virginia	12			305,364	164,609	140,146	609	24,463 R	53.9%	45.9%	54.0%	46.0%
Washington	7			500,840	335,844	156,772	8,224	179,072 R	67.1%	31.3%	68.2%	31.8%
West Virginia	8			642,752	375,551	263,784	3,417	111,767 R	58.4%	41.0%	58.7%	41.3%
Wisconsin	13			1,016,831	544,205	450,259	22,367	93,946 R	53.5%	44.3%	54.7%	45.3%
Wyoming	3			82,835	52,748	29,299	788	23,449 R	63.7%	35.4%	64.3%	35.7%
United States	444	87	—	36,805,951	21,437,277	15,007,698	360,976	6,429,579 R	58.2%	40.8%	58.8%	41.2%

PRESIDENT 1924

The Progressive party carried Wisconsin and its thirteen Electoral College votes were cast for the Progressive nominees. The Progressive party candidates ran second in eleven other states in the Midwest and West and in several states the Progressive total includes votes cast for more than one elector ticket.

The candidates listed below include all those who appeared on the ballot in at least one state.

15,719,921	Calvin Coolidge and Charles G. Dawes, *Republican.*
8,386,704	John W. Davis and Charles W. Bryan, *Democratic.*
4,832,532	Robert M. LaFollette and Burton K. Wheeler, *Progressive.*
56,292	Herman P. Faris and Marie Caroline Brehm, *Prohibition.*
34,174	Frank T. Johns and Verne L. Reynolds, *Socialist Labor.*
33,360	William Z. Foster and Benjamin Gitlow, *Communist.*
24,340	Gilbert O. Nations and Leander L. Pickett, *American.*
2,948	William J. Wallace and John C. Lincoln, *Commonwealth Land.*

In addition, 4,752 scattered write-in votes were reported from various states.

UNITED STATES

PRESIDENT 1924

State	Electoral Vote			Total Vote	Republican	Democratic	Progressive	Other	Plurality	Percentage Total Vote		
	Rep.	Dem.	Other							Rep.	Dem.	Prog.
Alabama		12		164,563	42,823	113,138	8,040	562	70,315 D	26.0%	68.8%	4.9%
Arizona	3			73,961	30,516	26,235	17,210		4,281 R	41.3%	35.5%	23.3%
Arkansas		9		138,540	40,583	84,790	13,167		44,207 D	29.3%	61.2%	9.5%
California	13			1,281,778	733,250	105,514	424,649	18,365	308,601 R	57.2%	8.2%	33.1%
Colorado	6			342,261	195,171	75,238	69,946	1,906	119,933 R	57.0%	22.0%	20.4%
Connecticut	7			400,396	246,322	110,184	42,416	1,474	136,138 R	61.5%	27.5%	10.6%
Delaware	3			90,885	52,441	33,445	4,979	20	18,996 R	57.7%	36.8%	5.5%
Florida		6		109,158	30,633	62,083	8,625	7,817	31,450 D	28.1%	56.9%	7.9%
Georgia		14		166,635	30,300	123,262	12,687	386	92,962 D	18.2%	74.0%	7.6%
Idaho	4			147,690	69,791	23,951	53,948		15,843 R	47.3%	16.2%	36.5%
Illinois	29			2,470,067	1,453,321	576,975	432,027	7,744	876,346 R	58.8%	23.4%	17.5%
Indiana	15			1,272,390	703,042	492,245	71,700	5,403	210,797 R	55.3%	38.7%	5.6%
Iowa	13			976,770	537,458	160,382	274,448	4,482	263,010 R	55.0%	16.4%	28.1%
Kansas	10			662,456	407,671	156,320	98,461	4	251,351 R	61.5%	23.6%	14.9%
Kentucky	13			813,843	396,758	375,593	38,465	3,027	21,165 R	48.8%	46.2%	4.7%
Louisiana		10		121,951	24,670	93,218		4,063	68,548 D	20.2%	76.4%	
Maine	6			192,192	138,440	41,964	11,382	406	96,476 R	72.0%	21.8%	5.9%
Maryland	8			358,630	162,414	148,072	47,157	987	14,342 R	45.3%	41.3%	13.1%
Massachusetts	18			1,129,837	703,476	280,831	141,225	4,305	422,645 R	62.3%	24.9%	12.5%
Michigan	15			1,160,419	874,631	152,359	122,014	11,415	722,272 R	75.4%	13.1%	10.5%
Minnesota	12			822,146	420,759	55,913	339,192	6,282	81,567 R	51.2%	6.8%	41.3%
Mississippi		10		112,442	8,494	100,474	3,474		91,980 D	7.6%	89.4%	3.1%
Missouri	18			1,310,095	648,488	574,962	83,996	2,649	73,526 R	49.5%	43.9%	6.4%
Montana	4			174,425	74,138	33,805	66,124	358	8,014 R	42.5%	19.4%	37.9%
Nebraska	8			463,559	218,985	137,299	105,681	1,594	81,686 R	47.2%	29.6%	22.8%
Nevada	3			26,921	11,243	5,909	9,769		1,474 R	41.8%	21.9%	36.3%
New Hampshire	4			164,769	98,575	57,201	8,993		41,374 R	59.8%	34.7%	5.5%
New Jersey	14			1,088,054	676,277	298,043	109,028	4,706	378,234 R	62.2%	27.4%	10.0%
New Mexico	3			112,830	54,745	48,542	9,543		6,203 R	48.5%	43.0%	8.5%
New York	45			3,263,939	1,820,058	950,796	474,913	18,172	869,262 R	55.8%	29.1%	14.6%
North Carolina		12		481,608	190,754	284,190	6,651	13	93,436 D	39.6%	59.0%	1.4%
North Dakota	5			199,081	94,931	13,858	89,922	370	5,009 R	47.7%	7.0%	45.2%
Ohio	24			2,016,296	1,176,130	477,887	358,008	4,271	698,243 R	58.3%	23.7%	17.8%
Oklahoma		10		527,828	225,756	255,798	46,274		30,042 D	42.8%	48.5%	8.8%
Oregon	5			279,488	142,579	67,589	68,403	917	74,176 R	51.0%	24.2%	24.5%
Pennsylvania	38			2,144,850	1,401,481	409,192	307,567	26,610	992,289 R	65.3%	19.1%	14.3%
Rhode Island	5			210,115	125,286	76,606	7,628	595	48,680 R	59.6%	36.5%	3.6%
South Carolina		9		50,755	1,123	49,008	623	1	47,885 D	2.2%	96.6%	1.2%
South Dakota	5			203,868	101,299	27,214	75,355		25,944 R	49.7%	13.3%	37.0%
Tennessee		12		301,030	130,831	159,339	10,666	194	28,508 D	43.5%	52.9%	3.5%
Texas		20		657,054	130,794	483,381	42,879		352,587 D	19.9%	73.6%	6.5%
Utah	4			156,990	77,327	47,001	32,662		30,326 R	49.3%	29.9%	20.8%
Vermont	4			102,917	80,498	16,124	5,964	331	64,374 R	78.2%	15.7%	5.8%
Virginia		12		223,603	73,328	139,717	10,369	189	66,389 D	32.8%	62.5%	4.6%
Washington	7			421,549	220,224	42,842	150,727	7,756	69,497 R	52.2%	10.2%	35.8%
West Virginia	8			583,662	288,635	257,232	36,723	1,072	31,403 R	49.5%	44.1%	6.3%
Wisconsin			13	840,827	311,614	68,115	453,678	7,420	142,064 P	37.1%	8.1%	54.0%
Wyoming	3			79,900	41,858	12,868	25,174		16,684 R	52.4%	16.1%	31.5%
United States	382	136	13	29,095,023	15,719,921	8,386,704	4,832,532	155,866	7,333,217 R	54.0%	28.8%	16.6%

PRESIDENT 1920

The Republican figures in South Carolina include votes cast for two elector tickets; the figures in Florida are the votes cast for the single elector candidate who ran on both the regular Republican ticket and the White Republican ticket. In Washington, the total vote for minor party candidates exceeded that for the Democratic candidates, but the Democratic total was greater than that for any one of the minor party nominees.

The candidates listed below include all those who appeared on the ballot in at least one state.

16,153,115	Warren G. Harding and Calvin Coolidge, *Republican.*
9,133,092	James M. Cox and Franklin D. Roosevelt, *Democratic.*
915,490	Eugene V. Debs and Seymour Stedman, *Socialist.*
265,229	Parley P. Christensen and Max S. Hayes, *Farmer-Labor.*
189,339	Aaron S. Watkins and D. Leigh Colvin, *Prohibition.*
48,098	James Ferguson and William J. Hough, *American.*
30,594	William W. Cox and August Gillhaus, *Socialist Labor.*
5,833	Robert C. Macauley and Richard C. Barnum, *Single Tax.*

In Texas, 27,309 votes were cast for a Black-and-Tan Republican elector ticket. In addition, 514 scattered write-in votes were reported from various states.

UNITED STATES

PRESIDENT 1920

State	Electoral Vote Rep.	Electoral Vote Dem.	Electoral Vote Other	Total Vote	Republican	Democratic	Other	Plurality	Total Vote Rep.	Total Vote Dem.	Major Vote Rep.	Major Vote Dem.
Alabama		12		233,951	74,719	156,064	3,168	81,345 D	31.9%	66.7%	32.4%	67.6%
Arizona	3			66,803	37,016	29,546	241	7,470 R	55.4%	44.2%	55.6%	44.4%
Arkansas		9		183,871	72,316	106,427	5,128	34,111 D	39.3%	57.9%	40.5%	59.5%
California	13			943,463	624,992	229,191	89,280	395,801 R	66.2%	24.3%	73.2%	26.8%
Colorado	6			292,053	173,248	104,936	13,869	68,312 R	59.3%	35.9%	62.3%	37.7%
Connecticut	7			365,518	229,238	120,721	15,559	108,517 R	62.7%	33.0%	65.5%	34.5%
Delaware	3			94,875	52,858	39,911	2,106	12,947 R	55.7%	42.1%	57.0%	43.0%
Florida		6		145,684	44,853	90,515	10,316	45,662 D	30.8%	62.1%	33.1%	66.9%
Georgia		14		149,558	42,981	106,112	465	63,131 D	28.7%	71.0%	28.8%	71.2%
Idaho	4			138,281	91,351	46,930		44,421 R	66.1%	33.9%	66.1%	33.9%
Illinois	29			2,094,714	1,420,480	534,395	139,839	886,085 R	67.8%	25.5%	72.7%	27.3%
Indiana	15			1,262,974	696,370	511,364	55,240	185,006 R	55.1%	40.5%	57.7%	42.3%
Iowa	13			894,959	634,674	227,804	32,481	406,870 R	70.9%	25.5%	73.6%	26.4%
Kansas	10			570,243	369,268	185,464	15,511	183,804 R	64.8%	32.5%	66.6%	33.4%
Kentucky		13		918,636	452,480	456,497	9,659	4,017 D	49.3%	49.7%	49.8%	50.2%
Louisiana		10		126,397	38,539	87,519	339	48,980 D	30.5%	69.2%	30.6%	69.4%
Maine	6			197,840	136,355	58,961	2,524	77,394 R	68.9%	29.8%	69.8%	30.2%
Maryland	8			428,443	236,117	180,626	11,700	55,491 R	55.1%	42.2%	56.7%	43.3%
Massachusetts	18			993,718	681,153	276,691	35,874	404,462 R	68.5%	27.8%	71.1%	28.9%
Michigan	15			1,048,411	762,865	233,450	52,096	529,415 R	72.8%	22.3%	76.6%	23.4%
Minnesota	12			735,838	519,421	142,994	73,423	376,427 R	70.6%	19.4%	78.4%	21.6%
Mississippi		10		82,351	11,576	69,136	1,639	57,560 D	14.1%	84.0%	14.3%	85.7%
Missouri	18			1,332,140	727,252	574,699	30,189	152,553 R	54.6%	43.1%	55.9%	44.1%
Montana	4			179,006	109,430	57,372	12,204	52,058 R	61.1%	32.1%	65.6%	34.4%
Nebraska	8			382,743	247,498	119,608	15,637	127,890 R	64.7%	31.3%	67.4%	32.6%
Nevada	3			27,194	15,479	9,851	1,864	5,628 R	56.9%	36.2%	61.1%	38.9%
New Hampshire	4			159,092	95,196	62,662	1,234	32,534 R	59.8%	39.4%	60.3%	39.7%
New Jersey	14			910,251	615,333	258,761	36,157	356,572 R	67.6%	28.4%	70.4%	29.6%
New Mexico	3			105,412	57,634	46,668	1,110	10,966 R	54.7%	44.3%	55.3%	44.7%
New York	45			2,898,513	1,871,167	781,238	246,108	1,089,929 R	64.6%	27.0%	70.5%	29.5%
North Carolina		12		538,649	232,819	305,367	463	72,548 D	43.2%	56.7%	43.3%	56.7%
North Dakota	5			205,786	160,082	37,422	8,282	122,660 R	77.8%	18.2%	81.1%	18.9%
Ohio	24			2,021,653	1,182,022	780,037	59,594	401,985 R	58.5%	38.6%	60.2%	39.8%
Oklahoma	10			485,678	243,840	216,122	25,716	27,718 R	50.2%	44.5%	53.0%	47.0%
Oregon	5			238,522	143,592	80,019	14,911	63,573 R	60.2%	33.5%	64.2%	35.8%
Pennsylvania	38			1,851,248	1,218,215	503,202	129,831	715,013 R	65.8%	27.2%	70.8%	29.2%
Rhode Island	5			167,981	107,463	55,062	5,456	52,401 R	64.0%	32.8%	66.1%	33.9%
South Carolina		9		66,808	2,610	64,170	28	61,560 D	3.9%	96.1%	3.9%	96.1%
South Dakota	5			182,237	110,692	35,938	35,607	74,754 R	60.7%	19.7%	75.5%	24.5%
Tennessee	12			428,036	219,229	206,558	2,249	12,671 R	51.2%	48.3%	51.5%	48.5%
Texas		20		486,109	114,658	287,920	83,531	173,262 D	23.6%	59.2%	28.5%	71.5%
Utah	4			145,828	81,555	56,639	7,634	24,916 R	55.9%	38.8%	59.0%	41.0%
Vermont	4			89,961	68,212	20,919	830	47,293 R	75.8%	23.3%	76.5%	23.5%
Virginia		12		231,000	87,456	141,670	1,874	54,214 D	37.9%	61.3%	38.2%	61.8%
Washington	7			398,715	223,137	84,298	91,280	138,839 R	56.0%	21.1%	72.6%	27.4%
West Virginia	8			509,936	282,007	220,785	7,144	61,222 R	55.3%	43.3%	56.1%	43.9%
Wisconsin	13			701,281	498,576	113,422	89,283	385,154 R	71.1%	16.2%	81.5%	18.5%
Wyoming	3			56,253	35,091	17,429	3,733	17,662 R	62.4%	31.0%	66.8%	33.2%
United States	404	127	—	26,768,613	16,153,115	9,133,092	1,482,406	7,020,023 R	60.3%	34.1%	63.9%	36.1%

ALABAMA

POPULAR VOTE FOR PRESIDENT 1920 TO 1956

Year	Total Vote	Republican Vote	Republican Candidate	Democratic Vote	Democratic Candidate	Other Vote	Plurality	Percentage Total Vote Rep.	Percentage Total Vote Dem.	Percentage Major Vote Rep.	Percentage Major Vote Dem.
1956	496,861	195,694	Eisenhower, Dwight D.	280,844	Stevenson, Adlai E.	20,323	85,150 D	39.4%	56.5%	41.1%	58.9%
1952	426,120	149,231	Eisenhower, Dwight D.	275,075	Stevenson, Adlai E.	1,814	125,844 D	35.0%	64.6%	35.2%	64.8%
1948 **	214,980	40,930	Dewey, Thomas E.		Truman, Harry S.	174,050	130,513 SR	19.0%		100.0%	
1944	244,743	44,540	Dewey, Thomas E.	198,918	Roosevelt, Franklin D.	1,285	154,378 D	18.2%	81.3%	18.3%	81.7%
1940	294,219	42,184	Willkie, Wendell	250,726	Roosevelt, Franklin D.	1,309	208,542 D	14.3%	85.2%	14.4%	85.6%
1936	275,744	35,358	Landon, Alfred M.	238,196	Roosevelt, Franklin D.	2,190	202,838 D	12.8%	86.4%	12.9%	87.1%
1932	245,303	34,675	Hoover, Herbert C.	207,910	Roosevelt, Franklin D.	2,718	173,235 D	14.1%	84.8%	14.3%	85.7%
1928	248,981	120,725	Hoover, Herbert C.	127,796	Smith, Alfred E.	460	7,071 D	48.5%	51.3%	48.6%	51.4%
1924	164,563	42,823	Coolidge, Calvin	113,138	Davis, John W.	8,602	70,315 D	26.0%	68.8%	27.5%	72.5%
1920	233,951	74,719	Harding, Warren G.	156,064	Cox, James M.	3,168	81,345 D	31.9%	66.7%	32.4%	67.6%

In 1948 other vote was 171,443 States Rights; 1,522 Progressive and 1,085 Prohibition.

ELECTORAL COLLEGE VOTE 1920 TO 1956

Year	Total	Republican	Democratic	Other
1956 **	11	—	10	1 JONES
1952	11	—	11	—
1948	11	—	—	11 SR
1944	11	—	11	—
1940	11	—	11	—
1936	11	—	11	—
1932	11	—	11	—
1928	12	—	12	—
1924	12	—	12	—
1920	12	—	12	—

In 1956 one of the eleven Democratic electors voted in the Electoral College for Walter B. Jones and Herman Talmadge rather than for the national Democratic candidates.

ALABAMA

LAUDERDALE
LIMESTONE
MADISON
JACKSON
COLBERT
LAWRENCE
FRANKLIN
MORGAN
MARSHALL
DE KALB
MARION
WINSTON
CULLMAN
BLOUNT
ETOWAH
CHEROKEE
LAMAR
FAYETTE
WALKER
ST. CLAIR
CALHOUN
CLEBURNE
JEFFERSON
TALLADEGA
PICKENS
TUSCALOOSA
SHELBY
CLAY
RANDOLPH
BIBB
COOSA
TALLAPOOSA
CHAMBERS
GREENE
CHILTON
HALE
SUMTER
PERRY
AUTAUGA
ELMORE
LEE
MACON
RUSSELL
MARENGO
DALLAS
MONTGOMERY
LOWNDES
BULLOCK
CHOCTAW
WILCOX
BARBOUR
PIKE
BUTLER
CLARKE
CRENSHAW
MONROE
HENRY
CONECUH
DALE
WASHINGTON
COFFEE
COVINGTON
ESCAMBIA
HOUSTON
GENEVA
MOBILE
BALDWIN

ALABAMA

PRESIDENT 1956

1950 Census Population	County	Total Vote	Republican	Democratic	Other	Rep.-Dem. Plurality	Percentage Total Vote Rep.	Percentage Total Vote Dem.	Percentage Major Vote Rep.	Percentage Major Vote Dem.
18,186	AUTAUGA	2,287	857	1,161	269	304 D	37.5%	50.8%	42.5%	57.5%
40,997	BALDWIN	8,415	4,293	3,878	244	415 R	51.0%	46.1%	52.5%	47.5%
28,892	BARBOUR	3,449	777	2,530	142	1,753 D	22.5%	73.4%	23.5%	76.5%
17,987	BIBB	2,582	1,004	1,471	107	467 D	38.9%	57.0%	40.6%	59.4%
28,975	BLOUNT	5,922	2,628	3,208	86	580 D	44.4%	54.2%	45.0%	55.0%
16,054	BULLOCK	1,252	304	812	136	508 D	24.3%	64.9%	27.2%	72.8%
29,228	BUTLER	3,533	1,324	1,958	251	634 D	37.5%	55.4%	40.3%	59.7%
79,539	CALHOUN	13,900	4,473	9,069	358	4,596 D	32.2%	65.2%	33.0%	67.0%
39,528	CHAMBERS	6,737	1,448	5,165	124	3,717 D	21.5%	76.7%	21.9%	78.1%
17,634	CHEROKEE	3,513	845	2,661	7	1,816 D	24.1%	75.7%	24.1%	75.9%
26,922	CHILTON	5,148	3,139	1,891	118	1,248 R	61.0%	36.7%	62.4%	37.6%
19,152	CHOCTAW	1,779	457	1,250	72	793 D	25.7%	70.3%	26.8%	73.2%
26,548	CLARKE	3,388	1,246	1,962	180	716 D	36.8%	57.9%	38.8%	61.2%
13,929	CLAY	3,323	1,597	1,677	49	80 D	48.1%	50.5%	48.8%	51.2%
11,904	CLEBURNE	2,470	1,056	1,407	7	351 D	42.8%	57.0%	42.9%	57.1%
30,720	COFFEE	5,268	973	4,163	132	3,190 D	18.5%	79.0%	18.9%	81.1%
39,561	COLBERT	8,937	1,819	7,007	111	5,188 D	20.4%	78.4%	20.6%	79.4%
21,776	CONECUH	2,754	885	1,687	182	802 D	32.1%	61.3%	34.4%	65.6%
11,766	COOSA	2,519	1,070	1,411	38	341 D	42.5%	56.0%	43.1%	56.9%
40,373	COVINGTON	7,490	2,257	4,887	346	2,630 D	30.1%	65.2%	31.6%	68.4%
18,981	CRENSHAW	2,975	567	2,252	156	1,685 D	19.1%	75.7%	20.1%	79.9%
49,046	CULLMAN	9,929	4,381	5,510	38	1,129 D	44.1%	55.5%	44.3%	55.7%
20,828	DALE	3,712	1,284	2,318	110	1,034 D	34.6%	62.4%	35.6%	64.4%
56,270	DALLAS	5,358	2,324	2,121	913	203 R	43.4%	39.6%	52.3%	47.7%
45,048	DE KALB	11,468	5,684	5,768	16	84 D	49.6%	50.3%	49.6%	50.4%
31,649	ELMORE	5,394	1,619	3,353	422	1,734 D	30.0%	62.2%	32.6%	67.4%
31,443	ESCAMBIA	5,299	1,529	3,437	333	1,908 D	28.9%	64.9%	30.8%	69.2%
93,892	ETOWAH	19,886	7,198	12,374	314	5,176 D	36.2%	62.2%	36.8%	63.2%
19,388	FAYETTE	3,928	1,948	1,956	24	8 D	49.6%	49.8%	49.9%	50.1%
25,705	FRANKLIN	6,769	3,399	3,354	16	45 R	50.2%	49.5%	50.3%	49.7%
25,899	GENEVA	4,118	1,179	2,841	98	1,662 D	28.6%	69.0%	29.3%	70.7%
16,482	GREENE	1,044	309	691	44	382 D	29.6%	66.2%	30.9%	69.1%
20,832	HALE	1,917	504	1,314	99	810 D	26.3%	68.5%	27.7%	72.3%
18,674	HENRY	2,713	429	2,127	157	1,698 D	15.8%	78.4%	16.8%	83.2%
46,522	HOUSTON	6,841	2,632	3,630	579	998 D	38.5%	53.1%	42.0%	58.0%
38,998	JACKSON	6,647	1,868	4,758	21	2,890 D	28.1%	71.6%	28.2%	71.8%
558,928	JEFFERSON	87,513	43,695	38,604	5,214	5,091 R	49.9%	44.1%	53.1%	46.9%
16,441	LAMAR	3,399	867	2,501	31	1,634 D	25.5%	73.6%	25.7%	74.3%
54,179	LAUDERDALE	11,692	2,458	9,150	84	6,692 D	21.0%	78.3%	21.2%	78.8%
27,128	LAWRENCE	4,185	1,197	2,961	27	1,764 D	28.6%	70.8%	28.8%	71.2%
45,073	LEE	5,051	1,586	3,302	163	1,716 D	31.4%	65.4%	32.4%	67.6%
35,766	LIMESTONE	4,750	589	4,145	16	3,556 D	12.4%	87.3%	12.4%	87.6%
18,018	LOWNDES	1,192	326	623	243	297 D	27.3%	52.3%	34.4%	65.6%
30,561	MACON	2,193	1,067	1,024	102	43 R	48.7%	46.7%	51.0%	49.0%
72,903	MADISON	12,150	2,993	9,054	103	6,061 D	24.6%	74.5%	24.8%	75.2%
29,494	MARENGO	3,052	1,009	1,858	185	849 D	33.1%	60.9%	35.2%	64.8%
27,264	MARION	5,409	2,536	2,849	24	313 D	46.9%	52.7%	47.1%	52.9%
45,090	MARSHALL	9,495	3,071	6,329	95	3,258 D	32.3%	66.7%	32.7%	67.3%
231,105	MOBILE	39,534	20,639	17,163	1,732	3,476 R	52.2%	43.4%	54.6%	45.4%
25,732	MONROE	2,958	759	2,069	130	1,310 D	25.7%	69.9%	26.8%	73.2%
138,965	MONTGOMERY	18,841	8,727	6,890	3,224	1,837 R	46.3%	36.6%	55.9%	44.1%
52,924	MORGAN	10,872	2,974	7,671	227	4,697 D	27.4%	70.6%	27.9%	72.1%
20,439	PERRY	1,812	613	974	225	361 D	33.8%	53.8%	38.6%	61.4%
24,349	PICKENS	2,824	993	1,660	171	667 D	35.2%	58.8%	37.4%	62.6%
30,608	PIKE	3,839	997	2,631	211	1,634 D	26.0%	68.5%	27.5%	72.5%
22,513	RANDOLPH	4,761	1,584	3,151	26	1,567 D	33.3%	66.2%	33.5%	66.5%
40,364	RUSSELL	4,479	1,265	3,060	154	1,795 D	28.2%	68.3%	29.2%	70.8%
26,687	ST. CLAIR	4,975	2,441	2,420	114	21 R	49.1%	48.6%	50.2%	49.8%
30,362	SHELBY	5,581	2,901	2,502	178	399 R	52.0%	44.8%	53.7%	46.3%
23,610	SUMTER	1,671	578	981	112	403 D	34.6%	58.7%	37.1%	62.9%

ALABAMA

PRESIDENT 1956

1950 Census Population	County	Total Vote	Republican	Democratic	Other	Rep.-Dem. Plurality	Percentage Total Vote Rep.	Percentage Total Vote Dem.	Percentage Major Vote Rep.	Percentage Major Vote Dem.
63,639	TALLADEGA	9,597	4,197	5,243	157	1,046 D	43.7%	54.6%	44.5%	55.5%
35,074	TALLAPOOSA	7,042	1,879	5,070	93	3,191 D	26.7%	72.0%	27.0%	73.0%
94,092	TUSCALOOSA	13,798	4,994	8,186	618	3,192 D	36.2%	59.3%	37.9%	62.1%
63,769	WALKER	12,919	5,179	7,661	79	2,482 D	40.1%	59.3%	40.3%	59.7%
15,612	WASHINGTON	2,569	777	1,705	87	928 D	30.2%	66.4%	31.3%	68.7%
23,476	WILCOX	1,474	499	778	197	279 D	33.9%	52.8%	39.1%	60.9%
18,250	WINSTON	4,570	2,998	1,570	2	1,428 R	65.6%	34.4%	65.6%	34.4%
3,061,743	TOTAL	496,861	195,694	280,844	20,323	85,150 D	39.4%	56.5%	41.1%	58.9%

ALABAMA

PRESIDENT 1952

1950 Census Population	County	Total Vote	Republican	Democratic	Other	Rep.-Dem. Plurality	Percentage: Total Vote Rep.	Percentage: Total Vote Dem.	Percentage: Major Vote Rep.	Percentage: Major Vote Dem.
18,186	AUTAUGA	2,308	787	1,505	16	718 D	34.1%	65.2%	34.3%	65.7%
40,997	BALDWIN	6,617	3,179	3,386	52	207 D	48.0%	51.2%	48.4%	51.6%
28,892	BARBOUR	3,050	798	2,250	2	1,452 D	26.2%	73.8%	26.2%	73.8%
17,987	BIBB	2,769	784	1,971	14	1,187 D	28.3%	71.2%	28.5%	71.5%
28,975	BLOUNT	4,888	1,720	3,161	7	1,441 D	35.2%	64.7%	35.2%	64.8%
16,054	BULLOCK	1,360	442	918		476 D	32.5%	67.5%	32.5%	67.5%
29,228	BUTLER	3,528	1,087	2,440	1	1,353 D	30.8%	69.2%	30.8%	69.2%
79,539	CALHOUN	11,193	3,064	8,023	106	4,959 D	27.4%	71.7%	27.6%	72.4%
39,528	CHAMBERS	7,190	990	6,155	45	5,165 D	13.8%	85.6%	13.9%	86.1%
17,634	CHEROKEE	3,211	539	2,664	8	2,125 D	16.8%	83.0%	16.8%	83.2%
26,922	CHILTON	4,844	2,563	2,269	12	294 R	52.9%	46.8%	53.0%	47.0%
19,152	CHOCTAW	2,185	593	1,583	9	990 D	27.1%	72.4%	27.3%	72.7%
26,548	CLARKE	4,425	1,303	3,121	1	1,818 D	29.4%	70.5%	29.5%	70.5%
13,929	CLAY	3,164	1,183	1,972	9	789 D	37.4%	62.3%	37.5%	62.5%
11,904	CLEBURNE	2,354	792	1,557	5	765 D	33.6%	66.1%	33.7%	66.3%
30,720	COFFEE	4,620	699	3,919	2	3,220 D	15.1%	84.8%	15.1%	84.9%
39,561	COLBERT	7,308	1,381	5,920	7	4,539 D	18.9%	81.0%	18.9%	81.1%
21,776	CONECUH	2,458	749	1,678	31	929 D	30.5%	68.3%	30.9%	69.1%
11,766	COOSA	2,291	788	1,501	2	713 D	34.4%	65.5%	34.4%	65.6%
40,373	COVINGTON	6,558	1,581	4,956	21	3,375 D	24.1%	75.6%	24.2%	75.8%
18,981	CRENSHAW	3,032	544	2,485	3	1,941 D	17.9%	82.0%	18.0%	82.0%
49,046	CULLMAN	8,667	3,391	5,254	22	1,863 D	39.1%	60.6%	39.2%	60.8%
20,828	DALE	3,763	1,073	2,669	21	1,596 D	28.5%	70.9%	28.7%	71.3%
56,270	DALLAS	4,632	2,550	2,082		468 R	55.1%	44.9%	55.1%	44.9%
45,048	DE KALB	9,217	3,997	5,209	11	1,212 D	43.4%	56.5%	43.4%	56.6%
31,649	ELMORE	5,518	1,315	4,199	4	2,884 D	23.8%	76.1%	23.8%	76.2%
31,443	ESCAMBIA	4,583	1,187	3,385	11	2,198 D	25.9%	73.9%	26.0%	74.0%
93,892	ETOWAH	15,697	4,634	10,997	66	6,363 D	29.5%	70.1%	29.6%	70.4%
19,388	FAYETTE	3,779	1,481	2,287	11	806 D	39.2%	60.5%	39.3%	60.7%
25,705	FRANKLIN	5,893	2,424	3,461	8	1,037 D	41.1%	58.7%	41.2%	58.8%
25,899	GENEVA	3,656	950	2,703	3	1,753 D	26.0%	73.9%	26.0%	74.0%
16,482	GREENE	1,105	430	674	1	244 D	38.9%	61.0%	38.9%	61.1%
20,832	HALE	1,972	758	1,210	4	452 D	38.4%	61.4%	38.5%	61.5%
18,674	HENRY	2,392	421	1,966	5	1,545 D	17.6%	82.2%	17.6%	82.4%
46,522	HOUSTON	6,364	2,517	3,779	68	1,262 D	39.6%	59.4%	40.0%	60.0%
38,998	JACKSON	4,959	1,272	3,677	10	2,405 D	25.7%	74.1%	25.7%	74.3%
558,928	JEFFERSON	70,766	32,254	38,111	401	5,857 D	45.6%	53.9%	45.8%	54.2%
16,441	LAMAR	3,118	605	2,512	1	1,907 D	19.4%	80.6%	19.4%	80.6%
54,179	LAUDERDALE	9,027	1,910	7,097	20	5,187 D	21.2%	78.6%	21.2%	78.8%
27,128	LAWRENCE	3,466	809	2,651	6	1,842 D	23.3%	76.5%	23.4%	76.6%
45,073	LEE	4,434	1,626	2,803	5	1,177 D	36.7%	63.2%	36.7%	63.3%
35,766	LIMESTONE	4,406	549	3,844	13	3,295 D	12.5%	87.2%	12.5%	87.5%
18,018	LOWNDES	1,443	631	809	3	178 D	43.7%	56.1%	43.8%	56.2%
30,561	MACON	2,079	621	1,457	1	836 D	29.9%	70.1%	29.9%	70.1%
72,903	MADISON	9,920	1,623	8,216	81	6,593 D	16.4%	82.8%	16.5%	83.5%
29,494	MARENGO	3,152	1,362	1,790		428 D	43.2%	56.8%	43.2%	56.8%
27,264	MARION	4,348	1,489	2,850	9	1,361 D	34.2%	65.5%	34.3%	65.7%
45,090	MARSHALL	8,099	2,069	6,011	19	3,942 D	25.5%	74.2%	25.6%	74.4%
231,105	MOBILE	28,715	14,153	14,473	89	320 D	49.3%	50.4%	49.4%	50.6%
25,732	MONROE	3,231	637	2,587	7	1,950 D	19.7%	80.1%	19.8%	80.2%
138,965	MONTGOMERY	17,529	8,102	9,234	193	1,132 D	46.2%	52.7%	46.7%	53.3%
52,924	MORGAN	9,380	2,335	7,029	16	4,694 D	24.9%	74.9%	24.9%	75.1%
20,439	PERRY	2,112	756	1,352	4	596 D	35.8%	64.0%	35.9%	64.1%
24,349	PICKENS	2,442	905	1,519	18	614 D	37.1%	62.2%	37.3%	62.7%
30,608	PIKE	3,514	965	2,546	3	1,581 D	27.5%	72.5%	27.5%	72.5%
22,513	RANDOLPH	4,018	1,047	2,964	7	1,917 D	26.1%	73.8%	26.1%	73.9%
40,364	RUSSELL	4,434	867	3,564	3	2,697 D	19.6%	80.4%	19.6%	80.4%
26,687	ST. CLAIR	3,922	1,590	2,326	6	736 D	40.5%	59.3%	40.6%	59.4%
30,362	SHELBY	4,636	2,156	2,473	7	317 D	46.5%	53.3%	46.6%	53.4%
23,610	SUMTER	1,599	702	894	3	192 D	43.9%	55.9%	44.0%	56.0%

ALABAMA

PRESIDENT 1952

1950 Census Population	County	Total Vote	Republican	Democratic	Other	Rep.-Dem. Plurality	Percentage Total Vote Rep.	Percentage Total Vote Dem.	Percentage Major Vote Rep.	Percentage Major Vote Dem.
63,639	TALLADEGA	8,642	3,588	5,028	26	1,440 D	41.5%	58.2%	41.6%	58.4%
35,074	TALLAPOOSA	6,249	1,187	5,055	7	3,868 D	19.0%	80.9%	19.0%	81.0%
94,092	TUSCALOOSA	11,720	3,872	7,677	171	3,805 D	33.0%	65.5%	33.5%	66.5%
63,769	WALKER	10,432	3,490	6,862	80	3,372 D	33.5%	65.8%	33.7%	66.3%
15,612	WASHINGTON	2,607	623	1,977	7	1,354 D	23.9%	75.8%	24.0%	76.0%
23,476	WILCOX	1,714	725	988	1	263 D	42.3%	57.6%	42.3%	57.7%
18,250	WINSTON	3,416	2,017	1,390	9	627 R	59.0%	40.7%	59.2%	40.8%
3,061,743	TOTAL	426,120	149,231	275,075	1,814	125,844 D	35.0%	64.6%	35.2%	64.8%

ALABAMA

PRESIDENT 1948

1940 Census Population	County	Total Vote	Republican	Democratic	States Rights	Other	Plurality	Percentage Total Vote Rep.	Dem.	St. Rgts.
20,977	AUTAUGA	1,302	110		1,160	16	1,066 SR	8.4%		90.3%
32,324	BALDWIN	3,546	767		2,577	101	1,911 SR	21.6%		75.5%
32,722	BARBOUR	1,796	101		1,679	8	1,586 SR	5.6%		93.9%
20,155	BIBB	1,375	123		1,188	32	1,097 SR	8.9%		88.7%
29,490	BLOUNT	2,587	771		1,768	24	1,021 SR	29.8%		69.3%
19,810	BULLOCK	809	10		799		789 SR	1.2%		98.8%
32,447	BUTLER	1,414	91		1,313	5	1,227 SR	6.4%		93.2%
63,319	CALHOUN	4,270	856		3,236	89	2,469 SR	20.0%		77.9%
42,146	CHAMBERS	1,796	218		1,520	29	1,331 SR	12.1%		86.2%
19,928	CHEROKEE	1,314	217		1,055	21	859 SR	16.5%		81.9%
27,955	CHILTON	3,588	1,584		1,966	19	401 SR	44.1%		55.3%
20,195	CHOCTAW	1,458	16		1,440	1	1,425 SR	1.1%		98.8%
27,636	CLARKE	2,114	47		2,059	4	2,016 SR	2.2%		97.6%
16,907	CLAY	1,511	387		1,106	9	728 SR	25.6%		73.8%
13,629	CLEBURNE	1,037	317		700	10	393 SR	30.6%		68.5%
31,987	COFFEE	2,160	113		2,031	8	1,926 SR	5.2%		94.4%
34,093	COLBERT	3,153	488		2,609	28	2,149 SR	15.5%		83.6%
25,489	CONECUH	1,415	64		1,339	6	1,281 SR	4.5%		95.1%
13,460	COOSA	1,133	275		840	9	574 SR	24.3%		74.9%
42,417	COVINGTON	2,954	154		2,764	18	2,628 SR	5.2%		94.2%
23,631	CRENSHAW	1,440	38		1,386	8	1,356 SR	2.6%		96.8%
47,343	CULLMAN	5,386	1,755		3,587	22	1,854 SR	32.6%		67.0%
22,685	DALE	1,622	230		1,352	20	1,142 SR	14.2%		84.6%
55,245	DALLAS	2,888	132		2,720	18	2,606 SR	4.6%		94.8%
43,075	DE KALB	6,350	2,743		3,573	17	847 SR	43.2%		56.5%
34,546	ELMORE	2,586	167		2,387	16	2,236 SR	6.5%		92.9%
30,671	ESCAMBIA	1,895	188		1,681	13	1,506 SR	9.9%		89.4%
72,580	ETOWAH	7,812	1,615		5,895	151	4,431 SR	20.7%		77.4%
21,651	FAYETTE	1,641	580		1,023	19	462 SR	35.3%		63.5%
27,552	FRANKLIN	5,807	2,555		3,226	13	684 SR	44.0%		55.8%
29,172	GENEVA	2,137	286		1,823	14	1,551 SR	13.4%		86.0%
19,185	GREENE	660	31		621	4	594 SR	4.7%		94.7%
25,533	HALE	1,090	43		1,041	3	1,001 SR	3.9%		95.8%
21,912	HENRY	1,089	47		1,040	1	994 SR	4.3%		95.6%
45,665	HOUSTON	3,189	426		2,715	24	2,313 SR	13.4%		85.9%
41,802	JACKSON	2,365	603		1,726	18	1,141 SR	25.5%		73.7%
459,930	JEFFERSON	38,418	7,261		30,043	557	23,339 SR	18.9%		79.7%
19,708	LAMAR	1,630	180		1,434	8	1,262 SR	11.0%		88.5%
46,230	LAUDERDALE	3,840	546		3,258	18	2,730 SR	14.2%		85.3%
27,880	LAWRENCE	1,819	357		1,436	13	1,092 SR	19.6%		79.7%
36,455	LEE	2,025	258		1,731	18	1,491 SR	12.7%		86.4%
35,642	LIMESTONE	1,999	112		1,853	17	1,758 SR	5.6%		93.5%
22,661	LOWNDES	819	13		752	27	766 SR	1.6%		95.1%
27,654	MACON	1,214	110		1,098	3	991 SR	9.1%		90.7%
66,317	MADISON	3,639	466		2,947	113	2,594 SR	12.8%		84.1%
35,736	MARENGO	1,946	67		1,873	3	1,809 SR	3.4%		96.4%
28,776	MARION	2,493	813		1,646	17	850 SR	32.6%		66.7%
42,395	MARSHALL	3,404	870		2,500	17	1,647 SR	25.6%		73.9%
141,974	MOBILE	14,154	2,685		10,831	319	8,465 SR	19.0%		78.8%
29,465	MONROE	1,731	31		1,688	6	1,663 SR	1.8%		97.9%
114,420	MONTGOMERY	7,410	802		6,196	206	5,600 SR	10.8%		86.4%
48,148	MORGAN	4,411	512		3,841	29	3,358 SR	11.6%		87.7%
26,610	PERRY	1,100	30		1,032	19	1,021 SR	2.7%		95.5%
27,671	PICKENS	1,534	91		1,423	10	1,342 SR	5.9%		93.4%
32,493	PIKE	1,840	87		1,741	6	1,660 SR	4.7%		94.9%
25,516	RANDOLPH	1,742	469		1,249	12	792 SR	26.9%		72.4%
35,775	RUSSELL	1,792	94		1,666	16	1,588 SR	5.2%		93.9%
27,336	ST. CLAIR	2,994	1,063		1,903	14	854 SR	35.5%		64.0%
28,962	SHELBY	2,841	921		1,878	21	978 SR	32.4%		66.8%
27,321	SUMTER	1,116	52		1,058	3	1,009 SR	4.7%		95.1%

ALABAMA

PRESIDENT 1948

1940 Census Population	County	Total Vote	Republican	Democratic	States Rights	Other	Plurality	Rep.	Dem.	St. Rgts.
								Percentage Total Vote		
51,832	TALLADEGA	3,740	593		3,077	35	2,519 SR	15.9%		83.2%
35,270	TALLAPOOSA	2,483	156		2,309	9	2,162 SR	6.3%		93.4%
76,036	TUSCALOOSA	5,555	658		4,697	100	4,139 SR	11.8%		86.4%
64,201	WALKER	6,197	1,852		4,007	169	2,324 SR	29.9%		67.4%
16,188	WASHINGTON	1,353	31		1,304	9	1,282 SR	2.3%		97.0%
26,279	WILCOX	1,176	14		1,162		1,148 SR	1.2%		98.8%
18,746	WINSTON	2,483	1,588		865	15	708 R	64.0%		35.4%
2,832,961	TOTAL	214,980	40,930		171,443	2,607	130,513 SR	19.0%		79.7%

ALABAMA

PRESIDENT 1944

1940 Census Population	County	Total Vote	Republican	Democratic	Other	Rep.-Dem. Plurality	Percentage Total Vote Rep.	Percentage Total Vote Dem.	Percentage Major Vote Rep.	Percentage Major Vote Dem.
20,977	AUTAUGA	1,364	117	1,242	5	1,125 D	8.6%	91.1%	8.6%	91.4%
32,324	BALDWIN	2,727	695	2,002	30	1,307 D	25.5%	73.4%	25.8%	74.2%
32,722	BARBOUR	2,357	67	2,237	53	2,170 D	2.8%	94.9%	2.9%	97.1%
20,155	BIBB	1,546	244	1,287	15	1,043 D	15.8%	83.2%	15.9%	84.1%
29,490	BLOUNT	3,145	998	2,134	13	1,136 D	31.7%	67.9%	31.9%	68.1%
19,810	BULLOCK	1,080	24	1,056		1,032 D	2.2%	97.8%	2.2%	97.8%
32,447	BUTLER	2,000	80	1,915	5	1,835 D	4.0%	95.8%	4.0%	96.0%
63,319	CALHOUN	5,030	694	4,308	28	3,614 D	13.8%	85.6%	13.9%	86.1%
42,146	CHAMBERS	3,662	194	3,458	10	3,264 D	5.3%	94.4%	5.3%	94.7%
19,928	CHEROKEE	2,200	408	1,774	18	1,366 D	18.5%	80.6%	18.7%	81.3%
27,955	CHILTON	3,376	1,385	1,984	7	599 D	41.0%	58.8%	41.1%	58.9%
20,195	CHOCTAW	1,332	86	1,243	3	1,157 D	6.5%	93.3%	6.5%	93.5%
27,636	CLARKE	2,408	142	2,263	3	2,121 D	5.9%	94.0%	5.9%	94.1%
16,907	CLAY	2,290	741	1,535	14	794 D	32.4%	67.0%	32.6%	67.4%
13,629	CLEBURNE	1,458	504	948	6	444 D	34.6%	65.0%	34.7%	65.3%
31,987	COFFEE	2,964	115	2,846	3	2,731 D	3.9%	96.0%	3.9%	96.1%
34,093	COLBERT	3,889	496	3,386	7	2,890 D	12.8%	87.1%	12.8%	87.2%
25,489	CONECUH	1,640	127	1,498	15	1,371 D	7.7%	91.3%	7.8%	92.2%
13,460	COOSA	1,481	394	1,079	8	685 D	26.6%	72.9%	26.7%	73.3%
42,417	COVINGTON	3,231	256	2,972	3	2,716 D	7.9%	92.0%	7.9%	92.1%
23,631	CRENSHAW	2,105	118	1,980	7	1,862 D	5.6%	94.1%	5.6%	94.4%
47,343	CULLMAN	6,145	2,202	3,898	45	1,696 D	35.8%	63.4%	36.1%	63.9%
22,685	DALE	2,447	325	2,094	28	1,769 D	13.3%	85.6%	13.4%	86.6%
55,245	DALLAS	3,043	149	2,883	11	2,734 D	4.9%	94.7%	4.9%	95.1%
43,075	DE KALB	7,002	2,627	4,366	9	1,739 D	37.5%	62.4%	37.6%	62.4%
34,546	ELMORE	3,295	184	3,108	3	2,924 D	5.6%	94.3%	5.6%	94.4%
30,671	ESCAMBIA	2,355	266	2,077	12	1,811 D	11.3%	88.2%	11.4%	88.6%
72,580	ETOWAH	7,521	1,525	5,895	101	4,370 D	20.3%	78.4%	20.6%	79.4%
21,651	FAYETTE	2,571	913	1,648	10	735 D	35.5%	64.1%	35.7%	64.3%
27,552	FRANKLIN	4,568	1,853	2,709	6	856 D	40.6%	59.3%	40.6%	59.4%
29,172	GENEVA	2,404	385	2,004	15	1,619 D	16.0%	83.4%	16.1%	83.9%
19,185	GREENE	722	45	676	1	631 D	6.2%	93.6%	6.2%	93.8%
25,533	HALE	1,298	33	1,265		1,232 D	2.5%	97.5%	2.5%	97.5%
21,912	HENRY	1,683	46	1,635	2	1,589 D	2.7%	97.1%	2.7%	97.3%
45,665	HOUSTON	3,648	282	3,349	17	3,067 D	7.7%	91.8%	7.8%	92.2%
41,802	JACKSON	4,000	1,026	2,967	7	1,941 D	25.7%	74.2%	25.7%	74.3%
459,930	JEFFERSON	38,684	7,409	31,101	174	23,692 D	19.2%	80.4%	19.2%	80.8%
19,708	LAMAR	2,352	310	2,025	17	1,715 D	13.2%	86.1%	13.3%	86.7%
46,230	LAUDERDALE	4,611	590	4,001	20	3,411 D	12.8%	86.8%	12.9%	87.1%
27,880	LAWRENCE	2,463	565	1,893	5	1,328 D	22.9%	76.9%	23.0%	77.0%
36,455	LEE	2,151	134	2,011	6	1,877 D	6.2%	93.5%	6.2%	93.8%
35,642	LIMESTONE	2,744	129	2,605	10	2,476 D	4.7%	94.9%	4.7%	95.3%
22,661	LOWNDES	819	16	802	1	786 D	2.0%	97.9%	2.0%	98.0%
27,654	MACON	1,115	82	1,032	1	950 D	7.4%	92.6%	7.4%	92.6%
66,317	MADISON	5,421	455	4,951	15	4,496 D	8.4%	91.3%	8.4%	91.6%
35,736	MARENGO	1,844	89	1,746	9	1,657 D	4.8%	94.7%	4.9%	95.1%
28,776	MARION	3,137	1,260	1,866	11	606 D	40.2%	59.5%	40.3%	59.7%
42,395	MARSHALL	4,561	1,200	3,356	5	2,156 D	26.3%	73.6%	26.3%	73.7%
141,974	MOBILE	12,423	2,867	9,439	117	6,572 D	23.1%	76.0%	23.3%	76.7%
29,465	MONROE	2,041	46	1,991	4	1,945 D	2.3%	97.6%	2.3%	97.7%
114,420	MONTGOMERY	9,562	381	9,143	38	8,762 D	4.0%	95.6%	4.0%	96.0%
48,148	MORGAN	4,838	664	4,124	50	3,460 D	13.7%	85.2%	13.9%	86.1%
26,610	PERRY	1,053	47	1,004	2	957 D	4.5%	95.3%	4.5%	95.5%
27,671	PICKENS	1,699	209	1,482	8	1,273 D	12.3%	87.2%	12.4%	87.6%
32,493	PIKE	2,480	90	2,328	62	2,238 D	3.6%	93.9%	3.7%	96.3%
25,516	RANDOLPH	2,512	702	1,785	25	1,083 D	27.9%	71.1%	28.2%	71.8%
35,775	RUSSELL	2,228	115	2,109	4	1,994 D	5.2%	94.7%	5.2%	94.8%
27,336	ST. CLAIR	2,950	1,117	1,819	14	702 D	37.9%	61.7%	38.0%	62.0%
28,962	SHELBY	2,913	945	1,955	13	1,010 D	32.4%	67.1%	32.6%	67.4%
27,321	SUMTER	1,131	53	1,075	3	1,022 D	4.7%	95.0%	4.7%	95.3%

ALABAMA

PRESIDENT 1944

1940 Census Population	County	Total Vote	Republican	Democratic	Other	Rep.-Dem. Plurality	Percentage Total Vote Rep.	Percentage Total Vote Dem.	Percentage Major Vote Rep.	Percentage Major Vote Dem.
51,832	TALLADEGA	3,806	675	3,102	29	2,427 D	17.7%	81.5%	17.9%	82.1%
35,270	TALLAPOOSA	3,469	136	3,326	7	3,190 D	3.9%	95.9%	3.9%	96.1%
76,036	TUSCALOOSA	5,573	584	4,939	50	4,355 D	10.5%	88.6%	10.6%	89.4%
64,201	WALKER	6,907	2,241	4,619	47	2,378 D	32.4%	66.9%	32.7%	67.3%
16,188	WASHINGTON	1,568	115	1,447	6	1,332 D	7.3%	92.3%	7.4%	92.6%
26,279	WILCOX	1,241	30	1,209	2	1,179 D	2.4%	97.4%	2.4%	97.6%
18,746	WINSTON	2,460	1,538	912	10	626 R	62.5%	37.1%	62.8%	37.2%
2,832,961	TOTAL	244,743	44,540	198,918	1,285	154,378 D	18.2%	81.3%	18.3%	81.7%

ALABAMA

PRESIDENT 1940

1940 Census Population	County	Total Vote	Republican	Democratic	Other	Rep.-Dem. Plurality	Percentage: Total Vote Rep.	Total Vote Dem.	Major Vote Rep.	Major Vote Dem.
20,977	AUTAUGA	1,741	99	1,630	12	1,531 D	5.7%	93.6%	5.7%	94.3%
32,324	BALDWIN	3,501	617	2,681	203	2,064 D	17.6%	76.6%	18.7%	81.3%
32,722	BARBOUR	2,428	90	2,328	10	2,238 D	3.7%	95.9%	3.7%	96.3%
20,155	BIBB	2,012	173	1,821	18	1,648 D	8.6%	90.5%	8.7%	91.3%
29,490	BLOUNT	3,677	855	2,784	38	1,929 D	23.3%	75.7%	23.5%	76.5%
19,810	BULLOCK	1,319	18	1,301		1,283 D	1.4%	98.6%	1.4%	98.6%
32,447	BUTLER	2,788	52	2,732	4	2,680 D	1.9%	98.0%	1.9%	98.1%
63,319	CALHOUN	5,073	645	4,408	20	3,763 D	12.7%	86.9%	12.8%	87.2%
42,146	CHAMBERS	4,262	110	4,141	11	4,031 D	2.6%	97.2%	2.6%	97.4%
19,928	CHEROKEE	3,010	381	2,617	12	2,236 D	12.7%	86.9%	12.7%	87.3%
27,955	CHILTON	4,751	1,995	2,746	10	751 D	42.0%	57.8%	42.1%	57.9%
20,195	CHOCTAW	2,096	73	2,023		1,950 D	3.5%	96.5%	3.5%	96.5%
27,636	CLARKE	3,802	48	3,753	1	3,705 D	1.3%	98.7%	1.3%	98.7%
16,907	CLAY	3,023	854	2,153	16	1,299 D	28.3%	71.2%	28.4%	71.6%
13,629	CLEBURNE	1,808	434	1,369	5	935 D	24.0%	75.7%	24.1%	75.9%
31,987	COFFEE	2,371	145	2,226		2,081 D	6.1%	93.9%	6.1%	93.9%
34,093	COLBERT	4,371	365	3,998	8	3,633 D	8.4%	91.5%	8.4%	91.6%
25,489	CONECUH	2,400	50	2,345	5	2,295 D	2.1%	97.7%	2.1%	97.9%
13,460	COOSA	1,677	317	1,347	13	1,030 D	18.9%	80.3%	19.1%	80.9%
42,417	COVINGTON	4,824	186	4,635	3	4,449 D	3.9%	96.1%	3.9%	96.1%
23,631	CRENSHAW	2,773	84	2,680	9	2,596 D	3.0%	96.6%	3.0%	97.0%
47,343	CULLMAN	8,686	3,057	5,603	26	2,546 D	35.2%	64.5%	35.3%	64.7%
22,685	DALE	2,922	374	2,543	5	2,169 D	12.8%	87.0%	12.8%	87.2%
55,245	DALLAS	3,266	157	3,106	3	2,949 D	4.8%	95.1%	4.8%	95.2%
43,075	DE KALB	8,259	2,810	5,432	17	2,622 D	34.0%	65.8%	34.1%	65.9%
34,546	ELMORE	4,420	144	4,267	9	4,123 D	3.3%	96.5%	3.3%	96.7%
30,671	ESCAMBIA	2,917	137	2,772	8	2,635 D	4.7%	95.0%	4.7%	95.3%
72,580	ETOWAH	8,315	1,270	7,012	33	5,742 D	15.3%	84.3%	15.3%	84.7%
21,651	FAYETTE	2,848	737	2,091	20	1,354 D	25.9%	73.4%	26.1%	73.9%
27,552	FRANKLIN	5,533	1,989	3,523	21	1,534 D	35.9%	63.7%	36.1%	63.9%
29,172	GENEVA	2,942	364	2,565	13	2,201 D	12.4%	87.2%	12.4%	87.6%
19,185	GREENE	971	77	894		817 D	7.9%	92.1%	7.9%	92.1%
25,533	HALE	1,723	32	1,691		1,659 D	1.9%	98.1%	1.9%	98.1%
21,912	HENRY	2,031	69	1,960	2	1,891 D	3.4%	96.5%	3.4%	96.6%
45,665	HOUSTON	4,439	483	3,941	15	3,458 D	10.9%	88.8%	10.9%	89.1%
41,802	JACKSON	4,772	945	3,818	9	2,873 D	19.8%	80.0%	19.8%	80.2%
459,930	JEFFERSON	44,001	6,714	37,110	177	30,396 D	15.3%	84.3%	15.3%	84.7%
19,708	LAMAR	2,952	275	2,665	12	2,390 D	9.3%	90.3%	9.4%	90.6%
46,230	LAUDERDALE	5,606	507	5,065	34	4,558 D	9.0%	90.3%	9.1%	90.9%
27,880	LAWRENCE	2,769	480	2,277	12	1,797 D	17.3%	82.2%	17.4%	82.6%
36,455	LEE	2,674	103	2,566	5	2,463 D	3.9%	96.0%	3.9%	96.1%
35,642	LIMESTONE	3,045	95	2,941	9	2,846 D	3.1%	96.6%	3.1%	96.9%
22,661	LOWNDES	1,145	12	1,132	1	1,120 D	1.0%	98.9%	1.0%	99.0%
27,654	MACON	1,301	41	1,259	1	1,218 D	3.2%	96.8%	3.2%	96.8%
66,317	MADISON	6,098	566	5,515	17	4,949 D	9.3%	90.4%	9.3%	90.7%
35,736	MARENGO	2,356	70	2,284	2	2,214 D	3.0%	96.9%	3.0%	97.0%
28,776	MARION	3,811	1,081	2,654	76	1,573 D	28.4%	69.6%	28.9%	71.1%
42,395	MARSHALL	5,079	913	4,142	24	3,229 D	18.0%	81.6%	18.1%	81.9%
141,974	MOBILE	13,493	1,887	11,480	126	9,593 D	14.0%	85.1%	14.1%	85.9%
29,465	MONROE	3,008	40	2,953	15	2,913 D	1.3%	98.2%	1.3%	98.7%
114,420	MONTGOMERY	11,573	230	11,311	32	11,081 D	2.0%	97.7%	2.0%	98.0%
48,148	MORGAN	5,878	500	5,345	33	4,845 D	8.5%	90.9%	8.6%	91.4%
26,610	PERRY	1,553	39	1,509	5	1,470 D	2.5%	97.2%	2.5%	97.5%
27,671	PICKENS	1,863	140	1,714	9	1,574 D	7.5%	92.0%	7.6%	92.4%
32,493	PIKE	3,178	121	3,049	8	2,928 D	3.8%	95.9%	3.8%	96.2%
25,516	RANDOLPH	3,089	670	2,407	12	1,737 D	21.7%	77.9%	21.8%	78.2%
35,775	RUSSELL	2,486	48	2,435	3	2,387 D	1.9%	97.9%	1.9%	98.1%
27,336	ST. CLAIR	4,024	1,540	2,462	22	922 D	38.3%	61.2%	38.5%	61.5%
28,962	SHELBY	3,722	938	2,777	7	1,839 D	25.2%	74.6%	25.2%	74.8%
27,321	SUMTER	1,451	46	1,404	1	1,358 D	3.2%	96.8%	3.2%	96.8%

ALABAMA

PRESIDENT 1940

1940 Census Population	County	Total Vote	Republican	Democratic	Other	Rep.-Dem. Plurality	Percentage Total Vote Rep.	Percentage Total Vote Dem.	Percentage Major Vote Rep.	Percentage Major Vote Dem.
51,832	TALLADEGA	4,512	534	3,965	13	3,431 D	11.8%	87.9%	11.9%	88.1%
35,270	TALLAPOOSA	4,475	139	4,325	11	4,186 D	3.1%	96.6%	3.1%	96.9%
76,036	TUSCALOOSA	6,732	426	6,284	22	5,858 D	6.3%	93.3%	6.3%	93.7%
64,201	WALKER	7,971	2,007	5,940	24	3,933 D	25.2%	74.5%	25.3%	74.7%
16,188	WASHINGTON	1,978	80	1,892	6	1,812 D	4.0%	95.7%	4.1%	95.9%
26,279	WILCOX	1,554	20	1,534		1,514 D	1.3%	98.7%	1.3%	98.7%
18,746	WINSTON	3,091	1,686	1,394	11	292 R	54.5%	45.1%	54.7%	45.3%
2,832,961	TOTAL	294,219	42,184	250,726	1,309	208,542 D	14.3%	85.2%	14.4%	85.6%

ALABAMA

PRESIDENT 1936

1930 Census Population	County	Total Vote	Republican	Democratic	Other	Rep.-Dem. Plurality	Percentage Total Vote Rep.	Percentage Total Vote Dem.	Percentage Major Vote Rep.	Percentage Major Vote Dem.
19,694	AUTAUGA	1,617	84	1,525	8	1,441 D	5.2%	94.3%	5.2%	94.8%
28,289	BALDWIN	2,967	434	2,338	195	1,904 D	14.6%	78.8%	15.7%	84.3%
32,425	BARBOUR	2,448	50	2,386	12	2,336 D	2.0%	97.5%	2.1%	97.9%
20,780	BIBB	2,066	190	1,868	8	1,678 D	9.2%	90.4%	9.2%	90.8%
28,020	BLOUNT	3,564	744	2,788	32	2,044 D	20.9%	78.2%	21.1%	78.9%
20,016	BULLOCK	1,194	5	1,188	1	1,183 D	0.4%	99.5%	0.4%	99.6%
30,195	BUTLER	2,448	83	2,358	7	2,275 D	3.4%	96.3%	3.4%	96.6%
55,611	CALHOUN	4,961	581	4,322	58	3,741 D	11.7%	87.1%	11.8%	88.2%
39,313	CHAMBERS	3,742	112	3,626	4	3,514 D	3.0%	96.9%	3.0%	97.0%
20,219	CHEROKEE	2,507	374	2,114	19	1,740 D	14.9%	84.3%	15.0%	85.0%
24,579	CHILTON	4,055	1,469	2,565	21	1,096 D	36.2%	63.3%	36.4%	63.6%
20,513	CHOCTAW	1,581	74	1,507		1,433 D	4.7%	95.3%	4.7%	95.3%
26,016	CLARKE	2,735	60	2,673	2	2,613 D	2.2%	97.7%	2.2%	97.8%
17,768	CLAY	2,978	700	2,138	140	1,438 D	23.5%	71.8%	24.7%	75.3%
12,877	CLEBURNE	1,766	543	1,212	11	669 D	30.7%	68.6%	30.9%	69.1%
32,556	COFFEE	3,305	110	3,178	17	3,068 D	3.3%	96.2%	3.3%	96.7%
29,860	COLBERT	3,628	251	3,365	12	3,114 D	6.9%	92.8%	6.9%	93.1%
25,429	CONECUH	2,296	89	2,195	12	2,106 D	3.9%	95.6%	3.9%	96.1%
12,460	COOSA	1,617	239	1,346	32	1,107 D	14.8%	83.2%	15.1%	84.9%
41,356	COVINGTON	4,447	167	4,265	15	4,098 D	3.8%	95.9%	3.8%	96.2%
23,656	CRENSHAW	2,471	96	2,371	4	2,275 D	3.9%	96.0%	3.9%	96.1%
41,051	CULLMAN	5,505	1,703	3,781	21	2,078 D	30.9%	68.7%	31.1%	68.9%
23,175	DALE	2,599	193	2,404	2	2,211 D	7.4%	92.5%	7.4%	92.6%
55,094	DALLAS	3,258	49	3,205	4	3,156 D	1.5%	98.4%	1.5%	98.5%
40,104	DE KALB	10,764	4,620	6,121	23	1,501 D	42.9%	56.9%	43.0%	57.0%
34,280	ELMORE	4,297	182	3,967	148	3,785 D	4.2%	92.3%	4.4%	95.6%
27,963	ESCAMBIA	2,698	103	2,585	10	2,482 D	3.8%	95.8%	3.8%	96.2%
63,399	ETOWAH	6,978	1,207	5,739	32	4,532 D	17.3%	82.2%	17.4%	82.6%
18,443	FAYETTE	2,999	732	2,244	23	1,512 D	24.4%	74.8%	24.6%	75.4%
25,372	FRANKLIN	4,964	1,875	3,059	30	1,184 D	37.8%	61.6%	38.0%	62.0%
30,104	GENEVA	2,949	295	2,652	2	2,357 D	10.0%	89.9%	10.0%	90.0%
19,745	GREENE	884	20	861	3	841 D	2.3%	97.4%	2.3%	97.7%
26,265	HALE	1,654	20	1,626	8	1,606 D	1.2%	98.3%	1.2%	98.8%
22,820	HENRY	1,963	35	1,925	3	1,890 D	1.8%	98.1%	1.8%	98.2%
45,935	HOUSTON	3,783	230	3,538	15	3,308 D	6.1%	93.5%	6.1%	93.9%
36,881	JACKSON	4,383	926	3,450	7	2,524 D	21.1%	78.7%	21.2%	78.8%
431,493	JEFFERSON	40,198	3,813	35,982	403	32,169 D	9.5%	89.5%	9.6%	90.4%
18,001	LAMAR	2,594	195	2,393	6	2,198 D	7.5%	92.3%	7.5%	92.5%
41,130	LAUDERDALE	5,125	390	4,685	50	4,295 D	7.6%	91.4%	7.7%	92.3%
26,942	LAWRENCE	2,663	444	2,213	6	1,769 D	16.7%	83.1%	16.7%	83.3%
36,063	LEE	2,283	93	2,183	7	2,090 D	4.1%	95.6%	4.1%	95.9%
36,629	LIMESTONE	2,990	108	2,861	21	2,753 D	3.6%	95.7%	3.6%	96.4%
22,878	LOWNDES	1,217	10	1,205	2	1,195 D	0.8%	99.0%	0.8%	99.2%
27,103	MACON	1,185	39	1,146		1,107 D	3.3%	96.7%	3.3%	96.7%
64,623	MADISON	6,220	514	5,661	45	5,147 D	8.3%	91.0%	8.3%	91.7%
36,426	MARENGO	2,321	33	2,287	1	2,254 D	1.4%	98.5%	1.4%	98.6%
25,967	MARION	3,609	911	2,655	43	1,744 D	25.2%	73.6%	25.5%	74.5%
39,802	MARSHALL	5,152	925	4,208	19	3,283 D	18.0%	81.7%	18.0%	82.0%
118,363	MOBILE	12,412	1,072	11,165	175	10,093 D	8.6%	90.0%	8.8%	91.2%
30,070	MONROE	2,596	29	2,558	9	2,529 D	1.1%	98.5%	1.1%	98.9%
98,671	MONTGOMERY	12,332	223	12,061	48	11,838 D	1.8%	97.8%	1.8%	98.2%
46,176	MORGAN	6,058	432	5,597	29	5,165 D	7.1%	92.4%	7.2%	92.8%
26,385	PERRY	1,551	24	1,527		1,503 D	1.5%	98.5%	1.5%	98.5%
24,902	PICKENS	1,781	107	1,665	9	1,558 D	6.0%	93.5%	6.0%	94.0%
32,240	PIKE	3,157	55	3,100	2	3,045 D	1.7%	98.2%	1.7%	98.3%
26,861	RANDOLPH	3,574	793	2,766	15	1,973 D	22.2%	77.4%	22.3%	77.7%
27,377	RUSSELL	2,256	66	2,181	9	2,115 D	2.9%	96.7%	2.9%	97.1%
24,510	ST. CLAIR	3,880	1,464	2,399	17	935 D	37.7%	61.8%	37.9%	62.1%
27,576	SHELBY	3,181	777	2,371	33	1,594 D	24.4%	74.5%	24.7%	75.3%
26,929	SUMTER	1,393	24	1,369		1,345 D	1.7%	98.3%	1.7%	98.3%

ALABAMA

PRESIDENT 1936

1930 Census Population	County	Total Vote	Republican	Democratic	Other	Rep.-Dem. Plurality	Percentage Total Vote Rep.	Percentage Total Vote Dem.	Percentage Major Vote Rep.	Percentage Major Vote Dem.
45,241	TALLADEGA	4,391	489	3,751	151	3,262 D	11.1%	85.4%	11.5%	88.5%
31,188	TALLAPOOSA	3,772	141	3,625	6	3,484 D	3.7%	96.1%	3.7%	96.3%
64,153	TUSCALOOSA	6,393	332	6,029	32	5,697 D	5.2%	94.3%	5.2%	94.8%
59,445	WALKER	7,484	1,699	5,697	88	3,998 D	22.7%	76.1%	23.0%	77.0%
16,365	WASHINGTON	1,822	72	1,736	14	1,664 D	4.0%	95.3%	4.0%	96.0%
24,880	WILCOX	1,377	11	1,365	1	1,354 D	0.8%	99.1%	0.8%	99.2%
15,596	WINSTON	2,706	1,428	1,270	8	158 R	52.8%	46.9%	52.9%	47.1%
2,646,248	TOTAL	275,744	35,358	238,196	2,190	202,838 D	12.8%	86.4%	12.9%	87.1%

ALABAMA

PRESIDENT 1932

1930 Census Population	County	Total Vote	Republican	Democratic	Other	Rep.-Dem. Plurality	Percentage Total Vote Rep.	Percentage Total Vote Dem.	Percentage Major Vote Rep.	Percentage Major Vote Dem.
19,694	AUTAUGA	1,474	138	1,322	14	1,184 D	9.4%	89.7%	9.5%	90.5%
28,289	BALDWIN	2,781	544	2,098	139	1,554 D	19.6%	75.4%	20.6%	79.4%
32,425	BARBOUR	2,278	64	2,207	7	2,143 D	2.8%	96.9%	2.8%	97.2%
20,780	BIBB	1,812	145	1,636	31	1,491 D	8.0%	90.3%	8.1%	91.9%
28,020	BLOUNT	2,962	582	2,332	48	1,750 D	19.6%	78.7%	20.0%	80.0%
20,016	BULLOCK	1,017	12	1,004	1	992 D	1.2%	98.7%	1.2%	98.8%
30,195	BUTLER	2,364	74	2,280	10	2,206 D	3.1%	96.4%	3.1%	96.9%
55,611	CALHOUN	5,107	684	4,392	31	3,708 D	13.4%	86.0%	13.5%	86.5%
39,313	CHAMBERS	2,903	342	2,550	11	2,208 D	11.8%	87.8%	11.8%	88.2%
20,219	CHEROKEE	2,282	359	1,897	26	1,538 D	15.7%	83.1%	15.9%	84.1%
24,579	CHILTON	3,253	1,532	1,664	57	132 D	47.1%	51.2%	47.9%	52.1%
20,513	CHOCTAW	1,582	48	1,533	1	1,485 D	3.0%	96.9%	3.0%	97.0%
26,016	CLARKE	2,465	53	2,408	4	2,355 D	2.2%	97.7%	2.2%	97.8%
17,768	CLAY	3,050	931	2,103	16	1,172 D	30.5%	69.0%	30.7%	69.3%
12,877	CLEBURNE	1,812	405	1,403	4	998 D	22.4%	77.4%	22.4%	77.6%
32,556	COFFEE	2,965	95	2,868	2	2,773 D	3.2%	96.7%	3.2%	96.8%
29,860	COLBERT	3,244	312	2,908	24	2,596 D	9.6%	89.6%	9.7%	90.3%
25,429	CONECUH	2,239	114	2,125		2,011 D	5.1%	94.9%	5.1%	94.9%
12,460	COOSA	1,531	250	1,265	16	1,015 D	16.3%	82.6%	16.5%	83.5%
41,356	COVINGTON	3,968	99	3,855	14	3,756 D	2.5%	97.2%	2.5%	97.5%
23,656	CRENSHAW	2,340	127	2,200	13	2,073 D	5.4%	94.0%	5.5%	94.5%
41,051	CULLMAN	3,944	956	2,910	78	1,954 D	24.2%	73.8%	24.7%	75.3%
23,175	DALE	2,455	155	2,300		2,145 D	6.3%	93.7%	6.3%	93.7%
55,094	DALLAS	3,134	93	3,027	14	2,934 D	3.0%	96.6%	3.0%	97.0%
40,104	DE KALB	7,790	3,496	4,217	77	721 D	44.9%	54.1%	45.3%	54.7%
34,280	ELMORE	3,641	160	3,198	283	3,038 D	4.4%	87.8%	4.8%	95.2%
27,963	ESCAMBIA	2,184	157	2,024	3	1,867 D	7.2%	92.7%	7.2%	92.8%
63,399	ETOWAH	6,322	1,093	5,167	62	4,074 D	17.3%	81.7%	17.5%	82.5%
18,443	FAYETTE	2,769	733	2,013	23	1,280 D	26.5%	72.7%	26.7%	73.3%
25,372	FRANKLIN	4,457	1,547	2,876	34	1,329 D	34.7%	64.5%	35.0%	65.0%
30,104	GENEVA	2,852	270	2,559	23	2,289 D	9.5%	89.7%	9.5%	90.5%
19,745	GREENE	675	9	665	1	656 D	1.3%	98.5%	1.3%	98.7%
26,265	HALE	1,348	70	1,275	3	1,205 D	5.2%	94.6%	5.2%	94.8%
22,820	HENRY	1,787	42	1,741	4	1,699 D	2.4%	97.4%	2.4%	97.6%
45,935	HOUSTON	4,031	157	3,863	11	3,706 D	3.9%	95.8%	3.9%	96.1%
36,881	JACKSON	4,056	938	3,110	8	2,172 D	23.1%	76.7%	23.2%	76.8%
431,493	JEFFERSON	36,541	4,572	31,156	813	26,584 D	12.5%	85.3%	12.8%	87.2%
18,001	LAMAR	2,473	258	2,207	8	1,949 D	10.4%	89.2%	10.5%	89.5%
41,130	LAUDERDALE	3,789	432	3,336	21	2,904 D	11.4%	88.0%	11.5%	88.5%
26,942	LAWRENCE	2,219	299	1,920		1,621 D	13.5%	86.5%	13.5%	86.5%
36,063	LEE	2,102	103	1,988	11	1,885 D	4.9%	94.6%	4.9%	95.1%
36,629	LIMESTONE	2,780	107	2,667	6	2,560 D	3.8%	95.9%	3.9%	96.1%
22,878	LOWNDES	1,091	18	1,073		1,055 D	1.6%	98.4%	1.6%	98.4%
27,103	MACON	962	56	905	1	849 D	5.8%	94.1%	5.8%	94.2%
64,623	MADISON	5,399	559	4,792	48	4,233 D	10.4%	88.8%	10.4%	89.6%
36,426	MARENGO	2,197	50	2,097	50	2,047 D	2.3%	95.4%	2.3%	97.7%
25,967	MARION	2,883	545	2,325	13	1,780 D	18.9%	80.6%	19.0%	81.0%
39,802	MARSHALL	4,850	904	3,836	110	2,932 D	18.6%	79.1%	19.1%	80.9%
118,363	MOBILE	11,442	1,705	9,658	79	7,953 D	14.9%	84.4%	15.0%	85.0%
30,070	MONROE	2,043	66	1,972	5	1,906 D	3.2%	96.5%	3.2%	96.8%
98,671	MONTGOMERY	10,533	441	10,066	26	9,625 D	4.2%	95.6%	4.2%	95.8%
46,176	MORGAN	5,744	656	4,986	102	4,330 D	11.4%	86.8%	11.6%	88.4%
26,385	PERRY	1,454	37	1,382	35	1,345 D	2.5%	95.0%	2.6%	97.4%
24,902	PICKENS	1,697	128	1,479	90	1,351 D	7.5%	87.2%	8.0%	92.0%
32,240	PIKE	2,599	52	2,545	2	2,493 D	2.0%	97.9%	2.0%	98.0%
26,861	RANDOLPH	3,005	767	2,226	12	1,459 D	25.5%	74.1%	25.6%	74.4%
27,377	RUSSELL	2,037	46	1,984	7	1,938 D	2.3%	97.4%	2.3%	97.7%
24,510	ST. CLAIR	3,675	1,449	2,185	41	736 D	39.4%	59.5%	39.9%	60.1%
27,576	SHELBY	3,263	864	2,365	34	1,501 D	26.5%	72.5%	26.8%	73.2%
26,929	SUMTER	1,319	26	1,293		1,267 D	2.0%	98.0%	2.0%	98.0%

ALABAMA

PRESIDENT 1932

1930 Census Population	County	Total Vote	Republican	Democratic	Other	Rep.-Dem. Plurality	Percentage Total Vote Rep.	Percentage Total Vote Dem.	Percentage Major Vote Rep.	Percentage Major Vote Dem.
45,241	TALLADEGA	3,978	617	3,354	7	2,737 D	15.5%	84.3%	15.5%	84.5%
31,188	TALLAPOOSA	3,537	138	3,391	8	3,253 D	3.9%	95.9%	3.9%	96.1%
64,153	TUSCALOOSA	5,657	302	5,322	33	5,020 D	5.3%	94.1%	5.4%	94.6%
59,445	WALKER	6,371	1,583	4,734	54	3,151 D	24.8%	74.3%	25.1%	74.9%
16,365	WASHINGTON	1,389	81	1,307	1	1,226 D	5.8%	94.1%	5.8%	94.2%
24,880	WILCOX	1,381	23	1,358		1,335 D	1.7%	98.3%	1.7%	98.3%
15,596	WINSTON	2,019	1,005	1,006	8	1 D	49.8%	49.8%	50.0%	50.0%
2,646,248	TOTAL	245,303	34,675	207,910	2,718	173,235 D	14.1%	84.8%	14.3%	85.7%

ALABAMA

PRESIDENT 1928

1920 Census Population	County	Total Vote	Republican	Democratic	Other	Rep.-Dem. Plurality	Percentage: Total Vote Rep.	Percentage: Total Vote Dem.	Percentage: Major Vote Rep.	Percentage: Major Vote Dem.
18,908	AUTAUGA	1,566	683	883		200 D	43.6%	56.4%	43.6%	56.4%
20,730	BALDWIN	2,719	1,388	1,317	14	71 R	51.0%	48.4%	51.3%	48.7%
32,067	BARBOUR	2,374	845	1,506	23	661 D	35.6%	63.4%	35.9%	64.1%
23,144	BIBB	2,199	1,003	1,188	8	185 D	45.6%	54.0%	45.8%	54.2%
25,538	BLOUNT	3,352	1,745	1,607		138 R	52.1%	47.9%	52.1%	47.9%
25,333	BULLOCK	948	249	699		450 D	26.3%	73.7%	26.3%	73.7%
29,531	BUTLER	1,934	699	1,235		536 D	36.1%	63.9%	36.1%	63.9%
47,822	CALHOUN	4,655	2,537	2,117	1	420 R	54.5%	45.5%	54.5%	45.5%
41,201	CHAMBERS	2,731	1,732	999		733 R	63.4%	36.6%	63.4%	36.6%
20,862	CHEROKEE	2,413	1,515	894	4	621 R	62.8%	37.0%	62.9%	37.1%
22,770	CHILTON	4,593	3,186	1,402	5	1,784 R	69.4%	30.5%	69.4%	30.6%
20,753	CHOCTAW	1,671	429	1,242		813 D	25.7%	74.3%	25.7%	74.3%
26,409	CLARKE	2,598	936	1,662		726 D	36.0%	64.0%	36.0%	64.0%
22,645	CLAY	2,868	1,889	978	1	911 R	65.9%	34.1%	65.9%	34.1%
13,360	CLEBURNE	1,902	1,108	794		314 R	58.3%	41.7%	58.3%	41.7%
30,070	COFFEE	2,645	1,036	1,609		573 D	39.2%	60.8%	39.2%	60.8%
31,997	COLBERT	3,948	1,249	2,596	103	1,347 D	31.6%	65.8%	32.5%	67.5%
24,593	CONECUH	1,971	1,113	858		255 R	56.5%	43.5%	56.5%	43.5%
14,839	COOSA	1,778	1,078	699	1	379 R	60.6%	39.3%	60.7%	39.3%
38,103	COVINGTON	3,686	1,681	2,000	5	319 D	45.6%	54.3%	45.7%	54.3%
23,017	CRENSHAW	2,292	978	1,314		336 D	42.7%	57.3%	42.7%	57.3%
33,034	CULLMAN	4,533	2,959	1,574		1,385 R	65.3%	34.7%	65.3%	34.7%
22,711	DALE	2,234	1,000	1,233	1	233 D	44.8%	55.2%	44.8%	55.2%
54,697	DALLAS	2,611	705	1,905	1	1,200 D	27.0%	73.0%	27.0%	73.0%
34,426	DE KALB	9,720	5,761	3,957	2	1,804 R	59.3%	40.7%	59.3%	40.7%
28,085	ELMORE	3,081	1,770	1,309	2	461 R	57.4%	42.5%	57.5%	42.5%
22,464	ESCAMBIA	2,832	1,754	1,077	1	677 R	61.9%	38.0%	62.0%	38.0%
47,275	ETOWAH	6,134	3,612	2,484	38	1,128 R	58.9%	40.5%	59.3%	40.7%
18,365	FAYETTE	2,818	1,686	1,131	1	555 R	59.8%	40.1%	59.9%	40.1%
22,011	FRANKLIN	5,222	2,937	2,279	6	658 R	56.2%	43.6%	56.3%	43.7%
29,315	GENEVA	3,018	1,533	1,485		48 R	50.8%	49.2%	50.8%	49.2%
18,133	GREENE	640	39	601		562 D	6.1%	93.9%	6.1%	93.9%
24,289	HALE	1,451	403	1,048		645 D	27.8%	72.2%	27.8%	72.2%
21,547	HENRY	1,613	796	815	2	19 D	49.3%	50.5%	49.4%	50.6%
37,334	HOUSTON	4,256	1,963	2,290	3	327 D	46.1%	53.8%	46.2%	53.8%
35,864	JACKSON	5,247	3,081	2,153	13	928 R	58.7%	41.0%	58.9%	41.1%
310,054	JEFFERSON	34,907	18,060	16,735	112	1,325 R	51.7%	47.9%	51.9%	48.1%
18,149	LAMAR	2,216	804	1,412		608 D	36.3%	63.7%	36.3%	63.7%
39,556	LAUDERDALE	4,174	1,410	2,763	1	1,353 D	33.8%	66.2%	33.8%	66.2%
24,307	LAWRENCE	2,046	1,008	1,035	3	27 D	49.3%	50.6%	49.3%	50.7%
32,821	LEE	2,455	1,016	1,436	3	420 D	41.4%	58.5%	41.4%	58.6%
31,341	LIMESTONE	2,096	407	1,689		1,282 D	19.4%	80.6%	19.4%	80.6%
25,406	LOWNDES	883	180	703		523 D	20.4%	79.6%	20.4%	79.6%
23,561	MACON	877	348	526	3	178 D	39.7%	60.0%	39.8%	60.2%
51,268	MADISON	5,378	2,695	2,681	2	14 R	50.1%	49.9%	50.1%	49.9%
36,065	MARENGO	2,650	752	1,898		1,146 D	28.4%	71.6%	28.4%	71.6%
22,008	MARION	3,029	1,488	1,541		53 D	49.1%	50.9%	49.1%	50.9%
32,669	MARSHALL	4,844	2,511	2,322	11	189 R	51.8%	47.9%	52.0%	48.0%
100,117	MOBILE	11,033	5,058	5,965	10	907 D	45.8%	54.1%	45.9%	54.1%
28,884	MONROE	2,417	1,074	1,343		269 D	44.4%	55.6%	44.4%	55.6%
80,853	MONTGOMERY	9,464	3,114	6,347	3	3,233 D	32.9%	67.1%	32.9%	67.1%
40,196	MORGAN	7,460	4,085	3,366	9	719 R	54.8%	45.1%	54.8%	45.2%
25,373	PERRY	1,702	459	1,242	1	783 D	27.0%	73.0%	27.0%	73.0%
25,353	PICKENS	1,662	634	1,028		394 D	38.1%	61.9%	38.1%	61.9%
31,631	PIKE	2,375	552	1,819	4	1,267 D	23.2%	76.6%	23.3%	76.7%
27,064	RANDOLPH	3,074	1,815	1,257	2	558 R	59.0%	40.9%	59.1%	40.9%
27,448	RUSSELL	1,197	333	846	18	513 D	27.8%	70.7%	28.2%	71.8%
23,383	ST. CLAIR	3,896	2,581	1,313	2	1,268 R	66.2%	33.7%	66.3%	33.7%
27,097	SHELBY	4,203	2,502	1,679	22	823 R	59.5%	39.9%	59.8%	40.2%
25,569	SUMTER	1,206	191	1,015		824 D	15.8%	84.2%	15.8%	84.2%

ALABAMA

PRESIDENT 1928

1920 Census Population	County	Total Vote	Republican	Democratic	Other	Rep.-Dem. Plurality	Percentage Total Vote Rep.	Percentage Total Vote Dem.	Percentage Major Vote Rep.	Percentage Major Vote Dem.
41,005	TALLADEGA	3,308	1,602	1,693	13	91 D	48.4%	51.2%	48.6%	51.4%
29,744	TALLAPOOSA	3,107	1,257	1,849	1	592 D	40.5%	59.5%	40.5%	59.5%
53,680	TUSCALOOSA	3,981	1,210	2,769	2	1,559 D	30.4%	69.6%	30.4%	69.6%
50,593	WALKER	7,863	3,635	4,228		593 D	46.2%	53.8%	46.2%	53.8%
14,279	WASHINGTON	1,234	515	718	1	203 D	41.7%	58.2%	41.8%	58.2%
31,080	WILCOX	1,246	266	979	1	713 D	21.3%	78.6%	21.4%	78.6%
14,378	WINSTON	2,745	2,085	659	1	1,426 R	76.0%	24.0%	76.0%	24.0%
2,348,174	TOTAL	248,981	120,725	127,796	460	7,071 D	48.5%	51.3%	48.6%	51.4%

ALABAMA

PRESIDENT 1924

1920 Census Population	County	Total Vote	Republican	Democratic	Other	Rep.-Dem. Plurality	Percentage Total Vote Rep.	Total Vote Dem.	Major Vote Rep.	Major Vote Dem.
18,908	AUTAUGA	954	146	781	27	635 D	15.3%	81.9%	15.7%	84.3%
20,730	BALDWIN	1,978	549	1,023	406	474 D	27.8%	51.7%	34.9%	65.1%
32,067	BARBOUR	1,463	78	1,340	45	1,262 D	5.3%	91.6%	5.5%	94.5%
23,144	BIBB	1,374	251	875	248	624 D	18.3%	63.7%	22.3%	77.7%
25,538	BLOUNT	3,710	1,518	2,083	109	565 D	40.9%	56.1%	42.2%	57.8%
25,333	BULLOCK	772	8	763	1	755 D	1.0%	98.8%	1.0%	99.0%
29,531	BUTLER	1,260	95	1,050	115	955 D	7.5%	83.3%	8.3%	91.7%
47,822	CALHOUN	2,819	766	1,907	146	1,141 D	27.2%	67.6%	28.7%	71.3%
41,201	CHAMBERS	2,112	146	1,922	44	1,776 D	6.9%	91.0%	7.1%	92.9%
20,862	CHEROKEE	2,276	845	1,380	51	535 D	37.1%	60.6%	38.0%	62.0%
22,770	CHILTON	2,524	1,595	848	81	747 R	63.2%	33.6%	65.3%	34.7%
20,753	CHOCTAW	1,044	19	1,021	4	1,002 D	1.8%	97.8%	1.8%	98.2%
26,409	CLARKE	1,152	78	1,059	15	981 D	6.8%	91.9%	6.9%	93.1%
22,645	CLAY	2,667	1,017	1,597	53	580 D	38.1%	59.9%	38.9%	61.1%
13,360	CLEBURNE	1,360	696	622	42	74 R	51.2%	45.7%	52.8%	47.2%
30,070	COFFEE	1,945	323	1,597	25	1,274 D	16.6%	82.1%	16.8%	83.2%
31,997	COLBERT	2,278	576	1,503	199	927 D	25.3%	66.0%	27.7%	72.3%
24,593	CONECUH	1,084	92	955	37	863 D	8.5%	88.1%	8.8%	91.2%
14,839	COOSA	1,314	508	790	16	282 D	38.7%	60.1%	39.1%	60.9%
38,103	COVINGTON	2,068	156	1,776	136	1,620 D	7.5%	85.9%	8.1%	91.9%
23,017	CRENSHAW	1,243	117	1,107	19	990 D	9.4%	89.1%	9.6%	90.4%
33,034	CULLMAN	3,633	1,639	1,809	185	170 D	45.1%	49.8%	47.5%	52.5%
22,711	DALE	1,441	297	1,117	27	820 D	20.6%	77.5%	21.0%	79.0%
54,697	DALLAS	2,123	50	1,948	125	1,898 D	2.4%	91.8%	2.5%	97.5%
34,426	DE KALB	6,437	3,434	3,003		431 R	53.3%	46.7%	53.3%	46.7%
28,085	ELMORE	1,333	219	1,088	26	869 D	16.4%	81.6%	16.8%	83.2%
22,464	ESCAMBIA	1,420	152	1,217	51	1,065 D	10.7%	85.7%	11.1%	88.9%
47,275	ETOWAH	5,017	1,664	3,081	272	1,417 D	33.2%	61.4%	35.1%	64.9%
18,365	FAYETTE	2,368	977	1,358	33	381 D	41.3%	57.3%	41.8%	58.2%
22,011	FRANKLIN	4,283	2,230	1,985	68	245 R	52.1%	46.3%	52.9%	47.1%
29,315	GENEVA	1,713	477	1,191	45	714 D	27.8%	69.5%	28.6%	71.4%
18,133	GREENE	415	5	408	2	403 D	1.2%	98.3%	1.2%	98.8%
24,289	HALE	885	23	856	6	833 D	2.6%	96.7%	2.6%	97.4%
21,547	HENRY	1,035	179	816	40	637 D	17.3%	78.8%	18.0%	82.0%
37,334	HOUSTON	2,064	242	1,731	91	1,489 D	11.7%	83.9%	12.3%	87.7%
35,864	JACKSON	2,909	885	1,923	101	1,038 D	30.4%	66.1%	31.5%	68.5%
310,054	JEFFERSON	23,780	5,678	15,133	2,969	9,455 D	23.9%	63.6%	27.3%	72.7%
18,149	LAMAR	1,369	262	1,087	20	825 D	19.1%	79.4%	19.4%	80.6%
39,556	LAUDERDALE	3,178	823	2,266	89	1,443 D	25.9%	71.3%	26.6%	73.4%
24,307	LAWRENCE	1,472	468	990	14	522 D	31.8%	67.3%	32.1%	67.9%
32,821	LEE	1,504	98	1,290	116	1,192 D	6.5%	85.8%	7.1%	92.9%
31,341	LIMESTONE	1,620	136	1,415	69	1,279 D	8.4%	87.3%	8.8%	91.2%
25,406	LOWNDES	628	5	602	21	597 D	0.8%	95.9%	0.8%	99.2%
23,561	MACON	589	48	538	3	490 D	8.1%	91.3%	8.2%	91.8%
51,268	MADISON	2,586	368	2,166	52	1,798 D	14.2%	83.8%	14.5%	85.5%
36,065	MARENGO	1,263	17	1,243	3	1,226 D	1.3%	98.4%	1.3%	98.7%
22,008	MARION	1,372		1,359	13	1,359 D		99.1%		100.0%
32,669	MARSHALL	4,433	1,718	2,629	86	911 D	38.8%	59.3%	39.5%	60.5%
100,117	MOBILE	6,355	1,814	4,125	416	2,311 D	28.5%	64.9%	30.5%	69.5%
28,884	MONROE	1,202	22	1,155	25	1,133 D	1.8%	96.1%	1.9%	98.1%
80,853	MONTGOMERY	5,042	233	4,422	387	4,189 D	4.6%	87.7%	5.0%	95.0%
40,196	MORGAN	3,139	519	2,247	373	1,728 D	16.5%	71.6%	18.8%	81.2%
25,373	PERRY	965	25	928	12	903 D	2.6%	96.2%	2.6%	97.4%
25,353	PICKENS	1,195	132	1,045	18	913 D	11.0%	87.4%	11.2%	88.8%
31,631	PIKE	1,882	30	1,832	20	1,802 D	1.6%	97.3%	1.6%	98.4%
27,064	RANDOLPH	2,001	669	1,307	25	638 D	33.4%	65.3%	33.9%	66.1%
27,448	RUSSELL	519	14	474	31	460 D	2.7%	91.3%	2.9%	97.1%
23,383	ST. CLAIR	2,828	1,432	1,281	115	151 R	50.6%	45.3%	52.8%	47.2%
27,097	SHELBY	3,827	1,753	1,882	192	129 D	45.8%	49.2%	48.2%	51.8%
25,569	SUMTER	884	28	837	19	809 D	3.2%	94.7%	3.2%	96.8%

ALABAMA

PRESIDENT 1924

1920 Census Population	County	Total Vote	Republican	Democratic	Other	Rep.-Dem. Plurality	Percentage Total Vote Rep.	Total Vote Dem.	Major Vote Rep.	Major Vote Dem.
41,005	TALLADEGA	2,412	628	1,730	54	1,102 D	26.0%	71.7%	26.6%	73.4%
29,744	TALLAPOOSA	1,720	1	1,713	6	1,712 D	0.1%	99.6%	0.1%	99.9%
53,680	TUSCALOOSA	2,754	247	2,363	144	2,116 D	9.0%	85.8%	9.5%	90.5%
50,593	WALKER	6,138	2,446	3,351	341	905 D	39.9%	54.6%	42.2%	57.8%
14,279	WASHINGTON	678	55	610	13	555 D	8.1%	90.0%	8.3%	91.7%
31,080	WILCOX	959	6	938	15	932 D	0.6%	97.8%	0.6%	99.4%
14,378	WINSTON	1,796	1,096	650	50	446 R	61.0%	36.2%	62.8%	37.2%
2,348,174	TOTAL	164,563	42,823	113,138	8,602	70,315 D	26.0%	68.8%	27.5%	72.5%

ALABAMA

PRESIDENT 1920

1920 Census Population	County	Total Vote	Republican	Democratic	Other	Rep.-Dem. Plurality	Percentage Total Vote Rep.	Total Vote Dem.	Major Vote Rep.	Major Vote Dem.
18,908	AUTAUGA	1,139	210	918	11	708 D	18.4%	80.6%	18.6%	81.4%
20,730	BALDWIN	1,937	556	1,230	151	674 D	28.7%	63.5%	31.1%	68.9%
32,067	BARBOUR	1,786	203	1,568	15	1,365 D	11.4%	87.8%	11.5%	88.5%
23,144	BIBB	2,148	364	1,643	141	1,279 D	16.9%	76.5%	18.1%	81.9%
25,538	BLOUNT	7,050	3,465	3,535	50	70 D	49.1%	50.1%	49.5%	50.5%
25,333	BULLOCK	880	2	877	1	875 D	0.2%	99.7%	0.2%	99.8%
29,531	BUTLER	1,471	153	1,299	19	1,146 D	10.4%	88.3%	10.5%	89.5%
47,822	CALHOUN	4,601	1,139	3,423	39	2,284 D	24.8%	74.4%	25.0%	75.0%
41,201	CHAMBERS	2,330	322	1,994	14	1,672 D	13.8%	85.6%	13.9%	86.1%
20,862	CHEROKEE	3,603	1,576	1,969	58	393 D	43.7%	54.6%	44.5%	55.5%
22,770	CHILTON	3,289	2,273	962	54	1,311 R	69.1%	29.2%	70.3%	29.7%
20,753	CHOCTAW	1,156	82	1,071	3	989 D	7.1%	92.6%	7.1%	92.9%
26,409	CLARKE	1,302	43	1,253	6	1,210 D	3.3%	96.2%	3.3%	96.7%
22,645	CLAY	4,301	2,133	2,165	3	32 D	49.6%	50.3%	49.6%	50.4%
13,360	CLEBURNE	1,657	971	684	2	287 R	58.6%	41.3%	58.7%	41.3%
30,070	COFFEE	2,408	673	1,721	14	1,048 D	27.9%	71.5%	28.1%	71.9%
31,997	COLBERT	2,581	650	1,869	62	1,219 D	25.2%	72.4%	25.8%	74.2%
24,593	CONECUH	1,504	189	1,315		1,126 D	12.6%	87.4%	12.6%	87.4%
14,839	COOSA	1,764	741	1,007	16	266 D	42.0%	57.1%	42.4%	57.6%
38,103	COVINGTON	2,654	548	2,039	67	1,491 D	20.6%	76.8%	21.2%	78.8%
23,017	CRENSHAW	1,729	310	1,411	8	1,101 D	17.9%	81.6%	18.0%	82.0%
33,034	CULLMAN	6,101	3,492	2,566	43	926 R	57.2%	42.1%	57.6%	42.4%
22,711	DALE	2,175	768	1,386	21	618 D	35.3%	63.7%	35.7%	64.3%
54,697	DALLAS	2,780	78	2,702		2,624 D	2.8%	97.2%	2.8%	97.2%
34,426	DE KALB	8,795	4,852	3,894	49	958 R	55.2%	44.3%	55.5%	44.5%
28,085	ELMORE	2,121	353	1,762	6	1,409 D	16.6%	83.1%	16.7%	83.3%
22,464	ESCAMBIA	1,637	178	1,455	4	1,277 D	10.9%	88.9%	10.9%	89.1%
47,275	ETOWAH	9,238	3,218	5,917	103	2,699 D	34.8%	64.1%	35.2%	64.8%
18,365	FAYETTE	3,309	1,865	1,413	31	452 R	56.4%	42.7%	56.9%	43.1%
22,011	FRANKLIN	5,089	2,930	2,094	65	836 R	57.6%	41.1%	58.3%	41.7%
29,315	GENEVA	2,612	1,088	1,488	36	400 D	41.7%	57.0%	42.2%	57.8%
18,133	GREENE	531	10	520	1	510 D	1.9%	97.9%	1.9%	98.1%
24,289	HALE	975	18	953	4	935 D	1.8%	97.7%	1.9%	98.1%
21,547	HENRY	1,205	489	715	1	226 D	40.6%	59.3%	40.6%	59.4%
37,334	HOUSTON	2,656	571	2,045	40	1,474 D	21.5%	77.0%	21.8%	78.2%
35,864	JACKSON	4,013	1,483	2,513	17	1,030 D	37.0%	62.6%	37.1%	62.9%
310,054	JEFFERSON	32,939	7,124	24,982	833	17,858 D	21.6%	75.8%	22.2%	77.8%
18,149	LAMAR	2,220	576	1,628	16	1,052 D	25.9%	73.3%	26.1%	73.9%
39,556	LAUDERDALE	3,870	1,164	2,644	62	1,480 D	30.1%	68.3%	30.6%	69.4%
24,307	LAWRENCE	1,782	831	935	16	104 D	46.6%	52.5%	47.1%	52.9%
32,821	LEE	1,893	155	1,620	118	1,465 D	8.2%	85.6%	8.7%	91.3%
31,341	LIMESTONE	2,114	285	1,812	17	1,527 D	13.5%	85.7%	13.6%	86.4%
25,406	LOWNDES	733	6	727		721 D	0.8%	99.2%	0.8%	99.2%
23,561	MACON	759	64	693	2	629 D	8.4%	91.3%	8.5%	91.5%
51,268	MADISON	3,340	489	2,822	29	2,333 D	14.6%	84.5%	14.8%	85.2%
36,065	MARENGO	1,412	42	1,370		1,328 D	3.0%	97.0%	3.0%	97.0%
22,008	MARION	4,329	1,865	2,461	3	596 D	43.1%	56.8%	43.1%	56.9%
32,669	MARSHALL	7,958	3,879	4,041	38	162 D	48.7%	50.8%	49.0%	51.0%
100,117	MOBILE	9,023	2,681	6,171	171	3,490 D	29.7%	68.4%	30.3%	69.7%
28,884	MONROE	1,328	20	1,295	13	1,275 D	1.5%	97.5%	1.5%	98.5%
80,853	MONTGOMERY	6,775	314	6,411	50	6,097 D	4.6%	94.6%	4.7%	95.3%
40,196	MORGAN	5,329	1,201	4,057	71	2,856 D	22.5%	76.1%	22.8%	77.2%
25,373	PERRY	1,243	34	1,195	14	1,161 D	2.7%	96.1%	2.8%	97.2%
25,353	PICKENS	1,702	263	1,419	20	1,156 D	15.5%	83.4%	15.6%	84.4%
31,631	PIKE	1,802	204	1,586	12	1,382 D	11.3%	88.0%	11.4%	88.6%
27,064	RANDOLPH	2,479	1,113	1,357	9	244 D	44.9%	54.7%	45.1%	54.9%
27,448	RUSSELL	748	29	671	48	642 D	3.9%	89.7%	4.1%	95.9%
23,383	ST. CLAIR	4,653	2,561	1,934	158	627 R	55.0%	41.6%	57.0%	43.0%
27,097	SHELBY	5,782	3,235	2,523	24	712 R	55.9%	43.6%	56.2%	43.8%
25,569	SUMTER	1,106	15	1,088	3	1,073 D	1.4%	98.4%	1.4%	98.6%

ALABAMA

PRESIDENT 1920

1920 Census Population	County	Total Vote	Republican	Democratic	Other	Rep.-Dem. Plurality	Percentage Total Vote Rep.	Percentage Total Vote Dem.	Percentage Major Vote Rep.	Percentage Major Vote Dem.
41,005	TALLADEGA	3,089	931	2,137	21	1,206 D	30.1%	69.2%	30.3%	69.7%
29,744	TALLAPOOSA	2,552	269	2,257	26	1,988 D	10.5%	88.4%	10.6%	89.4%
53,680	TUSCALOOSA	3,956	491	3,438	27	2,947 D	12.4%	86.9%	12.5%	87.5%
50,593	WALKER	9,399	4,488	4,703	208	215 D	47.7%	50.0%	48.8%	51.2%
14,279	WASHINGTON	663	85	575	3	490 D	12.8%	86.7%	12.9%	87.1%
31,080	WILCOX	1,102	2	1,099	1	1,097 D	0.2%	99.7%	0.2%	99.8%
14,378	WINSTON	3,344	2,307	1,037		1,270 R	69.0%	31.0%	69.0%	31.0%
2,348,174	TOTAL	233,951	74,719	156,064	3,168	81,345 D	31.9%	66.7%	32.4%	67.6%

ALABAMA

ELECTION NOTES

1956 Other vote was Independent electors.

1952 Other vote was Hamblen (Prohibition).

1948 The national Democratic candidates were not represented on the ballot. A special four-column table which gives the Thurmond (States Rights) vote is used to detail this election. Other vote was 1,522 Wallace (Progressive); 1,085 Watson (Prohibition).

1944 Other vote was 1,095 Watson (Prohibition); 190 Thomas (Socialist).

1940 Other vote was 700 Babson (Prohibition); 509 Browder (Communist); 100 Thomas (Socialist).

1936 Other vote was 719 Colvin (Prohibition); 678 Browder (Communist); 551 Lemke (Union); 242 Thomas (Socialist).

1932 Other vote was 2,030 Thomas (Socialist); 675 Foster (Communist); 13 Upshaw (Prohibition).

1928 Other vote was Thomas (Socialist).

1924 Other vote was 8,040 LaFollette (Progressive); 562 Faris (Prohibition).

1920 Other vote was 2,402 Debs (Socialist); 766 Watkins (Prohibition).

ARIZONA

POPULAR VOTE FOR PRESIDENT 1920 TO 1956

Year	Total Vote	Republican Vote	Republican Candidate	Democratic Vote	Democratic Candidate	Other Vote	Plurality	Percentage Total Vote Rep.	Percentage Total Vote Dem.	Percentage Major Vote Rep.	Percentage Major Vote Dem.
1956	290,173	176,990	Eisenhower, Dwight D.	112,880	Stevenson, Adlai E.	303	64,110 R	61.0%	38.9%	61.1%	38.9%
1952	260,570	152,042	Eisenhower, Dwight D.	108,528	Stevenson, Adlai E.		43,514 R	58.3%	41.7%	58.3%	41.7%
1948	177,065	77,597	Dewey, Thomas E.	95,251	Truman, Harry S.	4,217	17,654 D	43.8%	53.8%	44.9%	55.1%
1944	137,634	56,287	Dewey, Thomas E.	80,926	Roosevelt, Franklin D.	421	24,639 D	40.9%	58.8%	41.0%	59.0%
1940	150,039	54,030	Willkie, Wendell	95,267	Roosevelt, Franklin D.	742	41,237 D	36.0%	63.5%	36.2%	63.8%
1936	124,163	33,433	Landon, Alfred M.	86,722	Roosevelt, Franklin D.	4,008	53,289 D	26.9%	69.8%	27.8%	72.2%
1932	118,251	36,104	Hoover, Herbert C.	79,264	Roosevelt, Franklin D.	2,883	43,160 D	30.5%	67.0%	31.3%	68.7%
1928	91,254	52,533	Hoover, Herbert C.	38,537	Smith, Alfred E.	184	13,996 R	57.6%	42.2%	57.7%	42.3%
1924	73,961	30,516	Coolidge, Calvin	26,235	Davis, John W.	17,210	4,281 R	41.3%	35.5%	53.8%	46.2%
1920	66,803	37,016	Harding, Warren G.	29,546	Cox, James M.	241	7,470 R	55.4%	44.2%	55.6%	44.4%

ELECTORAL COLLEGE VOTE 1920 TO 1956

Year	Total	Republican	Democratic	Other
1956	4	4	—	—
1952	4	4	—	—
1948	4	—	4	—
1944	4	—	4	—
1940	3	—	3	—
1936	3	—	3	—
1932	3	—	3	—
1928	3	3	—	—
1924	3	3	—	—
1920	3	3	—	—

ARIZONA

COCONINO
MOHAVE
NAVAJO
APACHE
YAVAPAI
GILA
LA PAZ
MARICOPA
GREENLEE
PINAL
GRAHAM
YUMA
PIMA
COCHISE
SANTA CRUZ

ARIZONA

PRESIDENT 1956

1950 Census Population	County	Total Vote	Republican	Democratic	Other	Rep.-Dem. Plurality	Percentage Total Vote Rep.	Total Vote Dem.	Major Vote Rep.	Major Vote Dem.
27,767	APACHE	2,667	1,685	981	1	704 R	63.2%	36.8%	63.2%	36.8%
31,488	COCHISE	12,230	6,893	5,328	9	1,565 R	56.4%	43.6%	56.4%	43.6%
23,910	COCONINO	6,369	4,044	2,314	11	1,730 R	63.5%	36.3%	63.6%	36.4%
24,158	GILA	8,260	4,234	4,026		208 R	51.3%	48.7%	51.3%	48.7%
12,985	GRAHAM	4,072	2,384	1,688		696 R	58.5%	41.5%	58.5%	41.5%
12,805	GREENLEE	4,495	1,784	2,711		927 D	39.7%	60.3%	39.7%	60.3%
331,770	MARICOPA	146,341	92,140	54,010	191	38,130 R	63.0%	36.9%	63.0%	37.0%
8,510	MOHAVE	2,497	1,523	968	6	555 R	61.0%	38.8%	61.1%	38.9%
29,446	NAVAJO	5,970	3,928	2,033	9	1,895 R	65.8%	34.1%	65.9%	34.1%
141,216	PIMA	62,885	39,298	23,536	51	15,762 R	62.5%	37.4%	62.5%	37.5%
43,191	PINAL	10,842	5,762	5,063	17	699 R	53.1%	46.7%	53.2%	46.8%
9,344	SANTA CRUZ	2,778	1,646	1,131	1	515 R	59.3%	40.7%	59.3%	40.7%
24,991	YAVAPAI	9,654	6,339	3,315		3,024 R	65.7%	34.3%	65.7%	34.3%
28,006	YUMA	11,113	5,330	5,776	7	446 D	48.0%	52.0%	48.0%	52.0%
749,587	TOTAL	290,173	176,990	112,880	303	64,110 R	61.0%	38.9%	61.1%	38.9%

ARIZONA

PRESIDENT 1952

1950 Census Population	County	Total Vote	Republican	Democratic	Other	Rep.-Dem. Plurality	Percentage Total Vote Rep.	Total Vote Dem.	Major Vote Rep.	Major Vote Dem.
27,767	APACHE	2,960	1,767	1,193		574 R	59.7%	40.3%	59.7%	40.3%
31,488	COCHISE	12,135	6,495	5,640		855 R	53.5%	46.5%	53.5%	46.5%
23,910	COCONINO	6,235	3,827	2,408		1,419 R	61.4%	38.6%	61.4%	38.6%
24,158	GILA	8,698	3,770	4,928		1,158 D	43.3%	56.7%	43.3%	56.7%
12,985	GRAHAM	4,391	2,191	2,200		9 D	49.9%	50.1%	49.9%	50.1%
12,805	GREENLEE	4,396	1,377	3,019		1,642 D	31.3%	68.7%	31.3%	68.7%
331,770	MARICOPA	127,534	77,249	50,285		26,964 R	60.6%	39.4%	60.6%	39.4%
8,510	MOHAVE	2,812	1,746	1,066		680 R	62.1%	37.9%	62.1%	37.9%
29,446	NAVAJO	6,071	3,478	2,593		885 R	57.3%	42.7%	57.3%	42.7%
141,216	PIMA	53,350	32,113	21,237		10,876 R	60.2%	39.8%	60.2%	39.8%
43,191	PINAL	9,507	4,985	4,522		463 R	52.4%	47.6%	52.4%	47.6%
9,344	SANTA CRUZ	3,081	1,716	1,365		351 R	55.7%	44.3%	55.7%	44.3%
24,991	YAVAPAI	10,195	6,567	3,628		2,939 R	64.4%	35.6%	64.4%	35.6%
28,006	YUMA	9,205	4,761	4,444		317 R	51.7%	48.3%	51.7%	48.3%
749,587	TOTAL	260,570	152,042	108,528		43,514 R	58.3%	41.7%	58.3%	41.7%

ARIZONA

PRESIDENT 1948

1940 Census Population	County	Total Vote	Republican	Democratic	Other	Rep.-Dem. Plurality	Percentage Total Vote Rep.	Percentage Total Vote Dem.	Percentage Major Vote Rep.	Percentage Major Vote Dem.
24,095	APACHE	2,455	970	1,480	5	510 D	39.5%	60.3%	39.6%	60.4%
34,627	COCHISE	10,370	3,854	6,198	318	2,344 D	37.2%	59.8%	38.3%	61.7%
18,770	COCONINO	4,441	2,093	2,309	39	216 D	47.1%	52.0%	47.5%	52.5%
23,867	GILA	7,265	2,329	4,780	156	2,451 D	32.1%	65.8%	32.8%	67.2%
12,113	GRAHAM	3,386	1,209	2,139	38	930 D	35.7%	63.2%	36.1%	63.9%
8,698	GREENLEE	2,961	680	2,069	212	1,389 D	23.0%	69.9%	24.7%	75.3%
186,193	MARICOPA	78,992	36,585	40,498	1,909	3,913 D	46.3%	51.3%	47.5%	52.5%
8,591	MOHAVE	2,712	1,167	1,499	46	332 D	43.0%	55.3%	43.8%	56.2%
25,309	NAVAJO	4,566	1,841	2,669	56	828 D	40.3%	58.5%	40.8%	59.2%
72,838	PIMA	35,625	16,968	17,692	965	724 D	47.6%	49.7%	49.0%	51.0%
28,841	PINAL	5,887	2,232	3,572	83	1,340 D	37.9%	60.7%	38.5%	61.5%
9,482	SANTA CRUZ	2,519	1,058	1,424	37	366 D	42.0%	56.5%	42.6%	57.4%
26,511	YAVAPAI	8,922	4,287	4,439	196	152 D	48.0%	49.8%	49.1%	50.9%
19,326	YUMA	6,964	2,324	4,483	157	2,159 D	33.4%	64.4%	34.1%	65.9%
499,261	TOTAL	177,065	77,597	95,251	4,217	17,654 D	43.8%	53.8%	44.9%	55.1%

ARIZONA

PRESIDENT 1944

1940 Census Population	County	Total Vote	Republican	Democratic	Other	Rep.-Dem. Plurality	Percentage Total Vote Rep.	Percentage Total Vote Dem.	Percentage Major Vote Rep.	Percentage Major Vote Dem.
24,095	APACHE	1,968	728	1,238	2	510 D	37.0%	62.9%	37.0%	63.0%
34,627	COCHISE	10,319	3,371	6,935	13	3,564 D	32.7%	67.2%	32.7%	67.3%
18,770	COCONINO	4,028	1,786	2,236	6	450 D	44.3%	55.5%	44.4%	55.6%
23,867	GILA	7,107	2,260	4,818	29	2,558 D	31.8%	67.8%	31.9%	68.1%
12,113	GRAHAM	3,549	1,151	2,393	5	1,242 D	32.4%	67.4%	32.5%	67.5%
8,698	GREENLEE	2,704	739	1,956	9	1,217 D	27.3%	72.3%	27.4%	72.6%
186,193	MARICOPA	57,258	24,853	32,197	208	7,344 D	43.4%	56.2%	43.6%	56.4%
8,591	MOHAVE	2,284	974	1,303	7	329 D	42.6%	57.0%	42.8%	57.2%
25,309	NAVAJO	4,252	1,579	2,660	13	1,081 D	37.1%	62.6%	37.2%	62.8%
72,838	PIMA	23,913	10,850	13,006	57	2,156 D	45.4%	54.4%	45.5%	54.5%
28,841	PINAL	4,957	1,909	3,026	22	1,117 D	38.5%	61.0%	38.7%	61.3%
9,482	SANTA CRUZ	2,022	727	1,291	4	564 D	36.0%	63.8%	36.0%	64.0%
26,511	YAVAPAI	7,960	3,529	4,395	36	866 D	44.3%	55.2%	44.5%	55.5%
19,326	YUMA	5,313	1,831	3,472	10	1,641 D	34.5%	65.3%	34.5%	65.5%
499,261	TOTAL	137,634	56,287	80,926	421	24,639 D	40.9%	58.8%	41.0%	59.0%

ARIZONA

PRESIDENT 1940

1940 Census Population	County	Total Vote	Republican	Democratic	Other	Rep.-Dem. Plurality	Percentage Total Vote Rep.	Total Vote Dem.	Major Vote Rep.	Major Vote Dem.
24,095	APACHE	2,898	926	1,969	3	1,043 D	32.0%	67.9%	32.0%	68.0%
34,627	COCHISE	11,950	3,170	8,748	32	5,578 D	26.5%	73.2%	26.6%	73.4%
18,770	COCONINO	4,951	1,913	3,025	13	1,112 D	38.6%	61.1%	38.7%	61.3%
23,867	GILA	8,407	2,624	5,752	31	3,128 D	31.2%	68.4%	31.3%	68.7%
12,113	GRAHAM	4,310	1,161	3,130	19	1,969 D	26.9%	72.6%	27.1%	72.9%
8,698	GREENLEE	2,803	619	2,175	9	1,556 D	22.1%	77.6%	22.2%	77.8%
186,193	MARICOPA	58,079	22,610	35,055	414	12,445 D	38.9%	60.4%	39.2%	60.8%
8,591	MOHAVE	3,224	1,198	2,024	2	826 D	37.2%	62.8%	37.2%	62.8%
25,309	NAVAJO	4,597	1,533	3,052	12	1,519 D	33.3%	66.4%	33.4%	66.6%
72,838	PIMA	23,562	9,445	14,035	82	4,590 D	40.1%	59.6%	40.2%	59.8%
28,841	PINAL	6,429	1,996	4,411	22	2,415 D	31.0%	68.6%	31.2%	68.8%
9,482	SANTA CRUZ	2,516	978	1,536	2	558 D	38.9%	61.0%	38.9%	61.1%
26,511	YAVAPAI	10,282	3,987	6,217	78	2,230 D	38.8%	60.5%	39.1%	60.9%
19,326	YUMA	6,031	1,870	4,138	23	2,268 D	31.0%	68.6%	31.1%	68.9%
499,261	TOTAL	150,039	54,030	95,267	742	41,237 D	36.0%	63.5%	36.2%	63.8%

ARIZONA

PRESIDENT 1936

1930 Census Population	County	Total Vote	Republican	Democratic	Other	Rep.-Dem. Plurality	Percentage Total Vote Rep.	Total Vote Dem.	Major Vote Rep.	Major Vote Dem.
17,765	APACHE	2,327	638	1,674	15	1,036 D	27.4%	71.9%	27.6%	72.4%
40,998	COCHISE	10,499	2,092	8,130	277	6,038 D	19.9%	77.4%	20.5%	79.5%
14,064	COCONINO	3,829	1,140	2,578	111	1,438 D	29.8%	67.3%	30.7%	69.3%
31,016	GILA	6,568	1,526	4,859	183	3,333 D	23.2%	74.0%	23.9%	76.1%
10,373	GRAHAM	4,375	680	3,541	154	2,861 D	15.5%	80.9%	16.1%	83.9%
9,886	GREENLEE	1,771	218	1,526	27	1,308 D	12.3%	86.2%	12.5%	87.5%
150,970	MARICOPA	47,610	13,671	32,031	1,908	18,360 D	28.7%	67.3%	29.9%	70.1%
5,572	MOHAVE	2,529	609	1,814	106	1,205 D	24.1%	71.7%	25.1%	74.9%
21,202	NAVAJO	4,142	1,052	3,037	53	1,985 D	25.4%	73.3%	25.7%	74.3%
55,676	PIMA	18,590	6,079	12,249	262	6,170 D	32.7%	65.9%	33.2%	66.8%
22,081	PINAL	4,868	1,216	3,498	154	2,282 D	25.0%	71.9%	25.8%	74.2%
9,684	SANTA CRUZ	2,530	742	1,729	59	987 D	29.3%	68.3%	30.0%	70.0%
28,470	YAVAPAI	9,926	2,794	6,628	504	3,834 D	28.1%	66.8%	29.7%	70.3%
17,816	YUMA	4,599	976	3,428	195	2,452 D	21.2%	74.5%	22.2%	77.8%
435,573	TOTAL	124,163	33,433	86,722	4,008	53,289 D	26.9%	69.8%	27.8%	72.2%

ARIZONA

PRESIDENT 1932

1930 Census Population	County	Total Vote	Republican	Democratic	Other	Rep.-Dem. Plurality	Percentage Total Vote Rep.	Percentage Total Vote Dem.	Percentage Major Vote Rep.	Percentage Major Vote Dem.
17,765	APACHE	2,034	760	1,271	3	511 D	37.4%	62.5%	37.4%	62.6%
40,998	COCHISE	11,216	2,838	7,798	580	4,960 D	25.3%	69.5%	26.7%	73.3%
14,064	COCONINO	3,853	1,110	2,689	54	1,579 D	28.8%	69.8%	29.2%	70.8%
31,016	GILA	6,718	1,865	4,625	228	2,760 D	27.8%	68.8%	28.7%	71.3%
10,373	GRAHAM	3,625	718	2,867	40	2,149 D	19.8%	79.1%	20.0%	80.0%
9,886	GREENLEE	1,954	377	1,558	19	1,181 D	19.3%	79.7%	19.5%	80.5%
150,970	MARICOPA	44,280	15,086	28,601	593	13,515 D	34.1%	64.6%	34.5%	65.5%
5,572	MOHAVE	2,283	537	1,660	86	1,123 D	23.5%	72.7%	24.4%	75.6%
21,202	NAVAJO	4,146	1,248	2,602	296	1,354 D	30.1%	62.8%	32.4%	67.6%
55,676	PIMA	17,727	6,152	11,061	514	4,909 D	34.7%	62.4%	35.7%	64.3%
22,081	PINAL	4,184	1,000	3,137	47	2,137 D	23.9%	75.0%	24.2%	75.8%
9,684	SANTA CRUZ	2,260	625	1,606	29	981 D	27.7%	71.1%	28.0%	72.0%
28,470	YAVAPAI	9,141	2,626	6,326	189	3,700 D	28.7%	69.2%	29.3%	70.7%
17,816	YUMA	4,830	1,162	3,463	205	2,301 D	24.1%	71.7%	25.1%	74.9%
435,573	TOTAL	118,251	36,104	79,264	2,883	43,160 D	30.5%	67.0%	31.3%	68.7%

ARIZONA

PRESIDENT 1928

1920 Census Population	County	Total Vote	Republican	Democratic	Other	Rep.-Dem. Plurality	Percentage Total Vote Rep.	Percentage Total Vote Dem.	Percentage Major Vote Rep.	Percentage Major Vote Dem.
13,196	APACHE	1,628	837	791		46 R	51.4%	48.6%	51.4%	48.6%
46,465	COCHISE	10,083	5,776	4,262	45	1,514 R	57.3%	42.3%	57.5%	42.5%
9,982	COCONINO	2,901	1,717	1,172	12	545 R	59.2%	40.4%	59.4%	40.6%
25,678	GILA	6,790	3,436	3,341	13	95 R	50.6%	49.2%	50.7%	49.3%
10,148	GRAHAM	2,861	1,238	1,615	8	377 D	43.3%	56.4%	43.4%	56.6%
15,362	GREENLEE	1,628	685	935	8	250 D	42.1%	57.4%	42.3%	57.7%
89,576	MARICOPA	32,269	20,089	12,146	34	7,943 R	62.3%	37.6%	62.3%	37.7%
5,259	MOHAVE	1,868	1,127	728	13	399 R	60.3%	39.0%	60.8%	39.2%
16,077	NAVAJO	2,924	1,608	1,316		292 R	55.0%	45.0%	55.0%	45.0%
34,680	PIMA	11,653	6,635	4,976	42	1,659 R	56.9%	42.7%	57.1%	42.9%
16,130	PINAL	3,054	1,631	1,419	4	212 R	53.4%	46.5%	53.5%	46.5%
12,689	SANTA CRUZ	1,884	919	962	3	43 D	48.8%	51.1%	48.9%	51.1%
24,016	YAVAPAI	7,794	4,507	3,285	2	1,222 R	57.8%	42.1%	57.8%	42.2%
14,904	YUMA	3,917	2,328	1,589		739 R	59.4%	40.6%	59.4%	40.6%
334,162	TOTAL	91,254	52,533	38,537	184	13,996 R	57.6%	42.2%	57.7%	42.3%

ARIZONA

PRESIDENT 1924

1920 Census Population	County	Total Vote	Republican	Democratic	Progressive	Other	Plurality	Percentage Total Vote Rep.	Dem.	Prog.
13,196	APACHE	1,278	620	548	110		72 R	48.5%	42.9%	8.6%
46,465	COCHISE	9,699	3,712	3,496	2,491		216 R	38.3%	36.0%	25.7%
9,982	COCONINO	2,317	1,045	711	561		334 R	45.1%	30.7%	24.2%
25,678	GILA	6,348	2,193	2,218	1,937		25 D	34.5%	34.9%	30.5%
10,148	GRAHAM	2,451	813	1,252	386		439 D	33.2%	51.1%	15.7%
15,362	GREENLEE	1,348	404	768	176		364 D	30.0%	57.0%	13.1%
89,576	MARICOPA	23,758	10,611	9,177	3,970		1,434 R	44.7%	38.6%	16.7%
5,259	MOHAVE	1,942	738	475	729		9 R	38.0%	24.5%	37.5%
16,077	NAVAJO	2,471	1,060	684	727		333 R	42.9%	27.7%	29.4%
34,680	PIMA	8,439	3,559	2,594	2,286		965 R	42.2%	30.7%	27.1%
16,130	PINAL	2,631	1,075	988	568		87 R	40.9%	37.6%	21.6%
12,689	SANTA CRUZ	1,450	579	673	198		94 D	39.9%	46.4%	13.7%
24,016	YAVAPAI	6,763	2,827	1,800	2,136		691 R	41.8%	26.6%	31.6%
14,904	YUMA	3,066	1,280	851	935		345 R	41.7%	27.8%	30.5%
334,162	TOTAL	73,961	30,516	26,235	17,210		4,281 R	41.3%	35.5%	23.3%

ARIZONA

PRESIDENT 1920

1920 Census Population	County	Total Vote	Republican	Democratic	Other	Rep.-Dem. Plurality	Percentage Total Vote Rep.	Total Vote Dem.	Major Vote Rep.	Major Vote Dem.
13,196	APACHE	1,302	679	618	5	61 R	52.2%	47.5%	52.4%	47.6%
46,465	COCHISE	9,771	5,341	4,430		911 R	54.7%	45.3%	54.7%	45.3%
9,982	COCONINO	2,123	1,342	781		561 R	63.2%	36.8%	63.2%	36.8%
25,678	GILA	6,330	3,311	2,894	125	417 R	52.3%	45.7%	53.4%	46.6%
10,148	GRAHAM	2,323	1,062	1,261		199 D	45.7%	54.3%	45.7%	54.3%
15,362	GREENLEE	2,058	905	1,131	22	226 D	44.0%	55.0%	44.4%	55.6%
89,576	MARICOPA	20,161	11,336	8,825		2,511 R	56.2%	43.8%	56.2%	43.8%
5,259	MOHAVE	1,791	996	722	73	274 R	55.6%	40.3%	58.0%	42.0%
16,077	NAVAJO	2,115	1,078	1,031	6	47 R	51.0%	48.7%	51.1%	48.9%
34,680	PIMA	5,847	3,392	2,455		937 R	58.0%	42.0%	58.0%	42.0%
16,130	PINAL	2,767	1,493	1,264	10	229 R	54.0%	45.7%	54.2%	45.8%
12,689	SANTA CRUZ	1,556	850	706		144 R	54.6%	45.4%	54.6%	45.4%
24,016	YAVAPAI	5,876	3,625	2,251		1,374 R	61.7%	38.3%	61.7%	38.3%
14,904	YUMA	2,783	1,606	1,177		429 R	57.7%	42.3%	57.7%	42.3%
334,162	TOTAL	66,803	37,016	29,546	241	7,470 R	55.4%	44.2%	55.6%	44.4%

ARIZONA

ELECTION NOTES

1956 Other vote was Andrews (States Rights).

1952

1948 Other vote was 3,310 Wallace (Progressive); 786 Watson (Prohibition); 121 Teichert (Socialist Labor).

1944 Other vote was Watson (Prohibition).

1940 Other vote was Babson (Prohibition).

1936 Other vote was 3,307 Lemke (Union); 384 Colvin (Prohibition); 317 Thomas (Socialist).

1932 Other vote was 2,618 Thomas (Socialist); 256 Foster (Communist); 9 Arizona Progressive Democratic ticket (no candidate listed).

1928 Other vote was Foster (Communist).

1924 A special four-column table which gives the LaFollette (Progressive) vote is used to detail this election.

1920 Other vote was 222 Debs (Socialist); 15 Christensen (Farmer-Labor); 4 Watkins (Prohibition).

ARKANSAS

POPULAR VOTE FOR PRESIDENT 1920 TO 1956

		Republican		Democratic				Percentage			
								Total Vote		Major Vote	
Year	Total Vote	Vote	Candidate	Vote	Candidate	Other Vote	Plurality	Rep.	Dem.	Rep.	Dem.
1956	406,572	186,287	Eisenhower, Dwight D.	213,277	Stevenson, Adlai E.	7,008	26,990 D	45.8%	52.5%	46.6%	53.4%
1952	404,800	177,155	Eisenhower, Dwight D.	226,300	Stevenson, Adlai E.	1,345	49,145 D	43.8%	55.9%	43.9%	56.1%
1948	242,475	50,959	Dewey, Thomas E.	149,659	Truman, Harry S.	41,857	98,700 D	21.0%	61.7%	25.4%	74.6%
1944	212,954	63,551	Dewey, Thomas E.	148,965	Roosevelt, Franklin D.	438	85,414 D	29.8%	70.0%	29.9%	70.1%
1940	200,429	42,122	Willkie, Wendell	157,213	Roosevelt, Franklin D.	1,094	115,091 D	21.0%	78.4%	21.1%	78.9%
1936	179,431	32,049	Landon, Alfred M.	146,765	Roosevelt, Franklin D.	617	114,716 D	17.9%	81.8%	17.9%	82.1%
1932	216,569	27,465	Hoover, Herbert C.	186,829	Roosevelt, Franklin D.	2,275	159,364 D	12.7%	86.3%	12.8%	87.2%
1928	197,726	77,784	Hoover, Herbert C.	119,196	Smith, Alfred E.	746	41,412 D	39.3%	60.3%	39.5%	60.5%
1924	138,540	40,583	Coolidge, Calvin	84,790	Davis, John W.	13,167	44,207 D	29.3%	61.2%	32.4%	67.6%
1920	183,871	72,316	Harding, Warren G.	106,427	Cox, James M.	5,128	34,111 D	39.3%	57.9%	40.5%	59.5%

ELECTORAL COLLEGE VOTE 1920 TO 1956

Year	Total	Republican	Democratic	Other
1956	8	—	8	—
1952	8	—	8	—
1948	9	—	9	—
1944	9	—	9	—
1940	9	—	9	—
1936	9	—	9	—
1932	9	—	9	—
1928	9	—	9	—
1924	9	—	9	—
1920	9	—	9	—

ARKANSAS

BENTON
CARROLL
BOONE
MARION
BAXTER
FULTON
RANDOLPH
CLAY
WASHINGTON
MADISON
NEWTON
SEARCY
STONE
IZARD
SHARP
LAWRENCE
GREENE
INDEPENDENCE
CRAIGHEAD
MISSISSIPPI
CRAWFORD
FRANKLIN
JOHNSON
POPE
VAN BUREN
CLEBURNE
JACKSON
POINSETT
SEBASTIAN
LOGAN
CONWAY
FAULKNER
WHITE
WOODRUFF
CROSS
CRITTENDEN
SCOTT
YELL
PERRY
ST. FRANCIS
PULASKI
LONOKE
PRAIRIE
LEE
MONROE
POLK
MONTGOMERY
GARLAND
SALINE
PHILLIPS
HOWARD
HOT SPRING
GRANT
JEFFERSON
ARKANSAS
PIKE
SEVIER
CLARK
DALLAS
CLEVELAND
LINCOLN
DESHA
LITTLE RIVER
HEMPSTEAD
NEVADA
OUACHITA
CALHOUN
BRADLEY
DREW
MILLER
COLUMBIA
UNION
ASHLEY
CHICOT
LAFAYETTE

ARKANSAS

PRESIDENT 1956

1950 Census Population	County	Total Vote	Republican	Democratic	Other	Rep.-Dem. Plurality	Percentage: Total Vote Rep.	Total Vote Dem.	Major Vote Rep.	Major Vote Dem.
23,665	ARKANSAS	5,635	2,826	2,736	73	90 R	50.2%	48.6%	50.8%	49.2%
25,660	ASHLEY	4,270	1,183	2,820	267	1,637 D	27.7%	66.0%	29.6%	70.4%
11,683	BAXTER	3,192	1,721	1,451	20	270 R	53.9%	45.5%	54.3%	45.7%
38,076	BENTON	10,305	6,500	3,744	61	2,756 R	63.1%	36.3%	63.5%	36.5%
16,260	BOONE	6,006	3,153	2,829	24	324 R	52.5%	47.1%	52.7%	47.3%
15,987	BRADLEY	4,426	1,361	3,010	55	1,649 D	30.8%	68.0%	31.1%	68.9%
7,132	CALHOUN	1,762	445	1,303	14	858 D	25.3%	74.0%	25.5%	74.5%
13,244	CARROLL	3,980	2,310	1,651	19	659 R	58.0%	41.5%	58.3%	41.7%
22,306	CHICOT	3,455	1,043	2,273	139	1,230 D	30.2%	65.8%	31.5%	68.5%
22,998	CLARK	4,840	1,973	2,809	58	836 D	40.8%	58.0%	41.3%	58.7%
26,674	CLAY	4,113	1,711	2,368	34	657 D	41.6%	57.6%	41.9%	58.1%
11,487	CLEBURNE	2,048	947	1,094	7	147 D	46.2%	53.4%	46.4%	53.6%
8,956	CLEVELAND	1,592	423	1,149	20	726 D	26.6%	72.2%	26.9%	73.1%
28,770	COLUMBIA	5,394	2,342	2,845	207	503 D	43.4%	52.7%	45.2%	54.8%
18,137	CONWAY	4,281	1,636	2,618	27	982 D	38.2%	61.2%	38.5%	61.5%
50,613	CRAIGHEAD	10,060	4,035	5,876	149	1,841 D	40.1%	58.4%	40.7%	59.3%
22,727	CRAWFORD	5,843	3,090	2,723	30	367 R	52.9%	46.6%	53.2%	46.8%
47,184	CRITTENDEN	4,873	2,476	2,120	277	356 R	50.8%	43.5%	53.9%	46.1%
24,757	CROSS	3,417	1,176	2,165	76	989 D	34.4%	63.4%	35.2%	64.8%
12,416	DALLAS	2,762	984	1,726	52	742 D	35.6%	62.5%	36.3%	63.7%
25,155	DESHA	4,191	1,204	2,935	52	1,731 D	28.7%	70.0%	29.1%	70.9%
17,959	DREW	3,586	1,265	2,234	87	969 D	35.3%	62.3%	36.2%	63.8%
25,289	FAULKNER	5,860	2,399	3,428	33	1,029 D	40.9%	58.5%	41.2%	58.8%
12,358	FRANKLIN	2,771	1,137	1,614	20	477 D	41.0%	58.2%	41.3%	58.7%
9,187	FULTON	1,771	799	958	14	159 D	45.1%	54.1%	45.5%	54.5%
47,102	GARLAND	15,076	9,427	5,437	212	3,990 R	62.5%	36.1%	63.4%	36.6%
9,024	GRANT	2,139	818	1,272	49	454 D	38.2%	59.5%	39.1%	60.9%
29,149	GREENE	5,389	1,898	3,454	37	1,556 D	35.2%	64.1%	35.5%	64.5%
25,080	HEMPSTEAD	4,997	2,227	2,694	76	467 D	44.6%	53.9%	45.3%	54.7%
22,181	HOT SPRING	6,502	2,923	3,525	54	602 D	45.0%	54.2%	45.3%	54.7%
13,342	HOWARD	2,785	1,329	1,428	28	99 D	47.7%	51.3%	48.2%	51.8%
23,488	INDEPENDENCE	4,683	2,333	2,316	34	17 R	49.8%	49.5%	50.2%	49.8%
9,953	IZARD	1,716	511	1,200	5	689 D	29.8%	69.9%	29.9%	70.1%
25,912	JACKSON	5,061	1,323	3,699	39	2,376 D	26.1%	73.1%	26.3%	73.7%
76,075	JEFFERSON	12,558	5,743	6,426	389	683 D	45.7%	51.2%	47.2%	52.8%
16,138	JOHNSON	3,245	1,520	1,697	28	177 D	46.8%	52.3%	47.2%	52.8%
13,203	LAFAYETTE	2,280	836	1,348	96	512 D	36.7%	59.1%	38.3%	61.7%
21,303	LAWRENCE	3,948	1,584	2,303	61	719 D	40.1%	58.3%	40.8%	59.2%
24,322	LEE	2,814	974	1,719	121	745 D	34.6%	61.1%	36.2%	63.8%
17,079	LINCOLN	2,405	767	1,616	22	849 D	31.9%	67.2%	32.2%	67.8%
11,690	LITTLE RIVER	2,198	828	1,308	62	480 D	37.7%	59.5%	38.8%	61.2%
20,260	LOGAN	4,412	2,081	2,307	24	226 D	47.2%	52.3%	47.4%	52.6%
27,278	LONOKE	5,336	1,932	3,234	170	1,302 D	36.2%	60.6%	37.4%	62.6%
11,734	MADISON	4,716	2,525	2,186	5	339 R	53.5%	46.4%	53.6%	46.4%
8,609	MARION	1,922	857	1,061	4	204 D	44.6%	55.2%	44.7%	55.3%
32,614	MILLER	9,987	4,307	5,402	278	1,095 D	43.1%	54.1%	44.4%	55.6%
82,375	MISSISSIPPI	10,955	4,269	6,428	258	2,159 D	39.0%	58.7%	39.9%	60.1%
19,540	MONROE	2,634	1,099	1,460	75	361 D	41.7%	55.4%	42.9%	57.1%
6,680	MONTGOMERY	1,829	965	846	18	119 R	52.8%	46.3%	53.3%	46.7%
14,781	NEVADA	2,943	1,039	1,871	33	832 D	35.3%	63.6%	35.7%	64.3%
8,685	NEWTON	2,316	1,481	832	3	649 R	63.9%	35.9%	64.0%	36.0%
33,051	OUACHITA	8,129	2,819	5,188	122	2,369 D	34.7%	63.8%	35.2%	64.8%
5,978	PERRY	1,304	572	719	13	147 D	43.9%	55.1%	44.3%	55.7%
46,254	PHILLIPS	6,940	2,826	3,917	197	1,091 D	40.7%	56.4%	41.9%	58.1%
10,032	PIKE	1,903	905	985	13	80 D	47.6%	51.8%	47.9%	52.1%
39,311	POINSETT	6,006	2,117	3,817	72	1,700 D	35.2%	63.6%	35.7%	64.3%
14,182	POLK	3,143	1,832	1,287	24	545 R	58.3%	40.9%	58.7%	41.3%
23,291	POPE	5,045	2,267	2,753	25	486 D	44.9%	54.6%	45.2%	54.8%
13,768	PRAIRIE	2,440	917	1,504	19	587 D	37.6%	61.6%	37.9%	62.1%
196,685	PULASKI	50,301	25,702	23,372	1,227	2,330 R	51.1%	46.5%	52.4%	47.6%

ARKANSAS

PRESIDENT 1956

1950 Census Population	County	Total Vote	Republican	Democratic	Other	Rep.-Dem. Plurality	Percentage Total Vote Rep.	Percentage Total Vote Dem.	Percentage Major Vote Rep.	Percentage Major Vote Dem.
15,982	RANDOLPH	2,893	1,117	1,763	13	646 D	38.6%	60.9%	38.8%	61.2%
36,841	ST. FRANCIS	4,199	1,884	2,114	201	230 D	44.9%	50.3%	47.1%	52.9%
23,816	SALINE	6,378	2,603	3,705	70	1,102 D	40.8%	58.1%	41.3%	58.7%
10,057	SCOTT	2,899	1,637	1,248	14	389 R	56.5%	43.0%	56.7%	43.3%
10,424	SEARCY	3,374	2,441	909	24	1,532 R	72.3%	26.9%	72.9%	27.1%
64,202	SEBASTIAN	17,841	10,234	7,489	118	2,745 R	57.4%	42.0%	57.7%	42.3%
12,293	SEVIER	2,678	1,159	1,500	19	341 D	43.3%	56.0%	43.6%	56.4%
8,999	SHARP	1,600	645	927	28	282 D	40.3%	57.9%	41.0%	59.0%
7,662	STONE	1,411	651	756	4	105 D	46.1%	53.6%	46.3%	53.7%
49,686	UNION	12,726	5,059	7,055	612	1,996 D	39.8%	55.4%	41.8%	58.2%
9,687	VAN BUREN	2,642	1,296	1,331	15	35 D	49.1%	50.4%	49.3%	50.7%
49,979	WASHINGTON	12,623	7,683	4,857	83	2,826 R	60.9%	38.5%	61.3%	38.7%
38,040	WHITE	8,750	3,813	4,895	42	1,082 D	43.6%	55.9%	43.8%	56.2%
18,957	WOODRUFF	2,675	992	1,630	53	638 D	37.1%	60.9%	37.8%	62.2%
14,057	YELL	3,393	1,381	2,008	4	627 D	40.7%	59.2%	40.7%	59.3%
1,909,511	TOTAL	406,572	186,287	213,277	7,008	26,990 D	45.8%	52.5%	46.6%	53.4%

ARKANSAS

PRESIDENT 1952

1950 Census Population	County	Total Vote	Republican	Democratic	Other	Rep.-Dem. Plurality	Percentage Total Vote Rep.	Total Vote Dem.	Major Vote Rep.	Major Vote Dem.
23,665	ARKANSAS	5,358	2,697	2,648	13	49 R	50.3%	49.4%	50.5%	49.5%
25,660	ASHLEY	4,729	1,249	3,471	9	2,222 D	26.4%	73.4%	26.5%	73.5%
11,683	BAXTER	2,793	1,387	1,388	18	1 D	49.7%	49.7%	50.0%	50.0%
38,076	BENTON	11,500	7,916	3,558	26	4,358 R	68.8%	30.9%	69.0%	31.0%
16,260	BOONE	6,155	3,361	2,786	8	575 R	54.6%	45.3%	54.7%	45.3%
15,987	BRADLEY	3,297	869	2,417	11	1,548 D	26.4%	73.3%	26.4%	73.6%
7,132	CALHOUN	1,607	272	1,332	3	1,060 D	16.9%	82.9%	17.0%	83.0%
13,244	CARROLL	4,258	2,752	1,493	13	1,259 R	64.6%	35.1%	64.8%	35.2%
22,306	CHICOT	3,663	1,191	2,458	14	1,267 D	32.5%	67.1%	32.6%	67.4%
22,998	CLARK	4,647	1,679	2,963	5	1,284 D	36.1%	63.8%	36.2%	63.8%
26,674	CLAY	4,408	2,105	2,277	26	172 D	47.8%	51.7%	48.0%	52.0%
11,487	CLEBURNE	1,971	918	1,045	8	127 D	46.6%	53.0%	46.8%	53.2%
8,956	CLEVELAND	1,728	477	1,248	3	771 D	27.6%	72.2%	27.7%	72.3%
28,770	COLUMBIA	5,299	1,931	3,359	9	1,428 D	36.4%	63.4%	36.5%	63.5%
18,137	CONWAY	5,317	2,133	3,174	10	1,041 D	40.1%	59.7%	40.2%	59.8%
50,613	CRAIGHEAD	10,202	4,199	5,975	28	1,776 D	41.2%	58.6%	41.3%	58.7%
22,727	CRAWFORD	5,269	2,782	2,477	10	305 R	52.8%	47.0%	52.9%	47.1%
47,184	CRITTENDEN	4,864	1,865	2,982	17	1,117 D	38.3%	61.3%	38.5%	61.5%
24,757	CROSS	3,817	1,461	2,344	12	883 D	38.3%	61.4%	38.4%	61.6%
12,416	DALLAS	2,944	737	2,202	5	1,465 D	25.0%	74.8%	25.1%	74.9%
25,155	DESHA	4,192	1,037	3,150	5	2,113 D	24.7%	75.1%	24.8%	75.2%
17,959	DREW	3,306	1,040	2,261	5	1,221 D	31.5%	68.4%	31.5%	68.5%
25,289	FAULKNER	5,470	1,995	3,461	14	1,466 D	36.5%	63.3%	36.6%	63.4%
12,358	FRANKLIN	2,982	1,215	1,762	5	547 D	40.7%	59.1%	40.8%	59.2%
9,187	FULTON	1,938	890	1,048		158 D	45.9%	54.1%	45.9%	54.1%
47,102	GARLAND	13,065	7,848	5,165	52	2,683 R	60.1%	39.5%	60.3%	39.7%
9,024	GRANT	2,135	637	1,487	11	850 D	29.8%	69.6%	30.0%	70.0%
29,149	GREENE	5,458	1,875	3,571	12	1,696 D	34.4%	65.4%	34.4%	65.6%
25,080	HEMPSTEAD	4,887	2,115	2,771	1	656 D	43.3%	56.7%	43.3%	56.7%
22,181	HOT SPRING	5,331	1,842	3,474	15	1,632 D	34.6%	65.2%	34.7%	65.3%
13,342	HOWARD	2,443	944	1,492	7	548 D	38.6%	61.1%	38.8%	61.2%
23,488	INDEPENDENCE	5,003	2,499	2,485	19	14 R	50.0%	49.7%	50.1%	49.9%
9,953	IZARD	1,715	629	1,085	1	456 D	36.7%	63.3%	36.7%	63.3%
25,912	JACKSON	5,917	1,516	4,401		2,885 D	25.6%	74.4%	25.6%	74.4%
76,075	JEFFERSON	14,252	5,925	8,300	27	2,375 D	41.6%	58.2%	41.7%	58.3%
16,138	JOHNSON	3,765	1,728	2,021	16	293 D	45.9%	53.7%	46.1%	53.9%
13,203	LAFAYETTE	2,386	733	1,637	16	904 D	30.7%	68.6%	30.9%	69.1%
21,303	LAWRENCE	3,844	1,570	2,206	68	636 D	40.8%	57.4%	41.6%	58.4%
24,322	LEE	2,988	1,054	1,923	11	869 D	35.3%	64.4%	35.4%	64.6%
17,079	LINCOLN	2,472	595	1,871	6	1,276 D	24.1%	75.7%	24.1%	75.9%
11,690	LITTLE RIVER	2,308	783	1,522	3	739 D	33.9%	65.9%	34.0%	66.0%
20,260	LOGAN	4,689	2,103	2,567	19	464 D	44.8%	54.7%	45.0%	55.0%
27,278	LONOKE	5,094	1,570	3,517	7	1,947 D	30.8%	69.0%	30.9%	69.1%
11,734	MADISON	4,987	2,868	2,110	9	758 R	57.5%	42.3%	57.6%	42.4%
8,609	MARION	1,960	844	1,099	17	255 D	43.1%	56.1%	43.4%	56.6%
32,614	MILLER	8,509	3,137	5,337	35	2,200 D	36.9%	62.7%	37.0%	63.0%
82,375	MISSISSIPPI	11,567	4,586	6,968	13	2,382 D	39.6%	60.2%	39.7%	60.3%
19,540	MONROE	2,781	947	1,834		887 D	34.1%	65.9%	34.1%	65.9%
6,680	MONTGOMERY	1,622	815	807		8 R	50.2%	49.8%	50.2%	49.8%
14,781	NEVADA	3,014	1,037	1,972	5	935 D	34.4%	65.4%	34.5%	65.5%
8,685	NEWTON	2,838	1,728	1,107	3	621 R	60.9%	39.0%	61.0%	39.0%
33,051	OUACHITA	8,136	2,171	5,936	29	3,765 D	26.7%	73.0%	26.8%	73.2%
5,978	PERRY	1,310	502	802	6	300 D	38.3%	61.2%	38.5%	61.5%
46,254	PHILLIPS	6,340	2,592	3,741	7	1,149 D	40.9%	59.0%	40.9%	59.1%
10,032	PIKE	1,938	742	1,163	33	421 D	38.3%	60.0%	39.0%	61.0%
39,311	POINSETT	6,321	2,010	4,303	8	2,293 D	31.8%	68.1%	31.8%	68.2%
14,182	POLK	3,141	1,756	1,379	6	377 R	55.9%	43.9%	56.0%	44.0%
23,291	POPE	5,266	2,226	3,036	4	810 D	42.3%	57.7%	42.3%	57.7%
13,768	PRAIRIE	2,541	871	1,664	6	793 D	34.3%	65.5%	34.4%	65.6%
196,685	PULASKI	48,286	23,460	24,448	378	988 D	48.6%	50.6%	49.0%	51.0%

ARKANSAS

PRESIDENT 1952

1950 Census Population	County	Total Vote	Republican	Democratic	Other	Rep.-Dem. Plurality	Percentage Total Vote Rep.	Percentage Total Vote Dem.	Percentage Major Vote Rep.	Percentage Major Vote Dem.
15,982	RANDOLPH	3,254	1,302	1,941	11	639 D	40.0%	59.6%	40.1%	59.9%
36,841	ST. FRANCIS	4,259	1,792	2,466	1	674 D	42.1%	57.9%	42.1%	57.9%
23,816	SALINE	5,863	1,766	4,045	52	2,279 D	30.1%	69.0%	30.4%	69.6%
10,057	SCOTT	2,101	893	1,197	11	304 D	42.5%	57.0%	42.7%	57.3%
10,424	SEARCY	3,004	1,996	1,007	1	989 R	66.4%	33.5%	66.5%	33.5%
64,202	SEBASTIAN	17,944	10,114	7,802	28	2,312 R	56.4%	43.5%	56.5%	43.5%
12,293	SEVIER	2,805	1,130	1,673	2	543 D	40.3%	59.6%	40.3%	59.7%
8,999	SHARP	1,697	655	1,039	3	384 D	38.6%	61.2%	38.7%	61.3%
7,662	STONE	1,274	700	573	1	127 R	54.9%	45.0%	55.0%	45.0%
49,686	UNION	12,810	5,266	7,515	29	2,249 D	41.1%	58.7%	41.2%	58.8%
9,687	VAN BUREN	3,102	1,530	1,559	13	29 D	49.3%	50.3%	49.5%	50.5%
49,979	WASHINGTON	13,611	8,650	4,923	38	3,727 R	63.6%	36.2%	63.7%	36.3%
38,040	WHITE	7,070	2,884	4,179	7	1,295 D	40.8%	59.1%	40.8%	59.2%
18,957	WOODRUFF	2,839	818	2,017	4	1,199 D	28.8%	71.0%	28.9%	71.1%
14,057	YELL	3,144	1,243	1,884	17	641 D	39.5%	59.9%	39.8%	60.2%
1,909,511	TOTAL	404,800	177,155	226,300	1,345	49,145 D	43.8%	55.9%	43.9%	56.1%

ARKANSAS

PRESIDENT 1948

1940 Census Population	County	Total Vote	Republican	Democratic	Other	Rep.-Dem. Plurality	Percentage: Total Vote Rep.	Percentage: Total Vote Dem.	Percentage: Major Vote Rep.	Percentage: Major Vote Dem.
24,437	ARKANSAS	3,356	737	1,781	838	1,044 D	22.0%	53.1%	29.3%	70.7%
26,785	ASHLEY	2,408	197	1,844	367	1,647 D	8.2%	76.6%	9.7%	90.3%
10,281	BAXTER	1,760	553	1,098	109	545 D	31.4%	62.4%	33.5%	66.5%
36,148	BENTON	6,513	2,911	3,281	321	370 D	44.7%	50.4%	47.0%	53.0%
15,860	BOONE	4,995	1,499	3,190	306	1,691 D	30.0%	63.9%	32.0%	68.0%
18,097	BRADLEY	2,187	213	1,426	548	1,213 D	9.7%	65.2%	13.0%	87.0%
9,636	CALHOUN	918	45	768	105	723 D	4.9%	83.7%	5.5%	94.5%
14,737	CARROLL	3,688	1,525	2,032	131	507 D	41.4%	55.1%	42.9%	57.1%
27,452	CHICOT	1,762	203	952	607	749 D	11.5%	54.0%	17.6%	82.4%
24,402	CLARK	2,509	383	1,750	376	1,367 D	15.3%	69.7%	18.0%	82.0%
28,386	CLAY	3,091	878	2,069	144	1,191 D	28.4%	66.9%	29.8%	70.2%
13,134	CLEBURNE	1,447	312	1,061	74	749 D	21.6%	73.3%	22.7%	77.3%
12,570	CLEVELAND	1,006	79	679	248	600 D	7.9%	67.5%	10.4%	89.6%
29,822	COLUMBIA	2,981	217	1,788	976	1,571 D	7.3%	60.0%	10.8%	89.2%
21,536	CONWAY	2,454	425	1,771	258	1,346 D	17.3%	72.2%	19.4%	80.6%
47,200	CRAIGHEAD	5,110	759	3,238	1,113	2,479 D	14.9%	63.4%	19.0%	81.0%
23,920	CRAWFORD	2,952	1,002	1,730	220	728 D	33.9%	58.6%	36.7%	63.3%
42,473	CRITTENDEN	2,392	137	594	1,661	457 D	5.7%	24.8%	18.7%	81.3%
26,046	CROSS	2,265	213	1,100	952	887 D	9.4%	48.6%	16.2%	83.8%
14,471	DALLAS	1,702	152	1,174	376	1,022 D	8.9%	69.0%	11.5%	88.5%
27,160	DESHA	3,033	233	2,122	678	1,889 D	7.7%	70.0%	9.9%	90.1%
19,831	DREW	2,027	182	1,204	641	1,022 D	9.0%	59.4%	13.1%	86.9%
25,880	FAULKNER	3,597	626	2,653	318	2,027 D	17.4%	73.8%	19.1%	80.9%
15,683	FRANKLIN	2,092	391	1,591	110	1,200 D	18.7%	76.1%	19.7%	80.3%
10,253	FULTON	1,227	339	850	38	511 D	27.6%	69.3%	28.5%	71.5%
41,664	GARLAND	7,154	2,286	3,764	1,104	1,478 D	32.0%	52.6%	37.8%	62.2%
10,477	GRANT	1,235	121	883	231	762 D	9.8%	71.5%	12.1%	87.9%
30,204	GREENE	3,390	502	2,657	231	2,155 D	14.8%	78.4%	15.9%	84.1%
32,770	HEMPSTEAD	3,069	386	1,683	1,000	1,297 D	12.6%	54.8%	18.7%	81.3%
18,916	HOT SPRING	2,764	555	1,932	277	1,377 D	20.1%	69.9%	22.3%	77.7%
16,621	HOWARD	1,652	199	1,250	203	1,051 D	12.0%	75.7%	13.7%	86.3%
25,643	INDEPENDENCE	3,541	855	2,340	346	1,485 D	24.1%	66.1%	26.8%	73.2%
12,834	IZARD	1,566	240	1,283	43	1,043 D	15.3%	81.9%	15.8%	84.2%
26,427	JACKSON	3,270	338	2,696	236	2,358 D	10.3%	82.4%	11.1%	88.9%
65,101	JEFFERSON	8,214	1,176	5,086	1,952	3,910 D	14.3%	61.9%	18.8%	81.2%
18,795	JOHNSON	2,249	523	1,565	161	1,042 D	23.3%	69.6%	25.0%	75.0%
16,851	LAFAYETTE	1,424	113	700	611	587 D	7.9%	49.2%	13.9%	86.1%
22,651	LAWRENCE	2,672	497	2,001	174	1,504 D	18.6%	74.9%	19.9%	80.1%
26,810	LEE	1,491	95	528	868	433 D	6.4%	35.4%	15.2%	84.8%
19,709	LINCOLN	1,681	378	1,108	195	730 D	22.5%	65.9%	25.4%	74.6%
15,932	LITTLE RIVER	1,524	169	900	455	731 D	11.1%	59.1%	15.8%	84.2%
25,967	LOGAN	3,192	902	2,130	160	1,228 D	28.3%	66.7%	29.7%	70.3%
29,802	LONOKE	2,991	383	2,065	543	1,682 D	12.8%	69.0%	15.6%	84.4%
14,531	MADISON	4,297	2,201	2,041	55	160 R	51.2%	47.5%	51.9%	48.1%
9,464	MARION	1,561	381	1,133	47	752 D	24.4%	72.6%	25.2%	74.8%
31,874	MILLER	4,579	488	2,850	1,241	2,362 D	10.7%	62.2%	14.6%	85.4%
80,217	MISSISSIPPI	6,335	771	3,763	1,801	2,992 D	12.2%	59.4%	17.0%	83.0%
21,133	MONROE	2,350	299	1,431	620	1,132 D	12.7%	60.9%	17.3%	82.7%
8,876	MONTGOMERY	1,243	236	935	72	699 D	19.0%	75.2%	20.2%	79.8%
19,869	NEVADA	1,772	202	1,140	430	938 D	11.4%	64.3%	15.1%	84.9%
10,881	NEWTON	1,748	879	848	21	31 R	50.3%	48.5%	50.9%	49.1%
31,151	OUACHITA	4,818	476	3,315	1,027	2,839 D	9.9%	68.8%	12.6%	87.4%
8,392	PERRY	1,091	201	731	159	530 D	18.4%	67.0%	21.6%	78.4%
45,970	PHILLIPS	3,099	351	1,018	1,730	667 D	11.3%	32.8%	25.6%	74.4%
11,786	PIKE	1,351	256	997	98	741 D	18.9%	73.8%	20.4%	79.6%
37,670	POINSETT	3,702	435	2,415	852	1,980 D	11.8%	65.2%	15.3%	84.7%
15,832	POLK	2,140	554	1,417	169	863 D	25.9%	66.2%	28.1%	71.9%
25,682	POPE	3,716	764	2,525	427	1,761 D	20.6%	67.9%	23.2%	76.8%
15,304	PRAIRIE	1,678	260	1,020	398	760 D	15.5%	60.8%	20.3%	79.7%
156,085	PULASKI	24,639	5,910	13,120	5,609	7,210 D	24.0%	53.2%	31.1%	68.9%

ARKANSAS

PRESIDENT 1948

1940 Census Population	County	Total Vote	Republican	Democratic	Other	Rep.-Dem. Plurality	Percentage Total Vote Rep.	Percentage Total Vote Dem.	Percentage Major Vote Rep.	Percentage Major Vote Dem.
18,319	RANDOLPH	2,633	377	2,139	117	1,762 D	14.3%	81.2%	15.0%	85.0%
36,043	ST. FRANCIS	2,155	178	1,011	966	833 D	8.3%	46.9%	15.0%	85.0%
19,163	SALINE	2,868	390	2,070	408	1,680 D	13.6%	72.2%	15.9%	84.1%
13,300	SCOTT	1,408	260	1,093	55	833 D	18.5%	77.6%	19.2%	80.8%
11,942	SEARCY	2,326	1,064	1,205	57	141 D	45.7%	51.8%	46.9%	53.1%
62,809	SEBASTIAN	8,848	2,928	5,075	845	2,147 D	33.1%	57.4%	36.6%	63.4%
15,248	SEVIER	1,837	267	1,314	256	1,047 D	14.5%	71.5%	16.9%	83.1%
11,497	SHARP	1,453	295	1,078	80	783 D	20.3%	74.2%	21.5%	78.5%
8,603	STONE	1,919	644	1,186	89	542 D	33.6%	61.8%	35.2%	64.8%
50,461	UNION	8,339	1,039	5,588	1,712	4,549 D	12.5%	67.0%	15.7%	84.3%
12,518	VAN BUREN	2,070	617	1,324	129	707 D	29.8%	64.0%	31.8%	68.2%
41,114	WASHINGTON	7,074	2,859	3,493	722	634 D	40.4%	49.4%	45.0%	55.0%
37,176	WHITE	4,625	833	3,193	599	2,360 D	18.0%	69.0%	20.7%	79.3%
22,133	WOODRUFF	1,829	207	1,008	614	801 D	11.3%	55.1%	17.0%	83.0%
20,970	YELL	2,421	408	1,866	147	1,458 D	16.9%	77.1%	17.9%	82.1%
1,949,387	TOTAL	242,475	50,959	149,659	41,857	98,700 D	21.0%	61.7%	25.4%	74.6%

ARKANSAS

PRESIDENT 1944

1940 Census Population	County	Total Vote	Republican	Democratic	Other	Rep.-Dem. Plurality	Percentage Total Vote Rep.	Total Vote Dem.	Major Vote Rep.	Major Vote Dem.
24,437	ARKANSAS	2,751	1,031	1,711	9	680 D	37.5%	62.2%	37.6%	62.4%
26,785	ASHLEY	2,460	285	2,169	6	1,884 D	11.6%	88.2%	11.6%	88.4%
10,281	BAXTER	1,372	572	796	4	224 D	41.7%	58.0%	41.8%	58.2%
36,148	BENTON	6,175	3,305	2,861	9	444 R	53.5%	46.3%	53.6%	46.4%
15,860	BOONE	3,481	1,349	2,132		783 D	38.8%	61.2%	38.8%	61.2%
18,097	BRADLEY	1,877	162	1,710	5	1,548 D	8.6%	91.1%	8.7%	91.3%
9,636	CALHOUN	1,028	122	906		784 D	11.9%	88.1%	11.9%	88.1%
14,737	CARROLL	2,640	1,176	1,464		288 D	44.5%	55.5%	44.5%	55.5%
27,452	CHICOT	1,826	270	1,552	4	1,282 D	14.8%	85.0%	14.8%	85.2%
24,402	CLARK	2,621	637	1,981	3	1,344 D	24.3%	75.6%	24.3%	75.7%
28,386	CLAY	3,361	1,422	1,934	5	512 D	42.3%	57.5%	42.4%	57.6%
13,134	CLEBURNE	1,437	582	839	16	257 D	40.5%	58.4%	41.0%	59.0%
12,570	CLEVELAND	1,110	150	960		810 D	13.5%	86.5%	13.5%	86.5%
29,822	COLUMBIA	2,543	394	2,145	4	1,751 D	15.5%	84.3%	15.5%	84.5%
21,536	CONWAY	2,221	639	1,579	3	940 D	28.8%	71.1%	28.8%	71.2%
47,200	CRAIGHEAD	5,074	1,474	3,582	18	2,108 D	29.1%	70.6%	29.2%	70.8%
23,920	CRAWFORD	2,862	1,141	1,702	19	561 D	39.9%	59.5%	40.1%	59.9%
42,473	CRITTENDEN	1,920	372	1,548		1,176 D	19.4%	80.6%	19.4%	80.6%
26,046	CROSS	2,182	452	1,724	6	1,272 D	20.7%	79.0%	20.8%	79.2%
14,471	DALLAS	1,507	266	1,238	3	972 D	17.7%	82.1%	17.7%	82.3%
27,160	DESHA	1,362	186	1,175	1	989 D	13.7%	86.3%	13.7%	86.3%
19,831	DREW	1,691	320	1,370	1	1,050 D	18.9%	81.0%	18.9%	81.1%
25,880	FAULKNER	3,239	897	2,332	10	1,435 D	27.7%	72.0%	27.8%	72.2%
15,683	FRANKLIN	1,647	457	1,188	2	731 D	27.7%	72.1%	27.8%	72.2%
10,253	FULTON	1,187	525	660	2	135 D	44.2%	55.6%	44.3%	55.7%
41,664	GARLAND	5,669	2,069	3,596	4	1,527 D	36.5%	63.4%	36.5%	63.5%
10,477	GRANT	1,422	334	1,088		754 D	23.5%	76.5%	23.5%	76.5%
30,204	GREENE	3,501	928	2,565	8	1,637 D	26.5%	73.3%	26.6%	73.4%
32,770	HEMPSTEAD	2,789	624	2,157	8	1,533 D	22.4%	77.3%	22.4%	77.6%
18,916	HOT SPRING	2,510	853	1,646	11	793 D	34.0%	65.6%	34.1%	65.9%
16,621	HOWARD	2,118	576	1,538	4	962 D	27.2%	72.6%	27.2%	72.8%
25,643	INDEPENDENCE	2,980	1,192	1,779	9	587 D	40.0%	59.7%	40.1%	59.9%
12,834	IZARD	1,259	402	853	4	451 D	31.9%	67.8%	32.0%	68.0%
26,427	JACKSON	2,732	414	2,318		1,904 D	15.2%	84.8%	15.2%	84.8%
65,101	JEFFERSON	5,676	1,578	4,095	3	2,517 D	27.8%	72.1%	27.8%	72.2%
18,795	JOHNSON	1,911	593	1,311	7	718 D	31.0%	68.6%	31.1%	68.9%
16,851	LAFAYETTE	1,327	177	1,150		973 D	13.3%	86.7%	13.3%	86.7%
22,651	LAWRENCE	2,740	927	1,810	3	883 D	33.8%	66.1%	33.9%	66.1%
26,810	LEE	1,396	275	1,118	3	843 D	19.7%	80.1%	19.7%	80.3%
19,709	LINCOLN	1,175	141	1,034		893 D	12.0%	88.0%	12.0%	88.0%
15,932	LITTLE RIVER	1,289	326	961	2	635 D	25.3%	74.6%	25.3%	74.7%
25,967	LOGAN	3,555	1,279	2,269	7	990 D	36.0%	63.8%	36.0%	64.0%
29,802	LONOKE	2,763	697	2,064	2	1,367 D	25.2%	74.7%	25.2%	74.8%
14,531	MADISON	3,908	2,120	1,788		332 R	54.2%	45.8%	54.2%	45.8%
9,464	MARION	1,268	414	842	12	428 D	32.6%	66.4%	33.0%	67.0%
31,874	MILLER	3,851	972	2,873	6	1,901 D	25.2%	74.6%	25.3%	74.7%
80,217	MISSISSIPPI	5,235	1,292	3,938	5	2,646 D	24.7%	75.2%	24.7%	75.3%
21,133	MONROE	1,606	291	1,311	4	1,020 D	18.1%	81.6%	18.2%	81.8%
8,876	MONTGOMERY	924	349	573	2	224 D	37.8%	62.0%	37.9%	62.1%
19,869	NEVADA	1,771	415	1,353	3	938 D	23.4%	76.4%	23.5%	76.5%
10,881	NEWTON	1,650	934	710	6	224 R	56.6%	43.0%	56.8%	43.2%
31,151	OUACHITA	3,628	473	3,154	1	2,681 D	13.0%	86.9%	13.0%	87.0%
8,392	PERRY	995	285	710		425 D	28.6%	71.4%	28.6%	71.4%
45,970	PHILLIPS	2,548	501	2,046	1	1,545 D	19.7%	80.3%	19.7%	80.3%
11,786	PIKE	1,292	405	877	10	472 D	31.3%	67.9%	31.6%	68.4%
37,670	POINSETT	2,818	311	2,506	1	2,195 D	11.0%	88.9%	11.0%	89.0%
15,832	POLK	1,773	764	999	10	235 D	43.1%	56.3%	43.3%	56.7%
25,682	POPE	2,861	805	2,048	8	1,243 D	28.1%	71.6%	28.2%	71.8%
15,304	PRAIRIE	1,585	465	1,117	3	652 D	29.3%	70.5%	29.4%	70.6%
156,085	PULASKI	22,589	6,069	16,470	50	10,401 D	26.9%	72.9%	26.9%	73.1%

ARKANSAS

PRESIDENT 1944

1940 Census Population	County	Total Vote	Republican	Democratic	Other	Rep.-Dem. Plurality	Percentage Total Vote Rep.	Percentage Total Vote Dem.	Percentage Major Vote Rep.	Percentage Major Vote Dem.
18,319	RANDOLPH	2,049	529	1,514	6	985 D	25.8%	73.9%	25.9%	74.1%
36,043	ST. FRANCIS	2,108	446	1,654	8	1,208 D	21.2%	78.5%	21.2%	78.8%
19,163	SALINE	3,217	643	2,556	18	1,913 D	20.0%	79.5%	20.1%	79.9%
13,300	SCOTT	1,246	348	898		550 D	27.9%	72.1%	27.9%	72.1%
11,942	SEARCY	2,307	1,409	891	7	518 R	61.1%	38.6%	61.3%	38.7%
62,809	SEBASTIAN	9,467	3,452	6,008	7	2,556 D	36.5%	63.5%	36.5%	63.5%
15,248	SEVIER	1,746	389	1,356	1	967 D	22.3%	77.7%	22.3%	77.7%
11,497	SHARP	1,893	664	1,217	12	553 D	35.1%	64.3%	35.3%	64.7%
8,603	STONE	1,154	549	592	13	43 D	47.6%	51.3%	48.1%	51.9%
50,461	UNION	5,459	833	4,624	2	3,791 D	15.3%	84.7%	15.3%	84.7%
12,518	VAN BUREN	1,747	655	1,090	2	435 D	37.5%	62.4%	37.5%	62.5%
41,114	WASHINGTON	6,201	3,084	3,089	28	5 D	49.7%	49.8%	50.0%	50.0%
37,176	WHITE	3,878	1,346	2,532		1,186 D	34.7%	65.3%	34.7%	65.3%
22,133	WOODRUFF	1,662	279	1,377	6	1,098 D	16.8%	82.9%	16.8%	83.2%
20,970	YELL	2,132	489	1,642	1	1,153 D	22.9%	77.0%	22.9%	77.1%
1,949,387	TOTAL	212,954	63,551	148,965	438	85,414 D	29.8%	70.0%	29.9%	70.1%

ARKANSAS

PRESIDENT 1940

1940 Census Population	County	Total Vote	Republican	Democratic	Other	Rep.-Dem. Plurality	Percentage Total Vote Rep.	Total Vote Dem.	Major Vote Rep.	Major Vote Dem.
24,437	ARKANSAS	3,132	742	2,345	45	1,603 D	23.7%	74.9%	24.0%	76.0%
26,785	ASHLEY	2,023	184	1,835	4	1,651 D	9.1%	90.7%	9.1%	90.9%
10,281	BAXTER	1,355	489	859	7	370 D	36.1%	63.4%	36.3%	63.7%
36,148	BENTON	4,473	1,962	2,442	69	480 D	43.9%	54.6%	44.6%	55.4%
15,860	BOONE	2,869	786	2,054	29	1,268 D	27.4%	71.6%	27.7%	72.3%
18,097	BRADLEY	2,066	123	1,939	4	1,816 D	6.0%	93.9%	6.0%	94.0%
9,636	CALHOUN	862	44	818		774 D	5.1%	94.9%	5.1%	94.9%
14,737	CARROLL	2,687	1,081	1,604	2	523 D	40.2%	59.7%	40.3%	59.7%
27,452	CHICOT	1,755	161	1,592	2	1,431 D	9.2%	90.7%	9.2%	90.8%
24,402	CLARK	2,327	311	2,008	8	1,697 D	13.4%	86.3%	13.4%	86.6%
28,386	CLAY	2,779	1,029	1,676	74	647 D	37.0%	60.3%	38.0%	62.0%
13,134	CLEBURNE	1,218	374	834	10	460 D	30.7%	68.5%	31.0%	69.0%
12,570	CLEVELAND	1,048	58	989	1	931 D	5.5%	94.4%	5.5%	94.5%
29,822	COLUMBIA	2,422	149	2,270	3	2,121 D	6.2%	93.7%	6.2%	93.8%
21,536	CONWAY	2,340	272	2,067	1	1,795 D	11.6%	88.3%	11.6%	88.4%
47,200	CRAIGHEAD	4,262	935	3,300	27	2,365 D	21.9%	77.4%	22.1%	77.9%
23,920	CRAWFORD	2,318	691	1,581	46	890 D	29.8%	68.2%	30.4%	69.6%
42,473	CRITTENDEN	2,040	72	1,966	2	1,894 D	3.5%	96.4%	3.5%	96.5%
26,046	CROSS	2,035	285	1,746	4	1,461 D	14.0%	85.8%	14.0%	86.0%
14,471	DALLAS	1,467	118	1,295	54	1,177 D	8.0%	88.3%	8.4%	91.6%
27,160	DESHA	1,526	146	1,370	10	1,224 D	9.6%	89.8%	9.6%	90.4%
19,831	DREW	1,511	152	1,329	30	1,177 D	10.1%	88.0%	10.3%	89.7%
25,880	FAULKNER	3,066	519	2,535	12	2,016 D	16.9%	82.7%	17.0%	83.0%
15,683	FRANKLIN	1,922	319	1,601	2	1,282 D	16.6%	83.3%	16.6%	83.4%
10,253	FULTON	1,183	333	838	12	505 D	28.1%	70.8%	28.4%	71.6%
41,664	GARLAND	4,772	1,424	3,335	13	1,911 D	29.8%	69.9%	29.9%	70.1%
10,477	GRANT	1,203	160	1,043		883 D	13.3%	86.7%	13.3%	86.7%
30,204	GREENE	2,735	510	2,220	5	1,710 D	18.6%	81.2%	18.7%	81.3%
32,770	HEMPSTEAD	3,229	415	2,814		2,399 D	12.9%	87.1%	12.9%	87.1%
18,916	HOT SPRING	2,217	482	1,730	5	1,248 D	21.7%	78.0%	21.8%	78.2%
16,621	HOWARD	1,973	419	1,540	14	1,121 D	21.2%	78.1%	21.4%	78.6%
25,643	INDEPENDENCE	3,220	928	2,276	16	1,348 D	28.8%	70.7%	29.0%	71.0%
12,834	IZARD	1,426	366	1,058	2	692 D	25.7%	74.2%	25.7%	74.3%
26,427	JACKSON	2,628	382	2,223	23	1,841 D	14.5%	84.6%	14.7%	85.3%
65,101	JEFFERSON	4,429	587	3,829	13	3,242 D	13.3%	86.5%	13.3%	86.7%
18,795	JOHNSON	1,756	318	1,429	9	1,111 D	18.1%	81.4%	18.2%	81.8%
16,851	LAFAYETTE	1,536	159	1,352	25	1,193 D	10.4%	88.0%	10.5%	89.5%
22,651	LAWRENCE	3,360	852	2,484	24	1,632 D	25.4%	73.9%	25.5%	74.5%
26,810	LEE	1,212	109	1,100	3	991 D	9.0%	90.8%	9.0%	91.0%
19,709	LINCOLN	1,025	99	916	10	817 D	9.7%	89.4%	9.8%	90.2%
15,932	LITTLE RIVER	1,392	276	1,104	12	828 D	19.8%	79.3%	20.0%	80.0%
25,967	LOGAN	3,896	1,065	2,831		1,766 D	27.3%	72.7%	27.3%	72.7%
29,802	LONOKE	2,225	323	1,899	3	1,576 D	14.5%	85.3%	14.5%	85.5%
14,531	MADISON	4,308	2,107	2,196	5	89 D	48.9%	51.0%	49.0%	51.0%
9,464	MARION	1,201	320	864	17	544 D	26.6%	71.9%	27.0%	73.0%
31,874	MILLER	3,599	563	3,019	17	2,456 D	15.6%	83.9%	15.7%	84.3%
80,217	MISSISSIPPI	5,891	616	5,257	18	4,641 D	10.5%	89.2%	10.5%	89.5%
21,133	MONROE	1,624	128	1,494	2	1,366 D	7.9%	92.0%	7.9%	92.1%
8,876	MONTGOMERY	1,417	400	1,012	5	612 D	28.2%	71.4%	28.3%	71.7%
19,869	NEVADA	1,630	224	1,399	7	1,175 D	13.7%	85.8%	13.8%	86.2%
10,881	NEWTON	2,618	1,392	1,202	24	190 R	53.2%	45.9%	53.7%	46.3%
31,151	OUACHITA	3,240	284	2,951	5	2,667 D	8.8%	91.1%	8.8%	91.2%
8,392	PERRY	990	206	783	1	577 D	20.8%	79.1%	20.8%	79.2%
45,970	PHILLIPS	2,480	245	2,235		1,990 D	9.9%	90.1%	9.9%	90.1%
11,786	PIKE	1,409	424	974	11	550 D	30.1%	69.1%	30.3%	69.7%
37,670	POINSETT	4,817	670	4,138	9	3,468 D	13.9%	85.9%	13.9%	86.1%
15,832	POLK	1,858	585	1,255	18	670 D	31.5%	67.5%	31.8%	68.2%
25,682	POPE	4,561	770	3,765	26	2,995 D	16.9%	82.5%	17.0%	83.0%
15,304	PRAIRIE	1,408	336	1,069	3	733 D	23.9%	75.9%	23.9%	76.1%
156,085	PULASKI	17,230	2,955	14,219	56	11,264 D	17.2%	82.5%	17.2%	82.8%

ARKANSAS

PRESIDENT 1940

1940 Census Population	County	Total Vote	Republican	Democratic	Other	Rep.-Dem. Plurality	Percentage Total Vote Rep.	Percentage Total Vote Dem.	Percentage Major Vote Rep.	Percentage Major Vote Dem.
18,319	RANDOLPH	2,179	474	1,687	18	1,213 D	21.8%	77.4%	21.9%	78.1%
36,043	ST. FRANCIS	1,894	192	1,671	31	1,479 D	10.1%	88.2%	10.3%	89.7%
19,163	SALINE	2,251	274	1,963	14	1,689 D	12.2%	87.2%	12.2%	87.8%
13,300	SCOTT	1,353	353	992	8	639 D	26.1%	73.3%	26.2%	73.8%
11,942	SEARCY	2,278	1,292	982	4	310 R	56.7%	43.1%	56.8%	43.2%
62,809	SEBASTIAN	7,246	1,968	5,249	29	3,281 D	27.2%	72.4%	27.3%	72.7%
15,248	SEVIER	1,675	293	1,374	8	1,081 D	17.5%	82.0%	17.6%	82.4%
11,497	SHARP	1,537	433	1,099	5	666 D	28.2%	71.5%	28.3%	71.7%
8,603	STONE	1,057	406	644	7	238 D	38.4%	60.9%	38.7%	61.3%
50,461	UNION	5,345	489	4,842	14	4,353 D	9.1%	90.6%	9.2%	90.8%
12,518	VAN BUREN	1,470	402	1,068		666 D	27.3%	72.7%	27.3%	72.7%
41,114	WASHINGTON	4,750	1,819	2,873	58	1,054 D	38.3%	60.5%	38.8%	61.2%
37,176	WHITE	4,245	876	3,345	24	2,469 D	20.6%	78.8%	20.8%	79.2%
22,133	WOODRUFF	1,481	193	1,280	8	1,087 D	13.0%	86.4%	13.1%	86.9%
20,970	YELL	2,467	224	2,236	7	2,012 D	9.1%	90.6%	9.1%	90.9%
1,949,387	TOTAL	200,429	42,122	157,213	1,094	115,091 D	21.0%	78.4%	21.1%	78.9%

ARKANSAS

PRESIDENT 1936

1930 Census Population	County	Total Vote	Republican	Democratic	Other	Rep.-Dem. Plurality	Percentage Total Vote Rep.	Percentage Total Vote Dem.	Percentage Major Vote Rep.	Percentage Major Vote Dem.
22,300	ARKANSAS	2,357	341	2,008	8	1,667 D	14.5%	85.2%	14.5%	85.5%
25,151	ASHLEY	1,477	95	1,382		1,287 D	6.4%	93.6%	6.4%	93.6%
9,519	BAXTER	1,155	375	773	7	398 D	32.5%	66.9%	32.7%	67.3%
35,253	BENTON	4,114	1,672	2,418	24	746 D	40.6%	58.8%	40.9%	59.1%
14,937	BOONE	3,448	1,052	2,386	10	1,334 D	30.5%	69.2%	30.6%	69.4%
17,494	BRADLEY	1,637	65	1,571	1	1,506 D	4.0%	96.0%	4.0%	96.0%
9,752	CALHOUN	735	30	704	1	674 D	4.1%	95.8%	4.1%	95.9%
15,820	CARROLL	2,595	940	1,649	6	709 D	36.2%	63.5%	36.3%	63.7%
22,646	CHICOT	1,221	75	1,145	1	1,070 D	6.1%	93.8%	6.1%	93.9%
24,932	CLARK	2,163	193	1,962	8	1,769 D	8.9%	90.7%	9.0%	91.0%
27,278	CLAY	2,579	795	1,778	6	983 D	30.8%	68.9%	30.9%	69.1%
11,373	CLEBURNE	1,271	336	927	8	591 D	26.4%	72.9%	26.6%	73.4%
12,744	CLEVELAND	1,136	45	1,088	3	1,043 D	4.0%	95.8%	4.0%	96.0%
27,320	COLUMBIA	1,911	64	1,847		1,783 D	3.3%	96.7%	3.3%	96.7%
21,949	CONWAY	2,320	305	2,013	2	1,708 D	13.1%	86.8%	13.2%	86.8%
44,740	CRAIGHEAD	4,066	710	3,335	21	2,625 D	17.5%	82.0%	17.6%	82.4%
22,549	CRAWFORD	2,672	697	1,963	12	1,266 D	26.1%	73.5%	26.2%	73.8%
39,717	CRITTENDEN	1,880	22	1,858		1,836 D	1.2%	98.8%	1.2%	98.8%
25,723	CROSS	1,797	133	1,644	20	1,511 D	7.4%	91.5%	7.5%	92.5%
14,671	DALLAS	1,536	103	1,433		1,330 D	6.7%	93.3%	6.7%	93.3%
21,814	DESHA	1,468	55	1,411	2	1,356 D	3.7%	96.1%	3.8%	96.2%
19,928	DREW	1,301	70	1,229	2	1,159 D	5.4%	94.5%	5.4%	94.6%
28,381	FAULKNER	3,044	511	2,521	12	2,010 D	16.8%	82.8%	16.9%	83.1%
15,762	FRANKLIN	2,247	345	1,890	12	1,545 D	15.4%	84.1%	15.4%	84.6%
10,834	FULTON	1,386	437	946	3	509 D	31.5%	68.3%	31.6%	68.4%
36,031	GARLAND	4,183	1,217	2,931	35	1,714 D	29.1%	70.1%	29.3%	70.7%
9,834	GRANT	1,126	147	978	1	831 D	13.1%	86.9%	13.1%	86.9%
26,127	GREENE	2,229	412	1,811	6	1,399 D	18.5%	81.2%	18.5%	81.5%
30,847	HEMPSTEAD	2,623	190	2,431	2	2,241 D	7.2%	92.7%	7.2%	92.8%
18,105	HOT SPRING	2,033	444	1,581	8	1,137 D	21.8%	77.8%	21.9%	78.1%
17,489	HOWARD	1,717	275	1,437	5	1,162 D	16.0%	83.7%	16.1%	83.9%
24,225	INDEPENDENCE	2,792	685	2,101	6	1,416 D	24.5%	75.3%	24.6%	75.4%
12,872	IZARD	1,766	416	1,350		934 D	23.6%	76.4%	23.6%	76.4%
27,943	JACKSON	2,479	327	2,151	1	1,824 D	13.2%	86.8%	13.2%	86.8%
64,154	JEFFERSON	3,645	224	3,414	7	3,190 D	6.1%	93.7%	6.2%	93.8%
19,289	JOHNSON	1,772	318	1,432	22	1,114 D	17.9%	80.8%	18.2%	81.8%
16,934	LAFAYETTE	1,382	100	1,279	3	1,179 D	7.2%	92.5%	7.3%	92.7%
21,663	LAWRENCE	2,703	457	2,230	16	1,773 D	16.9%	82.5%	17.0%	83.0%
26,637	LEE	1,325	66	1,257	2	1,191 D	5.0%	94.9%	5.0%	95.0%
20,250	LINCOLN	952	39	913		874 D	4.1%	95.9%	4.1%	95.9%
15,515	LITTLE RIVER	1,255	192	1,056	7	864 D	15.3%	84.1%	15.4%	84.6%
24,110	LOGAN	3,440	770	2,663	7	1,893 D	22.4%	77.4%	22.4%	77.6%
33,759	LONOKE	3,047	310	2,735	2	2,425 D	10.2%	89.8%	10.2%	89.8%
13,334	MADISON	3,167	1,484	1,679	4	195 D	46.9%	53.0%	46.9%	53.1%
8,876	MARION	1,440	435	989	16	554 D	30.2%	68.7%	30.5%	69.5%
30,586	MILLER	3,021	323	2,689	9	2,366 D	10.7%	89.0%	10.7%	89.3%
69,289	MISSISSIPPI	5,147	303	4,835	9	4,532 D	5.9%	93.9%	5.9%	94.1%
20,651	MONROE	1,187	82	1,102	3	1,020 D	6.9%	92.8%	6.9%	93.1%
10,768	MONTGOMERY	1,519	465	1,034	20	569 D	30.6%	68.1%	31.0%	69.0%
20,407	NEVADA	1,461	204	1,252	5	1,048 D	14.0%	85.7%	14.0%	86.0%
10,564	NEWTON	1,991	1,053	938		115 R	52.9%	47.1%	52.9%	47.1%
29,890	OUACHITA	3,070	262	2,808		2,546 D	8.5%	91.5%	8.5%	91.5%
7,695	PERRY	1,148	249	899		650 D	21.7%	78.3%	21.7%	78.3%
40,683	PHILLIPS	2,363	94	2,259	10	2,165 D	4.0%	95.6%	4.0%	96.0%
11,792	PIKE	1,278	283	994	1	711 D	22.1%	77.8%	22.2%	77.8%
29,695	POINSETT	4,049	563	3,457	29	2,894 D	13.9%	85.4%	14.0%	86.0%
14,857	POLK	1,735	537	1,170	28	633 D	31.0%	67.4%	31.5%	68.5%
26,547	POPE	3,030	348	2,678	4	2,330 D	11.5%	88.4%	11.5%	88.5%
15,187	PRAIRIE	1,606	282	1,321	3	1,039 D	17.6%	82.3%	17.6%	82.4%
137,727	PULASKI	12,830	1,320	11,482	28	10,162 D	10.3%	89.5%	10.3%	89.7%

ARKANSAS

PRESIDENT 1936

1930 Census Population	County	Total Vote	Republican	Democratic	Other	Rep.-Dem. Plurality	Percentage Total Vote Rep.	Percentage Total Vote Dem.	Percentage Major Vote Rep.	Percentage Major Vote Dem.
16,871	RANDOLPH	2,110	414	1,693	3	1,279 D	19.6%	80.2%	19.6%	80.4%
33,394	ST. FRANCIS	2,046	94	1,938	14	1,844 D	4.6%	94.7%	4.6%	95.4%
15,660	SALINE	1,903	359	1,520	24	1,161 D	18.9%	79.9%	19.1%	80.9%
11,803	SCOTT	1,502	363	1,137	2	774 D	24.2%	75.7%	24.2%	75.8%
11,056	SEARCY	1,778	1,010	767	1	243 R	56.8%	43.1%	56.8%	43.2%
54,426	SEBASTIAN	5,720	1,161	4,539	20	3,378 D	20.3%	79.4%	20.4%	79.6%
16,364	SEVIER	1,500	289	1,200	11	911 D	19.3%	80.0%	19.4%	80.6%
10,715	SHARP	1,235	289	934	12	645 D	23.4%	75.6%	23.6%	76.4%
7,993	STONE	772	248	521	3	273 D	32.1%	67.5%	32.2%	67.8%
55,800	UNION	4,408	254	4,141	13	3,887 D	5.8%	93.9%	5.8%	94.2%
11,962	VAN BUREN	1,969	541	1,422	6	881 D	27.5%	72.2%	27.6%	72.4%
39,255	WASHINGTON	4,977	1,579	3,378	20	1,799 D	31.7%	67.9%	31.9%	68.1%
38,269	WHITE	3,045	535	2,503	7	1,968 D	17.6%	82.2%	17.6%	82.4%
22,682	WOODRUFF	1,739	253	1,473	13	1,220 D	14.5%	84.7%	14.7%	85.3%
21,313	YELL	2,700	318	2,382		2,064 D	11.8%	88.2%	11.8%	88.2%
1,854,482	TOTAL	179,431	32,049	146,765	617	114,716 D	17.9%	81.8%	17.9%	82.1%

ARKANSAS

PRESIDENT 1932

1930 Census Population	County	Total Vote	Republican	Democratic	Other	Rep.-Dem. Plurality	Percentage Total Vote Rep.	Percentage Total Vote Dem.	Percentage Major Vote Rep.	Percentage Major Vote Dem.
22,300	ARKANSAS	3,395	494	2,867	34	2,373 D	14.6%	84.4%	14.7%	85.3%
25,151	ASHLEY	2,733	188	2,537	8	2,349 D	6.9%	92.8%	6.9%	93.1%
9,519	BAXTER	1,254	194	1,039	21	845 D	15.5%	82.9%	15.7%	84.3%
35,253	BENTON	5,198	1,275	3,775	148	2,500 D	24.5%	72.6%	25.2%	74.8%
14,937	BOONE	3,385	697	2,644	44	1,947 D	20.6%	78.1%	20.9%	79.1%
17,494	BRADLEY	2,117	125	1,985	7	1,860 D	5.9%	93.8%	5.9%	94.1%
9,752	CALHOUN	1,302	59	1,235	8	1,176 D	4.5%	94.9%	4.6%	95.4%
15,820	CARROLL	2,941	758	2,150	33	1,392 D	25.8%	73.1%	26.1%	73.9%
22,646	CHICOT	1,780	98	1,680	2	1,582 D	5.5%	94.4%	5.5%	94.5%
24,932	CLARK	3,235	183	3,037	15	2,854 D	5.7%	93.9%	5.7%	94.3%
27,278	CLAY	2,306	397	1,891	18	1,494 D	17.2%	82.0%	17.4%	82.6%
11,373	CLEBURNE	1,982	204	1,750	28	1,546 D	10.3%	88.3%	10.4%	89.6%
12,744	CLEVELAND	1,534	92	1,440	2	1,348 D	6.0%	93.9%	6.0%	94.0%
27,320	COLUMBIA	2,515	85	2,420	10	2,335 D	3.4%	96.2%	3.4%	96.6%
21,949	CONWAY	2,835	285	2,530	20	2,245 D	10.1%	89.2%	10.1%	89.9%
44,740	CRAIGHEAD	5,066	606	4,412	48	3,806 D	12.0%	87.1%	12.1%	87.9%
22,549	CRAWFORD	3,824	809	2,962	53	2,153 D	21.2%	77.5%	21.5%	78.5%
39,717	CRITTENDEN	2,454	37	2,411	6	2,374 D	1.5%	98.2%	1.5%	98.5%
25,723	CROSS	2,164	87	2,066	11	1,979 D	4.0%	95.5%	4.0%	96.0%
14,671	DALLAS	2,296	150	2,139	7	1,989 D	6.5%	93.2%	6.6%	93.4%
21,814	DESHA	1,639	81	1,549	9	1,468 D	4.9%	94.5%	5.0%	95.0%
19,928	DREW	1,969	198	1,760	11	1,562 D	10.1%	89.4%	10.1%	89.9%
28,381	FAULKNER	3,243	437	2,749	57	2,312 D	13.5%	84.8%	13.7%	86.3%
15,762	FRANKLIN	2,235	275	1,896	64	1,621 D	12.3%	84.8%	12.7%	87.3%
10,834	FULTON	1,473	237	1,235	1	998 D	16.1%	83.8%	16.1%	83.9%
36,031	GARLAND	5,086	833	4,252	1	3,419 D	16.4%	83.6%	16.4%	83.6%
9,834	GRANT	1,685	55	1,626	4	1,571 D	3.3%	96.5%	3.3%	96.7%
26,127	GREENE	3,584	274	3,277	33	3,003 D	7.6%	91.4%	7.7%	92.3%
30,847	HEMPSTEAD	3,159	317	2,840	2	2,523 D	10.0%	89.9%	10.0%	90.0%
18,105	HOT SPRING	2,806	237	2,542	27	2,305 D	8.4%	90.6%	8.5%	91.5%
17,489	HOWARD	1,871	165	1,703	3	1,538 D	8.8%	91.0%	8.8%	91.2%
24,225	INDEPENDENCE	2,811	371	2,427	13	2,056 D	13.2%	86.3%	13.3%	86.7%
12,872	IZARD	1,439	200	1,227	12	1,027 D	13.9%	85.3%	14.0%	86.0%
27,943	JACKSON	2,723	193	2,521	9	2,328 D	7.1%	92.6%	7.1%	92.9%
64,154	JEFFERSON	2,990	419	2,548	23	2,129 D	14.0%	85.2%	14.1%	85.9%
19,289	JOHNSON	1,908	284	1,557	67	1,273 D	14.9%	81.6%	15.4%	84.6%
16,934	LAFAYETTE	1,652	151	1,495	6	1,344 D	9.1%	90.5%	9.2%	90.8%
21,663	LAWRENCE	3,413	293	3,056	64	2,763 D	8.6%	89.5%	8.7%	91.3%
26,637	LEE	1,678	39	1,635	4	1,596 D	2.3%	97.4%	2.3%	97.7%
20,250	LINCOLN	1,351	49	1,301	1	1,252 D	3.6%	96.3%	3.6%	96.4%
15,515	LITTLE RIVER	1,524	118	1,399	7	1,281 D	7.7%	91.8%	7.8%	92.2%
24,110	LOGAN	3,174	645	2,493	36	1,848 D	20.3%	78.5%	20.6%	79.4%
33,759	LONOKE	3,138	175	2,951	12	2,776 D	5.6%	94.0%	5.6%	94.4%
13,334	MADISON	5,095	2,197	2,803	95	606 D	43.1%	55.0%	43.9%	56.1%
8,876	MARION	1,599	235	1,282	82	1,047 D	14.7%	80.2%	15.5%	84.5%
30,586	MILLER	4,233	322	3,876	35	3,554 D	7.6%	91.6%	7.7%	92.3%
69,289	MISSISSIPPI	6,203	364	5,776	63	5,412 D	5.9%	93.1%	5.9%	94.1%
20,651	MONROE	1,935	170	1,753	12	1,583 D	8.8%	90.6%	8.8%	91.2%
10,768	MONTGOMERY	1,739	211	1,495	33	1,284 D	12.1%	86.0%	12.4%	87.6%
20,407	NEVADA	2,564	197	2,358	9	2,161 D	7.7%	92.0%	7.7%	92.3%
10,564	NEWTON	1,510	540	941	29	401 D	35.8%	62.3%	36.5%	63.5%
29,890	OUACHITA	3,557	432	3,118	7	2,686 D	12.1%	87.7%	12.2%	87.8%
7,695	PERRY	1,474	123	1,347	4	1,224 D	8.3%	91.4%	8.4%	91.6%
40,683	PHILLIPS	3,144	142	2,976	26	2,834 D	4.5%	94.7%	4.6%	95.4%
11,792	PIKE	1,659	176	1,480	3	1,304 D	10.6%	89.2%	10.6%	89.4%
29,695	POINSETT	4,636	252	4,312	72	4,060 D	5.4%	93.0%	5.5%	94.5%
14,857	POLK	1,874	223	1,568	83	1,345 D	11.9%	83.7%	12.5%	87.5%
26,547	POPE	2,702	280	2,391	31	2,111 D	10.4%	88.5%	10.5%	89.5%
15,187	PRAIRIE	1,911	158	1,743	10	1,585 D	8.3%	91.2%	8.3%	91.7%
137,727	PULASKI	16,440	2,281	14,049	110	11,768 D	13.9%	85.5%	14.0%	86.0%

ARKANSAS

PRESIDENT 1932

1930 Census Population	County	Total Vote	Republican	Democratic	Other	Rep.-Dem. Plurality	Percentage Total Vote Rep.	Percentage Total Vote Dem.	Percentage Major Vote Rep.	Percentage Major Vote Dem.
16,871	RANDOLPH	2,243	206	2,021	16	1,815 D	9.2%	90.1%	9.3%	90.7%
33,394	ST. FRANCIS	2,367	130	2,191	46	2,061 D	5.5%	92.6%	5.6%	94.4%
15,660	SALINE	2,129	107	1,990	32	1,883 D	5.0%	93.5%	5.1%	94.9%
11,803	SCOTT	1,312	174	1,042	96	868 D	13.3%	79.4%	14.3%	85.7%
11,056	SEARCY	1,808	846	947	15	101 D	46.8%	52.4%	47.2%	52.8%
54,426	SEBASTIAN	6,260	1,268	4,937	55	3,669 D	20.3%	78.9%	20.4%	79.6%
16,364	SEVIER	2,193	162	2,009	22	1,847 D	7.4%	91.6%	7.5%	92.5%
10,715	SHARP	1,484	142	1,334	8	1,192 D	9.6%	89.9%	9.6%	90.4%
7,993	STONE	1,390	261	1,100	29	839 D	18.8%	79.1%	19.2%	80.8%
55,800	UNION	5,738	245	5,429	64	5,184 D	4.3%	94.6%	4.3%	95.7%
11,962	VAN BUREN	1,890	413	1,456	21	1,043 D	21.9%	77.0%	22.1%	77.9%
39,255	WASHINGTON	6,596	1,502	4,971	123	3,469 D	22.8%	75.4%	23.2%	76.8%
38,269	WHITE	3,705	430	3,251	24	2,821 D	11.6%	87.7%	11.7%	88.3%
22,682	WOODRUFF	2,022	135	1,864	23	1,729 D	6.7%	92.2%	6.8%	93.2%
21,313	YELL	2,290	272	2,010	8	1,738 D	11.9%	87.8%	11.9%	88.1%
1,854,482	TOTAL	216,569	27,465	186,829	2,275	159,364 D	12.7%	86.3%	12.8%	87.2%

ARKANSAS

PRESIDENT 1928

1920 Census Population	County	Total Vote	Republican	Democratic	Other	Rep.-Dem. Plurality	Percentage Total Vote Rep.	Percentage Total Vote Dem.	Percentage Major Vote Rep.	Percentage Major Vote Dem.
21,483	ARKANSAS	2,545	1,046	1,491	8	445 D	41.1%	58.6%	41.2%	58.8%
23,410	ASHLEY	2,182	786	1,393	3	607 D	36.0%	63.8%	36.1%	63.9%
10,216	BAXTER	1,180	504	665	11	161 D	42.7%	56.4%	43.1%	56.9%
36,253	BENTON	5,669	3,248	2,348	73	900 R	57.3%	41.4%	58.0%	42.0%
16,098	BOONE	3,264	1,543	1,708	13	165 D	47.3%	52.3%	47.5%	52.5%
15,970	BRADLEY	1,934	447	1,487		1,040 D	23.1%	76.9%	23.1%	76.9%
11,807	CALHOUN	1,033	262	765	6	503 D	25.4%	74.1%	25.5%	74.5%
17,786	CARROLL	3,312	1,757	1,540	15	217 R	53.0%	46.5%	53.3%	46.7%
21,749	CHICOT	1,468	445	1,021	2	576 D	30.3%	69.6%	30.4%	69.6%
25,632	CLARK	2,736	913	1,817	6	904 D	33.4%	66.4%	33.4%	66.6%
27,276	CLAY	2,708	1,254	1,435	19	181 D	46.3%	53.0%	46.6%	53.4%
12,696	CLEBURNE	1,442	574	856	12	282 D	39.8%	59.4%	40.1%	59.9%
12,260	CLEVELAND	1,167	476	690	1	214 D	40.8%	59.1%	40.8%	59.2%
27,670	COLUMBIA	2,370	617	1,752	1	1,135 D	26.0%	73.9%	26.0%	74.0%
22,578	CONWAY	2,182	665	1,514	3	849 D	30.5%	69.4%	30.5%	69.5%
37,541	CRAIGHEAD	4,118	1,958	2,132	28	174 D	47.5%	51.8%	47.9%	52.1%
25,739	CRAWFORD	3,302	1,559	1,743		184 D	47.2%	52.8%	47.2%	52.8%
29,309	CRITTENDEN	1,939	304	1,635		1,331 D	15.7%	84.3%	15.7%	84.3%
18,579	CROSS	1,610	324	1,282	4	958 D	20.1%	79.6%	20.2%	79.8%
14,424	DALLAS	1,537	503	1,030	4	527 D	32.7%	67.0%	32.8%	67.2%
20,297	DESHA	1,415	331	1,082	2	751 D	23.4%	76.5%	23.4%	76.6%
21,822	DREW	1,956	500	1,452	4	952 D	25.6%	74.2%	25.6%	74.4%
27,681	FAULKNER	3,664	992	2,659	13	1,667 D	27.1%	72.6%	27.2%	72.8%
19,364	FRANKLIN	2,119	774	1,329	16	555 D	36.5%	62.7%	36.8%	63.2%
11,182	FULTON	1,622	686	934	2	248 D	42.3%	57.6%	42.3%	57.7%
25,785	GARLAND	5,558	2,720	2,823	15	103 D	48.9%	50.8%	49.1%	50.9%
10,710	GRANT	1,486	439	1,045	2	606 D	29.5%	70.3%	29.6%	70.4%
26,105	GREENE	2,450	1,011	1,426	13	415 D	41.3%	58.2%	41.5%	58.5%
31,602	HEMPSTEAD	2,929	886	2,038	5	1,152 D	30.2%	69.6%	30.3%	69.7%
17,784	HOT SPRING	2,130	1,126	999	5	127 R	52.9%	46.9%	53.0%	47.0%
18,565	HOWARD	1,827	763	1,055	9	292 D	41.8%	57.7%	42.0%	58.0%
23,976	INDEPENDENCE	2,668	1,150	1,511	7	361 D	43.1%	56.6%	43.2%	56.8%
13,871	IZARD	1,602	696	902	4	206 D	43.4%	56.3%	43.6%	56.4%
25,446	JACKSON	2,234	698	1,527	9	829 D	31.2%	68.4%	31.4%	68.6%
60,330	JEFFERSON	4,450	1,830	2,611	9	781 D	41.1%	58.7%	41.2%	58.8%
21,062	JOHNSON	2,074	766	1,292	16	526 D	36.9%	62.3%	37.2%	62.8%
15,522	LAFAYETTE	1,427	435	991	1	556 D	30.5%	69.4%	30.5%	69.5%
22,098	LAWRENCE	1,983	774	1,204	5	430 D	39.0%	60.7%	39.1%	60.9%
28,852	LEE	1,195	149	1,046		897 D	12.5%	87.5%	12.5%	87.5%
18,774	LINCOLN	1,021	151	869	1	718 D	14.8%	85.1%	14.8%	85.2%
16,301	LITTLE RIVER	1,375	457	916	2	459 D	33.2%	66.6%	33.3%	66.7%
25,866	LOGAN	3,430	1,455	1,967	8	512 D	42.4%	57.3%	42.5%	57.5%
33,400	LONOKE	2,536	676	1,857	3	1,181 D	26.7%	73.2%	26.7%	73.3%
14,918	MADISON	4,500	2,760	1,717	23	1,043 R	61.3%	38.2%	61.6%	38.4%
10,154	MARION	1,173	436	731	6	295 D	37.2%	62.3%	37.4%	62.6%
24,021	MILLER	2,911	1,150	1,752	9	602 D	39.5%	60.2%	39.6%	60.4%
47,320	MISSISSIPPI	5,799	1,324	4,451	24	3,127 D	22.8%	76.8%	22.9%	77.1%
21,601	MONROE	1,263	411	851	1	440 D	32.5%	67.4%	32.6%	67.4%
11,112	MONTGOMERY	1,715	976	726	13	250 R	56.9%	42.3%	57.3%	42.7%
21,934	NEVADA	2,192	946	1,242	4	296 D	43.2%	56.7%	43.2%	56.8%
11,199	NEWTON	1,857	1,316	533	8	783 R	70.9%	28.7%	71.2%	28.8%
20,636	OUACHITA	2,633	1,051	1,582		531 D	39.9%	60.1%	39.9%	60.1%
9,905	PERRY	1,113	474	636	3	162 D	42.6%	57.1%	42.7%	57.3%
44,530	PHILLIPS	2,552	487	2,061	4	1,574 D	19.1%	80.8%	19.1%	80.9%
12,397	PIKE	1,483	698	779	6	81 D	47.1%	52.5%	47.3%	52.7%
20,848	POINSETT	3,518	1,182	2,324	12	1,142 D	33.6%	66.1%	33.7%	66.3%
16,412	POLK	1,916	1,022	870	24	152 R	53.3%	45.4%	54.0%	46.0%
27,153	POPE	4,317	1,559	2,735	23	1,176 D	36.1%	63.4%	36.3%	63.7%
17,447	PRAIRIE	1,621	613	1,000	8	387 D	37.8%	61.7%	38.0%	62.0%
109,464	PULASKI	14,124	4,880	9,215	29	4,335 D	34.6%	65.2%	34.6%	65.4%

ARKANSAS

PRESIDENT 1928

1920 Census Population	County	Total Vote	Republican	Democratic	Other	Rep.-Dem. Plurality	Percentage Total Vote Rep.	Percentage Total Vote Dem.	Percentage Major Vote Rep.	Percentage Major Vote Dem.
17,713	RANDOLPH	2,311	776	1,527	8	751 D	33.6%	66.1%	33.7%	66.3%
28,385	ST. FRANCIS	2,002	617	1,376	9	759 D	30.8%	68.7%	31.0%	69.0%
16,781	SALINE	1,786	520	1,261	5	741 D	29.1%	70.6%	29.2%	70.8%
13,232	SCOTT	1,475	573	891	11	318 D	38.8%	60.4%	39.1%	60.9%
14,590	SEARCY	2,046	1,425	606	15	819 R	69.6%	29.6%	70.2%	29.8%
56,739	SEBASTIAN	6,684	3,465	3,186	33	279 R	51.8%	47.7%	52.1%	47.9%
18,301	SEVIER	1,783	524	1,259		735 D	29.4%	70.6%	29.4%	70.6%
11,132	SHARP	1,310	501	808	1	307 D	38.2%	61.7%	38.3%	61.7%
8,779	STONE	1,144	499	628	17	129 D	43.6%	54.9%	44.3%	55.7%
29,691	UNION	4,748	1,612	3,128	8	1,516 D	34.0%	65.9%	34.0%	66.0%
13,666	VAN BUREN	2,537	994	1,539	4	545 D	39.2%	60.7%	39.2%	60.8%
35,468	WASHINGTON	5,567	3,132	2,395	40	737 R	56.3%	43.0%	56.7%	43.3%
34,603	WHITE	4,279	1,957	2,299	23	342 D	45.7%	53.7%	46.0%	54.0%
21,547	WOODRUFF	1,617	452	1,163	2	711 D	28.0%	71.9%	28.0%	72.0%
25,655	YELL	2,901	802	2,086	13	1,284 D	27.6%	71.9%	27.8%	72.2%
1,752,204	TOTAL	197,726	77,784	119,196	746	41,412 D	39.3%	60.3%	39.5%	60.5%

ARKANSAS

PRESIDENT 1924

							Percentage			
							Total Vote		Major Vote	
1920 Census Population	County	Total Vote	Republican	Democratic	Other	Rep.-Dem. Plurality	Rep.	Dem.	Rep.	Dem.
21,483	ARKANSAS	1,350	488	772	90	284 D	36.1%	57.2%	38.7%	61.3%
23,410	ASHLEY	1,649	506	1,048	95	542 D	30.7%	63.6%	32.6%	67.4%
10,216	BAXTER	1,103	301	640	162	339 D	27.3%	58.0%	32.0%	68.0%
36,253	BENTON	4,573	1,694	2,313	566	619 D	37.0%	50.6%	42.3%	57.7%
16,098	BOONE	2,499	937	1,350	212	413 D	37.5%	54.0%	41.0%	59.0%
15,970	BRADLEY	1,555	453	1,002	100	549 D	29.1%	64.4%	31.1%	68.9%
11,807	CALHOUN	745	150	553	42	403 D	20.1%	74.2%	21.3%	78.7%
17,786	CARROLL	2,524	969	1,421	134	452 D	38.4%	56.3%	40.5%	59.5%
21,749	CHICOT	1,050	325	708	17	383 D	31.0%	67.4%	31.5%	68.5%
25,632	CLARK	1,910	483	1,223	204	740 D	25.3%	64.0%	28.3%	71.7%
27,276	CLAY	2,720	1,084	1,429	207	345 D	39.9%	52.5%	43.1%	56.9%
12,696	CLEBURNE	900	238	569	93	331 D	26.4%	63.2%	29.5%	70.5%
12,260	CLEVELAND	818	174	613	31	439 D	21.3%	74.9%	22.1%	77.9%
27,670	COLUMBIA	1,795	350	1,382	63	1,032 D	19.5%	77.0%	20.2%	79.8%
22,578	CONWAY	1,560	526	909	125	383 D	33.7%	58.3%	36.7%	63.3%
37,541	CRAIGHEAD	2,794	812	1,711	271	899 D	29.1%	61.2%	32.2%	67.8%
25,739	CRAWFORD	2,910	996	1,445	469	449 D	34.2%	49.7%	40.8%	59.2%
29,309	CRITTENDEN	874	77	777	20	700 D	8.8%	88.9%	9.0%	91.0%
18,579	CROSS	911	192	625	94	433 D	21.1%	68.6%	23.5%	76.5%
14,424	DALLAS	1,503	401	1,068	34	667 D	26.7%	71.1%	27.3%	72.7%
20,297	DESHA	970	209	540	221	331 D	21.5%	55.7%	27.9%	72.1%
21,822	DREW	1,603	563	1,018	22	455 D	35.1%	63.5%	35.6%	64.4%
27,681	FAULKNER	2,132	536	1,436	160	900 D	25.1%	67.4%	27.2%	72.8%
19,364	FRANKLIN	1,831	422	1,188	221	766 D	23.0%	64.9%	26.2%	73.8%
11,182	FULTON	1,007	292	678	37	386 D	29.0%	67.3%	30.1%	69.9%
25,785	GARLAND	2,837	1,064	1,501	272	437 D	37.5%	52.9%	41.5%	58.5%
10,710	GRANT	858	133	628	97	495 D	15.5%	73.2%	17.5%	82.5%
26,105	GREENE	1,935	456	1,148	331	692 D	23.6%	59.3%	28.4%	71.6%
31,602	HEMPSTEAD	2,354	715	1,459	180	744 D	30.4%	62.0%	32.9%	67.1%
17,784	HOT SPRING	1,340	392	793	155	401 D	29.3%	59.2%	33.1%	66.9%
18,565	HOWARD	1,462	338	954	170	616 D	23.1%	65.3%	26.2%	73.8%
23,976	INDEPENDENCE	2,042	534	1,313	195	779 D	26.2%	64.3%	28.9%	71.1%
13,871	IZARD	1,000	241	728	31	487 D	24.1%	72.8%	24.9%	75.1%
25,446	JACKSON	1,541	392	1,069	80	677 D	25.4%	69.4%	26.8%	73.2%
60,330	JEFFERSON	3,172	707	1,950	515	1,243 D	22.3%	61.5%	26.6%	73.4%
21,062	JOHNSON	1,572	311	1,029	232	718 D	19.8%	65.5%	23.2%	76.8%
15,522	LAFAYETTE	1,215	298	788	129	490 D	24.5%	64.9%	27.4%	72.6%
22,098	LAWRENCE	1,126	261	689	176	428 D	23.2%	61.2%	27.5%	72.5%
28,852	LEE	1,703	596	1,103	4	507 D	35.0%	64.8%	35.1%	64.9%
18,774	LINCOLN	738	170	563	5	393 D	23.0%	76.3%	23.2%	76.8%
16,301	LITTLE RIVER	868	276	546	46	270 D	31.8%	62.9%	33.6%	66.4%
25,866	LOGAN	2,923	937	1,457	529	520 D	32.1%	49.8%	39.1%	60.9%
33,400	LONOKE	1,345	321	962	62	641 D	23.9%	71.5%	25.0%	75.0%
14,918	MADISON	2,696	1,263	1,335	98	72 D	46.8%	49.5%	48.6%	51.4%
10,154	MARION	1,308	282	825	201	543 D	21.6%	63.1%	25.5%	74.5%
24,021	MILLER	2,297	397	1,460	440	1,063 D	17.3%	63.6%	21.4%	78.6%
47,320	MISSISSIPPI	2,828	703	2,039	86	1,336 D	24.9%	72.1%	25.6%	74.4%
21,601	MONROE	1,269	330	838	101	508 D	26.0%	66.0%	28.3%	71.7%
11,112	MONTGOMERY	882	360	431	91	71 D	40.8%	48.9%	45.5%	54.5%
21,934	NEVADA	1,291	386	719	186	333 D	29.9%	55.7%	34.9%	65.1%
11,199	NEWTON	944	578	298	68	280 R	61.2%	31.6%	66.0%	34.0%
20,636	OUACHITA	2,312	952	1,318	42	366 D	41.2%	57.0%	41.9%	58.1%
9,905	PERRY	790	260	386	144	126 D	32.9%	48.9%	40.2%	59.8%
44,530	PHILLIPS	2,310	454	1,785	71	1,331 D	19.7%	77.3%	20.3%	79.7%
12,397	PIKE	1,184	378	732	74	354 D	31.9%	61.8%	34.1%	65.9%
20,848	POINSETT	1,723	393	1,182	148	789 D	22.8%	68.6%	25.0%	75.0%
16,412	POLK	1,594	502	863	229	361 D	31.5%	54.1%	36.8%	63.2%
27,153	POPE	2,256	479	1,581	196	1,102 D	21.2%	70.1%	23.3%	76.7%
17,447	PRAIRIE	1,181	386	730	65	344 D	32.7%	61.8%	34.6%	65.4%
109,464	PULASKI	9,622	2,729	5,706	1,187	2,977 D	28.4%	59.3%	32.4%	67.6%

ARKANSAS

PRESIDENT 1924

1920 Census Population	County	Total Vote	Republican	Democratic	Other	Rep.-Dem. Plurality	Percentage Total Vote Rep.	Percentage Total Vote Dem.	Percentage Major Vote Rep.	Percentage Major Vote Dem.
17,713	RANDOLPH	1,208	389	772	47	383 D	32.2%	63.9%	33.5%	66.5%
28,385	ST. FRANCIS	1,467	433	972	62	539 D	29.5%	66.3%	30.8%	69.2%
16,781	SALINE	1,055	144	770	141	626 D	13.6%	73.0%	15.8%	84.2%
13,232	SCOTT	1,128	375	607	146	232 D	33.2%	53.8%	38.2%	61.8%
14,590	SEARCY	1,321	797	415	109	382 R	60.3%	31.4%	65.8%	34.2%
56,739	SEBASTIAN	5,992	1,985	3,148	859	1,163 D	33.1%	52.5%	38.7%	61.3%
18,301	SEVIER	1,477	270	931	276	661 D	18.3%	63.0%	22.5%	77.5%
11,132	SHARP	995	210	729	56	519 D	21.1%	73.3%	22.4%	77.6%
8,779	STONE	650	210	386	54	176 D	32.3%	59.4%	35.2%	64.8%
29,691	UNION	2,673	450	1,967	256	1,517 D	16.8%	73.6%	18.6%	81.4%
13,666	VAN BUREN	1,444	435	922	87	487 D	30.1%	63.9%	32.1%	67.9%
35,468	WASHINGTON	4,083	1,466	2,281	336	815 D	35.9%	55.9%	39.1%	60.9%
34,603	WHITE	2,452	679	1,488	285	809 D	27.7%	60.7%	31.3%	68.7%
21,547	WOODRUFF	1,047	254	762	31	508 D	24.3%	72.8%	25.0%	75.0%
25,655	YELL	1,744	334	1,314	96	980 D	19.2%	75.3%	20.3%	79.7%
1,752,204	TOTAL	138,540	40,583	84,790	13,167	44,207 D	29.3%	61.2%	32.4%	67.6%

ARKANSAS

PRESIDENT 1920

1920 Census Population	County	Total Vote	Republican	Democratic	Other	Rep.-Dem. Plurality	Percentage Total Vote Rep.	Percentage Total Vote Dem.	Percentage Major Vote Rep.	Percentage Major Vote Dem.
21,483	ARKANSAS	2,387	1,199	1,156	32	43 R	50.2%	48.4%	50.9%	49.1%
23,410	ASHLEY	2,069	725	1,312	32	587 D	35.0%	63.4%	35.6%	64.4%
10,216	BAXTER	1,261	484	707	70	223 D	38.4%	56.1%	40.6%	59.4%
36,253	BENTON	4,870	1,916	2,838	116	922 D	39.3%	58.3%	40.3%	59.7%
16,098	BOONE	1,817	647	1,106	64	459 D	35.6%	60.9%	36.9%	63.1%
15,970	BRADLEY	1,757	540	1,146	71	606 D	30.7%	65.2%	32.0%	68.0%
11,807	CALHOUN	1,139	337	736	66	399 D	29.6%	64.6%	31.4%	68.6%
17,786	CARROLL	2,747	1,338	1,344	65	6 D	48.7%	48.9%	49.9%	50.1%
21,749	CHICOT	1,386	489	887	10	398 D	35.3%	64.0%	35.5%	64.5%
25,632	CLARK	2,546	1,020	1,507	19	487 D	40.1%	59.2%	40.4%	59.6%
27,276	CLAY	3,492	1,536	1,775	181	239 D	44.0%	50.8%	46.4%	53.6%
12,696	CLEBURNE	1,206	459	678	69	219 D	38.1%	56.2%	40.4%	59.6%
12,260	CLEVELAND	1,299	475	809	15	334 D	36.6%	62.3%	37.0%	63.0%
27,670	COLUMBIA	2,926	857	2,052	17	1,195 D	29.3%	70.1%	29.5%	70.5%
22,578	CONWAY	3,071	1,243	1,791	37	548 D	40.5%	58.3%	41.0%	59.0%
37,541	CRAIGHEAD	3,241	1,058	2,079	104	1,021 D	32.6%	64.1%	33.7%	66.3%
25,739	CRAWFORD	3,398	1,497	1,861	40	364 D	44.1%	54.8%	44.6%	55.4%
29,309	CRITTENDEN	1,080	167	905	8	738 D	15.5%	83.8%	15.6%	84.4%
18,579	CROSS	1,344	457	845	42	388 D	34.0%	62.9%	35.1%	64.9%
14,424	DALLAS	1,821	659	1,140	22	481 D	36.2%	62.6%	36.6%	63.4%
20,297	DESHA	1,314	360	931	23	571 D	27.4%	70.9%	27.9%	72.1%
21,822	DREW	2,198	773	1,397	28	624 D	35.2%	63.6%	35.6%	64.4%
27,681	FAULKNER	3,251	1,148	1,971	132	823 D	35.3%	60.6%	36.8%	63.2%
19,364	FRANKLIN	2,392	769	1,502	121	733 D	32.1%	62.8%	33.9%	66.1%
11,182	FULTON	1,283	502	763	18	261 D	39.1%	59.5%	39.7%	60.3%
25,785	GARLAND	3,131	1,423	1,619	89	196 D	45.4%	51.7%	46.8%	53.2%
10,710	GRANT	865	230	619	16	389 D	26.6%	71.6%	27.1%	72.9%
26,105	GREENE	3,017	1,072	1,865	80	793 D	35.5%	61.8%	36.5%	63.5%
31,602	HEMPSTEAD	4,018	1,754	2,239	25	485 D	43.7%	55.7%	43.9%	56.1%
17,784	HOT SPRING	2,024	910	1,061	53	151 D	45.0%	52.4%	46.2%	53.8%
18,565	HOWARD	2,688	1,208	1,452	28	244 D	44.9%	54.0%	45.4%	54.6%
23,976	INDEPENDENCE	2,710	1,077	1,546	87	469 D	39.7%	57.0%	41.1%	58.9%
13,871	IZARD	1,352	485	841	26	356 D	35.9%	62.2%	36.6%	63.4%
25,446	JACKSON	2,804	1,131	1,575	98	444 D	40.3%	56.2%	41.8%	58.2%
60,330	JEFFERSON	3,783	1,048	2,670	65	1,622 D	27.7%	70.6%	28.2%	71.8%
21,062	JOHNSON	2,755	996	1,579	180	583 D	36.2%	57.3%	38.7%	61.3%
15,522	LAFAYETTE	1,460	500	954	6	454 D	34.2%	65.3%	34.4%	65.6%
22,098	LAWRENCE	2,434	699	1,686	49	987 D	28.7%	69.3%	29.3%	70.7%
28,852	LEE	1,500	354	1,108	38	754 D	23.6%	73.9%	24.2%	75.8%
18,774	LINCOLN	1,885	988	888	9	100 R	52.4%	47.1%	52.7%	47.3%
16,301	LITTLE RIVER	1,521	618	853	50	235 D	40.6%	56.1%	42.0%	58.0%
25,866	LOGAN	3,779	1,871	1,840	68	31 R	49.5%	48.7%	50.4%	49.6%
33,400	LONOKE	2,481	697	1,711	73	1,014 D	28.1%	69.0%	28.9%	71.1%
14,918	MADISON	3,230	1,715	1,463	52	252 R	53.1%	45.3%	54.0%	46.0%
10,154	MARION	1,297	371	744	182	373 D	28.6%	57.4%	33.3%	66.7%
24,021	MILLER	2,466	836	1,545	85	709 D	33.9%	62.7%	35.1%	64.9%
47,320	MISSISSIPPI	2,980	1,050	1,809	121	759 D	35.2%	60.7%	36.7%	63.3%
21,601	MONROE	1,776	912	834	30	78 R	51.4%	47.0%	52.2%	47.8%
11,112	MONTGOMERY	1,119	615	430	74	185 R	55.0%	38.4%	58.9%	41.1%
21,934	NEVADA	2,551	1,292	1,220	39	72 R	50.6%	47.8%	51.4%	48.6%
11,199	NEWTON	1,374	828	486	60	342 R	60.3%	35.4%	63.0%	37.0%
20,636	OUACHITA	2,474	1,141	1,307	26	166 D	46.1%	52.8%	46.6%	53.4%
9,905	PERRY	1,367	592	738	37	146 D	43.3%	54.0%	44.5%	55.5%
44,530	PHILLIPS	2,842	868	1,965	9	1,097 D	30.5%	69.1%	30.6%	69.4%
12,397	PIKE	1,817	921	849	47	72 R	50.7%	46.7%	52.0%	48.0%
20,848	POINSETT	1,922	633	1,201	88	568 D	32.9%	62.5%	34.5%	65.5%
16,412	POLK	2,535	1,173	1,208	154	35 D	46.3%	47.7%	49.3%	50.7%
27,153	POPE	3,271	1,120	2,082	69	962 D	34.2%	63.7%	35.0%	65.0%
17,447	PRAIRIE	1,845	842	962	41	120 D	45.6%	52.1%	46.7%	53.3%
109,464	PULASKI	10,367	3,711	6,506	150	2,795 D	35.8%	62.8%	36.3%	63.7%

ARKANSAS

PRESIDENT 1920

1920 Census Population	County	Total Vote	Republican	Democratic	Other	Rep.-Dem. Plurality	Percentage Total Vote Rep.	Total Vote Dem.	Major Vote Rep.	Major Vote Dem.
17,713	RANDOLPH	2,092	652	1,412	28	760 D	31.2%	67.5%	31.6%	68.4%
28,385	ST. FRANCIS	2,212	903	1,252	57	349 D	40.8%	56.6%	41.9%	58.1%
16,781	SALINE	1,670	403	1,206	61	803 D	24.1%	72.2%	25.0%	75.0%
13,232	SCOTT	1,602	751	771	80	20 D	46.9%	48.1%	49.3%	50.7%
14,590	SEARCY	1,760	1,070	594	96	476 R	60.8%	33.8%	64.3%	35.7%
56,739	SEBASTIAN	7,586	3,492	3,852	242	360 D	46.0%	50.8%	47.5%	52.5%
18,301	SEVIER	1,997	599	1,236	162	637 D	30.0%	61.9%	32.6%	67.4%
11,132	SHARP	1,514	400	995	119	595 D	26.4%	65.7%	28.7%	71.3%
8,779	STONE	935	367	516	52	149 D	39.3%	55.2%	41.6%	58.4%
29,691	UNION	2,316	493	1,763	60	1,270 D	21.3%	76.1%	21.9%	78.1%
13,666	VAN BUREN	1,902	1,388	440	74	948 R	73.0%	23.1%	75.9%	24.1%
35,468	WASHINGTON	4,879	2,118	2,637	124	519 D	43.4%	54.0%	44.5%	55.5%
34,603	WHITE	3,593	1,359	2,086	148	727 D	37.8%	58.1%	39.4%	60.6%
21,547	WOODRUFF	2,032	943	1,049	40	106 D	46.4%	51.6%	47.3%	52.7%
25,655	YELL	3,046	1,042	1,925	79	883 D	34.2%	63.2%	35.1%	64.9%
1,752,204	TOTAL	183,871	72,316	106,427	5,128	34,111 D	39.3%	57.9%	40.5%	59.5%

ARKANSAS

ELECTION NOTES

1956 Other vote was Andrews (States Rights).

1952 Other vote was 886 Hamblen (Prohibition); 458 MacArthur (Christian Nationalist); 1 Hass (Socialist Labor).

1948 Other vote was 40,068 Thurmond (States Rights); 1,037 Thomas (Socialist); 751 Wallace (Progressive); 1 Watson (Prohibition). States Rights candidates carried Crittenden, Lee and Phillips counties and ran second in a number of other counties.

1944 Other vote was Thomas (Socialist).

1940 Other vote was 793 Babson (Prohibition); 301 Thomas (Socialist).

1936 Other vote was 446 Thomas (Socialist); 167 Browder (Communist); 4 Union (Lemke).

1932 Other vote was 1,166 Thomas (Socialist); 952 Harvey (Liberty); 157 Foster (Communist).

1928 Other vote was 429 Thomas (Socialist); 317 Foster (Communist).

1924 State canvass report was not available for this election; data have been taken from Edgar Eugene Robinson's studies. Other vote was LaFollette (Progressive).

1920 State canvass report was not available for this election; data have been taken from Edgar Eugene Robinson's studies with the addition of unofficial figures for Logan county. Other vote was Debs (Socialist).

CALIFORNIA

POPULAR VOTE FOR PRESIDENT 1920 TO 1956

Year	Total Vote	Republican		Democratic		Other Vote	Plurality	Percentage			
								Total Vote		Major Vote	
		Vote	Candidate	Vote	Candidate			Rep.	Dem.	Rep.	Dem.
1956	5,466,355	3,027,668	Eisenhower, Dwight D.	2,420,135	Stevenson, Adlai E.	18,552	607,533 R	55.4%	44.3%	55.6%	44.4%
1952	5,141,849	2,897,310	Eisenhower, Dwight D.	2,197,548	Stevenson, Adlai E.	46,991	699,762 R	56.3%	42.7%	56.9%	43.1%
1948	4,021,538	1,895,269	Dewey, Thomas E.	1,913,134	Truman, Harry S.	213,135	17,865 D	47.1%	47.6%	49.8%	50.2%
1944	3,520,875	1,512,965	Dewey, Thomas E.	1,988,564	Roosevelt, Franklin D.	19,346	475,599 D	43.0%	56.5%	43.2%	56.8%
1940	3,268,791	1,351,419	Willkie, Wendell	1,877,618	Roosevelt, Franklin D.	39,754	526,199 D	41.3%	57.4%	41.9%	58.1%
1936	2,638,882	836,431	Landon, Alfred M.	1,766,836	Roosevelt, Franklin D.	35,615	930,405 D	31.7%	67.0%	32.1%	67.9%
1932	2,266,972	847,902	Hoover, Herbert C.	1,324,157	Roosevelt, Franklin D.	94,913	476,255 D	37.4%	58.4%	39.0%	61.0%
1928	1,796,656	1,162,323	Hoover, Herbert C.	614,365	Smith, Alfred E.	19,968	547,958 R	64.7%	34.2%	65.4%	34.6%
1924 **	1,281,778	733,250	Coolidge, Calvin	105,514	Davis, John W.	443,014	308,601 R	57.2%	8.2%	87.4%	12.6%
1920	943,463	624,992	Harding, Warren G.	229,191	Cox, James M.	89,280	395,801 R	66.2%	24.3%	73.2%	26.8%

In 1924 other vote was 424,649 Progressive and 18,365 Prohibition.

ELECTORAL COLLEGE VOTE 1920 TO 1956

Year	Total	Republican	Democratic	Other
1956	32	32	—	—
1952	32	32	—	—
1948	25	—	25	—
1944	25	—	25	—
1940	22	—	22	—
1936	22	—	22	—
1932	22	—	22	—
1928	13	13	—	—
1924	13	13	—	—
1920	13	13	—	—

CALIFORNIA

DEL NORTE
SISKIYOU
MODOC
HUMBOLDT
TRINITY
SHASTA
LASSEN
TEHAMA
PLUMAS
MENDOCINO
GLENN
BUTTE
SIERRA
NEVADA
LAKE
COLUSA
SUTTER
YUBA
PLACER
EL DORADO
YOLO
SONOMA
NAPA
SACRAMENTO
ALPINE
AMADOR
SOLANO
MARIN
CALAVERAS
TUOLUMNE
CONTRA COSTA
SAN JOAQUIN
MONO
SAN FRANCISCO
ALAMEDA
STANISLAUS
MARIPOSA
SAN MATEO
SANTA CLARA
MERCED
MADERA
SANTA CRUZ
INYO
SAN BENITO
FRESNO
TULARE
MONTEREY
KINGS
SAN LUIS OBISPO
KERN
SAN BERNARDINO
SANTA BARBARA (PART)
VENTURA (PART)
LOS ANGELES (PART)
VENTURA (PART)
SANTA BARBARA (PART)
ORANGE
RIVERSIDE
SANTA BARBARA (PART)
LOS ANGELES (PART)
VENTURA (PART)
SAN DIEGO
IMPERIAL

CALIFORNIA

PRESIDENT 1956

1950 Census Population	County	Total Vote	Republican	Democratic	Other	Rep.-Dem. Plurality	Percentage Total Vote Rep.	Total Vote Dem.	Major Vote Rep.	Major Vote Dem.
740,315	ALAMEDA	368,131	192,911	174,033	1,187	18,878 R	52.4%	47.3%	52.6%	47.4%
241	ALPINE	143	114	29		85 R	79.7%	20.3%	79.7%	20.3%
9,151	AMADOR	4,325	2,126	2,181	18	55 D	49.2%	50.4%	49.4%	50.6%
64,930	BUTTE	31,462	18,382	12,933	147	5,449 R	58.4%	41.1%	58.7%	41.3%
9,902	CALAVERAS	4,909	2,843	2,049	17	794 R	57.9%	41.7%	58.1%	41.9%
11,651	COLUSA	4,648	2,474	2,171	3	303 R	53.2%	46.7%	53.3%	46.7%
298,984	CONTRA COSTA	147,051	74,971	71,733	347	3,238 R	51.0%	48.8%	51.1%	48.9%
8,078	DEL NORTE	5,487	2,918	2,552	17	366 R	53.2%	46.5%	53.3%	46.7%
16,207	EL DORADO	8,607	4,613	3,957	37	656 R	53.6%	46.0%	53.8%	46.2%
276,515	FRESNO	119,115	51,611	67,234	270	15,623 D	43.3%	56.4%	43.4%	56.6%
15,448	GLENN	6,665	3,463	3,192	10	271 R	52.0%	47.9%	52.0%	48.0%
69,241	HUMBOLDT	36,177	19,019	17,025	133	1,994 R	52.6%	47.1%	52.8%	47.2%
62,975	IMPERIAL	18,781	10,526	8,197	58	2,329 R	56.0%	43.6%	56.2%	43.8%
11,658	INYO	5,324	3,524	1,782	18	1,742 R	66.2%	33.5%	66.4%	33.6%
228,309	KERN	90,075	46,220	43,533	322	2,687 R	51.3%	48.3%	51.5%	48.5%
46,768	KINGS	14,652	6,195	8,417	40	2,222 D	42.3%	57.4%	42.4%	57.6%
11,481	LAKE	6,282	4,073	2,185	24	1,888 R	64.8%	34.8%	65.1%	34.9%
18,474	LASSEN	5,963	2,533	3,412	18	879 D	42.5%	57.2%	42.6%	57.4%
4,151,687	LOS ANGELES	2,275,424	1,260,206	1,007,887	7,331	252,319 R	55.4%	44.3%	55.6%	44.4%
36,964	MADERA	12,439	5,239	7,162	38	1,923 D	42.1%	57.6%	42.2%	57.8%
85,619	MARIN	51,244	33,792	17,301	151	16,491 R	65.9%	33.8%	66.1%	33.9%
5,145	MARIPOSA	2,615	1,577	1,031	7	546 R	60.3%	39.4%	60.5%	39.5%
40,854	MENDOCINO	18,137	10,327	7,767	43	2,560 R	56.9%	42.8%	57.1%	42.9%
69,780	MERCED	24,852	11,430	13,366	56	1,936 D	46.0%	53.8%	46.1%	53.9%
9,678	MODOC	3,723	1,981	1,729	13	252 R	53.2%	46.4%	53.4%	46.6%
2,115	MONO	912	673	237	2	436 R	73.8%	26.0%	74.0%	26.0%
130,498	MONTEREY	49,573	29,514	19,932	127	9,582 R	59.5%	40.2%	59.7%	40.3%
46,603	NAPA	24,333	13,610	10,623	100	2,987 R	55.9%	43.7%	56.2%	43.8%
19,888	NEVADA	9,173	5,475	3,667	31	1,808 R	59.7%	40.0%	59.9%	40.1%
216,224	ORANGE	169,879	113,510	54,895	1,474	58,615 R	66.8%	32.3%	67.4%	32.6%
41,649	PLACER	19,739	9,059	10,611	69	1,552 D	45.9%	53.8%	46.1%	53.9%
13,519	PLUMAS	5,415	2,267	3,127	21	860 D	41.9%	57.7%	42.0%	58.0%
170,046	RIVERSIDE	91,329	56,766	34,098	465	22,668 R	62.2%	37.3%	62.5%	37.5%
277,140	SACRAMENTO	150,080	67,686	82,134	260	14,448 D	45.1%	54.7%	45.2%	54.8%
14,370	SAN BENITO	5,463	3,252	2,201	10	1,051 R	59.5%	40.3%	59.6%	40.4%
281,642	SAN BERNARDINO	151,650	86,263	64,946	441	21,317 R	56.9%	42.8%	57.0%	43.0%
556,808	SAN DIEGO	303,576	195,742	106,716	1,118	89,026 R	64.5%	35.2%	64.7%	35.3%
775,357	SAN FRANCISCO	336,998	173,648	161,766	1,584	11,882 R	51.5%	48.0%	51.8%	48.2%
200,750	SAN JOAQUIN	81,600	44,491	36,941	168	7,550 R	54.5%	45.3%	54.6%	45.4%
51,417	SAN LUIS OBISPO	27,748	16,223	11,407	118	4,816 R	58.5%	41.1%	58.7%	41.3%
235,659	SAN MATEO	163,903	100,049	63,637	217	36,412 R	61.0%	38.8%	61.1%	38.9%
98,220	SANTA BARBARA	48,484	31,294	16,925	265	14,369 R	64.5%	34.9%	64.9%	35.1%
290,547	SANTA CLARA	178,818	105,657	72,528	633	33,129 R	59.1%	40.6%	59.3%	40.7%
66,534	SANTA CRUZ	34,776	22,109	12,574	93	9,535 R	63.6%	36.2%	63.7%	36.3%
36,413	SHASTA	20,149	8,833	11,239	77	2,406 D	43.8%	55.8%	44.0%	56.0%
2,410	SIERRA	1,262	638	620	4	18 R	50.6%	49.1%	50.7%	49.3%
30,733	SISKIYOU	13,741	6,841	6,837	63	4 R	49.8%	49.8%	50.0%	50.0%
104,833	SOLANO	42,863	17,865	24,903	95	7,038 D	41.7%	58.1%	41.8%	58.2%
103,405	SONOMA	54,361	33,659	20,616	86	13,043 R	61.9%	37.9%	62.0%	38.0%
127,231	STANISLAUS	54,927	26,695	28,040	192	1,345 D	48.6%	51.0%	48.8%	51.2%
26,239	SUTTER	10,077	6,327	3,673	77	2,654 R	62.8%	36.4%	63.3%	36.7%
19,276	TEHAMA	9,042	4,866	4,143	33	723 R	53.8%	45.8%	54.0%	46.0%
5,087	TRINITY	2,870	1,447	1,406	17	41 R	50.4%	49.0%	50.7%	49.3%
149,264	TULARE	49,618	26,051	23,407	160	2,644 R	52.5%	47.2%	52.7%	47.3%
12,584	TUOLUMNE	6,943	3,619	3,310	14	309 R	52.1%	47.7%	52.2%	47.8%
114,647	VENTURA	52,767	26,342	26,276	149	66 R	49.9%	49.8%	50.1%	49.9%
40,640	YOLO	19,479	9,347	10,075	57	728 D	48.0%	51.7%	48.1%	51.9%
24,420	YUBA	8,576	4,782	3,767	27	1,015 R	55.8%	43.9%	55.9%	44.1%
10,586,223	TOTAL	5,466,355	3,027,668	2,420,135	18,552	607,533 R	55.4%	44.3%	55.6%	44.4%

CALIFORNIA

PRESIDENT 1952

1950 Census Population	County	Total Vote	Republican	Democratic	Other	Rep.-Dem. Plurality	Percentage: Total Vote Rep.	Total Vote Dem.	Major Vote Rep.	Major Vote Dem.
740,315	ALAMEDA	369,776	192,941	173,853	2,982	19,088 R	52.2%	47.0%	52.6%	47.4%
241	ALPINE	148	129	19		110 R	87.2%	12.8%	87.2%	12.8%
9,151	AMADOR	4,416	2,303	2,070	43	233 R	52.2%	46.9%	52.7%	47.3%
64,930	BUTTE	29,133	18,390	10,491	252	7,899 R	63.1%	36.0%	63.7%	36.3%
9,902	CALAVERAS	4,824	2,942	1,838	44	1,104 R	61.0%	38.1%	61.5%	38.5%
11,651	COLUSA	4,513	2,678	1,818	17	860 R	59.3%	40.3%	59.6%	40.4%
298,984	CONTRA COSTA	137,281	67,453	69,060	768	1,607 D	49.1%	50.3%	49.4%	50.6%
8,078	DEL NORTE	4,384	2,757	1,578	49	1,179 R	62.9%	36.0%	63.6%	36.4%
16,207	EL DORADO	8,073	4,828	3,152	93	1,676 R	59.8%	39.0%	60.5%	39.5%
276,515	FRESNO	107,376	52,025	54,541	810	2,516 D	48.5%	50.8%	48.8%	51.2%
15,448	GLENN	6,600	4,224	2,342	34	1,882 R	64.0%	35.5%	64.3%	35.7%
69,241	HUMBOLDT	31,687	18,913	12,490	284	6,423 R	59.7%	39.4%	60.2%	39.8%
62,975	IMPERIAL	16,903	10,462	6,333	108	4,129 R	61.9%	37.5%	62.3%	37.7%
11,658	INYO	5,162	3,549	1,585	28	1,964 R	68.8%	30.7%	69.1%	30.9%
228,309	KERN	81,332	44,600	36,151	581	8,449 R	54.8%	44.4%	55.2%	44.8%
46,768	KINGS	15,083	7,336	7,639	108	303 D	48.6%	50.6%	49.0%	51.0%
11,481	LAKE	6,087	4,113	1,911	63	2,202 R	67.6%	31.4%	68.3%	31.7%
18,474	LASSEN	7,262	3,119	4,104	39	985 D	42.9%	56.5%	43.2%	56.8%
4,151,687	LOS ANGELES	2,201,212	1,226,971	950,093	24,148	276,878 R	55.7%	43.2%	56.4%	43.6%
36,964	MADERA	12,091	5,933	6,042	116	109 D	49.1%	50.0%	49.5%	50.5%
85,619	MARIN	44,278	29,574	14,236	468	15,338 R	66.8%	32.2%	67.5%	32.5%
5,145	MARIPOSA	2,946	1,941	969	36	972 R	65.9%	32.9%	66.7%	33.3%
40,854	MENDOCINO	17,157	10,388	6,580	189	3,808 R	60.5%	38.4%	61.2%	38.8%
69,780	MERCED	24,395	12,865	11,316	214	1,549 R	52.7%	46.4%	53.2%	46.8%
9,678	MODOC	4,047	2,475	1,548	24	927 R	61.2%	38.3%	61.5%	38.5%
2,115	MONO	982	754	220	8	534 R	76.8%	22.4%	77.4%	22.6%
130,498	MONTEREY	46,451	28,786	17,411	254	11,375 R	62.0%	37.5%	62.3%	37.7%
46,603	NAPA	21,747	13,273	8,316	158	4,957 R	61.0%	38.2%	61.5%	38.5%
19,888	NEVADA	9,818	6,252	3,476	90	2,776 R	63.7%	35.4%	64.3%	35.7%
216,224	ORANGE	110,904	77,548	32,530	826	45,018 R	69.9%	29.3%	70.4%	29.6%
41,649	PLACER	18,153	9,104	8,887	162	217 R	50.2%	49.0%	50.6%	49.4%
13,519	PLUMAS	5,721	2,491	3,174	56	683 D	43.5%	55.5%	44.0%	56.0%
170,046	RIVERSIDE	75,649	48,874	26,016	759	22,858 R	64.6%	34.4%	65.3%	34.7%
277,140	SACRAMENTO	131,641	63,788	67,053	800	3,265 D	48.5%	50.9%	48.8%	51.2%
14,370	SAN BENITO	5,415	3,503	1,891	21	1,612 R	64.7%	34.9%	64.9%	35.1%
281,642	SAN BERNARDINO	129,631	73,921	54,615	1,095	19,306 R	57.0%	42.1%	57.5%	42.5%
556,808	SAN DIEGO	278,751	175,281	101,880	1,590	73,401 R	62.9%	36.5%	63.2%	36.8%
775,357	SAN FRANCISCO	359,949	188,531	167,282	4,136	21,249 R	52.4%	46.5%	53.0%	47.0%
200,750	SAN JOAQUIN	79,107	44,033	34,510	564	9,523 R	55.7%	43.6%	56.1%	43.9%
51,417	SAN LUIS OBISPO	25,691	16,733	8,761	197	7,972 R	65.1%	34.1%	65.6%	34.4%
235,659	SAN MATEO	139,222	87,780	50,802	640	36,978 R	63.1%	36.5%	63.3%	36.7%
98,220	SANTA BARBARA	44,943	29,984	14,793	166	15,191 R	66.7%	32.9%	67.0%	33.0%
290,547	SANTA CLARA	147,807	87,554	59,350	903	28,204 R	59.2%	40.2%	59.6%	40.4%
66,534	SANTA CRUZ	34,361	22,910	11,080	371	11,830 R	66.7%	32.2%	67.4%	32.6%
36,413	SHASTA	17,013	9,507	7,386	120	2,121 R	55.9%	43.4%	56.3%	43.7%
2,410	SIERRA	1,363	723	632	8	91 R	53.0%	46.4%	53.4%	46.6%
30,733	SISKIYOU	14,684	8,195	6,346	143	1,849 R	55.8%	43.2%	56.4%	43.6%
104,833	SOLANO	44,238	18,456	25,569	213	7,113 D	41.7%	57.8%	41.9%	58.1%
103,405	SONOMA	51,717	34,088	17,046	583	17,042 R	65.9%	33.0%	66.7%	33.3%
127,231	STANISLAUS	50,913	28,090	22,271	552	5,819 R	55.2%	43.7%	55.8%	44.2%
26,239	SUTTER	10,071	6,780	3,250	41	3,530 R	67.3%	32.3%	67.6%	32.4%
19,276	TEHAMA	8,465	5,436	2,953	76	2,483 R	64.2%	34.9%	64.8%	35.2%
5,087	TRINITY	2,674	1,526	1,120	28	406 R	57.1%	41.9%	57.7%	42.3%
149,264	TULARE	50,827	28,802	21,603	422	7,199 R	56.7%	42.5%	57.1%	42.9%
12,584	TUOLUMNE	6,402	3,753	2,593	56	1,160 R	58.6%	40.5%	59.1%	40.9%
114,647	VENTURA	45,137	23,392	21,489	256	1,903 R	51.8%	47.6%	52.1%	47.9%
40,640	YOLO	16,999	8,967	7,895	137	1,072 R	52.8%	46.4%	53.2%	46.8%
24,420	YUBA	9,237	5,586	3,589	62	1,997 R	60.5%	38.9%	60.9%	39.1%
10,586,223	TOTAL	5,141,849	2,897,310	2,197,548	46,991	699,762 R	56.3%	42.7%	56.9%	43.1%

CALIFORNIA

PRESIDENT 1948

1940 Census Population	County	Total Vote	Republican	Democratic	Other	Rep.-Dem. Plurality	Percentage Total Vote Rep.	Total Vote Dem.	Major Vote Rep.	Major Vote Dem.
513,011	ALAMEDA	323,331	150,588	154,549	18,194	3,961 D	46.6%	47.8%	49.4%	50.6%
323	ALPINE	138	106	25	7	81 R	76.8%	18.1%	80.9%	19.1%
8,973	AMADOR	4,063	1,578	2,334	151	756 D	38.8%	57.4%	40.3%	59.7%
42,840	BUTTE	22,181	10,948	10,133	1,100	815 R	49.4%	45.7%	51.9%	48.1%
8,221	CALAVERAS	4,037	1,888	1,995	154	107 D	46.8%	49.4%	48.6%	51.4%
9,788	COLUSA	3,901	1,803	2,020	78	217 D	46.2%	51.8%	47.2%	52.8%
100,450	CONTRA COSTA	91,376	36,958	50,277	4,141	13,319 D	40.4%	55.0%	42.4%	57.6%
4,745	DEL NORTE	2,840	1,541	1,172	127	369 R	54.3%	41.3%	56.8%	43.2%
13,229	EL DORADO	6,724	2,894	3,493	337	599 D	43.0%	51.9%	45.3%	54.7%
178,565	FRESNO	81,665	30,379	47,762	3,524	17,383 D	37.2%	58.5%	38.9%	61.1%
12,195	GLENN	5,528	2,819	2,578	131	241 R	51.0%	46.6%	52.2%	47.8%
45,812	HUMBOLDT	23,266	10,979	11,268	1,019	289 D	47.2%	48.4%	49.4%	50.6%
59,740	IMPERIAL	11,810	6,217	5,301	292	916 R	52.6%	44.9%	54.0%	46.0%
7,625	INYO	3,827	2,135	1,539	153	596 R	55.8%	40.2%	58.1%	41.9%
135,124	KERN	58,811	24,464	33,029	1,318	8,565 D	41.6%	56.2%	42.6%	57.4%
35,168	KINGS	11,521	4,289	6,909	323	2,620 D	37.2%	60.0%	38.3%	61.7%
8,069	LAKE	5,333	3,054	1,999	280	1,055 R	57.3%	37.5%	60.4%	39.6%
14,479	LASSEN	5,773	1,960	3,632	181	1,672 D	34.0%	62.9%	35.1%	64.9%
2,785,643	LOS ANGELES	1,729,082	804,232	812,690	112,160	8,458 D	46.5%	47.0%	49.7%	50.3%
23,314	MADERA	8,982	3,416	5,226	340	1,810 D	38.0%	58.2%	39.5%	60.5%
52,907	MARIN	32,855	18,747	12,540	1,568	6,207 R	57.1%	38.2%	59.9%	40.1%
5,605	MARIPOSA	2,467	1,378	983	106	395 R	55.9%	39.8%	58.4%	41.6%
27,864	MENDOCINO	12,603	6,368	5,553	682	815 R	50.5%	44.1%	53.4%	46.6%
46,988	MERCED	18,124	7,721	9,959	444	2,238 D	42.6%	54.9%	43.7%	56.3%
8,713	MODOC	3,180	1,480	1,607	93	127 D	46.5%	50.5%	47.9%	52.1%
2,299	MONO	835	541	255	39	286 R	64.8%	30.5%	68.0%	32.0%
73,032	MONTEREY	34,063	17,233	15,704	1,126	1,529 R	50.6%	46.1%	52.3%	47.7%
28,503	NAPA	16,516	8,724	7,207	585	1,517 R	52.8%	43.6%	54.8%	45.2%
19,283	NEVADA	8,326	3,917	3,914	495	3 R	47.0%	47.0%	50.0%	50.0%
130,760	ORANGE	79,814	48,587	29,018	2,209	19,569 R	60.9%	36.4%	62.6%	37.4%
28,108	PLACER	15,109	5,570	8,837	702	3,267 D	36.9%	58.5%	38.7%	61.3%
11,548	PLUMAS	5,058	1,657	3,125	276	1,468 D	32.8%	61.8%	34.7%	65.3%
105,524	RIVERSIDE	57,864	32,209	23,305	2,350	8,904 R	55.7%	40.3%	58.0%	42.0%
170,333	SACRAMENTO	92,842	35,074	54,197	3,571	19,123 D	37.8%	58.4%	39.3%	60.7%
11,392	SAN BENITO	4,987	2,775	2,096	116	679 R	55.6%	42.0%	57.0%	43.0%
161,108	SAN BERNARDINO	95,838	46,570	45,691	3,577	879 R	48.6%	47.7%	50.5%	49.5%
289,348	SAN DIEGO	205,459	101,552	98,217	5,690	3,335 R	49.4%	47.8%	50.8%	49.2%
634,536	SAN FRANCISCO	350,709	160,135	167,726	22,848	7,591 D	45.7%	47.8%	48.8%	51.2%
134,207	SAN JOAQUIN	59,361	29,135	27,908	2,318	1,227 R	49.1%	47.0%	51.1%	48.9%
33,246	SAN LUIS OBISPO	19,304	10,325	8,135	844	2,190 R	53.5%	42.1%	55.9%	44.1%
111,782	SAN MATEO	86,272	48,909	34,215	3,148	14,694 R	56.7%	39.7%	58.8%	41.2%
70,555	SANTA BARBARA	34,400	19,998	13,085	1,317	6,913 R	58.1%	38.0%	60.4%	39.6%
174,949	SANTA CLARA	99,502	52,982	41,905	4,615	11,077 R	53.2%	42.1%	55.8%	44.2%
45,057	SANTA CRUZ	26,690	15,395	9,862	1,433	5,533 R	57.7%	37.0%	61.0%	39.0%
28,800	SHASTA	12,623	5,010	7,177	436	2,167 D	39.7%	56.9%	41.1%	58.9%
3,025	SIERRA	1,258	546	660	52	114 D	43.4%	52.5%	45.3%	54.7%
28,598	SISKIYOU	12,498	5,315	6,749	434	1,434 D	42.5%	54.0%	44.1%	55.9%
49,118	SOLANO	36,624	12,345	23,257	1,022	10,912 D	33.7%	63.5%	34.7%	65.3%
69,052	SONOMA	39,984	22,077	16,026	1,881	6,051 R	55.2%	40.1%	57.9%	42.1%
74,866	STANISLAUS	38,371	18,564	18,350	1,457	214 R	48.4%	47.8%	50.3%	49.7%
18,680	SUTTER	7,458	3,913	3,362	183	551 R	52.5%	45.1%	53.8%	46.2%
14,316	TEHAMA	6,530	3,348	2,920	262	428 R	51.3%	44.7%	53.4%	46.6%
3,970	TRINITY	2,163	975	1,053	135	78 D	45.1%	48.7%	48.1%	51.9%
107,152	TULARE	39,192	18,414	19,681	1,097	1,267 D	47.0%	50.2%	48.3%	51.7%
10,887	TUOLUMNE	5,474	2,639	2,561	274	78 R	48.2%	46.8%	50.7%	49.3%
69,685	VENTURA	33,049	13,930	18,100	1,019	4,170 D	42.1%	54.8%	43.5%	56.5%
27,243	YOLO	12,684	5,560	6,655	469	1,095 D	43.8%	52.5%	45.5%	54.5%
17,034	YUBA	7,263	3,403	3,608	252	205 D	46.9%	49.7%	48.5%	51.5%
6,907,387	TOTAL	4,021,538	1,895,269	1,913,134	213,135	17,865 D	47.1%	47.6%	49.8%	50.2%

CALIFORNIA

PRESIDENT 1944

1940 Census Population	County	Total Vote	Republican	Democratic	Other	Rep.-Dem. Plurality	Percentage: Total Vote Rep.	Total Vote Dem.	Major Vote Rep.	Major Vote Dem.
513,011	ALAMEDA	293,987	122,982	169,631	1,374	46,649 D	41.8%	57.7%	42.0%	58.0%
323	ALPINE	143	98	45		53 R	68.5%	31.5%	68.5%	31.5%
8,973	AMADOR	3,203	1,191	1,976	36	785 D	37.2%	61.7%	37.6%	62.4%
42,840	BUTTE	16,768	7,852	8,811	105	959 D	46.8%	52.5%	47.1%	52.9%
8,221	CALAVERAS	3,369	1,455	1,893	21	438 D	43.2%	56.2%	43.5%	56.5%
9,788	COLUSA	3,679	1,579	2,090	10	511 D	42.9%	56.8%	43.0%	57.0%
100,450	CONTRA COSTA	74,785	26,816	47,831	138	21,015 D	35.9%	64.0%	35.9%	64.1%
4,745	DEL NORTE	1,830	1,011	818	1	193 R	55.2%	44.7%	55.3%	44.7%
13,229	EL DORADO	5,031	1,990	3,016	25	1,026 D	39.6%	59.9%	39.8%	60.2%
178,565	FRESNO	63,862	22,668	40,769	425	18,101 D	35.5%	63.8%	35.7%	64.3%
12,195	GLENN	4,884	2,409	2,452	23	43 D	49.3%	50.2%	49.6%	50.4%
45,812	HUMBOLDT	21,260	9,127	12,083	50	2,956 D	42.9%	56.8%	43.0%	57.0%
59,740	IMPERIAL	11,112	5,979	5,085	48	894 R	53.8%	45.8%	54.0%	46.0%
7,625	INYO	3,355	1,699	1,647	9	52 R	50.6%	49.1%	50.8%	49.2%
135,124	KERN	47,161	20,730	26,205	226	5,475 D	44.0%	55.6%	44.2%	55.8%
35,168	KINGS	10,134	3,468	6,591	75	3,123 D	34.2%	65.0%	34.5%	65.5%
8,069	LAKE	3,746	2,059	1,671	16	388 R	55.0%	44.6%	55.2%	44.8%
14,479	LASSEN	5,589	1,896	3,678	15	1,782 D	33.9%	65.8%	34.0%	66.0%
2,785,643	LOS ANGELES	1,561,564	666,441	886,252	8,871	219,811 D	42.7%	56.8%	42.9%	57.1%
23,314	MADERA	7,190	2,865	4,276	49	1,411 D	39.8%	59.5%	40.1%	59.9%
52,907	MARIN	27,896	13,304	14,516	76	1,212 D	47.7%	52.0%	47.8%	52.2%
5,605	MARIPOSA	2,185	965	1,203	17	238 D	44.2%	55.1%	44.5%	55.5%
27,864	MENDOCINO	10,143	4,655	5,452	36	797 D	45.9%	53.8%	46.1%	53.9%
46,988	MERCED	15,779	6,518	9,192	69	2,674 D	41.3%	58.3%	41.5%	58.5%
8,713	MODOC	2,837	1,288	1,540	9	252 D	45.4%	54.3%	45.5%	54.5%
2,299	MONO	621	378	242	1	136 R	60.9%	39.0%	61.0%	39.0%
73,032	MONTEREY	26,728	12,246	14,342	140	2,096 D	45.8%	53.7%	46.1%	53.9%
28,503	NAPA	14,936	7,092	7,748	96	656 D	47.5%	51.9%	47.8%	52.2%
19,283	NEVADA	5,961	2,648	3,266	47	618 D	44.4%	54.8%	44.8%	55.2%
130,760	ORANGE	67,450	38,394	28,649	407	9,745 R	56.9%	42.5%	57.3%	42.7%
28,108	PLACER	11,409	4,196	7,149	64	2,953 D	36.8%	62.7%	37.0%	63.0%
11,548	PLUMAS	3,759	1,126	2,625	8	1,499 D	30.0%	69.8%	30.0%	70.0%
105,524	RIVERSIDE	42,953	23,168	19,439	346	3,729 R	53.9%	45.3%	54.4%	45.6%
170,333	SACRAMENTO	74,218	24,611	49,204	403	24,593 D	33.2%	66.3%	33.3%	66.7%
11,392	SAN BENITO	4,267	2,253	1,998	16	255 R	52.8%	46.8%	53.0%	47.0%
161,108	SAN BERNARDINO	73,260	34,084	38,530	646	4,446 D	46.5%	52.6%	46.9%	53.1%
289,348	SAN DIEGO	166,764	75,746	89,959	1,059	14,213 D	45.4%	53.9%	45.7%	54.3%
634,536	SAN FRANCISCO	344,731	134,163	208,609	1,959	74,446 D	38.9%	60.5%	39.1%	60.9%
134,207	SAN JOAQUIN	51,588	24,357	27,074	157	2,717 D	47.2%	52.5%	47.4%	52.6%
33,246	SAN LUIS OBISPO	15,936	7,793	8,068	75	275 D	48.9%	50.6%	49.1%	50.9%
111,782	SAN MATEO	68,342	33,590	34,594	158	1,004 D	49.1%	50.6%	49.3%	50.7%
70,555	SANTA BARBARA	29,457	13,647	15,721	89	2,074 D	46.3%	53.4%	46.5%	53.5%
174,949	SANTA CLARA	83,777	39,409	43,869	499	4,460 D	47.0%	52.4%	47.3%	52.7%
45,057	SANTA CRUZ	20,637	11,102	9,357	178	1,745 R	53.8%	45.3%	54.3%	45.7%
28,800	SHASTA	9,843	4,023	5,798	22	1,775 D	40.9%	58.9%	41.0%	59.0%
3,025	SIERRA	1,110	443	662	5	219 D	39.9%	59.6%	40.1%	59.9%
28,598	SISKIYOU	10,323	4,351	5,914	58	1,563 D	42.1%	57.3%	42.4%	57.6%
49,118	SOLANO	34,801	10,361	24,335	105	13,974 D	29.8%	69.9%	29.9%	70.1%
69,052	SONOMA	32,369	16,309	15,949	111	360 R	50.4%	49.3%	50.6%	49.4%
74,866	STANISLAUS	30,271	14,297	15,537	437	1,240 D	47.2%	51.3%	47.9%	52.1%
18,680	SUTTER	6,223	3,111	3,083	29	28 R	50.0%	49.5%	50.2%	49.8%
14,316	TEHAMA	6,074	2,903	3,130	41	227 D	47.8%	51.5%	48.1%	51.9%
3,970	TRINITY	1,343	567	770	6	203 D	42.2%	57.3%	42.4%	57.6%
107,152	TULARE	32,464	16,005	16,221	238	216 D	49.3%	50.0%	49.7%	50.3%
10,887	TUOLUMNE	4,462	1,864	2,566	32	702 D	41.8%	57.5%	42.1%	57.9%
69,685	VENTURA	27,544	11,071	16,342	131	5,271 D	40.2%	59.3%	40.4%	59.6%
27,243	YOLO	10,116	4,233	5,837	46	1,604 D	41.8%	57.7%	42.0%	58.0%
17,034	YUBA	5,646	2,379	3,254	13	875 D	42.1%	57.6%	42.2%	57.8%
6,907,387	TOTAL	3,520,875	1,512,965	1,988,564	19,346	475,599 D	43.0%	56.5%	43.2%	56.8%

CALIFORNIA

PRESIDENT 1940

1940 Census Population	County	Total Vote	Republican	Democratic	Other	Rep.-Dem. Plurality	Percentage Total Vote Rep.	Total Vote Dem.	Major Vote Rep.	Major Vote Dem.
513,011	ALAMEDA	268,496	116,961	148,224	3,311	31,263 D	43.6%	55.2%	44.1%	55.9%
323	ALPINE	188	125	62	1	63 R	66.5%	33.0%	66.8%	33.2%
8,973	AMADOR	4,176	1,372	2,762	42	1,390 D	32.9%	66.1%	33.2%	66.8%
42,840	BUTTE	18,372	7,433	10,684	255	3,251 D	40.5%	58.2%	41.0%	59.0%
8,221	CALAVERAS	4,083	1,649	2,405	29	756 D	40.4%	58.9%	40.7%	59.3%
9,788	COLUSA	4,464	1,774	2,655	35	881 D	39.7%	59.5%	40.1%	59.9%
100,450	CONTRA COSTA	50,040	18,627	30,900	513	12,273 D	37.2%	61.8%	37.6%	62.4%
4,745	DEL NORTE	2,302	1,233	1,034	35	199 R	53.6%	44.9%	54.4%	45.6%
13,229	EL DORADO	6,237	2,019	4,144	74	2,125 D	32.4%	66.4%	32.8%	67.2%
178,565	FRESNO	70,750	21,079	48,866	805	27,787 D	29.8%	69.1%	30.1%	69.9%
12,195	GLENN	5,631	2,473	3,095	63	622 D	43.9%	55.0%	44.4%	55.6%
45,812	HUMBOLDT	22,024	9,470	12,329	225	2,859 D	43.0%	56.0%	43.4%	56.6%
59,740	IMPERIAL	14,712	6,854	7,728	130	874 D	46.6%	52.5%	47.0%	53.0%
7,625	INYO	3,330	1,483	1,820	27	337 D	44.5%	54.7%	44.9%	55.1%
135,124	KERN	52,126	19,445	32,202	479	12,757 D	37.3%	61.8%	37.6%	62.4%
35,168	KINGS	12,320	3,911	8,307	102	4,396 D	31.7%	67.4%	32.0%	68.0%
8,069	LAKE	4,151	2,215	1,897	39	318 R	53.4%	45.7%	53.9%	46.1%
14,479	LASSEN	6,313	1,902	4,367	44	2,465 D	30.1%	69.2%	30.3%	69.7%
2,785,643	LOS ANGELES	1,415,269	574,266	822,718	18,285	248,452 D	40.6%	58.1%	41.1%	58.9%
23,314	MADERA	8,503	2,653	5,749	101	3,096 D	31.2%	67.6%	31.6%	68.4%
52,907	MARIN	22,640	10,974	11,365	301	391 D	48.5%	50.2%	49.1%	50.9%
5,605	MARIPOSA	3,003	1,035	1,935	33	900 D	34.5%	64.4%	34.8%	65.2%
27,864	MENDOCINO	12,569	5,345	7,055	169	1,710 D	42.5%	56.1%	43.1%	56.9%
46,988	MERCED	16,784	6,101	10,501	182	4,400 D	36.4%	62.6%	36.7%	63.3%
8,713	MODOC	3,630	1,371	2,232	27	861 D	37.8%	61.5%	38.1%	61.9%
2,299	MONO	995	459	523	13	64 D	46.1%	52.6%	46.7%	53.3%
73,032	MONTEREY	26,833	11,810	14,758	265	2,948 D	44.0%	55.0%	44.5%	55.5%
28,503	NAPA	12,853	5,924	6,771	158	847 D	46.1%	52.7%	46.7%	53.3%
19,283	NEVADA	8,759	2,863	5,782	114	2,919 D	32.7%	66.0%	33.1%	66.9%
130,760	ORANGE	64,997	36,070	28,236	691	7,834 R	55.5%	43.4%	56.1%	43.9%
28,108	PLACER	12,436	3,887	8,402	147	4,515 D	31.3%	67.6%	31.6%	68.4%
11,548	PLUMAS	4,740	1,270	3,418	52	2,148 D	26.8%	72.1%	27.1%	72.9%
105,524	RIVERSIDE	42,380	21,779	20,003	598	1,776 R	51.4%	47.2%	52.1%	47.9%
170,333	SACRAMENTO	75,416	23,201	51,351	864	28,150 D	30.8%	68.1%	31.1%	68.9%
11,392	SAN BENITO	4,883	2,407	2,441	35	34 D	49.3%	50.0%	49.6%	50.4%
161,108	SAN BERNARDINO	68,878	30,511	37,520	847	7,009 D	44.3%	54.5%	44.8%	55.2%
289,348	SAN DIEGO	128,110	55,434	71,188	1,488	15,754 D	43.3%	55.6%	43.8%	56.2%
634,536	SAN FRANCISCO	311,878	122,449	185,607	3,822	63,158 D	39.3%	59.5%	39.7%	60.3%
134,207	SAN JOAQUIN	50,498	23,403	26,536	559	3,133 D	46.3%	52.5%	46.9%	53.1%
33,246	SAN LUIS OBISPO	15,920	7,204	8,499	217	1,295 D	45.3%	53.4%	45.9%	54.1%
111,782	SAN MATEO	56,951	26,539	29,831	581	3,292 D	46.6%	52.4%	47.1%	52.9%
70,555	SANTA BARBARA	31,678	14,107	17,237	334	3,130 D	44.5%	54.4%	45.0%	55.0%
174,949	SANTA CLARA	81,496	40,100	40,449	947	349 D	49.2%	49.6%	49.8%	50.2%
45,057	SANTA CRUZ	22,486	11,453	10,683	350	770 R	50.9%	47.5%	51.7%	48.3%
28,800	SHASTA	12,733	3,909	8,662	162	4,753 D	30.7%	68.0%	31.1%	68.9%
3,025	SIERRA	1,578	511	1,057	10	546 D	32.4%	67.0%	32.6%	67.4%
28,598	SISKIYOU	12,212	4,387	7,714	111	3,327 D	35.9%	63.2%	36.3%	63.7%
49,118	SOLANO	21,328	6,081	15,054	193	8,973 D	28.5%	70.6%	28.8%	71.2%
69,052	SONOMA	32,379	16,819	15,230	330	1,589 R	51.9%	47.0%	52.5%	47.5%
74,866	STANISLAUS	31,746	14,803	16,494	449	1,691 D	46.6%	52.0%	47.3%	52.7%
18,680	SUTTER	7,345	3,089	4,195	61	1,106 D	42.1%	57.1%	42.4%	57.6%
14,316	TEHAMA	6,628	2,913	3,618	97	705 D	43.9%	54.6%	44.6%	55.4%
3,970	TRINITY	2,242	780	1,431	31	651 D	34.8%	63.8%	35.3%	64.7%
107,152	TULARE	35,971	15,414	20,129	428	4,715 D	42.9%	56.0%	43.4%	56.6%
10,887	TUOLUMNE	5,624	2,004	3,541	79	1,537 D	35.6%	63.0%	36.1%	63.9%
69,685	VENTURA	26,634	11,225	15,182	227	3,957 D	42.1%	57.0%	42.5%	57.5%
27,243	YOLO	10,854	4,373	6,380	101	2,007 D	40.3%	58.8%	40.7%	59.3%
17,034	YUBA	7,217	2,471	4,660	86	2,189 D	34.2%	64.6%	34.7%	65.3%
6,907,387	TOTAL	3,268,791	1,351,419	1,877,618	39,754	526,199 D	41.3%	57.4%	41.9%	58.1%

CALIFORNIA

PRESIDENT 1936

1930 Census Population	County	Total Vote	Republican	Democratic	Other	Rep.-Dem. Plurality	Percentage Total Vote Rep.	Total Vote Dem.	Major Vote Rep.	Major Vote Dem.
474,883	ALAMEDA	234,686	82,352	149,323	3,011	66,971 D	35.1%	63.6%	35.5%	64.5%
241	ALPINE	159	74	85		11 D	46.5%	53.5%	46.5%	53.5%
8,494	AMADOR	3,323	777	2,506	40	1,729 D	23.4%	75.4%	23.7%	76.3%
34,093	BUTTE	15,928	5,103	10,490	335	5,387 D	32.0%	65.9%	32.7%	67.3%
6,008	CALAVERAS	3,534	960	2,520	54	1,560 D	27.2%	71.3%	27.6%	72.4%
10,258	COLUSA	4,213	1,186	2,965	62	1,779 D	28.2%	70.4%	28.6%	71.4%
78,608	CONTRA COSTA	35,975	9,604	26,007	364	16,403 D	26.7%	72.3%	27.0%	73.0%
4,739	DEL NORTE	2,174	853	1,292	29	439 D	39.2%	59.4%	39.8%	60.2%
8,325	EL DORADO	5,312	1,228	4,019	65	2,791 D	23.1%	75.7%	23.4%	76.6%
144,379	FRESNO	55,126	11,545	42,859	722	31,314 D	20.9%	77.7%	21.2%	78.8%
10,935	GLENN	4,984	1,620	3,288	76	1,668 D	32.5%	66.0%	33.0%	67.0%
43,233	HUMBOLDT	18,925	6,808	11,909	208	5,101 D	36.0%	62.9%	36.4%	63.6%
60,903	IMPERIAL	12,444	4,771	7,560	113	2,789 D	38.3%	60.8%	38.7%	61.3%
6,555	INYO	2,501	912	1,560	29	648 D	36.5%	62.4%	36.9%	63.1%
82,570	KERN	34,479	8,345	25,726	408	17,381 D	24.2%	74.6%	24.5%	75.5%
25,385	KINGS	9,404	2,226	7,062	116	4,836 D	23.7%	75.1%	24.0%	76.0%
7,166	LAKE	3,687	1,797	1,837	53	40 D	48.7%	49.8%	49.4%	50.6%
12,589	LASSEN	5,276	1,035	4,193	48	3,158 D	19.6%	79.5%	19.8%	80.2%
2,208,492	LOS ANGELES	1,130,415	357,401	757,351	15,663	399,950 D	31.6%	67.0%	32.1%	67.9%
17,164	MADERA	6,134	1,387	4,646	101	3,259 D	22.6%	75.7%	23.0%	77.0%
41,648	MARIN	18,572	6,211	12,152	209	5,941 D	33.4%	65.4%	33.8%	66.2%
3,233	MARIPOSA	2,563	621	1,907	35	1,286 D	24.2%	74.4%	24.6%	75.4%
23,505	MENDOCINO	10,266	3,670	6,432	164	2,762 D	35.7%	62.7%	36.3%	63.7%
36,748	MERCED	12,668	3,230	9,208	230	5,978 D	25.5%	72.7%	26.0%	74.0%
8,038	MODOC	2,831	968	1,828	35	860 D	34.2%	64.6%	34.6%	65.4%
1,360	MONO	707	241	458	8	217 D	34.1%	64.8%	34.5%	65.5%
53,705	MONTEREY	20,067	7,565	12,267	235	4,702 D	37.7%	61.1%	38.1%	61.9%
22,897	NAPA	10,390	3,973	6,270	147	2,297 D	38.2%	60.3%	38.8%	61.2%
10,596	NEVADA	7,131	1,913	5,128	90	3,215 D	26.8%	71.9%	27.2%	72.8%
118,674	ORANGE	54,251	23,494	29,836	921	6,342 D	43.3%	55.0%	44.1%	55.9%
24,468	PLACER	10,388	2,321	7,959	108	5,638 D	22.3%	76.6%	22.6%	77.4%
7,913	PLUMAS	3,435	680	2,707	48	2,027 D	19.8%	78.8%	20.1%	79.9%
81,024	RIVERSIDE	34,107	16,674	17,011	422	337 D	48.9%	49.9%	49.5%	50.5%
141,999	SACRAMENTO	60,184	12,119	47,265	800	35,146 D	20.1%	78.5%	20.4%	79.6%
11,311	SAN BENITO	4,142	1,515	2,565	62	1,050 D	36.6%	61.9%	37.1%	62.9%
133,900	SAN BERNARDINO	57,016	22,219	33,955	842	11,736 D	39.0%	59.6%	39.6%	60.4%
209,659	SAN DIEGO	101,854	35,686	64,628	1,540	28,942 D	35.0%	63.5%	35.6%	64.4%
634,394	SAN FRANCISCO	265,001	65,436	196,197	3,368	130,761 D	24.7%	74.0%	25.0%	75.0%
102,940	SAN JOAQUIN	39,723	10,172	29,078	473	18,906 D	25.6%	73.2%	25.9%	74.1%
29,613	SAN LUIS OBISPO	12,906	4,812	7,889	205	3,077 D	37.3%	61.1%	37.9%	62.1%
77,405	SAN MATEO	41,248	13,650	27,087	511	13,437 D	33.1%	65.7%	33.5%	66.5%
65,167	SANTA BARBARA	26,045	9,728	15,923	394	6,195 D	37.4%	61.1%	37.9%	62.1%
145,118	SANTA CLARA	65,576	26,498	38,346	732	11,848 D	40.4%	58.5%	40.9%	59.1%
37,433	SANTA CRUZ	17,908	8,260	9,326	322	1,066 D	46.1%	52.1%	47.0%	53.0%
13,927	SHASTA	7,510	2,159	5,236	115	3,077 D	28.7%	69.7%	29.2%	70.8%
2,422	SIERRA	1,507	340	1,152	15	812 D	22.6%	76.4%	22.8%	77.2%
25,480	SISKIYOU	9,909	2,919	6,865	125	3,946 D	29.5%	69.3%	29.8%	70.2%
40,834	SOLANO	17,244	3,603	13,459	182	9,856 D	20.9%	78.1%	21.1%	78.9%
62,222	SONOMA	28,706	11,185	17,273	248	6,088 D	39.0%	60.2%	39.3%	60.7%
56,641	STANISLAUS	24,302	8,613	15,341	348	6,728 D	35.4%	63.1%	36.0%	64.0%
14,618	SUTTER	5,738	1,613	4,019	106	2,406 D	28.1%	70.0%	28.6%	71.4%
13,866	TEHAMA	6,178	2,376	3,687	115	1,311 D	38.5%	59.7%	39.2%	60.8%
2,809	TRINITY	2,122	655	1,424	43	769 D	30.9%	67.1%	31.5%	68.5%
77,442	TULARE	28,015	8,624	18,956	435	10,332 D	30.8%	67.7%	31.3%	68.7%
9,271	TUOLUMNE	4,542	1,199	3,303	40	2,104 D	26.4%	72.7%	26.6%	73.4%
54,976	VENTURA	21,198	7,579	13,384	235	5,805 D	35.8%	63.1%	36.2%	63.8%
23,644	YOLO	8,692	2,594	5,992	106	3,398 D	29.8%	68.9%	30.2%	69.8%
11,331	YUBA	5,561	1,332	4,125	104	2,793 D	24.0%	74.2%	24.4%	75.6%
5,677,251	TOTAL	2,638,882	836,431	1,766,836	35,615	930,405 D	31.7%	67.0%	32.1%	67.9%

CALIFORNIA

PRESIDENT 1932

1930 Census Population	County	Total Vote	Republican	Democratic	Other	Rep.-Dem. Plurality	Percentage Total Vote Rep.	Percentage Total Vote Dem.	Percentage Major Vote Rep.	Percentage Major Vote Dem.
474,883	ALAMEDA	204,344	89,303	106,388	8,653	17,085 D	43.7%	52.1%	45.6%	54.4%
241	ALPINE	112	53	56	3	3 D	47.3%	50.0%	48.6%	51.4%
8,494	AMADOR	3,244	822	2,367	55	1,545 D	25.3%	73.0%	25.8%	74.2%
34,093	BUTTE	14,832	4,322	9,645	865	5,323 D	29.1%	65.0%	30.9%	69.1%
6,008	CALAVERAS	2,599	754	1,744	101	990 D	29.0%	67.1%	30.2%	69.8%
10,258	COLUSA	3,982	1,095	2,752	135	1,657 D	27.5%	69.1%	28.5%	71.5%
78,608	CONTRA COSTA	29,192	10,907	17,218	1,067	6,311 D	37.4%	59.0%	38.8%	61.2%
4,739	DEL NORTE	2,059	637	1,319	103	682 D	30.9%	64.1%	32.6%	67.4%
8,325	EL DORADO	4,135	956	3,034	145	2,078 D	23.1%	73.4%	24.0%	76.0%
144,379	FRESNO	46,537	12,134	32,528	1,875	20,394 D	26.1%	69.9%	27.2%	72.8%
10,935	GLENN	4,569	1,432	2,973	164	1,541 D	31.3%	65.1%	32.5%	67.5%
43,233	HUMBOLDT	16,073	6,795	8,723	555	1,928 D	42.3%	54.3%	43.8%	56.2%
60,903	IMPERIAL	13,039	3,783	8,772	484	4,989 D	29.0%	67.3%	30.1%	69.9%
6,555	INYO	2,258	698	1,459	101	761 D	30.9%	64.6%	32.4%	67.6%
82,570	KERN	27,920	7,011	19,634	1,275	12,623 D	25.1%	70.3%	26.3%	73.7%
25,385	KINGS	7,518	2,009	5,191	318	3,182 D	26.7%	69.0%	27.9%	72.1%
7,166	LAKE	3,744	1,301	2,344	99	1,043 D	34.7%	62.6%	35.7%	64.3%
12,589	LASSEN	4,340	1,167	3,056	117	1,889 D	26.9%	70.4%	27.6%	72.4%
2,208,492	LOS ANGELES	969,148	373,738	554,476	40,934	180,738 D	38.6%	57.2%	40.3%	59.7%
17,164	MADERA	4,928	1,243	3,457	228	2,214 D	25.2%	70.2%	26.4%	73.6%
41,648	MARIN	16,993	6,480	9,764	749	3,284 D	38.1%	57.5%	39.9%	60.1%
3,233	MARIPOSA	2,038	560	1,386	92	826 D	27.5%	68.0%	28.8%	71.2%
23,505	MENDOCINO	9,551	3,365	5,867	319	2,502 D	35.2%	61.4%	36.4%	63.6%
36,748	MERCED	10,734	2,920	7,202	612	4,282 D	27.2%	67.1%	28.8%	71.2%
8,038	MODOC	2,386	655	1,643	88	988 D	27.5%	68.9%	28.5%	71.5%
1,360	MONO	581	199	374	8	175 D	34.3%	64.4%	34.7%	65.3%
53,705	MONTEREY	15,750	6,200	8,942	608	2,742 D	39.4%	56.8%	40.9%	59.1%
22,897	NAPA	9,524	3,521	5,745	258	2,224 D	37.0%	60.3%	38.0%	62.0%
10,596	NEVADA	5,596	1,842	3,544	210	1,702 D	32.9%	63.3%	34.2%	65.8%
118,674	ORANGE	49,274	22,623	23,835	2,816	1,212 D	45.9%	48.4%	48.7%	51.3%
24,468	PLACER	8,683	2,242	6,200	241	3,958 D	25.8%	71.4%	26.6%	73.4%
7,913	PLUMAS	2,684	582	2,035	67	1,453 D	21.7%	75.8%	22.2%	77.8%
81,024	RIVERSIDE	28,112	14,112	12,755	1,245	1,357 R	50.2%	45.4%	52.5%	47.5%
141,999	SACRAMENTO	52,465	14,553	36,370	1,542	21,817 D	27.7%	69.3%	28.6%	71.4%
11,311	SAN BENITO	3,744	1,269	2,283	192	1,014 D	33.9%	61.0%	35.7%	64.3%
133,900	SAN BERNARDINO	49,548	22,094	24,889	2,565	2,795 D	44.6%	50.2%	47.0%	53.0%
209,659	SAN DIEGO	85,150	35,305	45,622	4,223	10,317 D	41.5%	53.6%	43.6%	56.4%
634,394	SAN FRANCISCO	222,828	70,152	144,236	8,440	74,084 D	31.5%	64.7%	32.7%	67.3%
102,940	SAN JOAQUIN	34,622	11,145	21,929	1,548	10,784 D	32.2%	63.3%	33.7%	66.3%
29,613	SAN LUIS OBISPO	12,062	3,449	7,933	680	4,484 D	28.6%	65.8%	30.3%	69.7%
77,405	SAN MATEO	33,879	13,442	19,094	1,343	5,652 D	39.7%	56.4%	41.3%	58.7%
65,167	SANTA BARBARA	23,291	8,864	13,373	1,054	4,509 D	38.1%	57.4%	39.9%	60.1%
145,118	SANTA CLARA	57,525	27,353	28,272	1,900	919 D	47.5%	49.1%	49.2%	50.8%
37,433	SANTA CRUZ	14,990	6,005	8,246	739	2,241 D	40.1%	55.0%	42.1%	57.9%
13,927	SHASTA	5,782	1,382	4,170	230	2,788 D	23.9%	72.1%	24.9%	75.1%
2,422	SIERRA	1,147	292	796	59	504 D	25.5%	69.4%	26.8%	73.2%
25,480	SISKIYOU	9,184	2,458	6,367	359	3,909 D	26.8%	69.3%	27.9%	72.1%
40,834	SOLANO	14,461	4,382	9,712	367	5,330 D	30.3%	67.2%	31.1%	68.9%
62,222	SONOMA	25,657	9,161	15,686	810	6,525 D	35.7%	61.1%	36.9%	63.1%
56,641	STANISLAUS	21,042	7,614	12,336	1,092	4,722 D	36.2%	58.6%	38.2%	61.8%
14,618	SUTTER	5,407	1,392	3,807	208	2,415 D	25.7%	70.4%	26.8%	73.2%
13,866	TEHAMA	5,851	2,001	3,534	316	1,533 D	34.2%	60.4%	36.2%	63.8%
2,809	TRINITY	1,508	318	1,101	89	783 D	21.1%	73.0%	22.4%	77.6%
77,442	TULARE	24,999	8,066	15,631	1,302	7,565 D	32.3%	62.5%	34.0%	66.0%
9,271	TUOLUMNE	3,794	1,145	2,521	128	1,376 D	30.2%	66.4%	31.2%	68.8%
54,976	VENTURA	18,535	6,908	10,903	724	3,995 D	37.3%	58.8%	38.8%	61.2%
23,644	YOLO	8,529	2,515	5,780	234	3,265 D	29.5%	67.8%	30.3%	69.7%
11,331	YUBA	4,493	1,176	3,138	179	1,962 D	26.2%	69.8%	27.3%	72.7%
5,677,251	TOTAL	2,266,972	847,902	1,324,157	94.913	476,255 D	37.4%	58.4%	39.0%	61.0%

CALIFORNIA

PRESIDENT 1928

1920 Census Population	County	Total Vote	Republican	Democratic	Other	Rep.-Dem. Plurality	Percentage Total Vote Rep.	Total Vote Dem.	Major Vote Rep.	Major Vote Dem.
344,177	ALAMEDA	181,194	118,539	60,875	1,780	57,664 R	65.4%	33.6%	66.1%	33.9%
243	ALPINE	52	49	3		46 R	94.2%	5.8%	94.2%	5.8%
7,793	AMADOR	2,244	990	1,246	8	256 D	44.1%	55.5%	44.3%	55.7%
30,030	BUTTE	10,432	6,306	3,946	180	2,360 R	60.4%	37.8%	61.5%	38.5%
6,183	CALAVERAS	2,346	1,262	1,066	18	196 R	53.8%	45.4%	54.2%	45.8%
9,290	COLUSA	3,112	1,752	1,338	22	414 R	56.3%	43.0%	56.7%	43.3%
53,889	CONTRA COSTA	22,349	13,495	8,573	281	4,922 R	60.4%	38.4%	61.2%	38.8%
2,759	DEL NORTE	1,380	771	599	10	172 R	55.9%	43.4%	56.3%	43.7%
6,426	EL DORADO	2,775	1,228	1,516	31	288 D	44.3%	54.6%	44.8%	55.2%
128,779	FRESNO	38,098	20,687	16,884	527	3,803 R	54.3%	44.3%	55.1%	44.9%
11,853	GLENN	3,792	2,466	1,297	29	1,169 R	65.0%	34.2%	65.5%	34.5%
37,413	HUMBOLDT	13,135	9,162	3,726	247	5,436 R	69.8%	28.4%	71.1%	28.9%
43,453	IMPERIAL	8,012	5,417	2,486	109	2,931 R	67.6%	31.0%	68.5%	31.5%
7,031	INYO	2,102	1,206	861	35	345 R	57.4%	41.0%	58.3%	41.7%
54,843	KERN	23,445	14,692	8,541	212	6,151 R	62.7%	36.4%	63.2%	36.8%
22,031	KINGS	5,721	2,947	2,701	73	246 R	51.5%	47.2%	52.2%	47.8%
5,402	LAKE	2,784	1,820	926	38	894 R	65.4%	33.3%	66.3%	33.7%
8,507	LASSEN	3,721	2,111	1,597	13	514 R	56.7%	42.9%	56.9%	43.1%
936,455	LOS ANGELES	731,301	513,526	209,945	7,830	303,581 R	70.2%	28.7%	71.0%	29.0%
12,203	MADERA	4,289	2,354	1,896	39	458 R	54.9%	44.2%	55.4%	44.6%
27,342	MARIN	13,688	7,862	5,686	140	2,176 R	57.4%	41.5%	58.0%	42.0%
2,775	MARIPOSA	1,192	656	517	19	139 R	55.0%	43.4%	55.9%	44.1%
24,116	MENDOCINO	7,588	4,810	2,628	150	2,182 R	63.4%	34.6%	64.7%	35.3%
24,579	MERCED	7,718	4,644	2,970	104	1,674 R	60.2%	38.5%	61.0%	39.0%
5,425	MODOC	1,660	942	711	7	231 R	56.7%	42.8%	57.0%	43.0%
960	MONO	356	220	127	9	93 R	61.8%	35.7%	63.4%	36.6%
27,980	MONTEREY	11,452	7,228	4,138	86	3,090 R	63.1%	36.1%	63.6%	36.4%
20,678	NAPA	8,175	4,699	3,422	54	1,277 R	57.5%	41.9%	57.9%	42.1%
10,850	NEVADA	4,179	2,173	1,959	47	214 R	52.0%	46.9%	52.6%	47.4%
61,375	ORANGE	38,527	30,572	7,611	344	22,961 R	79.4%	19.8%	80.1%	19.9%
18,584	PLACER	7,450	3,669	3,685	96	16 D	49.2%	49.5%	49.9%	50.1%
5,681	PLUMAS	2,075	947	1,079	49	132 D	45.6%	52.0%	46.7%	53.3%
50,297	RIVERSIDE	22,581	17,600	4,769	212	12,831 R	77.9%	21.1%	78.7%	21.3%
91,029	SACRAMENTO	40,849	20,762	19,684	403	1,078 R	50.8%	48.2%	51.3%	48.7%
8,995	SAN BENITO	3,348	1,971	1,366	11	605 R	58.9%	40.8%	59.1%	40.9%
73,401	SAN BERNARDINO	39,112	29,229	9,436	447	19,793 R	74.7%	24.1%	75.6%	24.4%
112,248	SAN DIEGO	71,151	47,769	22,749	633	25,020 R	67.1%	32.0%	67.7%	32.3%
506,676	SAN FRANCISCO	195,468	95,987	96,632	2,849	645 D	49.1%	49.4%	49.8%	50.2%
79,905	SAN JOAQUIN	27,326	16,695	10,343	288	6,352 R	61.1%	37.9%	61.7%	38.3%
21,893	SAN LUIS OBISPO	8,920	5,425	3,336	159	2,089 R	60.8%	37.4%	61.9%	38.1%
36,781	SAN MATEO	24,392	14,360	9,755	277	4,605 R	58.9%	40.0%	59.5%	40.5%
41,097	SANTA BARBARA	16,799	11,666	4,954	179	6,712 R	69.4%	29.5%	70.2%	29.8%
100,676	SANTA CLARA	49,694	31,710	17,589	395	14,121 R	63.8%	35.4%	64.3%	35.7%
26,269	SANTA CRUZ	12,075	8,275	3,688	112	4,587 R	68.5%	30.5%	69.2%	30.8%
13,361	SHASTA	4,408	2,301	2,025	82	276 R	52.2%	45.9%	53.2%	46.8%
1,783	SIERRA	887	457	420	10	37 R	51.5%	47.4%	52.1%	47.9%
18,545	SISKIYOU	6,772	3,758	2,916	98	842 R	55.5%	43.1%	56.3%	43.7%
40,602	SOLANO	13,497	7,061	6,278	158	783 R	52.3%	46.5%	52.9%	47.1%
52,090	SONOMA	21,591	12,891	8,506	194	4,385 R	59.7%	39.4%	60.2%	39.8%
43,557	STANISLAUS	16,019	10,753	5,063	203	5,690 R	67.1%	31.6%	68.0%	32.0%
10,115	SUTTER	4,148	2,239	1,875	34	364 R	54.0%	45.2%	54.4%	45.6%
12,882	TEHAMA	5,174	3,393	1,650	131	1,743 R	65.6%	31.9%	67.3%	32.7%
2,551	TRINITY	915	447	433	35	14 R	48.9%	47.3%	50.8%	49.2%
59,031	TULARE	18,910	12,057	6,635	218	5,422 R	63.8%	35.1%	64.5%	35.5%
7,768	TUOLUMNE	3,159	1,731	1,360	68	371 R	54.8%	43.1%	56.0%	44.0%
28,724	VENTURA	12,851	9,017	3,717	117	5,300 R	70.2%	28.9%	70.8%	29.2%
17,105	YOLO	6,224	3,545	2,641	38	904 R	57.0%	42.4%	57.3%	42.7%
10,375	YUBA	4,042	2,022	1,990	30	32 R	50.0%	49.2%	50.4%	49.6%
3,426,861	TOTAL	1,796,656	1,162,323	614,365	19,968	547,958 R	64.7%	34.2%	65.4%	34.6%

CALIFORNIA

PRESIDENT 1924

1920 Census Population	County	Total Vote	Republican	Democratic	Progressive	Other	Plurality	Percentage Total Vote		
								Rep.	Dem.	Prog.
344,177	ALAMEDA	132,490	81,454	8,020	41,434	1,582	40,020 R	61.5%	6.1%	31.3%
243	ALPINE	59	52	5	1	1	47 R	88.1%	8.5%	1.7%
7,793	AMADOR	1,847	719	316	787	25	68 P	38.9%	17.1%	42.6%
30,030	BUTTE	10,372	4,382	1,299	4,582	109	200 P	42.2%	12.5%	44.2%
6,183	CALAVERAS	2,211	872	333	975	31	103 P	39.4%	15.1%	44.1%
9,290	COLUSA	2,571	1,127	495	889	60	238 R	43.8%	19.3%	34.6%
53,889	CONTRA COSTA	16,573	9,061	1,114	6,231	167	2,830 R	54.7%	6.7%	37.6%
2,759	DEL NORTE	1,007	530	122	322	33	208 R	52.6%	12.1%	32.0%
6,426	EL DORADO	2,991	852	361	1,749	29	897 P	28.5%	12.1%	58.5%
128,779	FRESNO	35,527	15,635	4,610	14,836	446	799 R	44.0%	13.0%	41.8%
11,853	GLENN	3,220	1,444	367	1,330	79	114 R	44.8%	11.4%	41.3%
37,413	HUMBOLDT	11,910	6,767	845	4,148	150	2,619 R	56.8%	7.1%	34.8%
43,453	IMPERIAL	6,872	3,455	759	2,549	109	906 R	50.3%	11.0%	37.1%
7,031	INYO	1,999	950	256	779	14	171 R	47.5%	12.8%	39.0%
54,843	KERN	18,763	8,646	3,159	6,754	204	1,892 R	46.1%	16.8%	36.0%
22,031	KINGS	5,624	2,812	1,109	1,611	92	1,201 R	50.0%	19.7%	28.6%
5,402	LAKE	1,769	795	261	658	55	137 R	44.9%	14.8%	37.2%
8,507	LASSEN	2,629	1,072	356	1,164	37	92 P	40.8%	13.5%	44.3%
936,455	LOS ANGELES	457,457	299,675	33,554	117,249	6,979	182,426 R	65.5%	7.3%	25.6%
12,203	MADERA	3,558	1,518	450	1,514	76	4 R	42.7%	12.6%	42.6%
27,342	MARIN	10,800	5,780	656	4,230	134	1,550 R	53.5%	6.1%	39.2%
2,775	MARIPOSA	855	344	168	332	11	12 R	40.2%	19.6%	38.8%
24,116	MENDOCINO	6,137	3,465	739	1,850	83	1,615 R	56.5%	12.0%	30.1%
24,579	MERCED	6,749	3,573	710	2,301	165	1,272 R	52.9%	10.5%	34.1%
5,425	MODOC	1,672	731	374	547	20	184 R	43.7%	22.4%	32.7%
960	MONO	310	166	45	98	1	68 R	53.5%	14.5%	31.6%
27,980	MONTEREY	7,768	4,744	886	2,035	103	2,709 R	61.1%	11.4%	26.2%
20,678	NAPA	6,576	3,605	670	2,237	64	1,368 R	54.8%	10.2%	34.0%
10,850	NEVADA	3,583	1,513	307	1,682	81	169 P	42.2%	8.6%	46.9%
61,375	ORANGE	29,566	19,913	2,565	6,480	608	13,433 R	67.4%	8.7%	21.9%
18,584	PLACER	5,984	2,192	390	3,290	112	1,098 P	36.6%	6.5%	55.0%
5,681	PLUMAS	1,713	564	182	956	11	392 P	32.9%	10.6%	55.8%
50,297	RIVERSIDE	15,516	9,619	1,318	4,204	375	5,415 R	62.0%	8.5%	27.1%
91,029	SACRAMENTO	32,617	13,400	2,285	16,570	362	3,170 P	41.1%	7.0%	50.8%
8,995	SAN BENITO	2,695	1,443	361	857	34	586 R	53.5%	13.4%	31.8%
73,401	SAN BERNARDINO	28,061	15,974	2,634	8,720	733	7,254 R	56.9%	9.4%	31.1%
112,248	SAN DIEGO	46,391	22,726	2,944	20,200	521	2,526 R	49.0%	6.3%	43.5%
506,676	SAN FRANCISCO	153,920	73,494	9,811	68,864	1,751	4,630 R	47.7%	6.4%	44.7%
79,905	SAN JOAQUIN	22,607	11,056	2,397	8,885	269	2,171 R	48.9%	10.6%	39.3%
21,893	SAN LUIS OBISPO	7,761	3,804	731	3,061	165	743 R	49.0%	9.4%	39.4%
36,781	SAN MATEO	14,702	8,126	771	5,694	111	2,432 R	55.3%	5.2%	38.7%
41,097	SANTA BARBARA	13,318	8,615	1,242	3,292	169	5,323 R	64.7%	9.3%	24.7%
100,676	SANTA CLARA	34,568	20,056	2,560	11,474	478	8,582 R	58.0%	7.4%	33.2%
26,269	SANTA CRUZ	8,879	5,402	801	2,557	119	2,845 R	60.8%	9.0%	28.8%
13,361	SHASTA	4,651	1,951	598	2,049	53	98 P	41.9%	12.9%	44.1%
1,783	SIERRA	709	276	73	350	10	74 P	38.9%	10.3%	49.4%
18,545	SISKIYOU	6,005	2,437	584	2,844	140	407 P	40.6%	9.7%	47.4%
40,602	SOLANO	9,962	4,782	957	4,123	100	659 R	48.0%	9.6%	41.4%
52,090	SONOMA	17,028	9,535	1,767	5,469	257	4,066 R	56.0%	10.4%	32.1%
43,557	STANISLAUS	13,312	7,569	1,274	4,125	344	3,444 R	56.9%	9.6%	31.0%
10,115	SUTTER	3,239	1,617	367	1,219	36	398 R	49.9%	11.3%	37.6%
12,882	TEHAMA	4,227	1,943	486	1,667	131	276 R	46.0%	11.5%	39.4%
2,551	TRINITY	921	336	154	414	17	78 P	36.5%	16.7%	45.0%
59,031	TULARE	18,674	9,484	3,425	5,504	261	3,980 R	50.8%	18.3%	29.5%
7,768	TUOLUMNE	2,991	1,287	357	1,327	20	40 P	43.0%	11.9%	44.4%
28,724	VENTURA	8,755	5,705	911	2,029	110	3,676 R	65.2%	10.4%	23.2%
17,105	YOLO	5,447	2,470	797	2,097	83	373 R	45.3%	14.6%	38.5%
10,375	YUBA	3,660	1,735	426	1,454	45	281 R	47.4%	11.6%	39.7%
3,426,861	TOTAL	1,281,778	733,250	105,514	424,649	18,365	308,601 R	57.2%	8.2%	33.1%

CALIFORNIA

PRESIDENT 1920

1920 Census Population	County	Total Vote	Republican	Democratic	Other	Rep.-Dem. Plurality	Percentage Total Vote Rep.	Total Vote Dem.	Major Vote Rep.	Major Vote Dem.
344,177	ALAMEDA	105,889	73,177	21,468	11,244	51,709 R	69.1%	20.3%	77.3%	22.7%
243	ALPINE	70	64	6		58 R	91.4%	8.6%	91.4%	8.6%
7,793	AMADOR	2,105	1,350	639	116	711 R	64.1%	30.4%	67.9%	32.1%
30,030	BUTTE	8,234	5,409	2,262	563	3,147 R	65.7%	27.5%	70.5%	29.5%
6,183	CALAVERAS	2,314	1,480	641	193	839 R	64.0%	27.7%	69.8%	30.2%
9,290	COLUSA	2,686	1,645	907	134	738 R	61.2%	33.8%	64.5%	35.5%
53,889	CONTRA COSTA	14,182	9,041	3,483	1,658	5,558 R	63.7%	24.6%	72.2%	27.8%
2,759	DEL NORTE	952	596	279	77	317 R	62.6%	29.3%	68.1%	31.9%
6,426	EL DORADO	2,542	1,636	726	180	910 R	64.4%	28.6%	69.3%	30.7%
128,779	FRESNO	26,413	14,621	9,613	2,179	5,008 R	55.4%	36.4%	60.3%	39.7%
11,853	GLENN	2,985	1,916	902	167	1,014 R	64.2%	30.2%	68.0%	32.0%
37,413	HUMBOLDT	9,340	6,528	1,778	1,034	4,750 R	69.9%	19.0%	78.6%	21.4%
43,453	IMPERIAL	7,284	4,699	2,022	563	2,677 R	64.5%	27.8%	69.9%	30.1%
7,031	INYO	2,089	1,195	682	212	513 R	57.2%	32.6%	63.7%	36.3%
54,843	KERN	14,444	7,079	6,095	1,270	984 R	49.0%	42.2%	53.7%	46.3%
22,031	KINGS	4,707	2,806	1,604	297	1,202 R	59.6%	34.1%	63.6%	36.4%
5,402	LAKE	1,735	993	571	171	422 R	57.2%	32.9%	63.5%	36.5%
8,507	LASSEN	2,389	1,582	643	164	939 R	66.2%	26.9%	71.1%	28.9%
936,455	LOS ANGELES	257,264	178,117	55,661	23,486	122,456 R	69.2%	21.6%	76.2%	23.8%
12,203	MADERA	3,208	1,779	1,145	284	634 R	55.5%	35.7%	60.8%	39.2%
27,342	MARIN	7,813	5,375	1,688	750	3,687 R	68.8%	21.6%	76.1%	23.9%
2,775	MARIPOSA	874	484	320	70	164 R	55.4%	36.6%	60.2%	39.8%
24,116	MENDOCINO	6,749	4,443	1,789	517	2,654 R	65.8%	26.5%	71.3%	28.7%
24,579	MERCED	5,488	3,457	1,537	494	1,920 R	63.0%	28.0%	69.2%	30.8%
5,425	MODOC	1,585	992	535	58	457 R	62.6%	33.8%	65.0%	35.0%
960	MONO	251	170	56	25	114 R	67.7%	22.3%	75.2%	24.8%
27,980	MONTEREY	7,109	4,817	1,771	521	3,046 R	67.8%	24.9%	73.1%	26.9%
20,678	NAPA	6,266	4,448	1,444	374	3,004 R	71.0%	23.0%	75.5%	24.5%
10,850	NEVADA	3,163	2,055	747	361	1,308 R	65.0%	23.6%	73.3%	26.7%
61,375	ORANGE	17,893	12,797	3,502	1,594	9,295 R	71.5%	19.6%	78.5%	21.5%
18,584	PLACER	4,869	2,894	1,559	416	1,335 R	59.4%	32.0%	65.0%	35.0%
5,681	PLUMAS	1,562	999	403	160	596 R	64.0%	25.8%	71.3%	28.7%
50,297	RIVERSIDE	13,118	9,124	2,798	1,196	6,326 R	69.6%	21.3%	76.5%	23.5%
91,029	SACRAMENTO	24,100	15,634	7,150	1,316	8,484 R	64.9%	29.7%	68.6%	31.4%
8,995	SAN BENITO	3,023	1,965	900	158	1,065 R	65.0%	29.8%	68.6%	31.4%
73,401	SAN BERNARDINO	19,921	12,518	5,620	1,783	6,898 R	62.8%	28.2%	69.0%	31.0%
112,248	SAN DIEGO	31,087	19,826	8,478	2,783	11,348 R	63.8%	27.3%	70.0%	30.0%
506,676	SAN FRANCISCO	147,421	96,105	32,637	18,679	63,468 R	65.2%	22.1%	74.6%	25.4%
79,905	SAN JOAQUIN	19,698	12,003	6,487	1,208	5,516 R	60.9%	32.9%	64.9%	35.1%
21,893	SAN LUIS OBISPO	6,673	4,123	1,606	944	2,517 R	61.8%	24.1%	72.0%	28.0%
36,781	SAN MATEO	10,217	7,205	1,958	1,054	5,247 R	70.5%	19.2%	78.6%	21.4%
41,097	SANTA BARBARA	10,329	6,970	2,586	773	4,384 R	67.5%	25.0%	72.9%	27.1%
100,676	SANTA CLARA	28,732	19,565	6,485	2,682	13,080 R	68.1%	22.6%	75.1%	24.9%
26,269	SANTA CRUZ	7,974	5,285	1,957	732	3,328 R	66.3%	24.5%	73.0%	27.0%
13,361	SHASTA	3,396	2,108	1,028	260	1,080 R	62.1%	30.3%	67.2%	32.8%
1,783	SIERRA	701	506	158	37	348 R	72.2%	22.5%	76.2%	23.8%
18,545	SISKIYOU	4,844	2,909	1,502	433	1,407 R	60.1%	31.0%	65.9%	34.1%
40,602	SOLANO	10,965	7,102	2,954	909	4,148 R	64.8%	26.9%	70.6%	29.4%
52,090	SONOMA	15,512	10,377	4,070	1,065	6,307 R	66.9%	26.2%	71.8%	28.2%
43,557	STANISLAUS	11,423	7,038	3,055	1,330	3,983 R	61.6%	26.7%	69.7%	30.3%
10,115	SUTTER	2,648	1,862	636	150	1,226 R	70.3%	24.0%	74.5%	25.5%
12,882	TEHAMA	3,983	2,462	1,079	442	1,383 R	61.8%	27.1%	69.5%	30.5%
2,551	TRINITY	989	622	285	82	337 R	62.9%	28.8%	68.6%	31.4%
59,031	TULARE	14,914	9,136	4,837	941	4,299 R	61.3%	32.4%	65.4%	34.6%
7,768	TUOLUMNE	2,164	1,285	659	220	626 R	59.4%	30.5%	66.1%	33.9%
28,724	VENTURA	6,883	5,231	1,305	347	3,926 R	76.0%	19.0%	80.0%	20.0%
17,105	YOLO	5,448	3,375	1,787	286	1,588 R	61.9%	32.8%	65.4%	34.6%
10,375	YUBA	2,846	2,012	696	138	1,316 R	70.7%	24.5%	74.3%	25.7%
3,426,861	TOTAL	943,463	624,992	229,191	89,280	395,801 R	66.2%	24.3%	73.2%	26.8%

CALIFORNIA

ELECTION NOTES

1956 Other vote was 11,119 Holtwick (Prohibition); 6,087 Andrews (States Rights); 300 Hass (Socialist Labor); 123 Hoopes (Socialist); 96 Dobbs (Socialist Workers); 8 Smith (Christian Nationalist); 819 scattered write-in.

1952 Other vote was 24,106 Hallinan (Progressive); 15,653 Hamblen (Prohibition); 3,504 MacArthur (3,326 Christian Nationalist and 178 Constitution); 273 Hass (Socialist Labor); 206 Hoopes (Socialist); 3,249 scattered write-in.

1948 Other vote was 190,381 Wallace (Progressive); 16,926 Watson (Prohibition); 3,459 Thomas (Socialist); 1,228 Thurmond (States Rights); 195 Teichert (Socialist Labor); 133 Dobbs (Socialist Workers); 813 scattered write-in.

1944 Other vote was 14,770 Watson (Prohibition); 2,515 Thomas (Socialist); 180 Teichert (Socialist Labor); 1,881 scattered write-in.

1940 Other vote was 16,506 Thomas (Socialist); 13,586 Browder (Communist); 9,400 Babson (Prohibition); 262 scattered write-in.

1936 Other vote was 12,917 Colvin (Prohibition); 11,331 Thomas (Socialist); 10,877 Browder (Communist); 490 scattered write-in.

1932 Other vote was 63,299 Thomas (Socialist); 20,637 Upshaw (Prohibition); 9,827 Harvey (Liberty); 1,023 Foster (Communist); 127 scattered write-in.

1928 Other vote was 19,595 Thomas (Socialist); 373 scattered write-in.

1924 A special four-column table which gives the LaFollette (Progressive) vote is used to detail this election. Other vote was Faris (Prohibition).

1920 Other vote was 64,076 Debs (Socialist); 25,204 Watkins (Prohibition).

COLORADO

POPULAR VOTE FOR PRESIDENT 1920 TO 1956

Year	Total Vote	Republican Vote	Republican Candidate	Democratic Vote	Democratic Candidate	Other Vote	Plurality	Percentage Total Vote Rep.	Total Vote Dem.	Major Vote Rep.	Major Vote Dem.
1956	657,074	394,479	Eisenhower, Dwight D.	257,997	Stevenson, Adlai E.	4,598	136,482 R	60.0%	39.3%	60.5%	39.5%
1952	630,103	379,782	Eisenhower, Dwight D.	245,504	Stevenson, Adlai E.	4,817	134,278 R	60.3%	39.0%	60.7%	39.3%
1948	515,237	239,714	Dewey, Thomas E.	267,288	Truman, Harry S.	8,235	27,574 D	46.5%	51.9%	47.3%	52.7%
1944	505,039	268,731	Dewey, Thomas E.	234,331	Roosevelt, Franklin D.	1,977	34,400 R	53.2%	46.4%	53.4%	46.6%
1940	549,004	279,576	Willkie, Wendell	265,554	Roosevelt, Franklin D.	3,874	14,022 R	50.9%	48.4%	51.3%	48.7%
1936	488,685	181,267	Landon, Alfred M.	295,021	Roosevelt, Franklin D.	12,397	113,754 D	37.1%	60.4%	38.1%	61.9%
1932	457,696	189,617	Hoover, Herbert C.	250,877	Roosevelt, Franklin D.	17,202	61,260 D	41.4%	54.8%	43.0%	57.0%
1928	392,242	253,872	Hoover, Herbert C.	133,131	Smith, Alfred E.	5,239	120,741 R	64.7%	33.9%	65.6%	34.4%
1924 **	342,261	195,171	Coolidge, Calvin	75,238	Davis, John W.	71,852	119,933 R	57.0%	22.0%	72.2%	27.8%
1920	292,053	173,248	Harding, Warren G.	104,936	Cox, James M.	13,869	68,312 R	59.3%	35.9%	62.3%	37.7%

In 1924 other vote was 69,946 Progressive; 966 Prohibition; 562 Communist and 378 Socialist Labor.

ELECTORAL COLLEGE VOTE 1920 TO 1956

Year	Total	Republican	Democratic	Other
1956	6	6	—	—
1952	6	6	—	—
1948	6	—	6	—
1944	6	6	—	—
1940	6	6	—	—
1936	6	—	6	—
1932	6	—	6	—
1928	6	6	—	—
1924	6	6	—	—
1920	6	6	—	—

COLORADO

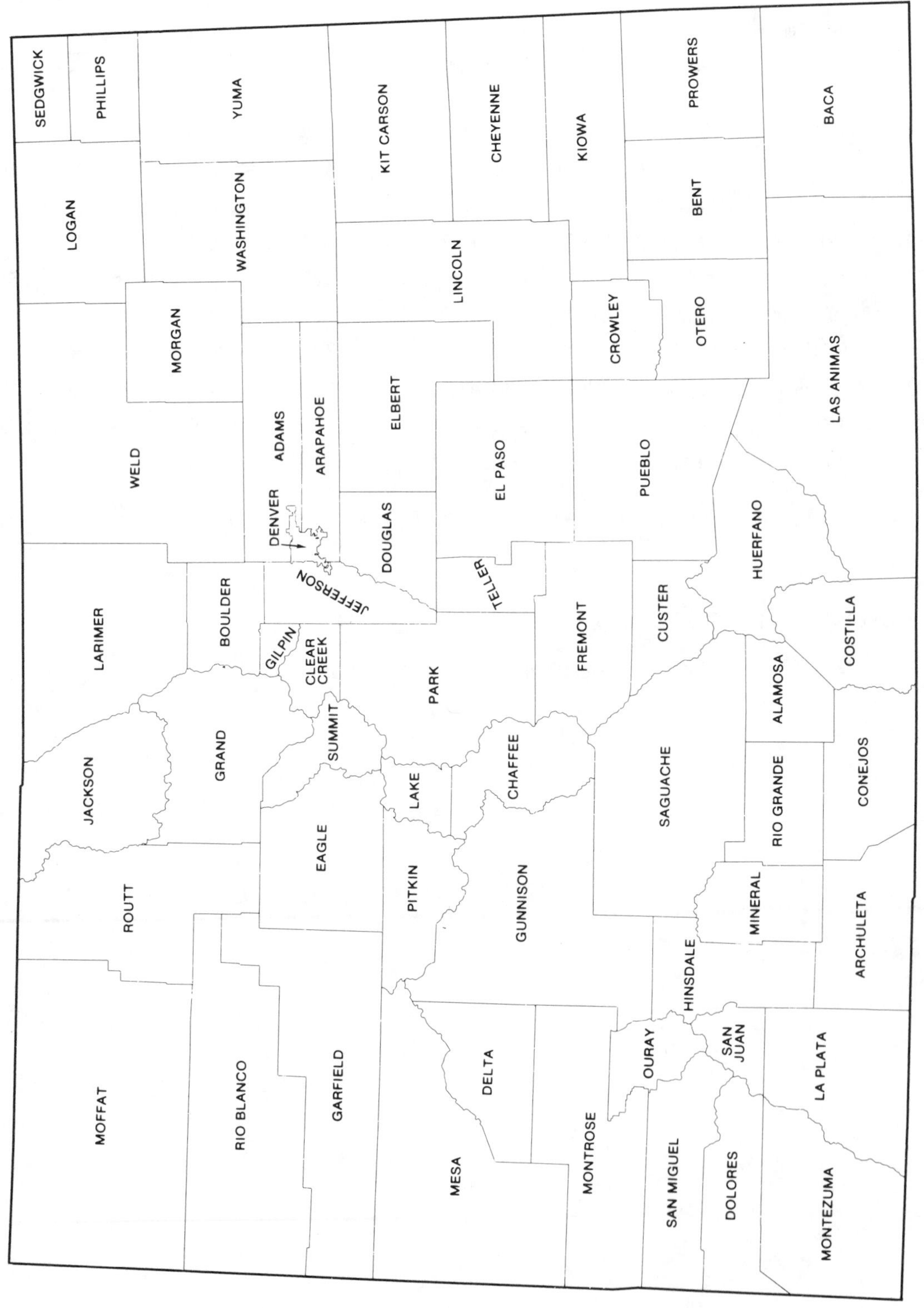
SEDGWICK
PHILLIPS
YUMA
KIT CARSON
CHEYENNE
KIOWA
PROWERS
BACA
LOGAN
WASHINGTON
LINCOLN
BENT
CROWLEY
OTERO
MORGAN
ELBERT
LAS ANIMAS
WELD
ADAMS
ARAPAHOE
EL PASO
PUEBLO
DENVER
DOUGLAS
HUERFANO
JEFFERSON
TELLER
LARIMER
BOULDER
FREMONT
CUSTER
COSTILLA
GILPIN
CLEAR CREEK
PARK
ALAMOSA
SUMMIT
GRAND
JACKSON
CHAFFEE
LAKE
SAGUACHE
RIO GRANDE
CONEJOS
EAGLE
PITKIN
GUNNISON
ROUTT
MINERAL
ARCHULETA
HINSDALE
SAN JUAN
OURAY
DELTA
LA PLATA
MOFFAT
RIO BLANCO
GARFIELD
MESA
MONTROSE
SAN MIGUEL
DOLORES
MONTEZUMA

COLORADO

PRESIDENT 1956

1950 Census Population	County	Total Vote	Republican	Democratic	Other	Rep.-Dem. Plurality	Percentage Total Vote Rep.	Percentage Total Vote Dem.	Percentage Major Vote Rep.	Percentage Major Vote Dem.
40,234	ADAMS	24,463	12,778	11,470	215	1,308 R	52.2%	46.9%	52.7%	47.3%
10,531	ALAMOSA	3,918	2,442	1,465	11	977 R	62.3%	37.4%	62.5%	37.5%
52,125	ARAPAHOE	31,243	19,716	11,351	176	8,365 R	63.1%	36.3%	63.5%	36.5%
3,030	ARCHULETA	1,060	635	423	2	212 R	59.9%	39.9%	60.0%	40.0%
7,964	BACA	2,876	1,715	1,150	11	565 R	59.6%	40.0%	59.9%	40.1%
8,775	BENT	3,001	1,718	1,283		435 R	57.2%	42.8%	57.2%	42.8%
48,296	BOULDER	25,039	16,748	8,149	142	8,599 R	66.9%	32.5%	67.3%	32.7%
7,168	CHAFFEE	3,587	2,284	1,303		981 R	63.7%	36.3%	63.7%	36.3%
3,453	CHEYENNE	1,329	820	507	2	313 R	61.7%	38.1%	61.8%	38.2%
3,289	CLEAR CREEK	1,500	973	520	7	453 R	64.9%	34.7%	65.2%	34.8%
10,171	CONEJOS	3,371	1,884	1,471	16	413 R	55.9%	43.6%	56.2%	43.8%
6,067	COSTILLA	2,254	958	1,256	40	298 D	42.5%	55.7%	43.3%	56.7%
5,222	CROWLEY	1,966	1,220	745	1	475 R	62.1%	37.9%	62.1%	37.9%
1,573	CUSTER	799	534	264	1	270 R	66.8%	33.0%	66.9%	33.1%
17,365	DELTA	7,002	4,531	2,458	13	2,073 R	64.7%	35.1%	64.8%	35.2%
415,786	DENVER	217,121	121,402	93,812	1,907	27,590 R	55.9%	43.2%	56.4%	43.6%
1,966	DOLORES	901	544	354	3	190 R	60.4%	39.3%	60.6%	39.4%
3,507	DOUGLAS	2,215	1,508	697	10	811 R	68.1%	31.5%	68.4%	31.6%
4,488	EAGLE	2,012	1,154	852	6	302 R	57.4%	42.3%	57.5%	42.5%
4,477	ELBERT	2,000	1,295	702	3	593 R	64.8%	35.1%	64.8%	35.2%
74,523	EL PASO	39,666	27,282	11,879	505	15,403 R	68.8%	29.9%	69.7%	30.3%
18,366	FREMONT	8,962	6,040	2,896	26	3,144 R	67.4%	32.3%	67.6%	32.4%
11,625	GARFIELD	5,297	3,332	1,953	12	1,379 R	62.9%	36.9%	63.0%	37.0%
850	GILPIN	639	394	244	1	150 R	61.7%	38.2%	61.8%	38.2%
3,963	GRAND	1,737	1,239	496	2	743 R	71.3%	28.6%	71.4%	28.6%
5,716	GUNNISON	2,247	1,400	846	1	554 R	62.3%	37.7%	62.3%	37.7%
263	HINSDALE	202	155	47		108 R	76.7%	23.3%	76.7%	23.3%
10,549	HUERFANO	4,365	2,091	2,262	12	171 D	47.9%	51.8%	48.0%	52.0%
1,976	JACKSON	892	594	297	1	297 R	66.6%	33.3%	66.7%	33.3%
55,687	JEFFERSON	39,865	25,398	14,270	197	11,128 R	63.7%	35.8%	64.0%	36.0%
3,003	KIOWA	1,253	810	443		367 R	64.6%	35.4%	64.6%	35.4%
8,600	KIT CARSON	3,161	2,243	911	7	1,332 R	71.0%	28.8%	71.1%	28.9%
6,150	LAKE	2,793	1,433	1,355	5	78 R	51.3%	48.5%	51.4%	48.6%
14,880	LA PLATA	7,140	4,770	2,366	4	2,404 R	66.8%	33.1%	66.8%	33.2%
43,554	LARIMER	20,015	14,364	5,612	39	8,752 R	71.8%	28.0%	71.9%	28.1%
25,902	LAS ANIMAS	10,414	5,290	5,099	25	191 R	50.8%	49.0%	50.9%	49.1%
5,909	LINCOLN	2,617	1,603	1,012	2	591 R	61.3%	38.7%	61.3%	38.7%
17,187	LOGAN	8,060	5,199	2,841	20	2,358 R	64.5%	35.2%	64.7%	35.3%
38,974	MESA	20,496	12,869	7,567	60	5,302 R	62.8%	36.9%	63.0%	37.0%
698	MINERAL	268	168	99	1	69 R	62.7%	36.9%	62.9%	37.1%
5,946	MOFFAT	2,561	1,762	797	2	965 R	68.8%	31.1%	68.9%	31.1%
9,991	MONTEZUMA	3,919	2,492	1,402	25	1,090 R	63.6%	35.8%	64.0%	36.0%
15,220	MONTROSE	6,534	4,054	2,461	19	1,593 R	62.0%	37.7%	62.2%	37.8%
18,074	MORGAN	8,298	5,325	2,956	17	2,369 R	64.2%	35.6%	64.3%	35.7%
25,275	OTERO	9,693	5,964	3,722	7	2,242 R	61.5%	38.4%	61.6%	38.4%
2,103	OURAY	962	634	322	6	312 R	65.9%	33.5%	66.3%	33.7%
1,870	PARK	1,013	715	297	1	418 R	70.6%	29.3%	70.7%	29.3%
4,924	PHILLIPS	2,423	1,535	887	1	648 R	63.4%	36.6%	63.4%	36.6%
1,646	PITKIN	885	550	334	1	216 R	62.1%	37.7%	62.2%	37.8%
14,836	PROWERS	5,815	3,350	2,460	5	890 R	57.6%	42.3%	57.7%	42.3%
90,188	PUEBLO	44,814	23,454	20,433	927	3,021 R	52.3%	45.6%	53.4%	46.6%
4,719	RIO BLANCO	2,229	1,593	635	1	958 R	71.5%	28.5%	71.5%	28.5%
12,832	RIO GRANDE	4,264	2,816	1,441	7	1,375 R	66.0%	33.8%	66.1%	33.9%
8,940	ROUTT	3,147	1,811	1,330	6	481 R	57.5%	42.3%	57.7%	42.3%
5,664	SAGUACHE	1,980	1,149	823	8	326 R	58.0%	41.6%	58.3%	41.7%
1,471	SAN JUAN	555	324	231		93 R	58.4%	41.6%	58.4%	41.6%
2,693	SAN MIGUEL	1,120	648	469	3	179 R	57.9%	41.9%	58.0%	42.0%
5,095	SEDGWICK	2,099	1,334	760	5	574 R	63.6%	36.2%	63.7%	36.3%
1,135	SUMMIT	664	429	235		194 R	64.6%	35.4%	64.6%	35.4%
2,754	TELLER	1,471	977	494		483 R	66.4%	33.6%	66.4%	33.6%

COLORADO

PRESIDENT 1956

1950 Census Population	County	Total Vote	Republican	Democratic	Other	Rep.-Dem. Plurality	Percentage Total Vote Rep.	Percentage Total Vote Dem.	Percentage Major Vote Rep.	Percentage Major Vote Dem.
7,520	WASHINGTON	3,098	2,020	1,067	11	953 R	65.2%	34.4%	65.4%	34.6%
67,504	WELD	27,455	17,228	10,170	57	7,058 R	62.7%	37.0%	62.9%	37.1%
10,827	YUMA	4,329	2,782	1,544	3	1,238 R	64.3%	35.7%	64.3%	35.7%
1,325,089	TOTAL	657,074	394,479	257,997	4,598	136,482 R	60.0%	39.3%	60.5%	39.5%

COLORADO

PRESIDENT 1952

1950 Census Population	County	Total Vote	Republican	Democratic	Other	Rep.-Dem. Plurality	Percentage Total Vote Rep.	Total Vote Dem.	Major Vote Rep.	Major Vote Dem.
40,234	ADAMS	16,387	8,995	7,321	71	1,674 R	54.9%	44.7%	55.1%	44.9%
10,531	ALAMOSA	4,391	2,728	1,626	37	1,102 R	62.1%	37.0%	62.7%	37.3%
52,125	ARAPAHOE	25,534	15,402	9,843	289	5,559 R	60.3%	38.5%	61.0%	39.0%
3,030	ARCHULETA	1,070	691	377	2	314 R	64.6%	35.2%	64.7%	35.3%
7,964	BACA	3,236	2,122	1,094	20	1,028 R	65.6%	33.8%	66.0%	34.0%
8,775	BENT	3,283	1,950	1,317	16	633 R	59.4%	40.1%	59.7%	40.3%
48,296	BOULDER	23,079	15,069	7,767	243	7,302 R	65.3%	33.7%	66.0%	34.0%
7,168	CHAFFEE	3,829	2,171	1,643	15	528 R	56.7%	42.9%	56.9%	43.1%
3,453	CHEYENNE	1,522	1,004	515	3	489 R	66.0%	33.8%	66.1%	33.9%
3,289	CLEAR CREEK	1,691	1,145	540	6	605 R	67.7%	31.9%	68.0%	32.0%
10,171	CONEJOS	3,902	2,194	1,610	98	584 R	56.2%	41.3%	57.7%	42.3%
6,067	COSTILLA	2,447	1,070	1,369	8	299 D	43.7%	55.9%	43.9%	56.1%
5,222	CROWLEY	2,281	1,546	726	9	820 R	67.8%	31.8%	68.0%	32.0%
1,573	CUSTER	899	662	231	6	431 R	73.6%	25.7%	74.1%	25.9%
17,365	DELTA	7,441	4,986	2,389	66	2,597 R	67.0%	32.1%	67.6%	32.4%
415,786	DENVER	213,563	119,792	92,237	1,534	27,555 R	56.1%	43.2%	56.5%	43.5%
1,966	DOLORES	871	542	323	6	219 R	62.2%	37.1%	62.7%	37.3%
3,507	DOUGLAS	2,068	1,427	637	4	790 R	69.0%	30.8%	69.1%	30.9%
4,488	EAGLE	2,313	1,242	1,058	13	184 R	53.7%	45.7%	54.0%	46.0%
4,477	ELBERT	2,176	1,579	586	11	993 R	72.6%	26.9%	72.9%	27.1%
74,523	EL PASO	36,778	25,272	11,203	303	14,069 R	68.7%	30.5%	69.3%	30.7%
18,366	FREMONT	9,199	5,964	3,176	59	2,788 R	64.8%	34.5%	65.3%	34.7%
11,625	GARFIELD	5,719	3,914	1,777	28	2,137 R	68.4%	31.1%	68.8%	31.2%
850	GILPIN	591	357	228	6	129 R	60.4%	38.6%	61.0%	39.0%
3,963	GRAND	1,895	1,333	554	8	779 R	70.3%	29.2%	70.6%	29.4%
5,716	GUNNISON	2,578	1,533	1,045		488 R	59.5%	40.5%	59.5%	40.5%
263	HINSDALE	208	154	54		100 R	74.0%	26.0%	74.0%	26.0%
10,549	HUERFANO	4,968	2,178	2,773	17	595 D	43.8%	55.8%	44.0%	56.0%
1,976	JACKSON	886	579	305	2	274 R	65.3%	34.4%	65.5%	34.5%
55,687	JEFFERSON	31,674	19,971	11,509	194	8,462 R	63.1%	36.3%	63.4%	36.6%
3,003	KIOWA	1,478	1,047	412	19	635 R	70.8%	27.9%	71.8%	28.2%
8,600	KIT CARSON	3,535	2,511	998	26	1,513 R	71.0%	28.2%	71.6%	28.4%
6,150	LAKE	2,897	1,303	1,585	9	282 D	45.0%	54.7%	45.1%	54.9%
14,880	LA PLATA	6,701	4,425	2,210	66	2,215 R	66.0%	33.0%	66.7%	33.3%
43,554	LARIMER	19,860	14,484	5,266	110	9,218 R	72.9%	26.5%	73.3%	26.7%
25,902	LAS ANIMAS	10,964	4,467	6,446	51	1,979 D	40.7%	58.8%	40.9%	59.1%
5,909	LINCOLN	2,773	1,843	927	3	916 R	66.5%	33.4%	66.5%	33.5%
17,187	LOGAN	7,739	5,237	2,459	43	2,778 R	67.7%	31.8%	68.0%	32.0%
38,974	MESA	18,845	11,883	6,883	79	5,000 R	63.1%	36.5%	63.3%	36.7%
698	MINERAL	308	209	98	1	111 R	67.9%	31.8%	68.1%	31.9%
5,946	MOFFAT	2,741	1,922	808	11	1,114 R	70.1%	29.5%	70.4%	29.6%
9,991	MONTEZUMA	3,626	2,466	1,127	33	1,339 R	68.0%	31.1%	68.6%	31.4%
15,220	MONTROSE	6,371	4,279	2,037	55	2,242 R	67.2%	32.0%	67.7%	32.3%
18,074	MORGAN	7,714	5,371	2,297	46	3,074 R	69.6%	29.8%	70.0%	30.0%
25,275	OTERO	10,307	6,552	3,721	34	2,831 R	63.6%	36.1%	63.8%	36.2%
2,103	OURAY	1,127	697	413	17	284 R	61.8%	36.6%	62.8%	37.2%
1,870	PARK	1,125	775	343	7	432 R	68.9%	30.5%	69.3%	30.7%
4,924	PHILLIPS	2,466	1,670	789	7	881 R	67.7%	32.0%	67.9%	32.1%
1,646	PITKIN	867	556	309	2	247 R	64.1%	35.6%	64.3%	35.7%
14,836	PROWERS	6,108	3,978	2,087	43	1,891 R	65.1%	34.2%	65.6%	34.4%
90,188	PUEBLO	41,659	20,333	20,613	713	280 D	48.8%	49.5%	49.7%	50.3%
4,719	RIO BLANCO	2,257	1,612	633	12	979 R	71.4%	28.0%	71.8%	28.2%
12,832	RIO GRANDE	4,566	3,201	1,350	15	1,851 R	70.1%	29.6%	70.3%	29.7%
8,940	ROUTT	3,739	2,143	1,575	21	568 R	57.3%	42.1%	57.6%	42.4%
5,664	SAGUACHE	2,065	1,344	714	7	630 R	65.1%	34.6%	65.3%	34.7%
1,471	SAN JUAN	761	432	327	2	105 R	56.8%	43.0%	56.9%	43.1%
2,693	SAN MIGUEL	1,185	654	524	7	130 R	55.2%	44.2%	55.5%	44.5%
5,095	SEDGWICK	2,223	1,528	686	9	842 R	68.7%	30.9%	69.0%	31.0%
1,135	SUMMIT	714	442	271	1	171 R	61.9%	38.0%	62.0%	38.0%
2,754	TELLER	1,631	1,042	572	17	470 R	63.9%	35.1%	64.6%	35.4%

COLORADO

PRESIDENT 1952

1950 Census Population	County	Total Vote	Republican	Democratic	Other	Rep.-Dem. Plurality	Percentage: Total Vote Rep.	Percentage: Total Vote Dem.	Percentage: Major Vote Rep.	Percentage: Major Vote Dem.
7,520	WASHINGTON	3,443	2,398	1,009	36	1,389 R	69.6%	29.3%	70.4%	29.6%
67,504	WELD	27,096	18,002	8,890	204	9,112 R	66.4%	32.8%	66.9%	33.1%
10,827	YUMA	4,733	3,404	1,292	37	2,112 R	71.9%	27.3%	72.5%	27.5%
1,325,089	TOTAL	630,103	379,782	245,504	4,817	134,278 R	60.3%	39.0%	60.7%	39.3%

COLORADO

PRESIDENT 1948

							Percentage			
							Total Vote		Major Vote	
1940 Census Population	County	Total Vote	Republican	Democratic	Other	Rep.-Dem. Plurality	Rep.	Dem.	Rep.	Dem.
22,481	ADAMS	10,791	4,419	6,240	132	1,821 D	41.0%	57.8%	41.5%	58.5%
10,484	ALAMOSA	4,374	1,950	2,395	29	445 D	44.6%	54.8%	44.9%	55.1%
32,150	ARAPAHOE	15,080	6,962	7,943	175	981 D	46.2%	52.7%	46.7%	53.3%
3,806	ARCHULETA	1,084	479	597	8	118 D	44.2%	55.1%	44.5%	55.5%
6,207	BACA	2,652	1,260	1,368	24	108 D	47.5%	51.6%	47.9%	52.1%
9,653	BENT	2,984	1,296	1,658	30	362 D	43.4%	55.6%	43.9%	56.1%
37,438	BOULDER	19,839	10,335	8,792	712	1,543 R	52.1%	44.3%	54.0%	46.0%
8,109	CHAFFEE	3,580	1,476	2,065	39	589 D	41.2%	57.7%	41.7%	58.3%
2,964	CHEYENNE	1,386	713	657	16	56 R	51.4%	47.4%	52.0%	48.0%
3,784	CLEAR CREEK	1,664	836	810	18	26 R	50.2%	48.7%	50.8%	49.2%
11,648	CONEJOS	3,827	1,532	2,236	59	704 D	40.0%	58.4%	40.7%	59.3%
7,533	COSTILLA	2,532	921	1,563	48	642 D	36.4%	61.7%	37.1%	62.9%
5,398	CROWLEY	2,040	1,027	1,004	9	23 R	50.3%	49.2%	50.6%	49.4%
2,270	CUSTER	943	547	384	12	163 R	58.0%	40.7%	58.8%	41.2%
16,470	DELTA	6,469	3,158	3,171	140	13 D	48.8%	49.0%	49.9%	50.1%
322,412	DENVER	169,067	76,364	89,489	3,214	13,125 D	45.2%	52.9%	46.0%	54.0%
1,958	DOLORES	801	352	435	14	83 D	43.9%	54.3%	44.7%	55.3%
3,496	DOUGLAS	1,756	979	767	10	212 R	55.8%	43.7%	56.1%	43.9%
5,361	EAGLE	1,831	738	1,008	85	270 D	40.3%	55.1%	42.3%	57.7%
5,460	ELBERT	2,049	1,155	873	21	282 R	56.4%	42.6%	57.0%	43.0%
54,025	EL PASO	28,419	15,705	12,291	423	3,414 R	55.3%	43.2%	56.1%	43.9%
19,742	FREMONT	8,627	4,421	4,077	129	344 R	51.2%	47.3%	52.0%	48.0%
10,560	GARFIELD	4,822	2,416	2,364	42	52 R	50.1%	49.0%	50.5%	49.5%
1,625	GILPIN	611	302	296	13	6 R	49.4%	48.4%	50.5%	49.5%
3,587	GRAND	1,562	777	763	22	14 R	49.7%	48.8%	50.5%	49.5%
6,192	GUNNISON	2,494	1,103	1,326	65	223 D	44.2%	53.2%	45.4%	54.6%
349	HINSDALE	208	133	75		58 R	63.9%	36.1%	63.9%	36.1%
16,088	HUERFANO	5,410	1,841	3,448	121	1,607 D	34.0%	63.7%	34.8%	65.2%
1,798	JACKSON	618	327	291		36 R	52.9%	47.1%	52.9%	47.1%
30,725	JEFFERSON	19,308	9,903	9,145	260	758 R	51.3%	47.4%	52.0%	48.0%
2,793	KIOWA	1,431	758	659	14	99 R	53.0%	46.1%	53.5%	46.5%
7,512	KIT CARSON	3,181	1,873	1,281	27	592 R	58.9%	40.3%	59.4%	40.6%
6,883	LAKE	2,502	838	1,581	83	743 D	33.5%	63.2%	34.6%	65.4%
15,494	LA PLATA	5,360	2,735	2,536	89	199 R	51.0%	47.3%	51.9%	48.1%
35,539	LARIMER	17,029	9,813	7,062	154	2,751 R	57.6%	41.5%	58.2%	41.8%
32,369	LAS ANIMAS	11,210	3,452	7,586	172	4,134 D	30.8%	67.7%	31.3%	68.7%
5,882	LINCOLN	2,516	1,271	1,231	14	40 R	50.5%	48.9%	50.8%	49.2%
18,370	LOGAN	6,448	3,223	3,179	46	44 R	50.0%	49.3%	50.3%	49.7%
33,791	MESA	15,185	6,586	8,401	198	1,815 D	43.4%	55.3%	43.9%	56.1%
975	MINERAL	335	144	190	1	46 D	43.0%	56.7%	43.1%	56.9%
5,086	MOFFAT	2,391	1,261	1,101	29	160 R	52.7%	46.0%	53.4%	46.6%
10,463	MONTEZUMA	3,313	1,630	1,653	30	23 D	49.2%	49.9%	49.6%	50.4%
15,418	MONTROSE	5,116	2,473	2,544	99	71 D	48.3%	49.7%	49.3%	50.7%
17,214	MORGAN	6,382	3,417	2,912	53	505 R	53.5%	45.6%	54.0%	46.0%
23,571	OTERO	13,032	4,311	8,640	81	4,329 D	33.1%	66.3%	33.3%	66.7%
2,089	OURAY	1,045	574	461	10	113 R	54.9%	44.1%	55.5%	44.5%
3,272	PARK	1,152	637	505	10	132 R	55.3%	43.8%	55.8%	44.2%
4,948	PHILLIPS	2,049	1,076	932	41	144 R	52.5%	45.5%	53.6%	46.4%
1,836	PITKIN	751	319	409	23	90 D	42.5%	54.5%	43.8%	56.2%
12,304	PROWERS	5,047	2,505	2,497	45	8 R	49.6%	49.5%	50.1%	49.9%
68,870	PUEBLO	35,041	12,756	21,637	648	8,881 D	36.4%	61.7%	37.1%	62.9%
2,943	RIO BLANCO	1,751	981	752	18	229 R	56.0%	42.9%	56.6%	43.4%
12,404	RIO GRANDE	3,876	2,049	1,814	13	235 R	52.9%	46.8%	53.0%	47.0%
10,525	ROUTT	3,651	1,492	2,088	71	596 D	40.9%	57.2%	41.7%	58.3%
6,173	SAGUACHE	1,937	914	1,009	14	95 D	47.2%	52.1%	47.5%	52.5%
1,439	SAN JUAN	700	329	348	23	19 D	47.0%	49.7%	48.6%	51.4%
3,664	SAN MIGUEL	1,079	451	613	15	162 D	41.8%	56.8%	42.4%	57.6%
5,294	SEDGWICK	1,867	1,020	834	13	186 R	54.6%	44.7%	55.0%	45.0%
1,754	SUMMIT	675	292	378	5	86 D	43.3%	56.0%	43.6%	56.4%
6,463	TELLER	1,547	748	779	20	31 D	48.4%	50.4%	49.0%	51.0%

COLORADO

PRESIDENT 1948

1940 Census Population	County	Total Vote	Republican	Democratic	Other	Rep.-Dem. Plurality	Percentage Total Vote Rep.	Percentage Total Vote Dem.	Percentage Major Vote Rep.	Percentage Major Vote Dem.
8,336	WASHINGTON	2,958	1,636	1,304	18	332 R	55.3%	44.1%	55.6%	44.4%
63,747	WELD	23,639	12,446	10,934	259	1,512 R	52.7%	46.3%	53.2%	46.8%
12,102	YUMA	4,213	2,277	1,907	29	370 R	54.0%	45.3%	54.4%	45.6%
1,123,296	TOTAL	515,237	239,714	267,288	8,235	27,574 D	46.5%	51.9%	47.3%	52.7%

COLORADO

PRESIDENT 1944

1940 Census Population	County	Total Vote	Republican	Democratic	Other	Rep.-Dem. Plurality	Percentage Total Vote Rep.	Percentage Total Vote Dem.	Percentage Major Vote Rep.	Percentage Major Vote Dem.
22,481	ADAMS	9,063	4,933	4,101	29	832 R	54.4%	45.2%	54.6%	45.4%
10,484	ALAMOSA	3,749	1,933	1,806	10	127 R	51.6%	48.2%	51.7%	48.3%
32,150	ARAPAHOE	16,611	9,057	7,485	69	1,572 R	54.5%	45.1%	54.8%	45.2%
3,806	ARCHULETA	1,030	602	427	1	175 R	58.4%	41.5%	58.5%	41.5%
6,207	BACA	2,469	1,528	941		587 R	61.9%	38.1%	61.9%	38.1%
9,653	BENT	3,021	1,556	1,456	9	100 R	51.5%	48.2%	51.7%	48.3%
37,438	BOULDER	17,610	10,054	7,442	114	2,612 R	57.1%	42.3%	57.5%	42.5%
8,109	CHAFFEE	3,430	1,675	1,731	24	56 D	48.8%	50.5%	49.2%	50.8%
2,964	CHEYENNE	1,521	923	594	4	329 R	60.7%	39.1%	60.8%	39.2%
3,784	CLEAR CREEK	1,438	795	636	7	159 R	55.3%	44.2%	55.6%	44.4%
11,648	CONEJOS	3,768	1,740	2,028		288 D	46.2%	53.8%	46.2%	53.8%
7,533	COSTILLA	2,416	896	1,515	5	619 D	37.1%	62.7%	37.2%	62.8%
5,398	CROWLEY	1,929	1,214	710	5	504 R	62.9%	36.8%	63.1%	36.9%
2,270	CUSTER	943	601	333	9	268 R	63.7%	35.3%	64.3%	35.7%
16,470	DELTA	5,838	3,462	2,351	25	1,111 R	59.3%	40.3%	59.6%	40.4%
322,412	DENVER	177,091	86,331	90,001	759	3,670 D	48.7%	50.8%	49.0%	51.0%
1,958	DOLORES	729	429	300		129 R	58.8%	41.2%	58.8%	41.2%
3,496	DOUGLAS	1,857	1,214	638	5	576 R	65.4%	34.4%	65.6%	34.4%
5,361	EAGLE	1,879	922	952	5	30 D	49.1%	50.7%	49.2%	50.8%
5,460	ELBERT	2,044	1,413	628	3	785 R	69.1%	30.7%	69.2%	30.8%
54,025	EL PASO	28,186	16,392	11,679	115	4,713 R	58.2%	41.4%	58.4%	41.6%
19,742	FREMONT	8,166	4,953	3,180	33	1,773 R	60.7%	38.9%	60.9%	39.1%
10,560	GARFIELD	4,464	2,588	1,865	11	723 R	58.0%	41.8%	58.1%	41.9%
1,625	GILPIN	487	272	213	2	59 R	55.9%	43.7%	56.1%	43.9%
3,587	GRAND	1,524	968	554	2	414 R	63.5%	36.4%	63.6%	36.4%
6,192	GUNNISON	2,637	1,221	1,411	5	190 D	46.3%	53.5%	46.4%	53.6%
349	HINSDALE	185	124	61		63 R	67.0%	33.0%	67.0%	33.0%
16,088	HUERFANO	5,427	2,119	3,290	18	1,171 D	39.0%	60.6%	39.2%	60.8%
1,798	JACKSON	715	463	252		211 R	64.8%	35.2%	64.8%	35.2%
30,725	JEFFERSON	17,160	9,815	7,277	68	2,538 R	57.2%	42.4%	57.4%	42.6%
2,793	KIOWA	1,498	970	522	6	448 R	64.8%	34.8%	65.0%	35.0%
7,512	KIT CARSON	3,419	2,471	937	11	1,534 R	72.3%	27.4%	72.5%	27.5%
6,883	LAKE	2,937	1,236	1,687	14	451 D	42.1%	57.4%	42.3%	57.7%
15,494	LA PLATA	5,069	3,023	2,031	15	992 R	59.6%	40.1%	59.8%	40.2%
35,539	LARIMER	15,144	9,914	5,172	58	4,742 R	65.5%	34.2%	65.7%	34.3%
32,369	LAS ANIMAS	11,034	4,179	6,800	55	2,621 D	37.9%	61.6%	38.1%	61.9%
5,882	LINCOLN	2,839	1,689	1,147	3	542 R	59.5%	40.4%	59.6%	40.4%
18,370	LOGAN	6,487	3,998	2,471	18	1,527 R	61.6%	38.1%	61.8%	38.2%
33,791	MESA	13,598	6,653	6,870	75	217 D	48.9%	50.5%	49.2%	50.8%
975	MINERAL	322	170	150	2	20 R	52.8%	46.6%	53.1%	46.9%
5,086	MOFFAT	2,374	1,445	923	6	522 R	60.9%	38.9%	61.0%	39.0%
10,463	MONTEZUMA	2,825	1,610	1,207	8	403 R	57.0%	42.7%	57.2%	42.8%
15,418	MONTROSE	5,237	2,952	2,258	27	694 R	56.4%	43.1%	56.7%	43.3%
17,214	MORGAN	6,026	4,166	1,839	21	2,327 R	69.1%	30.5%	69.4%	30.6%
23,571	OTERO	8,816	5,002	3,791	23	1,211 R	56.7%	43.0%	56.9%	43.1%
2,089	OURAY	807	503	303	1	200 R	62.3%	37.5%	62.4%	37.6%
3,272	PARK	1,102	670	426	6	244 R	60.8%	38.7%	61.1%	38.9%
4,948	PHILLIPS	2,233	1,455	761	17	694 R	65.2%	34.1%	65.7%	34.3%
1,836	PITKIN	724	368	355	1	13 R	50.8%	49.0%	50.9%	49.1%
12,304	PROWERS	4,762	2,796	1,948	18	848 R	58.7%	40.9%	58.9%	41.1%
68,870	PUEBLO	32,983	13,848	19,039	96	5,191 D	42.0%	57.7%	42.1%	57.9%
2,943	RIO BLANCO	1,337	881	451	5	430 R	65.9%	33.7%	66.1%	33.9%
12,404	RIO GRANDE	3,900	2,567	1,325	8	1,242 R	65.8%	34.0%	66.0%	34.0%
10,525	ROUTT	3,831	1,869	1,940	22	71 D	48.8%	50.6%	49.1%	50.9%
6,173	SAGUACHE	1,938	1,204	729	5	475 R	62.1%	37.6%	62.3%	37.7%
1,439	SAN JUAN	587	328	258	1	70 R	55.9%	44.0%	56.0%	44.0%
3,664	SAN MIGUEL	1,173	536	630	7	94 D	45.7%	53.7%	46.0%	54.0%
5,294	SEDGWICK	1,799	1,228	568	3	660 R	68.3%	31.6%	68.4%	31.6%
1,754	SUMMIT	566	326	237	3	89 R	57.6%	41.9%	57.9%	42.1%
6,463	TELLER	1,650	829	808	13	21 R	50.2%	49.0%	50.6%	49.4%

COLORADO

PRESIDENT 1944

1940 Census Population	County	Total Vote	Republican	Democratic	Other	Rep.-Dem. Plurality	Percentage Total Vote Rep.	Total Vote Dem.	Major Vote Rep.	Major Vote Dem.
8,336	WASHINGTON	3,328	2,259	1,058	11	1,201 R	67.9%	31.8%	68.1%	31.9%
63,747	WELD	23,086	14,546	8,459	81	6,087 R	63.0%	36.6%	63.2%	36.8%
12,102	YUMA	4,221	2,847	1,374		1,473 R	67.4%	32.6%	67.4%	32.6%
1,123,296	TOTAL	505,039	268,731	234,331	1,977	34,400 R	53.2%	46.4%	53.4%	46.6%

COLORADO

PRESIDENT 1940

1940 Census Population	County	Total Vote	Republican	Democratic	Other	Rep.-Dem. Plurality	Percentage Total Vote Rep.	Total Vote Dem.	Major Vote Rep.	Major Vote Dem.
22,481	ADAMS	9,503	4,767	4,674	62	93 R	50.2%	49.2%	50.5%	49.5%
10,484	ALAMOSA	4,733	2,243	2,467	23	224 D	47.4%	52.1%	47.6%	52.4%
32,150	ARAPAHOE	15,696	7,988	7,571	137	417 R	50.9%	48.2%	51.3%	48.7%
3,806	ARCHULETA	1,618	869	744	5	125 R	53.7%	46.0%	53.9%	46.1%
6,207	BACA	2,772	1,567	1,167	38	400 R	56.5%	42.1%	57.3%	42.7%
9,653	BENT	3,675	1,899	1,759	17	140 R	51.7%	47.9%	51.9%	48.1%
37,438	BOULDER	19,776	10,525	9,039	212	1,486 R	53.2%	45.7%	53.8%	46.2%
8,109	CHAFFEE	4,121	1,933	2,153	35	220 D	46.9%	52.2%	47.3%	52.7%
2,964	CHEYENNE	1,681	915	758	8	157 R	54.4%	45.1%	54.7%	45.3%
3,784	CLEAR CREEK	2,306	1,018	1,281	7	263 D	44.1%	55.6%	44.3%	55.7%
11,648	CONEJOS	4,526	2,028	2,481	17	453 D	44.8%	54.8%	45.0%	55.0%
7,533	COSTILLA	2,845	1,121	1,698	26	577 D	39.4%	59.7%	39.8%	60.2%
5,398	CROWLEY	2,281	1,419	850	12	569 R	62.2%	37.3%	62.5%	37.5%
2,270	CUSTER	1,194	685	495	14	190 R	57.4%	41.5%	58.1%	41.9%
16,470	DELTA	7,315	4,175	3,044	96	1,131 R	57.1%	41.6%	57.8%	42.2%
322,412	DENVER	173,371	81,328	90,938	1,105	9,610 D	46.9%	52.5%	47.2%	52.8%
1,958	DOLORES	873	478	379	16	99 R	54.8%	43.4%	55.8%	44.2%
3,496	DOUGLAS	2,108	1,298	801	9	497 R	61.6%	38.0%	61.8%	38.2%
5,361	EAGLE	2,564	1,077	1,474	13	397 D	42.0%	57.5%	42.2%	57.8%
5,460	ELBERT	2,700	1,756	934	10	822 R	65.0%	34.6%	65.3%	34.7%
54,025	EL PASO	30,315	16,766	13,320	229	3,446 R	55.3%	43.9%	55.7%	44.3%
19,742	FREMONT	9,394	5,150	4,186	58	964 R	54.8%	44.6%	55.2%	44.8%
10,560	GARFIELD	5,061	2,894	2,141	26	753 R	57.2%	42.3%	57.5%	42.5%
1,625	GILPIN	849	413	431	5	18 D	48.6%	50.8%	48.9%	51.1%
3,587	GRAND	1,946	1,074	863	9	211 R	55.2%	44.3%	55.4%	44.6%
6,192	GUNNISON	3,351	1,556	1,771	24	215 D	46.4%	52.8%	46.8%	53.2%
349	HINSDALE	255	150	103	2	47 R	58.8%	40.4%	59.3%	40.7%
16,088	HUERFANO	6,736	2,738	3,974	24	1,236 D	40.6%	59.0%	40.8%	59.2%
1,798	JACKSON	888	526	357	5	169 R	59.2%	40.2%	59.6%	40.4%
30,725	JEFFERSON	16,625	8,780	7,745	100	1,035 R	52.8%	46.6%	53.1%	46.9%
2,793	KIOWA	1,594	986	598	10	388 R	61.9%	37.5%	62.2%	37.8%
7,512	KIT CARSON	3,612	2,481	1,100	31	1,381 R	68.7%	30.5%	69.3%	30.7%
6,883	LAKE	3,481	1,403	2,063	15	660 D	40.3%	59.3%	40.5%	59.5%
15,494	LA PLATA	6,745	3,871	2,835	39	1,036 R	57.4%	42.0%	57.7%	42.3%
35,539	LARIMER	17,248	10,720	6,402	126	4,318 R	62.2%	37.1%	62.6%	37.4%
32,369	LAS ANIMAS	13,675	4,859	8,766	50	3,907 D	35.5%	64.1%	35.7%	64.3%
5,882	LINCOLN	2,988	1,780	1,185	23	595 R	59.6%	39.7%	60.0%	40.0%
18,370	LOGAN	7,515	4,613	2,819	83	1,794 R	61.4%	37.5%	62.1%	37.9%
33,791	MESA	14,912	7,049	7,694	169	645 D	47.3%	51.6%	47.8%	52.2%
975	MINERAL	508	229	273	6	44 D	45.1%	53.7%	45.6%	54.4%
5,086	MOFFAT	2,627	1,556	1,056	15	500 R	59.2%	40.2%	59.6%	40.4%
10,463	MONTEZUMA	3,904	2,313	1,573	18	740 R	59.2%	40.3%	59.5%	40.5%
15,418	MONTROSE	6,855	3,744	3,013	98	731 R	54.6%	44.0%	55.4%	44.6%
17,214	MORGAN	7,238	4,654	2,527	57	2,127 R	64.3%	34.9%	64.8%	35.2%
23,571	OTERO	10,088	5,459	4,567	62	892 R	54.1%	45.3%	54.4%	45.6%
2,089	OURAY	1,199	589	606	4	17 D	49.1%	50.5%	49.3%	50.7%
3,272	PARK	1,861	986	869	6	117 R	53.0%	46.7%	53.2%	46.8%
4,948	PHILLIPS	2,151	1,168	919	64	249 R	54.3%	42.7%	56.0%	44.0%
1,836	PITKIN	998	484	503	11	19 D	48.5%	50.4%	49.0%	51.0%
12,304	PROWERS	5,477	3,115	2,309	53	806 R	56.9%	42.2%	57.4%	42.6%
68,870	PUEBLO	33,115	14,185	18,805	125	4,620 D	42.8%	56.8%	43.0%	57.0%
2,943	RIO BLANCO	1,559	1,021	530	8	491 R	65.5%	34.0%	65.8%	34.2%
12,404	RIO GRANDE	5,357	3,075	2,242	40	833 R	57.4%	41.9%	57.8%	42.2%
10,525	ROUTT	5,019	2,212	2,775	32	563 D	44.1%	55.3%	44.4%	55.6%
6,173	SAGUACHE	2,631	1,462	1,142	27	320 R	55.6%	43.4%	56.1%	43.9%
1,439	SAN JUAN	834	452	378	4	74 R	54.2%	45.3%	54.5%	45.5%
3,664	SAN MIGUEL	1,587	729	851	7	122 D	45.9%	53.6%	46.1%	53.9%
5,294	SEDGWICK	2,419	1,448	959	12	489 R	59.9%	39.6%	60.2%	39.8%
1,754	SUMMIT	1,024	479	540	5	61 D	46.8%	52.7%	47.0%	53.0%
6,463	TELLER	3,372	1,268	2,084	20	816 D	37.6%	61.8%	37.8%	62.2%

COLORADO

PRESIDENT 1940

1940 Census Population	County	Total Vote	Republican	Democratic	Other	Rep.-Dem. Plurality	Percentage Total Vote Rep.	Percentage Total Vote Dem.	Percentage Major Vote Rep.	Percentage Major Vote Dem.
8,336	WASHINGTON	3,816	2,390	1,403	23	987 R	62.6%	36.8%	63.0%	37.0%
63,747	WELD	27,009	16,129	10,653	227	5,476 R	59.7%	39.4%	60.2%	39.8%
12,102	YUMA	5,508	3,531	1,917	60	1,614 R	64.1%	34.8%	64.8%	35.2%
1,123,296	TOTAL	549,004	279,576	265,554	3,874	14,022 R	50.9%	48.4%	51.3%	48.7%

COLORADO

PRESIDENT 1936

1930 Census Population	County	Total Vote	Republican	Democratic	Other	Rep.-Dem. Plurality	Total Vote Rep.	Total Vote Dem.	Major Vote Rep.	Major Vote Dem.
20,245	ADAMS	8,151	3,124	4,865	162	1,741 D	38.3%	59.7%	39.1%	60.9%
8,602	ALAMOSA	3,999	1,188	2,754	57	1,566 D	29.7%	68.9%	30.1%	69.9%
22,647	ARAPAHOE	11,171	4,272	6,489	410	2,217 D	38.2%	58.1%	39.7%	60.3%
3,204	ARCHULETA	1,333	541	761	31	220 D	40.6%	57.1%	41.6%	58.4%
10,570	BACA	3,264	1,288	1,797	179	509 D	39.5%	55.1%	41.8%	58.2%
9,134	BENT	3,181	1,299	1,821	61	522 D	40.8%	57.2%	41.6%	58.4%
32,456	BOULDER	17,501	7,244	9,788	469	2,544 D	41.4%	55.9%	42.5%	57.5%
8,126	CHAFFEE	3,664	1,069	2,447	148	1,378 D	29.2%	66.8%	30.4%	69.6%
3,723	CHEYENNE	1,710	767	903	40	136 D	44.9%	52.8%	45.9%	54.1%
2,155	CLEAR CREEK	2,076	720	1,340	16	620 D	34.7%	64.5%	35.0%	65.0%
9,803	CONEJOS	3,710	1,305	2,347	58	1,042 D	35.2%	63.3%	35.7%	64.3%
5,779	COSTILLA	2,504	930	1,518	56	588 D	37.1%	60.6%	38.0%	62.0%
5,934	CROWLEY	2,134	920	1,163	51	243 D	43.1%	54.5%	44.2%	55.8%
2,124	CUSTER	1,220	526	674	20	148 D	43.1%	55.2%	43.8%	56.2%
14,204	DELTA	6,468	2,661	3,230	577	569 D	41.1%	49.9%	45.2%	54.8%
287,861	DENVER	152,492	50,743	99,263	2,486	48,520 D	33.3%	65.1%	33.8%	66.2%
1,412	DOLORES	582	225	323	34	98 D	38.7%	55.5%	41.1%	58.9%
3,498	DOUGLAS	1,968	895	1,044	29	149 D	45.5%	53.0%	46.2%	53.8%
3,924	EAGLE	2,347	776	1,541	30	765 D	33.1%	65.7%	33.5%	66.5%
6,580	ELBERT	2,776	1,374	1,319	83	55 R	49.5%	47.5%	51.0%	49.0%
49,570	EL PASO	27,537	10,965	15,652	920	4,687 D	39.8%	56.8%	41.2%	58.8%
18,896	FREMONT	8,461	3,631	4,471	359	840 D	42.9%	52.8%	44.8%	55.2%
9,975	GARFIELD	4,528	1,945	2,406	177	461 D	43.0%	53.1%	44.7%	55.3%
1,212	GILPIN	1,077	321	736	20	415 D	29.8%	68.3%	30.4%	69.6%
2,108	GRAND	1,568	714	846	8	132 D	45.5%	54.0%	45.8%	54.2%
5,527	GUNNISON	3,215	978	2,179	58	1,201 D	30.4%	67.8%	31.0%	69.0%
449	HINSDALE	270	129	137	4	8 D	47.8%	50.7%	48.5%	51.5%
17,062	HUERFANO	7,136	2,299	4,793	44	2,494 D	32.2%	67.2%	32.4%	67.6%
1,386	JACKSON	886	419	433	34	14 D	47.3%	48.9%	49.2%	50.8%
21,810	JEFFERSON	12,825	5,271	7,283	271	2,012 D	41.1%	56.8%	42.0%	58.0%
3,786	KIOWA	1,732	772	918	42	146 D	44.6%	53.0%	45.7%	54.3%
9,725	KIT CARSON	3,901	1,980	1,730	191	250 R	50.8%	44.3%	53.4%	46.6%
4,899	LAKE	2,823	650	2,146	27	1,496 D	23.0%	76.0%	23.2%	76.8%
12,975	LA PLATA	5,579	2,354	3,040	185	686 D	42.2%	54.5%	43.6%	56.4%
33,137	LARIMER	15,221	7,243	7,521	457	278 D	47.6%	49.4%	49.1%	50.9%
36,008	LAS ANIMAS	13,612	3,333	10,220	59	6,887 D	24.5%	75.1%	24.6%	75.4%
7,850	LINCOLN	3,163	1,420	1,660	83	240 D	44.9%	52.5%	46.1%	53.9%
19,946	LOGAN	7,360	3,136	4,070	154	934 D	42.6%	55.3%	43.5%	56.5%
25,908	MESA	12,399	3,654	7,824	921	4,170 D	29.5%	63.1%	31.8%	68.2%
640	MINERAL	417	126	285	6	159 D	30.2%	68.3%	30.7%	69.3%
4,861	MOFFAT	2,264	954	1,090	220	136 D	42.1%	48.1%	46.7%	53.3%
7,798	MONTEZUMA	2,795	1,087	1,579	129	492 D	38.9%	56.5%	40.8%	59.2%
11,742	MONTROSE	5,425	2,248	2,938	239	690 D	41.4%	54.2%	43.3%	56.7%
18,284	MORGAN	6,481	3,058	3,146	277	88 D	47.2%	48.5%	49.3%	50.7%
24,390	OTERO	9,772	3,859	5,775	138	1,916 D	39.5%	59.1%	40.1%	59.9%
1,784	OURAY	1,116	428	677	11	249 D	38.4%	60.7%	38.7%	61.3%
2,052	PARK	2,110	746	1,336	28	590 D	35.4%	63.3%	35.8%	64.2%
5,797	PHILLIPS	2,603	941	1,602	60	661 D	36.2%	61.5%	37.0%	63.0%
1,770	PITKIN	1,017	305	659	53	354 D	30.0%	64.8%	31.6%	68.4%
14,762	PROWERS	5,539	2,432	2,896	211	464 D	43.9%	52.3%	45.6%	54.4%
66,038	PUEBLO	29,224	10,071	18,660	493	8,589 D	34.5%	63.9%	35.1%	64.9%
2,980	RIO BLANCO	1,488	830	587	71	243 R	55.8%	39.4%	58.6%	41.4%
9,953	RIO GRANDE	4,524	1,884	2,574	66	690 D	41.6%	56.9%	42.3%	57.7%
9,352	ROUTT	4,575	1,541	2,817	217	1,276 D	33.7%	61.6%	35.4%	64.6%
6,250	SAGUACHE	2,446	1,071	1,321	54	250 D	43.8%	54.0%	44.8%	55.2%
1,935	SAN JUAN	830	196	622	12	426 D	23.6%	74.9%	24.0%	76.0%
2,184	SAN MIGUEL	1,348	433	860	55	427 D	32.1%	63.8%	33.5%	66.5%
5,580	SEDGWICK	2,408	977	1,358	73	381 D	40.6%	56.4%	41.8%	58.2%
987	SUMMIT	769	268	496	5	228 D	34.9%	64.5%	35.1%	64.9%
4,141	TELLER	3,368	940	2,349	79	1,409 D	27.9%	69.7%	28.6%	71.4%

COLORADO

PRESIDENT 1936

1930 Census Population	County	Total Vote	Republican	Democratic	Other	Rep.-Dem. Plurality	Percentage Total Vote Rep.	Total Vote Dem.	Major Vote Rep.	Major Vote Dem.
9,591	WASHINGTON	3,886	1,723	2,071	92	348 D	44.3%	53.3%	45.4%	54.6%
65,097	WELD	23,296	9,606	12,993	697	3,387 D	41.2%	55.8%	42.5%	57.5%
13,613	YUMA	5,440	2,462	2,878	100	416 D	45.3%	52.9%	46.1%	53.9%
1,035,791	TOTAL	488,685	181,267	295,021	12,397	113,754 D	37.1%	60.4%	38.1%	61.9%

COLORADO

PRESIDENT 1932

1930 Census Population	County	Total Vote	Republican	Democratic	Other	Rep.-Dem. Plurality	Percentage: Total Vote Rep.	Total Vote Dem.	Major Vote Rep.	Major Vote Dem.
20,245	ADAMS	7,665	2,812	4,554	299	1,742 D	36.7%	59.4%	38.2%	61.8%
8,602	ALAMOSA	3,534	1,306	2,141	87	835 D	37.0%	60.6%	37.9%	62.1%
22,647	ARAPAHOE	10,642	4,287	5,796	559	1,509 D	40.3%	54.5%	42.5%	57.5%
3,204	ARCHULETA	1,410	462	928	20	466 D	32.8%	65.8%	33.2%	66.8%
10,570	BACA	3,965	1,349	2,247	369	898 D	34.0%	56.7%	37.5%	62.5%
9,134	BENT	3,353	1,327	1,948	78	621 D	39.6%	58.1%	40.5%	59.5%
32,456	BOULDER	16,707	7,487	8,412	808	925 D	44.8%	50.4%	47.1%	52.9%
8,126	CHAFFEE	3,628	1,061	2,393	174	1,332 D	29.2%	66.0%	30.7%	69.3%
3,723	CHEYENNE	1,893	746	1,042	105	296 D	39.4%	55.0%	41.7%	58.3%
2,155	CLEAR CREEK	1,564	597	939	28	342 D	38.2%	60.0%	38.9%	61.1%
9,803	CONEJOS	3,851	1,190	2,641	20	1,451 D	30.9%	68.6%	31.1%	68.9%
5,779	COSTILLA	2,215	707	1,475	33	768 D	31.9%	66.6%	32.4%	67.6%
5,934	CROWLEY	2,117	811	1,266	40	455 D	38.3%	59.8%	39.0%	61.0%
2,124	CUSTER	1,199	413	729	57	316 D	34.4%	60.8%	36.2%	63.8%
14,204	DELTA	6,327	2,341	3,467	519	1,126 D	37.0%	54.8%	40.3%	59.7%
287,861	DENVER	136,558	59,372	72,868	4,318	13,496 D	43.5%	53.4%	44.9%	55.1%
1,412	DOLORES	691	183	464	44	281 D	26.5%	67.1%	28.3%	71.7%
3,498	DOUGLAS	1,946	836	1,061	49	225 D	43.0%	54.5%	44.1%	55.9%
3,924	EAGLE	2,106	712	1,348	46	636 D	33.8%	64.0%	34.6%	65.4%
6,580	ELBERT	3,074	1,277	1,649	148	372 D	41.5%	53.6%	43.6%	56.4%
49,570	EL PASO	24,350	12,017	11,353	980	664 R	49.4%	46.6%	51.4%	48.6%
18,896	FREMONT	8,029	3,294	4,295	440	1,001 D	41.0%	53.5%	43.4%	56.6%
9,975	GARFIELD	4,810	1,734	2,946	130	1,212 D	36.0%	61.2%	37.1%	62.9%
1,212	GILPIN	835	271	539	25	268 D	32.5%	64.6%	33.5%	66.5%
2,108	GRAND	1,395	598	771	26	173 D	42.9%	55.3%	43.7%	56.3%
5,527	GUNNISON	2,916	985	1,807	124	822 D	33.8%	62.0%	35.3%	64.7%
449	HINSDALE	246	94	138	14	44 D	38.2%	56.1%	40.5%	59.5%
17,062	HUERFANO	6,744	2,490	4,159	95	1,669 D	36.9%	61.7%	37.4%	62.6%
1,386	JACKSON	822	390	415	17	25 D	47.4%	50.5%	48.4%	51.6%
21,810	JEFFERSON	12,048	5,522	6,023	503	501 D	45.8%	50.0%	47.8%	52.2%
3,786	KIOWA	1,968	769	1,113	86	344 D	39.1%	56.6%	40.9%	59.1%
9,725	KIT CARSON	4,313	1,835	2,289	189	454 D	42.5%	53.1%	44.5%	55.5%
4,899	LAKE	2,296	801	1,436	59	635 D	34.9%	62.5%	35.8%	64.2%
12,975	LA PLATA	5,517	2,124	3,156	237	1,032 D	38.5%	57.2%	40.2%	59.8%
33,137	LARIMER	14,118	7,040	6,494	584	546 R	49.9%	46.0%	52.0%	48.0%
36,008	LAS ANIMAS	12,877	3,651	8,964	262	5,313 D	28.4%	69.6%	28.9%	71.1%
7,850	LINCOLN	3,536	1,453	1,979	104	526 D	41.1%	56.0%	42.3%	57.7%
19,946	LOGAN	6,947	3,157	3,641	149	484 D	45.4%	52.4%	46.4%	53.6%
25,908	MESA	11,807	4,388	6,682	737	2,294 D	37.2%	56.6%	39.6%	60.4%
640	MINERAL	379	112	210	57	98 D	29.6%	55.4%	34.8%	65.2%
4,861	MOFFAT	2,407	880	1,388	139	508 D	36.6%	57.7%	38.8%	61.2%
7,798	MONTEZUMA	2,786	887	1,779	120	892 D	31.8%	63.9%	33.3%	66.7%
11,742	MONTROSE	4,858	1,992	2,516	350	524 D	41.0%	51.8%	44.2%	55.8%
18,284	MORGAN	6,765	3,370	3,181	214	189 R	49.8%	47.0%	51.4%	48.6%
24,390	OTERO	9,287	3,974	5,107	206	1,133 D	42.8%	55.0%	43.8%	56.2%
1,784	OURAY	1,152	398	706	48	308 D	34.5%	61.3%	36.1%	63.9%
2,052	PARK	1,735	577	1,057	101	480 D	33.3%	60.9%	35.3%	64.7%
5,797	PHILLIPS	2,592	903	1,453	236	550 D	34.8%	56.1%	38.3%	61.7%
1,770	PITKIN	1,012	239	727	46	488 D	23.6%	71.8%	24.7%	75.3%
14,762	PROWERS	5,726	2,568	3,020	138	452 D	44.8%	52.7%	46.0%	54.0%
66,038	PUEBLO	26,354	10,414	15,325	615	4,911 D	39.5%	58.2%	40.5%	59.5%
2,980	RIO BLANCO	1,545	687	826	32	139 D	44.5%	53.5%	45.4%	54.6%
9,953	RIO GRANDE	4,258	1,557	2,539	162	982 D	36.6%	59.6%	38.0%	62.0%
9,352	ROUTT	4,409	1,568	2,643	198	1,075 D	35.6%	59.9%	37.2%	62.8%
6,250	SAGUACHE	2,458	931	1,427	100	496 D	37.9%	58.1%	39.5%	60.5%
1,935	SAN JUAN	713	160	544	9	384 D	22.4%	76.3%	22.7%	77.3%
2,184	SAN MIGUEL	1,288	383	862	43	479 D	29.7%	66.9%	30.8%	69.2%
5,580	SEDGWICK	2,261	884	1,288	89	404 D	39.1%	57.0%	40.7%	59.3%
987	SUMMIT	644	224	397	23	173 D	34.8%	61.6%	36.1%	63.9%
4,141	TELLER	2,489	752	1,534	203	782 D	30.2%	61.6%	32.9%	67.1%

COLORADO

PRESIDENT 1932

1930 Census Population	County	Total Vote	Republican	Democratic	Other	Rep.-Dem. Plurality	Percentage Total Vote Rep.	Percentage Total Vote Dem.	Percentage Major Vote Rep.	Percentage Major Vote Dem.
9,591	WASHINGTON	3,913	1,385	2,378	150	993 D	35.4%	60.8%	36.8%	63.2%
65,097	WELD	22,945	10,754	11,182	1,009	428 D	46.9%	48.7%	49.0%	51.0%
13,613	YUMA	5,701	2,129	3,220	352	1,091 D	37.3%	56.5%	39.8%	60.2%
1,035,791	TOTAL	457,696	189,617	250,877	17,202	61,260 D	41.4%	54.8%	43.0%	57.0%

COLORADO

PRESIDENT 1928

1920 Census Population	County	Total Vote	Republican	Democratic	Other	Rep.-Dem. Plurality	Percentage: Total Vote Rep.	Percentage: Total Vote Dem.	Percentage: Major Vote Rep.	Percentage: Major Vote Dem.
14,430	ADAMS	6,388	4,031	2,265	92	1,766 R	63.1%	35.5%	64.0%	36.0%
5,148	ALAMOSA	3,021	1,759	1,239	23	520 R	58.2%	41.0%	58.7%	41.3%
13,766	ARAPAHOE	8,659	6,086	2,463	110	3,623 R	70.3%	28.4%	71.2%	28.8%
3,590	ARCHULETA	1,080	610	447	23	163 R	56.5%	41.4%	57.7%	42.3%
8,721	BACA	2,686	2,108	524	54	1,584 R	78.5%	19.5%	80.1%	19.9%
9,705	BENT	2,713	1,957	741	15	1,216 R	72.1%	27.3%	72.5%	27.5%
31,861	BOULDER	14,015	9,457	4,363	195	5,094 R	67.5%	31.1%	68.4%	31.6%
7,753	CHAFFEE	3,160	1,880	1,230	50	650 R	59.5%	38.9%	60.5%	39.5%
3,746	CHEYENNE	1,480	945	500	35	445 R	63.9%	33.8%	65.4%	34.6%
2,891	CLEAR CREEK	1,294	790	481	23	309 R	61.1%	37.2%	62.2%	37.8%
8,416	CONEJOS	3,234	1,463	1,692	79	229 D	45.2%	52.3%	46.4%	53.6%
5,032	COSTILLA	1,760	657	1,070	33	413 D	37.3%	60.8%	38.0%	62.0%
6,383	CROWLEY	1,900	1,243	635	22	608 R	65.4%	33.4%	66.2%	33.8%
2,172	CUSTER	1,019	600	389	30	211 R	58.9%	38.2%	60.7%	39.3%
13,668	DELTA	5,542	3,731	1,672	139	2,059 R	67.3%	30.2%	69.1%	30.9%
256,491	DENVER	116,002	73,543	41,238	1,221	32,305 R	63.4%	35.5%	64.1%	35.9%
1,243	DOLORES	692	387	278	27	109 R	55.9%	40.2%	58.2%	41.8%
3,517	DOUGLAS	1,723	1,107	603	13	504 R	64.2%	35.0%	64.7%	35.3%
3,385	EAGLE	1,605	1,014	570	21	444 R	63.2%	35.5%	64.0%	36.0%
6,980	ELBERT	2,708	1,933	738	37	1,195 R	71.4%	27.3%	72.4%	27.6%
44,027	EL PASO	21,578	16,243	5,069	266	11,174 R	75.3%	23.5%	76.2%	23.8%
17,883	FREMONT	7,799	5,365	2,352	82	3,013 R	68.8%	30.2%	69.5%	30.5%
9,304	GARFIELD	4,056	2,435	1,562	59	873 R	60.0%	38.5%	60.9%	39.1%
1,364	GILPIN	542	299	236	7	63 R	55.2%	43.5%	55.9%	44.1%
2,659	GRAND	1,239	770	451	18	319 R	62.1%	36.4%	63.1%	36.9%
5,590	GUNNISON	2,637	1,456	1,135	46	321 R	55.2%	43.0%	56.2%	43.8%
538	HINSDALE	238	128	106	4	22 R	53.8%	44.5%	54.7%	45.3%
16,879	HUERFANO	6,633	3,260	3,343	30	83 D	49.1%	50.4%	49.4%	50.6%
1,340	JACKSON	666	401	249	16	152 R	60.2%	37.4%	61.7%	38.3%
14,400	JEFFERSON	9,775	6,754	2,880	141	3,874 R	69.1%	29.5%	70.1%	29.9%
3,755	KIOWA	1,515	1,024	458	33	566 R	67.6%	30.2%	69.1%	30.9%
8,915	KIT CARSON	3,690	2,486	1,137	67	1,349 R	67.4%	30.8%	68.6%	31.4%
6,630	LAKE	2,469	990	1,449	30	459 D	40.1%	58.7%	40.6%	59.4%
11,218	LA PLATA	4,762	2,837	1,872	53	965 R	59.6%	39.3%	60.2%	39.8%
27,872	LARIMER	11,578	8,213	3,203	162	5,010 R	70.9%	27.7%	71.9%	28.1%
38,975	LAS ANIMAS	11,995	5,367	6,459	169	1,092 D	44.7%	53.8%	45.4%	54.6%
8,273	LINCOLN	3,053	2,110	888	55	1,222 R	69.1%	29.1%	70.4%	29.6%
18,427	LOGAN	6,086	4,377	1,620	89	2,757 R	71.9%	26.6%	73.0%	27.0%
22,281	MESA	9,802	6,446	3,223	133	3,223 R	65.8%	32.9%	66.7%	33.3%
779	MINERAL	350	144	187	19	43 D	41.1%	53.4%	43.5%	56.5%
5,129	MOFFAT	2,085	1,346	710	29	636 R	64.6%	34.1%	65.5%	34.5%
6,260	MONTEZUMA	2,150	1,341	772	37	569 R	62.4%	35.9%	63.5%	36.5%
11,852	MONTROSE	4,271	2,873	1,297	101	1,576 R	67.3%	30.4%	68.9%	31.1%
16,124	MORGAN	5,515	4,197	1,242	76	2,955 R	76.1%	22.5%	77.2%	22.8%
22,623	OTERO	7,730	5,788	1,876	66	3,912 R	74.9%	24.3%	75.5%	24.5%
2,620	OURAY	1,039	535	479	25	56 R	51.5%	46.1%	52.8%	47.2%
1,977	PARK	1,178	740	419	19	321 R	62.8%	35.6%	63.8%	36.2%
5,499	PHILLIPS	2,210	1,440	705	65	735 R	65.2%	31.9%	67.1%	32.9%
2,707	PITKIN	952	485	454	13	31 R	50.9%	47.7%	51.7%	48.3%
13,845	PROWERS	4,515	3,228	1,216	71	2,012 R	71.5%	26.9%	72.6%	27.4%
57,638	PUEBLO	23,673	15,541	7,881	251	7,660 R	65.6%	33.3%	66.4%	33.6%
3,135	RIO BLANCO	1,313	860	429	24	431 R	65.5%	32.7%	66.7%	33.3%
7,855	RIO GRANDE	3,520	2,254	1,226	40	1,028 R	64.0%	34.8%	64.8%	35.2%
8,948	ROUTT	4,017	2,304	1,645	68	659 R	57.4%	41.0%	58.3%	41.7%
4,638	SAGUACHE	2,381	1,491	854	36	637 R	62.6%	35.9%	63.6%	36.4%
1,700	SAN JUAN	746	277	436	33	159 D	37.1%	58.4%	38.8%	61.2%
5,281	SAN MIGUEL	1,313	721	554	38	167 R	54.9%	42.2%	56.5%	43.5%
4,207	SEDGWICK	1,847	1,247	580	20	667 R	67.5%	31.4%	68.3%	31.7%
1,724	SUMMIT	681	362	306	13	56 R	53.2%	44.9%	54.2%	45.8%
6,696	TELLER	2,275	1,184	1,037	54	147 R	52.0%	45.6%	53.3%	46.7%

COLORADO

PRESIDENT 1928

1920 Census Population	County	Total Vote	Republican	Democratic	Other	Rep.-Dem. Plurality	Percentage Total Vote Rep.	Percentage Total Vote Dem.	Percentage Major Vote Rep.	Percentage Major Vote Dem.
11,208	WASHINGTON	3,046	2,132	851	63	1,281 R	70.0%	27.9%	71.5%	28.5%
54,059	WELD	19,717	13,719	5,762	236	7,957 R	69.6%	29.2%	70.4%	29.6%
13,897	YUMA	4,924	3,401	1,383	140	2,018 R	69.1%	28.1%	71.1%	28.9%
939,629	TOTAL	392,242	253,872	133,131	5,239	120,741 R	64.7%	33.9%	65.6%	34.4%

COLORADO

PRESIDENT 1924

1920 Census Population	County	Total Vote	Republican	Democratic	Progressive	Other	Plurality	Percentage Total Vote Rep.	Dem.	Prog.
14,430	ADAMS	5,203	2,931	1,209	1,026	37	1,722 R	56.3%	23.2%	19.7%
5,148	ALAMOSA	2,486	1,009	625	841	11	168 R	40.6%	25.1%	33.8%
13,766	ARAPAHOE	6,643	4,267	1,209	1,141	26	3,058 R	64.2%	18.2%	17.2%
3,590	ARCHULETA	1,046	451	269	316	10	135 R	43.1%	25.7%	30.2%
8,721	BACA	2,533	1,174	653	654	52	520 R	46.3%	25.8%	25.8%
9,705	BENT	2,791	1,511	804	462	14	707 R	54.1%	28.8%	16.6%
31,861	BOULDER	12,927	7,595	3,273	2,007	52	4,322 R	58.8%	25.3%	15.5%
7,753	CHAFFEE	3,078	1,336	612	1,116	14	220 R	43.4%	19.9%	36.3%
3,746	CHEYENNE	1,571	875	236	450	10	425 R	55.7%	15.0%	28.6%
2,891	CLEAR CREEK	1,167	722	284	157	4	438 R	61.9%	24.3%	13.5%
8,416	CONEJOS	2,626	1,475	995	152	4	480 R	56.2%	37.9%	5.8%
5,032	COSTILLA	1,561	755	665	127	14	90 R	48.4%	42.6%	8.1%
6,383	CROWLEY	2,164	1,087	667	397	13	420 R	50.2%	30.8%	18.3%
2,172	CUSTER	966	429	281	246	10	148 R	44.4%	29.1%	25.5%
13,668	DELTA	5,063	2,752	1,345	927	39	1,407 R	54.4%	26.6%	18.3%
256,491	DENVER	93,123	59,077	15,764	17,876	406	41,201 R	63.4%	16.9%	19.2%
1,243	DOLORES	446	95	157	189	5	32 P	21.3%	35.2%	42.4%
3,517	DOUGLAS	1,572	870	383	313	6	487 R	55.3%	24.4%	19.9%
3,385	EAGLE	1,625	722	431	459	13	263 R	44.4%	26.5%	28.2%
6,980	ELBERT	2,598	1,428	506	643	21	785 R	55.0%	19.5%	24.7%
44,027	EL PASO	18,344	10,215	4,140	3,887	102	6,075 R	55.7%	22.6%	21.2%
17,883	FREMONT	7,252	4,433	1,550	1,229	40	2,883 R	61.1%	21.4%	16.9%
9,304	GARFIELD	3,772	1,934	917	897	24	1,017 R	51.3%	24.3%	23.8%
1,364	GILPIN	659	361	161	135	2	200 R	54.8%	24.4%	20.5%
2,659	GRAND	1,254	681	308	263	2	373 R	54.3%	24.6%	21.0%
5,590	GUNNISON	2,510	1,122	598	779	11	343 R	44.7%	23.8%	31.0%
538	HINSDALE	276	138	79	57	2	59 R	50.0%	28.6%	20.7%
16,879	HUERFANO	5,672	2,784	1,219	1,645	24	1,139 R	49.1%	21.5%	29.0%
1,340	JACKSON	585	394	111	75	5	283 R	67.4%	19.0%	12.8%
14,400	JEFFERSON	7,645	4,869	1,271	1,485	20	3,384 R	63.7%	16.6%	19.4%
3,755	KIOWA	1,695	805	431	456	3	349 R	47.5%	25.4%	26.9%
8,915	KIT CARSON	3,501	2,108	720	645	28	1,388 R	60.2%	20.6%	18.4%
6,630	LAKE	2,337	1,005	613	693	26	312 R	43.0%	26.2%	29.7%
11,218	LA PLATA	4,182	1,469	1,516	1,175	22	47 D	35.1%	36.3%	28.1%
27,872	LARIMER	9,809	6,538	1,970	1,222	79	4,568 R	66.7%	20.1%	12.5%
38,975	LAS ANIMAS	11,706	5,698	2,758	3,193	57	2,505 R	48.7%	23.6%	27.3%
8,273	LINCOLN	3,002	1,642	634	714	12	928 R	54.7%	21.1%	23.8%
18,427	LOGAN	5,581	3,103	946	1,484	48	1,619 R	55.6%	17.0%	26.6%
22,281	MESA	8,902	4,053	2,388	2,422	39	1,631 R	45.5%	26.8%	27.2%
779	MINERAL	326	150	101	73	2	49 R	46.0%	31.0%	22.4%
5,129	MOFFAT	1,990	1,009	647	330	4	362 R	50.7%	32.5%	16.6%
6,260	MONTEZUMA	2,033	703	721	595	14	18 D	34.6%	35.5%	29.3%
11,852	MONTROSE	4,533	2,077	1,239	1,186	31	838 R	45.8%	27.3%	26.2%
16,124	MORGAN	4,745	3,321	757	636	31	2,564 R	70.0%	16.0%	13.4%
22,623	OTERO	7,930	4,694	1,938	1,226	72	2,756 R	59.2%	24.4%	15.5%
2,620	OURAY	1,093	484	256	345	8	139 R	44.3%	23.4%	31.6%
1,977	PARK	1,176	660	316	177	23	344 R	56.1%	26.9%	15.1%
5,499	PHILLIPS	2,169	1,076	397	688	8	388 R	49.6%	18.3%	31.7%
2,707	PITKIN	935	442	204	286	3	156 R	47.3%	21.8%	30.6%
13,845	PROWERS	4,330	2,564	1,042	684	40	1,522 R	59.2%	24.1%	15.8%
57,638	PUEBLO	20,009	10,577	4,917	4,406	109	5,660 R	52.9%	24.6%	22.0%
3,135	RIO BLANCO	1,259	766	407	79	7	359 R	60.8%	32.3%	6.3%
7,855	RIO GRANDE	2,938	1,572	922	417	27	650 R	53.5%	31.4%	14.2%
8,948	ROUTT	3,405	1,822	1,116	449	18	706 R	53.5%	32.8%	13.2%
4,638	SAGUACHE	2,066	1,205	591	257	13	614 R	58.3%	28.6%	12.4%
1,700	SAN JUAN	548	218	206	124		12 R	39.8%	37.6%	22.6%
5,281	SAN MIGUEL	1,552	677	567	288	20	110 R	43.6%	36.5%	18.6%
4,207	SEDGWICK	1,499	779	372	337	11	407 R	52.0%	24.8%	22.5%
1,724	SUMMIT	745	354	241	144	6	113 R	47.5%	32.3%	19.3%
6,696	TELLER	2,630	1,283	592	739	16	544 R	48.8%	22.5%	28.1%

COLORADO

PRESIDENT 1924

1920 Census Population	County	Total Vote	Republican	Democratic	Progressive	Other	Plurality	Percentage Total Vote Rep.	Dem.	Prog.
11,208	WASHINGTON	3,411	1,851	720	822	18	1,029 R	54.3%	21.1%	24.1%
54,059	WELD	16,250	10,185	3,406	2,565	94	6,779 R	62.7%	21.0%	15.8%
13,897	YUMA	4,816	2,789	865	1,138	24	1,651 R	57.9%	18.0%	23.6%
939,629	TOTAL	342,261	195,171	75,238	69,946	1,906	119,933 R	57.0%	22.0%	20.4%

COLORADO

PRESIDENT 1920

1920 Census Population	County	Total Vote	Republican	Democratic	Other	Rep.-Dem. Plurality	Percentage Total Vote Rep.	Total Vote Dem.	Major Vote Rep.	Major Vote Dem.
14,430	ADAMS	4,360	2,510	1,633	217	877 R	57.6%	37.5%	60.6%	39.4%
5,148	ALAMOSA	2,084	1,081	949	54	132 R	51.9%	45.5%	53.3%	46.7%
13,766	ARAPAHOE	4,900	2,930	1,752	218	1,178 R	59.8%	35.8%	62.6%	37.4%
3,590	ARCHULETA	1,109	700	379	30	321 R	63.1%	34.2%	64.9%	35.1%
8,721	BACA	2,555	1,615	695	245	920 R	63.2%	27.2%	69.9%	30.1%
9,705	BENT	2,611	1,584	937	90	647 R	60.7%	35.9%	62.8%	37.2%
31,861	BOULDER	11,148	6,456	4,200	492	2,256 R	57.9%	37.7%	60.6%	39.4%
7,753	CHAFFEE	2,837	1,501	1,233	103	268 R	52.9%	43.5%	54.9%	45.1%
3,746	CHEYENNE	1,301	840	358	103	482 R	64.6%	27.5%	70.1%	29.9%
2,891	CLEAR CREEK	1,312	765	518	29	247 R	58.3%	39.5%	59.6%	40.4%
8,416	CONEJOS	2,512	1,595	886	31	709 R	63.5%	35.3%	64.3%	35.7%
5,032	COSTILLA	1,571	778	750	43	28 R	49.5%	47.7%	50.9%	49.1%
6,383	CROWLEY	2,223	1,348	792	83	556 R	60.6%	35.6%	63.0%	37.0%
2,172	CUSTER	885	560	289	36	271 R	63.3%	32.7%	66.0%	34.0%
13,668	DELTA	4,603	2,596	1,750	257	846 R	56.4%	38.0%	59.7%	40.3%
256,491	DENVER	70,258	43,581	22,839	3,838	20,742 R	62.0%	32.5%	65.6%	34.4%
1,243	DOLORES	408	197	153	58	44 R	48.3%	37.5%	56.3%	43.7%
3,517	DOUGLAS	1,544	948	561	35	387 R	61.4%	36.3%	62.8%	37.2%
3,385	EAGLE	1,549	854	649	46	205 R	55.1%	41.9%	56.8%	43.2%
6,980	ELBERT	2,493	1,654	673	166	981 R	66.3%	27.0%	71.1%	28.9%
44,027	EL PASO	15,189	9,535	5,073	581	4,462 R	62.8%	33.4%	65.3%	34.7%
17,883	FREMONT	5,676	3,027	2,339	310	688 R	53.3%	41.2%	56.4%	43.6%
9,304	GARFIELD	3,520	1,912	1,489	119	423 R	54.3%	42.3%	56.2%	43.8%
1,364	GILPIN	621	416	189	16	227 R	67.0%	30.4%	68.8%	31.2%
2,659	GRAND	1,236	649	553	34	96 R	52.5%	44.7%	54.0%	46.0%
5,590	GUNNISON	2,223	1,055	1,022	146	33 R	47.5%	46.0%	50.8%	49.2%
538	HINSDALE	252	149	67	36	82 R	59.1%	26.6%	69.0%	31.0%
16,879	HUERFANO	4,938	2,539	2,291	108	248 R	51.4%	46.4%	52.6%	47.4%
1,340	JACKSON	527	402	113	12	289 R	76.3%	21.4%	78.1%	21.9%
14,400	JEFFERSON	5,840	3,593	1,941	306	1,652 R	61.5%	33.2%	64.9%	35.1%
3,755	KIOWA	1,449	864	521	64	343 R	59.6%	36.0%	62.4%	37.6%
8,915	KIT CARSON	2,859	1,872	796	191	1,076 R	65.5%	27.8%	70.2%	29.8%
6,630	LAKE	2,421	1,287	992	142	295 R	53.2%	41.0%	56.5%	43.5%
11,218	LA PLATA	3,365	1,711	1,445	209	266 R	50.8%	42.9%	54.2%	45.8%
27,872	LARIMER	8,528	5,487	2,708	333	2,779 R	64.3%	31.8%	67.0%	33.0%
38,975	LAS ANIMAS	9,196	4,707	4,167	322	540 R	51.2%	45.3%	53.0%	47.0%
8,273	LINCOLN	2,963	1,815	1,013	135	802 R	61.3%	34.2%	64.2%	35.8%
18,427	LOGAN	5,230	3,123	1,893	214	1,230 R	59.7%	36.2%	62.3%	37.7%
22,281	MESA	7,271	3,621	3,138	512	483 R	49.8%	43.2%	53.6%	46.4%
779	MINERAL	371	183	146	42	37 R	49.3%	39.4%	55.6%	44.4%
5,129	MOFFAT	1,978	1,294	589	95	705 R	65.4%	29.8%	68.7%	31.3%
6,260	MONTEZUMA	1,793	936	727	130	209 R	52.2%	40.5%	56.3%	43.7%
11,852	MONTROSE	4,058	2,225	1,522	311	703 R	54.8%	37.5%	59.4%	40.6%
16,124	MORGAN	4,420	3,114	1,105	201	2,009 R	70.5%	25.0%	73.8%	26.2%
22,623	OTERO	6,876	3,846	2,727	303	1,119 R	55.9%	39.7%	58.5%	41.5%
2,620	OURAY	1,195	735	402	58	333 R	61.5%	33.6%	64.6%	35.4%
1,977	PARK	878	511	320	47	191 R	58.2%	36.4%	61.5%	38.5%
5,499	PHILLIPS	1,783	1,191	480	112	711 R	66.8%	26.9%	71.3%	28.7%
2,707	PITKIN	968	478	417	73	61 R	49.4%	43.1%	53.4%	46.6%
13,845	PROWERS	4,077	2,650	1,247	180	1,403 R	65.0%	30.6%	68.0%	32.0%
57,638	PUEBLO	18,109	9,621	7,863	625	1,758 R	53.1%	43.4%	55.0%	45.0%
3,135	RIO BLANCO	1,274	793	455	26	338 R	62.2%	35.7%	63.5%	36.5%
7,855	RIO GRANDE	2,721	1,660	985	76	675 R	61.0%	36.2%	62.8%	37.2%
8,948	ROUTT	3,224	1,854	1,224	146	630 R	57.5%	38.0%	60.2%	39.8%
4,638	SAGUACHE	1,981	1,195	717	69	478 R	60.3%	36.2%	62.5%	37.5%
1,700	SAN JUAN	654	330	290	34	40 R	50.5%	44.3%	53.2%	46.8%
5,281	SAN MIGUEL	1,709	928	688	93	240 R	54.3%	40.3%	57.4%	42.6%
4,207	SEDGWICK	1,254	819	372	63	447 R	65.3%	29.7%	68.8%	31.2%
1,724	SUMMIT	830	418	388	24	30 R	50.4%	46.7%	51.9%	48.1%
6,696	TELLER	2,681	1,552	1,010	119	542 R	57.9%	37.7%	60.6%	39.4%

COLORADO

PRESIDENT 1920

1920 Census Population	County	Total Vote	Republican	Democratic	Other	Rep.-Dem. Plurality	Percentage Total Vote Rep.	Percentage Total Vote Dem.	Percentage Major Vote Rep.	Percentage Major Vote Dem.
11,208	WASHINGTON	3,337	2,117	1,060	160	1,057 R	63.4%	31.8%	66.6%	33.4%
54,059	WELD	16,100	10,268	5,202	630	5,066 R	63.8%	32.3%	66.4%	33.6%
13,897	YUMA	4,215	2,673	1,254	288	1,419 R	63.4%	29.8%	68.1%	31.9%
939,629	TOTAL	292,053	173,248	104,936	13,869	68,312 R	59.3%	35.9%	62.3%	37.7%

COLORADO

ELECTION NOTES

1956 Other vote was 3,308 Hass (Socialist Labor); 759 Andrews (States Rights); 531 Hoopes (Socialist).

1952 Other vote was 2,181 MacArthur (Constitution); 1,919 Hallinan (Progressive); 365 Hoopes (Socialist); 352 Hass (Socialist).

1948 Other vote was 6,115 Wallace (Progressive); 1,678 Thomas (Socialist); 228 Dobbs (Socialist Workers); 214 Teichert (Socialist Labor).

1944 Other vote was Thomas (Socialist).

1940 Other vote was 1,899 Thomas (Socialist); 1,597 Babson (Prohibition); 378 Browder (Communist).

1936 Other vote was 9,962 Lemke (Union); 1,594 Thomas (Socialist); 497 Browder (Communist); 344 Aiken (Socialist Labor).

1932 Other vote was 13,591 Thomas (Socialist); 1,928 Upshaw (Prohibition); 787 Foster (Communist); 469 Coxey (Farmer-Labor); 427 Reynolds (Socialist Labor).

1928 Other vote was 3,472 Thomas (Socialist); 1,092 Webb (Farmer-Labor); 675 Foster (Communist).

1924 A special four-column table which gives the LaFollette (Progressive) vote is used to detail this election. The Progressive figures include 57,368 votes cast on the LaFollette-Wheeler ticket and 12,578 votes cast on the Farmer-Labor-LaFollette ticket. Other vote was 966 Faris (Prohibition); 562 Foster (Communist); 378 Johns (Socialist Labor).

1920 Other vote was 8,046 Debs (Socialist); 3,016 Christensen (Farmer-Labor); 2,807 Watkins (Prohibition).

CONNECTICUT

POPULAR VOTE FOR PRESIDENT 1920 TO 1956

Year	Total Vote	Republican Vote	Republican Candidate	Democratic Vote	Democratic Candidate	Other Vote	Plurality	Percentage Total Vote Rep.	Percentage Total Vote Dem.	Percentage Major Vote Rep.	Percentage Major Vote Dem.
1956	1,117,121	711,837	Eisenhower, Dwight D.	405,079	Stevenson, Adlai E.	205	306,758 R	63.7%	36.3%	63.7%	36.3%
1952	1,096,911	611,012	Eisenhower, Dwight D.	481,649	Stevenson, Adlai E.	4,250	129,363 R	55.7%	43.9%	55.9%	44.1%
1948	883,518	437,754	Dewey, Thomas E.	423,297	Truman, Harry S.	22,467	14,457 R	49.5%	47.9%	50.8%	49.2%
1944	831,990	390,527	Dewey, Thomas E.	435,146	Roosevelt, Franklin D.	6,317	44,619 D	46.9%	52.3%	47.3%	52.7%
1940	781,502	361,819	Willkie, Wendell	417,621	Roosevelt, Franklin D.	2,062	55,802 D	46.3%	53.4%	46.4%	53.6%
1936	690,723	278,685	Landon, Alfred M.	382,129	Roosevelt, Franklin D.	29,909	103,444 D	40.3%	55.3%	42.2%	57.8%
1932	594,183	288,420	Hoover, Herbert C.	281,632	Roosevelt, Franklin D.	24,131	6,788 R	48.5%	47.4%	50.6%	49.4%
1928	553,118	296,641	Hoover, Herbert C.	252,085	Smith, Alfred E.	4,392	44,556 R	53.6%	45.6%	54.1%	45.9%
1924	400,396	246,322	Coolidge, Calvin	110,184	Davis, John W.	43,890	136,138 R	61.5%	27.5%	69.1%	30.9%
1920	365,518	229,238	Harding, Warren G.	120,721	Cox, James M.	15,559	108,517 R	62.7%	33.0%	65.5%	34.5%

ELECTORAL COLLEGE VOTE 1920 TO 1956

Year	Total	Republican	Democratic	Other
1956	8	8	—	—
1952	8	8	—	—
1948	8	8	—	—
1944	8	—	8	—
1940	8	—	8	—
1936	8	—	8	—
1932	8	8	—	—
1928	7	7	—	—
1924	7	7	—	—
1920	7	7	—	—

CONNECTICUT

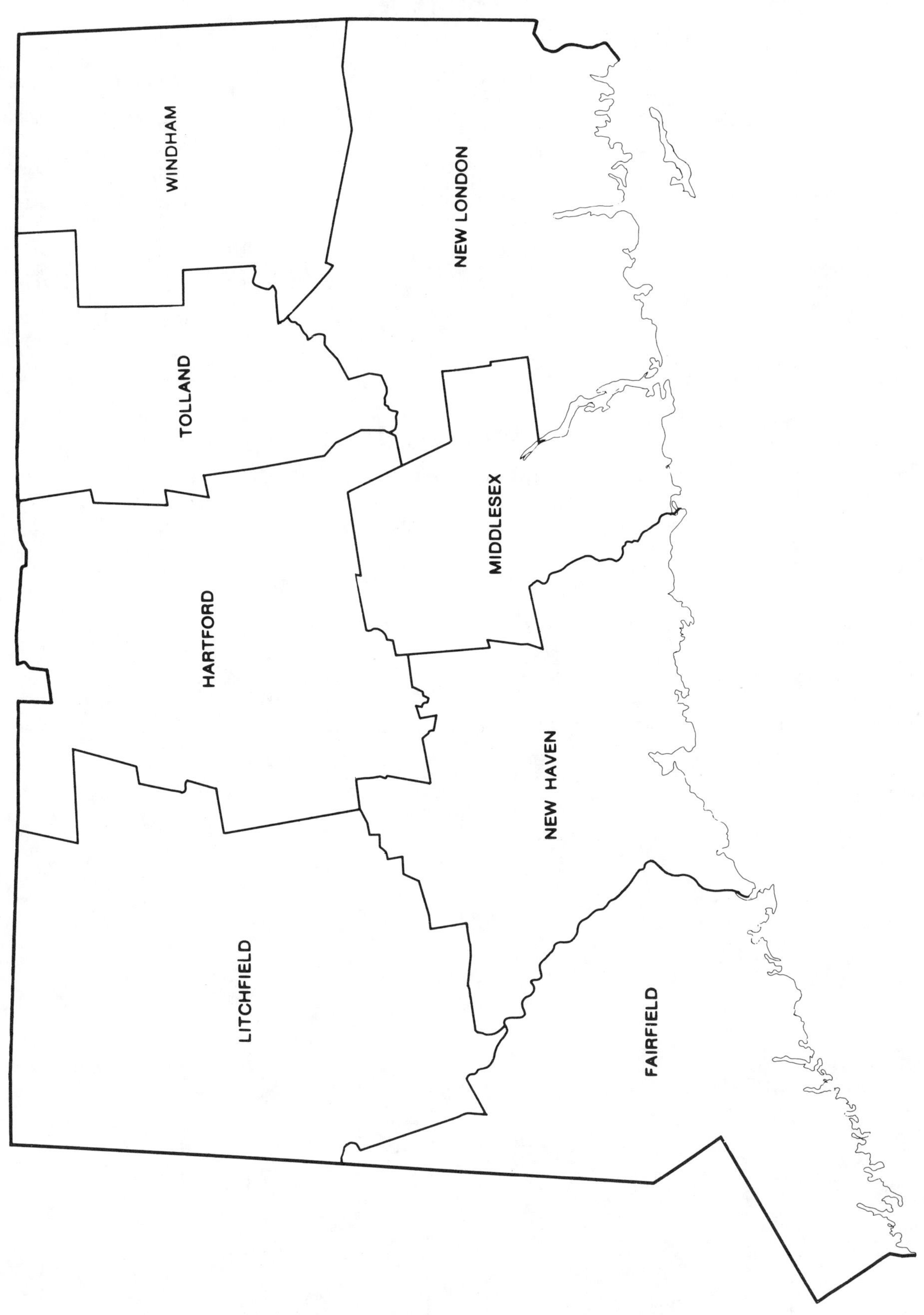

CONNECTICUT

PRESIDENT 1956

1950 Census Population	County	Total Vote	Republican	Democratic	Other	Rep.-Dem. Plurality	Percentage Total Vote Rep.	Percentage Total Vote Dem.	Percentage Major Vote Rep.	Percentage Major Vote Dem.
504,342	FAIRFIELD	284,847	199,841	84,890	116	114,951 R	70.2%	29.8%	70.2%	29.8%
539,661	HARTFORD	302,842	175,894	126,923	25	48,971 R	58.1%	41.9%	58.1%	41.9%
98,872	LITCHFIELD	57,261	40,029	17,226	6	22,803 R	69.9%	30.1%	69.9%	30.1%
67,332	MIDDLESEX	39,355	25,496	13,851	8	11,645 R	64.8%	35.2%	64.8%	35.2%
545,784	NEW HAVEN	303,459	191,215	112,208	36	79,007 R	63.0%	37.0%	63.0%	37.0%
144,821	NEW LONDON	70,781	43,453	27,317	11	16,136 R	61.4%	38.6%	61.4%	38.6%
44,709	TOLLAND	24,992	15,880	9,111	1	6,769 R	63.5%	36.5%	63.5%	36.5%
61,759	WINDHAM	33,584	20,029	13,553	2	6,476 R	59.6%	40.4%	59.6%	40.4%
2,007,280	TOTAL	1,117,121	711,837	405,079	205	306,758 R	63.7%	36.3%	63.7%	36.3%

CONNECTICUT

PRESIDENT 1952

1950 Census Population	County	Total Vote	Republican	Democratic	Other	Rep.-Dem. Plurality	Percentage Total Vote Rep.	Percentage Total Vote Dem.	Percentage Major Vote Rep.	Percentage Major Vote Dem.
504,342	FAIRFIELD	275,495	167,278	106,403	1,814	60,875 R	60.7%	38.6%	61.1%	38.9%
539,661	HARTFORD	297,715	150,332	146,551	832	3,781 R	50.5%	49.2%	50.6%	49.4%
98,872	LITCHFIELD	56,005	35,735	20,163	107	15,572 R	63.8%	36.0%	63.9%	36.1%
67,332	MIDDLESEX	37,953	22,157	15,722	74	6,435 R	58.4%	41.4%	58.5%	41.5%
545,784	NEW HAVEN	303,542	165,917	136,476	1,149	29,441 R	54.7%	45.0%	54.9%	45.1%
144,821	NEW LONDON	69,670	38,148	31,374	148	6,774 R	54.8%	45.0%	54.9%	45.1%
44,709	TOLLAND	22,943	13,466	9,425	52	4,041 R	58.7%	41.1%	58.8%	41.2%
61,759	WINDHAM	33,588	17,979	15,535	74	2,444 R	53.5%	46.3%	53.6%	46.4%
2,007,280	TOTAL	1,096,911	611,012	481,649	4,250	129,363 R	55.7%	43.9%	55.9%	44.1%

CONNECTICUT

PRESIDENT 1948

1940 Census Population	County	Total Vote	Republican	Democratic	Other	Rep.-Dem. Plurality	Percentage Total Vote Rep.	Total Vote Dem.	Major Vote Rep.	Major Vote Dem.
418,384	FAIRFIELD	217,072	118,636	90,767	7,669	27,869 R	54.7%	41.8%	56.7%	43.3%
450,189	HARTFORD	235,293	105,262	124,874	5,157	19,612 D	44.7%	53.1%	45.7%	54.3%
87,041	LITCHFIELD	46,299	26,848	18,628	823	8,220 R	58.0%	40.2%	59.0%	41.0%
55,999	MIDDLESEX	31,265	16,119	14,609	537	1,510 R	51.6%	46.7%	52.5%	47.5%
484,316	NEW HAVEN	248,993	120,769	121,591	6,633	822 D	48.5%	48.8%	49.8%	50.2%
125,224	NEW LONDON	57,814	27,416	29,425	973	2,009 D	47.4%	50.9%	48.2%	51.8%
31,866	TOLLAND	17,329	9,012	7,970	347	1,042 R	52.0%	46.0%	53.1%	46.9%
56,223	WINDHAM	29,453	13,692	15,433	328	1,741 D	46.5%	52.4%	47.0%	53.0%
1,709,242	TOTAL	883,518	437,754	423,297	22,467	14,457 R	49.5%	47.9%	50.8%	49.2%

CONNECTICUT

PRESIDENT 1944

1940 Census Population	County	Total Vote	Republican	Democratic	Other	Rep.-Dem. Plurality	Percentage Total Vote Rep.	Total Vote Dem.	Major Vote Rep.	Major Vote Dem.
418,384	FAIRFIELD	205,297	103,693	99,181	2,423	4,512 R	50.5%	48.3%	51.1%	48.9%
450,189	HARTFORD	224,218	95,224	127,841	1,153	32,617 D	42.5%	57.0%	42.7%	57.3%
87,041	LITCHFIELD	43,479	24,019	19,212	248	4,807 R	55.2%	44.2%	55.6%	44.4%
55,999	MIDDLESEX	28,042	14,315	13,551	176	764 R	51.0%	48.3%	51.4%	48.6%
484,316	NEW HAVEN	234,144	108,883	123,450	1,811	14,567 D	46.5%	52.7%	46.9%	53.1%
125,224	NEW LONDON	53,742	24,153	29,304	285	5,151 D	44.9%	54.5%	45.2%	54.8%
31,866	TOLLAND	16,046	8,208	7,721	117	487 R	51.2%	48.1%	51.5%	48.5%
56,223	WINDHAM	27,022	12,032	14,886	104	2,854 D	44.5%	55.1%	44.7%	55.3%
1,709,242	TOTAL	831,990	390,527	435,146	6,317	44,619 D	46.9%	52.3%	47.3%	52.7%

CONNECTICUT

PRESIDENT 1940

1940 Census Population	County	Total Vote	Republican	Democratic	Other	Rep.-Dem. Plurality	Percentage Total Vote Rep.	Percentage Total Vote Dem.	Percentage Major Vote Rep.	Percentage Major Vote Dem.
418,384	FAIRFIELD	185,707	91,190	93,688	829	2,498 D	49.1%	50.4%	49.3%	50.7%
450,189	HARTFORD	202,953	88,155	114,336	462	26,181 D	43.4%	56.3%	43.5%	56.5%
87,041	LITCHFIELD	42,542	22,956	19,537	49	3,419 R	54.0%	45.9%	54.0%	46.0%
55,999	MIDDLESEX	26,530	13,447	13,044	39	403 R	50.7%	49.2%	50.8%	49.2%
484,316	NEW HAVEN	229,689	103,100	126,072	517	22,972 D	44.9%	54.9%	45.0%	55.0%
125,224	NEW LONDON	51,773	23,389	28,286	98	4,897 D	45.2%	54.6%	45.3%	54.7%
31,866	TOLLAND	15,197	7,503	7,669	25	166 D	49.4%	50.5%	49.5%	50.5%
56,223	WINDHAM	27,111	12,079	14,989	43	2,910 D	44.6%	55.3%	44.6%	55.4%
1,709,242	TOTAL	781,502	361,819	417,621	2,062	55,802 D	46.3%	53.4%	46.4%	53.6%

CONNECTICUT

PRESIDENT 1936

1930 Census Population	County	Total Vote	Republican	Democratic	Other	Rep.-Dem. Plurality	Percentage Total Vote Rep.	Percentage Total Vote Dem.	Percentage Major Vote Rep.	Percentage Major Vote Dem.
386,702	FAIRFIELD	163,263	67,846	87,329	8,088	19,483 D	41.6%	53.5%	43.7%	56.3%
421,097	HARTFORD	176,318	65,652	103,450	7,216	37,798 D	37.2%	58.7%	38.8%	61.2%
82,556	LITCHFIELD	37,193	18,850	17,468	875	1,382 R	50.7%	47.0%	51.9%	48.1%
51,388	MIDDLESEX	23,578	10,925	12,294	359	1,369 D	46.3%	52.1%	47.1%	52.9%
463,449	NEW HAVEN	204,611	76,614	117,308	10,689	40,694 D	37.4%	57.3%	39.5%	60.5%
118,966	NEW LONDON	47,703	21,367	24,999	1,337	3,632 D	44.8%	52.4%	46.1%	53.9%
28,659	TOLLAND	13,129	5,965	6,676	488	711 D	45.4%	50.8%	47.2%	52.8%
54,086	WINDHAM	24,928	11,466	12,605	857	1,139 D	46.0%	50.6%	47.6%	52.4%
1,606,903	TOTAL	690,723	278,685	382,129	29,909	103,444 D	40.3%	55.3%	42.2%	57.8%

CONNECTICUT

PRESIDENT 1932

1930 Census Population	County	Total Vote	Republican	Democratic	Other	Rep.-Dem. Plurality	Percentage Total Vote Rep.	Total Vote Dem.	Major Vote Rep.	Major Vote Dem.
386,702	FAIRFIELD	144,697	72,238	64,367	8,092	7,871 R	49.9%	44.5%	52.9%	47.1%
421,097	HARTFORD	150,153	72,611	72,322	5,220	289 R	48.4%	48.2%	50.1%	49.9%
82,556	LITCHFIELD	32,811	18,682	13,469	660	5,213 R	56.9%	41.1%	58.1%	41.9%
51,388	MIDDLESEX	20,400	10,770	9,286	344	1,484 R	52.8%	45.5%	53.7%	46.3%
463,449	NEW HAVEN	174,141	79,019	86,826	8,296	7,807 D	45.4%	49.9%	47.6%	52.4%
118,966	NEW LONDON	40,155	19,721	19,576	858	145 R	49.1%	48.8%	50.2%	49.8%
28,659	TOLLAND	11,297	5,857	4,985	455	872 R	51.8%	44.1%	54.0%	46.0%
54,086	WINDHAM	20,529	9,522	10,801	206	1,279 D	46.4%	52.6%	46.9%	53.1%
1,606,903	TOTAL	594,183	288,420	281,632	24,131	6,788 R	48.5%	47.4%	50.6%	49.4%

CONNECTICUT

PRESIDENT 1928

1920 Census Population	County	Total Vote	Republican	Democratic	Other	Rep.-Dem. Plurality	Percentage Total Vote Rep.	Total Vote Dem.	Major Vote Rep.	Major Vote Dem.
320,936	FAIRFIELD	127,948	71,410	55,491	1,047	15,919 R	55.8%	43.4%	56.3%	43.7%
336,027	HARTFORD	142,955	75,997	65,789	1,169	10,208 R	53.2%	46.0%	53.6%	46.4%
76,262	LITCHFIELD	30,061	19,157	10,766	138	8,391 R	63.7%	35.8%	64.0%	36.0%
47,550	MIDDLESEX	18,700	11,205	7,380	115	3,825 R	59.9%	39.5%	60.3%	39.7%
415,214	NEW HAVEN	165,048	80,952	82,657	1,439	1,705 D	49.0%	50.1%	49.5%	50.5%
104,611	NEW LONDON	37,969	21,378	16,299	292	5,079 R	56.3%	42.9%	56.7%	43.3%
27,216	TOLLAND	10,884	6,502	4,256	126	2,246 R	59.7%	39.1%	60.4%	39.6%
52,815	WINDHAM	19,553	10,040	9,447	66	593 R	51.3%	48.3%	51.5%	48.5%
1,380,631	TOTAL	553,118	296,641	252,085	4,392	44,556 R	53.6%	45.6%	54.1%	45.9%

CONNECTICUT

PRESIDENT 1924

1920 Census Population	County	Total Vote	Republican	Democratic	Other	Rep.-Dem. Plurality	Percentage Total Vote Rep.	Total Vote Dem.	Major Vote Rep.	Major Vote Dem.
320,936	FAIRFIELD	87,647	58,041	18,815	10,791	39,226 R	66.2%	21.5%	75.5%	24.5%
336,027	HARTFORD	99,142	61,381	28,139	9,622	33,242 R	61.9%	28.4%	68.6%	31.4%
76,262	LITCHFIELD	25,273	15,499	6,645	3,129	8,854 R	61.3%	26.3%	70.0%	30.0%
47,550	MIDDLESEX	14,387	9,383	4,009	995	5,374 R	65.2%	27.9%	70.1%	29.9%
415,214	NEW HAVEN	120,519	69,164	36,247	15,108	32,917 R	57.4%	30.1%	65.6%	34.4%
104,611	NEW LONDON	29,206	18,205	8,615	2,386	9,590 R	62.3%	29.5%	67.9%	32.1%
27,216	TOLLAND	8,285	5,161	2,239	885	2,922 R	62.3%	27.0%	69.7%	30.3%
52,815	WINDHAM	15,937	9,488	5,475	974	4,013 R	59.5%	34.4%	63.4%	36.6%
1,380,631	TOTAL	400,396	246,322	110,184	43,890	136,138 R	61.5%	27.5%	69.1%	30.9%

CONNECTICUT

PRESIDENT 1920

1920 Census Population	County	Total Vote	Republican	Democratic	Other	Rep.-Dem. Plurality	Percentage Total Vote Rep.	Total Vote Dem.	Major Vote Rep.	Major Vote Dem.
320,936	FAIRFIELD	83,113	55,251	24,761	3,101	30,490 R	66.5%	29.8%	69.1%	30.9%
336,027	HARTFORD	88,979	54,046	30,287	4,646	23,759 R	60.7%	34.0%	64.1%	35.9%
76,262	LITCHFIELD	21,847	14,405	6,938	504	7,467 R	65.9%	31.8%	67.5%	32.5%
47,550	MIDDLESEX	12,948	8,447	4,170	331	4,277 R	65.2%	32.2%	66.9%	33.1%
415,214	NEW HAVEN	109,474	65,938	37,977	5,559	27,961 R	60.2%	34.7%	63.5%	36.5%
104,611	NEW LONDON	27,520	17,422	9,209	889	8,213 R	63.3%	33.5%	65.4%	34.6%
27,216	TOLLAND	7,765	5,135	2,308	322	2,827 R	66.1%	29.7%	69.0%	31.0%
52,815	WINDHAM	13,872	8,594	5,071	207	3,523 R	62.0%	36.6%	62.9%	37.1%
1,380,631	TOTAL	365,518	229,238	120,721	15,559	108,517 R	62.7%	33.0%	65.5%	34.5%

CONNECTICUT

ELECTION NOTES

1956 Other vote was scattered write-in.

1952 Other vote was 2,244 Hoopes (Socialist); 1,466 Hallinan (Progressive); 535 Hass (Socialist Labor); 5 scattered write-in.

1948 Other vote was 13,713 Wallace (Progressive); 6,964 Thomas (Socialist); 1,184 Teichert (Socialist Labor); 606 Dobbs (Socialist Workers).

1944 Other vote was 5,097 Thomas (Socialist); 1,220 Teichert (Socialist Labor).

1940 Other vote was 1,091 Browder (Communist); 971 Aiken (Socialist Labor). The Republican figures include 361,021 votes cast on the Republican ticket and 798 votes cast on the Union ticket.

1936 Other vote was 21,805 Lemke (Union); 5,683 Thomas (Socialist); 1,228 Aiken (Socialist Labor); 1,193 Browder (Communist).

1932 Other vote was 20,480 Thomas (Socialist); 2,287 Reynolds (Socialist Labor); 1,364 Foster (Communist).

1928 Other vote was 3,029 Thomas (Socialist); 738 Foster (Communist); 625 Reynolds (Socialist Labor).

1924 Other vote was 42,416 LaFollette (Progressive); 1,373 Johns (Socialist Labor); 101 scattered write-in.

1920 Other vote was 10,350 Debs (Socialist); 1,947 Christensen (Farmer-Labor); 1,771 Watkins (Prohibition); 1,491 Cox (Socialist Labor).

DELAWARE

POPULAR VOTE FOR PRESIDENT 1920 TO 1956

Year	Total Vote	Republican Vote	Republican Candidate	Democratic Vote	Democratic Candidate	Other Vote	Plurality	Percentage Total Vote Rep.	Percentage Total Vote Dem.	Percentage Major Vote Rep.	Percentage Major Vote Dem.
1956	177,988	98,057	Eisenhower, Dwight D.	79,421	Stevenson, Adlai E.	510	18,636 R	55.1%	44.6%	55.3%	44.7%
1952	174,025	90,059	Eisenhower, Dwight D.	83,315	Stevenson, Adlai E.	651	6,744 R	51.8%	47.9%	51.9%	48.1%
1948	139,073	69,588	Dewey, Thomas E.	67,813	Truman, Harry S.	1,672	1,775 R	50.0%	48.8%	50.6%	49.4%
1944	125,361	56,747	Dewey, Thomas E.	68,166	Roosevelt, Franklin D.	448	11,419 D	45.3%	54.4%	45.4%	54.6%
1940	136,374	61,440	Willkie, Wendell	74,599	Roosevelt, Franklin D.	335	13,159 D	45.1%	54.7%	45.2%	54.8%
1936	127,603	57,236	Landon, Alfred M.	69,702	Roosevelt, Franklin D.	665	12,466 D	44.9%	54.6%	45.1%	54.9%
1932	112,901	57,073	Hoover, Herbert C.	54,319	Roosevelt, Franklin D.	1,509	2,754 R	50.6%	48.1%	51.2%	48.8%
1928	104,602	68,860	Hoover, Herbert C.	35,354	Smith, Alfred E.	388	33,506 R	65.8%	33.8%	66.1%	33.9%
1924	90,885	52,441	Coolidge, Calvin	33,445	Davis, John W.	4,999	18,996 R	57.7%	36.8%	61.1%	38.9%
1920	94,875	52,858	Harding, Warren G.	39,911	Cox, James M.	2,106	12,947 R	55.7%	42.1%	57.0%	43.0%

ELECTORAL COLLEGE VOTE 1920 TO 1956

Year	Total	Republican	Democratic	Other
1956	3	3	—	—
1952	3	3	—	—
1948	3	3	—	—
1944	3	—	3	—
1940	3	—	3	—
1936	3	—	3	—
1932	3	3	—	—
1928	3	3	—	—
1924	3	3	—	—
1920	3	3	—	—

DELAWARE

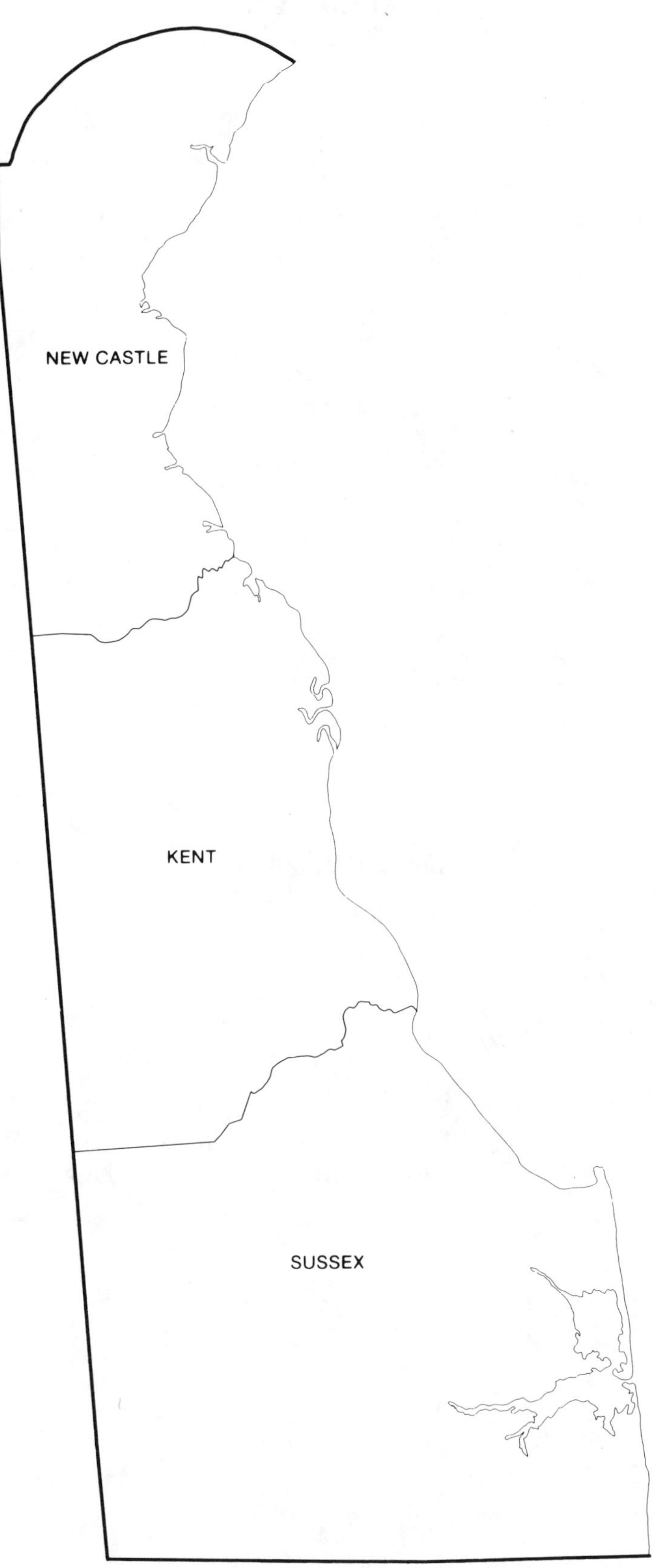

DELAWARE

PRESIDENT 1956

1950 Census Population	County	Total Vote	Republican	Democratic	Other	Rep.-Dem. Plurality	Percentage Total Vote Rep.	Total Vote Dem.	Major Vote Rep.	Major Vote Dem.
37,870	KENT	19,745	10,303	9,319	123	984 R	52.2%	47.2%	52.5%	47.5%
218,879	NEW CASTLE	127,813	71,133	56,405	275	14,728 R	55.7%	44.1%	55.8%	44.2%
61,336	SUSSEX	30,430	16,621	13,697	112	2,924 R	54.6%	45.0%	54.8%	45.2%
318,085	TOTAL	177,988	98,057	79,421	510	18,636 R	55.1%	44.6%	55.3%	44.7%

DELAWARE

PRESIDENT 1952

1950 Census Population	County	Total Vote	Republican	Democratic	Other	Rep.-Dem. Plurality	Percentage Total Vote Rep.	Total Vote Dem.	Major Vote Rep.	Major Vote Dem.
37,870	KENT	20,108	10,144	9,874	90	270 R	50.4%	49.1%	50.7%	49.3%
218,879	NEW CASTLE	121,396	62,658	58,387	351	4,271 R	51.6%	48.1%	51.8%	48.2%
61,336	SUSSEX	32,521	17,257	15,054	210	2,203 R	53.1%	46.3%	53.4%	46.6%
318,085	TOTAL	174,025	90,059	83,315	651	6,744 R	51.8%	47.9%	51.9%	48.1%

DELAWARE

PRESIDENT 1948

1940 Census Population	County	Total Vote	Republican	Democratic	Other	Rep.-Dem. Plurality	Percentage Total Vote Rep.	Total Vote Dem.	Major Vote Rep.	Major Vote Dem.
34,441	KENT	16,790	8,501	8,174	115	327 R	50.6%	48.7%	51.0%	49.0%
179,562	NEW CASTLE	97,001	47,451	48,117	1,433	666 D	48.9%	49.6%	49.7%	50.3%
52,502	SUSSEX	25,282	13,636	11,522	124	2,114 R	53.9%	45.6%	54.2%	45.8%
266,505	TOTAL	139,073	69,588	67,813	1,672	1,775 R	50.0%	48.8%	50.6%	49.4%

DELAWARE

PRESIDENT 1944

1940 Census Population	County	Total Vote	Republican	Democratic	Other	Rep.-Dem. Plurality	Percentage Total Vote Rep.	Percentage Total Vote Dem.	Percentage Major Vote Rep.	Percentage Major Vote Dem.
34,441	KENT	15,026	7,069	7,900	57	831 D	47.0%	52.6%	47.2%	52.8%
179,562	NEW CASTLE	87,689	37,783	49,588	318	11,805 D	43.1%	56.5%	43.2%	56.8%
52,502	SUSSEX	22,646	11,895	10,678	73	1,217 R	52.5%	47.2%	52.7%	47.3%
266,505	TOTAL	125,361	56,747	68,166	448	11,419 D	45.3%	54.4%	45.4%	54.6%

DELAWARE

PRESIDENT 1940

1940 Census Population	County	Total Vote	Republican	Democratic	Other	Rep.-Dem. Plurality	Percentage Total Vote Rep.	Percentage Total Vote Dem.	Percentage Major Vote Rep.	Percentage Major Vote Dem.
34,441	KENT	17,353	8,079	9,226	48	1,147 D	46.6%	53.2%	46.7%	53.3%
179,562	NEW CASTLE	93,936	41,508	52,167	261	10,659 D	44.2%	55.5%	44.3%	55.7%
52,502	SUSSEX	25,085	11,853	13,206	26	1,353 D	47.3%	52.6%	47.3%	52.7%
266,505	TOTAL	136,374	61,440	74,599	335	13,159 D	45.1%	54.7%	45.2%	54.8%

DELAWARE

PRESIDENT 1936

1930 Census Population	County	Total Vote	Republican	Democratic	Other	Rep.-Dem. Plurality	Percentage Total Vote Rep.	Percentage Total Vote Dem.	Percentage Major Vote Rep.	Percentage Major Vote Dem.
31,841	KENT	17,005	7,389	9,588	28	2,199 D	43.5%	56.4%	43.5%	56.5%
161,032	NEW CASTLE	85,766	37,851	47,315	600	9,464 D	44.1%	55.2%	44.4%	55.6%
45,507	SUSSEX	24,832	11,996	12,799	37	803 D	48.3%	51.5%	48.4%	51.6%
238,380	TOTAL	127,603	57,236	69,702	665	12,466 D	44.9%	54.6%	45.1%	54.9%

DELAWARE

PRESIDENT 1932

1930 Census Population	County	Total Vote	Republican	Democratic	Other	Rep.-Dem. Plurality	Percentage Total Vote Rep.	Percentage Total Vote Dem.	Percentage Major Vote Rep.	Percentage Major Vote Dem.
31,841	KENT	15,490	6,597	8,829	64	2,232 D	42.6%	57.0%	42.8%	57.2%
161,032	NEW CASTLE	74,109	39,844	32,872	1,393	6,972 R	53.8%	44.4%	54.8%	45.2%
45,507	SUSSEX	23,302	10,632	12,618	52	1,986 D	45.6%	54.1%	45.7%	54.3%
238,380	TOTAL	112,901	57,073	54,319	1,509	2,754 R	50.6%	48.1%	51.2%	48.8%

DELAWARE

PRESIDENT 1928

1920 Census Population	County	Total Vote	Republican	Democratic	Other	Rep.-Dem. Plurality	Percentage Total Vote Rep.	Percentage Total Vote Dem.	Percentage Major Vote Rep.	Percentage Major Vote Dem.
31,023	KENT	14,089	8,335	5,727	27	2,608 R	59.2%	40.6%	59.3%	40.7%
148,239	NEW CASTLE	70,412	47,641	22,464	307	25,177 R	67.7%	31.9%	68.0%	32.0%
43,741	SUSSEX	20,101	12,884	7,163	54	5,721 R	64.1%	35.6%	64.3%	35.7%
223,003	TOTAL	104,602	68,860	35,354	388	33,506 R	65.8%	33.8%	66.1%	33.9%

DELAWARE

PRESIDENT 1924

1920 Census Population	County	Total Vote	Republican	Democratic	Other	Rep.-Dem. Plurality	Percentage Total Vote Rep.	Percentage Total Vote Dem.	Percentage Major Vote Rep.	Percentage Major Vote Dem.
31,023	KENT	14,021	6,894	6,935	192	41 D	49.2%	49.5%	49.9%	50.1%
148,239	NEW CASTLE	57,851	35,427	17,842	4,582	17,585 R	61.2%	30.8%	66.5%	33.5%
43,741	SUSSEX	19,013	10,120	8,668	225	1,452 R	53.2%	45.6%	53.9%	46.1%
223,003	TOTAL	90,885	52,441	33,445	4,999	18,996 R	57.7%	36.8%	61.1%	38.9%

DELAWARE

PRESIDENT 1920

1920 Census Population	County	Total Vote	Republican	Democratic	Other	Rep.-Dem. Plurality	Percentage Total Vote Rep.	Total Vote Dem.	Major Vote Rep.	Major Vote Dem.
31,023	KENT	13,889	6,511	7,211	167	700 D	46.9%	51.9%	47.4%	52.6%
148,239	NEW CASTLE	62,791	36,600	24,252	1,939	12,348 R	58.3%	38.6%	60.1%	39.9%
43,741	SUSSEX	18,195	9,747	8,448		1,299 R	53.6%	46.4%	53.6%	46.4%
223,003	TOTAL	94,875	52,858	39,911	2,106	12,947 R	55.7%	42.1%	57.0%	43.0%

DELAWARE

ELECTION NOTES

1956 Other vote was 400 Holtwick (Prohibition); 110 Hass (Socialist Labor).

1952 Other vote was 242 Hass (Socialist Labor); 234 Hamblen (Prohibition); 155 Hallinan (Progressive); 20 Hoopes (Socialist).

1948 Other vote was 1,050 Wallace (Progressive); 343 Watson (Prohibition); 250 Thomas (Socialist); 29 Teichert (Socialist Labor).

1944 Other vote was 294 Watson (Prohibition); 154 Thomas (Socialist).

1940 Other vote was 220 Babson (Prohibition); 115 Thomas (Socialist).

1936 Other vote was 442 Lemke (Union); 172 Thomas (Socialist); 51 Browder (Communist). The Republican figures include 54,014 votes cast on the Republican ticket and 3,222 votes cast on the Independent Republican ticket.

1932 Other vote was 1,376 Thomas (Socialist); 133 Foster (Communist).

1928 Other vote was 329 Thomas (Socialist); 59 Foster (Communist).

1924 Other vote was 4,979 LaFollette (Progressive); 20 Wallace (Commonwealth Land).

1920 Other vote was 988 Debs (Socialist); 986 Watkins (Prohibition); 93 Christensen (Farmer-Labor); 39 Macauley (Single Tax).

FLORIDA

POPULAR VOTE FOR PRESIDENT 1920 TO 1956

		Republican		Democratic				Percentage			
								Total Vote		Major Vote	
Year	Total Vote	Vote	Candidate	Vote	Candidate	Other Vote	Plurality	Rep.	Dem.	Rep.	Dem.
1956	1,125,762	643,849	Eisenhower, Dwight D.	480,371	Stevenson, Adlai E.	1,542	163,478 R	57.2%	42.7%	57.3%	42.7%
1952	989,337	544,036	Eisenhower, Dwight D.	444,950	Stevenson, Adlai E.	351	99,086 R	55.0%	45.0%	55.0%	45.0%
1948 **	577,643	194,280	Dewey, Thomas E.	281,988	Truman, Harry S.	101,375	87,708 D	33.6%	48.8%	40.8%	59.2%
1944	482,803	143,215	Dewey, Thomas E.	339,377	Roosevelt, Franklin D.	211	196,162 D	29.7%	70.3%	29.7%	70.3%
1940	485,640	126,158	Willkie, Wendell	359,334	Roosevelt, Franklin D.	148	233,176 D	26.0%	74.0%	26.0%	74.0%
1936	327,436	78,248	Landon, Alfred M.	249,117	Roosevelt, Franklin D.	71	170,869 D	23.9%	76.1%	23.9%	76.1%
1932	276,943	69,170	Hoover, Herbert C.	206,307	Roosevelt, Franklin D.	1,466	137,137 D	25.0%	74.5%	25.1%	74.9%
1928	252,068	145,860	Hoover, Herbert C.	101,764	Smith, Alfred E.	4,444	44,096 R	57.9%	40.4%	58.9%	41.1%
1924	109,158	30,633	Coolidge, Calvin	62,083	Davis, John W.	16,442	31,450 D	28.1%	56.9%	33.0%	67.0%
1920	145,684	44,853	Harding, Warren G.	90,515	Cox, James M.	10,316	45,662 D	30.8%	62.1%	33.1%	66.9%

In 1948 other vote was 89,755 States Rights and 11,620 Progressive.

ELECTORAL COLLEGE VOTE 1920 TO 1956

Year	Total	Republican	Democratic	Other
1956	10	10	—	—
1952	10	10	—	—
1948	8	—	8	—
1944	8	—	8	—
1940	7	—	7	—
1936	7	—	7	—
1932	7	—	7	—
1928	6	6	—	—
1924	6	—	6	—
1920	6	—	6	—

FLORIDA

ESCAMBIA
SANTA ROSA
OKALOOSA
WALTON
HOLMES
WASHINGTON
BAY
JACKSON
CALHOUN
GULF
LIBERTY
FRANKLIN
GADSDEN
LEON
WAKULLA
JEFFERSON
MADISON
TAYLOR
HAMILTON
SUWANNEE
LAFAYETTE
DIXIE
COLUMBIA
GILCHRIST
LEVY
BAKER
UNION
BRADFORD
ALACHUA
NASSAU
DUVAL
CLAY
ST. JOHNS
PUTNAM
FLAGLER
MARION
VOLUSIA
LAKE
SEMINOLE
ORANGE
SUMTER
CITRUS
HERNANDO
PASCO
PINELLAS
HILLSBOROUGH
OSCEOLA
BREVARD
POLK
INDIAN RIVER
OKEECHOBEE
ST. LUCIE
MARTIN
HIGHLANDS
HARDEE
MANATEE
DE SOTO
SARASOTA
GLADES
CHARLOTTE
PALM BEACH
HENDRY
LEE
BROWARD
COLLIER
DADE
MONROE (PART)
MONROE (PART)

FLORIDA

PRESIDENT 1956

1950 Census Population	County	Total Vote	Republican	Democratic	Other	Rep.-Dem. Plurality	Percentage Total Vote Rep.	Total Vote Dem.	Major Vote Rep.	Major Vote Dem.
57,026	ALACHUA	14,846	7,939	6,889	18	1,050 R	53.5%	46.4%	53.5%	46.5%
6,313	BAKER	1,811	366	1,443	2	1,077 D	20.2%	79.7%	20.2%	79.8%
42,689	BAY	13,653	4,971	8,645	37	3,674 D	36.4%	63.3%	36.5%	63.5%
11,457	BRADFORD	3,540	1,203	2,328	9	1,125 D	34.0%	65.8%	34.1%	65.9%
23,653	BREVARD	13,932	10,004	3,928		6,076 R	71.8%	28.2%	71.8%	28.2%
83,933	BROWARD	60,289	43,552	16,561	176	26,991 R	72.2%	27.5%	72.5%	27.5%
7,922	CALHOUN	2,255	554	1,701		1,147 D	24.6%	75.4%	24.6%	75.4%
4,286	CHARLOTTE	2,518	1,589	929		660 R	63.1%	36.9%	63.1%	36.9%
6,111	CITRUS	3,117	1,570	1,527	20	43 R	50.4%	49.0%	50.7%	49.3%
14,323	CLAY	4,420	2,372	2,048		324 R	53.7%	46.3%	53.7%	46.3%
6,488	COLLIER	3,238	1,934	1,304		630 R	59.7%	40.3%	59.7%	40.3%
18,216	COLUMBIA	5,095	1,841	3,246	8	1,405 D	36.1%	63.7%	36.2%	63.8%
495,084	DADE	236,522	130,938	105,559	25	25,379 R	55.4%	44.6%	55.4%	44.6%
9,242	DESOTO	2,549	1,234	1,315		81 D	48.4%	51.6%	48.4%	51.6%
3,928	DIXIE	1,278	370	904	4	534 D	29.0%	70.7%	29.0%	71.0%
304,029	DUVAL	106,772	53,481	53,127	164	354 R	50.1%	49.8%	50.2%	49.8%
112,706	ESCAMBIA	35,558	13,227	22,320	11	9,093 D	37.2%	62.8%	37.2%	62.8%
3,367	FLAGLER	1,204	498	690	16	192 D	41.4%	57.3%	41.9%	58.1%
5,814	FRANKLIN	1,529	571	958		387 D	37.3%	62.7%	37.3%	62.7%
36,457	GADSDEN	3,607	1,321	2,262	24	941 D	36.6%	62.7%	36.9%	63.1%
3,499	GILCHRIST	1,062	137	925		788 D	12.9%	87.1%	12.9%	87.1%
2,199	GLADES	648	309	339		30 D	47.7%	52.3%	47.7%	52.3%
7,460	GULF	2,363	570	1,793		1,223 D	24.1%	75.9%	24.1%	75.9%
8,981	HAMILTON	1,960	464	1,493	3	1,029 D	23.7%	76.2%	23.7%	76.3%
10,073	HARDEE	3,479	1,589	1,890		301 D	45.7%	54.3%	45.7%	54.3%
6,051	HENDRY	2,076	1,071	1,003	2	68 R	51.6%	48.3%	51.6%	48.4%
6,693	HERNANDO	2,788	1,295	1,435	58	140 D	46.4%	51.5%	47.4%	52.6%
13,636	HIGHLANDS	5,776	3,480	2,296		1,184 R	60.2%	39.8%	60.2%	39.8%
249,894	HILLSBOROUGH	80,599	41,889	38,610	100	3,279 R	52.0%	47.9%	52.0%	48.0%
13,988	HOLMES	3,552	1,036	2,516		1,480 D	29.2%	70.8%	29.2%	70.8%
11,872	INDIAN RIVER	5,758	4,059	1,699		2,360 R	70.5%	29.5%	70.5%	29.5%
34,645	JACKSON	8,516	2,543	5,973		3,430 D	29.9%	70.1%	29.9%	70.1%
10,413	JEFFERSON	1,757	540	1,201	16	661 D	30.7%	68.4%	31.0%	69.0%
3,440	LAFAYETTE	1,241	187	1,054		867 D	15.1%	84.9%	15.1%	84.9%
36,340	LAKE	15,372	10,888	4,326	158	6,562 R	70.8%	28.1%	71.6%	28.4%
23,404	LEE	12,085	7,565	4,520		3,045 R	62.6%	37.4%	62.6%	37.4%
51,590	LEON	13,922	6,828	7,022	72	194 D	49.0%	50.4%	49.3%	50.7%
10,637	LEVY	2,770	934	1,821	15	887 D	33.7%	65.7%	33.9%	66.1%
3,182	LIBERTY	1,112	238	870	4	632 D	21.4%	78.2%	21.5%	78.5%
14,197	MADISON	3,089	1,017	2,064	8	1,047 D	32.9%	66.8%	33.0%	67.0%
34,704	MANATEE	17,362	11,904	5,394	64	6,510 R	68.6%	31.1%	68.8%	31.2%
38,187	MARION	12,499	6,362	6,114	23	248 R	50.9%	48.9%	51.0%	49.0%
7,807	MARTIN	4,387	2,997	1,387	3	1,610 R	68.3%	31.6%	68.4%	31.6%
29,957	MONROE	7,668	3,337	4,327	4	990 D	43.5%	56.4%	43.5%	56.5%
12,811	NASSAU	4,497	1,717	2,765	15	1,048 D	38.2%	61.5%	38.3%	61.7%
27,533	OKALOOSA	8,536	2,788	5,748		2,960 D	32.7%	67.3%	32.7%	67.3%
3,454	OKEECHOBEE	1,410	575	835		260 D	40.8%	59.2%	40.8%	59.2%
114,950	ORANGE	52,066	37,482	14,532	52	22,950 R	72.0%	27.9%	72.1%	27.9%
11,406	OSCEOLA	5,527	3,602	1,923	2	1,679 R	65.2%	34.8%	65.2%	34.8%
114,688	PALM BEACH	50,147	35,746	14,321	80	21,425 R	71.3%	28.6%	71.4%	28.6%
20,529	PASCO	9,742	5,501	4,181	60	1,320 R	56.5%	42.9%	56.8%	43.2%
159,249	PINELLAS	102,532	74,314	28,113	105	46,201 R	72.5%	27.4%	72.6%	27.4%
123,997	POLK	42,332	23,682	18,626	24	5,056 R	55.9%	44.0%	56.0%	44.0%
23,615	PUTNAM	7,485	4,212	3,232	41	980 R	56.3%	43.2%	56.6%	43.4%
24,998	ST. JOHNS	9,073	5,104	3,940	29	1,164 R	56.3%	43.4%	56.4%	43.6%
20,180	ST. LUCIE	8,192	5,435	2,731	26	2,704 R	66.3%	33.3%	66.6%	33.4%
18,554	SANTA ROSA	6,053	1,909	4,144		2,235 D	31.5%	68.5%	31.5%	68.5%
28,827	SARASOTA	19,003	13,937	5,052	14	8,885 R	73.3%	26.6%	73.4%	26.6%
26,883	SEMINOLE	8,977	5,841	3,125	11	2,716 R	65.1%	34.8%	65.1%	34.9%
11,330	SUMTER	3,390	1,061	2,329		1,268 D	31.3%	68.7%	31.3%	68.7%

FLORIDA

PRESIDENT 1956

1950 Census Population	County	Total Vote	Republican	Democratic	Other	Rep.-Dem. Plurality	Percentage Total Vote Rep.	Percentage Total Vote Dem.	Percentage Major Vote Rep.	Percentage Major Vote Dem.
16,986	SUWANNEE	4,209	1,046	3,163		2,117 D	24.9%	75.1%	24.9%	75.1%
10,416	TAYLOR	2,721	776	1,945		1,169 D	28.5%	71.5%	28.5%	71.5%
8,906	UNION	1,176	218	958		740 D	18.5%	81.5%	18.5%	81.5%
74,229	VOLUSIA	39,614	25,103	14,489	22	10,614 R	63.4%	36.6%	63.4%	36.6%
5,258	WAKULLA	1,467	393	1,074		681 D	26.8%	73.2%	26.8%	73.2%
14,725	WALTON	4,831	1,606	3,225		1,619 D	33.2%	66.8%	33.2%	66.8%
11,888	WASHINGTON	3,208	1,027	2,164	17	1,137 D	32.0%	67.5%	32.2%	67.8%
2,771,305	TOTAL	1,125,762	643,849	480,371	1,542	163,478 R	57.2%	42.7%	57.3%	42.7%

FLORIDA

PRESIDENT 1952

1950 Census Population	County	Total Vote	Republican	Democratic	Other	Rep.-Dem. Plurality	Percentage Total Vote Rep.	Total Vote Dem.	Major Vote Rep.	Major Vote Dem.
57,026	ALACHUA	14,422	8,432	5,990		2,442 R	58.5%	41.5%	58.5%	41.5%
6,313	BAKER	1,901	419	1,482		1,063 D	22.0%	78.0%	22.0%	78.0%
42,689	BAY	13,601	4,812	8,789		3,977 D	35.4%	64.6%	35.4%	64.6%
11,457	BRADFORD	3,288	976	2,312		1,336 D	29.7%	70.3%	29.7%	70.3%
23,653	BREVARD	10,913	6,756	4,157		2,599 R	61.9%	38.1%	61.9%	38.1%
83,933	BROWARD	38,360	26,506	11,854		14,652 R	69.1%	30.9%	69.1%	30.9%
7,922	CALHOUN	2,417	590	1,827		1,237 D	24.4%	75.6%	24.4%	75.6%
4,286	CHARLOTTE	1,929	1,134	795		339 R	58.8%	41.2%	58.8%	41.2%
6,111	CITRUS	2,610	1,249	1,361		112 D	47.9%	52.1%	47.9%	52.1%
14,323	CLAY	4,312	2,116	2,196		80 D	49.1%	50.9%	49.1%	50.9%
6,488	COLLIER	2,190	1,086	1,104		18 D	49.6%	50.4%	49.6%	50.4%
18,216	COLUMBIA	5,270	2,041	3,229		1,188 D	38.7%	61.3%	38.7%	61.3%
495,084	DADE	215,196	122,174	93,022		29,152 R	56.8%	43.2%	56.8%	43.2%
9,242	DESOTO	3,048	1,256	1,792		536 D	41.2%	58.8%	41.2%	58.8%
3,928	DIXIE	1,264	440	824		384 D	34.8%	65.2%	34.8%	65.2%
304,029	DUVAL	104,295	50,346	53,949		3,603 D	48.3%	51.7%	48.3%	51.7%
112,706	ESCAMBIA	32,671	12,176	20,495		8,319 D	37.3%	62.7%	37.3%	62.7%
3,367	FLAGLER	998	512	486		26 R	51.3%	48.7%	51.3%	48.7%
5,814	FRANKLIN	1,849	611	1,238		627 D	33.0%	67.0%	33.0%	67.0%
36,457	GADSDEN	4,541	1,835	2,706		871 D	40.4%	59.6%	40.4%	59.6%
3,499	GILCHRIST	1,187	195	992		797 D	16.4%	83.6%	16.4%	83.6%
2,199	GLADES	665	264	401		137 D	39.7%	60.3%	39.7%	60.3%
7,460	GULF	2,259	490	1,769		1,279 D	21.7%	78.3%	21.7%	78.3%
8,981	HAMILTON	2,110	658	1,452		794 D	31.2%	68.8%	31.2%	68.8%
10,073	HARDEE	3,871	1,802	2,069		267 D	46.6%	53.4%	46.6%	53.4%
6,051	HENDRY	1,970	918	1,052		134 D	46.6%	53.4%	46.6%	53.4%
6,693	HERNANDO	2,383	1,279	1,104		175 R	53.7%	46.3%	53.7%	46.3%
13,636	HIGHLANDS	5,688	2,952	2,736		216 R	51.9%	48.1%	51.9%	48.1%
249,894	HILLSBOROUGH	69,568	36,316	33,252		3,064 R	52.2%	47.8%	52.2%	47.8%
13,988	HOLMES	4,446	1,230	3,216		1,986 D	27.7%	72.3%	27.7%	72.3%
11,872	INDIAN RIVER	4,633	3,055	1,578		1,477 R	65.9%	34.1%	65.9%	34.1%
34,645	JACKSON	8,120	2,398	5,722		3,324 D	29.5%	70.5%	29.5%	70.5%
10,413	JEFFERSON	1,836	665	1,171		506 D	36.2%	63.8%	36.2%	63.8%
3,440	LAFAYETTE	1,250	269	981		712 D	21.5%	78.5%	21.5%	78.5%
36,340	LAKE	12,929	9,132	3,797		5,335 R	70.6%	29.4%	70.6%	29.4%
23,404	LEE	9,356	5,528	3,828		1,700 R	59.1%	40.9%	59.1%	40.9%
51,590	LEON	13,604	5,604	8,000		2,396 D	41.2%	58.8%	41.2%	58.8%
10,637	LEVY	3,076	1,066	2,010		944 D	34.7%	65.3%	34.7%	65.3%
3,182	LIBERTY	1,274	237	1,037		800 D	18.6%	81.4%	18.6%	81.4%
14,197	MADISON	2,834	1,209	1,625		416 D	42.7%	57.3%	42.7%	57.3%
34,704	MANATEE	13,638	9,055	4,583		4,472 R	66.4%	33.6%	66.4%	33.6%
38,187	MARION	11,988	6,134	5,854		280 R	51.2%	48.8%	51.2%	48.8%
7,807	MARTIN	3,570	2,308	1,262		1,046 R	64.6%	35.4%	64.6%	35.4%
29,957	MONROE	7,884	2,943	4,941		1,998 D	37.3%	62.7%	37.3%	62.7%
12,811	NASSAU	4,241	1,731	2,510		779 D	40.8%	59.2%	40.8%	59.2%
27,533	OKALOOSA	7,730	2,355	5,375		3,020 D	30.5%	69.5%	30.5%	69.5%
3,454	OKEECHOBEE	1,420	539	881		342 D	38.0%	62.0%	38.0%	62.0%
114,950	ORANGE	41,954	29,813	12,141		17,672 R	71.1%	28.9%	71.1%	28.9%
11,406	OSCEOLA	5,033	3,133	1,900		1,233 R	62.2%	37.8%	62.2%	37.8%
114,688	PALM BEACH	42,318	28,595	13,723		14,872 R	67.6%	32.4%	67.6%	32.4%
20,529	PASCO	8,111	4,562	3,549		1,013 R	56.2%	43.8%	56.2%	43.8%
159,249	PINELLAS	78,056	55,691	22,365		33,326 R	71.3%	28.7%	71.3%	28.7%
123,997	POLK	40,430	20,874	19,556		1,318 R	51.6%	48.4%	51.6%	48.4%
23,615	PUTNAM	7,291	3,766	3,525		241 R	51.7%	48.3%	51.7%	48.3%
24,998	ST. JOHNS	9,068	4,702	4,366		336 R	51.9%	48.1%	51.9%	48.1%
20,180	ST. LUCIE	7,449	4,667	2,782		1,885 R	62.7%	37.3%	62.7%	37.3%
18,554	SANTA ROSA	6,119	1,744	4,375		2,631 D	28.5%	71.5%	28.5%	71.5%
28,827	SARASOTA	13,483	9,538	3,945		5,593 R	70.7%	29.3%	70.7%	29.3%
26,883	SEMINOLE	7,803	4,683	3,120		1,563 R	60.0%	40.0%	60.0%	40.0%
11,330	SUMTER	3,331	1,054	2,277		1,223 D	31.6%	68.4%	31.6%	68.4%

FLORIDA

PRESIDENT 1952

1950 Census Population	County	Total Vote	Republican	Democratic	Other	Rep.-Dem. Plurality	Percentage Total Vote Rep.	Percentage Total Vote Dem.	Percentage Major Vote Rep.	Percentage Major Vote Dem.
16,986	SUWANNEE	4,438	1,611	2,827		1,216 D	36.3%	63.7%	36.3%	63.7%
10,416	TAYLOR	2,531	744	1,787		1,043 D	29.4%	70.6%	29.4%	70.6%
8,906	UNION	1,236	268	968		700 D	21.7%	78.3%	21.7%	78.3%
74,229	VOLUSIA	31,725	19,815	11,910		7,905 R	62.5%	37.5%	62.5%	37.5%
5,258	WAKULLA	1,547	375	1,172		797 D	24.2%	75.8%	24.2%	75.8%
14,725	WALTON	5,095	1,502	3,593		2,091 D	29.5%	70.5%	29.5%	70.5%
11,888	WASHINGTON	3,363	1,100	2,263		1,163 D	32.7%	67.3%	32.7%	67.3%
2,771,305	TOTAL	989,337	544,036	444,950	351	99,086 R	55.0%	45.0%	55.0%	45.0%

FLORIDA

PRESIDENT 1948

1940 Census Population	County	Total Vote	Republican	Democratic	Other	Rep.-Dem. Plurality	Percentage: Total Vote Rep.	Percentage: Total Vote Dem.	Percentage: Major Vote Rep.	Percentage: Major Vote Dem.
38,607	ALACHUA	10,182	2,403	3,745	4,034	1,342 D	23.6%	36.8%	39.1%	60.9%
6,510	BAKER	1,176	112	849	215	737 D	9.5%	72.2%	11.7%	88.3%
20,686	BAY	7,312	928	5,168	1,216	4,240 D	12.7%	70.7%	15.2%	84.8%
8,717	BRADFORD	2,190	357	1,228	605	871 D	16.3%	56.1%	22.5%	77.5%
16,142	BREVARD	5,564	2,315	2,348	901	33 D	41.6%	42.2%	49.6%	50.4%
39,794	BROWARD	19,521	9,933	7,096	2,492	2,837 R	50.9%	36.4%	58.3%	41.7%
8,218	CALHOUN	1,794	128	1,404	262	1,276 D	7.1%	78.3%	8.4%	91.6%
3,663	CHARLOTTE	1,268	559	520	189	39 R	44.1%	41.0%	51.8%	48.2%
5,846	CITRUS	1,652	461	940	251	479 D	27.9%	56.9%	32.9%	67.1%
6,468	CLAY	2,742	722	1,544	476	822 D	26.3%	56.3%	31.9%	68.1%
5,102	COLLIER	880	247	362	271	115 D	28.1%	41.1%	40.6%	59.4%
16,859	COLUMBIA	3,332	553	1,797	982	1,244 D	16.6%	53.9%	23.5%	76.5%
267,739	DADE	111,512	41,301	59,681	10,530	18,380 D	37.0%	53.5%	40.9%	59.1%
7,792	DESOTO	2,082	569	1,157	356	588 D	27.3%	55.6%	33.0%	67.0%
7,018	DIXIE	1,271	111	862	298	751 D	8.7%	67.8%	11.4%	88.6%
210,143	DUVAL	59,695	15,379	28,567	15,749	13,188 D	25.8%	47.9%	35.0%	65.0%
74,667	ESCAMBIA	22,156	3,267	13,982	4,907	10,715 D	14.7%	63.1%	18.9%	81.1%
3,008	FLAGLER	648	154	153	341	1 R	23.8%	23.6%	50.2%	49.8%
5,991	FRANKLIN	1,062	130	635	297	505 D	12.2%	59.8%	17.0%	83.0%
31,450	GADSDEN	2,802	376	1,427	999	1,051 D	13.4%	50.9%	20.9%	79.1%
4,250	GILCHRIST	1,061	46	884	131	838 D	4.3%	83.3%	4.9%	95.1%
2,745	GLADES	555	150	274	131	124 D	27.0%	49.4%	35.4%	64.6%
6,951	GULF	1,579	146	1,219	214	1,073 D	9.2%	77.2%	10.7%	89.3%
9,778	HAMILTON	1,612	202	1,071	339	869 D	12.5%	66.4%	15.9%	84.1%
10,158	HARDEE	2,857	689	1,871	297	1,182 D	24.1%	65.5%	26.9%	73.1%
5,237	HENDRY	1,297	340	699	258	359 D	26.2%	53.9%	32.7%	67.3%
5,641	HERNANDO	1,672	441	825	406	384 D	26.4%	49.3%	34.8%	65.2%
9,246	HIGHLANDS	4,260	1,471	2,257	532	786 D	34.5%	53.0%	39.5%	60.5%
180,148	HILLSBOROUGH	41,286	13,529	18,854	8,903	5,325 D	32.8%	45.7%	41.8%	58.2%
15,447	HOLMES	3,196	492	1,799	905	1,307 D	15.4%	56.3%	21.5%	78.5%
8,957	INDIAN RIVER	2,448	1,134	1,055	259	79 R	46.3%	43.1%	51.8%	48.2%
34,428	JACKSON	5,750	648	3,169	1,933	2,521 D	11.3%	55.1%	17.0%	83.0%
12,032	JEFFERSON	1,323	153	700	470	547 D	11.6%	52.9%	17.9%	82.1%
4,405	LAFAYETTE	1,145	52	975	118	923 D	4.5%	85.2%	5.1%	94.9%
27,255	LAKE	8,279	3,579	3,474	1,226	105 R	43.2%	42.0%	50.7%	49.3%
17,488	LEE	5,797	2,276	1,883	1,638	393 R	39.3%	32.5%	54.7%	45.3%
31,646	LEON	6,161	1,149	3,607	1,405	2,458 D	18.6%	58.5%	24.2%	75.8%
12,550	LEVY	2,023	225	1,128	670	903 D	11.1%	55.8%	16.6%	83.4%
3,752	LIBERTY	849	30	737	82	707 D	3.5%	86.8%	3.9%	96.1%
16,190	MADISON	2,300	207	1,189	904	982 D	9.0%	51.7%	14.8%	85.2%
26,098	MANATEE	7,610	3,371	2,766	1,473	605 R	44.3%	36.3%	54.9%	45.1%
31,243	MARION	8,156	1,829	4,650	1,677	2,821 D	22.4%	57.0%	28.2%	71.8%
6,295	MARTIN	2,114	948	815	351	133 R	44.8%	38.6%	53.8%	46.2%
14,078	MONROE	4,503	548	3,759	196	3,211 D	12.2%	83.5%	12.7%	87.3%
10,826	NASSAU	2,755	540	1,518	697	978 D	19.6%	55.1%	26.2%	73.8%
12,900	OKALOOSA	4,007	486	2,519	1,002	2,033 D	12.1%	62.9%	16.2%	83.8%
3,000	OKEECHOBEE	1,048	179	784	85	605 D	17.1%	74.8%	18.6%	81.4%
70,074	ORANGE	25,652	11,971	10,063	3,618	1,908 R	46.7%	39.2%	54.3%	45.7%
10,119	OSCEOLA	3,532	1,575	1,577	380	2 D	44.6%	44.6%	50.0%	50.0%
79,989	PALM BEACH	24,115	10,996	9,408	3,711	1,588 R	45.6%	39.0%	53.9%	46.1%
13,981	PASCO	4,881	1,839	2,375	667	536 D	37.7%	48.7%	43.6%	56.4%
91,852	PINELLAS	44,524	24,900	15,724	3,900	9,176 R	55.9%	35.3%	61.3%	38.7%
86,665	POLK	22,892	7,692	12,034	3,166	4,342 D	33.6%	52.6%	39.0%	61.0%
18,698	PUTNAM	4,835	1,435	1,947	1,453	512 D	29.7%	40.3%	42.4%	57.6%
20,012	ST. JOHNS	6,305	1,840	1,994	2,471	154 D	29.2%	31.6%	48.0%	52.0%
11,871	ST. LUCIE	4,440	1,689	1,704	1,047	15 D	38.0%	38.4%	49.8%	50.2%
16,085	SANTA ROSA	3,524	549	2,316	659	1,767 D	15.6%	65.7%	19.2%	80.8%
16,106	SARASOTA	7,125	3,559	2,302	1,264	1,257 R	50.0%	32.3%	60.7%	39.3%
22,304	SEMINOLE	5,007	1,665	2,261	1,081	596 D	33.3%	45.2%	42.4%	57.6%
11,041	SUMTER	2,152	251	1,411	490	1,160 D	11.7%	65.6%	15.1%	84.9%

FLORIDA

PRESIDENT 1948

1940 Census Population	County	Total Vote	Republican	Democratic	Other	Rep.-Dem. Plurality	Percentage Total Vote Rep.	Percentage Total Vote Dem.	Percentage Major Vote Rep.	Percentage Major Vote Dem.
17,073	SUWANNEE	4,235	398	3,033	804	2,635 D	9.4%	71.6%	11.6%	88.4%
11,565	TAYLOR	1,999	216	1,354	429	1,138 D	10.8%	67.7%	13.8%	86.2%
7,094	UNION	874	55	594	225	539 D	6.3%	68.0%	8.5%	91.5%
53,710	VOLUSIA	19,678	7,764	9,202	2,712	1,438 D	39.5%	46.8%	45.8%	54.2%
5,463	WAKULLA	1,379	72	997	310	925 D	5.2%	72.3%	6.7%	93.3%
14,246	WALTON	3,799	652	2,366	781	1,714 D	17.2%	62.3%	21.6%	78.4%
12,302	WASHINGTON	2,211	297	1,380	534	1,083 D	13.4%	62.4%	17.7%	82.3%
1,897,414	TOTAL	577,643	194,280	281,988	101,375	87,708 D	33.6%	48.8%	40.8%	59.2%

FLORIDA

PRESIDENT 1944

1940 Census Population	County	Total Vote	Republican	Democratic	Other	Rep.-Dem. Plurality	Percentage Total Vote Rep.	Percentage Total Vote Dem.	Percentage Major Vote Rep.	Percentage Major Vote Dem.
38,607	ALACHUA	7,445	1,690	5,755		4,065 D	22.7%	77.3%	22.7%	77.3%
6,510	BAKER	1,264	127	1,137		1,010 D	10.0%	90.0%	10.0%	90.0%
20,686	BAY	7,443	1,126	6,317		5,191 D	15.1%	84.9%	15.1%	84.9%
8,717	BRADFORD	2,130	355	1,775		1,420 D	16.7%	83.3%	16.7%	83.3%
16,142	BREVARD	4,420	1,769	2,651		882 D	40.0%	60.0%	40.0%	60.0%
39,794	BROWARD	11,766	5,583	6,183		600 D	47.5%	52.5%	47.5%	52.5%
8,218	CALHOUN	1,711	207	1,504		1,297 D	12.1%	87.9%	12.1%	87.9%
3,663	CHARLOTTE	1,193	404	789		385 D	33.9%	66.1%	33.9%	66.1%
5,846	CITRUS	1,592	264	1,328		1,064 D	16.6%	83.4%	16.6%	83.4%
6,468	CLAY	1,771	520	1,251		731 D	29.4%	70.6%	29.4%	70.6%
5,102	COLLIER	820	180	640		460 D	22.0%	78.0%	22.0%	78.0%
16,859	COLUMBIA	3,004	537	2,467		1,930 D	17.9%	82.1%	17.9%	82.1%
267,739	DADE	90,457	30,357	60,100		29,743 D	33.6%	66.4%	33.6%	66.4%
7,792	DESOTO	2,265	543	1,722		1,179 D	24.0%	76.0%	24.0%	76.0%
7,018	DIXIE	1,188	84	1,104		1,020 D	7.1%	92.9%	7.1%	92.9%
210,143	DUVAL	49,087	12,220	36,867		24,647 D	24.9%	75.1%	24.9%	75.1%
74,667	ESCAMBIA	19,431	3,191	16,240		13,049 D	16.4%	83.6%	16.4%	83.6%
3,008	FLAGLER	515	114	401		287 D	22.1%	77.9%	22.1%	77.9%
5,991	FRANKLIN	1,278	102	1,176		1,074 D	8.0%	92.0%	8.0%	92.0%
31,450	GADSDEN	3,036	462	2,574		2,112 D	15.2%	84.8%	15.2%	84.8%
4,250	GILCHRIST	943	81	862		781 D	8.6%	91.4%	8.6%	91.4%
2,745	GLADES	537	164	373		209 D	30.5%	69.5%	30.5%	69.5%
6,951	GULF	1,350	83	1,267		1,184 D	6.1%	93.9%	6.1%	93.9%
9,778	HAMILTON	1,462	262	1,200		938 D	17.9%	82.1%	17.9%	82.1%
10,158	HARDEE	2,864	708	2,156		1,448 D	24.7%	75.3%	24.7%	75.3%
5,237	HENDRY	1,280	347	933		586 D	27.1%	72.9%	27.1%	72.9%
5,641	HERNANDO	1,348	346	1,002		656 D	25.7%	74.3%	25.7%	74.3%
9,246	HIGHLANDS	2,987	874	2,113		1,239 D	29.3%	70.7%	29.3%	70.7%
180,148	HILLSBOROUGH	41,398	10,252	31,146		20,894 D	24.8%	75.2%	24.8%	75.2%
15,447	HOLMES	3,560	908	2,652		1,744 D	25.5%	74.5%	25.5%	74.5%
8,957	INDIAN RIVER	2,051	759	1,292		533 D	37.0%	63.0%	37.0%	63.0%
34,428	JACKSON	5,584	951	4,633		3,682 D	17.0%	83.0%	17.0%	83.0%
12,032	JEFFERSON	1,259	188	1,071		883 D	14.9%	85.1%	14.9%	85.1%
4,405	LAFAYETTE	965	140	825		685 D	14.5%	85.5%	14.5%	85.5%
27,255	LAKE	7,016	2,693	4,323		1,630 D	38.4%	61.6%	38.4%	61.6%
17,488	LEE	5,218	1,865	3,353		1,488 D	35.7%	64.3%	35.7%	64.3%
31,646	LEON	5,340	835	4,505		3,670 D	15.6%	84.4%	15.6%	84.4%
12,550	LEVY	2,332	225	2,107		1,882 D	9.6%	90.4%	9.6%	90.4%
3,752	LIBERTY	664	38	626		588 D	5.7%	94.3%	5.7%	94.3%
16,190	MADISON	2,207	293	1,914		1,621 D	13.3%	86.7%	13.3%	86.7%
26,098	MANATEE	6,762	2,218	4,544		2,326 D	32.8%	67.2%	32.8%	67.2%
31,243	MARION	7,239	1,642	5,597		3,955 D	22.7%	77.3%	22.7%	77.3%
6,295	MARTIN	1,490	530	960		430 D	35.6%	64.4%	35.6%	64.4%
14,078	MONROE	4,448	566	3,882		3,316 D	12.7%	87.3%	12.7%	87.3%
10,826	NASSAU	2,419	527	1,892		1,365 D	21.8%	78.2%	21.8%	78.2%
12,900	OKALOOSA	3,503	626	2,877		2,251 D	17.9%	82.1%	17.9%	82.1%
3,000	OKEECHOBEE	872	119	753		634 D	13.6%	86.4%	13.6%	86.4%
70,074	ORANGE	20,834	8,826	12,008		3,182 D	42.4%	57.6%	42.4%	57.6%
10,119	OSCEOLA	3,163	1,400	1,763		363 D	44.3%	55.7%	44.3%	55.7%
79,989	PALM BEACH	18,721	7,628	11,093		3,465 D	40.7%	59.3%	40.7%	59.3%
13,981	PASCO	3,875	1,352	2,523		1,171 D	34.9%	65.1%	34.9%	65.1%
91,852	PINELLAS	33,914	14,340	19,574		5,234 D	42.3%	57.7%	42.3%	57.7%
86,665	POLK	18,302	5,150	13,152		8,002 D	28.1%	71.9%	28.1%	71.9%
18,698	PUTNAM	4,089	1,163	2,926		1,763 D	28.4%	71.6%	28.4%	71.6%
20,012	ST. JOHNS	5,346	1,582	3,764		2,182 D	29.6%	70.4%	29.6%	70.4%
11,871	ST. LUCIE	3,049	920	2,129		1,209 D	30.2%	69.8%	30.2%	69.8%
16,085	SANTA ROSA	3,469	862	2,607		1,745 D	24.8%	75.2%	24.8%	75.2%
16,106	SARASOTA	5,552	2,109	3,443		1,334 D	38.0%	62.0%	38.0%	62.0%
22,304	SEMINOLE	4,292	1,352	2,940		1,588 D	31.5%	68.5%	31.5%	68.5%
11,041	SUMTER	2,114	276	1,838		1,562 D	13.1%	86.9%	13.1%	86.9%

FLORIDA

PRESIDENT 1944

1940 Census Population	County	Total Vote	Republican	Democratic	Other	Rep.-Dem. Plurality	Percentage Total Vote Rep.	Total Vote Dem.	Major Vote Rep.	Major Vote Dem.
17,073	SUWANNEE	3,009	483	2,526		2,043 D	16.1%	83.9%	16.1%	83.9%
11,565	TAYLOR	1,993	165	1,828		1,663 D	8.3%	91.7%	8.3%	91.7%
7,094	UNION	1,007	102	905		803 D	10.1%	89.9%	10.1%	89.9%
53,710	VOLUSIA	14,394	6,161	8,233		2,072 D	42.8%	57.2%	42.8%	57.2%
5,463	WAKULLA	1,091	73	1,018		945 D	6.7%	93.3%	6.7%	93.3%
14,246	WALTON	3,258	689	2,569		1,880 D	21.1%	78.9%	21.1%	78.9%
12,302	WASHINGTON	2,206	507	1,699		1,192 D	23.0%	77.0%	23.0%	77.0%
1,897,414	TOTAL	482,803	143,215	339,377	211	196,162 D	29.7%	70.3%	29.7%	70.3%

FLORIDA

PRESIDENT 1940

1940 Census Population	County	Total Vote	Republican	Democratic	Other	Rep.-Dem. Plurality	Percentage Total Vote Rep.	Total Vote Dem.	Major Vote Rep.	Major Vote Dem.
38,607	ALACHUA	8,086	1,372	6,714		5,342 D	17.0%	83.0%	17.0%	83.0%
6,510	BAKER	1,466	114	1,352		1,238 D	7.8%	92.2%	7.8%	92.2%
20,686	BAY	5,837	684	5,153		4,469 D	11.7%	88.3%	11.7%	88.3%
8,717	BRADFORD	1,849	261	1,588		1,327 D	14.1%	85.9%	14.1%	85.9%
16,142	BREVARD	4,979	1,984	2,995		1,011 D	39.8%	60.2%	39.8%	60.2%
39,794	BROWARD	10,410	3,988	6,422		2,434 D	38.3%	61.7%	38.3%	61.7%
8,218	CALHOUN	1,893	171	1,722		1,551 D	9.0%	91.0%	9.0%	91.0%
3,663	CHARLOTTE	1,317	407	910		503 D	30.9%	69.1%	30.9%	69.1%
5,846	CITRUS	1,755	194	1,561		1,367 D	11.1%	88.9%	11.1%	88.9%
6,468	CLAY	1,986	498	1,488		990 D	25.1%	74.9%	25.1%	74.9%
5,102	COLLIER	965	156	809		653 D	16.2%	83.8%	16.2%	83.8%
16,859	COLUMBIA	3,331	443	2,888		2,445 D	13.3%	86.7%	13.3%	86.7%
267,739	DADE	77,145	25,224	51,921		26,697 D	32.7%	67.3%	32.7%	67.3%
7,792	DESOTO	2,414	526	1,888		1,362 D	21.8%	78.2%	21.8%	78.2%
7,018	DIXIE	1,504	84	1,420		1,336 D	5.6%	94.4%	5.6%	94.4%
210,143	DUVAL	50,180	9,177	41,003		31,826 D	18.3%	81.7%	18.3%	81.7%
74,667	ESCAMBIA	18,450	2,249	16,201		13,952 D	12.2%	87.8%	12.2%	87.8%
3,008	FLAGLER	689	136	553		417 D	19.7%	80.3%	19.7%	80.3%
5,991	FRANKLIN	1,502	102	1,400		1,298 D	6.8%	93.2%	6.8%	93.2%
31,450	GADSDEN	3,635	417	3,218		2,801 D	11.5%	88.5%	11.5%	88.5%
4,250	GILCHRIST	1,099	88	1,011		923 D	8.0%	92.0%	8.0%	92.0%
2,745	GLADES	644	180	464		284 D	28.0%	72.0%	28.0%	72.0%
6,951	GULF	1,747	105	1,642		1,537 D	6.0%	94.0%	6.0%	94.0%
9,778	HAMILTON	1,609	185	1,424		1,239 D	11.5%	88.5%	11.5%	88.5%
10,158	HARDEE	3,253	694	2,559		1,865 D	21.3%	78.7%	21.3%	78.7%
5,237	HENDRY	1,357	317	1,040		723 D	23.4%	76.6%	23.4%	76.6%
5,641	HERNANDO	1,532	381	1,151		770 D	24.9%	75.1%	24.9%	75.1%
9,246	HIGHLANDS	3,093	878	2,215		1,337 D	28.4%	71.6%	28.4%	71.6%
180,148	HILLSBOROUGH	38,543	7,805	30,738		22,933 D	20.3%	79.7%	20.3%	79.7%
15,447	HOLMES	3,571	887	2,684		1,797 D	24.8%	75.2%	24.8%	75.2%
8,957	INDIAN RIVER	2,391	904	1,487		583 D	37.8%	62.2%	37.8%	62.2%
34,428	JACKSON	6,473	866	5,607		4,741 D	13.4%	86.6%	13.4%	86.6%
12,032	JEFFERSON	1,627	215	1,412		1,197 D	13.2%	86.8%	13.2%	86.8%
4,405	LAFAYETTE	1,212	122	1,090		968 D	10.1%	89.9%	10.1%	89.9%
27,255	LAKE	7,981	2,659	5,322		2,663 D	33.3%	66.7%	33.3%	66.7%
17,488	LEE	5,153	1,622	3,531		1,909 D	31.5%	68.5%	31.5%	68.5%
31,646	LEON	6,042	583	5,459		4,876 D	9.6%	90.4%	9.6%	90.4%
12,550	LEVY	2,793	266	2,527		2,261 D	9.5%	90.5%	9.5%	90.5%
3,752	LIBERTY	1,066	119	947		828 D	11.2%	88.8%	11.2%	88.8%
16,190	MADISON	2,861	440	2,421		1,981 D	15.4%	84.6%	15.4%	84.6%
26,098	MANATEE	7,114	1,983	5,131		3,148 D	27.9%	72.1%	27.9%	72.1%
31,243	MARION	7,424	1,297	6,127		4,830 D	17.5%	82.5%	17.5%	82.5%
6,295	MARTIN	1,614	596	1,018		422 D	36.9%	63.1%	36.9%	63.1%
14,078	MONROE	4,565	463	4,102		3,639 D	10.1%	89.9%	10.1%	89.9%
10,826	NASSAU	2,309	421	1,888		1,467 D	18.2%	81.8%	18.2%	81.8%
12,900	OKALOOSA	3,693	690	3,003		2,313 D	18.7%	81.3%	18.7%	81.3%
3,000	OKEECHOBEE	944	122	822		700 D	12.9%	87.1%	12.9%	87.1%
70,074	ORANGE	21,019	8,198	12,821		4,623 D	39.0%	61.0%	39.0%	61.0%
10,119	OSCEOLA	3,443	1,428	2,015		587 D	41.5%	58.5%	41.5%	58.5%
79,989	PALM BEACH	19,255	7,371	11,884		4,513 D	38.3%	61.7%	38.3%	61.7%
13,981	PASCO	4,453	1,362	3,091		1,729 D	30.6%	69.4%	30.6%	69.4%
91,852	PINELLAS	32,268	13,327	18,941		5,614 D	41.3%	58.7%	41.3%	58.7%
86,665	POLK	23,254	5,564	17,690		12,126 D	23.9%	76.1%	23.9%	76.1%
18,698	PUTNAM	4,485	1,008	3,477		2,469 D	22.5%	77.5%	22.5%	77.5%
20,012	ST. JOHNS	5,425	1,303	4,122		2,819 D	24.0%	76.0%	24.0%	76.0%
11,871	ST. LUCIE	3,131	962	2,169		1,207 D	30.7%	69.3%	30.7%	69.3%
16,085	SANTA ROSA	3,566	656	2,910		2,254 D	18.4%	81.6%	18.4%	81.6%
16,106	SARASOTA	5,445	1,672	3,773		2,101 D	30.7%	69.3%	30.7%	69.3%
22,304	SEMINOLE	4,519	1,369	3,150		1,781 D	30.3%	69.7%	30.3%	69.7%
11,041	SUMTER	2,635	253	2,382		2,129 D	9.6%	90.4%	9.6%	90.4%

FLORIDA

PRESIDENT 1940

1940 Census Population	County	Total Vote	Republican	Democratic	Other	Rep.-Dem. Plurality	Percentage Total Vote Rep.	Percentage Total Vote Dem.	Percentage Major Vote Rep.	Percentage Major Vote Dem.
17,073	SUWANNEE	3,267	401	2,866		2,465 D	12.3%	87.7%	12.3%	87.7%
11,565	TAYLOR	2,697	198	2,499		2,301 D	7.3%	92.7%	7.3%	92.7%
7,094	UNION	1,119	95	1,024		929 D	8.5%	91.5%	8.5%	91.5%
53,710	VOLUSIA	16,533	6,509	10,024		3,515 D	39.4%	60.6%	39.4%	60.6%
5,463	WAKULLA	1,406	70	1,336		1,266 D	5.0%	95.0%	5.0%	95.0%
14,246	WALTON	3,911	694	3,217		2,523 D	17.7%	82.3%	17.7%	82.3%
12,302	WASHINGTON	2,558	643	1,915		1,272 D	25.1%	74.9%	25.1%	74.9%
1,897,414	TOTAL	485,640	126,158	359,334	148	233,176 D	26.0%	74.0%	26.0%	74.0%

FLORIDA

PRESIDENT 1936

1930 Census Population	County	Total Vote	Republican	Democratic	Other	Rep.-Dem. Plurality	Percentage: Total Vote Rep.	Total Vote Dem.	Major Vote Rep.	Major Vote Dem.
34,365	ALACHUA	5,678	890	4,788		3,898 D	15.7%	84.3%	15.7%	84.3%
6,273	BAKER	1,671	116	1,555		1,439 D	6.9%	93.1%	6.9%	93.1%
12,091	BAY	3,743	541	3,202		2,661 D	14.5%	85.5%	14.5%	85.5%
9,405	BRADFORD	1,787	293	1,494		1,201 D	16.4%	83.6%	16.4%	83.6%
13,283	BREVARD	3,447	1,147	2,300		1,153 D	33.3%	66.7%	33.3%	66.7%
20,094	BROWARD	6,291	1,906	4,385		2,479 D	30.3%	69.7%	30.3%	69.7%
7,298	CALHOUN	1,224	181	1,043		862 D	14.8%	85.2%	14.8%	85.2%
4,013	CHARLOTTE	1,330	548	782		234 D	41.2%	58.8%	41.2%	58.8%
5,516	CITRUS	1,525	159	1,366		1,207 D	10.4%	89.6%	10.4%	89.6%
6,859	CLAY	1,813	562	1,251		689 D	31.0%	69.0%	31.0%	69.0%
2,883	COLLIER	990	88	902		814 D	8.9%	91.1%	8.9%	91.1%
14,638	COLUMBIA	2,979	196	2,783		2,587 D	6.6%	93.4%	6.6%	93.4%
142,955	DADE	38,323	10,295	28,007	21	17,712 D	26.9%	73.1%	26.9%	73.1%
7,745	DESOTO	2,154	560	1,594		1,034 D	26.0%	74.0%	26.0%	74.0%
6,419	DIXIE	1,234	64	1,170		1,106 D	5.2%	94.8%	5.2%	94.8%
155,503	DUVAL	31,357	5,368	25,989		20,621 D	17.1%	82.9%	17.1%	82.9%
53,594	ESCAMBIA	10,705	1,567	9,138		7,571 D	14.6%	85.4%	14.6%	85.4%
2,466	FLAGLER	613	106	507		401 D	17.3%	82.7%	17.3%	82.7%
6,283	FRANKLIN	1,538	125	1,413		1,288 D	8.1%	91.9%	8.1%	91.9%
29,890	GADSDEN	2,770	198	2,572		2,374 D	7.1%	92.9%	7.1%	92.9%
4,137	GILCHRIST	892	56	836		780 D	6.3%	93.7%	6.3%	93.7%
2,762	GLADES	758	235	523		288 D	31.0%	69.0%	31.0%	69.0%
3,182	GULF	915	71	844		773 D	7.8%	92.2%	7.8%	92.2%
9,454	HAMILTON	1,627	73	1,554		1,481 D	4.5%	95.5%	4.5%	95.5%
10,348	HARDEE	2,986	844	2,142		1,298 D	28.3%	71.7%	28.3%	71.7%
3,492	HENDRY	975	234	741		507 D	24.0%	76.0%	24.0%	76.0%
4,948	HERNANDO	1,428	313	1,115		802 D	21.9%	78.1%	21.9%	78.1%
9,192	HIGHLANDS	2,752	842	1,898	12	1,056 D	30.6%	69.0%	30.7%	69.3%
153,519	HILLSBOROUGH	25,563	5,361	20,202		14,841 D	21.0%	79.0%	21.0%	79.0%
12,924	HOLMES	3,985	772	3,213		2,441 D	19.4%	80.6%	19.4%	80.6%
6,724	INDIAN RIVER	1,802	532	1,270		738 D	29.5%	70.5%	29.5%	70.5%
31,969	JACKSON	4,108	351	3,757		3,406 D	8.5%	91.5%	8.5%	91.5%
13,408	JEFFERSON	1,370	127	1,243		1,116 D	9.3%	90.7%	9.3%	90.7%
4,361	LAFAYETTE	1,164	80	1,084		1,004 D	6.9%	93.1%	6.9%	93.1%
23,161	LAKE	6,080	2,034	4,045	1	2,011 D	33.5%	66.5%	33.5%	66.5%
14,990	LEE	3,688	1,137	2,549	2	1,412 D	30.8%	69.1%	30.8%	69.2%
23,476	LEON	4,047	277	3,770		3,493 D	6.8%	93.2%	6.8%	93.2%
12,456	LEVY	2,186	183	2,003		1,820 D	8.4%	91.6%	8.4%	91.6%
4,067	LIBERTY	864	64	800		736 D	7.4%	92.6%	7.4%	92.6%
15,614	MADISON	2,462	184	2,278		2,094 D	7.5%	92.5%	7.5%	92.5%
22,502	MANATEE	4,942	1,455	3,487		2,032 D	29.4%	70.6%	29.4%	70.6%
29,578	MARION	5,424	760	4,664		3,904 D	14.0%	86.0%	14.0%	86.0%
5,111	MARTIN	1,105	327	778		451 D	29.6%	70.4%	29.6%	70.4%
13,624	MONROE	2,887	282	2,605		2,323 D	9.8%	90.2%	9.8%	90.2%
9,375	NASSAU	1,337	242	1,095		853 D	18.1%	81.9%	18.1%	81.9%
9,897	OKALOOSA	2,890	457	2,433		1,976 D	15.8%	84.2%	15.8%	84.2%
4,129	OKEECHOBEE	841	186	655		469 D	22.1%	77.9%	22.1%	77.9%
49,737	ORANGE	11,717	4,394	7,314	9	2,920 D	37.5%	62.4%	37.5%	62.5%
10,699	OSCEOLA	2,723	1,101	1,622		521 D	40.4%	59.6%	40.4%	59.6%
51,781	PALM BEACH	14,117	4,478	9,635	4	5,157 D	31.7%	68.3%	31.7%	68.3%
10,574	PASCO	3,388	1,159	2,229		1,070 D	34.2%	65.8%	34.2%	65.8%
62,149	PINELLAS	20,265	8,183	12,072	10	3,889 D	40.4%	59.6%	40.4%	59.6%
72,291	POLK	14,614	4,164	10,441	9	6,277 D	28.5%	71.4%	28.5%	71.5%
18,096	PUTNAM	3,684	975	2,709		1,734 D	26.5%	73.5%	26.5%	73.5%
18,676	ST. JOHNS	4,496	1,085	3,411		2,326 D	24.1%	75.9%	24.1%	75.9%
7,057	ST. LUCIE	2,443	497	1,946		1,449 D	20.3%	79.7%	20.3%	79.7%
14,083	SANTA ROSA	3,678	744	2,934		2,190 D	20.2%	79.8%	20.2%	79.8%
12,440	SARASOTA	3,473	1,055	2,418		1,363 D	30.4%	69.6%	30.4%	69.6%
18,735	SEMINOLE	3,477	897	2,580		1,683 D	25.8%	74.2%	25.8%	74.2%
10,644	SUMTER	2,458	734	1,724		990 D	29.9%	70.1%	29.9%	70.1%

FLORIDA

PRESIDENT 1936

1930 Census Population	County	Total Vote	Republican	Democratic	Other	Rep.-Dem. Plurality	Percentage Total Vote Rep.	Total Vote Dem.	Major Vote Rep.	Major Vote Dem.
15,731	SUWANNEE	3,065	202	2,863		2,661 D	6.6%	93.4%	6.6%	93.4%
13,136	TAYLOR	2,024	127	1,897		1,770 D	6.3%	93.7%	6.3%	93.7%
7,428	UNION	1,178	89	1,089		1,000 D	7.6%	92.4%	7.6%	92.4%
42,757	VOLUSIA	12,858	4,934	7,924		2,990 D	38.4%	61.6%	38.4%	61.6%
5,468	WAKULLA	1,462	45	1,417		1,372 D	3.1%	96.9%	3.1%	96.9%
14,576	WALTON	3,288	510	2,778		2,268 D	15.5%	84.5%	15.5%	84.5%
12,180	WASHINGTON	2,778	486	2,289	3	1,803 D	17.5%	82.4%	17.5%	82.5%
1,468,211	TOTAL	327,436	78,248	249,117	71	170,869 D	23.9%	76.1%	23.9%	76.1%

FLORIDA

PRESIDENT 1932

1930 Census Population	County	Total Vote	Republican	Democratic	Other	Rep.-Dem. Plurality	Percentage Total Vote Rep.	Total Vote Dem.	Major Vote Rep.	Major Vote Dem.
34,365	ALACHUA	4,489	983	3,506		2,523 D	21.9%	78.1%	21.9%	78.1%
6,273	BAKER	1,365	87	1,278		1,191 D	6.4%	93.6%	6.4%	93.6%
12,091	BAY	3,121	429	2,692		2,263 D	13.7%	86.3%	13.7%	86.3%
9,405	BRADFORD	1,527	210	1,317		1,107 D	13.8%	86.2%	13.8%	86.2%
13,283	BREVARD	2,808	956	1,852		896 D	34.0%	66.0%	34.0%	66.0%
20,094	BROWARD	5,010	1,717	3,293		1,576 D	34.3%	65.7%	34.3%	65.7%
7,298	CALHOUN	1,460	129	1,331		1,202 D	8.8%	91.2%	8.8%	91.2%
4,013	CHARLOTTE	1,350	396	954		558 D	29.3%	70.7%	29.3%	70.7%
5,516	CITRUS	1,356	147	1,209		1,062 D	10.8%	89.2%	10.8%	89.2%
6,859	CLAY	1,841	556	1,285		729 D	30.2%	69.8%	30.2%	69.8%
2,883	COLLIER	461	37	424		387 D	8.0%	92.0%	8.0%	92.0%
14,638	COLUMBIA	2,671	174	2,497		2,323 D	6.5%	93.5%	6.5%	93.5%
142,955	DADE	27,064	9,244	17,820		8,576 D	34.2%	65.8%	34.2%	65.8%
7,745	DESOTO	2,130	506	1,624		1,118 D	23.8%	76.2%	23.8%	76.2%
6,419	DIXIE	1,151	55	1,096		1,041 D	4.8%	95.2%	4.8%	95.2%
155,503	DUVAL	25,134	6,096	19,038		12,942 D	24.3%	75.7%	24.3%	75.7%
53,594	ESCAMBIA	7,840	1,658	6,182		4,524 D	21.1%	78.9%	21.1%	78.9%
2,466	FLAGLER	569	94	475		381 D	16.5%	83.5%	16.5%	83.5%
6,283	FRANKLIN	1,057	99	958		859 D	9.4%	90.6%	9.4%	90.6%
29,890	GADSDEN	1,970	105	1,865		1,760 D	5.3%	94.7%	5.3%	94.7%
4,137	GILCHRIST	871	57	814		757 D	6.5%	93.5%	6.5%	93.5%
2,762	GLADES	676	148	528		380 D	21.9%	78.1%	21.9%	78.1%
3,182	GULF	678	30	648		618 D	4.4%	95.6%	4.4%	95.6%
9,454	HAMILTON	1,271	110	1,161		1,051 D	8.7%	91.3%	8.7%	91.3%
10,348	HARDEE	3,051	566	2,485		1,919 D	18.6%	81.4%	18.6%	81.4%
3,492	HENDRY	846	163	683		520 D	19.3%	80.7%	19.3%	80.7%
4,948	HERNANDO	1,355	258	1,097		839 D	19.0%	81.0%	19.0%	81.0%
9,192	HIGHLANDS	2,376	851	1,525		674 D	35.8%	64.2%	35.8%	64.2%
153,519	HILLSBOROUGH	23,854	4,711	19,143		14,432 D	19.7%	80.3%	19.7%	80.3%
12,924	HOLMES	3,130	429	2,701		2,272 D	13.7%	86.3%	13.7%	86.3%
6,724	INDIAN RIVER	1,754	446	1,308		862 D	25.4%	74.6%	25.4%	74.6%
31,969	JACKSON	5,431	599	4,832		4,233 D	11.0%	89.0%	11.0%	89.0%
13,408	JEFFERSON	1,499	81	1,418		1,337 D	5.4%	94.6%	5.4%	94.6%
4,361	LAFAYETTE	956	27	929		902 D	2.8%	97.2%	2.8%	97.2%
23,161	LAKE	4,937	1,867	3,070		1,203 D	37.8%	62.2%	37.8%	62.2%
14,990	LEE	3,530	973	2,557		1,584 D	27.6%	72.4%	27.6%	72.4%
23,476	LEON	3,202	252	2,950		2,698 D	7.9%	92.1%	7.9%	92.1%
12,456	LEVY	1,744	123	1,621		1,498 D	7.1%	92.9%	7.1%	92.9%
4,067	LIBERTY	713	31	682		651 D	4.3%	95.7%	4.3%	95.7%
15,614	MADISON	1,823	221	1,602		1,381 D	12.1%	87.9%	12.1%	87.9%
22,502	MANATEE	4,174	1,280	2,894		1,614 D	30.7%	69.3%	30.7%	69.3%
29,578	MARION	4,170	962	3,208		2,246 D	23.1%	76.9%	23.1%	76.9%
5,111	MARTIN	1,204	379	825		446 D	31.5%	68.5%	31.5%	68.5%
13,624	MONROE	3,174	336	2,838		2,502 D	10.6%	89.4%	10.6%	89.4%
9,375	NASSAU	1,502	296	1,206		910 D	19.7%	80.3%	19.7%	80.3%
9,897	OKALOOSA	2,369	232	2,137		1,905 D	9.8%	90.2%	9.8%	90.2%
4,129	OKEECHOBEE	892	90	802		712 D	10.1%	89.9%	10.1%	89.9%
49,737	ORANGE	8,399	3,522	4,877		1,355 D	41.9%	58.1%	41.9%	58.1%
10,699	OSCEOLA	2,562	906	1,656		750 D	35.4%	64.6%	35.4%	64.6%
51,781	PALM BEACH	11,740	4,006	7,734		3,728 D	34.1%	65.9%	34.1%	65.9%
10,574	PASCO	3,310	806	2,504		1,698 D	24.4%	75.6%	24.4%	75.6%
62,149	PINELLAS	16,694	7,024	9,670		2,646 D	42.1%	57.9%	42.1%	57.9%
72,291	POLK	12,953	3,490	9,463		5,973 D	26.9%	73.1%	26.9%	73.1%
18,096	PUTNAM	3,220	911	2,309		1,398 D	28.3%	71.7%	28.3%	71.7%
18,676	ST. JOHNS	4,609	1,265	3,344		2,079 D	27.4%	72.6%	27.4%	72.6%
7,057	ST. LUCIE	1,992	390	1,602		1,212 D	19.6%	80.4%	19.6%	80.4%
14,083	SANTA ROSA	3,121	315	2,806		2,491 D	10.1%	89.9%	10.1%	89.9%
12,440	SARASOTA	2,579	667	1,912		1,245 D	25.9%	74.1%	25.9%	74.1%
18,735	SEMINOLE	3,090	948	2,142		1,194 D	30.7%	69.3%	30.7%	69.3%
10,644	SUMTER	2,414	276	2,138		1,862 D	11.4%	88.6%	11.4%	88.6%

FLORIDA

PRESIDENT 1932

1930 Census Population	County	Total Vote	Republican	Democratic	Other	Rep.-Dem. Plurality	Percentage Total Vote Rep.	Percentage Total Vote Dem.	Percentage Major Vote Rep.	Percentage Major Vote Dem.
15,731	SUWANNEE	2,286	163	2,123		1,960 D	7.1%	92.9%	7.1%	92.9%
13,136	TAYLOR	1,577	130	1,447		1,317 D	8.2%	91.8%	8.2%	91.8%
7,428	UNION	957	60	897		837 D	6.3%	93.7%	6.3%	93.7%
42,757	VOLUSIA	11,811	4,425	7,386		2,961 D	37.5%	62.5%	37.5%	62.5%
5,468	WAKULLA	1,056	20	1,036		1,016 D	1.9%	98.1%	1.9%	98.1%
14,576	WALTON	2,782	305	2,477		2,172 D	11.0%	89.0%	11.0%	89.0%
12,180	WASHINGTON	2,769	345	2,424		2,079 D	12.5%	87.5%	12.5%	87.5%
1,468,211	TOTAL	276,943	69,170	206,307	1,466	137,137 D	25.0%	74.5%	25.1%	74.9%

FLORIDA

PRESIDENT 1928

1920 Census Population	County	Total Vote	Republican	Democratic	Other	Rep.-Dem. Plurality	Percentage: Total Vote Rep.	Total Vote Dem.	Major Vote Rep.	Major Vote Dem.
31,689	ALACHUA	4,008	1,824	1,965	219	141 D	45.5%	49.0%	48.1%	51.9%
5,622	BAKER	934	676	242	16	434 R	72.4%	25.9%	73.6%	26.4%
11,407	BAY	2,200	974	1,190	36	216 D	44.3%	54.1%	45.0%	55.0%
12,503	BRADFORD	1,221	534	679	8	145 D	43.7%	55.6%	44.0%	56.0%
8,505	BREVARD	2,946	1,830	1,063	53	767 R	62.1%	36.1%	63.3%	36.7%
5,135	BROWARD	4,540	2,889	1,564	87	1,325 R	63.6%	34.4%	64.9%	35.1%
8,775	CALHOUN	1,168	409	727	32	318 D	35.0%	62.2%	36.0%	64.0%
	CHARLOTTE	1,064	593	441	30	152 R	55.7%	41.4%	57.4%	42.6%
5,220	CITRUS	1,337	505	816	16	311 D	37.8%	61.0%	38.2%	61.8%
5,621	CLAY	1,510	1,088	394	28	694 R	72.1%	26.1%	73.4%	26.6%
	COLLIER	408	151	256	1	105 D	37.0%	62.7%	37.1%	62.9%
14,290	COLUMBIA	1,716	418	1,276	22	858 D	24.4%	74.4%	24.7%	75.3%
42,753	DADE	26,368	15,860	10,136	372	5,724 R	60.1%	38.4%	61.0%	39.0%
25,434	DESOTO	2,158	1,382	748	28	634 R	64.0%	34.7%	64.9%	35.1%
	DIXIE	805	463	342		121 R	57.5%	42.5%	57.5%	42.5%
113,540	DUVAL	26,689	16,919	9,316	454	7,603 R	63.4%	34.9%	64.5%	35.5%
49,386	ESCAMBIA	8,333	4,443	3,772	118	671 R	53.3%	45.3%	54.1%	45.9%
2,442	FLAGLER	559	325	219	15	106 R	58.1%	39.2%	59.7%	40.3%
5,318	FRANKLIN	754	334	417	3	83 D	44.3%	55.3%	44.5%	55.5%
23,539	GADSDEN	1,551	346	1,184	21	838 D	22.3%	76.3%	22.6%	77.4%
	GILCHRIST	550	125	392	33	267 D	22.7%	71.3%	24.2%	75.8%
	GLADES	616	331	281	4	50 R	53.7%	45.6%	54.1%	45.9%
	GULF	446	156	275	15	119 D	35.0%	61.7%	36.2%	63.8%
9,873	HAMILTON	992	167	741	84	574 D	16.8%	74.7%	18.4%	81.6%
	HARDEE	2,979	2,087	826	66	1,261 R	70.1%	27.7%	71.6%	28.4%
	HENDRY	622	337	266	19	71 R	54.2%	42.8%	55.9%	44.1%
4,548	HERNANDO	1,383	661	701	21	40 D	47.8%	50.7%	48.5%	51.5%
	HIGHLANDS	2,094	1,393	669	32	724 R	66.5%	31.9%	67.6%	32.4%
88,257	HILLSBOROUGH	22,088	11,703	9,993	392	1,710 R	53.0%	45.2%	53.9%	46.1%
12,850	HOLMES	3,036	2,260	735	41	1,525 R	74.4%	24.2%	75.5%	24.5%
	INDIAN RIVER	1,523	847	657	19	190 R	55.6%	43.1%	56.3%	43.7%
31,224	JACKSON	3,946	1,398	2,516	32	1,118 D	35.4%	63.8%	35.7%	64.3%
14,502	JEFFERSON	1,162	235	919	8	684 D	20.2%	79.1%	20.4%	79.6%
6,242	LAFAYETTE	575	135	435	5	300 D	23.5%	75.7%	23.7%	76.3%
12,744	LAKE	4,969	3,383	1,474	112	1,909 R	68.1%	29.7%	69.7%	30.3%
9,540	LEE	3,258	2,058	1,154	46	904 R	63.2%	35.4%	64.1%	35.9%
18,059	LEON	2,549	630	1,888	31	1,258 D	24.7%	74.1%	25.0%	75.0%
9,921	LEVY	1,538	711	797	30	86 D	46.2%	51.8%	47.1%	52.9%
5,006	LIBERTY	375	147	226	2	79 D	39.2%	60.3%	39.4%	60.6%
16,516	MADISON	1,035	266	769		503 D	25.7%	74.3%	25.7%	74.3%
18,712	MANATEE	4,235	2,705	1,472	58	1,233 R	63.9%	34.8%	64.8%	35.2%
23,968	MARION	3,873	1,927	1,863	83	64 R	49.8%	48.1%	50.8%	49.2%
	MARTIN	1,211	703	474	34	229 R	58.1%	39.1%	59.7%	40.3%
19,550	MONROE	3,092	1,142	1,899	51	757 D	36.9%	61.4%	37.6%	62.4%
11,340	NASSAU	1,325	863	445	17	418 R	65.1%	33.6%	66.0%	34.0%
9,360	OKALOOSA	1,905	1,385	503	17	882 R	72.7%	26.4%	73.4%	26.6%
2,132	OKEECHOBEE	954	657	287	10	370 R	68.9%	30.1%	69.6%	30.4%
19,890	ORANGE	9,315	6,524	2,616	175	3,908 R	70.0%	28.1%	71.4%	28.6%
7,195	OSCEOLA	2,921	1,760	1,127	34	633 R	60.3%	38.6%	61.0%	39.0%
18,654	PALM BEACH	8,248	5,298	2,652	298	2,646 R	64.2%	32.2%	66.6%	33.4%
8,802	PASCO	2,932	1,591	1,308	33	283 R	54.3%	44.6%	54.9%	45.1%
28,265	PINELLAS	14,151	10,545	3,439	167	7,106 R	74.5%	24.3%	75.4%	24.6%
38,661	POLK	12,386	7,460	4,576	350	2,884 R	60.2%	36.9%	62.0%	38.0%
14,568	PUTNAM	3,341	2,105	1,156	80	949 R	63.0%	34.6%	64.6%	35.4%
13,061	ST. JOHNS	5,291	1,939	3,307	45	1,368 D	36.6%	62.5%	37.0%	63.0%
7,886	ST. LUCIE	1,759	983	741	35	242 R	55.9%	42.1%	57.0%	43.0%
13,670	SANTA ROSA	2,201	1,628	541	32	1,087 R	74.0%	24.6%	75.1%	24.9%
	SARASOTA	2,839	1,603	1,181	55	422 R	56.5%	41.6%	57.6%	42.4%
10,986	SEMINOLE	3,036	1,788	1,187	61	601 R	58.9%	39.1%	60.1%	39.9%
7,851	SUMTER	2,072	1,152	909	11	243 R	55.6%	43.9%	55.9%	44.1%

FLORIDA

PRESIDENT 1928

1920 Census Population	County	Total Vote	Republican	Democratic	Other	Rep.-Dem. Plurality	Percentage Total Vote Rep.	Total Vote Dem.	Major Vote Rep.	Major Vote Dem.
19,789	SUWANNEE	1,913	606	1,286	21	680 D	31.7%	67.2%	32.0%	68.0%
11,219	TAYLOR	1,222	465	739	18	274 D	38.1%	60.5%	38.6%	61.4%
	UNION	689	177	503	9	326 D	25.7%	73.0%	26.0%	74.0%
23,374	VOLUSIA	9,808	6,648	3,043	117	3,605 R	67.8%	31.0%	68.6%	31.4%
5,129	WAKULLA	542	66	470	6	404 D	12.2%	86.7%	12.3%	87.7%
12,119	WALTON	2,404	1,475	908	21	567 R	61.4%	37.8%	61.9%	38.1%
11,828	WASHINGTON	2,398	1,672	671	55	1,001 R	69.7%	28.0%	71.4%	28.6%
968,470	TOTAL	252,068	145,860	101,764	4,444	44,096 R	57.9%	40.4%	58.9%	41.1%

FLORIDA

PRESIDENT 1924

1920 Census Population	County	Total Vote	Republican	Democratic	Other	Rep.-Dem. Plurality	Percentage Total Vote Rep.	Total Vote Dem.	Major Vote Rep.	Major Vote Dem.
31,689	ALACHUA	2,794	528	1,995	271	1,467 D	18.9%	71.4%	20.9%	79.1%
5,622	BAKER	379	124	215	40	91 D	32.7%	56.7%	36.6%	63.4%
11,407	BAY	1,248	318	838	92	520 D	25.5%	67.1%	27.5%	72.5%
12,503	BRADFORD	660	94	539	27	445 D	14.2%	81.7%	14.8%	85.2%
8,505	BREVARD	1,505	515	872	118	357 D	34.2%	57.9%	37.1%	62.9%
5,135	BROWARD	982	407	421	154	14 D	41.4%	42.9%	49.2%	50.8%
8,775	CALHOUN	519	56	406	57	350 D	10.8%	78.2%	12.1%	87.9%
	CHARLOTTE	535	167	321	47	154 D	31.2%	60.0%	34.2%	65.8%
5,220	CITRUS	505	30	423	52	393 D	5.9%	83.8%	6.6%	93.4%
5,621	CLAY	593	171	339	83	168 D	28.8%	57.2%	33.5%	66.5%
	COLLIER	180	15	148	17	133 D	8.3%	82.2%	9.2%	90.8%
14,290	COLUMBIA	951	85	776	90	691 D	8.9%	81.6%	9.9%	90.1%
42,753	DADE	10,583	2,753	3,474	4,356	721 D	26.0%	32.8%	44.2%	55.8%
25,434	DESOTO	915	230	641	44	411 D	25.1%	70.1%	26.4%	73.6%
	DIXIE	273	14	257	2	243 D	5.1%	94.1%	5.2%	94.8%
113,540	DUVAL	11,376	3,291	5,908	2,177	2,617 D	28.9%	51.9%	35.8%	64.2%
49,386	ESCAMBIA	4,342	1,274	2,290	778	1,016 D	29.3%	52.7%	35.7%	64.3%
2,442	FLAGLER	372	75	202	95	127 D	20.2%	54.3%	27.1%	72.9%
5,318	FRANKLIN	545	109	417	19	308 D	20.0%	76.5%	20.7%	79.3%
23,539	GADSDEN	802	47	681	74	634 D	5.9%	84.9%	6.5%	93.5%
	GILCHRIST	—	—	—	—	—	—	—	—	—
	GLADES	347	83	212	52	129 D	23.9%	61.1%	28.1%	71.9%
	GULF	—	—	—	—	—	—	—	—	—
9,873	HAMILTON	822	143	619	60	476 D	17.4%	75.3%	18.8%	81.2%
	HARDEE	1,165	264	795	106	531 D	22.7%	68.2%	24.9%	75.1%
	HENDRY	172	21	132	19	111 D	12.2%	76.7%	13.7%	86.3%
4,548	HERNANDO	401	59	300	42	241 D	14.7%	74.8%	16.4%	83.6%
	HIGHLANDS	794	265	457	72	192 D	33.4%	57.6%	36.7%	63.3%
88,257	HILLSBOROUGH	7,180	1,585	4,470	1,125	2,885 D	22.1%	62.3%	26.2%	73.8%
12,850	HOLMES	1,177	377	658	142	281 D	32.0%	55.9%	36.4%	63.6%
	INDIAN RIVER	—	—	—	—	—	—	—	—	—
31,224	JACKSON	2,193	320	1,771	102	1,451 D	14.6%	80.8%	15.3%	84.7%
14,502	JEFFERSON	681	66	566	49	500 D	9.7%	83.1%	10.4%	89.6%
6,242	LAFAYETTE	406	33	358	15	325 D	8.1%	88.2%	8.4%	91.6%
12,744	LAKE	2,600	948	1,381	271	433 D	36.5%	53.1%	40.7%	59.3%
9,540	LEE	1,622	552	845	225	293 D	34.0%	52.1%	39.5%	60.5%
18,059	LEON	1,110	92	947	71	855 D	8.3%	85.3%	8.9%	91.1%
9,921	LEVY	816	214	524	78	310 D	26.2%	64.2%	29.0%	71.0%
5,006	LIBERTY	224	18	193	13	175 D	8.0%	86.2%	8.5%	91.5%
16,516	MADISON	593	23	538	32	515 D	3.9%	90.7%	4.1%	95.9%
18,712	MANATEE	1,933	629	1,064	240	435 D	32.5%	55.0%	37.2%	62.8%
23,968	MARION	2,081	359	1,528	194	1,169 D	17.3%	73.4%	19.0%	81.0%
	MARTIN	—	—	—	—	—	—	—	—	—
19,550	MONROE	1,232	262	835	135	573 D	21.3%	67.8%	23.9%	76.1%
11,340	NASSAU	765	106	617	42	511 D	13.9%	80.7%	14.7%	85.3%
9,360	OKALOOSA	953	183	642	128	459 D	19.2%	67.4%	22.2%	77.8%
2,132	OKEECHOBEE	272	57	182	33	125 D	21.0%	66.9%	23.8%	76.2%
19,890	ORANGE	4,108	1,653	1,883	572	230 D	40.2%	45.8%	46.7%	53.3%
7,195	OSCEOLA	1,761	589	884	288	295 D	33.4%	50.2%	40.0%	60.0%
18,654	PALM BEACH	3,741	1,726	1,543	472	183 R	46.1%	41.2%	52.8%	47.2%
8,802	PASCO	1,456	472	780	204	308 D	32.4%	53.6%	37.7%	62.3%
28,265	PINELLAS	6,043	2,872	2,633	538	239 R	47.5%	43.6%	52.2%	47.8%
38,661	POLK	5,296	1,530	3,070	696	1,540 D	28.9%	58.0%	33.3%	66.7%
14,568	PUTNAM	1,634	574	889	171	315 D	35.1%	54.4%	39.2%	60.8%
13,061	ST. JOHNS	1,884	517	1,023	344	506 D	27.4%	54.3%	33.6%	66.4%
7,886	ST. LUCIE	1,418	524	722	172	198 D	37.0%	50.9%	42.1%	57.9%
13,670	SANTA ROSA	981	229	693	59	464 D	23.3%	70.6%	24.8%	75.2%
	SARASOTA	462	187	204	71	17 D	40.5%	44.2%	47.8%	52.2%
10,986	SEMINOLE	1,586	372	945	269	573 D	23.5%	59.6%	28.2%	71.8%
7,851	SUMTER	678	108	481	89	373 D	15.9%	70.9%	18.3%	81.7%

FLORIDA

PRESIDENT 1924

1920 Census Population	County	Total Vote	Republican	Democratic	Other	Rep.-Dem. Plurality	Percentage Total Vote Rep.	Percentage Total Vote Dem.	Percentage Major Vote Rep.	Percentage Major Vote Dem.
19,789	SUWANNEE	1,168	111	977	80	866 D	9.5%	83.6%	10.2%	89.8%
11,219	TAYLOR	608	100	476	32	376 D	16.4%	78.3%	17.4%	82.6%
	UNION	348	16	322	10	306 D	4.6%	92.5%	4.7%	95.3%
23,374	VOLUSIA	3,995	1,631	2,042	322	411 D	40.8%	51.1%	44.4%	55.6%
5,129	WAKULLA	389	34	332	23	298 D	8.7%	85.3%	9.3%	90.7%
12,119	WALTON	1,172	220	825	127	605 D	18.8%	70.4%	21.1%	78.9%
11,828	WASHINGTON	832	206	562	64	356 D	24.8%	67.5%	26.8%	73.2%
968,470	TOTAL	109,158	30,633	62,083	16,442	31,450 D	28.1%	56.9%	33.0%	67.0%

FLORIDA

PRESIDENT 1920

1920 Census Population	County	Total Vote	Republican	Democratic	Other	Rep.-Dem. Plurality	Percentage Total Vote Rep.	Total Vote Dem.	Major Vote Rep.	Major Vote Dem.
31,689	ALACHUA	4,564	1,119	3,310	135	2,191 D	24.5%	72.5%	25.3%	74.7%
5,622	BAKER	508	115	346	47	231 D	22.6%	68.1%	24.9%	75.1%
11,407	BAY	1,490	551	818	121	267 D	37.0%	54.9%	40.2%	59.8%
12,503	BRADFORD	1,610	248	1,269	93	1,021 D	15.4%	78.8%	16.3%	83.7%
8,505	BREVARD	1,677	659	894	124	235 D	39.3%	53.3%	42.4%	57.6%
5,135	BROWARD	999	442	415	142	27 R	44.2%	41.5%	51.6%	48.4%
8,775	CALHOUN	1,098	99	861	138	762 D	9.0%	78.4%	10.3%	89.7%
	CHARLOTTE	—	—	—	—	—	—	—	—	—
5,220	CITRUS	788	94	651	43	557 D	11.9%	82.6%	12.6%	87.4%
5,621	CLAY	1,123	486	558	79	72 D	43.3%	49.7%	46.6%	53.4%
	COLLIER	—	—	—	—	—	—	—	—	—
14,290	COLUMBIA	1,543	162	1,248	133	1,086 D	10.5%	80.9%	11.5%	88.5%
42,753	DADE	8,078	3,077	4,288	713	1,211 D	38.1%	53.1%	41.8%	58.2%
25,434	DESOTO	3,844	1,077	2,496	271	1,419 D	28.0%	64.9%	30.1%	69.9%
	DIXIE	—	—	—	—	—	—	—	—	—
113,540	DUVAL	21,257	6,628	13,650	979	7,022 D	31.2%	64.2%	32.7%	67.3%
49,386	ESCAMBIA	5,345	1,227	3,485	633	2,258 D	23.0%	65.2%	26.0%	74.0%
2,442	FLAGLER	374	74	206	94	132 D	19.8%	55.1%	26.4%	73.6%
5,318	FRANKLIN	946	276	587	83	311 D	29.2%	62.1%	32.0%	68.0%
23,539	GADSDEN	1,988	38	1,922	28	1,884 D	1.9%	96.7%	1.9%	98.1%
	GILCHRIST	—	—	—	—	—	—	—	—	—
	GLADES	—	—	—	—	—	—	—	—	—
	GULF	—	—	—	—	—	—	—	—	—
9,873	HAMILTON	949	151	706	92	555 D	15.9%	74.4%	17.6%	82.4%
	HARDEE	—	—	—	—	—	—	—	—	—
	HENDRY	—	—	—	—	—	—	—	—	—
4,548	HERNANDO	818	132	622	64	490 D	16.1%	76.0%	17.5%	82.5%
	HIGHLANDS	—	—	—	—	—	—	—	—	—
88,257	HILLSBOROUGH	12,349	3,772	6,976	1,601	3,204 D	30.5%	56.5%	35.1%	64.9%
12,850	HOLMES	1,600	537	869	194	332 D	33.6%	54.3%	38.2%	61.8%
	INDIAN RIVER	—	—	—	—	—	—	—	—	—
31,224	JACKSON	3,104	508	2,443	153	1,935 D	16.4%	78.7%	17.2%	82.8%
14,502	JEFFERSON	1,046	239	754	53	515 D	22.8%	72.1%	24.1%	75.9%
6,242	LAFAYETTE	714	69	618	27	549 D	9.7%	86.6%	10.0%	90.0%
12,744	LAKE	2,540	734	1,720	86	986 D	28.9%	67.7%	29.9%	70.1%
9,540	LEE	1,694	626	938	130	312 D	37.0%	55.4%	40.0%	60.0%
18,059	LEON	1,968	452	1,412	104	960 D	23.0%	71.7%	24.2%	75.8%
9,921	LEVY	1,278	377	882	19	505 D	29.5%	69.0%	29.9%	70.1%
5,006	LIBERTY	454	5	416	33	411 D	1.1%	91.6%	1.2%	98.8%
16,516	MADISON	986	30	920	36	890 D	3.0%	93.3%	3.2%	96.8%
18,712	MANATEE	2,867	884	1,790	193	906 D	30.8%	62.4%	33.1%	66.9%
23,968	MARION	3,902	1,232	2,436	234	1,204 D	31.6%	62.4%	33.6%	66.4%
	MARTIN	—	—	—	—	—	—	—	—	—
19,550	MONROE	1,747	510	979	258	469 D	29.2%	56.0%	34.3%	65.7%
11,340	NASSAU	1,248	281	900	67	619 D	22.5%	72.1%	23.8%	76.2%
9,360	OKALOOSA	1,003	411	568	24	157 D	41.0%	56.6%	42.0%	58.0%
2,132	OKEECHOBEE	364	58	237	69	179 D	15.9%	65.1%	19.7%	80.3%
19,890	ORANGE	3,668	1,447	2,035	186	588 D	39.4%	55.5%	41.6%	58.4%
7,195	OSCEOLA	1,871	1,035	728	108	307 R	55.3%	38.9%	58.7%	41.3%
18,654	PALM BEACH	3,886	1,892	1,488	506	404 R	48.7%	38.3%	56.0%	44.0%
8,802	PASCO	1,884	630	1,166	88	536 D	33.4%	61.9%	35.1%	64.9%
28,265	PINELLAS	5,819	2,529	2,848	442	319 D	43.5%	48.9%	47.0%	53.0%
38,661	POLK	5,949	1,782	3,918	249	2,136 D	30.0%	65.9%	31.3%	68.7%
14,568	PUTNAM	2,915	1,181	1,557	177	376 D	40.5%	53.4%	43.1%	56.9%
13,061	ST. JOHNS	3,215	1,221	1,810	184	589 D	38.0%	56.3%	40.3%	59.7%
7,886	ST. LUCIE	1,997	707	1,167	123	460 D	35.4%	58.4%	37.7%	62.3%
13,670	SANTA ROSA	1,153	333	813	7	480 D	28.9%	70.5%	29.1%	70.9%
	SARASOTA	—	—	—	—	—	—	—	—	—
10,986	SEMINOLE	2,376	767	1,485	124	718 D	32.3%	62.5%	34.1%	65.9%
7,851	SUMTER	1,155	219	921	15	702 D	19.0%	79.7%	19.2%	80.8%

FLORIDA

PRESIDENT 1920

1920 Census Population	County	Total Vote	Republican	Democratic	Other	Rep.-Dem. Plurality	Percentage Total Vote Rep.	Total Vote Dem.	Major Vote Rep.	Major Vote Dem.
19,789	SUWANNEE	2,048	382	1,486	180	1,104 D	18.7%	72.6%	20.4%	79.6%
11,219	TAYLOR	722	128	563	31	435 D	17.7%	78.0%	18.5%	81.5%
	UNION	—	—	—	—	—	—	—	—	—
23,374	VOLUSIA	5,266	2,175	2,763	328	588 D	41.3%	52.5%	44.0%	56.0%
5,129	WAKULLA	668	119	530	19	411 D	17.8%	79.3%	18.3%	81.7%
12,119	WALTON	2,019	619	1,297	103	678 D	30.7%	64.2%	32.3%	67.7%
11,828	WASHINGTON	1,210	307	750	153	443 D	25.4%	62.0%	29.0%	71.0%
968,470	TOTAL	145,684	44,853	90,515	10,316	45,662 D	30.8%	62.1%	33.1%	66.9%

FLORIDA

In 1921 Charlotte, Glades, Hardee and Highlands counties were organized from parts of De Soto county; Union county was organized from part of Bradford county; Dixie county was organized from part of Lafayette county; Sarasota county was organized from part of Manatee county. In 1923 Collier and Hendry counties were organized from parts of Lee county. In 1925 Gulf county was organized from part of Calhoun county; Indian River county was organized from part of St. Lucie county; Martin county was organized from parts of Palm Beach and St. Lucie counties. In 1926 Gilchrist county was organized from part of Alachua county. Population figures are not available for these counties created between the 1920 and 1930 Census.

ELECTION NOTES

1956 Other vote was scattered write-in.

1952 Other vote was scattered write-in. The statewide total in the other vote column is these write-in votes which were not available by county.

1948 Other vote was 89,755 Thurmond (States Rights); 11,620 Wallace (Progressive). States Rights candidates carried Alachua, Flagler and St. Johns counties and ran second in almost all counties in the "Panhandle".

1944 Other vote was scattered write-in. The statewide total in the other vote column is these write-in votes which were not available by county.

1940 Other vote was scattered write-in. The statewide total in the other vote column is these write-in votes which were not available by county..

1936 Other vote was scattered write-in.

1932 Other vote was 775 Thomas (Socialist); 691 scattered write-in. The statewide total in the other vote column is the Socialist and write-in votes which were not reported by county.

1928 Other vote was 2,284 Thomas (Socialist); 2,160 Foster (Communist).

1924 Other vote was 8,625 LaFollette (Progressive); 5,498 Faris (Prohibition); 2,319 Nations (American).

1920 Other vote was 5,189 Debs (Socialist); 5,127 Watkins (Prohibition). The Republican vote is the vote cast for the single elector candidate who ran on both the regular Republican and White Republican elector tickets.

GEORGIA

POPULAR VOTE FOR PRESIDENT 1920 TO 1956

		Republican		Democratic				Percentage			
								Total Vote		Major Vote	
Year	Total Vote	Vote	Candidate	Vote	Candidate	Other Vote	Plurality	Rep.	Dem.	Rep.	Dem.
1956	669,655	222,778	Eisenhower, Dwight D.	444,688	Stevenson, Adlai E.	2,189	221,910 D	33.3%	66.4%	33.4%	66.6%
1952	655,785	198,961	Eisenhower, Dwight D.	456,823	Stevenson, Adlai E.	1	257,862 D	30.3%	69.7%	30.3%	69.7%
1948 **	418,844	76,691	Dewey, Thomas E.	254,646	Truman, Harry S.	87,507	169,511 D	18.3%	60.8%	23.1%	76.9%
1944	328,129	59,900	Dewey, Thomas E.	268,187	Roosevelt, Franklin D.	42	208,287 D	18.3%	81.7%	18.3%	81.7%
1940	312,686	46,495	Willkie, Wendell	265,194	Roosevelt, Franklin D.	997	218,699 D	14.9%	84.8%	14.9%	85.1%
1936	293,170	36,943	Landon, Alfred M.	255,363	Roosevelt, Franklin D.	864	218,420 D	12.6%	87.1%	12.6%	87.4%
1932	255,590	19,863	Hoover, Herbert C.	234,118	Roosevelt, Franklin D.	1,609	214,255 D	7.8%	91.6%	7.8%	92.2%
1928	231,592	101,800	Hoover, Herbert C.	129,604	Smith, Alfred E.	188	27,804 D	44.0%	56.0%	44.0%	56.0%
1924	166,635	30,300	Coolidge, Calvin	123,262	Davis, John W.	13,073	92,962 D	18.2%	74.0%	19.7%	80.3%
1920	149,558	42,981	Harding, Warren G.	106,112	Cox, James M.	465	63,131 D	28.7%	71.0%	28.8%	71.2%

In 1948 other vote was 85,135 States Rights; 1,636 Progressive; 732 Prohibition; 3 Socialist and 1 scattered.

ELECTORAL COLLEGE VOTE 1920 TO 1956

Year	Total	Republican	Democratic	Other
1956	12	—	12	—
1952	12	—	12	—
1948	12	—	12	—
1944	12	—	12	—
1940	12	—	12	—
1936	12	—	12	—
1932	12	—	12	—
1928	14	—	14	—
1924	14	—	14	—
1920	14	—	14	—

GEORGIA

DADE
CATOOSA
WHITFIELD
MURRAY
FANNIN
UNION
TOWNS
RABUN
WALKER
GILMER
HABERSHAM
WHITE
LUMPKIN
CHATTOOGA
GORDON
PICKENS
DAWSON
STEPHENS
FRANKLIN
HART
FLOYD
BARTOW
CHEROKEE
FORSYTH
HALL
BANKS
JACKSON
MADISON
ELBERT
POLK
PAULDING
COBB
GWINNETT
BARROW
CLARKE
OCONEE
OGLETHORPE
WILKES
LINCOLN
HARALSON
DOUGLAS
FULTON
DE KALB
ROCK-DALE
WALTON
CARROLL
CLAYTON
NEWTON
MORGAN
GREENE
TALIA-FERRO
McDUFFIE
COLUMBIA
FAYETTE
HENRY
COWETA
HEARD
SPALDING
BUTTS
JASPER
PUTNAM
HANCOCK
WARREN
RICHMOND
GLAS-COCK
JEFFERSON
TROUP
MERIWETHER
PIKE
LAMAR
MONROE
JONES
BALDWIN
WASHINGTON
BURKE
UPSON
HARRIS
TALBOT
CRAWFORD
BIBB
TWIGGS
WILKINSON
JOHNSON
JENKINS
SCREVEN
MUSCOGEE
TAYLOR
PEACH
HOUSTON
BLECKLEY
LAURENS
EMANUEL
EFFINGHAM
CHATTA-HOOCHEE
MARION
SCHLEY
MACON
TREUTLEN
CANDLER
BULLOCH
STEWART
WEBSTER
SUMTER
DOOLY
PULASKI
DODGE
WHEELER
MONTGOMERY
TOOMBS
EVANS
TATTNALL
BRYAN
CHATHAM
QUIT-MAN
WILCOX
CRISP
TELFAIR
RANDOLPH
TERRELL
LEE
TURNER
BEN HILL
JEFF DAVIS
APPLING
LIBERTY
LONG
CLAY
CALHOUN
DOUGHERTY
WORTH
IRWIN
COFFEE
BACON
WAYNE
McINTOSH
TIFT
EARLY
BAKER
MITCHELL
PIERCE
BERRIEN
ATKINSON
MILLER
COLQUITT
COOK
WARE
BRANTLEY
GLYNN
SEMINOLE
LANIER
DECATUR
GRADY
THOMAS
BROOKS
CLINCH
CHARLTON
CAMDEN
LOWNDES
ECHOLS

GEORGIA

PRESIDENT 1956

1950 Census Population	County	Total Vote	Republican	Democratic	Other	Rep.-Dem. Plurality	Percentage Total Vote Rep.	Total Vote Dem.	Major Vote Rep.	Major Vote Dem.
14,003	APPLING	2,369	506	1,719	144	1,213 D	21.4%	72.6%	22.7%	77.3%
7,362	ATKINSON	1,841	122	1,719		1,597 D	6.6%	93.4%	6.6%	93.4%
8,940	BACON	2,839	394	2,445		2,051 D	13.9%	86.1%	13.9%	86.1%
5,952	BAKER	815	32	783		751 D	3.9%	96.1%	3.9%	96.1%
29,706	BALDWIN	3,361	1,080	2,275	6	1,195 D	32.1%	67.7%	32.2%	67.8%
6,935	BANKS	1,179	187	990	2	803 D	15.9%	84.0%	15.9%	84.1%
13,115	BARROW	2,708	442	2,266		1,824 D	16.3%	83.7%	16.3%	83.7%
27,370	BARTOW	5,176	1,536	3,640		2,104 D	29.7%	70.3%	29.7%	70.3%
14,879	BEN HILL	2,708	554	2,150	4	1,596 D	20.5%	79.4%	20.5%	79.5%
13,966	BERRIEN	2,571	167	2,403	1	2,236 D	6.5%	93.5%	6.5%	93.5%
114,079	BIBB	22,750	7,368	15,382		8,014 D	32.4%	67.6%	32.4%	67.6%
9,218	BLECKLEY	1,673	136	1,537		1,401 D	8.1%	91.9%	8.1%	91.9%
6,387	BRANTLEY	1,436	228	1,208		980 D	15.9%	84.1%	15.9%	84.1%
18,169	BROOKS	2,487	534	1,936	17	1,402 D	21.5%	77.8%	21.6%	78.4%
5,965	BRYAN	1,576	331	1,242	3	911 D	21.0%	78.8%	21.0%	79.0%
24,740	BULLOCH	4,315	901	3,414		2,513 D	20.9%	79.1%	20.9%	79.1%
23,458	BURKE	2,049	721	1,300	28	579 D	35.2%	63.4%	35.7%	64.3%
9,079	BUTTS	2,208	323	1,885		1,562 D	14.6%	85.4%	14.6%	85.4%
8,578	CALHOUN	1,206	107	1,094	5	987 D	8.9%	90.7%	8.9%	91.1%
7,322	CAMDEN	2,194	1,014	1,178	2	164 D	46.2%	53.7%	46.3%	53.7%
	CAMPBELL	—	—	—	—	—	—	—	—	—
8,063	CANDLER	1,318	308	996	14	688 D	23.4%	75.6%	23.6%	76.4%
34,112	CARROLL	6,567	1,712	4,855		3,143 D	26.1%	73.9%	26.1%	73.9%
15,146	CATOOSA	3,583	1,336	2,163	84	827 D	37.3%	60.4%	38.2%	61.8%
4,821	CHARLTON	954	204	750		546 D	21.4%	78.6%	21.4%	78.6%
151,481	CHATHAM	26,099	16,512	9,587		6,925 R	63.3%	36.7%	63.3%	36.7%
12,149	CHATTAHOOCHEE	150	43	107		64 D	28.7%	71.3%	28.7%	71.3%
21,197	CHATTOOGA	5,506	1,682	3,823	1	2,141 D	30.5%	69.4%	30.6%	69.4%
20,750	CHEROKEE	3,939	1,829	2,110		281 D	46.4%	53.6%	46.4%	53.6%
36,550	CLARKE	6,371	2,107	4,257	7	2,150 D	33.1%	66.8%	33.1%	66.9%
5,844	CLAY	499	103	390	6	287 D	20.6%	78.2%	20.9%	79.1%
22,872	CLAYTON	7,115	1,593	5,522		3,929 D	22.4%	77.6%	22.4%	77.6%
6,007	CLINCH	2,097	518	1,579		1,061 D	24.7%	75.3%	24.7%	75.3%
61,830	COBB	18,510	6,798	11,696	16	4,898 D	36.7%	63.2%	36.8%	63.2%
23,961	COFFEE	3,774	574	3,199	1	2,625 D	15.2%	84.8%	15.2%	84.8%
33,999	COLQUITT	5,765	1,336	4,412	17	3,076 D	23.2%	76.5%	23.2%	76.8%
9,525	COLUMBIA	1,329	463	866		403 D	34.8%	65.2%	34.8%	65.2%
12,201	COOK	2,346	245	2,100	1	1,855 D	10.4%	89.5%	10.4%	89.6%
27,786	COWETA	3,855	850	3,003	2	2,153 D	22.0%	77.9%	22.1%	77.9%
6,080	CRAWFORD	893	109	779	5	670 D	12.2%	87.2%	12.3%	87.7%
17,663	CRISP	3,366	835	2,526	5	1,691 D	24.8%	75.0%	24.8%	75.2%
7,364	DADE	1,586	723	863		140 D	45.6%	54.4%	45.6%	54.4%
3,712	DAWSON	1,334	613	721		108 D	46.0%	54.0%	46.0%	54.0%
23,620	DECATUR	4,761	1,062	3,699		2,637 D	22.3%	77.7%	22.3%	77.7%
136,395	DE KALB	46,341	15,979	30,336	26	14,357 D	34.5%	65.5%	34.5%	65.5%
17,865	DODGE	4,219	738	3,479	2	2,741 D	17.5%	82.5%	17.5%	82.5%
14,159	DOOLY	2,025	174	1,851		1,677 D	8.6%	91.4%	8.6%	91.4%
43,617	DOUGHERTY	7,513	3,248	4,126	139	878 D	43.2%	54.9%	44.0%	56.0%
12,173	DOUGLAS	3,112	1,001	2,111		1,110 D	32.2%	67.8%	32.2%	67.8%
17,413	EARLY	2,014	193	1,818	3	1,625 D	9.6%	90.3%	9.6%	90.4%
2,494	ECHOLS	666	134	530	2	396 D	20.1%	79.6%	20.2%	79.8%
9,133	EFFINGHAM	1,369	637	611	121	26 R	46.5%	44.6%	51.0%	49.0%
18,585	ELBERT	4,085	447	3,635	3	3,188 D	10.9%	89.0%	11.0%	89.0%
19,789	EMANUEL	3,052	679	2,373		1,694 D	22.2%	77.8%	22.2%	77.8%
6,653	EVANS	1,513	356	1,154	3	798 D	23.5%	76.3%	23.6%	76.4%
15,192	FANNIN	5,466	3,521	1,945		1,576 R	64.4%	35.6%	64.4%	35.6%
7,978	FAYETTE	1,446	138	1,308		1,170 D	9.5%	90.5%	9.5%	90.5%
62,899	FLOYD	12,588	5,955	6,633		678 D	47.3%	52.7%	47.3%	52.7%
11,005	FORSYTH	3,129	1,131	1,998		867 D	36.1%	63.9%	36.1%	63.9%
14,446	FRANKLIN	3,225	253	2,968	4	2,715 D	7.8%	92.0%	7.9%	92.1%

GEORGIA

PRESIDENT 1956

1950 Census Population	County	Total Vote	Republican	Democratic	Other	Rep.-Dem. Plurality	Percentage: Total Vote Rep.	Percentage: Total Vote Dem.	Percentage: Major Vote Rep.	Percentage: Major Vote Dem.
473,572	FULTON	93,219	40,966	52,062	191	11,096 D	43.9%	55.8%	44.0%	56.0%
9,963	GILMER	3,134	1,857	1,275	2	582 R	59.3%	40.7%	59.3%	40.7%
3,579	GLASCOCK	425	110	314	1	204 D	25.9%	73.9%	25.9%	74.1%
29,046	GLYNN	6,169	3,098	3,071		27 R	50.2%	49.8%	50.2%	49.8%
18,922	GORDON	3,003	1,025	1,972	6	947 D	34.1%	65.7%	34.2%	65.8%
18,928	GRADY	3,193	496	2,697		2,201 D	15.5%	84.5%	15.5%	84.5%
12,843	GREENE	2,555	541	2,012	2	1,471 D	21.2%	78.7%	21.2%	78.8%
32,320	GWINNETT	7,130	1,443	5,687		4,244 D	20.2%	79.8%	20.2%	79.8%
16,553	HABERSHAM	3,131	855	2,276		1,421 D	27.3%	72.7%	27.3%	72.7%
40,113	HALL	8,741	2,752	5,989		3,237 D	31.5%	68.5%	31.5%	68.5%
11,052	HANCOCK	1,214	354	860		506 D	29.2%	70.8%	29.2%	70.8%
14,663	HARALSON	4,690	2,218	2,472		254 D	47.3%	52.7%	47.3%	52.7%
11,265	HARRIS	1,901	563	1,328	10	765 D	29.6%	69.9%	29.8%	70.2%
14,495	HART	2,133	117	2,016		1,899 D	5.5%	94.5%	5.5%	94.5%
6,975	HEARD	1,300	194	1,106		912 D	14.9%	85.1%	14.9%	85.1%
15,857	HENRY	3,484	848	2,636		1,788 D	24.3%	75.7%	24.3%	75.7%
20,964	HOUSTON	5,551	1,060	4,483	8	3,423 D	19.1%	80.8%	19.1%	80.9%
11,973	IRWIN	1,866	312	1,554		1,242 D	16.7%	83.3%	16.7%	83.3%
18,997	JACKSON	3,547	438	3,100	9	2,662 D	12.3%	87.4%	12.4%	87.6%
7,473	JASPER	1,250	288	962		674 D	23.0%	77.0%	23.0%	77.0%
9,299	JEFF DAVIS	1,907	247	1,656	4	1,409 D	13.0%	86.8%	13.0%	87.0%
18,855	JEFFERSON	1,883	515	1,356	12	841 D	27.3%	72.0%	27.5%	72.5%
10,264	JENKINS	1,272	261	1,000	11	739 D	20.5%	78.6%	20.7%	79.3%
9,893	JOHNSON	1,869	179	1,607	83	1,428 D	9.6%	86.0%	10.0%	90.0%
7,538	JONES	1,596	382	1,208	6	826 D	23.9%	75.7%	24.0%	76.0%
10,242	LAMAR	2,086	555	1,531		976 D	26.6%	73.4%	26.6%	73.4%
5,151	LANIER	1,044	152	890	2	738 D	14.6%	85.2%	14.6%	85.4%
33,123	LAURENS	6,274	1,189	5,085		3,896 D	19.0%	81.0%	19.0%	81.0%
6,674	LEE	620	79	532	9	453 D	12.7%	85.8%	12.9%	87.1%
8,444	LIBERTY	1,859	967	892		75 R	52.0%	48.0%	52.0%	48.0%
6,462	LINCOLN	851	155	696		541 D	18.2%	81.8%	18.2%	81.8%
3,598	LONG	1,476	281	1,195		914 D	19.0%	81.0%	19.0%	81.0%
35,211	LOWNDES	6,087	2,135	3,936	16	1,801 D	35.1%	64.7%	35.2%	64.8%
6,574	LUMPKIN	1,179	486	693		207 D	41.2%	58.8%	41.2%	58.8%
11,443	MCDUFFIE	1,690	649	1,039	2	390 D	38.4%	61.5%	38.4%	61.6%
6,008	MCINTOSH	1,510	886	624		262 R	58.7%	41.3%	58.7%	41.3%
14,213	MACON	2,354	363	1,984	7	1,621 D	15.4%	84.3%	15.5%	84.5%
12,238	MADISON	2,383	161	2,222		2,061 D	6.8%	93.2%	6.8%	93.2%
6,521	MARION	776	158	618		460 D	20.4%	79.6%	20.4%	79.6%
21,055	MERIWETHER	3,736	592	3,137	7	2,545 D	15.8%	84.0%	15.9%	84.1%
9,023	MILLER	2,004	441	1,563		1,122 D	22.0%	78.0%	22.0%	78.0%
	MILTON	—	—	—	—	—	—	—	—	—
22,528	MITCHELL	3,131	382	2,735	14	2,353 D	12.2%	87.4%	12.3%	87.7%
10,523	MONROE	2,051	506	1,545		1,039 D	24.7%	75.3%	24.7%	75.3%
7,901	MONTGOMERY	1,325	271	1,052	2	781 D	20.5%	79.4%	20.5%	79.5%
11,899	MORGAN	1,738	246	1,492		1,246 D	14.2%	85.8%	14.2%	85.8%
10,676	MURRAY	2,963	1,144	1,819		675 D	38.6%	61.4%	38.6%	61.4%
118,028	MUSCOGEE	16,523	8,176	8,160	187	16 R	49.5%	49.4%	50.0%	50.0%
20,185	NEWTON	3,764	532	3,232		2,700 D	14.1%	85.9%	14.1%	85.9%
7,009	OCONEE	1,478	314	1,159	5	845 D	21.2%	78.4%	21.3%	78.7%
9,958	OGLETHORPE	1,572	167	1,404	1	1,237 D	10.6%	89.3%	10.6%	89.4%
11,752	PAULDING	2,539	940	1,599		659 D	37.0%	63.0%	37.0%	63.0%
11,705	PEACH	2,005	461	1,541	3	1,080 D	23.0%	76.9%	23.0%	77.0%
8,855	PICKENS	3,577	2,341	1,236		1,105 R	65.4%	34.6%	65.4%	34.6%
11,112	PIERCE	2,152	386	1,766		1,380 D	17.9%	82.1%	17.9%	82.1%
8,459	PIKE	1,277	210	1,067		857 D	16.4%	83.6%	16.4%	83.6%
30,976	POLK	6,601	2,098	4,502	1	2,404 D	31.8%	68.2%	31.8%	68.2%
8,808	PULASKI	1,593	171	1,422		1,251 D	10.7%	89.3%	10.7%	89.3%
7,731	PUTNAM	1,361	268	1,093		825 D	19.7%	80.3%	19.7%	80.3%
3,015	QUITMAN	386	31	355		324 D	8.0%	92.0%	8.0%	92.0%

GEORGIA

PRESIDENT 1956

1950 Census Population	County	Total Vote	Republican	Democratic	Other	Rep.-Dem. Plurality	Percentage Total Vote Rep.	Percentage Total Vote Dem.	Percentage Major Vote Rep.	Percentage Major Vote Dem.
7,424	RABUN	1,808	413	1,391	4	978 D	22.8%	76.9%	22.9%	77.1%
13,804	RANDOLPH	2,129	547	1,582		1,035 D	25.7%	74.3%	25.7%	74.3%
108,876	RICHMOND	17,365	10,251	6,819	295	3,432 R	59.0%	39.3%	60.1%	39.9%
8,464	ROCKDALE	2,263	484	1,779		1,295 D	21.4%	78.6%	21.4%	78.6%
4,036	SCHLEY	565	117	441	7	324 D	20.7%	78.1%	21.0%	79.0%
18,000	SCREVEN	1,865	521	1,332	12	811 D	27.9%	71.4%	28.1%	71.9%
7,904	SEMINOLE	1,474	129	1,343	2	1,214 D	8.8%	91.1%	8.8%	91.2%
31,045	SPALDING	6,329	1,458	4,853	18	3,395 D	23.0%	76.7%	23.1%	76.9%
16,647	STEPHENS	3,279	684	2,595		1,911 D	20.9%	79.1%	20.9%	79.1%
9,194	STEWART	939	235	692	12	457 D	25.0%	73.7%	25.4%	74.6%
24,208	SUMTER	3,234	730	2,149	355	1,419 D	22.6%	66.5%	25.4%	74.6%
7,687	TALBOT	848	136	710	2	574 D	16.0%	83.7%	16.1%	83.9%
4,515	TALIAFERRO	759	160	599		439 D	21.1%	78.9%	21.1%	78.9%
15,939	TATTNALL	2,321	440	1,881		1,441 D	19.0%	81.0%	19.0%	81.0%
9,113	TAYLOR	1,642	276	1,359	7	1,083 D	16.8%	82.8%	16.9%	83.1%
13,221	TELFAIR	2,359	284	2,075		1,791 D	12.0%	88.0%	12.0%	88.0%
14,314	TERRELL	1,508	203	1,301	4	1,098 D	13.5%	86.3%	13.5%	86.5%
33,932	THOMAS	5,762	2,240	3,522		1,282 D	38.9%	61.1%	38.9%	61.1%
22,645	TIFT	4,083	960	3,123		2,163 D	23.5%	76.5%	23.5%	76.5%
17,382	TOOMBS	2,963	565	2,397	1	1,832 D	19.1%	80.9%	19.1%	80.9%
4,803	TOWNS	1,981	1,096	885		211 R	55.3%	44.7%	55.3%	44.7%
6,522	TREUTLEN	1,077	117	960		843 D	10.9%	89.1%	10.9%	89.1%
49,841	TROUP	8,386	2,214	6,162	10	3,948 D	26.4%	73.5%	26.4%	73.6%
10,479	TURNER	1,752	354	1,398		1,044 D	20.2%	79.8%	20.2%	79.8%
8,308	TWIGGS	1,164	158	1,002	4	844 D	13.6%	86.1%	13.6%	86.4%
7,318	UNION	2,746	1,360	1,386		26 D	49.5%	50.5%	49.5%	50.5%
25,078	UPSON	4,134	712	3,422		2,710 D	17.2%	82.8%	17.2%	82.8%
38,198	WALKER	7,368	3,552	3,693	123	141 D	48.2%	50.1%	49.0%	51.0%
20,230	WALTON	3,744	470	3,271	3	2,801 D	12.6%	87.4%	12.6%	87.4%
30,289	WARE	8,164	2,276	5,888		3,612 D	27.9%	72.1%	27.9%	72.1%
8,779	WARREN	853	152	675	26	523 D	17.8%	79.1%	18.4%	81.6%
21,012	WASHINGTON	3,135	602	2,530	3	1,928 D	19.2%	80.7%	19.2%	80.8%
14,248	WAYNE	3,034	950	2,084		1,134 D	31.3%	68.7%	31.3%	68.7%
4,081	WEBSTER	346	51	295		244 D	14.7%	85.3%	14.7%	85.3%
6,712	WHEELER	1,143	150	993		843 D	13.1%	86.9%	13.1%	86.9%
5,951	WHITE	1,569	469	1,100		631 D	29.9%	70.1%	29.9%	70.1%
34,432	WHITFIELD	8,469	4,205	4,264		59 D	49.7%	50.3%	49.7%	50.3%
10,167	WILCOX	1,918	232	1,686		1,454 D	12.1%	87.9%	12.1%	87.9%
12,388	WILKES	2,039	305	1,714	20	1,409 D	15.0%	84.1%	15.1%	84.9%
9,781	WILKINSON	1,694	393	1,299	2	906 D	23.2%	76.7%	23.2%	76.8%
19,357	WORTH	2,375	293	2,078	4	1,785 D	12.3%	87.5%	12.4%	87.6%
3,444,578	TOTAL	669,655	222,778	444,688	2,189	221,910 D	33.3%	66.4%	33.4%	66.6%

GEORGIA

PRESIDENT 1952

1950 Census Population	County	Total Vote	Republican	Democratic	Other	Rep.-Dem. Plurality	Percentage Total Vote Rep.	Total Vote Dem.	Major Vote Rep.	Major Vote Dem.
14,003	APPLING	2,892	713	2,179		1,466 D	24.7%	75.3%	24.7%	75.3%
7,362	ATKINSON	1,754	194	1,560		1,366 D	11.1%	88.9%	11.1%	88.9%
8,940	BACON	2,055	543	1,512		969 D	26.4%	73.6%	26.4%	73.6%
5,952	BAKER	1,160	155	1,005		850 D	13.4%	86.6%	13.4%	86.6%
29,706	BALDWIN	3,341	1,023	2,318		1,295 D	30.6%	69.4%	30.6%	69.4%
6,935	BANKS	1,459	204	1,255		1,051 D	14.0%	86.0%	14.0%	86.0%
13,115	BARROW	2,603	236	2,367		2,131 D	9.1%	90.9%	9.1%	90.9%
27,370	BARTOW	5,156	1,183	3,973		2,790 D	22.9%	77.1%	22.9%	77.1%
14,879	BEN HILL	2,745	697	2,048		1,351 D	25.4%	74.6%	25.4%	74.6%
13,966	BERRIEN	2,551	364	2,187		1,823 D	14.3%	85.7%	14.3%	85.7%
114,079	BIBB	20,808	6,121	14,687		8,566 D	29.4%	70.6%	29.4%	70.6%
9,218	BLECKLEY	1,704	187	1,517		1,330 D	11.0%	89.0%	11.0%	89.0%
6,387	BRANTLEY	1,358	276	1,082		806 D	20.3%	79.7%	20.3%	79.7%
18,169	BROOKS	2,666	800	1,866		1,066 D	30.0%	70.0%	30.0%	70.0%
5,965	BRYAN	1,302	331	971		640 D	25.4%	74.6%	25.4%	74.6%
24,740	BULLOCH	4,528	909	3,619		2,710 D	20.1%	79.9%	20.1%	79.9%
23,458	BURKE	2,092	932	1,160		228 D	44.6%	55.4%	44.6%	55.4%
9,079	BUTTS	2,099	189	1,910		1,721 D	9.0%	91.0%	9.0%	91.0%
8,578	CALHOUN	957	147	810		663 D	15.4%	84.6%	15.4%	84.6%
7,322	CAMDEN	1,904	619	1,285		666 D	32.5%	67.5%	32.5%	67.5%
	CAMPBELL	—	—	—		—	—	—	—	—
8,063	CANDLER	1,870	422	1,448		1,026 D	22.6%	77.4%	22.6%	77.4%
34,112	CARROLL	6,401	1,194	5,207		4,013 D	18.7%	81.3%	18.7%	81.3%
15,146	CATOOSA	3,598	1,371	2,227		856 D	38.1%	61.9%	38.1%	61.9%
4,821	CHARLTON	1,103	288	815		527 D	26.1%	73.9%	26.1%	73.9%
151,481	CHATHAM	29,902	15,532	14,370		1,162 R	51.9%	48.1%	51.9%	48.1%
12,149	CHATTAHOOCHEE	189	73	116		43 D	38.6%	61.4%	38.6%	61.4%
21,197	CHATTOOGA	4,387	771	3,616		2,845 D	17.6%	82.4%	17.6%	82.4%
20,750	CHEROKEE	4,070	1,618	2,452		834 D	39.8%	60.2%	39.8%	60.2%
36,550	CLARKE	6,492	1,588	4,904		3,316 D	24.5%	75.5%	24.5%	75.5%
5,844	CLAY	657	176	481		305 D	26.8%	73.2%	26.8%	73.2%
22,872	CLAYTON	5,288	1,230	4,058		2,828 D	23.3%	76.7%	23.3%	76.7%
6,007	CLINCH	1,518	350	1,168		818 D	23.1%	76.9%	23.1%	76.9%
61,830	COBB	14,345	4,163	10,182		6,019 D	29.0%	71.0%	29.0%	71.0%
23,961	COFFEE	4,370	1,078	3,292		2,214 D	24.7%	75.3%	24.7%	75.3%
33,999	COLQUITT	5,928	1,411	4,517		3,106 D	23.8%	76.2%	23.8%	76.2%
9,525	COLUMBIA	1,379	530	849		319 D	38.4%	61.6%	38.4%	61.6%
12,201	COOK	2,742	395	2,347		1,952 D	14.4%	85.6%	14.4%	85.6%
27,786	COWETA	4,489	652	3,837		3,185 D	14.5%	85.5%	14.5%	85.5%
6,080	CRAWFORD	1,093	145	948		803 D	13.3%	86.7%	13.3%	86.7%
17,663	CRISP	3,065	949	2,116		1,167 D	31.0%	69.0%	31.0%	69.0%
7,364	DADE	1,982	686	1,296		610 D	34.6%	65.4%	34.6%	65.4%
3,712	DAWSON	1,240	470	770		300 D	37.9%	62.1%	37.9%	62.1%
23,620	DECATUR	3,582	1,001	2,581		1,580 D	27.9%	72.1%	27.9%	72.1%
136,395	DE KALB	36,453	15,588	20,865		5,277 D	42.8%	57.2%	42.8%	57.2%
17,865	DODGE	3,899	454	3,445		2,991 D	11.6%	88.4%	11.6%	88.4%
14,159	DOOLY	1,961	197	1,764		1,567 D	10.0%	90.0%	10.0%	90.0%
43,617	DOUGHERTY	6,970	2,535	4,435		1,900 D	36.4%	63.6%	36.4%	63.6%
12,173	DOUGLAS	2,747	645	2,102		1,457 D	23.5%	76.5%	23.5%	76.5%
17,413	EARLY	2,110	307	1,803		1,496 D	14.5%	85.5%	14.5%	85.5%
2,494	ECHOLS	626	94	532		438 D	15.0%	85.0%	15.0%	85.0%
9,133	EFFINGHAM	1,629	829	800		29 R	50.9%	49.1%	50.9%	49.1%
18,585	ELBERT	3,831	552	3,279		2,727 D	14.4%	85.6%	14.4%	85.6%
19,789	EMANUEL	3,303	661	2,642		1,981 D	20.0%	80.0%	20.0%	80.0%
6,653	EVANS	1,657	433	1,224		791 D	26.1%	73.9%	26.1%	73.9%
15,192	FANNIN	4,817	2,904	1,913		991 R	60.3%	39.7%	60.3%	39.7%
7,978	FAYETTE	1,409	195	1,214		1,019 D	13.8%	86.2%	13.8%	86.2%
62,899	FLOYD	13,009	4,532	8,477		3,945 D	34.8%	65.2%	34.8%	65.2%
11,005	FORSYTH	1,927	536	1,391		855 D	27.8%	72.2%	27.8%	72.2%
14,446	FRANKLIN	3,275	373	2,902		2,529 D	11.4%	88.6%	11.4%	88.6%

GEORGIA

PRESIDENT 1952

1950 Census Population	County	Total Vote	Republican	Democratic	Other	Rep.-Dem. Plurality	Percentage Total Vote Rep.	Percentage Total Vote Dem.	Percentage Major Vote Rep.	Percentage Major Vote Dem.
473,572	FULTON	87,656	35,197	52,459		17,262 D	40.2%	59.8%	40.2%	59.8%
9,963	GILMER	2,683	1,324	1,359		35 D	49.3%	50.7%	49.3%	50.7%
3,579	GLASCOCK	614	233	381		148 D	37.9%	62.1%	37.9%	62.1%
29,046	GLYNN	5,923	2,575	3,348		773 D	43.5%	56.5%	43.5%	56.5%
18,922	GORDON	3,083	880	2,203		1,323 D	28.5%	71.5%	28.5%	71.5%
18,928	GRADY	3,425	643	2,782		2,139 D	18.8%	81.2%	18.8%	81.2%
12,843	GREENE	2,720	397	2,323		1,926 D	14.6%	85.4%	14.6%	85.4%
32,320	GWINNETT	7,041	1,015	6,026		5,011 D	14.4%	85.6%	14.4%	85.6%
16,553	HABERSHAM	3,568	921	2,647		1,726 D	25.8%	74.2%	25.8%	74.2%
40,113	HALL	7,966	1,845	6,121		4,276 D	23.2%	76.8%	23.2%	76.8%
11,052	HANCOCK	1,512	267	1,245		978 D	17.7%	82.3%	17.7%	82.3%
14,663	HARALSON	3,547	1,264	2,283		1,019 D	35.6%	64.4%	35.6%	64.4%
11,265	HARRIS	1,918	544	1,374		830 D	28.4%	71.6%	28.4%	71.6%
14,495	HART	3,448	204	3,244		3,040 D	5.9%	94.1%	5.9%	94.1%
6,975	HEARD	1,373	184	1,189		1,005 D	13.4%	86.6%	13.4%	86.6%
15,857	HENRY	3,142	553	2,589		2,036 D	17.6%	82.4%	17.6%	82.4%
20,964	HOUSTON	3,300	511	2,789		2,278 D	15.5%	84.5%	15.5%	84.5%
11,973	IRWIN	1,991	516	1,475		959 D	25.9%	74.1%	25.9%	74.1%
18,997	JACKSON	3,750	409	3,341		2,932 D	10.9%	89.1%	10.9%	89.1%
7,473	JASPER	1,333	228	1,105		877 D	17.1%	82.9%	17.1%	82.9%
9,299	JEFF DAVIS	1,690	367	1,323		956 D	21.7%	78.3%	21.7%	78.3%
18,855	JEFFERSON	2,220	744	1,476		732 D	33.5%	66.5%	33.5%	66.5%
10,264	JENKINS	1,534	368	1,166		798 D	24.0%	76.0%	24.0%	76.0%
9,893	JOHNSON	2,152	344	1,808		1,464 D	16.0%	84.0%	16.0%	84.0%
7,538	JONES	1,705	278	1,427		1,149 D	16.3%	83.7%	16.3%	83.7%
10,242	LAMAR	1,981	429	1,552		1,123 D	21.7%	78.3%	21.7%	78.3%
5,151	LANIER	1,015	170	845		675 D	16.7%	83.3%	16.7%	83.3%
33,123	LAURENS	6,047	1,046	5,001		3,955 D	17.3%	82.7%	17.3%	82.7%
6,674	LEE	595	205	390		185 D	34.5%	65.5%	34.5%	65.5%
8,444	LIBERTY	1,965	517	1,448		931 D	26.3%	73.7%	26.3%	73.7%
6,462	LINCOLN	971	327	644		317 D	33.7%	66.3%	33.7%	66.3%
3,598	LONG	1,111	420	691		271 D	37.8%	62.2%	37.8%	62.2%
35,211	LOWNDES	5,324	2,079	3,245		1,166 D	39.0%	61.0%	39.0%	61.0%
6,574	LUMPKIN	1,367	370	997		627 D	27.1%	72.9%	27.1%	72.9%
11,443	MCDUFFIE	2,105	933	1,172		239 D	44.3%	55.7%	44.3%	55.7%
6,008	MCINTOSH	1,227	503	724		221 D	41.0%	59.0%	41.0%	59.0%
14,213	MACON	1,791	319	1,472		1,153 D	17.8%	82.2%	17.8%	82.2%
12,238	MADISON	2,124	225	1,899		1,674 D	10.6%	89.4%	10.6%	89.4%
6,521	MARION	833	182	651		469 D	21.8%	78.2%	21.8%	78.2%
21,055	MERIWETHER	4,082	531	3,551		3,020 D	13.0%	87.0%	13.0%	87.0%
9,023	MILLER	1,840	223	1,617		1,394 D	12.1%	87.9%	12.1%	87.9%
	MILTON	—	—	—		—	—	—	—	—
22,528	MITCHELL	3,655	601	3,054		2,453 D	16.4%	83.6%	16.4%	83.6%
10,523	MONROE	2,907	501	2,406		1,905 D	17.2%	82.8%	17.2%	82.8%
7,901	MONTGOMERY	2,048	290	1,758		1,468 D	14.2%	85.8%	14.2%	85.8%
11,899	MORGAN	1,896	247	1,649		1,402 D	13.0%	87.0%	13.0%	87.0%
10,676	MURRAY	2,596	756	1,840		1,084 D	29.1%	70.9%	29.1%	70.9%
118,028	MUSCOGEE	19,034	7,814	11,220		3,406 D	41.1%	58.9%	41.1%	58.9%
20,185	NEWTON	3,960	431	3,529		3,098 D	10.9%	89.1%	10.9%	89.1%
7,009	OCONEE	1,519	337	1,182		845 D	22.2%	77.8%	22.2%	77.8%
9,958	OGLETHORPE	1,669	208	1,461		1,253 D	12.5%	87.5%	12.5%	87.5%
11,752	PAULDING	2,940	788	2,152		1,364 D	26.8%	73.2%	26.8%	73.2%
11,705	PEACH	1,898	374	1,523	1	1,149 D	19.7%	80.2%	19.7%	80.3%
8,855	PICKENS	2,640	1,328	1,312		16 R	50.3%	49.7%	50.3%	49.7%
11,112	PIERCE	2,495	592	1,903		1,311 D	23.7%	76.3%	23.7%	76.3%
8,459	PIKE	1,534	286	1,248		962 D	18.6%	81.4%	18.6%	81.4%
30,976	POLK	5,746	1,299	4,447		3,148 D	22.6%	77.4%	22.6%	77.4%
8,808	PULASKI	1,737	165	1,572		1,407 D	9.5%	90.5%	9.5%	90.5%
7,731	PUTNAM	1,501	250	1,251		1,001 D	16.7%	83.3%	16.7%	83.3%
3,015	QUITMAN	425	93	332		239 D	21.9%	78.1%	21.9%	78.1%

GEORGIA

PRESIDENT 1952

1950 Census Population	County	Total Vote	Republican	Democratic	Other	Rep.-Dem. Plurality	Percentage Total Vote Rep.	Total Vote Dem.	Major Vote Rep.	Major Vote Dem.
7,424	RABUN	1,769	449	1,320		871 D	25.4%	74.6%	25.4%	74.6%
13,804	RANDOLPH	1,926	507	1,419		912 D	26.3%	73.7%	26.3%	73.7%
108,876	RICHMOND	17,931	9,347	8,584		763 R	52.1%	47.9%	52.1%	47.9%
8,464	ROCKDALE	1,986	321	1,665		1,344 D	16.2%	83.8%	16.2%	83.8%
4,036	SCHLEY	584	148	436		288 D	25.3%	74.7%	25.3%	74.7%
18,000	SCREVEN	2,276	692	1,584		892 D	30.4%	69.6%	30.4%	69.6%
7,904	SEMINOLE	1,302	176	1,126		950 D	13.5%	86.5%	13.5%	86.5%
31,045	SPALDING	6,545	1,249	5,296		4,047 D	19.1%	80.9%	19.1%	80.9%
16,647	STEPHENS	4,200	661	3,539		2,878 D	15.7%	84.3%	15.7%	84.3%
9,194	STEWART	1,127	311	816		505 D	27.6%	72.4%	27.6%	72.4%
24,208	SUMTER	3,523	1,068	2,455		1,387 D	30.3%	69.7%	30.3%	69.7%
7,687	TALBOT	853	175	678		503 D	20.5%	79.5%	20.5%	79.5%
4,515	TALIAFERRO	976	103	873		770 D	10.6%	89.4%	10.6%	89.4%
15,939	TATTNALL	3,547	1,114	2,433		1,319 D	31.4%	68.6%	31.4%	68.6%
9,113	TAYLOR	1,956	277	1,679		1,402 D	14.2%	85.8%	14.2%	85.8%
13,221	TELFAIR	2,938	243	2,695		2,452 D	8.3%	91.7%	8.3%	91.7%
14,314	TERRELL	1,744	369	1,375		1,006 D	21.2%	78.8%	21.2%	78.8%
33,932	THOMAS	6,244	2,273	3,971		1,698 D	36.4%	63.6%	36.4%	63.6%
22,645	TIFT	4,272	1,318	2,954		1,636 D	30.9%	69.1%	30.9%	69.1%
17,382	TOOMBS	3,364	723	2,641		1,918 D	21.5%	78.5%	21.5%	78.5%
4,803	TOWNS	2,094	983	1,111		128 D	46.9%	53.1%	46.9%	53.1%
6,522	TREUTLEN	1,517	101	1,416		1,315 D	6.7%	93.3%	6.7%	93.3%
49,841	TROUP	9,017	1,887	7,130		5,243 D	20.9%	79.1%	20.9%	79.1%
10,479	TURNER	1,759	402	1,357		955 D	22.9%	77.1%	22.9%	77.1%
8,308	TWIGGS	1,271	191	1,080		889 D	15.0%	85.0%	15.0%	85.0%
7,318	UNION	2,690	1,330	1,360		30 D	49.4%	50.6%	49.4%	50.6%
25,078	UPSON	4,485	648	3,837		3,189 D	14.4%	85.6%	14.4%	85.6%
38,198	WALKER	7,232	2,866	4,366		1,500 D	39.6%	60.4%	39.6%	60.4%
20,230	WALTON	3,996	324	3,672		3,348 D	8.1%	91.9%	8.1%	91.9%
30,289	WARE	8,045	2,418	5,627		3,209 D	30.1%	69.9%	30.1%	69.9%
8,779	WARREN	1,067	374	693		319 D	35.1%	64.9%	35.1%	64.9%
21,012	WASHINGTON	3,176	795	2,381		1,586 D	25.0%	75.0%	25.0%	75.0%
14,248	WAYNE	2,761	832	1,929		1,097 D	30.1%	69.9%	30.1%	69.9%
4,081	WEBSTER	473	138	335		197 D	29.2%	70.8%	29.2%	70.8%
6,712	WHEELER	1,541	261	1,280		1,019 D	16.9%	83.1%	16.9%	83.1%
5,951	WHITE	1,421	282	1,139		857 D	19.8%	80.2%	19.8%	80.2%
34,432	WHITFIELD	7,456	2,795	4,661		1,866 D	37.5%	62.5%	37.5%	62.5%
10,167	WILCOX	2,179	301	1,878		1,577 D	13.8%	86.2%	13.8%	86.2%
12,388	WILKES	1,786	286	1,500		1,214 D	16.0%	84.0%	16.0%	84.0%
9,781	WILKINSON	2,007	378	1,629		1,251 D	18.8%	81.2%	18.8%	81.2%
19,357	WORTH	2,430	444	1,986		1,542 D	18.3%	81.7%	18.3%	81.7%
3,444,578	TOTAL	655,785	198,961	456,823	1	257,862 D	30.3%	69.7%	30.3%	69.7%

GEORGIA

PRESIDENT 1948

1940 Census Population	County	Total Vote	Republican	Democratic	Other	Rep.-Dem. Plurality	Percentage Total Vote Rep.	Total Vote Dem.	Major Vote Rep.	Major Vote Dem.
14,497	APPLING	3,207	289	2,268	650	1,979 D	9.0%	70.7%	11.3%	88.7%
7,093	ATKINSON	1,120	66	938	116	872 D	5.9%	83.8%	6.6%	93.4%
8,096	BACON	1,235	104	785	346	681 D	8.4%	63.6%	11.7%	88.3%
7,344	BAKER	283	7	218	58	211 D	2.5%	77.0%	3.1%	96.9%
24,190	BALDWIN	2,095	559	1,132	404	573 D	26.7%	54.0%	33.1%	66.9%
8,733	BANKS	598	38	533	27	495 D	6.4%	89.1%	6.7%	93.3%
13,064	BARROW	2,053	155	1,554	344	1,399 D	7.5%	75.7%	9.1%	90.9%
25,283	BARTOW	3,068	440	2,384	244	1,944 D	14.3%	77.7%	15.6%	84.4%
14,523	BEN HILL	1,896	223	1,438	235	1,215 D	11.8%	75.8%	13.4%	86.6%
15,370	BERRIEN	2,127	107	1,772	248	1,665 D	5.0%	83.3%	5.7%	94.3%
83,783	BIBB	14,077	3,043	7,011	4,023	3,968 D	21.6%	49.8%	30.3%	69.7%
9,655	BLECKLEY	838	71	536	231	465 D	8.5%	64.0%	11.7%	88.3%
6,871	BRANTLEY	766	79	463	224	384 D	10.3%	60.4%	14.6%	85.4%
20,497	BROOKS	1,677	188	975	514	787 D	11.2%	58.1%	16.2%	83.8%
6,288	BRYAN	1,759	135	1,147	477	1,012 D	7.7%	65.2%	10.5%	89.5%
26,010	BULLOCH	2,953	276	2,036	641	1,760 D	9.3%	68.9%	11.9%	88.1%
26,520	BURKE	1,496	107	357	1,032	250 D	7.2%	23.9%	23.1%	76.9%
9,182	BUTTS	1,168	61	987	120	926 D	5.2%	84.5%	5.8%	94.2%
10,438	CALHOUN	514	36	399	79	363 D	7.0%	77.6%	8.3%	91.7%
5,910	CAMDEN	1,085	208	552	325	344 D	19.2%	50.9%	27.4%	72.6%
	CAMPBELL	—	—	—	—	—	—	—	—	—
9,103	CANDLER	1,007	125	589	293	464 D	12.4%	58.5%	17.5%	82.5%
34,156	CARROLL	3,671	526	2,671	474	2,145 D	14.3%	72.8%	16.5%	83.5%
12,199	CATOOSA	1,538	268	1,051	219	783 D	17.4%	68.3%	20.3%	79.7%
5,256	CHARLTON	568	70	339	159	269 D	12.3%	59.7%	17.1%	82.9%
117,970	CHATHAM	23,897	5,966	10,864	7,067	4,898 D	25.0%	45.5%	35.4%	64.6%
15,138	CHATTAHOOCHEE	116	1	46	69	45 D	0.9%	39.7%	2.1%	97.9%
18,532	CHATTOOGA	3,950	362	3,396	192	3,034 D	9.2%	86.0%	9.6%	90.4%
20,126	CHEROKEE	2,153	631	1,267	255	636 D	29.3%	58.8%	33.2%	66.8%
28,398	CLARKE	4,317	707	3,095	515	2,388 D	16.4%	71.7%	18.6%	81.4%
7,064	CLAY	367	39	295	33	256 D	10.6%	80.4%	11.7%	88.3%
11,655	CLAYTON	3,296	339	2,192	765	1,853 D	10.3%	66.5%	13.4%	86.6%
6,437	CLINCH	1,744	168	1,283	293	1,115 D	9.6%	73.6%	11.6%	88.4%
38,272	COBB	7,098	1,524	4,766	808	3,242 D	21.5%	67.1%	24.2%	75.8%
21,541	COFFEE	4,144	309	3,168	667	2,859 D	7.5%	76.4%	8.9%	91.1%
33,012	COLQUITT	3,465	537	2,255	673	1,718 D	15.5%	65.1%	19.2%	80.8%
9,433	COLUMBIA	1,060	59	164	837	105 D	5.6%	15.5%	26.5%	73.5%
11,919	COOK	1,574	123	1,192	259	1,069 D	7.8%	75.7%	9.4%	90.6%
26,972	COWETA	2,649	219	2,214	216	1,995 D	8.3%	83.6%	9.0%	91.0%
7,128	CRAWFORD	710	64	389	257	325 D	9.0%	54.8%	14.1%	85.9%
17,540	CRISP	1,973	221	1,225	527	1,004 D	11.2%	62.1%	15.3%	84.7%
5,894	DADE	2,026	338	1,488	200	1,150 D	16.7%	73.4%	18.5%	81.5%
4,479	DAWSON	1,488	786	660	42	126 R	52.8%	44.4%	54.4%	45.6%
22,234	DECATUR	2,272	296	1,209	767	913 D	13.0%	53.2%	19.7%	80.3%
86,942	DE KALB	19,521	5,758	10,826	2,937	5,068 D	29.5%	55.5%	34.7%	65.3%
21,022	DODGE	2,473	210	1,725	538	1,515 D	8.5%	69.8%	10.9%	89.1%
16,886	DOOLY	652	22	577	53	555 D	3.4%	88.5%	3.7%	96.3%
28,565	DOUGHERTY	3,921	614	2,517	790	1,903 D	15.7%	64.2%	19.6%	80.4%
10,053	DOUGLAS	3,346	1,019	1,336	991	317 D	30.5%	39.9%	43.3%	56.7%
18,679	EARLY	1,353	94	1,110	149	1,016 D	6.9%	82.0%	7.8%	92.2%
2,964	ECHOLS	623	32	332	259	300 D	5.1%	53.3%	8.8%	91.2%
9,646	EFFINGHAM	1,293	160	347	786	187 D	12.4%	26.8%	31.6%	68.4%
19,618	ELBERT	2,123	152	1,617	354	1,465 D	7.2%	76.2%	8.6%	91.4%
23,517	EMANUEL	2,398	241	1,436	721	1,195 D	10.1%	59.9%	14.4%	85.6%
7,401	EVANS	1,402	118	953	331	835 D	8.4%	68.0%	11.0%	89.0%
14,752	FANNIN	4,870	2,789	1,998	83	791 R	57.3%	41.0%	58.3%	41.7%
8,170	FAYETTE	1,144	54	825	265	771 D	4.7%	72.1%	6.1%	93.9%
56,141	FLOYD	7,611	1,689	5,247	675	3,558 D	22.2%	68.9%	24.4%	75.6%
11,322	FORSYTH	2,662	573	1,813	276	1,240 D	21.5%	68.1%	24.0%	76.0%
15,612	FRANKLIN	1,329	138	1,036	155	898 D	10.4%	78.0%	11.8%	88.2%

GEORGIA

PRESIDENT 1948

1940 Census Population	County	Total Vote	Republican	Democratic	Other	Rep.-Dem. Plurality	Percentage Total Vote Rep.	Percentage Total Vote Dem.	Percentage Major Vote Rep.	Percentage Major Vote Dem.
392,886	FULTON	51,054	14,976	29,318	6,760	14,342 D	29.3%	57.4%	33.8%	66.2%
9,001	GILMER	2,540	1,203	1,275	62	72 D	47.4%	50.2%	48.5%	51.5%
4,547	GLASCOCK	504	13	123	368	110 D	2.6%	24.4%	9.6%	90.4%
21,920	GLYNN	4,580	1,090	2,444	1,046	1,354 D	23.8%	53.4%	30.8%	69.2%
18,445	GORDON	2,065	377	1,523	165	1,146 D	18.3%	73.8%	19.8%	80.2%
19,654	GRADY	2,180	244	1,516	420	1,272 D	11.2%	69.5%	13.9%	86.1%
13,709	GREENE	1,590	92	1,213	285	1,121 D	5.8%	76.3%	7.0%	93.0%
29,087	GWINNETT	3,727	413	2,832	482	2,419 D	11.1%	76.0%	12.7%	87.3%
14,771	HABERSHAM	2,071	368	1,477	226	1,109 D	17.8%	71.3%	19.9%	80.1%
34,822	HALL	4,159	606	3,093	460	2,487 D	14.6%	74.4%	16.4%	83.6%
12,764	HANCOCK	772	111	441	220	330 D	14.4%	57.1%	20.1%	79.9%
14,377	HARALSON	3,563	831	2,263	469	1,432 D	23.3%	63.5%	26.9%	73.1%
11,428	HARRIS	1,137	138	759	240	621 D	12.1%	66.8%	15.4%	84.6%
15,512	HART	1,530	78	1,363	89	1,285 D	5.1%	89.1%	5.4%	94.6%
8,610	HEARD	800	77	670	53	593 D	9.6%	83.8%	10.3%	89.7%
15,119	HENRY	1,846	229	1,400	217	1,171 D	12.4%	75.8%	14.1%	85.9%
11,303	HOUSTON	2,072	204	1,437	431	1,233 D	9.8%	69.4%	12.4%	87.6%
12,936	IRWIN	1,355	146	946	263	800 D	10.8%	69.8%	13.4%	86.6%
20,089	JACKSON	2,222	145	1,866	211	1,721 D	6.5%	84.0%	7.2%	92.8%
8,772	JASPER	865	87	562	216	475 D	10.1%	65.0%	13.4%	86.6%
8,841	JEFF DAVIS	905	70	611	224	541 D	7.7%	67.5%	10.3%	89.7%
20,040	JEFFERSON	1,716	137	544	1,035	407 D	8.0%	31.7%	20.1%	79.9%
11,843	JENKINS	969	98	595	276	497 D	10.1%	61.4%	14.1%	85.9%
12,953	JOHNSON	1,256	67	685	504	618 D	5.3%	54.5%	8.9%	91.1%
8,331	JONES	1,114	103	588	423	485 D	9.2%	52.8%	14.9%	85.1%
10,091	LAMAR	1,269	164	909	196	745 D	12.9%	71.6%	15.3%	84.7%
5,632	LANIER	680	92	486	102	394 D	13.5%	71.5%	15.9%	84.1%
33,606	LAURENS	3,804	268	2,325	1,211	2,057 D	7.0%	61.1%	10.3%	89.7%
7,837	LEE	468	36	215	217	179 D	7.7%	45.9%	14.3%	85.7%
8,595	LIBERTY	1,212	121	820	271	699 D	10.0%	67.7%	12.9%	87.1%
7,042	LINCOLN	729	32	99	598	67 D	4.4%	13.6%	24.4%	75.6%
4,086	LONG	513	25	337	151	312 D	4.9%	65.7%	6.9%	93.1%
31,860	LOWNDES	3,958	634	1,867	1,457	1,233 D	16.0%	47.2%	25.3%	74.7%
6,223	LUMPKIN	739	142	547	50	405 D	19.2%	74.0%	20.6%	79.4%
10,878	MCDUFFIE	1,500	51	182	1,267	131 D	3.4%	12.1%	21.9%	78.1%
5,292	MCINTOSH	870	233	425	212	192 D	26.8%	48.9%	35.4%	64.6%
15,947	MACON	1,182	127	675	380	548 D	10.7%	57.1%	15.8%	84.2%
13,431	MADISON	1,439	62	1,160	217	1,098 D	4.3%	80.6%	5.1%	94.9%
6,954	MARION	541	45	283	213	238 D	8.3%	52.3%	13.7%	86.3%
22,055	MERIWETHER	2,409	204	1,967	238	1,763 D	8.5%	81.7%	9.4%	90.6%
9,998	MILLER	861	32	723	106	691 D	3.7%	84.0%	4.2%	95.8%
	MILTON	—	—	—	—	—	—	—	—	—
23,261	MITCHELL	2,067	152	1,453	462	1,301 D	7.4%	70.3%	9.5%	90.5%
10,749	MONROE	1,420	169	881	370	712 D	11.9%	62.0%	16.1%	83.9%
9,668	MONTGOMERY	1,693	117	1,048	528	931 D	6.9%	61.9%	10.0%	90.0%
12,713	MORGAN	1,406	115	1,147	144	1,032 D	8.2%	81.6%	9.1%	90.9%
11,137	MURRAY	2,424	616	1,653	155	1,037 D	25.4%	68.2%	27.1%	72.9%
75,494	MUSCOGEE	10,203	2,443	5,920	1,840	3,477 D	23.9%	58.0%	29.2%	70.8%
18,576	NEWTON	2,500	243	2,113	144	1,870 D	9.7%	84.5%	10.3%	89.7%
7,576	OCONEE	935	94	579	262	485 D	10.1%	61.9%	14.0%	86.0%
12,430	OGLETHORPE	1,118	62	819	237	757 D	5.5%	73.3%	7.0%	93.0%
12,832	PAULDING	1,456	333	981	142	648 D	22.9%	67.4%	25.3%	74.7%
10,378	PEACH	1,193	166	642	385	476 D	13.9%	53.8%	20.5%	79.5%
9,136	PICKENS	2,722	1,255	1,239	228	16 R	46.1%	45.5%	50.3%	49.7%
11,800	PIERCE	1,514	108	908	498	800 D	7.1%	60.0%	10.6%	89.4%
10,375	PIKE	472	72	256	144	184 D	15.3%	54.2%	22.0%	78.0%
28,467	POLK	3,706	491	2,918	297	2,427 D	13.2%	78.7%	14.4%	85.6%
9,829	PULASKI	794	64	567	163	503 D	8.1%	71.4%	10.1%	89.9%
8,514	PUTNAM	854	110	609	135	499 D	12.9%	71.3%	15.3%	84.7%
3,435	QUITMAN	361	19	246	96	227 D	5.3%	68.1%	7.2%	92.8%

GEORGIA

PRESIDENT 1948

1940 Census Population	County	Total Vote	Republican	Democratic	Other	Rep.-Dem. Plurality	Percentage Total Vote Rep.	Percentage Total Vote Dem.	Percentage Major Vote Rep.	Percentage Major Vote Dem.
7,821	RABUN	969	165	747	57	582 D	17.0%	77.1%	18.1%	81.9%
16,609	RANDOLPH	970	134	575	261	441 D	13.8%	59.3%	18.9%	81.1%
81,863	RICHMOND	12,846	1,528	2,450	8,868	922 D	11.9%	19.1%	38.4%	61.6%
7,724	ROCKDALE	1,481	126	1,209	146	1,083 D	8.5%	81.6%	9.4%	90.6%
5,033	SCHLEY	375	43	257	75	214 D	11.5%	68.5%	14.3%	85.7%
20,353	SCREVEN	1,513	172	838	503	666 D	11.4%	55.4%	17.0%	83.0%
8,492	SEMINOLE	899	105	722	72	617 D	11.7%	80.3%	12.7%	87.3%
28,427	SPALDING	4,626	506	3,441	679	2,935 D	10.9%	74.4%	12.8%	87.2%
12,972	STEPHENS	1,323	278	912	133	634 D	21.0%	68.9%	23.4%	76.6%
10,603	STEWART	588	46	276	266	230 D	7.8%	46.9%	14.3%	85.7%
24,502	SUMTER	2,144	256	1,018	870	762 D	11.9%	47.5%	20.1%	79.9%
8,141	TALBOT	812	92	582	138	490 D	11.3%	71.7%	13.6%	86.4%
6,278	TALIAFERRO	599	21	504	74	483 D	3.5%	84.1%	4.0%	96.0%
16,243	TATTNALL	1,864	216	1,071	577	855 D	11.6%	57.5%	16.8%	83.2%
10,768	TAYLOR	1,101	99	638	364	539 D	9.0%	57.9%	13.4%	86.6%
15,145	TELFAIR	1,127	75	712	340	637 D	6.7%	63.2%	9.5%	90.5%
16,675	TERRELL	951	100	608	243	508 D	10.5%	63.9%	14.1%	85.9%
31,289	THOMAS	3,667	925	1,429	1,313	504 D	25.2%	39.0%	39.3%	60.7%
18,599	TIFT	4,644	637	3,158	849	2,521 D	13.7%	68.0%	16.8%	83.2%
16,952	TOOMBS	2,016	193	1,161	662	968 D	9.6%	57.6%	14.3%	85.7%
4,925	TOWNS	824	302	516	6	214 D	36.7%	62.6%	36.9%	63.1%
7,632	TREUTLEN	673	26	413	234	387 D	3.9%	61.4%	5.9%	94.1%
43,879	TROUP	5,169	536	3,896	737	3,360 D	10.4%	75.4%	12.1%	87.9%
10,846	TURNER	1,143	147	774	222	627 D	12.9%	67.7%	16.0%	84.0%
9,117	TWIGGS	815	52	359	404	307 D	6.4%	44.0%	12.7%	87.3%
7,680	UNION	2,778	1,274	1,420	84	146 D	45.9%	51.1%	47.3%	52.7%
25,064	UPSON	2,993	262	2,432	299	2,170 D	8.8%	81.3%	9.7%	90.3%
31,024	WALKER	4,895	980	3,418	497	2,438 D	20.0%	69.8%	22.3%	77.7%
20,777	WALTON	2,871	164	2,440	267	2,276 D	5.7%	85.0%	6.3%	93.7%
27,929	WARE	4,650	655	2,611	1,384	1,956 D	14.1%	56.2%	20.1%	79.9%
10,236	WARREN	814	33	256	525	223 D	4.1%	31.4%	11.4%	88.6%
24,230	WASHINGTON	1,379	204	1,169	6	965 D	14.8%	84.8%	14.9%	85.1%
13,122	WAYNE	1,752	190	1,277	285	1,087 D	10.8%	72.9%	13.0%	87.0%
4,726	WEBSTER	314	79	118	117	39 D	25.2%	37.6%	40.1%	59.9%
8,535	WHEELER	885	39	560	286	521 D	4.4%	63.3%	6.5%	93.5%
6,417	WHITE	630	59	497	74	438 D	9.4%	78.9%	10.6%	89.4%
26,105	WHITFIELD	5,391	1,249	3,419	723	2,170 D	23.2%	63.4%	26.8%	73.2%
12,755	WILCOX	1,115	75	791	249	716 D	6.7%	70.9%	8.7%	91.3%
15,084	WILKES	1,212	95	771	346	676 D	7.8%	63.6%	11.0%	89.0%
11,025	WILKINSON	1,099	96	501	502	405 D	8.7%	45.6%	16.1%	83.9%
21,374	WORTH	1,504	124	1,159	221	1,035 D	8.2%	77.1%	9.7%	90.3%
3,123,723	TOTAL	418,844	76,691	254,646	87,507	177,955 D	18.3%	60.8%	23.1%	76.9%

GEORGIA

PRESIDENT 1944

1940 Census Population	County	Total Vote	Republican	Democratic	Other	Rep.-Dem. Plurality	Percentage Total Vote Rep.	Total Vote Dem.	Major Vote Rep.	Major Vote Dem.
14,497	APPLING	1,705	387	1,318		931 D	22.7%	77.3%	22.7%	77.3%
7,093	ATKINSON	856	90	766		676 D	10.5%	89.5%	10.5%	89.5%
8,096	BACON	983	220	763		543 D	22.4%	77.6%	22.4%	77.6%
7,344	BAKER	509	31	478		447 D	6.1%	93.9%	6.1%	93.9%
24,190	BALDWIN	1,614	307	1,307		1,000 D	19.0%	81.0%	19.0%	81.0%
8,733	BANKS	619	125	490	4	365 D	20.2%	79.2%	20.3%	79.7%
13,064	BARROW	1,770	257	1,513		1,256 D	14.5%	85.5%	14.5%	85.5%
25,283	BARTOW	2,421	506	1,915		1,409 D	20.9%	79.1%	20.9%	79.1%
14,523	BEN HILL	1,237	190	1,046	1	856 D	15.4%	84.6%	15.4%	84.6%
15,370	BERRIEN	1,698	217	1,481		1,264 D	12.8%	87.2%	12.8%	87.2%
83,783	BIBB	7,236	1,884	5,352		3,468 D	26.0%	74.0%	26.0%	74.0%
9,655	BLECKLEY	1,028	213	815		602 D	20.7%	79.3%	20.7%	79.3%
6,871	BRANTLEY	664	124	540		416 D	18.7%	81.3%	18.7%	81.3%
20,497	BROOKS	1,660	279	1,381		1,102 D	16.8%	83.2%	16.8%	83.2%
6,288	BRYAN	778	90	688		598 D	11.6%	88.4%	11.6%	88.4%
26,010	BULLOCH	2,195	274	1,921		1,647 D	12.5%	87.5%	12.5%	87.5%
26,520	BURKE	1,062	153	909		756 D	14.4%	85.6%	14.4%	85.6%
9,182	BUTTS	1,415	85	1,330		1,245 D	6.0%	94.0%	6.0%	94.0%
10,438	CALHOUN	773	37	736		699 D	4.8%	95.2%	4.8%	95.2%
5,910	CAMDEN	632	76	556		480 D	12.0%	88.0%	12.0%	88.0%
	CAMPBELL	—	—	—		—	—	—	—	—
9,103	CANDLER	791	138	653		515 D	17.4%	82.6%	17.4%	82.6%
34,156	CARROLL	4,035	704	3,331		2,627 D	17.4%	82.6%	17.4%	82.6%
12,199	CATOOSA	1,848	395	1,453		1,058 D	21.4%	78.6%	21.4%	78.6%
5,256	CHARLTON	551	89	462		373 D	16.2%	83.8%	16.2%	83.8%
117,970	CHATHAM	10,783	2,058	8,725		6,667 D	19.1%	80.9%	19.1%	80.9%
15,138	CHATTAHOOCHEE	119	19	100		81 D	16.0%	84.0%	16.0%	84.0%
18,532	CHATTOOGA	2,782	287	2,495		2,208 D	10.3%	89.7%	10.3%	89.7%
20,126	CHEROKEE	2,407	1,059	1,348		289 D	44.0%	56.0%	44.0%	56.0%
28,398	CLARKE	3,386	274	3,112		2,838 D	8.1%	91.9%	8.1%	91.9%
7,064	CLAY	477	35	442		407 D	7.3%	92.7%	7.3%	92.7%
11,655	CLAYTON	2,074	245	1,828	1	1,583 D	11.8%	88.1%	11.8%	88.2%
6,437	CLINCH	646	64	582		518 D	9.9%	90.1%	9.9%	90.1%
38,272	COBB	6,349	1,349	5,000		3,651 D	21.2%	78.8%	21.2%	78.8%
21,541	COFFEE	1,991	366	1,625		1,259 D	18.4%	81.6%	18.4%	81.6%
33,012	COLQUITT	3,004	696	2,308		1,612 D	23.2%	76.8%	23.2%	76.8%
9,433	COLUMBIA	580	72	508		436 D	12.4%	87.6%	12.4%	87.6%
11,919	COOK	1,359	204	1,155		951 D	15.0%	85.0%	15.0%	85.0%
26,972	COWETA	2,779	130	2,649		2,519 D	4.7%	95.3%	4.7%	95.3%
7,128	CRAWFORD	524	149	375		226 D	28.4%	71.6%	28.4%	71.6%
17,540	CRISP	1,416	217	1,199		982 D	15.3%	84.7%	15.3%	84.7%
5,894	DADE	1,112	169	943		774 D	15.2%	84.8%	15.2%	84.8%
4,479	DAWSON	811	342	469		127 D	42.2%	57.8%	42.2%	57.8%
22,234	DECATUR	1,900	294	1,606		1,312 D	15.5%	84.5%	15.5%	84.5%
86,942	DE KALB	14,625	2,555	12,069	1	9,514 D	17.5%	82.5%	17.5%	82.5%
21,022	DODGE	1,674	237	1,437		1,200 D	14.2%	85.8%	14.2%	85.8%
16,886	DOOLY	932	87	845		758 D	9.3%	90.7%	9.3%	90.7%
28,565	DOUGHERTY	3,537	338	3,199		2,861 D	9.6%	90.4%	9.6%	90.4%
10,053	DOUGLAS	1,108	280	828		548 D	25.3%	74.7%	25.3%	74.7%
18,679	EARLY	1,830	77	1,753		1,676 D	4.2%	95.8%	4.2%	95.8%
2,964	ECHOLS	508	42	466		424 D	8.3%	91.7%	8.3%	91.7%
9,646	EFFINGHAM	798	365	433		68 D	45.7%	54.3%	45.7%	54.3%
19,618	ELBERT	1,936	370	1,564	2	1,194 D	19.1%	80.8%	19.1%	80.9%
23,517	EMANUEL	1,953	317	1,635	1	1,318 D	16.2%	83.7%	16.2%	83.8%
7,401	EVANS	874	117	756	1	639 D	13.4%	86.5%	13.4%	86.6%
14,752	FANNIN	3,278	1,980	1,298		682 R	60.4%	39.6%	60.4%	39.6%
8,170	FAYETTE	880	98	782		684 D	11.1%	88.9%	11.1%	88.9%
56,141	FLOYD	5,887	1,123	4,764		3,641 D	19.1%	80.9%	19.1%	80.9%
11,322	FORSYTH	1,742	695	1,047		352 D	39.9%	60.1%	39.9%	60.1%
15,612	FRANKLIN	1,705	328	1,377		1,049 D	19.2%	80.8%	19.2%	80.8%

GEORGIA

PRESIDENT 1944

1940 Census Population	County	Total Vote	Republican	Democratic	Other	Rep.-Dem. Plurality	Percentage Total Vote Rep.	Total Vote Dem.	Major Vote Rep.	Major Vote Dem.
392,886	FULTON	44,848	7,687	37,161		29,474 D	17.1%	82.9%	17.1%	82.9%
9,001	GILMER	1,677	793	884		91 D	47.3%	52.7%	47.3%	52.7%
4,547	GLASCOCK	479	161	318		157 D	33.6%	66.4%	33.6%	66.4%
21,920	GLYNN	2,380	385	1,995		1,610 D	16.2%	83.8%	16.2%	83.8%
18,445	GORDON	2,075	617	1,457	1	840 D	29.7%	70.2%	29.7%	70.3%
19,654	GRADY	1,884	223	1,661		1,438 D	11.8%	88.2%	11.8%	88.2%
13,709	GREENE	1,394	144	1,246	4	1,102 D	10.3%	89.4%	10.4%	89.6%
29,087	GWINNETT	4,052	713	3,339		2,626 D	17.6%	82.4%	17.6%	82.4%
14,771	HABERSHAM	2,346	504	1,842		1,338 D	21.5%	78.5%	21.5%	78.5%
34,822	HALL	3,863	796	3,066	1	2,270 D	20.6%	79.4%	20.6%	79.4%
12,764	HANCOCK	489	109	380		271 D	22.3%	77.7%	22.3%	77.7%
14,377	HARALSON	2,159	911	1,248		337 D	42.2%	57.8%	42.2%	57.8%
11,428	HARRIS	972	79	893		814 D	8.1%	91.9%	8.1%	91.9%
15,512	HART	1,344	183	1,161		978 D	13.6%	86.4%	13.6%	86.4%
8,610	HEARD	742	185	557		372 D	24.9%	75.1%	24.9%	75.1%
15,119	HENRY	1,613	152	1,461		1,309 D	9.4%	90.6%	9.4%	90.6%
11,303	HOUSTON	725	190	535		345 D	26.2%	73.8%	26.2%	73.8%
12,936	IRWIN	1,121	259	862		603 D	23.1%	76.9%	23.1%	76.9%
20,089	JACKSON	1,975	221	1,754		1,533 D	11.2%	88.8%	11.2%	88.8%
8,772	JASPER	863	86	777		691 D	10.0%	90.0%	10.0%	90.0%
8,841	JEFF DAVIS	857	120	737		617 D	14.0%	86.0%	14.0%	86.0%
20,040	JEFFERSON	1,317	274	1,043		769 D	20.8%	79.2%	20.8%	79.2%
11,843	JENKINS	799	101	698		597 D	12.6%	87.4%	12.6%	87.4%
12,953	JOHNSON	1,282	304	978		674 D	23.7%	76.3%	23.7%	76.3%
8,331	JONES	859	196	661	2	465 D	22.8%	76.9%	22.9%	77.1%
10,091	LAMAR	1,158	143	1,015		872 D	12.3%	87.7%	12.3%	87.7%
5,632	LANIER	665	40	625		585 D	6.0%	94.0%	6.0%	94.0%
33,606	LAURENS	3,042	498	2,544		2,046 D	16.4%	83.6%	16.4%	83.6%
7,837	LEE	474	27	447		420 D	5.7%	94.3%	5.7%	94.3%
8,595	LIBERTY	603	122	481		359 D	20.2%	79.8%	20.2%	79.8%
7,042	LINCOLN	609	165	444		279 D	27.1%	72.9%	27.1%	72.9%
4,086	LONG	447	129	318		189 D	28.9%	71.1%	28.9%	71.1%
31,860	LOWNDES	2,493	401	2,092		1,691 D	16.1%	83.9%	16.1%	83.9%
6,223	LUMPKIN	1,108	212	896		684 D	19.1%	80.9%	19.1%	80.9%
10,878	MCDUFFIE	982	187	795		608 D	19.0%	81.0%	19.0%	81.0%
5,292	MCINTOSH	558	149	406	3	257 D	26.7%	72.8%	26.8%	73.2%
15,947	MACON	1,057	168	889		721 D	15.9%	84.1%	15.9%	84.1%
13,431	MADISON	1,502	265	1,235	2	970 D	17.6%	82.2%	17.7%	82.3%
6,954	MARION	571	70	501		431 D	12.3%	87.7%	12.3%	87.7%
22,055	MERIWETHER	2,376	189	2,187		1,998 D	8.0%	92.0%	8.0%	92.0%
9,998	MILLER	868	59	809		750 D	6.8%	93.2%	6.8%	93.2%
	MILTON	—	—	—		—	—	—	—	—
23,261	MITCHELL	2,405	226	2,179		1,953 D	9.4%	90.6%	9.4%	90.6%
10,749	MONROE	1,542	410	1,132		722 D	26.6%	73.4%	26.6%	73.4%
9,668	MONTGOMERY	670	94	575	1	481 D	14.0%	85.8%	14.1%	85.9%
12,713	MORGAN	1,221	51	1,166	4	1,115 D	4.2%	95.5%	4.2%	95.8%
11,137	MURRAY	2,046	671	1,375		704 D	32.8%	67.2%	32.8%	67.2%
75,494	MUSCOGEE	7,842	1,344	6,498		5,154 D	17.1%	82.9%	17.1%	82.9%
18,576	NEWTON	2,145	123	2,022		1,899 D	5.7%	94.3%	5.7%	94.3%
7,576	OCONEE	765	195	570		375 D	25.5%	74.5%	25.5%	74.5%
12,430	OGLETHORPE	1,095	173	922		749 D	15.8%	84.2%	15.8%	84.2%
12,832	PAULDING	2,133	775	1,355	3	580 D	36.3%	63.5%	36.4%	63.6%
10,378	PEACH	1,155	236	919		683 D	20.4%	79.6%	20.4%	79.6%
9,136	PICKENS	1,575	795	780		15 R	50.5%	49.5%	50.5%	49.5%
11,800	PIERCE	1,234	165	1,069		904 D	13.4%	86.6%	13.4%	86.6%
10,375	PIKE	875	133	742		609 D	15.2%	84.8%	15.2%	84.8%
28,467	POLK	3,161	463	2,698		2,235 D	14.6%	85.4%	14.6%	85.4%
9,829	PULASKI	647	55	592		537 D	8.5%	91.5%	8.5%	91.5%
8,514	PUTNAM	775	74	701		627 D	9.5%	90.5%	9.5%	90.5%
3,435	QUITMAN	371	16	355		339 D	4.3%	95.7%	4.3%	95.7%

GEORGIA

PRESIDENT 1944

1940 Census Population	County	Total Vote	Republican	Democratic	Other	Rep.-Dem. Plurality	Percentage Total Vote Rep.	Total Vote Dem.	Major Vote Rep.	Major Vote Dem.
7,821	RABUN	1,432	185	1,247		1,062 D	12.9%	87.1%	12.9%	87.1%
16,609	RANDOLPH	1,265	106	1,159		1,053 D	8.4%	91.6%	8.4%	91.6%
81,863	RICHMOND	8,070	1,152	6,918		5,766 D	14.3%	85.7%	14.3%	85.7%
7,724	ROCKDALE	1,042	96	946		850 D	9.2%	90.8%	9.2%	90.8%
5,033	SCHLEY	366	37	329		292 D	10.1%	89.9%	10.1%	89.9%
20,353	SCREVEN	1,092	197	895		698 D	18.0%	82.0%	18.0%	82.0%
8,492	SEMINOLE	1,159	83	1,076		993 D	7.2%	92.8%	7.2%	92.8%
28,427	SPALDING	3,023	217	2,805	1	2,588 D	7.2%	92.8%	7.2%	92.8%
12,972	STEPHENS	1,370	212	1,158		946 D	15.5%	84.5%	15.5%	84.5%
10,603	STEWART	675	78	597		519 D	11.6%	88.4%	11.6%	88.4%
24,502	SUMTER	1,744	194	1,550		1,356 D	11.1%	88.9%	11.1%	88.9%
8,141	TALBOT	877	45	832		787 D	5.1%	94.9%	5.1%	94.9%
6,278	TALIAFERRO	395	6	389		383 D	1.5%	98.5%	1.5%	98.5%
16,243	TATTNALL	1,709	494	1,215		721 D	28.9%	71.1%	28.9%	71.1%
10,768	TAYLOR	1,042	269	773		504 D	25.8%	74.2%	25.8%	74.2%
15,145	TELFAIR	1,361	174	1,187		1,013 D	12.8%	87.2%	12.8%	87.2%
16,675	TERRELL	1,688	49	1,639		1,590 D	2.9%	97.1%	2.9%	97.1%
31,289	THOMAS	2,305	557	1,747	1	1,190 D	24.2%	75.8%	24.2%	75.8%
18,599	TIFT	2,026	396	1,630		1,234 D	19.5%	80.5%	19.5%	80.5%
16,952	TOOMBS	2,062	237	1,825		1,588 D	11.5%	88.5%	11.5%	88.5%
4,925	TOWNS	1,811	674	1,137		463 D	37.2%	62.8%	37.2%	62.8%
7,632	TREUTLEN	947	54	893		839 D	5.7%	94.3%	5.7%	94.3%
43,879	TROUP	3,575	342	3,233		2,891 D	9.6%	90.4%	9.6%	90.4%
10,846	TURNER	1,132	334	797	1	463 D	29.5%	70.4%	29.5%	70.5%
9,117	TWIGGS	627	170	457		287 D	27.1%	72.9%	27.1%	72.9%
7,680	UNION	2,048	760	1,288		528 D	37.1%	62.9%	37.1%	62.9%
25,064	UPSON	2,605	243	2,362		2,119 D	9.3%	90.7%	9.3%	90.7%
31,024	WALKER	3,519	765	2,753	1	1,988 D	21.7%	78.2%	21.7%	78.3%
20,777	WALTON	2,218	172	2,046		1,874 D	7.8%	92.2%	7.8%	92.2%
27,929	WARE	2,767	459	2,306	2	1,847 D	16.6%	83.3%	16.6%	83.4%
10,236	WARREN	603	152	449	2	297 D	25.2%	74.5%	25.3%	74.7%
24,230	WASHINGTON	1,445	351	1,094		743 D	24.3%	75.7%	24.3%	75.7%
13,122	WAYNE	1,230	252	978		726 D	20.5%	79.5%	20.5%	79.5%
4,726	WEBSTER	349	65	284		219 D	18.6%	81.4%	18.6%	81.4%
8,535	WHEELER	668	151	517		366 D	22.6%	77.4%	22.6%	77.4%
6,417	WHITE	869	161	706	2	545 D	18.5%	81.2%	18.6%	81.4%
26,105	WHITFIELD	3,859	1,032	2,827		1,795 D	26.7%	73.3%	26.7%	73.3%
12,755	WILCOX	1,570	206	1,364		1,158 D	13.1%	86.9%	13.1%	86.9%
15,084	WILKES	1,105	159	946		787 D	14.4%	85.6%	14.4%	85.6%
11,025	WILKINSON	1,034	271	763		492 D	26.2%	73.8%	26.2%	73.8%
21,374	WORTH	1,314	218	1,096		878 D	16.6%	83.4%	16.6%	83.4%
3,123,723	TOTAL	328,129	59,900	268,187	42	208,287 D	18.3%	81.7%	18.3%	81.7%

GEORGIA

PRESIDENT 1940

1940 Census Population	County	Total Vote	Republican	Democratic	Other	Rep.-Dem. Plurality	Percentage: Total Vote Rep.	Total Vote Dem.	Major Vote Rep.	Major Vote Dem.
14,497	APPLING	1,842	312	1,514	16	1,202 D	16.9%	82.2%	17.1%	82.9%
7,093	ATKINSON	770	66	703	1	637 D	8.6%	91.3%	8.6%	91.4%
8,096	BACON	923	97	821	5	724 D	10.5%	88.9%	10.6%	89.4%
7,344	BAKER	588	30	557	1	527 D	5.1%	94.7%	5.1%	94.9%
24,190	BALDWIN	1,520	203	1,313	4	1,110 D	13.4%	86.4%	13.4%	86.6%
8,733	BANKS	838	164	668	6	504 D	19.6%	79.7%	19.7%	80.3%
13,064	BARROW	1,839	219	1,615	5	1,396 D	11.9%	87.8%	11.9%	88.1%
25,283	BARTOW	2,060	318	1,734	8	1,416 D	15.4%	84.2%	15.5%	84.5%
14,523	BEN HILL	1,392	181	1,206	5	1,025 D	13.0%	86.6%	13.0%	87.0%
15,370	BERRIEN	1,180	23	1,156	1	1,133 D	1.9%	98.0%	2.0%	98.0%
83,783	BIBB	8,137	1,371	6,729	37	5,358 D	16.8%	82.7%	16.9%	83.1%
9,655	BLECKLEY	888	100	785	3	685 D	11.3%	88.4%	11.3%	88.7%
6,871	BRANTLEY	1,030	67	960	3	893 D	6.5%	93.2%	6.5%	93.5%
20,497	BROOKS	1,549	248	1,300	1	1,052 D	16.0%	83.9%	16.0%	84.0%
6,288	BRYAN	925	49	874	2	825 D	5.3%	94.5%	5.3%	94.7%
26,010	BULLOCH	2,210	141	2,063	6	1,922 D	6.4%	93.3%	6.4%	93.6%
26,520	BURKE	1,077	42	1,029	6	987 D	3.9%	95.5%	3.9%	96.1%
9,182	BUTTS	1,101	87	1,012	2	925 D	7.9%	91.9%	7.9%	92.1%
10,438	CALHOUN	643	33	610		577 D	5.1%	94.9%	5.1%	94.9%
5,910	CAMDEN	625	60	564	1	504 D	9.6%	90.2%	9.6%	90.4%
	CAMPBELL	—	—	—	—	—	—	—	—	—
9,103	CANDLER	813	63	748	2	685 D	7.7%	92.0%	7.8%	92.2%
34,156	CARROLL	4,432	616	3,808	8	3,192 D	13.9%	85.9%	13.9%	86.1%
12,199	CATOOSA	1,689	249	1,440		1,191 D	14.7%	85.3%	14.7%	85.3%
5,256	CHARLTON	622	60	562		502 D	9.6%	90.4%	9.6%	90.4%
117,970	CHATHAM	12,052	1,985	10,048	19	8,063 D	16.5%	83.4%	16.5%	83.5%
15,138	CHATTAHOOCHEE	224	20	204		184 D	8.9%	91.1%	8.9%	91.1%
18,532	CHATTOOGA	2,697	273	2,413	11	2,140 D	10.1%	89.5%	10.2%	89.8%
20,126	CHEROKEE	2,582	1,017	1,552	13	535 D	39.4%	60.1%	39.6%	60.4%
28,398	CLARKE	3,150	246	2,894	10	2,648 D	7.8%	91.9%	7.8%	92.2%
7,064	CLAY	523	33	488	2	455 D	6.3%	93.3%	6.3%	93.7%
11,655	CLAYTON	1,545	161	1,382	2	1,221 D	10.4%	89.4%	10.4%	89.6%
6,437	CLINCH	1,112	63	1,049		986 D	5.7%	94.3%	5.7%	94.3%
38,272	COBB	5,448	992	4,447	9	3,455 D	18.2%	81.6%	18.2%	81.8%
21,541	COFFEE	1,694	128	1,561	5	1,433 D	7.6%	92.1%	7.6%	92.4%
33,012	COLQUITT	2,361	525	1,819	17	1,294 D	22.2%	77.0%	22.4%	77.6%
9,433	COLUMBIA	677	46	627	4	581 D	6.8%	92.6%	6.8%	93.2%
11,919	COOK	1,084	143	941		798 D	13.2%	86.8%	13.2%	86.8%
26,972	COWETA	2,957	103	2,846	8	2,743 D	3.5%	96.2%	3.5%	96.5%
7,128	CRAWFORD	437	74	362	1	288 D	16.9%	82.8%	17.0%	83.0%
17,540	CRISP	1,182	129	1,049	4	920 D	10.9%	88.7%	11.0%	89.0%
5,894	DADE	1,133	151	982		831 D	13.3%	86.7%	13.3%	86.7%
4,479	DAWSON	763	276	484	3	208 D	36.2%	63.4%	36.3%	63.7%
22,234	DECATUR	2,000	217	1,781	2	1,564 D	10.9%	89.1%	10.9%	89.1%
86,942	DE KALB	10,988	2,081	8,862	45	6,781 D	18.9%	80.7%	19.0%	81.0%
21,022	DODGE	1,456	171	1,280	5	1,109 D	11.7%	87.9%	11.8%	88.2%
16,886	DOOLY	1,337	124	1,209	4	1,085 D	9.3%	90.4%	9.3%	90.7%
28,565	DOUGHERTY	2,356	180	2,175	1	1,995 D	7.6%	92.3%	7.6%	92.4%
10,053	DOUGLAS	1,033	195	833	5	638 D	18.9%	80.6%	19.0%	81.0%
18,679	EARLY	1,857	104	1,751	2	1,647 D	5.6%	94.3%	5.6%	94.4%
2,964	ECHOLS	460	18	441	1	423 D	3.9%	95.9%	3.9%	96.1%
9,646	EFFINGHAM	860	227	633		406 D	26.4%	73.6%	26.4%	73.6%
19,618	ELBERT	2,429	357	2,052	20	1,695 D	14.7%	84.5%	14.8%	85.2%
23,517	EMANUEL	1,511	81	1,428	2	1,347 D	5.4%	94.5%	5.4%	94.6%
7,401	EVANS	1,520	112	1,399	9	1,287 D	7.4%	92.0%	7.4%	92.6%
14,752	FANNIN	4,027	2,256	1,771		485 R	56.0%	44.0%	56.0%	44.0%
8,170	FAYETTE	621	44	577		533 D	7.1%	92.9%	7.1%	92.9%
56,141	FLOYD	6,461	912	5,528	21	4,616 D	14.1%	85.6%	14.2%	85.8%
11,322	FORSYTH	2,012	634	1,378		744 D	31.5%	68.5%	31.5%	68.5%
15,612	FRANKLIN	1,822	222	1,579	21	1,357 D	12.2%	86.7%	12.3%	87.7%

GEORGIA

PRESIDENT 1940

1940 Census Population	County	Total Vote	Republican	Democratic	Other	Rep.-Dem. Plurality	Percentage: Total Vote Rep.	Total Vote Dem.	Major Vote Rep.	Major Vote Dem.
392,886	FULTON	37,466	6,033	31,311	122	25,278 D	16.1%	83.6%	16.2%	83.8%
9,001	GILMER	1,521	653	865	3	212 D	42.9%	56.9%	43.0%	57.0%
4,547	GLASCOCK	410	76	332	2	256 D	18.5%	81.0%	18.6%	81.4%
21,920	GLYNN	2,295	274	2,014	7	1,740 D	11.9%	87.8%	12.0%	88.0%
18,445	GORDON	2,159	527	1,623	9	1,096 D	24.4%	75.2%	24.5%	75.5%
19,654	GRADY	1,697	224	1,461	12	1,237 D	13.2%	86.1%	13.3%	86.7%
13,709	GREENE	1,658	148	1,497	13	1,349 D	8.9%	90.3%	9.0%	91.0%
29,087	GWINNETT	4,771	728	4,023	20	3,295 D	15.3%	84.3%	15.3%	84.7%
14,771	HABERSHAM	2,270	421	1,840	9	1,419 D	18.5%	81.1%	18.6%	81.4%
34,822	HALL	3,482	513	2,943	26	2,430 D	14.7%	84.5%	14.8%	85.2%
12,764	HANCOCK	655	153	501	1	348 D	23.4%	76.5%	23.4%	76.6%
14,377	HARALSON	1,858	457	1,397	4	940 D	24.6%	75.2%	24.6%	75.4%
11,428	HARRIS	993	71	914	8	843 D	7.2%	92.0%	7.2%	92.8%
15,512	HART	1,441	97	1,328	16	1,231 D	6.7%	92.2%	6.8%	93.2%
8,610	HEARD	870	221	647	2	426 D	25.4%	74.4%	25.5%	74.5%
15,119	HENRY	1,654	101	1,551	2	1,450 D	6.1%	93.8%	6.1%	93.9%
11,303	HOUSTON	772	149	622	1	473 D	19.3%	80.6%	19.3%	80.7%
12,936	IRWIN	1,162	197	962	3	765 D	17.0%	82.8%	17.0%	83.0%
20,089	JACKSON	1,771	166	1,599	6	1,433 D	9.4%	90.3%	9.4%	90.6%
8,772	JASPER	763	72	689	2	617 D	9.4%	90.3%	9.5%	90.5%
8,841	JEFF DAVIS	799	101	696	2	595 D	12.6%	87.1%	12.7%	87.3%
20,040	JEFFERSON	1,246	171	1,068	7	897 D	13.7%	85.7%	13.8%	86.2%
11,843	JENKINS	1,011	69	940	2	871 D	6.8%	93.0%	6.8%	93.2%
12,953	JOHNSON	2,704	306	2,386	12	2,080 D	11.3%	88.2%	11.4%	88.6%
8,331	JONES	715	101	613	1	512 D	14.1%	85.7%	14.1%	85.9%
10,091	LAMAR	959	85	869	5	784 D	8.9%	90.6%	8.9%	91.1%
5,632	LANIER	625	16	607	2	591 D	2.6%	97.1%	2.6%	97.4%
33,606	LAURENS	2,755	435	2,316	4	1,881 D	15.8%	84.1%	15.8%	84.2%
7,837	LEE	435	17	416	2	399 D	3.9%	95.6%	3.9%	96.1%
8,595	LIBERTY	510	102	407	1	305 D	20.0%	79.8%	20.0%	80.0%
7,042	LINCOLN	538	67	466	5	399 D	12.5%	86.6%	12.6%	87.4%
4,086	LONG	397	76	319	2	243 D	19.1%	80.4%	19.2%	80.8%
31,860	LOWNDES	2,822	260	2,551	11	2,291 D	9.2%	90.4%	9.2%	90.8%
6,223	LUMPKIN	1,067	165	899	3	734 D	15.5%	84.3%	15.5%	84.5%
10,878	MCDUFFIE	1,041	75	959	7	884 D	7.2%	92.1%	7.3%	92.7%
5,292	MCINTOSH	574	106	468		362 D	18.5%	81.5%	18.5%	81.5%
15,947	MACON	928	72	852	4	780 D	7.8%	91.8%	7.8%	92.2%
13,431	MADISON	1,359	185	1,160	14	975 D	13.6%	85.4%	13.8%	86.2%
6,954	MARION	683	77	605	1	528 D	11.3%	88.6%	11.3%	88.7%
22,055	MERIWETHER	2,908	174	2,726	8	2,552 D	6.0%	93.7%	6.0%	94.0%
9,998	MILLER	825	50	775		725 D	6.1%	93.9%	6.1%	93.9%
	MILTON	—	—	—	—	—	—	—	—	—
23,261	MITCHELL	2,286	155	2,131		1,976 D	6.8%	93.2%	6.8%	93.2%
10,749	MONROE	1,069	49	1,014	6	965 D	4.6%	94.9%	4.6%	95.4%
9,668	MONTGOMERY	767	75	686	6	611 D	9.8%	89.4%	9.9%	90.1%
12,713	MORGAN	508	24	484		460 D	4.7%	95.3%	4.7%	95.3%
11,137	MURRAY	1,946	545	1,399	2	854 D	28.0%	71.9%	28.0%	72.0%
75,494	MUSCOGEE	6,101	702	5,392	7	4,690 D	11.5%	88.4%	11.5%	88.5%
18,576	NEWTON	1,611	95	1,512	4	1,417 D	5.9%	93.9%	5.9%	94.1%
7,576	OCONEE	817	177	635	5	458 D	21.7%	77.7%	21.8%	78.2%
12,430	OGLETHORPE	950	131	818	1	687 D	13.8%	86.1%	13.8%	86.2%
12,832	PAULDING	2,435	770	1,653	12	883 D	31.6%	67.9%	31.8%	68.2%
10,378	PEACH	899	155	738	6	583 D	17.2%	82.1%	17.4%	82.6%
9,136	PICKENS	2,020	884	1,124	12	240 D	43.8%	55.6%	44.0%	56.0%
11,800	PIERCE	1,030	84	943	3	859 D	8.2%	91.6%	8.2%	91.8%
10,375	PIKE	1,038	209	829		620 D	20.1%	79.9%	20.1%	79.9%
28,467	POLK	3,104	401	2,693	10	2,292 D	12.9%	86.8%	13.0%	87.0%
9,829	PULASKI	520	38	478	4	440 D	7.3%	91.9%	7.4%	92.6%
8,514	PUTNAM	792	61	730	1	669 D	7.7%	92.2%	7.7%	92.3%
3,435	QUITMAN	343	19	324		305 D	5.5%	94.5%	5.5%	94.5%

GEORGIA

PRESIDENT 1940

1940 Census Population	County	Total Vote	Republican	Democratic	Other	Rep.-Dem. Plurality	Percentage Total Vote Rep.	Percentage Total Vote Dem.	Percentage Major Vote Rep.	Percentage Major Vote Dem.
7,821	RABUN	1,043	82	958	3	876 D	7.9%	91.9%	7.9%	92.1%
16,609	RANDOLPH	1,443	143	1,298	2	1,155 D	9.9%	90.0%	9.9%	90.1%
81,863	RICHMOND	6,508	641	5,855	12	5,214 D	9.8%	90.0%	9.9%	90.1%
7,724	ROCKDALE	1,380	86	1,291	3	1,205 D	6.2%	93.6%	6.2%	93.8%
5,033	SCHLEY	542	69	471	2	402 D	12.7%	86.9%	12.8%	87.2%
20,353	SCREVEN	1,279	100	1,174	5	1,074 D	7.8%	91.8%	7.8%	92.2%
8,492	SEMINOLE	946	58	884	4	826 D	6.1%	93.4%	6.2%	93.8%
28,427	SPALDING	3,223	197	3,022	4	2,825 D	6.1%	93.8%	6.1%	93.9%
12,972	STEPHENS	1,182	90	1,084	8	994 D	7.6%	91.7%	7.7%	92.3%
10,603	STEWART	652	52	600		548 D	8.0%	92.0%	8.0%	92.0%
24,502	SUMTER	1,692	118	1,561	13	1,443 D	7.0%	92.3%	7.0%	93.0%
8,141	TALBOT	706	49	656	1	607 D	6.9%	92.9%	7.0%	93.0%
6,278	TALIAFERRO	526	19	507		488 D	3.6%	96.4%	3.6%	96.4%
16,243	TATTNALL	1,674	421	1,246	7	825 D	25.1%	74.4%	25.3%	74.7%
10,768	TAYLOR	1,011	213	796	2	583 D	21.1%	78.7%	21.1%	78.9%
15,145	TELFAIR	1,508	104	1,391	13	1,287 D	6.9%	92.2%	7.0%	93.0%
16,675	TERRELL	1,040		1,040		1,040 D		100.0%		100.0%
31,289	THOMAS	2,448	371	2,072	5	1,701 D	15.2%	84.6%	15.2%	84.8%
18,599	TIFT	1,711	226	1,463	22	1,237 D	13.2%	85.5%	13.4%	86.6%
16,952	TOOMBS	1,195	134	1,061		927 D	11.2%	88.8%	11.2%	88.8%
4,925	TOWNS	1,724	830	894		64 D	48.1%	51.9%	48.1%	51.9%
7,632	TREUTLEN	1,222	38	1,184		1,146 D	3.1%	96.9%	3.1%	96.9%
43,879	TROUP	3,477	288	3,176	13	2,888 D	8.3%	91.3%	8.3%	91.7%
10,846	TURNER	1,147	351	791	5	440 D	30.6%	69.0%	30.7%	69.3%
9,117	TWIGGS	814	91	723		632 D	11.2%	88.8%	11.2%	88.8%
7,680	UNION	1,509	557	950	2	393 D	36.9%	63.0%	37.0%	63.0%
25,064	UPSON	2,394	159	2,235		2,076 D	6.6%	93.4%	6.6%	93.4%
31,024	WALKER	3,424	558	2,859	7	2,301 D	16.3%	83.5%	16.3%	83.7%
20,777	WALTON	2,288	104	2,179	5	2,075 D	4.5%	95.2%	4.6%	95.4%
27,929	WARE	2,986	308	2,672	6	2,364 D	10.3%	89.5%	10.3%	89.7%
10,236	WARREN	703	95	606	2	511 D	13.5%	86.2%	13.6%	86.4%
24,230	WASHINGTON	1,374	253	1,112	9	859 D	18.4%	80.9%	18.5%	81.5%
13,122	WAYNE	1,725	179	1,542	4	1,363 D	10.4%	89.4%	10.4%	89.6%
4,726	WEBSTER	330	50	280		230 D	15.2%	84.8%	15.2%	84.8%
8,535	WHEELER	615	117	495	3	378 D	19.0%	80.5%	19.1%	80.9%
6,417	WHITE	865	111	754		643 D	12.8%	87.2%	12.8%	87.2%
26,105	WHITFIELD	4,159	991	3,162	6	2,171 D	23.8%	76.0%	23.9%	76.1%
12,755	WILCOX	1,017	118	890	9	772 D	11.6%	87.5%	11.7%	88.3%
15,084	WILKES	1,152	123	1,022	7	899 D	10.7%	88.7%	10.7%	89.3%
11,025	WILKINSON	1,054	147	906	1	759 D	13.9%	86.0%	14.0%	86.0%
21,374	WORTH	1,129	190	936	3	746 D	16.8%	82.9%	16.9%	83.1%
3,123,723	TOTAL	312,686	46,495	265,194	997	218,699 D	14.9%	84.8%	14.9%	85.1%

GEORGIA

PRESIDENT 1936

1930 Census Population	County	Total Vote	Republican	Democratic	Other	Rep.-Dem. Plurality	Percentage Total Vote Rep.	Percentage Total Vote Dem.	Percentage Major Vote Rep.	Percentage Major Vote Dem.
13,314	APPLING	1,457	140	1,309	8	1,169 D	9.6%	89.8%	9.7%	90.3%
6,894	ATKINSON	987	29	958		929 D	2.9%	97.1%	2.9%	97.1%
7,055	BACON	991	62	929		867 D	6.3%	93.7%	6.3%	93.7%
7,818	BAKER	613	13	599	1	586 D	2.1%	97.7%	2.1%	97.9%
22,878	BALDWIN	926	113	811	2	698 D	12.2%	87.6%	12.2%	87.8%
9,703	BANKS	822	181	641		460 D	22.0%	78.0%	22.0%	78.0%
12,401	BARROW	1,355	172	1,181	2	1,009 D	12.7%	87.2%	12.7%	87.3%
25,364	BARTOW	2,680	444	2,228	8	1,784 D	16.6%	83.1%	16.6%	83.4%
13,047	BEN HILL	1,294	146	1,147	1	1,001 D	11.3%	88.6%	11.3%	88.7%
14,646	BERRIEN	1,753	53	1,700		1,647 D	3.0%	97.0%	3.0%	97.0%
77,042	BIBB	6,197	452	5,722	23	5,270 D	7.3%	92.3%	7.3%	92.7%
9,133	BLECKLEY	720	69	649	2	580 D	9.6%	90.1%	9.6%	90.4%
6,895	BRANTLEY	572	40	527	5	487 D	7.0%	92.1%	7.1%	92.9%
21,330	BROOKS	1,377	94	1,277	6	1,183 D	6.8%	92.7%	6.9%	93.1%
5,952	BRYAN	699	63	632	4	569 D	9.0%	90.4%	9.1%	90.9%
26,509	BULLOCH	2,049	66	1,978	5	1,912 D	3.2%	96.5%	3.2%	96.8%
29,224	BURKE	1,094	51	1,040	3	989 D	4.7%	95.1%	4.7%	95.3%
9,345	BUTTS	853	28	820	5	792 D	3.3%	96.1%	3.3%	96.7%
10,576	CALHOUN	793	14	777	2	763 D	1.8%	98.0%	1.8%	98.2%
6,338	CAMDEN	571	53	515	3	462 D	9.3%	90.2%	9.3%	90.7%
	CAMPBELL	—	—	—	—	—	—	—	—	—
8,991	CANDLER	1,075	80	992	3	912 D	7.4%	92.3%	7.5%	92.5%
34,272	CARROLL	4,374	653	3,717	4	3,064 D	14.9%	85.0%	14.9%	85.1%
9,421	CATOOSA	1,239	218	1,018	3	800 D	17.6%	82.2%	17.6%	82.4%
4,381	CHARLTON	497	28	468	1	440 D	5.6%	94.2%	5.6%	94.4%
105,431	CHATHAM	11,270	1,227	10,019	24	8,792 D	10.9%	88.9%	10.9%	89.1%
8,894	CHATTAHOOCHEE	226	20	206		186 D	8.8%	91.2%	8.8%	91.2%
15,407	CHATTOOGA	3,232	231	2,999	2	2,768 D	7.1%	92.8%	7.2%	92.8%
20,003	CHEROKEE	2,060	842	1,211	7	369 D	40.9%	58.8%	41.0%	59.0%
25,613	CLARKE	2,796	160	2,632	4	2,472 D	5.7%	94.1%	5.7%	94.3%
6,943	CLAY	499	13	484	2	471 D	2.6%	97.0%	2.6%	97.4%
10,260	CLAYTON	1,530	175	1,352	3	1,177 D	11.4%	88.4%	11.5%	88.5%
7,015	CLINCH	1,075	71	1,002	2	931 D	6.6%	93.2%	6.6%	93.4%
35,408	COBB	3,515	707	2,802	6	2,095 D	20.1%	79.7%	20.1%	79.9%
19,739	COFFEE	1,819	116	1,702	1	1,586 D	6.4%	93.6%	6.4%	93.6%
30,622	COLQUITT	2,901	448	2,449	4	2,001 D	15.4%	84.4%	15.5%	84.5%
8,793	COLUMBIA	700	34	659	7	625 D	4.9%	94.1%	4.9%	95.1%
11,311	COOK	1,816	117	1,697	2	1,580 D	6.4%	93.4%	6.4%	93.6%
25,127	COWETA	2,336	73	2,260	3	2,187 D	3.1%	96.7%	3.1%	96.9%
7,020	CRAWFORD	437	22	413	2	391 D	5.0%	94.5%	5.1%	94.9%
17,343	CRISP	1,110	79	1,029	2	950 D	7.1%	92.7%	7.1%	92.9%
4,146	DADE	985	127	857	1	730 D	12.9%	87.0%	12.9%	87.1%
3,502	DAWSON	699	322	377		55 D	46.1%	53.9%	46.1%	53.9%
23,622	DECATUR	2,053	79	1,965	9	1,886 D	3.8%	95.7%	3.9%	96.1%
70,278	DE KALB	8,560	1,137	7,391	32	6,254 D	13.3%	86.3%	13.3%	86.7%
21,599	DODGE	1,336	71	1,259	6	1,188 D	5.3%	94.2%	5.3%	94.7%
18,025	DOOLY	1,380	41	1,339		1,298 D	3.0%	97.0%	3.0%	97.0%
22,306	DOUGHERTY	2,716	122	2,591	3	2,469 D	4.5%	95.4%	4.5%	95.5%
9,461	DOUGLAS	1,255	237	1,015	3	778 D	18.9%	80.9%	18.9%	81.1%
18,273	EARLY	1,157	46	1,107	4	1,061 D	4.0%	95.7%	4.0%	96.0%
2,744	ECHOLS	331	30	300	1	270 D	9.1%	90.6%	9.1%	90.9%
10,164	EFFINGHAM	755	142	612	1	470 D	18.8%	81.1%	18.8%	81.2%
18,485	ELBERT	2,232	438	1,772	22	1,334 D	19.6%	79.4%	19.8%	80.2%
24,101	EMANUEL	2,081	125	1,943	13	1,818 D	6.0%	93.4%	6.0%	94.0%
7,102	EVANS	771	35	733	3	698 D	4.5%	95.1%	4.6%	95.4%
12,969	FANNIN	3,430	1,890	1,540		350 R	55.1%	44.9%	55.1%	44.9%
8,665	FAYETTE	819	70	748	1	678 D	8.5%	91.3%	8.6%	91.4%
48,667	FLOYD	6,119	612	5,499	8	4,887 D	10.0%	89.9%	10.0%	90.0%
10,624	FORSYTH	1,331	551	780		229 D	41.4%	58.6%	41.4%	58.6%
15,902	FRANKLIN	1,869	238	1,621	10	1,383 D	12.7%	86.7%	12.8%	87.2%

GEORGIA

PRESIDENT 1936

1930 Census Population	County	Total Vote	Republican	Democratic	Other	Rep.-Dem. Plurality	Percentage Total Vote Rep.	Percentage Total Vote Dem.	Percentage Major Vote Rep.	Percentage Major Vote Dem.
335,220	FULTON	30,829	3,552	27,183	94	23,631 D	11.5%	88.2%	11.6%	88.4%
7,344	GILMER	2,175	1,047	1,128		81 D	48.1%	51.9%	48.1%	51.9%
4,388	GLASCOCK	440	68	369	3	301 D	15.5%	83.9%	15.6%	84.4%
19,400	GLYNN	2,188	260	1,925	3	1,665 D	11.9%	88.0%	11.9%	88.1%
16,846	GORDON	2,537	504	2,026	7	1,522 D	19.9%	79.9%	19.9%	80.1%
19,200	GRADY	1,829	163	1,659	7	1,496 D	8.9%	90.7%	8.9%	91.1%
12,616	GREENE	1,444	86	1,348	10	1,262 D	6.0%	93.4%	6.0%	94.0%
27,853	GWINNETT	2,926	541	2,382	3	1,841 D	18.5%	81.4%	18.5%	81.5%
12,748	HABERSHAM	2,328	424	1,884	20	1,460 D	18.2%	80.9%	18.4%	81.6%
30,313	HALL	3,181	444	2,731	6	2,287 D	14.0%	85.9%	14.0%	86.0%
13,070	HANCOCK	570	57	504	9	447 D	10.0%	88.4%	10.2%	89.8%
13,263	HARALSON	2,438	787	1,643	8	856 D	32.3%	67.4%	32.4%	67.6%
11,140	HARRIS	1,008	54	953	1	899 D	5.4%	94.5%	5.4%	94.6%
15,174	HART	1,741	222	1,514	5	1,292 D	12.8%	87.0%	12.8%	87.2%
9,102	HEARD	883	155	725	3	570 D	17.6%	82.1%	17.6%	82.4%
15,924	HENRY	1,482	116	1,362	4	1,246 D	7.8%	91.9%	7.8%	92.2%
11,280	HOUSTON	833	37	796		759 D	4.4%	95.6%	4.4%	95.6%
12,199	IRWIN	1,141	110	1,025	6	915 D	9.6%	89.8%	9.7%	90.3%
21,609	JACKSON	2,638	187	2,447	4	2,260 D	7.1%	92.8%	7.1%	92.9%
8,594	JASPER	956	33	923		890 D	3.5%	96.5%	3.5%	96.5%
8,118	JEFF DAVIS	724	93	631		538 D	12.8%	87.2%	12.8%	87.2%
20,727	JEFFERSON	1,418	168	1,238	12	1,070 D	11.8%	87.3%	11.9%	88.1%
12,908	JENKINS	912	32	880		848 D	3.5%	96.5%	3.5%	96.5%
12,681	JOHNSON	2,205	334	1,861	10	1,527 D	15.1%	84.4%	15.2%	84.8%
8,992	JONES	531	23	508		485 D	4.3%	95.7%	4.3%	95.7%
9,745	LAMAR	909	69	839	1	770 D	7.6%	92.3%	7.6%	92.4%
5,190	LANIER	835	30	800	5	770 D	3.6%	95.8%	3.6%	96.4%
32,693	LAURENS	2,931	304	2,620	7	2,316 D	10.4%	89.4%	10.4%	89.6%
8,328	LEE	492	1	490	1	489 D	0.2%	99.6%	0.2%	99.8%
8,153	LIBERTY	421	49	369	3	320 D	11.6%	87.6%	11.7%	88.3%
7,847	LINCOLN	666	88	561	17	473 D	13.2%	84.2%	13.6%	86.4%
4,180	LONG	359	51	305	3	254 D	14.2%	85.0%	14.3%	85.7%
29,994	LOWNDES	3,266	130	3,099	37	2,969 D	4.0%	94.9%	4.0%	96.0%
4,927	LUMPKIN	777	160	617		457 D	20.6%	79.4%	20.6%	79.4%
9,014	MCDUFFIE	809	98	705	6	607 D	12.1%	87.1%	12.2%	87.8%
5,763	MCINTOSH	361	53	308		255 D	14.7%	85.3%	14.7%	85.3%
16,643	MACON	1,053	92	958	3	866 D	8.7%	91.0%	8.8%	91.2%
14,921	MADISON	2,098	393	1,697	8	1,304 D	18.7%	80.9%	18.8%	81.2%
6,968	MARION	483	62	420	1	358 D	12.8%	87.0%	12.9%	87.1%
22,437	MERIWETHER	2,577	138	2,438	1	2,300 D	5.4%	94.6%	5.4%	94.6%
9,076	MILLER	690	36	653	1	617 D	5.2%	94.6%	5.2%	94.8%
	MILTON	—	—	—	—	—	—	—	—	—
23,620	MITCHELL	2,381	79	2,297	5	2,218 D	3.3%	96.5%	3.3%	96.7%
11,606	MONROE	1,431	147	1,277	7	1,130 D	10.3%	89.2%	10.3%	89.7%
10,020	MONTGOMERY	1,034	81	945	8	864 D	7.8%	91.4%	7.9%	92.1%
12,488	MORGAN	1,169	37	1,130	2	1,093 D	3.2%	96.7%	3.2%	96.8%
9,215	MURRAY	2,404	806	1,597	1	791 D	33.5%	66.4%	33.5%	66.5%
57,558	MUSCOGEE	5,471	455	5,009	7	4,554 D	8.3%	91.6%	8.3%	91.7%
17,290	NEWTON	2,126	123	1,994	9	1,871 D	5.8%	93.8%	5.8%	94.2%
8,082	OCONEE	659	173	483	3	310 D	26.3%	73.3%	26.4%	73.6%
12,927	OGLETHORPE	964	115	845	4	730 D	11.9%	87.7%	12.0%	88.0%
12,327	PAULDING	2,034	645	1,386	3	741 D	31.7%	68.1%	31.8%	68.2%
10,268	PEACH	829	49	767	13	718 D	5.9%	92.5%	6.0%	94.0%
9,687	PICKENS	2,276	1,053	1,223		170 D	46.3%	53.7%	46.3%	53.7%
12,522	PIERCE	1,549	45	1,494	10	1,449 D	2.9%	96.4%	2.9%	97.1%
10,853	PIKE	1,062	149	910	3	761 D	14.0%	85.7%	14.1%	85.9%
25,141	POLK	3,147	389	2,754	4	2,365 D	12.4%	87.5%	12.4%	87.6%
9,005	PULASKI	854	38	808	8	770 D	4.4%	94.6%	4.5%	95.5%
8,367	PUTNAM	755	51	703	1	652 D	6.8%	93.1%	6.8%	93.2%
3,820	QUITMAN	374	19	355		336 D	5.1%	94.9%	5.1%	94.9%

GEORGIA

PRESIDENT 1936

1930 Census Population	County	Total Vote	Republican	Democratic	Other	Rep.-Dem. Plurality	Percentage Total Vote Rep.	Total Vote Dem.	Major Vote Rep.	Major Vote Dem.
6,331	RABUN	1,111	162	948	1	786 D	14.6%	85.3%	14.6%	85.4%
17,174	RANDOLPH	1,287	74	1,208	5	1,134 D	5.7%	93.9%	5.8%	94.2%
72,990	RICHMOND	7,810	551	7,239	20	6,688 D	7.1%	92.7%	7.1%	92.9%
7,247	ROCKDALE	911	73	837	1	764 D	8.0%	91.9%	8.0%	92.0%
5,347	SCHLEY	462	43	419		376 D	9.3%	90.7%	9.3%	90.7%
20,503	SCREVEN	1,009	61	933	15	872 D	6.0%	92.5%	6.1%	93.9%
7,389	SEMINOLE	843	82	761		679 D	9.7%	90.3%	9.7%	90.3%
23,495	SPALDING	2,500	36	2,457	7	2,421 D	1.4%	98.3%	1.4%	98.6%
11,740	STEPHENS	1,212	68	1,142	2	1,074 D	5.6%	94.2%	5.6%	94.4%
11,114	STEWART	681	49	628	4	579 D	7.2%	92.2%	7.2%	92.8%
26,800	SUMTER	1,934	58	1,870	6	1,812 D	3.0%	96.7%	3.0%	97.0%
8,458	TALBOT	843	41	796	6	755 D	4.9%	94.4%	4.9%	95.1%
6,172	TALIAFERRO	573	14	552	7	538 D	2.4%	96.3%	2.5%	97.5%
15,411	TATTNALL	1,272	214	1,047	11	833 D	16.8%	82.3%	17.0%	83.0%
10,617	TAYLOR	921	147	771	3	624 D	16.0%	83.7%	16.0%	84.0%
14,997	TELFAIR	1,279	121	1,158		1,037 D	9.5%	90.5%	9.5%	90.5%
18,290	TERRELL	1,399	61	1,336	2	1,275 D	4.4%	95.5%	4.4%	95.6%
32,612	THOMAS	2,645	222	2,409	14	2,187 D	8.4%	91.1%	8.4%	91.6%
16,068	TIFT	1,798	161	1,627	10	1,466 D	9.0%	90.5%	9.0%	91.0%
17,165	TOOMBS	1,083	78	1,001	4	923 D	7.2%	92.4%	7.2%	92.8%
4,346	TOWNS	1,495	732	763		31 D	49.0%	51.0%	49.0%	51.0%
7,488	TREUTLEN	936	23	912	1	889 D	2.5%	97.4%	2.5%	97.5%
36,752	TROUP	2,898	167	2,728	3	2,561 D	5.8%	94.1%	5.8%	94.2%
11,196	TURNER	1,048	188	860		672 D	17.9%	82.1%	17.9%	82.1%
8,372	TWIGGS	549	57	491	1	434 D	10.4%	89.4%	10.4%	89.6%
6,340	UNION	1,931	783	1,148		365 D	40.5%	59.5%	40.5%	59.5%
19,509	UPSON	1,610	138	1,471	1	1,333 D	8.6%	91.4%	8.6%	91.4%
26,206	WALKER	2,776	458	2,313	5	1,855 D	16.5%	83.3%	16.5%	83.5%
21,118	WALTON	2,086	132	1,952	2	1,820 D	6.3%	93.6%	6.3%	93.7%
26,558	WARE	2,827	256	2,566	5	2,310 D	9.1%	90.8%	9.1%	90.9%
11,181	WARREN	682	129	545	8	416 D	18.9%	79.9%	19.1%	80.9%
25,030	WASHINGTON	1,441	149	1,286	6	1,137 D	10.3%	89.2%	10.4%	89.6%
12,647	WAYNE	899	105	788	6	683 D	11.7%	87.7%	11.8%	88.2%
5,032	WEBSTER	351	40	310	1	270 D	11.4%	88.3%	11.4%	88.6%
9,149	WHEELER	689	94	594	1	500 D	13.6%	86.2%	13.7%	86.3%
6,056	WHITE	760	161	599		438 D	21.2%	78.8%	21.2%	78.8%
20,808	WHITFIELD	3,367	877	2,481	9	1,604 D	26.0%	73.7%	26.1%	73.9%
13,439	WILCOX	1,263	195	1,066	2	871 D	15.4%	84.4%	15.5%	84.5%
15,944	WILKES	1,122	78	1,031	13	953 D	7.0%	91.9%	7.0%	93.0%
10,844	WILKINSON	818	118	695	5	577 D	14.4%	85.0%	14.5%	85.5%
21,094	WORTH	1,257	132	1,124	1	992 D	10.5%	89.4%	10.5%	89.5%
2,908,506	TOTAL	293,170	36,943	255,363	864	218,420 D	12.6%	87.1%	12.6%	87.4%

GEORGIA

PRESIDENT 1932

1930 Census Population	County	Total Vote	Republican	Democratic	Other	Rep.-Dem. Plurality	Percentage: Total Vote Rep.	Total Vote Dem.	Major Vote Rep.	Major Vote Dem.
13,314	APPLING	665	64	601		537 D	9.6%	90.4%	9.6%	90.4%
6,894	ATKINSON	793	41	747	5	706 D	5.2%	94.2%	5.2%	94.8%
7,055	BACON	528	11	515	2	504 D	2.1%	97.5%	2.1%	97.9%
7,818	BAKER	652	2	647	3	645 D	0.3%	99.2%	0.3%	99.7%
22,878	BALDWIN	854	45	801	8	756 D	5.3%	93.8%	5.3%	94.7%
9,703	BANKS	1,361	58	1,283	20	1,225 D	4.3%	94.3%	4.3%	95.7%
12,401	BARROW	1,145	23	1,111	11	1,088 D	2.0%	97.0%	2.0%	98.0%
25,364	BARTOW	1,677	121	1,546	10	1,425 D	7.2%	92.2%	7.3%	92.7%
13,047	BEN HILL	1,116	85	1,026	5	941 D	7.6%	91.9%	7.7%	92.3%
14,646	BERRIEN	1,485	19	1,447	19	1,428 D	1.3%	97.4%	1.3%	98.7%
77,042	BIBB	4,808	405	4,372	31	3,967 D	8.4%	90.9%	8.5%	91.5%
9,133	BLECKLEY	1,376	37	1,338	1	1,301 D	2.7%	97.2%	2.7%	97.3%
6,895	BRANTLEY	717	22	693	2	671 D	3.1%	96.7%	3.1%	96.9%
21,330	BROOKS	1,506	75	1,426	5	1,351 D	5.0%	94.7%	5.0%	95.0%
5,952	BRYAN	373	17	353	3	336 D	4.6%	94.6%	4.6%	95.4%
26,509	BULLOCH	2,231	17	2,203	11	2,186 D	0.8%	98.7%	0.8%	99.2%
29,224	BURKE	522	18	498	6	480 D	3.4%	95.4%	3.5%	96.5%
9,345	BUTTS	1,725	21	1,693	11	1,672 D	1.2%	98.1%	1.2%	98.8%
10,576	CALHOUN	497	10	483	4	473 D	2.0%	97.2%	2.0%	98.0%
6,338	CAMDEN	469	49	417	3	368 D	10.4%	88.9%	10.5%	89.5%
	CAMPBELL	—	—	—	—	—	—	—	—	—
8,991	CANDLER	490	13	476	1	463 D	2.7%	97.1%	2.7%	97.3%
34,272	CARROLL	3,546	284	3,232	30	2,948 D	8.0%	91.1%	8.1%	91.9%
9,421	CATOOSA	1,117	123	985	9	862 D	11.0%	88.2%	11.1%	88.9%
4,381	CHARLTON	363	32	330	1	298 D	8.8%	90.9%	8.8%	91.2%
105,431	CHATHAM	9,744	1,669	8,020	55	6,351 D	17.1%	82.3%	17.2%	82.8%
8,894	CHATTAHOOCHEE	187	1	186		185 D	0.5%	99.5%	0.5%	99.5%
15,407	CHATTOOGA	2,411	188	2,200	23	2,012 D	7.8%	91.2%	7.9%	92.1%
20,003	CHEROKEE	2,059	314	1,727	18	1,413 D	15.3%	83.9%	15.4%	84.6%
25,613	CLARKE	2,164	159	1,992	13	1,833 D	7.3%	92.1%	7.4%	92.6%
6,943	CLAY	448	12	433	3	421 D	2.7%	96.7%	2.7%	97.3%
10,260	CLAYTON	1,403	35	1,361	7	1,326 D	2.5%	97.0%	2.5%	97.5%
7,015	CLINCH	474	11	461	2	450 D	2.3%	97.3%	2.3%	97.7%
35,408	COBB	3,321	218	3,079	24	2,861 D	6.6%	92.7%	6.6%	93.4%
19,739	COFFEE	1,702	29	1,652	21	1,623 D	1.7%	97.1%	1.7%	98.3%
30,622	COLQUITT	3,652	101	3,534	17	3,433 D	2.8%	96.8%	2.8%	97.2%
8,793	COLUMBIA	539	11	528		517 D	2.0%	98.0%	2.0%	98.0%
11,311	COOK	1,440	25	1,408	7	1,383 D	1.7%	97.8%	1.7%	98.3%
25,127	COWETA	2,235	46	2,183	6	2,137 D	2.1%	97.7%	2.1%	97.9%
7,020	CRAWFORD	281	9	272		263 D	3.2%	96.8%	3.2%	96.8%
17,343	CRISP	740	10	725	5	715 D	1.4%	98.0%	1.4%	98.6%
4,146	DADE	887	103	770	14	667 D	11.6%	86.8%	11.8%	88.2%
3,502	DAWSON	676	105	567	4	462 D	15.5%	83.9%	15.6%	84.4%
23,622	DECATUR	1,257	65	1,169	23	1,104 D	5.2%	93.0%	5.3%	94.7%
70,278	DE KALB	6,039	633	5,323	83	4,690 D	10.5%	88.1%	10.6%	89.4%
21,599	DODGE	2,843	33	2,809	1	2,776 D	1.2%	98.8%	1.2%	98.8%
18,025	DOOLY	1,151	8	1,139	4	1,131 D	0.7%	99.0%	0.7%	99.3%
22,306	DOUGHERTY	2,117	95	2,012	10	1,917 D	4.5%	95.0%	4.5%	95.5%
9,461	DOUGLAS	1,087	57	1,013	17	956 D	5.2%	93.2%	5.3%	94.7%
18,273	EARLY	1,152	19	1,131	2	1,112 D	1.6%	98.2%	1.7%	98.3%
2,744	ECHOLS	419	5	414		409 D	1.2%	98.8%	1.2%	98.8%
10,164	EFFINGHAM	610	90	518	2	428 D	14.8%	84.9%	14.8%	85.2%
18,485	ELBERT	2,119	77	2,023	19	1,946 D	3.6%	95.5%	3.7%	96.3%
24,101	EMANUEL	2,457	33	2,420	4	2,387 D	1.3%	98.5%	1.3%	98.7%
7,102	EVANS	576	21	548	7	527 D	3.6%	95.1%	3.7%	96.3%
12,969	FANNIN	3,342	1,967	1,375		592 R	58.9%	41.1%	58.9%	41.1%
8,665	FAYETTE	753	6	746	1	740 D	0.8%	99.1%	0.8%	99.2%
48,667	FLOYD	4,672	300	4,342	30	4,042 D	6.4%	92.9%	6.5%	93.5%
10,624	FORSYTH	1,750	117	1,627	6	1,510 D	6.7%	93.0%	6.7%	93.3%
15,902	FRANKLIN	1,461	78	1,361	22	1,283 D	5.3%	93.2%	5.4%	94.6%

GEORGIA

PRESIDENT 1932

1930 Census Population	County	Total Vote	Republican	Democratic	Other	Rep.-Dem. Plurality	Percentage Total Vote Rep.	Percentage Total Vote Dem.	Percentage Major Vote Rep.	Percentage Major Vote Dem.
335,220	FULTON	22,453	2,063	20,137	253	18,074 D	9.2%	89.7%	9.3%	90.7%
7,344	GILMER	1,826	616	1,210		594 D	33.7%	66.3%	33.7%	66.3%
4,388	GLASCOCK	400	7	393		386 D	1.8%	98.3%	1.8%	98.3%
19,400	GLYNN	1,452	186	1,262	4	1,076 D	12.8%	86.9%	12.8%	87.2%
16,846	GORDON	1,848	122	1,708	18	1,586 D	6.6%	92.4%	6.7%	93.3%
19,200	GRADY	2,254	60	2,184	10	2,124 D	2.7%	96.9%	2.7%	97.3%
12,616	GREENE	972	52	918	2	866 D	5.3%	94.4%	5.4%	94.6%
27,853	GWINNETT	2,708	91	2,616	1	2,525 D	3.4%	96.6%	3.4%	96.6%
12,748	HABERSHAM	1,947	225	1,693	29	1,468 D	11.6%	87.0%	11.7%	88.3%
30,313	HALL	2,780	120	2,649	11	2,529 D	4.3%	95.3%	4.3%	95.7%
13,070	HANCOCK	551	18	529	4	511 D	3.3%	96.0%	3.3%	96.7%
13,263	HARALSON	1,501	223	1,278		1,055 D	14.9%	85.1%	14.9%	85.1%
11,140	HARRIS	875	21	851	3	830 D	2.4%	97.3%	2.4%	97.6%
15,174	HART	1,274	12	1,261	1	1,249 D	0.9%	99.0%	0.9%	99.1%
9,102	HEARD	1,016	24	989	3	965 D	2.4%	97.3%	2.4%	97.6%
15,924	HENRY	1,532	21	1,496	15	1,475 D	1.4%	97.7%	1.4%	98.6%
11,280	HOUSTON	487	27	460		433 D	5.5%	94.5%	5.5%	94.5%
12,199	IRWIN	1,439	22	1,416	1	1,394 D	1.5%	98.4%	1.5%	98.5%
21,609	JACKSON	1,485	80	1,389	16	1,309 D	5.4%	93.5%	5.4%	94.6%
8,594	JASPER	790	14	773	3	759 D	1.8%	97.8%	1.8%	98.2%
8,118	JEFF DAVIS	1,232	50	1,179	3	1,129 D	4.1%	95.7%	4.1%	95.9%
20,727	JEFFERSON	1,536	65	1,454	17	1,389 D	4.2%	94.7%	4.3%	95.7%
12,908	JENKINS	530	20	510		490 D	3.8%	96.2%	3.8%	96.2%
12,681	JOHNSON	1,340	18	1,314	8	1,296 D	1.3%	98.1%	1.4%	98.6%
8,992	JONES	556		553	3	553 D		99.5%		100.0%
9,745	LAMAR	754	33	714	7	681 D	4.4%	94.7%	4.4%	95.6%
5,190	LANIER	217	3	211	3	208 D	1.4%	97.2%	1.4%	98.6%
32,693	LAURENS	2,227	38	2,188	1	2,150 D	1.7%	98.2%	1.7%	98.3%
8,328	LEE	258	6	252		246 D	2.3%	97.7%	2.3%	97.7%
8,153	LIBERTY	308	18	289	1	271 D	5.8%	93.8%	5.9%	94.1%
7,847	LINCOLN	664	3	660	1	657 D	0.5%	99.4%	0.5%	99.5%
4,180	LONG	449	14	430	5	416 D	3.1%	95.8%	3.2%	96.8%
29,994	LOWNDES	1,944	97	1,840	7	1,743 D	5.0%	94.7%	5.0%	95.0%
4,927	LUMPKIN	1,005	81	924		843 D	8.1%	91.9%	8.1%	91.9%
9,014	MCDUFFIE	604	29	568	7	539 D	4.8%	94.0%	4.9%	95.1%
5,763	MCINTOSH	290	19	271		252 D	6.6%	93.4%	6.6%	93.4%
16,643	MACON	1,497	55	1,438	4	1,383 D	3.7%	96.1%	3.7%	96.3%
14,921	MADISON	2,170	38	2,124	8	2,086 D	1.8%	97.9%	1.8%	98.2%
6,968	MARION	479	24	455		431 D	5.0%	95.0%	5.0%	95.0%
22,437	MERIWETHER	2,662	53	2,604	5	2,551 D	2.0%	97.8%	2.0%	98.0%
9,076	MILLER	396		392	4	392 D		99.0%		100.0%
	MILTON	—	—	—	—	—	—	—	—	—
23,620	MITCHELL	2,117	15	2,097	5	2,082 D	0.7%	99.1%	0.7%	99.3%
11,606	MONROE	1,246	45	1,200	1	1,155 D	3.6%	96.3%	3.6%	96.4%
10,020	MONTGOMERY	893	17	868	8	851 D	1.9%	97.2%	1.9%	98.1%
12,488	MORGAN	1,006	74	923	9	849 D	7.4%	91.7%	7.4%	92.6%
9,215	MURRAY	2,233	350	1,874	9	1,524 D	15.7%	83.9%	15.7%	84.3%
57,558	MUSCOGEE	3,667	230	3,413	24	3,183 D	6.3%	93.1%	6.3%	93.7%
17,290	NEWTON	1,727	45	1,672	10	1,627 D	2.6%	96.8%	2.6%	97.4%
8,082	OCONEE	718	39	664	15	625 D	5.4%	92.5%	5.5%	94.5%
12,927	OGLETHORPE	1,276	34	1,240	2	1,206 D	2.7%	97.2%	2.7%	97.3%
12,327	PAULDING	2,228	276	1,914	38	1,638 D	12.4%	85.9%	12.6%	87.4%
10,268	PEACH	656	56	595	5	539 D	8.5%	90.7%	8.6%	91.4%
9,687	PICKENS	2,215	743	1,472		729 D	33.5%	66.5%	33.5%	66.5%
12,522	PIERCE	1,129	29	1,094	6	1,065 D	2.6%	96.9%	2.6%	97.4%
10,853	PIKE	1,064	33	1,021	10	988 D	3.1%	96.0%	3.1%	96.9%
25,141	POLK	2,381	211	2,170		1,959 D	8.9%	91.1%	8.9%	91.1%
9,005	PULASKI	987	14	973		959 D	1.4%	98.6%	1.4%	98.6%
8,367	PUTNAM	806	33	770	3	737 D	4.1%	95.5%	4.1%	95.9%
3,820	QUITMAN	243		239	4	239 D		98.4%		100.0%

GEORGIA

PRESIDENT 1932

1930 Census Population	County	Total Vote	Republican	Democratic	Other	Rep.-Dem. Plurality	Percentage Total Vote Rep.	Total Vote Dem.	Major Vote Rep.	Major Vote Dem.
6,331	RABUN	979	78	893	8	815 D	8.0%	91.2%	8.0%	92.0%
17,174	RANDOLPH	1,383	31	1,344	8	1,313 D	2.2%	97.2%	2.3%	97.7%
72,990	RICHMOND	5,694	738	4,873	83	4,135 D	13.0%	85.6%	13.2%	86.8%
7,247	ROCKDALE	483	18	461	4	443 D	3.7%	95.4%	3.8%	96.2%
5,347	SCHLEY	408	8	398	2	390 D	2.0%	97.5%	2.0%	98.0%
20,503	SCREVEN	557	46	508	3	462 D	8.3%	91.2%	8.3%	91.7%
7,389	SEMINOLE	806	20	776	10	756 D	2.5%	96.3%	2.5%	97.5%
23,495	SPALDING	2,251	54	2,185	12	2,131 D	2.4%	97.1%	2.4%	97.6%
11,740	STEPHENS	1,052	18	1,026	8	1,008 D	1.7%	97.5%	1.7%	98.3%
11,114	STEWART	606	15	588	3	573 D	2.5%	97.0%	2.5%	97.5%
26,800	SUMTER	1,692	57	1,619	16	1,562 D	3.4%	95.7%	3.4%	96.6%
8,458	TALBOT	960	45	912	3	867 D	4.7%	95.0%	4.7%	95.3%
6,172	TALIAFERRO	506	3	503		500 D	0.6%	99.4%	0.6%	99.4%
15,411	TATTNALL	2,176	37	2,133	6	2,096 D	1.7%	98.0%	1.7%	98.3%
10,617	TAYLOR	732	44	685	3	641 D	6.0%	93.6%	6.0%	94.0%
14,997	TELFAIR	797	45	746	6	701 D	5.6%	93.6%	5.7%	94.3%
18,290	TERRELL	1,027	24	1,000	3	976 D	2.3%	97.4%	2.3%	97.7%
32,612	THOMAS	2,710	90	2,607	13	2,517 D	3.3%	96.2%	3.3%	96.7%
16,068	TIFT	1,466	65	1,394	7	1,329 D	4.4%	95.1%	4.5%	95.5%
17,165	TOOMBS	1,936	54	1,868	14	1,814 D	2.8%	96.5%	2.8%	97.2%
4,346	TOWNS	1,532	790	742		48 R	51.6%	48.4%	51.6%	48.4%
7,488	TREUTLEN	885	36	849		813 D	4.1%	95.9%	4.1%	95.9%
36,752	TROUP	2,454	81	2,371	2	2,290 D	3.3%	96.6%	3.3%	96.7%
11,196	TURNER	977	59	909	9	850 D	6.0%	93.0%	6.1%	93.9%
8,372	TWIGGS	664	15	646	3	631 D	2.3%	97.3%	2.3%	97.7%
6,340	UNION	2,154	810	1,344		534 D	37.6%	62.4%	37.6%	62.4%
19,509	UPSON	1,684	20	1,660	4	1,640 D	1.2%	98.6%	1.2%	98.8%
26,206	WALKER	2,691	405	2,255	31	1,850 D	15.1%	83.8%	15.2%	84.8%
21,118	WALTON	2,172	36	2,136		2,100 D	1.7%	98.3%	1.7%	98.3%
26,558	WARE	2,723	205	2,504	14	2,299 D	7.5%	92.0%	7.6%	92.4%
11,181	WARREN	697	18	676	3	658 D	2.6%	97.0%	2.6%	97.4%
25,030	WASHINGTON	1,936	9	1,923	4	1,914 D	0.5%	99.3%	0.5%	99.5%
12,647	WAYNE	1,111	60	1,044	7	984 D	5.4%	94.0%	5.4%	94.6%
5,032	WEBSTER	240	5	235		230 D	2.1%	97.9%	2.1%	97.9%
9,149	WHEELER	1,157	29	1,127	1	1,098 D	2.5%	97.4%	2.5%	97.5%
6,056	WHITE	991	53	936	2	883 D	5.3%	94.5%	5.4%	94.6%
20,808	WHITFIELD	2,912	483	2,384	45	1,901 D	16.6%	81.9%	16.8%	83.2%
13,439	WILCOX	645	25	619	1	594 D	3.9%	96.0%	3.9%	96.1%
15,944	WILKES	1,224	42	1,172	10	1,130 D	3.4%	95.8%	3.5%	96.5%
10,844	WILKINSON	726		726		726 D		100.0%		100.0%
21,094	WORTH	2,310	38	2,269	3	2,231 D	1.6%	98.2%	1.6%	98.4%
2,908,506	TOTAL	255,590	19,863	234,118	1,609	214,255 D	7.8%	91.6%	7.8%	92.2%

GEORGIA

PRESIDENT 1928

1920 Census Population	County	Total Vote	Republican	Democratic	Other	Rep.-Dem. Plurality	Percentage: Total Vote Rep.	Total Vote Dem.	Major Vote Rep.	Major Vote Dem.
10,594	APPLING	994	579	415		164 R	58.2%	41.8%	58.2%	41.8%
7,656	ATKINSON	471	121	350		229 D	25.7%	74.3%	25.7%	74.3%
6,460	BACON	508	203	305		102 D	40.0%	60.0%	40.0%	60.0%
8,298	BAKER	561	99	462		363 D	17.6%	82.4%	17.6%	82.4%
19,791	BALDWIN	982	270	712		442 D	27.5%	72.5%	27.5%	72.5%
11,814	BANKS	785	363	422		59 D	46.2%	53.8%	46.2%	53.8%
13,188	BARROW	1,163	684	479		205 R	58.8%	41.2%	58.8%	41.2%
24,527	BARTOW	1,668	838	830		8 R	50.2%	49.8%	50.2%	49.8%
14,599	BEN HILL	1,466	460	1,006		546 D	31.4%	68.6%	31.4%	68.6%
15,573	BERRIEN	840	105	735		630 D	12.5%	87.5%	12.5%	87.5%
71,304	BIBB	4,367	2,078	2,289		211 D	47.6%	52.4%	47.6%	52.4%
10,532	BLECKLEY	712	71	641		570 D	10.0%	90.0%	10.0%	90.0%
	BRANTLEY	338	172	166		6 R	50.9%	49.1%	50.9%	49.1%
24,538	BROOKS	962	192	770		578 D	20.0%	80.0%	20.0%	80.0%
6,343	BRYAN	370	151	219		68 D	40.8%	59.2%	40.8%	59.2%
26,133	BULLOCH	1,645	387	1,258		871 D	23.5%	76.5%	23.5%	76.5%
30,836	BURKE	947	260	687		427 D	27.5%	72.5%	27.5%	72.5%
12,327	BUTTS	994	148	846		698 D	14.9%	85.1%	14.9%	85.1%
10,225	CALHOUN	662	91	571		480 D	13.7%	86.3%	13.7%	86.3%
6,969	CAMDEN	541	267	274		7 D	49.4%	50.6%	49.4%	50.6%
11,709	CAMPBELL	752	327	425		98 D	43.5%	56.5%	43.5%	56.5%
9,228	CANDLER	544	133	411		278 D	24.4%	75.6%	24.4%	75.6%
34,752	CARROLL	4,025	2,112	1,913		199 R	52.5%	47.5%	52.5%	47.5%
6,677	CATOOSA	1,167	605	562		43 R	51.8%	48.2%	51.8%	48.2%
4,536	CHARLTON	575	160	415		255 D	27.8%	72.2%	27.8%	72.2%
100,032	CHATHAM	10,822	5,288	5,534		246 D	48.9%	51.1%	48.9%	51.1%
5,266	CHATTAHOOCHEE	159	18	141		123 D	11.3%	88.7%	11.3%	88.7%
14,312	CHATTOOGA	2,016	1,096	920		176 R	54.4%	45.6%	54.4%	45.6%
18,569	CHEROKEE	2,260	1,679	581		1,098 R	74.3%	25.7%	74.3%	25.7%
26,111	CLARKE	2,131	724	1,407		683 D	34.0%	66.0%	34.0%	66.0%
7,557	CLAY	461	56	405		349 D	12.1%	87.9%	12.1%	87.9%
11,159	CLAYTON	1,231	619	612		7 R	50.3%	49.7%	50.3%	49.7%
7,984	CLINCH	860	143	717		574 D	16.6%	83.4%	16.6%	83.4%
30,437	COBB	3,137	1,711	1,426		285 R	54.5%	45.5%	54.5%	45.5%
18,653	COFFEE	1,767	591	1,176		585 D	33.4%	66.6%	33.4%	66.6%
29,332	COLQUITT	1,766	796	970		174 D	45.1%	54.9%	45.1%	54.9%
11,718	COLUMBIA	513	234	279		45 D	45.6%	54.4%	45.6%	54.4%
11,180	COOK	926	237	689		452 D	25.6%	74.4%	25.6%	74.4%
29,047	COWETA	1,885	229	1,656		1,427 D	12.1%	87.9%	12.1%	87.9%
8,893	CRAWFORD	406	48	358		310 D	11.8%	88.2%	11.8%	88.2%
18,914	CRISP	925	402	523		121 D	43.5%	56.5%	43.5%	56.5%
3,918	DADE	781	328	453		125 D	42.0%	58.0%	42.0%	58.0%
4,204	DAWSON	622	290	332		42 D	46.6%	53.4%	46.6%	53.4%
31,785	DECATUR	1,890	1,156	734		422 R	61.2%	38.8%	61.2%	38.8%
44,051	DE KALB	4,671	2,378	2,293		85 R	50.9%	49.1%	50.9%	49.1%
22,540	DODGE	950	273	677		404 D	28.7%	71.3%	28.7%	71.3%
20,522	DOOLY	900	156	744		588 D	17.3%	82.7%	17.3%	82.7%
20,063	DOUGHERTY	1,361	379	982		603 D	27.8%	72.2%	27.8%	72.2%
10,477	DOUGLAS	1,058	606	452		154 R	57.3%	42.7%	57.3%	42.7%
18,983	EARLY	905	231	674		443 D	25.5%	74.5%	25.5%	74.5%
3,313	ECHOLS	343	29	314		285 D	8.5%	91.5%	8.5%	91.5%
9,985	EFFINGHAM	790	627	163		464 R	79.4%	20.6%	79.4%	20.6%
23,905	ELBERT	1,983	931	1,052		121 D	46.9%	53.1%	46.9%	53.1%
25,862	EMANUEL	1,431	355	1,076		721 D	24.8%	75.2%	24.8%	75.2%
6,594	EVANS	681	192	489		297 D	28.2%	71.8%	28.2%	71.8%
12,103	FANNIN	2,541	1,730	811		919 R	68.1%	31.9%	68.1%	31.9%
11,396	FAYETTE	557	190	367		177 D	34.1%	65.9%	34.1%	65.9%
39,841	FLOYD	3,224	1,730	1,494		236 R	53.7%	46.3%	53.7%	46.3%
11,755	FORSYTH	1,221	934	287		647 R	76.5%	23.5%	76.5%	23.5%
19,957	FRANKLIN	1,571	801	770		31 R	51.0%	49.0%	51.0%	49.0%

GEORGIA

PRESIDENT 1928

1920 Census Population	County	Total Vote	Republican	Democratic	Other	Rep.-Dem. Plurality	Percentage Total Vote Rep.	Total Vote Dem.	Major Vote Rep.	Major Vote Dem.
232,606	FULTON	18,240	9,368	8,872		496 R	51.4%	48.6%	51.4%	48.6%
8,406	GILMER	1,541	1,012	529		483 R	65.7%	34.3%	65.7%	34.3%
4,192	GLASCOCK	348	225	123		102 R	64.7%	35.3%	64.7%	35.3%
19,370	GLYNN	1,348	799	549		250 R	59.3%	40.7%	59.3%	40.7%
17,736	GORDON	1,779	1,039	740		299 R	58.4%	41.6%	58.4%	41.6%
20,306	GRADY	1,611	439	1,172		733 D	27.3%	72.7%	27.3%	72.7%
18,972	GREENE	872	245	627		382 D	28.1%	71.9%	28.1%	71.9%
30,327	GWINNETT	2,032	1,062	970		92 R	52.3%	47.7%	52.3%	47.7%
10,730	HABERSHAM	2,509	1,404	1,105		299 R	56.0%	44.0%	56.0%	44.0%
26,822	HALL	3,096	1,573	1,523		50 R	50.8%	49.2%	50.8%	49.2%
18,357	HANCOCK	670	118	552		434 D	17.6%	82.4%	17.6%	82.4%
14,440	HARALSON	2,237	1,547	690		857 R	69.2%	30.8%	69.2%	30.8%
15,775	HARRIS	695	144	551		407 D	20.7%	79.3%	20.7%	79.3%
17,944	HART	1,522	603	919		316 D	39.6%	60.4%	39.6%	60.4%
11,126	HEARD	883	390	493		103 D	44.2%	55.8%	44.2%	55.8%
20,420	HENRY	1,123	360	763		403 D	32.1%	67.9%	32.1%	67.9%
21,964	HOUSTON	415	92	323		231 D	22.2%	77.8%	22.2%	77.8%
12,670	IRWIN	1,079	162	917		755 D	15.0%	85.0%	15.0%	85.0%
24,654	JACKSON	1,677	818	859		41 D	48.8%	51.2%	48.8%	51.2%
16,362	JASPER	772	140	632		492 D	18.1%	81.9%	18.1%	81.9%
7,322	JEFF DAVIS	495	180	315		135 D	36.4%	63.6%	36.4%	63.6%
22,602	JEFFERSON	1,855	1,057	798		259 R	57.0%	43.0%	57.0%	43.0%
14,328	JENKINS	741	332	409		77 D	44.8%	55.2%	44.8%	55.2%
13,546	JOHNSON	916	284	632		348 D	31.0%	69.0%	31.0%	69.0%
13,269	JONES	514	100	414		314 D	19.5%	80.5%	19.5%	80.5%
	LAMAR	798	126	672		546 D	15.8%	84.2%	15.8%	84.2%
	LANIER	441	138	303		165 D	31.3%	68.7%	31.3%	68.7%
39,605	LAURENS	2,457	470	1,987		1,517 D	19.1%	80.9%	19.1%	80.9%
10,904	LEE	332	45	287		242 D	13.6%	86.4%	13.6%	86.4%
12,707	LIBERTY	404	203	201		2 R	50.2%	49.8%	50.2%	49.8%
9,739	LINCOLN	858	413	445		32 D	48.1%	51.9%	48.1%	51.9%
	LONG	567	401	166		235 R	70.7%	29.3%	70.7%	29.3%
26,521	LOWNDES	2,009	596	1,413		817 D	29.7%	70.3%	29.7%	70.3%
5,240	LUMPKIN	941	381	560		179 D	40.5%	59.5%	40.5%	59.5%
11,509	MCDUFFIE	685	381	304		77 R	55.6%	44.4%	55.6%	44.4%
5,119	MCINTOSH	321	180	141		39 R	56.1%	43.9%	56.1%	43.9%
17,667	MACON	1,077	258	819		561 D	24.0%	76.0%	24.0%	76.0%
18,803	MADISON	1,001	527	474		53 R	52.6%	47.4%	52.6%	47.4%
7,604	MARION	479	114	365		251 D	23.8%	76.2%	23.8%	76.2%
26,168	MERIWETHER	1,802	287	1,515		1,228 D	15.9%	84.1%	15.9%	84.1%
9,565	MILLER	423	101	322		221 D	23.9%	76.1%	23.9%	76.1%
6,885	MILTON	627	444	183		261 R	70.8%	29.2%	70.8%	29.2%
25,588	MITCHELL	1,501	143	1,358		1,215 D	9.5%	90.5%	9.5%	90.5%
20,138	MONROE	1,130	329	801		472 D	29.1%	70.9%	29.1%	70.9%
9,167	MONTGOMERY	435	98	337		239 D	22.5%	77.5%	22.5%	77.5%
20,143	MORGAN	1,011	208	803		595 D	20.6%	79.4%	20.6%	79.4%
9,490	MURRAY	2,088	1,106	982		124 R	53.0%	47.0%	53.0%	47.0%
44,195	MUSCOGEE	3,672	1,574	2,098		524 D	42.9%	57.1%	42.9%	57.1%
21,680	NEWTON	1,571	698	873		175 D	44.4%	55.6%	44.4%	55.6%
11,067	OCONEE	644	300	344		44 D	46.6%	53.4%	46.6%	53.4%
20,287	OGLETHORPE	1,018	205	813		608 D	20.1%	79.9%	20.1%	79.9%
14,025	PAULDING	1,991	1,301	690		611 R	65.3%	34.7%	65.3%	34.7%
	PEACH	780	208	572		364 D	26.7%	73.3%	26.7%	73.3%
8,222	PICKENS	1,862	1,319	543		776 R	70.8%	29.2%	70.8%	29.2%
11,934	PIERCE	808	285	523		238 D	35.3%	64.7%	35.3%	64.7%
21,212	PIKE	952	238	714		476 D	25.0%	75.0%	25.0%	75.0%
20,357	POLK	2,348	1,462	886		576 R	62.3%	37.7%	62.3%	37.7%
11,587	PULASKI	744	105	639		534 D	14.1%	85.9%	14.1%	85.9%
15,151	PUTNAM	739	57	682		625 D	7.7%	92.3%	7.7%	92.3%
3,417	QUITMAN	215	41	174		133 D	19.1%	80.9%	19.1%	80.9%

GEORGIA

PRESIDENT 1928

1920 Census Population	County	Total Vote	Republican	Democratic	Other	Rep.-Dem. Plurality	Percentage Total Vote Rep.	Total Vote Dem.	Major Vote Rep.	Major Vote Dem.
5,746	RABUN	896	306	590		284 D	34.2%	65.8%	34.2%	65.8%
16,721	RANDOLPH	980	177	803		626 D	18.1%	81.9%	18.1%	81.9%
63,692	RICHMOND	7,190	5,104	2,086		3,018 R	71.0%	29.0%	71.0%	29.0%
9,521	ROCKDALE	628	156	472		316 D	24.8%	75.2%	24.8%	75.2%
5,243	SCHLEY	405	77	328		251 D	19.0%	81.0%	19.0%	81.0%
23,552	SCREVEN	1,006	706	300		406 R	70.2%	29.8%	70.2%	29.8%
	SEMINOLE	481	110	371		261 D	22.9%	77.1%	22.9%	77.1%
21,908	SPALDING	2,146	412	1,734		1,322 D	19.2%	80.8%	19.2%	80.8%
11,215	STEPHENS	708	270	438		168 D	38.1%	61.9%	38.1%	61.9%
12,089	STEWART	820	88	732		644 D	10.7%	89.3%	10.7%	89.3%
29,640	SUMTER	1,531	294	1,237		943 D	19.2%	80.8%	19.2%	80.8%
11,158	TALBOT	610	74	536		462 D	12.1%	87.9%	12.1%	87.9%
8,841	TALIAFERRO	504	58	446		388 D	11.5%	88.5%	11.5%	88.5%
14,502	TATTNALL	1,251	791	460		331 R	63.2%	36.8%	63.2%	36.8%
11,473	TAYLOR	943	353	590		237 D	37.4%	62.6%	37.4%	62.6%
15,291	TELFAIR	2,389	332	2,057		1,725 D	13.9%	86.1%	13.9%	86.1%
19,601	TERRELL	1,013	116	897		781 D	11.5%	88.5%	11.5%	88.5%
33,044	THOMAS	2,054	814	1,240		426 D	39.6%	60.4%	39.6%	60.4%
14,493	TIFT	1,247	511	736		225 D	41.0%	59.0%	41.0%	59.0%
13,897	TOOMBS	1,166	551	615		64 D	47.3%	52.7%	47.3%	52.7%
3,937	TOWNS	1,374	857	517		340 R	62.4%	37.6%	62.4%	37.6%
7,664	TREUTLEN	456	64	392		328 D	14.0%	86.0%	14.0%	86.0%
36,097	TROUP	2,524	967	1,557		590 D	38.3%	61.7%	38.3%	61.7%
12,466	TURNER	854	526	328		198 R	61.6%	38.4%	61.6%	38.4%
10,407	TWIGGS	645	74	571		497 D	11.5%	88.5%	11.5%	88.5%
6,455	UNION	3,496	2,873	623		2,250 R	82.2%	17.8%	82.2%	17.8%
14,786	UPSON	942	221	721		500 D	23.5%	76.5%	23.5%	76.5%
23,370	WALKER	2,839	1,786	1,053		733 R	62.9%	37.1%	62.9%	37.1%
24,216	WALTON	1,559	424	1,135		711 D	27.2%	72.8%	27.2%	72.8%
28,361	WARE	2,755	1,339	1,416		77 D	48.6%	51.4%	48.6%	51.4%
11,828	WARREN	502	255	247		8 R	50.8%	49.2%	50.8%	49.2%
28,147	WASHINGTON	1,614	472	1,142		670 D	29.2%	70.8%	29.2%	70.8%
14,381	WAYNE	901	413	488		75 D	45.8%	54.2%	45.8%	54.2%
5,342	WEBSTER	235	61	174		113 D	26.0%	74.0%	26.0%	74.0%
9,817	WHEELER	413	101	312		211 D	24.5%	75.5%	24.5%	75.5%
6,105	WHITE	842	568	274		294 R	67.5%	32.5%	67.5%	32.5%
16,897	WHITFIELD	2,804	1,650	1,154		496 R	58.8%	41.2%	58.8%	41.2%
15,511	WILCOX	675	216	459		243 D	32.0%	68.0%	32.0%	68.0%
24,210	WILKES	1,545	798	747		51 R	51.7%	48.3%	51.7%	48.3%
11,376	WILKINSON	714	227	487		260 D	31.8%	68.2%	31.8%	68.2%
23,863	WORTH	1,262	310	952		642 D	24.6%	75.4%	24.6%	75.4%
2,895,832	TOTAL	231,592	101,800	129,604	188	27,804 D	44.0%	56.0%	44.0%	56.0%

GEORGIA

PRESIDENT 1924

1920 Census Population	County	Total Vote	Republican	Democratic	Other	Rep.-Dem. Plurality	Percentage: Total Vote Rep.	Total Vote Dem.	Major Vote Rep.	Major Vote Dem.
10,594	APPLING	257	44	212	1	168 D	17.1%	82.5%	17.2%	82.8%
7,656	ATKINSON	436	25	394	17	369 D	5.7%	90.4%	6.0%	94.0%
6,460	BACON	1,055	79	961	15	882 D	7.5%	91.1%	7.6%	92.4%
8,298	BAKER	273	21	245	7	224 D	7.7%	89.7%	7.9%	92.1%
19,791	BALDWIN	984	107	826	51	719 D	10.9%	83.9%	11.5%	88.5%
11,814	BANKS	393	86	291	16	205 D	21.9%	74.0%	22.8%	77.2%
13,188	BARROW	762	88	501	173	413 D	11.5%	65.7%	14.9%	85.1%
24,527	BARTOW	1,393	482	846	65	364 D	34.6%	60.7%	36.3%	63.7%
14,599	BEN HILL	847	150	507	190	357 D	17.7%	59.9%	22.8%	77.2%
15,573	BERRIEN	432	13	409	10	396 D	3.0%	94.7%	3.1%	96.9%
71,304	BIBB	4,385	455	3,647	283	3,192 D	10.4%	83.2%	11.1%	88.9%
10,532	BLECKLEY	405	21	367	17	346 D	5.2%	90.6%	5.4%	94.6%
	BRANTLEY	279	9	238	32	229 D	3.2%	85.3%	3.6%	96.4%
24,538	BROOKS	1,321	128	1,179	14	1,051 D	9.7%	89.3%	9.8%	90.2%
6,343	BRYAN	208	9	196	3	187 D	4.3%	94.2%	4.4%	95.6%
26,133	BULLOCH	1,052	37	989	26	952 D	3.5%	94.0%	3.6%	96.4%
30,836	BURKE	541	76	449	16	373 D	14.0%	83.0%	14.5%	85.5%
12,327	BUTTS	581	50	493	38	443 D	8.6%	84.9%	9.2%	90.8%
10,225	CALHOUN	412	66	343	3	277 D	16.0%	83.3%	16.1%	83.9%
6,969	CAMDEN	175	1	172	2	171 D	0.6%	98.3%	0.6%	99.4%
11,709	CAMPBELL	508	18	477	13	459 D	3.5%	93.9%	3.6%	96.4%
9,228	CANDLER	269	14	241	14	227 D	5.2%	89.6%	5.5%	94.5%
34,752	CARROLL	2,538	526	1,784	228	1,258 D	20.7%	70.3%	22.8%	77.2%
6,677	CATOOSA	932	242	661	29	419 D	26.0%	70.9%	26.8%	73.2%
4,536	CHARLTON	178	20	151	7	131 D	11.2%	84.8%	11.7%	88.3%
100,032	CHATHAM	8,815	1,800	6,158	857	4,358 D	20.4%	69.9%	22.6%	77.4%
5,266	CHATTAHOOCHEE	227	14	208	5	194 D	6.2%	91.6%	6.3%	93.7%
14,312	CHATTOOGA	2,061	412	1,615	34	1,203 D	20.0%	78.4%	20.3%	79.7%
18,569	CHEROKEE	1,503	601	848	54	247 D	40.0%	56.4%	41.5%	58.5%
26,111	CLARKE	1,860	267	1,530	63	1,263 D	14.4%	82.3%	14.9%	85.1%
7,557	CLAY	331	51	246	34	195 D	15.4%	74.3%	17.2%	82.8%
11,159	CLAYTON	394	46	273	75	227 D	11.7%	69.3%	14.4%	85.6%
7,984	CLINCH	265	13	235	17	222 D	4.9%	88.7%	5.2%	94.8%
30,437	COBB	1,910	362	1,360	188	998 D	19.0%	71.2%	21.0%	79.0%
18,653	COFFEE	650	62	510	78	448 D	9.5%	78.5%	10.8%	89.2%
29,332	COLQUITT	1,922	205	1,572	145	1,367 D	10.7%	81.8%	11.5%	88.5%
11,718	COLUMBIA	300	47	213	40	166 D	15.7%	71.0%	18.1%	81.9%
11,180	COOK	581	44	502	35	458 D	7.6%	86.4%	8.1%	91.9%
29,047	COWETA	1,117	67	1,010	40	943 D	6.0%	90.4%	6.2%	93.8%
8,893	CRAWFORD	374	7	352	15	345 D	1.9%	94.1%	1.9%	98.1%
18,914	CRISP	476	21	439	16	418 D	4.4%	92.2%	4.6%	95.4%
3,918	DADE	741	119	563	59	444 D	16.1%	76.0%	17.4%	82.6%
4,204	DAWSON	546	264	279	3	15 D	48.4%	51.1%	48.6%	51.4%
31,785	DECATUR	922	151	637	134	486 D	16.4%	69.1%	19.2%	80.8%
44,051	DE KALB	3,241	590	2,277	374	1,687 D	18.2%	70.3%	20.6%	79.4%
22,540	DODGE	1,754	91	1,654	9	1,563 D	5.2%	94.3%	5.2%	94.8%
20,522	DOOLY	637	45	590	2	545 D	7.1%	92.6%	7.1%	92.9%
20,063	DOUGHERTY	1,314	167	1,065	82	898 D	12.7%	81.1%	13.6%	86.4%
10,477	DOUGLAS	575	86	355	134	269 D	15.0%	61.7%	19.5%	80.5%
18,983	EARLY	435	22	351	62	329 D	5.1%	80.7%	5.9%	94.1%
3,313	ECHOLS	495	11	482	2	471 D	2.2%	97.4%	2.2%	97.8%
9,985	EFFINGHAM	406	39	337	30	298 D	9.6%	83.0%	10.4%	89.6%
23,905	ELBERT	1,287	72	1,024	191	952 D	5.6%	79.6%	6.6%	93.4%
25,862	EMANUEL	774	39	710	25	671 D	5.0%	91.7%	5.2%	94.8%
6,594	EVANS	828	21	790	17	769 D	2.5%	95.4%	2.6%	97.4%
12,103	FANNIN	2,732	1,650	1,079	3	571 R	60.4%	39.5%	60.5%	39.5%
11,396	FAYETTE	323	24	257	42	233 D	7.4%	79.6%	8.5%	91.5%
39,841	FLOYD	2,604	470	1,922	212	1,452 D	18.0%	73.8%	19.6%	80.4%
11,755	FORSYTH	1,030	298	715	17	417 D	28.9%	69.4%	29.4%	70.6%
19,957	FRANKLIN	843	109	618	116	509 D	12.9%	73.3%	15.0%	85.0%

GEORGIA

PRESIDENT 1924

1920 Census Population	County	Total Vote	Republican	Democratic	Other	Rep.-Dem. Plurality	Percentage Total Vote Rep.	Total Vote Dem.	Major Vote Rep.	Major Vote Dem.
232,606	FULTON	12,638	3,229	7,830	1,579	4,601 D	25.5%	62.0%	29.2%	70.8%
8,406	GILMER	1,688	912	776		136 R	54.0%	46.0%	54.0%	46.0%
4,192	GLASCOCK	205	26	111	68	85 D	12.7%	54.1%	19.0%	81.0%
19,370	GLYNN	970	283	612	75	329 D	29.2%	63.1%	31.6%	68.4%
17,736	GORDON	1,340	397	875	68	478 D	29.6%	65.3%	31.2%	68.8%
20,306	GRADY	1,574	100	1,449	25	1,349 D	6.4%	92.1%	6.5%	93.5%
18,972	GREENE	781	77	558	146	481 D	9.9%	71.4%	12.1%	87.9%
30,327	GWINNETT	1,334	207	1,011	116	804 D	15.5%	75.8%	17.0%	83.0%
10,730	HABERSHAM	1,192	322	808	62	486 D	27.0%	67.8%	28.5%	71.5%
26,822	HALL	1,863	290	1,398	175	1,108 D	15.6%	75.0%	17.2%	82.8%
18,357	HANCOCK	308	22	272	14	250 D	7.1%	88.3%	7.5%	92.5%
14,440	HARALSON	1,235	667	447	121	220 R	54.0%	36.2%	59.9%	40.1%
15,775	HARRIS	517	20	457	40	437 D	3.9%	88.4%	4.2%	95.8%
17,944	HART	1,117	65	857	195	792 D	5.8%	76.7%	7.0%	93.0%
11,126	HEARD	369	35	327	7	292 D	9.5%	88.6%	9.7%	90.3%
20,420	HENRY	714	53	594	67	541 D	7.4%	83.2%	8.2%	91.8%
21,964	HOUSTON	1,709	75	1,611	23	1,536 D	4.4%	94.3%	4.4%	95.6%
12,670	IRWIN	324	35	268	21	233 D	10.8%	82.7%	11.6%	88.4%
24,654	JACKSON	1,214	142	993	79	851 D	11.7%	81.8%	12.5%	87.5%
16,362	JASPER	525	68	448	9	380 D	13.0%	85.3%	13.2%	86.8%
7,322	JEFF DAVIS	167	39	122	6	83 D	23.4%	73.1%	24.2%	75.8%
22,602	JEFFERSON	682	103	502	77	399 D	15.1%	73.6%	17.0%	83.0%
14,328	JENKINS	240	16	200	24	184 D	6.7%	83.3%	7.4%	92.6%
13,546	JOHNSON	1,368	194	1,058	116	864 D	14.2%	77.3%	15.5%	84.5%
13,269	JONES	443	26	414	3	388 D	5.9%	93.5%	5.9%	94.1%
	LAMAR	664	38	594	32	556 D	5.7%	89.5%	6.0%	94.0%
	LANIER	403	46	356	1	310 D	11.4%	88.3%	11.4%	88.6%
39,605	LAURENS	1,299	121	1,127	51	1,006 D	9.3%	86.8%	9.7%	90.3%
10,904	LEE	245	23	211	11	188 D	9.4%	86.1%	9.8%	90.2%
12,707	LIBERTY	416	39	334	43	295 D	9.4%	80.3%	10.5%	89.5%
9,739	LINCOLN	1,264	121	847	296	726 D	9.6%	67.0%	12.5%	87.5%
	LONG	564	19	499	46	480 D	3.4%	88.5%	3.7%	96.3%
26,521	LOWNDES	1,211	57	1,095	59	1,038 D	4.7%	90.4%	4.9%	95.1%
5,240	LUMPKIN	478	111	357	10	246 D	23.2%	74.7%	23.7%	76.3%
11,509	MCDUFFIE	560	37	267	256	230 D	6.6%	47.7%	12.2%	87.8%
5,119	MCINTOSH	173	44	127	2	83 D	25.4%	73.4%	25.7%	74.3%
17,667	MACON	750	52	649	49	597 D	6.9%	86.5%	7.4%	92.6%
18,803	MADISON	686	121	504	61	383 D	17.6%	73.5%	19.4%	80.6%
7,604	MARION	321	31	272	18	241 D	9.7%	84.7%	10.2%	89.8%
26,168	MERIWETHER	1,331	103	886	342	783 D	7.7%	66.6%	10.4%	89.6%
9,565	MILLER	183	45	126	12	81 D	24.6%	68.9%	26.3%	73.7%
6,885	MILTON	328	53	224	51	171 D	16.2%	68.3%	19.1%	80.9%
25,588	MITCHELL	838	51	736	51	685 D	6.1%	87.8%	6.5%	93.5%
20,138	MONROE	767	64	672	31	608 D	8.3%	87.6%	8.7%	91.3%
9,167	MONTGOMERY	453	87	353	13	266 D	19.2%	77.9%	19.8%	80.2%
20,143	MORGAN	768	126	598	44	472 D	16.4%	77.9%	17.4%	82.6%
9,490	MURRAY	1,531	648	818	65	170 D	42.3%	53.4%	44.2%	55.8%
44,195	MUSCOGEE	2,415	218	2,067	130	1,849 D	9.0%	85.6%	9.5%	90.5%
21,680	NEWTON	950	139	716	95	577 D	14.6%	75.4%	16.3%	83.7%
11,067	OCONEE	387	46	279	62	233 D	11.9%	72.1%	14.2%	85.8%
20,287	OGLETHORPE	1,965	129	1,748	88	1,619 D	6.6%	89.0%	6.9%	93.1%
14,025	PAULDING	923	378	419	126	41 D	41.0%	45.4%	47.4%	52.6%
	PEACH	—	—	—	—	—	—	—	—	—
8,222	PICKENS	1,907	1,149	754	4	395 R	60.3%	39.5%	60.4%	39.6%
11,934	PIERCE	501	83	397	21	314 D	16.6%	79.2%	17.3%	82.7%
21,212	PIKE	1,008	41	895	72	854 D	4.1%	88.8%	4.4%	95.6%
20,357	POLK	1,441	481	803	157	322 D	33.4%	55.7%	37.5%	62.5%
11,587	PULASKI	492	29	442	21	413 D	5.9%	89.8%	6.2%	93.8%
15,151	PUTNAM	468	7	457	4	450 D	1.5%	97.6%	1.5%	98.5%
3,417	QUITMAN	150	8	138	4	130 D	5.3%	92.0%	5.5%	94.5%

GEORGIA

PRESIDENT 1924

1920 Census Population	County	Total Vote	Republican	Democratic	Other	Rep.-Dem. Plurality	Percentage Total Vote Rep.	Total Vote Dem.	Major Vote Rep.	Major Vote Dem.
5,746	RABUN	593	117	454	22	337 D	19.7%	76.6%	20.5%	79.5%
16,721	RANDOLPH	656	88	518	50	430 D	13.4%	79.0%	14.5%	85.5%
63,692	RICHMOND	3,844	1,296	2,169	379	873 D	33.7%	56.4%	37.4%	62.6%
9,521	ROCKDALE	434	24	382	28	358 D	5.5%	88.0%	5.9%	94.1%
5,243	SCHLEY	281	12	266	3	254 D	4.3%	94.7%	4.3%	95.7%
23,552	SCREVEN	1,145	288	821	36	533 D	25.2%	71.7%	26.0%	74.0%
	SEMINOLE	245	24	201	20	177 D	9.8%	82.0%	10.7%	89.3%
21,908	SPALDING	1,420	75	1,257	88	1,182 D	5.3%	88.5%	5.6%	94.4%
11,215	STEPHENS	599	40	523	36	483 D	6.7%	87.3%	7.1%	92.9%
12,089	STEWART	465	24	408	33	384 D	5.2%	87.7%	5.6%	94.4%
29,640	SUMTER	1,462	124	1,225	113	1,101 D	8.5%	83.8%	9.2%	90.8%
11,158	TALBOT	526	33	491	2	458 D	6.3%	93.3%	6.3%	93.7%
8,841	TALIAFERRO	293	4	228	61	224 D	1.4%	77.8%	1.7%	98.3%
14,502	TATTNALL	1,315	66	1,100	149	1,034 D	5.0%	83.7%	5.7%	94.3%
11,473	TAYLOR	486	96	370	20	274 D	19.8%	76.1%	20.6%	79.4%
15,291	TELFAIR	1,757	264	1,382	111	1,118 D	15.0%	78.7%	16.0%	84.0%
19,601	TERRELL	696	45	630	21	585 D	6.5%	90.5%	6.7%	93.3%
33,044	THOMAS	1,463	115	1,280	68	1,165 D	7.9%	87.5%	8.2%	91.8%
14,493	TIFT	595	33	522	40	489 D	5.5%	87.7%	5.9%	94.1%
13,897	TOOMBS	378	32	314	32	282 D	8.5%	83.1%	9.2%	90.8%
3,937	TOWNS	1,372	765	604	3	161 R	55.8%	44.0%	55.9%	44.1%
7,664	TREUTLEN	252	27	222	3	195 D	10.7%	88.1%	10.8%	89.2%
36,097	TROUP	1,684	165	1,422	97	1,257 D	9.8%	84.4%	10.4%	89.6%
12,466	TURNER	536	166	338	32	172 D	31.0%	63.1%	32.9%	67.1%
10,407	TWIGGS	486	39	417	30	378 D	8.0%	85.8%	8.6%	91.4%
6,455	UNION	1,567	719	793	55	74 D	45.9%	50.6%	47.6%	52.4%
14,786	UPSON	581	37	484	60	447 D	6.4%	83.3%	7.1%	92.9%
23,370	WALKER	2,672	878	1,740	54	862 D	32.9%	65.1%	33.5%	66.5%
24,216	WALTON	1,025	90	873	62	783 D	8.8%	85.2%	9.3%	90.7%
28,361	WARE	1,996	216	1,497	283	1,281 D	10.8%	75.0%	12.6%	87.4%
11,828	WARREN	387	36	253	98	217 D	9.3%	65.4%	12.5%	87.5%
28,147	WASHINGTON	965	130	758	77	628 D	13.5%	78.5%	14.6%	85.4%
14,381	WAYNE	503	33	409	61	376 D	6.6%	81.3%	7.5%	92.5%
5,342	WEBSTER	160	10	140	10	130 D	6.3%	87.5%	6.7%	93.3%
9,817	WHEELER	869		772	97	772 D		88.8%		100.0%
6,105	WHITE	650	158	476	16	318 D	24.3%	73.2%	24.9%	75.1%
16,897	WHITFIELD	1,996	668	1,236	92	568 D	33.5%	61.9%	35.1%	64.9%
15,511	WILCOX	490	21	431	38	410 D	4.3%	88.0%	4.6%	95.4%
24,210	WILKES	1,075	44	836	195	792 D	4.1%	77.8%	5.0%	95.0%
11,376	WILKINSON	353	56	284	13	228 D	15.9%	80.5%	16.5%	83.5%
23,863	WORTH	731	40	616	75	576 D	5.5%	84.3%	6.1%	93.9%
2,895,832	TOTAL	166,635	30,300	123,262	13,073	92,962 D	18.2%	74.0%	19.7%	80.3%

GEORGIA

PRESIDENT 1920

1920 Census Population	County	Total Vote	Republican	Democratic	Other	Rep.-Dem. Plurality	Percentage: Total Vote Rep.	Percentage: Total Vote Dem.	Percentage: Major Vote Rep.	Percentage: Major Vote Dem.
10,594	APPLING	509	196	313		117 D	38.5%	61.5%	38.5%	61.5%
7,656	ATKINSON	572	119	453		334 D	20.8%	79.2%	20.8%	79.2%
6,460	BACON	526	219	307		88 D	41.6%	58.4%	41.6%	58.4%
8,298	BAKER	221	80	141		61 D	36.2%	63.8%	36.2%	63.8%
19,791	BALDWIN	646	92	554		462 D	14.2%	85.8%	14.2%	85.8%
11,814	BANKS	821	342	479		137 D	41.7%	58.3%	41.7%	58.3%
13,188	BARROW	1,143	412	731		319 D	36.0%	64.0%	36.0%	64.0%
24,527	BARTOW	1,676	754	922		168 D	45.0%	55.0%	45.0%	55.0%
14,599	BEN HILL	775	232	543		311 D	29.9%	70.1%	29.9%	70.1%
15,573	BERRIEN	681	58	623		565 D	8.5%	91.5%	8.5%	91.5%
71,304	BIBB	2,488	458	2,030		1,572 D	18.4%	81.6%	18.4%	81.6%
10,532	BLECKLEY	262		262		262 D		100.0%		100.0%
	BRANTLEY	—	—	—		—	—	—	—	—
24,538	BROOKS	673	76	597		521 D	11.3%	88.7%	11.3%	88.7%
6,343	BRYAN	196	21	175		154 D	10.7%	89.3%	10.7%	89.3%
26,133	BULLOCH	1,346	248	1,098		850 D	18.4%	81.6%	18.4%	81.6%
30,836	BURKE	426	39	387		348 D	9.2%	90.8%	9.2%	90.8%
12,327	BUTTS	643	141	502		361 D	21.9%	78.1%	21.9%	78.1%
10,225	CALHOUN	454	5	449		444 D	1.1%	98.9%	1.1%	98.9%
6,969	CAMDEN	166	14	152		138 D	8.4%	91.6%	8.4%	91.6%
11,709	CAMPBELL	370	107	263		156 D	28.9%	71.1%	28.9%	71.1%
9,228	CANDLER	741	68	673		605 D	9.2%	90.8%	9.2%	90.8%
34,752	CARROLL	2,859	1,227	1,632		405 D	42.9%	57.1%	42.9%	57.1%
6,677	CATOOSA	88	33	55		22 D	37.5%	62.5%	37.5%	62.5%
4,536	CHARLTON	185	28	157		129 D	15.1%	84.9%	15.1%	84.9%
100,032	CHATHAM	5,238	995	4,243		3,248 D	19.0%	81.0%	19.0%	81.0%
5,266	CHATTAHOOCHEE	92	5	87		82 D	5.4%	94.6%	5.4%	94.6%
14,312	CHATTOOGA	1,401	514	887		373 D	36.7%	63.3%	36.7%	63.3%
18,569	CHEROKEE	1,682	1,138	544		594 R	67.7%	32.3%	67.7%	32.3%
26,111	CLARKE	1,636	217	1,419		1,202 D	13.3%	86.7%	13.3%	86.7%
7,557	CLAY	293	63	230		167 D	21.5%	78.5%	21.5%	78.5%
11,159	CLAYTON	509	34	475		441 D	6.7%	93.3%	6.7%	93.3%
7,984	CLINCH	371	77	294		217 D	20.8%	79.2%	20.8%	79.2%
30,437	COBB	2,303	1,095	1,208		113 D	47.5%	52.5%	47.5%	52.5%
18,653	COFFEE	656	230	426		196 D	35.1%	64.9%	35.1%	64.9%
29,332	COLQUITT	1,291	523	768		245 D	40.5%	59.5%	40.5%	59.5%
11,718	COLUMBIA	476		476		476 D		100.0%		100.0%
11,180	COOK	563	303	260		43 R	53.8%	46.2%	53.8%	46.2%
29,047	COWETA	1,263	169	1,094		925 D	13.4%	86.6%	13.4%	86.6%
8,893	CRAWFORD	300	65	235		170 D	21.7%	78.3%	21.7%	78.3%
18,914	CRISP	648	83	565		482 D	12.8%	87.2%	12.8%	87.2%
3,918	DADE	608	114	494		380 D	18.8%	81.3%	18.8%	81.3%
4,204	DAWSON	608	354	254		100 R	58.2%	41.8%	58.2%	41.8%
31,785	DECATUR	1,282	300	982		682 D	23.4%	76.6%	23.4%	76.6%
44,051	DE KALB	2,650	803	1,847		1,044 D	30.3%	69.7%	30.3%	69.7%
22,540	DODGE	804	177	627		450 D	22.0%	78.0%	22.0%	78.0%
20,522	DOOLY	583	39	544		505 D	6.7%	93.3%	6.7%	93.3%
20,063	DOUGHERTY	726	105	621		516 D	14.5%	85.5%	14.5%	85.5%
10,477	DOUGLAS	902	475	427		48 R	52.7%	47.3%	52.7%	47.3%
18,983	EARLY	415	34	381		347 D	8.2%	91.8%	8.2%	91.8%
3,313	ECHOLS	—	—	—		—	—	—	—	—
9,985	EFFINGHAM	844	118	726		608 D	14.0%	86.0%	14.0%	86.0%
23,905	ELBERT	1,434	187	1,247		1,060 D	13.0%	87.0%	13.0%	87.0%
25,862	EMANUEL	1,634	190	1,444		1,254 D	11.6%	88.4%	11.6%	88.4%
6,594	EVANS	448	16	432		416 D	3.6%	96.4%	3.6%	96.4%
12,103	FANNIN	1,632	1,083	549		534 R	66.4%	33.6%	66.4%	33.6%
11,396	FAYETTE	311	80	231		151 D	25.7%	74.3%	25.7%	74.3%
39,841	FLOYD	2,590	667	1,923		1,256 D	25.8%	74.2%	25.8%	74.2%
11,755	FORSYTH	1,554	741	813		72 D	47.7%	52.3%	47.7%	52.3%
19,957	FRANKLIN	1,336	447	889		442 D	33.5%	66.5%	33.5%	66.5%

GEORGIA

PRESIDENT 1920

1920 Census Population	County	Total Vote	Republican	Democratic	Other	Rep.-Dem. Plurality	Percentage Total Vote Rep.	Percentage Total Vote Dem.	Percentage Major Vote Rep.	Percentage Major Vote Dem.
232,606	FULTON	9,971	3,336	6,635		3,299 D	33.5%	66.5%	33.5%	66.5%
8,406	GILMER	1,208	662	546		116 R	54.8%	45.2%	54.8%	45.2%
4,192	GLASCOCK	315	83	232		149 D	26.3%	73.7%	26.3%	73.7%
19,370	GLYNN	554	132	422		290 D	23.8%	76.2%	23.8%	76.2%
17,736	GORDON	1,642	929	713		216 R	56.6%	43.4%	56.6%	43.4%
20,306	GRADY	1,119	232	887		655 D	20.7%	79.3%	20.7%	79.3%
18,972	GREENE	859	178	681		503 D	20.7%	79.3%	20.7%	79.3%
30,327	GWINNETT	2,785	1,140	1,645		505 D	40.9%	59.1%	40.9%	59.1%
10,730	HABERSHAM	1,129	626	503		123 R	55.4%	44.6%	55.4%	44.6%
26,822	HALL	2,327	852	1,475		623 D	36.6%	63.4%	36.6%	63.4%
18,357	HANCOCK	551	53	498		445 D	9.6%	90.4%	9.6%	90.4%
14,440	HARALSON	1,546	1,108	438		670 R	71.7%	28.3%	71.7%	28.3%
15,775	HARRIS	407	9	398		389 D	2.2%	97.8%	2.2%	97.8%
17,944	HART	1,017	323	694		371 D	31.8%	68.2%	31.8%	68.2%
11,126	HEARD	475	14	461		447 D	2.9%	97.1%	2.9%	97.1%
20,420	HENRY	608		608		608 D		100.0%		100.0%
21,964	HOUSTON	762	39	723		684 D	5.1%	94.9%	5.1%	94.9%
12,670	IRWIN	639	114	525		411 D	17.8%	82.2%	17.8%	82.2%
24,654	JACKSON	1,403	334	1,069		735 D	23.8%	76.2%	23.8%	76.2%
16,362	JASPER	471	42	429		387 D	8.9%	91.1%	8.9%	91.1%
7,322	JEFF DAVIS	563	303	260		43 R	53.8%	46.2%	53.8%	46.2%
22,602	JEFFERSON	919	82	837		755 D	8.9%	91.1%	8.9%	91.1%
14,328	JENKINS	380	49	331		282 D	12.9%	87.1%	12.9%	87.1%
13,546	JOHNSON	380	74	306		232 D	19.5%	80.5%	19.5%	80.5%
13,269	JONES	118	31	87		56 D	26.3%	73.7%	26.3%	73.7%
	LAMAR	—	—	—		—	—	—	—	—
	LANIER	—	—	—		—	—	—	—	—
39,605	LAURENS	1,517	350	1,167		817 D	23.1%	76.9%	23.1%	76.9%
10,904	LEE	270	19	251		232 D	7.0%	93.0%	7.0%	93.0%
12,707	LIBERTY	478	175	303		128 D	36.6%	63.4%	36.6%	63.4%
9,739	LINCOLN	512	3	509		506 D	0.6%	99.4%	0.6%	99.4%
	LONG	—	—	—		—	—	—	—	—
26,521	LOWNDES	1,528	220	1,308		1,088 D	14.4%	85.6%	14.4%	85.6%
5,240	LUMPKIN	360	205	155		50 R	56.9%	43.1%	56.9%	43.1%
11,509	MCDUFFIE	491	109	382		273 D	22.2%	77.8%	22.2%	77.8%
5,119	MCINTOSH	158	39	119		80 D	24.7%	75.3%	24.7%	75.3%
17,667	MACON	551	68	483		415 D	12.3%	87.7%	12.3%	87.7%
18,803	MADISON	974	281	693		412 D	28.9%	71.1%	28.9%	71.1%
7,604	MARION	416	180	236		56 D	43.3%	56.7%	43.3%	56.7%
26,168	MERIWETHER	1,245	186	1,059		873 D	14.9%	85.1%	14.9%	85.1%
9,565	MILLER	185	30	155		125 D	16.2%	83.8%	16.2%	83.8%
6,885	MILTON	509	231	278		47 D	45.4%	54.6%	45.4%	54.6%
25,588	MITCHELL	1,074	144	930		786 D	13.4%	86.6%	13.4%	86.6%
20,138	MONROE	920	83	837		754 D	9.0%	91.0%	9.0%	91.0%
9,167	MONTGOMERY	317	148	169		21 D	46.7%	53.3%	46.7%	53.3%
20,143	MORGAN	626	176	450		274 D	28.1%	71.9%	28.1%	71.9%
9,490	MURRAY	1,579	851	728		123 R	53.9%	46.1%	53.9%	46.1%
44,195	MUSCOGEE	1,473	101	1,372		1,271 D	6.9%	93.1%	6.9%	93.1%
21,680	NEWTON	1,102	349	753		404 D	31.7%	68.3%	31.7%	68.3%
11,067	OCONEE	449	108	341		233 D	24.1%	75.9%	24.1%	75.9%
20,287	OGLETHORPE	886	42	844		802 D	4.7%	95.3%	4.7%	95.3%
14,025	PAULDING	1,294	954	340		614 R	73.7%	26.3%	73.7%	26.3%
	PEACH	—	—	—		—	—	—	—	—
8,222	PICKENS	1,267	830	437		393 R	65.5%	34.5%	65.5%	34.5%
11,934	PIERCE	529	122	407		285 D	23.1%	76.9%	23.1%	76.9%
21,212	PIKE	1,557	280	1,277		997 D	18.0%	82.0%	18.0%	82.0%
20,357	POLK	1,662	1,004	658		346 R	60.4%	39.6%	60.4%	39.6%
11,587	PULASKI	395	57	338		281 D	14.4%	85.6%	14.4%	85.6%
15,151	PUTNAM	425	5	420		415 D	1.2%	98.8%	1.2%	98.8%
3,417	QUITMAN	139	4	135		131 D	2.9%	97.1%	2.9%	97.1%

GEORGIA

PRESIDENT 1920

1920 Census Population	County	Total Vote	Republican	Democratic	Other	Rep.-Dem. Plurality	Percentage Total Vote Rep.	Total Vote Dem.	Major Vote Rep.	Major Vote Dem.
5,746	RABUN	459	147	312		165 D	32.0%	68.0%	32.0%	68.0%
16,721	RANDOLPH	585	51	534		483 D	8.7%	91.3%	8.7%	91.3%
63,692	RICHMOND	3,167	511	2,656		2,145 D	16.1%	83.9%	16.1%	83.9%
9,521	ROCKDALE	689	201	488		287 D	29.2%	70.8%	29.2%	70.8%
5,243	SCHLEY	288	53	235		182 D	18.4%	81.6%	18.4%	81.6%
23,552	SCREVEN	899	260	639		379 D	28.9%	71.1%	28.9%	71.1%
	SEMINOLE	—	—	—		—	—	—	—	—
21,908	SPALDING	1,011	181	830		649 D	17.9%	82.1%	17.9%	82.1%
11,215	STEPHENS	667	252	415		163 D	37.8%	62.2%	37.8%	62.2%
12,089	STEWART	375	31	344		313 D	8.3%	91.7%	8.3%	91.7%
29,640	SUMTER	1,372	296	1,076		780 D	21.6%	78.4%	21.6%	78.4%
11,158	TALBOT	422	43	379		336 D	10.2%	89.8%	10.2%	89.8%
8,841	TALIAFERRO	342	12	330		318 D	3.5%	96.5%	3.5%	96.5%
14,502	TATTNALL	748	301	447		146 D	40.2%	59.8%	40.2%	59.8%
11,473	TAYLOR	702	211	491		280 D	30.1%	69.9%	30.1%	69.9%
15,291	TELFAIR	1,106	37	1,069		1,032 D	3.3%	96.7%	3.3%	96.7%
19,601	TERRELL	548	48	500		452 D	8.8%	91.2%	8.8%	91.2%
33,044	THOMAS	1,298	168	1,130		962 D	12.9%	87.1%	12.9%	87.1%
14,493	TIFT	730	154	576		422 D	21.1%	78.9%	21.1%	78.9%
13,897	TOOMBS	643	246	397		151 D	38.3%	61.7%	38.3%	61.7%
3,937	TOWNS	654	398	256		142 R	60.9%	39.1%	60.9%	39.1%
7,664	TREUTLEN	370	107	263		156 D	28.9%	71.1%	28.9%	71.1%
36,097	TROUP	1,793	342	1,451		1,109 D	19.1%	80.9%	19.1%	80.9%
12,466	TURNER	575	182	393		211 D	31.7%	68.3%	31.7%	68.3%
10,407	TWIGGS	317	44	273		229 D	13.9%	86.1%	13.9%	86.1%
6,455	UNION	1,031	562	469		93 R	54.5%	45.5%	54.5%	45.5%
14,786	UPSON	1,127	170	957		787 D	15.1%	84.9%	15.1%	84.9%
23,370	WALKER	2,416	1,069	1,347		278 D	44.2%	55.8%	44.2%	55.8%
24,216	WALTON	1,312	123	1,189		1,066 D	9.4%	90.6%	9.4%	90.6%
28,361	WARE	1,116	215	901		686 D	19.3%	80.7%	19.3%	80.7%
11,828	WARREN	485	83	402		319 D	17.1%	82.9%	17.1%	82.9%
28,147	WASHINGTON	1,252	118	1,134		1,016 D	9.4%	90.6%	9.4%	90.6%
14,381	WAYNE	432	25	407		382 D	5.8%	94.2%	5.8%	94.2%
5,342	WEBSTER	209	24	185		161 D	11.5%	88.5%	11.5%	88.5%
9,817	WHEELER	451	101	350		249 D	22.4%	77.6%	22.4%	77.6%
6,105	WHITE	473	264	209		55 R	55.8%	44.2%	55.8%	44.2%
16,897	WHITFIELD	1,835	1,073	762		311 R	58.5%	41.5%	58.5%	41.5%
15,511	WILCOX	587	106	481		375 D	18.1%	81.9%	18.1%	81.9%
24,210	WILKES	888	12	876		864 D	1.4%	98.6%	1.4%	98.6%
11,376	WILKINSON	293	37	256		219 D	12.6%	87.4%	12.6%	87.4%
23,863	WORTH	840	214	626		412 D	25.5%	74.5%	25.5%	74.5%
2,895,832	TOTAL	149,558	42,981	106,112	465	63,131 D	28.7%	71.0%	28.8%	71.2%

GEORGIA

In 1921 Brantley county was organized from parts of Charlton, Pierce and Wayne counties; Lamar county was organized from parts of Monroe and Pike counties; Lanier county was organized from parts of Berrien, Clinch and Lowndes counties; Long county was organized from part of Liberty county; Seminole county was organized from part of Decatur county. In 1925 Peach county was organized from parts of Houston and Macon counties. In 1932 Campbell and Milton counties were merged with Fulton county. Population figures are not available for these counties created between the 1920 and 1930 Census.

ELECTION NOTES

1956 Other vote was 2,096 States Rights (Andrews); 93 scattered write-in.

1952 Other vote was scattered write-in.

1948 Other vote was 85,135 Thurmond (States Rights); 1,636 Wallace (Progressive); 732 Watson (Prohibition); 3 Thomas (Socialist); 1 scattered write-in. States Rights candidates carried Burke, Chattahoochee, Columbia, Effingham, Glascock, Jefferson, Lee, Lincoln, McDuffie, Richmond, Twiggs, Warren and Wilkinson counties and ran second statewide and in a number of counties. It should be noted that the plurality in the county-by-county table is a Republican-Democratic plurality and the plurality in the state summary table is a first-second party plurality.

1944 Other vote was 36 Watson (Prohibition); 6 Thomas (Socialist). The Republican figures include 56,527 votes cast on the Republican ticket and 3,373 votes cast on the Independent Democratic ticket.

1940 Other vote was 983 Babson (Prohibition); 14 scattered write-in. The Republican figures include 23,934 votes cast on the Republican ticket and 22,561 cast on the Independent Democratic ticket.

1936 Other vote was 660 Colvin (Prohibition); 136 Lemke (Union); 68 Thomas (Socialist).

1932 Other vote was 1,125 Upshaw (Prohibition); 461 Thomas (Socialist); 23 Foster (Communist). Prohibition or Socialist candidates ran second in several counties where there was no Republican vote and in one county in which the Republican vote was two.

1928 Other vote was 124 Thomas (Socialist); 64 Foster (Communist). The minor party vote was not reported by county. The Republican figures include 65,423 votes cast on the Republican ticket and 36,377 votes cast on the anti-Smith ticket.

1924 Other vote was 12,687 LaFollette (Progressive); 231 Faris (Prohibition); 155 Nations (American). The statewide total in the other vote column includes the Prohibition and American votes which were not available by county. Progressive candidates ran second in a number of counties.

1920 Other vote was Debs (Socialist). The statewide total in the other vote column is the Socialist vote which was not reported by county. No returns were canvassed for Echols county.

IDAHO

POPULAR VOTE FOR PRESIDENT 1920 TO 1956

Year	Total Vote	Republican Vote	Republican Candidate	Democratic Vote	Democratic Candidate	Other Vote	Plurality	Percentage Total Vote Rep.	Percentage Total Vote Dem.	Percentage Major Vote Rep.	Percentage Major Vote Dem.
1956	272,989	166,979	Eisenhower, Dwight D.	105,868	Stevenson, Adlai E.	142	61,111 R	61.2%	38.8%	61.2%	38.8%
1952	276,254	180,707	Eisenhower, Dwight D.	95,081	Stevenson, Adlai E.	466	85,626 R	65.4%	34.4%	65.5%	34.5%
1948	214,816	101,514	Dewey, Thomas E.	107,370	Truman, Harry S.	5,932	5,856 D	47.3%	50.0%	48.6%	51.4%
1944	208,321	100,137	Dewey, Thomas E.	107,399	Roosevelt, Franklin D.	785	7,262 D	48.1%	51.6%	48.3%	51.7%
1940	235,168	106,553	Willkie, Wendell	127,842	Roosevelt, Franklin D.	773	21,289 D	45.3%	54.4%	45.5%	54.5%
1936	199,617	66,256	Landon, Alfred M.	125,683	Roosevelt, Franklin D.	7,678	59,427 D	33.2%	63.0%	34.5%	65.5%
1932	186,520	71,312	Hoover, Herbert C.	109,479	Roosevelt, Franklin D.	5,729	38,167 D	38.2%	58.7%	39.4%	60.6%
1928	151,541	97,322	Hoover, Herbert C.	52,926	Smith, Alfred E.	1,293	44,396 R	64.2%	34.9%	64.8%	35.2%
1924 **	147,690	69,791	Coolidge, Calvin	23,951	Davis, John W.	53,948	15,843 R	47.3%	16.2%	74.5%	25.5%
1920	138,281	91,351	Harding, Warren G.	46,930	Cox, James M.		44,421 R	66.1%	33.9%	66.1%	33.9%

In 1924 other vote was Progressive.

ELECTORAL COLLEGE VOTE 1920 TO 1956

Year	Total	Republican	Democratic	Other
1956	4	4	—	—
1952	4	4	—	—
1948	4	—	4	—
1944	4	—	4	—
1940	4	—	4	—
1936	4	—	4	—
1932	4	—	4	—
1928	4	4	—	—
1924	4	4	—	—
1920	4	4	—	—

IDAHO

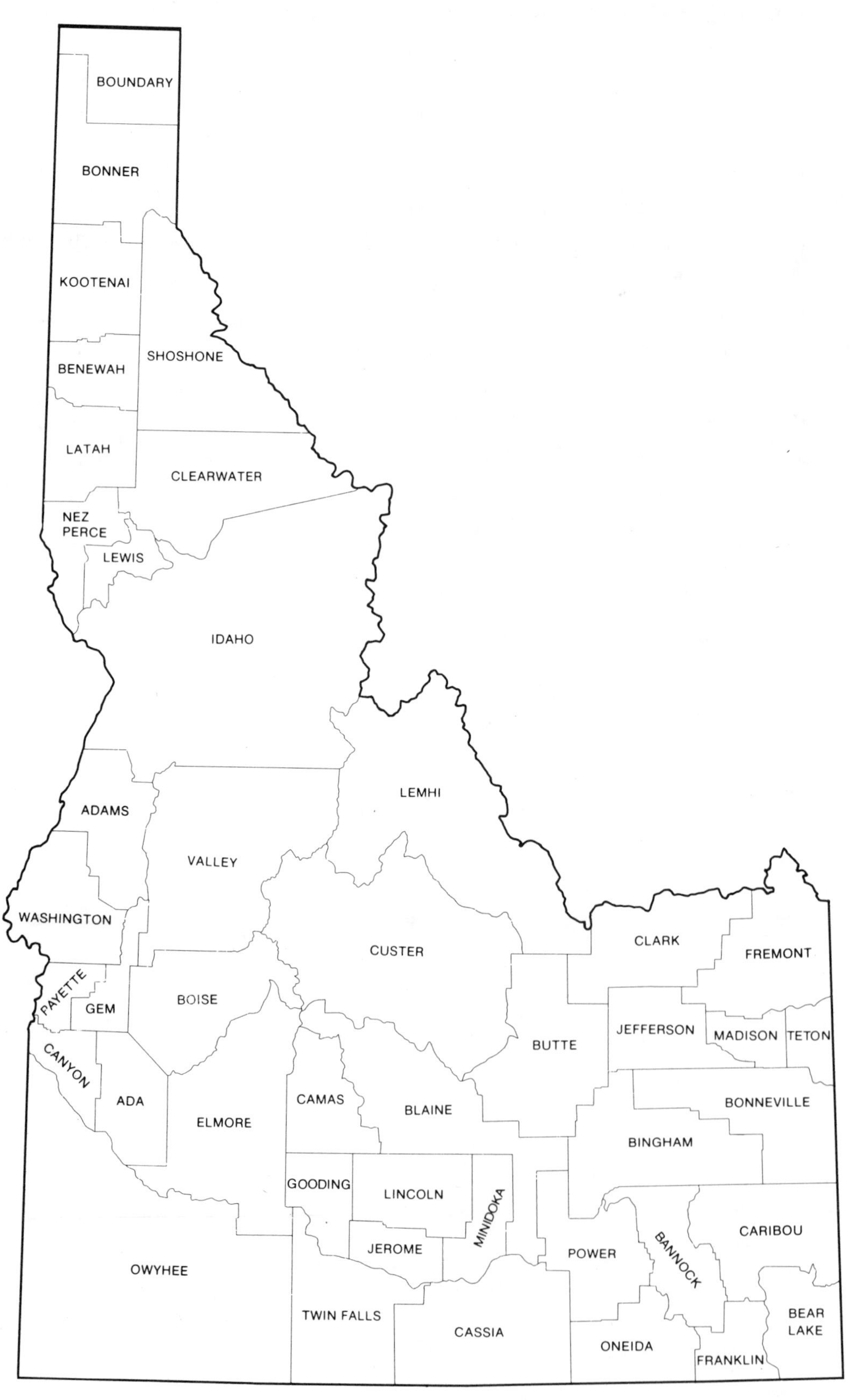

BOUNDARY
BONNER
KOOTENAI
SHOSHONE
BENEWAH
LATAH
CLEARWATER
NEZ PERCE
LEWIS
IDAHO
LEMHI
ADAMS
VALLEY
WASHINGTON
CUSTER
CLARK
FREMONT
PAYETTE
GEM
BOISE
JEFFERSON
MADISON
TETON
BUTTE
CANYON
ADA
CAMAS
ELMORE
BLAINE
BONNEVILLE
BINGHAM
GOODING
LINCOLN
MINIDOKA
CARIBOU
JEROME
POWER
BANNOCK
OWYHEE
TWIN FALLS
CASSIA
ONEIDA
FRANKLIN
BEAR LAKE

IDAHO

PRESIDENT 1956

1950 Census Population	County	Total Vote	Republican	Democratic	Other	Rep.-Dem. Plurality	Percentage Total Vote Rep.	Total Vote Dem.	Major Vote Rep.	Major Vote Dem.
70,649	ADA	37,750	26,387	11,328	35	15,059 R	69.9%	30.0%	70.0%	30.0%
3,347	ADAMS	1,384	842	542		300 R	60.8%	39.2%	60.8%	39.2%
41,745	BANNOCK	19,584	10,476	9,101	7	1,375 R	53.5%	46.5%	53.5%	46.5%
6,834	BEAR LAKE	3,399	2,181	1,218		963 R	64.2%	35.8%	64.2%	35.8%
6,173	BENEWAH	2,903	1,460	1,442	1	18 R	50.3%	49.7%	50.3%	49.7%
23,271	BINGHAM	9,265	5,853	3,412		2,441 R	63.2%	36.8%	63.2%	36.8%
5,384	BLAINE	2,367	1,384	978	5	406 R	58.5%	41.3%	58.6%	41.4%
1,776	BOISE	855	570	285		285 R	66.7%	33.3%	66.7%	33.3%
14,853	BONNER	7,464	3,937	3,514	13	423 R	52.7%	47.1%	52.8%	47.2%
30,210	BONNEVILLE	16,778	11,099	5,676	3	5,423 R	66.2%	33.8%	66.2%	33.8%
5,908	BOUNDARY	2,571	1,419	1,150	2	269 R	55.2%	44.7%	55.2%	44.8%
2,722	BUTTE	1,443	774	669		105 R	53.6%	46.4%	53.6%	46.4%
1,079	CAMAS	603	337	266		71 R	55.9%	44.1%	55.9%	44.1%
53,597	CANYON	23,052	15,483	7,540	29	7,943 R	67.2%	32.7%	67.3%	32.7%
5,576	CARIBOU	2,618	1,668	950		718 R	63.7%	36.3%	63.7%	36.3%
14,629	CASSIA	5,733	3,944	1,789		2,155 R	68.8%	31.2%	68.8%	31.2%
918	CLARK	469	318	151		167 R	67.8%	32.2%	67.8%	32.2%
8,217	CLEARWATER	3,532	1,508	2,024		516 D	42.7%	57.3%	42.7%	57.3%
3,318	CUSTER	1,344	811	533		278 R	60.3%	39.7%	60.3%	39.7%
6,687	ELMORE	3,609	1,849	1,759	1	90 R	51.2%	48.7%	51.2%	48.8%
9,867	FRANKLIN	3,976	2,795	1,181		1,614 R	70.3%	29.7%	70.3%	29.7%
9,351	FREMONT	4,048	2,513	1,535		978 R	62.1%	37.9%	62.1%	37.9%
8,730	GEM	4,164	2,445	1,717	2	728 R	58.7%	41.2%	58.7%	41.3%
11,101	GOODING	4,620	2,835	1,783	2	1,052 R	61.4%	38.6%	61.4%	38.6%
11,423	IDAHO	5,263	2,703	2,546	14	157 R	51.4%	48.4%	51.5%	48.5%
10,495	JEFFERSON	4,571	2,748	1,823		925 R	60.1%	39.9%	60.1%	39.9%
12,080	JEROME	4,832	3,127	1,705		1,422 R	64.7%	35.3%	64.7%	35.3%
24,947	KOOTENAI	13,502	7,330	6,149	23	1,181 R	54.3%	45.5%	54.4%	45.6%
20,971	LATAH	8,706	5,024	3,682		1,342 R	57.7%	42.3%	57.7%	42.3%
6,278	LEMHI	2,832	1,794	1,038		756 R	63.3%	36.7%	63.3%	36.7%
4,208	LEWIS	2,125	833	1,292		459 D	39.2%	60.8%	39.2%	60.8%
4,256	LINCOLN	1,729	1,069	660		409 R	61.8%	38.2%	61.8%	38.2%
9,156	MADISON	3,961	2,538	1,423		1,115 R	64.1%	35.9%	64.1%	35.9%
9,785	MINIDOKA	4,646	2,954	1,692		1,262 R	63.6%	36.4%	63.6%	36.4%
22,658	NEZ PERCE	12,083	5,635	6,448		813 D	46.6%	53.4%	46.6%	53.4%
4,387	ONEIDA	2,062	1,324	738		586 R	64.2%	35.8%	64.2%	35.8%
6,307	OWYHEE	2,332	1,468	864		604 R	63.0%	37.0%	63.0%	37.0%
11,921	PAYETTE	5,114	3,342	1,767	5	1,575 R	65.4%	34.6%	65.4%	34.6%
3,988	POWER	1,877	1,108	769		339 R	59.0%	41.0%	59.0%	41.0%
22,806	SHOSHONE	9,046	4,598	4,448		150 R	50.8%	49.2%	50.8%	49.2%
3,204	TETON	1,293	842	451		391 R	65.1%	34.9%	65.1%	34.9%
40,979	TWIN FALLS	17,763	12,097	5,666		6,431 R	68.1%	31.9%	68.1%	31.9%
4,270	VALLEY	1,796	1,285	511		774 R	71.5%	28.5%	71.5%	28.5%
8,576	WASHINGTON	3,925	2,272	1,653		619 R	57.9%	42.1%	57.9%	42.1%
588,637	TOTAL	272,989	166,979	105,868	142	61,111 R	61.2%	38.8%	61.2%	38.8%

IDAHO

PRESIDENT 1952

1950 Census Population	County	Total Vote	Republican	Democratic	Other	Rep.-Dem. Plurality	Percentage: Total Vote Rep.	Total Vote Dem.	Major Vote Rep.	Major Vote Dem.
70,649	ADA	37,736	27,415	10,281	40	17,134 R	72.6%	27.2%	72.7%	27.3%
3,347	ADAMS	1,452	933	517	2	416 R	64.3%	35.6%	64.3%	35.7%
41,745	BANNOCK	19,662	10,864	8,771	27	2,093 R	55.3%	44.6%	55.3%	44.7%
6,834	BEAR LAKE	3,574	2,300	1,274		1,026 R	64.4%	35.6%	64.4%	35.6%
6,173	BENEWAH	3,011	1,568	1,436	7	132 R	52.1%	47.7%	52.2%	47.8%
23,271	BINGHAM	9,143	6,114	3,024	5	3,090 R	66.9%	33.1%	66.9%	33.1%
5,384	BLAINE	2,642	1,609	1,033		576 R	60.9%	39.1%	60.9%	39.1%
1,776	BOISE	970	655	309	6	346 R	67.5%	31.9%	67.9%	32.1%
14,853	BONNER	7,645	4,309	3,293	43	1,016 R	56.4%	43.1%	56.7%	43.3%
30,210	BONNEVILLE	14,993	10,252	4,737	4	5,515 R	68.4%	31.6%	68.4%	31.6%
5,908	BOUNDARY	2,691	1,641	1,040	10	601 R	61.0%	38.6%	61.2%	38.8%
2,722	BUTTE	1,389	916	473		443 R	65.9%	34.1%	65.9%	34.1%
1,079	CAMAS	650	425	224	1	201 R	65.4%	34.5%	65.5%	34.5%
53,597	CANYON	23,942	17,065	6,810	67	10,255 R	71.3%	28.4%	71.5%	28.5%
5,576	CARIBOU	2,598	1,788	809	1	979 R	68.8%	31.1%	68.8%	31.2%
14,629	CASSIA	6,159	4,481	1,676	2	2,805 R	72.8%	27.2%	72.8%	27.2%
918	CLARK	508	382	126		256 R	75.2%	24.8%	75.2%	24.8%
8,217	CLEARWATER	3,327	1,494	1,826	7	332 D	44.9%	54.9%	45.0%	55.0%
3,318	CUSTER	1,517	1,058	452	7	606 R	69.7%	29.8%	70.1%	29.9%
6,687	ELMORE	3,143	1,653	1,484	6	169 R	52.6%	47.2%	52.7%	47.3%
9,867	FRANKLIN	4,436	3,252	1,181	3	2,071 R	73.3%	26.6%	73.4%	26.6%
9,351	FREMONT	4,213	2,710	1,500	3	1,210 R	64.3%	35.6%	64.4%	35.6%
8,730	GEM	4,128	2,568	1,555	5	1,013 R	62.2%	37.7%	62.3%	37.7%
11,101	GOODING	4,860	3,452	1,404	4	2,048 R	71.0%	28.9%	71.1%	28.9%
11,423	IDAHO	5,330	3,054	2,269	7	785 R	57.3%	42.6%	57.4%	42.6%
10,495	JEFFERSON	4,446	2,970	1,474	2	1,496 R	66.8%	33.2%	66.8%	33.2%
12,080	JEROME	5,130	3,807	1,318	5	2,489 R	74.2%	25.7%	74.3%	25.7%
24,947	KOOTENAI	12,774	7,272	5,414	88	1,858 R	56.9%	42.4%	57.3%	42.7%
20,971	LATAH	8,702	5,440	3,254	8	2,186 R	62.5%	37.4%	62.6%	37.4%
6,278	LEMHI	2,950	2,100	848	2	1,252 R	71.2%	28.7%	71.2%	28.8%
4,208	LEWIS	2,280	1,004	1,276		272 D	44.0%	56.0%	44.0%	56.0%
4,256	LINCOLN	1,945	1,383	562		821 R	71.1%	28.9%	71.1%	28.9%
9,156	MADISON	4,106	2,756	1,348	2	1,408 R	67.1%	32.8%	67.2%	32.8%
9,785	MINIDOKA	4,381	3,128	1,253		1,875 R	71.4%	28.6%	71.4%	28.6%
22,658	NEZ PERCE	11,231	5,659	5,552	20	107 R	50.4%	49.4%	50.5%	49.5%
4,387	ONEIDA	2,287	1,547	739	1	808 R	67.6%	32.3%	67.7%	32.3%
6,307	OWYHEE	2,575	1,813	759	3	1,054 R	70.4%	29.5%	70.5%	29.5%
11,921	PAYETTE	5,439	3,936	1,491	12	2,445 R	72.4%	27.4%	72.5%	27.5%
3,988	POWER	1,911	1,308	603		705 R	68.4%	31.6%	68.4%	31.6%
22,806	SHOSHONE	9,862	5,119	4,684	59	435 R	51.9%	47.5%	52.2%	47.8%
3,204	TETON	1,455	964	491		473 R	66.3%	33.7%	66.3%	33.7%
40,979	TWIN FALLS	19,023	14,471	4,548	4	9,923 R	76.1%	23.9%	76.1%	23.9%
4,270	VALLEY	2,008	1,456	552		904 R	72.5%	27.5%	72.5%	27.5%
8,576	WASHINGTON	4,030	2,616	1,411	3	1,205 R	64.9%	35.0%	65.0%	35.0%
588,637	TOTAL	276,254	180,707	95,081	466	85,626 R	65.4%	34.4%	65.5%	34.5%

IDAHO

PRESIDENT 1948

1940 Census Population	County	Total Vote	Republican	Democratic	Other	Rep.-Dem. Plurality	Percentage Total Vote Rep.	Total Vote Dem.	Major Vote Rep.	Major Vote Dem.
50,401	ADA	26,705	14,972	11,253	480	3,719 R	56.1%	42.1%	57.1%	42.9%
3,407	ADAMS	1,274	603	647	24	44 D	47.3%	50.8%	48.2%	51.8%
34,759	BANNOCK	15,560	5,580	9,679	301	4,099 D	35.9%	62.2%	36.6%	63.4%
7,911	BEAR LAKE	3,280	1,590	1,664	26	74 D	48.5%	50.7%	48.9%	51.1%
7,332	BENEWAH	2,731	1,038	1,590	103	552 D	38.0%	58.2%	39.5%	60.5%
21,044	BINGHAM	6,448	3,162	3,197	89	35 D	49.0%	49.6%	49.7%	50.3%
5,295	BLAINE	2,162	945	1,182	35	237 D	43.7%	54.7%	44.4%	55.6%
2,333	BOISE	940	437	479	24	42 D	46.5%	51.0%	47.7%	52.3%
15,667	BONNER	5,867	2,666	2,916	285	250 D	45.4%	49.7%	47.8%	52.2%
25,697	BONNEVILLE	10,001	4,499	5,382	120	883 D	45.0%	53.8%	45.5%	54.5%
5,987	BOUNDARY	2,099	910	1,029	160	119 D	43.4%	49.0%	46.9%	53.1%
1,877	BUTTE	846	412	426	8	14 D	48.7%	50.4%	49.2%	50.8%
1,360	CAMAS	575	289	278	8	11 R	50.3%	48.3%	51.0%	49.0%
40,987	CANYON	18,363	9,700	7,903	760	1,797 R	52.8%	43.0%	55.1%	44.9%
2,284	CARIBOU	930	447	475	8	28 D	48.1%	51.1%	48.5%	51.5%
14,430	CASSIA	4,671	2,424	2,178	69	246 R	51.9%	46.6%	52.7%	47.3%
1,005	CLARK	432	262	165	5	97 R	60.6%	38.2%	61.4%	38.6%
8,243	CLEARWATER	2,549	820	1,571	158	751 D	32.2%	61.6%	34.3%	65.7%
3,549	CUSTER	1,257	612	625	20	13 D	48.7%	49.7%	49.5%	50.5%
5,518	ELMORE	2,503	854	1,589	60	735 D	34.1%	63.5%	35.0%	65.0%
10,229	FRANKLIN	3,813	2,028	1,763	22	265 R	53.2%	46.2%	53.5%	46.5%
10,304	FREMONT	3,811	1,777	2,014	20	237 D	46.6%	52.8%	46.9%	53.1%
9,544	GEM	3,426	1,585	1,724	117	139 D	46.3%	50.3%	47.9%	52.1%
9,257	GOODING	4,015	2,111	1,844	60	267 R	52.6%	45.9%	53.4%	46.6%
12,691	IDAHO	4,218	1,790	2,300	128	510 D	42.4%	54.5%	43.8%	56.2%
10,762	JEFFERSON	3,568	1,490	2,017	61	527 D	41.8%	56.5%	42.5%	57.5%
9,900	JEROME	4,305	2,128	2,124	53	4 R	49.4%	49.3%	50.0%	50.0%
22,283	KOOTENAI	10,262	4,265	5,284	713	1,019 D	41.6%	51.5%	44.7%	55.3%
18,804	LATAH	7,889	3,805	3,810	274	5 D	48.2%	48.3%	50.0%	50.0%
6,521	LEMHI	1,938	1,037	864	37	173 R	53.5%	44.6%	54.6%	45.4%
4,666	LEWIS	1,763	487	1,224	52	737 D	27.6%	69.4%	28.5%	71.5%
4,230	LINCOLN	1,617	851	748	18	103 R	52.6%	46.3%	53.2%	46.8%
9,186	MADISON	3,647	1,602	2,024	21	422 D	43.9%	55.5%	44.2%	55.8%
9,870	MINIDOKA	3,432	1,654	1,668	110	14 D	48.2%	48.6%	49.8%	50.2%
18,873	NEZ PERCE	9,322	3,168	5,747	407	2,579 D	34.0%	61.6%	35.5%	64.5%
5,417	ONEIDA	1,982	962	1,008	12	46 D	48.5%	50.9%	48.8%	51.2%
5,652	OWYHEE	1,937	969	925	43	44 R	50.0%	47.8%	51.2%	48.8%
9,511	PAYETTE	4,081	2,430	1,568	83	862 R	59.5%	38.4%	60.8%	39.2%
3,965	POWER	1,681	875	795	11	80 R	52.1%	47.3%	52.4%	47.6%
21,230	SHOSHONE	8,261	3,200	4,472	589	1,272 D	38.7%	54.1%	41.7%	58.3%
3,601	TETON	1,272	593	672	7	79 D	46.6%	52.8%	46.9%	53.1%
36,403	TWIN FALLS	14,061	7,833	6,019	209	1,814 R	55.7%	42.8%	56.5%	43.5%
4,035	VALLEY	1,841	939	828	74	111 R	51.0%	45.0%	53.1%	46.9%
8,853	WASHINGTON	3,481	1,713	1,700	68	13 R	49.2%	48.8%	50.2%	49.8%
524,873	TOTAL	214,816	101,514	107,370	5,932	5,856 D	47.3%	50.0%	48.6%	51.4%

IDAHO

PRESIDENT 1944

1940 Census Population	County	Total Vote	Republican	Democratic	Other	Rep.-Dem. Plurality	Percentage Total Vote Rep.	Total Vote Dem.	Major Vote Rep.	Major Vote Dem.
50,401	ADA	24,144	13,410	10,667	67	2,743 R	55.5%	44.2%	55.7%	44.3%
3,407	ADAMS	1,364	642	721	1	79 D	47.1%	52.9%	47.1%	52.9%
34,759	BANNOCK	15,105	5,413	9,681	11	4,268 D	35.8%	64.1%	35.9%	64.1%
7,911	BEAR LAKE	3,347	1,613	1,732	2	119 D	48.2%	51.7%	48.2%	51.8%
7,332	BENEWAH	2,643	1,173	1,446	24	273 D	44.4%	54.7%	44.8%	55.2%
21,044	BINGHAM	6,658	3,223	3,428	7	205 D	48.4%	51.5%	48.5%	51.5%
5,295	BLAINE	1,916	874	1,037	5	163 D	45.6%	54.1%	45.7%	54.3%
2,333	BOISE	1,031	464	564	3	100 D	45.0%	54.7%	45.1%	54.9%
15,667	BONNER	6,063	2,924	3,116	23	192 D	48.2%	51.4%	48.4%	51.6%
25,697	BONNEVILLE	8,999	4,048	4,935	16	887 D	45.0%	54.8%	45.1%	54.9%
5,987	BOUNDARY	2,160	1,064	1,053	43	11 R	49.3%	48.8%	50.3%	49.7%
1,877	BUTTE	849	431	416	2	15 R	50.8%	49.0%	50.9%	49.1%
1,360	CAMAS	618	301	317		16 D	48.7%	51.3%	48.7%	51.3%
40,987	CANYON	16,762	9,215	7,306	241	1,909 R	55.0%	43.6%	55.8%	44.2%
2,284	CARIBOU	978	462	516		54 D	47.2%	52.8%	47.2%	52.8%
14,430	CASSIA	4,896	2,563	2,325	8	238 R	52.3%	47.5%	52.4%	47.6%
1,005	CLARK	499	317	180	2	137 R	63.5%	36.1%	63.8%	36.2%
8,243	CLEARWATER	2,626	865	1,744	17	879 D	32.9%	66.4%	33.2%	66.8%
3,549	CUSTER	1,178	565	613		48 D	48.0%	52.0%	48.0%	52.0%
5,518	ELMORE	2,667	1,030	1,627	10	597 D	38.6%	61.0%	38.8%	61.2%
10,229	FRANKLIN	3,925	1,950	1,971	4	21 D	49.7%	50.2%	49.7%	50.3%
10,304	FREMONT	3,871	1,755	2,116		361 D	45.3%	54.7%	45.3%	54.7%
9,544	GEM	3,265	1,363	1,866	36	503 D	41.7%	57.2%	42.2%	57.8%
9,257	GOODING	3,716	2,049	1,659	8	390 R	55.1%	44.6%	55.3%	44.7%
12,691	IDAHO	4,063	1,977	2,071	15	94 D	48.7%	51.0%	48.8%	51.2%
10,762	JEFFERSON	3,665	1,458	2,198	9	740 D	39.8%	60.0%	39.9%	60.1%
9,900	JEROME	3,898	2,157	1,741		416 R	55.3%	44.7%	55.3%	44.7%
22,283	KOOTENAI	10,222	4,388	5,792	42	1,404 D	42.9%	56.7%	43.1%	56.9%
18,804	LATAH	7,083	3,526	3,514	43	12 R	49.8%	49.6%	50.1%	49.9%
6,521	LEMHI	2,040	1,048	988	4	60 R	51.4%	48.4%	51.5%	48.5%
4,666	LEWIS	1,811	589	1,222		633 D	32.5%	67.5%	32.5%	67.5%
4,230	LINCOLN	1,720	934	784	2	150 R	54.3%	45.6%	54.4%	45.6%
9,186	MADISON	3,458	1,527	1,927	4	400 D	44.2%	55.7%	44.2%	55.8%
9,870	MINIDOKA	3,424	1,781	1,635	8	146 R	52.0%	47.8%	52.1%	47.9%
18,873	NEZ PERCE	8,649	3,159	5,453	37	2,294 D	36.5%	63.0%	36.7%	63.3%
5,417	ONEIDA	2,163	935	1,227	1	292 D	43.2%	56.7%	43.2%	56.8%
5,652	OWYHEE	1,819	983	824	12	159 R	54.0%	45.3%	54.4%	45.6%
9,511	PAYETTE	3,885	2,485	1,382	18	1,103 R	64.0%	35.6%	64.3%	35.7%
3,965	POWER	1,696	895	801		94 R	52.8%	47.2%	52.8%	47.2%
21,230	SHOSHONE	8,463	3,162	5,290	11	2,128 D	37.4%	62.5%	37.4%	62.6%
3,601	TETON	1,193	552	641		89 D	46.3%	53.7%	46.3%	53.7%
36,403	TWIN FALLS	14,116	7,946	6,128	42	1,818 R	56.3%	43.4%	56.5%	43.5%
4,035	VALLEY	1,819	919	896	4	23 R	50.5%	49.3%	50.6%	49.4%
8,853	WASHINGTON	3,854	2,002	1,849	3	153 R	51.9%	48.0%	52.0%	48.0%
524,873	TOTAL	208,321	100,137	107,399	785	7,262 D	48.1%	51.6%	48.3%	51.7%

IDAHO

PRESIDENT 1940

1940 Census Population	County	Total Vote	Republican	Democratic	Other	Rep.-Dem. Plurality	Percentage Total Vote Rep.	Percentage Total Vote Dem.	Percentage Major Vote Rep.	Percentage Major Vote Dem.
50,401	ADA	25,293	12,861	12,381	51	480 R	50.8%	49.0%	51.0%	49.0%
3,407	ADAMS	1,711	779	929	3	150 D	45.5%	54.3%	45.6%	54.4%
34,759	BANNOCK	15,913	5,419	10,493	1	5,074 D	34.1%	65.9%	34.1%	65.9%
7,911	BEAR LAKE	3,787	1,761	2,026		265 D	46.5%	53.5%	46.5%	53.5%
7,332	BENEWAH	3,250	1,304	1,924	22	620 D	40.1%	59.2%	40.4%	59.6%
21,044	BINGHAM	7,488	3,662	3,815	11	153 D	48.9%	50.9%	49.0%	51.0%
5,295	BLAINE	2,687	1,124	1,559	4	435 D	41.8%	58.0%	41.9%	58.1%
2,333	BOISE	1,167	489	677	1	188 D	41.9%	58.0%	41.9%	58.1%
15,667	BONNER	6,940	3,072	3,834	34	762 D	44.3%	55.2%	44.5%	55.5%
25,697	BONNEVILLE	9,900	3,999	5,891	10	1,892 D	40.4%	59.5%	40.4%	59.6%
5,987	BOUNDARY	2,684	1,221	1,393	70	172 D	45.5%	51.9%	46.7%	53.3%
1,877	BUTTE	871	423	448		25 D	48.6%	51.4%	48.6%	51.4%
1,360	CAMAS	748	367	381		14 D	49.1%	50.9%	49.1%	50.9%
40,987	CANYON	17,478	8,776	8,639	63	137 R	50.2%	49.4%	50.4%	49.6%
2,284	CARIBOU	1,049	390	658	1	268 D	37.2%	62.7%	37.2%	62.8%
14,430	CASSIA	5,689	2,748	2,930	11	182 D	48.3%	51.5%	48.4%	51.6%
1,005	CLARK	611	399	212		187 R	65.3%	34.7%	65.3%	34.7%
8,243	CLEARWATER	3,429	1,128	2,284	17	1,156 D	32.9%	66.6%	33.1%	66.9%
3,549	CUSTER	1,659	760	894	5	134 D	45.8%	53.9%	45.9%	54.1%
5,518	ELMORE	2,713	1,077	1,632	4	555 D	39.7%	60.2%	39.8%	60.2%
10,229	FRANKLIN	4,227	2,069	2,158		89 D	48.9%	51.1%	48.9%	51.1%
10,304	FREMONT	4,554	1,996	2,556	2	560 D	43.8%	56.1%	43.8%	56.2%
9,544	GEM	4,132	1,462	2,666	4	1,204 D	35.4%	64.5%	35.4%	64.6%
9,257	GOODING	4,275	2,352	1,919	4	433 R	55.0%	44.9%	55.1%	44.9%
12,691	IDAHO	5,545	2,641	2,888	16	247 D	47.6%	52.1%	47.8%	52.2%
10,762	JEFFERSON	4,364	1,717	2,631	16	914 D	39.3%	60.3%	39.5%	60.5%
9,900	JEROME	4,408	2,520	1,881	7	639 R	57.2%	42.7%	57.3%	42.7%
22,283	KOOTENAI	10,462	4,333	5,997	132	1,664 D	41.4%	57.3%	41.9%	58.1%
18,804	LATAH	8,500	3,971	4,494	35	523 D	46.7%	52.9%	46.9%	53.1%
6,521	LEMHI	3,077	1,412	1,664	1	252 D	45.9%	54.1%	45.9%	54.1%
4,666	LEWIS	2,198	729	1,462	7	733 D	33.2%	66.5%	33.3%	66.7%
4,230	LINCOLN	1,902	1,009	886	7	123 R	53.0%	46.6%	53.2%	46.8%
9,186	MADISON	3,851	1,632	2,218	1	586 D	42.4%	57.6%	42.4%	57.6%
9,870	MINIDOKA	3,974	1,979	1,982	13	3 D	49.8%	49.9%	50.0%	50.0%
18,873	NEZ PERCE	9,413	3,409	5,963	41	2,554 D	36.2%	63.3%	36.4%	63.6%
5,417	ONEIDA	2,584	1,140	1,440	4	300 D	44.1%	55.7%	44.2%	55.8%
5,652	OWYHEE	2,205	1,031	1,160	14	129 D	46.8%	52.6%	47.1%	52.9%
9,511	PAYETTE	4,364	2,554	1,790	20	764 R	58.5%	41.0%	58.8%	41.2%
3,965	POWER	1,885	951	931	3	20 R	50.5%	49.4%	50.5%	49.5%
21,230	SHOSHONE	10,172	3,525	6,565	82	3,040 D	34.7%	64.5%	34.9%	65.1%
3,601	TETON	1,511	667	844		177 D	44.1%	55.9%	44.1%	55.9%
36,403	TWIN FALLS	16,351	9,031	7,286	34	1,745 R	55.2%	44.6%	55.3%	44.7%
4,035	VALLEY	1,943	761	1,165	17	404 D	39.2%	60.0%	39.5%	60.5%
8,853	WASHINGTON	4,204	1,903	2,296	5	393 D	45.3%	54.6%	45.3%	54.7%
524,873	TOTAL	235,168	106,553	127,842	773	21,289 D	45.3%	54.4%	45.5%	54.5%

IDAHO

PRESIDENT 1936

1930 Census Population	County	Total Vote	Republican	Democratic	Other	Rep.-Dem. Plurality	Percentage Total Vote Rep.	Total Vote Dem.	Major Vote Rep.	Major Vote Dem.
37,925	ADA	20,574	7,581	12,027	966	4,446 D	36.8%	58.5%	38.7%	61.3%
2,867	ADAMS	1,296	434	770	92	336 D	33.5%	59.4%	36.0%	64.0%
31,266	BANNOCK	13,393	3,830	9,443	120	5,613 D	28.6%	70.5%	28.9%	71.1%
7,872	BEAR LAKE	3,486	1,404	2,078	4	674 D	40.3%	59.6%	40.3%	59.7%
6,371	BENEWAH	2,901	897	1,906	98	1,009 D	30.9%	65.7%	32.0%	68.0%
18,561	BINGHAM	6,753	2,354	4,215	184	1,861 D	34.9%	62.4%	35.8%	64.2%
3,768	BLAINE	2,107	735	1,361	11	626 D	34.9%	64.6%	35.1%	64.9%
1,847	BOISE	1,190	368	780	42	412 D	30.9%	65.5%	32.1%	67.9%
13,152	BONNER	5,993	2,016	3,521	456	1,505 D	33.6%	58.8%	36.4%	63.6%
19,664	BONNEVILLE	7,787	2,213	5,439	135	3,226 D	28.4%	69.8%	28.9%	71.1%
4,555	BOUNDARY	2,162	732	1,304	126	572 D	33.9%	60.3%	36.0%	64.0%
1,934	BUTTE	869	312	546	11	234 D	35.9%	62.8%	36.4%	63.6%
1,411	CAMAS	731	274	442	15	168 D	37.5%	60.5%	38.3%	61.7%
30,930	CANYON	14,547	4,910	8,290	1,347	3,380 D	33.8%	57.0%	37.2%	62.8%
2,121	CARIBOU	962	321	640	1	319 D	33.4%	66.5%	33.4%	66.6%
13,116	CASSIA	4,797	1,629	3,100	68	1,471 D	34.0%	64.6%	34.4%	65.6%
1,122	CLARK	580	304	272	4	32 R	52.4%	46.9%	52.8%	47.2%
6,599	CLEARWATER	2,926	812	1,959	155	1,147 D	27.8%	67.0%	29.3%	70.7%
3,162	CUSTER	1,421	530	875	16	345 D	37.3%	61.6%	37.7%	62.3%
4,491	ELMORE	2,380	688	1,567	125	879 D	28.9%	65.8%	30.5%	69.5%
9,379	FRANKLIN	3,670	1,396	2,255	19	859 D	38.0%	61.4%	38.2%	61.8%
9,924	FREMONT	4,366	1,423	2,904	39	1,481 D	32.6%	66.5%	32.9%	67.1%
7,419	GEM	3,568	879	2,468	221	1,589 D	24.6%	69.2%	26.3%	73.7%
7,580	GOODING	3,705	1,505	2,100	100	595 D	40.6%	56.7%	41.7%	58.3%
10,107	IDAHO	4,929	1,535	3,104	290	1,569 D	31.1%	63.0%	33.1%	66.9%
9,171	JEFFERSON	3,864	1,037	2,776	51	1,739 D	26.8%	71.8%	27.2%	72.8%
8,358	JEROME	3,778	1,297	2,374	107	1,077 D	34.3%	62.8%	35.3%	64.7%
19,469	KOOTENAI	8,999	2,586	5,752	661	3,166 D	28.7%	63.9%	31.0%	69.0%
17,798	LATAH	7,458	2,838	4,359	261	1,521 D	38.1%	58.4%	39.4%	60.6%
4,643	LEMHI	2,666	943	1,648	75	705 D	35.4%	61.8%	36.4%	63.6%
5,238	LEWIS	2,168	507	1,612	49	1,105 D	23.4%	74.4%	23.9%	76.1%
3,242	LINCOLN	1,721	766	916	39	150 D	44.5%	53.2%	45.5%	54.5%
8,316	MADISON	3,592	1,114	2,455	23	1,341 D	31.0%	68.3%	31.2%	68.8%
8,403	MINIDOKA	3,097	948	2,095	54	1,147 D	30.6%	67.6%	31.2%	68.8%
17,591	NEZ PERCE	7,985	1,988	5,705	292	3,717 D	24.9%	71.4%	25.8%	74.2%
5,870	ONEIDA	2,638	955	1,673	10	718 D	36.2%	63.4%	36.3%	63.7%
4,103	OWYHEE	1,728	500	1,106	122	606 D	28.9%	64.0%	31.1%	68.9%
7,318	PAYETTE	3,663	1,524	1,677	462	153 D	41.6%	45.8%	47.6%	52.4%
4,457	POWER	1,812	708	1,075	29	367 D	39.1%	59.3%	39.7%	60.3%
19,060	SHOSHONE	7,582	2,146	5,377	59	3,231 D	28.3%	70.9%	28.5%	71.5%
3,573	TETON	1,409	542	834	33	292 D	38.5%	59.2%	39.4%	60.6%
29,828	TWIN FALLS	12,828	4,966	7,476	386	2,510 D	38.7%	58.3%	39.9%	60.1%
3,488	VALLEY	1,980	575	1,260	145	685 D	29.0%	63.6%	31.3%	68.7%
7,962	WASHINGTON	3,556	1,234	2,147	175	913 D	34.7%	60.4%	36.5%	63.5%
445,032	TOTAL	199,617	66,256	125,683	7,678	59,427 D	33.2%	63.0%	34.5%	65.5%

IDAHO

PRESIDENT 1932

1930 Census Population	County	Total Vote	Republican	Democratic	Other	Rep.-Dem. Plurality	Percentage Total Vote Rep.	Total Vote Dem.	Major Vote Rep.	Major Vote Dem.
37,925	ADA	17,529	8,062	8,836	631	774 D	46.0%	50.4%	47.7%	52.3%
2,867	ADAMS	1,242	318	854	70	536 D	25.6%	68.8%	27.1%	72.9%
31,266	BANNOCK	12,932	4,549	8,271	112	3,722 D	35.2%	64.0%	35.5%	64.5%
7,872	BEAR LAKE	3,509	1,785	1,721	3	64 R	50.9%	49.0%	50.9%	49.1%
6,371	BENEWAH	2,720	979	1,602	139	623 D	36.0%	58.9%	37.9%	62.1%
18,561	BINGHAM	6,810	2,897	3,802	111	905 D	42.5%	55.8%	43.2%	56.8%
3,768	BLAINE	1,846	696	1,133	17	437 D	37.7%	61.4%	38.1%	61.9%
1,847	BOISE	1,059	342	679	38	337 D	32.3%	64.1%	33.5%	66.5%
13,152	BONNER	5,794	1,951	3,695	148	1,744 D	33.7%	63.8%	34.6%	65.4%
19,664	BONNEVILLE	7,190	2,759	4,298	133	1,539 D	38.4%	59.8%	39.1%	60.9%
4,555	BOUNDARY	2,290	765	1,451	74	686 D	33.4%	63.4%	34.5%	65.5%
1,934	BUTTE	981	395	581	5	186 D	40.3%	59.2%	40.5%	59.5%
1,411	CAMAS	690	234	441	15	207 D	33.9%	63.9%	34.7%	65.3%
30,930	CANYON	13,074	5,085	6,940	1,049	1,855 D	38.9%	53.1%	42.3%	57.7%
2,121	CARIBOU	908	397	499	12	102 D	43.7%	55.0%	44.3%	55.7%
13,116	CASSIA	4,666	2,025	2,598	43	573 D	43.4%	55.7%	43.8%	56.2%
1,122	CLARK	602	276	325	1	49 D	45.8%	54.0%	45.9%	54.1%
6,599	CLEARWATER	2,553	822	1,699	32	877 D	32.2%	66.5%	32.6%	67.4%
3,162	CUSTER	1,306	443	839	24	396 D	33.9%	64.2%	34.6%	65.4%
4,491	ELMORE	2,489	797	1,615	77	818 D	32.0%	64.9%	33.0%	67.0%
9,379	FRANKLIN	3,637	1,760	1,871	6	111 D	48.4%	51.4%	48.5%	51.5%
9,924	FREMONT	4,340	1,509	2,830	1	1,321 D	34.8%	65.2%	34.8%	65.2%
7,419	GEM	3,261	898	2,007	356	1,109 D	27.5%	61.5%	30.9%	69.1%
7,580	GOODING	3,540	1,451	1,911	178	460 D	41.0%	54.0%	43.2%	56.8%
10,107	IDAHO	4,196	1,089	3,005	102	1,916 D	26.0%	71.6%	26.6%	73.4%
9,171	JEFFERSON	3,729	1,174	2,501	54	1,327 D	31.5%	67.1%	31.9%	68.1%
8,358	JEROME	3,682	1,396	2,219	67	823 D	37.9%	60.3%	38.6%	61.4%
19,469	KOOTENAI	8,269	2,820	4,743	706	1,923 D	34.1%	57.4%	37.3%	62.7%
17,798	LATAH	6,763	3,091	3,554	118	463 D	45.7%	52.6%	46.5%	53.5%
4,643	LEMHI	2,167	793	1,332	42	539 D	36.6%	61.5%	37.3%	62.7%
5,238	LEWIS	1,957	526	1,390	41	864 D	26.9%	71.0%	27.5%	72.5%
3,242	LINCOLN	1,589	692	869	28	177 D	43.5%	54.7%	44.3%	55.7%
8,316	MADISON	3,400	1,265	2,112	23	847 D	37.2%	62.1%	37.5%	62.5%
8,403	MINIDOKA	3,363	1,126	2,164	73	1,038 D	33.5%	64.3%	34.2%	65.8%
17,591	NEZ PERCE	7,416	2,215	5,077	124	2,862 D	29.9%	68.5%	30.4%	69.6%
5,870	ONEIDA	2,512	1,045	1,449	18	404 D	41.6%	57.7%	41.9%	58.1%
4,103	OWYHEE	1,614	587	959	68	372 D	36.4%	59.4%	38.0%	62.0%
7,318	PAYETTE	3,596	1,538	1,836	222	298 D	42.8%	51.1%	45.6%	54.4%
4,457	POWER	1,726	593	1,126	7	533 D	34.4%	65.2%	34.5%	65.5%
19,060	SHOSHONE	7,354	2,907	4,347	100	1,440 D	39.5%	59.1%	40.1%	59.9%
3,573	TETON	1,539	672	860	7	188 D	43.7%	55.9%	43.9%	56.1%
29,828	TWIN FALLS	11,717	4,926	6,395	396	1,469 D	42.0%	54.6%	43.5%	56.5%
3,488	VALLEY	1,460	447	921	92	474 D	30.6%	63.1%	32.7%	67.3%
7,962	WASHINGTON	3,503	1,215	2,122	166	907 D	34.7%	60.6%	36.4%	63.6%
445,032	TOTAL	186,520	71,312	109,479	5,729	38,167 D	38.2%	58.7%	39.4%	60.6%

IDAHO

PRESIDENT 1928

1920 Census Population	County	Total Vote	Republican	Democratic	Other	Rep.-Dem. Plurality	Percentage Total Vote Rep.	Total Vote Dem.	Major Vote Rep.	Major Vote Dem.
35,213	ADA	14,308	10,279	3,921	108	6,358 R	71.8%	27.4%	72.4%	27.6%
2,966	ADAMS	905	521	374	10	147 R	57.6%	41.3%	58.2%	41.8%
27,532	BANNOCK	9,953	5,297	4,602	54	695 R	53.2%	46.2%	53.5%	46.5%
8,783	BEAR LAKE	2,955	1,802	1,146	7	656 R	61.0%	38.8%	61.1%	38.9%
6,997	BENEWAH	2,338	1,343	958	37	385 R	57.4%	41.0%	58.4%	41.6%
18,310	BINGHAM	5,035	3,236	1,778	21	1,458 R	64.3%	35.3%	64.5%	35.5%
4,473	BLAINE	1,634	849	780	5	69 R	52.0%	47.7%	52.1%	47.9%
1,822	BOISE	919	521	389	9	132 R	56.7%	42.3%	57.3%	42.7%
12,957	BONNER	4,524	2,861	1,603	60	1,258 R	63.2%	35.4%	64.1%	35.9%
17,501	BONNEVILLE	5,336	3,218	2,110	8	1,108 R	60.3%	39.5%	60.4%	39.6%
4,474	BOUNDARY	1,646	1,015	607	24	408 R	61.7%	36.9%	62.6%	37.4%
2,940	BUTTE	797	493	301	3	192 R	61.9%	37.8%	62.1%	37.9%
1,730	CAMAS	653	413	230	10	183 R	63.2%	35.2%	64.2%	35.8%
26,932	CANYON	9,619	7,293	2,187	139	5,106 R	75.8%	22.7%	76.9%	23.1%
2,191	CARIBOU	766	471	291	4	180 R	61.5%	38.0%	61.8%	38.2%
15,659	CASSIA	3,402	2,388	994	20	1,394 R	70.2%	29.2%	70.6%	29.4%
1,886	CLARK	518	388	129	1	259 R	74.9%	24.9%	75.0%	25.0%
4,993	CLEARWATER	2,074	1,195	852	27	343 R	57.6%	41.1%	58.4%	41.6%
3,550	CUSTER	1,171	647	516	8	131 R	55.3%	44.1%	55.6%	44.4%
5,087	ELMORE	1,877	1,125	739	13	386 R	59.9%	39.4%	60.4%	39.6%
8,650	FRANKLIN	2,926	1,718	1,193	15	525 R	58.7%	40.8%	59.0%	41.0%
10,380	FREMONT	3,619	1,674	1,933	12	259 D	46.3%	53.4%	46.4%	53.6%
6,427	GEM	2,332	1,656	646	30	1,010 R	71.0%	27.7%	71.9%	28.1%
7,548	GOODING	2,689	1,852	821	16	1,031 R	68.9%	30.5%	69.3%	30.7%
11,749	IDAHO	3,812	2,099	1,676	37	423 R	55.1%	44.0%	55.6%	44.4%
9,441	JEFFERSON	3,028	1,671	1,350	7	321 R	55.2%	44.6%	55.3%	44.7%
5,729	JEROME	2,831	2,050	759	22	1,291 R	72.4%	26.8%	73.0%	27.0%
17,878	KOOTENAI	7,114	4,973	2,020	121	2,953 R	69.9%	28.4%	71.1%	28.9%
18,092	LATAH	6,225	4,472	1,681	72	2,791 R	71.8%	27.0%	72.7%	27.3%
5,164	LEMHI	1,994	1,139	837	18	302 R	57.1%	42.0%	57.6%	42.4%
5,851	LEWIS	1,964	1,146	793	25	353 R	58.4%	40.4%	59.1%	40.9%
3,446	LINCOLN	1,227	865	358	4	507 R	70.5%	29.2%	70.7%	29.3%
9,167	MADISON	2,900	1,670	1,228	2	442 R	57.6%	42.3%	57.6%	42.4%
9,035	MINIDOKA	2,996	1,832	1,132	32	700 R	61.1%	37.8%	61.8%	38.2%
15,253	NEZ PERCE	6,644	4,054	2,535	55	1,519 R	61.0%	38.2%	61.5%	38.5%
6,723	ONEIDA	2,211	1,184	1,020	7	164 R	53.6%	46.1%	53.7%	46.3%
4,694	OWYHEE	1,476	918	533	25	385 R	62.2%	36.1%	63.3%	36.7%
7,021	PAYETTE	2,890	2,203	621	66	1,582 R	76.2%	21.5%	78.0%	22.0%
5,105	POWER	1,508	852	653	3	199 R	56.5%	43.3%	56.6%	43.4%
14,250	SHOSHONE	6,117	3,648	2,430	39	1,218 R	59.6%	39.7%	60.0%	40.0%
3,921	TETON	1,103	753	348	2	405 R	68.3%	31.6%	68.4%	31.6%
28,398	TWIN FALLS	9,338	6,791	2,471	76	4,320 R	72.7%	26.5%	73.3%	26.7%
2,524	VALLEY	1,195	774	407	14	367 R	64.8%	34.1%	65.5%	34.5%
9,424	WASHINGTON	2,972	1,973	974	25	999 R	66.4%	32.8%	66.9%	33.1%
431,866	TOTAL	151,541	97,322	52,926	1,293	44,396 R	64.2%	34.9%	64.8%	35.2%

IDAHO

PRESIDENT 1924

1920 Census Population	County	Total Vote	Republican	Democratic	Progressive	Other	Plurality	Percentage Total Vote Rep.	Dem.	Prog.
35,213	ADA	13,189	7,181	2,253	3,755		3,426 R	54.4%	17.1%	28.5%
2,966	ADAMS	971	419	195	357		62 R	43.2%	20.1%	36.8%
27,532	BANNOCK	10,027	4,521	1,598	3,908		613 R	45.1%	15.9%	39.0%
8,783	BEAR LAKE	2,956	1,607	873	476		734 R	54.4%	29.5%	16.1%
6,997	BENEWAH	2,449	1,154	310	985		169 R	47.1%	12.7%	40.2%
18,310	BINGHAM	5,013	2,683	689	1,641		1,042 R	53.5%	13.7%	32.7%
4,473	BLAINE	1,780	774	527	479		247 R	43.5%	29.6%	26.9%
1,822	BOISE	874	379	189	306		73 R	43.4%	21.6%	35.0%
12,957	BONNER	4,222	1,707	529	1,986		279 P	40.4%	12.5%	47.0%
17,501	BONNEVILLE	5,332	2,865	425	2,042		823 R	53.7%	8.0%	38.3%
4,474	BOUNDARY	1,771	839	240	692		147 R	47.4%	13.6%	39.1%
2,940	BUTTE	879	404	192	283		121 R	46.0%	21.8%	32.2%
1,730	CAMAS	625	215	110	300		85 P	34.4%	17.6%	48.0%
26,932	CANYON	9,943	3,821	964	5,158		1,337 P	38.4%	9.7%	51.9%
2,191	CARIBOU	856	507	142	207		300 R	59.2%	16.6%	24.2%
15,659	CASSIA	3,888	2,038	519	1,331		707 R	52.4%	13.3%	34.2%
1,886	CLARK	709	494	43	172		322 R	69.7%	6.1%	24.3%
4,993	CLEARWATER	1,975	937	318	720		217 R	47.4%	16.1%	36.5%
3,550	CUSTER	1,256	584	385	287		199 R	46.5%	30.7%	22.9%
5,087	ELMORE	2,064	785	375	904		119 P	38.0%	18.2%	43.8%
8,650	FRANKLIN	2,615	1,360	536	719		641 R	52.0%	20.5%	27.5%
10,380	FREMONT	3,662	1,660	527	1,475		185 R	45.3%	14.4%	40.3%
6,427	GEM	2,583	1,068	376	1,139		71 P	41.3%	14.6%	44.1%
7,548	GOODING	2,465	1,101	418	946		155 R	44.7%	17.0%	38.4%
11,749	IDAHO	3,543	1,355	768	1,420		65 P	38.2%	21.7%	40.1%
9,441	JEFFERSON	2,767	1,391	297	1,079		312 R	50.3%	10.7%	39.0%
5,729	JEROME	2,358	1,107	362	889		218 R	46.9%	15.4%	37.7%
17,878	KOOTENAI	7,274	3,272	756	3,246		26 R	45.0%	10.4%	44.6%
18,092	LATAH	5,795	3,028	835	1,932		1,096 R	52.3%	14.4%	33.3%
5,164	LEMHI	1,926	1,096	434	396		662 R	56.9%	22.5%	20.6%
5,851	LEWIS	1,998	646	590	762		116 P	32.3%	29.5%	38.1%
3,446	LINCOLN	1,272	690	156	426		264 R	54.2%	12.3%	33.5%
9,167	MADISON	2,728	1,418	693	617		725 R	52.0%	25.4%	22.6%
9,035	MINIDOKA	2,612	1,043	198	1,371		328 P	39.9%	7.6%	52.5%
15,253	NEZ PERCE	5,283	2,244	1,199	1,840		404 R	42.5%	22.7%	34.8%
6,723	ONEIDA	2,149	939	463	747		192 R	43.7%	21.5%	34.8%
4,694	OWYHEE	1,536	562	305	669		107 P	36.6%	19.9%	43.6%
7,021	PAYETTE	2,416	1,145	389	882		263 R	47.4%	16.1%	36.5%
5,105	POWER	1,744	757	307	680		77 R	43.4%	17.6%	39.0%
14,250	SHOSHONE	5,927	3,035	825	2,067		968 R	51.2%	13.9%	34.9%
3,921	TETON	1,182	664	180	338		326 R	56.2%	15.2%	28.6%
28,398	TWIN FALLS	9,046	4,637	1,630	2,779		1,858 R	51.3%	18.0%	30.7%
2,524	VALLEY	1,198	486	214	498		12 P	40.6%	17.9%	41.6%
9,424	WASHINGTON	2,832	1,173	617	1,042		131 R	41.4%	21.8%	36.8%
431,866	TOTAL	147,690	69,791	23,951	53,948		15,843 R	47.3%	16.2%	36.5%

IDAHO

PRESIDENT 1920

1920 Census Population	County	Total Vote	Republican	Democratic	Other	Rep.-Dem. Plurality	Percentage Total Vote Rep.	Total Vote Dem.	Major Vote Rep.	Major Vote Dem.
35,213	ADA	12,730	8,535	4,195		4,340 R	67.0%	33.0%	67.0%	33.0%
2,966	ADAMS	1,118	721	397		324 R	64.5%	35.5%	64.5%	35.5%
27,532	BANNOCK	7,909	4,908	3,001		1,907 R	62.1%	37.9%	62.1%	37.9%
8,783	BEAR LAKE	3,022	1,845	1,177		668 R	61.1%	38.9%	61.1%	38.9%
6,997	BENEWAH	2,186	1,390	796		594 R	63.6%	36.4%	63.6%	36.4%
18,310	BINGHAM	4,544	3,355	1,189		2,166 R	73.8%	26.2%	73.8%	26.2%
4,473	BLAINE	1,786	1,222	564		658 R	68.4%	31.6%	68.4%	31.6%
1,822	BOISE	991	613	378		235 R	61.9%	38.1%	61.9%	38.1%
12,957	BONNER	3,829	2,272	1,557		715 R	59.3%	40.7%	59.3%	40.7%
17,501	BONNEVILLE	4,882	3,440	1,442		1,998 R	70.5%	29.5%	70.5%	29.5%
4,474	BOUNDARY	1,430	904	526		378 R	63.2%	36.8%	63.2%	36.8%
2,940	BUTTE	999	680	319		361 R	68.1%	31.9%	68.1%	31.9%
1,730	CAMAS	681	406	275		131 R	59.6%	40.4%	59.6%	40.4%
26,932	CANYON	9,139	5,754	3,385		2,369 R	63.0%	37.0%	63.0%	37.0%
2,191	CARIBOU	750	568	182		386 R	75.7%	24.3%	75.7%	24.3%
15,659	CASSIA	3,928	2,741	1,187		1,554 R	69.8%	30.2%	69.8%	30.2%
1,886	CLARK	793	611	182		429 R	77.0%	23.0%	77.0%	23.0%
4,993	CLEARWATER	1,509	1,021	488		533 R	67.7%	32.3%	67.7%	32.3%
3,550	CUSTER	1,237	844	393		451 R	68.2%	31.8%	68.2%	31.8%
5,087	ELMORE	1,972	1,103	869		234 R	55.9%	44.1%	55.9%	44.1%
8,650	FRANKLIN	2,539	1,630	909		721 R	64.2%	35.8%	64.2%	35.8%
10,380	FREMONT	3,118	2,040	1,078		962 R	65.4%	34.6%	65.4%	34.6%
6,427	GEM	2,268	1,433	835		598 R	63.2%	36.8%	63.2%	36.8%
7,548	GOODING	2,703	1,913	790		1,123 R	70.8%	29.2%	70.8%	29.2%
11,749	IDAHO	3,637	2,501	1,136		1,365 R	68.8%	31.2%	68.8%	31.2%
9,441	JEFFERSON	2,578	1,831	747		1,084 R	71.0%	29.0%	71.0%	29.0%
5,729	JEROME	2,591	1,803	788		1,015 R	69.6%	30.4%	69.6%	30.4%
17,878	KOOTENAI	5,481	3,640	1,841		1,799 R	66.4%	33.6%	66.4%	33.6%
18,092	LATAH	5,559	3,991	1,568		2,423 R	71.8%	28.2%	71.8%	28.2%
5,164	LEMHI	2,034	1,333	701		632 R	65.5%	34.5%	65.5%	34.5%
5,851	LEWIS	1,808	1,089	719		370 R	60.2%	39.8%	60.2%	39.8%
3,446	LINCOLN	1,207	781	426		355 R	64.7%	35.3%	64.7%	35.3%
9,167	MADISON	2,913	1,932	981		951 R	66.3%	33.7%	66.3%	33.7%
9,035	MINIDOKA	2,735	1,629	1,106		523 R	59.6%	40.4%	59.6%	40.4%
15,253	NEZ PERCE	4,396	2,840	1,556		1,284 R	64.6%	35.4%	64.6%	35.4%
6,723	ONEIDA	2,275	1,519	756		763 R	66.8%	33.2%	66.8%	33.2%
4,694	OWYHEE	1,540	1,022	518		504 R	66.4%	33.6%	66.4%	33.6%
7,021	PAYETTE	2,515	1,727	788		939 R	68.7%	31.3%	68.7%	31.3%
5,105	POWER	1,754	1,188	566		622 R	67.7%	32.3%	67.7%	32.3%
14,250	SHOSHONE	4,926	3,194	1,732		1,462 R	64.8%	35.2%	64.8%	35.2%
3,921	TETON	1,345	932	413		519 R	69.3%	30.7%	69.3%	30.7%
28,398	TWIN FALLS	8,893	6,011	2,882		3,129 R	67.6%	32.4%	67.6%	32.4%
2,524	VALLEY	843	519	324		195 R	61.6%	38.4%	61.6%	38.4%
9,424	WASHINGTON	3,188	1,920	1,268		652 R	60.2%	39.8%	60.2%	39.8%
431,866	TOTAL	138,281	91,351	46,930		44,421 R	66.1%	33.9%	66.1%	33.9%

IDAHO

ELECTION NOTES

1956 Other vote was 126 Andrews (States Rights); 16 scattered write-in.

1952 Other vote was 443 Hallinan (Progressive); 23 scattered write-in.

1948 Other vote was 4,972 Wallace (Progressive); 628 Watson (Prohibition); 332 Thomas (Socialist).

1944 Other vote was 503 Watson (Prohibition); 282 Thomas (Socialist).

1940 Other vote was 497 Thomas (Socialist); 276 Browder (Communist).

1936 Other vote was Lemke (Union).

1932 Other vote was 4,712 Harvey (Liberty); 526 Thomas (Socialist); 491 Foster (Communist).

1928 Other vote was Thomas (Socialist).

1924 A special four-column table which gives the LaFollette (Progressive) vote is used to detail this election.

1920

ILLINOIS

POPULAR VOTE FOR PRESIDENT 1920 TO 1956

Year	Total Vote	Republican Vote	Republican Candidate	Democratic Vote	Democratic Candidate	Other Vote	Plurality	Percentage Total Vote Rep.	Percentage Total Vote Dem.	Percentage Major Vote Rep.	Percentage Major Vote Dem.
1956	4,407,407	2,623,327	Eisenhower, Dwight D.	1,775,682	Stevenson, Adlai E.	8,398	847,645 R	59.5%	40.3%	59.6%	40.4%
1952	4,481,058	2,457,327	Eisenhower, Dwight D.	2,013,920	Stevenson, Adlai E.	9,811	443,407 R	54.8%	44.9%	55.0%	45.0%
1948	3,984,046	1,961,103	Dewey, Thomas E.	1,994,715	Truman, Harry S.	28,228	33,612 D	49.2%	50.1%	49.6%	50.4%
1944	4,036,061	1,939,314	Dewey, Thomas E.	2,079,479	Roosevelt, Franklin D.	17,268	140,165 D	48.0%	51.5%	48.3%	51.7%
1940	4,217,935	2,047,240	Willkie, Wendell	2,149,934	Roosevelt, Franklin D.	20,761	102,694 D	48.5%	51.0%	48.8%	51.2%
1936	3,956,522	1,570,393	Landon, Alfred M.	2,282,999	Roosevelt, Franklin D.	103,130	712,606 D	39.7%	57.7%	40.8%	59.2%
1932	3,407,926	1,432,756	Hoover, Herbert C.	1,882,304	Roosevelt, Franklin D.	92,866	449,548 D	42.0%	55.2%	43.2%	56.8%
1928	3,107,489	1,769,141	Hoover, Herbert C.	1,313,817	Smith, Alfred E.	24,531	455,324 R	56.9%	42.3%	57.4%	42.6%
1924 **	2,470,067	1,453,321	Coolidge, Calvin	576,975	Davis, John W.	439,771	876,346 R	58.8%	23.4%	71.6%	28.4%
1920	2,094,714	1,420,480	Harding, Warren G.	534,395	Cox, James M.	139,839	886,085 R	67.8%	25.5%	72.7%	27.3%

In 1924 other vote was 432,027 Progressive; 2,622 Communist; 2,367 Prohibition; 2,334 Socialist Labor and 421 Commonwealth Land.

ELECTORAL COLLEGE VOTE 1920 TO 1956

Year	Total	Republican	Democratic	Other
1956	27	27	—	—
1952	27	27	—	—
1948	28	—	28	—
1944	28	—	28	—
1940	29	—	29	—
1936	29	—	29	—
1932	29	—	29	—
1928	29	29	—	—
1924	29	29	—	—
1920	29	29	—	—

ILLINOIS

JO DAVIESS
STEPHENSON
WINNEBAGO
BOONE
McHENRY
LAKE
CARROLL
OGLE
DE KALB
KANE
DU PAGE
COOK
WHITESIDE
LEE
KENDALL
WILL
ROCK ISLAND
HENRY
BUREAU
LA SALLE
GRUNDY
MERCER
PUTNAM
KANKAKEE
STARK
MARSHALL
HENDERSON
WARREN
KNOX
PEORIA
WOODFORD
LIVINGSTON
IROQUOIS
HANCOCK
McDONOUGH
FULTON
TAZEWELL
McLEAN
FORD
MASON
SCHUYLER
LOGAN
DE WITT
CHAMPAIGN
VERMILION
ADAMS
BROWN
CASS
MENARD
PIATT
MACON
DOUGLAS
EDGAR
MORGAN
SANGAMON
MOULTRIE
PIKE
SCOTT
CHRISTIAN
COLES
SHELBY
GREENE
CLARK
CALHOUN
MACOUPIN
MONTGOMERY
CUMBER-
LAND
JERSEY
FAYETTE
EFFINGHAM
JASPER
CRAWFORD
BOND
MADISON
CLAY
RICHLAND
LAWRENCE
MARION
CLINTON
ST. CLAIR
EDWARDS
WABASH
WAYNE
WASHINGTON
JEFFERSON
MONROE
RANDOLPH
PERRY
HAMILTON
WHITE
FRANKLIN
JACKSON
WILLIAMSON
SALINE
GALLATIN
HARDIN
UNION
JOHNSON
POPE
ALEX-
ANDER
PULASKI
MASSAC

ILLINOIS

PRESIDENT 1956

1950 Census Population	County	Total Vote	Republican	Democratic	Other	Rep.-Dem. Plurality	Percentage Total Vote Rep.	Percentage Total Vote Dem.	Percentage Major Vote Rep.	Percentage Major Vote Dem.
64,690	ADAMS	31,003	19,569	11,402	32	8,167 R	63.1%	36.8%	63.2%	36.8%
20,316	ALEXANDER	8,613	4,425	4,167	21	258 R	51.4%	48.4%	51.5%	48.5%
14,157	BOND	7,187	4,342	2,834	11	1,508 R	60.4%	39.4%	60.5%	39.5%
17,070	BOONE	8,602	6,706	1,890	6	4,816 R	78.0%	22.0%	78.0%	22.0%
7,132	BROWN	3,775	2,026	1,748	1	278 R	53.7%	46.3%	53.7%	46.3%
37,711	BUREAU	19,711	13,909	5,781	21	8,128 R	70.6%	29.3%	70.6%	29.4%
6,898	CALHOUN	3,391	1,892	1,498	1	394 R	55.8%	44.2%	55.8%	44.2%
18,976	CARROLL	9,211	6,503	2,693	15	3,810 R	70.6%	29.2%	70.7%	29.3%
15,097	CASS	7,504	4,125	3,368	11	757 R	55.0%	44.9%	55.1%	44.9%
106,100	CHAMPAIGN	42,040	28,190	13,799	51	14,391 R	67.1%	32.8%	67.1%	32.9%
38,816	CHRISTIAN	19,434	10,282	9,093	59	1,189 R	52.9%	46.8%	53.1%	46.9%
17,362	CLARK	8,974	5,451	3,519	4	1,932 R	60.7%	39.2%	60.8%	39.2%
17,445	CLAY	8,648	5,079	3,553	16	1,526 R	58.7%	41.1%	58.8%	41.2%
22,594	CLINTON	11,627	7,378	4,242	7	3,136 R	63.5%	36.5%	63.5%	36.5%
40,328	COLES	20,015	12,436	7,569	10	4,867 R	62.1%	37.8%	62.2%	37.8%
4,508,792	COOK	2,276,844	1,293,223	977,821	5,800	315,402 R	56.8%	42.9%	56.9%	43.1%
21,137	CRAWFORD	10,662	6,747	3,906	9	2,841 R	63.3%	36.6%	63.3%	36.7%
10,496	CUMBERLAND	5,512	3,235	2,272	5	963 R	58.7%	41.2%	58.7%	41.3%
40,781	DE KALB	19,929	15,078	4,826	25	10,252 R	75.7%	24.2%	75.8%	24.2%
16,894	DE WITT	8,404	5,307	3,093	4	2,214 R	63.1%	36.8%	63.2%	36.8%
16,706	DOUGLAS	8,339	5,559	2,774	6	2,785 R	66.7%	33.3%	66.7%	33.3%
154,599	DU PAGE	115,144	91,834	23,103	207	68,731 R	79.8%	20.1%	79.9%	20.1%
23,407	EDGAR	12,309	7,942	4,362	5	3,580 R	64.5%	35.4%	64.5%	35.5%
9,056	EDWARDS	4,550	3,339	1,210	1	2,129 R	73.4%	26.6%	73.4%	26.6%
21,675	EFFINGHAM	11,380	6,904	4,455	21	2,449 R	60.7%	39.1%	60.8%	39.2%
24,582	FAYETTE	11,658	6,739	4,914	5	1,825 R	57.8%	42.2%	57.8%	42.2%
15,901	FORD	8,182	6,027	2,152	3	3,875 R	73.7%	26.3%	73.7%	26.3%
48,685	FRANKLIN	23,069	11,761	11,308		453 R	51.0%	49.0%	51.0%	49.0%
43,716	FULTON	21,125	12,375	8,702	48	3,673 R	58.6%	41.2%	58.7%	41.3%
9,818	GALLATIN	4,415	2,179	2,230	6	51 D	49.4%	50.5%	49.4%	50.6%
18,852	GREENE	8,646	4,718	3,909	19	809 R	54.6%	45.2%	54.7%	45.3%
19,217	GRUNDY	10,261	7,640	2,618	3	5,022 R	74.5%	25.5%	74.5%	25.5%
12,256	HAMILTON	6,364	3,675	2,685	4	990 R	57.7%	42.2%	57.8%	42.2%
25,790	HANCOCK	13,297	8,431	4,854	12	3,577 R	63.4%	36.5%	63.5%	36.5%
7,530	HARDIN	3,371	1,919	1,444	8	475 R	56.9%	42.8%	57.1%	42.9%
8,416	HENDERSON	4,215	2,743	1,469	3	1,274 R	65.1%	34.9%	65.1%	34.9%
46,492	HENRY	24,284	15,896	8,349	39	7,547 R	65.5%	34.4%	65.6%	34.4%
32,348	IROQUOIS	16,609	12,104	4,487	18	7,617 R	72.9%	27.0%	73.0%	27.0%
38,124	JACKSON	17,927	10,526	7,391	10	3,135 R	58.7%	41.2%	58.7%	41.3%
12,266	JASPER	6,002	3,107	2,895		212 R	51.8%	48.2%	51.8%	48.2%
35,892	JEFFERSON	17,727	9,637	8,090		1,547 R	54.4%	45.6%	54.4%	45.6%
15,264	JERSEY	7,640	4,220	3,415	5	805 R	55.2%	44.7%	55.3%	44.7%
21,459	JO DAVIESS	9,686	6,762	2,906	18	3,856 R	69.8%	30.0%	69.9%	30.1%
8,729	JOHNSON	4,524	2,973	1,549	2	1,424 R	65.7%	34.2%	65.7%	34.3%
150,388	KANE	76,916	56,009	20,848	59	35,161 R	72.8%	27.1%	72.9%	27.1%
73,524	KANKAKEE	33,128	21,993	11,088	47	10,905 R	66.4%	33.5%	66.5%	33.5%
12,115	KENDALL	6,471	5,057	1,407	7	3,650 R	78.1%	21.7%	78.2%	21.8%
54,366	KNOX	28,251	18,656	9,558	37	9,098 R	66.0%	33.8%	66.1%	33.9%
179,097	LAKE	99,189	66,781	32,279	129	34,502 R	67.3%	32.5%	67.4%	32.6%
100,610	LA SALLE	51,862	33,461	18,318	83	15,143 R	64.5%	35.3%	64.6%	35.4%
20,539	LAWRENCE	9,862	6,104	3,751	7	2,353 R	61.9%	38.0%	61.9%	38.1%
36,451	LEE	16,189	11,653	4,531	5	7,122 R	72.0%	28.0%	72.0%	28.0%
37,809	LIVINGSTON	19,143	13,939	5,197	7	8,742 R	72.8%	27.1%	72.8%	27.2%
30,671	LOGAN	14,396	9,589	4,793	14	4,796 R	66.6%	33.3%	66.7%	33.3%
28,199	MCDONOUGH	13,605	9,725	3,872	8	5,853 R	71.5%	28.5%	71.5%	28.5%
50,656	MCHENRY	31,798	24,912	6,820	66	18,092 R	78.3%	21.4%	78.5%	21.5%
76,577	MCLEAN	38,111	25,758	12,332	21	13,426 R	67.6%	32.4%	67.6%	32.4%
98,853	MACON	50,771	27,673	23,066	32	4,607 R	54.5%	45.4%	54.5%	45.5%
44,210	MACOUPIN	24,627	12,290	12,303	34	13 D	49.9%	50.0%	50.0%	50.0%
182,307	MADISON	87,398	39,413	47,897	88	8,484 D	45.1%	54.8%	45.1%	54.9%

ILLINOIS

PRESIDENT 1956

1950 Census Population	County	Total Vote	Republican	Democratic	Other	Rep.-Dem. Plurality	Percentage Total Vote Rep.	Total Vote Dem.	Major Vote Rep.	Major Vote Dem.
41,700	MARION	19,385	10,813	8,551	21	2,262 R	55.8%	44.1%	55.8%	44.2%
13,025	MARSHALL	7,014	4,764	2,245	5	2,519 R	67.9%	32.0%	68.0%	32.0%
15,326	MASON	7,889	4,677	3,199	13	1,478 R	59.3%	40.6%	59.4%	40.6%
13,594	MASSAC	6,629	4,265	2,359	5	1,906 R	64.3%	35.6%	64.4%	35.6%
9,639	MENARD	5,025	3,188	1,833	4	1,355 R	63.4%	36.5%	63.5%	36.5%
17,374	MERCER	8,708	5,732	2,969	7	2,763 R	65.8%	34.1%	65.9%	34.1%
13,282	MONROE	7,364	4,715	2,648	1	2,067 R	64.0%	36.0%	64.0%	36.0%
32,460	MONTGOMERY	17,645	9,945	7,692	8	2,253 R	56.4%	43.6%	56.4%	43.6%
35,568	MORGAN	16,600	10,262	6,327	11	3,935 R	61.8%	38.1%	61.9%	38.1%
13,171	MOULTRIE	6,515	3,756	2,751	8	1,005 R	57.7%	42.2%	57.7%	42.3%
33,429	OGLE	16,870	13,194	3,660	16	9,534 R	78.2%	21.7%	78.3%	21.7%
174,347	PEORIA	81,141	50,888	30,145	108	20,743 R	62.7%	37.2%	62.8%	37.2%
21,684	PERRY	11,414	6,513	4,901		1,612 R	57.1%	42.9%	57.1%	42.9%
13,970	PIATT	6,979	4,622	2,356	1	2,266 R	66.2%	33.8%	66.2%	33.8%
22,155	PIKE	11,318	5,920	5,382	16	538 R	52.3%	47.6%	52.4%	47.6%
5,779	POPE	2,765	1,842	922	1	920 R	66.6%	33.3%	66.6%	33.4%
13,639	PULASKI	5,227	2,966	2,246	15	720 R	56.7%	43.0%	56.9%	43.1%
4,746	PUTNAM	2,641	1,724	913	4	811 R	65.3%	34.6%	65.4%	34.6%
31,673	RANDOLPH	15,221	8,439	6,778	4	1,661 R	55.4%	44.5%	55.5%	44.5%
16,889	RICHLAND	7,794	5,304	2,485	5	2,819 R	68.1%	31.9%	68.1%	31.9%
133,558	ROCK ISLAND	60,605	31,342	29,145	118	2,197 R	51.7%	48.1%	51.8%	48.2%
205,995	ST. CLAIR	97,106	41,528	55,295	283	13,767 D	42.8%	56.9%	42.9%	57.1%
33,420	SALINE	15,716	8,481	7,215	20	1,266 R	54.0%	45.9%	54.0%	46.0%
131,484	SANGAMON	71,935	42,951	28,949	35	14,002 R	59.7%	40.2%	59.7%	40.3%
9,613	SCHUYLER	5,270	3,068	2,189	13	879 R	58.2%	41.5%	58.4%	41.6%
7,245	SCOTT	3,781	2,303	1,478		825 R	60.9%	39.1%	60.9%	39.1%
24,434	SHELBY	12,425	7,075	5,337	13	1,738 R	56.9%	43.0%	57.0%	43.0%
8,721	STARK	4,361	3,241	1,118	2	2,123 R	74.3%	25.6%	74.4%	25.6%
41,595	STEPHENSON	20,614	14,245	6,349	20	7,896 R	69.1%	30.8%	69.2%	30.8%
76,165	TAZEWELL	39,970	23,690	16,230	50	7,460 R	59.3%	40.6%	59.3%	40.7%
20,500	UNION	8,569	4,204	4,359	6	155 D	49.1%	50.9%	49.1%	50.9%
87,079	VERMILION	44,585	26,534	17,991	60	8,543 R	59.5%	40.4%	59.6%	40.4%
14,651	WABASH	7,146	4,425	2,713	8	1,712 R	61.9%	38.0%	62.0%	38.0%
21,981	WARREN	10,582	7,580	2,996	6	4,584 R	71.6%	28.3%	71.7%	28.3%
14,460	WASHINGTON	8,135	5,299	2,820	16	2,479 R	65.1%	34.7%	65.3%	34.7%
20,933	WAYNE	10,242	6,286	3,942	14	2,344 R	61.4%	38.5%	61.5%	38.5%
20,935	WHITE	10,917	6,128	4,778	11	1,350 R	56.1%	43.8%	56.2%	43.8%
49,336	WHITESIDE	23,784	17,589	6,158	37	11,431 R	74.0%	25.9%	74.1%	25.9%
134,336	WILL	70,916	45,628	25,188	100	20,440 R	64.3%	35.5%	64.4%	35.6%
48,621	WILLIAMSON	23,810	13,438	10,345	27	3,093 R	56.4%	43.4%	56.5%	43.5%
152,385	WINNEBAGO	77,484	48,332	29,063	89	19,269 R	62.4%	37.5%	62.4%	37.6%
21,335	WOODFORD	11,783	8,505	3,257	21	5,248 R	72.2%	27.6%	72.3%	27.7%
8,712,176	TOTAL	4,407,407	2,623,327	1,775,682	8,398	847,645 R	59.5%	40.3%	59.6%	40.4%

ILLINOIS

PRESIDENT 1952

1950 Census Population	County	Total Vote	Republican	Democratic	Other	Rep.-Dem. Plurality	Percentage Total Vote Rep.	Total Vote Dem.	Major Vote Rep.	Major Vote Dem.
64,690	ADAMS	32,974	19,652	13,301	21	6,351 R	59.6%	40.3%	59.6%	40.4%
20,316	ALEXANDER	9,553	5,219	4,305	29	914 R	54.6%	45.1%	54.8%	45.2%
14,157	BOND	7,359	4,565	2,776	18	1,789 R	62.0%	37.7%	62.2%	37.8%
17,070	BOONE	8,932	6,628	2,287	17	4,341 R	74.2%	25.6%	74.3%	25.7%
7,132	BROWN	3,699	2,137	1,557	5	580 R	57.8%	42.1%	57.9%	42.1%
37,711	BUREAU	20,498	14,300	6,173	25	8,127 R	69.8%	30.1%	69.8%	30.2%
6,898	CALHOUN	3,371	1,915	1,454	2	461 R	56.8%	43.1%	56.8%	43.2%
18,976	CARROLL	9,576	6,978	2,584	14	4,394 R	72.9%	27.0%	73.0%	27.0%
15,097	CASS	7,565	4,152	3,405	8	747 R	54.9%	45.0%	54.9%	45.1%
106,100	CHAMPAIGN	41,251	27,188	13,951	112	13,237 R	65.9%	33.8%	66.1%	33.9%
38,816	CHRISTIAN	19,767	9,906	9,844	17	62 R	50.1%	49.8%	50.2%	49.8%
17,362	CLARK	9,326	5,700	3,621	5	2,079 R	61.1%	38.8%	61.2%	38.8%
17,445	CLAY	8,701	5,254	3,432	15	1,822 R	60.4%	39.4%	60.5%	39.5%
22,594	CLINTON	11,620	6,760	4,853	7	1,907 R	58.2%	41.8%	58.2%	41.8%
40,328	COLES	20,556	12,660	7,876	20	4,784 R	61.6%	38.3%	61.6%	38.4%
4,508,792	COOK	2,367,939	1,188,973	1,172,454	6,512	16,519 R	50.2%	49.5%	50.3%	49.7%
21,137	CRAWFORD	10,724	6,768	3,947	9	2,821 R	63.1%	36.8%	63.2%	36.8%
10,496	CUMBERLAND	5,514	3,302	2,200	12	1,102 R	59.9%	39.9%	60.0%	40.0%
40,781	DE KALB	19,947	14,807	5,110	30	9,697 R	74.2%	25.6%	74.3%	25.7%
16,894	DE WITT	8,436	5,212	3,221	3	1,991 R	61.8%	38.2%	61.8%	38.2%
16,706	DOUGLAS	8,241	5,530	2,706	5	2,824 R	67.1%	32.8%	67.1%	32.9%
154,599	DU PAGE	93,840	71,134	22,489	217	48,645 R	75.8%	24.0%	76.0%	24.0%
23,407	EDGAR	12,891	8,323	4,558	10	3,765 R	64.6%	35.4%	64.6%	35.4%
9,056	EDWARDS	4,669	3,502	1,162	5	2,340 R	75.0%	24.9%	75.1%	24.9%
21,675	EFFINGHAM	11,300	6,530	4,745	25	1,785 R	57.8%	42.0%	57.9%	42.1%
24,582	FAYETTE	12,339	7,028	5,299	12	1,729 R	57.0%	42.9%	57.0%	43.0%
15,901	FORD	8,345	6,216	2,121	8	4,095 R	74.5%	25.4%	74.6%	25.4%
48,685	FRANKLIN	23,766	11,723	11,981	62	258 D	49.3%	50.4%	49.5%	50.5%
43,716	FULTON	21,760	13,302	8,414	44	4,888 R	61.1%	38.7%	61.3%	38.7%
9,818	GALLATIN	4,461	2,300	2,153	8	147 R	51.6%	48.3%	51.7%	48.3%
18,852	GREENE	9,132	5,019	4,106	7	913 R	55.0%	45.0%	55.0%	45.0%
19,217	GRUNDY	10,478	7,347	3,118	13	4,229 R	70.1%	29.8%	70.2%	29.8%
12,256	HAMILTON	6,717	4,047	2,662	8	1,385 R	60.3%	39.6%	60.3%	39.7%
25,790	HANCOCK	13,881	9,181	4,681	19	4,500 R	66.1%	33.7%	66.2%	33.8%
7,530	HARDIN	3,553	1,984	1,563	6	421 R	55.8%	44.0%	55.9%	44.1%
8,416	HENDERSON	4,303	2,839	1,458	6	1,381 R	66.0%	33.9%	66.1%	33.9%
46,492	HENRY	24,892	16,301	8,558	33	7,743 R	65.5%	34.4%	65.6%	34.4%
32,348	IROQUOIS	17,107	12,456	4,634	17	7,822 R	72.8%	27.1%	72.9%	27.1%
38,124	JACKSON	17,674	10,193	7,457	24	2,736 R	57.7%	42.2%	57.8%	42.2%
12,266	JASPER	6,491	3,753	2,728	10	1,025 R	57.8%	42.0%	57.9%	42.1%
35,892	JEFFERSON	18,558	9,841	8,698	19	1,143 R	53.0%	46.9%	53.1%	46.9%
15,264	JERSEY	7,461	4,031	3,424	6	607 R	54.0%	45.9%	54.1%	45.9%
21,459	JO DAVIESS	10,003	7,132	2,858	13	4,274 R	71.3%	28.6%	71.4%	28.6%
8,729	JOHNSON	4,947	3,327	1,614	6	1,713 R	67.3%	32.6%	67.3%	32.7%
150,388	KANE	74,955	50,801	24,058	96	26,743 R	67.8%	32.1%	67.9%	32.1%
73,524	KANKAKEE	33,005	20,279	12,636	90	7,643 R	61.4%	38.3%	61.6%	38.4%
12,115	KENDALL	6,461	4,982	1,476	3	3,506 R	77.1%	22.8%	77.1%	22.9%
54,366	KNOX	28,940	18,569	10,354	17	8,215 R	64.2%	35.8%	64.2%	35.8%
179,097	LAKE	87,427	54,929	32,353	145	22,576 R	62.8%	37.0%	62.9%	37.1%
100,610	LA SALLE	54,277	32,857	21,321	99	11,536 R	60.5%	39.3%	60.6%	39.4%
20,539	LAWRENCE	10,086	6,207	3,875	4	2,332 R	61.5%	38.4%	61.6%	38.4%
36,451	LEE	16,651	11,941	4,700	10	7,241 R	71.7%	28.2%	71.8%	28.2%
37,809	LIVINGSTON	19,727	14,095	5,612	20	8,483 R	71.5%	28.4%	71.5%	28.5%
30,671	LOGAN	14,229	9,162	5,048	19	4,114 R	64.4%	35.5%	64.5%	35.5%
28,199	MCDONOUGH	14,053	10,126	3,922	5	6,204 R	72.1%	27.9%	72.1%	27.9%
50,656	MCHENRY	28,257	20,975	7,218	64	13,757 R	74.2%	25.5%	74.4%	25.6%
76,577	MCLEAN	37,826	24,494	13,296	36	11,198 R	64.8%	35.2%	64.8%	35.2%
98,853	MACON	48,066	25,744	22,277	45	3,467 R	53.6%	46.3%	53.6%	46.4%
44,210	MACOUPIN	25,348	12,336	12,944	68	608 D	48.7%	51.1%	48.8%	51.2%
182,307	MADISON	87,039	36,206	50,734	99	14,528 D	41.6%	58.3%	41.6%	58.4%

ILLINOIS

PRESIDENT 1952

1950 Census Population	County	Total Vote	Republican	Democratic	Other	Rep.-Dem. Plurality	Total Vote Rep.	Total Vote Dem.	Major Vote Rep.	Major Vote Dem.
41,700	MARION	20,140	10,804	9,317	19	1,487 R	53.6%	46.3%	53.7%	46.3%
13,025	MARSHALL	7,201	4,850	2,343	8	2,507 R	67.4%	32.5%	67.4%	32.6%
15,326	MASON	8,047	4,982	3,061	4	1,921 R	61.9%	38.0%	61.9%	38.1%
13,594	MASSAC	6,930	4,212	2,711	7	1,501 R	60.8%	39.1%	60.8%	39.2%
9,639	MENARD	5,256	3,307	1,946	3	1,361 R	62.9%	37.0%	63.0%	37.0%
17,374	MERCER	9,097	6,416	2,679	2	3,737 R	70.5%	29.4%	70.5%	29.5%
13,282	MONROE	6,959	4,528	2,430	1	2,098 R	65.1%	34.9%	65.1%	34.9%
32,460	MONTGOMERY	18,225	10,014	8,195	16	1,819 R	54.9%	45.0%	55.0%	45.0%
35,568	MORGAN	17,046	10,405	6,637	4	3,768 R	61.0%	38.9%	61.1%	38.9%
13,171	MOULTRIE	6,563	3,880	2,675	8	1,205 R	59.1%	40.8%	59.2%	40.8%
33,429	OGLE	17,163	13,351	3,796	16	9,555 R	77.8%	22.1%	77.9%	22.1%
174,347	PEORIA	83,339	49,245	33,955	139	15,290 R	59.1%	40.7%	59.2%	40.8%
21,684	PERRY	11,923	6,580	5,340	3	1,240 R	55.2%	44.8%	55.2%	44.8%
13,970	PIATT	6,932	4,701	2,220	11	2,481 R	67.8%	32.0%	67.9%	32.1%
22,155	PIKE	11,611	6,382	5,219	10	1,163 R	55.0%	44.9%	55.0%	45.0%
5,779	POPE	2,883	1,947	933	3	1,014 R	67.5%	32.4%	67.6%	32.4%
13,639	PULASKI	5,854	3,447	2,397	10	1,050 R	58.9%	40.9%	59.0%	41.0%
4,746	PUTNAM	2,703	1,691	1,010	2	681 R	62.6%	37.4%	62.6%	37.4%
31,673	RANDOLPH	15,438	8,427	6,998	13	1,429 R	54.6%	45.3%	54.6%	45.4%
16,889	RICHLAND	8,139	5,569	2,565	5	3,004 R	68.4%	31.5%	68.5%	31.5%
133,558	ROCK ISLAND	60,912	32,933	27,879	100	5,054 R	54.1%	45.8%	54.2%	45.8%
205,995	ST. CLAIR	100,503	39,713	60,311	479	20,598 D	39.5%	60.0%	39.7%	60.3%
33,420	SALINE	17,006	9,206	7,771	29	1,435 R	54.1%	45.7%	54.2%	45.8%
131,484	SANGAMON	72,968	39,392	33,526	50	5,866 R	54.0%	45.9%	54.0%	46.0%
9,613	SCHUYLER	5,375	3,295	2,076	4	1,219 R	61.3%	38.6%	61.3%	38.7%
7,245	SCOTT	3,807	2,298	1,506	3	792 R	60.4%	39.6%	60.4%	39.6%
24,434	SHELBY	12,469	7,189	5,268	12	1,921 R	57.7%	42.2%	57.7%	42.3%
8,721	STARK	4,500	3,398	1,100	2	2,298 R	75.5%	24.4%	75.5%	24.5%
41,595	STEPHENSON	21,086	14,446	6,605	35	7,841 R	68.5%	31.3%	68.6%	31.4%
76,165	TAZEWELL	37,653	20,763	16,862	28	3,901 R	55.1%	44.8%	55.2%	44.8%
20,500	UNION	8,963	4,658	4,296	9	362 R	52.0%	47.9%	52.0%	48.0%
87,079	VERMILION	44,226	25,367	18,771	88	6,596 R	57.4%	42.4%	57.5%	42.5%
14,651	WABASH	6,917	4,246	2,661	10	1,585 R	61.4%	38.5%	61.5%	38.5%
21,981	WARREN	11,004	8,020	2,973	11	5,047 R	72.9%	27.0%	73.0%	27.0%
14,460	WASHINGTON	8,381	5,546	2,824	11	2,722 R	66.2%	33.7%	66.3%	33.7%
20,933	WAYNE	10,418	6,495	3,911	12	2,584 R	62.3%	37.5%	62.4%	37.6%
20,935	WHITE	10,431	6,141	4,284	6	1,857 R	58.9%	41.1%	58.9%	41.1%
49,336	WHITESIDE	23,599	17,294	6,238	67	11,056 R	73.3%	26.4%	73.5%	26.5%
134,336	WILL	68,392	38,533	29,749	110	8,784 R	56.3%	43.5%	56.4%	43.6%
48,621	WILLIAMSON	24,223	13,348	10,838	37	2,510 R	55.1%	44.7%	55.2%	44.8%
152,385	WINNEBAGO	75,004	43,468	31,409	127	12,059 R	58.0%	41.9%	58.1%	41.9%
21,335	WOODFORD	11,308	8,022	3,273	13	4,749 R	70.9%	28.9%	71.0%	29.0%
8,712,176	TOTAL	4,481,058	2,457,327	2,013,920	9,811	443,407 R	54.8%	44.9%	55.0%	45.0%

ILLINOIS

PRESIDENT 1948

1940 Census Population	County	Total Vote	Republican	Democratic	Other	Rep.-Dem. Plurality	Percentage Total Vote Rep.	Percentage Total Vote Dem.	Percentage Major Vote Rep.	Percentage Major Vote Dem.
65,229	ADAMS	29,441	14,329	14,960	152	631 D	48.7%	50.8%	48.9%	51.1%
25,496	ALEXANDER	9,298	4,561	4,641	96	80 D	49.1%	49.9%	49.6%	50.4%
14,540	BOND	6,483	3,438	2,837	208	601 R	53.0%	43.8%	54.8%	45.2%
15,202	BOONE	6,882	4,916	1,941	25	2,975 R	71.4%	28.2%	71.7%	28.3%
8,053	BROWN	3,389	1,562	1,805	22	243 D	46.1%	53.3%	46.4%	53.6%
37,600	BUREAU	17,748	11,207	6,463	78	4,744 R	63.1%	36.4%	63.4%	36.6%
8,207	CALHOUN	2,923	1,526	1,377	20	149 R	52.2%	47.1%	52.6%	47.4%
17,987	CARROLL	8,189	5,318	2,809	62	2,509 R	64.9%	34.3%	65.4%	34.6%
16,425	CASS	7,217	3,391	3,776	50	385 D	47.0%	52.3%	47.3%	52.7%
70,578	CHAMPAIGN	31,465	19,156	11,572	737	7,584 R	60.9%	36.8%	62.3%	37.7%
38,564	CHRISTIAN	17,062	7,576	9,366	120	1,790 D	44.4%	54.9%	44.7%	55.3%
18,842	CLARK	8,303	4,477	3,714	112	763 R	53.9%	44.7%	54.7%	45.3%
18,947	CLAY	7,108	3,782	3,160	166	622 R	53.2%	44.5%	54.5%	45.5%
22,912	CLINTON	9,963	5,128	4,773	62	355 R	51.5%	47.9%	51.8%	48.2%
38,470	COLES	17,084	8,638	8,393	53	245 R	50.6%	49.1%	50.7%	49.3%
4,063,342	COOK	2,245,899	1,015,800	1,216,636	13,463	200,836 D	45.2%	54.2%	45.5%	54.5%
21,294	CRAWFORD	9,364	5,111	4,150	103	961 R	54.6%	44.3%	55.2%	44.8%
11,698	CUMBERLAND	4,832	2,451	2,353	28	98 R	50.7%	48.7%	51.0%	49.0%
34,388	DE KALB	16,567	11,380	5,082	105	6,298 R	68.7%	30.7%	69.1%	30.9%
18,244	DE WITT	7,513	4,178	3,290	45	888 R	55.6%	43.8%	55.9%	44.1%
17,590	DOUGLAS	7,129	4,181	2,893	55	1,288 R	58.6%	40.6%	59.1%	40.9%
103,480	DU PAGE	62,238	45,794	15,528	916	30,266 R	73.6%	24.9%	74.7%	25.3%
24,430	EDGAR	11,470	6,282	5,121	67	1,161 R	54.8%	44.6%	55.1%	44.9%
8,974	EDWARDS	3,770	2,491	1,206	73	1,285 R	66.1%	32.0%	67.4%	32.6%
22,034	EFFINGHAM	9,859	4,823	4,940	96	117 D	48.9%	50.1%	49.4%	50.6%
29,159	FAYETTE	11,608	5,717	5,771	120	54 D	49.3%	49.7%	49.8%	50.2%
15,007	FORD	7,015	4,903	2,079	33	2,824 R	69.9%	29.6%	70.2%	29.8%
53,137	FRANKLIN	21,444	9,407	11,750	287	2,343 D	43.9%	54.8%	44.5%	55.5%
44,627	FULTON	17,933	9,504	8,226	203	1,278 R	53.0%	45.9%	53.6%	46.4%
11,414	GALLATIN	4,200	1,789	2,385	26	596 D	42.6%	56.8%	42.9%	57.1%
20,292	GREENE	7,727	3,639	4,035	53	396 D	47.1%	52.2%	47.4%	52.6%
18,398	GRUNDY	9,240	5,954	3,255	31	2,699 R	64.4%	35.2%	64.7%	35.3%
13,454	HAMILTON	5,669	2,887	2,750	32	137 R	50.9%	48.5%	51.2%	48.8%
26,297	HANCOCK	12,779	7,098	5,559	122	1,539 R	55.5%	43.5%	56.1%	43.9%
7,759	HARDIN	3,087	1,713	1,358	16	355 R	55.5%	44.0%	55.8%	44.2%
8,949	HENDERSON	3,838	2,336	1,465	37	871 R	60.9%	38.2%	61.5%	38.5%
43,798	HENRY	21,011	12,363	8,489	159	3,874 R	58.8%	40.4%	59.3%	40.7%
32,496	IROQUOIS	14,001	9,051	4,823	127	4,228 R	64.6%	34.4%	65.2%	34.8%
37,920	JACKSON	15,408	8,288	6,939	181	1,349 R	53.8%	45.0%	54.4%	45.6%
13,431	JASPER	5,943	2,957	2,936	50	21 R	49.8%	49.4%	50.2%	49.8%
34,375	JEFFERSON	16,321	7,393	8,928		1,535 D	45.3%	54.7%	45.3%	54.7%
13,636	JERSEY	6,139	3,021	3,092	26	71 D	49.2%	50.4%	49.4%	50.6%
19,989	JO DAVIESS	8,570	5,299	3,220	51	2,079 R	61.8%	37.6%	62.2%	37.8%
10,727	JOHNSON	4,309	2,778	1,510	21	1,268 R	64.5%	35.0%	64.8%	35.2%
130,206	KANE	60,992	39,284	21,176	532	18,108 R	64.4%	34.7%	65.0%	35.0%
60,877	KANKAKEE	27,201	15,699	11,305	197	4,394 R	57.7%	41.6%	58.1%	41.9%
11,105	KENDALL	5,469	3,925	1,517	27	2,408 R	71.8%	27.7%	72.1%	27.9%
52,250	KNOX	24,952	15,016	9,772	164	5,244 R	60.2%	39.2%	60.6%	39.4%
121,094	LAKE	62,368	39,456	22,192	720	17,264 R	63.3%	35.6%	64.0%	36.0%
97,801	LA SALLE	44,440	24,453	19,666	321	4,787 R	55.0%	44.3%	55.4%	44.6%
21,075	LAWRENCE	9,057	4,472	4,391	194	81 R	49.4%	48.5%	50.5%	49.5%
34,604	LEE	13,441	9,001	4,368	72	4,633 R	67.0%	32.5%	67.3%	32.7%
38,838	LIVINGSTON	16,876	11,184	5,618	74	5,566 R	66.3%	33.3%	66.6%	33.4%
29,438	LOGAN	12,312	7,431	4,832	49	2,599 R	60.4%	39.2%	60.6%	39.4%
26,944	MCDONOUGH	12,373	8,058	4,206	109	3,852 R	65.1%	34.0%	65.7%	34.3%
37,311	MCHENRY	20,949	15,387	5,459	103	9,928 R	73.4%	26.1%	73.8%	26.2%
73,930	MCLEAN	31,517	18,430	12,904	183	5,526 R	58.5%	40.9%	58.8%	41.2%
84,693	MACON	40,456	18,719	21,487	250	2,768 D	46.3%	53.1%	46.6%	53.4%
46,304	MACOUPIN	22,298	10,198	11,742	358	1,544 D	45.7%	52.7%	46.5%	53.5%
149,349	MADISON	66,306	25,059	40,897	350	15,838 D	37.8%	61.7%	38.0%	62.0%

ILLINOIS

PRESIDENT 1948

1940 Census Population	County	Total Vote	Republican	Democratic	Other	Rep.-Dem. Plurality	Percentage Total Vote Rep.	Percentage Total Vote Dem.	Percentage Major Vote Rep.	Percentage Major Vote Dem.
47,989	MARION	16,884	7,798	8,878	208	1,080 D	46.2%	52.6%	46.8%	53.2%
13,179	MARSHALL	6,318	3,785	2,514	19	1,271 R	59.9%	39.8%	60.1%	39.9%
15,358	MASON	7,074	3,525	3,503	46	22 R	49.8%	49.5%	50.2%	49.8%
14,937	MASSAC	5,125	3,201	1,842	82	1,359 R	62.5%	35.9%	63.5%	36.5%
10,663	MENARD	4,968	2,899	2,043	26	856 R	58.4%	41.1%	58.7%	41.3%
17,701	MERCER	8,420	5,267	3,117	36	2,150 R	62.6%	37.0%	62.8%	37.2%
12,754	MONROE	5,432	3,403	2,026	3	1,377 R	62.6%	37.3%	62.7%	37.3%
34,499	MONTGOMERY	16,455	8,348	7,902	205	446 R	50.7%	48.0%	51.4%	48.6%
36,378	MORGAN	15,255	8,398	6,798	59	1,600 R	55.1%	44.6%	55.3%	44.7%
13,477	MOULTRIE	6,161	3,043	3,037	81	6 R	49.4%	49.3%	50.0%	50.0%
29,869	OGLE	13,378	9,519	3,796	63	5,723 R	71.2%	28.4%	71.5%	28.5%
153,374	PEORIA	66,352	35,018	31,026	308	3,992 R	52.8%	46.8%	53.0%	47.0%
23,438	PERRY	10,226	5,109	5,043	74	66 R	50.0%	49.3%	50.3%	49.7%
14,659	PIATT	6,064	3,646	2,361	57	1,285 R	60.1%	38.9%	60.7%	39.3%
25,340	PIKE	10,494	4,722	5,674	98	952 D	45.0%	54.1%	45.4%	54.6%
7,999	POPE	2,696	1,764	916	16	848 R	65.4%	34.0%	65.8%	34.2%
15,875	PULASKI	5,033	2,658	2,344	31	314 R	52.8%	46.6%	53.1%	46.9%
5,289	PUTNAM	2,336	1,405	905	26	500 R	60.1%	38.7%	60.8%	39.2%
33,608	RANDOLPH	13,781	6,867	6,852	62	15 R	49.8%	49.7%	50.1%	49.9%
17,137	RICHLAND	6,413	3,884	2,438	91	1,446 R	60.6%	38.0%	61.4%	38.6%
113,323	ROCK ISLAND	47,211	22,192	24,542	477	2,350 D	47.0%	52.0%	47.5%	52.5%
166,899	ST. CLAIR	85,617	30,883	54,260	474	23,377 D	36.1%	63.4%	36.3%	63.7%
38,066	SALINE	15,485	7,676	7,718	91	42 D	49.6%	49.8%	49.9%	50.1%
117,912	SANGAMON	63,273	33,714	29,196	363	4,518 R	53.3%	46.1%	53.6%	46.4%
11,430	SCHUYLER	5,074	2,519	2,464	91	55 R	49.6%	48.6%	50.6%	49.4%
8,176	SCOTT	3,588	1,840	1,735	13	105 R	51.3%	48.4%	51.5%	48.5%
26,290	SHELBY	11,029	5,282	5,589	158	307 D	47.9%	50.7%	48.6%	51.4%
8,881	STARK	3,707	2,537	1,163	7	1,374 R	68.4%	31.4%	68.6%	31.4%
40,646	STEPHENSON	18,122	10,564	7,409	149	3,155 R	58.3%	40.9%	58.8%	41.2%
58,362	TAZEWELL	26,778	12,504	14,131	143	1,627 D	46.7%	52.8%	46.9%	53.1%
21,528	UNION	8,398	3,864	4,479	55	615 D	46.0%	53.3%	46.3%	53.7%
86,791	VERMILION	35,646	18,994	16,173	479	2,821 R	53.3%	45.4%	54.0%	46.0%
13,724	WABASH	5,898	2,916	2,857	125	59 R	49.4%	48.4%	50.5%	49.5%
21,286	WARREN	10,179	6,738	3,367	74	3,371 R	66.2%	33.1%	66.7%	33.3%
15,801	WASHINGTON	7,330	4,544	2,737	49	1,807 R	62.0%	37.3%	62.4%	37.6%
22,092	WAYNE	9,114	4,984	4,070	60	914 R	54.7%	44.7%	55.0%	45.0%
20,027	WHITE	9,338	4,498	4,761	79	263 D	48.2%	51.0%	48.6%	51.4%
43,338	WHITESIDE	18,375	12,922	5,299	154	7,623 R	70.3%	28.8%	70.9%	29.1%
114,210	WILL	55,628	28,601	26,430	597	2,171 R	51.4%	47.5%	52.0%	48.0%
51,424	WILLIAMSON	20,357	10,386	9,841	130	545 R	51.0%	48.3%	51.3%	48.7%
121,178	WINNEBAGO	57,313	29,537	27,145	631	2,392 R	51.5%	47.4%	52.1%	47.9%
19,124	WOODFORD	9,276	5,784	3,446	46	2,338 R	62.4%	37.1%	62.7%	37.3%
7,897,241	TOTAL	3,984,046	1,961,103	1,994,715	28,228	33,612 D	49.2%	50.1%	49.6%	50.4%

ILLINOIS

PRESIDENT 1944

1940 Census Population	County	Total Vote	Republican	Democratic	Other	Rep.-Dem. Plurality	Percentage Total Vote Rep.	Percentage Total Vote Dem.	Percentage Major Vote Rep.	Percentage Major Vote Dem.
65,229	ADAMS	29,439	15,564	13,733	142	1,831 R	52.9%	46.6%	53.1%	46.9%
25,496	ALEXANDER	9,637	4,792	4,767	78	25 R	49.7%	49.5%	50.1%	49.9%
14,540	BOND	6,708	3,907	2,607	194	1,300 R	58.2%	38.9%	60.0%	40.0%
15,202	BOONE	7,800	5,708	2,074	18	3,634 R	73.2%	26.6%	73.3%	26.7%
8,053	BROWN	3,607	1,738	1,849	20	111 D	48.2%	51.3%	48.5%	51.5%
37,600	BUREAU	18,829	11,802	6,976	51	4,826 R	62.7%	37.0%	62.9%	37.1%
8,207	CALHOUN	3,241	1,956	1,271	14	685 R	60.4%	39.2%	60.6%	39.4%
17,987	CARROLL	8,962	6,101	2,843	18	3,258 R	68.1%	31.7%	68.2%	31.8%
16,425	CASS	7,585	3,641	3,909	35	268 D	48.0%	51.5%	48.2%	51.8%
70,578	CHAMPAIGN	32,954	18,935	13,842	177	5,093 R	57.5%	42.0%	57.8%	42.2%
38,564	CHRISTIAN	18,437	8,995	9,360	82	365 D	48.8%	50.8%	49.0%	51.0%
18,842	CLARK	9,044	5,373	3,619	52	1,754 R	59.4%	40.0%	59.8%	40.2%
18,947	CLAY	8,110	4,484	3,531	95	953 R	55.3%	43.5%	55.9%	44.1%
22,912	CLINTON	10,750	6,753	3,944	53	2,809 R	62.8%	36.7%	63.1%	36.9%
38,470	COLES	18,463	9,473	8,936	54	537 R	51.3%	48.4%	51.5%	48.5%
4,063,342	COOK	2,206,191	924,659	1,275,367	6,165	350,708 D	41.9%	57.8%	42.0%	58.0%
21,294	CRAWFORD	10,617	6,056	4,482	79	1,574 R	57.0%	42.2%	57.5%	42.5%
11,698	CUMBERLAND	5,106	2,700	2,391	15	309 R	52.9%	46.8%	53.0%	47.0%
34,388	DE KALB	18,210	12,157	6,004	49	6,153 R	66.8%	33.0%	66.9%	33.1%
18,244	DE WITT	8,357	4,630	3,658	69	972 R	55.4%	43.8%	55.9%	44.1%
17,590	DOUGLAS	8,035	4,684	3,323	28	1,361 R	58.3%	41.4%	58.5%	41.5%
103,480	DU PAGE	60,775	41,890	18,711	174	23,179 R	68.9%	30.8%	69.1%	30.9%
24,430	EDGAR	12,069	6,961	5,054	54	1,907 R	57.7%	41.9%	57.9%	42.1%
8,974	EDWARDS	4,250	3,016	1,197	37	1,819 R	71.0%	28.2%	71.6%	28.4%
22,034	EFFINGHAM	10,119	5,441	4,587	91	854 R	53.8%	45.3%	54.3%	45.7%
29,159	FAYETTE	11,887	6,332	5,435	120	897 R	53.3%	45.7%	53.8%	46.2%
15,007	FORD	7,605	5,317	2,270	18	3,047 R	69.9%	29.8%	70.1%	29.9%
53,137	FRANKLIN	23,213	11,377	11,663	173	286 D	49.0%	50.2%	49.4%	50.6%
44,627	FULTON	20,229	11,117	8,946	166	2,171 R	55.0%	44.2%	55.4%	44.6%
11,414	GALLATIN	4,295	2,073	2,175	47	102 D	48.3%	50.6%	48.8%	51.2%
20,292	GREENE	8,574	4,261	4,268	45	7 D	49.7%	49.8%	50.0%	50.0%
18,398	GRUNDY	9,876	6,310	3,544	22	2,766 R	63.9%	35.9%	64.0%	36.0%
13,454	HAMILTON	6,551	3,582	2,914	55	668 R	54.7%	44.5%	55.1%	44.9%
26,297	HANCOCK	13,378	7,972	5,338	68	2,634 R	59.6%	39.9%	59.9%	40.1%
7,759	HARDIN	3,438	2,037	1,370	31	667 R	59.2%	39.8%	59.8%	40.2%
8,949	HENDERSON	4,255	2,695	1,550	10	1,145 R	63.3%	36.4%	63.5%	36.5%
43,798	HENRY	22,761	13,539	9,130	92	4,409 R	59.5%	40.1%	59.7%	40.3%
32,496	IROQUOIS	15,648	10,389	5,168	91	5,221 R	66.4%	33.0%	66.8%	33.2%
37,920	JACKSON	16,791	10,002	6,735	54	3,267 R	59.6%	40.1%	59.8%	40.2%
13,431	JASPER	6,624	3,453	3,142	29	311 R	52.1%	47.4%	52.4%	47.6%
34,375	JEFFERSON	16,551	7,916	8,496	139	580 D	47.8%	51.3%	48.2%	51.8%
13,636	JERSEY	6,486	3,546	2,910	30	636 R	54.7%	44.9%	54.9%	45.1%
19,989	JO DAVIESS	9,797	6,465	3,298	34	3,167 R	66.0%	33.7%	66.2%	33.8%
10,727	JOHNSON	4,833	3,298	1,522	13	1,776 R	68.2%	31.5%	68.4%	31.6%
130,206	KANE	62,236	38,689	23,362	185	15,327 R	62.2%	37.5%	62.4%	37.6%
60,877	KANKAKEE	26,688	15,256	11,342	90	3,914 R	57.2%	42.5%	57.4%	42.6%
11,105	KENDALL	5,701	4,022	1,673	6	2,349 R	70.5%	29.3%	70.6%	29.4%
52,250	KNOX	26,160	15,964	10,070	126	5,894 R	61.0%	38.5%	61.3%	38.7%
121,094	LAKE	61,310	35,674	25,453	183	10,221 R	58.2%	41.5%	58.4%	41.6%
97,801	LA SALLE	51,878	28,179	21,489	2,210	6,690 R	54.3%	41.4%	56.7%	43.3%
21,075	LAWRENCE	9,305	5,191	4,003	111	1,188 R	55.8%	43.0%	56.5%	43.5%
34,604	LEE	15,317	10,397	4,899	21	5,498 R	67.9%	32.0%	68.0%	32.0%
38,838	LIVINGSTON	18,719	12,436	6,231	52	6,205 R	66.4%	33.3%	66.6%	33.4%
29,438	LOGAN	12,852	7,955	4,868	29	3,087 R	61.9%	37.9%	62.0%	38.0%
26,944	MCDONOUGH	13,616	9,028	4,497	91	4,531 R	66.3%	33.0%	66.8%	33.2%
37,311	MCHENRY	21,299	15,666	5,567	66	10,099 R	73.6%	26.1%	73.8%	26.2%
73,930	MCLEAN	33,562	19,366	14,011	185	5,355 R	57.7%	41.7%	58.0%	42.0%
84,693	MACON	42,569	19,608	22,808	153	3,200 D	46.1%	53.6%	46.2%	53.8%
46,304	MACOUPIN	23,683	11,572	11,951	160	379 D	48.9%	50.5%	49.2%	50.8%
149,349	MADISON	68,872	28,399	40,114	359	11,715 D	41.2%	58.2%	41.5%	58.5%

ILLINOIS

PRESIDENT 1944

1940 Census Population	County	Total Vote	Republican	Democratic	Other	Rep.-Dem. Plurality	Percentage Total Vote Rep.	Total Vote Dem.	Major Vote Rep.	Major Vote Dem.
47,989	MARION	19,640	9,408	10,079	153	671 D	47.9%	51.3%	48.3%	51.7%
13,179	MARSHALL	6,801	4,195	2,596	10	1,599 R	61.7%	38.2%	61.8%	38.2%
15,358	MASON	7,262	3,959	3,282	21	677 R	54.5%	45.2%	54.7%	45.3%
14,937	MASSAC	5,648	3,814	1,758	76	2,056 R	67.5%	31.1%	68.4%	31.6%
10,663	MENARD	4,926	3,013	1,888	25	1,125 R	61.2%	38.3%	61.5%	38.5%
17,701	MERCER	8,978	5,667	3,277	34	2,390 R	63.1%	36.5%	63.4%	36.6%
12,754	MONROE	6,109	4,032	2,068	9	1,964 R	66.0%	33.9%	66.1%	33.9%
34,499	MONTGOMERY	17,045	8,989	7,855	201	1,134 R	52.7%	46.1%	53.4%	46.6%
36,378	MORGAN	15,930	8,923	6,965	42	1,958 R	56.0%	43.7%	56.2%	43.8%
13,477	MOULTRIE	6,079	3,180	2,853	46	327 R	52.3%	46.9%	52.7%	47.3%
29,869	OGLE	14,712	10,680	3,951	81	6,729 R	72.6%	26.9%	73.0%	27.0%
153,374	PEORIA	67,251	34,171	32,837	243	1,334 R	50.8%	48.8%	51.0%	49.0%
23,438	PERRY	10,946	6,236	4,677	33	1,559 R	57.0%	42.7%	57.1%	42.9%
14,659	PIATT	6,588	3,912	2,641	35	1,271 R	59.4%	40.1%	59.7%	40.3%
25,340	PIKE	11,532	5,633	5,833	66	200 D	48.8%	50.6%	49.1%	50.9%
7,999	POPE	3,158	2,305	813	40	1,492 R	73.0%	25.7%	73.9%	26.1%
15,875	PULASKI	5,598	3,248	2,311	39	937 R	58.0%	41.3%	58.4%	41.6%
5,289	PUTNAM	2,396	1,521	865	10	656 R	63.5%	36.1%	63.7%	36.3%
33,608	RANDOLPH	13,756	7,518	6,199	39	1,319 R	54.7%	45.1%	54.8%	45.2%
17,137	RICHLAND	7,514	4,577	2,858	79	1,719 R	60.9%	38.0%	61.6%	38.4%
113,323	ROCK ISLAND	54,262	23,980	30,102	180	6,122 D	44.2%	55.5%	44.3%	55.7%
166,899	ST. CLAIR	82,209	33,557	48,325	327	14,768 D	40.8%	58.8%	41.0%	59.0%
38,066	SALINE	16,539	9,083	7,351	105	1,732 R	54.9%	44.4%	55.3%	44.7%
117,912	SANGAMON	61,745	32,871	28,713	161	4,158 R	53.2%	46.5%	53.4%	46.6%
11,430	SCHUYLER	5,405	2,801	2,555	49	246 R	51.8%	47.3%	52.3%	47.7%
8,176	SCOTT	4,058	2,185	1,864	9	321 R	53.8%	45.9%	54.0%	46.0%
26,290	SHELBY	12,243	6,201	5,919	123	282 R	50.6%	48.3%	51.2%	48.8%
8,881	STARK	4,458	3,050	1,401	7	1,649 R	68.4%	31.4%	68.5%	31.5%
40,646	STEPHENSON	19,821	11,948	7,755	118	4,193 R	60.3%	39.1%	60.6%	39.4%
58,362	TAZEWELL	27,039	12,531	14,412	96	1,881 D	46.3%	53.3%	46.5%	53.5%
21,528	UNION	8,527	4,114	4,367	46	253 D	48.2%	51.2%	48.5%	51.5%
86,791	VERMILION	39,454	20,794	18,387	273	2,407 R	52.7%	46.6%	53.1%	46.9%
13,724	WABASH	6,603	3,496	3,026	81	470 R	52.9%	45.8%	53.6%	46.4%
21,286	WARREN	11,050	7,085	3,926	39	3,159 R	64.1%	35.5%	64.3%	35.7%
15,801	WASHINGTON	8,186	5,428	2,723	35	2,705 R	66.3%	33.3%	66.6%	33.4%
22,092	WAYNE	9,763	5,683	4,019	61	1,664 R	58.2%	41.2%	58.6%	41.4%
20,027	WHITE	10,052	5,139	4,822	91	317 R	51.1%	48.0%	51.6%	48.4%
43,338	WHITESIDE	19,888	14,162	5,555	171	8,607 R	71.2%	27.9%	71.8%	28.2%
114,210	WILL	57,453	30,058	27,085	310	2,973 R	52.3%	47.1%	52.6%	47.4%
51,424	WILLIAMSON	22,671	12,594	9,974	103	2,620 R	55.6%	44.0%	55.8%	44.2%
121,178	WINNEBAGO	58,945	30,837	27,831	277	3,006 R	52.3%	47.2%	52.6%	47.4%
19,124	WOODFORD	9,787	6,237	3,514	36	2,723 R	63.7%	35.9%	64.0%	36.0%
7,897,241	TOTAL	4,036,061	1,939,314	2,079,479	17,268	140,165 D	48.0%	51.5%	48.3%	51.7%

ILLINOIS

PRESIDENT 1940

1940 Census Population	County	Total Vote	Republican	Democratic	Other	Rep.-Dem. Plurality	Percentage Total Vote Rep.	Percentage Total Vote Dem.	Percentage Major Vote Rep.	Percentage Major Vote Dem.
65,229	ADAMS	36,333	18,480	17,361	492	1,119 R	50.9%	47.8%	51.6%	48.4%
25,496	ALEXANDER	12,988	6,260	6,591	137	331 D	48.2%	50.7%	48.7%	51.3%
14,540	BOND	8,285	4,754	3,376	155	1,378 R	57.4%	40.7%	58.5%	41.5%
15,202	BOONE	8,632	6,330	2,277	25	4,053 R	73.3%	26.4%	73.5%	26.5%
8,053	BROWN	4,648	2,101	2,478	69	377 D	45.2%	53.3%	45.9%	54.1%
37,600	BUREAU	21,607	13,258	8,274	75	4,984 R	61.4%	38.3%	61.6%	38.4%
8,207	CALHOUN	4,158	2,516	1,625	17	891 R	60.5%	39.1%	60.8%	39.2%
17,987	CARROLL	10,013	6,398	3,592	23	2,806 R	63.9%	35.9%	64.0%	36.0%
16,425	CASS	9,416	4,490	4,854	72	364 D	47.7%	51.6%	48.1%	51.9%
70,578	CHAMPAIGN	38,144	20,314	17,563	267	2,751 R	53.3%	46.0%	53.6%	46.4%
38,564	CHRISTIAN	21,862	10,255	11,457	150	1,202 D	46.9%	52.4%	47.2%	52.8%
18,842	CLARK	10,836	5,976	4,807	53	1,169 R	55.1%	44.4%	55.4%	44.6%
18,947	CLAY	10,222	5,185	4,934	103	251 R	50.7%	48.3%	51.2%	48.8%
22,912	CLINTON	12,230	7,582	4,558	90	3,024 R	62.0%	37.3%	62.5%	37.5%
38,470	COLES	22,014	10,528	11,409	77	881 D	47.8%	51.8%	48.0%	52.0%
4,063,342	COOK	2,114,807	938,454	1,168,141	8,212	229,687 D	44.4%	55.2%	44.5%	55.5%
21,294	CRAWFORD	12,805	7,036	5,703	66	1,333 R	54.9%	44.5%	55.2%	44.8%
11,698	CUMBERLAND	6,451	3,330	3,091	30	239 R	51.6%	47.9%	51.9%	48.1%
34,388	DE KALB	19,668	12,577	6,989	102	5,588 R	63.9%	35.5%	64.3%	35.7%
18,244	DE WITT	10,574	5,477	5,052	45	425 R	51.8%	47.8%	52.0%	48.0%
17,590	DOUGLAS	10,031	5,451	4,513	67	938 R	54.3%	45.0%	54.7%	45.3%
103,480	DU PAGE	60,049	40,746	18,923	380	21,823 R	67.9%	31.5%	68.3%	31.7%
24,430	EDGAR	14,780	7,985	6,713	82	1,272 R	54.0%	45.4%	54.3%	45.7%
8,974	EDWARDS	5,182	3,361	1,770	51	1,591 R	64.9%	34.2%	65.5%	34.5%
22,034	EFFINGHAM	12,006	5,941	5,988	77	47 D	49.5%	49.9%	49.8%	50.2%
29,159	FAYETTE	14,915	7,486	7,286	143	200 R	50.2%	48.9%	50.7%	49.3%
15,007	FORD	8,862	5,770	3,062	30	2,708 R	65.1%	34.6%	65.3%	34.7%
53,137	FRANKLIN	28,660	12,936	15,523	201	2,587 D	45.1%	54.2%	45.5%	54.5%
44,627	FULTON	25,228	12,816	12,198	214	618 R	50.8%	48.4%	51.2%	48.8%
11,414	GALLATIN	5,929	2,588	3,293	48	705 D	43.6%	55.5%	44.0%	56.0%
20,292	GREENE	10,925	4,840	6,015	70	1,175 D	44.3%	55.1%	44.6%	55.4%
18,398	GRUNDY	10,741	6,593	4,105	43	2,488 R	61.4%	38.2%	61.6%	38.4%
13,454	HAMILTON	7,748	4,005	3,691	52	314 R	51.7%	47.6%	52.0%	48.0%
26,297	HANCOCK	15,961	9,108	6,688	165	2,420 R	57.1%	41.9%	57.7%	42.3%
7,759	HARDIN	4,333	2,333	1,974	26	359 R	53.8%	45.6%	54.2%	45.8%
8,949	HENDERSON	5,281	3,264	1,977	40	1,287 R	61.8%	37.4%	62.3%	37.7%
43,798	HENRY	25,648	14,971	10,481	196	4,490 R	58.4%	40.9%	58.8%	41.2%
32,496	IROQUOIS	18,191	11,047	7,036	108	4,011 R	60.7%	38.7%	61.1%	38.9%
37,920	JACKSON	21,708	11,980	9,600	128	2,380 R	55.2%	44.2%	55.5%	44.5%
13,431	JASPER	7,815	4,082	3,689	44	393 R	52.2%	47.2%	52.5%	47.5%
34,375	JEFFERSON	19,715	8,692	10,887	136	2,195 D	44.1%	55.2%	44.4%	55.6%
13,636	JERSEY	7,694	3,958	3,692	44	266 R	51.4%	48.0%	51.7%	48.3%
19,989	JO DAVIESS	11,192	7,285	3,864	43	3,421 R	65.1%	34.5%	65.3%	34.7%
10,727	JOHNSON	6,094	3,827	2,254	13	1,573 R	62.8%	37.0%	62.9%	37.1%
130,206	KANE	67,914	41,949	25,676	289	16,273 R	61.8%	37.8%	62.0%	38.0%
60,877	KANKAKEE	29,838	15,998	13,716	124	2,282 R	53.6%	46.0%	53.8%	46.2%
11,105	KENDALL	6,196	4,200	1,978	18	2,222 R	67.8%	31.9%	68.0%	32.0%
52,250	KNOX	30,224	17,459	12,597	168	4,862 R	57.8%	41.7%	58.1%	41.9%
121,094	LAKE	63,461	38,242	24,965	254	13,277 R	60.3%	39.3%	60.5%	39.5%
97,801	LA SALLE	55,399	25,296	29,704	399	4,408 D	45.7%	53.6%	46.0%	54.0%
21,075	LAWRENCE	11,833	6,061	5,625	147	436 R	51.2%	47.5%	51.9%	48.1%
34,604	LEE	17,285	11,228	6,005	52	5,223 R	65.0%	34.7%	65.2%	34.8%
38,838	LIVINGSTON	21,686	13,909	7,722	55	6,187 R	64.1%	35.6%	64.3%	35.7%
29,438	LOGAN	15,725	8,929	6,753	43	2,176 R	56.8%	42.9%	56.9%	43.1%
26,944	MCDONOUGH	16,217	10,326	5,783	108	4,543 R	63.7%	35.7%	64.1%	35.9%
37,311	MCHENRY	22,795	16,480	6,170	145	10,310 R	72.3%	27.1%	72.8%	27.2%
73,930	MCLEAN	40,166	21,865	18,024	277	3,841 R	54.4%	44.9%	54.8%	45.2%
84,693	MACON	47,864	19,998	27,589	277	7,591 D	41.8%	57.6%	42.0%	58.0%
46,304	MACOUPIN	27,610	13,000	14,356	254	1,356 D	47.1%	52.0%	47.5%	52.5%
149,349	MADISON	75,929	30,445	44,803	681	14,358 D	40.1%	59.0%	40.5%	59.5%

ILLINOIS

PRESIDENT 1940

1940 Census Population	County	Total Vote	Republican	Democratic	Other	Rep.-Dem. Plurality	Percentage Total Vote Rep.	Percentage Total Vote Dem.	Percentage Major Vote Rep.	Percentage Major Vote Dem.
47,989	MARION	24,476	10,461	13,807	208	3,346 D	42.7%	56.4%	43.1%	56.9%
13,179	MARSHALL	7,910	4,527	3,343	40	1,184 R	57.2%	42.3%	57.5%	42.5%
15,358	MASON	8,998	4,541	4,416	41	125 R	50.5%	49.1%	50.7%	49.3%
14,937	MASSAC	7,574	4,722	2,813	39	1,909 R	62.3%	37.1%	62.7%	37.3%
10,663	MENARD	6,458	3,531	2,894	33	637 R	54.7%	44.8%	55.0%	45.0%
17,701	MERCER	10,204	6,336	3,830	38	2,506 R	62.1%	37.5%	62.3%	37.7%
12,754	MONROE	7,602	4,754	2,826	22	1,928 R	62.5%	37.2%	62.7%	37.3%
34,499	MONTGOMERY	20,325	10,497	9,654	174	843 R	51.6%	47.5%	52.1%	47.9%
36,378	MORGAN	19,283	10,137	9,082	64	1,055 R	52.6%	47.1%	52.7%	47.3%
13,477	MOULTRIE	7,373	3,636	3,696	41	60 D	49.3%	50.1%	49.6%	50.4%
29,869	OGLE	16,742	11,838	4,833	71	7,005 R	70.7%	28.9%	71.0%	29.0%
153,374	PEORIA	77,221	34,911	42,009	301	7,098 D	45.2%	54.4%	45.4%	54.6%
23,438	PERRY	13,837	7,243	6,539	55	704 R	52.3%	47.3%	52.6%	47.4%
14,659	PIATT	8,159	4,564	3,564	31	1,000 R	55.9%	43.7%	56.2%	43.8%
25,340	PIKE	14,441	6,619	7,676	146	1,057 D	45.8%	53.2%	46.3%	53.7%
7,999	POPE	4,430	2,914	1,499	17	1,415 R	65.8%	33.8%	66.0%	34.0%
15,875	PULASKI	8,085	4,589	3,456	40	1,133 R	56.8%	42.7%	57.0%	43.0%
5,289	PUTNAM	2,985	1,778	1,195	12	583 R	59.6%	40.0%	59.8%	40.2%
33,608	RANDOLPH	17,215	9,333	7,802	80	1,531 R	54.2%	45.3%	54.5%	45.5%
17,137	RICHLAND	9,446	5,022	4,335	89	687 R	53.2%	45.9%	53.7%	46.3%
113,323	ROCK ISLAND	61,101	25,629	35,240	232	9,611 D	41.9%	57.7%	42.1%	57.9%
166,899	ST. CLAIR	89,891	35,998	53,482	411	17,484 D	40.0%	59.5%	40.2%	59.8%
38,066	SALINE	21,377	10,567	10,692	118	125 D	49.4%	50.0%	49.7%	50.3%
117,912	SANGAMON	67,628	35,464	31,943	221	3,521 R	52.4%	47.2%	52.6%	47.4%
11,430	SCHUYLER	6,803	3,318	3,404	81	86 D	48.8%	50.0%	49.4%	50.6%
8,176	SCOTT	5,099	2,585	2,492	22	93 R	50.7%	48.9%	50.9%	49.1%
26,290	SHELBY	15,197	7,250	7,704	243	454 D	47.7%	50.7%	48.5%	51.5%
8,881	STARK	5,225	3,393	1,818	14	1,575 R	64.9%	34.8%	65.1%	34.9%
40,646	STEPHENSON	23,045	14,040	8,911	94	5,129 R	60.9%	38.7%	61.2%	38.8%
58,362	TAZEWELL	30,159	12,419	17,624	116	5,205 D	41.2%	58.4%	41.3%	58.7%
21,528	UNION	10,800	4,915	5,804	81	889 D	45.5%	53.7%	45.9%	54.1%
86,791	VERMILION	46,242	23,059	22,891	292	168 R	49.9%	49.5%	50.2%	49.8%
13,724	WABASH	7,965	3,659	4,187	119	528 D	45.9%	52.6%	46.6%	53.4%
21,286	WARREN	12,735	7,790	4,878	67	2,912 R	61.2%	38.3%	61.5%	38.5%
15,801	WASHINGTON	9,222	5,701	3,479	42	2,222 R	61.8%	37.7%	62.1%	37.9%
22,092	WAYNE	12,192	6,556	5,569	67	987 R	53.8%	45.7%	54.1%	45.9%
20,027	WHITE	11,493	5,459	5,909	125	450 D	47.5%	51.4%	48.0%	52.0%
43,338	WHITESIDE	23,242	15,752	7,356	134	8,396 R	67.8%	31.6%	68.2%	31.8%
114,210	WILL	61,946	32,291	29,442	213	2,849 R	52.1%	47.5%	52.3%	47.7%
51,424	WILLIAMSON	29,217	14,433	14,645	139	212 D	49.4%	50.1%	49.6%	50.4%
121,178	WINNEBAGO	59,127	30,683	28,061	383	2,622 R	51.9%	47.5%	52.2%	47.8%
19,124	WOODFORD	10,942	6,575	4,314	53	2,261 R	60.1%	39.4%	60.4%	39.6%
7,897,241	TOTAL	4,217,935	2,047,240	2,149,934	20,761	102,694 D	48.5%	51.0%	48.8%	51.2%

ILLINOIS

PRESIDENT 1936

1930 Census Population	County	Total Vote	Republican	Democratic	Other	Rep.-Dem. Plurality	Percentage Total Vote Rep.	Percentage Total Vote Dem.	Percentage Major Vote Rep.	Percentage Major Vote Dem.
62,784	ADAMS	33,473	13,114	18,857	1,502	5,743 D	39.2%	56.3%	41.0%	59.0%
22,542	ALEXANDER	12,653	5,553	6,972	128	1,419 D	43.9%	55.1%	44.3%	55.7%
14,406	BOND	7,836	4,046	3,541	249	505 R	51.6%	45.2%	53.3%	46.7%
15,078	BOONE	8,022	5,375	2,383	264	2,992 R	67.0%	29.7%	69.3%	30.7%
7,892	BROWN	4,549	1,591	2,873	85	1,282 D	35.0%	63.2%	35.6%	64.4%
38,845	BUREAU	20,322	10,462	9,516	344	946 R	51.5%	46.8%	52.4%	47.6%
8,034	CALHOUN	4,102	1,883	2,058	161	175 D	45.9%	50.2%	47.8%	52.2%
18,433	CARROLL	9,328	4,886	4,368	74	518 R	52.4%	46.8%	52.8%	47.2%
16,537	CASS	9,090	3,209	5,786	95	2,577 D	35.3%	63.7%	35.7%	64.3%
64,273	CHAMPAIGN	34,535	15,808	18,203	524	2,395 D	45.8%	52.7%	46.5%	53.5%
37,538	CHRISTIAN	20,521	8,145	11,400	976	3,255 D	39.7%	55.6%	41.7%	58.3%
17,872	CLARK	11,314	5,426	5,836	52	410 D	48.0%	51.6%	48.2%	51.8%
16,155	CLAY	9,384	4,528	4,752	104	224 D	48.3%	50.6%	48.8%	51.2%
21,369	CLINTON	11,145	3,653	5,355	2,137	1,702 D	32.8%	48.0%	40.6%	59.4%
37,315	COLES	20,868	8,800	11,931	137	3,131 D	42.2%	57.2%	42.4%	57.6%
3,982,123	COOK	2,009,457	701,206	1,253,164	55,087	551,958 D	34.9%	62.4%	35.9%	64.1%
21,085	CRAWFORD	12,099	5,823	6,164	112	341 D	48.1%	50.9%	48.6%	51.4%
10,419	CUMBERLAND	6,356	3,016	3,290	50	274 D	47.5%	51.8%	47.8%	52.2%
32,644	DE KALB	18,275	9,826	7,899	550	1,927 R	53.8%	43.2%	55.4%	44.6%
18,598	DE WITT	10,280	4,544	5,676	60	1,132 D	44.2%	55.2%	44.5%	55.5%
17,914	DOUGLAS	9,694	4,606	5,029	59	423 D	47.5%	51.9%	47.8%	52.2%
91,998	DU PAGE	51,632	28,380	21,684	1,568	6,696 R	55.0%	42.0%	56.7%	43.3%
24,966	EDGAR	14,898	6,929	7,822	147	893 D	46.5%	52.5%	47.0%	53.0%
8,303	EDWARDS	5,100	2,813	2,211	76	602 R	55.2%	43.4%	56.0%	44.0%
19,013	EFFINGHAM	10,583	4,293	6,030	260	1,737 D	40.6%	57.0%	41.6%	58.4%
23,487	FAYETTE	13,371	6,419	6,824	128	405 D	48.0%	51.0%	48.5%	51.5%
15,489	FORD	8,410	4,524	3,715	171	809 R	53.8%	44.2%	54.9%	45.1%
59,442	FRANKLIN	26,625	10,708	15,254	663	4,546 D	40.2%	57.3%	41.2%	58.8%
43,983	FULTON	23,422	10,130	12,864	428	2,734 D	43.2%	54.9%	44.1%	55.9%
10,091	GALLATIN	5,774	2,004	3,701	69	1,697 D	34.7%	64.1%	35.1%	64.9%
20,417	GREENE	10,544	3,916	6,510	118	2,594 D	37.1%	61.7%	37.6%	62.4%
18,678	GRUNDY	10,185	5,360	4,481	344	879 R	52.6%	44.0%	54.5%	45.5%
12,995	HAMILTON	7,535	3,321	4,152	62	831 D	44.1%	55.1%	44.4%	55.6%
26,420	HANCOCK	15,507	7,383	7,726	398	343 D	47.6%	49.8%	48.9%	51.1%
6,955	HARDIN	4,011	2,008	1,984	19	24 R	50.1%	49.5%	50.3%	49.7%
8,778	HENDERSON	5,220	2,663	2,496	61	167 R	51.0%	47.8%	51.6%	48.4%
43,851	HENRY	24,094	11,953	11,490	651	463 R	49.6%	47.7%	51.0%	49.0%
32,913	IROQUOIS	17,173	7,908	8,654	611	746 D	46.0%	50.4%	47.7%	52.3%
35,680	JACKSON	20,546	10,363	9,971	212	392 R	50.4%	48.5%	51.0%	49.0%
12,809	JASPER	7,502	3,221	4,149	132	928 D	42.9%	55.3%	43.7%	56.3%
31,034	JEFFERSON	17,668	7,290	10,240	138	2,950 D	41.3%	58.0%	41.6%	58.4%
12,556	JERSEY	7,061	3,023	3,955	83	932 D	42.8%	56.0%	43.3%	56.7%
20,235	JO DAVIESS	10,950	5,619	5,079	252	540 R	51.3%	46.4%	52.5%	47.5%
10,203	JOHNSON	6,050	3,537	2,497	16	1,040 R	58.5%	41.3%	58.6%	41.4%
125,327	KANE	63,729	33,491	28,187	2,051	5,304 R	52.6%	44.2%	54.3%	45.7%
50,095	KANKAKEE	26,538	10,935	13,162	2,441	2,227 D	41.2%	49.6%	45.4%	54.6%
10,555	KENDALL	5,720	3,138	2,374	208	764 R	54.9%	41.5%	56.9%	43.1%
51,336	KNOX	29,124	14,712	13,697	715	1,015 R	50.5%	47.0%	51.8%	48.2%
104,387	LAKE	53,675	27,548	24,524	1,603	3,024 R	51.3%	45.7%	52.9%	47.1%
97,695	LA SALLE	51,201	22,240	26,926	2,035	4,686 D	43.4%	52.6%	45.2%	54.8%
21,885	LAWRENCE	11,398	5,060	6,168	170	1,108 D	44.4%	54.1%	45.1%	54.9%
32,329	LEE	16,232	8,914	6,845	473	2,069 R	54.9%	42.2%	56.6%	43.4%
39,092	LIVINGSTON	20,334	10,801	9,190	343	1,611 R	53.1%	45.2%	54.0%	46.0%
28,863	LOGAN	15,087	7,019	7,886	182	867 D	46.5%	52.3%	47.1%	52.9%
27,329	MCDONOUGH	16,012	8,723	7,138	151	1,585 R	54.5%	44.6%	55.0%	45.0%
35,079	MCHENRY	19,866	12,031	6,893	942	5,138 R	60.6%	34.7%	63.6%	36.4%
73,117	MCLEAN	39,132	16,826	21,508	798	4,682 D	43.0%	55.0%	43.9%	56.1%
81,731	MACON	43,486	15,585	27,360	541	11,775 D	35.8%	62.9%	36.3%	63.7%
48,703	MACOUPIN	25,851	9,502	14,896	1,453	5,394 D	36.8%	57.6%	38.9%	61.1%
143,830	MADISON	65,686	22,073	42,172	1,441	20,099 D	33.6%	64.2%	34.4%	65.6%

ILLINOIS

PRESIDENT 1936

1930 Census Population	County	Total Vote	Republican	Democratic	Other	Rep.-Dem. Plurality	Percentage Total Vote Rep.	Total Vote Dem.	Major Vote Rep.	Major Vote Dem.
35,635	MARION	19,446	8,321	10,820	305	2,499 D	42.8%	55.6%	43.5%	56.5%
13,023	MARSHALL	7,760	3,544	4,149	67	605 D	45.7%	53.5%	46.1%	53.9%
15,115	MASON	8,731	3,395	5,278	58	1,883 D	38.9%	60.5%	39.1%	60.9%
14,081	MASSAC	6,983	3,894	3,039	50	855 R	55.8%	43.5%	56.2%	43.8%
10,575	MENARD	6,277	3,067	3,152	58	85 D	48.9%	50.2%	49.3%	50.7%
16,641	MERCER	9,884	5,028	4,751	105	277 R	50.9%	48.1%	51.4%	48.6%
12,369	MONROE	6,850	3,226	3,477	147	251 D	47.1%	50.8%	48.1%	51.9%
35,278	MONTGOMERY	18,964	8,140	10,132	692	1,992 D	42.9%	53.4%	44.5%	55.5%
34,240	MORGAN	18,811	8,844	9,800	167	956 D	47.0%	52.1%	47.4%	52.6%
13,247	MOULTRIE	7,249	3,074	4,110	65	1,036 D	42.4%	56.7%	42.8%	57.2%
28,118	OGLE	15,546	9,576	5,776	194	3,800 R	61.6%	37.2%	62.4%	37.6%
141,344	PEORIA	74,865	25,425	48,063	1,377	22,638 D	34.0%	64.2%	34.6%	65.4%
22,767	PERRY	12,768	5,482	7,043	243	1,561 D	42.9%	55.2%	43.8%	56.2%
15,588	PIATT	8,061	3,931	4,084	46	153 D	48.8%	50.7%	49.0%	51.0%
24,357	PIKE	13,974	5,589	8,187	198	2,598 D	40.0%	58.6%	40.6%	59.4%
7,996	POPE	4,548	2,787	1,728	33	1,059 R	61.3%	38.0%	61.7%	38.3%
14,834	PULASKI	7,645	3,774	3,804	67	30 D	49.4%	49.8%	49.8%	50.2%
5,235	PUTNAM	2,901	1,435	1,437	29	2 D	49.5%	49.5%	50.0%	50.0%
29,313	RANDOLPH	15,701	7,057	8,247	397	1,190 D	44.9%	52.5%	46.1%	53.9%
14,053	RICHLAND	8,492	4,040	4,268	184	228 D	47.6%	50.3%	48.6%	51.4%
98,191	ROCK ISLAND	53,027	19,487	32,741	799	13,254 D	36.7%	61.7%	37.3%	62.7%
157,775	ST. CLAIR	83,762	26,684	54,238	2,840	27,554 D	31.9%	64.8%	33.0%	67.0%
37,100	SALINE	19,616	9,055	10,253	308	1,198 D	46.2%	52.3%	46.9%	53.1%
111,733	SANGAMON	63,670	29,562	32,281	1,827	2,719 D	46.4%	50.7%	47.8%	52.2%
11,676	SCHUYLER	6,957	3,029	3,885	43	856 D	43.5%	55.8%	43.8%	56.2%
8,539	SCOTT	5,138	2,165	2,945	28	780 D	42.1%	57.3%	42.4%	57.6%
25,471	SHELBY	14,201	5,795	8,186	220	2,391 D	40.8%	57.6%	41.4%	58.6%
9,184	STARK	4,958	2,696	2,220	42	476 R	54.4%	44.8%	54.8%	45.2%
40,064	STEPHENSON	21,342	9,943	10,567	832	624 D	46.6%	49.5%	48.5%	51.5%
46,082	TAZEWELL	24,774	7,946	16,487	341	8,541 D	32.1%	66.5%	32.5%	67.5%
19,883	UNION	10,461	4,165	6,260	36	2,095 D	39.8%	59.8%	40.0%	60.0%
89,339	VERMILION	44,156	18,350	25,016	790	6,666 D	41.6%	56.7%	42.3%	57.7%
13,197	WABASH	7,224	2,860	4,214	150	1,354 D	39.6%	58.3%	40.4%	59.6%
21,745	WARREN	12,465	6,919	5,409	137	1,510 R	55.5%	43.4%	56.1%	43.9%
16,286	WASHINGTON	8,868	4,540	4,119	209	421 R	51.2%	46.4%	52.4%	47.6%
19,130	WAYNE	11,330	5,528	5,752	50	224 D	48.8%	50.8%	49.0%	51.0%
18,149	WHITE	10,909	4,322	6,511	76	2,189 D	39.6%	59.7%	39.9%	60.1%
39,019	WHITESIDE	21,243	12,666	7,982	595	4,684 R	59.6%	37.6%	61.3%	38.7%
110,732	WILL	55,314	25,028	28,135	2,151	3,107 D	45.2%	50.9%	47.1%	52.9%
53,880	WILLIAMSON	27,334	12,319	14,663	352	2,344 D	45.1%	53.6%	45.7%	54.3%
117,373	WINNEBAGO	53,989	24,997	27,200	1,792	2,203 D	46.3%	50.4%	47.9%	52.1%
18,792	WOODFORD	10,093	4,845	5,122	126	277 D	48.0%	50.7%	48.6%	51.4%
7,630,654	TOTAL	3,956,522	1,570,393	2,282,999	103,130	712,606 D	39.7%	57.7%	40.8%	59.2%

ILLINOIS

PRESIDENT 1932

1930 Census Population	County	Total Vote	Republican	Democratic	Other	Rep.-Dem. Plurality	Percentage: Total Vote		Percentage: Major Vote	
							Rep.	Dem.	Rep.	Dem.
62,784	ADAMS	31,669	10,134	21,098	437	10,964 D	32.0%	66.6%	32.4%	67.6%
22,542	ALEXANDER	10,533	4,729	5,653	151	924 D	44.9%	53.7%	45.5%	54.5%
14,406	BOND	6,958	3,171	3,630	157	459 D	45.6%	52.2%	46.6%	53.4%
15,078	BOONE	7,575	5,244	2,239	92	3,005 R	69.2%	29.6%	70.1%	29.9%
7,892	BROWN	3,993	1,148	2,822	23	1,674 D	28.8%	70.7%	28.9%	71.1%
38,845	BUREAU	19,280	8,721	10,309	250	1,588 D	45.2%	53.5%	45.8%	54.2%
8,034	CALHOUN	3,504	1,239	2,229	36	990 D	35.4%	63.6%	35.7%	64.3%
18,433	CARROLL	8,495	4,571	3,812	112	759 R	53.8%	44.9%	54.5%	45.5%
16,537	CASS	8,507	2,745	5,669	93	2,924 D	32.3%	66.6%	32.6%	67.4%
64,273	CHAMPAIGN	31,070	13,995	16,474	601	2,479 D	45.0%	53.0%	45.9%	54.1%
37,538	CHRISTIAN	18,242	6,096	11,515	631	5,419 D	33.4%	63.1%	34.6%	65.4%
17,872	CLARK	9,881	4,148	5,659	74	1,511 D	42.0%	57.3%	42.3%	57.7%
16,155	CLAY	8,064	3,373	4,565	126	1,192 D	41.8%	56.6%	42.5%	57.5%
21,369	CLINTON	10,466	2,548	7,736	182	5,188 D	24.3%	73.9%	24.8%	75.2%
37,315	COLES	18,559	7,313	11,081	165	3,768 D	39.4%	59.7%	39.8%	60.2%
3,982,123	COOK	1,664,232	690,146	919,231	54,855	229,085 D	41.5%	55.2%	42.9%	57.1%
21,085	CRAWFORD	10,800	4,550	6,081	169	1,531 D	42.1%	56.3%	42.8%	57.2%
10,419	CUMBERLAND	5,324	2,166	3,128	30	962 D	40.7%	58.8%	40.9%	59.1%
32,644	DE KALB	16,594	9,356	6,923	315	2,433 R	56.4%	41.7%	57.5%	42.5%
18,598	DE WITT	9,673	4,207	5,339	127	1,132 D	43.5%	55.2%	44.1%	55.9%
17,914	DOUGLAS	8,236	3,108	4,954	174	1,846 D	37.7%	60.2%	38.6%	61.4%
91,998	DU PAGE	45,809	25,758	18,547	1,504	7,211 R	56.2%	40.5%	58.1%	41.9%
24,966	EDGAR	13,836	5,953	7,745	138	1,792 D	43.0%	56.0%	43.5%	56.5%
8,303	EDWARDS	4,216	2,203	1,956	57	247 R	52.3%	46.4%	53.0%	47.0%
19,013	EFFINGHAM	9,569	2,933	6,503	133	3,570 D	30.7%	68.0%	31.1%	68.9%
23,487	FAYETTE	12,360	5,122	7,053	185	1,931 D	41.4%	57.1%	42.1%	57.9%
15,489	FORD	7,616	3,342	4,175	99	833 D	43.9%	54.8%	44.5%	55.5%
59,442	FRANKLIN	23,290	7,560	14,754	976	7,194 D	32.5%	63.3%	33.9%	66.1%
43,983	FULTON	20,611	7,579	12,144	888	4,565 D	36.8%	58.9%	38.4%	61.6%
10,091	GALLATIN	4,813	1,279	3,469	65	2,190 D	26.6%	72.1%	26.9%	73.1%
20,417	GREENE	9,335	2,857	6,347	131	3,490 D	30.6%	68.0%	31.0%	69.0%
18,678	GRUNDY	9,315	4,491	4,755	69	264 D	48.2%	51.0%	48.6%	51.4%
12,995	HAMILTON	6,617	2,513	4,059	45	1,546 D	38.0%	61.3%	38.2%	61.8%
26,420	HANCOCK	13,734	4,789	8,808	137	4,019 D	34.9%	64.1%	35.2%	64.8%
6,955	HARDIN	3,223	1,559	1,610	54	51 D	48.4%	50.0%	49.2%	50.8%
8,778	HENDERSON	4,266	1,815	2,372	79	557 D	42.5%	55.6%	43.3%	56.7%
43,851	HENRY	22,199	11,376	10,122	701	1,254 R	51.2%	45.6%	52.9%	47.1%
32,913	IROQUOIS	15,898	6,303	9,434	161	3,131 D	39.6%	59.3%	40.1%	59.9%
35,680	JACKSON	17,715	7,636	9,730	349	2,094 D	43.1%	54.9%	44.0%	56.0%
12,809	JASPER	6,726	2,300	4,390	36	2,090 D	34.2%	65.3%	34.4%	65.6%
31,034	JEFFERSON	15,005	5,333	9,495	177	4,162 D	35.5%	63.3%	36.0%	64.0%
12,556	JERSEY	6,069	2,157	3,807	105	1,650 D	35.5%	62.7%	36.2%	63.8%
20,235	JO DAVIESS	10,177	4,520	5,497	160	977 D	44.4%	54.0%	45.1%	54.9%
10,203	JOHNSON	4,861	2,424	2,387	50	37 R	49.9%	49.1%	50.4%	49.6%
125,327	KANE	58,656	32,934	24,638	1,084	8,296 R	56.1%	42.0%	57.2%	42.8%
50,095	KANKAKEE	24,792	10,873	13,555	364	2,682 D	43.9%	54.7%	44.5%	55.5%
10,555	KENDALL	5,209	2,749	2,398	62	351 R	52.8%	46.0%	53.4%	46.6%
51,336	KNOX	24,918	12,244	12,282	392	38 D	49.1%	49.3%	49.9%	50.1%
104,387	LAKE	47,122	23,994	21,139	1,989	2,855 R	50.9%	44.9%	53.2%	46.8%
97,695	LA SALLE	47,587	19,179	27,500	908	8,321 D	40.3%	57.8%	41.1%	58.9%
21,885	LAWRENCE	10,441	4,194	6,100	147	1,906 D	40.2%	58.4%	40.7%	59.3%
32,329	LEE	15,161	7,802	7,182	177	620 R	51.5%	47.4%	52.1%	47.9%
39,092	LIVINGSTON	18,589	8,403	10,024	162	1,621 D	45.2%	53.9%	45.6%	54.4%
28,863	LOGAN	14,116	5,850	8,119	147	2,269 D	41.4%	57.5%	41.9%	58.1%
27,329	MCDONOUGH	14,105	6,329	7,608	168	1,279 D	44.9%	53.9%	45.4%	54.6%
35,079	MCHENRY	18,594	9,880	8,260	454	1,620 R	53.1%	44.4%	54.5%	45.5%
73,117	MCLEAN	35,871	15,450	19,535	886	4,085 D	43.1%	54.5%	44.2%	55.8%
81,731	MACON	39,346	16,868	21,638	840	4,770 D	42.9%	55.0%	43.8%	56.2%
48,703	MACOUPIN	23,640	7,031	14,810	1,799	7,779 D	29.7%	62.6%	32.2%	67.8%
143,830	MADISON	57,238	19,774	35,211	2,253	15,437 D	34.5%	61.5%	36.0%	64.0%

ILLINOIS

PRESIDENT 1932

1930 Census Population	County	Total Vote	Republican	Democratic	Other	Rep.-Dem. Plurality	Percentage Total Vote Rep.	Total Vote Dem.	Major Vote Rep.	Major Vote Dem.
35,635	MARION	17,380	6,276	10,791	313	4,515 D	36.1%	62.1%	36.8%	63.2%
13,023	MARSHALL	7,345	3,166	4,133	46	967 D	43.1%	56.3%	43.4%	56.6%
15,115	MASON	8,300	2,551	5,681	68	3,130 D	30.7%	68.4%	31.0%	69.0%
14,081	MASSAC	5,525	2,851	2,593	81	258 R	51.6%	46.9%	52.4%	47.6%
10,575	MENARD	5,823	2,327	3,453	43	1,126 D	40.0%	59.3%	40.3%	59.7%
16,641	MERCER	8,835	4,436	4,309	90	127 R	50.2%	48.8%	50.7%	49.3%
12,369	MONROE	6,259	2,186	3,993	80	1,807 D	34.9%	63.8%	35.4%	64.6%
35,278	MONTGOMERY	17,126	5,945	10,456	725	4,511 D	34.7%	61.1%	36.2%	63.8%
34,240	MORGAN	18,130	7,787	10,170	173	2,383 D	43.0%	56.1%	43.4%	56.6%
13,247	MOULTRIE	6,646	2,353	4,219	74	1,866 D	35.4%	63.5%	35.8%	64.2%
28,118	OGLE	13,912	8,224	5,416	272	2,808 R	59.1%	38.9%	60.3%	39.7%
141,344	PEORIA	63,716	25,166	37,605	945	12,439 D	39.5%	59.0%	40.1%	59.9%
22,767	PERRY	11,502	3,778	7,400	324	3,622 D	32.8%	64.3%	33.8%	66.2%
15,588	PIATT	7,443	3,179	4,200	64	1,021 D	42.7%	56.4%	43.1%	56.9%
24,357	PIKE	12,452	4,181	8,013	258	3,832 D	33.6%	64.4%	34.3%	65.7%
7,996	POPE	3,732	2,011	1,697	24	314 R	53.9%	45.5%	54.2%	45.8%
14,834	PULASKI	6,726	3,225	3,446	55	221 D	47.9%	51.2%	48.3%	51.7%
5,235	PUTNAM	2,651	1,050	1,554	47	504 D	39.6%	58.6%	40.3%	59.7%
29,313	RANDOLPH	13,647	4,747	8,634	266	3,887 D	34.8%	63.3%	35.5%	64.5%
14,053	RICHLAND	7,182	2,765	4,318	99	1,553 D	38.5%	60.1%	39.0%	61.0%
98,191	ROCK ISLAND	46,549	21,205	24,676	668	3,471 D	45.6%	53.0%	46.2%	53.8%
157,775	ST. CLAIR	72,571	22,744	47,305	2,522	24,561 D	31.3%	65.2%	32.5%	67.5%
37,100	SALINE	16,473	6,294	9,725	454	3,431 D	38.2%	59.0%	39.3%	60.7%
111,733	SANGAMON	60,643	26,856	32,745	1,042	5,889 D	44.3%	54.0%	45.1%	54.9%
11,676	SCHUYLER	5,930	2,075	3,782	73	1,707 D	35.0%	63.8%	35.4%	64.6%
8,539	SCOTT	4,804	1,740	3,012	52	1,272 D	36.2%	62.7%	36.6%	63.4%
25,471	SHELBY	12,969	4,657	8,093	219	3,436 D	35.9%	62.4%	36.5%	63.5%
9,184	STARK	4,533	2,119	2,369	45	250 D	46.7%	52.3%	47.2%	52.8%
40,064	STEPHENSON	20,198	8,963	10,728	507	1,765 D	44.4%	53.1%	45.5%	54.5%
46,082	TAZEWELL	21,055	7,260	13,591	204	6,331 D	34.5%	64.5%	34.8%	65.2%
19,883	UNION	9,085	2,859	6,157	69	3,298 D	31.5%	67.8%	31.7%	68.3%
89,339	VERMILION	40,677	15,643	24,032	1,002	8,389 D	38.5%	59.1%	39.4%	60.6%
13,197	WABASH	6,695	2,309	4,280	106	1,971 D	34.5%	63.9%	35.0%	65.0%
21,745	WARREN	11,258	5,498	5,610	150	112 D	48.8%	49.8%	49.5%	50.5%
16,286	WASHINGTON	7,926	3,076	4,696	154	1,620 D	38.8%	59.2%	39.6%	60.4%
19,130	WAYNE	9,656	4,097	5,488	71	1,391 D	42.4%	56.8%	42.7%	57.3%
18,149	WHITE	9,298	3,320	5,909	69	2,589 D	35.7%	63.6%	36.0%	64.0%
39,019	WHITESIDE	18,626	11,388	7,010	228	4,378 R	61.1%	37.6%	61.9%	38.1%
110,732	WILL	52,266	25,173	25,798	1,295	625 D	48.2%	49.4%	49.4%	50.6%
53,880	WILLIAMSON	22,265	8,714	12,961	590	4,247 D	39.1%	58.2%	40.2%	59.8%
117,373	WINNEBAGO	46,625	26,632	17,707	2,286	8,925 R	57.1%	38.0%	60.1%	39.9%
18,792	WOODFORD	9,192	3,866	5,244	82	1,378 D	42.1%	57.0%	42.4%	57.6%
7,630,654	TOTAL	3,407,926	1,432,756	1,882,304	92,866	449,548 D	42.0%	55.2%	43.2%	56.8%

ILLINOIS

PRESIDENT 1928

1920 Census Population	County	Total Vote	Republican	Democratic	Other	Rep.-Dem. Plurality	Percentage Total Vote Rep.	Total Vote Dem.	Major Vote Rep.	Major Vote Dem.
62,188	ADAMS	29,093	15,590	13,215	288	2,375 R	53.6%	45.4%	54.1%	45.9%
23,980	ALEXANDER	9,252	5,666	3,558	28	2,108 R	61.2%	38.5%	61.4%	38.6%
16,045	BOND	6,494	4,160	2,298	36	1,862 R	64.1%	35.4%	64.4%	35.6%
15,322	BOONE	7,369	5,965	1,371	33	4,594 R	80.9%	18.6%	81.3%	18.7%
9,336	BROWN	4,165	2,289	1,867	9	422 R	55.0%	44.8%	55.1%	44.9%
42,648	BUREAU	18,133	11,557	6,486	90	5,071 R	63.7%	35.8%	64.1%	35.9%
8,245	CALHOUN	3,178	1,594	1,551	33	43 R	50.2%	48.8%	50.7%	49.3%
19,345	CARROLL	8,118	6,197	1,876	45	4,321 R	76.3%	23.1%	76.8%	23.2%
17,896	CASS	7,494	4,009	3,461	24	548 R	53.5%	46.2%	53.7%	46.3%
56,959	CHAMPAIGN	28,550	19,494	8,915	141	10,579 R	68.3%	31.2%	68.6%	31.4%
38,458	CHRISTIAN	17,431	9,896	7,345	190	2,551 R	56.8%	42.1%	57.4%	42.6%
21,165	CLARK	9,288	5,632	3,621	35	2,011 R	60.6%	39.0%	60.9%	39.1%
17,684	CLAY	6,940	4,522	2,418		2,104 R	65.2%	34.8%	65.2%	34.8%
22,947	CLINTON	9,852	3,031	6,774	47	3,743 D	30.8%	68.8%	30.9%	69.1%
35,108	COLES	16,607	11,479	5,071	57	6,408 R	69.1%	30.5%	69.4%	30.6%
3,053,017	COOK	1,540,171	812,063	716,283	11,825	95,780 R	52.7%	46.5%	53.1%	46.9%
22,771	CRAWFORD	9,522	5,989	3,495	38	2,494 R	62.9%	36.7%	63.1%	36.9%
12,858	CUMBERLAND	5,143	3,242	1,873	28	1,369 R	63.0%	36.4%	63.4%	36.6%
31,339	DE KALB	15,503	11,501	3,940	62	7,561 R	74.2%	25.4%	74.5%	25.5%
19,252	DE WITT	8,790	6,100	2,631	59	3,469 R	69.4%	29.9%	69.9%	30.1%
19,604	DOUGLAS	7,171	4,890	2,239	42	2,651 R	68.2%	31.2%	68.6%	31.4%
42,120	DU PAGE	38,712	28,016	10,479	217	17,537 R	72.4%	27.1%	72.8%	27.2%
25,769	EDGAR	12,886	7,509	5,325	52	2,184 R	58.3%	41.3%	58.5%	41.5%
9,431	EDWARDS	3,826	2,861	950	15	1,911 R	74.8%	24.8%	75.1%	24.9%
19,556	EFFINGHAM	8,214	3,882	4,239	93	357 D	47.3%	51.6%	47.8%	52.2%
26,187	FAYETTE	10,616	6,545	3,998	73	2,547 R	61.7%	37.7%	62.1%	37.9%
16,466	FORD	6,793	4,668	2,098	27	2,570 R	68.7%	30.9%	69.0%	31.0%
57,293	FRANKLIN	21,622	9,900	11,369	353	1,469 D	45.8%	52.6%	46.5%	53.5%
48,163	FULTON	17,680	10,600	6,591	489	4,009 R	60.0%	37.3%	61.7%	38.3%
12,856	GALLATIN	4,373	2,002	2,343	28	341 D	45.8%	53.6%	46.1%	53.9%
22,883	GREENE	8,421	4,299	4,076	46	223 R	51.1%	48.4%	51.3%	48.7%
18,580	GRUNDY	8,329	5,126	3,174	29	1,952 R	61.5%	38.1%	61.8%	38.2%
15,920	HAMILTON	6,412	3,275	3,037	100	238 R	51.1%	47.4%	51.9%	48.1%
28,523	HANCOCK	13,290	7,795	5,447	48	2,348 R	58.7%	41.0%	58.9%	41.1%
7,533	HARDIN	2,732	1,758	933	41	825 R	64.3%	34.2%	65.3%	34.7%
9,770	HENDERSON	3,790	2,695	1,065	30	1,630 R	71.1%	28.1%	71.7%	28.3%
45,162	HENRY	20,707	14,666	5,858	183	8,808 R	70.8%	28.3%	71.5%	28.5%
34,841	IROQUOIS	13,923	8,453	5,421	49	3,032 R	60.7%	38.9%	60.9%	39.1%
37,091	JACKSON	15,102	9,180	5,836	86	3,344 R	60.8%	38.6%	61.1%	38.9%
16,064	JASPER	6,272	3,201	3,055	16	146 R	51.0%	48.7%	51.2%	48.8%
28,480	JEFFERSON	13,301	7,326	5,905	70	1,421 R	55.1%	44.4%	55.4%	44.6%
12,682	JERSEY	5,480	2,993	2,473	14	520 R	54.6%	45.1%	54.8%	45.2%
21,917	JO DAVIESS	10,283	6,333	3,856	94	2,477 R	61.6%	37.5%	62.2%	37.8%
12,022	JOHNSON	4,091	2,892	1,163	36	1,729 R	70.7%	28.4%	71.3%	28.7%
99,499	KANE	54,673	38,236	16,184	253	22,052 R	69.9%	29.6%	70.3%	29.7%
44,940	KANKAKEE	22,279	11,905	10,247	127	1,658 R	53.4%	46.0%	53.7%	46.3%
10,074	KENDALL	4,752	3,589	1,154	9	2,435 R	75.5%	24.3%	75.7%	24.3%
46,727	KNOX	22,330	16,151	5,993	186	10,158 R	72.3%	26.8%	72.9%	27.1%
74,285	LAKE	39,587	26,814	12,252	521	14,562 R	67.7%	30.9%	68.6%	31.4%
92,925	LA SALLE	45,228	24,039	20,807	382	3,232 R	53.2%	46.0%	53.6%	46.4%
21,380	LAWRENCE	9,726	5,851	3,806	69	2,045 R	60.2%	39.1%	60.6%	39.4%
28,004	LEE	13,760	9,238	4,476	46	4,762 R	67.1%	32.5%	67.4%	32.6%
39,070	LIVINGSTON	16,992	11,161	5,737	94	5,424 R	65.7%	33.8%	66.0%	34.0%
29,562	LOGAN	12,725	7,631	5,019	75	2,612 R	60.0%	39.4%	60.3%	39.7%
27,074	MCDONOUGH	13,138	8,953	4,104	81	4,849 R	68.1%	31.2%	68.6%	31.4%
33,164	MCHENRY	16,319	10,661	5,596	62	5,065 R	65.3%	34.3%	65.6%	34.4%
70,107	MCLEAN	31,789	20,780	10,742	267	10,038 R	65.4%	33.8%	65.9%	34.1%
65,175	MACON	34,654	24,492	9,932	230	14,560 R	70.7%	28.7%	71.1%	28.9%
57,274	MACOUPIN	22,438	10,699	11,290	449	591 D	47.7%	50.3%	48.7%	51.3%
106,895	MADISON	52,406	28,028	23,658	720	4,370 R	53.5%	45.1%	54.2%	45.8%

ILLINOIS

PRESIDENT 1928

1920 Census Population	County	Total Vote	Republican	Democratic	Other	Rep.-Dem. Plurality	Percentage Total Vote Rep.	Total Vote Dem.	Major Vote Rep.	Major Vote Dem.
37,497	MARION	15,052	9,110	5,823	119	3,287 R	60.5%	38.7%	61.0%	39.0%
14,760	MARSHALL	6,865	4,029	2,828	8	1,201 R	58.7%	41.2%	58.8%	41.2%
16,634	MASON	7,221	3,956	3,246	19	710 R	54.8%	45.0%	54.9%	45.1%
13,559	MASSAC	4,673	3,405	1,241	27	2,164 R	72.9%	26.6%	73.3%	26.7%
11,694	MENARD	5,025	3,243	1,742	40	1,501 R	64.5%	34.7%	65.1%	34.9%
18,800	MERCER	8,073	5,699	2,316	58	3,383 R	70.6%	28.7%	71.1%	28.9%
12,839	MONROE	5,665	2,721	2,934	10	213 D	48.0%	51.8%	48.1%	51.9%
41,403	MONTGOMERY	16,575	8,999	7,392	184	1,607 R	54.3%	44.6%	54.9%	45.1%
33,567	MORGAN	16,046	10,192	5,805	49	4,387 R	63.5%	36.2%	63.7%	36.3%
14,839	MOULTRIE	5,488	3,310	2,168	10	1,142 R	60.3%	39.5%	60.4%	39.6%
26,830	OGLE	12,546	9,808	2,691	47	7,117 R	78.2%	21.4%	78.5%	21.5%
111,710	PEORIA	54,913	31,024	23,150	739	7,874 R	56.5%	42.2%	57.3%	42.7%
22,901	PERRY	9,766	4,636	5,029	101	393 D	47.5%	51.5%	48.0%	52.0%
15,714	PIATT	6,557	4,565	1,959	33	2,606 R	69.6%	29.9%	70.0%	30.0%
26,866	PIKE	10,836	6,705	4,008	123	2,697 R	61.9%	37.0%	62.6%	37.4%
9,625	POPE	2,706	2,004	679	23	1,325 R	74.1%	25.1%	74.7%	25.3%
14,629	PULASKI	5,092	3,319	1,726	47	1,593 R	65.2%	33.9%	65.8%	34.2%
7,579	PUTNAM	2,270	1,387	869	14	518 R	61.1%	38.3%	61.5%	38.5%
29,109	RANDOLPH	12,093	5,739	6,251	103	512 D	47.5%	51.7%	47.9%	52.1%
14,044	RICHLAND	6,623	4,042	2,550	31	1,492 R	61.0%	38.5%	61.3%	38.7%
92,297	ROCK ISLAND	41,776	27,246	14,334	196	12,912 R	65.2%	34.3%	65.5%	34.5%
136,520	ST. CLAIR	68,037	31,026	36,374	637	5,348 D	45.6%	53.5%	46.0%	54.0%
38,353	SALINE	13,983	7,525	6,337	121	1,188 R	53.8%	45.3%	54.3%	45.7%
100,262	SANGAMON	53,271	31,957	21,026	288	10,931 R	60.0%	39.5%	60.3%	39.7%
13,285	SCHUYLER	5,576	3,011	2,542	23	469 R	54.0%	45.6%	54.2%	45.8%
9,489	SCOTT	4,338	2,601	1,730	7	871 R	60.0%	39.9%	60.1%	39.9%
29,601	SHELBY	11,528	7,214	4,071	243	3,143 R	62.6%	35.3%	63.9%	36.1%
9,693	STARK	4,293	2,966	1,306	21	1,660 R	69.1%	30.4%	69.4%	30.6%
37,743	STEPHENSON	17,643	11,992	5,579	72	6,413 R	68.0%	31.6%	68.2%	31.8%
38,540	TAZEWELL	16,586	9,409	6,910	267	2,499 R	56.7%	41.7%	57.7%	42.3%
20,249	UNION	7,530	3,352	4,149	29	797 D	44.5%	55.1%	44.7%	55.3%
86,162	VERMILION	34,717	21,616	12,728	373	8,888 R	62.3%	36.7%	62.9%	37.1%
14,034	WABASH	6,369	2,373	3,955	41	1,582 D	37.3%	62.1%	37.5%	62.5%
21,488	WARREN	10,753	7,915	2,681	157	5,234 R	73.6%	24.9%	74.7%	25.3%
18,035	WASHINGTON	6,508	3,638	2,848	22	790 R	55.9%	43.8%	56.1%	43.9%
22,772	WAYNE	8,364	5,189	3,108	67	2,081 R	62.0%	37.2%	62.5%	37.5%
20,081	WHITE	7,879	4,177	3,666	36	511 R	53.0%	46.5%	53.3%	46.7%
36,174	WHITESIDE	17,728	13,580	4,079	69	9,501 R	76.6%	23.0%	76.9%	23.1%
92,911	WILL	47,405	26,081	20,877	447	5,204 R	55.0%	44.0%	55.5%	44.5%
61,092	WILLIAMSON	21,309	10,913	10,139	257	774 R	51.2%	47.6%	51.8%	48.2%
90,929	WINNEBAGO	41,372	33,258	7,684	430	25,574 R	80.4%	18.6%	81.2%	18.8%
19,340	WOODFORD	8,524	5,140	3,311	73	1,829 R	60.3%	38.8%	60.8%	39.2%
6,485,280	TOTAL	3,107,489	1,769,141	1,313,817	24,531	455,324 R	56.9%	42.3%	57.4%	42.6%

ILLINOIS

PRESIDENT 1924

1920 Census Population	County	Total Vote	Republican	Democratic	Progressive	Other	Plurality	Percentage Total Vote Rep.	Dem.	Prog.
62,188	ADAMS	24,404	9,985	8,628	5,693	98	1,357 R	40.9%	35.4%	23.3%
23,980	ALEXANDER	7,685	4,465	2,639	573	8	1,826 R	58.1%	34.3%	7.5%
16,045	BOND	6,407	3,644	2,143	585	35	1,501 R	56.9%	33.4%	9.1%
15,322	BOONE	6,464	4,872	348	1,235	9	3,637 R	75.4%	5.4%	19.1%
9,336	BROWN	3,946	1,637	2,149	139	21	512 D	41.5%	54.5%	3.5%
42648	BUREAU	15,663	9,457	1,995	4,169	42	5,288 R	60.4%	12.7%	26.6%
8,245	CALHOUN	2,361	1,136	1,115	100	10	21 R	48.1%	47.2%	4.2%
19345	CARROLL	7,482	4,559	603	2,301	19	2,258 R	60.9%	8.1%	30.8%
17,896	CASS	7,613	3,139	2,909	1,547	18	230 R	41.2%	38.2%	20.3%
56,959	CHAMPAIGN	22,677	14,244	5,221	3,149	63	9,023 R	62.8%	23.0%	13.9%
38,458	CHRISTIAN	16,056	7,398	5,826	2,741	91	1,572 R	46.1%	36.3%	17.1%
21,165	CLARK	9,178	4,731	4,203	211	33	528 R	51.5%	45.8%	2.3%
17,684	CLAY	6,919	3,432	2,987	479	21	445 R	49.6%	43.2%	6.9%
22,947	CLINTON	7,942	2,358	1,693	3,876	15	1,518 P	29.7%	21.3%	48.8%
35,108	COLES	15,194	8,342	5,544	1,275	33	2,798 R	54.9%	36.5%	8.4%
3,053,017	COOK	1,113,652	688,973	226,141	196,149	2,389	462,832 R	61.9%	20.3%	17.6%
22,771	CRAWFORD	9,425	4,830	4,223	364	8	607 R	51.2%	44.8%	3.9%
12,858	CUMBERLAND	5,281	2,698	2,384	190	9	314 R	51.1%	45.1%	3.6%
31,339	DE KALB	13,744	10,500	1,540	1,654	50	8,846 R	76.4%	11.2%	12.0%
19,252	DE WITT	8,802	5,173	2,752	846	31	2,421 R	58.8%	31.3%	9.6%
19,604	DOUGLAS	7,270	4,046	2,315	874	35	1,731 R	55.7%	31.8%	12.0%
42,120	DU PAGE	23,233	16,917	1,893	4,378	45	12,539 R	72.8%	8.1%	18.8%
25,769	EDGAR	12,037	6,297	5,222	500	18	1,075 R	52.3%	43.4%	4.2%
9,431	EDWARDS	3,952	2,750	1,047	140	15	1,703 R	69.6%	26.5%	3.5%
19,556	EFFINGHAM	8,063	3,159	3,814	1,070	20	655 D	39.2%	47.3%	13.3%
26,187	FAYETTE	10,344	5,010	4,668	627	39	342 R	48.4%	45.1%	6.1%
16,466	FORD	6,624	4,672	1,093	849	10	3,579 R	70.5%	16.5%	12.8%
57,293	FRANKLIN	17,121	6,779	5,791	4,304	247	988 R	39.6%	33.8%	25.1%
48,163	FULTON	17,921	8,664	5,011	4,150	96	3,653 R	48.3%	28.0%	23.2%
12,856	GALLATIN	4,576	1,792	2,385	368	31	593 D	39.2%	52.1%	8.0%
22,883	GREENE	8,878	3,527	4,648	687	16	1,121 D	39.7%	52.4%	7.7%
18,580	GRUNDY	6,780	4,337	742	1,681	20	2,656 R	64.0%	10.9%	24.8%
15,920	HAMILTON	6,041	2,659	3,168	200	14	509 D	44.0%	52.4%	3.3%
28,523	HANCOCK	12,885	6,678	5,189	963	55	1,489 R	51.8%	40.3%	7.5%
7,533	HARDIN	2,809	1,378	1,358	70	3	20 R	49.1%	48.3%	2.5%
9,770	HENDERSON	3,951	2,879	803	257	12	2,076 R	72.9%	20.3%	6.5%
45,162	HENRY	18,179	13,159	1,944	3,027	49	10,132 R	72.4%	10.7%	16.7%
34,841	IROQUOIS	11,702	7,498	2,303	1,873	28	5,195 R	64.1%	19.7%	16.0%
37,091	JACKSON	13,030	6,424	4,707	1,845	54	1,717 R	49.3%	36.1%	14.2%
16,064	JASPER	6,397	3,030	3,144	201	22	114 D	47.4%	49.1%	3.1%
28,480	JEFFERSON	12,130	5,406	6,258	436	30	852 D	44.6%	51.6%	3.6%
12,682	JERSEY	5,536	2,460	2,723	335	18	263 D	44.4%	49.2%	6.1%
21,917	JO DAVIESS	9,659	4,864	1,477	3,279	39	1,585 R	50.4%	15.3%	33.9%
12,022	JOHNSON	4,073	2,468	1,408	188	9	1,060 R	60.6%	34.6%	4.6%
99,499	KANE	42,858	32,717	3,517	6,517	107	26,200 R	76.3%	8.2%	15.2%
44,940	KANKAKEE	18,471	12,462	2,488	3,438	83	9,024 R	67.5%	13.5%	18.6%
10,074	KENDALL	4,409	3,513	432	455	9	3,058 R	79.7%	9.8%	10.3%
46,727	KNOX	19,680	12,968	2,617	4,044	51	8,924 R	65.9%	13.3%	20.5%
74,285	LAKE	24,150	18,229	2,008	3,671	242	14,558 R	75.5%	8.3%	15.2%
92,925	LA SALLE	35,417	21,417	6,216	7,686	98	13,731 R	60.5%	17.6%	21.7%
21,380	LAWRENCE	8,945	4,607	4,103	167	68	504 R	51.5%	45.9%	1.9%
28,004	LEE	12,057	8,363	2,367	1,289	38	5,996 R	69.4%	19.6%	10.7%
39,070	LIVINGSTON	15,025	9,695	2,911	2,387	32	6,784 R	64.5%	19.4%	15.9%
29,562	LOGAN	12,356	7,063	3,708	1,537	48	3,355 R	57.2%	30.0%	12.4%
27,074	MCDONOUGH	12,306	7,505	4,016	746	39	3,489 R	61.0%	32.6%	6.1%
33,164	MCHENRY	13,015	8,751	1,372	2,864	28	5,887 R	67.2%	10.5%	22.0%
70,107	MCLEAN	29,582	16,550	6,826	6,132	74	9,724 R	55.9%	23.1%	20.7%
65,175	MACON	27,331	16,458	6,670	4,120	83	9,788 R	60.2%	24.4%	15.1%
57,274	MACOUPIN	21,841	8,571	6,134	6,959	177	1,612 R	39.2%	28.1%	31.9%
106,895	MADISON	41,851	19,926	12,863	8,965	97	7,063 R	47.6%	30.7%	21.4%

ILLINOIS

PRESIDENT 1924

1920 Census Population	County	Total Vote	Republican	Democratic	Progressive	Other	Plurality	Percentage Total Vote Rep.	Dem.	Prog.
37,497	MARION	13,381	5,889	4,768	2,671	53	1,121 R	44.0%	35.6%	20.0%
14,760	MARSHALL	6,465	3,776	1,836	823	30	1,940 R	58.4%	28.4%	12.7%
16,634	MASON	6,680	3,522	2,536	604	18	986 R	52.7%	38.0%	9.0%
13,559	MASSAC	4,517	3,227	920	350	20	2,307 R	71.4%	20.4%	7.7%
11,694	MENARD	5,217	2,931	1,954	319	13	977 R	56.2%	37.5%	6.1%
18,800	MERCER	8,225	5,618	1,699	890	18	3,919 R	68.3%	20.7%	10.8%
12,839	MONROE	4,943	2,390	1,369	1,173	11	1,021 R	48.4%	27.7%	23.7%
41,403	MONTGOMERY	16,975	8,022	5,622	3,225	106	2,400 R	47.3%	33.1%	19.0%
33,567	MORGAN	14,844	8,223	5,721	877	23	2,502 R	55.4%	38.5%	5.9%
14,839	MOULTRIE	5,652	3,001	2,403	225	23	598 R	53.1%	42.5%	4.0%
26,830	OGLE	11,799	8,449	1,591	1,727	32	6,722 R	71.6%	13.5%	14.6%
111,710	PEORIA	43,112	25,243	6,343	11,306	220	13,937 R	58.6%	14.7%	26.2%
22,901	PERRY	9,289	3,693	3,007	2,536	53	686 R	39.8%	32.4%	27.3%
15,714	PIATT	5,907	3,799	1,733	354	21	2,066 R	64.3%	29.3%	6.0%
26,866	PIKE	10,943	4,989	5,424	481	49	435 D	45.6%	49.6%	4.4%
9,625	POPE	3,249	2,161	978	106	4	1,183 R	66.5%	30.1%	3.3%
14,629	PULASKI	5,449	3,355	1,700	390	4	1,655 R	61.6%	31.2%	7.2%
7,579	PUTNAM	2,218	1,364	260	586	8	778 R	61.5%	11.7%	26.4%
29,109	RANDOLPH	10,880	4,527	3,734	2,591	28	793 R	41.6%	34.3%	23.8%
14,044	RICHLAND	6,155	3,082	2,749	295	29	333 R	50.1%	44.7%	4.8%
92,297	ROCK ISLAND	35,647	20,563	3,631	11,320	133	9,243 R	57.7%	10.2%	31.8%
136,520	ST. CLAIR	50,994	23,380	14,921	12,468	225	8,459 R	45.8%	29.3%	24.4%
38,353	SALINE	12,937	6,084	4,037	2,743	73	2,047 R	47.0%	31.2%	21.2%
100,262	SANGAMON	45,446	23,443	12,640	9,054	309	10,803 R	51.6%	27.8%	19.9%
13,285	SCHUYLER	5,906	2,729	2,860	298	19	131 D	46.2%	48.4%	5.0%
9,489	SCOTT	4,411	2,227	1,994	180	10	233 R	50.5%	45.2%	4.1%
29,601	SHELBY	11,646	5,605	5,265	717	59	340 R	48.1%	45.2%	6.2%
9,693	STARK	3,796	2,698	784	310	4	1,914 R	71.1%	20.7%	8.2%
37,743	STEPHENSON	16,216	8,638	2,452	5,088	38	3,550 R	53.3%	15.1%	31.4%
38,540	TAZEWELL	14,370	7,488	3,375	3,470	37	4,018 R	52.1%	23.5%	24.1%
20,249	UNION	6,586	2,579	3,783	216	8	1,204 D	39.2%	57.4%	3.3%
86,162	VERMILION	32,615	17,822	6,424	8,073	296	9,749 R	54.6%	19.7%	24.8%
14,034	WABASH	5,621	2,564	2,442	589	26	122 R	45.6%	43.4%	10.5%
21,488	WARREN	10,623	6,912	2,440	1,225	46	4,472 R	65.1%	23.0%	11.5%
18,035	WASHINGTON	6,103	3,444	1,717	917	25	1,727 R	56.4%	28.1%	15.0%
22,772	WAYNE	9,368	4,937	4,247	164	20	690 R	52.7%	45.3%	1.8%
20,081	WHITE	8,454	3,780	4,377	278	19	597 D	44.7%	51.8%	3.3%
36,174	WHITESIDE	15,576	11,532	1,957	2,057	30	9,475 R	74.0%	12.6%	13.2%
92,911	WILL	35,505	22,780	4,707	7,902	116	14,878 R	64.2%	13.3%	22.3%
61,092	WILLIAMSON	20,689	9,366	6,117	5,114	92	3,249 R	45.3%	29.6%	24.7%
90,929	WINNEBAGO	30,814	21,978	2,228	6,434	174	15,544 R	71.3%	7.2%	20.9%
19,340	WOODFORD	7,464	4,290	1,828	1,326	20	2,462 R	57.5%	24.5%	17.8%
6,485,280	TOTAL	2,470,067	1,453,321	576,975	432,027	7,744	876,346 R	58.8%	23.4%	17.5%

ILLINOIS

PRESIDENT 1920

1920 Census Population	County	Total Vote	Republican	Democratic	Other	Rep.-Dem. Plurality	Percentage Total Vote Rep.	Percentage Total Vote Dem.	Percentage Major Vote Rep.	Percentage Major Vote Dem.
62,188	ADAMS	22,521	12,852	7,222	2,447	5,630 R	57.1%	32.1%	64.0%	36.0%
23,980	ALEXANDER	8,539	5,287	3,167	85	2,120 R	61.9%	37.1%	62.5%	37.5%
16,045	BOND	5,663	3,662	1,533	468	2,129 R	64.7%	27.1%	70.5%	29.5%
15,322	BOONE	6,025	5,386	496	143	4,890 R	89.4%	8.2%	91.6%	8.4%
9,336	BROWN	3,527	1,590	1,866	71	276 D	45.1%	52.9%	46.0%	54.0%
42,648	BUREAU	13,302	9,968	2,354	980	7,614 R	74.9%	17.7%	80.9%	19.1%
8,245	CALHOUN	2,109	1,367	703	39	664 R	64.8%	33.3%	66.0%	34.0%
19,345	CARROLL	5,994	5,194	606	194	4,588 R	86.7%	10.1%	89.6%	10.4%
17,896	CASS	7,318	3,956	2,861	501	1,095 R	54.1%	39.1%	58.0%	42.0%
56,959	CHAMPAIGN	21,681	15,573	5,247	861	10,326 R	71.8%	24.2%	74.8%	25.2%
38,458	CHRISTIAN	14,285	7,535	5,398	1,352	2,137 R	52.7%	37.8%	58.3%	41.7%
21,165	CLARK	9,597	5,312	4,181	104	1,131 R	55.4%	43.6%	56.0%	44.0%
17,684	CLAY	6,149	3,683	2,358	108	1,325 R	59.9%	38.3%	61.0%	39.0%
22,947	CLINTON	7,164	4,564	1,661	939	2,903 R	63.7%	23.2%	73.3%	26.7%
35,108	COLES	14,574	8,563	5,811	200	2,752 R	58.8%	39.9%	59.6%	40.4%
3,053,017	COOK	893,137	635,197	197,499	60,441	437,698 R	71.1%	22.1%	76.3%	23.7%
22,771	CRAWFORD	9,430	5,188	4,092	150	1,096 R	55.0%	43.4%	55.9%	44.1%
12,858	CUMBERLAND	5,320	3,095	2,162	63	933 R	58.2%	40.6%	58.9%	41.1%
31,339	DE KALB	12,361	10,374	1,700	287	8,674 R	83.9%	13.8%	85.9%	14.1%
19,252	DE WITT	8,242	5,001	3,079	162	1,922 R	60.7%	37.4%	61.9%	38.1%
19,604	DOUGLAS	7,491	4,885	2,308	298	2,577 R	65.2%	30.8%	67.9%	32.1%
42,120	DU PAGE	14,976	12,280	2,084	612	10,196 R	82.0%	13.9%	85.5%	14.5%
25,769	EDGAR	12,667	6,750	5,694	223	1,056 R	53.3%	45.0%	54.2%	45.8%
9,431	EDWARDS	3,790	3,002	742	46	2,260 R	79.2%	19.6%	80.2%	19.8%
19,556	EFFINGHAM	7,267	4,176	2,985	106	1,191 R	57.5%	41.1%	58.3%	41.7%
26,187	FAYETTE	9,846	5,758	3,824	264	1,934 R	58.5%	38.8%	60.1%	39.9%
16,466	FORD	6,062	4,995	958	109	4,037 R	82.4%	15.8%	83.9%	16.1%
57,293	FRANKLIN	14,886	7,608	4,894	2,384	2,714 R	51.1%	32.9%	60.9%	39.1%
48,163	FULTON	16,072	9,523	5,293	1,256	4,230 R	59.3%	32.9%	64.3%	35.7%
12,856	GALLATIN	4,373	2,184	2,000	189	184 R	49.9%	45.7%	52.2%	47.8%
22,883	GREENE	7,683	3,685	3,776	222	91 D	48.0%	49.1%	49.4%	50.6%
18,580	GRUNDY	5,805	4,647	803	355	3,844 R	80.1%	13.8%	85.3%	14.7%
15,920	HAMILTON	5,886	3,220	2,591	75	629 R	54.7%	44.0%	55.4%	44.6%
28,523	HANCOCK	12,778	7,379	5,125	274	2,254 R	57.7%	40.1%	59.0%	41.0%
7,533	HARDIN	2,527	1,555	943	29	612 R	61.5%	37.3%	62.2%	37.8%
9,770	HENDERSON	3,584	2,747	740	97	2,007 R	76.6%	20.6%	78.8%	21.2%
45,162	HENRY	15,677	12,379	2,530	768	9,849 R	79.0%	16.1%	83.0%	17.0%
34,841	IROQUOIS	11,809	9,186	2,429	194	6,757 R	77.8%	20.6%	79.1%	20.9%
37,091	JACKSON	13,347	8,003	4,575	769	3,428 R	60.0%	34.3%	63.6%	36.4%
16,064	JASPER	6,351	3,279	2,971	101	308 R	51.6%	46.8%	52.5%	47.5%
28,480	JEFFERSON	10,660	5,711	4,772	177	939 R	53.6%	44.8%	54.5%	45.5%
12,682	JERSEY	4,962	2,873	1,999	90	874 R	57.9%	40.3%	59.0%	41.0%
21,917	JO DAVIESS	7,997	6,098	1,604	295	4,494 R	76.3%	20.1%	79.2%	20.8%
12,022	JOHNSON	4,191	2,972	1,137	82	1,835 R	70.9%	27.1%	72.3%	27.7%
99,499	KANE	32,398	26,832	4,323	1,243	22,509 R	82.8%	13.3%	86.1%	13.9%
44,940	KANKAKEE	16,201	12,853	2,828	520	10,025 R	79.3%	17.5%	82.0%	18.0%
10,074	KENDALL	3,931	3,459	439	33	3,020 R	88.0%	11.2%	88.7%	11.3%
46,727	KNOX	17,005	12,559	2,852	1,594	9,707 R	73.9%	16.8%	81.5%	18.5%
74,285	LAKE	19,096	15,712	2,321	1,063	13,391 R	82.3%	12.2%	87.1%	12.9%
92,925	LA SALLE	32,434	23,751	6,626	2,057	17,125 R	73.2%	20.4%	78.2%	21.8%
21,380	LAWRENCE	8,714	4,720	3,707	287	1,013 R	54.2%	42.5%	56.0%	44.0%
28,004	LEE	9,646	7,615	1,715	316	5,900 R	78.9%	17.8%	81.6%	18.4%
39,070	LIVINGSTON	13,874	10,382	3,101	391	7,281 R	74.8%	22.4%	77.0%	23.0%
29,562	LOGAN	10,738	6,957	3,232	549	3,725 R	64.8%	30.1%	68.3%	31.7%
27,074	MCDONOUGH	11,430	7,221	3,930	279	3,291 R	63.2%	34.4%	64.8%	35.2%
33,164	MCHENRY	11,616	9,885	1,536	195	8,349 R	85.1%	13.2%	86.6%	13.4%
70,107	MCLEAN	25,555	16,680	6,411	2,464	10,269 R	65.3%	25.1%	72.2%	27.8%
65,175	MACON	25,257	16,486	7,917	854	8,569 R	65.3%	31.3%	67.6%	32.4%
57,274	MACOUPIN	19,470	8,700	5,936	4,834	2,764 R	44.7%	30.5%	59.4%	40.6%
106,895	MADISON	33,292	19,249	10,149	3,894	9,100 R	57.8%	30.5%	65.5%	34.5%

ILLINOIS

PRESIDENT 1920

1920 Census Population	County	Total Vote	Republican	Democratic	Other	Rep.-Dem. Plurality	Percentage Total Vote Rep.	Percentage Total Vote Dem.	Percentage Major Vote Rep.	Percentage Major Vote Dem.
37,497	MARION	12,715	6,620	4,351	1,744	2,269 R	52.1%	34.2%	60.3%	39.7%
14,760	MARSHALL	5,523	3,734	1,568	221	2,166 R	67.6%	28.4%	70.4%	29.6%
16,634	MASON	6,579	3,842	2,595	142	1,247 R	58.4%	39.4%	59.7%	40.3%
13,559	MASSAC	4,496	3,731	688	77	3,043 R	83.0%	15.3%	84.4%	15.6%
11,694	MENARD	4,869	2,882	1,864	123	1,018 R	59.2%	38.3%	60.7%	39.3%
18,800	MERCER	7,416	5,531	1,574	311	3,957 R	74.6%	21.2%	77.8%	22.2%
12,839	MONROE	4,215	2,955	932	328	2,023 R	70.1%	22.1%	76.0%	24.0%
41,403	MONTGOMERY	14,039	7,429	4,756	1,854	2,673 R	52.9%	33.9%	61.0%	39.0%
33,567	MORGAN	12,993	8,169	4,447	377	3,722 R	62.9%	34.2%	64.8%	35.2%
14,839	MOULTRIE	5,881	3,279	2,513	89	766 R	55.8%	42.7%	56.6%	43.4%
26,830	OGLE	11,233	9,322	1,720	191	7,602 R	83.0%	15.3%	84.4%	15.6%
111,710	PEORIA	37,182	24,541	9,453	3,188	15,088 R	66.0%	25.4%	72.2%	27.8%
22,901	PERRY	7,864	4,598	2,478	788	2,120 R	58.5%	31.5%	65.0%	35.0%
15,714	PIATT	6,284	4,283	1,903	98	2,380 R	68.2%	30.3%	69.2%	30.8%
26,866	PIKE	10,280	5,564	4,279	437	1,285 R	54.1%	41.6%	56.5%	43.5%
9,625	POPE	3,211	2,486	687	38	1,799 R	77.4%	21.4%	78.3%	21.7%
14,629	PULASKI	6,368	4,002	2,276	90	1,726 R	62.8%	35.7%	63.7%	36.3%
7,579	PUTNAM	2,192	1,623	362	207	1,261 R	74.0%	16.5%	81.8%	18.2%
29,109	RANDOLPH	9,882	6,180	3,181	521	2,999 R	62.5%	32.2%	66.0%	34.0%
14,044	RICHLAND	5,304	3,026	2,174	104	852 R	57.1%	41.0%	58.2%	41.8%
92,297	ROCK ISLAND	30,719	21,908	5,208	3,603	16,700 R	71.3%	17.0%	80.8%	19.2%
136,520	ST. CLAIR	42,231	21,681	14,032	6,518	7,649 R	51.3%	33.2%	60.7%	39.3%
38,353	SALINE	12,692	6,722	3,500	2,470	3,222 R	53.0%	27.6%	65.8%	34.2%
100,262	SANGAMON	36,723	21,820	11,000	3,903	10,820 R	59.4%	30.0%	66.5%	33.5%
13,285	SCHUYLER	5,199	2,800	2,258	141	542 R	53.9%	43.4%	55.4%	44.6%
9,489	SCOTT	3,971	2,075	1,786	110	289 R	52.3%	45.0%	53.7%	46.3%
29,601	SHELBY	11,776	6,351	5,113	312	1,238 R	53.9%	43.4%	55.4%	44.6%
9,693	STARK	3,456	2,750	661	45	2,089 R	79.6%	19.1%	80.6%	19.4%
37,743	STEPHENSON	12,821	9,570	2,772	479	6,798 R	74.6%	21.6%	77.5%	22.5%
38,540	TAZEWELL	12,250	7,679	3,640	931	4,039 R	62.7%	29.7%	67.8%	32.2%
20,249	UNION	6,847	3,119	3,660	68	541 D	45.6%	53.5%	46.0%	54.0%
86,162	VERMILION	29,439	18,175	8,634	2,630	9,541 R	61.7%	29.3%	67.8%	32.2%
14,034	WABASH	5,479	2,871	2,514	94	357 R	52.4%	45.9%	53.3%	46.7%
21,488	WARREN	9,090	6,309	2,236	545	4,073 R	69.4%	24.6%	73.8%	26.2%
18,035	WASHINGTON	6,386	4,519	1,102	765	3,417 R	70.8%	17.3%	80.4%	19.6%
22,772	WAYNE	8,113	4,908	3,137	68	1,771 R	60.5%	38.7%	61.0%	39.0%
20,081	WHITE	8,772	4,494	4,148	130	346 R	51.2%	47.3%	52.0%	48.0%
36,174	WHITESIDE	13,363	10,923	1,927	513	8,996 R	81.7%	14.4%	85.0%	15.0%
92,911	WILL	28,474	21,746	5,410	1,318	16,336 R	76.4%	19.0%	80.1%	19.9%
61,092	WILLIAMSON	17,834	10,118	4,728	2,988	5,390 R	56.7%	26.5%	68.2%	31.8%
90,929	WINNEBAGO	25,134	19,913	3,355	1,866	16,558 R	79.2%	13.3%	85.6%	14.4%
19,340	WOODFORD	7,137	4,929	1,977	231	2,952 R	69.1%	27.7%	71.4%	28.6%
6,485,280	TOTAL	2,094,714	1,420,480	534,395	139,839	886,085 R	67.8%	25.5%	72.7%	27.3%

ILLINOIS

ELECTION NOTES

1956 Other vote was 8,342 Hass (Socialist Labor); 56 scattered write-in.

1952 Other vote was 9,363 Hass (Socialist Labor); 448 scattered write-in.

1948 Other vote was 11,959 Watson (Prohibition); 11,522 Thomas (Socialist); 3,118 Teichert (Socialist Labor); 1,629 scattered write-in.

1944 Other vote was 9,677 Teichert (Socialist Labor); 7,411 Watson (Prohibition); 180 Thomas (Socialist write-in). The statewide total in the other vote column includes the Socialist votes which were not reported by county.

1940 Other vote was 10,914 Thomas (Socialist); 9,190 Babson (Prohibition); 657 scattered write-in.

1936 Other vote was 89,439 Lemke (Union); 7,530 Thomas (Socialist); 3,439 Colvin (Prohibition); 1,921 Aiken (Socialist Labor); 801 Browder (Communist).

1932 Other vote was 67,258 Thomas (Socialist); 15,582 Foster (Communist); 6,388 Upshaw (Prohibition); 3,638 Reynolds (Socialist Labor).

1928 Other vote was 19,138 Thomas (Socialist); 3,581 Foster (Communist); 1,812 Reynolds (Socialist Labor).

1924 A special four-column table which gives the LaFollette (Progressive) vote is used to detail this election. Other vote was 2,622 Foster (Communist); 2,367 Faris (Prohibition); 2,334 Johns (Socialist Labor); 421 Wallace (Commonwealth Land).

1920 Other vote was 74,747 Debs (Socialist); 49,630 Christensen (Farmer-Labor); 11,216 Watkins (Prohibition); 3,471 Cox (Socialist Labor); 775 Macauley (Single Tax).

INDIANA

POPULAR VOTE FOR PRESIDENT 1920 TO 1956

Year	Total Vote	Republican Vote	Republican Candidate	Democratic Vote	Democratic Candidate	Other Vote	Plurality	Percentage Total Vote Rep.	Percentage Total Vote Dem.	Percentage Major Vote Rep.	Percentage Major Vote Dem.
1956	1,974,607	1,182,811	Eisenhower, Dwight D.	783,908	Stevenson, Adlai E.	7,888	398,903 R	59.9%	39.7%	60.1%	39.9%
1952	1,955,049	1,136,259	Eisenhower, Dwight D.	801,530	Stevenson, Adlai E.	17,260	334,729 R	58.1%	41.0%	58.6%	41.4%
1948	1,656,212	821,079	Dewey, Thomas E.	807,831	Truman, Harry S.	27,302	13,248 R	49.6%	48.8%	50.4%	49.6%
1944	1,672,091	875,891	Dewey, Thomas E.	781,403	Roosevelt, Franklin D.	14,797	94,488 R	52.4%	46.7%	52.9%	47.1%
1940	1,782,747	899,466	Willkie, Wendell	874,063	Roosevelt, Franklin D.	9,218	25,403 R	50.5%	49.0%	50.7%	49.3%
1936	1,650,897	691,570	Landon, Alfred M.	934,974	Roosevelt, Franklin D.	24,353	243,404 D	41.9%	56.6%	42.5%	57.5%
1932	1,576,927	677,184	Hoover, Herbert C.	862,054	Roosevelt, Franklin D.	37,689	184,870 D	42.9%	54.7%	44.0%	56.0%
1928	1,421,314	848,290	Hoover, Herbert C.	562,691	Smith, Alfred E.	10,333	285,599 R	59.7%	39.6%	60.1%	39.9%
1924	1,272,390	703,042	Coolidge, Calvin	492,245	Davis, John W.	77,103	210,797 R	55.3%	38.7%	58.8%	41.2%
1920	1,262,974	696,370	Harding, Warren G.	511,364	Cox, James M.	55,240	185,006 R	55.1%	40.5%	57.7%	42.3%

ELECTORAL COLLEGE VOTE 1920 TO 1956

Year	Total	Republican	Democratic	Other
1956	13	13	—	—
1952	13	13	—	—
1948	13	13	—	—
1944	13	13	—	—
1940	14	14	—	—
1936	14	—	14	—
1932	14	—	14	—
1928	15	15	—	—
1924	15	15	—	—
1920	15	15	—	—

INDIANA

ST. JOSEPH
ELKHART
LAGRANGE
STEUBEN
LA PORTE
LAKE
PORTER
NOBLE
DE KALB
MARSHALL
STARKE
KOSCIUSKO
WHITLEY
ALLEN
JASPER
PULASKI
FULTON
NEWTON
WABASH
HUNTINGTON
MIAMI
CASS
WHITE
WELLS
ADAMS
BENTON
CARROLL
GRANT
HOWARD
BLACK-FORD
JAY
WARREN
TIPPECANOE
CLINTON
TIPTON
DELAWARE
RANDOLPH
FOUNTAIN
MADISON
BOONE
HAMILTON
MONTGOMERY
VERMILLION
HENRY
WAYNE
PARKE
HENDRICKS
MARION
HANCOCK
PUTNAM
RUSH
FAYETTE
UNION
SHELBY
MORGAN
JOHNSON
VIGO
CLAY
FRANKLIN
OWEN
DECATUR
BARTHOLOMEW
BROWN
MONROE
SULLIVAN
RIPLEY
DEARBORN
GREENE
JENNINGS
OHIO
JACKSON
LAWRENCE
SWITZER-LAND
JEFFERSON
KNOX
DAVIESS
MARTIN
SCOTT
WASHINGTON
ORANGE
CLARK
GIBSON
PIKE
DUBOIS
FLOYD
CRAWFORD
HARRISON
PERRY
WARRICK
VANDER-BURGH
SPENCER
POSEY

INDIANA

PRESIDENT 1956

1950 Census Population	County	Total Vote	Republican	Democratic	Other	Rep.-Dem. Plurality	Percentage Total Vote Rep.	Total Vote Dem.	Major Vote Rep.	Major Vote Dem.
22,393	ADAMS	10,708	7,079	3,520	109	3,559 R	66.1%	32.9%	66.8%	33.2%
183,722	ALLEN	83,844	58,210	25,444	190	32,766 R	69.4%	30.3%	69.6%	30.4%
36,108	BARTHOLOMEW	20,453	12,227	8,134	92	4,093 R	59.8%	39.8%	60.1%	39.9%
11,462	BENTON	5,974	4,004	1,961	9	2,043 R	67.0%	32.8%	67.1%	32.9%
14,026	BLACKFORD	7,071	3,855	3,152	64	703 R	54.5%	44.6%	55.0%	45.0%
23,993	BOONE	13,926	8,573	5,318	35	3,255 R	61.6%	38.2%	61.7%	38.3%
6,209	BROWN	3,219	1,649	1,555	15	94 R	51.2%	48.3%	51.5%	48.5%
16,010	CARROLL	9,086	5,748	3,312	26	2,436 R	63.3%	36.5%	63.4%	36.6%
38,793	CASS	20,299	12,624	7,594	81	5,030 R	62.2%	37.4%	62.4%	37.6%
48,330	CLARK	24,433	12,483	11,871	79	612 R	51.1%	48.6%	51.3%	48.7%
23,918	CLAY	13,061	7,302	5,720	39	1,582 R	55.9%	43.8%	56.1%	43.9%
29,734	CLINTON	16,032	9,690	6,268	74	3,422 R	60.4%	39.1%	60.7%	39.3%
9,289	CRAWFORD	5,185	2,694	2,433	58	261 R	52.0%	46.9%	52.5%	47.5%
26,762	DAVIESS	13,707	8,608	5,057	42	3,551 R	62.8%	36.9%	63.0%	37.0%
25,141	DEARBORN	12,746	7,189	5,535	22	1,654 R	56.4%	43.4%	56.5%	43.5%
18,218	DECATUR	9,851	6,390	3,427	34	2,963 R	64.9%	34.8%	65.1%	34.9%
26,023	DE KALB	13,575	9,061	4,435	79	4,626 R	66.7%	32.7%	67.1%	32.9%
90,252	DELAWARE	45,827	24,792	20,818	217	3,974 R	54.1%	45.4%	54.4%	45.6%
23,785	DUBOIS	12,139	6,942	5,177	20	1,765 R	57.2%	42.6%	57.3%	42.7%
84,512	ELKHART	40,677	28,088	12,363	226	15,725 R	69.1%	30.4%	69.4%	30.6%
23,391	FAYETTE	11,862	6,673	5,156	33	1,517 R	56.3%	43.5%	56.4%	43.6%
43,955	FLOYD	18,865	10,410	8,378	77	2,032 R	55.2%	44.4%	55.4%	44.6%
17,836	FOUNTAIN	10,230	6,456	3,751	23	2,705 R	63.1%	36.7%	63.3%	36.7%
16,034	FRANKLIN	7,028	4,429	2,573	26	1,856 R	63.0%	36.6%	63.3%	36.7%
16,565	FULTON	9,259	6,258	2,945	56	3,313 R	67.6%	31.8%	68.0%	32.0%
30,720	GIBSON	16,653	9,256	7,318	79	1,938 R	55.6%	43.9%	55.8%	44.2%
62,156	GRANT	27,206	17,548	9,455	203	8,093 R	64.5%	34.8%	65.0%	35.0%
27,886	GREENE	15,969	8,722	7,186	61	1,536 R	54.6%	45.0%	54.8%	45.2%
28,491	HAMILTON	16,271	11,220	4,974	77	6,246 R	69.0%	30.6%	69.3%	30.7%
20,332	HANCOCK	11,617	6,962	4,600	55	2,362 R	59.9%	39.6%	60.2%	39.8%
17,858	HARRISON	9,648	5,299	4,266	83	1,033 R	54.9%	44.2%	55.4%	44.6%
24,594	HENDRICKS	16,129	10,578	5,521	30	5,057 R	65.6%	34.2%	65.7%	34.3%
45,505	HENRY	22,418	13,750	8,502	166	5,248 R	61.3%	37.9%	61.8%	38.2%
54,498	HOWARD	29,581	17,234	12,159	188	5,075 R	58.3%	41.1%	58.6%	41.4%
31,400	HUNTINGTON	17,184	11,024	6,027	133	4,997 R	64.2%	35.1%	64.7%	35.3%
28,237	JACKSON	14,617	8,375	6,185	57	2,190 R	57.3%	42.3%	57.5%	42.5%
17,031	JASPER	7,399	5,374	2,004	21	3,370 R	72.6%	27.1%	72.8%	27.2%
23,157	JAY	11,454	6,767	4,571	116	2,196 R	59.1%	39.9%	59.7%	40.3%
21,613	JEFFERSON	11,004	6,632	4,344	28	2,288 R	60.3%	39.5%	60.4%	39.6%
15,250	JENNINGS	7,414	4,502	2,879	33	1,623 R	60.7%	38.8%	61.0%	39.0%
26,183	JOHNSON	16,291	10,125	6,125	41	4,000 R	62.2%	37.6%	62.3%	37.7%
43,415	KNOX	21,801	13,047	8,691	63	4,356 R	59.8%	39.9%	60.0%	40.0%
33,002	KOSCIUSKO	17,824	12,777	4,904	143	7,873 R	71.7%	27.5%	72.3%	27.7%
15,347	LAGRANGE	5,414	3,815	1,562	37	2,253 R	70.5%	28.9%	71.0%	29.0%
368,152	LAKE	178,460	92,803	85,000	657	7,803 R	52.0%	47.6%	52.2%	47.8%
76,808	LA PORTE	39,142	24,622	14,417	103	10,205 R	62.9%	36.8%	63.1%	36.9%
34,346	LAWRENCE	17,346	11,090	6,197	59	4,893 R	63.9%	35.7%	64.2%	35.8%
103,911	MADISON	55,943	30,329	25,408	206	4,921 R	54.2%	45.4%	54.4%	45.6%
551,777	MARION	262,347	162,566	99,102	679	63,464 R	62.0%	37.8%	62.1%	37.9%
29,468	MARSHALL	15,982	10,504	5,398	80	5,106 R	65.7%	33.8%	66.1%	33.9%
10,678	MARTIN	5,296	2,946	2,343	7	603 R	55.6%	44.2%	55.7%	44.3%
28,201	MIAMI	15,372	9,574	5,724	74	3,850 R	62.3%	37.2%	62.6%	37.4%
50,080	MONROE	21,015	13,223	7,732	60	5,491 R	62.9%	36.8%	63.1%	36.9%
29,122	MONTGOMERY	15,927	10,418	5,443	66	4,975 R	65.4%	34.2%	65.7%	34.3%
23,726	MORGAN	13,103	8,318	4,735	50	3,583 R	63.5%	36.1%	63.7%	36.3%
11,006	NEWTON	5,222	3,890	1,316	16	2,574 R	74.5%	25.2%	74.7%	25.3%
25,075	NOBLE	12,267	8,175	4,028	64	4,147 R	66.6%	32.8%	67.0%	33.0%
4,223	OHIO	2,331	1,237	1,087	7	150 R	53.1%	46.6%	53.2%	46.8%
16,879	ORANGE	9,221	5,751	3,438	32	2,313 R	62.4%	37.3%	62.6%	37.4%
11,763	OWEN	6,301	3,685	2,581	35	1,104 R	58.5%	41.0%	58.8%	41.2%

INDIANA

PRESIDENT 1956

1950 Census Population	County	Total Vote	Republican	Democratic	Other	Rep.-Dem. Plurality	Percentage Total Vote Rep.	Total Vote Dem.	Major Vote Rep.	Major Vote Dem.
15,674	PARKE	8,604	5,080	3,502	22	1,578 R	59.0%	40.7%	59.2%	40.8%
17,367	PERRY	8,993	4,946	4,037	10	909 R	55.0%	44.9%	55.1%	44.9%
14,995	PIKE	8,015	4,596	3,353	66	1,243 R	57.3%	41.8%	57.8%	42.2%
40,076	PORTER	20,589	14,970	5,574	45	9,396 R	72.7%	27.1%	72.9%	27.1%
19,818	POSEY	9,724	5,780	3,919	25	1,861 R	59.4%	40.3%	59.6%	40.4%
12,493	PULASKI	6,633	4,117	2,424	92	1,693 R	62.1%	36.5%	62.9%	37.1%
22,950	PUTNAM	11,280	6,684	4,572	24	2,112 R	59.3%	40.5%	59.4%	40.6%
27,141	RANDOLPH	13,873	9,020	4,701	152	4,319 R	65.0%	33.9%	65.7%	34.3%
18,763	RIPLEY	10,633	6,577	4,026	30	2,551 R	61.9%	37.9%	62.0%	38.0%
19,799	RUSH	9,587	6,202	3,346	39	2,856 R	64.7%	34.9%	65.0%	35.0%
205,058	ST. JOSEPH	112,472	57,827	54,152	493	3,675 R	51.4%	48.1%	51.6%	48.4%
11,519	SCOTT	6,156	3,117	3,011	28	106 R	50.6%	48.9%	50.9%	49.1%
28,026	SHELBY	15,811	9,170	6,561	80	2,609 R	58.0%	41.5%	58.3%	41.7%
16,174	SPENCER	8,960	5,404	3,530	26	1,874 R	60.3%	39.4%	60.5%	39.5%
15,282	STARKE	8,447	5,063	3,349	35	1,714 R	59.9%	39.6%	60.2%	39.8%
17,087	STEUBEN	7,739	5,538	2,171	30	3,367 R	71.6%	28.1%	71.8%	28.2%
23,667	SULLIVAN	11,946	5,829	6,048	69	219 D	48.8%	50.6%	49.1%	50.9%
7,599	SWITZERLAND	4,209	2,074	2,114	21	40 D	49.3%	50.2%	49.5%	50.5%
74,473	TIPPECANOE	33,843	23,776	9,995	72	13,781 R	70.3%	29.5%	70.4%	29.6%
15,566	TIPTON	8,305	4,939	3,320	46	1,619 R	59.5%	40.0%	59.8%	40.2%
6,412	UNION	3,192	2,026	1,157	9	869 R	63.5%	36.2%	63.7%	36.3%
160,422	VANDERBURGH	73,619	42,462	30,860	297	11,602 R	57.7%	41.9%	57.9%	42.1%
19,723	VERMILLION	10,533	5,352	5,149	32	203 R	50.8%	48.9%	51.0%	49.0%
105,160	VIGO	50,068	25,253	24,680	135	573 R	50.4%	49.3%	50.6%	49.4%
29,047	WABASH	14,496	10,318	4,085	93	6,233 R	71.2%	28.2%	71.6%	28.4%
8,535	WARREN	4,406	2,979	1,408	19	1,571 R	67.6%	32.0%	67.9%	32.1%
21,527	WARRICK	10,987	6,286	4,668	33	1,618 R	57.2%	42.5%	57.4%	42.6%
16,520	WASHINGTON	8,739	4,864	3,849	26	1,015 R	55.7%	44.0%	55.8%	44.2%
68,566	WAYNE	32,638	20,157	12,337	144	7,820 R	61.8%	37.8%	62.0%	38.0%
19,564	WELLS	9,778	5,703	3,984	91	1,719 R	58.3%	40.7%	58.9%	41.1%
18,042	WHITE	9,949	6,708	3,219	22	3,489 R	67.4%	32.4%	67.6%	32.4%
18,828	WHITLEY	10,157	6,422	3,688	47	2,734 R	63.2%	36.3%	63.5%	36.5%
3,934,224	TOTAL	1,974,607	1,182,811	783,908	7,888	398,903 R	59.9%	39.7%	60.1%	39.9%

INDIANA

PRESIDENT 1952

1950 Census Population	County	Total Vote	Republican	Democratic	Other	Rep.-Dem. Plurality	Percentage Total Vote Rep.	Percentage Total Vote Dem.	Percentage Major Vote Rep.	Percentage Major Vote Dem.
22,393	ADAMS	10,408	6,204	3,744	460	2,460 R	59.6%	36.0%	62.4%	37.6%
183,722	ALLEN	82,941	54,877	27,506	558	27,371 R	66.2%	33.2%	66.6%	33.4%
36,108	BARTHOLOMEW	19,502	11,462	7,844	196	3,618 R	58.8%	40.2%	59.4%	40.6%
11,462	BENTON	5,957	4,125	1,815	17	2,310 R	69.2%	30.5%	69.4%	30.6%
14,026	BLACKFORD	7,066	3,759	3,144	163	615 R	53.2%	44.5%	54.5%	45.5%
23,993	BOONE	13,673	8,619	4,986	68	3,633 R	63.0%	36.5%	63.4%	36.6%
6,209	BROWN	2,964	1,517	1,414	33	103 R	51.2%	47.7%	51.8%	48.2%
16,010	CARROLL	9,178	5,902	3,208	68	2,694 R	64.3%	35.0%	64.8%	35.2%
38,793	CASS	20,385	12,296	7,982	107	4,314 R	60.3%	39.2%	60.6%	39.4%
48,330	CLARK	23,025	11,190	11,703	132	513 D	48.6%	50.8%	48.9%	51.1%
23,918	CLAY	13,351	7,118	6,078	155	1,040 R	53.3%	45.5%	53.9%	46.1%
29,734	CLINTON	16,724	10,057	6,469	198	3,588 R	60.1%	38.7%	60.9%	39.1%
9,289	CRAWFORD	5,304	2,750	2,457	97	293 R	51.8%	46.3%	52.8%	47.2%
26,762	DAVIESS	13,676	8,328	5,247	101	3,081 R	60.9%	38.4%	61.3%	38.7%
25,141	DEARBORN	12,934	7,091	5,810	33	1,281 R	54.8%	44.9%	55.0%	45.0%
18,218	DECATUR	9,961	6,490	3,393	78	3,097 R	65.2%	34.1%	65.7%	34.3%
26,023	DE KALB	13,476	8,713	4,347	416	4,366 R	64.7%	32.3%	66.7%	33.3%
90,252	DELAWARE	43,590	24,272	18,733	585	5,539 R	55.7%	43.0%	56.4%	43.6%
23,785	DUBOIS	12,227	6,538	5,658	31	880 R	53.5%	46.3%	53.6%	46.4%
84,512	ELKHART	38,108	25,277	12,002	829	13,275 R	66.3%	31.5%	67.8%	32.2%
23,391	FAYETTE	12,270	7,000	5,178	92	1,822 R	57.0%	42.2%	57.5%	42.5%
43,955	FLOYD	22,139	11,608	10,368	163	1,240 R	52.4%	46.8%	52.8%	47.2%
17,836	FOUNTAIN	10,119	6,208	3,871	40	2,337 R	61.3%	38.3%	61.6%	38.4%
16,034	FRANKLIN	7,230	4,630	2,548	52	2,082 R	64.0%	35.2%	64.5%	35.5%
16,565	FULTON	9,175	6,247	2,799	129	3,448 R	68.1%	30.5%	69.1%	30.9%
30,720	GIBSON	16,986	9,171	7,617	198	1,554 R	54.0%	44.8%	54.6%	45.4%
62,156	GRANT	27,923	16,678	10,646	599	6,032 R	59.7%	38.1%	61.0%	39.0%
27,886	GREENE	16,189	8,620	7,417	152	1,203 R	53.2%	45.8%	53.8%	46.2%
28,491	HAMILTON	15,560	10,843	4,564	153	6,279 R	69.7%	29.3%	70.4%	29.6%
20,332	HANCOCK	11,619	6,964	4,539	116	2,425 R	59.9%	39.1%	60.5%	39.5%
17,858	HARRISON	9,454	5,069	4,213	172	856 R	53.6%	44.6%	54.6%	45.4%
24,594	HENDRICKS	14,586	9,712	4,793	81	4,919 R	66.6%	32.9%	67.0%	33.0%
45,505	HENRY	22,882	14,184	8,378	320	5,806 R	62.0%	36.6%	62.9%	37.1%
54,498	HOWARD	28,517	15,212	12,938	367	2,274 R	53.3%	45.4%	54.0%	46.0%
31,400	HUNTINGTON	16,953	10,508	6,114	331	4,394 R	62.0%	36.1%	63.2%	36.8%
28,237	JACKSON	14,630	8,067	6,460	103	1,607 R	55.1%	44.2%	55.5%	44.5%
17,031	JASPER	7,692	5,556	2,102	34	3,454 R	72.2%	27.3%	72.6%	27.4%
23,157	JAY	12,331	7,270	4,764	297	2,506 R	59.0%	38.6%	60.4%	39.6%
21,613	JEFFERSON	10,473	6,169	4,251	53	1,918 R	58.9%	40.6%	59.2%	40.8%
15,250	JENNINGS	7,286	4,460	2,777	49	1,683 R	61.2%	38.1%	61.6%	38.4%
26,183	JOHNSON	15,082	9,119	5,909	54	3,210 R	60.5%	39.2%	60.7%	39.3%
43,415	KNOX	22,316	12,786	9,384	146	3,402 R	57.3%	42.1%	57.7%	42.3%
33,002	KOSCIUSKO	16,710	11,521	4,677	512	6,844 R	68.9%	28.0%	71.1%	28.9%
15,347	LAGRANGE	5,555	3,822	1,604	129	2,218 R	68.8%	28.9%	70.4%	29.6%
368,152	LAKE	165,845	74,073	90,721	1,051	16,648 D	44.7%	54.7%	44.9%	55.1%
76,808	LA PORTE	37,733	22,576	15,011	146	7,565 R	59.8%	39.8%	60.1%	39.9%
34,346	LAWRENCE	17,475	11,296	6,044	135	5,252 R	64.6%	34.6%	65.1%	34.9%
103,911	MADISON	54,374	28,730	25,125	519	3,605 R	52.8%	46.2%	53.3%	46.7%
551,777	MARION	271,939	164,466	106,387	1,086	58,079 R	60.5%	39.1%	60.7%	39.3%
29,468	MARSHALL	15,828	9,990	5,538	300	4,452 R	63.1%	35.0%	64.3%	35.7%
10,678	MARTIN	5,332	2,757	2,546	29	211 R	51.7%	47.7%	52.0%	48.0%
28,201	MIAMI	15,694	9,254	6,264	176	2,990 R	59.0%	39.9%	59.6%	40.4%
50,080	MONROE	19,925	12,072	7,745	108	4,327 R	60.6%	38.9%	60.9%	39.1%
29,122	MONTGOMERY	16,041	10,569	5,386	86	5,183 R	65.9%	33.6%	66.2%	33.8%
23,726	MORGAN	13,072	8,222	4,755	95	3,467 R	62.9%	36.4%	63.4%	36.6%
11,006	NEWTON	5,561	4,159	1,373	29	2,786 R	74.8%	24.7%	75.2%	24.8%
25,075	NOBLE	12,544	8,203	4,151	190	4,052 R	65.4%	33.1%	66.4%	33.6%
4,223	OHIO	2,348	1,219	1,119	10	100 R	51.9%	47.7%	52.1%	47.9%
16,879	ORANGE	8,898	5,551	3,272	75	2,279 R	62.4%	36.8%	62.9%	37.1%
11,763	OWEN	6,361	3,713	2,577	71	1,136 R	58.4%	40.5%	59.0%	41.0%

INDIANA

PRESIDENT 1952

1950 Census Population	County	Total Vote	Republican	Democratic	Other	Rep.-Dem. Plurality	Percentage Total Vote Rep.	Percentage Total Vote Dem.	Percentage Major Vote Rep.	Percentage Major Vote Dem.
15,674	PARKE	8,690	5,069	3,574	47	1,495 R	58.3%	41.1%	58.6%	41.4%
17,367	PERRY	8,832	4,816	4,001	15	815 R	54.5%	45.3%	54.6%	45.4%
14,995	PIKE	7,838	4,253	3,478	107	775 R	54.3%	44.4%	55.0%	45.0%
40,076	PORTER	19,190	13,194	5,909	87	7,285 R	68.8%	30.8%	69.1%	30.9%
19,818	POSEY	9,187	5,293	3,835	59	1,458 R	57.6%	41.7%	58.0%	42.0%
12,493	PULASKI	6,387	4,030	2,244	113	1,786 R	63.1%	35.1%	64.2%	35.8%
22,950	PUTNAM	11,118	6,632	4,446	40	2,186 R	59.7%	40.0%	59.9%	40.1%
27,141	RANDOLPH	13,986	9,150	4,461	375	4,689 R	65.4%	31.9%	67.2%	32.8%
18,763	RIPLEY	10,725	6,650	4,031	44	2,619 R	62.0%	37.6%	62.3%	37.7%
19,799	RUSH	10,353	6,918	3,348	87	3,570 R	66.8%	32.3%	67.4%	32.6%
205,058	ST. JOSEPH	107,632	53,537	53,269	826	268 R	49.7%	49.5%	50.1%	49.9%
11,519	SCOTT	5,959	2,984	2,931	44	53 R	50.1%	49.2%	50.4%	49.6%
28,026	SHELBY	15,671	8,961	6,552	158	2,409 R	57.2%	41.8%	57.8%	42.2%
16,174	SPENCER	8,941	5,497	3,401	43	2,096 R	61.5%	38.0%	61.8%	38.2%
15,282	STARKE	8,196	4,871	3,274	51	1,597 R	59.4%	39.9%	59.8%	40.2%
17,087	STEUBEN	7,288	5,322	1,886	80	3,436 R	73.0%	25.9%	73.8%	26.2%
23,667	SULLIVAN	12,988	5,929	6,964	95	1,035 D	45.6%	53.6%	46.0%	54.0%
7,599	SWITZERLAND	4,275	2,070	2,167	38	97 D	48.4%	50.7%	48.9%	51.1%
74,473	TIPPECANOE	33,246	23,447	9,678	121	13,769 R	70.5%	29.1%	70.8%	29.2%
15,566	TIPTON	8,745	5,299	3,362	84	1,937 R	60.6%	38.4%	61.2%	38.8%
6,412	UNION	3,211	2,159	1,029	23	1,130 R	67.2%	32.0%	67.7%	32.3%
160,422	VANDERBURGH	72,187	42,010	29,718	459	12,292 R	58.2%	41.2%	58.6%	41.4%
19,723	VERMILLION	11,043	5,283	5,708	52	425 D	47.8%	51.7%	48.1%	51.9%
105,160	VIGO	51,878	25,806	25,841	231	35 D	49.7%	49.8%	50.0%	50.0%
29,047	WABASH	14,690	9,980	4,395	315	5,585 R	67.9%	29.9%	69.4%	30.6%
8,535	WARREN	4,548	3,191	1,332	25	1,859 R	70.2%	29.3%	70.6%	29.4%
21,527	WARRICK	10,762	6,064	4,639	59	1,425 R	56.3%	43.1%	56.7%	43.3%
16,520	WASHINGTON	8,745	4,849	3,844	52	1,005 R	55.4%	44.0%	55.8%	44.2%
68,566	WAYNE	32,180	20,068	11,819	293	8,249 R	62.4%	36.7%	62.9%	37.1%
19,564	WELLS	9,633	5,380	3,963	290	1,417 R	55.8%	41.1%	57.6%	42.4%
18,042	WHITE	10,052	6,795	3,211	46	3,584 R	67.6%	31.9%	67.9%	32.1%
18,828	WHITLEY	9,776	5,893	3,755	128	2,138 R	60.3%	38.4%	61.1%	38.9%
3,934,224	TOTAL	1,955,049	1,136,259	801,530	17,260	334,729 R	58.1%	41.0%	58.6%	41.4%

INDIANA

PRESIDENT 1948

1940 Census Population	County	Total Vote	Republican	Democratic	Other	Rep.-Dem. Plurality	Percentage Total Vote Rep.	Total Vote Dem.	Major Vote Rep.	Major Vote Dem.
21,254	ADAMS	9,645	4,832	4,640	173	192 R	50.1%	48.1%	51.0%	49.0%
155,084	ALLEN	69,436	37,494	31,239	703	6,255 R	54.0%	45.0%	54.6%	45.4%
28,276	BARTHOLOMEW	16,012	7,804	7,960	248	156 D	48.7%	49.7%	49.5%	50.5%
11,117	BENTON	5,570	3,224	2,317	29	907 R	57.9%	41.6%	58.2%	41.8%
13,783	BLACKFORD	6,641	2,840	3,611	190	771 D	42.8%	54.4%	44.0%	56.0%
22,081	BOONE	11,586	6,450	5,037	99	1,413 R	55.7%	43.5%	56.2%	43.8%
6,189	BROWN	2,629	1,092	1,459	78	367 D	41.5%	55.5%	42.8%	57.2%
15,410	CARROLL	8,514	4,597	3,845	72	752 R	54.0%	45.2%	54.5%	45.5%
36,908	CASS	19,385	9,105	10,086	194	981 D	47.0%	52.0%	47.4%	52.6%
31,020	CLARK	18,153	7,001	10,953	199	3,952 D	38.6%	60.3%	39.0%	61.0%
25,365	CLAY	11,905	5,654	5,965	286	311 D	47.5%	50.1%	48.7%	51.3%
28,411	CLINTON	14,921	7,762	7,001	158	761 R	52.0%	46.9%	52.6%	47.4%
10,171	CRAWFORD	5,167	2,427	2,625	115	198 D	47.0%	50.8%	48.0%	52.0%
26,163	DAVIESS	13,044	7,030	5,867	147	1,163 R	53.9%	45.0%	54.5%	45.5%
23,053	DEARBORN	11,462	5,353	6,040	69	687 D	46.7%	52.7%	47.0%	53.0%
17,722	DECATUR	9,066	5,163	3,808	95	1,355 R	56.9%	42.0%	57.6%	42.4%
24,756	DE KALB	12,652	6,941	5,439	272	1,502 R	54.9%	43.0%	56.1%	43.9%
74,963	DELAWARE	33,525	15,662	17,060	803	1,398 D	46.7%	50.9%	47.9%	52.1%
22,579	DUBOIS	10,928	4,295	6,564	69	2,269 D	39.3%	60.1%	39.6%	60.4%
72,634	ELKHART	33,517	18,999	13,703	815	5,296 R	56.7%	40.9%	58.1%	41.9%
19,411	FAYETTE	11,338	5,399	5,876	63	477 D	47.6%	51.8%	47.9%	52.1%
35,061	FLOYD	19,121	8,367	10,593	161	2,226 D	43.8%	55.4%	44.1%	55.9%
18,299	FOUNTAIN	9,471	5,186	4,215	70	971 R	54.8%	44.5%	55.2%	44.8%
14,412	FRANKLIN	6,468	3,566	2,860	42	706 R	55.1%	44.2%	55.5%	44.5%
15,577	FULTON	8,398	4,930	3,233	235	1,697 R	58.7%	38.5%	60.4%	39.6%
30,709	GIBSON	15,709	7,431	7,988	290	557 D	47.3%	50.8%	48.2%	51.8%
55,813	GRANT	26,115	13,138	12,212	765	926 R	50.3%	46.8%	51.8%	48.2%
31,330	GREENE	15,463	7,453	7,709	301	256 D	48.2%	49.9%	49.2%	50.8%
24,614	HAMILTON	12,107	7,521	4,384	202	3,137 R	62.1%	36.2%	63.2%	36.8%
17,302	HANCOCK	9,826	4,721	4,948	157	227 D	48.0%	50.4%	48.8%	51.2%
17,106	HARRISON	8,751	4,104	4,465	182	361 D	46.9%	51.0%	47.9%	52.1%
20,151	HENDRICKS	10,682	6,327	4,280	75	2,047 R	59.2%	40.1%	59.6%	40.4%
40,208	HENRY	19,421	10,487	8,523	411	1,964 R	54.0%	43.9%	55.2%	44.8%
47,752	HOWARD	24,362	10,874	12,937	551	2,063 D	44.6%	53.1%	45.7%	54.3%
29,931	HUNTINGTON	15,723	8,178	7,202	343	976 R	52.0%	45.8%	53.2%	46.8%
26,612	JACKSON	13,471	6,062	7,258	151	1,196 D	45.0%	53.9%	45.5%	54.5%
14,397	JASPER	6,603	4,320	2,216	67	2,104 R	65.4%	33.6%	66.1%	33.9%
22,601	JAY	11,442	5,635	5,520	287	115 R	49.2%	48.2%	50.5%	49.5%
19,912	JEFFERSON	9,604	5,166	4,302	136	864 R	53.8%	44.8%	54.6%	45.4%
13,680	JENNINGS	6,636	3,485	3,084	67	401 R	52.5%	46.5%	53.1%	46.9%
22,493	JOHNSON	12,454	6,151	6,216	87	65 D	49.4%	49.9%	49.7%	50.3%
43,973	KNOX	21,182	9,250	11,650	282	2,400 D	43.7%	55.0%	44.3%	55.7%
29,561	KOSCIUSKO	14,855	9,327	5,102	426	4,225 R	62.8%	34.3%	64.6%	35.4%
14,352	LAGRANGE	4,867	3,106	1,628	133	1,478 R	63.8%	33.4%	65.6%	34.4%
293,195	LAKE	132,595	51,413	77,025	4,157	25,612 D	38.8%	58.1%	40.0%	60.0%
63,660	LA PORTE	29,859	15,661	13,923	275	1,738 R	52.4%	46.6%	52.9%	47.1%
35,045	LAWRENCE	14,869	8,643	6,131	95	2,512 R	58.1%	41.2%	58.5%	41.5%
88,575	MADISON	43,948	18,917	24,439	592	5,522 D	43.0%	55.6%	43.6%	56.4%
460,926	MARION	204,013	103,603	97,915	2,495	5,688 R	50.8%	48.0%	51.4%	48.6%
25,935	MARSHALL	13,819	7,873	5,661	285	2,212 R	57.0%	41.0%	58.2%	41.8%
10,300	MARTIN	5,073	2,230	2,788	55	558 D	44.0%	55.0%	44.4%	55.6%
27,926	MIAMI	13,863	7,083	6,538	242	545 R	51.1%	47.2%	52.0%	48.0%
36,534	MONROE	17,532	9,579	7,375	578	2,204 R	54.6%	42.1%	56.5%	43.5%
27,231	MONTGOMERY	13,537	7,890	5,492	155	2,398 R	58.3%	40.6%	59.0%	41.0%
19,801	MORGAN	10,297	5,677	4,428	192	1,249 R	55.1%	43.0%	56.2%	43.8%
10,775	NEWTON	4,845	3,312	1,483	50	1,829 R	68.4%	30.6%	69.1%	30.9%
22,776	NOBLE	11,344	6,503	4,676	165	1,827 R	57.3%	41.2%	58.2%	41.8%
3,782	OHIO	2,215	1,031	1,173	11	142 D	46.5%	53.0%	46.8%	53.2%
17,311	ORANGE	8,021	4,574	3,359	88	1,215 R	57.0%	41.9%	57.7%	42.3%
12,090	OWEN	5,870	3,002	2,738	130	264 R	51.1%	46.6%	52.3%	47.7%

INDIANA

PRESIDENT 1948

1940 Census Population	County	Total Vote	Republican	Democratic	Other	Rep.-Dem. Plurality	Percentage Total Vote Rep.	Percentage Total Vote Dem.	Percentage Major Vote Rep.	Percentage Major Vote Dem.
17,358	PARKE	8,112	4,326	3,681	105	645 R	53.3%	45.4%	54.0%	46.0%
17,770	PERRY	8,354	3,761	4,569	24	808 D	45.0%	54.7%	45.2%	54.8%
17,045	PIKE	7,452	3,696	3,596	160	100 R	49.6%	48.3%	50.7%	49.3%
27,836	PORTER	14,318	8,907	5,161	250	3,746 R	62.2%	36.0%	63.3%	36.7%
19,183	POSEY	8,731	3,879	4,729	123	850 D	44.4%	54.2%	45.1%	54.9%
12,056	PULASKI	5,992	3,039	2,736	217	303 R	50.7%	45.7%	52.6%	47.4%
20,839	PUTNAM	9,963	5,072	4,814	77	258 R	50.9%	48.3%	51.3%	48.7%
26,766	RANDOLPH	12,287	7,122	4,655	510	2,467 R	58.0%	37.9%	60.5%	39.5%
18,898	RIPLEY	9,961	5,313	4,574	74	739 R	53.3%	45.9%	53.7%	46.3%
18,927	RUSH	9,321	5,362	3,814	145	1,548 R	57.5%	40.9%	58.4%	41.6%
161,823	ST. JOSEPH	90,846	39,593	49,866	1,387	10,273 D	43.6%	54.9%	44.3%	55.7%
8,978	SCOTT	5,635	2,429	3,128	78	699 D	43.1%	55.5%	43.7%	56.3%
25,953	SHELBY	13,324	6,068	6,992	264	924 D	45.5%	52.5%	46.5%	53.5%
16,211	SPENCER	8,726	4,496	4,163	67	333 R	51.5%	47.7%	51.9%	48.1%
12,258	STARKE	6,960	3,518	3,312	130	206 R	50.5%	47.6%	51.5%	48.5%
13,740	STEUBEN	6,452	4,341	1,996	115	2,345 R	67.3%	30.9%	68.5%	31.5%
27,014	SULLIVAN	11,801	4,824	6,705	272	1,881 D	40.9%	56.8%	41.8%	58.2%
8,167	SWITZERLAND	4,247	1,839	2,375	33	536 D	43.3%	55.9%	43.6%	56.4%
51,020	TIPPECANOE	28,107	17,034	10,825	248	6,209 R	60.6%	38.5%	61.1%	38.9%
15,135	TIPTON	8,210	4,169	3,925	116	244 R	50.8%	47.8%	51.5%	48.5%
6,017	UNION	2,939	1,859	1,049	31	810 R	63.3%	35.7%	63.9%	36.1%
130,783	VANDERBURGH	60,956	27,584	32,640	732	5,056 D	45.3%	53.5%	45.8%	54.2%
21,787	VERMILLION	10,404	4,685	5,426	293	741 D	45.0%	52.2%	46.3%	53.7%
99,709	VIGO	45,564	19,049	25,906	609	6,857 D	41.8%	56.9%	42.4%	57.6%
26,601	WABASH	13,245	8,149	4,692	404	3,457 R	61.5%	35.4%	63.5%	36.5%
9,055	WARREN	3,869	2,444	1,391	34	1,053 R	63.2%	36.0%	63.7%	36.3%
19,435	WARRICK	9,440	4,602	4,750	88	148 D	48.8%	50.3%	49.2%	50.8%
17,008	WASHINGTON	7,757	3,660	4,033	64	373 D	47.2%	52.0%	47.6%	52.4%
59,229	WAYNE	26,716	15,445	10,749	522	4,696 R	57.8%	40.2%	59.0%	41.0%
19,099	WELLS	9,094	4,288	4,726	80	438 D	47.2%	52.0%	47.6%	52.4%
17,037	WHITE	8,813	4,911	3,849	53	1,062 R	55.7%	43.7%	56.1%	43.9%
17,001	WHITLEY	9,089	4,715	4,240	134	475 R	51.9%	46.6%	52.7%	47.3%
3,427,796	TOTAL	1,656,212	821,079	807,831	27,302	13,248 R	49.6%	48.8%	50.4%	49.6%

INDIANA

PRESIDENT 1944

1940 Census Population	County	Total Vote	Republican	Democratic	Other	Rep.-Dem. Plurality	Percentage Total Vote Rep.	Total Vote Dem.	Major Vote Rep.	Major Vote Dem.
21,254	ADAMS	9,601	5,648	3,804	149	1,844 R	58.8%	39.6%	59.8%	40.2%
155,084	ALLEN	72,709	41,907	30,445	357	11,462 R	57.6%	41.9%	57.9%	42.1%
28,276	BARTHOLOMEW	15,080	7,689	7,139	252	550 R	51.0%	47.3%	51.9%	48.1%
11,117	BENTON	5,713	3,621	2,065	27	1,556 R	63.4%	36.1%	63.7%	36.3%
13,783	BLACKFORD	6,439	3,079	3,207	153	128 D	47.8%	49.8%	49.0%	51.0%
22,081	BOONE	12,185	6,823	5,292	70	1,531 R	56.0%	43.4%	56.3%	43.7%
6,189	BROWN	2,571	1,174	1,352	45	178 D	45.7%	52.6%	46.5%	53.5%
15,410	CARROLL	8,505	4,872	3,578	55	1,294 R	57.3%	42.1%	57.7%	42.3%
36,908	CASS	18,506	9,788	8,615	103	1,173 R	52.9%	46.6%	53.2%	46.8%
31,020	CLARK	17,081	7,241	9,778	62	2,537 D	42.4%	57.2%	42.5%	57.5%
25,365	CLAY	12,553	6,688	5,721	144	967 R	53.3%	45.6%	53.9%	46.1%
28,411	CLINTON	14,605	8,087	6,381	137	1,706 R	55.4%	43.7%	55.9%	44.1%
10,171	CRAWFORD	4,927	2,488	2,335	104	153 R	50.5%	47.4%	51.6%	48.4%
26,163	DAVIESS	13,052	7,458	5,523	71	1,935 R	57.1%	42.3%	57.5%	42.5%
23,053	DEARBORN	10,691	5,487	5,157	47	330 R	51.3%	48.2%	51.6%	48.4%
17,722	DECATUR	9,003	5,479	3,471	53	2,008 R	60.9%	38.6%	61.2%	38.8%
24,756	DE KALB	12,387	7,479	4,810	98	2,669 R	60.4%	38.8%	60.9%	39.1%
74,963	DELAWARE	36,575	17,340	18,780	455	1,440 D	47.4%	51.3%	48.0%	52.0%
22,579	DUBOIS	10,162	4,855	5,273	34	418 D	47.8%	51.9%	47.9%	52.1%
72,634	ELKHART	34,208	20,659	12,991	558	7,668 R	60.4%	38.0%	61.4%	38.6%
19,411	FAYETTE	10,938	5,603	5,299	36	304 R	51.2%	48.4%	51.4%	48.6%
35,061	FLOYD	19,071	8,410	10,541	120	2,131 D	44.1%	55.3%	44.4%	55.6%
18,299	FOUNTAIN	9,625	5,557	4,022	46	1,535 R	57.7%	41.8%	58.0%	42.0%
14,412	FRANKLIN	6,346	3,796	2,530	20	1,266 R	59.8%	39.9%	60.0%	40.0%
15,577	FULTON	8,469	5,190	3,201	78	1,989 R	61.3%	37.8%	61.9%	38.1%
30,709	GIBSON	15,525	7,895	7,462	168	433 R	50.9%	48.1%	51.4%	48.6%
55,813	GRANT	26,379	14,527	11,031	821	3,496 R	55.1%	41.8%	56.8%	43.2%
31,330	GREENE	15,086	8,213	6,744	129	1,469 R	54.4%	44.7%	54.9%	45.1%
24,614	HAMILTON	12,560	8,297	4,101	162	4,196 R	66.1%	32.7%	66.9%	33.1%
17,302	HANCOCK	9,938	5,139	4,652	147	487 R	51.7%	46.8%	52.5%	47.5%
17,106	HARRISON	8,786	4,397	4,285	104	112 R	50.0%	48.8%	50.6%	49.4%
20,151	HENDRICKS	11,039	6,673	4,297	69	2,376 R	60.4%	38.9%	60.8%	39.2%
40,208	HENRY	19,296	10,583	8,297	416	2,286 R	54.8%	43.0%	56.1%	43.9%
47,752	HOWARD	23,265	11,515	11,224	526	291 R	49.5%	48.2%	50.6%	49.4%
29,931	HUNTINGTON	15,166	8,668	6,128	370	2,540 R	57.2%	40.4%	58.6%	41.4%
26,612	JACKSON	12,426	6,321	5,982	123	339 R	50.9%	48.1%	51.4%	48.6%
14,397	JASPER	6,550	4,364	2,168	18	2,196 R	66.6%	33.1%	66.8%	33.2%
22,601	JAY	11,629	6,207	5,166	256	1,041 R	53.4%	44.4%	54.6%	45.4%
19,912	JEFFERSON	10,234	5,748	4,376	110	1,372 R	56.2%	42.8%	56.8%	43.2%
13,680	JENNINGS	6,219	3,643	2,537	39	1,106 R	58.6%	40.8%	58.9%	41.1%
22,493	JOHNSON	11,673	6,194	5,426	53	768 R	53.1%	46.5%	53.3%	46.7%
43,973	KNOX	20,463	10,023	10,297	143	274 D	49.0%	50.3%	49.3%	50.7%
29,561	KOSCIUSKO	14,708	9,577	4,865	266	4,712 R	65.1%	33.1%	66.3%	33.7%
14,352	LAGRANGE	5,095	3,501	1,539	55	1,962 R	68.7%	30.2%	69.5%	30.5%
293,195	LAKE	123,950	48,147	75,066	737	26,919 D	38.8%	60.6%	39.1%	60.9%
63,660	LA PORTE	30,568	16,543	13,896	129	2,647 R	54.1%	45.5%	54.3%	45.7%
35,045	LAWRENCE	14,515	9,200	5,246	69	3,954 R	63.4%	36.1%	63.7%	36.3%
88,575	MADISON	46,383	21,381	24,488	514	3,107 D	46.1%	52.8%	46.6%	53.4%
460,926	MARION	223,837	116,421	106,382	1,034	10,039 R	52.0%	47.5%	52.3%	47.7%
25,935	MARSHALL	13,736	8,225	5,254	257	2,971 R	59.9%	38.2%	61.0%	39.0%
10,300	MARTIN	4,997	2,467	2,515	15	48 D	49.4%	50.3%	49.5%	50.5%
27,926	MIAMI	14,777	8,207	6,379	191	1,828 R	55.5%	43.2%	56.3%	43.7%
36,534	MONROE	16,125	8,993	6,809	323	2,184 R	55.8%	42.2%	56.9%	43.1%
27,231	MONTGOMERY	13,999	8,319	5,620	60	2,699 R	59.4%	40.1%	59.7%	40.3%
19,801	MORGAN	10,348	6,115	4,156	77	1,959 R	59.1%	40.2%	59.5%	40.5%
10,775	NEWTON	5,004	3,398	1,583	23	1,815 R	67.9%	31.6%	68.2%	31.8%
22,776	NOBLE	11,448	7,200	4,174	74	3,026 R	62.9%	36.5%	63.3%	36.7%
3,782	OHIO	2,184	1,126	1,043	15	83 R	51.6%	47.8%	51.9%	48.1%
17,311	ORANGE	7,966	4,784	3,130	52	1,654 R	60.1%	39.3%	60.4%	39.6%
12,090	OWEN	5,975	3,318	2,602	55	716 R	55.5%	43.5%	56.0%	44.0%

INDIANA

PRESIDENT 1944

1940 Census Population	County	Total Vote	Republican	Democratic	Other	Rep.-Dem. Plurality	Percentage Total Vote Rep.	Percentage Total Vote Dem.	Percentage Major Vote Rep.	Percentage Major Vote Dem.
17,358	PARKE	8,048	4,751	3,241	56	1,510 R	59.0%	40.3%	59.4%	40.6%
17,770	PERRY	8,102	4,087	3,996	19	91 R	50.4%	49.3%	50.6%	49.4%
17,045	PIKE	7,886	4,267	3,513	106	754 R	54.1%	44.5%	54.8%	45.2%
27,836	PORTER	14,146	8,561	5,528	57	3,033 R	60.5%	39.1%	60.8%	39.2%
19,183	POSEY	8,619	4,374	4,183	62	191 R	50.7%	48.5%	51.1%	48.9%
12,056	PULASKI	5,826	3,206	2,509	111	697 R	55.0%	43.1%	56.1%	43.9%
20,839	PUTNAM	10,283	5,386	4,857	40	529 R	52.4%	47.2%	52.6%	47.4%
26,766	RANDOLPH	12,758	7,805	4,590	363	3,215 R	61.2%	36.0%	63.0%	37.0%
18,898	RIPLEY	9,544	5,642	3,835	67	1,807 R	59.1%	40.2%	59.5%	40.5%
18,927	RUSH	9,821	5,853	3,891	77	1,962 R	59.6%	39.6%	60.1%	39.9%
161,823	ST. JOSEPH	87,589	39,875	47,149	565	7,274 D	45.5%	53.8%	45.8%	54.2%
8,978	SCOTT	5,054	2,379	2,621	54	242 D	47.1%	51.9%	47.6%	52.4%
25,953	SHELBY	13,733	6,816	6,798	119	18 R	49.6%	49.5%	50.1%	49.9%
16,211	SPENCER	8,686	4,986	3,647	53	1,339 R	57.4%	42.0%	57.8%	42.2%
12,258	STARKE	6,415	3,574	2,791	50	783 R	55.7%	43.5%	56.2%	43.8%
13,740	STEUBEN	6,618	4,739	1,837	42	2,902 R	71.6%	27.8%	72.1%	27.9%
27,014	SULLIVAN	12,397	5,855	6,420	122	565 D	47.2%	51.8%	47.7%	52.3%
8,167	SWITZERLAND	4,267	2,019	2,191	57	172 D	47.3%	51.3%	48.0%	52.0%
51,020	TIPPECANOE	26,212	15,888	10,229	95	5,659 R	60.6%	39.0%	60.8%	39.2%
15,135	TIPTON	7,843	4,296	3,427	120	869 R	54.8%	43.7%	55.6%	44.4%
6,017	UNION	3,169	1,998	1,154	17	844 R	63.0%	36.4%	63.4%	36.6%
130,783	VANDERBURGH	65,462	30,684	34,440	338	3,756 D	46.9%	52.6%	47.1%	52.9%
21,787	VERMILLION	9,963	4,998	4,912	53	86 R	50.2%	49.3%	50.4%	49.6%
99,709	VIGO	46,223	21,493	24,649	81	3,156 D	46.5%	53.3%	46.6%	53.4%
26,601	WABASH	13,415	8,357	4,665	393	3,692 R	62.3%	34.8%	64.2%	35.8%
9,055	WARREN	4,434	2,870	1,555	9	1,315 R	64.7%	35.1%	64.9%	35.1%
19,435	WARRICK	9,166	5,042	4,049	75	993 R	55.0%	44.2%	55.5%	44.5%
17,008	WASHINGTON	8,015	4,033	3,940	42	93 R	50.3%	49.2%	50.6%	49.4%
59,229	WAYNE	28,059	15,295	12,432	332	2,863 R	54.5%	44.3%	55.2%	44.8%
19,099	WELLS	9,410	4,708	4,475	227	233 R	50.0%	47.6%	51.3%	48.7%
17,037	WHITE	8,650	5,039	3,570	41	1,469 R	58.3%	41.3%	58.5%	41.5%
17,001	WHITLEY	9,427	5,268	4,079	80	1,189 R	55.9%	43.3%	56.4%	43.6%
3,427,796	TOTAL	1,672,091	875,891	781,403	14,797	94,488 R	52.4%	46.7%	52.9%	47.1%

INDIANA

PRESIDENT 1940

1940 Census Population	County	Total Vote	Republican	Democratic	Other	Rep.-Dem. Plurality	Percentage Total Vote Rep.	Total Vote Dem.	Major Vote Rep.	Major Vote Dem.
21,254	ADAMS	9,730	5,247	4,382	101	865 R	53.9%	45.0%	54.5%	45.5%
155,084	ALLEN	70,709	40,430	29,967	312	10,463 R	57.2%	42.4%	57.4%	42.6%
28,276	BARTHOLOMEW	16,156	7,890	8,180	86	290 D	48.8%	50.6%	49.1%	50.9%
11,117	BENTON	6,384	3,675	2,689	20	986 R	57.6%	42.1%	57.7%	42.3%
13,783	BLACKFORD	7,530	3,352	4,095	83	743 D	44.5%	54.4%	45.0%	55.0%
22,081	BOONE	13,267	7,066	6,152	49	914 R	53.3%	46.4%	53.5%	46.5%
6,189	BROWN	3,160	1,477	1,662	21	185 D	46.7%	52.6%	47.1%	52.9%
15,410	CARROLL	9,273	5,012	4,214	47	798 R	54.0%	45.4%	54.3%	45.7%
36,908	CASS	20,386	10,057	10,268	61	211 D	49.3%	50.4%	49.5%	50.5%
31,020	CLARK	15,104	6,044	9,015	45	2,971 D	40.0%	59.7%	40.1%	59.9%
25,365	CLAY	15,114	7,768	7,255	91	513 R	51.4%	48.0%	51.7%	48.3%
28,411	CLINTON	16,444	8,610	7,732	102	878 R	52.4%	47.0%	52.7%	47.3%
10,171	CRAWFORD	5,529	2,652	2,836	41	184 D	48.0%	51.3%	48.3%	51.7%
26,163	DAVIESS	14,075	7,615	6,401	59	1,214 R	54.1%	45.5%	54.3%	45.7%
23,053	DEARBORN	11,987	5,908	6,038	41	130 D	49.3%	50.4%	49.5%	50.5%
17,722	DECATUR	10,547	6,087	4,417	43	1,670 R	57.7%	41.9%	57.9%	42.1%
24,756	DE KALB	13,426	7,676	5,690	60	1,986 R	57.2%	42.4%	57.4%	42.6%
74,963	DELAWARE	38,691	17,616	20,836	239	3,220 D	45.5%	53.9%	45.8%	54.2%
22,579	DUBOIS	10,745	4,729	5,992	24	1,263 D	44.0%	55.8%	44.1%	55.9%
72,634	ELKHART	33,716	19,735	13,620	361	6,115 R	58.5%	40.4%	59.2%	40.8%
19,411	FAYETTE	11,147	5,567	5,542	38	25 R	49.9%	49.7%	50.1%	49.9%
35,061	FLOYD	18,944	8,056	10,799	89	2,743 D	42.5%	57.0%	42.7%	57.3%
18,299	FOUNTAIN	10,572	5,771	4,783	18	988 R	54.6%	45.2%	54.7%	45.3%
14,412	FRANKLIN	7,539	4,381	3,142	16	1,239 R	58.1%	41.7%	58.2%	41.8%
15,577	FULTON	9,472	5,532	3,879	61	1,653 R	58.4%	41.0%	58.8%	41.2%
30,709	GIBSON	17,223	8,326	8,709	188	383 D	48.3%	50.6%	48.9%	51.1%
55,813	GRANT	28,779	15,187	13,257	335	1,930 R	52.8%	46.1%	53.4%	46.6%
31,330	GREENE	17,889	9,071	8,718	100	353 R	50.7%	48.7%	51.0%	49.0%
24,614	HAMILTON	13,797	8,931	4,791	75	4,140 R	64.7%	34.7%	65.1%	34.9%
17,302	HANCOCK	10,785	5,283	5,417	85	134 D	49.0%	50.2%	49.4%	50.6%
17,106	HARRISON	9,439	4,650	4,725	64	75 D	49.3%	50.1%	49.6%	50.4%
20,151	HENDRICKS	11,710	6,782	4,883	45	1,899 R	57.9%	41.7%	58.1%	41.9%
40,208	HENRY	20,858	11,051	9,623	184	1,428 R	53.0%	46.1%	53.5%	46.5%
47,752	HOWARD	24,793	11,855	12,655	283	800 D	47.8%	51.0%	48.4%	51.6%
29,931	HUNTINGTON	16,497	9,110	7,220	167	1,890 R	55.2%	43.8%	55.8%	44.2%
26,612	JACKSON	13,917	6,281	7,557	79	1,276 D	45.1%	54.3%	45.4%	54.6%
14,397	JASPER	7,241	4,462	2,751	28	1,711 R	61.6%	38.0%	61.9%	38.1%
22,601	JAY	13,149	6,478	6,554	117	76 D	49.3%	49.8%	49.7%	50.3%
19,912	JEFFERSON	10,676	5,957	4,688	31	1,269 R	55.8%	43.9%	56.0%	44.0%
13,680	JENNINGS	6,939	3,921	2,989	29	932 R	56.5%	43.1%	56.7%	43.3%
22,493	JOHNSON	12,857	6,451	6,350	56	101 R	50.2%	49.4%	50.4%	49.6%
43,973	KNOX	23,590	11,211	12,265	114	1,054 D	47.5%	52.0%	47.8%	52.2%
29,561	KOSCIUSKO	15,760	9,879	5,768	113	4,111 R	62.7%	36.6%	63.1%	36.9%
14,352	LAGRANGE	5,882	3,731	2,124	27	1,607 R	63.4%	36.1%	63.7%	36.3%
293,195	LAKE	118,330	45,898	71,985	447	26,087 D	38.8%	60.8%	38.9%	61.1%
63,660	LA PORTE	29,593	15,771	13,732	90	2,039 R	53.3%	46.4%	53.5%	46.5%
35,045	LAWRENCE	17,308	10,717	6,553	38	4,164 R	61.9%	37.9%	62.1%	37.9%
88,575	MADISON	48,754	22,382	26,111	261	3,729 D	45.9%	53.6%	46.2%	53.8%
460,926	MARION	247,539	124,845	121,907	787	2,938 R	50.4%	49.2%	50.6%	49.4%
25,935	MARSHALL	13,681	7,718	5,852	111	1,866 R	56.4%	42.8%	56.9%	43.1%
10,300	MARTIN	5,551	2,902	2,638	11	264 R	52.3%	47.5%	52.4%	47.6%
27,926	MIAMI	15,575	8,217	7,252	106	965 R	52.8%	46.6%	53.1%	46.9%
36,534	MONROE	18,499	10,311	8,117	71	2,194 R	55.7%	43.9%	56.0%	44.0%
27,231	MONTGOMERY	15,616	8,554	6,994	68	1,560 R	54.8%	44.8%	55.0%	45.0%
19,801	MORGAN	11,544	6,613	4,895	36	1,718 R	57.3%	42.4%	57.5%	42.5%
10,775	NEWTON	5,674	3,536	2,116	22	1,420 R	62.3%	37.3%	62.6%	37.4%
22,776	NOBLE	12,517	7,443	5,014	60	2,429 R	59.5%	40.1%	59.7%	40.3%
3,782	OHIO	2,404	1,186	1,210	8	24 D	49.3%	50.3%	49.5%	50.5%
17,311	ORANGE	9,553	5,519	4,003	31	1,516 R	57.8%	41.9%	58.0%	42.0%
12,090	OWEN	6,868	3,709	3,121	38	588 R	54.0%	45.4%	54.3%	45.7%

INDIANA

PRESIDENT 1940

1940 Census Population	County	Total Vote	Republican	Democratic	Other	Rep.-Dem. Plurality	Percentage Total Vote Rep.	Total Vote Dem.	Major Vote Rep.	Major Vote Dem.
17,358	PARKE	9,683	5,242	4,384	57	858 R	54.1%	45.3%	54.5%	45.5%
17,770	PERRY	8,978	4,489	4,475	14	14 R	50.0%	49.8%	50.1%	49.9%
17,045	PIKE	9,177	4,672	4,449	56	223 R	50.9%	48.5%	51.2%	48.8%
27,836	PORTER	14,161	8,270	5,840	51	2,430 R	58.4%	41.2%	58.6%	41.4%
19,183	POSEY	9,593	4,514	5,022	57	508 D	47.1%	52.4%	47.3%	52.7%
12,056	PULASKI	6,588	3,472	3,021	95	451 R	52.7%	45.9%	53.5%	46.5%
20,839	PUTNAM	11,901	5,832	6,020	49	188 D	49.0%	50.6%	49.2%	50.8%
26,766	RANDOLPH	14,046	8,033	5,787	226	2,246 R	57.2%	41.2%	58.1%	41.9%
18,898	RIPLEY	10,933	6,061	4,834	38	1,227 R	55.4%	44.2%	55.6%	44.4%
18,927	RUSH	10,807	6,486	4,282	39	2,204 R	60.0%	39.6%	60.2%	39.8%
161,823	ST. JOSEPH	82,158	36,164	45,620	374	9,456 D	44.0%	55.5%	44.2%	55.8%
8,978	SCOTT	4,972	2,285	2,668	19	383 D	46.0%	53.7%	46.1%	53.9%
25,953	SHELBY	15,348	7,216	8,015	117	799 D	47.0%	52.2%	47.4%	52.6%
16,211	SPENCER	9,889	5,667	4,180	42	1,487 R	57.3%	42.3%	57.6%	42.4%
12,258	STARKE	6,412	3,473	2,917	22	556 R	54.2%	45.5%	54.4%	45.6%
13,740	STEUBEN	7,620	5,056	2,524	40	2,532 R	66.4%	33.1%	66.7%	33.3%
27,014	SULLIVAN	15,289	6,471	8,667	151	2,196 D	42.3%	56.7%	42.7%	57.3%
8,167	SWITZERLAND	4,966	2,285	2,659	22	374 D	46.0%	53.5%	46.2%	53.8%
51,020	TIPPECANOE	28,350	16,148	12,129	73	4,019 R	57.0%	42.8%	57.1%	42.9%
15,135	TIPTON	8,978	4,749	4,173	56	576 R	52.9%	46.5%	53.2%	46.8%
6,017	UNION	3,443	2,009	1,415	19	594 R	58.4%	41.1%	58.7%	41.3%
130,783	VANDERBURGH	67,267	28,417	38,567	283	10,150 D	42.2%	57.3%	42.4%	57.6%
21,787	VERMILLION	11,973	5,716	6,174	83	458 D	47.7%	51.6%	48.1%	51.9%
99,709	VIGO	52,684	23,177	29,308	199	6,131 D	44.0%	55.6%	44.2%	55.8%
26,601	WABASH	14,327	8,755	5,431	141	3,324 R	61.1%	37.9%	61.7%	38.3%
9,055	WARREN	4,940	2,999	1,927	14	1,072 R	60.7%	39.0%	60.9%	39.1%
19,435	WARRICK	10,517	5,456	5,019	42	437 R	51.9%	47.7%	52.1%	47.9%
17,008	WASHINGTON	8,716	4,216	4,471	29	255 D	48.4%	51.3%	48.5%	51.5%
59,229	WAYNE	29,370	15,058	14,139	173	919 R	51.3%	48.1%	51.6%	48.4%
19,099	WELLS	10,257	4,898	5,236	123	338 D	47.8%	51.0%	48.3%	51.7%
17,037	WHITE	9,409	5,189	4,176	44	1,013 R	55.1%	44.4%	55.4%	44.6%
17,001	WHITLEY	9,561	5,100	4,404	57	696 R	53.3%	46.1%	53.7%	46.3%
3,427,796	TOTAL	1,782,747	899,466	874,063	9,218	25,403 R	50.5%	49.0%	50.7%	49.3%

INDIANA

PRESIDENT 1936

1930 Census Population	County	Total Vote	Republican	Democratic	Other	Rep.-Dem. Plurality	Percentage Total Vote Rep.	Total Vote Dem.	Major Vote Rep.	Major Vote Dem.
19,957	ADAMS	9,208	3,249	5,822	137	2,573 D	35.3%	63.2%	35.8%	64.2%
146,743	ALLEN	66,146	24,765	39,151	2,230	14,386 D	37.4%	59.2%	38.7%	61.3%
24,864	BARTHOLOMEW	15,107	6,484	8,536	87	2,052 D	42.9%	56.5%	43.2%	56.8%
11,886	BENTON	6,331	2,989	3,211	131	222 D	47.2%	50.7%	48.2%	51.8%
13,617	BLACKFORD	7,145	2,845	4,217	83	1,372 D	39.8%	59.0%	40.3%	59.7%
22,290	BOONE	12,593	5,739	6,775	79	1,036 D	45.6%	53.8%	45.9%	54.1%
5,168	BROWN	2,844	1,244	1,585	15	341 D	43.7%	55.7%	44.0%	56.0%
15,049	CARROLL	9,167	4,426	4,676	65	250 D	48.3%	51.0%	48.6%	51.4%
34,518	CASS	19,422	8,528	10,475	419	1,947 D	43.9%	53.9%	44.9%	55.1%
30,764	CLARK	15,896	5,536	10,116	244	4,580 D	34.8%	63.6%	35.4%	64.6%
26,479	CLAY	14,683	6,335	8,235	113	1,900 D	43.1%	56.1%	43.5%	56.5%
27,329	CLINTON	15,730	7,265	8,340	125	1,075 D	46.2%	53.0%	46.6%	53.4%
10,160	CRAWFORD	5,519	2,589	2,919	11	330 D	46.9%	52.9%	47.0%	53.0%
25,832	DAVIESS	13,470	6,459	6,848	163	389 D	48.0%	50.8%	48.5%	51.5%
21,056	DEARBORN	11,256	4,669	6,366	221	1,697 D	41.5%	56.6%	42.3%	57.7%
17,308	DECATUR	10,107	5,126	4,887	94	239 R	50.7%	48.4%	51.2%	48.8%
24,911	DE KALB	13,027	5,848	6,970	209	1,122 D	44.9%	53.5%	45.6%	54.4%
67,270	DELAWARE	33,527	14,207	19,048	272	4,841 D	42.4%	56.8%	42.7%	57.3%
20,553	DUBOIS	10,359	3,011	6,927	421	3,916 D	29.1%	66.9%	30.3%	69.7%
68,875	ELKHART	30,371	14,896	14,473	1,002	423 R	49.0%	47.7%	50.7%	49.3%
19,243	FAYETTE	10,922	5,067	5,756	99	689 D	46.4%	52.7%	46.8%	53.2%
34,655	FLOYD	18,121	6,976	10,654	491	3,678 D	38.5%	58.8%	39.6%	60.4%
17,971	FOUNTAIN	10,316	4,663	5,617	36	954 D	45.2%	54.4%	45.4%	54.6%
14,498	FRANKLIN	7,164	2,952	3,891	321	939 D	41.2%	54.3%	43.1%	56.9%
15,038	FULTON	9,004	4,541	4,322	141	219 R	50.4%	48.0%	51.2%	48.8%
29,202	GIBSON	16,710	7,078	9,392	240	2,314 D	42.4%	56.2%	43.0%	57.0%
51,066	GRANT	26,260	11,774	13,655	831	1,881 D	44.8%	52.0%	46.3%	53.7%
31,481	GREENE	17,344	7,460	9,730	154	2,270 D	43.0%	56.1%	43.4%	56.6%
23,444	HAMILTON	12,870	7,323	5,396	151	1,927 R	56.9%	41.9%	57.6%	42.4%
16,605	HANCOCK	10,180	4,174	5,962	44	1,788 D	41.0%	58.6%	41.2%	58.8%
17,254	HARRISON	8,986	3,885	5,025	76	1,140 D	43.2%	55.9%	43.6%	56.4%
19,725	HENDRICKS	11,097	5,776	5,237	84	539 R	52.1%	47.2%	52.4%	47.6%
35,238	HENRY	19,420	9,099	10,172	149	1,073 D	46.9%	52.4%	47.2%	52.8%
46,696	HOWARD	22,346	9,534	12,288	524	2,754 D	42.7%	55.0%	43.7%	56.3%
29,073	HUNTINGTON	15,697	7,024	8,361	312	1,337 D	44.7%	53.3%	45.7%	54.3%
23,731	JACKSON	13,037	4,951	8,018	68	3,067 D	38.0%	61.5%	38.2%	61.8%
13,388	JASPER	6,721	3,540	3,109	72	431 R	52.7%	46.3%	53.2%	46.8%
20,846	JAY	11,967	5,233	6,535	199	1,302 D	43.7%	54.6%	44.5%	55.5%
19,182	JEFFERSON	10,207	5,320	4,805	82	515 R	52.1%	47.1%	52.5%	47.5%
11,800	JENNINGS	6,823	3,594	3,157	72	437 R	52.7%	46.3%	53.2%	46.8%
21,706	JOHNSON	12,329	5,315	6,934	80	1,619 D	43.1%	56.2%	43.4%	56.6%
43,813	KNOX	22,400	8,589	13,669	142	5,080 D	38.3%	61.0%	38.6%	61.4%
27,488	KOSCIUSKO	15,179	8,182	6,890	107	1,292 R	53.9%	45.4%	54.3%	45.7%
13,780	LAGRANGE	6,042	3,125	2,821	96	304 R	51.7%	46.7%	52.6%	47.4%
261,310	LAKE	103,750	33,689	68,551	1,510	34,862 D	32.5%	66.1%	33.0%	67.0%
60,490	LA PORTE	27,392	11,722	15,359	311	3,637 D	42.8%	56.1%	43.3%	56.7%
35,583	LAWRENCE	18,178	9,982	8,062	134	1,920 R	54.9%	44.4%	55.3%	44.7%
82,888	MADISON	44,495	16,644	27,347	504	10,703 D	37.4%	61.5%	37.8%	62.2%
422,666	MARION	216,550	87,798	124,961	3,791	37,163 D	40.5%	57.7%	41.3%	58.7%
25,077	MARSHALL	12,971	6,118	6,651	202	533 D	47.2%	51.3%	47.9%	52.1%
10,103	MARTIN	5,546	2,583	2,923	40	340 D	46.6%	52.7%	46.9%	53.1%
29,032	MIAMI	15,122	6,747	8,173	202	1,426 D	44.6%	54.0%	45.2%	54.8%
35,974	MONROE	18,110	8,842	9,220	48	378 D	48.8%	50.9%	49.0%	51.0%
26,980	MONTGOMERY	15,549	7,369	8,053	127	684 D	47.4%	51.8%	47.8%	52.2%
19,424	MORGAN	11,328	5,793	5,451	84	342 R	51.1%	48.1%	51.5%	48.5%
9,841	NEWTON	5,408	2,937	2,430	41	507 R	54.3%	44.9%	54.7%	45.3%
22,404	NOBLE	11,936	5,760	5,990	186	230 D	48.3%	50.2%	49.0%	51.0%
3,747	OHIO	2,384	1,022	1,362		340 D	42.9%	57.1%	42.9%	57.1%
17,459	ORANGE	9,692	5,106	4,549	37	557 R	52.7%	46.9%	52.9%	47.1%
11,351	OWEN	6,648	3,091	3,498	59	407 D	46.5%	52.6%	46.9%	53.1%

INDIANA

PRESIDENT 1936

1930 Census Population	County	Total Vote	Republican	Democratic	Other	Rep.-Dem. Plurality	Percentage Total Vote Rep.	Percentage Total Vote Dem.	Percentage Major Vote Rep.	Percentage Major Vote Dem.
16,561	PARKE	9,542	4,665	4,811	66	146 D	48.9%	50.4%	49.2%	50.8%
16,625	PERRY	8,619	3,619	4,752	248	1,133 D	42.0%	55.1%	43.2%	56.8%
16,361	PIKE	8,882	3,885	4,952	45	1,067 D	43.7%	55.8%	44.0%	56.0%
22,821	PORTER	11,936	6,278	5,560	98	718 R	52.6%	46.6%	53.0%	47.0%
17,853	POSEY	8,888	3,088	5,630	170	2,542 D	34.7%	63.3%	35.4%	64.6%
11,195	PULASKI	6,120	2,780	3,274	66	494 D	45.4%	53.5%	45.9%	54.1%
20,448	PUTNAM	11,207	4,961	6,177	69	1,216 D	44.3%	55.1%	44.5%	55.5%
24,859	RANDOLPH	13,283	6,682	6,487	114	195 R	50.3%	48.8%	50.7%	49.3%
18,078	RIPLEY	10,698	4,919	5,546	233	627 D	46.0%	51.8%	47.0%	53.0%
19,412	RUSH	11,500	5,457	5,999	44	542 D	47.5%	52.2%	47.6%	52.4%
160,033	ST. JOSEPH	70,339	25,807	43,131	1,401	17,324 D	36.7%	61.3%	37.4%	62.6%
6,664	SCOTT	4,746	2,034	2,696	16	662 D	42.9%	56.8%	43.0%	57.0%
26,552	SHELBY	14,717	6,026	8,552	139	2,526 D	40.9%	58.1%	41.3%	58.7%
16,713	SPENCER	9,676	4,567	4,966	143	399 D	47.2%	51.3%	47.9%	52.1%
10,620	STARKE	6,032	2,846	3,143	43	297 D	47.2%	52.1%	47.5%	52.5%
13,386	STEUBEN	7,545	3,998	3,402	145	596 R	53.0%	45.1%	54.0%	46.0%
28,133	SULLIVAN	15,154	4,685	10,203	266	5,518 D	30.9%	67.3%	31.5%	68.5%
8,432	SWITZERLAND	5,066	2,212	2,840	14	628 D	43.7%	56.1%	43.8%	56.2%
47,535	TIPPECANOE	26,122	13,081	12,732	309	349 R	50.1%	48.7%	50.7%	49.3%
15,208	TIPTON	8,739	3,842	4,796	101	954 D	44.0%	54.9%	44.5%	55.5%
5,880	UNION	3,313	1,630	1,662	21	32 D	49.2%	50.2%	49.5%	50.5%
113,320	VANDERBURGH	57,085	14,725	41,490	870	26,765 D	25.8%	72.7%	26.2%	73.8%
23,238	VERMILLION	11,635	4,320	7,188	127	2,868 D	37.1%	61.8%	37.5%	62.5%
98,861	VIGO	50,738	17,278	33,018	442	15,740 D	34.1%	65.1%	34.4%	65.6%
25,170	WABASH	13,623	7,223	6,200	200	1,023 R	53.0%	45.5%	53.8%	46.2%
9,167	WARREN	5,045	2,780	2,242	23	538 R	55.1%	44.4%	55.4%	44.6%
18,230	WARRICK	9,429	3,968	5,343	118	1,375 D	42.1%	56.7%	42.6%	57.4%
16,285	WASHINGTON	8,482	3,690	4,766	26	1,076 D	43.5%	56.2%	43.6%	56.4%
54,809	WAYNE	26,373	12,126	13,696	551	1,570 D	46.0%	51.9%	47.0%	53.0%
18,411	WELLS	9,854	3,606	6,189	59	2,583 D	36.6%	62.8%	36.8%	63.2%
15,831	WHITE	9,250	4,245	4,863	142	618 D	45.9%	52.6%	46.6%	53.4%
15,931	WHITLEY	9,150	3,959	5,115	76	1,156 D	43.3%	55.9%	43.6%	56.4%
3,238,503	TOTAL	1,650,897	691,570	934,974	24,353	243,404 D	41.9%	56.6%	42.5%	57.5%

INDIANA

PRESIDENT 1932

1930 Census Population	County	Total Vote	Republican	Democratic	Other	Rep.-Dem. Plurality	Percentage Total Vote Rep.	Total Vote Dem.	Major Vote Rep.	Major Vote Dem.
19,957	ADAMS	8,913	2,910	5,892	111	2,982 D	32.6%	66.1%	33.1%	66.9%
146,743	ALLEN	66,562	27,065	38,447	1,050	11,382 D	40.7%	57.8%	41.3%	58.7%
24,864	BARTHOLOMEW	13,938	6,015	7,533	390	1,518 D	43.2%	54.0%	44.4%	55.6%
11,886	BENTON	5,983	2,433	3,496	54	1,063 D	40.7%	58.4%	41.0%	59.0%
13,617	BLACKFORD	7,130	2,890	4,088	152	1,198 D	40.5%	57.3%	41.4%	58.6%
22,290	BOONE	12,440	5,309	6,900	231	1,591 D	42.7%	55.5%	43.5%	56.5%
5,168	BROWN	2,527	790	1,676	61	886 D	31.3%	66.3%	32.0%	68.0%
15,049	CARROLL	8,799	3,853	4,866	80	1,013 D	43.8%	55.3%	44.2%	55.8%
34,518	CASS	19,248	7,980	10,987	281	3,007 D	41.5%	57.1%	42.1%	57.9%
30,764	CLARK	15,522	5,881	9,501	140	3,620 D	37.9%	61.2%	38.2%	61.8%
26,479	CLAY	13,818	5,343	8,151	324	2,808 D	38.7%	59.0%	39.6%	60.4%
27,329	CLINTON	14,776	6,288	8,314	174	2,026 D	42.6%	56.3%	43.1%	56.9%
10,160	CRAWFORD	5,528	2,175	3,272	81	1,097 D	39.3%	59.2%	39.9%	60.1%
25,832	DAVIESS	12,889	5,838	6,772	279	934 D	45.3%	52.5%	46.3%	53.7%
21,056	DEARBORN	11,275	4,716	6,429	130	1,713 D	41.8%	57.0%	42.3%	57.7%
17,308	DECATUR	10,198	4,646	5,437	115	791 D	45.6%	53.3%	46.1%	53.9%
24,911	DE KALB	12,981	5,590	7,235	156	1,645 D	43.1%	55.7%	43.6%	56.4%
67,270	DELAWARE	31,245	16,012	14,346	887	1,666 R	51.2%	45.9%	52.7%	47.3%
20,553	DUBOIS	9,996	2,357	7,547	92	5,190 D	23.6%	75.5%	23.8%	76.2%
68,875	ELKHART	29,566	13,826	14,885	855	1,059 D	46.8%	50.3%	48.2%	51.8%
19,243	FAYETTE	10,154	4,867	5,148	139	281 D	47.9%	50.7%	48.6%	51.4%
34,655	FLOYD	18,153	7,333	10,497	323	3,164 D	40.4%	57.8%	41.1%	58.9%
17,971	FOUNTAIN	9,950	4,162	5,665	123	1,503 D	41.8%	56.9%	42.4%	57.6%
14,498	FRANKLIN	7,459	2,687	4,704	68	2,017 D	36.0%	63.1%	36.4%	63.6%
15,038	FULTON	8,722	3,787	4,794	141	1,007 D	43.4%	55.0%	44.1%	55.9%
29,202	GIBSON	15,863	6,237	9,162	464	2,925 D	39.3%	57.8%	40.5%	59.5%
51,066	GRANT	25,961	11,398	13,390	1,173	1,992 D	43.9%	51.6%	46.0%	54.0%
31,481	GREENE	15,933	6,397	8,845	691	2,448 D	40.1%	55.5%	42.0%	58.0%
23,444	HAMILTON	13,376	7,100	5,999	277	1,101 R	53.1%	44.8%	54.2%	45.8%
16,605	HANCOCK	10,081	4,055	5,836	190	1,781 D	40.2%	57.9%	41.0%	59.0%
17,254	HARRISON	8,804	3,553	5,128	123	1,575 D	40.4%	58.2%	40.9%	59.1%
19,725	HENDRICKS	10,817	5,317	5,293	207	24 R	49.2%	48.9%	50.1%	49.9%
35,238	HENRY	17,319	8,430	8,255	634	175 R	48.7%	47.7%	50.5%	49.5%
46,696	HOWARD	20,744	9,257	10,541	946	1,284 D	44.6%	50.8%	46.8%	53.2%
29,073	HUNTINGTON	15,821	6,791	8,697	333	1,906 D	42.9%	55.0%	43.8%	56.2%
23,731	JACKSON	12,086	3,996	7,882	208	3,886 D	33.1%	65.2%	33.6%	66.4%
13,388	JASPER	6,504	2,897	3,538	69	641 D	44.5%	54.4%	45.0%	55.0%
20,846	JAY	11,711	5,018	6,693		1,675 D	42.8%	57.2%	42.8%	57.2%
19,182	JEFFERSON	10,164	4,670	5,305	189	635 D	45.9%	52.2%	46.8%	53.2%
11,800	JENNINGS	6,717	3,020	3,603	94	583 D	45.0%	53.6%	45.6%	54.4%
21,706	JOHNSON	11,718	4,593	6,940	185	2,347 D	39.2%	59.2%	39.8%	60.2%
43,813	KNOX	21,140	6,590	14,084	466	7,494 D	31.2%	66.6%	31.9%	68.1%
27,488	KOSCIUSKO	14,791	7,063	7,475	253	412 D	47.8%	50.5%	48.6%	51.4%
13,780	LAGRANGE	5,820	2,461	3,261	98	800 D	42.3%	56.0%	43.0%	57.0%
261,310	LAKE	91,492	42,596	46,060	2,836	3,464 D	46.6%	50.3%	48.0%	52.0%
60,490	LA PORTE	25,995	10,739	14,890	366	4,151 D	41.3%	57.3%	41.9%	58.1%
35,583	LAWRENCE	16,741	8,314	8,215	212	99 R	49.7%	49.1%	50.3%	49.7%
82,888	MADISON	41,860	18,803	22,069	988	3,266 D	44.9%	52.7%	46.0%	54.0%
422,666	MARION	212,664	98,256	106,661	7,747	8,405 D	46.2%	50.2%	47.9%	52.1%
25,077	MARSHALL	12,407	4,943	7,212	252	2,269 D	39.8%	58.1%	40.7%	59.3%
10,103	MARTIN	5,225	2,106	3,072	47	966 D	40.3%	58.8%	40.7%	59.3%
29,032	MIAMI	15,191	5,987	8,892	312	2,905 D	39.4%	58.5%	40.2%	59.8%
35,974	MONROE	16,497	7,759	8,478	260	719 D	47.0%	51.4%	47.8%	52.2%
26,980	MONTGOMERY	14,704	6,417	8,077	210	1,660 D	43.6%	54.9%	44.3%	55.7%
19,424	MORGAN	10,795	4,825	5,775	195	950 D	44.7%	53.5%	45.5%	54.5%
9,841	NEWTON	5,102	2,380	2,654	68	274 D	46.6%	52.0%	47.3%	52.7%
22,404	NOBLE	11,968	5,304	6,538	126	1,234 D	44.3%	54.6%	44.8%	55.2%
3,747	OHIO	2,305	997	1,288	20	291 D	43.3%	55.9%	43.6%	56.4%
17,459	ORANGE	9,487	4,561	4,844	82	283 D	48.1%	51.1%	48.5%	51.5%
11,351	OWEN	6,236	2,423	3,639	174	1,216 D	38.9%	58.4%	40.0%	60.0%

INDIANA

PRESIDENT 1932

1930 Census Population	County	Total Vote	Republican	Democratic	Other	Rep.-Dem. Plurality	Percentage Total Vote Rep.	Total Vote Dem.	Major Vote Rep.	Major Vote Dem.
16,561	PARKE	8,864	3,926	4,703	235	777 D	44.3%	53.1%	45.5%	54.5%
16,625	PERRY	8,357	3,253	5,053	51	1,800 D	38.9%	60.5%	39.2%	60.8%
16,361	PIKE	7,931	3,193	4,547	191	1,354 D	40.3%	57.3%	41.3%	58.7%
22,821	PORTER	11,382	5,631	5,542	209	89 R	49.5%	48.7%	50.4%	49.6%
17,853	POSEY	8,644	2,876	5,641	127	2,765 D	33.3%	65.3%	33.8%	66.2%
11,195	PULASKI	5,641	2,226	3,286	129	1,060 D	39.5%	58.3%	40.4%	59.6%
20,448	PUTNAM	10,968	4,438	6,168	362	1,730 D	40.5%	56.2%	41.8%	58.2%
24,859	RANDOLPH	13,166	6,509	6,223	434	286 R	49.4%	47.3%	51.1%	48.9%
18,078	RIPLEY	10,348	4,240	5,987	121	1,747 D	41.0%	57.9%	41.5%	58.5%
19,412	RUSH	10,290	5,094	5,056	140	38 R	49.5%	49.1%	50.2%	49.8%
160,033	ST. JOSEPH	68,563	28,198	38,026	2,339	9,828 D	41.1%	55.5%	42.6%	57.4%
6,664	SCOTT	4,008	1,722	2,240	46	518 D	43.0%	55.9%	43.5%	56.5%
26,552	SHELBY	14,219	5,410	8,552	257	3,142 D	38.0%	60.1%	38.7%	61.3%
16,713	SPENCER	9,503	4,014	5,422	67	1,408 D	42.2%	57.1%	42.5%	57.5%
10,620	STARKE	6,010	2,449	3,420	141	971 D	40.7%	56.9%	41.7%	58.3%
13,386	STEUBEN	7,428	3,594	3,717	117	123 D	48.4%	50.0%	49.2%	50.8%
28,133	SULLIVAN	12,477	3,667	7,835	975	4,168 D	29.4%	62.8%	31.9%	68.1%
8,432	SWITZERLAND	5,035	1,953	2,981	101	1,028 D	38.8%	59.2%	39.6%	60.4%
47,535	TIPPECANOE	25,663	11,818	13,609	236	1,791 D	46.1%	53.0%	46.5%	53.5%
15,208	TIPTON	8,723	3,680	4,898	145	1,218 D	42.2%	56.2%	42.9%	57.1%
5,880	UNION	3,289	1,658	1,587	44	71 R	50.4%	48.3%	51.1%	48.9%
113,320	VANDERBURGH	49,752	16,873	31,828	1,051	14,955 D	33.9%	64.0%	34.6%	65.4%
23,238	VERMILLION	10,872	4,115	6,390	367	2,275 D	37.8%	58.8%	39.2%	60.8%
98,861	VIGO	45,187	18,310	25,886	991	7,576 D	40.5%	57.3%	41.4%	58.6%
25,170	WABASH	13,476	6,652	6,553	271	99 R	49.4%	48.6%	50.4%	49.6%
9,167	WARREN	4,544	2,223	2,256	65	33 D	48.9%	49.6%	49.6%	50.4%
18,230	WARRICK	9,086	3,429	5,409	248	1,980 D	37.7%	59.5%	38.8%	61.2%
16,285	WASHINGTON	8,181	3,316	4,809	56	1,493 D	40.5%	58.8%	40.8%	59.2%
54,809	WAYNE	26,506	12,683	13,287	536	604 D	47.8%	50.1%	48.8%	51.2%
18,411	WELLS	9,528	3,073	6,236	219	3,163 D	32.3%	65.4%	33.0%	67.0%
15,831	WHITE	8,592	3,484	4,976	132	1,492 D	40.5%	57.9%	41.2%	58.8%
15,931	WHITLEY	8,853	3,471	5,058	324	1,587 D	39.2%	57.1%	40.7%	59.3%
3,238,503	TOTAL	1,576,927	677,184	862,054	37,689	184,870 D	42.9%	54.7%	44.0%	56.0%

INDIANA

PRESIDENT 1928

1920 Census Population	County	Total Vote	Republican	Democratic	Other	Rep.-Dem. Plurality	Percentage Total Vote Rep.	Percentage Total Vote Dem.	Percentage Major Vote Rep.	Percentage Major Vote Dem.
20,503	ADAMS	8,139	4,045	4,066	28	21 D	49.7%	50.0%	49.9%	50.1%
114,303	ALLEN	60,720	34,234	26,292	194	7,942 R	56.4%	43.3%	56.6%	43.4%
23,887	BARTHOLOMEW	11,752	6,788	4,881	83	1,907 R	57.8%	41.5%	58.2%	41.8%
12,206	BENTON	5,756	3,360	2,368	28	992 R	58.4%	41.1%	58.7%	41.3%
14,084	BLACKFORD	6,541	3,882	2,576	83	1,306 R	59.3%	39.4%	60.1%	39.9%
23,575	BOONE	11,147	6,556	4,500	91	2,056 R	58.8%	40.4%	59.3%	40.7%
7,019	BROWN	1,977	959	999	19	40 D	48.5%	50.5%	49.0%	51.0%
16,315	CARROLL	8,028	4,780	3,182	66	1,598 R	59.5%	39.6%	60.0%	40.0%
38,333	CASS	17,163	10,522	6,522	119	4,000 R	61.3%	38.0%	61.7%	38.3%
29,381	CLARK	14,285	8,056	6,193	36	1,863 R	56.4%	43.4%	56.5%	43.5%
29,447	CLAY	12,641	7,103	5,358	180	1,745 R	56.2%	42.4%	57.0%	43.0%
27,737	CLINTON	13,610	7,606	5,895	109	1,711 R	55.9%	43.3%	56.3%	43.7%
11,201	CRAWFORD	4,656	2,672	1,933	51	739 R	57.4%	41.5%	58.0%	42.0%
26,856	DAVIESS	12,543	7,116	5,324	103	1,792 R	56.7%	42.4%	57.2%	42.8%
20,033	DEARBORN	10,829	6,334	4,459	36	1,875 R	58.5%	41.2%	58.7%	41.3%
17,813	DECATUR	9,246	5,400	3,791	55	1,609 R	58.4%	41.0%	58.8%	41.2%
25,600	DE KALB	11,514	7,373	4,077	64	3,296 R	64.0%	35.4%	64.4%	35.6%
56,377	DELAWARE	27,770	19,102	8,532	136	10,570 R	68.8%	30.7%	69.1%	30.9%
19,915	DUBOIS	9,384	3,301	6,044	39	2,743 D	35.2%	64.4%	35.3%	64.7%
56,384	ELKHART	27,924	20,876	6,900	148	13,976 R	74.8%	24.7%	75.2%	24.8%
17,142	FAYETTE	9,379	5,874	3,455	50	2,419 R	62.6%	36.8%	63.0%	37.0%
30,661	FLOYD	17,902	10,471	7,327	104	3,144 R	58.5%	40.9%	58.8%	41.2%
18,823	FOUNTAIN	8,921	4,960	3,894	67	1,066 R	55.6%	43.6%	56.0%	44.0%
14,806	FRANKLIN	7,260	3,426	3,817	17	391 D	47.2%	52.6%	47.3%	52.7%
16,478	FULTON	7,574	4,627	2,881	66	1,746 R	61.1%	38.0%	61.6%	38.4%
29,201	GIBSON	14,259	8,137	5,882	240	2,255 R	57.1%	41.3%	58.0%	42.0%
51,353	GRANT	22,216	14,659	7,273	284	7,386 R	66.0%	32.7%	66.8%	33.2%
36,770	GREENE	14,291	8,262	5,761	268	2,501 R	57.8%	40.3%	58.9%	41.1%
24,222	HAMILTON	11,645	7,960	3,611	74	4,349 R	68.4%	31.0%	68.8%	31.2%
17,210	HANCOCK	8,476	4,788	3,626	62	1,162 R	56.5%	42.8%	56.9%	43.1%
18,656	HARRISON	8,158	4,440	3,664	54	776 R	54.4%	44.9%	54.8%	45.2%
20,291	HENDRICKS	9,190	5,954	3,181	55	2,773 R	64.8%	34.6%	65.2%	34.8%
34,682	HENRY	15,324	10,502	4,554	268	5,948 R	68.5%	29.7%	69.8%	30.2%
43,965	HOWARD	18,885	12,632	5,930	323	6,702 R	66.9%	31.4%	68.1%	31.9%
31,671	HUNTINGTON	14,136	8,323	5,678	135	2,645 R	58.9%	40.2%	59.4%	40.6%
24,228	JACKSON	10,347	5,151	5,130	66	21 R	49.8%	49.6%	50.1%	49.9%
13,961	JASPER	5,636	3,700	1,915	21	1,785 R	65.6%	34.0%	65.9%	34.1%
23,318	JAY	10,844	5,998	4,759	87	1,239 R	55.3%	43.9%	55.8%	44.2%
20,709	JEFFERSON	9,251	5,295	3,906	50	1,389 R	57.2%	42.2%	57.5%	42.5%
13,280	JENNINGS	6,098	3,705	2,369	24	1,336 R	60.8%	38.8%	61.0%	39.0%
20,739	JOHNSON	10,152	5,513	4,548	91	965 R	54.3%	44.8%	54.8%	45.2%
46,195	KNOX	20,104	10,035	9,837	232	198 R	49.9%	48.9%	50.5%	49.5%
27,120	KOSCIUSKO	12,620	7,973	4,537	110	3,436 R	63.2%	36.0%	63.7%	36.3%
14,009	LAGRANGE	4,924	3,171	1,720	33	1,451 R	64.4%	34.9%	64.8%	35.2%
159,957	LAKE	81,719	48,768	32,321	630	16,447 R	59.7%	39.6%	60.1%	39.9%
50,443	LA PORTE	24,075	14,763	9,254	58	5,509 R	61.3%	38.4%	61.5%	38.5%
28,228	LAWRENCE	14,329	9,844	4,428	57	5,416 R	68.7%	30.9%	69.0%	31.0%
69,151	MADISON	35,814	23,083	12,496	235	10,587 R	64.5%	34.9%	64.9%	35.1%
348,061	MARION	184,100	109,630	73,309	1,161	36,321 R	59.5%	39.8%	59.9%	40.1%
23,744	MARSHALL	11,185	6,738	4,377	70	2,361 R	60.2%	39.1%	60.6%	39.4%
11,865	MARTIN	4,722	2,450	2,245	27	205 R	51.9%	47.5%	52.2%	47.8%
28,668	MIAMI	14,052	8,318	5,592	142	2,726 R	59.2%	39.8%	59.8%	40.2%
24,519	MONROE	13,259	8,883	4,317	59	4,566 R	67.0%	32.6%	67.3%	32.7%
28,490	MONTGOMERY	13,915	8,863	4,960	92	3,903 R	63.7%	35.6%	64.1%	35.9%
20,010	MORGAN	9,460	5,464	3,933	63	1,531 R	57.8%	41.6%	58.1%	41.9%
10,144	NEWTON	4,735	3,053	1,649	33	1,404 R	64.5%	34.8%	64.9%	35.1%
22,470	NOBLE	10,605	6,338	4,207	60	2,131 R	59.8%	39.7%	60.1%	39.9%
4,024	OHIO	2,154	1,230	911	13	319 R	57.1%	42.3%	57.4%	42.6%
16,974	ORANGE	8,234	5,086	3,112	36	1,974 R	61.8%	37.8%	62.0%	38.0%
12,760	OWEN	5,517	3,036	2,420	61	616 R	55.0%	43.9%	55.6%	44.4%

INDIANA

PRESIDENT 1928

1920 Census Population	County	Total Vote	Republican	Democratic	Other	Rep.-Dem. Plurality	Percentage Total Vote Rep.	Percentage Total Vote Dem.	Percentage Major Vote Rep.	Percentage Major Vote Dem.
18,875	PARKE	7,981	4,729	3,165	87	1,564 R	59.3%	39.7%	59.9%	40.1%
16,692	PERRY	7,561	3,772	3,782	7	10 D	49.9%	50.0%	49.9%	50.1%
18,684	PIKE	7,673	4,190	3,409	74	781 R	54.6%	44.4%	55.1%	44.9%
20,256	PORTER	10,090	7,107	2,921	62	4,186 R	70.4%	28.9%	70.9%	29.1%
19,334	POSEY	8,487	4,396	4,052	39	344 R	51.8%	47.7%	52.0%	48.0%
12,385	PULASKI	4,852	2,738	2,040	74	698 R	56.4%	42.0%	57.3%	42.7%
19,880	PUTNAM	9,603	5,351	4,177	75	1,174 R	55.7%	43.5%	56.2%	43.8%
26,484	RANDOLPH	11,733	8,368	3,264	101	5,104 R	71.3%	27.8%	71.9%	28.1%
18,694	RIPLEY	9,476	5,059	4,387	30	672 R	53.4%	46.3%	53.6%	46.4%
19,241	RUSH	9,711	6,640	2,996	75	3,644 R	68.4%	30.9%	68.9%	31.1%
103,304	ST. JOSEPH	64,006	36,844	26,846	316	9,998 R	57.6%	41.9%	57.8%	42.2%
7,424	SCOTT	3,263	1,719	1,527	17	192 R	52.7%	46.8%	53.0%	47.0%
25,982	SHELBY	13,389	7,516	5,790	83	1,726 R	56.1%	43.2%	56.5%	43.5%
18,400	SPENCER	8,844	4,672	4,152	20	520 R	52.8%	46.9%	52.9%	47.1%
10,278	STARKE	4,813	2,759	2,016	38	743 R	57.3%	41.9%	57.8%	42.2%
13,360	STEUBEN	6,216	4,435	1,730	51	2,705 R	71.3%	27.8%	71.9%	28.1%
31,630	SULLIVAN	12,134	6,199	5,642	293	557 R	51.1%	46.5%	52.4%	47.6%
9,311	SWITZERLAND	4,464	2,617	1,805	42	812 R	58.6%	40.4%	59.2%	40.8%
42,813	TIPPECANOE	23,978	15,165	8,720	93	6,445 R	63.2%	36.4%	63.5%	36.5%
16,152	TIPTON	8,050	4,774	3,186	90	1,588 R	59.3%	39.6%	60.0%	40.0%
6,021	UNION	3,184	2,101	1,069	14	1,032 R	66.0%	33.6%	66.3%	33.7%
92,293	VANDERBURGH	48,905	29,067	19,646	192	9,421 R	59.4%	40.2%	59.7%	40.3%
27,625	VERMILLION	10,100	5,192	4,793	115	399 R	51.4%	47.5%	52.0%	48.0%
100,212	VIGO	41,968	22,962	18,509	497	4,453 R	54.7%	44.1%	55.4%	44.6%
27,231	WABASH	12,508	8,537	3,872	99	4,665 R	68.3%	31.0%	68.8%	31.2%
9,699	WARREN	3,856	2,644	1,188	24	1,456 R	68.6%	30.8%	69.0%	31.0%
19,862	WARRICK	8,505	4,603	3,744	158	859 R	54.1%	44.0%	55.1%	44.9%
16,645	WASHINGTON	7,381	3,835	3,518	28	317 R	52.0%	47.7%	52.2%	47.8%
48,136	WAYNE	23,601	15,936	7,547	118	8,389 R	67.5%	32.0%	67.9%	32.1%
20,509	WELLS	8,465	4,142	4,246	77	104 D	48.9%	50.2%	49.4%	50.6%
17,351	WHITE	7,556	4,534	2,980	42	1,554 R	60.0%	39.4%	60.3%	39.7%
15,660	WHITLEY	7,869	4,519	3,294	56	1,225 R	57.4%	41.9%	57.8%	42.2%
2,930,390	TOTAL	1,421,314	848,290	562,691	10,333	285,599 R	59.7%	39.6%	60.1%	39.9%

INDIANA

PRESIDENT 1924

1920 Census Population	County	Total Vote	Republican	Democratic	Other	Rep.-Dem. Plurality	Percentage: Total Vote Rep.	Total Vote Dem.	Major Vote Rep.	Major Vote Dem.
20,503	ADAMS	8,055	3,330	4,300	425	970 D	41.3%	53.4%	43.6%	56.4%
114,303	ALLEN	46,573	25,207	17,244	4,122	7,963 R	54.1%	37.0%	59.4%	40.6%
23,887	BARTHOLOMEW	11,668	6,606	4,760	302	1,846 R	56.6%	40.8%	58.1%	41.9%
12,206	BENTON	5,590	3,250	2,104	236	1,146 R	58.1%	37.6%	60.7%	39.3%
14,084	BLACKFORD	6,953	3,553	3,094	306	459 R	51.1%	44.5%	53.5%	46.5%
23,575	BOONE	11,900	6,256	5,466	178	790 R	52.6%	45.9%	53.4%	46.6%
7,019	BROWN	2,047	756	1,229	62	473 D	36.9%	60.0%	38.1%	61.9%
16,315	CARROLL	8,489	4,543	3,660	286	883 R	53.5%	43.1%	55.4%	44.6%
38,333	CASS	17,783	9,939	5,276	2,568	4,663 R	55.9%	29.7%	65.3%	34.7%
29,381	CLARK	11,498	5,944	5,218	336	726 R	51.7%	45.4%	53.3%	46.7%
29,447	CLAY	12,189	5,955	5,349	885	606 R	48.9%	43.9%	52.7%	47.3%
27,737	CLINTON	13,862	7,469	6,070	323	1,399 R	53.9%	43.8%	55.2%	44.8%
11,201	CRAWFORD	4,450	1,917	2,384	149	467 D	43.1%	53.6%	44.6%	55.4%
26,856	DAVIESS	12,500	6,427	5,558	515	869 R	51.4%	44.5%	53.6%	46.4%
20,033	DEARBORN	9,536	4,588	4,330	618	258 R	48.1%	45.4%	51.4%	48.6%
17,813	DECATUR	9,269	4,907	4,092	270	815 R	52.9%	44.1%	54.5%	45.5%
25,600	DE KALB	11,154	6,093	4,133	928	1,960 R	54.6%	37.1%	59.6%	40.4%
56,377	DELAWARE	23,340	14,411	7,830	1,099	6,581 R	61.7%	33.5%	64.8%	35.2%
19,915	DUBOIS	8,870	2,708	5,651	511	2,943 D	30.5%	63.7%	32.4%	67.6%
56,384	ELKHART	20,304	13,096	4,729	2,479	8,367 R	64.5%	23.3%	73.5%	26.5%
17,142	FAYETTE	8,501	5,284	2,940	277	2,344 R	62.2%	34.6%	64.3%	35.7%
30,661	FLOYD	14,479	6,733	6,971	775	238 D	46.5%	48.1%	49.1%	50.9%
18,823	FOUNTAIN	9,353	4,796	4,282	275	514 R	51.3%	45.8%	52.8%	47.2%
14,806	FRANKLIN	7,418	3,296	3,915	207	619 D	44.4%	52.8%	45.7%	54.3%
16,478	FULTON	7,796	4,329	3,244	223	1,085 R	55.5%	41.6%	57.2%	42.8%
29,201	GIBSON	14,308	7,100	6,149	1,059	951 R	49.6%	43.0%	53.6%	46.4%
51,353	GRANT	20,276	11,173	7,086	2,017	4,087 R	55.1%	34.9%	61.2%	38.8%
36,770	GREENE	14,521	6,670	5,966	1,885	704 R	45.9%	41.1%	52.8%	47.2%
24,222	HAMILTON	11,498	7,463	3,785	250	3,678 R	64.9%	32.9%	66.3%	33.7%
17,210	HANCOCK	8,595	4,063	4,364	168	301 D	47.3%	50.8%	48.2%	51.8%
18,656	HARRISON	8,064	3,896	4,005	163	109 D	48.3%	49.7%	49.3%	50.7%
20,291	HENDRICKS	9,449	5,766	3,489	194	2,277 R	61.0%	36.9%	62.3%	37.7%
34,682	HENRY	14,461	8,800	5,376	285	3,424 R	60.9%	37.2%	62.1%	37.9%
43,965	HOWARD	17,383	10,438	5,451	1,494	4,987 R	60.0%	31.4%	65.7%	34.3%
31,671	HUNTINGTON	14,462	7,437	5,506	1,519	1,931 R	51.4%	38.1%	57.5%	42.5%
24,228	JACKSON	10,057	4,187	5,332	538	1,145 D	41.6%	53.0%	44.0%	56.0%
13,961	JASPER	5,716	3,679	1,744	293	1,935 R	64.4%	30.5%	67.8%	32.2%
23,318	JAY	10,890	5,753	4,812	325	941 R	52.8%	44.2%	54.5%	45.5%
20,709	JEFFERSON	9,355	5,192	3,914	249	1,278 R	55.5%	41.8%	57.0%	43.0%
13,280	JENNINGS	6,444	3,506	2,730	208	776 R	54.4%	42.4%	56.2%	43.8%
20,739	JOHNSON	9,757	4,954	4,699	104	255 R	50.8%	48.2%	51.3%	48.7%
46,195	KNOX	19,168	8,493	8,603	2,072	110 D	44.3%	44.9%	49.7%	50.3%
27,120	KOSCIUSKO	11,690	6,819	4,384	487	2,435 R	58.3%	37.5%	60.9%	39.1%
14,009	LAGRANGE	4,864	3,081	1,566	217	1,515 R	63.3%	32.2%	66.3%	33.7%
159,957	LAKE	47,968	30,990	10,918	6,060	20,072 R	64.6%	22.8%	73.9%	26.1%
50,443	LA PORTE	18,943	11,597	5,214	2,132	6,383 R	61.2%	27.5%	69.0%	31.0%
28,228	LAWRENCE	12,254	7,438	4,414	402	3,024 R	60.7%	36.0%	62.8%	37.2%
69,151	MADISON	32,003	18,447	12,061	1,495	6,386 R	57.6%	37.7%	60.5%	39.5%
348,061	MARION	160,880	95,135	59,498	6,247	35,637 R	59.1%	37.0%	61.5%	38.5%
23,744	MARSHALL	10,060	5,354	4,277	429	1,077 R	53.2%	42.5%	55.6%	44.4%
11,865	MARTIN	5,281	2,470	2,669	142	199 D	46.8%	50.5%	48.1%	51.9%
28,668	MIAMI	13,199	6,796	4,976	1,427	1,820 R	51.5%	37.7%	57.7%	42.3%
24,519	MONROE	11,312	6,247	4,689	376	1,558 R	55.2%	41.5%	57.1%	42.9%
28,490	MONTGOMERY	14,295	8,366	5,708	221	2,658 R	58.5%	39.9%	59.4%	40.6%
20,010	MORGAN	9,586	5,328	4,042	216	1,286 R	55.6%	42.2%	56.9%	43.1%
10,144	NEWTON	4,481	2,705	1,523	253	1,182 R	60.4%	34.0%	64.0%	36.0%
22,470	NOBLE	10,397	5,793	4,163	441	1,630 R	55.7%	40.0%	58.2%	41.8%
4,024	OHIO	2,105	989	1,058	58	69 D	47.0%	50.3%	48.3%	51.7%
16,974	ORANGE	8,098	4,538	3,374	186	1,164 R	56.0%	41.7%	57.4%	42.6%
12,760	OWEN	5,541	2,627	2,670	244	43 D	47.4%	48.2%	49.6%	50.4%

INDIANA

PRESIDENT 1924

1920 Census Population	County	Total Vote	Republican	Democratic	Other	Rep.-Dem. Plurality	Percentage Total Vote Rep.	Percentage Total Vote Dem.	Percentage Major Vote Rep.	Percentage Major Vote Dem.
18,875	PARKE	8,249	4,877	2,898	474	1,979 R	59.1%	35.1%	62.7%	37.3%
16,692	PERRY	7,314	3,240	3,895	179	655 D	44.3%	53.3%	45.4%	54.6%
18,684	PIKE	7,965	3,885	3,604	476	281 R	48.8%	45.2%	51.9%	48.1%
20,256	PORTER	8,284	5,613	1,640	1,031	3,973 R	67.8%	19.8%	77.4%	22.6%
19,334	POSEY	8,548	4,173	4,115	260	58 R	48.8%	48.1%	50.3%	49.7%
12,385	PULASKI	4,952	2,725	1,953	274	772 R	55.0%	39.4%	58.3%	41.7%
19,880	PUTNAM	10,032	4,930	4,759	343	171 R	49.1%	47.4%	50.9%	49.1%
26,484	RANDOLPH	11,539	7,397	3,768	374	3,629 R	64.1%	32.7%	66.3%	33.7%
18,694	RIPLEY	9,576	4,694	4,257	625	437 R	49.0%	44.5%	52.4%	47.6%
19,241	RUSH	9,521	5,958	3,415	148	2,543 R	62.6%	35.9%	63.6%	36.4%
103,304	ST. JOSEPH	41,082	23,682	15,056	2,344	8,626 R	57.6%	36.6%	61.1%	38.9%
7,424	SCOTT	3,436	1,532	1,824	80	292 D	44.6%	53.1%	45.6%	54.4%
25,982	SHELBY	12,936	6,664	5,976	296	688 R	51.5%	46.2%	52.7%	47.3%
18,400	SPENCER	9,045	4,395	4,409	241	14 D	48.6%	48.7%	49.9%	50.1%
10,278	STARKE	4,394	2,329	1,555	510	774 R	53.0%	35.4%	60.0%	40.0%
13,360	STEUBEN	5,905	4,046	1,610	249	2,436 R	68.5%	27.3%	71.5%	28.5%
31,630	SULLIVAN	12,053	5,139	5,213	1,701	74 D	42.6%	43.3%	49.6%	50.4%
9,311	SWITZERLAND	4,858	2,346	2,414	98	68 D	48.3%	49.7%	49.3%	50.7%
42,813	TIPPECANOE	20,823	12,161	7,619	1,043	4,542 R	58.4%	36.6%	61.5%	38.5%
16,152	TIPTON	8,150	4,183	3,660	307	523 R	51.3%	44.9%	53.3%	46.7%
6,021	UNION	3,245	1,907	1,284	54	623 R	58.8%	39.6%	59.8%	40.2%
92,293	VANDERBURGH	46,856	25,907	17,186	3,763	8,721 R	55.3%	36.7%	60.1%	39.9%
27,625	VERMILLION	9,135	4,489	2,779	1,867	1,710 R	49.1%	30.4%	61.8%	38.2%
100,212	VIGO	37,059	19,545	12,999	4,515	6,546 R	52.7%	35.1%	60.1%	39.9%
27,231	WABASH	12,040	7,277	4,054	709	3,223 R	60.4%	33.7%	64.2%	35.8%
9,699	WARREN	4,357	3,035	1,150	172	1,885 R	69.7%	26.4%	72.5%	27.5%
19,862	WARRICK	8,617	4,437	3,797	383	640 R	51.5%	44.1%	53.9%	46.1%
16,645	WASHINGTON	7,502	3,479	3,942	81	463 D	46.4%	52.5%	46.9%	53.1%
48,136	WAYNE	19,225	11,487	6,211	1,527	5,276 R	59.8%	32.3%	64.9%	35.1%
20,509	WELLS	8,754	3,932	4,537	285	605 D	44.9%	51.8%	46.4%	53.6%
17,351	WHITE	7,940	4,475	3,138	327	1,337 R	56.4%	39.5%	58.8%	41.2%
15,660	WHITLEY	8,060	4,420	3,484	156	936 R	54.8%	43.2%	55.9%	44.1%
2,930,390	TOTAL	1,272,390	703,042	492,245	77,103	210,797 R	55.3%	38.7%	58.8%	41.2%

INDIANA

PRESIDENT 1920

1920 Census Population	County	Total Vote	Republican	Democratic	Other	Rep.-Dem. Plurality	Total Vote Rep.	Total Vote Dem.	Major Vote Rep.	Major Vote Dem.
20,503	ADAMS	7,998	4,144	3,653	201	491 R	51.8%	45.7%	53.1%	46.9%
114,303	ALLEN	42,177	24,208	13,804	4,165	10,404 R	57.4%	32.7%	63.7%	36.3%
23,887	BARTHOLOMEW	12,210	6,585	5,420	205	1,165 R	53.9%	44.4%	54.9%	45.1%
12,206	BENTON	6,081	3,900	2,098	83	1,802 R	64.1%	34.5%	65.0%	35.0%
14,084	BLACKFORD	6,073	3,145	2,555	373	590 R	51.8%	42.1%	55.2%	44.8%
23,575	BOONE	13,058	6,650	6,178	230	472 R	50.9%	47.3%	51.8%	48.2%
7,019	BROWN	2,144	788	1,316	40	528 D	36.8%	61.4%	37.5%	62.5%
16,315	CARROLL	9,284	5,006	4,186	92	820 R	53.9%	45.1%	54.5%	45.5%
38,333	CASS	18,314	9,545	8,194	575	1,351 R	52.1%	44.7%	53.8%	46.2%
29,381	CLARK	13,357	6,466	6,729	162	263 D	48.4%	50.4%	49.0%	51.0%
29,447	CLAY	12,716	6,129	5,612	975	517 R	48.2%	44.1%	52.2%	47.8%
27,737	CLINTON	14,717	7,739	6,721	257	1,018 R	52.6%	45.7%	53.5%	46.5%
11,201	CRAWFORD	4,669	2,290	2,213	166	77 R	49.0%	47.4%	50.9%	49.1%
26,856	DAVIESS	12,633	6,748	5,587	298	1,161 R	53.4%	44.2%	54.7%	45.3%
20,033	DEARBORN	10,183	5,159	4,884	140	275 R	50.7%	48.0%	51.4%	48.6%
17,813	DECATUR	9,566	5,516	3,896	154	1,620 R	57.7%	40.7%	58.6%	41.4%
25,600	DE KALB	11,560	6,514	4,750	296	1,764 R	56.3%	41.1%	57.8%	42.2%
56,377	DELAWARE	24,030	14,845	8,329	856	6,516 R	61.8%	34.7%	64.1%	35.9%
19,915	DUBOIS	8,095	3,738	4,238	119	500 D	46.2%	52.4%	46.9%	53.1%
56,384	ELKHART	20,461	12,297	5,770	2,394	6,527 R	60.1%	28.2%	68.1%	31.9%
17,142	FAYETTE	8,738	4,742	3,768	228	974 R	54.3%	43.1%	55.7%	44.3%
30,661	FLOYD	15,447	7,669	7,391	387	278 R	49.6%	47.8%	50.9%	49.1%
18,823	FOUNTAIN	9,647	5,218	4,088	341	1,130 R	54.1%	42.4%	56.1%	43.9%
14,806	FRANKLIN	6,893	3,137	3,671	85	534 D	45.5%	53.3%	46.1%	53.9%
16,478	FULTON	8,554	4,618	3,602	334	1,016 R	54.0%	42.1%	56.2%	43.8%
29,201	GIBSON	14,610	7,498	6,384	728	1,114 R	51.3%	43.7%	54.0%	46.0%
51,353	GRANT	22,405	12,349	7,900	2,156	4,449 R	55.1%	35.3%	61.0%	39.0%
36,770	GREENE	15,388	7,486	6,335	1,567	1,151 R	48.6%	41.2%	54.2%	45.8%
24,222	HAMILTON	12,527	7,897	4,280	350	3,617 R	63.0%	34.2%	64.9%	35.1%
17,210	HANCOCK	9,579	4,422	4,958	199	536 D	46.2%	51.8%	47.1%	52.9%
18,656	HARRISON	8,301	4,271	3,898	132	373 R	51.5%	47.0%	52.3%	47.7%
20,291	HENDRICKS	10,630	6,293	4,192	145	2,101 R	59.2%	39.4%	60.0%	40.0%
34,682	HENRY	15,328	8,742	5,824	762	2,918 R	57.0%	38.0%	60.0%	40.0%
43,965	HOWARD	17,730	10,379	5,767	1,584	4,612 R	58.5%	32.5%	64.3%	35.7%
31,671	HUNTINGTON	15,093	8,100	6,506	487	1,594 R	53.7%	43.1%	55.5%	44.5%
24,228	JACKSON	10,552	5,069	5,319	164	250 D	48.0%	50.4%	48.8%	51.2%
13,961	JASPER	5,895	3,942	1,872	81	2,070 R	66.9%	31.8%	67.8%	32.2%
23,318	JAY	11,414	6,089	4,759	566	1,330 R	53.3%	41.7%	56.1%	43.9%
20,709	JEFFERSON	9,880	5,732	4,000	148	1,732 R	58.0%	40.5%	58.9%	41.1%
13,280	JENNINGS	6,117	3,404	2,603	110	801 R	55.6%	42.6%	56.7%	43.3%
20,739	JOHNSON	10,722	4,863	5,452	407	589 D	45.4%	50.8%	47.1%	52.9%
46,195	KNOX	19,479	10,011	8,052	1,416	1,959 R	51.4%	41.3%	55.4%	44.6%
27,120	KOSCIUSKO	13,504	8,326	4,836	342	3,490 R	61.7%	35.8%	63.3%	36.7%
14,009	LAGRANGE	5,663	3,852	1,687	124	2,165 R	68.0%	29.8%	69.5%	30.5%
159,957	LAKE	38,028	26,296	7,136	4,596	19,160 R	69.1%	18.8%	78.7%	21.3%
50,443	LA PORTE	17,238	11,204	5,459	575	5,745 R	65.0%	31.7%	67.2%	32.8%
28,228	LAWRENCE	11,708	6,808	4,709	191	2,099 R	58.1%	40.2%	59.1%	40.9%
69,151	MADISON	31,562	15,704	13,325	2,533	2,379 R	49.8%	42.2%	54.1%	45.9%
348,061	MARION	145,571	79,957	61,460	4,154	18,497 R	54.9%	42.2%	56.5%	43.5%
23,744	MARSHALL	10,642	5,708	4,631	303	1,077 R	53.6%	43.5%	55.2%	44.8%
11,865	MARTIN	5,255	2,747	2,443	65	304 R	52.3%	46.5%	52.9%	47.1%
28,668	MIAMI	14,124	7,336	6,259	529	1,077 R	51.9%	44.3%	54.0%	46.0%
24,519	MONROE	10,500	5,633	4,751	116	882 R	53.6%	45.2%	54.2%	45.8%
28,490	MONTGOMERY	16,135	8,792	7,159	184	1,633 R	54.5%	44.4%	55.1%	44.9%
20,010	MORGAN	10,069	5,634	4,254	181	1,380 R	56.0%	42.2%	57.0%	43.0%
10,144	NEWTON	4,861	3,129	1,664	68	1,465 R	64.4%	34.2%	65.3%	34.7%
22,470	NOBLE	11,213	6,820	4,148	245	2,672 R	60.8%	37.0%	62.2%	37.8%
4,024	OHIO	2,312	1,177	1,097	38	80 R	50.9%	47.4%	51.8%	48.2%
16,974	ORANGE	8,029	4,726	3,222	81	1,504 R	58.9%	40.1%	59.5%	40.5%
12,760	OWEN	6,094	2,997	2,948	149	49 R	49.2%	48.4%	50.4%	49.6%

INDIANA

PRESIDENT 1920

1920 Census Population	County	Total Vote	Republican	Democratic	Other	Rep.-Dem. Plurality	Percentage Total Vote Rep.	Total Vote Dem.	Major Vote Rep.	Major Vote Dem.
18,875	PARKE	8,888	4,989	3,543	356	1,446 R	56.1%	39.9%	58.5%	41.5%
16,692	PERRY	7,465	3,864	3,560	41	304 R	51.8%	47.7%	52.0%	48.0%
18,684	PIKE	7,863	4,069	3,067	727	1,002 R	51.7%	39.0%	57.0%	43.0%
20,256	PORTER	7,664	5,570	1,671	423	3,899 R	72.7%	21.8%	76.9%	23.1%
19,334	POSEY	9,658	4,802	4,695	161	107 R	49.7%	48.6%	50.6%	49.4%
12,385	PULASKI	5,085	2,740	2,228	117	512 R	53.9%	43.8%	55.2%	44.8%
19,880	PUTNAM	10,746	5,140	5,417	189	277 D	47.8%	50.4%	48.7%	51.3%
26,484	RANDOLPH	13,439	8,773	4,198	468	4,575 R	65.3%	31.2%	67.6%	32.4%
18,694	RIPLEY	9,452	5,372	3,976	104	1,396 R	56.8%	42.1%	57.5%	42.5%
19,241	RUSH	10,803	6,113	4,513	177	1,600 R	56.6%	41.8%	57.5%	42.5%
103,304	ST. JOSEPH	31,305	17,675	12,355	1,275	5,320 R	56.5%	39.5%	58.9%	41.1%
7,424	SCOTT	3,597	1,709	1,848	40	139 D	47.5%	51.4%	48.0%	52.0%
25,982	SHELBY	13,437	6,336	6,845	256	509 D	47.2%	50.9%	48.1%	51.9%
18,400	SPENCER	9,240	5,270	3,855	115	1,415 R	57.0%	41.7%	57.8%	42.2%
10,278	STARKE	4,264	2,683	1,467	114	1,216 R	62.9%	34.4%	64.7%	35.3%
13,360	STEUBEN	6,848	4,963	1,676	209	3,287 R	72.5%	24.5%	74.8%	25.2%
31,630	SULLIVAN	12,991	5,376	6,160	1,455	784 D	41.4%	47.4%	46.6%	53.4%
9,311	SWITZERLAND	5,038	2,525	2,412	101	113 R	50.1%	47.9%	51.1%	48.9%
42,813	TIPPECANOE	20,639	12,730	7,562	347	5,168 R	61.7%	36.6%	62.7%	37.3%
16,152	TIPTON	8,472	4,357	3,956	159	401 R	51.4%	46.7%	52.4%	47.6%
6,021	UNION	3,403	1,984	1,375	44	609 R	58.3%	40.4%	59.1%	40.9%
92,293	VANDERBURGH	36,946	19,357	13,904	3,685	5,453 R	52.4%	37.6%	58.2%	41.8%
27,625	VERMILLION	9,439	4,916	3,218	1,305	1,698 R	52.1%	34.1%	60.4%	39.6%
100,212	VIGO	37,114	18,668	15,739	2,707	2,929 R	50.3%	42.4%	54.3%	45.7%
27,231	WABASH	13,290	8,018	4,827	445	3,191 R	60.3%	36.3%	62.4%	37.6%
9,699	WARREN	4,707	3,337	1,311	59	2,026 R	70.9%	27.9%	71.8%	28.2%
19,862	WARRICK	9,033	4,675	3,915	443	760 R	51.8%	43.3%	54.4%	45.6%
16,645	WASHINGTON	7,913	3,708	4,157	48	449 D	46.9%	52.5%	47.1%	52.9%
48,136	WAYNE	21,221	12,631	8,015	575	4,616 R	59.5%	37.8%	61.2%	38.8%
20,509	WELLS	9,305	4,430	4,653	222	223 D	47.6%	50.0%	48.8%	51.2%
17,351	WHITE	8,317	4,871	3,375	71	1,496 R	58.6%	40.6%	59.1%	40.9%
15,660	WHITLEY	8,629	4,530	3,929	170	601 R	52.5%	45.5%	53.6%	46.4%
2,930,390	TOTAL	1,262,974	696,370	511,364	55,240	185,006 R	55.1%	40.5%	57.7%	42.3%

INDIANA

ELECTION NOTES

1956 Other vote was 6,554 Holtwick (Prohibition); 1,334 Hass (Socialist Labor).

1952 Other vote was 15,335 Hamblen (Prohibition); 1,085 Hallinan (Progressive); 840 Hass (Socialist Labor).

1948 Other vote was 14,711 Watson (Prohibition); 9,649 Wallace (Progressive); 2,179 Thomas (Socialist); 763 Teichert (Socialist Labor).

1944 Other vote was 12,574 Watson (Prohibition); 2,223 Thomas (Socialist).

1940 Other vote was 6,437 Babson (Prohibition); 2,075 Thomas (Socialist); 706 Aiken (Socialist Labor).

1936 Other vote was 19,407 Lemke (Union); 3,856 Thomas (Socialist); 1,090 Browder (Communist).

1932 Other vote was 21,388 Thomas (Socialist); 10,399 Upshaw (Prohibition); 2,187 Foster (Communist); 2,070 Reynolds (Socialist Labor); 1,645 Zahnd (National). The total vote (1,645) for the National candidate is the vote for the highest elector; the county-by-county figures are for the average vote in each county which totals 1,615; therefore, the statewide total in the other vote column is 30 above the sum of the counties.

1928 Other vote was 5,496 Varney (Prohibition); 3,871 Thomas (Socialist); 645 Reynolds (Socialist Labor); 321 Foster (Communist).

1924 Other vote was 71,700 LaFollette (Progressive); 4,416 Faris (Prohibition); 987 Foster (Communist).

1920 Other vote was 24,713 Debs (Socialist); 16,499 Christensen (Farmer-Labor); 13,462 Watkins (Prohibition); 566 Macauley (Single Tax).

IOWA

POPULAR VOTE FOR PRESIDENT 1920 TO 1956

Year	Total Vote	Republican Vote	Republican Candidate	Democratic Vote	Democratic Candidate	Other Vote	Plurality	Percentage Total Vote Rep.	Percentage Total Vote Dem.	Percentage Major Vote Rep.	Percentage Major Vote Dem.
1956	1,234,564	729,187	Eisenhower, Dwight D.	501,858	Stevenson, Adlai E.	3,519	227,329 R	59.1%	40.7%	59.2%	40.8%
1952	1,268,773	808,906	Eisenhower, Dwight D.	451,513	Stevenson, Adlai E.	8,354	357,393 R	63.8%	35.6%	64.2%	35.8%
1948	1,038,264	494,018	Dewey, Thomas E.	522,380	Truman, Harry S.	21,866	28,362 D	47.6%	50.3%	48.6%	51.4%
1944	1,052,599	547,267	Dewey, Thomas E.	499,876	Roosevelt, Franklin D.	5,456	47,391 R	52.0%	47.5%	52.3%	47.7%
1940	1,215,432	632,370	Willkie, Wendell	578,802	Roosevelt, Franklin D.	4,260	53,568 R	52.0%	47.6%	52.2%	47.8%
1936	1,142,737	487,977	Landon, Alfred M.	621,756	Roosevelt, Franklin D.	33,004	133,779 D	42.7%	54.4%	44.0%	56.0%
1932	1,036,687	414,433	Hoover, Herbert C.	598,019	Roosevelt, Franklin D.	24,235	183,586 D	40.0%	57.7%	40.9%	59.1%
1928	1,009,189	623,570	Hoover, Herbert C.	379,011	Smith, Alfred E.	6,608	244,559 R	61.8%	37.6%	62.2%	37.8%
1924 **	976,770	537,458	Coolidge, Calvin	160,382	Davis, John W.	278,930	263,010 R	55.0%	16.4%	77.0%	23.0%
1920	894,959	634,674	Harding, Warren G.	227,804	Cox, James M.	32,481	406,870 R	70.9%	25.5%	73.6%	26.4%

In 1924 other vote was 274,448 Progressive; 4,037 Communist and 445 scattered.

ELECTORAL COLLEGE VOTE 1920 TO 1956

Year	Total	Republican	Democratic	Other
1956	10	10	—	—
1952	10	10	—	—
1948	10	—	10	—
1944	10	10	—	—
1940	11	11	—	—
1936	11	—	11	—
1932	11	—	11	—
1928	13	13	—	—
1924	13	13	—	—
1920	13	13	—	—

IOWA

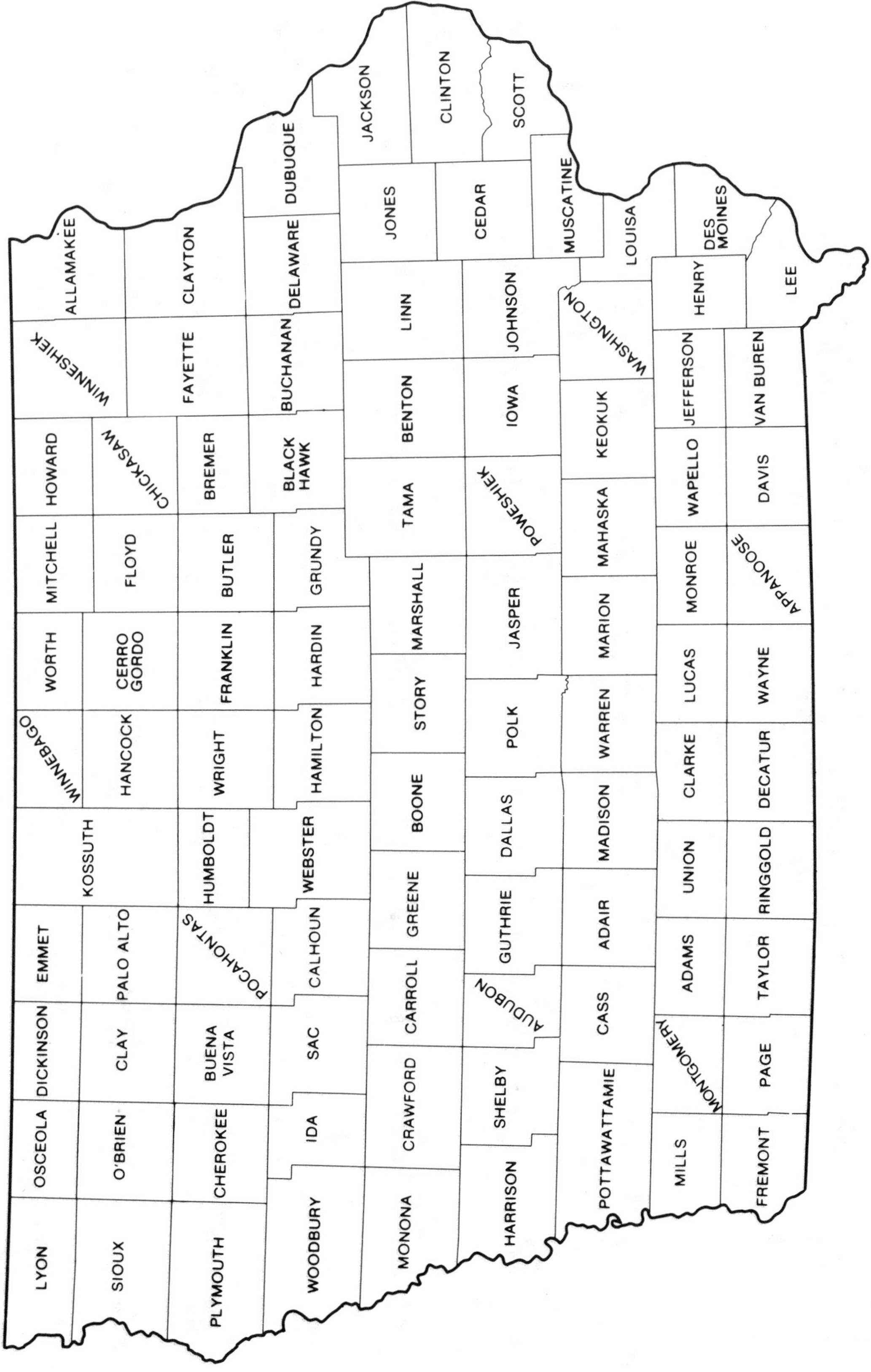

ALLAMAKEE
CLAYTON
DUBUQUE
JACKSON
CLINTON
SCOTT
WINNESHIEK
FAYETTE
DELAWARE
JONES
CEDAR
MUSCATINE
LOUISA
DES MOINES
LEE
HOWARD
CHICKASAW
BREMER
BUCHANAN
LINN
JOHNSON
WASHINGTON
HENRY
MITCHELL
FLOYD
BUTLER
BLACK HAWK
BENTON
IOWA
KEOKUK
JEFFERSON
VAN BUREN
WORTH
CERRO GORDO
FRANKLIN
GRUNDY
TAMA
POWESHIEK
MAHASKA
WAPELLO
DAVIS
WINNEBAGO
HANCOCK
WRIGHT
HARDIN
MARSHALL
JASPER
MARION
MONROE
APPANOOSE
KOSSUTH
HUMBOLDT
HAMILTON
STORY
POLK
WARREN
LUCAS
WAYNE
EMMET
PALO ALTO
POCAHONTAS
WEBSTER
BOONE
DALLAS
MADISON
CLARKE
DECATUR
DICKINSON
CLAY
BUENA VISTA
CALHOUN
GREENE
GUTHRIE
ADAIR
UNION
RINGGOLD
OSCEOLA
O'BRIEN
CHEROKEE
SAC
CARROLL
AUDUBON
CASS
ADAMS
TAYLOR
LYON
SIOUX
PLYMOUTH
IDA
CRAWFORD
SHELBY
POTTAWATTAMIE
MONTGOMERY
PAGE
WOODBURY
MONONA
HARRISON
MILLS
FREMONT

IOWA

PRESIDENT 1956

1950 Census Population	County	Total Vote	Republican	Democratic	Other	Rep.-Dem. Plurality	Percentage: Total Vote Rep.	Total Vote Dem.	Major Vote Rep.	Major Vote Dem.
12,292	ADAIR	5,791	3,426	2,362	3	1,064 R	59.2%	40.8%	59.2%	40.8%
8,753	ADAMS	4,020	2,248	1,756	16	492 R	55.9%	43.7%	56.1%	43.9%
16,351	ALLAMAKEE	7,824	5,182	2,622	20	2,560 R	66.2%	33.5%	66.4%	33.6%
19,683	APPANOOSE	9,054	4,980	4,064	10	916 R	55.0%	44.9%	55.1%	44.9%
11,579	AUDUBON	5,644	3,057	2,585	2	472 R	54.2%	45.8%	54.2%	45.8%
22,656	BENTON	10,006	5,634	3,946	426	1,688 R	56.3%	39.4%	58.8%	41.2%
100,448	BLACK HAWK	48,719	28,250	20,403	66	7,847 R	58.0%	41.9%	58.1%	41.9%
28,139	BOONE	12,564	6,740	5,815	9	925 R	53.6%	46.3%	53.7%	46.3%
18,884	BREMER	8,831	5,930	2,892	9	3,038 R	67.1%	32.7%	67.2%	32.8%
21,927	BUCHANAN	9,035	5,512	3,513	10	1,999 R	61.0%	38.9%	61.1%	38.9%
21,113	BUENA VISTA	10,563	6,470	4,083	10	2,387 R	61.3%	38.7%	61.3%	38.7%
17,394	BUTLER	7,961	5,669	2,289	3	3,380 R	71.2%	28.8%	71.2%	28.8%
16,925	CALHOUN	7,669	4,409	2,972	288	1,437 R	57.5%	38.8%	59.7%	40.3%
23,065	CARROLL	10,913	5,816	5,085	12	731 R	53.3%	46.6%	53.4%	46.6%
18,532	CASS	8,930	6,103	2,818	9	3,285 R	68.3%	31.6%	68.4%	31.6%
16,910	CEDAR	8,258	5,344	2,912	2	2,432 R	64.7%	35.3%	64.7%	35.3%
46,053	CERRO GORDO	21,841	12,449	9,362	30	3,087 R	57.0%	42.9%	57.1%	42.9%
19,052	CHEROKEE	8,079	4,821	3,254	4	1,567 R	59.7%	40.3%	59.7%	40.3%
15,228	CHICKASAW	7,495	4,205	3,275	15	930 R	56.1%	43.7%	56.2%	43.8%
9,369	CLARKE	4,397	2,462	1,929	6	533 R	56.0%	43.9%	56.1%	43.9%
18,103	CLAY	8,190	5,107	2,970	113	2,137 R	62.4%	36.3%	63.2%	36.8%
22,522	CLAYTON	10,926	6,529	4,384	13	2,145 R	59.8%	40.1%	59.8%	40.2%
49,664	CLINTON	23,208	14,765	8,394	49	6,371 R	63.6%	36.2%	63.8%	36.2%
19,741	CRAWFORD	8,374	4,608	3,749	17	859 R	55.0%	44.8%	55.1%	44.9%
23,661	DALLAS	11,806	6,619	5,185	2	1,434 R	56.1%	43.9%	56.1%	43.9%
9,959	DAVIS	5,129	2,661	2,458	10	203 R	51.9%	47.9%	52.0%	48.0%
12,601	DECATUR	5,725	2,912	2,806	7	106 R	50.9%	49.0%	50.9%	49.1%
17,734	DELAWARE	8,369	5,732	2,621	16	3,111 R	68.5%	31.3%	68.6%	31.4%
42,056	DES MOINES	19,958	11,152	8,781	25	2,371 R	55.9%	44.0%	55.9%	44.1%
12,756	DICKINSON	6,157	3,641	2,498	18	1,143 R	59.1%	40.6%	59.3%	40.7%
71,337	DUBUQUE	31,247	17,923	13,174	150	4,749 R	57.4%	42.2%	57.6%	42.4%
14,102	EMMET	6,584	4,193	2,386	5	1,807 R	63.7%	36.2%	63.7%	36.3%
28,294	FAYETTE	12,866	7,914	4,935	17	2,979 R	61.5%	38.4%	61.6%	38.4%
21,505	FLOYD	9,927	6,172	3,739	16	2,433 R	62.2%	37.7%	62.3%	37.7%
16,268	FRANKLIN	7,084	4,563	2,513	8	2,050 R	64.4%	35.5%	64.5%	35.5%
12,323	FREMONT	5,511	3,241	2,254	16	987 R	58.8%	40.9%	59.0%	41.0%
15,544	GREENE	7,162	4,255	2,802	105	1,453 R	59.4%	39.1%	60.3%	39.7%
13,722	GRUNDY	6,827	4,915	1,908	4	3,007 R	72.0%	27.9%	72.0%	28.0%
15,197	GUTHRIE	7,270	4,283	2,981	6	1,302 R	58.9%	41.0%	59.0%	41.0%
19,660	HAMILTON	9,514	5,667	3,829	18	1,838 R	59.6%	40.2%	59.7%	40.3%
15,077	HANCOCK	7,114	4,305	2,803	6	1,502 R	60.5%	39.4%	60.6%	39.4%
22,218	HARDIN	10,432	6,642	3,775	15	2,867 R	63.7%	36.2%	63.8%	36.2%
19,560	HARRISON	8,935	5,209	3,709	17	1,500 R	58.3%	41.5%	58.4%	41.6%
18,708	HENRY	8,495	5,818	2,667	10	3,151 R	68.5%	31.4%	68.6%	31.4%
13,105	HOWARD	6,605	3,491	3,106	8	385 R	52.9%	47.0%	52.9%	47.1%
13,117	HUMBOLDT	6,507	3,747	2,756	4	991 R	57.6%	42.4%	57.6%	42.4%
10,697	IDA	5,310	3,226	2,083	1	1,143 R	60.8%	39.2%	60.8%	39.2%
15,835	IOWA	7,777	4,875	2,753	149	2,122 R	62.7%	35.4%	63.9%	36.1%
18,622	JACKSON	8,905	5,575	3,181	149	2,394 R	62.6%	35.7%	63.7%	36.3%
32,305	JASPER	16,428	9,310	7,098	20	2,212 R	56.7%	43.2%	56.7%	43.3%
15,696	JEFFERSON	7,659	4,807	2,845	7	1,962 R	62.8%	37.1%	62.8%	37.2%
45,756	JOHNSON	20,076	11,298	8,767	11	2,531 R	56.3%	43.7%	56.3%	43.7%
19,401	JONES	8,967	5,605	3,352	10	2,253 R	62.5%	37.4%	62.6%	37.4%
16,797	KEOKUK	8,338	4,680	3,649	9	1,031 R	56.1%	43.8%	56.2%	43.8%
26,241	KOSSUTH	12,204	6,680	5,514	10	1,166 R	54.7%	45.2%	54.8%	45.2%
43,102	LEE	19,829	11,571	8,226	32	3,345 R	58.4%	41.5%	58.4%	41.6%
104,274	LINN	55,116	33,402	21,667	47	11,735 R	60.6%	39.3%	60.7%	39.3%
11,101	LOUISA	5,048	3,184	1,858	6	1,326 R	63.1%	36.8%	63.1%	36.9%
12,069	LUCAS	5,832	3,397	2,431	4	966 R	58.2%	41.7%	58.3%	41.7%
14,697	LYON	6,150	4,356	1,790	4	2,566 R	70.8%	29.1%	70.9%	29.1%

IOWA

PRESIDENT 1956

1950 Census Population	County	Total Vote	Republican	Democratic	Other	Rep.-Dem. Plurality	Percentage Total Vote Rep.	Total Vote Dem.	Major Vote Rep.	Major Vote Dem.
13,131	MADISON	6,544	3,883	2,652	9	1,231 R	59.3%	40.5%	59.4%	40.6%
24,672	MAHASKA	11,034	6,864	3,965	205	2,899 R	62.2%	35.9%	63.4%	36.6%
25,930	MARION	12,168	6,830	5,316	22	1,514 R	56.1%	43.7%	56.2%	43.8%
35,611	MARSHALL	16,425	10,305	5,755	365	4,550 R	62.7%	35.0%	64.2%	35.8%
14,064	MILLS	5,454	3,539	1,897	18	1,642 R	64.9%	34.8%	65.1%	34.9%
13,945	MITCHELL	6,812	4,175	2,630	7	1,545 R	61.3%	38.6%	61.4%	38.6%
16,303	MONONA	7,345	3,854	3,477	14	377 R	52.5%	47.3%	52.6%	47.4%
11,814	MONROE	5,612	2,984	2,616	12	368 R	53.2%	46.6%	53.3%	46.7%
15,685	MONTGOMERY	7,643	5,027	2,597	19	2,430 R	65.8%	34.0%	65.9%	34.1%
32,148	MUSCATINE	14,298	8,552	5,718	28	2,834 R	59.8%	40.0%	59.9%	40.1%
18,970	O'BRIEN	9,118	6,138	2,970	10	3,168 R	67.3%	32.6%	67.4%	32.6%
10,181	OSCEOLA	4,772	2,986	1,779	7	1,207 R	62.6%	37.3%	62.7%	37.3%
23,921	PAGE	10,397	7,380	3,001	16	4,379 R	71.0%	28.9%	71.1%	28.9%
15,891	PALO ALTO	7,421	3,795	3,624	2	171 R	51.1%	48.8%	51.2%	48.8%
23,252	PLYMOUTH	10,748	7,246	3,502		3,744 R	67.4%	32.6%	67.4%	32.6%
15,496	POCAHONTAS	6,818	3,606	3,201	11	405 R	52.9%	46.9%	53.0%	47.0%
226,010	POLK	115,491	62,392	53,025	74	9,367 R	54.0%	45.9%	54.1%	45.9%
69,682	POTTAWATTAMIE	30,468	17,632	12,731	105	4,901 R	57.9%	41.8%	58.1%	41.9%
19,344	POWESHIEK	8,749	5,145	3,602	2	1,543 R	58.8%	41.2%	58.8%	41.2%
9,528	RINGGOLD	4,490	2,713	1,775	2	938 R	60.4%	39.5%	60.5%	39.5%
17,518	SAC	8,125	4,874	3,248	3	1,626 R	60.0%	40.0%	60.0%	40.0%
100,698	SCOTT	47,104	27,965	18,969	170	8,996 R	59.4%	40.3%	59.6%	40.4%
15,942	SHELBY	7,793	4,425	3,300	68	1,125 R	56.8%	42.3%	57.3%	42.7%
26,381	SIOUX	12,328	9,651	2,666	11	6,985 R	78.3%	21.6%	78.4%	21.6%
44,294	STORY	19,640	13,264	6,352	24	6,912 R	67.5%	32.3%	67.6%	32.4%
21,688	TAMA	10,773	5,952	4,795	26	1,157 R	55.2%	44.5%	55.4%	44.6%
12,420	TAYLOR	5,978	3,533	2,436	9	1,097 R	59.1%	40.7%	59.2%	40.8%
15,651	UNION	7,501	4,666	2,828	7	1,838 R	62.2%	37.7%	62.3%	37.7%
11,007	VAN BUREN	5,068	3,233	1,833	2	1,400 R	63.8%	36.2%	63.8%	36.2%
47,397	WAPELLO	21,381	10,401	10,960	20	559 D	48.6%	51.3%	48.7%	51.3%
17,758	WARREN	9,174	5,430	3,729	15	1,701 R	59.2%	40.6%	59.3%	40.7%
19,557	WASHINGTON	8,876	5,844	3,022	10	2,822 R	65.8%	34.0%	65.9%	34.1%
11,737	WAYNE	5,897	3,340	2,553	4	787 R	56.6%	43.3%	56.7%	43.3%
44,241	WEBSTER	21,049	11,097	9,901	51	1,196 R	52.7%	47.0%	52.8%	47.2%
13,450	WINNEBAGO	6,453	3,926	2,521	6	1,405 R	60.8%	39.1%	60.9%	39.1%
21,639	WINNESHIEK	10,460	6,192	4,251	17	1,941 R	59.2%	40.6%	59.3%	40.7%
103,917	WOODBURY	45,445	25,399	19,997	49	5,402 R	55.9%	44.0%	55.9%	44.1%
11,068	WORTH	5,167	2,700	2,465	2	235 R	52.3%	47.7%	52.3%	47.7%
19,652	WRIGHT	9,390	5,512	3,865	13	1,647 R	58.7%	41.2%	58.8%	41.2%
2,621,073	TOTAL	1,234,564	729,187	501,858	3,519	227,329 R	59.1%	40.7%	59.2%	40.8%

IOWA

PRESIDENT 1952

							Percentage			
							Total Vote		Major Vote	
1950 Census Population	County	Total Vote	Republican	Democratic	Other	Rep.-Dem. Plurality	Rep.	Dem.	Rep.	Dem.
12,292	ADAIR	6,326	4,497	1,817	12	2,680 R	71.1%	28.7%	71.2%	28.8%
8,753	ADAMS	4,531	3,129	1,383	19	1,746 R	69.1%	30.5%	69.3%	30.7%
16,351	ALLAMAKEE	8,438	6,087	2,341	10	3,746 R	72.1%	27.7%	72.2%	27.8%
19,683	APPANOOSE	9,804	5,429	4,276	99	1,153 R	55.4%	43.6%	55.9%	44.1%
11,579	AUDUBON	5,829	3,605	2,220	4	1,385 R	61.8%	38.1%	61.9%	38.1%
22,656	BENTON	10,689	6,316	3,831	542	2,485 R	59.1%	35.8%	62.2%	37.8%
100,448	BLACK HAWK	46,234	28,671	17,360	203	11,311 R	62.0%	37.5%	62.3%	37.7%
28,139	BOONE	12,947	7,901	4,896	150	3,005 R	61.0%	37.8%	61.7%	38.3%
18,884	BREMER	9,183	6,806	2,363	14	4,443 R	74.1%	25.7%	74.2%	25.8%
21,927	BUCHANAN	9,484	6,431	3,019	34	3,412 R	67.8%	31.8%	68.1%	31.9%
21,113	BUENA VISTA	10,813	7,539	3,254	20	4,285 R	69.7%	30.1%	69.9%	30.1%
17,394	BUTLER	8,210	6,360	1,836	14	4,524 R	77.5%	22.4%	77.6%	22.4%
16,925	CALHOUN	7,966	5,391	2,411	164	2,980 R	67.7%	30.3%	69.1%	30.9%
23,065	CARROLL	11,628	7,473	4,139	16	3,334 R	64.3%	35.6%	64.4%	35.6%
18,532	CASS	9,727	7,355	2,349	23	5,006 R	75.6%	24.1%	75.8%	24.2%
16,910	CEDAR	8,640	6,176	2,447	17	3,729 R	71.5%	28.3%	71.6%	28.4%
46,053	CERRO GORDO	21,608	13,207	8,354	47	4,853 R	61.1%	38.7%	61.3%	38.7%
19,052	CHEROKEE	8,541	6,018	2,502	21	3,516 R	70.5%	29.3%	70.6%	29.4%
15,228	CHICKASAW	7,949	5,022	2,921	6	2,101 R	63.2%	36.7%	63.2%	36.8%
9,369	CLARKE	4,894	3,215	1,653	26	1,562 R	65.7%	33.8%	66.0%	34.0%
18,103	CLAY	8,641	6,271	2,258	112	4,013 R	72.6%	26.1%	73.5%	26.5%
22,522	CLAYTON	11,408	7,669	3,730	9	3,939 R	67.2%	32.7%	67.3%	32.7%
49,664	CLINTON	23,385	15,372	7,975	38	7,397 R	65.7%	34.1%	65.8%	34.2%
19,741	CRAWFORD	8,868	5,646	3,107	115	2,539 R	63.7%	35.0%	64.5%	35.5%
23,661	DALLAS	12,610	8,008	4,501	101	3,507 R	63.5%	35.7%	64.0%	36.0%
9,959	DAVIS	5,495	3,195	2,283	17	912 R	58.1%	41.5%	58.3%	41.7%
12,601	DECATUR	6,168	3,621	2,521	26	1,100 R	58.7%	40.9%	59.0%	41.0%
17,734	DELAWARE	8,810	6,449	2,351	10	4,098 R	73.2%	26.7%	73.3%	26.7%
42,056	DES MOINES	20,957	12,182	8,686	89	3,496 R	58.1%	41.4%	58.4%	41.6%
12,756	DICKINSON	6,194	4,401	1,748	45	2,653 R	71.1%	28.2%	71.6%	28.4%
71,337	DUBUQUE	32,845	18,075	14,542	228	3,533 R	55.0%	44.3%	55.4%	44.6%
14,102	EMMET	6,904	4,935	1,947	22	2,988 R	71.5%	28.2%	71.7%	28.3%
28,294	FAYETTE	13,589	9,152	4,403	34	4,749 R	67.3%	32.4%	67.5%	32.5%
21,505	FLOYD	10,054	7,042	2,999	13	4,043 R	70.0%	29.8%	70.1%	29.9%
16,268	FRANKLIN	7,470	5,432	1,941	97	3,491 R	72.7%	26.0%	73.7%	26.3%
12,323	FREMONT	5,894	3,802	2,085	7	1,717 R	64.5%	35.4%	64.6%	35.4%
15,544	GREENE	7,725	5,378	2,228	119	3,150 R	69.6%	28.8%	70.7%	29.3%
13,722	GRUNDY	7,156	5,652	1,483	21	4,169 R	79.0%	20.7%	79.2%	20.8%
15,197	GUTHRIE	7,671	5,377	2,281	13	3,096 R	70.1%	29.7%	70.2%	29.8%
19,660	HAMILTON	9,828	7,006	2,788	34	4,218 R	71.3%	28.4%	71.5%	28.5%
15,077	HANCOCK	7,178	5,115	2,053	10	3,062 R	71.3%	28.6%	71.4%	28.6%
22,218	HARDIN	11,132	7,880	3,205	47	4,675 R	70.8%	28.8%	71.1%	28.9%
19,560	HARRISON	9,366	5,972	3,370	24	2,602 R	63.8%	36.0%	63.9%	36.1%
18,708	HENRY	8,931	6,424	2,438	69	3,986 R	71.9%	27.3%	72.5%	27.5%
13,105	HOWARD	6,881	4,305	2,564	12	1,741 R	62.6%	37.3%	62.7%	37.3%
13,117	HUMBOLDT	6,674	4,534	2,124	16	2,410 R	67.9%	31.8%	68.1%	31.9%
10,697	IDA	5,418	3,800	1,603	15	2,197 R	70.1%	29.6%	70.3%	29.7%
15,835	IOWA	8,362	5,625	2,514	223	3,111 R	67.3%	30.1%	69.1%	30.9%
18,622	JACKSON	9,127	5,867	3,074	186	2,793 R	64.3%	33.7%	65.6%	34.4%
32,305	JASPER	16,465	9,610	6,756	99	2,854 R	58.4%	41.0%	58.7%	41.3%
15,696	JEFFERSON	8,149	5,630	2,470	49	3,160 R	69.1%	30.3%	69.5%	30.5%
45,756	JOHNSON	19,350	11,231	8,067	52	3,164 R	58.0%	41.7%	58.2%	41.8%
19,401	JONES	9,073	6,070	2,991	12	3,079 R	66.9%	33.0%	67.0%	33.0%
16,797	KEOKUK	8,897	5,712	3,135	50	2,577 R	64.2%	35.2%	64.6%	35.4%
26,241	KOSSUTH	12,105	7,765	4,330	10	3,435 R	64.1%	35.8%	64.2%	35.8%
43,102	LEE	20,969	12,289	8,625	55	3,664 R	58.6%	41.1%	58.8%	41.2%
104,274	LINN	53,441	31,383	21,818	240	9,565 R	58.7%	40.8%	59.0%	41.0%
11,101	LOUISA	5,369	3,675	1,673	21	2,002 R	68.4%	31.2%	68.7%	31.3%
12,069	LUCAS	6,215	3,921	2,217	77	1,704 R	63.1%	35.7%	63.9%	36.1%
14,697	LYON	6,226	4,893	1,324	9	3,569 R	78.6%	21.3%	78.7%	21.3%

IOWA

PRESIDENT 1952

1950 Census Population	County	Total Vote	Republican	Democratic	Other	Rep.-Dem. Plurality	Percentage Total Vote Rep.	Total Vote Dem.	Major Vote Rep.	Major Vote Dem.
13,131	MADISON	7,149	4,967	2,131	51	2,836 R	69.5%	29.8%	70.0%	30.0%
24,672	MAHASKA	11,523	7,369	3,745	409	3,624 R	64.0%	32.5%	66.3%	33.7%
25,930	MARION	12,516	7,165	5,196	155	1,969 R	57.2%	41.5%	58.0%	42.0%
35,611	MARSHALL	16,890	11,135	5,314	441	5,821 R	65.9%	31.5%	67.7%	32.3%
14,064	MILLS	5,834	4,028	1,792	14	2,236 R	69.0%	30.7%	69.2%	30.8%
13,945	MITCHELL	7,237	5,050	2,175	12	2,875 R	69.8%	30.1%	69.9%	30.1%
16,303	MONONA	7,784	4,849	2,918	17	1,931 R	62.3%	37.5%	62.4%	37.6%
11,814	MONROE	6,042	3,219	2,785	38	434 R	53.3%	46.1%	53.6%	46.4%
15,685	MONTGOMERY	8,334	6,074	2,235	25	3,839 R	72.9%	26.8%	73.1%	26.9%
32,148	MUSCATINE	15,196	9,361	5,772	63	3,589 R	61.6%	38.0%	61.9%	38.1%
18,970	O'BRIEN	9,360	7,130	2,192	38	4,938 R	76.2%	23.4%	76.5%	23.5%
10,181	OSCEOLA	4,981	3,573	1,396	12	2,177 R	71.7%	28.0%	71.9%	28.1%
23,921	PAGE	11,553	8,840	2,669	44	6,171 R	76.5%	23.1%	76.8%	23.2%
15,891	PALO ALTO	7,597	4,595	2,993	9	1,602 R	60.5%	39.4%	60.6%	39.4%
23,252	PLYMOUTH	10,957	8,140	2,768	49	5,372 R	74.3%	25.3%	74.6%	25.4%
15,496	POCAHONTAS	7,245	4,472	2,517	256	1,955 R	61.7%	34.7%	64.0%	36.0%
226,010	POLK	112,783	60,934	50,867	982	10,067 R	54.0%	45.1%	54.5%	45.5%
69,682	POTTAWATTAMIE	30,854	18,894	11,897	63	6,997 R	61.2%	38.6%	61.4%	38.6%
19,344	POWESHIEK	9,498	6,105	3,318	75	2,787 R	64.3%	34.9%	64.8%	35.2%
9,528	RINGGOLD	4,871	3,442	1,408	21	2,034 R	70.7%	28.9%	71.0%	29.0%
17,518	SAC	8,894	6,417	2,451	26	3,966 R	72.1%	27.6%	72.4%	27.6%
100,698	SCOTT	48,026	29,719	17,807	500	11,912 R	61.9%	37.1%	62.5%	37.5%
15,942	SHELBY	7,939	5,135	2,762	42	2,373 R	64.7%	34.8%	65.0%	35.0%
26,381	SIOUX	12,349	10,275	2,050	24	8,225 R	83.2%	16.6%	83.4%	16.6%
44,294	STORY	19,296	13,857	5,299	140	8,558 R	71.8%	27.5%	72.3%	27.7%
21,688	TAMA	11,154	7,061	4,076	17	2,985 R	63.3%	36.5%	63.4%	36.6%
12,420	TAYLOR	6,423	4,608	1,784	31	2,824 R	71.7%	27.8%	72.1%	27.9%
15,651	UNION	8,332	5,742	2,566	24	3,176 R	68.9%	30.8%	69.1%	30.9%
11,007	VAN BUREN	5,480	3,870	1,577	33	2,293 R	70.6%	28.8%	71.0%	29.0%
47,397	WAPELLO	22,150	11,571	10,449	130	1,122 R	52.2%	47.2%	52.5%	47.5%
17,758	WARREN	9,017	5,911	3,042	64	2,869 R	65.6%	33.7%	66.0%	34.0%
19,557	WASHINGTON	9,585	6,946	2,604	35	4,342 R	72.5%	27.2%	72.7%	27.3%
11,737	WAYNE	6,525	3,995	2,497	33	1,498 R	61.2%	38.3%	61.5%	38.5%
44,241	WEBSTER	21,385	12,336	8,681	368	3,655 R	57.7%	40.6%	58.7%	41.3%
13,450	WINNEBAGO	6,499	4,574	1,905	20	2,669 R	70.4%	29.3%	70.6%	29.4%
21,639	WINNESHIEK	10,736	7,154	3,560	22	3,594 R	66.6%	33.2%	66.8%	33.2%
103,917	WOODBURY	47,151	27,518	19,474	159	8,044 R	58.4%	41.3%	58.6%	41.4%
11,068	WORTH	5,404	3,315	2,075	14	1,240 R	61.3%	38.4%	61.5%	38.5%
19,652	WRIGHT	9,783	6,566	3,186	31	3,380 R	67.1%	32.6%	67.3%	32.7%
2,621,073	TOTAL	1,268,773	808,906	451,513	8,354	357,393 R	63.8%	35.6%	64.2%	35.8%

IOWA

PRESIDENT 1948

1940 Census Population	County	Total Vote	Republican	Democratic	Other	Rep.-Dem. Plurality	Percentage Total Vote Rep.	Percentage Total Vote Dem.	Percentage Major Vote Rep.	Percentage Major Vote Dem.
13,196	ADAIR	5,523	2,879	2,567	77	312 R	52.1%	46.5%	52.9%	47.1%
10,156	ADAMS	4,012	2,142	1,817	53	325 R	53.4%	45.3%	54.1%	45.9%
17,184	ALLAMAKEE	7,726	4,474	3,172	80	1,302 R	57.9%	41.1%	58.5%	41.5%
24,245	APPANOOSE	9,296	4,078	4,998	220	920 D	43.9%	53.8%	44.9%	55.1%
11,790	AUDUBON	5,153	2,177	2,840	136	663 D	42.2%	55.1%	43.4%	56.6%
22,879	BENTON	8,367	3,770	4,209	388	439 D	45.1%	50.3%	47.2%	52.8%
79,946	BLACK HAWK	36,230	16,041	19,603	586	3,562 D	44.3%	54.1%	45.0%	55.0%
29,782	BOONE	10,222	4,183	5,541	498	1,358 D	40.9%	54.2%	43.0%	57.0%
17,932	BREMER	7,433	3,837	3,502	94	335 R	51.6%	47.1%	52.3%	47.7%
20,991	BUCHANAN	8,523	4,310	4,127	86	183 R	50.6%	48.4%	51.1%	48.9%
19,838	BUENA VISTA	8,493	3,959	4,340	194	381 D	46.6%	51.1%	47.7%	52.3%
17,986	BUTLER	6,513	3,380	3,008	125	372 R	51.9%	46.2%	52.9%	47.1%
17,584	CALHOUN	6,398	3,083	3,164	151	81 D	48.2%	49.5%	49.4%	50.6%
22,770	CARROLL	9,786	3,974	5,711	101	1,737 D	40.6%	58.4%	41.0%	59.0%
18,647	CASS	8,559	5,106	3,372	81	1,734 R	59.7%	39.4%	60.2%	39.8%
16,884	CEDAR	7,016	3,957	2,958	101	999 R	56.4%	42.2%	57.2%	42.8%
43,845	CERRO GORDO	17,682	7,840	9,544	298	1,704 D	44.3%	54.0%	45.1%	54.9%
19,258	CHEROKEE	7,144	3,318	3,739	87	421 D	46.4%	52.3%	47.0%	53.0%
15,227	CHICKASAW	7,589	3,449	4,071	69	622 D	45.4%	53.6%	45.9%	54.1%
10,233	CLARKE	4,379	2,195	2,101	83	94 R	50.1%	48.0%	51.1%	48.9%
17,762	CLAY	6,961	3,036	3,649	276	613 D	43.6%	52.4%	45.4%	54.6%
24,334	CLAYTON	10,111	5,151	4,857	103	294 R	50.9%	48.0%	51.5%	48.5%
44,722	CLINTON	18,665	9,859	8,534	272	1,325 R	52.8%	45.7%	53.6%	46.4%
20,538	CRAWFORD	7,485	3,267	3,983	235	716 D	43.6%	53.2%	45.1%	54.9%
24,649	DALLAS	10,819	4,810	5,661	348	851 D	44.5%	52.3%	45.9%	54.1%
11,136	DAVIS	5,305	2,276	2,982	47	706 D	42.9%	56.2%	43.3%	56.7%
14,012	DECATUR	5,803	2,547	3,172	84	625 D	43.9%	54.7%	44.5%	55.5%
18,487	DELAWARE	7,498	4,555	2,876	67	1,679 R	60.7%	38.4%	61.3%	38.7%
36,804	DES MOINES	16,729	7,621	8,792	316	1,171 D	45.6%	52.6%	46.4%	53.6%
12,185	DICKINSON	4,766	2,304	2,324	138	20 D	48.3%	48.8%	49.8%	50.2%
63,768	DUBUQUE	25,913	10,111	15,521	281	5,410 D	39.0%	59.9%	39.4%	60.6%
13,406	EMMET	5,313	2,464	2,752	97	288 D	46.4%	51.8%	47.2%	52.8%
29,151	FAYETTE	11,760	6,296	5,303	161	993 R	53.5%	45.1%	54.3%	45.7%
20,169	FLOYD	8,497	4,644	3,688	165	956 R	54.7%	43.4%	55.7%	44.3%
16,379	FRANKLIN	6,021	2,716	2,871	434	155 D	45.1%	47.7%	48.6%	51.4%
14,645	FREMONT	5,378	2,698	2,637	43	61 R	50.2%	49.0%	50.6%	49.4%
16,599	GREENE	6,290	3,059	2,946	285	113 R	48.6%	46.8%	50.9%	49.1%
13,518	GRUNDY	5,647	3,154	2,344	149	810 R	55.9%	41.5%	57.4%	42.6%
17,210	GUTHRIE	6,891	3,389	3,392	110	3 D	49.2%	49.2%	50.0%	50.0%
19,922	HAMILTON	7,345	3,535	3,613	197	78 D	48.1%	49.2%	49.5%	50.5%
15,402	HANCOCK	6,051	2,802	3,096	153	294 D	46.3%	51.2%	47.5%	52.5%
22,530	HARDIN	8,854	4,553	4,023	278	530 R	51.4%	45.4%	53.1%	46.9%
22,767	HARRISON	9,016	4,341	4,608	67	267 D	48.1%	51.1%	48.5%	51.5%
17,994	HENRY	7,805	4,620	3,042	143	1,578 R	59.2%	39.0%	60.3%	39.7%
13,531	HOWARD	6,090	2,630	3,378	82	748 D	43.2%	55.5%	43.8%	56.2%
13,459	HUMBOLDT	5,432	2,498	2,855	79	357 D	46.0%	52.6%	46.7%	53.3%
11,047	IDA	4,698	2,257	2,365	76	108 D	48.0%	50.3%	48.8%	51.2%
17,016	IOWA	6,978	3,659	3,030	289	629 R	52.4%	43.4%	54.7%	45.3%
19,181	JACKSON	7,005	3,597	3,263	145	334 R	51.3%	46.6%	52.4%	47.6%
31,496	JASPER	12,786	5,710	6,684	392	974 D	44.7%	52.3%	46.1%	53.9%
15,762	JEFFERSON	7,088	3,906	3,033	149	873 R	55.1%	42.8%	56.3%	43.7%
33,191	JOHNSON	16,303	7,139	8,611	553	1,472 D	43.8%	52.8%	45.3%	54.7%
19,950	JONES	8,322	4,290	3,915	117	375 R	51.6%	47.0%	52.3%	47.7%
18,406	KEOKUK	8,475	4,201	4,118	156	83 R	49.6%	48.6%	50.5%	49.5%
26,630	KOSSUTH	10,353	4,186	6,039	128	1,853 D	40.4%	58.3%	40.9%	59.1%
41,074	LEE	17,212	7,801	9,201	210	1,400 D	45.3%	53.5%	45.9%	54.1%
89,142	LINN	43,098	20,881	20,995	1,222	114 D	48.5%	48.7%	49.9%	50.1%
11,384	LOUISA	4,429	2,420	1,945	64	475 R	54.6%	43.9%	55.4%	44.6%
14,571	LUCAS	5,475	2,656	2,697	122	41 D	48.5%	49.3%	49.6%	50.4%
15,374	LYON	4,740	2,500	2,174	66	326 R	52.7%	45.9%	53.5%	46.5%

IOWA

PRESIDENT 1948

1940 Census Population	County	Total Vote	Republican	Democratic	Other	Rep.-Dem. Plurality	Percentage Total Vote Rep.	Total Vote Dem.	Major Vote Rep.	Major Vote Dem.
14,525	MADISON	6,123	3,207	2,827	89	380 R	52.4%	46.2%	53.1%	46.9%
26,485	MAHASKA	9,030	4,238	4,327	465	89 D	46.9%	47.9%	49.5%	50.5%
27,019	MARION	10,870	4,312	6,300	258	1,988 D	39.7%	58.0%	40.6%	59.4%
35,406	MARSHALL	12,833	6,698	5,602	533	1,096 R	52.2%	43.7%	54.5%	45.5%
15,064	MILLS	5,107	2,921	2,155	31	766 R	57.2%	42.2%	57.5%	42.5%
14,121	MITCHELL	6,119	3,021	2,873	225	148 R	49.4%	47.0%	51.3%	48.7%
18,238	MONONA	7,346	3,179	4,098	69	919 D	43.3%	55.8%	43.7%	56.3%
14,553	MONROE	5,926	2,371	3,445	110	1,074 D	40.0%	58.1%	40.8%	59.2%
15,697	MONTGOMERY	6,910	4,084	2,751	75	1,333 R	59.1%	39.8%	59.8%	40.2%
31,296	MUSCATINE	11,615	6,003	5,466	146	537 R	51.7%	47.1%	52.3%	47.7%
19,293	O'BRIEN	7,326	3,697	3,421	208	276 R	50.5%	46.7%	51.9%	48.1%
10,607	OSCEOLA	3,939	1,772	2,123	44	351 D	45.0%	53.9%	45.5%	54.5%
24,887	PAGE	9,374	5,638	3,567	169	2,071 R	60.1%	38.1%	61.2%	38.8%
16,170	PALO ALTO	6,601	2,594	3,858	149	1,264 D	39.3%	58.4%	40.2%	59.8%
23,502	PLYMOUTH	9,416	5,002	4,339	75	663 R	53.1%	46.1%	53.5%	46.5%
16,266	POCAHONTAS	6,051	2,397	3,500	154	1,103 D	39.6%	57.8%	40.6%	59.4%
195,835	POLK	81,379	33,742	45,289	2,348	11,547 D	41.5%	55.7%	42.7%	57.3%
66,756	POTTAWATTAMIE	24,095	12,384	11,430	281	954 R	51.4%	47.4%	52.0%	48.0%
18,758	POWESHIEK	8,385	3,888	4,324	173	436 D	46.4%	51.6%	47.3%	52.7%
11,137	RINGGOLD	4,459	2,487	1,922	50	565 R	55.8%	43.1%	56.4%	43.6%
17,639	SAC	7,363	3,505	3,699	159	194 D	47.6%	50.2%	48.7%	51.3%
84,748	SCOTT	34,081	16,842	16,661	578	181 R	49.4%	48.9%	50.3%	49.7%
16,720	SHELBY	6,935	3,301	3,499	135	198 D	47.6%	50.5%	48.5%	51.5%
27,209	SIOUX	9,801	5,597	4,042	162	1,555 R	57.1%	41.2%	58.1%	41.9%
33,434	STORY	15,251	8,307	6,152	792	2,155 R	54.5%	40.3%	57.5%	42.5%
22,428	TAMA	10,028	4,763	5,115	150	352 D	47.5%	51.0%	48.2%	51.8%
14,258	TAYLOR	5,698	3,244	2,402	52	842 R	56.9%	42.2%	57.5%	42.5%
16,280	UNION	7,414	4,138	3,218	58	920 R	55.8%	43.4%	56.3%	43.7%
12,053	VAN BUREN	4,688	2,702	1,917	69	785 R	57.6%	40.9%	58.5%	41.5%
44,280	WAPELLO	18,976	7,875	10,841	260	2,966 D	41.5%	57.1%	42.1%	57.9%
17,695	WARREN	7,605	3,876	3,481	248	395 R	51.0%	45.8%	52.7%	47.3%
20,055	WASHINGTON	8,245	4,680	3,485	80	1,195 R	56.8%	42.3%	57.3%	42.7%
13,308	WAYNE	6,123	2,738	3,314	71	576 D	44.7%	54.1%	45.2%	54.8%
41,521	WEBSTER	17,066	6,951	9,508	607	2,557 D	40.7%	55.7%	42.2%	57.8%
13,972	WINNEBAGO	5,451	2,636	2,626	189	10 R	48.4%	48.2%	50.1%	49.9%
22,263	WINNESHIEK	9,663	4,594	4,905	164	311 D	47.5%	50.8%	48.4%	51.6%
103,627	WOODBURY	39,084	16,655	22,056	373	5,401 D	42.6%	56.4%	43.0%	57.0%
11,449	WORTH	4,637	1,878	2,623	136	745 D	40.5%	56.6%	41.7%	58.3%
20,038	WRIGHT	7,800	3,810	3,866	124	56 D	48.8%	49.6%	49.6%	50.4%
2,538,268	TOTAL	1,038,264	494,018	522,380	21,866	28,362 D	47.6%	50.3%	48.6%	51.4%

IOWA

PRESIDENT 1944

1940 Census Population	County	Total Vote	Republican	Democratic	Other	Rep.-Dem. Plurality	Percentage Total Vote Rep.	Total Vote Dem.	Major Vote Rep.	Major Vote Dem.
13,196	ADAIR	5,743	3,428	2,297	18	1,131 R	59.7%	40.0%	59.9%	40.1%
10,156	ADAMS	4,413	2,540	1,868	5	672 R	57.6%	42.3%	57.6%	42.4%
17,184	ALLAMAKEE	7,929	5,017	2,893	19	2,124 R	63.3%	36.5%	63.4%	36.6%
24,245	APPANOOSE	10,020	4,928	5,015	77	87 D	49.2%	50.0%	49.6%	50.4%
11,790	AUDUBON	5,447	2,346	3,094	7	748 D	43.1%	56.8%	43.1%	56.9%
22,879	BENTON	9,039	4,378	4,619	42	241 D	48.4%	51.1%	48.7%	51.3%
79,946	BLACK HAWK	32,434	15,687	16,593	154	906 D	48.4%	51.2%	48.6%	51.4%
29,782	BOONE	11,003	4,868	6,062	73	1,194 D	44.2%	55.1%	44.5%	55.5%
17,932	BREMER	7,642	4,861	2,764	17	2,097 R	63.6%	36.2%	63.8%	36.2%
20,991	BUCHANAN	8,508	4,653	3,841	14	812 R	54.7%	45.1%	54.8%	45.2%
19,838	BUENA VISTA	8,309	3,993	4,277	39	284 D	48.1%	51.5%	48.3%	51.7%
17,986	BUTLER	6,431	4,182	2,225	24	1,957 R	65.0%	34.6%	65.3%	34.7%
17,584	CALHOUN	6,946	3,375	3,544	27	169 D	48.6%	51.0%	48.8%	51.2%
22,770	CARROLL	9,659	4,833	4,799	27	34 R	50.0%	49.7%	50.2%	49.8%
18,647	CASS	8,561	5,610	2,928	23	2,682 R	65.5%	34.2%	65.7%	34.3%
16,884	CEDAR	7,307	4,673	2,610	24	2,063 R	64.0%	35.7%	64.2%	35.8%
43,845	CERRO GORDO	17,459	8,311	9,088	60	777 D	47.6%	52.1%	47.8%	52.2%
19,258	CHEROKEE	6,949	3,723	3,197	29	526 R	53.6%	46.0%	53.8%	46.2%
15,227	CHICKASAW	6,929	3,575	3,328	26	247 R	51.6%	48.0%	51.8%	48.2%
10,233	CLARKE	4,584	2,603	1,946	35	657 R	56.8%	42.5%	57.2%	42.8%
17,762	CLAY	6,724	3,055	3,639	30	584 D	45.4%	54.1%	45.6%	54.4%
24,334	CLAYTON	10,163	5,855	4,259	49	1,596 R	57.6%	41.9%	57.9%	42.1%
44,722	CLINTON	19,624	11,533	8,028	63	3,505 R	58.8%	40.9%	59.0%	41.0%
20,538	CRAWFORD	7,509	4,242	3,218	49	1,024 R	56.5%	42.9%	56.9%	43.1%
24,649	DALLAS	10,864	5,413	5,316	135	97 R	49.8%	48.9%	50.5%	49.5%
11,136	DAVIS	5,318	2,559	2,727	32	168 D	48.1%	51.3%	48.4%	51.6%
14,012	DECATUR	6,268	2,934	3,316	18	382 D	46.8%	52.9%	46.9%	53.1%
18,487	DELAWARE	7,682	5,164	2,498	20	2,666 R	67.2%	32.5%	67.4%	32.6%
36,804	DES MOINES	17,177	9,488	7,543	146	1,945 R	55.2%	43.9%	55.7%	44.3%
12,185	DICKINSON	4,627	2,133	2,473	21	340 D	46.1%	53.4%	46.3%	53.7%
63,768	DUBUQUE	25,458	12,502	12,867	89	365 D	49.1%	50.5%	49.3%	50.7%
13,406	EMMET	5,286	2,668	2,577	41	91 R	50.5%	48.8%	50.9%	49.1%
29,151	FAYETTE	11,846	6,693	5,105	48	1,588 R	56.5%	43.1%	56.7%	43.3%
20,169	FLOYD	8,731	5,248	3,446	37	1,802 R	60.1%	39.5%	60.4%	39.6%
16,379	FRANKLIN	6,062	3,150	2,851	61	299 R	52.0%	47.0%	52.5%	47.5%
14,645	FREMONT	5,877	3,113	2,747	17	366 R	53.0%	46.7%	53.1%	46.9%
16,599	GREENE	6,263	3,437	2,797	29	640 R	54.9%	44.7%	55.1%	44.9%
13,518	GRUNDY	5,834	3,625	2,191	18	1,434 R	62.1%	37.6%	62.3%	37.7%
17,210	GUTHRIE	6,977	4,042	2,899	36	1,143 R	57.9%	41.6%	58.2%	41.8%
19,922	HAMILTON	8,180	3,837	4,302	41	465 D	46.9%	52.6%	47.1%	52.9%
15,402	HANCOCK	6,003	3,114	2,855	34	259 R	51.9%	47.6%	52.2%	47.8%
22,530	HARDIN	9,094	5,059	3,975	60	1,084 R	55.6%	43.7%	56.0%	44.0%
22,767	HARRISON	9,309	5,059	4,201	49	858 R	54.3%	45.1%	54.6%	45.4%
17,994	HENRY	7,998	5,208	2,741	49	2,467 R	65.1%	34.3%	65.5%	34.5%
13,531	HOWARD	6,114	2,961	3,132	21	171 D	48.4%	51.2%	48.6%	51.4%
13,459	HUMBOLDT	5,290	2,525	2,749	16	224 D	47.7%	52.0%	47.9%	52.1%
11,047	IDA	4,601	2,640	1,943	18	697 R	57.4%	42.2%	57.6%	42.4%
17,016	IOWA	7,340	3,959	3,119	262	840 R	53.9%	42.5%	55.9%	44.1%
19,181	JACKSON	7,886	4,341	3,537	8	804 R	55.0%	44.9%	55.1%	44.9%
31,496	JASPER	13,479	6,413	6,978	88	565 D	47.6%	51.8%	47.9%	52.1%
15,762	JEFFERSON	7,344	4,335	2,926	83	1,409 R	59.0%	39.8%	59.7%	40.3%
33,191	JOHNSON	14,897	6,396	8,434	67	2,038 D	42.9%	56.6%	43.1%	56.9%
19,950	JONES	8,032	4,453	3,563	16	890 R	55.4%	44.4%	55.6%	44.4%
18,406	KEOKUK	8,606	4,644	3,900	62	744 R	54.0%	45.3%	54.4%	45.6%
26,630	KOSSUTH	10,433	4,918	5,488	27	570 D	47.1%	52.6%	47.3%	52.7%
41,074	LEE	17,736	9,406	8,252	78	1,154 R	53.0%	46.5%	53.3%	46.7%
89,142	LINN	42,562	21,293	21,123	146	170 R	50.0%	49.6%	50.2%	49.8%
11,384	LOUISA	4,679	2,745	1,894	40	851 R	58.7%	40.5%	59.2%	40.8%
14,571	LUCAS	5,713	3,139	2,526	48	613 R	54.9%	44.2%	55.4%	44.6%
15,374	LYON	5,042	3,065	1,970	7	1,095 R	60.8%	39.1%	60.9%	39.1%

IOWA

PRESIDENT 1944

1940 Census Population	County	Total Vote	Republican	Democratic	Other	Rep.-Dem. Plurality	Percentage Total Vote Rep.	Total Vote Dem.	Major Vote Rep.	Major Vote Dem.
14,525	MADISON	6,313	3,737	2,550	26	1,187 R	59.2%	40.4%	59.4%	40.6%
26,485	MAHASKA	10,072	5,123	4,652	297	471 R	50.9%	46.2%	52.4%	47.6%
27,019	MARION	11,338	4,874	6,365	99	1,491 D	43.0%	56.1%	43.4%	56.6%
35,406	MARSHALL	13,157	7,325	5,598	234	1,727 R	55.7%	42.5%	56.7%	43.3%
15,064	MILLS	5,421	3,288	2,106	27	1,182 R	60.7%	38.8%	61.0%	39.0%
14,121	MITCHELL	6,132	3,406	2,696	30	710 R	55.5%	44.0%	55.8%	44.2%
18,238	MONONA	7,366	3,583	3,761	22	178 D	48.6%	51.1%	48.8%	51.2%
14,553	MONROE	5,929	2,625	3,258	46	633 D	44.3%	55.0%	44.6%	55.4%
15,697	MONTGOMERY	6,783	4,165	2,572	46	1,593 R	61.4%	37.9%	61.8%	38.2%
31,296	MUSCATINE	11,963	7,104	4,801	58	2,303 R	59.4%	40.1%	59.7%	40.3%
19,293	O'BRIEN	7,201	4,033	3,138	30	895 R	56.0%	43.6%	56.2%	43.8%
10,607	OSCEOLA	3,798	2,100	1,689	9	411 R	55.3%	44.5%	55.4%	44.6%
24,887	PAGE	9,682	6,300	3,297	85	3,003 R	65.1%	34.1%	65.6%	34.4%
16,170	PALO ALTO	6,533	2,772	3,726	35	954 D	42.4%	57.0%	42.7%	57.3%
23,502	PLYMOUTH	9,076	6,085	2,970	21	3,115 R	67.0%	32.7%	67.2%	32.8%
16,266	POCAHONTAS	6,199	2,600	3,577	22	977 D	41.9%	57.7%	42.1%	57.9%
195,835	POLK	83,118	36,629	46,072	417	9,443 D	44.1%	55.4%	44.3%	55.7%
66,756	POTTAWATTAMIE	25,818	14,007	11,752	59	2,255 R	54.3%	45.5%	54.4%	45.6%
18,758	POWESHIEK	8,461	4,186	4,234	41	48 D	49.5%	50.0%	49.7%	50.3%
11,137	RINGGOLD	4,662	2,767	1,867	28	900 R	59.4%	40.0%	59.7%	40.3%
17,639	SAC	7,030	3,770	3,223	37	547 R	53.6%	45.8%	53.9%	46.1%
84,748	SCOTT	37,081	18,015	18,962	104	947 D	48.6%	51.1%	48.7%	51.3%
16,720	SHELBY	6,933	3,873	2,978	82	895 R	55.9%	43.0%	56.5%	43.5%
27,209	SIOUX	9,940	6,552	3,369	19	3,183 R	65.9%	33.9%	66.0%	34.0%
33,434	STORY	13,818	7,163	6,554	101	609 R	51.8%	47.4%	52.2%	47.8%
22,428	TAMA	10,567	5,249	5,286	32	37 D	49.7%	50.0%	49.8%	50.2%
14,258	TAYLOR	6,200	3,804	2,376	20	1,428 R	61.4%	38.3%	61.6%	38.4%
16,280	UNION	7,450	4,566	2,861	23	1,705 R	61.3%	38.4%	61.5%	38.5%
12,053	VAN BUREN	5,122	3,095	1,997	30	1,098 R	60.4%	39.0%	60.8%	39.2%
44,280	WAPELLO	19,089	8,244	10,732	113	2,488 D	43.2%	56.2%	43.4%	56.6%
17,695	WARREN	7,641	4,266	3,319	56	947 R	55.8%	43.4%	56.2%	43.8%
20,055	WASHINGTON	8,763	5,308	3,423	32	1,885 R	60.6%	39.1%	60.8%	39.2%
13,308	WAYNE	6,158	3,098	3,025	35	73 R	50.3%	49.1%	50.6%	49.4%
41,521	WEBSTER	16,468	6,935	9,477	56	2,542 D	42.1%	57.5%	42.3%	57.7%
13,972	WINNEBAGO	5,480	2,808	2,654	18	154 R	51.2%	48.4%	51.4%	48.6%
22,263	WINNESHIEK	9,893	5,318	4,557	18	761 R	53.8%	46.1%	53.9%	46.1%
103,627	WOODBURY	39,096	18,544	20,448	104	1,904 D	47.4%	52.3%	47.6%	52.4%
11,449	WORTH	4,725	2,086	2,629	10	543 D	44.1%	55.6%	44.2%	55.8%
20,038	WRIGHT	8,183	3,916	4,232	35	316 D	47.9%	51.7%	48.1%	51.9%
2,538,268	TOTAL	1,052,599	547,267	499,876	5,456	47,391 R	52.0%	47.5%	52.3%	47.7%

IOWA

PRESIDENT 1940

1940 Census Population	County	Total Vote	Republican	Democratic	Other	Rep.-Dem. Plurality	Percentage Total Vote Rep.	Percentage Total Vote Dem.	Percentage Major Vote Rep.	Percentage Major Vote Dem.
13,196	ADAIR	6,648	3,907	2,734	7	1,173 R	58.8%	41.1%	58.8%	41.2%
10,156	ADAMS	5,292	3,182	2,088	22	1,094 R	60.1%	39.5%	60.4%	39.6%
17,184	ALLAMAKEE	9,122	5,840	3,258	24	2,582 R	64.0%	35.7%	64.2%	35.8%
24,245	APPANOOSE	12,202	6,032	6,069	101	37 D	49.4%	49.7%	49.8%	50.2%
11,790	AUDUBON	5,875	2,632	3,236	7	604 D	44.8%	55.1%	44.9%	55.1%
22,879	BENTON	10,693	5,298	5,363	32	65 D	49.5%	50.2%	49.7%	50.3%
79,946	BLACK HAWK	34,532	17,132	17,305	95	173 D	49.6%	50.1%	49.7%	50.3%
29,782	BOONE	12,469	5,227	7,168	74	1,941 D	41.9%	57.5%	42.2%	57.8%
17,932	BREMER	8,495	5,374	3,103	18	2,271 R	63.3%	36.5%	63.4%	36.6%
20,991	BUCHANAN	10,309	5,630	4,649	30	981 R	54.6%	45.1%	54.8%	45.2%
19,838	BUENA VISTA	9,399	4,576	4,784	39	208 D	48.7%	50.9%	48.9%	51.1%
17,986	BUTLER	7,628	4,848	2,760	20	2,088 R	63.6%	36.2%	63.7%	36.3%
17,584	CALHOUN	8,161	3,792	4,344	25	552 D	46.5%	53.2%	46.6%	53.4%
22,770	CARROLL	10,923	5,376	5,526	21	150 D	49.2%	50.6%	49.3%	50.7%
18,647	CASS	10,172	6,377	3,763	32	2,614 R	62.7%	37.0%	62.9%	37.1%
16,884	CEDAR	8,840	5,521	3,293	26	2,228 R	62.5%	37.3%	62.6%	37.4%
43,845	CERRO GORDO	20,612	9,728	10,839	45	1,111 D	47.2%	52.6%	47.3%	52.7%
19,258	CHEROKEE	8,332	4,458	3,855	19	603 R	53.5%	46.3%	53.6%	46.4%
15,227	CHICKASAW	8,423	4,440	3,981	2	459 R	52.7%	47.3%	52.7%	47.3%
10,233	CLARKE	5,510	2,962	2,513	35	449 R	53.8%	45.6%	54.1%	45.9%
17,762	CLAY	8,025	3,673	4,328	24	655 D	45.8%	53.9%	45.9%	54.1%
24,334	CLAYTON	12,434	7,443	4,973	18	2,470 R	59.9%	40.0%	59.9%	40.1%
44,722	CLINTON	22,478	12,177	10,251	50	1,926 R	54.2%	45.6%	54.3%	45.7%
20,538	CRAWFORD	9,449	5,284	4,130	35	1,154 R	55.9%	43.7%	56.1%	43.9%
24,649	DALLAS	12,628	6,218	6,279	131	61 D	49.2%	49.7%	49.8%	50.2%
11,136	DAVIS	6,377	2,975	3,374	28	399 D	46.7%	52.9%	46.9%	53.1%
14,012	DECATUR	7,448	3,494	3,938	16	444 D	46.9%	52.9%	47.0%	53.0%
18,487	DELAWARE	9,176	6,175	2,985	16	3,190 R	67.3%	32.5%	67.4%	32.6%
36,804	DES MOINES	17,625	10,988	6,578	59	4,410 R	62.3%	37.3%	62.6%	37.4%
12,185	DICKINSON	5,742	2,736	2,985	21	249 D	47.6%	52.0%	47.8%	52.2%
63,768	DUBUQUE	28,441	14,590	13,805	46	785 R	51.3%	48.5%	51.4%	48.6%
13,406	EMMET	6,197	3,053	3,097	47	44 D	49.3%	50.0%	49.6%	50.4%
29,151	FAYETTE	14,342	8,237	6,066	39	2,171 R	57.4%	42.3%	57.6%	42.4%
20,169	FLOYD	10,031	5,829	4,167	35	1,662 R	58.1%	41.5%	58.3%	41.7%
16,379	FRANKLIN	7,310	3,623	3,540	147	83 R	49.6%	48.4%	50.6%	49.4%
14,645	FREMONT	7,764	3,825	3,914	25	89 D	49.3%	50.4%	49.4%	50.6%
16,599	GREENE	7,506	3,920	3,566	20	354 R	52.2%	47.5%	52.4%	47.6%
13,518	GRUNDY	6,674	3,908	2,745	21	1,163 R	58.6%	41.1%	58.7%	41.3%
17,210	GUTHRIE	8,255	4,733	3,489	33	1,244 R	57.3%	42.3%	57.6%	42.4%
19,922	HAMILTON	9,501	4,183	5,279	39	1,096 D	44.0%	55.6%	44.2%	55.8%
15,402	HANCOCK	7,173	3,632	3,514	27	118 R	50.6%	49.0%	50.8%	49.2%
22,530	HARDIN	10,491	5,692	4,764	35	928 R	54.3%	45.4%	54.4%	45.6%
22,767	HARRISON	11,428	6,094	5,317	17	777 R	53.3%	46.5%	53.4%	46.6%
17,994	HENRY	8,749	5,893	2,837	19	3,056 R	67.4%	32.4%	67.5%	32.5%
13,531	HOWARD	7,405	3,714	3,675	16	39 R	50.2%	49.6%	50.3%	49.7%
13,459	HUMBOLDT	6,143	2,853	3,268	22	415 D	46.4%	53.2%	46.6%	53.4%
11,047	IDA	5,487	3,166	2,306	15	860 R	57.7%	42.0%	57.9%	42.1%
17,016	IOWA	8,488	4,696	3,649	143	1,047 R	55.3%	43.0%	56.3%	43.7%
19,181	JACKSON	9,661	5,417	4,218	26	1,199 R	56.1%	43.7%	56.2%	43.8%
31,496	JASPER	15,421	7,240	8,129	52	889 D	46.9%	52.7%	47.1%	52.9%
15,762	JEFFERSON	8,336	4,891	3,402	43	1,489 R	58.7%	40.8%	59.0%	41.0%
33,191	JOHNSON	16,278	7,206	9,017	55	1,811 D	44.3%	55.4%	44.4%	55.6%
19,950	JONES	9,929	5,630	4,273	26	1,357 R	56.7%	43.0%	56.9%	43.1%
18,406	KEOKUK	9,988	5,394	4,552	42	842 R	54.0%	45.6%	54.2%	45.8%
26,630	KOSSUTH	12,165	5,639	6,502	24	863 D	46.4%	53.4%	46.4%	53.6%
41,074	LEE	19,766	10,616	9,117	33	1,499 R	53.7%	46.1%	53.8%	46.2%
89,142	LINN	43,235	23,581	19,531	123	4,050 R	54.5%	45.2%	54.7%	45.3%
11,384	LOUISA	5,627	3,330	2,247	50	1,083 R	59.2%	39.9%	59.7%	40.3%
14,571	LUCAS	7,149	3,806	3,255	88	551 R	53.2%	45.5%	53.9%	46.1%
15,374	LYON	6,540	3,880	2,648	12	1,232 R	59.3%	40.5%	59.4%	40.6%

IOWA

PRESIDENT 1940

1940 Census Population	County	Total Vote	Republican	Democratic	Other	Rep.-Dem. Plurality	Percentage Total Vote Rep.	Total Vote Dem.	Major Vote Rep.	Major Vote Dem.
14,525	MADISON	7,600	4,477	3,094	29	1,383 R	58.9%	40.7%	59.1%	40.9%
26,485	MAHASKA	11,977	6,123	5,757	97	366 R	51.1%	48.1%	51.5%	48.5%
27,019	MARION	12,753	5,763	6,915	75	1,152 D	45.2%	54.2%	45.5%	54.5%
35,406	MARSHALL	15,065	8,503	6,497	65	2,006 R	56.4%	43.1%	56.7%	43.3%
15,064	MILLS	6,749	3,873	2,862	14	1,011 R	57.4%	42.4%	57.5%	42.5%
14,121	MITCHELL	6,987	3,947	3,025	15	922 R	56.5%	43.3%	56.6%	43.4%
18,238	MONONA	8,990	4,192	4,783	15	591 D	46.6%	53.2%	46.7%	53.3%
14,553	MONROE	7,336	3,270	3,994	72	724 D	44.6%	54.4%	45.0%	55.0%
15,697	MONTGOMERY	8,220	4,848	3,332	40	1,516 R	59.0%	40.5%	59.3%	40.7%
31,296	MUSCATINE	14,421	8,543	5,825	53	2,718 R	59.2%	40.4%	59.5%	40.5%
19,293	O'BRIEN	8,931	4,760	4,133	38	627 R	53.3%	46.3%	53.5%	46.5%
10,607	OSCEOLA	4,742	2,425	2,288	29	137 R	51.1%	48.2%	51.5%	48.5%
24,887	PAGE	11,566	7,407	4,102	57	3,305 R	64.0%	35.5%	64.4%	35.6%
16,170	PALO ALTO	7,822	3,322	4,482	18	1,160 D	42.5%	57.3%	42.6%	57.4%
23,502	PLYMOUTH	11,579	7,725	3,831	23	3,894 R	66.7%	33.1%	66.8%	33.2%
16,266	POCAHONTAS	7,121	2,985	4,118	18	1,133 D	41.9%	57.8%	42.0%	58.0%
195,835	POLK	93,193	41,245	51,647	301	10,402 D	44.3%	55.4%	44.4%	55.6%
66,756	POTTAWATTAMIE	31,188	15,929	15,221	38	708 R	51.1%	48.8%	51.1%	48.9%
18,758	POWESHIEK	9,611	4,773	4,794	44	21 D	49.7%	49.9%	49.9%	50.1%
11,137	RINGGOLD	5,894	3,507	2,374	13	1,133 R	59.5%	40.3%	59.6%	40.4%
17,639	SAC	8,121	4,358	3,754	9	604 R	53.7%	46.2%	53.7%	46.3%
84,748	SCOTT	39,630	18,504	20,996	130	2,492 D	46.7%	53.0%	46.8%	53.2%
16,720	SHELBY	8,460	4,613	3,811	36	802 R	54.5%	45.0%	54.8%	45.2%
27,209	SIOUX	11,750	7,585	4,144	21	3,441 R	64.6%	35.3%	64.7%	35.3%
33,434	STORY	15,070	7,853	7,152	65	701 R	52.1%	47.5%	52.3%	47.7%
22,428	TAMA	11,893	5,865	5,996	32	131 D	49.3%	50.4%	49.4%	50.6%
14,258	TAYLOR	7,421	4,420	2,976	25	1,444 R	59.6%	40.1%	59.8%	40.2%
16,280	UNION	8,668	5,421	3,229	18	2,192 R	62.5%	37.3%	62.7%	37.3%
12,053	VAN BUREN	6,550	4,108	2,416	26	1,692 R	62.7%	36.9%	63.0%	37.0%
44,280	WAPELLO	21,006	9,039	11,880	87	2,841 D	43.0%	56.6%	43.2%	56.8%
17,695	WARREN	8,923	5,016	3,856	51	1,160 R	56.2%	43.2%	56.5%	43.5%
20,055	WASHINGTON	9,721	5,649	4,030	42	1,619 R	58.1%	41.5%	58.4%	41.6%
13,308	WAYNE	7,401	3,748	3,625	28	123 R	50.6%	49.0%	50.8%	49.2%
41,521	WEBSTER	18,366	7,583	10,731	52	3,148 D	41.3%	58.4%	41.4%	58.6%
13,972	WINNEBAGO	6,388	3,308	3,051	29	257 R	51.8%	47.8%	52.0%	48.0%
22,263	WINNESHIEK	11,637	6,208	5,405	24	803 R	53.3%	46.4%	53.5%	46.5%
103,627	WOODBURY	47,378	22,832	24,457	89	1,625 D	48.2%	51.6%	48.3%	51.7%
11,449	WORTH	5,455	2,434	3,007	14	573 D	44.6%	55.1%	44.7%	55.3%
20,038	WRIGHT	9,350	4,443	4,871	36	428 D	47.5%	52.1%	47.7%	52.3%
2,538,268	TOTAL	1,215,432	632,370	578,802	4,260	53,568 R	52.0%	47.6%	52.2%	47.8%

IOWA

PRESIDENT 1936

1930 Census Population	County	Total Vote	Republican	Democratic	Other	Rep.-Dem. Plurality	Percentage Total Vote Rep.	Percentage Total Vote Dem.	Percentage Major Vote Rep.	Percentage Major Vote Dem.
13,891	ADAIR	6,763	3,436	3,243	84	193 R	50.8%	48.0%	51.4%	48.6%
10,437	ADAMS	5,268	2,953	2,249	66	704 R	56.1%	42.7%	56.8%	43.2%
16,328	ALLAMAKEE	8,763	4,053	4,327	383	274 D	46.3%	49.4%	48.4%	51.6%
24,835	APPANOOSE	12,203	5,511	6,599	93	1,088 D	45.2%	54.1%	45.5%	54.5%
12,264	AUDUBON	5,839	2,344	3,448	47	1,104 D	40.1%	59.1%	40.5%	59.5%
22,851	BENTON	9,934	4,144	5,606	184	1,462 D	41.7%	56.4%	42.5%	57.5%
69,146	BLACK HAWK	31,681	13,666	16,793	1,222	3,127 D	43.1%	53.0%	44.9%	55.1%
29,271	BOONE	11,629	4,110	7,080	439	2,970 D	35.3%	60.9%	36.7%	63.3%
17,046	BREMER	8,470	3,220	5,058	192	1,838 D	38.0%	59.7%	38.9%	61.1%
19,550	BUCHANAN	9,894	4,734	5,025	135	291 D	47.8%	50.8%	48.5%	51.5%
18,667	BUENA VISTA	8,785	3,334	5,287	164	1,953 D	38.0%	60.2%	38.7%	61.3%
17,617	BUTLER	7,551	3,604	3,786	161	182 D	47.7%	50.1%	48.8%	51.2%
17,605	CALHOUN	7,699	3,027	4,544	128	1,517 D	39.3%	59.0%	40.0%	60.0%
22,326	CARROLL	10,503	3,259	6,285	959	3,026 D	31.0%	59.8%	34.1%	65.9%
19,422	CASS	9,962	5,622	4,284	56	1,338 R	56.4%	43.0%	56.8%	43.2%
16,760	CEDAR	8,235	3,686	4,385	164	699 D	44.8%	53.2%	45.7%	54.3%
38,476	CERRO GORDO	17,794	7,599	9,694	501	2,095 D	42.7%	54.5%	43.9%	56.1%
18,737	CHEROKEE	7,845	2,902	4,716	227	1,814 D	37.0%	60.1%	38.1%	61.9%
14,637	CHICKASAW	7,866	3,143	4,458	265	1,315 D	40.0%	56.7%	41.3%	58.7%
10,384	CLARKE	5,263	2,571	2,613	79	42 D	48.9%	49.6%	49.6%	50.4%
16,107	CLAY	7,586	2,774	4,691	121	1,917 D	36.6%	61.8%	37.2%	62.8%
24,559	CLAYTON	12,236	5,017	6,731	488	1,714 D	41.0%	55.0%	42.7%	57.3%
44,377	CLINTON	23,042	10,016	12,269	757	2,253 D	43.5%	53.2%	44.9%	55.1%
21,028	CRAWFORD	9,502	3,514	5,720	268	2,206 D	37.0%	60.2%	38.1%	61.9%
25,493	DALLAS	11,973	5,442	6,341	190	899 D	45.5%	53.0%	46.2%	53.8%
11,150	DAVIS	6,313	2,815	3,463	35	648 D	44.6%	54.9%	44.8%	55.2%
14,903	DECATUR	7,494	3,327	4,131	36	804 D	44.4%	55.1%	44.6%	55.4%
18,122	DELAWARE	9,046	4,483	4,350	213	133 R	49.6%	48.1%	50.8%	49.2%
38,162	DES MOINES	15,705	6,763	7,011	1,931	248 D	43.1%	44.6%	49.1%	50.9%
10,982	DICKINSON	5,791	2,322	3,399	70	1,077 D	40.1%	58.7%	40.6%	59.4%
61,214	DUBUQUE	27,378	8,275	16,291	2,812	8,016 D	30.2%	59.5%	33.7%	66.3%
12,856	EMMET	5,645	2,362	3,158	125	796 D	41.8%	55.9%	42.8%	57.2%
29,145	FAYETTE	13,397	5,891	7,210	296	1,319 D	44.0%	53.8%	45.0%	55.0%
19,524	FLOYD	9,031	4,267	4,242	522	25 R	47.2%	47.0%	50.1%	49.9%
16,382	FRANKLIN	6,705	2,530	3,993	182	1,463 D	37.7%	59.6%	38.8%	61.2%
15,533	FREMONT	7,617	3,291	4,301	25	1,010 D	43.2%	56.5%	43.3%	56.7%
16,528	GREENE	7,559	3,384	3,961	214	577 D	44.8%	52.4%	46.1%	53.9%
14,133	GRUNDY	6,703	2,656	3,918	129	1,262 D	39.6%	58.5%	40.4%	59.6%
17,324	GUTHRIE	8,070	4,155	3,619	296	536 R	51.5%	44.8%	53.4%	46.6%
20,978	HAMILTON	8,758	3,174	5,432	152	2,258 D	36.2%	62.0%	36.9%	63.1%
14,802	HANCOCK	6,629	2,585	3,930	114	1,345 D	39.0%	59.3%	39.7%	60.3%
22,947	HARDIN	9,933	4,306	5,429	198	1,123 D	43.4%	54.7%	44.2%	55.8%
24,897	HARRISON	11,678	5,314	6,206	158	892 D	45.5%	53.1%	46.1%	53.9%
17,660	HENRY	8,271	4,480	3,542	249	938 R	54.2%	42.8%	55.8%	44.2%
13,082	HOWARD	7,098	2,947	3,861	290	914 D	41.5%	54.4%	43.3%	56.7%
13,202	HUMBOLDT	5,797	2,262	3,420	115	1,158 D	39.0%	59.0%	39.8%	60.2%
11,933	IDA	5,333	1,834	3,397	102	1,563 D	34.4%	63.7%	35.1%	64.9%
17,332	IOWA	7,712	3,360	4,163	189	803 D	43.6%	54.0%	44.7%	55.3%
18,481	JACKSON	8,823	3,581	4,889	353	1,308 D	40.6%	55.4%	42.3%	57.7%
32,936	JASPER	14,395	5,875	8,315	205	2,440 D	40.8%	57.8%	41.4%	58.6%
16,241	JEFFERSON	7,941	4,037	3,690	214	347 R	50.8%	46.5%	52.2%	47.8%
30,276	JOHNSON	14,743	5,629	8,794	320	3,165 D	38.2%	59.6%	39.0%	61.0%
19,206	JONES	9,356	4,141	5,052	163	911 D	44.3%	54.0%	45.0%	55.0%
19,148	KEOKUK	9,878	4,491	5,162	225	671 D	45.5%	52.3%	46.5%	53.5%
25,452	KOSSUTH	11,863	3,569	8,071	223	4,502 D	30.1%	68.0%	30.7%	69.3%
41,268	LEE	19,317	8,955	9,630	732	675 D	46.4%	49.9%	48.2%	51.8%
82,336	LINN	39,806	19,129	19,724	953	595 D	48.1%	49.6%	49.2%	50.8%
11,575	LOUISA	5,615	2,655	2,859	101	204 D	47.3%	50.9%	48.2%	51.8%
15,114	LUCAS	7,382	3,414	3,773	195	359 D	46.2%	51.1%	47.5%	52.5%
15,293	LYON	5,944	2,264	3,590	90	1,326 D	38.1%	60.4%	38.7%	61.3%

IOWA

PRESIDENT 1936

1930 Census Population	County	Total Vote	Republican	Democratic	Other	Rep.-Dem. Plurality	Percentage Total Vote Rep.	Total Vote Dem.	Major Vote Rep.	Major Vote Dem.
14,331	MADISON	7,609	4,188	3,365	56	823 R	55.0%	44.2%	55.4%	44.6%
25,804	MAHASKA	11,726	5,270	6,094	362	824 D	44.9%	52.0%	46.4%	53.6%
25,727	MARION	11,986	4,975	6,745	266	1,770 D	41.5%	56.3%	42.4%	57.6%
33,727	MARSHALL	14,008	7,377	6,297	334	1,080 R	52.7%	45.0%	53.9%	46.1%
15,866	MILLS	7,075	3,424	3,610	41	186 D	48.4%	51.0%	48.7%	51.3%
14,065	MITCHELL	6,603	2,765	3,610	228	845 D	41.9%	54.7%	43.4%	56.6%
18,213	MONONA	8,500	3,008	5,346	146	2,338 D	35.4%	62.9%	36.0%	64.0%
15,010	MONROE	7,461	3,001	4,205	255	1,204 D	40.2%	56.4%	41.6%	58.4%
16,752	MONTGOMERY	8,386	4,395	3,920	71	475 R	52.4%	46.7%	52.9%	47.1%
29,385	MUSCATINE	13,313	6,332	6,593	388	261 D	47.6%	49.5%	49.0%	51.0%
18,409	O'BRIEN	8,612	3,350	5,139	123	1,789 D	38.9%	59.7%	39.5%	60.5%
10,182	OSCEOLA	4,453	1,539	2,812	102	1,273 D	34.6%	63.1%	35.4%	64.6%
25,904	PAGE	11,323	6,624	4,646	53	1,978 R	58.5%	41.0%	58.8%	41.2%
15,398	PALO ALTO	7,333	2,613	4,515	205	1,902 D	35.6%	61.6%	36.7%	63.3%
24,159	PLYMOUTH	11,445	4,133	5,994	1,318	1,861 D	36.1%	52.4%	40.8%	59.2%
15,687	POCAHONTAS	6,819	2,277	4,357	185	2,080 D	33.4%	63.9%	34.3%	65.7%
172,837	POLK	79,460	33,819	44,274	1,367	10,455 D	42.6%	55.7%	43.3%	56.7%
69,888	POTTAWATTAMIE	28,913	12,223	16,259	431	4,036 D	42.3%	56.2%	42.9%	57.1%
18,727	POWESHIEK	8,996	4,037	4,745	214	708 D	44.9%	52.7%	46.0%	54.0%
11,966	RINGGOLD	5,995	3,316	2,615	64	701 R	55.3%	43.6%	55.9%	44.1%
17,641	SAC	8,023	3,437	4,472	114	1,035 D	42.8%	55.7%	43.5%	56.5%
77,332	SCOTT	34,145	12,691	20,737	717	8,046 D	37.2%	60.7%	38.0%	62.0%
17,131	SHELBY	8,231	3,490	4,264	477	774 D	42.4%	51.8%	45.0%	55.0%
26,806	SIOUX	10,669	4,543	5,553	573	1,010 D	42.6%	52.0%	45.0%	55.0%
31,141	STORY	13,588	6,358	6,933	297	575 D	46.8%	51.0%	47.8%	52.2%
21,987	TAMA	11,522	4,737	6,625	160	1,888 D	41.1%	57.5%	41.7%	58.3%
14,859	TAYLOR	7,545	4,145	3,337	63	808 R	54.9%	44.2%	55.4%	44.6%
17,435	UNION	8,699	4,647	3,938	114	709 R	53.4%	45.3%	54.1%	45.9%
12,603	VAN BUREN	6,422	3,535	2,804	83	731 R	55.0%	43.7%	55.8%	44.2%
40,480	WAPELLO	18,512	7,647	10,578	287	2,931 D	41.3%	57.1%	42.0%	58.0%
17,700	WARREN	8,805	4,642	4,011	152	631 R	52.7%	45.6%	53.6%	46.4%
19,822	WASHINGTON	9,118	4,619	4,379	120	240 R	50.7%	48.0%	51.3%	48.7%
13,787	WAYNE	7,452	3,609	3,778	65	169 D	48.4%	50.7%	48.9%	51.1%
40,425	WEBSTER	17,174	6,494	9,885	795	3,391 D	37.8%	57.6%	39.6%	60.4%
13,143	WINNEBAGO	5,927	2,592	3,133	202	541 D	43.7%	52.9%	45.3%	54.7%
21,630	WINNESHIEK	11,181	4,489	5,980	712	1,491 D	40.1%	53.5%	42.9%	57.1%
101,669	WOODBURY	43,002	14,157	26,847	1,998	12,690 D	32.9%	62.4%	34.5%	65.5%
11,164	WORTH	4,984	1,964	2,976	44	1,012 D	39.4%	59.7%	39.8%	60.2%
20,216	WRIGHT	8,710	3,311	5,177	222	1,866 D	38.0%	59.4%	39.0%	61.0%
2,470,939	TOTAL	1,142,737	487,977	621,756	33,004	133,779 D	42.7%	54.4%	44.0%	56.0%

IOWA

PRESIDENT 1932

1930 Census Population	County	Total Vote	Republican	Democratic	Other	Rep.-Dem. Plurality	Percentage Total Vote Rep.	Total Vote Dem.	Major Vote Rep.	Major Vote Dem.
13,891	ADAIR	4,949	2,305	2,607	37	302 D	46.6%	52.7%	46.9%	53.1%
10,437	ADAMS	3,939	1,795	2,097	47	302 D	45.6%	53.2%	46.1%	53.9%
16,328	ALLAMAKEE	7,848	3,009	4,783	56	1,774 D	38.3%	60.9%	38.6%	61.4%
24,835	APPANOOSE	10,017	4,229	5,519	269	1,290 D	42.2%	55.1%	43.4%	56.6%
12,264	AUDUBON	4,633	1,604	2,986	43	1,382 D	34.6%	64.5%	34.9%	65.1%
22,851	BENTON	9,819	3,424	6,070	325	2,646 D	34.9%	61.8%	36.1%	63.9%
69,146	BLACK HAWK	29,765	14,746	14,660	359	86 R	49.5%	49.3%	50.1%	49.9%
29,271	BOONE	9,722	3,694	5,293	735	1,599 D	38.0%	54.4%	41.1%	58.9%
17,046	BREMER	7,994	2,520	5,411	63	2,891 D	31.5%	67.7%	31.8%	68.2%
19,550	BUCHANAN	9,500	4,401	5,004	95	603 D	46.3%	52.7%	46.8%	53.2%
18,667	BUENA VISTA	8,210	3,162	4,835	213	1,673 D	38.5%	58.9%	39.5%	60.5%
17,617	BUTLER	7,116	3,012	4,028	76	1,016 D	42.3%	56.6%	42.8%	57.2%
17,605	CALHOUN	6,977	2,404	4,368	205	1,964 D	34.5%	62.6%	35.5%	64.5%
22,326	CARROLL	9,499	2,265	7,174	60	4,909 D	23.8%	75.5%	24.0%	76.0%
19,422	CASS	8,645	4,215	4,339	91	124 D	48.8%	50.2%	49.3%	50.7%
16,760	CEDAR	8,068	3,277	4,718	73	1,441 D	40.6%	58.5%	41.0%	59.0%
38,476	CERRO GORDO	16,218	7,317	8,752	149	1,435 D	45.1%	54.0%	45.5%	54.5%
18,737	CHEROKEE	7,382	2,570	4,701	111	2,131 D	34.8%	63.7%	35.3%	64.7%
14,637	CHICKASAW	7,676	2,585	5,047	44	2,462 D	33.7%	65.8%	33.9%	66.1%
10,384	CLARKE	4,030	1,608	2,342	80	734 D	39.9%	58.1%	40.7%	59.3%
16,107	CLAY	6,769	2,599	3,944	226	1,345 D	38.4%	58.3%	39.7%	60.3%
24,559	CLAYTON	11,134	3,725	7,347	62	3,622 D	33.5%	66.0%	33.6%	66.4%
44,377	CLINTON	21,880	9,085	12,587	208	3,502 D	41.5%	57.5%	41.9%	58.1%
21,028	CRAWFORD	8,942	2,334	6,084	524	3,750 D	26.1%	68.0%	27.7%	72.3%
25,493	DALLAS	9,611	4,516	4,887	208	371 D	47.0%	50.8%	48.0%	52.0%
11,150	DAVIS	5,195	1,757	3,351	87	1,594 D	33.8%	64.5%	34.4%	65.6%
14,903	DECATUR	5,830	2,148	3,591	91	1,443 D	36.8%	61.6%	37.4%	62.6%
18,122	DELAWARE	8,754	4,088	4,559	107	471 D	46.7%	52.1%	47.3%	52.7%
38,162	DES MOINES	15,675	5,590	9,395	690	3,805 D	35.7%	59.9%	37.3%	62.7%
10,982	DICKINSON	4,706	2,074	2,500	132	426 D	44.1%	53.1%	45.3%	54.7%
61,214	DUBUQUE	26,999	6,747	19,210	1,042	12,463 D	25.0%	71.2%	26.0%	74.0%
12,856	EMMET	4,709	2,129	2,486	94	357 D	45.2%	52.8%	46.1%	53.9%
29,145	FAYETTE	13,022	5,166	7,690	166	2,524 D	39.7%	59.1%	40.2%	59.8%
19,524	FLOYD	8,781	4,083	4,563	135	480 D	46.5%	52.0%	47.2%	52.8%
16,382	FRANKLIN	6,110	2,013	3,782	315	1,769 D	32.9%	61.9%	34.7%	65.3%
15,533	FREMONT	6,989	2,339	4,585	65	2,246 D	33.5%	65.6%	33.8%	66.2%
16,528	GREENE	5,278	2,360	2,747	171	387 D	44.7%	52.0%	46.2%	53.8%
14,133	GRUNDY	6,134	2,419	3,661	54	1,242 D	39.4%	59.7%	39.8%	60.2%
17,324	GUTHRIE	5,812	2,637	3,099	76	462 D	45.4%	53.3%	46.0%	54.0%
20,978	HAMILTON	7,624	2,330	5,191	103	2,861 D	30.6%	68.1%	31.0%	69.0%
14,802	HANCOCK	6,254	2,355	3,822	77	1,467 D	37.7%	61.1%	38.1%	61.9%
22,947	HARDIN	9,246	3,523	5,022	701	1,499 D	38.1%	54.3%	41.2%	58.8%
24,897	HARRISON	11,008	3,513	7,427	68	3,914 D	31.9%	67.5%	32.1%	67.9%
17,660	HENRY	8,074	3,398	4,518	158	1,120 D	42.1%	56.0%	42.9%	57.1%
13,082	HOWARD	6,658	2,426	4,176	56	1,750 D	36.4%	62.7%	36.7%	63.3%
13,202	HUMBOLDT	4,889	2,028	2,804	57	776 D	41.5%	57.4%	42.0%	58.0%
11,933	IDA	5,187	1,452	3,661	74	2,209 D	28.0%	70.6%	28.4%	71.6%
17,332	IOWA	7,499	2,628	4,376	495	1,748 D	35.0%	58.4%	37.5%	62.5%
18,481	JACKSON	8,499	2,892	5,094	513	2,202 D	34.0%	59.9%	36.2%	63.8%
32,936	JASPER	12,401	5,399	6,781	221	1,382 D	43.5%	54.7%	44.3%	55.7%
16,241	JEFFERSON	7,110	2,955	4,056	99	1,101 D	41.6%	57.0%	42.1%	57.9%
30,276	JOHNSON	14,483	5,484	8,764	235	3,280 D	37.9%	60.5%	38.5%	61.5%
19,206	JONES	8,501	3,500	4,952	49	1,452 D	41.2%	58.3%	41.4%	58.6%
19,148	KEOKUK	9,369	3,442	5,839	88	2,397 D	36.7%	62.3%	37.1%	62.9%
25,452	KOSSUTH	10,148	3,075	6,925	148	3,850 D	30.3%	68.2%	30.8%	69.3%
41,268	LEE	17,902	7,084	10,624	194	3,540 D	39.6%	59.3%	40.0%	60.0%
82,336	LINN	36,915	18,733	17,693	489	1,040 R	50.7%	47.9%	51.4%	48.6%
11,575	LOUISA	4,989	2,045	2,856	88	811 D	41.0%	57.2%	41.7%	58.3%
15,114	LUCAS	5,976	2,381	3,434	161	1,053 D	39.8%	57.5%	40.9%	59.1%
15,293	LYON	5,297	1,684	3,543	70	1,859 D	31.8%	66.9%	32.2%	67.8%

IOWA

PRESIDENT 1932

1930 Census Population	County	Total Vote	Republican	Democratic	Other	Rep.-Dem. Plurality	Percentage Total Vote Rep.	Percentage Total Vote Dem.	Percentage Major Vote Rep.	Percentage Major Vote Dem.
14,331	MADISON	5,655	2,663	2,923	69	260 D	47.1%	51.7%	47.7%	52.3%
25,804	MAHASKA	10,713	4,655	5,586	472	931 D	43.5%	52.1%	45.5%	54.5%
25,727	MARION	11,034	3,695	7,067	272	3,372 D	33.5%	64.0%	34.3%	65.7%
33,727	MARSHALL	13,483	6,604	6,385	494	219 R	49.0%	47.4%	50.8%	49.2%
15,866	MILLS	6,356	2,420	3,861	75	1,441 D	38.1%	60.7%	38.5%	61.5%
14,065	MITCHELL	6,549	2,527	3,940	82	1,413 D	38.6%	60.2%	39.1%	60.9%
18,213	MONONA	7,812	2,181	5,537	94	3,356 D	27.9%	70.9%	28.3%	71.7%
15,010	MONROE	6,426	2,458	3,716	252	1,258 D	38.3%	57.8%	39.8%	60.2%
16,752	MONTGOMERY	7,401	3,507	3,760	134	253 D	47.4%	50.8%	48.3%	51.7%
29,385	MUSCATINE	12,917	6,160	6,423	334	263 D	47.7%	49.7%	49.0%	51.0%
18,409	O'BRIEN	7,848	3,213	4,503	132	1,290 D	40.9%	57.4%	41.6%	58.4%
10,182	OSCEOLA	3,829	1,190	2,590	49	1,400 D	31.1%	67.6%	31.5%	68.5%
25,904	PAGE	9,507	4,512	4,863	132	351 D	47.5%	51.2%	48.1%	51.9%
15,398	PALO ALTO	6,568	2,378	4,094	96	1,716 D	36.2%	62.3%	36.7%	63.3%
24,159	PLYMOUTH	10,563	2,888	7,565	110	4,677 D	27.3%	71.6%	27.6%	72.4%
15,687	POCAHONTAS	6,321	1,800	4,245	276	2,445 D	28.5%	67.2%	29.8%	70.2%
172,837	POLK	68,672	34,023	31,517	3,132	2,506 R	49.5%	45.9%	51.9%	48.1%
69,888	POTTAWATTAMIE	26,616	9,565	16,674	377	7,109 D	35.9%	62.6%	36.5%	63.5%
18,727	POWESHIEK	8,355	3,490	4,649	216	1,159 D	41.8%	55.6%	42.9%	57.1%
11,966	RINGGOLD	4,623	2,082	2,480	61	398 D	45.0%	53.6%	45.6%	54.4%
17,641	SAC	7,369	3,131	4,165	73	1,034 D	42.5%	56.5%	42.9%	57.1%
77,332	SCOTT	32,455	14,218	16,887	1,350	2,669 D	43.8%	52.0%	45.7%	54.3%
17,131	SHELBY	7,540	2,478	4,940	122	2,462 D	32.9%	65.5%	33.4%	66.6%
26,806	SIOUX	10,202	3,943	6,170	89	2,227 D	38.6%	60.5%	39.0%	61.0%
31,141	STORY	12,992	6,735	5,638	619	1,097 R	51.8%	43.4%	54.4%	45.6%
21,987	TAMA	10,920	4,051	6,704	165	2,653 D	37.1%	61.4%	37.7%	62.3%
14,859	TAYLOR	5,924	2,670	3,159	95	489 D	45.1%	53.3%	45.8%	54.2%
17,435	UNION	7,083	3,043	3,967	73	924 D	43.0%	56.0%	43.4%	56.6%
12,603	VAN BUREN	5,581	2,375	3,135	71	760 D	42.6%	56.2%	43.1%	56.9%
40,480	WAPELLO	17,076	7,256	9,504	316	2,248 D	42.5%	55.7%	43.3%	56.7%
17,700	WARREN	7,408	3,725	3,542	141	183 R	50.3%	47.8%	51.3%	48.7%
19,822	WASHINGTON	8,595	3,889	4,554	152	665 D	45.2%	53.0%	46.1%	53.9%
13,787	WAYNE	6,328	2,311	3,896	121	1,585 D	36.5%	61.6%	37.2%	62.8%
40,425	WEBSTER	15,117	5,243	8,957	917	3,714 D	34.7%	59.3%	36.9%	63.1%
13,143	WINNEBAGO	5,499	2,012	3,281	206	1,269 D	36.6%	59.7%	38.0%	62.0%
21,630	WINNESHIEK	10,333	3,348	6,823	162	3,475 D	32.4%	66.0%	32.9%	67.1%
101,669	WOODBURY	39,922	12,764	26,397	761	13,633 D	32.0%	66.1%	32.6%	67.4%
11,164	WORTH	4,395	1,690	2,640	65	950 D	38.5%	60.1%	39.0%	61.0%
20,216	WRIGHT	8,334	3,262	4,922	150	1,660 D	39.1%	59.1%	39.9%	60.1%
2,470,939	TOTAL	1,036,687	414,433	598,019	24,235	183,586 D	40.0%	57.7%	40.9%	59.1%

IOWA

PRESIDENT 1928

1920 Census Population	County	Total Vote	Republican	Democratic	Other	Rep.-Dem. Plurality	Percentage Total Vote Rep.	Total Vote Dem.	Major Vote Rep.	Major Vote Dem.
14,259	ADAIR	6,030	4,176	1,854		2,322 R	69.3%	30.7%	69.3%	30.7%
10,521	ADAMS	4,437	2,958	1,479		1,479 R	66.7%	33.3%	66.7%	33.3%
17,285	ALLAMAKEE	8,012	4,785	3,227		1,558 R	59.7%	40.3%	59.7%	40.3%
30,535	APPANOOSE	10,204	6,864	3,340		3,524 R	67.3%	32.7%	67.3%	32.7%
12,520	AUDUBON	4,704	2,340	2,364		24 D	49.7%	50.3%	49.7%	50.3%
24,080	BENTON	8,976	5,669	3,307		2,362 R	63.2%	36.8%	63.2%	36.8%
56,570	BLACK HAWK	27,876	19,409	8,467		10,942 R	69.6%	30.4%	69.6%	30.4%
29,892	BOONE	10,570	7,521	3,049		4,472 R	71.2%	28.8%	71.2%	28.8%
16,728	BREMER	7,025	3,879	3,146		733 R	55.2%	44.8%	55.2%	44.8%
19,890	BUCHANAN	8,984	5,885	3,099		2,786 R	65.5%	34.5%	65.5%	34.5%
18,556	BUENA VISTA	7,696	5,087	2,609		2,478 R	66.1%	33.9%	66.1%	33.9%
17,845	BUTLER	6,665	4,789	1,876		2,913 R	71.9%	28.1%	71.9%	28.1%
17,783	CALHOUN	6,817	4,136	2,681		1,455 R	60.7%	39.3%	60.7%	39.3%
21,549	CARROLL	10,148	4,014	6,134		2,120 D	39.6%	60.4%	39.6%	60.4%
19,421	CASS	8,760	6,120	2,640		3,480 R	69.9%	30.1%	69.9%	30.1%
17,560	CEDAR	7,373	4,856	2,517		2,339 R	65.9%	34.1%	65.9%	34.1%
34,675	CERRO GORDO	14,490	9,582	4,908		4,674 R	66.1%	33.9%	66.1%	33.9%
17,760	CHEROKEE	6,610	3,909	2,701		1,208 R	59.1%	40.9%	59.1%	40.9%
15,431	CHICKASAW	7,377	3,712	3,665		47 R	50.3%	49.7%	50.3%	49.7%
10,506	CLARKE	4,422	2,780	1,642		1,138 R	62.9%	37.1%	62.9%	37.1%
15,660	CLAY	6,050	3,986	2,064		1,922 R	65.9%	34.1%	65.9%	34.1%
25,032	CLAYTON	11,005	6,774	4,231		2,543 R	61.6%	38.4%	61.6%	38.4%
43,371	CLINTON	20,938	12,295	8,643		3,652 R	58.7%	41.3%	58.7%	41.3%
20,614	CRAWFORD	7,931	3,436	4,495		1,059 D	43.3%	56.7%	43.3%	56.7%
25,120	DALLAS	10,402	7,294	3,108		4,186 R	70.1%	29.9%	70.1%	29.9%
12,574	DAVIS	5,656	3,097	2,559		538 R	54.8%	45.2%	54.8%	45.2%
16,566	DECATUR	6,617	3,942	2,675		1,267 R	59.6%	40.4%	59.6%	40.4%
18,183	DELAWARE	8,433	5,390	3,043		2,347 R	63.9%	36.1%	63.9%	36.1%
35,520	DES MOINES	16,125	10,547	5,578		4,969 R	65.4%	34.6%	65.4%	34.6%
10,241	DICKINSON	4,296	3,045	1,251		1,794 R	70.9%	29.1%	70.9%	29.1%
58,262	DUBUQUE	29,181	9,744	19,437		9,693 D	33.4%	66.6%	33.4%	66.6%
12,627	EMMET	4,590	3,218	1,372		1,846 R	70.1%	29.9%	70.1%	29.9%
29,251	FAYETTE	12,399	8,338	4,061		4,277 R	67.2%	32.8%	67.2%	32.8%
18,860	FLOYD	7,749	5,675	2,074		3,601 R	73.2%	26.8%	73.2%	26.8%
15,807	FRANKLIN	5,112	3,424	1,688		1,736 R	67.0%	33.0%	67.0%	33.0%
15,447	FREMONT	6,419	3,597	2,822		775 R	56.0%	44.0%	56.0%	44.0%
16,467	GREENE	6,306	4,299	2,007		2,292 R	68.2%	31.8%	68.2%	31.8%
14,420	GRUNDY	5,291	3,671	1,620		2,051 R	69.4%	30.6%	69.4%	30.6%
17,596	GUTHRIE	7,007	4,772	2,235		2,537 R	68.1%	31.9%	68.1%	31.9%
19,531	HAMILTON	7,146	4,171	2,975		1,196 R	58.4%	41.6%	58.4%	41.6%
14,723	HANCOCK	5,047	3,114	1,933		1,181 R	61.7%	38.3%	61.7%	38.3%
23,337	HARDIN	8,104	5,731	2,373		3,358 R	70.7%	29.3%	70.7%	29.3%
24,488	HARRISON	10,011	5,605	4,406		1,199 R	56.0%	44.0%	56.0%	44.0%
18,298	HENRY	7,213	5,160	2,053		3,107 R	71.5%	28.5%	71.5%	28.5%
13,705	HOWARD	6,568	3,375	3,193		182 R	51.4%	48.6%	51.4%	48.6%
12,951	HUMBOLDT	4,507	2,828	1,679		1,149 R	62.7%	37.3%	62.7%	37.3%
11,689	IDA	4,658	2,486	2,172		314 R	53.4%	46.6%	53.4%	46.6%
18,600	IOWA	7,166	4,091	3,075		1,016 R	57.1%	42.9%	57.1%	42.9%
19,931	JACKSON	8,469	4,740	3,729		1,011 R	56.0%	44.0%	56.0%	44.0%
27,855	JASPER	13,001	9,144	3,857		5,287 R	70.3%	29.7%	70.3%	29.7%
16,440	JEFFERSON	7,078	4,919	2,159		2,760 R	69.5%	30.5%	69.5%	30.5%
26,462	JOHNSON	14,469	7,288	7,181		107 R	50.4%	49.6%	50.4%	49.6%
18,607	JONES	8,066	5,090	2,976		2,114 R	63.1%	36.9%	63.1%	36.9%
20,983	KEOKUK	9,076	5,304	3,772		1,532 R	58.4%	41.6%	58.4%	41.6%
25,082	KOSSUTH	9,614	4,878	4,736		142 R	50.7%	49.3%	50.7%	49.3%
39,676	LEE	19,430	11,645	7,785		3,860 R	59.9%	40.1%	59.9%	40.1%
74,004	LINN	37,167	25,452	11,715		13,737 R	68.5%	31.5%	68.5%	31.5%
12,179	LOUISA	4,732	3,275	1,457		1,818 R	69.2%	30.8%	69.2%	30.8%
15,686	LUCAS	5,699	3,811	1,888		1,923 R	66.9%	33.1%	66.9%	33.1%
15,431	LYON	4,802	3,170	1,632		1,538 R	66.0%	34.0%	66.0%	34.0%

IOWA

PRESIDENT 1928

1920 Census Population	County	Total Vote	Republican	Democratic	Other	Rep.-Dem. Plurality	Percentage Total Vote Rep.	Total Vote Dem.	Major Vote Rep.	Major Vote Dem.
15,020	MADISON	6,542	4,364	2,178		2,186 R	66.7%	33.3%	66.7%	33.3%
26,270	MAHASKA	10,568	7,368	3,200		4,168 R	69.7%	30.3%	69.7%	30.3%
24,957	MARION	10,338	6,225	4,113		2,112 R	60.2%	39.8%	60.2%	39.8%
32,630	MARSHALL	12,710	9,326	3,384		5,942 R	73.4%	26.6%	73.4%	26.6%
15,422	MILLS	5,608	3,429	2,179		1,250 R	61.1%	38.9%	61.1%	38.9%
13,921	MITCHELL	5,842	3,534	2,308		1,226 R	60.5%	39.5%	60.5%	39.5%
17,125	MONONA	6,581	3,745	2,836		909 R	56.9%	43.1%	56.9%	43.1%
23,467	MONROE	6,879	4,060	2,819		1,241 R	59.0%	41.0%	59.0%	41.0%
17,048	MONTGOMERY	7,234	5,155	2,079		3,076 R	71.3%	28.7%	71.3%	28.7%
29,042	MUSCATINE	12,659	8,604	4,055		4,549 R	68.0%	32.0%	68.0%	32.0%
19,051	O'BRIEN	7,242	4,845	2,397		2,448 R	66.9%	33.1%	66.9%	33.1%
10,223	OSCEOLA	3,652	2,085	1,567		518 R	57.1%	42.9%	57.1%	42.9%
24,137	PAGE	9,659	7,181	2,478		4,703 R	74.3%	25.7%	74.3%	25.7%
15,486	PALO ALTO	6,306	3,463	2,843		620 R	54.9%	45.1%	54.9%	45.1%
23,584	PLYMOUTH	9,863	4,848	5,015		167 D	49.2%	50.8%	49.2%	50.8%
15,602	POCAHONTAS	6,146	3,322	2,824		498 R	54.1%	45.9%	54.1%	45.9%
154,029	POLK	62,015	42,290	19,725		22,565 R	68.2%	31.8%	68.2%	31.8%
61,550	POTTAWATTAMIE	24,259	14,354	9,905		4,449 R	59.2%	40.8%	59.2%	40.8%
19,910	POWESHIEK	7,999	5,212	2,787		2,425 R	65.2%	34.8%	65.2%	34.8%
12,919	RINGGOLD	5,246	3,674	1,572		2,102 R	70.0%	30.0%	70.0%	30.0%
17,500	SAC	6,875	4,461	2,414		2,047 R	64.9%	35.1%	64.9%	35.1%
73,952	SCOTT	29,916	16,974	12,942		4,032 R	56.7%	43.3%	56.7%	43.3%
16,065	SHELBY	7,063	3,459	3,604		145 D	49.0%	51.0%	49.0%	51.0%
26,458	SIOUX	9,217	6,378	2,839		3,539 R	69.2%	30.8%	69.2%	30.8%
26,185	STORY	11,749	9,035	2,714		6,321 R	76.9%	23.1%	76.9%	23.1%
21,861	TAMA	10,387	5,589	4,798		791 R	53.8%	46.2%	53.8%	46.2%
15,514	TAYLOR	6,774	4,700	2,074		2,626 R	69.4%	30.6%	69.4%	30.6%
17,268	UNION	8,083	5,432	2,651		2,781 R	67.2%	32.8%	67.2%	32.8%
14,060	VAN BUREN	5,848	3,904	1,944		1,960 R	66.8%	33.2%	66.8%	33.2%
37,937	WAPELLO	17,379	11,586	5,793		5,793 R	66.7%	33.3%	66.7%	33.3%
18,047	WARREN	7,533	5,294	2,239		3,055 R	70.3%	29.7%	70.3%	29.7%
20,421	WASHINGTON	8,702	5,948	2,754		3,194 R	68.4%	31.6%	68.4%	31.6%
15,378	WAYNE	6,490	3,911	2,579		1,332 R	60.3%	39.7%	60.3%	39.7%
37,611	WEBSTER	15,022	8,525	6,497		2,028 R	56.8%	43.2%	56.8%	43.2%
13,489	WINNEBAGO	4,654	3,386	1,268		2,118 R	72.8%	27.2%	72.8%	27.2%
22,091	WINNESHIEK	9,619	5,084	4,535		549 R	52.9%	47.1%	52.9%	47.1%
92,171	WOODBURY	37,418	20,587	16,831		3,756 R	55.0%	45.0%	55.0%	45.0%
11,630	WORTH	4,231	2,921	1,310		1,611 R	69.0%	31.0%	69.0%	31.0%
20,348	WRIGHT	7,567	5,020	2,547		2,473 R	66.3%	33.7%	66.3%	33.7%
2,404,021	TOTAL	1,009,189	623,570	379,011	6,608	244,559 R	61.8%	37.6%	62.2%	37.8%

IOWA

PRESIDENT 1924

1920 Census Population	County	Total Vote	Republican	Democratic	Progressive	Other	Plurality	Percentage Total Vote Rep.	Dem.	Prog.
14,259	ADAIR	6,006	4,043	688	1,275		2,768 R	67.3%	11.5%	21.2%
10,521	ADAMS	4,691	2,547	897	1,247		1,300 R	54.3%	19.1%	26.6%
17,285	ALLAMAKEE	7,154	2,755	1,289	3,110		355 P	38.5%	18.0%	43.5%
30,535	APPANOOSE	11,175	6,421	2,032	2,722		3,699 R	57.5%	18.2%	24.4%
12,520	AUDUBON	4,592	2,475	965	1,152		1,323 R	53.9%	21.0%	25.1%
24,080	BENTON	9,102	5,314	1,459	2,329		2,985 R	58.4%	16.0%	25.6%
56,570	BLACK HAWK	24,191	15,813	2,981	5,397		10,416 R	65.4%	12.3%	22.3%
29,892	BOONE	10,635	4,980	702	4,953		27 R	46.8%	6.6%	46.6%
16,728	BREMER	7,302	3,532	911	2,859		673 R	48.4%	12.5%	39.2%
19,890	BUCHANAN	8,648	5,459	1,780	1,409		3,679 R	63.1%	20.6%	16.3%
18,556	BUENA VISTA	7,266	3,812	683	2,771		1,041 R	52.5%	9.4%	38.1%
17,845	BUTLER	6,411	3,823	667	1,921		1,902 R	59.6%	10.4%	30.0%
17,783	CALHOUN	6,601	3,529	714	2,358		1,171 R	53.5%	10.8%	35.7%
21,549	CARROLL	8,743	3,590	1,994	3,159		431 R	41.1%	22.8%	36.1%
19,421	CASS	8,308	5,721	1,099	1,488		4,233 R	68.9%	13.2%	17.9%
17,560	CEDAR	7,613	4,625	1,478	1,510		3,115 R	60.8%	19.4%	19.8%
34,675	CERRO GORDO	14,269	8,410	1,345	4,514		3,896 R	58.9%	9.4%	31.6%
17,760	CHEROKEE	6,172	3,240	904	2,028		1,212 R	52.5%	14.6%	32.9%
15,431	CHICKASAW	7,340	3,416	1,736	2,188		1,228 R	46.5%	23.7%	29.8%
10,506	CLARKE	4,860	2,554	743	1,563		991 R	52.6%	15.3%	32.2%
15,660	CLAY	5,780	3,549	378	1,853		1,696 R	61.4%	6.5%	32.1%
25,032	CLAYTON	10,038	4,168	1,556	4,314		146 P	41.5%	15.5%	43.0%
43,371	CLINTON	19,636	10,359	3,811	5,466		4,893 R	52.8%	19.4%	27.8%
20,614	CRAWFORD	7,775	2,882	1,255	3,638		756 P	37.1%	16.1%	46.8%
25,120	DALLAS	10,251	6,359	933	2,959		3,400 R	62.0%	9.1%	28.9%
12,574	DAVIS	5,748	2,804	1,802	1,142		1,002 R	48.8%	31.4%	19.9%
16,566	DECATUR	6,831	3,221	1,693	1,917		1,304 R	47.2%	24.8%	28.1%
18,183	DELAWARE	7,630	4,938	1,146	1,546		3,392 R	64.7%	15.0%	20.3%
35,520	DES MOINES	14,739	7,995	2,616	4,128		3,867 R	54.2%	17.7%	28.0%
10,241	DICKINSON	4,419	2,967	435	1,017		1,950 R	67.1%	9.8%	23.0%
58,262	DUBUQUE	24,566	8,280	5,718	10,568		2,288 P	33.7%	23.3%	43.0%
12,627	EMMET	5,133	2,739	407	1,987		752 R	53.4%	7.9%	38.7%
29,251	FAYETTE	11,880	5,974	1,272	4,634		1,340 R	50.3%	10.7%	39.0%
18,860	FLOYD	7,589	5,012	529	2,048		2,964 R	66.0%	7.0%	27.0%
15,807	FRANKLIN	5,128	3,064	360	1,704		1,360 R	59.8%	7.0%	33.2%
15,447	FREMONT	6,220	3,313	2,525	382		788 R	53.3%	40.6%	6.1%
16,467	GREENE	6,886	4,599	790	1,497		3,102 R	66.8%	11.5%	21.7%
14,420	GRUNDY	5,738	3,322	615	1,801		1,521 R	57.9%	10.7%	31.4%
17,596	GUTHRIE	7,181	4,314	840	2,027		2,287 R	60.1%	11.7%	28.2%
19,531	HAMILTON	7,239	4,401	490	2,348		2,053 R	60.8%	6.8%	32.4%
14,723	HANCOCK	5,338	3,183	550	1,605		1,578 R	59.6%	10.3%	30.1%
23,337	HARDIN	7,833	4,714	634	2,485		2,229 R	60.2%	8.1%	31.7%
24,488	HARRISON	9,915	5,062	3,179	1,674		1,883 R	51.1%	32.1%	16.9%
18,298	HENRY	7,293	4,536	1,344	1,413		3,123 R	62.2%	18.4%	19.4%
13,705	HOWARD	5,975	2,850	1,604	1,521		1,246 R	47.7%	26.8%	25.5%
12,951	HUMBOLDT	4,754	2,841	370	1,543		1,298 R	59.8%	7.8%	32.5%
11,689	IDA	4,674	2,033	685	1,956		77 R	43.5%	14.7%	41.8%
18,600	IOWA	6,813	3,549	1,458	1,806		1,743 R	52.1%	21.4%	26.5%
19,931	JACKSON	8,325	4,218	2,352	1,755		1,866 R	50.7%	28.3%	21.1%
27,855	JASPER	11,543	6,565	1,214	3,764		2,801 R	56.9%	10.5%	32.6%
16,440	JEFFERSON	6,590	4,062	1,249	1,279		2,783 R	61.6%	19.0%	19.4%
26,462	JOHNSON	12,864	5,741	4,570	2,553		1,171 R	44.6%	35.5%	19.8%
18,607	JONES	7,918	4,524	2,212	1,182		2,312 R	57.1%	27.9%	14.9%
20,983	KEOKUK	9,329	4,795	2,568	1,966		2,227 R	51.4%	27.5%	21.1%
25,082	KOSSUTH	8,737	3,806	1,369	3,562		244 R	43.6%	15.7%	40.8%
39,676	LEE	18,350	9,999	4,903	3,448		5,096 R	54.5%	26.7%	18.8%
74,004	LINN	34,647	22,371	5,941	6,335		16,036 R	64.6%	17.1%	18.3%
12,179	LOUISA	4,540	2,952	643	945		2,007 R	65.0%	14.2%	20.8%
15,686	LUCAS	6,242	3,288	824	2,130		1,158 R	52.7%	13.2%	34.1%
15,431	LYON	4,725	2,082	481	2,162		80 P	44.1%	10.2%	45.8%

IOWA

PRESIDENT 1924

1920 Census Population	County	Total Vote	Republican	Democratic	Progressive	Other	Plurality	Percentage Total Vote Rep.	Dem.	Prog.
15,020	MADISON	6,888	4,191	1,367	1,330		2,824 R	60.8%	19.8%	19.3%
26,270	MAHASKA	10,493	5,810	1,673	3,010		2,800 R	55.4%	15.9%	28.7%
24,957	MARION	10,595	5,058	2,383	3,154		1,904 R	47.7%	22.5%	29.8%
32,630	MARSHALL	13,110	9,010	1,516	2,584		6,426 R	68.7%	11.6%	19.7%
15,422	MILLS	5,825	3,348	1,750	727		1,598 R	57.5%	30.0%	12.5%
13,921	MITCHELL	6,150	2,892	400	2,858		34 R	47.0%	6.5%	46.5%
17,125	MONONA	6,268	3,195	1,271	1,802		1,393 R	51.0%	20.3%	28.7%
23,467	MONROE	8,000	4,098	1,388	2,514		1,584 R	51.2%	17.4%	31.4%
17,048	MONTGOMERY	7,154	4,617	805	1,732		2,885 R	64.5%	11.3%	24.2%
29,042	MUSCATINE	11,785	7,731	1,963	2,091		5,640 R	65.6%	16.7%	17.7%
19,051	O'BRIEN	7,128	4,172	756	2,200		1,972 R	58.5%	10.6%	30.9%
10,223	OSCEOLA	3,716	1,876	386	1,454		422 R	50.5%	10.4%	39.1%
24,137	PAGE	9,177	6,023	1,643	1,511		4,380 R	65.6%	17.9%	16.5%
15,486	PALO ALTO	5,929	2,943	593	2,393		550 R	49.6%	10.0%	40.4%
23,584	PLYMOUTH	9,036	3,803	1,605	3,628		175 R	42.1%	17.8%	40.2%
15,602	POCAHONTAS	6,290	2,537	819	2,934		397 P	40.3%	13.0%	46.6%
154,029	POLK	59,723	37,491	6,665	15,567		21,924 R	62.8%	11.2%	26.1%
61,550	POTTAWATTAMIE	25,322	13,380	5,305	6,637		6,743 R	52.8%	21.0%	26.2%
19,910	POWESHIEK	8,221	4,414	1,428	2,379		2,035 R	53.7%	17.4%	28.9%
12,919	RINGGOLD	5,186	3,147	882	1,157		1,990 R	60.7%	17.0%	22.3%
17,500	SAC	6,533	3,970	674	1,889		2,081 R	60.8%	10.3%	28.9%
73,952	SCOTT	30,194	18,360	4,347	7,487		10,873 R	60.8%	14.4%	24.8%
16,065	SHELBY	6,750	3,252	2,297	1,201		955 R	48.2%	34.0%	17.8%
26,458	SIOUX	8,416	4,960	900	2,556		2,404 R	58.9%	10.7%	30.4%
26,185	STORY	10,780	6,916	1,310	2,554		4,362 R	64.2%	12.2%	23.7%
21,861	TAMA	9,360	5,177	2,180	2,003		2,997 R	55.3%	23.3%	21.4%
15,514	TAYLOR	6,971	4,254	1,138	1,579		2,675 R	61.0%	16.3%	22.7%
17,268	UNION	7,841	4,250	1,166	2,425		1,825 R	54.2%	14.9%	30.9%
14,060	VAN BUREN	5,964	3,623	1,209	1,132		2,414 R	60.7%	20.3%	19.0%
37,937	WAPELLO	17,307	9,870	3,039	4,398		5,472 R	57.0%	17.6%	25.4%
18,047	WARREN	7,536	4,683	1,274	1,579		3,104 R	62.1%	16.9%	21.0%
20,421	WASHINGTON	8,371	5,053	1,868	1,450		3,185 R	60.4%	22.3%	17.3%
15,378	WAYNE	6,634	3,322	1,826	1,486		1,496 R	50.1%	27.5%	22.4%
37,611	WEBSTER	13,996	6,641	2,076	5,279		1,362 R	47.4%	14.8%	37.7%
13,489	WINNEBAGO	5,167	2,445	225	2,497		52 P	47.3%	4.4%	48.3%
22,091	WINNESHIEK	9,427	4,154	1,510	3,763		391 R	44.1%	16.0%	39.9%
92,171	WOODBURY	35,034	16,639	5,676	12,719		3,920 R	47.5%	16.2%	36.3%
11,630	WORTH	4,589	2,340	180	2,069		271 R	51.0%	3.9%	45.1%
20,348	WRIGHT	7,531	4,323	501	2,707		1,616 R	57.4%	6.7%	35.9%
2,404,021	TOTAL	976,770	537,458	160,382	274,448	4,482	263,010 R	55.0%	16.4%	28.1%

IOWA

PRESIDENT 1920

1920 Census Population	County	Total Vote	Republican	Democratic	Other	Rep.-Dem. Plurality	Percentage Total Vote Rep.	Percentage Total Vote Dem.	Percentage Major Vote Rep.	Percentage Major Vote Dem.
14,259	ADAIR	5,563	4,133	1,358	72	2,775 R	74.3%	24.4%	75.3%	24.7%
10,521	ADAMS	4,557	2,845	1,670	42	1,175 R	62.4%	36.6%	63.0%	37.0%
17,285	ALLAMAKEE	7,090	5,192	1,833	65	3,359 R	73.2%	25.9%	73.9%	26.1%
30,535	APPANOOSE	9,743	6,382	2,952	409	3,430 R	65.5%	30.3%	68.4%	31.6%
12,520	AUDUBON	4,378	2,963	1,405	10	1,558 R	67.7%	32.1%	67.8%	32.2%
24,080	BENTON	9,207	6,539	2,343	325	4,196 R	71.0%	25.4%	73.6%	26.4%
56,570	BLACK HAWK	22,101	16,920	4,000	1,181	12,920 R	76.6%	18.1%	80.9%	19.1%
29,892	BOONE	9,980	7,093	2,240	647	4,853 R	71.1%	22.4%	76.0%	24.0%
16,728	BREMER	7,269	6,287	902	80	5,385 R	86.5%	12.4%	87.5%	12.5%
19,890	BUCHANAN	7,997	6,334	1,600	63	4,734 R	79.2%	20.0%	79.8%	20.2%
18,556	BUENA VISTA	6,270	4,927	1,204	139	3,723 R	78.6%	19.2%	80.4%	19.6%
17,845	BUTLER	6,806	5,900	830	76	5,070 R	86.7%	12.2%	87.7%	12.3%
17,783	CALHOUN	6,858	5,277	1,479	102	3,798 R	76.9%	21.6%	78.1%	21.9%
21,549	CARROLL	8,671	6,320	2,174	177	4,146 R	72.9%	25.1%	74.4%	25.6%
19,421	CASS	8,382	6,558	1,668	156	4,890 R	78.2%	19.9%	79.7%	20.3%
17,560	CEDAR	7,315	5,697	1,420	198	4,277 R	77.9%	19.4%	80.0%	20.0%
34,675	CERRO GORDO	10,951	8,293	2,302	356	5,991 R	75.7%	21.0%	78.3%	21.7%
17,760	CHEROKEE	5,849	4,544	1,211	94	3,333 R	77.7%	20.7%	79.0%	21.0%
15,431	CHICKASAW	6,744	4,517	2,171	56	2,346 R	67.0%	32.2%	67.5%	32.5%
10,506	CLARKE	4,450	3,150	1,257	43	1,893 R	70.8%	28.2%	71.5%	28.5%
15,660	CLAY	5,585	4,471	1,001	113	3,470 R	80.1%	17.9%	81.7%	18.3%
25,032	CLAYTON	8,706	6,747	1,808	151	4,939 R	77.5%	20.8%	78.9%	21.1%
43,371	CLINTON	17,536	11,746	3,153	2,637	8,593 R	67.0%	18.0%	78.8%	21.2%
20,614	CRAWFORD	7,972	5,473	2,151	348	3,322 R	68.7%	27.0%	71.8%	28.2%
25,120	DALLAS	9,454	6,677	2,577	200	4,100 R	70.6%	27.3%	72.2%	27.8%
12,574	DAVIS	5,535	3,117	2,353	65	764 R	56.3%	42.5%	57.0%	43.0%
16,566	DECATUR	6,845	4,187	2,592	66	1,595 R	61.2%	37.9%	61.8%	38.2%
18,183	DELAWARE	7,088	5,880	1,111	97	4,769 R	83.0%	15.7%	84.1%	15.9%
35,520	DES MOINES	12,997	8,287	3,449	1,261	4,838 R	63.8%	26.5%	70.6%	29.4%
10,241	DICKINSON	4,101	3,298	760	43	2,538 R	80.4%	18.5%	81.3%	18.7%
58,262	DUBUQUE	21,000	12,436	7,636	928	4,800 R	59.2%	36.4%	62.0%	38.0%
12,627	EMMET	4,421	3,360	991	70	2,369 R	76.0%	22.4%	77.2%	22.8%
29,251	FAYETTE	10,444	8,265	1,941	238	6,324 R	79.1%	18.6%	81.0%	19.0%
18,860	FLOYD	7,197	6,106	933	158	5,173 R	84.8%	13.0%	86.7%	13.3%
15,807	FRANKLIN	5,109	4,397	601	111	3,796 R	86.1%	11.8%	88.0%	12.0%
15,447	FREMONT	6,364	3,776	2,524	64	1,252 R	59.3%	39.7%	59.9%	40.1%
16,467	GREENE	6,460	5,102	1,303	55	3,799 R	79.0%	20.2%	79.7%	20.3%
14,420	GRUNDY	5,432	4,662	714	56	3,948 R	85.8%	13.1%	86.7%	13.3%
17,596	GUTHRIE	7,099	5,338	1,647	114	3,691 R	75.2%	23.2%	76.4%	23.6%
19,531	HAMILTON	7,148	5,924	1,126	98	4,798 R	82.9%	15.8%	84.0%	16.0%
14,723	HANCOCK	4,474	3,617	725	132	2,892 R	80.8%	16.2%	83.3%	16.7%
23,337	HARDIN	7,915	6,646	1,076	193	5,570 R	84.0%	13.6%	86.1%	13.9%
24,488	HARRISON	9,742	6,127	3,479	136	2,648 R	62.9%	35.7%	63.8%	36.2%
18,298	HENRY	7,306	5,254	1,939	113	3,315 R	71.9%	26.5%	73.0%	27.0%
13,705	HOWARD	5,418	3,601	1,717	100	1,884 R	66.5%	31.7%	67.7%	32.3%
12,951	HUMBOLDT	4,319	3,577	681	61	2,896 R	82.8%	15.8%	84.0%	16.0%
11,689	IDA	4,684	3,547	1,090	47	2,457 R	75.7%	23.3%	76.5%	23.5%
18,600	IOWA	6,997	4,892	2,019	86	2,873 R	69.9%	28.9%	70.8%	29.2%
19,931	JACKSON	7,005	4,763	1,954	288	2,809 R	68.0%	27.9%	70.9%	29.1%
27,855	JASPER	11,029	7,417	3,390	222	4,027 R	67.2%	30.7%	68.6%	31.4%
16,440	JEFFERSON	6,108	4,558	1,450	100	3,108 R	74.6%	23.7%	75.9%	24.1%
26,462	JOHNSON	10,923	5,696	5,032	195	664 R	52.1%	46.1%	53.1%	46.9%
18,607	JONES	8,461	5,962	2,436	63	3,526 R	70.5%	28.8%	71.0%	29.0%
20,983	KEOKUK	9,135	6,207	2,800	128	3,407 R	67.9%	30.7%	68.9%	31.1%
25,082	KOSSUTH	7,769	6,018	1,682	69	4,336 R	77.5%	21.7%	78.2%	21.8%
39,676	LEE	16,322	10,763	5,177	382	5,586 R	65.9%	31.7%	67.5%	32.5%
74,004	LINN	27,818	20,036	6,932	850	13,104 R	72.0%	24.9%	74.3%	25.7%
12,179	LOUISA	4,594	3,560	932	102	2,628 R	77.5%	20.3%	79.3%	20.7%
15,686	LUCAS	5,506	3,775	1,463	268	2,312 R	68.6%	26.6%	72.1%	27.9%
15,431	LYON	4,459	3,633	729	97	2,904 R	81.5%	16.3%	83.3%	16.7%

IOWA

PRESIDENT 1920

1920 Census Population	County	Total Vote	Republican	Democratic	Other	Rep.-Dem. Plurality	Percentage Total Vote Rep.	Total Vote Dem.	Major Vote Rep.	Major Vote Dem.
15,020	MADISON	6,487	4,465	1,899	123	2,566 R	68.8%	29.3%	70.2%	29.8%
26,270	MAHASKA	10,440	6,739	3,339	362	3,400 R	64.5%	32.0%	66.9%	33.1%
24,957	MARION	9,599	5,435	3,861	303	1,574 R	56.6%	40.2%	58.5%	41.5%
32,630	MARSHALL	11,800	9,334	2,166	300	7,168 R	79.1%	18.4%	81.2%	18.8%
15,422	MILLS	5,338	3,683	1,592	63	2,091 R	69.0%	29.8%	69.8%	30.2%
13,921	MITCHELL	5,332	4,476	773	83	3,703 R	83.9%	14.5%	85.3%	14.7%
17,125	MONONA	6,575	4,569	1,960	46	2,609 R	69.5%	29.8%	70.0%	30.0%
23,467	MONROE	7,352	4,500	2,081	771	2,419 R	61.2%	28.3%	68.4%	31.6%
17,048	MONTGOMERY	6,510	4,980	1,404	126	3,576 R	76.5%	21.6%	78.0%	22.0%
29,042	MUSCATINE	11,544	8,115	2,293	1,136	5,822 R	70.3%	19.9%	78.0%	22.0%
19,051	O'BRIEN	6,714	5,137	1,468	109	3,669 R	76.5%	21.9%	77.8%	22.2%
10,223	OSCEOLA	3,541	2,717	754	70	1,963 R	76.7%	21.3%	78.3%	21.7%
24,137	PAGE	9,131	6,949	1,931	251	5,018 R	76.1%	21.1%	78.3%	21.7%
15,486	PALO ALTO	5,466	3,904	1,467	95	2,437 R	71.4%	26.8%	72.7%	27.3%
23,584	PLYMOUTH	7,996	6,090	1,801	105	4,289 R	76.2%	22.5%	77.2%	22.8%
15,602	POCAHONTAS	5,774	4,046	1,639	89	2,407 R	70.1%	28.4%	71.2%	28.8%
154,029	POLK	53,986	36,073	16,281	1,632	19,792 R	66.8%	30.2%	68.9%	31.1%
61,550	POTTAWATTAMIE	20,887	13,506	6,659	722	6,847 R	64.7%	31.9%	67.0%	33.0%
19,910	POWESHIEK	8,130	5,806	2,125	199	3,681 R	71.4%	26.1%	73.2%	26.8%
12,919	RINGGOLD	5,095	3,702	1,327	66	2,375 R	72.7%	26.0%	73.6%	26.4%
17,500	SAC	6,334	4,984	1,268	82	3,716 R	78.7%	20.0%	79.7%	20.3%
73,952	SCOTT	27,631	16,233	5,473	5,925	10,760 R	58.7%	19.8%	74.8%	25.2%
16,065	SHELBY	6,550	4,621	1,882	47	2,739 R	70.5%	28.7%	71.1%	28.9%
26,458	SIOUX	7,653	6,068	1,510	75	4,558 R	79.3%	19.7%	80.1%	19.9%
26,185	STORY	10,784	8,713	1,909	162	6,804 R	80.8%	17.7%	82.0%	18.0%
21,861	TAMA	9,073	6,352	2,552	169	3,800 R	70.0%	28.1%	71.3%	28.7%
15,514	TAYLOR	6,901	4,997	1,757	147	3,240 R	72.4%	25.5%	74.0%	26.0%
17,268	UNION	6,805	4,466	2,228	111	2,238 R	65.6%	32.7%	66.7%	33.3%
14,060	VAN BUREN	6,086	4,321	1,682	83	2,639 R	71.0%	27.6%	72.0%	28.0%
37,937	WAPELLO	14,537	9,884	4,131	522	5,753 R	68.0%	28.4%	70.5%	29.5%
18,047	WARREN	7,548	5,323	2,066	159	3,257 R	70.5%	27.4%	72.0%	28.0%
20,421	WASHINGTON	8,177	5,813	2,257	107	3,556 R	71.1%	27.6%	72.0%	28.0%
15,378	WAYNE	6,773	4,234	2,434	105	1,800 R	62.5%	35.9%	63.5%	36.5%
37,611	WEBSTER	12,988	8,312	2,804	1,872	5,508 R	64.0%	21.6%	74.8%	25.2%
13,489	WINNEBAGO	4,514	3,931	469	114	3,462 R	87.1%	10.4%	89.3%	10.7%
22,091	WINNESHIEK	8,797	6,684	1,933	180	4,751 R	76.0%	22.0%	77.6%	22.4%
92,171	WOODBURY	28,362	17,603	9,815	944	7,788 R	62.1%	34.6%	64.2%	35.8%
11,630	WORTH	4,009	3,401	516	92	2,885 R	84.8%	12.9%	86.8%	13.2%
20,348	WRIGHT	7,082	5,739	1,205	138	4,534 R	81.0%	17.0%	82.6%	17.4%
2,404,021	TOTAL	894,959	634,674	227,804	32,481	406,870 R	70.9%	25.5%	73.6%	26.4%

IOWA

ELECTION NOTES

1956 Other vote was 3,202 Andrews (States Rights); 192 Hoopes (Socialist); 125 Hass (Socialist Labor).

1952 Other vote was 5,085 Hallinan (Progressive); 2,882 Hamblen (Prohibition); 219 Hoopes (Socialist); 139 Hass (Socialist Labor); 29 scattered write-in.

1948 Other vote was 12,125 Wallace (Progressive); 4,274 Teichert (Socialist Labor); 3,382 Watson (Prohibition); 1,829 Thomas (Socialist); 256 Dobbs (Socialist Workers).

1944 Other vote was 3,752 Watson (Prohibition); 1,511 Thomas (Socialist); 193 Teichert (Socialist Labor).

1940 Other vote was 2,284 Babson (Prohibition); 1,524 Browder (Communist); 452 Aiken (Socialist Labor).

1936 Other vote was 29,687 Lemke (Union); 1,373 Thomas (Socialist); 1,182 Colvin (Prohibition); 506 Browder (Communist); 252 Aiken (Socialist Labor); 4 scattered write-in.

1932 Other vote was 20,467 Thomas (Socialist); 2,111 Upshaw (Prohibition); 1,094 Coxey (Farmer-Labor); 559 Foster (Communist); 4 scattered write-in.

1928 Other vote was 3,088 Webb (Farmer-Labor); 2,960 Thomas (Socialist); 328 Foster (Communist); 230 Reynolds (Socialist Labor; 2 scattered write-in. The statewide total in the other vote column represents these votes for minor party candidates which were not available by county.

1924 A special four-column table which gives the LaFollette (Progressive) vote is used to detail this election. Other vote was 4,037 Foster (Communist); 445 scattered write-in. The statewide total in the other vote column represents these votes for minor party candidates which were not available by county.

1920 Other vote was 16,981 Debs (Socialist); 10,321 Christensen (Farmer-Labor); 4,197 Watkins (Prohibition); 982 Cox (Socialist Labor).

KANSAS

POPULAR VOTE FOR PRESIDENT 1920 TO 1956

Year	Total Vote	Republican		Democratic		Other Vote	Plurality	Percentage			
								Total Vote		Major Vote	
		Vote	Candidate	Vote	Candidate			Rep.	Dem.	Rep.	Dem.
1956	866,243	566,878	Eisenhower, Dwight D.	296,317	Stevenson, Adlai E.	3,048	270,561 R	65.4%	34.2%	65.7%	34.3%
1952	896,166	616,302	Eisenhower, Dwight D.	273,296	Stevenson, Adlai E.	6,568	343,006 R	68.8%	30.5%	69.3%	30.7%
1948	788,819	423,039	Dewey, Thomas E.	351,902	Truman, Harry S.	13,878	71,137 R	53.6%	44.6%	54.6%	45.4%
1944	733,776	442,096	Dewey, Thomas E.	287,458	Roosevelt, Franklin D.	4,222	154,638 R	60.2%	39.2%	60.6%	39.4%
1940	860,297	489,169	Willkie, Wendell	364,725	Roosevelt, Franklin D.	6,403	124,444 R	56.9%	42.4%	57.3%	42.7%
1936	865,507	397,727	Landon, Alfred M.	464,520	Roosevelt, Franklin D.	3,260	66,793 D	46.0%	53.7%	46.1%	53.9%
1932	791,978	349,498	Hoover, Herbert C.	424,204	Roosevelt, Franklin D.	18,276	74,706 D	44.1%	53.6%	45.2%	54.8%
1928	713,200	513,672	Hoover, Herbert C.	193,003	Smith, Alfred E.	6,525	320,669 R	72.0%	27.1%	72.7%	27.3%
1924 **	662,456	407,671	Coolidge, Calvin	156,320	Davis, John W.	98,465	251,351 R	61.5%	23.6%	72.3%	27.7%
1920	570,243	369,268	Harding, Warren G.	185,464	Cox, James M.	15,511	183,804 R	64.8%	32.5%	66.6%	33.4%

In 1924 other vote was 98,461 Progressive and 4 scattered.

ELECTORAL COLLEGE VOTE 1920 TO 1956

Year	Total	Republican	Democratic	Other
1956	8	8	—	—
1952	8	8	—	—
1948	8	8	—	—
1944	8	8	—	—
1940	9	9	—	—
1936	9	—	9	—
1932	9	—	9	—
1928	10	10	—	—
1924	10	10	—	—
1920	10	10	—	—

KANSAS

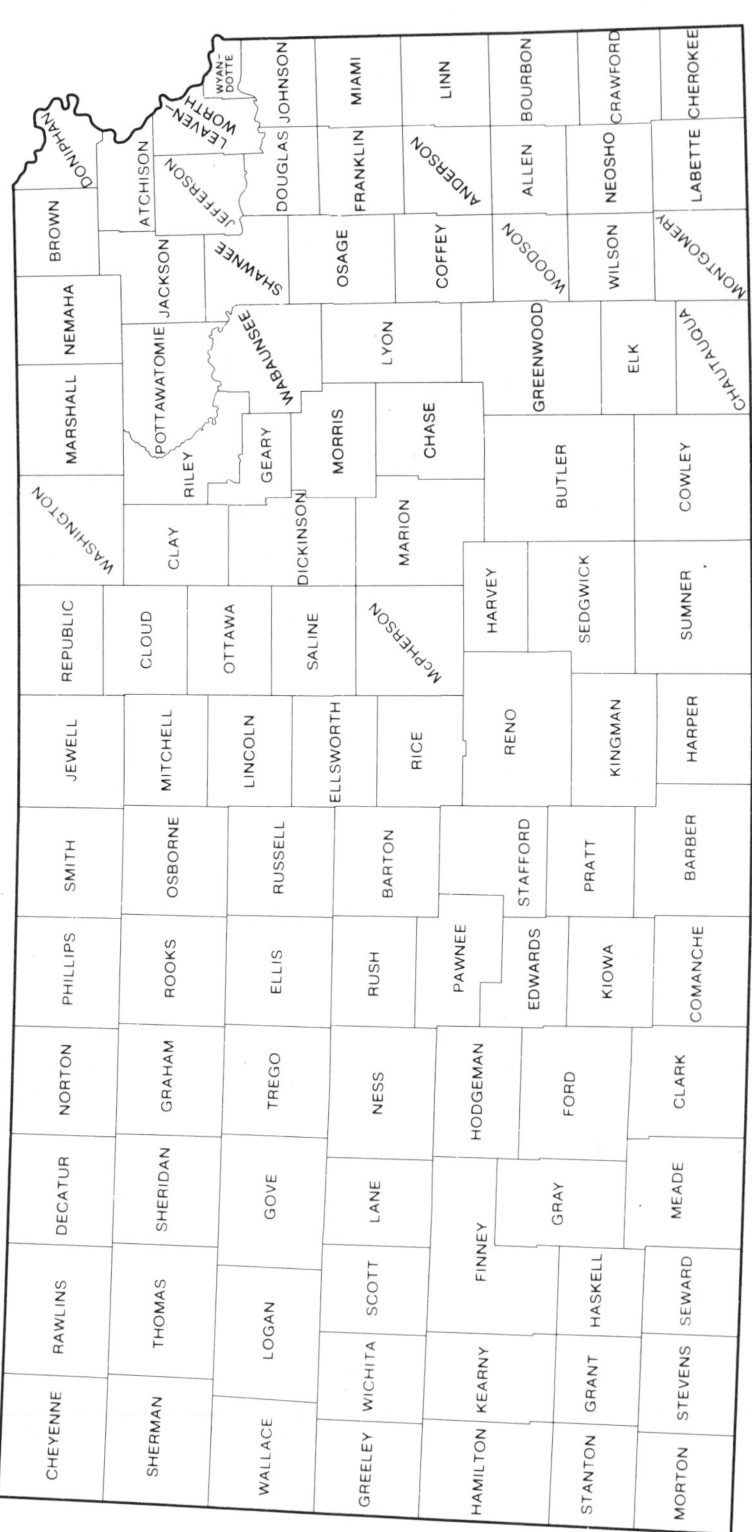

WYAN-DOTTE
JOHNSON
MIAMI
LINN
BOURBON
CRAWFORD
CHEROKEE
DONIPHAN
LEAVEN-WORTH
ATCHISON
JEFFERSON
DOUGLAS
FRANKLIN
ANDERSON
ALLEN
NEOSHO
LABETTE
BROWN
JACKSON
SHAWNEE
OSAGE
COFFEY
WOODSON
WILSON
MONTGOMERY
NEMAHA
POTTAWATOMIE
WABAUNSEE
LYON
GREENWOOD
ELK
CHAUTAUQUA
MARSHALL
RILEY
GEARY
MORRIS
CHASE
BUTLER
COWLEY
WASHINGTON
CLAY
DICKINSON
MARION
HARVEY
SEDGWICK
SUMNER
REPUBLIC
CLOUD
OTTAWA
SALINE
McPHERSON
JEWELL
MITCHELL
LINCOLN
ELLSWORTH
RICE
RENO
KINGMAN
HARPER
SMITH
OSBORNE
RUSSELL
BARTON
STAFFORD
PRATT
BARBER
PHILLIPS
ROOKS
ELLIS
RUSH
PAWNEE
EDWARDS
KIOWA
COMANCHE
NORTON
GRAHAM
TREGO
NESS
HODGEMAN
FORD
CLARK
DECATUR
SHERIDAN
GOVE
LANE
FINNEY
GRAY
MEADE
RAWLINS
THOMAS
LOGAN
SCOTT
HASKELL
SEWARD
WICHITA
KEARNY
GRANT
STEVENS
CHEYENNE
SHERMAN
WALLACE
GREELEY
HAMILTON
STANTON
MORTON

KANSAS

PRESIDENT 1956

1950 Census Population	County	Total Vote	Republican	Democratic	Other	Rep.-Dem. Plurality	Percentage: Total Vote Rep.	Total Vote Dem.	Major Vote Rep.	Major Vote Dem.
18,187	ALLEN	7,508	5,342	2,143	23	3,199 R	71.2%	28.5%	71.4%	28.6%
10,267	ANDERSON	4,463	3,080	1,369	14	1,711 R	69.0%	30.7%	69.2%	30.8%
21,496	ATCHISON	8,751	5,608	3,134	9	2,474 R	64.1%	35.8%	64.2%	35.8%
8,521	BARBER	3,949	2,698	1,241	10	1,457 R	68.3%	31.4%	68.5%	31.5%
29,909	BARTON	13,063	8,644	4,378	41	4,266 R	66.2%	33.5%	66.4%	33.6%
19,153	BOURBON	8,504	5,306	3,151	47	2,155 R	62.4%	37.1%	62.7%	37.3%
14,651	BROWN	6,677	5,138	1,519	20	3,619 R	77.0%	22.7%	77.2%	22.8%
31,001	BUTLER	15,794	9,591	6,158	45	3,433 R	60.7%	39.0%	60.9%	39.1%
4,831	CHASE	2,086	1,553	529	4	1,024 R	74.4%	25.4%	74.6%	25.4%
7,376	CHAUTAUQUA	3,077	2,180	887	10	1,293 R	70.8%	28.8%	71.1%	28.9%
25,144	CHEROKEE	9,975	5,824	4,112	39	1,712 R	58.4%	41.2%	58.6%	41.4%
5,668	CHEYENNE	2,150	1,479	663	8	816 R	68.8%	30.8%	69.0%	31.0%
3,946	CLARK	1,780	1,243	529	8	714 R	69.8%	29.7%	70.1%	29.9%
11,697	CLAY	5,461	4,378	1,034	49	3,344 R	80.2%	18.9%	80.9%	19.1%
16,104	CLOUD	6,509	4,466	2,008	35	2,458 R	68.6%	30.8%	69.0%	31.0%
10,408	COFFEY	4,549	3,286	1,247	16	2,039 R	72.2%	27.4%	72.5%	27.5%
3,888	COMANCHE	1,710	1,238	461	11	777 R	72.4%	27.0%	72.9%	27.1%
36,905	COWLEY	10,533	6,734	3,753	46	2,981 R	63.9%	35.6%	64.2%	35.8%
40,231	CRAWFORD	17,437	9,578	7,799	60	1,779 R	54.9%	44.7%	55.1%	44.9%
6,185	DECATUR	2,957	2,028	920	9	1,108 R	68.6%	31.1%	68.8%	31.2%
21,190	DICKINSON	9,908	7,422	2,452	34	4,970 R	74.9%	24.7%	75.2%	24.8%
10,499	DONIPHAN	4,339	3,130	1,197	12	1,933 R	72.1%	27.6%	72.3%	27.7%
34,086	DOUGLAS	15,351	11,029	4,283	39	6,746 R	71.8%	27.9%	72.0%	28.0%
5,936	EDWARDS	2,597	1,816	771	10	1,045 R	69.9%	29.7%	70.2%	29.8%
6,679	ELK	2,731	1,909	812	10	1,097 R	69.9%	29.7%	70.2%	29.8%
19,043	ELLIS	7,528	4,466	3,058	4	1,408 R	59.3%	40.6%	59.4%	40.6%
8,465	ELLSWORTH	3,889	2,524	1,351	14	1,173 R	64.9%	34.7%	65.1%	34.9%
15,092	FINNEY	5,348	3,576	1,752	20	1,824 R	66.9%	32.8%	67.1%	32.9%
19,670	FORD	8,320	5,561	2,710	49	2,851 R	66.8%	32.6%	67.2%	32.8%
19,928	FRANKLIN	9,181	6,557	2,591	33	3,966 R	71.4%	28.2%	71.7%	28.3%
21,671	GEARY	6,123	4,013	2,078	32	1,935 R	65.5%	33.9%	65.9%	34.1%
4,447	GOVE	1,819	1,315	492	12	823 R	72.3%	27.0%	72.8%	27.2%
5,020	GRAHAM	2,412	1,676	725	11	951 R	69.5%	30.1%	69.8%	30.2%
4,638	GRANT	1,523	1,058	459	6	599 R	69.5%	30.1%	69.7%	30.3%
4,894	GRAY	1,914	1,278	627	9	651 R	66.8%	32.8%	67.1%	32.9%
2,010	GREELEY	777	599	174	4	425 R	77.1%	22.4%	77.5%	22.5%
13,574	GREENWOOD	5,948	4,164	1,763	21	2,401 R	70.0%	29.6%	70.3%	29.7%
3,696	HAMILTON	1,426	865	552	9	313 R	60.7%	38.7%	61.0%	39.0%
10,263	HARPER	4,445	3,111	1,311	23	1,800 R	70.0%	29.5%	70.4%	29.6%
21,698	HARVEY	10,494	7,367	3,084	43	4,283 R	70.2%	29.4%	70.5%	29.5%
2,606	HASKELL	1,176	829	341	6	488 R	70.5%	29.0%	70.9%	29.1%
3,310	HODGEMAN	1,554	1,113	435	6	678 R	71.6%	28.0%	71.9%	28.1%
11,098	JACKSON	4,837	3,469	1,356	12	2,113 R	71.7%	28.0%	71.9%	28.1%
11,084	JEFFERSON	5,235	3,677	1,536	22	2,141 R	70.2%	29.3%	70.5%	29.5%
9,698	JEWELL	4,496	3,395	1,034	67	2,361 R	75.5%	23.0%	76.7%	23.3%
62,783	JOHNSON	49,733	35,511	14,185	37	21,326 R	71.4%	28.5%	71.5%	28.5%
3,492	KEARNY	1,275	854	418	3	436 R	67.0%	32.8%	67.1%	32.9%
10,324	KINGMAN	4,670	3,226	1,428	16	1,798 R	69.1%	30.6%	69.3%	30.7%
4,743	KIOWA	2,254	1,717	517	20	1,200 R	76.2%	22.9%	76.9%	23.1%
29,285	LABETTE	12,936	7,677	5,202	57	2,475 R	59.3%	40.2%	59.6%	40.4%
2,808	LANE	1,376	992	380	4	612 R	72.1%	27.6%	72.3%	27.7%
42,361	LEAVENWORTH	14,339	8,826	5,480	33	3,346 R	61.6%	38.2%	61.7%	38.3%
6,643	LINCOLN	2,912	2,219	681	12	1,538 R	76.2%	23.4%	76.5%	23.5%
10,053	LINN	4,175	2,991	1,177	7	1,814 R	71.6%	28.2%	71.8%	28.2%
4,206	LOGAN	1,829	1,328	493	8	835 R	72.6%	27.0%	72.9%	27.1%
26,576	LYON	11,911	8,021	3,831	59	4,190 R	67.3%	32.2%	67.7%	32.3%
23,670	MCPHERSON	10,198	7,521	2,603	74	4,918 R	73.7%	25.5%	74.3%	25.7%
16,307	MARION	6,998	5,318	1,644	36	3,674 R	76.0%	23.5%	76.4%	23.6%
17,926	MARSHALL	8,179	5,664	2,487	28	3,177 R	69.3%	30.4%	69.5%	30.5%
5,710	MEADE	2,315	1,720	575	20	1,145 R	74.3%	24.8%	74.9%	25.1%

KANSAS

PRESIDENT 1956

1950 Census Population	County	Total Vote	Republican	Democratic	Other	Rep.-Dem. Plurality	Percentage Total Vote Rep.	Total Vote Dem.	Major Vote Rep.	Major Vote Dem.
19,698	MIAMI	8,484	5,031	3,428	25	1,603 R	59.3%	40.4%	59.5%	40.5%
10,320	MITCHELL	4,432	3,198	1,214	20	1,984 R	72.2%	27.4%	72.5%	27.5%
46,487	MONTGOMERY	20,598	13,252	7,265	81	5,987 R	64.3%	35.3%	64.6%	35.4%
8,485	MORRIS	3,905	2,677	1,208	20	1,469 R	68.6%	30.9%	68.9%	31.1%
2,610	MORTON	1,257	814	436	7	378 R	64.8%	34.7%	65.1%	34.9%
14,341	NEMAHA	6,251	4,195	2,038	18	2,157 R	67.1%	32.6%	67.3%	32.7%
20,348	NEOSHO	8,920	5,886	3,005	29	2,881 R	66.0%	33.7%	66.2%	33.8%
6,322	NESS	2,650	1,876	758	16	1,118 R	70.8%	28.6%	71.2%	28.8%
8,808	NORTON	4,264	3,052	1,194	18	1,858 R	71.6%	28.0%	71.9%	28.1%
12,811	OSAGE	6,147	4,136	1,979	32	2,157 R	67.3%	32.2%	67.6%	32.4%
8,558	OSBORNE	3,999	2,948	1,023	28	1,925 R	73.7%	25.6%	74.2%	25.8%
7,265	OTTAWA	3,385	2,329	1,037	19	1,292 R	68.8%	30.6%	69.2%	30.8%
11,041	PAWNEE	4,375	2,788	1,567	20	1,221 R	63.7%	35.8%	64.0%	36.0%
9,273	PHILLIPS	4,129	3,117	985	27	2,132 R	75.5%	23.9%	76.0%	24.0%
12,344	POTTAWATOMIE	5,782	4,335	1,422	25	2,913 R	75.0%	24.6%	75.3%	24.7%
12,156	PRATT	5,610	3,620	1,956	34	1,664 R	64.5%	34.9%	64.9%	35.1%
5,728	RAWLINS	2,387	1,668	711	8	957 R	69.9%	29.8%	70.1%	29.9%
54,058	RENO	22,620	15,057	7,461	102	7,596 R	66.6%	33.0%	66.9%	33.1%
11,478	REPUBLIC	5,266	3,621	1,613	32	2,008 R	68.8%	30.6%	69.2%	30.8%
15,635	RICE	6,581	4,638	1,926	17	2,712 R	70.5%	29.3%	70.7%	29.3%
33,405	RILEY	12,213	9,385	2,784	44	6,601 R	76.8%	22.8%	77.1%	22.9%
9,043	ROOKS	4,316	3,059	1,238	19	1,821 R	70.9%	28.7%	71.2%	28.8%
7,231	RUSH	3,094	2,007	1,080	7	927 R	64.9%	34.9%	65.0%	35.0%
13,406	RUSSELL	5,461	3,920	1,528	13	2,392 R	71.8%	28.0%	72.0%	28.0%
33,409	SALINE	16,117	11,172	4,908	37	6,264 R	69.3%	30.5%	69.5%	30.5%
4,921	SCOTT	1,832	1,376	451	5	925 R	75.1%	24.6%	75.3%	24.7%
222,290	SEDGWICK	118,360	72,292	45,732	336	26,560 R	61.1%	38.6%	61.3%	38.7%
9,972	SEWARD	4,066	2,885	1,162	19	1,723 R	71.0%	28.6%	71.3%	28.7%
105,418	SHAWNEE	49,075	32,647	16,298	130	16,349 R	66.5%	33.2%	66.7%	33.3%
4,607	SHERIDAN	1,964	1,324	633	7	691 R	67.4%	32.2%	67.7%	32.3%
7,373	SHERMAN	2,809	1,825	962	22	863 R	65.0%	34.2%	65.5%	34.5%
8,846	SMITH	4,307	3,142	1,139	26	2,003 R	73.0%	26.4%	73.4%	26.6%
8,816	STAFFORD	3,990	2,728	1,242	20	1,486 R	68.4%	31.1%	68.7%	31.3%
2,263	STANTON	782	549	226	7	323 R	70.2%	28.9%	70.8%	29.2%
4,516	STEVENS	1,845	1,273	565	7	708 R	69.0%	30.6%	69.3%	30.7%
23,646	SUMNER	11,158	7,024	4,088	46	2,936 R	63.0%	36.6%	63.2%	36.8%
7,572	THOMAS	3,042	1,888	1,138	16	750 R	62.1%	37.4%	62.4%	37.6%
5,868	TREGO	2,403	1,668	726	9	942 R	69.4%	30.2%	69.7%	30.3%
7,212	WABAUNSEE	3,458	2,650	802	6	1,848 R	76.6%	23.2%	76.8%	23.2%
2,508	WALLACE	941	684	251	6	433 R	72.7%	26.7%	73.2%	26.8%
12,977	WASHINGTON	5,641	4,220	1,389	32	2,831 R	74.8%	24.6%	75.2%	24.8%
2,640	WICHITA	1,061	747	312	2	435 R	70.4%	29.4%	70.5%	29.5%
14,815	WILSON	6,167	4,502	1,645	20	2,857 R	73.0%	26.7%	73.2%	26.8%
6,711	WOODSON	3,063	2,171	870	22	1,301 R	70.9%	28.4%	71.4%	28.6%
165,318	WYANDOTTE	72,632	34,604	37,842	186	3,238 D	47.6%	52.1%	47.8%	52.2%
1,905,299	TOTAL	866,243	566,878	296,317	3,048	270,561 R	65.4%	34.2%	65.7%	34.3%

KANSAS

PRESIDENT 1952

1950 Census Population	County	Total Vote	Republican	Democratic	Other	Rep.-Dem. Plurality	Percentage Total Vote Rep.	Total Vote Dem.	Major Vote Rep.	Major Vote Dem.
18,187	ALLEN	8,236	6,045	2,160	31	3,885 R	73.4%	26.2%	73.7%	26.3%
10,267	ANDERSON	5,018	3,672	1,333	13	2,339 R	73.2%	26.6%	73.4%	26.6%
21,496	ATCHISON	9,296	6,004	3,283	9	2,721 R	64.6%	35.3%	64.6%	35.4%
8,521	BARBER	4,145	3,071	1,028	46	2,043 R	74.1%	24.8%	74.9%	25.1%
29,909	BARTON	13,319	9,380	3,847	92	5,533 R	70.4%	28.9%	70.9%	29.1%
19,153	BOURBON	8,864	5,785	3,023	56	2,762 R	65.3%	34.1%	65.7%	34.3%
14,651	BROWN	7,491	6,031	1,440	20	4,591 R	80.5%	19.2%	80.7%	19.3%
31,001	BUTLER	15,651	10,179	5,359	113	4,820 R	65.0%	34.2%	65.5%	34.5%
4,831	CHASE	2,334	1,815	513	6	1,302 R	77.8%	22.0%	78.0%	22.0%
7,376	CHAUTAUQUA	3,400	2,542	837	21	1,705 R	74.8%	24.6%	75.2%	24.8%
25,144	CHEROKEE	10,914	6,261	4,597	56	1,664 R	57.4%	42.1%	57.7%	42.3%
5,668	CHEYENNE	2,532	1,915	597	20	1,318 R	75.6%	23.6%	76.2%	23.8%
3,946	CLARK	1,924	1,410	479	35	931 R	73.3%	24.9%	74.6%	25.4%
11,697	CLAY	5,961	5,059	831	71	4,228 R	84.9%	13.9%	85.9%	14.1%
16,104	CLOUD	7,417	5,580	1,793	44	3,787 R	75.2%	24.2%	75.7%	24.3%
10,408	COFFEY	4,989	3,731	1,239	19	2,492 R	74.8%	24.8%	75.1%	24.9%
3,888	COMANCHE	1,827	1,443	374	10	1,069 R	79.0%	20.5%	79.4%	20.6%
36,905	COWLEY	16,812	11,454	5,242	116	6,212 R	68.1%	31.2%	68.6%	31.4%
40,231	CRAWFORD	19,074	10,646	8,349	79	2,297 R	55.8%	43.8%	56.0%	44.0%
6,185	DECATUR	3,288	2,451	821	16	1,630 R	74.5%	25.0%	74.9%	25.1%
21,190	DICKINSON	10,967	8,969	1,967	31	7,002 R	81.8%	17.9%	82.0%	18.0%
10,499	DONIPHAN	4,902	3,711	1,175	16	2,536 R	75.7%	24.0%	76.0%	24.0%
34,086	DOUGLAS	14,924	11,095	3,765	64	7,330 R	74.3%	25.2%	74.7%	25.3%
5,936	EDWARDS	2,869	2,192	647	30	1,545 R	76.4%	22.6%	77.2%	22.8%
6,679	ELK	3,116	2,380	717	19	1,663 R	76.4%	23.0%	76.8%	23.2%
19,043	ELLIS	7,413	4,882	2,528	3	2,354 R	65.9%	34.1%	65.9%	34.1%
8,465	ELLSWORTH	4,311	3,219	1,068	24	2,151 R	74.7%	24.8%	75.1%	24.9%
15,092	FINNEY	5,932	4,290	1,597	45	2,693 R	72.3%	26.9%	72.9%	27.1%
19,670	FORD	9,221	6,359	2,748	114	3,611 R	69.0%	29.8%	69.8%	30.2%
19,928	FRANKLIN	9,584	6,983	2,532	69	4,451 R	72.9%	26.4%	73.4%	26.6%
21,671	GEARY	6,116	4,314	1,750	52	2,564 R	70.5%	28.6%	71.1%	28.9%
4,447	GOVE	1,916	1,453	453	10	1,000 R	75.8%	23.6%	76.2%	23.8%
5,020	GRAHAM	2,560	1,859	686	15	1,173 R	72.6%	26.8%	73.0%	27.0%
4,638	GRANT	1,798	1,277	502	19	775 R	71.0%	27.9%	71.8%	28.2%
4,894	GRAY	2,061	1,515	537	9	978 R	73.5%	26.1%	73.8%	26.2%
2,010	GREELEY	917	725	181	11	544 R	79.1%	19.7%	80.0%	20.0%
13,574	GREENWOOD	6,749	4,974	1,743	32	3,231 R	73.7%	25.8%	74.1%	25.9%
3,696	HAMILTON	1,663	1,209	437	17	772 R	72.7%	26.3%	73.5%	26.5%
10,263	HARPER	4,547	3,575	927	45	2,648 R	78.6%	20.4%	79.4%	20.6%
21,698	HARVEY	10,095	7,154	2,726	215	4,428 R	70.9%	27.0%	72.4%	27.6%
2,606	HASKELL	1,171	870	283	18	587 R	74.3%	24.2%	75.5%	24.5%
3,310	HODGEMAN	1,740	1,330	392	18	938 R	76.4%	22.5%	77.2%	22.8%
11,098	JACKSON	5,527	4,161	1,358	8	2,803 R	75.3%	24.6%	75.4%	24.6%
11,084	JEFFERSON	5,417	3,980	1,411	26	2,569 R	73.5%	26.0%	73.8%	26.2%
9,698	JEWELL	5,147	4,162	885	100	3,277 R	80.9%	17.2%	82.5%	17.5%
62,783	JOHNSON	40,163	29,103	10,990	70	18,113 R	72.5%	27.4%	72.6%	27.4%
3,492	KEARNY	1,390	1,012	362	16	650 R	72.8%	26.0%	73.7%	26.3%
10,324	KINGMAN	4,992	3,820	1,096	76	2,724 R	76.5%	22.0%	77.7%	22.3%
4,743	KIOWA	2,338	1,838	432	68	1,406 R	78.6%	18.5%	81.0%	19.0%
29,285	LABETTE	13,913	8,624	5,219	70	3,405 R	62.0%	37.5%	62.3%	37.7%
2,808	LANE	1,467	1,142	311	14	831 R	77.8%	21.2%	78.6%	21.4%
42,361	LEAVENWORTH	14,783	9,046	5,698	39	3,348 R	61.2%	38.5%	61.4%	38.6%
6,643	LINCOLN	3,357	2,841	507	9	2,334 R	84.6%	15.1%	84.9%	15.1%
10,053	LINN	4,767	3,527	1,220	20	2,307 R	74.0%	25.6%	74.3%	25.7%
4,206	LOGAN	1,931	1,544	369	18	1,175 R	80.0%	19.1%	80.7%	19.3%
26,576	LYON	12,568	8,544	3,944	80	4,600 R	68.0%	31.4%	68.4%	31.6%
23,670	MCPHERSON	10,798	8,053	2,371	374	5,682 R	74.6%	22.0%	77.3%	22.7%
16,307	MARION	7,767	6,228	1,361	178	4,867 R	80.2%	17.5%	82.1%	17.9%
17,926	MARSHALL	9,092	6,851	2,215	26	4,636 R	75.4%	24.4%	75.6%	24.4%
5,710	MEADE	2,680	2,061	568	51	1,493 R	76.9%	21.2%	78.4%	21.6%

KANSAS

PRESIDENT 1952

1950 Census Population	County	Total Vote	Republican	Democratic	Other	Rep.-Dem. Plurality	Percentage Total Vote Rep.	Percentage Total Vote Dem.	Percentage Major Vote Rep.	Percentage Major Vote Dem.
19,698	MIAMI	9,022	5,623	3,374	25	2,249 R	62.3%	37.4%	62.5%	37.5%
10,320	MITCHELL	5,146	4,167	961	18	3,206 R	81.0%	18.7%	81.3%	18.7%
46,487	MONTGOMERY	22,070	14,261	7,679	130	6,582 R	64.6%	34.8%	65.0%	35.0%
8,485	MORRIS	4,403	3,263	1,124	16	2,139 R	74.1%	25.5%	74.4%	25.6%
2,610	MORTON	1,277	893	362	22	531 R	69.9%	28.3%	71.2%	28.8%
14,341	NEMAHA	6,812	5,175	1,618	19	3,557 R	76.0%	23.8%	76.2%	23.8%
20,348	NEOSHO	9,614	6,595	2,987	32	3,608 R	68.6%	31.1%	68.8%	31.2%
6,322	NESS	3,000	2,288	664	48	1,624 R	76.3%	22.1%	77.5%	22.5%
8,808	NORTON	4,631	3,530	1,047	54	2,483 R	76.2%	22.6%	77.1%	22.9%
12,811	OSAGE	6,666	4,589	2,036	41	2,553 R	68.8%	30.5%	69.3%	30.7%
8,558	OSBORNE	4,403	3,577	754	72	2,823 R	81.2%	17.1%	82.6%	17.4%
7,265	OTTAWA	3,755	2,916	801	38	2,115 R	77.7%	21.3%	78.5%	21.5%
11,041	PAWNEE	4,824	3,431	1,340	53	2,091 R	71.1%	27.8%	71.9%	28.1%
9,273	PHILLIPS	4,631	3,713	884	34	2,829 R	80.2%	19.1%	80.8%	19.2%
12,344	POTTAWATOMIE	6,343	4,944	1,387	12	3,557 R	77.9%	21.9%	78.1%	21.9%
12,156	PRATT	5,805	3,998	1,743	64	2,255 R	68.9%	30.0%	69.6%	30.4%
5,728	RAWLINS	2,796	2,120	670	6	1,450 R	75.8%	24.0%	76.0%	24.0%
54,058	RENO	22,983	15,762	6,555	666	9,207 R	68.6%	28.5%	70.6%	29.4%
11,478	REPUBLIC	5,961	4,573	1,358	30	3,215 R	76.7%	22.8%	77.1%	22.9%
15,635	RICE	7,478	5,572	1,832	74	3,740 R	74.5%	24.5%	75.3%	24.7%
33,405	RILEY	12,201	9,799	2,352	50	7,447 R	80.3%	19.3%	80.6%	19.4%
9,043	ROOKS	4,482	3,331	1,105	46	2,226 R	74.3%	24.7%	75.1%	24.9%
7,231	RUSH	3,510	2,650	843	17	1,807 R	75.5%	24.0%	75.9%	24.1%
13,406	RUSSELL	6,333	4,813	1,499	21	3,314 R	76.0%	23.7%	76.3%	23.7%
33,409	SALINE	16,409	12,326	4,003	80	8,323 R	75.1%	24.4%	75.5%	24.5%
4,921	SCOTT	2,146	1,681	443	22	1,238 R	78.3%	20.6%	79.1%	20.9%
222,290	SEDGWICK	106,788	70,983	34,926	879	36,057 R	66.5%	32.7%	67.0%	33.0%
9,972	SEWARD	4,308	3,136	1,146	26	1,990 R	72.8%	26.6%	73.2%	26.8%
105,418	SHAWNEE	51,067	33,201	17,651	215	15,550 R	65.0%	34.6%	65.3%	34.7%
4,607	SHERIDAN	2,140	1,581	555	4	1,026 R	73.9%	25.9%	74.0%	26.0%
7,373	SHERMAN	3,413	2,403	941	69	1,462 R	70.4%	27.6%	71.9%	28.1%
8,846	SMITH	4,660	3,623	986	51	2,637 R	77.7%	21.2%	78.6%	21.4%
8,816	STAFFORD	4,436	3,162	1,174	100	1,988 R	71.3%	26.5%	72.9%	27.1%
2,263	STANTON	890	664	215	11	449 R	74.6%	24.2%	75.5%	24.5%
4,516	STEVENS	1,918	1,480	423	15	1,057 R	77.2%	22.1%	77.8%	22.2%
23,646	SUMNER	11,797	8,134	3,567	96	4,567 R	68.9%	30.2%	69.5%	30.5%
7,572	THOMAS	3,585	2,490	1,069	26	1,421 R	69.5%	29.8%	70.0%	30.0%
5,868	TREGO	2,533	1,915	608	10	1,307 R	75.6%	24.0%	75.9%	24.1%
7,212	WABAUNSEE	3,927	3,182	736	9	2,446 R	81.0%	18.7%	81.2%	18.8%
2,508	WALLACE	1,199	945	249	5	696 R	78.8%	20.8%	79.1%	20.9%
12,977	WASHINGTON	6,309	5,135	1,148	26	3,987 R	81.4%	18.2%	81.7%	18.3%
2,640	WICHITA	1,199	910	276	13	634 R	75.9%	23.0%	76.7%	23.3%
14,815	WILSON	7,078	5,180	1,845	53	3,335 R	73.2%	26.1%	73.7%	26.3%
6,711	WOODSON	3,400	2,594	786	20	1,808 R	76.3%	23.1%	76.7%	23.3%
165,318	WYANDOTTE	73,657	34,648	38,751	258	4,103 D	47.0%	52.6%	47.2%	52.8%
1,905,299	TOTAL	896,166	616,302	273,296	6,568	343,006 R	68.8%	30.5%	69.3%	30.7%

KANSAS

PRESIDENT 1948

1940 Census Population	County	Total Vote	Republican	Democratic	Other	Rep.-Dem. Plurality	Percentage Total Vote Rep.	Percentage Total Vote Dem.	Percentage Major Vote Rep.	Percentage Major Vote Dem.
19,874	ALLEN	7,685	4,704	2,891	90	1,813 R	61.2%	37.6%	61.9%	38.1%
11,658	ANDERSON	4,902	2,787	2,071	44	716 R	56.9%	42.2%	57.4%	42.6%
22,222	ATCHISON	8,113	4,141	3,910	62	231 R	51.0%	48.2%	51.4%	48.6%
9,073	BARBER	3,953	2,013	1,891	49	122 R	50.9%	47.8%	51.6%	48.4%
25,010	BARTON	11,600	6,191	5,307	102	884 R	53.4%	45.8%	53.8%	46.2%
20,944	BOURBON	8,215	4,225	3,879	111	346 R	51.4%	47.2%	52.1%	47.9%
17,395	BROWN	6,646	4,518	2,060	68	2,458 R	68.0%	31.0%	68.7%	31.3%
32,013	BUTLER	12,952	6,551	6,269	132	282 R	50.6%	48.4%	51.1%	48.9%
6,345	CHASE	2,430	1,432	961	37	471 R	58.9%	39.5%	59.8%	40.2%
9,233	CHAUTAUQUA	3,244	1,925	1,261	58	664 R	59.3%	38.9%	60.4%	39.6%
29,817	CHEROKEE	9,663	4,616	4,854	193	238 D	47.8%	50.2%	48.7%	51.3%
6,221	CHEYENNE	2,278	1,219	978	81	241 R	53.5%	42.9%	55.5%	44.5%
4,081	CLARK	1,807	999	777	31	222 R	55.3%	43.0%	56.3%	43.8%
13,281	CLAY	5,711	3,763	1,804	144	1,959 R	65.9%	31.6%	67.6%	32.4%
17,247	CLOUD	7,155	4,018	2,891	246	1,127 R	56.2%	40.4%	58.2%	41.8%
12,278	COFFEY	4,812	2,945	1,796	71	1,149 R	61.2%	37.3%	62.1%	37.9%
4,412	COMANCHE	1,740	1,077	650	13	427 R	61.9%	37.4%	62.4%	37.6%
38,139	COWLEY	15,541	8,102	7,042	397	1,060 R	52.1%	45.3%	53.5%	46.5%
44,191	CRAWFORD	17,815	8,229	9,005	581	776 D	46.2%	50.5%	47.7%	52.3%
7,434	DECATUR	3,005	1,545	1,402	58	143 R	51.4%	46.7%	52.4%	47.6%
22,929	DICKINSON	9,867	5,918	3,815	134	2,103 R	60.0%	38.7%	60.8%	39.2%
12,936	DONIPHAN	4,369	2,785	1,555	29	1,230 R	63.7%	35.6%	64.2%	35.8%
25,171	DOUGLAS	14,454	9,287	4,778	389	4,509 R	64.3%	33.1%	66.0%	34.0%
6,377	EDWARDS	2,798	1,627	1,083	88	544 R	58.1%	38.7%	60.0%	40.0%
8,180	ELK	3,075	1,962	1,087	26	875 R	63.8%	35.3%	64.3%	35.7%
17,508	ELLIS	6,606	2,676	3,863	67	1,187 D	40.5%	58.5%	40.9%	59.1%
9,855	ELLSWORTH	4,079	2,155	1,879	45	276 R	52.8%	46.1%	53.4%	46.6%
10,092	FINNEY	5,015	2,508	2,367	140	141 R	50.0%	47.2%	51.4%	48.6%
17,254	FORD	8,662	4,089	4,396	177	307 D	47.2%	50.8%	48.2%	51.8%
20,889	FRANKLIN	8,834	5,145	3,467	222	1,678 R	58.2%	39.2%	59.7%	40.3%
15,222	GEARY	5,760	2,864	2,810	86	54 R	49.7%	48.8%	50.5%	49.5%
4,793	GOVE	1,792	1,030	719	43	311 R	57.5%	40.1%	58.9%	41.1%
6,071	GRAHAM	2,328	1,380	913	35	467 R	59.3%	39.2%	60.2%	39.8%
1,946	GRANT	1,391	742	625	24	117 R	53.3%	44.9%	54.3%	45.7%
4,773	GRAY	1,928	1,035	869	24	166 R	53.7%	45.1%	54.4%	45.6%
1,638	GREELEY	733	391	326	16	65 R	53.3%	44.5%	54.5%	45.5%
16,495	GREENWOOD	6,200	3,553	2,574	73	979 R	57.3%	41.5%	58.0%	42.0%
2,645	HAMILTON	1,479	749	722	8	27 R	50.6%	48.8%	50.9%	49.1%
12,068	HARPER	4,560	2,702	1,752	106	950 R	59.3%	38.4%	60.7%	39.3%
21,712	HARVEY	9,130	5,270	3,615	245	1,655 R	57.7%	39.6%	59.3%	40.7%
2,088	HASKELL	1,083	592	466	25	126 R	54.7%	43.0%	56.0%	44.0%
3,535	HODGEMAN	1,555	945	590	20	355 R	60.8%	37.9%	61.6%	38.4%
13,382	JACKSON	5,165	3,166	1,958	41	1,208 R	61.3%	37.9%	61.8%	38.2%
12,718	JEFFERSON	5,058	2,986	2,010	62	976 R	59.0%	39.7%	59.8%	40.2%
11,970	JEWELL	4,975	3,143	1,574	258	1,569 R	63.2%	31.6%	66.6%	33.4%
33,327	JOHNSON	23,378	14,191	8,982	205	5,209 R	60.7%	38.4%	61.2%	38.8%
2,525	KEARNY	1,242	676	541	25	135 R	54.4%	43.6%	55.5%	44.5%
12,001	KINGMAN	4,724	2,640	2,008	76	632 R	55.9%	42.5%	56.8%	43.2%
5,112	KIOWA	2,104	1,258	722	124	536 R	59.8%	34.3%	63.5%	36.5%
30,352	LABETTE	12,565	6,298	6,113	154	185 R	50.1%	48.7%	50.7%	49.3%
2,821	LANE	1,328	764	525	39	239 R	57.5%	39.5%	59.3%	40.7%
41,112	LEAVENWORTH	13,317	6,474	6,740	103	266 D	48.6%	50.6%	49.0%	51.0%
8,338	LINCOLN	3,318	2,181	1,094	43	1,087 R	65.7%	33.0%	66.6%	33.4%
11,969	LINN	4,354	2,632	1,673	49	959 R	60.5%	38.4%	61.1%	38.9%
3,688	LOGAN	1,734	1,105	579	50	526 R	63.7%	33.4%	65.6%	34.4%
26,424	LYON	11,876	5,941	5,708	227	233 R	50.0%	48.1%	51.0%	49.0%
24,152	MCPHERSON	10,344	5,952	3,879	513	2,073 R	57.5%	37.5%	60.5%	39.5%
18,951	MARION	7,285	4,724	2,421	140	2,303 R	64.8%	33.2%	66.1%	33.9%
20,986	MARSHALL	8,329	5,122	3,148	59	1,974 R	61.5%	37.8%	61.9%	38.1%
5,522	MEADE	2,336	1,406	834	96	572 R	60.2%	35.7%	62.8%	37.2%

KANSAS

PRESIDENT 1948

1940 Census Population	County	Total Vote	Republican	Democratic	Other	Rep.-Dem. Plurality	Percentage Total Vote Rep.	Total Vote Dem.	Major Vote Rep.	Major Vote Dem.
19,489	MIAMI	7,388	3,650	3,660	78	10 D	49.4%	49.5%	49.9%	50.1%
11,339	MITCHELL	4,823	2,998	1,750	75	1,248 R	62.2%	36.3%	63.1%	36.9%
49,729	MONTGOMERY	19,444	10,636	8,621	187	2,015 R	54.7%	44.3%	55.2%	44.8%
10,363	MORRIS	4,047	2,285	1,701	61	584 R	56.5%	42.0%	57.3%	42.7%
2,186	MORTON	1,186	624	545	17	79 R	52.6%	46.0%	53.4%	46.6%
16,761	NEMAHA	6,371	3,529	2,810	32	719 R	55.4%	44.1%	55.7%	44.3%
22,210	NEOSHO	8,947	5,072	3,770	105	1,302 R	56.7%	42.1%	57.4%	42.6%
6,864	NESS	2,907	1,689	1,130	88	559 R	58.1%	38.9%	59.9%	40.1%
9,831	NORTON	4,036	2,461	1,414	161	1,047 R	61.0%	35.0%	63.5%	36.5%
15,118	OSAGE	6,254	3,474	2,659	121	815 R	55.5%	42.5%	56.6%	43.4%
9,835	OSBORNE	4,140	2,603	1,420	117	1,183 R	62.9%	34.3%	64.7%	35.3%
9,224	OTTAWA	3,734	2,203	1,424	107	779 R	59.0%	38.1%	60.7%	39.3%
10,300	PAWNEE	4,235	2,221	1,945	69	276 R	52.4%	45.9%	53.3%	46.7%
10,435	PHILLIPS	4,094	2,715	1,223	156	1,492 R	66.3%	29.9%	68.9%	31.1%
14,015	POTTAWATOMIE	5,921	3,709	2,167	45	1,542 R	62.6%	36.6%	63.1%	36.9%
12,348	PRATT	5,731	2,878	2,751	102	127 R	50.2%	48.0%	51.1%	48.9%
6,618	RAWLINS	2,522	1,389	1,095	38	294 R	55.1%	43.4%	55.9%	44.1%
52,165	RENO	21,567	11,187	9,957	423	1,230 R	51.9%	46.2%	52.9%	47.1%
13,124	REPUBLIC	5,586	3,375	2,109	102	1,266 R	60.4%	37.8%	61.5%	38.5%
17,213	RICE	6,882	4,002	2,752	128	1,250 R	58.2%	40.0%	59.3%	40.7%
20,617	RILEY	13,567	9,227	4,052	288	5,175 R	68.0%	29.9%	69.5%	30.5%
8,497	ROOKS	3,882	2,197	1,636	49	561 R	56.6%	42.1%	57.3%	42.7%
8,285	RUSH	3,262	1,840	1,360	62	480 R	56.4%	41.7%	57.5%	42.5%
13,464	RUSSELL	5,512	3,113	2,343	56	770 R	56.5%	42.5%	57.1%	42.9%
29,535	SALINE	14,920	7,928	6,798	194	1,130 R	53.1%	45.6%	53.8%	46.2%
3,773	SCOTT	1,829	1,040	739	50	301 R	56.9%	40.4%	58.5%	41.5%
143,311	SEDGWICK	79,029	39,165	38,621	1,243	544 R	49.6%	48.9%	50.3%	49.7%
6,540	SEWARD	3,517	1,829	1,614	74	215 R	52.0%	45.9%	53.1%	46.9%
91,247	SHAWNEE	44,808	23,673	20,346	789	3,327 R	52.8%	45.4%	53.8%	46.2%
5,312	SHERIDAN	2,082	1,097	966	19	131 R	52.7%	46.4%	53.2%	46.8%
6,421	SHERMAN	2,760	1,380	1,289	91	91 R	50.0%	46.7%	51.7%	48.3%
10,582	SMITH	4,456	2,760	1,590	106	1,170 R	61.9%	35.7%	63.4%	36.6%
10,487	STAFFORD	4,453	2,304	2,049	100	255 R	51.7%	46.0%	52.9%	47.1%
1,443	STANTON	720	407	300	13	107 R	56.5%	41.7%	57.6%	42.4%
3,193	STEVENS	1,521	822	666	33	156 R	54.0%	43.8%	55.2%	44.8%
26,163	SUMNER	10,685	5,922	4,571	192	1,351 R	55.4%	42.8%	56.4%	43.6%
6,425	THOMAS	3,030	1,497	1,476	57	21 R	49.4%	48.7%	50.4%	49.6%
5,822	TREGO	2,387	1,237	1,117	33	120 R	51.8%	46.8%	52.5%	47.5%
9,219	WABAUNSEE	3,648	2,437	1,162	49	1,275 R	66.8%	31.9%	67.7%	32.3%
2,216	WALLACE	1,094	637	439	18	198 R	58.2%	40.1%	59.2%	40.8%
15,921	WASHINGTON	5,883	3,894	1,894	95	2,000 R	66.2%	32.2%	67.3%	32.7%
2,185	WICHITA	1,077	606	443	28	163 R	56.3%	41.1%	57.8%	42.2%
17,723	WILSON	6,506	3,868	2,538	100	1,330 R	59.5%	39.0%	60.4%	39.6%
8,014	WOODSON	3,191	1,997	1,145	49	852 R	62.6%	35.9%	63.6%	36.4%
145,071	WYANDOTTE	66,788	24,398	41,366	1,024	16,968 D	36.5%	61.9%	37.1%	62.9%
1,801,028	TOTAL	788,819	423,039	351,902	13,878	71,137 R	53.6%	44.6%	54.6%	45.4%

KANSAS

PRESIDENT 1944

1940 Census Population	County	Total Vote	Republican	Democratic	Other	Rep.-Dem. Plurality	Percentage: Total Vote Rep.	Total Vote Dem.	Major Vote Rep.	Major Vote Dem.
19,874	ALLEN	7,340	5,032	2,262	46	2,770 R	68.6%	30.8%	69.0%	31.0%
11,658	ANDERSON	4,716	3,060	1,649	7	1,411 R	64.9%	35.0%	65.0%	35.0%
22,222	ATCHISON	8,076	4,731	3,325	20	1,406 R	58.6%	41.2%	58.7%	41.3%
9,073	BARBER	3,672	2,140	1,501	31	639 R	58.3%	40.9%	58.8%	41.2%
25,010	BARTON	9,345	5,547	3,761	37	1,786 R	59.4%	40.2%	59.6%	40.4%
20,944	BOURBON	8,451	4,790	3,622	39	1,168 R	56.7%	42.9%	56.9%	43.1%
17,395	BROWN	6,779	4,947	1,817	15	3,130 R	73.0%	26.8%	73.1%	26.9%
32,013	BUTLER	13,203	7,064	6,084	55	980 R	53.5%	46.1%	53.7%	46.3%
6,345	CHASE	2,517	1,510	998	9	512 R	60.0%	39.7%	60.2%	39.8%
9,233	CHAUTAUQUA	3,421	2,305	1,106	10	1,199 R	67.4%	32.3%	67.6%	32.4%
29,817	CHEROKEE	9,988	5,458	4,468	62	990 R	54.6%	44.7%	55.0%	45.0%
6,221	CHEYENNE	2,368	1,610	736	22	874 R	68.0%	31.1%	68.6%	31.4%
4,081	CLARK	1,706	950	741	15	209 R	55.7%	43.4%	56.2%	43.8%
13,281	CLAY	5,541	4,101	1,391	49	2,710 R	74.0%	25.1%	74.7%	25.3%
17,247	CLOUD	6,875	4,377	2,391	107	1,986 R	63.7%	34.8%	64.7%	35.3%
12,278	COFFEY	5,144	3,461	1,660	23	1,801 R	67.3%	32.3%	67.6%	32.4%
4,412	COMANCHE	1,705	1,048	642	15	406 R	61.5%	37.7%	62.0%	38.0%
38,139	COWLEY	15,120	8,453	6,577	90	1,876 R	55.9%	43.5%	56.2%	43.8%
44,191	CRAWFORD	17,311	9,017	8,211	83	806 R	52.1%	47.4%	52.3%	47.7%
7,434	DECATUR	2,934	1,758	1,159	17	599 R	59.9%	39.5%	60.3%	39.7%
22,929	DICKINSON	9,446	6,227	3,190	29	3,037 R	65.9%	33.8%	66.1%	33.9%
12,936	DONIPHAN	4,491	3,230	1,261		1,969 R	71.9%	28.1%	71.9%	28.1%
25,171	DOUGLAS	12,189	8,224	3,886	79	4,338 R	67.5%	31.9%	67.9%	32.1%
6,377	EDWARDS	2,564	1,669	876	19	793 R	65.1%	34.2%	65.6%	34.4%
8,180	ELK	3,246	2,283	954	9	1,329 R	70.3%	29.4%	70.5%	29.5%
17,508	ELLIS	5,603	3,369	2,218	16	1,151 R	60.1%	39.6%	60.3%	39.7%
9,855	ELLSWORTH	3,974	2,290	1,678	6	612 R	57.6%	42.2%	57.7%	42.3%
10,092	FINNEY	4,065	2,366	1,667	32	699 R	58.2%	41.0%	58.7%	41.3%
17,254	FORD	7,181	4,110	2,994	77	1,116 R	57.2%	41.7%	57.9%	42.1%
20,889	FRANKLIN	8,310	5,375	2,880	55	2,495 R	64.7%	34.7%	65.1%	34.9%
15,222	GEARY	4,973	2,833	2,107	33	726 R	57.0%	42.4%	57.3%	42.7%
4,793	GOVE	1,562	1,125	420	17	705 R	72.0%	26.9%	72.8%	27.2%
6,071	GRAHAM	2,482	1,651	814	17	837 R	66.5%	32.8%	67.0%	33.0%
1,946	GRANT	853	566	282	5	284 R	66.4%	33.1%	66.7%	33.3%
4,773	GRAY	1,854	1,057	775	22	282 R	57.0%	41.8%	57.7%	42.3%
1,638	GREELEY	600	378	215	7	163 R	63.0%	35.8%	63.7%	36.3%
16,495	GREENWOOD	6,187	3,959	2,187	41	1,772 R	64.0%	35.3%	64.4%	35.6%
2,645	HAMILTON	1,275	795	471	9	324 R	62.4%	36.9%	62.8%	37.2%
12,068	HARPER	4,468	2,849	1,573	46	1,276 R	63.8%	35.2%	64.4%	35.6%
21,712	HARVEY	8,703	5,339	3,300	64	2,039 R	61.3%	37.9%	61.8%	38.2%
2,088	HASKELL	868	520	342	6	178 R	59.9%	39.4%	60.3%	39.7%
3,535	HODGEMAN	1,481	982	490	9	492 R	66.3%	33.1%	66.7%	33.3%
13,382	JACKSON	5,257	3,665	1,567	25	2,098 R	69.7%	29.8%	70.0%	30.0%
12,718	JEFFERSON	5,098	3,504	1,575	19	1,929 R	68.7%	30.9%	69.0%	31.0%
11,970	JEWELL	5,059	3,754	1,216	89	2,538 R	74.2%	24.0%	75.5%	24.5%
33,327	JOHNSON	17,773	11,951	5,771	51	6,180 R	67.2%	32.5%	67.4%	32.6%
2,525	KEARNY	980	612	365	3	247 R	62.4%	37.2%	62.6%	37.4%
12,001	KINGMAN	4,435	2,827	1,579	29	1,248 R	63.7%	35.6%	64.2%	35.8%
5,112	KIOWA	2,125	1,479	618	28	861 R	69.6%	29.1%	70.5%	29.5%
30,352	LABETTE	12,926	7,480	5,398	48	2,082 R	57.9%	41.8%	58.1%	41.9%
2,821	LANE	1,173	773	388	12	385 R	65.9%	33.1%	66.6%	33.4%
41,112	LEAVENWORTH	12,438	7,282	5,097	59	2,185 R	58.5%	41.0%	58.8%	41.2%
8,338	LINCOLN	3,339	2,405	910	24	1,495 R	72.0%	27.3%	72.5%	27.5%
11,969	LINN	4,647	3,185	1,442	20	1,743 R	68.5%	31.0%	68.8%	31.2%
3,688	LOGAN	1,518	1,107	406	5	701 R	72.9%	26.7%	73.2%	26.8%
26,424	LYON	10,799	5,710	4,984	105	726 R	52.9%	46.2%	53.4%	46.6%
24,152	MCPHERSON	9,372	5,840	3,321	211	2,519 R	62.3%	35.4%	63.7%	36.3%
18,951	MARION	7,185	5,219	1,925	41	3,294 R	72.6%	26.8%	73.1%	26.9%
20,986	MARSHALL	8,886	6,184	2,681	21	3,503 R	69.6%	30.2%	69.8%	30.2%
5,522	MEADE	2,087	1,424	631	32	793 R	68.2%	30.2%	69.3%	30.7%

KANSAS

PRESIDENT 1944

1940 Census Population	County	Total Vote	Republican	Democratic	Other	Rep.-Dem. Plurality	Percentage Total Vote Rep.	Total Vote Dem.	Major Vote Rep.	Major Vote Dem.
19,489	MIAMI	7,552	4,326	3,217	9	1,109 R	57.3%	42.6%	57.4%	42.6%
11,339	MITCHELL	4,857	3,238	1,579	40	1,659 R	66.7%	32.5%	67.2%	32.8%
49,729	MONTGOMERY	18,844	11,738	7,063	43	4,675 R	62.3%	37.5%	62.4%	37.6%
10,363	MORRIS	4,231	2,628	1,584	19	1,044 R	62.1%	37.4%	62.4%	37.6%
2,186	MORTON	987	617	367	3	250 R	62.5%	37.2%	62.7%	37.3%
16,761	NEMAHA	6,437	4,277	2,149	11	2,128 R	66.4%	33.4%	66.6%	33.4%
22,210	NEOSHO	8,679	5,420	3,233	26	2,187 R	62.4%	37.3%	62.6%	37.4%
6,864	NESS	2,666	1,745	876	45	869 R	65.5%	32.9%	66.6%	33.4%
9,831	NORTON	4,078	2,890	1,159	29	1,731 R	70.9%	28.4%	71.4%	28.6%
15,118	OSAGE	6,377	4,107	2,212	58	1,895 R	64.4%	34.7%	65.0%	35.0%
9,835	OSBORNE	3,953	2,827	1,078	48	1,749 R	71.5%	27.3%	72.4%	27.6%
9,224	OTTAWA	3,847	2,428	1,378	41	1,050 R	63.1%	35.8%	63.8%	36.2%
10,300	PAWNEE	3,806	2,057	1,727	22	330 R	54.0%	45.4%	54.4%	45.6%
10,435	PHILLIPS	4,197	3,053	1,098	46	1,955 R	72.7%	26.2%	73.5%	26.5%
14,015	POTTAWATOMIE	5,819	4,074	1,727	18	2,347 R	70.0%	29.7%	70.2%	29.8%
12,348	PRATT	5,029	2,658	2,334	37	324 R	52.9%	46.4%	53.2%	46.8%
6,618	RAWLINS	2,542	1,569	955	18	614 R	61.7%	37.6%	62.2%	37.8%
52,165	RENO	18,743	11,004	7,604	135	3,400 R	58.7%	40.6%	59.1%	40.9%
13,124	REPUBLIC	5,715	3,802	1,891	22	1,911 R	66.5%	33.1%	66.8%	33.2%
17,213	RICE	6,584	4,024	2,505	55	1,519 R	61.1%	38.0%	61.6%	38.4%
20,617	RILEY	9,244	6,511	2,659	74	3,852 R	70.4%	28.8%	71.0%	29.0%
8,497	ROOKS	3,549	2,361	1,166	22	1,195 R	66.5%	32.9%	66.9%	33.1%
8,285	RUSH	3,283	2,193	1,076	14	1,117 R	66.8%	32.8%	67.1%	32.9%
13,464	RUSSELL	4,950	3,344	1,583	23	1,761 R	67.6%	32.0%	67.9%	32.1%
29,535	SALINE	12,723	7,571	5,097	55	2,474 R	59.5%	40.1%	59.8%	40.2%
3,773	SCOTT	1,482	903	565	14	338 R	60.9%	38.1%	61.5%	38.5%
143,311	SEDGWICK	73,698	38,896	34,442	360	4,454 R	52.8%	46.7%	53.0%	47.0%
6,540	SEWARD	2,949	1,590	1,342	17	248 R	53.9%	45.5%	54.2%	45.8%
91,247	SHAWNEE	36,247	21,396	14,678	173	6,718 R	59.0%	40.5%	59.3%	40.7%
5,312	SHERIDAN	2,007	1,342	658	7	684 R	66.9%	32.8%	67.1%	32.9%
6,421	SHERMAN	2,677	1,608	1,021	48	587 R	60.1%	38.1%	61.2%	38.8%
10,582	SMITH	4,693	3,282	1,377	34	1,905 R	69.9%	29.3%	70.4%	29.6%
10,487	STAFFORD	4,432	2,493	1,908	31	585 R	56.3%	43.1%	56.6%	43.4%
1,443	STANTON	645	398	240	7	158 R	61.7%	37.2%	62.4%	37.6%
3,193	STEVENS	1,176	760	414	2	346 R	64.6%	35.2%	64.7%	35.3%
26,163	SUMNER	10,594	6,343	4,187	64	2,156 R	59.9%	39.5%	60.2%	39.8%
6,425	THOMAS	2,758	1,631	1,097	30	534 R	59.1%	39.8%	59.8%	40.2%
5,822	TREGO	2,354	1,459	883	12	576 R	62.0%	37.5%	62.3%	37.7%
9,219	WABAUNSEE	3,738	2,839	873	26	1,966 R	75.9%	23.4%	76.5%	23.5%
2,216	WALLACE	1,017	720	292	5	428 R	70.8%	28.7%	71.1%	28.9%
15,921	WASHINGTON	6,536	5,040	1,455	41	3,585 R	77.1%	22.3%	77.6%	22.4%
2,185	WICHITA	939	604	329	6	275 R	64.3%	35.0%	64.7%	35.3%
17,723	WILSON	6,195	4,248	1,912	35	2,336 R	68.6%	30.9%	69.0%	31.0%
8,014	WOODSON	3,318	2,308	999	11	1,309 R	69.6%	30.1%	69.8%	30.2%
145,071	WYANDOTTE	59,945	26,817	32,914	214	6,097 D	44.7%	54.9%	44.9%	55.1%
1,801,028	TOTAL	733,776	442,096	287,458	4,222	154,638 R	60.2%	39.2%	60.6%	39.4%

KANSAS

PRESIDENT 1940

1940 Census Population	County	Total Vote	Republican	Democratic	Other	Rep.-Dem. Plurality	Percentage Total Vote Rep.	Total Vote Dem.	Major Vote Rep.	Major Vote Dem.
19,874	ALLEN	9,600	6,376	3,178	46	3,198 R	66.4%	33.1%	66.7%	33.3%
11,658	ANDERSON	6,033	3,886	2,114	33	1,772 R	64.4%	35.0%	64.8%	35.2%
22,222	ATCHISON	10,560	5,921	4,557	82	1,364 R	56.1%	43.2%	56.5%	43.5%
9,073	BARBER	4,521	2,389	2,074	58	315 R	52.8%	45.9%	53.5%	46.5%
25,010	BARTON	11,043	6,011	4,982	50	1,029 R	54.4%	45.1%	54.7%	45.3%
20,944	BOURBON	10,727	5,751	4,898	78	853 R	53.6%	45.7%	54.0%	46.0%
17,395	BROWN	8,684	6,008	2,633	43	3,375 R	69.2%	30.3%	69.5%	30.5%
32,013	BUTLER	15,360	7,619	7,615	126	4 R	49.6%	49.6%	50.0%	50.0%
6,345	CHASE	3,238	1,871	1,344	23	527 R	57.8%	41.5%	58.2%	41.8%
9,233	CHAUTAUQUA	4,606	2,888	1,679	39	1,209 R	62.7%	36.5%	63.2%	36.8%
29,817	CHEROKEE	13,396	6,600	6,670	126	70 D	49.3%	49.8%	49.7%	50.3%
6,221	CHEYENNE	2,744	1,760	971	13	789 R	64.1%	35.4%	64.4%	35.6%
4,081	CLARK	2,167	1,072	1,079	16	7 D	49.5%	49.8%	49.8%	50.2%
13,281	CLAY	6,836	4,699	2,067	70	2,632 R	68.7%	30.2%	69.5%	30.5%
17,247	CLOUD	8,728	5,275	3,327	126	1,948 R	60.4%	38.1%	61.3%	38.7%
12,278	COFFEY	6,480	4,164	2,272	44	1,892 R	64.3%	35.1%	64.7%	35.3%
4,412	COMANCHE	2,222	1,322	880	20	442 R	59.5%	39.6%	60.0%	40.0%
38,139	COWLEY	17,935	9,684	8,115	136	1,569 R	54.0%	45.2%	54.4%	45.6%
44,191	CRAWFORD	21,275	10,143	11,002	130	859 D	47.7%	51.7%	48.0%	52.0%
7,434	DECATUR	3,593	2,018	1,546	29	472 R	56.2%	43.0%	56.6%	43.4%
22,929	DICKINSON	10,958	6,931	3,957	70	2,974 R	63.3%	36.1%	63.7%	36.3%
12,936	DONIPHAN	6,210	4,204	1,986	20	2,218 R	67.7%	32.0%	67.9%	32.1%
25,171	DOUGLAS	13,014	9,146	3,727	141	5,419 R	70.3%	28.6%	71.0%	29.0%
6,377	EDWARDS	3,136	1,886	1,219	31	667 R	60.1%	38.9%	60.7%	39.3%
8,180	ELK	4,283	2,774	1,478	31	1,296 R	64.8%	34.5%	65.2%	34.8%
17,508	ELLIS	6,946	3,622	3,299	25	323 R	52.1%	47.5%	52.3%	47.7%
9,855	ELLSWORTH	4,910	2,658	2,237	15	421 R	54.1%	45.6%	54.3%	45.7%
10,092	FINNEY	4,400	2,349	2,027	24	322 R	53.4%	46.1%	53.7%	46.3%
17,254	FORD	8,382	4,356	3,954	72	402 R	52.0%	47.2%	52.4%	47.6%
20,889	FRANKLIN	10,020	6,393	3,542	85	2,851 R	63.8%	35.3%	64.3%	35.7%
15,222	GEARY	5,394	2,840	2,504	50	336 R	52.7%	46.4%	53.1%	46.9%
4,793	GOVE	2,039	1,352	659	28	693 R	66.3%	32.3%	67.2%	32.8%
6,071	GRAHAM	2,959	1,804	1,135	20	669 R	61.0%	38.4%	61.4%	38.6%
1,946	GRANT	1,006	614	382	10	232 R	61.0%	38.0%	61.6%	38.4%
4,773	GRAY	2,036	1,056	962	18	94 R	51.9%	47.2%	52.3%	47.7%
1,638	GREELEY	770	497	268	5	229 R	64.5%	34.8%	65.0%	35.0%
16,495	GREENWOOD	8,109	4,893	3,160	56	1,733 R	60.3%	39.0%	60.8%	39.2%
2,645	HAMILTON	1,377	798	569	10	229 R	58.0%	41.3%	58.4%	41.6%
12,068	HARPER	5,751	3,205	2,478	68	727 R	55.7%	43.1%	56.4%	43.6%
21,712	HARVEY	9,759	5,539	4,087	133	1,452 R	56.8%	41.9%	57.5%	42.5%
2,088	HASKELL	1,038	607	425	6	182 R	58.5%	40.9%	58.8%	41.2%
3,535	HODGEMAN	1,794	1,092	690	12	402 R	60.9%	38.5%	61.3%	38.7%
13,382	JACKSON	6,737	4,306	2,397	34	1,909 R	63.9%	35.6%	64.2%	35.8%
12,718	JEFFERSON	6,580	4,330	2,212	38	2,118 R	65.8%	33.6%	66.2%	33.8%
11,970	JEWELL	6,415	4,591	1,719	105	2,872 R	71.6%	26.8%	72.8%	27.2%
33,327	JOHNSON	16,142	10,326	5,770	46	4,556 R	64.0%	35.7%	64.2%	35.8%
2,525	KEARNY	1,243	721	519	3	202 R	58.0%	41.8%	58.1%	41.9%
12,001	KINGMAN	5,645	3,068	2,528	49	540 R	54.3%	44.8%	54.8%	45.2%
5,112	KIOWA	2,451	1,571	844	36	727 R	64.1%	34.4%	65.1%	34.9%
30,352	LABETTE	15,157	8,210	6,860	87	1,350 R	54.2%	45.3%	54.5%	45.5%
2,821	LANE	1,461	888	557	16	331 R	60.8%	38.1%	61.5%	38.5%
41,112	LEAVENWORTH	14,598	8,503	6,053	42	2,450 R	58.2%	41.5%	58.4%	41.6%
8,338	LINCOLN	4,169	2,822	1,301	46	1,521 R	67.7%	31.2%	68.4%	31.6%
11,969	LINN	6,187	4,086	2,067	34	2,019 R	66.0%	33.4%	66.4%	33.6%
3,688	LOGAN	1,797	1,201	584	12	617 R	66.8%	32.5%	67.3%	32.7%
26,424	LYON	13,219	6,918	6,170	131	748 R	52.3%	46.7%	52.9%	47.1%
24,152	MCPHERSON	11,176	6,732	4,240	204	2,492 R	60.2%	37.9%	61.4%	38.6%
18,951	MARION	8,547	5,764	2,724	59	3,040 R	67.4%	31.9%	67.9%	32.1%
20,986	MARSHALL	10,931	7,286	3,588	57	3,698 R	66.7%	32.8%	67.0%	33.0%
5,522	MEADE	2,647	1,618	970	59	648 R	61.1%	36.6%	62.5%	37.5%

KANSAS

PRESIDENT 1940

1940 Census Population	County	Total Vote	Republican	Democratic	Other	Rep.-Dem. Plurality	Percentage: Total Vote Rep.	Total Vote Dem.	Major Vote Rep.	Major Vote Dem.
19,489	MIAMI	9,121	5,178	3,900	43	1,278 R	56.8%	42.8%	57.0%	43.0%
11,339	MITCHELL	5,792	3,681	2,060	51	1,621 R	63.6%	35.6%	64.1%	35.9%
49,729	MONTGOMERY	23,894	13,781	9,999	114	3,782 R	57.7%	41.8%	58.0%	42.0%
10,363	MORRIS	5,315	3,276	1,992	47	1,284 R	61.6%	37.5%	62.2%	37.8%
2,186	MORTON	1,154	643	503	8	140 R	55.7%	43.6%	56.1%	43.9%
16,761	NEMAHA	7,889	5,178	2,679	32	2,499 R	65.6%	34.0%	65.9%	34.1%
22,210	NEOSHO	11,031	6,556	4,419	56	2,137 R	59.4%	40.1%	59.7%	40.3%
6,864	NESS	3,112	1,826	1,230	56	596 R	58.7%	39.5%	59.8%	40.2%
9,831	NORTON	4,859	3,415	1,378	66	2,037 R	70.3%	28.4%	71.2%	28.8%
15,118	OSAGE	8,247	4,991	3,186	70	1,805 R	60.5%	38.6%	61.0%	39.0%
9,835	OSBORNE	4,995	3,424	1,488	83	1,936 R	68.5%	29.8%	69.7%	30.3%
9,224	OTTAWA	4,925	2,810	2,065	50	745 R	57.1%	41.9%	57.6%	42.4%
10,300	PAWNEE	4,587	2,329	2,216	42	113 R	50.8%	48.3%	51.2%	48.8%
10,435	PHILLIPS	5,290	3,676	1,563	51	2,113 R	69.5%	29.5%	70.2%	29.8%
14,015	POTTAWATOMIE	7,299	5,045	2,226	28	2,819 R	69.1%	30.5%	69.4%	30.6%
12,348	PRATT	5,867	2,930	2,870	67	60 R	49.9%	48.9%	50.5%	49.5%
6,618	RAWLINS	3,030	1,758	1,247	25	511 R	58.0%	41.2%	58.5%	41.5%
52,165	RENO	23,208	12,448	10,543	217	1,905 R	53.6%	45.4%	54.1%	45.9%
13,124	REPUBLIC	7,003	4,450	2,511	42	1,939 R	63.5%	35.9%	63.9%	36.1%
17,213	RICE	8,483	4,792	3,635	56	1,157 R	56.5%	42.9%	56.9%	43.1%
20,617	RILEY	10,818	7,420	3,293	105	4,127 R	68.6%	30.4%	69.3%	30.7%
8,497	ROOKS	4,273	2,590	1,650	33	940 R	60.6%	38.6%	61.1%	38.9%
8,285	RUSH	4,001	2,394	1,588	19	806 R	59.8%	39.7%	60.1%	39.9%
13,464	RUSSELL	6,342	3,714	2,579	49	1,135 R	58.6%	40.7%	59.0%	41.0%
29,535	SALINE	14,581	7,975	6,514	92	1,461 R	54.7%	44.7%	55.0%	45.0%
3,773	SCOTT	1,726	988	717	21	271 R	57.2%	41.5%	57.9%	42.1%
143,311	SEDGWICK	66,926	32,160	34,219	547	2,059 D	48.1%	51.1%	48.4%	51.6%
6,540	SEWARD	3,027	1,503	1,474	50	29 R	49.7%	48.7%	50.5%	49.5%
91,247	SHAWNEE	43,454	23,882	19,375	197	4,507 R	55.0%	44.6%	55.2%	44.8%
5,312	SHERIDAN	2,404	1,492	903	9	589 R	62.1%	37.6%	62.3%	37.7%
6,421	SHERMAN	3,008	1,569	1,399	40	170 R	52.2%	46.5%	52.9%	47.1%
10,582	SMITH	5,535	3,630	1,855	50	1,775 R	65.6%	33.5%	66.2%	33.8%
10,487	STAFFORD	5,357	2,795	2,509	53	286 R	52.2%	46.8%	52.7%	47.3%
1,443	STANTON	692	378	301	13	77 R	54.6%	43.5%	55.7%	44.3%
3,193	STEVENS	1,546	851	674	21	177 R	55.0%	43.6%	55.8%	44.2%
26,163	SUMNER	12,698	6,585	5,988	125	597 R	51.9%	47.2%	52.4%	47.6%
6,425	THOMAS	3,175	1,721	1,423	31	298 R	54.2%	44.8%	54.7%	45.3%
5,822	TREGO	2,728	1,571	1,140	17	431 R	57.6%	41.8%	57.9%	42.1%
9,219	WABAUNSEE	4,727	3,481	1,212	34	2,269 R	73.6%	25.6%	74.2%	25.8%
2,216	WALLACE	1,127	756	361	10	395 R	67.1%	32.0%	67.7%	32.3%
15,921	WASHINGTON	7,903	5,792	2,061	50	3,731 R	73.3%	26.1%	73.8%	26.2%
2,185	WICHITA	1,090	644	433	13	211 R	59.1%	39.7%	59.8%	40.2%
17,723	WILSON	8,209	5,288	2,859	62	2,429 R	64.4%	34.8%	64.9%	35.1%
8,014	WOODSON	4,065	2,637	1,398	30	1,239 R	64.9%	34.4%	65.4%	34.6%
145,071	WYANDOTTE	66,643	28,152	38,239	252	10,087 D	42.2%	57.4%	42.4%	57.6%
1,801,028	TOTAL	860,297	489,169	364,725	6,403	124,444 R	56.9%	42.4%	57.3%	42.7%

KANSAS

PRESIDENT 1936

1930 Census Population	County	Total Vote	Republican	Democratic	Other	Rep.-Dem. Plurality	Percentage Total Vote Rep.	Percentage Total Vote Dem.	Percentage Major Vote Rep.	Percentage Major Vote Dem.
21,391	ALLEN	9,945	6,071	3,869	5	2,202 R	61.0%	38.9%	61.1%	38.9%
13,355	ANDERSON	6,318	3,452	2,767	99	685 R	54.6%	43.8%	55.5%	44.5%
23,945	ATCHISON	11,160	5,312	5,817	31	505 D	47.6%	52.1%	47.7%	52.3%
10,178	BARBER	4,608	1,816	2,774	18	958 D	39.4%	60.2%	39.6%	60.4%
19,776	BARTON	9,517	3,534	5,978	5	2,444 D	37.1%	62.8%	37.2%	62.8%
22,386	BOURBON	11,120	5,402	5,714	4	312 D	48.6%	51.4%	48.6%	51.4%
20,553	BROWN	9,320	5,814	3,495	11	2,319 R	62.4%	37.5%	62.5%	37.5%
35,904	BUTLER	15,514	6,204	9,283	27	3,079 D	40.0%	59.8%	40.1%	59.9%
6,952	CHASE	3,325	1,610	1,706	9	96 D	48.4%	51.3%	48.6%	51.4%
10,352	CHAUTAUQUA	4,599	2,506	2,080	13	426 R	54.5%	45.2%	54.6%	45.4%
31,457	CHEROKEE	13,408	5,445	7,894	69	2,449 D	40.6%	58.9%	40.8%	59.2%
6,948	CHEYENNE	2,925	1,241	1,673	11	432 D	42.4%	57.2%	42.6%	57.4%
4,796	CLARK	2,358	899	1,457	2	558 D	38.1%	61.8%	38.2%	61.8%
14,556	CLAY	6,987	3,525	3,441	21	84 R	50.5%	49.2%	50.6%	49.4%
18,006	CLOUD	8,785	4,208	4,546	31	338 D	47.9%	51.7%	48.1%	51.9%
13,653	COFFEY	6,578	3,900	2,662	16	1,238 R	59.3%	40.5%	59.4%	40.6%
5,238	COMANCHE	2,363	932	1,428	3	496 D	39.4%	60.4%	39.5%	60.5%
40,903	COWLEY	19,255	8,378	10,805	72	2,427 D	43.5%	56.1%	43.7%	56.3%
49,329	CRAWFORD	21,636	8,596	12,974	66	4,378 D	39.7%	60.0%	39.9%	60.1%
8,866	DECATUR	4,104	1,727	2,362	15	635 D	42.1%	57.6%	42.2%	57.8%
25,870	DICKINSON	11,283	5,936	5,313	34	623 R	52.6%	47.1%	52.8%	47.2%
14,063	DONIPHAN	6,559	3,791	2,749	19	1,042 R	57.8%	41.9%	58.0%	42.0%
25,143	DOUGLAS	13,379	8,324	4,961	94	3,363 R	62.2%	37.1%	62.7%	37.3%
7,295	EDWARDS	3,383	1,394	1,986	3	592 D	41.2%	58.7%	41.2%	58.8%
9,210	ELK	4,423	2,355	2,059	9	296 R	53.2%	46.6%	53.4%	46.6%
15,907	ELLIS	6,469	1,622	4,834	13	3,212 D	25.1%	74.7%	25.1%	74.9%
10,132	ELLSWORTH	5,055	2,058	2,990	7	932 D	40.7%	59.1%	40.8%	59.2%
11,014	FINNEY	4,557	1,863	2,682	12	819 D	40.9%	58.9%	41.0%	59.0%
20,647	FORD	8,730	3,378	5,335	17	1,957 D	38.7%	61.1%	38.8%	61.2%
22,024	FRANKLIN	10,538	6,007	4,503	28	1,504 R	57.0%	42.7%	57.2%	42.8%
14,366	GEARY	5,367	2,382	2,973	12	591 D	44.4%	55.4%	44.5%	55.5%
5,643	GOVE	2,222	1,107	1,090	25	17 R	49.8%	49.1%	50.4%	49.6%
7,772	GRAHAM	3,202	1,462	1,734	6	272 D	45.7%	54.2%	45.7%	54.3%
3,092	GRANT	1,092	476	616		140 D	43.6%	56.4%	43.6%	56.4%
6,211	GRAY	2,225	764	1,459	2	695 D	34.3%	65.6%	34.4%	65.6%
1,712	GREELEY	785	396	388	1	8 R	50.4%	49.4%	50.5%	49.5%
19,235	GREENWOOD	8,345	4,146	4,176	23	30 D	49.7%	50.0%	49.8%	50.2%
3,328	HAMILTON	1,616	720	885	11	165 D	44.6%	54.8%	44.9%	55.1%
12,823	HARPER	5,854	2,441	3,391	22	950 D	41.7%	57.9%	41.9%	58.1%
22,120	HARVEY	9,841	4,456	5,357	28	901 D	45.3%	54.4%	45.4%	54.6%
2,805	HASKELL	1,069	442	626	1	184 D	41.3%	58.6%	41.4%	58.6%
4,157	HODGEMAN	1,946	781	1,162	3	381 D	40.1%	59.7%	40.2%	59.8%
14,776	JACKSON	6,959	3,680	3,265	14	415 R	52.9%	46.9%	53.0%	47.0%
14,129	JEFFERSON	6,841	3,711	3,105	25	606 R	54.2%	45.4%	54.4%	45.6%
14,462	JEWELL	6,664	3,849	2,780	35	1,069 R	57.8%	41.7%	58.1%	41.9%
27,179	JOHNSON	14,554	8,399	6,108	47	2,291 R	57.7%	42.0%	57.9%	42.1%
3,196	KEARNY	1,313	586	716	11	130 D	44.6%	54.5%	45.0%	55.0%
11,674	KINGMAN	5,732	2,014	3,705	13	1,691 D	35.1%	64.6%	35.2%	64.8%
6,035	KIOWA	2,705	1,280	1,417	8	137 D	47.3%	52.4%	47.5%	52.5%
31,346	LABETTE	14,716	6,610	8,050	56	1,440 D	44.9%	54.7%	45.1%	54.9%
3,372	LANE	1,558	682	853	23	171 D	43.8%	54.7%	44.4%	55.6%
42,673	LEAVENWORTH	16,601	8,532	7,996	73	536 R	51.4%	48.2%	51.6%	48.4%
9,707	LINCOLN	4,220	2,001	2,209	10	208 D	47.4%	52.3%	47.5%	52.5%
13,534	LINN	6,587	3,872	2,682	33	1,190 R	58.8%	40.7%	59.1%	40.9%
4,145	LOGAN	1,867	955	908	4	47 R	51.2%	48.6%	51.3%	48.7%
29,240	LYON	13,423	6,005	7,340	78	1,335 D	44.7%	54.7%	45.0%	55.0%
23,588	MCPHERSON	11,044	4,744	6,256	44	1,512 D	43.0%	56.6%	43.1%	56.9%
20,739	MARION	8,426	4,185	4,207	34	22 D	49.7%	49.9%	49.9%	50.1%
23,056	MARSHALL	11,190	5,929	5,238	23	691 R	53.0%	46.8%	53.1%	46.9%
6,858	MEADE	2,615	1,218	1,394	3	176 D	46.6%	53.3%	46.6%	53.4%

KANSAS

PRESIDENT 1936

1930 Census Population	County	Total Vote	Republican	Democratic	Other	Rep.-Dem. Plurality	Percentage Total Vote Rep.	Total Vote Dem.	Major Vote Rep.	Major Vote Dem.
21,243	MIAMI	9,291	4,676	4,601	14	75 R	50.3%	49.5%	50.4%	49.6%
12,774	MITCHELL	6,111	2,781	3,289	41	508 D	45.5%	53.8%	45.8%	54.2%
51,411	MONTGOMERY	23,167	11,565	11,535	67	30 R	49.9%	49.8%	50.1%	49.9%
11,859	MORRIS	5,575	2,751	2,805	19	54 D	49.3%	50.3%	49.5%	50.5%
4,092	MORTON	1,521	636	876	9	240 D	41.8%	57.6%	42.1%	57.9%
18,342	NEMAHA	8,172	3,903	4,175	94	272 D	47.8%	51.1%	48.3%	51.7%
22,665	NEOSHO	11,428	5,777	5,611	40	166 R	50.6%	49.1%	50.7%	49.3%
8,358	NESS	3,322	1,302	2,002	18	700 D	39.2%	60.3%	39.4%	60.6%
11,701	NORTON	5,160	2,829	2,307	24	522 R	54.8%	44.7%	55.1%	44.9%
17,538	OSAGE	8,486	4,232	4,224	30	8 R	49.9%	49.8%	50.0%	50.0%
11,568	OSBORNE	4,978	2,765	2,200	13	565 R	55.5%	44.2%	55.7%	44.3%
9,819	OTTAWA	5,033	2,230	2,785	18	555 D	44.3%	55.3%	44.5%	55.5%
10,510	PAWNEE	4,576	1,753	2,814	9	1,061 D	38.3%	61.5%	38.4%	61.6%
12,159	PHILLIPS	5,358	3,193	2,154	11	1,039 R	59.6%	40.2%	59.7%	40.3%
15,862	POTTAWATOMIE	7,398	3,977	3,284	137	693 R	53.8%	44.4%	54.8%	45.2%
13,312	PRATT	5,827	1,946	3,871	10	1,925 D	33.4%	66.4%	33.5%	66.5%
7,362	RAWLINS	3,404	1,364	2,029	11	665 D	40.1%	59.6%	40.2%	59.8%
47,785	RENO	22,896	8,607	14,203	86	5,596 D	37.6%	62.0%	37.7%	62.3%
14,745	REPUBLIC	7,280	3,830	3,427	23	403 R	52.6%	47.1%	52.8%	47.2%
13,800	RICE	8,245	3,318	4,905	22	1,587 D	40.2%	59.5%	40.4%	59.6%
19,882	RILEY	10,278	6,077	4,104	97	1,973 R	59.1%	39.9%	59.7%	40.3%
9,534	ROOKS	4,385	2,150	2,235		85 D	49.0%	51.0%	49.0%	51.0%
9,093	RUSH	4,219	1,733	2,482	4	749 D	41.1%	58.8%	41.1%	58.9%
11,045	RUSSELL	5,984	2,241	3,736	7	1,495 D	37.4%	62.4%	37.5%	62.5%
29,337	SALINE	13,983	6,061	7,872	50	1,811 D	43.3%	56.3%	43.5%	56.5%
3,976	SCOTT	1,724	625	1,096	3	471 D	36.3%	63.6%	36.3%	63.7%
136,330	SEDGWICK	61,353	21,654	39,503	196	17,849 D	35.3%	64.4%	35.4%	64.6%
8,075	SEWARD	3,109	1,108	1,997	4	889 D	35.6%	64.2%	35.7%	64.3%
85,200	SHAWNEE	42,888	19,785	22,942	161	3,157 D	46.1%	53.5%	46.3%	53.7%
6,038	SHERIDAN	2,501	1,007	1,442	52	435 D	40.3%	57.7%	41.1%	58.9%
7,400	SHERMAN	3,029	1,159	1,814	56	655 D	38.3%	59.9%	39.0%	61.0%
13,545	SMITH	6,156	3,292	2,847	17	445 R	53.5%	46.2%	53.6%	46.4%
10,460	STAFFORD	5,171	1,939	3,212	20	1,273 D	37.5%	62.1%	37.6%	62.4%
2,152	STANTON	770	311	458	1	147 D	40.4%	59.5%	40.4%	59.6%
4,655	STEVENS	1,730	701	1,023	6	322 D	40.5%	59.1%	40.7%	59.3%
28,960	SUMNER	12,939	4,946	7,966	27	3,020 D	38.2%	61.6%	38.3%	61.7%
7,334	THOMAS	3,388	1,200	2,168	20	968 D	35.4%	64.0%	35.6%	64.4%
6,470	TREGO	2,811	1,012	1,783	16	771 D	36.0%	63.4%	36.2%	63.8%
10,830	WABAUNSEE	5,059	2,809	2,235	15	574 R	55.5%	44.2%	55.7%	44.3%
2,882	WALLACE	1,161	658	492	11	166 R	56.7%	42.4%	57.2%	42.8%
17,112	WASHINGTON	8,192	4,809	3,355	28	1,454 R	58.7%	41.0%	58.9%	41.1%
2,579	WICHITA	1,091	448	637	6	189 D	41.1%	58.4%	41.3%	58.7%
18,646	WILSON	8,687	4,829	3,816	42	1,013 R	55.6%	43.9%	55.9%	44.1%
8,526	WOODSON	4,277	2,374	1,884	19	490 R	55.5%	44.0%	55.8%	44.2%
141,211	WYANDOTTE	64,596	26,239	38,101	256	11,862 D	40.6%	59.0%	40.8%	59.2%
1,880,999	TOTAL	865,507	397,727	464,520	3,260	66,793 D	46.0%	53.7%	46.1%	53.9%

KANSAS

PRESIDENT 1932

1930 Census Population	County	Total Vote	Republican	Democratic	Other	Rep.-Dem. Plurality	Percentage: Total Vote Rep.	Total Vote Dem.	Major Vote Rep.	Major Vote Dem.
21,391	ALLEN	8,936	4,510	4,249	177	261 R	50.5%	47.5%	51.5%	48.5%
13,355	ANDERSON	6,076	2,408	3,580	88	1,172 D	39.6%	58.9%	40.2%	59.8%
23,945	ATCHISON	10,575	4,778	5,640	157	862 D	45.2%	53.3%	45.9%	54.1%
10,178	BARBER	4,088	1,671	2,321	96	650 D	40.9%	56.8%	41.9%	58.1%
19,776	BARTON	8,238	3,365	4,776	97	1,411 D	40.8%	58.0%	41.3%	58.7%
22,386	BOURBON	10,035	4,277	5,577	181	1,300 D	42.6%	55.6%	43.4%	56.6%
20,553	BROWN	8,669	5,005	3,604	60	1,401 R	57.7%	41.6%	58.1%	41.9%
35,904	BUTLER	13,994	6,116	7,447	431	1,331 D	43.7%	53.2%	45.1%	54.9%
6,952	CHASE	3,231	1,485	1,703	43	218 D	46.0%	52.7%	46.6%	53.4%
10,352	CHAUTAUQUA	4,360	1,893	2,263	204	370 D	43.4%	51.9%	45.5%	54.5%
31,457	CHEROKEE	11,880	4,045	7,442	393	3,397 D	34.0%	62.6%	35.2%	64.8%
6,948	CHEYENNE	2,829	979	1,716	134	737 D	34.6%	60.7%	36.3%	63.7%
4,796	CLARK	2,106	938	1,152	16	214 D	44.5%	54.7%	44.9%	55.1%
14,556	CLAY	6,591	3,115	3,289	187	174 D	47.3%	49.9%	48.6%	51.4%
18,006	CLOUD	7,812	3,120	4,457	235	1,337 D	39.9%	57.1%	41.2%	58.8%
13,653	COFFEY	6,184	2,707	3,389	88	682 D	43.8%	54.8%	44.4%	55.6%
5,238	COMANCHE	2,152	945	1,175	32	230 D	43.9%	54.6%	44.6%	55.4%
40,903	COWLEY	17,126	7,657	8,681	788	1,024 D	44.7%	50.7%	46.9%	53.1%
49,329	CRAWFORD	18,401	6,884	10,994	523	4,110 D	37.4%	59.7%	38.5%	61.5%
8,866	DECATUR	3,969	1,439	2,422	108	983 D	36.3%	61.0%	37.3%	62.7%
25,870	DICKINSON	10,849	5,320	5,339	190	19 D	49.0%	49.2%	49.9%	50.1%
14,063	DONIPHAN	5,349	2,748	2,532	69	216 R	51.4%	47.3%	52.0%	48.0%
25,143	DOUGLAS	12,521	7,346	4,833	342	2,513 R	58.7%	38.6%	60.3%	39.7%
7,295	EDWARDS	3,198	1,420	1,693	85	273 D	44.4%	52.9%	45.6%	54.4%
9,210	ELK	4,057	1,746	2,239	72	493 D	43.0%	55.2%	43.8%	56.2%
15,907	ELLIS	5,970	1,465	4,449	56	2,984 D	24.5%	74.5%	24.8%	75.2%
10,132	ELLSWORTH	4,598	1,607	2,928	63	1,321 D	34.9%	63.7%	35.4%	64.6%
11,014	FINNEY	4,500	2,116	2,300	84	184 D	47.0%	51.1%	47.9%	52.1%
20,647	FORD	8,015	3,335	4,442	238	1,107 D	41.6%	55.4%	42.9%	57.1%
22,024	FRANKLIN	9,742	4,887	4,690	165	197 R	50.2%	48.1%	51.0%	49.0%
14,366	GEARY	4,783	1,957	2,705	121	748 D	40.9%	56.6%	42.0%	58.0%
5,643	GOVE	2,280	1,043	1,186	51	143 D	45.7%	52.0%	46.8%	53.2%
7,772	GRAHAM	3,464	1,284	2,082	98	798 D	37.1%	60.1%	38.1%	61.9%
3,092	GRANT	1,172	395	737	40	342 D	33.7%	62.9%	34.9%	65.1%
6,211	GRAY	2,317	910	1,348	59	438 D	39.3%	58.2%	40.3%	59.7%
1,712	GREELEY	842	359	440	43	81 D	42.6%	52.3%	44.9%	55.1%
19,235	GREENWOOD	7,747	3,592	4,002	153	410 D	46.4%	51.7%	47.3%	52.7%
3,328	HAMILTON	1,775	651	1,021	103	370 D	36.7%	57.5%	38.9%	61.1%
12,823	HARPER	5,145	2,116	2,860	169	744 D	41.1%	55.6%	42.5%	57.5%
22,120	HARVEY	8,507	4,192	4,091	224	101 R	49.3%	48.1%	50.6%	49.4%
2,805	HASKELL	1,126	456	639	31	183 D	40.5%	56.7%	41.6%	58.4%
4,157	HODGEMAN	1,859	847	988	24	141 D	45.6%	53.1%	46.2%	53.8%
14,776	JACKSON	6,799	3,271	3,442	86	171 D	48.1%	50.6%	48.7%	51.3%
14,129	JEFFERSON	6,271	2,974	3,185	112	211 D	47.4%	50.8%	48.3%	51.7%
14,462	JEWELL	6,896	3,324	3,367	205	43 D	48.2%	48.8%	49.7%	50.3%
27,179	JOHNSON	13,096	6,487	6,485	124	2 R	49.5%	49.5%	50.0%	50.0%
3,196	KEARNY	1,359	529	771	59	242 D	38.9%	56.7%	40.7%	59.3%
11,674	KINGMAN	5,065	1,923	3,050	92	1,127 D	38.0%	60.2%	38.7%	61.3%
6,035	KIOWA	2,500	1,306	1,159	35	147 R	52.2%	46.4%	53.0%	47.0%
31,346	LABETTE	13,755	5,794	7,667	294	1,873 D	42.1%	55.7%	43.0%	57.0%
3,372	LANE	1,567	672	866	29	194 D	42.9%	55.3%	43.7%	56.3%
42,673	LEAVENWORTH	16,114	6,484	9,507	123	3,023 D	40.2%	59.0%	40.5%	59.5%
9,707	LINCOLN	4,051	1,653	2,297	101	644 D	40.8%	56.7%	41.8%	58.2%
13,534	LINN	5,953	2,647	3,216	90	569 D	44.5%	54.0%	45.1%	54.9%
4,145	LOGAN	1,959	867	1,025	67	158 D	44.3%	52.3%	45.8%	54.2%
29,240	LYON	12,756	6,044	6,365	347	321 D	47.4%	49.9%	48.7%	51.3%
23,588	MCPHERSON	9,377	4,098	5,003	276	905 D	43.7%	53.4%	45.0%	55.0%
20,739	MARION	7,715	3,220	4,366	129	1,146 D	41.7%	56.6%	42.4%	57.6%
23,056	MARSHALL	10,544	4,455	5,970	119	1,515 D	42.3%	56.6%	42.7%	57.3%
6,858	MEADE	2,521	1,248	1,231	42	17 R	49.5%	48.8%	50.3%	49.7%

KANSAS

PRESIDENT 1932

1930 Census Population	County	Total Vote	Republican	Democratic	Other	Rep.-Dem. Plurality	Percentage Total Vote Rep.	Total Vote Dem.	Major Vote Rep.	Major Vote Dem.
21,243	MIAMI	8,520	3,667	4,739	114	1,072 D	43.0%	55.6%	43.6%	56.4%
12,774	MITCHELL	5,859	2,502	3,176	181	674 D	42.7%	54.2%	44.1%	55.9%
51,411	MONTGOMERY	20,339	9,958	9,941	440	17 R	49.0%	48.9%	50.0%	50.0%
11,859	MORRIS	5,164	2,566	2,452	146	114 R	49.7%	47.5%	51.1%	48.9%
4,092	MORTON	1,793	621	1,093	79	472 D	34.6%	61.0%	36.2%	63.8%
18,342	NEMAHA	7,800	3,167	4,578	55	1,411 D	40.6%	58.7%	40.9%	59.1%
22,665	NEOSHO	9,965	4,212	5,616	137	1,404 D	42.3%	56.4%	42.9%	57.1%
8,358	NESS	3,304	1,409	1,772	123	363 D	42.6%	53.6%	44.3%	55.7%
11,701	NORTON	5,145	2,272	2,705	168	433 D	44.2%	52.6%	45.6%	54.4%
17,538	OSAGE	8,165	3,707	4,199	259	492 D	45.4%	51.4%	46.9%	53.1%
11,568	OSBORNE	4,919	2,555	2,231	133	324 R	51.9%	45.4%	53.4%	46.6%
9,819	OTTAWA	4,559	1,884	2,505	170	621 D	41.3%	54.9%	42.9%	57.1%
10,510	PAWNEE	4,443	1,889	2,451	103	562 D	42.5%	55.2%	43.5%	56.5%
12,159	PHILLIPS	5,327	2,165	3,007	155	842 D	40.6%	56.4%	41.9%	58.1%
15,862	POTTAWATOMIE	7,346	3,339	3,910	97	571 D	45.5%	53.2%	46.1%	53.9%
13,312	PRATT	5,397	2,167	3,109	121	942 D	40.2%	57.6%	41.1%	58.9%
7,362	RAWLINS	3,423	1,064	2,245	114	1,181 D	31.1%	65.6%	32.2%	67.8%
47,785	RENO	18,970	8,972	9,351	647	379 D	47.3%	49.3%	49.0%	51.0%
14,745	REPUBLIC	6,887	2,655	4,105	127	1,450 D	38.6%	59.6%	39.3%	60.7%
13,800	RICE	6,298	3,107	3,037	154	70 R	49.3%	48.2%	50.6%	49.4%
19,882	RILEY	9,765	5,337	4,101	327	1,236 R	54.7%	42.0%	56.5%	43.5%
9,534	ROOKS	4,322	2,005	2,229	88	224 D	46.4%	51.6%	47.4%	52.6%
9,093	RUSH	3,774	1,433	2,275	66	842 D	38.0%	60.3%	38.6%	61.4%
11,045	RUSSELL	4,631	1,805	2,723	103	918 D	39.0%	58.8%	39.9%	60.1%
29,337	SALINE	12,772	5,265	7,118	389	1,853 D	41.2%	55.7%	42.5%	57.5%
3,976	SCOTT	1,748	595	1,092	61	497 D	34.0%	62.5%	35.3%	64.7%
136,330	SEDGWICK	52,594	21,815	29,344	1,435	7,529 D	41.5%	55.8%	42.6%	57.4%
8,075	SEWARD	2,972	1,297	1,576	99	279 D	43.6%	53.0%	45.1%	54.9%
85,200	SHAWNEE	37,141	19,847	16,471	823	3,376 R	53.4%	44.3%	54.6%	45.4%
6,038	SHERIDAN	2,707	878	1,773	56	895 D	32.4%	65.5%	33.1%	66.9%
7,400	SHERMAN	3,454	1,112	2,110	232	998 D	32.2%	61.1%	34.5%	65.5%
13,545	SMITH	6,169	2,870	3,155	144	285 D	46.5%	51.1%	47.6%	52.4%
10,460	STAFFORD	4,718	1,945	2,651	122	706 D	41.2%	56.2%	42.3%	57.7%
2,152	STANTON	1,024	412	598	14	186 D	40.2%	58.4%	40.8%	59.2%
4,655	STEVENS	1,860	578	1,225	57	647 D	31.1%	65.9%	32.1%	67.9%
28,960	SUMNER	11,619	4,926	6,353	340	1,427 D	42.4%	54.7%	43.7%	56.3%
7,334	THOMAS	3,438	1,158	2,103	177	945 D	33.7%	61.2%	35.5%	64.5%
6,470	TREGO	2,719	918	1,751	50	833 D	33.8%	64.4%	34.4%	65.6%
10,830	WABAUNSEE	4,862	2,304	2,465	93	161 D	47.4%	50.7%	48.3%	51.7%
2,882	WALLACE	1,393	561	761	71	200 D	40.3%	54.6%	42.4%	57.6%
17,112	WASHINGTON	7,653	3,324	4,234	95	910 D	43.4%	55.3%	44.0%	56.0%
2,579	WICHITA	1,139	375	732	32	357 D	32.9%	64.3%	33.9%	66.1%
18,646	WILSON	7,616	3,422	4,001	193	579 D	44.9%	52.5%	46.1%	53.9%
8,526	WOODSON	4,078	1,842	2,119	117	277 D	45.2%	52.0%	46.5%	53.5%
141,211	WYANDOTTE	58,821	25,471	32,629	721	7,158 D	43.3%	55.5%	43.8%	56.2%
1,880,999	TOTAL	791,978	349,498	424,204	18,276	74,706 D	44.1%	53.6%	45.2%	54.8%

KANSAS

PRESIDENT 1928

1920 Census Population	County	Total Vote	Republican	Democratic	Other	Rep.-Dem. Plurality	Percentage: Total Vote Rep.	Percentage: Total Vote Dem.	Percentage: Major Vote Rep.	Percentage: Major Vote Dem.
23,509	ALLEN	8,550	6,695	1,803	52	4,892 R	78.3%	21.1%	78.8%	21.2%
12,986	ANDERSON	5,485	3,562	1,874	49	1,688 R	64.9%	34.2%	65.5%	34.5%
23,411	ATCHISON	10,440	6,647	3,756	37	2,891 R	63.7%	36.0%	63.9%	36.1%
9,739	BARBER	3,904	2,984	871	49	2,113 R	76.4%	22.3%	77.4%	22.6%
18,422	BARTON	7,767	4,966	2,777	24	2,189 R	63.9%	35.8%	64.1%	35.9%
23,198	BOURBON	9,556	7,251	2,223	82	5,028 R	75.9%	23.3%	76.5%	23.5%
20,949	BROWN	8,717	6,692	2,005	20	4,687 R	76.8%	23.0%	76.9%	23.1%
43,842	BUTLER	12,802	10,168	2,533	101	7,635 R	79.4%	19.8%	80.1%	19.9%
7,144	CHASE	2,856	2,079	739	38	1,340 R	72.8%	25.9%	73.8%	26.2%
11,598	CHAUTAUQUA	4,348	3,303	944	101	2,359 R	76.0%	21.7%	77.8%	22.2%
33,609	CHEROKEE	11,296	7,478	3,442	376	4,036 R	66.2%	30.5%	68.5%	31.5%
5,587	CHEYENNE	2,106	1,466	586	54	880 R	69.6%	27.8%	71.4%	28.6%
4,989	CLARK	1,810	1,383	419	8	964 R	76.4%	23.1%	76.7%	23.3%
14,365	CLAY	6,044	4,457	1,515	72	2,942 R	73.7%	25.1%	74.6%	25.4%
17,714	CLOUD	7,745	5,286	2,376	83	2,910 R	68.3%	30.7%	69.0%	31.0%
14,254	COFFEY	5,883	4,342	1,514	27	2,828 R	73.8%	25.7%	74.1%	25.9%
5,302	COMANCHE	1,943	1,554	385	4	1,169 R	80.0%	19.8%	80.1%	19.9%
35,155	COWLEY	15,721	12,701	2,818	202	9,883 R	80.8%	17.9%	81.8%	18.2%
61,800	CRAWFORD	17,642	10,992	6,351	299	4,641 R	62.3%	36.0%	63.4%	36.6%
8,121	DECATUR	3,478	2,314	1,129	35	1,185 R	66.5%	32.5%	67.2%	32.8%
25,777	DICKINSON	10,070	7,758	2,246	66	5,512 R	77.0%	22.3%	77.5%	22.5%
13,438	DONIPHAN	5,509	4,002	1,496	11	2,506 R	72.6%	27.2%	72.8%	27.2%
23,998	DOUGLAS	11,292	8,887	2,297	108	6,590 R	78.7%	20.3%	79.5%	20.5%
7,057	EDWARDS	2,959	2,171	768	20	1,403 R	73.4%	26.0%	73.9%	26.1%
9,034	ELK	3,880	3,007	831	42	2,176 R	77.5%	21.4%	78.3%	21.7%
14,138	ELLIS	5,075	1,700	3,364	11	1,664 D	33.5%	66.3%	33.6%	66.4%
10,379	ELLSWORTH	4,068	2,450	1,588	30	862 R	60.2%	39.0%	60.7%	39.3%
7,674	FINNEY	3,174	2,433	709	32	1,724 R	76.7%	22.3%	77.4%	22.6%
14,273	FORD	6,835	4,893	1,870	72	3,023 R	71.6%	27.4%	72.3%	27.7%
21,946	FRANKLIN	9,370	7,346	1,951	73	5,395 R	78.4%	20.8%	79.0%	21.0%
13,452	GEARY	3,971	2,746	1,203	22	1,543 R	69.2%	30.3%	69.5%	30.5%
4,748	GOVE	2,072	1,470	590	12	880 R	70.9%	28.5%	71.4%	28.6%
7,624	GRAHAM	2,970	1,832	1,087	51	745 R	61.7%	36.6%	62.8%	37.2%
1,087	GRANT	831	635	185	11	450 R	76.4%	22.3%	77.4%	22.6%
4,711	GRAY	1,918	1,294	606	18	688 R	67.5%	31.6%	68.1%	31.9%
1,028	GREELEY	561	439	121	1	318 R	78.3%	21.6%	78.4%	21.6%
14,715	GREENWOOD	7,466	5,863	1,554	49	4,309 R	78.5%	20.8%	79.0%	21.0%
2,586	HAMILTON	1,226	839	363	24	476 R	68.4%	29.6%	69.8%	30.2%
13,656	HARPER	4,768	3,712	1,005	51	2,707 R	77.9%	21.1%	78.7%	21.3%
20,744	HARVEY	8,155	6,330	1,748	77	4,582 R	77.6%	21.4%	78.4%	21.6%
1,455	HASKELL	880	646	222	12	424 R	73.4%	25.2%	74.4%	25.6%
3,734	HODGEMAN	1,661	1,122	528	11	594 R	67.5%	31.8%	68.0%	32.0%
15,495	JACKSON	6,453	4,811	1,602	40	3,209 R	74.6%	24.8%	75.0%	25.0%
14,750	JEFFERSON	6,433	4,810	1,601	22	3,209 R	74.8%	24.9%	75.0%	25.0%
16,240	JEWELL	5,960	4,583	1,289	88	3,294 R	76.9%	21.6%	78.0%	22.0%
18,314	JOHNSON	11,627	8,185	3,373	69	4,812 R	70.4%	29.0%	70.8%	29.2%
2,617	KEARNY	1,106	854	229	23	625 R	77.2%	20.7%	78.9%	21.1%
12,119	KINGMAN	4,721	3,287	1,408	26	1,879 R	69.6%	29.8%	70.0%	30.0%
6,164	KIOWA	2,350	1,929	406	15	1,523 R	82.1%	17.3%	82.6%	17.4%
34,047	LABETTE	12,191	9,048	2,969	174	6,079 R	74.2%	24.4%	75.3%	24.7%
2,848	LANE	1,338	954	364	20	590 R	71.3%	27.2%	72.4%	27.6%
38,402	LEAVENWORTH	15,056	8,472	6,539	45	1,933 R	56.3%	43.4%	56.4%	43.6%
9,894	LINCOLN	3,631	2,655	953	23	1,702 R	73.1%	26.2%	73.6%	26.4%
13,815	LINN	5,627	4,231	1,328	68	2,903 R	75.2%	23.6%	76.1%	23.9%
3,223	LOGAN	1,488	1,066	405	17	661 R	71.6%	27.2%	72.5%	27.5%
26,154	LYON	11,595	8,753	2,761	81	5,992 R	75.5%	23.8%	76.0%	24.0%
21,845	MCPHERSON	7,789	6,230	1,457	102	4,773 R	80.0%	18.7%	81.0%	19.0%
22,923	MARION	7,410	5,446	1,938	26	3,508 R	73.5%	26.2%	73.8%	26.2%
22,730	MARSHALL	10,316	6,918	3,329	69	3,589 R	67.1%	32.3%	67.5%	32.5%
5,542	MEADE	2,336	1,709	618	9	1,091 R	73.2%	26.5%	73.4%	26.6%

KANSAS

PRESIDENT 1928

1920 Census Population	County	Total Vote	Republican	Democratic	Other	Rep.-Dem. Plurality	Percentage Total Vote Rep.	Total Vote Dem.	Major Vote Rep.	Major Vote Dem.
19,809	MIAMI	8,157	5,931	2,148	78	3,783 R	72.7%	26.3%	73.4%	26.6%
13,886	MITCHELL	5,164	3,245	1,855	64	1,390 R	62.8%	35.9%	63.6%	36.4%
49,645	MONTGOMERY	18,760	14,316	4,205	239	10,111 R	76.3%	22.4%	77.3%	22.7%
12,005	MORRIS	4,815	3,830	929	56	2,901 R	79.5%	19.3%	80.5%	19.5%
3,177	MORTON	1,282	1,010	259	13	751 R	78.8%	20.2%	79.6%	20.4%
18,487	NEMAHA	7,592	4,639	2,919	34	1,720 R	61.1%	38.4%	61.4%	38.6%
24,000	NEOSHO	9,136	6,603	2,459	74	4,144 R	72.3%	26.9%	72.9%	27.1%
7,490	NESS	2,878	2,058	784	36	1,274 R	71.5%	27.2%	72.4%	27.6%
11,423	NORTON	4,548	3,365	1,087	96	2,278 R	74.0%	23.9%	75.6%	24.4%
18,621	OSAGE	8,056	5,900	2,058	98	3,842 R	73.2%	25.5%	74.1%	25.9%
12,441	OSBORNE	4,528	3,683	821	24	2,862 R	81.3%	18.1%	81.8%	18.2%
10,714	OTTAWA	4,354	3,158	1,131	65	2,027 R	72.5%	26.0%	73.6%	26.4%
9,323	PAWNEE	3,763	2,829	918	16	1,911 R	75.2%	24.4%	75.5%	24.5%
12,505	PHILLIPS	4,595	3,206	1,332	57	1,874 R	69.8%	29.0%	70.6%	29.4%
16,154	POTTAWATOMIE	6,816	4,451	2,341	24	2,110 R	65.3%	34.3%	65.5%	34.5%
12,909	PRATT	5,032	4,055	934	43	3,121 R	80.6%	18.6%	81.3%	18.7%
6,799	RAWLINS	2,887	1,668	1,164	55	504 R	57.8%	40.3%	58.9%	41.1%
44,423	RENO	16,868	12,872	3,843	153	9,029 R	76.3%	22.8%	77.0%	23.0%
15,855	REPUBLIC	6,341	4,324	1,956	61	2,368 R	68.2%	30.8%	68.9%	31.1%
14,832	RICE	5,835	4,321	1,462	52	2,859 R	74.1%	25.1%	74.7%	25.3%
20,650	RILEY	8,461	6,592	1,791	78	4,801 R	77.9%	21.2%	78.6%	21.4%
9,966	ROOKS	3,652	2,583	1,044	25	1,539 R	70.7%	28.6%	71.2%	28.8%
8,360	RUSH	3,307	1,985	1,296	26	689 R	60.0%	39.2%	60.5%	39.5%
10,748	RUSSELL	4,180	2,782	1,366	32	1,416 R	66.6%	32.7%	67.1%	32.9%
25,103	SALINE	11,056	7,872	3,108	76	4,764 R	71.2%	28.1%	71.7%	28.3%
3,121	SCOTT	1,347	886	450	11	436 R	65.8%	33.4%	66.3%	33.7%
92,234	SEDGWICK	43,186	32,132	10,649	405	21,483 R	74.4%	24.7%	75.1%	24.9%
6,220	SEWARD	2,433	1,873	538	22	1,335 R	77.0%	22.1%	77.7%	22.3%
69,159	SHAWNEE	32,336	24,723	7,433	180	17,290 R	76.5%	23.0%	76.9%	23.1%
5,484	SHERIDAN	2,396	1,450	930	16	520 R	60.5%	38.8%	60.9%	39.1%
5,592	SHERMAN	2,718	2,028	630	60	1,398 R	74.6%	23.2%	76.3%	23.7%
14,985	SMITH	5,409	4,021	1,338	50	2,683 R	74.3%	24.7%	75.0%	25.0%
11,559	STAFFORD	4,355	3,278	1,025	52	2,253 R	75.3%	23.5%	76.2%	23.8%
908	STANTON	664	497	164	3	333 R	74.8%	24.7%	75.2%	24.8%
3,943	STEVENS	1,443	1,133	300	10	833 R	78.5%	20.8%	79.1%	20.9%
29,213	SUMNER	11,240	8,951	2,108	181	6,843 R	79.6%	18.8%	80.9%	19.1%
5,517	THOMAS	2,771	1,828	899	44	929 R	66.0%	32.4%	67.0%	33.0%
5,880	TREGO	2,354	1,359	982	13	377 R	57.7%	41.7%	58.1%	41.9%
11,424	WABAUNSEE	4,311	3,099	1,189	23	1,910 R	71.9%	27.6%	72.3%	27.7%
2,424	WALLACE	1,115	738	356	21	382 R	66.2%	31.9%	67.5%	32.5%
17,984	WASHINGTON	7,097	4,781	2,267	49	2,514 R	67.4%	31.9%	67.8%	32.2%
1,856	WICHITA	845	464	370	11	94 R	54.9%	43.8%	55.6%	44.4%
21,157	WILSON	7,141	5,603	1,465	73	4,138 R	78.5%	20.5%	79.3%	20.7%
8,984	WOODSON	3,767	2,885	855	27	2,030 R	76.6%	22.7%	77.1%	22.9%
122,218	WYANDOTTE	49,978	32,829	16,884	265	15,945 R	65.7%	33.8%	66.0%	34.0%
1,769,257	TOTAL	713,200	513,672	193,003	6,525	320,669 R	72.0%	27.1%	72.7%	27.3%

KANSAS

PRESIDENT 1924

1920 Census Population	County	Total Vote	Republican	Democratic	Other	Rep.-Dem. Plurality	Percentage Total Vote Rep.	Percentage Total Vote Dem.	Percentage Major Vote Rep.	Percentage Major Vote Dem.
23,509	ALLEN	8,723	6,101	2,181	441	3,920 R	69.9%	25.0%	73.7%	26.3%
12,986	ANDERSON	5,085	3,101	1,421	563	1,680 R	61.0%	27.9%	68.6%	31.4%
23,411	ATCHISON	9,786	6,246	2,199	1,341	4,047 R	63.8%	22.5%	74.0%	26.0%
9,739	BARBER	3,808	2,218	909	681	1,309 R	58.2%	23.9%	70.9%	29.1%
18,422	BARTON	7,274	4,109	1,605	1,560	2,504 R	56.5%	22.1%	71.9%	28.1%
23,198	BOURBON	8,598	4,210	2,850	1,538	1,360 R	49.0%	33.1%	59.6%	40.4%
20,949	BROWN	8,191	5,647	1,866	678	3,781 R	68.9%	22.8%	75.2%	24.8%
43,842	BUTLER	12,716	7,367	3,642	1,707	3,725 R	57.9%	28.6%	66.9%	33.1%
7,144	CHASE	2,910	1,822	758	330	1,064 R	62.6%	26.0%	70.6%	29.4%
11,598	CHAUTAUQUA	4,066	2,439	1,087	540	1,352 R	60.0%	26.7%	69.2%	30.8%
33,609	CHEROKEE	10,278	5,437	3,071	1,770	2,366 R	52.9%	29.9%	63.9%	36.1%
5,587	CHEYENNE	2,221	1,119	485	617	634 R	50.4%	21.8%	69.8%	30.2%
4,989	CLARK	1,638	969	410	259	559 R	59.2%	25.0%	70.3%	29.7%
14,365	CLAY	5,986	3,767	1,417	802	2,350 R	62.9%	23.7%	72.7%	27.3%
17,714	CLOUD	6,939	4,342	1,238	1,359	3,104 R	62.6%	17.8%	77.8%	22.2%
14,254	COFFEY	5,686	3,552	1,631	503	1,921 R	62.5%	28.7%	68.5%	31.5%
5,302	COMANCHE	1,741	1,049	432	260	617 R	60.3%	24.8%	70.8%	29.2%
35,155	COWLEY	14,577	8,529	3,161	2,887	5,368 R	58.5%	21.7%	73.0%	27.0%
61,800	CRAWFORD	18,005	9,063	3,433	5,509	5,630 R	50.3%	19.1%	72.5%	27.5%
8,121	DECATUR	3,457	1,621	1,218	618	403 R	46.9%	35.2%	57.1%	42.9%
25,777	DICKINSON	9,566	6,178	1,690	1,698	4,488 R	64.6%	17.7%	78.5%	21.5%
13,438	DONIPHAN	5,206	3,789	1,072	345	2,717 R	72.8%	20.6%	77.9%	22.1%
23,998	DOUGLAS	10,700	8,052	1,922	726	6,130 R	75.3%	18.0%	80.7%	19.3%
7,057	EDWARDS	2,880	1,929	548	403	1,381 R	67.0%	19.0%	77.9%	22.1%
9,034	ELK	3,802	2,443	1,104	255	1,339 R	64.3%	29.0%	68.9%	31.1%
14,138	ELLIS	3,802	1,763	842	1,197	921 R	46.4%	22.1%	67.7%	32.3%
10,379	ELLSWORTH	3,890	2,286	950	654	1,336 R	58.8%	24.4%	70.6%	29.4%
7,674	FINNEY	2,843	1,753	614	476	1,139 R	61.7%	21.6%	74.1%	25.9%
14,273	FORD	5,948	3,449	1,551	948	1,898 R	58.0%	26.1%	69.0%	31.0%
21,946	FRANKLIN	8,960	6,008	2,324	628	3,684 R	67.1%	25.9%	72.1%	27.9%
13,452	GEARY	4,037	2,678	723	636	1,955 R	66.3%	17.9%	78.7%	21.3%
4,748	GOVE	1,787	1,211	400	176	811 R	67.8%	22.4%	75.2%	24.8%
7,624	GRAHAM	3,033	1,631	629	773	1,002 R	53.8%	20.7%	72.2%	27.8%
1,087	GRANT	684	459	148	77	311 R	67.1%	21.6%	75.6%	24.4%
4,711	GRAY	1,616	959	463	194	496 R	59.3%	28.7%	67.4%	32.6%
1,028	GREELEY	556	357	75	124	282 R	64.2%	13.5%	82.6%	17.4%
14,715	GREENWOOD	6,532	4,181	1,795	556	2,386 R	64.0%	27.5%	70.0%	30.0%
2,586	HAMILTON	1,167	610	307	250	303 R	52.3%	26.3%	66.5%	33.5%
13,656	HARPER	4,282	2,280	1,321	681	959 R	53.2%	30.9%	63.3%	36.7%
20,744	HARVEY	7,630	4,499	1,744	1,387	2,755 R	59.0%	22.9%	72.1%	27.9%
1,455	HASKELL	757	493	167	97	326 R	65.1%	22.1%	74.7%	25.3%
3,734	HODGEMAN	1,482	899	367	216	532 R	60.7%	24.8%	71.0%	29.0%
15,495	JACKSON	6,177	4,391	1,419	367	2,972 R	71.1%	23.0%	75.6%	24.4%
14,750	JEFFERSON	6,082	4,422	1,320	340	3,102 R	72.7%	21.7%	77.0%	23.0%
16,240	JEWELL	6,698	4,342	1,861	495	2,481 R	64.8%	27.8%	70.0%	30.0%
18,314	JOHNSON	9,224	6,102	2,519	603	3,583 R	66.2%	27.3%	70.8%	29.2%
2,617	KEARNY	1,103	635	199	269	436 R	57.6%	18.0%	76.1%	23.9%
12,119	KINGMAN	4,447	2,416	1,077	954	1,339 R	54.3%	24.2%	69.2%	30.8%
6,164	KIOWA	2,199	1,541	498	160	1,043 R	70.1%	22.6%	75.6%	24.4%
34,047	LABETTE	11,933	6,593	2,971	2,369	3,622 R	55.3%	24.9%	68.9%	31.1%
2,848	LANE	1,173	693	281	199	412 R	59.1%	24.0%	71.1%	28.9%
38,402	LEAVENWORTH	13,856	9,429	2,982	1,445	6,447 R	68.0%	21.5%	76.0%	24.0%
9,894	LINCOLN	3,833	2,277	615	941	1,662 R	59.4%	16.0%	78.7%	21.3%
13,815	LINN	5,458	3,161	1,683	614	1,478 R	57.9%	30.8%	65.3%	34.7%
3,223	LOGAN	1,475	942	286	247	656 R	63.9%	19.4%	76.7%	23.3%
26,154	LYON	10,974	6,290	2,750	1,934	3,540 R	57.3%	25.1%	69.6%	30.4%
21,845	MCPHERSON	7,771	5,128	1,530	1,113	3,598 R	66.0%	19.7%	77.0%	23.0%
22,923	MARION	7,109	4,008	1,520	1,581	2,488 R	56.4%	21.4%	72.5%	27.5%
22,730	MARSHALL	9,317	5,809	2,369	1,139	3,440 R	62.3%	25.4%	71.0%	29.0%
5,542	MEADE	1,927	1,290	472	165	818 R	66.9%	24.5%	73.2%	26.8%

KANSAS

PRESIDENT 1924

1920 Census Population	County	Total Vote	Republican	Democratic	Other	Rep.-Dem. Plurality	Percentage Total Vote Rep.	Total Vote Dem.	Major Vote Rep.	Major Vote Dem.
19,809	MIAMI	7,753	4,788	1,994	971	2,794 R	61.8%	25.7%	70.6%	29.4%
13,886	MITCHELL	5,287	3,161	1,470	656	1,691 R	59.8%	27.8%	68.3%	31.7%
49,645	MONTGOMERY	17,163	11,160	4,178	1,825	6,982 R	65.0%	24.3%	72.8%	27.2%
12,005	MORRIS	4,774	3,089	1,040	645	2,049 R	64.7%	21.8%	74.8%	25.2%
3,177	MORTON	1,216	669	286	261	383 R	55.0%	23.5%	70.1%	29.9%
18,487	NEMAHA	6,799	4,096	1,846	857	2,250 R	60.2%	27.2%	68.9%	31.1%
24,000	NEOSHO	8,699	5,106	2,274	1,319	2,832 R	58.7%	26.1%	69.2%	30.8%
7,490	NESS	2,520	1,629	541	350	1,088 R	64.6%	21.5%	75.1%	24.9%
11,423	NORTON	4,682	2,778	1,261	643	1,517 R	59.3%	26.9%	68.8%	31.2%
18,621	OSAGE	7,843	4,957	2,050	836	2,907 R	63.2%	26.1%	70.7%	29.3%
12,441	OSBORNE	4,658	3,333	905	420	2,428 R	71.6%	19.4%	78.6%	21.4%
10,714	OTTAWA	4,108	2,475	854	779	1,621 R	60.2%	20.8%	74.3%	25.7%
9,323	PAWNEE	3,849	2,407	1,111	331	1,296 R	62.5%	28.9%	68.4%	31.6%
12,505	PHILLIPS	4,815	2,647	1,376	792	1,271 R	55.0%	28.6%	65.8%	34.2%
16,154	POTTAWATOMIE	6,356	4,340	1,471	545	2,869 R	68.3%	23.1%	74.7%	25.3%
12,909	PRATT	4,815	2,762	1,205	848	1,557 R	57.4%	25.0%	69.6%	30.4%
6,799	RAWLINS	2,649	1,213	742	694	471 R	45.8%	28.0%	62.0%	38.0%
44,423	RENO	15,851	10,339	3,675	1,837	6,664 R	65.2%	23.2%	73.8%	26.2%
15,855	REPUBLIC	6,122	3,671	1,616	835	2,055 R	60.0%	26.4%	69.4%	30.6%
14,832	RICE	5,720	3,920	1,303	497	2,617 R	68.5%	22.8%	75.1%	24.9%
20,650	RILEY	7,790	5,455	1,646	689	3,809 R	70.0%	21.1%	76.8%	23.2%
9,966	ROOKS	3,699	2,442	930	327	1,512 R	66.0%	25.1%	72.4%	27.6%
8,360	RUSH	3,109	1,780	787	542	993 R	57.3%	25.3%	69.3%	30.7%
10,748	RUSSELL	4,101	2,637	687	777	1,950 R	64.3%	16.8%	79.3%	20.7%
25,103	SALINE	10,505	6,534	1,966	2,005	4,568 R	62.2%	18.7%	76.9%	23.1%
3,121	SCOTT	1,443	734	445	264	289 R	50.9%	30.8%	62.3%	37.7%
92,234	SEDGWICK	36,943	21,144	8,712	7,087	12,432 R	57.2%	23.6%	70.8%	29.2%
6,220	SEWARD	2,277	1,184	676	417	508 R	52.0%	29.7%	63.7%	36.3%
69,159	SHAWNEE	27,878	20,132	5,099	2,647	15,033 R	72.2%	18.3%	79.8%	20.2%
5,484	SHERIDAN	2,233	1,320	542	371	778 R	59.1%	24.3%	70.9%	29.1%
5,592	SHERMAN	2,445	1,122	528	795	594 R	45.9%	21.6%	68.0%	32.0%
14,985	SMITH	5,637	3,226	1,634	777	1,592 R	57.2%	29.0%	66.4%	33.6%
11,559	STAFFORD	4,520	3,100	957	463	2,143 R	68.6%	21.2%	76.4%	23.6%
908	STANTON	607	379	158	70	221 R	62.4%	26.0%	70.6%	29.4%
3,943	STEVENS	1,372	913	302	157	611 R	66.5%	22.0%	75.1%	24.9%
29,213	SUMNER	10,108	5,552	2,556	2,000	2,996 R	54.9%	25.3%	68.5%	31.5%
5,517	THOMAS	2,735	1,436	822	477	614 R	52.5%	30.1%	63.6%	36.4%
5,880	TREGO	1,928	1,121	399	408	722 R	58.1%	20.7%	73.8%	26.3%
11,424	WABAUNSEE	4,161	2,742	633	786	2,109 R	65.9%	15.2%	81.2%	18.8%
2,424	WALLACE	1,123	603	171	349	432 R	53.7%	15.2%	77.9%	22.1%
17,984	WASHINGTON	6,756	4,120	1,528	1,108	2,592 R	61.0%	22.6%	72.9%	27.1%
1,856	WICHITA	769	482	147	140	335 R	62.7%	19.1%	76.6%	23.4%
21,157	WILSON	7,071	4,596	1,736	739	2,860 R	65.0%	24.6%	72.6%	27.4%
8,984	WOODSON	3,818	2,412	1,026	380	1,386 R	63.2%	26.9%	70.2%	29.8%
122,218	WYANDOTTE	40,148	23,881	8,913	7,354	14,968 R	59.5%	22.2%	72.8%	27.2%
1,769,257	TOTAL	662,456	407,671	156,320	98,465	251,351 R	61.5%	23.6%	72.3%	27.7%

KANSAS

PRESIDENT 1920

1920 Census Population	County	Total Vote	Republican	Democratic	Other	Rep.-Dem. Plurality	Percentage Total Vote Rep.	Total Vote Dem.	Major Vote Rep.	Major Vote Dem.
23,509	ALLEN	7,522	5,091	2,272	159	2,819 R	67.7%	30.2%	69.1%	30.9%
12,986	ANDERSON	4,884	3,068	1,708	108	1,360 R	62.8%	35.0%	64.2%	35.8%
23,411	ATCHISON	9,031	5,872	3,082	77	2,790 R	65.0%	34.1%	65.6%	34.4%
9,739	BARBER	3,612	2,400	1,098	114	1,302 R	66.4%	30.4%	68.6%	31.4%
18,422	BARTON	5,806	3,993	1,688	125	2,305 R	68.8%	29.1%	70.3%	29.7%
23,198	BOURBON	8,051	4,194	3,632	225	562 R	52.1%	45.1%	53.6%	46.4%
20,949	BROWN	7,262	5,249	1,937	76	3,312 R	72.3%	26.7%	73.0%	27.0%
43,842	BUTLER	11,264	6,821	4,112	331	2,709 R	60.6%	36.5%	62.4%	37.6%
7,144	CHASE	2,622	1,659	904	59	755 R	63.3%	34.5%	64.7%	35.3%
11,598	CHAUTAUQUA	3,702	2,539	936	227	1,603 R	68.6%	25.3%	73.1%	26.9%
33,609	CHEROKEE	9,790	5,466	3,832	492	1,634 R	55.8%	39.1%	58.8%	41.2%
5,587	CHEYENNE	1,710	1,079	471	160	608 R	63.1%	27.5%	69.6%	30.4%
4,989	CLARK	1,588	923	610	55	313 R	58.1%	38.4%	60.2%	39.8%
14,365	CLAY	4,844	3,521	1,155	168	2,366 R	72.7%	23.8%	75.3%	24.7%
17,714	CLOUD	5,858	4,090	1,534	234	2,556 R	69.8%	26.2%	72.7%	27.3%
14,254	COFFEY	5,249	3,370	1,785	94	1,585 R	64.2%	34.0%	65.4%	34.6%
5,302	COMANCHE	1,778	1,121	612	45	509 R	63.0%	34.4%	64.7%	35.3%
35,155	COWLEY	12,414	7,352	4,733	329	2,619 R	59.2%	38.1%	60.8%	39.2%
61,800	CRAWFORD	14,553	7,957	5,362	1,234	2,595 R	54.7%	36.8%	59.7%	40.3%
8,121	DECATUR	2,809	1,448	1,221	140	227 R	51.5%	43.5%	54.3%	45.7%
25,777	DICKINSON	8,337	5,761	2,387	189	3,374 R	69.1%	28.6%	70.7%	29.3%
13,438	DONIPHAN	4,406	3,369	978	59	2,391 R	76.5%	22.2%	77.5%	22.5%
23,998	DOUGLAS	8,557	6,266	2,197	94	4,069 R	73.2%	25.7%	74.0%	26.0%
7,057	EDWARDS	2,540	1,782	681	77	1,101 R	70.2%	26.8%	72.4%	27.6%
9,034	ELK	3,452	2,253	1,110	89	1,143 R	65.3%	32.2%	67.0%	33.0%
14,138	ELLIS	3,173	2,385	740	48	1,645 R	75.2%	23.3%	76.3%	23.7%
10,379	ELLSWORTH	3,451	2,264	1,090	97	1,174 R	65.6%	31.6%	67.5%	32.5%
7,674	FINNEY	2,281	1,573	619	89	954 R	69.0%	27.1%	71.8%	28.2%
14,273	FORD	5,339	3,305	1,879	155	1,426 R	61.9%	35.2%	63.8%	36.2%
21,946	FRANKLIN	8,005	5,216	2,606	183	2,610 R	65.2%	32.6%	66.7%	33.3%
13,452	GEARY	3,456	2,404	962	90	1,442 R	69.6%	27.8%	71.4%	28.6%
4,748	GOVE	1,268	950	285	33	665 R	74.9%	22.5%	76.9%	23.1%
7,624	GRAHAM	2,588	1,658	762	168	896 R	64.1%	29.4%	68.5%	31.5%
1,087	GRANT	460	339	108	13	231 R	73.7%	23.5%	75.8%	24.2%
4,711	GRAY	1,547	962	507	78	455 R	62.2%	32.8%	65.5%	34.5%
1,028	GREELEY	393	273	93	27	180 R	69.5%	23.7%	74.6%	25.4%
14,715	GREENWOOD	5,007	3,422	1,478	107	1,944 R	68.3%	29.5%	69.8%	30.2%
2,586	HAMILTON	1,025	591	371	63	220 R	57.7%	36.2%	61.4%	38.6%
13,656	HARPER	4,206	2,593	1,486	127	1,107 R	61.7%	35.3%	63.6%	36.4%
20,744	HARVEY	7,060	4,454	2,457	149	1,997 R	63.1%	34.8%	64.4%	35.6%
1,455	HASKELL	638	444	150	44	294 R	69.6%	23.5%	74.7%	25.3%
3,734	HODGEMAN	1,289	945	306	38	639 R	73.3%	23.7%	75.5%	24.5%
15,495	JACKSON	5,346	3,753	1,562	31	2,191 R	70.2%	29.2%	70.6%	29.4%
14,750	JEFFERSON	5,029	3,463	1,535	31	1,928 R	68.9%	30.5%	69.3%	30.7%
16,240	JEWELL	5,940	3,925	1,899	116	2,026 R	66.1%	32.0%	67.4%	32.6%
18,314	JOHNSON	6,729	4,325	2,303	101	2,022 R	64.3%	34.2%	65.3%	34.7%
2,617	KEARNY	968	617	266	85	351 R	63.7%	27.5%	69.9%	30.1%
12,119	KINGMAN	4,460	2,818	1,557	85	1,261 R	63.2%	34.9%	64.4%	35.6%
6,164	KIOWA	2,030	1,411	587	32	824 R	69.5%	28.9%	70.6%	29.4%
34,047	LABETTE	11,384	6,596	4,328	460	2,268 R	57.9%	38.0%	60.4%	39.6%
2,848	LANE	1,026	656	298	72	358 R	63.9%	29.0%	68.8%	31.2%
38,402	LEAVENWORTH	10,524	6,846	3,409	269	3,437 R	65.1%	32.4%	66.8%	33.2%
9,894	LINCOLN	3,306	2,298	935	73	1,363 R	69.5%	28.3%	71.1%	28.9%
13,815	LINN	5,075	3,189	1,764	122	1,425 R	62.8%	34.8%	64.4%	35.6%
3,223	LOGAN	1,138	781	312	45	469 R	68.6%	27.4%	71.5%	28.5%
26,154	LYON	8,990	5,492	3,303	195	2,189 R	61.1%	36.7%	62.4%	37.6%
21,845	MCPHERSON	7,007	4,870	1,926	211	2,944 R	69.5%	27.5%	71.7%	28.3%
22,923	MARION	5,834	3,840	1,713	281	2,127 R	65.8%	29.4%	69.2%	30.8%
22,730	MARSHALL	7,984	5,706	2,026	252	3,680 R	71.5%	25.4%	73.8%	26.2%
5,542	MEADE	1,742	1,236	483	23	753 R	71.0%	27.7%	71.9%	28.1%

KANSAS

PRESIDENT 1920

1920 Census Population	County	Total Vote	Republican	Democratic	Other	Rep.-Dem. Plurality	Percentage: Total Vote Rep.	Total Vote Dem.	Major Vote Rep.	Major Vote Dem.
19,809	MIAMI	6,664	4,060	2,450	154	1,610 R	60.9%	36.8%	62.4%	37.6%
13,886	MITCHELL	4,845	3,310	1,409	126	1,901 R	68.3%	29.1%	70.1%	29.9%
49,645	MONTGOMERY	16,145	10,044	5,657	444	4,387 R	62.2%	35.0%	64.0%	36.0%
12,005	MORRIS	4,534	3,001	1,467	66	1,534 R	66.2%	32.4%	67.2%	32.8%
3,177	MORTON	1,073	783	266	24	517 R	73.0%	24.8%	74.6%	25.4%
18,487	NEMAHA	6,437	4,655	1,731	51	2,924 R	72.3%	26.9%	72.9%	27.1%
24,000	NEOSHO	8,467	5,150	3,195	122	1,955 R	60.8%	37.7%	61.7%	38.3%
7,490	NESS	2,005	1,402	492	111	910 R	69.9%	24.5%	74.0%	26.0%
11,423	NORTON	3,507	2,288	1,082	137	1,206 R	65.2%	30.9%	67.9%	32.1%
18,621	OSAGE	7,177	4,507	2,414	256	2,093 R	62.8%	33.6%	65.1%	34.9%
12,441	OSBORNE	4,110	3,060	980	70	2,080 R	74.5%	23.8%	75.7%	24.3%
10,714	OTTAWA	3,991	2,512	1,358	121	1,154 R	62.9%	34.0%	64.9%	35.1%
9,323	PAWNEE	3,326	2,128	1,138	60	990 R	64.0%	34.2%	65.2%	34.8%
12,505	PHILLIPS	4,172	2,862	1,230	80	1,632 R	68.6%	29.5%	69.9%	30.1%
16,154	POTTAWATOMIE	5,823	4,481	1,293	49	3,188 R	77.0%	22.2%	77.6%	22.4%
12,909	PRATT	4,243	2,722	1,433	88	1,289 R	64.2%	33.8%	65.5%	34.5%
6,799	RAWLINS	1,907	1,236	495	176	741 R	64.8%	26.0%	71.4%	28.6%
44,423	RENO	14,375	9,649	4,385	341	5,264 R	67.1%	30.5%	68.8%	31.2%
15,855	REPUBLIC	5,440	3,661	1,672	107	1,989 R	67.3%	30.7%	68.6%	31.4%
14,832	RICE	5,289	3,651	1,532	106	2,119 R	69.0%	29.0%	70.4%	29.6%
20,650	RILEY	6,626	4,875	1,610	141	3,265 R	73.6%	24.3%	75.2%	24.8%
9,966	ROOKS	3,064	2,143	843	78	1,300 R	69.9%	27.5%	71.8%	28.2%
8,360	RUSH	2,747	2,017	605	125	1,412 R	73.4%	22.0%	76.9%	23.1%
10,748	RUSSELL	3,198	2,407	724	67	1,683 R	75.3%	22.6%	76.9%	23.1%
25,103	SALINE	8,622	5,554	2,808	260	2,746 R	64.4%	32.6%	66.4%	33.6%
3,121	SCOTT	1,078	636	379	63	257 R	59.0%	35.2%	62.7%	37.3%
92,234	SEDGWICK	28,134	16,642	10,998	494	5,644 R	59.2%	39.1%	60.2%	39.8%
6,220	SEWARD	2,097	1,290	722	85	568 R	61.5%	34.4%	64.1%	35.9%
69,159	SHAWNEE	22,349	14,814	7,217	318	7,597 R	66.3%	32.3%	67.2%	32.8%
5,484	SHERIDAN	1,715	1,194	477	44	717 R	69.6%	27.8%	71.5%	28.5%
5,592	SHERMAN	1,962	1,066	789	107	277 R	54.3%	40.2%	57.5%	42.5%
14,985	SMITH	4,918	3,251	1,535	132	1,716 R	66.1%	31.2%	67.9%	32.1%
11,559	STAFFORD	3,968	2,779	1,057	132	1,722 R	70.0%	26.6%	72.4%	27.6%
908	STANTON	368	269	89	10	180 R	73.1%	24.2%	75.1%	24.9%
3,943	STEVENS	1,261	876	346	39	530 R	69.5%	27.4%	71.7%	28.3%
29,213	SUMNER	9,638	5,830	3,454	354	2,376 R	60.5%	35.8%	62.8%	37.2%
5,517	THOMAS	1,917	1,046	747	124	299 R	54.6%	39.0%	58.3%	41.7%
5,880	TREGO	1,731	1,299	395	37	904 R	75.0%	22.8%	76.7%	23.3%
11,424	WABAUNSEE	3,683	2,859	782	42	2,077 R	77.6%	21.2%	78.5%	21.5%
2,424	WALLACE	898	632	203	63	429 R	70.4%	22.6%	75.7%	24.3%
17,984	WASHINGTON	5,772	4,390	1,287	95	3,103 R	76.1%	22.3%	77.3%	22.7%
1,856	WICHITA	571	422	127	22	295 R	73.9%	22.2%	76.9%	23.1%
21,157	WILSON	6,076	4,024	1,768	284	2,256 R	66.2%	29.1%	69.5%	30.5%
8,984	WOODSON	3,279	2,253	944	82	1,309 R	68.7%	28.8%	70.5%	29.5%
122,218	WYANDOTTE	33,702	19,294	13,737	671	5,557 R	57.2%	40.8%	58.4%	41.6%
1,769,257	TOTAL	570,243	369,268	185,464	15,511	183,804 R	64.8%	32.5%	66.6%	33.4%

KANSAS

ELECTION NOTES

1956 Other vote was Holtwick (Prohibition).

1952 Other vote was 6,038 Hamblen (Prohibition); 530 Hoopes (Socialist).

1948 Other vote was 6,468 Watson (Prohibition); 4,603 Wallace (Progressive); 2,807 Thomas (Socialist).

1944 Other vote was 2,609 Watson (Prohibition); 1,613 Thomas (Socialist).

1940 Other vote was 4,056 Babson (Prohibition); 2,347 Thomas (Socialist).

1936 Other vote was 2,766 Thomas (Socialist); 494 Lemke (Union). The statewide total in the other vote column includes 18 absentee Socialist votes cast outside the state and not reported by counties.

1932 Other vote was Thomas (Socialist).

1928 Other vote was 6,205 Thomas (Socialist); 320 Foster (Communist).

1924 Other vote was 98,461 LaFollette (Progressive); 4 scattered write-in. Progressive candidates ran second in Cheyenne, Cloud, Crawford, Dickinson, Ellis, Graham, Greeley, Kearny, Lincoln, Marion, Russell, Saline, Sherman, Trego, Wabaunsee and Wallace counties.

1920 Other vote was Debs (Socialist).

KENTUCKY

POPULAR VOTE FOR PRESIDENT 1920 TO 1956

		Republican		Democratic				Percentage			
								Total Vote		Major Vote	
Year	Total Vote	Vote	Candidate	Vote	Candidate	Other Vote	Plurality	Rep.	Dem.	Rep.	Dem.
1956	1,053,805	572,192	Eisenhower, Dwight D.	476,453	Stevenson, Adlai E.	5,160	95,739 R	54.3%	45.2%	54.6%	45.4%
1952	993,148	495,029	Eisenhower, Dwight D.	495,729	Stevenson, Adlai E.	2,390	700 D	49.8%	49.9%	50.0%	50.0%
1948	822,658	341,210	Dewey, Thomas E.	466,756	Truman, Harry S.	14,692	125,546 D	41.5%	56.7%	42.2%	57.8%
1944	867,924	392,448	Dewey, Thomas E.	472,589	Roosevelt, Franklin D.	2,887	80,141 D	45.2%	54.5%	45.4%	54.6%
1940	970,163	410,384	Willkie, Wendell	557,322	Roosevelt, Franklin D.	2,457	146,938 D	42.3%	57.4%	42.4%	57.6%
1936	926,214	369,702	Landon, Alfred M.	541,944	Roosevelt, Franklin D.	14,568	172,242 D	39.9%	58.5%	40.6%	59.4%
1932	983,059	394,716	Hoover, Herbert C.	580,574	Roosevelt, Franklin D.	7,769	185,858 D	40.2%	59.1%	40.5%	59.5%
1928	940,521	558,064	Hoover, Herbert C.	381,070	Smith, Alfred E.	1,387	176,994 R	59.3%	40.5%	59.4%	40.6%
1924	813,843	396,758	Coolidge, Calvin	375,593	Davis, John W.	41,492	21,165 R	48.8%	46.2%	51.4%	48.6%
1920	918,636	452,480	Harding, Warren G.	456,497	Cox, James M.	9,659	4,017 D	49.3%	49.7%	49.8%	50.2%

ELECTORAL COLLEGE VOTE 1920 TO 1956

Year	Total	Republican	Democratic	Other
1956	10	10	—	—
1952	10	—	10	—
1948	11	—	11	—
1944	11	—	11	—
1940	11	—	11	—
1936	11	—	11	—
1932	11	—	11	—
1928	13	13	—	—
1924	13	13	—	—
1920	13	—	13	—

KENTUCKY

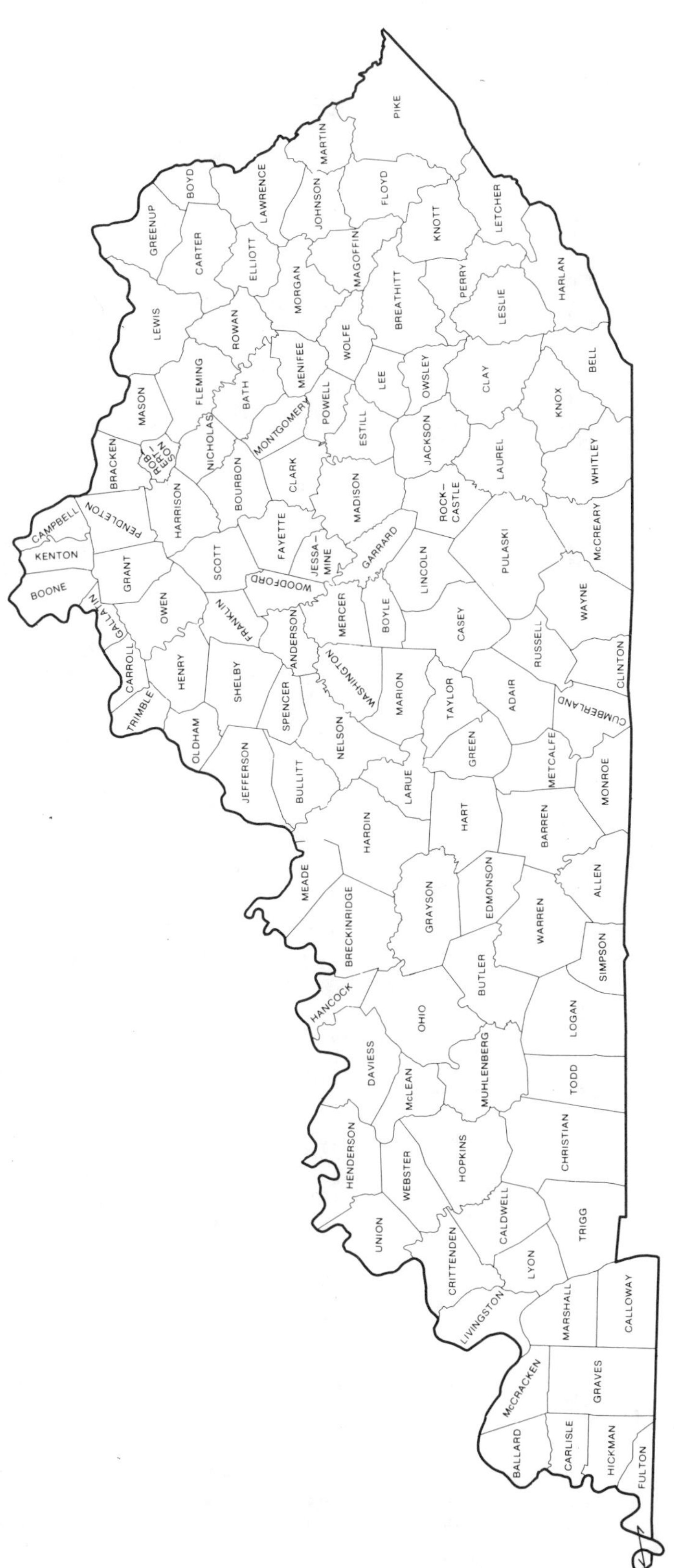
PIKE
MARTIN
BOYD
LAWRENCE
JOHNSON
FLOYD
LETCHER
KNOTT
GREENUP
CARTER
ELLIOTT
MAGOFFIN
MORGAN
PERRY
HARLAN
LESLIE
BREATHITT
LEWIS
ROWAN
WOLFE
MENIFEE
BELL
CLAY
OWSLEY
LEE
FLEMING
BATH
MASON
POWELL
KNOX
ESTILL
MONTGOMERY
NICHOLAS
ROBERTSON
BRACKEN
JACKSON
LAUREL
WHITLEY
CLARK
MADISON
BOURBON
HARRISON
ROCK-CASTLE
PENDLETON
CAMPBELL
FAYETTE
McCREARY
PULASKI
GARRARD
JESSAMINE
KENTON
GRANT
SCOTT
LINCOLN
WOODFORD
BOONE
GALLATIN
OWEN
FRANKLIN
MERCER
BOYLE
WAYNE
CASEY
ANDERSON
RUSSELL
CLINTON
CARROLL
HENRY
WASHINGTON
SHELBY
MARION
TAYLOR
ADAIR
CUMBERLAND
TRIMBLE
SPENCER
OLDHAM
NELSON
GREEN
METCALFE
MONROE
JEFFERSON
BULLITT
LARUE
HART
HARDIN
BARREN
MEADE
ALLEN
EDMONSON
BRECKINRIDGE
GRAYSON
WARREN
SIMPSON
BUTLER
HANCOCK
OHIO
LOGAN
DAVIESS
MUHLENBERG
TODD
McLEAN
HENDERSON
HOPKINS
CHRISTIAN
WEBSTER
CALDWELL
TRIGG
UNION
CRITTENDEN
LYON
LIVINGSTON
MARSHALL
CALLOWAY
McCRACKEN
GRAVES
BALLARD
CARLISLE
HICKMAN
FULTON

KENTUCKY

PRESIDENT 1956

1950 Census Population	County	Total Vote	Republican	Democratic	Other	Rep.-Dem. Plurality	Percentage Total Vote Rep.	Percentage Total Vote Dem.	Percentage Major Vote Rep.	Percentage Major Vote Dem.
17,603	ADAIR	6,651	4,157	2,491	3	1,666 R	62.5%	37.5%	62.5%	37.5%
13,787	ALLEN	5,193	3,200	1,975	18	1,225 R	61.6%	38.0%	61.8%	38.2%
8,984	ANDERSON	3,973	1,878	2,089	6	211 D	47.3%	52.6%	47.3%	52.7%
8,545	BALLARD	3,936	838	3,088	10	2,250 D	21.3%	78.5%	21.3%	78.7%
28,461	BARREN	9,414	4,206	5,206	2	1,000 D	44.7%	55.3%	44.7%	55.3%
10,410	BATH	4,125	1,889	2,221	15	332 D	45.8%	53.8%	46.0%	54.0%
47,602	BELL	11,319	6,824	4,477	18	2,347 R	60.3%	39.6%	60.4%	39.6%
13,015	BOONE	6,090	3,139	2,933	18	206 R	51.5%	48.2%	51.7%	48.3%
17,752	BOURBON	5,790	2,475	3,263	52	788 D	42.7%	56.4%	43.1%	56.9%
49,949	BOYD	20,082	11,502	8,546	34	2,956 R	57.3%	42.6%	57.4%	42.6%
20,532	BOYLE	6,880	3,427	3,436	17	9 D	49.8%	49.9%	49.9%	50.1%
8,424	BRACKEN	3,276	1,754	1,515	7	239 R	53.5%	46.2%	53.7%	46.3%
19,964	BREATHITT	5,673	2,423	3,246	4	823 D	42.7%	57.2%	42.7%	57.3%
15,528	BRECKINRIDGE	6,671	3,784	2,867	20	917 R	56.7%	43.0%	56.9%	43.1%
11,349	BULLITT	4,290	2,007	2,279	4	272 D	46.8%	53.1%	46.8%	53.2%
11,309	BUTLER	4,513	3,303	1,202	8	2,101 R	73.2%	26.6%	73.3%	26.7%
13,199	CALDWELL	5,124	2,681	2,417	26	264 R	52.3%	47.2%	52.6%	47.4%
20,147	CALLOWAY	8,460	2,292	6,152	16	3,860 D	27.1%	72.7%	27.1%	72.9%
76,196	CAMPBELL	29,171	18,617	10,359	195	8,258 R	63.8%	35.5%	64.2%	35.8%
6,206	CARLISLE	2,676	608	2,063	5	1,455 D	22.7%	77.1%	22.8%	77.2%
8,517	CARROLL	3,316	1,130	2,169	17	1,039 D	34.1%	65.4%	34.3%	65.7%
22,559	CARTER	8,258	5,127	3,112	19	2,015 R	62.1%	37.7%	62.2%	37.8%
17,446	CASEY	5,749	4,167	1,570	12	2,597 R	72.5%	27.3%	72.6%	27.4%
42,359	CHRISTIAN	11,495	4,963	6,487	45	1,524 D	43.2%	56.4%	43.3%	56.7%
18,898	CLARK	6,663	3,030	3,609	24	579 D	45.5%	54.2%	45.6%	54.4%
23,116	CLAY	5,934	4,897	1,027	10	3,870 R	82.5%	17.3%	82.7%	17.3%
10,605	CLINTON	4,147	3,396	747	4	2,649 R	81.9%	18.0%	82.0%	18.0%
10,818	CRITTENDEN	4,068	2,548	1,494	26	1,054 R	62.6%	36.7%	63.0%	37.0%
9,309	CUMBERLAND	3,601	2,584	1,000	17	1,584 R	71.8%	27.8%	72.1%	27.9%
57,241	DAVIESS	18,373	11,491	6,674	208	4,817 R	62.5%	36.3%	63.3%	36.7%
9,376	EDMONSON	3,897	2,800	1,092	5	1,708 R	71.9%	28.0%	71.9%	28.1%
7,085	ELLIOTT	3,176	1,033	2,143		1,110 D	32.5%	67.5%	32.5%	67.5%
14,677	ESTILL	4,868	2,946	1,912	10	1,034 R	60.5%	39.3%	60.6%	39.4%
100,746	FAYETTE	35,683	21,904	13,547	232	8,357 R	61.4%	38.0%	61.8%	38.2%
11,962	FLEMING	5,280	2,744	2,519	17	225 R	52.0%	47.7%	52.1%	47.9%
53,500	FLOYD	14,088	6,166	7,907	15	1,741 D	43.8%	56.1%	43.8%	56.2%
25,933	FRANKLIN	10,553	4,047	6,412	94	2,365 D	38.3%	60.8%	38.7%	61.3%
13,668	FULTON	4,128	1,147	2,953	28	1,806 D	27.8%	71.5%	28.0%	72.0%
3,969	GALLATIN	1,771	547	1,223	1	676 D	30.9%	69.1%	30.9%	69.1%
11,029	GARRARD	4,133	2,311	1,798	24	513 R	55.9%	43.5%	56.2%	43.8%
9,809	GRANT	3,996	1,680	2,300	16	620 D	42.0%	57.6%	42.2%	57.8%
31,364	GRAVES	13,815	3,711	10,090	14	6,379 D	26.9%	73.0%	26.9%	73.1%
17,063	GRAYSON	6,592	4,565	2,021	6	2,544 R	69.3%	30.7%	69.3%	30.7%
11,261	GREEN	4,689	2,951	1,726	12	1,225 R	62.9%	36.8%	63.1%	36.9%
24,887	GREENUP	10,538	5,464	5,045	29	419 R	51.9%	47.9%	52.0%	48.0%
6,009	HANCOCK	2,346	1,317	1,022	7	295 R	56.1%	43.6%	56.3%	43.7%
50,312	HARDIN	9,430	5,050	4,325	55	725 R	53.6%	45.9%	53.9%	46.1%
71,751	HARLAN	15,761	8,820	6,915	26	1,905 R	56.0%	43.9%	56.1%	43.9%
13,736	HARRISON	5,657	2,128	3,515	14	1,387 D	37.6%	62.1%	37.7%	62.3%
15,321	HART	6,506	3,276	3,207	23	69 R	50.4%	49.3%	50.5%	49.5%
30,715	HENDERSON	10,838	5,085	5,501	252	416 D	46.9%	50.8%	48.0%	52.0%
11,394	HENRY	4,838	1,670	3,157	11	1,487 D	34.5%	65.3%	34.6%	65.4%
7,778	HICKMAN	3,163	785	2,367	11	1,582 D	24.8%	74.8%	24.9%	75.1%
38,815	HOPKINS	11,917	5,300	6,535	82	1,235 D	44.5%	54.8%	44.8%	55.2%
13,101	JACKSON	4,471	3,950	501	20	3,449 R	88.3%	11.2%	88.7%	11.3%
484,615	JEFFERSON	203,917	119,262	83,483	1,172	35,779 R	58.5%	40.9%	58.8%	41.2%
12,458	JESSAMINE	4,553	2,340	2,072	141	268 R	51.4%	45.5%	53.0%	47.0%
23,846	JOHNSON	8,165	5,802	2,356	7	3,446 R	71.1%	28.9%	71.1%	28.9%
104,254	KENTON	36,070	20,895	14,923	252	5,972 R	57.9%	41.4%	58.3%	41.7%
20,320	KNOTT	5,712	1,715	3,987	10	2,272 D	30.0%	69.8%	30.1%	69.9%

KENTUCKY

PRESIDENT 1956

1950 Census Population	County	Total Vote	Republican	Democratic	Other	Rep.-Dem. Plurality	Percentage: Total Vote Rep.	Total Vote Dem.	Major Vote Rep.	Major Vote Dem.
30,409	KNOX	8,882	6,341	2,539	2	3,802 R	71.4%	28.6%	71.4%	28.6%
9,956	LARUE	4,259	2,387	1,859	13	528 R	56.0%	43.6%	56.2%	43.8%
25,797	LAUREL	8,916	6,586	2,316	14	4,270 R	73.9%	26.0%	74.0%	26.0%
14,418	LAWRENCE	5,438	2,932	2,495	11	437 R	53.9%	45.9%	54.0%	46.0%
8,739	LEE	2,716	1,774	938	4	836 R	65.3%	34.5%	65.4%	34.6%
15,537	LESLIE	4,315	3,770	531	14	3,239 R	87.4%	12.3%	87.7%	12.3%
39,522	LETCHER	9,904	5,741	4,133	30	1,608 R	58.0%	41.7%	58.1%	41.9%
13,520	LEWIS	4,927	3,333	1,585	9	1,748 R	67.6%	32.2%	67.8%	32.2%
18,668	LINCOLN	6,510	3,535	2,953	22	582 R	54.3%	45.4%	54.5%	45.5%
7,184	LIVINGSTON	3,046	1,247	1,795	4	548 D	40.9%	58.9%	41.0%	59.0%
22,335	LOGAN	8,174	2,855	5,299	20	2,444 D	34.9%	64.8%	35.0%	65.0%
6,853	LYON	2,535	989	1,527	19	538 D	39.0%	60.2%	39.3%	60.7%
49,137	MCCRACKEN	21,258	7,076	14,103	79	7,027 D	33.3%	66.3%	33.4%	66.6%
16,660	MCCREARY	4,630	3,812	814	4	2,998 R	82.3%	17.6%	82.4%	17.6%
10,021	MCLEAN	3,870	1,886	1,965	19	79 D	48.7%	50.8%	49.0%	51.0%
31,179	MADISON	11,710	5,955	5,670	85	285 R	50.9%	48.4%	51.2%	48.8%
13,839	MAGOFFIN	4,509	2,343	2,162	4	181 R	52.0%	47.9%	52.0%	48.0%
17,212	MARION	5,892	2,945	2,927	20	18 R	50.0%	49.7%	50.2%	49.8%
13,387	MARSHALL	6,382	2,015	4,358	9	2,343 D	31.6%	68.3%	31.6%	68.4%
11,677	MARTIN	3,633	2,927	694	12	2,233 R	80.6%	19.1%	80.8%	19.2%
18,486	MASON	7,490	3,880	3,572	38	308 R	51.8%	47.7%	52.1%	47.9%
9,422	MEADE	3,692	1,670	2,016	6	346 D	45.2%	54.6%	45.3%	54.7%
4,798	MENIFEE	1,985	799	1,185	1	386 D	40.3%	59.7%	40.3%	59.7%
14,643	MERCER	5,952	3,168	2,767	17	401 R	53.2%	46.5%	53.4%	46.6%
9,851	METCALFE	4,438	2,412	2,014	12	398 R	54.3%	45.4%	54.5%	45.5%
13,770	MONROE	5,014	3,759	1,255		2,504 R	75.0%	25.0%	75.0%	25.0%
13,025	MONTGOMERY	4,895	2,220	2,656	19	436 D	45.4%	54.3%	45.5%	54.5%
13,624	MORGAN	5,048	1,878	3,164	6	1,286 D	37.2%	62.7%	37.2%	62.8%
32,501	MUHLENBERG	10,113	5,323	4,752	38	571 R	52.6%	47.0%	52.8%	47.2%
19,521	NELSON	7,365	4,107	3,240	18	867 R	55.8%	44.0%	55.9%	44.1%
7,532	NICHOLAS	2,695	999	1,667	29	668 D	37.1%	61.9%	37.5%	62.5%
20,840	OHIO	7,649	4,901	2,726	22	2,175 R	64.1%	35.6%	64.3%	35.7%
11,018	OLDHAM	3,909	2,128	1,769	12	359 R	54.4%	45.3%	54.6%	45.4%
9,755	OWEN	3,791	857	2,928	6	2,071 D	22.6%	77.2%	22.6%	77.4%
7,324	OWSLEY	2,347	2,013	331	3	1,682 R	85.8%	14.1%	85.9%	14.1%
9,610	PENDLETON	4,174	2,273	1,889	12	384 R	54.5%	45.3%	54.6%	45.4%
46,566	PERRY	11,161	6,591	4,545	25	2,046 R	59.1%	40.7%	59.2%	40.8%
81,154	PIKE	23,185	11,678	11,466	41	212 R	50.4%	49.5%	50.5%	49.5%
6,812	POWELL	2,685	1,339	1,343	3	4 D	49.9%	50.0%	49.9%	50.1%
38,452	PULASKI	14,572	10,636	3,899	37	6,737 R	73.0%	26.8%	73.2%	26.8%
2,881	ROBERTSON	1,412	617	793	2	176 D	43.7%	56.2%	43.8%	56.2%
13,925	ROCKCASTLE	5,112	3,787	1,313	12	2,474 R	74.1%	25.7%	74.3%	25.7%
12,708	ROWAN	4,857	2,470	2,380	7	90 R	50.9%	49.0%	50.9%	49.1%
13,717	RUSSELL	4,358	3,065	1,284	9	1,781 R	70.3%	29.5%	70.5%	29.5%
15,141	SCOTT	4,848	1,940	2,860	48	920 D	40.0%	59.0%	40.4%	59.6%
17,912	SHELBY	6,799	2,768	4,017	14	1,249 D	40.7%	59.1%	40.8%	59.2%
11,678	SIMPSON	4,350	1,454	2,879	17	1,425 D	33.4%	66.2%	33.6%	66.4%
6,157	SPENCER	2,117	896	1,214	7	318 D	42.3%	57.3%	42.5%	57.5%
14,403	TAYLOR	6,342	3,892	2,433	17	1,459 R	61.4%	38.4%	61.5%	38.5%
12,890	TODD	4,585	1,480	3,087	18	1,607 D	32.3%	67.3%	32.4%	67.6%
9,683	TRIGG	3,855	1,329	2,517	9	1,188 D	34.5%	65.3%	34.6%	65.4%
5,148	TRIMBLE	2,310	506	1,792	12	1,286 D	21.9%	77.6%	22.0%	78.0%
14,893	UNION	5,193	1,956	2,863	374	907 D	37.7%	55.1%	40.6%	59.4%
42,758	WARREN	15,310	8,123	7,143	44	980 R	53.1%	46.7%	53.2%	46.8%
12,777	WASHINGTON	4,637	2,536	2,084	17	452 R	54.7%	44.9%	54.9%	45.1%
16,475	WAYNE	5,902	3,609	2,263	30	1,346 R	61.1%	38.3%	61.5%	38.5%
15,555	WEBSTER	5,253	1,948	3,050	255	1,102 D	37.1%	58.1%	39.0%	61.0%
31,940	WHITLEY	10,438	7,759	2,656	23	5,103 R	74.3%	25.4%	74.5%	25.5%
7,615	WOLFE	2,742	1,059	1,683		624 D	38.6%	61.4%	38.6%	61.4%
11,212	WOODFORD	4,257	2,170	2,027	60	143 R	51.0%	47.6%	51.7%	48.3%
2,944,806	TOTAL	1,053,805	572,192	476,453	5,160	95,739 R	54.3%	45.2%	54.6%	45.4%

KENTUCKY

PRESIDENT 1952

1950 Census Population	County	Total Vote	Republican	Democratic	Other	Rep.-Dem. Plurality	Percentage: Total Vote Rep.	Total Vote Dem.	Major Vote Rep.	Major Vote Dem.
17,603	ADAIR	5,927	3,737	2,184	6	1,553 R	63.1%	36.8%	63.1%	36.9%
13,787	ALLEN	4,717	2,946	1,750	21	1,196 R	62.5%	37.1%	62.7%	37.3%
8,984	ANDERSON	3,607	1,445	2,153	9	708 D	40.1%	59.7%	40.2%	59.8%
8,545	BALLARD	3,767	851	2,910	6	2,059 D	22.6%	77.2%	22.6%	77.4%
28,461	BARREN	8,365	3,743	4,618	4	875 D	44.7%	55.2%	44.8%	55.2%
10,410	BATH	4,142	1,737	2,400	5	663 D	41.9%	57.9%	42.0%	58.0%
47,602	BELL	11,761	6,461	5,276	24	1,185 R	54.9%	44.9%	55.0%	45.0%
13,015	BOONE	4,946	2,309	2,620	17	311 D	46.7%	53.0%	46.8%	53.2%
17,752	BOURBON	5,570	2,229	3,339	2	1,110 D	40.0%	59.9%	40.0%	60.0%
49,949	BOYD	20,720	10,426	10,245	49	181 R	50.3%	49.4%	50.4%	49.6%
20,532	BOYLE	6,763	2,969	3,771	23	802 D	43.9%	55.8%	44.1%	55.9%
8,424	BRACKEN	3,444	1,690	1,753	1	63 D	49.1%	50.9%	49.1%	50.9%
19,964	BREATHITT	4,764	1,381	3,383		2,002 D	29.0%	71.0%	29.0%	71.0%
15,528	BRECKINRIDGE	5,922	3,078	2,828	16	250 R	52.0%	47.8%	52.1%	47.9%
11,349	BULLITT	3,418	1,292	2,121	5	829 D	37.8%	62.1%	37.9%	62.1%
11,309	BUTLER	4,165	2,996	1,157	12	1,839 R	71.9%	27.8%	72.1%	27.9%
13,199	CALDWELL	4,650	2,507	2,133	10	374 R	53.9%	45.9%	54.0%	46.0%
20,147	CALLOWAY	7,275	1,829	5,434	12	3,605 D	25.1%	74.7%	25.2%	74.8%
76,196	CAMPBELL	30,716	17,705	12,976	35	4,729 R	57.6%	42.2%	57.7%	42.3%
6,206	CARLISLE	2,524	656	1,867	1	1,211 D	26.0%	74.0%	26.0%	74.0%
8,517	CARROLL	3,632	1,019	2,605	8	1,586 D	28.1%	71.7%	28.1%	71.9%
22,559	CARTER	7,262	4,221	3,019	22	1,202 R	58.1%	41.6%	58.3%	41.7%
17,446	CASEY	5,366	3,831	1,522	13	2,309 R	71.4%	28.4%	71.6%	28.4%
42,359	CHRISTIAN	11,672	4,858	6,787	27	1,929 D	41.6%	58.1%	41.7%	58.3%
18,898	CLARK	6,212	2,592	3,620		1,028 D	41.7%	58.3%	41.7%	58.3%
23,116	CLAY	5,544	4,161	1,365	18	2,796 R	75.1%	24.6%	75.3%	24.7%
10,605	CLINTON	3,546	2,856	678	12	2,178 R	80.5%	19.1%	80.8%	19.2%
10,818	CRITTENDEN	3,914	2,471	1,427	16	1,044 R	63.1%	36.5%	63.4%	36.6%
9,309	CUMBERLAND	3,349	2,426	909	14	1,517 R	72.4%	27.1%	72.7%	27.3%
57,241	DAVIESS	18,010	10,462	7,522	26	2,940 R	58.1%	41.8%	58.2%	41.8%
9,376	EDMONSON	3,273	2,279	992	2	1,287 R	69.6%	30.3%	69.7%	30.3%
7,085	ELLIOTT	2,703	629	2,074		1,445 D	23.3%	76.7%	23.3%	76.7%
14,677	ESTILL	4,550	2,630	1,900	20	730 R	57.8%	41.8%	58.1%	41.9%
100,746	FAYETTE	31,789	17,376	14,275	138	3,101 R	54.7%	44.9%	54.9%	45.1%
11,962	FLEMING	5,050	2,592	2,446	12	146 R	51.3%	48.4%	51.4%	48.6%
53,500	FLOYD	13,189	4,238	8,940	11	4,702 D	32.1%	67.8%	32.2%	67.8%
25,933	FRANKLIN	10,411	3,097	7,309	5	4,212 D	29.7%	70.2%	29.8%	70.2%
13,668	FULTON	3,942	1,266	2,673	3	1,407 D	32.1%	67.8%	32.1%	67.9%
3,969	GALLATIN	1,851	465	1,383	3	918 D	25.1%	74.7%	25.2%	74.8%
11,029	GARRARD	4,331	2,398	1,927	6	471 R	55.4%	44.5%	55.4%	44.6%
9,809	GRANT	4,161	1,609	2,545	7	936 D	38.7%	61.2%	38.7%	61.3%
31,364	GRAVES	12,530	2,925	9,592	13	6,667 D	23.3%	76.6%	23.4%	76.6%
17,063	GRAYSON	6,362	4,011	2,341	10	1,670 R	63.0%	36.8%	63.1%	36.9%
11,261	GREEN	4,641	2,773	1,857	11	916 R	59.8%	40.0%	59.9%	40.1%
24,887	GREENUP	9,078	4,354	4,716	8	362 D	48.0%	51.9%	48.0%	52.0%
6,009	HANCOCK	2,525	1,341	1,177	7	164 R	53.1%	46.6%	53.3%	46.7%
50,312	HARDIN	8,558	3,914	4,599	45	685 D	45.7%	53.7%	46.0%	54.0%
71,751	HARLAN	17,330	7,284	10,025	21	2,741 D	42.0%	57.8%	42.1%	57.9%
13,736	HARRISON	5,240	1,866	3,367	7	1,501 D	35.6%	64.3%	35.7%	64.3%
15,321	HART	5,903	2,934	2,952	17	18 D	49.7%	50.0%	49.8%	50.2%
30,715	HENDERSON	10,893	4,929	5,913	51	984 D	45.2%	54.3%	45.5%	54.5%
11,394	HENRY	5,062	1,584	3,468	10	1,884 D	31.3%	68.5%	31.4%	68.6%
7,778	HICKMAN	2,865	871	1,988	6	1,117 D	30.4%	69.4%	30.5%	69.5%
38,815	HOPKINS	11,469	4,285	7,157	27	2,872 D	37.4%	62.4%	37.4%	62.6%
13,101	JACKSON	3,578	3,104	471	3	2,633 R	86.8%	13.2%	86.8%	13.2%
484,615	JEFFERSON	181,447	99,069	81,642	736	17,427 R	54.6%	45.0%	54.8%	45.2%
12,458	JESSAMINE	4,792	2,193	2,578	21	385 D	45.8%	53.8%	46.0%	54.0%
23,846	JOHNSON	7,856	5,199	2,654	3	2,545 R	66.2%	33.8%	66.2%	33.8%
104,254	KENTON	38,709	19,200	19,457	52	257 D	49.6%	50.3%	49.7%	50.3%
20,320	KNOTT	5,582	1,124	4,437	21	3,313 D	20.1%	79.5%	20.2%	79.8%

KENTUCKY

PRESIDENT 1952

1950 Census Population	County	Total Vote	Republican	Democratic	Other	Rep.-Dem. Plurality	Percentage Total Vote Rep.	Total Vote Dem.	Major Vote Rep.	Major Vote Dem.
30,409	KNOX	8,253	5,470	2,766	17	2,704 R	66.3%	33.5%	66.4%	33.6%
9,956	LARUE	3,862	1,701	2,161		460 D	44.0%	56.0%	44.0%	56.0%
25,797	LAUREL	8,051	5,776	2,263	12	3,513 R	71.7%	28.1%	71.8%	28.2%
14,418	LAWRENCE	5,302	2,696	2,597	9	99 R	50.8%	49.0%	50.9%	49.1%
8,739	LEE	2,678	1,572	1,100	6	472 R	58.7%	41.1%	58.8%	41.2%
15,537	LESLIE	3,959	3,239	705	15	2,534 R	81.8%	17.8%	82.1%	17.9%
39,522	LETCHER	9,786	4,689	5,097		408 D	47.9%	52.1%	47.9%	52.1%
13,520	LEWIS	4,888	3,317	1,556	15	1,761 R	67.9%	31.8%	68.1%	31.9%
18,668	LINCOLN	6,114	3,186	2,910	18	276 R	52.1%	47.6%	52.3%	47.7%
7,184	LIVINGSTON	2,657	1,102	1,554	1	452 D	41.5%	58.5%	41.5%	58.5%
22,335	LOGAN	7,690	2,758	4,917	15	2,159 D	35.9%	63.9%	35.9%	64.1%
6,853	LYON	2,158	746	1,404	8	658 D	34.6%	65.1%	34.7%	65.3%
49,137	MCCRACKEN	18,375	6,051	12,302	22	6,251 D	32.9%	66.9%	33.0%	67.0%
16,660	MCCREARY	4,309	3,360	937	12	2,423 R	78.0%	21.7%	78.2%	21.8%
10,021	MCLEAN	3,763	1,791	1,961	11	170 D	47.6%	52.1%	47.7%	52.3%
31,179	MADISON	11,815	5,886	5,901	28	15 D	49.8%	49.9%	49.9%	50.1%
13,839	MAGOFFIN	4,342	2,093	2,243	6	150 D	48.2%	51.7%	48.3%	51.7%
17,212	MARION	5,429	2,262	3,159	8	897 D	41.7%	58.2%	41.7%	58.3%
13,387	MARSHALL	4,934	1,474	3,445	15	1,971 D	29.9%	69.8%	30.0%	70.0%
11,677	MARTIN	3,815	2,641	1,174		1,467 R	69.2%	30.8%	69.2%	30.8%
18,486	MASON	7,228	3,606	3,614	8	8 D	49.9%	50.0%	49.9%	50.1%
9,422	MEADE	3,310	1,265	2,040	5	775 D	38.2%	61.6%	38.3%	61.7%
4,798	MENIFEE	1,863	638	1,219	6	581 D	34.2%	65.4%	34.4%	65.6%
14,643	MERCER	5,312	2,545	2,740	27	195 D	47.9%	51.6%	48.2%	51.8%
9,851	METCALFE	4,037	2,176	1,848	13	328 R	53.9%	45.8%	54.1%	45.9%
13,770	MONROE	4,759	3,675	1,084		2,591 R	77.2%	22.8%	77.2%	22.8%
13,025	MONTGOMERY	4,648	1,981	2,653	14	672 D	42.6%	57.1%	42.7%	57.3%
13,624	MORGAN	4,476	1,311	3,161	4	1,850 D	29.3%	70.6%	29.3%	70.7%
32,501	MUHLENBERG	9,812	4,761	5,037	14	276 D	48.5%	51.3%	48.6%	51.4%
19,521	NELSON	6,494	3,064	3,417	13	353 D	47.2%	52.6%	47.3%	52.7%
7,532	NICHOLAS	2,979	1,156	1,819	4	663 D	38.8%	61.1%	38.9%	61.1%
20,840	OHIO	7,142	4,428	2,700	14	1,728 R	62.0%	37.8%	62.1%	37.9%
11,018	OLDHAM	3,476	1,723	1,735	18	12 D	49.6%	49.9%	49.8%	50.2%
9,755	OWEN	4,000	819	3,174	7	2,355 D	20.5%	79.4%	20.5%	79.5%
7,324	OWSLEY	2,387	1,954	419	14	1,535 R	81.9%	17.6%	82.3%	17.7%
9,610	PENDLETON	3,892	1,895	1,993	4	98 D	48.7%	51.2%	48.7%	51.3%
46,566	PERRY	10,762	5,210	5,538	14	328 D	48.4%	51.5%	48.5%	51.5%
81,154	PIKE	22,576	9,778	12,761	37	2,983 D	43.3%	56.5%	43.4%	56.6%
6,812	POWELL	2,213	992	1,218	3	226 D	44.8%	55.0%	44.9%	55.1%
38,452	PULASKI	13,707	9,651	4,032	24	5,619 R	70.4%	29.4%	70.5%	29.5%
2,881	ROBERTSON	1,451	623	827	1	204 D	42.9%	57.0%	43.0%	57.0%
13,925	ROCKCASTLE	4,842	3,503	1,326	13	2,177 R	72.3%	27.4%	72.5%	27.5%
12,708	ROWAN	4,216	1,985	2,220	11	235 D	47.1%	52.7%	47.2%	52.8%
13,717	RUSSELL	4,095	2,913	1,171	11	1,742 R	71.1%	28.6%	71.3%	28.7%
15,141	SCOTT	5,261	2,077	3,171	13	1,094 D	39.5%	60.3%	39.6%	60.4%
17,912	SHELBY	6,562	2,474	4,076	12	1,602 D	37.7%	62.1%	37.8%	62.2%
11,678	SIMPSON	4,040	1,310	2,724	6	1,414 D	32.4%	67.4%	32.5%	67.5%
6,157	SPENCER	2,007	723	1,283	1	560 D	36.0%	63.9%	36.0%	64.0%
14,403	TAYLOR	5,592	3,126	2,439	27	687 R	55.9%	43.6%	56.2%	43.8%
12,890	TODD	4,416	1,401	2,995	20	1,594 D	31.7%	67.8%	31.9%	68.1%
9,683	TRIGG	3,725	1,134	2,585	6	1,451 D	30.4%	69.4%	30.5%	69.5%
5,148	TRIMBLE	2,240	370	1,855	15	1,485 D	16.5%	82.8%	16.6%	83.4%
14,893	UNION	5,422	1,967	3,445	10	1,478 D	36.3%	63.5%	36.3%	63.7%
42,758	WARREN	14,407	7,267	7,106	34	161 R	50.4%	49.3%	50.6%	49.4%
12,777	WASHINGTON	4,415	2,290	2,114	11	176 R	51.9%	47.9%	52.0%	48.0%
16,475	WAYNE	5,861	3,396	2,461	4	935 R	57.9%	42.0%	58.0%	42.0%
15,555	WEBSTER	5,386	1,858	3,516	12	1,658 D	34.5%	65.3%	34.6%	65.4%
31,940	WHITLEY	10,011	7,030	2,958	23	4,072 R	70.2%	29.5%	70.4%	29.6%
7,615	WOLFE	2,435	876	1,557	2	681 D	36.0%	63.9%	36.0%	64.0%
11,212	WOODFORD	4,171	1,845	2,319	7	474 D	44.2%	55.6%	44.3%	55.7%
2,944,806	TOTAL	993,148	495,029	495,729	2,390	700 D	49.8%	49.9%	50.0%	50.0%

KENTUCKY

PRESIDENT 1948

1940 Census Population	County	Total Vote	Republican	Democratic	Other	Rep.-Dem. Plurality	Percentage Total Vote Rep.	Total Vote Dem.	Major Vote Rep.	Major Vote Dem.
18,566	ADAIR	5,036	2,839	2,144	53	695 R	56.4%	42.6%	57.0%	43.0%
15,496	ALLEN	3,985	2,280	1,605	100	675 R	57.2%	40.3%	58.7%	41.3%
8,936	ANDERSON	3,154	971	2,135	48	1,164 D	30.8%	67.7%	31.3%	68.7%
9,480	BALLARD	3,195	454	2,702	39	2,248 D	14.2%	84.6%	14.4%	85.6%
27,559	BARREN	6,715	2,437	4,095	183	1,658 D	36.3%	61.0%	37.3%	62.7%
11,451	BATH	3,591	1,276	2,287	28	1,011 D	35.5%	63.7%	35.8%	64.2%
43,812	BELL	10,124	4,327	5,708	89	1,381 D	42.7%	56.4%	43.1%	56.9%
10,820	BOONE	3,523	1,151	2,320	52	1,169 D	32.7%	65.9%	33.2%	66.8%
17,932	BOURBON	5,302	1,610	3,562	130	1,952 D	30.4%	67.2%	31.1%	68.9%
45,938	BOYD	15,844	6,707	9,006	131	2,299 D	42.3%	56.8%	42.7%	57.3%
17,075	BOYLE	5,336	1,897	3,338	101	1,441 D	35.6%	62.6%	36.2%	63.8%
9,389	BRACKEN	3,134	1,239	1,863	32	624 D	39.5%	59.4%	39.9%	60.1%
23,946	BREATHITT	4,264	957	3,295	12	2,338 D	22.4%	77.3%	22.5%	77.5%
17,744	BRECKINRIDGE	5,110	2,407	2,623	80	216 D	47.1%	51.3%	47.9%	52.1%
9,511	BULLITT	2,385	673	1,681	31	1,008 D	28.2%	70.5%	28.6%	71.4%
14,371	BUTLER	3,658	2,494	1,105	59	1,389 R	68.2%	30.2%	69.3%	30.7%
14,499	CALDWELL	3,985	1,626	2,210	149	584 D	40.8%	55.5%	42.4%	57.6%
19,041	CALLOWAY	5,668	681	4,896	91	4,215 D	12.0%	86.4%	12.2%	87.8%
71,918	CAMPBELL	25,231	11,851	13,008	372	1,157 D	47.0%	51.6%	47.7%	52.3%
7,650	CARLISLE	2,199	279	1,899	21	1,620 D	12.7%	86.4%	12.8%	87.2%
8,657	CARROLL	3,345	639	2,626	80	1,987 D	19.1%	78.5%	19.6%	80.4%
25,545	CARTER	6,577	3,472	3,082	23	390 R	52.8%	46.9%	53.0%	47.0%
19,962	CASEY	4,911	3,380	1,495	36	1,885 R	68.8%	30.4%	69.3%	30.7%
36,129	CHRISTIAN	9,502	3,242	5,582	678	2,340 D	34.1%	58.7%	36.7%	63.3%
17,988	CLARK	4,908	1,508	3,292	108	1,784 D	30.7%	67.1%	31.4%	68.6%
23,901	CLAY	4,676	3,142	1,468	66	1,674 R	67.2%	31.4%	68.2%	31.8%
10,279	CLINTON	3,048	2,295	709	44	1,586 R	75.3%	23.3%	76.4%	23.6%
12,115	CRITTENDEN	3,461	1,927	1,497	37	430 R	55.7%	43.3%	56.3%	43.7%
11,923	CUMBERLAND	2,775	1,947	794	34	1,153 R	70.2%	28.6%	71.0%	29.0%
52,335	DAVIESS	13,727	4,873	8,682	172	3,809 D	35.5%	63.2%	35.9%	64.1%
11,344	EDMONSON	3,048	1,984	1,031	33	953 R	65.1%	33.8%	65.8%	34.2%
8,713	ELLIOTT	2,512	410	2,095	7	1,685 D	16.3%	83.4%	16.4%	83.6%
17,978	ESTILL	4,045	2,056	1,937	52	119 R	50.8%	47.9%	51.5%	48.5%
78,899	FAYETTE	25,155	10,959	13,202	994	2,243 D	43.6%	52.5%	45.4%	54.6%
13,327	FLEMING	4,852	2,088	2,722	42	634 D	43.0%	56.1%	43.4%	56.6%
52,986	FLOYD	12,016	3,127	8,823	66	5,696 D	26.0%	73.4%	26.2%	73.8%
23,308	FRANKLIN	8,822	1,962	6,679	181	4,717 D	22.2%	75.7%	22.7%	77.3%
15,413	FULTON	3,110	450	2,497	163	2,047 D	14.5%	80.3%	15.3%	84.7%
4,307	GALLATIN	1,731	342	1,381	8	1,039 D	19.8%	79.8%	19.8%	80.2%
11,910	GARRARD	3,656	1,890	1,725	41	165 R	51.7%	47.2%	52.3%	47.7%
9,876	GRANT	3,803	1,154	2,633	16	1,479 D	30.3%	69.2%	30.5%	69.5%
31,763	GRAVES	10,276	1,442	8,682	152	7,240 D	14.0%	84.5%	14.2%	85.8%
17,562	GRAYSON	5,092	2,880	2,174	38	706 R	56.6%	42.7%	57.0%	43.0%
12,321	GREEN	3,860	2,186	1,628	46	558 R	56.6%	42.2%	57.3%	42.7%
24,917	GREENUP	7,406	3,168	4,186	52	1,018 D	42.8%	56.5%	43.1%	56.9%
6,807	HANCOCK	2,147	985	1,146	16	161 D	45.9%	53.4%	46.2%	53.8%
29,108	HARDIN	6,447	2,297	3,990	160	1,693 D	35.6%	61.9%	36.5%	63.5%
75,275	HARLAN	13,710	4,402	9,158	150	4,756 D	32.1%	66.8%	32.5%	67.5%
15,124	HARRISON	4,802	1,224	3,494	84	2,270 D	25.5%	72.8%	25.9%	74.1%
17,239	HART	4,865	2,311	2,495	59	184 D	47.5%	51.3%	48.1%	51.9%
27,020	HENDERSON	7,646	1,904	5,499	243	3,595 D	24.9%	71.9%	25.7%	74.3%
12,220	HENRY	4,640	1,193	3,398	49	2,205 D	25.7%	73.2%	26.0%	74.0%
9,142	HICKMAN	2,564	326	2,143	95	1,817 D	12.7%	83.6%	13.2%	86.8%
37,789	HOPKINS	9,366	2,608	6,149	609	3,541 D	27.8%	65.7%	29.8%	70.2%
16,339	JACKSON	3,222	2,781	429	12	2,352 R	86.3%	13.3%	86.6%	13.4%
385,392	JEFFERSON	143,629	69,645	70,756	3,228	1,111 D	48.5%	49.3%	49.6%	50.4%
12,174	JESSAMINE	3,878	1,414	2,301	163	887 D	36.5%	59.3%	38.1%	61.9%
25,771	JOHNSON	6,392	3,993	2,378	21	1,615 R	62.5%	37.2%	62.7%	37.3%
93,139	KENTON	30,200	10,771	18,918	511	8,147 D	35.7%	62.6%	36.3%	63.7%
20,007	KNOTT	5,414	754	4,660		3,906 D	13.9%	86.1%	13.9%	86.1%

KENTUCKY

PRESIDENT 1948

1940 Census Population	County	Total Vote	Republican	Democratic	Other	Rep.-Dem. Plurality	Percentage Total Vote Rep.	Percentage Total Vote Dem.	Percentage Major Vote Rep.	Percentage Major Vote Dem.
31,029	KNOX	7,123	4,241	2,814	68	1,427 R	59.5%	39.5%	60.1%	39.9%
9,622	LARUE	3,206	1,277	1,864	65	587 D	39.8%	58.1%	40.7%	59.3%
25,640	LAUREL	6,326	4,107	2,187	32	1,920 R	64.9%	34.6%	65.3%	34.7%
17,275	LAWRENCE	4,521	2,117	2,372	32	255 D	46.8%	52.5%	47.2%	52.8%
10,860	LEE	2,317	1,233	1,058	26	175 R	53.2%	45.7%	53.8%	46.2%
14,981	LESLIE	3,211	2,397	783	31	1,614 R	74.6%	24.4%	75.4%	24.6%
40,592	LETCHER	8,324	3,560	4,741	23	1,181 D	42.8%	57.0%	42.9%	57.1%
15,686	LEWIS	4,172	2,708	1,449	15	1,259 R	64.9%	34.7%	65.1%	34.9%
19,859	LINCOLN	5,614	2,593	2,920	101	327 D	46.2%	52.0%	47.0%	53.0%
9,127	LIVINGSTON	2,311	671	1,622	18	951 D	29.0%	70.2%	29.3%	70.7%
23,345	LOGAN	5,865	1,352	4,355	158	3,003 D	23.1%	74.3%	23.7%	76.3%
9,067	LYON	2,155	582	1,505	68	923 D	27.0%	69.8%	27.9%	72.1%
48,534	MCCRACKEN	14,754	3,251	11,183	320	7,932 D	22.0%	75.8%	22.5%	77.5%
16,451	MCCREARY	3,978	3,031	933	14	2,098 R	76.2%	23.5%	76.5%	23.5%
11,446	MCLEAN	3,272	1,112	2,104	56	992 D	34.0%	64.3%	34.6%	65.4%
28,541	MADISON	10,156	4,619	5,344	193	725 D	45.5%	52.6%	46.4%	53.6%
17,490	MAGOFFIN	4,135	1,882	2,253		371 D	45.5%	54.5%	45.5%	54.5%
16,913	MARION	4,225	1,171	3,008	46	1,837 D	27.7%	71.2%	28.0%	72.0%
16,602	MARSHALL	3,673	711	2,942	20	2,231 D	19.4%	80.1%	19.5%	80.5%
10,970	MARTIN	2,898	1,964	911	23	1,053 R	67.8%	31.4%	68.3%	31.7%
19,066	MASON	6,208	2,519	3,620	69	1,101 D	40.6%	58.3%	41.0%	59.0%
8,827	MEADE	2,725	773	1,915	37	1,142 D	28.4%	70.3%	28.8%	71.2%
5,691	MENIFEE	1,564	435	1,112	17	677 D	27.8%	71.1%	28.1%	71.9%
14,629	MERCER	4,363	1,599	2,682	82	1,083 D	36.6%	61.5%	37.4%	62.6%
10,853	METCALFE	3,346	1,640	1,683	23	43 D	49.0%	50.3%	49.4%	50.6%
14,070	MONROE	4,097	2,812	1,249	36	1,563 R	68.6%	30.5%	69.2%	30.8%
12,280	MONTGOMERY	3,960	1,083	2,731	146	1,648 D	27.3%	69.0%	28.4%	71.6%
16,827	MORGAN	4,487	987	3,488	12	2,501 D	22.0%	77.7%	22.1%	77.9%
37,554	MUHLENBERG	8,031	3,478	4,426	127	948 D	43.3%	55.1%	44.0%	56.0%
18,004	NELSON	5,336	1,715	3,556	65	1,841 D	32.1%	66.6%	32.5%	67.5%
8,617	NICHOLAS	2,742	815	1,885	42	1,070 D	29.7%	68.7%	30.2%	69.8%
24,421	OHIO	6,106	3,300	2,721	85	579 R	54.0%	44.6%	54.8%	45.2%
10,716	OLDHAM	2,829	1,036	1,703	90	667 D	36.6%	60.2%	37.8%	62.2%
10,942	OWEN	3,583	504	3,056	23	2,552 D	14.1%	85.3%	14.2%	85.8%
8,957	OWSLEY	2,161	1,718	437	6	1,281 R	79.5%	20.2%	79.7%	20.3%
10,392	PENDLETON	3,374	1,373	1,958	43	585 D	40.7%	58.0%	41.2%	58.8%
47,828	PERRY	9,453	3,755	5,614	84	1,859 D	39.7%	59.4%	40.1%	59.9%
71,122	PIKE	19,642	8,097	11,423	122	3,326 D	41.2%	58.2%	41.5%	58.5%
7,671	POWELL	1,713	719	975	19	256 D	42.0%	56.9%	42.4%	57.6%
39,863	PULASKI	11,510	7,549	3,844	117	3,705 R	65.6%	33.4%	66.3%	33.7%
3,419	ROBERTSON	1,314	442	864	8	422 D	33.6%	65.8%	33.8%	66.2%
17,165	ROCKCASTLE	4,564	3,236	1,309	19	1,927 R	70.9%	28.7%	71.2%	28.8%
12,734	ROWAN	3,622	1,502	2,097	23	595 D	41.5%	57.9%	41.7%	58.3%
13,615	RUSSELL	3,613	2,404	1,191	18	1,213 R	66.5%	33.0%	66.9%	33.1%
14,314	SCOTT	5,014	1,352	3,548	114	2,196 D	27.0%	70.8%	27.6%	72.4%
17,759	SHELBY	5,622	1,626	3,840	156	2,214 D	28.9%	68.3%	29.7%	70.3%
11,752	SIMPSON	3,619	762	2,752	105	1,990 D	21.1%	76.0%	21.7%	78.3%
6,757	SPENCER	1,812	493	1,298	21	805 D	27.2%	71.6%	27.5%	72.5%
13,556	TAYLOR	4,581	2,087	2,415	79	328 D	45.6%	52.7%	46.4%	53.6%
14,234	TODD	3,900	827	2,929	144	2,102 D	21.2%	75.1%	22.0%	78.0%
12,784	TRIGG	3,383	816	2,485	82	1,669 D	24.1%	73.5%	24.7%	75.3%
5,601	TRIMBLE	1,968	194	1,746	28	1,552 D	9.9%	88.7%	10.0%	90.0%
17,411	UNION	4,406	744	3,607	55	2,863 D	16.9%	81.9%	17.1%	82.9%
36,631	WARREN	11,189	3,919	6,768	502	2,849 D	35.0%	60.5%	36.7%	63.3%
12,965	WASHINGTON	3,962	1,813	2,121	28	308 D	45.8%	53.5%	46.1%	53.9%
17,204	WAYNE	4,548	2,480	2,029	39	451 R	54.5%	44.6%	55.0%	45.0%
19,198	WEBSTER	4,459	1,087	3,288	84	2,201 D	24.4%	73.7%	24.8%	75.2%
33,186	WHITLEY	8,653	5,611	2,932	110	2,679 R	64.8%	33.9%	65.7%	34.3%
9,997	WOLFE	2,733	813	1,918	2	1,105 D	29.7%	70.2%	29.8%	70.2%
11,847	WOODFORD	3,555	1,229	2,175	151	946 D	34.6%	61.2%	36.1%	63.9%
2,845,627	TOTAL	822,658	341,210	466,756	14,692	125,546 D	41.5%	56.7%	42.2%	57.8%

KENTUCKY

PRESIDENT 1944

1940 Census Population	County	Total Vote	Republican	Democratic	Other	Rep.-Dem. Plurality	Percentage Total Vote Rep.	Total Vote Dem.	Major Vote Rep.	Major Vote Dem.
18,566	ADAIR	5,847	3,414	2,411	22	1,003 R	58.4%	41.2%	58.6%	41.4%
15,496	ALLEN	4,886	3,120	1,742	24	1,378 R	63.9%	35.7%	64.2%	35.8%
8,936	ANDERSON	3,579	1,409	2,148	22	739 D	39.4%	60.0%	39.6%	60.4%
9,480	BALLARD	3,491	637	2,845	9	2,208 D	18.2%	81.5%	18.3%	81.7%
27,559	BARREN	7,701	3,262	4,439		1,177 D	42.4%	57.6%	42.4%	57.6%
11,451	BATH	3,773	1,581	2,184	8	603 D	41.9%	57.9%	42.0%	58.0%
43,812	BELL	9,474	4,822	4,616	36	206 R	50.9%	48.7%	51.1%	48.9%
10,820	BOONE	3,921	1,457	2,451	13	994 D	37.2%	62.5%	37.3%	62.7%
17,932	BOURBON	5,803	1,957	3,828	18	1,871 D	33.7%	66.0%	33.8%	66.2%
45,938	BOYD	15,040	6,868	8,130	42	1,262 D	45.7%	54.1%	45.8%	54.2%
17,075	BOYLE	5,719	2,195	3,490	34	1,295 D	38.4%	61.0%	38.6%	61.4%
9,389	BRACKEN	3,417	1,483	1,915	19	432 D	43.4%	56.0%	43.6%	56.4%
23,946	BREATHITT	4,183	1,230	2,922	31	1,692 D	29.4%	69.9%	29.6%	70.4%
17,744	BRECKINRIDGE	6,218	3,292	2,889	37	403 R	52.9%	46.5%	53.3%	46.7%
9,511	BULLITT	2,976	876	2,092	8	1,216 D	29.4%	70.3%	29.5%	70.5%
14,371	BUTLER	4,514	3,354	1,153	7	2,201 R	74.3%	25.5%	74.4%	25.6%
14,499	CALDWELL	4,696	2,242	2,444	10	202 D	47.7%	52.0%	47.8%	52.2%
19,041	CALLOWAY	6,026	1,121	4,888	17	3,767 D	18.6%	81.1%	18.7%	81.3%
71,918	CAMPBELL	26,670	13,647	12,959	64	688 R	51.2%	48.6%	51.3%	48.7%
7,650	CARLISLE	2,568	505	2,057	6	1,552 D	19.7%	80.1%	19.7%	80.3%
8,657	CARROLL	3,428	755	2,662	11	1,907 D	22.0%	77.7%	22.1%	77.9%
25,545	CARTER	6,860	4,117	2,733	10	1,384 R	60.0%	39.8%	60.1%	39.9%
19,962	CASEY	5,409	3,869	1,520	20	2,349 R	71.5%	28.1%	71.8%	28.2%
36,129	CHRISTIAN	10,801	4,506	6,260	35	1,754 D	41.7%	58.0%	41.9%	58.1%
17,988	CLARK	5,564	1,929	3,608	27	1,679 D	34.7%	64.8%	34.8%	65.2%
23,901	CLAY	5,495	4,307	1,185	3	3,122 R	78.4%	21.6%	78.4%	21.6%
10,279	CLINTON	3,185	2,618	564	3	2,054 R	82.2%	17.7%	82.3%	17.7%
12,115	CRITTENDEN	4,259	2,690	1,544	25	1,146 R	63.2%	36.3%	63.5%	36.5%
11,923	CUMBERLAND	3,346	2,619	717	10	1,902 R	78.3%	21.4%	78.5%	21.5%
52,335	DAVIESS	14,355	6,135	8,143	77	2,008 D	42.7%	56.7%	43.0%	57.0%
11,344	EDMONSON	3,458	2,433	1,016	9	1,417 R	70.4%	29.4%	70.5%	29.5%
8,713	ELLIOTT	2,235	514	1,721		1,207 D	23.0%	77.0%	23.0%	77.0%
17,978	ESTILL	4,517	2,493	2,000	24	493 R	55.2%	44.3%	55.5%	44.5%
78,899	FAYETTE	24,598	10,857	13,567	174	2,710 D	44.1%	55.2%	44.5%	55.5%
13,327	FLEMING	5,292	2,666	2,612	14	54 R	50.4%	49.4%	50.5%	49.5%
52,986	FLOYD	10,926	3,197	7,729		4,532 D	29.3%	70.7%	29.3%	70.7%
23,308	FRANKLIN	8,448	2,050	6,356	42	4,306 D	24.3%	75.2%	24.4%	75.6%
15,413	FULTON	3,640	654	2,973	13	2,319 D	18.0%	81.7%	18.0%	82.0%
4,307	GALLATIN	1,888	516	1,360	12	844 D	27.3%	72.0%	27.5%	72.5%
11,910	GARRARD	3,820	2,042	1,764	14	278 R	53.5%	46.2%	53.7%	46.3%
9,876	GRANT	4,047	1,621	2,413	13	792 D	40.1%	59.6%	40.2%	59.8%
31,763	GRAVES	10,238	2,172	8,057	9	5,885 D	21.2%	78.7%	21.2%	78.8%
17,562	GRAYSON	6,085	3,629	2,436	20	1,193 R	59.6%	40.0%	59.8%	40.2%
12,321	GREEN	4,219	2,379	1,809	31	570 R	56.4%	42.9%	56.8%	43.2%
24,917	GREENUP	7,542	3,718	3,821	3	103 D	49.3%	50.7%	49.3%	50.7%
6,807	HANCOCK	2,509	1,365	1,129	15	236 R	54.4%	45.0%	54.7%	45.3%
29,108	HARDIN	7,294	2,831	4,436	27	1,605 D	38.8%	60.8%	39.0%	61.0%
75,275	HARLAN	13,838	5,815	8,000	23	2,185 D	42.0%	57.8%	42.1%	57.9%
15,124	HARRISON	5,192	1,466	3,706	20	2,240 D	28.2%	71.4%	28.3%	71.7%
17,239	HART	6,162	3,014	3,138	10	124 D	48.9%	50.9%	49.0%	51.0%
27,020	HENDERSON	8,595	2,683	5,887	25	3,204 D	31.2%	68.5%	31.3%	68.7%
12,220	HENRY	5,063	1,497	3,548	18	2,051 D	29.6%	70.1%	29.7%	70.3%
9,142	HICKMAN	2,602	588	2,005	9	1,417 D	22.6%	77.1%	22.7%	77.3%
37,789	HOPKINS	11,174	3,795	7,352	27	3,557 D	34.0%	65.8%	34.0%	66.0%
16,339	JACKSON	3,908	3,578	328	2	3,250 R	91.6%	8.4%	91.6%	8.4%
385,392	JEFFERSON	141,621	60,905	80,236	480	19,331 D	43.0%	56.7%	43.2%	56.8%
12,174	JESSAMINE	4,248	1,790	2,426	32	636 D	42.1%	57.1%	42.5%	57.5%
25,771	JOHNSON	6,874	4,642	2,222	10	2,420 R	67.5%	32.3%	67.6%	32.4%
93,139	KENTON	30,236	12,654	17,524	58	4,870 D	41.9%	58.0%	41.9%	58.1%
20,007	KNOTT	4,670	803	3,867		3,064 D	17.2%	82.8%	17.2%	82.8%

KENTUCKY

PRESIDENT 1944

1940 Census Population	County	Total Vote	Republican	Democratic	Other	Rep.-Dem. Plurality	Percentage Total Vote Rep.	Total Vote Dem.	Major Vote Rep.	Major Vote Dem.
31,029	KNOX	7,570	5,178	2,385	7	2,793 R	68.4%	31.5%	68.5%	31.5%
9,622	LARUE	3,641	1,550	2,065	26	515 D	42.6%	56.7%	42.9%	57.1%
25,640	LAUREL	7,160	5,051	2,104	5	2,947 R	70.5%	29.4%	70.6%	29.4%
17,275	LAWRENCE	5,135	2,715	2,408	12	307 R	52.9%	46.9%	53.0%	47.0%
10,860	LEE	2,550	1,468	1,072	10	396 R	57.6%	42.0%	57.8%	42.2%
14,981	LESLIE	3,178	2,679	499		2,180 R	84.3%	15.7%	84.3%	15.7%
40,592	LETCHER	8,670	4,055	4,599	16	544 D	46.8%	53.0%	46.9%	53.1%
15,686	LEWIS	4,717	3,275	1,434	8	1,841 R	69.4%	30.4%	69.5%	30.5%
19,859	LINCOLN	5,922	2,793	3,087	42	294 D	47.2%	52.1%	47.5%	52.5%
9,127	LIVINGSTON	2,892	1,202	1,686	4	484 D	41.6%	58.3%	41.6%	58.4%
23,345	LOGAN	7,339	2,211	5,110	18	2,899 D	30.1%	69.6%	30.2%	69.8%
9,067	LYON	2,679	924	1,743	12	819 D	34.5%	65.1%	34.6%	65.4%
48,534	MCCRACKEN	15,120	4,190	10,846	84	6,656 D	27.7%	71.7%	27.9%	72.1%
16,451	MCCREARY	4,301	3,419	880	2	2,539 R	79.5%	20.5%	79.5%	20.5%
11,446	MCLEAN	3,997	1,752	2,222	23	470 D	43.8%	55.6%	44.1%	55.9%
28,541	MADISON	11,307	5,468	5,769	70	301 D	48.4%	51.0%	48.7%	51.3%
17,490	MAGOFFIN	4,166	2,135	2,031		104 R	51.2%	48.8%	51.2%	48.8%
16,913	MARION	4,694	1,673	2,996	25	1,323 D	35.6%	63.8%	35.8%	64.2%
16,602	MARSHALL	4,274	1,316	2,947	11	1,631 D	30.8%	69.0%	30.9%	69.1%
10,970	MARTIN	2,639	2,067	571	1	1,496 R	78.3%	21.6%	78.4%	21.6%
19,066	MASON	7,105	3,256	3,810	39	554 D	45.8%	53.6%	46.1%	53.9%
8,827	MEADE	2,880	1,040	1,828	12	788 D	36.1%	63.5%	36.3%	63.7%
5,691	MENIFEE	1,547	568	976	3	408 D	36.7%	63.1%	36.8%	63.2%
14,629	MERCER	5,146	2,039	3,086	21	1,047 D	39.6%	60.0%	39.8%	60.2%
10,853	METCALFE	4,012	2,306	1,694	12	612 R	57.5%	42.2%	57.7%	42.4%
14,070	MONROE	4,749	3,648	1,101		2,547 R	76.8%	23.2%	76.8%	23.2%
12,280	MONTGOMERY	3,823	1,481	2,334	8	853 D	38.7%	61.1%	38.8%	61.2%
16,827	MORGAN	4,464	1,217	3,242	5	2,025 D	27.3%	72.6%	27.3%	72.7%
37,554	MUHLENBERG	8,304	4,618	3,657	29	961 R	55.6%	44.0%	55.8%	44.2%
18,004	NELSON	5,811	2,136	3,648	27	1,512 D	36.8%	62.8%	36.9%	63.1%
8,617	NICHOLAS	2,885	1,059	1,813	13	754 D	36.7%	62.8%	36.9%	63.1%
24,421	OHIO	7,657	4,494	3,131	32	1,363 R	58.7%	40.9%	58.9%	41.1%
10,716	OLDHAM	2,947	1,021	1,908	18	887 D	34.6%	64.7%	34.9%	65.1%
10,942	OWEN	3,800	627	3,157	16	2,530 D	16.5%	83.1%	16.6%	83.4%
8,957	OWSLEY	2,361	2,033	325	3	1,708 R	86.1%	13.8%	86.2%	13.8%
10,392	PENDLETON	4,090	1,977	2,096	17	119 D	48.3%	51.2%	48.5%	51.5%
47,828	PERRY	9,862	4,333	5,527	2	1,194 D	43.9%	56.0%	43.9%	56.1%
71,122	PIKE	17,897	8,092	9,757	48	1,665 D	45.2%	54.5%	45.3%	54.7%
7,671	POWELL	1,931	902	1,023	6	121 D	46.7%	53.0%	46.9%	53.1%
39,863	PULASKI	12,328	8,318	3,934	76	4,384 R	67.5%	31.9%	67.9%	32.1%
3,419	ROBERTSON	1,413	556	855	2	299 D	39.3%	60.5%	39.4%	60.6%
17,165	ROCKCASTLE	5,136	3,802	1,327	7	2,475 R	74.0%	25.8%	74.1%	25.9%
12,734	ROWAN	3,774	1,815	1,944	15	129 D	48.1%	51.5%	48.3%	51.7%
13,615	RUSSELL	4,219	3,019	1,185	15	1,834 R	71.6%	28.1%	71.8%	28.2%
14,314	SCOTT	5,248	1,589	3,627	32	2,038 D	30.3%	69.1%	30.5%	69.5%
17,759	SHELBY	6,446	1,997	4,415	34	2,418 D	31.0%	68.5%	31.1%	68.9%
11,752	SIMPSON	3,850	1,012	2,821	17	1,809 D	26.3%	73.3%	26.4%	73.6%
6,757	SPENCER	2,096	646	1,443	7	797 D	30.8%	68.8%	30.9%	69.1%
13,556	TAYLOR	5,136	2,622	2,475	39	147 R	51.1%	48.2%	51.4%	48.6%
14,234	TODD	4,374	1,363	2,990	21	1,627 D	31.2%	68.4%	31.3%	68.7%
12,784	TRIGG	3,857	1,332	2,511	14	1,179 D	34.5%	65.1%	34.7%	65.3%
5,601	TRIMBLE	2,210	264	1,916	30	1,652 D	11.9%	86.7%	12.1%	87.9%
17,411	UNION	4,436	935	3,489	12	2,554 D	21.1%	78.7%	21.1%	78.9%
36,631	WARREN	12,509	4,944	7,528	37	2,584 D	39.5%	60.2%	39.6%	60.4%
12,965	WASHINGTON	4,654	2,353	2,283	18	70 R	50.6%	49.1%	50.8%	49.2%
17,204	WAYNE	5,070	3,048	2,022		1,026 R	60.1%	39.9%	60.1%	39.9%
19,198	WEBSTER	5,189	1,840	3,324	25	1,484 D	35.5%	64.1%	35.6%	64.4%
33,186	WHITLEY	8,731	6,378	2,352	1	4,026 R	73.1%	26.9%	73.1%	26.9%
9,997	WOLFE	2,341	889	1,450	2	561 D	38.0%	61.9%	38.0%	62.0%
11,847	WOODFORD	3,542	1,374	2,154	14	780 D	38.8%	60.8%	38.9%	61.1%
2,845,627	TOTAL	867,924	392,448	472,589	2,887	80,141 D	45.2%	54.5%	45.4%	54.6%

KENTUCKY

PRESIDENT 1940

1940 Census Population	County	Total Vote	Republican	Democratic	Other	Rep.-Dem. Plurality	Percentage Total Vote Rep.	Total Vote Dem.	Major Vote Rep.	Major Vote Dem.
18,566	ADAIR	6,398	3,674	2,711	13	963 R	57.4%	42.4%	57.5%	42.5%
15,496	ALLEN	5,289	3,232	2,036	21	1,196 R	61.1%	38.5%	61.4%	38.6%
8,936	ANDERSON	3,769	1,244	2,515	10	1,271 D	33.0%	66.7%	33.1%	66.9%
9,480	BALLARD	3,971	758	3,212	1	2,454 D	19.1%	80.9%	19.1%	80.9%
27,559	BARREN	8,132	3,233	4,888	11	1,655 D	39.8%	60.1%	39.8%	60.2%
11,451	BATH	4,176	1,636	2,528	12	892 D	39.2%	60.5%	39.3%	60.7%
43,812	BELL	10,899	4,962	5,910	27	948 D	45.5%	54.2%	45.6%	54.4%
10,820	BOONE	3,888	1,357	2,518	13	1,161 D	34.9%	64.8%	35.0%	65.0%
17,932	BOURBON	6,931	2,673	4,254	4	1,581 D	38.6%	61.4%	38.6%	61.4%
45,938	BOYD	17,265	7,322	9,868	75	2,546 D	42.4%	57.2%	42.6%	57.4%
17,075	BOYLE	6,349	2,257	4,081	11	1,824 D	35.5%	64.3%	35.6%	64.4%
9,389	BRACKEN	3,521	1,551	1,961	9	410 D	44.0%	55.7%	44.2%	55.8%
23,946	BREATHITT	5,590	1,602	3,977	11	2,375 D	28.7%	71.1%	28.7%	71.3%
17,744	BRECKINRIDGE	6,591	3,258	3,296	37	38 D	49.4%	50.0%	49.7%	50.3%
9,511	BULLITT	3,207	813	2,388	6	1,575 D	25.4%	74.5%	25.4%	74.6%
14,371	BUTLER	4,624	3,163	1,455	6	1,708 R	68.4%	31.5%	68.5%	31.5%
14,499	CALDWELL	5,130	2,246	2,858	26	612 D	43.8%	55.7%	44.0%	56.0%
19,041	CALLOWAY	6,698	896	5,793	9	4,897 D	13.4%	86.5%	13.4%	86.6%
71,918	CAMPBELL	29,820	14,916	14,801	103	115 R	50.0%	49.6%	50.2%	49.8%
7,650	CARLISLE	2,878	500	2,366	12	1,866 D	17.4%	82.2%	17.4%	82.6%
8,657	CARROLL	3,730	804	2,915	11	2,111 D	21.6%	78.2%	21.6%	78.4%
25,545	CARTER	7,946	4,520	3,403	23	1,117 R	56.9%	42.8%	57.0%	43.0%
19,962	CASEY	5,753	3,874	1,862	17	2,012 R	67.3%	32.4%	67.5%	32.5%
36,129	CHRISTIAN	12,181	5,566	6,599	16	1,033 D	45.7%	54.2%	45.8%	54.2%
17,988	CLARK	6,125	2,136	3,970	19	1,834 D	34.9%	64.8%	35.0%	65.0%
23,901	CLAY	6,027	4,395	1,632		2,763 R	72.9%	27.1%	72.9%	27.1%
10,279	CLINTON	3,328	2,573	755		1,818 R	77.3%	22.7%	77.3%	22.7%
12,115	CRITTENDEN	4,472	2,624	1,834	14	790 R	58.7%	41.0%	58.9%	41.1%
11,923	CUMBERLAND	3,409	2,533	872	4	1,661 R	74.3%	25.6%	74.4%	25.6%
52,335	DAVIESS	15,026	5,633	9,344	49	3,711 D	37.5%	62.2%	37.6%	62.4%
11,344	EDMONSON	3,934	2,589	1,332	13	1,257 R	65.8%	33.9%	66.0%	34.0%
8,713	ELLIOTT	2,647	634	2,013		1,379 D	24.0%	76.0%	24.0%	76.0%
17,978	ESTILL	5,486	2,889	2,587	10	302 R	52.7%	47.2%	52.8%	47.2%
78,899	FAYETTE	28,432	12,514	15,834	84	3,320 D	44.0%	55.7%	44.1%	55.9%
13,327	FLEMING	5,868	2,855	2,999	14	144 D	48.7%	51.1%	48.8%	51.2%
52,986	FLOYD	12,811	3,711	9,100		5,389 D	29.0%	71.0%	29.0%	71.0%
23,308	FRANKLIN	8,897	1,927	6,956	14	5,029 D	21.7%	78.2%	21.7%	78.3%
15,413	FULTON	4,392	791	3,592	9	2,801 D	18.0%	81.8%	18.0%	82.0%
4,307	GALLATIN	1,972	495	1,473	4	978 D	25.1%	74.7%	25.2%	74.8%
11,910	GARRARD	4,318	2,148	2,162	8	14 D	49.7%	50.1%	49.8%	50.2%
9,876	GRANT	4,269	1,535	2,729	5	1,194 D	36.0%	63.9%	36.0%	64.0%
31,763	GRAVES	11,935	2,122	9,786	27	7,664 D	17.8%	82.0%	17.8%	82.2%
17,562	GRAYSON	5,861	3,156	2,678	27	478 R	53.8%	45.7%	54.1%	45.9%
12,321	GREEN	4,508	2,497	1,993	18	504 R	55.4%	44.2%	55.6%	44.4%
24,917	GREENUP	8,825	4,059	4,742	24	683 D	46.0%	53.7%	46.1%	53.9%
6,807	HANCOCK	2,764	1,424	1,338	2	86 R	51.5%	48.4%	51.6%	48.4%
29,108	HARDIN	7,090	2,351	4,718	21	2,367 D	33.2%	66.5%	33.3%	66.7%
75,275	HARLAN	16,483	5,859	10,582	42	4,723 D	35.5%	64.2%	35.6%	64.4%
15,124	HARRISON	5,954	1,707	4,228	19	2,521 D	28.7%	71.0%	28.8%	71.2%
17,239	HART	6,155	2,866	3,280	9	414 D	46.6%	53.3%	46.6%	53.4%
27,020	HENDERSON	9,211	2,455	6,727	29	4,272 D	26.7%	73.0%	26.7%	73.3%
12,220	HENRY	5,329	1,445	3,862	22	2,417 D	27.1%	72.5%	27.2%	72.8%
9,142	HICKMAN	3,255	490	2,758	7	2,268 D	15.1%	84.7%	15.1%	84.9%
37,789	HOPKINS	12,609	3,884	8,695	30	4,811 D	30.8%	69.0%	30.9%	69.1%
16,339	JACKSON	4,200	3,722	465	13	3,257 R	88.6%	11.1%	88.9%	11.1%
385,392	JEFFERSON	161,218	66,052	94,710	456	28,658 D	41.0%	58.7%	41.1%	58.9%
12,174	JESSAMINE	4,692	1,837	2,815	40	978 D	39.2%	60.0%	39.5%	60.5%
25,771	JOHNSON	8,094	5,042	3,042	10	2,000 R	62.3%	37.6%	62.4%	37.6%
93,139	KENTON	32,482	13,147	19,261	74	6,114 D	40.5%	59.3%	40.6%	59.4%
20,007	KNOTT	5,193	759	4,434		3,675 D	14.6%	85.4%	14.6%	85.4%

KENTUCKY

PRESIDENT 1940

1940 Census Population	County	Total Vote	Republican	Democratic	Other	Rep.-Dem. Plurality	Percentage Total Vote Rep.	Total Vote Dem.	Major Vote Rep.	Major Vote Dem.
31,029	KNOX	8,330	5,003	3,319	8	1,684 R	60.1%	39.8%	60.1%	39.9%
9,622	LARUE	3,781	1,309	2,463	9	1,154 D	34.6%	65.1%	34.7%	65.3%
25,640	LAUREL	8,060	5,180	2,860	20	2,320 R	64.3%	35.5%	64.4%	35.6%
17,275	LAWRENCE	6,252	3,055	3,178	19	123 D	48.9%	50.8%	49.0%	51.0%
10,860	LEE	3,495	1,866	1,622	7	244 R	53.4%	46.4%	53.5%	46.5%
14,981	LESLIE	3,921	3,292	626	3	2,666 R	84.0%	16.0%	84.0%	16.0%
40,592	LETCHER	10,579	4,433	6,127	19	1,694 D	41.9%	57.9%	42.0%	58.0%
15,686	LEWIS	5,249	3,371	1,878		1,493 R	64.2%	35.8%	64.2%	35.8%
19,859	LINCOLN	6,783	3,090	3,657	36	567 D	45.6%	53.9%	45.8%	54.2%
9,127	LIVINGSTON	3,213	1,184	2,013	16	829 D	36.9%	62.7%	37.0%	63.0%
23,345	LOGAN	8,908	2,268	6,631	9	4,363 D	25.5%	74.4%	25.5%	74.5%
9,067	LYON	2,917	921	1,979	17	1,058 D	31.6%	67.8%	31.8%	68.2%
48,534	MCCRACKEN	15,168	3,554	11,562	52	8,008 D	23.4%	76.2%	23.5%	76.5%
16,451	MCCREARY	4,429	3,172	1,248	9	1,924 R	71.6%	28.2%	71.8%	28.2%
11,446	MCLEAN	4,417	1,698	2,709	10	1,011 D	38.4%	61.3%	38.5%	61.5%
28,541	MADISON	12,340	5,789	6,484	67	695 D	46.9%	52.5%	47.2%	52.8%
17,490	MAGOFFIN	5,481	2,668	2,812	1	144 D	48.7%	51.3%	48.7%	51.3%
16,913	MARION	5,264	1,763	3,482	19	1,719 D	33.5%	66.1%	33.6%	66.4%
16,602	MARSHALL	4,662	1,100	3,549	13	2,449 D	23.6%	76.1%	23.7%	76.3%
10,970	MARTIN	3,102	2,275	826	1	1,449 R	73.3%	26.6%	73.4%	26.6%
19,066	MASON	8,117	3,704	4,386	27	682 D	45.6%	54.0%	45.8%	54.2%
8,827	MEADE	3,121	995	2,114	12	1,119 D	31.9%	67.7%	32.0%	68.0%
5,691	MENIFEE	1,692	511	1,176	5	665 D	30.2%	69.5%	30.3%	69.7%
14,629	MERCER	5,470	1,845	3,606	19	1,761 D	33.7%	65.9%	33.8%	66.2%
10,853	METCALFE	4,044	2,206	1,826	12	380 R	54.5%	45.2%	54.7%	45.3%
14,070	MONROE	4,722	3,321	1,390	11	1,931 R	70.3%	29.4%	70.5%	29.5%
12,280	MONTGOMERY	4,439	1,671	2,755	13	1,084 D	37.6%	62.1%	37.8%	62.2%
16,827	MORGAN	5,657	1,509	4,148		2,639 D	26.7%	73.3%	26.7%	73.3%
37,554	MUHLENBERG	10,500	5,332	5,140	28	192 R	50.8%	49.0%	50.9%	49.1%
18,004	NELSON	6,310	2,109	4,193	8	2,084 D	33.4%	66.5%	33.5%	66.5%
8,617	NICHOLAS	3,345	1,207	2,124	14	917 D	36.1%	63.5%	36.2%	63.8%
24,421	OHIO	8,204	4,451	3,729	24	722 R	54.3%	45.5%	54.4%	45.6%
10,716	OLDHAM	2,841	848	1,983	10	1,135 D	29.8%	69.8%	30.0%	70.0%
10,942	OWEN	4,231	569	3,655	7	3,086 D	13.4%	86.4%	13.5%	86.5%
8,957	OWSLEY	3,266	2,672	591	3	2,081 R	81.8%	18.1%	81.9%	18.1%
10,392	PENDLETON	4,208	2,029	2,165	14	136 D	48.2%	51.4%	48.4%	51.6%
47,828	PERRY	11,563	4,693	6,852	18	2,159 D	40.6%	59.3%	40.6%	59.4%
71,122	PIKE	21,161	8,985	12,160	16	3,175 D	42.5%	57.5%	42.5%	57.5%
7,671	POWELL	2,270	989	1,266	15	277 D	43.6%	55.8%	43.9%	56.1%
39,863	PULASKI	13,468	8,533	4,896	39	3,637 R	63.4%	36.4%	63.5%	36.5%
3,419	ROBERTSON	1,414	578	829	7	251 D	40.9%	58.6%	41.1%	58.9%
17,165	ROCKCASTLE	5,194	3,536	1,652	6	1,884 R	68.1%	31.8%	68.2%	31.8%
12,734	ROWAN	4,240	1,944	2,294	2	350 D	45.8%	54.1%	45.9%	54.1%
13,615	RUSSELL	4,334	3,069	1,250	15	1,819 R	70.8%	28.8%	71.1%	28.9%
14,314	SCOTT	5,849	1,795	4,039	15	2,244 D	30.7%	69.1%	30.8%	69.2%
17,759	SHELBY	6,702	1,861	4,823	18	2,962 D	27.8%	72.0%	27.8%	72.2%
11,752	SIMPSON	3,945	987	2,950	8	1,963 D	25.0%	74.8%	25.1%	74.9%
6,757	SPENCER	2,300	567	1,728	5	1,161 D	24.7%	75.1%	24.7%	75.3%
13,556	TAYLOR	5,606	2,792	2,790	24	2 R	49.8%	49.8%	50.0%	50.0%
14,234	TODD	4,792	1,436	3,337	19	1,901 D	30.0%	69.6%	30.1%	69.9%
12,784	TRIGG	4,388	1,494	2,883	11	1,389 D	34.0%	65.7%	34.1%	65.9%
5,601	TRIMBLE	2,155	242	1,909	4	1,667 D	11.2%	88.6%	11.3%	88.7%
17,411	UNION	5,474	1,111	4,355	8	3,244 D	20.3%	79.6%	20.3%	79.7%
36,631	WARREN	11,800	4,195	7,569	36	3,374 D	35.6%	64.1%	35.7%	64.3%
12,965	WASHINGTON	4,976	2,362	2,612	2	250 D	47.5%	52.5%	47.5%	52.5%
17,204	WAYNE	5,702	3,177	2,519	6	658 R	55.7%	44.2%	55.8%	44.2%
19,198	WEBSTER	6,321	2,107	4,197	17	2,090 D	33.3%	66.4%	33.4%	66.6%
33,186	WHITLEY	10,596	6,502	4,078	16	2,424 R	61.4%	38.5%	61.5%	38.5%
9,997	WOLFE	3,237	1,032	2,205		1,173 D	31.9%	68.1%	31.9%	68.1%
11,847	WOODFORD	4,151	1,514	2,630	7	1,116 D	36.5%	63.4%	36.5%	63.5%
2,845,627	TOTAL	970,163	410,384	557,322	2,457	146,938 D	42.3%	57.4%	42.4%	57.6%

KENTUCKY

PRESIDENT 1936

1930 Census Population	County	Total Vote	Republican	Democratic	Other	Rep.-Dem. Plurality	Percentage: Total Vote Rep.	Percentage: Total Vote Dem.	Percentage: Major Vote Rep.	Percentage: Major Vote Dem.
16,401	ADAIR	6,050	3,371	2,669	10	702 R	55.7%	44.1%	55.8%	44.2%
15,180	ALLEN	5,505	3,070	2,422	13	648 R	55.8%	44.0%	55.9%	44.1%
8,494	ANDERSON	3,825	1,360	2,454	11	1,094 D	35.6%	64.2%	35.7%	64.3%
9,910	BALLARD	4,303	773	3,523	7	2,750 D	18.0%	81.9%	18.0%	82.0%
25,844	BARREN	8,513	3,352	5,137	24	1,785 D	39.4%	60.3%	39.5%	60.5%
11,075	BATH	4,530	1,725	2,795	10	1,070 D	38.1%	61.7%	38.2%	61.8%
38,747	BELL	10,461	4,573	5,853	35	1,280 D	43.7%	56.0%	43.9%	56.1%
9,595	BOONE	3,915	1,042	2,785	88	1,743 D	26.6%	71.1%	27.2%	72.8%
18,060	BOURBON	6,364	2,471	3,872	21	1,401 D	38.8%	60.8%	39.0%	61.0%
43,849	BOYD	16,492	6,650	9,762	80	3,112 D	40.3%	59.2%	40.5%	59.5%
16,282	BOYLE	6,606	2,431	4,148	27	1,717 D	36.8%	62.8%	37.0%	63.0%
9,616	BRACKEN	3,444	1,436	1,956	52	520 D	41.7%	56.8%	42.3%	57.7%
21,143	BREATHITT	5,781	1,790	3,980	11	2,190 D	31.0%	68.8%	31.0%	69.0%
17,368	BRECKINRIDGE	6,225	2,898	3,233	94	335 D	46.6%	51.9%	47.3%	52.7%
8,868	BULLITT	3,136	647	2,474	15	1,827 D	20.6%	78.9%	20.7%	79.3%
12,620	BUTLER	3,835	2,594	1,237	4	1,357 R	67.6%	32.3%	67.7%	32.3%
13,781	CALDWELL	4,848	2,121	2,699	28	578 D	43.8%	55.7%	44.0%	56.0%
17,662	CALLOWAY	6,472	939	5,523	10	4,584 D	14.5%	85.3%	14.5%	85.5%
73,391	CAMPBELL	30,194	10,327	16,780	3,087	6,453 D	34.2%	55.6%	38.1%	61.9%
7,363	CARLISLE	2,600	420	2,150	30	1,730 D	16.2%	82.7%	16.3%	83.7%
8,155	CARROLL	3,547	794	2,718	35	1,924 D	22.4%	76.6%	22.6%	77.4%
23,839	CARTER	7,810	4,372	3,403	35	969 R	56.0%	43.6%	56.2%	43.8%
16,747	CASEY	5,536	3,588	1,925	23	1,663 R	64.8%	34.8%	65.1%	34.9%
34,283	CHRISTIAN	12,030	5,370	6,660		1,290 D	44.6%	55.4%	44.6%	55.4%
17,640	CLARK	6,659	2,246	4,396	17	2,150 D	33.7%	66.0%	33.8%	66.2%
18,526	CLAY	5,659	4,087	1,572		2,515 R	72.2%	27.8%	72.2%	27.8%
9,004	CLINTON	2,848	2,147	701		1,446 R	75.4%	24.6%	75.4%	24.6%
11,931	CRITTENDEN	4,375	2,441	1,926	8	515 R	55.8%	44.0%	55.9%	44.1%
10,204	CUMBERLAND	3,065	2,127	935	3	1,192 R	69.4%	30.5%	69.5%	30.5%
43,779	DAVIESS	15,347	4,636	9,957	754	5,321 D	30.2%	64.9%	31.8%	68.2%
11,475	EDMONSON	3,860	2,526	1,329	5	1,197 R	65.4%	34.4%	65.5%	34.5%
7,571	ELLIOTT	2,019	480	1,539		1,059 D	23.8%	76.2%	23.8%	76.2%
17,079	ESTILL	5,590	2,931	2,646	13	285 R	52.4%	47.3%	52.6%	47.4%
68,543	FAYETTE	26,175	11,544	14,428	203	2,884 D	44.1%	55.1%	44.4%	55.6%
12,931	FLEMING	5,649	2,749	2,879	21	130 D	48.7%	51.0%	48.8%	51.2%
41,942	FLOYD	11,337	3,375	7,962		4,587 D	29.8%	70.2%	29.8%	70.2%
21,064	FRANKLIN	8,258	2,010	6,222	26	4,212 D	24.3%	75.3%	24.4%	75.6%
14,927	FULTON	4,526	782	3,727	17	2,945 D	17.3%	82.3%	17.3%	82.7%
4,437	GALLATIN	1,875	404	1,456	15	1,052 D	21.5%	77.7%	21.7%	78.3%
11,562	GARRARD	4,535	2,252	2,276	7	24 D	49.7%	50.2%	49.7%	50.3%
9,876	GRANT	3,939	1,353	2,560	26	1,207 D	34.3%	65.0%	34.6%	65.4%
30,778	GRAVES	11,065	1,692	9,231	142	7,539 D	15.3%	83.4%	15.5%	84.5%
17,055	GRAYSON	5,603	2,907	2,676	20	231 R	51.9%	47.8%	52.1%	47.9%
11,401	GREEN	4,312	2,336	1,970	6	366 R	54.2%	45.7%	54.2%	45.8%
24,554	GREENUP	8,659	3,973	4,686		713 D	45.9%	54.1%	45.9%	54.1%
6,147	HANCOCK	2,422	1,087	1,317	18	230 D	44.9%	54.4%	45.2%	54.8%
20,913	HARDIN	6,814	2,284	4,480	50	2,196 D	33.5%	65.7%	33.8%	66.2%
64,557	HARLAN	18,570	7,510	11,060		3,550 D	40.4%	59.6%	40.4%	59.6%
14,859	HARRISON	6,149	1,756	4,378	15	2,622 D	28.6%	71.2%	28.6%	71.4%
16,169	HART	6,511	3,147	3,341	23	194 D	48.3%	51.3%	48.5%	51.5%
26,295	HENDERSON	8,833	1,811	6,835	187	5,024 D	20.5%	77.4%	20.9%	79.1%
12,564	HENRY	5,065	1,516	3,545	4	2,029 D	29.9%	70.0%	30.0%	70.0%
8,725	HICKMAN	2,952	385	2,548	19	2,163 D	13.0%	86.3%	13.1%	86.9%
37,449	HOPKINS	11,838	3,602	8,193	43	4,591 D	30.4%	69.2%	30.5%	69.5%
10,467	JACKSON	3,863	3,440	420	3	3,020 R	89.0%	10.9%	89.1%	10.9%
355,350	JEFFERSON	142,369	53,043	85,748	3,578	32,705 D	37.3%	60.2%	38.2%	61.8%
12,431	JESSAMINE	4,902	2,066	2,813	23	747 D	42.1%	57.4%	42.3%	57.7%
22,968	JOHNSON	7,429	4,305	3,106	18	1,199 R	57.9%	41.8%	58.1%	41.9%
93,534	KENTON	34,666	8,885	21,879	3,902	12,994 D	25.6%	63.1%	28.9%	71.1%
15,230	KNOTT	4,353	865	3,488		2,623 D	19.9%	80.1%	19.9%	80.1%

KENTUCKY

PRESIDENT 1936

1930 Census Population	County	Total Vote	Republican	Democratic	Other	Rep.-Dem. Plurality	Percentage Total Vote Rep.	Percentage Total Vote Dem.	Percentage Major Vote Rep.	Percentage Major Vote Dem.
26,266	KNOX	8,345	4,921	3,419	5	1,502 R	59.0%	41.0%	59.0%	41.0%
9,093	LARUE	3,467	1,151	2,305	11	1,154 D	33.2%	66.5%	33.3%	66.7%
21,109	LAUREL	7,487	4,798	2,677	12	2,121 R	64.1%	35.8%	64.2%	35.8%
16,713	LAWRENCE	6,128	2,944	3,175	9	231 D	48.0%	51.8%	48.1%	51.9%
9,729	LEE	3,254	1,812	1,440	2	372 R	55.7%	44.3%	55.7%	44.3%
10,765	LESLIE	3,337	2,716	618	3	2,098 R	81.4%	18.5%	81.5%	18.5%
35,702	LETCHER	10,122	3,871	6,240	11	2,369 D	38.2%	61.6%	38.3%	61.7%
14,315	LEWIS	5,257	3,255	1,985	17	1,270 R	61.9%	37.8%	62.1%	37.9%
17,687	LINCOLN	6,826	3,211	3,575	40	364 D	47.0%	52.4%	47.3%	52.7%
8,608	LIVINGSTON	2,947	1,039	1,897	11	858 D	35.3%	64.4%	35.4%	64.6%
21,875	LOGAN	6,745	1,812	4,912	21	3,100 D	26.9%	72.8%	26.9%	73.1%
8,530	LYON	2,799	929	1,861	9	932 D	33.2%	66.5%	33.3%	66.7%
46,271	MCCRACKEN	13,829	3,160	10,557	112	7,397 D	22.9%	76.3%	23.0%	77.0%
14,627	MCCREARY	4,069	2,953	1,105	11	1,848 R	72.6%	27.2%	72.8%	27.2%
11,072	MCLEAN	3,879	1,338	2,496	45	1,158 D	34.5%	64.3%	34.9%	65.1%
27,621	MADISON	12,376	6,034	6,259	83	225 D	48.8%	50.6%	49.1%	50.9%
15,719	MAGOFFIN	5,137	2,577	2,554	6	23 R	50.2%	49.7%	50.2%	49.8%
15,499	MARION	5,146	1,567	3,526	53	1,959 D	30.5%	68.5%	30.8%	69.2%
12,889	MARSHALL	4,624	1,141	3,472	11	2,331 D	24.7%	75.1%	24.7%	75.3%
8,584	MARTIN	2,855	2,037	817	1	1,220 R	71.3%	28.6%	71.4%	28.6%
18,862	MASON	7,967	3,317	4,503	147	1,186 D	41.6%	56.5%	42.4%	57.6%
8,042	MEADE	2,967	785	2,102	80	1,317 D	26.5%	70.8%	27.2%	72.8%
4,958	MENIFEE	1,686	559	1,123	4	564 D	33.2%	66.6%	33.2%	66.8%
14,471	MERCER	5,846	2,161	3,659	26	1,498 D	37.0%	62.6%	37.1%	62.9%
9,373	METCALFE	3,530	1,777	1,748	5	29 R	50.3%	49.5%	50.4%	49.6%
13,077	MONROE	3,706	2,345	1,352	9	993 R	63.3%	36.5%	63.4%	36.6%
11,660	MONTGOMERY	4,267	1,649	2,594	24	945 D	38.6%	60.8%	38.9%	61.1%
15,130	MORGAN	4,531	1,269	3,256	6	1,987 D	28.0%	71.9%	28.0%	72.0%
37,784	MUHLENBERG	10,628	4,168	6,385	75	2,217 D	39.2%	60.1%	39.5%	60.5%
16,551	NELSON	6,358	1,913	4,234	211	2,321 D	30.1%	66.6%	31.1%	68.9%
8,571	NICHOLAS	3,620	1,277	2,325	18	1,048 D	35.3%	64.2%	35.5%	64.5%
24,469	OHIO	8,589	4,532	4,030	27	502 R	52.8%	46.9%	52.9%	47.1%
7,402	OLDHAM	2,794	760	2,020	14	1,260 D	27.2%	72.3%	27.3%	72.7%
10,710	OWEN	4,065	661	3,392	12	2,731 D	16.3%	83.4%	16.3%	83.7%
7,223	OWSLEY	2,738	2,273	464	1	1,809 R	83.0%	16.9%	83.0%	17.0%
10,876	PENDLETON	4,311	1,837	2,432	42	595 D	42.6%	56.4%	43.0%	57.0%
42,186	PERRY	11,359	4,595	6,753	11	2,158 D	40.5%	59.5%	40.5%	59.5%
63,267	PIKE	19,603	8,210	11,382	11	3,172 D	41.9%	58.1%	41.9%	58.1%
5,800	POWELL	2,197	998	1,185	14	187 D	45.4%	53.9%	45.7%	54.3%
35,640	PULASKI	12,305	7,570	4,711	24	2,859 R	61.5%	38.3%	61.6%	38.4%
3,344	ROBERTSON	1,403	498	897	8	399 D	35.5%	63.9%	35.7%	64.3%
15,149	ROCKCASTLE	5,443	3,875	1,568		2,307 R	71.2%	28.8%	71.2%	28.8%
10,893	ROWAN	3,684	1,687	1,989	8	302 D	45.8%	54.0%	45.9%	54.1%
11,930	RUSSELL	3,942	2,688	1,235	19	1,453 R	68.2%	31.3%	68.5%	31.5%
14,400	SCOTT	5,838	1,861	3,966	11	2,105 D	31.9%	67.9%	31.9%	68.1%
17,679	SHELBY	6,317	1,898	4,384	35	2,486 D	30.0%	69.4%	30.2%	69.8%
11,336	SIMPSON	4,280	1,240	3,027	13	1,787 D	29.0%	70.7%	29.1%	70.9%
6,606	SPENCER	2,294	638	1,647	9	1,009 D	27.8%	71.8%	27.9%	72.1%
12,047	TAYLOR	5,491	2,738	2,732	21	6 R	49.9%	49.8%	50.1%	49.9%
13,520	TODD	4,176	1,178	2,987	11	1,809 D	28.2%	71.5%	28.3%	71.7%
12,531	TRIGG	4,468	1,521	2,928	19	1,407 D	34.0%	65.5%	34.2%	65.8%
5,348	TRIMBLE	1,948	271	1,659	18	1,388 D	13.9%	85.2%	14.0%	86.0%
17,053	UNION	5,785	965	4,713	107	3,748 D	16.7%	81.5%	17.0%	83.0%
33,676	WARREN	12,514	4,347	8,113	54	3,766 D	34.7%	64.8%	34.9%	65.1%
12,623	WASHINGTON	4,943	2,391	2,516	36	125 D	48.4%	50.9%	48.7%	51.3%
15,848	WAYNE	5,480	2,924	2,546	10	378 R	53.4%	46.5%	53.5%	46.5%
20,534	WEBSTER	6,792	1,983	4,788	21	2,805 D	29.2%	70.5%	29.3%	70.7%
29,730	WHITLEY	8,920	5,733	3,175	12	2,558 R	64.3%	35.6%	64.4%	35.6%
8,425	WOLFE	2,549	972	1,577		605 D	38.1%	61.9%	38.1%	61.9%
10,981	WOODFORD	4,138	1,558	2,574	6	1,016 D	37.7%	62.2%	37.7%	62.3%
2,614,589	TOTAL	926,214	369,702	541,944	14,568	172,242 D	39.9%	58.5%	40.6%	59.4%

KENTUCKY

PRESIDENT 1932

1930 Census Population	County	Total Vote	Republican	Democratic	Other	Rep.-Dem. Plurality	Percentage Total Vote Rep.	Total Vote Dem.	Major Vote Rep.	Major Vote Dem.
16,401	ADAIR	6,347	3,084	3,251	12	167 D	48.6%	51.2%	48.7%	51.3%
15,180	ALLEN	6,368	3,219	3,116	33	103 R	50.5%	48.9%	50.8%	49.2%
8,494	ANDERSON	3,634	1,184	2,415	35	1,231 D	32.6%	66.5%	32.9%	67.1%
9,910	BALLARD	4,584	572	3,987	25	3,415 D	12.5%	87.0%	12.5%	87.5%
25,844	BARREN	10,181	3,622	6,518	41	2,896 D	35.6%	64.0%	35.7%	64.3%
11,075	BATH	4,505	1,576	2,909	20	1,333 D	35.0%	64.6%	35.1%	64.9%
38,747	BELL	10,213	4,695	5,440	78	745 D	46.0%	53.3%	46.3%	53.7%
9,595	BOONE	4,923	1,355	3,536	32	2,181 D	27.5%	71.8%	27.7%	72.3%
18,060	BOURBON	7,604	2,820	4,759	25	1,939 D	37.1%	62.6%	37.2%	62.8%
43,849	BOYD	15,343	6,853	8,315	175	1,462 D	44.7%	54.2%	45.2%	54.8%
16,282	BOYLE	6,711	2,208	4,473	30	2,265 D	32.9%	66.7%	33.0%	67.0%
9,616	BRACKEN	3,921	1,471	2,407	43	936 D	37.5%	61.4%	37.9%	62.1%
21,143	BREATHITT	5,902	1,371	4,524	7	3,153 D	23.2%	76.7%	23.3%	76.7%
17,368	BRECKINRIDGE	7,085	3,237	3,814	34	577 D	45.7%	53.8%	45.9%	54.1%
8,868	BULLITT	4,014	1,088	2,918	8	1,830 D	27.1%	72.7%	27.2%	72.8%
12,620	BUTLER	4,331	2,586	1,736	9	850 R	59.7%	40.1%	59.8%	40.2%
13,781	CALDWELL	5,039	2,020	2,971	48	951 D	40.1%	59.0%	40.5%	59.5%
17,662	CALLOWAY	7,184	813	6,335	36	5,522 D	11.3%	88.2%	11.4%	88.6%
73,391	CAMPBELL	30,208	11,665	17,776	767	6,111 D	38.6%	58.8%	39.6%	60.4%
7,363	CARLISLE	3,253	402	2,840	11	2,438 D	12.4%	87.3%	12.4%	87.6%
8,155	CARROLL	3,795	761	3,015	19	2,254 D	20.1%	79.4%	20.2%	79.8%
23,839	CARTER	9,020	4,376	4,565	79	189 D	48.5%	50.6%	48.9%	51.1%
16,747	CASEY	6,516	3,840	2,651	25	1,189 R	58.9%	40.7%	59.2%	40.8%
34,283	CHRISTIAN	12,920	5,235	7,618	67	2,383 D	40.5%	59.0%	40.7%	59.3%
17,640	CLARK	6,936	1,981	4,920	35	2,939 D	28.6%	70.9%	28.7%	71.3%
18,526	CLAY	5,620	3,474	2,133	13	1,341 R	61.8%	38.0%	62.0%	38.0%
9,004	CLINTON	3,330	2,422	908		1,514 R	72.7%	27.3%	72.7%	27.3%
11,931	CRITTENDEN	4,320	2,185	2,119	16	66 R	50.6%	49.1%	50.8%	49.2%
10,204	CUMBERLAND	3,615	2,369	1,235	11	1,134 R	65.5%	34.2%	65.7%	34.3%
43,779	DAVIESS	15,685	5,059	10,527	99	5,468 D	32.3%	67.1%	32.5%	67.5%
11,475	EDMONSON	4,499	2,690	1,796	13	894 R	59.8%	39.9%	60.0%	40.0%
7,571	ELLIOTT	2,532	382	2,150		1,768 D	15.1%	84.9%	15.1%	84.9%
17,079	ESTILL	6,136	2,963	3,150	23	187 D	48.3%	51.3%	48.5%	51.5%
68,543	FAYETTE	27,869	11,847	15,765	257	3,918 D	42.5%	56.6%	42.9%	57.1%
12,931	FLEMING	6,124	2,638	3,442	44	804 D	43.1%	56.2%	43.4%	56.6%
41,942	FLOYD	11,986	3,415	8,537	34	5,122 D	28.5%	71.2%	28.6%	71.4%
21,064	FRANKLIN	8,404	2,034	6,331	39	4,297 D	24.2%	75.3%	24.3%	75.7%
14,927	FULTON	4,845	837	3,985	23	3,148 D	17.3%	82.2%	17.4%	82.6%
4,437	GALLATIN	2,163	365	1,792	6	1,427 D	16.9%	82.8%	16.9%	83.1%
11,562	GARRARD	4,859	2,276	2,582	1	306 D	46.8%	53.1%	46.9%	53.1%
9,876	GRANT	4,592	1,407	3,148	37	1,741 D	30.6%	68.6%	30.9%	69.1%
30,778	GRAVES	11,764	1,825	9,888	51	8,063 D	15.5%	84.1%	15.6%	84.4%
17,055	GRAYSON	7,624	3,721	3,872	31	151 D	48.8%	50.8%	49.0%	51.0%
11,401	GREEN	4,583	2,281	2,277	25	4 R	49.8%	49.7%	50.0%	50.0%
24,554	GREENUP	8,492	3,422	4,963	107	1,541 D	40.3%	58.4%	40.8%	59.2%
6,147	HANCOCK	2,826	1,174	1,623	29	449 D	41.5%	57.4%	42.0%	58.0%
20,913	HARDIN	8,920	2,801	6,047	72	3,246 D	31.4%	67.8%	31.7%	68.3%
64,557	HARLAN	20,254	11,118	9,091	45	2,027 R	54.9%	44.9%	55.0%	45.0%
14,859	HARRISON	6,790	1,833	4,909	48	3,076 D	27.0%	72.3%	27.2%	72.8%
16,169	HART	6,642	2,601	4,008	33	1,407 D	39.2%	60.3%	39.4%	60.6%
26,295	HENDERSON	8,881	2,485	6,100	296	3,615 D	28.0%	68.7%	28.9%	71.1%
12,564	HENRY	5,987	1,643	4,303	41	2,660 D	27.4%	71.9%	27.6%	72.4%
8,725	HICKMAN	3,789	446	3,327	16	2,881 D	11.8%	87.8%	11.8%	88.2%
37,449	HOPKINS	13,085	3,817	9,158	110	5,341 D	29.2%	70.0%	29.4%	70.6%
10,467	JACKSON	3,416	2,879	529	8	2,350 R	84.3%	15.5%	84.5%	15.5%
355,350	JEFFERSON	141,096	67,137	72,402	1,557	5,265 D	47.6%	51.3%	48.1%	51.9%
12,431	JESSAMINE	4,595	1,710	2,873	12	1,163 D	37.2%	62.5%	37.3%	62.7%
22,968	JOHNSON	8,025	4,871	3,134	20	1,737 R	60.7%	39.1%	60.8%	39.2%
93,534	KENTON	34,263	11,202	22,311	750	11,109 D	32.7%	65.1%	33.4%	66.6%
15,230	KNOTT	5,190	747	4,443		3,696 D	14.4%	85.6%	14.4%	85.6%

KENTUCKY

PRESIDENT 1932

1930 Census Population	County	Total Vote	Republican	Democratic	Other	Rep.-Dem. Plurality	Percentage Total Vote Rep.	Percentage Total Vote Dem.	Percentage Major Vote Rep.	Percentage Major Vote Dem.
26,266	KNOX	7,938	4,513	3,375	50	1,138 R	56.9%	42.5%	57.2%	42.8%
9,093	LARUE	3,899	1,235	2,650	14	1,415 D	31.7%	68.0%	31.8%	68.2%
21,109	LAUREL	8,430	4,827	3,569	34	1,258 R	57.3%	42.3%	57.5%	42.5%
16,713	LAWRENCE	6,494	2,766	3,701	27	935 D	42.6%	57.0%	42.8%	57.2%
9,729	LEE	3,604	1,628	1,970	6	342 D	45.2%	54.7%	45.2%	54.8%
10,765	LESLIE	3,387	2,810	569	8	2,241 R	83.0%	16.8%	83.2%	16.8%
35,702	LETCHER	9,975	4,732	5,190	53	458 D	47.4%	52.0%	47.7%	52.3%
14,315	LEWIS	5,748	3,212	2,488	48	724 R	55.9%	43.3%	56.4%	43.6%
17,687	LINCOLN	7,695	3,063	4,574	58	1,511 D	39.8%	59.4%	40.1%	59.9%
8,608	LIVINGSTON	3,312	1,070	2,231	11	1,161 D	32.3%	67.4%	32.4%	67.6%
21,875	LOGAN	9,917	2,778	7,072	67	4,294 D	28.0%	71.3%	28.2%	71.8%
8,530	LYON	2,979	873	2,099	7	1,226 D	29.3%	70.5%	29.4%	70.6%
46,271	MCCRACKEN	12,499	3,140	9,188	171	6,048 D	25.1%	73.5%	25.5%	74.5%
14,627	MCCREARY	4,576	3,360	1,194	22	2,166 R	73.4%	26.1%	73.8%	26.2%
11,072	MCLEAN	4,224	1,412	2,771	41	1,359 D	33.4%	65.6%	33.8%	66.2%
27,621	MADISON	12,884	5,811	6,957	116	1,146 D	45.1%	54.0%	45.5%	54.5%
15,719	MAGOFFIN	5,395	2,661	2,721	13	60 D	49.3%	50.4%	49.4%	50.6%
15,499	MARION	6,021	1,571	4,427	23	2,856 D	26.1%	73.5%	26.2%	73.8%
12,889	MARSHALL	5,129	863	4,246	20	3,383 D	16.8%	82.8%	16.9%	83.1%
8,584	MARTIN	2,559	1,774	770	15	1,004 R	69.3%	30.1%	69.7%	30.3%
18,862	MASON	8,334	3,213	5,065	56	1,852 D	38.6%	60.8%	38.8%	61.2%
8,042	MEADE	3,564	1,050	2,488	26	1,438 D	29.5%	69.8%	29.7%	70.3%
4,958	MENIFEE	1,910	474	1,425	11	951 D	24.8%	74.6%	25.0%	75.0%
14,471	MERCER	5,745	1,950	3,759	36	1,809 D	33.9%	65.4%	34.2%	65.8%
9,373	METCALFE	3,730	1,729	1,985	16	256 D	46.4%	53.2%	46.6%	53.4%
13,077	MONROE	4,190	2,559	1,620	11	939 R	61.1%	38.7%	61.2%	38.8%
11,660	MONTGOMERY	4,338	1,515	2,810	13	1,295 D	34.9%	64.8%	35.0%	65.0%
15,130	MORGAN	5,584	1,435	4,137	12	2,702 D	25.7%	74.1%	25.8%	74.2%
37,784	MUHLENBERG	11,630	4,349	7,162	119	2,813 D	37.4%	61.6%	37.8%	62.2%
16,551	NELSON	7,401	2,100	5,272	29	3,172 D	28.4%	71.2%	28.5%	71.5%
8,571	NICHOLAS	3,988	1,219	2,728	41	1,509 D	30.6%	68.4%	30.9%	69.1%
24,469	OHIO	9,934	4,880	4,870	184	10 R	49.1%	49.0%	50.1%	49.9%
7,402	OLDHAM	3,233	888	2,319	26	1,431 D	27.5%	71.7%	27.7%	72.3%
10,710	OWEN	4,960	658	4,240	62	3,582 D	13.3%	85.5%	13.4%	86.6%
7,223	OWSLEY	2,510	1,985	520	5	1,465 R	79.1%	20.7%	79.2%	20.8%
10,876	PENDLETON	4,620	1,812	2,745	63	933 D	39.2%	59.4%	39.8%	60.2%
42,186	PERRY	11,655	5,240	6,393	22	1,153 D	45.0%	54.9%	45.0%	55.0%
63,267	PIKE	20,674	7,914	12,686	74	4,772 D	38.3%	61.4%	38.4%	61.6%
5,800	POWELL	2,135	826	1,300	9	474 D	38.7%	60.9%	38.9%	61.1%
35,640	PULASKI	11,861	6,905	4,931	25	1,974 R	58.2%	41.6%	58.3%	41.7%
3,344	ROBERTSON	1,604	538	1,056	10	518 D	33.5%	65.8%	33.8%	66.2%
15,149	ROCKCASTLE	5,564	3,577	1,976	11	1,601 R	64.3%	35.5%	64.4%	35.6%
10,893	ROWAN	4,490	1,622	2,844	24	1,222 D	36.1%	63.3%	36.3%	63.7%
11,930	RUSSELL	4,216	2,490	1,699	27	791 R	59.1%	40.3%	59.4%	40.6%
14,400	SCOTT	6,551	1,943	4,572	36	2,629 D	29.7%	69.8%	29.8%	70.2%
17,679	SHELBY	7,325	2,108	5,180	37	3,072 D	28.8%	70.7%	28.9%	71.1%
11,336	SIMPSON	4,827	1,203	3,603	21	2,400 D	24.9%	74.6%	25.0%	75.0%
6,606	SPENCER	2,515	736	1,773	6	1,037 D	29.3%	70.5%	29.3%	70.7%
12,047	TAYLOR	5,454	2,592	2,823	39	231 D	47.5%	51.8%	47.9%	52.1%
13,520	TODD	5,556	1,562	3,966	28	2,404 D	28.1%	71.4%	28.3%	71.7%
12,531	TRIGG	5,078	1,452	3,611	15	2,159 D	28.6%	71.1%	28.7%	71.3%
5,348	TRIMBLE	2,354	257	2,083	14	1,826 D	10.9%	88.5%	11.0%	89.0%
17,053	UNION	5,991	1,063	4,892	36	3,829 D	17.7%	81.7%	17.9%	82.1%
33,676	WARREN	13,578	4,569	8,932	77	4,363 D	33.7%	65.8%	33.8%	66.2%
12,623	WASHINGTON	5,203	2,340	2,841	22	501 D	45.0%	54.6%	45.2%	54.8%
15,848	WAYNE	5,646	2,682	2,929	35	247 D	47.5%	51.9%	47.8%	52.2%
20,534	WEBSTER	7,138	2,257	4,833	48	2,576 D	31.6%	67.7%	31.8%	68.2%
29,730	WHITLEY	9,820	6,186	3,576	58	2,610 R	63.0%	36.4%	63.4%	36.6%
8,425	WOLFE	3,232	909	2,321	2	1,412 D	28.1%	71.8%	28.1%	71.9%
10,981	WOODFORD	4,918	1,720	3,180	18	1,460 D	35.0%	64.7%	35.1%	64.9%
2,614,589	TOTAL	983,059	394,716	580,574	7,769	185,858 D	40.2%	59.1%	40.5%	59.5%

KENTUCKY

PRESIDENT 1928

1920 Census Population	County	Total Vote	Republican	Democratic	Other	Rep.-Dem. Plurality	Percentage Total Vote Rep.	Percentage Total Vote Dem.	Percentage Major Vote Rep.	Percentage Major Vote Dem.
17,289	ADAIR	5,588	3,856	1,732		2,124 R	69.0%	31.0%	69.0%	31.0%
16,761	ALLEN	5,815	4,253	1,562		2,691 R	73.1%	26.9%	73.1%	26.9%
9,982	ANDERSON	3,578	1,859	1,718	1	141 R	52.0%	48.0%	52.0%	48.0%
12,045	BALLARD	3,839	940	2,896	3	1,956 D	24.5%	75.4%	24.5%	75.5%
25,356	BARREN	8,636	5,101	3,530	5	1,571 R	59.1%	40.9%	59.1%	40.9%
11,996	BATH	4,061	2,223	1,830	8	393 R	54.7%	45.1%	54.8%	45.2%
33,988	BELL	9,145	6,570	2,551	24	4,019 R	71.8%	27.9%	72.0%	28.0%
9,572	BOONE	4,466	2,604	1,855	7	749 R	58.3%	41.5%	58.4%	41.6%
18,418	BOURBON	7,734	4,512	3,218	4	1,294 R	58.3%	41.6%	58.4%	41.6%
29,281	BOYD	13,736	9,118	4,611	7	4,507 R	66.4%	33.6%	66.4%	33.6%
14,998	BOYLE	6,512	3,517	2,992	3	525 R	54.0%	45.9%	54.0%	46.0%
10,210	BRACKEN	4,030	2,820	1,201	9	1,619 R	70.0%	29.8%	70.1%	29.9%
20,614	BREATHITT	5,326	2,309	3,017		708 D	43.4%	56.6%	43.4%	56.6%
19,652	BRECKINRIDGE	7,773	4,783	2,987	3	1,796 R	61.5%	38.4%	61.6%	38.4%
9,328	BULLITT	3,554	1,793	1,758	3	35 R	50.5%	49.5%	50.5%	49.5%
15,197	BUTLER	3,963	3,272	684	7	2,588 R	82.6%	17.3%	82.7%	17.3%
13,975	CALDWELL	4,560	2,855	1,695	10	1,160 R	62.6%	37.2%	62.7%	37.3%
20,802	CALLOWAY	5,002	1,557	3,431	14	1,874 D	31.1%	68.6%	31.2%	68.8%
61,868	CAMPBELL	31,920	17,317	14,508	95	2,809 R	54.3%	45.5%	54.4%	45.6%
8,231	CARLISLE	2,783	787	1,994	2	1,207 D	28.3%	71.6%	28.3%	71.7%
8,346	CARROLL	3,515	1,649	1,863	3	214 D	46.9%	53.0%	47.0%	53.0%
22,474	CARTER	7,773	5,342	2,392	39	2,950 R	68.7%	30.8%	69.1%	30.9%
17,213	CASEY	5,330	3,805	1,519	6	2,286 R	71.4%	28.5%	71.5%	28.5%
35,883	CHRISTIAN	12,771	7,069	5,702		1,367 R	55.4%	44.6%	55.4%	44.6%
17,901	CLARK	6,955	3,495	3,460		35 R	50.3%	49.7%	50.3%	49.7%
19,795	CLAY	5,104	4,439	651	14	3,788 R	87.0%	12.8%	87.2%	12.8%
8,589	CLINTON	2,905	2,580	325		2,255 R	88.8%	11.2%	88.8%	11.2%
13,125	CRITTENDEN	4,382	3,000	1,376	6	1,624 R	68.5%	31.4%	68.6%	31.4%
10,648	CUMBERLAND	3,132	2,593	538	1	2,055 R	82.8%	17.2%	82.8%	17.2%
40,733	DAVIESS	16,243	8,896	7,332	15	1,564 R	54.8%	45.1%	54.8%	45.2%
10,894	EDMONSON	4,186	3,104	1,076	6	2,028 R	74.2%	25.7%	74.3%	25.7%
8,887	ELLIOTT	1,918	601	1,317		716 D	31.3%	68.7%	31.3%	68.7%
15,569	ESTILL	5,532	3,641	1,886	5	1,755 R	65.8%	34.1%	65.9%	34.1%
54,664	FAYETTE	26,092	16,988	9,065	39	7,923 R	65.1%	34.7%	65.2%	34.8%
15,614	FLEMING	5,888	3,798	2,086	4	1,712 R	64.5%	35.4%	64.5%	35.5%
27,427	FLOYD	10,830	5,109	5,721		612 D	47.2%	52.8%	47.2%	52.8%
19,357	FRANKLIN	7,345	3,485	3,853	7	368 D	47.4%	52.5%	47.5%	52.5%
15,197	FULTON	4,503	1,366	3,132	5	1,766 D	30.3%	69.6%	30.4%	69.6%
4,664	GALLATIN	1,835	1,010	823	2	187 R	55.0%	44.9%	55.1%	44.9%
12,503	GARRARD	4,591	2,862	1,729		1,133 R	62.3%	37.7%	62.3%	37.7%
10,435	GRANT	4,116	2,448	1,662	6	786 R	59.5%	40.4%	59.6%	40.4%
32,483	GRAVES	9,484	3,223	6,237	24	3,014 D	34.0%	65.8%	34.1%	65.9%
19,927	GRAYSON	6,242	3,937	2,295	10	1,642 R	63.1%	36.8%	63.2%	36.8%
11,391	GREEN	4,096	2,824	1,272		1,552 R	68.9%	31.1%	68.9%	31.1%
20,062	GREENUP	6,845	4,410	2,435		1,975 R	64.4%	35.6%	64.4%	35.6%
6,945	HANCOCK	2,767	1,614	1,151	2	463 R	58.3%	41.6%	58.4%	41.6%
24,287	HARDIN	7,848	4,624	3,210	14	1,414 R	58.9%	40.9%	59.0%	41.0%
31,546	HARLAN	16,246	12,251	3,958	37	8,293 R	75.4%	24.4%	75.6%	24.4%
15,798	HARRISON	6,078	2,909	3,164	5	255 D	47.9%	52.1%	47.9%	52.1%
18,544	HART	5,833	3,480	2,339	14	1,141 R	59.7%	40.1%	59.8%	40.2%
27,609	HENDERSON	9,544	5,443	4,068	33	1,375 R	57.0%	42.6%	57.2%	42.8%
13,411	HENRY	5,270	2,334	2,929	7	595 D	44.3%	55.6%	44.3%	55.7%
10,244	HICKMAN	2,936	767	2,163	6	1,396 D	26.1%	73.7%	26.2%	73.8%
34,133	HOPKINS	13,000	6,330	6,640	30	310 D	48.7%	51.1%	48.8%	51.2%
11,687	JACKSON	3,680	3,552	123	5	3,429 R	96.5%	3.3%	96.7%	3.3%
286,369	JEFFERSON	162,613	97,803	64,472	338	33,331 R	60.1%	39.6%	60.3%	39.7%
12,205	JESSAMINE	5,152	2,857	2,295		562 R	55.5%	44.5%	55.5%	44.5%
19,622	JOHNSON	7,217	5,339	1,869	9	3,470 R	74.0%	25.9%	74.1%	25.9%
73,453	KENTON	39,208	21,043	18,165		2,878 R	53.7%	46.3%	53.7%	46.3%
11,655	KNOTT	3,826	1,004	2,822		1,818 D	26.2%	73.8%	26.2%	73.8%

KENTUCKY

PRESIDENT 1928

1920 Census Population	County	Total Vote	Republican	Democratic	Other	Rep.-Dem. Plurality	Percentage: Total Vote Rep.	Total Vote Dem.	Major Vote Rep.	Major Vote Dem.
24,172	KNOX	7,432	5,928	1,497	7	4,431 R	79.8%	20.1%	79.8%	20.2%
10,004	LARUE	3,625	1,892	1,727	6	165 R	52.2%	47.6%	52.3%	47.7%
19,814	LAUREL	6,052	4,906	1,141	5	3,765 R	81.1%	18.9%	81.1%	18.9%
17,643	LAWRENCE	5,499	3,277	2,217	5	1,060 R	59.6%	40.3%	59.6%	40.4%
11,918	LEE	3,137	2,005	1,131	1	874 R	63.9%	36.1%	63.9%	36.1%
10,097	LESLIE	2,969	2,806	159	4	2,647 R	94.5%	5.4%	94.6%	5.4%
24,467	LETCHER	8,918	5,400	3,502	16	1,898 R	60.6%	39.3%	60.7%	39.3%
15,829	LEWIS	5,203	4,077	1,120	6	2,957 R	78.4%	21.5%	78.4%	21.6%
16,481	LINCOLN	6,227	3,903	2,314	10	1,589 R	62.7%	37.2%	62.8%	37.2%
9,732	LIVINGSTON	2,989	1,767	1,217	5	550 R	59.1%	40.7%	59.2%	40.8%
23,633	LOGAN	8,708	4,858	3,843	7	1,015 R	55.8%	44.1%	55.8%	44.2%
8,795	LYON	2,509	1,215	1,286	8	71 D	48.4%	51.3%	48.6%	51.4%
37,246	MCCRACKEN	12,943	7,368	5,535	40	1,833 R	56.9%	42.8%	57.1%	42.9%
11,676	MCCREARY	4,065	3,622	435	8	3,187 R	89.1%	10.7%	89.3%	10.7%
12,502	MCLEAN	4,147	2,408	1,728	11	680 R	58.1%	41.7%	58.2%	41.8%
26,284	MADISON	11,090	6,325	4,736	29	1,589 R	57.0%	42.7%	57.2%	42.8%
13,859	MAGOFFIN	4,622	2,816	1,806		1,010 R	60.9%	39.1%	60.9%	39.1%
15,527	MARION	5,863	2,395	3,461	7	1,066 D	40.8%	59.0%	40.9%	59.1%
15,215	MARSHALL	3,925	1,879	2,036	10	157 D	47.9%	51.9%	48.0%	52.0%
7,654	MARTIN	2,081	1,674	404	3	1,270 R	80.4%	19.4%	80.6%	19.4%
17,760	MASON	8,382	5,012	3,364	6	1,648 R	59.8%	40.1%	59.8%	40.2%
9,442	MEADE	3,317	1,610	1,700	7	90 D	48.5%	51.3%	48.6%	51.4%
5,779	MENIFEE	1,457	732	725		7 R	50.2%	49.8%	50.2%	49.8%
14,795	MERCER	5,606	3,462	2,140	4	1,322 R	61.8%	38.2%	61.8%	38.2%
10,075	METCALFE	3,458	2,314	1,144		1,170 R	66.9%	33.1%	66.9%	33.1%
14,214	MONROE	3,979	3,127	843	9	2,284 R	78.6%	21.2%	78.8%	21.2%
12,245	MONTGOMERY	4,699	2,742	1,938	19	804 R	58.4%	41.2%	58.6%	41.4%
16,518	MORGAN	4,600	2,025	2,575		550 D	44.0%	56.0%	44.0%	56.0%
33,353	MUHLENBERG	11,830	6,651	5,130	49	1,521 R	56.2%	43.4%	56.5%	43.5%
16,137	NELSON	6,960	2,926	4,031	3	1,105 D	42.0%	57.9%	42.1%	57.9%
9,894	NICHOLAS	3,707	1,867	1,836	4	31 R	50.4%	49.5%	50.4%	49.6%
26,473	OHIO	8,514	5,690	2,784	40	2,906 R	66.8%	32.7%	67.1%	32.9%
7,689	OLDHAM	2,969	1,604	1,359	6	245 R	54.0%	45.8%	54.1%	45.9%
12,554	OWEN	4,135	1,573	2,552	10	979 D	38.0%	61.7%	38.1%	61.9%
7,820	OWSLEY	2,353	2,107	241	5	1,866 R	89.5%	10.2%	89.7%	10.3%
11,719	PENDLETON	4,768	3,196	1,567	5	1,629 R	67.0%	32.9%	67.1%	32.9%
26,042	PERRY	9,927	6,099	3,814	14	2,285 R	61.4%	38.4%	61.5%	38.5%
49,477	PIKE	17,335	9,386	7,930	19	1,456 R	54.1%	45.7%	54.2%	45.8%
6,745	POWELL	1,892	1,160	732		428 R	61.3%	38.7%	61.3%	38.7%
34,010	PULASKI	11,857	9,348	2,494	15	6,854 R	78.8%	21.0%	78.9%	21.1%
3,871	ROBERTSON	1,382	742	640		102 R	53.7%	46.3%	53.7%	46.3%
15,406	ROCKCASTLE	4,766	3,858	908		2,950 R	80.9%	19.1%	80.9%	19.1%
9,467	ROWAN	3,032	1,857	1,170	5	687 R	61.2%	38.6%	61.3%	38.7%
11,854	RUSSELL	3,860	3,028	823	9	2,205 R	78.4%	21.3%	78.6%	21.4%
15,318	SCOTT	6,043	3,192	2,843	8	349 R	52.8%	47.0%	52.9%	47.1%
18,532	SHELBY	7,165	3,933	3,232		701 R	54.9%	45.1%	54.9%	45.1%
11,150	SIMPSON	4,125	1,635	2,490		855 D	39.6%	60.4%	39.6%	60.4%
7,785	SPENCER	2,516	1,565	947	4	618 R	62.2%	37.6%	62.3%	37.7%
12,236	TAYLOR	4,841	3,149	1,684	8	1,465 R	65.0%	34.8%	65.2%	34.8%
15,694	TODD	4,915	2,496	2,416	3	80 R	50.8%	49.2%	50.8%	49.2%
14,208	TRIGG	4,381	2,346	2,031	4	315 R	53.5%	46.4%	53.6%	46.4%
6,011	TRIMBLE	1,897	573	1,317	7	744 D	30.2%	69.4%	30.3%	69.7%
18,040	UNION	6,243	2,350	3,884	9	1,534 D	37.6%	62.2%	37.7%	62.3%
30,858	WARREN	13,024	7,931	5,092	1	2,839 R	60.9%	39.1%	60.9%	39.1%
14,773	WASHINGTON	5,204	2,933	2,266	5	667 R	56.4%	43.5%	56.4%	43.6%
16,208	WAYNE	4,542	2,907	1,635		1,272 R	64.0%	36.0%	64.0%	36.0%
20,762	WEBSTER	7,127	3,527	3,591	9	64 D	49.5%	50.4%	49.6%	50.4%
27,749	WHITLEY	9,680	8,060	1,610	10	6,450 R	83.3%	16.6%	83.4%	16.6%
8,783	WOLFE	2,626	1,270	1,356		86 D	48.4%	51.6%	48.4%	51.6%
11,784	WOODFORD	4,551	2,490	2,056	5	434 R	54.7%	45.2%	54.8%	45.2%
2,416,630	TOTAL	940,521	558,064	381,070	1,387	176,994 R	59.3%	40.5%	59.4%	40.6%

KENTUCKY

PRESIDENT 1924

1920 Census Population	County	Total Vote	Republican	Democratic	Other	Rep.-Dem. Plurality	Percentage Total Vote Rep.	Total Vote Dem.	Major Vote Rep.	Major Vote Dem.
17,289	ADAIR	5,032	2,725	2,269	38	456 R	54.2%	45.1%	54.6%	45.4%
16,761	ALLEN	5,501	3,092	2,373	36	719 R	56.2%	43.1%	56.6%	43.4%
9,982	ANDERSON	3,541	1,398	2,089	54	691 D	39.5%	59.0%	40.1%	59.9%
12,045	BALLARD	3,983	751	3,128	104	2,377 D	18.9%	78.5%	19.4%	80.6%
25,356	BARREN	7,965	3,431	4,449	85	1,018 D	43.1%	55.9%	43.5%	56.5%
11,996	BATH	3,839	1,723	2,095	21	372 D	44.9%	54.6%	45.1%	54.9%
33,988	BELL	7,896	5,371	2,166	359	3,205 R	68.0%	27.4%	71.3%	28.7%
9,572	BOONE	3,515	1,173	2,204	138	1,031 D	33.4%	62.7%	34.7%	65.3%
18,418	BOURBON	7,831	3,679	4,034	118	355 D	47.0%	51.5%	47.7%	52.3%
29,281	BOYD	10,893	6,042	4,079	772	1,963 R	55.5%	37.4%	59.7%	40.3%
14,998	BOYLE	6,200	2,656	3,197	347	541 D	42.8%	51.6%	45.4%	54.6%
10,210	BRACKEN	3,413	1,749	1,485	179	264 R	51.2%	43.5%	54.1%	45.9%
20,614	BREATHITT	4,544	1,708	2,826	10	1,118 D	37.6%	62.2%	37.7%	62.3%
19,652	BRECKINRIDGE	7,162	3,814	3,230	118	584 R	53.3%	45.1%	54.1%	45.9%
9,328	BULLITT	2,859	942	1,789	128	847 D	32.9%	62.6%	34.5%	65.5%
15,197	BUTLER	3,831	2,597	1,177	57	1,420 R	67.8%	30.7%	68.8%	31.2%
13,975	CALDWELL	4,832	2,475	2,183	174	292 R	51.2%	45.2%	53.1%	46.9%
20,802	CALLOWAY	4,882	936	3,790	156	2,854 D	19.2%	77.6%	19.8%	80.2%
61,868	CAMPBELL	24,849	12,242	5,564	7,043	6,678 R	49.3%	22.4%	68.8%	31.2%
8,231	CARLISLE	2,758	467	2,250	41	1,783 D	16.9%	81.6%	17.2%	82.8%
8,346	CARROLL	3,561	1,298	2,243	20	945 D	36.5%	63.0%	36.7%	63.3%
22,474	CARTER	7,213	4,414	2,552	247	1,862 R	61.2%	35.4%	63.4%	36.6%
17,213	CASEY	4,920	3,090	1,797	33	1,293 R	62.8%	36.5%	63.2%	36.8%
35,883	CHRISTIAN	13,850	7,150	6,585	115	565 R	51.6%	47.5%	52.1%	47.9%
17,901	CLARK	6,612	2,686	3,857	69	1,171 D	40.6%	58.3%	41.1%	58.9%
19,795	CLAY	4,815	3,551	1,144	120	2,407 R	73.7%	23.8%	75.6%	24.4%
8,589	CLINTON	2,607	2,047	543	17	1,504 R	78.5%	20.8%	79.0%	21.0%
13,125	CRITTENDEN	4,421	2,486	1,869	66	617 R	56.2%	42.3%	57.1%	42.9%
10,648	CUMBERLAND	3,049	2,113	918	18	1,195 R	69.3%	30.1%	69.7%	30.3%
40,733	DAVIESS	15,510	7,202	8,116	192	914 D	46.4%	52.3%	47.0%	53.0%
10,894	EDMONSON	3,188	2,005	1,183		822 R	62.9%	37.1%	62.9%	37.1%
8,887	ELLIOTT	2,324	591	1,702	31	1,111 D	25.4%	73.2%	25.8%	74.2%
15,569	ESTILL	4,343	2,071	2,052	220	19 R	47.7%	47.2%	50.2%	49.8%
54,664	FAYETTE	22,396	11,632	10,433	331	1,199 R	51.9%	46.6%	52.7%	47.3%
15,614	FLEMING	5,180	2,543	2,590	47	47 D	49.1%	50.0%	49.5%	50.5%
27,427	FLOYD	8,484	3,685	4,220	579	535 D	43.4%	49.7%	46.6%	53.4%
19,357	FRANKLIN	7,591	2,811	4,678	102	1,867 D	37.0%	61.6%	37.5%	62.5%
15,197	FULTON	4,292	891	3,336	65	2,445 D	20.8%	77.7%	21.1%	78.9%
4,664	GALLATIN	1,779	749	1,007	23	258 D	42.1%	56.6%	42.7%	57.3%
12,503	GARRARD	4,728	2,575	2,126	27	449 R	54.5%	45.0%	54.8%	45.2%
10,435	GRANT	3,579	1,424	1,923	232	499 D	39.8%	53.7%	42.5%	57.5%
32,483	GRAVES	9,813	2,279	7,266	268	4,987 D	23.2%	74.0%	23.9%	76.1%
19,927	GRAYSON	6,068	3,149	2,858	61	291 R	51.9%	47.1%	52.4%	47.6%
11,391	GREEN	3,470	1,909	1,548	13	361 R	55.0%	44.6%	55.2%	44.8%
20,062	GREENUP	5,286	2,490	1,932	864	558 R	47.1%	36.5%	56.3%	43.7%
6,945	HANCOCK	2,706	1,313	1,323	70	10 D	48.5%	48.9%	49.8%	50.2%
24,287	HARDIN	7,175	2,712	4,296	167	1,584 D	37.8%	59.9%	38.7%	61.3%
31,546	HARLAN	13,206	9,632	2,133	1,441	7,499 R	72.9%	16.2%	81.9%	18.1%
15,798	HARRISON	6,153	2,129	3,924	100	1,795 D	34.6%	63.8%	35.2%	64.8%
18,544	HART	5,642	2,687	2,862	93	175 D	47.6%	50.7%	48.4%	51.6%
27,609	HENDERSON	9,060	4,828	4,046	186	782 R	53.3%	44.7%	54.4%	45.6%
13,411	HENRY	5,656	1,910	3,706	40	1,796 D	33.8%	65.5%	34.0%	66.0%
10,244	HICKMAN	2,901	614	2,270	17	1,656 D	21.2%	78.2%	21.3%	78.7%
34,133	HOPKINS	11,793	5,231	5,864	698	633 D	44.4%	49.7%	47.1%	52.9%
11,687	JACKSON	3,046	2,686	284	76	2,402 R	88.2%	9.3%	90.4%	9.6%
286,369	JEFFERSON	117,293	61,475	50,409	5,409	11,066 R	52.4%	43.0%	54.9%	45.1%
12,205	JESSAMINE	4,764	2,144	2,470	150	326 D	45.0%	51.8%	46.5%	53.5%
19,622	JOHNSON	4,938	3,025	1,480	433	1,545 R	61.3%	30.0%	67.1%	32.9%
73,453	KENTON	30,446	13,444	7,948	9,054	5,496 R	44.2%	26.1%	62.8%	37.2%
11,655	KNOTT	3,173	866	2,286	21	1,420 D	27.3%	72.0%	27.5%	72.5%

KENTUCKY

PRESIDENT 1924

1920 Census Population	County	Total Vote	Republican	Democratic	Other	Rep.-Dem. Plurality	Percentage			
							Total Vote		Major Vote	
							Rep.	Dem.	Rep.	Dem.
24,172	KNOX	5,638	3,761	1,587	290	2,174 R	66.7%	28.1%	70.3%	29.7%
10,004	LARUE	3,390	1,368	1,993	29	625 D	40.4%	58.8%	40.7%	59.3%
19,814	LAUREL	4,880	3,211	1,451	218	1,760 R	65.8%	29.7%	68.9%	31.1%
17,643	LAWRENCE	5,040	2,509	2,445	86	64 R	49.8%	48.5%	50.6%	49.4%
11,918	LEE	2,708	1,319	1,348	41	29 D	48.7%	49.8%	49.5%	50.5%
10,097	LESLIE	2,291	2,035	223	33	1,812 R	88.8%	9.7%	90.1%	9.9%
24,467	LETCHER	5,711	3,112	1,912	687	1,200 R	54.5%	33.5%	61.9%	38.1%
15,829	LEWIS	4,642	3,002	1,445	195	1,557 R	64.7%	31.1%	67.5%	32.5%
16,481	LINCOLN	6,356	3,002	3,100	254	98 D	47.2%	48.8%	49.2%	50.8%
9,732	LIVINGSTON	3,085	1,250	1,768	67	518 D	40.5%	57.3%	41.4%	58.6%
23,633	LOGAN	8,637	3,686	4,772	179	1,086 D	42.7%	55.3%	43.6%	56.4%
8,795	LYON	2,716	976	1,696	44	720 D	35.9%	62.4%	36.5%	63.5%
37,246	MCCRACKEN	12,258	4,956	6,028	1,274	1,072 D	40.4%	49.2%	45.1%	54.9%
11,676	MCCREARY	3,056	2,283	533	240	1,750 R	74.7%	17.4%	81.1%	18.9%
12,502	MCLEAN	4,239	1,838	2,284	117	446 D	43.4%	53.9%	44.6%	55.4%
26,284	MADISON	10,269	5,253	4,895	121	358 R	51.2%	47.7%	51.8%	48.2%
13,859	MAGOFFIN	3,961	2,182	1,757	22	425 R	55.1%	44.4%	55.4%	44.6%
15,527	MARION	5,107	1,956	3,055	96	1,099 D	38.3%	59.8%	39.0%	61.0%
15,215	MARSHALL	3,993	1,175	2,752	66	1,577 D	29.4%	68.9%	29.9%	70.1%
7,654	MARTIN	2,042	1,481	364	197	1,117 R	72.5%	17.8%	80.3%	19.7%
17,760	MASON	7,021	3,372	3,525	124	153 D	48.0%	50.2%	48.9%	51.1%
9,442	MEADE	2,931	1,082	1,802	47	720 D	36.9%	61.5%	37.5%	62.5%
5,779	MENIFEE	1,339	445	873	21	428 D	33.2%	65.2%	33.8%	66.2%
14,795	MERCER	5,267	2,510	2,698	59	188 D	47.7%	51.2%	48.2%	51.8%
10,075	METCALFE	2,708	1,430	1,262	16	168 R	52.8%	46.6%	53.1%	46.9%
14,214	MONROE	3,442	2,434	970	38	1,464 R	70.7%	28.2%	71.5%	28.5%
12,245	MONTGOMERY	4,340	1,942	2,347	51	405 D	44.7%	54.1%	45.3%	54.7%
16,518	MORGAN	5,131	1,792	3,311	28	1,519 D	34.9%	64.5%	35.1%	64.9%
33,353	MUHLENBERG	10,471	5,210	4,379	882	831 R	49.8%	41.8%	54.3%	45.7%
16,137	NELSON	6,008	2,066	3,863	79	1,797 D	34.4%	64.3%	34.8%	65.2%
9,894	NICHOLAS	3,610	1,333	2,235	42	902 D	36.9%	61.9%	37.4%	62.6%
26,473	OHIO	9,067	4,909	3,817	341	1,092 R	54.1%	42.1%	56.3%	43.7%
7,689	OLDHAM	2,888	899	1,954	35	1,055 D	31.1%	67.7%	31.5%	68.5%
12,554	OWEN	4,107	914	3,155	38	2,241 D	22.3%	76.8%	22.5%	77.5%
7,820	OWSLEY	1,759	1,409	323	27	1,086 R	80.1%	18.4%	81.4%	18.6%
11,719	PENDLETON	4,290	2,117	2,028	145	89 R	49.3%	47.3%	51.1%	48.9%
26,042	PERRY	7,324	4,307	2,658	359	1,649 R	58.8%	36.3%	61.8%	38.2%
49,477	PIKE	13,471	6,990	5,835	646	1,155 R	51.9%	43.3%	54.5%	45.5%
6,745	POWELL	1,689	724	939	26	215 D	42.9%	55.6%	43.5%	56.5%
34,010	PULASKI	10,298	6,464	3,158	676	3,306 R	62.8%	30.7%	67.2%	32.8%
3,871	ROBERTSON	1,177	485	680	12	195 D	41.2%	57.8%	41.6%	58.4%
15,406	ROCKCASTLE	4,061	2,679	1,277	105	1,402 R	66.0%	31.4%	67.7%	32.3%
9,467	ROWAN	2,453	1,305	1,092	56	213 R	53.2%	44.5%	54.4%	45.6%
11,854	RUSSELL	3,506	2,258	1,224	24	1,034 R	64.4%	34.9%	64.8%	35.2%
15,318	SCOTT	6,188	2,315	3,805	68	1,490 D	37.4%	61.5%	37.8%	62.2%
18,532	SHELBY	7,100	2,936	4,092	72	1,156 D	41.4%	57.6%	41.8%	58.2%
11,150	SIMPSON	4,025	1,285	2,688	52	1,403 D	31.9%	66.8%	32.3%	67.7%
7,785	SPENCER	2,273	943	1,320	10	377 D	41.5%	58.1%	41.7%	58.3%
12,236	TAYLOR	4,312	2,227	2,052	33	175 R	51.6%	47.6%	52.0%	48.0%
15,694	TODD	4,673	1,935	2,679	59	744 D	41.4%	57.3%	41.9%	58.1%
14,208	TRIGG	4,769	2,108	2,625	36	517 D	44.2%	55.0%	44.5%	55.5%
6,011	TRIMBLE	2,028	335	1,676	17	1,341 D	16.5%	82.6%	16.7%	83.3%
18,040	UNION	5,537	1,768	3,493	276	1,725 D	31.9%	63.1%	33.6%	66.4%
30,858	WARREN	12,705	5,568	7,005	132	1,437 D	43.8%	55.1%	44.3%	55.7%
14,773	WASHINGTON	4,519	2,268	2,238	13	30 R	50.2%	49.5%	50.3%	49.7%
16,208	WAYNE	4,446	2,397	2,020	29	377 R	53.9%	45.4%	54.3%	45.7%
20,762	WEBSTER	6,680	3,160	3,449	71	289 D	47.3%	51.6%	47.8%	52.2%
27,749	WHITLEY	6,857	4,676	1,413	768	3,263 R	68.2%	20.6%	76.8%	23.2%
8,783	WOLFE	2,435	821	1,597	17	776 D	33.7%	65.6%	34.0%	66.0%
11,784	WOODFORD	4,562	2,077	2,472	13	395 D	45.5%	54.2%	45.7%	54.3%
2,416,630	TOTAL	813,843	396,758	375,593	41,492	21,165 R	48.8%	46.2%	51.4%	48.6%

KENTUCKY

PRESIDENT 1920

1920 Census Population	County	Total Vote	Republican	Democratic	Other	Rep.-Dem. Plurality	Percentage Total Vote Rep.	Percentage Total Vote Dem.	Percentage Major Vote Rep.	Percentage Major Vote Dem.
17,289	ADAIR	6,265	3,526	2,725	14	801 R	56.3%	43.5%	56.4%	43.6%
16,761	ALLEN	5,770	3,476	2,255	39	1,221 R	60.2%	39.1%	60.7%	39.3%
9,982	ANDERSON	4,330	1,819	2,499	12	680 D	42.0%	57.7%	42.1%	57.9%
12,045	BALLARD	5,213	1,107	3,987	119	2,880 D	21.2%	76.5%	21.7%	78.3%
25,356	BARREN	9,531	3,972	5,499	60	1,527 D	41.7%	57.7%	41.9%	58.1%
11,996	BATH	4,459	1,997	2,440	22	443 D	44.8%	54.7%	45.0%	55.0%
33,988	BELL	9,014	6,691	2,277	46	4,414 R	74.2%	25.3%	74.6%	25.4%
9,572	BOONE	4,480	973	3,472	35	2,499 D	21.7%	77.5%	21.9%	78.1%
18,418	BOURBON	9,524	4,029	5,452	43	1,423 D	42.3%	57.2%	42.5%	57.5%
29,281	BOYD	11,563	6,334	5,103	126	1,231 R	54.8%	44.1%	55.4%	44.6%
14,998	BOYLE	7,342	3,205	4,099	38	894 D	43.7%	55.8%	43.9%	56.1%
10,210	BRACKEN	4,468	1,791	2,621	56	830 D	40.1%	58.7%	40.6%	59.4%
20,614	BREATHITT	5,232	2,464	2,737	31	273 D	47.1%	52.3%	47.4%	52.6%
19,652	BRECKINRIDGE	8,099	4,368	3,702	29	666 R	53.9%	45.7%	54.1%	45.9%
9,328	BULLITT	3,954	1,393	2,548	13	1,155 D	35.2%	64.4%	35.3%	64.7%
15,197	BUTLER	5,466	4,097	1,356	13	2,741 R	75.0%	24.8%	75.1%	24.9%
13,975	CALDWELL	5,792	2,958	2,746	88	212 R	51.1%	47.4%	51.9%	48.1%
20,802	CALLOWAY	6,284	1,520	4,574	190	3,054 D	24.2%	72.8%	24.9%	75.1%
61,868	CAMPBELL	23,976	12,210	10,597	1,169	1,613 R	50.9%	44.2%	53.5%	46.5%
8,231	CARLISLE	3,442	688	2,688	66	2,000 D	20.0%	78.1%	20.4%	79.6%
8,346	CARROLL	4,141	906	3,209	26	2,303 D	21.9%	77.5%	22.0%	78.0%
22,474	CARTER	7,414	4,595	2,757	62	1,838 R	62.0%	37.2%	62.5%	37.5%
17,213	CASEY	5,533	3,543	1,951	39	1,592 R	64.0%	35.3%	64.5%	35.5%
35,883	CHRISTIAN	16,057	8,743	7,209	105	1,534 R	54.4%	44.9%	54.8%	45.2%
17,901	CLARK	7,987	3,105	4,846	36	1,741 D	38.9%	60.7%	39.1%	60.9%
19,795	CLAY	5,008	4,015	960	33	3,055 R	80.2%	19.2%	80.7%	19.3%
8,589	CLINTON	2,798	2,356	431	11	1,925 R	84.2%	15.4%	84.5%	15.5%
13,125	CRITTENDEN	5,311	3,149	2,138	24	1,011 R	59.3%	40.3%	59.6%	40.4%
10,648	CUMBERLAND	3,324	2,380	931	13	1,449 R	71.6%	28.0%	71.9%	28.1%
40,733	DAVIESS	17,359	7,584	9,669	106	2,085 D	43.7%	55.7%	44.0%	56.0%
10,894	EDMONSON	3,535	2,348	1,171	16	1,177 R	66.4%	33.1%	66.7%	33.3%
8,887	ELLIOTT	2,637	860	1,764	13	904 D	32.6%	66.9%	32.8%	67.2%
15,569	ESTILL	4,387	2,552	1,823	12	729 R	58.2%	41.6%	58.3%	41.7%
54,664	FAYETTE	24,139	11,032	12,926	181	1,894 D	45.7%	53.5%	46.0%	54.0%
15,614	FLEMING	6,474	2,960	3,488	26	528 D	45.7%	53.9%	45.9%	54.1%
27,427	FLOYD	6,468	2,825	3,597	46	772 D	43.7%	55.6%	44.0%	56.0%
19,357	FRANKLIN	8,609	2,710	5,878	21	3,168 D	31.5%	68.3%	31.6%	68.4%
15,197	FULTON	5,239	1,365	3,843	31	2,478 D	26.1%	73.4%	26.2%	73.8%
4,664	GALLATIN	2,327	536	1,782	9	1,246 D	23.0%	76.6%	23.1%	76.9%
12,503	GARRARD	5,469	2,994	2,434	41	560 R	54.7%	44.5%	55.2%	44.8%
10,435	GRANT	4,337	1,613	2,686	38	1,073 D	37.2%	61.9%	37.5%	62.5%
32,483	GRAVES	12,500	3,241	9,018	241	5,777 D	25.9%	72.1%	26.4%	73.6%
19,927	GRAYSON	7,049	4,174	2,830	45	1,344 R	59.2%	40.1%	59.6%	40.4%
11,391	GREEN	4,050	2,310	1,723	17	587 R	57.0%	42.5%	57.3%	42.7%
20,062	GREENUP	5,963	3,111	2,754	98	357 R	52.2%	46.2%	53.0%	47.0%
6,945	HANCOCK	2,879	1,446	1,384	49	62 R	50.2%	48.1%	51.1%	48.9%
24,287	HARDIN	8,782	3,334	5,382	66	2,048 D	38.0%	61.3%	38.3%	61.7%
31,546	HARLAN	9,351	7,493	1,805	53	5,688 R	80.1%	19.3%	80.6%	19.4%
15,798	HARRISON	7,239	2,378	4,804	57	2,426 D	32.8%	66.4%	33.1%	66.9%
18,544	HART	6,313	3,264	2,972	77	292 R	51.7%	47.1%	52.3%	47.7%
27,609	HENDERSON	11,718	4,161	7,272	285	3,111 D	35.5%	62.1%	36.4%	63.6%
13,411	HENRY	6,897	2,208	4,640	49	2,432 D	32.0%	67.3%	32.2%	67.8%
10,244	HICKMAN	3,934	866	3,045	23	2,179 D	22.0%	77.4%	22.1%	77.9%
34,133	HOPKINS	14,836	6,732	7,829	275	1,097 D	45.4%	52.8%	46.2%	53.8%
11,687	JACKSON	3,444	3,174	260	10	2,914 R	92.2%	7.5%	92.4%	7.6%
286,369	JEFFERSON	125,549	68,202	56,046	1,301	12,156 R	54.3%	44.6%	54.9%	45.1%
12,205	JESSAMINE	5,689	2,349	3,206	134	857 D	41.3%	56.4%	42.3%	57.7%
19,622	JOHNSON	6,137	4,373	1,714	50	2,659 R	71.3%	27.9%	71.8%	28.2%
73,453	KENTON	28,730	11,411	16,300	1,019	4,889 D	39.7%	56.7%	41.2%	58.8%
11,655	KNOTT	3,108	802	2,295	11	1,493 D	25.8%	73.8%	25.9%	74.1%

KENTUCKY

PRESIDENT 1920

1920 Census Population	County	Total Vote	Republican	Democratic	Other	Rep.-Dem. Plurality	Percentage: Total Vote Rep.	Total Vote Dem.	Major Vote Rep.	Major Vote Dem.
24,172	KNOX	6,818	5,228	1,534	56	3,694 R	76.7%	22.5%	77.3%	22.7%
10,004	LARUE	4,211	1,838	2,361	12	523 D	43.6%	56.1%	43.8%	56.2%
19,814	LAUREL	5,909	4,252	1,621	36	2,631 R	72.0%	27.4%	72.4%	27.6%
17,643	LAWRENCE	5,433	2,849	2,558	26	291 R	52.4%	47.1%	52.7%	47.3%
11,918	LEE	3,116	1,856	1,246	14	610 R	59.6%	40.0%	59.8%	40.2%
10,097	LESLIE	2,734	2,576	142	16	2,434 R	94.2%	5.2%	94.8%	5.2%
24,467	LETCHER	6,301	4,317	1,960	24	2,357 R	68.5%	31.1%	68.8%	31.2%
15,829	LEWIS	5,827	4,186	1,550	91	2,636 R	71.8%	26.6%	73.0%	27.0%
16,481	LINCOLN	7,566	3,710	3,787	69	77 D	49.0%	50.1%	49.5%	50.5%
9,732	LIVINGSTON	3,784	1,790	1,933	61	143 D	47.3%	51.1%	48.1%	51.9%
23,633	LOGAN	10,125	3,948	6,111	66	2,163 D	39.0%	60.4%	39.2%	60.8%
8,795	LYON	3,282	1,275	1,968	39	693 D	38.8%	60.0%	39.3%	60.7%
37,246	MCCRACKEN	14,880	6,085	8,496	299	2,411 D	40.9%	57.1%	41.7%	58.3%
11,676	MCCREARY	3,439	2,889	525	25	2,364 R	84.0%	15.3%	84.6%	15.4%
12,502	MCLEAN	5,221	2,408	2,754	59	346 D	46.1%	52.7%	46.6%	53.4%
26,284	MADISON	11,739	6,012	5,647	80	365 R	51.2%	48.1%	51.6%	48.4%
13,859	MAGOFFIN	3,715	2,347	1,352	16	995 R	63.2%	36.4%	63.4%	36.6%
15,527	MARION	6,258	2,431	3,807	20	1,376 D	38.8%	60.8%	39.0%	61.0%
15,215	MARSHALL	5,492	1,883	3,569	40	1,686 D	34.3%	65.0%	34.5%	65.5%
7,654	MARTIN	2,077	1,726	330	21	1,396 R	83.1%	15.9%	83.9%	16.1%
17,760	MASON	8,476	3,743	4,691	42	948 D	44.2%	55.3%	44.4%	55.6%
9,442	MEADE	3,693	1,468	2,195	30	727 D	39.8%	59.4%	40.1%	59.9%
5,779	MENIFEE	1,746	581	1,149	16	568 D	33.3%	65.8%	33.6%	66.4%
14,795	MERCER	6,442	2,786	3,623	33	837 D	43.2%	56.2%	43.5%	56.5%
10,075	METCALFE	3,259	1,809	1,442	8	367 R	55.5%	44.2%	55.6%	44.4%
14,214	MONROE	4,549	3,426	1,108	15	2,318 R	75.3%	24.4%	75.6%	24.4%
12,245	MONTGOMERY	5,260	2,163	3,069	28	906 D	41.1%	58.3%	41.3%	58.7%
16,518	MORGAN	5,166	1,802	3,347	17	1,545 D	34.9%	64.8%	35.0%	65.0%
33,353	MUHLENBERG	11,753	6,667	4,824	262	1,843 R	56.7%	41.0%	58.0%	42.0%
16,137	NELSON	8,033	2,945	5,061	27	2,116 D	36.7%	63.0%	36.8%	63.2%
9,894	NICHOLAS	4,494	1,496	2,953	45	1,457 D	33.3%	65.7%	33.6%	66.4%
26,473	OHIO	9,571	5,371	4,011	189	1,360 R	56.1%	41.9%	57.2%	42.8%
7,689	OLDHAM	3,684	1,014	2,655	15	1,641 D	27.5%	72.1%	27.6%	72.4%
12,554	OWEN	5,689	1,049	4,623	17	3,574 D	18.4%	81.3%	18.5%	81.5%
7,820	OWSLEY	2,180	1,914	257	9	1,657 R	87.8%	11.8%	88.2%	11.8%
11,719	PENDLETON	4,752	2,105	2,598	49	493 D	44.3%	54.7%	44.8%	55.2%
26,042	PERRY	6,573	4,345	2,203	25	2,142 R	66.1%	33.5%	66.4%	33.6%
49,477	PIKE	13,622	7,911	5,619	92	2,292 R	58.1%	41.2%	58.5%	41.5%
6,745	POWELL	1,884	835	1,038	11	203 D	44.3%	55.1%	44.6%	55.4%
34,010	PULASKI	11,059	7,262	3,749	48	3,513 R	65.7%	33.9%	66.0%	34.0%
3,871	ROBERTSON	1,570	623	940	7	317 D	39.7%	59.9%	39.9%	60.1%
15,406	ROCKCASTLE	5,018	3,561	1,438	19	2,123 R	71.0%	28.7%	71.2%	28.8%
9,467	ROWAN	2,847	1,564	1,264	19	300 R	54.9%	44.4%	55.3%	44.7%
11,854	RUSSELL	3,751	2,587	1,157	7	1,430 R	69.0%	30.8%	69.1%	30.9%
15,318	SCOTT	7,679	2,661	4,993	25	2,332 D	34.7%	65.0%	34.8%	65.2%
18,532	SHELBY	8,879	3,402	5,446	31	2,044 D	38.3%	61.3%	38.4%	61.6%
11,150	SIMPSON	4,907	1,680	3,206	21	1,526 D	34.2%	65.3%	34.4%	65.6%
7,785	SPENCER	3,253	1,102	2,135	16	1,033 D	33.9%	65.6%	34.0%	66.0%
12,236	TAYLOR	4,898	2,493	2,380	25	113 R	50.9%	48.6%	51.2%	48.8%
15,694	TODD	6,010	2,663	3,292	55	629 D	44.3%	54.8%	44.7%	55.3%
14,208	TRIGG	5,548	2,420	3,056	72	636 D	43.6%	55.1%	44.2%	55.8%
6,011	TRIMBLE	2,434	361	2,057	16	1,696 D	14.8%	84.5%	14.9%	85.1%
18,040	UNION	6,947	1,943	4,919	85	2,976 D	28.0%	70.8%	28.3%	71.7%
30,858	WARREN	12,599	5,474	7,010	115	1,536 D	43.4%	55.6%	43.8%	56.2%
14,773	WASHINGTON	5,502	2,892	2,600	10	292 R	52.6%	47.3%	52.7%	47.3%
16,208	WAYNE	4,849	2,992	1,827	30	1,165 R	61.7%	37.7%	62.1%	37.9%
20,762	WEBSTER	8,415	3,554	4,831	30	1,277 D	42.2%	57.4%	42.4%	57.6%
27,749	WHITLEY	8,819	7,235	1,556	28	5,679 R	82.0%	17.6%	82.3%	17.7%
8,783	WOLFE	2,432	939	1,476	17	537 D	38.6%	60.7%	38.9%	61.1%
11,784	WOODFORD	5,542	2,218	3,299	25	1,081 D	40.0%	59.5%	40.2%	59.8%
2,416,630	TOTAL	918,636	452,480	456,497	9,659	4,017 D	49.3%	49.7%	49.8%	50.2%

KENTUCKY

ELECTION NOTES

1956 Other vote was 2,657 Byrd (States Rights); 2,145 Holtwick (Prohibition); 358 Hass (Socialist Labor). Kentucky was the only state where the States Rights candidate was Harry Flood Byrd.

1952 Other vote was 1,161 Hamblen (Prohibition); 893 Hass (Socialist Labor); 336 Hallinan (Progressive).

1948 Other vote was 10,411 Thurmond (States Rights); 1,567 Wallace (Progressive); 1,284 Thomas (Socialist); 1,245 Watson (Prohibition); 185 Teichert (Socialist Labor).

1944 Other vote was 2,023 Watson (Prohibition); 535 Thomas (Socialist); 329 Teichert (Socialist Labor).

1940 Other vote was 1,443 Babson (Prohibition); 1,014 Thomas (Socialist).

1936 Other vote was 12,501 Lemke (Union); 939 Colvin (Prohibition); 627 Thomas (Socialist); 294 Aiken (Socialist Labor); 207 Browder (Communist).

1932 Other vote was 3,853 Thomas (Socialist); 2,252 Upshaw (Prohibition); 1,393 Reynolds (Socialist Labor); 271 Foster (Communist).

1928 Other vote was 783 Thomas (Socialist); 316 Reynolds (Socialist Labor); 288 Foster (Communist).

1924 Other vote was 38,465 LaFollette (Progressive); 1,501 Johns (Socialist Labor); 1,300 Nations (American); 226 Wallace (Commonwealth Land).

1920 Other vote was 6,409 Debs (Socialist); 3,250 Watkins (Prohibition).

LOUISIANA

POPULAR VOTE FOR PRESIDENT 1920 TO 1956

	Total	Republican		Democratic		Other		Percentage			
								Total Vote		Major Vote	
Year	Vote	Vote	Candidate	Vote	Candidate	Vote	Plurality	Rep.	Dem.	Rep.	Dem.
1956	617,544	329,047	Eisenhower, Dwight D.	243,977	Stevenson, Adlai E.	44,520	85,070 R	53.3%	39.5%	57.4%	42.6%
1952	651,952	306,925	Eisenhower, Dwight D.	345,027	Stevenson, Adlai E.		38,102 D	47.1%	52.9%	47.1%	52.9%
1948 **	416,336	72,657	Dewey, Thomas E.	136,344	Truman, Harry S.	207,335	67,946 SR	17.5%	32.7%	34.8%	65.2%
1944	349,383	67,750	Dewey, Thomas E.	281,564	Roosevelt, Franklin D.	69	213,814 D	19.4%	80.6%	19.4%	80.6%
1940	372,305	52,446	Willkie, Wendell	319,751	Roosevelt, Franklin D.	108	267,305 D	14.1%	85.9%	14.1%	85.9%
1936	329,778	36,791	Landon, Alfred M.	292,894	Roosevelt, Franklin D.	93	256,103 D	11.2%	88.8%	11.2%	88.8%
1932	268,804	18,853	Hoover, Herbert C.	249,418	Roosevelt, Franklin D.	533	230,565 D	7.0%	92.8%	7.0%	93.0%
1928	215,833	51,160	Hoover, Herbert C.	164,655	Smith, Alfred E.	18	113,495 D	23.7%	76.3%	23.7%	76.3%
1924	121,951	24,670	Coolidge, Calvin	93,218	Davis, John W.	4,063	68,548 D	20.2%	76.4%	20.9%	79.1%
1920	126,397	38,539	Harding, Warren G.	87,519	Cox, James M.	339	48,980 D	30.5%	69.2%	30.6%	69.4%

In 1948 other vote was 204,290 States Rights; 3,035 Progressive and 10 scattered.

ELECTORAL COLLEGE VOTE 1920 TO 1956

Year	Total	Republican	Democratic	Other
1956	10	10	—	—
1952	10	—	10	—
1948	10	—	—	10 SR
1944	10	—	10	—
1940	10	—	10	—
1936	10	—	10	—
1932	10	—	10	—
1928	10	—	10	—
1924	10	—	10	—
1920	10	—	10	—

LOUISIANA

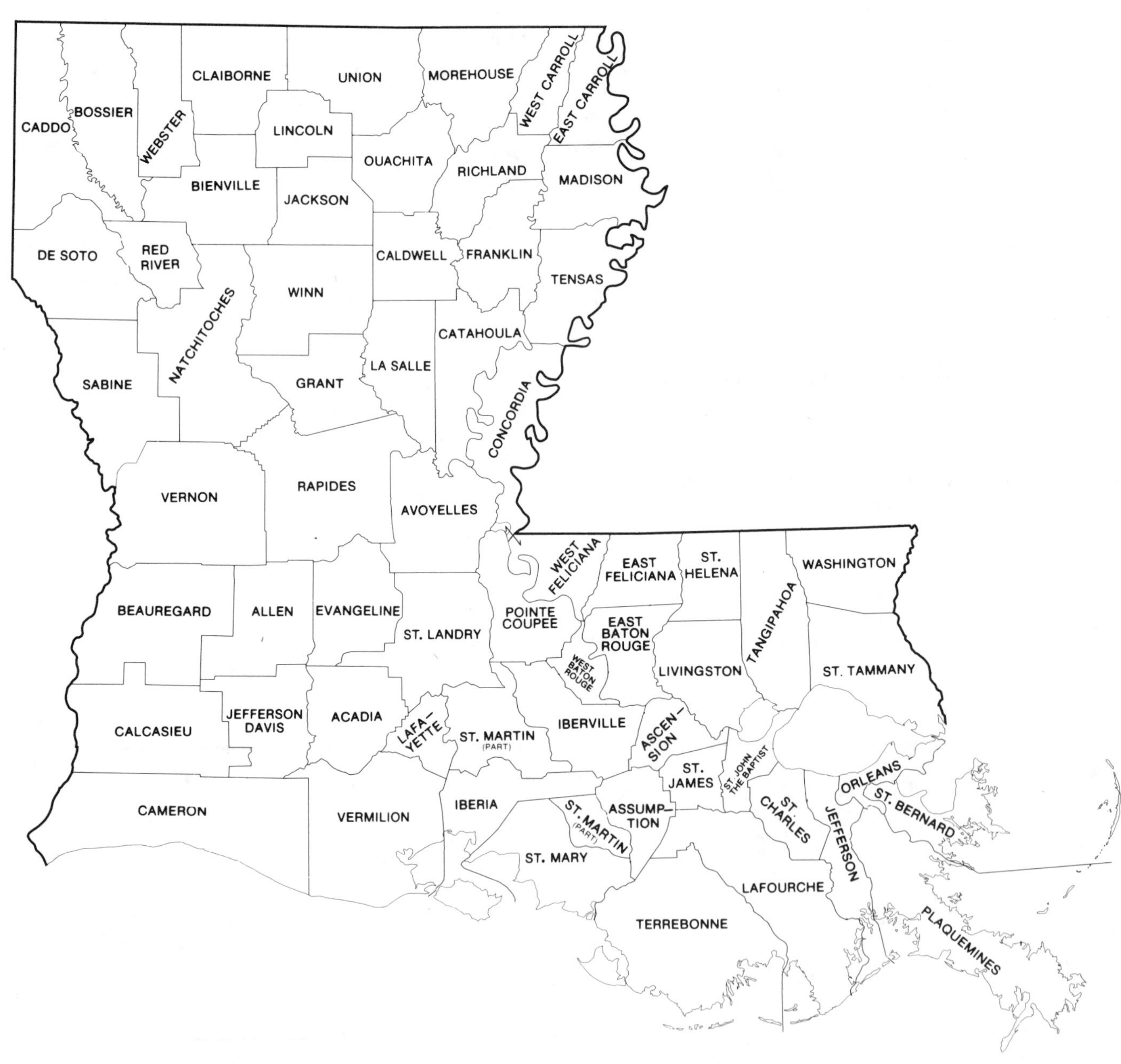
CADDO
BOSSIER
WEBSTER
CLAIBORNE
UNION
MOREHOUSE
WEST CARROLL
EAST CARROLL
LINCOLN
OUACHITA
RICHLAND
MADISON
BIENVILLE
JACKSON
DE SOTO
RED RIVER
CALDWELL
FRANKLIN
TENSAS
NATCHITOCHES
WINN
CATAHOULA
LA SALLE
SABINE
GRANT
CONCORDIA
VERNON
RAPIDES
AVOYELLES
WEST FELICIANA
EAST FELICIANA
ST. HELENA
WASHINGTON
BEAUREGARD
ALLEN
EVANGELINE
ST. LANDRY
POINTE COUPEE
EAST BATON ROUGE
TANGIPAHOA
WEST BATON ROUGE
LIVINGSTON
ST. TAMMANY
CALCASIEU
JEFFERSON DAVIS
ACADIA
LAFAYETTE
ST. MARTIN (PART)
IBERVILLE
ASCENSION
ST. JAMES
ST. JOHN THE BAPTIST
ORLEANS
ST. BERNARD
CAMERON
VERMILION
IBERIA
ST. MARTIN (PART)
ASSUMPTION
ST. CHARLES
JEFFERSON
ST. MARY
LAFOURCHE
TERREBONNE
PLAQUEMINES

LOUISIANA

PRESIDENT 1956

1950 Census Population	Parish	Total Vote	Republican	Democratic	Other	Rep.-Dem. Plurality	Percentage Total Vote Rep.	Percentage Total Vote Dem.	Percentage Major Vote Rep.	Percentage Major Vote Dem.
47,050	ACADIA	10,517	4,204	6,122	191	1,918 D	40.0%	58.2%	40.7%	59.3%
18,835	ALLEN	4,893	2,469	2,284	140	185 R	50.5%	46.7%	51.9%	48.1%
22,387	ASCENSION	4,535	1,853	2,606	76	753 D	40.9%	57.5%	41.6%	58.4%
17,278	ASSUMPTION	3,096	1,708	1,282	106	426 R	55.2%	41.4%	57.1%	42.9%
38,031	AVOYELLES	7,319	3,255	3,628	436	373 D	44.5%	49.6%	47.3%	52.7%
17,766	BEAUREGARD	5,146	2,711	2,276	159	435 R	52.7%	44.2%	54.4%	45.6%
19,105	BIENVILLE	3,100	1,515	815	770	700 R	48.9%	26.3%	65.0%	35.0%
40,139	BOSSIER	6,345	3,107	1,954	1,284	1,153 R	49.0%	30.8%	61.4%	38.6%
176,547	CADDO	38,849	23,432	10,780	4,637	12,652 R	60.3%	27.7%	68.5%	31.5%
89,635	CALCASIEU	26,733	13,760	12,255	718	1,505 R	51.5%	45.8%	52.9%	47.1%
10,293	CALDWELL	1,669	587	468	614	119 R	35.2%	28.0%	55.6%	44.4%
6,244	CAMERON	1,360	547	794	19	247 D	40.2%	58.4%	40.8%	59.2%
11,834	CATAHOULA	1,802	845	707	250	138 R	46.9%	39.2%	54.4%	45.6%
25,063	CLAIBORNE	3,886	2,084	810	992	1,274 R	53.6%	20.8%	72.0%	28.0%
14,398	CONCORDIA	2,116	841	699	576	142 R	39.7%	33.0%	54.6%	45.4%
24,398	DE SOTO	3,771	2,011	1,206	554	805 R	53.3%	32.0%	62.5%	37.5%
158,236	EAST BATON ROUGE	42,331	24,018	17,072	1,241	6,946 R	56.7%	40.3%	58.5%	41.5%
16,302	EAST CARROLL	1,347	415	545	387	130 D	30.8%	40.5%	43.2%	56.8%
19,133	EAST FELICIANA	2,435	912	1,304	219	392 D	37.5%	53.6%	41.2%	58.8%
31,629	EVANGELINE	5,680	2,170	3,336	174	1,166 D	38.2%	58.7%	39.4%	60.6%
29,376	FRANKLIN	3,457	1,130	1,352	975	222 D	32.7%	39.1%	45.5%	54.5%
14,263	GRANT	3,539	1,630	1,542	367	88 R	46.1%	43.6%	51.4%	48.6%
40,059	IBERIA	10,615	6,733	3,544	338	3,189 R	63.4%	33.4%	65.5%	34.5%
26,750	IBERVILLE	3,924	1,843	2,018	63	175 D	47.0%	51.4%	47.7%	52.3%
15,434	JACKSON	2,862	1,553	916	393	637 R	54.3%	32.0%	62.9%	37.1%
103,873	JEFFERSON	42,499	24,324	16,577	1,598	7,747 R	57.2%	39.0%	59.5%	40.5%
26,298	JEFFERSON DAVIS	6,626	4,170	2,346	110	1,824 R	62.9%	35.4%	64.0%	36.0%
57,743	LAFAYETTE	11,753	6,711	4,695	347	2,016 R	57.1%	39.9%	58.8%	41.2%
42,209	LAFOURCHE	9,528	5,741	3,466	321	2,275 R	60.3%	36.4%	62.4%	37.6%
12,717	LA SALLE	3,062	1,885	951	226	934 R	61.6%	31.1%	66.5%	33.5%
25,782	LINCOLN	4,520	2,676	1,014	830	1,662 R	59.2%	22.4%	72.5%	27.5%
20,054	LIVINGSTON	4,372	1,628	2,571	173	943 D	37.2%	58.8%	38.8%	61.2%
17,451	MADISON	1,692	461	276	955	185 R	27.2%	16.3%	62.6%	37.4%
32,038	MOREHOUSE	5,182	1,850	1,512	1,820	338 R	35.7%	29.2%	55.0%	45.0%
38,144	NATCHITOCHES	5,770	3,203	2,028	539	1,175 R	55.5%	35.1%	61.2%	38.8%
570,445	ORLEANS	164,634	93,082	64,958	6,594	28,124 R	56.5%	39.5%	58.9%	41.1%
74,713	OUACHITA	15,158	7,094	4,372	3,692	2,722 R	46.8%	28.8%	61.9%	38.1%
14,239	PLAQUEMINES	3,692	2,998	534	160	2,464 R	81.2%	14.5%	84.9%	15.1%
21,841	POINTE COUPEE	2,958	1,332	1,542	84	210 D	45.0%	52.1%	46.3%	53.7%
90,648	RAPIDES	16,911	9,105	5,961	1,845	3,144 R	53.8%	35.2%	60.4%	39.6%
12,113	RED RIVER	1,788	661	803	324	142 D	37.0%	44.9%	45.2%	54.8%
26,672	RICHLAND	3,557	1,063	1,094	1,400	31 D	29.9%	30.8%	49.3%	50.7%
20,880	SABINE	4,134	2,086	1,800	248	286 R	50.5%	43.5%	53.7%	46.3%
11,087	ST. BERNARD	7,217	3,648	3,283	286	365 R	50.5%	45.5%	52.6%	47.4%
13,363	ST. CHARLES	4,177	2,417	1,671	89	746 R	57.9%	40.0%	59.1%	40.9%
9,013	ST. HELENA	1,689	545	997	147	452 D	32.3%	59.0%	35.3%	64.7%
15,334	ST. JAMES	3,759	1,849	1,832	78	17 R	49.2%	48.7%	50.2%	49.8%
14,861	ST. JOHN THE BAPTIST	2,714	1,372	1,278	64	94 R	50.6%	47.1%	51.8%	48.2%
78,476	ST. LANDRY	9,970	5,141	4,435	394	706 R	51.6%	44.5%	53.7%	46.3%
26,353	ST. MARTIN	3,780	1,615	2,069	96	454 D	42.7%	54.7%	43.8%	56.2%
35,848	ST. MARY	6,663	4,097	2,395	171	1,702 R	61.5%	35.9%	63.1%	36.9%
26,988	ST. TAMMANY	7,639	3,965	3,373	301	592 R	51.9%	44.2%	54.0%	46.0%
53,218	TANGIPAHOA	11,185	5,788	4,831	566	957 R	51.7%	43.2%	54.5%	45.5%
13,209	TENSAS	1,026	359	324	343	35 R	35.0%	31.6%	52.6%	47.4%
43,328	TERREBONNE	7,684	4,983	2,460	241	2,523 R	64.8%	32.0%	66.9%	33.1%
19,141	UNION	3,418	1,384	878	1,156	506 R	40.5%	25.7%	61.2%	38.8%
36,929	VERMILION	8,695	3,877	4,564	254	687 D	44.6%	52.5%	45.9%	54.1%
18,974	VERNON	4,762	2,372	2,158	232	214 R	49.8%	45.3%	52.4%	47.6%
38,371	WASHINGTON	8,047	3,081	4,658	308	1,577 D	38.3%	57.9%	39.8%	60.2%
35,704	WEBSTER	6,733	3,280	2,352	1,101	928 R	48.7%	34.9%	58.2%	41.8%

LOUISIANA

PRESIDENT 1956

1950 Census Population	Parish	Total Vote	Republican	Democratic	Other	Rep.-Dem. Plurality	Percentage Total Vote Rep.	Percentage Total Vote Dem.	Percentage Major Vote Rep.	Percentage Major Vote Dem.
11,738	WEST BATON ROUGE	2,314	1,035	1,208	71	173 D	44.7%	52.2%	46.1%	53.9%
17,248	WEST CARROLL	2,622	658	875	1,089	217 D	25.1%	33.4%	42.9%	57.1%
10,169	WEST FELICIANA	784	442	296	46	146 R	56.4%	37.8%	59.9%	40.1%
16,119	WINN	3,503	1,736	1,225	542	511 R	49.6%	35.0%	58.6%	41.4%
2,683,516	TOTAL	617,544	329,047	243,977	44,520	85,070 R	53.3%	39.5%	57.4%	42.6%

LOUISIANA

PRESIDENT 1952

1950 Census Population	Parish	Total Vote	Republican	Democratic	Other	Rep.-Dem. Plurality	Percentage Total Vote Rep.	Percentage Total Vote Dem.	Percentage Major Vote Rep.	Percentage Major Vote Dem.
47,050	ACADIA	10,030	4,167	5,863		1,696 D	41.5%	58.5%	41.5%	58.5%
18,835	ALLEN	5,215	1,461	3,754		2,293 D	28.0%	72.0%	28.0%	72.0%
22,387	ASCENSION	5,380	1,787	3,593		1,806 D	33.2%	66.8%	33.2%	66.8%
17,278	ASSUMPTION	2,857	1,210	1,647		437 D	42.4%	57.6%	42.4%	57.6%
38,031	AVOYELLES	6,884	2,479	4,405		1,926 D	36.0%	64.0%	36.0%	64.0%
17,766	BEAUREGARD	1,785	789	996		207 D	44.2%	55.8%	44.2%	55.8%
19,105	BIENVILLE	3,740	1,986	1,754		232 R	53.1%	46.9%	53.1%	46.9%
40,139	BOSSIER	6,360	3,677	2,683		994 R	57.8%	42.2%	57.8%	42.2%
176,547	CADDO	42,404	27,850	14,554		13,296 R	65.7%	34.3%	65.7%	34.3%
89,635	CALCASIEU	26,916	11,102	15,814		4,712 D	41.2%	58.8%	41.2%	58.8%
10,293	CALDWELL	2,123	961	1,162		201 D	45.3%	54.7%	45.3%	54.7%
6,244	CAMERON	1,689	684	1,005		321 D	40.5%	59.5%	40.5%	59.5%
11,834	CATAHOULA	2,220	884	1,336		452 D	39.8%	60.2%	39.8%	60.2%
25,063	CLAIBORNE	4,326	2,796	1,530		1,266 R	64.6%	35.4%	64.6%	35.4%
14,398	CONCORDIA	2,362	1,110	1,252		142 D	47.0%	53.0%	47.0%	53.0%
24,398	DE SOTO	3,981	2,303	1,678		625 R	57.8%	42.2%	57.8%	42.2%
158,236	EAST BATON ROUGE	42,798	19,693	23,105		3,412 D	46.0%	54.0%	46.0%	54.0%
16,302	EAST CARROLL	1,675	757	918		161 D	45.2%	54.8%	45.2%	54.8%
19,133	EAST FELICIANA	1,895	876	1,019		143 D	46.2%	53.8%	46.2%	53.8%
31,629	EVANGELINE	5,843	2,445	3,398		953 D	41.8%	58.2%	41.8%	58.2%
29,376	FRANKLIN	4,447	1,614	2,833		1,219 D	36.3%	63.7%	36.3%	63.7%
14,263	GRANT	4,089	1,443	2,646		1,203 D	35.3%	64.7%	35.3%	64.7%
40,059	IBERIA	9,709	5,669	4,040		1,629 R	58.4%	41.6%	58.4%	41.6%
26,750	IBERVILLE	5,207	1,710	3,497		1,787 D	32.8%	67.2%	32.8%	67.2%
15,434	JACKSON	4,431	1,614	2,817		1,203 D	36.4%	63.6%	36.4%	63.6%
103,873	JEFFERSON	36,455	17,090	19,365		2,275 D	46.9%	53.1%	46.9%	53.1%
26,298	JEFFERSON DAVIS	7,031	3,447	3,584		137 D	49.0%	51.0%	49.0%	51.0%
57,743	LAFAYETTE	12,913	6,470	6,443		27 R	50.1%	49.9%	50.1%	49.9%
42,209	LAFOURCHE	9,135	3,739	5,396		1,657 D	40.9%	59.1%	40.9%	59.1%
12,717	LA SALLE	3,693	1,692	2,001		309 D	45.8%	54.2%	45.8%	54.2%
25,782	LINCOLN	5,083	3,074	2,009		1,065 R	60.5%	39.5%	60.5%	39.5%
20,054	LIVINGSTON	5,014	1,436	3,578		2,142 D	28.6%	71.4%	28.6%	71.4%
17,451	MADISON	1,948	1,253	695		558 R	64.3%	35.7%	64.3%	35.7%
32,038	MOREHOUSE	5,573	2,567	3,006		439 D	46.1%	53.9%	46.1%	53.9%
38,144	NATCHITOCHES	6,980	3,104	3,876		772 D	44.5%	55.5%	44.5%	55.5%
570,445	ORLEANS	175,571	85,572	89,999		4,427 D	48.7%	51.3%	48.7%	51.3%
74,713	OUACHITA	18,617	8,842	9,775		933 D	47.5%	52.5%	47.5%	52.5%
14,239	PLAQUEMINES	3,625	3,370	255		3,115 R	93.0%	7.0%	93.0%	7.0%
21,841	POINTE COUPEE	2,559	1,174	1,385		211 D	45.9%	54.1%	45.9%	54.1%
90,648	RAPIDES	23,325	9,749	13,576		3,827 D	41.8%	58.2%	41.8%	58.2%
12,113	RED RIVER	2,596	774	1,822		1,048 D	29.8%	70.2%	29.8%	70.2%
26,672	RICHLAND	4,144	1,645	2,499		854 D	39.7%	60.3%	39.7%	60.3%
20,880	SABINE	5,321	2,039	3,282		1,243 D	38.3%	61.7%	38.3%	61.7%
11,087	ST. BERNARD	4,384	2,267	2,117		150 R	51.7%	48.3%	51.7%	48.3%
13,363	ST. CHARLES	3,765	1,086	2,679		1,593 D	28.8%	71.2%	28.8%	71.2%
9,013	ST. HELENA	1,481	586	895		309 D	39.6%	60.4%	39.6%	60.4%
15,334	ST. JAMES	3,518	1,353	2,165		812 D	38.5%	61.5%	38.5%	61.5%
14,861	ST. JOHN THE BAPTIST	2,786	654	2,132		1,478 D	23.5%	76.5%	23.5%	76.5%
78,476	ST. LANDRY	10,064	5,303	4,761		542 R	52.7%	47.3%	52.7%	47.3%
26,353	ST. MARTIN	3,566	1,554	2,012		458 D	43.6%	56.4%	43.6%	56.4%
35,848	ST. MARY	8,666	4,417	4,249		168 R	51.0%	49.0%	51.0%	49.0%
26,988	ST. TAMMANY	8,063	3,598	4,465		867 D	44.6%	55.4%	44.6%	55.4%
53,218	TANGIPAHOA	11,016	5,166	5,850		684 D	46.9%	53.1%	46.9%	53.1%
13,209	TENSAS	1,391	703	688		15 R	50.5%	49.5%	50.5%	49.5%
43,328	TERREBONNE	8,100	3,848	4,252		404 D	47.5%	52.5%	47.5%	52.5%
19,141	UNION	3,949	1,894	2,055		161 D	48.0%	52.0%	48.0%	52.0%
36,929	VERMILION	9,129	3,868	5,261		1,393 D	42.4%	57.6%	42.4%	57.6%
18,974	VERNON	5,962	2,130	3,832		1,702 D	35.7%	64.3%	35.7%	64.3%
38,371	WASHINGTON	9,852	2,432	7,420		4,988 D	24.7%	75.3%	24.7%	75.3%
35,704	WEBSTER	7,986	3,442	4,544		1,102 D	43.1%	56.9%	43.1%	56.9%

LOUISIANA

PRESIDENT 1952

1950 Census Population	Parish	Total Vote	Republican	Democratic	Other	Rep.-Dem. Plurality	Percentage Total Vote Rep.	Total Vote Dem.	Major Vote Rep.	Major Vote Dem.
11,738	WEST BATON ROUGE	1,984	704	1,280		576 D	35.5%	64.5%	35.5%	64.5%
17,248	WEST CARROLL	3,438	1,398	2,040		642 D	40.7%	59.3%	40.7%	59.3%
10,169	WEST FELICIANA	782	503	279		224 R	64.3%	35.7%	64.3%	35.7%
16,119	WINN	4,121	1,915	2,206		291 D	46.5%	53.5%	46.5%	53.5%
2,683,516	TOTAL	651,952	306,925	345,027		38,102 D	47.1%	52.9%	47.1%	52.9%

LOUISIANA

PRESIDENT 1948

1940 Census Population	Parish	Total Vote	Republican	Democratic	States Rights	Other	Plurality	Percentage Total Vote Rep.	Dem.	St. Rgts.
46,260	ACADIA	6,678	784	2,382	3,497	15	1,115 SR	11.7%	35.7%	52.4%
17,540	ALLEN	3,219	241	1,996	980	2	1,016 D	7.5%	62.0%	30.4%
21,215	ASCENSION	2,983	433	1,126	1,420	4	294 SR	14.5%	37.7%	47.6%
18,541	ASSUMPTION	1,834	469	362	1,000	3	531 SR	25.6%	19.7%	54.5%
39,256	AVOYELLES	7,105	285	1,356	5,417	47	4,061 SR	4.0%	19.1%	76.2%
14,847	BEAUREGARD	3,473	449	1,653	1,365	6	288 D	12.9%	47.6%	39.3%
23,933	BIENVILLE	2,977	191	421	2,362	3	1,941 SR	6.4%	14.1%	79.3%
33,162	BOSSIER	3,876	338	1,147	2,390	1	1,243 SR	8.7%	29.6%	61.7%
150,203	CADDO	22,117	4,777	5,985	11,292	63	5,307 SR	21.6%	27.1%	51.1%
56,506	CALCASIEU	12,438	1,940	7,074	3,400	24	3,674 D	15.6%	56.9%	27.3%
12,046	CALDWELL	1,748	151	777	818	2	41 SR	8.6%	44.5%	46.8%
7,203	CAMERON	1,123	87	742	293	1	449 D	7.7%	66.1%	26.1%
14,618	CATAHOULA	1,666	86	515	1,062	3	547 SR	5.2%	30.9%	63.7%
29,855	CLAIBORNE	2,786	265	457	2,061	3	1,604 SR	9.5%	16.4%	74.0%
14,562	CONCORDIA	1,567	98	329	1,140		811 SR	6.3%	21.0%	72.8%
31,803	DE SOTO	2,778	270	617	1,889	2	1,272 SR	9.7%	22.2%	68.0%
88,415	EAST BATON ROUGE	21,464	4,585	8,560	8,166	153	394 D	21.4%	39.9%	38.0%
19,023	EAST CARROLL	1,104	116	323	663	2	340 SR	10.5%	29.3%	60.1%
18,039	EAST FELICIANA	1,234	127	267	839	1	572 SR	10.3%	21.6%	68.0%
30,497	EVANGELINE	5,773	206	1,149	4,415	3	3,266 SR	3.6%	19.9%	76.5%
32,382	FRANKLIN	3,885	149	1,857	1,872	7	15 SR	3.8%	47.8%	48.2%
15,933	GRANT	2,840	273	1,120	1,439	8	319 SR	9.6%	39.4%	50.7%
37,183	IBERIA	6,157	2,910	1,015	2,224	8	686 R	47.3%	16.5%	36.1%
27,721	IBERVILLE	3,067	506	1,697	856	8	841 D	16.5%	55.3%	27.9%
17,807	JACKSON	2,289	169	713	1,400	7	687 SR	7.4%	31.1%	61.2%
50,427	JEFFERSON	16,168	2,620	4,654	8,822	72	4,168 SR	16.2%	28.8%	54.6%
24,191	JEFFERSON DAVIS	3,641	793	1,717	1,122	9	595 D	21.8%	47.2%	30.8%
43,941	LAFAYETTE	7,599	2,068	1,787	3,724	20	1,656 SR	27.2%	23.5%	49.0%
38,615	LAFOURCHE	5,913	1,247	1,586	3,052	28	1,466 SR	21.1%	26.8%	51.6%
10,959	LA SALLE	2,751	266	716	1,767	2	1,051 SR	9.7%	26.0%	64.2%
24,790	LINCOLN	3,201	353	625	2,196	27	1,571 SR	11.0%	19.5%	68.6%
17,790	LIVINGSTON	3,471	264	1,841	1,351	15	490 D	7.6%	53.0%	38.9%
18,443	MADISON	1,366	127	197	1,033	9	836 SR	9.3%	14.4%	75.6%
27,571	MOREHOUSE	2,814	242	1,177	1,391	4	214 SR	8.6%	41.8%	49.4%
40,997	NATCHITOCHES	5,352	763	1,692	2,887	10	1,195 SR	14.3%	31.6%	53.9%
494,537	ORLEANS	123,785	29,442	41,900	50,234	2,209	8,334 SR	23.8%	33.8%	40.6%
59,168	OUACHITA	10,802	1,729	4,213	4,848	12	635 SR	16.0%	39.0%	44.9%
12,318	PLAQUEMINES	2,774	90	77	2,597	10	2,507 SR	3.2%	2.8%	93.6%
24,004	POINTE COUPEE	1,979	198	402	1,375	4	973 SR	10.0%	20.3%	69.5%
73,370	RAPIDES	13,060	1,707	4,730	6,581	42	1,851 SR	13.1%	36.2%	50.4%
15,881	RED RIVER	2,106	113	452	1,535	6	1,083 SR	5.4%	21.5%	72.9%
28,829	RICHLAND	2,535	119	960	1,448	8	488 SR	4.7%	37.9%	57.1%
23,586	SABINE	4,126	469	1,405	2,249	3	844 SR	11.4%	34.1%	54.5%
7,280	ST. BERNARD	2,445	107	91	2,242	5	2,135 SR	4.4%	3.7%	91.7%
12,321	ST. CHARLES	2,410	286	914	1,206	4	292 SR	11.9%	37.9%	50.0%
9,542	ST. HELENA	1,191	59	469	662	1	193 SR	5.0%	39.4%	55.6%
16,596	ST. JAMES	2,117	453	859	800	5	59 D	21.4%	40.6%	37.8%
14,766	ST. JOHN THE BAPTIST	1,880	379	799	695	7	104 D	20.2%	42.5%	37.0%
71,481	ST. LANDRY	7,747	829	1,179	5,730	9	4,551 SR	10.7%	15.2%	74.0%
26,394	ST. MARTIN	3,824	688	307	2,822	7	2,134 SR	18.0%	8.0%	73.8%
31,458	ST. MARY	3,503	824	918	1,751	10	833 SR	23.5%	26.2%	50.0%
23,624	ST. TAMMANY	5,041	790	1,164	3,063	24	1,899 SR	15.7%	23.1%	60.8%
45,519	TANGIPAHOA	7,408	1,287	2,184	3,919	18	1,735 SR	17.4%	29.5%	52.9%
15,940	TENSAS	1,045	72	239	732	2	493 SR	6.9%	22.9%	70.0%
35,880	TERREBONNE	4,334	1,048	1,262	2,011	13	749 SR	24.2%	29.1%	46.4%
20,943	UNION	2,856	259	724	1,870	3	1,146 SR	9.1%	25.4%	65.5%
37,750	VERMILION	6,261	1,212	1,806	3,236	7	1,430 SR	19.4%	28.8%	51.7%
19,142	VERNON	4,582	296	1,939	2,331	16	392 SR	6.5%	42.3%	50.9%
34,443	WASHINGTON	7,801	371	3,267	4,141	22	874 SR	4.8%	41.9%	53.1%
33,676	WEBSTER	5,291	455	1,933	2,895	8	962 SR	8.6%	36.5%	54.7%

LOUISIANA

PRESIDENT 1948

1940 Census Population	Parish	Total Vote	Republican	Democratic	States Rights	Other	Plurality	Percentage Total Vote Rep.	Dem.	St. Rgts.
11,263	WEST BATON ROUGE	1,167	141	557	466	3	91 D	12.1%	47.7%	39.9%
19,252	WEST CARROLL	2,297	151	921	1,221	4	300 SR	6.6%	40.1%	53.2%
11,720	WEST FELICIANA	582	102	101	377	2	275 SR	17.5%	17.4%	64.8%
16,923	WINN	2,930	333	940	1,648	9	708 SR	11.4%	32.1%	56.2%
2,363,880	TOTAL	416,336	72,657	136,344	204,290	3,045	67,946 SR	17.5%	32.7%	49.1%

LOUISIANA

PRESIDENT 1944

1940 Census Population	Parish	Total Vote	Republican	Democratic	Other	Rep.-Dem. Plurality	Percentage Total Vote Rep.	Total Vote Dem.	Major Vote Rep.	Major Vote Dem.
46,260	ACADIA	5,462	1,023	4,439		3,416 D	18.7%	81.3%	18.7%	81.3%
17,540	ALLEN	2,541	336	2,205		1,869 D	13.2%	86.8%	13.2%	86.8%
21,215	ASCENSION	2,655	364	2,291		1,927 D	13.7%	86.3%	13.7%	86.3%
18,541	ASSUMPTION	1,845	426	1,419		993 D	23.1%	76.9%	23.1%	76.9%
39,256	AVOYELLES	4,095	306	3,789		3,483 D	7.5%	92.5%	7.5%	92.5%
14,847	BEAUREGARD	2,985	759	2,226		1,467 D	25.4%	74.6%	25.4%	74.6%
23,933	BIENVILLE	2,506	705	1,801		1,096 D	28.1%	71.9%	28.1%	71.9%
33,162	BOSSIER	3,053	622	2,430	1	1,808 D	20.4%	79.6%	20.4%	79.6%
150,203	CADDO	18,810	5,885	12,896	29	7,011 D	31.3%	68.6%	31.3%	68.7%
56,506	CALCASIEU	9,728	1,867	7,861		5,994 D	19.2%	80.8%	19.2%	80.8%
12,046	CALDWELL	1,647	505	1,142		637 D	30.7%	69.3%	30.7%	69.3%
7,203	CAMERON	1,111	86	1,025		939 D	7.7%	92.3%	7.7%	92.3%
14,618	CATAHOULA	1,499	291	1,208		917 D	19.4%	80.6%	19.4%	80.6%
29,855	CLAIBORNE	2,844	578	2,266		1,688 D	20.3%	79.7%	20.3%	79.7%
14,562	CONCORDIA	1,175	201	974		773 D	17.1%	82.9%	17.1%	82.9%
31,803	DE SOTO	2,396	538	1,858		1,320 D	22.5%	77.5%	22.5%	77.5%
88,415	EAST BATON ROUGE	17,782	3,025	14,757		11,732 D	17.0%	83.0%	17.0%	83.0%
19,023	EAST CARROLL	1,282	357	925		568 D	27.8%	72.2%	27.8%	72.2%
18,039	EAST FELICIANA	1,089	220	869		649 D	20.2%	79.8%	20.2%	79.8%
30,497	EVANGELINE	3,304	275	3,029		2,754 D	8.3%	91.7%	8.3%	91.7%
32,382	FRANKLIN	3,073	597	2,476		1,879 D	19.4%	80.6%	19.4%	80.6%
15,933	GRANT	2,495	556	1,939		1,383 D	22.3%	77.7%	22.3%	77.7%
37,183	IBERIA	4,802	1,141	3,661		2,520 D	23.8%	76.2%	23.8%	76.2%
27,721	IBERVILLE	2,697	432	2,265		1,833 D	16.0%	84.0%	16.0%	84.0%
17,807	JACKSON	2,257	414	1,840	3	1,426 D	18.3%	81.5%	18.4%	81.6%
50,427	JEFFERSON	12,050	1,782	10,268		8,486 D	14.8%	85.2%	14.8%	85.2%
24,191	JEFFERSON DAVIS	3,485	1,156	2,329		1,173 D	33.2%	66.8%	33.2%	66.8%
43,941	LAFAYETTE	5,543	742	4,801		4,059 D	13.4%	86.6%	13.4%	86.6%
38,615	LAFOURCHE	5,855	875	4,980		4,105 D	14.9%	85.1%	14.9%	85.1%
10,959	LA SALLE	2,548	504	2,018	26	1,514 D	19.8%	79.2%	20.0%	80.0%
24,790	LINCOLN	2,737	1,032	1,705		673 D	37.7%	62.3%	37.7%	62.3%
17,790	LIVINGSTON	2,803	343	2,460		2,117 D	12.2%	87.8%	12.2%	87.8%
18,443	MADISON	1,102	338	764		426 D	30.7%	69.3%	30.7%	69.3%
27,571	MOREHOUSE	2,337	478	1,859		1,381 D	20.5%	79.5%	20.5%	79.5%
40,997	NATCHITOCHES	3,644	1,105	2,536	3	1,431 D	30.3%	69.6%	30.3%	69.7%
494,537	ORLEANS	110,608	20,190	90,411	7	70,221 D	18.3%	81.7%	18.3%	81.7%
59,168	OUACHITA	8,956	2,627	6,329		3,702 D	29.3%	70.7%	29.3%	70.7%
12,318	PLAQUEMINES	2,090	335	1,755		1,420 D	16.0%	84.0%	16.0%	84.0%
24,004	POINTE COUPEE	1,707	271	1,436		1,165 D	15.9%	84.1%	15.9%	84.1%
73,370	RAPIDES	10,844	1,712	9,132		7,420 D	15.8%	84.2%	15.8%	84.2%
15,881	RED RIVER	1,384	409	975		566 D	29.6%	70.4%	29.6%	70.4%
28,829	RICHLAND	2,575	488	2,087		1,599 D	19.0%	81.0%	19.0%	81.0%
23,586	SABINE	3,087	1,039	2,048		1,009 D	33.7%	66.3%	33.7%	66.3%
7,280	ST. BERNARD	2,124	80	2,044		1,964 D	3.8%	96.2%	3.8%	96.2%
12,321	ST. CHARLES	2,119	174	1,945		1,771 D	8.2%	91.8%	8.2%	91.8%
9,542	ST. HELENA	791	108	683		575 D	13.7%	86.3%	13.7%	86.3%
16,596	ST. JAMES	1,652	265	1,387		1,122 D	16.0%	84.0%	16.0%	84.0%
14,766	ST. JOHN THE BAPTIST	1,519	195	1,324		1,129 D	12.8%	87.2%	12.8%	87.2%
71,481	ST. LANDRY	5,207	784	4,423		3,639 D	15.1%	84.9%	15.1%	84.9%
26,394	ST. MARTIN	2,537	153	2,384		2,231 D	6.0%	94.0%	6.0%	94.0%
31,458	ST. MARY	4,129	538	3,591		3,053 D	13.0%	87.0%	13.0%	87.0%
23,624	ST. TAMMANY	4,153	703	3,450		2,747 D	16.9%	83.1%	16.9%	83.1%
45,519	TANGIPAHOA	5,991	1,572	4,419		2,847 D	26.2%	73.8%	26.2%	73.8%
15,940	TENSAS	798	160	638		478 D	20.1%	79.9%	20.1%	79.9%
35,880	TERREBONNE	4,089	550	3,539		2,989 D	13.5%	86.5%	13.5%	86.5%
20,943	UNION	2,568	803	1,765		962 D	31.3%	68.7%	31.3%	68.7%
37,750	VERMILION	5,360	676	4,684		4,008 D	12.6%	87.4%	12.6%	87.4%
19,142	VERNON	4,097	1,022	3,075		2,053 D	24.9%	75.1%	24.9%	75.1%
34,443	WASHINGTON	5,216	406	4,810		4,404 D	7.8%	92.2%	7.8%	92.2%
33,676	WEBSTER	4,554	899	3,655		2,756 D	19.7%	80.3%	19.7%	80.3%

LOUISIANA

PRESIDENT 1944

1940 Census Population	Parish	Total Vote	Republican	Democratic	Other	Rep.-Dem. Plurality	Percentage Total Vote Rep.	Percentage Total Vote Dem.	Percentage Major Vote Rep.	Percentage Major Vote Dem.
11,263	WEST BATON ROUGE	1,132	87	1,045		958 D	7.7%	92.3%	7.7%	92.3%
19,252	WEST CARROLL	1,971	581	1,390		809 D	29.5%	70.5%	29.5%	70.5%
11,720	WEST FELICIANA	604	178	426		248 D	29.5%	70.5%	29.5%	70.5%
16,923	WINN	2,284	881	1,403		522 D	38.6%	61.4%	38.6%	61.4%
2,363,880	TOTAL	349,383	67,750	281,564	69	213,814 D	19.4%	80.6%	19.4%	80.6%

LOUISIANA

PRESIDENT 1940

1940 Census Population	Parish	Total Vote	Republican	Democratic	Other	Rep.-Dem. Plurality	Percentage Total Vote Rep.	Percentage Total Vote Dem.	Percentage Major Vote Rep.	Percentage Major Vote Dem.
46,260	ACADIA	5,779	719	5,058	2	4,339 D	12.4%	87.5%	12.4%	87.6%
17,540	ALLEN	2,869	277	2,592		2,315 D	9.7%	90.3%	9.7%	90.3%
21,215	ASCENSION	2,836	385	2,451		2,066 D	13.6%	86.4%	13.6%	86.4%
18,541	ASSUMPTION	2,481	722	1,759		1,037 D	29.1%	70.9%	29.1%	70.9%
39,256	AVOYELLES	5,066	183	4,883		4,700 D	3.6%	96.4%	3.6%	96.4%
14,847	BEAUREGARD	3,205	528	2,677		2,149 D	16.5%	83.5%	16.5%	83.5%
23,933	BIENVILLE	3,246	362	2,883	1	2,521 D	11.2%	88.8%	11.2%	88.8%
33,162	BOSSIER	3,340	275	3,045	20	2,770 D	8.2%	91.2%	8.3%	91.7%
150,203	CADDO	20,345	3,124	17,192	29	14,068 D	15.4%	84.5%	15.4%	84.6%
56,506	CALCASIEU	8,429	1,425	6,993	11	5,568 D	16.9%	83.0%	16.9%	83.1%
12,046	CALDWELL	1,986	318	1,668		1,350 D	16.0%	84.0%	16.0%	84.0%
7,203	CAMERON	1,223	48	1,175		1,127 D	3.9%	96.1%	3.9%	96.1%
14,618	CATAHOULA	1,646	134	1,512		1,378 D	8.1%	91.9%	8.1%	91.9%
29,855	CLAIBORNE	3,236	187	3,049		2,862 D	5.8%	94.2%	5.8%	94.2%
14,562	CONCORDIA	1,292	119	1,173		1,054 D	9.2%	90.8%	9.2%	90.8%
31,803	DE SOTO	3,083	211	2,872		2,661 D	6.8%	93.2%	6.8%	93.2%
88,415	EAST BATON ROUGE	15,065	1,762	13,303		11,541 D	11.7%	88.3%	11.7%	88.3%
19,023	EAST CARROLL	1,295	270	1,025		755 D	20.8%	79.2%	20.8%	79.2%
18,039	EAST FELICIANA	1,223	164	1,059		895 D	13.4%	86.6%	13.4%	86.6%
30,497	EVANGELINE	3,789	220	3,569		3,349 D	5.8%	94.2%	5.8%	94.2%
32,382	FRANKLIN	3,451	292	3,159		2,867 D	8.5%	91.5%	8.5%	91.5%
15,933	GRANT	2,766	232	2,534		2,302 D	8.4%	91.6%	8.4%	91.6%
37,183	IBERIA	5,797	1,706	4,091		2,385 D	29.4%	70.6%	29.4%	70.6%
27,721	IBERVILLE	3,001	496	2,505		2,009 D	16.5%	83.5%	16.5%	83.5%
17,807	JACKSON	3,014	280	2,734		2,454 D	9.3%	90.7%	9.3%	90.7%
50,427	JEFFERSON	9,316	982	8,334		7,352 D	10.5%	89.5%	10.5%	89.5%
24,191	JEFFERSON DAVIS	3,585	1,054	2,531		1,477 D	29.4%	70.6%	29.4%	70.6%
43,941	LAFAYETTE	8,173	1,850	6,323		4,473 D	22.6%	77.4%	22.6%	77.4%
38,615	LAFOURCHE	4,596	1,065	3,531		2,466 D	23.2%	76.8%	23.2%	76.8%
10,959	LA SALLE	2,307	258	2,039	10	1,781 D	11.2%	88.4%	11.2%	88.8%
24,790	LINCOLN	3,418	449	2,969		2,520 D	13.1%	86.9%	13.1%	86.9%
17,790	LIVINGSTON	3,223	252	2,971		2,719 D	7.8%	92.2%	7.8%	92.2%
18,443	MADISON	1,199	182	1,017		835 D	15.2%	84.8%	15.2%	84.8%
27,571	MOREHOUSE	2,639	222	2,417		2,195 D	8.4%	91.6%	8.4%	91.6%
40,997	NATCHITOCHES	4,508	684	3,824		3,140 D	15.2%	84.8%	15.2%	84.8%
494,537	ORLEANS	114,364	16,406	97,930	28	81,524 D	14.3%	85.6%	14.3%	85.7%
59,168	OUACHITA	10,015	1,509	8,506		6,997 D	15.1%	84.9%	15.1%	84.9%
12,318	PLAQUEMINES	2,183	204	1,979		1,775 D	9.3%	90.7%	9.3%	90.7%
24,004	POINTE COUPEE	2,124	247	1,877		1,630 D	11.6%	88.4%	11.6%	88.4%
73,370	RAPIDES	9,969	869	9,100		8,231 D	8.7%	91.3%	8.7%	91.3%
15,881	RED RIVER	2,123	231	1,892		1,661 D	10.9%	89.1%	10.9%	89.1%
28,829	RICHLAND	2,727	310	2,417		2,107 D	11.4%	88.6%	11.4%	88.6%
23,586	SABINE	3,614	588	3,026		2,438 D	16.3%	83.7%	16.3%	83.7%
7,280	ST. BERNARD	1,825	110	1,715		1,605 D	6.0%	94.0%	6.0%	94.0%
12,321	ST. CHARLES	1,703	153	1,550		1,397 D	9.0%	91.0%	9.0%	91.0%
9,542	ST. HELENA	1,087	80	1,007		927 D	7.4%	92.6%	7.4%	92.6%
16,596	ST. JAMES	1,969	506	1,463		957 D	25.7%	74.3%	25.7%	74.3%
14,766	ST. JOHN THE BAPTIST	1,477	285	1,192		907 D	19.3%	80.7%	19.3%	80.7%
71,481	ST. LANDRY	6,919	561	6,358		5,797 D	8.1%	91.9%	8.1%	91.9%
26,394	ST. MARTIN	3,854	602	3,252		2,650 D	15.6%	84.4%	15.6%	84.4%
31,458	ST. MARY	4,425	739	3,686		2,947 D	16.7%	83.3%	16.7%	83.3%
23,624	ST. TAMMANY	5,143	668	4,475		3,807 D	13.0%	87.0%	13.0%	87.0%
45,519	TANGIPAHOA	7,187	1,284	5,900	3	4,616 D	17.9%	82.1%	17.9%	82.1%
15,940	TENSAS	1,052	95	957		862 D	9.0%	91.0%	9.0%	91.0%
35,880	TERREBONNE	3,818	601	3,217		2,616 D	15.7%	84.3%	15.7%	84.3%
20,943	UNION	3,213	371	2,842		2,471 D	11.5%	88.5%	11.5%	88.5%
37,750	VERMILION	7,590	2,621	4,969		2,348 D	34.5%	65.5%	34.5%	65.5%
19,142	VERNON	3,750	311	3,439		3,128 D	8.3%	91.7%	8.3%	91.7%
34,443	WASHINGTON	6,376	314	6,062		5,748 D	4.9%	95.1%	4.9%	95.1%
33,676	WEBSTER	4,113	332	3,777	4	3,445 D	8.1%	91.8%	8.1%	91.9%

LOUISIANA

PRESIDENT 1940

1940 Census Population	Parish	Total Vote	Republican	Democratic	Other	Rep.-Dem. Plurality	Percentage Total Vote Rep.	Percentage Total Vote Dem.	Percentage Major Vote Rep.	Percentage Major Vote Dem.
11,263	WEST BATON ROUGE	1,326	141	1,185		1,044 D	10.6%	89.4%	10.6%	89.4%
19,252	WEST CARROLL	2,238	362	1,876		1,514 D	16.2%	83.8%	16.2%	83.8%
11,720	WEST FELICIANA	760	127	633		506 D	16.7%	83.3%	16.7%	83.3%
16,923	WINN	2,934	382	2,552		2,170 D	13.0%	87.0%	13.0%	87.0%
2,363,880	TOTAL	372,305	52,446	319,751	108	267,305 D	14.1%	85.9%	14.1%	85.9%

LOUISIANA

PRESIDENT 1936

1930 Census Population	Parish	Total Vote	Republican	Democratic	Other	Rep.-Dem. Plurality	Percentage Total Vote Rep.	Total Vote Dem.	Major Vote Rep.	Major Vote Dem.
39,326	ACADIA	4,945	441	4,504		4,063 D	8.9%	91.1%	8.9%	91.1%
15,261	ALLEN	2,531	324	2,207		1,883 D	12.8%	87.2%	12.8%	87.2%
18,438	ASCENSION	2,710	350	2,359	1	2,009 D	12.9%	87.0%	12.9%	87.1%
15,990	ASSUMPTION	1,823	1,111	712		399 R	60.9%	39.1%	60.9%	39.1%
34,926	AVOYELLES	4,860	452	4,408		3,956 D	9.3%	90.7%	9.3%	90.7%
14,569	BEAUREGARD	2,730	549	2,181		1,632 D	20.1%	79.9%	20.1%	79.9%
23,789	BIENVILLE	2,807	213	2,593	1	2,380 D	7.6%	92.4%	7.6%	92.4%
28,388	BOSSIER	2,170	193	1,975	2	1,782 D	8.9%	91.0%	8.9%	91.1%
124,670	CADDO	13,857	1,697	12,156	4	10,459 D	12.2%	87.7%	12.3%	87.7%
41,963	CALCASIEU	7,309	1,037	6,259	13	5,222 D	14.2%	85.6%	14.2%	85.8%
10,430	CALDWELL	1,606	235	1,371		1,136 D	14.6%	85.4%	14.6%	85.4%
6,054	CAMERON	1,083	16	1,067		1,051 D	1.5%	98.5%	1.5%	98.5%
12,451	CATAHOULA	1,461	98	1,363		1,265 D	6.7%	93.3%	6.7%	93.3%
32,285	CLAIBORNE	2,711	146	2,563	2	2,417 D	5.4%	94.5%	5.4%	94.6%
12,778	CONCORDIA	1,211	58	1,152	1	1,094 D	4.8%	95.1%	4.8%	95.2%
31,016	DE SOTO	2,430	93	2,337		2,244 D	3.8%	96.2%	3.8%	96.2%
68,208	EAST BATON ROUGE	10,980	1,069	9,911		8,842 D	9.7%	90.3%	9.7%	90.3%
15,815	EAST CARROLL	906	95	811		716 D	10.5%	89.5%	10.5%	89.5%
17,449	EAST FELICIANA	1,159	102	1,057		955 D	8.8%	91.2%	8.8%	91.2%
25,483	EVANGELINE	3,815	331	3,484		3,153 D	8.7%	91.3%	8.7%	91.3%
30,530	FRANKLIN	3,187	231	2,948	8	2,717 D	7.2%	92.5%	7.3%	92.7%
15,709	GRANT	2,358	511	1,847		1,336 D	21.7%	78.3%	21.7%	78.3%
28,192	IBERIA	3,829	1,234	2,595		1,361 D	32.2%	67.8%	32.2%	67.8%
24,638	IBERVILLE	2,216	263	1,953		1,690 D	11.9%	88.1%	11.9%	88.1%
13,808	JACKSON	1,976	169	1,807		1,638 D	8.6%	91.4%	8.6%	91.4%
40,032	JEFFERSON	9,767	705	9,056	6	8,351 D	7.2%	92.7%	7.2%	92.8%
19,765	JEFFERSON DAVIS	3,175	608	2,567		1,959 D	19.1%	80.9%	19.1%	80.9%
38,827	LAFAYETTE	4,876	306	4,570		4,264 D	6.3%	93.7%	6.3%	93.7%
32,419	LAFOURCHE	3,827	1,630	2,195	2	565 D	42.6%	57.4%	42.6%	57.4%
11,668	LA SALLE	1,899	256	1,643		1,387 D	13.5%	86.5%	13.5%	86.5%
22,822	LINCOLN	2,356	201	2,154	1	1,953 D	8.5%	91.4%	8.5%	91.5%
18,206	LIVINGSTON	2,910	496	2,414		1,918 D	17.0%	83.0%	17.0%	83.0%
14,829	MADISON	1,156	71	1,085		1,014 D	6.1%	93.9%	6.1%	93.9%
23,689	MOREHOUSE	2,688	172	2,514	2	2,342 D	6.4%	93.5%	6.4%	93.6%
38,477	NATCHITOCHES	3,978	502	3,476		2,974 D	12.6%	87.4%	12.6%	87.4%
458,762	ORLEANS	118,282	10,254	108,012	16	97,758 D	8.7%	91.3%	8.7%	91.3%
54,337	OUACHITA	8,748	1,113	7,635		6,522 D	12.7%	87.3%	12.7%	87.3%
9,608	PLAQUEMINES	2,303	94	2,209		2,115 D	4.1%	95.9%	4.1%	95.9%
21,007	POINTE COUPEE	1,535	116	1,419		1,303 D	7.6%	92.4%	7.6%	92.4%
65,455	RAPIDES	9,274	1,257	8,017		6,760 D	13.6%	86.4%	13.6%	86.4%
16,078	RED RIVER	1,773	132	1,641		1,509 D	7.4%	92.6%	7.4%	92.6%
26,374	RICHLAND	2,594	165	2,425	4	2,260 D	6.4%	93.5%	6.4%	93.6%
24,110	SABINE	2,865	417	2,447	1	2,030 D	14.6%	85.4%	14.6%	85.4%
6,512	ST. BERNARD	2,294	25	2,269		2,244 D	1.1%	98.9%	1.1%	98.9%
12,111	ST. CHARLES	1,599	96	1,503		1,407 D	6.0%	94.0%	6.0%	94.0%
8,492	ST. HELENA	1,301	102	1,199		1,097 D	7.8%	92.2%	7.8%	92.2%
15,338	ST. JAMES	1,834	259	1,575		1,316 D	14.1%	85.9%	14.1%	85.9%
14,078	ST. JOHN THE BAPTIST	2,004	262	1,742		1,480 D	13.1%	86.9%	13.1%	86.9%
60,074	ST. LANDRY	6,080	441	5,639		5,198 D	7.3%	92.7%	7.3%	92.7%
21,767	ST. MARTIN	2,738	100	2,638		2,538 D	3.7%	96.3%	3.7%	96.3%
29,397	ST. MARY	2,429	487	1,942		1,455 D	20.0%	80.0%	20.0%	80.0%
20,929	ST. TAMMANY	4,071	594	3,477		2,883 D	14.6%	85.4%	14.6%	85.4%
46,227	TANGIPAHOA	6,000	1,374	4,624	2	3,250 D	22.9%	77.1%	22.9%	77.1%
15,096	TENSAS	835	23	812		789 D	2.8%	97.2%	2.8%	97.2%
29,816	TERREBONNE	2,420	526	1,894		1,368 D	21.7%	78.3%	21.7%	78.3%
20,731	UNION	2,050	272	1,778		1,506 D	13.3%	86.7%	13.3%	86.7%
33,684	VERMILION	4,652	496	4,141	15	3,645 D	10.7%	89.0%	10.7%	89.3%
20,047	VERNON	3,764	928	2,831	5	1,903 D	24.7%	75.2%	24.7%	75.3%
29,904	WASHINGTON	6,017	350	5,667		5,317 D	5.8%	94.2%	5.8%	94.2%
29,458	WEBSTER	3,106	301	2,799	6	2,498 D	9.7%	90.1%	9.7%	90.3%

LOUISIANA

PRESIDENT 1936

1930 Census Population	Parish	Total Vote	Republican	Democratic	Other	Rep.-Dem. Plurality	Percentage Total Vote Rep.	Percentage Total Vote Dem.	Percentage Major Vote Rep.	Percentage Major Vote Dem.
9,716	WEST BATON ROUGE	949	80	868	1	788 D	8.4%	91.5%	8.4%	91.6%
13,895	WEST CARROLL	1,672	232	1,440		1,208 D	13.9%	86.1%	13.9%	86.1%
10,924	WEST FELICIANA	640	76	564		488 D	11.9%	88.1%	11.9%	88.1%
14,766	WINN	2,647	254	2,393		2,139 D	9.6%	90.4%	9.6%	90.4%
2,101,593	TOTAL	329,778	36,791	292,894	93	256,103 D	11.2%	88.8%	11.2%	88.8%

LOUISIANA

PRESIDENT 1932

1930 Census Population	Parish	Total Vote	Republican	Democratic	Other	Rep.-Dem. Plurality	Percentage Total Vote Rep.	Percentage Total Vote Dem.	Percentage Major Vote Rep.	Percentage Major Vote Dem.
39,326	ACADIA	3,934	351	3,583		3,232 D	8.9%	91.1%	8.9%	91.1%
15,261	ALLEN	2,209	130	2,075	4	1,945 D	5.9%	93.9%	5.9%	94.1%
18,438	ASCENSION	2,079	279	1,800		1,521 D	13.4%	86.6%	13.4%	86.6%
15,990	ASSUMPTION	1,924	386	1,538		1,152 D	20.1%	79.9%	20.1%	79.9%
34,926	AVOYELLES	3,278	130	3,148		3,018 D	4.0%	96.0%	4.0%	96.0%
14,569	BEAUREGARD	2,465	146	2,319		2,173 D	5.9%	94.1%	5.9%	94.1%
23,789	BIENVILLE	2,713	41	2,671	1	2,630 D	1.5%	98.5%	1.5%	98.5%
28,388	BOSSIER	2,247	56	2,191		2,135 D	2.5%	97.5%	2.5%	97.5%
124,670	CADDO	13,553	1,309	12,159	85	10,850 D	9.7%	89.7%	9.7%	90.3%
41,963	CALCASIEU	6,805	678	6,105	22	5,427 D	10.0%	89.7%	10.0%	90.0%
10,430	CALDWELL	1,541	86	1,448	7	1,362 D	5.6%	94.0%	5.6%	94.4%
6,054	CAMERON	948	10	938		928 D	1.1%	98.9%	1.1%	98.9%
12,451	CATAHOULA	1,369	29	1,340		1,311 D	2.1%	97.9%	2.1%	97.9%
32,285	CLAIBORNE	2,826	61	2,765		2,704 D	2.2%	97.8%	2.2%	97.8%
12,778	CONCORDIA	1,019	20	999		979 D	2.0%	98.0%	2.0%	98.0%
31,016	DE SOTO	2,505	87	2,416	2	2,329 D	3.5%	96.4%	3.5%	96.5%
68,208	EAST BATON ROUGE	7,441	1,045	6,363	33	5,318 D	14.0%	85.5%	14.1%	85.9%
15,815	EAST CARROLL	775	24	751		727 D	3.1%	96.9%	3.1%	96.9%
17,449	EAST FELICIANA	1,243	65	1,178		1,113 D	5.2%	94.8%	5.2%	94.8%
25,483	EVANGELINE	3,167	52	3,115		3,063 D	1.6%	98.4%	1.6%	98.4%
30,530	FRANKLIN	3,010	78	2,930	2	2,852 D	2.6%	97.3%	2.6%	97.4%
15,709	GRANT	2,048	81	1,966	1	1,885 D	4.0%	96.0%	4.0%	96.0%
28,192	IBERIA	3,210	798	2,412		1,614 D	24.9%	75.1%	24.9%	75.1%
24,638	IBERVILLE	1,738	430	1,308		878 D	24.7%	75.3%	24.7%	75.3%
13,808	JACKSON	1,782	34	1,748		1,714 D	1.9%	98.1%	1.9%	98.1%
40,032	JEFFERSON	7,875	466	7,395	14	6,929 D	5.9%	93.9%	5.9%	94.1%
19,765	JEFFERSON DAVIS	2,824	512	2,308	4	1,796 D	18.1%	81.7%	18.2%	81.8%
38,827	LAFAYETTE	4,312	291	4,019	2	3,728 D	6.7%	93.2%	6.8%	93.2%
32,419	LAFOURCHE	2,988	364	2,623	1	2,259 D	12.2%	87.8%	12.2%	87.8%
11,668	LA SALLE	1,856	117	1,738	1	1,621 D	6.3%	93.6%	6.3%	93.7%
22,822	LINCOLN	2,071	163	1,908		1,745 D	7.9%	92.1%	7.9%	92.1%
18,206	LIVINGSTON	2,042	89	1,953		1,864 D	4.4%	95.6%	4.4%	95.6%
14,829	MADISON	615	67	548		481 D	10.9%	89.1%	10.9%	89.1%
23,689	MOREHOUSE	2,097	83	2,014		1,931 D	4.0%	96.0%	4.0%	96.0%
38,477	NATCHITOCHES	3,633	173	3,458	2	3,285 D	4.8%	95.2%	4.8%	95.2%
458,762	ORLEANS	90,860	5,407	85,288	165	79,881 D	6.0%	93.9%	6.0%	94.0%
54,337	OUACHITA	6,427	423	5,968	36	5,545 D	6.6%	92.9%	6.6%	93.4%
9,608	PLAQUEMINES	1,956	38	1,918		1,880 D	1.9%	98.1%	1.9%	98.1%
21,007	POINTE COUPEE	1,092	65	1,027		962 D	6.0%	94.0%	6.0%	94.0%
65,455	RAPIDES	8,258	680	7,578		6,898 D	8.2%	91.8%	8.2%	91.8%
16,078	RED RIVER	1,689	24	1,661	4	1,637 D	1.4%	98.3%	1.4%	98.6%
26,374	RICHLAND	1,820	46	1,773	1	1,727 D	2.5%	97.4%	2.5%	97.5%
24,110	SABINE	3,128	110	3,008	10	2,898 D	3.5%	96.2%	3.5%	96.5%
6,512	ST. BERNARD	1,631	106	1,525		1,419 D	6.5%	93.5%	6.5%	93.5%
12,111	ST. CHARLES	1,519	86	1,429	4	1,343 D	5.7%	94.1%	5.7%	94.3%
8,492	ST. HELENA	988	26	962		936 D	2.6%	97.4%	2.6%	97.4%
15,338	ST. JAMES	1,955	240	1,715		1,475 D	12.3%	87.7%	12.3%	87.7%
14,078	ST. JOHN THE BAPTIST	1,004	176	799	29	623 D	17.5%	79.6%	18.1%	81.9%
60,074	ST. LANDRY	4,063	297	3,766		3,469 D	7.3%	92.7%	7.3%	92.7%
21,767	ST. MARTIN	1,527	107	1,420		1,313 D	7.0%	93.0%	7.0%	93.0%
29,397	ST. MARY	2,545	473	2,072		1,599 D	18.6%	81.4%	18.6%	81.4%
20,929	ST. TAMMANY	3,389	178	3,206	5	3,028 D	5.3%	94.6%	5.3%	94.7%
46,227	TANGIPAHOA	4,862	455	4,404	3	3,949 D	9.4%	90.6%	9.4%	90.6%
15,096	TENSAS	665	29	635	1	606 D	4.4%	95.5%	4.4%	95.6%
29,816	TERREBONNE	2,341	215	2,126		1,911 D	9.2%	90.8%	9.2%	90.8%
20,731	UNION	2,343	58	2,285		2,227 D	2.5%	97.5%	2.5%	97.5%
33,684	VERMILION	3,214	269	2,945		2,676 D	8.4%	91.6%	8.4%	91.6%
20,047	VERNON	2,969	46	2,868	55	2,822 D	1.5%	96.6%	1.6%	98.4%
29,904	WASHINGTON	4,281	283	3,997	1	3,714 D	6.6%	93.4%	6.6%	93.4%
29,458	WEBSTER	3,093	73	3,020		2,947 D	2.4%	97.6%	2.4%	97.6%

LOUISIANA

PRESIDENT 1932

1930 Census Population	Parish	Total Vote	Republican	Democratic	Other	Rep.-Dem. Plurality	Percentage Total Vote Rep.	Total Vote Dem.	Major Vote Rep.	Major Vote Dem.
9,716	WEST BATON ROUGE	689	96	593		497 D	13.9%	86.1%	13.9%	86.1%
13,895	WEST CARROLL	1,502	31	1,471		1,440 D	2.1%	97.9%	2.1%	97.9%
10,924	WEST FELICIANA	606	49	557		508 D	8.1%	91.9%	8.1%	91.9%
14,766	WINN	2,246	36	2,172	38	2,136 D	1.6%	96.7%	1.6%	98.4%
2,101,593	TOTAL	268,804	18,853	249,418	533	230,565 D	7.0%	92.8%	7.0%	93.0%

LOUISIANA

PRESIDENT 1928

1920 Census Population	Parish	Total Vote	Republican	Democratic	Other	Rep.-Dem. Plurality	Percentage Total Vote Rep.	Total Vote Dem.	Major Vote Rep.	Major Vote Dem.
34,820	ACADIA	4,704	1,071	3,633		2,562 D	22.8%	77.2%	22.8%	77.2%
18,382	ALLEN	2,033	725	1,308		583 D	35.7%	64.3%	35.7%	64.3%
22,155	ASCENSION	1,838	436	1,402		966 D	23.7%	76.3%	23.7%	76.3%
17,912	ASSUMPTION	1,255	307	948		641 D	24.5%	75.5%	24.5%	75.5%
35,300	AVOYELLES	3,315	419	2,896		2,477 D	12.6%	87.4%	12.6%	87.4%
20,767	BEAUREGARD	1,981	468	1,513		1,045 D	23.6%	76.4%	23.6%	76.4%
20,977	BIENVILLE	1,668	367	1,301		934 D	22.0%	78.0%	22.0%	78.0%
22,266	BOSSIER	1,412	225	1,187		962 D	15.9%	84.1%	15.9%	84.1%
83,265	CADDO	10,599	3,665	6,934		3,269 D	34.6%	65.4%	34.6%	65.4%
32,807	CALCASIEU	5,532	1,997	3,532	3	1,535 D	36.1%	63.8%	36.1%	63.9%
9,514	CALDWELL	1,090	288	802		514 D	26.4%	73.6%	26.4%	73.6%
3,952	CAMERON	431	41	390		349 D	9.5%	90.5%	9.5%	90.5%
11,074	CATAHOULA	1,051	341	710		369 D	32.4%	67.6%	32.4%	67.6%
27,885	CLAIBORNE	1,809	249	1,560		1,311 D	13.8%	86.2%	13.8%	86.2%
12,466	CONCORDIA	724	133	591		458 D	18.4%	81.6%	18.4%	81.6%
29,376	DE SOTO	1,964	517	1,445	2	928 D	26.3%	73.6%	26.4%	73.6%
44,513	EAST BATON ROUGE	7,570	2,995	4,575		1,580 D	39.6%	60.4%	39.6%	60.4%
11,231	EAST CARROLL	566	130	436		306 D	23.0%	77.0%	23.0%	77.0%
17,487	EAST FELICIANA	782	160	622		462 D	20.5%	79.5%	20.5%	79.5%
23,485	EVANGELINE	2,173	300	1,873		1,573 D	13.8%	86.2%	13.8%	86.2%
24,100	FRANKLIN	1,633	492	1,141		649 D	30.1%	69.9%	30.1%	69.9%
14,403	GRANT	1,528	505	1,023		518 D	33.0%	67.0%	33.0%	67.0%
26,855	IBERIA	2,974	413	2,561		2,148 D	13.9%	86.1%	13.9%	86.1%
26,806	IBERVILLE	1,908	278	1,630		1,352 D	14.6%	85.4%	14.6%	85.4%
14,486	JACKSON	907		907		907 D		100.0%		100.0%
21,563	JEFFERSON	6,068	742	5,326		4,584 D	12.2%	87.8%	12.2%	87.8%
18,999	JEFFERSON DAVIS	2,823	1,120	1,703		583 D	39.7%	60.3%	39.7%	60.3%
30,841	LAFAYETTE	3,789	592	3,197		2,605 D	15.6%	84.4%	15.6%	84.4%
30,344	LAFOURCHE	2,237	243	1,994		1,751 D	10.9%	89.1%	10.9%	89.1%
9,856	LA SALLE	1,331	450	881		431 D	33.8%	66.2%	33.8%	66.2%
16,962	LINCOLN	1,711	670	1,041		371 D	39.2%	60.8%	39.2%	60.8%
11,643	LIVINGSTON	2,022	975	1,047		72 D	48.2%	51.8%	48.2%	51.8%
10,829	MADISON	469	151	318		167 D	32.2%	67.8%	32.2%	67.8%
19,311	MOREHOUSE	1,180	340	840		500 D	28.8%	71.2%	28.8%	71.2%
38,602	NATCHITOCHES	2,625	526	2,099		1,573 D	20.0%	80.0%	20.0%	80.0%
387,219	ORLEANS	70,343	14,424	55,919		41,495 D	20.5%	79.5%	20.5%	79.5%
30,319	OUACHITA	4,119	1,380	2,739		1,359 D	33.5%	66.5%	33.5%	66.5%
10,194	PLAQUEMINES	1,154	98	1,056		958 D	8.5%	91.5%	8.5%	91.5%
24,697	POINTE COUPEE	1,432	102	1,330		1,228 D	7.1%	92.9%	7.1%	92.9%
59,444	RAPIDES	6,964	2,494	4,470		1,976 D	35.8%	64.2%	35.8%	64.2%
15,301	RED RIVER	1,219	317	891	11	574 D	26.0%	73.1%	26.2%	73.8%
20,860	RICHLAND	1,325	242	1,083		841 D	18.3%	81.7%	18.3%	81.7%
20,713	SABINE	2,149	735	1,414		679 D	34.2%	65.8%	34.2%	65.8%
4,968	ST. BERNARD	2,436	77	2,359		2,282 D	3.2%	96.8%	3.2%	96.8%
8,586	ST. CHARLES	1,224	108	1,116		1,008 D	8.8%	91.2%	8.8%	91.2%
8,427	ST. HELENA	754	145	609		464 D	19.2%	80.8%	19.2%	80.8%
21,228	ST. JAMES	1,614	128	1,486		1,358 D	7.9%	92.1%	7.9%	92.1%
11,896	ST. JOHN THE BAPTIST	1,089	118	971		853 D	10.8%	89.2%	10.8%	89.2%
51,697	ST. LANDRY	4,112	718	3,394		2,676 D	17.5%	82.5%	17.5%	82.5%
21,990	ST. MARTIN	2,134	242	1,892		1,650 D	11.3%	88.7%	11.3%	88.7%
30,754	ST. MARY	2,359	605	1,754		1,149 D	25.6%	74.4%	25.6%	74.4%
20,645	ST. TAMMANY	2,756	945	1,811		866 D	34.3%	65.7%	34.3%	65.7%
31,440	TANGIPAHOA	4,249	1,415	2,834		1,419 D	33.3%	66.7%	33.3%	66.7%
12,085	TENSAS	446	96	350		254 D	21.5%	78.5%	21.5%	78.5%
26,974	TERREBONNE	1,910	268	1,642		1,374 D	14.0%	86.0%	14.0%	86.0%
19,621	UNION	1,509	422	1,085	2	663 D	28.0%	71.9%	28.0%	72.0%
26,482	VERMILION	3,031	451	2,580		2,129 D	14.9%	85.1%	14.9%	85.1%
20,493	VERNON	2,691	500	2,191		1,691 D	18.6%	81.4%	18.6%	81.4%
24,164	WASHINGTON	3,548	1,528	2,020		492 D	43.1%	56.9%	43.1%	56.9%
24,707	WEBSTER	1,786	356	1,430		1,074 D	19.9%	80.1%	19.9%	80.1%

LOUISIANA

PRESIDENT 1928

1920 Census Population	Parish	Total Vote	Republican	Democratic	Other	Rep.-Dem. Plurality	Percentage Total Vote Rep.	Percentage Total Vote Dem.	Percentage Major Vote Rep.	Percentage Major Vote Dem.
11,092	WEST BATON ROUGE	686	78	608		530 D	11.4%	88.6%	11.4%	88.6%
8,857	WEST CARROLL	887	214	673		459 D	24.1%	75.9%	24.1%	75.9%
12,303	WEST FELICIANA	511	90	421		331 D	17.6%	82.4%	17.6%	82.4%
16,119	WINN	1,694	533	1,161		628 D	31.5%	68.5%	31.5%	68.5%
1,798,509	TOTAL	215,833	51,160	164,655	18	113,495 D	23.7%	76.3%	23.7%	76.3%

LOUISIANA

PRESIDENT 1924

1920 Census Population	Parish	Total Vote	Republican	Democratic	Other	Rep.-Dem. Plurality	Percentage Total Vote Rep.	Percentage Total Vote Dem.	Percentage Major Vote Rep.	Percentage Major Vote Dem.
34,820	ACADIA	2,288	691	1,481	116	790 D	30.2%	64.7%	31.8%	68.2%
18,382	ALLEN	1,422	410	1,012		602 D	28.8%	71.2%	28.8%	71.2%
22,155	ASCENSION	956	277	679		402 D	29.0%	71.0%	29.0%	71.0%
17,912	ASSUMPTION	906	601	305		296 R	66.3%	33.7%	66.3%	33.7%
35,300	AVOYELLES	1,324	314	1,010		696 D	23.7%	76.3%	23.7%	76.3%
20,767	BEAUREGARD	1,427	235	1,191	1	956 D	16.5%	83.5%	16.5%	83.5%
20,977	BIENVILLE	844	67	774	3	707 D	7.9%	91.7%	8.0%	92.0%
22,266	BOSSIER	822	48	751	23	703 D	5.8%	91.4%	6.0%	94.0%
83,265	CADDO	5,990	1,062	4,517	411	3,455 D	17.7%	75.4%	19.0%	81.0%
32,807	CALCASIEU	3,656	1,129	2,494	33	1,365 D	30.9%	68.2%	31.2%	68.8%
9,514	CALDWELL	523	77	442	4	365 D	14.7%	84.5%	14.8%	85.2%
3,952	CAMERON	373	20	353		333 D	5.4%	94.6%	5.4%	94.6%
11,074	CATAHOULA	296	78	218		140 D	26.4%	73.6%	26.4%	73.6%
27,885	CLAIBORNE	1,306	54	1,252		1,198 D	4.1%	95.9%	4.1%	95.9%
12,466	CONCORDIA	365	46	319		273 D	12.6%	87.4%	12.6%	87.4%
29,376	DE SOTO	1,275	118	1,146	11	1,028 D	9.3%	89.9%	9.3%	90.7%
44,513	EAST BATON ROUGE	3,394	611	2,764	19	2,153 D	18.0%	81.4%	18.1%	81.9%
11,231	EAST CARROLL	348	71	277		206 D	20.4%	79.6%	20.4%	79.6%
17,487	EAST FELICIANA	529	25	504		479 D	4.7%	95.3%	4.7%	95.3%
23,485	EVANGELINE	757	153	603	1	450 D	20.2%	79.7%	20.2%	79.8%
24,100	FRANKLIN	830	143	687		544 D	17.2%	82.8%	17.2%	82.8%
14,403	GRANT	762	167	595		428 D	21.9%	78.1%	21.9%	78.1%
26,855	IBERIA	1,419	679	740		61 D	47.9%	52.1%	47.9%	52.1%
26,806	IBERVILLE	954	391	556	7	165 D	41.0%	58.3%	41.3%	58.7%
14,486	JACKSON	770	88	682		594 D	11.4%	88.6%	11.4%	88.6%
21,563	JEFFERSON	2,175	296	1,663	216	1,367 D	13.6%	76.5%	15.1%	84.9%
18,999	JEFFERSON DAVIS	1,856	883	973		90 D	47.6%	52.4%	47.6%	52.4%
30,841	LAFAYETTE	1,833	531	978	324	447 D	29.0%	53.4%	35.2%	64.8%
30,344	LAFOURCHE	1,289	611	678		67 D	47.4%	52.6%	47.4%	52.6%
9,856	LA SALLE	569	102	456	11	354 D	17.9%	80.1%	18.3%	81.7%
16,962	LINCOLN	1,166	157	1,005	4	848 D	13.5%	86.2%	13.5%	86.5%
11,643	LIVINGSTON	767	110	657		547 D	14.3%	85.7%	14.3%	85.7%
10,829	MADISON	287	13	274		261 D	4.5%	95.5%	4.5%	95.5%
19,311	MOREHOUSE	723	141	582		441 D	19.5%	80.5%	19.5%	80.5%
38,602	NATCHITOCHES	1,346	200	1,132	14	932 D	14.9%	84.1%	15.0%	85.0%
387,219	ORLEANS	47,791	7,865	37,785	2,141	29,920 D	16.5%	79.1%	17.2%	82.8%
30,319	OUACHITA	2,108	480	1,542	86	1,062 D	22.8%	73.1%	23.7%	76.3%
10,194	PLAQUEMINES	571	119	432	20	313 D	20.8%	75.7%	21.6%	78.4%
24,697	POINTE COUPEE	528	146	369	13	223 D	27.7%	69.9%	28.3%	71.7%
59,444	RAPIDES	3,290	1,022	2,159	109	1,137 D	31.1%	65.6%	32.1%	67.9%
15,301	RED RIVER	647	34	579	34	545 D	5.3%	89.5%	5.5%	94.5%
20,860	RICHLAND	794	116	678		562 D	14.6%	85.4%	14.6%	85.4%
20,713	SABINE	1,403	217	1,176	10	959 D	15.5%	83.8%	15.6%	84.4%
4,968	ST. BERNARD	539	13	526		513 D	2.4%	97.6%	2.4%	97.6%
8,586	ST. CHARLES	620	132	488		356 D	21.3%	78.7%	21.3%	78.7%
8,427	ST. HELENA	203	18	185		167 D	8.9%	91.1%	8.9%	91.1%
21,228	ST. JAMES	896	278	615	3	337 D	31.0%	68.6%	31.1%	68.9%
11,896	ST. JOHN THE BAPTIST	530	194	336		142 D	36.6%	63.4%	36.6%	63.4%
51,697	ST. LANDRY	1,711	357	1,354		997 D	20.9%	79.1%	20.9%	79.1%
21,990	ST. MARTIN	656	172	461	23	289 D	26.2%	70.3%	27.2%	72.8%
30,754	ST. MARY	1,300	633	639	28	6 D	48.7%	49.2%	49.8%	50.2%
20,645	ST. TAMMANY	1,311	269	969	73	700 D	20.5%	73.9%	21.7%	78.3%
31,440	TANGIPAHOA	2,105	479	1,626		1,147 D	22.8%	77.2%	22.8%	77.2%
12,085	TENSAS	359	21	338		317 D	5.8%	94.2%	5.8%	94.2%
26,974	TERREBONNE	897	415	482		67 D	46.3%	53.7%	46.3%	53.7%
19,621	UNION	883	7	875	1	868 D	0.8%	99.1%	0.8%	99.2%
26,482	VERMILION	1,014	416	598		182 D	41.0%	59.0%	41.0%	59.0%
20,493	VERNON	1,547	142	1,372	33	1,230 D	9.2%	88.7%	9.4%	90.6%
24,164	WASHINGTON	1,646	179	1,278	189	1,099 D	10.9%	77.6%	12.3%	87.7%
24,707	WEBSTER	1,033	52	929	52	877 D	5.0%	89.9%	5.3%	94.7%

LOUISIANA

PRESIDENT 1924

1920 Census Population	Parish	Total Vote	Republican	Democratic	Other	Rep.-Dem. Plurality	Percentage Total Vote Rep.	Percentage Total Vote Dem.	Percentage Major Vote Rep.	Percentage Major Vote Dem.
11,092	WEST BATON ROUGE	324	92	191	41	99 D	28.4%	59.0%	32.5%	67.5%
8,857	WEST CARROLL	419	68	342	9	274 D	16.2%	81.6%	16.6%	83.4%
12,303	WEST FELICIANA	362	15	347		332 D	4.1%	95.9%	4.1%	95.9%
16,119	WINN	917	120	797		677 D	13.1%	86.9%	13.1%	86.9%
1,798,509	TOTAL	121,951	24,670	93,218	4,063	68,548 D	20.2%	76.4%	20.9%	79.1%

LOUISIANA

PRESIDENT 1920

1920 Census Population	Parish	Total Vote	Republican	Democratic	Other	Rep.-Dem. Plurality	Percentage Total Vote Rep.	Total Vote Dem.	Major Vote Rep.	Major Vote Dem.
34,820	ACADIA	2,205	1,141	1,058	6	83 R	51.7%	48.0%	51.9%	48.1%
18,382	ALLEN	1,250	242	1,008		766 D	19.4%	80.6%	19.4%	80.6%
22,155	ASCENSION	1,118	496	622		126 D	44.4%	55.6%	44.4%	55.6%
17,912	ASSUMPTION	927	725	202		523 R	78.2%	21.8%	78.2%	21.8%
35,300	AVOYELLES	2,146	724	1,422		698 D	33.7%	66.3%	33.7%	66.3%
20,767	BEAUREGARD	1,362	202	1,146	14	944 D	14.8%	84.1%	15.0%	85.0%
20,977	BIENVILLE	1,704	257	1,419	28	1,162 D	15.1%	83.3%	15.3%	84.7%
22,266	BOSSIER	775	44	731		687 D	5.7%	94.3%	5.7%	94.3%
83,265	CADDO	4,665	401	4,264		3,863 D	8.6%	91.4%	8.6%	91.4%
32,807	CALCASIEU	2,976	483	2,480	13	1,997 D	16.2%	83.3%	16.3%	83.7%
9,514	CALDWELL	667	128	539		411 D	19.2%	80.8%	19.2%	80.8%
3,952	CAMERON	157	11	146		135 D	7.0%	93.0%	7.0%	93.0%
11,074	CATAHOULA	693	176	517		341 D	25.4%	74.6%	25.4%	74.6%
27,885	CLAIBORNE	1,264	48	1,216		1,168 D	3.8%	96.2%	3.8%	96.2%
12,466	CONCORDIA	392	12	380		368 D	3.1%	96.9%	3.1%	96.9%
29,376	DE SOTO	1,275	56	1,219		1,163 D	4.4%	95.6%	4.4%	95.6%
44,513	EAST BATON ROUGE	2,778	442	2,336		1,894 D	15.9%	84.1%	15.9%	84.1%
11,231	EAST CARROLL	255	8	247		239 D	3.1%	96.9%	3.1%	96.9%
17,487	EAST FELICIANA	559	30	529		499 D	5.4%	94.6%	5.4%	94.6%
23,485	EVANGELINE	1,129	587	542		45 R	52.0%	48.0%	52.0%	48.0%
24,100	FRANKLIN	1,071	173	898		725 D	16.2%	83.8%	16.2%	83.8%
14,403	GRANT	783	109	674		565 D	13.9%	86.1%	13.9%	86.1%
26,855	IBERIA	1,713	1,275	438		837 R	74.4%	25.6%	74.4%	25.6%
26,806	IBERVILLE	850	465	385		80 R	54.7%	45.3%	54.7%	45.3%
14,486	JACKSON	1,395	166	1,229		1,063 D	11.9%	88.1%	11.9%	88.1%
21,563	JEFFERSON	1,430	192	1,238		1,046 D	13.4%	86.6%	13.4%	86.6%
18,999	JEFFERSON DAVIS	1,623	895	728		167 R	55.1%	44.9%	55.1%	44.9%
30,841	LAFAYETTE	1,868	1,045	823		222 R	55.9%	44.1%	55.9%	44.1%
30,344	LAFOURCHE	1,381	1,044	337		707 R	75.6%	24.4%	75.6%	24.4%
9,856	LA SALLE	694	109	570	15	461 D	15.7%	82.1%	16.1%	83.9%
16,962	LINCOLN	1,172	183	989		806 D	15.6%	84.4%	15.6%	84.4%
11,643	LIVINGSTON	893	218	674	1	456 D	24.4%	75.5%	24.4%	75.6%
10,829	MADISON	335	4	331		327 D	1.2%	98.8%	1.2%	98.8%
19,311	MOREHOUSE	660	38	622		584 D	5.8%	94.2%	5.8%	94.2%
38,602	NATCHITOCHES	1,798	203	1,595		1,392 D	11.3%	88.7%	11.3%	88.7%
387,219	ORLEANS	50,543	17,819	32,724		14,905 D	35.3%	64.7%	35.3%	64.7%
30,319	OUACHITA	1,646	164	1,481	1	1,317 D	10.0%	90.0%	10.0%	90.0%
10,194	PLAQUEMINES	469	124	329	16	205 D	26.4%	70.1%	27.4%	72.6%
24,697	POINTE COUPEE	550	143	407		264 D	26.0%	74.0%	26.0%	74.0%
59,444	RAPIDES	3,211	445	2,765	1	2,320 D	13.9%	86.1%	13.9%	86.1%
15,301	RED RIVER	953	187	766		579 D	19.6%	80.4%	19.6%	80.4%
20,860	RICHLAND	714	50	664		614 D	7.0%	93.0%	7.0%	93.0%
20,713	SABINE	1,356	111	1,245		1,134 D	8.2%	91.8%	8.2%	91.8%
4,968	ST. BERNARD	414	56	358		302 D	13.5%	86.5%	13.5%	86.5%
8,586	ST. CHARLES	275	92	183		91 D	33.5%	66.5%	33.5%	66.5%
8,427	ST. HELENA	402	36	366		330 D	9.0%	91.0%	9.0%	91.0%
21,228	ST. JAMES	875	533	342		191 R	60.9%	39.1%	60.9%	39.1%
11,896	ST. JOHN THE BAPTIST	489	250	239		11 R	51.1%	48.9%	51.1%	48.9%
51,697	ST. LANDRY	1,959	942	1,017		75 D	48.1%	51.9%	48.1%	51.9%
21,990	ST. MARTIN	738	419	319		100 R	56.8%	43.2%	56.8%	43.2%
30,754	ST. MARY	1,327	788	539		249 R	59.4%	40.6%	59.4%	40.6%
20,645	ST. TAMMANY	1,243	276	967		691 D	22.2%	77.8%	22.2%	77.8%
31,440	TANGIPAHOA	1,941	440	1,501		1,061 D	22.7%	77.3%	22.7%	77.3%
12,085	TENSAS	258	15	243		228 D	5.8%	94.2%	5.8%	94.2%
26,974	TERREBONNE	1,190	713	477		236 R	59.9%	40.1%	59.9%	40.1%
19,621	UNION	1,319	98	1,221		1,123 D	7.4%	92.6%	7.4%	92.6%
26,482	VERMILION	1,970	1,420	549	1	871 R	72.1%	27.9%	72.1%	27.9%
20,493	VERNON	1,348	205	1,143		938 D	15.2%	84.8%	15.2%	84.8%
24,164	WASHINGTON	1,259	165	1,094		929 D	13.1%	86.9%	13.1%	86.9%
24,707	WEBSTER	1,121	112	1,009		897 D	10.0%	90.0%	10.0%	90.0%

LOUISIANA

PRESIDENT 1920

1920 Census Population	Parish	Total Vote	Republican	Democratic	Other	Rep.-Dem. Plurality	Percentage Total Vote Rep.	Percentage Total Vote Dem.	Percentage Major Vote Rep.	Percentage Major Vote Dem.
11,092	WEST BATON ROUGE	527	175	352		177 D	33.2%	66.8%	33.2%	66.8%
8,857	WEST CARROLL	470	104	346	20	242 D	22.1%	73.6%	23.1%	76.9%
12,303	WEST FELICIANA	390	34	356		322 D	8.7%	91.3%	8.7%	91.3%
16,119	WINN	1,477	291	963	223	672 D	19.7%	65.2%	23.2%	76.8%
1,798,509	TOTAL	126,397	38,539	87,519	339	48,980 D	30.5%	69.2%	30.6%	69.4%

LOUISIANA

ELECTION NOTES

1956 Other vote was Unpledged States Rights. The Unpledged States Rights electors carried Caldwell, Madison, Richland and West Carroll parishes in the northeast section of the state and ran second in other parishes in that area.

1952

1948 A special four-column table which gives the Thurmond (States Rights) vote is used to detail this election. Other vote was 3,035 Wallace (Progressive); 10 scattered write-in.

1944 Other vote was scattered write-in.

1940 Other vote was scattered write-in.

1936 Other vote was scattered write-in.

1932 Other vote was scattered write-in.

1928 Other vote was scattered write-in.

1924 Other vote was scattered write-in. Many of these write-in votes were for the Progressive candidate LaFollette but the division of votes among individuals was not reported.

1920 Other vote was scattered write-in.

MAINE

POPULAR VOTE FOR PRESIDENT 1920 TO 1956

		Republican		Democratic				Percentage			
								Total Vote		Major Vote	
Year	Total Vote	Vote	Candidate	Vote	Candidate	Other Vote	Plurality	Rep.	Dem.	Rep.	Dem.
1956	351,706	249,238	Eisenhower, Dwight D.	102,468	Stevenson, Adlai E.		146,770 R	70.9%	29.1%	70.9%	29.1%
1952	351,786	232,353	Eisenhower, Dwight D.	118,806	Stevenson, Adlai E.	627	113,547 R	66.0%	33.8%	66.2%	33.8%
1948	264,787	150,234	Dewey, Thomas E.	111,916	Truman, Harry S.	2,637	38,318 R	56.7%	42.3%	57.3%	42.7%
1944	296,400	155,434	Dewey, Thomas E.	140,631	Roosevelt, Franklin D.	335	14,803 R	52.4%	47.4%	52.5%	47.5%
1940	320,840	163,951	Willkie, Wendell	156,478	Roosevelt, Franklin D.	411	7,473 R	51.1%	48.8%	51.2%	48.8%
1936	304,240	168,823	Landon, Alfred M.	126,333	Roosevelt, Franklin D.	9,084	42,490 R	55.5%	41.5%	57.2%	42.8%
1932	298,444	166,631	Hoover, Herbert C.	128,907	Roosevelt, Franklin D.	2,906	37,724 R	55.8%	43.2%	56.4%	43.6%
1928	262,170	179,923	Hoover, Herbert C.	81,179	Smith, Alfred E.	1,068	98,744 R	68.6%	31.0%	68.9%	31.1%
1924	192,192	138,440	Coolidge, Calvin	41,964	Davis, John W.	11,788	96,476 R	72.0%	21.8%	76.7%	23.3%
1920	197,840	136,355	Harding, Warren G.	58,961	Cox, James M.	2,524	77,394 R	68.9%	29.8%	69.8%	30.2%

ELECTORAL COLLEGE VOTE 1920 TO 1956

Year	Total	Republican	Democratic	Other
1956	5	5	—	—
1952	5	5	—	—
1948	5	5	—	—
1944	5	5	—	—
1940	5	5	—	—
1936	5	5	—	—
1932	5	5	—	—
1928	6	6	—	—
1924	6	6	—	—
1920	6	6	—	—

MAINE

AROOSTOOK
PISCATAQUIS
SOMERSET
PENOBSCOT
WASHINGTON
FRANKLIN
HANCOCK
OXFORD
WALDO
KENNEBEC
ANDROSCOGGIN
KNOX
SAGADAHOC
LINCOLN
CUMBERLAND
YORK

MAINE

PRESIDENT 1956

1950 Census Population	County	Total Vote	Republican	Democratic	Other	Rep.-Dem. Plurality	Percentage Total Vote Rep.	Total Vote Dem.	Major Vote Rep.	Major Vote Dem.
83,594	ANDROSCOGGIN	36,227	20,385	15,842		4,543 R	56.3%	43.7%	56.3%	43.7%
96,039	AROOSTOOK	22,090	16,001	6,089		9,912 R	72.4%	27.6%	72.4%	27.6%
169,201	CUMBERLAND	69,134	49,696	19,438		30,258 R	71.9%	28.1%	71.9%	28.1%
20,682	FRANKLIN	7,987	6,307	1,680		4,627 R	79.0%	21.0%	79.0%	21.0%
32,105	HANCOCK	13,020	11,316	1,704		9,612 R	86.9%	13.1%	86.9%	13.1%
83,881	KENNEBEC	34,511	23,028	11,483		11,545 R	66.7%	33.3%	66.7%	33.3%
28,121	KNOX	10,903	8,866	2,037		6,829 R	81.3%	18.7%	81.3%	18.7%
18,004	LINCOLN	8,355	7,191	1,164		6,027 R	86.1%	13.9%	86.1%	13.9%
44,221	OXFORD	17,260	12,607	4,653		7,954 R	73.0%	27.0%	73.0%	27.0%
108,198	PENOBSCOT	36,374	27,806	8,568		19,238 R	76.4%	23.6%	76.4%	23.6%
18,617	PISCATAQUIS	6,877	5,336	1,541		3,795 R	77.6%	22.4%	77.6%	22.4%
20,911	SAGADAHOC	8,502	6,201	2,301		3,900 R	72.9%	27.1%	72.9%	27.1%
39,785	SOMERSET	14,590	10,471	4,119		6,352 R	71.8%	28.2%	71.8%	28.2%
21,687	WALDO	7,974	6,590	1,384		5,206 R	82.6%	17.4%	82.6%	17.4%
35,187	WASHINGTON	10,736	8,181	2,555		5,626 R	76.2%	23.8%	76.2%	23.8%
93,541	YORK	47,166	29,256	17,910		11,346 R	62.0%	38.0%	62.0%	38.0%
913,774	TOTAL	351,706	249,238	102,468		146,770 R	70.9%	29.1%	70.9%	29.1%

MAINE

PRESIDENT 1952

1950 Census Population	County	Total Vote	Republican	Democratic	Other	Rep.-Dem. Plurality	Percentage Total Vote Rep.	Total Vote Dem.	Major Vote Rep.	Major Vote Dem.
83,594	ANDROSCOGGIN	35,676	18,049	17,560	67	489 R	50.6%	49.2%	50.7%	49.3%
96,039	AROOSTOOK	24,476	16,851	7,561	64	9,290 R	68.8%	30.9%	69.0%	31.0%
169,201	CUMBERLAND	67,898	46,957	20,831	110	26,126 R	69.2%	30.7%	69.3%	30.7%
20,682	FRANKLIN	8,036	5,885	2,137	14	3,748 R	73.2%	26.6%	73.4%	26.6%
32,105	HANCOCK	12,734	10,596	2,111	27	8,485 R	83.2%	16.6%	83.4%	16.6%
83,881	KENNEBEC	33,351	21,207	12,113	31	9,094 R	63.6%	36.3%	63.6%	36.4%
28,121	KNOX	11,227	8,793	2,414	20	6,379 R	78.3%	21.5%	78.5%	21.5%
18,004	LINCOLN	8,074	6,766	1,299	9	5,467 R	83.8%	16.1%	83.9%	16.1%
44,221	OXFORD	17,375	11,575	5,757	43	5,818 R	66.6%	33.1%	66.8%	33.2%
108,198	PENOBSCOT	35,885	24,614	11,222	49	13,392 R	68.6%	31.3%	68.7%	31.3%
18,617	PISCATAQUIS	6,923	4,652	2,261	10	2,391 R	67.2%	32.7%	67.3%	32.7%
20,911	SAGADAHOC	8,668	5,799	2,850	19	2,949 R	66.9%	32.9%	67.0%	33.0%
39,785	SOMERSET	14,649	9,805	4,815	29	4,990 R	66.9%	32.9%	67.1%	32.9%
21,687	WALDO	7,925	6,363	1,545	17	4,818 R	80.3%	19.5%	80.5%	19.5%
35,187	WASHINGTON	11,225	7,396	3,806	23	3,590 R	65.9%	33.9%	66.0%	34.0%
93,541	YORK	47,664	27,045	20,524	95	6,521 R	56.7%	43.1%	56.9%	43.1%
913,774	TOTAL	351,786	232,353	118,806	627	113,547 R	66.0%	33.8%	66.2%	33.8%

MAINE

PRESIDENT 1948

1940 Census Population	County	Total Vote	Republican	Democratic	Other	Rep.-Dem. Plurality	Percentage: Total Vote Rep.	Total Vote Dem.	Major Vote Rep.	Major Vote Dem.
76,679	ANDROSCOGGIN	29,165	11,443	17,405	317	5,962 D	39.2%	59.7%	39.7%	60.3%
94,436	AROOSTOOK	16,740	9,459	7,183	98	2,276 R	56.5%	42.9%	56.8%	43.2%
146,000	CUMBERLAND	49,885	30,284	18,913	688	11,371 R	60.7%	37.9%	61.6%	38.4%
19,896	FRANKLIN	5,920	3,741	2,135	44	1,606 R	63.2%	36.1%	63.7%	36.3%
32,422	HANCOCK	8,830	6,863	1,878	89	4,985 R	77.7%	21.3%	78.5%	21.5%
77,231	KENNEBEC	25,260	13,923	11,163	174	2,760 R	55.1%	44.2%	55.5%	44.5%
27,191	KNOX	7,395	5,374	1,924	97	3,450 R	72.7%	26.0%	73.6%	26.4%
16,294	LINCOLN	5,893	4,743	1,095	55	3,648 R	80.5%	18.6%	81.2%	18.8%
42,662	OXFORD	12,782	7,444	5,183	155	2,261 R	58.2%	40.5%	59.0%	41.0%
97,104	PENOBSCOT	27,315	16,367	10,705	243	5,662 R	59.9%	39.2%	60.5%	39.5%
18,467	PISCATAQUIS	5,438	3,227	2,181	30	1,046 R	59.3%	40.1%	59.7%	40.3%
19,123	SAGADAHOC	6,371	3,745	2,556	70	1,189 R	58.8%	40.1%	59.4%	40.6%
38,245	SOMERSET	10,418	6,301	4,034	83	2,267 R	60.5%	38.7%	61.0%	39.0%
21,159	WALDO	5,890	4,371	1,469	50	2,902 R	74.2%	24.9%	74.8%	25.2%
37,767	WASHINGTON	8,748	5,130	3,538	80	1,592 R	58.6%	40.4%	59.2%	40.8%
82,550	YORK	38,737	17,819	20,554	364	2,735 D	46.0%	53.1%	46.4%	53.6%
847,226	TOTAL	264,787	150,234	111,916	2,637	38,318 R	56.7%	42.3%	57.3%	42.7%

MAINE

PRESIDENT 1944

1940 Census Population	County	Total Vote	Republican	Democratic	Other	Rep.-Dem. Plurality	Percentage: Total Vote Rep.	Total Vote Dem.	Major Vote Rep.	Major Vote Dem.
76,679	ANDROSCOGGIN	30,039	10,927	19,078	34	8,151 D	36.4%	63.5%	36.4%	63.6%
94,436	AROOSTOOK	19,717	11,678	8,017	22	3,661 R	59.2%	40.7%	59.3%	40.7%
146,000	CUMBERLAND	56,278	29,349	26,857	72	2,492 R	52.2%	47.7%	52.2%	47.8%
19,896	FRANKLIN	6,777	4,127	2,646	4	1,481 R	60.9%	39.0%	60.9%	39.1%
32,422	HANCOCK	10,396	7,143	3,241	12	3,902 R	68.7%	31.2%	68.8%	31.2%
77,231	KENNEBEC	28,430	14,335	14,070	25	265 R	50.4%	49.5%	50.5%	49.5%
27,191	KNOX	9,363	5,590	3,758	15	1,832 R	59.7%	40.1%	59.8%	40.2%
16,294	LINCOLN	7,030	4,919	2,102	9	2,817 R	70.0%	29.9%	70.1%	29.9%
42,662	OXFORD	14,442	8,053	6,377	12	1,676 R	55.8%	44.2%	55.8%	44.2%
97,104	PENOBSCOT	30,264	16,934	13,292	38	3,642 R	56.0%	43.9%	56.0%	44.0%
18,467	PISCATAQUIS	6,494	3,536	2,957	1	579 R	54.5%	45.5%	54.5%	45.5%
19,123	SAGADAHOC	7,889	3,883	4,003	3	120 D	49.2%	50.7%	49.2%	50.8%
38,245	SOMERSET	12,523	7,167	5,331	25	1,836 R	57.2%	42.6%	57.3%	42.7%
21,159	WALDO	6,104	4,291	1,807	6	2,484 R	70.3%	29.6%	70.4%	29.6%
37,767	WASHINGTON	11,107	5,380	5,709	18	329 D	48.4%	51.4%	48.5%	51.5%
82,550	YORK	39,547	18,122	21,386	39	3,264 D	45.8%	54.1%	45.9%	54.1%
847,226	TOTAL	296,400	155,434	140,631	335	14,803 R	52.4%	47.4%	52.5%	47.5%

MAINE

PRESIDENT 1940

1940 Census Population	County	Total Vote	Republican	Democratic	Other	Rep.-Dem. Plurality	Percentage Total Vote Rep.	Total Vote Dem.	Major Vote Rep.	Major Vote Dem.
76,679	ANDROSCOGGIN	29,707	10,394	19,273	40	8,879 D	35.0%	64.9%	35.0%	65.0%
94,436	AROOSTOOK	23,804	13,888	9,877	39	4,011 R	58.3%	41.5%	58.4%	41.6%
146,000	CUMBERLAND	56,782	29,795	26,911	76	2,884 R	52.5%	47.4%	52.5%	47.5%
19,896	FRANKLIN	7,779	4,548	3,224	7	1,324 R	58.5%	41.4%	58.5%	41.5%
32,422	HANCOCK	12,867	8,539	4,315	13	4,224 R	66.4%	33.5%	66.4%	33.6%
77,231	KENNEBEC	30,765	14,877	15,861	27	984 D	48.4%	51.6%	48.4%	51.6%
27,191	KNOX	10,747	6,530	4,197	20	2,333 R	60.8%	39.1%	60.9%	39.1%
16,294	LINCOLN	7,664	5,244	2,415	5	2,829 R	68.4%	31.5%	68.5%	31.5%
42,662	OXFORD	16,183	8,656	7,502	25	1,154 R	53.5%	46.4%	53.6%	46.4%
97,104	PENOBSCOT	33,471	18,674	14,757	40	3,917 R	55.8%	44.1%	55.9%	44.1%
18,467	PISCATAQUIS	7,312	3,806	3,499	7	307 R	52.1%	47.9%	52.1%	47.9%
19,123	SAGADAHOC	8,092	3,504	4,575	13	1,071 D	43.3%	56.5%	43.4%	56.6%
38,245	SOMERSET	14,088	7,526	6,534	28	992 R	53.4%	46.4%	53.5%	46.5%
21,159	WALDO	8,398	5,170	3,214	14	1,956 R	61.6%	38.3%	61.7%	38.3%
37,767	WASHINGTON	14,326	6,253	8,048	25	1,795 D	43.6%	56.2%	43.7%	56.3%
82,550	YORK	38,855	16,547	22,276	32	5,729 D	42.6%	57.3%	42.6%	57.4%
847,226	TOTAL	320,840	163,951	156,478	411	7,473 R	51.1%	48.8%	51.2%	48.8%

MAINE

PRESIDENT 1936

1930 Census Population	County	Total Vote	Republican	Democratic	Other	Rep.-Dem. Plurality	Percentage Total Vote Rep.	Total Vote Dem.	Major Vote Rep.	Major Vote Dem.
71,214	ANDROSCOGGIN	27,477	10,480	16,657	340	6,177 D	38.1%	60.6%	38.6%	61.4%
87,843	AROOSTOOK	22,736	14,708	7,704	324	7,004 R	64.7%	33.9%	65.6%	34.4%
134,645	CUMBERLAND	54,030	30,021	22,895	1,114	7,126 R	55.6%	42.4%	56.7%	43.3%
19,941	FRANKLIN	7,928	4,957	2,859	112	2,098 R	62.5%	36.1%	63.4%	36.6%
30,721	HANCOCK	12,700	9,151	3,315	234	5,836 R	72.1%	26.1%	73.4%	26.6%
70,691	KENNEBEC	27,081	14,987	11,268	826	3,719 R	55.3%	41.6%	57.1%	42.9%
27,693	KNOX	10,879	6,567	3,991	321	2,576 R	60.4%	36.7%	62.2%	37.8%
15,498	LINCOLN	7,232	5,252	1,850	130	3,402 R	72.6%	25.6%	74.0%	26.0%
41,483	OXFORD	15,366	8,778	5,836	752	2,942 R	57.1%	38.0%	60.1%	39.9%
92,379	PENOBSCOT	31,368	19,077	9,732	2,559	9,345 R	60.8%	31.0%	66.2%	33.8%
18,231	PISCATAQUIS	7,295	4,057	3,051	187	1,006 R	55.6%	41.8%	57.1%	42.9%
16,927	SAGADAHOC	7,130	3,707	3,273	150	434 R	52.0%	45.9%	53.1%	46.9%
39,111	SOMERSET	13,281	7,558	5,282	441	2,276 R	56.9%	39.8%	58.9%	41.1%
20,286	WALDO	8,172	5,309	2,678	185	2,631 R	65.0%	32.8%	66.5%	33.5%
37,826	WASHINGTON	14,495	6,387	7,925	183	1,538 D	44.1%	54.7%	44.6%	55.4%
72,934	YORK	37,070	17,827	18,017	1,226	190 D	48.1%	48.6%	49.7%	50.3%
797,423	TOTAL	304,240	168,823	126,333	9,084	42,490 R	55.5%	41.5%	57.2%	42.8%

MAINE

PRESIDENT 1932

1930 Census Population	County	Total Vote	Republican	Democratic	Other	Rep.-Dem. Plurality	Percentage Total Vote Rep.	Percentage Total Vote Dem.	Percentage Major Vote Rep.	Percentage Major Vote Dem.
71,214	ANDROSCOGGIN	24,562	9,838	14,441	283	4,603 D	40.1%	58.8%	40.5%	59.5%
87,843	AROOSTOOK	23,631	14,054	9,409	168	4,645 R	59.5%	39.8%	59.9%	40.1%
134,645	CUMBERLAND	54,033	32,864	20,655	514	12,209 R	60.8%	38.2%	61.4%	38.6%
19,941	FRANKLIN	7,733	4,521	3,171	41	1,350 R	58.5%	41.0%	58.8%	41.2%
30,721	HANCOCK	12,396	7,942	4,369	85	3,573 R	64.1%	35.2%	64.5%	35.5%
70,691	KENNEBEC	26,797	14,451	12,110	236	2,341 R	53.9%	45.2%	54.4%	45.6%
27,693	KNOX	11,159	6,169	4,765	225	1,404 R	55.3%	42.7%	56.4%	43.6%
15,498	LINCOLN	7,309	4,666	2,602	41	2,064 R	63.8%	35.6%	64.2%	35.8%
41,483	OXFORD	15,673	8,264	7,179	230	1,085 R	52.7%	45.8%	53.5%	46.5%
92,379	PENOBSCOT	32,317	18,987	13,058	272	5,929 R	58.8%	40.4%	59.3%	40.7%
18,231	PISCATAQUIS	7,099	4,198	2,849	52	1,349 R	59.1%	40.1%	59.6%	40.4%
16,927	SAGADAHOC	7,037	4,220	2,763	54	1,457 R	60.0%	39.3%	60.4%	39.6%
39,111	SOMERSET	13,461	7,144	6,040	277	1,104 R	53.1%	44.9%	54.2%	45.8%
20,286	WALDO	8,467	4,505	3,907	55	598 R	53.2%	46.1%	53.6%	46.4%
37,826	WASHINGTON	14,451	7,507	6,829	115	678 R	51.9%	47.3%	52.4%	47.6%
72,934	YORK	32,319	17,301	14,760	258	2,541 R	53.5%	45.7%	54.0%	46.0%
797,423	TOTAL	298,444	166,631	128,907	2,906	37,724 R	55.8%	43.2%	56.4%	43.6%

MAINE

PRESIDENT 1928

1920 Census Population	County	Total Vote	Republican	Democratic	Other	Rep.-Dem. Plurality	Percentage Total Vote Rep.	Percentage Total Vote Dem.	Percentage Major Vote Rep.	Percentage Major Vote Dem.
65,796	ANDROSCOGGIN	22,854	11,790	10,940	124	850 R	51.6%	47.9%	51.9%	48.1%
81,728	AROOSTOOK	20,357	14,545	5,771	41	8,774 R	71.4%	28.3%	71.6%	28.4%
124,376	CUMBERLAND	48,995	33,190	15,648	157	17,542 R	67.7%	31.9%	68.0%	32.0%
19,825	FRANKLIN	6,432	4,923	1,487	22	3,436 R	76.5%	23.1%	76.8%	23.2%
30,361	HANCOCK	9,946	8,140	1,773	33	6,367 R	81.8%	17.8%	82.1%	17.9%
63,844	KENNEBEC	23,859	15,541	8,226	92	7,315 R	65.1%	34.5%	65.4%	34.6%
26,245	KNOX	9,080	6,660	2,332	88	4,328 R	73.3%	25.7%	74.1%	25.9%
15,976	LINCOLN	5,669	4,470	1,181	18	3,289 R	78.8%	20.8%	79.1%	20.9%
37,700	OXFORD	13,490	9,409	4,015	66	5,394 R	69.7%	29.8%	70.1%	29.9%
87,684	PENOBSCOT	30,960	21,750	9,114	96	12,636 R	70.3%	29.4%	70.5%	29.5%
20,554	PISCATAQUIS	6,161	4,792	1,353	16	3,439 R	77.8%	22.0%	78.0%	22.0%
23,021	SAGADAHOC	6,208	4,605	1,583	20	3,022 R	74.2%	25.5%	74.4%	25.6%
37,171	SOMERSET	11,406	8,055	3,251	100	4,804 R	70.6%	28.5%	71.2%	28.8%
21,328	WALDO	6,294	4,851	1,402	41	3,449 R	77.1%	22.3%	77.6%	22.4%
41,709	WASHINGTON	11,639	8,531	3,073	35	5,458 R	73.3%	26.4%	73.5%	26.5%
70,696	YORK	28,820	18,671	10,030	119	8,641 R	64.8%	34.8%	65.1%	34.9%
768,014	TOTAL	262,170	179,923	81,179	1,068	98,744 R	68.6%	31.0%	68.9%	31.1%

MAINE

PRESIDENT 1924

1920 Census Population	County	Total Vote	Republican	Democratic	Other	Rep.-Dem. Plurality	Percentage Total Vote Rep.	Total Vote Dem.	Major Vote Rep.	Major Vote Dem.
65,796	ANDROSCOGGIN	16,187	9,680	4,733	1,774	4,947 R	59.8%	29.2%	67.2%	32.8%
81,728	AROOSTOOK	11,707	9,554	1,510	643	8,044 R	81.6%	12.9%	86.4%	13.6%
124,376	CUMBERLAND	35,719	26,187	7,078	2,454	19,109 R	73.3%	19.8%	78.7%	21.3%
19,825	FRANKLIN	4,681	3,389	1,123	169	2,266 R	72.4%	24.0%	75.1%	24.9%
30,361	HANCOCK	7,075	5,474	1,392	209	4,082 R	77.4%	19.7%	79.7%	20.3%
63,844	KENNEBEC	18,159	13,122	4,184	853	8,938 R	72.3%	23.0%	75.8%	24.2%
26,245	KNOX	7,028	4,919	1,770	339	3,149 R	70.0%	25.2%	73.5%	26.5%
15,976	LINCOLN	4,280	3,311	878	91	2,433 R	77.4%	20.5%	79.0%	21.0%
37,700	OXFORD	10,103	7,062	2,563	478	4,499 R	69.9%	25.4%	73.4%	26.6%
87,684	PENOBSCOT	20,128	15,081	3,618	1,429	11,463 R	74.9%	18.0%	80.7%	19.3%
20,554	PISCATAQUIS	5,308	4,031	974	303	3,057 R	75.9%	18.3%	80.5%	19.5%
23,021	SAGADAHOC	4,802	3,518	1,084	200	2,434 R	73.3%	22.6%	76.4%	23.6%
37,171	SOMERSET	9,285	6,855	1,822	608	5,033 R	73.8%	19.6%	79.0%	21.0%
21,328	WALDO	5,281	4,003	1,125	153	2,878 R	75.8%	21.3%	78.1%	21.9%
41,709	WASHINGTON	8,621	6,010	2,106	505	3,904 R	69.7%	24.4%	74.1%	25.9%
70,696	YORK	23,828	16,244	6,004	1,580	10,240 R	68.2%	25.2%	73.0%	27.0%
768,014	TOTAL	192,192	138,440	41,964	11,788	96,476 R	72.0%	21.8%	76.7%	23.3%

MAINE

PRESIDENT 1920

1920 Census Population	County	Total Vote	Republican	Democratic	Other	Rep.-Dem. Plurality	Percentage Total Vote Rep.	Total Vote Dem.	Major Vote Rep.	Major Vote Dem.
65,796	ANDROSCOGGIN	15,724	9,565	5,757	402	3,808 R	60.8%	36.6%	62.4%	37.6%
81,728	AROOSTOOK	12,648	11,191	1,407	50	9,784 R	88.5%	11.1%	88.8%	11.2%
124,376	CUMBERLAND	35,585	24,623	10,484	478	14,139 R	69.2%	29.5%	70.1%	29.9%
19,825	FRANKLIN	5,526	3,820	1,668	38	2,152 R	69.1%	30.2%	69.6%	30.4%
30,361	HANCOCK	7,818	5,604	2,154	60	3,450 R	71.7%	27.6%	72.2%	27.8%
63,844	KENNEBEC	17,973	12,333	5,466	174	6,867 R	68.6%	30.4%	69.3%	30.7%
26,245	KNOX	8,183	4,979	2,971	233	2,008 R	60.8%	36.3%	62.6%	37.4%
15,976	LINCOLN	4,983	3,668	1,256	59	2,412 R	73.6%	25.2%	74.5%	25.5%
37,700	OXFORD	11,304	7,301	3,906	97	3,395 R	64.6%	34.6%	65.1%	34.9%
87,684	PENOBSCOT	20,398	14,145	6,110	143	8,035 R	69.3%	30.0%	69.8%	30.2%
20,554	PISCATAQUIS	5,886	4,049	1,788	49	2,261 R	68.8%	30.4%	69.4%	30.6%
23,021	SAGADAHOC	5,642	3,857	1,709	76	2,148 R	68.4%	30.3%	69.3%	30.7%
37,171	SOMERSET	9,592	6,533	2,770	289	3,763 R	68.1%	28.9%	70.2%	29.8%
21,328	WALDO	6,128	4,383	1,666	79	2,717 R	71.5%	27.2%	72.5%	27.5%
41,709	WASHINGTON	9,870	6,768	2,997	105	3,771 R	68.6%	30.4%	69.3%	30.7%
70,696	YORK	20,580	13,536	6,852	192	6,684 R	65.8%	33.3%	66.4%	33.6%
768,014	TOTAL	197,840	136,355	58,961	2,524	77,394 R	68.9%	29.8%	69.8%	30.2%

MAINE

ELECTION NOTES

1956

1952 Other vote was 332 Hallinan (Progressive); 156 Hass (Socialist Labor); 138 Hoopes (Socialist); 1 write-in.

1948 Other vote was 1,884 Wallace (Progressive); 547 Thomas (Socialist); 206 Teichert (Socialist Labor).

1944 Other vote was Teichert (Socialist Labor).

1940 Other vote was Browder (Communist).

1936 Other vote was 7,581 Lemke (Union); 783 Thomas (Socialist); 334 Colvin (Prohibition); 257 Browder (Communist); 129 Aiken (Socialist Labor).

1932 Other vote was 2,489 Thomas (Socialist); 255 Reynolds (Socialist Labor); 162 Foster (Communist).

1928 Other vote was Thomas (Socialist).

1924 Other vote was 11,382 LaFollette (Progressive); 406 Johns (Socialist Labor).

1920 Other vote was 2,214 Debs (Socialist); 310 Macauley (Single Tax).

MARYLAND

POPULAR VOTE FOR PRESIDENT 1920 TO 1956

Year	Total Vote	Republican Vote	Republican Candidate	Democratic Vote	Democratic Candidate	Other Vote	Plurality	Percentage Total Vote Rep.	Percentage Total Vote Dem.	Percentage Major Vote Rep.	Percentage Major Vote Dem.
1956	932,827	559,738	Eisenhower, Dwight D.	372,613	Stevenson, Adlai E.	476	187,125 R	60.0%	39.9%	60.0%	40.0%
1952	902,074	499,424	Eisenhower, Dwight D.	395,337	Stevenson, Adlai E.	7,313	104,087 R	55.4%	43.8%	55.8%	44.2%
1948	596,748	294,814	Dewey, Thomas E.	286,521	Truman, Harry S.	15,413	8,293 R	49.4%	48.0%	50.7%	49.3%
1944	608,439	292,949	Dewey, Thomas E.	315,490	Roosevelt, Franklin D.		22,541 D	48.1%	51.9%	48.1%	51.9%
1940	660,104	269,534	Willkie, Wendell	384,546	Roosevelt, Franklin D.	6,024	115,012 D	40.8%	58.3%	41.2%	58.8%
1936	624,896	231,435	Landon, Alfred M.	389,612	Roosevelt, Franklin D.	3,849	158,177 D	37.0%	62.3%	37.3%	62.7%
1932	511,054	184,184	Hoover, Herbert C.	314,314	Roosevelt, Franklin D.	12,556	130,130 D	36.0%	61.5%	36.9%	63.1%
1928	528,348	301,479	Hoover, Herbert C.	223,626	Smith, Alfred E.	3,243	77,853 R	57.1%	42.3%	57.4%	42.6%
1924	358,630	162,414	Coolidge, Calvin	148,072	Davis, John W.	48,144	14,342 R	45.3%	41.3%	52.3%	47.7%
1920	428,443	236,117	Harding, Warren G.	180,626	Cox, James M.	11,700	55,491 R	55.1%	42.2%	56.7%	43.3%

ELECTORAL COLLEGE VOTE 1920 TO 1956

Year	Total	Republican	Democratic	Other
1956	9	9	—	—
1952	9	9	—	—
1948	8	8	—	—
1944	8	—	8	—
1940	8	—	8	—
1936	8	—	8	—
1932	8	—	8	—
1928	8	8	—	—
1924	8	8	—	—
1920	8	8	—	—

MARYLAND

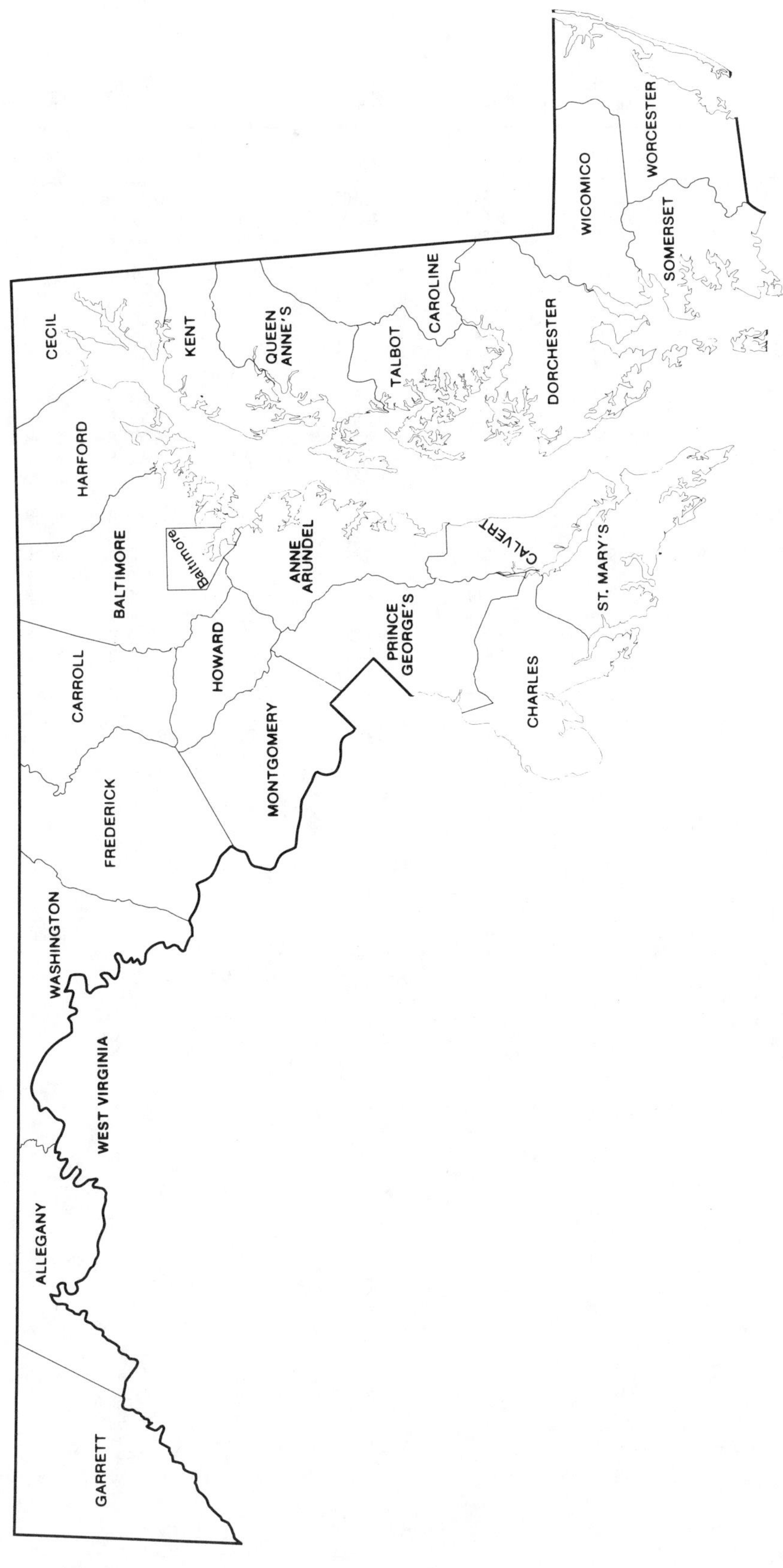
CECIL
KENT
QUEEN ANNE'S
CAROLINE
TALBOT
DORCHESTER
WICOMICO
WORCESTER
SOMERSET
HARFORD
BALTIMORE
Baltimore
ANNE ARUNDEL
CALVERT
ST. MARY'S
PRINCE GEORGE'S
CHARLES
HOWARD
CARROLL
MONTGOMERY
FREDERICK
WASHINGTON
WEST VIRGINIA
ALLEGANY
GARRETT

MARYLAND

PRESIDENT 1956

1950 Census Population	County	Total Vote	Republican	Democratic	Other	Rep.-Dem. Plurality	Percentage Total Vote Rep.	Percentage Total Vote Dem.	Percentage Major Vote Rep.	Percentage Major Vote Dem.
89,556	ALLEGANY	31,014	20,239	10,775		9,464 R	65.3%	34.7%	65.3%	34.7%
117,392	ANNE ARUNDEL	44,696	28,622	15,888	186	12,734 R	64.0%	35.5%	64.3%	35.7%
949,708	BALTIMORE CITY	318,847	178,244	140,603		37,641 R	55.9%	44.1%	55.9%	44.1%
270,273	BALTIMORE COUNTY	152,386	104,021	48,270	95	55,751 R	68.3%	31.7%	68.3%	31.7%
12,100	CALVERT	4,756	2,764	1,966	26	798 R	58.1%	41.3%	58.4%	41.6%
18,234	CAROLINE	6,912	4,208	2,702	2	1,506 R	60.9%	39.1%	60.9%	39.1%
44,907	CARROLL	16,183	11,749	4,423	11	7,326 R	72.6%	27.3%	72.7%	27.3%
33,356	CECIL	12,153	7,217	4,936		2,281 R	59.4%	40.6%	59.4%	40.6%
23,415	CHARLES	9,019	5,088	3,931		1,157 R	56.4%	43.6%	56.4%	43.6%
27,815	DORCHESTER	9,556	5,809	3,733	14	2,076 R	60.8%	39.1%	60.9%	39.1%
62,287	FREDERICK	22,010	14,387	7,619	4	6,768 R	65.4%	34.6%	65.4%	34.6%
21,259	GARRETT	7,600	5,555	2,045		3,510 R	73.1%	26.9%	73.1%	26.9%
51,782	HARFORD	19,245	12,657	6,588		6,069 R	65.8%	34.2%	65.8%	34.2%
23,119	HOWARD	10,182	6,534	3,599	49	2,935 R	64.2%	35.3%	64.5%	35.5%
13,677	KENT	6,125	3,747	2,378		1,369 R	61.2%	38.8%	61.2%	38.8%
164,401	MONTGOMERY	99,107	56,501	42,606		13,895 R	57.0%	43.0%	57.0%	43.0%
194,182	PRINCE GEORGES	79,955	40,654	39,280	21	1,374 R	50.8%	49.1%	50.9%	49.1%
14,579	QUEEN ANNES	5,962	3,321	2,641		680 R	55.7%	44.3%	55.7%	44.3%
29,111	ST. MARYS	7,784	4,336	3,443	5	893 R	55.7%	44.2%	55.7%	44.3%
20,745	SOMERSET	7,801	4,770	3,031		1,739 R	61.1%	38.9%	61.1%	38.9%
19,428	TALBOT	8,810	6,018	2,735	57	3,283 R	68.3%	31.0%	68.8%	31.2%
78,886	WASHINGTON	31,023	19,455	11,562	6	7,893 R	62.7%	37.3%	62.7%	37.3%
39,641	WICOMICO	14,666	9,377	5,289		4,088 R	63.9%	36.1%	63.9%	36.1%
23,148	WORCESTER	7,035	4,465	2,570		1,895 R	63.5%	36.5%	63.5%	36.5%
2,343,001	TOTAL	932,827	559,738	372,613	476	187,125 R	60.0%	39.9%	60.0%	40.0%

MARYLAND

PRESIDENT 1952

1950 Census Population	County	Total Vote	Republican	Democratic	Other	Rep.-Dem. Plurality	Percentage Total Vote Rep.	Total Vote Dem.	Major Vote Rep.	Major Vote Dem.
89,556	ALLEGANY	33,762	19,186	14,529	47	4,657 R	56.8%	43.0%	56.9%	43.1%
117,392	ANNE ARUNDEL	38,300	23,273	14,739	288	8,534 R	60.8%	38.5%	61.2%	38.8%
949,708	BALTIMORE CITY	349,858	166,605	178,469	4,784	11,864 D	47.6%	51.0%	48.3%	51.7%
270,273	BALTIMORE COUNTY	130,858	81,898	48,476	484	33,422 R	62.6%	37.0%	62.8%	37.2%
12,100	CALVERT	5,012	2,769	2,209	34	560 R	55.2%	44.1%	55.6%	44.4%
18,234	CAROLINE	6,899	4,155	2,733	11	1,422 R	60.2%	39.6%	60.3%	39.7%
44,907	CARROLL	16,522	11,563	4,934	25	6,629 R	70.0%	29.9%	70.1%	29.9%
33,356	CECIL	12,098	6,482	5,590	26	892 R	53.6%	46.2%	53.7%	46.3%
23,415	CHARLES	7,721	4,334	3,338	49	996 R	56.1%	43.2%	56.5%	43.5%
27,815	DORCHESTER	10,499	5,524	4,823	152	701 R	52.6%	45.9%	53.4%	46.6%
62,287	FREDERICK	22,451	14,562	7,851	38	6,711 R	64.9%	35.0%	65.0%	35.0%
21,259	GARRETT	7,279	4,980	2,281	18	2,699 R	68.4%	31.3%	68.6%	31.4%
51,782	HARFORD	17,659	10,770	6,809	80	3,961 R	61.0%	38.6%	61.3%	38.7%
23,119	HOWARD	9,302	5,497	3,693	112	1,804 R	59.1%	39.7%	59.8%	40.2%
13,677	KENT	6,171	3,656	2,504	11	1,152 R	59.2%	40.6%	59.4%	40.6%
164,401	MONTGOMERY	76,653	47,805	28,381	467	19,424 R	62.4%	37.0%	62.7%	37.3%
194,182	PRINCE GEORGES	67,602	38,060	29,119	423	8,941 R	56.3%	43.1%	56.7%	43.3%
14,579	QUEEN ANNES	6,265	3,170	3,058	37	112 R	50.6%	48.8%	50.9%	49.1%
29,111	ST. MARYS	7,891	4,270	3,588	33	682 R	54.1%	45.5%	54.3%	45.7%
20,745	SOMERSET	8,103	4,113	3,951	39	162 R	50.8%	48.8%	51.0%	49.0%
19,428	TALBOT	8,395	5,357	3,019	19	2,338 R	63.8%	36.0%	64.0%	36.0%
78,886	WASHINGTON	30,394	17,653	12,657	84	4,996 R	58.1%	41.6%	58.2%	41.8%
39,641	WICOMICO	14,965	9,061	5,878	26	3,183 R	60.5%	39.3%	60.7%	39.3%
23,148	WORCESTER	7,415	4,681	2,708	26	1,973 R	63.1%	36.5%	63.4%	36.6%
2,343,001	TOTAL	902,074	499,424	395,337	7,313	104,087 R	55.4%	43.8%	55.8%	44.2%

MARYLAND

PRESIDENT 1948

1940 Census Population	County	Total Vote	Republican	Democratic	Other	Rep.-Dem. Plurality	Percentage Total Vote Rep.	Total Vote Dem.	Major Vote Rep.	Major Vote Dem.
86,973	ALLEGANY	29,348	14,375	14,398	575	23 D	49.0%	49.1%	50.0%	50.0%
68,375	ANNE ARUNDEL	20,475	10,973	8,713	789	2,260 R	53.6%	42.6%	55.7%	44.3%
859,100	BALTIMORE CITY	255,363	110,879	134,615	9,869	23,736 D	43.4%	52.7%	45.2%	54.8%
155,825	BALTIMORE COUNTY	74,715	41,846	31,883	986	9,963 R	56.0%	42.7%	56.8%	43.2%
10,484	CALVERT	3,820	1,919	1,851	50	68 R	50.2%	48.5%	50.9%	49.1%
17,549	CAROLINE	5,223	2,746	2,430	47	316 R	52.6%	46.5%	53.1%	46.9%
39,054	CARROLL	12,333	8,003	4,226	104	3,777 R	64.9%	34.3%	65.4%	34.6%
26,407	CECIL	8,237	3,866	4,323	48	457 D	46.9%	52.5%	47.2%	52.8%
17,612	CHARLES	4,684	2,703	1,878	103	825 R	57.7%	40.1%	59.0%	41.0%
28,006	DORCHESTER	8,389	3,751	4,507	131	756 D	44.7%	53.7%	45.4%	54.6%
57,312	FREDERICK	17,197	9,934	7,142	121	2,792 R	57.8%	41.5%	58.2%	41.8%
21,981	GARRETT	5,498	3,536	1,909	53	1,627 R	64.3%	34.7%	64.9%	35.1%
35,060	HARFORD	11,834	6,168	5,494	172	674 R	52.1%	46.4%	52.9%	47.1%
17,175	HOWARD	6,028	3,113	2,725	190	388 R	51.6%	45.2%	53.3%	46.7%
13,465	KENT	5,048	2,489	2,524	35	35 D	49.3%	50.0%	49.7%	50.3%
83,912	MONTGOMERY	38,407	23,174	14,336	897	8,838 R	60.3%	37.3%	61.8%	38.2%
89,490	PRINCE GEORGES	30,164	14,718	14,874	572	156 D	48.8%	49.3%	49.7%	50.3%
14,476	QUEEN ANNES	4,786	2,038	2,660	88	622 D	42.6%	55.6%	43.4%	56.6%
14,626	ST. MARYS	4,641	2,247	2,293	101	46 D	48.4%	49.4%	49.5%	50.5%
20,965	SOMERSET	6,307	3,129	3,112	66	17 R	49.6%	49.3%	50.1%	49.9%
18,784	TALBOT	6,001	3,585	2,344	72	1,241 R	59.7%	39.1%	60.5%	39.5%
68,838	WASHINGTON	22,645	11,887	10,588	170	1,299 R	52.5%	46.8%	52.9%	47.1%
34,530	WICOMICO	10,571	5,062	5,415	94	353 D	47.9%	51.2%	48.3%	51.7%
21,245	WORCESTER	5,034	2,673	2,281	80	392 R	53.1%	45.3%	54.0%	46.0%
1,821,244	TOTAL	596,748	294,814	286,521	15,413	8,293 R	49.4%	48.0%	50.7%	49.3%

MARYLAND

PRESIDENT 1944

1940 Census Population	County	Total Vote	Republican	Democratic	Other	Rep.-Dem. Plurality	Percentage Total Vote Rep.	Percentage Total Vote Dem.	Percentage Major Vote Rep.	Percentage Major Vote Dem.
86,973	ALLEGANY	30,934	15,589	15,345		244 R	50.4%	49.6%	50.4%	49.6%
68,375	ANNE ARUNDEL	21,129	10,860	10,269		591 R	51.4%	48.6%	51.4%	48.6%
859,100	BALTIMORE CITY	276,310	112,817	163,493		50,676 D	40.8%	59.2%	40.8%	59.2%
155,825	BALTIMORE COUNTY	60,322	34,047	26,275		7,772 R	56.4%	43.6%	56.4%	43.6%
10,484	CALVERT	3,733	2,184	1,549		635 R	58.5%	41.5%	58.5%	41.5%
17,549	CAROLINE	5,133	3,073	2,060		1,013 R	59.9%	40.1%	59.9%	40.1%
39,054	CARROLL	13,482	8,999	4,483		4,516 R	66.7%	33.3%	66.7%	33.3%
26,407	CECIL	8,342	3,680	4,662		982 D	44.1%	55.9%	44.1%	55.9%
17,612	CHARLES	4,630	2,755	1,875		880 R	59.5%	40.5%	59.5%	40.5%
28,006	DORCHESTER	9,005	4,241	4,764		523 D	47.1%	52.9%	47.1%	52.9%
57,312	FREDERICK	19,895	11,367	8,528		2,839 R	57.1%	42.9%	57.1%	42.9%
21,981	GARRETT	6,123	4,162	1,961		2,201 R	68.0%	32.0%	68.0%	32.0%
35,060	HARFORD	11,590	6,751	4,839		1,912 R	58.2%	41.8%	58.2%	41.8%
17,175	HOWARD	6,484	3,344	3,140		204 R	51.6%	48.4%	51.6%	48.4%
13,465	KENT	4,805	2,351	2,454		103 D	48.9%	51.1%	48.9%	51.1%
83,912	MONTGOMERY	35,724	20,400	15,324		5,076 R	57.1%	42.9%	57.1%	42.9%
89,490	PRINCE GEORGES	27,756	13,750	14,006		256 D	49.5%	50.5%	49.5%	50.5%
14,476	QUEEN ANNES	5,146	2,119	3,027		908 D	41.2%	58.8%	41.2%	58.8%
14,626	ST. MARYS	4,564	2,673	1,891		782 R	58.6%	41.4%	58.6%	41.4%
20,965	SOMERSET	6,915	3,790	3,125		665 R	54.8%	45.2%	54.8%	45.2%
18,784	TALBOT	6,480	3,712	2,768		944 R	57.3%	42.7%	57.3%	42.7%
68,838	WASHINGTON	23,592	12,227	11,365		862 R	51.8%	48.2%	51.8%	48.2%
34,530	WICOMICO	10,714	5,040	5,674		634 D	47.0%	53.0%	47.0%	53.0%
21,245	WORCESTER	5,631	3,018	2,613		405 R	53.6%	46.4%	53.6%	46.4%
1,821,244	TOTAL	608,439	292,949	315,490		22,541 D	48.1%	51.9%	48.1%	51.9%

MARYLAND

PRESIDENT 1940

1940 Census Population	County	Total Vote	Republican	Democratic	Other	Rep.-Dem. Plurality	Percentage Total Vote Rep.	Percentage Total Vote Dem.	Percentage Major Vote Rep.	Percentage Major Vote Dem.
86,973	ALLEGANY	33,448	14,804	18,456	188	3,652 D	44.3%	55.2%	44.5%	55.5%
68,375	ANNE ARUNDEL	22,405	9,204	13,116	85	3,912 D	41.1%	58.5%	41.2%	58.8%
859,100	BALTIMORE CITY	315,996	112,364	199,715	3,917	87,351 D	35.6%	63.2%	36.0%	64.0%
155,825	BALTIMORE COUNTY	57,198	26,652	30,360	186	3,708 D	46.6%	53.1%	46.7%	53.3%
10,484	CALVERT	4,246	2,067	2,149	30	82 D	48.7%	50.6%	49.0%	51.0%
17,549	CAROLINE	6,401	3,087	3,284	30	197 D	48.2%	51.3%	48.5%	51.5%
39,054	CARROLL	14,178	8,300	5,833	45	2,467 R	58.5%	41.1%	58.7%	41.3%
26,407	CECIL	9,288	3,878	5,360	50	1,482 D	41.8%	57.7%	42.0%	58.0%
17,612	CHARLES	5,464	2,716	2,692	56	24 R	49.7%	49.3%	50.2%	49.8%
28,006	DORCHESTER	10,128	3,953	6,088	87	2,135 D	39.0%	60.1%	39.4%	60.6%
57,312	FREDERICK	21,833	10,485	11,255	93	770 D	48.0%	51.6%	48.2%	51.8%
21,981	GARRETT	7,230	4,387	2,805	38	1,582 R	60.7%	38.8%	61.0%	39.0%
35,060	HARFORD	12,060	6,501	5,500	59	1,001 R	53.9%	45.6%	54.2%	45.8%
17,175	HOWARD	7,069	3,082	3,957	30	875 D	43.6%	56.0%	43.8%	56.2%
13,465	KENT	5,681	2,639	3,014	28	375 D	46.5%	53.1%	46.7%	53.3%
83,912	MONTGOMERY	29,521	13,831	15,177	513	1,346 D	46.9%	51.4%	47.7%	52.3%
89,490	PRINCE GEORGES	26,251	9,523	16,592	136	7,069 D	36.3%	63.2%	36.5%	63.5%
14,476	QUEEN ANNES	6,126	2,508	3,581	37	1,073 D	40.9%	58.5%	41.2%	58.8%
14,626	ST. MARYS	5,205	2,301	2,860	44	559 D	44.2%	54.9%	44.6%	55.4%
20,965	SOMERSET	8,390	3,954	4,352	84	398 D	47.1%	51.9%	47.6%	52.4%
18,784	TALBOT	8,106	4,368	3,689	49	679 R	53.9%	45.5%	54.2%	45.8%
68,838	WASHINGTON	25,262	11,054	14,125	83	3,071 D	43.8%	55.9%	43.9%	56.1%
34,530	WICOMICO	12,012	4,741	7,198	73	2,457 D	39.5%	59.9%	39.7%	60.3%
21,245	WORCESTER	6,606	3,135	3,388	83	253 D	47.5%	51.3%	48.1%	51.9%
1,821,244	TOTAL	660,104	269,534	384,546	6,024	115,012 D	40.8%	58.3%	41.2%	58.8%

MARYLAND

PRESIDENT 1936

1930 Census Population	County	Total Vote	Republican	Democratic	Other	Rep.-Dem. Plurality	Percentage Total Vote Rep.	Percentage Total Vote Dem.	Percentage Major Vote Rep.	Percentage Major Vote Dem.
79,098	ALLEGANY	31,203	11,191	19,721	291	8,530 D	35.9%	63.2%	36.2%	63.8%
55,167	ANNE ARUNDEL	20,033	8,478	11,413	142	2,935 D	42.3%	57.0%	42.6%	57.4%
804,874	BALTIMORE CITY	310,294	97,667	210,668	1,959	113,001 D	31.5%	67.9%	31.7%	68.3%
124,565	BALTIMORE COUNTY	47,576	18,893	28,367	316	9,474 D	39.7%	59.6%	40.0%	60.0%
9,528	CALVERT	3,979	2,082	1,872	25	210 R	52.3%	47.0%	52.7%	47.3%
17,387	CAROLINE	6,206	2,611	3,579	16	968 D	42.1%	57.7%	42.2%	57.8%
35,978	CARROLL	13,957	7,383	6,496	78	887 R	52.9%	46.5%	53.2%	46.8%
25,827	CECIL	8,582	3,617	4,914	51	1,297 D	42.1%	57.3%	42.4%	57.6%
16,166	CHARLES	5,284	2,623	2,597	64	26 R	49.6%	49.1%	50.2%	49.8%
26,813	DORCHESTER	9,039	3,735	5,293	11	1,558 D	41.3%	58.6%	41.4%	58.6%
54,440	FREDERICK	20,286	9,500	10,722	64	1,222 D	46.8%	52.9%	47.0%	53.0%
19,908	GARRETT	7,373	4,057	3,252	64	805 R	55.0%	44.1%	55.5%	44.5%
31,603	HARFORD	11,531	5,327	6,165	39	838 D	46.2%	53.5%	46.4%	53.6%
16,169	HOWARD	6,825	2,638	4,138	49	1,500 D	38.7%	60.6%	38.9%	61.1%
14,242	KENT	5,507	2,543	2,931	33	388 D	46.2%	53.2%	46.5%	53.5%
49,206	MONTGOMERY	23,532	10,133	13,246	153	3,113 D	43.1%	56.3%	43.3%	56.7%
60,095	PRINCE GEORGES	23,295	8,107	15,087	101	6,980 D	34.8%	64.8%	35.0%	65.0%
14,571	QUEEN ANNES	5,503	1,946	3,548	9	1,602 D	35.4%	64.5%	35.4%	64.6%
15,189	ST. MARYS	5,239	2,286	2,829	124	543 D	43.6%	54.0%	44.7%	55.3%
23,382	SOMERSET	8,958	4,770	4,116	72	654 R	53.2%	45.9%	53.7%	46.3%
18,583	TALBOT	7,365	3,578	3,768	19	190 D	48.6%	51.2%	48.7%	51.3%
65,882	WASHINGTON	24,718	10,619	14,050	49	3,431 D	43.0%	56.8%	43.0%	57.0%
31,229	WICOMICO	11,913	4,545	7,273	95	2,728 D	38.2%	61.1%	38.5%	61.5%
21,624	WORCESTER	6,698	3,106	3,567	25	461 D	46.4%	53.3%	46.5%	53.5%
1,631,526	TOTAL	624,896	231,435	389,612	3,849	158,177 D	37.0%	62.3%	37.3%	62.7%

MARYLAND

PRESIDENT 1932

1930 Census Population	County	Total Vote	Republican	Democratic	Other	Rep.-Dem. Plurality	Percentage Total Vote Rep.	Percentage Total Vote Dem.	Percentage Major Vote Rep.	Percentage Major Vote Dem.
79,098	ALLEGANY	26,322	12,911	12,033	1,378	878 R	49.1%	45.7%	51.8%	48.2%
55,167	ANNE ARUNDEL	15,933	5,778	9,761	394	3,983 D	36.3%	61.3%	37.2%	62.8%
804,874	BALTIMORE CITY	247,232	78,954	160,309	7,969	81,355 D	31.9%	64.8%	33.0%	67.0%
124,565	BALTIMORE COUNTY	39,494	13,938	24,626	930	10,688 D	35.3%	62.4%	36.1%	63.9%
9,528	CALVERT	3,577	1,838	1,696	43	142 R	51.4%	47.4%	52.0%	48.0%
17,387	CAROLINE	5,671	1,998	3,651	22	1,653 D	35.2%	64.4%	35.4%	64.6%
35,978	CARROLL	12,306	5,732	6,482	92	750 D	46.6%	52.7%	46.9%	53.1%
25,827	CECIL	7,959	3,569	4,282	108	713 D	44.8%	53.8%	45.5%	54.5%
16,166	CHARLES	4,371	1,851	2,473	47	622 D	42.3%	56.6%	42.8%	57.2%
26,813	DORCHESTER	8,052	3,466	4,547	39	1,081 D	43.0%	56.5%	43.3%	56.7%
54,440	FREDERICK	18,024	7,144	10,686	194	3,542 D	39.6%	59.3%	40.1%	59.9%
19,908	GARRETT	5,443	3,048	2,232	163	816 R	56.0%	41.0%	57.7%	42.3%
31,603	HARFORD	10,134	3,954	6,073	107	2,119 D	39.0%	59.9%	39.4%	60.6%
16,169	HOWARD	6,190	1,970	4,161	59	2,191 D	31.8%	67.2%	32.1%	67.9%
14,242	KENT	3,854	1,468	2,370	16	902 D	38.1%	61.5%	38.2%	61.8%
49,206	MONTGOMERY	15,763	5,698	9,882	183	4,184 D	36.1%	62.7%	36.6%	63.4%
60,095	PRINCE GEORGES	18,556	6,696	11,580	280	4,884 D	36.1%	62.4%	36.6%	63.4%
14,571	QUEEN ANNES	5,294	1,583	3,683	28	2,100 D	29.9%	69.6%	30.1%	69.9%
15,189	ST. MARYS	4,300	1,322	2,885	93	1,563 D	30.7%	67.1%	31.4%	68.6%
23,382	SOMERSET	8,545	3,675	4,811	59	1,136 D	43.0%	56.3%	43.3%	56.7%
18,583	TALBOT	6,950	2,672	4,233	45	1,561 D	38.4%	60.9%	38.7%	61.3%
65,882	WASHINGTON	20,527	8,929	11,370	228	2,441 D	43.5%	55.4%	44.0%	56.0%
31,229	WICOMICO	10,755	3,812	6,895	48	3,083 D	35.4%	64.1%	35.6%	64.4%
21,624	WORCESTER	5,802	2,178	3,593	31	1,415 D	37.5%	61.9%	37.7%	62.3%
1,631,526	TOTAL	511,054	184,184	314,314	12,556	130,130 D	36.0%	61.5%	36.9%	63.1%

MARYLAND

PRESIDENT 1928

1920 Census Population	County	Total Vote	Republican	Democratic	Other	Rep.-Dem. Plurality	Percentage Total Vote Rep.	Total Vote Dem.	Major Vote Rep.	Major Vote Dem.
69,938	ALLEGANY	28,703	19,443	9,026	234	10,417 R	67.7%	31.4%	68.3%	31.7%
43,408	ANNE ARUNDEL	16,486	10,145	6,259	82	3,886 R	61.5%	38.0%	61.8%	38.2%
733,826	BALTIMORE CITY	263,058	135,182	126,106	1,770	9,076 R	51.4%	47.9%	51.7%	48.3%
74,817	BALTIMORE COUNTY	39,701	23,889	15,632	180	8,257 R	60.2%	39.4%	60.4%	39.6%
9,744	CALVERT	3,262	2,085	1,144	33	941 R	63.9%	35.1%	64.6%	35.4%
18,652	CAROLINE	5,322	3,270	2,030	22	1,240 R	61.4%	38.1%	61.7%	38.3%
34,245	CARROLL	12,419	8,644	3,731	44	4,913 R	69.6%	30.0%	69.9%	30.1%
23,612	CECIL	7,962	5,706	2,201	55	3,505 R	71.7%	27.6%	72.2%	27.8%
17,705	CHARLES	4,391	2,522	1,860	9	662 R	57.4%	42.4%	57.6%	42.4%
27,895	DORCHESTER	8,535	6,333	2,180	22	4,153 R	74.2%	25.5%	74.4%	25.6%
52,541	FREDERICK	20,089	12,569	7,406	114	5,163 R	62.6%	36.9%	62.9%	37.1%
19,678	GARRETT	5,577	4,371	1,168	38	3,203 R	78.4%	20.9%	78.9%	21.1%
29,291	HARFORD	10,040	6,479	3,506	55	2,973 R	64.5%	34.9%	64.9%	35.1%
15,826	HOWARD	6,417	3,296	3,088	33	208 R	51.4%	48.1%	51.6%	48.4%
15,026	KENT	5,257	2,777	2,450	30	327 R	52.8%	46.6%	53.1%	46.9%
34,921	MONTGOMERY	16,139	9,318	6,739	82	2,579 R	57.7%	41.8%	58.0%	42.0%
43,347	PRINCE GEORGES	16,562	9,782	6,658	122	3,124 R	59.1%	40.2%	59.5%	40.5%
16,001	QUEEN ANNES	5,389	2,666	2,700	23	34 D	49.5%	50.1%	49.7%	50.3%
16,112	ST. MARYS	4,733	1,609	3,006	118	1,397 D	34.0%	63.5%	34.9%	65.1%
24,602	SOMERSET	7,395	5,071	2,277	47	2,794 R	68.6%	30.8%	69.0%	31.0%
18,306	TALBOT	6,443	3,990	2,432	21	1,558 R	61.9%	37.7%	62.1%	37.9%
59,694	WASHINGTON	18,301	12,404	5,816	81	6,588 R	67.8%	31.8%	68.1%	31.9%
28,165	WICOMICO	10,033	5,923	4,095	15	1,828 R	59.0%	40.8%	59.1%	40.9%
22,309	WORCESTER	6,134	4,005	2,116	13	1,889 R	65.3%	34.5%	65.4%	34.6%
1,449,661	TOTAL	528,348	301,479	223,626	3,243	77,853 R	57.1%	42.3%	57.4%	42.6%

MARYLAND

PRESIDENT 1924

1920 Census Population	County	Total Vote	Republican	Democratic	Other	Rep.-Dem. Plurality	Percentage Total Vote Rep.	Percentage Total Vote Dem.	Percentage Major Vote Rep.	Percentage Major Vote Dem.
69,938	ALLEGANY	16,370	9,042	4,442	2,886	4,600 R	55.2%	27.1%	67.1%	32.9%
43,408	ANNE ARUNDEL	8,255	3,670	3,766	819	96 D	44.5%	45.6%	49.4%	50.6%
733,826	BALTIMORE CITY	163,252	69,588	60,222	33,442	9,366 R	42.6%	36.9%	53.6%	46.4%
74,817	BALTIMORE COUNTY	21,661	9,383	9,424	2,854	41 D	43.3%	43.5%	49.9%	50.1%
9,744	CALVERT	2,893	1,564	1,242	87	322 R	54.1%	42.9%	55.7%	44.3%
18,652	CAROLINE	4,888	2,210	2,493	185	283 D	45.2%	51.0%	47.0%	53.0%
34,245	CARROLL	10,263	5,301	4,616	346	685 R	51.7%	45.0%	53.5%	46.5%
23,612	CECIL	6,266	3,156	2,863	247	293 R	50.4%	45.7%	52.4%	47.6%
17,705	CHARLES	3,914	2,215	1,491	208	724 R	56.6%	38.1%	59.8%	40.2%
27,895	DORCHESTER	6,612	3,356	3,047	209	309 R	50.8%	46.1%	52.4%	47.6%
52,541	FREDERICK	17,106	8,441	7,740	925	701 R	49.3%	45.2%	52.2%	47.8%
19,678	GARRETT	4,198	2,594	1,226	378	1,368 R	61.8%	29.2%	67.9%	32.1%
29,291	HARFORD	7,758	3,545	3,841	372	296 D	45.7%	49.5%	48.0%	52.0%
15,826	HOWARD	5,169	1,989	2,786	394	797 D	38.5%	53.9%	41.7%	58.3%
15,026	KENT	4,749	2,019	2,628	102	609 D	42.5%	55.3%	43.4%	56.6%
34,921	MONTGOMERY	12,894	5,675	6,639	580	964 D	44.0%	51.5%	46.1%	53.9%
43,347	PRINCE GEORGES	12,490	5,868	5,088	1,534	780 R	47.0%	40.7%	53.6%	46.4%
16,001	QUEEN ANNES	4,908	1,656	3,155	97	1,499 D	33.7%	64.3%	34.4%	65.6%
16,112	ST. MARYS	3,703	1,653	1,949	101	296 D	44.6%	52.6%	45.9%	54.1%
24,602	SOMERSET	6,310	3,230	2,903	177	327 R	51.2%	46.0%	52.7%	47.3%
18,306	TALBOT	5,488	2,451	2,859	178	408 D	44.7%	52.1%	46.2%	53.8%
59,694	WASHINGTON	15,106	7,460	5,964	1,682	1,496 R	49.4%	39.5%	55.6%	44.4%
28,165	WICOMICO	8,635	3,744	4,620	271	876 D	43.4%	53.5%	44.8%	55.2%
22,309	WORCESTER	5,742	2,604	3,068	70	464 D	45.4%	53.4%	45.9%	54.1%
1,449,661	TOTAL	358,630	162,414	148,072	48,144	14,342 R	45.3%	41.3%	52.3%	47.7%

MARYLAND

PRESIDENT 1920

1920 Census Population	County	Total Vote	Republican	Democratic	Other	Rep.-Dem. Plurality	Percentage Total Vote Rep.	Percentage Total Vote Dem.	Percentage Major Vote Rep.	Percentage Major Vote Dem.
69,938	ALLEGANY	16,726	9,595	5,643	1,488	3,952 R	57.4%	33.7%	63.0%	37.0%
43,408	ANNE ARUNDEL	11,370	6,199	5,053	118	1,146 R	54.5%	44.4%	55.1%	44.9%
733,826	BALTIMORE CITY	220,146	125,526	86,748	7,872	38,778 R	57.0%	39.4%	59.1%	40.9%
74,817	BALTIMORE COUNTY	22,183	12,432	9,365	386	3,067 R	56.0%	42.2%	57.0%	43.0%
9,744	CALVERT	3,001	1,741	1,230	30	511 R	58.0%	41.0%	58.6%	41.4%
18,652	CAROLINE	5,990	2,929	3,012	49	83 D	48.9%	50.3%	49.3%	50.7%
34,245	CARROLL	10,125	5,784	4,273	68	1,511 R	57.1%	42.2%	57.5%	42.5%
23,612	CECIL	6,957	3,435	3,468	54	33 D	49.4%	49.8%	49.8%	50.2%
17,705	CHARLES	4,270	2,585	1,642	43	943 R	60.5%	38.5%	61.2%	38.8%
27,895	DORCHESTER	8,210	4,218	3,950	42	268 R	51.4%	48.1%	51.6%	48.4%
52,541	FREDERICK	17,518	9,559	7,747	212	1,812 R	54.6%	44.2%	55.2%	44.8%
19,678	GARRETT	3,993	2,805	1,070	118	1,735 R	70.2%	26.8%	72.4%	27.6%
29,291	HARFORD	8,374	4,175	4,134	65	41 R	49.9%	49.4%	50.2%	49.8%
15,826	HOWARD	5,068	2,608	2,397	63	211 R	51.5%	47.3%	52.1%	47.9%
15,026	KENT	5,886	2,838	3,034	14	196 D	48.2%	51.5%	48.3%	51.7%
34,921	MONTGOMERY	12,402	5,948	6,277	177	329 D	48.0%	50.6%	48.7%	51.3%
43,347	PRINCE GEORGES	11,663	6,628	4,857	178	1,771 R	56.8%	41.6%	57.7%	42.3%
16,001	QUEEN ANNES	5,762	2,157	3,519	86	1,362 D	37.4%	61.1%	38.0%	62.0%
16,112	ST. MARYS	4,094	2,175	1,861	58	314 R	53.1%	45.5%	53.9%	46.1%
24,602	SOMERSET	6,354	3,658	2,634	62	1,024 R	57.6%	41.5%	58.1%	41.9%
18,306	TALBOT	6,200	3,050	3,130	20	80 D	49.2%	50.5%	49.4%	50.6%
59,694	WASHINGTON	15,995	8,757	6,852	386	1,905 R	54.7%	42.8%	56.1%	43.9%
28,165	WICOMICO	9,309	4,225	5,054	30	829 D	45.4%	54.3%	45.5%	54.5%
22,309	WORCESTER	6,847	3,090	3,676	81	586 D	45.1%	53.7%	45.7%	54.3%
1,449,661	TOTAL	428,443	236,117	180,626	11,700	55,491 R	55.1%	42.2%	56.7%	43.3%

MARYLAND

ELECTION NOTES

1956 Other vote was scattered write-in.

1952 Other vote was Hallinan (Progressive).

1948 Other vote was 9,983 Wallace (Progressive); 2,941 Thomas (Socialist); 2,489 Thurmond (States Rights).

1944

1940 Other vote was 4,093 Thomas (Socialist); 1,274 Browder (Communist); 657 Aiken (Socialist Labor).

1936 Other vote was 1,629 Thomas (Socialist); 1,305 Aiken (Socialist Labor); 915 Browder (Communist).

1932 Other vote was 10,489 Thomas (Socialist); 1,036 Reynolds (Socialist Labor); 1,031 Foster (Communist).

1928 Other vote was 1,701 Thomas (Socialist); 906 Reynolds (Socialist Labor); 636 Foster (Communist).

1924 Other vote was 47,157 LaFollette (Progressive); 987 Johns (Socialist Labor).

1920 Other vote was 8,876 Debs (Socialist); 1,645 Christensen (Farmer-Labor); 1,178 Cox (Socialist Labor); 1 write-in.

MASSACHUSETTS

POPULAR VOTE FOR PRESIDENT 1920 TO 1956

Year	Total Vote	Republican Vote	Republican Candidate	Democratic Vote	Democratic Candidate	Other Vote	Plurality	Total Vote Rep.	Total Vote Dem.	Major Vote Rep.	Major Vote Dem.
1956	2,348,506	1,393,197	Eisenhower, Dwight D.	948,190	Stevenson, Adlai E.	7,119	445,007 R	59.3%	40.4%	59.5%	40.5%
1952	2,383,398	1,292,325	Eisenhower, Dwight D.	1,083,525	Stevenson, Adlai E.	7,548	208,800 R	54.2%	45.5%	54.4%	45.6%
1948	2,107,146	909,370	Dewey, Thomas E.	1,151,788	Truman, Harry S.	45,988	242,418 D	43.2%	54.7%	44.1%	55.9%
1944	1,960,665	921,350	Dewey, Thomas E.	1,035,296	Roosevelt, Franklin D.	4,019	113,946 D	47.0%	52.8%	47.1%	52.9%
1940	2,026,993	939,700	Willkie, Wendell	1,076,522	Roosevelt, Franklin D.	10,771	136,822 D	46.4%	53.1%	46.6%	53.4%
1936	1,840,357	768,613	Landon, Alfred M.	942,716	Roosevelt, Franklin D.	129,028	174,103 D	41.8%	51.2%	44.9%	55.1%
1932	1,580,114	736,959	Hoover, Herbert C.	800,148	Roosevelt, Franklin D.	43,007	63,189 D	46.6%	50.6%	47.9%	52.1%
1928	1,577,823	775,566	Hoover, Herbert C.	792,758	Smith, Alfred E.	9,499	17,192 D	49.2%	50.2%	49.5%	50.5%
1924	1,129,837	703,476	Coolidge, Calvin	280,831	Davis, John W.	145,530	422,645 R	62.3%	24.9%	71.5%	28.5%
1920	993,718	681,153	Harding, Warren G.	276,691	Cox, James M.	35,874	404,462 R	68.5%	27.8%	71.1%	28.9%

ELECTORAL COLLEGE VOTE 1920 TO 1956

Year	Total	Republican	Democratic	Other
1956	16	16	—	—
1952	16	16	—	—
1948	16	—	16	—
1944	16	—	16	—
1940	17	—	17	—
1936	17	—	17	—
1932	17	—	17	—
1928	18	—	18	—
1924	18	18	—	—
1920	18	18	—	—

MASSACHUSETTS

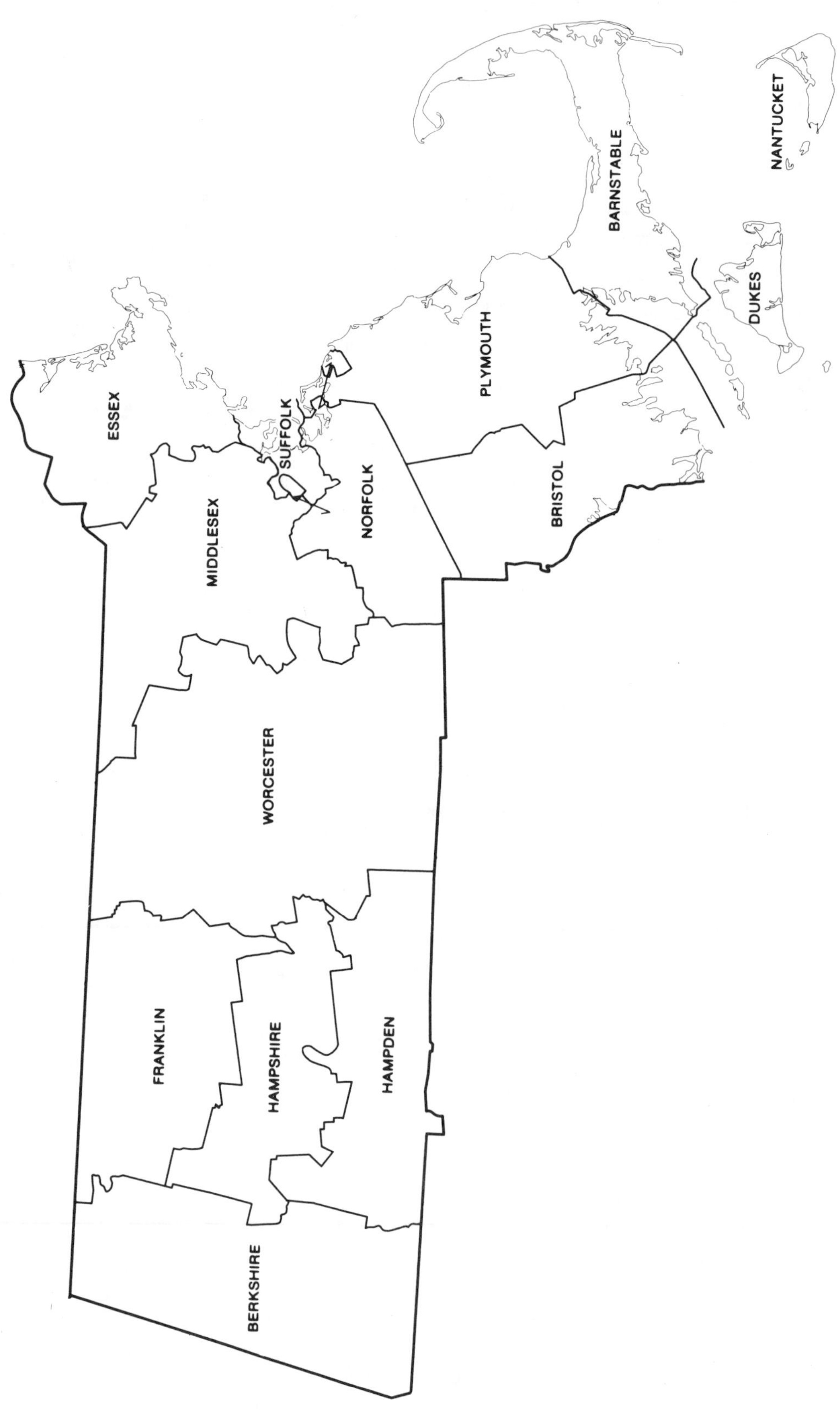

MASSACHUSETTS

PRESIDENT 1956

1950 Census Population	County	Total Vote	Republican	Democratic	Other	Rep.-Dem. Plurality	Percentage Total Vote Rep.	Total Vote Dem.	Major Vote Rep.	Major Vote Dem.
46,805	BARNSTABLE	28,202	23,472	4,672	58	18,800 R	83.2%	16.6%	83.4%	16.6%
132,966	BERKSHIRE	66,973	41,355	25,361	257	15,994 R	61.7%	37.9%	62.0%	38.0%
381,569	BRISTOL	189,365	109,542	79,357	466	30,185 R	57.8%	41.9%	58.0%	42.0%
5,633	DUKES	3,160	2,618	541	1	2,077 R	82.8%	17.1%	82.9%	17.1%
522,384	ESSEX	276,453	166,115	109,671	667	56,444 R	60.1%	39.7%	60.2%	39.8%
52,747	FRANKLIN	27,436	19,779	7,574	83	12,205 R	72.1%	27.6%	72.3%	27.7%
367,971	HAMPDEN	187,367	104,689	81,743	935	22,946 R	55.9%	43.6%	56.2%	43.8%
87,594	HAMPSHIRE	42,564	26,361	16,119	84	10,242 R	61.9%	37.9%	62.1%	37.9%
1,064,569	MIDDLESEX	561,373	343,125	216,668	1,580	126,457 R	61.1%	38.6%	61.3%	38.7%
3,484	NANTUCKET	1,900	1,582	317	1	1,265 R	83.3%	16.7%	83.3%	16.7%
392,308	NORFOLK	229,996	152,747	76,656	593	76,091 R	66.4%	33.3%	66.6%	33.4%
189,468	PLYMOUTH	106,161	75,575	30,377	209	45,198 R	71.2%	28.6%	71.3%	28.7%
896,615	SUFFOLK	355,686	162,836	191,245	1,605	28,409 D	45.8%	53.8%	46.0%	54.0%
546,401	WORCESTER	271,870	163,401	107,889	580	55,512 R	60.1%	39.7%	60.2%	39.8%
4,690,514	TOTAL	2,348,506	1,393,197	948,190	7,119	445,007 R	59.3%	40.4%	59.5%	40.5%

MASSACHUSETTS

PRESIDENT 1952

1950 Census Population	County	Total Vote	Republican	Democratic	Other	Rep.-Dem. Plurality	Percentage Total Vote Rep.	Total Vote Dem.	Major Vote Rep.	Major Vote Dem.
46,805	BARNSTABLE	25,971	20,943	4,984	44	15,959 R	80.6%	19.2%	80.8%	19.2%
132,966	BERKSHIRE	68,441	38,413	29,785	243	8,628 R	56.1%	43.5%	56.3%	43.7%
381,569	BRISTOL	192,011	98,105	93,444	462	4,661 R	51.1%	48.7%	51.2%	48.8%
5,633	DUKES	3,198	2,432	760	6	1,672 R	76.0%	23.8%	76.2%	23.8%
522,384	ESSEX	280,409	156,030	123,334	1,045	32,696 R	55.6%	44.0%	55.9%	44.1%
52,747	FRANKLIN	28,268	19,489	8,729	50	10,760 R	68.9%	30.9%	69.1%	30.9%
367,971	HAMPDEN	190,193	98,641	90,936	616	7,705 R	51.9%	47.8%	52.0%	48.0%
87,594	HAMPSHIRE	41,486	24,141	17,247	98	6,894 R	58.2%	41.6%	58.3%	41.7%
1,064,569	MIDDLESEX	554,605	316,069	236,910	1,626	79,159 R	57.0%	42.7%	57.2%	42.8%
3,484	NANTUCKET	1,897	1,490	405	2	1,085 R	78.5%	21.3%	78.6%	21.4%
392,308	NORFOLK	215,361	140,409	74,321	631	66,088 R	65.2%	34.5%	65.4%	34.6%
189,468	PLYMOUTH	101,042	67,922	32,815	305	35,107 R	67.2%	32.5%	67.4%	32.6%
896,615	SUFFOLK	404,879	162,147	240,957	1,775	78,810 D	40.0%	59.5%	40.2%	59.8%
546,401	WORCESTER	275,637	146,094	128,898	645	17,196 R	53.0%	46.8%	53.1%	46.9%
4,690,514	TOTAL	2,383,398	1,292,325	1,083,525	7,548	208,800 R	54.2%	45.5%	54.4%	45.6%

MASSACHUSETTS

PRESIDENT 1948

1940 Census Population	County	Total Vote	Republican	Democratic	Other	Rep.-Dem. Plurality	Percentage Total Vote Rep.	Total Vote Dem.	Major Vote Rep.	Major Vote Dem.
37,295	BARNSTABLE	19,490	14,633	4,616	241	10,017 R	75.1%	23.7%	76.0%	24.0%
122,273	BERKSHIRE	59,267	27,482	30,668	1,117	3,186 D	46.4%	51.7%	47.3%	52.7%
364,637	BRISTOL	172,551	63,216	106,741	2,594	43,525 D	36.6%	61.9%	37.2%	62.8%
5,669	DUKES	2,484	1,731	720	33	1,011 R	69.7%	29.0%	70.6%	29.4%
496,313	ESSEX	246,371	108,894	132,016	5,461	23,122 D	44.2%	53.6%	45.2%	54.8%
49,453	FRANKLIN	24,373	14,919	9,231	223	5,688 R	61.2%	37.9%	61.8%	38.2%
332,107	HAMPDEN	167,720	70,256	94,609	2,855	24,353 D	41.9%	56.4%	42.6%	57.4%
72,461	HAMPSHIRE	35,833	17,331	18,012	490	681 D	48.4%	50.3%	49.0%	51.0%
971,390	MIDDLESEX	485,908	228,262	248,240	9,406	19,978 D	47.0%	51.1%	47.9%	52.1%
3,401	NANTUCKET	1,442	1,013	409	20	604 R	70.2%	28.4%	71.2%	28.8%
325,180	NORFOLK	176,737	100,280	72,327	4,130	27,953 R	56.7%	40.9%	58.1%	41.9%
168,824	PLYMOUTH	85,146	48,925	34,765	1,456	14,160 R	57.5%	40.8%	58.5%	41.5%
863,248	SUFFOLK	385,067	105,671	265,611	13,785	159,940 D	27.4%	69.0%	28.5%	71.5%
504,470	WORCESTER	244,757	106,757	133,823	4,177	27,066 D	43.6%	54.7%	44.4%	55.6%
4,316,721	TOTAL	2,107,146	909,370	1,151,788	45,988	242,418 D	43.2%	54.7%	44.1%	55.9%

MASSACHUSETTS

PRESIDENT 1944

1940 Census Population	County	Total Vote	Republican	Democratic	Other	Rep.-Dem. Plurality	Percentage Total Vote Rep.	Total Vote Dem.	Major Vote Rep.	Major Vote Dem.
37,295	BARNSTABLE	16,525	11,543	4,938	44	6,605 R	69.9%	29.9%	70.0%	30.0%
122,273	BERKSHIRE	56,227	24,830	31,212	185	6,382 D	44.2%	55.5%	44.3%	55.7%
364,637	BRISTOL	151,692	60,880	90,529	283	29,649 D	40.1%	59.7%	40.2%	59.8%
5,669	DUKES	2,234	1,372	861	1	511 R	61.4%	38.5%	61.4%	38.6%
496,313	ESSEX	230,756	111,958	118,228	570	6,270 D	48.5%	51.2%	48.6%	51.4%
49,453	FRANKLIN	22,703	13,252	9,400	51	3,852 R	58.4%	41.4%	58.5%	41.5%
332,107	HAMPDEN	155,486	63,293	91,819	374	28,526 D	40.7%	59.1%	40.8%	59.2%
72,461	HAMPSHIRE	32,680	14,907	17,676	97	2,769 D	45.6%	54.1%	45.8%	54.2%
971,390	MIDDLESEX	447,080	236,102	210,253	725	25,849 R	52.8%	47.0%	52.9%	47.1%
3,401	NANTUCKET	1,349	779	569	1	210 R	57.7%	42.2%	57.8%	42.2%
325,180	NORFOLK	167,479	97,490	69,606	383	27,884 R	58.2%	41.6%	58.3%	41.7%
168,824	PLYMOUTH	79,709	47,245	32,290	174	14,955 R	59.3%	40.5%	59.4%	40.6%
863,248	SUFFOLK	374,487	139,285	234,475	727	95,190 D	37.2%	62.6%	37.3%	62.7%
504,470	WORCESTER	222,258	98,414	123,440	404	25,026 D	44.3%	55.5%	44.4%	55.6%
4,316,721	TOTAL	1,960,665	921,350	1,035,296	4,019	113,946 D	47.0%	52.8%	47.1%	52.9%

MASSACHUSETTS

PRESIDENT 1940

1940 Census Population	County	Total Vote	Republican	Democratic	Other	Rep.-Dem. Plurality	Percentage Total Vote Rep.	Total Vote Dem.	Major Vote Rep.	Major Vote Dem.
37,295	BARNSTABLE	18,118	12,659	5,351	108	7,308 R	69.9%	29.5%	70.3%	29.7%
122,273	BERKSHIRE	58,880	25,973	32,620	287	6,647 D	44.1%	55.4%	44.3%	55.7%
364,637	BRISTOL	158,391	60,143	97,571	677	37,428 D	38.0%	61.6%	38.1%	61.9%
5,669	DUKES	2,670	1,643	1,014	13	629 R	61.5%	38.0%	61.8%	38.2%
496,313	ESSEX	243,735	116,134	125,998	1,603	9,864 D	47.6%	51.7%	48.0%	52.0%
49,453	FRANKLIN	23,728	14,137	9,472	119	4,665 R	59.6%	39.9%	59.9%	40.1%
332,107	HAMPDEN	154,796	64,502	89,477	817	24,975 D	41.7%	57.8%	41.9%	58.1%
72,461	HAMPSHIRE	33,715	15,651	17,823	241	2,172 D	46.4%	52.9%	46.8%	53.2%
971,390	MIDDLESEX	463,437	242,658	218,663	2,116	23,995 R	52.4%	47.2%	52.6%	47.4%
3,401	NANTUCKET	1,647	1,015	624	8	391 R	61.6%	37.9%	61.9%	38.1%
325,180	NORFOLK	166,017	97,525	67,654	838	29,871 R	58.7%	40.8%	59.0%	41.0%
168,824	PLYMOUTH	83,606	48,617	34,481	508	14,136 R	58.2%	41.2%	58.5%	41.5%
863,248	SUFFOLK	384,145	138,575	243,233	2,337	104,658 D	36.1%	63.3%	36.3%	63.7%
504,470	WORCESTER	234,108	100,468	132,541	1,099	32,073 D	42.9%	56.6%	43.1%	56.9%
4,316,721	TOTAL	2,026,993	939,700	1,076,522	10,771	136,822 D	46.4%	53.1%	46.6%	53.4%

MASSACHUSETTS

PRESIDENT 1936

1930 Census Population	County	Total Vote	Republican	Democratic	Other	Rep.-Dem. Plurality	Percentage Total Vote Rep.	Total Vote Dem.	Major Vote Rep.	Major Vote Dem.
32,305	BARNSTABLE	16,485	11,337	4,751	397	6,586 R	68.8%	28.8%	70.5%	29.5%
120,700	BERKSHIRE	53,568	22,607	29,087	1,874	6,480 D	42.2%	54.3%	43.7%	56.3%
364,590	BRISTOL	141,145	49,754	80,805	10,586	31,051 D	35.3%	57.2%	38.1%	61.9%
4,953	DUKES	2,615	1,655	931	29	724 R	63.3%	35.6%	64.0%	36.0%
498,040	ESSEX	222,999	97,310	106,078	19,611	8,768 D	43.6%	47.6%	47.8%	52.2%
49,612	FRANKLIN	23,721	13,756	9,324	641	4,432 R	58.0%	39.3%	59.6%	40.4%
335,496	HAMPDEN	140,180	51,288	80,164	8,728	28,876 D	36.6%	57.2%	39.0%	61.0%
72,801	HAMPSHIRE	30,906	14,012	15,412	1,482	1,400 D	45.3%	49.9%	47.6%	52.4%
934,924	MIDDLESEX	419,520	199,704	189,512	30,304	10,192 R	47.6%	45.2%	51.3%	48.7%
3,678	NANTUCKET	1,544	969	548	27	421 R	62.8%	35.5%	63.9%	36.1%
299,426	NORFOLK	148,890	82,545	57,770	8,575	24,775 R	55.4%	38.8%	58.8%	41.2%
162,311	PLYMOUTH	78,010	41,942	30,466	5,602	11,476 R	53.8%	39.1%	57.9%	42.1%
879,536	SUFFOLK	350,010	96,418	223,732	29,860	127,314 D	27.5%	63.9%	30.1%	69.9%
491,242	WORCESTER	210,764	85,316	114,136	11,312	28,820 D	40.5%	54.2%	42.8%	57.2%
4,249,614	TOTAL	1,840,357	768,613	942,716	129,028	174,103 D	41.8%	51.2%	44.9%	55.1%

MASSACHUSETTS

PRESIDENT 1932

1930 Census Population	County	Total Vote	Republican	Democratic	Other	Rep.-Dem. Plurality	Percentage Total Vote Rep.	Percentage Total Vote Dem.	Percentage Major Vote Rep.	Percentage Major Vote Dem.
32,305	BARNSTABLE	13,527	9,476	3,829	222	5,647 R	70.1%	28.3%	71.2%	28.8%
120,700	BERKSHIRE	48,220	23,186	23,252	1,782	66 D	48.1%	48.2%	49.9%	50.1%
364,590	BRISTOL	116,675	50,846	62,474	3,355	11,628 D	43.6%	53.5%	44.9%	55.1%
4,953	DUKES	1,933	1,330	583	20	747 R	68.8%	30.2%	69.5%	30.5%
498,040	ESSEX	193,018	95,277	91,787	5,954	3,490 R	49.4%	47.6%	50.9%	49.1%
49,612	FRANKLIN	19,748	13,040	6,248	460	6,792 R	66.0%	31.6%	67.6%	32.4%
335,496	HAMPDEN	123,629	55,032	63,189	5,408	8,157 D	44.5%	51.1%	46.6%	53.4%
72,801	HAMPSHIRE	26,869	13,241	12,332	1,296	909 R	49.3%	45.9%	51.8%	48.2%
934,924	MIDDLESEX	365,751	184,486	174,257	7,008	10,229 R	50.4%	47.6%	51.4%	48.6%
3,678	NANTUCKET	1,380	812	561	7	251 R	58.8%	40.7%	59.1%	40.9%
299,426	NORFOLK	127,146	75,232	49,121	2,793	26,111 R	59.2%	38.6%	60.5%	39.5%
162,311	PLYMOUTH	65,744	37,729	26,137	1,878	11,592 R	57.4%	39.8%	59.1%	40.9%
879,536	SUFFOLK	296,072	88,737	198,792	8,543	110,055 D	30.0%	67.1%	30.9%	69.1%
491,242	WORCESTER	180,402	88,535	87,586	4,281	949 R	49.1%	48.6%	50.3%	49.7%
4,249,614	TOTAL	1,580,114	736,959	800,148	43,007	63,189 D	46.6%	50.6%	47.9%	52.1%

MASSACHUSETTS

PRESIDENT 1928

1920 Census Population	County	Total Vote	Republican	Democratic	Other	Rep.-Dem. Plurality	Percentage Total Vote Rep.	Percentage Total Vote Dem.	Percentage Major Vote Rep.	Percentage Major Vote Dem.
26,670	BARNSTABLE	12,845	9,886	2,899	60	6,987 R	77.0%	22.6%	77.3%	22.7%
113,033	BERKSHIRE	48,174	23,855	24,075	244	220 D	49.5%	50.0%	49.8%	50.2%
359,005	BRISTOL	115,755	55,205	59,257	1,293	4,052 D	47.7%	51.2%	48.2%	51.8%
4,372	DUKES	1,958	1,487	470	1	1,017 R	75.9%	24.0%	76.0%	24.0%
482,156	ESSEX	192,810	102,008	89,508	1,294	12,500 R	52.9%	46.4%	53.3%	46.7%
49,361	FRANKLIN	20,324	14,333	5,842	149	8,491 R	70.5%	28.7%	71.0%	29.0%
300,305	HAMPDEN	118,822	56,063	62,056	703	5,993 D	47.2%	52.2%	47.5%	52.5%
69,599	HAMPSHIRE	27,051	14,101	12,695	255	1,406 R	52.1%	46.9%	52.6%	47.4%
778,352	MIDDLESEX	363,841	189,189	173,339	1,313	15,850 R	52.0%	47.6%	52.2%	47.8%
2,797	NANTUCKET	1,261	865	395	1	470 R	68.6%	31.3%	68.7%	31.3%
219,081	NORFOLK	121,076	73,530	47,057	489	26,473 R	60.7%	38.9%	61.0%	39.0%
156,968	PLYMOUTH	66,766	41,362	24,887	517	16,475 R	62.0%	37.3%	62.4%	37.6%
835,522	SUFFOLK	306,130	99,392	204,603	2,135	105,211 D	32.5%	66.8%	32.7%	67.3%
455,135	WORCESTER	181,010	94,290	85,675	1,045	8,615 R	52.1%	47.3%	52.4%	47.6%
3,852,356	TOTAL	1,577,823	775,566	792,758	9,499	17,192 D	49.2%	50.2%	49.5%	50.5%

MASSACHUSETTS

PRESIDENT 1924

1920 Census Population	County	Total Vote	Republican	Democratic	Other	Rep.-Dem. Plurality	Percentage Total Vote Rep.	Total Vote Dem.	Major Vote Rep.	Major Vote Dem.
26,670	BARNSTABLE	8,577	7,333	881	363	6,452 R	85.5%	10.3%	89.3%	10.7%
113,033	BERKSHIRE	34,571	21,106	9,712	3,753	11,394 R	61.1%	28.1%	68.5%	31.5%
359,005	BRISTOL	88,980	58,929	19,802	10,249	39,127 R	66.2%	22.3%	74.8%	25.2%
4,372	DUKES	1,360	1,182	108	70	1,074 R	86.9%	7.9%	91.6%	8.4%
482,156	ESSEX	139,550	92,918	25,635	20,997	67,283 R	66.6%	18.4%	78.4%	21.6%
49,361	FRANKLIN	14,717	11,350	2,089	1,278	9,261 R	77.1%	14.2%	84.5%	15.5%
300,305	HAMPDEN	77,515	46,489	19,079	11,947	27,410 R	60.0%	24.6%	70.9%	29.1%
69,599	HAMPSHIRE	21,014	13,918	5,037	2,059	8,881 R	66.2%	24.0%	73.4%	26.6%
778,352	MIDDLESEX	255,235	162,530	64,544	28,161	97,986 R	63.7%	25.3%	71.6%	28.4%
2,797	NANTUCKET	889	708	167	14	541 R	79.6%	18.8%	80.9%	19.1%
219,081	NORFOLK	81,505	57,948	15,041	8,516	42,907 R	71.1%	18.5%	79.4%	20.6%
156,968	PLYMOUTH	50,355	34,728	8,863	6,764	25,865 R	69.0%	17.6%	79.7%	20.3%
835,522	SUFFOLK	221,993	104,658	78,702	38,633	25,956 R	47.1%	35.5%	57.1%	42.9%
455,135	WORCESTER	133,576	89,679	31,171	12,726	58,508 R	67.1%	23.3%	74.2%	25.8%
3,852,356	TOTAL	1,129,837	703,476	280,831	145,530	422,645 R	62.3%	24.9%	71.5%	28.5%

MASSACHUSETTS

PRESIDENT 1920

1920 Census Population	County	Total Vote	Republican	Democratic	Other	Rep.-Dem. Plurality	Percentage Total Vote Rep.	Total Vote Dem.	Major Vote Rep.	Major Vote Dem.
26,670	BARNSTABLE	7,562	6,383	1,125	54	5,258 R	84.4%	14.9%	85.0%	15.0%
113,033	BERKSHIRE	31,910	20,138	10,956	816	9,182 R	63.1%	34.3%	64.8%	35.2%
359,005	BRISTOL	77,032	56,734	17,719	2,579	39,015 R	73.6%	23.0%	76.2%	23.8%
4,372	DUKES	1,168	1,013	150	5	863 R	86.7%	12.8%	87.1%	12.9%
482,156	ESSEX	132,264	95,057	30,560	6,647	64,497 R	71.9%	23.1%	75.7%	24.3%
49,361	FRANKLIN	12,757	9,931	2,542	284	7,389 R	77.8%	19.9%	79.6%	20.4%
300,305	HAMPDEN	67,820	46,741	19,156	1,923	27,585 R	68.9%	28.2%	70.9%	29.1%
69,599	HAMPSHIRE	18,793	13,174	5,305	314	7,869 R	70.1%	28.2%	71.3%	28.7%
778,352	MIDDLESEX	224,078	156,636	61,661	5,781	94,975 R	69.9%	27.5%	71.8%	28.2%
2,797	NANTUCKET	816	608	205	3	403 R	74.5%	25.1%	74.8%	25.2%
219,081	NORFOLK	69,385	51,826	15,720	1,839	36,106 R	74.7%	22.7%	76.7%	23.3%
156,968	PLYMOUTH	45,663	33,582	9,373	2,708	24,209 R	73.5%	20.5%	78.2%	21.8%
835,522	SUFFOLK	186,098	108,089	67,552	10,457	40,537 R	58.1%	36.3%	61.5%	38.5%
455,135	WORCESTER	118,372	81,241	34,667	2,464	46,574 R	68.6%	29.3%	70.1%	29.9%
3,852,356	TOTAL	993,718	681,153	276,691	35,874	404,462 R	68.5%	27.8%	71.1%	28.9%

MASSACHUSETTS

ELECTION NOTES

1956 Other vote was 5,573 Hass (Socialist Labor); 1,205 Holtwick (Prohibition); 341 scattered write-in.

1952 Other vote was 4,636 Hallinan (Progressive); 1,957 Hass (Socialist Labor); 886 Hamblen (Prohibition); 69 scattered write-in.

1948 Other vote was 38,157 Wallace (Progressive); 5,535 Teichert (Socialist Labor); 1,663 Watson (Prohibition); 633 scattered write-in.

1944 Other vote was 2,780 Teichert (Socialist Labor); 973 Watson (Prohibition); 266 scattered write-in.

1940 Other vote was 4,091 Thomas (Socialist); 3,806 Browder (Communist); 1,492 Aiken (Socialist Labor); 1,370 Babson (Prohibition); 12 scattered write-in.

1936 Other vote was 118,639 Lemke (Union); 5,111 Thomas (Socialist); 2,930 Browder (Communist); 1,305 Aiken (Socialist Labor); 1,032 Colvin (Prohibition); 11 scattered write-in.

1932 Other vote was 34,305 Thomas (Socialist); 4,821 Foster (Communist); 2,668 Reynolds (Socialist Labor); 1,142 Upshaw (Prohibition); 71 scattered write-in.

1928 Other vote was 6,262 Thomas (Socialist); 2,461 Foster (Communist); 772 Reyonlds (Socialist Labor); 4 scattered write-in.

1924 Other vote was 141,225 LaFollette (Progressive); 2,635 Foster (Communist); 1,668 Johns (Socialist Labor); 2 scattered write-in.

1920 Other vote was 32,267 Debs (Socialist); 3,583 Cox (Socialist Labor); 24 scattered write-in.

MICHIGAN

POPULAR VOTE FOR PRESIDENT 1920 TO 1956

Year	Total Vote	Republican		Democratic		Other Vote	Plurality	Percentage			
								Total Vote		Major Vote	
		Vote	Candidate	Vote	Candidate			Rep.	Dem.	Rep.	Dem.
1956	3,080,468	1,713,647	Eisenhower, Dwight D.	1,359,898	Stevenson, Adlai E.	6,923	353,749 R	55.6%	44.1%	55.8%	44.2%
1952	2,798,592	1,551,529	Eisenhower, Dwight D.	1,230,657	Stevenson, Adlai E.	16,406	320,872 R	55.4%	44.0%	55.8%	44.2%
1948	2,109,609	1,038,595	Dewey, Thomas E.	1,003,448	Truman, Harry S.	67,566	35,147 R	49.2%	47.6%	50.9%	49.1%
1944	2,205,223	1,084,423	Dewey, Thomas E.	1,106,899	Roosevelt, Franklin D.	13,901	22,476 D	49.2%	50.2%	49.5%	50.5%
1940	2,085,929	1,039,917	Willkie, Wendell	1,032,991	Roosevelt, Franklin D.	13,021	6,926 R	49.9%	49.5%	50.2%	49.8%
1936	1,805,098	699,733	Landon, Alfred M.	1,016,794	Roosevelt, Franklin D.	88,571	317,061 D	38.8%	56.3%	40.8%	59.2%
1932	1,664,765	739,894	Hoover, Herbert C.	871,700	Roosevelt, Franklin D.	53,171	131,806 D	44.4%	52.4%	45.9%	54.1%
1928	1,372,082	965,396	Hoover, Herbert C.	396,762	Smith, Alfred E.	9,924	568,634 R	70.4%	28.9%	70.9%	29.1%
1924 * *	1,160,419	874,631	Coolidge, Calvin	152,359	Davis, John W.	133,429	722,272 R	75.4%	13.1%	85.2%	14.8%
1920	1,048,411	762,865	Harding, Warren G.	233,450	Cox, James M.	52,096	529,415 R	72.8%	22.3%	76.6%	23.4%

In 1924 other vote was 122,014 Progressive; 6,085 Prohibition and 5,330 Socialist Labor.

ELECTORAL COLLEGE VOTE 1920 TO 1956

Year	Total	Republican	Democratic	Other
1956	20	20	—	—
1952	20	20	—	—
1948	19	19	—	—
1944	19	—	19	—
1940	19	19	—	—
1936	19	—	19	—
1932	19	—	19	—
1928	15	15	—	—
1924	15	15	—	—
1920	15	15	—	—

MICHIGAN

KEWEENAW (PART)
KEWEENAW (PART)
HOUGHTON
ONTONAGON
BARAGA
GOGEBIC
IRON
MARQUETTE
ALGER
LUCE
CHIPPEWA
SCHOOLCRAFT
DICKINSON
DELTA
MACKINAC
MENOMINEE
EMMET
CHEBOYGAN
PRESQUE ISLE
CHARLEVOIX
ANTRIM
OTSEGO
MONTMORENCY
ALPENA
LEELANAU
BENZIE
GRAND TRAVERSE
KALKASKA
CRAWFORD
OSCODA
ALCONA
MANISTEE
WEXFORD
MISSAUKEE
ROSCOMMON
OGEMAW
IOSCO
MASON
LAKE
OSCEOLA
CLARE
GLADWIN
ARENAC
HURON
OCEANA
NEWAYGO
MECOSTA
ISABELLA
MIDLAND
BAY
TUSCOLA
SANILAC
MUSKEGON
MONTCALM
GRATIOT
SAGINAW
OTTAWA
KENT
IONIA
CLINTON
SHIAWASSEE
GENESEE
LAPEER
ST. CLAIR
ALLEGAN
BARRY
EATON
INGHAM
LIVINGSTON
OAKLAND
MACOMB
VAN BUREN
KALAMAZOO
CALHOUN
JACKSON
WASHTENAW
WAYNE
BERRIEN
CASS
ST. JOSEPH
BRANCH
HILLSDALE
LENAWEE
MONROE

MICHIGAN

PRESIDENT 1956

1950 Census Population	County	Total Vote	Republican	Democratic	Other	Rep.-Dem. Plurality	Percentage Total Vote Rep.	Total Vote Dem.	Major Vote Rep.	Major Vote Dem.
5,856	ALCONA	2,784	1,991	788	5	1,203 R	71.5%	28.3%	71.6%	28.4%
10,007	ALGER	4,193	2,070	2,105	18	35 D	49.4%	50.2%	49.6%	50.4%
47,493	ALLEGAN	22,177	16,509	5,617	51	10,892 R	74.4%	25.3%	74.6%	25.4%
22,189	ALPENA	10,177	7,142	3,033	2	4,109 R	70.2%	29.8%	70.2%	29.8%
10,721	ANTRIM	5,008	3,623	1,376	9	2,247 R	72.3%	27.5%	72.5%	27.5%
9,644	ARENAC	4,155	2,631	1,520	4	1,111 R	63.3%	36.6%	63.4%	36.6%
8,037	BARAGA	3,545	1,968	1,574	3	394 R	55.5%	44.4%	55.6%	44.4%
26,183	BARRY	13,329	9,359	3,907	63	5,452 R	70.2%	29.3%	70.5%	29.5%
88,461	BAY	38,948	23,519	15,301	128	8,218 R	60.4%	39.3%	60.6%	39.4%
8,306	BENZIE	3,681	2,620	1,046	15	1,574 R	71.2%	28.4%	71.5%	28.5%
115,702	BERRIEN	54,045	35,397	18,454	194	16,943 R	65.5%	34.1%	65.7%	34.3%
30,202	BRANCH	12,744	8,856	3,827	61	5,029 R	69.5%	30.0%	69.8%	30.2%
120,813	CALHOUN	52,643	32,284	20,184	175	12,100 R	61.3%	38.3%	61.5%	38.5%
28,185	CASS	13,788	8,899	4,842	47	4,057 R	64.5%	35.1%	64.8%	35.2%
13,475	CHARLEVOIX	5,874	3,924	1,935	15	1,989 R	66.8%	32.9%	67.0%	33.0%
13,731	CHEBOYGAN	6,296	4,379	1,910	7	2,469 R	69.6%	30.3%	69.6%	30.4%
29,206	CHIPPEWA	11,077	6,957	4,106	14	2,851 R	62.8%	37.1%	62.9%	37.1%
10,253	CLARE	4,928	3,721	1,194	13	2,527 R	75.5%	24.2%	75.7%	24.3%
31,195	CLINTON	14,474	10,770	3,673	31	7,097 R	74.4%	25.4%	74.6%	25.4%
4,151	CRAWFORD	1,930	1,380	547	3	833 R	71.5%	28.3%	71.6%	28.4%
32,913	DELTA	14,300	7,766	6,489	45	1,277 R	54.3%	45.4%	54.5%	45.5%
24,844	DICKINSON	11,330	6,200	5,113	17	1,087 R	54.7%	45.1%	54.8%	45.2%
40,023	EATON	19,850	13,762	6,053	35	7,709 R	69.3%	30.5%	69.5%	30.5%
16,534	EMMET	6,695	4,764	1,903	28	2,861 R	71.2%	28.4%	71.5%	28.5%
270,963	GENESEE	138,474	75,431	62,808	235	12,623 R	54.5%	45.4%	54.6%	45.4%
9,451	GLADWIN	4,248	3,121	1,117	10	2,004 R	73.5%	26.3%	73.6%	26.4%
27,053	GOGEBIC	13,032	6,865	6,142	25	723 R	52.7%	47.1%	52.8%	47.2%
28,598	GRAND TRAVERSE	12,388	9,102	3,256	30	5,846 R	73.5%	26.3%	73.7%	26.3%
33,429	GRATIOT	13,630	10,319	3,267	44	7,052 R	75.7%	24.0%	76.0%	24.0%
31,916	HILLSDALE	13,806	10,311	3,428	67	6,883 R	74.7%	24.8%	75.0%	25.0%
39,771	HOUGHTON	16,511	9,620	6,866	25	2,754 R	58.3%	41.6%	58.4%	41.6%
33,149	HURON	13,704	10,493	3,192	19	7,301 R	76.6%	23.3%	76.7%	23.3%
172,941	INGHAM	82,654	55,211	27,323	120	27,888 R	66.8%	33.1%	66.9%	33.1%
38,158	IONIA	15,999	11,001	4,952	46	6,049 R	68.8%	31.0%	69.0%	31.0%
10,906	IOSCO	6,048	4,385	1,660	3	2,725 R	72.5%	27.4%	72.5%	27.5%
17,692	IRON	9,458	4,955	4,490	13	465 R	52.4%	47.5%	52.5%	47.5%
28,964	ISABELLA	11,621	8,415	3,183	23	5,232 R	72.4%	27.4%	72.6%	27.4%
107,925	JACKSON	51,079	35,453	15,479	147	19,974 R	69.4%	30.3%	69.6%	30.4%
126,707	KALAMAZOO	61,433	43,305	17,808	320	25,497 R	70.5%	29.0%	70.9%	29.1%
4,597	KALKASKA	2,088	1,443	636	9	807 R	69.1%	30.5%	69.4%	30.6%
288,292	KENT	144,482	94,969	48,871	642	46,098 R	65.7%	33.8%	66.0%	34.0%
2,918	KEWEENAW	1,523	834	689		145 R	54.8%	45.2%	54.8%	45.2%
5,257	LAKE	2,699	1,614	1,083	2	531 R	59.8%	40.1%	59.8%	40.2%
35,794	LAPEER	14,459	10,527	3,913	19	6,614 R	72.8%	27.1%	72.9%	27.1%
8,647	LEELANAU	4,278	2,987	1,287	4	1,700 R	69.8%	30.1%	69.9%	30.1%
64,629	LENAWEE	29,031	21,100	7,857	74	13,243 R	72.7%	27.1%	72.9%	27.1%
26,725	LIVINGSTON	14,205	10,315	3,845	45	6,470 R	72.6%	27.1%	72.8%	27.2%
8,147	LUCE	2,390	1,734	651	5	1,083 R	72.6%	27.2%	72.7%	27.3%
9,287	MACKINAC	4,823	3,279	1,540	4	1,739 R	68.0%	31.9%	68.0%	32.0%
184,961	MACOMB	121,419	58,337	62,816	266	4,479 D	48.0%	51.7%	48.2%	51.8%
18,524	MANISTEE	8,336	5,313	3,014	9	2,299 R	63.7%	36.2%	63.8%	36.2%
47,654	MARQUETTE	22,084	12,504	9,543	37	2,961 R	56.6%	43.2%	56.7%	43.3%
20,474	MASON	9,428	6,142	3,274	12	2,868 R	65.1%	34.7%	65.2%	34.8%
18,968	MECOSTA	7,279	5,492	1,768	19	3,724 R	75.4%	24.3%	75.6%	24.4%
25,299	MENOMINEE	10,757	6,137	4,610	10	1,527 R	57.1%	42.9%	57.1%	42.9%
35,662	MIDLAND	17,662	13,207	4,422	33	8,785 R	74.8%	25.0%	74.9%	25.1%
7,458	MISSAUKEE	3,168	2,433	727	8	1,706 R	76.8%	22.9%	77.0%	23.0%
75,666	MONROE	33,305	18,782	14,414	109	4,368 R	56.4%	43.3%	56.6%	43.4%
31,013	MONTCALM	13,981	9,759	4,189	33	5,570 R	69.8%	30.0%	70.0%	30.0%
4,125	MONTMORENCY	1,996	1,385	608	3	777 R	69.4%	30.5%	69.5%	30.5%

MICHIGAN

PRESIDENT 1956

1950 Census Population	County	Total Vote	Republican	Democratic	Other	Rep.-Dem. Plurality	Percentage Total Vote Rep.	Percentage Total Vote Dem.	Percentage Major Vote Rep.	Percentage Major Vote Dem.
121,545	MUSKEGON	56,246	30,395	25,679	172	4,716 R	54.0%	45.7%	54.2%	45.8%
21,567	NEWAYGO	9,916	7,088	2,808	20	4,280 R	71.5%	28.3%	71.6%	28.4%
396,001	OAKLAND	253,418	152,990	99,901	527	53,089 R	60.4%	39.4%	60.5%	39.5%
16,105	OCEANA	6,372	4,479	1,868	25	2,611 R	70.3%	29.3%	70.6%	29.4%
9,345	OGEMAW	4,237	2,931	1,300	6	1,631 R	69.2%	30.7%	69.3%	30.7%
10,282	ONTONAGON	5,155	2,976	2,175	4	801 R	57.7%	42.2%	57.8%	42.2%
13,797	OSCEOLA	5,811	4,549	1,236	26	3,313 R	78.3%	21.3%	78.6%	21.4%
3,134	OSCODA	1,338	1,044	294		750 R	78.0%	22.0%	78.0%	22.0%
6,435	OTSEGO	3,028	1,930	1,095	3	835 R	63.7%	36.2%	63.8%	36.2%
73,751	OTTAWA	38,200	28,611	9,459	130	19,152 R	74.9%	24.8%	75.2%	24.8%
11,996	PRESQUE ISLE	4,978	3,058	1,917	3	1,141 R	61.4%	38.5%	61.5%	38.5%
5,916	ROSCOMMON	3,509	2,674	827	8	1,847 R	76.2%	23.6%	76.4%	23.6%
153,515	SAGINAW	69,361	43,470	25,681	210	17,789 R	62.7%	37.0%	62.9%	37.1%
91,599	ST. CLAIR	41,920	29,116	12,753	51	16,363 R	69.5%	30.4%	69.5%	30.5%
35,071	ST. JOSEPH	16,634	12,328	4,242	64	8,086 R	74.1%	25.5%	74.4%	25.6%
30,837	SANILAC	14,066	11,095	2,954	17	8,141 R	78.9%	21.0%	79.0%	21.0%
9,148	SCHOOLCRAFT	4,177	2,453	1,723	1	730 R	58.7%	41.2%	58.7%	41.3%
45,967	SHIAWASSEE	21,551	14,600	6,873	78	7,727 R	67.7%	31.9%	68.0%	32.0%
38,258	TUSCOLA	15,935	12,052	3,864	19	8,188 R	75.6%	24.2%	75.7%	24.3%
39,184	VAN BUREN	19,063	13,291	5,678	94	7,613 R	69.7%	29.8%	70.1%	29.9%
134,606	WASHTENAW	58,176	38,911	19,124	141	19,787 R	66.9%	32.9%	67.0%	33.0%
2,435,235	WAYNE	1,148,245	481,783	664,618	1,844	182,835 D	42.0%	57.9%	42.0%	58.0%
18,628	WEXFORD	7,683	5,052	2,604	27	2,448 R	65.8%	33.9%	66.0%	34.0%
6,371,766	TOTAL	3,080,468	1,713,647	1,359,898	6,923	353,749 R	55.6%	44.1%	55.8%	44.2%

MICHIGAN

PRESIDENT 1952

1950 Census Population	County	Total Vote	Republican	Democratic	Other	Rep.-Dem. Plurality	Percentage: Total Vote Rep.	Percentage: Total Vote Dem.	Percentage: Major Vote Rep.	Percentage: Major Vote Dem.
5,856	ALCONA	2,215	1,441	766	8	675 R	65.1%	34.6%	65.3%	34.7%
10,007	ALGER	4,159	2,066	2,058	35	8 R	49.7%	49.5%	50.1%	49.9%
47,493	ALLEGAN	21,338	15,663	5,437	238	10,226 R	73.4%	25.5%	74.2%	25.8%
22,189	ALPENA	9,421	6,248	3,134	39	3,114 R	66.3%	33.3%	66.6%	33.4%
10,721	ANTRIM	4,618	3,533	1,046	39	2,487 R	76.5%	22.7%	77.2%	22.8%
9,644	ARENAC	4,064	2,753	1,290	21	1,463 R	67.7%	31.7%	68.1%	31.9%
8,037	BARAGA	3,671	2,103	1,540	28	563 R	57.3%	42.0%	57.7%	42.3%
26,183	BARRY	12,287	8,933	3,230	124	5,703 R	72.7%	26.3%	73.4%	26.6%
88,461	BAY	34,396	20,087	14,113	196	5,974 R	58.4%	41.0%	58.7%	41.3%
8,306	BENZIE	3,768	2,752	980	36	1,772 R	73.0%	26.0%	73.7%	26.3%
115,702	BERRIEN	52,320	32,932	19,088	300	13,844 R	62.9%	36.5%	63.3%	36.7%
30,202	BRANCH	12,884	9,215	3,564	105	5,651 R	71.5%	27.7%	72.1%	27.9%
120,813	CALHOUN	51,447	31,941	19,171	335	12,770 R	62.1%	37.3%	62.5%	37.5%
28,185	CASS	13,072	8,479	4,500	93	3,979 R	64.9%	34.4%	65.3%	34.7%
13,475	CHARLEVOIX	5,722	3,895	1,778	49	2,117 R	68.1%	31.1%	68.7%	31.3%
13,731	CHEBOYGAN	6,309	4,385	1,900	24	2,485 R	69.5%	30.1%	69.8%	30.2%
29,206	CHIPPEWA	11,389	7,075	4,257	57	2,818 R	62.1%	37.4%	62.4%	37.6%
10,253	CLARE	4,630	3,529	1,059	42	2,470 R	76.2%	22.9%	76.9%	23.1%
31,195	CLINTON	13,566	10,510	2,977	79	7,533 R	77.5%	21.9%	77.9%	22.1%
4,151	CRAWFORD	1,835	1,331	490	14	841 R	72.5%	26.7%	73.1%	26.9%
32,913	DELTA	14,458	7,488	6,921	49	567 R	51.8%	47.9%	52.0%	48.0%
24,844	DICKINSON	11,811	6,045	5,710	56	335 R	51.2%	48.3%	51.4%	48.6%
40,023	EATON	19,018	13,723	5,170	125	8,553 R	72.2%	27.2%	72.6%	27.4%
16,534	EMMET	7,014	5,113	1,871	30	3,242 R	72.9%	26.7%	73.2%	26.8%
270,963	GENESEE	119,712	62,220	56,753	739	5,467 R	52.0%	47.4%	52.3%	47.7%
9,451	GLADWIN	3,996	3,031	936	29	2,095 R	75.9%	23.4%	76.4%	23.6%
27,053	GOGEBIC	13,051	6,195	6,803	53	608 D	47.5%	52.1%	47.7%	52.3%
28,598	GRAND TRAVERSE	11,711	9,034	2,639	38	6,395 R	77.1%	22.5%	77.4%	22.6%
33,429	GRATIOT	13,021	10,034	2,887	100	7,147 R	77.1%	22.2%	77.7%	22.3%
31,916	HILLSDALE	14,143	10,680	3,340	123	7,340 R	75.5%	23.6%	76.2%	23.8%
39,771	HOUGHTON	17,733	10,563	7,100	70	3,463 R	59.6%	40.0%	59.8%	40.2%
33,149	HURON	13,089	10,639	2,421	29	8,218 R	81.3%	18.5%	81.5%	18.5%
172,941	INGHAM	76,161	51,503	24,125	533	27,378 R	67.6%	31.7%	68.1%	31.9%
38,158	IONIA	15,819	10,970	4,722	127	6,248 R	69.3%	29.9%	69.9%	30.1%
10,906	IOSCO	5,059	3,772	1,274	13	2,498 R	74.6%	25.2%	74.8%	25.2%
17,692	IRON	9,216	4,564	4,597	55	33 D	49.5%	49.9%	49.8%	50.2%
28,964	ISABELLA	11,180	8,222	2,881	77	5,341 R	73.5%	25.8%	74.1%	25.9%
107,925	JACKSON	48,105	32,810	15,065	230	17,745 R	68.2%	31.3%	68.5%	31.5%
126,707	KALAMAZOO	58,185	38,847	18,967	371	19,880 R	66.8%	32.6%	67.2%	32.8%
4,597	KALKASKA	1,823	1,326	483	14	843 R	72.7%	26.5%	73.3%	26.7%
288,292	KENT	128,315	79,647	47,221	1,447	32,426 R	62.1%	36.8%	62.8%	37.2%
2,918	KEWEENAW	1,559	801	747	11	54 R	51.4%	47.9%	51.7%	48.3%
5,257	LAKE	2,696	1,549	1,127	20	422 R	57.5%	41.8%	57.9%	42.1%
35,794	LAPEER	13,656	9,940	3,644	72	6,296 R	72.8%	26.7%	73.2%	26.8%
8,647	LEELANAU	3,934	2,926	999	9	1,927 R	74.4%	25.4%	74.5%	25.5%
64,629	LENAWEE	27,549	20,035	7,397	117	12,638 R	72.7%	26.9%	73.0%	27.0%
26,725	LIVINGSTON	12,955	9,790	3,086	79	6,704 R	75.6%	23.8%	76.0%	24.0%
8,147	LUCE	2,159	1,603	553	3	1,050 R	74.2%	25.6%	74.4%	25.6%
9,287	MACKINAC	4,354	3,058	1,285	11	1,773 R	70.2%	29.5%	70.4%	29.6%
184,961	MACOMB	74,364	37,474	36,544	346	930 R	50.4%	49.1%	50.6%	49.4%
18,524	MANISTEE	8,376	5,235	3,114	27	2,121 R	62.5%	37.2%	62.7%	37.3%
47,654	MARQUETTE	21,655	11,618	9,949	88	1,669 R	53.7%	45.9%	53.9%	46.1%
20,474	MASON	9,558	6,179	3,298	81	2,881 R	64.6%	34.5%	65.2%	34.8%
18,968	MECOSTA	7,102	5,436	1,587	79	3,849 R	76.5%	22.3%	77.4%	22.6%
25,299	MENOMINEE	11,068	6,147	4,884	37	1,263 R	55.5%	44.1%	55.7%	44.3%
35,662	MIDLAND	14,570	10,508	3,945	117	6,563 R	72.1%	27.1%	72.7%	27.3%
7,458	MISSAUKEE	3,156	2,525	600	31	1,925 R	80.0%	19.0%	80.8%	19.2%
75,666	MONROE	30,074	17,159	12,758	157	4,401 R	57.1%	42.4%	57.4%	42.6%
31,013	MONTCALM	13,926	9,946	3,844	136	6,102 R	71.4%	27.6%	72.1%	27.9%
4,125	MONTMORENCY	2,015	1,449	544	22	905 R	71.9%	27.0%	72.7%	27.3%

MICHIGAN

PRESIDENT 1952

1950 Census Population	County	Total Vote	Republican	Democratic	Other	Rep.-Dem. Plurality	Percentage Total Vote Rep.	Total Vote Dem.	Major Vote Rep.	Major Vote Dem.
121,545	MUSKEGON	50,446	25,967	23,826	653	2,141 R	51.5%	47.2%	52.1%	47.9%
21,567	NEWAYGO	9,351	6,715	2,541	95	4,174 R	71.8%	27.2%	72.5%	27.5%
396,001	OAKLAND	190,179	115,503	73,871	805	41,632 R	60.7%	38.8%	61.0%	39.0%
16,105	OCEANA	6,622	4,704	1,799	119	2,905 R	71.0%	27.2%	72.3%	27.7%
9,345	OGEMAW	4,036	2,983	1,030	23	1,953 R	73.9%	25.5%	74.3%	25.7%
10,282	ONTONAGON	5,159	2,961	2,134	64	827 R	57.4%	41.4%	58.1%	41.9%
13,797	OSCEOLA	5,842	4,607	1,160	75	3,447 R	78.9%	19.9%	79.9%	20.1%
3,134	OSCODA	1,297	1,047	246	4	801 R	80.7%	19.0%	81.0%	19.0%
6,435	OTSEGO	2,818	1,941	865	12	1,076 R	68.9%	30.7%	69.2%	30.8%
73,751	OTTAWA	30,657	22,328	7,835	494	14,493 R	72.8%	25.6%	74.0%	26.0%
11,996	PRESQUE ISLE	4,822	2,982	1,825	15	1,157 R	61.8%	37.8%	62.0%	38.0%
5,916	ROSCOMMON	3,239	2,547	676	16	1,871 R	78.6%	20.9%	79.0%	21.0%
153,515	SAGINAW	60,100	38,604	20,983	513	17,621 R	64.2%	34.9%	64.8%	35.2%
91,599	ST. CLAIR	40,256	27,894	12,268	94	15,626 R	69.3%	30.5%	69.5%	30.5%
35,071	ST. JOSEPH	16,887	12,191	4,509	187	7,682 R	72.2%	26.7%	73.0%	27.0%
30,837	SANILAC	13,557	11,181	2,298	78	8,883 R	82.5%	17.0%	83.0%	17.0%
9,148	SCHOOLCRAFT	4,052	2,352	1,692	8	660 R	58.0%	41.8%	58.2%	41.8%
45,967	SHIAWASSEE	19,824	13,562	6,056	206	7,506 R	68.4%	30.5%	69.1%	30.9%
38,258	TUSCOLA	15,119	11,788	3,251	80	8,537 R	78.0%	21.5%	78.4%	21.6%
39,184	VAN BUREN	18,659	13,231	5,309	119	7,922 R	70.9%	28.5%	71.4%	28.6%
134,606	WASHTENAW	53,759	35,826	17,671	262	18,155 R	66.6%	32.9%	67.0%	33.0%
2,435,235	WAYNE	1,083,381	456,371	622,236	4,774	165,865 D	42.1%	57.4%	42.3%	57.7%
18,628	WEXFORD	8,073	5,569	2,407	97	3,162 R	69.0%	29.8%	69.8%	30.2%
6,371,766	TOTAL	2,798,592	1,551,529	1,230,657	16,406	320,872 R	55.4%	44.0%	55.8%	44.2%

MICHIGAN

PRESIDENT 1948

1940 Census Population	County	Total Vote	Republican	Democratic	Other	Rep.-Dem. Plurality	Percentage Total Vote Rep.	Total Vote Dem.	Major Vote Rep.	Major Vote Dem.
5,463	ALCONA	2,168	1,425	708	35	717 R	65.7%	32.7%	66.8%	33.2%
10,167	ALGER	3,983	1,702	2,009	272	307 D	42.7%	50.4%	45.9%	54.1%
41,839	ALLEGAN	15,424	10,439	4,594	391	5,845 R	67.7%	29.8%	69.4%	30.6%
20,766	ALPENA	7,152	4,313	2,743	96	1,570 R	60.3%	38.4%	61.1%	38.9%
10,964	ANTRIM	3,849	2,588	1,129	132	1,459 R	67.2%	29.3%	69.6%	30.4%
9,233	ARENAC	3,041	1,790	1,203	48	587 R	58.9%	39.6%	59.8%	40.2%
9,356	BARAGA	3,748	1,878	1,656	214	222 R	50.1%	44.2%	53.1%	46.9%
22,613	BARRY	8,768	5,677	2,726	365	2,951 R	64.7%	31.1%	67.6%	32.4%
74,981	BAY	27,997	13,321	14,349	327	1,028 D	47.6%	51.3%	48.1%	51.9%
7,800	BENZIE	3,089	2,013	964	112	1,049 R	65.2%	31.2%	67.6%	32.4%
89,117	BERRIEN	37,361	22,003	14,516	842	7,487 R	58.9%	38.9%	60.3%	39.7%
25,845	BRANCH	10,027	6,323	3,405	299	2,918 R	63.1%	34.0%	65.0%	35.0%
94,206	CALHOUN	35,096	19,285	15,077	734	4,208 R	54.9%	43.0%	56.1%	43.9%
21,910	CASS	9,032	5,615	3,201	216	2,414 R	62.2%	35.4%	63.7%	36.3%
13,031	CHARLEVOIX	4,895	2,911	1,847	137	1,064 R	59.5%	37.7%	61.2%	38.8%
13,644	CHEBOYGAN	5,109	3,184	1,842	83	1,342 R	62.3%	36.1%	63.4%	36.6%
27,807	CHIPPEWA	9,331	4,977	3,860	494	1,117 R	53.3%	41.4%	56.3%	43.7%
9,163	CLARE	3,805	2,512	1,197	96	1,315 R	66.0%	31.5%	67.7%	32.3%
26,671	CLINTON	10,191	7,510	2,523	158	4,987 R	73.7%	24.8%	74.9%	25.1%
3,765	CRAWFORD	1,328	849	455	24	394 R	63.9%	34.3%	65.1%	34.9%
34,037	DELTA	12,633	5,414	6,943	276	1,529 D	42.9%	55.0%	43.8%	56.2%
28,731	DICKINSON	11,309	4,417	6,295	597	1,878 D	39.1%	55.7%	41.2%	58.8%
34,124	EATON	13,320	8,637	4,264	419	4,373 R	64.8%	32.0%	66.9%	33.1%
15,791	EMMET	5,621	3,565	1,922	134	1,643 R	63.4%	34.2%	65.0%	35.0%
227,944	GENESEE	86,228	38,270	45,032	2,926	6,762 D	44.4%	52.2%	45.9%	54.1%
9,385	GLADWIN	3,104	2,062	963	79	1,099 R	66.4%	31.0%	68.2%	31.8%
31,797	GOGEBIC	12,569	5,204	6,722	643	1,518 D	41.4%	53.5%	43.6%	56.4%
23,390	GRAND TRAVERSE	8,015	5,473	2,365	177	3,108 R	68.3%	29.5%	69.8%	30.2%
32,205	GRATIOT	10,027	7,035	2,659	333	4,376 R	70.2%	26.5%	72.6%	27.4%
29,092	HILLSDALE	10,760	7,232	3,095	433	4,137 R	67.2%	28.8%	70.0%	30.0%
47,631	HOUGHTON	17,471	9,541	6,925	1,005	2,616 R	54.6%	39.6%	57.9%	42.1%
32,584	HURON	10,648	7,978	2,562	108	5,416 R	74.9%	24.1%	75.7%	24.3%
130,616	INGHAM	52,575	31,868	19,366	1,341	12,502 R	60.6%	36.8%	62.2%	37.8%
35,710	IONIA	12,731	7,970	4,450	311	3,520 R	62.6%	35.0%	64.2%	35.8%
8,560	IOSCO	3,772	2,599	1,115	58	1,484 R	68.9%	29.6%	70.0%	30.0%
20,243	IRON	8,212	3,659	4,125	428	466 D	44.6%	50.2%	47.0%	53.0%
25,982	ISABELLA	8,158	5,485	2,487	186	2,998 R	67.2%	30.5%	68.8%	31.2%
93,108	JACKSON	35,037	21,449	12,809	779	8,640 R	61.2%	36.6%	62.6%	37.4%
100,085	KALAMAZOO	41,517	23,799	16,393	1,325	7,406 R	57.3%	39.5%	59.2%	40.8%
5,159	KALKASKA	1,277	837	400	40	437 R	65.5%	31.3%	67.7%	32.3%
246,338	KENT	98,776	53,669	43,205	1,902	10,464 R	54.3%	43.7%	55.4%	44.6%
4,004	KEWEENAW	1,625	814	647	164	167 R	50.1%	39.8%	55.7%	44.3%
4,798	LAKE	2,490	1,348	1,077	65	271 R	54.1%	43.3%	55.6%	44.4%
32,116	LAPEER	13,298	8,358	4,668	272	3,690 R	62.9%	35.1%	64.2%	35.8%
8,436	LEELANAU	2,794	1,928	835	31	1,093 R	69.0%	29.9%	69.8%	30.2%
53,110	LENAWEE	21,291	14,369	6,529	393	7,840 R	67.5%	30.7%	68.8%	31.2%
20,863	LIVINGSTON	10,379	7,368	2,813	198	4,555 R	71.0%	27.1%	72.4%	27.6%
7,423	LUCE	1,887	1,273	570	44	703 R	67.5%	30.2%	69.1%	30.9%
9,438	MACKINAC	3,362	2,182	1,138	42	1,044 R	64.9%	33.8%	65.7%	34.3%
107,638	MACOMB	47,660	21,205	25,265	1,190	4,060 D	44.5%	53.0%	45.6%	54.4%
18,450	MANISTEE	7,399	3,913	3,339	147	574 R	52.9%	45.1%	54.0%	46.0%
47,144	MARQUETTE	19,064	8,591	10,003	470	1,412 D	45.1%	52.5%	46.2%	53.8%
19,378	MASON	7,407	4,147	2,988	272	1,159 R	56.0%	40.3%	58.1%	41.9%
16,902	MECOSTA	5,557	3,803	1,572	182	2,231 R	68.4%	28.3%	70.8%	29.2%
24,883	MENOMINEE	9,667	4,420	5,094	153	674 D	45.7%	52.7%	46.5%	53.5%
27,094	MIDLAND	9,196	5,811	3,204	181	2,607 R	63.2%	34.8%	64.5%	35.5%
8,034	MISSAUKEE	2,554	1,742	750	62	992 R	68.2%	29.4%	69.9%	30.1%
58,620	MONROE	21,824	11,070	10,434	320	636 R	50.7%	47.8%	51.5%	48.5%
28,581	MONTCALM	9,335	6,081	2,999	255	3,082 R	65.1%	32.1%	67.0%	33.0%
3,840	MONTMORENCY	1,644	1,054	553	37	501 R	64.1%	33.6%	65.6%	34.4%

MICHIGAN

PRESIDENT 1948

1940 Census Population	County	Total Vote	Republican	Democratic	Other	Rep.-Dem. Plurality	Percentage Total Vote Rep.	Percentage Total Vote Dem.	Percentage Major Vote Rep.	Percentage Major Vote Dem.
94,501	MUSKEGON	37,107	15,382	20,631	1,094	5,249 D	41.5%	55.6%	42.7%	57.3%
19,286	NEWAYGO	6,566	4,394	2,027	145	2,367 R	66.9%	30.9%	68.4%	31.6%
254,068	OAKLAND	116,866	62,516	51,491	2,859	11,025 R	53.5%	44.1%	54.8%	45.2%
14,812	OCEANA	4,899	2,943	1,714	242	1,229 R	60.1%	35.0%	63.2%	36.8%
8,720	OGEMAW	3,187	2,062	1,038	87	1,024 R	64.7%	32.6%	66.5%	33.5%
11,359	ONTONAGON	5,104	2,561	2,163	380	398 R	50.2%	42.4%	54.2%	45.8%
13,309	OSCEOLA	4,555	3,122	1,276	157	1,846 R	68.5%	28.0%	71.0%	29.0%
2,543	OSCODA	1,089	785	285	19	500 R	72.1%	26.2%	73.4%	26.6%
5,827	OTSEGO	2,320	1,392	888	40	504 R	60.0%	38.3%	61.1%	38.9%
59,660	OTTAWA	25,288	16,028	8,789	471	7,239 R	63.4%	34.8%	64.6%	35.4%
12,250	PRESQUE ISLE	4,165	2,271	1,872	22	399 R	54.5%	44.9%	54.8%	45.2%
3,668	ROSCOMMON	2,781	2,055	687	39	1,368 R	73.9%	24.7%	74.9%	25.1%
130,468	SAGINAW	40,733	22,923	16,995	815	5,928 R	56.3%	41.7%	57.4%	42.6%
76,222	ST. CLAIR	28,942	17,883	10,647	412	7,236 R	61.8%	36.8%	62.7%	37.3%
31,749	ST. JOSEPH	12,436	8,166	3,928	342	4,238 R	65.7%	31.6%	67.5%	32.5%
30,114	SANILAC	10,606	8,237	2,167	202	6,070 R	77.7%	20.4%	79.2%	20.8%
9,524	SCHOOLCRAFT	3,447	1,713	1,651	83	62 R	49.7%	47.9%	50.9%	49.1%
41,207	SHIAWASSEE	15,496	10,377	4,852	267	5,525 R	67.0%	31.3%	68.1%	31.9%
35,694	TUSCOLA	11,041	8,125	2,676	240	5,449 R	73.6%	24.2%	75.2%	24.8%
35,111	VAN BUREN	14,004	9,511	4,082	411	5,429 R	67.9%	29.1%	70.0%	30.0%
80,810	WASHTENAW	38,567	24,588	12,721	1,258	11,867 R	63.8%	33.0%	65.9%	34.1%
2,015,623	WAYNE	846,106	321,773	489,654	34,679	167,881 D	38.0%	57.9%	39.7%	60.3%
17,976	WEXFORD	6,717	3,833	2,635	249	1,198 R	57.1%	39.2%	59.3%	40.7%
5,256,106	TOTAL	2,109,609	1,038,595	1,003,448	67,566	35,147 R	49.2%	47.6%	50.9%	49.1%

MICHIGAN

PRESIDENT 1944

1940 Census Population	County	Total Vote	Republican	Democratic	Other	Rep.-Dem. Plurality	Percentage: Total Vote Rep.	Total Vote Dem.	Major Vote Rep.	Major Vote Dem.
5,463	ALCONA	2,230	1,503	716	11	787 R	67.4%	32.1%	67.7%	32.3%
10,167	ALGER	4,036	1,504	2,519	13	1,015 D	37.3%	62.4%	37.4%	62.6%
41,839	ALLEGAN	16,878	12,327	4,480	71	7,847 R	73.0%	26.5%	73.3%	26.7%
20,766	ALPENA	7,327	4,453	2,856	18	1,597 R	60.8%	39.0%	60.9%	39.1%
10,964	ANTRIM	3,881	2,626	1,206	49	1,420 R	67.7%	31.1%	68.5%	31.5%
9,233	ARENAC	3,271	1,978	1,280	13	698 R	60.5%	39.1%	60.7%	39.3%
9,356	BARAGA	3,714	1,829	1,874	11	45 D	49.2%	50.5%	49.4%	50.6%
22,613	BARRY	10,203	7,057	3,010	136	4,047 R	69.2%	29.5%	70.1%	29.9%
74,981	BAY	31,204	15,459	15,602	143	143 D	49.5%	50.0%	49.8%	50.2%
7,800	BENZIE	3,142	2,026	1,084	32	942 R	64.5%	34.5%	65.1%	34.9%
89,117	BERRIEN	40,934	24,832	15,886	216	8,946 R	60.7%	38.8%	61.0%	39.0%
25,845	BRANCH	10,609	7,155	3,406	48	3,749 R	67.4%	32.1%	67.7%	32.3%
94,206	CALHOUN	37,693	20,664	16,611	418	4,053 R	54.8%	44.1%	55.4%	44.6%
21,910	CASS	10,051	6,566	3,417	68	3,149 R	65.3%	34.0%	65.8%	34.2%
13,031	CHARLEVOIX	4,974	3,039	1,893	42	1,146 R	61.1%	38.1%	61.6%	38.4%
13,644	CHEBOYGAN	5,116	2,943	2,141	32	802 R	57.5%	41.8%	57.9%	42.1%
27,807	CHIPPEWA	9,725	5,335	4,344	46	991 R	54.9%	44.7%	55.1%	44.9%
9,163	CLARE	3,735	2,636	1,078	21	1,558 R	70.6%	28.9%	71.0%	29.0%
26,671	CLINTON	10,984	8,422	2,533	29	5,889 R	76.7%	23.1%	76.9%	23.1%
3,765	CRAWFORD	1,355	797	550	8	247 R	58.8%	40.6%	59.2%	40.8%
34,037	DELTA	12,644	5,213	7,375	56	2,162 D	41.2%	58.3%	41.4%	58.6%
28,731	DICKINSON	11,842	4,987	6,740	115	1,753 D	42.1%	56.9%	42.5%	57.5%
34,124	EATON	15,140	9,975	5,049	116	4,926 R	65.9%	33.3%	66.4%	33.6%
15,791	EMMET	5,782	3,538	2,206	38	1,332 R	61.2%	38.2%	61.6%	38.4%
227,944	GENESEE	94,116	41,145	52,444	527	11,299 D	43.7%	55.7%	44.0%	56.0%
9,385	GLADWIN	3,464	2,457	985	22	1,472 R	70.9%	28.4%	71.4%	28.6%
31,797	GOGEBIC	13,268	5,283	7,938	47	2,655 D	39.8%	59.8%	40.0%	60.0%
23,390	GRAND TRAVERSE	8,075	5,413	2,607	55	2,806 R	67.0%	32.3%	67.5%	32.5%
32,205	GRATIOT	11,244	7,987	3,160	97	4,827 R	71.0%	28.1%	71.7%	28.3%
29,092	HILLSDALE	12,598	9,364	3,153	81	6,211 R	74.3%	25.0%	74.8%	25.2%
47,631	HOUGHTON	19,238	9,110	10,066	62	956 D	47.4%	52.3%	47.5%	52.5%
32,584	HURON	11,898	9,538	2,301	59	7,237 R	80.2%	19.3%	80.6%	19.4%
130,616	INGHAM	58,313	34,255	23,655	403	10,600 R	58.7%	40.6%	59.2%	40.8%
35,710	IONIA	13,914	9,331	4,437	146	4,894 R	67.1%	31.9%	67.8%	32.2%
8,560	IOSCO	3,479	2,340	1,127	12	1,213 R	67.3%	32.4%	67.5%	32.5%
20,243	IRON	8,546	3,945	4,537	64	592 D	46.2%	53.1%	46.5%	53.5%
25,982	ISABELLA	8,949	6,356	2,522	71	3,834 R	71.0%	28.2%	71.6%	28.4%
93,108	JACKSON	37,100	22,992	13,859	249	9,133 R	62.0%	37.4%	62.4%	37.6%
100,085	KALAMAZOO	41,654	24,974	16,223	457	8,751 R	60.0%	38.9%	60.6%	39.4%
5,159	KALKASKA	1,412	992	409	11	583 R	70.3%	29.0%	70.8%	29.2%
246,338	KENT	99,116	54,163	43,679	1,274	10,484 R	54.6%	44.1%	55.4%	44.6%
4,004	KEWEENAW	1,837	866	965	6	99 D	47.1%	52.5%	47.3%	52.7%
4,798	LAKE	1,946	1,145	794	7	351 R	58.8%	40.8%	59.1%	40.9%
32,116	LAPEER	10,821	7,769	3,002	50	4,767 R	71.8%	27.7%	72.1%	27.9%
8,436	LEELANAU	3,023	2,063	944	16	1,119 R	68.2%	31.2%	68.6%	31.4%
53,110	LENAWEE	23,243	16,382	6,750	111	9,632 R	70.5%	29.0%	70.8%	29.2%
20,863	LIVINGSTON	10,391	7,417	2,910	64	4,507 R	71.4%	28.0%	71.8%	28.2%
7,423	LUCE	1,993	1,195	790	8	405 R	60.0%	39.6%	60.2%	39.8%
9,438	MACKINAC	3,776	2,268	1,488	20	780 R	60.1%	39.4%	60.4%	39.6%
107,638	MACOMB	45,135	21,305	23,506	324	2,201 D	47.2%	52.1%	47.5%	52.5%
18,450	MANISTEE	7,530	4,095	3,398	37	697 R	54.4%	45.1%	54.7%	45.3%
47,144	MARQUETTE	19,944	8,163	11,707	74	3,544 D	40.9%	58.7%	41.1%	58.9%
19,378	MASON	7,630	4,446	3,137	47	1,309 R	58.3%	41.1%	58.6%	41.4%
16,902	MECOSTA	5,995	4,217	1,708	70	2,509 R	70.3%	28.5%	71.2%	28.8%
24,883	MENOMINEE	9,573	4,869	4,632	72	237 R	50.9%	48.4%	51.2%	48.8%
27,094	MIDLAND	10,482	6,850	3,569	63	3,281 R	65.4%	34.0%	65.7%	34.3%
8,034	MISSAUKEE	2,763	1,979	759	25	1,220 R	71.6%	27.5%	72.3%	27.7%
58,620	MONROE	23,836	13,478	10,275	83	3,203 R	56.5%	43.1%	56.7%	43.3%
28,581	MONTCALM	10,790	7,525	3,168	97	4,357 R	69.7%	29.4%	70.4%	29.6%
3,840	MONTMORENCY	1,586	1,034	541	11	493 R	65.2%	34.1%	65.7%	34.3%

MICHIGAN

PRESIDENT 1944

1940 Census Population	County	Total Vote	Republican	Democratic	Other	Rep.-Dem. Plurality	Percentage Total Vote Rep.	Percentage Total Vote Dem.	Percentage Major Vote Rep.	Percentage Major Vote Dem.
94,501	MUSKEGON	36,786	16,536	19,963	287	3,427 D	45.0%	54.3%	45.3%	54.7%
19,286	NEWAYGO	7,434	5,250	2,156	28	3,094 R	70.6%	29.0%	70.9%	29.1%
254,068	OAKLAND	115,813	59,627	55,272	914	4,355 R	51.5%	47.7%	51.9%	48.1%
14,812	OCEANA	5,335	3,534	1,738	63	1,796 R	66.2%	32.6%	67.0%	33.0%
8,720	OGEMAW	3,363	2,339	1,006	18	1,333 R	69.6%	29.9%	69.9%	30.1%
11,359	ONTONAGON	5,061	2,433	2,611	17	178 D	48.1%	51.6%	48.2%	51.8%
13,309	OSCEOLA	5,178	3,787	1,338	53	2,449 R	73.1%	25.8%	73.9%	26.1%
2,543	OSCODA	950	615	332	3	283 R	64.7%	34.9%	64.9%	35.1%
5,827	OTSEGO	2,182	1,259	912	11	347 R	57.7%	41.8%	58.0%	42.0%
59,660	OTTAWA	25,786	17,077	8,511	198	8,566 R	66.2%	33.0%	66.7%	33.3%
12,250	PRESQUE ISLE	4,314	2,209	2,092	13	117 R	51.2%	48.5%	51.4%	48.6%
3,668	ROSCOMMON	1,789	1,292	484	13	808 R	72.2%	27.1%	72.7%	27.3%
130,468	SAGINAW	48,402	27,289	20,383	730	6,906 R	56.4%	42.1%	57.2%	42.8%
76,222	ST. CLAIR	31,123	19,175	11,813	135	7,362 R	61.6%	38.0%	61.9%	38.1%
31,749	ST. JOSEPH	14,089	9,785	4,235	69	5,550 R	69.5%	30.1%	69.8%	30.2%
30,114	SANILAC	11,587	9,512	2,015	60	7,497 R	82.1%	17.4%	82.5%	17.5%
9,524	SCHOOLCRAFT	3,447	1,704	1,724	19	20 D	49.4%	50.0%	49.7%	50.3%
41,207	SHIAWASSEE	16,957	11,601	5,292	64	6,309 R	68.4%	31.2%	68.7%	31.3%
35,694	TUSCOLA	12,787	9,789	2,938	60	6,851 R	76.6%	23.0%	76.9%	23.1%
35,111	VAN BUREN	16,037	10,951	5,002	84	5,949 R	68.3%	31.2%	68.6%	31.4%
80,810	WASHTENAW	39,906	24,740	14,922	244	9,818 R	62.0%	37.4%	62.4%	37.6%
2,015,623	WAYNE	875,093	316,270	554,670	4,153	238,400 D	36.1%	63.4%	36.3%	63.7%
17,976	WEXFORD	6,656	4,074	2,489	93	1,585 R	61.2%	37.4%	62.1%	37.9%
5,256,106	TOTAL	2,205,223	1,084,423	1,106,899	13,901	22,476 D	49.2%	50.2%	49.5%	50.5%

MICHIGAN

PRESIDENT 1940

1940 Census Population	County	Total Vote	Republican	Democratic	Other	Rep.-Dem. Plurality	Percentage Total Vote Rep.	Total Vote Dem.	Major Vote Rep.	Major Vote Dem.
5,463	ALCONA	2,501	1,648	847	6	801 R	65.9%	33.9%	66.1%	33.9%
10,167	ALGER	4,675	1,629	2,984	62	1,355 D	34.8%	63.8%	35.3%	64.7%
41,839	ALLEGAN	17,792	12,347	5,385	60	6,962 R	69.4%	30.3%	69.6%	30.4%
20,766	ALPENA	8,432	4,822	3,597	13	1,225 R	57.2%	42.7%	57.3%	42.7%
10,964	ANTRIM	4,553	3,027	1,497	29	1,530 R	66.5%	32.9%	66.9%	33.1%
9,233	ARENAC	3,807	2,293	1,499	15	794 R	60.2%	39.4%	60.5%	39.5%
9,356	BARAGA	4,697	2,512	2,152	33	360 R	53.5%	45.8%	53.9%	46.1%
22,613	BARRY	10,025	6,872	3,091	62	3,781 R	68.5%	30.8%	69.0%	31.0%
74,981	BAY	29,587	14,618	14,902	67	284 D	49.4%	50.4%	49.5%	50.5%
7,800	BENZIE	3,765	2,320	1,429	16	891 R	61.6%	38.0%	61.9%	38.1%
89,117	BERRIEN	39,947	22,778	16,961	208	5,817 R	57.0%	42.5%	57.3%	42.7%
25,845	BRANCH	11,764	7,400	4,318	46	3,082 R	62.9%	36.7%	63.2%	36.8%
94,206	CALHOUN	40,610	21,633	18,682	295	2,951 R	53.3%	46.0%	53.7%	46.3%
21,910	CASS	11,268	6,868	4,340	60	2,528 R	61.0%	38.5%	61.3%	38.7%
13,031	CHARLEVOIX	5,736	3,522	2,163	51	1,359 R	61.4%	37.7%	62.0%	38.0%
13,644	CHEBOYGAN	6,523	3,646	2,856	21	790 R	55.9%	43.8%	56.1%	43.9%
27,807	CHIPPEWA	11,353	5,851	5,473	29	378 R	51.5%	48.2%	51.7%	48.3%
9,163	CLARE	4,300	3,004	1,277	19	1,727 R	69.9%	29.7%	70.2%	29.8%
26,671	CLINTON	11,081	8,311	2,745	25	5,566 R	75.0%	24.8%	75.2%	24.8%
3,765	CRAWFORD	1,662	873	777	12	96 R	52.5%	46.8%	52.9%	47.1%
34,037	DELTA	15,101	6,218	8,802	81	2,584 D	41.2%	58.3%	41.4%	58.6%
28,731	DICKINSON	13,859	6,188	7,582	89	1,394 D	44.6%	54.7%	44.9%	55.1%
34,124	EATON	15,594	9,864	5,645	85	4,219 R	63.3%	36.2%	63.6%	36.4%
15,791	EMMET	7,071	4,216	2,831	24	1,385 R	59.6%	40.0%	59.8%	40.2%
227,944	GENESEE	89,283	38,495	50,300	488	11,805 D	43.1%	56.3%	43.4%	56.6%
9,385	GLADWIN	4,044	2,741	1,294	9	1,447 R	67.8%	32.0%	67.9%	32.1%
31,797	GOGEBIC	15,734	6,431	9,104	199	2,673 D	40.9%	57.9%	41.4%	58.6%
23,390	GRAND TRAVERSE	8,745	5,620	3,095	30	2,525 R	64.3%	35.4%	64.5%	35.5%
32,205	GRATIOT	12,551	8,661	3,825	65	4,836 R	69.0%	30.5%	69.4%	30.6%
29,092	HILLSDALE	13,007	9,398	3,538	71	5,860 R	72.3%	27.2%	72.6%	27.4%
47,631	HOUGHTON	21,926	11,030	10,815	81	215 R	50.3%	49.3%	50.5%	49.5%
32,584	HURON	13,258	10,570	2,654	34	7,916 R	79.7%	20.0%	79.9%	20.1%
130,616	INGHAM	57,382	32,565	24,375	442	8,190 R	56.8%	42.5%	57.2%	42.8%
35,710	IONIA	14,916	9,439	5,399	78	4,040 R	63.3%	36.2%	63.6%	36.4%
8,560	IOSCO	3,825	2,504	1,303	18	1,201 R	65.5%	34.1%	65.8%	34.2%
20,243	IRON	9,661	4,766	4,808	87	42 D	49.3%	49.8%	49.8%	50.2%
25,982	ISABELLA	9,891	7,019	2,828	44	4,191 R	71.0%	28.6%	71.3%	28.7%
93,108	JACKSON	39,941	24,558	15,170	213	9,388 R	61.5%	38.0%	61.8%	38.2%
100,085	KALAMAZOO	43,622	25,596	17,733	293	7,863 R	58.7%	40.7%	59.1%	40.9%
5,159	KALKASKA	1,885	1,155	718	12	437 R	61.3%	38.1%	61.7%	38.3%
246,338	KENT	102,076	53,131	48,196	749	4,935 R	52.1%	47.2%	52.4%	47.6%
4,004	KEWEENAW	2,060	1,080	967	13	113 R	52.4%	46.9%	52.8%	47.2%
4,798	LAKE	2,495	1,413	1,070	12	343 R	56.6%	42.9%	56.9%	43.1%
32,116	LAPEER	11,044	7,714	3,299	31	4,415 R	69.8%	29.9%	70.0%	30.0%
8,436	LEELANAU	3,639	2,405	1,223	11	1,182 R	66.1%	33.6%	66.3%	33.7%
53,110	LENAWEE	24,166	16,963	7,132	71	9,831 R	70.2%	29.5%	70.4%	29.6%
20,863	LIVINGSTON	10,356	7,068	3,254	34	3,814 R	68.3%	31.4%	68.5%	31.5%
7,423	LUCE	2,617	1,542	1,069	6	473 R	58.9%	40.8%	59.1%	40.9%
9,438	MACKINAC	4,679	2,591	2,075	13	516 R	55.4%	44.3%	55.5%	44.5%
107,638	MACOMB	39,054	17,848	21,003	203	3,155 D	45.7%	53.8%	45.9%	54.1%
18,450	MANISTEE	8,892	4,630	4,242	20	388 R	52.1%	47.7%	52.2%	47.8%
47,144	MARQUETTE	21,982	9,034	12,854	94	3,820 D	41.1%	58.5%	41.3%	58.7%
19,378	MASON	8,763	4,874	3,836	53	1,038 R	55.6%	43.8%	56.0%	44.0%
16,902	MECOSTA	6,932	4,759	2,153	20	2,606 R	68.7%	31.1%	68.9%	31.1%
24,883	MENOMINEE	11,208	5,409	5,727	72	318 D	48.3%	51.1%	48.6%	51.4%
27,094	MIDLAND	10,157	6,269	3,834	54	2,435 R	61.7%	37.7%	62.1%	37.9%
8,034	MISSAUKEE	3,223	2,154	1,037	32	1,117 R	66.8%	32.2%	67.5%	32.5%
58,620	MONROE	23,945	13,517	10,368	60	3,149 R	56.5%	43.3%	56.6%	43.4%
28,581	MONTCALM	11,855	7,633	4,119	103	3,514 R	64.4%	34.7%	65.0%	35.0%
3,840	MONTMORENCY	1,966	1,189	768	9	421 R	60.5%	39.1%	60.8%	39.2%

MICHIGAN

PRESIDENT 1940

1940 Census Population	County	Total Vote	Republican	Democratic	Other	Rep.-Dem. Plurality	Percentage Total Vote Rep.	Percentage Total Vote Dem.	Percentage Major Vote Rep.	Percentage Major Vote Dem.
94,501	MUSKEGON	34,424	14,957	19,257	210	4,300 D	43.4%	55.9%	43.7%	56.3%
19,286	NEWAYGO	8,145	5,418	2,693	34	2,725 R	66.5%	33.1%	66.8%	33.2%
254,068	OAKLAND	96,623	49,002	47,022	599	1,980 R	50.7%	48.7%	51.0%	49.0%
14,812	OCEANA	6,127	3,711	2,379	37	1,332 R	60.6%	38.8%	60.9%	39.1%
8,720	OGEMAW	3,739	2,447	1,278	14	1,169 R	65.4%	34.2%	65.7%	34.3%
11,359	ONTONAGON	6,116	2,880	3,103	133	223 D	47.1%	50.7%	48.1%	51.9%
13,309	OSCEOLA	5,789	4,217	1,555	17	2,662 R	72.8%	26.9%	73.1%	26.9%
2,543	OSCODA	1,073	661	409	3	252 R	61.6%	38.1%	61.8%	38.2%
5,827	OTSEGO	2,480	1,353	1,119	8	234 R	54.6%	45.1%	54.7%	45.3%
59,660	OTTAWA	24,784	15,462	9,152	170	6,310 R	62.4%	36.9%	62.8%	37.2%
12,250	PRESQUE ISLE	5,160	2,552	2,595	13	43 D	49.5%	50.3%	49.6%	50.4%
3,668	ROSCOMMON	2,118	1,360	739	19	621 R	64.2%	34.9%	64.8%	35.2%
130,468	SAGINAW	49,753	27,042	22,490	221	4,552 R	54.4%	45.2%	54.6%	45.4%
76,222	ST. CLAIR	30,976	18,635	12,259	82	6,376 R	60.2%	39.6%	60.3%	39.7%
31,749	ST. JOSEPH	15,115	10,025	5,045	45	4,980 R	66.3%	33.4%	66.5%	33.5%
30,114	SANILAC	12,527	10,289	2,195	43	8,094 R	82.1%	17.5%	82.4%	17.6%
9,524	SCHOOLCRAFT	4,334	2,003	2,320	11	317 D	46.2%	53.5%	46.3%	53.7%
41,207	SHIAWASSEE	15,804	9,995	5,727	82	4,268 R	63.2%	36.2%	63.6%	36.4%
35,694	TUSCOLA	13,448	10,146	3,257	45	6,889 R	75.4%	24.2%	75.7%	24.3%
35,111	VAN BUREN	17,297	11,571	5,625	101	5,946 R	66.9%	32.5%	67.3%	32.7%
80,810	WASHTENAW	33,719	21,664	11,802	253	9,862 R	64.2%	35.0%	64.7%	35.3%
2,015,623	WAYNE	732,569	275,974	451,003	5,592	175,029 D	37.7%	61.6%	38.0%	62.0%
17,976	WEXFORD	7,326	4,322	2,947	57	1,375 R	59.0%	40.2%	59.5%	40.5%
5,256,106	TOTAL	2,085,929	1,039,917	1,032,991	13,021	6,926 R	49.9%	49.5%	50.2%	49.8%

MICHIGAN

PRESIDENT 1936

1930 Census Population	County	Total Vote	Republican	Democratic	Other	Rep.-Dem. Plurality	Percentage Total Vote Rep.	Total Vote Dem.	Major Vote Rep.	Major Vote Dem.
4,989	ALCONA	2,410	1,276	919	215	357 R	52.9%	38.1%	58.1%	41.9%
9,327	ALGER	4,209	1,291	2,824	94	1,533 D	30.7%	67.1%	31.4%	68.6%
38,974	ALLEGAN	16,106	9,247	5,922	937	3,325 R	57.4%	36.8%	61.0%	39.0%
18,574	ALPENA	7,076	3,536	3,231	309	305 R	50.0%	45.7%	52.3%	47.7%
9,979	ANTRIM	4,608	2,391	2,032	185	359 R	51.9%	44.1%	54.1%	45.9%
8,007	ARENAC	3,460	1,505	1,761	194	256 D	43.5%	50.9%	46.1%	53.9%
9,168	BARAGA	4,335	2,035	2,218	82	183 D	46.9%	51.2%	47.8%	52.2%
20,928	BARRY	9,255	4,950	3,880	425	1,070 R	53.5%	41.9%	56.1%	43.9%
69,474	BAY	24,885	8,729	13,789	2,367	5,060 D	35.1%	55.4%	38.8%	61.2%
6,587	BENZIE	3,658	1,742	1,686	230	56 R	47.6%	46.1%	50.8%	49.2%
81,066	BERRIEN	37,125	15,321	20,822	982	5,501 D	41.3%	56.1%	42.4%	57.6%
23,950	BRANCH	11,375	5,528	5,425	422	103 R	48.6%	47.7%	50.5%	49.5%
87,043	CALHOUN	36,153	14,667	20,231	1,255	5,564 D	40.6%	56.0%	42.0%	58.0%
20,888	CASS	10,345	4,525	5,114	706	589 D	43.7%	49.4%	46.9%	53.1%
11,981	CHARLEVOIX	5,722	2,814	2,669	239	145 R	49.2%	46.6%	51.3%	48.7%
11,502	CHEBOYGAN	6,009	2,584	3,016	409	432 D	43.0%	50.2%	46.1%	53.9%
25,047	CHIPPEWA	10,398	4,901	5,259	238	358 D	47.1%	50.6%	48.2%	51.8%
7,032	CLARE	3,708	1,979	1,494	235	485 R	53.4%	40.3%	57.0%	43.0%
24,174	CLINTON	9,823	4,915	4,296	612	619 R	50.0%	43.7%	53.4%	46.6%
3,097	CRAWFORD	1,493	580	876	37	296 D	38.8%	58.7%	39.8%	60.2%
32,280	DELTA	13,791	4,527	8,954	310	4,427 D	32.8%	64.9%	33.6%	66.4%
29,941	DICKINSON	12,934	4,563	7,952	419	3,389 D	35.3%	61.5%	36.5%	63.5%
31,728	EATON	14,031	6,649	6,780	602	131 D	47.4%	48.3%	49.5%	50.5%
15,109	EMMET	6,489	2,893	3,075	521	182 D	44.6%	47.4%	48.5%	51.5%
211,641	GENESEE	73,931	21,097	49,891	2,943	28,794 D	28.5%	67.5%	29.7%	70.3%
7,424	GLADWIN	3,343	1,645	1,533	165	112 R	49.2%	45.9%	51.8%	48.2%
31,577	GOGEBIC	13,257	4,649	8,461	147	3,812 D	35.1%	63.8%	35.5%	64.5%
20,011	GRAND TRAVERSE	7,980	3,676	3,827	477	151 D	46.1%	48.0%	49.0%	51.0%
30,252	GRATIOT	11,298	5,322	5,457	519	135 D	47.1%	48.3%	49.4%	50.6%
27,417	HILLSDALE	12,217	6,723	5,023	471	1,700 R	55.0%	41.1%	57.2%	42.8%
52,851	HOUGHTON	21,206	9,345	11,642	219	2,297 D	44.1%	54.9%	44.5%	55.5%
31,132	HURON	11,207	5,240	3,949	2,018	1,291 R	46.8%	35.2%	57.0%	43.0%
116,587	INGHAM	48,313	19,434	27,086	1,793	7,652 D	40.2%	56.1%	41.8%	58.2%
35,093	IONIA	14,782	6,487	7,140	1,155	653 D	43.9%	48.3%	47.6%	52.4%
7,517	IOSCO	3,475	1,768	1,547	160	221 R	50.9%	44.5%	53.3%	46.7%
20,805	IRON	9,130	3,834	5,216	80	1,382 D	42.0%	57.1%	42.4%	57.6%
21,126	ISABELLA	8,658	4,051	3,871	736	180 R	46.8%	44.7%	51.1%	48.9%
92,304	JACKSON	36,486	16,350	19,288	848	2,938 D	44.8%	52.9%	45.9%	54.1%
91,368	KALAMAZOO	37,380	17,824	17,870	1,686	46 D	47.7%	47.8%	49.9%	50.1%
3,799	KALKASKA	1,870	855	952	63	97 D	45.7%	50.9%	47.3%	52.7%
240,511	KENT	85,304	36,633	44,823	3,848	8,190 D	42.9%	52.5%	45.0%	55.0%
5,076	KEWEENAW	2,154	1,070	1,060	24	10 R	49.7%	49.2%	50.2%	49.8%
4,066	LAKE	2,493	1,091	1,337	65	246 D	43.8%	53.6%	44.9%	55.1%
28,348	LAPEER	9,364	5,081	3,868	415	1,213 R	54.3%	41.3%	56.8%	43.2%
8,206	LEELANAU	3,405	1,692	1,542	171	150 R	49.7%	45.3%	52.3%	47.7%
49,849	LENAWEE	21,435	12,154	8,299	982	3,855 R	56.7%	38.7%	59.4%	40.6%
19,274	LIVINGSTON	9,563	5,117	4,117	329	1,000 R	53.5%	43.1%	55.4%	44.6%
6,528	LUCE	2,515	1,199	1,297	19	98 D	47.7%	51.6%	48.0%	52.0%
8,783	MACKINAC	4,346	1,984	2,286	76	302 D	45.7%	52.6%	46.5%	53.5%
77,146	MACOMB	29,299	9,383	17,593	2,323	8,210 D	32.0%	60.0%	34.8%	65.2%
17,409	MANISTEE	8,350	3,509	4,542	299	1,033 D	42.0%	54.4%	43.6%	56.4%
44,076	MARQUETTE	19,844	7,607	11,994	243	4,387 D	38.3%	60.4%	38.8%	61.2%
18,756	MASON	8,190	3,224	4,598	368	1,374 D	39.4%	56.1%	41.2%	58.8%
15,738	MECOSTA	6,341	3,176	2,621	544	555 R	50.1%	41.3%	54.8%	45.2%
23,652	MENOMINEE	10,546	3,556	6,447	543	2,891 D	33.7%	61.1%	35.5%	64.5%
19,150	MIDLAND	7,957	3,829	3,751	377	78 R	48.1%	47.1%	50.5%	49.5%
6,992	MISSAUKEE	3,163	1,730	1,385	48	345 R	54.7%	43.8%	55.5%	44.5%
52,485	MONROE	21,284	8,330	11,075	1,879	2,745 D	39.1%	52.0%	42.9%	57.1%
27,471	MONTCALM	10,925	5,031	4,950	944	81 R	46.1%	45.3%	50.4%	49.6%
2,814	MONTMORENCY	1,798	792	958	48	166 D	44.0%	53.3%	45.3%	54.7%

MICHIGAN

PRESIDENT 1936

1930 Census Population	County	Total Vote	Republican	Democratic	Other	Rep.-Dem. Plurality	Percentage Total Vote Rep.	Percentage Total Vote Dem.	Percentage Major Vote Rep.	Percentage Major Vote Dem.
84,630	MUSKEGON	27,133	9,366	17,252	515	7,886 D	34.5%	63.6%	35.2%	64.8%
17,029	NEWAYGO	7,644	3,930	3,288	426	642 R	51.4%	43.0%	54.4%	45.6%
211,251	OAKLAND	73,997	30,071	40,329	3,597	10,258 D	40.6%	54.5%	42.7%	57.3%
13,805	OCEANA	5,861	2,663	2,902	296	239 D	45.4%	49.5%	47.9%	52.1%
6,595	OGEMAW	3,605	1,631	1,774	200	143 D	45.2%	49.2%	47.9%	52.1%
11,114	ONTONAGON	5,563	2,162	3,233	168	1,071 D	38.9%	58.1%	40.1%	59.9%
12,806	OSCEOLA	5,520	3,107	1,992	421	1,115 R	56.3%	36.1%	60.9%	39.1%
1,728	OSCODA	956	456	492	8	36 D	47.7%	51.5%	48.1%	51.9%
5,554	OTSEGO	2,447	1,102	1,280	65	178 D	45.0%	52.3%	46.3%	53.7%
54,858	OTTAWA	21,645	11,114	9,579	952	1,535 R	51.3%	44.3%	53.7%	46.3%
11,330	PRESQUE ISLE	4,605	1,621	2,905	79	1,284 D	35.2%	63.1%	35.8%	64.2%
2,055	ROSCOMMON	1,684	836	782	66	54 R	49.6%	46.4%	51.7%	48.3%
120,717	SAGINAW	41,410	15,527	22,592	3,291	7,065 D	37.5%	54.6%	40.7%	59.3%
67,563	ST. CLAIR	27,782	12,760	12,663	2,359	97 R	45.9%	45.6%	50.2%	49.8%
30,618	ST. JOSEPH	13,809	7,160	6,048	601	1,112 R	51.9%	43.8%	54.2%	45.8%
27,751	SANILAC	11,036	6,975	3,285	776	3,690 R	63.2%	29.8%	68.0%	32.0%
8,451	SCHOOLCRAFT	3,885	1,430	2,333	122	903 D	36.8%	60.1%	38.0%	62.0%
39,517	SHIAWASSEE	13,878	6,017	6,666	1,195	649 D	43.4%	48.0%	47.4%	52.6%
32,934	TUSCOLA	11,037	6,188	3,743	1,106	2,445 R	56.1%	33.9%	62.3%	37.7%
32,637	VAN BUREN	16,655	9,110	6,720	825	2,390 R	54.7%	40.3%	57.5%	42.5%
65,530	WASHTENAW	29,510	14,986	13,589	935	1,397 R	50.8%	46.0%	52.4%	47.6%
1,888,946	WAYNE	626,120	190,732	404,055	31,333	213,323 D	30.5%	64.5%	32.1%	67.9%
16,827	WEXFORD	7,109	3,153	3,771	185	618 D	44.4%	53.0%	45.5%	54.5%
4,842,325	TOTAL	1,805,098	699,733	1,016,794	88,571	317,061 D	38.8%	56.3%	40.8%	59.2%

MICHIGAN

PRESIDENT 1932

1930 Census Population	County	Total Vote	Republican	Democratic	Other	Rep.-Dem. Plurality	Total Vote Rep.	Total Vote Dem.	Major Vote Rep.	Major Vote Dem.
4,989	ALCONA	1,842	881	884	77	3 D	47.8%	48.0%	49.9%	50.1%
9,327	ALGER	3,690	1,354	2,111	225	757 D	36.7%	57.2%	39.1%	60.9%
38,974	ALLEGAN	16,082	8,705	7,030	347	1,675 R	54.1%	43.7%	55.3%	44.7%
18,574	ALPENA	7,006	3,222	3,562	222	340 D	46.0%	50.8%	47.5%	52.5%
9,979	ANTRIM	4,158	2,308	1,686	164	622 R	55.5%	40.5%	57.8%	42.2%
8,007	ARENAC	3,666	1,471	2,086	109	615 D	40.1%	56.9%	41.4%	58.6%
9,168	BARAGA	4,086	1,917	2,016	153	99 D	46.9%	49.3%	48.7%	51.3%
20,928	BARRY	9,258	4,556	4,416	286	140 R	49.2%	47.7%	50.8%	49.2%
69,474	BAY	25,092	9,816	14,708	568	4,892 D	39.1%	58.6%	40.0%	60.0%
6,587	BENZIE	3,176	1,595	1,432	149	163 R	50.2%	45.1%	52.7%	47.3%
81,066	BERRIEN	33,264	14,123	18,447	694	4,324 D	42.5%	55.5%	43.4%	56.6%
23,950	BRANCH	10,640	4,663	5,685	292	1,022 D	43.8%	53.4%	45.1%	54.9%
87,043	CALHOUN	33,563	16,255	16,281	1,027	26 D	48.4%	48.5%	50.0%	50.0%
20,888	CASS	9,636	3,994	5,349	293	1,355 D	41.4%	55.5%	42.7%	57.3%
11,981	CHARLEVOIX	5,291	2,623	2,344	324	279 R	49.6%	44.3%	52.8%	47.2%
11,502	CHEBOYGAN	5,811	2,309	3,431	71	1,122 D	39.7%	59.0%	40.2%	59.8%
25,047	CHIPPEWA	9,665	5,252	4,221	192	1,031 R	54.3%	43.7%	55.4%	44.6%
7,032	CLARE	3,324	1,474	1,741	109	267 D	44.3%	52.4%	45.8%	54.2%
24,174	CLINTON	9,853	4,647	5,098	108	451 D	47.2%	51.7%	47.7%	52.3%
3,097	CRAWFORD	1,337	559	755	23	196 D	41.8%	56.5%	42.5%	57.5%
32,280	DELTA	12,285	4,386	7,363	536	2,977 D	35.7%	59.9%	37.3%	62.7%
29,941	DICKINSON	12,031	5,120	6,482	429	1,362 D	42.6%	53.9%	44.1%	55.9%
31,728	EATON	13,172	5,840	6,887	445	1,047 D	44.3%	52.3%	45.9%	54.1%
15,109	EMMET	6,275	2,890	3,110	275	220 D	46.1%	49.6%	48.2%	51.8%
211,641	GENESEE	67,267	28,231	36,860	2,176	8,629 D	42.0%	54.8%	43.4%	56.6%
7,424	GLADWIN	3,142	1,378	1,661	103	283 D	43.9%	52.9%	45.3%	54.7%
31,577	GOGEBIC	11,521	5,379	5,531	611	152 D	46.7%	48.0%	49.3%	50.7%
20,011	GRAND TRAVERSE	7,531	3,442	3,907	182	465 D	45.7%	51.9%	46.8%	53.2%
30,252	GRATIOT	11,538	5,123	6,124	291	1,001 D	44.4%	53.1%	45.5%	54.5%
27,417	HILLSDALE	11,867	5,879	5,696	292	183 R	49.5%	48.0%	50.8%	49.2%
52,851	HOUGHTON	20,780	12,308	7,838	634	4,470 R	59.2%	37.7%	61.1%	38.9%
31,132	HURON	11,690	5,707	5,770	213	63 D	48.8%	49.4%	49.7%	50.3%
116,587	INGHAM	44,545	21,044	22,370	1,131	1,326 D	47.2%	50.2%	48.5%	51.5%
35,093	IONIA	15,100	6,074	8,695	331	2,621 D	40.2%	57.6%	41.1%	58.9%
7,517	IOSCO	3,186	1,581	1,500	105	81 R	49.6%	47.1%	51.3%	48.7%
20,805	IRON	8,116	4,347	3,416	353	931 R	53.6%	42.1%	56.0%	44.0%
21,126	ISABELLA	8,645	4,211	4,272	162	61 D	48.7%	49.4%	49.6%	50.4%
92,304	JACKSON	33,730	16,150	16,584	996	434 D	47.9%	49.2%	49.3%	50.7%
91,368	KALAMAZOO	33,785	18,584	13,974	1,227	4,610 R	55.0%	41.4%	57.1%	42.9%
3,799	KALKASKA	1,485	705	649	131	56 R	47.5%	43.7%	52.1%	47.9%
240,511	KENT	86,723	42,186	41,601	2,936	585 R	48.6%	48.0%	50.3%	49.7%
5,076	KEWEENAW	2,007	1,454	527	26	927 R	72.4%	26.3%	73.4%	26.6%
4,066	LAKE	2,312	991	1,241	80	250 D	42.9%	53.7%	44.4%	55.6%
28,348	LAPEER	9,412	4,882	4,315	215	567 R	51.9%	45.8%	53.1%	46.9%
8,206	LEELANAU	3,313	1,527	1,746	40	219 D	46.1%	52.7%	46.7%	53.3%
49,849	LENAWEE	21,607	10,912	10,420	275	492 R	50.5%	48.2%	51.2%	48.8%
19,274	LIVINGSTON	9,357	4,534	4,684	139	150 D	48.5%	50.1%	49.2%	50.8%
6,528	LUCE	2,235	1,259	928	48	331 R	56.3%	41.5%	57.6%	42.4%
8,783	MACKINAC	4,109	1,504	2,578	27	1,074 D	36.6%	62.7%	36.8%	63.2%
77,146	MACOMB	25,984	8,649	16,539	796	7,890 D	33.3%	63.7%	34.3%	65.7%
17,409	MANISTEE	8,115	3,256	4,475	384	1,219 D	40.1%	55.1%	42.1%	57.9%
44,076	MARQUETTE	17,629	9,810	7,221	598	2,589 R	55.6%	41.0%	57.6%	42.4%
18,756	MASON	7,292	3,098	3,854	340	756 D	42.5%	52.9%	44.6%	55.4%
15,738	MECOSTA	6,635	3,336	3,152	147	184 R	50.3%	47.5%	51.4%	48.6%
23,652	MENOMINEE	9,473	3,374	5,782	317	2,408 D	35.6%	61.0%	36.9%	63.1%
19,150	MIDLAND	7,489	3,791	3,553	145	238 R	50.6%	47.4%	51.6%	48.4%
6,992	MISSAUKEE	2,789	1,439	1,282	68	157 R	51.6%	46.0%	52.9%	47.1%
52,485	MONROE	20,010	7,255	12,417	338	5,162 D	36.3%	62.1%	36.9%	63.1%
27,471	MONTCALM	11,403	5,166	5,704	533	538 D	45.3%	50.0%	47.5%	52.5%
2,814	MONTMORENCY	1,564	595	903	66	308 D	38.0%	57.7%	39.7%	60.3%

MICHIGAN

PRESIDENT 1932

1930 Census Population	County	Total Vote	Republican	Democratic	Other	Rep.-Dem. Plurality	Percentage Total Vote Rep.	Percentage Total Vote Dem.	Percentage Major Vote Rep.	Percentage Major Vote Dem.
84,630	MUSKEGON	26,265	11,971	13,497	797	1,526 D	45.6%	51.4%	47.0%	53.0%
17,029	NEWAYGO	6,953	3,458	3,275	220	183 R	49.7%	47.1%	51.4%	48.6%
211,251	OAKLAND	67,928	32,462	33,135	2,331	673 D	47.8%	48.8%	49.5%	50.5%
13,805	OCEANA	5,707	2,481	3,051	175	570 D	43.5%	53.5%	44.8%	55.2%
6,595	OGEMAW	3,204	1,472	1,645	87	173 D	45.9%	51.3%	47.2%	52.8%
11,114	ONTONAGON	5,023	2,287	2,337	399	50 D	45.5%	46.5%	49.5%	50.5%
12,806	OSCEOLA	5,381	2,969	2,321	91	648 R	55.2%	43.1%	56.1%	43.9%
1,728	OSCODA	775	410	349	16	61 R	52.9%	45.0%	54.0%	46.0%
5,554	OTSEGO	2,493	1,006	1,377	110	371 D	40.4%	55.2%	42.2%	57.8%
54,858	OTTAWA	20,700	12,076	7,981	643	4,095 R	58.3%	38.6%	60.2%	39.8%
11,330	PRESQUE ISLE	3,865	1,560	2,217	88	657 D	40.4%	57.4%	41.3%	58.7%
2,055	ROSCOMMON	1,410	601	757	52	156 D	42.6%	53.7%	44.3%	55.7%
120,717	SAGINAW	41,414	17,794	22,643	977	4,849 D	43.0%	54.7%	44.0%	56.0%
67,563	ST. CLAIR	28,041	14,883	12,776	382	2,107 R	53.1%	45.6%	53.8%	46.2%
30,618	ST. JOSEPH	12,852	5,626	6,917	309	1,291 D	43.8%	53.8%	44.9%	55.1%
27,751	SANILAC	11,205	6,860	4,077	268	2,783 R	61.2%	36.4%	62.7%	37.3%
8,451	SCHOOLCRAFT	3,511	1,722	1,660	129	62 R	49.0%	47.3%	50.9%	49.1%
39,517	SHIAWASSEE	14,936	6,600	8,002	334	1,402 D	44.2%	53.6%	45.2%	54.8%
32,934	TUSCOLA	11,367	6,110	5,077	180	1,033 R	53.8%	44.7%	54.6%	45.4%
32,637	VAN BUREN	14,641	6,954	7,223	464	269 D	47.5%	49.3%	49.1%	50.9%
65,530	WASHTENAW	29,100	15,368	12,552	1,180	2,816 R	52.8%	43.1%	55.0%	45.0%
1,888,946	WAYNE	543,601	212,678	310,686	20,237	98,008 D	39.1%	57.2%	40.6%	59.4%
16,827	WEXFORD	6,804	3,425	3,251	128	174 R	50.3%	47.8%	51.3%	48.7%
4,842,325	TOTAL	1,664,765	739,894	871,700	53,171	131,806 D	44.4%	52.4%	45.9%	54.1%

MICHIGAN

PRESIDENT 1928

1920 Census Population	County	Total Vote	Republican	Democratic	Other	Rep.-Dem. Plurality	Percentage Total Vote Rep.	Percentage Total Vote Dem.	Percentage Major Vote Rep.	Percentage Major Vote Dem.
5,912	ALCONA	1,458	1,149	302	7	847 R	78.8%	20.7%	79.2%	20.8%
9,983	ALGER	2,906	1,716	1,053	137	663 R	59.1%	36.2%	62.0%	38.0%
37,540	ALLEGAN	13,217	10,792	2,358	67	8,434 R	81.7%	17.8%	82.1%	17.9%
17,869	ALPENA	5,466	3,467	1,984	15	1,483 R	63.4%	36.3%	63.6%	36.4%
11,543	ANTRIM	3,263	2,756	484	23	2,272 R	84.5%	14.8%	85.1%	14.9%
9,460	ARENAC	2,375	1,612	749	14	863 R	67.9%	31.5%	68.3%	31.7%
7,662	BARAGA	3,375	2,203	1,046	126	1,157 R	65.3%	31.0%	67.8%	32.2%
21,383	BARRY	7,561	6,044	1,459	58	4,585 R	79.9%	19.3%	80.6%	19.4%
69,548	BAY	21,917	12,467	9,395	55	3,072 R	56.9%	42.9%	57.0%	43.0%
6,947	BENZIE	2,194	1,849	321	24	1,528 R	84.3%	14.6%	85.2%	14.8%
62,653	BERRIEN	27,791	19,064	8,555	172	10,509 R	68.6%	30.8%	69.0%	31.0%
23,997	BRANCH	9,150	6,818	2,266	66	4,552 R	74.5%	24.8%	75.1%	24.9%
72,918	CALHOUN	30,321	24,379	5,769	173	18,610 R	80.4%	19.0%	80.9%	19.1%
20,395	CASS	8,143	5,720	2,346	77	3,374 R	70.2%	28.8%	70.9%	29.1%
15,788	CHARLEVOIX	4,363	3,489	842	32	2,647 R	80.0%	19.3%	80.6%	19.4%
13,991	CHEBOYGAN	4,546	2,743	1,784	19	959 R	60.3%	39.2%	60.6%	39.4%
24,818	CHIPPEWA	7,755	5,326	2,355	74	2,971 R	68.7%	30.4%	69.3%	30.7%
8,250	CLARE	2,324	1,920	381	23	1,539 R	82.6%	16.4%	83.4%	16.6%
23,110	CLINTON	8,210	6,161	2,013	36	4,148 R	75.0%	24.5%	75.4%	24.6%
4,049	CRAWFORD	1,017	776	237	4	539 R	76.3%	23.3%	76.6%	23.4%
30,909	DELTA	10,930	5,420	5,419	91	1 R	49.6%	49.6%	50.0%	50.0%
19,456	DICKINSON	10,509	5,840	4,626	43	1,214 R	55.6%	44.0%	55.8%	44.2%
29,377	EATON	10,836	8,493	2,285	58	6,208 R	78.4%	21.1%	78.8%	21.2%
15,639	EMMET	4,882	3,679	1,166	37	2,513 R	75.4%	23.9%	75.9%	24.1%
125,668	GENESEE	53,853	42,743	10,910	200	31,833 R	79.4%	20.3%	79.7%	20.3%
8,827	GLADWIN	2,143	1,795	341	7	1,454 R	83.8%	15.9%	84.0%	16.0%
33,225	GOGEBIC	9,362	6,061	3,134	167	2,927 R	64.7%	33.5%	65.9%	34.1%
19,518	GRAND TRAVERSE	5,940	4,429	1,489	22	2,940 R	74.6%	25.1%	74.8%	25.2%
33,914	GRATIOT	10,741	8,823	1,854	64	6,969 R	82.1%	17.3%	82.6%	17.4%
28,161	HILLSDALE	10,226	8,282	1,893	51	6,389 R	81.0%	18.5%	81.4%	18.6%
71,930	HOUGHTON	18,042	11,240	6,573	229	4,667 R	62.3%	36.4%	63.1%	36.9%
32,786	HURON	10,875	7,046	3,797	32	3,249 R	64.8%	34.9%	65.0%	35.0%
81,554	INGHAM	37,243	29,383	7,654	206	21,729 R	78.9%	20.6%	79.3%	20.7%
33,087	IONIA	12,643	9,471	3,089	83	6,382 R	74.9%	24.4%	75.4%	24.6%
8,199	IOSCO	2,439	1,873	552	14	1,321 R	76.8%	22.6%	77.2%	22.8%
22,107	IRON	6,415	4,103	2,262	50	1,841 R	64.0%	35.3%	64.5%	35.5%
22,610	ISABELLA	6,736	4,926	1,762	48	3,164 R	73.1%	26.2%	73.7%	26.3%
72,539	JACKSON	32,693	25,080	7,462	151	17,618 R	76.7%	22.8%	77.1%	22.9%
71,225	KALAMAZOO	29,830	23,626	5,946	258	17,680 R	79.2%	19.9%	79.9%	20.1%
5,577	KALKASKA	1,168	988	160	20	828 R	84.6%	13.7%	86.1%	13.9%
183,041	KENT	75,310	56,573	18,229	508	38,344 R	75.1%	24.2%	75.6%	24.4%
6,322	KEWEENAW	1,704	1,305	360	39	945 R	76.6%	21.1%	78.4%	21.6%
4,437	LAKE	1,570	1,147	409	14	738 R	73.1%	26.1%	73.7%	26.3%
25,782	LAPEER	7,867	6,514	1,312	41	5,202 R	82.8%	16.7%	83.2%	16.8%
9,061	LEELANAU	2,437	1,521	903	13	618 R	62.4%	37.1%	62.7%	37.3%
47,767	LENAWEE	19,227	14,794	4,321	112	10,473 R	76.9%	22.5%	77.4%	22.6%
17,522	LIVINGSTON	7,741	5,642	2,075	24	3,567 R	72.9%	26.8%	73.1%	26.9%
6,149	LUCE	1,827	1,466	350	11	1,116 R	80.2%	19.2%	80.7%	19.3%
8,026	MACKINAC	3,243	1,879	1,355	9	524 R	57.9%	41.8%	58.1%	41.9%
38,103	MACOMB	20,299	12,845	7,363	91	5,482 R	63.3%	36.3%	63.6%	36.4%
20,899	MANISTEE	6,799	4,129	2,624	46	1,505 R	60.7%	38.6%	61.1%	38.9%
45,786	MARQUETTE	15,811	10,879	4,716	216	6,163 R	68.8%	29.8%	69.8%	30.2%
19,831	MASON	5,936	4,318	1,567	51	2,751 R	72.7%	26.4%	73.4%	26.6%
17,765	MECOSTA	5,463	4,422	1,004	37	3,418 R	80.9%	18.4%	81.5%	18.5%
23,778	MENOMINEE	8,507	4,255	4,198	54	57 R	50.0%	49.3%	50.3%	49.7%
17,237	MIDLAND	5,538	4,555	964	19	3,591 R	82.2%	17.4%	82.5%	17.5%
9,004	MISSAUKEE	2,014	1,756	247	11	1,509 R	87.2%	12.3%	87.7%	12.3%
37,115	MONROE	17,507	10,202	7,242	63	2,960 R	58.3%	41.4%	58.5%	41.5%
30,441	MONTCALM	9,318	7,691	1,572	55	6,119 R	82.5%	16.9%	83.0%	17.0%
4,089	MONTMORENCY	1,064	787	270	7	517 R	74.0%	25.4%	74.5%	25.5%

MICHIGAN

PRESIDENT 1928

1920 Census Population	County	Total Vote	Republican	Democratic	Other	Rep.-Dem. Plurality	Percentage Total Vote Rep.	Percentage Total Vote Dem.	Percentage Major Vote Rep.	Percentage Major Vote Dem.
62,362	MUSKEGON	22,281	16,997	5,158	126	11,839 R	76.3%	23.1%	76.7%	23.3%
17,378	NEWAYGO	5,465	4,552	888	25	3,664 R	83.3%	16.2%	83.7%	16.3%
90,050	OAKLAND	55,618	45,343	10,011	264	35,332 R	81.5%	18.0%	81.9%	18.1%
15,601	OCEANA	4,469	3,555	871	43	2,684 R	79.5%	19.5%	80.3%	19.7%
7,786	OGEMAW	2,221	1,630	579	12	1,051 R	73.4%	26.1%	73.8%	26.2%
12,428	ONTONAGON	4,013	2,394	1,353	266	1,041 R	59.7%	33.7%	63.9%	36.1%
15,221	OSCEOLA	4,527	3,923	582	22	3,341 R	86.7%	12.9%	87.1%	12.9%
1,783	OSCODA	551	476	73	2	403 R	86.4%	13.2%	86.7%	13.3%
6,043	OTSEGO	1,531	1,049	476	6	573 R	68.5%	31.1%	68.8%	31.2%
47,660	OTTAWA	18,035	15,417	2,524	94	12,893 R	85.5%	14.0%	85.9%	14.1%
12,131	PRESQUE ISLE	3,041	1,992	1,029	20	963 R	65.5%	33.8%	65.9%	34.1%
2,032	ROSCOMMON	1,023	780	236	7	544 R	76.2%	23.1%	76.8%	23.2%
100,286	SAGINAW	34,242	22,467	11,555	220	10,912 R	65.6%	33.7%	66.0%	34.0%
58,009	ST. CLAIR	25,399	18,177	7,151	71	11,026 R	71.6%	28.2%	71.8%	28.2%
26,818	ST. JOSEPH	11,546	8,781	2,698	67	6,083 R	76.1%	23.4%	76.5%	23.5%
31,237	SANILAC	9,668	7,888	1,736	44	6,152 R	81.6%	18.0%	82.0%	18.0%
9,977	SCHOOLCRAFT	2,733	1,826	877	30	949 R	66.8%	32.1%	67.6%	32.4%
35,924	SHIAWASSEE	12,407	9,851	2,496	60	7,355 R	79.4%	20.1%	79.8%	20.2%
33,320	TUSCOLA	9,703	8,188	1,464	51	6,724 R	84.4%	15.1%	84.8%	15.2%
30,715	VAN BUREN	12,050	9,325	2,643	82	6,682 R	77.4%	21.9%	77.9%	22.1%
49,520	WASHTENAW	25,093	19,676	5,308	109	14,368 R	78.4%	21.2%	78.8%	21.2%
1,177,645	WAYNE	426,718	265,852	157,047	3,819	108,805 R	62.3%	36.8%	62.9%	37.1%
18,207	WEXFORD	5,708	4,825	853	30	3,972 R	84.5%	14.9%	85.0%	15.0%
3,668,412	TOTAL	1,372,082	965,396	396,762	9,924	568,634 R	70.4%	28.9%	70.9%	29.1%

MICHIGAN

PRESIDENT 1924

1920 Census Population	County	Total Vote	Republican	Democratic	Other	Rep.-Dem. Plurality	Percentage Total Vote Rep.	Percentage Total Vote Dem.	Percentage Major Vote Rep.	Percentage Major Vote Dem.
5,912	ALCONA	1,420	1,027	184	209	843 R	72.3%	13.0%	84.8%	15.2%
9,983	ALGER	2,440	1,623	228	589	1,395 R	66.5%	9.3%	87.7%	12.3%
37,540	ALLEGAN	11,872	9,417	1,562	893	7,855 R	79.3%	13.2%	85.8%	14.2%
17,869	ALPENA	6,107	4,628	948	531	3,680 R	75.8%	15.5%	83.0%	17.0%
11,543	ANTRIM	2,925	2,246	371	308	1,875 R	76.8%	12.7%	85.8%	14.2%
9,460	ARENAC	2,615	1,767	575	273	1,192 R	67.6%	22.0%	75.4%	24.6%
7,662	BARAGA	2,386	1,714	208	464	1,506 R	71.8%	8.7%	89.2%	10.8%
21,383	BARRY	7,998	5,656	2,046	296	3,610 R	70.7%	25.6%	73.4%	26.6%
69,548	BAY	22,951	14,861	5,881	2,209	8,980 R	64.8%	25.6%	71.6%	28.4%
6,947	BENZIE	2,603	1,922	198	483	1,724 R	73.8%	7.6%	90.7%	9.3%
62,653	BERRIEN	24,497	15,612	4,445	4,440	11,167 R	63.7%	18.1%	77.8%	22.2%
23,997	BRANCH	9,302	6,016	2,253	1,033	3,763 R	64.7%	24.2%	72.8%	27.2%
72,918	CALHOUN	25,262	18,165	4,020	3,077	14,145 R	71.9%	15.9%	81.9%	18.1%
20,395	CASS	7,584	4,545	2,328	711	2,217 R	59.9%	30.7%	66.1%	33.9%
15,788	CHARLEVOIX	4,201	3,346	406	449	2,940 R	79.6%	9.7%	89.2%	10.8%
13,991	CHEBOYGAN	4,182	2,683	994	505	1,689 R	64.2%	23.8%	73.0%	27.0%
24,818	CHIPPEWA	7,029	5,443	516	1,070	4,927 R	77.4%	7.3%	91.3%	8.7%
8,250	CLARE	2,472	1,920	358	194	1,562 R	77.7%	14.5%	84.3%	15.7%
23,110	CLINTON	8,641	6,637	1,359	645	5,278 R	76.8%	15.7%	83.0%	17.0%
4,049	CRAWFORD	1,152	840	163	149	677 R	72.9%	14.1%	83.7%	16.3%
30,909	DELTA	9,554	4,761	463	4,330	4,298 R	49.8%	4.8%	91.1%	8.9%
19,456	DICKINSON	6,609	4,538	400	1,671	4,138 R	68.7%	6.1%	91.9%	8.1%
29,377	EATON	11,175	8,232	2,462	481	5,770 R	73.7%	22.0%	77.0%	23.0%
15,639	EMMET	4,362	3,020	773	569	2,247 R	69.2%	17.7%	79.6%	20.4%
125,668	GENESEE	40,878	34,264	4,225	2,389	30,039 R	83.8%	10.3%	89.0%	11.0%
8,827	GLADWIN	2,435	1,908	255	272	1,653 R	78.4%	10.5%	88.2%	11.8%
33,225	GOGEBIC	7,707	5,128	487	2,092	4,641 R	66.5%	6.3%	91.3%	8.7%
19,518	GRAND TRAVERSE	5,358	4,011	558	789	3,453 R	74.9%	10.4%	87.8%	12.2%
33,914	GRATIOT	8,832	6,720	1,839	273	4,881 R	76.1%	20.8%	78.5%	21.5%
28,161	HILLSDALE	9,578	6,556	1,980	1,042	4,576 R	68.4%	20.7%	76.8%	23.2%
71,930	HOUGHTON	16,662	13,833	1,045	1,784	12,788 R	83.0%	6.3%	93.0%	7.0%
32,786	HURON	10,898	8,843	988	1,067	7,855 R	81.1%	9.1%	90.0%	10.0%
81,554	INGHAM	34,505	28,005	4,814	1,686	23,191 R	81.2%	14.0%	85.3%	14.7%
33,087	IONIA	12,979	9,502	2,821	656	6,681 R	73.2%	21.7%	77.1%	22.9%
8,199	IOSCO	2,398	1,713	304	381	1,409 R	71.4%	12.7%	84.9%	15.1%
22,107	IRON	4,307	2,802	247	1,258	2,555 R	65.1%	5.7%	91.9%	8.1%
22,610	ISABELLA	6,805	5,245	1,208	352	4,037 R	77.1%	17.8%	81.3%	18.7%
72,539	JACKSON	28,390	19,640	5,639	3,111	14,001 R	69.2%	19.9%	77.7%	22.3%
71,225	KALAMAZOO	24,500	18,451	3,587	2,462	14,864 R	75.3%	14.6%	83.7%	16.3%
5,577	KALKASKA	1,371	966	205	200	761 R	70.5%	15.0%	82.5%	17.5%
183,041	KENT	59,008	45,207	7,982	5,819	37,225 R	76.6%	13.5%	85.0%	15.0%
6,322	KEWEENAW	1,559	1,421	50	88	1,371 R	91.1%	3.2%	96.6%	3.4%
4,437	LAKE	1,554	1,069	313	172	756 R	68.8%	20.1%	77.4%	22.6%
25,782	LAPEER	7,528	6,297	929	302	5,368 R	83.6%	12.3%	87.1%	12.9%
9,061	LEELANAU	2,378	1,792	301	285	1,491 R	75.4%	12.7%	85.6%	14.4%
47,767	LENAWEE	18,388	13,358	3,950	1,080	9,408 R	72.6%	21.5%	77.2%	22.8%
17,522	LIVINGSTON	7,252	4,886	2,037	329	2,849 R	67.4%	28.1%	70.6%	29.4%
6,149	LUCE	1,054	850	112	92	738 R	80.6%	10.6%	88.4%	11.6%
8,026	MACKINAC	3,111	1,606	998	507	608 R	51.6%	32.1%	61.7%	38.3%
38,103	MACOMB	15,933	11,147	3,191	1,595	7,956 R	70.0%	20.0%	77.7%	22.3%
20,899	MANISTEE	6,371	3,701	1,314	1,356	2,387 R	58.1%	20.6%	73.8%	26.2%
45,786	MARQUETTE	13,820	9,771	845	3,204	8,926 R	70.7%	6.1%	92.0%	8.0%
19,831	MASON	5,310	3,567	815	928	2,752 R	67.2%	15.3%	81.4%	18.6%
17,765	MECOSTA	5,047	3,884	794	369	3,090 R	77.0%	15.7%	83.0%	17.0%
23,778	MENOMINEE	7,764	4,142	1,055	2,567	3,087 R	53.3%	13.6%	79.7%	20.3%
17,237	MIDLAND	5,063	4,004	625	434	3,379 R	79.1%	12.3%	86.5%	13.5%
9,004	MISSAUKEE	2,025	1,723	208	94	1,515 R	85.1%	10.3%	89.2%	10.8%
37,115	MONROE	15,383	8,940	4,981	1,462	3,959 R	58.1%	32.4%	64.2%	35.8%
30,441	MONTCALM	8,791	6,942	1,396	453	5,546 R	79.0%	15.9%	83.3%	16.7%
4,089	MONTMORENCY	1,170	748	140	282	608 R	63.9%	12.0%	84.2%	15.8%

MICHIGAN

PRESIDENT 1924

1920 Census Population	County	Total Vote	Republican	Democratic	Other	Rep.-Dem. Plurality	Percentage Total Vote Rep.	Total Vote Dem.	Major Vote Rep.	Major Vote Dem.
62,362	MUSKEGON	18,206	14,422	1,462	2,322	12,960 R	79.2%	8.0%	90.8%	9.2%
17,378	NEWAYGO	5,356	4,243	720	393	3,523 R	79.2%	13.4%	85.5%	14.5%
90,050	OAKLAND	35,196	28,603	4,105	2,488	24,498 R	81.3%	11.7%	87.4%	12.6%
15,601	OCEANA	4,450	3,335	650	465	2,685 R	74.9%	14.6%	83.7%	16.3%
7,786	OGEMAW	2,161	1,714	258	189	1,456 R	79.3%	11.9%	86.9%	13.1%
12,428	ONTONAGON	3,149	2,249	417	483	1,832 R	71.4%	13.2%	84.4%	15.6%
15,221	OSCEOLA	3,921	3,050	566	305	2,484 R	77.8%	14.4%	84.3%	15.7%
1,783	OSCODA	473	389	52	32	337 R	82.2%	11.0%	88.2%	11.8%
6,043	OTSEGO	1,550	1,144	249	157	895 R	73.8%	16.1%	82.1%	17.9%
47,660	OTTAWA	14,880	11,688	1,871	1,321	9,817 R	78.5%	12.6%	86.2%	13.8%
12,131	PRESQUE ISLE	3,432	2,315	431	686	1,884 R	67.5%	12.6%	84.3%	15.7%
2,032	ROSCOMMON	695	484	99	112	385 R	69.6%	14.2%	83.0%	17.0%
100,286	SAGINAW	34,738	23,618	6,206	4,914	17,412 R	68.0%	17.9%	79.2%	20.8%
58,009	ST. CLAIR	22,780	17,435	3,600	1,745	13,835 R	76.5%	15.8%	82.9%	17.1%
26,818	ST. JOSEPH	10,137	6,633	2,649	855	3,984 R	65.4%	26.1%	71.5%	28.5%
31,237	SANILAC	9,188	7,767	983	438	6,784 R	84.5%	10.7%	88.8%	11.2%
9,977	SCHOOLCRAFT	2,470	1,515	190	765	1,325 R	61.3%	7.7%	88.9%	11.1%
35,924	SHIAWASSEE	12,313	8,987	1,738	1,588	7,249 R	73.0%	14.1%	83.8%	16.2%
33,320	TUSCOLA	9,319	7,490	1,076	753	6,414 R	80.4%	11.5%	87.4%	12.6%
30,715	VAN BUREN	10,320	7,384	1,646	1,290	5,738 R	71.6%	15.9%	81.8%	18.2%
49,520	WASHTENAW	19,830	14,326	3,603	1,901	10,723 R	72.2%	18.2%	79.9%	20.1%
1,177,645	WAYNE	335,336	268,653	23,817	42,866	244,836 R	80.1%	7.1%	91.9%	8.1%
18,207	WEXFORD	5,068	3,926	592	550	3,334 R	77.5%	11.7%	86.9%	13.1%
3,668,412	TOTAL	1,160,419	874,631	152,359	133,429	722,272 R	75.4%	13.1%	85.2%	14.8%

MICHIGAN

PRESIDENT 1920

1920 Census Population	County	Total Vote	Republican	Democratic	Other	Rep.-Dem. Plurality	Percentage: Total Vote Rep.	Total Vote Dem.	Major Vote Rep.	Major Vote Dem.
5,912	ALCONA	1,375	1,043	264	68	779 R	75.9%	19.2%	79.8%	20.2%
9,983	ALGER	1,911	1,263	468	180	795 R	66.1%	24.5%	73.0%	27.0%
37,540	ALLEGAN	10,311	7,825	2,154	332	5,671 R	75.9%	20.9%	78.4%	21.6%
17,869	ALPENA	5,470	3,467	1,893	110	1,574 R	63.4%	34.6%	64.7%	35.3%
11,543	ANTRIM	2,915	2,260	518	137	1,742 R	77.5%	17.8%	81.4%	18.6%
9,460	ARENAC	2,292	1,521	669	102	852 R	66.4%	29.2%	69.5%	30.5%
7,662	BARAGA	1,832	1,368	304	160	1,064 R	74.7%	16.6%	81.8%	18.2%
21,383	BARRY	7,291	5,154	1,874	263	3,280 R	70.7%	25.7%	73.3%	26.7%
69,548	BAY	21,460	13,933	7,011	516	6,922 R	64.9%	32.7%	66.5%	33.5%
6,947	BENZIE	2,111	1,520	422	169	1,098 R	72.0%	20.0%	78.3%	21.7%
62,653	BERRIEN	21,265	15,748	4,855	662	10,893 R	74.1%	22.8%	76.4%	23.6%
23,997	BRANCH	8,181	5,704	2,181	296	3,523 R	69.7%	26.7%	72.3%	27.7%
72,918	CALHOUN	24,193	16,722	6,291	1,180	10,431 R	69.1%	26.0%	72.7%	27.3%
20,395	CASS	6,058	4,498	1,286	274	3,212 R	74.2%	21.2%	77.8%	22.2%
15,788	CHARLEVOIX	3,995	3,079	704	212	2,375 R	77.1%	17.6%	81.4%	18.6%
13,991	CHEBOYGAN	3,895	2,472	1,281	142	1,191 R	63.5%	32.9%	65.9%	34.1%
24,818	CHIPPEWA	6,364	4,732	1,266	366	3,466 R	74.4%	19.9%	78.9%	21.1%
8,250	CLARE	2,398	1,762	511	125	1,251 R	73.5%	21.3%	77.5%	22.5%
23,110	CLINTON	7,628	6,019	1,464	145	4,555 R	78.9%	19.2%	80.4%	19.6%
4,049	CRAWFORD	1,127	726	361	40	365 R	64.4%	32.0%	66.8%	33.2%
30,909	DELTA	7,550	4,938	1,985	627	2,953 R	65.4%	26.3%	71.3%	28.7%
19,456	DICKINSON	4,617	3,539	580	498	2,959 R	76.7%	12.6%	85.9%	14.1%
29,377	EATON	10,344	7,343	2,727	274	4,616 R	71.0%	26.4%	72.9%	27.1%
15,639	EMMET	4,441	3,059	1,070	312	1,989 R	68.9%	24.1%	74.1%	25.9%
125,668	GENESEE	32,873	24,543	7,408	922	17,135 R	74.7%	22.5%	76.8%	23.2%
8,827	GLADWIN	2,144	1,687	313	144	1,374 R	78.7%	14.6%	84.4%	15.7%
33,225	GOGEBIC	6,882	5,486	823	573	4,663 R	79.7%	12.0%	87.0%	13.0%
19,518	GRAND TRAVERSE	5,478	4,056	1,158	264	2,898 R	74.0%	21.1%	77.8%	22.2%
33,914	GRATIOT	8,498	6,578	1,846	74	4,732 R	77.4%	21.7%	78.1%	21.9%
28,161	HILLSDALE	9,406	6,690	2,467	249	4,223 R	71.1%	26.2%	73.1%	26.9%
71,930	HOUGHTON	18,625	14,938	3,088	599	11,850 R	80.2%	16.6%	82.9%	17.1%
32,786	HURON	10,117	8,354	1,581	182	6,773 R	82.6%	15.6%	84.1%	15.9%
81,554	INGHAM	26,480	18,437	7,061	982	11,376 R	69.6%	26.7%	72.3%	27.7%
33,087	IONIA	11,802	7,977	3,395	430	4,582 R	67.6%	28.8%	70.1%	29.9%
8,199	IOSCO	2,624	2,013	548	63	1,465 R	76.7%	20.9%	78.6%	21.4%
22,107	IRON	4,245	3,515	497	233	3,018 R	82.8%	11.7%	87.6%	12.4%
22,610	ISABELLA	6,894	5,089	1,627	178	3,462 R	73.8%	23.6%	75.8%	24.2%
72,539	JACKSON	24,534	15,922	7,789	823	8,133 R	64.9%	31.7%	67.2%	32.8%
71,225	KALAMAZOO	20,384	13,765	5,271	1,348	8,494 R	67.5%	25.9%	72.3%	27.7%
5,577	KALKASKA	1,216	890	224	102	666 R	73.2%	18.4%	79.9%	20.1%
183,041	KENT	58,175	40,802	14,763	2,610	26,039 R	70.1%	25.4%	73.4%	26.6%
6,322	KEWEENAW	1,411	1,272	89	50	1,183 R	90.1%	6.3%	93.5%	6.5%
4,437	LAKE	1,238	926	261	51	665 R	74.8%	21.1%	78.0%	22.0%
25,782	LAPEER	7,026	5,523	1,298	205	4,225 R	78.6%	18.5%	81.0%	19.0%
9,061	LEELANAU	2,621	2,156	406	59	1,750 R	82.3%	15.5%	84.2%	15.8%
47,767	LENAWEE	17,379	11,973	5,095	311	6,878 R	68.9%	29.3%	70.1%	29.9%
17,522	LIVINGSTON	7,237	4,639	2,437	161	2,202 R	64.1%	33.7%	65.6%	34.4%
6,149	LUCE	925	708	187	30	521 R	76.5%	20.2%	79.1%	20.9%
8,026	MACKINAC	2,680	1,685	932	63	753 R	62.9%	34.8%	64.4%	35.6%
38,103	MACOMB	13,161	9,735	3,023	403	6,712 R	74.0%	23.0%	76.3%	23.7%
20,899	MANISTEE	4,570	2,179	2,184	207	5 D	47.7%	47.8%	49.9%	50.1%
45,786	MARQUETTE	13,103	9,233	3,012	858	6,221 R	70.5%	23.0%	75.4%	24.6%
19,831	MASON	5,263	3,652	1,338	273	2,314 R	69.4%	25.4%	73.2%	26.8%
17,765	MECOSTA	5,258	3,932	1,145	181	2,787 R	74.8%	21.8%	77.4%	22.6%
23,778	MENOMINEE	6,967	5,045	1,560	362	3,485 R	72.4%	22.4%	76.4%	23.6%
17,237	MIDLAND	5,217	4,115	959	143	3,156 R	78.9%	18.4%	81.1%	18.9%
9,004	MISSAUKEE	2,184	1,801	345	38	1,456 R	82.5%	15.8%	83.9%	16.1%
37,115	MONROE	14,096	8,646	5,224	226	3,422 R	61.3%	37.1%	62.3%	37.7%
30,441	MONTCALM	8,598	6,644	1,695	259	4,949 R	77.3%	19.7%	79.7%	20.3%
4,089	MONTMORENCY	1,101	832	199	70	633 R	75.6%	18.1%	80.7%	19.3%

MICHIGAN

PRESIDENT 1920

1920 Census Population	County	Total Vote	Republican	Democratic	Other	Rep.-Dem. Plurality	Percentage Total Vote Rep.	Percentage Total Vote Dem.	Percentage Major Vote Rep.	Percentage Major Vote Dem.
62,362	MUSKEGON	15,877	11,702	3,468	707	8,234 R	73.7%	21.8%	77.1%	22.9%
17,378	NEWAYGO	5,307	4,188	929	190	3,259 R	78.9%	17.5%	81.8%	18.2%
90,050	OAKLAND	27,220	19,321	6,421	1,478	12,900 R	71.0%	23.6%	75.1%	24.9%
15,601	OCEANA	4,541	3,535	785	221	2,750 R	77.8%	17.3%	81.8%	18.2%
7,786	OGEMAW	2,233	1,687	444	102	1,243 R	75.5%	19.9%	79.2%	20.8%
12,428	ONTONAGON	2,920	1,977	657	286	1,320 R	67.7%	22.5%	75.1%	24.9%
15,221	OSCEOLA	4,457	3,603	769	85	2,834 R	80.8%	17.3%	82.4%	17.6%
1,783	OSCODA	524	439	75	10	364 R	83.8%	14.3%	85.4%	14.6%
6,043	OTSEGO	1,365	874	466	25	408 R	64.0%	34.1%	65.2%	34.8%
47,660	OTTAWA	13,370	10,528	2,391	451	8,137 R	78.7%	17.9%	81.5%	18.5%
12,131	PRESQUE ISLE	3,123	2,522	525	76	1,997 R	80.8%	16.8%	82.8%	17.2%
2,032	ROSCOMMON	866	652	182	32	470 R	75.3%	21.0%	78.2%	21.8%
100,286	SAGINAW	29,932	20,425	8,494	1,013	11,931 R	68.2%	28.4%	70.6%	29.4%
58,009	ST. CLAIR	19,879	14,938	4,566	375	10,372 R	75.1%	23.0%	76.6%	23.4%
26,818	ST. JOSEPH	9,063	6,035	2,725	303	3,310 R	66.6%	30.1%	68.9%	31.1%
31,237	SANILAC	8,571	7,256	1,146	169	6,110 R	84.7%	13.4%	86.4%	13.6%
9,977	SCHOOLCRAFT	2,490	1,776	428	286	1,348 R	71.3%	17.2%	80.6%	19.4%
35,924	SHIAWASSEE	10,287	7,194	2,595	498	4,599 R	69.9%	25.2%	73.5%	26.5%
33,320	TUSCOLA	8,809	7,282	1,269	258	6,013 R	82.7%	14.4%	85.2%	14.8%
30,715	VAN BUREN	9,192	6,904	1,988	300	4,916 R	75.1%	21.6%	77.6%	22.4%
49,520	WASHTENAW	18,912	14,082	4,468	362	9,614 R	74.5%	23.6%	75.9%	24.1%
1,177,645	WAYNE	294,943	220,482	51,773	22,688	168,709 R	74.8%	17.6%	81.0%	19.0%
18,207	WEXFORD	4,664	3,406	1,095	163	2,311 R	73.0%	23.5%	75.7%	24.3%
3,668,412	TOTAL	1,048,411	762,865	233,450	52,096	529,415 R	72.8%	22.3%	76.6%	23.4%

MICHIGAN

ELECTION NOTES

1956 Other vote was Holtwick (Prohibition).

1952 Other vote was 10,331 Hamblen (Prohibition); 3,922 Hallinan (Progressive); 1,495 Hass (Socialist Labor); 655 Dobbs (Socialist Workers); 3 scattered write-in.

1948 Other vote was 46,515 Wallace (Progressive); 13,052 Watson (Prohibition); 6,063 Thomas (Socialist); 1,263 Teichert (Socialist Labor); 672 Dobbs (Socialist Workers); 1 write-in.

1944 Other vote was 6,503 Watson (Prohibition); 4,598 Thomas (Socialist); 1,530 Smith (America First); 1,264 Teichert (Socialist Labor); 6 scattered write-in.

1940 Other vote was 7,593 Thomas (Socialist); 2,834 Browder (Communist); 1,795 Babson (Prohibition); 795 Aiken (Socialist Labor); 4 scattered write-in.

1936 Other vote was 75,795 Lemke (Union); 8,208 Thomas (Socialist); 3,384 Browder (Communist); 600 Aiken (Socialist Labor); 579 Colvin (Prohibition); 5 scattered write-in.

1932 Other vote was 39,205 Thomas (Socialist); 9,318 Foster (Communist); 2,893 Upshaw (Prohibition); 1,401 Reynolds (Socialist Labor); 217 Harvey (Liberty); 137 Coxey (Farmer-Labor).

1928 Other vote was 3,516 Thomas (Socialist); 2,881 Foster (Communist); 2,728 Varney (Prohibition); 799 Reynolds (Socialist Labor).

1924 Other vote was 122,014 LaFollette (Progressive); 6,085 Faris (Prohibition); 5,330 Johns (Socialist Labor). Progressive candidates ran second in a number of counties.

1920 Other vote was 28,947 Debs (Socialist); 10,480 Christensen (Farmer-Labor); 9,646 Watkins (Prohibition); 2,539 Cox (Socialist Labor); 484 Macauley (Single Tax). The statewide figures on the total line are for the highest elector in each party and the county-by-county figures are the average elector vote as reported by the state canvass; therefore, the addition of the individual counties will produce a smaller total than that on the statewide total line.

MINNESOTA

POPULAR VOTE FOR PRESIDENT 1920 TO 1956

Year	Total Vote	Republican		Democratic		Other Vote	Plurality	Percentage			
								Total Vote		Major Vote	
		Vote	Candidate	Vote	Candidate			Rep.	Dem.	Rep.	Dem.
1956	1,340,005	719,302	Eisenhower, Dwight D.	617,525	Stevenson, Adlai E.	3,178	101,777 R	53.7%	46.1%	53.8%	46.2%
1952	1,379,483	763,211	Eisenhower, Dwight D.	608,458	Stevenson, Adlai E.	7,814	154,753 R	55.3%	44.1%	55.6%	44.4%
1948	1,212,226	483,617	Dewey, Thomas E.	692,966	Truman, Harry S.	35,643	209,349 D	39.9%	57.2%	41.1%	58.9%
1944	1,125,504	527,416	Dewey, Thomas E.	589,864	Roosevelt, Franklin D.	8,224	62,448 D	46.9%	52.4%	47.2%	52.8%
1940	1,251,188	596,274	Willkie, Wendell	644,196	Roosevelt, Franklin D.	10,718	47,922 D	47.7%	51.5%	48.1%	51.9%
1936	1,129,975	350,461	Landon, Alfred M.	698,811	Roosevelt, Franklin D.	80,703	348,350 D	31.0%	61.8%	33.4%	66.6%
1932	1,002,843	363,959	Hoover, Herbert C.	600,806	Roosevelt, Franklin D.	38,078	236,847 D	36.3%	59.9%	37.7%	62.3%
1928	970,976	560,977	Hoover, Herbert C.	396,451	Smith, Alfred E.	13,548	164,526 R	57.8%	40.8%	58.6%	41.4%
1924 **	822,146	420,759	Coolidge, Calvin	55,913	Davis, John W.	345,474	81,567 R	51.2%	6.8%	88.3%	11.7%
1920	735,838	519,421	Harding, Warren G.	142,994	Cox, James M.	73,423	376,427 R	70.6%	19.4%	78.4%	21.6%

In 1924 other vote was 339,192 Progressive; 4,427 Communist and 1,855 Socialist Labor.

ELECTORAL COLLEGE VOTE 1920 TO 1956

Year	Total	Republican	Democratic	Other
1956	11	11	—	—
1952	11	11	—	—
1948	11	—	11	—
1944	11	—	11	—
1940	11	—	11	—
1936	11	—	11	—
1932	11	—	11	—
1928	12	12	—	—
1924	12	12	—	—
1920	12	12	—	—

MINNESOTA

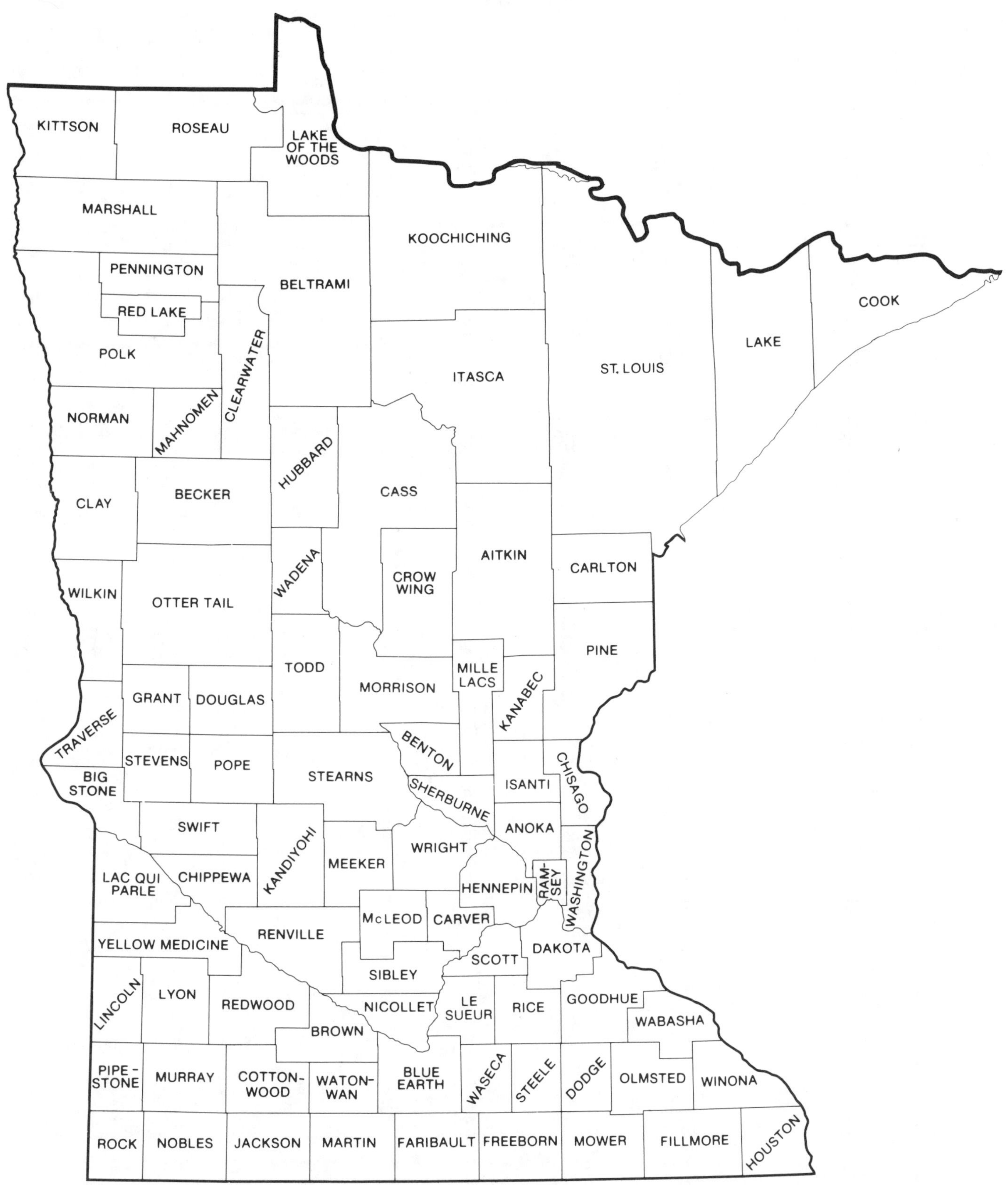
KITTSON
ROSEAU
LAKE OF THE WOODS
MARSHALL
KOOCHICHING
PENNINGTON
BELTRAMI
RED LAKE
COOK
POLK
CLEARWATER
LAKE
ST. LOUIS
ITASCA
NORMAN
MAHNOMEN
HUBBARD
CASS
CLAY
BECKER
AITKIN
CARLTON
WADENA
CROW WING
WILKIN
OTTER TAIL
PINE
TODD
MILLE LACS
GRANT
DOUGLAS
MORRISON
KANABEC
TRAVERSE
BENTON
STEVENS
POPE
STEARNS
ISANTI
CHISAGO
BIG STONE
SHERBURNE
SWIFT
ANOKA
WRIGHT
KANDIYOHI
MEEKER
WASHINGTON
LAC QUI PARLE
CHIPPEWA
HENNEPIN
RAM-SEY
McLEOD
CARVER
RENVILLE
YELLOW MEDICINE
DAKOTA
SCOTT
SIBLEY
LYON
REDWOOD
GOODHUE
NICOLLET
LE SUEUR
RICE
LINCOLN
WABASHA
BROWN
PIPE-STONE
MURRAY
COTTON-WOOD
WATON-WAN
BLUE EARTH
WASECA
STEELE
DODGE
OLMSTED
WINONA
ROCK
NOBLES
JACKSON
MARTIN
FARIBAULT
FREEBORN
MOWER
FILLMORE
HOUSTON

MINNESOTA

PRESIDENT 1956

1950 Census Population	County	Total Vote	Republican	Democratic	Other	Rep.-Dem. Plurality	Percentage: Total Vote Rep.	Percentage: Total Vote Dem.	Percentage: Major Vote Rep.	Percentage: Major Vote Dem.
14,327	AITKIN	5,504	2,762	2,733	9	29 R	50.2%	49.7%	50.3%	49.7%
35,579	ANOKA	21,092	9,359	11,697	36	2,338 D	44.4%	55.5%	44.4%	55.6%
24,836	BECKER	9,251	4,608	4,619	24	11 D	49.8%	49.9%	49.9%	50.1%
24,962	BELTRAMI	7,797	3,974	3,807	16	167 R	51.0%	48.8%	51.1%	48.9%
15,911	BENTON	6,216	3,591	2,609	16	982 R	57.8%	42.0%	57.9%	42.1%
9,607	BIG STONE	3,925	1,737	2,180	8	443 D	44.3%	55.5%	44.3%	55.7%
38,327	BLUE EARTH	16,886	11,398	5,467	21	5,931 R	67.5%	32.4%	67.6%	32.4%
25,895	BROWN	11,059	7,965	3,067	27	4,898 R	72.0%	27.7%	72.2%	27.8%
24,584	CARLTON	10,677	4,168	6,484	25	2,316 D	39.0%	60.7%	39.1%	60.9%
18,155	CARVER	8,589	6,226	2,334	29	3,892 R	72.5%	27.2%	72.7%	27.3%
19,468	CASS	6,765	4,007	2,748	10	1,259 R	59.2%	40.6%	59.3%	40.7%
16,739	CHIPPEWA	7,060	3,623	3,434	3	189 R	51.3%	48.6%	51.3%	48.7%
12,669	CHISAGO	6,153	3,413	2,731	9	682 R	55.5%	44.4%	55.6%	44.4%
30,363	CLAY	12,855	6,783	6,057	15	726 R	52.8%	47.1%	52.8%	47.2%
10,204	CLEARWATER	3,650	1,464	2,171	15	707 D	40.1%	59.5%	40.3%	59.7%
2,900	COOK	1,748	1,078	668	2	410 R	61.7%	38.2%	61.7%	38.3%
15,763	COTTONWOOD	6,968	4,619	2,344	5	2,275 R	66.3%	33.6%	66.3%	33.7%
30,875	CROW WING	12,243	6,657	5,556	30	1,101 R	54.4%	45.4%	54.5%	45.5%
49,019	DAKOTA	25,839	13,112	12,672	55	440 R	50.7%	49.0%	50.9%	49.1%
12,624	DODGE	5,025	3,205	1,814	6	1,391 R	63.8%	36.1%	63.9%	36.1%
21,304	DOUGLAS	9,320	5,114	4,194	12	920 R	54.9%	45.0%	54.9%	45.1%
23,879	FARIBAULT	10,465	6,886	3,554	25	3,332 R	65.8%	34.0%	66.0%	34.0%
24,465	FILLMORE	10,440	7,004	3,427	9	3,577 R	67.1%	32.8%	67.1%	32.9%
34,517	FREEBORN	14,781	7,632	7,138	11	494 R	51.6%	48.3%	51.7%	48.3%
32,118	GOODHUE	14,353	9,365	4,969	19	4,396 R	65.2%	34.6%	65.3%	34.7%
9,542	GRANT	4,177	2,064	2,107	6	43 D	49.4%	50.4%	49.5%	50.5%
676,579	HENNEPIN	333,112	183,248	149,341	523	33,907 R	55.0%	44.8%	55.1%	44.9%
14,435	HOUSTON	6,680	4,538	2,133	9	2,405 R	67.9%	31.9%	68.0%	32.0%
11,085	HUBBARD	3,913	2,453	1,454	6	999 R	62.7%	37.2%	62.8%	37.2%
12,123	ISANTI	4,959	2,348	2,605	6	257 D	47.3%	52.5%	47.4%	52.6%
33,321	ITASCA	15,178	6,408	8,737	33	2,329 D	42.2%	57.6%	42.3%	57.7%
16,306	JACKSON	6,784	3,543	3,232	9	311 R	52.2%	47.6%	52.3%	47.7%
9,192	KANABEC	3,693	1,950	1,736	7	214 R	52.8%	47.0%	52.9%	47.1%
28,644	KANDIYOHI	12,305	5,445	6,834	26	1,389 D	44.3%	55.5%	44.3%	55.7%
9,649	KITTSON	3,798	1,569	2,222	7	653 D	41.3%	58.5%	41.4%	58.6%
16,910	KOOCHICHING	6,468	2,757	3,695	16	938 D	42.6%	57.1%	42.7%	57.3%
14,545	LAC QUI PARLE	6,108	3,276	2,826	6	450 R	53.6%	46.3%	53.7%	46.3%
7,781	LAKE	5,143	2,055	3,079	9	1,024 D	40.0%	59.9%	40.0%	60.0%
4,955	LAKE OF THE WOODS	1,777	723	1,048	6	325 D	40.7%	59.0%	40.8%	59.2%
19,088	LE SUEUR	8,599	5,026	3,556	17	1,470 R	58.4%	41.4%	58.6%	41.4%
10,150	LINCOLN	4,390	2,060	2,316	14	256 D	46.9%	52.8%	47.1%	52.9%
22,253	LYON	9,386	5,188	4,190	8	998 R	55.3%	44.6%	55.3%	44.7%
22,198	MCLEOD	9,828	6,743	3,068	17	3,675 R	68.6%	31.2%	68.7%	31.3%
7,059	MAHNOMEN	2,392	875	1,513	4	638 D	36.6%	63.3%	36.6%	63.4%
16,125	MARSHALL	6,007	2,519	3,478	10	959 D	41.9%	57.9%	42.0%	58.0%
25,655	MARTIN	11,456	8,152	3,289	15	4,863 R	71.2%	28.7%	71.3%	28.7%
18,966	MEEKER	8,097	4,738	3,348	11	1,390 R	58.5%	41.3%	58.6%	41.4%
15,165	MILLE LACS	5,941	3,315	2,619	7	696 R	55.8%	44.1%	55.9%	44.1%
25,832	MORRISON	9,727	5,042	4,653	32	389 R	51.8%	47.8%	52.0%	48.0%
42,277	MOWER	18,890	9,570	9,219	101	351 R	50.7%	48.8%	50.9%	49.1%
14,801	MURRAY	5,971	3,261	2,695	15	566 R	54.6%	45.1%	54.8%	45.2%
20,929	NICOLLET	7,966	5,322	2,636	8	2,686 R	66.8%	33.1%	66.9%	33.1%
22,435	NOBLES	9,241	5,196	4,036	9	1,160 R	56.2%	43.7%	56.3%	43.7%
12,909	NORMAN	5,081	2,338	2,740	3	402 D	46.0%	53.9%	46.0%	54.0%
48,228	OLMSTED	21,012	13,789	7,172	51	6,617 R	65.6%	34.1%	65.8%	34.2%
51,320	OTTER TAIL	19,375	12,764	6,571	40	6,193 R	65.9%	33.9%	66.0%	34.0%
12,965	PENNINGTON	5,359	2,408	2,947	4	539 D	44.9%	55.0%	45.0%	55.0%
18,223	PINE	7,041	3,204	3,829	8	625 D	45.5%	54.4%	45.6%	54.4%
14,003	PIPESTONE	5,533	3,362	2,165	6	1,197 R	60.8%	39.1%	60.8%	39.2%
35,900	POLK	14,853	6,847	7,980	26	1,133 D	46.1%	53.7%	46.2%	53.8%

MINNESOTA

PRESIDENT 1956

1950 Census Population	County	Total Vote	Republican	Democratic	Other	Rep.-Dem. Plurality	Percentage Total Vote Rep.	Percentage Total Vote Dem.	Percentage Major Vote Rep.	Percentage Major Vote Dem.
12,862	POPE	5,309	2,725	2,577	7	148 R	51.3%	48.5%	51.4%	48.6%
355,332	RAMSEY	169,039	80,701	87,784	554	7,083 D	47.7%	51.9%	47.9%	52.1%
6,806	RED LAKE	2,345	782	1,555	8	773 D	33.3%	66.3%	33.5%	66.5%
22,127	REDWOOD	9,006	5,956	3,039	11	2,917 R	66.1%	33.7%	66.2%	33.8%
23,954	RENVILLE	9,958	5,728	4,213	17	1,515 R	57.5%	42.3%	57.6%	42.4%
36,235	RICE	12,984	8,471	4,489	24	3,982 R	65.2%	34.6%	65.4%	34.6%
11,278	ROCK	4,862	3,267	1,591	4	1,676 R	67.2%	32.7%	67.2%	32.8%
14,505	ROSEAU	4,973	1,901	3,062	10	1,161 D	38.2%	61.6%	38.3%	61.7%
206,062	ST. LOUIS	102,723	39,902	62,190	631	22,288 D	38.8%	60.5%	39.1%	60.9%
16,486	SCOTT	7,598	4,148	3,431	19	717 R	54.6%	45.2%	54.7%	45.3%
10,661	SHERBURNE	4,487	2,681	1,796	10	885 R	59.8%	40.0%	59.9%	40.1%
15,816	SIBLEY	6,842	4,737	2,099	6	2,638 R	69.2%	30.7%	69.3%	30.7%
70,681	STEARNS	27,257	17,364	9,829	64	7,535 R	63.7%	36.1%	63.9%	36.1%
21,155	STEELE	9,764	6,435	3,293	36	3,142 R	65.9%	33.7%	66.1%	33.9%
11,106	STEVENS	4,430	2,606	1,822	2	784 R	58.8%	41.1%	58.9%	41.1%
15,837	SWIFT	6,365	2,637	3,720	8	1,083 D	41.4%	58.4%	41.5%	58.5%
25,420	TODD	8,981	5,075	3,882	24	1,193 R	56.5%	43.2%	56.7%	43.3%
8,053	TRAVERSE	3,198	1,467	1,724	7	257 D	45.9%	53.9%	46.0%	54.0%
16,878	WABASHA	7,068	4,728	2,301	39	2,427 R	66.9%	32.6%	67.3%	32.7%
12,806	WADENA	4,767	3,028	1,733	6	1,295 R	63.5%	36.4%	63.6%	36.4%
14,957	WASECA	6,889	4,663	2,215	11	2,448 R	67.7%	32.2%	67.8%	32.2%
34,544	WASHINGTON	17,056	9,562	7,462	32	2,100 R	56.1%	43.8%	56.2%	43.8%
13,881	WATONWAN	5,861	3,963	1,886	12	2,077 R	67.6%	32.2%	67.8%	32.2%
10,567	WILKIN	4,218	2,335	1,881	2	454 R	55.4%	44.6%	55.4%	44.6%
39,841	WINONA	15,893	9,743	6,048	102	3,695 R	61.3%	38.1%	61.7%	38.3%
27,716	WRIGHT	12,213	7,257	4,944	12	2,313 R	59.4%	40.5%	59.5%	40.5%
16,279	YELLOW MEDICINE	7,018	3,594	3,416	8	178 R	51.2%	48.7%	51.3%	48.7%
2,982,483	TOTAL	1,340,005	719,302	617,525	3,178	101,777 R	53.7%	46.1%	53.8%	46.2%

MINNESOTA

PRESIDENT 1952

1950 Census Population	County	Total Vote	Republican	Democratic	Other	Rep.-Dem. Plurality	Percentage Total Vote Rep.	Percentage Total Vote Dem.	Percentage Major Vote Rep.	Percentage Major Vote Dem.
14,327	AITKIN	6,050	3,384	2,577	89	807 R	55.9%	42.6%	56.8%	43.2%
35,579	ANOKA	16,839	7,425	9,344	70	1,919 D	44.1%	55.5%	44.3%	55.7%
24,836	BECKER	10,414	5,815	4,539	60	1,276 R	55.8%	43.6%	56.2%	43.8%
24,962	BELTRAMI	8,962	4,817	4,092	53	725 R	53.7%	45.7%	54.1%	45.9%
15,911	BENTON	6,476	3,856	2,587	33	1,269 R	59.5%	39.9%	59.8%	40.2%
9,607	BIG STONE	4,392	2,260	2,107	25	153 R	51.5%	48.0%	51.8%	48.2%
38,327	BLUE EARTH	16,870	11,867	4,952	51	6,915 R	70.3%	29.4%	70.6%	29.4%
25,895	BROWN	11,308	8,152	3,129	27	5,023 R	72.1%	27.7%	72.3%	27.7%
24,584	CARLTON	10,698	4,175	6,432	91	2,257 D	39.0%	60.1%	39.4%	60.6%
18,155	CARVER	8,848	6,674	2,159	15	4,515 R	75.4%	24.4%	75.6%	24.4%
19,468	CASS	7,486	4,601	2,818	67	1,783 R	61.5%	37.6%	62.0%	38.0%
16,739	CHIPPEWA	7,618	4,411	3,171	36	1,240 R	57.9%	41.6%	58.2%	41.8%
12,669	CHISAGO	6,460	3,892	2,536	32	1,356 R	60.2%	39.3%	60.5%	39.5%
30,363	CLAY	12,234	7,178	5,036	20	2,142 R	58.7%	41.2%	58.8%	41.2%
10,204	CLEARWATER	4,116	1,971	2,089	56	118 D	47.9%	50.8%	48.5%	51.5%
2,900	COOK	1,454	946	503	5	443 R	65.1%	34.6%	65.3%	34.7%
15,763	COTTONWOOD	7,674	5,488	2,130	56	3,358 R	71.5%	27.8%	72.0%	28.0%
30,875	CROW WING	12,956	6,992	5,883	81	1,109 R	54.0%	45.4%	54.3%	45.7%
49,019	DAKOTA	23,879	11,871	11,890	118	19 D	49.7%	49.8%	50.0%	50.0%
12,624	DODGE	5,508	3,893	1,582	33	2,311 R	70.7%	28.7%	71.1%	28.9%
21,304	DOUGLAS	9,848	6,037	3,768	43	2,269 R	61.3%	38.3%	61.6%	38.4%
23,879	FARIBAULT	10,930	7,763	3,120	47	4,643 R	71.0%	28.5%	71.3%	28.7%
24,465	FILLMORE	11,057	8,405	2,612	40	5,793 R	76.0%	23.6%	76.3%	23.7%
34,517	FREEBORN	15,021	8,450	6,525	46	1,925 R	56.3%	43.4%	56.4%	43.6%
32,118	GOODHUE	15,494	10,422	5,037	35	5,385 R	67.3%	32.5%	67.4%	32.6%
9,542	GRANT	4,478	2,665	1,791	22	874 R	59.5%	40.0%	59.8%	40.2%
676,579	HENNEPIN	337,141	180,338	155,388	1,415	24,950 R	53.5%	46.1%	53.7%	46.3%
14,435	HOUSTON	7,223	5,365	1,830	28	3,535 R	74.3%	25.3%	74.6%	25.4%
11,085	HUBBARD	4,493	3,099	1,360	34	1,739 R	69.0%	30.3%	69.5%	30.5%
12,123	ISANTI	5,142	2,682	2,393	67	289 R	52.2%	46.5%	52.8%	47.2%
33,321	ITASCA	15,782	6,573	9,128	81	2,555 D	41.6%	57.8%	41.9%	58.1%
16,306	JACKSON	7,342	4,558	2,771	13	1,787 R	62.1%	37.7%	62.2%	37.8%
9,192	KANABEC	3,948	2,205	1,714	29	491 R	55.9%	43.4%	56.3%	43.7%
28,644	KANDIYOHI	12,747	6,370	6,264	113	106 R	50.0%	49.1%	50.4%	49.6%
9,649	KITTSON	4,264	1,837	2,387	40	550 D	43.1%	56.0%	43.5%	56.5%
16,910	KOOCHICHING	6,851	2,742	4,078	31	1,336 D	40.0%	59.5%	40.2%	59.8%
14,545	LAC QUI PARLE	6,705	3,924	2,753	28	1,171 R	58.5%	41.1%	58.8%	41.2%
7,781	LAKE	4,289	1,451	2,814	24	1,363 D	33.8%	65.6%	34.0%	66.0%
4,955	LAKE OF THE WOODS	2,027	898	1,117	12	219 D	44.3%	55.1%	44.6%	55.4%
19,088	LE SUEUR	9,140	5,776	3,348	16	2,428 R	63.2%	36.6%	63.3%	36.7%
10,150	LINCOLN	4,657	2,746	1,892	19	854 R	59.0%	40.6%	59.2%	40.8%
22,253	LYON	10,069	6,015	4,030	24	1,985 R	59.7%	40.0%	59.9%	40.1%
22,198	MCLEOD	10,048	7,246	2,781	21	4,465 R	72.1%	27.7%	72.3%	27.7%
7,059	MAHNOMEN	2,660	1,220	1,436	4	216 D	45.9%	54.0%	45.9%	54.1%
16,125	MARSHALL	6,733	3,516	3,132	85	384 R	52.2%	46.5%	52.9%	47.1%
25,655	MARTIN	12,123	9,411	2,673	39	6,738 R	77.6%	22.0%	77.9%	22.1%
18,966	MEEKER	8,608	5,750	2,833	25	2,917 R	66.8%	32.9%	67.0%	33.0%
15,165	MILLE LACS	6,446	3,766	2,639	41	1,127 R	58.4%	40.9%	58.8%	41.2%
25,832	MORRISON	10,639	6,050	4,551	38	1,499 R	56.9%	42.8%	57.1%	42.9%
42,277	MOWER	18,551	9,862	8,551	138	1,311 R	53.2%	46.1%	53.6%	46.4%
14,801	MURRAY	6,223	4,054	2,145	24	1,909 R	65.1%	34.5%	65.4%	34.6%
20,929	NICOLLET	8,398	5,775	2,584	39	3,191 R	68.8%	30.8%	69.1%	30.9%
22,435	NOBLES	9,717	6,340	3,351	26	2,989 R	65.2%	34.5%	65.4%	34.6%
12,909	NORMAN	5,573	3,069	2,465	39	604 R	55.1%	44.2%	55.5%	44.5%
48,228	OLMSTED	21,447	14,566	6,792	89	7,774 R	67.9%	31.7%	68.2%	31.8%
51,320	OTTER TAIL	21,921	16,447	5,388	86	11,059 R	75.0%	24.6%	75.3%	24.7%
12,965	PENNINGTON	5,615	2,726	2,802	87	76 D	48.5%	49.9%	49.3%	50.7%
18,223	PINE	8,038	4,255	3,692	91	563 R	52.9%	45.9%	53.5%	46.5%
14,003	PIPESTONE	6,221	4,507	1,701	13	2,806 R	72.4%	27.3%	72.6%	27.4%
35,900	POLK	15,683	8,326	7,244	113	1,082 R	53.1%	46.2%	53.5%	46.5%

MINNESOTA

PRESIDENT 1952

1950 Census Population	County	Total Vote	Republican	Democratic	Other	Rep.-Dem. Plurality	Percentage Total Vote Rep.	Total Vote Dem.	Major Vote Rep.	Major Vote Dem.
12,862	POPE	5,988	3,593	2,381	14	1,212 R	60.0%	39.8%	60.1%	39.9%
355,332	RAMSEY	171,370	76,093	93,783	1,494	17,690 D	44.4%	54.7%	44.8%	55.2%
6,806	RED LAKE	2,491	1,034	1,431	26	397 D	41.5%	57.4%	41.9%	58.1%
22,127	REDWOOD	9,810	7,093	2,695	22	4,398 R	72.3%	27.5%	72.5%	27.5%
23,954	RENVILLE	10,626	6,742	3,828	56	2,914 R	63.4%	36.0%	63.8%	36.2%
36,235	RICE	13,693	9,334	4,330	29	5,004 R	68.2%	31.6%	68.3%	31.7%
11,278	ROCK	5,067	3,774	1,286	7	2,488 R	74.5%	25.4%	74.6%	25.4%
14,505	ROSEAU	5,727	2,596	3,062	69	466 D	45.3%	53.5%	45.9%	54.1%
206,062	ST. LOUIS	103,286	38,900	63,032	1,354	24,132 D	37.7%	61.0%	38.2%	61.8%
16,486	SCOTT	7,606	4,277	3,315	14	962 R	56.2%	43.6%	56.3%	43.7%
10,661	SHERBURNE	4,478	2,839	1,630	9	1,209 R	63.4%	36.4%	63.5%	36.5%
15,816	SIBLEY	7,214	5,323	1,871	20	3,452 R	73.8%	25.9%	74.0%	26.0%
70,681	STEARNS	28,213	18,267	9,907	39	8,360 R	64.7%	35.1%	64.8%	35.2%
21,155	STEELE	9,804	6,956	2,819	29	4,137 R	71.0%	28.8%	71.2%	28.8%
11,106	STEVENS	4,879	3,288	1,579	12	1,709 R	67.4%	32.4%	67.6%	32.4%
15,837	SWIFT	6,871	3,532	3,291	48	241 R	51.4%	47.9%	51.8%	48.2%
25,420	TODD	10,211	6,731	3,439	41	3,292 R	65.9%	33.7%	66.2%	33.8%
8,053	TRAVERSE	3,573	1,809	1,756	8	53 R	50.6%	49.1%	50.7%	49.3%
16,878	WABASHA	7,843	5,461	2,356	26	3,105 R	69.6%	30.0%	69.9%	30.1%
12,806	WADENA	5,343	3,662	1,665	16	1,997 R	68.5%	31.2%	68.7%	31.3%
14,957	WASECA	7,113	4,962	2,132	19	2,830 R	69.8%	30.0%	69.9%	30.1%
34,544	WASHINGTON	17,240	9,408	7,768	64	1,640 R	54.6%	45.1%	54.8%	45.2%
13,881	WATONWAN	6,316	4,549	1,752	15	2,797 R	72.0%	27.7%	72.2%	27.8%
10,567	WILKIN	4,556	2,979	1,564	13	1,415 R	65.4%	34.3%	65.6%	34.4%
39,841	WINONA	16,621	10,723	5,834	64	4,889 R	64.5%	35.1%	64.8%	35.2%
27,716	WRIGHT	12,524	8,089	4,373	62	3,716 R	64.6%	34.9%	64.9%	35.1%
16,279	YELLOW MEDICINE	7,486	4,322	3,143	21	1,179 R	57.7%	42.0%	57.9%	42.1%
2,982,483	TOTAL	1,379,483	763,211	608,458	7,814	154,753 R	55.3%	44.1%	55.6%	44.4%

MINNESOTA

PRESIDENT 1948

1940 Census Population	County	Total Vote	Republican	Democratic	Other	Rep.-Dem. Plurality	Percentage Total Vote Rep.	Percentage Total Vote Dem.	Percentage Major Vote Rep.	Percentage Major Vote Dem.
17,865	AITKIN	6,007	2,466	3,277	264	811 D	41.1%	54.6%	42.9%	57.1%
22,443	ANOKA	11,929	3,853	7,730	346	3,877 D	32.3%	64.8%	33.3%	66.7%
26,562	BECKER	9,727	3,495	5,885	347	2,390 D	35.9%	60.5%	37.3%	62.7%
26,107	BELTRAMI	9,580	3,126	6,020	434	2,894 D	32.6%	62.8%	34.2%	65.8%
16,106	BENTON	6,015	2,297	3,632	86	1,335 D	38.2%	60.4%	38.7%	61.3%
10,447	BIG STONE	3,886	1,321	2,466	99	1,145 D	34.0%	63.5%	34.9%	65.1%
36,203	BLUE EARTH	14,954	7,520	7,272	162	248 R	50.3%	48.6%	50.8%	49.2%
25,544	BROWN	10,016	5,068	4,804	144	264 R	50.6%	48.0%	51.3%	48.7%
24,212	CARLTON	10,157	2,742	6,967	448	4,225 D	27.0%	68.6%	28.2%	71.8%
17,606	CARVER	7,482	4,582	2,816	84	1,766 R	61.2%	37.6%	61.9%	38.1%
20,646	CASS	7,278	3,179	3,933	166	754 D	43.7%	54.0%	44.7%	55.3%
16,927	CHIPPEWA	6,646	2,569	3,888	189	1,319 D	38.7%	58.5%	39.8%	60.2%
13,124	CHISAGO	6,065	2,704	3,184	177	480 D	44.6%	52.5%	45.9%	54.1%
25,337	CLAY	11,145	4,302	6,624	219	2,322 D	38.6%	59.4%	39.4%	60.6%
11,153	CLEARWATER	4,212	1,171	2,793	248	1,622 D	27.8%	66.3%	29.5%	70.5%
3,030	COOK	1,406	674	688	44	14 D	47.9%	48.9%	49.5%	50.5%
16,143	COTTONWOOD	6,632	3,222	3,333	77	111 D	48.6%	50.3%	49.2%	50.8%
30,226	CROW WING	11,845	4,702	6,773	370	2,071 D	39.7%	57.2%	41.0%	59.0%
39,660	DAKOTA	19,623	6,819	12,487	317	5,668 D	34.8%	63.6%	35.3%	64.7%
12,931	DODGE	4,961	2,381	2,523	57	142 D	48.0%	50.9%	48.6%	51.4%
20,369	DOUGLAS	8,973	3,744	5,022	207	1,278 D	41.7%	56.0%	42.7%	57.3%
23,941	FARIBAULT	10,014	4,619	5,261	134	642 D	46.1%	52.5%	46.8%	53.2%
25,830	FILLMORE	10,128	5,587	4,414	127	1,173 R	55.2%	43.6%	55.9%	44.1%
31,780	FREEBORN	13,276	5,238	7,825	213	2,587 D	39.5%	58.9%	40.1%	59.9%
31,564	GOODHUE	14,222	6,704	7,313	205	609 D	47.1%	51.4%	47.8%	52.2%
9,828	GRANT	4,388	1,789	2,378	221	589 D	40.8%	54.2%	42.9%	57.1%
568,899	HENNEPIN	282,234	121,169	151,920	9,145	30,751 D	42.9%	53.8%	44.4%	55.6%
14,735	HOUSTON	6,231	3,540	2,623	68	917 R	56.8%	42.1%	57.4%	42.6%
11,085	HUBBARD	4,241	2,071	2,044	126	27 R	48.8%	48.2%	50.3%	49.7%
12,950	ISANTI	4,994	1,918	2,758	318	840 D	38.4%	55.2%	41.0%	59.0%
32,996	ITASCA	14,716	4,334	9,653	729	5,319 D	29.5%	65.6%	31.0%	69.0%
16,805	JACKSON	6,969	2,288	4,541	140	2,253 D	32.8%	65.2%	33.5%	66.5%
9,651	KANABEC	3,970	1,531	2,305	134	774 D	38.6%	58.1%	39.9%	60.1%
26,524	KANDIYOHI	11,593	3,666	7,204	723	3,538 D	31.6%	62.1%	33.7%	66.3%
10,717	KITTSON	4,183	1,035	2,970	178	1,935 D	24.7%	71.0%	25.8%	74.2%
16,930	KOOCHICHING	6,968	1,718	4,968	282	3,250 D	24.7%	71.3%	25.7%	74.3%
15,509	LAC QUI PARLE	6,100	2,330	3,690	80	1,360 D	38.2%	60.5%	38.7%	61.3%
6,956	LAKE	3,729	924	2,555	250	1,631 D	24.8%	68.5%	26.6%	73.4%
5,975	LAKE OF THE WOODS	2,005	583	1,302	120	719 D	29.1%	64.9%	30.9%	69.1%
19,227	LE SUEUR	8,828	3,858	4,890	80	1,032 D	43.7%	55.4%	44.1%	55.9%
10,797	LINCOLN	4,090	1,312	2,694	84	1,382 D	32.1%	65.9%	32.8%	67.2%
21,569	LYON	9,286	3,054	6,144	88	3,090 D	32.9%	66.2%	33.2%	66.8%
21,380	MCLEOD	8,716	4,623	3,987	106	636 R	53.0%	45.7%	53.7%	46.3%
8,054	MAHNOMEN	2,775	579	2,125	71	1,546 D	20.9%	76.6%	21.4%	78.6%
18,364	MARSHALL	6,507	2,090	4,126	291	2,036 D	32.1%	63.4%	33.6%	66.4%
24,656	MARTIN	10,764	4,662	6,015	87	1,353 D	43.3%	55.9%	43.7%	56.3%
19,277	MEEKER	8,065	3,620	4,333	112	713 D	44.9%	53.7%	45.5%	54.5%
15,558	MILLE LACS	6,039	2,502	3,343	194	841 D	41.4%	55.4%	42.8%	57.2%
27,473	MORRISON	10,092	3,922	6,026	144	2,104 D	38.9%	59.7%	39.4%	60.6%
36,113	MOWER	15,301	5,672	9,468	161	3,796 D	37.1%	61.9%	37.5%	62.5%
15,060	MURRAY	5,602	1,951	3,594	57	1,643 D	34.8%	64.2%	35.2%	64.8%
18,282	NICOLLET	7,325	3,576	3,663	86	87 D	48.8%	50.0%	49.4%	50.6%
21,215	NOBLES	8,382	3,203	5,090	89	1,887 D	38.2%	60.7%	38.6%	61.4%
14,746	NORMAN	5,157	1,695	3,245	217	1,550 D	32.9%	62.9%	34.3%	65.7%
42,658	OLMSTED	17,467	8,131	9,155	181	1,024 D	46.6%	52.4%	47.0%	53.0%
53,192	OTTER TAIL	18,172	11,131	6,546	495	4,585 R	61.3%	36.0%	63.0%	37.0%
12,913	PENNINGTON	5,608	1,759	3,402	447	1,643 D	31.4%	60.7%	34.1%	65.9%
21,478	PINE	8,407	3,069	4,978	360	1,909 D	36.5%	59.2%	38.1%	61.9%
13,794	PIPESTONE	5,180	2,281	2,804	95	523 D	44.0%	54.1%	44.9%	55.1%
37,734	POLK	14,580	4,662	9,279	639	4,617 D	32.0%	63.6%	33.4%	66.6%

MINNESOTA

PRESIDENT 1948

1940 Census Population	County	Total Vote	Republican	Democratic	Other	Rep.-Dem. Plurality	Percentage Total Vote Rep.	Total Vote Dem.	Major Vote Rep.	Major Vote Dem.
13,544	POPE	5,462	2,114	3,251	97	1,137 D	38.7%	59.5%	39.4%	60.6%
309,935	RAMSEY	140,887	48,142	88,528	4,217	40,386 D	34.2%	62.8%	35.2%	64.8%
7,413	RED LAKE	2,468	592	1,771	105	1,179 D	24.0%	71.8%	25.1%	74.9%
22,290	REDWOOD	8,445	4,160	4,182	103	22 D	49.3%	49.5%	49.9%	50.1%
24,625	RENVILLE	9,679	4,297	5,227	155	930 D	44.4%	54.0%	45.1%	54.9%
32,160	RICE	12,321	6,301	5,832	188	469 R	51.1%	47.3%	51.9%	48.1%
10,933	ROCK	4,234	2,035	2,134	65	99 D	48.1%	50.4%	48.8%	51.2%
15,103	ROSEAU	5,528	1,458	3,674	396	2,216 D	26.4%	66.5%	28.4%	71.6%
206,917	ST. LOUIS	97,292	28,490	62,553	6,249	34,063 D	29.3%	64.3%	31.3%	68.7%
15,585	SCOTT	6,935	2,583	4,278	74	1,695 D	37.2%	61.7%	37.6%	62.4%
10,456	SHERBURNE	3,895	1,828	1,958	109	130 D	46.9%	50.3%	48.3%	51.7%
16,625	SIBLEY	6,157	3,260	2,818	79	442 R	52.9%	45.8%	53.6%	46.4%
67,200	STEARNS	25,706	10,153	15,261	292	5,108 D	39.5%	59.4%	40.0%	60.0%
19,749	STEELE	8,816	4,451	4,305	60	146 R	50.5%	48.8%	50.8%	49.2%
11,039	STEVENS	4,283	1,928	2,313	42	385 D	45.0%	54.0%	45.5%	54.5%
15,469	SWIFT	6,468	2,109	4,082	277	1,973 D	32.6%	63.1%	34.1%	65.9%
27,438	TODD	9,535	4,166	5,157	212	991 D	43.7%	54.1%	44.7%	55.3%
8,283	TRAVERSE	3,223	1,008	2,151	64	1,143 D	31.3%	66.7%	31.9%	68.1%
17,653	WABASHA	7,102	3,297	3,730	75	433 D	46.4%	52.5%	46.9%	53.1%
12,772	WADENA	4,917	2,272	2,556	89	284 D	46.2%	52.0%	47.1%	52.9%
15,186	WASECA	6,680	3,511	3,120	49	391 R	52.6%	46.7%	52.9%	47.1%
26,430	WASHINGTON	13,970	5,686	8,039	245	2,353 D	40.7%	57.5%	41.4%	58.6%
13,902	WATONWAN	5,698	2,581	3,039	78	458 D	45.3%	53.3%	45.9%	54.1%
10,475	WILKIN	4,060	1,700	2,291	69	591 D	41.9%	56.4%	42.6%	57.4%
37,795	WINONA	15,313	6,880	8,281	152	1,401 D	44.9%	54.1%	45.4%	54.6%
27,550	WRIGHT	11,297	5,589	5,523	185	66 R	49.5%	48.9%	50.3%	49.7%
16,917	YELLOW MEDICINE	7,012	2,693	4,164	155	1,471 D	38.4%	59.4%	39.3%	60.7%
2,792,300	TOTAL	1,212,226	483,617	692,966	35,643	209,349 D	39.9%	57.2%	41.1%	58.9%

MINNESOTA

PRESIDENT 1944

1940 Census Population	County	Total Vote	Republican	Democratic	Other	Rep.-Dem. Plurality	Percentage Total Vote Rep.	Percentage Total Vote Dem.	Percentage Major Vote Rep.	Percentage Major Vote Dem.
17,865	AITKIN	5,509	2,720	2,743	46	23 D	49.4%	49.8%	49.8%	50.2%
22,443	ANOKA	9,468	3,958	5,431	79	1,473 D	41.8%	57.4%	42.2%	57.8%
26,562	BECKER	8,750	3,803	4,889	58	1,086 D	43.5%	55.9%	43.8%	56.2%
26,107	BELTRAMI	8,256	2,705	5,490	61	2,785 D	32.8%	66.5%	33.0%	67.0%
16,106	BENTON	5,264	2,988	2,258	18	730 R	56.8%	42.9%	57.0%	43.0%
10,447	BIG STONE	3,752	1,608	2,120	24	512 D	42.9%	56.5%	43.1%	56.9%
36,203	BLUE EARTH	14,581	9,429	5,098	54	4,331 R	64.7%	35.0%	64.9%	35.1%
25,544	BROWN	9,949	7,018	2,842	89	4,176 R	70.5%	28.6%	71.2%	28.8%
24,212	CARLTON	8,856	2,653	6,153	50	3,500 D	30.0%	69.5%	30.1%	69.9%
17,606	CARVER	7,427	5,823	1,565	39	4,258 R	78.4%	21.1%	78.8%	21.2%
20,646	CASS	6,547	3,135	3,377	35	242 D	47.9%	51.6%	48.1%	51.9%
16,927	CHIPPEWA	6,279	2,967	3,264	48	297 D	47.3%	52.0%	47.6%	52.4%
13,124	CHISAGO	5,434	3,020	2,376	38	644 R	55.6%	43.7%	56.0%	44.0%
25,337	CLAY	9,674	4,392	5,230	52	838 D	45.4%	54.1%	45.6%	54.4%
11,153	CLEARWATER	3,817	1,125	2,658	34	1,533 D	29.5%	69.6%	29.7%	70.3%
3,030	COOK	1,066	513	545	8	32 D	48.1%	51.1%	48.5%	51.5%
16,143	COTTONWOOD	6,308	3,916	2,354	38	1,562 R	62.1%	37.3%	62.5%	37.5%
30,226	CROW WING	10,067	4,500	5,504	63	1,004 D	44.7%	54.7%	45.0%	55.0%
39,660	DAKOTA	16,403	7,731	8,562	110	831 D	47.1%	52.2%	47.4%	52.6%
12,931	DODGE	4,725	2,902	1,808	15	1,094 R	61.4%	38.3%	61.6%	38.4%
20,369	DOUGLAS	7,867	4,140	3,681	46	459 R	52.6%	46.8%	52.9%	47.1%
23,941	FARIBAULT	9,487	5,822	3,640	25	2,182 R	61.4%	38.4%	61.5%	38.5%
25,830	FILLMORE	9,562	6,339	3,183	40	3,156 R	66.3%	33.3%	66.6%	33.4%
31,780	FREEBORN	12,246	5,728	6,486	32	758 D	46.8%	53.0%	46.9%	53.1%
31,564	GOODHUE	13,679	7,820	5,791	68	2,029 R	57.2%	42.3%	57.5%	42.5%
9,828	GRANT	3,879	1,898	1,969	12	71 D	48.9%	50.8%	49.1%	50.9%
568,899	HENNEPIN	267,320	116,781	148,792	1,747	32,011 D	43.7%	55.7%	44.0%	56.0%
14,735	HOUSTON	5,908	4,036	1,847	25	2,189 R	68.3%	31.3%	68.6%	31.4%
11,085	HUBBARD	3,740	2,114	1,613	13	501 R	56.5%	43.1%	56.7%	43.3%
12,950	ISANTI	4,487	2,205	2,225	57	20 D	49.1%	49.6%	49.8%	50.2%
32,996	ITASCA	13,095	4,227	8,787	81	4,560 D	32.3%	67.1%	32.5%	67.5%
16,805	JACKSON	6,230	2,789	3,417	24	628 D	44.8%	54.8%	44.9%	55.1%
9,651	KANABEC	3,713	1,913	1,776	24	137 R	51.5%	47.8%	51.9%	48.1%
26,524	KANDIYOHI	10,353	3,784	6,482	87	2,698 D	36.5%	62.6%	36.9%	63.1%
10,717	KITTSON	3,757	983	2,752	22	1,769 D	26.2%	73.2%	26.3%	73.7%
16,930	KOOCHICHING	5,639	1,607	3,981	51	2,374 D	28.5%	70.6%	28.8%	71.2%
15,509	LAC QUI PARLE	5,900	3,104	2,779	17	325 R	52.6%	47.1%	52.8%	47.2%
6,956	LAKE	3,239	792	2,401	46	1,609 D	24.5%	74.1%	24.8%	75.2%
5,975	LAKE OF THE WOODS	1,811	642	1,168	1	526 D	35.5%	64.5%	35.5%	64.5%
19,227	LE SUEUR	7,967	4,560	3,358	49	1,202 R	57.2%	42.1%	57.6%	42.4%
10,797	LINCOLN	3,917	1,600	2,302	15	702 D	40.8%	58.8%	41.0%	59.0%
21,569	LYON	8,295	3,617	4,640	38	1,023 D	43.6%	55.9%	43.8%	56.2%
21,380	MCLEOD	8,361	5,756	2,557	48	3,199 R	68.8%	30.6%	69.2%	30.8%
8,054	MAHNOMEN	2,260	748	1,494	18	746 D	33.1%	66.1%	33.4%	66.6%
18,364	MARSHALL	5,864	2,029	3,808	27	1,779 D	34.6%	64.9%	34.8%	65.2%
24,656	MARTIN	9,654	5,182	4,443	29	739 R	53.7%	46.0%	53.8%	46.2%
19,277	MEEKER	7,506	4,302	3,159	45	1,143 R	57.3%	42.1%	57.7%	42.3%
15,558	MILLE LACS	5,707	2,798	2,872	37	74 D	49.0%	50.3%	49.3%	50.7%
27,473	MORRISON	9,002	5,035	3,920	47	1,115 R	55.9%	43.5%	56.2%	43.8%
36,113	MOWER	13,835	6,588	7,199	48	611 D	47.6%	52.0%	47.8%	52.2%
15,060	MURRAY	5,102	2,585	2,495	22	90 R	50.7%	48.9%	50.9%	49.1%
18,282	NICOLLET	6,702	4,345	2,321	36	2,024 R	64.8%	34.6%	65.2%	34.8%
21,215	NOBLES	7,597	4,149	3,413	35	736 R	54.6%	44.9%	54.9%	45.1%
14,746	NORMAN	4,768	1,884	2,846	38	962 D	39.5%	59.7%	39.8%	60.2%
42,658	OLMSTED	15,274	8,355	6,873	46	1,482 R	54.7%	45.0%	54.9%	45.1%
53,192	OTTER TAIL	18,284	12,351	5,823	110	6,528 R	67.6%	31.8%	68.0%	32.0%
12,913	PENNINGTON	4,905	1,525	3,330	50	1,805 D	31.1%	67.9%	31.4%	68.6%
21,478	PINE	7,829	3,433	4,332	64	899 D	43.8%	55.3%	44.2%	55.8%
13,794	PIPESTONE	4,994	2,844	2,129	21	715 R	56.9%	42.6%	57.2%	42.8%
37,734	POLK	13,310	4,402	8,808	100	4,406 D	33.1%	66.2%	33.3%	66.7%

MINNESOTA

PRESIDENT 1944

1940 Census Population	County	Total Vote	Republican	Democratic	Other	Rep.-Dem. Plurality	Percentage Total Vote Rep.	Percentage Total Vote Dem.	Percentage Major Vote Rep.	Percentage Major Vote Dem.
13,544	POPE	5,401	2,607	2,781	13	174 D	48.3%	51.5%	48.4%	51.6%
309,935	RAMSEY	133,744	53,052	78,759	1,933	25,707 D	39.7%	58.9%	40.2%	59.8%
7,413	RED LAKE	2,414	757	1,642	15	885 D	31.4%	68.0%	31.6%	68.4%
22,290	REDWOOD	8,343	5,428	2,886	29	2,542 R	65.1%	34.6%	65.3%	34.7%
24,625	RENVILLE	8,976	5,160	3,747	69	1,413 R	57.5%	41.7%	57.9%	42.1%
32,160	RICE	11,322	6,824	4,470	28	2,354 R	60.3%	39.5%	60.4%	39.6%
10,933	ROCK	4,260	2,584	1,649	27	935 R	60.7%	38.7%	61.0%	39.0%
15,103	ROSEAU	5,250	1,513	3,697	40	2,184 D	28.8%	70.4%	29.0%	71.0%
206,917	ST. LOUIS	91,942	27,493	63,369	1,080	35,876 D	29.9%	68.9%	30.3%	69.7%
15,585	SCOTT	6,150	3,326	2,786	38	540 R	54.1%	45.3%	54.4%	45.6%
10,456	SHERBURNE	3,518	2,046	1,447	25	599 R	58.2%	41.1%	58.6%	41.4%
16,625	SIBLEY	6,024	4,311	1,683	30	2,628 R	71.6%	27.9%	71.9%	28.1%
67,200	STEARNS	22,029	13,298	8,647	84	4,651 R	60.4%	39.3%	60.6%	39.4%
19,749	STEELE	8,082	4,760	3,307	15	1,453 R	58.9%	40.9%	59.0%	41.0%
11,039	STEVENS	4,082	2,377	1,693	12	684 R	58.2%	41.5%	58.4%	41.6%
15,469	SWIFT	5,876	2,519	3,310	47	791 D	42.9%	56.3%	43.2%	56.8%
27,438	TODD	9,493	5,636	3,803	54	1,833 R	59.4%	40.1%	59.7%	40.3%
8,283	TRAVERSE	3,031	1,296	1,721	14	425 D	42.8%	56.8%	43.0%	57.0%
17,653	WABASHA	6,728	4,213	2,482	33	1,731 R	62.6%	36.9%	62.9%	37.1%
12,772	WADENA	4,537	2,653	1,868	16	785 R	58.5%	41.2%	58.7%	41.3%
15,186	WASECA	6,375	4,146	2,207	22	1,939 R	65.0%	34.6%	65.3%	34.7%
26,430	WASHINGTON	11,679	6,014	5,599	66	415 R	51.5%	47.9%	51.8%	48.2%
13,902	WATONWAN	5,493	3,146	2,324	23	822 R	57.3%	42.3%	57.5%	42.5%
10,475	WILKIN	3,776	1,945	1,819	12	126 R	51.5%	48.2%	51.7%	48.3%
37,795	WINONA	14,506	8,296	6,117	93	2,179 R	57.2%	42.2%	57.6%	42.4%
27,550	WRIGHT	10,711	6,961	3,678	72	3,283 R	65.0%	34.3%	65.4%	34.6%
16,917	YELLOW MEDICINE	6,585	3,337	3,214	34	123 R	50.7%	48.8%	50.9%	49.1%
2,792,300	TOTAL	1,125,504	527,416	589,864	8,224	62,448 D	46.9%	52.4%	47.2%	52.8%

MINNESOTA

PRESIDENT 1940

1940 Census Population	County	Total Vote	Republican	Democratic	Other	Rep.-Dem. Plurality	Percentage Total Vote Rep.	Percentage Total Vote Dem.	Percentage Major Vote Rep.	Percentage Major Vote Dem.
17,865	AITKIN	7,470	3,744	3,610	116	134 R	50.1%	48.3%	50.9%	49.1%
22,443	ANOKA	9,883	4,302	5,501	80	1,199 D	43.5%	55.7%	43.9%	56.1%
26,562	BECKER	10,816	4,292	6,432	92	2,140 D	39.7%	59.5%	40.0%	60.0%
26,107	BELTRAMI	10,713	3,511	7,036	166	3,525 D	32.8%	65.7%	33.3%	66.7%
16,106	BENTON	6,261	3,491	2,742	28	749 R	55.8%	43.8%	56.0%	44.0%
10,447	BIG STONE	4,482	1,925	2,517	40	592 D	42.9%	56.2%	43.3%	56.7%
36,203	BLUE EARTH	15,584	9,642	5,880	62	3,762 R	61.9%	37.7%	62.1%	37.9%
25,544	BROWN	11,301	7,533	3,678	90	3,855 R	66.7%	32.5%	67.2%	32.8%
24,212	CARLTON	10,670	3,400	7,159	111	3,759 D	31.9%	67.1%	32.2%	67.8%
17,606	CARVER	8,303	6,528	1,753	22	4,775 R	78.6%	21.1%	78.8%	21.2%
20,646	CASS	8,533	4,089	4,392	52	303 D	47.9%	51.5%	48.2%	51.8%
16,927	CHIPPEWA	7,340	3,307	3,969	64	662 D	45.1%	54.1%	45.5%	54.5%
13,124	CHISAGO	6,377	3,569	2,746	62	823 R	56.0%	43.1%	56.5%	43.5%
25,337	CLAY	10,793	4,450	6,295	48	1,845 D	41.2%	58.3%	41.4%	58.6%
11,153	CLEARWATER	4,678	1,354	3,289	35	1,935 D	28.9%	70.3%	29.2%	70.8%
3,030	COOK	1,366	673	686	7	13 D	49.3%	50.2%	49.5%	50.5%
16,143	COTTONWOOD	7,255	4,228	2,991	36	1,237 R	58.3%	41.2%	58.6%	41.4%
30,226	CROW WING	12,550	5,524	6,876	150	1,352 D	44.0%	54.8%	44.5%	55.5%
39,660	DAKOTA	17,743	8,339	9,327	77	988 D	47.0%	52.6%	47.2%	52.8%
12,931	DODGE	5,625	3,257	2,357	11	900 R	57.9%	41.9%	58.0%	42.0%
20,369	DOUGLAS	9,207	4,652	4,507	48	145 R	50.5%	49.0%	50.8%	49.2%
23,941	FARIBAULT	10,971	6,816	4,099	56	2,717 R	62.1%	37.4%	62.4%	37.6%
25,830	FILLMORE	11,704	7,839	3,826	39	4,013 R	67.0%	32.7%	67.2%	32.8%
31,780	FREEBORN	13,680	6,683	6,942	55	259 D	48.9%	50.7%	49.0%	51.0%
31,564	GOODHUE	15,656	9,095	6,475	86	2,620 R	58.1%	41.4%	58.4%	41.6%
9,828	GRANT	4,764	2,443	2,291	30	152 R	51.3%	48.1%	51.6%	48.4%
568,899	HENNEPIN	270,358	122,960	145,168	2,230	22,208 D	45.5%	53.7%	45.9%	54.1%
14,735	HOUSTON	6,944	4,825	2,082	37	2,743 R	69.5%	30.0%	69.9%	30.1%
11,085	HUBBARD	4,711	2,544	2,141	26	403 R	54.0%	45.4%	54.3%	45.7%
12,950	ISANTI	5,361	2,617	2,654	90	37 D	48.8%	49.5%	49.6%	50.4%
32,996	ITASCA	15,254	5,196	9,899	159	4,703 D	34.1%	64.9%	34.4%	65.6%
16,805	JACKSON	7,482	3,387	4,065	30	678 D	45.3%	54.3%	45.5%	54.5%
9,651	KANABEC	4,545	2,311	2,185	49	126 R	50.8%	48.1%	51.4%	48.6%
26,524	KANDIYOHI	11,540	4,263	7,187	90	2,924 D	36.9%	62.3%	37.2%	62.8%
10,717	KITTSON	4,480	1,279	3,167	34	1,888 D	28.5%	70.7%	28.8%	71.2%
16,930	KOOCHICHING	7,353	2,095	5,219	39	3,124 D	28.5%	71.0%	28.6%	71.4%
15,509	LAC QUI PARLE	6,923	3,789	3,106	28	683 R	54.7%	44.9%	55.0%	45.0%
6,956	LAKE	3,733	933	2,750	50	1,817 D	25.0%	73.7%	25.3%	74.7%
5,975	LAKE OF THE WOODS	2,528	850	1,638	40	788 D	33.6%	64.8%	34.2%	65.8%
19,227	LE SUEUR	9,313	5,543	3,750	20	1,793 R	59.5%	40.3%	59.6%	40.4%
10,797	LINCOLN	4,789	2,220	2,536	33	316 D	46.4%	53.0%	46.7%	53.3%
21,569	LYON	9,575	4,305	5,234	36	929 D	45.0%	54.7%	45.1%	54.9%
21,380	MCLEOD	9,420	6,474	2,884	62	3,590 R	68.7%	30.6%	69.2%	30.8%
8,054	MAHNOMEN	3,042	1,069	1,959	14	890 D	35.1%	64.4%	35.3%	64.7%
18,364	MARSHALL	7,034	2,441	4,549	44	2,108 D	34.7%	64.7%	34.9%	65.1%
24,656	MARTIN	10,720	6,409	4,290	21	2,119 R	59.8%	40.0%	59.9%	40.1%
19,277	MEEKER	8,686	5,026	3,615	45	1,411 R	57.9%	41.6%	58.2%	41.8%
15,558	MILLE LACS	7,151	3,459	3,619	73	160 D	48.4%	50.6%	48.9%	51.1%
27,473	MORRISON	10,936	5,734	5,144	58	590 R	52.4%	47.0%	52.7%	47.3%
36,113	MOWER	15,217	7,169	7,988	60	819 D	47.1%	52.5%	47.3%	52.7%
15,060	MURRAY	6,281	3,044	3,203	34	159 D	48.5%	51.0%	48.7%	51.3%
18,282	NICOLLET	7,537	4,674	2,832	31	1,842 R	62.0%	37.6%	62.3%	37.7%
21,215	NOBLES	9,059	5,104	3,919	36	1,185 R	56.3%	43.3%	56.6%	43.4%
14,746	NORMAN	5,916	2,161	3,716	39	1,555 D	36.5%	62.8%	36.8%	63.2%
42,658	OLMSTED	17,551	9,096	8,393	62	703 R	51.8%	47.8%	52.0%	48.0%
53,192	OTTER TAIL	21,629	13,737	7,705	187	6,032 R	63.5%	35.6%	64.1%	35.9%
12,913	PENNINGTON	5,841	1,857	3,886	98	2,029 D	31.8%	66.5%	32.3%	67.7%
21,478	PINE	9,526	4,106	5,263	157	1,157 D	43.1%	55.2%	43.8%	56.2%
13,794	PIPESTONE	5,842	3,423	2,390	29	1,033 R	58.6%	40.9%	58.9%	41.1%
37,734	POLK	15,985	5,200	10,652	133	5,452 D	32.5%	66.6%	32.8%	67.2%

MINNESOTA

PRESIDENT 1940

1940 Census Population	County	Total Vote	Republican	Democratic	Other	Rep.-Dem. Plurality	Percentage Total Vote Rep.	Percentage Total Vote Dem.	Percentage Major Vote Rep.	Percentage Major Vote Dem.
13,544	POPE	6,090	2,805	3,266	19	461 D	46.1%	53.6%	46.2%	53.8%
309,935	RAMSEY	138,165	57,093	78,990	2,082	21,897 D	41.3%	57.2%	42.0%	58.0%
7,413	RED LAKE	2,915	876	2,023	16	1,147 D	30.1%	69.4%	30.2%	69.8%
22,290	REDWOOD	9,782	6,105	3,637	40	2,468 R	62.4%	37.2%	62.7%	37.3%
24,625	RENVILLE	10,842	6,196	4,588	58	1,608 R	57.1%	42.3%	57.5%	42.5%
32,160	RICE	12,875	8,143	4,687	45	3,456 R	63.2%	36.4%	63.5%	36.5%
10,933	ROCK	4,951	2,944	1,983	24	961 R	59.5%	40.1%	59.8%	40.2%
15,103	ROSEAU	6,123	1,730	4,289	104	2,559 D	28.3%	70.0%	28.7%	71.3%
206,917	ST. LOUIS	102,623	32,243	68,620	1,760	36,377 D	31.4%	66.9%	32.0%	68.0%
15,585	SCOTT	7,172	4,241	2,910	21	1,331 R	59.1%	40.6%	59.3%	40.7%
10,456	SHERBURNE	4,040	2,450	1,570	20	880 R	60.6%	38.9%	60.9%	39.1%
16,625	SIBLEY	7,589	5,564	1,986	39	3,578 R	73.3%	26.2%	73.7%	26.3%
67,200	STEARNS	25,434	16,027	9,305	102	6,722 R	63.0%	36.6%	63.3%	36.7%
19,749	STEELE	9,199	5,517	3,668	14	1,849 R	60.0%	39.9%	60.1%	39.9%
11,039	STEVENS	4,652	2,619	2,018	15	601 R	56.3%	43.4%	56.5%	43.5%
15,469	SWIFT	6,768	2,815	3,899	54	1,084 D	41.6%	57.6%	41.9%	58.1%
27,438	TODD	10,916	6,302	4,553	61	1,749 R	57.7%	41.7%	58.1%	41.9%
8,283	TRAVERSE	3,541	1,434	2,094	13	660 D	40.5%	59.1%	40.6%	59.4%
17,653	WABASHA	8,324	5,656	2,655	13	3,001 R	67.9%	31.9%	68.1%	31.9%
12,772	WADENA	5,340	2,898	2,405	37	493 R	54.3%	45.0%	54.6%	45.4%
15,186	WASECA	7,213	4,515	2,673	25	1,842 R	62.6%	37.1%	62.8%	37.2%
26,430	WASHINGTON	13,052	6,710	6,288	54	422 R	51.4%	48.2%	51.6%	48.4%
13,902	WATONWAN	6,289	3,478	2,783	28	695 R	55.3%	44.3%	55.6%	44.4%
10,475	WILKIN	4,249	2,067	2,176	6	109 D	48.6%	51.2%	48.7%	51.3%
37,795	WINONA	16,891	9,599	7,187	105	2,412 R	56.8%	42.5%	57.2%	42.8%
27,550	WRIGHT	12,377	8,297	3,993	87	4,304 R	67.0%	32.3%	67.5%	32.5%
16,917	YELLOW MEDICINE	7,789	3,964	3,786	39	178 R	50.9%	48.6%	51.1%	48.9%
2,792,300	TOTAL	1,251,188	596,274	644,196	10,718	47,922 D	47.7%	51.5%	48.1%	51.9%

MINNESOTA

PRESIDENT 1936

1930 Census Population	County	Total Vote	Republican	Democratic	Other	Rep.-Dem. Plurality	Percentage: Total Vote Rep.	Total Vote Dem.	Major Vote Rep.	Major Vote Dem.
							Rep.	Dem.	Rep.	Dem.
15,009	AITKIN	6,611	2,466	3,806	339	1,340 D	37.3%	57.6%	39.3%	60.7%
18,415	ANOKA	7,909	2,586	4,501	822	1,915 D	32.7%	56.9%	36.5%	63.5%
22,503	BECKER	9,466	2,683	6,473	310	3,790 D	28.3%	68.4%	29.3%	70.7%
20,707	BELTRAMI	8,957	2,182	6,507	268	4,325 D	24.4%	72.6%	25.1%	74.9%
15,056	BENTON	5,813	1,783	3,111	919	1,328 D	30.7%	53.5%	36.4%	63.6%
9,838	BIG STONE	3,999	1,116	2,648	235	1,532 D	27.9%	66.2%	29.6%	70.4%
33,847	BLUE EARTH	14,769	5,550	8,255	964	2,705 D	37.6%	55.9%	40.2%	59.8%
23,428	BROWN	10,267	2,679	6,637	951	3,958 D	26.1%	64.6%	28.8%	71.2%
21,232	CARLTON	9,478	2,163	7,136	179	4,973 D	22.8%	75.3%	23.3%	76.7%
16,936	CARVER	7,292	3,095	2,814	1,383	281 R	42.4%	38.6%	52.4%	47.6%
15,591	CASS	7,334	2,634	4,440	260	1,806 D	35.9%	60.5%	37.2%	62.8%
15,762	CHIPPEWA	6,559	2,223	4,027	309	1,804 D	33.9%	61.4%	35.6%	64.4%
13,189	CHISAGO	6,080	2,462	3,360	258	898 D	40.5%	55.3%	42.3%	57.7%
23,120	CLAY	9,621	2,880	6,282	459	3,402 D	29.9%	65.3%	31.4%	68.6%
9,546	CLEARWATER	4,258	939	3,208	111	2,269 D	22.1%	75.3%	22.6%	77.4%
2,435	COOK	1,204	387	793	24	406 D	32.1%	65.9%	32.8%	67.2%
14,782	COTTONWOOD	6,623	2,509	3,929	185	1,420 D	37.9%	59.3%	39.0%	61.0%
25,627	CROW WING	10,673	3,611	6,561	501	2,950 D	33.8%	61.5%	35.5%	64.5%
34,592	DAKOTA	15,398	4,043	8,890	2,465	4,847 D	26.3%	57.7%	31.3%	68.7%
12,127	DODGE	5,138	2,138	2,812	188	674 D	41.6%	54.7%	43.2%	56.8%
18,813	DOUGLAS	7,364	2,681	4,186	497	1,505 D	36.4%	56.8%	39.0%	61.0%
21,642	FARIBAULT	9,847	3,773	5,603	471	1,830 D	38.3%	56.9%	40.2%	59.8%
24,748	FILLMORE	10,404	5,054	4,764	586	290 R	48.6%	45.8%	51.5%	48.5%
28,741	FREEBORN	12,305	4,653	7,378	274	2,725 D	37.8%	60.0%	38.7%	61.3%
31,317	GOODHUE	14,361	5,682	8,257	422	2,575 D	39.6%	57.5%	40.8%	59.2%
9,558	GRANT	4,075	1,566	2,358	151	792 D	38.4%	57.9%	39.9%	60.1%
517,785	HENNEPIN	245,480	81,206	144,289	19,985	63,083 D	33.1%	58.8%	36.0%	64.0%
13,845	HOUSTON	6,100	2,701	3,156	243	455 D	44.3%	51.7%	46.1%	53.9%
9,596	HUBBARD	4,062	1,618	2,312	132	694 D	39.8%	56.9%	41.2%	58.8%
12,081	ISANTI	5,123	1,437	3,442	244	2,005 D	28.0%	67.2%	29.5%	70.5%
27,224	ITASCA	12,819	3,594	8,896	329	5,302 D	28.0%	69.4%	28.8%	71.2%
15,863	JACKSON	7,195	1,676	5,187	332	3,511 D	23.3%	72.1%	24.4%	75.6%
8,558	KANABEC	4,088	1,350	2,579	159	1,229 D	33.0%	63.1%	34.4%	65.6%
23,574	KANDIYOHI	9,524	2,500	6,595	429	4,095 D	26.2%	69.2%	27.5%	72.5%
9,688	KITTSON	4,269	1,080	3,127	62	2,047 D	25.3%	73.2%	25.7%	74.3%
14,078	KOOCHICHING	6,513	1,316	5,065	132	3,749 D	20.2%	77.8%	20.6%	79.4%
15,398	LAC QUI PARLE	5,996	2,066	3,243	687	1,177 D	34.5%	54.1%	38.9%	61.1%
7,068	LAKE	3,390	617	2,717	56	2,100 D	18.2%	80.1%	18.5%	81.5%
4,194	LAKE OF THE WOODS	2,052	385	1,566	101	1,181 D	18.8%	76.3%	19.7%	80.3%
17,990	LE SUEUR	8,865	2,849	5,077	939	2,228 D	32.1%	57.3%	35.9%	64.1%
11,303	LINCOLN	4,334	1,199	2,662	473	1,463 D	27.7%	61.4%	31.1%	68.9%
19,326	LYON	8,424	2,551	5,163	710	2,612 D	30.3%	61.3%	33.1%	66.9%
20,522	MCLEOD	8,058	2,941	4,449	668	1,508 D	36.5%	55.2%	39.8%	60.2%
6,153	MAHNOMEN	2,634	474	2,025	135	1,551 D	18.0%	76.9%	19.0%	81.0%
17,003	MARSHALL	6,852	1,904	4,802	146	2,898 D	27.8%	70.1%	28.4%	71.6%
22,401	MARTIN	9,825	3,090	6,492	243	3,402 D	31.5%	66.1%	32.2%	67.8%
17,914	MEEKER	7,542	2,479	4,242	821	1,763 D	32.9%	56.2%	36.9%	63.1%
14,076	MILLE LACS	6,220	2,091	3,767	362	1,676 D	33.6%	60.6%	35.7%	64.3%
25,442	MORRISON	9,848	2,682	6,112	1,054	3,430 D	27.2%	62.1%	30.5%	69.5%
28,065	MOWER	13,487	4,743	8,228	516	3,485 D	35.2%	61.0%	36.6%	63.4%
13,902	MURRAY	5,855	1,601	3,926	328	2,325 D	27.3%	67.1%	29.0%	71.0%
16,550	NICOLLET	7,003	2,360	4,136	507	1,776 D	33.7%	59.1%	36.3%	63.7%
18,618	NOBLES	8,072	2,601	4,919	552	2,318 D	32.2%	60.9%	34.6%	65.4%
14,061	NORMAN	5,502	1,570	3,778	154	2,208 D	28.5%	68.7%	29.4%	70.6%
35,426	OLMSTED	14,919	5,316	8,958	645	3,642 D	35.6%	60.0%	37.2%	62.8%
51,006	OTTER TAIL	18,110	8,899	8,642	569	257 R	49.1%	47.7%	50.7%	49.3%
10,487	PENNINGTON	5,155	1,258	3,736	161	2,478 D	24.4%	72.5%	25.2%	74.8%
20,264	PINE	8,638	2,452	5,797	389	3,345 D	28.4%	67.1%	29.7%	70.3%
12,238	PIPESTONE	5,170	1,881	3,026	263	1,145 D	36.4%	58.5%	38.3%	61.7%
36,019	POLK	15,437	3,751	11,337	349	7,586 D	24.3%	73.4%	24.9%	75.1%

MINNESOTA

PRESIDENT 1936

1930 Census Population	County	Total Vote	Republican	Democratic	Other	Rep.-Dem. Plurality	Percentage Total Vote Rep.	Percentage Total Vote Dem.	Percentage Major Vote Rep.	Percentage Major Vote Dem.
13,085	POPE	5,242	1,869	3,200	173	1,331 D	35.7%	61.0%	36.9%	63.1%
286,721	RAMSEY	130,728	30,553	86,286	13,889	55,733 D	23.4%	66.0%	26.1%	73.9%
6,887	RED LAKE	2,653	487	2,057	109	1,570 D	18.4%	77.5%	19.1%	80.9%
20,620	REDWOOD	8,972	3,286	4,965	721	1,679 D	36.6%	55.3%	39.8%	60.2%
23,645	RENVILLE	9,453	3,049	5,344	1,060	2,295 D	32.3%	56.5%	36.3%	63.7%
29,974	RICE	12,327	4,888	5,928	1,511	1,040 D	39.7%	48.1%	45.2%	54.8%
10,962	ROCK	4,838	1,752	2,910	176	1,158 D	36.2%	60.1%	37.6%	62.4%
12,621	ROSEAU	5,266	1,326	3,761	179	2,435 D	25.2%	71.4%	26.1%	73.9%
204,596	ST. LOUIS	93,510	22,332	69,365	1,813	47,033 D	23.9%	74.2%	24.4%	75.6%
14,116	SCOTT	6,559	1,528	3,861	1,170	2,333 D	23.3%	58.9%	28.4%	71.6%
9,709	SHERBURNE	3,737	1,623	1,881	233	258 D	43.4%	50.3%	46.3%	53.7%
15,865	SIBLEY	6,735	2,184	4,140	411	1,956 D	32.4%	61.5%	34.5%	65.5%
62,121	STEARNS	22,580	5,262	12,760	4,558	7,498 D	23.3%	56.5%	29.2%	70.8%
18,475	STEELE	8,224	3,373	4,481	370	1,108 D	41.0%	54.5%	42.9%	57.1%
10,185	STEVENS	3,958	1,431	2,352	175	921 D	36.2%	59.4%	37.8%	62.2%
14,735	SWIFT	5,986	1,618	3,749	619	2,131 D	27.0%	62.6%	30.1%	69.9%
26,170	TODD	10,002	3,780	5,627	595	1,847 D	37.8%	56.3%	40.2%	59.8%
7,938	TRAVERSE	3,144	761	2,297	86	1,536 D	24.2%	73.1%	24.9%	75.1%
17,613	WABASHA	7,697	2,663	4,122	912	1,459 D	34.6%	53.6%	39.2%	60.8%
10,990	WADENA	4,649	1,898	2,605	146	707 D	40.8%	56.0%	42.1%	57.9%
14,412	WASECA	6,348	2,482	3,520	346	1,038 D	39.1%	55.5%	41.4%	58.6%
24,753	WASHINGTON	11,710	3,863	6,768	1,079	2,905 D	33.0%	57.8%	36.3%	63.7%
12,802	WATONWAN	5,772	1,930	3,668	174	1,738 D	33.4%	63.5%	34.5%	65.5%
9,791	WILKIN	3,938	1,278	2,428	232	1,150 D	32.5%	61.7%	34.5%	65.5%
35,144	WINONA	15,551	5,353	9,268	930	3,915 D	34.4%	59.6%	36.6%	63.4%
27,119	WRIGHT	11,351	4,087	5,363	1,901	1,276 D	36.0%	47.2%	43.2%	56.8%
16,625	YELLOW MEDICINE	6,679	2,029	3,921	729	1,892 D	30.4%	58.7%	34.1%	65.9%
2,563,953	TOTAL	1,129,975	350,461	698,811	80,703	348,350 D	31.0%	61.8%	33.4%	66.6%

MINNESOTA

PRESIDENT 1932

1930 Census Population	County	Total Vote	Republican	Democratic	Other	Rep.-Dem. Plurality	Percentage: Total Vote		Percentage: Major Vote	
							Rep.	Dem.	Rep.	Dem.
15,009	AITKIN	5,743	2,341	2,945	457	604 D	40.8%	51.3%	44.3%	55.7%
18,415	ANOKA	7,152	2,718	4,253	181	1,535 D	38.0%	59.5%	39.0%	61.0%
22,503	BECKER	8,210	2,299	5,547	364	3,248 D	28.0%	67.6%	29.3%	70.7%
20,707	BELTRAMI	7,222	2,318	4,386	518	2,068 D	32.1%	60.7%	34.6%	65.4%
15,056	BENTON	5,350	1,329	3,901	120	2,572 D	24.8%	72.9%	25.4%	74.6%
9,838	BIG STONE	4,136	868	3,200	68	2,332 D	21.0%	77.4%	21.3%	78.7%
33,847	BLUE EARTH	13,691	5,550	7,925	216	2,375 D	40.5%	57.9%	41.2%	58.8%
23,428	BROWN	8,955	2,027	6,716	212	4,689 D	22.6%	75.0%	23.2%	76.8%
21,232	CARLTON	7,838	3,336	3,586	916	250 D	42.6%	45.8%	48.2%	51.8%
16,936	CARVER	6,902	2,508	4,328	66	1,820 D	36.3%	62.7%	36.7%	63.3%
15,591	CASS	6,043	2,302	3,494	247	1,192 D	38.1%	57.8%	39.7%	60.3%
15,762	CHIPPEWA	5,986	1,940	3,888	158	1,948 D	32.4%	65.0%	33.3%	66.7%
13,189	CHISAGO	5,755	2,524	3,047	184	523 D	43.9%	52.9%	45.3%	54.7%
23,120	CLAY	8,764	2,556	5,938	270	3,382 D	29.2%	67.8%	30.1%	69.9%
9,546	CLEARWATER	3,692	845	2,688	159	1,843 D	22.9%	72.8%	23.9%	76.1%
2,435	COOK	966	418	492	56	74 D	43.3%	50.9%	45.9%	54.1%
14,782	COTTONWOOD	4,876	1,921	2,877	78	956 D	39.4%	59.0%	40.0%	60.0%
25,627	CROW WING	9,578	3,991	5,068	519	1,077 D	41.7%	52.9%	44.1%	55.9%
34,592	DAKOTA	13,635	4,439	8,958	238	4,519 D	32.6%	65.7%	33.1%	66.9%
12,127	DODGE	4,891	2,129	2,675	87	546 D	43.5%	54.7%	44.3%	55.7%
18,813	DOUGLAS	7,656	2,325	5,101	230	2,776 D	30.4%	66.6%	31.3%	68.7%
21,642	FARIBAULT	8,892	4,148	4,590	154	442 D	46.6%	51.6%	47.5%	52.5%
24,748	FILLMORE	10,325	4,979	5,166	180	187 D	48.2%	50.0%	49.1%	50.9%
28,741	FREEBORN	11,052	4,931	5,838	283	907 D	44.6%	52.8%	45.8%	54.2%
31,317	GOODHUE	13,310	5,486	7,450	374	1,964 D	41.2%	56.0%	42.4%	57.6%
9,558	GRANT	3,935	1,148	2,702	85	1,554 D	29.2%	68.7%	29.8%	70.2%
517,785	HENNEPIN	217,566	91,087	119,234	7,245	28,147 D	41.9%	54.8%	43.3%	56.7%
13,845	HOUSTON	5,478	2,335	3,052	91	717 D	42.6%	55.7%	43.3%	56.7%
9,596	HUBBARD	3,751	1,349	2,230	172	881 D	36.0%	59.5%	37.7%	62.3%
12,081	ISANTI	4,877	1,484	3,147	246	1,663 D	30.4%	64.5%	32.0%	68.0%
27,224	ITASCA	10,237	3,782	5,616	839	1,834 D	36.9%	54.9%	40.2%	59.8%
15,863	JACKSON	5,761	1,524	4,129	108	2,605 D	26.5%	71.7%	27.0%	73.0%
8,558	KANABEC	3,605	1,268	2,106	231	838 D	35.2%	58.4%	37.6%	62.4%
23,574	KANDIYOHI	8,901	2,674	5,813	414	3,139 D	30.0%	65.3%	31.5%	68.5%
9,688	KITTSON	3,416	950	2,332	134	1,382 D	27.8%	68.3%	28.9%	71.1%
14,078	KOOCHICHING	4,974	1,427	3,148	399	1,721 D	28.7%	63.3%	31.2%	68.8%
15,398	LAC QUI PARLE	6,000	1,911	3,992	97	2,081 D	31.9%	66.5%	32.4%	67.6%
7,068	LAKE	3,002	1,290	1,059	653	231 R	43.0%	35.3%	54.9%	45.1%
4,194	LAKE OF THE WOODS	1,567	369	972	226	603 D	23.5%	62.0%	27.5%	72.5%
17,990	LE SUEUR	8,100	2,121	5,878	101	3,757 D	26.2%	72.6%	26.5%	73.5%
11,303	LINCOLN	4,064	974	2,963	127	1,989 D	24.0%	72.9%	24.7%	75.3%
19,326	LYON	7,383	2,264	4,989	130	2,725 D	30.7%	67.6%	31.2%	68.8%
20,522	MCLEOD	7,608	2,293	5,187	128	2,894 D	30.1%	68.2%	30.7%	69.3%
6,153	MAHNOMEN	2,069	264	1,734	71	1,470 D	12.8%	83.8%	13.2%	86.8%
17,003	MARSHALL	5,463	1,866	3,259	338	1,393 D	34.2%	59.7%	36.4%	63.6%
22,401	MARTIN	7,851	3,004	4,731	116	1,727 D	38.3%	60.3%	38.8%	61.2%
17,914	MEEKER	7,147	2,273	4,723	151	2,450 D	31.8%	66.1%	32.5%	67.5%
14,076	MILLE LACS	5,836	1,986	3,538	312	1,552 D	34.0%	60.6%	36.0%	64.0%
25,442	MORRISON	9,123	2,198	6,712	213	4,514 D	24.1%	73.6%	24.7%	75.3%
28,065	MOWER	10,599	4,005	6,421	173	2,416 D	37.8%	60.6%	38.4%	61.6%
13,902	MURRAY	4,658	1,314	3,264	80	1,950 D	28.2%	70.1%	28.7%	71.3%
16,550	NICOLLET	6,328	2,217	3,960	151	1,743 D	35.0%	62.6%	35.9%	64.1%
18,618	NOBLES	6,838	2,417	4,343	78	1,926 D	35.3%	63.5%	35.8%	64.2%
14,061	NORMAN	5,234	1,313	3,601	320	2,288 D	25.1%	68.8%	26.7%	73.3%
35,426	OLMSTED	12,874	5,254	7,340	280	2,086 D	40.8%	57.0%	41.7%	58.3%
51,006	OTTER TAIL	16,964	7,416	8,805	743	1,389 D	43.7%	51.9%	45.7%	54.3%
10,487	PENNINGTON	4,310	1,212	2,743	355	1,531 D	28.1%	63.6%	30.6%	69.4%
20,264	PINE	7,801	2,304	4,862	635	2,558 D	29.5%	62.3%	32.2%	67.8%
12,238	PIPESTONE	4,578	1,509	2,996	73	1,487 D	33.0%	65.4%	33.5%	66.5%
36,019	POLK	13,190	3,604	8,751	835	5,147 D	27.3%	66.3%	29.2%	70.8%

MINNESOTA

PRESIDENT 1932

1930 Census Population	County	Total Vote	Republican	Democratic	Other	Rep.-Dem. Plurality	Percentage Total Vote Rep.	Total Vote Dem.	Major Vote Rep.	Major Vote Dem.
13,085	POPE	5,365	1,688	3,571	106	1,883 D	31.5%	66.6%	32.1%	67.9%
286,721	RAMSEY	107,980	38,589	66,128	3,263	27,539 D	35.7%	61.2%	36.9%	63.1%
6,887	RED LAKE	2,341	351	1,893	97	1,542 D	15.0%	80.9%	15.6%	84.4%
20,620	REDWOOD	7,480	2,634	4,727	119	2,093 D	35.2%	63.2%	35.8%	64.2%
23,645	RENVILLE	8,761	2,631	5,967	163	3,336 D	30.0%	68.1%	30.6%	69.4%
29,974	RICE	11,215	4,743	6,289	183	1,546 D	42.3%	56.1%	43.0%	57.0%
10,962	ROCK	4,201	1,452	2,695	54	1,243 D	34.6%	64.2%	35.0%	65.0%
12,621	ROSEAU	4,224	1,078	2,805	341	1,727 D	25.5%	66.4%	27.8%	72.2%
204,596	ST. LOUIS	83,729	34,883	40,181	8,665	5,298 D	41.7%	48.0%	46.5%	53.5%
14,116	SCOTT	6,049	1,134	4,878	37	3,744 D	18.7%	80.6%	18.9%	81.1%
9,709	SHERBURNE	3,625	1,601	1,938	86	337 D	44.2%	53.5%	45.2%	54.8%
15,865	SIBLEY	6,236	1,398	4,756	82	3,358 D	22.4%	76.3%	22.7%	77.3%
62,121	STEARNS	23,050	4,499	18,293	258	13,794 D	19.5%	79.4%	19.7%	80.3%
18,475	STEELE	7,790	3,365	4,318	107	953 D	43.2%	55.4%	43.8%	56.2%
10,185	STEVENS	3,990	1,396	2,552	42	1,156 D	35.0%	64.0%	35.4%	64.6%
14,735	SWIFT	5,782	1,308	4,339	135	3,031 D	22.6%	75.0%	23.2%	76.8%
26,170	TODD	9,387	3,114	6,023	250	2,909 D	33.2%	64.2%	34.1%	65.9%
7,938	TRAVERSE	3,282	608	2,633	41	2,025 D	18.5%	80.2%	18.8%	81.2%
17,613	WABASHA	6,978	2,319	4,540	119	2,221 D	33.2%	65.1%	33.8%	66.2%
10,990	WADENA	4,030	1,585	2,300	145	715 D	39.3%	57.1%	40.8%	59.2%
14,412	WASECA	5,903	2,012	3,805	86	1,793 D	34.1%	64.5%	34.6%	65.4%
24,753	WASHINGTON	10,656	3,996	6,413	247	2,417 D	37.5%	60.2%	38.4%	61.6%
12,802	WATONWAN	4,843	1,919	2,795	129	876 D	39.6%	57.7%	40.7%	59.3%
9,791	WILKIN	3,662	1,126	2,488	48	1,362 D	30.7%	67.9%	31.2%	68.8%
35,144	WINONA	13,308	4,751	8,305	252	3,554 D	35.7%	62.4%	36.4%	63.6%
27,119	WRIGHT	10,830	3,406	7,205	219	3,799 D	31.4%	66.5%	32.1%	67.9%
16,625	YELLOW MEDICINE	6,438	1,739	4,580	119	2,841 D	27.0%	71.1%	27.5%	72.5%
2,563,953	TOTAL	1,002,843	363,959	600,806	38,078	236,847 D	36.3%	59.9%	37.7%	62.3%

MINNESOTA

PRESIDENT 1928

1920 Census Population	County	Total Vote	Republican	Democratic	Other	Rep.-Dem. Plurality	Percentage Total Vote Rep.	Percentage Total Vote Dem.	Percentage Major Vote Rep.	Percentage Major Vote Dem.
15,043	AITKIN	5,636	3,951	1,428	257	2,523 R	70.1%	25.3%	73.5%	26.5%
15,626	ANOKA	6,462	3,816	2,571	75	1,245 R	59.1%	39.8%	59.7%	40.3%
22,851	BECKER	7,703	4,273	3,253	177	1,020 R	55.5%	42.2%	56.8%	43.2%
27,079	BELTRAMI	6,522	4,062	2,221	239	1,841 R	62.3%	34.1%	64.7%	35.3%
14,073	BENTON	5,126	2,373	2,732	21	359 D	46.3%	53.3%	46.5%	53.5%
9,766	BIG STONE	3,799	1,641	2,133	25	492 D	43.2%	56.1%	43.5%	56.5%
31,477	BLUE EARTH	13,376	8,120	5,177	79	2,943 R	60.7%	38.7%	61.1%	38.9%
22,421	BROWN	9,016	3,611	5,341	64	1,730 D	40.1%	59.2%	40.3%	59.7%
19,391	CARLTON	7,158	4,582	2,138	438	2,444 R	64.0%	29.9%	68.2%	31.8%
16,946	CARVER	6,901	3,983	2,885	33	1,098 R	57.7%	41.8%	58.0%	42.0%
15,897	CASS	5,642	3,781	1,747	114	2,034 R	67.0%	31.0%	68.4%	31.6%
15,720	CHIPPEWA	5,651	3,547	2,032	72	1,515 R	62.8%	36.0%	63.6%	36.4%
14,445	CHISAGO	5,582	4,215	1,297	70	2,918 R	75.5%	23.2%	76.5%	23.5%
21,780	CLAY	8,272	5,057	3,128	87	1,929 R	61.1%	37.8%	61.8%	38.2%
8,569	CLEARWATER	3,163	1,898	1,189	76	709 R	60.0%	37.6%	61.5%	38.5%
1,841	COOK	839	609	219	11	390 R	72.6%	26.1%	73.6%	26.4%
14,570	COTTONWOOD	5,048	3,405	1,604	39	1,801 R	67.5%	31.8%	68.0%	32.0%
24,566	CROW WING	9,483	6,436	2,851	196	3,585 R	67.9%	30.1%	69.3%	30.7%
28,967	DAKOTA	13,323	6,019	7,215	89	1,196 D	45.2%	54.2%	45.5%	54.5%
12,552	DODGE	4,791	3,569	1,196	26	2,373 R	74.5%	25.0%	74.9%	25.1%
19,039	DOUGLAS	7,191	4,262	2,829	100	1,433 R	59.3%	39.3%	60.1%	39.9%
20,998	FARIBAULT	8,506	5,885	2,545	76	3,340 R	69.2%	29.9%	69.8%	30.2%
25,330	FILLMORE	9,925	7,719	2,143	63	5,576 R	77.8%	21.6%	78.3%	21.7%
24,692	FREEBORN	10,750	7,815	2,859	76	4,956 R	72.7%	26.6%	73.2%	26.8%
30,799	GOODHUE	13,372	9,752	3,520	100	6,232 R	72.9%	26.3%	73.5%	26.5%
9,788	GRANT	3,786	2,057	1,687	42	370 R	54.3%	44.6%	54.9%	45.1%
415,419	HENNEPIN	208,447	125,472	80,851	2,124	44,621 R	60.2%	38.8%	60.8%	39.2%
14,013	HOUSTON	5,573	3,615	1,937	21	1,678 R	64.9%	34.8%	65.1%	34.9%
10,136	HUBBARD	3,484	2,291	1,120	73	1,171 R	65.8%	32.1%	67.2%	32.8%
13,278	ISANTI	4,410	3,137	1,191	82	1,946 R	71.1%	27.0%	72.5%	27.5%
23,876	ITASCA	8,656	5,103	3,122	431	1,981 R	59.0%	36.1%	62.0%	38.0%
15,955	JACKSON	5,628	3,099	2,503	26	596 R	55.1%	44.5%	55.3%	44.7%
9,086	KANABEC	3,482	2,380	1,040	62	1,340 R	68.4%	29.9%	69.6%	30.4%
22,060	KANDIYOHI	8,522	5,780	2,481	261	3,299 R	67.8%	29.1%	70.0%	30.0%
10,638	KITTSON	3,445	1,957	1,383	105	574 R	56.8%	40.1%	58.6%	41.4%
13,520	KOOCHICHING	4,843	2,599	2,110	134	489 R	53.7%	43.6%	55.2%	44.8%
15,554	LAC QUI PARLE	5,710	3,406	2,245	59	1,161 R	59.6%	39.3%	60.3%	39.7%
8,251	LAKE	2,765	2,014	618	133	1,396 R	72.8%	22.4%	76.5%	23.5%
	LAKE OF THE WOODS	1,508	781	671	56	110 R	51.8%	44.5%	53.8%	46.2%
17,870	LE SUEUR	8,054	3,401	4,615	38	1,214 D	42.2%	57.3%	42.4%	57.6%
11,268	LINCOLN	4,050	1,952	2,064	34	112 D	48.2%	51.0%	48.6%	51.4%
18,837	LYON	7,388	4,058	3,274	56	784 R	54.9%	44.3%	55.3%	44.7%
20,444	MCLEOD	7,757	4,252	3,445	60	807 R	54.8%	44.4%	55.2%	44.8%
6,197	MAHNOMEN	2,027	606	1,378	43	772 D	29.9%	68.0%	30.5%	69.5%
19,443	MARSHALL	6,070	3,738	2,200	132	1,538 R	61.6%	36.2%	63.0%	37.0%
21,085	MARTIN	7,972	5,110	2,822	40	2,288 R	64.1%	35.4%	64.4%	35.6%
18,103	MEEKER	7,002	4,175	2,761	66	1,414 R	59.6%	39.4%	60.2%	39.8%
14,180	MILLE LACS	5,552	3,998	1,436	118	2,562 R	72.0%	25.9%	73.6%	26.4%
25,841	MORRISON	9,119	3,846	5,222	51	1,376 D	42.2%	57.3%	42.4%	57.6%
25,993	MOWER	9,842	6,209	3,587	46	2,622 R	63.1%	36.4%	63.4%	36.6%
13,631	MURRAY	4,709	2,602	2,078	29	524 R	55.3%	44.1%	55.6%	44.4%
15,036	NICOLLET	6,136	3,628	2,466	42	1,162 R	59.1%	40.2%	59.5%	40.5%
17,917	NOBLES	6,563	3,676	2,862	25	814 R	56.0%	43.6%	56.2%	43.8%
14,880	NORMAN	4,909	3,308	1,401	200	1,907 R	67.4%	28.5%	70.2%	29.8%
28,014	OLMSTED	13,098	8,334	4,720	44	3,614 R	63.6%	36.0%	63.8%	36.2%
50,818	OTTER TAIL	17,025	11,624	4,990	411	6,634 R	68.3%	29.3%	70.0%	30.0%
12,091	PENNINGTON	3,838	2,506	1,198	134	1,308 R	65.3%	31.2%	67.7%	32.3%
21,117	PINE	7,568	4,278	3,185	105	1,093 R	56.5%	42.1%	57.3%	42.7%
12,050	PIPESTONE	4,207	2,578	1,591	38	987 R	61.3%	37.8%	61.8%	38.2%
37,090	POLK	12,866	7,215	5,357	294	1,858 R	56.1%	41.6%	57.4%	42.6%

MINNESOTA

PRESIDENT 1928

1920 Census Population	County	Total Vote	Republican	Democratic	Other	Rep.-Dem. Plurality	Percentage Total Vote Rep.	Percentage Total Vote Dem.	Percentage Major Vote Rep.	Percentage Major Vote Dem.
13,631	POPE	5,114	3,382	1,667	65	1,715 R	66.1%	32.6%	67.0%	33.0%
244,554	RAMSEY	110,910	53,054	56,807	1,049	3,753 D	47.8%	51.2%	48.3%	51.7%
7,263	RED LAKE	2,256	712	1,507	37	795 D	31.6%	66.8%	32.1%	67.9%
20,908	REDWOOD	8,089	5,111	2,899	79	2,212 R	63.2%	35.8%	63.8%	36.2%
23,634	RENVILLE	8,932	5,107	3,731	94	1,376 R	57.2%	41.8%	57.8%	42.2%
28,307	RICE	11,639	6,576	5,014	49	1,562 R	56.5%	43.1%	56.7%	43.3%
10,965	ROCK	4,053	2,433	1,607	13	826 R	60.0%	39.6%	60.2%	39.8%
13,305	ROSEAU	4,145	2,618	1,342	185	1,276 R	63.2%	32.4%	66.1%	33.9%
206,391	ST. LOUIS	72,517	44,331	25,401	2,785	18,930 R	61.1%	35.0%	63.6%	36.4%
14,245	SCOTT	6,162	1,732	4,419	11	2,687 D	28.1%	71.7%	28.2%	71.8%
9,651	SHERBURNE	3,528	2,437	1,064	27	1,373 R	69.1%	30.2%	69.6%	30.4%
15,635	SIBLEY	5,901	3,301	2,553	47	748 R	55.9%	43.3%	56.4%	43.6%
55,741	STEARNS	22,615	6,459	16,104	52	9,645 D	28.6%	71.2%	28.6%	71.4%
18,061	STEELE	7,595	4,744	2,826	25	1,918 R	62.5%	37.2%	62.7%	37.3%
9,778	STEVENS	3,748	2,275	1,457	16	818 R	60.7%	38.9%	61.0%	39.0%
15,093	SWIFT	5,613	2,791	2,733	89	58 R	49.7%	48.7%	50.5%	49.5%
26,059	TODD	9,500	5,682	3,733	85	1,949 R	59.8%	39.3%	60.4%	39.6%
7,943	TRAVERSE	3,130	1,214	1,899	17	685 D	38.8%	60.7%	39.0%	61.0%
17,919	WABASHA	7,063	3,944	3,087	32	857 R	55.8%	43.7%	56.1%	43.9%
10,699	WADENA	4,044	2,592	1,343	109	1,249 R	64.1%	33.2%	65.9%	34.1%
14,133	WASECA	5,710	3,251	2,418	41	833 R	56.9%	42.3%	57.3%	42.7%
23,761	WASHINGTON	10,351	6,113	4,158	80	1,955 R	59.1%	40.2%	59.5%	40.5%
12,457	WATONWAN	4,744	3,306	1,412	26	1,894 R	69.7%	29.8%	70.1%	29.9%
10,187	WILKIN	3,477	1,874	1,578	25	296 R	53.9%	45.4%	54.3%	45.7%
33,653	WINONA	14,031	7,459	6,484	88	975 R	53.2%	46.2%	53.5%	46.5%
28,685	WRIGHT	10,626	6,011	4,483	132	1,528 R	56.6%	42.2%	57.3%	42.7%
16,550	YELLOW MEDICINE	6,235	3,302	2,861	72	441 R	53.0%	45.9%	53.6%	46.4%
2,387,125	TOTAL	970,976	560,977	396,451	13,548	164,526 R	57.8%	40.8%	58.6%	41.4%

MINNESOTA

PRESIDENT 1924

1920 Census Population	County	Total Vote	Republican	Democratic	Progressive	Other	Plurality	Percentage Total Vote Rep.	Dem.	Prog.
15,043	AITKIN	5,068	2,720	212	1,959	177	761 R	53.7%	4.2%	38.7%
15,626	ANOKA	5,505	3,146	458	1,883	18	1,263 R	57.1%	8.3%	34.2%
22,851	BECKER	6,452	2,936	429	2,963	124	27 P	45.5%	6.6%	45.9%
27,079	BELTRAMI	6,404	2,960	323	3,053	68	93 P	46.2%	5.0%	47.7%
14,073	BENTON	3,888	1,629	572	1,644	43	15 P	41.9%	14.7%	42.3%
9,766	BIG STONE	3,303	1,524	260	1,508	11	16 R	46.1%	7.9%	45.7%
31,477	BLUE EARTH	12,295	6,773	1,123	4,360	39	2,413 R	55.1%	9.1%	35.5%
22,421	BROWN	7,076	2,255	270	4,515	36	2,260 P	31.9%	3.8%	63.8%
19,391	CARLTON	6,314	3,142	303	2,552	317	590 R	49.8%	4.8%	40.4%
16,946	CARVER	5,508	2,214	358	2,907	29	693 P	40.2%	6.5%	52.8%
15,897	CASS	5,173	2,800	270	2,052	51	748 R	54.1%	5.2%	39.7%
15,720	CHIPPEWA	5,060	2,140	140	2,761	19	621 P	42.3%	2.8%	54.6%
14,445	CHISAGO	5,072	2,678	135	2,236	23	442 R	52.8%	2.7%	44.1%
21,780	CLAY	6,916	3,081	439	3,357	39	276 P	44.5%	6.3%	48.5%
8,569	CLEARWATER	2,717	1,020	86	1,592	19	572 P	37.5%	3.2%	58.6%
1,841	COOK	693	471	29	189	4	282 R	68.0%	4.2%	27.3%
14,570	COTTONWOOD	4,776	2,722	217	1,818	19	904 R	57.0%	4.5%	38.1%
24,566	CROW WING	8,449	4,230	417	3,725	77	505 R	50.1%	4.9%	44.1%
28,967	DAKOTA	9,284	3,931	929	4,378	46	447 P	42.3%	10.0%	47.2%
12,552	DODGE	4,329	2,856	215	1,239	19	1,617 R	66.0%	5.0%	28.6%
19,039	DOUGLAS	6,192	2,424	315	3,430	23	1,006 P	39.1%	5.1%	55.4%
20,998	FARIBAULT	8,057	4,682	578	2,776	21	1,906 R	58.1%	7.2%	34.5%
25,330	FILLMORE	8,845	5,550	460	2,797	38	2,753 R	62.7%	5.2%	31.6%
24,692	FREEBORN	9,630	6,139	480	2,991	20	3,148 R	63.7%	5.0%	31.1%
30,799	GOODHUE	11,599	6,849	615	4,113	22	2,736 R	59.0%	5.3%	35.5%
9,788	GRANT	3,402	1,674	118	1,601	9	73 R	49.2%	3.5%	47.1%
415,419	HENNEPIN	171,327	101,120	10,806	58,846	555	42,274 R	59.0%	6.3%	34.3%
14,013	HOUSTON	5,192	2,782	402	1,992	16	790 R	53.6%	7.7%	38.4%
10,136	HUBBARD	3,259	1,884	191	1,166	18	718 R	57.8%	5.9%	35.8%
13,278	ISANTI	4,016	1,588	79	2,332	17	744 P	39.5%	2.0%	58.1%
23,876	ITASCA	8,255	4,961	496	2,532	266	2,429 R	60.1%	6.0%	30.7%
15,955	JACKSON	5,637	2,760	407	2,446	24	314 R	49.0%	7.2%	43.4%
9,086	KANABEC	3,168	1,507	128	1,521	12	14 P	47.6%	4.0%	48.0%
22,060	KANDIYOHI	8,022	3,222	222	4,552	26	1,330 P	40.2%	2.8%	56.7%
10,638	KITTSON	3,109	1,333	249	1,503	24	170 P	42.9%	8.0%	48.3%
13,520	KOOCHICHING	4,105	1,536	222	2,304	43	768 P	37.4%	5.4%	56.1%
15,554	LAC QUI PARLE	5,473	2,860	106	2,481	26	379 R	52.3%	1.9%	45.3%
8,251	LAKE	2,683	1,251	60	1,319	53	68 P	46.6%	2.2%	49.2%
	LAKE OF THE WOODS	1,646	703	92	832	19	129 P	42.7%	5.6%	50.5%
17,870	LE SUEUR	6,481	2,475	1,199	2,756	51	281 P	38.2%	18.5%	42.5%
11,268	LINCOLN	3,450	1,657	252	1,511	30	146 R	48.0%	7.3%	43.8%
18,837	LYON	6,553	3,519	334	2,674	26	845 R	53.7%	5.1%	40.8%
20,444	MCLEOD	6,329	2,841	563	2,893	32	52 P	44.9%	8.9%	45.7%
6,197	MAHNOMEN	1,867	629	122	1,094	22	465 P	33.7%	6.5%	58.6%
19,443	MARSHALL	5,246	2,100	290	2,812	44	712 P	40.0%	5.5%	53.6%
21,085	MARTIN	7,535	4,238	751	2,529	17	1,709 R	56.2%	10.0%	33.6%
18,103	MEEKER	6,064	2,757	365	2,910	32	153 P	45.5%	6.0%	48.0%
14,180	MILLE LACS	4,946	2,413	167	2,348	18	65 R	48.8%	3.4%	47.5%
25,841	MORRISON	7,514	3,128	769	3,546	71	418 P	41.6%	10.2%	47.2%
25,993	MOWER	9,088	5,061	564	3,436	27	1,625 R	55.7%	6.2%	37.8%
13,631	MURRAY	4,441	2,034	334	2,048	25	14 P	45.8%	7.5%	46.1%
15,036	NICOLLET	5,031	2,518	287	2,208	18	310 R	50.0%	5.7%	43.9%
17,917	NOBLES	6,150	2,835	421	2,875	19	40 P	46.1%	6.8%	46.7%
14,880	NORMAN	4,363	1,997	171	2,174	21	177 P	45.8%	3.9%	49.8%
28,014	OLMSTED	10,127	5,722	857	3,508	40	2,214 R	56.5%	8.5%	34.6%
50,818	OTTER TAIL	13,629	7,557	568	5,346	158	2,211 R	55.4%	4.2%	39.2%
12,091	PENNINGTON	3,609	1,126	146	2,320	17	1,194 P	31.2%	4.0%	64.3%
21,117	PINE	6,438	2,706	469	3,196	67	490 P	42.0%	7.3%	49.6%
12,050	PIPESTONE	4,290	2,066	219	1,984	21	82 R	48.2%	5.1%	46.2%
37,090	POLK	11,440	5,027	663	5,695	55	668 P	43.9%	5.8%	49.8%

MINNESOTA

PRESIDENT 1924

1920 Census Population	County	Total Vote	Republican	Democratic	Progressive	Other	Plurality	Percentage Total Vote Rep.	Dem.	Prog.
13,631	POPE	4,531	2,079	151	2,284	17	205 P	45.9%	3.3%	50.4%
244,554	RAMSEY	83,019	39,566	8,407	34,684	362	4,882 R	47.7%	10.1%	41.8%
7,263	RED LAKE	1,827	643	213	956	15	313 P	35.2%	11.7%	52.3%
20,908	REDWOOD	6,597	3,342	443	2,778	34	564 R	50.7%	6.7%	42.1%
23,634	RENVILLE	7,981	3,405	641	3,898	37	493 P	42.7%	8.0%	48.8%
28,307	RICE	9,603	5,883	1,199	2,454	67	3,429 R	61.3%	12.5%	25.6%
10,965	ROCK	3,973	2,065	261	1,637	10	428 R	52.0%	6.6%	41.2%
13,305	ROSEAU	3,334	1,300	148	1,862	24	562 P	39.0%	4.4%	55.8%
206,391	ST. LOUIS	64,623	37,033	2,577	23,166	1,847	13,867 R	57.3%	4.0%	35.8%
14,245	SCOTT	4,520	1,324	829	2,327	40	1,003 P	29.3%	18.3%	51.5%
9,651	SHERBURNE	3,081	1,961	180	925	15	1,036 R	63.6%	5.8%	30.0%
15,635	SIBLEY	5,060	1,749	341	2,935	35	1,186 P	34.6%	6.7%	58.0%
55,741	STEARNS	17,314	6,469	1,354	9,385	106	2,916 P	37.4%	7.8%	54.2%
18,061	STEELE	6,047	3,598	796	1,632	21	1,966 R	59.5%	13.2%	27.0%
9,778	STEVENS	3,170	1,553	238	1,362	17	191 R	49.0%	7.5%	43.0%
15,093	SWIFT	4,922	1,654	334	2,918	16	1,264 P	33.6%	6.8%	59.3%
26,059	TODD	8,379	4,441	557	3,339	42	1,102 R	53.0%	6.6%	39.8%
7,943	TRAVERSE	2,548	1,002	202	1,330	14	328 P	39.3%	7.9%	52.2%
17,919	WABASHA	6,307	2,834	644	2,811	18	23 R	44.9%	10.2%	44.6%
10,699	WADENA	3,465	1,900	182	1,265	118	635 R	54.8%	5.3%	36.5%
14,133	WASECA	5,605	2,081	442	3,057	25	976 P	37.1%	7.9%	54.5%
23,761	WASHINGTON	8,553	4,482	699	3,351	21	1,131 R	52.4%	8.2%	39.2%
12,457	WATONWAN	4,288	2,297	279	1,703	9	594 R	53.6%	6.5%	39.7%
10,187	WILKIN	2,845	1,342	245	1,250	8	92 R	47.2%	8.6%	43.9%
33,653	WINONA	13,026	5,670	1,111	6,183	62	513 P	43.5%	8.5%	47.5%
28,685	WRIGHT	9,151	4,349	567	4,172	63	177 R	47.5%	6.2%	45.6%
16,550	YELLOW MEDICINE	5,887	2,278	151	3,440	18	1,162 P	38.7%	2.6%	58.4%
2,387,125	TOTAL	822,146	420,759	55,913	339,192	6,282	81,567 R	51.2%	6.8%	41.3%

MINNESOTA

PRESIDENT 1920

1920 Census Population	County	Total Vote	Republican	Democratic	Other	Rep.-Dem. Plurality	Percentage: Total Vote Rep.	Total Vote Dem.	Major Vote Rep.	Major Vote Dem.
15,043	AITKIN	4,181	2,933	613	635	2,320 R	70.2%	14.7%	82.7%	17.3%
15,626	ANOKA	4,859	3,505	865	489	2,640 R	72.1%	17.8%	80.2%	19.8%
22,851	BECKER	6,349	4,811	901	637	3,910 R	75.8%	14.2%	84.2%	15.8%
27,079	BELTRAMI	7,375	4,518	1,427	1,430	3,091 R	61.3%	19.3%	76.0%	24.0%
14,073	BENTON	3,704	2,920	554	230	2,366 R	78.8%	15.0%	84.1%	15.9%
9,766	BIG STONE	3,090	2,415	451	224	1,964 R	78.2%	14.6%	84.3%	15.7%
31,477	BLUE EARTH	11,251	8,894	1,974	383	6,920 R	79.1%	17.5%	81.8%	18.2%
22,421	BROWN	7,240	5,841	796	603	5,045 R	80.7%	11.0%	88.0%	12.0%
19,391	CARLTON	4,764	2,833	1,152	779	1,681 R	59.5%	24.2%	71.1%	28.9%
16,946	CARVER	5,810	5,073	562	175	4,511 R	87.3%	9.7%	90.0%	10.0%
15,897	CASS	4,598	3,242	710	646	2,532 R	70.5%	15.4%	82.0%	18.0%
15,720	CHIPPEWA	5,064	3,532	960	572	2,572 R	69.7%	19.0%	78.6%	21.4%
14,445	CHISAGO	5,450	4,361	484	605	3,877 R	80.0%	8.9%	90.0%	10.0%
21,780	CLAY	6,771	4,943	1,335	493	3,608 R	73.0%	19.7%	78.7%	21.3%
8,569	CLEARWATER	2,528	1,788	340	400	1,448 R	70.7%	13.4%	84.0%	16.0%
1,841	COOK	641	467	98	76	369 R	72.9%	15.3%	82.7%	17.3%
14,570	COTTONWOOD	4,500	3,882	451	167	3,431 R	86.3%	10.0%	89.6%	10.4%
24,566	CROW WING	7,481	5,262	1,077	1,142	4,185 R	70.3%	14.4%	83.0%	17.0%
28,967	DAKOTA	8,086	5,373	2,190	523	3,183 R	66.4%	27.1%	71.0%	29.0%
12,552	DODGE	4,060	3,386	516	158	2,870 R	83.4%	12.7%	86.8%	13.2%
19,039	DOUGLAS	6,696	4,428	733	1,535	3,695 R	66.1%	10.9%	85.8%	14.2%
20,998	FARIBAULT	7,775	6,687	869	219	5,818 R	86.0%	11.2%	88.5%	11.5%
25,330	FILLMORE	8,544	7,341	899	304	6,442 R	85.9%	10.5%	89.1%	10.9%
24,692	FREEBORN	8,263	6,772	1,131	360	5,641 R	82.0%	13.7%	85.7%	14.3%
30,799	GOODHUE	10,968	9,330	1,118	520	8,212 R	85.1%	10.2%	89.3%	10.7%
9,788	GRANT	3,202	2,427	533	242	1,894 R	75.8%	16.6%	82.0%	18.0%
415,419	HENNEPIN	140,169	90,517	28,911	20,741	61,606 R	64.6%	20.6%	75.8%	24.2%
14,013	HOUSTON	4,787	4,101	598	88	3,503 R	85.7%	12.5%	87.3%	12.7%
10,136	HUBBARD	3,031	2,238	453	340	1,785 R	73.8%	14.9%	83.2%	16.8%
13,278	ISANTI	4,450	3,007	405	1,038	2,602 R	67.6%	9.1%	88.1%	11.9%
23,876	ITASCA	6,813	3,973	1,930	910	2,043 R	58.3%	28.3%	67.3%	32.7%
15,955	JACKSON	5,158	4,313	715	130	3,598 R	83.6%	13.9%	85.8%	14.2%
9,086	KANABEC	3,219	2,436	332	451	2,104 R	75.7%	10.3%	88.0%	12.0%
22,060	KANDIYOHI	7,474	4,759	1,282	1,433	3,477 R	63.7%	17.2%	78.8%	21.2%
10,638	KITTSON	3,329	2,485	599	245	1,886 R	74.6%	18.0%	80.6%	19.4%
13,520	KOOCHICHING	3,230	1,786	859	585	927 R	55.3%	26.6%	67.5%	32.5%
15,554	LAC QUI PARLE	5,127	4,219	653	255	3,566 R	82.3%	12.7%	86.6%	13.4%
8,251	LAKE	2,419	990	594	835	396 R	40.9%	24.6%	62.5%	37.5%
	LAKE OF THE WOODS	—	—	—	—	—	—	—	—	—
17,870	LE SUEUR	6,130	4,059	1,853	218	2,206 R	66.2%	30.2%	68.7%	31.3%
11,268	LINCOLN	3,384	2,548	673	163	1,875 R	75.3%	19.9%	79.1%	20.9%
18,837	LYON	6,229	4,557	1,232	440	3,325 R	73.2%	19.8%	78.7%	21.3%
20,444	MCLEOD	6,996	5,430	1,139	427	4,291 R	77.6%	16.3%	82.7%	17.3%
6,197	MAHNOMEN	1,495	1,076	215	204	861 R	72.0%	14.4%	83.3%	16.7%
19,443	MARSHALL	6,283	4,738	885	660	3,853 R	75.4%	14.1%	84.3%	15.7%
21,085	MARTIN	6,554	5,142	1,221	191	3,921 R	78.5%	18.6%	80.8%	19.2%
18,103	MEEKER	5,986	4,693	878	415	3,815 R	78.4%	14.7%	84.2%	15.8%
14,180	MILLE LACS	4,812	3,521	526	765	2,995 R	73.2%	10.9%	87.0%	13.0%
25,841	MORRISON	6,924	5,371	1,131	422	4,240 R	77.6%	16.3%	82.6%	17.4%
25,993	MOWER	7,725	6,339	1,061	325	5,278 R	82.1%	13.7%	85.7%	14.3%
13,631	MURRAY	4,131	3,270	698	163	2,572 R	79.2%	16.9%	82.4%	17.6%
15,036	NICOLLET	4,931	4,115	556	260	3,559 R	83.5%	11.3%	88.1%	11.9%
17,917	NOBLES	5,550	4,420	982	148	3,438 R	79.6%	17.7%	81.8%	18.2%
14,880	NORMAN	4,653	3,451	481	721	2,970 R	74.2%	10.3%	87.8%	12.2%
28,014	OLMSTED	9,245	7,130	1,756	359	5,374 R	77.1%	19.0%	80.2%	19.8%
50,818	OTTER TAIL	14,119	11,084	1,741	1,294	9,343 R	78.5%	12.3%	86.4%	13.6%
12,091	PENNINGTON	3,822	2,320	768	734	1,552 R	60.7%	20.1%	75.1%	24.9%
21,117	PINE	5,804	3,879	1,127	798	2,752 R	66.8%	19.4%	77.5%	22.5%
12,050	PIPESTONE	3,888	3,106	490	292	2,616 R	79.9%	12.6%	86.4%	13.6%
37,090	POLK	11,800	8,197	2,111	1,492	6,086 R	69.5%	17.9%	79.5%	20.5%

MINNESOTA

PRESIDENT 1920

1920 Census Population	County	Total Vote	Republican	Democratic	Other	Rep.-Dem. Plurality	Percentage Total Vote Rep.	Percentage Total Vote Dem.	Percentage Major Vote Rep.	Percentage Major Vote Dem.
13,631	POPE	4,540	3,466	709	365	2,757 R	76.3%	15.6%	83.0%	17.0%
244,554	RAMSEY	68,587	40,204	21,110	7,273	19,094 R	58.6%	30.8%	65.6%	34.4%
7,263	RED LAKE	2,097	1,308	558	231	750 R	62.4%	26.6%	70.1%	29.9%
20,908	REDWOOD	6,728	5,589	880	259	4,709 R	83.1%	13.1%	86.4%	13.6%
23,634	RENVILLE	8,141	5,995	1,283	863	4,712 R	73.6%	15.8%	82.4%	17.6%
28,307	RICE	8,715	6,500	2,040	175	4,460 R	74.6%	23.4%	76.1%	23.9%
10,965	ROCK	3,692	3,121	442	129	2,679 R	84.5%	12.0%	87.6%	12.4%
13,305	ROSEAU	3,722	2,387	500	835	1,887 R	64.1%	13.4%	82.7%	17.3%
206,391	ST. LOUIS	49,115	27,987	14,767	6,361	13,220 R	57.0%	30.1%	65.5%	34.5%
14,245	SCOTT	4,372	3,015	1,253	104	1,762 R	69.0%	28.7%	70.6%	29.4%
9,651	SHERBURNE	3,225	2,747	307	171	2,440 R	85.2%	9.5%	89.9%	10.1%
15,635	SIBLEY	4,885	4,198	502	185	3,696 R	85.9%	10.3%	89.3%	10.7%
55,741	STEARNS	15,714	13,566	1,616	532	11,950 R	86.3%	10.3%	89.4%	10.6%
18,061	STEELE	5,550	4,243	1,167	140	3,076 R	76.5%	21.0%	78.4%	21.6%
9,778	STEVENS	2,930	2,339	457	134	1,882 R	79.8%	15.6%	83.7%	16.3%
15,093	SWIFT	5,060	3,553	985	522	2,568 R	70.2%	19.5%	78.3%	21.7%
26,059	TODD	7,662	5,448	1,464	750	3,984 R	71.1%	19.1%	78.8%	21.2%
7,943	TRAVERSE	2,403	1,759	550	94	1,209 R	73.2%	22.9%	76.2%	23.8%
17,919	WABASHA	6,364	4,907	1,275	182	3,632 R	77.1%	20.0%	79.4%	20.6%
10,699	WADENA	3,487	2,635	503	349	2,132 R	75.6%	14.4%	84.0%	16.0%
14,133	WASECA	5,051	3,626	1,257	168	2,369 R	71.8%	24.9%	74.3%	25.7%
23,761	WASHINGTON	7,819	5,852	1,558	409	4,294 R	74.8%	19.9%	79.0%	21.0%
12,457	WATONWAN	4,312	3,510	647	155	2,863 R	81.4%	15.0%	84.4%	15.6%
10,187	WILKIN	2,801	2,106	561	134	1,545 R	75.2%	20.0%	79.0%	21.0%
33,653	WINONA	11,300	7,888	2,896	516	4,992 R	69.8%	25.6%	73.1%	26.9%
28,685	WRIGHT	8,820	7,013	1,299	508	5,714 R	79.5%	14.7%	84.4%	15.6%
16,550	YELLOW MEDICINE	5,829	4,225	814	790	3,411 R	72.5%	14.0%	83.8%	16.2%
2,387,125	TOTAL	735,838	519,421	142,994	73,423	376,427 R	70.6%	19.4%	78.4%	21.6%

MINNESOTA

In 1922 Lake of the Woods county was organized from part of Beltrami county. Population data for the years between the 1920 and 1930 Census are not available.

ELECTION NOTES

1956 Other vote was 2,080 Hass (Socialist Labor); 1,098 Dobbs (Socialist Workers).

1952 Other vote was 2,666 Hallinan (Progressive); 2,383 Hass (Socialist Labor); 2,147 Hamblen (Prohibition); 618 Dobbs (Socialist Workers).

1948 Other vote was 27,866 Wallace (Progressive); 4,646 Thomas (Socialist); 2,525 Teichert (Socialist Labor); 606 Dobbs (Socialist Workers).

1944 Other vote was 5,048 Thomas (Socialist); 3,176 Teichert (Socialist Labor).

1940 Other vote was 5,454 Thomas (Socialist); 2,711 Browder (Communist); 2,553 Aiken (Socialist Labor).

1936 Other vote was 74,296 Lemke (Union); 2,872 Thomas (Socialist); 2,574 Browder (Communist); 961 Aiken (Socialist Labor).

1932 Other vote was 25,476 Thomas (Socialist); 6,101 Foster (Communist); 5,731 Coxey (Farmer-Labor); 770 Reynolds (Socialist Labor).

1928 Other vote was 6,774 Thomas (Socialist); 4,853 Foster (Communist); 1,921 Reynolds (Socialist Labor).

1924 A special four-column table which gives the LaFollette (Progressive) vote is used to detail this election. Other vote was 4,427 Foster (Communist); 1,855 Johns (Socialist Labor).

1920 Other vote was 56,106 Debs (Socialist); 11,489 Watkins (Prohibition); 5,828 Cox (Socialist Labor). Socialist candidates ran second in several counties.

MISSISSIPPI

POPULAR VOTE FOR PRESIDENT 1920 TO 1956

		Republican		Democratic				Percentage			
								Total Vote		Major Vote	
Year	Total Vote	Vote	Candidate	Vote	Candidate	Other Vote	Plurality	Rep.	Dem.	Rep.	Dem.
1956	248,104	60,685	Eisenhower, Dwight D.	144,453	Stevenson, Adlai E.	42,966	83,768 D	24.5%	58.2%	29.6%	70.4%
1952	285,532	112,966	Eisenhower, Dwight D.	172,566	Stevenson, Adlai E.		59,600 D	39.6%	60.4%	39.6%	60.4%
1948 **	192,190	5,043	Dewey, Thomas E.	19,384	Truman, Harry S.	167,763	148,154 SR	2.6%	10.1%	20.6%	79.4%
1944	180,234	11,613	Dewey, Thomas E.	168,621	Roosevelt, Franklin D.		157,008 D	6.4%	93.6%	6.4%	93.6%
1940	175,824	7,364	Willkie, Wendell	168,267	Roosevelt, Franklin D.	193	160,903 D	4.2%	95.7%	4.2%	95.8%
1936	162,142	4,467	Landon, Alfred M.	157,333	Roosevelt, Franklin D.	342	152,866 D	2.8%	97.0%	2.8%	97.2%
1932	146,034	5,180	Hoover, Herbert C.	140,168	Roosevelt, Franklin D.	686	134,988 D	3.5%	96.0%	3.6%	96.4%
1928	151,568	27,030	Hoover, Herbert C.	124,538	Smith, Alfred E.		97,508 D	17.8%	82.2%	17.8%	82.2%
1924	112,442	8,494	Coolidge, Calvin	100,474	Davis, John W.	3,474	91,980 D	7.6%	89.4%	7.8%	92.2%
1920	82,351	11,576	Harding, Warren G.	69,136	Cox, James M.	1,639	57,560 D	14.1%	84.0%	14.3%	85.7%

In 1948 other vote was 167,538 States Rights and 225 Progressive.

ELECTORAL COLLEGE VOTE 1920 TO 1956

Year	Total	Republican	Democratic	Other
1956	8	—	8	—
1952	8	—	8	—
1948	9	—	—	9 SR
1944	9	—	9	—
1940	9	—	9	—
1936	9	—	9	—
1932	9	—	9	—
1928	10	—	10	—
1924	10	—	10	—
1920	10	—	10	—

MISSISSIPPI

MISSISSIPPI

PRESIDENT 1956

1950 Census Population	County	Total Vote	Republican	Democratic	Independent	Other	Plurality	Percentage Total Vote Rep.	Dem.	Ind.
32,256	ADAMS	4,094	1,664	1,279	1,151		385 R	40.6%	31.2%	28.1%
27,158	ALCORN	4,072	827	3,143	102		2,316 D	20.3%	77.2%	2.5%
19,261	AMITE	1,716	255	802	659		143 D	14.9%	46.7%	38.4%
26,652	ATTALA	2,658	445	1,793	420		1,348 D	16.7%	67.5%	15.8%
8,793	BENTON	944	108	786	50		678 D	11.4%	83.3%	5.3%
63,004	BOLIVAR	3,511	754	1,176	1,581		405 I	21.5%	33.5%	45.0%
18,369	CALHOUN	2,217	301	1,763	153		1,462 D	13.6%	79.5%	6.9%
15,499	CARROLL	1,551	234	1,080	237		843 D	15.1%	69.6%	15.3%
18,951	CHICKASAW	2,056	231	1,650	175		1,419 D	11.2%	80.3%	8.5%
11,009	CHOCTAW	1,404	221	1,117	66		896 D	15.7%	79.6%	4.7%
11,944	CLAIBORNE	822	191	339	292		47 D	23.2%	41.2%	35.5%
19,362	CLARKE	2,407	500	1,763	144		1,263 D	20.8%	73.2%	6.0%
17,757	CLAY	2,247	410	1,225	612		613 D	18.2%	54.5%	27.2%
49,361	COAHOMA	3,299	1,082	1,677	540		595 D	32.8%	50.8%	16.4%
30,493	COPIAH	2,304	387	1,270	647		623 D	16.8%	55.1%	28.1%
16,036	COVINGTON	2,051	386	1,382	283		996 D	18.8%	67.4%	13.8%
24,599	DE SOTO	1,846	398	1,236	212		838 D	21.6%	67.0%	11.5%
45,055	FORREST	6,013	2,256	1,928	1,829		328 R	37.5%	32.1%	30.4%
10,929	FRANKLIN	1,544	177	862	505		357 D	11.5%	55.8%	32.7%
10,012	GEORGE	1,661	403	1,150	108		747 D	24.3%	69.2%	6.5%
8,215	GREENE	1,229	351	734	144		383 D	28.6%	59.7%	11.7%
18,830	GRENADA	2,188	407	949	832		117 D	18.6%	43.4%	38.0%
11,891	HANCOCK	2,674	1,421	1,179	74		242 R	53.1%	44.1%	2.8%
84,073	HARRISON	13,001	5,742	6,549	710		807 D	44.2%	50.4%	5.5%
142,164	HINDS	20,278	7,015	7,104	6,159		89 D	34.6%	35.0%	30.4%
33,301	HOLMES	2,139	215	872	1,052		180 I	10.1%	40.8%	49.2%
23,115	HUMPHREYS	1,294	127	576	591		15 I	9.8%	44.5%	45.7%
4,966	ISSAQUENA	289	42	172	75		97 D	14.5%	59.5%	26.0%
17,216	ITAWAMBA	2,665	298	2,310	57		2,012 D	11.2%	86.7%	2.1%
31,401	JACKSON	6,906	2,692	3,882	332		1,190 D	39.0%	56.2%	4.8%
18,912	JASPER	2,445	287	1,958	200		1,671 D	11.7%	80.1%	8.2%
11,306	JEFFERSON	962	189	440	333		107 D	19.6%	45.7%	34.6%
15,500	JEFFERSON DAVIS	1,429	156	1,049	224		825 D	10.9%	73.4%	15.7%
57,235	JONES	8,263	2,463	5,137	663		2,674 D	29.8%	62.2%	8.0%
15,893	KEMPER	1,823	173	1,586	64		1,413 D	9.5%	87.0%	3.5%
22,798	LAFAYETTE	2,701	575	1,968	158		1,393 D	21.3%	72.9%	5.8%
13,225	LAMAR	1,718	429	805	484		321 D	25.0%	46.9%	28.2%
64,171	LAUDERDALE	9,127	2,817	5,414	896		2,597 D	30.9%	59.3%	9.8%
12,639	LAWRENCE	1,519	276	1,025	218		749 D	18.2%	67.5%	14.4%
21,610	LEAKE	2,999	220	2,475	304		2,171 D	7.3%	82.5%	10.1%
38,237	LEE	5,157	929	3,883	345		2,954 D	18.0%	75.3%	6.7%
51,813	LEFLORE	3,588	887	1,769	932		837 D	24.7%	49.3%	26.0%
27,899	LINCOLN	3,773	848	1,942	983		959 D	22.5%	51.5%	26.1%
37,852	LOWNDES	4,126	1,205	2,308	613		1,103 D	29.2%	55.9%	14.9%
33,860	MADISON	2,395	377	996	1,022		26 I	15.7%	41.6%	42.7%
23,967	MARION	3,032	611	1,751	670		1,081 D	20.2%	57.8%	22.1%
25,106	MARSHALL	1,694	287	1,192	215		905 D	16.9%	70.4%	12.7%
36,543	MONROE	4,624	705	3,630	289		2,925 D	15.2%	78.5%	6.3%
14,470	MONTGOMERY	1,779	278	1,134	367		767 D	15.6%	63.7%	20.6%
25,730	NESHOBA	3,629	502	2,827	300		2,325 D	13.8%	77.9%	8.3%
22,681	NEWTON	3,126	360	2,359	407		1,952 D	11.5%	75.5%	13.0%
20,022	NOXUBEE	1,320	257	690	373		317 D	19.5%	52.3%	28.3%
24,569	OKTIBBEHA	2,640	702	1,552	386		850 D	26.6%	58.8%	14.6%
31,271	PANOLA	2,631	519	1,741	371		1,222 D	19.7%	66.2%	14.1%
20,641	PEARL RIVER	2,848	1,129	1,274	445		145 D	39.6%	44.7%	15.6%
9,108	PERRY	1,100	347	581	172		234 D	31.5%	52.8%	15.6%
35,137	PIKE	4,106	1,210	1,714	1,182		504 D	29.5%	41.7%	28.8%
19,994	PONTOTOC	2,812	335	2,320	157		1,985 D	11.9%	82.5%	5.6%
19,810	PRENTISS	2,399	383	1,942	74		1,559 D	16.0%	81.0%	3.1%
25,885	QUITMAN	1,499	276	954	269		678 D	18.4%	63.6%	17.9%

MISSISSIPPI

PRESIDENT 1956

1950 Census Population	County	Total Vote	Republican	Democratic	Independent	Other	Plurality	Rep.	Dem.	Ind.
								Percentage Total Vote		
28,881	RANKIN	3,089	556	1,537	996		541 D	18.0%	49.8%	32.2%
21,681	SCOTT	3,171	503	2,077	591		1,486 D	15.9%	65.5%	18.6%
12,903	SHARKEY	832	211	308	313		5 I	25.4%	37.0%	37.6%
21,819	SIMPSON	3,189	467	2,140	582		1,558 D	14.6%	67.1%	18.3%
16,740	SMITH	2,543	277	2,055	211		1,778 D	10.9%	80.8%	8.3%
6,264	STONE	1,168	293	761	114		468 D	25.1%	65.2%	9.8%
56,031	SUNFLOWER	3,120	520	1,585	1,015		570 D	16.7%	50.8%	32.5%
30,486	TALLAHATCHIE	2,687	341	1,969	377		1,592 D	12.7%	73.3%	14.0%
18,011	TATE	1,749	171	1,414	164		1,243 D	9.8%	80.8%	9.4%
17,522	TIPPAH	2,955	287	2,569	99		2,282 D	9.7%	86.9%	3.4%
15,544	TISHOMINGO	2,170	516	1,577	77		1,061 D	23.8%	72.7%	3.5%
21,664	TUNICA	836	200	470	166		270 D	23.9%	56.2%	19.9%
20,262	UNION	3,494	427	2,882	185		2,455 D	12.2%	82.5%	5.3%
15,563	WALTHALL	1,725	306	1,143	276		837 D	17.7%	66.3%	16.0%
39,616	WARREN	5,328	2,419	1,857	1,052		562 R	45.4%	34.9%	19.7%
70,504	WASHINGTON	5,490	1,973	2,722	795		749 D	35.9%	49.6%	14.5%
17,010	WAYNE	2,129	373	1,493	263		1,120 D	17.5%	70.1%	12.4%
11,607	WEBSTER	1,745	188	1,412	145		1,224 D	10.8%	80.9%	8.3%
14,116	WILKINSON	851	240	260	351		91 I	28.2%	30.6%	41.2%
22,231	WINSTON	2,705	361	2,132	212		1,771 D	13.3%	78.8%	7.8%
15,191	YALOBUSHA	1,696	414	1,015	267		601 D	24.4%	59.8%	15.7%
35,712	YAZOO	3,088	370	911	1,807		896 I	12.0%	29.5%	58.5%
2,178,914	TOTAL	248,104	60,685	144,453	42,966		83,768 D	24.5%	58.2%	17.3%

MISSISSIPPI

PRESIDENT 1952

1950 Census Population	County	Total Vote	Republican	Democratic	Other	Rep.-Dem. Plurality	Percentage Total Vote Rep.	Total Vote Dem.	Major Vote Rep.	Major Vote Dem.
32,256	ADAMS	4,069	2,372	1,697		675 R	58.3%	41.7%	58.3%	41.7%
27,158	ALCORN	4,430	1,155	3,275		2,120 D	26.1%	73.9%	26.1%	73.9%
19,261	AMITE	1,898	777	1,121		344 D	40.9%	59.1%	40.9%	59.1%
26,652	ATTALA	3,436	1,178	2,258		1,080 D	34.3%	65.7%	34.3%	65.7%
8,793	BENTON	1,179	216	963		747 D	18.3%	81.7%	18.3%	81.7%
63,004	BOLIVAR	3,939	2,096	1,843		253 R	53.2%	46.8%	53.2%	46.8%
18,369	CALHOUN	2,975	691	2,284		1,593 D	23.2%	76.8%	23.2%	76.8%
15,499	CARROLL	1,703	535	1,168		633 D	31.4%	68.6%	31.4%	68.6%
18,951	CHICKASAW	2,490	685	1,805		1,120 D	27.5%	72.5%	27.5%	72.5%
11,009	CHOCTAW	1,911	524	1,387		863 D	27.4%	72.6%	27.4%	72.6%
11,944	CLAIBORNE	1,056	560	496		64 R	53.0%	47.0%	53.0%	47.0%
19,362	CLARKE	2,754	754	2,000		1,246 D	27.4%	72.6%	27.4%	72.6%
17,757	CLAY	2,307	1,077	1,230		153 D	46.7%	53.3%	46.7%	53.3%
49,361	COAHOMA	3,734	1,619	2,115		496 D	43.4%	56.6%	43.4%	56.6%
30,493	COPIAH	3,577	1,527	2,050		523 D	42.7%	57.3%	42.7%	57.3%
16,036	COVINGTON	2,305	770	1,535		765 D	33.4%	66.6%	33.4%	66.6%
24,599	DE SOTO	2,042	754	1,288		534 D	36.9%	63.1%	36.9%	63.1%
45,055	FORREST	7,416	4,480	2,936		1,544 R	60.4%	39.6%	60.4%	39.6%
10,929	FRANKLIN	1,680	514	1,166		652 D	30.6%	69.4%	30.6%	69.4%
10,012	GEORGE	1,954	603	1,351		748 D	30.9%	69.1%	30.9%	69.1%
8,215	GREENE	1,753	506	1,247		741 D	28.9%	71.1%	28.9%	71.1%
18,830	GRENADA	2,174	1,000	1,174		174 D	46.0%	54.0%	46.0%	54.0%
11,891	HANCOCK	2,925	1,347	1,578		231 D	46.1%	53.9%	46.1%	53.9%
84,073	HARRISON	13,141	5,960	7,181		1,221 D	45.4%	54.6%	45.4%	54.6%
142,164	HINDS	23,453	12,520	10,933		1,587 R	53.4%	46.6%	53.4%	46.6%
33,301	HOLMES	2,728	1,305	1,423		118 D	47.8%	52.2%	47.8%	52.2%
23,115	HUMPHREYS	1,447	589	858		269 D	40.7%	59.3%	40.7%	59.3%
4,966	ISSAQUENA	297	127	170		43 D	42.8%	57.2%	42.8%	57.2%
17,216	ITAWAMBA	2,792	556	2,236		1,680 D	19.9%	80.1%	19.9%	80.1%
31,401	JACKSON	6,316	2,170	4,146		1,976 D	34.4%	65.6%	34.4%	65.6%
18,912	JASPER	2,540	668	1,872		1,204 D	26.3%	73.7%	26.3%	73.7%
11,306	JEFFERSON	1,149	610	539		71 R	53.1%	46.9%	53.1%	46.9%
15,500	JEFFERSON DAVIS	2,099	473	1,626		1,153 D	22.5%	77.5%	22.5%	77.5%
57,235	JONES	9,923	4,039	5,884		1,845 D	40.7%	59.3%	40.7%	59.3%
15,893	KEMPER	1,965	372	1,593		1,221 D	18.9%	81.1%	18.9%	81.1%
22,798	LAFAYETTE	3,231	868	2,363		1,495 D	26.9%	73.1%	26.9%	73.1%
13,225	LAMAR	2,294	1,034	1,260		226 D	45.1%	54.9%	45.1%	54.9%
64,171	LAUDERDALE	9,978	4,137	5,841		1,704 D	41.5%	58.5%	41.5%	58.5%
12,639	LAWRENCE	1,673	556	1,117		561 D	33.2%	66.8%	33.2%	66.8%
21,610	LEAKE	3,270	603	2,667		2,064 D	18.4%	81.6%	18.4%	81.6%
38,237	LEE	6,176	2,002	4,174		2,172 D	32.4%	67.6%	32.4%	67.6%
51,813	LEFLORE	4,279	2,434	1,845		589 R	56.9%	43.1%	56.9%	43.1%
27,899	LINCOLN	4,299	2,028	2,271		243 D	47.2%	52.8%	47.2%	52.8%
37,852	LOWNDES	4,288	2,670	1,618		1,052 R	62.3%	37.7%	62.3%	37.7%
33,860	MADISON	2,921	1,496	1,425		71 R	51.2%	48.8%	51.2%	48.8%
23,967	MARION	4,017	1,420	2,597		1,177 D	35.3%	64.7%	35.3%	64.7%
25,106	MARSHALL	2,451	604	1,847		1,243 D	24.6%	75.4%	24.6%	75.4%
36,543	MONROE	4,929	1,417	3,512		2,095 D	28.7%	71.3%	28.7%	71.3%
14,470	MONTGOMERY	2,196	840	1,356		516 D	38.3%	61.7%	38.3%	61.7%
25,730	NESHOBA	4,648	1,081	3,567		2,486 D	23.3%	76.7%	23.3%	76.7%
22,681	NEWTON	3,311	851	2,460		1,609 D	25.7%	74.3%	25.7%	74.3%
20,022	NOXUBEE	1,645	887	758		129 R	53.9%	46.1%	53.9%	46.1%
24,569	OKTIBBEHA	3,101	1,435	1,666		231 D	46.3%	53.7%	46.3%	53.7%
31,271	PANOLA	3,079	1,032	2,047		1,015 D	33.5%	66.5%	33.5%	66.5%
20,641	PEARL RIVER	3,801	1,741	2,060		319 D	45.8%	54.2%	45.8%	54.2%
9,108	PERRY	1,293	511	782		271 D	39.5%	60.5%	39.5%	60.5%
35,137	PIKE	5,403	2,908	2,495		413 R	53.8%	46.2%	53.8%	46.2%
19,994	PONTOTOC	2,929	648	2,281		1,633 D	22.1%	77.9%	22.1%	77.9%
19,810	PRENTISS	3,403	731	2,672		1,941 D	21.5%	78.5%	21.5%	78.5%
25,885	QUITMAN	1,650	492	1,158		666 D	29.8%	70.2%	29.8%	70.2%

MISSISSIPPI

PRESIDENT 1952

1950 Census Population	County	Total Vote	Republican	Democratic	Other	Rep.-Dem. Plurality	Percentage Total Vote Rep.	Total Vote Dem.	Major Vote Rep.	Major Vote Dem.
28,881	RANKIN	3,622	1,545	2,077		532 D	42.7%	57.3%	42.7%	57.3%
21,681	SCOTT	3,331	1,123	2,208		1,085 D	33.7%	66.3%	33.7%	66.3%
12,903	SHARKEY	988	600	388		212 R	60.7%	39.3%	60.7%	39.3%
21,819	SIMPSON	3,645	878	2,767		1,889 D	24.1%	75.9%	24.1%	75.9%
16,740	SMITH	3,026	738	2,288		1,550 D	24.4%	75.6%	24.4%	75.6%
6,264	STONE	1,534	569	965		396 D	37.1%	62.9%	37.1%	62.9%
56,031	SUNFLOWER	4,056	2,007	2,049		42 D	49.5%	50.5%	49.5%	50.5%
30,486	TALLAHATCHIE	3,098	748	2,350		1,602 D	24.1%	75.9%	24.1%	75.9%
18,011	TATE	1,962	387	1,575		1,188 D	19.7%	80.3%	19.7%	80.3%
17,522	TIPPAH	3,389	511	2,878		2,367 D	15.1%	84.9%	15.1%	84.9%
15,544	TISHOMINGO	2,274	679	1,595		916 D	29.9%	70.1%	29.9%	70.1%
21,664	TUNICA	913	383	530		147 D	41.9%	58.1%	41.9%	58.1%
20,262	UNION	3,666	917	2,749		1,832 D	25.0%	75.0%	25.0%	75.0%
15,563	WALTHALL	1,848	491	1,357		866 D	26.6%	73.4%	26.6%	73.4%
39,616	WARREN	5,824	3,458	2,366		1,092 R	59.4%	40.6%	59.4%	40.6%
70,504	WASHINGTON	5,919	3,301	2,618		683 R	55.8%	44.2%	55.8%	44.2%
17,010	WAYNE	2,321	717	1,604		887 D	30.9%	69.1%	30.9%	69.1%
11,607	WEBSTER	2,218	453	1,765		1,312 D	20.4%	79.6%	20.4%	79.6%
14,116	WILKINSON	1,262	699	563		136 R	55.4%	44.6%	55.4%	44.6%
22,231	WINSTON	3,330	771	2,559		1,788 D	23.2%	76.8%	23.2%	76.8%
15,191	YALOBUSHA	2,099	753	1,346		593 D	35.9%	64.1%	35.9%	64.1%
35,712	YAZOO	3,385	1,683	1,702		19 D	49.7%	50.3%	49.7%	50.3%
2,178,914	TOTAL	285,532	112,966	172,566		59,600 D	39.6%	60.4%	39.6%	60.4%

MISSISSIPPI

PRESIDENT 1948

1940 Census Population	County	Total Vote	Republican	Democratic	States Rights	Other	Plurality	Percentage Total Vote Rep.	Dem.	St. Rgts.
27,238	ADAMS	2,200	95	71	2,032	2	1,937 SR	4.3%	3.2%	92.4%
26,969	ALCORN	3,091	91	1,013	1,984	3	971 SR	2.9%	32.8%	64.2%
21,892	AMITE	1,631	17	55	1,559		1,504 SR	1.0%	3.4%	95.6%
30,227	ATTALA	2,467	32	130	2,299	6	2,169 SR	1.3%	5.3%	93.2%
10,429	BENTON	810	11	118	679	2	561 SR	1.4%	14.6%	83.8%
67,574	BOLIVAR	2,914	115	219	2,579	1	2,360 SR	3.9%	7.5%	88.5%
20,893	CALHOUN	1,898	36	786	1,074	2	288 SR	1.9%	41.4%	56.6%
20,651	CARROLL	1,226	14	74	1,138		1,064 SR	1.1%	6.0%	92.8%
21,427	CHICKASAW	1,954	12	115	1,826	1	1,711 SR	0.6%	5.9%	93.4%
13,548	CHOCTAW	1,286	43	131	1,110	2	979 SR	3.3%	10.2%	86.3%
12,810	CLAIBORNE	775	14	19	741	1	722 SR	1.8%	2.5%	95.6%
20,596	CLARKE	1,928	17	144	1,763	4	1,619 SR	0.9%	7.5%	91.4%
19,030	CLAY	1,686	22	59	1,604	1	1,545 SR	1.3%	3.5%	95.1%
48,333	COAHOMA	2,319	113	246	1,959	1	1,713 SR	4.9%	10.6%	84.5%
33,974	COPIAH	2,631	19	89	2,523		2,434 SR	0.7%	3.4%	95.9%
17,030	COVINGTON	1,687	16	135	1,532	4	1,397 SR	0.9%	8.0%	90.8%
26,663	DE SOTO	1,450	14	137	1,299		1,162 SR	1.0%	9.4%	89.6%
34,901	FORREST	5,880	167	406	5,296	11	4,890 SR	2.8%	6.9%	90.1%
12,504	FRANKLIN	1,227	12	55	1,160		1,105 SR	1.0%	4.5%	94.5%
8,704	GEORGE	1,166	25	108	1,032	1	924 SR	2.1%	9.3%	88.5%
9,512	GREENE	1,018	14	118	885	1	767 SR	1.4%	11.6%	86.9%
19,052	GRENADA	1,541	26	109	1,405	1	1,296 SR	1.7%	7.1%	91.2%
11,328	HANCOCK	1,775	151	222	1,400	2	1,178 SR	8.5%	12.5%	78.9%
50,799	HARRISON	7,458	415	692	6,325	26	5,633 SR	5.6%	9.3%	84.8%
107,273	HINDS	15,255	492	1,041	13,705	17	12,664 SR	3.2%	6.8%	89.8%
39,710	HOLMES	2,224	24	61	2,139		2,078 SR	1.1%	2.7%	96.2%
26,257	HUMPHREYS	1,144	11	17	1,116		1,099 SR	1.0%	1.5%	97.6%
6,433	ISSAQUENA	225	5	11	209		198 SR	2.2%	4.9%	92.9%
19,922	ITAWAMBA	1,735	50	634	1,050	1	416 SR	2.9%	36.5%	60.5%
20,601	JACKSON	3,713	238	783	2,671	21	1,888 SR	6.4%	21.1%	71.9%
19,484	JASPER	1,942	26	121	1,795		1,674 SR	1.3%	6.2%	92.4%
13,969	JEFFERSON	996	14	15	967		952 SR	1.4%	1.5%	97.1%
15,869	JEFFERSON DAVIS	1,544	51	41	1,452		1,401 SR	3.3%	2.7%	94.0%
49,227	JONES	6,528	193	599	5,709	27	5,110 SR	3.0%	9.2%	87.5%
21,867	KEMPER	1,517	29	98	1,389	1	1,291 SR	1.9%	6.5%	91.6%
21,257	LAFAYETTE	1,980	48	744	1,184	4	440 SR	2.4%	37.6%	59.8%
12,096	LAMAR	1,469	36	91	1,342		1,251 SR	2.5%	6.2%	91.4%
58,247	LAUDERDALE	6,079	171	578	5,322	8	4,744 SR	2.8%	9.5%	87.5%
13,983	LAWRENCE	1,341	13	66	1,261	1	1,195 SR	1.0%	4.9%	94.0%
24,570	LEAKE	2,584	12	180	2,387	5	2,207 SR	0.5%	7.0%	92.4%
38,838	LEE	3,846	82	636	3,127	1	2,491 SR	2.1%	16.5%	81.3%
53,406	LEFLORE	2,973	80	139	2,749	5	2,610 SR	2.7%	4.7%	92.5%
27,506	LINCOLN	3,177	40	52	3,082	3	3,030 SR	1.3%	1.6%	97.0%
35,245	LOWNDES	2,937	66	116	2,755		2,639 SR	2.2%	3.9%	93.8%
37,504	MADISON	1,965	51	81	1,831	2	1,750 SR	2.6%	4.1%	93.2%
24,085	MARION	2,745	49	205	2,491		2,286 SR	1.8%	7.5%	90.7%
25,522	MARSHALL	1,397	29	152	1,215	1	1,063 SR	2.1%	10.9%	87.0%
37,648	MONROE	2,959	54	624	2,281		1,657 SR	1.8%	21.1%	77.1%
15,703	MONTGOMERY	1,714	35	105	1,573	1	1,468 SR	2.0%	6.1%	91.8%
27,882	NESHOBA	3,130	33	260	2,833	4	2,573 SR	1.1%	8.3%	90.5%
24,249	NEWTON	2,650	39	169	2,439	3	2,270 SR	1.5%	6.4%	92.0%
25,669	NOXUBEE	1,122	17	74	1,031		957 SR	1.5%	6.6%	91.9%
22,151	OKTIBBEHA	2,004	58	158	1,786	2	1,628 SR	2.9%	7.9%	89.1%
34,421	PANOLA	2,170	38	195	1,935	2	1,740 SR	1.8%	9.0%	89.2%
19,125	PEARL RIVER	2,121	46	146	1,925	4	1,779 SR	2.2%	6.9%	90.8%
9,292	PERRY	877	25	87	764	1	677 SR	2.9%	9.9%	87.1%
35,002	PIKE	3,940	69	221	3,648	2	3,427 SR	1.8%	5.6%	92.6%
22,904	PONTOTOC	1,915	28	348	1,535	4	1,187 SR	1.5%	18.2%	80.2%
20,921	PRENTISS	1,665	74	602	988	1	386 SR	4.4%	36.2%	59.3%
27,191	QUITMAN	1,160	21	91	1,046	2	955 SR	1.8%	7.8%	90.2%

MISSISSIPPI

PRESIDENT 1948

1940 Census Population	County	Total Vote	Republican	Democratic	States Rights	Other	Plurality	Percentage Total Vote Rep.	Dem.	St. Rgts.
27,934	RANKIN	2,759	23	57	2,677	2	2,620 SR	0.8%	2.1%	97.0%
23,144	SCOTT	2,526	15	170	2,339	2	2,169 SR	0.6%	6.7%	92.6%
15,433	SHARKEY	778	10	23	745		722 SR	1.3%	3.0%	95.8%
22,024	SIMPSON	2,572	59	171	2,342		2,171 SR	2.3%	6.6%	91.1%
19,403	SMITH	2,229	33	295	1,900	1	1,605 SR	1.5%	13.2%	85.2%
6,155	STONE	1,123	17	50	1,053	3	1,003 SR	1.5%	4.5%	93.8%
61,007	SUNFLOWER	2,673	55	136	2,482		2,346 SR	2.1%	5.1%	92.9%
34,166	TALLAHATCHIE	2,446	37	287	2,122		1,835 SR	1.5%	11.7%	86.8%
19,309	TATE	1,412	16	199	1,196	1	997 SR	1.1%	14.1%	84.7%
19,680	TIPPAH	2,152	66	425	1,658	3	1,233 SR	3.1%	19.7%	77.0%
16,974	TISHOMINGO	1,884	98	711	1,073	2	362 SR	5.2%	37.7%	57.0%
22,610	TUNICA	750	12	23	715		692 SR	1.6%	3.1%	95.3%
21,867	UNION	1,964	63	478	1,420	3	942 SR	3.2%	24.3%	72.3%
17,534	WALTHALL	1,292	5	85	1,202		1,117 SR	0.4%	6.6%	93.0%
39,595	WARREN	4,170	245	320	3,602	3	3,282 SR	5.9%	7.7%	86.4%
67,576	WASHINGTON	2,979	271	260	2,447	1	2,176 SR	9.1%	8.7%	82.1%
16,928	WAYNE	1,376	4	137	1,235		1,098 SR	0.3%	10.0%	89.8%
14,160	WEBSTER	1,404	47	277	1,078	2	801 SR	3.3%	19.7%	76.8%
15,955	WILKINSON	874	21	43	809	1	766 SR	2.4%	4.9%	92.6%
22,751	WINSTON	2,105	33	240	1,828	4	1,588 SR	1.6%	11.4%	86.8%
18,387	YALOBUSHA	1,568	49	135	1,382	2	1,247 SR	3.1%	8.6%	88.1%
40,091	YAZOO	2,393	26	70	2,297		2,227 SR	1.1%	2.9%	96.0%
2,183,796	TOTAL	192,190	5,043	19,384	167,538	225	148,154 SR	2.6%	10.1%	87.2%

MISSISSIPPI

PRESIDENT 1944

1940 Census Population	County	Total Vote	Republican	Democratic	Other	Rep.-Dem. Plurality	Percentage Total Vote Rep.	Total Vote Dem.	Major Vote Rep.	Major Vote Dem.
27,238	ADAMS	1,920	282	1,638		1,356 D	14.7%	85.3%	14.7%	85.3%
26,969	ALCORN	2,875	206	2,669		2,463 D	7.2%	92.8%	7.2%	92.8%
21,892	AMITE	1,513	87	1,426		1,339 D	5.8%	94.2%	5.8%	94.2%
30,227	ATTALA	2,274	87	2,187		2,100 D	3.8%	96.2%	3.8%	96.2%
10,429	BENTON	894	42	852		810 D	4.7%	95.3%	4.7%	95.3%
67,574	BOLIVAR	2,822	378	2,444		2,066 D	13.4%	86.6%	13.4%	86.6%
20,893	CALHOUN	2,169	97	2,072		1,975 D	4.5%	95.5%	4.5%	95.5%
20,651	CARROLL	1,506	68	1,438		1,370 D	4.5%	95.5%	4.5%	95.5%
21,427	CHICKASAW	2,115	180	1,935		1,755 D	8.5%	91.5%	8.5%	91.5%
13,548	CHOCTAW	1,195	76	1,119		1,043 D	6.4%	93.6%	6.4%	93.6%
12,810	CLAIBORNE	755	45	710		665 D	6.0%	94.0%	6.0%	94.0%
20,596	CLARKE	1,789	95	1,694		1,599 D	5.3%	94.7%	5.3%	94.7%
19,030	CLAY	1,267	109	1,158		1,049 D	8.6%	91.4%	8.6%	91.4%
48,333	COAHOMA	2,583	191	2,392		2,201 D	7.4%	92.6%	7.4%	92.6%
33,974	COPIAH	2,494	85	2,409		2,324 D	3.4%	96.6%	3.4%	96.6%
17,030	COVINGTON	1,730	58	1,672		1,614 D	3.4%	96.6%	3.4%	96.6%
26,663	DE SOTO	1,684	123	1,561		1,438 D	7.3%	92.7%	7.3%	92.7%
34,901	FORREST	4,085	436	3,649		3,213 D	10.7%	89.3%	10.7%	89.3%
12,504	FRANKLIN	1,260	49	1,211		1,162 D	3.9%	96.1%	3.9%	96.1%
8,704	GEORGE	1,143	92	1,051		959 D	8.0%	92.0%	8.0%	92.0%
9,512	GREENE	1,016	109	907		798 D	10.7%	89.3%	10.7%	89.3%
19,052	GRENADA	1,490	117	1,373		1,256 D	7.9%	92.1%	7.9%	92.1%
11,328	HANCOCK	1,779	137	1,642		1,505 D	7.7%	92.3%	7.7%	92.3%
50,799	HARRISON	6,598	622	5,976		5,354 D	9.4%	90.6%	9.4%	90.6%
107,273	HINDS	11,428	962	10,466		9,504 D	8.4%	91.6%	8.4%	91.6%
39,710	HOLMES	2,076	122	1,954		1,832 D	5.9%	94.1%	5.9%	94.1%
26,257	HUMPHREYS	1,185	35	1,150		1,115 D	3.0%	97.0%	3.0%	97.0%
6,433	ISSAQUENA	220	5	215		210 D	2.3%	97.7%	2.3%	97.7%
19,922	ITAWAMBA	1,533	183	1,350		1,167 D	11.9%	88.1%	11.9%	88.1%
20,601	JACKSON	2,849	213	2,636		2,423 D	7.5%	92.5%	7.5%	92.5%
19,484	JASPER	1,714	47	1,667		1,620 D	2.7%	97.3%	2.7%	97.3%
13,969	JEFFERSON	791	25	766		741 D	3.2%	96.8%	3.2%	96.8%
15,869	JEFFERSON DAVIS	1,460	88	1,372		1,284 D	6.0%	94.0%	6.0%	94.0%
49,227	JONES	5,119	337	4,782		4,445 D	6.6%	93.4%	6.6%	93.4%
21,867	KEMPER	1,382	37	1,345		1,308 D	2.7%	97.3%	2.7%	97.3%
21,257	LAFAYETTE	2,235	87	2,148		2,061 D	3.9%	96.1%	3.9%	96.1%
12,096	LAMAR	1,158	93	1,065		972 D	8.0%	92.0%	8.0%	92.0%
58,247	LAUDERDALE	6,415	379	6,036		5,657 D	5.9%	94.1%	5.9%	94.1%
13,983	LAWRENCE	1,580	45	1,535		1,490 D	2.8%	97.2%	2.8%	97.2%
24,570	LEAKE	2,824	24	2,800		2,776 D	0.8%	99.2%	0.8%	99.2%
38,838	LEE	3,739	230	3,509		3,279 D	6.2%	93.8%	6.2%	93.8%
53,406	LEFLORE	2,599	200	2,399		2,199 D	7.7%	92.3%	7.7%	92.3%
27,506	LINCOLN	2,548	103	2,445		2,342 D	4.0%	96.0%	4.0%	96.0%
35,245	LOWNDES	2,576	360	2,216		1,856 D	14.0%	86.0%	14.0%	86.0%
37,504	MADISON	2,025	104	1,921		1,817 D	5.1%	94.9%	5.1%	94.9%
24,085	MARION	2,495	54	2,441		2,387 D	2.2%	97.8%	2.2%	97.8%
25,522	MARSHALL	1,504	63	1,441		1,378 D	4.2%	95.8%	4.2%	95.8%
37,648	MONROE	3,263	159	3,104		2,945 D	4.9%	95.1%	4.9%	95.1%
15,703	MONTGOMERY	1,445	74	1,371		1,297 D	5.1%	94.9%	5.1%	94.9%
27,882	NESHOBA	3,156	131	3,025		2,894 D	4.2%	95.8%	4.2%	95.8%
24,249	NEWTON	2,572	56	2,516		2,460 D	2.2%	97.8%	2.2%	97.8%
25,669	NOXUBEE	1,097	103	994		891 D	9.4%	90.6%	9.4%	90.6%
22,151	OKTIBBEHA	2,058	110	1,948		1,838 D	5.3%	94.7%	5.3%	94.7%
34,421	PANOLA	2,021	90	1,931		1,841 D	4.5%	95.5%	4.5%	95.5%
19,125	PEARL RIVER	2,215	84	2,131		2,047 D	3.8%	96.2%	3.8%	96.2%
9,292	PERRY	840	44	796		752 D	5.2%	94.8%	5.2%	94.8%
35,002	PIKE	3,220	248	2,972		2,724 D	7.7%	92.3%	7.7%	92.3%
22,904	PONTOTOC	1,803	87	1,716		1,629 D	4.8%	95.2%	4.8%	95.2%
20,921	PRENTISS	1,827	175	1,652		1,477 D	9.6%	90.4%	9.6%	90.4%
27,191	QUITMAN	1,165	59	1,106		1,047 D	5.1%	94.9%	5.1%	94.9%

MISSISSIPPI

PRESIDENT 1944

1940 Census Population	County	Total Vote	Republican	Democratic	Other	Rep.-Dem. Plurality	Percentage Total Vote Rep.	Total Vote Dem.	Major Vote Rep.	Major Vote Dem.
27,934	RANKIN	2,472	98	2,374		2,276 D	4.0%	96.0%	4.0%	96.0%
23,144	SCOTT	2,225	60	2,165		2,105 D	2.7%	97.3%	2.7%	97.3%
15,433	SHARKEY	722	24	698		674 D	3.3%	96.7%	3.3%	96.7%
22,024	SIMPSON	2,548	78	2,470		2,392 D	3.1%	96.9%	3.1%	96.9%
19,403	SMITH	2,621	165	2,456		2,291 D	6.3%	93.7%	6.3%	93.7%
6,155	STONE	1,032	43	989		946 D	4.2%	95.8%	4.2%	95.8%
61,007	SUNFLOWER	2,954	155	2,799		2,644 D	5.2%	94.8%	5.2%	94.8%
34,166	TALLAHATCHIE	2,441	40	2,401		2,361 D	1.6%	98.4%	1.6%	98.4%
19,309	TATE	1,484	29	1,455		1,426 D	2.0%	98.0%	2.0%	98.0%
19,680	TIPPAH	2,665	126	2,539		2,413 D	4.7%	95.3%	4.7%	95.3%
16,974	TISHOMINGO	1,708	296	1,412		1,116 D	17.3%	82.7%	17.3%	82.7%
22,610	TUNICA	756	35	721		686 D	4.6%	95.4%	4.6%	95.4%
21,867	UNION	2,323	183	2,140		1,957 D	7.9%	92.1%	7.9%	92.1%
17,534	WALTHALL	1,298	68	1,230		1,162 D	5.2%	94.8%	5.2%	94.8%
39,595	WARREN	3,506	304	3,202		2,898 D	8.7%	91.3%	8.7%	91.3%
67,576	WASHINGTON	2,466	454	2,012		1,558 D	18.4%	81.6%	18.4%	81.6%
16,928	WAYNE	1,415	35	1,380		1,345 D	2.5%	97.5%	2.5%	97.5%
14,160	WEBSTER	1,631	127	1,504		1,377 D	7.8%	92.2%	7.8%	92.2%
15,955	WILKINSON	943	80	863		783 D	8.5%	91.5%	8.5%	91.5%
22,751	WINSTON	1,873	51	1,822		1,771 D	2.7%	97.3%	2.7%	97.3%
18,387	YALOBUSHA	1,679	97	1,582		1,485 D	5.8%	94.2%	5.8%	94.2%
40,091	YAZOO	2,379	78	2,301		2,223 D	3.3%	96.7%	3.3%	96.7%
2,183,796	TOTAL	180,234	11,613	168,621		157,008 D	6.4%	93.6%	6.4%	93.6%

MISSISSIPPI

PRESIDENT 1940

1940 Census Population	County	Total Vote	Republican	Democratic	Other	Rep.-Dem. Plurality	Percentage Total Vote Rep.	Total Vote Dem.	Major Vote Rep.	Major Vote Dem.
27,238	ADAMS	2,036	166	1,869	1	1,703 D	8.2%	91.8%	8.2%	91.8%
26,969	ALCORN	3,068	133	2,934	1	2,801 D	4.3%	95.6%	4.3%	95.7%
21,892	AMITE	1,499	64	1,435		1,371 D	4.3%	95.7%	4.3%	95.7%
30,227	ATTALA	2,120	63	2,049	8	1,986 D	3.0%	96.7%	3.0%	97.0%
10,429	BENTON	959	24	935		911 D	2.5%	97.5%	2.5%	97.5%
67,574	BOLIVAR	3,209	234	2,974	1	2,740 D	7.3%	92.7%	7.3%	92.7%
20,893	CALHOUN	2,032	74	1,958		1,884 D	3.6%	96.4%	3.6%	96.4%
20,651	CARROLL	1,446	38	1,408		1,370 D	2.6%	97.4%	2.6%	97.4%
21,427	CHICKASAW	1,823	58	1,764	1	1,706 D	3.2%	96.8%	3.2%	96.8%
13,548	CHOCTAW	1,278	66	1,212		1,146 D	5.2%	94.8%	5.2%	94.8%
12,810	CLAIBORNE	779	32	737	10	705 D	4.1%	94.6%	4.2%	95.8%
20,596	CLARKE	1,753	42	1,711		1,669 D	2.4%	97.6%	2.4%	97.6%
19,030	CLAY	1,336	103	1,232	1	1,129 D	7.7%	92.2%	7.7%	92.3%
48,333	COAHOMA	2,577	137	2,440		2,303 D	5.3%	94.7%	5.3%	94.7%
33,974	COPIAH	2,384	49	2,335		2,286 D	2.1%	97.9%	2.1%	97.9%
17,030	COVINGTON	1,471	52	1,419		1,367 D	3.5%	96.5%	3.5%	96.5%
26,663	DE SOTO	1,535	40	1,491	4	1,451 D	2.6%	97.1%	2.6%	97.4%
34,901	FORREST	3,313	228	3,075	10	2,847 D	6.9%	92.8%	6.9%	93.1%
12,504	FRANKLIN	1,405	29	1,376		1,347 D	2.1%	97.9%	2.1%	97.9%
8,704	GEORGE	983	38	945		907 D	3.9%	96.1%	3.9%	96.1%
9,512	GREENE	992	66	926		860 D	6.7%	93.3%	6.7%	93.3%
19,052	GRENADA	1,425	62	1,354	9	1,292 D	4.4%	95.0%	4.4%	95.6%
11,328	HANCOCK	1,748	197	1,550	1	1,353 D	11.3%	88.7%	11.3%	88.7%
50,799	HARRISON	6,214	633	5,577	4	4,944 D	10.2%	89.7%	10.2%	89.8%
107,273	HINDS	10,459	538	9,917	4	9,379 D	5.1%	94.8%	5.1%	94.9%
39,710	HOLMES	2,078	37	2,041		2,004 D	1.8%	98.2%	1.8%	98.2%
26,257	HUMPHREYS	1,081	20	1,061		1,041 D	1.9%	98.1%	1.9%	98.1%
6,433	ISSAQUENA	227	9	218		209 D	4.0%	96.0%	4.0%	96.0%
19,922	ITAWAMBA	1,758	119	1,627	12	1,508 D	6.8%	92.5%	6.8%	93.2%
20,601	JACKSON	2,300	171	2,124	5	1,953 D	7.4%	92.3%	7.5%	92.5%
19,484	JASPER	1,748	35	1,713		1,678 D	2.0%	98.0%	2.0%	98.0%
13,969	JEFFERSON	808	7	801		794 D	0.9%	99.1%	0.9%	99.1%
15,869	JEFFERSON DAVIS	1,330	38	1,289	3	1,251 D	2.9%	96.9%	2.9%	97.1%
49,227	JONES	4,759	242	4,517		4,275 D	5.1%	94.9%	5.1%	94.9%
21,867	KEMPER	1,464	42	1,422		1,380 D	2.9%	97.1%	2.9%	97.1%
21,257	LAFAYETTE	2,255	65	2,188	2	2,123 D	2.9%	97.0%	2.9%	97.1%
12,096	LAMAR	1,203	55	1,148		1,093 D	4.6%	95.4%	4.6%	95.4%
58,247	LAUDERDALE	6,246	303	5,936	7	5,633 D	4.9%	95.0%	4.9%	95.1%
13,983	LAWRENCE	1,255	37	1,218		1,181 D	2.9%	97.1%	2.9%	97.1%
24,570	LEAKE	2,823	17	2,802	4	2,785 D	0.6%	99.3%	0.6%	99.4%
38,838	LEE	3,935	120	3,814	1	3,694 D	3.0%	96.9%	3.1%	96.9%
53,406	LEFLORE	2,515	111	2,404		2,293 D	4.4%	95.6%	4.4%	95.6%
27,506	LINCOLN	2,440	97	2,332	11	2,235 D	4.0%	95.6%	4.0%	96.0%
35,245	LOWNDES	2,418	147	2,268	3	2,121 D	6.1%	93.8%	6.1%	93.9%
37,504	MADISON	2,104	66	2,038		1,972 D	3.1%	96.9%	3.1%	96.9%
24,085	MARION	2,128	45	2,083		2,038 D	2.1%	97.9%	2.1%	97.9%
25,522	MARSHALL	1,451	48	1,403		1,355 D	3.3%	96.7%	3.3%	96.7%
37,648	MONROE	3,360	94	3,263	3	3,169 D	2.8%	97.1%	2.8%	97.2%
15,703	MONTGOMERY	1,554	44	1,509	1	1,465 D	2.8%	97.1%	2.8%	97.2%
27,882	NESHOBA	2,967	77	2,880	10	2,803 D	2.6%	97.1%	2.6%	97.4%
24,249	NEWTON	2,539	41	2,495	3	2,454 D	1.6%	98.3%	1.6%	98.4%
25,669	NOXUBEE	1,203	51	1,152		1,101 D	4.2%	95.8%	4.2%	95.8%
22,151	OKTIBBEHA	2,044	79	1,951	14	1,872 D	3.9%	95.5%	3.9%	96.1%
34,421	PANOLA	2,034	45	1,988	1	1,943 D	2.2%	97.7%	2.2%	97.8%
19,125	PEARL RIVER	2,118	88	2,022	8	1,934 D	4.2%	95.5%	4.2%	95.8%
9,292	PERRY	846	18	828		810 D	2.1%	97.9%	2.1%	97.9%
35,002	PIKE	3,147	185	2,956	6	2,771 D	5.9%	93.9%	5.9%	94.1%
22,904	PONTOTOC	2,244	70	2,171	3	2,101 D	3.1%	96.7%	3.1%	96.9%
20,921	PRENTISS	2,235	118	2,117		1,999 D	5.3%	94.7%	5.3%	94.7%
27,191	QUITMAN	1,182	29	1,152	1	1,123 D	2.5%	97.5%	2.5%	97.5%

MISSISSIPPI

PRESIDENT 1940

1940 Census Population	County	Total Vote	Republican	Democratic	Other	Rep.-Dem. Plurality	Percentage Total Vote Rep.	Percentage Total Vote Dem.	Percentage Major Vote Rep.	Percentage Major Vote Dem.
27,934	RANKIN	2,151	35	2,110	6	2,075 D	1.6%	98.1%	1.6%	98.4%
23,144	SCOTT	2,407	30	2,377		2,347 D	1.2%	98.8%	1.2%	98.8%
15,433	SHARKEY	765	18	747		729 D	2.4%	97.6%	2.4%	97.6%
22,024	SIMPSON	2,357	40	2,316	1	2,276 D	1.7%	98.3%	1.7%	98.3%
19,403	SMITH	1,854	27	1,826	1	1,799 D	1.5%	98.5%	1.5%	98.5%
6,155	STONE	830	28	802		774 D	3.4%	96.6%	3.4%	96.6%
61,007	SUNFLOWER	3,142	71	3,071		3,000 D	2.3%	97.7%	2.3%	97.7%
34,166	TALLAHATCHIE	2,328	33	2,288	7	2,255 D	1.4%	98.3%	1.4%	98.6%
19,309	TATE	1,612	3	1,609		1,606 D	0.2%	99.8%	0.2%	99.8%
19,680	TIPPAH	2,311	63	2,248		2,185 D	2.7%	97.3%	2.7%	97.3%
16,974	TISHOMINGO	1,630	159	1,463	8	1,304 D	9.8%	89.8%	9.8%	90.2%
22,610	TUNICA	808	13	795		782 D	1.6%	98.4%	1.6%	98.4%
21,867	UNION	2,726	108	2,609	9	2,501 D	4.0%	95.7%	4.0%	96.0%
17,534	WALTHALL	1,247	40	1,206	1	1,166 D	3.2%	96.7%	3.2%	96.8%
39,595	WARREN	3,241	192	3,048	1	2,856 D	5.9%	94.0%	5.9%	94.1%
67,576	WASHINGTON	2,642	292	2,349	1	2,057 D	11.1%	88.9%	11.1%	88.9%
16,928	WAYNE	1,410	22	1,388		1,366 D	1.6%	98.4%	1.6%	98.4%
14,160	WEBSTER	1,687	87	1,595	5	1,508 D	5.2%	94.5%	5.2%	94.8%
15,955	WILKINSON	988	46	942		896 D	4.7%	95.3%	4.7%	95.3%
22,751	WINSTON	2,005	26	1,979		1,953 D	1.3%	98.7%	1.3%	98.7%
18,387	YALOBUSHA	1,605	50	1,555		1,505 D	3.1%	96.9%	3.1%	96.9%
40,091	YAZOO	2,435	45	2,390		2,345 D	1.8%	98.2%	1.8%	98.2%
2,183,796	TOTAL	175,824	7,364	168,267	193	160,903 D	4.2%	95.7%	4.2%	95.8%

MISSISSIPPI

PRESIDENT 1936

1930 Census Population	County	Total Vote	Republican	Democratic	Other	Rep.-Dem. Plurality	Percentage: Total Vote Rep.	Total Vote Dem.	Major Vote Rep.	Major Vote Dem.
23,564	ADAMS	1,860	124	1,732	4	1,608 D	6.7%	93.1%	6.7%	93.3%
23,653	ALCORN	2,457	53	2,396	8	2,343 D	2.2%	97.5%	2.2%	97.8%
19,712	AMITE	1,492	56	1,421	15	1,365 D	3.8%	95.2%	3.8%	96.2%
26,035	ATTALA	1,897	36	1,855	6	1,819 D	1.9%	97.8%	1.9%	98.1%
9,813	BENTON	1,727	10	1,717		1,707 D	0.6%	99.4%	0.6%	99.4%
71,051	BOLIVAR	2,397	101	2,296		2,195 D	4.2%	95.8%	4.2%	95.8%
18,080	CALHOUN	1,733	40	1,691	2	1,651 D	2.3%	97.6%	2.3%	97.7%
19,765	CARROLL	1,050	19	1,030	1	1,011 D	1.8%	98.1%	1.8%	98.2%
20,835	CHICKASAW	1,578	18	1,559	1	1,541 D	1.1%	98.8%	1.1%	98.9%
12,339	CHOCTAW	1,386	41	1,342	3	1,301 D	3.0%	96.8%	3.0%	97.0%
12,152	CLAIBORNE	806	31	774	1	743 D	3.8%	96.0%	3.9%	96.1%
19,679	CLARKE	2,123	31	2,089	3	2,058 D	1.5%	98.4%	1.5%	98.5%
17,931	CLAY	1,303	32	1,271		1,239 D	2.5%	97.5%	2.5%	97.5%
46,327	COAHOMA	2,108	49	2,059		2,010 D	2.3%	97.7%	2.3%	97.7%
31,614	COPIAH	2,443	45	2,397	1	2,352 D	1.8%	98.1%	1.8%	98.2%
15,028	COVINGTON	1,644	52	1,589	3	1,537 D	3.2%	96.7%	3.2%	96.8%
25,438	DE SOTO	1,356	13	1,343		1,330 D	1.0%	99.0%	1.0%	99.0%
30,115	FORREST	3,841	234	3,596	11	3,362 D	6.1%	93.6%	6.1%	93.9%
12,268	FRANKLIN	1,134	33	1,098	3	1,065 D	2.9%	96.8%	2.9%	97.1%
7,523	GEORGE	918	24	892	2	868 D	2.6%	97.2%	2.6%	97.4%
10,644	GREENE	879	46	830	3	784 D	5.2%	94.4%	5.3%	94.7%
16,802	GRENADA	1,258	13	1,245		1,232 D	1.0%	99.0%	1.0%	99.0%
11,415	HANCOCK	1,464	164	1,284	16	1,120 D	11.2%	87.7%	11.3%	88.7%
44,143	HARRISON	4,740	495	4,208	37	3,713 D	10.4%	88.8%	10.5%	89.5%
85,118	HINDS	8,976	313	8,647	16	8,334 D	3.5%	96.3%	3.5%	96.5%
38,534	HOLMES	1,897	12	1,885		1,873 D	0.6%	99.4%	0.6%	99.4%
24,729	HUMPHREYS	1,171	7	1,164		1,157 D	0.6%	99.4%	0.6%	99.4%
5,734	ISSAQUENA	214		214		214 D		100.0%		100.0%
18,225	ITAWAMBA	1,512	47	1,465		1,418 D	3.1%	96.9%	3.1%	96.9%
15,973	JACKSON	1,831	120	1,704	7	1,584 D	6.6%	93.1%	6.6%	93.4%
18,634	JASPER	2,027	21	2,004	2	1,983 D	1.0%	98.9%	1.0%	99.0%
14,291	JEFFERSON	894	9	884	1	875 D	1.0%	98.9%	1.0%	99.0%
14,281	JEFFERSON DAVIS	1,394	67	1,325	2	1,258 D	4.8%	95.1%	4.8%	95.2%
41,492	JONES	4,695	185	4,461	49	4,276 D	3.9%	95.0%	4.0%	96.0%
21,881	KEMPER	1,485	8	1,477		1,469 D	0.5%	99.5%	0.5%	99.5%
19,978	LAFAYETTE	1,683	26	1,652	5	1,626 D	1.5%	98.2%	1.5%	98.5%
12,848	LAMAR	1,306	91	1,210	5	1,119 D	7.0%	92.6%	7.0%	93.0%
52,748	LAUDERDALE	6,154	67	6,075	12	6,008 D	1.1%	98.7%	1.1%	98.9%
12,471	LAWRENCE	1,321	34	1,286	1	1,252 D	2.6%	97.4%	2.6%	97.4%
21,803	LEAKE	2,584	8	2,566	10	2,558 D	0.3%	99.3%	0.3%	99.7%
35,313	LEE	3,627	42	3,585		3,543 D	1.2%	98.8%	1.2%	98.8%
53,506	LEFLORE	2,173	35	2,137	1	2,102 D	1.6%	98.3%	1.6%	98.4%
26,357	LINCOLN	2,549	74	2,465	10	2,391 D	2.9%	96.7%	2.9%	97.1%
29,987	LOWNDES	2,394	56	2,328	10	2,272 D	2.3%	97.2%	2.3%	97.7%
35,796	MADISON	1,871	32	1,838	1	1,806 D	1.7%	98.2%	1.7%	98.3%
19,923	MARION	1,970	37	1,932	1	1,895 D	1.9%	98.1%	1.9%	98.1%
24,869	MARSHALL	1,134	22	1,111	1	1,089 D	1.9%	98.0%	1.9%	98.1%
36,141	MONROE	3,257	55	3,199	3	3,144 D	1.7%	98.2%	1.7%	98.3%
15,009	MONTGOMERY	1,388	5	1,383		1,378 D	0.4%	99.6%	0.4%	99.6%
26,691	NESHOBA	3,565	67	3,495	3	3,428 D	1.9%	98.0%	1.9%	98.1%
22,910	NEWTON	2,666	39	2,624	3	2,585 D	1.5%	98.4%	1.5%	98.5%
25,560	NOXUBEE	1,360	27	1,332	1	1,305 D	2.0%	97.9%	2.0%	98.0%
19,119	OKTIBBEHA	1,734	19	1,714	1	1,695 D	1.1%	98.8%	1.1%	98.9%
28,648	PANOLA	1,484	3	1,481		1,478 D	0.2%	99.8%	0.2%	99.8%
19,405	PEARL RIVER	1,240	81	1,156	3	1,075 D	6.5%	93.2%	6.5%	93.5%
8,197	PERRY	753	16	737		721 D	2.1%	97.9%	2.1%	97.9%
32,201	PIKE	3,261	86	3,170	5	3,084 D	2.6%	97.2%	2.6%	97.4%
22,034	PONTOTOC	2,388	93	2,286	9	2,193 D	3.9%	95.7%	3.9%	96.1%
19,265	PRENTISS	1,863	50	1,809	4	1,759 D	2.7%	97.1%	2.7%	97.3%
25,304	QUITMAN	1,035	9	1,025	1	1,016 D	0.9%	99.0%	0.9%	99.1%

MISSISSIPPI

PRESIDENT 1936

1930 Census Population	County	Total Vote	Republican	Democratic	Other	Rep.-Dem. Plurality	Percentage Total Vote Rep.	Total Vote Dem.	Major Vote Rep.	Major Vote Dem.
20,353	RANKIN	1,941	54	1,884	3	1,830 D	2.8%	97.1%	2.8%	97.2%
20,914	SCOTT	2,131	33	2,097	1	2,064 D	1.5%	98.4%	1.5%	98.5%
13,877	SHARKEY	574	7	567		560 D	1.2%	98.8%	1.2%	98.8%
20,897	SIMPSON	2,494	48	2,445	1	2,397 D	1.9%	98.0%	1.9%	98.1%
18,405	SMITH	1,694	17	1,676	1	1,659 D	1.0%	98.9%	1.0%	99.0%
5,704	STONE	700	23	675	2	652 D	3.3%	96.4%	3.3%	96.7%
66,364	SUNFLOWER	2,529	21	2,508		2,487 D	0.8%	99.2%	0.8%	99.2%
35,568	TALLAHATCHIE	1,572	4	1,567	1	1,563 D	0.3%	99.7%	0.3%	99.7%
17,671	TATE	1,095	7	1,088		1,081 D	0.6%	99.4%	0.6%	99.4%
18,658	TIPPAH	1,644	19	1,625		1,606 D	1.2%	98.8%	1.2%	98.8%
16,411	TISHOMINGO	1,744	115	1,619	10	1,504 D	6.6%	92.8%	6.6%	93.4%
21,233	TUNICA	706	5	701		696 D	0.7%	99.3%	0.7%	99.3%
21,268	UNION	2,316	63	2,249	4	2,186 D	2.7%	97.1%	2.7%	97.3%
13,871	WALTHALL	1,263	28	1,234	1	1,206 D	2.2%	97.7%	2.2%	97.8%
35,785	WARREN	3,361	122	3,233	6	3,111 D	3.6%	96.2%	3.6%	96.4%
54,310	WASHINGTON	2,241	94	2,143	4	2,049 D	4.2%	95.6%	4.2%	95.8%
15,295	WAYNE	1,412	44	1,367	1	1,323 D	3.1%	96.8%	3.1%	96.9%
12,128	WEBSTER	1,507	56	1,439	12	1,383 D	3.7%	95.5%	3.7%	96.3%
13,957	WILKINSON	790	21	767	2	746 D	2.7%	97.1%	2.7%	97.3%
21,239	WINSTON	2,440	21	2,418	1	2,397 D	0.9%	99.1%	0.9%	99.1%
17,750	YALOBUSHA	1,377	25	1,350	2	1,325 D	1.8%	98.0%	1.8%	98.2%
37,262	YAZOO	2,161	17	2,141	3	2,124 D	0.8%	99.1%	0.8%	99.2%
2,009,821	TOTAL	162,142	4,467	157,333	342	152,866 D	2.8%	97.0%	2.8%	97.2%

MISSISSIPPI

PRESIDENT 1932

1930 Census Population	County	Total Vote	Republican	Democratic	Other	Rep.-Dem. Plurality	Percentage Total Vote Rep.	Percentage Total Vote Dem.	Percentage Major Vote Rep.	Percentage Major Vote Dem.
23,564	ADAMS	1,819	384	1,420	15	1,036 D	21.1%	78.1%	21.3%	78.7%
23,653	ALCORN	2,544	73	2,461	10	2,388 D	2.9%	96.7%	2.9%	97.1%
19,712	AMITE	1,318	73	1,237	8	1,164 D	5.5%	93.9%	5.6%	94.4%
26,035	ATTALA	2,419	38	2,370	11	2,332 D	1.6%	98.0%	1.6%	98.4%
9,813	BENTON	823	8	814	1	806 D	1.0%	98.9%	1.0%	99.0%
71,051	BOLIVAR	2,151	204	1,941	6	1,737 D	9.5%	90.2%	9.5%	90.5%
18,080	CALHOUN	1,954	27	1,923	4	1,896 D	1.4%	98.4%	1.4%	98.6%
19,765	CARROLL	1,199	9	1,189	1	1,180 D	0.8%	99.2%	0.8%	99.2%
20,835	CHICKASAW	1,475	16	1,455	4	1,439 D	1.1%	98.6%	1.1%	98.9%
12,339	CHOCTAW	1,134	23	1,110	1	1,087 D	2.0%	97.9%	2.0%	98.0%
12,152	CLAIBORNE	730	16	713	1	697 D	2.2%	97.7%	2.2%	97.8%
19,679	CLARKE	1,542	53	1,482	7	1,429 D	3.4%	96.1%	3.5%	96.5%
17,931	CLAY	1,407	34	1,371	2	1,337 D	2.4%	97.4%	2.4%	97.6%
46,327	COAHOMA	1,737	62	1,672	3	1,610 D	3.6%	96.3%	3.6%	96.4%
31,614	COPIAH	2,403	28	2,371	4	2,343 D	1.2%	98.7%	1.2%	98.8%
15,028	COVINGTON	1,380	22	1,352	6	1,330 D	1.6%	98.0%	1.6%	98.4%
25,438	DE SOTO	1,413	13	1,396	4	1,383 D	0.9%	98.8%	0.9%	99.1%
30,115	FORREST	2,280	182	2,068	30	1,886 D	8.0%	90.7%	8.1%	91.9%
12,268	FRANKLIN	990	25	965		940 D	2.5%	97.5%	2.5%	97.5%
7,523	GEORGE	844	19	824	1	805 D	2.3%	97.6%	2.3%	97.7%
10,644	GREENE	848	29	818	1	789 D	3.4%	96.5%	3.4%	96.6%
16,802	GRENADA	1,112	11	1,101		1,090 D	1.0%	99.0%	1.0%	99.0%
11,415	HANCOCK	1,472	109	1,349	14	1,240 D	7.4%	91.6%	7.5%	92.5%
44,143	HARRISON	4,619	449	4,124	46	3,675 D	9.7%	89.3%	9.8%	90.2%
85,118	HINDS	6,983	403	6,541	39	6,138 D	5.8%	93.7%	5.8%	94.2%
38,534	HOLMES	1,852	45	1,799	8	1,754 D	2.4%	97.1%	2.4%	97.6%
24,729	HUMPHREYS	785	10	775		765 D	1.3%	98.7%	1.3%	98.7%
5,734	ISSAQUENA	160	1	159		158 D	0.6%	99.4%	0.6%	99.4%
18,225	ITAWAMBA	1,895	40	1,851	4	1,811 D	2.1%	97.7%	2.1%	97.9%
15,973	JACKSON	1,770	126	1,634	10	1,508 D	7.1%	92.3%	7.2%	92.8%
18,634	JASPER	1,579	38	1,526	15	1,488 D	2.4%	96.6%	2.4%	97.6%
14,291	JEFFERSON	782	24	753	5	729 D	3.1%	96.3%	3.1%	96.9%
14,281	JEFFERSON DAVIS	972	30	940	2	910 D	3.1%	96.7%	3.1%	96.9%
41,492	JONES	4,172	173	3,816	183	3,643 D	4.1%	91.5%	4.3%	95.7%
21,881	KEMPER	1,449	27	1,420	2	1,393 D	1.9%	98.0%	1.9%	98.1%
19,978	LAFAYETTE	1,861	26	1,831	4	1,805 D	1.4%	98.4%	1.4%	98.6%
12,848	LAMAR	1,069	31	1,033	5	1,002 D	2.9%	96.6%	2.9%	97.1%
52,748	LAUDERDALE	5,039	191	4,830	18	4,639 D	3.8%	95.9%	3.8%	96.2%
12,471	LAWRENCE	965	31	933	1	902 D	3.2%	96.7%	3.2%	96.8%
21,803	LEAKE	1,926	14	1,903	9	1,889 D	0.7%	98.8%	0.7%	99.3%
35,313	LEE	3,838	129	3,704	5	3,575 D	3.4%	96.5%	3.4%	96.6%
53,506	LEFLORE	1,915	34	1,877	4	1,843 D	1.8%	98.0%	1.8%	98.2%
26,357	LINCOLN	2,479	92	2,379	8	2,287 D	3.7%	96.0%	3.7%	96.3%
29,987	LOWNDES	2,364	50	2,305	9	2,255 D	2.1%	97.5%	2.1%	97.9%
35,796	MADISON	1,533	51	1,474	8	1,423 D	3.3%	96.2%	3.3%	96.7%
19,923	MARION	2,531	94	2,429	8	2,335 D	3.7%	96.0%	3.7%	96.3%
24,869	MARSHALL	1,320	38	1,281	1	1,243 D	2.9%	97.0%	2.9%	97.1%
36,141	MONROE	3,533	82	3,448	3	3,366 D	2.3%	97.6%	2.3%	97.7%
15,009	MONTGOMERY	1,384	17	1,366	1	1,349 D	1.2%	98.7%	1.2%	98.8%
26,691	NESHOBA	2,300	56	2,236	8	2,180 D	2.4%	97.2%	2.4%	97.6%
22,910	NEWTON	2,320	56	2,253	11	2,197 D	2.4%	97.1%	2.4%	97.6%
25,560	NOXUBEE	1,096	41	1,052	3	1,011 D	3.7%	96.0%	3.8%	96.2%
19,119	OKTIBBEHA	1,600	26	1,574		1,548 D	1.6%	98.4%	1.6%	98.4%
28,648	PANOLA	1,341	20	1,318	3	1,298 D	1.5%	98.3%	1.5%	98.5%
19,405	PEARL RIVER	1,613	99	1,500	14	1,401 D	6.1%	93.0%	6.2%	93.8%
8,197	PERRY	542	15	523	4	508 D	2.8%	96.5%	2.8%	97.2%
32,201	PIKE	2,528	118	2,400	10	2,282 D	4.7%	94.9%	4.7%	95.3%
22,034	PONTOTOC	1,900	31	1,862	7	1,831 D	1.6%	98.0%	1.6%	98.4%
19,265	PRENTISS	2,052	76	1,976		1,900 D	3.7%	96.3%	3.7%	96.3%
25,304	QUITMAN	742	18	720	4	702 D	2.4%	97.0%	2.4%	97.6%

MISSISSIPPI

PRESIDENT 1932

1930 Census Population	County	Total Vote	Republican	Democratic	Other	Rep.-Dem. Plurality	Percentage Total Vote Rep.	Total Vote Dem.	Major Vote Rep.	Major Vote Dem.
20,353	RANKIN	1,590	52	1,536	2	1,484 D	3.3%	96.6%	3.3%	96.7%
20,914	SCOTT	1,554	17	1,537		1,520 D	1.1%	98.9%	1.1%	98.9%
13,877	SHARKEY	552		551	1	551 D		99.8%		100.0%
20,897	SIMPSON	1,989	47	1,941	1	1,894 D	2.4%	97.6%	2.4%	97.6%
18,405	SMITH	1,595	17	1,576	2	1,559 D	1.1%	98.8%	1.1%	98.9%
5,704	STONE	458	32	424	2	392 D	7.0%	92.6%	7.0%	93.0%
66,364	SUNFLOWER	2,450	34	2,411	5	2,377 D	1.4%	98.4%	1.4%	98.6%
35,568	TALLAHATCHIE	2,471	16	2,453	2	2,437 D	0.6%	99.3%	0.6%	99.4%
17,671	TATE	996	9	986	1	977 D	0.9%	99.0%	0.9%	99.1%
18,658	TIPPAH	2,028	52	1,972	4	1,920 D	2.6%	97.2%	2.6%	97.4%
16,411	TISHOMINGO	1,754	112	1,636	6	1,524 D	6.4%	93.3%	6.4%	93.6%
21,233	TUNICA	581	8	573		565 D	1.4%	98.6%	1.4%	98.6%
21,268	UNION	2,346	74	2,264	8	2,190 D	3.2%	96.5%	3.2%	96.8%
13,871	WALTHALL	1,101	30	1,069	2	1,039 D	2.7%	97.1%	2.7%	97.3%
35,785	WARREN	2,611	169	2,422	20	2,253 D	6.5%	92.8%	6.5%	93.5%
54,310	WASHINGTON	1,795	100	1,691	4	1,591 D	5.6%	94.2%	5.6%	94.4%
15,295	WAYNE	1,050	23	1,023	4	1,000 D	2.2%	97.4%	2.2%	97.8%
12,128	WEBSTER	1,133	35	1,092	6	1,057 D	3.1%	96.4%	3.1%	96.9%
13,957	WILKINSON	834	18	813	3	795 D	2.2%	97.5%	2.2%	97.8%
21,239	WINSTON	1,736	12	1,720	4	1,708 D	0.7%	99.1%	0.7%	99.3%
17,750	YALOBUSHA	1,583	39	1,536	8	1,497 D	2.5%	97.0%	2.5%	97.5%
37,262	YAZOO	2,024	24	1,995	5	1,971 D	1.2%	98.6%	1.2%	98.8%
2,009,821	TOTAL	146,034	5,180	140,168	686	134,988 D	3.5%	96.0%	3.6%	96.4%

MISSISSIPPI

PRESIDENT 1928

1920 Census Population	County	Total Vote	Republican	Democratic	Other	Rep.-Dem. Plurality	Percentage Total Vote Rep.	Total Vote Dem.	Major Vote Rep.	Major Vote Dem.
22,183	ADAMS	2,177	840	1,337		497 D	38.6%	61.4%	38.6%	61.4%
21,369	ALCORN	1,866	335	1,531		1,196 D	18.0%	82.0%	18.0%	82.0%
18,960	AMITE	1,514	325	1,189		864 D	21.5%	78.5%	21.5%	78.5%
24,831	ATTALA	2,371	113	2,258		2,145 D	4.8%	95.2%	4.8%	95.2%
9,851	BENTON	840	47	793		746 D	5.6%	94.4%	5.6%	94.4%
57,669	BOLIVAR	2,205	266	1,939		1,673 D	12.1%	87.9%	12.1%	87.9%
16,823	CALHOUN	1,560	283	1,277		994 D	18.1%	81.9%	18.1%	81.9%
20,324	CARROLL	1,151	49	1,102		1,053 D	4.3%	95.7%	4.3%	95.7%
22,212	CHICKASAW	1,666	171	1,495		1,324 D	10.3%	89.7%	10.3%	89.7%
12,491	CHOCTAW	1,126	118	1,008		890 D	10.5%	89.5%	10.5%	89.5%
13,019	CLAIBORNE	751	43	708		665 D	5.7%	94.3%	5.7%	94.3%
17,927	CLARKE	1,694	563	1,131		568 D	33.2%	66.8%	33.2%	66.8%
17,490	CLAY	1,584	128	1,456		1,328 D	8.1%	91.9%	8.1%	91.9%
41,511	COAHOMA	2,001	223	1,778		1,555 D	11.1%	88.9%	11.1%	88.9%
28,672	COPIAH	2,894	161	2,733		2,572 D	5.6%	94.4%	5.6%	94.4%
14,869	COVINGTON	1,320	189	1,131		942 D	14.3%	85.7%	14.3%	85.7%
24,359	DE SOTO	1,421	64	1,357		1,293 D	4.5%	95.5%	4.5%	95.5%
21,238	FORREST	3,240	1,447	1,793		346 D	44.7%	55.3%	44.7%	55.3%
14,156	FRANKLIN	1,086	181	905		724 D	16.7%	83.3%	16.7%	83.3%
5,564	GEORGE	705	369	336		33 R	52.3%	47.7%	52.3%	47.7%
10,430	GREENE	935	342	593		251 D	36.6%	63.4%	36.6%	63.4%
13,607	GRENADA	1,195	40	1,155		1,115 D	3.3%	96.7%	3.3%	96.7%
10,380	HANCOCK	1,720	436	1,284		848 D	25.3%	74.7%	25.3%	74.7%
32,855	HARRISON	5,197	1,485	3,712		2,227 D	28.6%	71.4%	28.6%	71.4%
57,110	HINDS	6,683	976	5,707		4,731 D	14.6%	85.4%	14.6%	85.4%
34,513	HOLMES	2,138	134	2,004		1,870 D	6.3%	93.7%	6.3%	93.7%
19,192	HUMPHREYS	1,021	1	1,020		1,019 D	0.1%	99.9%	0.1%	99.9%
7,618	ISSAQUENA	140	6	134		128 D	4.3%	95.7%	4.3%	95.7%
15,647	ITAWAMBA	1,185	331	854		523 D	27.9%	72.1%	27.9%	72.1%
19,208	JACKSON	1,828	567	1,261		694 D	31.0%	69.0%	31.0%	69.0%
18,508	JASPER	1,604	625	979		354 D	39.0%	61.0%	39.0%	61.0%
15,946	JEFFERSON	891	61	830		769 D	6.8%	93.2%	6.8%	93.2%
12,755	JEFFERSON DAVIS	1,019	163	856		693 D	16.0%	84.0%	16.0%	84.0%
32,919	JONES	4,088	1,804	2,284		480 D	44.1%	55.9%	44.1%	55.9%
19,619	KEMPER	1,562	141	1,421		1,280 D	9.0%	91.0%	9.0%	91.0%
19,243	LAFAYETTE	1,783	131	1,652		1,521 D	7.3%	92.7%	7.3%	92.7%
12,869	LAMAR	1,128	410	718		308 D	36.3%	63.7%	36.3%	63.7%
45,897	LAUDERDALE	5,356	1,798	3,558		1,760 D	33.6%	66.4%	33.6%	66.4%
12,663	LAWRENCE	969	210	759		549 D	21.7%	78.3%	21.7%	78.3%
16,973	LEAKE	1,907	212	1,695		1,483 D	11.1%	88.9%	11.1%	88.9%
29,618	LEE	3,124	367	2,757		2,390 D	11.7%	88.3%	11.7%	88.3%
37,256	LEFLORE	2,324	105	2,219		2,114 D	4.5%	95.5%	4.5%	95.5%
24,652	LINCOLN	2,613	422	2,191		1,769 D	16.2%	83.8%	16.2%	83.8%
27,632	LOWNDES	2,321	185	2,136		1,951 D	8.0%	92.0%	8.0%	92.0%
29,292	MADISON	1,643	124	1,519		1,395 D	7.5%	92.5%	7.5%	92.5%
17,144	MARION	1,448	526	922		396 D	36.3%	63.7%	36.3%	63.7%
26,105	MARSHALL	1,522	100	1,422		1,322 D	6.6%	93.4%	6.6%	93.4%
32,613	MONROE	3,409	376	3,033		2,657 D	11.0%	89.0%	11.0%	89.0%
13,805	MONTGOMERY	1,705	98	1,607		1,509 D	5.7%	94.3%	5.7%	94.3%
19,303	NESHOBA	2,422	516	1,906		1,390 D	21.3%	78.7%	21.3%	78.7%
20,727	NEWTON	2,442	368	2,074		1,706 D	15.1%	84.9%	15.1%	84.9%
23,710	NOXUBEE	1,255	102	1,153		1,051 D	8.1%	91.9%	8.1%	91.9%
16,872	OKTIBBEHA	1,688	111	1,577		1,466 D	6.6%	93.4%	6.6%	93.4%
27,845	PANOLA	1,711	142	1,569		1,427 D	8.3%	91.7%	8.3%	91.7%
15,468	PEARL RIVER	1,797	918	879		39 R	51.1%	48.9%	51.1%	48.9%
8,987	PERRY	560	277	283		6 D	49.5%	50.5%	49.5%	50.5%
28,725	PIKE	3,351	920	2,431		1,511 D	27.5%	72.5%	27.5%	72.5%
19,962	PONTOTOC	1,798	261	1,537		1,276 D	14.5%	85.5%	14.5%	85.5%
17,606	PRENTISS	1,635	269	1,366		1,097 D	16.5%	83.5%	16.5%	83.5%
19,861	QUITMAN	879	86	793		707 D	9.8%	90.2%	9.8%	90.2%

MISSISSIPPI

PRESIDENT 1928

1920 Census Population	County	Total Vote	Republican	Democratic	Other	Rep.-Dem. Plurality	Percentage Total Vote Rep.	Percentage Total Vote Dem.	Percentage Major Vote Rep.	Percentage Major Vote Dem.
20,272	RANKIN	1,505	180	1,325		1,145 D	12.0%	88.0%	12.0%	88.0%
16,420	SCOTT	2,214	164	2,050		1,886 D	7.4%	92.6%	7.4%	92.6%
14,190	SHARKEY	511	36	475		439 D	7.0%	93.0%	7.0%	93.0%
18,109	SIMPSON	2,123	231	1,892		1,661 D	10.9%	89.1%	10.9%	89.1%
16,178	SMITH	1,869	419	1,450		1,031 D	22.4%	77.6%	22.4%	77.6%
6,528	STONE	694	436	258		178 R	62.8%	37.2%	62.8%	37.2%
46,374	SUNFLOWER	2,764	88	2,676		2,588 D	3.2%	96.8%	3.2%	96.8%
35,953	TALLAHATCHIE	2,317	33	2,284		2,251 D	1.4%	98.6%	1.4%	98.6%
19,636	TATE	1,316	42	1,274		1,232 D	3.2%	96.8%	3.2%	96.8%
15,419	TIPPAH	1,755	298	1,457		1,159 D	17.0%	83.0%	17.0%	83.0%
15,091	TISHOMINGO	1,550	585	965		380 D	37.7%	62.3%	37.7%	62.3%
20,386	TUNICA	680	26	654		628 D	3.8%	96.2%	3.8%	96.2%
20,044	UNION	2,182	324	1,858		1,534 D	14.8%	85.2%	14.8%	85.2%
13,455	WALTHALL	1,082	218	864		646 D	20.1%	79.9%	20.1%	79.9%
33,362	WARREN	3,299	530	2,769		2,239 D	16.1%	83.9%	16.1%	83.9%
51,092	WASHINGTON	1,742	246	1,496		1,250 D	14.1%	85.9%	14.1%	85.9%
15,467	WAYNE	1,206	289	917		628 D	24.0%	76.0%	24.0%	76.0%
12,644	WEBSTER	1,440	338	1,102		764 D	23.5%	76.5%	23.5%	76.5%
15,319	WILKINSON	840	73	767		694 D	8.7%	91.3%	8.7%	91.3%
18,139	WINSTON	1,717	97	1,620		1,523 D	5.6%	94.4%	5.6%	94.4%
18,738	YALOBUSHA	1,453	204	1,249		1,045 D	14.0%	86.0%	14.0%	86.0%
37,149	YAZOO	2,141	112	2,029		1,917 D	5.2%	94.8%	5.2%	94.8%
1,790,618	TOTAL	151,568	27,030	124,538		97,508 D	17.8%	82.2%	17.8%	82.2%

MISSISSIPPI

PRESIDENT 1924

1920 Census Population	County	Total Vote	Republican	Democratic	Other	Rep.-Dem. Plurality	Percentage: Total Vote Rep.	Total Vote Dem.	Major Vote Rep.	Major Vote Dem.
22,183	ADAMS	1,156	304	836	16	532 D	26.3%	72.3%	26.7%	73.3%
21,369	ALCORN	2,053	223	1,828	2	1,605 D	10.9%	89.0%	10.9%	89.1%
18,960	AMITE	1,012	86	926		840 D	8.5%	91.5%	8.5%	91.5%
24,831	ATTALA	1,766	119	1,600	47	1,481 D	6.7%	90.6%	6.9%	93.1%
9,851	BENTON	579	35	541	3	506 D	6.0%	93.4%	6.1%	93.9%
57,669	BOLIVAR	1,574	266	1,212	96	946 D	16.9%	77.0%	18.0%	82.0%
16,823	CALHOUN	1,397	69	1,129	199	1,060 D	4.9%	80.8%	5.8%	94.2%
20,324	CARROLL	965	70	895		825 D	7.3%	92.7%	7.3%	92.7%
22,212	CHICKASAW	1,416	86	1,301	29	1,215 D	6.1%	91.9%	6.2%	93.8%
12,491	CHOCTAW	1,317	98	1,219		1,121 D	7.4%	92.6%	7.4%	92.6%
13,019	CLAIBORNE	619	14	605		591 D	2.3%	97.7%	2.3%	97.7%
17,927	CLARKE	1,395	87	1,306	2	1,219 D	6.2%	93.6%	6.2%	93.8%
17,490	CLAY	1,218	82	1,136		1,054 D	6.7%	93.3%	6.7%	93.3%
41,511	COAHOMA	1,483	121	1,362		1,241 D	8.2%	91.8%	8.2%	91.8%
28,672	COPIAH	2,130	43	2,087		2,044 D	2.0%	98.0%	2.0%	98.0%
14,869	COVINGTON	963	48	822	93	774 D	5.0%	85.4%	5.5%	94.5%
24,359	DE SOTO	1,082	17	1,065		1,048 D	1.6%	98.4%	1.6%	98.4%
21,238	FORREST	2,134	156	1,826	152	1,670 D	7.3%	85.6%	7.9%	92.1%
14,156	FRANKLIN	627	36	591		555 D	5.7%	94.3%	5.7%	94.3%
5,564	GEORGE	570	68	502		434 D	11.9%	88.1%	11.9%	88.1%
10,430	GREENE	487	31	456		425 D	6.4%	93.6%	6.4%	93.6%
13,607	GRENADA	950	17	933		916 D	1.8%	98.2%	1.8%	98.2%
10,380	HANCOCK	709	192	467	50	275 D	27.1%	65.9%	29.1%	70.9%
32,855	HARRISON	3,739	523	3,044	172	2,521 D	14.0%	81.4%	14.7%	85.3%
57,110	HINDS	4,498	245	4,083	170	3,838 D	5.4%	90.8%	5.7%	94.3%
34,513	HOLMES	1,265	92	1,173		1,081 D	7.3%	92.7%	7.3%	92.7%
19,192	HUMPHREYS	661	33	628		595 D	5.0%	95.0%	5.0%	95.0%
7,618	ISSAQUENA	143	17	126		109 D	11.9%	88.1%	11.9%	88.1%
15,647	ITAWAMBA	950	62	888		826 D	6.5%	93.5%	6.5%	93.5%
19,208	JACKSON	1,170	158	1,010	2	852 D	13.5%	86.3%	13.5%	86.5%
18,508	JASPER	1,319	61	1,257	1	1,196 D	4.6%	95.3%	4.6%	95.4%
15,946	JEFFERSON	547	50	497		447 D	9.1%	90.9%	9.1%	90.9%
12,755	JEFFERSON DAVIS	820	88	732		644 D	10.7%	89.3%	10.7%	89.3%
32,919	JONES	3,155	318	2,373	464	2,055 D	10.1%	75.2%	11.8%	88.2%
19,619	KEMPER	967	56	911		855 D	5.8%	94.2%	5.8%	94.2%
19,243	LAFAYETTE	1,974	89	1,848	37	1,759 D	4.5%	93.6%	4.6%	95.4%
12,869	LAMAR	911	80	795	36	715 D	8.8%	87.3%	9.1%	90.9%
45,897	LAUDERDALE	4,113	320	3,204	589	2,884 D	7.8%	77.9%	9.1%	90.9%
12,663	LAWRENCE	729	55	674		619 D	7.5%	92.5%	7.5%	92.5%
16,973	LEAKE	1,303	48	1,255		1,207 D	3.7%	96.3%	3.7%	96.3%
29,618	LEE	2,773	152	2,621		2,469 D	5.5%	94.5%	5.5%	94.5%
37,256	LEFLORE	1,279	135	1,144		1,009 D	10.6%	89.4%	10.6%	89.4%
24,652	LINCOLN	1,502	154	1,278	70	1,124 D	10.3%	85.1%	10.8%	89.2%
27,632	LOWNDES	1,717	62	1,655		1,593 D	3.6%	96.4%	3.6%	96.4%
29,292	MADISON	1,707	109	1,598		1,489 D	6.4%	93.6%	6.4%	93.6%
17,144	MARION	1,138	99	1,039		940 D	8.7%	91.3%	8.7%	91.3%
26,105	MARSHALL	1,182	40	1,142		1,102 D	3.4%	96.6%	3.4%	96.6%
32,613	MONROE	2,479	121	2,326	32	2,205 D	4.9%	93.8%	4.9%	95.1%
13,805	MONTGOMERY	1,170	60	1,015	95	955 D	5.1%	86.8%	5.6%	94.4%
19,303	NESHOBA	1,831	228	1,603		1,375 D	12.5%	87.5%	12.5%	87.5%
20,727	NEWTON	1,822	72	1,657	93	1,585 D	4.0%	90.9%	4.2%	95.8%
23,710	NOXUBEE	1,010	44	966		922 D	4.4%	95.6%	4.4%	95.6%
16,872	OKTIBBEHA	1,442	30	1,370	42	1,340 D	2.1%	95.0%	2.1%	97.9%
27,845	PANOLA	1,348	53	1,264	31	1,211 D	3.9%	93.8%	4.0%	96.0%
15,468	PEARL RIVER	1,118	164	855	99	691 D	14.7%	76.5%	16.1%	83.9%
8,987	PERRY	455	55	383	17	328 D	12.1%	84.2%	12.6%	87.4%
28,725	PIKE	2,289	197	1,640	452	1,443 D	8.6%	71.6%	10.7%	89.3%
19,962	PONTOTOC	1,292	86	1,206		1,120 D	6.7%	93.3%	6.7%	93.3%
17,606	PRENTISS	1,406	179	1,225	2	1,046 D	12.7%	87.1%	12.7%	87.3%
19,861	QUITMAN	610	36	574		538 D	5.9%	94.1%	5.9%	94.1%

MISSISSIPPI

PRESIDENT 1924

1920 Census Population	County	Total Vote	Republican	Democratic	Other	Rep.-Dem. Plurality	Percentage: Total Vote Rep.	Total Vote Dem.	Major Vote Rep.	Major Vote Dem.
20,272	RANKIN	1,449	34	1,415		1,381 D	2.3%	97.7%	2.3%	97.7%
16,420	SCOTT	1,322	53	1,179	90	1,126 D	4.0%	89.2%	4.3%	95.7%
14,190	SHARKEY	393	34	353	6	319 D	8.7%	89.8%	8.8%	91.2%
18,109	SIMPSON	1,625	100	1,518	7	1,418 D	6.2%	93.4%	6.2%	93.8%
16,178	SMITH	1,161	49	1,081	31	1,032 D	4.2%	93.1%	4.3%	95.7%
6,528	STONE	468	56	412		356 D	12.0%	88.0%	12.0%	88.0%
46,374	SUNFLOWER	1,770	76	1,694		1,618 D	4.3%	95.7%	4.3%	95.7%
35,953	TALLAHATCHIE	1,401	15	1,386		1,371 D	1.1%	98.9%	1.1%	98.9%
19,636	TATE	1,014	6	1,002	6	996 D	0.6%	98.8%	0.6%	99.4%
15,419	TIPPAH	1,552	96	1,411	45	1,315 D	6.2%	90.9%	6.4%	93.6%
15,091	TISHOMINGO	1,460	279	1,181		902 D	19.1%	80.9%	19.1%	80.9%
20,386	TUNICA	508	13	495		482 D	2.6%	97.4%	2.6%	97.4%
20,044	UNION	1,971	135	1,750	86	1,615 D	6.8%	88.8%	7.2%	92.8%
13,455	WALTHALL	724	64	660		596 D	8.8%	91.2%	8.8%	91.2%
33,362	WARREN	2,122	328	1,794		1,466 D	15.5%	84.5%	15.5%	84.5%
51,092	WASHINGTON	1,422	143	1,277	2	1,134 D	10.1%	89.8%	10.1%	89.9%
15,467	WAYNE	961	56	905		849 D	5.8%	94.2%	5.8%	94.2%
12,644	WEBSTER	1,130	115	918	97	803 D	10.2%	81.2%	11.1%	88.9%
15,319	WILKINSON	395	40	355		315 D	10.1%	89.9%	10.1%	89.9%
18,139	WINSTON	1,397	53	1,344		1,291 D	3.8%	96.2%	3.8%	96.2%
18,738	YALOBUSHA	1,356	53	1,292	11	1,239 D	3.9%	95.3%	3.9%	96.1%
37,149	YAZOO	1,405	57	1,348		1,291 D	4.1%	95.9%	4.1%	95.9%
1,790,618	TOTAL	112,442	8,494	100,474	3,474	91,980 D	7.6%	89.4%	7.8%	92.2%

MISSISSIPPI

PRESIDENT 1920

1920 Census Population	County	Total Vote	Republican	Democratic	Other	Rep.-Dem. Plurality	Percentage Total Vote Rep.	Percentage Total Vote Dem.	Percentage Major Vote Rep.	Percentage Major Vote Dem.
22,183	ADAMS	759	114	642	3	528 D	15.0%	84.6%	15.1%	84.9%
21,369	ALCORN	1,731	354	1,336	41	982 D	20.5%	77.2%	20.9%	79.1%
18,960	AMITE	673	90	578	5	488 D	13.4%	85.9%	13.5%	86.5%
24,831	ATTALA	1,478	270	1,187	21	917 D	18.3%	80.3%	18.5%	81.5%
9,851	BENTON	535	124	405	6	281 D	23.2%	75.7%	23.4%	76.6%
57,669	BOLIVAR	1,370	326	1,039	5	713 D	23.8%	75.8%	23.9%	76.1%
16,823	CALHOUN	1,088	160	887	41	727 D	14.7%	81.5%	15.3%	84.7%
20,324	CARROLL	865	184	670	11	486 D	21.3%	77.5%	21.5%	78.5%
22,212	CHICKASAW	1,165	194	945	26	751 D	16.7%	81.1%	17.0%	83.0%
12,491	CHOCTAW	984	191	779	14	588 D	19.4%	79.2%	19.7%	80.3%
13,019	CLAIBORNE	416	14	401	1	387 D	3.4%	96.4%	3.4%	96.6%
17,927	CLARKE	880	47	809	24	762 D	5.3%	91.9%	5.5%	94.5%
17,490	CLAY	821	48	770	3	722 D	5.8%	93.8%	5.9%	94.1%
41,511	COAHOMA	954	61	883	10	822 D	6.4%	92.6%	6.5%	93.5%
28,672	COPIAH	1,371	60	1,297	14	1,237 D	4.4%	94.6%	4.4%	95.6%
14,869	COVINGTON	936	257	650	29	393 D	27.5%	69.4%	28.3%	71.7%
24,359	DE SOTO	845	27	816	2	789 D	3.2%	96.6%	3.2%	96.8%
21,238	FORREST	1,357	140	1,151	66	1,011 D	10.3%	84.8%	10.8%	89.2%
14,156	FRANKLIN	860	203	654	3	451 D	23.6%	76.0%	23.7%	76.3%
5,564	GEORGE	335	56	262	17	206 D	16.7%	78.2%	17.6%	82.4%
10,430	GREENE	364	24	337	3	313 D	6.6%	92.6%	6.6%	93.4%
13,607	GRENADA	552	12	532	8	520 D	2.2%	96.4%	2.2%	97.8%
10,380	HANCOCK	439	130	306	3	176 D	29.6%	69.7%	29.8%	70.2%
32,855	HARRISON	1,625	314	1,267	44	953 D	19.3%	78.0%	19.9%	80.1%
57,110	HINDS	2,737	151	2,519	67	2,368 D	5.5%	92.0%	5.7%	94.3%
34,513	HOLMES	1,001	69	917	15	848 D	6.9%	91.6%	7.0%	93.0%
19,192	HUMPHREYS	340	21	317	2	296 D	6.2%	93.2%	6.2%	93.8%
7,618	ISSAQUENA	96	13	83		70 D	13.5%	86.5%	13.5%	86.5%
15,647	ITAWAMBA	1,224	198	1,023	3	825 D	16.2%	83.6%	16.2%	83.8%
19,208	JACKSON	703	121	578	4	457 D	17.2%	82.2%	17.3%	82.7%
18,508	JASPER	1,012	98	899	15	801 D	9.7%	88.8%	9.8%	90.2%
15,946	JEFFERSON	445	14	430	1	416 D	3.1%	96.6%	3.2%	96.8%
12,755	JEFFERSON DAVIS	670	179	486	5	307 D	26.7%	72.5%	26.9%	73.1%
32,919	JONES	2,057	419	1,398	240	979 D	20.4%	68.0%	23.1%	76.9%
19,619	KEMPER	889	129	734	26	605 D	14.5%	82.6%	14.9%	85.1%
19,243	LAFAYETTE	1,209	321	876	12	555 D	26.6%	72.5%	26.8%	73.2%
12,869	LAMAR	883	192	672	19	480 D	21.7%	76.1%	22.2%	77.8%
45,897	LAUDERDALE	2,893	228	2,539	126	2,311 D	7.9%	87.8%	8.2%	91.8%
12,663	LAWRENCE	662	131	529	2	398 D	19.8%	79.9%	19.8%	80.2%
16,973	LEAKE	1,227	121	1,081	25	960 D	9.9%	88.1%	10.1%	89.9%
29,618	LEE	1,967	302	1,655	10	1,353 D	15.4%	84.1%	15.4%	84.6%
37,256	LEFLORE	1,012	39	969	4	930 D	3.9%	95.8%	3.9%	96.1%
24,652	LINCOLN	1,208	421	774	13	353 D	34.9%	64.1%	35.2%	64.8%
27,632	LOWNDES	991	51	931	9	880 D	5.1%	93.9%	5.2%	94.8%
29,292	MADISON	896	57	831	8	774 D	6.4%	92.7%	6.4%	93.6%
17,144	MARION	772	143	613	16	470 D	18.5%	79.4%	18.9%	81.1%
26,105	MARSHALL	856	30	823	3	793 D	3.5%	96.1%	3.5%	96.5%
32,613	MONROE	2,034	139	1,881	14	1,742 D	6.8%	92.5%	6.9%	93.1%
13,805	MONTGOMERY	918	57	847	14	790 D	6.2%	92.3%	6.3%	93.7%
19,303	NESHOBA	1,326	182	1,089	55	907 D	13.7%	82.1%	14.3%	85.7%
20,727	NEWTON	1,399	108	1,209	82	1,101 D	7.7%	86.4%	8.2%	91.8%
23,710	NOXUBEE	724	24	699	1	675 D	3.3%	96.5%	3.3%	96.7%
16,872	OKTIBBEHA	850	70	779	1	709 D	8.2%	91.6%	8.2%	91.8%
27,845	PANOLA	926	80	843	3	763 D	8.6%	91.0%	8.7%	91.3%
15,468	PEARL RIVER	519	53	464	2	411 D	10.2%	89.4%	10.3%	89.7%
8,987	PERRY	345	69	271	5	202 D	20.0%	78.6%	20.3%	79.7%
28,725	PIKE	1,312	153	1,114	45	961 D	11.7%	84.9%	12.1%	87.9%
19,962	PONTOTOC	1,447	439	991	17	552 D	30.3%	68.5%	30.7%	69.3%
17,606	PRENTISS	1,538	496	993	49	497 D	32.2%	64.6%	33.3%	66.7%
19,861	QUITMAN	417	39	377	1	338 D	9.4%	90.4%	9.4%	90.6%

MISSISSIPPI

PRESIDENT 1920

1920 Census Population	County	Total Vote	Republican	Democratic	Other	Rep.-Dem. Plurality	Percentage Total Vote Rep.	Percentage Total Vote Dem.	Percentage Major Vote Rep.	Percentage Major Vote Dem.
20,272	RANKIN	952	43	904	5	861 D	4.5%	95.0%	4.5%	95.5%
16,420	SCOTT	1,141	64	1,055	22	991 D	5.6%	92.5%	5.7%	94.3%
14,190	SHARKEY	235	7	228		221 D	3.0%	97.0%	3.0%	97.0%
18,109	SIMPSON	1,025	109	902	14	793 D	10.6%	88.0%	10.8%	89.2%
16,178	SMITH	1,256	265	968	23	703 D	21.1%	77.1%	21.5%	78.5%
6,528	STONE	320	16	299	5	283 D	5.0%	93.4%	5.1%	94.9%
46,374	SUNFLOWER	1,117	47	1,061	9	1,014 D	4.2%	95.0%	4.2%	95.8%
35,953	TALLAHATCHIE	1,174	69	1,092	13	1,023 D	5.9%	93.0%	5.9%	94.1%
19,636	TATE	1,004	117	876	11	759 D	11.7%	87.3%	11.8%	88.2%
15,419	TIPPAH	1,214	237	955	22	718 D	19.5%	78.7%	19.9%	80.1%
15,091	TISHOMINGO	1,249	387	841	21	454 D	31.0%	67.3%	31.5%	68.5%
20,386	TUNICA	259	2	256	1	254 D	0.8%	98.8%	0.8%	99.2%
20,044	UNION	1,665	429	1,224	12	795 D	25.8%	73.5%	26.0%	74.0%
13,455	WALTHALL	600	139	446	15	307 D	23.2%	74.3%	23.8%	76.2%
33,362	WARREN	1,258	161	1,082	15	921 D	12.8%	86.0%	13.0%	87.0%
51,092	WASHINGTON	837	60	776	1	716 D	7.2%	92.7%	7.2%	92.8%
15,467	WAYNE	707	112	547	48	435 D	15.8%	77.4%	17.0%	83.0%
12,644	WEBSTER	925	299	580	46	281 D	32.3%	62.7%	34.0%	66.0%
15,319	WILKINSON	433	15	416	2	401 D	3.5%	96.1%	3.5%	96.5%
18,139	WINSTON	1,080	113	950	17	837 D	10.5%	88.0%	10.6%	89.4%
18,738	YALOBUSHA	985	82	893	10	811 D	8.3%	90.7%	8.4%	91.6%
37,149	YAZOO	1,007	46	948	13	902 D	4.6%	94.1%	4.6%	95.4%
1,790,618	TOTAL	82,351	11,576	69,136	1,639	57,560 D	14.1%	84.0%	14.3%	85.7%

MISSISSIPPI

ELECTION NOTES

1956 A special four-column table which gives the Independent elector ticket vote is used to detail this election. Republican figures include 56,372 Republican and 4,313 Mississippi Black-and-Tan Grand Old Party votes.

1952 Republican votes are those cast for a group of electors officially listed as Independent "pledged to vote for the nominees of the National Republican Party".

1948 A special four-column table which gives the Thurmond (States Rights) vote is used to detail this election. Other vote was Wallace (Progressive). Republican figures include 2,595 Republican and 2,448 Independent Republican votes.

1944 The Democratic figures include 158,657 votes cast for a special elector ticket designated by the Legislature and 9,964 Convention votes. Republican figures include 7,860 Independent Republican and 3,753 Republican votes.

1940 Other vote was Thomas (Socialist). The Republican figures include 4,550 Independent Republican and 2,814 Republican votes.

1936 Other vote was Thomas (Socialist). The Republican figures include 2,772 Black-and-Tan and 1,695 Lily White votes.

1932 Other vote was Thomas (Socialist). The Republican figures include 3,210 Lily White and 1,970 Black-and-Tan votes.

1928 The Republican figures include 26,222 Republican, 544 Ligon elector ticket and 264 Rogers elector ticket votes. Ligon votes represented the Howard group of Republicans. Some sources identify the Rogers votes as Socialist, though they are included with the Republican total in the report of the Clerk of the House of Representatives and are so listed here.

1924 Other vote was LaFollette (Progressive).

1920 Other vote was Debs (Socialist).

MISSOURI

POPULAR VOTE FOR PRESIDENT 1920 TO 1956

Year	Total Vote	Republican Vote	Republican Candidate	Democratic Vote	Democratic Candidate	Other Vote	Plurality	Percentage Total Vote Rep.	Percentage Total Vote Dem.	Percentage Major Vote Rep.	Percentage Major Vote Dem.
1956	1,832,562	914,289	Eisenhower, Dwight D.	918,273	Stevenson, Adlai E.		3,984 D	49.9%	50.1%	49.9%	50.1%
1952	1,892,062	959,429	Eisenhower, Dwight D.	929,830	Stevenson, Adlai E.	2,803	29,599 R	50.7%	49.1%	50.8%	49.2%
1948	1,578,628	655,039	Dewey, Thomas E.	917,315	Truman, Harry S.	6,274	262,276 D	41.5%	58.1%	41.7%	58.3%
1944	1,571,697	761,175	Dewey, Thomas E.	807,356	Roosevelt, Franklin D.	3,166	46,181 D	48.4%	51.4%	48.5%	51.5%
1940	1,833,729	871,009	Willkie, Wendell	958,476	Roosevelt, Franklin D.	4,244	87,467 D	47.5%	52.3%	47.6%	52.4%
1936	1,828,635	697,891	Landon, Alfred M.	1,111,043	Roosevelt, Franklin D.	19,701	413,152 D	38.2%	60.8%	38.6%	61.4%
1932	1,609,894	564,713	Hoover, Herbert C.	1,025,406	Roosevelt, Franklin D.	19,775	460,693 D	35.1%	63.7%	35.5%	64.5%
1928	1,500,845	834,080	Hoover, Herbert C.	662,684	Smith, Alfred E.	4,081	171,396 R	55.6%	44.2%	55.7%	44.3%
1924	1,310,095	648,488	Coolidge, Calvin	574,962	Davis, John W.	86,645	73,526 R	49.5%	43.9%	53.0%	47.0%
1920	1,332,140	727,252	Harding, Warren G.	574,699	Cox, James M.	30,189	152,553 R	54.6%	43.1%	55.9%	44.1%

ELECTORAL COLLEGE VOTE 1920 TO 1956

Year	Total	Republican	Democratic	Other
1956	13	—	13	—
1952	13	13	—	—
1948	15	—	15	—
1944	15	—	15	—
1940	15	—	15	—
1936	15	—	15	—
1932	15	—	15	—
1928	18	18	—	—
1924	18	18	—	—
1920	18	18	—	—

MISSOURI

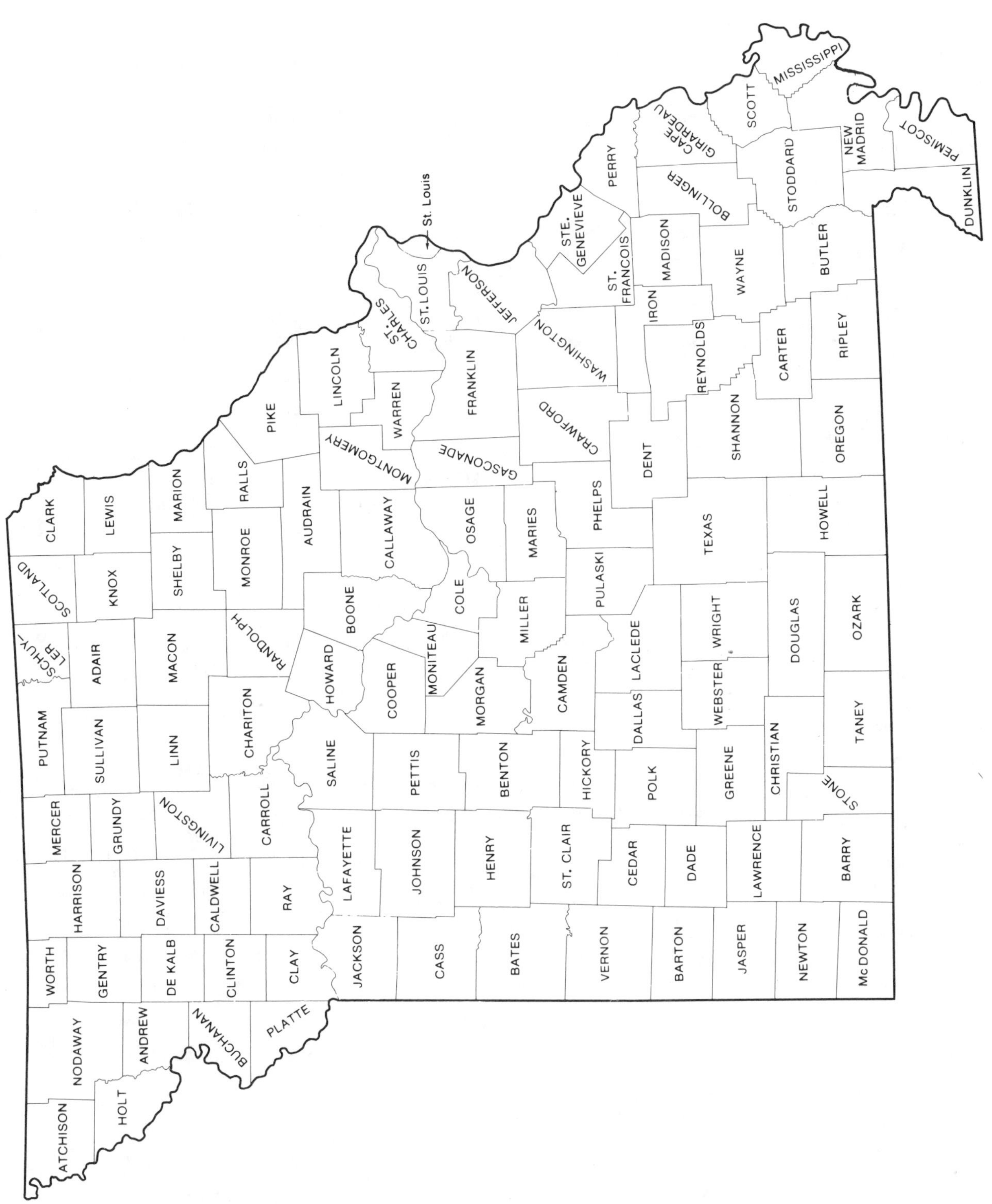
St. Louis
MISSISSIPPI
SCOTT
CAPE GIRARDEAU
NEW MADRID
PEMISCOT
PERRY
BOLLINGER
STODDARD
DUNKLIN
STE. GENEVIEVE
ST. FRANCOIS
MADISON
WAYNE
BUTLER
ST. LOUIS
JEFFERSON
ST. CHARLES
IRON
REYNOLDS
CARTER
RIPLEY
WASHINGTON
LINCOLN
FRANKLIN
WARREN
PIKE
CRAWFORD
SHANNON
OREGON
DENT
MONTGOMERY
GASCONADE
RALLS
MARION
LEWIS
CLARK
AUDRAIN
CALLAWAY
OSAGE
MARIES
PHELPS
TEXAS
HOWELL
MONROE
SHELBY
KNOX
SCOTLAND
PULASKI
BOONE
COLE
MILLER
WRIGHT
DOUGLAS
OZARK
RANDOLPH
MACON
ADAIR
SCHUYLER
HOWARD
MONITEAU
LACLEDE
CAMDEN
COOPER
MORGAN
CHARITON
WEBSTER
DALLAS
TANEY
PUTNAM
SULLIVAN
LINN
SALINE
PETTIS
BENTON
HICKORY
POLK
GREENE
CHRISTIAN
STONE
MERCER
GRUNDY
LIVINGSTON
CARROLL
LAFAYETTE
JOHNSON
HENRY
ST. CLAIR
CEDAR
DADE
LAWRENCE
BARRY
HARRISON
DAVIESS
CALDWELL
RAY
WORTH
GENTRY
DE KALB
CLINTON
CLAY
JACKSON
CASS
BATES
VERNON
BARTON
JASPER
NEWTON
McDONALD
NODAWAY
ANDREW
BUCHANAN
PLATTE
ATCHISON
HOLT

MISSOURI

PRESIDENT 1956

1950 Census Population	County	Total Vote	Republican	Democratic	Other	Rep.-Dem. Plurality	Percentage Total Vote Rep.	Total Vote Dem.	Major Vote Rep.	Major Vote Dem.
19,689	ADAIR	8,740	5,322	3,418		1,904 R	60.9%	39.1%	60.9%	39.1%
11,727	ANDREW	6,002	3,609	2,393		1,216 R	60.1%	39.9%	60.1%	39.9%
11,127	ATCHISON	5,095	2,774	2,321		453 R	54.4%	45.6%	54.4%	45.6%
23,829	AUDRAIN	10,615	4,664	5,951		1,287 D	43.9%	56.1%	43.9%	56.1%
21,755	BARRY	10,586	6,063	4,523		1,540 R	57.3%	42.7%	57.3%	42.7%
12,678	BARTON	6,428	3,547	2,881		666 R	55.2%	44.8%	55.2%	44.8%
17,534	BATES	9,767	5,467	4,300		1,167 R	56.0%	44.0%	56.0%	44.0%
9,080	BENTON	4,708	3,145	1,563		1,582 R	66.8%	33.2%	66.8%	33.2%
11,019	BOLLINGER	5,030	2,845	2,185		660 R	56.6%	43.4%	56.6%	43.4%
48,432	BOONE	18,601	8,197	10,404		2,207 D	44.1%	55.9%	44.1%	55.9%
96,826	BUCHANAN	38,695	20,311	18,384		1,927 R	52.5%	47.5%	52.5%	47.5%
37,707	BUTLER	13,085	7,216	5,869		1,347 R	55.1%	44.9%	55.1%	44.9%
9,929	CALDWELL	5,145	3,216	1,929		1,287 R	62.5%	37.5%	62.5%	37.5%
23,316	CALLAWAY	8,737	3,572	5,165		1,593 D	40.9%	59.1%	40.9%	59.1%
7,861	CAMDEN	4,277	2,817	1,460		1,357 R	65.9%	34.1%	65.9%	34.1%
38,397	CAPE GIRARDEAU	18,271	10,638	7,633		3,005 R	58.2%	41.8%	58.2%	41.8%
15,589	CARROLL	8,183	4,751	3,432		1,319 R	58.1%	41.9%	58.1%	41.9%
4,777	CARTER	2,100	1,033	1,067		34 D	49.2%	50.8%	49.2%	50.8%
19,325	CASS	11,164	5,589	5,575		14 R	50.1%	49.9%	50.1%	49.9%
10,663	CEDAR	4,996	3,276	1,720		1,556 R	65.6%	34.4%	65.6%	34.4%
14,944	CHARITON	7,130	3,459	3,671		212 D	48.5%	51.5%	48.5%	51.5%
12,412	CHRISTIAN	5,462	3,732	1,730		2,002 R	68.3%	31.7%	68.3%	31.7%
9,003	CLARK	4,816	2,623	2,193		430 R	54.5%	45.5%	54.5%	45.5%
45,221	CLAY	27,041	13,436	13,605		169 D	49.7%	50.3%	49.7%	50.3%
11,726	CLINTON	6,002	3,026	2,976		50 R	50.4%	49.6%	50.4%	49.6%
35,464	COLE	16,711	9,323	7,388		1,935 R	55.8%	44.2%	55.8%	44.2%
16,608	COOPER	8,506	4,995	3,511		1,484 R	58.7%	41.3%	58.7%	41.3%
11,615	CRAWFORD	6,049	3,594	2,455		1,139 R	59.4%	40.6%	59.4%	40.6%
9,324	DADE	4,120	2,641	1,479		1,162 R	64.1%	35.9%	64.1%	35.9%
10,392	DALLAS	4,587	2,987	1,600		1,387 R	65.1%	34.9%	65.1%	34.9%
11,180	DAVIESS	5,937	3,326	2,611		715 R	56.0%	44.0%	56.0%	44.0%
8,047	DE KALB	4,410	2,538	1,872		666 R	57.6%	42.4%	57.6%	42.4%
10,936	DENT	5,619	2,658	2,961		303 D	47.3%	52.7%	47.3%	52.7%
12,638	DOUGLAS	4,043	2,910	1,133		1,777 R	72.0%	28.0%	72.0%	28.0%
45,329	DUNKLIN	13,641	4,943	8,698		3,755 D	36.2%	63.8%	36.2%	63.8%
36,046	FRANKLIN	19,996	11,605	8,391		3,214 R	58.0%	42.0%	58.0%	42.0%
12,342	GASCONADE	6,433	5,080	1,353		3,727 R	79.0%	21.0%	79.0%	21.0%
11,036	GENTRY	5,682	3,020	2,662		358 R	53.2%	46.8%	53.2%	46.8%
104,823	GREENE	50,150	29,944	20,206		9,738 R	59.7%	40.3%	59.7%	40.3%
13,220	GRUNDY	6,891	4,139	2,752		1,387 R	60.1%	39.9%	60.1%	39.9%
14,107	HARRISON	6,659	4,141	2,518		1,623 R	62.2%	37.8%	62.2%	37.8%
20,043	HENRY	10,689	5,789	4,900		889 R	54.2%	45.8%	54.2%	45.8%
5,387	HICKORY	2,356	1,661	695		966 R	70.5%	29.5%	70.5%	29.5%
9,833	HOLT	4,601	2,888	1,713		1,175 R	62.8%	37.2%	62.8%	37.2%
11,857	HOWARD	5,719	2,177	3,542		1,365 D	38.1%	61.9%	38.1%	61.9%
22,725	HOWELL	8,539	5,473	3,066		2,407 R	64.1%	35.9%	64.1%	35.9%
9,458	IRON	3,780	1,810	1,970		160 D	47.9%	52.1%	47.9%	52.1%
541,035	JACKSON	255,704	122,182	133,522		11,340 D	47.8%	52.2%	47.8%	52.2%
79,106	JASPER	33,818	20,414	13,404		7,010 R	60.4%	39.6%	60.4%	39.6%
38,007	JEFFERSON	24,580	10,712	13,868		3,156 D	43.6%	56.4%	43.6%	56.4%
20,716	JOHNSON	11,129	6,599	4,530		2,069 R	59.3%	40.7%	59.3%	40.7%
7,617	KNOX	3,784	1,934	1,850		84 R	51.1%	48.9%	51.1%	48.9%
19,010	LACLEDE	8,366	5,079	3,287		1,792 R	60.7%	39.3%	60.7%	39.3%
25,272	LAFAYETTE	14,214	8,133	6,081		2,052 R	57.2%	42.8%	57.2%	42.8%
23,420	LAWRENCE	12,161	7,372	4,789		2,583 R	60.6%	39.4%	60.6%	39.4%
10,733	LEWIS	5,029	2,301	2,728		427 D	45.8%	54.2%	45.8%	54.2%
13,478	LINCOLN	7,104	3,114	3,990		876 D	43.8%	56.2%	43.8%	56.2%
18,865	LINN	10,083	5,028	5,055		27 D	49.9%	50.1%	49.9%	50.1%
16,532	LIVINGSTON	8,950	5,165	3,785		1,380 R	57.7%	42.3%	57.7%	42.3%
14,144	MCDONALD	6,403	3,646	2,757		889 R	56.9%	43.1%	56.9%	43.1%

MISSOURI

PRESIDENT 1956

1950 Census Population	County	Total Vote	Republican	Democratic	Other	Rep.-Dem. Plurality	Percentage Total Vote Rep.	Total Vote Dem.	Major Vote Rep.	Major Vote Dem.
18,332	MACON	9,031	4,694	4,337		357 R	52.0%	48.0%	52.0%	48.0%
10,380	MADISON	5,043	2,763	2,280		483 R	54.8%	45.2%	54.8%	45.2%
7,423	MARIES	3,277	1,392	1,885		493 D	42.5%	57.5%	42.5%	57.5%
29,765	MARION	12,531	5,657	6,874		1,217 D	45.1%	54.9%	45.1%	54.9%
7,235	MERCER	3,144	2,035	1,109		926 R	64.7%	35.3%	64.7%	35.3%
13,734	MILLER	6,620	4,085	2,535		1,550 R	61.7%	38.3%	61.7%	38.3%
22,551	MISSISSIPPI	5,764	2,111	3,653		1,542 D	36.6%	63.4%	36.6%	63.4%
10,840	MONITEAU	5,791	3,239	2,552		687 R	55.9%	44.1%	55.9%	44.1%
11,314	MONROE	5,743	1,331	4,412		3,081 D	23.2%	76.8%	23.2%	76.8%
11,555	MONTGOMERY	6,287	3,443	2,844		599 R	54.8%	45.2%	54.8%	45.2%
10,207	MORGAN	5,294	3,163	2,131		1,032 R	59.7%	40.3%	59.7%	40.3%
39,444	NEW MADRID	11,971	3,552	8,419		4,867 D	29.7%	70.3%	29.7%	70.3%
28,240	NEWTON	13,321	7,792	5,529		2,263 R	58.5%	41.5%	58.5%	41.5%
24,033	NODAWAY	11,752	6,381	5,371		1,010 R	54.3%	45.7%	54.3%	45.7%
11,978	OREGON	3,908	1,436	2,472		1,036 D	36.7%	63.3%	36.7%	63.3%
11,301	OSAGE	5,522	3,077	2,445		632 R	55.7%	44.3%	55.7%	44.3%
8,856	OZARK	3,028	2,141	887		1,254 R	70.7%	29.3%	70.7%	29.3%
45,624	PEMISCOT	12,033	3,969	8,064		4,095 D	33.0%	67.0%	33.0%	67.0%
14,890	PERRY	6,746	4,400	2,346		2,054 R	65.2%	34.8%	65.2%	34.8%
31,577	PETTIS	15,852	8,766	7,086		1,680 R	55.3%	44.7%	55.3%	44.7%
21,504	PHELPS	9,534	4,773	4,761		12 R	50.1%	49.9%	50.1%	49.9%
16,844	PIKE	7,706	3,474	4,232		758 D	45.1%	54.9%	45.1%	54.9%
14,973	PLATTE	8,867	3,596	5,271		1,675 D	40.6%	59.4%	40.6%	59.4%
16,062	POLK	7,378	4,410	2,968		1,442 R	59.8%	40.2%	59.8%	40.2%
10,392	PULASKI	5,468	2,532	2,936		404 D	46.3%	53.7%	46.3%	53.7%
9,166	PUTNAM	3,789	2,674	1,115		1,559 R	70.6%	29.4%	70.6%	29.4%
8,686	RALLS	4,005	1,373	2,632		1,259 D	34.3%	65.7%	34.3%	65.7%
22,918	RANDOLPH	10,506	3,709	6,797		3,088 D	35.3%	64.7%	35.3%	64.7%
15,932	RAY	7,677	3,041	4,636		1,595 D	39.6%	60.4%	39.6%	60.4%
6,918	REYNOLDS	2,513	917	1,596		679 D	36.5%	63.5%	36.5%	63.5%
11,414	RIPLEY	4,338	2,189	2,149		40 R	50.5%	49.5%	50.5%	49.5%
29,834	ST. CHARLES	17,080	9,462	7,618		1,844 R	55.4%	44.6%	55.4%	44.6%
10,482	ST. CLAIR	5,218	3,018	2,200		818 R	57.8%	42.2%	57.8%	42.2%
35,276	ST. FRANCOIS	17,534	9,968	7,566		2,402 R	56.8%	43.2%	56.8%	43.2%
856,796	ST. LOUIS CITY	332,255	130,045	202,210		72,165 D	39.1%	60.9%	39.1%	60.9%
406,349	ST. LOUIS COUNTY	259,992	138,111	121,881		16,230 R	53.1%	46.9%	53.1%	46.9%
11,237	STE. GENEVIEVE	4,996	2,633	2,363		270 R	52.7%	47.3%	52.7%	47.3%
26,694	SALINE	11,811	5,970	5,841		129 R	50.5%	49.5%	50.5%	49.5%
5,760	SCHUYLER	3,148	1,500	1,648		148 D	47.6%	52.4%	47.6%	52.4%
7,332	SCOTLAND	3,779	1,735	2,044		309 D	45.9%	54.1%	45.9%	54.1%
32,842	SCOTT	11,337	4,654	6,683		2,029 D	41.1%	58.9%	41.1%	58.9%
8,377	SHANNON	2,993	1,171	1,822		651 D	39.1%	60.9%	39.1%	60.9%
9,730	SHELBY	5,034	1,990	3,044		1,054 D	39.5%	60.5%	39.5%	60.5%
33,463	STODDARD	11,201	4,832	6,369		1,537 D	43.1%	56.9%	43.1%	56.9%
9,748	STONE	3,988	2,939	1,049		1,890 R	73.7%	26.3%	73.7%	26.3%
11,299	SULLIVAN	6,162	3,357	2,805		552 R	54.5%	45.5%	54.5%	45.5%
9,863	TANEY	4,695	3,218	1,477		1,741 R	68.5%	31.5%	68.5%	31.5%
18,992	TEXAS	8,858	4,352	4,506		154 D	49.1%	50.9%	49.1%	50.9%
22,685	VERNON	9,731	5,184	4,547		637 R	53.3%	46.7%	53.3%	46.7%
7,666	WARREN	4,063	2,852	1,211		1,641 R	70.2%	29.8%	70.2%	29.8%
14,689	WASHINGTON	5,763	3,383	2,380		1,003 R	58.7%	41.3%	58.7%	41.3%
10,514	WAYNE	4,964	2,513	2,451		62 R	50.6%	49.4%	50.6%	49.4%
15,072	WEBSTER	7,072	3,940	3,132		808 R	55.7%	44.3%	55.7%	44.3%
5,120	WORTH	2,692	1,338	1,354		16 D	49.7%	50.3%	49.7%	50.3%
15,834	WRIGHT	6,638	4,360	2,278		2,082 R	65.7%	34.3%	65.7%	34.3%
3,954,653	TOTAL	1,832,562	914,289	918,273		3,984 D	49.9%	50.1%	49.9%	50.1%

MISSOURI

PRESIDENT 1952

1950 Census Population	County	Total Vote	Republican	Democratic	Other	Rep.-Dem. Plurality	Percentage Total Vote Rep.	Percentage Total Vote Dem.	Percentage Major Vote Rep.	Percentage Major Vote Dem.
19,689	ADAIR	9,120	5,748	3,339	33	2,409 R	63.0%	36.6%	63.3%	36.7%
11,727	ANDREW	6,562	4,452	2,104	6	2,348 R	67.8%	32.1%	67.9%	32.1%
11,127	ATCHISON	5,297	3,259	2,028	10	1,231 R	61.5%	38.3%	61.6%	38.4%
23,829	AUDRAIN	11,554	4,767	6,775	12	2,008 D	41.3%	58.6%	41.3%	58.7%
21,755	BARRY	10,788	6,664	4,124		2,540 R	61.8%	38.2%	61.8%	38.2%
12,678	BARTON	6,741	4,056	2,661	24	1,395 R	60.2%	39.5%	60.4%	39.6%
17,534	BATES	9,999	6,002	3,995	2	2,007 R	60.0%	40.0%	60.0%	40.0%
9,080	BENTON	4,799	3,470	1,303	26	2,167 R	72.3%	27.2%	72.7%	27.3%
11,019	BOLLINGER	5,245	3,060	2,182	3	878 R	58.3%	41.6%	58.4%	41.6%
48,432	BOONE	17,785	7,545	10,206	34	2,661 D	42.4%	57.4%	42.5%	57.5%
96,826	BUCHANAN	41,985	22,087	19,854	44	2,233 R	52.6%	47.3%	52.7%	47.3%
37,707	BUTLER	14,285	7,843	6,426	16	1,417 R	54.9%	45.0%	55.0%	45.0%
9,929	CALDWELL	5,619	3,755	1,860	4	1,895 R	66.8%	33.1%	66.9%	33.1%
23,316	CALLAWAY	9,321	3,818	5,484	19	1,666 D	41.0%	58.8%	41.0%	59.0%
7,861	CAMDEN	4,025	2,789	1,226	10	1,563 R	69.3%	30.5%	69.5%	30.5%
38,397	CAPE GIRARDEAU	18,684	10,729	7,933	22	2,796 R	57.4%	42.5%	57.5%	42.5%
15,589	CARROLL	8,568	5,410	3,146	12	2,264 R	63.1%	36.7%	63.2%	36.8%
4,777	CARTER	2,223	1,100	1,123		23 D	49.5%	50.5%	49.5%	50.5%
19,325	CASS	11,102	6,000	5,089	13	911 R	54.0%	45.8%	54.1%	45.9%
10,663	CEDAR	5,319	3,814	1,483	22	2,331 R	71.7%	27.9%	72.0%	28.0%
14,944	CHARITON	7,627	3,883	3,730	14	153 R	50.9%	48.9%	51.0%	49.0%
12,412	CHRISTIAN	5,824	4,440	1,374	10	3,066 R	76.2%	23.6%	76.4%	23.6%
9,003	CLARK	4,918	2,850	2,045	23	805 R	58.0%	41.6%	58.2%	41.8%
45,221	CLAY	25,598	13,043	12,502	53	541 R	51.0%	48.8%	51.1%	48.9%
11,726	CLINTON	6,742	3,685	3,048	9	637 R	54.7%	45.2%	54.7%	45.3%
35,464	COLE	17,210	9,700	7,507	3	2,193 R	56.4%	43.6%	56.4%	43.6%
16,608	COOPER	8,695	5,208	3,475	12	1,733 R	59.9%	40.0%	60.0%	40.0%
11,615	CRAWFORD	6,220	3,753	2,453	14	1,300 R	60.3%	39.4%	60.5%	39.5%
9,324	DADE	4,747	3,395	1,340	12	2,055 R	71.5%	28.2%	71.7%	28.3%
10,392	DALLAS	4,726	3,459	1,258	9	2,201 R	73.2%	26.6%	73.3%	26.7%
11,180	DAVIESS	6,282	3,845	2,424	13	1,421 R	61.2%	38.6%	61.3%	38.7%
8,047	DE KALB	4,856	3,073	1,773	10	1,300 R	63.3%	36.5%	63.4%	36.6%
10,936	DENT	5,497	2,755	2,738	4	17 R	50.1%	49.8%	50.2%	49.8%
12,638	DOUGLAS	4,971	4,051	909	11	3,142 R	81.5%	18.3%	81.7%	18.3%
45,329	DUNKLIN	14,924	5,400	9,515	9	4,115 D	36.2%	63.8%	36.2%	63.8%
36,046	FRANKLIN	20,004	11,367	8,610	27	2,757 R	56.8%	43.0%	56.9%	43.1%
12,342	GASCONADE	6,633	5,339	1,285	9	4,054 R	80.5%	19.4%	80.6%	19.4%
11,036	GENTRY	5,937	3,429	2,508		921 R	57.8%	42.2%	57.8%	42.2%
104,823	GREENE	48,988	29,673	19,234	81	10,439 R	60.6%	39.3%	60.7%	39.3%
13,220	GRUNDY	7,555	4,790	2,747	18	2,043 R	63.4%	36.4%	63.6%	36.4%
14,107	HARRISON	7,465	5,191	2,261	13	2,930 R	69.5%	30.3%	69.7%	30.3%
20,043	HENRY	11,220	6,628	4,576	16	2,052 R	59.1%	40.8%	59.2%	40.8%
5,387	HICKORY	2,686	2,054	622	10	1,432 R	76.5%	23.2%	76.8%	23.2%
9,833	HOLT	4,985	3,476	1,487	22	1,989 R	69.7%	29.8%	70.0%	30.0%
11,857	HOWARD	5,982	2,340	3,635	7	1,295 D	39.1%	60.8%	39.2%	60.8%
22,725	HOWELL	9,983	6,608	3,349	26	3,259 R	66.2%	33.5%	66.4%	33.6%
9,458	IRON	4,124	1,831	2,286	7	455 D	44.4%	55.4%	44.5%	55.5%
541,035	JACKSON	272,297	133,093	138,792	412	5,699 D	48.9%	51.0%	49.0%	51.0%
79,106	JASPER	37,812	23,065	14,665	82	8,400 R	61.0%	38.8%	61.1%	38.9%
38,007	JEFFERSON	22,437	9,607	12,808	22	3,201 D	42.8%	57.1%	42.9%	57.1%
20,716	JOHNSON	11,307	6,990	4,294	23	2,696 R	61.8%	38.0%	61.9%	38.1%
7,617	KNOX	4,224	2,229	1,988	7	241 R	52.8%	47.1%	52.9%	47.1%
19,010	LACLEDE	8,155	5,312	2,839	4	2,473 R	65.1%	34.8%	65.2%	34.8%
25,272	LAFAYETTE	14,857	8,805	6,020	32	2,785 R	59.3%	40.5%	59.4%	40.6%
23,420	LAWRENCE	12,295	8,029	4,232	34	3,797 R	65.3%	34.4%	65.5%	34.5%
10,733	LEWIS	5,320	2,416	2,896	8	480 D	45.4%	54.4%	45.5%	54.5%
13,478	LINCOLN	7,487	3,458	4,020	9	562 D	46.2%	53.7%	46.2%	53.8%
18,865	LINN	10,751	5,551	5,189	11	362 R	51.6%	48.3%	51.7%	48.3%
16,532	LIVINGSTON	9,359	5,594	3,757	8	1,837 R	59.8%	40.1%	59.8%	40.2%
14,144	MCDONALD	6,657	4,121	2,525	11	1,596 R	61.9%	37.9%	62.0%	38.0%

MISSOURI

PRESIDENT 1952

1950 Census Population	County	Total Vote	Republican	Democratic	Other	Rep.-Dem. Plurality	Percentage Total Vote Rep.	Percentage Total Vote Dem.	Percentage Major Vote Rep.	Percentage Major Vote Dem.
18,332	MACON	10,129	5,537	4,577	15	960 R	54.7%	45.2%	54.7%	45.3%
10,380	MADISON	5,051	2,676	2,375		301 R	53.0%	47.0%	53.0%	47.0%
7,423	MARIES	3,290	1,501	1,783	6	282 D	45.6%	54.2%	45.7%	54.3%
29,765	MARION	14,637	6,162	8,457	18	2,295 D	42.1%	57.8%	42.2%	57.8%
7,235	MERCER	3,428	2,482	936	10	1,546 R	72.4%	27.3%	72.6%	27.4%
13,734	MILLER	6,681	4,237	2,426	18	1,811 R	63.4%	36.3%	63.6%	36.4%
22,551	MISSISSIPPI	6,730	2,380	4,331	19	1,951 D	35.4%	64.4%	35.5%	64.5%
10,840	MONITEAU	6,081	3,658	2,416	7	1,242 R	60.2%	39.7%	60.2%	39.8%
11,314	MONROE	6,259	1,488	4,760	11	3,272 D	23.8%	76.1%	23.8%	76.2%
11,555	MONTGOMERY	6,510	3,670	2,835	5	835 R	56.4%	43.5%	56.4%	43.6%
10,207	MORGAN	5,147	3,390	1,750	7	1,640 R	65.9%	34.0%	66.0%	34.0%
39,444	NEW MADRID	12,329	3,809	8,504	16	4,695 D	30.9%	69.0%	30.9%	69.1%
28,240	NEWTON	13,677	8,577	5,070	30	3,507 R	62.7%	37.1%	62.8%	37.2%
24,033	NODAWAY	12,441	7,614	4,805	22	2,809 R	61.2%	38.6%	61.3%	38.7%
11,978	OREGON	4,744	1,804	2,926	14	1,122 D	38.0%	61.7%	38.1%	61.9%
11,301	OSAGE	5,605	3,404	2,191	10	1,213 R	60.7%	39.1%	60.8%	39.2%
8,856	OZARK	3,309	2,572	734	3	1,838 R	77.7%	22.2%	77.8%	22.2%
45,624	PEMISCOT	13,043	4,118	8,913	12	4,795 D	31.6%	68.3%	31.6%	68.4%
14,890	PERRY	6,960	4,633	2,324	3	2,309 R	66.6%	33.4%	66.6%	33.4%
31,577	PETTIS	16,636	9,261	7,363	12	1,898 R	55.7%	44.3%	55.7%	44.3%
21,504	PHELPS	9,554	4,694	4,846	14	152 D	49.1%	50.7%	49.2%	50.8%
16,844	PIKE	8,436	3,836	4,582	18	746 D	45.5%	54.3%	45.6%	54.4%
14,973	PLATTE	8,003	3,390	4,604	9	1,214 D	42.4%	57.5%	42.4%	57.6%
16,062	POLK	7,761	5,263	2,474	24	2,789 R	67.8%	31.9%	68.0%	32.0%
10,392	PULASKI	5,712	2,678	3,026	8	348 D	46.9%	53.0%	46.9%	53.1%
9,166	PUTNAM	4,368	3,202	1,149	17	2,053 R	73.3%	26.3%	73.6%	26.4%
8,686	RALLS	4,465	1,437	3,020	8	1,583 D	32.2%	67.6%	32.2%	67.8%
22,918	RANDOLPH	11,496	3,968	7,501	27	3,533 D	34.5%	65.2%	34.6%	65.4%
15,932	RAY	8,240	3,349	4,869	22	1,520 D	40.6%	59.1%	40.8%	59.2%
6,918	REYNOLDS	3,079	949	2,124	6	1,175 D	30.8%	69.0%	30.9%	69.1%
11,414	RIPLEY	4,650	2,444	2,194	12	250 R	52.6%	47.2%	52.7%	47.3%
29,834	ST. CHARLES	14,964	8,451	6,493	20	1,958 R	56.5%	43.4%	56.6%	43.4%
10,482	ST. CLAIR	5,400	3,465	1,914	21	1,551 R	64.2%	35.4%	64.4%	35.6%
35,276	ST. FRANCOIS	17,729	9,672	8,040	17	1,632 R	54.6%	45.3%	54.6%	45.4%
856,796	ST. LOUIS CITY	381,148	144,828	235,893	427	91,065 D	38.0%	61.9%	38.0%	62.0%
406,349	ST. LOUIS COUNTY	212,480	116,821	95,457	202	21,364 R	55.0%	44.9%	55.0%	45.0%
11,237	STE. GENEVIEVE	5,069	2,682	2,385	2	297 R	52.9%	47.1%	52.9%	47.1%
26,694	SALINE	13,271	6,926	6,318	27	608 R	52.2%	47.6%	52.3%	47.7%
5,760	SCHUYLER	3,323	1,636	1,680	7	44 D	49.2%	50.6%	49.3%	50.7%
7,332	SCOTLAND	4,226	2,123	2,093	10	30 R	50.2%	49.5%	50.4%	49.6%
32,842	SCOTT	11,814	4,661	7,127	26	2,466 D	39.5%	60.3%	39.5%	60.5%
8,377	SHANNON	3,327	1,291	2,028	8	737 D	38.8%	61.0%	38.9%	61.1%
9,730	SHELBY	5,424	2,163	3,237	24	1,074 D	39.9%	59.7%	40.1%	59.9%
33,463	STODDARD	11,649	5,514	6,110	25	596 D	47.3%	52.5%	47.4%	52.6%
9,748	STONE	3,931	3,172	748	11	2,424 R	80.7%	19.0%	80.9%	19.1%
11,299	SULLIVAN	6,792	3,746	3,041	5	705 R	55.2%	44.8%	55.2%	44.8%
9,863	TANEY	4,148	3,037	1,099	12	1,938 R	73.2%	26.5%	73.4%	26.6%
18,992	TEXAS	9,225	4,824	4,372	29	452 R	52.3%	47.4%	52.5%	47.5%
22,685	VERNON	10,408	5,924	4,450	34	1,474 R	56.9%	42.8%	57.1%	42.9%
7,666	WARREN	4,097	2,977	1,112	8	1,865 R	72.7%	27.1%	72.8%	27.2%
14,689	WASHINGTON	6,033	3,338	2,684	11	654 R	55.3%	44.5%	55.4%	44.6%
10,514	WAYNE	4,937	2,423	2,500	14	77 D	49.1%	50.6%	49.2%	50.8%
15,072	WEBSTER	7,615	4,701	2,894	20	1,807 R	61.7%	38.0%	61.9%	38.1%
5,120	WORTH	2,914	1,682	1,227	5	455 R	57.7%	42.1%	57.8%	42.2%
15,834	WRIGHT	7,309	5,285	2,006	18	3,279 R	72.3%	27.4%	72.5%	27.5%
3,954,653	TOTAL	1,892,062	959,429	929,830	2,803	29,599 R	50.7%	49.1%	50.8%	49.2%

MISSOURI

PRESIDENT 1948

1940 Census Population	County	Total Vote	Republican	Democratic	Other	Rep.-Dem. Plurality	Percentage Total Vote Rep.	Percentage Total Vote Dem.	Percentage Major Vote Rep.	Percentage Major Vote Dem.
20,246	ADAIR	8,201	4,024	4,136	41	112 D	49.1%	50.4%	49.3%	50.7%
13,015	ANDREW	5,729	3,142	2,576	11	566 R	54.8%	45.0%	54.9%	45.1%
12,897	ATCHISON	4,693	2,190	2,498	5	308 D	46.7%	53.2%	46.7%	53.3%
22,673	AUDRAIN	10,250	2,739	7,495	16	4,756 D	26.7%	73.1%	26.8%	73.2%
23,546	BARRY	9,536	4,812	4,724		88 R	50.5%	49.5%	50.5%	49.5%
14,148	BARTON	5,592	2,577	3,008	7	431 D	46.1%	53.8%	46.1%	53.9%
19,531	BATES	8,533	4,156	4,371	6	215 D	48.7%	51.2%	48.7%	51.3%
11,142	BENTON	4,131	2,768	1,360	3	1,408 R	67.0%	32.9%	67.1%	32.9%
12,898	BOLLINGER	4,267	2,187	2,075	5	112 R	51.3%	48.6%	51.3%	48.7%
34,991	BOONE	14,653	4,289	10,200	164	5,911 D	29.3%	69.6%	29.6%	70.4%
94,067	BUCHANAN	36,034	13,002	22,975	57	9,973 D	36.1%	63.8%	36.1%	63.9%
34,276	BUTLER	9,630	4,276	5,319	35	1,043 D	44.4%	55.2%	44.6%	55.4%
11,629	CALDWELL	4,676	2,687	1,985	4	702 R	57.5%	42.5%	57.5%	42.5%
23,094	CALLAWAY	8,658	2,433	6,215	10	3,782 D	28.1%	71.8%	28.1%	71.9%
8,971	CAMDEN	3,291	2,020	1,264	7	756 R	61.4%	38.4%	61.5%	38.5%
37,775	CAPE GIRARDEAU	14,971	7,084	7,872	15	788 D	47.3%	52.6%	47.4%	52.6%
17,814	CARROLL	7,618	4,212	3,401	5	811 R	55.3%	44.6%	55.3%	44.7%
6,226	CARTER	2,237	964	1,255	18	291 D	43.1%	56.1%	43.4%	56.6%
19,534	CASS	9,045	3,614	5,415	16	1,801 D	40.0%	59.9%	40.0%	60.0%
11,697	CEDAR	5,000	2,928	2,062	10	866 R	58.6%	41.2%	58.7%	41.3%
18,084	CHARITON	6,791	2,615	4,170	6	1,555 D	38.5%	61.4%	38.5%	61.5%
13,538	CHRISTIAN	4,735	3,129	1,600	6	1,529 R	66.1%	33.8%	66.2%	33.8%
10,166	CLARK	4,619	2,264	2,352	3	88 D	49.0%	50.9%	49.0%	51.0%
30,417	CLAY	18,304	6,408	11,855	41	5,447 D	35.0%	64.8%	35.1%	64.9%
13,261	CLINTON	5,715	2,227	3,481	7	1,254 D	39.0%	60.9%	39.0%	61.0%
34,912	COLE	14,825	6,909	7,891	25	982 D	46.6%	53.2%	46.7%	53.3%
18,075	COOPER	7,968	4,094	3,865	9	229 R	51.4%	48.5%	51.4%	48.6%
12,693	CRAWFORD	4,949	2,650	2,289	10	361 R	53.5%	46.3%	53.7%	46.3%
11,248	DADE	4,521	2,783	1,733	5	1,050 R	61.6%	38.3%	61.6%	38.4%
11,523	DALLAS	4,296	2,695	1,590	11	1,105 R	62.7%	37.0%	62.9%	37.1%
13,398	DAVIESS	5,693	2,823	2,868	2	45 D	49.6%	50.4%	49.6%	50.4%
9,751	DE KALB	4,135	2,098	2,033	4	65 R	50.7%	49.2%	50.8%	49.2%
11,763	DENT	4,990	2,003	2,973	14	970 D	40.1%	59.6%	40.3%	59.7%
15,600	DOUGLAS	3,914	2,734	1,163	17	1,571 R	69.9%	29.7%	70.2%	29.8%
44,957	DUNKLIN	13,461	2,466	10,979	16	8,513 D	18.3%	81.6%	18.3%	81.7%
33,868	FRANKLIN	15,585	7,725	7,822	38	97 D	49.6%	50.2%	49.7%	50.3%
12,414	GASCONADE	5,485	4,268	1,204	13	3,064 R	77.8%	22.0%	78.0%	22.0%
13,359	GENTRY	6,044	2,633	3,410	1	777 D	43.6%	56.4%	43.6%	56.4%
90,541	GREENE	39,664	18,836	20,762	66	1,926 D	47.5%	52.3%	47.6%	52.4%
15,716	GRUNDY	6,512	3,331	3,177	4	154 R	51.2%	48.8%	51.2%	48.8%
16,525	HARRISON	6,513	3,646	2,854	13	792 R	56.0%	43.8%	56.1%	43.9%
22,313	HENRY	10,174	4,619	5,551	4	932 D	45.4%	54.6%	45.4%	54.6%
6,506	HICKORY	2,462	1,728	733	1	995 R	70.2%	29.8%	70.2%	29.8%
12,476	HOLT	4,651	2,607	2,040	4	567 R	56.1%	43.9%	56.1%	43.9%
13,026	HOWARD	5,693	1,538	4,143	12	2,605 D	27.0%	72.8%	27.1%	72.9%
22,270	HOWELL	8,060	4,427	3,599	34	828 R	54.9%	44.7%	55.2%	44.8%
10,440	IRON	3,994	1,435	2,552	7	1,117 D	35.9%	63.9%	36.0%	64.0%
477,828	JACKSON	226,527	86,471	139,186	870	52,715 D	38.2%	61.4%	38.3%	61.7%
78,705	JASPER	30,078	14,593	15,404	81	811 D	48.5%	51.2%	48.6%	51.4%
32,023	JEFFERSON	16,435	6,085	10,280	70	4,195 D	37.0%	62.5%	37.2%	62.8%
21,617	JOHNSON	9,805	4,903	4,888	14	15 R	50.0%	49.9%	50.1%	49.9%
8,878	KNOX	3,889	1,620	2,268	1	648 D	41.7%	58.3%	41.7%	58.3%
18,718	LACLEDE	7,015	3,773	3,221	21	552 R	53.8%	45.9%	53.9%	46.1%
27,856	LAFAYETTE	12,642	6,634	5,988	20	646 R	52.5%	47.4%	52.6%	47.4%
24,637	LAWRENCE	10,058	5,392	4,649	17	743 R	53.6%	46.2%	53.7%	46.3%
11,490	LEWIS	4,731	1,564	3,155	12	1,591 D	33.1%	66.7%	33.1%	66.9%
14,395	LINCOLN	6,336	2,135	4,190	11	2,055 D	33.7%	66.1%	33.8%	66.2%
21,416	LINN	9,833	4,034	5,788	11	1,754 D	41.0%	58.9%	41.1%	58.9%
18,000	LIVINGSTON	8,031	3,835	4,182	14	347 D	47.8%	52.1%	47.8%	52.2%
15,749	MCDONALD	5,915	2,979	2,925	11	54 R	50.4%	49.5%	50.5%	49.5%

MISSOURI

PRESIDENT 1948

1940 Census Population	County	Total Vote	Republican	Democratic	Other	Rep.-Dem. Plurality	Percentage Total Vote Rep.	Percentage Total Vote Dem.	Percentage Major Vote Rep.	Percentage Major Vote Dem.
21,396	MACON	9,039	3,833	5,193	13	1,360 D	42.4%	57.5%	42.5%	57.5%
9,656	MADISON	4,599	2,086	2,509	4	423 D	45.4%	54.6%	45.4%	54.6%
8,638	MARIES	2,846	894	1,948	4	1,054 D	31.4%	68.4%	31.5%	68.5%
31,576	MARION	12,944	3,802	9,122	20	5,320 D	29.4%	70.5%	29.4%	70.6%
8,766	MERCER	2,605	1,595	1,008	2	587 R	61.2%	38.7%	61.3%	38.7%
14,798	MILLER	5,611	3,088	2,514	9	574 R	55.0%	44.8%	55.1%	44.9%
23,149	MISSISSIPPI	5,915	1,293	4,592	30	3,299 D	21.9%	77.6%	22.0%	78.0%
11,775	MONITEAU	5,385	2,594	2,787	4	193 D	48.2%	51.8%	48.2%	51.8%
13,195	MONROE	5,585	809	4,769	7	3,960 D	14.5%	85.4%	14.5%	85.5%
12,442	MONTGOMERY	5,693	2,889	2,792	12	97 R	50.7%	49.0%	50.9%	49.1%
11,140	MORGAN	4,238	2,365	1,862	11	503 R	55.8%	43.9%	55.9%	44.1%
39,787	NEW MADRID	11,018	2,082	8,925	11	6,843 D	18.9%	81.0%	18.9%	81.1%
29,039	NEWTON	11,443	5,820	5,598	25	222 R	50.9%	48.9%	51.0%	49.0%
25,556	NODAWAY	11,161	4,886	6,253	22	1,367 D	43.8%	56.0%	43.9%	56.1%
13,390	OREGON	4,357	1,214	3,133	10	1,919 D	27.9%	71.9%	27.9%	72.1%
12,375	OSAGE	5,170	2,488	2,672	10	184 D	48.1%	51.7%	48.2%	51.8%
10,766	OZARK	2,832	1,967	859	6	1,108 R	69.5%	30.3%	69.6%	30.4%
46,857	PEMISCOT	12,526	2,249	10,269	8	8,020 D	18.0%	82.0%	18.0%	82.0%
15,358	PERRY	5,043	2,903	2,133	7	770 R	57.6%	42.3%	57.6%	42.4%
33,336	PETTIS	15,069	6,657	8,388	24	1,731 D	44.2%	55.7%	44.2%	55.8%
17,437	PHELPS	8,277	3,053	5,202	22	2,149 D	36.9%	62.8%	37.0%	63.0%
18,327	PIKE	7,400	2,448	4,934	18	2,486 D	33.1%	66.7%	33.2%	66.8%
13,862	PLATTE	6,014	1,644	4,354	16	2,710 D	27.3%	72.4%	27.4%	72.6%
17,400	POLK	7,107	4,026	3,079	2	947 R	56.6%	43.3%	56.7%	43.3%
10,775	PULASKI	4,513	1,644	2,858	11	1,214 D	36.4%	63.3%	36.5%	63.5%
11,327	PUTNAM	3,977	2,499	1,463	15	1,036 R	62.8%	36.8%	63.1%	36.9%
10,040	RALLS	3,922	908	3,013	1	2,105 D	23.2%	76.8%	23.2%	76.8%
24,458	RANDOLPH	10,178	2,256	7,912	10	5,656 D	22.2%	77.7%	22.2%	77.8%
18,584	RAY	6,937	2,102	4,826	9	2,724 D	30.3%	69.6%	30.3%	69.7%
9,370	REYNOLDS	2,748	692	2,050	6	1,358 D	25.2%	74.6%	25.2%	74.8%
12,606	RIPLEY	3,858	1,533	2,304	21	771 D	39.7%	59.7%	40.0%	60.0%
25,562	ST. CHARLES	12,064	5,976	6,049	39	73 D	49.5%	50.1%	49.7%	50.3%
13,146	ST. CLAIR	5,044	2,548	2,489	7	59 R	50.5%	49.3%	50.6%	49.4%
35,950	ST. FRANCOIS	13,542	6,234	7,276	32	1,042 D	46.0%	53.7%	46.1%	53.9%
816,048	ST. LOUIS CITY	343,770	120,656	220,654	2,460	99,998 D	35.1%	64.2%	35.4%	64.6%
274,230	ST. LOUIS COUNTY	133,383	69,592	62,684	1,107	6,908 R	52.2%	47.0%	52.6%	47.4%
10,905	STE. GENEVIEVE	3,568	1,567	1,984	17	417 D	43.9%	55.6%	44.1%	55.9%
29,416	SALINE	12,029	4,822	7,185	22	2,363 D	40.1%	59.7%	40.2%	59.8%
6,627	SCHUYLER	3,277	1,377	1,892	8	515 D	42.0%	57.7%	42.1%	57.9%
8,557	SCOTLAND	4,153	1,693	2,451	9	758 D	40.8%	59.0%	40.9%	59.1%
30,377	SCOTT	10,803	2,519	8,266	18	5,747 D	23.3%	76.5%	23.4%	76.6%
11,831	SHANNON	3,174	805	2,352	17	1,547 D	25.4%	74.1%	25.5%	74.5%
11,224	SHELBY	4,760	1,348	3,400	12	2,052 D	28.3%	71.4%	28.4%	71.6%
33,009	STODDARD	10,169	3,117	7,029	23	3,912 D	30.7%	69.1%	30.7%	69.3%
11,298	STONE	3,121	2,222	892	7	1,330 R	71.2%	28.6%	71.4%	28.6%
13,701	SULLIVAN	6,592	3,140	3,443	9	303 D	47.6%	52.2%	47.7%	52.3%
10,323	TANEY	3,797	2,361	1,427	9	934 R	62.2%	37.6%	62.3%	37.7%
19,813	TEXAS	7,994	3,320	4,664	10	1,344 D	41.5%	58.3%	41.6%	58.4%
25,586	VERNON	9,164	3,808	5,342	14	1,534 D	41.6%	58.3%	41.6%	58.4%
7,734	WARREN	3,468	2,380	1,071	17	1,309 R	68.6%	30.9%	69.0%	31.0%
17,492	WASHINGTON	4,585	2,200	2,370	15	170 D	48.0%	51.7%	48.1%	51.9%
12,794	WAYNE	4,634	1,937	2,695	2	758 D	41.8%	58.2%	41.8%	58.2%
17,226	WEBSTER	6,890	3,581	3,292	17	289 R	52.0%	47.8%	52.1%	47.9%
6,345	WORTH	2,732	1,162	1,563	7	401 D	42.5%	57.2%	42.6%	57.4%
17,967	WRIGHT	6,058	3,542	2,505	11	1,037 R	58.5%	41.4%	58.6%	41.4%
3,784,664	TOTAL	1,578,628	655,039	917,315	6,274	262,276 D	41.5%	58.1%	41.7%	58.3%

MISSOURI

PRESIDENT 1944

1940 Census Population	County	Total Vote	Republican	Democratic	Other	Rep.-Dem. Plurality	Percentage Total Vote Rep.	Total Vote Dem.	Major Vote Rep.	Major Vote Dem.
20,246	ADAIR	8,541	4,909	3,606	26	1,303 R	57.5%	42.2%	57.7%	42.3%
13,015	ANDREW	5,995	3,734	2,254	7	1,480 R	62.3%	37.6%	62.4%	37.6%
12,897	ATCHISON	5,021	2,803	2,214	4	589 R	55.8%	44.1%	55.9%	44.1%
22,673	AUDRAIN	9,939	3,455	6,471	13	3,016 D	34.8%	65.1%	34.8%	65.2%
23,546	BARRY	9,848	5,796	4,029	23	1,767 R	58.9%	40.9%	59.0%	41.0%
14,148	BARTON	6,067	3,356	2,688	23	668 R	55.3%	44.3%	55.5%	44.5%
19,531	BATES	9,236	5,122	4,096	18	1,026 R	55.5%	44.3%	55.6%	44.4%
11,142	BENTON	4,408	3,294	1,108	6	2,186 R	74.7%	25.1%	74.8%	25.2%
12,898	BOLLINGER	4,694	2,850	1,841	3	1,009 R	60.7%	39.2%	60.8%	39.2%
34,991	BOONE	13,929	4,195	9,704	30	5,509 D	30.1%	69.7%	30.2%	69.8%
94,067	BUCHANAN	35,224	15,113	20,091	20	4,978 D	42.9%	57.0%	42.9%	57.1%
34,276	BUTLER	10,626	6,375	4,219	32	2,156 R	60.0%	39.7%	60.2%	39.8%
11,629	CALDWELL	5,393	3,384	2,001	8	1,383 R	62.7%	37.1%	62.8%	37.2%
23,094	CALLAWAY	8,924	3,143	5,757	24	2,614 D	35.2%	64.5%	35.3%	64.7%
8,971	CAMDEN	3,175	2,180	990	5	1,190 R	68.7%	31.2%	68.8%	31.2%
37,775	CAPE GIRARDEAU	15,195	8,339	6,845	11	1,494 R	54.9%	45.0%	54.9%	45.1%
17,814	CARROLL	8,430	5,127	3,283	20	1,844 R	60.8%	38.9%	61.0%	39.0%
6,226	CARTER	2,252	1,033	1,207	12	174 D	45.9%	53.6%	46.1%	53.9%
19,534	CASS	9,041	4,687	4,347	7	340 R	51.8%	48.1%	51.9%	48.1%
11,697	CEDAR	5,059	3,576	1,478	5	2,098 R	70.7%	29.2%	70.8%	29.2%
18,084	CHARITON	7,740	3,802	3,930	8	128 D	49.1%	50.8%	49.2%	50.8%
13,538	CHRISTIAN	5,310	4,167	1,134	9	3,033 R	78.5%	21.4%	78.6%	21.4%
10,166	CLARK	4,868	2,707	2,155	6	552 R	55.6%	44.3%	55.7%	44.3%
30,417	CLAY	15,446	6,724	8,682	40	1,958 D	43.5%	56.2%	43.6%	56.4%
13,261	CLINTON	5,996	2,912	3,079	5	167 D	48.6%	51.4%	48.6%	51.4%
34,912	COLE	14,507	7,364	7,139	4	225 R	50.8%	49.2%	50.8%	49.2%
18,075	COOPER	8,677	4,928	3,729	20	1,199 R	56.8%	43.0%	56.9%	43.1%
12,693	CRAWFORD	5,264	3,077	2,177	10	900 R	58.5%	41.4%	58.6%	41.4%
11,248	DADE	4,786	3,316	1,462	8	1,854 R	69.3%	30.5%	69.4%	30.6%
11,523	DALLAS	4,306	3,232	1,064	10	2,168 R	75.1%	24.7%	75.2%	24.8%
13,398	DAVIESS	6,169	3,597	2,567	5	1,030 R	58.3%	41.6%	58.4%	41.6%
9,751	DE KALB	4,625	2,658	1,961	6	697 R	57.5%	42.4%	57.5%	42.5%
11,763	DENT	5,162	2,456	2,699	7	243 D	47.6%	52.3%	47.6%	52.4%
15,600	DOUGLAS	4,330	3,570	746	14	2,824 R	82.4%	17.2%	82.7%	17.3%
44,957	DUNKLIN	12,732	4,274	8,431	27	4,157 D	33.6%	66.2%	33.6%	66.4%
33,868	FRANKLIN	15,326	9,325	5,958	43	3,367 R	60.8%	38.9%	61.0%	39.0%
12,414	GASCONADE	6,013	5,007	994	12	4,013 R	83.3%	16.5%	83.4%	16.6%
13,359	GENTRY	6,000	2,970	3,022	8	52 D	49.5%	50.4%	49.6%	50.4%
90,541	GREENE	38,886	21,531	17,287	68	4,244 R	55.4%	44.5%	55.5%	44.5%
15,716	GRUNDY	7,167	4,158	2,997	12	1,161 R	58.0%	41.8%	58.1%	41.9%
16,525	HARRISON	6,964	4,330	2,623	11	1,707 R	62.2%	37.7%	62.3%	37.7%
22,313	HENRY	10,174	5,564	4,587	23	977 R	54.7%	45.1%	54.8%	45.2%
6,506	HICKORY	2,734	2,171	560	3	1,611 R	79.4%	20.5%	79.5%	20.5%
12,476	HOLT	4,946	3,152	1,785	9	1,367 R	63.7%	36.1%	63.8%	36.2%
13,026	HOWARD	5,918	1,951	3,958	9	2,007 D	33.0%	66.9%	33.0%	67.0%
22,270	HOWELL	8,185	5,151	3,020	14	2,131 R	62.9%	36.9%	63.0%	37.0%
10,440	IRON	3,854	1,649	2,205		556 D	42.8%	57.2%	42.8%	57.2%
477,828	JACKSON	209,632	95,406	113,803	423	18,397 D	45.5%	54.3%	45.6%	54.4%
78,705	JASPER	30,475	17,301	13,111	63	4,190 R	56.8%	43.0%	56.9%	43.1%
32,023	JEFFERSON	14,745	6,758	7,953	34	1,195 D	45.8%	53.9%	45.9%	54.1%
21,617	JOHNSON	10,378	5,949	4,419	10	1,530 R	57.3%	42.6%	57.4%	42.6%
8,878	KNOX	4,008	2,057	1,943	8	114 R	51.3%	48.5%	51.4%	48.6%
18,718	LACLEDE	7,687	4,670	3,011	6	1,659 R	60.8%	39.2%	60.8%	39.2%
27,856	LAFAYETTE	13,561	7,951	5,603	7	2,348 R	58.6%	41.3%	58.7%	41.3%
24,637	LAWRENCE	10,722	6,836	3,859	27	2,977 R	63.8%	36.0%	63.9%	36.1%
11,490	LEWIS	4,882	1,988	2,883	11	895 D	40.7%	59.1%	40.8%	59.2%
14,395	LINCOLN	6,698	2,910	3,773	15	863 D	43.4%	56.3%	43.5%	56.5%
21,416	LINN	10,193	4,942	5,242	9	300 D	48.5%	51.4%	48.5%	51.5%
18,000	LIVINGSTON	8,610	4,697	3,887	26	810 R	54.6%	45.1%	54.7%	45.3%
15,749	MCDONALD	6,056	3,520	2,523	13	997 R	58.1%	41.7%	58.2%	41.8%

MISSOURI

PRESIDENT 1944

1940 Census Population	County	Total Vote	Republican	Democratic	Other	Rep.-Dem. Plurality	Percentage Total Vote Rep.	Total Vote Dem.	Major Vote Rep.	Major Vote Dem.
21,396	MACON	9,581	4,796	4,772	13	24 R	50.1%	49.8%	50.1%	49.9%
9,656	MADISON	4,488	2,277	2,203	8	74 R	50.7%	49.1%	50.8%	49.2%
8,638	MARIES	3,366	1,519	1,824	23	305 D	45.1%	54.2%	45.4%	54.6%
31,576	MARION	13,149	4,560	8,575	14	4,015 D	34.7%	65.2%	34.7%	65.3%
8,766	MERCER	3,288	2,249	1,035	4	1,214 R	68.4%	31.5%	68.5%	31.5%
14,798	MILLER	5,850	3,609	2,229	12	1,380 R	61.7%	38.1%	61.8%	38.2%
23,149	MISSISSIPPI	6,153	1,944	4,182	27	2,238 D	31.6%	68.0%	31.7%	68.3%
11,775	MONITEAU	5,577	3,237	2,327	13	910 R	58.0%	41.7%	58.2%	41.8%
13,195	MONROE	6,106	1,098	5,000	8	3,902 D	18.0%	81.9%	18.0%	82.0%
12,442	MONTGOMERY	6,276	3,527	2,743	6	784 R	56.2%	43.7%	56.3%	43.7%
11,140	MORGAN	4,641	2,896	1,735	10	1,161 R	62.4%	37.4%	62.5%	37.5%
39,787	NEW MADRID	11,752	4,108	7,626	18	3,518 D	35.0%	64.9%	35.0%	65.0%
29,039	NEWTON	12,154	6,985	5,146	23	1,839 R	57.5%	42.3%	57.6%	42.4%
25,556	NODAWAY	11,180	5,766	5,407	7	359 R	51.6%	48.4%	51.6%	48.4%
13,390	OREGON	4,314	1,573	2,734	7	1,161 D	36.5%	63.4%	36.5%	63.5%
12,375	OSAGE	5,412	3,284	2,121	7	1,163 R	60.7%	39.2%	60.8%	39.2%
10,766	OZARK	3,338	2,707	628	3	2,079 R	81.1%	18.8%	81.2%	18.8%
46,857	PEMISCOT	11,733	4,333	7,380	20	3,047 D	36.9%	62.9%	37.0%	63.0%
15,358	PERRY	6,226	4,207	2,014	5	2,193 R	67.6%	32.3%	67.6%	32.4%
33,336	PETTIS	14,894	7,696	7,176	22	520 R	51.7%	48.2%	51.7%	48.3%
17,437	PHELPS	7,449	3,180	4,256	13	1,076 D	42.7%	57.1%	42.8%	57.2%
18,327	PIKE	8,032	3,351	4,659	22	1,308 D	41.7%	58.0%	41.8%	58.2%
13,862	PLATTE	6,093	2,344	3,741	8	1,397 D	38.5%	61.4%	38.5%	61.5%
17,400	POLK	7,585	5,040	2,527	18	2,513 R	66.4%	33.3%	66.6%	33.4%
10,775	PULASKI	5,400	2,345	3,048	7	703 D	43.4%	56.4%	43.5%	56.5%
11,327	PUTNAM	4,281	3,106	1,168	7	1,938 R	72.6%	27.3%	72.7%	27.3%
10,040	RALLS	3,966	1,164	2,799	3	1,635 D	29.3%	70.6%	29.4%	70.6%
24,458	RANDOLPH	10,525	2,879	7,629	17	4,750 D	27.4%	72.5%	27.4%	72.6%
18,584	RAY	7,627	3,094	4,521	12	1,427 D	40.6%	59.3%	40.6%	59.4%
9,370	REYNOLDS	2,833	951	1,877	5	926 D	33.6%	66.3%	33.6%	66.4%
12,606	RIPLEY	3,779	1,841	1,923	15	82 D	48.7%	50.9%	48.9%	51.1%
25,562	ST. CHARLES	11,966	7,050	4,880	36	2,170 R	58.9%	40.8%	59.1%	40.9%
13,146	ST. CLAIR	5,431	3,306	2,119	6	1,187 R	60.9%	39.0%	60.9%	39.1%
35,950	ST. FRANCOIS	14,076	7,320	6,745	11	575 R	52.0%	47.9%	52.0%	48.0%
816,048	ST. LOUIS CITY	339,919	134,411	204,687	821	70,276 D	39.5%	60.2%	39.6%	60.4%
274,230	ST. LOUIS COUNTY	122,266	64,131	57,780	355	6,351 R	52.5%	47.3%	52.6%	47.4%
10,905	STE. GENEVIEVE	4,098	2,214	1,878	6	336 R	54.0%	45.8%	54.1%	45.9%
29,416	SALINE	12,753	6,022	6,715	16	693 D	47.2%	52.7%	47.3%	52.7%
6,627	SCHUYLER	3,264	1,526	1,729	9	203 D	46.8%	53.0%	46.9%	53.1%
8,557	SCOTLAND	4,222	2,058	2,158	6	100 D	48.7%	51.1%	48.8%	51.2%
30,377	SCOTT	11,168	3,995	7,132	41	3,137 D	35.8%	63.9%	35.9%	64.1%
11,831	SHANNON	3,214	1,110	2,093	11	983 D	34.5%	65.1%	34.7%	65.3%
11,224	SHELBY	5,387	1,934	3,435	18	1,501 D	35.9%	63.8%	36.0%	64.0%
33,009	STODDARD	11,086	5,079	5,982	25	903 D	45.8%	54.0%	45.9%	54.1%
11,298	STONE	3,818	3,080	737	1	2,343 R	80.7%	19.3%	80.7%	19.3%
13,701	SULLIVAN	6,147	3,262	2,880	5	382 R	53.1%	46.9%	53.1%	46.9%
10,323	TANEY	3,444	2,499	936	9	1,563 R	72.6%	27.2%	72.8%	27.2%
19,813	TEXAS	7,938	3,916	4,011	11	95 D	49.3%	50.5%	49.4%	50.6%
25,586	VERNON	10,062	5,171	4,885	6	286 R	51.4%	48.5%	51.4%	48.6%
7,734	WARREN	3,847	3,017	815	15	2,202 R	78.4%	21.2%	78.7%	21.3%
17,492	WASHINGTON	4,974	2,900	2,065	9	835 R	58.3%	41.5%	58.4%	41.6%
12,794	WAYNE	4,349	2,171	2,169	9	2 R	49.9%	49.9%	50.0%	50.0%
17,226	WEBSTER	7,073	4,281	2,777	15	1,504 R	60.5%	39.3%	60.7%	39.3%
6,345	WORTH	2,881	1,444	1,437		7 R	50.1%	49.9%	50.1%	49.9%
17,967	WRIGHT	6,537	4,413	2,116	8	2,297 R	67.5%	32.4%	67.6%	32.4%
3,784,664	TOTAL	1,571,697	761,175	807,356	3,166	46,181 D	48.4%	51.4%	48.5%	51.5%

MISSOURI

PRESIDENT 1940

1940 Census Population	County	Total Vote	Republican	Democratic	Other	Rep.-Dem. Plurality	Percentage Total Vote Rep.	Total Vote Dem.	Major Vote Rep.	Major Vote Dem.
20,246	ADAIR	10,566	5,688	4,813	65	875 R	53.8%	45.6%	54.2%	45.8%
13,015	ANDREW	7,454	4,384	3,059	11	1,325 R	58.8%	41.0%	58.9%	41.1%
12,897	ATCHISON	6,358	3,322	3,025	11	297 R	52.2%	47.6%	52.3%	47.7%
22,673	AUDRAIN	11,224	3,447	7,768	9	4,321 D	30.7%	69.2%	30.7%	69.3%
23,546	BARRY	11,804	6,573	5,207	24	1,366 R	55.7%	44.1%	55.8%	44.2%
14,148	BARTON	7,315	3,737	3,539	39	198 R	51.1%	48.4%	51.4%	48.6%
19,531	BATES	10,738	5,727	4,978	33	749 R	53.3%	46.4%	53.5%	46.5%
11,142	BENTON	5,695	3,912	1,765	18	2,147 R	68.7%	31.0%	68.9%	31.1%
12,898	BOLLINGER	5,934	3,415	2,511	8	904 R	57.5%	42.3%	57.6%	42.4%
34,991	BOONE	16,543	4,869	11,615	59	6,746 D	29.4%	70.2%	29.5%	70.5%
94,067	BUCHANAN	41,995	17,484	24,482	29	6,998 D	41.6%	58.3%	41.7%	58.3%
34,276	BUTLER	14,275	8,024	6,213	38	1,811 R	56.2%	43.5%	56.4%	43.6%
11,629	CALDWELL	6,713	3,976	2,728	9	1,248 R	59.2%	40.6%	59.3%	40.7%
23,094	CALLAWAY	10,757	3,574	7,162	21	3,588 D	33.2%	66.6%	33.3%	66.7%
8,971	CAMDEN	4,246	2,692	1,549	5	1,143 R	63.4%	36.5%	63.5%	36.5%
37,775	CAPE GIRARDEAU	17,978	9,297	8,642	39	655 R	51.7%	48.1%	51.8%	48.2%
17,814	CARROLL	10,457	6,000	4,446	11	1,554 R	57.4%	42.5%	57.4%	42.6%
6,226	CARTER	2,697	1,195	1,499	3	304 D	44.3%	55.6%	44.4%	55.6%
19,534	CASS	10,479	4,983	5,479	17	496 D	47.6%	52.3%	47.6%	52.4%
11,697	CEDAR	6,073	4,068	1,973	32	2,095 R	67.0%	32.5%	67.3%	32.7%
18,084	CHARITON	9,497	4,439	5,053	5	614 D	46.7%	53.2%	46.8%	53.2%
13,538	CHRISTIAN	6,253	4,509	1,729	15	2,780 R	72.1%	27.7%	72.3%	27.7%
10,166	CLARK	5,917	3,171	2,728	18	443 R	53.6%	46.1%	53.8%	46.2%
30,417	CLAY	15,861	6,159	9,672	30	3,513 D	38.8%	61.0%	38.9%	61.1%
13,261	CLINTON	6,847	3,030	3,800	17	770 D	44.3%	55.5%	44.4%	55.6%
34,912	COLE	15,892	7,664	8,219	9	555 D	48.2%	51.7%	48.3%	51.7%
18,075	COOPER	10,343	5,720	4,606	17	1,114 R	55.3%	44.5%	55.4%	44.6%
12,693	CRAWFORD	6,365	3,615	2,736	14	879 R	56.8%	43.0%	56.9%	43.1%
11,248	DADE	5,761	3,910	1,835	16	2,075 R	67.9%	31.9%	68.1%	31.9%
11,523	DALLAS	5,435	3,859	1,566	10	2,293 R	71.0%	28.8%	71.1%	28.9%
13,398	DAVIESS	7,625	4,289	3,325	11	964 R	56.2%	43.6%	56.3%	43.7%
9,751	DE KALB	5,593	3,072	2,505	16	567 R	54.9%	44.8%	55.1%	44.9%
11,763	DENT	5,766	2,652	3,101	13	449 D	46.0%	53.8%	46.1%	53.9%
15,600	DOUGLAS	6,252	4,870	1,350	32	3,520 R	77.9%	21.6%	78.3%	21.7%
44,957	DUNKLIN	16,680	5,516	11,132	32	5,616 D	33.1%	66.7%	33.1%	66.9%
33,868	FRANKLIN	17,555	10,283	7,237	35	3,046 R	58.6%	41.2%	58.7%	41.3%
12,414	GASCONADE	6,501	5,333	1,163	5	4,170 R	82.0%	17.9%	82.1%	17.9%
13,359	GENTRY	7,154	3,446	3,689	19	243 D	48.2%	51.6%	48.3%	51.7%
90,541	GREENE	43,695	21,456	22,130	109	674 D	49.1%	50.6%	49.2%	50.8%
15,716	GRUNDY	8,404	4,558	3,813	33	745 R	54.2%	45.4%	54.4%	45.6%
16,525	HARRISON	8,636	5,304	3,325	7	1,979 R	61.4%	38.5%	61.5%	38.5%
22,313	HENRY	12,423	6,332	6,069	22	263 R	51.0%	48.9%	51.1%	48.9%
6,506	HICKORY	3,291	2,496	787	8	1,709 R	75.8%	23.9%	76.0%	24.0%
12,476	HOLT	6,422	3,739	2,677	6	1,062 R	58.2%	41.7%	58.3%	41.7%
13,026	HOWARD	7,123	2,333	4,770	20	2,437 D	32.8%	67.0%	32.8%	67.2%
22,270	HOWELL	10,397	6,158	4,218	21	1,940 R	59.2%	40.6%	59.3%	40.7%
10,440	IRON	4,565	2,062	2,495	8	433 D	45.2%	54.7%	45.2%	54.8%
477,828	JACKSON	239,219	101,568	137,285	366	35,717 D	42.5%	57.4%	42.5%	57.5%
78,705	JASPER	37,111	18,755	18,249	107	506 R	50.5%	49.2%	50.7%	49.3%
32,023	JEFFERSON	17,115	7,517	9,553	45	2,036 D	43.9%	55.8%	44.0%	56.0%
21,617	JOHNSON	11,928	6,468	5,441	19	1,027 R	54.2%	45.6%	54.3%	45.7%
8,878	KNOX	4,983	2,370	2,594	19	224 D	47.6%	52.1%	47.7%	52.3%
18,718	LACLEDE	8,278	4,941	3,323	14	1,618 R	59.7%	40.1%	59.8%	40.2%
27,856	LAFAYETTE	15,744	8,802	6,913	29	1,889 R	55.9%	43.9%	56.0%	44.0%
24,637	LAWRENCE	12,641	7,317	5,279	45	2,038 R	57.9%	41.8%	58.1%	41.9%
11,490	LEWIS	5,942	2,428	3,484	30	1,056 D	40.9%	58.6%	41.1%	58.9%
14,395	LINCOLN	7,480	3,035	4,420	25	1,385 D	40.6%	59.1%	40.7%	59.3%
21,416	LINN	11,934	5,664	6,246	24	582 D	47.5%	52.3%	47.6%	52.4%
18,000	LIVINGSTON	9,956	5,298	4,633	25	665 R	53.2%	46.5%	53.3%	46.7%
15,749	MCDONALD	7,394	4,063	3,312	19	751 R	54.9%	44.8%	55.1%	44.9%

MISSOURI

PRESIDENT 1940

1940 Census Population	County	Total Vote	Republican	Democratic	Other	Rep.-Dem. Plurality	Percentage Total Vote Rep.	Total Vote Dem.	Major Vote Rep.	Major Vote Dem.
21,396	MACON	11,519	5,384	6,120	15	736 D	46.7%	53.1%	46.8%	53.2%
9,656	MADISON	4,905	2,495	2,405	5	90 R	50.9%	49.0%	50.9%	49.1%
8,638	MARIES	3,836	1,749	2,078	9	329 D	45.6%	54.2%	45.7%	54.3%
31,576	MARION	15,660	5,892	9,723	45	3,831 D	37.6%	62.1%	37.7%	62.3%
8,766	MERCER	4,161	2,787	1,364	10	1,423 R	67.0%	32.8%	67.1%	32.9%
14,798	MILLER	7,107	3,971	3,113	23	858 R	55.9%	43.8%	56.1%	43.9%
23,149	MISSISSIPPI	7,462	3,073	4,362	27	1,289 D	41.2%	58.5%	41.3%	58.7%
11,775	MONITEAU	6,556	3,627	2,922	7	705 R	55.3%	44.6%	55.4%	44.6%
13,195	MONROE	7,231	1,200	6,018	13	4,818 D	16.6%	83.2%	16.6%	83.4%
12,442	MONTGOMERY	7,151	3,930	3,205	16	725 R	55.0%	44.8%	55.1%	44.9%
11,140	MORGAN	5,556	3,166	2,376	14	790 R	57.0%	42.8%	57.1%	42.9%
39,787	NEW MADRID	15,933	6,318	9,591	24	3,273 D	39.7%	60.2%	39.7%	60.3%
29,039	NEWTON	14,364	8,064	6,256	44	1,808 R	56.1%	43.6%	56.3%	43.7%
25,556	NODAWAY	13,461	6,759	6,696	6	63 R	50.2%	49.7%	50.2%	49.8%
13,390	OREGON	5,434	1,826	3,593	15	1,767 D	33.6%	66.1%	33.7%	66.3%
12,375	OSAGE	6,086	3,743	2,332	11	1,411 R	61.5%	38.3%	61.6%	38.4%
10,766	OZARK	4,405	3,421	965	19	2,456 R	77.7%	21.9%	78.0%	22.0%
46,857	PEMISCOT	15,453	6,011	9,391	51	3,380 D	38.9%	60.8%	39.0%	61.0%
15,358	PERRY	7,019	4,656	2,354	9	2,302 R	66.3%	33.5%	66.4%	33.6%
33,336	PETTIS	17,492	8,905	8,570	17	335 R	50.9%	49.0%	51.0%	49.0%
17,437	PHELPS	8,114	3,319	4,780	15	1,461 D	40.9%	58.9%	41.0%	59.0%
18,327	PIKE	9,489	3,707	5,742	40	2,035 D	39.1%	60.5%	39.2%	60.8%
13,862	PLATTE	7,193	2,545	4,635	13	2,090 D	35.4%	64.4%	35.4%	64.6%
17,400	POLK	8,928	5,534	3,380	14	2,154 R	62.0%	37.9%	62.1%	37.9%
10,775	PULASKI	5,127	2,367	2,752	8	385 D	46.2%	53.7%	46.2%	53.8%
11,327	PUTNAM	5,561	3,828	1,708	25	2,120 R	68.8%	30.7%	69.1%	30.9%
10,040	RALLS	4,980	1,412	3,562	6	2,150 D	28.4%	71.5%	28.4%	71.6%
24,458	RANDOLPH	12,497	3,319	9,155	23	5,836 D	26.6%	73.3%	26.6%	73.4%
18,584	RAY	9,201	3,399	5,786	16	2,387 D	36.9%	62.9%	37.0%	63.0%
9,370	REYNOLDS	3,600	1,187	2,406	7	1,219 D	33.0%	66.8%	33.0%	67.0%
12,606	RIPLEY	4,725	2,291	2,419	15	128 D	48.5%	51.2%	48.6%	51.4%
25,562	ST. CHARLES	13,176	7,792	5,334	50	2,458 R	59.1%	40.5%	59.4%	40.6%
13,146	ST. CLAIR	6,834	3,950	2,859	25	1,091 R	57.8%	41.8%	58.0%	42.0%
35,950	ST. FRANCOIS	16,851	8,687	8,132	32	555 R	51.6%	48.3%	51.6%	48.4%
816,048	ST. LOUIS CITY	402,451	168,165	233,338	948	65,173 D	41.8%	58.0%	41.9%	58.1%
274,230	ST. LOUIS COUNTY	119,747	66,909	52,380	458	14,529 R	55.9%	43.7%	56.1%	43.9%
10,905	STE. GENEVIEVE	4,856	2,750	2,098	8	652 R	56.6%	43.2%	56.7%	43.3%
29,416	SALINE	15,352	7,336	7,988	28	652 D	47.8%	52.0%	47.9%	52.1%
6,627	SCHUYLER	3,748	1,732	1,998	18	266 D	46.2%	53.3%	46.4%	53.6%
8,557	SCOTLAND	4,787	2,329	2,435	23	106 D	48.7%	50.9%	48.9%	51.1%
30,377	SCOTT	12,342	4,401	7,899	42	3,498 D	35.7%	64.0%	35.8%	64.2%
11,831	SHANNON	4,423	1,589	2,806	28	1,217 D	35.9%	63.4%	36.2%	63.8%
11,224	SHELBY	6,221	2,167	4,028	26	1,861 D	34.8%	64.7%	35.0%	65.0%
33,009	STODDARD	12,818	6,055	6,725	38	670 D	47.2%	52.5%	47.4%	52.6%
11,298	STONE	4,647	3,598	1,041	8	2,557 R	77.4%	22.4%	77.6%	22.4%
13,701	SULLIVAN	7,836	4,080	3,743	13	337 R	52.1%	47.8%	52.2%	47.8%
10,323	TANEY	4,684	3,167	1,497	20	1,670 R	67.6%	32.0%	67.9%	32.1%
19,813	TEXAS	9,239	4,730	4,497	12	233 R	51.2%	48.7%	51.3%	48.7%
25,586	VERNON	11,735	5,443	6,271	21	828 D	46.4%	53.4%	46.5%	53.5%
7,734	WARREN	4,344	3,403	914	27	2,489 R	78.3%	21.0%	78.8%	21.2%
17,492	WASHINGTON	6,706	3,817	2,881	8	936 R	56.9%	43.0%	57.0%	43.0%
12,794	WAYNE	5,739	2,735	2,991	13	256 D	47.7%	52.1%	47.8%	52.2%
17,226	WEBSTER	8,352	4,818	3,518	16	1,300 R	57.7%	42.1%	57.8%	42.2%
6,345	WORTH	3,513	1,807	1,702	4	105 R	51.4%	48.4%	51.5%	48.5%
17,967	WRIGHT	7,843	5,096	2,727	20	2,369 R	65.0%	34.8%	65.1%	34.9%
3,784,664	TOTAL	1,833,729	871,009	958,476	4,244	87,467 D	47.5%	52.3%	47.6%	52.4%

MISSOURI

PRESIDENT 1936

1930 Census Population	County	Total Vote	Republican	Democratic	Other	Rep.-Dem. Plurality	Percentage Total Vote Rep.	Total Vote Dem.	Major Vote Rep.	Major Vote Dem.
19,436	ADAIR	10,127	4,685	5,315	127	630 D	46.3%	52.5%	46.9%	53.2%
13,469	ANDREW	7,693	3,987	3,702	4	285 R	51.8%	48.1%	51.9%	48.1%
13,421	ATCHISON	6,503	3,044	3,452	7	408 D	46.8%	53.1%	46.9%	53.1%
22,077	AUDRAIN	9,994	2,508	7,455	31	4,947 D	25.1%	74.6%	25.2%	74.8%
22,803	BARRY	11,699	5,906	5,744	49	162 R	50.5%	49.1%	50.7%	49.3%
14,560	BARTON	7,249	3,164	4,048	37	884 D	43.6%	55.8%	43.9%	56.1%
22,068	BATES	10,777	5,022	5,681	74	659 D	46.6%	52.7%	46.9%	53.1%
11,708	BENTON	5,346	3,375	1,950	21	1,425 R	63.1%	36.5%	63.4%	36.6%
12,269	BOLLINGER	5,869	2,988	2,816	65	172 R	50.9%	48.0%	51.5%	48.5%
30,995	BOONE	14,926	3,624	11,241	61	7,617 D	24.3%	75.3%	24.4%	75.6%
98,633	BUCHANAN	44,933	15,912	28,825	196	12,913 D	35.4%	64.2%	35.6%	64.4%
23,697	BUTLER	12,631	6,355	6,234	42	121 R	50.3%	49.4%	50.5%	49.5%
12,509	CALDWELL	6,813	3,792	3,014	7	778 R	55.7%	44.2%	55.7%	44.3%
19,923	CALLAWAY	10,293	3,112	7,160	21	4,048 D	30.2%	69.6%	30.3%	69.7%
9,142	CAMDEN	4,195	2,281	1,908	6	373 R	54.4%	45.5%	54.5%	45.5%
33,203	CAPE GIRARDEAU	16,330	7,374	8,892	64	1,518 D	45.2%	54.5%	45.3%	54.7%
19,940	CARROLL	10,605	5,432	5,141	32	291 R	51.2%	48.5%	51.4%	48.6%
5,503	CARTER	2,689	1,073	1,590	26	517 D	39.9%	59.1%	40.3%	59.7%
20,962	CASS	9,853	4,070	5,731	52	1,661 D	41.3%	58.2%	41.5%	58.5%
11,136	CEDAR	6,012	3,535	2,443	34	1,092 R	58.8%	40.6%	59.1%	40.9%
19,588	CHARITON	8,957	3,433	5,490	34	2,057 D	38.3%	61.3%	38.5%	61.5%
13,169	CHRISTIAN	6,501	4,022	2,462	17	1,560 R	61.9%	37.9%	62.0%	38.0%
10,254	CLARK	5,840	2,812	3,003	25	191 D	48.2%	51.4%	48.4%	51.6%
26,811	CLAY	14,084	4,491	9,535	58	5,044 D	31.9%	67.7%	32.0%	68.0%
13,505	CLINTON	6,727	2,512	4,166	49	1,654 D	37.3%	61.9%	37.6%	62.4%
30,848	COLE	15,106	6,180	8,831	95	2,651 D	40.9%	58.5%	41.2%	58.8%
19,522	COOPER	10,197	4,980	5,188	29	208 D	48.8%	50.9%	49.0%	51.0%
11,287	CRAWFORD	5,961	3,041	2,879	41	162 R	51.0%	48.3%	51.4%	48.6%
11,764	DADE	5,669	3,326	2,312	31	1,014 R	58.7%	40.8%	59.0%	41.0%
10,541	DALLAS	4,828	3,066	1,749	13	1,317 R	63.5%	36.2%	63.7%	36.3%
14,424	DAVIESS	7,902	3,924	3,953	25	29 D	49.7%	50.0%	49.8%	50.2%
10,270	DE KALB	5,570	2,872	2,680	18	192 R	51.6%	48.1%	51.7%	48.3%
10,974	DENT	5,514	2,313	3,168	33	855 D	41.9%	57.5%	42.2%	57.8%
13,959	DOUGLAS	6,187	4,031	2,118	38	1,913 R	65.2%	34.2%	65.6%	34.4%
35,799	DUNKLIN	14,066	3,775	10,233	58	6,458 D	26.8%	72.7%	26.9%	73.1%
30,519	FRANKLIN	15,920	7,708	7,565	647	143 R	48.4%	47.5%	50.5%	49.5%
12,172	GASCONADE	5,716	4,202	1,492	22	2,710 R	73.5%	26.1%	73.8%	26.2%
14,348	GENTRY	7,306	3,115	4,173	18	1,058 D	42.6%	57.1%	42.7%	57.3%
82,929	GREENE	38,906	17,298	21,489	119	4,191 D	44.5%	55.2%	44.6%	55.4%
16,135	GRUNDY	8,763	4,521	4,187	55	334 R	51.6%	47.8%	51.9%	48.1%
17,233	HARRISON	8,852	4,888	3,942	22	946 R	55.2%	44.5%	55.4%	44.6%
22,931	HENRY	12,111	4,927	7,145	39	2,218 D	40.7%	59.0%	40.8%	59.2%
6,430	HICKORY	3,247	2,329	910	8	1,419 R	71.7%	28.0%	71.9%	28.1%
12,720	HOLT	6,499	3,409	3,076	14	333 R	52.5%	47.3%	52.6%	47.4%
13,490	HOWARD	7,092	1,745	5,326	21	3,581 D	24.6%	75.1%	24.7%	75.3%
19,672	HOWELL	10,064	5,297	4,725	42	572 R	52.6%	46.9%	52.9%	47.1%
9,642	IRON	4,029	1,605	2,413	11	808 D	39.8%	59.9%	39.9%	60.1%
470,454	JACKSON	295,319	79,119	215,120	1,080	136,001 D	26.8%	72.8%	26.9%	73.1%
73,810	JASPER	34,585	14,440	19,822	323	5,382 D	41.8%	57.3%	42.1%	57.9%
27,563	JEFFERSON	14,974	5,575	9,158	241	3,583 D	37.2%	61.2%	37.8%	62.2%
22,413	JOHNSON	12,113	5,797	6,294	22	497 D	47.9%	52.0%	47.9%	52.1%
9,658	KNOX	5,193	2,134	3,030	29	896 D	41.1%	58.3%	41.3%	58.7%
16,320	LACLEDE	7,977	4,258	3,691	28	567 R	53.4%	46.3%	53.6%	46.4%
29,259	LAFAYETTE	14,861	7,535	7,275	51	260 R	50.7%	49.0%	50.9%	49.1%
23,774	LAWRENCE	12,439	6,185	6,184	70	1 R	49.7%	49.7%	50.0%	50.0%
12,093	LEWIS	5,903	1,994	3,859	50	1,865 D	33.8%	65.4%	34.1%	65.9%
13,929	LINCOLN	6,924	2,258	4,625	41	2,367 D	32.6%	66.8%	32.8%	67.2%
23,339	LINN	11,915	5,118	6,744	53	1,626 D	43.0%	56.6%	43.1%	56.9%
18,615	LIVINGSTON	9,944	4,678	5,226	40	548 D	47.0%	52.6%	47.2%	52.8%
13,936	MCDONALD	6,819	3,312	3,503	4	191 D	48.6%	51.4%	48.6%	51.4%

MISSOURI

PRESIDENT 1936

1930 Census Population	County	Total Vote	Republican	Democratic	Other	Rep.-Dem. Plurality	Percentage Total Vote Rep.	Total Vote Dem.	Major Vote Rep.	Major Vote Dem.
23,070	MACON	11,262	4,808	6,417	37	1,609 D	42.7%	57.0%	42.8%	57.2%
9,418	MADISON	4,342	2,013	2,323	6	310 D	46.4%	53.5%	46.4%	53.6%
8,368	MARIES	3,740	1,306	2,414	20	1,108 D	34.9%	64.5%	35.1%	64.9%
33,493	MARION	15,747	4,628	11,068	51	6,440 D	29.4%	70.3%	29.5%	70.5%
9,350	MERCER	4,605	2,757	1,834	14	923 R	59.9%	39.8%	60.1%	39.9%
16,728	MILLER	7,086	3,607	3,436	43	171 R	50.9%	48.5%	51.2%	48.8%
15,762	MISSISSIPPI	6,737	2,552	4,160	25	1,608 D	37.9%	61.7%	38.0%	62.0%
12,173	MONITEAU	6,466	3,238	3,210	18	28 R	50.1%	49.6%	50.2%	49.8%
13,466	MONROE	7,340	939	6,376	25	5,437 D	12.8%	86.9%	12.8%	87.2%
13,011	MONTGOMERY	6,937	3,468	3,458	11	10 R	50.0%	49.8%	50.1%	49.9%
10,968	MORGAN	5,596	2,993	2,585	18	408 R	53.5%	46.2%	53.7%	46.3%
30,262	NEW MADRID	12,872	5,056	7,791	25	2,735 D	39.3%	60.5%	39.4%	60.6%
26,959	NEWTON	13,448	6,437	6,929	82	492 D	47.9%	51.5%	48.2%	51.8%
26,371	NODAWAY	13,399	5,817	7,499	83	1,682 D	43.4%	56.0%	43.7%	56.3%
12,220	OREGON	4,970	1,461	3,504	5	2,043 D	29.4%	70.5%	29.4%	70.6%
12,462	OSAGE	5,899	2,836	2,995	68	159 D	48.1%	50.8%	48.6%	51.4%
9,537	OZARK	4,354	2,981	1,359	14	1,622 R	68.5%	31.2%	68.7%	31.3%
37,284	PEMISCOT	12,324	4,139	8,171	14	4,032 D	33.6%	66.3%	33.6%	66.4%
13,707	PERRY	6,606	3,382	3,098	126	284 R	51.2%	46.9%	52.2%	47.8%
34,664	PETTIS	16,821	7,435	9,265	121	1,830 D	44.2%	55.1%	44.5%	55.5%
15,308	PHELPS	7,381	2,690	4,658	33	1,968 D	36.4%	63.1%	36.6%	63.4%
18,001	PIKE	8,827	2,871	5,898	58	3,027 D	32.5%	66.8%	32.7%	67.3%
13,819	PLATTE	6,691	1,787	4,884	20	3,097 D	26.7%	73.0%	26.8%	73.2%
17,803	POLK	9,048	5,126	3,899	23	1,227 R	56.7%	43.1%	56.8%	43.2%
10,755	PULASKI	5,076	2,177	2,886	13	709 D	42.9%	56.9%	43.0%	57.0%
11,503	PUTNAM	5,402	3,458	1,902	42	1,556 R	64.0%	35.2%	64.5%	35.5%
10,704	RALLS	4,885	1,051	3,822	12	2,771 D	21.5%	78.2%	21.6%	78.4%
26,431	RANDOLPH	12,491	2,723	9,733	35	7,010 D	21.8%	77.9%	21.9%	78.1%
19,846	RAY	9,124	2,805	6,300	19	3,495 D	30.7%	69.0%	30.8%	69.2%
8,923	REYNOLDS	3,396	915	2,476	5	1,561 D	26.9%	72.9%	27.0%	73.0%
11,176	RIPLEY	4,397	1,911	2,466	20	555 D	43.5%	56.1%	43.7%	56.3%
24,354	ST. CHARLES	12,068	5,156	5,903	1,009	747 D	42.7%	48.9%	46.6%	53.4%
13,289	ST. CLAIR	6,684	3,351	3,302	31	49 R	50.1%	49.4%	50.4%	49.6%
35,832	ST. FRANCOIS	15,213	7,271	7,876	66	605 D	47.8%	51.8%	48.0%	52.0%
821,960	ST. LOUIS CITY	396,830	127,887	260,063	8,880	132,176 D	32.2%	65.5%	33.0%	67.0%
211,593	ST. LOUIS COUNTY	112,100	45,541	63,226	3,333	17,685 D	40.6%	56.4%	41.9%	58.1%
10,097	STE. GENEVIEVE	4,182	1,664	2,446	72	782 D	39.8%	58.5%	40.5%	59.5%
30,598	SALINE	14,776	6,108	8,622	46	2,514 D	41.3%	58.4%	41.5%	58.5%
6,951	SCHUYLER	3,629	1,447	2,173	9	726 D	39.9%	59.9%	40.0%	60.0%
8,853	SCOTLAND	4,772	1,940	2,768	64	828 D	40.7%	58.0%	41.2%	58.8%
24,913	SCOTT	10,941	3,126	7,763	52	4,637 D	28.6%	71.0%	28.7%	71.3%
10,894	SHANNON	4,349	1,225	3,069	55	1,844 D	28.2%	70.6%	28.5%	71.5%
11,983	SHELBY	6,102	1,697	4,367	38	2,670 D	27.8%	71.6%	28.0%	72.0%
27,452	STODDARD	11,491	4,828	6,608	55	1,780 D	42.0%	57.5%	42.2%	57.8%
11,614	STONE	4,745	3,366	1,366	13	2,000 R	70.9%	28.8%	71.1%	28.9%
15,212	SULLIVAN	8,025	4,019	3,986	20	33 R	50.1%	49.7%	50.2%	49.8%
8,867	TANEY	4,560	2,827	1,710	23	1,117 R	62.0%	37.5%	62.3%	37.7%
18,580	TEXAS	8,884	4,132	4,718	34	586 D	46.5%	53.1%	46.7%	53.3%
25,031	VERNON	11,478	4,546	6,872	60	2,326 D	39.6%	59.9%	39.8%	60.2%
8,082	WARREN	3,941	2,639	1,277	25	1,362 R	67.0%	32.4%	67.4%	32.6%
14,450	WASHINGTON	5,902	2,909	2,942	51	33 D	49.3%	49.8%	49.7%	50.3%
12,243	WAYNE	5,745	2,494	3,235	16	741 D	43.4%	56.3%	43.5%	56.5%
16,148	WEBSTER	8,102	4,469	3,612	21	857 R	55.2%	44.6%	55.3%	44.7%
6,535	WORTH	3,556	1,581	1,944	31	363 D	44.5%	54.7%	44.9%	55.1%
16,741	WRIGHT	8,174	4,837	3,296	41	1,541 R	59.2%	40.3%	59.5%	40.5%
3,629,367	TOTAL	1,828,635	697,891	1,111,043	19,701	413,152 D	38.2%	60.8%	38.6%	61.4%

MISSOURI

PRESIDENT 1932

1930 Census Population	County	Total Vote	Republican	Democratic	Other	Rep.-Dem. Plurality	Percentage Total Vote Rep.	Percentage Total Vote Dem.	Percentage Major Vote Rep.	Percentage Major Vote Dem.
19,436	ADAIR	7,760	2,991	4,623	146	1,632 D	38.5%	59.6%	39.3%	60.7%
13,469	ANDREW	6,138	2,826	3,280	32	454 D	46.0%	53.4%	46.3%	53.7%
13,421	ATCHISON	5,806	2,155	3,617	34	1,462 D	37.1%	62.3%	37.3%	62.7%
22,077	AUDRAIN	10,392	3,037	7,301	54	4,264 D	29.2%	70.3%	29.4%	70.6%
22,803	BARRY	10,588	4,497	5,957	134	1,460 D	42.5%	56.3%	43.0%	57.0%
14,560	BARTON	6,104	2,092	3,897	115	1,805 D	34.3%	63.8%	34.9%	65.1%
22,068	BATES	9,694	3,395	6,220	79	2,825 D	35.0%	64.2%	35.3%	64.7%
11,708	BENTON	4,672	2,038	2,596	38	558 D	43.6%	55.6%	44.0%	56.0%
12,269	BOLLINGER	5,444	2,411	2,994	39	583 D	44.3%	55.0%	44.6%	55.4%
30,995	BOONE	14,979	3,241	11,554	184	8,313 D	21.6%	77.1%	21.9%	78.1%
98,633	BUCHANAN	40,922	14,602	26,060	260	11,458 D	35.7%	63.7%	35.9%	64.1%
23,697	BUTLER	10,303	4,155	6,058	90	1,903 D	40.3%	58.8%	40.7%	59.3%
12,509	CALDWELL	5,677	2,688	2,949	40	261 D	47.3%	51.9%	47.7%	52.3%
19,923	CALLAWAY	9,172	2,079	7,042	51	4,963 D	22.7%	76.8%	22.8%	77.2%
9,142	CAMDEN	3,313	1,497	1,801	15	304 D	45.2%	54.4%	45.4%	54.6%
33,203	CAPE GIRARDEAU	14,307	5,796	8,394	117	2,598 D	40.5%	58.7%	40.8%	59.2%
19,940	CARROLL	9,003	3,894	5,072	37	1,178 D	43.3%	56.3%	43.4%	56.6%
5,503	CARTER	2,309	750	1,522	37	772 D	32.5%	65.9%	33.0%	67.0%
20,962	CASS	8,847	3,009	5,772	66	2,763 D	34.0%	65.2%	34.3%	65.7%
11,136	CEDAR	5,412	2,515	2,834	63	319 D	46.5%	52.4%	47.0%	53.0%
19,588	CHARITON	7,367	1,835	5,498	34	3,663 D	24.9%	74.6%	25.0%	75.0%
13,169	CHRISTIAN	5,055	2,395	2,577	83	182 D	47.4%	51.0%	48.2%	51.8%
10,254	CLARK	5,324	2,223	3,072	29	849 D	41.8%	57.7%	42.0%	58.0%
26,811	CLAY	12,612	3,117	9,398	97	6,281 D	24.7%	74.5%	24.9%	75.1%
13,505	CLINTON	5,867	1,805	4,042	20	2,237 D	30.8%	68.9%	30.9%	69.1%
30,848	COLE	14,731	5,636	9,068	27	3,432 D	38.3%	61.6%	38.3%	61.7%
19,522	COOPER	9,226	3,695	5,493	38	1,798 D	40.0%	59.5%	40.2%	59.8%
11,287	CRAWFORD	5,425	2,213	3,166	46	953 D	40.8%	58.4%	41.1%	58.9%
11,764	DADE	5,228	2,340	2,833	55	493 D	44.8%	54.2%	45.2%	54.8%
10,541	DALLAS	4,136	1,958	2,143	35	185 D	47.3%	51.8%	47.7%	52.3%
14,424	DAVIESS	5,906	2,351	3,523	32	1,172 D	39.8%	59.7%	40.0%	60.0%
10,270	DE KALB	4,288	1,747	2,519	22	772 D	40.7%	58.7%	41.0%	59.0%
10,974	DENT	5,017	1,701	3,293	23	1,592 D	33.9%	65.6%	34.1%	65.9%
13,959	DOUGLAS	4,415	2,362	1,922	131	440 R	53.5%	43.5%	55.1%	44.9%
35,799	DUNKLIN	11,211	1,977	9,141	93	7,164 D	17.6%	81.5%	17.8%	82.2%
30,519	FRANKLIN	13,992	5,369	8,479	144	3,110 D	38.4%	60.6%	38.8%	61.2%
12,172	GASCONADE	4,610	2,571	1,998	41	573 R	55.8%	43.3%	56.3%	43.7%
14,348	GENTRY	5,563	1,877	3,677	9	1,800 D	33.7%	66.1%	33.8%	66.2%
82,929	GREENE	32,794	13,943	18,255	596	4,312 D	42.5%	55.7%	43.3%	56.7%
16,135	GRUNDY	7,020	2,953	4,006	61	1,053 D	42.1%	57.1%	42.4%	57.6%
17,233	HARRISON	5,883	2,476	3,376	31	900 D	42.1%	57.4%	42.3%	57.7%
22,931	HENRY	10,500	3,631	6,809	60	3,178 D	34.6%	64.8%	34.8%	65.2%
6,430	HICKORY	2,479	1,586	878	15	708 R	64.0%	35.4%	64.4%	35.6%
12,720	HOLT	5,394	2,253	3,117	24	864 D	41.8%	57.8%	42.0%	58.0%
13,490	HOWARD	6,737	1,337	5,354	46	4,017 D	19.8%	79.5%	20.0%	80.0%
19,672	HOWELL	8,540	3,660	4,775	105	1,115 D	42.9%	55.9%	43.4%	56.6%
9,642	IRON	4,172	1,439	2,689	44	1,250 D	34.5%	64.5%	34.9%	65.1%
470,454	JACKSON	256,885	83,214	172,456	1,215	89,242 D	32.4%	67.1%	32.5%	67.5%
73,810	JASPER	29,604	11,788	17,349	467	5,561 D	39.8%	58.6%	40.5%	59.5%
27,563	JEFFERSON	12,844	4,559	8,130	155	3,571 D	35.5%	63.3%	35.9%	64.1%
22,413	JOHNSON	10,645	4,088	6,481	76	2,393 D	38.4%	60.9%	38.7%	61.3%
9,658	KNOX	4,562	1,465	3,045	52	1,580 D	32.1%	66.7%	32.5%	67.5%
16,320	LACLEDE	6,823	2,804	3,960	59	1,156 D	41.1%	58.0%	41.5%	58.5%
29,259	LAFAYETTE	13,613	5,670	7,906	37	2,236 D	41.7%	58.1%	41.8%	58.2%
23,774	LAWRENCE	10,732	4,146	6,411	175	2,265 D	38.6%	59.7%	39.3%	60.7%
12,093	LEWIS	5,143	1,341	3,746	56	2,405 D	26.1%	72.8%	26.4%	73.6%
13,929	LINCOLN	6,061	1,604	4,428	29	2,824 D	26.5%	73.1%	26.6%	73.4%
23,339	LINN	9,858	3,611	6,177	70	2,566 D	36.6%	62.7%	36.9%	63.1%
18,615	LIVINGSTON	8,431	3,659	4,742	30	1,083 D	43.4%	56.2%	43.6%	56.4%
13,936	MCDONALD	6,465	2,464	3,943	58	1,479 D	38.1%	61.0%	38.5%	61.5%

MISSOURI

PRESIDENT 1932

1930 Census Population	County	Total Vote	Republican	Democratic	Other	Rep.-Dem. Plurality	Percentage Total Vote Rep.	Percentage Total Vote Dem.	Percentage Major Vote Rep.	Percentage Major Vote Dem.
23,070	MACON	9,718	3,266	6,370	82	3,104 D	33.6%	65.5%	33.9%	66.1%
9,418	MADISON	3,788	1,428	2,347	13	919 D	37.7%	62.0%	37.8%	62.2%
8,368	MARIES	3,521	745	2,758	18	2,013 D	21.2%	78.3%	21.3%	78.7%
33,493	MARION	14,519	4,123	10,293	103	6,170 D	28.4%	70.9%	28.6%	71.4%
9,350	MERCER	2,901	1,357	1,520	24	163 D	46.8%	52.4%	47.2%	52.8%
16,728	MILLER	6,435	2,615	3,776	44	1,161 D	40.6%	58.7%	40.9%	59.1%
15,762	MISSISSIPPI	4,858	1,687	3,136	35	1,449 D	34.7%	64.6%	35.0%	65.0%
12,173	MONITEAU	6,114	2,331	3,767	16	1,436 D	38.1%	61.6%	38.2%	61.8%
13,466	MONROE	6,968	714	6,210	44	5,496 D	10.2%	89.1%	10.3%	89.7%
13,011	MONTGOMERY	6,241	2,607	3,600	34	993 D	41.8%	57.7%	42.0%	58.0%
10,968	MORGAN	4,807	2,000	2,768	39	768 D	41.6%	57.6%	41.9%	58.1%
30,262	NEW MADRID	11,652	3,768	7,837	47	4,069 D	32.3%	67.3%	32.5%	67.5%
26,959	NEWTON	12,209	4,806	7,224	179	2,418 D	39.4%	59.2%	40.0%	60.0%
26,371	NODAWAY	10,602	3,584	6,959	59	3,375 D	33.8%	65.6%	34.0%	66.0%
12,220	OREGON	4,423	786	3,599	38	2,813 D	17.8%	81.4%	17.9%	82.1%
12,462	OSAGE	5,387	1,798	3,567	22	1,769 D	33.4%	66.2%	33.5%	66.5%
9,537	OZARK	3,106	1,730	1,358	18	372 R	55.7%	43.7%	56.0%	44.0%
37,284	PEMISCOT	12,356	4,415	7,909	32	3,494 D	35.7%	64.0%	35.8%	64.2%
13,707	PERRY	5,917	2,396	3,502	19	1,106 D	40.5%	59.2%	40.6%	59.4%
34,664	PETTIS	15,545	5,982	9,474	89	3,492 D	38.5%	60.9%	38.7%	61.3%
15,308	PHELPS	6,720	1,794	4,858	68	3,064 D	26.7%	72.3%	27.0%	73.0%
18,001	PIKE	8,379	2,462	5,783	134	3,321 D	29.4%	69.0%	29.9%	70.1%
13,819	PLATTE	6,358	1,160	5,179	19	4,019 D	18.2%	81.5%	18.3%	81.7%
17,803	POLK	8,213	3,811	4,355	47	544 D	46.4%	53.0%	46.7%	53.3%
10,755	PULASKI	4,766	1,489	3,260	17	1,771 D	31.2%	68.4%	31.4%	68.6%
11,503	PUTNAM	4,315	2,180	1,987	148	193 R	50.5%	46.0%	52.3%	47.7%
10,704	RALLS	4,307	761	3,526	20	2,765 D	17.7%	81.9%	17.8%	82.2%
26,431	RANDOLPH	11,935	2,575	9,294	66	6,719 D	21.6%	77.9%	21.7%	78.3%
19,846	RAY	7,846	1,706	6,088	52	4,382 D	21.7%	77.6%	21.9%	78.1%
8,923	REYNOLDS	3,252	792	2,439	21	1,647 D	24.4%	75.0%	24.5%	75.5%
11,176	RIPLEY	3,834	1,139	2,600	95	1,461 D	29.7%	67.8%	30.5%	69.5%
24,354	ST. CHARLES	10,737	3,664	6,911	162	3,247 D	34.1%	64.4%	34.6%	65.4%
13,289	ST. CLAIR	6,022	2,271	3,681	70	1,410 D	37.7%	61.1%	38.2%	61.8%
35,832	ST. FRANCOIS	13,804	6,017	7,613	174	1,596 D	43.6%	55.2%	44.1%	55.9%
821,960	ST. LOUIS CITY	357,105	123,448	226,338	7,319	102,890 D	34.6%	63.4%	35.3%	64.7%
211,593	ST. LOUIS COUNTY	98,257	35,872	59,044	3,341	23,172 D	36.5%	60.1%	37.8%	62.2%
10,097	STE. GENEVIEVE	4,215	1,109	3,087	19	1,978 D	26.3%	73.2%	26.4%	73.6%
30,598	SALINE	12,245	3,783	8,389	73	4,606 D	30.9%	68.5%	31.1%	68.9%
6,951	SCHUYLER	3,372	1,109	2,239	24	1,130 D	32.9%	66.4%	33.1%	66.9%
8,853	SCOTLAND	4,205	1,410	2,738	57	1,328 D	33.5%	65.1%	34.0%	66.0%
24,913	SCOTT	9,333	2,310	6,948	75	4,638 D	24.8%	74.4%	25.0%	75.0%
10,894	SHANNON	3,924	879	2,949	96	2,070 D	22.4%	75.2%	23.0%	77.0%
11,983	SHELBY	5,344	1,104	4,215	25	3,111 D	20.7%	78.9%	20.8%	79.2%
27,452	STODDARD	10,485	3,234	7,139	112	3,905 D	30.8%	68.1%	31.2%	68.8%
11,614	STONE	3,688	1,748	1,911	29	163 D	47.4%	51.8%	47.8%	52.2%
15,212	SULLIVAN	7,453	3,373	4,053	27	680 D	45.3%	54.4%	45.4%	54.6%
8,867	TANEY	3,987	2,045	1,911	31	134 R	51.3%	47.9%	51.7%	48.3%
18,580	TEXAS	7,675	2,621	4,996	58	2,375 D	34.1%	65.1%	34.4%	65.6%
25,031	VERNON	9,681	2,856	6,687	138	3,831 D	29.5%	69.1%	29.9%	70.1%
8,082	WARREN	3,516	1,974	1,513	29	461 R	56.1%	43.0%	56.6%	43.4%
14,450	WASHINGTON	5,559	2,246	3,275	38	1,029 D	40.4%	58.9%	40.7%	59.3%
12,243	WAYNE	5,169	1,955	3,172	42	1,217 D	37.8%	61.4%	38.1%	61.9%
16,148	WEBSTER	7,357	3,083	4,211	63	1,128 D	41.9%	57.2%	42.3%	57.7%
6,535	WORTH	2,821	1,041	1,763	17	722 D	36.9%	62.5%	37.1%	62.9%
16,741	WRIGHT	6,948	3,023	3,862	63	839 D	43.5%	55.6%	43.9%	56.1%
3,629,367	TOTAL	1,609,894	564,713	1,025,406	19,775	460,693 D	35.1%	63.7%	35.5%	64.5%

MISSOURI

PRESIDENT 1928

1920 Census Population	County	Total Vote	Republican	Democratic	Other	Rep.-Dem. Plurality	Percentage: Total Vote Rep.	Percentage: Total Vote Dem.	Percentage: Major Vote Rep.	Percentage: Major Vote Dem.
21,404	ADAIR	8,429	5,538	2,841	50	2,697 R	65.7%	33.7%	66.1%	33.9%
14,075	ANDREW	6,373	4,243	2,118	12	2,125 R	66.6%	33.2%	66.7%	33.3%
13,008	ATCHISON	5,786	3,239	2,535	12	704 R	56.0%	43.8%	56.1%	43.9%
20,589	AUDRAIN	9,222	4,141	5,067	14	926 D	44.9%	54.9%	45.0%	55.0%
23,473	BARRY	9,383	5,901	3,431	51	2,470 R	62.9%	36.6%	63.2%	36.8%
16,879	BARTON	5,985	3,662	2,275	48	1,387 R	61.2%	38.0%	61.7%	38.3%
23,933	BATES	9,781	6,133	3,594	54	2,539 R	62.7%	36.7%	63.1%	36.9%
12,989	BENTON	4,716	3,411	1,296	9	2,115 R	72.3%	27.5%	72.5%	27.5%
13,909	BOLLINGER	4,846	3,014	1,824	8	1,190 R	62.2%	37.6%	62.3%	37.7%
29,672	BOONE	13,319	4,876	8,422	21	3,546 D	36.6%	63.2%	36.7%	63.3%
93,684	BUCHANAN	32,624	20,459	12,110	55	8,349 R	62.7%	37.1%	62.8%	37.2%
24,106	BUTLER	8,949	5,591	3,320	38	2,271 R	62.5%	37.1%	62.7%	37.3%
13,849	CALDWELL	6,331	4,167	2,164		2,003 R	65.8%	34.2%	65.8%	34.2%
23,007	CALLAWAY	8,437	3,269	5,153	15	1,884 D	38.7%	61.1%	38.8%	61.2%
10,474	CAMDEN	2,695	2,085	606	4	1,479 R	77.4%	22.5%	77.5%	22.5%
29,839	CAPE GIRARDEAU	12,829	7,344	5,464	21	1,880 R	57.2%	42.6%	57.3%	42.7%
20,480	CARROLL	9,624	5,875	3,735	14	2,140 R	61.0%	38.8%	61.1%	38.9%
7,482	CARTER	1,962	989	963	10	26 R	50.4%	49.1%	50.7%	49.3%
21,536	CASS	8,964	5,299	3,647	18	1,652 R	59.1%	40.7%	59.2%	40.8%
13,933	CEDAR	5,080	3,340	1,728	12	1,612 R	65.7%	34.0%	65.9%	34.1%
21,769	CHARITON	8,501	3,929	4,559	13	630 D	46.2%	53.6%	46.3%	53.7%
15,252	CHRISTIAN	4,721	3,576	1,124	21	2,452 R	75.7%	23.8%	76.1%	23.9%
11,874	CLARK	5,447	3,259	2,170	18	1,089 R	59.8%	39.8%	60.0%	40.0%
20,455	CLAY	11,185	5,584	5,574	27	10 R	49.9%	49.8%	50.0%	50.0%
14,461	CLINTON	6,229	3,736	2,485	8	1,251 R	60.0%	39.9%	60.1%	39.9%
24,680	COLE	13,133	6,637	6,481	15	156 R	50.5%	49.3%	50.6%	49.4%
19,308	COOPER	9,216	4,794	4,413	9	381 R	52.0%	47.9%	52.1%	47.9%
12,355	CRAWFORD	4,428	2,926	1,476	26	1,450 R	66.1%	33.3%	66.5%	33.5%
14,173	DADE	4,957	3,497	1,453	7	2,044 R	70.5%	29.3%	70.6%	29.4%
12,033	DALLAS	3,783	2,835	931	17	1,904 R	74.9%	24.6%	75.3%	24.7%
16,641	DAVIESS	7,057	4,254	2,789	14	1,465 R	60.3%	39.5%	60.4%	39.6%
11,694	DE KALB	5,254	3,338	1,898	18	1,440 R	63.5%	36.1%	63.8%	36.2%
12,318	DENT	4,266	2,367	1,871	28	496 R	55.5%	43.9%	55.9%	44.1%
15,436	DOUGLAS	4,474	3,758	681	35	3,077 R	84.0%	15.2%	84.7%	15.3%
32,773	DUNKLIN	8,501	3,602	4,879	20	1,277 D	42.4%	57.4%	42.5%	57.5%
28,427	FRANKLIN	13,292	7,831	5,429	32	2,402 R	58.9%	40.8%	59.1%	40.9%
12,381	GASCONADE	5,242	4,171	1,058	13	3,113 R	79.6%	20.2%	79.8%	20.2%
15,634	GENTRY	6,256	3,506	2,735	15	771 R	56.0%	43.7%	56.2%	43.8%
68,698	GREENE	33,151	22,166	10,901	84	11,265 R	66.9%	32.9%	67.0%	33.0%
17,554	GRUNDY	7,604	5,226	2,332	46	2,894 R	68.7%	30.7%	69.1%	30.9%
19,719	HARRISON	7,153	4,818	2,319	16	2,499 R	67.4%	32.4%	67.5%	32.5%
25,116	HENRY	10,603	6,263	4,319	21	1,944 R	59.1%	40.7%	59.2%	40.8%
7,033	HICKORY	2,637	2,233	399	5	1,834 R	84.7%	15.1%	84.8%	15.2%
14,084	HOLT	5,776	3,845	1,919	12	1,926 R	66.6%	33.2%	66.7%	33.3%
13,997	HOWARD	6,720	2,254	4,452	14	2,198 D	33.5%	66.3%	33.6%	66.4%
21,102	HOWELL	7,461	4,869	2,543	49	2,326 R	65.3%	34.1%	65.7%	34.3%
9,458	IRON	3,255	1,910	1,342	3	568 R	58.7%	41.2%	58.7%	41.3%
367,846	JACKSON	223,677	126,589	96,703	385	29,886 R	56.6%	43.2%	56.7%	43.3%
75,941	JASPER	29,059	20,587	8,292	180	12,295 R	70.8%	28.5%	71.3%	28.7%
26,555	JEFFERSON	11,538	6,285	5,231	22	1,054 R	54.5%	45.3%	54.6%	45.4%
24,899	JOHNSON	11,367	7,032	4,316	19	2,716 R	61.9%	38.0%	62.0%	38.0%
10,783	KNOX	4,848	2,628	2,213	7	415 R	54.2%	45.6%	54.3%	45.7%
16,857	LACLEDE	6,025	3,971	2,031	23	1,940 R	65.9%	33.7%	66.2%	33.8%
30,006	LAFAYETTE	13,658	7,687	5,939	32	1,748 R	56.3%	43.5%	56.4%	43.6%
24,211	LAWRENCE	10,017	6,328	3,646	43	2,682 R	63.2%	36.4%	63.4%	36.6%
13,465	LEWIS	5,646	2,741	2,882	23	141 D	48.5%	51.0%	48.7%	51.3%
15,956	LINCOLN	6,088	2,722	3,356	10	634 D	44.7%	55.1%	44.8%	55.2%
24,778	LINN	11,411	6,996	4,395	20	2,601 R	61.3%	38.5%	61.4%	38.6%
18,857	LIVINGSTON	8,980	5,742	3,221	17	2,521 R	63.9%	35.9%	64.1%	35.9%
14,690	MCDONALD	5,686	3,684	1,986	16	1,698 R	64.8%	34.9%	65.0%	35.0%

MISSOURI

PRESIDENT 1928

1920 Census Population	County	Total Vote	Republican	Democratic	Other	Rep.-Dem. Plurality	Percentage: Total Vote Rep.	Total Vote Dem.	Major Vote Rep.	Major Vote Dem.
27,518	MACON	10,510	5,618	4,838	54	780 R	53.5%	46.0%	53.7%	46.3%
10,721	MADISON	3,491	2,165	1,326		839 R	62.0%	38.0%	62.0%	38.0%
9,500	MARIES	3,231	1,415	1,808	8	393 D	43.8%	56.0%	43.9%	56.1%
30,226	MARION	13,367	7,664	5,679	24	1,985 R	57.3%	42.5%	57.4%	42.6%
11,281	MERCER	3,798	2,869	925	4	1,944 R	75.5%	24.4%	75.6%	24.4%
15,567	MILLER	5,376	3,379	1,979	18	1,400 R	62.9%	36.8%	63.1%	36.9%
12,860	MISSISSIPPI	4,609	1,999	2,602	8	603 D	43.4%	56.5%	43.4%	56.6%
13,532	MONITEAU	5,839	3,496	2,310	33	1,186 R	59.9%	39.6%	60.2%	39.8%
16,414	MONROE	6,354	1,378	4,957	19	3,579 D	21.7%	78.0%	21.8%	78.2%
15,233	MONTGOMERY	6,203	3,910	2,285	8	1,625 R	63.0%	36.8%	63.1%	36.9%
12,015	MORGAN	4,458	3,017	1,432	9	1,585 R	67.7%	32.1%	67.8%	32.2%
25,180	NEW MADRID	8,925	4,750	4,153	22	597 R	53.2%	46.5%	53.4%	46.6%
24,886	NEWTON	10,408	7,054	3,269	85	3,785 R	67.8%	31.4%	68.3%	31.7%
27,744	NODAWAY	12,474	7,160	5,297	17	1,863 R	57.4%	42.5%	57.5%	42.5%
12,889	OREGON	3,550	1,662	1,884	4	222 D	46.8%	53.1%	46.9%	53.1%
13,559	OSAGE	5,572	2,474	3,092	6	618 D	44.4%	55.5%	44.4%	55.6%
11,125	OZARK	3,164	2,616	529	19	2,087 R	82.7%	16.7%	83.2%	16.8%
26,634	PEMISCOT	11,515	6,256	5,259		997 R	54.3%	45.7%	54.3%	45.7%
14,434	PERRY	5,245	2,648	2,591	6	57 R	50.5%	49.4%	50.5%	49.5%
35,813	PETTIS	15,939	10,346	5,554	39	4,792 R	64.9%	34.8%	65.1%	34.9%
14,941	PHELPS	5,874	2,967	2,896	11	71 R	50.5%	49.3%	50.6%	49.4%
20,345	PIKE	8,347	4,569	3,749	29	820 R	54.7%	44.9%	54.9%	45.1%
13,990	PLATTE	5,777	2,423	3,344	10	921 D	41.9%	57.9%	42.0%	58.0%
20,351	POLK	7,622	5,307	2,303	12	3,004 R	69.6%	30.2%	69.7%	30.3%
10,490	PULASKI	4,171	2,229	1,934	8	295 R	53.4%	46.4%	53.5%	46.5%
13,115	PUTNAM	4,755	3,498	1,247	10	2,251 R	73.6%	26.2%	73.7%	26.3%
10,412	RALLS	4,071	1,794	2,273	4	479 D	44.1%	55.8%	44.1%	55.9%
27,633	RANDOLPH	10,842	4,825	6,008	9	1,183 D	44.5%	55.4%	44.5%	55.5%
20,508	RAY	7,866	3,280	4,570	16	1,290 D	41.7%	58.1%	41.8%	58.2%
10,106	REYNOLDS	2,835	1,247	1,582	6	335 D	44.0%	55.8%	44.1%	55.9%
12,061	RIPLEY	3,631	2,226	1,395	10	831 R	61.3%	38.4%	61.5%	38.5%
22,828	ST. CHARLES	10,507	5,404	5,081	22	323 R	51.4%	48.4%	51.5%	48.5%
15,341	ST. CLAIR	5,584	3,846	1,701	37	2,145 R	68.9%	30.5%	69.3%	30.7%
31,403	ST. FRANCOIS	13,228	9,040	4,171	17	4,869 R	68.3%	31.5%	68.4%	31.6%
772,897	ST. LOUIS CITY	339,194	161,701	176,428	1,065	14,727 D	47.7%	52.0%	47.8%	52.2%
100,737	ST. LOUIS COUNTY	76,667	42,572	33,802	293	8,770 R	55.5%	44.1%	55.7%	44.3%
9,809	STE. GENEVIEVE	3,652	1,099	2,547	6	1,448 D	30.1%	69.7%	30.1%	69.9%
28,826	SALINE	13,044	6,780	6,251	13	529 R	52.0%	47.9%	52.0%	48.0%
8,383	SCHUYLER	3,628	1,822	1,797	9	25 R	50.2%	49.5%	50.3%	49.7%
10,700	SCOTLAND	4,566	2,350	2,194	22	156 R	51.5%	48.1%	51.7%	48.3%
23,409	SCOTT	8,944	3,779	5,159	6	1,380 D	42.3%	57.7%	42.3%	57.7%
11,865	SHANNON	3,456	1,542	1,884	30	342 D	44.6%	54.5%	45.0%	55.0%
13,617	SHELBY	5,468	2,303	3,158	7	855 D	42.1%	57.8%	42.2%	57.8%
29,755	STODDARD	8,951	4,906	4,016	29	890 R	54.8%	44.9%	55.0%	45.0%
11,941	STONE	3,543	2,972	559	12	2,413 R	83.9%	15.8%	84.2%	15.8%
17,781	SULLIVAN	7,496	4,183	3,292	21	891 R	55.8%	43.9%	56.0%	44.0%
8,178	TANEY	3,302	2,319	971	12	1,348 R	70.2%	29.4%	70.5%	29.5%
20,548	TEXAS	7,133	4,050	3,067	16	983 R	56.8%	43.0%	56.9%	43.1%
26,069	VERNON	9,490	5,783	3,676	31	2,107 R	60.9%	38.7%	61.1%	38.9%
8,490	WARREN	3,620	2,610	999	11	1,611 R	72.1%	27.6%	72.3%	27.7%
13,803	WASHINGTON	5,120	3,019	2,091	10	928 R	59.0%	40.8%	59.1%	40.9%
13,012	WAYNE	4,685	2,662	2,011	12	651 R	56.8%	42.9%	57.0%	43.0%
16,609	WEBSTER	6,353	4,002	2,343	8	1,659 R	63.0%	36.9%	63.1%	36.9%
7,642	WORTH	3,257	1,839	1,407	11	432 R	56.5%	43.2%	56.7%	43.3%
17,733	WRIGHT	6,501	4,504	1,973	24	2,531 R	69.3%	30.3%	69.5%	30.5%
3,404,049	TOTAL	1,500,845	834,080	662,684	4,081	171,396 R	55.6%	44.2%	55.7%	44.3%

MISSOURI

PRESIDENT 1924

1920 Census Population	County	Total Vote	Republican	Democratic	Other	Rep.-Dem. Plurality	Percentage Total Vote Rep.	Total Vote Dem.	Major Vote Rep.	Major Vote Dem.
21,404	ADAIR	8,183	4,383	2,800	1,000	1,583 R	53.6%	34.2%	61.0%	39.0%
14,075	ANDREW	6,385	3,535	2,648	202	887 R	55.4%	41.5%	57.2%	42.8%
13,008	ATCHISON	5,501	2,710	2,617	174	93 R	49.3%	47.6%	50.9%	49.1%
20,589	AUDRAIN	9,142	3,125	5,866	151	2,741 D	34.2%	64.2%	34.8%	65.2%
23,473	BARRY	8,481	4,065	3,606	810	459 R	47.9%	42.5%	53.0%	47.0%
16,879	BARTON	6,075	2,952	2,682	441	270 R	48.6%	44.1%	52.4%	47.6%
23,933	BATES	9,663	4,552	4,722	389	170 D	47.1%	48.9%	49.1%	50.9%
12,989	BENTON	4,436	2,693	1,588	155	1,105 R	60.7%	35.8%	62.9%	37.1%
13,909	BOLLINGER	4,390	2,204	2,075	111	129 R	50.2%	47.3%	51.5%	48.5%
29,672	BOONE	12,373	3,547	8,657	169	5,110 D	28.7%	70.0%	29.1%	70.9%
93,684	BUCHANAN	34,926	17,509	14,759	2,658	2,750 R	50.1%	42.3%	54.3%	45.7%
24,106	BUTLER	8,019	4,489	2,953	577	1,536 R	56.0%	36.8%	60.3%	39.7%
13,849	CALDWELL	6,043	3,545	2,383	115	1,162 R	58.7%	39.4%	59.8%	40.2%
23,007	CALLAWAY	8,836	2,799	5,904	133	3,105 D	31.7%	66.8%	32.2%	67.8%
10,474	CAMDEN	3,031	1,732	1,196	103	536 R	57.1%	39.5%	59.2%	40.8%
29,839	CAPE GIRARDEAU	11,666	6,076	4,967	623	1,109 R	52.1%	42.6%	55.0%	45.0%
20,480	CARROLL	9,613	4,907	4,502	204	405 R	51.0%	46.8%	52.2%	47.8%
7,482	CARTER	1,903	772	1,051	80	279 D	40.6%	55.2%	42.3%	57.7%
21,536	CASS	8,561	3,610	4,709	242	1,099 D	42.2%	55.0%	43.4%	56.6%
13,933	CEDAR	5,019	2,802	2,007	210	795 R	55.8%	40.0%	58.3%	41.7%
21,769	CHARITON	8,194	3,173	4,795	226	1,622 D	38.7%	58.5%	39.8%	60.2%
15,252	CHRISTIAN	4,289	2,692	1,281	316	1,411 R	62.8%	29.9%	67.8%	32.2%
11,874	CLARK	5,853	2,948	2,770	135	178 R	50.4%	47.3%	51.6%	48.4%
20,455	CLAY	9,459	2,998	6,076	385	3,078 D	31.7%	64.2%	33.0%	67.0%
14,461	CLINTON	6,162	2,848	3,177	137	329 D	46.2%	51.6%	47.3%	52.7%
24,680	COLE	11,821	6,205	5,033	583	1,172 R	52.5%	42.6%	55.2%	44.8%
19,308	COOPER	9,012	4,755	4,070	187	685 R	52.8%	45.2%	53.9%	46.1%
12,355	CRAWFORD	4,189	2,336	1,697	156	639 R	55.8%	40.5%	57.9%	42.1%
14,173	DADE	4,850	2,651	2,007	192	644 R	54.7%	41.4%	56.9%	43.1%
12,033	DALLAS	3,585	2,188	1,304	93	884 R	61.0%	36.4%	62.7%	37.3%
16,641	DAVIESS	7,524	3,869	3,520	135	349 R	51.4%	46.8%	52.4%	47.6%
11,694	DE KALB	5,192	2,730	2,368	94	362 R	52.6%	45.6%	53.6%	46.4%
12,318	DENT	4,153	1,779	2,263	111	484 D	42.8%	54.5%	44.0%	56.0%
15,436	DOUGLAS	3,784	2,617	909	258	1,708 R	69.2%	24.0%	74.2%	25.8%
32,773	DUNKLIN	8,052	3,436	4,357	259	921 D	42.7%	54.1%	44.1%	55.9%
28,427	FRANKLIN	10,543	6,253	3,384	906	2,869 R	59.3%	32.1%	64.9%	35.1%
12,381	GASCONADE	4,357	3,306	577	474	2,729 R	75.9%	13.2%	85.1%	14.9%
15,634	GENTRY	7,222	3,318	3,555	349	237 D	45.9%	49.2%	48.3%	51.7%
68,698	GREENE	29,771	13,618	13,084	3,069	534 R	45.7%	43.9%	51.0%	49.0%
17,554	GRUNDY	7,467	3,782	2,367	1,318	1,415 R	50.6%	31.7%	61.5%	38.5%
19,719	HARRISON	7,300	4,247	2,792	261	1,455 R	58.2%	38.2%	60.3%	39.7%
25,116	HENRY	9,871	4,616	4,706	549	90 D	46.8%	47.7%	49.5%	50.5%
7,033	HICKORY	2,680	1,895	722	63	1,173 R	70.7%	26.9%	72.4%	27.6%
14,084	HOLT	5,719	3,316	2,255	148	1,061 R	58.0%	39.4%	59.5%	40.5%
13,997	HOWARD	6,860	1,873	4,759	228	2,886 D	27.3%	69.4%	28.2%	71.8%
21,102	HOWELL	6,493	3,130	2,681	682	449 R	48.2%	41.3%	53.9%	46.1%
9,458	IRON	3,071	1,328	1,675	68	347 D	43.2%	54.5%	44.2%	55.8%
367,846	JACKSON	175,982	91,141	76,002	8,839	15,139 R	51.8%	43.2%	54.5%	45.5%
75,941	JASPER	24,860	13,701	9,176	1,983	4,525 R	55.1%	36.9%	59.9%	40.1%
26,555	JEFFERSON	9,963	4,870	4,356	737	514 R	48.9%	43.7%	52.8%	47.2%
24,899	JOHNSON	11,006	5,248	5,526	232	278 D	47.7%	50.2%	48.7%	51.3%
10,783	KNOX	5,220	2,288	2,722	210	434 D	43.8%	52.1%	45.7%	54.3%
16,857	LACLEDE	5,735	2,960	2,500	275	460 R	51.6%	43.6%	54.2%	45.8%
30,006	LAFAYETTE	12,923	6,517	5,877	529	640 R	50.4%	45.5%	52.6%	47.4%
24,211	LAWRENCE	9,116	4,499	3,768	849	731 R	49.4%	41.3%	54.4%	45.6%
13,465	LEWIS	6,120	2,416	3,481	223	1,065 D	39.5%	56.9%	41.0%	59.0%
15,956	LINCOLN	6,157	2,563	3,419	175	856 D	41.6%	55.5%	42.8%	57.2%
24,778	LINN	11,246	5,155	5,386	705	231 D	45.8%	47.9%	48.9%	51.1%
18,857	LIVINGSTON	8,988	4,517	4,316	155	201 R	50.3%	48.0%	51.1%	48.9%
14,690	MCDONALD	4,916	2,374	2,301	241	73 R	48.3%	46.8%	50.8%	49.2%

MISSOURI

PRESIDENT 1924

1920 Census Population	County	Total Vote	Republican	Democratic	Other	Rep.-Dem. Plurality	Percentage Total Vote Rep.	Total Vote Dem.	Major Vote Rep.	Major Vote Dem.
27,518	MACON	10,950	4,909	5,538	503	629 D	44.8%	50.6%	47.0%	53.0%
10,721	MADISON	3,265	1,569	1,665	31	96 D	48.1%	51.0%	48.5%	51.5%
9,500	MARIES	3,042	1,004	1,913	125	909 D	33.0%	62.9%	34.4%	65.6%
30,226	MARION	12,297	5,408	5,739	1,150	331 D	44.0%	46.7%	48.5%	51.5%
11,281	MERCER	4,010	2,508	1,209	293	1,299 R	62.5%	30.1%	67.5%	32.5%
15,567	MILLER	5,361	3,011	1,962	388	1,049 R	56.2%	36.6%	60.5%	39.5%
12,860	MISSISSIPPI	4,310	1,797	2,360	153	563 D	41.7%	54.8%	43.2%	56.8%
13,532	MONITEAU	5,902	3,138	2,601	163	537 R	53.2%	44.1%	54.7%	45.3%
16,414	MONROE	6,910	1,141	5,597	172	4,456 D	16.5%	81.0%	16.9%	83.1%
15,233	MONTGOMERY	6,648	3,563	2,938	147	625 R	53.6%	44.2%	54.8%	45.2%
12,015	MORGAN	4,397	2,489	1,842	66	647 R	56.6%	41.9%	57.5%	42.5%
25,180	NEW MADRID	8,312	4,018	4,167	127	149 D	48.3%	50.1%	49.1%	50.9%
24,886	NEWTON	9,011	4,592	3,970	449	622 R	51.0%	44.1%	53.6%	46.4%
27,744	NODAWAY	12,521	6,242	5,803	476	439 R	49.9%	46.3%	51.8%	48.2%
12,889	OREGON	3,487	896	2,231	360	1,335 D	25.7%	64.0%	28.7%	71.3%
13,559	OSAGE	4,802	2,496	1,986	320	510 R	52.0%	41.4%	55.7%	44.3%
11,125	OZARK	2,546	1,758	688	100	1,070 R	69.0%	27.0%	71.9%	28.1%
26,634	PEMISCOT	10,573	4,811	5,616	146	805 D	45.5%	53.1%	46.1%	53.9%
14,434	PERRY	4,771	2,656	1,826	289	830 R	55.7%	38.3%	59.3%	40.7%
35,813	PETTIS	15,236	7,280	6,568	1,388	712 R	47.8%	43.1%	52.6%	47.4%
14,941	PHELPS	5,500	2,085	2,918	497	833 D	37.9%	53.1%	41.7%	58.3%
20,345	PIKE	7,999	3,715	4,040	244	325 D	46.4%	50.5%	47.9%	52.1%
13,990	PLATTE	5,744	1,999	3,674	71	1,675 D	34.8%	64.0%	35.2%	64.8%
20,351	POLK	7,291	4,097	3,033	161	1,064 R	56.2%	41.6%	57.5%	42.5%
10,490	PULASKI	3,867	1,578	2,127	162	549 D	40.8%	55.0%	42.6%	57.4%
13,115	PUTNAM	5,108	3,340	1,495	273	1,845 R	65.4%	29.3%	69.1%	30.9%
10,412	RALLS	4,072	1,365	2,617	90	1,252 D	33.5%	64.3%	34.3%	65.7%
27,633	RANDOLPH	11,569	2,991	7,372	1,206	4,381 D	25.9%	63.7%	28.9%	71.1%
20,508	RAY	8,041	2,753	4,989	299	2,236 D	34.2%	62.0%	35.6%	64.4%
10,106	REYNOLDS	2,724	873	1,822	29	949 D	32.0%	66.9%	32.4%	67.6%
12,061	RIPLEY	3,424	1,428	1,863	133	435 D	41.7%	54.4%	43.4%	56.6%
22,828	ST. CHARLES	7,897	4,668	2,364	865	2,304 R	59.1%	29.9%	66.4%	33.6%
15,341	ST. CLAIR	5,849	2,907	2,640	302	267 R	49.7%	45.1%	52.4%	47.6%
31,403	ST. FRANCOIS	11,956	6,117	5,542	297	575 R	51.2%	46.4%	52.5%	47.5%
772,897	ST. LOUIS CITY	264,597	139,433	95,888	29,276	43,545 R	52.7%	36.2%	59.3%	40.7%
100,737	ST. LOUIS COUNTY	47,834	26,669	16,075	5,090	10,594 R	55.8%	33.6%	62.4%	37.6%
9,809	STE. GENEVIEVE	2,703	1,330	1,257	116	73 R	49.2%	46.5%	51.4%	48.6%
28,826	SALINE	12,125	4,990	6,564	571	1,574 D	41.2%	54.1%	43.2%	56.8%
8,383	SCHUYLER	3,592	1,522	1,982	88	460 D	42.4%	55.2%	43.4%	56.6%
10,700	SCOTLAND	5,092	2,282	2,595	215	313 D	44.8%	51.0%	46.8%	53.2%
23,409	SCOTT	8,226	3,335	3,633	1,258	298 D	40.5%	44.2%	47.9%	52.1%
11,865	SHANNON	3,415	1,174	2,107	134	933 D	34.4%	61.7%	35.8%	64.2%
13,617	SHELBY	5,788	1,737	3,957	94	2,220 D	30.0%	68.4%	30.5%	69.5%
29,755	STODDARD	8,680	3,844	4,348	488	504 D	44.3%	50.1%	46.9%	53.1%
11,941	STONE	2,860	1,871	626	363	1,245 R	65.4%	21.9%	74.9%	25.1%
17,781	SULLIVAN	7,875	3,885	3,703	287	182 R	49.3%	47.0%	51.2%	48.8%
8,178	TANEY	2,781	1,710	981	90	729 R	61.5%	35.3%	63.5%	36.5%
20,548	TEXAS	6,400	2,787	3,421	192	634 D	43.5%	53.5%	44.9%	55.1%
26,069	VERNON	9,239	3,593	4,839	807	1,246 D	38.9%	52.4%	42.6%	57.4%
8,490	WARREN	3,508	2,667	644	197	2,023 R	76.0%	18.4%	80.5%	19.5%
13,803	WASHINGTON	4,405	2,397	1,955	53	442 R	54.4%	44.4%	55.1%	44.9%
13,012	WAYNE	4,439	1,958	2,283	198	325 D	44.1%	51.4%	46.2%	53.8%
16,609	WEBSTER	6,197	3,168	2,730	299	438 R	51.1%	44.1%	53.7%	46.3%
7,642	WORTH	3,355	1,666	1,650	39	16 R	49.7%	49.2%	50.2%	49.8%
17,733	WRIGHT	5,641	3,105	2,303	233	802 R	55.0%	40.8%	57.4%	42.6%
3,404,049	TOTAL	1,310,095	648,488	574,962	86,645	73,526 R	49.5%	43.9%	53.0%	47.0%

MISSOURI

PRESIDENT 1920

1920 Census Population	County	Total Vote	Republican	Democratic	Other	Rep.-Dem. Plurality	Percentage Total Vote Rep.	Total Vote Dem.	Major Vote Rep.	Major Vote Dem.
21,404	ADAIR	7,878	4,861	2,534	483	2,327 R	61.7%	32.2%	65.7%	34.3%
14,075	ANDREW	6,429	3,913	2,466	50	1,447 R	60.9%	38.4%	61.3%	38.7%
13,008	ATCHISON	5,514	3,236	2,227	51	1,009 R	58.7%	40.4%	59.2%	40.8%
20,589	AUDRAIN	9,409	3,827	5,514	68	1,687 D	40.7%	58.6%	41.0%	59.0%
23,473	BARRY	9,049	5,162	3,729	158	1,433 R	57.0%	41.2%	58.1%	41.9%
16,879	BARTON	6,814	3,480	3,040	294	440 R	51.1%	44.6%	53.4%	46.6%
23,933	BATES	9,708	5,039	4,433	236	606 R	51.9%	45.7%	53.2%	46.8%
12,989	BENTON	4,915	3,367	1,506	42	1,861 R	68.5%	30.6%	69.1%	30.9%
13,909	BOLLINGER	4,949	2,869	2,019	61	850 R	58.0%	40.8%	58.7%	41.3%
29,672	BOONE	12,890	4,077	8,748	65	4,671 D	31.6%	67.9%	31.8%	68.2%
93,684	BUCHANAN	33,714	17,191	16,188	335	1,003 R	51.0%	48.0%	51.5%	48.5%
24,106	BUTLER	7,442	4,601	2,662	179	1,939 R	61.8%	35.8%	63.3%	36.7%
13,849	CALDWELL	6,688	4,168	2,498	22	1,670 R	62.3%	37.4%	62.5%	37.5%
23,007	CALLAWAY	9,339	3,274	6,035	30	2,761 D	35.1%	64.6%	35.2%	64.8%
10,474	CAMDEN	3,349	2,276	1,034	39	1,242 R	68.0%	30.9%	68.8%	31.2%
29,839	CAPE GIRARDEAU	12,273	7,537	4,584	152	2,953 R	61.4%	37.4%	62.2%	37.8%
20,480	CARROLL	9,780	5,609	4,075	96	1,534 R	57.4%	41.7%	57.9%	42.1%
7,482	CARTER	2,047	1,057	930	60	127 R	51.6%	45.4%	53.2%	46.8%
21,536	CASS	9,185	4,055	5,030	100	975 D	44.1%	54.8%	44.6%	55.4%
13,933	CEDAR	5,495	3,488	1,936	71	1,552 R	63.5%	35.2%	64.3%	35.7%
21,769	CHARITON	9,084	4,331	4,675	78	344 D	47.7%	51.5%	48.1%	51.9%
15,252	CHRISTIAN	4,857	3,795	919	143	2,876 R	78.1%	18.9%	80.5%	19.5%
11,874	CLARK	5,761	3,310	2,383	68	927 R	57.5%	41.4%	58.1%	41.9%
20,455	CLAY	9,118	2,804	6,283	31	3,479 D	30.8%	68.9%	30.9%	69.1%
14,461	CLINTON	6,514	3,165	3,304	45	139 D	48.6%	50.7%	48.9%	51.1%
24,680	COLE	10,081	5,878	4,167	36	1,711 R	58.3%	41.3%	58.5%	41.5%
19,308	COOPER	8,856	5,151	3,657	48	1,494 R	58.2%	41.3%	58.5%	41.5%
12,355	CRAWFORD	4,358	2,634	1,658	66	976 R	60.4%	38.0%	61.4%	38.6%
14,173	DADE	5,507	3,520	1,892	95	1,628 R	63.9%	34.4%	65.0%	35.0%
12,033	DALLAS	3,811	2,665	1,100	46	1,565 R	69.9%	28.9%	70.8%	29.2%
16,641	DAVIESS	8,118	4,458	3,560	100	898 R	54.9%	43.9%	55.6%	44.4%
11,694	DE KALB	5,189	3,001	2,121	67	880 R	57.8%	40.9%	58.6%	41.4%
12,318	DENT	4,264	2,204	1,970	90	234 R	51.7%	46.2%	52.8%	47.2%
15,436	DOUGLAS	4,053	3,327	577	149	2,750 R	82.1%	14.2%	85.2%	14.8%
32,773	DUNKLIN	9,963	4,455	5,199	309	744 D	44.7%	52.2%	46.1%	53.9%
28,427	FRANKLIN	11,733	8,712	2,814	207	5,898 R	74.3%	24.0%	75.6%	24.4%
12,381	GASCONADE	4,978	4,481	454	43	4,027 R	90.0%	9.1%	90.8%	9.2%
15,634	GENTRY	6,929	3,442	3,374	113	68 R	49.7%	48.7%	50.5%	49.5%
68,698	GREENE	28,126	15,755	11,514	857	4,241 R	56.0%	40.9%	57.8%	42.2%
17,554	GRUNDY	7,973	5,123	2,721	129	2,402 R	64.3%	34.1%	65.3%	34.7%
19,719	HARRISON	7,740	5,151	2,502	87	2,649 R	66.6%	32.3%	67.3%	32.7%
25,116	HENRY	10,813	5,313	5,367	133	54 D	49.1%	49.6%	49.7%	50.3%
7,033	HICKORY	2,713	2,131	532	50	1,599 R	78.5%	19.6%	80.0%	20.0%
14,084	HOLT	6,556	4,153	2,329	74	1,824 R	63.3%	35.5%	64.1%	35.9%
13,997	HOWARD	6,888	2,125	4,735	28	2,610 D	30.9%	68.7%	31.0%	69.0%
21,102	HOWELL	6,869	4,344	2,323	202	2,021 R	63.2%	33.8%	65.2%	34.8%
9,458	IRON	3,071	1,463	1,554	54	91 D	47.6%	50.6%	48.5%	51.5%
367,846	JACKSON	158,214	79,875	76,791	1,548	3,084 R	50.5%	48.5%	51.0%	49.0%
75,941	JASPER	29,225	17,074	11,006	1,145	6,068 R	58.4%	37.7%	60.8%	39.2%
26,555	JEFFERSON	10,595	5,730	4,684	181	1,046 R	54.1%	44.2%	55.0%	45.0%
24,899	JOHNSON	11,252	5,700	5,444	108	256 R	50.7%	48.4%	51.1%	48.9%
10,783	KNOX	5,061	2,749	2,250	62	499 R	54.3%	44.5%	55.0%	45.0%
16,857	LACLEDE	5,754	3,469	2,183	102	1,286 R	60.3%	37.9%	61.4%	38.6%
30,006	LAFAYETTE	13,734	7,471	6,169	94	1,302 R	54.4%	44.9%	54.8%	45.2%
24,211	LAWRENCE	9,935	6,093	3,532	310	2,561 R	61.3%	35.6%	63.3%	36.7%
13,465	LEWIS	6,405	2,810	3,542	53	732 D	43.9%	55.3%	44.2%	55.8%
15,956	LINCOLN	6,909	3,209	3,660	40	451 D	46.4%	53.0%	46.7%	53.3%
24,778	LINN	10,878	5,557	5,184	137	373 R	51.1%	47.7%	51.7%	48.3%
18,857	LIVINGSTON	8,856	5,093	3,666	97	1,427 R	57.5%	41.4%	58.1%	41.9%
14,690	MCDONALD	5,291	2,921	2,242	128	679 R	55.2%	42.4%	56.6%	43.4%

MISSOURI

PRESIDENT 1920

1920 Census Population	County	Total Vote	Republican	Democratic	Other	Rep.-Dem. Plurality	Percentage: Total Vote Rep.	Total Vote Dem.	Major Vote Rep.	Major Vote Dem.
27,518	MACON	12,192	6,309	5,626	257	683 R	51.7%	46.1%	52.9%	47.1%
10,721	MADISON	3,876	2,023	1,830	23	193 R	52.2%	47.2%	52.5%	47.5%
9,500	MARIES	3,150	1,445	1,677	28	232 D	45.9%	53.2%	46.3%	53.7%
30,226	MARION	11,545	4,660	6,719	166	2,059 D	40.4%	58.2%	41.0%	59.0%
11,281	MERCER	4,274	3,170	1,044	60	2,126 R	74.2%	24.4%	75.2%	24.8%
15,567	MILLER	5,474	3,555	1,833	86	1,722 R	64.9%	33.5%	66.0%	34.0%
12,860	MISSISSIPPI	4,679	2,193	2,442	44	249 D	46.9%	52.2%	47.3%	52.7%
13,532	MONITEAU	5,994	3,535	2,405	54	1,130 R	59.0%	40.1%	59.5%	40.5%
16,414	MONROE	7,635	1,406	6,136	93	4,730 D	18.4%	80.4%	18.6%	81.4%
15,233	MONTGOMERY	7,088	3,910	3,103	75	807 R	55.2%	43.8%	55.8%	44.2%
12,015	MORGAN	4,780	2,911	1,834	35	1,077 R	60.9%	38.4%	61.3%	38.7%
25,180	NEW MADRID	7,498	3,745	3,637	116	108 R	49.9%	48.5%	50.7%	49.3%
24,886	NEWTON	9,912	5,541	4,078	293	1,463 R	55.9%	41.1%	57.6%	42.4%
27,744	NODAWAY	12,493	6,971	5,404	118	1,567 R	55.8%	43.3%	56.3%	43.7%
12,889	OREGON	3,333	1,319	1,961	53	642 D	39.6%	58.8%	40.2%	59.8%
13,559	OSAGE	4,856	3,699	1,118	39	2,581 R	76.2%	23.0%	76.8%	23.2%
11,125	OZARK	3,082	2,457	569	56	1,888 R	79.7%	18.5%	81.2%	18.8%
26,634	PEMISCOT	8,453	4,443	3,901	109	542 R	52.6%	46.1%	53.2%	46.8%
14,434	PERRY	5,181	3,652	1,504	25	2,148 R	70.5%	29.0%	70.8%	29.2%
35,813	PETTIS	15,355	8,595	6,561	199	2,034 R	56.0%	42.7%	56.7%	43.3%
14,941	PHELPS	5,152	2,692	2,422	38	270 R	52.3%	47.0%	52.6%	47.4%
20,345	PIKE	8,963	3,860	5,034	69	1,174 D	43.1%	56.2%	43.4%	56.6%
13,990	PLATTE	6,102	1,724	4,361	17	2,637 D	28.3%	71.5%	28.3%	71.7%
20,351	POLK	7,907	4,967	2,847	93	2,120 R	62.8%	36.0%	63.6%	36.4%
10,490	PULASKI	3,870	1,853	1,978	39	125 D	47.9%	51.1%	48.4%	51.6%
13,115	PUTNAM	5,321	3,880	1,315	126	2,565 R	72.9%	24.7%	74.7%	25.3%
10,412	RALLS	4,197	1,362	2,803	32	1,441 D	32.5%	66.8%	32.7%	67.3%
27,633	RANDOLPH	11,968	3,768	8,115	85	4,347 D	31.5%	67.8%	31.7%	68.3%
20,508	RAY	8,165	3,228	4,865	72	1,637 D	39.5%	59.6%	39.9%	60.1%
10,106	REYNOLDS	3,046	1,173	1,837	36	664 D	38.5%	60.3%	39.0%	61.0%
12,061	RIPLEY	3,676	1,752	1,735	189	17 R	47.7%	47.2%	50.2%	49.8%
22,828	ST. CHARLES	9,213	6,645	2,472	96	4,173 R	72.1%	26.8%	72.9%	27.1%
15,341	ST. CLAIR	5,706	3,249	2,296	161	953 R	56.9%	40.2%	58.6%	41.4%
31,403	ST. FRANCOIS	11,039	5,504	5,300	235	204 R	49.9%	48.0%	50.9%	49.1%
772,897	ST. LOUIS CITY	282,652	163,280	106,047	13,325	57,233 R	57.8%	37.5%	60.6%	39.4%
100,737	ST. LOUIS COUNTY	39,342	25,008	12,438	1,896	12,570 R	63.6%	31.6%	66.8%	33.2%
9,809	STE. GENEVIEVE	3,088	1,917	1,149	22	768 R	62.1%	37.2%	62.5%	37.5%
28,826	SALINE	12,812	5,613	7,114	85	1,501 D	43.8%	55.5%	44.1%	55.9%
8,383	SCHUYLER	3,637	1,806	1,793	38	13 R	49.7%	49.3%	50.2%	49.8%
10,700	SCOTLAND	4,724	2,509	2,124	91	385 R	53.1%	45.0%	54.2%	45.8%
23,409	SCOTT	8,579	4,204	4,157	218	47 R	49.0%	48.5%	50.3%	49.7%
11,865	SHANNON	3,371	1,639	1,661	71	22 D	48.6%	49.3%	49.7%	50.3%
13,617	SHELBY	6,134	2,128	3,935	71	1,807 D	34.7%	64.2%	35.1%	64.9%
29,755	STODDARD	9,441	4,641	4,428	372	213 R	49.2%	46.9%	51.2%	48.8%
11,941	STONE	3,500	2,749	672	79	2,077 R	78.5%	19.2%	80.4%	19.6%
17,781	SULLIVAN	8,121	4,576	3,475	70	1,101 R	56.3%	42.8%	56.8%	43.2%
8,178	TANEY	2,956	2,001	913	42	1,088 R	67.7%	30.9%	68.7%	31.3%
20,548	TEXAS	6,585	3,552	2,965	68	587 R	53.9%	45.0%	54.5%	45.5%
26,069	VERNON	10,246	4,645	5,419	182	774 D	45.3%	52.9%	46.2%	53.8%
8,490	WARREN	4,133	3,512	545	76	2,967 R	85.0%	13.2%	86.6%	13.4%
13,803	WASHINGTON	4,486	2,618	1,837	31	781 R	58.4%	40.9%	58.8%	41.2%
13,012	WAYNE	4,552	2,380	2,072	100	308 R	52.3%	45.5%	53.5%	46.5%
16,609	WEBSTER	6,509	4,000	2,428	81	1,572 R	61.5%	37.3%	62.2%	37.8%
7,642	WORTH	3,450	1,888	1,532	30	356 R	54.7%	44.4%	55.2%	44.8%
17,733	WRIGHT	5,748	3,661	2,008	79	1,653 R	63.7%	34.9%	64.6%	35.4%
3,404,049	TOTAL	1,332,140	727,252	574,699	30,189	152,553 R	54.6%	43.1%	55.9%	44.1%

MISSOURI

ELECTION NOTES

1956

1952 Other vote was 987 Hallinan (Progressive); 885 Hamblen (Prohibition); 535 MacArthur (302 Christian Nationalist and 233 America First); 227 Hoopes (Socialist); 169 Hass (Socialist Labor).

1948 Other vote was 3,998 Wallace (Progressive); 2,222 Thomas (Socialist); 54 scattered write-in. The statewide total in the other vote column includes the scattered write-in votes which were not reported by county.

1944 Other vote was 1,751 Thomas (Socialist); 1,195 Watson (Prohibition); 220 Teichert (Socialist Labor).

1940 Other vote was 2,226 Thomas (Socialist); 1,809 Babson (Prohibition); 209 Aiken (Socialist Labor).

1936 Other vote was 14,630 Lemke (Union); 3,454 Thomas (Socialist); 908 Colvin (Prohibition); 417 Browder (Communist); 292 Aiken (Socialist Labor).

1932 Other vote was 16,374 Thomas (Socialist); 2,429 Upshaw (Prohibition); 568 Foster (Communist); 404 Reynolds (Socialist Labor).

1928 Other vote was 3,739 Thomas (Socialist); 342 Reynolds (Socialist Labor).

1924 Other vote was 83,996 LaFollette (56,733 Socialist and 27,263 Liberal); 1,418 Faris (Prohibition); 1,066 Johns (Socialist Labor); 165 Wallace (Commonwealth Land).

1920 Other vote was 20,342 Debs (Socialist); 5,152 Watkins (Prohibition); 3,108 Christensen (Farmer-Labor); 1,587 Cox (Socialist Labor).

MONTANA

POPULAR VOTE FOR PRESIDENT 1920 TO 1956

Year	Total Vote	Republican Vote	Republican Candidate	Democratic Vote	Democratic Candidate	Other Vote	Plurality	Percentage Total Vote Rep.	Percentage Total Vote Dem.	Percentage Major Vote Rep.	Percentage Major Vote Dem.
1956	271,171	154,933	Eisenhower, Dwight D.	116,238	Stevenson, Adlai E.		38,695 R	57.1%	42.9%	57.1%	42.9%
1952	265,037	157,394	Eisenhower, Dwight D.	106,213	Stevenson, Adlai E.	1,430	51,181 R	59.4%	40.1%	59.7%	40.3%
1948	224,278	96,770	Dewey, Thomas E.	119,071	Truman, Harry S.	8,437	22,301 D	43.1%	53.1%	44.8%	55.2%
1944	207,355	93,163	Dewey, Thomas E.	112,556	Roosevelt, Franklin D.	1,636	19,393 D	44.9%	54.3%	45.3%	54.7%
1940	247,873	99,579	Willkie, Wendell	145,698	Roosevelt, Franklin D.	2,596	46,119 D	40.2%	58.8%	40.6%	59.4%
1936	230,502	63,598	Landon, Alfred M.	159,690	Roosevelt, Franklin D.	7,214	96,092 D	27.6%	69.3%	28.5%	71.5%
1932	216,479	78,078	Hoover, Herbert C.	127,286	Roosevelt, Franklin D.	11,115	49,208 D	36.1%	58.8%	38.0%	62.0%
1928	194,108	113,300	Hoover, Herbert C.	78,578	Smith, Alfred E.	2,230	34,722 R	58.4%	40.5%	59.0%	41.0%
1924 **	174,425	74,138	Coolidge, Calvin	33,805	Davis, John W.	66,482	8,014 R	42.5%	19.4%	68.7%	31.3%
1920	179,006	109,430	Harding, Warren G.	57,372	Cox, James M.	12,204	52,058 R	61.1%	32.1%	65.6%	34.4%

In 1924 other vote was 66,124 Progressive and 358 Communist.

ELECTORAL COLLEGE VOTE 1920 TO 1956

Year	Total	Republican	Democratic	Other
1956	4	4	—	—
1952	4	4	—	—
1948	4	—	4	—
1944	4	—	4	—
1940	4	—	4	—
1936	4	—	4	—
1932	4	—	4	—
1928	4	4	—	—
1924	4	4	—	—
1920	4	4	—	—

MONTANA

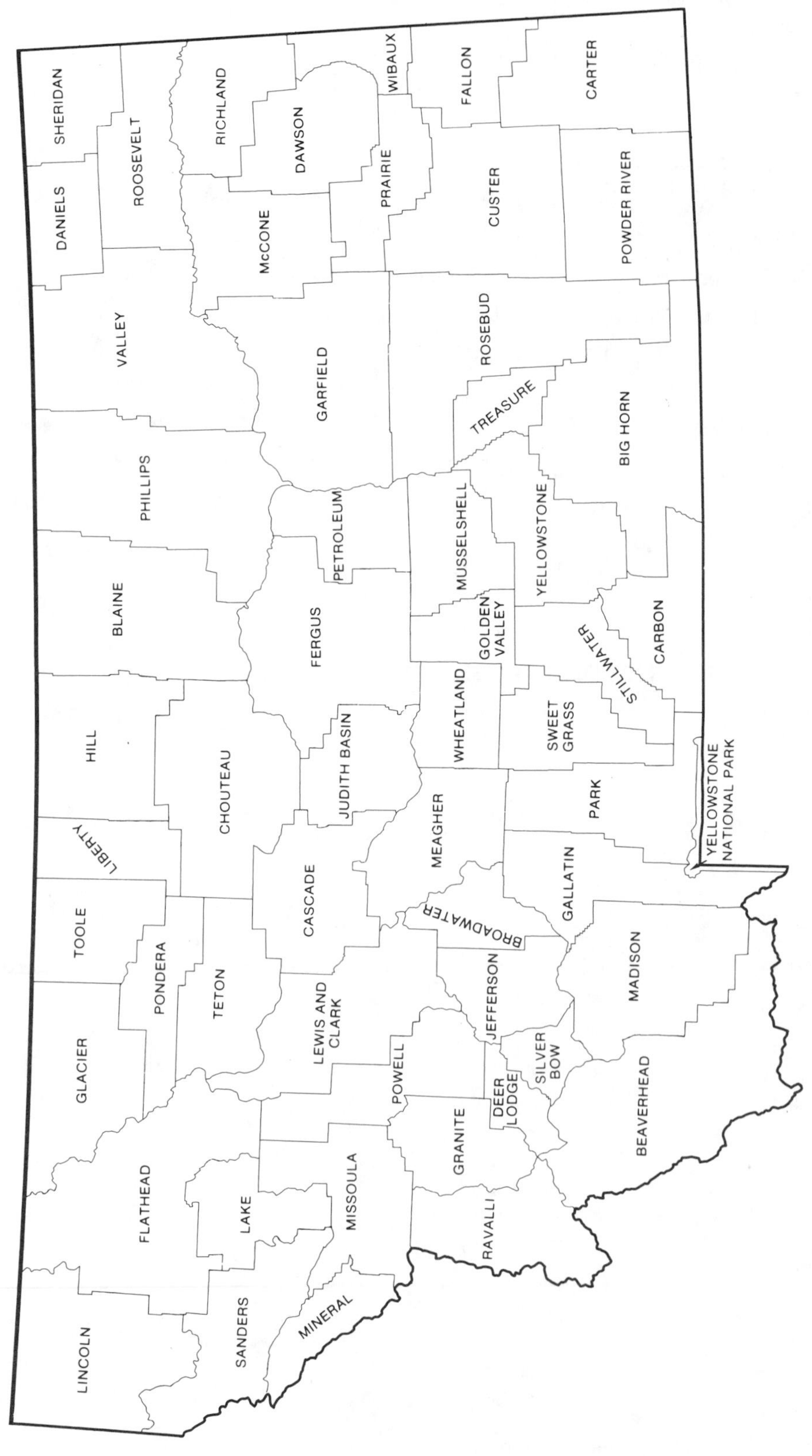
SHERIDAN
DANIELS
ROOSEVELT
RICHLAND
DAWSON
McCONE
WIBAUX
PRAIRIE
FALLON
CARTER
CUSTER
POWDER RIVER
VALLEY
GARFIELD
ROSEBUD
TREASURE
BIG HORN
PHILLIPS
PETROLEUM
MUSSELSHELL
YELLOWSTONE
BLAINE
FERGUS
GOLDEN VALLEY
STILLWATER
CARBON
HILL
CHOUTEAU
JUDITH BASIN
WHEATLAND
SWEET GRASS
PARK
YELLOWSTONE NATIONAL PARK
LIBERTY
CASCADE
MEAGHER
GALLATIN
BROADWATER
TOOLE
PONDERA
TETON
LEWIS AND CLARK
JEFFERSON
MADISON
GLACIER
POWELL
SILVER BOW
DEER LODGE
BEAVERHEAD
GRANITE
FLATHEAD
LAKE
MISSOULA
RAVALLI
MINERAL
SANDERS
LINCOLN

MONTANA

PRESIDENT 1956

1950 Census Population	County	Total Vote	Republican	Democratic	Other	Rep.-Dem. Plurality	Percentage Total Vote Rep.	Total Vote Dem.	Major Vote Rep.	Major Vote Dem.
6,671	BEAVERHEAD	2,984	1,955	1,029		926 R	65.5%	34.5%	65.5%	34.5%
9,824	BIG HORN	3,081	1,739	1,342		397 R	56.4%	43.6%	56.4%	43.6%
8,516	BLAINE	2,898	1,460	1,438		22 R	50.4%	49.6%	50.4%	49.6%
2,922	BROADWATER	1,318	869	449		420 R	65.9%	34.1%	65.9%	34.1%
10,241	CARBON	4,165	2,345	1,820		525 R	56.3%	43.7%	56.3%	43.7%
2,798	CARTER	1,134	698	436		262 R	61.6%	38.4%	61.6%	38.4%
53,027	CASCADE	23,553	12,455	11,098		1,357 R	52.9%	47.1%	52.9%	47.1%
6,974	CHOUTEAU	3,515	1,721	1,794		73 D	49.0%	51.0%	49.0%	51.0%
12,661	CUSTER	5,557	3,240	2,317		923 R	58.3%	41.7%	58.3%	41.7%
3,946	DANIELS	1,928	982	946		36 R	50.9%	49.1%	50.9%	49.1%
9,092	DAWSON	4,392	2,463	1,929		534 R	56.1%	43.9%	56.1%	43.9%
16,553	DEER LODGE	7,343	3,551	3,792		241 D	48.4%	51.6%	48.4%	51.6%
3,660	FALLON	1,579	967	612		355 R	61.2%	38.8%	61.2%	38.8%
14,015	FERGUS	6,528	3,771	2,757		1,014 R	57.8%	42.2%	57.8%	42.2%
31,495	FLATHEAD	14,091	8,088	6,003		2,085 R	57.4%	42.6%	57.4%	42.6%
21,902	GALLATIN	9,940	6,680	3,260		3,420 R	67.2%	32.8%	67.2%	32.8%
2,172	GARFIELD	982	558	424		134 R	56.8%	43.2%	56.8%	43.2%
9,645	GLACIER	3,876	2,054	1,822		232 R	53.0%	47.0%	53.0%	47.0%
1,337	GOLDEN VALLEY	639	383	256		127 R	59.9%	40.1%	59.9%	40.1%
2,773	GRANITE	1,429	896	533		363 R	62.7%	37.3%	62.7%	37.3%
14,285	HILL	6,414	3,415	2,999		416 R	53.2%	46.8%	53.2%	46.8%
4,014	JEFFERSON	1,709	1,049	660		389 R	61.4%	38.6%	61.4%	38.6%
3,200	JUDITH BASIN	1,637	789	848		59 D	48.2%	51.8%	48.2%	51.8%
13,835	LAKE	5,616	3,363	2,253		1,110 R	59.9%	40.1%	59.9%	40.1%
24,540	LEWIS AND CLARK	12,356	7,959	4,397		3,562 R	64.4%	35.6%	64.4%	35.6%
2,180	LIBERTY	1,089	601	488		113 R	55.2%	44.8%	55.2%	44.8%
8,693	LINCOLN	4,607	2,321	2,286		35 R	50.4%	49.6%	50.4%	49.6%
3,258	MCCONE	1,641	752	889		137 D	45.8%	54.2%	45.8%	54.2%
5,998	MADISON	2,587	1,662	925		737 R	64.2%	35.8%	64.2%	35.8%
2,079	MEAGHER	1,067	712	355		357 R	66.7%	33.3%	66.7%	33.3%
2,081	MINERAL	1,158	606	552		54 R	52.3%	47.7%	52.3%	47.7%
35,493	MISSOULA	17,387	10,627	6,760		3,867 R	61.1%	38.9%	61.1%	38.9%
5,408	MUSSELSHELL	2,280	1,165	1,115		50 R	51.1%	48.9%	51.1%	48.9%
11,999	PARK	5,884	3,733	2,151		1,582 R	63.4%	36.6%	63.4%	36.6%
1,026	PETROLEUM	463	258	205		53 R	55.7%	44.3%	55.7%	44.3%
6,334	PHILLIPS	3,032	1,605	1,427		178 R	52.9%	47.1%	52.9%	47.1%
6,392	PONDERA	3,089	1,651	1,438		213 R	53.4%	46.6%	53.4%	46.6%
2,693	POWDER RIVER	1,156	700	456		244 R	60.6%	39.4%	60.6%	39.4%
6,301	POWELL	2,897	1,683	1,214		469 R	58.1%	41.9%	58.1%	41.9%
2,377	PRAIRIE	1,040	637	403		234 R	61.3%	38.8%	61.3%	38.8%
13,101	RAVALLI	5,598	3,437	2,161		1,276 R	61.4%	38.6%	61.4%	38.6%
10,366	RICHLAND	4,250	2,366	1,884		482 R	55.7%	44.3%	55.7%	44.3%
9,580	ROOSEVELT	4,190	1,985	2,205		220 D	47.4%	52.6%	47.4%	52.6%
6,570	ROSEBUD	2,406	1,516	890		626 R	63.0%	37.0%	63.0%	37.0%
6,983	SANDERS	3,168	1,649	1,519		130 R	52.1%	47.9%	52.1%	47.9%
6,674	SHERIDAN	3,010	1,153	1,857		704 D	38.3%	61.7%	38.3%	61.7%
48,422	SILVER BOW	23,094	11,619	11,475		144 R	50.3%	49.7%	50.3%	49.7%
5,416	STILLWATER	2,553	1,540	1,013		527 R	60.3%	39.7%	60.3%	39.7%
3,621	SWEET GRASS	1,584	1,129	455		674 R	71.3%	28.7%	71.3%	28.7%
7,232	TETON	3,350	1,728	1,622		106 R	51.6%	48.4%	51.6%	48.4%
6,867	TOOLE	3,387	1,927	1,460		467 R	56.9%	43.1%	56.9%	43.1%
1,402	TREASURE	589	337	252		85 R	57.2%	42.8%	57.2%	42.8%
11,353	VALLEY	4,868	2,357	2,511		154 D	48.4%	51.6%	48.4%	51.6%
3,187	WHEATLAND	1,510	932	578		354 R	61.7%	38.3%	61.7%	38.3%
1,907	WIBAUX	821	431	390		41 R	52.5%	47.5%	52.5%	47.5%
55,875	YELLOWSTONE	28,752	18,664	10,088		8,576 R	64.9%	35.1%	64.9%	35.1%
591,024	TOTAL	271,171	154,933	116,238		38,695 R	57.1%	42.9%	57.1%	42.9%

MONTANA

PRESIDENT 1952

1950 Census Population	County	Total Vote	Republican	Democratic	Other	Rep.-Dem. Plurality	Percentage Total Vote Rep.	Total Vote Dem.	Major Vote Rep.	Major Vote Dem.
6,671	BEAVERHEAD	3,128	2,196	920	12	1,276 R	70.2%	29.4%	70.5%	29.5%
9,824	BIG HORN	3,285	2,165	1,114	6	1,051 R	65.9%	33.9%	66.0%	34.0%
8,516	BLAINE	3,106	1,890	1,207	9	683 R	60.8%	38.9%	61.0%	39.0%
2,922	BROADWATER	1,397	962	435		527 R	68.9%	31.1%	68.9%	31.1%
10,241	CARBON	4,470	2,734	1,713	23	1,021 R	61.2%	38.3%	61.5%	38.5%
2,798	CARTER	1,277	921	351	5	570 R	72.1%	27.5%	72.4%	27.6%
53,027	CASCADE	23,373	12,176	11,051	146	1,125 R	52.1%	47.3%	52.4%	47.6%
6,974	CHOUTEAU	3,535	2,098	1,423	14	675 R	59.3%	40.3%	59.6%	40.4%
12,661	CUSTER	5,535	3,461	2,050	24	1,411 R	62.5%	37.0%	62.8%	37.2%
3,946	DANIELS	1,748	1,092	649	7	443 R	62.5%	37.1%	62.7%	37.3%
9,092	DAWSON	3,658	2,396	1,247	15	1,149 R	65.5%	34.1%	65.8%	34.2%
16,553	DEER LODGE	7,217	3,001	4,162	54	1,161 D	41.6%	57.7%	41.9%	58.1%
3,660	FALLON	1,494	1,046	440	8	606 R	70.0%	29.5%	70.4%	29.6%
14,015	FERGUS	6,691	4,402	2,271	18	2,131 R	65.8%	33.9%	66.0%	34.0%
31,495	FLATHEAD	12,476	7,372	4,994	110	2,378 R	59.1%	40.0%	59.6%	40.4%
21,902	GALLATIN	9,729	6,998	2,697	34	4,301 R	71.9%	27.7%	72.2%	27.8%
2,172	GARFIELD	994	723	269	2	454 R	72.7%	27.1%	72.9%	27.1%
9,645	GLACIER	3,769	2,061	1,698	10	363 R	54.7%	45.1%	54.8%	45.2%
1,337	GOLDEN VALLEY	669	471	198		273 R	70.4%	29.6%	70.4%	29.6%
2,773	GRANITE	1,401	923	473	5	450 R	65.9%	33.8%	66.1%	33.9%
14,285	HILL	6,266	3,474	2,748	44	726 R	55.4%	43.9%	55.8%	44.2%
4,014	JEFFERSON	1,784	1,084	687	13	397 R	60.8%	38.5%	61.2%	38.8%
3,200	JUDITH BASIN	1,853	1,074	746	33	328 R	58.0%	40.3%	59.0%	41.0%
13,835	LAKE	5,609	3,651	1,893	65	1,758 R	65.1%	33.7%	65.9%	34.1%
24,540	LEWIS AND CLARK	12,246	7,663	4,563	20	3,100 R	62.6%	37.3%	62.7%	37.3%
2,180	LIBERTY	1,088	671	411	6	260 R	61.7%	37.8%	62.0%	38.0%
8,693	LINCOLN	3,821	1,881	1,907	33	26 D	49.2%	49.9%	49.7%	50.3%
3,258	MCCONE	1,598	900	674	24	226 R	56.3%	42.2%	57.2%	42.8%
5,998	MADISON	2,752	1,993	751	8	1,242 R	72.4%	27.3%	72.6%	27.4%
2,079	MEAGHER	1,120	792	326	2	466 R	70.7%	29.1%	70.8%	29.2%
2,081	MINERAL	1,054	553	491	10	62 R	52.5%	46.6%	53.0%	47.0%
35,493	MISSOULA	17,041	10,053	6,901	87	3,152 R	59.0%	40.5%	59.3%	40.7%
5,408	MUSSELSHELL	2,502	1,253	1,240	9	13 R	50.1%	49.6%	50.3%	49.7%
11,999	PARK	6,150	4,152	1,969	29	2,183 R	67.5%	32.0%	67.8%	32.2%
1,026	PETROLEUM	474	319	155		164 R	67.3%	32.7%	67.3%	32.7%
6,334	PHILLIPS	3,017	1,771	1,224	22	547 R	58.7%	40.6%	59.1%	40.9%
6,392	PONDERA	2,992	1,719	1,246	27	473 R	57.5%	41.6%	58.0%	42.0%
2,693	POWDER RIVER	1,222	888	327	7	561 R	72.7%	26.8%	73.1%	26.9%
6,301	POWELL	3,082	1,783	1,281	18	502 R	57.9%	41.6%	58.2%	41.8%
2,377	PRAIRIE	1,114	771	338	5	433 R	69.2%	30.3%	69.5%	30.5%
13,101	RAVALLI	5,329	3,537	1,750	42	1,787 R	66.4%	32.8%	66.9%	33.1%
10,366	RICHLAND	3,725	2,506	1,196	23	1,310 R	67.3%	32.1%	67.7%	32.3%
9,580	ROOSEVELT	3,483	1,998	1,466	19	532 R	57.4%	42.1%	57.7%	42.3%
6,570	ROSEBUD	2,553	1,734	805	14	929 R	67.9%	31.5%	68.3%	31.7%
6,983	SANDERS	3,078	1,724	1,311	43	413 R	56.0%	42.6%	56.8%	43.2%
6,674	SHERIDAN	2,711	1,339	1,347	25	8 D	49.4%	49.7%	49.9%	50.1%
48,422	SILVER BOW	23,458	10,196	13,114	148	2,918 D	43.5%	55.9%	43.7%	56.3%
5,416	STILLWATER	2,520	1,689	816	15	873 R	67.0%	32.4%	67.4%	32.6%
3,621	SWEET GRASS	1,704	1,315	372	17	943 R	77.2%	21.8%	77.9%	22.1%
7,232	TETON	3,378	1,978	1,389	11	589 R	58.6%	41.1%	58.7%	41.3%
6,867	TOOLE	3,294	1,853	1,426	15	427 R	56.3%	43.3%	56.5%	43.5%
1,402	TREASURE	597	392	205		187 R	65.7%	34.3%	65.7%	34.3%
11,353	VALLEY	4,621	2,462	2,130	29	332 R	53.3%	46.1%	53.6%	46.4%
3,187	WHEATLAND	1,607	1,026	572	9	454 R	63.8%	35.6%	64.2%	35.8%
1,907	WIBAUX	885	556	324	5	232 R	62.8%	36.6%	63.2%	36.8%
55,875	YELLOWSTONE	26,357	17,556	8,750	51	8,806 R	66.6%	33.2%	66.7%	33.3%
591,024	TOTAL	265,037	157,394	106,213	1,430	51,181 R	59.4%	40.1%	59.7%	40.3%

MONTANA

PRESIDENT 1948

1940 Census Population	County	Total Vote	Republican	Democratic	Other	Rep.-Dem. Plurality	Percentage Total Vote Rep.	Percentage Total Vote Dem.	Percentage Major Vote Rep.	Percentage Major Vote Dem.
6,943	BEAVERHEAD	3,005	1,583	1,356	66	227 R	52.7%	45.1%	53.9%	46.1%
10,419	BIG HORN	2,702	1,334	1,328	40	6 R	49.4%	49.1%	50.1%	49.9%
9,566	BLAINE	2,748	997	1,669	82	672 D	36.3%	60.7%	37.4%	62.6%
3,451	BROADWATER	1,266	704	536	26	168 R	55.6%	42.3%	56.8%	43.2%
11,865	CARBON	4,169	1,901	1,997	271	96 D	45.6%	47.9%	48.8%	51.2%
3,280	CARTER	1,084	501	568	15	67 D	46.2%	52.4%	46.9%	53.1%
41,999	CASCADE	19,817	6,830	12,082	905	5,252 D	34.5%	61.0%	36.1%	63.9%
7,316	CHOUTEAU	3,138	1,181	1,832	125	651 D	37.6%	58.4%	39.2%	60.8%
10,422	CUSTER	4,263	1,845	2,359	59	514 D	43.3%	55.3%	43.9%	56.1%
4,563	DANIELS	1,523	624	826	73	202 D	41.0%	54.2%	43.0%	57.0%
8,618	DAWSON	3,017	1,555	1,397	65	158 R	51.5%	46.3%	52.7%	47.3%
13,627	DEER LODGE	6,212	2,036	3,862	314	1,826 D	32.8%	62.2%	34.5%	65.5%
3,719	FALLON	1,329	678	623	28	55 R	51.0%	46.9%	52.1%	47.9%
14,040	FERGUS	5,652	2,411	3,059	182	648 D	42.7%	54.1%	44.1%	55.9%
24,271	FLATHEAD	9,193	4,240	4,546	407	306 D	46.1%	49.5%	48.3%	51.7%
18,269	GALLATIN	7,950	4,220	3,548	182	672 R	53.1%	44.6%	54.3%	45.7%
2,641	GARFIELD	973	501	451	21	50 R	51.5%	46.4%	52.6%	47.4%
9,034	GLACIER	3,508	1,238	2,238	32	1,000 D	35.3%	63.8%	35.6%	64.4%
1,607	GOLDEN VALLEY	663	352	295	16	57 R	53.1%	44.5%	54.4%	45.6%
3,401	GRANITE	1,268	659	567	42	92 R	52.0%	44.7%	53.8%	46.2%
13,304	HILL	5,181	1,645	3,321	215	1,676 D	31.8%	64.1%	33.1%	66.9%
4,664	JEFFERSON	1,644	750	836	58	86 D	45.6%	50.9%	47.3%	52.7%
3,655	JUDITH BASIN	1,662	609	934	119	325 D	36.6%	56.2%	39.5%	60.5%
13,490	LAKE	4,650	2,295	2,177	178	118 R	49.4%	46.8%	51.3%	48.7%
22,131	LEWIS AND CLARK	10,176	5,174	4,745	257	429 R	50.8%	46.6%	52.2%	47.8%
2,209	LIBERTY	926	354	542	30	188 D	38.2%	58.5%	39.5%	60.5%
7,882	LINCOLN	2,893	1,079	1,689	125	610 D	37.3%	58.4%	39.0%	61.0%
3,798	MCCONE	1,371	518	702	151	184 D	37.8%	51.2%	42.5%	57.5%
7,294	MADISON	2,357	1,300	1,006	51	294 R	55.2%	42.7%	56.4%	43.6%
2,237	MEAGHER	1,035	518	497	20	21 R	50.0%	48.0%	51.0%	49.0%
2,135	MINERAL	860	338	475	47	137 D	39.3%	55.2%	41.6%	58.4%
29,038	MISSOULA	13,873	6,426	7,005	442	579 D	46.3%	50.5%	47.8%	52.2%
5,717	MUSSELSHELL	2,496	1,010	1,188	298	178 D	40.5%	47.6%	46.0%	54.0%
11,566	PARK	4,845	2,461	2,222	162	239 R	50.8%	45.9%	52.6%	47.4%
1,083	PETROLEUM	461	214	235	12	21 D	46.4%	51.0%	47.7%	52.3%
7,892	PHILLIPS	2,569	964	1,506	99	542 D	37.5%	58.6%	39.0%	61.0%
6,716	PONDERA	2,550	902	1,555	93	653 D	35.4%	61.0%	36.7%	63.3%
3,159	POWDER RIVER	1,303	784	480	39	304 R	60.2%	36.8%	62.0%	38.0%
6,152	POWELL	2,674	1,163	1,427	84	264 D	43.5%	53.4%	44.9%	55.1%
2,410	PRAIRIE	1,042	499	527	16	28 D	47.9%	50.6%	48.6%	51.4%
12,978	RAVALLI	4,723	2,354	2,159	210	195 R	49.8%	45.7%	52.2%	47.8%
10,209	RICHLAND	3,090	1,332	1,673	85	341 D	43.1%	54.1%	44.3%	55.7%
9,806	ROOSEVELT	3,128	1,142	1,820	166	678 D	36.5%	58.2%	38.6%	61.4%
6,477	ROSEBUD	2,181	1,106	1,031	44	75 R	50.7%	47.3%	51.8%	48.2%
6,926	SANDERS	2,767	1,191	1,425	151	234 D	43.0%	51.5%	45.5%	54.5%
7,814	SHERIDAN	2,453	699	1,515	239	816 D	28.5%	61.8%	31.6%	68.4%
53,207	SILVER BOW	21,335	7,305	12,715	1,315	5,410 D	34.2%	59.6%	36.5%	63.5%
5,694	STILLWATER	2,087	1,137	890	60	247 R	54.5%	42.6%	56.1%	43.9%
3,719	SWEET GRASS	1,366	843	499	24	344 R	61.7%	36.5%	62.8%	37.2%
6,922	TETON	2,720	1,005	1,632	83	627 D	36.9%	60.0%	38.1%	61.9%
6,769	TOOLE	2,888	1,092	1,756	40	664 D	37.8%	60.8%	38.3%	61.7%
1,499	TREASURE	560	253	291	16	38 D	45.2%	52.0%	46.5%	53.5%
15,181	VALLEY	4,110	1,375	2,535	200	1,160 D	33.5%	61.7%	35.2%	64.8%
3,286	WHEATLAND	1,533	780	733	20	47 R	50.9%	47.8%	51.6%	48.4%
2,161	WIBAUX	905	421	471	13	50 D	46.5%	52.0%	47.2%	52.8%
41,182	YELLOWSTONE	20,384	10,342	9,718	324	624 R	50.7%	47.7%	51.6%	48.4%
559,456	TOTAL	224,278	96,770	119,071	8,437	22,301 D	43.1%	53.1%	44.8%	55.2%

MONTANA

PRESIDENT 1944

1940 Census Population	County	Total Vote	Republican	Democratic	Other	Rep.-Dem. Plurality	Percentage Total Vote Rep.	Percentage Total Vote Dem.	Percentage Major Vote Rep.	Percentage Major Vote Dem.
6,943	BEAVERHEAD	2,832	1,556	1,263	13	293 R	54.9%	44.6%	55.2%	44.8%
10,419	BIG HORN	2,695	1,394	1,289	12	105 R	51.7%	47.8%	52.0%	48.0%
9,566	BLAINE	2,479	990	1,469	20	479 D	39.9%	59.3%	40.3%	59.7%
3,451	BROADWATER	1,323	760	558	5	202 R	57.4%	42.2%	57.7%	42.3%
11,865	CARBON	4,230	2,126	2,073	31	53 R	50.3%	49.0%	50.6%	49.4%
3,280	CARTER	1,118	507	610	1	103 D	45.3%	54.6%	45.4%	54.6%
41,999	CASCADE	17,437	6,372	10,924	141	4,552 D	36.5%	62.6%	36.8%	63.2%
7,316	CHOUTEAU	3,153	1,220	1,906	27	686 D	38.7%	60.5%	39.0%	61.0%
10,422	CUSTER	3,897	1,830	2,038	29	208 D	47.0%	52.3%	47.3%	52.7%
4,563	DANIELS	1,516	680	824	12	144 D	44.9%	54.4%	45.2%	54.8%
8,618	DAWSON	2,927	1,549	1,362	16	187 R	52.9%	46.5%	53.2%	46.8%
13,627	DEER LODGE	6,556	2,176	4,347	33	2,171 D	33.2%	66.3%	33.4%	66.6%
3,719	FALLON	1,371	870	494	7	376 R	63.5%	36.0%	63.8%	36.2%
14,040	FERGUS	5,422	2,229	3,164	29	935 D	41.1%	58.4%	41.3%	58.7%
24,271	FLATHEAD	7,786	4,066	3,608	112	458 R	52.2%	46.3%	53.0%	47.0%
18,269	GALLATIN	6,632	3,120	3,479	33	359 D	47.0%	52.5%	47.3%	52.7%
2,641	GARFIELD	1,033	553	478	2	75 R	53.5%	46.3%	53.6%	46.4%
9,034	GLACIER	3,379	1,228	2,142	9	914 D	36.3%	63.4%	36.4%	63.6%
1,607	GOLDEN VALLEY	662	395	266	1	129 R	59.7%	40.2%	59.8%	40.2%
3,401	GRANITE	1,288	702	574	12	128 R	54.5%	44.6%	55.0%	45.0%
13,304	HILL	4,669	1,646	2,986	37	1,340 D	35.3%	64.0%	35.5%	64.5%
4,664	JEFFERSON	1,603	797	803	3	6 D	49.7%	50.1%	49.8%	50.2%
3,655	JUDITH BASIN	1,747	691	1,049	7	358 D	39.6%	60.0%	39.7%	60.3%
13,490	LAKE	4,059	2,265	1,750	44	515 R	55.8%	43.1%	56.4%	43.6%
22,131	LEWIS AND CLARK	9,258	4,482	4,737	39	255 D	48.4%	51.2%	48.6%	51.4%
2,209	LIBERTY	842	393	440	9	47 D	46.7%	52.3%	47.2%	52.8%
7,882	LINCOLN	2,589	1,109	1,445	35	336 D	42.8%	55.8%	43.4%	56.6%
3,798	MCCONE	1,320	526	763	31	237 D	39.8%	57.8%	40.8%	59.2%
7,294	MADISON	2,313	1,278	1,022	13	256 R	55.3%	44.2%	55.6%	44.4%
2,237	MEAGHER	993	509	482	2	27 R	51.3%	48.5%	51.4%	48.6%
2,135	MINERAL	792	380	401	11	21 D	48.0%	50.6%	48.7%	51.3%
29,038	MISSOULA	11,028	5,371	5,558	99	187 D	48.7%	50.4%	49.1%	50.9%
5,717	MUSSELSHELL	2,375	1,004	1,342	29	338 D	42.3%	56.5%	42.8%	57.2%
11,566	PARK	4,677	2,396	2,245	36	151 R	51.2%	48.0%	51.6%	48.4%
1,083	PETROLEUM	481	253	225	3	28 R	52.6%	46.8%	52.9%	47.1%
7,892	PHILLIPS	2,543	1,089	1,435	19	346 D	42.8%	56.4%	43.1%	56.9%
6,716	PONDERA	2,361	890	1,448	23	558 D	37.7%	61.3%	38.1%	61.9%
3,159	POWDER RIVER	1,137	650	476	11	174 R	57.2%	41.9%	57.7%	42.3%
6,152	POWELL	2,645	1,100	1,527	18	427 D	41.6%	57.7%	41.9%	58.1%
2,410	PRAIRIE	1,074	598	468	8	130 R	55.7%	43.6%	56.1%	43.9%
12,978	RAVALLI	4,311	2,342	1,926	43	416 R	54.3%	44.7%	54.9%	45.1%
10,209	RICHLAND	3,161	1,347	1,777	37	430 D	42.6%	56.2%	43.1%	56.9%
9,806	ROOSEVELT	3,168	1,281	1,848	39	567 D	40.4%	58.3%	40.9%	59.1%
6,477	ROSEBUD	2,301	1,154	1,114	33	40 R	50.2%	48.4%	50.9%	49.1%
6,926	SANDERS	2,278	1,070	1,184	24	114 D	47.0%	52.0%	47.5%	52.5%
7,814	SHERIDAN	2,548	791	1,713	44	922 D	31.0%	67.2%	31.6%	68.4%
53,207	SILVER BOW	21,040	7,610	13,228	202	5,618 D	36.2%	62.9%	36.5%	63.5%
5,694	STILLWATER	2,142	1,201	934	7	267 R	56.1%	43.6%	56.3%	43.7%
3,719	SWEET GRASS	1,440	897	533	10	364 R	62.3%	37.0%	62.7%	37.3%
6,922	TETON	2,601	1,074	1,508	19	434 D	41.3%	58.0%	41.6%	58.4%
6,769	TOOLE	2,668	1,113	1,545	10	432 D	41.7%	57.9%	41.9%	58.1%
1,499	TREASURE	573	287	282	4	5 R	50.1%	49.2%	50.4%	49.6%
15,181	VALLEY	3,582	1,341	2,196	45	855 D	37.4%	61.3%	37.9%	62.1%
3,286	WHEATLAND	1,516	767	733	16	34 R	50.6%	48.4%	51.1%	48.9%
2,161	WIBAUX	859	432	425	2	7 R	50.3%	49.5%	50.4%	49.6%
41,182	YELLOWSTONE	16,925	8,706	8,140	79	566 R	51.4%	48.1%	51.7%	48.3%
559,456	TOTAL	207,355	93,163	112,556	1,636	19,393 D	44.9%	54.3%	45.3%	54.7%

MONTANA

PRESIDENT 1940

1940 Census Population	County	Total Vote	Republican	Democratic	Other	Rep.-Dem. Plurality	Percentage Total Vote Rep.	Percentage Total Vote Dem.	Percentage Major Vote Rep.	Percentage Major Vote Dem.
6,943	BEAVERHEAD	3,371	1,725	1,632	14	93 R	51.2%	48.4%	51.4%	48.6%
10,419	BIG HORN	3,560	1,616	1,926	18	310 D	45.4%	54.1%	45.6%	54.4%
9,566	BLAINE	3,327	1,165	2,129	33	964 D	35.0%	64.0%	35.4%	64.6%
3,451	BROADWATER	1,613	755	854	4	99 D	46.8%	52.9%	46.9%	53.1%
11,865	CARBON	5,161	2,421	2,678	62	257 D	46.9%	51.9%	47.5%	52.5%
3,280	CARTER	1,292	556	734	2	178 D	43.0%	56.8%	43.1%	56.9%
41,999	CASCADE	20,324	6,443	13,637	244	7,194 D	31.7%	67.1%	32.1%	67.9%
7,316	CHOUTEAU	3,475	1,235	2,213	27	978 D	35.5%	63.7%	35.8%	64.2%
10,422	CUSTER	4,834	2,017	2,782	35	765 D	41.7%	57.6%	42.0%	58.0%
4,563	DANIELS	1,921	807	1,086	28	279 D	42.0%	56.5%	42.6%	57.4%
8,618	DAWSON	3,392	1,612	1,765	15	153 D	47.5%	52.0%	47.7%	52.3%
13,627	DEER LODGE	7,345	2,397	4,916	32	2,519 D	32.6%	66.9%	32.8%	67.2%
3,719	FALLON	1,624	925	686	13	239 R	57.0%	42.2%	57.4%	42.6%
14,040	FERGUS	6,619	2,706	3,873	40	1,167 D	40.9%	58.5%	41.1%	58.9%
24,271	FLATHEAD	9,771	4,403	5,217	151	814 D	45.1%	53.4%	45.8%	54.2%
18,269	GALLATIN	8,198	3,430	4,718	50	1,288 D	41.8%	57.6%	42.1%	57.9%
2,641	GARFIELD	1,271	625	644	2	19 D	49.2%	50.7%	49.3%	50.7%
9,034	GLACIER	3,760	1,352	2,399	9	1,047 D	36.0%	63.8%	36.0%	64.0%
1,607	GOLDEN VALLEY	759	402	351	6	51 R	53.0%	46.2%	53.4%	46.6%
3,401	GRANITE	1,710	784	917	9	133 D	45.8%	53.6%	46.1%	53.9%
13,304	HILL	5,617	1,842	3,700	75	1,858 D	32.8%	65.9%	33.2%	66.8%
4,664	JEFFERSON	2,097	830	1,259	8	429 D	39.6%	60.0%	39.7%	60.3%
3,655	JUDITH BASIN	1,913	670	1,215	28	545 D	35.0%	63.5%	35.5%	64.5%
13,490	LAKE	5,181	2,718	2,379	84	339 R	52.5%	45.9%	53.3%	46.7%
22,131	LEWIS AND CLARK	10,683	4,762	5,814	107	1,052 D	44.6%	54.4%	45.0%	55.0%
2,209	LIBERTY	994	434	550	10	116 D	43.7%	55.3%	44.1%	55.9%
7,882	LINCOLN	3,448	1,250	2,150	48	900 D	36.3%	62.4%	36.8%	63.2%
3,798	MCCONE	1,501	529	928	44	399 D	35.2%	61.8%	36.3%	63.7%
7,294	MADISON	3,256	1,557	1,674	25	117 D	47.8%	51.4%	48.2%	51.8%
2,237	MEAGHER	1,157	520	621	16	101 D	44.9%	53.7%	45.6%	54.4%
2,135	MINERAL	1,068	402	645	21	243 D	37.6%	60.4%	38.4%	61.6%
29,038	MISSOULA	13,537	5,640	7,747	150	2,107 D	41.7%	57.2%	42.1%	57.9%
5,717	MUSSELSHELL	2,952	1,086	1,807	59	721 D	36.8%	61.2%	37.5%	62.5%
11,566	PARK	5,319	2,433	2,833	53	400 D	45.7%	53.3%	46.2%	53.8%
1,083	PETROLEUM	631	313	316	2	3 D	49.6%	50.1%	49.8%	50.2%
7,892	PHILLIPS	3,366	1,110	2,225	31	1,115 D	33.0%	66.1%	33.3%	66.7%
6,716	PONDERA	2,980	1,038	1,899	43	861 D	34.8%	63.7%	35.3%	64.7%
3,159	POWDER RIVER	1,212	633	561	18	72 R	52.2%	46.3%	53.0%	47.0%
6,152	POWELL	2,902	1,116	1,765	21	649 D	38.5%	60.8%	38.7%	61.3%
2,410	PRAIRIE	1,161	597	554	10	43 R	51.4%	47.7%	51.9%	48.1%
12,978	RAVALLI	5,313	2,483	2,773	57	290 D	46.7%	52.2%	47.2%	52.8%
10,209	RICHLAND	3,645	1,497	2,095	53	598 D	41.1%	57.5%	41.7%	58.3%
9,806	ROOSEVELT	3,982	1,503	2,418	61	915 D	37.7%	60.7%	38.3%	61.7%
6,477	ROSEBUD	2,677	1,252	1,399	26	147 D	46.8%	52.3%	47.2%	52.8%
6,926	SANDERS	2,794	1,088	1,634	72	546 D	38.9%	58.5%	40.0%	60.0%
7,814	SHERIDAN	3,052	892	2,108	52	1,216 D	29.2%	69.1%	29.7%	70.3%
53,207	SILVER BOW	25,734	7,932	17,467	335	9,535 D	30.8%	67.9%	31.2%	68.8%
5,694	STILLWATER	2,475	1,255	1,201	19	54 R	50.7%	48.5%	51.1%	48.9%
3,719	SWEET GRASS	1,611	861	741	9	120 R	53.4%	46.0%	53.7%	46.3%
6,922	TETON	2,894	1,132	1,735	27	603 D	39.1%	60.0%	39.5%	60.5%
6,769	TOOLE	3,182	1,218	1,954	10	736 D	38.3%	61.4%	38.4%	61.6%
1,499	TREASURE	610	287	321	2	34 D	47.0%	52.6%	47.2%	52.8%
15,181	VALLEY	5,162	1,597	3,493	72	1,896 D	30.9%	67.7%	31.4%	68.6%
3,286	WHEATLAND	1,742	786	948	8	162 D	45.1%	54.4%	45.3%	54.7%
2,161	WIBAUX	1,043	461	576	6	115 D	44.2%	55.2%	44.5%	55.5%
41,182	YELLOWSTONE	17,655	8,479	9,036	140	557 D	48.0%	51.2%	48.4%	51.6%
559,456	TOTAL	247,873	99,579	145,698	2,596	46,119 D	40.2%	58.8%	40.6%	59.4%

MONTANA

PRESIDENT 1936

1930 Census Population	County	Total Vote	Republican	Democratic	Other	Rep.-Dem. Plurality	Percentage Total Vote Rep.	Total Vote Dem.	Major Vote Rep.	Major Vote Dem.
6,654	BEAVERHEAD	3,538	1,304	2,153	81	849 D	36.9%	60.9%	37.7%	62.3%
8,543	BIG HORN	3,186	1,087	2,037	62	950 D	34.1%	63.9%	34.8%	65.2%
9,006	BLAINE	3,074	851	2,166	57	1,315 D	27.7%	70.5%	28.2%	71.8%
2,738	BROADWATER	1,597	502	1,071	24	569 D	31.4%	67.1%	31.9%	68.1%
12,571	CARBON	4,876	1,617	3,116	143	1,499 D	33.2%	63.9%	34.2%	65.8%
4,136	CARTER	1,414	464	929	21	465 D	32.8%	65.7%	33.3%	66.7%
41,146	CASCADE	17,789	4,077	13,325	387	9,248 D	22.9%	74.9%	23.4%	76.6%
8,635	CHOUTEAU	3,657	878	2,734	45	1,856 D	24.0%	74.8%	24.3%	75.7%
11,242	CUSTER	4,713	1,381	3,196	136	1,815 D	29.3%	67.8%	30.2%	69.8%
5,553	DANIELS	2,115	467	1,596	52	1,129 D	22.1%	75.5%	22.6%	77.4%
9,881	DAWSON	3,410	1,221	2,169	20	948 D	35.8%	63.6%	36.0%	64.0%
16,293	DEER LODGE	6,549	1,640	4,813	96	3,173 D	25.0%	73.5%	25.4%	74.6%
4,568	FALLON	1,661	598	1,015	48	417 D	36.0%	61.1%	37.1%	62.9%
16,531	FERGUS	6,745	1,821	4,675	249	2,854 D	27.0%	69.3%	28.0%	72.0%
19,200	FLATHEAD	8,532	2,460	5,408	664	2,948 D	28.8%	63.4%	31.3%	68.7%
16,124	GALLATIN	7,168	2,151	4,697	320	2,546 D	30.0%	65.5%	31.4%	68.6%
4,252	GARFIELD	1,577	548	991	38	443 D	34.7%	62.8%	35.6%	64.4%
5,297	GLACIER	3,265	781	2,453	31	1,672 D	23.9%	75.1%	24.1%	75.9%
2,126	GOLDEN VALLEY	821	331	474	16	143 D	40.3%	57.7%	41.1%	58.9%
3,013	GRANITE	1,724	475	1,227	22	752 D	27.6%	71.2%	27.9%	72.1%
13,775	HILL	5,520	1,014	4,328	178	3,314 D	18.4%	78.4%	19.0%	81.0%
4,133	JEFFERSON	2,063	573	1,409	81	836 D	27.8%	68.3%	28.9%	71.1%
5,238	JUDITH BASIN	2,231	645	1,534	52	889 D	28.9%	68.8%	29.6%	70.4%
9,541	LAKE	4,422	1,401	2,656	365	1,255 D	31.7%	60.1%	34.5%	65.5%
18,224	LEWIS AND CLARK	8,725	2,951	5,614	160	2,663 D	33.8%	64.3%	34.5%	65.5%
2,198	LIBERTY	1,065	276	758	31	482 D	25.9%	71.2%	26.7%	73.3%
7,089	LINCOLN	3,050	745	2,117	188	1,372 D	24.4%	69.4%	26.0%	74.0%
4,790	MCCONE	1,739	332	1,366	41	1,034 D	19.1%	78.6%	19.6%	80.4%
6,323	MADISON	2,890	1,006	1,819	65	813 D	34.8%	62.9%	35.6%	64.4%
2,272	MEAGHER	1,280	495	767	18	272 D	38.7%	59.9%	39.2%	60.8%
1,626	MINERAL	960	215	657	88	442 D	22.4%	68.4%	24.7%	75.3%
21,782	MISSOULA	10,803	2,697	7,690	416	4,993 D	25.0%	71.2%	26.0%	74.0%
7,242	MUSSELSHELL	3,014	771	2,092	151	1,321 D	25.6%	69.4%	26.9%	73.1%
10,922	PARK	4,793	1,583	2,968	242	1,385 D	33.0%	61.9%	34.8%	65.2%
2,045	PETROLEUM	806	258	523	25	265 D	32.0%	64.9%	33.0%	67.0%
8,208	PHILLIPS	3,494	850	2,555	89	1,705 D	24.3%	73.1%	25.0%	75.0%
6,964	PONDERA	2,934	658	2,213	63	1,555 D	22.4%	75.4%	22.9%	77.1%
3,909	POWDER RIVER	1,349	545	758	46	213 D	40.4%	56.2%	41.8%	58.2%
6,202	POWELL	2,914	799	2,060	55	1,261 D	27.4%	70.7%	27.9%	72.1%
3,941	PRAIRIE	1,363	454	877	32	423 D	33.3%	64.3%	34.1%	65.9%
10,315	RAVALLI	4,732	1,580	2,859	293	1,279 D	33.4%	60.4%	35.6%	64.4%
9,633	RICHLAND	3,677	1,066	2,516	95	1,450 D	29.0%	68.4%	29.8%	70.2%
10,672	ROOSEVELT	4,109	1,052	2,923	134	1,871 D	25.6%	71.1%	26.5%	73.5%
7,347	ROSEBUD	2,670	866	1,624	180	758 D	32.4%	60.8%	34.8%	65.2%
5,692	SANDERS	2,735	718	1,788	229	1,070 D	26.3%	65.4%	28.7%	71.3%
9,869	SHERIDAN	3,168	513	2,503	152	1,990 D	16.2%	79.0%	17.0%	83.0%
56,969	SILVER BOW	22,623	4,528	17,697	398	13,169 D	20.0%	78.2%	20.4%	79.6%
6,253	STILLWATER	2,422	1,034	1,292	96	258 D	42.7%	53.3%	44.5%	55.5%
3,944	SWEET GRASS	1,544	664	783	97	119 D	43.0%	50.7%	45.9%	54.1%
6,068	TETON	2,550	604	1,917	29	1,313 D	23.7%	75.2%	24.0%	76.0%
6,714	TOOLE	2,884	654	2,120	110	1,466 D	22.7%	73.5%	23.6%	76.4%
1,661	TREASURE	669	244	398	27	154 D	36.5%	59.5%	38.0%	62.0%
11,181	VALLEY	7,057	996	5,862	199	4,866 D	14.1%	83.1%	14.5%	85.5%
3,751	WHEATLAND	1,659	602	1,037	20	435 D	36.3%	62.5%	36.7%	63.3%
2,767	WIBAUX	1,161	362	790	9	428 D	31.2%	68.0%	31.4%	68.6%
30,785	YELLOWSTONE	14,016	5,193	8,575	248	3,382 D	37.1%	61.2%	37.7%	62.3%
537,606	TOTAL	230,502	63,598	159,690	7,214	96,092 D	27.6%	69.3%	28.5%	71.5%

MONTANA

PRESIDENT 1932

1930 Census Population	County	Total Vote	Republican	Democratic	Other	Rep.-Dem. Plurality	Percentage Total Vote Rep.	Total Vote Dem.	Major Vote Rep.	Major Vote Dem.
6,654	BEAVERHEAD	3,291	1,418	1,834	39	416 D	43.1%	55.7%	43.6%	56.4%
8,543	BIG HORN	2,628	957	1,637	34	680 D	36.4%	62.3%	36.9%	63.1%
9,006	BLAINE	3,160	1,063	1,977	120	914 D	33.6%	62.6%	35.0%	65.0%
2,738	BROADWATER	1,519	512	988	19	476 D	33.7%	65.0%	34.1%	65.9%
12,571	CARBON	5,076	1,942	2,872	262	930 D	38.3%	56.6%	40.3%	59.7%
4,136	CARTER	1,511	565	915	31	350 D	37.4%	60.6%	38.2%	61.8%
41,146	CASCADE	16,823	5,800	10,047	976	4,247 D	34.5%	59.7%	36.6%	63.4%
8,635	CHOUTEAU	3,477	1,232	2,093	152	861 D	35.4%	60.2%	37.1%	62.9%
11,242	CUSTER	4,528	1,675	2,729	124	1,054 D	37.0%	60.3%	38.0%	62.0%
5,553	DANIELS	1,886	482	1,172	232	690 D	25.6%	62.1%	29.1%	70.9%
9,881	DAWSON	3,457	1,470	1,929	58	459 D	42.5%	55.8%	43.2%	56.8%
16,293	DEER LODGE	6,204	2,198	3,893	113	1,695 D	35.4%	62.7%	36.1%	63.9%
4,568	FALLON	1,734	690	973	71	283 D	39.8%	56.1%	41.5%	58.5%
16,531	FERGUS	7,136	2,400	4,470	266	2,070 D	33.6%	62.6%	34.9%	65.1%
19,200	FLATHEAD	7,683	2,978	4,026	679	1,048 D	38.8%	52.4%	42.5%	57.5%
16,124	GALLATIN	7,095	2,553	4,359	183	1,806 D	36.0%	61.4%	36.9%	63.1%
4,252	GARFIELD	1,785	678	1,044	63	366 D	38.0%	58.5%	39.4%	60.6%
5,297	GLACIER	2,439	702	1,717	20	1,015 D	28.8%	70.4%	29.0%	71.0%
2,126	GOLDEN VALLEY	912	423	469	20	46 D	46.4%	51.4%	47.4%	52.6%
3,013	GRANITE	1,439	536	855	48	319 D	37.2%	59.4%	38.5%	61.5%
13,775	HILL	5,054	1,589	3,257	208	1,668 D	31.4%	64.4%	32.8%	67.2%
4,133	JEFFERSON	2,114	784	1,246	84	462 D	37.1%	58.9%	38.6%	61.4%
5,238	JUDITH BASIN	2,131	720	1,280	131	560 D	33.8%	60.1%	36.0%	64.0%
9,541	LAKE	4,082	1,361	2,514	207	1,153 D	33.3%	61.6%	35.1%	64.9%
18,224	LEWIS AND CLARK	8,596	3,671	4,714	211	1,043 D	42.7%	54.8%	43.8%	56.2%
2,198	LIBERTY	1,010	252	731	27	479 D	25.0%	72.4%	25.6%	74.4%
7,089	LINCOLN	2,906	833	1,867	206	1,034 D	28.7%	64.2%	30.9%	69.1%
4,790	MCCONE	1,731	456	1,020	255	564 D	26.3%	58.9%	30.9%	69.1%
6,323	MADISON	2,976	1,097	1,764	115	667 D	36.9%	59.3%	38.3%	61.7%
2,272	MEAGHER	1,101	462	621	18	159 D	42.0%	56.4%	42.7%	57.3%
1,626	MINERAL	955	260	578	117	318 D	27.2%	60.5%	31.0%	69.0%
21,782	MISSOULA	9,616	3,819	5,242	555	1,423 D	39.7%	54.5%	42.1%	57.9%
7,242	MUSSELSHELL	2,840	1,021	1,584	235	563 D	36.0%	55.8%	39.2%	60.8%
10,922	PARK	4,609	1,895	2,533	181	638 D	41.1%	55.0%	42.8%	57.2%
2,045	PETROLEUM	924	351	544	29	193 D	38.0%	58.9%	39.2%	60.8%
8,208	PHILLIPS	3,324	1,127	2,054	143	927 D	33.9%	61.8%	35.4%	64.6%
6,964	PONDERA	2,875	930	1,805	140	875 D	32.3%	62.8%	34.0%	66.0%
3,909	POWDER RIVER	1,450	515	875	60	360 D	35.5%	60.3%	37.1%	62.9%
6,202	POWELL	2,995	1,031	1,869	95	838 D	34.4%	62.4%	35.6%	64.4%
3,941	PRAIRIE	1,387	634	732	21	98 D	45.7%	52.8%	46.4%	53.6%
10,315	RAVALLI	4,311	1,714	2,292	305	578 D	39.8%	53.2%	42.8%	57.2%
9,633	RICHLAND	3,116	1,216	1,768	132	552 D	39.0%	56.7%	40.8%	59.2%
10,672	ROOSEVELT	3,500	965	2,263	272	1,298 D	27.6%	64.7%	29.9%	70.1%
7,347	ROSEBUD	2,804	1,027	1,646	131	619 D	36.6%	58.7%	38.4%	61.6%
5,692	SANDERS	2,601	760	1,577	264	817 D	29.2%	60.6%	32.5%	67.5%
9,869	SHERIDAN	3,246	739	1,450	1,057	711 D	22.8%	44.7%	33.8%	66.2%
56,969	SILVER BOW	21,834	6,792	13,626	1,416	6,834 D	31.1%	62.4%	33.3%	66.7%
6,253	STILLWATER	2,453	1,085	1,281	87	196 D	44.2%	52.2%	45.9%	54.1%
3,944	SWEET GRASS	1,594	784	761	49	23 R	49.2%	47.7%	50.7%	49.3%
6,068	TETON	2,428	875	1,496	57	621 D	36.0%	61.6%	36.9%	63.1%
6,714	TOOLE	2,874	862	1,917	95	1,055 D	30.0%	66.7%	31.0%	69.0%
1,661	TREASURE	596	276	310	10	34 D	46.3%	52.0%	47.1%	52.9%
11,181	VALLEY	4,092	1,242	2,499	351	1,257 D	30.4%	61.1%	33.2%	66.8%
3,751	WHEATLAND	1,836	828	996	12	168 D	45.1%	54.2%	45.4%	54.6%
2,767	WIBAUX	1,252	445	798	9	353 D	35.5%	63.7%	35.8%	64.2%
30,785	YELLOWSTONE	11,483	5,386	5,777	320	391 D	46.9%	50.3%	48.2%	51.8%
537,606	TOTAL	216,479	78,078	127,286	11,115	49,208 D	36.1%	58.8%	38.0%	62.0%

MONTANA

PRESIDENT 1928

1920 Census Population	County	Total Vote	Republican	Democratic	Other	Rep.-Dem. Plurality	Percentage Total Vote Rep.	Total Vote Dem.	Major Vote Rep.	Major Vote Dem.
7,369	BEAVERHEAD	3,064	1,906	1,144	14	762 R	62.2%	37.3%	62.5%	37.5%
7,015	BIG HORN	2,297	1,274	1,017	6	257 R	55.5%	44.3%	55.6%	44.4%
9,057	BLAINE	2,714	1,537	1,160	17	377 R	56.6%	42.7%	57.0%	43.0%
3,239	BROADWATER	1,415	743	663	9	80 R	52.5%	46.9%	52.8%	47.2%
15,279	CARBON	4,327	2,514	1,674	139	840 R	58.1%	38.7%	60.0%	40.0%
3,972	CARTER	1,192	763	420	9	343 R	64.0%	35.2%	64.5%	35.5%
38,836	CASCADE	14,856	8,183	6,540	133	1,643 R	55.1%	44.0%	55.6%	44.4%
11,051	CHOUTEAU	3,106	1,837	1,232	37	605 R	59.1%	39.7%	59.9%	40.1%
12,194	CUSTER	3,906	2,503	1,386	17	1,117 R	64.1%	35.5%	64.4%	35.6%
	DANIELS	1,736	936	780	20	156 R	53.9%	44.9%	54.5%	45.5%
9,239	DAWSON	3,286	2,207	1,065	14	1,142 R	67.2%	32.4%	67.5%	32.5%
15,323	DEER LODGE	5,901	2,695	3,184	22	489 D	45.7%	54.0%	45.8%	54.2%
4,548	FALLON	1,500	1,036	454	10	582 R	69.1%	30.3%	69.5%	30.5%
28,344	FERGUS	6,838	4,109	2,667	62	1,442 R	60.1%	39.0%	60.6%	39.4%
21,705	FLATHEAD	6,152	4,098	1,972	82	2,126 R	66.6%	32.1%	67.5%	32.5%
15,864	GALLATIN	6,318	3,861	2,423	34	1,438 R	61.1%	38.4%	61.4%	38.6%
5,368	GARFIELD	1,688	1,176	499	13	677 R	69.7%	29.6%	70.2%	29.8%
4,178	GLACIER	1,826	847	976	3	129 D	46.4%	53.5%	46.5%	53.5%
	GOLDEN VALLEY	978	625	346	7	279 R	63.9%	35.4%	64.4%	35.6%
4,167	GRANITE	1,366	849	509	8	340 R	62.2%	37.3%	62.5%	37.5%
13,958	HILL	4,377	2,336	2,022	19	314 R	53.4%	46.2%	53.6%	46.4%
5,203	JEFFERSON	1,778	1,013	751	14	262 R	57.0%	42.2%	57.4%	42.6%
	JUDITH BASIN	2,364	1,342	978	44	364 R	56.8%	41.4%	57.8%	42.2%
	LAKE	3,157	1,876	1,256	25	620 R	59.4%	39.8%	59.9%	40.1%
18,660	LEWIS AND CLARK	7,744	4,441	3,278	25	1,163 R	57.3%	42.3%	57.5%	42.5%
2,416	LIBERTY	786	446	332	8	114 R	56.7%	42.2%	57.3%	42.7%
7,797	LINCOLN	2,327	1,217	1,067	43	150 R	52.3%	45.9%	53.3%	46.7%
4,747	MCCONE	1,529	946	554	29	392 R	61.9%	36.2%	63.1%	36.9%
7,495	MADISON	2,611	1,785	812	14	973 R	68.4%	31.1%	68.7%	31.3%
2,622	MEAGHER	1,051	714	335	2	379 R	67.9%	31.9%	68.1%	31.9%
2,327	MINERAL	832	443	370	19	73 R	53.2%	44.5%	54.5%	45.5%
24,041	MISSOULA	8,467	5,056	3,291	120	1,765 R	59.7%	38.9%	60.6%	39.4%
12,030	MUSSELSHELL	3,181	1,608	1,444	129	164 R	50.6%	45.4%	52.7%	47.3%
11,330	PARK	4,496	3,095	1,338	63	1,757 R	68.8%	29.8%	69.8%	30.2%
	PETROLEUM	963	586	372	5	214 R	60.9%	38.6%	61.2%	38.8%
9,311	PHILLIPS	2,828	1,671	1,135	22	536 R	59.1%	40.1%	59.6%	40.4%
5,741	PONDERA	2,283	1,324	944	15	380 R	58.0%	41.3%	58.4%	41.6%
3,357	POWDER RIVER	1,199	780	410	9	370 R	65.1%	34.2%	65.5%	34.5%
6,909	POWELL	2,622	1,568	1,031	23	537 R	59.8%	39.3%	60.3%	39.7%
3,684	PRAIRIE	1,379	968	405	6	563 R	70.2%	29.4%	70.5%	29.5%
10,098	RAVALLI	3,724	2,551	1,112	61	1,439 R	68.5%	29.9%	69.6%	30.4%
8,989	RICHLAND	2,594	1,648	917	29	731 R	63.5%	35.4%	64.2%	35.8%
10,347	ROOSEVELT	2,949	1,630	1,296	23	334 R	55.3%	43.9%	55.7%	44.3%
8,002	ROSEBUD	2,558	1,519	1,025	14	494 R	59.4%	40.1%	59.7%	40.3%
4,903	SANDERS	2,128	1,142	873	113	269 R	53.7%	41.0%	56.7%	43.3%
13,847	SHERIDAN	2,971	1,624	1,190	157	434 R	54.7%	40.1%	57.7%	42.3%
60,313	SILVER BOW	21,103	9,456	11,228	419	1,772 D	44.8%	53.2%	45.7%	54.3%
7,630	STILLWATER	2,408	1,687	711	10	976 R	70.1%	29.5%	70.4%	29.6%
4,926	SWEET GRASS	1,605	1,163	435	7	728 R	72.5%	27.1%	72.8%	27.2%
5,870	TETON	2,085	1,263	804	18	459 R	60.6%	38.6%	61.1%	38.9%
3,724	TOOLE	2,422	1,325	1,076	21	249 R	54.7%	44.4%	55.2%	44.8%
1,990	TREASURE	541	354	186	1	168 R	65.4%	34.4%	65.6%	34.4%
11,542	VALLEY	3,649	2,330	1,294	25	1,036 R	63.9%	35.5%	64.3%	35.7%
5,619	WHEATLAND	1,754	1,207	542	5	665 R	68.8%	30.9%	69.0%	31.0%
3,113	WIBAUX	1,036	583	448	5	135 R	56.3%	43.2%	56.5%	43.5%
29,600	YELLOWSTONE	10,141	6,904	3,205	32	3,699 R	68.1%	31.6%	68.3%	31.7%
548,889	TOTAL	194,108	113,300	78,578	2,230	34,722 R	58.4%	40.5%	59.0%	41.0%

MONTANA

PRESIDENT 1924

1920 Census Population	County	Total Vote	Republican	Democratic	Progressive	Other	Plurality	Percentage Total Vote Rep.	Dem.	Prog.
7,369	BEAVERHEAD	2,742	1,386	766	587	3	620 R	50.5%	27.9%	21.4%
7,015	BIG HORN	1,874	1,082	327	465		617 R	57.7%	17.4%	24.8%
9,057	BLAINE	1,808	827	337	642	2	185 R	45.7%	18.6%	35.5%
3,239	BROADWATER	1,408	531	486	390	1	45 R	37.7%	34.5%	27.7%
15,279	CARBON	4,266	1,891	698	1,648	29	243 R	44.3%	16.4%	38.6%
3,972	CARTER	1,235	669	283	283		386 R	54.2%	22.9%	22.9%
38,836	CASCADE	11,706	5,081	2,220	4,373	32	708 R	43.4%	19.0%	37.4%
11,051	CHOUTEAU	2,919	1,347	706	857	9	490 R	46.1%	24.2%	29.4%
12,194	CUSTER	3,778	1,654	412	1,707	5	53 P	43.8%	10.9%	45.2%
	DANIELS	1,435	505	185	740	5	235 P	35.2%	12.9%	51.6%
9,239	DAWSON	2,619	1,326	346	941	6	385 R	50.6%	13.2%	35.9%
15,323	DEER LODGE	5,467	1,937	1,611	1,918	1	19 R	35.4%	29.5%	35.1%
4,548	FALLON	1,314	731	220	363		368 R	55.6%	16.7%	27.6%
28,344	FERGUS	7,642	2,942	1,580	3,119	1	177 P	38.5%	20.7%	40.8%
21,705	FLATHEAD	5,871	2,541	788	2,537	5	4 R	43.3%	13.4%	43.2%
15,864	GALLATIN	5,623	2,494	1,564	1,564	1	930 R	44.4%	27.8%	27.8%
5,368	GARFIELD	1,733	876	355	502		374 R	50.5%	20.5%	29.0%
4,178	GLACIER	1,406	586	511	309		75 R	41.7%	36.3%	22.0%
	GOLDEN VALLEY	1,114	422	118	573	1	151 P	37.9%	10.6%	51.4%
4,167	GRANITE	1,339	582	353	402	2	180 R	43.5%	26.4%	30.0%
13,958	HILL	3,628	1,110	602	1,906	10	796 P	30.6%	16.6%	52.5%
5,203	JEFFERSON	1,776	648	434	689	5	41 P	36.5%	24.4%	38.8%
	JUDITH BASIN	2,148	888	480	763	17	125 R	41.3%	22.3%	35.5%
	LAKE	3,157	884	340	1,932	1	1,048 P	28.0%	10.8%	61.2%
18,660	LEWIS AND CLARK	6,875	3,433	1,869	1,570	3	1,564 R	49.9%	27.2%	22.8%
2,416	LIBERTY	709	239	141	329		90 P	33.7%	19.9%	46.4%
7,797	LINCOLN	2,387	976	374	1,030	7	54 P	40.9%	15.7%	43.2%
4,747	MCCONE	1,294	494	143	627	30	133 P	38.2%	11.1%	48.5%
7,495	MADISON	2,480	1,137	672	665	6	465 R	45.8%	27.1%	26.8%
2,622	MEAGHER	1,047	624	257	166		367 R	59.6%	24.5%	15.9%
2,327	MINERAL	1,032	223	123	686		463 P	21.6%	11.9%	66.5%
24,041	MISSOULA	8,104	2,386	1,012	4,704	2	2,318 P	29.4%	12.5%	58.0%
12,030	MUSSELSHELL	3,267	1,488	247	1,512	20	24 P	45.5%	7.6%	46.3%
11,330	PARK	4,337	2,199	688	1,447	3	752 R	50.7%	15.9%	33.4%
	PETROLEUM	—	—	—	—		—	—	—	—
9,311	PHILLIPS	2,647	1,236	473	935	3	301 R	46.7%	17.9%	35.3%
5,741	PONDERA	2,028	764	414	849	1	85 P	37.7%	20.4%	41.9%
3,357	POWDER RIVER	986	480	123	380	3	100 R	48.7%	12.5%	38.5%
6,909	POWELL	2,431	982	559	889	1	93 R	40.4%	23.0%	36.6%
3,684	PRAIRIE	1,215	683	162	367	3	316 R	56.2%	13.3%	30.2%
10,098	RAVALLI	3,469	1,311	562	1,594	2	283 P	37.8%	16.2%	45.9%
8,989	RICHLAND	1,854	926	238	688	2	238 R	49.9%	12.8%	37.1%
10,347	ROOSEVELT	2,468	965	389	1,111	3	146 P	39.1%	15.8%	45.0%
8,002	ROSEBUD	2,270	1,115	259	892	4	223 R	49.1%	11.4%	39.3%
4,903	SANDERS	2,052	588	188	1,275	1	687 P	28.7%	9.2%	62.1%
13,847	SHERIDAN	2,562	905	176	1,464	17	559 P	35.3%	6.9%	57.1%
60,313	SILVER BOW	18,814	6,520	5,393	6,813	88	293 P	34.7%	28.7%	36.2%
7,630	STILLWATER	2,358	1,412	375	567	4	845 R	59.9%	15.9%	24.0%
4,926	SWEET GRASS	1,432	853	248	331		522 R	59.6%	17.3%	23.1%
5,870	TETON	1,920	775	396	746	3	29 R	40.4%	20.6%	38.9%
3,724	TOOLE	1,859	697	439	720	3	23 P	37.5%	23.6%	38.7%
1,990	TREASURE	522	289	84	148	1	141 R	55.4%	16.1%	28.4%
11,542	VALLEY	3,043	1,555	497	986	5	569 R	51.1%	16.3%	32.4%
5,619	WHEATLAND	1,635	723	221	691		32 R	44.2%	13.5%	42.3%
3,113	WIBAUX	887	505	189	191	2	314 R	56.9%	21.3%	21.5%
29,600	YELLOWSTONE	8,433	4,715	1,172	2,541	5	2,174 R	55.9%	13.9%	30.1%
548,889	TOTAL	174,425	74,138	33,805	66,124	358	8,014 R	42.5%	19.4%	37.9%

MONTANA

PRESIDENT 1920

1920 Census Population	County	Total Vote	Republican	Democratic	Other	Rep.-Dem. Plurality	Percentage Total Vote Rep.	Total Vote Dem.	Major Vote Rep.	Major Vote Dem.
7,369	BEAVERHEAD	2,978	2,049	833	96	1,216 R	68.8%	28.0%	71.1%	28.9%
7,015	BIG HORN	1,605	1,062	475	68	587 R	66.2%	29.6%	69.1%	30.9%
9,057	BLAINE	2,753	1,720	848	185	872 R	62.5%	30.8%	67.0%	33.0%
3,239	BROADWATER	1,404	723	622	59	101 R	51.5%	44.3%	53.8%	46.2%
15,279	CARBON	4,214	2,700	1,107	407	1,593 R	64.1%	26.3%	70.9%	29.1%
3,972	CARTER	1,170	782	342	46	440 R	66.8%	29.2%	69.6%	30.4%
38,836	CASCADE	11,572	6,808	3,938	826	2,870 R	58.8%	34.0%	63.4%	36.6%
11,051	CHOUTEAU	4,348	2,646	1,436	266	1,210 R	60.9%	33.0%	64.8%	35.2%
12,194	CUSTER	3,637	2,347	1,127	163	1,220 R	64.5%	31.0%	67.6%	32.4%
	DANIELS	1,349	811	289	249	522 R	60.1%	21.4%	73.7%	26.3%
9,239	DAWSON	2,791	1,784	875	132	909 R	63.9%	31.4%	67.1%	32.9%
15,323	DEER LODGE	5,219	3,130	1,567	522	1,563 R	60.0%	30.0%	66.6%	33.4%
4,548	FALLON	1,491	1,064	381	46	683 R	71.4%	25.6%	73.6%	26.4%
28,344	FERGUS	9,727	5,858	3,371	498	2,487 R	60.2%	34.7%	63.5%	36.5%
21,705	FLATHEAD	6,581	3,900	2,241	440	1,659 R	59.3%	34.1%	63.5%	36.5%
15,864	GALLATIN	5,920	3,238	2,370	312	868 R	54.7%	40.0%	57.7%	42.3%
5,368	GARFIELD	1,798	1,226	484	88	742 R	68.2%	26.9%	71.7%	28.3%
4,178	GLACIER	1,876	1,297	531	48	766 R	69.1%	28.3%	71.0%	29.0%
	GOLDEN VALLEY	1,633	1,185	381	67	804 R	72.6%	23.3%	75.7%	24.3%
4,167	GRANITE	1,478	949	439	90	510 R	64.2%	29.7%	68.4%	31.6%
13,958	HILL	4,004	2,220	1,388	396	832 R	55.4%	34.7%	61.5%	38.5%
5,203	JEFFERSON	1,779	969	688	122	281 R	54.5%	38.7%	58.5%	41.5%
	JUDITH BASIN	—	—	—	—	—	—	—	—	—
	LAKE	—	—	—	—	—	—	—	—	—
18,660	LEWIS AND CLARK	6,913	4,348	2,413	152	1,935 R	62.9%	34.9%	64.3%	35.7%
2,416	LIBERTY	1,190	757	331	102	426 R	63.6%	27.8%	69.6%	30.4%
7,797	LINCOLN	2,063	1,187	683	193	504 R	57.5%	33.1%	63.5%	36.5%
4,747	MCCONE	1,898	1,177	537	184	640 R	62.0%	28.3%	68.7%	31.3%
7,495	MADISON	2,646	1,672	877	97	795 R	63.2%	33.1%	65.6%	34.4%
2,622	MEAGHER	1,077	744	314	19	430 R	69.1%	29.2%	70.3%	29.7%
2,327	MINERAL	889	347	362	180	15 D	39.0%	40.7%	48.9%	51.1%
24,041	MISSOULA	8,314	4,374	3,292	648	1,082 R	52.6%	39.6%	57.1%	42.9%
12,030	MUSSELSHELL	3,225	1,910	951	364	959 R	59.2%	29.5%	66.8%	33.2%
11,330	PARK	4,020	2,537	1,155	328	1,382 R	63.1%	28.7%	68.7%	31.3%
	PETROLEUM	—	—	—	—	—	—	—	—	—
9,311	PHILLIPS	2,522	1,693	648	181	1,045 R	67.1%	25.7%	72.3%	27.7%
5,741	PONDERA	2,647	1,654	893	100	761 R	62.5%	33.7%	64.9%	35.1%
3,357	POWDER RIVER	1,340	955	330	55	625 R	71.3%	24.6%	74.3%	25.7%
6,909	POWELL	2,352	1,345	787	220	558 R	57.2%	33.5%	63.1%	36.9%
3,684	PRAIRIE	1,149	881	242	26	639 R	76.7%	21.1%	78.5%	21.5%
10,098	RAVALLI	3,488	2,110	1,224	154	886 R	60.5%	35.1%	63.3%	36.7%
8,989	RICHLAND	2,687	1,759	744	184	1,015 R	65.5%	27.7%	70.3%	29.7%
10,347	ROOSEVELT	3,282	2,239	873	170	1,366 R	68.2%	26.6%	71.9%	28.1%
8,002	ROSEBUD	2,279	1,624	555	100	1,069 R	71.3%	24.4%	74.5%	25.5%
4,903	SANDERS	2,010	1,035	741	234	294 R	51.5%	36.9%	58.3%	41.7%
13,847	SHERIDAN	2,497	1,335	610	552	725 R	53.5%	24.4%	68.6%	31.4%
60,313	SILVER BOW	18,198	10,074	6,394	1,730	3,680 R	55.4%	35.1%	61.2%	38.8%
7,630	STILLWATER	2,441	1,721	664	56	1,057 R	70.5%	27.2%	72.2%	27.8%
4,926	SWEET GRASS	1,408	1,035	349	24	686 R	73.5%	24.8%	74.8%	25.2%
5,870	TETON	2,119	1,319	671	129	648 R	62.2%	31.7%	66.3%	33.7%
3,724	TOOLE	1,405	861	405	139	456 R	61.3%	28.8%	68.0%	32.0%
1,990	TREASURE	724	517	174	33	343 R	71.4%	24.0%	74.8%	25.2%
11,542	VALLEY	3,333	2,096	895	342	1,201 R	62.9%	26.9%	70.1%	29.9%
5,619	WHEATLAND	1,817	1,250	520	47	730 R	68.8%	28.6%	70.6%	29.4%
3,113	WIBAUX	966	692	223	51	469 R	71.6%	23.1%	75.6%	24.4%
29,600	YELLOWSTONE	8,780	5,714	2,782	284	2,932 R	65.1%	31.7%	67.3%	32.7%
548,889	TOTAL	179,006	109,430	57,372	12,204	52,058 R	61.1%	32.1%	65.6%	34.4%

MONTANA

In 1920 Daniels county was organized from parts of Sheridan and Valle counties; Golden Valley county was organized from parts of Musselshell and Sweet Grass counties; Judith Basin county was organized from parts of Cascade and Fergus counties. In 1923 Lake county was organized from parts of Flathead and Missoula counties. In 1925 Petroleum county was organized from part of Fergus county. Population data for counties created between the 1920 and 1930 Census are not available. Population totals include persons living in Yellowstone National Park and not under any county jurisdiction: 52 in 1930, 43 in 1940 and 58 in 1950.

ELECTION NOTES

1956

1952 Other vote was 723 Hallinan (Progressive); 548 Hamblen (Prohibition); 159 Hoopes (Socialist).

1948 Other vote was 7,313 Wallace (Progressive); 695 Thomas (Socialist); 429 Watson (Prohibition).

1944 Other vote was 1,296 Thomas (Socialist); 340 Watson (Prohibition).

1940 Other vote was 1,443 Thomas (Socialist); 664 Babson (Prohibition); 489 Browder (Communist).

1936 Other vote was 5,539 Lemke (Union); 1,066 Thomas (Socialist); 385 Browder (Communist); 224 Colvin (Prohibition).

1932 Other vote was 7,891 Thomas (Socialist); 1,775 Foster (Communist); 1,449 Harvey (Liberty).

1928 Other vote was 1,667 Thomas (Socialist); 563 Foster (Communist).

1924 A special four-column table which gives the LaFollette (Progressive) vote is used to detail this election. The LaFollette vote is a combination of 61,105 LaFollette-Wheeler Independent; 4,771 Farmer-Labor and 248 Socialist votes. Other vote was Foster (Communist).

1920 Other vote was Christensen (Farmer-Labor).

NEBRASKA

POPULAR VOTE FOR PRESIDENT 1920 TO 1956

Year	Total Vote	Republican Vote	Republican Candidate	Democratic Vote	Democratic Candidate	Other Vote	Plurality	Percentage Total Vote Rep.	Percentage Total Vote Dem.	Percentage Major Vote Rep.	Percentage Major Vote Dem.
1956	577,137	378,108	Eisenhower, Dwight D.	199,029	Stevenson, Adlai E.		179,079 R	65.5%	34.5%	65.5%	34.5%
1952	609,660	421,603	Eisenhower, Dwight D.	188,057	Stevenson, Adlai E.		233,546 R	69.2%	30.8%	69.2%	30.8%
1948	488,940	264,774	Dewey, Thomas E.	224,165	Truman, Harry S.	1	40,609 R	54.2%	45.8%	54.2%	45.8%
1944	563,126	329,880	Dewey, Thomas E.	233,246	Roosevelt, Franklin D.		96,634 R	58.6%	41.4%	58.6%	41.4%
1940	615,878	352,201	Willkie, Wendell	263,677	Roosevelt, Franklin D.		88,524 R	57.2%	42.8%	57.2%	42.8%
1936	608,023	247,731	Landon, Alfred M.	347,445	Roosevelt, Franklin D.	12,847	99,714 D	40.7%	57.1%	41.6%	58.4%
1932	570,135	201,177	Hoover, Herbert C.	359,082	Roosevelt, Franklin D.	9,876	157,905 D	35.3%	63.0%	35.9%	64.1%
1928	547,128	345,745	Hoover, Herbert C.	197,950	Smith, Alfred E.	3,433	147,795 R	63.2%	36.2%	63.6%	36.4%
1924 **	463,559	218,985	Coolidge, Calvin	137,299	Davis, John W.	107,275	81,686 R	47.2%	29.6%	61.5%	38.5%
1920	382,743	247,498	Harding, Warren G.	119,608	Cox, James M.	15,637	127,890 R	64.7%	31.3%	67.4%	32.6%

In 1924 other vote was 105,681 Progressive and 1,594 Prohibition.

ELECTORAL COLLEGE VOTE 1920 TO 1956

Year	Total	Republican	Democratic	Other
1956	6	6	—	—
1952	6	6	—	—
1948	6	6	—	—
1944	6	6	—	—
1940	7	7	—	—
1936	7	—	7	—
1932	7	—	7	—
1928	8	8	—	—
1924	8	8	—	—
1920	8	8	—	—

NEBRASKA

RICHARDSON
NEMAHA
PAWNEE
JOHNSON
OTOE
CASS
SARPY
DOUGLAS
WASHING-TON
BURT
THURSTON
DAKOTA
DIXON
CEDAR
WAYNE
CUMING
DODGE
SAUNDERS
LANCASTER
GAGE
JEFFERSON
SALINE
SEWARD
BUTLER
COLFAX
STANTON
PIERCE
MADISON
PLATTE
POLK
YORK
FILLMORE
THAYER
NUCKOLLS
CLAY
HAMILTON
MERRICK
NANCE
BOONE
ANTELOPE
KNOX
BOYD
HOLT
WHEELER
GREELEY
HOWARD
HALL
ADAMS
WEBSTER
FRANKLIN
KEARNEY
BUFFALO
SHERMAN
VALLEY
GARFIELD
KEYA PAHA
ROCK
LOUP
CUSTER
DAWSON
PHELPS
HARLAN
GOSPER
FURNAS
BROWN
BLAINE
CHERRY
THOMAS
LOGAN
LINCOLN
FRONTIER
RED WILLOW
HOOKER
McPHERSON
HAYES
HITCHCOCK
GRANT
ARTHUR
KEITH
PERKINS
CHASE
DUNDY
SHERIDAN
GARDEN
DEUEL
DAWES
BOX BUTTE
MORRILL
CHEYENNE
SIOUX
SCOTTS BLUFF
BANNER
KIMBALL

NEBRASKA

PRESIDENT 1956

1950 Census Population	County	Total Vote	Republican	Democratic	Other	Rep.-Dem. Plurality	Percentage Total Vote Rep.	Total Vote Dem.	Major Vote Rep.	Major Vote Dem.
28,855	ADAMS	12,231	8,186	4,045		4,141 R	66.9%	33.1%	66.9%	33.1%
11,624	ANTELOPE	4,941	3,607	1,334		2,273 R	73.0%	27.0%	73.0%	27.0%
803	ARTHUR	316	248	68		180 R	78.5%	21.5%	78.5%	21.5%
1,325	BANNER	514	329	185		144 R	64.0%	36.0%	64.0%	36.0%
1,203	BLAINE	565	416	149		267 R	73.6%	26.4%	73.6%	26.4%
10,721	BOONE	4,298	3,021	1,277		1,744 R	70.3%	29.7%	70.3%	29.7%
12,279	BOX BUTTE	4,353	2,991	1,362		1,629 R	68.7%	31.3%	68.7%	31.3%
4,911	BOYD	2,262	1,414	848		566 R	62.5%	37.5%	62.5%	37.5%
5,164	BROWN	2,114	1,566	548		1,018 R	74.1%	25.9%	74.1%	25.9%
25,134	BUFFALO	10,442	7,342	3,100		4,242 R	70.3%	29.7%	70.3%	29.7%
11,536	BURT	4,978	3,459	1,519		1,940 R	69.5%	30.5%	69.5%	30.5%
11,432	BUTLER	5,108	2,864	2,244		620 R	56.1%	43.9%	56.1%	43.9%
16,361	CASS	7,537	4,814	2,723		2,091 R	63.9%	36.1%	63.9%	36.1%
13,843	CEDAR	5,887	3,809	2,078		1,731 R	64.7%	35.3%	64.7%	35.3%
5,176	CHASE	2,114	1,444	670		774 R	68.3%	31.7%	68.3%	31.7%
8,397	CHERRY	3,298	2,414	884		1,530 R	73.2%	26.8%	73.2%	26.8%
12,081	CHEYENNE	5,991	3,809	2,182		1,627 R	63.6%	36.4%	63.6%	36.4%
8,700	CLAY	4,339	3,099	1,240		1,859 R	71.4%	28.6%	71.4%	28.6%
10,010	COLFAX	4,369	2,843	1,526		1,317 R	65.1%	34.9%	65.1%	34.9%
12,994	CUMING	5,525	4,223	1,302		2,921 R	76.4%	23.6%	76.4%	23.6%
19,170	CUSTER	8,223	5,798	2,425		3,373 R	70.5%	29.5%	70.5%	29.5%
10,401	DAKOTA	4,740	2,516	2,224		292 R	53.1%	46.9%	53.1%	46.9%
9,708	DAWES	3,416	2,523	893		1,630 R	73.9%	26.1%	73.9%	26.1%
19,393	DAWSON	8,542	6,503	2,039		4,464 R	76.1%	23.9%	76.1%	23.9%
3,330	DEUEL	1,459	1,165	294		871 R	79.8%	20.2%	79.8%	20.2%
9,129	DIXON	4,219	2,493	1,726		767 R	59.1%	40.9%	59.1%	40.9%
26,265	DODGE	13,298	9,210	4,088		5,122 R	69.3%	30.7%	69.3%	30.7%
281,020	DOUGLAS	123,380	73,270	50,110		23,160 R	59.4%	40.6%	59.4%	40.6%
4,354	DUNDY	1,691	1,196	495		701 R	70.7%	29.3%	70.7%	29.3%
9,610	FILLMORE	4,686	3,137	1,549		1,588 R	66.9%	33.1%	66.9%	33.1%
7,096	FRANKLIN	2,843	1,955	888		1,067 R	68.8%	31.2%	68.8%	31.2%
5,282	FRONTIER	2,236	1,602	634		968 R	71.6%	28.4%	71.6%	28.4%
9,385	FURNAS	4,005	2,894	1,111		1,783 R	72.3%	27.7%	72.3%	27.7%
28,052	GAGE	11,109	7,514	3,595		3,919 R	67.6%	32.4%	67.6%	32.4%
4,114	GARDEN	1,502	1,167	335		832 R	77.7%	22.3%	77.7%	22.3%
2,912	GARFIELD	1,198	936	262		674 R	78.1%	21.9%	78.1%	21.9%
2,734	GOSPER	1,139	814	325		489 R	71.5%	28.5%	71.5%	28.5%
1,057	GRANT	520	433	87		346 R	83.3%	16.7%	83.3%	16.7%
5,575	GREELEY	2,150	1,240	910		330 R	57.7%	42.3%	57.7%	42.3%
32,186	HALL	14,351	9,536	4,815		4,721 R	66.4%	33.6%	66.4%	33.6%
8,778	HAMILTON	4,292	3,217	1,075		2,142 R	75.0%	25.0%	75.0%	25.0%
7,189	HARLAN	2,698	1,850	848		1,002 R	68.6%	31.4%	68.6%	31.4%
2,404	HAYES	1,037	726	311		415 R	70.0%	30.0%	70.0%	30.0%
5,867	HITCHCOCK	2,311	1,570	741		829 R	67.9%	32.1%	67.9%	32.1%
14,859	HOLT	6,111	4,237	1,874		2,363 R	69.3%	30.7%	69.3%	30.7%
1,061	HOOKER	432	368	64		304 R	85.2%	14.8%	85.2%	14.8%
7,226	HOWARD	3,150	1,701	1,449		252 R	54.0%	46.0%	54.0%	46.0%
13,623	JEFFERSON	5,989	4,267	1,722		2,545 R	71.2%	28.8%	71.2%	28.8%
7,251	JOHNSON	3,300	2,160	1,140		1,020 R	65.5%	34.5%	65.5%	34.5%
6,409	KEARNEY	3,330	2,158	1,172		986 R	64.8%	35.2%	64.8%	35.2%
7,449	KEITH	3,554	2,624	930		1,694 R	73.8%	26.2%	73.8%	26.2%
2,160	KEYA PAHA	898	635	263		372 R	70.7%	29.3%	70.7%	29.3%
4,283	KIMBALL	2,246	1,590	656		934 R	70.8%	29.2%	70.8%	29.2%
14,820	KNOX	5,924	3,814	2,110		1,704 R	64.4%	35.6%	64.4%	35.6%
119,742	LANCASTER	54,808	35,591	19,217		16,374 R	64.9%	35.1%	64.9%	35.1%
27,380	LINCOLN	11,998	7,523	4,475		3,048 R	62.7%	37.3%	62.7%	37.3%
1,357	LOGAN	515	367	148		219 R	71.3%	28.7%	71.3%	28.7%
1,348	LOUP	580	441	139		302 R	76.0%	24.0%	76.0%	24.0%
825	MCPHERSON	379	281	98		183 R	74.1%	25.9%	74.1%	25.9%
24,338	MADISON	10,917	7,968	2,949		5,019 R	73.0%	27.0%	73.0%	27.0%

NEBRASKA

PRESIDENT 1956

1950 Census Population	County	Total Vote	Republican	Democratic	Other	Rep.-Dem. Plurality	Percentage Total Vote Rep.	Total Vote Dem.	Major Vote Rep.	Major Vote Dem.
8,812	MERRICK	3,983	2,857	1,126		1,731 R	71.7%	28.3%	71.7%	28.3%
8,263	MORRILL	2,839	1,810	1,029		781 R	63.8%	36.2%	63.8%	36.2%
6,512	NANCE	2,558	1,779	779		1,000 R	69.5%	30.5%	69.5%	30.5%
10,973	NEMAHA	4,575	3,141	1,434		1,707 R	68.7%	31.3%	68.7%	31.3%
9,609	NUCKOLLS	4,157	2,672	1,485		1,187 R	64.3%	35.7%	64.3%	35.7%
17,056	OTOE	7,571	5,275	2,296		2,979 R	69.7%	30.3%	69.7%	30.3%
6,744	PAWNEE	2,852	1,830	1,022		808 R	64.2%	35.8%	64.2%	35.8%
4,809	PERKINS	1,962	1,296	666		630 R	66.1%	33.9%	66.1%	33.9%
9,048	PHELPS	4,815	3,502	1,313		2,189 R	72.7%	27.3%	72.7%	27.3%
9,405	PIERCE	3,952	2,800	1,152		1,648 R	70.9%	29.1%	70.9%	29.1%
19,910	PLATTE	9,496	6,574	2,922		3,652 R	69.2%	30.8%	69.2%	30.8%
8,044	POLK	3,617	2,482	1,135		1,347 R	68.6%	31.4%	68.6%	31.4%
12,977	RED WILLOW	5,431	3,806	1,625		2,181 R	70.1%	29.9%	70.1%	29.9%
16,886	RICHARDSON	6,994	4,480	2,514		1,966 R	64.1%	35.9%	64.1%	35.9%
3,026	ROCK	1,209	928	281		647 R	76.8%	23.2%	76.8%	23.2%
14,046	SALINE	6,643	3,248	3,395		147 D	48.9%	51.1%	48.9%	51.1%
15,693	SARPY	6,327	3,826	2,501		1,325 R	60.5%	39.5%	60.5%	39.5%
16,923	SAUNDERS	8,308	4,973	3,335		1,638 R	59.9%	40.1%	59.9%	40.1%
33,939	SCOTTS BLUFF	12,717	8,027	4,690		3,337 R	63.1%	36.9%	63.1%	36.9%
13,155	SEWARD	5,598	3,688	1,910		1,778 R	65.9%	34.1%	65.9%	34.1%
9,539	SHERIDAN	3,511	2,618	893		1,725 R	74.6%	25.4%	74.6%	25.4%
6,421	SHERMAN	2,648	1,429	1,219		210 R	54.0%	46.0%	54.0%	46.0%
3,124	SIOUX	759	499	260		239 R	65.7%	34.3%	65.7%	34.3%
6,387	STANTON	2,573	1,676	897		779 R	65.1%	34.9%	65.1%	34.9%
10,563	THAYER	4,793	3,346	1,447		1,899 R	69.8%	30.2%	69.8%	30.2%
1,206	THOMAS	543	422	121		301 R	77.7%	22.3%	77.7%	22.3%
8,590	THURSTON	3,128	1,722	1,406		316 R	55.1%	44.9%	55.1%	44.9%
7,252	VALLEY	3,278	2,189	1,089		1,100 R	66.8%	33.2%	66.8%	33.2%
11,511	WASHINGTON	5,262	3,531	1,731		1,800 R	67.1%	32.9%	67.1%	32.9%
10,129	WAYNE	4,183	3,040	1,143		1,897 R	72.7%	27.3%	72.7%	27.3%
7,395	WEBSTER	3,254	2,298	956		1,342 R	70.6%	29.4%	70.6%	29.4%
1,526	WHEELER	609	391	218		173 R	64.2%	35.8%	64.2%	35.8%
14,346	YORK	6,634	5,065	1,569		3,496 R	76.3%	23.7%	76.3%	23.7%
1,325,510	TOTAL	577,137	378,108	199,029		179,079 R	65.5%	34.5%	65.5%	34.5%

NEBRASKA

PRESIDENT 1952

1950 Census Population	County	Total Vote	Republican	Democratic	Other	Rep.-Dem. Plurality	Percentage Total Vote Rep.	Percentage Total Vote Dem.	Percentage Major Vote Rep.	Percentage Major Vote Dem.
28,855	ADAMS	12,778	9,033	3,745		5,288 R	70.7%	29.3%	70.7%	29.3%
11,624	ANTELOPE	5,445	4,377	1,068		3,309 R	80.4%	19.6%	80.4%	19.6%
803	ARTHUR	369	307	62		245 R	83.2%	16.8%	83.2%	16.8%
1,325	BANNER	623	484	139		345 R	77.7%	22.3%	77.7%	22.3%
1,203	BLAINE	595	458	137		321 R	77.0%	23.0%	77.0%	23.0%
10,721	BOONE	4,736	3,453	1,283		2,170 R	72.9%	27.1%	72.9%	27.1%
12,279	BOX BUTTE	5,665	4,426	1,239		3,187 R	78.1%	21.9%	78.1%	21.9%
4,911	BOYD	2,413	1,656	757		899 R	68.6%	31.4%	68.6%	31.4%
5,164	BROWN	2,493	1,950	543		1,407 R	78.2%	21.8%	78.2%	21.8%
25,134	BUFFALO	10,968	8,467	2,501		5,966 R	77.2%	22.8%	77.2%	22.8%
11,536	BURT	5,397	4,154	1,243		2,911 R	77.0%	23.0%	77.0%	23.0%
11,432	BUTLER	5,413	3,459	1,954		1,505 R	63.9%	36.1%	63.9%	36.1%
16,361	CASS	7,690	5,088	2,602		2,486 R	66.2%	33.8%	66.2%	33.8%
13,843	CEDAR	6,170	4,753	1,417		3,336 R	77.0%	23.0%	77.0%	23.0%
5,176	CHASE	2,404	1,941	463		1,478 R	80.7%	19.3%	80.7%	19.3%
8,397	CHERRY	4,108	3,148	960		2,188 R	76.6%	23.4%	76.6%	23.4%
12,081	CHEYENNE	6,423	4,206	2,217		1,989 R	65.5%	34.5%	65.5%	34.5%
8,700	CLAY	4,674	3,559	1,115		2,444 R	76.1%	23.9%	76.1%	23.9%
10,010	COLFAX	4,790	3,332	1,458		1,874 R	69.6%	30.4%	69.6%	30.4%
12,994	CUMING	5,652	4,557	1,095		3,462 R	80.6%	19.4%	80.6%	19.4%
19,170	CUSTER	9,256	7,143	2,113		5,030 R	77.2%	22.8%	77.2%	22.8%
10,401	DAKOTA	4,606	2,643	1,963		680 R	57.4%	42.6%	57.4%	42.6%
9,708	DAWES	4,740	3,583	1,157		2,426 R	75.6%	24.4%	75.6%	24.4%
19,393	DAWSON	8,950	7,130	1,820		5,310 R	79.7%	20.3%	79.7%	20.3%
3,330	DEUEL	1,613	1,372	241		1,131 R	85.1%	14.9%	85.1%	14.9%
9,129	DIXON	4,226	2,977	1,249		1,728 R	70.4%	29.6%	70.4%	29.6%
26,265	DODGE	12,938	9,256	3,682		5,574 R	71.5%	28.5%	71.5%	28.5%
281,020	DOUGLAS	127,048	71,457	55,591		15,866 R	56.2%	43.8%	56.2%	43.8%
4,354	DUNDY	2,067	1,670	397		1,273 R	80.8%	19.2%	80.8%	19.2%
9,610	FILLMORE	4,819	3,603	1,216		2,387 R	74.8%	25.2%	74.8%	25.2%
7,096	FRANKLIN	3,213	2,438	775		1,663 R	75.9%	24.1%	75.9%	24.1%
5,282	FRONTIER	2,569	1,980	589		1,391 R	77.1%	22.9%	77.1%	22.9%
9,385	FURNAS	4,482	3,464	1,018		2,446 R	77.3%	22.7%	77.3%	22.7%
28,052	GAGE	12,071	8,917	3,154		5,763 R	73.9%	26.1%	73.9%	26.1%
4,114	GARDEN	1,798	1,457	341		1,116 R	81.0%	19.0%	81.0%	19.0%
2,912	GARFIELD	1,295	1,042	253		789 R	80.5%	19.5%	80.5%	19.5%
2,734	GOSPER	1,310	1,017	293		724 R	77.6%	22.4%	77.6%	22.4%
1,057	GRANT	557	452	105		347 R	81.1%	18.9%	81.1%	18.9%
5,575	GREELEY	2,467	1,543	924		619 R	62.5%	37.5%	62.5%	37.5%
32,186	HALL	15,043	10,435	4,608		5,827 R	69.4%	30.6%	69.4%	30.6%
8,778	HAMILTON	4,709	3,579	1,130		2,449 R	76.0%	24.0%	76.0%	24.0%
7,189	HARLAN	3,030	2,300	730		1,570 R	75.9%	24.1%	75.9%	24.1%
2,404	HAYES	1,152	932	220		712 R	80.9%	19.1%	80.9%	19.1%
5,867	HITCHCOCK	2,677	2,008	669		1,339 R	75.0%	25.0%	75.0%	25.0%
14,859	HOLT	6,814	5,088	1,726		3,362 R	74.7%	25.3%	74.7%	25.3%
1,061	HOOKER	483	411	72		339 R	85.1%	14.9%	85.1%	14.9%
7,226	HOWARD	3,571	2,115	1,456		659 R	59.2%	40.8%	59.2%	40.8%
13,623	JEFFERSON	6,491	4,941	1,550		3,391 R	76.1%	23.9%	76.1%	23.9%
7,251	JOHNSON	3,765	2,787	978		1,809 R	74.0%	26.0%	74.0%	26.0%
6,409	KEARNEY	3,352	2,422	930		1,492 R	72.3%	27.7%	72.3%	27.7%
7,449	KEITH	3,559	2,790	769		2,021 R	78.4%	21.6%	78.4%	21.6%
2,160	KEYA PAHA	993	785	208		577 R	79.1%	20.9%	79.1%	20.9%
4,283	KIMBALL	2,121	1,646	475		1,171 R	77.6%	22.4%	77.6%	22.4%
14,820	KNOX	6,413	4,840	1,573		3,267 R	75.5%	24.5%	75.5%	24.5%
119,742	LANCASTER	54,525	36,797	17,728		19,069 R	67.5%	32.5%	67.5%	32.5%
27,380	LINCOLN	12,018	8,292	3,726		4,566 R	69.0%	31.0%	69.0%	31.0%
1,357	LOGAN	603	447	156		291 R	74.1%	25.9%	74.1%	25.9%
1,348	LOUP	616	507	109		398 R	82.3%	17.7%	82.3%	17.7%
825	MCPHERSON	408	355	53		302 R	87.0%	13.0%	87.0%	13.0%
24,338	MADISON	10,883	8,294	2,589		5,705 R	76.2%	23.8%	76.2%	23.8%

NEBRASKA

PRESIDENT 1952

1950 Census Population	County	Total Vote	Republican	Democratic	Other	Rep.-Dem. Plurality	Percentage Total Vote Rep.	Total Vote Dem.	Major Vote Rep.	Major Vote Dem.
8,812	MERRICK	4,253	3,288	965		2,323 R	77.3%	22.7%	77.3%	22.7%
8,263	MORRILL	3,382	2,485	897		1,588 R	73.5%	26.5%	73.5%	26.5%
6,512	NANCE	2,863	2,112	751		1,361 R	73.8%	26.2%	73.8%	26.2%
10,973	NEMAHA	5,167	3,735	1,432		2,303 R	72.3%	27.7%	72.3%	27.7%
9,609	NUCKOLLS	4,622	3,251	1,371		1,880 R	70.3%	29.7%	70.3%	29.7%
17,056	OTOE	8,021	6,082	1,939		4,143 R	75.8%	24.2%	75.8%	24.2%
6,744	PAWNEE	3,242	2,432	810		1,622 R	75.0%	25.0%	75.0%	25.0%
4,809	PERKINS	2,088	1,637	451		1,186 R	78.4%	21.6%	78.4%	21.6%
9,048	PHELPS	4,901	3,822	1,079		2,743 R	78.0%	22.0%	78.0%	22.0%
9,405	PIERCE	4,143	3,234	909		2,325 R	78.1%	21.9%	78.1%	21.9%
19,910	PLATTE	9,340	6,695	2,645		4,050 R	71.7%	28.3%	71.7%	28.3%
8,044	POLK	3,924	3,008	916		2,092 R	76.7%	23.3%	76.7%	23.3%
12,977	RED WILLOW	6,064	4,433	1,631		2,802 R	73.1%	26.9%	73.1%	26.9%
16,886	RICHARDSON	8,050	5,688	2,362		3,326 R	70.7%	29.3%	70.7%	29.3%
3,026	ROCK	1,493	1,226	267		959 R	82.1%	17.9%	82.1%	17.9%
14,046	SALINE	7,013	4,221	2,792		1,429 R	60.2%	39.8%	60.2%	39.8%
15,693	SARPY	6,178	3,649	2,529		1,120 R	59.1%	40.9%	59.1%	40.9%
16,923	SAUNDERS	8,487	5,525	2,962		2,563 R	65.1%	34.9%	65.1%	34.9%
33,939	SCOTTS BLUFF	13,263	9,674	3,589		6,085 R	72.9%	27.1%	72.9%	27.1%
13,155	SEWARD	5,942	4,257	1,685		2,572 R	71.6%	28.4%	71.6%	28.4%
9,539	SHERIDAN	4,353	3,512	841		2,671 R	80.7%	19.3%	80.7%	19.3%
6,421	SHERMAN	2,950	1,784	1,166		618 R	60.5%	39.5%	60.5%	39.5%
3,124	SIOUX	1,393	1,093	300		793 R	78.5%	21.5%	78.5%	21.5%
6,387	STANTON	2,655	1,983	672		1,311 R	74.7%	25.3%	74.7%	25.3%
10,563	THAYER	5,258	3,992	1,266		2,726 R	75.9%	24.1%	75.9%	24.1%
1,206	THOMAS	610	490	120		370 R	80.3%	19.7%	80.3%	19.7%
8,590	THURSTON	3,092	1,918	1,174		744 R	62.0%	38.0%	62.0%	38.0%
7,252	VALLEY	3,657	2,630	1,027		1,603 R	71.9%	28.1%	71.9%	28.1%
11,511	WASHINGTON	5,455	3,770	1,685		2,085 R	69.1%	30.9%	69.1%	30.9%
10,129	WAYNE	4,204	3,338	866		2,472 R	79.4%	20.6%	79.4%	20.6%
7,395	WEBSTER	3,644	2,719	925		1,794 R	74.6%	25.4%	74.6%	25.4%
1,526	WHEELER	686	455	231		224 R	66.3%	33.7%	66.3%	33.7%
14,346	YORK	7,210	5,742	1,468		4,274 R	79.6%	20.4%	79.6%	20.4%
1,325,510	TOTAL	609,660	421,603	188,057		233,546 R	69.2%	30.8%	69.2%	30.8%

NEBRASKA

PRESIDENT 1948

1940 Census Population	County	Total Vote	Republican	Democratic	Other	Rep.-Dem. Plurality	Percentage Total Vote Rep.	Percentage Total Vote Dem.	Percentage Major Vote Rep.	Percentage Major Vote Dem.
24,576	ADAMS	10,212	5,560	4,652		908 R	54.4%	45.6%	54.4%	45.6%
13,289	ANTELOPE	4,741	2,868	1,873		995 R	60.5%	39.5%	60.5%	39.5%
1,045	ARTHUR	346	199	147		52 R	57.5%	42.5%	57.5%	42.5%
1,403	BANNER	538	309	229		80 R	57.4%	42.6%	57.4%	42.6%
1,538	BLAINE	500	252	248		4 R	50.4%	49.6%	50.4%	49.6%
12,127	BOONE	4,013	2,235	1,778		457 R	55.7%	44.3%	55.7%	44.3%
10,736	BOX BUTTE	4,374	2,351	2,023		328 R	53.7%	46.3%	53.7%	46.3%
6,060	BOYD	2,095	1,060	1,035		25 R	50.6%	49.4%	50.6%	49.4%
5,962	BROWN	1,874	1,174	700		474 R	62.6%	37.4%	62.6%	37.4%
23,655	BUFFALO	8,578	4,862	3,716		1,146 R	56.7%	43.3%	56.7%	43.3%
12,546	BURT	4,556	2,656	1,900		756 R	58.3%	41.7%	58.3%	41.7%
13,106	BUTLER	4,710	2,105	2,605		500 D	44.7%	55.3%	44.7%	55.3%
16,992	CASS	6,568	3,527	3,041		486 R	53.7%	46.3%	53.7%	46.3%
15,126	CEDAR	5,194	2,616	2,578		38 R	50.4%	49.6%	50.4%	49.6%
5,310	CHASE	1,830	1,094	736		358 R	59.8%	40.2%	59.8%	40.2%
9,637	CHERRY	3,633	2,141	1,492		649 R	58.9%	41.1%	58.9%	41.1%
9,505	CHEYENNE	4,300	2,161	2,139		22 R	50.3%	49.7%	50.3%	49.7%
10,445	CLAY	4,100	2,511	1,589		922 R	61.2%	38.8%	61.2%	38.8%
10,627	COLFAX	3,825	1,928	1,897		31 R	50.4%	49.6%	50.4%	49.6%
13,562	CUMING	4,587	2,930	1,657		1,273 R	63.9%	36.1%	63.9%	36.1%
22,591	CUSTER	7,413	4,057	3,356		701 R	54.7%	45.3%	54.7%	45.3%
9,836	DAKOTA	3,751	1,379	2,372		993 D	36.8%	63.2%	36.8%	63.2%
10,128	DAWES	3,898	2,399	1,499		900 R	61.5%	38.5%	61.5%	38.5%
17,890	DAWSON	6,806	4,203	2,603		1,600 R	61.8%	38.2%	61.8%	38.2%
3,580	DEUEL	1,455	1,043	412		631 R	71.7%	28.3%	71.7%	28.3%
10,413	DIXON	3,621	1,899	1,722		177 R	52.4%	47.6%	52.4%	47.6%
23,799	DODGE	10,718	5,848	4,870		978 R	54.6%	45.4%	54.6%	45.4%
247,562	DOUGLAS	96,433	47,175	49,258		2,083 D	48.9%	51.1%	48.9%	51.1%
5,122	DUNDY	1,581	935	646		289 R	59.1%	40.9%	59.1%	40.9%
11,417	FILLMORE	4,573	2,677	1,896		781 R	58.5%	41.5%	58.5%	41.5%
7,740	FRANKLIN	2,895	1,555	1,340		215 R	53.7%	46.3%	53.7%	46.3%
6,417	FRONTIER	2,154	1,307	846	1	461 R	60.7%	39.3%	60.7%	39.3%
10,098	FURNAS	3,752	2,258	1,494		764 R	60.2%	39.8%	60.2%	39.8%
29,588	GAGE	9,435	5,311	4,124		1,187 R	56.3%	43.7%	56.3%	43.7%
4,680	GARDEN	1,442	923	519		404 R	64.0%	36.0%	64.0%	36.0%
3,444	GARFIELD	1,244	702	542		160 R	56.4%	43.6%	56.4%	43.6%
3,687	GOSPER	1,193	621	572		49 R	52.1%	47.9%	52.1%	47.9%
1,327	GRANT	412	273	139		134 R	66.3%	33.7%	66.3%	33.7%
6,845	GREELEY	2,094	829	1,265		436 D	39.6%	60.4%	39.6%	60.4%
27,523	HALL	10,284	5,694	4,590		1,104 R	55.4%	44.6%	55.4%	44.6%
9,982	HAMILTON	3,915	2,406	1,509		897 R	61.5%	38.5%	61.5%	38.5%
7,130	HARLAN	2,710	1,490	1,220		270 R	55.0%	45.0%	55.0%	45.0%
2,958	HAYES	947	529	418		111 R	55.9%	44.1%	55.9%	44.1%
6,404	HITCHCOCK	2,131	1,208	923		285 R	56.7%	43.3%	56.7%	43.3%
16,552	HOLT	5,769	3,147	2,622		525 R	54.6%	45.4%	54.6%	45.4%
1,253	HOOKER	335	249	86		163 R	74.3%	25.7%	74.3%	25.7%
8,422	HOWARD	3,026	1,133	1,893		760 D	37.4%	62.6%	37.4%	62.6%
15,532	JEFFERSON	5,560	3,352	2,208		1,144 R	60.3%	39.7%	60.3%	39.7%
8,662	JOHNSON	3,108	1,817	1,291		526 R	58.5%	41.5%	58.5%	41.5%
6,854	KEARNEY	2,840	1,440	1,400		40 R	50.7%	49.3%	50.7%	49.3%
8,333	KEITH	2,709	1,600	1,109		491 R	59.1%	40.9%	59.1%	40.9%
3,235	KEYA PAHA	935	538	397		141 R	57.5%	42.5%	57.5%	42.5%
3,913	KIMBALL	1,696	1,024	672		352 R	60.4%	39.6%	60.4%	39.6%
16,478	KNOX	5,375	2,778	2,597		181 R	51.7%	48.3%	51.7%	48.3%
100,585	LANCASTER	41,958	23,620	18,338		5,282 R	56.3%	43.7%	56.3%	43.7%
25,425	LINCOLN	8,550	4,419	4,131		288 R	51.7%	48.3%	51.7%	48.3%
1,742	LOGAN	487	254	233		21 R	52.2%	47.8%	52.2%	47.8%
1,777	LOUP	557	294	263		31 R	52.8%	47.2%	52.8%	47.2%
1,175	MCPHERSON	307	209	98		111 R	68.1%	31.9%	68.1%	31.9%
24,269	MADISON	8,790	5,486	3,304		2,182 R	62.4%	37.6%	62.4%	37.6%

NEBRASKA

PRESIDENT 1948

1940 Census Population	County	Total Vote	Republican	Democratic	Other	Rep.-Dem. Plurality	Total Vote Rep.	Total Vote Dem.	Major Vote Rep.	Major Vote Dem.
9,354	MERRICK	3,341	2,074	1,267		807 R	62.1%	37.9%	62.1%	37.9%
9,436	MORRILL	2,798	1,478	1,320		158 R	52.8%	47.2%	52.8%	47.2%
7,653	NANCE	2,358	1,339	1,019		320 R	56.8%	43.2%	56.8%	43.2%
12,781	NEMAHA	4,100	2,413	1,687		726 R	58.9%	41.1%	58.9%	41.1%
10,446	NUCKOLLS	3,863	2,036	1,827		209 R	52.7%	47.3%	52.7%	47.3%
18,994	OTOE	6,575	4,060	2,515		1,545 R	61.7%	38.3%	61.7%	38.3%
8,514	PAWNEE	2,996	1,725	1,271		454 R	57.6%	42.4%	57.6%	42.4%
5,197	PERKINS	1,767	904	863		41 R	51.2%	48.8%	51.2%	48.8%
8,452	PHELPS	4,304	2,489	1,815		674 R	57.8%	42.2%	57.8%	42.2%
10,211	PIERCE	3,249	1,866	1,383		483 R	57.4%	42.6%	57.4%	42.6%
20,191	PLATTE	7,129	3,812	3,317		495 R	53.5%	46.5%	53.5%	46.5%
8,748	POLK	3,422	2,026	1,396		630 R	59.2%	40.8%	59.2%	40.8%
11,951	RED WILLOW	4,848	2,610	2,238		372 R	53.8%	46.2%	53.8%	46.2%
19,178	RICHARDSON	7,297	3,778	3,519		259 R	51.8%	48.2%	51.8%	48.2%
3,977	ROCK	1,264	809	455		354 R	64.0%	36.0%	64.0%	36.0%
15,010	SALINE	6,239	2,641	3,598		957 D	42.3%	57.7%	42.3%	57.7%
10,835	SARPY	5,002	2,367	2,635		268 D	47.3%	52.7%	47.3%	52.7%
17,892	SAUNDERS	7,639	3,660	3,979		319 D	47.9%	52.1%	47.9%	52.1%
33,917	SCOTTS BLUFF	9,795	5,409	4,386		1,023 R	55.2%	44.8%	55.2%	44.8%
14,167	SEWARD	5,190	2,916	2,274		642 R	56.2%	43.8%	56.2%	43.8%
9,869	SHERIDAN	3,361	2,180	1,181		999 R	64.9%	35.1%	64.9%	35.1%
7,764	SHERMAN	2,611	1,003	1,608		605 D	38.4%	61.6%	38.4%	61.6%
4,001	SIOUX	1,177	657	520		137 R	55.8%	44.2%	55.8%	44.2%
6,887	STANTON	2,248	1,259	989		270 R	56.0%	44.0%	56.0%	44.0%
12,262	THAYER	4,532	2,601	1,931		670 R	57.4%	42.6%	57.4%	42.6%
1,553	THOMAS	550	312	238		74 R	56.7%	43.3%	56.7%	43.3%
10,243	THURSTON	3,039	1,149	1,890		741 D	37.8%	62.2%	37.8%	62.2%
8,163	VALLEY	3,055	1,670	1,385		285 R	54.7%	45.3%	54.7%	45.3%
11,578	WASHINGTON	4,306	2,400	1,906		494 R	55.7%	44.3%	55.7%	44.3%
9,880	WAYNE	3,481	2,323	1,158		1,165 R	66.7%	33.3%	66.7%	33.3%
8,071	WEBSTER	3,329	1,964	1,365		599 R	59.0%	41.0%	59.0%	41.0%
2,170	WHEELER	591	264	327		63 D	44.7%	55.3%	44.7%	55.3%
14,874	YORK	6,051	3,960	2,091		1,869 R	65.4%	34.6%	65.4%	34.6%
1,315,834	TOTAL	488,940	264,774	224,165	1	40,609 R	54.2%	45.8%	54.2%	45.8%

NEBRASKA

PRESIDENT 1944

1940 Census Population	County	Total Vote	Republican	Democratic	Other	Rep.-Dem. Plurality	Percentage: Total Vote Rep.	Total Vote Dem.	Major Vote Rep.	Major Vote Dem.
24,576	ADAMS	11,777	7,165	4,612		2,553 R	60.8%	39.2%	60.8%	39.2%
13,289	ANTELOPE	5,506	3,888	1,618		2,270 R	70.6%	29.4%	70.6%	29.4%
1,045	ARTHUR	421	268	153		115 R	63.7%	36.3%	63.7%	36.3%
1,403	BANNER	532	378	154		224 R	71.1%	28.9%	71.1%	28.9%
1,538	BLAINE	614	366	248		118 R	59.6%	40.4%	59.6%	40.4%
12,127	BOONE	4,530	2,865	1,665		1,200 R	63.2%	36.8%	63.2%	36.8%
10,736	BOX BUTTE	4,730	2,994	1,736		1,258 R	63.3%	36.7%	63.3%	36.7%
6,060	BOYD	2,351	1,456	895		561 R	61.9%	38.1%	61.9%	38.1%
5,962	BROWN	2,294	1,549	745		804 R	67.5%	32.5%	67.5%	32.5%
23,655	BUFFALO	9,925	6,073	3,852		2,221 R	61.2%	38.8%	61.2%	38.8%
12,546	BURT	5,351	3,189	2,162		1,027 R	59.6%	40.4%	59.6%	40.4%
13,106	BUTLER	5,415	2,493	2,922		429 D	46.0%	54.0%	46.0%	54.0%
16,992	CASS	7,732	4,588	3,144		1,444 R	59.3%	40.7%	59.3%	40.7%
15,126	CEDAR	5,455	3,616	1,839		1,777 R	66.3%	33.7%	66.3%	33.7%
5,310	CHASE	2,092	1,444	648		796 R	69.0%	31.0%	69.0%	31.0%
9,637	CHERRY	3,685	2,314	1,371		943 R	62.8%	37.2%	62.8%	37.2%
9,505	CHEYENNE	4,406	2,654	1,752		902 R	60.2%	39.8%	60.2%	39.8%
10,445	CLAY	4,905	3,375	1,530		1,845 R	68.8%	31.2%	68.8%	31.2%
10,627	COLFAX	4,492	2,314	2,178		136 R	51.5%	48.5%	51.5%	48.5%
13,562	CUMING	5,409	4,008	1,401		2,607 R	74.1%	25.9%	74.1%	25.9%
22,591	CUSTER	8,651	5,330	3,321		2,009 R	61.6%	38.4%	61.6%	38.4%
9,836	DAKOTA	3,692	1,703	1,989		286 D	46.1%	53.9%	46.1%	53.9%
10,128	DAWES	4,194	2,747	1,447		1,300 R	65.5%	34.5%	65.5%	34.5%
17,890	DAWSON	7,287	5,017	2,270		2,747 R	68.8%	31.2%	68.8%	31.2%
3,580	DEUEL	1,531	1,125	406		719 R	73.5%	26.5%	73.5%	26.5%
10,413	DIXON	3,845	2,382	1,463		919 R	62.0%	38.0%	62.0%	38.0%
23,799	DODGE	11,081	6,803	4,278		2,525 R	61.4%	38.6%	61.4%	38.6%
247,562	DOUGLAS	117,205	53,443	63,762		10,319 D	45.6%	54.4%	45.6%	54.4%
5,122	DUNDY	1,933	1,320	613		707 R	68.3%	31.7%	68.3%	31.7%
11,417	FILLMORE	5,150	3,362	1,788		1,574 R	65.3%	34.7%	65.3%	34.7%
7,740	FRANKLIN	3,054	2,085	969		1,116 R	68.3%	31.7%	68.3%	31.7%
6,417	FRONTIER	2,613	1,855	758		1,097 R	71.0%	29.0%	71.0%	29.0%
10,098	FURNAS	4,199	2,870	1,329		1,541 R	68.3%	31.7%	68.3%	31.7%
29,588	GAGE	11,590	7,352	4,238		3,114 R	63.4%	36.6%	63.4%	36.6%
4,680	GARDEN	1,789	1,248	541		707 R	69.8%	30.2%	69.8%	30.2%
3,444	GARFIELD	1,304	896	408		488 R	68.7%	31.3%	68.7%	31.3%
3,687	GOSPER	1,419	935	484		451 R	65.9%	34.1%	65.9%	34.1%
1,327	GRANT	499	327	172		155 R	65.5%	34.5%	65.5%	34.5%
6,845	GREELEY	2,507	1,242	1,265		23 D	49.5%	50.5%	49.5%	50.5%
27,523	HALL	12,419	7,651	4,768		2,883 R	61.6%	38.4%	61.6%	38.4%
9,982	HAMILTON	4,387	3,057	1,330		1,727 R	69.7%	30.3%	69.7%	30.3%
7,130	HARLAN	2,997	1,991	1,006		985 R	66.4%	33.6%	66.4%	33.6%
2,958	HAYES	1,169	782	387		395 R	66.9%	33.1%	66.9%	33.1%
6,404	HITCHCOCK	2,433	1,556	877		679 R	64.0%	36.0%	64.0%	36.0%
16,552	HOLT	6,763	4,198	2,565		1,633 R	62.1%	37.9%	62.1%	37.9%
1,253	HOOKER	433	330	103		227 R	76.2%	23.8%	76.2%	23.8%
8,422	HOWARD	3,598	1,556	2,042		486 D	43.2%	56.8%	43.2%	56.8%
15,532	JEFFERSON	6,444	4,257	2,187		2,070 R	66.1%	33.9%	66.1%	33.9%
8,662	JOHNSON	3,668	2,649	1,019		1,630 R	72.2%	27.8%	72.2%	27.8%
6,854	KEARNEY	3,049	1,782	1,267		515 R	58.4%	41.6%	58.4%	41.6%
8,333	KEITH	2,886	1,739	1,147		592 R	60.3%	39.7%	60.3%	39.7%
3,235	KEYA PAHA	1,115	781	334		447 R	70.0%	30.0%	70.0%	30.0%
3,913	KIMBALL	1,745	1,169	576		593 R	67.0%	33.0%	67.0%	33.0%
16,478	KNOX	6,249	3,762	2,487		1,275 R	60.2%	39.8%	60.2%	39.8%
100,585	LANCASTER	46,053	26,715	19,338		7,377 R	58.0%	42.0%	58.0%	42.0%
25,425	LINCOLN	10,313	5,969	4,344		1,625 R	57.9%	42.1%	57.9%	42.1%
1,742	LOGAN	694	450	244		206 R	64.8%	35.2%	64.8%	35.2%
1,777	LOUP	670	488	182		306 R	72.8%	27.2%	72.8%	27.2%
1,175	MCPHERSON	428	310	118		192 R	72.4%	27.6%	72.4%	27.6%
24,269	MADISON	10,265	6,892	3,373		3,519 R	67.1%	32.9%	67.1%	32.9%

NEBRASKA

PRESIDENT 1944

1940 Census Population	County	Total Vote	Republican	Democratic	Other	Rep.-Dem. Plurality	Percentage Total Vote Rep.	Total Vote Dem.	Major Vote Rep.	Major Vote Dem.
9,354	MERRICK	4,081	2,691	1,390		1,301 R	65.9%	34.1%	65.9%	34.1%
9,436	MORRILL	3,106	1,998	1,108		890 R	64.3%	35.7%	64.3%	35.7%
7,653	NANCE	2,810	1,697	1,113		584 R	60.4%	39.6%	60.4%	39.6%
12,781	NEMAHA	5,052	3,267	1,785		1,482 R	64.7%	35.3%	64.7%	35.3%
10,446	NUCKOLLS	4,292	2,685	1,607		1,078 R	62.6%	37.4%	62.6%	37.4%
18,994	OTOE	7,955	5,291	2,664		2,627 R	66.5%	33.5%	66.5%	33.5%
8,514	PAWNEE	3,529	2,254	1,275		979 R	63.9%	36.1%	63.9%	36.1%
5,197	PERKINS	2,107	1,301	806		495 R	61.7%	38.3%	61.7%	38.3%
8,452	PHELPS	3,911	2,460	1,451		1,009 R	62.9%	37.1%	62.9%	37.1%
10,211	PIERCE	4,160	2,956	1,204		1,752 R	71.1%	28.9%	71.1%	28.9%
20,191	PLATTE	7,957	4,509	3,448		1,061 R	56.7%	43.3%	56.7%	43.3%
8,748	POLK	3,874	2,357	1,517		840 R	60.8%	39.2%	60.8%	39.2%
11,951	RED WILLOW	5,239	3,107	2,132		975 R	59.3%	40.7%	59.3%	40.7%
19,178	RICHARDSON	7,965	4,482	3,483		999 R	56.3%	43.7%	56.3%	43.7%
3,977	ROCK	1,490	984	506		478 R	66.0%	34.0%	66.0%	34.0%
15,010	SALINE	7,154	3,255	3,899		644 D	45.5%	54.5%	45.5%	54.5%
10,835	SARPY	5,295	2,641	2,654		13 D	49.9%	50.1%	49.9%	50.1%
17,892	SAUNDERS	10,814	6,615	4,199		2,416 R	61.2%	38.8%	61.2%	38.8%
33,917	SCOTTS BLUFF	10,680	6,947	3,733		3,214 R	65.0%	35.0%	65.0%	35.0%
14,167	SEWARD	5,804	3,721	2,083		1,638 R	64.1%	35.9%	64.1%	35.9%
9,869	SHERIDAN	3,601	2,570	1,031		1,539 R	71.4%	28.6%	71.4%	28.6%
7,764	SHERMAN	2,893	1,309	1,584		275 D	45.2%	54.8%	45.2%	54.8%
4,001	SIOUX	1,284	876	408		468 R	68.2%	31.8%	68.2%	31.8%
6,887	STANTON	2,556	1,682	874		808 R	65.8%	34.2%	65.8%	34.2%
12,262	THAYER	5,198	3,554	1,644		1,910 R	68.4%	31.6%	68.4%	31.6%
1,553	THOMAS	552	338	214		124 R	61.2%	38.8%	61.2%	38.8%
10,243	THURSTON	3,216	1,584	1,632		48 D	49.3%	50.7%	49.3%	50.7%
8,163	VALLEY	3,571	2,096	1,475		621 R	58.7%	41.3%	58.7%	41.3%
11,578	WASHINGTON	5,118	2,844	2,274		570 R	55.6%	44.4%	55.6%	44.4%
9,880	WAYNE	3,907	2,886	1,021		1,865 R	73.9%	26.1%	73.9%	26.1%
8,071	WEBSTER	3,617	2,523	1,094		1,429 R	69.8%	30.2%	69.8%	30.2%
2,170	WHEELER	702	392	310		82 R	55.8%	44.2%	55.8%	44.2%
14,874	YORK	6,693	4,885	1,808		3,077 R	73.0%	27.0%	73.0%	27.0%
1,315,834	TOTAL	563,126	329,880	233,246		96,634 R	58.6%	41.4%	58.6%	41.4%

NEBRASKA

PRESIDENT 1940

1940 Census Population	County	Total Vote	Republican	Democratic	Other	Rep.-Dem. Plurality	Percentage Total Vote Rep.	Total Vote Dem.	Major Vote Rep.	Major Vote Dem.
24,576	ADAMS	10,941	6,630	4,311		2,319 R	60.6%	39.4%	60.6%	39.4%
13,289	ANTELOPE	6,486	4,331	2,155		2,176 R	66.8%	33.2%	66.8%	33.2%
1,045	ARTHUR	542	348	194		154 R	64.2%	35.8%	64.2%	35.8%
1,403	BANNER	676	450	226		224 R	66.6%	33.4%	66.6%	33.4%
1,538	BLAINE	765	454	311		143 R	59.3%	40.7%	59.3%	40.7%
12,127	BOONE	5,348	3,334	2,014		1,320 R	62.3%	37.7%	62.3%	37.7%
10,736	BOX BUTTE	5,137	2,942	2,195		747 R	57.3%	42.7%	57.3%	42.7%
6,060	BOYD	2,791	1,734	1,057		677 R	62.1%	37.9%	62.1%	37.9%
5,962	BROWN	2,758	1,783	975		808 R	64.6%	35.4%	64.6%	35.4%
23,655	BUFFALO	10,447	6,387	4,060		2,327 R	61.1%	38.9%	61.1%	38.9%
12,546	BURT	6,032	3,443	2,589		854 R	57.1%	42.9%	57.1%	42.9%
13,106	BUTLER	6,212	2,966	3,246		280 D	47.7%	52.3%	47.7%	52.3%
16,992	CASS	8,331	4,704	3,627		1,077 R	56.5%	43.5%	56.5%	43.5%
15,126	CEDAR	7,016	4,397	2,619		1,778 R	62.7%	37.3%	62.7%	37.3%
5,310	CHASE	2,461	1,557	904		653 R	63.3%	36.7%	63.3%	36.7%
9,637	CHERRY	4,486	2,705	1,781		924 R	60.3%	39.7%	60.3%	39.7%
9,505	CHEYENNE	4,337	2,394	1,943		451 R	55.2%	44.8%	55.2%	44.8%
10,445	CLAY	5,339	3,576	1,763		1,813 R	67.0%	33.0%	67.0%	33.0%
10,627	COLFAX	4,948	2,587	2,361		226 R	52.3%	47.7%	52.3%	47.7%
13,562	CUMING	5,978	4,383	1,595		2,788 R	73.3%	26.7%	73.3%	26.7%
22,591	CUSTER	10,507	6,269	4,238		2,031 R	59.7%	40.3%	59.7%	40.3%
9,836	DAKOTA	4,562	2,140	2,422		282 D	46.9%	53.1%	46.9%	53.1%
10,128	DAWES	4,955	3,184	1,771		1,413 R	64.3%	35.7%	64.3%	35.7%
17,890	DAWSON	8,248	5,445	2,803		2,642 R	66.0%	34.0%	66.0%	34.0%
3,580	DEUEL	1,721	1,156	565		591 R	67.2%	32.8%	67.2%	32.8%
10,413	DIXON	4,950	3,038	1,912		1,126 R	61.4%	38.6%	61.4%	38.6%
23,799	DODGE	11,423	7,141	4,282		2,859 R	62.5%	37.5%	62.5%	37.5%
247,562	DOUGLAS	120,165	53,325	66,840		13,515 D	44.4%	55.6%	44.4%	55.6%
5,122	DUNDY	2,244	1,441	803		638 R	64.2%	35.8%	64.2%	35.8%
11,417	FILLMORE	5,646	3,677	1,969		1,708 R	65.1%	34.9%	65.1%	34.9%
7,740	FRANKLIN	3,732	2,354	1,378		976 R	63.1%	36.9%	63.1%	36.9%
6,417	FRONTIER	3,131	2,069	1,062		1,007 R	66.1%	33.9%	66.1%	33.9%
10,098	FURNAS	5,113	3,316	1,797		1,519 R	64.9%	35.1%	64.9%	35.1%
29,588	GAGE	13,252	8,156	5,096		3,060 R	61.5%	38.5%	61.5%	38.5%
4,680	GARDEN	2,087	1,351	736		615 R	64.7%	35.3%	64.7%	35.3%
3,444	GARFIELD	1,586	1,053	533		520 R	66.4%	33.6%	66.4%	33.6%
3,687	GOSPER	1,629	1,001	628		373 R	61.4%	38.6%	61.4%	38.6%
1,327	GRANT	666	423	243		180 R	63.5%	36.5%	63.5%	36.5%
6,845	GREELEY	3,032	1,530	1,502		28 R	50.5%	49.5%	50.5%	49.5%
27,523	HALL	12,099	7,412	4,687		2,725 R	61.3%	38.7%	61.3%	38.7%
9,982	HAMILTON	4,952	3,286	1,666		1,620 R	66.4%	33.6%	66.4%	33.6%
7,130	HARLAN	3,535	2,182	1,353		829 R	61.7%	38.3%	61.7%	38.3%
2,958	HAYES	1,357	759	598		161 R	55.9%	44.1%	55.9%	44.1%
6,404	HITCHCOCK	2,851	1,663	1,188		475 R	58.3%	41.7%	58.3%	41.7%
16,552	HOLT	7,856	4,840	3,016		1,824 R	61.6%	38.4%	61.6%	38.4%
1,253	HOOKER	550	403	147		256 R	73.3%	26.7%	73.3%	26.7%
8,422	HOWARD	3,934	1,696	2,238		542 D	43.1%	56.9%	43.1%	56.9%
15,532	JEFFERSON	7,739	4,980	2,759		2,221 R	64.3%	35.7%	64.3%	35.7%
8,662	JOHNSON	4,276	2,919	1,357		1,562 R	68.3%	31.7%	68.3%	31.7%
6,854	KEARNEY	3,353	1,792	1,561		231 R	53.4%	46.6%	53.4%	46.6%
8,333	KEITH	3,781	2,022	1,759		263 R	53.5%	46.5%	53.5%	46.5%
3,235	KEYA PAHA	1,506	1,004	502		502 R	66.7%	33.3%	66.7%	33.3%
3,913	KIMBALL	1,925	1,190	735		455 R	61.8%	38.2%	61.8%	38.2%
16,478	KNOX	7,531	4,352	3,179		1,173 R	57.8%	42.2%	57.8%	42.2%
100,585	LANCASTER	46,705	27,384	19,321		8,063 R	58.6%	41.4%	58.6%	41.4%
25,425	LINCOLN	10,868	5,908	4,960		948 R	54.4%	45.6%	54.4%	45.6%
1,742	LOGAN	823	498	325		173 R	60.5%	39.5%	60.5%	39.5%
1,777	LOUP	828	539	289		250 R	65.1%	34.9%	65.1%	34.9%
1,175	MCPHERSON	578	414	164		250 R	71.6%	28.4%	71.6%	28.4%
24,269	MADISON	11,335	7,353	3,982		3,371 R	64.9%	35.1%	64.9%	35.1%

NEBRASKA

PRESIDENT 1940

1940 Census Population	County	Total Vote	Republican	Democratic	Other	Rep.-Dem. Plurality	Percentage Total Vote Rep.	Total Vote Dem.	Major Vote Rep.	Major Vote Dem.
9,354	MERRICK	4,352	2,886	1,466		1,420 R	66.3%	33.7%	66.3%	33.7%
9,436	MORRILL	3,685	2,214	1,471		743 R	60.1%	39.9%	60.1%	39.9%
7,653	NANCE	3,398	1,963	1,435		528 R	57.8%	42.2%	57.8%	42.2%
12,781	NEMAHA	6,366	3,817	2,549		1,268 R	60.0%	40.0%	60.0%	40.0%
10,446	NUCKOLLS	4,890	3,017	1,873		1,144 R	61.7%	38.3%	61.7%	38.3%
18,994	OTOE	8,726	5,799	2,927		2,872 R	66.5%	33.5%	66.5%	33.5%
8,514	PAWNEE	4,239	2,643	1,596		1,047 R	62.3%	37.7%	62.3%	37.7%
5,197	PERKINS	2,467	1,413	1,054		359 R	57.3%	42.7%	57.3%	42.7%
8,452	PHELPS	4,359	2,512	1,847		665 R	57.6%	42.4%	57.6%	42.4%
10,211	PIERCE	4,720	3,271	1,449		1,822 R	69.3%	30.7%	69.3%	30.7%
20,191	PLATTE	8,791	4,929	3,862		1,067 R	56.1%	43.9%	56.1%	43.9%
8,748	POLK	4,288	2,653	1,635		1,018 R	61.9%	38.1%	61.9%	38.1%
11,951	RED WILLOW	5,600	3,119	2,481		638 R	55.7%	44.3%	55.7%	44.3%
19,178	RICHARDSON	8,938	4,833	4,105		728 R	54.1%	45.9%	54.1%	45.9%
3,977	ROCK	1,704	1,104	600		504 R	64.8%	35.2%	64.8%	35.2%
15,010	SALINE	7,902	3,673	4,229		556 D	46.5%	53.5%	46.5%	53.5%
10,835	SARPY	4,702	2,165	2,537		372 D	46.0%	54.0%	46.0%	54.0%
17,892	SAUNDERS	9,079	4,917	4,162		755 R	54.2%	45.8%	54.2%	45.8%
33,917	SCOTTS BLUFF	12,444	7,989	4,455		3,534 R	64.2%	35.8%	64.2%	35.8%
14,167	SEWARD	6,646	4,117	2,529		1,588 R	61.9%	38.1%	61.9%	38.1%
9,869	SHERIDAN	4,727	3,161	1,566		1,595 R	66.9%	33.1%	66.9%	33.1%
7,764	SHERMAN	3,382	1,494	1,888		394 D	44.2%	55.8%	44.2%	55.8%
4,001	SIOUX	1,690	1,072	618		454 R	63.4%	36.6%	63.4%	36.6%
6,887	STANTON	3,155	2,074	1,081		993 R	65.7%	34.3%	65.7%	34.3%
12,262	THAYER	5,970	3,893	2,077		1,816 R	65.2%	34.8%	65.2%	34.8%
1,553	THOMAS	763	486	277		209 R	63.7%	36.3%	63.7%	36.3%
10,243	THURSTON	4,012	1,973	2,039		66 D	49.2%	50.8%	49.2%	50.8%
8,163	VALLEY	4,039	2,449	1,590		859 R	60.6%	39.4%	60.6%	39.4%
11,578	WASHINGTON	5,558	2,922	2,636		286 R	52.6%	47.4%	52.6%	47.4%
9,880	WAYNE	4,604	3,209	1,395		1,814 R	69.7%	30.3%	69.7%	30.3%
8,071	WEBSTER	4,176	2,847	1,329		1,518 R	68.2%	31.8%	68.2%	31.8%
2,170	WHEELER	922	495	427		68 R	53.7%	46.3%	53.7%	46.3%
14,874	YORK	7,522	5,322	2,200		3,122 R	70.8%	29.2%	70.8%	29.2%
1,315,834	TOTAL	615,878	352,201	263,677		88,524 R	57.2%	42.8%	57.2%	42.8%

NEBRASKA

PRESIDENT 1936

1930 Census Population	County	Total Vote	Republican	Democratic	Other	Rep.-Dem. Plurality	Percentage Total Vote Rep.	Percentage Total Vote Dem.	Percentage Major Vote Rep.	Percentage Major Vote Dem.
26,275	ADAMS	10,621	4,094	6,126	401	2,032 D	38.5%	57.7%	40.1%	59.9%
15,206	ANTELOPE	6,672	3,304	3,165	203	139 R	49.5%	47.4%	51.1%	48.9%
1,344	ARTHUR	550	312	235	3	77 R	56.7%	42.7%	57.0%	43.0%
1,676	BANNER	650	277	367	6	90 D	42.6%	56.5%	43.0%	57.0%
1,584	BLAINE	716	342	365	9	23 D	47.8%	51.0%	48.4%	51.6%
14,738	BOONE	6,025	2,728	3,095	202	367 D	45.3%	51.4%	46.8%	53.2%
11,861	BOX BUTTE	4,663	1,711	2,900	52	1,189 D	36.7%	62.2%	37.1%	62.9%
7,169	BOYD	2,900	1,290	1,555	55	265 D	44.5%	53.6%	45.3%	54.7%
5,772	BROWN	2,638	1,419	1,188	31	231 R	53.8%	45.0%	54.4%	45.6%
24,338	BUFFALO	10,972	4,595	6,002	375	1,407 D	41.9%	54.7%	43.4%	56.6%
13,062	BURT	5,901	2,710	3,120	71	410 D	45.9%	52.9%	46.5%	53.5%
14,410	BUTLER	6,926	2,442	4,360	124	1,918 D	35.3%	63.0%	35.9%	64.1%
17,684	CASS	8,645	3,669	4,922	54	1,253 D	42.4%	56.9%	42.7%	57.3%
16,427	CEDAR	6,793	2,394	3,781	618	1,387 D	35.2%	55.7%	38.8%	61.2%
5,484	CHASE	2,587	1,031	1,493	63	462 D	39.9%	57.7%	40.8%	59.2%
10,898	CHERRY	3,939	1,874	2,010	55	136 D	47.6%	51.0%	48.2%	51.8%
10,187	CHEYENNE	4,442	1,374	2,950	118	1,576 D	30.9%	66.4%	31.8%	68.2%
13,571	CLAY	5,918	2,856	2,932	130	76 D	48.3%	49.5%	49.3%	50.7%
11,434	COLFAX	5,075	1,644	3,210	221	1,566 D	32.4%	63.3%	33.9%	66.1%
14,327	CUMING	5,840	2,275	3,114	451	839 D	39.0%	53.3%	42.2%	57.8%
26,189	CUSTER	11,495	5,250	5,907	338	657 D	45.7%	51.4%	47.1%	52.9%
9,505	DAKOTA	4,282	1,264	2,741	277	1,477 D	29.5%	64.0%	31.6%	68.4%
11,493	DAWES	5,122	2,083	2,784	255	701 D	40.7%	54.4%	42.8%	57.2%
17,875	DAWSON	7,702	3,573	4,021	108	448 D	46.4%	52.2%	47.1%	52.9%
3,992	DEUEL	1,808	747	1,020	41	273 D	41.3%	56.4%	42.3%	57.7%
11,586	DIXON	4,870	2,108	2,640	122	532 D	43.3%	54.2%	44.4%	55.6%
25,273	DODGE	11,339	4,561	6,317	461	1,756 D	40.2%	55.7%	41.9%	58.1%
232,982	DOUGLAS	107,076	35,349	70,245	1,482	34,896 D	33.0%	65.6%	33.5%	66.5%
5,610	DUNDY	2,408	1,054	1,328	26	274 D	43.8%	55.1%	44.2%	55.8%
12,971	FILLMORE	6,062	2,858	3,154	50	296 D	47.1%	52.0%	47.5%	52.5%
9,094	FRANKLIN	4,165	1,685	2,350	130	665 D	40.5%	56.4%	41.8%	58.2%
8,114	FRONTIER	3,509	1,576	1,883	50	307 D	44.9%	53.7%	45.6%	54.4%
12,140	FURNAS	5,424	2,842	2,482	100	360 R	52.4%	45.8%	53.4%	46.6%
30,242	GAGE	12,745	5,291	7,227	227	1,936 D	41.5%	56.7%	42.3%	57.7%
5,099	GARDEN	2,007	996	986	25	10 R	49.6%	49.1%	50.3%	49.7%
3,207	GARFIELD	1,476	744	697	35	47 R	50.4%	47.2%	51.6%	48.4%
4,287	GOSPER	1,783	647	1,118	18	471 D	36.3%	62.7%	36.7%	63.3%
1,427	GRANT	590	267	321	2	54 D	45.3%	54.4%	45.4%	54.6%
8,442	GREELEY	3,525	1,107	1,988	430	881 D	31.4%	56.4%	35.8%	64.2%
27,117	HALL	11,810	5,146	6,295	369	1,149 D	43.6%	53.3%	45.0%	55.0%
12,159	HAMILTON	5,449	2,748	2,653	48	95 R	50.4%	48.7%	50.9%	49.1%
8,957	HARLAN	3,814	1,692	2,084	38	392 D	44.4%	54.6%	44.8%	55.2%
3,603	HAYES	1,482	654	818	10	164 D	44.1%	55.2%	44.4%	55.6%
7,269	HITCHCOCK	3,045	1,285	1,738	22	453 D	42.2%	57.1%	42.5%	57.5%
16,509	HOLT	7,764	3,714	3,902	148	188 D	47.8%	50.3%	48.8%	51.2%
1,180	HOOKER	482	288	191	3	97 R	59.8%	39.6%	60.1%	39.9%
10,020	HOWARD	4,494	1,223	3,148	123	1,925 D	27.2%	70.0%	28.0%	72.0%
16,409	JEFFERSON	7,624	3,048	4,526	50	1,478 D	40.0%	59.4%	40.2%	59.8%
9,157	JOHNSON	4,525	2,126	2,359	40	233 D	47.0%	52.1%	47.4%	52.6%
8,094	KEARNEY	3,711	1,214	2,445	52	1,231 D	32.7%	65.9%	33.2%	66.8%
6,721	KEITH	3,152	1,094	2,000	58	906 D	34.7%	63.5%	35.4%	64.6%
3,203	KEYA PAHA	1,393	830	556	7	274 R	59.6%	39.9%	59.9%	40.1%
4,675	KIMBALL	2,032	842	1,137	53	295 D	41.4%	56.0%	42.5%	57.5%
19,110	KNOX	7,583	2,949	4,449	185	1,500 D	38.9%	58.7%	39.9%	60.1%
100,324	LANCASTER	44,106	20,902	22,366	838	1,464 D	47.4%	50.7%	48.3%	51.7%
25,627	LINCOLN	10,796	3,857	6,742	197	2,885 D	35.7%	62.4%	36.4%	63.6%
2,014	LOGAN	874	410	456	8	46 D	46.9%	52.2%	47.3%	52.7%
1,818	LOUP	787	438	335	14	103 R	55.7%	42.6%	56.7%	43.3%
1,358	MCPHERSON	584	326	250	8	76 R	55.8%	42.8%	56.6%	43.4%
26,037	MADISON	11,340	5,149	6,044	147	895 D	45.4%	53.3%	46.0%	54.0%

NEBRASKA

PRESIDENT 1936

1930 Census Population	County	Total Vote	Republican	Democratic	Other	Rep.-Dem. Plurality	Percentage Total Vote Rep.	Percentage Total Vote Dem.	Percentage Major Vote Rep.	Percentage Major Vote Dem.
10,619	MERRICK	4,887	2,367	2,401	119	34 D	48.4%	49.1%	49.6%	50.4%
9,950	MORRILL	3,404	1,354	1,999	51	645 D	39.8%	58.7%	40.4%	59.6%
8,718	NANCE	3,831	1,770	2,012	49	242 D	46.2%	52.5%	46.8%	53.2%
12,356	NEMAHA	6,202	2,720	3,459	23	739 D	43.9%	55.8%	44.0%	56.0%
12,629	NUCKOLLS	5,171	2,317	2,778	76	461 D	44.8%	53.7%	45.5%	54.5%
19,901	OTOE	8,634	4,399	4,173	62	226 R	50.9%	48.3%	51.3%	48.7%
9,423	PAWNEE	4,404	2,074	2,297	33	223 D	47.1%	52.2%	47.4%	52.6%
5,834	PERKINS	2,460	861	1,584	15	723 D	35.0%	64.4%	35.2%	64.8%
9,261	PHELPS	4,490	1,884	2,587	19	703 D	42.0%	57.6%	42.1%	57.9%
11,080	PIERCE	4,495	2,016	2,357	122	341 D	44.8%	52.4%	46.1%	53.9%
21,181	PLATTE	9,512	2,850	6,249	413	3,399 D	30.0%	65.7%	31.3%	68.7%
10,092	POLK	4,823	2,256	2,519	48	263 D	46.8%	52.2%	47.2%	52.8%
13,859	RED WILLOW	5,692	2,078	3,445	169	1,367 D	36.5%	60.5%	37.6%	62.4%
19,826	RICHARDSON	9,758	3,908	5,813	37	1,905 D	40.0%	59.6%	40.2%	59.8%
3,366	ROCK	1,672	944	710	18	234 R	56.5%	42.5%	57.1%	42.9%
16,356	SALINE	8,206	2,637	5,480	89	2,843 D	32.1%	66.8%	32.5%	67.5%
10,402	SARPY	4,649	1,569	3,030	50	1,461 D	33.7%	65.2%	34.1%	65.9%
20,167	SAUNDERS	9,587	3,773	5,514	300	1,741 D	39.4%	57.5%	40.6%	59.4%
28,644	SCOTTS BLUFF	9,996	4,051	5,768	177	1,717 D	40.5%	57.7%	41.3%	58.7%
15,938	SEWARD	7,039	3,123	3,866	50	743 D	44.4%	54.9%	44.7%	55.3%
10,793	SHERIDAN	4,485	1,907	2,428	150	521 D	42.5%	54.1%	44.0%	56.0%
9,122	SHERMAN	4,043	1,294	2,701	48	1,407 D	32.0%	66.8%	32.4%	67.6%
4,667	SIOUX	1,658	674	956	28	282 D	40.7%	57.7%	41.3%	58.7%
7,809	STANTON	3,198	1,169	1,917	112	748 D	36.6%	59.9%	37.9%	62.1%
13,684	THAYER	6,125	2,628	3,418	79	790 D	42.9%	55.8%	43.5%	56.5%
1,510	THOMAS	753	366	374	13	8 D	48.6%	49.7%	49.5%	50.5%
10,462	THURSTON	4,062	1,195	2,676	191	1,481 D	29.4%	65.9%	30.9%	69.1%
9,533	VALLEY	4,095	2,033	1,960	102	73 R	49.6%	47.9%	50.9%	49.1%
12,095	WASHINGTON	5,734	2,263	3,426	45	1,163 D	39.5%	59.7%	39.8%	60.2%
10,566	WAYNE	4,547	2,149	2,322	76	173 D	47.3%	51.1%	48.1%	51.9%
10,210	WEBSTER	4,368	1,912	2,408	48	496 D	43.8%	55.1%	44.3%	55.7%
2,335	WHEELER	920	358	484	78	126 D	38.9%	52.6%	42.5%	57.5%
17,239	YORK	8,415	4,554	3,741	120	813 R	54.1%	44.5%	54.9%	45.1%
1,377,963	TOTAL	608,023	247,731	347,445	12,847	99,714 D	40.7%	57.1%	41.6%	58.4%

NEBRASKA

PRESIDENT 1932

1930 Census Population	County	Total Vote	Republican	Democratic	Other	Rep.-Dem. Plurality	Percentage: Total Vote Rep.	Percentage: Total Vote Dem.	Percentage: Major Vote Rep.	Percentage: Major Vote Dem.
26,275	ADAMS	9,934	3,915	5,611	408	1,696 D	39.4%	56.5%	41.1%	58.9%
15,206	ANTELOPE	6,416	2,270	4,053	93	1,783 D	35.4%	63.2%	35.9%	64.1%
1,344	ARTHUR	596	237	338	21	101 D	39.8%	56.7%	41.2%	58.8%
1,676	BANNER	651	285	357	9	72 D	43.8%	54.8%	44.4%	55.6%
1,584	BLAINE	689	244	431	14	187 D	35.4%	62.6%	36.1%	63.9%
14,738	BOONE	6,291	1,862	4,360	69	2,498 D	29.6%	69.3%	29.9%	70.1%
11,861	BOX BUTTE	4,525	1,772	2,688	65	916 D	39.2%	59.4%	39.7%	60.3%
7,169	BOYD	2,957	808	2,098	51	1,290 D	27.3%	71.0%	27.8%	72.2%
5,772	BROWN	2,750	1,174	1,565	11	391 D	42.7%	56.9%	42.9%	57.1%
24,338	BUFFALO	9,923	3,773	5,872	278	2,099 D	38.0%	59.2%	39.1%	60.9%
13,062	BURT	5,656	1,857	3,734	65	1,877 D	32.8%	66.0%	33.2%	66.8%
14,410	BUTLER	6,203	1,712	4,456	35	2,744 D	27.6%	71.8%	27.8%	72.2%
17,684	CASS	8,072	2,756	5,155	161	2,399 D	34.1%	63.9%	34.8%	65.2%
16,427	CEDAR	6,732	1,696	4,981	55	3,285 D	25.2%	74.0%	25.4%	74.6%
5,484	CHASE	2,455	948	1,408	99	460 D	38.6%	57.4%	40.2%	59.8%
10,898	CHERRY	4,703	1,754	2,912	37	1,158 D	37.3%	61.9%	37.6%	62.4%
10,187	CHEYENNE	4,465	1,285	3,068	112	1,783 D	28.8%	68.7%	29.5%	70.5%
13,571	CLAY	6,376	2,320	3,878	178	1,558 D	36.4%	60.8%	37.4%	62.6%
11,434	COLFAX	4,779	648	4,076	55	3,428 D	13.6%	85.3%	13.7%	86.3%
14,327	CUMING	5,639	1,191	4,391	57	3,200 D	21.1%	77.9%	21.3%	78.7%
26,189	CUSTER	11,086	3,953	6,844	289	2,891 D	35.7%	61.7%	36.6%	63.4%
9,505	DAKOTA	3,937	863	3,044	30	2,181 D	21.9%	77.3%	22.1%	77.9%
11,493	DAWES	4,672	2,095	2,457	120	362 D	44.8%	52.6%	46.0%	54.0%
17,875	DAWSON	7,505	2,859	4,513	133	1,654 D	38.1%	60.1%	38.8%	61.2%
3,992	DEUEL	1,765	630	1,093	42	463 D	35.7%	61.9%	36.6%	63.4%
11,586	DIXON	4,653	1,620	2,953	80	1,333 D	34.8%	63.5%	35.4%	64.6%
25,273	DODGE	10,855	3,489	7,247	119	3,758 D	32.1%	66.8%	32.5%	67.5%
232,982	DOUGLAS	94,768	33,938	59,347	1,483	25,409 D	35.8%	62.6%	36.4%	63.6%
5,610	DUNDY	2,354	974	1,344	36	370 D	41.4%	57.1%	42.0%	58.0%
12,971	FILLMORE	5,881	2,178	3,655	48	1,477 D	37.0%	62.1%	37.3%	62.7%
9,094	FRANKLIN	4,091	1,404	2,633	54	1,229 D	34.3%	64.4%	34.8%	65.2%
8,114	FRONTIER	3,595	1,353	2,188	54	835 D	37.6%	60.9%	38.2%	61.8%
12,140	FURNAS	5,477	2,087	3,303	87	1,216 D	38.1%	60.3%	38.7%	61.3%
30,242	GAGE	11,585	4,315	7,036	234	2,721 D	37.2%	60.7%	38.0%	62.0%
5,099	GARDEN	2,010	768	1,204	38	436 D	38.2%	59.9%	38.9%	61.1%
3,207	GARFIELD	1,417	622	775	20	153 D	43.9%	54.7%	44.5%	55.5%
4,287	GOSPER	1,758	477	1,263	18	786 D	27.1%	71.8%	27.4%	72.6%
1,427	GRANT	671	251	395	25	144 D	37.4%	58.9%	38.9%	61.1%
8,442	GREELEY	3,743	817	2,832	94	2,015 D	21.8%	75.7%	22.4%	77.6%
27,117	HALL	10,492	3,743	6,266	483	2,523 D	35.7%	59.7%	37.4%	62.6%
12,159	HAMILTON	5,051	2,003	2,969	79	966 D	39.7%	58.8%	40.3%	59.7%
8,957	HARLAN	3,879	1,272	2,486	121	1,214 D	32.8%	64.1%	33.8%	66.2%
3,603	HAYES	1,508	506	962	40	456 D	33.6%	63.8%	34.5%	65.5%
7,269	HITCHCOCK	2,983	1,168	1,772	43	604 D	39.2%	59.4%	39.7%	60.3%
16,509	HOLT	7,200	2,375	4,761	64	2,386 D	33.0%	66.1%	33.3%	66.7%
1,180	HOOKER	511	162	342	7	180 D	31.7%	66.9%	32.1%	67.9%
10,020	HOWARD	4,306	734	3,409	163	2,675 D	17.0%	79.2%	17.7%	82.3%
16,409	JEFFERSON	7,402	2,453	4,819	130	2,366 D	33.1%	65.1%	33.7%	66.3%
9,157	JOHNSON	4,181	1,644	2,505	32	861 D	39.3%	59.9%	39.6%	60.4%
8,094	KEARNEY	3,569	1,129	2,367	73	1,238 D	31.6%	66.3%	32.3%	67.7%
6,721	KEITH	2,991	946	2,009	36	1,063 D	31.6%	67.2%	32.0%	68.0%
3,203	KEYA PAHA	1,336	675	645	16	30 R	50.5%	48.3%	51.1%	48.9%
4,675	KIMBALL	2,110	793	1,268	49	475 D	37.6%	60.1%	38.5%	61.5%
19,110	KNOX	7,128	1,830	5,229	69	3,399 D	25.7%	73.4%	25.9%	74.1%
100,324	LANCASTER	39,723	20,772	18,190	761	2,582 R	52.3%	45.8%	53.3%	46.7%
25,627	LINCOLN	9,431	3,082	6,047	302	2,965 D	32.7%	64.1%	33.8%	66.2%
2,014	LOGAN	927	346	564	17	218 D	37.3%	60.8%	38.0%	62.0%
1,818	LOUP	703	287	389	27	102 D	40.8%	55.3%	42.5%	57.5%
1,358	MCPHERSON	669	291	367	11	76 D	43.5%	54.9%	44.2%	55.8%
26,037	MADISON	10,954	3,489	7,366	99	3,877 D	31.9%	67.2%	32.1%	67.9%

NEBRASKA

PRESIDENT 1932

1930 Census Population	County	Total Vote	Republican	Democratic	Other	Rep.-Dem. Plurality	Percentage Total Vote Rep.	Percentage Total Vote Dem.	Percentage Major Vote Rep.	Percentage Major Vote Dem.
10,619	MERRICK	4,696	1,698	2,881	117	1,183 D	36.2%	61.4%	37.1%	62.9%
9,950	MORRILL	3,476	1,406	2,008	62	602 D	40.4%	57.8%	41.2%	58.8%
8,718	NANCE	3,661	1,156	2,479	26	1,323 D	31.6%	67.7%	31.8%	68.2%
12,356	NEMAHA	5,709	2,075	3,593	41	1,518 D	36.3%	62.9%	36.6%	63.4%
12,629	NUCKOLLS	5,333	1,812	3,420	101	1,608 D	34.0%	64.1%	34.6%	65.4%
19,901	OTOE	7,959	3,119	4,752	88	1,633 D	39.2%	59.7%	39.6%	60.4%
9,423	PAWNEE	4,249	1,568	2,641	40	1,073 D	36.9%	62.2%	37.3%	62.7%
5,834	PERKINS	2,398	674	1,669	55	995 D	28.1%	69.6%	28.8%	71.2%
9,261	PHELPS	4,372	1,709	2,589	74	880 D	39.1%	59.2%	39.8%	60.2%
11,080	PIERCE	4,143	1,128	2,980	35	1,852 D	27.2%	71.9%	27.5%	72.5%
21,181	PLATTE	8,627	1,864	6,691	72	4,827 D	21.6%	77.6%	21.8%	78.2%
10,092	POLK	4,628	1,636	2,939	53	1,303 D	35.4%	63.5%	35.8%	64.2%
13,859	RED WILLOW	5,592	1,972	3,479	141	1,507 D	35.3%	62.2%	36.2%	63.8%
19,826	RICHARDSON	8,249	2,802	5,383	64	2,581 D	34.0%	65.3%	34.2%	65.8%
3,366	ROCK	1,445	613	810	22	197 D	42.4%	56.1%	43.1%	56.9%
16,356	SALINE	7,896	1,993	5,831	72	3,838 D	25.2%	73.8%	25.5%	74.5%
10,402	SARPY	4,329	1,148	3,112	69	1,964 D	26.5%	71.9%	26.9%	73.1%
20,167	SAUNDERS	9,134	2,772	6,134	228	3,362 D	30.3%	67.2%	31.1%	68.9%
28,644	SCOTTS BLUFF	9,011	4,108	4,792	111	684 D	45.6%	53.2%	46.2%	53.8%
15,938	SEWARD	6,571	2,298	4,208	65	1,910 D	35.0%	64.0%	35.3%	64.7%
10,793	SHERIDAN	4,865	1,820	2,945	100	1,125 D	37.4%	60.5%	38.2%	61.8%
9,122	SHERMAN	3,692	952	2,670	70	1,718 D	25.8%	72.3%	26.3%	73.7%
4,667	SIOUX	1,704	667	1,006	31	339 D	39.1%	59.0%	39.9%	60.1%
7,809	STANTON	2,879	568	2,302	9	1,734 D	19.7%	80.0%	19.8%	80.2%
13,684	THAYER	5,809	1,878	3,841	90	1,963 D	32.3%	66.1%	32.8%	67.2%
1,510	THOMAS	721	262	437	22	175 D	36.3%	60.6%	37.5%	62.5%
10,462	THURSTON	4,056	739	3,273	44	2,534 D	18.2%	80.7%	18.4%	81.6%
9,533	VALLEY	4,057	1,584	2,400	73	816 D	39.0%	59.2%	39.8%	60.2%
12,095	WASHINGTON	5,157	1,382	3,709	66	2,327 D	26.8%	71.9%	27.1%	72.9%
10,566	WAYNE	4,154	1,455	2,608	91	1,153 D	35.0%	62.8%	35.8%	64.2%
10,210	WEBSTER	4,389	1,627	2,632	130	1,005 D	37.1%	60.0%	38.2%	61.8%
2,335	WHEELER	906	219	658	29	439 D	24.2%	72.6%	25.0%	75.0%
17,239	YORK	7,579	3,573	3,920	86	347 D	47.1%	51.7%	47.7%	52.3%
1,377,963	TOTAL	570,135	201,177	359,082	9,876	157,905 D	35.3%	63.0%	35.9%	64.1%

NEBRASKA

PRESIDENT 1928

1920 Census Population	County	Total Vote	Republican	Democratic	Other	Rep.-Dem. Plurality	Percentage			
							Total Vote		Major Vote	
							Rep.	Dem.	Rep.	Dem.
22,621	ADAMS	10,186	7,194	2,926	66	4,268 R	70.6%	28.7%	71.1%	28.9%
15,243	ANTELOPE	6,308	4,277	2,016	15	2,261 R	67.8%	32.0%	68.0%	32.0%
1,412	ARTHUR	579	402	169	8	233 R	69.4%	29.2%	70.4%	29.6%
1,435	BANNER	635	548	81	6	467 R	86.3%	12.8%	87.1%	12.9%
1,778	BLAINE	662	484	175	3	309 R	73.1%	26.4%	73.4%	26.6%
14,146	BOONE	6,099	3,816	2,260	23	1,556 R	62.6%	37.1%	62.8%	37.2%
8,407	BOX BUTTE	4,282	3,028	1,238	16	1,790 R	70.7%	28.9%	71.0%	29.0%
8,243	BOYD	2,815	1,653	1,143	19	510 R	58.7%	40.6%	59.1%	40.9%
6,749	BROWN	2,575	1,907	636	32	1,271 R	74.1%	24.7%	75.0%	25.0%
23,787	BUFFALO	10,329	7,460	2,801	68	4,659 R	72.2%	27.1%	72.7%	27.3%
12,559	BURT	5,353	3,551	1,783	19	1,768 R	66.3%	33.3%	66.6%	33.4%
14,606	BUTLER	6,418	2,930	3,465	23	535 D	45.7%	54.0%	45.8%	54.2%
18,029	CASS	7,777	4,970	2,739	68	2,231 R	63.9%	35.2%	64.5%	35.5%
16,225	CEDAR	6,467	3,206	3,241	20	35 D	49.6%	50.1%	49.7%	50.3%
4,939	CHASE	2,142	1,540	579	23	961 R	71.9%	27.0%	72.7%	27.3%
11,753	CHERRY	4,208	2,905	1,285	18	1,620 R	69.0%	30.5%	69.3%	30.7%
8,405	CHEYENNE	4,203	2,618	1,563	22	1,055 R	62.3%	37.2%	62.6%	37.4%
14,486	CLAY	5,926	4,105	1,767	54	2,338 R	69.3%	29.8%	69.9%	30.1%
11,624	COLFAX	4,194	1,432	2,746	16	1,314 D	34.1%	65.5%	34.3%	65.7%
13,769	CUMING	5,043	2,418	2,597	28	179 D	47.9%	51.5%	48.2%	51.8%
26,407	CUSTER	10,967	8,379	2,506	82	5,873 R	76.4%	22.9%	77.0%	23.0%
7,694	DAKOTA	3,463	1,709	1,754		45 D	49.4%	50.6%	49.4%	50.6%
10,160	DAWES	4,468	3,276	1,173	19	2,103 R	73.3%	26.3%	73.6%	26.4%
16,004	DAWSON	6,902	5,125	1,718	59	3,407 R	74.3%	24.9%	74.9%	25.1%
3,282	DEUEL	1,609	1,197	403	9	794 R	74.4%	25.0%	74.8%	25.2%
11,815	DIXON	4,601	2,982	1,607	12	1,375 R	64.8%	34.9%	65.0%	35.0%
23,197	DODGE	10,315	6,250	4,030	35	2,220 R	60.6%	39.1%	60.8%	39.2%
204,524	DOUGLAS	90,405	47,551	42,267	587	5,284 R	52.6%	46.8%	52.9%	47.1%
4,869	DUNDY	2,061	1,575	472	14	1,103 R	76.4%	22.9%	76.9%	23.1%
13,671	FILLMORE	5,746	3,479	2,235	32	1,244 R	60.5%	38.9%	60.9%	39.1%
10,067	FRANKLIN	3,993	2,533	1,443	17	1,090 R	63.4%	36.1%	63.7%	36.3%
8,540	FRONTIER	3,254	2,335	879	40	1,456 R	71.8%	27.0%	72.7%	27.3%
11,657	FURNAS	5,139	3,760	1,339	40	2,421 R	73.2%	26.1%	73.7%	26.3%
29,721	GAGE	11,998	8,378	3,526	94	4,852 R	69.8%	29.4%	70.4%	29.6%
4,572	GARDEN	1,889	1,470	404	15	1,066 R	77.8%	21.4%	78.4%	21.6%
3,496	GARFIELD	1,421	1,180	235	6	945 R	83.0%	16.5%	83.4%	16.6%
4,669	GOSPER	1,465	975	480	10	495 R	66.6%	32.8%	67.0%	33.0%
1,486	GRANT	561	398	160	3	238 R	70.9%	28.5%	71.3%	28.7%
8,685	GREELEY	3,564	1,457	2,098	9	641 D	40.9%	58.9%	41.0%	59.0%
23,720	HALL	10,306	6,862	3,391	53	3,471 R	66.6%	32.9%	66.9%	33.1%
13,237	HAMILTON	5,284	3,634	1,606	44	2,028 R	68.8%	30.4%	69.4%	30.6%
9,220	HARLAN	3,861	2,702	1,055	104	1,647 R	70.0%	27.3%	71.9%	28.1%
3,327	HAYES	1,393	917	440	36	477 R	65.8%	31.6%	67.6%	32.4%
6,045	HITCHCOCK	2,743	2,022	698	23	1,324 R	73.7%	25.4%	74.3%	25.7%
17,151	HOLT	6,882	3,746	3,126	10	620 R	54.4%	45.4%	54.5%	45.5%
1,378	HOOKER	467	355	110	2	245 R	76.0%	23.6%	76.3%	23.7%
10,739	HOWARD	4,157	1,937	2,197	23	260 D	46.6%	52.9%	46.9%	53.1%
16,140	JEFFERSON	6,609	4,359	2,193	57	2,166 R	66.0%	33.2%	66.5%	33.5%
8,940	JOHNSON	4,134	2,632	1,485	17	1,147 R	63.7%	35.9%	63.9%	36.1%
8,583	KEARNEY	3,553	2,426	1,093	34	1,333 R	68.3%	30.8%	68.9%	31.1%
5,294	KEITH	2,556	1,715	832	9	883 R	67.1%	32.6%	67.3%	32.7%
3,594	KEYA PAHA	1,240	989	232	19	757 R	79.8%	18.7%	81.0%	19.0%
4,498	KIMBALL	1,751	1,296	438	17	858 R	74.0%	25.0%	74.7%	25.3%
18,894	KNOX	6,614	3,668	2,914	32	754 R	55.5%	44.1%	55.7%	44.3%
85,902	LANCASTER	40,605	30,523	9,840	242	20,683 R	75.2%	24.2%	75.6%	24.4%
23,420	LINCOLN	8,425	5,946	2,381	98	3,565 R	70.6%	28.3%	71.4%	28.6%
1,596	LOGAN	800	595	195	10	400 R	74.4%	24.4%	75.3%	24.7%
1,946	LOUP	709	594	106	9	488 R	83.8%	15.0%	84.9%	15.1%
1,692	MCPHERSON	497	419	69	9	350 R	84.3%	13.9%	85.9%	14.1%
22,511	MADISON	9,684	6,229	3,407	48	2,822 R	64.3%	35.2%	64.6%	35.4%

NEBRASKA

PRESIDENT 1928

1920 Census Population	County	Total Vote	Republican	Democratic	Other	Rep.-Dem. Plurality	Percentage Total Vote Rep.	Total Vote Dem.	Major Vote Rep.	Major Vote Dem.
10,763	MERRICK	4,699	3,269	1,403	27	1,866 R	69.6%	29.9%	70.0%	30.0%
9,151	MORRILL	3,112	2,318	756	38	1,562 R	74.5%	24.3%	75.4%	24.6%
8,712	NANCE	3,632	2,299	1,318	15	981 R	63.3%	36.3%	63.6%	36.4%
12,547	NEMAHA	5,548	3,777	1,767	4	2,010 R	68.1%	31.8%	68.1%	31.9%
13,236	NUCKOLLS	5,027	3,299	1,684	44	1,615 R	65.6%	33.5%	66.2%	33.8%
19,494	OTOE	8,077	5,063	2,959	55	2,104 R	62.7%	36.6%	63.1%	36.9%
9,578	PAWNEE	4,394	2,825	1,547	22	1,278 R	64.3%	35.2%	64.6%	35.4%
3,967	PERKINS	2,106	1,461	631	14	830 R	69.4%	30.0%	69.8%	30.2%
9,900	PHELPS	4,251	3,297	927	27	2,370 R	77.6%	21.8%	78.1%	21.9%
10,681	PIERCE	4,137	2,542	1,586	9	956 R	61.4%	38.3%	61.6%	38.4%
19,464	PLATTE	8,210	3,435	4,748	27	1,313 D	41.8%	57.8%	42.0%	58.0%
10,714	POLK	4,609	3,096	1,494	19	1,602 R	67.2%	32.4%	67.5%	32.5%
11,434	RED WILLOW	5,384	3,559	1,770	55	1,789 R	66.1%	32.9%	66.8%	33.2%
18,968	RICHARDSON	8,962	5,833	3,072	57	2,761 R	65.1%	34.3%	65.5%	34.5%
3,703	ROCK	1,341	1,034	305	2	729 R	77.1%	22.7%	77.2%	22.8%
16,514	SALINE	7,328	3,347	3,955	26	608 D	45.7%	54.0%	45.8%	54.2%
9,370	SARPY	3,940	2,011	1,900	29	111 R	51.0%	48.2%	51.4%	48.6%
20,589	SAUNDERS	9,186	5,356	3,793	37	1,563 R	58.3%	41.3%	58.5%	41.5%
20,710	SCOTTS BLUFF	8,167	6,677	1,403	87	5,274 R	81.8%	17.2%	82.6%	17.4%
15,867	SEWARD	5,930	3,539	2,367	24	1,172 R	59.7%	39.9%	59.9%	40.1%
9,625	SHERIDAN	4,315	3,030	1,226	59	1,804 R	70.2%	28.4%	71.2%	28.8%
8,877	SHERMAN	3,435	1,675	1,733	27	58 D	48.8%	50.5%	49.1%	50.9%
4,528	SIOUX	1,624	1,178	435	11	743 R	72.5%	26.8%	73.0%	27.0%
7,756	STANTON	2,514	1,211	1,296	7	85 D	48.2%	51.6%	48.3%	51.7%
13,976	THAYER	5,748	3,552	2,173	23	1,379 R	61.8%	37.8%	62.0%	38.0%
1,773	THOMAS	562	406	152	4	254 R	72.2%	27.0%	72.8%	27.2%
9,589	THURSTON	3,393	1,538	1,837	18	299 D	45.3%	54.1%	45.6%	54.4%
9,823	VALLEY	3,996	2,768	1,205	23	1,563 R	69.3%	30.2%	69.7%	30.3%
12,180	WASHINGTON	4,684	2,750	1,912	22	838 R	58.7%	40.8%	59.0%	41.0%
9,725	WAYNE	3,628	2,354	1,235	39	1,119 R	64.9%	34.0%	65.6%	34.4%
10,922	WEBSTER	4,286	2,924	1,342	20	1,582 R	68.2%	31.3%	68.5%	31.5%
2,531	WHEELER	832	534	293	5	241 R	64.2%	35.2%	64.6%	35.4%
17,146	YORK	7,779	5,769	1,979	31	3,790 R	74.2%	25.4%	74.5%	25.5%
1,296,372	TOTAL	547,128	345,745	197,950	3,433	147,795 R	63.2%	36.2%	63.6%	36.4%

NEBRASKA

PRESIDENT 1924

1920 Census Population	County	Total Vote	Republican	Democratic	Progressive	Other	Plurality	Percentage Total Vote Rep.	Dem.	Prog.
22,621	ADAMS	8,516	4,824	2,353	1,311	28	2,471 R	56.6%	27.6%	15.4%
15,243	ANTELOPE	4,913	2,998	1,150	745	20	1,848 R	61.0%	23.4%	15.2%
1,412	ARTHUR	410	143	101	164	2	21 P	34.9%	24.6%	40.0%
1,435	BANNER	492	245	88	153	6	92 R	49.8%	17.9%	31.1%
1,778	BLAINE	583	253	132	197	1	56 R	43.4%	22.6%	33.8%
14,146	BOONE	5,537	2,013	1,782	1,717	25	231 R	36.4%	32.2%	31.0%
8,407	BOX BUTTE	3,545	1,506	814	1,216	9	290 R	42.5%	23.0%	34.3%
8,243	BOYD	2,648	991	532	1,114	11	123 P	37.4%	20.1%	42.1%
6,749	BROWN	2,452	1,104	714	616	18	390 R	45.0%	29.1%	25.1%
23,787	BUFFALO	8,771	4,746	2,337	1,641	47	2,409 R	54.1%	26.6%	18.7%
12,559	BURT	5,179	2,813	1,870	484	12	943 R	54.3%	36.1%	9.3%
14,606	BUTLER	5,434	2,435	2,444	544	11	9 D	44.8%	45.0%	10.0%
18,029	CASS	7,344	3,639	2,352	1,327	26	1,287 R	49.6%	32.0%	18.1%
16,225	CEDAR	6,115	2,441	1,747	1,917	10	524 R	39.9%	28.6%	31.3%
4,939	CHASE	1,908	919	570	411	8	349 R	48.2%	29.9%	21.5%
11,753	CHERRY	3,806	1,663	1,169	967	7	494 R	43.7%	30.7%	25.4%
8,405	CHEYENNE	3,321	1,719	555	1,034	13	685 R	51.8%	16.7%	31.1%
14,486	CLAY	5,481	2,758	1,716	986	21	1,042 R	50.3%	31.3%	18.0%
11,624	COLFAX	3,716	1,450	1,293	965	8	157 R	39.0%	34.8%	26.0%
13,769	CUMING	4,473	1,642	981	1,840	10	198 P	36.7%	21.9%	41.1%
26,407	CUSTER	9,595	3,833	2,575	3,144	43	689 R	39.9%	26.8%	32.8%
7,694	DAKOTA	3,136	1,235	964	931	6	271 R	39.4%	30.7%	29.7%
10,160	DAWES	3,818	1,575	595	1,632	16	57 P	41.3%	15.6%	42.7%
16,004	DAWSON	5,952	3,016	1,526	1,386	24	1,490 R	50.7%	25.6%	23.3%
3,282	DEUEL	1,331	775	316	236	4	459 R	58.2%	23.7%	17.7%
11,815	DIXON	4,223	2,153	1,090	964	16	1,063 R	51.0%	25.8%	22.8%
23,197	DODGE	8,323	3,798	2,183	2,316	26	1,482 R	45.6%	26.2%	27.8%
204,524	DOUGLAS	65,340	29,390	18,672	17,184	94	10,718 R	45.0%	28.6%	26.3%
4,869	DUNDY	1,828	1,036	459	324	9	577 R	56.7%	25.1%	17.7%
13,671	FILLMORE	5,351	2,758	2,156	429	8	602 R	51.5%	40.3%	8.0%
10,067	FRANKLIN	3,745	1,920	1,331	476	18	589 R	51.3%	35.5%	12.7%
8,540	FRONTIER	2,864	1,497	599	745	23	752 R	52.3%	20.9%	26.0%
11,657	FURNAS	4,728	2,378	1,534	801	15	844 R	50.3%	32.4%	16.9%
29,721	GAGE	10,514	5,331	3,330	1,825	28	2,001 R	50.7%	31.7%	17.4%
4,572	GARDEN	1,553	725	459	361	8	266 R	46.7%	29.6%	23.2%
3,496	GARFIELD	1,280	757	251	268	4	489 R	59.1%	19.6%	20.9%
4,669	GOSPER	1,487	540	394	550	3	10 P	36.3%	26.5%	37.0%
1,486	GRANT	534	260	191	82	1	69 R	48.7%	35.8%	15.4%
8,685	GREELEY	2,919	773	1,220	908	18	312 D	26.5%	41.8%	31.1%
23,720	HALL	8,525	4,040	1,863	2,564	58	1,476 R	47.4%	21.9%	30.1%
13,237	HAMILTON	5,230	2,935	1,545	722	28	1,390 R	56.1%	29.5%	13.8%
9,220	HARLAN	3,689	1,845	1,216	604	24	629 R	50.0%	33.0%	16.4%
3,327	HAYES	1,115	475	288	347	5	128 R	42.6%	25.8%	31.1%
6,045	HITCHCOCK	2,155	987	633	528	7	354 R	45.8%	29.4%	24.5%
17,151	HOLT	5,943	2,207	1,529	2,176	31	31 R	37.1%	25.7%	36.6%
1,378	HOOKER	440	176	111	151	2	25 R	40.0%	25.2%	34.3%
10,739	HOWARD	3,455	1,091	1,434	914	16	343 D	31.6%	41.5%	26.5%
16,140	JEFFERSON	5,719	2,752	1,824	1,134	9	928 R	48.1%	31.9%	19.8%
8,940	JOHNSON	3,834	2,075	1,285	465	9	790 R	54.1%	33.5%	12.1%
8,583	KEARNEY	3,226	1,453	1,243	508	22	210 R	45.0%	38.5%	15.7%
5,294	KEITH	2,141	1,069	602	462	8	467 R	49.9%	28.1%	21.6%
3,594	KEYA PAHA	1,215	504	251	451	9	53 R	41.5%	20.7%	37.1%
4,498	KIMBALL	1,464	750	253	461		289 R	51.2%	17.3%	31.5%
18,894	KNOX	6,226	2,405	1,532	2,265	24	140 R	38.6%	24.6%	36.4%
85,902	LANCASTER	33,199	18,061	11,563	3,485	90	6,498 R	54.4%	34.8%	10.5%
23,420	LINCOLN	6,979	2,857	1,373	2,723	26	134 R	40.9%	19.7%	39.0%
1,596	LOGAN	683	277	165	234	7	43 R	40.6%	24.2%	34.3%
1,946	LOUP	594	285	105	200	4	85 R	48.0%	17.7%	33.7%
1,692	MCPHERSON	528	213	96	207	12	6 R	40.3%	18.2%	39.2%
22,511	MADISON	8,695	3,537	1,959	3,125	74	412 R	40.7%	22.5%	35.9%

NEBRASKA

PRESIDENT 1924

1920 Census Population	County	Total Vote	Republican	Democratic	Progressive	Other	Plurality	Percentage Total Vote Rep.	Dem.	Prog.
10,763	MERRICK	4,277	2,324	1,137	796	20	1,187 R	54.3%	26.6%	18.6%
9,151	MORRILL	2,519	1,153	734	623	9	419 R	45.8%	29.1%	24.7%
8,712	NANCE	3,319	1,574	1,130	603	12	444 R	47.4%	34.0%	18.2%
12,547	NEMAHA	4,856	2,378	1,871	604	3	507 R	49.0%	38.5%	12.4%
13,236	NUCKOLLS	4,804	2,595	1,596	600	13	999 R	54.0%	33.2%	12.5%
19,494	OTOE	6,475	3,245	2,208	1,003	19	1,037 R	50.1%	34.1%	15.5%
9,578	PAWNEE	3,844	2,147	1,365	328	4	782 R	55.9%	35.5%	8.5%
3,967	PERKINS	1,652	836	493	318	5	343 R	50.6%	29.8%	19.2%
9,900	PHELPS	3,944	1,928	993	1,015	8	913 R	48.9%	25.2%	25.7%
10,681	PIERCE	3,706	1,570	760	1,363	13	207 R	42.4%	20.5%	36.8%
19,464	PLATTE	6,867	2,108	2,173	2,576	10	403 P	30.7%	31.6%	37.5%
10,714	POLK	4,167	2,354	1,229	567	17	1,125 R	56.5%	29.5%	13.6%
11,434	RED WILLOW	4,329	1,931	1,122	1,264	12	667 R	44.6%	25.9%	29.2%
18,968	RICHARDSON	7,517	3,625	3,089	789	14	536 R	48.2%	41.1%	10.5%
3,703	ROCK	1,236	585	293	353	5	232 R	47.3%	23.7%	28.6%
16,514	SALINE	6,576	2,834	3,123	610	9	289 D	43.1%	47.5%	9.3%
9,370	SARPY	3,631	1,411	1,247	964	9	164 R	38.9%	34.3%	26.5%
20,589	SAUNDERS	7,749	3,499	2,823	1,414	13	676 R	45.2%	36.4%	18.2%
20,710	SCOTTS BLUFF	5,474	3,410	1,132	902	30	2,278 R	62.3%	20.7%	16.5%
15,867	SEWARD	5,684	2,797	1,848	1,023	16	949 R	49.2%	32.5%	18.0%
9,625	SHERIDAN	3,640	1,509	661	1,453	17	56 R	41.5%	18.2%	39.9%
8,877	SHERMAN	2,964	1,182	1,048	715	19	134 R	39.9%	35.4%	24.1%
4,528	SIOUX	1,333	480	149	697	7	217 P	36.0%	11.2%	52.3%
7,756	STANTON	2,440	962	596	874	8	88 R	39.4%	24.4%	35.8%
13,976	THAYER	5,399	2,847	1,719	818	15	1,128 R	52.7%	31.8%	15.2%
1,773	THOMAS	581	206	216	158	1	10 D	35.5%	37.2%	27.2%
9,589	THURSTON	3,239	1,210	1,191	829	9	19 R	37.4%	36.8%	25.6%
9,823	VALLEY	3,659	2,014	802	834	9	1,180 R	55.0%	21.9%	22.8%
12,180	WASHINGTON	4,154	1,876	1,231	961	86	645 R	45.2%	29.6%	23.1%
9,725	WAYNE	3,505	1,840	775	879	11	961 R	52.5%	22.1%	25.1%
10,922	WEBSTER	4,033	2,194	1,207	616	16	987 R	54.4%	29.9%	15.3%
2,531	WHEELER	759	205	145	404	5	199 P	27.0%	19.1%	53.2%
17,146	YORK	7,007	4,110	1,778	1,091	28	2,332 R	58.7%	25.4%	15.6%
1,296,372	TOTAL	463,559	218,985	137,299	105,681	1,594	81,686 R	47.2%	29.6%	22.8%

NEBRASKA

PRESIDENT 1920

1920 Census Population	County	Total Vote	Republican	Democratic	Other	Rep.-Dem. Plurality	Percentage: Total Vote Rep.	Total Vote Dem.	Major Vote Rep.	Major Vote Dem.
22,621	ADAMS	7,008	4,849	1,932	227	2,917 R	69.2%	27.6%	71.5%	28.5%
15,243	ANTELOPE	4,685	3,322	1,154	209	2,168 R	70.9%	24.6%	74.2%	25.8%
1,412	ARTHUR	293	167	94	32	73 R	57.0%	32.1%	64.0%	36.0%
1,435	BANNER	356	258	69	29	189 R	72.5%	19.4%	78.9%	21.1%
1,778	BLAINE	514	328	176	10	152 R	63.8%	34.2%	65.1%	34.9%
14,146	BOONE	4,711	3,108	1,461	142	1,647 R	66.0%	31.0%	68.0%	32.0%
8,407	BOX BUTTE	2,503	1,630	756	117	874 R	65.1%	30.2%	68.3%	31.7%
8,243	BOYD	2,116	1,482	527	107	955 R	70.0%	24.9%	73.8%	26.2%
6,749	BROWN	2,065	1,417	558	90	859 R	68.6%	27.0%	71.7%	28.3%
23,787	BUFFALO	7,557	4,954	2,258	345	2,696 R	65.6%	29.9%	68.7%	31.3%
12,559	BURT	4,228	2,969	1,194	65	1,775 R	70.2%	28.2%	71.3%	28.7%
14,606	BUTLER	4,486	2,478	1,918	90	560 R	55.2%	42.8%	56.4%	43.6%
18,029	CASS	6,127	3,575	2,192	360	1,383 R	58.3%	35.8%	62.0%	38.0%
16,225	CEDAR	5,243	3,906	1,279	58	2,627 R	74.5%	24.4%	75.3%	24.7%
4,939	CHASE	1,475	976	414	85	562 R	66.2%	28.1%	70.2%	29.8%
11,753	CHERRY	2,465	1,636	711	118	925 R	66.4%	28.8%	69.7%	30.3%
8,405	CHEYENNE	2,582	1,857	604	121	1,253 R	71.9%	23.4%	75.5%	24.5%
14,486	CLAY	5,008	3,392	1,466	150	1,926 R	67.7%	29.3%	69.8%	30.2%
11,624	COLFAX	3,005	1,992	957	56	1,035 R	66.3%	31.8%	67.5%	32.5%
13,769	CUMING	4,040	3,177	764	99	2,413 R	78.6%	18.9%	80.6%	19.4%
26,407	CUSTER	8,387	4,974	2,739	674	2,235 R	59.3%	32.7%	64.5%	35.5%
7,694	DAKOTA	2,437	1,525	873	39	652 R	62.6%	35.8%	63.6%	36.4%
10,160	DAWES	2,788	1,801	900	87	901 R	64.6%	32.3%	66.7%	33.3%
16,004	DAWSON	5,128	3,384	1,444	300	1,940 R	66.0%	28.2%	70.1%	29.9%
3,282	DEUEL	1,055	684	321	50	363 R	64.8%	30.4%	68.1%	31.9%
11,815	DIXON	3,409	2,435	911	63	1,524 R	71.4%	26.7%	72.8%	27.2%
23,197	DODGE	6,864	4,832	1,799	233	3,033 R	70.4%	26.2%	72.9%	27.1%
204,524	DOUGLAS	49,375	28,543	18,439	2,393	10,104 R	57.8%	37.3%	60.8%	39.2%
4,869	DUNDY	1,572	1,094	375	103	719 R	69.6%	23.9%	74.5%	25.5%
13,671	FILLMORE	4,419	2,803	1,549	67	1,254 R	63.4%	35.1%	64.4%	35.6%
10,067	FRANKLIN	3,403	2,294	1,030	79	1,264 R	67.4%	30.3%	69.0%	31.0%
8,540	FRONTIER	2,570	1,750	673	147	1,077 R	68.1%	26.2%	72.2%	27.8%
11,657	FURNAS	4,039	2,445	1,371	223	1,074 R	60.5%	33.9%	64.1%	35.9%
29,721	GAGE	8,786	6,059	2,477	250	3,582 R	69.0%	28.2%	71.0%	29.0%
4,572	GARDEN	1,395	924	421	50	503 R	66.2%	30.2%	68.7%	31.3%
3,496	GARFIELD	950	611	252	87	359 R	64.3%	26.5%	70.8%	29.2%
4,669	GOSPER	1,368	794	486	88	308 R	58.0%	35.5%	62.0%	38.0%
1,486	GRANT	399	256	141	2	115 R	64.2%	35.3%	64.5%	35.5%
8,685	GREELEY	2,618	1,345	1,180	93	165 R	51.4%	45.1%	53.3%	46.7%
23,720	HALL	7,123	4,719	1,724	680	2,995 R	66.3%	24.2%	73.2%	26.8%
13,237	HAMILTON	4,410	2,950	1,356	104	1,594 R	66.9%	30.7%	68.5%	31.5%
9,220	HARLAN	2,947	1,756	974	217	782 R	59.6%	33.1%	64.3%	35.7%
3,327	HAYES	771	512	207	52	305 R	66.4%	26.8%	71.2%	28.8%
6,045	HITCHCOCK	1,830	1,127	615	88	512 R	61.6%	33.6%	64.7%	35.3%
17,151	HOLT	4,898	3,163	1,577	158	1,586 R	64.6%	32.2%	66.7%	33.3%
1,378	HOOKER	362	230	117	15	113 R	63.5%	32.3%	66.3%	33.7%
10,739	HOWARD	2,971	1,508	1,311	152	197 R	50.8%	44.1%	53.5%	46.5%
16,140	JEFFERSON	5,134	3,488	1,408	238	2,080 R	67.9%	27.4%	71.2%	28.8%
8,940	JOHNSON	3,389	2,416	909	64	1,507 R	71.3%	26.8%	72.7%	27.3%
8,583	KEARNEY	3,043	1,683	1,273	87	410 R	55.3%	41.8%	56.9%	43.1%
5,294	KEITH	1,622	1,050	472	100	578 R	64.7%	29.1%	69.0%	31.0%
3,594	KEYA PAHA	740	479	218	43	261 R	64.7%	29.5%	68.7%	31.3%
4,498	KIMBALL	1,299	910	339	50	571 R	70.1%	26.1%	72.9%	27.1%
18,894	KNOX	5,264	3,678	1,470	116	2,208 R	69.9%	27.9%	71.4%	28.6%
85,902	LANCASTER	24,990	15,638	8,435	917	7,203 R	62.6%	33.8%	65.0%	35.0%
23,420	LINCOLN	5,822	3,342	1,896	584	1,446 R	57.4%	32.6%	63.8%	36.2%
1,596	LOGAN	540	312	180	48	132 R	57.8%	33.3%	63.4%	36.6%
1,946	LOUP	514	343	117	54	226 R	66.7%	22.8%	74.6%	25.4%
1,692	MCPHERSON	327	229	75	23	154 R	70.0%	22.9%	75.3%	24.7%
22,511	MADISON	7,056	5,171	1,716	169	3,455 R	73.3%	24.3%	75.1%	24.9%

NEBRASKA

PRESIDENT 1920

1920 Census Population	County	Total Vote	Republican	Democratic	Other	Rep.-Dem. Plurality	Percentage Total Vote Rep.	Percentage Total Vote Dem.	Percentage Major Vote Rep.	Percentage Major Vote Dem.
10,763	MERRICK	3,663	2,385	1,075	203	1,310 R	65.1%	29.3%	68.9%	31.1%
9,151	MORRILL	2,085	1,366	667	52	699 R	65.5%	32.0%	67.2%	32.8%
8,712	NANCE	2,701	1,877	746	78	1,131 R	69.5%	27.6%	71.6%	28.4%
12,547	NEMAHA	4,511	2,888	1,512	111	1,376 R	64.0%	33.5%	65.6%	34.4%
13,236	NUCKOLLS	4,116	2,637	1,337	142	1,300 R	64.1%	32.5%	66.4%	33.6%
19,494	OTOE	5,722	3,869	1,671	182	2,198 R	67.6%	29.2%	69.8%	30.2%
9,578	PAWNEE	3,592	2,510	972	110	1,538 R	69.9%	27.1%	72.1%	27.9%
3,967	PERKINS	1,180	722	387	71	335 R	61.2%	32.8%	65.1%	34.9%
9,900	PHELPS	3,754	2,324	1,169	261	1,155 R	61.9%	31.1%	66.5%	33.5%
10,681	PIERCE	3,299	2,478	743	78	1,735 R	75.1%	22.5%	76.9%	23.1%
19,464	PLATTE	5,493	4,058	1,367	68	2,691 R	73.9%	24.9%	74.8%	25.2%
10,714	POLK	3,751	2,393	1,236	122	1,157 R	63.8%	33.0%	65.9%	34.1%
11,434	RED WILLOW	3,385	1,993	1,133	259	860 R	58.9%	33.5%	63.8%	36.2%
18,968	RICHARDSON	7,284	4,496	2,679	109	1,817 R	61.7%	36.8%	62.7%	37.3%
3,703	ROCK	885	621	239	25	382 R	70.2%	27.0%	72.2%	27.8%
16,514	SALINE	5,449	3,197	2,172	80	1,025 R	58.7%	39.9%	59.5%	40.5%
9,370	SARPY	2,780	1,662	1,027	91	635 R	59.8%	36.9%	61.8%	38.2%
20,589	SAUNDERS	6,223	3,733	2,296	194	1,437 R	60.0%	36.9%	61.9%	38.1%
20,710	SCOTTS BLUFF	4,459	3,189	969	301	2,220 R	71.5%	21.7%	76.7%	23.3%
15,867	SEWARD	5,273	3,690	1,497	86	2,193 R	70.0%	28.4%	71.1%	28.9%
9,625	SHERIDAN	2,656	1,714	784	158	930 R	64.5%	29.5%	68.6%	31.4%
8,877	SHERMAN	2,595	1,582	848	165	734 R	61.0%	32.7%	65.1%	34.9%
4,528	SIOUX	965	627	252	86	375 R	65.0%	26.1%	71.3%	28.7%
7,756	STANTON	2,005	1,457	501	47	956 R	72.7%	25.0%	74.4%	25.6%
13,976	THAYER	4,714	3,456	1,120	138	2,336 R	73.3%	23.8%	75.5%	24.5%
1,773	THOMAS	546	305	207	34	98 R	55.9%	37.9%	59.6%	40.4%
9,589	THURSTON	2,632	1,667	925	40	742 R	63.3%	35.1%	64.3%	35.7%
9,823	VALLEY	2,986	1,935	912	139	1,023 R	64.8%	30.5%	68.0%	32.0%
12,180	WASHINGTON	3,788	2,409	1,295	84	1,114 R	63.6%	34.2%	65.0%	35.0%
9,725	WAYNE	3,105	2,312	681	112	1,631 R	74.5%	21.9%	77.2%	22.8%
10,922	WEBSTER	3,675	2,599	913	163	1,686 R	70.7%	24.8%	74.0%	26.0%
2,531	WHEELER	612	352	165	95	187 R	57.5%	27.0%	68.1%	31.9%
17,146	YORK	6,378	4,265	1,857	256	2,408 R	66.9%	29.1%	69.7%	30.3%
1,296,372	TOTAL	382,743	247,498	119,608	15,637	127,890 R	64.7%	31.3%	67.4%	32.6%

NEBRASKA

ELECTION NOTES

1956

1952

1948 Other vote was write-in.

1944

1940

1936 Other vote was Lemke (Union).

1932 Other vote was Thomas (Socialist).

1928 Other vote was Thomas (Socialist).

1924 A special four-column table which gives the LaFollette (Progressive) vote is used to detail this election. Other vote was Faris (Prohibition).

1920 Other vote was 9,600 Debs (Socialist); 5,947 Watkins (Prohibition); 90 scattered write-in.

NEVADA

POPULAR VOTE FOR PRESIDENT 1920 TO 1956

Year	Total Vote	Republican		Democratic		Other Vote	Plurality	Percentage			
								Total Vote		Major Vote	
		Vote	Candidate	Vote	Candidate			Rep.	Dem.	Rep.	Dem.
1956	96,689	56,049	Eisenhower, Dwight D.	40,640	Stevenson, Adlai E.		15,409 R	58.0%	42.0%	58.0%	42.0%
1952	82,190	50,502	Eisenhower, Dwight D.	31,688	Stevenson, Adlai E.		18,814 R	61.4%	38.6%	61.4%	38.6%
1948	62,117	29,357	Dewey, Thomas E.	31,291	Truman, Harry S.	1,469	1,934 D	47.3%	50.4%	48.4%	51.6%
1944	54,234	24,611	Dewey, Thomas E.	29,623	Roosevelt, Franklin D.		5,012 D	45.4%	54.6%	45.4%	54.6%
1940	53,174	21,229	Willkie, Wendell	31,945	Roosevelt, Franklin D.		10,716 D	39.9%	60.1%	39.9%	60.1%
1936	43,848	11,923	Landon, Alfred M.	31,925	Roosevelt, Franklin D.		20,002 D	27.2%	72.8%	27.2%	72.8%
1932	41,430	12,674	Hoover, Herbert C.	28,756	Roosevelt, Franklin D.		16,082 D	30.6%	69.4%	30.6%	69.4%
1928	32,417	18,327	Hoover, Herbert C.	14,090	Smith, Alfred E.		4,237 R	56.5%	43.5%	56.5%	43.5%
1924 **	26,921	11,243	Coolidge, Calvin	5,909	Davis, John W.	9,769	1,474 R	41.8%	21.9%	65.5%	34.5%
1920	27,194	15,479	Harding, Warren G.	9,851	Cox, James M.	1,864	5,628 R	56.9%	36.2%	61.1%	38.9%

In 1924 other vote was Progressive.

ELECTORAL COLLEGE VOTE 1920 TO 1956

Year	Total	Republican	Democratic	Other
1956	3	3	—	—
1952	3	3	—	—
1948	3	—	3	—
1944	3	—	3	—
1940	3	—	3	—
1936	3	—	3	—
1932	3	—	3	—
1928	3	3	—	—
1924	3	3	—	—
1920	3	3	—	—

NEVADA

HUMBOLDT
ELKO
WASHOE
PERSHING
LANDER
EUREKA
CHURCHILL
STOREY
WHITE PINE
Carson City
DOUGLAS
LYON
MINERAL
NYE
ESMERALDA
LINCOLN
CLARK

NEVADA

PRESIDENT 1956

1950 Census Population	County	Total Vote	Republican	Democratic	Other	Rep.-Dem. Plurality	Percentage Total Vote Rep.	Total Vote Dem.	Major Vote Rep.	Major Vote Dem.
6,161	CHURCHILL	3,082	2,013	1,069		944 R	65.3%	34.7%	65.3%	34.7%
48,289	CLARK	37,679	18,584	19,095		511 D	49.3%	50.7%	49.3%	50.7%
2,029	DOUGLAS	1,319	1,063	256		807 R	80.6%	19.4%	80.6%	19.4%
11,654	ELKO	4,717	2,981	1,736		1,245 R	63.2%	36.8%	63.2%	36.8%
614	ESMERALDA	288	164	124		40 R	56.9%	43.1%	56.9%	43.1%
896	EUREKA	513	330	183		147 R	64.3%	35.7%	64.3%	35.7%
4,838	HUMBOLDT	2,132	1,292	840		452 R	60.6%	39.4%	60.6%	39.4%
1,850	LANDER	823	540	283		257 R	65.6%	34.4%	65.6%	34.4%
3,837	LINCOLN	1,688	885	803		82 R	52.4%	47.6%	52.4%	47.6%
3,679	LYON	2,478	1,697	781		916 R	68.5%	31.5%	68.5%	31.5%
5,560	MINERAL	2,848	1,433	1,415		18 R	50.3%	49.7%	50.3%	49.7%
3,101	NYE	1,695	946	749		197 R	55.8%	44.2%	55.8%	44.2%
4,172	ORMSBY	2,571	1,749	822		927 R	68.0%	32.0%	68.0%	32.0%
3,103	PERSHING	1,457	895	562		333 R	61.4%	38.6%	61.4%	38.6%
671	STOREY	376	226	150		76 R	60.1%	39.9%	60.1%	39.9%
50,205	WASHOE	28,390	18,865	9,525		9,340 R	66.4%	33.6%	66.4%	33.6%
9,424	WHITE PINE	4,633	2,386	2,247		139 R	51.5%	48.5%	51.5%	48.5%
160,083	TOTAL	96,689	56,049	40,640		15,409 R	58.0%	42.0%	58.0%	42.0%

NEVADA

PRESIDENT 1952

1950 Census Population	County	Total Vote	Republican	Democratic	Other	Rep.-Dem. Plurality	Percentage Total Vote Rep.	Total Vote Dem.	Major Vote Rep.	Major Vote Dem.
6,161	CHURCHILL	2,851	1,948	903		1,045 R	68.3%	31.7%	68.3%	31.7%
48,289	CLARK	25,188	13,333	11,855		1,478 R	52.9%	47.1%	52.9%	47.1%
2,029	DOUGLAS	1,125	948	177		771 R	84.3%	15.7%	84.3%	15.7%
11,654	ELKO	4,859	3,104	1,755		1,349 R	63.9%	36.1%	63.9%	36.1%
614	ESMERALDA	313	174	139		35 R	55.6%	44.4%	55.6%	44.4%
896	EUREKA	536	379	157		222 R	70.7%	29.3%	70.7%	29.3%
4,838	HUMBOLDT	2,089	1,398	691		707 R	66.9%	33.1%	66.9%	33.1%
1,850	LANDER	738	501	237		264 R	67.9%	32.1%	67.9%	32.1%
3,837	LINCOLN	1,844	903	941		38 D	49.0%	51.0%	49.0%	51.0%
3,679	LYON	2,029	1,453	576		877 R	71.6%	28.4%	71.6%	28.4%
5,560	MINERAL	2,666	1,297	1,369		72 D	48.6%	51.4%	48.6%	51.4%
3,101	NYE	1,604	1,037	567		470 R	64.7%	35.3%	64.7%	35.3%
4,172	ORMSBY	2,232	1,653	579		1,074 R	74.1%	25.9%	74.1%	25.9%
3,103	PERSHING	1,441	919	522		397 R	63.8%	36.2%	63.8%	36.2%
671	STOREY	355	206	149		57 R	58.0%	42.0%	58.0%	42.0%
50,205	WASHOE	27,932	19,044	8,888		10,156 R	68.2%	31.8%	68.2%	31.8%
9,424	WHITE PINE	4,388	2,205	2,183		22 R	50.3%	49.7%	50.3%	49.7%
160,083	TOTAL	82,190	50,502	31,688		18,814 R	61.4%	38.6%	61.4%	38.6%

NEVADA

PRESIDENT 1948

1940 Census Population	County	Total Vote	Republican	Democratic	Other	Rep.-Dem. Plurality	Percentage Total Vote Rep.	Total Vote Dem.	Major Vote Rep.	Major Vote Dem.
5,317	CHURCHILL	2,372	1,206	1,055	111	151 R	50.8%	44.5%	53.3%	46.7%
16,414	CLARK	17,453	6,382	10,787	284	4,405 D	36.6%	61.8%	37.2%	62.8%
2,056	DOUGLAS	1,032	719	298	15	421 R	69.7%	28.9%	70.7%	29.3%
10,912	ELKO	3,771	1,683	2,026	62	343 D	44.6%	53.7%	45.4%	54.6%
1,554	ESMERALDA	365	164	183	18	19 D	44.9%	50.1%	47.3%	52.7%
1,361	EUREKA	603	312	278	13	34 R	51.7%	46.1%	52.9%	47.1%
4,743	HUMBOLDT	1,831	901	886	44	15 R	49.2%	48.4%	50.4%	49.6%
1,745	LANDER	704	397	298	9	99 R	56.4%	42.3%	57.1%	42.9%
4,130	LINCOLN	1,553	520	1,004	29	484 D	33.5%	64.6%	34.1%	65.9%
4,076	LYON	1,633	967	629	37	338 R	59.2%	38.5%	60.6%	39.4%
2,342	MINERAL	1,928	706	1,194	28	488 D	36.6%	61.9%	37.2%	62.8%
3,606	NYE	1,390	722	595	73	127 R	51.9%	42.8%	54.8%	45.2%
3,209	ORMSBY	1,801	1,095	681	25	414 R	60.8%	37.8%	61.7%	38.3%
2,713	PERSHING	1,262	677	541	44	136 R	53.6%	42.9%	55.6%	44.4%
1,216	STOREY	388	187	184	17	3 R	48.2%	47.4%	50.4%	49.6%
32,476	WASHOE	20,188	11,323	8,365	500	2,958 R	56.1%	41.4%	57.5%	42.5%
12,377	WHITE PINE	3,843	1,396	2,287	160	891 D	36.3%	59.5%	37.9%	62.1%
110,247	TOTAL	62,117	29,357	31,291	1,469	1,934 D	47.3%	50.4%	48.4%	51.6%

NEVADA

PRESIDENT 1944

1940 Census Population	County	Total Vote	Republican	Democratic	Other	Rep.-Dem. Plurality	Percentage Total Vote Rep.	Total Vote Dem.	Major Vote Rep.	Major Vote Dem.
5,317	CHURCHILL	2,176	1,130	1,046		84 R	51.9%	48.1%	51.9%	48.1%
16,414	CLARK	11,893	4,543	7,350		2,807 D	38.2%	61.8%	38.2%	61.8%
2,056	DOUGLAS	838	556	282		274 R	66.3%	33.7%	66.3%	33.7%
10,912	ELKO	3,922	1,642	2,280		638 D	41.9%	58.1%	41.9%	58.1%
1,554	ESMERALDA	373	150	223		73 D	40.2%	59.8%	40.2%	59.8%
1,361	EUREKA	534	317	217		100 R	59.4%	40.6%	59.4%	40.6%
4,743	HUMBOLDT	1,829	835	994		159 D	45.7%	54.3%	45.7%	54.3%
1,745	LANDER	808	425	383		42 R	52.6%	47.4%	52.6%	47.4%
4,130	LINCOLN	1,819	524	1,295		771 D	28.8%	71.2%	28.8%	71.2%
4,076	LYON	1,603	895	708		187 R	55.8%	44.2%	55.8%	44.2%
2,342	MINERAL	2,095	751	1,344		593 D	35.8%	64.2%	35.8%	64.2%
3,606	NYE	1,666	723	943		220 D	43.4%	56.6%	43.4%	56.6%
3,209	ORMSBY	1,506	841	665		176 R	55.8%	44.2%	55.8%	44.2%
2,713	PERSHING	1,062	538	524		14 R	50.7%	49.3%	50.7%	49.3%
1,216	STOREY	336	163	173		10 D	48.5%	51.5%	48.5%	51.5%
32,476	WASHOE	17,408	9,024	8,384		640 R	51.8%	48.2%	51.8%	48.2%
12,377	WHITE PINE	4,366	1,554	2,812		1,258 D	35.6%	64.4%	35.6%	64.4%
110,247	TOTAL	54,234	24,611	29,623		5,012 D	45.4%	54.6%	45.4%	54.6%

NEVADA

PRESIDENT 1940

1940 Census Population	County	Total Vote	Republican	Democratic	Other	Rep.-Dem. Plurality	Percentage Total Vote Rep.	Total Vote Dem.	Major Vote Rep.	Major Vote Dem.
5,317	CHURCHILL	2,438	1,171	1,267		96 D	48.0%	52.0%	48.0%	52.0%
16,414	CLARK	7,324	2,170	5,154		2,984 D	29.6%	70.4%	29.6%	70.4%
2,056	DOUGLAS	922	592	330		262 R	64.2%	35.8%	64.2%	35.8%
10,912	ELKO	4,799	1,783	3,016		1,233 D	37.2%	62.8%	37.2%	62.8%
1,554	ESMERALDA	931	292	639		347 D	31.4%	68.6%	31.4%	68.6%
1,361	EUREKA	637	284	353		69 D	44.6%	55.4%	44.6%	55.4%
4,743	HUMBOLDT	2,156	789	1,367		578 D	36.6%	63.4%	36.6%	63.4%
1,745	LANDER	868	393	475		82 D	45.3%	54.7%	45.3%	54.7%
4,130	LINCOLN	2,062	461	1,601		1,140 D	22.4%	77.6%	22.4%	77.6%
4,076	LYON	2,030	963	1,067		104 D	47.4%	52.6%	47.4%	52.6%
2,342	MINERAL	1,099	406	693		287 D	36.9%	63.1%	36.9%	63.1%
3,606	NYE	1,935	729	1,206		477 D	37.7%	62.3%	37.7%	62.3%
3,209	ORMSBY	1,533	748	785		37 D	48.8%	51.2%	48.8%	51.2%
2,713	PERSHING	1,290	594	696		102 D	46.0%	54.0%	46.0%	54.0%
1,216	STOREY	606	224	382		158 D	37.0%	63.0%	37.0%	63.0%
32,476	WASHOE	17,305	8,062	9,243		1,181 D	46.6%	53.4%	46.6%	53.4%
12,377	WHITE PINE	5,239	1,568	3,671		2,103 D	29.9%	70.1%	29.9%	70.1%
110,247	TOTAL	53,174	21,229	31,945		10,716 D	39.9%	60.1%	39.9%	60.1%

NEVADA

PRESIDENT 1936

1930 Census Population	County	Total Vote	Republican	Democratic	Other	Rep.-Dem. Plurality	Percentage Total Vote Rep.	Total Vote Dem.	Major Vote Rep.	Major Vote Dem.
5,075	CHURCHILL	2,049	759	1,290		531 D	37.0%	63.0%	37.0%	63.0%
8,532	CLARK	6,269	1,178	5,091		3,913 D	18.8%	81.2%	18.8%	81.2%
1,840	DOUGLAS	812	346	466		120 D	42.6%	57.4%	42.6%	57.4%
9,960	ELKO	3,953	1,065	2,888		1,823 D	26.9%	73.1%	26.9%	73.1%
1,077	ESMERALDA	722	156	566		410 D	21.6%	78.4%	21.6%	78.4%
1,333	EUREKA	576	180	396		216 D	31.3%	68.8%	31.3%	68.8%
3,795	HUMBOLDT	1,600	390	1,210		820 D	24.4%	75.6%	24.4%	75.6%
1,714	LANDER	822	237	585		348 D	28.8%	71.2%	28.8%	71.2%
3,601	LINCOLN	1,893	254	1,639		1,385 D	13.4%	86.6%	13.4%	86.6%
3,810	LYON	1,690	487	1,203		716 D	28.8%	71.2%	28.8%	71.2%
1,863	MINERAL	1,014	236	778		542 D	23.3%	76.7%	23.3%	76.7%
3,989	NYE	1,959	464	1,495		1,031 D	23.7%	76.3%	23.7%	76.3%
2,221	ORMSBY	1,278	533	745		212 D	41.7%	58.3%	41.7%	58.3%
2,652	PERSHING	1,130	269	861		592 D	23.8%	76.2%	23.8%	76.2%
667	STOREY	531	139	392		253 D	26.2%	73.8%	26.2%	73.8%
27,158	WASHOE	13,872	4,358	9,514		5,156 D	31.4%	68.6%	31.4%	68.6%
11,771	WHITE PINE	3,678	872	2,806		1,934 D	23.7%	76.3%	23.7%	76.3%
91,058	TOTAL	43,848	11,923	31,925		20,002 D	27.2%	72.8%	27.2%	72.8%

NEVADA

PRESIDENT 1932

1930 Census Population	County	Total Vote	Republican	Democratic	Other	Rep.-Dem. Plurality	Percentage Total Vote Rep.	Total Vote Dem.	Major Vote Rep.	Major Vote Dem.
5,075	CHURCHILL	2,192	674	1,518		844 D	30.7%	69.3%	30.7%	69.3%
8,532	CLARK	7,184	1,347	5,837		4,490 D	18.8%	81.3%	18.8%	81.3%
1,840	DOUGLAS	729	331	398		67 D	45.4%	54.6%	45.4%	54.6%
9,960	ELKO	3,887	1,325	2,562		1,237 D	34.1%	65.9%	34.1%	65.9%
1,077	ESMERALDA	573	147	426		279 D	25.7%	74.3%	25.7%	74.3%
1,333	EUREKA	521	136	385		249 D	26.1%	73.9%	26.1%	73.9%
3,795	HUMBOLDT	1,531	405	1,126		721 D	26.5%	73.5%	26.5%	73.5%
1,714	LANDER	808	272	536		264 D	33.7%	66.3%	33.7%	66.3%
3,601	LINCOLN	1,400	295	1,105		810 D	21.1%	78.9%	21.1%	78.9%
3,810	LYON	1,439	456	983		527 D	31.7%	68.3%	31.7%	68.3%
1,863	MINERAL	885	238	647		409 D	26.9%	73.1%	26.9%	73.1%
3,989	NYE	1,802	506	1,296		790 D	28.1%	71.9%	28.1%	71.9%
2,221	ORMSBY	1,065	486	579		93 D	45.6%	54.4%	45.6%	54.4%
2,652	PERSHING	1,039	247	792		545 D	23.8%	76.2%	23.8%	76.2%
667	STOREY	371	124	247		123 D	33.4%	66.6%	33.4%	66.6%
27,158	WASHOE	12,474	4,333	8,141		3,808 D	34.7%	65.3%	34.7%	65.3%
11,771	WHITE PINE	3,530	1,352	2,178		826 D	38.3%	61.7%	38.3%	61.7%
91,058	TOTAL	41,430	12,674	28,756		16,082 D	30.6%	69.4%	30.6%	69.4%

NEVADA

PRESIDENT 1928

1920 Census Population	County	Total Vote	Republican	Democratic	Other	Rep.-Dem. Plurality	Percentage Total Vote Rep.	Total Vote Dem.	Major Vote Rep.	Major Vote Dem.
4,649	CHURCHILL	1,877	1,126	751		375 R	60.0%	40.0%	60.0%	40.0%
4,859	CLARK	2,268	1,284	984		300 R	56.6%	43.4%	56.6%	43.4%
1,825	DOUGLAS	642	456	186		270 R	71.0%	29.0%	71.0%	29.0%
8,083	ELKO	3,318	1,876	1,442		434 R	56.5%	43.5%	56.5%	43.5%
2,410	ESMERALDA	646	305	341		36 D	47.2%	52.8%	47.2%	52.8%
1,350	EUREKA	512	251	261		10 D	49.0%	51.0%	49.0%	51.0%
3,743	HUMBOLDT	1,385	783	602		181 R	56.5%	43.5%	56.5%	43.5%
1,484	LANDER	770	456	314		142 R	59.2%	40.8%	59.2%	40.8%
2,287	LINCOLN	1,095	553	542		11 R	50.5%	49.5%	50.5%	49.5%
4,078	LYON	1,631	927	704		223 R	56.8%	43.2%	56.8%	43.2%
1,848	MINERAL	601	275	326		51 D	45.8%	54.2%	45.8%	54.2%
6,504	NYE	2,081	958	1,123		165 D	46.0%	54.0%	46.0%	54.0%
2,453	ORMSBY	1,016	590	426		164 R	58.1%	41.9%	58.1%	41.9%
2,803	PERSHING	995	543	452		91 R	54.6%	45.4%	54.6%	45.4%
1,469	STOREY	456	185	271		86 D	40.6%	59.4%	40.6%	59.4%
18,627	WASHOE	9,719	5,767	3,952		1,815 R	59.3%	40.7%	59.3%	40.7%
8,935	WHITE PINE	3,405	1,992	1,413		579 R	58.5%	41.5%	58.5%	41.5%
77,407	TOTAL	32,417	18,327	14,090		4,237 R	56.5%	43.5%	56.5%	43.5%

NEVADA

PRESIDENT 1924

1920 Census Population	County	Total Vote	Republican	Democratic	Progressive	Other	Plurality	Percentage Total Vote Rep.	Dem.	Prog.
4,649	CHURCHILL	1,573	655	310	608		47 R	41.6%	19.7%	38.7%
4,859	CLARK	1,636	533	288	815		282 P	32.6%	17.6%	49.8%
1,825	DOUGLAS	581	343	95	143		200 R	59.0%	16.4%	24.6%
8,083	ELKO	2,868	1,113	604	1,151		38 P	38.8%	21.1%	40.1%
2,410	ESMERALDA	726	241	150	335		94 P	33.2%	20.7%	46.1%
1,350	EUREKA	418	209	94	115		94 R	50.0%	22.5%	27.5%
3,743	HUMBOLDT	1,133	400	248	485		85 P	35.3%	21.9%	42.8%
1,484	LANDER	545	254	138	153		101 R	46.6%	25.3%	28.1%
2,287	LINCOLN	738	200	257	281		24 P	27.1%	34.8%	38.1%
4,078	LYON	1,303	618	231	454		164 R	47.4%	17.7%	34.8%
1,848	MINERAL	504	191	84	229		38 P	37.9%	16.7%	45.4%
6,504	NYE	2,227	884	454	889		5 P	39.7%	20.4%	39.9%
2,453	ORMSBY	932	413	415	104		2 D	44.3%	44.5%	11.2%
2,803	PERSHING	854	308	164	382		74 P	36.1%	19.2%	44.7%
1,469	STOREY	761	283	209	269		14 R	37.2%	27.5%	35.3%
18,627	WASHOE	7,766	3,549	1,669	2,548		1,001 R	45.7%	21.5%	32.8%
8,935	WHITE PINE	2,356	1,049	499	808		241 R	44.5%	21.2%	34.3%
77,407	TOTAL	26,921	11,243	5,909	9,769		1,474 R	41.8%	21.9%	36.3%

NEVADA

PRESIDENT 1920

1920 Census Population	County	Total Vote	Republican	Democratic	Other	Rep.-Dem. Plurality	Percentage Total Vote Rep.	Total Vote Dem.	Major Vote Rep.	Major Vote Dem.
4,649	CHURCHILL	1,616	873	506	237	367 R	54.0%	31.3%	63.3%	36.7%
4,859	CLARK	1,320	589	620	111	31 D	44.6%	47.0%	48.7%	51.3%
1,825	DOUGLAS	656	503	147	6	356 R	76.7%	22.4%	77.4%	22.6%
8,083	ELKO	2,521	1,369	1,029	123	340 R	54.3%	40.8%	57.1%	42.9%
2,410	ESMERALDA	940	466	347	127	119 R	49.6%	36.9%	57.3%	42.7%
1,350	EUREKA	491	313	157	21	156 R	63.7%	32.0%	66.6%	33.4%
3,743	HUMBOLDT	1,284	660	532	92	128 R	51.4%	41.4%	55.4%	44.6%
1,484	LANDER	709	416	254	39	162 R	58.7%	35.8%	62.1%	37.9%
2,287	LINCOLN	783	373	366	44	7 R	47.6%	46.7%	50.5%	49.5%
4,078	LYON	1,408	945	344	119	601 R	67.1%	24.4%	73.3%	26.7%
1,848	MINERAL	629	374	209	46	165 R	59.5%	33.2%	64.2%	35.8%
6,504	NYE	2,899	1,576	1,007	316	569 R	54.4%	34.7%	61.0%	39.0%
2,453	ORMSBY	1,024	592	413	19	179 R	57.8%	40.3%	58.9%	41.1%
2,803	PERSHING	996	563	389	44	174 R	56.5%	39.1%	59.1%	40.9%
1,469	STOREY	617	324	272	21	52 R	52.5%	44.1%	54.4%	45.6%
18,627	WASHOE	6,865	4,189	2,357	319	1,832 R	61.0%	34.3%	64.0%	36.0%
8,935	WHITE PINE	2,436	1,354	902	180	452 R	55.6%	37.0%	60.0%	40.0%
77,407	TOTAL	27,194	15,479	9,851	1,864	5,628 R	56.9%	36.2%	61.1%	38.9%

NEVADA

ELECTION NOTES

1956

1952

1948 Other vote was Wallace (Progressive).

1944

1940

1936

1932

1928

1924 A special four-column table which gives the LaFollette (Progressive) vote is used to detail this election.

1920 Other vote was Debs (Socialist).

NEW HAMPSHIRE

POPULAR VOTE FOR PRESIDENT 1920 TO 1956

		Republican		Democratic				Percentage			
								Total Vote		Major Vote	
Year	Total Vote	Vote	Candidate	Vote	Candidate	Other Vote	Plurality	Rep.	Dem.	Rep.	Dem.
1956	266,994	176,519	Eisenhower, Dwight D.	90,364	Stevenson, Adlai E.	111	86,155 R	66.1%	33.8%	66.1%	33.9%
1952	272,950	166,287	Eisenhower, Dwight D.	106,663	Stevenson, Adlai E.		59,624 R	60.9%	39.1%	60.9%	39.1%
1948	231,440	121,299	Dewey, Thomas E.	107,995	Truman, Harry S.	2,146	13,304 R	52.4%	46.7%	52.9%	47.1%
1944	229,625	109,916	Dewey, Thomas E.	119,663	Roosevelt, Franklin D.	46	9,747 D	47.9%	52.1%	47.9%	52.1%
1940	235,419	110,127	Willkie, Wendell	125,292	Roosevelt, Franklin D.		15,165 D	46.8%	53.2%	46.8%	53.2%
1936	218,114	104,642	Landon, Alfred M.	108,460	Roosevelt, Franklin D.	5,012	3,818 D	48.0%	49.7%	49.1%	50.9%
1932	205,520	103,629	Hoover, Herbert C.	100,680	Roosevelt, Franklin D.	1,211	2,949 R	50.4%	49.0%	50.7%	49.3%
1928	196,757	115,404	Hoover, Herbert C.	80,715	Smith, Alfred E.	638	34,689 R	58.7%	41.0%	58.8%	41.2%
1924	164,769	98,575	Coolidge, Calvin	57,201	Davis, John W.	8,993	41,374 R	59.8%	34.7%	63.3%	36.7%
1920	159,092	95,196	Harding, Warren G.	62,662	Cox, James M.	1,234	32,534 R	59.8%	39.4%	60.3%	39.7%

ELECTORAL COLLEGE VOTE 1920 TO 1956

Year	Total	Republican	Democratic	Other
1956	4	4	—	—
1952	4	4	—	—
1948	4	4	—	—
1944	4	—	4	—
1940	4	—	4	—
1936	4	—	4	—
1932	4	4	—	—
1928	4	4	—	—
1924	4	4	—	—
1920	4	4	—	—

NEW HAMPSHIRE

NEW HAMPSHIRE

PRESIDENT 1956

1950 Census Population	County	Total Vote	Republican	Democratic	Other	Rep.-Dem. Plurality	Percentage Total Vote Rep.	Total Vote Dem.	Major Vote Rep.	Major Vote Dem.
26,632	BELKNAP	13,038	9,902	3,131	5	6,771 R	75.9%	24.0%	76.0%	24.0%
15,868	CARROLL	8,816	7,527	1,281	8	6,246 R	85.4%	14.5%	85.5%	14.5%
38,811	CHESHIRE	18,170	12,585	5,574	11	7,011 R	69.3%	30.7%	69.3%	30.7%
35,932	COOS	17,338	11,465	5,871	2	5,594 R	66.1%	33.9%	66.1%	33.9%
47,923	GRAFTON	21,081	15,609	5,466	6	10,143 R	74.0%	25.9%	74.1%	25.9%
156,987	HILLSBOROUGH	81,528	45,248	36,234	46	9,014 R	55.5%	44.4%	55.5%	44.5%
63,022	MERRIMACK	30,774	22,060	8,711	3	13,349 R	71.7%	28.3%	71.7%	28.3%
70,059	ROCKINGHAM	38,442	28,226	10,198	18	18,028 R	73.4%	26.5%	73.5%	26.5%
51,567	STRAFFORD	25,160	15,494	9,659	7	5,835 R	61.6%	38.4%	61.6%	38.4%
26,441	SULLIVAN	12,647	8,403	4,239	5	4,164 R	66.4%	33.5%	66.5%	33.5%
533,242	TOTAL	266,994	176,519	90,364	111	86,155 R	66.1%	33.8%	66.1%	33.9%

NEW HAMPSHIRE

PRESIDENT 1952

1950 Census Population	County	Total Vote	Republican	Democratic	Other	Rep.-Dem. Plurality	Percentage Total Vote Rep.	Total Vote Dem.	Major Vote Rep.	Major Vote Dem.
26,632	BELKNAP	13,322	9,567	3,755		5,812 R	71.8%	28.2%	71.8%	28.2%
15,868	CARROLL	9,076	7,498	1,578		5,920 R	82.6%	17.4%	82.6%	17.4%
38,811	CHESHIRE	18,607	11,897	6,710		5,187 R	63.9%	36.1%	63.9%	36.1%
35,932	COOS	17,823	9,975	7,848		2,127 R	56.0%	44.0%	56.0%	44.0%
47,923	GRAFTON	22,061	15,937	6,124		9,813 R	72.2%	27.8%	72.2%	27.8%
156,987	HILLSBOROUGH	83,065	41,263	41,802		539 D	49.7%	50.3%	49.7%	50.3%
63,022	MERRIMACK	32,134	21,824	10,310		11,514 R	67.9%	32.1%	67.9%	32.1%
70,059	ROCKINGHAM	38,320	26,280	12,040		14,240 R	68.6%	31.4%	68.6%	31.4%
51,567	STRAFFORD	25,482	13,729	11,753		1,976 R	53.9%	46.1%	53.9%	46.1%
26,441	SULLIVAN	13,060	8,317	4,743		3,574 R	63.7%	36.3%	63.7%	36.3%
533,242	TOTAL	272,950	166,287	106,663		59,624 R	60.9%	39.1%	60.9%	39.1%

NEW HAMPSHIRE

PRESIDENT 1948

1940 Census Population	County	Total Vote	Republican	Democratic	Other	Rep.-Dem. Plurality	Percentage Total Vote Rep.	Percentage Total Vote Dem.	Percentage Major Vote Rep.	Percentage Major Vote Dem.
24,328	BELKNAP	11,039	7,152	3,822	65	3,330 R	64.8%	34.6%	65.2%	34.8%
15,589	CARROLL	8,050	6,127	1,869	54	4,258 R	76.1%	23.2%	76.6%	23.4%
34,953	CHESHIRE	15,506	9,043	6,337	126	2,706 R	58.3%	40.9%	58.8%	41.2%
39,274	COOS	15,165	7,005	7,930	230	925 D	46.2%	52.3%	46.9%	53.1%
44,645	GRAFTON	19,281	12,248	6,841	192	5,407 R	63.5%	35.5%	64.2%	35.8%
144,888	HILLSBOROUGH	70,742	28,257	41,789	696	13,532 D	39.9%	59.1%	40.3%	59.7%
60,710	MERRIMACK	27,935	16,586	11,171	178	5,415 R	59.4%	40.0%	59.8%	40.2%
58,142	ROCKINGHAM	31,128	18,890	11,937	301	6,953 R	60.7%	38.3%	61.3%	38.7%
43,553	STRAFFORD	21,776	9,988	11,603	185	1,615 D	45.9%	53.3%	46.3%	53.7%
25,442	SULLIVAN	10,818	6,003	4,696	119	1,307 R	55.5%	43.4%	56.1%	43.9%
491,524	TOTAL	231,440	121,299	107,995	2,146	13,304 R	52.4%	46.7%	52.9%	47.1%

NEW HAMPSHIRE

PRESIDENT 1944

1940 Census Population	County	Total Vote	Republican	Democratic	Other	Rep.-Dem. Plurality	Percentage Total Vote Rep.	Percentage Total Vote Dem.	Percentage Major Vote Rep.	Percentage Major Vote Dem.
24,328	BELKNAP	11,515	6,188	5,325	2	863 R	53.7%	46.2%	53.7%	46.3%
15,589	CARROLL	7,713	5,251	2,461	1	2,790 R	68.1%	31.9%	68.1%	31.9%
34,953	CHESHIRE	15,432	8,334	7,098		1,236 R	54.0%	46.0%	54.0%	46.0%
39,274	COOS	14,922	6,209	8,709	4	2,500 D	41.6%	58.4%	41.6%	58.4%
44,645	GRAFTON	19,697	10,947	8,743	7	2,204 R	55.6%	44.4%	55.6%	44.4%
144,888	HILLSBOROUGH	68,236	25,921	42,306	9	16,385 D	38.0%	62.0%	38.0%	62.0%
60,710	MERRIMACK	27,983	14,599	13,382	2	1,217 R	52.2%	47.8%	52.2%	47.8%
58,142	ROCKINGHAM	30,316	17,144	13,170	2	3,974 R	56.6%	43.4%	56.6%	43.4%
43,553	STRAFFORD	21,898	9,388	12,497	13	3,109 D	42.9%	57.1%	42.9%	57.1%
25,442	SULLIVAN	11,913	5,935	5,972	6	37 D	49.8%	50.1%	49.8%	50.2%
491,524	TOTAL	229,625	109,916	119,663	46	9,747 D	47.9%	52.1%	47.9%	52.1%

NEW HAMPSHIRE

PRESIDENT 1940

1940 Census Population	County	Total Vote	Republican	Democratic	Other	Rep.-Dem. Plurality	Percentage Total Vote Rep.	Percentage Total Vote Dem.	Percentage Major Vote Rep.	Percentage Major Vote Dem.
24,328	BELKNAP	11,768	6,115	5,653		462 R	52.0%	48.0%	52.0%	48.0%
15,589	CARROLL	8,526	5,656	2,870		2,786 R	66.3%	33.7%	66.3%	33.7%
34,953	CHESHIRE	15,218	8,302	6,916		1,386 R	54.6%	45.4%	54.6%	45.4%
39,274	COOS	16,750	6,650	10,100		3,450 D	39.7%	60.3%	39.7%	60.3%
44,645	GRAFTON	21,239	11,478	9,761		1,717 R	54.0%	46.0%	54.0%	46.0%
144,888	HILLSBOROUGH	68,781	26,201	42,580		16,379 D	38.1%	61.9%	38.1%	61.9%
60,710	MERRIMACK	29,615	14,923	14,692		231 R	50.4%	49.6%	50.4%	49.6%
58,142	ROCKINGHAM	30,224	16,223	14,001		2,222 R	53.7%	46.3%	53.7%	46.3%
43,553	STRAFFORD	21,843	8,996	12,847		3,851 D	41.2%	58.8%	41.2%	58.8%
25,442	SULLIVAN	11,455	5,583	5,872		289 D	48.7%	51.3%	48.7%	51.3%
491,524	TOTAL	235,419	110,127	125,292		15,165 D	46.8%	53.2%	46.8%	53.2%

NEW HAMPSHIRE

PRESIDENT 1936

1930 Census Population	County	Total Vote	Republican	Democratic	Other	Rep.-Dem. Plurality	Percentage Total Vote Rep.	Percentage Total Vote Dem.	Percentage Major Vote Rep.	Percentage Major Vote Dem.
22,623	BELKNAP	11,522	6,219	5,150	153	1,069 R	54.0%	44.7%	54.7%	45.3%
14,277	CARROLL	8,325	5,521	2,769	35	2,752 R	66.3%	33.3%	66.6%	33.4%
33,685	CHESHIRE	14,574	8,052	6,322	200	1,730 R	55.2%	43.4%	56.0%	44.0%
38,959	COOS	15,694	6,737	8,737	220	2,000 D	42.9%	55.7%	43.5%	56.5%
42,816	GRAFTON	20,016	11,336	8,520	160	2,816 R	56.6%	42.6%	57.1%	42.9%
140,165	HILLSBOROUGH	61,180	23,293	34,992	2,895	11,699 D	38.1%	57.2%	40.0%	60.0%
56,152	MERRIMACK	28,319	14,456	13,645	218	811 R	51.0%	48.2%	51.4%	48.6%
53,750	ROCKINGHAM	28,249	15,466	12,207	576	3,259 R	54.7%	43.2%	55.9%	44.1%
38,580	STRAFFORD	19,697	8,215	11,005	477	2,790 D	41.7%	55.9%	42.7%	57.3%
24,286	SULLIVAN	10,538	5,347	5,113	78	234 R	50.7%	48.5%	51.1%	48.9%
465,293	TOTAL	218,114	104,642	108,460	5,012	3,818 D	48.0%	49.7%	49.1%	50.9%

NEW HAMPSHIRE

PRESIDENT 1932

1930 Census Population	County	Total Vote	Republican	Democratic	Other	Rep.-Dem. Plurality	Percentage Total Vote Rep.	Total Vote Dem.	Major Vote Rep.	Major Vote Dem.
22,623	BELKNAP	10,988	6,048	4,911	29	1,137 R	55.0%	44.7%	55.2%	44.8%
14,277	CARROLL	8,161	5,269	2,873	19	2,396 R	64.6%	35.2%	64.7%	35.3%
33,685	CHESHIRE	13,692	7,904	5,662	126	2,242 R	57.7%	41.4%	58.3%	41.7%
38,959	COOS	15,205	7,189	7,928	88	739 D	47.3%	52.1%	47.6%	52.4%
42,816	GRAFTON	19,323	10,810	8,342	171	2,468 R	55.9%	43.2%	56.4%	43.6%
140,165	HILLSBOROUGH	56,161	23,308	32,458	395	9,150 D	41.5%	57.8%	41.8%	58.2%
56,152	MERRIMACK	26,908	13,986	12,805	117	1,181 R	52.0%	47.6%	52.2%	47.8%
53,750	ROCKINGHAM	26,405	14,902	11,363	140	3,539 R	56.4%	43.0%	56.7%	43.3%
38,580	STRAFFORD	19,098	9,060	9,970	68	910 D	47.4%	52.2%	47.6%	52.4%
24,286	SULLIVAN	9,579	5,153	4,368	58	785 R	53.8%	45.6%	54.1%	45.9%
465,293	TOTAL	205,520	103,629	100,680	1,211	2,949 R	50.4%	49.0%	50.7%	49.3%

NEW HAMPSHIRE

PRESIDENT 1928

1920 Census Population	County	Total Vote	Republican	Democratic	Other	Rep.-Dem. Plurality	Percentage Total Vote Rep.	Total Vote Dem.	Major Vote Rep.	Major Vote Dem.
21,178	BELKNAP	10,462	6,762	3,689	11	3,073 R	64.6%	35.3%	64.7%	35.3%
15,017	CARROLL	7,117	5,509	1,592	16	3,917 R	77.4%	22.4%	77.6%	22.4%
30,975	CHESHIRE	13,756	8,673	5,025	58	3,648 R	63.0%	36.5%	63.3%	36.7%
36,093	COOS	13,931	7,891	6,006	34	1,885 R	56.6%	43.1%	56.8%	43.2%
40,572	GRAFTON	18,759	12,566	6,035	158	6,531 R	67.0%	32.2%	67.6%	32.4%
135,512	HILLSBOROUGH	54,087	24,465	29,457	165	4,992 D	45.2%	54.5%	45.4%	54.6%
51,770	MERRIMACK	25,935	15,724	10,139	72	5,585 R	60.6%	39.1%	60.8%	39.2%
52,498	ROCKINGHAM	25,425	17,590	7,782	53	9,808 R	69.2%	30.6%	69.3%	30.7%
38,546	STRAFFORD	17,939	10,470	7,441	28	3,029 R	58.4%	41.5%	58.5%	41.5%
20,922	SULLIVAN	9,346	5,754	3,549	43	2,205 R	61.6%	38.0%	61.9%	38.1%
443,083	TOTAL	196,757	115,404	80,715	638	34,689 R	58.7%	41.0%	58.8%	41.2%

NEW HAMPSHIRE

PRESIDENT 1924

1920 Census Population	County	Total Vote	Republican	Democratic	Other	Rep.-Dem. Plurality	Percentage Total Vote Rep.	Percentage Total Vote Dem.	Percentage Major Vote Rep.	Percentage Major Vote Dem.
21,178	BELKNAP	9,399	5,996	3,217	186	2,779 R	63.8%	34.2%	65.1%	34.9%
15,017	CARROLL	6,685	4,372	2,213	100	2,159 R	65.4%	33.1%	66.4%	33.6%
30,975	CHESHIRE	10,156	7,008	2,720	428	4,288 R	69.0%	26.8%	72.0%	28.0%
36,093	COOS	11,651	6,137	4,620	894	1,517 R	52.7%	39.7%	57.1%	42.9%
40,572	GRAFTON	16,364	10,493	5,360	511	5,133 R	64.1%	32.8%	66.2%	33.8%
135,512	HILLSBOROUGH	42,773	22,098	16,002	4,673	6,096 R	51.7%	37.4%	58.0%	42.0%
51,770	MERRIMACK	22,692	13,587	8,283	822	5,304 R	59.9%	36.5%	62.1%	37.9%
52,498	ROCKINGHAM	21,237	14,530	6,073	634	8,457 R	68.4%	28.6%	70.5%	29.5%
38,546	STRAFFORD	16,187	9,167	6,445	575	2,722 R	56.6%	39.8%	58.7%	41.3%
20,922	SULLIVAN	7,625	5,187	2,268	170	2,919 R	68.0%	29.7%	69.6%	30.4%
443,083	TOTAL	164,769	98,575	57,201	8,993	41,374 R	59.8%	34.7%	63.3%	36.7%

NEW HAMPSHIRE

PRESIDENT 1920

1920 Census Population	County	Total Vote	Republican	Democratic	Other	Rep.-Dem. Plurality	Percentage Total Vote Rep.	Percentage Total Vote Dem.	Percentage Major Vote Rep.	Percentage Major Vote Dem.
21,178	BELKNAP	9,115	5,628	3,464	23	2,164 R	61.7%	38.0%	61.9%	38.1%
15,017	CARROLL	6,510	4,214	2,279	17	1,935 R	64.7%	35.0%	64.9%	35.1%
30,975	CHESHIRE	10,092	6,644	3,374	74	3,270 R	65.8%	33.4%	66.3%	33.7%
36,093	COOS	11,228	6,114	4,985	129	1,129 R	54.5%	44.4%	55.1%	44.9%
40,572	GRAFTON	15,794	9,650	6,102	42	3,548 R	61.1%	38.6%	61.3%	38.7%
135,512	HILLSBOROUGH	42,322	23,040	18,736	546	4,304 R	54.4%	44.3%	55.2%	44.8%
51,770	MERRIMACK	21,872	12,748	8,976	148	3,772 R	58.3%	41.0%	58.7%	41.3%
52,498	ROCKINGHAM	20,525	13,811	6,582	132	7,229 R	67.3%	32.1%	67.7%	32.3%
38,546	STRAFFORD	14,412	8,700	5,643	69	3,057 R	60.4%	39.2%	60.7%	39.3%
20,922	SULLIVAN	7,222	4,647	2,521	54	2,126 R	64.3%	34.9%	64.8%	35.2%
443,083	TOTAL	159,092	95,196	62,662	1,234	32,534 R	59.8%	39.4%	60.3%	39.7%

NEW HAMPSHIRE

ELECTION NOTES

1956 Other vote was Andrews (States Rights).

1952

1948 Other vote was 1,970 Wallace (Progressive); 86 Thomas (Socialist); 83 Teichert (Socialist Labor); 7 Thurmond (States Rights).

1944 Other vote was Thomas (Socialist).

1940

1936 Other vote was 4,819 Lemke (Union); 193 Browder (Communist).

1932 Other vote was 947 Thomas (Socialist); 264 Foster (Communist).

1928 Other vote was 465 Thomas (Socialist); 173 Foster (Communist).

1924 Other vote was LaFollette (Progressive).

1920 Other vote was Debs (Socialist).

NEW JERSEY

POPULAR VOTE FOR PRESIDENT 1920 TO 1956

Year	Total Vote	Republican Vote	Republican Candidate	Democratic Vote	Democratic Candidate	Other Vote	Plurality	Percentage Total Vote Rep.	Percentage Total Vote Dem.	Percentage Major Vote Rep.	Percentage Major Vote Dem.
1956	2,484,312	1,606,942	Eisenhower, Dwight D.	850,337	Stevenson, Adlai E.	27,033	756,605 R	64.7%	34.2%	65.4%	34.6%
1952	2,418,554	1,373,613	Eisenhower, Dwight D.	1,015,902	Stevenson, Adlai E.	29,039	357,711 R	56.8%	42.0%	57.5%	42.5%
1948	1,949,555	981,124	Dewey, Thomas E.	895,455	Truman, Harry S.	72,976	85,669 R	50.3%	45.9%	52.3%	47.7%
1944	1,963,761	961,335	Dewey, Thomas E.	987,874	Roosevelt, Franklin D.	14,552	26,539 D	49.0%	50.3%	49.3%	50.7%
1940	1,972,552	945,475	Willkie, Wendell	1,016,808	Roosevelt, Franklin D.	10,269	71,333 D	47.9%	51.5%	48.2%	51.8%
1936	1,820,437	720,322	Landon, Alfred M.	1,083,850	Roosevelt, Franklin D.	16,265	363,528 D	39.6%	59.5%	39.9%	60.1%
1932	1,630,063	775,684	Hoover, Herbert C.	806,630	Roosevelt, Franklin D.	47,749	30,946 D	47.6%	49.5%	49.0%	51.0%
1928	1,549,381	926,050	Hoover, Herbert C.	616,517	Smith, Alfred E.	6,814	309,533 R	59.8%	39.8%	60.0%	40.0%
1924 **	1,088,054	676,277	Coolidge, Calvin	298,043	Davis, John W.	113,734	378,234 R	62.2%	27.4%	69.4%	30.6%
1920	910,251	615,333	Harding, Warren G.	258,761	Cox, James M.	36,157	356,572 R	67.6%	28.4%	70.4%	29.6%

In 1924 other vote was 109,028 Progressive; 1,660 Prohibition; 1,560 Communist; 853 Socialist Labor; 368 American and 265 Commonwealth Land.

ELECTORAL COLLEGE VOTE 1920 TO 1956

Year	Total	Republican	Democratic	Other
1956	16	16	—	—
1952	16	16	—	—
1948	16	16	—	—
1944	16	—	16	—
1940	16	—	16	—
1936	16	—	16	—
1932	16	—	16	—
1928	14	14	—	—
1924	14	14	—	—
1920	14	14	—	—

NEW JERSEY

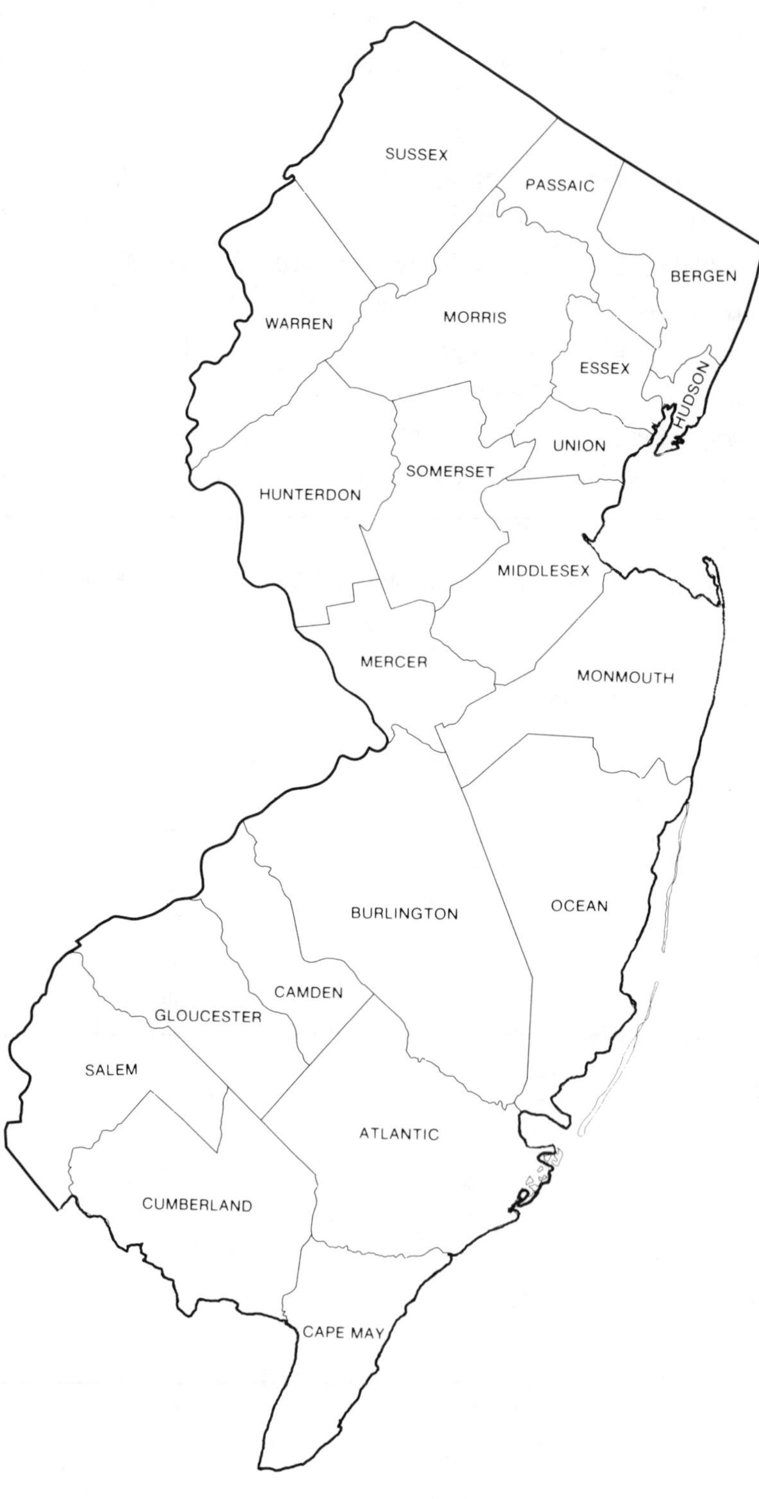
SUSSEX
PASSAIC
BERGEN
WARREN
MORRIS
ESSEX
HUDSON
UNION
SOMERSET
HUNTERDON
MIDDLESEX
MERCER
MONMOUTH
BURLINGTON
OCEAN
CAMDEN
GLOUCESTER
SALEM
ATLANTIC
CUMBERLAND
CAPE MAY

NEW JERSEY

PRESIDENT 1956

1950 Census Population	County	Total Vote	Republican	Democratic	Other	Rep.-Dem. Plurality	Percentage Total Vote Rep.	Percentage Total Vote Dem.	Percentage Major Vote Rep.	Percentage Major Vote Dem.
132,399	ATLANTIC	68,038	44,698	21,668	1,672	23,030 R	65.7%	31.8%	67.4%	32.6%
539,139	BERGEN	338,113	254,334	82,169	1,610	172,165 R	75.2%	24.3%	75.6%	24.4%
135,910	BURLINGTON	62,471	38,145	24,258	68	13,887 R	61.1%	38.8%	61.1%	38.9%
300,743	CAMDEN	160,953	85,067	75,152	734	9,915 R	52.9%	46.7%	53.1%	46.9%
37,131	CAPE MAY	22,815	16,887	5,897	31	10,990 R	74.0%	25.8%	74.1%	25.9%
88,597	CUMBERLAND	41,444	24,067	17,309	68	6,758 R	58.1%	41.8%	58.2%	41.8%
905,949	ESSEX	388,253	234,682	146,313	7,258	88,369 R	60.4%	37.7%	61.6%	38.4%
91,727	GLOUCESTER	50,728	30,646	20,007	75	10,639 R	60.4%	39.4%	60.5%	39.5%
647,437	HUDSON	297,585	183,919	107,098	6,568	76,821 R	61.8%	36.0%	63.2%	36.8%
42,736	HUNTERDON	22,193	16,150	5,957	86	10,193 R	72.8%	26.8%	73.1%	26.9%
229,781	MERCER	109,105	56,029	52,684	392	3,345 R	51.4%	48.3%	51.5%	48.5%
264,872	MIDDLESEX	165,286	100,071	64,538	677	35,533 R	60.5%	39.0%	60.8%	39.2%
225,327	MONMOUTH	116,751	83,828	32,329	594	51,499 R	71.8%	27.7%	72.2%	27.8%
164,371	MORRIS	96,469	76,571	19,503	395	57,068 R	79.4%	20.2%	79.7%	20.3%
56,622	OCEAN	37,479	28,033	9,367	79	18,666 R	74.8%	25.0%	75.0%	25.0%
337,093	PASSAIC	166,676	101,182	61,859	3,635	39,323 R	60.7%	37.1%	62.1%	37.9%
49,508	SALEM	23,423	14,091	9,276	56	4,815 R	60.2%	39.6%	60.3%	39.7%
99,052	SOMERSET	52,789	37,930	14,529	330	23,401 R	71.9%	27.5%	72.3%	27.7%
34,423	SUSSEX	19,669	15,867	3,756	46	12,111 R	80.7%	19.1%	80.9%	19.1%
398,138	UNION	216,414	146,228	67,540	2,646	78,688 R	67.6%	31.2%	68.4%	31.6%
54,374	WARREN	27,658	18,517	9,128	13	9,389 R	66.9%	33.0%	67.0%	33.0%
4,835,329	TOTAL	2,484,312	1,606,942	850,337	27,033	756,605 R	64.7%	34.2%	65.4%	34.6%

NEW JERSEY

PRESIDENT 1952

1950 Census Population	County	Total Vote	Republican	Democratic	Other	Rep.-Dem. Plurality	Percentage Total Vote Rep.	Total Vote Dem.	Major Vote Rep.	Major Vote Dem.
132,399	ATLANTIC	69,375	40,259	28,953	163	11,306 R	58.0%	41.7%	58.2%	41.8%
539,139	BERGEN	307,502	212,842	93,373	1,287	119,469 R	69.2%	30.4%	69.5%	30.5%
135,910	BURLINGTON	55,744	30,202	25,482	60	4,720 R	54.2%	45.7%	54.2%	45.8%
300,743	CAMDEN	154,541	72,335	81,444	762	9,109 D	46.8%	52.7%	47.0%	53.0%
37,131	CAPE MAY	22,209	15,218	6,984	7	8,234 R	68.5%	31.4%	68.5%	31.5%
88,597	CUMBERLAND	40,859	21,819	18,929	111	2,890 R	53.4%	46.3%	53.5%	46.5%
905,949	ESSEX	407,635	219,863	180,501	7,271	39,362 R	53.9%	44.3%	54.9%	45.1%
91,727	GLOUCESTER	45,737	25,103	20,536	98	4,567 R	54.9%	44.9%	55.0%	45.0%
647,437	HUDSON	324,280	153,583	161,469	9,228	7,886 D	47.4%	49.8%	48.7%	51.3%
42,736	HUNTERDON	21,400	14,439	6,878	83	7,561 R	67.5%	32.1%	67.7%	32.3%
229,781	MERCER	108,662	50,423	57,751	488	7,328 D	46.4%	53.1%	46.6%	53.4%
264,872	MIDDLESEX	146,224	73,577	70,234	2,413	3,343 R	50.3%	48.0%	51.2%	48.8%
225,327	MONMOUTH	110,491	73,228	37,006	257	36,222 R	66.3%	33.5%	66.4%	33.6%
164,371	MORRIS	86,629	62,847	23,662	120	39,185 R	72.5%	27.3%	72.6%	27.4%
56,622	OCEAN	32,267	23,490	8,660	117	14,830 R	72.8%	26.8%	73.1%	26.9%
337,093	PASSAIC	164,190	89,083	70,727	4,380	18,356 R	54.3%	43.1%	55.7%	44.3%
49,508	SALEM	23,442	12,026	11,362	54	664 R	51.3%	48.5%	51.4%	48.6%
99,052	SOMERSET	49,320	31,239	18,007	74	13,232 R	63.3%	36.5%	63.4%	36.6%
34,423	SUSSEX	17,963	13,415	4,534	14	8,881 R	74.7%	25.2%	74.7%	25.3%
398,138	UNION	203,245	122,885	78,336	2,024	44,549 R	60.5%	38.5%	61.1%	38.9%
54,374	WARREN	26,839	15,737	11,074	28	4,663 R	58.6%	41.3%	58.7%	41.3%
4,835,329	TOTAL	2,418,554	1,373,613	1,015,902	29,039	357,711 R	56.8%	42.0%	57.5%	42.5%

NEW JERSEY

PRESIDENT 1948

1940 Census Population	County	Total Vote	Republican	Democratic	Other	Rep.-Dem. Plurality	Percentage Total Vote Rep.	Percentage Total Vote Dem.	Percentage Major Vote Rep.	Percentage Major Vote Dem.
124,066	ATLANTIC	58,071	31,608	25,313	1,150	6,295 R	54.4%	43.6%	55.5%	44.5%
409,646	BERGEN	217,131	142,657	69,132	5,342	73,525 R	65.7%	31.8%	67.4%	32.6%
97,013	BURLINGTON	42,432	21,183	20,801	448	382 R	49.9%	49.0%	50.5%	49.5%
255,727	CAMDEN	121,132	51,977	66,388	2,767	14,411 D	42.9%	54.8%	43.9%	56.1%
28,919	CAPE MAY	17,417	11,227	6,031	159	5,196 R	64.5%	34.6%	65.1%	34.9%
73,184	CUMBERLAND	32,313	16,556	15,195	562	1,361 R	51.2%	47.0%	52.1%	47.9%
837,340	ESSEX	343,567	166,963	155,468	21,136	11,495 R	48.6%	45.3%	51.8%	48.2%
72,219	GLOUCESTER	35,765	19,477	15,785	503	3,692 R	54.5%	44.1%	55.2%	44.8%
652,040	HUDSON	304,653	111,113	182,979	10,561	71,866 D	36.5%	60.1%	37.8%	62.2%
36,766	HUNTERDON	17,509	10,654	6,515	340	4,139 R	60.8%	37.2%	62.1%	37.9%
197,318	MERCER	89,436	37,794	49,690	1,952	11,896 D	42.3%	55.6%	43.2%	56.8%
217,077	MIDDLESEX	116,210	49,810	61,634	4,766	11,824 D	42.9%	53.0%	44.7%	55.3%
161,238	MONMOUTH	85,033	52,908	30,507	1,618	22,401 R	62.2%	35.9%	63.4%	36.6%
125,732	MORRIS	62,574	42,558	18,864	1,152	23,694 R	68.0%	30.1%	69.3%	30.7%
37,706	OCEAN	23,767	16,740	6,366	661	10,374 R	70.4%	26.8%	72.4%	27.6%
309,353	PASSAIC	130,430	59,675	60,147	10,608	472 D	45.8%	46.1%	49.8%	50.2%
42,274	SALEM	18,418	8,961	9,278	179	317 D	48.7%	50.4%	49.1%	50.9%
74,390	SOMERSET	36,862	22,034	14,104	724	7,930 R	59.8%	38.3%	61.0%	39.0%
29,632	SUSSEX	13,939	9,269	4,527	143	4,742 R	66.5%	32.5%	67.2%	32.8%
328,344	UNION	162,180	87,402	66,759	8,019	20,643 R	53.9%	41.2%	56.7%	43.3%
50,181	WARREN	20,716	10,558	9,972	186	586 R	51.0%	48.1%	51.4%	48.6%
4,160,165	TOTAL	1,949,555	981,124	895,455	72,976	85,669 R	50.3%	45.9%	52.3%	47.7%

NEW JERSEY

PRESIDENT 1944

1940 Census Population	County	Total Vote	Republican	Democratic	Other	Rep.-Dem. Plurality	Percentage: Total Vote Rep.	Percentage: Total Vote Dem.	Percentage: Major Vote Rep.	Percentage: Major Vote Dem.
124,066	ATLANTIC	54,794	25,593	28,972	229	3,379 D	46.7%	52.9%	46.9%	53.1%
409,646	BERGEN	219,752	142,836	76,350	566	66,486 R	65.0%	34.7%	65.2%	34.8%
97,013	BURLINGTON	41,460	18,765	22,623	72	3,858 D	45.3%	54.6%	45.3%	54.7%
255,727	CAMDEN	128,357	42,197	85,691	469	43,494 D	32.9%	66.8%	33.0%	67.0%
28,919	CAPE MAY	15,114	8,252	6,835	27	1,417 R	54.6%	45.2%	54.7%	45.3%
73,184	CUMBERLAND	30,218	14,477	15,674	67	1,197 D	47.9%	51.9%	48.0%	52.0%
837,340	ESSEX	360,742	178,989	174,320	7,433	4,669 R	49.6%	48.3%	50.7%	49.3%
72,219	GLOUCESTER	34,555	16,684	17,758	113	1,074 D	48.3%	51.4%	48.4%	51.6%
652,040	HUDSON	309,135	117,087	191,354	694	74,267 D	37.9%	61.9%	38.0%	62.0%
36,766	HUNTERDON	16,652	9,843	6,774	35	3,069 R	59.1%	40.7%	59.2%	40.8%
197,318	MERCER	89,371	36,844	52,383	144	15,539 D	41.2%	58.6%	41.3%	58.7%
217,077	MIDDLESEX	107,378	45,232	60,504	1,642	15,272 D	42.1%	56.3%	42.8%	57.2%
161,238	MONMOUTH	84,122	49,349	34,720	53	14,629 R	58.7%	41.3%	58.7%	41.3%
125,732	MORRIS	61,372	39,732	21,454	186	18,278 R	64.7%	35.0%	64.9%	35.1%
37,706	OCEAN	21,032	13,317	7,683	32	5,634 R	63.3%	36.5%	63.4%	36.6%
309,353	PASSAIC	137,182	67,856	68,737	589	881 D	49.5%	50.1%	49.7%	50.3%
42,274	SALEM	18,310	7,942	10,345	23	2,403 D	43.4%	56.5%	43.4%	56.6%
74,390	SOMERSET	34,770	20,266	14,467	37	5,799 R	58.3%	41.6%	58.3%	41.7%
29,632	SUSSEX	14,066	8,817	5,237	12	3,580 R	62.7%	37.2%	62.7%	37.3%
328,344	UNION	164,625	86,543	75,969	2,113	10,574 R	52.6%	46.1%	53.3%	46.7%
50,181	WARREN	20,754	10,714	10,024	16	690 R	51.6%	48.3%	51.7%	48.3%
4,160,165	TOTAL	1,963,761	961,335	987,874	14,552	26,539 D	49.0%	50.3%	49.3%	50.7%

NEW JERSEY

PRESIDENT 1940

1940 Census Population	County	Total Vote	Republican	Democratic	Other	Rep.-Dem. Plurality	Percentage Total Vote Rep.	Total Vote Dem.	Major Vote Rep.	Major Vote Dem.
124,066	ATLANTIC	66,798	30,551	36,155	92	5,604 D	45.7%	54.1%	45.8%	54.2%
409,646	BERGEN	208,823	131,588	76,541	694	55,047 R	63.0%	36.7%	63.2%	36.8%
97,013	BURLINGTON	47,878	21,161	26,574	143	5,413 D	44.2%	55.5%	44.3%	55.7%
255,727	CAMDEN	128,919	43,480	84,837	602	41,357 D	33.7%	65.8%	33.9%	66.1%
28,919	CAPE MAY	17,944	9,429	8,485	30	944 R	52.5%	47.3%	52.6%	47.4%
73,184	CUMBERLAND	35,680	16,322	19,251	107	2,929 D	45.7%	54.0%	45.9%	54.1%
837,340	ESSEX	344,034	182,124	154,363	7,547	27,761 R	52.9%	44.9%	54.1%	45.9%
72,219	GLOUCESTER	38,111	17,674	20,284	153	2,610 D	46.4%	53.2%	46.6%	53.4%
652,040	HUDSON	316,508	107,552	208,429	527	100,877 D	34.0%	65.9%	34.0%	66.0%
36,766	HUNTERDON	18,203	10,284	7,872	47	2,412 R	56.5%	43.2%	56.6%	43.4%
197,318	MERCER	87,533	37,190	50,121	222	12,931 D	42.5%	57.3%	42.6%	57.4%
217,077	MIDDLESEX	109,013	41,709	67,140	164	25,431 D	38.3%	61.6%	38.3%	61.7%
161,238	MONMOUTH	86,047	49,675	36,298	74	13,377 R	57.7%	42.2%	57.8%	42.2%
125,732	MORRIS	64,612	39,720	24,698	194	15,022 R	61.5%	38.2%	61.7%	38.3%
37,706	OCEAN	22,182	13,394	8,762	26	4,632 R	60.4%	39.5%	60.5%	39.5%
309,353	PASSAIC	135,907	65,523	69,880	504	4,357 D	48.2%	51.4%	48.4%	51.6%
42,274	SALEM	20,433	8,132	12,244	57	4,112 D	39.8%	59.9%	39.9%	60.1%
74,390	SOMERSET	36,755	20,169	16,490	96	3,679 R	54.9%	44.9%	55.0%	45.0%
29,632	SUSSEX	14,984	8,642	6,314	28	2,328 R	57.7%	42.1%	57.8%	42.2%
328,344	UNION	152,296	79,962	70,737	1,597	9,225 R	52.5%	46.4%	53.1%	46.9%
50,181	WARREN	21,555	10,595	10,929	31	334 D	49.2%	50.7%	49.2%	50.8%
4,160,165	TOTAL	1,972,552	945,475	1,016,808	10,269	71,333 D	47.9%	51.5%	48.2%	51.8%

NEW JERSEY

PRESIDENT 1936

1930 Census Population	County	Total Vote	Republican	Democratic	Other	Rep.-Dem. Plurality	Percentage Total Vote Rep.	Percentage Total Vote Dem.	Percentage Major Vote Rep.	Percentage Major Vote Dem.
124,823	ATLANTIC	64,688	24,680	39,605	403	14,925 D	38.2%	61.2%	38.4%	61.6%
364,977	BERGEN	181,878	89,628	91,107	1,143	1,479 D	49.3%	50.1%	49.6%	50.4%
93,541	BURLINGTON	45,159	18,644	26,095	420	7,451 D	41.3%	57.8%	41.7%	58.3%
252,312	CAMDEN	123,742	35,874	86,300	1,568	50,426 D	29.0%	69.7%	29.4%	70.6%
29,486	CAPE MAY	17,952	8,531	9,363	58	832 D	47.5%	52.2%	47.7%	52.3%
69,895	CUMBERLAND	35,292	14,500	20,492	300	5,992 D	41.1%	58.1%	41.4%	58.6%
833,513	ESSEX	319,441	140,991	174,857	3,593	33,866 D	44.1%	54.7%	44.6%	55.4%
70,802	GLOUCESTER	36,622	15,813	20,516	293	4,703 D	43.2%	56.0%	43.5%	56.5%
690,730	HUDSON	300,559	65,110	233,390	2,059	168,280 D	21.7%	77.7%	21.8%	78.2%
34,728	HUNTERDON	18,409	8,832	9,526	51	694 D	48.0%	51.7%	48.1%	51.9%
187,143	MERCER	77,564	29,283	47,702	579	18,419 D	37.8%	61.5%	38.0%	62.0%
212,208	MIDDLESEX	95,340	32,959	61,679	702	28,720 D	34.6%	64.7%	34.8%	65.2%
147,209	MONMOUTH	80,767	41,460	38,914	393	2,546 R	51.3%	48.2%	51.6%	48.4%
110,445	MORRIS	57,943	32,365	24,978	600	7,387 R	55.9%	43.1%	56.4%	43.6%
33,069	OCEAN	21,372	11,293	9,889	190	1,404 R	52.8%	46.3%	53.3%	46.7%
302,129	PASSAIC	122,190	49,046	71,384	1,760	22,338 D	40.1%	58.4%	40.7%	59.3%
36,834	SALEM	19,402	7,671	11,614	117	3,943 D	39.5%	59.9%	39.8%	60.2%
65,132	SOMERSET	31,887	15,806	15,987	94	181 D	49.6%	50.1%	49.7%	50.3%
27,830	SUSSEX	14,861	7,945	6,862	54	1,083 R	53.5%	46.2%	53.7%	46.3%
305,209	UNION	132,097	59,553	70,813	1,731	11,260 D	45.1%	53.6%	45.7%	54.3%
49,319	WARREN	21,957	9,437	12,476	44	3,039 D	43.0%	56.8%	43.1%	56.9%
4,041,334	TOTAL	1,820,437	720,322	1,083,850	16,265	363,528 D	39.6%	59.5%	39.9%	60.1%

NEW JERSEY

PRESIDENT 1932

1930 Census Population	County	Total Vote	Republican	Democratic	Other	Rep.-Dem. Plurality	Percentage Total Vote Rep.	Total Vote Dem.	Major Vote Rep.	Major Vote Dem.
124,823	ATLANTIC	60,261	31,264	28,071	926	3,193 R	51.9%	46.6%	52.7%	47.3%
364,977	BERGEN	165,743	86,885	73,921	4,937	12,964 R	52.4%	44.6%	54.0%	46.0%
93,541	BURLINGTON	40,629	23,623	15,824	1,182	7,799 R	58.1%	38.9%	59.9%	40.1%
252,312	CAMDEN	109,847	55,856	48,825	5,166	7,031 R	50.8%	44.4%	53.4%	46.6%
29,486	CAPE MAY	17,482	10,112	7,160	210	2,952 R	57.8%	41.0%	58.5%	41.5%
69,895	CUMBERLAND	29,971	16,668	12,371	932	4,297 R	55.6%	41.3%	57.4%	42.6%
833,513	ESSEX	290,772	149,630	132,666	8,476	16,964 R	51.5%	45.6%	53.0%	47.0%
70,802	GLOUCESTER	33,561	18,782	13,817	962	4,965 R	56.0%	41.2%	57.6%	42.4%
690,730	HUDSON	257,019	66,937	184,676	5,406	117,739 D	26.0%	71.9%	26.6%	73.4%
34,728	HUNTERDON	16,326	8,476	7,531	319	945 R	51.9%	46.1%	53.0%	47.0%
187,143	MERCER	66,879	33,715	30,284	2,880	3,431 R	50.4%	45.3%	52.7%	47.3%
212,208	MIDDLESEX	80,781	32,673	45,997	2,111	13,324 D	40.4%	56.9%	41.5%	58.5%
147,209	MONMOUTH	76,741	40,467	35,219	1,055	5,248 R	52.7%	45.9%	53.5%	46.5%
110,445	MORRIS	53,202	31,481	20,117	1,604	11,364 R	59.2%	37.8%	61.0%	39.0%
33,069	OCEAN	18,460	10,513	7,508	439	3,005 R	57.0%	40.7%	58.3%	41.7%
302,129	PASSAIC	109,404	49,218	54,576	5,610	5,358 D	45.0%	49.9%	47.4%	52.6%
36,834	SALEM	17,425	9,870	7,357	198	2,513 R	56.6%	42.2%	57.3%	42.7%
65,132	SOMERSET	28,273	15,317	12,345	611	2,972 R	54.2%	43.7%	55.4%	44.6%
27,830	SUSSEX	13,408	7,130	6,136	142	994 R	53.2%	45.8%	53.7%	46.3%
305,209	UNION	122,961	67,512	51,357	4,092	16,155 R	54.9%	41.8%	56.8%	43.2%
49,319	WARREN	20,355	9,277	10,636	442	1,359 D	45.6%	52.3%	46.6%	53.4%
4,041,334	TOTAL	1,630,063	775,684	806,630	47,749	30,946 D	47.6%	49.5%	49.0%	51.0%

NEW JERSEY

PRESIDENT 1928

1920 Census Population	County	Total Vote	Republican	Democratic	Other	Rep.-Dem. Plurality	Percentage Total Vote Rep.	Total Vote Dem.	Major Vote Rep.	Major Vote Dem.
83,914	ATLANTIC	56,465	37,238	19,152	75	18,086 R	65.9%	33.9%	66.0%	34.0%
210,703	BERGEN	140,067	89,105	50,373	589	38,732 R	63.6%	36.0%	63.9%	36.1%
81,770	BURLINGTON	41,294	30,224	10,972	98	19,252 R	73.2%	26.6%	73.4%	26.6%
190,508	CAMDEN	108,228	75,517	32,151	560	43,366 R	69.8%	29.7%	70.1%	29.9%
19,460	CAPE MAY	15,978	12,207	3,731	40	8,476 R	76.4%	23.4%	76.6%	23.4%
61,348	CUMBERLAND	30,699	23,921	6,694	84	17,227 R	77.9%	21.8%	78.1%	21.9%
652,089	ESSEX	288,514	168,856	118,268	1,390	50,588 R	58.5%	41.0%	58.8%	41.2%
48,224	GLOUCESTER	32,302	25,627	6,594	81	19,033 R	79.3%	20.4%	79.5%	20.5%
629,154	HUDSON	254,071	99,972	153,009	1,090	53,037 D	39.3%	60.2%	39.5%	60.5%
32,885	HUNTERDON	16,076	11,820	4,225	31	7,595 R	73.5%	26.3%	73.7%	26.3%
159,881	MERCER	69,338	41,056	27,908	374	13,148 R	59.2%	40.2%	59.5%	40.5%
162,334	MIDDLESEX	73,950	38,714	34,908	328	3,806 R	52.4%	47.2%	52.6%	47.4%
104,925	MONMOUTH	71,454	47,046	24,286	122	22,760 R	65.8%	34.0%	66.0%	34.0%
82,694	MORRIS	48,859	33,489	15,188	182	18,301 R	68.5%	31.1%	68.8%	31.2%
22,155	OCEAN	12,800	12,301	445	54	11,856 R	96.1%	3.5%	96.5%	3.5%
259,174	PASSAIC	105,834	57,708	47,167	959	10,541 R	54.5%	44.6%	55.0%	45.0%
36,572	SALEM	15,360	12,323	3,001	36	9,322 R	80.2%	19.5%	80.4%	19.6%
47,991	SOMERSET	24,580	16,386	8,120	74	8,266 R	66.7%	33.0%	66.9%	33.1%
24,905	SUSSEX	12,032	8,964	3,043	25	5,921 R	74.5%	25.3%	74.7%	25.3%
200,157	UNION	106,092	68,119	37,476	497	30,643 R	64.2%	35.3%	64.5%	35.5%
45,057	WARREN	20,495	14,992	5,444	59	9,548 R	73.1%	26.6%	73.4%	26.6%
3,155,900	TOTAL	1,549,381	926,050	616,517	6,814	309,533 R	59.8%	39.8%	60.0%	40.0%

NEW JERSEY

PRESIDENT 1924

1920 Census Population	County	Total Vote	Republican	Democratic	Other	Rep.-Dem. Plurality	Percentage Total Vote Rep.	Percentage Total Vote Dem.	Percentage Major Vote Rep.	Percentage Major Vote Dem.
83,914	ATLANTIC	37,939	27,936	6,937	3,066	20,999 R	73.6%	18.3%	80.1%	19.9%
210,703	BERGEN	87,598	60,803	16,844	9,951	43,959 R	69.4%	19.2%	78.3%	21.7%
81,770	BURLINGTON	30,780	21,617	7,794	1,369	13,823 R	70.2%	25.3%	73.5%	26.5%
190,508	CAMDEN	72,622	48,154	17,577	6,891	30,577 R	66.3%	24.2%	73.3%	26.7%
19,460	CAPE MAY	11,246	8,139	2,611	496	5,528 R	72.4%	23.2%	75.7%	24.3%
61,348	CUMBERLAND	22,084	15,691	4,780	1,613	10,911 R	71.1%	21.6%	76.6%	23.4%
652,089	ESSEX	186,673	123,614	41,708	21,351	81,906 R	66.2%	22.3%	74.8%	25.2%
48,224	GLOUCESTER	21,328	15,513	4,167	1,648	11,346 R	72.7%	19.5%	78.8%	21.2%
629,154	HUDSON	193,952	80,892	91,094	21,966	10,202 D	41.7%	47.0%	47.0%	53.0%
32,885	HUNTERDON	14,747	8,940	5,103	704	3,837 R	60.6%	34.6%	63.7%	36.3%
159,881	MERCER	51,551	30,689	14,639	6,223	16,050 R	59.5%	28.4%	67.7%	32.3%
162,334	MIDDLESEX	55,482	34,556	16,373	4,553	18,183 R	62.3%	29.5%	67.9%	32.1%
104,925	MONMOUTH	52,482	34,451	14,931	3,100	19,520 R	65.6%	28.4%	69.8%	30.2%
82,694	MORRIS	35,655	24,812	8,042	2,801	16,770 R	69.6%	22.6%	75.5%	24.5%
22,155	OCEAN	12,222	8,677	2,594	951	6,083 R	71.0%	21.2%	77.0%	23.0%
259,174	PASSAIC	69,599	43,384	11,644	14,571	31,740 R	62.3%	16.7%	78.8%	21.2%
36,572	SALEM	11,657	8,027	3,206	424	4,821 R	68.9%	27.5%	71.5%	28.5%
47,991	SOMERSET	18,260	12,986	4,143	1,131	8,843 R	71.1%	22.7%	75.8%	24.2%
24,905	SUSSEX	10,298	6,319	3,632	347	2,687 R	61.4%	35.3%	63.5%	36.5%
200,157	UNION	74,060	50,356	14,738	8,966	35,618 R	68.0%	19.9%	77.4%	22.6%
45,057	WARREN	15,844	9,606	5,186	1,052	4,420 R	60.6%	32.7%	64.9%	35.1%
3,155,900	TOTAL	1,088,054	676,277	298,043	113,734	378,234 R	62.2%	27.4%	69.4%	30.6%

NEW JERSEY

PRESIDENT 1920

1920 Census Population	County	Total Vote	Republican	Democratic	Other	Rep.-Dem. Plurality	Percentage Total Vote Rep.	Percentage Total Vote Dem.	Percentage Major Vote Rep.	Percentage Major Vote Dem.
83,914	ATLANTIC	27,725	21,245	5,753	727	15,492 R	76.6%	20.8%	78.7%	21.3%
210,703	BERGEN	62,305	47,512	12,396	2,397	35,116 R	76.3%	19.9%	79.3%	20.7%
81,770	BURLINGTON	26,041	17,898	7,532	611	10,366 R	68.7%	28.9%	70.4%	29.6%
190,508	CAMDEN	62,087	40,771	17,893	3,423	22,878 R	65.7%	28.8%	69.5%	30.5%
19,460	CAPE MAY	8,175	5,785	2,198	192	3,587 R	70.8%	26.9%	72.5%	27.5%
61,348	CUMBERLAND	17,427	11,913	4,487	1,027	7,426 R	68.4%	25.7%	72.6%	27.4%
652,089	ESSEX	163,848	116,168	40,970	6,710	75,198 R	70.9%	25.0%	73.9%	26.1%
48,224	GLOUCESTER	17,557	11,693	4,869	995	6,824 R	66.6%	27.7%	70.6%	29.4%
629,154	HUDSON	170,793	101,759	62,637	6,397	39,122 R	59.6%	36.7%	61.9%	38.1%
32,885	HUNTERDON	13,686	7,443	6,067	176	1,376 R	54.4%	44.3%	55.1%	44.9%
159,881	MERCER	46,683	29,626	15,713	1,344	13,913 R	63.5%	33.7%	65.3%	34.7%
162,334	MIDDLESEX	42,088	29,334	11,618	1,136	17,716 R	69.7%	27.6%	71.6%	28.4%
104,925	MONMOUTH	42,336	28,818	12,975	543	15,843 R	68.1%	30.6%	69.0%	31.0%
82,694	MORRIS	28,931	20,686	7,256	989	13,430 R	71.5%	25.1%	74.0%	26.0%
22,155	OCEAN	9,139	6,840	2,138	161	4,702 R	74.8%	23.4%	76.2%	23.8%
259,174	PASSAIC	59,225	42,692	11,873	4,660	30,819 R	72.1%	20.0%	78.2%	21.8%
36,572	SALEM	11,485	7,638	3,483	364	4,155 R	66.5%	30.3%	68.7%	31.3%
47,991	SOMERSET	15,435	10,962	4,192	281	6,770 R	71.0%	27.2%	72.3%	27.7%
24,905	SUSSEX	8,892	5,224	3,516	152	1,708 R	58.7%	39.5%	59.8%	40.2%
200,157	UNION	54,303	39,409	12,103	2,791	27,306 R	72.6%	22.3%	76.5%	23.5%
45,057	WARREN	15,683	8,035	7,218	430	817 R	51.2%	46.0%	52.7%	47.3%
3,155,900	TOTAL	910,251	615,333	258,761	36,157	356,572 R	67.6%	28.4%	70.4%	29.6%

NEW JERSEY

In the six elections from 1920 to 1940, the figures on the statewide total line are for the highest elector in each party and the county-by-county figures are the average elector vote as reported by the state canvass; therefore, the addition of the individual counties will produce a smaller total than that on the statewide total line.

ELECTION NOTES

1956 Other vote was 9,147 Holtwick (Prohibition); 6,736 Hass (Socialist Labor); 5,317 Andrews (States Rights); 4,004 Dobbs (Socialist Workers); 1,829 Krajewski (American Third Party).

1952 Other vote was 8,593 Hoopes (Socialist); 5,815 Hass (Socialist Labor); 5,589 Hallinan (Progressive); 4,203 Krajewski (Poor Man's Party); 3,850 Dobbs (Socialist Workers); 989 Hamblen (Prohibition).

1948 Other vote was 42,683 Wallace (Progressive); 10,593 Watson (Prohibition); 10,521 Thomas (Socialist); 5,825 Dobbs (Socialist Workers); 3,354 Teichert (Socialist Labor).

1944 Other vote was 6,939 Teichert (Socialist Labor); 4,255 Watson (Prohibition); 3,358 Thomas (Socialist).

1940 Other vote was 6,508 Browder (Communist); 2,433 Thomas (Socialist); 873 Babson (Prohibition); 455 Aiken (Socialist Labor).

1936 Other vote was 9,407 Lemke (Union); 3,931 Thomas (Socialist); 1,639 Browder (Communist); 926 Colvin (Prohibition); 362 Aiken (Socialist Labor).

1932 Other vote was 42,998 Thomas (Socialist); 2,915 Foster (Communist); 1,062 Reynolds (Socialist Labor); 774 Upshaw (Prohibition).

1928 Other vote was 4,897 Thomas (Socialist); 1,257 Foster (Communist); 500 Reynolds (Socialist Labor); 160 Varney (Prohibition).

1924 Other vote was 109,028 LaFollette (Progressive); 1,660 Faris (Prohibition); 1,560 Foster (Communist); 853 Johns (Socialist Labor); 368 Nations (American); 265 Wallace (Commonwealth Land). Progressive candidates ran second in Passaic county.

1920 Other vote was 27,385 Debs (Socialist); 4,895 Watkins (Prohibition); 2,264 Christensen (Farmer-Labor); 1,010 Cox (Socialist Labor); 603 Macauley (Single Tax).

NEW MEXICO

POPULAR VOTE FOR PRESIDENT 1920 TO 1956

Year	Total Vote	Republican Vote	Republican Candidate	Democratic Vote	Democratic Candidate	Other Vote	Plurality	Percentage Total Vote Rep.	Percentage Total Vote Dem.	Percentage Major Vote Rep.	Percentage Major Vote Dem.
1956	253,926	146,788	Eisenhower, Dwight D.	106,098	Stevenson, Adlai E.	1,040	40,690 R	57.8%	41.8%	58.0%	42.0%
1952	238,608	132,170	Eisenhower, Dwight D.	105,661	Stevenson, Adlai E.	777	26,509 R	55.4%	44.3%	55.6%	44.4%
1948	187,063	80,303	Dewey, Thomas E.	105,464	Truman, Harry S.	1,296	25,161 D	42.9%	56.4%	43.2%	56.8%
1944	152,225	70,688	Dewey, Thomas E.	81,389	Roosevelt, Franklin D.	148	10,701 D	46.4%	53.5%	46.5%	53.5%
1940	183,258	79,315	Willkie, Wendell	103,699	Roosevelt, Franklin D.	244	24,384 D	43.3%	56.6%	43.3%	56.7%
1036	169,135	61,727	Landon, Alfred M.	106,037	Roosevelt, Franklin D.	1,371	44,310 D	36.5%	62.7%	36.8%	63.2%
1932	151,606	54,217	Hoover, Herbert C.	95,089	Roosevelt, Franklin D.	2,300	40,872 D	35.8%	62.7%	36.3%	63.7%
1928	118,077	69,708	Hoover, Herbert C.	48,211	Smith, Alfred E.	158	21,497 R	59.0%	40.8%	59.1%	40.9%
1924	112,830	54,745	Coolidge, Calvin	48,542	Davis, John W.	9,543	6,203 R	48.5%	43.0%	53.0%	47.0%
1920	105,412	57,634	Harding, Warren G.	46,668	Cox, James M.	1,110	10,966 R	54.7%	44.3%	55.3%	44.7%

ELECTORAL COLLEGE VOTE 1920 TO 1956

Year	Total	Republican	Democratic	Other
1956	4	4	—	—
1952	4	4	—	—
1948	4	—	4	—
1944	4	—	4	—
1940	3	—	3	—
1936	3	—	3	—
1932	3	—	3	—
1928	3	3	—	—
1924	3	3	—	—
1920	3	3	—	—

NEW MEXICO

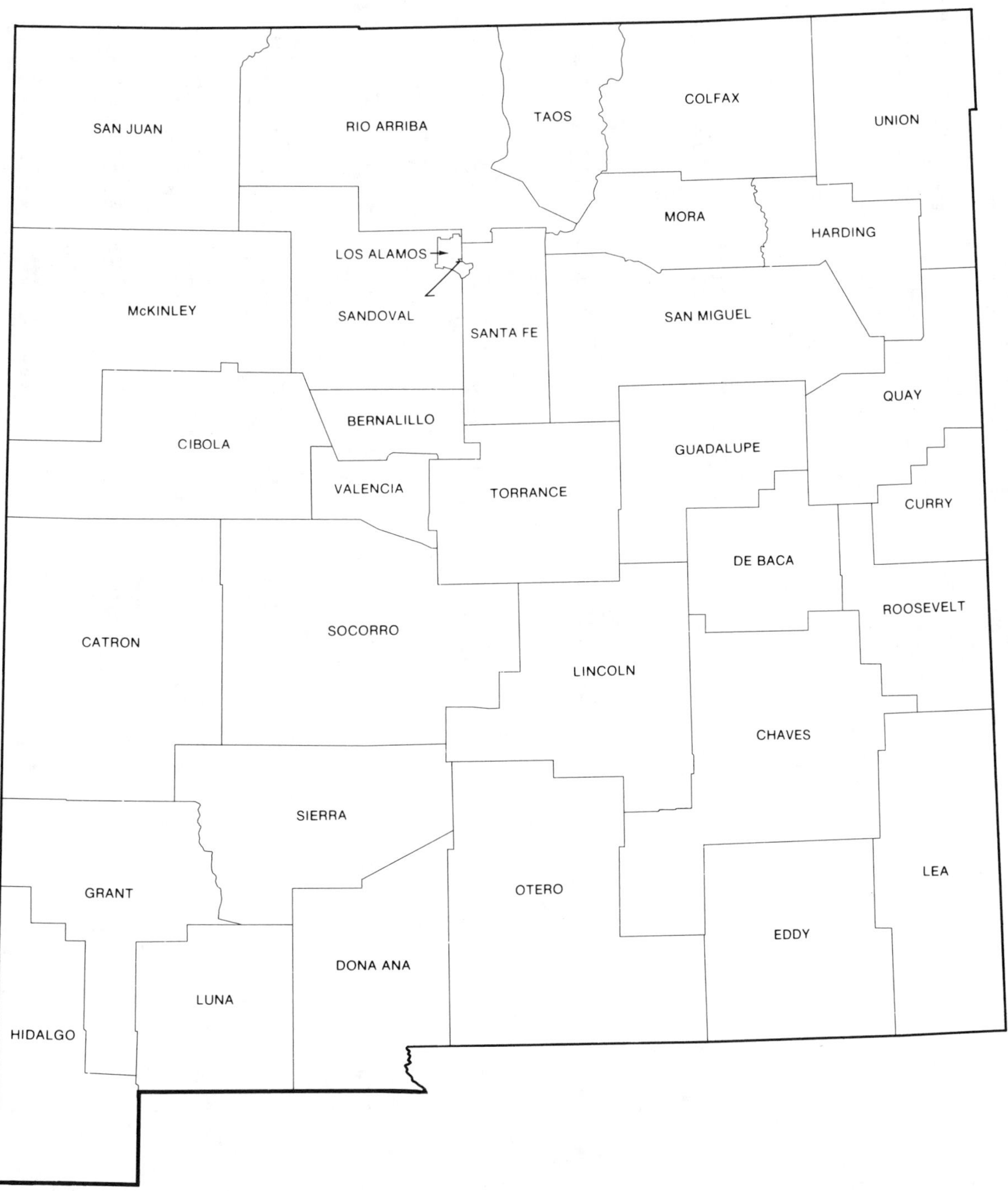

SAN JUAN
RIO ARRIBA
TAOS
COLFAX
UNION
MORA
HARDING
LOS ALAMOS
McKINLEY
SANDOVAL
SANTA FE
SAN MIGUEL
QUAY
CIBOLA
BERNALILLO
GUADALUPE
VALENCIA
TORRANCE
CURRY
DE BACA
ROOSEVELT
CATRON
SOCORRO
LINCOLN
CHAVES
SIERRA
GRANT
OTERO
LEA
EDDY
DONA ANA
LUNA
HIDALGO

NEW MEXICO

PRESIDENT 1956

1950 Census Population	County	Total Vote	Republican	Democratic	Other	Rep.-Dem. Plurality	Percentage Total Vote Rep.	Total Vote Dem.	Major Vote Rep.	Major Vote Dem.
145,673	BERNALILLO	65,143	41,893	22,954	296	18,939 R	64.3%	35.2%	64.6%	35.4%
3,533	CATRON	1,188	711	477		234 R	59.8%	40.2%	59.8%	40.2%
40,605	CHAVES	11,896	7,538	4,270	88	3,268 R	63.4%	35.9%	63.8%	36.2%
16,761	COLFAX	5,409	2,959	2,450		509 R	54.7%	45.3%	54.7%	45.3%
23,351	CURRY	8,427	4,826	3,545	56	1,281 R	57.3%	42.1%	57.7%	42.3%
3,464	DE BACA	1,313	779	528	6	251 R	59.3%	40.2%	59.6%	40.4%
39,557	DONA ANA	11,991	7,025	4,918	48	2,107 R	58.6%	41.0%	58.8%	41.2%
40,640	EDDY	14,618	6,691	7,820	107	1,129 D	45.8%	53.5%	46.1%	53.9%
21,649	GRANT	7,377	3,224	4,122	31	898 D	43.7%	55.9%	43.9%	56.1%
6,772	GUADALUPE	2,723	1,529	1,191	3	338 R	56.2%	43.7%	56.2%	43.8%
3,013	HARDING	1,083	671	412		259 R	62.0%	38.0%	62.0%	38.0%
5,095	HIDALGO	1,564	790	771	3	19 R	50.5%	49.3%	50.6%	49.4%
30,717	LEA	11,879	5,661	6,140	78	479 D	47.7%	51.7%	48.0%	52.0%
7,409	LINCOLN	3,020	1,956	1,059	5	897 R	64.8%	35.1%	64.9%	35.1%
10,476	LOS ALAMOS	4,629	2,406	2,214	9	192 R	52.0%	47.8%	52.1%	47.9%
8,753	LUNA	3,067	1,526	1,506	35	20 R	49.8%	49.1%	50.3%	49.7%
27,451	MCKINLEY	7,811	4,450	3,331	30	1,119 R	57.0%	42.6%	57.2%	42.8%
8,720	MORA	2,969	1,736	1,233		503 R	58.5%	41.5%	58.5%	41.5%
14,909	OTERO	6,483	3,919	2,558	6	1,361 R	60.5%	39.5%	60.5%	39.5%
13,971	QUAY	4,318	2,311	1,988	19	323 R	53.5%	46.0%	53.8%	46.2%
24,997	RIO ARRIBA	8,860	4,566	4,291	3	275 R	51.5%	48.4%	51.6%	48.4%
16,409	ROOSEVELT	4,963	2,708	2,247	8	461 R	54.6%	45.3%	54.7%	45.3%
12,438	SANDOVAL	3,554	1,979	1,574	1	405 R	55.7%	44.3%	55.7%	44.3%
18,292	SAN JUAN	7,690	5,194	2,425	71	2,769 R	67.5%	31.5%	68.2%	31.8%
26,512	SAN MIGUEL	9,100	5,083	4,014	3	1,069 R	55.9%	44.1%	55.9%	44.1%
38,153	SANTA FE	16,441	9,359	6,997	85	2,362 R	56.9%	42.6%	57.2%	42.8%
7,186	SIERRA	3,006	1,954	1,035	17	919 R	65.0%	34.4%	65.4%	34.6%
9,670	SOCORRO	3,841	2,365	1,476		889 R	61.6%	38.4%	61.6%	38.4%
17,146	TAOS	5,847	3,100	2,743	4	357 R	53.0%	46.9%	53.1%	46.9%
8,012	TORRANCE	2,787	1,567	1,201	19	366 R	56.2%	43.1%	56.6%	43.4%
7,372	UNION	2,711	1,649	1,061	1	588 R	60.8%	39.1%	60.8%	39.2%
22,481	VALENCIA	8,218	4,663	3,547	8	1,116 R	56.7%	43.2%	56.8%	43.2%
681,187	TOTAL	253,926	146,788	106,098	1,040	40,690 R	57.8%	41.8%	58.0%	42.0%

NEW MEXICO

PRESIDENT 1952

1950 Census Population	County	Total Vote	Republican	Democratic	Other	Rep.-Dem. Plurality	Percentage Total Vote Rep.	Total Vote Dem.	Major Vote Rep.	Major Vote Dem.
145,673	BERNALILLO	57,200	33,964	23,164	72	10,800 R	59.4%	40.5%	59.5%	40.5%
3,533	CATRON	1,205	741	464		277 R	61.5%	38.5%	61.5%	38.5%
40,605	CHAVES	10,979	7,018	3,880	81	3,138 R	63.9%	35.3%	64.4%	35.6%
16,761	COLFAX	6,586	3,397	3,184	5	213 R	51.6%	48.3%	51.6%	48.4%
23,351	CURRY	8,459	5,023	3,422	14	1,601 R	59.4%	40.5%	59.5%	40.5%
3,464	DE BACA	1,376	782	591	3	191 R	56.8%	43.0%	57.0%	43.0%
39,557	DONA ANA	10,478	5,902	4,556	20	1,346 R	56.3%	43.5%	56.4%	43.6%
40,640	EDDY	13,591	6,041	7,495	55	1,454 D	44.4%	55.1%	44.6%	55.4%
21,649	GRANT	7,922	3,421	4,315	186	894 D	43.2%	54.5%	44.2%	55.8%
6,772	GUADALUPE	2,922	1,575	1,347		228 R	53.9%	46.1%	53.9%	46.1%
3,013	HARDING	1,197	760	436	1	324 R	63.5%	36.4%	63.5%	36.5%
5,095	HIDALGO	1,544	781	757	6	24 R	50.6%	49.0%	50.8%	49.2%
30,717	LEA	9,971	4,738	5,204	29	466 D	47.5%	52.2%	47.7%	52.3%
7,409	LINCOLN	3,106	2,004	1,095	7	909 R	64.5%	35.3%	64.7%	35.3%
10,476	LOS ALAMOS	4,515	2,226	2,281	8	55 D	49.3%	50.5%	49.4%	50.6%
8,753	LUNA	3,095	1,729	1,332	34	397 R	55.9%	43.0%	56.5%	43.5%
27,451	MCKINLEY	6,207	3,091	3,097	19	6 D	49.8%	49.9%	50.0%	50.0%
8,720	MORA	3,266	1,849	1,413	4	436 R	56.6%	43.3%	56.7%	43.3%
14,909	OTERO	4,620	2,456	2,162	2	294 R	53.2%	46.8%	53.2%	46.8%
13,971	QUAY	5,115	2,711	2,375	29	336 R	53.0%	46.4%	53.3%	46.7%
24,997	RIO ARRIBA	8,905	4,336	4,564	5	228 D	48.7%	51.3%	48.7%	51.3%
16,409	ROOSEVELT	5,340	3,030	2,298	12	732 R	56.7%	43.0%	56.9%	43.1%
12,438	SANDOVAL	3,448	1,795	1,647	6	148 R	52.1%	47.8%	52.1%	47.9%
18,292	SAN JUAN	5,541	3,864	1,659	18	2,205 R	69.7%	29.9%	70.0%	30.0%
26,512	SAN MIGUEL	9,818	5,360	4,451	7	909 R	54.6%	45.3%	54.6%	45.4%
38,153	SANTA FE	15,916	9,011	6,786	119	2,225 R	56.6%	42.6%	57.0%	43.0%
7,186	SIERRA	3,196	2,033	1,158	5	875 R	63.6%	36.2%	63.7%	36.3%
9,670	SOCORRO	4,006	2,224	1,777	5	447 R	55.5%	44.4%	55.6%	44.4%
17,146	TAOS	5,646	2,763	2,877	6	114 D	48.9%	51.0%	49.0%	51.0%
8,012	TORRANCE	3,177	1,747	1,422	8	325 R	55.0%	44.8%	55.1%	44.9%
7,372	UNION	3,136	1,988	1,142	6	846 R	63.4%	36.4%	63.5%	36.5%
22,481	VALENCIA	7,125	3,810	3,310	5	500 R	53.5%	46.5%	53.5%	46.5%
681,187	TOTAL	238,608	132,170	105,661	777	26,509 R	55.4%	44.3%	55.6%	44.4%

NEW MEXICO

PRESIDENT 1948

1940 Census Population	County	Total Vote	Republican	Democratic	Other	Rep.-Dem. Plurality	Percentage Total Vote Rep.	Percentage Total Vote Dem.	Percentage Major Vote Rep.	Percentage Major Vote Dem.
69,391	BERNALILLO	35,364	16,668	18,305	391	1,637 D	47.1%	51.8%	47.7%	52.3%
4,881	CATRON	1,173	521	648	4	127 D	44.4%	55.2%	44.6%	55.4%
23,980	CHAVES	7,725	3,123	4,569	33	1,446 D	40.4%	59.1%	40.6%	59.4%
18,718	COLFAX	6,480	2,575	3,871	34	1,296 D	39.7%	59.7%	39.9%	60.1%
18,159	CURRY	7,941	2,132	5,759	50	3,627 D	26.8%	72.5%	27.0%	73.0%
3,725	DE BACA	1,131	458	670	3	212 D	40.5%	59.2%	40.6%	59.4%
30,411	DONA ANA	8,593	3,440	5,116	37	1,676 D	40.0%	59.5%	40.2%	59.8%
24,311	EDDY	10,021	2,305	7,593	123	5,288 D	23.0%	75.8%	23.3%	76.7%
20,050	GRANT	5,727	1,999	3,592	136	1,593 D	34.9%	62.7%	35.8%	64.2%
8,646	GUADALUPE	3,115	1,565	1,550		15 R	50.2%	49.8%	50.2%	49.8%
4,374	HARDING	1,307	649	653	5	4 D	49.7%	50.0%	49.8%	50.2%
4,821	HIDALGO	1,242	374	859	9	485 D	30.1%	69.2%	30.3%	69.7%
21,154	LEA	6,025	1,273	4,708	44	3,435 D	21.1%	78.1%	21.3%	78.7%
8,557	LINCOLN	3,005	1,575	1,406	24	169 R	52.4%	46.8%	52.8%	47.2%
	LOS ALAMOS	—	—	—	—	—	—	—	—	—
6,457	LUNA	2,584	941	1,629	14	688 D	36.4%	63.0%	36.6%	63.4%
23,641	MCKINLEY	5,149	2,109	2,995	45	886 D	41.0%	58.2%	41.3%	58.7%
10,981	MORA	3,437	1,893	1,541	3	352 R	55.1%	44.8%	55.1%	44.9%
10,522	OTERO	3,733	1,354	2,361	18	1,007 D	36.3%	63.2%	36.4%	63.6%
12,111	QUAY	4,493	1,392	3,063	38	1,671 D	31.0%	68.2%	31.2%	68.8%
25,352	RIO ARRIBA	9,043	4,273	4,753	17	480 D	47.3%	52.6%	47.3%	52.7%
14,549	ROOSEVELT	4,075	956	3,087	32	2,131 D	23.5%	75.8%	23.6%	76.4%
13,898	SANDOVAL	3,539	1,675	1,851	13	176 D	47.3%	52.3%	47.5%	52.5%
17,115	SAN JUAN	3,965	2,407	1,544	14	863 R	60.7%	38.9%	60.9%	39.1%
27,910	SAN MIGUEL	9,629	4,655	4,953	21	298 D	48.3%	51.4%	48.4%	51.6%
30,826	SANTA FE	13,731	7,491	6,172	68	1,319 R	54.6%	44.9%	54.8%	45.2%
6,962	SIERRA	2,680	1,274	1,389	17	115 D	47.5%	51.8%	47.8%	52.2%
11,422	SOCORRO	3,798	2,139	1,650	9	489 R	56.3%	43.4%	56.5%	43.5%
18,528	TAOS	5,870	2,852	2,977	41	125 D	48.6%	50.7%	48.9%	51.1%
11,026	TORRANCE	3,412	1,709	1,696	7	13 R	50.1%	49.7%	50.2%	49.8%
9,095	UNION	2,849	1,246	1,590	13	344 D	43.7%	55.8%	43.9%	56.1%
20,245	VALENCIA	6,227	3,280	2,914	33	366 R	52.7%	46.8%	53.0%	47.0%
531,818	TOTAL	187,063	80,303	105,464	1,296	25,161 D	42.9%	56.4%	43.2%	56.8%

NEW MEXICO

PRESIDENT 1944

1940 Census Population	County	Total Vote	Republican	Democratic	Other	Rep.-Dem. Plurality	Percentage: Total Vote Rep.	Percentage: Total Vote Dem.	Percentage: Major Vote Rep.	Percentage: Major Vote Dem.
69,391	BERNALILLO	23,904	11,662	12,229	13	567 D	48.8%	51.2%	48.8%	51.2%
4,881	CATRON	1,289	699	589	1	110 R	54.2%	45.7%	54.3%	45.7%
23,980	CHAVES	6,516	3,149	3,350	17	201 D	48.3%	51.4%	48.5%	51.5%
18,718	COLFAX	5,685	2,661	3,017	7	356 D	46.8%	53.1%	46.9%	53.1%
18,159	CURRY	5,609	2,326	3,271	12	945 D	41.5%	58.3%	41.6%	58.4%
3,725	DE BACA	1,216	554	660	2	106 D	45.6%	54.3%	45.6%	54.4%
30,411	DONA ANA	7,327	3,149	4,172	6	1,023 D	43.0%	56.9%	43.0%	57.0%
24,311	EDDY	7,327	2,083	5,228	16	3,145 D	28.4%	71.4%	28.5%	71.5%
20,050	GRANT	5,446	1,970	3,472	4	1,502 D	36.2%	63.8%	36.2%	63.8%
8,646	GUADALUPE	3,188	1,649	1,539		110 R	51.7%	48.3%	51.7%	48.3%
4,374	HARDING	1,467	820	647		173 R	55.9%	44.1%	55.9%	44.1%
4,821	HIDALGO	1,174	367	807		440 D	31.3%	68.7%	31.3%	68.7%
21,154	LEA	4,168	1,227	2,938	3	1,711 D	29.4%	70.5%	29.5%	70.5%
8,557	LINCOLN	2,801	1,455	1,342	4	113 R	51.9%	47.9%	52.0%	48.0%
	LOS ALAMOS	—	—	—	—	—	—	—	—	—
6,457	LUNA	2,459	1,074	1,383	2	309 D	43.7%	56.2%	43.7%	56.3%
23,641	MCKINLEY	3,760	1,547	2,210	3	663 D	41.1%	58.8%	41.2%	58.8%
10,981	MORA	3,209	1,783	1,425	1	358 R	55.6%	44.4%	55.6%	44.4%
10,522	OTERO	3,362	1,467	1,892	3	425 D	43.6%	56.3%	43.7%	56.3%
12,111	QUAY	3,732	1,449	2,272	11	823 D	38.8%	60.9%	38.9%	61.1%
25,352	RIO ARRIBA	7,327	3,532	3,792	3	260 D	48.2%	51.8%	48.2%	51.8%
14,549	ROOSEVELT	3,969	1,610	2,359		749 D	40.6%	59.4%	40.6%	59.4%
13,898	SANDOVAL	2,795	1,439	1,354	2	85 R	51.5%	48.4%	51.5%	48.5%
17,115	SAN JUAN	2,540	1,438	1,093	9	345 R	56.6%	43.0%	56.8%	43.2%
27,910	SAN MIGUEL	8,702	4,014	4,684	4	670 D	46.1%	53.8%	46.1%	53.9%
30,826	SANTA FE	10,397	5,482	4,915		567 R	52.7%	47.3%	52.7%	47.3%
6,962	SIERRA	2,128	1,112	1,008	8	104 R	52.3%	47.4%	52.5%	47.5%
11,422	SOCORRO	4,000	2,030	1,967	3	63 R	50.7%	49.2%	50.8%	49.2%
18,528	TAOS	5,084	2,557	2,525	2	32 R	50.3%	49.7%	50.3%	49.7%
11,026	TORRANCE	3,456	2,014	1,438	4	576 R	58.3%	41.6%	58.3%	41.7%
9,095	UNION	2,959	1,604	1,350	5	254 R	54.2%	45.6%	54.3%	45.7%
20,245	VALENCIA	5,229	2,765	2,461	3	304 R	52.9%	47.1%	52.9%	47.1%
531,818	TOTAL	152,225	70,688	81,389	148	10,701 D	46.4%	53.5%	46.5%	53.5%

NEW MEXICO

PRESIDENT 1940

1940 Census Population	County	Total Vote	Republican	Democratic	Other	Rep.-Dem. Plurality	Percentage Total Vote Rep.	Total Vote Dem.	Major Vote Rep.	Major Vote Dem.
69,391	BERNALILLO	26,461	11,999	14,428	34	2,429 D	45.3%	54.5%	45.4%	54.6%
4,881	CATRON	1,988	949	1,039		90 D	47.7%	52.3%	47.7%	52.3%
23,980	CHAVES	7,299	2,981	4,304	14	1,323 D	40.8%	59.0%	40.9%	59.1%
18,718	COLFAX	7,690	3,452	4,234	4	782 D	44.9%	55.1%	44.9%	55.1%
18,159	CURRY	6,319	1,629	4,670	20	3,041 D	25.8%	73.9%	25.9%	74.1%
3,725	DE BACA	1,449	479	970		491 D	33.1%	66.9%	33.1%	66.9%
30,411	DONA ANA	8,936	3,720	5,208	8	1,488 D	41.6%	58.3%	41.7%	58.3%
24,311	EDDY	6,604	1,625	4,968	11	3,343 D	24.6%	75.2%	24.6%	75.4%
20,050	GRANT	5,930	2,015	3,914	1	1,899 D	34.0%	66.0%	34.0%	66.0%
8,646	GUADALUPE	3,889	1,807	2,082		275 D	46.5%	53.5%	46.5%	53.5%
4,374	HARDING	2,011	998	1,004	9	6 D	49.6%	49.9%	49.9%	50.1%
4,821	HIDALGO	1,565	516	1,049		533 D	33.0%	67.0%	33.0%	67.0%
21,154	LEA	5,592	1,286	4,295	11	3,009 D	23.0%	76.8%	23.0%	77.0%
8,557	LINCOLN	3,570	1,794	1,763	13	31 R	50.3%	49.4%	50.4%	49.6%
	LOS ALAMOS	—	—	—	—	—	—	—	—	—
6,457	LUNA	2,460	1,066	1,388	6	322 D	43.3%	56.4%	43.4%	56.6%
23,641	MCKINLEY	4,232	1,701	2,525	6	824 D	40.2%	59.7%	40.3%	59.7%
10,981	MORA	4,401	2,440	1,960	1	480 R	55.4%	44.5%	55.5%	44.5%
10,522	OTERO	3,389	1,596	1,788	5	192 D	47.1%	52.8%	47.2%	52.8%
12,111	QUAY	4,650	1,413	3,215	22	1,802 D	30.4%	69.1%	30.5%	69.5%
25,352	RIO ARRIBA	9,247	4,289	4,952	6	663 D	46.4%	53.6%	46.4%	53.6%
14,549	ROOSEVELT	4,590	1,384	3,190	16	1,806 D	30.2%	69.5%	30.3%	69.7%
13,898	SANDOVAL	4,051	1,990	2,060	1	70 D	49.1%	50.9%	49.1%	50.9%
17,115	SAN JUAN	3,207	1,757	1,445	5	312 R	54.8%	45.1%	54.9%	45.1%
27,910	SAN MIGUEL	10,943	4,882	6,054	7	1,172 D	44.6%	55.3%	44.6%	55.4%
30,826	SANTA FE	12,770	6,285	6,482	3	197 D	49.2%	50.8%	49.2%	50.8%
6,962	SIERRA	2,910	1,372	1,534	4	162 D	47.1%	52.7%	47.2%	52.8%
11,422	SOCORRO	5,197	2,703	2,489	5	214 R	52.0%	47.9%	52.1%	47.9%
18,528	TAOS	6,810	3,342	3,463	5	121 D	49.1%	50.9%	49.1%	50.9%
11,026	TORRANCE	4,439	2,509	1,921	9	588 R	56.5%	43.3%	56.6%	43.4%
9,095	UNION	3,899	1,900	1,987	12	87 D	48.7%	51.0%	48.9%	51.1%
20,245	VALENCIA	6,760	3,436	3,318	6	118 R	50.8%	49.1%	50.9%	49.1%
531,818	TOTAL	183,258	79,315	103,699	244	24,384 D	43.3%	56.6%	43.3%	56.7%

NEW MEXICO

PRESIDENT 1936

1930 Census Population	County	Total Vote	Republican	Democratic	Other	Rep.-Dem. Plurality	Percentage Total Vote Rep.	Total Vote Dem.	Major Vote Rep.	Major Vote Dem.
45,430	BERNALILLO	22,582	7,107	15,305	170	8,198 D	31.5%	67.8%	31.7%	68.3%
3,282	CATRON	2,272	798	1,456	18	658 D	35.1%	64.1%	35.4%	64.6%
19,549	CHAVES	7,017	2,505	4,394	118	1,889 D	35.7%	62.6%	36.3%	63.7%
19,157	COLFAX	7,451	2,745	4,661	45	1,916 D	36.8%	62.6%	37.1%	62.9%
15,809	CURRY	5,797	1,023	4,689	85	3,666 D	17.6%	80.9%	17.9%	82.1%
2,893	DE BACA	1,460	444	1,010	6	566 D	30.4%	69.2%	30.5%	69.5%
27,455	DONA ANA	8,102	2,494	5,544	64	3,050 D	30.8%	68.4%	31.0%	69.0%
15,842	EDDY	5,425	1,027	4,349	49	3,322 D	18.9%	80.2%	19.1%	80.9%
19,050	GRANT	4,736	1,469	3,215	52	1,746 D	31.0%	67.9%	31.4%	68.6%
7,027	GUADALUPE	3,966	1,775	2,187	4	412 D	44.8%	55.1%	44.8%	55.2%
4,421	HARDING	2,169	888	1,276	5	388 D	40.9%	58.8%	41.0%	59.0%
5,023	HIDALGO	1,459	326	1,115	18	789 D	22.3%	76.4%	22.6%	77.4%
6,144	LEA	4,491	549	3,905	37	3,356 D	12.2%	87.0%	12.3%	87.7%
7,198	LINCOLN	3,641	1,579	2,021	41	442 D	43.4%	55.5%	43.9%	56.1%
	LOS ALAMOS	—	—	—	—	—	—	—	—	—
6,247	LUNA	2,367	806	1,500	61	694 D	34.1%	63.4%	35.0%	65.0%
20,643	MCKINLEY	3,944	1,404	2,526	14	1,122 D	35.6%	64.0%	35.7%	64.3%
10,322	MORA	4,725	2,259	2,460	6	201 D	47.8%	52.1%	47.9%	52.1%
9,779	OTERO	3,355	1,333	1,989	33	656 D	39.7%	59.3%	40.1%	59.9%
10,828	QUAY	4,290	816	3,423	51	2,607 D	19.0%	79.8%	19.2%	80.8%
21,381	RIO ARRIBA	8,802	4,093	4,691	18	598 D	46.5%	53.3%	46.6%	53.4%
11,109	ROOSEVELT	3,855	677	2,951	227	2,274 D	17.6%	76.5%	18.7%	81.3%
11,144	SANDOVAL	3,898	1,800	2,094	4	294 D	46.2%	53.7%	46.2%	53.8%
14,701	SAN JUAN	2,944	1,345	1,530	69	185 D	45.7%	52.0%	46.8%	53.2%
23,636	SAN MIGUEL	10,906	4,697	6,199	10	1,502 D	43.1%	56.8%	43.1%	56.9%
19,567	SANTA FE	11,132	4,960	6,145	27	1,185 D	44.6%	55.2%	44.7%	55.3%
5,184	SIERRA	2,562	951	1,587	24	636 D	37.1%	61.9%	37.5%	62.5%
9,611	SOCORRO	5,023	2,530	2,477	16	53 R	50.4%	49.3%	50.5%	49.5%
14,394	TAOS	5,979	2,918	3,051	10	133 D	48.8%	51.0%	48.9%	51.1%
9,269	TORRANCE	4,227	1,843	2,346	38	503 D	43.6%	55.5%	44.0%	56.0%
11,036	UNION	4,267	1,625	2,605	37	980 D	38.1%	61.0%	38.4%	61.6%
16,186	VALENCIA	6,291	2,941	3,336	14	395 D	46.7%	53.0%	46.9%	53.1%
423,317	TOTAL	169,135	61,727	106,037	1,371	44,310 D	36.5%	62.7%	36.8%	63.2%

NEW MEXICO

PRESIDENT 1932

1930 Census Population	County	Total Vote	Republican	Democratic	Other	Rep.-Dem. Plurality	Percentage Total Vote Rep.	Percentage Total Vote Dem.	Percentage Major Vote Rep.	Percentage Major Vote Dem.
45,430	BERNALILLO	18,243	7,309	10,722	212	3,413 D	40.1%	58.8%	40.5%	59.5%
3,282	CATRON	1,608	610	972	26	362 D	37.9%	60.4%	38.6%	61.4%
19,549	CHAVES	6,322	1,830	4,257	235	2,427 D	28.9%	67.3%	30.1%	69.9%
19,157	COLFAX	7,547	3,214	4,282	51	1,068 D	42.6%	56.7%	42.9%	57.1%
15,809	CURRY	5,079	932	3,738	409	2,806 D	18.4%	73.6%	20.0%	80.0%
2,893	DE BACA	1,305	264	1,023	18	759 D	20.2%	78.4%	20.5%	79.5%
27,455	DONA ANA	7,595	2,354	5,133	108	2,779 D	31.0%	67.6%	31.4%	68.6%
15,842	EDDY	4,459	818	3,565	76	2,747 D	18.3%	80.0%	18.7%	81.3%
19,050	GRANT	4,795	1,381	3,344	70	1,963 D	28.8%	69.7%	29.2%	70.8%
7,027	GUADALUPE	3,542	1,621	1,909	12	288 D	45.8%	53.9%	45.9%	54.1%
4,421	HARDING	2,293	779	1,478	36	699 D	34.0%	64.5%	34.5%	65.5%
5,023	HIDALGO	1,460	299	1,131	30	832 D	20.5%	77.5%	20.9%	79.1%
6,144	LEA	2,756	271	2,371	114	2,100 D	9.8%	86.0%	10.3%	89.7%
7,198	LINCOLN	3,418	1,172	2,225	21	1,053 D	34.3%	65.1%	34.5%	65.5%
	LOS ALAMOS	—	—	—	—	—	—	—	—	—
6,247	LUNA	2,286	641	1,605	40	964 D	28.0%	70.2%	28.5%	71.5%
20,643	MCKINLEY	3,489	1,373	2,096	20	723 D	39.4%	60.1%	39.6%	60.4%
10,322	MORA	4,407	1,444	2,962	1	1,518 D	32.8%	67.2%	32.8%	67.2%
9,779	OTERO	3,127	969	2,091	67	1,122 D	31.0%	66.9%	31.7%	68.3%
10,828	QUAY	4,077	852	3,058	167	2,206 D	20.9%	75.0%	21.8%	78.2%
21,381	RIO ARRIBA	8,229	2,880	5,337	12	2,457 D	35.0%	64.9%	35.0%	65.0%
11,109	ROOSEVELT	3,404	475	2,826	103	2,351 D	14.0%	83.0%	14.4%	85.6%
11,144	SANDOVAL	3,378	1,562	1,808	8	246 D	46.2%	53.5%	46.4%	53.6%
14,701	SAN JUAN	2,635	925	1,506	204	581 D	35.1%	57.2%	38.1%	61.9%
23,636	SAN MIGUEL	10,460	5,364	5,076	20	288 R	51.3%	48.5%	51.4%	48.6%
19,567	SANTA FE	9,390	3,625	5,739	26	2,114 D	38.6%	61.1%	38.7%	61.3%
5,184	SIERRA	2,210	667	1,515	28	848 D	30.2%	68.6%	30.6%	69.4%
9,611	SOCORRO	4,438	1,931	2,495	12	564 D	43.5%	56.2%	43.6%	56.4%
14,394	TAOS	5,723	2,416	3,277	30	861 D	42.2%	57.3%	42.4%	57.6%
9,269	TORRANCE	4,071	1,803	2,202	66	399 D	44.3%	54.1%	45.0%	55.0%
11,036	UNION	4,353	1,173	3,117	63	1,944 D	26.9%	71.6%	27.3%	72.7%
16,186	VALENCIA	5,507	3,263	2,229	15	1,034 R	59.3%	40.5%	59.4%	40.6%
423,317	TOTAL	151,606	54,217	95,089	2,300	40,872 D	35.8%	62.7%	36.3%	63.7%

NEW MEXICO

PRESIDENT 1928

1920 Census Population	County	Total Vote	Republican	Democratic	Other	Rep.-Dem. Plurality	Percentage: Total Vote Rep.	Total Vote Dem.	Major Vote Rep.	Major Vote Dem.
29,855	BERNALILLO	15,311	8,725	6,572	14	2,153 R	57.0%	42.9%	57.0%	43.0%
	CATRON	1,195	774	420	1	354 R	64.8%	35.1%	64.8%	35.2%
12,075	CHAVES	4,496	3,124	1,364	8	1,760 R	69.5%	30.3%	69.6%	30.4%
21,550	COLFAX	6,936	3,904	3,022	10	882 R	56.3%	43.6%	56.4%	43.6%
11,236	CURRY	3,504	1,968	1,530	6	438 R	56.2%	43.7%	56.3%	43.7%
3,196	DE BACA	991	474	514	3	40 D	47.8%	51.9%	48.0%	52.0%
16,548	DONA ANA	5,318	3,141	2,169	8	972 R	59.1%	40.8%	59.2%	40.8%
9,116	EDDY	2,833	1,618	1,212	3	406 R	57.1%	42.8%	57.2%	42.8%
21,939	GRANT	4,060	2,058	1,994	8	64 R	50.7%	49.1%	50.8%	49.2%
8,015	GUADALUPE	2,811	1,718	1,093		625 R	61.1%	38.9%	61.1%	38.9%
	HARDING	1,644	916	726	2	190 R	55.7%	44.2%	55.8%	44.2%
4,338	HIDALGO	1,071	561	509	1	52 R	52.4%	47.5%	52.4%	47.6%
3,545	LEA	1,014	537	474	3	63 R	53.0%	46.7%	53.1%	46.9%
7,823	LINCOLN	2,315	1,489	821	5	668 R	64.3%	35.5%	64.5%	35.5%
	LOS ALAMOS	—	—	—	—	—	—	—	—	—
12,270	LUNA	1,514	860	647	7	213 R	56.8%	42.7%	57.1%	42.9%
13,731	MCKINLEY	3,335	2,075	1,247	13	828 R	62.2%	37.4%	62.5%	37.5%
13,915	MORA	3,797	1,998	1,799		199 R	52.6%	47.4%	52.6%	47.4%
7,902	OTERO	2,408	1,250	1,148	10	102 R	51.9%	47.7%	52.1%	47.9%
10,444	QUAY	3,215	1,616	1,594	5	22 R	50.3%	49.6%	50.3%	49.7%
19,552	RIO ARRIBA	6,557	4,109	2,444	4	1,665 R	62.7%	37.3%	62.7%	37.3%
6,548	ROOSEVELT	2,264	1,157	1,098	9	59 R	51.1%	48.5%	51.3%	48.7%
8,863	SANDOVAL	2,860	1,700	1,159	1	541 R	59.4%	40.5%	59.5%	40.5%
8,333	SAN JUAN	2,164	1,436	724	4	712 R	66.4%	33.5%	66.5%	33.5%
22,867	SAN MIGUEL	8,748	5,184	3,560	4	1,624 R	59.3%	40.7%	59.3%	40.7%
15,030	SANTA FE	7,685	4,630	3,051	4	1,579 R	60.2%	39.7%	60.3%	39.7%
4,619	SIERRA	1,424	766	657	1	109 R	53.8%	46.1%	53.8%	46.2%
14,061	SOCORRO	3,507	1,940	1,564	3	376 R	55.3%	44.6%	55.4%	44.6%
12,773	TAOS	4,284	2,441	1,842	1	599 R	57.0%	43.0%	57.0%	43.0%
9,731	TORRANCE	3,034	1,958	1,070	6	888 R	64.5%	35.3%	64.7%	35.3%
16,680	UNION	3,400	2,081	1,306	13	775 R	61.2%	38.4%	61.4%	38.6%
13,795	VALENCIA	4,382	3,500	881	1	2,619 R	79.9%	20.1%	79.9%	20.1%
360,350	TOTAL	118,077	69,708	48,211	158	21,497 R	59.0%	40.8%	59.1%	40.9%

NEW MEXICO

PRESIDENT 1924

1920 Census Population	County	Total Vote	Republican	Democratic	Other	Rep.-Dem. Plurality	Percentage Total Vote Rep.	Percentage Total Vote Dem.	Percentage Major Vote Rep.	Percentage Major Vote Dem.
29,855	BERNALILLO	14,284	7,078	6,023	1,183	1,055 R	49.6%	42.2%	54.0%	46.0%
	CATRON	1,055	499	418	138	81 R	47.3%	39.6%	54.4%	45.6%
12,075	CHAVES	3,855	1,519	2,168	168	649 D	39.4%	56.2%	41.2%	58.8%
21,550	COLFAX	7,307	3,512	3,067	728	445 R	48.1%	42.0%	53.4%	46.6%
11,236	CURRY	3,255	669	1,738	848	1,069 D	20.6%	53.4%	27.8%	72.2%
3,196	DE BACA	930	270	574	86	304 D	29.0%	61.7%	32.0%	68.0%
16,548	DONA ANA	4,819	2,823	1,775	221	1,048 R	58.6%	36.8%	61.4%	38.6%
9,116	EDDY	2,320	658	1,524	138	866 D	28.4%	65.7%	30.2%	69.8%
21,939	GRANT	4,436	1,756	2,085	595	329 D	39.6%	47.0%	45.7%	54.3%
8,015	GUADALUPE	2,564	1,329	1,056	179	273 R	51.8%	41.2%	55.7%	44.3%
	HARDING	1,711	721	714	276	7 R	42.1%	41.7%	50.2%	49.8%
4,338	HIDALGO	926	261	476	189	215 D	28.2%	51.4%	35.4%	64.6%
3,545	LEA	736	138	552	46	414 D	18.8%	75.0%	20.0%	80.0%
7,823	LINCOLN	2,216	1,087	837	292	250 R	49.1%	37.8%	56.5%	43.5%
	LOS ALAMOS	—	—	—	—	—	—	—	—	—
12,270	LUNA	1,638	709	596	333	113 R	43.3%	36.4%	54.3%	45.7%
13,731	MCKINLEY	3,226	1,653	1,150	423	503 R	51.2%	35.6%	59.0%	41.0%
13,915	MORA	4,316	2,197	2,087	32	110 R	50.9%	48.4%	51.3%	48.7%
7,902	OTERO	2,021	832	886	303	54 D	41.2%	43.8%	48.4%	51.6%
10,444	QUAY	3,057	851	1,548	658	697 D	27.8%	50.6%	35.5%	64.5%
19,552	RIO ARRIBA	6,591	3,707	2,734	150	973 R	56.2%	41.5%	57.6%	42.4%
6,548	ROOSEVELT	2,037	398	1,340	299	942 D	19.5%	65.8%	22.9%	77.1%
8,863	SANDOVAL	2,712	1,587	1,096	29	491 R	58.5%	40.4%	59.2%	40.8%
8,333	SAN JUAN	1,981	889	819	273	70 R	44.9%	41.3%	52.0%	48.0%
22,867	SAN MIGUEL	7,702	3,894	3,543	265	351 R	50.6%	46.0%	52.4%	47.6%
15,030	SANTA FE	6,791	4,010	2,602	179	1,408 R	59.0%	38.3%	60.6%	39.4%
4,619	SIERRA	1,312	632	546	134	86 R	48.2%	41.6%	53.7%	46.3%
14,061	SOCORRO	3,742	2,332	1,251	159	1,081 R	62.3%	33.4%	65.1%	34.9%
12,773	TAOS	4,209	2,470	1,655	84	815 R	58.7%	39.3%	59.9%	40.1%
9,731	TORRANCE	3,255	1,666	1,269	320	397 R	51.2%	39.0%	56.8%	43.2%
16,680	UNION	3,746	1,415	1,735	596	320 D	37.8%	46.3%	44.9%	55.1%
13,795	VALENCIA	4,080	3,183	678	219	2,505 R	78.0%	16.6%	82.4%	17.6%
360,350	TOTAL	112,830	54,745	48,542	9,543	6,203 R	48.5%	43.0%	53.0%	47.0%

NEW MEXICO

PRESIDENT 1920

1920 Census Population	County	Total Vote	Republican	Democratic	Other	Rep.-Dem. Plurality	Percentage Total Vote Rep.	Percentage Total Vote Dem.	Percentage Major Vote Rep.	Percentage Major Vote Dem.
29,855	BERNALILLO	9,833	4,969	4,808	56	161 R	50.5%	48.9%	50.8%	49.2%
	CATRON	—	—	—	—	—	—	—	—	—
12,075	CHAVES	3,876	1,765	2,080	31	315 D	45.5%	53.7%	45.9%	54.1%
21,550	COLFAX	6,107	3,351	2,709	47	642 R	54.9%	44.4%	55.3%	44.7%
11,236	CURRY	3,179	884	2,143	152	1,259 D	27.8%	67.4%	29.2%	70.8%
3,196	DE BACA	1,121	412	693	16	281 D	36.8%	61.8%	37.3%	62.7%
16,548	DONA ANA	3,964	2,627	1,318	19	1,309 R	66.3%	33.2%	66.6%	33.4%
9,116	EDDY	2,624	982	1,611	31	629 D	37.4%	61.4%	37.9%	62.1%
21,939	GRANT	4,147	2,230	1,879	38	351 R	53.8%	45.3%	54.3%	45.7%
8,015	GUADALUPE	2,840	1,599	1,224	17	375 R	56.3%	43.1%	56.6%	43.4%
	HARDING	—	—	—	—	—	—	—	—	—
4,338	HIDALGO	1,003	443	551	9	108 D	44.2%	54.9%	44.6%	55.4%
3,545	LEA	1,011	255	733	23	478 D	25.2%	72.5%	25.8%	74.2%
7,823	LINCOLN	2,540	1,456	1,047	37	409 R	57.3%	41.2%	58.2%	41.8%
	LOS ALAMOS	—	—	—	—	—	—	—	—	—
12,270	LUNA	1,868	834	1,000	34	166 D	44.6%	53.5%	45.5%	54.5%
13,731	MCKINLEY	2,541	1,525	989	27	536 R	60.0%	38.9%	60.7%	39.3%
13,915	MORA	4,685	2,478	2,179	28	299 R	52.9%	46.5%	53.2%	46.8%
7,902	OTERO	2,393	1,229	1,095	69	134 R	51.4%	45.8%	52.9%	47.1%
10,444	QUAY	3,098	1,213	1,813	72	600 D	39.2%	58.5%	40.1%	59.9%
19,552	RIO ARRIBA	6,042	3,986	2,056		1,930 R	66.0%	34.0%	66.0%	34.0%
6,548	ROOSEVELT	1,817	571	1,178	68	607 D	31.4%	64.8%	32.6%	67.4%
8,863	SANDOVAL	2,078	1,194	884		310 R	57.5%	42.5%	57.5%	42.5%
8,333	SAN JUAN	1,845	985	831	29	154 R	53.4%	45.0%	54.2%	45.8%
22,867	SAN MIGUEL	9,525	5,535	3,990		1,545 R	58.1%	41.9%	58.1%	41.9%
15,030	SANTA FE	4,787	3,060	1,700	27	1,360 R	63.9%	35.5%	64.3%	35.7%
4,619	SIERRA	1,518	862	642	14	220 R	56.8%	42.3%	57.3%	42.7%
14,061	SOCORRO	4,987	3,150	1,807	30	1,343 R	63.2%	36.2%	63.5%	36.5%
12,773	TAOS	3,884	2,519	1,359	6	1,160 R	64.9%	35.0%	65.0%	35.0%
9,731	TORRANCE	2,905	1,751	1,125	29	626 R	60.3%	38.7%	60.9%	39.1%
16,680	UNION	5,388	2,930	2,273	185	657 R	54.4%	42.2%	56.3%	43.7%
13,795	VALENCIA	3,806	2,839	951	16	1,888 R	74.6%	25.0%	74.9%	25.1%
360,350	TOTAL	105,412	57,634	46,668	1,110	10,966 R	54.7%	44.3%	55.3%	44.7%

NEW MEXICO

In 1921 Catron county was organized from part of Socorro; Harding county was organized from parts of Mora and Union counties. In 1949 Los Alamos county was organized from part of Sandoval county.

ELECTION NOTES

1956 Other vote was 607 Holtwick (Prohibition); 364 Andrews (States Rights); 69 Hass (Socialist Labor).

1952 Other vote was 297 Hamblen (Prohibition); 225 Hallinan (Progressive); 220 MacArthur (Christian Nationalist); 35 Hass (Socialist Labor).

1948 Other vote was 1,037 Wallace (Progressive); 127 Watson (Prohibition); 83 Thomas (Socialist); 49 Teichert (Socialist Labor).

1944 Other vote was Watson (Prohibition).

1940 Other vote was 144 Thomas (Socialist); 100 Babson (Prohibition).

1936 Other vote was 924 Lemke (Union); 343 Thomas (Socialist); 61 Colvin (Prohibition); 43 Browder (Communist).

1932 Other vote was 1,776 Thomas (Socialist); 389 Harvey (Liberty); 135 Foster (Communist).

1928 Other vote was Foster (Communist).

1924 Other vote was LaFollette (Progressive). Progressive candidates ran second in Curry county.

1920 Other vote was 1,104 Christensen (Farmer-Labor); 2 Debs (Socialist); 4 scattered write-in.

NEW YORK

POPULAR VOTE FOR PRESIDENT 1920 TO 1956

Year	Total Vote	Republican		Democratic		Other Vote	Plurality	Percentage			
								Total Vote		Major Vote	
		Vote	Candidate	Vote	Candidate			Rep.	Dem.	Rep.	Dem.
1956	7,095,971	4,345,506	Eisenhower, Dwight D.	2,747,944	Stevenson, Adlai E.	2,521	1,597,562 R	61.2%	38.7%	61.3%	38.7%
1952	7,128,239	3,952,813	Eisenhower, Dwight D.	3,104,601	Stevenson, Adlai E.	70,825	848,212 R	55.5%	43.6%	56.0%	44.0%
1948	6,177,337	2,841,163	Dewey, Thomas E.	2,780,204	Truman, Harry S.	555,970	60,959 R	46.0%	45.0%	50.5%	49.5%
1944	6,316,790	2,987,647	Dewey, Thomas E.	3,304,238	Roosevelt, Franklin D.	24,905	316,591 D	47.3%	52.3%	47.5%	52.5%
1940	6,301,596	3,027,478	Willkie, Wendell	3,251,918	Roosevelt, Franklin D.	22,200	224,440 D	48.0%	51.6%	48.2%	51.8%
1936	5,596,398	2,180,670	Landon, Alfred M.	3,293,222	Roosevelt, Franklin D.	122,506	1,112,552 D	39.0%	58.8%	39.8%	60.2%
1932	4,688,614	1,937,963	Hoover, Herbert C.	2,534,959	Roosevelt, Franklin D.	215,692	596,996 D	41.3%	54.1%	43.3%	56.7%
1928	4,405,626	2,193,344	Hoover, Herbert C.	2,089,863	Smith, Alfred E.	122,419	103,481 R	49.8%	47.4%	51.2%	48.8%
1924 **	3,263,939	1,820,058	Coolidge, Calvin	950,796	Davis, John W.	493,085	869,262 R	55.8%	29.1%	65.7%	34.3%
1920	2,898,513	1,871,167	Harding, Warren G.	781,238	Cox, James M.	246,108	1,089,929 R	64.6%	27.0%	70.5%	29.5%

In 1924 other vote was 474,913 Progressive; 9,928 Socialist Labor and 8,244 Communist.

ELECTORAL COLLEGE VOTE 1920 TO 1956

Year	Total	Republican	Democratic	Other
1956	45	45	—	—
1952	45	45	—	—
1948	47	47	—	—
1944	47	—	47	—
1940	47	—	47	—
1936	47	—	47	—
1932	47	—	47	—
1928	45	45	—	—
1924	45	45	—	—
1920	45	45	—	—

NEW YORK

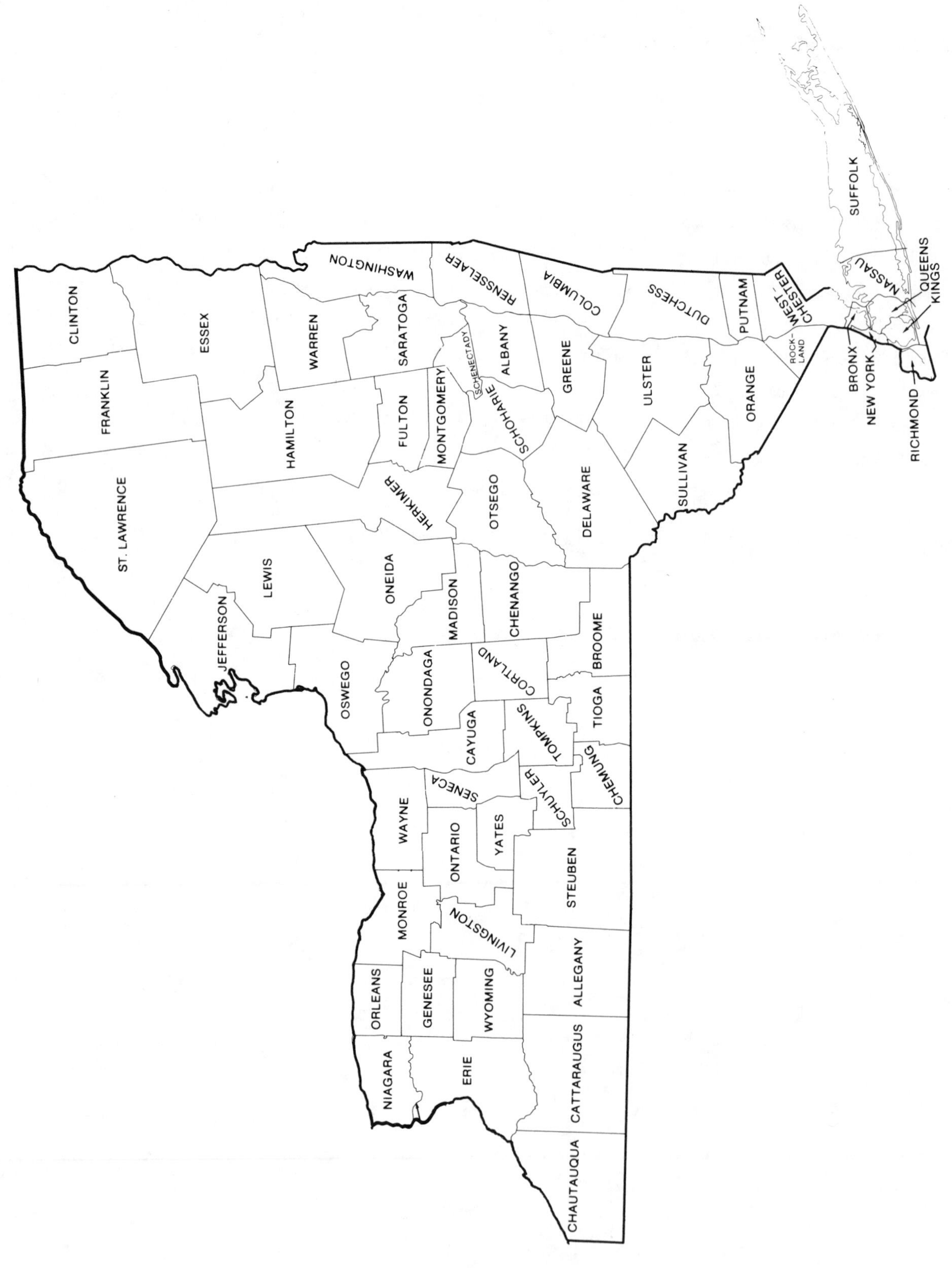
CLINTON
ESSEX
WASHINGTON
RENSSELAER
COLUMBIA
DUTCHESS
PUTNAM
WEST-CHESTER
SUFFOLK
NASSAU
QUEENS
KINGS
FRANKLIN
WARREN
SARATOGA
SCHENECTADY
ALBANY
GREENE
ULSTER
ROCK-LAND
ORANGE
BRONX
NEW YORK
RICHMOND
HAMILTON
FULTON
MONTGOMERY
SCHOHARIE
SULLIVAN
ST. LAWRENCE
HERKIMER
OTSEGO
DELAWARE
LEWIS
ONEIDA
MADISON
CHENANGO
JEFFERSON
BROOME
OSWEGO
ONONDAGA
CORTLAND
TIOGA
CAYUGA
TOMPKINS
CHEMUNG
SENECA
SCHUYLER
WAYNE
ONTARIO
YATES
STEUBEN
MONROE
LIVINGSTON
ALLEGANY
ORLEANS
GENESEE
WYOMING
NIAGARA
ERIE
CATTARAUGUS
CHAUTAUQUA

NEW YORK

PRESIDENT 1956

1950 Census Population	County	Total Vote	Republican	Democratic	Other	Rep.-Dem. Plurality	Percentage			
							Total Vote		Major Vote	
							Rep.	Dem.	Rep.	Dem.
239,386	ALBANY	152,193	86,202	65,982	9	20,220 R	56.6%	43.4%	56.6%	43.4%
43,784	ALLEGANY	19,736	16,068	3,668		12,400 R	81.4%	18.6%	81.4%	18.6%
1,451,277	BRONX	601,588	257,382	343,823	383	86,441 D	42.8%	57.2%	42.8%	57.2%
184,698	BROOME	90,241	67,024	23,217		43,807 R	74.3%	25.7%	74.3%	25.7%
77,901	CATTARAUGUS	34,895	25,282	9,613		15,669 R	72.5%	27.5%	72.5%	27.5%
70,136	CAYUGA	36,775	26,503	10,268	4	16,235 R	72.1%	27.9%	72.1%	27.9%
135,189	CHAUTAUQUA	64,432	44,149	20,269	14	23,880 R	68.5%	31.5%	68.5%	31.5%
86,827	CHEMUNG	44,862	33,270	11,592		21,678 R	74.2%	25.8%	74.2%	25.8%
39,138	CHENANGO	20,118	16,314	3,804		12,510 R	81.1%	18.9%	81.1%	18.9%
53,622	CLINTON	23,130	16,295	6,833	2	9,462 R	70.4%	29.5%	70.5%	29.5%
43,182	COLUMBIA	24,003	19,004	4,999		14,005 R	79.2%	20.8%	79.2%	20.8%
37,158	CORTLAND	17,697	14,085	3,612		10,473 R	79.6%	20.4%	79.6%	20.4%
44,420	DELAWARE	21,199	17,364	3,835		13,529 R	81.9%	18.1%	81.9%	18.1%
136,781	DUTCHESS	68,724	53,840	14,876	8	38,964 R	78.3%	21.6%	78.4%	21.6%
899,238	ERIE	459,649	292,657	166,930	62	125,727 R	63.7%	36.3%	63.7%	36.3%
35,086	ESSEX	16,965	13,930	3,035		10,895 R	82.1%	17.9%	82.1%	17.9%
44,830	FRANKLIN	18,229	13,003	5,226		7,777 R	71.3%	28.7%	71.3%	28.7%
51,021	FULTON	24,596	18,244	6,352		11,892 R	74.2%	25.8%	74.2%	25.8%
47,584	GENESEE	23,600	17,614	5,986		11,628 R	74.6%	25.4%	74.6%	25.4%
28,745	GREENE	18,073	14,262	3,811		10,451 R	78.9%	21.1%	78.9%	21.1%
4,105	HAMILTON	3,089	2,619	470		2,149 R	84.8%	15.2%	84.8%	15.2%
61,407	HERKIMER	31,035	22,246	8,789		13,457 R	71.7%	28.3%	71.7%	28.3%
85,521	JEFFERSON	38,389	28,429	9,959	1	18,470 R	74.1%	25.9%	74.1%	25.9%
2,738,175	KINGS	1,018,479	460,456	557,655	368	97,199 D	45.2%	54.8%	45.2%	54.8%
22,521	LEWIS	10,300	7,764	2,536		5,228 R	75.4%	24.6%	75.4%	24.6%
40,257	LIVINGSTON	20,513	15,523	4,989	1	10,534 R	75.7%	24.3%	75.7%	24.3%
46,214	MADISON	23,462	18,555	4,903	4	13,652 R	79.1%	20.9%	79.1%	20.9%
487,632	MONROE	274,931	183,747	91,161	23	92,586 R	66.8%	33.2%	66.8%	33.2%
59,594	MONTGOMERY	30,685	20,678	9,996	11	10,682 R	67.4%	32.6%	67.4%	32.6%
672,765	NASSAU	539,463	372,358	166,646	459	205,712 R	69.0%	30.9%	69.1%	30.9%
1,960,101	NEW YORK	678,317	300,004	377,856	457	77,852 D	44.2%	55.7%	44.3%	55.7%
189,992	NIAGARA	92,594	62,433	30,161		32,272 R	67.4%	32.6%	67.4%	32.6%
222,855	ONEIDA	114,827	80,178	34,649		45,529 R	69.8%	30.2%	69.8%	30.2%
341,719	ONONDAGA	187,770	137,852	49,918		87,934 R	73.4%	26.6%	73.4%	26.6%
60,172	ONTARIO	30,041	22,317	7,719	5	14,598 R	74.3%	25.7%	74.3%	25.7%
152,255	ORANGE	74,490	57,739	16,722	29	41,017 R	77.5%	22.4%	77.5%	22.5%
29,832	ORLEANS	15,359	11,895	3,464		8,431 R	77.4%	22.6%	77.4%	22.6%
77,181	OSWEGO	38,086	29,277	8,809		20,468 R	76.9%	23.1%	76.9%	23.1%
50,763	OTSEGO	25,128	19,484	5,644		13,840 R	77.5%	22.5%	77.5%	22.5%
20,307	PUTNAM	17,605	12,898	4,694	13	8,204 R	73.3%	26.7%	73.3%	26.7%
1,550,849	QUEENS	787,265	471,223	315,898	144	155,325 R	59.9%	40.1%	59.9%	40.1%
132,607	RENSSELAER	75,702	55,186	20,516		34,670 R	72.9%	27.1%	72.9%	27.1%
191,555	RICHMOND	83,936	64,233	19,644	59	44,589 R	76.5%	23.4%	76.6%	23.4%
89,276	ROCKLAND	47,940	34,049	13,881	10	20,168 R	71.0%	29.0%	71.0%	29.0%
98,897	ST. LAWRENCE	42,789	31,897	10,892		21,005 R	74.5%	25.5%	74.5%	25.5%
74,869	SARATOGA	41,866	32,522	9,338	6	23,184 R	77.7%	22.3%	77.7%	22.3%
142,497	SCHENECTADY	80,235	58,540	21,673	22	36,867 R	73.0%	27.0%	73.0%	27.0%
22,703	SCHOHARIE	12,078	8,851	3,227		5,624 R	73.3%	26.7%	73.3%	26.7%
14,182	SCHUYLER	7,408	5,795	1,613		4,182 R	78.2%	21.8%	78.2%	21.8%
29,253	SENECA	14,040	10,417	3,623		6,794 R	74.2%	25.8%	74.2%	25.8%
91,439	STEUBEN	43,342	33,902	9,440		24,462 R	78.2%	21.8%	78.2%	21.8%
276,129	SUFFOLK	216,232	167,805	48,323	104	119,482 R	77.6%	22.3%	77.6%	22.4%
40,731	SULLIVAN	24,782	15,845	8,937		6,908 R	63.9%	36.1%	63.9%	36.1%
30,166	TIOGA	15,149	11,958	3,188	3	8,770 R	78.9%	21.0%	79.0%	21.0%
59,122	TOMPKINS	25,224	19,749	5,475		14,274 R	78.3%	21.7%	78.3%	21.7%
92,621	ULSTER	56,360	43,034	13,321	5	29,713 R	76.4%	23.6%	76.4%	23.6%
39,205	WARREN	21,749	17,852	3,897		13,955 R	82.1%	17.9%	82.1%	17.9%
47,144	WASHINGTON	23,266	18,449	4,817		13,632 R	79.3%	20.7%	79.3%	20.7%
57,323	WAYNE	28,850	22,940	5,910		17,030 R	79.5%	20.5%	79.5%	20.5%
625,816	WESTCHESTER	377,078	271,906	104,857	315	167,049 R	72.1%	27.8%	72.2%	27.8%
32,822	WYOMING	15,896	12,499	3,397		9,102 R	78.6%	21.4%	78.6%	21.4%
17,615	YATES	9,516	7,910	1,606		6,304 R	83.1%	16.9%	83.1%	16.9%
14,830,192	TOTAL	7,095,971	4,345,506	2,747,944	2,521	1,597,562 R	61.2%	38.7%	61.3%	38.7%

NEW YORK

PRESIDENT 1952

1950 Census Population	County	Total Vote	Republican	Democratic	Other	Rep.-Dem. Plurality	Percentage Total Vote Rep.	Percentage Total Vote Dem.	Percentage Major Vote Rep.	Percentage Major Vote Dem.
239,386	ALBANY	152,806	79,871	72,633	302	7,238 R	52.3%	47.5%	52.4%	47.6%
43,784	ALLEGANY	20,324	16,365	3,943	16	12,422 R	80.5%	19.4%	80.6%	19.4%
1,451,277	BRONX	648,753	241,898	392,477	14,378	150,579 D	37.3%	60.5%	38.1%	61.9%
184,698	BROOME	90,717	64,738	25,833	146	38,905 R	71.4%	28.5%	71.5%	28.5%
77,901	CATTARAUGUS	36,195	24,808	11,333	54	13,475 R	68.5%	31.3%	68.6%	31.4%
70,136	CAYUGA	36,804	25,037	11,695	72	13,342 R	68.0%	31.8%	68.2%	31.8%
135,189	CHAUTAUQUA	65,620	42,043	23,427	150	18,616 R	64.1%	35.7%	64.2%	35.8%
86,827	CHEMUNG	44,022	30,188	13,729	105	16,459 R	68.6%	31.2%	68.7%	31.3%
39,138	CHENANGO	20,167	16,062	4,089	16	11,973 R	79.6%	20.3%	79.7%	20.3%
53,622	CLINTON	22,546	14,535	7,963	48	6,572 R	64.5%	35.3%	64.6%	35.4%
43,182	COLUMBIA	23,659	17,539	6,075	45	11,464 R	74.1%	25.7%	74.3%	25.7%
37,158	CORTLAND	18,093	13,985	4,079	29	9,906 R	77.3%	22.5%	77.4%	22.6%
44,420	DELAWARE	21,879	17,737	4,116	26	13,621 R	81.1%	18.8%	81.2%	18.8%
136,781	DUTCHESS	65,198	46,381	18,644	173	27,737 R	71.1%	28.6%	71.3%	28.7%
899,238	ERIE	451,249	253,927	196,378	944	57,549 R	56.3%	43.5%	56.4%	43.6%
35,086	ESSEX	16,959	12,800	4,130	29	8,670 R	75.5%	24.4%	75.6%	24.4%
44,830	FRANKLIN	18,828	12,212	6,591	25	5,621 R	64.9%	35.0%	64.9%	35.1%
51,021	FULTON	25,710	18,068	7,570	72	10,498 R	70.3%	29.4%	70.5%	29.5%
47,584	GENESEE	23,443	16,606	6,819	18	9,787 R	70.8%	29.1%	70.9%	29.1%
28,745	GREENE	17,435	12,907	4,504	24	8,403 R	74.0%	25.8%	74.1%	25.9%
4,105	HAMILTON	3,165	2,615	546	4	2,069 R	82.6%	17.3%	82.7%	17.3%
61,407	HERKIMER	32,668	20,980	11,599	89	9,381 R	64.2%	35.5%	64.4%	35.6%
85,521	JEFFERSON	39,983	27,932	12,026	25	15,906 R	69.9%	30.1%	69.9%	30.1%
2,738,175	KINGS	1,123,249	446,708	656,229	20,312	209,521 D	39.8%	58.4%	40.5%	59.5%
22,521	LEWIS	10,576	7,622	2,927	27	4,695 R	72.1%	27.7%	72.3%	27.7%
40,257	LIVINGSTON	20,690	14,760	5,901	29	8,859 R	71.3%	28.5%	71.4%	28.6%
46,214	MADISON	23,101	17,715	5,353	33	12,362 R	76.7%	23.2%	76.8%	23.2%
487,632	MONROE	270,400	159,172	110,723	505	48,449 R	58.9%	40.9%	59.0%	41.0%
59,594	MONTGOMERY	32,533	19,554	12,934	45	6,620 R	60.1%	39.8%	60.2%	39.8%
672,765	NASSAU	438,090	305,900	130,267	1,923	175,633 R	69.8%	29.7%	70.1%	29.9%
1,960,101	NEW YORK	765,183	300,284	446,727	18,172	146,443 D	39.2%	58.4%	40.2%	59.8%
189,992	NIAGARA	91,499	54,843	36,504	152	18,339 R	59.9%	39.9%	60.0%	40.0%
222,855	ONEIDA	114,283	69,652	44,438	193	25,214 R	60.9%	38.9%	61.1%	38.9%
341,719	ONONDAGA	183,714	119,268	64,022	424	55,246 R	64.9%	34.8%	65.1%	34.9%
60,172	ONTARIO	30,448	21,659	8,763	26	12,896 R	71.1%	28.8%	71.2%	28.8%
152,255	ORANGE	71,949	51,217	20,585	147	30,632 R	71.2%	28.6%	71.3%	28.7%
29,832	ORLEANS	15,590	11,686	3,893	11	7,793 R	75.0%	25.0%	75.0%	25.0%
77,181	OSWEGO	39,082	27,609	11,444	29	16,165 R	70.6%	29.3%	70.7%	29.3%
50,763	OTSEGO	26,458	20,304	6,115	39	14,189 R	76.7%	23.1%	76.9%	23.1%
20,307	PUTNAM	16,118	11,038	5,001	79	6,037 R	68.5%	31.0%	68.8%	31.2%
1,550,849	QUEENS	789,682	450,610	331,217	7,855	119,393 R	57.1%	41.9%	57.6%	42.4%
132,607	RENSSELAER	77,337	51,453	25,734	150	25,719 R	66.5%	33.3%	66.7%	33.3%
191,555	RICHMOND	84,606	55,991	28,280	335	27,711 R	66.2%	33.4%	66.4%	33.6%
89,276	ROCKLAND	42,973	27,657	15,084	232	12,573 R	64.4%	35.1%	64.7%	35.3%
98,897	ST. LAWRENCE	41,087	28,036	13,000	51	15,036 R	68.2%	31.6%	68.3%	31.7%
74,869	SARATOGA	41,186	29,712	11,413	61	18,299 R	72.1%	27.7%	72.2%	27.8%
142,497	SCHENECTADY	81,699	54,272	27,157	270	27,115 R	66.4%	33.2%	66.6%	33.4%
22,703	SCHOHARIE	12,509	8,972	3,509	28	5,463 R	71.7%	28.1%	71.9%	28.1%
14,182	SCHUYLER	7,409	5,604	1,784	21	3,820 R	75.6%	24.1%	75.9%	24.1%
29,253	SENECA	14,020	9,669	4,328	23	5,341 R	69.0%	30.9%	69.1%	30.9%
91,439	STEUBEN	43,342	32,123	11,154	65	20,969 R	74.1%	25.7%	74.2%	25.8%
276,129	SUFFOLK	155,050	115,570	39,120	360	76,450 R	74.5%	25.2%	74.7%	25.3%
40,731	SULLIVAN	23,626	14,926	8,421	279	6,505 R	63.2%	35.6%	63.9%	36.1%
30,166	TIOGA	15,095	11,799	3,259	37	8,540 R	78.2%	21.6%	78.4%	21.6%
59,122	TOMPKINS	25,019	18,673	6,285	61	12,388 R	74.6%	25.1%	74.8%	25.2%
92,621	ULSTER	52,085	36,141	15,733	211	20,408 R	69.4%	30.2%	69.7%	30.3%
39,205	WARREN	22,131	17,046	5,051	34	11,995 R	77.0%	22.8%	77.1%	22.9%
47,144	WASHINGTON	23,789	17,551	6,210	28	11,341 R	73.8%	26.1%	73.9%	26.1%
57,323	WAYNE	28,362	21,693	6,621	48	15,072 R	76.5%	23.3%	76.6%	23.4%
625,816	WESTCHESTER	352,170	237,105	113,358	1,707	123,747 R	67.3%	32.2%	67.7%	32.3%
32,822	WYOMING	16,206	12,154	4,038	14	8,116 R	75.0%	24.9%	75.1%	24.9%
17,615	YATES	9,670	7,831	1,820	19	6,011 R	81.0%	18.8%	81.1%	18.9%
14,830,192	TOTAL	7,128,239	3,952,813	3,104,601	70,825	848,212 R	55.5%	43.6%	56.0%	44.0%

NEW YORK

PRESIDENT 1948

1940 Census Population	County	Total Vote	Republican	Democratic	Other	Rep.-Dem. Plurality	Percentage Total Vote Rep.	Total Vote Dem.	Major Vote Rep.	Major Vote Dem.
221,315	ALBANY	140,730	59,965	75,419	5,346	15,454 D	42.6%	53.6%	44.3%	55.7%
39,681	ALLEGANY	17,639	12,689	4,711	239	7,978 R	71.9%	26.7%	72.9%	27.1%
1,394,711	BRONX	622,355	173,044	337,129	112,182	164,085 D	27.8%	54.2%	33.9%	66.1%
165,749	BROOME	70,986	43,110	25,654	2,222	17,456 R	60.7%	36.1%	62.7%	37.3%
72,652	CATTARAUGUS	30,393	18,246	11,289	858	6,957 R	60.0%	37.1%	61.8%	38.2%
65,508	CAYUGA	33,747	19,017	14,317	413	4,700 R	56.4%	42.4%	57.0%	43.0%
123,580	CHAUTAUQUA	52,144	29,969	20,683	1,492	9,286 R	57.5%	39.7%	59.2%	40.8%
73,718	CHEMUNG	36,919	22,754	13,352	813	9,402 R	61.6%	36.2%	63.0%	37.0%
36,454	CHENANGO	16,982	11,988	4,764	230	7,224 R	70.6%	28.1%	71.6%	28.4%
54,006	CLINTON	19,755	9,694	9,357	704	337 R	49.1%	47.4%	50.9%	49.1%
41,464	COLUMBIA	20,880	13,758	6,527	595	7,231 R	65.9%	31.3%	67.8%	32.2%
33,668	CORTLAND	15,283	10,433	4,614	236	5,819 R	68.3%	30.2%	69.3%	30.7%
40,989	DELAWARE	19,474	14,226	4,965	283	9,261 R	73.1%	25.5%	74.1%	25.9%
120,542	DUTCHESS	53,039	34,067	17,439	1,533	16,628 R	64.2%	32.9%	66.1%	33.9%
798,377	ERIE	383,372	175,118	197,618	10,636	22,500 D	45.7%	51.5%	47.0%	53.0%
34,178	ESSEX	14,717	10,287	4,088	342	6,199 R	69.9%	27.8%	71.6%	28.4%
44,286	FRANKLIN	16,302	8,993	6,799	510	2,194 R	55.2%	41.7%	56.9%	43.1%
48,597	FULTON	21,134	12,787	7,667	680	5,120 R	60.5%	36.3%	62.5%	37.5%
44,481	GENESEE	20,142	12,650	7,024	468	5,626 R	62.8%	34.9%	64.3%	35.7%
27,926	GREENE	15,883	10,566	4,955	362	5,611 R	66.5%	31.2%	68.1%	31.9%
4,188	HAMILTON	2,790	2,000	744	46	1,256 R	71.7%	26.7%	72.9%	27.1%
59,527	HERKIMER	28,338	14,688	12,577	1,073	2,111 R	51.8%	44.4%	53.9%	46.1%
84,003	JEFFERSON	33,351	19,661	13,176	514	6,485 R	59.0%	39.5%	59.9%	40.1%
2,698,285	KINGS	1,083,801	330,494	579,922	173,385	249,428 D	30.5%	53.5%	36.3%	63.7%
22,815	LEWIS	9,078	5,692	3,211	175	2,481 R	62.7%	35.4%	63.9%	36.1%
38,510	LIVINGSTON	18,062	11,310	6,409	343	4,901 R	62.6%	35.5%	63.8%	36.2%
39,598	MADISON	19,658	13,413	5,937	308	7,476 R	68.2%	30.2%	69.3%	30.7%
438,230	MONROE	227,790	109,608	110,641	7,541	1,033 D	48.1%	48.6%	49.8%	50.2%
59,142	MONTGOMERY	29,064	14,212	14,085	767	127 R	48.9%	48.5%	50.2%	49.8%
406,748	NASSAU	265,238	184,284	70,492	10,462	113,792 R	69.5%	26.6%	72.3%	27.7%
1,889,924	NEW YORK	738,237	241,752	380,310	116,175	138,558 D	32.7%	51.5%	38.9%	61.1%
160,110	NIAGARA	72,219	35,858	34,119	2,242	1,739 R	49.7%	47.2%	51.2%	48.8%
203,636	ONEIDA	97,613	46,755	48,332	2,526	1,577 D	47.9%	49.5%	49.2%	50.8%
295,108	ONONDAGA	156,648	84,370	66,295	5,983	18,075 R	53.9%	42.3%	56.0%	44.0%
55,307	ONTARIO	25,439	16,156	8,852	431	7,304 R	63.5%	34.8%	64.6%	35.4%
140,113	ORANGE	60,796	38,351	20,638	1,807	17,713 R	63.1%	33.9%	65.0%	35.0%
27,760	ORLEANS	13,834	9,566	4,009	259	5,557 R	69.1%	29.0%	70.5%	29.5%
71,275	OSWEGO	32,904	19,095	12,820	989	6,275 R	58.0%	39.0%	59.8%	40.2%
46,082	OTSEGO	23,197	15,437	7,174	586	8,263 R	66.5%	30.9%	68.3%	31.7%
16,555	PUTNAM	12,877	8,222	4,012	643	4,210 R	63.9%	31.2%	67.2%	32.8%
1,297,634	QUEENS	639,543	323,459	268,742	47,342	54,717 R	50.6%	42.0%	54.6%	45.4%
121,834	RENSSELAER	71,197	40,375	28,468	2,354	11,907 R	56.7%	40.0%	58.6%	41.4%
174,441	RICHMOND	73,134	39,539	30,442	3,153	9,097 R	54.1%	41.6%	56.5%	43.5%
74,261	ROCKLAND	35,681	20,661	13,066	1,954	7,595 R	57.9%	36.6%	61.3%	38.7%
91,098	ST. LAWRENCE	34,925	21,160	13,200	565	7,960 R	60.6%	37.8%	61.6%	38.4%
65,606	SARATOGA	33,666	20,706	11,457	1,503	9,249 R	61.5%	34.0%	64.4%	35.6%
122,494	SCHENECTADY	67,391	35,495	28,225	3,671	7,270 R	52.7%	41.9%	55.7%	44.3%
20,812	SCHOHARIE	11,019	6,751	4,032	236	2,719 R	61.3%	36.6%	62.6%	37.4%
12,979	SCHUYLER	6,431	4,452	1,868	111	2,584 R	69.2%	29.0%	70.4%	29.6%
25,732	SENECA	12,516	7,266	4,897	353	2,369 R	58.1%	39.1%	59.7%	40.3%
84,927	STEUBEN	36,736	22,938	12,895	903	10,043 R	62.4%	35.1%	64.0%	36.0%
197,355	SUFFOLK	108,265	75,519	29,104	3,642	46,415 R	69.8%	26.9%	72.2%	27.8%
37,901	SULLIVAN	21,152	11,253	7,654	2,245	3,599 R	53.2%	36.2%	59.5%	40.5%
27,072	TIOGA	12,362	8,673	3,385	304	5,288 R	70.2%	27.4%	71.9%	28.1%
42,340	TOMPKINS	20,444	13,719	5,721	1,004	7,998 R	67.1%	28.0%	70.6%	29.4%
87,017	ULSTER	45,012	28,941	14,441	1,630	14,500 R	64.3%	32.1%	66.7%	33.3%
36,035	WARREN	18,703	12,884	5,486	333	7,398 R	68.9%	29.3%	70.1%	29.9%
46,726	WASHINGTON	20,464	13,975	6,017	472	7,958 R	68.3%	29.4%	69.9%	30.1%
52,747	WAYNE	23,270	16,167	6,749	354	9,418 R	69.5%	29.0%	70.5%	29.5%
573,558	WESTCHESTER	289,765	177,077	95,681	17,007	81,396 R	61.1%	33.0%	64.9%	35.1%
31,394	WYOMING	14,564	9,871	4,508	185	5,363 R	67.8%	31.0%	68.6%	31.4%
16,381	YATES	8,159	5,997	2,040	122	3,957 R	73.5%	25.0%	74.6%	25.4%
13,479,142	TOTAL	6,177,337	2,841,163	2,780,204	555,970	60,959 R	46.0%	45.0%	50.5%	49.5%

NEW YORK

PRESIDENT 1944

1940 Census Population	County	Total Vote	Republican	Democratic	Other	Rep.-Dem. Plurality	Percentage Total Vote Rep.	Percentage Total Vote Dem.	Percentage Major Vote Rep.	Percentage Major Vote Dem.
221,315	ALBANY	131,960	60,543	71,128	289	10,585 D	45.9%	53.9%	46.0%	54.0%
39,681	ALLEGANY	18,279	13,454	4,786	39	8,668 R	73.6%	26.2%	73.8%	26.2%
1,394,711	BRONX	665,035	211,158	450,525	3,352	239,367 D	31.8%	67.7%	31.9%	68.1%
165,749	BROOME	75,206	44,013	31,056	137	12,957 R	58.5%	41.3%	58.6%	41.4%
72,652	CATTARAUGUS	31,795	19,907	11,787	101	8,120 R	62.6%	37.1%	62.8%	37.2%
65,508	CAYUGA	32,629	18,680	13,849	100	4,831 R	57.2%	42.4%	57.4%	42.6%
123,580	CHAUTAUQUA	55,174	32,824	22,086	264	10,738 R	59.5%	40.0%	59.8%	40.2%
73,718	CHEMUNG	37,357	22,198	15,064	95	7,134 R	59.4%	40.3%	59.6%	40.4%
36,454	CHENANGO	17,779	12,745	4,997	37	7,748 R	71.7%	28.1%	71.8%	28.2%
54,006	CLINTON	18,806	8,775	9,996	35	1,221 D	46.7%	53.2%	46.7%	53.3%
41,464	COLUMBIA	20,078	13,055	6,969	54	6,086 R	65.0%	34.7%	65.2%	34.8%
33,668	CORTLAND	15,441	10,450	4,967	24	5,483 R	67.7%	32.2%	67.8%	32.2%
40,989	DELAWARE	20,069	14,916	5,128	25	9,788 R	74.3%	25.6%	74.4%	25.6%
120,542	DUTCHESS	55,826	32,890	22,778	158	10,112 R	58.9%	40.8%	59.1%	40.9%
798,377	ERIE	383,235	185,975	195,905	1,355	9,930 D	48.5%	51.1%	48.7%	51.3%
34,178	ESSEX	14,798	10,128	4,637	33	5,491 R	68.4%	31.3%	68.6%	31.4%
44,286	FRANKLIN	17,324	9,225	8,060	39	1,165 R	53.2%	46.5%	53.4%	46.6%
48,597	FULTON	22,070	13,195	8,813	62	4,382 R	59.8%	39.9%	60.0%	40.0%
44,481	GENESEE	20,324	13,478	6,796	50	6,682 R	66.3%	33.4%	66.5%	33.5%
27,926	GREENE	15,064	9,807	5,231	26	4,576 R	65.1%	34.7%	65.2%	34.8%
4,188	HAMILTON	2,673	1,834	830	9	1,004 R	68.6%	31.1%	68.8%	31.2%
59,527	HERKIMER	28,085	15,656	12,381	48	3,275 R	55.7%	44.1%	55.8%	44.2%
84,003	JEFFERSON	36,329	21,834	14,449	46	7,385 R	60.1%	39.8%	60.2%	39.8%
2,698,285	KINGS	1,158,364	393,926	758,270	6,168	364,344 D	34.0%	65.5%	34.2%	65.8%
22,815	LEWIS	9,715	6,256	3,441	18	2,815 R	64.4%	35.4%	64.5%	35.5%
38,510	LIVINGSTON	17,775	11,383	6,351	41	5,032 R	64.0%	35.7%	64.2%	35.8%
39,598	MADISON	19,514	13,369	6,109	36	7,260 R	68.5%	31.3%	68.6%	31.4%
438,230	MONROE	232,273	111,725	119,672	876	7,947 D	48.1%	51.5%	48.3%	51.7%
59,142	MONTGOMERY	29,189	14,726	14,400	63	326 R	50.5%	49.3%	50.6%	49.4%
406,748	NASSAU	238,801	159,713	78,512	576	81,201 R	66.9%	32.9%	67.0%	33.0%
1,889,924	NEW YORK	772,761	258,650	509,263	4,848	250,613 D	33.5%	65.9%	33.7%	66.3%
160,110	NIAGARA	72,666	37,614	34,850	202	2,764 R	51.8%	48.0%	51.9%	48.1%
203,636	ONEIDA	97,344	48,749	48,371	224	378 R	50.1%	49.7%	50.2%	49.8%
295,108	ONONDAGA	154,638	80,507	73,562	569	6,945 R	52.1%	47.6%	52.3%	47.7%
55,307	ONTARIO	26,364	16,859	9,437	68	7,422 R	63.9%	35.8%	64.1%	35.9%
140,113	ORANGE	63,262	39,041	24,059	162	14,982 R	61.7%	38.0%	61.9%	38.1%
27,760	ORLEANS	14,026	9,998	4,006	22	5,992 R	71.3%	28.6%	71.4%	28.6%
71,275	OSWEGO	32,355	19,733	12,593	29	7,140 R	61.0%	38.9%	61.0%	39.0%
46,082	OTSEGO	23,313	15,427	7,849	37	7,578 R	66.2%	33.7%	66.3%	33.7%
16,555	PUTNAM	11,294	7,010	4,251	33	2,759 R	62.1%	37.6%	62.3%	37.7%
1,297,634	QUEENS	660,375	365,365	292,940	2,070	72,425 R	55.3%	44.4%	55.5%	44.5%
121,834	RENSSELAER	68,131	37,819	30,173	139	7,646 R	55.5%	44.3%	55.6%	44.4%
174,441	RICHMOND	73,915	42,188	31,502	225	10,686 R	57.1%	42.6%	57.3%	42.7%
74,261	ROCKLAND	32,998	19,471	13,437	90	6,034 R	59.0%	40.7%	59.2%	40.8%
91,098	ST. LAWRENCE	37,219	21,919	15,223	77	6,696 R	58.9%	40.9%	59.0%	41.0%
65,606	SARATOGA	34,083	20,197	13,788	98	6,409 R	59.3%	40.5%	59.4%	40.6%
122,494	SCHENECTADY	68,868	35,178	33,397	293	1,781 R	51.1%	48.5%	51.3%	48.7%
20,812	SCHOHARIE	10,801	6,546	4,219	36	2,327 R	60.6%	39.1%	60.8%	39.2%
12,979	SCHUYLER	6,279	4,506	1,767	6	2,739 R	71.8%	28.1%	71.8%	28.2%
25,732	SENECA	11,688	7,424	4,236	28	3,188 R	63.5%	36.2%	63.7%	36.3%
84,927	STEUBEN	39,072	25,538	13,461	73	12,077 R	65.4%	34.5%	65.5%	34.5%
197,355	SUFFOLK	97,133	65,650	31,231	252	34,419 R	67.6%	32.2%	67.8%	32.2%
37,901	SULLIVAN	20,167	11,258	8,836	73	2,422 R	55.8%	43.8%	56.0%	44.0%
27,072	TIOGA	12,790	8,934	3,831	25	5,103 R	69.9%	30.0%	70.0%	30.0%
42,340	TOMPKINS	20,053	12,805	7,174	74	5,631 R	63.9%	35.8%	64.1%	35.9%
87,017	ULSTER	43,763	26,703	16,943	117	9,760 R	61.0%	38.7%	61.2%	38.8%
36,035	WARREN	18,897	12,144	6,716	37	5,428 R	64.3%	35.5%	64.4%	35.6%
46,726	WASHINGTON	20,992	13,861	7,100	31	6,761 R	66.0%	33.8%	66.1%	33.9%
52,747	WAYNE	24,555	17,523	6,999	33	10,524 R	71.4%	28.5%	71.5%	28.5%
573,558	WESTCHESTER	282,980	174,635	107,591	754	67,044 R	61.7%	38.0%	61.9%	38.1%
31,394	WYOMING	14,689	10,219	4,455	15	5,764 R	69.6%	30.3%	69.6%	30.4%
16,381	YATES	8,352	6,338	2,005	9	4,333 R	75.9%	24.0%	76.0%	24.0%
13,479,142	TOTAL	6,316,790	2,987,647	3,304,238	24,905	316,591 D	47.3%	52.3%	47.5%	52.5%

NEW YORK

PRESIDENT 1940

1940 Census Population	County	Total Vote	Republican	Democratic	Other	Rep.-Dem. Plurality	Total Vote Rep.	Total Vote Dem.	Major Vote Rep.	Major Vote Dem.
221,315	ALBANY	136,167	58,912	77,052	203	18,140 D	43.3%	56.6%	43.3%	56.7%
39,681	ALLEGANY	20,767	15,611	5,077	79	10,534 R	75.2%	24.4%	75.5%	24.5%
1,394,711	BRONX	620,518	198,293	418,931	3,294	220,638 D	32.0%	67.5%	32.1%	67.9%
165,749	BROOME	76,284	44,013	32,092	179	11,921 R	57.7%	42.1%	57.8%	42.2%
72,652	CATTARAUGUS	35,055	22,987	11,924	144	11,063 R	65.6%	34.0%	65.8%	34.2%
65,508	CAYUGA	35,173	21,032	13,985	156	7,047 R	59.8%	39.8%	60.1%	39.9%
123,580	CHAUTAUQUA	57,316	35,536	21,524	256	14,012 R	62.0%	37.6%	62.3%	37.7%
73,718	CHEMUNG	37,497	22,156	15,203	138	6,953 R	59.1%	40.5%	59.3%	40.7%
36,454	CHENANGO	19,452	14,168	5,241	43	8,927 R	72.8%	26.9%	73.0%	27.0%
54,006	CLINTON	21,800	10,369	11,378	53	1,009 D	47.6%	52.2%	47.7%	52.3%
41,464	COLUMBIA	22,162	13,527	8,591	44	4,936 R	61.0%	38.8%	61.2%	38.8%
33,668	CORTLAND	17,411	12,233	5,147	31	7,086 R	70.3%	29.6%	70.4%	29.6%
40,989	DELAWARE	21,700	15,684	5,968	48	9,716 R	72.3%	27.5%	72.4%	27.6%
120,542	DUTCHESS	58,049	32,329	25,598	122	6,731 R	55.7%	44.1%	55.8%	44.2%
798,377	ERIE	374,435	183,664	189,779	992	6,115 D	49.1%	50.7%	49.2%	50.8%
34,178	ESSEX	17,451	11,868	5,545	38	6,323 R	68.0%	31.8%	68.2%	31.8%
44,286	FRANKLIN	20,958	11,446	9,479	33	1,967 R	54.6%	45.2%	54.7%	45.3%
48,597	FULTON	24,015	14,896	9,040	79	5,856 R	62.0%	37.6%	62.2%	37.8%
44,481	GENESEE	21,229	14,503	6,664	62	7,839 R	68.3%	31.4%	68.5%	31.5%
27,926	GREENE	16,616	10,153	6,425	38	3,728 R	61.1%	38.7%	61.2%	38.8%
4,188	HAMILTON	2,873	2,029	840	4	1,189 R	70.6%	29.2%	70.7%	29.3%
59,527	HERKIMER	30,657	17,590	13,013	54	4,577 R	57.4%	42.4%	57.5%	42.5%
84,003	JEFFERSON	40,262	25,584	14,581	97	11,003 R	63.5%	36.2%	63.7%	36.3%
2,698,285	KINGS	1,141,613	394,534	742,668	4,411	348,134 D	34.6%	65.1%	34.7%	65.3%
22,815	LEWIS	11,532	8,049	3,466	17	4,583 R	69.8%	30.1%	69.9%	30.1%
38,510	LIVINGSTON	19,084	12,629	6,397	58	6,232 R	66.2%	33.5%	66.4%	33.6%
39,598	MADISON	21,662	15,262	6,301	99	8,961 R	70.5%	29.1%	70.8%	29.2%
438,230	MONROE	236,064	114,383	120,613	1,068	6,230 D	48.5%	51.1%	48.7%	51.3%
59,142	MONTGOMERY	30,659	15,546	15,079	34	467 R	50.7%	49.2%	50.8%	49.2%
406,748	NASSAU	217,293	143,672	73,171	450	70,501 R	66.1%	33.7%	66.3%	33.7%
1,889,924	NEW YORK	774,507	292,480	478,153	3,874	185,673 D	37.8%	61.7%	38.0%	62.0%
160,110	NIAGARA	70,101	36,729	33,207	165	3,522 R	52.4%	47.4%	52.5%	47.5%
203,636	ONEIDA	101,742	52,362	49,109	271	3,253 R	51.5%	48.3%	51.6%	48.4%
295,108	ONONDAGA	159,022	91,056	67,481	485	23,575 R	57.3%	42.4%	57.4%	42.6%
55,307	ONTARIO	28,162	18,932	9,110	120	9,822 R	67.2%	32.3%	67.5%	32.5%
140,113	ORANGE	66,685	38,913	27,632	140	11,281 R	58.4%	41.4%	58.5%	41.5%
27,760	ORLEANS	15,519	10,958	4,525	36	6,433 R	70.6%	29.2%	70.8%	29.2%
71,275	OSWEGO	36,230	22,688	13,459	83	9,229 R	62.6%	37.1%	62.8%	37.2%
46,082	OTSEGO	24,647	16,771	7,798	78	8,973 R	68.0%	31.6%	68.3%	31.7%
16,555	PUTNAM	11,997	7,164	4,794	39	2,370 R	59.7%	40.0%	59.9%	40.1%
1,297,634	QUEENS	613,332	323,406	288,024	1,902	35,382 R	52.7%	47.0%	52.9%	47.1%
121,834	RENSSELAER	72,132	39,648	32,387	97	7,261 R	55.0%	44.9%	55.0%	45.0%
174,441	RICHMOND	77,448	38,911	38,307	230	604 R	50.2%	49.5%	50.4%	49.6%
74,261	ROCKLAND	35,064	20,040	14,897	127	5,143 R	57.2%	42.5%	57.4%	42.6%
91,098	ST. LAWRENCE	39,990	24,339	15,569	82	8,770 R	60.9%	38.9%	61.0%	39.0%
65,606	SARATOGA	36,433	21,298	15,037	98	6,261 R	58.5%	41.3%	58.6%	41.4%
122,494	SCHENECTADY	66,469	34,101	32,041	327	2,060 R	51.3%	48.2%	51.6%	48.4%
20,812	SCHOHARIE	11,414	7,316	4,073	25	3,243 R	64.1%	35.7%	64.2%	35.8%
12,979	SCHUYLER	7,171	4,936	2,211	24	2,725 R	68.8%	30.8%	69.1%	30.9%
25,732	SENECA	12,598	8,364	4,203	31	4,161 R	66.4%	33.4%	66.6%	33.4%
84,927	STEUBEN	42,365	27,587	14,651	127	12,936 R	65.1%	34.6%	65.3%	34.7%
197,355	SUFFOLK	97,835	63,712	33,853	270	29,859 R	65.1%	34.6%	65.3%	34.7%
37,901	SULLIVAN	21,738	11,877	9,785	76	2,092 R	54.6%	45.0%	54.8%	45.2%
27,072	TIOGA	13,758	9,618	4,081	59	5,537 R	69.9%	29.7%	70.2%	29.8%
42,340	TOMPKINS	21,552	14,325	7,118	109	7,207 R	66.5%	33.0%	66.8%	33.2%
87,017	ULSTER	47,696	27,186	20,403	107	6,783 R	57.0%	42.8%	57.1%	42.9%
36,035	WARREN	20,923	13,657	7,226	40	6,431 R	65.3%	34.5%	65.4%	34.6%
46,726	WASHINGTON	23,975	15,960	7,977	38	7,983 R	66.6%	33.3%	66.7%	33.3%
52,747	WAYNE	26,616	19,196	7,358	62	11,838 R	72.1%	27.6%	72.3%	27.7%
573,558	WESTCHESTER	293,691	182,883	110,114	694	72,769 R	62.3%	37.5%	62.4%	37.6%
31,394	WYOMING	15,755	11,323	4,393	39	6,930 R	71.9%	27.9%	72.0%	28.0%
16,381	YATES	9,275	7,084	2,170	21	4,914 R	76.4%	23.4%	76.6%	23.4%
13,479,142	TOTAL	6,301,596	3,027,478	3,251,918	22,200	224,440 D	48.0%	51.6%	48.2%	51.8%

NEW YORK

PRESIDENT 1936

							Percentage			
							Total Vote		Major Vote	
1930 Census Population	County	Total Vote	Republican	Democratic	Other	Rep.-Dem. Plurality	Rep.	Dem.	Rep.	Dem.
211,953	ALBANY	127,511	52,962	71,631	2,918	18,669 D	41.5%	56.2%	42.5%	57.5%
38,025	ALLEGANY	19,508	13,829	5,288	391	8,541 R	70.9%	27.1%	72.3%	27.7%
1,265,258	BRONX	528,818	93,151	419,625	16,042	326,474 D	17.6%	79.4%	18.2%	81.8%
147,022	BROOME	67,603	36,945	29,708	950	7,237 R	54.6%	43.9%	55.4%	44.6%
72,398	CATTARAUGUS	32,984	20,484	11,901	599	8,583 R	62.1%	36.1%	63.3%	36.7%
64,751	CAYUGA	33,200	20,203	12,158	839	8,045 R	60.9%	36.6%	62.4%	37.6%
126,457	CHAUTAUQUA	54,927	30,435	23,283	1,209	7,152 R	55.4%	42.4%	56.7%	43.3%
74,680	CHEMUNG	36,195	20,515	15,542	138	4,973 R	56.7%	42.9%	56.9%	43.1%
34,665	CHENANGO	18,995	13,772	5,143	80	8,629 R	72.5%	27.1%	72.8%	27.2%
46,687	CLINTON	21,538	10,521	10,898	119	377 D	48.8%	50.6%	49.1%	50.9%
41,617	COLUMBIA	21,673	13,034	8,375	264	4,659 R	60.1%	38.6%	60.9%	39.1%
31,709	CORTLAND	16,637	11,718	4,606	313	7,112 R	70.4%	27.7%	71.8%	28.2%
41,163	DELAWARE	21,364	15,164	6,142	58	9,022 R	71.0%	28.7%	71.2%	28.8%
105,462	DUTCHESS	54,345	28,868	24,467	1,010	4,401 R	53.1%	45.0%	54.1%	45.9%
762,408	ERIE	342,208	152,312	183,555	6,341	31,243 D	44.5%	53.6%	45.3%	54.7%
33,959	ESSEX	17,088	11,599	5,447	42	6,152 R	67.9%	31.9%	68.0%	32.0%
45,694	FRANKLIN	20,478	11,521	8,799	158	2,722 R	56.3%	43.0%	56.7%	43.3%
46,560	FULTON	23,737	14,253	8,977	507	5,276 R	60.0%	37.8%	61.4%	38.6%
44,468	GENESEE	20,069	13,292	6,177	600	7,115 R	66.2%	30.8%	68.3%	31.7%
25,808	GREENE	16,060	9,060	6,744	256	2,316 R	56.4%	42.0%	57.3%	42.7%
3,929	HAMILTON	2,629	1,695	934		761 R	64.5%	35.5%	64.5%	35.5%
64,006	HERKIMER	29,129	15,941	12,847	341	3,094 R	54.7%	44.1%	55.4%	44.6%
83,574	JEFFERSON	39,466	24,925	13,975	566	10,950 R	63.2%	35.4%	64.1%	35.9%
2,560,401	KINGS	974,301	212,852	738,306	23,143	525,454 D	21.8%	75.8%	22.4%	77.6%
23,447	LEWIS	11,426	8,048	3,263	115	4,785 R	70.4%	28.6%	71.2%	28.8%
37,560	LIVINGSTON	18,953	12,353	6,088	512	6,265 R	65.2%	32.1%	67.0%	33.0%
39,790	MADISON	20,590	14,353	5,867	370	8,486 R	69.7%	28.5%	71.0%	29.0%
423,881	MONROE	210,523	93,055	114,286	3,182	21,231 D	44.2%	54.3%	44.9%	55.1%
60,076	MONTGOMERY	29,139	14,127	14,698	314	571 D	48.5%	50.4%	49.0%	51.0%
303,053	NASSAU	172,779	94,968	74,232	3,579	20,736 R	55.0%	43.0%	56.1%	43.9%
1,867,312	NEW YORK	711,253	174,299	517,134	19,820	342,835 D	24.5%	72.7%	25.2%	74.8%
149,329	NIAGARA	61,415	30,144	29,207	2,064	937 R	49.1%	47.6%	50.8%	49.2%
198,763	ONEIDA	91,111	46,317	43,439	1,355	2,878 R	50.8%	47.7%	51.6%	48.4%
291,606	ONONDAGA	146,270	80,498	62,945	2,827	17,553 R	55.0%	43.0%	56.1%	43.9%
54,276	ONTARIO	27,215	17,812	8,787	616	9,025 R	65.4%	32.3%	67.0%	33.0%
130,383	ORANGE	63,276	34,428	27,528	1,320	6,900 R	54.4%	43.5%	55.6%	44.4%
28,795	ORLEANS	14,994	10,569	4,016	409	6,553 R	70.5%	26.8%	72.5%	27.5%
69,645	OSWEGO	34,376	22,803	11,068	505	11,735 R	66.3%	32.2%	67.3%	32.7%
46,710	OTSEGO	24,765	16,682	7,807	276	8,875 R	67.4%	31.5%	68.1%	31.9%
13,744	PUTNAM	10,633	5,761	4,682	190	1,079 R	54.2%	44.0%	55.2%	44.8%
1,079,129	QUEENS	493,009	162,797	320,053	10,159	157,256 D	33.0%	64.9%	33.7%	66.3%
119,781	RENSSELAER	68,621	34,772	31,754	2,095	3,018 R	50.7%	46.3%	52.3%	47.7%
158,346	RICHMOND	70,389	22,852	46,229	1,308	23,377 D	32.5%	65.7%	33.1%	66.9%
59,599	ROCKLAND	32,090	15,583	15,876	631	293 D	48.6%	49.5%	49.5%	50.5%
90,960	ST. LAWRENCE	39,556	26,031	12,763	762	13,268 R	65.8%	32.3%	67.1%	32.9%
63,314	SARATOGA	34,266	19,153	14,619	494	4,534 R	55.9%	42.7%	56.7%	43.3%
125,021	SCHENECTADY	59,407	26,914	31,027	1,466	4,113 D	45.3%	52.2%	46.5%	53.5%
19,667	SCHOHARIE	11,434	6,895	4,229	310	2,666 R	60.3%	37.0%	62.0%	38.0%
12,909	SCHUYLER	7,455	4,819	2,551	85	2,268 R	64.6%	34.2%	65.4%	34.6%
24,983	SENECA	12,454	7,919	4,295	240	3,624 R	63.6%	34.5%	64.8%	35.2%
82,671	STEUBEN	40,810	24,987	14,978	845	10,009 R	61.2%	36.7%	62.5%	37.5%
161,055	SUFFOLK	84,335	48,970	33,078	2,287	15,892 R	58.1%	39.2%	59.7%	40.3%
35,272	SULLIVAN	19,982	9,757	9,908	317	151 D	48.8%	49.6%	49.6%	50.4%
25,480	TIOGA	13,640	9,163	4,305	172	4,858 R	67.2%	31.6%	68.0%	32.0%
41,490	TOMPKINS	20,746	13,332	7,007	407	6,325 R	64.3%	33.8%	65.5%	34.5%
80,155	ULSTER	44,611	24,678	19,118	815	5,560 R	55.3%	42.9%	56.3%	43.7%
34,174	WARREN	19,871	12,873	6,807	191	6,066 R	64.8%	34.3%	65.4%	34.6%
46,482	WASHINGTON	23,317	15,186	7,713	418	7,473 R	65.1%	33.1%	66.3%	33.7%
49,995	WAYNE	25,534	17,901	7,099	534	10,802 R	70.1%	27.8%	71.6%	28.4%
520,947	WESTCHESTER	261,569	133,670	123,561	4,338	10,109 R	51.1%	47.2%	52.0%	48.0%
28,764	WYOMING	14,841	10,253	4,420	168	5,833 R	69.1%	29.8%	69.9%	30.1%
16,848	YATES	9,280	6,897	2,257	126	4,640 R	74.3%	24.3%	75.3%	24.7%
12,588,066	TOTAL	5,596,398	2,180,670	3,293,222	122,506	1,112,552 D	39.0%	58.8%	39.8%	60.2%

NEW YORK

PRESIDENT 1932

1930 Census Population	County	Total Vote	Republican	Democratic	Other	Rep.-Dem. Plurality	Percentage Total Vote Rep.	Percentage Total Vote Dem.	Percentage Major Vote Rep.	Percentage Major Vote Dem.
211,953	ALBANY	120,759	46,244	73,194	1,321	26,950 D	38.3%	60.6%	38.7%	61.3%
38,025	ALLEGANY	17,777	12,348	4,961	468	7,387 R	69.5%	27.9%	71.3%	28.7%
1,265,258	BRONX	399,919	76,587	281,330	42,002	204,743 D	19.2%	70.3%	21.4%	78.6%
147,022	BROOME	56,494	32,751	22,802	941	9,949 R	58.0%	40.4%	59.0%	41.0%
72,398	CATTARAUGUS	30,786	18,071	11,467	1,248	6,604 R	58.7%	37.2%	61.2%	38.8%
64,751	CAYUGA	31,043	17,280	12,989	774	4,291 R	55.7%	41.8%	57.1%	42.9%
126,457	CHAUTAUQUA	50,275	30,479	16,914	2,882	13,565 R	60.6%	33.6%	64.3%	35.7%
74,680	CHEMUNG	34,750	20,152	13,825	773	6,327 R	58.0%	39.8%	59.3%	40.7%
34,665	CHENANGO	17,719	11,566	5,953	200	5,613 R	65.3%	33.6%	66.0%	34.0%
46,687	CLINTON	19,365	8,263	11,027	75	2,764 D	42.7%	56.9%	42.8%	57.2%
41,617	COLUMBIA	20,931	11,667	9,083	181	2,584 R	55.7%	43.4%	56.2%	43.8%
31,709	CORTLAND	14,585	9,859	4,425	301	5,434 R	67.6%	30.3%	69.0%	31.0%
41,163	DELAWARE	19,980	13,050	6,723	207	6,327 R	65.3%	33.6%	66.0%	34.0%
105,462	DUTCHESS	46,871	25,757	20,374	740	5,383 R	55.0%	43.5%	55.8%	44.2%
762,408	ERIE	282,930	141,059	131,012	10,859	10,047 R	49.9%	46.3%	51.8%	48.2%
33,959	ESSEX	15,786	10,062	5,597	127	4,465 R	63.7%	35.5%	64.3%	35.7%
45,694	FRANKLIN	19,857	9,422	10,318	117	896 D	47.4%	52.0%	47.7%	52.3%
46,560	FULTON	20,988	14,984	5,678	326	9,306 R	71.4%	27.1%	72.5%	27.5%
44,468	GENESEE	18,335	11,881	6,152	302	5,729 R	64.8%	33.6%	65.9%	34.1%
25,808	GREENE	14,261	7,334	6,794	133	540 R	51.4%	47.6%	51.9%	48.1%
3,929	HAMILTON	2,728	1,603	1,107	18	496 R	58.8%	40.6%	59.2%	40.8%
64,006	HERKIMER	26,790	15,158	11,194	438	3,964 R	56.6%	41.8%	57.5%	42.5%
83,574	JEFFERSON	36,724	22,760	13,478	486	9,282 R	62.0%	36.7%	62.8%	37.2%
2,560,401	KINGS	769,008	192,536	514,172	62,300	321,636 D	25.0%	66.9%	27.2%	72.8%
23,447	LEWIS	10,424	6,258	4,086	80	2,172 R	60.0%	39.2%	60.5%	39.5%
37,560	LIVINGSTON	17,888	11,114	6,529	245	4,585 R	62.1%	36.5%	63.0%	37.0%
39,790	MADISON	19,272	11,931	6,896	445	5,035 R	61.9%	35.8%	63.4%	36.6%
423,881	MONROE	185,960	95,964	83,208	6,788	12,756 R	51.6%	44.7%	53.6%	46.4%
60,076	MONTGOMERY	26,076	14,104	11,700	272	2,404 R	54.1%	44.9%	54.7%	45.3%
303,053	NASSAU	144,100	78,544	61,752	3,804	16,792 R	54.5%	42.9%	56.0%	44.0%
1,867,312	NEW YORK	565,205	157,014	378,077	30,114	221,063 D	27.8%	66.9%	29.3%	70.7%
149,329	NIAGARA	52,891	30,852	20,765	1,274	10,087 R	58.3%	39.3%	59.8%	40.2%
198,763	ONEIDA	81,148	41,193	38,413	1,542	2,780 R	50.8%	47.3%	51.7%	48.3%
291,606	ONONDAGA	133,219	66,363	62,227	4,629	4,136 R	49.8%	46.7%	51.6%	48.4%
54,276	ONTARIO	25,320	15,624	9,273	423	6,351 R	61.7%	36.6%	62.8%	37.2%
130,383	ORANGE	54,423	30,687	22,971	765	7,716 R	56.4%	42.2%	57.2%	42.8%
28,795	ORLEANS	14,321	9,735	4,303	283	5,432 R	68.0%	30.0%	69.3%	30.7%
69,645	OSWEGO	32,201	18,322	13,314	565	5,008 R	56.9%	41.3%	57.9%	42.1%
46,710	OTSEGO	23,265	14,904	8,114	247	6,790 R	64.1%	34.9%	64.7%	35.3%
13,744	PUTNAM	8,512	4,633	3,730	149	903 R	54.4%	43.8%	55.4%	44.6%
1,079,129	QUEENS	398,141	136,641	244,740	16,760	108,099 D	34.3%	61.5%	35.8%	64.2%
119,781	RENSSELAER	64,217	30,606	32,783	828	2,177 D	47.7%	51.1%	48.3%	51.7%
158,346	RICHMOND	60,345	21,278	36,857	2,210	15,579 D	35.3%	61.1%	36.6%	63.4%
59,599	ROCKLAND	27,982	13,963	13,347	672	616 R	49.9%	47.7%	51.1%	48.9%
90,960	ST. LAWRENCE	35,680	22,650	12,687	343	9,963 R	63.5%	35.6%	64.1%	35.9%
63,314	SARATOGA	31,578	17,990	13,053	535	4,937 R	57.0%	41.3%	58.0%	42.0%
125,021	SCHENECTADY	53,371	28,187	22,230	2,954	5,957 R	52.8%	41.7%	55.9%	44.1%
19,667	SCHOHARIE	10,318	5,513	4,684	121	829 R	53.4%	45.4%	54.1%	45.9%
12,909	SCHUYLER	6,881	4,491	2,255	135	2,236 R	65.3%	32.8%	66.6%	33.4%
24,983	SENECA	11,486	6,502	4,764	220	1,738 R	56.6%	41.5%	57.7%	42.3%
82,671	STEUBEN	36,959	22,986	13,219	754	9,767 R	62.2%	35.8%	63.5%	36.5%
161,055	SUFFOLK	72,528	40,247	30,799	1,482	9,448 R	55.5%	42.5%	56.6%	43.4%
35,272	SULLIVAN	18,517	8,294	9,656	567	1,362 D	44.8%	52.1%	46.2%	53.8%
25,480	TIOGA	12,328	8,047	4,067	214	3,980 R	65.3%	33.0%	66.4%	33.6%
41,490	TOMPKINS	18,916	12,185	6,180	551	6,005 R	64.4%	32.7%	66.3%	33.7%
80,155	ULSTER	39,721	21,002	18,092	627	2,910 R	52.9%	45.5%	53.7%	46.3%
34,174	WARREN	18,392	11,585	6,661	146	4,924 R	63.0%	36.2%	63.5%	36.5%
46,482	WASHINGTON	22,184	14,478	7,512	194	6,966 R	65.3%	33.9%	65.8%	34.2%
49,995	WAYNE	22,675	15,031	7,122	522	7,909 R	66.3%	31.4%	67.9%	32.1%
520,947	WESTCHESTER	220,788	112,747	101,435	6,606	11,312 R	51.1%	45.9%	52.6%	47.4%
28,764	WYOMING	14,137	9,377	4,490	270	4,887 R	66.3%	31.8%	67.6%	32.4%
16,848	YATES	8,584	6,048	2,399	137	3,649 R	70.5%	27.9%	71.6%	28.4%
12,588,066	TOTAL	4,688,614	1,937,963	2,534,959	215,692	596,996 D	41.3%	54.1%	43.3%	56.7%

NEW YORK

PRESIDENT 1928

1920 Census Population	County	Total Vote	Republican	Democratic	Other	Rep.-Dem. Plurality	Percentage Total Vote Rep.	Total Vote Dem.	Major Vote Rep.	Major Vote Dem.
186,106	ALBANY	113,437	48,762	62,380	2,295	13,618 D	43.0%	55.0%	43.9%	56.1%
36,842	ALLEGANY	19,399	15,306	3,491	602	11,815 R	78.9%	18.0%	81.4%	18.6%
732,016	BRONX	343,947	98,636	232,766	12,545	134,130 D	28.7%	67.7%	29.8%	70.2%
113,610	BROOME	61,092	39,860	19,563	1,669	20,297 R	65.2%	32.0%	67.1%	32.9%
71,323	CATTARAUGUS	33,001	22,135	10,229	637	11,906 R	67.1%	31.0%	68.4%	31.6%
65,221	CAYUGA	32,525	20,202	11,787	536	8,415 R	62.1%	36.2%	63.2%	36.8%
115,348	CHAUTAUQUA	52,584	38,220	13,223	1,141	24,997 R	72.7%	25.1%	74.3%	25.7%
65,872	CHEMUNG	37,354	25,029	12,189	136	12,840 R	67.0%	32.6%	67.2%	32.8%
34,969	CHENANGO	18,073	13,955	3,986	132	9,969 R	77.2%	22.1%	77.8%	22.2%
43,898	CLINTON	18,771	7,824	10,888	59	3,064 D	41.7%	58.0%	41.8%	58.2%
38,930	COLUMBIA	20,612	14,000	6,403	209	7,597 R	67.9%	31.1%	68.6%	31.4%
29,625	CORTLAND	15,869	11,960	3,662	247	8,298 R	75.4%	23.1%	76.6%	23.4%
42,774	DELAWARE	20,645	16,225	4,362	58	11,863 R	78.6%	21.1%	78.8%	21.2%
91,747	DUTCHESS	46,801	28,687	16,748	1,366	11,939 R	61.3%	35.8%	63.1%	36.9%
634,688	ERIE	281,789	144,726	126,449	10,614	18,277 R	51.4%	44.9%	53.4%	46.6%
31,871	ESSEX	15,770	10,462	5,291	17	5,171 R	66.3%	33.6%	66.4%	33.6%
43,541	FRANKLIN	19,045	9,495	9,501	49	6 D	49.9%	49.9%	50.0%	50.0%
44,927	FULTON	21,139	15,043	5,728	368	9,315 R	71.2%	27.1%	72.4%	27.6%
37,976	GENESEE	19,195	13,251	5,181	763	8,070 R	69.0%	27.0%	71.9%	28.1%
25,796	GREENE	14,285	9,529	4,440	316	5,089 R	66.7%	31.1%	68.2%	31.8%
3,970	HAMILTON	2,351	1,399	952		447 R	59.5%	40.5%	59.5%	40.5%
64,962	HERKIMER	29,709	18,624	10,654	431	7,970 R	62.7%	35.9%	63.6%	36.4%
82,250	JEFFERSON	39,695	26,361	12,908	426	13,453 R	66.4%	32.5%	67.1%	32.9%
2,018,356	KINGS	679,837	245,622	404,393	29,822	158,771 D	36.1%	59.5%	37.8%	62.2%
23,704	LEWIS	11,344	7,175	4,161	8	3,014 R	63.2%	36.7%	63.3%	36.7%
36,830	LIVINGSTON	18,160	11,632	5,545	983	6,087 R	64.1%	30.5%	67.7%	32.3%
39,535	MADISON	19,851	14,333	5,217	301	9,116 R	72.2%	26.3%	73.3%	26.7%
352,034	MONROE	179,078	99,803	73,759	5,516	26,044 R	55.7%	41.2%	57.5%	42.5%
57,928	MONTGOMERY	25,309	15,257	9,845	207	5,412 R	60.3%	38.9%	60.8%	39.2%
126,120	NASSAU	113,140	71,015	40,079	2,046	30,936 R	62.8%	35.4%	63.9%	36.1%
2,284,103	NEW YORK	521,558	186,396	317,227	17,935	130,831 D	35.7%	60.8%	37.0%	63.0%
118,705	NIAGARA	52,453	33,229	16,881	2,343	16,348 R	63.4%	32.2%	66.3%	33.7%
182,833	ONEIDA	84,786	44,782	38,231	1,773	6,551 R	52.8%	45.1%	53.9%	46.1%
241,465	ONONDAGA	133,716	76,278	54,706	2,732	21,572 R	57.0%	40.9%	58.2%	41.8%
52,652	ONTARIO	27,225	17,769	8,491	965	9,278 R	65.3%	31.2%	67.7%	32.3%
119,844	ORANGE	58,240	37,334	19,047	1,859	18,287 R	64.1%	32.7%	66.2%	33.8%
28,619	ORLEANS	14,292	9,828	3,792	672	6,036 R	68.8%	26.5%	72.2%	27.8%
71,045	OSWEGO	33,930	21,849	11,639	442	10,210 R	64.4%	34.3%	65.2%	34.8%
46,200	OTSEGO	24,606	18,286	6,006	314	12,280 R	74.3%	24.4%	75.3%	24.7%
10,802	PUTNAM	6,981	4,534	2,278	169	2,256 R	64.9%	32.6%	66.6%	33.4%
469,042	QUEENS	345,556	158,505	184,640	2,411	26,135 D	45.9%	53.4%	46.2%	53.8%
113,129	RENSSELAER	66,191	32,370	33,094	727	724 D	48.9%	50.0%	49.4%	50.6%
116,531	RICHMOND	54,234	24,995	28,945	294	3,950 D	46.1%	53.4%	46.3%	53.7%
45,548	ROCKLAND	26,072	15,732	9,769	571	5,963 R	60.3%	37.5%	61.7%	38.3%
88,121	ST. LAWRENCE	38,960	25,804	12,567	589	13,237 R	66.2%	32.3%	67.2%	32.8%
60,029	SARATOGA	32,187	19,183	12,247	757	6,936 R	59.6%	38.0%	61.0%	39.0%
109,363	SCHENECTADY	52,009	29,428	21,277	1,304	8,151 R	56.6%	40.9%	58.0%	42.0%
21,303	SCHOHARIE	10,209	6,906	2,926	377	3,980 R	67.6%	28.7%	70.2%	29.8%
13,098	SCHUYLER	6,587	4,749	1,731	107	3,018 R	72.1%	26.3%	73.3%	26.7%
24,735	SENECA	11,938	7,911	3,873	154	4,038 R	66.3%	32.4%	67.1%	32.9%
80,627	STEUBEN	40,466	28,028	10,699	1,739	17,329 R	69.3%	26.4%	72.4%	27.6%
110,246	SUFFOLK	63,315	41,199	19,497	2,619	21,702 R	65.1%	30.8%	67.9%	32.1%
33,163	SULLIVAN	16,861	10,331	6,207	323	4,124 R	61.3%	36.8%	62.5%	37.5%
24,212	TIOGA	12,958	9,963	2,779	216	7,184 R	76.9%	21.4%	78.2%	21.8%
35,285	TOMPKINS	19,866	14,471	5,114	281	9,357 R	72.8%	25.7%	73.9%	26.1%
74,979	ULSTER	40,695	25,418	14,200	1,077	11,218 R	62.5%	34.9%	64.2%	35.8%
31,673	WARREN	18,519	11,697	6,793	29	4,904 R	63.2%	36.7%	63.3%	36.7%
44,888	WASHINGTON	23,163	15,499	7,221	443	8,278 R	66.9%	31.2%	68.2%	31.8%
48,827	WAYNE	24,155	18,187	5,338	630	12,849 R	75.3%	22.1%	77.3%	22.7%
344,436	WESTCHESTER	195,544	109,939	80,926	4,679	29,013 R	56.2%	41.4%	57.6%	42.4%
30,314	WYOMING	15,152	10,830	3,992	330	6,838 R	71.5%	26.3%	73.1%	26.9%
16,641	YATES	9,395	7,386	1,950	59	5,436 R	78.6%	20.8%	79.1%	20.9%
10,385,227	TOTAL	4,405,626	2,193,344	2,089,863	122,419	103,481 R	49.8%	47.4%	51.2%	48.8%

NEW YORK

PRESIDENT 1924

1920 Census Population	County	Total Vote	Republican	Democratic	Other	Rep.-Dem. Plurality	Percentage Total Vote Rep.	Total Vote Dem.	Major Vote Rep.	Major Vote Dem.
186,106	ALBANY	92,772	48,253	38,671	5,848	9,582 R	52.0%	41.7%	55.5%	44.5%
36,842	ALLEGANY	16,196	12,203	2,755	1,238	9,448 R	75.3%	17.0%	81.6%	18.4%
732,016	BRONX	216,657	79,583	72,840	64,234	6,743 R	36.7%	33.6%	52.2%	47.8%
113,610	BROOME	41,749	28,262	9,289	4,198	18,973 R	67.7%	22.2%	75.3%	24.7%
71,323	CATTARAUGUS	27,066	17,307	5,369	4,390	11,938 R	63.9%	19.8%	76.3%	23.7%
65,221	CAYUGA	27,100	17,252	7,369	2,479	9,883 R	63.7%	27.2%	70.1%	29.9%
115,348	CHAUTAUQUA	41,764	29,757	5,560	6,447	24,197 R	71.3%	13.3%	84.3%	15.7%
65,872	CHEMUNG	28,765	18,599	7,162	3,004	11,437 R	64.7%	24.9%	72.2%	27.8%
34,969	CHENANGO	15,596	11,323	3,392	881	7,931 R	72.6%	21.7%	76.9%	23.1%
43,898	CLINTON	13,698	7,918	5,138	642	2,780 R	57.8%	37.5%	60.6%	39.4%
38,930	COLUMBIA	16,914	10,774	5,466	674	5,308 R	63.7%	32.3%	66.3%	33.7%
29,625	CORTLAND	13,041	10,032	2,170	839	7,862 R	76.9%	16.6%	82.2%	17.8%
42,774	DELAWARE	17,919	13,020	4,158	741	8,862 R	72.7%	23.2%	75.8%	24.2%
91,747	DUTCHESS	34,303	22,173	8,864	3,266	13,309 R	64.6%	25.8%	71.4%	28.6%
634,688	ERIE	191,480	112,070	40,780	38,630	71,290 R	58.5%	21.3%	73.3%	26.7%
31,871	ESSEX	11,565	8,553	2,639	373	5,914 R	74.0%	22.8%	76.4%	23.6%
43,541	FRANKLIN	14,515	9,352	4,364	799	4,988 R	64.4%	30.1%	68.2%	31.8%
44,927	FULTON	16,358	11,858	3,143	1,357	8,715 R	72.5%	19.2%	79.0%	21.0%
37,976	GENESEE	15,542	11,101	3,384	1,057	7,717 R	71.4%	21.8%	76.6%	23.4%
25,796	GREENE	12,188	7,503	3,951	734	3,552 R	61.6%	32.4%	65.5%	34.5%
3,970	HAMILTON	1,736	1,063	631	42	432 R	61.2%	36.3%	62.8%	37.2%
64,962	HERKIMER	23,563	15,625	6,464	1,474	9,161 R	66.3%	27.4%	70.7%	29.3%
82,250	JEFFERSON	30,942	21,159	7,665	2,118	13,494 R	68.4%	24.8%	73.4%	26.6%
2,018,356	KINGS	498,687	236,877	158,907	102,903	77,970 R	47.5%	31.9%	59.9%	40.1%
23,704	LEWIS	9,057	6,066	2,801	190	3,265 R	67.0%	30.9%	68.4%	31.6%
36,830	LIVINGSTON	15,055	10,472	3,676	907	6,796 R	69.6%	24.4%	74.0%	26.0%
39,535	MADISON	16,321	11,589	3,430	1,302	8,159 R	71.0%	21.0%	77.2%	22.8%
352,034	MONROE	141,128	80,577	28,956	31,595	51,621 R	57.1%	20.5%	73.6%	26.4%
57,928	MONTGOMERY	20,362	12,869	5,939	1,554	6,930 R	63.2%	29.2%	68.4%	31.6%
126,120	NASSAU	65,031	45,825	14,322	4,884	31,503 R	70.5%	22.0%	76.2%	23.8%
2,284,103	NEW YORK	463,326	190,871	183,249	89,206	7,622 R	41.2%	39.6%	51.0%	49.0%
118,705	NIAGARA	38,062	25,874	7,993	4,195	17,881 R	68.0%	21.0%	76.4%	23.6%
182,833	ONEIDA	60,734	37,545	18,124	5,065	19,421 R	61.8%	29.8%	67.4%	32.6%
241,465	ONONDAGA	100,769	65,395	24,773	10,601	40,622 R	64.9%	24.6%	72.5%	27.5%
52,652	ONTARIO	22,523	15,013	5,933	1,577	9,080 R	66.7%	26.3%	71.7%	28.3%
119,844	ORANGE	43,083	29,184	9,765	4,134	19,419 R	67.7%	22.7%	74.9%	25.1%
28,619	ORLEANS	11,880	8,543	2,320	1,017	6,223 R	71.9%	19.5%	78.6%	21.4%
71,045	OSWEGO	28,542	18,576	7,864	2,102	10,712 R	65.1%	27.6%	70.3%	29.7%
46,200	OTSEGO	20,670	13,573	5,841	1,256	7,732 R	65.7%	28.3%	69.9%	30.1%
10,802	PUTNAM	5,605	3,796	1,472	337	2,324 R	67.7%	26.3%	72.1%	27.9%
469,042	QUEENS	188,169	100,793	58,402	28,974	42,391 R	53.6%	31.0%	63.3%	36.7%
113,129	RENSSELAER	54,673	30,549	19,783	4,341	10,766 R	55.9%	36.2%	60.7%	39.3%
116,531	RICHMOND	37,586	18,007	15,801	3,778	2,206 R	47.9%	42.0%	53.3%	46.7%
45,548	ROCKLAND	19,559	11,915	5,640	2,004	6,275 R	60.9%	28.8%	67.9%	32.1%
88,121	ST. LAWRENCE	31,584	22,583	7,103	1,898	15,480 R	71.5%	22.5%	76.1%	23.9%
60,029	SARATOGA	26,856	17,682	7,026	2,148	10,656 R	65.8%	26.2%	71.6%	28.4%
109,363	SCHENECTADY	39,699	24,514	9,167	6,018	15,347 R	61.7%	23.1%	72.8%	27.2%
21,303	SCHOHARIE	9,879	6,142	3,413	324	2,729 R	62.2%	34.5%	64.3%	35.7%
13,098	SCHUYLER	6,074	4,301	1,555	218	2,746 R	70.8%	25.6%	73.4%	26.6%
24,735	SENECA	9,974	6,598	2,727	649	3,871 R	66.2%	27.3%	70.8%	29.2%
80,627	STEUBEN	32,160	21,481	7,194	3,485	14,287 R	66.8%	22.4%	74.9%	25.1%
110,246	SUFFOLK	45,455	31,456	10,024	3,975	21,432 R	69.2%	22.1%	75.8%	24.2%
33,163	SULLIVAN	13,604	7,734	4,057	1,813	3,677 R	56.9%	29.8%	65.6%	34.4%
24,212	TIOGA	10,810	7,834	2,234	742	5,600 R	72.5%	20.7%	77.8%	22.2%
35,285	TOMPKINS	16,123	11,766	3,701	656	8,065 R	73.0%	23.0%	76.1%	23.9%
74,979	ULSTER	31,660	20,048	9,361	2,251	10,687 R	63.3%	29.6%	68.2%	31.8%
31,673	WARREN	14,168	9,627	3,663	878	5,964 R	67.9%	25.9%	72.4%	27.6%
44,888	WASHINGTON	19,264	13,774	4,321	1,169	9,453 R	71.5%	22.4%	76.1%	23.9%
48,827	WAYNE	19,485	14,358	3,991	1,136	10,367 R	73.7%	20.5%	78.2%	21.8%
344,436	WESTCHESTER	133,035	85,029	30,964	17,042	54,065 R	63.9%	23.3%	73.3%	26.7%
30,314	WYOMING	13,705	10,148	2,512	1,045	7,636 R	74.0%	18.3%	80.2%	19.8%
16,641	YATES	8,153	6,334	1,568	251	4,766 R	77.7%	19.2%	80.2%	19.8%
10,385,227	TOTAL	3,263,939	1,820,058	950,796	493,085	869,262 R	55.8%	29.1%	65.7%	34.3%

NEW YORK

PRESIDENT 1920

1920 Census Population	County	Total Vote	Republican	Democratic	Other	Rep.-Dem. Plurality	Percentage Total Vote Rep.	Percentage Total Vote Dem.	Percentage Major Vote Rep.	Percentage Major Vote Dem.
186,106	ALBANY	78,989	48,750	28,376	1,863	20,374 R	61.7%	35.9%	63.2%	36.8%
36,842	ALLEGANY	14,697	10,898	2,799	1,000	8,099 R	74.2%	19.0%	79.6%	20.4%
732,016	BRONX	187,329	106,050	45,741	35,538	60,309 R	56.6%	24.4%	69.9%	30.1%
113,610	BROOME	35,903	24,759	9,251	1,893	15,508 R	69.0%	25.8%	72.8%	27.2%
71,323	CATTARAUGUS	24,029	16,083	6,693	1,253	9,390 R	66.9%	27.9%	70.6%	29.4%
65,221	CAYUGA	22,510	15,234	6,343	933	8,891 R	67.7%	28.2%	70.6%	29.4%
115,348	CHAUTAUQUA	38,587	27,618	6,781	4,188	20,837 R	71.6%	17.6%	80.3%	19.7%
65,872	CHEMUNG	26,068	17,864	7,060	1,144	10,804 R	68.5%	27.1%	71.7%	28.3%
34,969	CHENANGO	14,224	10,116	3,735	373	6,381 R	71.1%	26.3%	73.0%	27.0%
43,898	CLINTON	13,385	9,062	4,110	213	4,952 R	67.7%	30.7%	68.8%	31.2%
38,930	COLUMBIA	14,823	9,284	5,203	336	4,081 R	62.6%	35.1%	64.1%	35.9%
29,625	CORTLAND	12,516	9,606	2,541	369	7,065 R	76.7%	20.3%	79.1%	20.9%
42,774	DELAWARE	16,701	11,719	4,528	454	7,191 R	70.2%	27.1%	72.1%	27.9%
91,747	DUTCHESS	32,246	21,152	9,938	1,156	11,214 R	65.6%	30.8%	68.0%	32.0%
634,688	ERIE	157,796	99,762	40,436	17,598	59,326 R	63.2%	25.6%	71.2%	28.8%
31,871	ESSEX	10,379	8,042	2,218	119	5,824 R	77.5%	21.4%	78.4%	21.6%
43,541	FRANKLIN	13,865	9,786	3,825	254	5,961 R	70.6%	27.6%	71.9%	28.1%
44,927	FULTON	15,539	10,946	3,192	1,401	7,754 R	70.4%	20.5%	77.4%	22.6%
37,976	GENESEE	12,923	9,628	2,570	725	7,058 R	74.5%	19.9%	78.9%	21.1%
25,796	GREENE	10,282	6,323	3,498	461	2,825 R	61.5%	34.0%	64.4%	35.6%
3,970	HAMILTON	1,406	881	516	9	365 R	62.7%	36.7%	63.1%	36.9%
64,962	HERKIMER	21,924	14,310	6,507	1,107	7,803 R	65.3%	29.7%	68.7%	31.3%
82,250	JEFFERSON	31,201	22,072	7,925	1,204	14,147 R	70.7%	25.4%	73.6%	26.4%
2,018,356	KINGS	462,248	292,692	119,612	49,944	173,080 R	63.3%	25.9%	71.0%	29.0%
23,704	LEWIS	8,692	5,906	2,673	113	3,233 R	67.9%	30.8%	68.8%	31.2%
36,830	LIVINGSTON	13,783	9,488	3,571	724	5,917 R	68.8%	25.9%	72.7%	27.3%
39,535	MADISON	15,348	11,094	3,797	457	7,297 R	72.3%	24.7%	74.5%	25.5%
352,034	MONROE	115,721	73,809	28,523	13,389	45,286 R	63.8%	24.6%	72.1%	27.9%
57,928	MONTGOMERY	19,425	12,835	5,911	679	6,924 R	66.1%	30.4%	68.5%	31.5%
126,120	NASSAU	43,331	33,099	8,595	1,637	24,504 R	76.4%	19.8%	79.4%	20.6%
2,284,103	NEW YORK	464,420	275,013	135,249	54,158	139,764 R	59.2%	29.1%	67.0%	33.0%
118,705	NIAGARA	31,032	21,193	7,416	2,423	13,777 R	68.3%	23.9%	74.1%	25.9%
182,833	ONEIDA	54,791	36,311	15,560	2,920	20,751 R	66.3%	28.4%	70.0%	30.0%
241,465	ONONDAGA	86,047	57,008	23,308	5,731	33,700 R	66.3%	27.1%	71.0%	29.0%
52,652	ONTARIO	20,184	13,361	5,678	1,145	7,683 R	66.2%	28.1%	70.2%	29.8%
119,844	ORANGE	37,135	24,558	10,567	2,010	13,991 R	66.1%	28.5%	69.9%	30.1%
28,619	ORLEANS	11,410	8,305	2,266	839	6,039 R	72.8%	19.9%	78.6%	21.4%
71,045	OSWEGO	26,979	17,905	8,045	1,029	9,860 R	66.4%	29.8%	69.0%	31.0%
46,200	OTSEGO	18,961	12,112	6,275	574	5,837 R	63.9%	33.1%	65.9%	34.1%
10,802	PUTNAM	4,911	3,447	1,405	59	2,042 R	70.2%	28.6%	71.0%	29.0%
469,042	QUEENS	137,324	94,360	35,296	7,668	59,064 R	68.7%	25.7%	72.8%	27.2%
113,129	RENSSELAER	51,371	28,810	20,224	2,337	8,586 R	56.1%	39.4%	58.8%	41.2%
116,531	RICHMOND	28,258	17,844	9,373	1,041	8,471 R	63.1%	33.2%	65.6%	34.4%
45,548	ROCKLAND	16,897	11,169	5,057	671	6,112 R	66.1%	29.9%	68.8%	31.2%
88,121	ST. LAWRENCE	32,606	24,651	7,213	742	17,438 R	75.6%	22.1%	77.4%	22.6%
60,029	SARATOGA	23,858	16,222	6,905	731	9,317 R	68.0%	28.9%	70.1%	29.9%
109,363	SCHENECTADY	33,582	19,208	8,741	5,633	10,467 R	57.2%	26.0%	68.7%	31.3%
21,303	SCHOHARIE	9,537	5,572	3,697	268	1,875 R	58.4%	38.8%	60.1%	39.9%
13,098	SCHUYLER	5,368	3,827	1,231	310	2,596 R	71.3%	22.9%	75.7%	24.3%
24,735	SENECA	9,696	6,260	3,023	413	3,237 R	64.6%	31.2%	67.4%	32.6%
80,627	STEUBEN	27,868	18,335	7,401	2,132	10,934 R	65.8%	26.6%	71.2%	28.8%
110,246	SUFFOLK	36,574	26,737	8,852	985	17,885 R	73.1%	24.2%	75.1%	24.9%
33,163	SULLIVAN	12,458	8,029	3,623	806	4,406 R	64.4%	29.1%	68.9%	31.1%
24,212	TIOGA	9,511	6,772	2,406	333	4,366 R	71.2%	25.3%	73.8%	26.2%
35,285	TOMPKINS	13,573	9,508	3,487	578	6,021 R	70.1%	25.7%	73.2%	26.8%
74,979	ULSTER	28,612	19,001	8,759	852	10,242 R	66.4%	30.6%	68.4%	31.6%
31,673	WARREN	12,555	9,009	3,227	319	5,782 R	71.8%	25.7%	73.6%	26.4%
44,888	WASHINGTON	18,093	13,647	4,124	322	9,523 R	75.4%	22.8%	76.8%	23.2%
48,827	WAYNE	18,205	13,333	4,289	583	9,044 R	73.2%	23.6%	75.7%	24.3%
344,436	WESTCHESTER	111,335	76,020	28,060	7,255	47,960 R	68.3%	25.2%	73.0%	27.0%
30,314	WYOMING	12,101	9,134	2,442	525	6,692 R	75.5%	20.2%	78.9%	21.1%
16,641	YATES	7,391	5,638	1,571	182	4,067 R	76.3%	21.3%	78.2%	21.8%
10,385,227	TOTAL	2,898,513	1,871,167	781,238	246,108	1,089,929 R	64.6%	27.0%	70.5%	29.5%

NEW YORK

ELECTION NOTES

1956 Other vote was 1,027 Andrews (States Rights); 150 Hass (Socialist Labor); 82 Hoopes (Socialist); 1,262 scattered write-in. The Democratic candidate was also the Liberal nominee and 292,487 of his votes were received as the Liberal candidate.

1952 Other vote was 64,211 Hallinan (Progressive); 2,664 Hoopes (Socialist); 2,212 Dobbs (Socialist Workers); 1,560 Hass (Socialist Labor); 178 scattered write-in. The Democratic candidate was also the Liberal nominee and 416,711 of his votes were received as the Liberal candidate.

1948 Other vote was 509,559 Wallace (Progressive); 40,879 Thomas (Socialist); 2,729 Teichert (Socialist Labor); 2,675 Dobbs (Socialist Workers); 128 scattered write-in. The statewide total in the other vote column includes the write-in votes which were not reported by county. The Democratic candidate was also the Liberal nominee and 222,562 of his votes were received as the Liberal candidate.

1944 Other vote was 14,352 Teichert (Socialist Labor); 10,553 Thomas (Socialist). The Democratic candidate was also the American Labor and Liberal nominee and 496,405 of his votes were received as the American Labor candidate and 329,235 of his votes were received as the Liberal candidate.

1940 Other vote was 18,950 Thomas (Socialist); 3,250 Babson (Prohibition). The Democratic candidate was also the American Labor nominee and 417,418 of his votes were received as the American Labor candidate.

1936 Other vote was 86,897 Thomas (Socialist); 35,609 Browder (Communist). The Democratic candidate was also the American Labor nominee and 274,924 of his votes were received as the American Labor candidate.

1932 Other vote was 177,397 Thomas (Socialist); 27,956 Foster (Communist); 10,339 Reynolds (Socialist Labor).

1928 Other vote was 107,332 Thomas (Socialist); 10,876 Foster (Communist); 4,211 Reynolds (Socialist Labor).

1924 Other vote was 474,913 LaFollette (268,518 Socialist and 206,395 Progressive); 9,928 Johns (Socialist Labor); 8,244 Foster (Communist). The LaFollette combined tickets ran second in Chautauqua and Monroe counties.

1920 Other vote was 203,201 Debs (Socialist); 19,653 Watkins (Prohibition); 18,413 Christensen (Farmer-Labor); 4,841 Cox (Socialist Labor).

NORTH CAROLINA

POPULAR VOTE FOR PRESIDENT 1920 TO 1956

Year	Total Vote	Republican Vote	Republican Candidate	Democratic Vote	Democratic Candidate	Other Vote	Plurality	Percentage Total Vote Rep.	Percentage Total Vote Dem.	Percentage Major Vote Rep.	Percentage Major Vote Dem.
1956	1,165,592	575,062	Eisenhower, Dwight D.	590,530	Stevenson, Adlai E.		15,468 D	49.3%	50.7%	49.3%	50.7%
1952	1,210,910	558,107	Eisenhower, Dwight D.	652,803	Stevenson, Adlai E.		94,696 D	46.1%	53.9%	46.1%	53.9%
1948	791,209	258,572	Dewey, Thomas E.	459,070	Truman, Harry S.	73,567	200,498 D	32.7%	58.0%	36.0%	64.0%
1944	790,554	263,155	Dewey, Thomas E.	527,399	Roosevelt, Franklin D.		264,244 D	33.3%	66.7%	33.3%	66.7%
1940	822,648	213,633	Willkie, Wendell	609,015	Roosevelt, Franklin D.		395,382 D	26.0%	74.0%	26.0%	74.0%
1936	839,475	223,294	Landon, Alfred M.	616,141	Roosevelt, Franklin D.	40	392,847 D	26.6%	73.4%	26.6%	73.4%
1932	711,498	208,344	Hoover, Herbert C.	497,566	Roosevelt, Franklin D.	5,588	289,222 D	29.3%	69.9%	29.5%	70.5%
1928	635,150	348,923	Hoover, Herbert C.	286,227	Smith, Alfred E.		62,696 R	54.9%	45.1%	54.9%	45.1%
1924	481,608	190,754	Coolidge, Calvin	284,190	Davis, John W.	6,664	93,436 D	39.6%	59.0%	40.2%	59.8%
1920	538,649	232,819	Harding, Warren G.	305,367	Cox, James M.	463	72,548 D	43.2%	56.7%	43.3%	56.7%

ELECTORAL COLLEGE VOTE 1920 TO 1956

Year	Total	Republican	Democratic	Other
1956	14	—	14	—
1952	14	—	14	—
1948	14	—	14	—
1944	14	—	14	—
1940	13	—	13	—
1936	13	—	13	—
1932	13	—	13	—
1928	12	12	—	—
1924	12	—	12	—
1920	12	—	12	—

NORTH CAROLINA

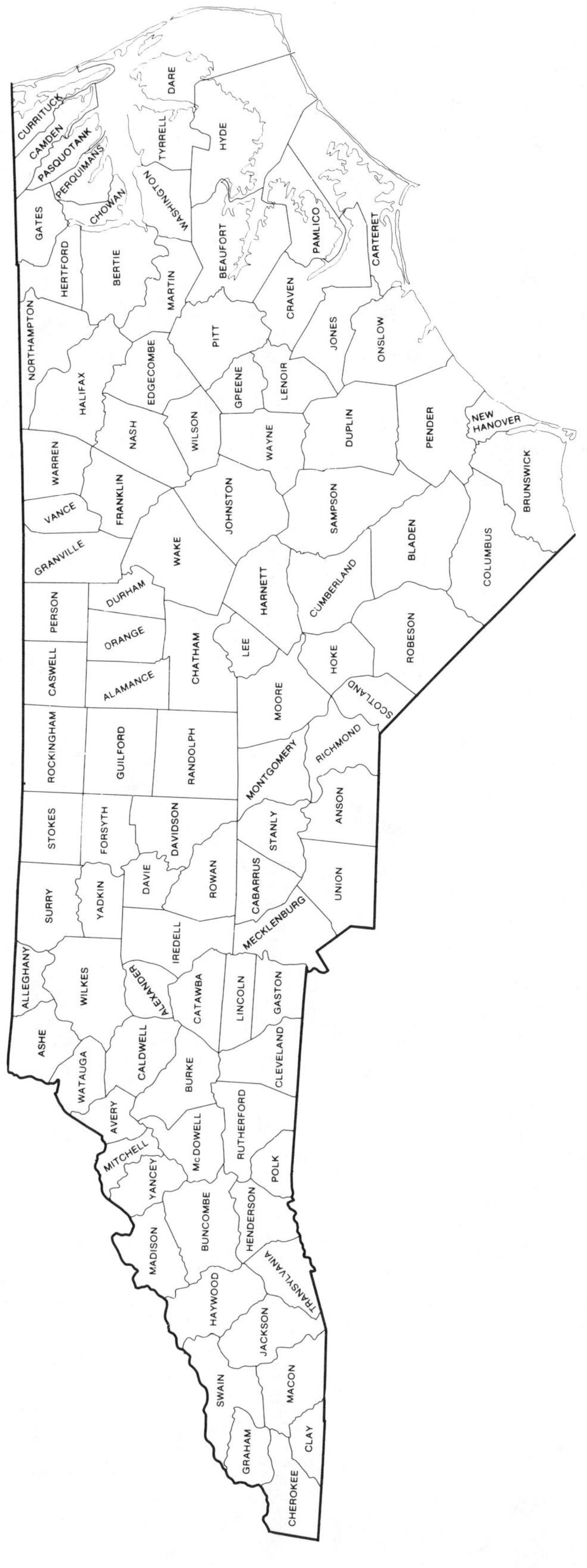

NORTH CAROLINA

PRESIDENT 1956

1950 Census Population	County	Total Vote	Republican	Democratic	Other	Rep.-Dem. Plurality	Percentage Total Vote Rep.	Total Vote Dem.	Major Vote Rep.	Major Vote Dem.
71,220	ALAMANCE	23,152	12,123	11,029		1,094 R	52.4%	47.6%	52.4%	47.6%
14,554	ALEXANDER	6,477	3,767	2,710		1,057 R	58.2%	41.8%	58.2%	41.8%
8,155	ALLEGHANY	3,369	1,699	1,670		29 R	50.4%	49.6%	50.4%	49.6%
26,781	ANSON	5,238	1,640	3,598		1,958 D	31.3%	68.7%	31.3%	68.7%
21,878	ASHE	8,570	4,588	3,982		606 R	53.5%	46.5%	53.5%	46.5%
13,352	AVERY	4,978	4,009	969		3,040 R	80.5%	19.5%	80.5%	19.5%
37,134	BEAUFORT	8,007	2,277	5,730		3,453 D	28.4%	71.6%	28.4%	71.6%
26,439	BERTIE	3,842	469	3,373		2,904 D	12.2%	87.8%	12.2%	87.8%
29,703	BLADEN	5,620	1,542	4,078		2,536 D	27.4%	72.6%	27.4%	72.6%
19,238	BRUNSWICK	6,596	3,299	3,297		2 R	50.0%	50.0%	50.0%	50.0%
124,403	BUNCOMBE	41,699	22,655	19,044		3,611 R	54.3%	45.7%	54.3%	45.7%
45,518	BURKE	19,822	11,823	7,999		3,824 R	59.6%	40.4%	59.6%	40.4%
63,783	CABARRUS	21,635	14,462	7,173		7,289 R	66.8%	33.2%	66.8%	33.2%
43,352	CALDWELL	17,694	10,833	6,861		3,972 R	61.2%	38.8%	61.2%	38.8%
5,223	CAMDEN	1,156	343	813		470 D	29.7%	70.3%	29.7%	70.3%
23,059	CARTERET	7,679	3,804	3,875		71 D	49.5%	50.5%	49.5%	50.5%
20,870	CASWELL	3,672	1,204	2,468		1,264 D	32.8%	67.2%	32.8%	67.2%
61,794	CATAWBA	30,670	19,246	11,424		7,822 R	62.8%	37.2%	62.8%	37.2%
25,392	CHATHAM	7,880	3,729	4,151		422 D	47.3%	52.7%	47.3%	52.7%
18,294	CHEROKEE	6,673	3,830	2,843		987 R	57.4%	42.6%	57.4%	42.6%
12,540	CHOWAN	2,041	556	1,485		929 D	27.2%	72.8%	27.2%	72.8%
6,006	CLAY	2,729	1,442	1,287		155 R	52.8%	47.2%	52.8%	47.2%
64,357	CLEVELAND	15,484	7,076	8,408		1,332 D	45.7%	54.3%	45.7%	54.3%
50,621	COLUMBUS	10,105	2,300	7,805		5,505 D	22.8%	77.2%	22.8%	77.2%
48,823	CRAVEN	9,273	2,956	6,317		3,361 D	31.9%	68.1%	31.9%	68.1%
96,006	CUMBERLAND	15,561	6,699	8,862		2,163 D	43.0%	57.0%	43.0%	57.0%
6,201	CURRITUCK	1,913	488	1,425		937 D	25.5%	74.5%	25.5%	74.5%
5,405	DARE	1,867	1,028	839		189 R	55.1%	44.9%	55.1%	44.9%
62,244	DAVIDSON	26,165	16,178	9,987		6,191 R	61.8%	38.2%	61.8%	38.2%
15,420	DAVIE	6,709	4,599	2,110		2,489 R	68.5%	31.5%	68.5%	31.5%
41,074	DUPLIN	9,041	2,110	6,931		4,821 D	23.3%	76.7%	23.3%	76.7%
101,639	DURHAM	27,061	13,226	13,835		609 D	48.9%	51.1%	48.9%	51.1%
51,634	EDGECOMBE	9,670	1,840	7,830		5,990 D	19.0%	81.0%	19.0%	81.0%
146,135	FORSYTH	45,187	29,368	15,819		13,549 R	65.0%	35.0%	65.0%	35.0%
31,341	FRANKLIN	6,090	792	5,298		4,506 D	13.0%	87.0%	13.0%	87.0%
110,836	GASTON	33,830	18,159	15,671		2,488 R	53.7%	46.3%	53.7%	46.3%
9,555	GATES	1,585	341	1,244		903 D	21.5%	78.5%	21.5%	78.5%
6,886	GRAHAM	3,248	1,762	1,486		276 R	54.2%	45.8%	54.2%	45.8%
31,793	GRANVILLE	5,476	1,463	4,013		2,550 D	26.7%	73.3%	26.7%	73.3%
18,024	GREENE	3,507	222	3,285		3,063 D	6.3%	93.7%	6.3%	93.7%
191,057	GUILFORD	54,699	32,751	21,948		10,803 R	59.9%	40.1%	59.9%	40.1%
58,377	HALIFAX	10,206	2,346	7,860		5,514 D	23.0%	77.0%	23.0%	77.0%
47,605	HARNETT	11,419	3,998	7,421		3,423 D	35.0%	65.0%	35.0%	65.0%
37,631	HAYWOOD	14,553	6,955	7,598		643 D	47.8%	52.2%	47.8%	52.2%
30,921	HENDERSON	13,246	9,243	4,003		5,240 R	69.8%	30.2%	69.8%	30.2%
21,453	HERTFORD	3,437	729	2,708		1,979 D	21.2%	78.8%	21.2%	78.8%
15,756	HOKE	2,457	513	1,944		1,431 D	20.9%	79.1%	20.9%	79.1%
6,479	HYDE	1,519	491	1,028		537 D	32.3%	67.7%	32.3%	67.7%
56,303	IREDELL	18,411	11,125	7,286		3,839 R	60.4%	39.6%	60.4%	39.6%
19,261	JACKSON	7,290	3,503	3,787		284 D	48.1%	51.9%	48.1%	51.9%
65,906	JOHNSTON	14,745	4,893	9,852		4,959 D	33.2%	66.8%	33.2%	66.8%
11,004	JONES	2,367	415	1,952		1,537 D	17.5%	82.5%	17.5%	82.5%
23,522	LEE	6,111	1,948	4,163		2,215 D	31.9%	68.1%	31.9%	68.1%
45,953	LENOIR	9,411	2,564	6,847		4,283 D	27.2%	72.8%	27.2%	72.8%
27,459	LINCOLN	12,475	6,637	5,838		799 R	53.2%	46.8%	53.2%	46.8%
25,720	MCDOWELL	9,860	5,468	4,392		1,076 R	55.5%	44.5%	55.5%	44.5%
16,174	MACON	6,433	3,408	3,025		383 R	53.0%	47.0%	53.0%	47.0%
20,522	MADISON	7,956	4,263	3,693		570 R	53.6%	46.4%	53.6%	46.4%
27,938	MARTIN	6,179	449	5,730		5,281 D	7.3%	92.7%	7.3%	92.7%
197,052	MECKLENBURG	71,696	44,469	27,227		17,242 R	62.0%	38.0%	62.0%	38.0%

NORTH CAROLINA

PRESIDENT 1956

1950 Census Population	County	Total Vote	Republican	Democratic	Other	Rep.-Dem. Plurality	Percentage Total Vote Rep.	Percentage Total Vote Dem.	Percentage Major Vote Rep.	Percentage Major Vote Dem.
15,143	MITCHELL	5,338	4,269	1,069		3,200 R	80.0%	20.0%	80.0%	20.0%
17,260	MONTGOMERY	6,447	3,359	3,088		271 R	52.1%	47.9%	52.1%	47.9%
33,129	MOORE	9,967	5,238	4,729		509 R	52.6%	47.4%	52.6%	47.4%
59,919	NASH	12,634	2,665	9,969		7,304 D	21.1%	78.9%	21.1%	78.9%
63,272	NEW HANOVER	19,717	9,470	10,247		777 D	48.0%	52.0%	48.0%	52.0%
28,432	NORTHAMPTON	4,989	747	4,242		3,495 D	15.0%	85.0%	15.0%	85.0%
42,047	ONSLOW	6,318	1,626	4,692		3,066 D	25.7%	74.3%	25.7%	74.3%
34,435	ORANGE	9,139	4,396	4,743		347 D	48.1%	51.9%	48.1%	51.9%
9,993	PAMLICO	2,330	954	1,376		422 D	40.9%	59.1%	40.9%	59.1%
24,347	PASQUOTANK	4,790	1,827	2,963		1,136 D	38.1%	61.9%	38.1%	61.9%
18,423	PENDER	3,205	1,009	2,196		1,187 D	31.5%	68.5%	31.5%	68.5%
9,602	PERQUIMANS	1,731	709	1,022		313 D	41.0%	59.0%	41.0%	59.0%
24,361	PERSON	5,173	1,740	3,433		1,693 D	33.6%	66.4%	33.6%	66.4%
63,789	PITT	14,388	2,515	11,873		9,358 D	17.5%	82.5%	17.5%	82.5%
11,627	POLK	5,350	2,823	2,527		296 R	52.8%	47.2%	52.8%	47.2%
50,804	RANDOLPH	21,578	13,174	8,404		4,770 R	61.1%	38.9%	61.1%	38.9%
39,597	RICHMOND	9,499	2,907	6,592		3,685 D	30.6%	69.4%	30.6%	69.4%
87,769	ROBESON	13,301	2,785	10,516		7,731 D	20.9%	79.1%	20.9%	79.1%
64,816	ROCKINGHAM	17,887	8,991	8,896		95 R	50.3%	49.7%	50.3%	49.7%
75,410	ROWAN	27,323	17,562	9,761		7,801 R	64.3%	35.7%	64.3%	35.7%
46,356	RUTHERFORD	15,408	8,200	7,208		992 R	53.2%	46.8%	53.2%	46.8%
49,780	SAMPSON	13,882	6,685	7,197		512 D	48.2%	51.8%	48.2%	51.8%
26,336	SCOTLAND	4,213	1,171	3,042		1,871 D	27.8%	72.2%	27.8%	72.2%
37,130	STANLY	17,360	10,667	6,693		3,974 R	61.4%	38.6%	61.4%	38.6%
21,520	STOKES	8,289	4,341	3,948		393 R	52.4%	47.6%	52.4%	47.6%
45,593	SURRY	16,021	9,001	7,020		1,981 R	56.2%	43.8%	56.2%	43.8%
9,921	SWAIN	3,820	2,026	1,794		232 R	53.0%	47.0%	53.0%	47.0%
15,194	TRANSYLVANIA	7,336	3,901	3,435		466 R	53.2%	46.8%	53.2%	46.8%
5,048	TYRRELL	1,035	420	615		195 D	40.6%	59.4%	40.6%	59.4%
42,034	UNION	9,745	3,362	6,383		3,021 D	34.5%	65.5%	34.5%	65.5%
32,101	VANCE	6,877	1,955	4,922		2,967 D	28.4%	71.6%	28.4%	71.6%
136,450	WAKE	37,621	15,194	22,427		7,233 D	40.4%	59.6%	40.4%	59.6%
23,539	WARREN	3,451	718	2,733		2,015 D	20.8%	79.2%	20.8%	79.2%
13,180	WASHINGTON	2,980	1,033	1,947		914 D	34.7%	65.3%	34.7%	65.3%
18,342	WATAUGA	7,859	4,636	3,223		1,413 R	59.0%	41.0%	59.0%	41.0%
64,267	WAYNE	10,976	4,220	6,756		2,536 D	38.4%	61.6%	38.4%	61.6%
45,243	WILKES	17,414	11,544	5,870		5,674 R	66.3%	33.7%	66.3%	33.7%
54,506	WILSON	11,158	2,830	8,328		5,498 D	25.4%	74.6%	25.4%	74.6%
22,133	YADKIN	7,830	5,469	2,361		3,108 R	69.8%	30.2%	69.8%	30.2%
16,306	YANCEY	5,772	2,808	2,964		156 D	48.6%	51.4%	48.6%	51.4%
4,061,929	TOTAL	1,165,592	575,062	590,530		15,468 D	49.3%	50.7%	49.3%	50.7%

NORTH CAROLINA

PRESIDENT 1952

1950 Census Population	County	Total Vote	Republican	Democratic	Other	Rep.-Dem. Plurality	Percentage Total Vote Rep.	Total Vote Dem.	Major Vote Rep.	Major Vote Dem.
71,220	ALAMANCE	24,790	11,388	13,402		2,014 D	45.9%	54.1%	45.9%	54.1%
14,554	ALEXANDER	6,262	3,597	2,665		932 R	57.4%	42.6%	57.4%	42.6%
8,155	ALLEGHANY	3,598	1,789	1,809		20 D	49.7%	50.3%	49.7%	50.3%
26,781	ANSON	5,986	1,843	4,143		2,300 D	30.8%	69.2%	30.8%	69.2%
21,878	ASHE	9,099	4,563	4,536		27 R	50.1%	49.9%	50.1%	49.9%
13,352	AVERY	4,689	3,725	964		2,761 R	79.4%	20.6%	79.4%	20.6%
37,134	BEAUFORT	7,833	2,404	5,429		3,025 D	30.7%	69.3%	30.7%	69.3%
26,439	BERTIE	3,941	384	3,557		3,173 D	9.7%	90.3%	9.7%	90.3%
29,703	BLADEN	5,216	1,710	3,506		1,796 D	32.8%	67.2%	32.8%	67.2%
19,238	BRUNSWICK	5,909	2,958	2,951		7 R	50.1%	49.9%	50.1%	49.9%
124,403	BUNCOMBE	46,869	24,444	22,425		2,019 R	52.2%	47.8%	52.2%	47.8%
45,518	BURKE	18,845	11,113	7,732		3,381 R	59.0%	41.0%	59.0%	41.0%
63,783	CABARRUS	24,193	15,053	9,140		5,913 R	62.2%	37.8%	62.2%	37.8%
43,352	CALDWELL	16,693	9,160	7,533		1,627 R	54.9%	45.1%	54.9%	45.1%
5,223	CAMDEN	1,336	340	996		656 D	25.4%	74.6%	25.4%	74.6%
23,059	CARTERET	7,247	2,967	4,280		1,313 D	40.9%	59.1%	40.9%	59.1%
20,870	CASWELL	3,570	973	2,597		1,624 D	27.3%	72.7%	27.3%	72.7%
61,794	CATAWBA	28,368	16,814	11,554		5,260 R	59.3%	40.7%	59.3%	40.7%
25,392	CHATHAM	7,909	3,606	4,303		697 D	45.6%	54.4%	45.6%	54.4%
18,294	CHEROKEE	6,591	3,228	3,363		135 D	49.0%	51.0%	49.0%	51.0%
12,540	CHOWAN	1,985	537	1,448		911 D	27.1%	72.9%	27.1%	72.9%
6,006	CLAY	2,882	1,443	1,439		4 R	50.1%	49.9%	50.1%	49.9%
64,357	CLEVELAND	17,315	7,606	9,709		2,103 D	43.9%	56.1%	43.9%	56.1%
50,621	COLUMBUS	9,942	3,001	6,941		3,940 D	30.2%	69.8%	30.2%	69.8%
48,823	CRAVEN	8,914	2,822	6,092		3,270 D	31.7%	68.3%	31.7%	68.3%
96,006	CUMBERLAND	16,313	7,474	8,839		1,365 D	45.8%	54.2%	45.8%	54.2%
6,201	CURRITUCK	1,885	414	1,471		1,057 D	22.0%	78.0%	22.0%	78.0%
5,405	DARE	1,726	767	959		192 D	44.4%	55.6%	44.4%	55.6%
62,244	DAVIDSON	25,230	14,299	10,931		3,368 R	56.7%	43.3%	56.7%	43.3%
15,420	DAVIE	6,416	4,010	2,406		1,604 R	62.5%	37.5%	62.5%	37.5%
41,074	DUPLIN	8,507	2,115	6,392		4,277 D	24.9%	75.1%	24.9%	75.1%
101,639	DURHAM	30,198	11,301	18,897		7,596 D	37.4%	62.6%	37.4%	62.6%
51,634	EDGECOMBE	10,431	1,927	8,504		6,577 D	18.5%	81.5%	18.5%	81.5%
146,135	FORSYTH	50,971	26,436	24,535		1,901 R	51.9%	48.1%	51.9%	48.1%
31,341	FRANKLIN	6,116	740	5,376		4,636 D	12.1%	87.9%	12.1%	87.9%
110,836	GASTON	36,938	19,157	17,781		1,376 R	51.9%	48.1%	51.9%	48.1%
9,555	GATES	1,611	364	1,247		883 D	22.6%	77.4%	22.6%	77.4%
6,886	GRAHAM	2,970	1,380	1,590		210 D	46.5%	53.5%	46.5%	53.5%
31,793	GRANVILLE	5,749	1,166	4,583		3,417 D	20.3%	79.7%	20.3%	79.7%
18,024	GREENE	3,162	186	2,976		2,790 D	5.9%	94.1%	5.9%	94.1%
191,057	GUILFORD	62,338	33,310	29,028		4,282 R	53.4%	46.6%	53.4%	46.6%
58,377	HALIFAX	11,017	2,210	8,807		6,597 D	20.1%	79.9%	20.1%	79.9%
47,605	HARNETT	11,901	4,306	7,595		3,289 D	36.2%	63.8%	36.2%	63.8%
37,631	HAYWOOD	14,885	6,124	8,761		2,637 D	41.1%	58.9%	41.1%	58.9%
30,921	HENDERSON	12,571	8,768	3,803		4,965 R	69.7%	30.3%	69.7%	30.3%
21,453	HERTFORD	3,438	579	2,859		2,280 D	16.8%	83.2%	16.8%	83.2%
15,756	HOKE	2,377	616	1,761		1,145 D	25.9%	74.1%	25.9%	74.1%
6,479	HYDE	1,325	406	919		513 D	30.6%	69.4%	30.6%	69.4%
56,303	IREDELL	20,384	11,804	8,580		3,224 R	57.9%	42.1%	57.9%	42.1%
19,261	JACKSON	7,976	3,680	4,296		616 D	46.1%	53.9%	46.1%	53.9%
65,906	JOHNSTON	15,426	5,429	9,997		4,568 D	35.2%	64.8%	35.2%	64.8%
11,004	JONES	2,004	331	1,673		1,342 D	16.5%	83.5%	16.5%	83.5%
23,522	LEE	6,793	2,105	4,688		2,583 D	31.0%	69.0%	31.0%	69.0%
45,953	LENOIR	8,946	2,223	6,723		4,500 D	24.8%	75.2%	24.8%	75.2%
27,459	LINCOLN	11,617	6,228	5,389		839 R	53.6%	46.4%	53.6%	46.4%
25,720	MCDOWELL	9,465	4,710	4,755		45 D	49.8%	50.2%	49.8%	50.2%
16,174	MACON	6,723	3,327	3,396		69 D	49.5%	50.5%	49.5%	50.5%
20,522	MADISON	8,417	4,751	3,666		1,085 R	56.4%	43.6%	56.4%	43.6%
27,938	MARTIN	5,908	415	5,493		5,078 D	7.0%	93.0%	7.0%	93.0%
197,052	MECKLENBURG	77,378	44,334	33,044		11,290 R	57.3%	42.7%	57.3%	42.7%

NORTH CAROLINA

PRESIDENT 1952

1950 Census Population	County	Total Vote	Republican	Democratic	Other	Rep.-Dem. Plurality	Percentage Total Vote Rep.	Total Vote Dem.	Major Vote Rep.	Major Vote Dem.
15,143	MITCHELL	5,245	4,009	1,236		2,773 R	76.4%	23.6%	76.4%	23.6%
17,260	MONTGOMERY	6,357	3,181	3,176		5 R	50.0%	50.0%	50.0%	50.0%
33,129	MOORE	10,508	5,442	5,066		376 R	51.8%	48.2%	51.8%	48.2%
59,919	NASH	13,060	2,636	10,424		7,788 D	20.2%	79.8%	20.2%	79.8%
63,272	NEW HANOVER	19,660	9,330	10,330		1,000 D	47.5%	52.5%	47.5%	52.5%
28,432	NORTHAMPTON	4,917	583	4,334		3,751 D	11.9%	88.1%	11.9%	88.1%
42,047	ONSLOW	5,536	1,261	4,275		3,014 D	22.8%	77.2%	22.8%	77.2%
34,435	ORANGE	8,969	3,813	5,156		1,343 D	42.5%	57.5%	42.5%	57.5%
9,993	PAMLICO	2,331	903	1,428		525 D	38.7%	61.3%	38.7%	61.3%
24,347	PASQUOTANK	5,680	2,101	3,579		1,478 D	37.0%	63.0%	37.0%	63.0%
18,423	PENDER	3,181	1,152	2,029		877 D	36.2%	63.8%	36.2%	63.8%
9,602	PERQUIMANS	1,889	644	1,245		601 D	34.1%	65.9%	34.1%	65.9%
24,361	PERSON	5,640	1,374	4,266		2,892 D	24.4%	75.6%	24.4%	75.6%
63,789	PITT	13,474	2,203	11,271		9,068 D	16.4%	83.6%	16.4%	83.6%
11,627	POLK	5,302	2,561	2,741		180 D	48.3%	51.7%	48.3%	51.7%
50,804	RANDOLPH	21,404	12,429	8,975		3,454 R	58.1%	41.9%	58.1%	41.9%
39,597	RICHMOND	10,701	3,361	7,340		3,979 D	31.4%	68.6%	31.4%	68.6%
87,769	ROBESON	13,438	4,127	9,311		5,184 D	30.7%	69.3%	30.7%	69.3%
64,816	ROCKINGHAM	19,308	6,885	12,423		5,538 D	35.7%	64.3%	35.7%	64.3%
75,410	ROWAN	28,831	17,535	11,296		6,239 R	60.8%	39.2%	60.8%	39.2%
46,356	RUTHERFORD	16,142	8,387	7,755		632 R	52.0%	48.0%	52.0%	48.0%
49,780	SAMPSON	13,405	6,449	6,956		507 D	48.1%	51.9%	48.1%	51.9%
26,336	SCOTLAND	4,502	1,590	2,912		1,322 D	35.3%	64.7%	35.3%	64.7%
37,130	STANLY	17,295	10,093	7,202		2,891 R	58.4%	41.6%	58.4%	41.6%
21,520	STOKES	8,296	3,792	4,504		712 D	45.7%	54.3%	45.7%	54.3%
45,593	SURRY	15,797	7,591	8,206		615 D	48.1%	51.9%	48.1%	51.9%
9,921	SWAIN	3,629	1,680	1,949		269 D	46.3%	53.7%	46.3%	53.7%
15,194	TRANSYLVANIA	7,688	4,047	3,641		406 R	52.6%	47.4%	52.6%	47.4%
5,048	TYRRELL	1,301	385	916		531 D	29.6%	70.4%	29.6%	70.4%
42,034	UNION	11,206	3,790	7,416		3,626 D	33.8%	66.2%	33.8%	66.2%
32,101	VANCE	7,418	1,721	5,697		3,976 D	23.2%	76.8%	23.2%	76.8%
136,450	WAKE	38,450	15,057	23,393		8,336 D	39.2%	60.8%	39.2%	60.8%
23,539	WARREN	3,624	664	2,960		2,296 D	18.3%	81.7%	18.3%	81.7%
13,180	WASHINGTON	2,748	774	1,974		1,200 D	28.2%	71.8%	28.2%	71.8%
18,342	WATAUGA	8,127	4,527	3,600		927 R	55.7%	44.3%	55.7%	44.3%
64,267	WAYNE	11,943	4,662	7,281		2,619 D	39.0%	61.0%	39.0%	61.0%
45,243	WILKES	18,589	11,446	7,143		4,303 R	61.6%	38.4%	61.6%	38.4%
54,506	WILSON	11,253	2,569	8,684		6,115 D	22.8%	77.2%	22.8%	77.2%
22,133	YADKIN	8,326	5,540	2,786		2,754 R	66.5%	33.5%	66.5%	33.5%
16,306	YANCEY	6,646	2,953	3,693		740 D	44.4%	55.6%	44.4%	55.6%
4,061,929	TOTAL	1,210,910	558,107	652,803		94,696 D	46.1%	53.9%	46.1%	53.9%

NORTH CAROLINA

PRESIDENT 1948

1940 Census Population	County	Total Vote	Republican	Democratic	Other	Rep.-Dem. Plurality	Percentage Total Vote Rep.	Total Vote Dem.	Major Vote Rep.	Major Vote Dem.
57,427	ALAMANCE	15,380	5,124	8,287	1,969	3,163 D	33.3%	53.9%	38.2%	61.8%
13,454	ALEXANDER	4,823	2,314	2,057	452	257 R	48.0%	42.6%	52.9%	47.1%
8,341	ALLEGHANY	3,241	1,374	1,667	200	293 D	42.4%	51.4%	45.2%	54.8%
28,443	ANSON	3,711	447	2,692	572	2,245 D	12.0%	72.5%	14.2%	85.8%
22,664	ASHE	9,127	4,266	4,633	228	367 D	46.7%	50.8%	47.9%	52.1%
13,561	AVERY	4,008	2,995	933	80	2,062 R	74.7%	23.3%	76.2%	23.8%
36,431	BEAUFORT	6,030	1,055	4,675	300	3,620 D	17.5%	77.5%	18.4%	81.6%
26,201	BERTIE	3,170	85	3,034	51	2,949 D	2.7%	95.7%	2.7%	97.3%
27,156	BLADEN	3,914	500	2,831	583	2,331 D	12.8%	72.3%	15.0%	85.0%
17,125	BRUNSWICK	4,683	1,896	2,052	735	156 D	40.5%	43.8%	48.0%	52.0%
108,755	BUNCOMBE	30,851	11,460	17,072	2,319	5,612 D	37.1%	55.3%	40.2%	59.8%
38,615	BURKE	13,488	6,374	6,226	888	148 R	47.3%	46.2%	50.6%	49.4%
59,393	CABARRUS	12,826	4,294	5,059	3,473	765 D	33.5%	39.4%	45.9%	54.1%
35,795	CALDWELL	10,785	4,987	5,033	765	46 D	46.2%	46.7%	49.8%	50.2%
5,440	CAMDEN	779	127	576	76	449 D	16.3%	73.9%	18.1%	81.9%
18,284	CARTERET	5,160	1,520	3,491	149	1,971 D	29.5%	67.7%	30.3%	69.7%
20,032	CASWELL	2,399	351	1,651	397	1,300 D	14.6%	68.8%	17.5%	82.5%
51,653	CATAWBA	19,937	9,471	8,844	1,622	627 R	47.5%	44.4%	51.7%	48.3%
24,726	CHATHAM	5,795	2,008	3,396	391	1,388 D	34.7%	58.6%	37.2%	62.8%
18,813	CHEROKEE	5,572	2,615	2,771	186	156 D	46.9%	49.7%	48.6%	51.4%
11,572	CHOWAN	1,274	124	1,070	80	946 D	9.7%	84.0%	10.4%	89.6%
6,405	CLAY	2,575	1,213	1,307	55	94 D	47.1%	50.8%	48.1%	51.9%
58,055	CLEVELAND	9,261	1,905	6,039	1,317	4,134 D	20.6%	65.2%	24.0%	76.0%
45,663	COLUMBUS	7,369	1,105	5,511	753	4,406 D	15.0%	74.8%	16.7%	83.3%
31,298	CRAVEN	6,278	745	5,039	494	4,294 D	11.9%	80.3%	12.9%	87.1%
59,320	CUMBERLAND	9,062	1,741	4,996	2,325	3,255 D	19.2%	55.1%	25.8%	74.2%
6,709	CURRITUCK	1,368	130	1,144	94	1,014 D	9.5%	83.6%	10.2%	89.8%
6,041	DARE	1,214	373	802	39	429 D	30.7%	66.1%	31.7%	68.3%
53,377	DAVIDSON	17,314	8,539	7,991	784	548 R	49.3%	46.2%	51.7%	48.3%
14,909	DAVIE	4,959	2,679	1,917	363	762 R	54.0%	38.7%	58.3%	41.7%
39,739	DUPLIN	7,220	1,024	5,866	330	4,842 D	14.2%	81.2%	14.9%	85.1%
80,244	DURHAM	17,613	4,531	11,530	1,552	6,999 D	25.7%	65.5%	28.2%	71.8%
49,162	EDGECOMBE	7,142	478	6,410	254	5,932 D	6.7%	89.8%	6.9%	93.1%
126,475	FORSYTH	24,725	10,147	12,201	2,377	2,054 D	41.0%	49.3%	45.4%	54.6%
30,382	FRANKLIN	4,957	234	4,538	185	4,304 D	4.7%	91.5%	4.9%	95.1%
87,531	GASTON	18,968	6,180	8,966	3,822	2,786 D	32.6%	47.3%	40.8%	59.2%
10,060	GATES	1,080	89	939	52	850 D	8.2%	86.9%	8.7%	91.3%
6,418	GRAHAM	2,715	1,115	1,527	73	412 D	41.1%	56.2%	42.2%	57.8%
29,344	GRANVILLE	4,121	334	3,513	274	3,179 D	8.1%	85.2%	8.7%	91.3%
18,548	GREENE	2,786	65	2,687	34	2,622 D	2.3%	96.4%	2.4%	97.6%
153,916	GUILFORD	35,349	14,167	17,224	3,958	3,057 D	40.1%	48.7%	45.1%	54.9%
56,512	HALIFAX	7,109	505	6,172	432	5,667 D	7.1%	86.8%	7.6%	92.4%
44,239	HARNETT	8,916	1,985	6,608	323	4,623 D	22.3%	74.1%	23.1%	76.9%
34,804	HAYWOOD	10,266	2,684	7,373	209	4,689 D	26.1%	71.8%	26.7%	73.3%
26,049	HENDERSON	9,632	4,971	3,311	1,350	1,660 R	51.6%	34.4%	60.0%	40.0%
19,352	HERTFORD	2,438	196	2,165	77	1,969 D	8.0%	88.8%	8.3%	91.7%
14,937	HOKE	1,659	142	1,339	178	1,197 D	8.6%	80.7%	9.6%	90.4%
7,860	HYDE	1,052	214	800	38	586 D	20.3%	76.0%	21.1%	78.9%
50,424	IREDELL	12,136	4,441	5,761	1,934	1,320 D	36.6%	47.5%	43.5%	56.5%
19,366	JACKSON	6,725	2,520	4,005	200	1,485 D	37.5%	59.6%	38.6%	61.4%
63,798	JOHNSTON	12,997	3,211	9,188	598	5,977 D	24.7%	70.7%	25.9%	74.1%
10,926	JONES	1,406	113	1,238	55	1,125 D	8.0%	88.1%	8.4%	91.6%
18,743	LEE	4,348	871	3,234	243	2,363 D	20.0%	74.4%	21.2%	78.8%
41,211	LENOIR	6,150	515	5,445	190	4,930 D	8.4%	88.5%	8.6%	91.4%
24,187	LINCOLN	8,358	3,635	3,570	1,153	65 R	43.5%	42.7%	50.5%	49.5%
22,996	MCDOWELL	7,152	2,709	3,805	638	1,096 D	37.9%	53.2%	41.6%	58.4%
15,880	MACON	5,309	2,388	2,785	136	397 D	45.0%	52.5%	46.2%	53.8%
22,522	MADISON	5,995	3,341	2,558	96	783 R	55.7%	42.7%	56.6%	43.4%
26,111	MARTIN	4,853	163	4,636	54	4,473 D	3.4%	95.5%	3.4%	96.6%
151,826	MECKLENBURG	33,185	11,518	14,353	7,314	2,835 D	34.7%	43.3%	44.5%	55.5%

NORTH CAROLINA

PRESIDENT 1948

1940 Census Population	County	Total Vote	Republican	Democratic	Other	Rep.-Dem. Plurality	Percentage Total Vote Rep.	Percentage Total Vote Dem.	Percentage Major Vote Rep.	Percentage Major Vote Dem.
15,980	MITCHELL	3,809	2,908	818	83	2,090 R	76.3%	21.5%	78.0%	22.0%
16,280	MONTGOMERY	4,558	1,975	2,165	418	190 D	43.3%	47.5%	47.7%	52.3%
30,969	MOORE	6,750	2,719	3,341	690	622 D	40.3%	49.5%	44.9%	55.1%
55,608	NASH	8,576	684	7,590	302	6,906 D	8.0%	88.5%	8.3%	91.7%
47,935	NEW HANOVER	11,193	3,162	5,364	2,667	2,202 D	28.2%	47.9%	37.1%	62.9%
28,299	NORTHAMPTON	3,896	179	3,591	126	3,412 D	4.6%	92.2%	4.7%	95.3%
17,939	ONSLOW	3,799	316	3,318	165	3,002 D	8.3%	87.3%	8.7%	91.3%
23,072	ORANGE	5,843	1,813	3,523	507	1,710 D	31.0%	60.3%	34.0%	66.0%
9,706	PAMLICO	2,197	685	1,370	142	685 D	31.2%	62.4%	33.3%	66.7%
20,568	PASQUOTANK	2,916	701	1,976	239	1,275 D	24.0%	67.8%	26.2%	73.8%
17,710	PENDER	2,138	304	1,334	500	1,030 D	14.2%	62.4%	18.6%	81.4%
9,773	PERQUIMANS	1,060	135	849	76	714 D	12.7%	80.1%	13.7%	86.3%
25,029	PERSON	3,752	480	3,087	185	2,607 D	12.8%	82.3%	13.5%	86.5%
61,244	PITT	9,522	602	8,519	401	7,917 D	6.3%	89.5%	6.6%	93.4%
11,874	POLK	3,991	1,636	2,078	277	442 D	41.0%	52.1%	44.0%	56.0%
44,554	RANDOLPH	15,682	8,372	6,567	743	1,805 R	53.4%	41.9%	56.0%	44.0%
36,810	RICHMOND	6,082	866	4,376	840	3,510 D	14.2%	72.0%	16.5%	83.5%
76,860	ROBESON	9,133	1,036	7,056	1,041	6,020 D	11.3%	77.3%	12.8%	87.2%
57,898	ROCKINGHAM	12,415	2,936	8,553	926	5,617 D	23.6%	68.9%	25.6%	74.4%
69,206	ROWAN	15,702	5,722	6,799	3,181	1,077 D	36.4%	43.3%	45.7%	54.3%
45,577	RUTHERFORD	11,750	4,342	5,992	1,416	1,650 D	37.0%	51.0%	42.0%	58.0%
47,440	SAMPSON	10,548	4,932	4,965	651	33 D	46.8%	47.1%	49.8%	50.2%
23,232	SCOTLAND	2,819	359	1,957	503	1,598 D	12.7%	69.4%	15.5%	84.5%
32,834	STANLY	11,674	5,902	4,415	1,357	1,487 R	50.6%	37.8%	57.2%	42.8%
22,656	STOKES	7,891	3,291	4,431	169	1,140 D	41.7%	56.2%	42.6%	57.4%
41,783	SURRY	12,253	4,643	6,956	654	2,313 D	37.9%	56.8%	40.0%	60.0%
12,177	SWAIN	3,367	1,389	1,908	70	519 D	41.3%	56.7%	42.1%	57.9%
12,241	TRANSYLVANIA	6,163	2,861	2,975	327	114 D	46.4%	48.3%	49.0%	51.0%
5,556	TYRRELL	1,113	336	732	45	396 D	30.2%	65.8%	31.5%	68.5%
39,097	UNION	5,144	738	3,407	999	2,669 D	14.3%	66.2%	17.8%	82.2%
29,961	VANCE	4,627	549	3,679	399	3,130 D	11.9%	79.5%	13.0%	87.0%
109,544	WAKE	24,423	4,850	17,939	1,634	13,089 D	19.9%	73.5%	21.3%	78.7%
23,145	WARREN	2,771	192	2,376	203	2,184 D	6.9%	85.7%	7.5%	92.5%
12,323	WASHINGTON	2,057	333	1,675	49	1,342 D	16.2%	81.4%	16.6%	83.4%
18,114	WATAUGA	7,400	3,851	3,379	170	472 R	52.0%	45.7%	53.3%	46.7%
58,328	WAYNE	8,348	1,658	6,111	579	4,453 D	19.9%	73.2%	21.3%	78.7%
43,003	WILKES	14,400	8,234	5,784	382	2,450 R	57.2%	40.2%	58.7%	41.3%
50,219	WILSON	6,966	665	6,008	293	5,343 D	9.5%	86.2%	10.0%	90.0%
20,657	YADKIN	5,934	3,631	2,083	220	1,548 R	61.2%	35.1%	63.5%	36.5%
17,202	YANCEY	5,832	2,282	3,481	69	1,199 D	39.1%	59.7%	39.6%	60.4%
3,571,623	TOTAL	791,209	258,572	459,070	73,567	200,498 D	32.7%	58.0%	36.0%	64.0%

NORTH CAROLINA

PRESIDENT 1944

1940 Census Population	County	Total Vote	Republican	Democratic	Other	Rep.-Dem. Plurality	Percentage Total Vote Rep.	Total Vote Dem.	Major Vote Rep.	Major Vote Dem.
57,427	ALAMANCE	14,160	4,976	9,184		4,208 D	35.1%	64.9%	35.1%	64.9%
13,454	ALEXANDER	5,253	2,971	2,282		689 R	56.6%	43.4%	56.6%	43.4%
8,341	ALLEGHANY	3,305	1,495	1,810		315 D	45.2%	54.8%	45.2%	54.8%
28,443	ANSON	4,092	510	3,582		3,072 D	12.5%	87.5%	12.5%	87.5%
22,664	ASHE	8,887	4,524	4,363		161 R	50.9%	49.1%	50.9%	49.1%
13,561	AVERY	4,016	3,178	838		2,340 R	79.1%	20.9%	79.1%	20.9%
36,431	BEAUFORT	5,839	1,133	4,706		3,573 D	19.4%	80.6%	19.4%	80.6%
26,201	BERTIE	3,266	124	3,142		3,018 D	3.8%	96.2%	3.8%	96.2%
27,156	BLADEN	3,273	731	2,542		1,811 D	22.3%	77.7%	22.3%	77.7%
17,125	BRUNSWICK	4,343	1,997	2,346		349 D	46.0%	54.0%	46.0%	54.0%
108,755	BUNCOMBE	30,276	9,398	20,878		11,480 D	31.0%	69.0%	31.0%	69.0%
38,615	BURKE	12,650	5,855	6,795		940 D	46.3%	53.7%	46.3%	53.7%
59,393	CABARRUS	13,297	4,233	9,064		4,831 D	31.8%	68.2%	31.8%	68.2%
35,795	CALDWELL	9,784	4,365	5,419		1,054 D	44.6%	55.4%	44.6%	55.4%
5,440	CAMDEN	915	193	722		529 D	21.1%	78.9%	21.1%	78.9%
18,284	CARTERET	5,055	1,566	3,489		1,923 D	31.0%	69.0%	31.0%	69.0%
20,032	CASWELL	2,415	492	1,923		1,431 D	20.4%	79.6%	20.4%	79.6%
51,653	CATAWBA	17,357	7,211	10,146		2,935 D	41.5%	58.5%	41.5%	58.5%
24,726	CHATHAM	6,287	2,431	3,856		1,425 D	38.7%	61.3%	38.7%	61.3%
18,813	CHEROKEE	5,207	2,625	2,582		43 R	50.4%	49.6%	50.4%	49.6%
11,572	CHOWAN	1,480	166	1,314		1,148 D	11.2%	88.8%	11.2%	88.8%
6,405	CLAY	2,508	1,263	1,245		18 R	50.4%	49.6%	50.4%	49.6%
58,055	CLEVELAND	10,806	2,636	8,170		5,534 D	24.4%	75.6%	24.4%	75.6%
45,663	COLUMBUS	7,269	1,552	5,717		4,165 D	21.4%	78.6%	21.4%	78.6%
31,298	CRAVEN	5,698	826	4,872		4,046 D	14.5%	85.5%	14.5%	85.5%
59,320	CUMBERLAND	8,629	2,014	6,615		4,601 D	23.3%	76.7%	23.3%	76.7%
6,709	CURRITUCK	1,280	231	1,049		818 D	18.0%	82.0%	18.0%	82.0%
6,041	DARE	1,225	259	966		707 D	21.1%	78.9%	21.1%	78.9%
53,377	DAVIDSON	18,900	9,445	9,455		10 D	50.0%	50.0%	50.0%	50.0%
14,909	DAVIE	5,510	3,244	2,266		978 R	58.9%	41.1%	58.9%	41.1%
39,739	DUPLIN	6,901	1,437	5,464		4,027 D	20.8%	79.2%	20.8%	79.2%
80,244	DURHAM	16,453	3,690	12,763		9,073 D	22.4%	77.6%	22.4%	77.6%
49,162	EDGECOMBE	7,210	448	6,762		6,314 D	6.2%	93.8%	6.2%	93.8%
126,475	FORSYTH	26,404	10,014	16,390		6,376 D	37.9%	62.1%	37.9%	62.1%
30,382	FRANKLIN	4,256	289	3,967		3,678 D	6.8%	93.2%	6.8%	93.2%
87,531	GASTON	19,767	6,023	13,744		7,721 D	30.5%	69.5%	30.5%	69.5%
10,060	GATES	1,258	153	1,105		952 D	12.2%	87.8%	12.2%	87.8%
6,418	GRAHAM	3,245	1,356	1,889		533 D	41.8%	58.2%	41.8%	58.2%
29,344	GRANVILLE	3,540	325	3,215		2,890 D	9.2%	90.8%	9.2%	90.8%
18,548	GREENE	2,641	113	2,528		2,415 D	4.3%	95.7%	4.3%	95.7%
153,916	GUILFORD	36,457	12,962	23,495		10,533 D	35.6%	64.4%	35.6%	64.4%
56,512	HALIFAX	7,429	440	6,989		6,549 D	5.9%	94.1%	5.9%	94.1%
44,239	HARNETT	9,770	3,191	6,579		3,388 D	32.7%	67.3%	32.7%	67.3%
34,804	HAYWOOD	10,674	2,919	7,755		4,836 D	27.3%	72.7%	27.3%	72.7%
26,049	HENDERSON	10,292	4,613	5,679		1,066 D	44.8%	55.2%	44.8%	55.2%
19,352	HERTFORD	2,121	125	1,996		1,871 D	5.9%	94.1%	5.9%	94.1%
14,937	HOKE	1,942	160	1,782		1,622 D	8.2%	91.8%	8.2%	91.8%
7,860	HYDE	1,247	323	924		601 D	25.9%	74.1%	25.9%	74.1%
50,424	IREDELL	13,222	4,864	8,358		3,494 D	36.8%	63.2%	36.8%	63.2%
19,366	JACKSON	6,803	2,694	4,109		1,415 D	39.6%	60.4%	39.6%	60.4%
63,798	JOHNSTON	12,705	4,423	8,282		3,859 D	34.8%	65.2%	34.8%	65.2%
10,926	JONES	1,432	211	1,221		1,010 D	14.7%	85.3%	14.7%	85.3%
18,743	LEE	4,256	808	3,448		2,640 D	19.0%	81.0%	19.0%	81.0%
41,211	LENOIR	5,807	554	5,253		4,699 D	9.5%	90.5%	9.5%	90.5%
24,187	LINCOLN	7,846	3,678	4,168		490 D	46.9%	53.1%	46.9%	53.1%
22,996	MCDOWELL	6,266	2,258	4,008		1,750 D	36.0%	64.0%	36.0%	64.0%
15,880	MACON	5,365	2,510	2,855		345 D	46.8%	53.2%	46.8%	53.2%
22,522	MADISON	6,679	4,388	2,291		2,097 R	65.7%	34.3%	65.7%	34.3%
26,111	MARTIN	4,541	133	4,408		4,275 D	2.9%	97.1%	2.9%	97.1%
151,826	MECKLENBURG	35,384	9,434	25,950		16,516 D	26.7%	73.3%	26.7%	73.3%

NORTH CAROLINA

PRESIDENT 1944

1940 Census Population	County	Total Vote	Republican	Democratic	Other	Rep.-Dem. Plurality	Percentage Total Vote Rep.	Total Vote Dem.	Major Vote Rep.	Major Vote Dem.
15,980	MITCHELL	4,216	3,192	1,024		2,168 R	75.7%	24.3%	75.7%	24.3%
16,280	MONTGOMERY	4,628	1,963	2,665		702 D	42.4%	57.6%	42.4%	57.6%
30,969	MOORE	6,374	2,663	3,711		1,048 D	41.8%	58.2%	41.8%	58.2%
55,608	NASH	8,453	876	7,577		6,701 D	10.4%	89.6%	10.4%	89.6%
47,935	NEW HANOVER	12,305	2,829	9,476		6,647 D	23.0%	77.0%	23.0%	77.0%
28,299	NORTHAMPTON	3,642	172	3,470		3,298 D	4.7%	95.3%	4.7%	95.3%
17,939	ONSLOW	3,144	433	2,711		2,278 D	13.8%	86.2%	13.8%	86.2%
23,072	ORANGE	4,741	1,467	3,274		1,807 D	30.9%	69.1%	30.9%	69.1%
9,706	PAMLICO	2,014	719	1,295		576 D	35.7%	64.3%	35.7%	64.3%
20,568	PASQUOTANK	3,400	860	2,540		1,680 D	25.3%	74.7%	25.3%	74.7%
17,710	PENDER	2,173	441	1,732		1,291 D	20.3%	79.7%	20.3%	79.7%
9,773	PERQUIMANS	1,226	266	960		694 D	21.7%	78.3%	21.7%	78.3%
25,029	PERSON	3,114	607	2,507		1,900 D	19.5%	80.5%	19.5%	80.5%
61,244	PITT	9,051	495	8,556		8,061 D	5.5%	94.5%	5.5%	94.5%
11,874	POLK	4,018	1,678	2,340		662 D	41.8%	58.2%	41.8%	58.2%
44,554	RANDOLPH	16,045	8,768	7,277		1,491 R	54.6%	45.4%	54.6%	45.4%
36,810	RICHMOND	6,332	938	5,394		4,456 D	14.8%	85.2%	14.8%	85.2%
76,860	ROBESON	8,396	1,118	7,278		6,160 D	13.3%	86.7%	13.3%	86.7%
57,898	ROCKINGHAM	11,779	3,024	8,755		5,731 D	25.7%	74.3%	25.7%	74.3%
69,206	ROWAN	15,583	5,862	9,721		3,859 D	37.6%	62.4%	37.6%	62.4%
45,577	RUTHERFORD	12,077	4,698	7,379		2,681 D	38.9%	61.1%	38.9%	61.1%
47,440	SAMPSON	10,282	6,062	4,220		1,842 R	59.0%	41.0%	59.0%	41.0%
23,232	SCOTLAND	2,675	303	2,372		2,069 D	11.3%	88.7%	11.3%	88.7%
32,834	STANLY	11,582	6,083	5,499		584 R	52.5%	47.5%	52.5%	47.5%
22,656	STOKES	7,486	3,376	4,110		734 D	45.1%	54.9%	45.1%	54.9%
41,783	SURRY	12,795	5,116	7,679		2,563 D	40.0%	60.0%	40.0%	60.0%
12,177	SWAIN	3,615	1,505	2,110		605 D	41.6%	58.4%	41.6%	58.4%
12,241	TRANSYLVANIA	5,270	2,251	3,019		768 D	42.7%	57.3%	42.7%	57.3%
5,556	TYRRELL	892	281	611		330 D	31.5%	68.5%	31.5%	68.5%
39,097	UNION	6,843	1,114	5,729		4,615 D	16.3%	83.7%	16.3%	83.7%
29,961	VANCE	4,638	528	4,110		3,582 D	11.4%	88.6%	11.4%	88.6%
109,544	WAKE	22,046	3,996	18,050		14,054 D	18.1%	81.9%	18.1%	81.9%
23,145	WARREN	2,722	242	2,480		2,238 D	8.9%	91.1%	8.9%	91.1%
12,323	WASHINGTON	2,279	497	1,782		1,285 D	21.8%	78.2%	21.8%	78.2%
18,114	WATAUGA	7,168	3,954	3,214		740 R	55.2%	44.8%	55.2%	44.8%
58,328	WAYNE	8,142	1,914	6,228		4,314 D	23.5%	76.5%	23.5%	76.5%
43,003	WILKES	14,699	9,121	5,578		3,543 R	62.1%	37.9%	62.1%	37.9%
50,219	WILSON	7,249	769	6,480		5,711 D	10.6%	89.4%	10.6%	89.4%
20,657	YADKIN	6,862	4,392	2,470		1,922 R	64.0%	36.0%	64.0%	36.0%
17,202	YANCEY	5,703	2,402	3,301		899 D	42.1%	57.9%	42.1%	57.9%
3,571,623	TOTAL	790,554	263,155	527,399		264,244 D	33.3%	66.7%	33.3%	66.7%

NORTH CAROLINA

PRESIDENT 1940

1940 Census Population	County	Total Vote	Republican	Democratic	Other	Rep.-Dem. Plurality	Percentage Total Vote Rep.	Percentage Total Vote Dem.	Percentage Major Vote Rep.	Percentage Major Vote Dem.
57,427	ALAMANCE	14,811	3,382	11,429		8,047 D	22.8%	77.2%	22.8%	77.2%
13,454	ALEXANDER	4,956	2,217	2,739		522 D	44.7%	55.3%	44.7%	55.3%
8,341	ALLEGHANY	3,169	1,217	1,952		735 D	38.4%	61.6%	38.4%	61.6%
28,443	ANSON	4,923	371	4,552		4,181 D	7.5%	92.5%	7.5%	92.5%
22,664	ASHE	8,891	4,175	4,716		541 D	47.0%	53.0%	47.0%	53.0%
13,561	AVERY	4,138	2,944	1,194		1,750 R	71.1%	28.9%	71.1%	28.9%
36,431	BEAUFORT	6,464	936	5,528		4,592 D	14.5%	85.5%	14.5%	85.5%
26,201	BERTIE	3,385	98	3,287		3,189 D	2.9%	97.1%	2.9%	97.1%
27,156	BLADEN	3,468	543	2,925		2,382 D	15.7%	84.3%	15.7%	84.3%
17,125	BRUNSWICK	4,239	1,522	2,717		1,195 D	35.9%	64.1%	35.9%	64.1%
108,755	BUNCOMBE	33,601	8,723	24,878		16,155 D	26.0%	74.0%	26.0%	74.0%
38,615	BURKE	12,131	4,889	7,242		2,353 D	40.3%	59.7%	40.3%	59.7%
59,393	CABARRUS	14,355	2,579	11,776		9,197 D	18.0%	82.0%	18.0%	82.0%
35,795	CALDWELL	9,339	3,005	6,334		3,329 D	32.2%	67.8%	32.2%	67.8%
5,440	CAMDEN	1,095	134	961		827 D	12.2%	87.8%	12.2%	87.8%
18,284	CARTERET	5,685	1,789	3,896		2,107 D	31.5%	68.5%	31.5%	68.5%
20,032	CASWELL	2,686	351	2,335		1,984 D	13.1%	86.9%	13.1%	86.9%
51,653	CATAWBA	16,889	5,656	11,233		5,577 D	33.5%	66.5%	33.5%	66.5%
24,726	CHATHAM	5,854	1,829	4,025		2,196 D	31.2%	68.8%	31.2%	68.8%
18,813	CHEROKEE	5,854	2,674	3,180		506 D	45.7%	54.3%	45.7%	54.3%
11,572	CHOWAN	1,634	87	1,547		1,460 D	5.3%	94.7%	5.3%	94.7%
6,405	CLAY	2,525	1,176	1,349		173 D	46.6%	53.4%	46.6%	53.4%
58,055	CLEVELAND	11,316	1,970	9,346		7,376 D	17.4%	82.6%	17.4%	82.6%
45,663	COLUMBUS	6,834	934	5,900		4,966 D	13.7%	86.3%	13.7%	86.3%
31,298	CRAVEN	5,542	626	4,916		4,290 D	11.3%	88.7%	11.3%	88.7%
59,320	CUMBERLAND	7,168	1,118	6,050		4,932 D	15.6%	84.4%	15.6%	84.4%
6,709	CURRITUCK	1,634	102	1,532		1,430 D	6.2%	93.8%	6.2%	93.8%
6,041	DARE	1,529	315	1,214		899 D	20.6%	79.4%	20.6%	79.4%
53,377	DAVIDSON	18,062	6,978	11,084		4,106 D	38.6%	61.4%	38.6%	61.4%
14,909	DAVIE	5,428	2,532	2,896		364 D	46.6%	53.4%	46.6%	53.4%
39,739	DUPLIN	6,654	1,260	5,394		4,134 D	18.9%	81.1%	18.9%	81.1%
80,244	DURHAM	17,301	2,491	14,810		12,319 D	14.4%	85.6%	14.4%	85.6%
49,162	EDGECOMBE	7,832	316	7,516		7,200 D	4.0%	96.0%	4.0%	96.0%
126,475	FORSYTH	27,789	7,125	20,664		13,539 D	25.6%	74.4%	25.6%	74.4%
30,382	FRANKLIN	4,951	227	4,724		4,497 D	4.6%	95.4%	4.6%	95.4%
87,531	GASTON	21,556	4,294	17,262		12,968 D	19.9%	80.1%	19.9%	80.1%
10,060	GATES	1,496	108	1,388		1,280 D	7.2%	92.8%	7.2%	92.8%
6,418	GRAHAM	2,493	1,089	1,404		315 D	43.7%	56.3%	43.7%	56.3%
29,344	GRANVILLE	4,137	213	3,924		3,711 D	5.1%	94.9%	5.1%	94.9%
18,548	GREENE	3,094	104	2,990		2,886 D	3.4%	96.6%	3.4%	96.6%
153,916	GUILFORD	36,335	9,770	26,565		16,795 D	26.9%	73.1%	26.9%	73.1%
56,512	HALIFAX	8,343	361	7,982		7,621 D	4.3%	95.7%	4.3%	95.7%
44,239	HARNETT	8,882	2,280	6,602		4,322 D	25.7%	74.3%	25.7%	74.3%
34,804	HAYWOOD	10,988	2,357	8,631		6,274 D	21.5%	78.5%	21.5%	78.5%
26,049	HENDERSON	10,048	3,712	6,336		2,624 D	36.9%	63.1%	36.9%	63.1%
19,352	HERTFORD	2,556	92	2,464		2,372 D	3.6%	96.4%	3.6%	96.4%
14,937	HOKE	2,021	117	1,904		1,787 D	5.8%	94.2%	5.8%	94.2%
7,860	HYDE	1,511	309	1,202		893 D	20.5%	79.5%	20.5%	79.5%
50,424	IREDELL	14,148	3,820	10,328		6,508 D	27.0%	73.0%	27.0%	73.0%
19,366	JACKSON	6,973	2,410	4,563		2,153 D	34.6%	65.4%	34.6%	65.4%
63,798	JOHNSTON	14,168	4,192	9,976		5,784 D	29.6%	70.4%	29.6%	70.4%
10,926	JONES	1,604	233	1,371		1,138 D	14.5%	85.5%	14.5%	85.5%
18,743	LEE	4,209	527	3,682		3,155 D	12.5%	87.5%	12.5%	87.5%
41,211	LENOIR	6,687	440	6,247		5,807 D	6.6%	93.4%	6.6%	93.4%
24,187	LINCOLN	8,000	3,099	4,901		1,802 D	38.7%	61.3%	38.7%	61.3%
22,996	MCDOWELL	7,506	2,216	5,290		3,074 D	29.5%	70.5%	29.5%	70.5%
15,880	MACON	5,253	2,312	2,941		629 D	44.0%	56.0%	44.0%	56.0%
22,522	MADISON	7,788	4,617	3,171		1,446 R	59.3%	40.7%	59.3%	40.7%
26,111	MARTIN	4,734	106	4,628		4,522 D	2.2%	97.8%	2.2%	97.8%
151,826	MECKLENBURG	35,781	7,013	28,768		21,755 D	19.6%	80.4%	19.6%	80.4%

NORTH CAROLINA

PRESIDENT 1940

1940 Census Population	County	Total Vote	Republican	Democratic	Other	Rep.-Dem. Plurality	Percentage Total Vote Rep.	Total Vote Dem.	Major Vote Rep.	Major Vote Dem.
15,980	MITCHELL	4,740	3,290	1,450		1,840 R	69.4%	30.6%	69.4%	30.6%
16,280	MONTGOMERY	4,796	1,789	3,007		1,218 D	37.3%	62.7%	37.3%	62.7%
30,969	MOORE	6,917	2,587	4,330		1,743 D	37.4%	62.6%	37.4%	62.6%
55,608	NASH	9,069	613	8,456		7,843 D	6.8%	93.2%	6.8%	93.2%
47,935	NEW HANOVER	10,235	1,635	8,600		6,965 D	16.0%	84.0%	16.0%	84.0%
28,299	NORTHAMPTON	3,931	105	3,826		3,721 D	2.7%	97.3%	2.7%	97.3%
17,939	ONSLOW	2,654	271	2,383		2,112 D	10.2%	89.8%	10.2%	89.8%
23,072	ORANGE	4,773	1,100	3,673		2,573 D	23.0%	77.0%	23.0%	77.0%
9,706	PAMLICO	2,178	730	1,448		718 D	33.5%	66.5%	33.5%	66.5%
20,568	PASQUOTANK	3,820	506	3,314		2,808 D	13.2%	86.8%	13.2%	86.8%
17,710	PENDER	2,554	305	2,249		1,944 D	11.9%	88.1%	11.9%	88.1%
9,773	PERQUIMANS	1,404	228	1,176		948 D	16.2%	83.8%	16.2%	83.8%
25,029	PERSON	3,671	432	3,239		2,807 D	11.8%	88.2%	11.8%	88.2%
61,244	PITT	10,436	369	10,067		9,698 D	3.5%	96.5%	3.5%	96.5%
11,874	POLK	3,982	1,528	2,454		926 D	38.4%	61.6%	38.4%	61.6%
44,554	RANDOLPH	15,511	7,056	8,455		1,399 D	45.5%	54.5%	45.5%	54.5%
36,810	RICHMOND	7,309	779	6,530		5,751 D	10.7%	89.3%	10.7%	89.3%
76,860	ROBESON	10,182	931	9,251		8,320 D	9.1%	90.9%	9.1%	90.9%
57,898	ROCKINGHAM	13,713	2,398	11,315		8,917 D	17.5%	82.5%	17.5%	82.5%
69,206	ROWAN	17,082	4,059	13,023		8,964 D	23.8%	76.2%	23.8%	76.2%
45,577	RUTHERFORD	13,073	4,204	8,869		4,665 D	32.2%	67.8%	32.2%	67.8%
47,440	SAMPSON	10,876	5,769	5,107		662 R	53.0%	47.0%	53.0%	47.0%
23,232	SCOTLAND	3,231	250	2,981		2,731 D	7.7%	92.3%	7.7%	92.3%
32,834	STANLY	10,890	4,569	6,321		1,752 D	42.0%	58.0%	42.0%	58.0%
22,656	STOKES	6,986	2,712	4,274		1,562 D	38.8%	61.2%	38.8%	61.2%
41,783	SURRY	13,049	4,178	8,871		4,693 D	32.0%	68.0%	32.0%	68.0%
12,177	SWAIN	3,847	1,425	2,422		997 D	37.0%	63.0%	37.0%	63.0%
12,241	TRANSYLVANIA	5,331	2,019	3,312		1,293 D	37.9%	62.1%	37.9%	62.1%
5,556	TYRRELL	1,555	415	1,140		725 D	26.7%	73.3%	26.7%	73.3%
39,097	UNION	7,813	634	7,179		6,545 D	8.1%	91.9%	8.1%	91.9%
29,961	VANCE	4,632	380	4,252		3,872 D	8.2%	91.8%	8.2%	91.8%
109,544	WAKE	20,748	2,665	18,083		15,418 D	12.8%	87.2%	12.8%	87.2%
23,145	WARREN	2,923	247	2,676		2,429 D	8.5%	91.5%	8.5%	91.5%
12,323	WASHINGTON	2,086	362	1,724		1,362 D	17.4%	82.6%	17.4%	82.6%
18,114	WATAUGA	7,354	3,739	3,615		124 R	50.8%	49.2%	50.8%	49.2%
58,328	WAYNE	8,871	1,649	7,222		5,573 D	18.6%	81.4%	18.6%	81.4%
43,003	WILKES	15,745	8,446	7,299		1,147 R	53.6%	46.4%	53.6%	46.4%
50,219	WILSON	8,496	584	7,912		7,328 D	6.9%	93.1%	6.9%	93.1%
20,657	YADKIN	7,737	4,077	3,660		417 R	52.7%	47.3%	52.7%	47.3%
17,202	YANCEY	6,005	2,516	3,489		973 D	41.9%	58.1%	41.9%	58.1%
3,571,623	TOTAL	822,648	213,633	609,015		395,382 D	26.0%	74.0%	26.0%	74.0%

NORTH CAROLINA

PRESIDENT 1936

1930 Census Population	County	Total Vote	Republican	Democratic	Other	Rep.-Dem. Plurality	Percentage Total Vote Rep.	Total Vote Dem.	Major Vote Rep.	Major Vote Dem.
42,140	ALAMANCE	14,872	3,847	11,025		7,178 D	25.9%	74.1%	25.9%	74.1%
12,922	ALEXANDER	5,713	2,451	3,262		811 D	42.9%	57.1%	42.9%	57.1%
7,186	ALLEGHANY	3,843	1,498	2,345		847 D	39.0%	61.0%	39.0%	61.0%
29,349	ANSON	5,010	381	4,629		4,248 D	7.6%	92.4%	7.6%	92.4%
21,019	ASHE	10,109	4,557	5,552		995 D	45.1%	54.9%	45.1%	54.9%
11,803	AVERY	3,810	2,971	839		2,132 R	78.0%	22.0%	78.0%	22.0%
35,026	BEAUFORT	7,097	964	6,133		5,169 D	13.6%	86.4%	13.6%	86.4%
25,844	BERTIE	3,943	115	3,828		3,713 D	2.9%	97.1%	2.9%	97.1%
22,389	BLADEN	3,911	551	3,360		2,809 D	14.1%	85.9%	14.1%	85.9%
15,818	BRUNSWICK	4,335	1,625	2,710		1,085 D	37.5%	62.5%	37.5%	62.5%
97,937	BUNCOMBE	33,116	9,470	23,646		14,176 D	28.6%	71.4%	28.6%	71.4%
29,410	BURKE	12,960	5,506	7,454		1,948 D	42.5%	57.5%	42.5%	57.5%
44,331	CABARRUS	15,122	2,825	12,297		9,472 D	18.7%	81.3%	18.7%	81.3%
28,016	CALDWELL	10,230	3,421	6,809		3,388 D	33.4%	66.6%	33.4%	66.6%
5,461	CAMDEN	1,125	117	1,008		891 D	10.4%	89.6%	10.4%	89.6%
16,900	CARTERET	5,669	1,889	3,780		1,891 D	33.3%	66.7%	33.3%	66.7%
18,214	CASWELL	2,700	207	2,493		2,286 D	7.7%	92.3%	7.7%	92.3%
43,991	CATAWBA	17,404	6,387	11,017		4,630 D	36.7%	63.3%	36.7%	63.3%
24,177	CHATHAM	6,555	2,182	4,373		2,191 D	33.3%	66.7%	33.3%	66.7%
16,151	CHEROKEE	6,687	3,214	3,473		259 D	48.1%	51.9%	48.1%	51.9%
11,282	CHOWAN	1,646	96	1,550		1,454 D	5.8%	94.2%	5.8%	94.2%
5,434	CLAY	2,865	1,525	1,340		185 R	53.2%	46.8%	53.2%	46.8%
51,914	CLEVELAND	13,509	2,116	11,393		9,277 D	15.7%	84.3%	15.7%	84.3%
37,720	COLUMBUS	7,573	1,214	6,359		5,145 D	16.0%	84.0%	16.0%	84.0%
30,665	CRAVEN	5,996	453	5,543		5,090 D	7.6%	92.4%	7.6%	92.4%
45,219	CUMBERLAND	7,529	1,024	6,505		5,481 D	13.6%	86.4%	13.6%	86.4%
6,710	CURRITUCK	1,753	128	1,625		1,497 D	7.3%	92.7%	7.3%	92.7%
5,202	DARE	1,931	542	1,389		847 D	28.1%	71.9%	28.1%	71.9%
47,865	DAVIDSON	18,500	7,656	10,844		3,188 D	41.4%	58.6%	41.4%	58.6%
14,386	DAVIE	4,978	2,502	2,476		26 R	50.3%	49.7%	50.3%	49.7%
35,103	DUPLIN	7,512	1,546	5,966		4,420 D	20.6%	79.4%	20.6%	79.4%
67,196	DURHAM	14,993	2,189	12,804		10,615 D	14.6%	85.4%	14.6%	85.4%
47,894	EDGECOMBE	6,950	266	6,684		6,418 D	3.8%	96.2%	3.8%	96.2%
111,681	FORSYTH	23,990	5,256	18,734		13,478 D	21.9%	78.1%	21.9%	78.1%
29,456	FRANKLIN	5,440	231	5,209		4,978 D	4.2%	95.8%	4.2%	95.8%
78,093	GASTON	22,327	4,772	17,555		12,783 D	21.4%	78.6%	21.4%	78.6%
10,551	GATES	1,612	128	1,484		1,356 D	7.9%	92.1%	7.9%	92.1%
5,841	GRAHAM	2,798	1,325	1,473		148 D	47.4%	52.6%	47.4%	52.6%
28,723	GRANVILLE	4,464	185	4,279		4,094 D	4.1%	95.9%	4.1%	95.9%
18,656	GREENE	3,213	116	3,097		2,981 D	3.6%	96.4%	3.6%	96.4%
133,010	GUILFORD	35,093	9,514	25,579		16,065 D	27.1%	72.9%	27.1%	72.9%
53,246	HALIFAX	8,538	308	8,230		7,922 D	3.6%	96.4%	3.6%	96.4%
37,911	HARNETT	10,282	2,264	8,018		5,754 D	22.0%	78.0%	22.0%	78.0%
28,273	HAYWOOD	11,506	3,331	8,175		4,844 D	29.0%	71.0%	29.0%	71.0%
23,404	HENDERSON	10,846	5,099	5,747		648 D	47.0%	53.0%	47.0%	53.0%
17,542	HERTFORD	2,411	84	2,327		2,243 D	3.5%	96.5%	3.5%	96.5%
14,244	HOKE	2,094	141	1,953		1,812 D	6.7%	93.3%	6.7%	93.3%
8,550	HYDE	1,459	302	1,157		855 D	20.7%	79.3%	20.7%	79.3%
46,693	IREDELL	15,125	3,817	11,308		7,491 D	25.2%	74.8%	25.2%	74.8%
17,519	JACKSON	7,641	3,061	4,580		1,519 D	40.1%	59.9%	40.1%	59.9%
57,621	JOHNSTON	15,592	4,339	11,253		6,914 D	27.8%	72.2%	27.8%	72.2%
10,428	JONES	1,751	188	1,563		1,375 D	10.7%	89.3%	10.7%	89.3%
16,996	LEE	4,393	670	3,723		3,053 D	15.3%	84.7%	15.3%	84.7%
35,716	LENOIR	6,205	351	5,854		5,503 D	5.7%	94.3%	5.7%	94.3%
22,872	LINCOLN	9,016	3,501	5,515		2,014 D	38.8%	61.2%	38.8%	61.2%
20,336	MCDOWELL	8,466	3,114	5,352		2,238 D	36.8%	63.2%	36.8%	63.2%
13,672	MACON	5,865	2,554	3,311		757 D	43.5%	56.5%	43.5%	56.5%
20,306	MADISON	8,232	5,099	3,133		1,966 R	61.9%	38.1%	61.9%	38.1%
23,400	MARTIN	4,588	111	4,477		4,366 D	2.4%	97.6%	2.4%	97.6%
127,971	MECKLENBURG	30,878	4,709	26,169		21,460 D	15.3%	84.7%	15.3%	84.7%

NORTH CAROLINA

PRESIDENT 1936

1930 Census Population	County	Total Vote	Republican	Democratic	Other	Rep.-Dem. Plurality	Percentage Total Vote Rep.	Percentage Total Vote Dem.	Percentage Major Vote Rep.	Percentage Major Vote Dem.
13,962	MITCHELL	5,067	3,380	1,687		1,693 R	66.7%	33.3%	66.7%	33.3%
16,218	MONTGOMERY	5,990	2,506	3,484		978 D	41.8%	58.2%	41.8%	58.2%
28,215	MOORE	6,947	2,481	4,466		1,985 D	35.7%	64.3%	35.7%	64.3%
52,782	NASH	9,199	517	8,682		8,165 D	5.6%	94.4%	5.6%	94.4%
43,010	NEW HANOVER	8,685	1,306	7,379		6,073 D	15.0%	85.0%	15.0%	85.0%
27,161	NORTHAMPTON	3,894	109	3,785		3,676 D	2.8%	97.2%	2.8%	97.2%
15,289	ONSLOW	2,993	235	2,758		2,523 D	7.9%	92.1%	7.9%	92.1%
21,171	ORANGE	5,335	1,446	3,860	29	2,414 D	27.1%	72.4%	27.3%	72.7%
9,299	PAMLICO	2,487	860	1,627		767 D	34.6%	65.4%	34.6%	65.4%
19,143	PASQUOTANK	3,555	324	3,226	5	2,902 D	9.1%	90.7%	9.1%	90.9%
15,686	PENDER	2,712	333	2,379		2,046 D	12.3%	87.7%	12.3%	87.7%
10,668	PERQUIMANS	1,131	161	970		809 D	14.2%	85.8%	14.2%	85.8%
22,039	PERSON	3,282	384	2,898		2,514 D	11.7%	88.3%	11.7%	88.3%
54,466	PITT	9,864	325	9,539		9,214 D	3.3%	96.7%	3.3%	96.7%
10,216	POLK	4,315	1,794	2,521		727 D	41.6%	58.4%	41.6%	58.4%
36,259	RANDOLPH	15,017	6,927	8,090		1,163 D	46.1%	53.9%	46.1%	53.9%
34,016	RICHMOND	7,316	607	6,709		6,102 D	8.3%	91.7%	8.3%	91.7%
66,512	ROBESON	11,012	732	10,280		9,548 D	6.6%	93.4%	6.6%	93.4%
51,083	ROCKINGHAM	13,888	2,522	11,366		8,844 D	18.2%	81.8%	18.2%	81.8%
56,665	ROWAN	17,114	4,306	12,808		8,502 D	25.2%	74.8%	25.2%	74.8%
40,452	RUTHERFORD	14,741	4,830	9,911		5,081 D	32.8%	67.2%	32.8%	67.2%
40,082	SAMPSON	10,885	4,948	5,937		989 D	45.5%	54.5%	45.5%	54.5%
20,174	SCOTLAND	3,497	314	3,183		2,869 D	9.0%	91.0%	9.0%	91.0%
30,216	STANLY	11,028	4,523	6,505		1,982 D	41.0%	59.0%	41.0%	59.0%
22,290	STOKES	7,643	3,259	4,384		1,125 D	42.6%	57.4%	42.6%	57.4%
39,749	SURRY	13,599	4,766	8,833		4,067 D	35.0%	65.0%	35.0%	65.0%
11,568	SWAIN	4,703	2,084	2,619		535 D	44.3%	55.7%	44.3%	55.7%
9,589	TRANSYLVANIA	4,846	2,001	2,845		844 D	41.3%	58.7%	41.3%	58.7%
5,164	TYRRELL	1,353	304	1,049		745 D	22.5%	77.5%	22.5%	77.5%
40,979	UNION	8,081	601	7,480		6,879 D	7.4%	92.6%	7.4%	92.6%
27,294	VANCE	4,851	315	4,536		4,221 D	6.5%	93.5%	6.5%	93.5%
94,757	WAKE	22,312	2,456	19,850	6	17,394 D	11.0%	89.0%	11.0%	89.0%
23,364	WARREN	3,187	140	3,047		2,907 D	4.4%	95.6%	4.4%	95.6%
11,603	WASHINGTON	2,410	535	1,875		1,340 D	22.2%	77.8%	22.2%	77.8%
15,165	WATAUGA	7,289	3,409	3,880		471 D	46.8%	53.2%	46.8%	53.2%
53,013	WAYNE	8,838	1,751	7,087		5,336 D	19.8%	80.2%	19.8%	80.2%
36,162	WILKES	14,864	8,358	6,506		1,852 R	56.2%	43.8%	56.2%	43.8%
44,914	WILSON	8,071	549	7,522		6,973 D	6.8%	93.2%	6.8%	93.2%
18,010	YADKIN	7,409	4,200	3,209		991 R	56.7%	43.3%	56.7%	43.3%
14,486	YANCEY	6,294	2,691	3,603		912 D	42.8%	57.2%	42.8%	57.2%
3,170,276	TOTAL	839,475	223,294	616,141	40	392,847 D	26.6%	73.4%	26.6%	73.4%

NORTH CAROLINA

PRESIDENT 1932

1930 Census Population	County	Total Vote	Republican	Democratic	Other	Rep.-Dem. Plurality	Percentage Total Vote Rep.	Total Vote Dem.	Major Vote Rep.	Major Vote Dem.
42,140	ALAMANCE	12,882	4,478	8,240	164	3,762 D	34.8%	64.0%	35.2%	64.8%
12,922	ALEXANDER	4,933	1,952	2,953	28	1,001 D	39.6%	59.9%	39.8%	60.2%
7,186	ALLEGHANY	2,776	810	1,951	15	1,141 D	29.2%	70.3%	29.3%	70.7%
29,349	ANSON	4,480	223	4,252	5	4,029 D	5.0%	94.9%	5.0%	95.0%
21,019	ASHE	8,660	3,871	4,751	38	880 D	44.7%	54.9%	44.9%	55.1%
11,803	AVERY	3,900	2,833	1,045	22	1,788 R	72.6%	26.8%	73.1%	26.9%
35,026	BEAUFORT	6,431	839	5,552	40	4,713 D	13.0%	86.3%	13.1%	86.9%
25,844	BERTIE	3,224	65	3,154	5	3,089 D	2.0%	97.8%	2.0%	98.0%
22,389	BLADEN	3,495	808	2,651	36	1,843 D	23.1%	75.9%	23.4%	76.6%
15,818	BRUNSWICK	4,060	1,798	2,245	17	447 D	44.3%	55.3%	44.5%	55.5%
97,937	BUNCOMBE	27,353	8,745	18,241	367	9,496 D	32.0%	66.7%	32.4%	67.6%
29,410	BURKE	10,736	4,823	5,866	47	1,043 D	44.9%	54.6%	45.1%	54.9%
44,331	CABARRUS	11,977	3,444	8,465	68	5,021 D	28.8%	70.7%	28.9%	71.1%
28,016	CALDWELL	9,275	3,750	5,479	46	1,729 D	40.4%	59.1%	40.6%	59.4%
5,461	CAMDEN	994	78	915	1	837 D	7.8%	92.1%	7.9%	92.1%
16,900	CARTERET	5,275	1,765	3,455	55	1,690 D	33.5%	65.5%	33.8%	66.2%
18,214	CASWELL	2,033	169	1,858	6	1,689 D	8.3%	91.4%	8.3%	91.7%
43,991	CATAWBA	14,340	5,817	8,446	77	2,629 D	40.6%	58.9%	40.8%	59.2%
24,177	CHATHAM	6,912	2,590	4,263	59	1,673 D	37.5%	61.7%	37.8%	62.2%
16,151	CHEROKEE	6,504	3,131	3,348	25	217 D	48.1%	51.5%	48.3%	51.7%
11,282	CHOWAN	1,708	64	1,639	5	1,575 D	3.7%	96.0%	3.8%	96.2%
5,434	CLAY	2,614	1,265	1,341	8	76 D	48.4%	51.3%	48.5%	51.5%
51,914	CLEVELAND	9,945	1,904	8,016	25	6,112 D	19.1%	80.6%	19.2%	80.8%
37,720	COLUMBUS	5,890	739	5,098	53	4,359 D	12.5%	86.6%	12.7%	87.3%
30,665	CRAVEN	4,860	466	4,375	19	3,909 D	9.6%	90.0%	9.6%	90.4%
45,219	CUMBERLAND	5,983	931	5,012	40	4,081 D	15.6%	83.8%	15.7%	84.3%
6,710	CURRITUCK	1,832	69	1,759	4	1,690 D	3.8%	96.0%	3.8%	96.2%
5,202	DARE	1,744	497	1,241	6	744 D	28.5%	71.2%	28.6%	71.4%
47,865	DAVIDSON	15,500	6,051	9,292	157	3,241 D	39.0%	59.9%	39.4%	60.6%
14,386	DAVIE	4,895	2,473	2,381	41	92 R	50.5%	48.6%	50.9%	49.1%
35,103	DUPLIN	5,882	1,173	4,674	35	3,501 D	19.9%	79.5%	20.1%	79.9%
67,196	DURHAM	10,680	2,770	7,559	351	4,789 D	25.9%	70.8%	26.8%	73.2%
47,894	EDGECOMBE	6,141	248	5,872	21	5,624 D	4.0%	95.6%	4.1%	95.9%
111,681	FORSYTH	20,100	5,727	14,016	357	8,289 D	28.5%	69.7%	29.0%	71.0%
29,456	FRANKLIN	4,504	199	4,294	11	4,095 D	4.4%	95.3%	4.4%	95.6%
78,093	GASTON	18,211	5,164	12,890	157	7,726 D	28.4%	70.8%	28.6%	71.4%
10,551	GATES	1,288	89	1,198	1	1,109 D	6.9%	93.0%	6.9%	93.1%
5,841	GRAHAM	2,558	1,183	1,364	11	181 D	46.2%	53.3%	46.4%	53.6%
28,723	GRANVILLE	4,029	212	3,808	9	3,596 D	5.3%	94.5%	5.3%	94.7%
18,656	GREENE	2,607	94	2,510	3	2,416 D	3.6%	96.3%	3.6%	96.4%
133,010	GUILFORD	29,059	9,263	19,301	495	10,038 D	31.9%	66.4%	32.4%	67.6%
53,246	HALIFAX	6,752	306	6,413	33	6,107 D	4.5%	95.0%	4.6%	95.4%
37,911	HARNETT	9,012	2,617	6,346	49	3,729 D	29.0%	70.4%	29.2%	70.8%
28,273	HAYWOOD	9,906	3,082	6,790	34	3,708 D	31.1%	68.5%	31.2%	68.8%
23,404	HENDERSON	9,490	4,172	5,255	63	1,083 D	44.0%	55.4%	44.3%	55.7%
17,542	HERTFORD	1,930	88	1,835	7	1,747 D	4.6%	95.1%	4.6%	95.4%
14,244	HOKE	1,850	65	1,780	5	1,715 D	3.5%	96.2%	3.5%	96.5%
8,550	HYDE	1,201	147	1,050	4	903 D	12.2%	87.4%	12.3%	87.7%
46,693	IREDELL	12,005	3,583	8,367	55	4,784 D	29.8%	69.7%	30.0%	70.0%
17,519	JACKSON	7,208	2,813	4,360	35	1,547 D	39.0%	60.5%	39.2%	60.8%
57,621	JOHNSTON	13,511	3,887	9,574	50	5,687 D	28.8%	70.9%	28.9%	71.1%
10,428	JONES	1,585	132	1,449	4	1,317 D	8.3%	91.4%	8.3%	91.7%
16,996	LEE	3,752	681	3,058	13	2,377 D	18.2%	81.5%	18.2%	81.8%
35,716	LENOIR	5,051	350	4,677	24	4,327 D	6.9%	92.6%	7.0%	93.0%
22,872	LINCOLN	7,996	3,563	4,399	34	836 D	44.6%	55.0%	44.8%	55.2%
20,336	MCDOWELL	7,323	2,478	4,810	35	2,332 D	33.8%	65.7%	34.0%	66.0%
13,672	MACON	5,560	2,307	3,223	30	916 D	41.5%	58.0%	41.7%	58.3%
20,306	MADISON	7,370	4,552	2,769	49	1,783 R	61.8%	37.6%	62.2%	37.8%
23,400	MARTIN	3,883	94	3,781	8	3,687 D	2.4%	97.4%	2.4%	97.6%
127,971	MECKLENBURG	23,321	4,973	18,167	181	13,194 D	21.3%	77.9%	21.5%	78.5%

NORTH CAROLINA

PRESIDENT 1932

1930 Census Population	County	Total Vote	Republican	Democratic	Other	Rep.-Dem. Plurality	Percentage			
							Total Vote		Major Vote	
							Rep.	Dem.	Rep.	Dem.
13,962	MITCHELL	5,580	3,798	1,773	9	2,025 R	68.1%	31.8%	68.2%	31.8%
16,218	MONTGOMERY	5,098	2,153	2,927	18	774 D	42.2%	57.4%	42.4%	57.6%
28,215	MOORE	6,793	2,459	4,287	47	1,828 D	36.2%	63.1%	36.5%	63.5%
52,782	NASH	8,053	532	7,472	49	6,940 D	6.6%	92.8%	6.6%	93.4%
43,010	NEW HANOVER	7,601	1,430	6,030	141	4,600 D	18.8%	79.3%	19.2%	80.8%
27,161	NORTHAMPTON	3,397	147	3,243	7	3,096 D	4.3%	95.5%	4.3%	95.7%
15,289	ONSLOW	2,877	253	2,615	9	2,362 D	8.8%	90.9%	8.8%	91.2%
21,171	ORANGE	4,203	1,114	2,924	165	1,810 D	26.5%	69.6%	27.6%	72.4%
9,299	PAMLICO	2,266	665	1,526	75	861 D	29.3%	67.3%	30.4%	69.6%
19,143	PASQUOTANK	3,292	328	2,946	18	2,618 D	10.0%	89.5%	10.0%	90.0%
15,686	PENDER	2,274	270	1,993	11	1,723 D	11.9%	87.6%	11.9%	88.1%
10,668	PERQUIMANS	1,507	225	1,280	2	1,055 D	14.9%	84.9%	15.0%	85.0%
22,039	PERSON	3,049	660	2,372	17	1,712 D	21.6%	77.8%	21.8%	78.2%
54,466	PITT	8,000	255	7,724	21	7,469 D	3.2%	96.6%	3.2%	96.8%
10,216	POLK	3,843	1,421	2,401	21	980 D	37.0%	62.5%	37.2%	62.8%
36,259	RANDOLPH	13,492	6,072	7,345	75	1,273 D	45.0%	54.4%	45.3%	54.7%
34,016	RICHMOND	5,591	693	4,862	36	4,169 D	12.4%	87.0%	12.5%	87.5%
66,512	ROBESON	8,687	783	7,860	44	7,077 D	9.0%	90.5%	9.1%	90.9%
51,083	ROCKINGHAM	10,771	2,896	7,795	80	4,899 D	26.9%	72.4%	27.1%	72.9%
56,665	ROWAN	14,426	4,464	9,782	180	5,318 D	30.9%	67.8%	31.3%	68.7%
40,452	RUTHERFORD	12,838	4,448	8,336	54	3,888 D	34.6%	64.9%	34.8%	65.2%
40,082	SAMPSON	9,152	4,127	4,911	114	784 D	45.1%	53.7%	45.7%	54.3%
20,174	SCOTLAND	2,822	208	2,608	6	2,400 D	7.4%	92.4%	7.4%	92.6%
30,216	STANLY	9,826	3,992	5,785	49	1,793 D	40.6%	58.9%	40.8%	59.2%
22,290	STOKES	6,333	2,577	3,721	35	1,144 D	40.7%	58.8%	40.9%	59.1%
39,749	SURRY	12,070	4,511	7,490	69	2,979 D	37.4%	62.1%	37.6%	62.4%
11,568	SWAIN	4,324	1,893	2,412	19	519 D	43.8%	55.8%	44.0%	56.0%
9,589	TRANSYLVANIA	4,216	1,671	2,523	22	852 D	39.6%	59.8%	39.8%	60.2%
5,164	TYRRELL	1,137	258	873	6	615 D	22.7%	76.8%	22.8%	77.2%
40,979	UNION	6,870	710	6,103	57	5,393 D	10.3%	88.8%	10.4%	89.6%
27,294	VANCE	4,165	318	3,833	14	3,515 D	7.6%	92.0%	7.7%	92.3%
94,757	WAKE	17,279	2,170	14,863	246	12,693 D	12.6%	86.0%	12.7%	87.3%
23,364	WARREN	2,777	110	2,661	6	2,551 D	4.0%	95.8%	4.0%	96.0%
11,603	WASHINGTON	2,312	619	1,681	12	1,062 D	26.8%	72.7%	26.9%	73.1%
15,165	WATAUGA	6,606	3,166	3,419	21	253 D	47.9%	51.8%	48.1%	51.9%
53,013	WAYNE	8,056	1,631	6,365	60	4,734 D	20.2%	79.0%	20.4%	79.6%
36,162	WILKES	12,159	6,522	5,598	39	924 R	53.6%	46.0%	53.8%	46.2%
44,914	WILSON	6,721	517	6,153	51	5,636 D	7.7%	91.5%	7.8%	92.2%
18,010	YADKIN	6,242	3,422	2,789	31	633 R	54.8%	44.7%	55.1%	44.9%
14,486	YANCEY	5,817	2,396	3,412	9	1,016 D	41.2%	58.7%	41.3%	58.7%
3,170,276	TOTAL	711,498	208,344	497,566	5,588	289,222 D	29.3%	69.9%	29.5%	70.5%

NORTH CAROLINA

PRESIDENT 1928

1920 Census Population	County	Total Vote	Republican	Democratic	Other	Rep.-Dem. Plurality	Percentage Total Vote Rep.	Total Vote Dem.	Major Vote Rep.	Major Vote Dem.
32,718	ALAMANCE	11,070	6,810	4,260		2,550 R	61.5%	38.5%	61.5%	38.5%
12,212	ALEXANDER	4,327	2,605	1,722		883 R	60.2%	39.8%	60.2%	39.8%
7,403	ALLEGHANY	2,782	1,368	1,414		46 D	49.2%	50.8%	49.2%	50.8%
28,334	ANSON	3,673	726	2,947		2,221 D	19.8%	80.2%	19.8%	80.2%
21,001	ASHE	7,795	4,337	3,458		879 R	55.6%	44.4%	55.6%	44.4%
10,335	AVERY	3,663	3,273	390		2,883 R	89.4%	10.6%	89.4%	10.6%
31,024	BEAUFORT	6,054	2,521	3,533		1,012 D	41.6%	58.4%	41.6%	58.4%
23,993	BERTIE	2,374	374	2,000		1,626 D	15.8%	84.2%	15.8%	84.2%
19,761	BLADEN	3,463	1,911	1,552		359 R	55.2%	44.8%	55.2%	44.8%
14,876	BRUNSWICK	2,949	1,931	1,018		913 R	65.5%	34.5%	65.5%	34.5%
64,148	BUNCOMBE	28,995	16,590	12,405		4,185 R	57.2%	42.8%	57.2%	42.8%
23,297	BURKE	7,989	5,108	2,881		2,227 R	63.9%	36.1%	63.9%	36.1%
33,730	CABARRUS	11,417	6,548	4,869		1,679 R	57.4%	42.6%	57.4%	42.6%
19,984	CALDWELL	6,498	4,207	2,291		1,916 R	64.7%	35.3%	64.7%	35.3%
5,382	CAMDEN	869	245	624		379 D	28.2%	71.8%	28.2%	71.8%
15,384	CARTERET	5,178	3,133	2,045		1,088 R	60.5%	39.5%	60.5%	39.5%
15,759	CASWELL	1,685	749	936		187 D	44.5%	55.5%	44.5%	55.5%
33,839	CATAWBA	12,472	7,556	4,916		2,640 R	60.6%	39.4%	60.6%	39.4%
23,814	CHATHAM	5,998	3,318	2,680		638 R	55.3%	44.7%	55.3%	44.7%
15,242	CHEROKEE	5,150	3,239	1,911		1,328 R	62.9%	37.1%	62.9%	37.1%
10,649	CHOWAN	1,288	352	936		584 D	27.3%	72.7%	27.3%	72.7%
4,646	CLAY	2,009	1,106	903		203 R	55.1%	44.9%	55.1%	44.9%
34,272	CLEVELAND	9,680	4,766	4,914		148 D	49.2%	50.8%	49.2%	50.8%
30,124	COLUMBUS	6,387	3,533	2,854		679 R	55.3%	44.7%	55.3%	44.7%
29,048	CRAVEN	4,731	2,237	2,494		257 D	47.3%	52.7%	47.3%	52.7%
35,064	CUMBERLAND	6,831	3,534	3,297		237 R	51.7%	48.3%	51.7%	48.3%
7,268	CURRITUCK	1,419	166	1,253		1,087 D	11.7%	88.3%	11.7%	88.3%
5,115	DARE	1,697	814	883		69 D	48.0%	52.0%	48.0%	52.0%
35,201	DAVIDSON	14,180	8,960	5,220		3,740 R	63.2%	36.8%	63.2%	36.8%
13,578	DAVIE	4,044	2,959	1,085		1,874 R	73.2%	26.8%	73.2%	26.8%
30,223	DUPLIN	5,558	2,911	2,647		264 R	52.4%	47.6%	52.4%	47.6%
42,219	DURHAM	13,205	8,723	4,482		4,241 R	66.1%	33.9%	66.1%	33.9%
37,995	EDGECOMBE	5,161	977	4,184		3,207 D	18.9%	81.1%	18.9%	81.1%
77,269	FORSYTH	19,897	13,258	6,639		6,619 R	66.6%	33.4%	66.6%	33.4%
26,667	FRANKLIN	3,560	729	2,831		2,102 D	20.5%	79.5%	20.5%	79.5%
51,242	GASTON	16,404	9,702	6,702		3,000 R	59.1%	40.9%	59.1%	40.9%
10,537	GATES	1,130	558	572		14 D	49.4%	50.6%	49.4%	50.6%
4,872	GRAHAM	2,223	1,260	963		297 R	56.7%	43.3%	56.7%	43.3%
26,846	GRANVILLE	3,820	858	2,962		2,104 D	22.5%	77.5%	22.5%	77.5%
16,212	GREENE	1,723	542	1,181		639 D	31.5%	68.5%	31.5%	68.5%
79,272	GUILFORD	26,413	16,541	9,872		6,669 R	62.6%	37.4%	62.6%	37.4%
43,766	HALIFAX	5,772	890	4,882		3,992 D	15.4%	84.6%	15.4%	84.6%
28,313	HARNETT	8,294	4,740	3,554		1,186 R	57.1%	42.9%	57.1%	42.9%
23,496	HAYWOOD	8,645	4,472	4,173		299 R	51.7%	48.3%	51.7%	48.3%
18,248	HENDERSON	8,359	5,210	3,149		2,061 R	62.3%	37.7%	62.3%	37.7%
16,294	HERTFORD	1,423	393	1,030		637 D	27.6%	72.4%	27.6%	72.4%
11,722	HOKE	1,465	311	1,154		843 D	21.2%	78.8%	21.2%	78.8%
8,386	HYDE	1,272	682	590		92 R	53.6%	46.4%	53.6%	46.4%
37,956	IREDELL	11,548	6,712	4,836		1,876 R	58.1%	41.9%	58.1%	41.9%
13,396	JACKSON	6,683	3,512	3,171		341 R	52.6%	47.4%	52.6%	47.4%
48,998	JOHNSTON	12,737	7,696	5,041		2,655 R	60.4%	39.6%	60.4%	39.6%
9,912	JONES	1,144	658	486		172 R	57.5%	42.5%	57.5%	42.5%
13,400	LEE	3,131	1,416	1,715		299 D	45.2%	54.8%	45.2%	54.8%
29,555	LENOIR	3,674	1,311	2,363		1,052 D	35.7%	64.3%	35.7%	64.3%
17,862	LINCOLN	6,843	3,930	2,913		1,017 R	57.4%	42.6%	57.4%	42.6%
16,763	MCDOWELL	6,853	3,423	3,430		7 D	49.9%	50.1%	49.9%	50.1%
12,887	MACON	5,094	2,903	2,191		712 R	57.0%	43.0%	57.0%	43.0%
20,083	MADISON	5,869	4,776	1,093		3,683 R	81.4%	18.6%	81.4%	18.6%
20,828	MARTIN	3,229	411	2,818		2,407 D	12.7%	87.3%	12.7%	87.3%
80,695	MECKLENBURG	21,731	12,041	9,690		2,351 R	55.4%	44.6%	55.4%	44.6%

NORTH CAROLINA

PRESIDENT 1928

1920 Census Population	County	Total Vote	Republican	Democratic	Other	Rep.-Dem. Plurality	Percentage Total Vote Rep.	Total Vote Dem.	Major Vote Rep.	Major Vote Dem.
11,278	MITCHELL	4,263	3,436	827		2,609 R	80.6%	19.4%	80.6%	19.4%
14,607	MONTGOMERY	4,669	2,653	2,016		637 R	56.8%	43.2%	56.8%	43.2%
21,388	MOORE	5,929	3,290	2,639		651 R	55.5%	44.5%	55.5%	44.5%
41,061	NASH	6,315	2,066	4,249		2,183 D	32.7%	67.3%	32.7%	67.3%
40,620	NEW HANOVER	7,008	4,248	2,760		1,488 R	60.6%	39.4%	60.6%	39.4%
23,184	NORTHAMPTON	2,179	456	1,723		1,267 D	20.9%	79.1%	20.9%	79.1%
14,703	ONSLOW	2,325	1,253	1,072		181 R	53.9%	46.1%	53.9%	46.1%
17,895	ORANGE	4,363	2,564	1,799		765 R	58.8%	41.2%	58.8%	41.2%
9,060	PAMLICO	1,977	1,099	878		221 R	55.6%	44.4%	55.6%	44.4%
17,670	PASQUOTANK	2,757	814	1,943		1,129 D	29.5%	70.5%	29.5%	70.5%
14,788	PENDER	2,298	1,300	998		302 R	56.6%	43.4%	56.6%	43.4%
11,137	PERQUIMANS	1,209	600	609		9 D	49.6%	50.4%	49.6%	50.4%
18,973	PERSON	2,358	1,123	1,235		112 D	47.6%	52.4%	47.6%	52.4%
45,569	PITT	6,041	1,395	4,646		3,251 D	23.1%	76.9%	23.1%	76.9%
8,832	POLK	3,489	1,873	1,616		257 R	53.7%	46.3%	53.7%	46.3%
30,856	RANDOLPH	11,602	7,414	4,188		3,226 R	63.9%	36.1%	63.9%	36.1%
25,567	RICHMOND	5,020	2,045	2,975		930 D	40.7%	59.3%	40.7%	59.3%
54,674	ROBESON	7,497	2,767	4,730		1,963 D	36.9%	63.1%	36.9%	63.1%
44,149	ROCKINGHAM	8,996	5,585	3,411		2,174 R	62.1%	37.9%	62.1%	37.9%
44,062	ROWAN	12,740	7,957	4,783		3,174 R	62.5%	37.5%	62.5%	37.5%
31,426	RUTHERFORD	9,908	5,762	4,146		1,616 R	58.2%	41.8%	58.2%	41.8%
36,002	SAMPSON	7,864	5,579	2,285		3,294 R	70.9%	29.1%	70.9%	29.1%
15,600	SCOTLAND	2,349	588	1,761		1,173 D	25.0%	75.0%	25.0%	75.0%
27,429	STANLY	7,597	4,597	3,000		1,597 R	60.5%	39.5%	60.5%	39.5%
20,575	STOKES	5,729	3,759	1,970		1,789 R	65.6%	34.4%	65.6%	34.4%
32,464	SURRY	10,662	7,015	3,647		3,368 R	65.8%	34.2%	65.8%	34.2%
13,224	SWAIN	4,207	2,484	1,723		761 R	59.0%	41.0%	59.0%	41.0%
9,303	TRANSYLVANIA	3,887	2,165	1,722		443 R	55.7%	44.3%	55.7%	44.3%
4,849	TYRRELL	980	505	475		30 R	51.5%	48.5%	51.5%	48.5%
36,029	UNION	5,288	2,448	2,840		392 D	46.3%	53.7%	46.3%	53.7%
22,799	VANCE	3,844	1,449	2,395		946 D	37.7%	62.3%	37.7%	62.3%
75,155	WAKE	16,061	6,720	9,341		2,621 D	41.8%	58.2%	41.8%	58.2%
21,593	WARREN	2,416	379	2,037		1,658 D	15.7%	84.3%	15.7%	84.3%
11,429	WASHINGTON	2,081	1,183	898		285 R	56.8%	43.2%	56.8%	43.2%
13,477	WATAUGA	5,750	3,159	2,591		568 R	54.9%	45.1%	54.9%	45.1%
43,640	WAYNE	8,060	4,340	3,720		620 R	53.8%	46.2%	53.8%	46.2%
32,644	WILKES	10,610	7,808	2,802		5,006 R	73.6%	26.4%	73.6%	26.4%
36,813	WILSON	5,468	1,933	3,535		1,602 D	35.4%	64.6%	35.4%	64.6%
16,391	YADKIN	4,639	3,878	761		3,117 R	83.6%	16.4%	83.6%	16.4%
15,093	YANCEY	5,188	2,712	2,476		236 R	52.3%	47.7%	52.3%	47.7%
2,559,123	TOTAL	635,150	348,923	286,227		62,696 R	54.9%	45.1%	54.9%	45.1%

NORTH CAROLINA

PRESIDENT 1924

1920 Census Population	County	Total Vote	Republican	Democratic	Other	Rep.-Dem. Plurality	Percentage Total Vote Rep.	Total Vote Dem.	Major Vote Rep.	Major Vote Dem.
32,718	ALAMANCE	8,169	3,217	4,859	93	1,642 D	39.4%	59.5%	39.8%	60.2%
12,212	ALEXANDER	4,748	2,437	2,291	20	146 R	51.3%	48.3%	51.5%	48.5%
7,403	ALLEGHANY	2,883	1,234	1,643	6	409 D	42.8%	57.0%	42.9%	57.1%
28,334	ANSON	2,622	225	2,372	25	2,147 D	8.6%	90.5%	8.7%	91.3%
21,001	ASHE	8,288	3,952	4,333	3	381 D	47.7%	52.3%	47.7%	52.3%
10,335	AVERY	2,560	2,189	357	14	1,832 R	85.5%	13.9%	86.0%	14.0%
31,024	BEAUFORT	4,643	1,502	3,048	93	1,546 D	32.3%	65.6%	33.0%	67.0%
23,993	BERTIE	1,949	159	1,785	5	1,626 D	8.2%	91.6%	8.2%	91.8%
19,761	BLADEN	2,360	786	1,551	23	765 D	33.3%	65.7%	33.6%	66.4%
14,876	BRUNSWICK	2,455	1,296	1,118	41	178 R	52.8%	45.5%	53.7%	46.3%
64,148	BUNCOMBE	16,850	6,285	10,098	467	3,813 D	37.3%	59.9%	38.4%	61.6%
23,297	BURKE	7,327	3,190	4,137		947 D	43.5%	56.5%	43.5%	56.5%
33,730	CABARRUS	8,148	3,510	4,449	189	939 D	43.1%	54.6%	44.1%	55.9%
19,984	CALDWELL	5,877	2,503	3,348	26	845 D	42.6%	57.0%	42.8%	57.2%
5,382	CAMDEN	577	132	436	9	304 D	22.9%	75.6%	23.2%	76.8%
15,384	CARTERET	4,130	1,854	2,261	15	407 D	44.9%	54.7%	45.1%	54.9%
15,759	CASWELL	1,546	467	1,075	4	608 D	30.2%	69.5%	30.3%	69.7%
33,839	CATAWBA	11,919	5,998	5,754	167	244 R	50.3%	48.3%	51.0%	49.0%
23,814	CHATHAM	6,216	2,755	3,446	15	691 D	44.3%	55.4%	44.4%	55.6%
15,242	CHEROKEE	4,079	2,314	1,742	23	572 R	56.7%	42.7%	57.1%	42.9%
10,649	CHOWAN	817	98	714	5	616 D	12.0%	87.4%	12.1%	87.9%
4,646	CLAY	2,061	1,090	953	18	137 R	52.9%	46.2%	53.4%	46.6%
34,272	CLEVELAND	5,529	1,743	3,749	37	2,006 D	31.5%	67.8%	31.7%	68.3%
30,124	COLUMBUS	4,412	1,629	2,757	26	1,128 D	36.9%	62.5%	37.1%	62.9%
29,048	CRAVEN	3,311	325	2,942	44	2,617 D	9.8%	88.9%	9.9%	90.1%
35,064	CUMBERLAND	4,332	1,372	2,923	37	1,551 D	31.7%	67.5%	31.9%	68.1%
7,268	CURRITUCK	735	52	670	13	618 D	7.1%	91.2%	7.2%	92.8%
5,115	DARE	1,457	629	826	2	197 D	43.2%	56.7%	43.2%	56.8%
35,201	DAVIDSON	12,790	6,227	6,507	56	280 D	48.7%	50.9%	48.9%	51.1%
13,578	DAVIE	4,480	2,672	1,795	13	877 R	59.6%	40.1%	59.8%	40.2%
30,223	DUPLIN	4,503	1,542	2,924	37	1,382 D	34.2%	64.9%	34.5%	65.5%
42,219	DURHAM	8,151	3,093	4,837	221	1,744 D	37.9%	59.3%	39.0%	61.0%
37,995	EDGECOMBE	2,554	171	2,274	109	2,103 D	6.7%	89.0%	7.0%	93.0%
77,269	FORSYTH	13,178	5,315	7,404	459	2,089 D	40.3%	56.2%	41.8%	58.2%
26,667	FRANKLIN	2,306	302	1,991	13	1,689 D	13.1%	86.3%	13.2%	86.8%
51,242	GASTON	10,202	3,566	6,554	82	2,988 D	35.0%	64.2%	35.2%	64.8%
10,537	GATES	895	215	679	1	464 D	24.0%	75.9%	24.0%	76.0%
4,872	GRAHAM	1,759	907	841	11	66 R	51.6%	47.8%	51.9%	48.1%
26,846	GRANVILLE	2,695	461	2,220	14	1,759 D	17.1%	82.4%	17.2%	82.8%
16,212	GREENE	1,308	182	1,119	7	937 D	13.9%	85.6%	14.0%	86.0%
79,272	GUILFORD	15,943	6,822	8,804	317	1,982 D	42.8%	55.2%	43.7%	56.3%
43,766	HALIFAX	3,583	268	3,232	83	2,964 D	7.5%	90.2%	7.7%	92.3%
28,313	HARNETT	6,202	2,895	3,296	11	401 D	46.7%	53.1%	46.8%	53.2%
23,496	HAYWOOD	7,030	2,440	4,582	8	2,142 D	34.7%	65.2%	34.7%	65.3%
18,248	HENDERSON	6,603	3,548	3,007	48	541 R	53.7%	45.5%	54.1%	45.9%
16,294	HERTFORD	1,099	164	932	3	768 D	14.9%	84.8%	15.0%	85.0%
11,722	HOKE	1,291	141	1,146	4	1,005 D	10.9%	88.8%	11.0%	89.0%
8,386	HYDE	974	305	653	16	348 D	31.3%	67.0%	31.8%	68.2%
37,956	IREDELL	10,150	3,565	6,449	136	2,884 D	35.1%	63.5%	35.6%	64.4%
13,396	JACKSON	5,905	2,788	3,100	17	312 D	47.2%	52.5%	47.4%	52.6%
48,998	JOHNSTON	9,589	4,910	4,656	23	254 R	51.2%	48.6%	51.3%	48.7%
9,912	JONES	873	179	692	2	513 D	20.5%	79.3%	20.6%	79.4%
13,400	LEE	2,554	710	1,834	10	1,124 D	27.8%	71.8%	27.9%	72.1%
29,555	LENOIR	2,730	514	2,191	25	1,677 D	18.8%	80.3%	19.0%	81.0%
17,862	LINCOLN	5,609	2,658	2,909	42	251 D	47.4%	51.9%	47.7%	52.3%
16,763	MCDOWELL	5,638	2,590	3,023	25	433 D	45.9%	53.6%	46.1%	53.9%
12,887	MACON	4,211	2,015	2,178	18	163 D	47.9%	51.7%	48.1%	51.9%
20,083	MADISON	4,797	3,252	1,471	74	1,781 R	67.8%	30.7%	68.9%	31.1%
20,828	MARTIN	2,224	216	1,999	9	1,783 D	9.7%	89.9%	9.8%	90.2%
80,695	MECKLENBURG	11,452	2,572	8,443	437	5,871 D	22.5%	73.7%	23.3%	76.7%

NORTH CAROLINA

PRESIDENT 1924

1920 Census Population	County	Total Vote	Republican	Democratic	Other	Rep.-Dem. Plurality	Percentage Total Vote Rep.	Total Vote Dem.	Major Vote Rep.	Major Vote Dem.
11,278	MITCHELL	2,237	1,540	689	8	851 R	68.8%	30.8%	69.1%	30.9%
14,607	MONTGOMERY	4,565	2,077	2,483	5	406 D	45.5%	54.4%	45.5%	54.5%
21,388	MOORE	4,783	1,974	2,771	38	797 D	41.3%	57.9%	41.6%	58.4%
41,061	NASH	4,083	823	3,129	131	2,306 D	20.2%	76.6%	20.8%	79.2%
40,620	NEW HANOVER	6,330	1,190	4,735	405	3,545 D	18.8%	74.8%	20.1%	79.9%
23,184	NORTHAMPTON	1,823	144	1,662	17	1,518 D	7.9%	91.2%	8.0%	92.0%
14,703	ONSLOW	1,576	423	1,122	31	699 D	26.8%	71.2%	27.4%	72.6%
17,895	ORANGE	3,010	1,065	1,879	66	814 D	35.4%	62.4%	36.2%	63.8%
9,060	PAMLICO	1,257	459	798		339 D	36.5%	63.5%	36.5%	63.5%
17,670	PASQUOTANK	1,553	305	1,236	12	931 D	19.6%	79.6%	19.8%	80.2%
14,788	PENDER	1,445	253	1,175	17	922 D	17.5%	81.3%	17.7%	82.3%
11,137	PERQUIMANS	853	295	550	8	255 D	34.6%	64.5%	34.9%	65.1%
18,973	PERSON	2,604	1,025	1,576	3	551 D	39.4%	60.5%	39.4%	60.6%
45,569	PITT	3,765	512	3,197	56	2,685 D	13.6%	84.9%	13.8%	86.2%
8,832	POLK	3,071	1,445	1,613	13	168 D	47.1%	52.5%	47.3%	52.7%
30,856	RANDOLPH	11,757	6,336	5,397	24	939 R	53.9%	45.9%	54.0%	46.0%
25,567	RICHMOND	3,237	599	2,475	163	1,876 D	18.5%	76.5%	19.5%	80.5%
54,674	ROBESON	4,392	314	4,064	14	3,750 D	7.1%	92.5%	7.2%	92.8%
44,149	ROCKINGHAM	7,122	2,566	4,467	89	1,901 D	36.0%	62.7%	36.5%	63.5%
44,062	ROWAN	9,114	3,560	4,816	738	1,256 D	39.1%	52.8%	42.5%	57.5%
31,426	RUTHERFORD	9,027	3,897	5,101	29	1,204 D	43.2%	56.5%	43.3%	56.7%
36,002	SAMPSON	5,244	3,188	2,021	35	1,167 R	60.8%	38.5%	61.2%	38.8%
15,600	SCOTLAND	1,685	205	1,469	11	1,264 D	12.2%	87.2%	12.2%	87.8%
27,429	STANLY	7,476	3,594	3,832	50	238 D	48.1%	51.3%	48.4%	51.6%
20,575	STOKES	4,835	2,482	2,309	44	173 R	51.3%	47.8%	51.8%	48.2%
32,464	SURRY	9,474	4,990	4,418	66	572 R	52.7%	46.6%	53.0%	47.0%
13,224	SWAIN	3,971	2,178	1,769	24	409 R	54.8%	44.5%	55.2%	44.8%
9,303	TRANSYLVANIA	3,612	1,814	1,776	22	38 R	50.2%	49.2%	50.5%	49.5%
4,849	TYRRELL	1,081	442	638	1	196 D	40.9%	59.0%	40.9%	59.1%
36,029	UNION	3,425	672	2,721	32	2,049 D	19.6%	79.4%	19.8%	80.2%
22,799	VANCE	2,504	470	2,013	21	1,543 D	18.8%	80.4%	18.9%	81.1%
75,155	WAKE	11,836	2,975	8,376	485	5,401 D	25.1%	70.8%	26.2%	73.8%
21,593	WARREN	1,970	166	1,742	62	1,576 D	8.4%	88.4%	8.7%	91.3%
11,429	WASHINGTON	1,723	834	883	6	49 D	48.4%	51.2%	48.6%	51.4%
13,477	WATAUGA	5,038	2,665	2,365	8	300 R	52.9%	46.9%	53.0%	47.0%
43,640	WAYNE	4,787	1,379	3,366	42	1,987 D	28.8%	70.3%	29.1%	70.9%
32,644	WILKES	9,728	6,131	3,586	11	2,545 R	63.0%	36.9%	63.1%	36.9%
36,813	WILSON	3,274	574	2,619	81	2,045 D	17.5%	80.0%	18.0%	82.0%
16,391	YADKIN	4,281	2,889	1,381	11	1,508 R	67.5%	32.3%	67.7%	32.3%
15,093	YANCEY	4,769	2,156	2,592	21	436 D	45.2%	54.4%	45.4%	54.6%
2,559,123	TOTAL	481,608	190,754	284,190	6,664	93,436 D	39.6%	59.0%	40.2%	59.8%

NORTH CAROLINA

PRESIDENT 1920

1920 Census Population	County	Total Vote	Republican	Democratic	Other	Rep.-Dem. Plurality	Percentage Total Vote Rep.	Total Vote Dem.	Major Vote Rep.	Major Vote Dem.
32,718	ALAMANCE	9,874	4,619	5,255		636 D	46.8%	53.2%	46.8%	53.2%
12,212	ALEXANDER	4,688	2,643	2,045		598 R	56.4%	43.6%	56.4%	43.6%
7,403	ALLEGHANY	2,610	1,201	1,409		208 D	46.0%	54.0%	46.0%	54.0%
28,334	ANSON	3,608	433	3,175		2,742 D	12.0%	88.0%	12.0%	88.0%
21,001	ASHE	7,239	3,808	3,431		377 R	52.6%	47.4%	52.6%	47.4%
10,335	AVERY	2,900	2,503	397		2,106 R	86.3%	13.7%	86.3%	13.7%
31,024	BEAUFORT	5,788	2,266	3,522		1,256 D	39.1%	60.9%	39.1%	60.9%
23,993	BERTIE	2,052	212	1,840		1,628 D	10.3%	89.7%	10.3%	89.7%
19,761	BLADEN	3,003	1,064	1,939		875 D	35.4%	64.6%	35.4%	64.6%
14,876	BRUNSWICK	2,615	1,362	1,253		109 R	52.1%	47.9%	52.1%	47.9%
64,148	BUNCOMBE	18,184	8,017	10,167		2,150 D	44.1%	55.9%	44.1%	55.9%
23,297	BURKE	6,854	3,592	3,262		330 R	52.4%	47.6%	52.4%	47.6%
33,730	CABARRUS	9,566	5,148	4,418		730 R	53.8%	46.2%	53.8%	46.2%
19,984	CALDWELL	6,229	3,298	2,931		367 R	52.9%	47.1%	52.9%	47.1%
5,382	CAMDEN	682	142	540		398 D	20.8%	79.2%	20.8%	79.2%
15,384	CARTERET	4,385	2,315	2,070		245 R	52.8%	47.2%	52.8%	47.2%
15,759	CASWELL	1,744	505	1,239		734 D	29.0%	71.0%	29.0%	71.0%
33,839	CATAWBA	11,339	5,935	5,404		531 R	52.3%	47.7%	52.3%	47.7%
23,814	CHATHAM	6,092	2,906	3,186		280 D	47.7%	52.3%	47.7%	52.3%
15,242	CHEROKEE	4,267	2,506	1,761		745 R	58.7%	41.3%	58.7%	41.3%
10,649	CHOWAN	1,300	209	1,091		882 D	16.1%	83.9%	16.1%	83.9%
4,646	CLAY	1,666	911	755		156 R	54.7%	45.3%	54.7%	45.3%
34,272	CLEVELAND	8,134	2,953	5,181		2,228 D	36.3%	63.7%	36.3%	63.7%
30,124	COLUMBUS	4,894	1,783	3,111		1,328 D	36.4%	63.6%	36.4%	63.6%
29,048	CRAVEN	4,144	731	3,413		2,682 D	17.6%	82.4%	17.6%	82.4%
35,064	CUMBERLAND	5,205	1,972	3,233		1,261 D	37.9%	62.1%	37.9%	62.1%
7,268	CURRITUCK	1,086	86	1,000		914 D	7.9%	92.1%	7.9%	92.1%
5,115	DARE	1,457	632	825		193 D	43.4%	56.6%	43.4%	56.6%
35,201	DAVIDSON	10,757	5,960	4,797		1,163 R	55.4%	44.6%	55.4%	44.6%
13,578	DAVIE	4,215	2,591	1,624		967 R	61.5%	38.5%	61.5%	38.5%
30,223	DUPLIN	6,095	2,697	3,398		701 D	44.2%	55.8%	44.2%	55.8%
42,219	DURHAM	8,196	3,550	4,646		1,096 D	43.3%	56.7%	43.3%	56.7%
37,995	EDGECOMBE	3,367	24	3,343		3,319 D	0.7%	99.3%	0.7%	99.3%
77,269	FORSYTH	14,915	6,792	8,123		1,331 D	45.5%	54.5%	45.5%	54.5%
26,667	FRANKLIN	3,331	589	2,742		2,153 D	17.7%	82.3%	17.7%	82.3%
51,242	GASTON	12,951	5,803	7,148		1,345 D	44.8%	55.2%	44.8%	55.2%
10,537	GATES	1,123	327	796		469 D	29.1%	70.9%	29.1%	70.9%
4,872	GRAHAM	1,559	915	644		271 R	58.7%	41.3%	58.7%	41.3%
26,846	GRANVILLE	3,455	833	2,622		1,789 D	24.1%	75.9%	24.1%	75.9%
16,212	GREENE	2,088	439	1,649		1,210 D	21.0%	79.0%	21.0%	79.0%
79,272	GUILFORD	17,535	7,920	9,615		1,695 D	45.2%	54.8%	45.2%	54.8%
43,766	HALIFAX	3,953	524	3,429		2,905 D	13.3%	86.7%	13.3%	86.7%
28,313	HARNETT	7,230	3,311	3,919		608 D	45.8%	54.2%	45.8%	54.2%
23,496	HAYWOOD	7,229	3,000	4,229		1,229 D	41.5%	58.5%	41.5%	58.5%
18,248	HENDERSON	5,833	3,337	2,496		841 R	57.2%	42.8%	57.2%	42.8%
16,294	HERTFORD	1,325	221	1,104		883 D	16.7%	83.3%	16.7%	83.3%
11,722	HOKE	1,432	166	1,266		1,100 D	11.6%	88.4%	11.6%	88.4%
8,386	HYDE	1,664	530	1,134		604 D	31.9%	68.1%	31.9%	68.1%
37,956	IREDELL	10,872	4,402	6,470		2,068 D	40.5%	59.5%	40.5%	59.5%
13,396	JACKSON	4,740	2,355	2,385		30 D	49.7%	50.3%	49.7%	50.3%
48,998	JOHNSTON	11,618	5,588	6,030		442 D	48.1%	51.9%	48.1%	51.9%
9,912	JONES	1,349	385	964		579 D	28.5%	71.5%	28.5%	71.5%
13,400	LEE	3,470	1,143	2,327		1,184 D	32.9%	67.1%	32.9%	67.1%
29,555	LENOIR	3,713	1,153	2,560		1,407 D	31.1%	68.9%	31.1%	68.9%
17,862	LINCOLN	6,468	3,137	3,331		194 D	48.5%	51.5%	48.5%	51.5%
16,763	MCDOWELL	5,370	2,561	2,809		248 D	47.7%	52.3%	47.7%	52.3%
12,887	MACON	4,227	2,050	2,177		127 D	48.5%	51.5%	48.5%	51.5%
20,083	MADISON	4,956	3,616	1,340		2,276 R	73.0%	27.0%	73.0%	27.0%
20,828	MARTIN	3,091	530	2,561		2,031 D	17.1%	82.9%	17.1%	82.9%
80,695	MECKLENBURG	14,734	3,421	11,313		7,892 D	23.2%	76.8%	23.2%	76.8%

NORTH CAROLINA

PRESIDENT 1920

1920 Census Population	County	Total Vote	Republican	Democratic	Other	Rep.-Dem. Plurality	Percentage Total Vote Rep.	Total Vote Dem.	Major Vote Rep.	Major Vote Dem.
11,278	MITCHELL	2,850	2,153	697		1,456 R	75.5%	24.5%	75.5%	24.5%
14,607	MONTGOMERY	4,625	2,304	2,321		17 D	49.8%	50.2%	49.8%	50.2%
21,388	MOORE	4,958	2,279	2,679		400 D	46.0%	54.0%	46.0%	54.0%
41,061	NASH	5,587	1,556	4,031		2,475 D	27.9%	72.1%	27.9%	72.1%
40,620	NEW HANOVER	4,814	712	4,102		3,390 D	14.8%	85.2%	14.8%	85.2%
23,184	NORTHAMPTON	2,470	165	2,305		2,140 D	6.7%	93.3%	6.7%	93.3%
14,703	ONSLOW	2,410	853	1,557		704 D	35.4%	64.6%	35.4%	64.6%
17,895	ORANGE	3,730	1,737	1,993		256 D	46.6%	53.4%	46.6%	53.4%
9,060	PAMLICO	2,294	1,008	1,286		278 D	43.9%	56.1%	43.9%	56.1%
17,670	PASQUOTANK	2,243	507	1,736		1,229 D	22.6%	77.4%	22.6%	77.4%
14,788	PENDER	2,279	699	1,580		881 D	30.7%	69.3%	30.7%	69.3%
11,137	PERQUIMANS	1,529	487	1,042		555 D	31.9%	68.1%	31.9%	68.1%
18,973	PERSON	3,212	1,566	1,646		80 D	48.8%	51.2%	48.8%	51.2%
45,569	PITT	5,060	864	4,196		3,332 D	17.1%	82.9%	17.1%	82.9%
8,832	POLK	2,687	1,326	1,361		35 D	49.3%	50.7%	49.3%	50.7%
30,856	RANDOLPH	11,407	6,297	5,110		1,187 R	55.2%	44.8%	55.2%	44.8%
25,567	RICHMOND	4,465	1,124	3,341		2,217 D	25.2%	74.8%	25.2%	74.8%
54,674	ROBESON	8,403	2,220	6,183		3,963 D	26.4%	73.6%	26.4%	73.6%
44,149	ROCKINGHAM	8,112	3,605	4,507		902 D	44.4%	55.6%	44.4%	55.6%
44,062	ROWAN	11,309	4,888	6,421		1,533 D	43.2%	56.8%	43.2%	56.8%
31,426	RUTHERFORD	9,116	4,015	5,101		1,086 D	44.0%	56.0%	44.0%	56.0%
36,002	SAMPSON	7,779	5,353	2,426		2,927 R	68.8%	31.2%	68.8%	31.2%
15,600	SCOTLAND	2,011	306	1,705		1,399 D	15.2%	84.8%	15.2%	84.8%
27,429	STANLY	8,155	4,312	3,843		469 R	52.9%	47.1%	52.9%	47.1%
20,575	STOKES	4,925	2,926	1,999		927 R	59.4%	40.6%	59.4%	40.6%
32,464	SURRY	8,717	5,170	3,547		1,623 R	59.3%	40.7%	59.3%	40.7%
13,224	SWAIN	3,673	2,239	1,434		805 R	61.0%	39.0%	61.0%	39.0%
9,303	TRANSYLVANIA	3,222	1,680	1,542		138 R	52.1%	47.9%	52.1%	47.9%
4,849	TYRRELL	1,250	532	718		186 D	42.6%	57.4%	42.6%	57.4%
36,029	UNION	5,572	1,404	4,168		2,764 D	25.2%	74.8%	25.2%	74.8%
22,799	VANCE	3,277	816	2,461		1,645 D	24.9%	75.1%	24.9%	75.1%
75,155	WAKE	11,673	3,653	8,020		4,367 D	31.3%	68.7%	31.3%	68.7%
21,593	WARREN	2,160	295	1,865		1,570 D	13.7%	86.3%	13.7%	86.3%
11,429	WASHINGTON	2,087	971	1,116		145 D	46.5%	53.5%	46.5%	53.5%
13,477	WATAUGA	4,352	2,631	1,721		910 R	60.5%	39.5%	60.5%	39.5%
43,640	WAYNE	7,616	2,822	4,794		1,972 D	37.1%	62.9%	37.1%	62.9%
32,644	WILKES	9,294	6,451	2,843		3,608 R	69.4%	30.6%	69.4%	30.6%
36,813	WILSON	4,870	1,374	3,496		2,122 D	28.2%	71.8%	28.2%	71.8%
16,391	YADKIN	4,651	3,301	1,350		1,951 R	71.0%	29.0%	71.0%	29.0%
15,093	YANCEY	4,876	2,596	2,280		316 R	53.2%	46.8%	53.2%	46.8%
2,559,123	TOTAL	538,649	232,819	305,367	463	72,548 D	43.2%	56.7%	43.3%	56.7%

NORTH CAROLINA

ELECTION NOTES

1956

1952

1948 Other vote was 69,652 Thurmond (States Rights); 3,915 Wallace (Progressive). States Rights candidates ran second in several counties.

1944

1940

1936 Other vote was 21 Thomas (Socialist); 11 Browder (Communist); 2 Lemke (Union); 6 scattered write-in.

1932 Other vote was Thomas (Socialist).

1928

1924 Other vote was 6,651 LaFollette (Progressive); 13 Faris (Prohibition). The statewide total in the other vote column includes the Prohibition vote which was not reported by county.

1920 Other vote was 446 Debs (Socialist); 17 Watkins (Prohibition). The statewide total in the other vote column is the minor party vote which was not reported by county.

NORTH DAKOTA

POPULAR VOTE FOR PRESIDENT 1920 TO 1956

		Republican		Democratic				Percentage			
								Total Vote		Major Vote	
Year	Total Vote	Vote	Candidate	Vote	Candidate	Other Vote	Plurality	Rep.	Dem.	Rep.	Dem.
1956	253,991	156,766	Eisenhower, Dwight D.	96,742	Stevenson, Adlai E.	483	60,024 R	61.7%	38.1%	61.8%	38.2%
1952	270,127	191,712	Eisenhower, Dwight D.	76,694	Stevenson, Adlai E.	1,721	115,018 R	71.0%	28.4%	71.4%	28.6%
1948	220,716	115,139	Dewey, Thomas E.	95,812	Truman, Harry S.	9,765	19,327 R	52.2%	43.4%	54.6%	45.4%
1944	220,182	118,535	Dewey, Thomas E.	100,144	Roosevelt, Franklin D.	1,503	18,391 R	53.8%	45.5%	54.2%	45.8%
1940	280,775	154,590	Willkie, Wendell	124,036	Roosevelt, Franklin D.	2,149	30,554 R	55.1%	44.2%	55.5%	44.5%
1936	273,716	72,751	Landon, Alfred M.	163,148	Roosevelt, Franklin D.	37,817	90,397 D	26.6%	59.6%	30.8%	69.2%
1932	256,290	71,772	Hoover, Herbert C.	178,350	Roosevelt, Franklin D.	6,168	106,578 D	28.0%	69.6%	28.7%	71.3%
1928	239,845	131,419	Hoover, Herbert C.	106,648	Smith, Alfred E.	1,778	24,771 R	54.8%	44.5%	55.2%	44.8%
1924 **	199,081	94,931	Coolidge, Calvin	13,858	Davis, John W.	90,292	5,009 R	47.7%	7.0%	87.3%	12.7%
1920	205,786	160,082	Harding, Warren G.	37,422	Cox, James M.	8,282	122,660 R	77.8%	18.2%	81.1%	18.9%

In 1924 other vote was 89,922 Progressive and 370 Communist.

ELECTORAL COLLEGE VOTE 1920 TO 1956

Year	Total	Republican	Democratic	Other
1956	4	4	—	—
1952	4	4	—	—
1948	4	4	—	—
1944	4	4	—	—
1940	4	4	—	—
1936	4	—	4	—
1932	4	—	4	—
1928	5	5	—	—
1924	5	5	—	—
1920	5	5	—	—

NORTH DAKOTA

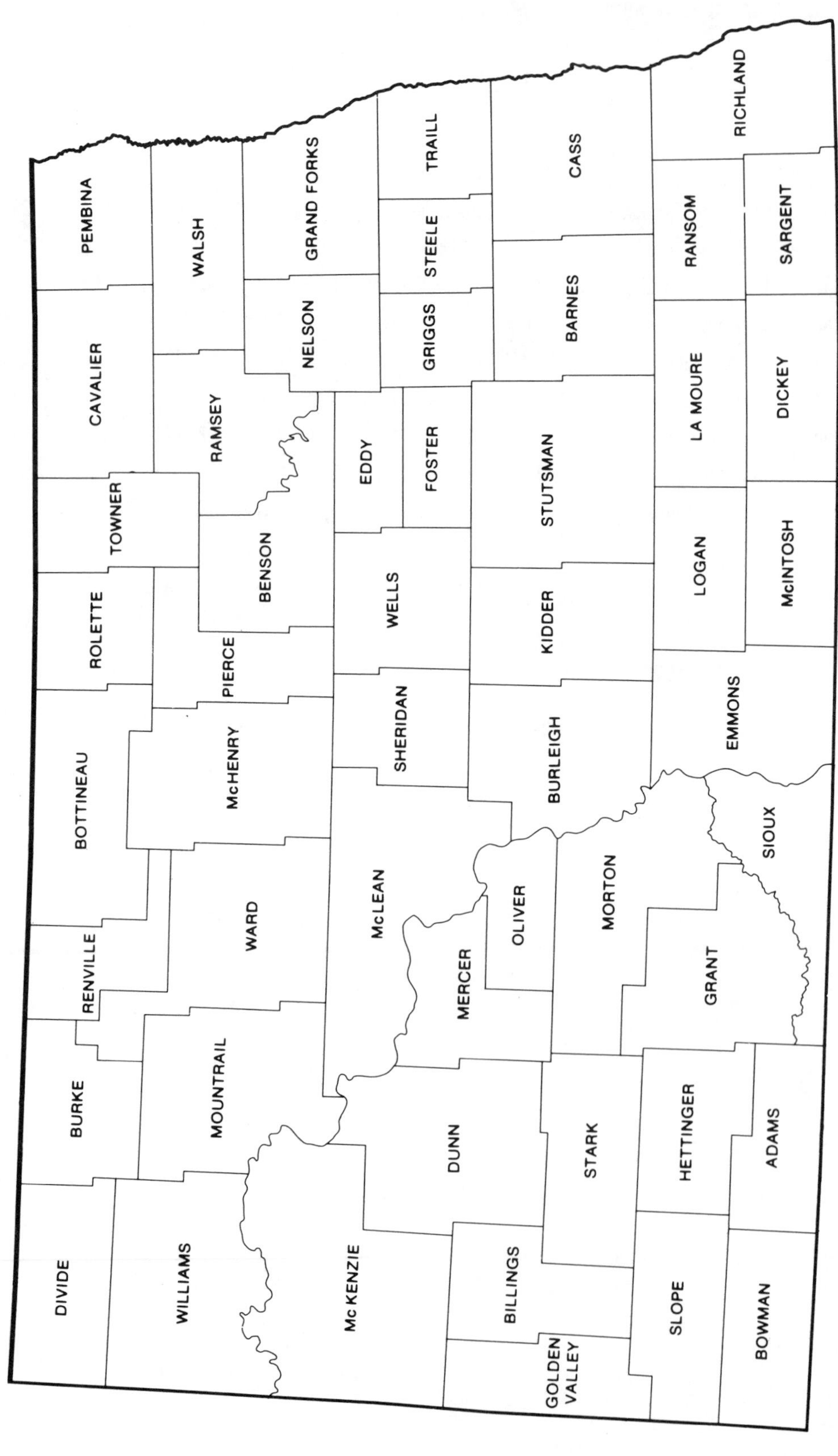

NORTH DAKOTA

PRESIDENT 1956

1950 Census Population	County	Total Vote	Republican	Democratic	Other	Rep.-Dem. Plurality	Percentage Total Vote Rep.	Percentage Total Vote Dem.	Percentage Major Vote Rep.	Percentage Major Vote Dem.
4,910	ADAMS	2,063	1,338	723	2	615 R	64.9%	35.0%	64.9%	35.1%
16,884	BARNES	7,219	4,475	2,730	14	1,745 R	62.0%	37.8%	62.1%	37.9%
10,675	BENSON	4,203	2,340	1,851	12	489 R	55.7%	44.0%	55.8%	44.2%
1,777	BILLINGS	689	437	248	4	189 R	63.4%	36.0%	63.8%	36.2%
12,140	BOTTINEAU	4,646	2,923	1,718	5	1,205 R	62.9%	37.0%	63.0%	37.0%
4,001	BOWMAN	1,726	1,007	715	4	292 R	58.3%	41.4%	58.5%	41.5%
6,621	BURKE	2,359	1,415	936	8	479 R	60.0%	39.7%	60.2%	39.8%
25,673	BURLEIGH	12,467	9,199	3,231	37	5,968 R	73.8%	25.9%	74.0%	26.0%
58,877	CASS	26,770	16,932	9,821	17	7,111 R	63.2%	36.7%	63.3%	36.7%
11,840	CAVALIER	4,295	2,450	1,836	9	614 R	57.0%	42.7%	57.2%	42.8%
9,121	DICKEY	3,770	2,327	1,435	8	892 R	61.7%	38.1%	61.9%	38.1%
5,967	DIVIDE	2,493	1,296	1,194	3	102 R	52.0%	47.9%	52.0%	48.0%
7,212	DUNN	2,628	1,567	1,055	6	512 R	59.6%	40.1%	59.8%	40.2%
5,372	EDDY	2,212	1,239	973		266 R	56.0%	44.0%	56.0%	44.0%
9,715	EMMONS	3,617	2,789	825	3	1,964 R	77.1%	22.8%	77.2%	22.8%
5,337	FOSTER	2,306	1,234	1,062	10	172 R	53.5%	46.1%	53.7%	46.3%
3,499	GOLDEN VALLEY	1,397	824	567	6	257 R	59.0%	40.6%	59.2%	40.8%
39,443	GRAND FORKS	16,550	10,289	6,231	30	4,058 R	62.2%	37.6%	62.3%	37.7%
7,114	GRANT	2,599	1,872	718	9	1,154 R	72.0%	27.6%	72.3%	27.7%
5,460	GRIGGS	2,387	1,212	1,173	2	39 R	50.8%	49.1%	50.8%	49.2%
7,100	HETTINGER	2,682	1,882	796	4	1,086 R	70.2%	29.7%	70.3%	29.7%
6,168	KIDDER	2,237	1,523	708	6	815 R	68.1%	31.6%	68.3%	31.7%
9,498	LA MOURE	4,134	2,433	1,694	7	739 R	58.9%	41.0%	59.0%	41.0%
6,357	LOGAN	2,358	1,807	547	4	1,260 R	76.6%	23.2%	76.8%	23.2%
12,556	MCHENRY	4,860	3,019	1,825	16	1,194 R	62.1%	37.6%	62.3%	37.7%
7,590	MCINTOSH	3,193	2,689	498	6	2,191 R	84.2%	15.6%	84.4%	15.6%
6,849	MCKENZIE	3,027	1,609	1,405	13	204 R	53.2%	46.4%	53.4%	46.6%
18,824	MCLEAN	6,280	3,653	2,609	18	1,044 R	58.2%	41.5%	58.3%	41.7%
8,686	MERCER	3,227	2,555	666	6	1,889 R	79.2%	20.6%	79.3%	20.7%
19,295	MORTON	7,890	5,232	2,628	30	2,604 R	66.3%	33.3%	66.6%	33.4%
9,418	MOUNTRAIL	3,597	1,699	1,891	7	192 D	47.2%	52.6%	47.3%	52.7%
8,090	NELSON	3,617	1,821	1,794	2	27 R	50.3%	49.6%	50.4%	49.6%
3,091	OLIVER	1,079	788	279	12	509 R	73.0%	25.9%	73.9%	26.1%
13,990	PEMBINA	4,977	3,077	1,887	13	1,190 R	61.8%	37.9%	62.0%	38.0%
8,326	PIERCE	3,342	1,997	1,340	5	657 R	59.8%	40.1%	59.8%	40.2%
14,373	RAMSEY	5,930	3,821	2,103	6	1,718 R	64.4%	35.5%	64.5%	35.5%
8,876	RANSOM	4,174	2,361	1,808	5	553 R	56.6%	43.3%	56.6%	43.4%
5,405	RENVILLE	2,061	1,035	1,025	1	10 R	50.2%	49.7%	50.2%	49.8%
19,865	RICHLAND	8,154	4,971	3,171	12	1,800 R	61.0%	38.9%	61.1%	38.9%
11,102	ROLETTE	3,178	1,444	1,728	6	284 D	45.4%	54.4%	45.5%	54.5%
7,616	SARGENT	3,142	1,662	1,473	7	189 R	52.9%	46.9%	53.0%	47.0%
5,253	SHERIDAN	2,118	1,646	472		1,174 R	77.7%	22.3%	77.7%	22.3%
3,696	SIOUX	1,197	718	476	3	242 R	60.0%	39.8%	60.1%	39.9%
2,315	SLOPE	833	433	397	3	36 R	52.0%	47.7%	52.2%	47.8%
16,137	STARK	6,040	4,251	1,778	11	2,473 R	70.4%	29.4%	70.5%	29.5%
5,145	STEELE	2,337	1,188	1,148	1	40 R	50.8%	49.1%	50.9%	49.1%
24,158	STUTSMAN	9,554	5,718	3,825	11	1,893 R	59.8%	40.0%	59.9%	40.1%
6,360	TOWNER	2,564	1,391	1,169	4	222 R	54.3%	45.6%	54.3%	45.7%
11,359	TRAILL	5,062	3,090	1,969	3	1,121 R	61.0%	38.9%	61.1%	38.9%
18,859	WALSH	7,200	3,946	3,238	16	708 R	54.8%	45.0%	54.9%	45.1%
34,782	WARD	14,832	9,042	5,762	28	3,280 R	61.0%	38.8%	61.1%	38.9%
10,417	WELLS	4,355	2,912	1,434	9	1,478 R	66.9%	32.9%	67.0%	33.0%
16,442	WILLIAMS	8,364	4,188	4,157	19	31 R	50.1%	49.7%	50.2%	49.8%
619,636	TOTAL	253,991	156,766	96,742	483	60,024 R	61.7%	38.1%	61.8%	38.2%

NORTH DAKOTA

PRESIDENT 1952

1950 Census Population	County	Total Vote	Republican	Democratic	Other	Rep.-Dem. Plurality	Percentage Total Vote Rep.	Total Vote Dem.	Major Vote Rep.	Major Vote Dem.
4,910	ADAMS	2,213	1,561	633	19	928 R	70.5%	28.6%	71.1%	28.9%
16,884	BARNES	7,703	5,534	2,120	49	3,414 R	71.8%	27.5%	72.3%	27.7%
10,675	BENSON	4,584	3,192	1,353	39	1,839 R	69.6%	29.5%	70.2%	29.8%
1,777	BILLINGS	822	674	143	5	531 R	82.0%	17.4%	82.5%	17.5%
12,140	BOTTINEAU	5,034	3,911	1,094	29	2,817 R	77.7%	21.7%	78.1%	21.9%
4,001	BOWMAN	1,931	1,375	540	16	835 R	71.2%	28.0%	71.8%	28.2%
6,621	BURKE	2,841	1,986	811	44	1,175 R	69.9%	28.5%	71.0%	29.0%
25,673	BURLEIGH	11,975	9,526	2,400	49	7,126 R	79.5%	20.0%	79.9%	20.1%
58,877	CASS	27,344	18,094	9,193	57	8,901 R	66.2%	33.6%	66.3%	33.7%
11,840	CAVALIER	5,052	3,519	1,496	37	2,023 R	69.7%	29.6%	70.2%	29.8%
9,121	DICKEY	4,095	2,917	1,150	28	1,767 R	71.2%	28.1%	71.7%	28.3%
5,967	DIVIDE	2,824	1,999	807	18	1,192 R	70.8%	28.6%	71.2%	28.8%
7,212	DUNN	2,924	2,237	664	23	1,573 R	76.5%	22.7%	77.1%	22.9%
5,372	EDDY	2,288	1,534	728	26	806 R	67.0%	31.8%	67.8%	32.2%
9,715	EMMONS	3,910	3,369	522	19	2,847 R	86.2%	13.4%	86.6%	13.4%
5,337	FOSTER	2,428	1,558	862	8	696 R	64.2%	35.5%	64.4%	35.6%
3,499	GOLDEN VALLEY	1,562	1,186	376		810 R	75.9%	24.1%	75.9%	24.1%
39,443	GRAND FORKS	16,662	10,939	5,639	84	5,300 R	65.7%	33.8%	66.0%	34.0%
7,114	GRANT	2,889	2,465	403	21	2,062 R	85.3%	13.9%	85.9%	14.1%
5,460	GRIGGS	2,609	1,727	872	10	855 R	66.2%	33.4%	66.4%	33.6%
7,100	HETTINGER	2,654	2,330	297	27	2,033 R	87.8%	11.2%	88.7%	11.3%
6,168	KIDDER	2,679	2,195	468	16	1,727 R	81.9%	17.5%	82.4%	17.6%
9,498	LA MOURE	4,379	3,202	1,145	32	2,057 R	73.1%	26.1%	73.7%	26.3%
6,357	LOGAN	2,544	2,165	369	10	1,796 R	85.1%	14.5%	85.4%	14.6%
12,556	MCHENRY	5,518	4,227	1,228	63	2,999 R	76.6%	22.3%	77.5%	22.5%
7,590	MCINTOSH	3,348	3,043	276	29	2,767 R	90.9%	8.2%	91.7%	8.3%
6,849	MCKENZIE	3,152	2,260	846	46	1,414 R	71.7%	26.8%	72.8%	27.2%
18,824	MCLEAN	7,555	5,184	2,295	76	2,889 R	68.6%	30.4%	69.3%	30.7%
8,686	MERCER	3,524	2,994	512	18	2,482 R	85.0%	14.5%	85.4%	14.6%
19,295	MORTON	8,426	6,309	2,079	38	4,230 R	74.9%	24.7%	75.2%	24.8%
9,418	MOUNTRAIL	3,998	2,516	1,437	45	1,079 R	62.9%	35.9%	63.6%	36.4%
8,090	NELSON	3,880	2,443	1,418	19	1,025 R	63.0%	36.5%	63.3%	36.7%
3,091	OLIVER	1,289	1,132	143	14	989 R	87.8%	11.1%	88.8%	11.2%
13,990	PEMBINA	5,944	4,012	1,891	41	2,121 R	67.5%	31.8%	68.0%	32.0%
8,326	PIERCE	3,608	2,806	773	29	2,033 R	77.8%	21.4%	78.4%	21.6%
14,373	RAMSEY	6,489	4,670	1,794	25	2,876 R	72.0%	27.6%	72.2%	27.8%
8,876	RANSOM	4,347	3,051	1,265	31	1,786 R	70.2%	29.1%	70.7%	29.3%
5,405	RENVILLE	2,360	1,571	767	22	804 R	66.6%	32.5%	67.2%	32.8%
19,865	RICHLAND	8,630	6,022	2,541	67	3,481 R	69.8%	29.4%	70.3%	29.7%
11,102	ROLETTE	3,365	2,188	1,160	17	1,028 R	65.0%	34.5%	65.4%	34.6%
7,616	SARGENT	3,230	2,124	1,090	16	1,034 R	65.8%	33.7%	66.1%	33.9%
5,253	SHERIDAN	2,309	2,016	267	26	1,749 R	87.3%	11.6%	88.3%	11.7%
3,696	SIOUX	1,322	968	336	18	632 R	73.2%	25.4%	74.2%	25.8%
2,315	SLOPE	983	682	290	11	392 R	69.4%	29.5%	70.2%	29.8%
16,137	STARK	6,688	5,322	1,332	34	3,990 R	79.6%	19.9%	80.0%	20.0%
5,145	STEELE	2,434	1,513	911	10	602 R	62.2%	37.4%	62.4%	37.6%
24,158	STUTSMAN	9,916	6,713	3,156	47	3,557 R	67.7%	31.8%	68.0%	32.0%
6,360	TOWNER	2,831	1,960	843	28	1,117 R	69.2%	29.8%	69.9%	30.1%
11,359	TRAILL	5,391	3,884	1,484	23	2,400 R	72.0%	27.5%	72.4%	27.6%
18,859	WALSH	8,304	4,761	3,494	49	1,267 R	57.3%	42.1%	57.7%	42.3%
34,782	WARD	15,211	10,130	4,966	115	5,164 R	66.6%	32.6%	67.1%	32.9%
10,417	WELLS	4,762	3,709	1,016	37	2,693 R	77.9%	21.3%	78.5%	21.5%
16,442	WILLIAMS	7,367	4,307	2,999	61	1,308 R	58.5%	40.7%	59.0%	41.0%
619,636	TOTAL	270,127	191,712	76,694	1,721	115,018 R	71.0%	28.4%	71.4%	28.6%

NORTH DAKOTA

PRESIDENT 1948

1940 Census Population	County	Total Vote	Republican	Democratic	Other	Rep.-Dem. Plurality	Total Vote Rep.	Total Vote Dem.	Major Vote Rep.	Major Vote Dem.
4,664	ADAMS	1,780	908	753	119	155 R	51.0%	42.3%	54.7%	45.3%
17,814	BARNES	6,594	3,385	2,892	317	493 R	51.3%	43.9%	53.9%	46.1%
12,629	BENSON	4,331	1,920	2,216	195	296 D	44.3%	51.2%	46.4%	53.6%
2,531	BILLINGS	736	372	311	53	61 R	50.5%	42.3%	54.5%	45.5%
13,253	BOTTINEAU	4,231	2,513	1,571	147	942 R	59.4%	37.1%	61.5%	38.5%
3,860	BOWMAN	1,451	723	597	131	126 R	49.8%	41.1%	54.8%	45.2%
7,653	BURKE	2,379	1,212	972	195	240 R	50.9%	40.9%	55.5%	44.5%
22,736	BURLEIGH	8,493	5,049	3,117	327	1,932 R	59.4%	36.7%	61.8%	38.2%
52,849	CASS	21,836	11,430	9,937	469	1,493 R	52.3%	45.5%	53.5%	46.5%
13,923	CAVALIER	4,158	1,864	2,198	96	334 D	44.8%	52.9%	45.9%	54.1%
9,696	DICKEY	3,232	1,774	1,264	194	510 R	54.9%	39.1%	58.4%	41.6%
7,086	DIVIDE	2,038	981	887	170	94 R	48.1%	43.5%	52.5%	47.5%
8,376	DUNN	2,423	1,244	1,074	105	170 R	51.3%	44.3%	53.7%	46.3%
5,741	EDDY	2,032	952	919	161	33 R	46.9%	45.2%	50.9%	49.1%
11,699	EMMONS	3,503	2,223	1,187	93	1,036 R	63.5%	33.9%	65.2%	34.8%
5,824	FOSTER	2,093	938	1,089	66	151 D	44.8%	52.0%	46.3%	53.7%
3,498	GOLDEN VALLEY	1,401	788	585	28	203 R	56.2%	41.8%	57.4%	42.6%
34,518	GRAND FORKS	13,789	6,374	6,996	419	622 D	46.2%	50.7%	47.7%	52.3%
8,264	GRANT	2,323	1,555	689	79	866 R	66.9%	29.7%	69.3%	30.7%
5,818	GRIGGS	2,338	1,036	1,180	122	144 D	44.3%	50.5%	46.8%	53.2%
7,457	HETTINGER	2,358	1,517	752	89	765 R	64.3%	31.9%	66.9%	33.1%
6,692	KIDDER	2,370	1,510	773	87	737 R	63.7%	32.6%	66.1%	33.9%
10,298	LA MOURE	3,708	1,999	1,481	228	518 R	53.9%	39.9%	57.4%	42.6%
7,561	LOGAN	2,218	1,585	557	76	1,028 R	71.5%	25.1%	74.0%	26.0%
14,034	MCHENRY	4,567	2,578	1,770	219	808 R	56.4%	38.8%	59.3%	40.7%
8,984	MCINTOSH	2,776	2,203	513	60	1,690 R	79.4%	18.5%	81.1%	18.9%
8,426	MCKENZIE	2,591	1,168	1,227	196	59 D	45.1%	47.4%	48.8%	51.2%
16,082	MCLEAN	5,513	2,762	2,283	468	479 R	50.1%	41.4%	54.7%	45.3%
9,611	MERCER	2,948	2,219	643	86	1,576 R	75.3%	21.8%	77.5%	22.5%
20,184	MORTON	6,394	3,607	2,521	266	1,086 R	56.4%	39.4%	58.9%	41.1%
10,482	MOUNTRAIL	3,304	1,395	1,521	388	126 D	42.2%	46.0%	47.8%	52.2%
9,129	NELSON	3,538	1,672	1,629	237	43 R	47.3%	46.0%	50.7%	49.3%
3,859	OLIVER	1,104	749	304	51	445 R	67.8%	27.5%	71.1%	28.9%
15,671	PEMBINA	5,155	2,406	2,666	83	260 D	46.7%	51.7%	47.4%	52.6%
9,208	PIERCE	2,953	1,738	1,147	68	591 R	58.9%	38.8%	60.2%	39.8%
15,626	RAMSEY	5,555	2,891	2,458	206	433 R	52.0%	44.2%	54.0%	46.0%
10,061	RANSOM	3,485	1,772	1,595	118	177 R	50.8%	45.8%	52.6%	47.4%
5,533	RENVILLE	1,742	812	838	92	26 D	46.6%	48.1%	49.2%	50.8%
20,519	RICHLAND	7,075	3,448	3,413	214	35 R	48.7%	48.2%	50.3%	49.7%
12,583	ROLETTE	2,869	1,179	1,565	125	386 D	41.1%	54.5%	43.0%	57.0%
8,693	SARGENT	3,033	1,387	1,506	140	119 D	45.7%	49.7%	47.9%	52.1%
6,616	SHERIDAN	1,969	1,554	372	43	1,182 R	78.9%	18.9%	80.7%	19.3%
4,419	SIOUX	1,166	667	465	34	202 R	57.2%	39.9%	58.9%	41.1%
2,932	SLOPE	885	447	388	50	59 R	50.5%	43.8%	53.5%	46.5%
15,414	STARK	5,357	3,222	2,017	118	1,205 R	60.1%	37.7%	61.5%	38.5%
6,193	STEELE	2,338	1,052	1,163	123	111 D	45.0%	49.7%	47.5%	52.5%
23,495	STUTSMAN	7,957	4,208	3,415	334	793 R	52.9%	42.9%	55.2%	44.8%
7,200	TOWNER	2,301	1,145	1,100	56	45 R	49.8%	47.8%	51.0%	49.0%
12,300	TRAILL	4,477	2,328	1,874	275	454 R	52.0%	41.9%	55.4%	44.6%
20,747	WALSH	7,031	2,646	4,170	215	1,524 D	37.6%	59.3%	38.8%	61.2%
31,981	WARD	11,337	5,514	5,189	634	325 R	48.6%	45.8%	51.5%	48.5%
11,198	WELLS	3,986	2,385	1,492	109	893 R	59.8%	37.4%	61.5%	38.5%
16,315	WILLIAMS	5,495	2,133	2,571	791	438 D	38.8%	46.8%	45.3%	54.7%
641,935	TOTAL	220,716	115,139	95,812	9,765	19,327 R	52.2%	43.4%	54.6%	45.4%

NORTH DAKOTA

PRESIDENT 1944

1940 Census Population	County	Total Vote	Republican	Democratic	Other	Rep.-Dem. Plurality	Percentage: Total Vote Rep.	Total Vote Dem.	Major Vote Rep.	Major Vote Dem.
4,664	ADAMS	1,648	966	668	14	298 R	58.6%	40.5%	59.1%	40.9%
17,814	BARNES	6,653	3,696	2,922	35	774 R	55.6%	43.9%	55.8%	44.2%
12,629	BENSON	4,010	1,726	2,261	23	535 D	43.0%	56.4%	43.3%	56.7%
2,531	BILLINGS	566	354	209	3	145 R	62.5%	36.9%	62.9%	37.1%
13,253	BOTTINEAU	4,660	2,663	1,953	44	710 R	57.1%	41.9%	57.7%	42.3%
3,860	BOWMAN	1,410	785	609	16	176 R	55.7%	43.2%	56.3%	43.7%
7,653	BURKE	2,827	1,540	1,226	61	314 R	54.5%	43.4%	55.7%	44.3%
22,736	BURLEIGH	7,700	4,616	3,061	23	1,555 R	59.9%	39.8%	60.1%	39.9%
52,849	CASS	21,167	10,661	10,390	116	271 R	50.4%	49.1%	50.6%	49.4%
13,923	CAVALIER	4,308	2,011	2,274	23	263 D	46.7%	52.8%	46.9%	53.1%
9,696	DICKEY	3,492	2,134	1,339	19	795 R	61.1%	38.3%	61.4%	38.6%
7,086	DIVIDE	2,772	1,225	1,513	34	288 D	44.2%	54.6%	44.7%	55.3%
8,376	DUNN	2,298	1,374	919	5	455 R	59.8%	40.0%	59.9%	40.1%
5,741	EDDY	2,048	974	1,042	32	68 D	47.6%	50.9%	48.3%	51.7%
11,699	EMMONS	2,929	2,255	656	18	1,599 R	77.0%	22.4%	77.5%	22.5%
5,824	FOSTER	2,007	891	1,102	14	211 D	44.4%	54.9%	44.7%	55.3%
3,498	GOLDEN VALLEY	1,158	709	443	6	266 R	61.2%	38.3%	61.5%	38.5%
34,518	GRAND FORKS	13,434	5,668	7,707	59	2,039 D	42.2%	57.4%	42.4%	57.6%
8,264	GRANT	2,164	1,745	410	9	1,335 R	80.6%	18.9%	81.0%	19.0%
5,818	GRIGGS	2,227	990	1,228	9	238 D	44.5%	55.1%	44.6%	55.4%
7,457	HETTINGER	2,371	1,812	554	5	1,258 R	76.4%	23.4%	76.6%	23.4%
6,692	KIDDER	2,103	1,397	693	13	704 R	66.4%	33.0%	66.8%	33.2%
10,298	LA MOURE	3,752	2,298	1,422	32	876 R	61.2%	37.9%	61.8%	38.2%
7,561	LOGAN	2,202	1,904	294	4	1,610 R	86.5%	13.4%	86.6%	13.4%
14,034	MCHENRY	5,112	3,141	1,934	37	1,207 R	61.4%	37.8%	61.9%	38.1%
8,984	MCINTOSH	2,916	2,682	226	8	2,456 R	92.0%	7.8%	92.2%	7.8%
8,426	MCKENZIE	2,863	1,241	1,592	30	351 D	43.3%	55.6%	43.8%	56.2%
16,082	MCLEAN	5,288	2,822	2,326	140	496 R	53.4%	44.0%	54.8%	45.2%
9,611	MERCER	2,956	2,504	445	7	2,059 R	84.7%	15.1%	84.9%	15.1%
20,184	MORTON	5,415	3,537	1,850	28	1,687 R	65.3%	34.2%	65.7%	34.3%
10,482	MOUNTRAIL	3,693	1,666	1,981	46	315 D	45.1%	53.6%	45.7%	54.3%
9,129	NELSON	3,441	1,506	1,925	10	419 D	43.8%	55.9%	43.9%	56.1%
3,859	OLIVER	984	756	219	9	537 R	76.8%	22.3%	77.5%	22.5%
15,671	PEMBINA	5,361	2,410	2,903	48	493 D	45.0%	54.2%	45.4%	54.6%
9,208	PIERCE	3,316	1,992	1,307	17	685 R	60.1%	39.4%	60.4%	39.6%
15,626	RAMSEY	5,083	2,505	2,539	39	34 D	49.3%	50.0%	49.7%	50.3%
10,061	RANSOM	3,712	2,044	1,639	29	405 R	55.1%	44.2%	55.5%	44.5%
5,533	RENVILLE	2,164	1,046	1,095	23	49 D	48.3%	50.6%	48.9%	51.1%
20,519	RICHLAND	7,624	4,402	3,192	30	1,210 R	57.7%	41.9%	58.0%	42.0%
12,583	ROLETTE	2,832	1,070	1,745	17	675 D	37.8%	61.6%	38.0%	62.0%
8,693	SARGENT	2,934	1,488	1,426	20	62 R	50.7%	48.6%	51.1%	48.9%
6,616	SHERIDAN	2,308	1,910	386	12	1,524 R	82.8%	16.7%	83.2%	16.8%
4,419	SIOUX	1,122	673	445	4	228 R	60.0%	39.7%	60.2%	39.8%
2,932	SLOPE	878	434	439	5	5 D	49.4%	50.0%	49.7%	50.3%
15,414	STARK	4,398	2,852	1,534	12	1,318 R	64.8%	34.9%	65.0%	35.0%
6,193	STEELE	2,374	1,042	1,320	12	278 D	43.9%	55.6%	44.1%	55.9%
23,495	STUTSMAN	7,509	4,220	3,243	46	977 R	56.2%	43.2%	56.5%	43.5%
7,200	TOWNER	2,286	1,097	1,185	4	88 D	48.0%	51.8%	48.1%	51.9%
12,300	TRAILL	4,869	2,370	2,479	20	109 D	48.7%	50.9%	48.9%	51.1%
20,747	WALSH	7,252	2,471	4,747	34	2,276 D	34.1%	65.5%	34.2%	65.8%
31,981	WARD	11,417	5,514	5,822	81	308 D	48.3%	51.0%	48.6%	51.4%
11,198	WELLS	4,106	2,529	1,557	20	972 R	61.6%	37.9%	61.9%	38.1%
16,315	WILLIAMS	6,063	2,217	3,748	98	1,531 D	36.6%	61.8%	37.2%	62.8%
641,935	TOTAL	220,182	118,535	100,144	1,503	18,391 R	53.8%	45.5%	54.2%	45.8%

NORTH DAKOTA

PRESIDENT 1940

1940 Census Population	County	Total Vote	Republican	Democratic	Other	Rep.-Dem. Plurality	Percentage Total Vote Rep.	Percentage Total Vote Dem.	Percentage Major Vote Rep.	Percentage Major Vote Dem.
4,664	ADAMS	2,095	1,231	837	27	394 R	58.8%	40.0%	59.5%	40.5%
17,814	BARNES	8,062	4,649	3,384	29	1,265 R	57.7%	42.0%	57.9%	42.1%
12,629	BENSON	5,420	2,485	2,898	37	413 D	45.8%	53.5%	46.2%	53.8%
2,531	BILLINGS	1,068	663	404	1	259 R	62.1%	37.8%	62.1%	37.9%
13,253	BOTTINEAU	5,628	3,129	2,469	30	660 R	55.6%	43.9%	55.9%	44.1%
3,860	BOWMAN	1,831	927	882	22	45 R	50.6%	48.2%	51.2%	48.8%
7,653	BURKE	3,391	1,951	1,342	98	609 R	57.5%	39.6%	59.2%	40.8%
22,736	BURLEIGH	10,266	5,858	4,350	58	1,508 R	57.1%	42.4%	57.4%	42.6%
52,849	CASS	24,586	12,567	11,911	108	656 R	51.1%	48.4%	51.3%	48.7%
13,923	CAVALIER	5,618	2,845	2,757	16	88 R	50.6%	49.1%	50.8%	49.2%
9,696	DICKEY	4,835	2,777	1,721	337	1,056 R	57.4%	35.6%	61.7%	38.3%
7,086	DIVIDE	3,242	1,437	1,771	34	334 D	44.3%	54.6%	44.8%	55.2%
8,376	DUNN	3,536	2,132	1,392	12	740 R	60.3%	39.4%	60.5%	39.5%
5,741	EDDY	2,724	1,319	1,368	37	49 D	48.4%	50.2%	49.1%	50.9%
11,699	EMMONS	4,548	3,515	1,004	29	2,511 R	77.3%	22.1%	77.8%	22.2%
5,824	FOSTER	2,567	1,109	1,446	12	337 D	43.2%	56.3%	43.4%	56.6%
3,498	GOLDEN VALLEY	1,571	873	689	9	184 R	55.6%	43.9%	55.9%	44.1%
34,518	GRAND FORKS	15,506	7,043	8,396	67	1,353 D	45.4%	54.1%	45.6%	54.4%
8,264	GRANT	3,453	2,815	627	11	2,188 R	81.5%	18.2%	81.8%	18.2%
5,818	GRIGGS	2,592	1,117	1,464	11	347 D	43.1%	56.5%	43.3%	56.7%
7,457	HETTINGER	3,151	2,468	671	12	1,797 R	78.3%	21.3%	78.6%	21.4%
6,692	KIDDER	3,062	2,214	837	11	1,377 R	72.3%	27.3%	72.6%	27.4%
10,298	LA MOURE	4,620	2,943	1,637	40	1,306 R	63.7%	35.4%	64.3%	35.7%
7,561	LOGAN	3,077	2,572	498	7	2,074 R	83.6%	16.2%	83.8%	16.2%
14,034	MCHENRY	6,174	3,894	2,225	55	1,669 R	63.1%	36.0%	63.6%	36.4%
8,984	MCINTOSH	3,812	3,494	318		3,176 R	91.7%	8.3%	91.7%	8.3%
8,426	MCKENZIE	4,046	1,563	2,440	43	877 D	38.6%	60.3%	39.0%	61.0%
16,082	MCLEAN	6,972	4,113	2,666	193	1,447 R	59.0%	38.2%	60.7%	39.3%
9,611	MERCER	3,914	3,341	567	6	2,774 R	85.4%	14.5%	85.5%	14.5%
20,184	MORTON	8,428	5,499	2,889	40	2,610 R	65.2%	34.3%	65.6%	34.4%
10,482	MOUNTRAIL	4,435	1,981	2,392	62	411 D	44.7%	53.9%	45.3%	54.7%
9,129	NELSON	4,316	1,859	2,435	22	576 D	43.1%	56.4%	43.3%	56.7%
3,859	OLIVER	1,623	1,356	266	1	1,090 R	83.5%	16.4%	83.6%	16.4%
15,671	PEMBINA	6,655	2,924	3,711	20	787 D	43.9%	55.8%	44.1%	55.9%
9,208	PIERCE	3,811	2,349	1,451	11	898 R	61.6%	38.1%	61.8%	38.2%
15,626	RAMSEY	7,194	3,629	3,530	35	99 R	50.4%	49.1%	50.7%	49.3%
10,061	RANSOM	4,589	2,579	1,986	24	593 R	56.2%	43.3%	56.5%	43.5%
5,533	RENVILLE	2,556	1,202	1,298	56	96 D	47.0%	50.8%	48.1%	51.9%
20,519	RICHLAND	8,734	5,102	3,584	48	1,518 R	58.4%	41.0%	58.7%	41.3%
12,583	ROLETTE	4,392	1,555	2,820	17	1,265 D	35.4%	64.2%	35.5%	64.5%
8,693	SARGENT	3,843	1,922	1,894	27	28 R	50.0%	49.3%	50.4%	49.6%
6,616	SHERIDAN	2,957	2,405	543	9	1,862 R	81.3%	18.4%	81.6%	18.4%
4,419	SIOUX	1,746	1,167	578	1	589 R	66.8%	33.1%	66.9%	33.1%
2,932	SLOPE	1,391	801	585	5	216 R	57.6%	42.1%	57.8%	42.2%
15,414	STARK	6,457	4,367	2,075	15	2,292 R	67.6%	32.1%	67.8%	32.2%
6,193	STEELE	2,784	1,328	1,434	22	106 D	47.7%	51.5%	48.1%	51.9%
23,495	STUTSMAN	9,562	5,634	3,897	31	1,737 R	58.9%	40.8%	59.1%	40.9%
7,200	TOWNER	3,241	1,630	1,596	15	34 R	50.3%	49.2%	50.5%	49.5%
12,300	TRAILL	5,390	2,882	2,476	32	406 R	53.5%	45.9%	53.8%	46.2%
20,747	WALSH	8,568	3,051	5,499	18	2,448 D	35.6%	64.2%	35.7%	64.3%
31,981	WARD	14,293	6,519	7,669	105	1,150 D	45.6%	53.7%	45.9%	54.1%
11,198	WELLS	5,232	3,335	1,878	19	1,457 R	63.7%	35.9%	64.0%	36.0%
16,315	WILLIAMS	7,211	2,470	4,579	162	2,109 D	34.3%	63.5%	35.0%	65.0%
641,935	TOTAL	280,775	154,590	124,036	2,149	30,554 R	55.1%	44.2%	55.5%	44.5%

NORTH DAKOTA

PRESIDENT 1936

1930 Census Population	County	Total Vote	Republican	Democratic	Other	Rep.-Dem. Plurality	Percentage Total Vote Rep.	Percentage Total Vote Dem.	Percentage Major Vote Rep.	Percentage Major Vote Dem.
6,343	ADAMS	2,404	746	1,321	337	575 D	31.0%	55.0%	36.1%	63.9%
18,804	BARNES	7,746	2,324	4,484	938	2,160 D	30.0%	57.9%	34.1%	65.9%
13,327	BENSON	5,363	1,020	3,343	1,000	2,323 D	19.0%	62.3%	23.4%	76.6%
3,140	BILLINGS	1,232	329	729	174	400 D	26.7%	59.2%	31.1%	68.9%
14,853	BOTTINEAU	5,779	1,224	3,286	1,269	2,062 D	21.2%	56.9%	27.1%	72.9%
5,119	BOWMAN	2,010	534	1,118	358	584 D	26.6%	55.6%	32.3%	67.7%
9,998	BURKE	3,731	684	1,821	1,226	1,137 D	18.3%	48.8%	27.3%	72.7%
19,769	BURLEIGH	9,723	2,447	6,314	962	3,867 D	25.2%	64.9%	27.9%	72.1%
48,735	CASS	21,670	7,632	12,400	1,638	4,768 D	35.2%	57.2%	38.1%	61.9%
14,554	CAVALIER	5,809	1,657	3,533	619	1,876 D	28.5%	60.8%	31.9%	68.1%
10,877	DICKEY	4,458	1,533	2,287	638	754 D	34.4%	51.3%	40.1%	59.9%
9,636	DIVIDE	3,536	585	2,212	739	1,627 D	16.5%	62.6%	20.9%	79.1%
9,566	DUNN	3,381	732	2,257	392	1,525 D	21.7%	66.8%	24.5%	75.5%
6,346	EDDY	2,711	579	1,729	403	1,150 D	21.4%	63.8%	25.1%	74.9%
12,467	EMMONS	4,183	1,117	2,424	642	1,307 D	26.7%	57.9%	31.5%	68.5%
6,353	FOSTER	2,759	685	1,894	180	1,209 D	24.8%	68.6%	26.6%	73.4%
4,122	GOLDEN VALLEY	1,659	581	991	87	410 D	35.0%	59.7%	37.0%	63.0%
31,956	GRAND FORKS	14,549	4,312	9,222	1,015	4,910 D	29.6%	63.4%	31.9%	68.1%
10,134	GRANT	3,456	1,022	1,858	576	836 D	29.6%	53.8%	35.5%	64.5%
6,889	GRIGGS	2,723	666	1,665	392	999 D	24.5%	61.1%	28.6%	71.4%
8,796	HETTINGER	3,317	989	1,383	945	394 D	29.8%	41.7%	41.7%	58.3%
8,031	KIDDER	2,932	872	1,492	568	620 D	29.7%	50.9%	36.9%	63.1%
11,517	LA MOURE	4,871	1,614	2,412	845	798 D	33.1%	49.5%	40.1%	59.9%
8,089	LOGAN	2,864	984	1,292	588	308 D	34.4%	45.1%	43.2%	56.8%
15,439	MCHENRY	6,169	1,619	3,294	1,256	1,675 D	26.2%	53.4%	33.0%	67.0%
9,621	MCINTOSH	3,629	1,469	1,900	260	431 D	40.5%	52.4%	43.6%	56.4%
9,709	MCKENZIE	3,888	570	2,885	433	2,315 D	14.7%	74.2%	16.5%	83.5%
17,991	MCLEAN	6,862	1,732	4,018	1,112	2,286 D	25.2%	58.6%	30.1%	69.9%
9,516	MERCER	3,619	1,142	1,924	553	782 D	31.6%	53.2%	37.2%	62.8%
19,647	MORTON	8,090	1,857	5,612	621	3,755 D	23.0%	69.4%	24.9%	75.1%
13,544	MOUNTRAIL	4,769	700	2,775	1,294	2,075 D	14.7%	58.2%	20.1%	79.9%
10,203	NELSON	4,491	1,002	2,954	535	1,952 D	22.3%	65.8%	25.3%	74.7%
4,262	OLIVER	1,573	469	906	198	437 D	29.8%	57.6%	34.1%	65.9%
14,757	PEMBINA	6,481	2,040	4,139	302	2,099 D	31.5%	63.9%	33.0%	67.0%
9,074	PIERCE	3,764	912	2,168	684	1,256 D	24.2%	57.6%	29.6%	70.4%
16,252	RAMSEY	6,993	1,784	4,559	650	2,775 D	25.5%	65.2%	28.1%	71.9%
10,983	RANSOM	4,298	1,303	2,385	610	1,082 D	30.3%	55.5%	35.3%	64.7%
7,263	RENVILLE	2,861	611	1,766	484	1,155 D	21.4%	61.7%	25.7%	74.3%
21,008	RICHLAND	7,596	2,386	3,792	1,418	1,406 D	31.4%	49.9%	38.6%	61.4%
10,760	ROLETTE	4,432	857	3,186	389	2,329 D	19.3%	71.9%	21.2%	78.8%
9,298	SARGENT	3,577	863	2,306	408	1,443 D	24.1%	64.5%	27.2%	72.8%
7,373	SHERIDAN	2,798	834	1,150	814	316 D	29.8%	41.1%	42.0%	58.0%
4,687	SIOUX	1,664	585	877	202	292 D	35.2%	52.7%	40.0%	60.0%
4,150	SLOPE	1,421	331	896	194	565 D	23.3%	63.1%	27.0%	73.0%
15,340	STARK	6,139	1,602	4,012	525	2,410 D	26.1%	65.4%	28.5%	71.5%
6,972	STEELE	2,873	724	1,444	705	720 D	25.2%	50.3%	33.4%	66.6%
26,100	STUTSMAN	9,369	2,725	5,564	1,080	2,839 D	29.1%	59.4%	32.9%	67.1%
8,393	TOWNER	3,214	720	1,744	750	1,024 D	22.4%	54.3%	29.2%	70.8%
12,600	TRAILL	5,269	1,807	2,780	682	973 D	34.3%	52.8%	39.4%	60.6%
20,047	WALSH	8,185	1,813	5,756	616	3,943 D	22.2%	70.3%	24.0%	76.0%
33,597	WARD	14,055	3,142	8,872	2,041	5,730 D	22.4%	63.1%	26.2%	73.8%
13,285	WELLS	5,298	1,263	3,114	921	1,851 D	23.8%	58.8%	28.9%	71.1%
19,553	WILLIAMS	7,473	1,021	4,903	1,549	3,882 D	13.7%	65.6%	17.2%	82.8%
680,845	TOTAL	273,716	72,751	163,148	37,817	90,397 D	26.6%	59.6%	30.8%	69.2%

NORTH DAKOTA

PRESIDENT 1932

1930 Census Population	County	Total Vote	Republican	Democratic	Other	Rep.-Dem. Plurality	Percentage Total Vote Rep.	Total Vote Dem.	Major Vote Rep.	Major Vote Dem.
6,343	ADAMS	2,606	915	1,514	177	599 D	35.1%	58.1%	37.7%	62.3%
18,804	BARNES	7,667	2,527	4,833	307	2,306 D	33.0%	63.0%	34.3%	65.7%
13,327	BENSON	4,917	1,170	3,650	97	2,480 D	23.8%	74.2%	24.3%	75.7%
3,140	BILLINGS	1,079	295	760	24	465 D	27.3%	70.4%	28.0%	72.0%
14,853	BOTTINEAU	5,567	1,201	4,178	188	2,977 D	21.6%	75.0%	22.3%	77.7%
5,119	BOWMAN	2,176	616	1,292	268	676 D	28.3%	59.4%	32.3%	67.7%
9,998	BURKE	3,594	906	2,473	215	1,567 D	25.2%	68.8%	26.8%	73.2%
19,769	BURLEIGH	8,439	2,687	5,621	131	2,934 D	31.8%	66.6%	32.3%	67.7%
48,735	CASS	20,394	8,937	11,094	363	2,157 D	43.8%	54.4%	44.6%	55.4%
14,554	CAVALIER	5,285	1,471	3,770	44	2,299 D	27.8%	71.3%	28.1%	71.9%
10,877	DICKEY	4,643	1,424	3,068	151	1,644 D	30.7%	66.1%	31.7%	68.3%
9,636	DIVIDE	3,402	817	2,374	211	1,557 D	24.0%	69.8%	25.6%	74.4%
9,566	DUNN	3,008	569	2,380	59	1,811 D	18.9%	79.1%	19.3%	80.7%
6,346	EDDY	2,527	537	1,888	102	1,351 D	21.3%	74.7%	22.1%	77.9%
12,467	EMMONS	4,049	916	3,089	44	2,173 D	22.6%	76.3%	22.9%	77.1%
6,353	FOSTER	2,471	609	1,838	24	1,229 D	24.6%	74.4%	24.9%	75.1%
4,122	GOLDEN VALLEY	1,695	653	1,023	19	370 D	38.5%	60.4%	39.0%	61.0%
31,956	GRAND FORKS	12,900	5,090	7,579	231	2,489 D	39.5%	58.8%	40.2%	59.8%
10,134	GRANT	3,654	657	2,912	85	2,255 D	18.0%	79.7%	18.4%	81.6%
6,889	GRIGGS	2,431	482	1,838	111	1,356 D	19.8%	75.6%	20.8%	79.2%
8,796	HETTINGER	3,358	921	2,336	101	1,415 D	27.4%	69.6%	28.3%	71.7%
8,031	KIDDER	2,792	709	2,042	41	1,333 D	25.4%	73.1%	25.8%	74.2%
11,517	LA MOURE	4,583	1,134	3,310	139	2,176 D	24.7%	72.2%	25.5%	74.5%
8,089	LOGAN	2,767	390	2,350	27	1,960 D	14.1%	84.9%	14.2%	85.8%
15,439	MCHENRY	5,566	1,396	3,937	233	2,541 D	25.1%	70.7%	26.2%	73.8%
9,621	MCINTOSH	3,543	465	3,078		2,613 D	13.1%	86.9%	13.1%	86.9%
9,709	MCKENZIE	3,547	710	2,655	182	1,945 D	20.0%	74.9%	21.1%	78.9%
17,991	MCLEAN	5,723	1,369	4,354		2,985 D	23.9%	76.1%	23.9%	76.1%
9,516	MERCER	2,993	480	2,491	22	2,011 D	16.0%	83.2%	16.2%	83.8%
19,647	MORTON	7,430	1,828	5,548	54	3,720 D	24.6%	74.7%	24.8%	75.2%
13,544	MOUNTRAIL	4,448	986	3,284	178	2,298 D	22.2%	73.8%	23.1%	76.9%
10,203	NELSON	4,132	956	3,176		2,220 D	23.1%	76.9%	23.1%	76.9%
4,262	OLIVER	1,469	302	1,152	15	850 D	20.6%	78.4%	20.8%	79.2%
14,757	PEMBINA	5,590	1,911	3,636	43	1,725 D	34.2%	65.0%	34.5%	65.5%
9,074	PIERCE	3,333	856	2,439	38	1,583 D	25.7%	73.2%	26.0%	74.0%
16,252	RAMSEY	6,329	1,917	4,337	75	2,420 D	30.3%	68.5%	30.7%	69.3%
10,983	RANSOM	4,563	1,445	3,025	93	1,580 D	31.7%	66.3%	32.3%	67.7%
7,263	RENVILLE	2,731	689	1,969	73	1,280 D	25.2%	72.1%	25.9%	74.1%
21,008	RICHLAND	8,183	2,304	5,663	216	3,359 D	28.2%	69.2%	28.9%	71.1%
10,760	ROLETTE	3,604	706	2,855	43	2,149 D	19.6%	79.2%	19.8%	80.2%
9,298	SARGENT	3,709	785	2,818	106	2,033 D	21.2%	76.0%	21.8%	78.2%
7,373	SHERIDAN	2,453	468	1,945	40	1,477 D	19.1%	79.3%	19.4%	80.6%
4,687	SIOUX	1,722	350	1,328	44	978 D	20.3%	77.1%	20.9%	79.1%
4,150	SLOPE	1,660	461	1,136	63	675 D	27.8%	68.4%	28.9%	71.1%
15,340	STARK	6,229	1,443	4,786		3,343 D	23.2%	76.8%	23.2%	76.8%
6,972	STEELE	2,685	695	1,925	65	1,230 D	25.9%	71.7%	26.5%	73.5%
26,100	STUTSMAN	8,878	2,577	6,182	119	3,605 D	29.0%	69.6%	29.4%	70.6%
8,393	TOWNER	2,999	765	2,190	44	1,425 D	25.5%	73.0%	25.9%	74.1%
12,600	TRAILL	5,074	1,893	3,112	69	1,219 D	37.3%	61.3%	37.8%	62.2%
20,047	WALSH	7,244	1,616	5,342	286	3,726 D	22.3%	73.7%	23.2%	76.8%
33,597	WARD	12,626	4,195	8,129	302	3,934 D	33.2%	64.4%	34.0%	66.0%
13,285	WELLS	4,939	1,062	3,823	54	2,761 D	21.5%	77.4%	21.7%	78.3%
19,553	WILLIAMS	6,884	1,509	4,823	552	3,314 D	21.9%	70.1%	23.8%	76.2%
680,845	TOTAL	256,290	71,772	178,350	6,168	106,578 D	28.0%	69.6%	28.7%	71.3%

NORTH DAKOTA

PRESIDENT 1928

1920 Census Population	County	Total Vote	Republican	Democratic	Other	Rep.-Dem. Plurality	Percentage Total Vote Rep.	Percentage Total Vote Dem.	Percentage Major Vote Rep.	Percentage Major Vote Dem.
5,593	ADAMS	2,250	1,590	644	16	946 R	70.7%	28.6%	71.2%	28.8%
18,678	BARNES	7,083	3,755	3,293	35	462 R	53.0%	46.5%	53.3%	46.7%
13,095	BENSON	4,872	2,621	2,194	57	427 R	53.8%	45.0%	54.4%	45.6%
3,126	BILLINGS	877	458	412	7	46 R	52.2%	47.0%	52.6%	47.4%
15,109	BOTTINEAU	5,383	2,680	2,648	55	32 R	49.8%	49.2%	50.3%	49.7%
4,768	BOWMAN	1,875	1,031	821	23	210 R	55.0%	43.8%	55.7%	44.3%
9,511	BURKE	3,429	2,002	1,336	91	666 R	58.4%	39.0%	60.0%	40.0%
15,578	BURLEIGH	7,115	3,955	3,076	84	879 R	55.6%	43.2%	56.3%	43.7%
41,477	CASS	18,858	12,480	6,315	63	6,165 R	66.2%	33.5%	66.4%	33.6%
15,555	CAVALIER	5,592	3,068	2,510	14	558 R	54.9%	44.9%	55.0%	45.0%
10,499	DICKEY	4,253	2,250	1,977	26	273 R	52.9%	46.5%	53.2%	46.8%
9,637	DIVIDE	3,252	1,963	1,250	39	713 R	60.4%	38.4%	61.1%	38.9%
8,828	DUNN	2,925	1,360	1,561	4	201 D	46.5%	53.4%	46.6%	53.4%
6,493	EDDY	2,322	1,071	1,240	11	169 D	46.1%	53.4%	46.3%	53.7%
11,288	EMMONS	3,875	1,792	2,066	17	274 D	46.2%	53.3%	46.4%	53.6%
6,108	FOSTER	2,321	1,137	1,178	6	41 D	49.0%	50.8%	49.1%	50.9%
4,832	GOLDEN VALLEY	1,499	937	552	10	385 R	62.5%	36.8%	62.9%	37.1%
28,795	GRAND FORKS	12,371	8,024	4,300	47	3,724 R	64.9%	34.8%	65.1%	34.9%
9,553	GRANT	3,222	1,759	1,434	29	325 R	54.6%	44.5%	55.1%	44.9%
7,402	GRIGGS	2,534	1,329	1,182	23	147 R	52.4%	46.6%	52.9%	47.1%
7,685	HETTINGER	2,883	1,553	1,323	7	230 R	53.9%	45.9%	54.0%	46.0%
7,798	KIDDER	2,403	1,200	1,190	13	10 R	49.9%	49.5%	50.2%	49.8%
11,564	LA MOURE	4,082	2,245	1,800	37	445 R	55.0%	44.1%	55.5%	44.5%
7,723	LOGAN	2,321	1,013	1,293	15	280 D	43.6%	55.7%	43.9%	56.1%
15,544	MCHENRY	5,494	2,914	2,535	45	379 R	53.0%	46.1%	53.5%	46.5%
9,010	MCINTOSH	2,670	1,196	1,474		278 D	44.8%	55.2%	44.8%	55.2%
9,544	MCKENZIE	3,435	2,100	1,289	46	811 R	61.1%	37.5%	62.0%	38.0%
17,266	MCLEAN	5,746	2,730	2,855	161	125 D	47.5%	49.7%	48.9%	51.1%
8,224	MERCER	2,593	971	1,619	3	648 D	37.4%	62.4%	37.5%	62.5%
18,714	MORTON	6,853	2,881	3,946	26	1,065 D	42.0%	57.6%	42.2%	57.8%
12,140	MOUNTRAIL	4,501	2,354	2,003	144	351 R	52.3%	44.5%	54.0%	46.0%
10,362	NELSON	3,928	2,364	1,542	22	822 R	60.2%	39.3%	60.5%	39.5%
4,425	OLIVER	1,316	680	631	5	49 R	51.7%	47.9%	51.9%	48.1%
15,177	PEMBINA	5,472	3,324	2,141	7	1,183 R	60.7%	39.1%	60.8%	39.2%
9,283	PIERCE	3,086	1,469	1,606	11	137 D	47.6%	52.0%	47.8%	52.2%
15,427	RAMSEY	5,943	3,246	2,672	25	574 R	54.6%	45.0%	54.8%	45.2%
11,618	RANSOM	4,145	2,613	1,505	27	1,108 R	63.0%	36.3%	63.5%	36.5%
7,776	RENVILLE	2,674	1,473	1,174	27	299 R	55.1%	43.9%	55.6%	44.4%
20,887	RICHLAND	7,889	4,251	3,604	34	647 R	53.9%	45.7%	54.1%	45.9%
10,061	ROLETTE	3,539	1,327	2,181	31	854 D	37.5%	61.6%	37.8%	62.2%
9,655	SARGENT	3,780	1,772	1,989	19	217 D	46.9%	52.6%	47.1%	52.9%
7,935	SHERIDAN	2,194	1,242	944	8	298 R	56.6%	43.0%	56.8%	43.2%
3,308	SIOUX	1,698	687	988	23	301 D	40.5%	58.2%	41.0%	59.0%
4,940	SLOPE	1,434	873	542	19	331 R	60.9%	37.8%	61.7%	38.3%
13,542	STARK	5,161	1,924	3,231	6	1,307 D	37.3%	62.6%	37.3%	62.7%
7,401	STEELE	2,745	1,574	1,152	19	422 R	57.3%	42.0%	57.7%	42.3%
24,575	STUTSMAN	8,684	4,782	3,873	29	909 R	55.1%	44.6%	55.3%	44.7%
8,327	TOWNER	2,928	1,588	1,324	16	264 R	54.2%	45.2%	54.5%	45.5%
12,210	TRAILL	5,098	3,638	1,447	13	2,191 R	71.4%	28.4%	71.5%	28.5%
19,078	WALSH	7,472	3,657	3,798	17	141 D	48.9%	50.8%	49.1%	50.9%
28,811	WARD	10,986	6,561	4,362	63	2,199 R	59.7%	39.7%	60.1%	39.9%
12,957	WELLS	4,512	2,364	2,123	25	241 R	52.4%	47.1%	52.7%	47.3%
17,980	WILLIAMS	6,272	3,591	2,503	178	1,088 R	57.3%	39.9%	58.9%	41.1%
646,872	TOTAL	239,845	131,419	106,648	1,778	24,771 R	54.8%	44.5%	55.2%	44.8%

NORTH DAKOTA

PRESIDENT 1924

1920 Census Population	County	Total Vote	Republican	Democratic	Progressive	Other	Plurality	Percentage Total Vote Rep.	Dem.	Prog.
5,593	ADAMS	1,928	776	106	1,045	1	269 P	40.2%	5.5%	54.2%
18,678	BARNES	6,228	3,205	346	2,675	2	530 R	51.5%	5.6%	43.0%
13,095	BENSON	4,156	1,870	246	2,038	2	168 P	45.0%	5.9%	49.0%
3,126	BILLINGS	871	421	32	418		3 R	48.3%	3.7%	48.0%
15,109	BOTTINEAU	4,182	1,338	221	2,621	2	1,283 P	32.0%	5.3%	62.7%
4,768	BOWMAN	1,718	776	67	875		99 P	45.2%	3.9%	50.9%
9,511	BURKE	2,514	996	135	1,376	7	380 P	39.6%	5.4%	54.7%
15,578	BURLEIGH	5,928	3,152	379	2,338	59	814 R	53.2%	6.4%	39.4%
41,477	CASS	15,041	9,906	1,352	3,769	14	6,137 R	65.9%	9.0%	25.1%
15,555	CAVALIER	4,443	2,428	539	1,471	5	957 R	54.6%	12.1%	33.1%
10,499	DICKEY	3,930	1,716	352	1,856	6	140 P	43.7%	9.0%	47.2%
9,637	DIVIDE	2,442	743	91	1,605	3	862 P	30.4%	3.7%	65.7%
8,828	DUNN	2,291	980	190	1,112	9	132 P	42.8%	8.3%	48.5%
6,493	EDDY	2,240	881	101	1,258		377 P	39.3%	4.5%	56.2%
11,288	EMMONS	3,021	1,198	123	1,695	5	497 P	39.7%	4.1%	56.1%
6,108	FOSTER	2,043	922	287	833	1	89 R	45.1%	14.0%	40.8%
4,832	GOLDEN VALLEY	1,487	718	140	628	1	90 R	48.3%	9.4%	42.2%
28,795	GRAND FORKS	10,651	6,690	943	3,011	7	3,679 R	62.8%	8.9%	28.3%
9,553	GRANT	2,867	1,120	125	1,618	4	498 P	39.1%	4.4%	56.4%
7,402	GRIGGS	2,214	738	116	1,360		622 P	33.3%	5.2%	61.4%
7,685	HETTINGER	2,356	936	128	1,291	1	355 P	39.7%	5.4%	54.8%
7,798	KIDDER	2,141	844	110	1,187		343 P	39.4%	5.1%	55.4%
11,564	LA MOURE	3,810	1,647	221	1,940	2	293 P	43.2%	5.8%	50.9%
7,723	LOGAN	1,816	787	29	994	6	207 P	43.3%	1.6%	54.7%
15,544	MCHENRY	4,587	1,692	264	2,630	1	938 P	36.9%	5.8%	57.3%
9,010	MCINTOSH	1,849	637	39	1,172	1	535 P	34.5%	2.1%	63.4%
9,544	MCKENZIE	2,918	1,113	137	1,661	7	548 P	38.1%	4.7%	56.9%
17,266	MCLEAN	4,583	1,651	194	2,718	20	1,067 P	36.0%	4.2%	59.3%
8,224	MERCER	2,086	522	70	1,489	5	967 P	25.0%	3.4%	71.4%
18,714	MORTON	5,370	2,377	265	2,716	12	339 P	44.3%	4.9%	50.6%
12,140	MOUNTRAIL	3,741	1,354	130	2,209	48	855 P	36.2%	3.5%	59.0%
10,362	NELSON	3,449	1,697	175	1,571	6	126 R	49.2%	5.1%	45.5%
4,425	OLIVER	1,141	367	31	739	4	372 P	32.2%	2.7%	64.8%
15,177	PEMBINA	4,715	2,783	588	1,341	3	1,442 R	59.0%	12.5%	28.4%
9,283	PIERCE	2,474	1,160	157	1,156	1	4 R	46.9%	6.3%	46.7%
15,427	RAMSEY	4,988	3,110	359	1,505	14	1,605 R	62.3%	7.2%	30.2%
11,618	RANSOM	4,084	1,862	303	1,919		57 P	45.6%	7.4%	47.0%
7,776	RENVILLE	2,017	649	120	1,247	1	598 P	32.2%	5.9%	61.8%
20,887	RICHLAND	6,624	3,235	769	2,617	3	618 R	48.8%	11.6%	39.5%
10,061	ROLETTE	2,419	869	137	1,410	3	541 P	35.9%	5.7%	58.3%
9,655	SARGENT	3,361	1,468	232	1,656	5	188 P	43.7%	6.9%	49.3%
7,935	SHERIDAN	1,714	594	49	1,069	2	475 P	34.7%	2.9%	62.4%
3,308	SIOUX	1,249	777	58	407	7	370 R	62.2%	4.6%	32.6%
4,940	SLOPE	1,576	616	47	913		297 P	39.1%	3.0%	57.9%
13,542	STARK	4,211	2,130	266	1,808	7	322 R	50.6%	6.3%	42.9%
7,401	STEELE	2,363	1,247	85	1,029	2	218 R	52.8%	3.6%	43.5%
24,575	STUTSMAN	6,973	3,952	463	2,552	6	1,400 R	56.7%	6.6%	36.6%
8,327	TOWNER	2,461	1,173	223	1,053	12	120 R	47.7%	9.1%	42.8%
12,210	TRAILL	4,583	2,596	234	1,752	1	844 R	56.6%	5.1%	38.2%
19,078	WALSH	5,770	2,837	917	2,009	7	828 R	49.2%	15.9%	34.8%
28,811	WARD	8,681	4,166	721	3,784	10	382 R	48.0%	8.3%	43.6%
12,957	WELLS	3,703	1,644	138	1,917	4	273 P	44.4%	3.7%	51.8%
17,980	WILLIAMS	5,073	1,865	308	2,859	41	994 P	36.8%	6.1%	56.4%
646,872	TOTAL	199,081	94,931	13,858	89,922	370	5,009 R	47.7%	7.0%	45.2%

NORTH DAKOTA

PRESIDENT 1920

1920 Census Population	County	Total Vote	Republican	Democratic	Other	Rep.-Dem. Plurality	Percentage Total Vote Rep.	Total Vote Dem.	Major Vote Rep.	Major Vote Dem.
5,593	ADAMS	1,768	1,377	347	44	1,030 R	77.9%	19.6%	79.9%	20.1%
18,678	BARNES	6,416	5,150	1,101	165	4,049 R	80.3%	17.2%	82.4%	17.6%
13,095	BENSON	4,365	3,540	680	145	2,860 R	81.1%	15.6%	83.9%	16.1%
3,126	BILLINGS	860	787	61	12	726 R	91.5%	7.1%	92.8%	7.2%
15,109	BOTTINEAU	4,808	3,487	970	351	2,517 R	72.5%	20.2%	78.2%	21.8%
4,768	BOWMAN	1,708	1,192	321	195	871 R	69.8%	18.8%	78.8%	21.2%
9,511	BURKE	2,694	1,911	456	327	1,455 R	70.9%	16.9%	80.7%	19.3%
15,578	BURLEIGH	5,564	4,300	943	321	3,357 R	77.3%	16.9%	82.0%	18.0%
41,477	CASS	13,938	10,735	2,817	386	7,918 R	77.0%	20.2%	79.2%	20.8%
15,555	CAVALIER	4,969	3,936	981	52	2,955 R	79.2%	19.7%	80.0%	20.0%
10,499	DICKEY	3,809	2,887	766	156	2,121 R	75.8%	20.1%	79.0%	21.0%
9,637	DIVIDE	3,017	2,438	462	117	1,976 R	80.8%	15.3%	84.1%	15.9%
8,828	DUNN	2,608	2,102	457	49	1,645 R	80.6%	17.5%	82.1%	17.9%
6,493	EDDY	2,218	1,525	577	116	948 R	68.8%	26.0%	72.5%	27.5%
11,288	EMMONS	3,160	2,900	238	22	2,662 R	91.8%	7.5%	92.4%	7.6%
6,108	FOSTER	2,004	1,583	371	50	1,212 R	79.0%	18.5%	81.0%	19.0%
4,832	GOLDEN VALLEY	1,527	1,177	286	64	891 R	77.1%	18.7%	80.5%	19.5%
28,795	GRAND FORKS	10,332	7,646	2,527	159	5,119 R	74.0%	24.5%	75.2%	24.8%
9,553	GRANT	2,626	2,184	296	146	1,888 R	83.2%	11.3%	88.1%	11.9%
7,402	GRIGGS	2,355	1,739	530	86	1,209 R	73.8%	22.5%	76.6%	23.4%
7,685	HETTINGER	2,216	1,849	327	40	1,522 R	83.4%	14.8%	85.0%	15.0%
7,798	KIDDER	2,299	1,855	336	108	1,519 R	80.7%	14.6%	84.7%	15.3%
11,564	LA MOURE	3,855	2,991	645	219	2,346 R	77.6%	16.7%	82.3%	17.7%
7,723	LOGAN	1,773	1,590	154	29	1,436 R	89.7%	8.7%	91.2%	8.8%
15,544	MCHENRY	4,770	3,534	848	388	2,686 R	74.1%	17.8%	80.6%	19.4%
9,010	MCINTOSH	1,889	1,782	79	28	1,703 R	94.3%	4.2%	95.8%	4.2%
9,544	MCKENZIE	3,254	2,587	511	156	2,076 R	79.5%	15.7%	83.5%	16.5%
17,266	MCLEAN	5,017	3,724	748	545	2,976 R	74.2%	14.9%	83.3%	16.7%
8,224	MERCER	2,047	1,786	172	89	1,614 R	87.2%	8.4%	91.2%	8.8%
18,714	MORTON	5,347	4,618	632	97	3,986 R	86.4%	11.8%	88.0%	12.0%
12,140	MOUNTRAIL	4,070	2,960	687	423	2,273 R	72.7%	16.9%	81.2%	18.8%
10,362	NELSON	3,701	3,127	501	73	2,626 R	84.5%	13.5%	86.2%	13.8%
4,425	OLIVER	1,287	1,105	111	71	994 R	85.9%	8.6%	90.9%	9.1%
15,177	PEMBINA	5,359	3,925	1,405	29	2,520 R	73.2%	26.2%	73.6%	26.4%
9,283	PIERCE	2,485	2,102	294	89	1,808 R	84.6%	11.8%	87.7%	12.3%
15,427	RAMSEY	5,037	3,996	937	104	3,059 R	79.3%	18.6%	81.0%	19.0%
11,618	RANSOM	3,894	3,010	802	82	2,208 R	77.3%	20.6%	79.0%	21.0%
7,776	RENVILLE	2,698	1,987	581	130	1,406 R	73.6%	21.5%	77.4%	22.6%
20,887	RICHLAND	6,900	5,483	1,339	78	4,144 R	79.5%	19.4%	80.4%	19.6%
10,061	ROLETTE	2,850	2,139	535	176	1,604 R	75.1%	18.8%	80.0%	20.0%
9,655	SARGENT	3,565	2,787	673	105	2,114 R	78.2%	18.9%	80.5%	19.5%
7,935	SHERIDAN	1,928	1,776	134	18	1,642 R	92.1%	7.0%	93.0%	7.0%
3,308	SIOUX	961	776	163	22	613 R	80.7%	17.0%	82.6%	17.4%
4,940	SLOPE	1,493	1,143	235	115	908 R	76.6%	15.7%	82.9%	17.1%
13,542	STARK	4,089	3,526	532	31	2,994 R	86.2%	13.0%	86.9%	13.1%
7,401	STEELE	2,609	2,222	337	50	1,885 R	85.2%	12.9%	86.8%	13.2%
24,575	STUTSMAN	7,145	5,531	1,394	220	4,137 R	77.4%	19.5%	79.9%	20.1%
8,327	TOWNER	2,763	2,192	476	95	1,716 R	79.3%	17.2%	82.2%	17.8%
12,210	TRAILL	4,263	3,666	523	74	3,143 R	86.0%	12.3%	87.5%	12.5%
19,078	WALSH	6,824	4,581	2,047	196	2,534 R	67.1%	30.0%	69.1%	30.9%
28,811	WARD	9,147	6,166	2,291	690	3,875 R	67.4%	25.0%	72.9%	27.1%
12,957	WELLS	3,736	3,202	456	78	2,746 R	85.7%	12.2%	87.5%	12.5%
17,980	WILLIAMS	5,769	3,768	1,330	671	2,438 R	65.3%	23.1%	73.9%	26.1%
646,872	TOTAL	205,786	160,082	37,422	8,282	122,660 R	77.8%	18.2%	81.1%	18.9%

NORTH DAKOTA

ELECTION NOTES

1956 Other vote was Andrews (States Rights).

1952 Other vote was 1,075 MacArthur (Christian Nationalist); 344 Hallinan (Progressive); 302 Hamblen (Prohibition).

1948 Other vote was 8,391 Wallace (Progressive); 1,000 Thomas (Socialist); 374 Thurmond (States Rights).

1944 Other vote was 954 Thomas (Socialist); 549 Watson (Prohibition).

1940 Other vote was 1,279 Thomas (Socialist); 545 Alfred Knutson (Peace-Jobs-Security-Civil Rights); 325 Babson (Prohibition). The Knutson vote is listed as Communist in some sources.

1936 Other vote was 36,708 Lemke (Union); 552 Thomas (Socialist); 360 Browder (Communist); 197 Colvin (Prohibition). Union candidates ran second in several counties.

1932 Other vote was 3,521 Thomas (Socialist); 1,817 Harvey (Liberty); 830 Foster (Communist).

1928 Other vote was 936 Thomas (Socialist); 842 Foster (Communist).

1924 A special four-column table which gives the LaFollette (Progressive) vote is used to detail this election. Other vote was Foster (Communist).

1920 Other vote was Debs (Socialist).

OHIO

POPULAR VOTE FOR PRESIDENT 1920 TO 1956

Year	Total Vote	Republican Vote	Republican Candidate	Democratic Vote	Democratic Candidate	Other Vote	Plurality	Total Vote Rep.	Total Vote Dem.	Major Vote Rep.	Major Vote Dem.
1956	3,702,265	2,262,610	Eisenhower, Dwight D.	1,439,655	Stevenson, Adlai E.		822,955 R	61.1%	38.9%	61.1%	38.9%
1952	3,700,758	2,100,391	Eisenhower, Dwight D.	1,600,367	Stevenson, Adlai E.		500,024 R	56.8%	43.2%	56.8%	43.2%
1948	2,936,071	1,445,684	Dewey, Thomas E.	1,452,791	Truman, Harry S.	37,596	7,107 D	49.2%	49.5%	49.9%	50.1%
1944	3,153,056	1,582,293	Dewey, Thomas E.	1,570,763	Roosevelt, Franklin D.		11,530 R	50.2%	49.8%	50.2%	49.8%
1940	3,319,912	1,586,773	Willkie, Wendell	1,733,139	Roosevelt, Franklin D.		146,366 D	47.8%	52.2%	47.8%	52.2%
1936	3,012,660	1,127,855	Landon, Alfred M.	1,747,140	Roosevelt, Franklin D.	137,665	619,285 D	37.4%	58.0%	39.2%	60.8%
1932	2,609,728	1,227,319	Hoover, Herbert C.	1,301,695	Roosevelt, Franklin D.	80,714	74,376 D	47.0%	49.9%	48.5%	51.5%
1928	2,508,346	1,627,546	Hoover, Herbert C.	864,210	Smith, Alfred E.	16,590	763,336 R	64.9%	34.5%	65.3%	34.7%
1924 **	2,016,296	1,176,130	Coolidge, Calvin	477,887	Davis, John W.	362,279	698,243 R	58.3%	23.7%	71.1%	28.9%
1920	2,021,653	1,182,022	Harding, Warren G.	780,037	Cox, James M.	59,594	401,985 R	58.5%	38.6%	60.2%	39.8%

In 1924 other vote was 358,008 Progressive; 3,025 Socialist Labor and 1,246 Commonwealth Land.

ELECTORAL COLLEGE VOTE 1920 TO 1956

Year	Total	Republican	Democratic	Other
1956	25	25	—	—
1952	25	25	—	—
1948	25	—	25	—
1944	25	25	—	—
1940	26	—	26	—
1936	26	—	26	—
1932	26	—	26	—
1928	24	24	—	—
1924	24	24	—	—
1920	24	24	—	—

OHIO

WILLIAMS
FULTON
LUCAS
OTTAWA
LAKE
ASHTABULA
GEAUGA
DEFIANCE
HENRY
WOOD
SANDUSKY
ERIE
LORAIN
CUYAHOGA
TRUMBULL
PAULDING
PUTNAM
HANCOCK
SENECA
HURON
MEDINA
SUMMIT
PORTAGE
MAHONING
VAN WERT
ALLEN
WYANDOT
CRAWFORD
ASHLAND
RICHLAND
WAYNE
STARK
COLUMBIANA
MERCER
AUGLAIZE
HARDIN
MARION
MORROW
HOLMES
CARROLL
SHELBY
LOGAN
UNION
DELAWARE
KNOX
TUSCARAWAS
COSHOCTON
HARRISON
JEFFERSON
DARKE
MIAMI
CHAMPAIGN
CLARK
MADISON
FRANKLIN
LICKING
MUSKINGUM
GUERNSEY
BELMONT
PREBLE
MONTGOMERY
GREENE
FAYETTE
PICKAWAY
FAIRFIELD
PERRY
MORGAN
NOBLE
MONROE
BUTLER
WARREN
CLINTON
ROSS
HOCKING
ATHENS
WASHINGTON
HAMILTON
CLERMONT
HIGHLAND
VINTON
MEIGS
BROWN
ADAMS
PIKE
JACKSON
GALLIA
SCIOTO
LAWRENCE

OHIO

PRESIDENT 1956

1950 Census Population	County	Total Vote	Republican	Democratic	Other	Rep.-Dem. Plurality	Percentage Total Vote Rep.	Percentage Total Vote Dem.	Percentage Major Vote Rep.	Percentage Major Vote Dem.
20,499	ADAMS	9,531	5,637	3,894		1,743 R	59.1%	40.9%	59.1%	40.9%
88,183	ALLEN	40,430	28,388	12,042		16,346 R	70.2%	29.8%	70.2%	29.8%
33,040	ASHLAND	17,426	12,792	4,634		8,158 R	73.4%	26.6%	73.4%	26.6%
78,695	ASHTABULA	37,360	24,165	13,195		10,970 R	64.7%	35.3%	64.7%	35.3%
45,839	ATHENS	16,753	10,794	5,959		4,835 R	64.4%	35.6%	64.4%	35.6%
30,637	AUGLAIZE	15,891	11,453	4,438		7,015 R	72.1%	27.9%	72.1%	27.9%
87,740	BELMONT	38,221	19,230	18,991		239 R	50.3%	49.7%	50.3%	49.7%
22,221	BROWN	10,036	5,690	4,346		1,344 R	56.7%	43.3%	56.7%	43.3%
147,203	BUTLER	66,116	41,785	24,331		17,454 R	63.2%	36.8%	63.2%	36.8%
19,039	CARROLL	8,506	5,916	2,590		3,326 R	69.6%	30.4%	69.6%	30.4%
26,793	CHAMPAIGN	12,618	8,767	3,851		4,916 R	69.5%	30.5%	69.5%	30.5%
111,661	CLARK	46,447	28,767	17,680		11,087 R	61.9%	38.1%	61.9%	38.1%
42,182	CLERMONT	23,940	14,914	9,026		5,888 R	62.3%	37.7%	62.3%	37.7%
25,572	CLINTON	11,301	7,919	3,382		4,537 R	70.1%	29.9%	70.1%	29.9%
98,920	COLUMBIANA	43,299	28,783	14,516		14,267 R	66.5%	33.5%	66.5%	33.5%
31,141	COSHOCTON	14,338	9,549	4,789		4,760 R	66.6%	33.4%	66.6%	33.4%
38,738	CRAWFORD	19,532	13,763	5,769		7,994 R	70.5%	29.5%	70.5%	29.5%
1,389,532	CUYAHOGA	658,032	353,474	304,558		48,916 R	53.7%	46.3%	53.7%	46.3%
41,799	DARKE	20,585	13,447	7,138		6,309 R	65.3%	34.7%	65.3%	34.7%
25,925	DEFIANCE	12,727	8,786	3,941		4,845 R	69.0%	31.0%	69.0%	31.0%
30,278	DELAWARE	14,736	10,739	3,997		6,742 R	72.9%	27.1%	72.9%	27.1%
52,565	ERIE	21,047	14,771	6,276		8,495 R	70.2%	29.8%	70.2%	29.8%
52,130	FAIRFIELD	23,984	15,647	8,337		7,310 R	65.2%	34.8%	65.2%	34.8%
22,554	FAYETTE	10,145	6,696	3,449		3,247 R	66.0%	34.0%	66.0%	34.0%
503,410	FRANKLIN	230,396	151,544	78,852		72,692 R	65.8%	34.2%	65.8%	34.2%
25,580	FULTON	11,652	9,030	2,622		6,408 R	77.5%	22.5%	77.5%	22.5%
24,910	GALLIA	9,917	7,040	2,877		4,163 R	71.0%	29.0%	71.0%	29.0%
26,646	GEAUGA	15,789	10,971	4,818		6,153 R	69.5%	30.5%	69.5%	30.5%
58,892	GREENE	25,332	15,471	9,861		5,610 R	61.1%	38.9%	61.1%	38.9%
38,452	GUERNSEY	15,373	10,224	5,149		5,075 R	66.5%	33.5%	66.5%	33.5%
723,952	HAMILTON	335,806	222,009	113,797		108,212 R	66.1%	33.9%	66.1%	33.9%
44,280	HANCOCK	21,002	15,713	5,289		10,424 R	74.8%	25.2%	74.8%	25.2%
28,673	HARDIN	13,605	9,049	4,556		4,493 R	66.5%	33.5%	66.5%	33.5%
19,054	HARRISON	8,275	5,444	2,831		2,613 R	65.8%	34.2%	65.8%	34.2%
22,423	HENRY	10,939	8,164	2,775		5,389 R	74.6%	25.4%	74.6%	25.4%
28,188	HIGHLAND	13,223	8,397	4,826		3,571 R	63.5%	36.5%	63.5%	36.5%
19,520	HOCKING	8,259	4,925	3,334		1,591 R	59.6%	40.4%	59.6%	40.4%
18,760	HOLMES	5,750	3,955	1,795		2,160 R	68.8%	31.2%	68.8%	31.2%
39,353	HURON	16,626	12,208	4,418		7,790 R	73.4%	26.6%	73.4%	26.6%
27,767	JACKSON	12,538	8,106	4,432		3,674 R	64.7%	35.3%	64.7%	35.3%
96,495	JEFFERSON	43,865	22,162	21,703		459 R	50.5%	49.5%	50.5%	49.5%
35,287	KNOX	17,305	12,347	4,958		7,389 R	71.3%	28.7%	71.3%	28.7%
75,979	LAKE	50,735	31,017	19,718		11,299 R	61.1%	38.9%	61.1%	38.9%
49,115	LAWRENCE	20,099	12,607	7,492		5,115 R	62.7%	37.3%	62.7%	37.3%
70,645	LICKING	32,493	21,912	10,581		11,331 R	67.4%	32.6%	67.4%	32.6%
31,329	LOGAN	15,455	11,229	4,226		7,003 R	72.7%	27.3%	72.7%	27.3%
148,162	LORAIN	67,114	40,340	26,774		13,566 R	60.1%	39.9%	60.1%	39.9%
395,551	LUCAS	189,099	100,501	88,598		11,903 R	53.1%	46.9%	53.1%	46.9%
22,300	MADISON	9,358	6,483	2,875		3,608 R	69.3%	30.7%	69.3%	30.7%
257,629	MAHONING	123,118	63,992	59,126		4,866 R	52.0%	48.0%	52.0%	48.0%
49,959	MARION	22,550	15,125	7,425		7,700 R	67.1%	32.9%	67.1%	32.9%
40,417	MEDINA	21,520	15,155	6,365		8,790 R	70.4%	29.6%	70.4%	29.6%
23,227	MEIGS	9,376	6,593	2,783		3,810 R	70.3%	29.7%	70.3%	29.7%
28,311	MERCER	13,728	9,456	4,272		5,184 R	68.9%	31.1%	68.9%	31.1%
61,309	MIAMI	29,364	20,135	9,229		10,906 R	68.6%	31.4%	68.6%	31.4%
15,362	MONROE	6,316	3,738	2,578		1,160 R	59.2%	40.8%	59.2%	40.8%
398,441	MONTGOMERY	183,548	107,278	76,270		31,008 R	58.4%	41.6%	58.4%	41.6%
12,836	MORGAN	5,600	4,134	1,466		2,668 R	73.8%	26.2%	73.8%	26.2%
17,168	MORROW	8,224	5,885	2,339		3,546 R	71.6%	28.4%	71.6%	28.4%
74,535	MUSKINGUM	32,898	22,788	10,110		12,678 R	69.3%	30.7%	69.3%	30.7%

OHIO

PRESIDENT 1956

1950 Census Population	County	Total Vote	Republican	Democratic	Other	Rep.-Dem. Plurality	Percentage Total Vote Rep.	Total Vote Dem.	Major Vote Rep.	Major Vote Dem.
11,750	NOBLE	5,804	3,861	1,943		1,918 R	66.5%	33.5%	66.5%	33.5%
29,469	OTTAWA	13,982	8,806	5,176		3,630 R	63.0%	37.0%	63.0%	37.0%
15,047	PAULDING	7,055	4,885	2,170		2,715 R	69.2%	30.8%	69.2%	30.8%
28,999	PERRY	11,634	7,511	4,123		3,388 R	64.6%	35.4%	64.6%	35.4%
29,352	PICKAWAY	11,465	6,956	4,509		2,447 R	60.7%	39.3%	60.7%	39.3%
14,607	PIKE	7,310	3,447	3,863		416 D	47.2%	52.8%	47.2%	52.8%
63,954	PORTAGE	32,071	18,943	13,128		5,815 R	59.1%	40.9%	59.1%	40.9%
27,081	PREBLE	12,673	8,099	4,574		3,525 R	63.9%	36.1%	63.9%	36.1%
25,248	PUTNAM	11,946	8,408	3,538		4,870 R	70.4%	29.6%	70.4%	29.6%
91,305	RICHLAND	39,676	26,098	13,578		12,520 R	65.8%	34.2%	65.8%	34.2%
54,424	ROSS	20,454	13,036	7,418		5,618 R	63.7%	36.3%	63.7%	36.3%
46,114	SANDUSKY	20,696	15,009	5,687		9,322 R	72.5%	27.5%	72.5%	27.5%
82,910	SCIOTO	37,095	22,110	14,985		7,125 R	59.6%	40.4%	59.6%	40.4%
52,978	SENECA	23,988	17,728	6,260		11,468 R	73.9%	26.1%	73.9%	26.1%
28,488	SHELBY	13,967	9,452	4,515		4,937 R	67.7%	32.3%	67.7%	32.3%
283,194	STARK	133,112	83,667	49,445		34,222 R	62.9%	37.1%	62.9%	37.1%
410,032	SUMMIT	196,250	102,872	93,378		9,494 R	52.4%	47.6%	52.4%	47.6%
158,915	TRUMBULL	76,849	43,936	32,913		11,023 R	57.2%	42.8%	57.2%	42.8%
70,320	TUSCARAWAS	32,784	19,876	12,908		6,968 R	60.6%	39.4%	60.6%	39.4%
20,687	UNION	10,228	7,575	2,653		4,922 R	74.1%	25.9%	74.1%	25.9%
26,971	VAN WERT	14,042	9,834	4,208		5,626 R	70.0%	30.0%	70.0%	30.0%
10,759	VINTON	4,914	2,998	1,916		1,082 R	61.0%	39.0%	61.0%	39.0%
38,505	WARREN	20,866	13,673	7,193		6,480 R	65.5%	34.5%	65.5%	34.5%
44,407	WASHINGTON	19,995	13,927	6,068		7,859 R	69.7%	30.3%	69.7%	30.3%
58,716	WAYNE	26,453	19,469	6,984		12,485 R	73.6%	26.4%	73.6%	26.4%
26,202	WILLIAMS	13,009	9,784	3,225		6,559 R	75.2%	24.8%	75.2%	24.8%
59,605	WOOD	25,397	16,844	8,553		8,291 R	66.3%	33.7%	66.3%	33.7%
19,785	WYANDOT	9,302	6,807	2,495		4,312 R	73.2%	26.8%	73.2%	26.8%
7,946,627	TOTAL	3,702,265	2,262,610	1,439,655		822,955 R	61.1%	38.9%	61.1%	38.9%

OHIO

PRESIDENT 1952

1950 Census Population	County	Total Vote	Republican	Democratic	Other	Rep.-Dem. Plurality	Percentage Total Vote Rep.	Total Vote Dem.	Major Vote Rep.	Major Vote Dem.
20,499	ADAMS	9,585	5,648	3,937		1,711 R	58.9%	41.1%	58.9%	41.1%
88,183	ALLEN	40,535	26,396	14,139		12,257 R	65.1%	34.9%	65.1%	34.9%
33,040	ASHLAND	17,703	12,459	5,244		7,215 R	70.4%	29.6%	70.4%	29.6%
78,695	ASHTABULA	37,861	23,185	14,676		8,509 R	61.2%	38.8%	61.2%	38.8%
45,839	ATHENS	17,937	10,829	7,108		3,721 R	60.4%	39.6%	60.4%	39.6%
30,637	AUGLAIZE	15,748	10,599	5,149		5,450 R	67.3%	32.7%	67.3%	32.7%
87,740	BELMONT	42,452	17,693	24,759		7,066 D	41.7%	58.3%	41.7%	58.3%
22,221	BROWN	10,463	5,635	4,828		807 R	53.9%	46.1%	53.9%	46.1%
147,203	BUTLER	66,520	35,769	30,751		5,018 R	53.8%	46.2%	53.8%	46.2%
19,039	CARROLL	8,841	5,707	3,134		2,573 R	64.6%	35.4%	64.6%	35.4%
26,793	CHAMPAIGN	13,443	8,880	4,563		4,317 R	66.1%	33.9%	66.1%	33.9%
111,661	CLARK	48,250	27,464	20,786		6,678 R	56.9%	43.1%	56.9%	43.1%
42,182	CLERMONT	22,923	13,221	9,702		3,519 R	57.7%	42.3%	57.7%	42.3%
25,572	CLINTON	12,076	8,191	3,885		4,306 R	67.8%	32.2%	67.8%	32.2%
98,920	COLUMBIANA	45,764	26,707	19,057		7,650 R	58.4%	41.6%	58.4%	41.6%
31,141	COSHOCTON	15,631	9,832	5,799		4,033 R	62.9%	37.1%	62.9%	37.1%
38,738	CRAWFORD	20,222	13,370	6,852		6,518 R	66.1%	33.9%	66.1%	33.9%
1,389,532	CUYAHOGA	654,427	329,465	324,962		4,503 R	50.3%	49.7%	50.3%	49.7%
41,799	DARKE	21,267	13,670	7,597		6,073 R	64.3%	35.7%	64.3%	35.7%
25,925	DEFIANCE	12,995	8,834	4,161		4,673 R	68.0%	32.0%	68.0%	32.0%
30,278	DELAWARE	14,921	10,682	4,239		6,443 R	71.6%	28.4%	71.6%	28.4%
52,565	ERIE	21,794	14,245	7,549		6,696 R	65.4%	34.6%	65.4%	34.6%
52,130	FAIRFIELD	24,167	15,027	9,140		5,887 R	62.2%	37.8%	62.2%	37.8%
22,554	FAYETTE	10,682	6,800	3,882		2,918 R	63.7%	36.3%	63.7%	36.3%
503,410	FRANKLIN	230,514	138,894	91,620		47,274 R	60.3%	39.7%	60.3%	39.7%
25,580	FULTON	11,756	9,191	2,565		6,626 R	78.2%	21.8%	78.2%	21.8%
24,910	GALLIA	9,916	6,763	3,153		3,610 R	68.2%	31.8%	68.2%	31.8%
26,646	GEAUGA	13,182	8,975	4,207		4,768 R	68.1%	31.9%	68.1%	31.9%
58,892	GREENE	22,023	12,900	9,123		3,777 R	58.6%	41.4%	58.6%	41.4%
38,452	GUERNSEY	16,380	9,749	6,631		3,118 R	59.5%	40.5%	59.5%	40.5%
723,952	HAMILTON	348,475	207,690	140,785		66,905 R	59.6%	40.4%	59.6%	40.4%
44,280	HANCOCK	20,365	14,999	5,366		9,633 R	73.7%	26.3%	73.7%	26.3%
28,673	HARDIN	14,299	9,235	5,064		4,171 R	64.6%	35.4%	64.6%	35.4%
19,054	HARRISON	8,920	5,306	3,614		1,692 R	59.5%	40.5%	59.5%	40.5%
22,423	HENRY	11,039	8,029	3,010		5,019 R	72.7%	27.3%	72.7%	27.3%
28,188	HIGHLAND	13,787	8,568	5,219		3,349 R	62.1%	37.9%	62.1%	37.9%
19,520	HOCKING	8,681	4,743	3,938		805 R	54.6%	45.4%	54.6%	45.4%
18,760	HOLMES	5,980	3,891	2,089		1,802 R	65.1%	34.9%	65.1%	34.9%
39,353	HURON	17,247	12,372	4,875		7,497 R	71.7%	28.3%	71.7%	28.3%
27,767	JACKSON	12,206	7,223	4,983		2,240 R	59.2%	40.8%	59.2%	40.8%
96,495	JEFFERSON	47,068	19,569	27,499		7,930 D	41.6%	58.4%	41.6%	58.4%
35,287	KNOX	18,399	12,705	5,694		7,011 R	69.1%	30.9%	69.1%	30.9%
75,979	LAKE	38,829	23,483	15,346		8,137 R	60.5%	39.5%	60.5%	39.5%
49,115	LAWRENCE	21,278	11,962	9,316		2,646 R	56.2%	43.8%	56.2%	43.8%
70,645	LICKING	32,103	20,385	11,718		8,667 R	63.5%	36.5%	63.5%	36.5%
31,329	LOGAN	15,877	11,084	4,793		6,291 R	69.8%	30.2%	69.8%	30.2%
148,162	LORAIN	60,019	33,825	26,194		7,631 R	56.4%	43.6%	56.4%	43.6%
395,551	LUCAS	188,533	97,490	91,043		6,447 R	51.7%	48.3%	51.7%	48.3%
22,300	MADISON	9,456	6,279	3,177		3,102 R	66.4%	33.6%	66.4%	33.6%
257,629	MAHONING	120,886	53,164	67,722		14,558 D	44.0%	56.0%	44.0%	56.0%
49,959	MARION	23,434	14,583	8,851		5,732 R	62.2%	37.8%	62.2%	37.8%
40,417	MEDINA	20,504	14,433	6,071		8,362 R	70.4%	29.6%	70.4%	29.6%
23,227	MEIGS	10,036	6,700	3,336		3,364 R	66.8%	33.2%	66.8%	33.2%
28,311	MERCER	13,783	9,058	4,725		4,333 R	65.7%	34.3%	65.7%	34.3%
61,309	MIAMI	29,987	19,525	10,462		9,063 R	65.1%	34.9%	65.1%	34.9%
15,362	MONROE	6,706	3,493	3,213		280 R	52.1%	47.9%	52.1%	47.9%
398,441	MONTGOMERY	171,765	91,905	79,860		12,045 R	53.5%	46.5%	53.5%	46.5%
12,836	MORGAN	5,981	4,303	1,678		2,625 R	71.9%	28.1%	71.9%	28.1%
17,168	MORROW	8,485	6,106	2,379		3,727 R	72.0%	28.0%	72.0%	28.0%
74,535	MUSKINGUM	33,734	21,244	12,490		8,754 R	63.0%	37.0%	63.0%	37.0%

OHIO

PRESIDENT 1952

1950 Census Population	County	Total Vote	Republican	Democratic	Other	Rep.-Dem. Plurality	Percentage Total Vote Rep.	Percentage Total Vote Dem.	Percentage Major Vote Rep.	Percentage Major Vote Dem.
11,750	NOBLE	6,100	4,046	2,054		1,992 R	66.3%	33.7%	66.3%	33.7%
29,469	OTTAWA	14,516	8,708	5,808		2,900 R	60.0%	40.0%	60.0%	40.0%
15,047	PAULDING	7,223	4,837	2,386		2,451 R	67.0%	33.0%	67.0%	33.0%
28,999	PERRY	12,700	7,425	5,275		2,150 R	58.5%	41.5%	58.5%	41.5%
29,352	PICKAWAY	11,945	6,836	5,109		1,727 R	57.2%	42.8%	57.2%	42.8%
14,607	PIKE	6,875	2,982	3,893		911 D	43.4%	56.6%	43.4%	56.6%
63,954	PORTAGE	30,721	17,168	13,553		3,615 R	55.9%	44.1%	55.9%	44.1%
27,081	PREBLE	13,241	8,405	4,836		3,569 R	63.5%	36.5%	63.5%	36.5%
25,248	PUTNAM	12,197	8,398	3,799		4,599 R	68.9%	31.1%	68.9%	31.1%
91,305	RICHLAND	40,609	25,829	14,780		11,049 R	63.6%	36.4%	63.6%	36.4%
54,424	ROSS	22,016	13,431	8,585		4,846 R	61.0%	39.0%	61.0%	39.0%
46,114	SANDUSKY	20,987	14,939	6,048		8,891 R	71.2%	28.8%	71.2%	28.8%
82,910	SCIOTO	38,548	20,403	18,145		2,258 R	52.9%	47.1%	52.9%	47.1%
52,978	SENECA	24,810	17,750	7,060		10,690 R	71.5%	28.5%	71.5%	28.5%
28,488	SHELBY	14,290	8,957	5,333		3,624 R	62.7%	37.3%	62.7%	37.3%
283,194	STARK	129,960	74,929	55,031		19,898 R	57.7%	42.3%	57.7%	42.3%
410,032	SUMMIT	188,611	91,168	97,443		6,275 D	48.3%	51.7%	48.3%	51.7%
158,915	TRUMBULL	76,855	37,793	39,062		1,269 D	49.2%	50.8%	49.2%	50.8%
70,320	TUSCARAWAS	34,952	18,620	16,332		2,288 R	53.3%	46.7%	53.3%	46.7%
20,687	UNION	10,604	7,761	2,843		4,918 R	73.2%	26.8%	73.2%	26.8%
26,971	VAN WERT	14,463	9,355	5,108		4,247 R	64.7%	35.3%	64.7%	35.3%
10,759	VINTON	4,932	2,903	2,029		874 R	58.9%	41.1%	58.9%	41.1%
38,505	WARREN	18,583	11,529	7,054		4,475 R	62.0%	38.0%	62.0%	38.0%
44,407	WASHINGTON	21,217	13,841	7,376		6,465 R	65.2%	34.8%	65.2%	34.8%
58,716	WAYNE	26,488	18,074	8,414		9,660 R	68.2%	31.8%	68.2%	31.8%
26,202	WILLIAMS	13,246	9,888	3,358		6,530 R	74.6%	25.4%	74.6%	25.4%
59,605	WOOD	26,437	17,269	9,168		8,101 R	65.3%	34.7%	65.3%	34.7%
19,785	WYANDOT	9,792	7,015	2,777		4,238 R	71.6%	28.4%	71.6%	28.4%
7,946,627	TOTAL	3,700,758	2,100,391	1,600,367		500,024 R	56.8%	43.2%	56.8%	43.2%

OHIO

PRESIDENT 1948

1940 Census Population	County	Total Vote	Republican	Democratic	Other	Rep.-Dem. Plurality	Percentage: Total Vote Rep.	Total Vote Dem.	Major Vote Rep.	Major Vote Dem.
21,705	ADAMS	9,408	5,103	4,293	12	810 R	54.2%	45.6%	54.3%	45.7%
73,303	ALLEN	30,668	17,380	13,161	127	4,219 R	56.7%	42.9%	56.9%	43.1%
29,785	ASHLAND	14,191	8,027	6,095	69	1,932 R	56.6%	42.9%	56.8%	43.2%
68,674	ASHTABULA	28,326	15,389	12,560	377	2,829 R	54.3%	44.3%	55.1%	44.9%
46,166	ATHENS	16,354	8,902	7,398	54	1,504 R	54.4%	45.2%	54.6%	45.4%
28,037	AUGLAIZE	12,522	6,818	5,670	34	1,148 R	54.4%	45.3%	54.6%	45.4%
95,614	BELMONT	37,143	13,283	23,217	643	9,934 D	35.8%	62.5%	36.4%	63.6%
21,638	BROWN	9,099	3,931	5,140	28	1,209 D	43.2%	56.5%	43.3%	56.7%
120,249	BUTLER	45,991	21,393	24,276	322	2,883 D	46.5%	52.8%	46.8%	53.2%
17,449	CARROLL	7,313	4,283	2,996	34	1,287 R	58.6%	41.0%	58.8%	41.2%
25,258	CHAMPAIGN	11,100	6,492	4,585	23	1,907 R	58.5%	41.3%	58.6%	41.4%
95,647	CLARK	35,917	18,548	17,236	133	1,312 R	51.6%	48.0%	51.8%	48.2%
34,109	CLERMONT	16,887	8,592	8,224	71	368 R	50.9%	48.7%	51.1%	48.9%
22,574	CLINTON	9,799	6,009	3,758	32	2,251 R	61.3%	38.4%	61.5%	38.5%
90,121	COLUMBIANA	34,538	17,724	16,588	226	1,136 R	51.3%	48.0%	51.7%	48.3%
30,594	COSHOCTON	13,634	7,096	6,457	81	639 R	52.0%	47.4%	52.4%	47.6%
35,571	CRAWFORD	16,503	8,862	7,600	41	1,262 R	53.7%	46.1%	53.8%	46.2%
1,217,250	CUYAHOGA	490,628	214,889	257,958	17,781	43,069 D	43.8%	52.6%	45.4%	54.6%
38,831	DARKE	17,813	8,956	8,770	87	186 R	50.3%	49.2%	50.5%	49.5%
24,367	DEFIANCE	10,409	5,927	4,454	28	1,473 R	56.9%	42.8%	57.1%	42.9%
26,780	DELAWARE	12,506	8,089	4,371	46	3,718 R	64.7%	35.0%	64.9%	35.1%
43,201	ERIE	18,302	9,568	8,644	90	924 R	52.3%	47.2%	52.5%	47.5%
48,490	FAIRFIELD	18,907	9,471	9,375	61	96 R	50.1%	49.6%	50.3%	49.7%
21,385	FAYETTE	8,395	4,865	3,513	17	1,352 R	58.0%	41.8%	58.1%	41.9%
388,712	FRANKLIN	184,999	98,707	84,806	1,486	13,901 R	53.4%	45.8%	53.8%	46.2%
23,626	FULTON	9,230	6,523	2,672	35	3,851 R	70.7%	28.9%	70.9%	29.1%
24,930	GALLIA	9,207	5,743	3,430	34	2,313 R	62.4%	37.3%	62.6%	37.4%
19,430	GEAUGA	8,622	5,535	2,960	127	2,575 R	64.2%	34.3%	65.2%	34.8%
35,863	GREENE	18,300	9,186	8,970	144	216 R	50.2%	49.0%	50.6%	49.4%
38,822	GUERNSEY	14,380	7,651	6,639	90	1,012 R	53.2%	46.2%	53.5%	46.5%
621,987	HAMILTON	288,413	151,055	135,290	2,068	15,765 R	52.4%	46.9%	52.8%	47.2%
40,793	HANCOCK	18,079	11,427	6,598	54	4,829 R	63.2%	36.5%	63.4%	36.6%
27,061	HARDIN	12,967	7,441	5,474	52	1,967 R	57.4%	42.2%	57.6%	42.4%
20,313	HARRISON	7,700	4,215	3,422	63	793 R	54.7%	44.4%	55.2%	44.8%
22,756	HENRY	8,724	5,024	3,689	11	1,335 R	57.6%	42.3%	57.7%	42.3%
27,099	HIGHLAND	12,540	6,849	5,675	16	1,174 R	54.6%	45.3%	54.7%	45.3%
21,504	HOCKING	8,212	3,733	4,462	17	729 D	45.5%	54.3%	45.6%	54.4%
17,876	HOLMES	4,982	2,496	2,480	6	16 R	50.1%	49.8%	50.2%	49.8%
34,800	HURON	15,134	9,004	6,073	57	2,931 R	59.5%	40.1%	59.7%	40.3%
27,004	JACKSON	10,874	5,782	5,059	33	723 R	53.2%	46.5%	53.3%	46.7%
98,129	JEFFERSON	38,409	14,230	23,725	454	9,495 D	37.0%	61.8%	37.5%	62.5%
31,024	KNOX	14,755	8,607	6,120	28	2,487 R	58.3%	41.5%	58.4%	41.6%
50,020	LAKE	24,108	12,973	10,844	291	2,129 R	53.8%	45.0%	54.5%	45.5%
46,705	LAWRENCE	17,684	8,113	9,495	76	1,382 D	45.9%	53.7%	46.1%	53.9%
62,279	LICKING	27,762	15,164	12,511	87	2,653 R	54.6%	45.1%	54.8%	45.2%
29,624	LOGAN	13,305	8,118	5,149	38	2,969 R	61.0%	38.7%	61.2%	38.8%
112,390	LORAIN	43,638	21,616	21,397	625	219 R	49.5%	49.0%	50.3%	49.7%
344,333	LUCAS	142,853	66,798	74,064	1,991	7,266 D	46.8%	51.8%	47.4%	52.6%
21,811	MADISON	8,094	4,730	3,356	8	1,374 R	58.4%	41.5%	58.5%	41.5%
240,251	MAHONING	101,146	37,365	62,468	1,313	25,103 D	36.9%	61.8%	37.4%	62.6%
44,898	MARION	18,606	10,333	8,223	50	2,110 R	55.5%	44.2%	55.7%	44.3%
33,034	MEDINA	14,717	9,462	5,133	122	4,329 R	64.3%	34.9%	64.8%	35.2%
24,104	MEIGS	9,193	5,564	3,595	34	1,969 R	60.5%	39.1%	60.7%	39.3%
26,256	MERCER	11,202	5,266	5,928	8	662 D	47.0%	52.9%	47.0%	53.0%
52,632	MIAMI	23,255	13,100	10,066	89	3,034 R	56.3%	43.3%	56.5%	43.5%
18,641	MONROE	6,454	2,574	3,873	7	1,299 D	39.9%	60.0%	39.9%	60.1%
295,480	MONTGOMERY	138,114	60,048	76,879	1,187	16,831 D	43.5%	55.7%	43.9%	56.1%
14,227	MORGAN	5,276	3,480	1,783	13	1,697 R	66.0%	33.8%	66.1%	33.9%
15,646	MORROW	6,955	4,327	2,616	12	1,711 R	62.2%	37.6%	62.3%	37.7%
69,795	MUSKINGUM	28,895	16,049	12,765	81	3,284 R	55.5%	44.2%	55.7%	44.3%

OHIO

PRESIDENT 1948

1940 Census Population	County	Total Vote	Republican	Democratic	Other	Rep.-Dem. Plurality	Percentage Total Vote Rep.	Total Vote Dem.	Major Vote Rep.	Major Vote Dem.
14,587	NOBLE	5,943	3,494	2,425	24	1,069 R	58.8%	40.8%	59.0%	41.0%
24,360	OTTAWA	11,783	5,591	6,157	35	566 D	47.4%	52.3%	47.6%	52.4%
15,527	PAULDING	6,110	3,579	2,512	19	1,067 R	58.6%	41.1%	58.8%	41.2%
31,087	PERRY	10,992	5,692	5,264	36	428 R	51.8%	47.9%	52.0%	48.0%
27,889	PICKAWAY	10,262	4,965	5,290	7	325 D	48.4%	51.5%	48.4%	51.6%
16,113	PIKE	7,161	2,639	4,516	6	1,877 D	36.9%	63.1%	36.9%	63.1%
46,660	PORTAGE	23,876	11,621	11,987	268	366 D	48.7%	50.2%	49.2%	50.8%
23,329	PREBLE	10,516	5,837	4,656	23	1,181 R	55.5%	44.3%	55.6%	44.4%
25,016	PUTNAM	10,148	5,006	5,114	28	108 D	49.3%	50.4%	49.5%	50.5%
73,853	RICHLAND	30,886	15,894	14,712	280	1,182 R	51.5%	47.6%	51.9%	48.1%
52,147	ROSS	19,964	10,398	9,524	42	874 R	52.1%	47.7%	52.2%	47.8%
41,014	SANDUSKY	18,099	10,847	7,216	36	3,631 R	59.9%	39.9%	60.1%	39.9%
86,565	SCIOTO	34,852	16,800	17,923	129	1,123 D	48.2%	51.4%	48.4%	51.6%
48,499	SENECA	19,524	11,493	7,954	77	3,539 R	58.9%	40.7%	59.1%	40.9%
26,071	SHELBY	12,377	5,406	6,939	32	1,533 D	43.7%	56.1%	43.8%	56.2%
234,887	STARK	100,150	51,482	47,533	1,135	3,949 R	51.4%	47.5%	52.0%	48.0%
339,405	SUMMIT	140,950	60,174	78,096	2,680	17,922 D	42.7%	55.4%	43.5%	56.5%
132,315	TRUMBULL	63,392	25,297	37,097	998	11,800 D	39.9%	58.5%	40.5%	59.5%
68,816	TUSCARAWAS	26,817	11,873	14,799	145	2,926 D	44.3%	55.2%	44.5%	55.5%
20,012	UNION	8,713	5,688	3,008	17	2,680 R	65.3%	34.5%	65.4%	34.6%
26,759	VAN WERT	11,936	6,785	5,127	24	1,658 R	56.8%	43.0%	57.0%	43.0%
11,573	VINTON	4,355	2,323	2,016	16	307 R	53.3%	46.3%	53.5%	46.5%
29,894	WARREN	13,409	7,584	5,793	32	1,791 R	56.6%	43.2%	56.7%	43.3%
43,537	WASHINGTON	17,936	10,349	7,542	45	2,807 R	57.7%	42.0%	57.8%	42.2%
50,520	WAYNE	21,090	12,152	8,868	70	3,284 R	57.6%	42.0%	57.8%	42.2%
25,510	WILLIAMS	10,470	6,784	3,662	24	3,122 R	64.8%	35.0%	64.9%	35.1%
51,796	WOOD	23,041	13,197	9,725	119	3,472 R	57.3%	42.2%	57.6%	42.4%
19,218	WYANDOT	8,182	4,849	3,308	25	1,541 R	59.3%	40.4%	59.4%	40.6%
6,907,612	TOTAL	2,936,071	1,445,684	1,452,791	37,596	7,107 D	49.2%	49.5%	49.9%	50.1%

OHIO

PRESIDENT 1944

1940 Census Population	County	Total Vote	Republican	Democratic	Other	Rep.-Dem. Plurality	Percentage Total Vote Rep.	Total Vote Dem.	Major Vote Rep.	Major Vote Dem.
21,705	ADAMS	9,588	5,590	3,998		1,592 R	58.3%	41.7%	58.3%	41.7%
73,303	ALLEN	33,588	21,024	12,564		8,460 R	62.6%	37.4%	62.6%	37.4%
29,785	ASHLAND	15,124	8,994	6,130		2,864 R	59.5%	40.5%	59.5%	40.5%
68,674	ASHTABULA	30,500	17,181	13,319		3,862 R	56.3%	43.7%	56.3%	43.7%
46,166	ATHENS	17,764	10,326	7,438		2,888 R	58.1%	41.9%	58.1%	41.9%
28,037	AUGLAIZE	13,868	8,980	4,888		4,092 R	64.8%	35.2%	64.8%	35.2%
95,614	BELMONT	39,578	15,485	24,093		8,608 D	39.1%	60.9%	39.1%	60.9%
21,638	BROWN	9,767	5,024	4,743		281 R	51.4%	48.6%	51.4%	48.6%
120,249	BUTLER	49,400	22,702	26,698		3,996 D	46.0%	54.0%	46.0%	54.0%
17,449	CARROLL	7,805	4,898	2,907		1,991 R	62.8%	37.2%	62.8%	37.2%
25,258	CHAMPAIGN	12,595	7,795	4,800		2,995 R	61.9%	38.1%	61.9%	38.1%
95,647	CLARK	44,569	22,207	22,362		155 D	49.8%	50.2%	49.8%	50.2%
34,109	CLERMONT	17,062	9,125	7,937		1,188 R	53.5%	46.5%	53.5%	46.5%
22,574	CLINTON	10,913	7,200	3,713		3,487 R	66.0%	34.0%	66.0%	34.0%
90,121	COLUMBIANA	38,772	19,976	18,796		1,180 R	51.5%	48.5%	51.5%	48.5%
30,594	COSHOCTON	14,043	7,917	6,126		1,791 R	56.4%	43.6%	56.4%	43.6%
35,571	CRAWFORD	17,543	10,464	7,079		3,385 R	59.6%	40.4%	59.6%	40.4%
1,217,250	CUYAHOGA	548,483	217,824	330,659		112,835 D	39.7%	60.3%	39.7%	60.3%
38,831	DARKE	19,171	11,135	8,036		3,099 R	58.1%	41.9%	58.1%	41.9%
24,367	DEFIANCE	11,084	7,450	3,634		3,816 R	67.2%	32.8%	67.2%	32.8%
26,780	DELAWARE	13,755	9,186	4,569		4,617 R	66.8%	33.2%	66.8%	33.2%
43,201	ERIE	18,416	10,663	7,753		2,910 R	57.9%	42.1%	57.9%	42.1%
48,490	FAIRFIELD	19,574	11,135	8,439		2,696 R	56.9%	43.1%	56.9%	43.1%
21,385	FAYETTE	9,878	5,933	3,945		1,988 R	60.1%	39.9%	60.1%	39.9%
388,712	FRANKLIN	188,686	99,292	89,394		9,898 R	52.6%	47.4%	52.6%	47.4%
23,626	FULTON	10,405	8,258	2,147		6,111 R	79.4%	20.6%	79.4%	20.6%
24,930	GALLIA	9,432	6,464	2,968		3,496 R	68.5%	31.5%	68.5%	31.5%
19,430	GEAUGA	8,559	5,295	3,264		2,031 R	61.9%	38.1%	61.9%	38.1%
35,863	GREENE	17,617	9,680	7,937		1,743 R	54.9%	45.1%	54.9%	45.1%
38,822	GUERNSEY	15,390	8,878	6,512		2,366 R	57.7%	42.3%	57.7%	42.3%
621,987	HAMILTON	299,430	154,960	144,470		10,490 R	51.8%	48.2%	51.8%	48.2%
40,793	HANCOCK	19,702	13,450	6,252		7,198 R	68.3%	31.7%	68.3%	31.7%
27,061	HARDIN	13,694	8,566	5,128		3,438 R	62.6%	37.4%	62.6%	37.4%
20,313	HARRISON	8,575	5,194	3,381		1,813 R	60.6%	39.4%	60.6%	39.4%
22,756	HENRY	9,846	7,241	2,605		4,636 R	73.5%	26.5%	73.5%	26.5%
27,099	HIGHLAND	13,299	7,963	5,336		2,627 R	59.9%	40.1%	59.9%	40.1%
21,504	HOCKING	8,301	4,535	3,766		769 R	54.6%	45.4%	54.6%	45.4%
17,876	HOLMES	5,656	3,093	2,563		530 R	54.7%	45.3%	54.7%	45.3%
34,800	HURON	17,321	11,442	5,879		5,563 R	66.1%	33.9%	66.1%	33.9%
27,004	JACKSON	11,452	6,786	4,666		2,120 R	59.3%	40.7%	59.3%	40.7%
98,129	JEFFERSON	40,323	15,496	24,827		9,331 D	38.4%	61.6%	38.4%	61.6%
31,024	KNOX	15,536	9,963	5,573		4,390 R	64.1%	35.9%	64.1%	35.9%
50,020	LAKE	26,410	13,697	12,713		984 R	51.9%	48.1%	51.9%	48.1%
46,705	LAWRENCE	17,278	9,312	7,966		1,346 R	53.9%	46.1%	53.9%	46.1%
62,279	LICKING	29,634	16,815	12,819		3,996 R	56.7%	43.3%	56.7%	43.3%
29,624	LOGAN	14,826	9,882	4,944		4,938 R	66.7%	33.3%	66.7%	33.3%
112,390	LORAIN	49,120	23,866	25,254		1,388 D	48.6%	51.4%	48.6%	51.4%
344,333	LUCAS	153,356	77,247	76,109		1,138 R	50.4%	49.6%	50.4%	49.6%
21,811	MADISON	8,920	5,546	3,374		2,172 R	62.2%	37.8%	62.2%	37.8%
240,251	MAHONING	105,286	35,184	70,102		34,918 D	33.4%	66.6%	33.4%	66.6%
44,898	MARION	20,700	11,925	8,775		3,150 R	57.6%	42.4%	57.6%	42.4%
33,034	MEDINA	16,378	10,375	6,003		4,372 R	63.3%	36.7%	63.3%	36.7%
24,104	MEIGS	9,800	6,401	3,399		3,002 R	65.3%	34.7%	65.3%	34.7%
26,256	MERCER	12,234	7,712	4,522		3,190 R	63.0%	37.0%	63.0%	37.0%
52,632	MIAMI	25,227	14,751	10,476		4,275 R	58.5%	41.5%	58.5%	41.5%
18,641	MONROE	7,191	3,617	3,574		43 R	50.3%	49.7%	50.3%	49.7%
295,480	MONTGOMERY	145,703	63,336	82,367		19,031 D	43.5%	56.5%	43.5%	56.5%
14,227	MORGAN	5,974	4,309	1,665		2,644 R	72.1%	27.9%	72.1%	27.9%
15,646	MORROW	7,795	5,439	2,356		3,083 R	69.8%	30.2%	69.8%	30.2%
69,795	MUSKINGUM	30,306	17,577	12,729		4,848 R	58.0%	42.0%	58.0%	42.0%

OHIO

PRESIDENT 1944

1940 Census Population	County	Total Vote	Republican	Democratic	Other	Rep.-Dem. Plurality	Percentage Total Vote Rep.	Total Vote Dem.	Major Vote Rep.	Major Vote Dem.
14,587	NOBLE	6,365	4,130	2,235		1,895 R	64.9%	35.1%	64.9%	35.1%
24,360	OTTAWA	11,863	6,922	4,941		1,981 R	58.3%	41.7%	58.3%	41.7%
15,527	PAULDING	6,870	4,515	2,355		2,160 R	65.7%	34.3%	65.7%	34.3%
31,087	PERRY	12,389	7,339	5,050		2,289 R	59.2%	40.8%	59.2%	40.8%
27,889	PICKAWAY	11,359	5,997	5,362		635 R	52.8%	47.2%	52.8%	47.2%
16,113	PIKE	7,085	3,117	3,968		851 D	44.0%	56.0%	44.0%	56.0%
46,660	PORTAGE	24,817	12,284	12,533		249 D	49.5%	50.5%	49.5%	50.5%
23,329	PREBLE	11,481	6,609	4,872		1,737 R	57.6%	42.4%	57.6%	42.4%
25,016	PUTNAM	11,149	8,004	3,145		4,859 R	71.8%	28.2%	71.8%	28.2%
73,853	RICHLAND	33,471	18,065	15,406		2,659 R	54.0%	46.0%	54.0%	46.0%
52,147	ROSS	21,352	11,424	9,928		1,496 R	53.5%	46.5%	53.5%	46.5%
41,014	SANDUSKY	19,892	13,763	6,129		7,634 R	69.2%	30.8%	69.2%	30.8%
86,565	SCIOTO	34,623	17,489	17,134		355 R	50.5%	49.5%	50.5%	49.5%
48,499	SENECA	21,361	15,137	6,224		8,913 R	70.9%	29.1%	70.9%	29.1%
26,071	SHELBY	12,706	7,084	5,622		1,462 R	55.8%	44.2%	55.8%	44.2%
234,887	STARK	108,899	51,506	57,393		5,887 D	47.3%	52.7%	47.3%	52.7%
339,405	SUMMIT	155,479	64,696	90,783		26,087 D	41.6%	58.4%	41.6%	58.4%
132,315	TRUMBULL	59,462	25,150	34,312		9,162 D	42.3%	57.7%	42.3%	57.7%
68,816	TUSCARAWAS	30,541	14,357	16,184		1,827 D	47.0%	53.0%	47.0%	53.0%
20,012	UNION	9,815	6,908	2,907		4,001 R	70.4%	29.6%	70.4%	29.6%
26,759	VAN WERT	13,575	8,529	5,046		3,483 R	62.8%	37.2%	62.8%	37.2%
11,573	VINTON	4,545	2,719	1,826		893 R	59.8%	40.2%	59.8%	40.2%
29,894	WARREN	14,363	8,598	5,765		2,833 R	59.9%	40.1%	59.9%	40.1%
43,537	WASHINGTON	18,699	11,676	7,023		4,653 R	62.4%	37.6%	62.4%	37.6%
50,520	WAYNE	23,122	13,616	9,506		4,110 R	58.9%	41.1%	58.9%	41.1%
25,510	WILLIAMS	12,155	8,738	3,417		5,321 R	71.9%	28.1%	71.9%	28.1%
51,796	WOOD	24,041	16,016	8,025		7,991 R	66.6%	33.4%	66.6%	33.4%
19,218	WYANDOT	9,375	6,144	3,231		2,913 R	65.5%	34.5%	65.5%	34.5%
6,907,612	TOTAL	3,153,056	1,582,293	1,570,763		11,530 R	50.2%	49.8%	50.2%	49.8%

OHIO

PRESIDENT 1940

1940 Census Population	County	Total Vote	Republican	Democratic	Other	Rep.-Dem. Plurality	Percentage: Total Vote Rep.	Total Vote Dem.	Major Vote Rep.	Major Vote Dem.
21,705	ADAMS	11,187	6,180	5,007		1,173 R	55.2%	44.8%	55.2%	44.8%
73,303	ALLEN	35,144	20,675	14,469		6,206 R	58.8%	41.2%	58.8%	41.2%
29,785	ASHLAND	16,459	8,624	7,835		789 R	52.4%	47.6%	52.4%	47.6%
68,674	ASHTABULA	32,945	18,491	14,454		4,037 R	56.1%	43.9%	56.1%	43.9%
46,166	ATHENS	22,662	11,213	11,449		236 D	49.5%	50.5%	49.5%	50.5%
28,037	AUGLAIZE	14,657	8,953	5,704		3,249 R	61.1%	38.9%	61.1%	38.9%
95,614	BELMONT	46,323	17,705	28,618		10,913 D	38.2%	61.8%	38.2%	61.8%
21,638	BROWN	11,121	5,477	5,644		167 D	49.2%	50.8%	49.2%	50.8%
120,249	BUTLER	54,201	23,380	30,821		7,441 D	43.1%	56.9%	43.1%	56.9%
17,449	CARROLL	8,749	5,160	3,589		1,571 R	59.0%	41.0%	59.0%	41.0%
25,258	CHAMPAIGN	13,770	7,841	5,929		1,912 R	56.9%	43.1%	56.9%	43.1%
95,647	CLARK	46,569	20,681	25,888		5,207 D	44.4%	55.6%	44.4%	55.6%
34,109	CLERMONT	18,309	9,367	8,942		425 R	51.2%	48.8%	51.2%	48.8%
22,574	CLINTON	11,991	7,027	4,964		2,063 R	58.6%	41.4%	58.6%	41.4%
90,121	COLUMBIANA	43,570	21,221	22,349		1,128 D	48.7%	51.3%	48.7%	51.3%
30,594	COSHOCTON	16,512	8,623	7,889		734 R	52.2%	47.8%	52.2%	47.8%
35,571	CRAWFORD	19,302	10,336	8,966		1,370 R	53.5%	46.5%	53.5%	46.5%
1,217,250	CUYAHOGA	556,188	209,070	347,118		138,048 D	37.6%	62.4%	37.6%	62.4%
38,831	DARKE	20,798	11,147	9,651		1,496 R	53.6%	46.4%	53.6%	46.4%
24,367	DEFIANCE	12,323	8,010	4,313		3,697 R	65.0%	35.0%	65.0%	35.0%
26,780	DELAWARE	15,236	9,570	5,666		3,904 R	62.8%	37.2%	62.8%	37.2%
43,201	ERIE	20,521	11,267	9,254		2,013 R	54.9%	45.1%	54.9%	45.1%
48,490	FAIRFIELD	22,111	10,813	11,298		485 D	48.9%	51.1%	48.9%	51.1%
21,385	FAYETTE	11,233	5,984	5,249		735 R	53.3%	46.7%	53.3%	46.7%
388,712	FRANKLIN	189,134	92,533	96,601		4,068 D	48.9%	51.1%	48.9%	51.1%
23,626	FULTON	11,183	8,653	2,530		6,123 R	77.4%	22.6%	77.4%	22.6%
24,930	GALLIA	11,228	7,285	3,943		3,342 R	64.9%	35.1%	64.9%	35.1%
19,430	GEAUGA	8,689	5,371	3,318		2,053 R	61.8%	38.2%	61.8%	38.2%
35,863	GREENE	18,154	9,273	8,881		392 R	51.1%	48.9%	51.1%	48.9%
38,822	GUERNSEY	18,835	10,125	8,710		1,415 R	53.8%	46.2%	53.8%	46.2%
621,987	HAMILTON	303,640	154,733	148,907		5,826 R	51.0%	49.0%	51.0%	49.0%
40,793	HANCOCK	21,929	14,174	7,755		6,419 R	64.6%	35.4%	64.6%	35.4%
27,061	HARDIN	15,739	9,192	6,547		2,645 R	58.4%	41.6%	58.4%	41.6%
20,313	HARRISON	10,288	5,729	4,559		1,170 R	55.7%	44.3%	55.7%	44.3%
22,756	HENRY	11,292	7,784	3,508		4,276 R	68.9%	31.1%	68.9%	31.1%
27,099	HIGHLAND	15,451	8,530	6,921		1,609 R	55.2%	44.8%	55.2%	44.8%
21,504	HOCKING	11,024	5,336	5,688		352 D	48.4%	51.6%	48.4%	51.6%
17,876	HOLMES	6,550	3,201	3,349		148 D	48.9%	51.1%	48.9%	51.1%
34,800	HURON	18,499	11,758	6,741		5,017 R	63.6%	36.4%	63.6%	36.4%
27,004	JACKSON	13,933	7,551	6,382		1,169 R	54.2%	45.8%	54.2%	45.8%
98,129	JEFFERSON	46,092	16,578	29,514		12,936 D	36.0%	64.0%	36.0%	64.0%
31,024	KNOX	17,384	10,303	7,081		3,222 R	59.3%	40.7%	59.3%	40.7%
50,020	LAKE	25,872	13,464	12,408		1,056 R	52.0%	48.0%	52.0%	48.0%
46,705	LAWRENCE	20,935	10,274	10,661		387 D	49.1%	50.9%	49.1%	50.9%
62,279	LICKING	32,667	16,288	16,379		91 D	49.9%	50.1%	49.9%	50.1%
29,624	LOGAN	16,212	9,861	6,351		3,510 R	60.8%	39.2%	60.8%	39.2%
112,390	LORAIN	49,253	23,422	25,831		2,409 D	47.6%	52.4%	47.6%	52.4%
344,333	LUCAS	154,353	76,405	77,948		1,543 D	49.5%	50.5%	49.5%	50.5%
21,811	MADISON	10,294	5,904	4,390		1,514 R	57.4%	42.6%	57.4%	42.6%
240,251	MAHONING	113,937	37,496	76,441		38,945 D	32.9%	67.1%	32.9%	67.1%
44,898	MARION	22,279	11,817	10,462		1,355 R	53.0%	47.0%	53.0%	47.0%
33,034	MEDINA	16,838	10,116	6,722		3,394 R	60.1%	39.9%	60.1%	39.9%
24,104	MEIGS	12,222	7,239	4,983		2,256 R	59.2%	40.8%	59.2%	40.8%
26,256	MERCER	13,019	7,905	5,114		2,791 R	60.7%	39.3%	60.7%	39.3%
52,632	MIAMI	26,524	14,725	11,799		2,926 R	55.5%	44.5%	55.5%	44.5%
18,641	MONROE	8,672	4,534	4,138		396 R	52.3%	47.7%	52.3%	47.7%
295,480	MONTGOMERY	143,950	57,866	86,084		28,218 D	40.2%	59.8%	40.2%	59.8%
14,227	MORGAN	7,603	4,966	2,637		2,329 R	65.3%	34.7%	65.3%	34.7%
15,646	MORROW	8,672	5,457	3,215		2,242 R	62.9%	37.1%	62.9%	37.1%
69,795	MUSKINGUM	35,148	19,395	15,753		3,642 R	55.2%	44.8%	55.2%	44.8%

OHIO

PRESIDENT 1940

1940 Census Population	County	Total Vote	Republican	Democratic	Other	Rep.-Dem. Plurality	Percentage Total Vote Rep.	Total Vote Dem.	Major Vote Rep.	Major Vote Dem.
14,587	NOBLE	7,959	4,922	3,037		1,885 R	61.8%	38.2%	61.8%	38.2%
24,360	OTTAWA	12,428	6,872	5,556		1,316 R	55.3%	44.7%	55.3%	44.7%
15,527	PAULDING	8,104	4,949	3,155		1,794 R	61.1%	38.9%	61.1%	38.9%
31,087	PERRY	15,609	8,656	6,953		1,703 R	55.5%	44.5%	55.5%	44.5%
27,889	PICKAWAY	12,869	5,974	6,895		921 D	46.4%	53.6%	46.4%	53.6%
16,113	PIKE	8,127	3,165	4,962		1,797 D	38.9%	61.1%	38.9%	61.1%
46,660	PORTAGE	24,464	11,777	12,687		910 D	48.1%	51.9%	48.1%	51.9%
23,329	PREBLE	12,246	6,511	5,735		776 R	53.2%	46.8%	53.2%	46.8%
25,016	PUTNAM	12,601	8,946	3,655		5,291 R	71.0%	29.0%	71.0%	29.0%
73,853	RICHLAND	35,802	17,157	18,645		1,488 D	47.9%	52.1%	47.9%	52.1%
52,147	ROSS	24,227	11,780	12,447		667 D	48.6%	51.4%	48.6%	51.4%
41,014	SANDUSKY	21,170	14,054	7,116		6,938 R	66.4%	33.6%	66.4%	33.6%
86,565	SCIOTO	41,388	19,462	21,926		2,464 D	47.0%	53.0%	47.0%	53.0%
48,499	SENECA	23,736	16,272	7,464		8,808 R	68.6%	31.4%	68.6%	31.4%
26,071	SHELBY	13,235	7,130	6,105		1,025 R	53.9%	46.1%	53.9%	46.1%
234,887	STARK	105,880	46,384	59,496		13,112 D	43.8%	56.2%	43.8%	56.2%
339,405	SUMMIT	152,960	63,405	89,555		26,150 D	41.5%	58.5%	41.5%	58.5%
132,315	TRUMBULL	59,641	25,026	34,615		9,589 D	42.0%	58.0%	42.0%	58.0%
68,816	TUSCARAWAS	33,679	14,675	19,004		4,329 D	43.6%	56.4%	43.6%	56.4%
20,012	UNION	11,161	7,214	3,947		3,267 R	64.6%	35.4%	64.6%	35.4%
26,759	VAN WERT	14,910	8,656	6,254		2,402 R	58.1%	41.9%	58.1%	41.9%
11,573	VINTON	5,594	3,190	2,404		786 R	57.0%	43.0%	57.0%	43.0%
29,894	WARREN	15,617	8,722	6,895		1,827 R	55.8%	44.2%	55.8%	44.2%
43,537	WASHINGTON	22,142	13,558	8,584		4,974 R	61.2%	38.8%	61.2%	38.8%
50,520	WAYNE	24,273	13,525	10,748		2,777 R	55.7%	44.3%	55.7%	44.3%
25,510	WILLIAMS	13,528	9,463	4,065		5,398 R	70.0%	30.0%	70.0%	30.0%
51,796	WOOD	26,709	16,998	9,711		7,287 R	63.6%	36.4%	63.6%	36.4%
19,218	WYANDOT	10,478	6,272	4,206		2,066 R	59.9%	40.1%	59.9%	40.1%
6,907,612	TOTAL	3,319,912	1,586,773	1,733,139		146,366 D	47.8%	52.2%	47.8%	52.2%

OHIO

PRESIDENT 1936

1930 Census Population	County	Total Vote	Republican	Democratic	Other	Rep.-Dem. Plurality	Percentage Total Vote Rep.	Percentage Total Vote Dem.	Percentage Major Vote Rep.	Percentage Major Vote Dem.
20,381	ADAMS	11,770	5,910	5,832	28	78 R	50.2%	49.5%	50.3%	49.7%
69,419	ALLEN	33,592	15,079	16,500	2,013	1,421 D	44.9%	49.1%	47.8%	52.2%
26,867	ASHLAND	15,352	6,154	8,818	380	2,664 D	40.1%	57.4%	41.1%	58.9%
68,361	ASHTABULA	30,010	14,025	14,468	1,517	443 D	46.7%	48.2%	49.2%	50.8%
44,175	ATHENS	22,922	9,509	13,205	208	3,696 D	41.5%	57.6%	41.9%	58.1%
28,034	AUGLAIZE	14,305	5,526	7,835	944	2,309 D	38.6%	54.8%	41.4%	58.6%
94,719	BELMONT	45,481	14,511	30,545	425	16,034 D	31.9%	67.2%	32.2%	67.8%
20,148	BROWN	11,088	4,511	6,316	261	1,805 D	40.7%	57.0%	41.7%	58.3%
114,084	BUTLER	49,832	17,842	29,892	2,098	12,050 D	35.8%	60.0%	37.4%	62.6%
16,057	CARROLL	8,337	4,440	3,801	96	639 R	53.3%	45.6%	53.9%	46.1%
24,103	CHAMPAIGN	13,719	6,872	6,485	362	387 R	50.1%	47.3%	51.4%	48.6%
90,936	CLARK	42,540	15,483	26,138	919	10,655 D	36.4%	61.4%	37.2%	62.8%
29,786	CLERMONT	17,270	7,608	9,204	458	1,596 D	44.1%	53.3%	45.3%	54.7%
21,547	CLINTON	12,127	6,265	5,785	77	480 R	51.7%	47.7%	52.0%	48.0%
86,484	COLUMBIANA	40,198	16,986	22,664	548	5,678 D	42.3%	56.4%	42.8%	57.2%
28,976	COSHOCTON	15,866	6,449	9,316	101	2,867 D	40.6%	58.7%	40.9%	59.1%
35,345	CRAWFORD	18,419	6,638	10,955	826	4,317 D	36.0%	59.5%	37.7%	62.3%
1,201,455	CUYAHOGA	475,418	128,947	311,117	35,354	182,170 D	27.1%	65.4%	29.3%	70.7%
38,009	DARKE	20,283	8,375	11,114	794	2,739 D	41.3%	54.8%	43.0%	57.0%
22,714	DEFIANCE	11,670	5,000	5,608	1,062	608 D	42.8%	48.1%	47.1%	52.9%
26,016	DELAWARE	14,709	7,364	7,045	300	319 R	50.1%	47.9%	51.1%	48.9%
42,133	ERIE	18,720	6,869	10,376	1,475	3,507 D	36.7%	55.4%	39.8%	60.2%
44,010	FAIRFIELD	20,830	8,062	12,322	446	4,260 D	38.7%	59.2%	39.6%	60.4%
20,755	FAYETTE	10,689	4,841	5,807	41	966 D	45.3%	54.3%	45.5%	54.5%
361,055	FRANKLIN	158,047	63,830	90,746	3,471	26,916 D	40.4%	57.4%	41.3%	58.7%
23,477	FULTON	10,224	6,152	3,582	490	2,570 R	60.2%	35.0%	63.2%	36.8%
23,050	GALLIA	11,275	6,700	4,548	27	2,152 R	59.4%	40.3%	59.6%	40.4%
15,414	GEAUGA	7,314	3,620	3,400	294	220 R	49.5%	46.5%	51.6%	48.4%
33,259	GREENE	16,712	7,449	8,946	317	1,497 D	44.6%	53.5%	45.4%	54.6%
41,486	GUERNSEY	20,070	8,532	11,404	134	2,872 D	42.5%	56.8%	42.8%	57.2%
589,356	HAMILTON	280,436	108,506	153,117	18,813	44,611 D	38.7%	54.6%	41.5%	58.5%
40,404	HANCOCK	20,784	9,816	9,929	1,039	113 D	47.2%	47.8%	49.7%	50.3%
27,635	HARDIN	16,283	7,631	8,441	211	810 D	46.9%	51.8%	47.5%	52.5%
18,844	HARRISON	10,045	4,779	5,231	35	452 D	47.6%	52.1%	47.7%	52.3%
22,524	HENRY	10,668	4,108	5,472	1,088	1,364 D	38.5%	51.3%	42.9%	57.1%
25,416	HIGHLAND	15,451	7,392	8,011	48	619 D	47.8%	51.8%	48.0%	52.0%
20,407	HOCKING	10,678	3,960	6,580	138	2,620 D	37.1%	61.6%	37.6%	62.4%
16,726	HOLMES	6,432	2,247	4,097	88	1,850 D	34.9%	63.7%	35.4%	64.6%
33,700	HURON	18,022	8,318	8,500	1,204	182 D	46.2%	47.2%	49.5%	50.5%
25,040	JACKSON	13,694	6,853	6,802	39	51 R	50.0%	49.7%	50.2%	49.8%
88,307	JEFFERSON	40,935	13,044	27,472	419	14,428 D	31.9%	67.1%	32.2%	67.8%
29,338	KNOX	16,641	7,956	8,315	370	359 D	47.8%	50.0%	48.9%	51.1%
41,674	LAKE	21,707	9,386	11,213	1,108	1,827 D	43.2%	51.7%	45.6%	54.4%
44,541	LAWRENCE	20,066	8,498	11,471	97	2,973 D	42.4%	57.2%	42.6%	57.4%
59,962	LICKING	30,372	11,958	17,785	629	5,827 D	39.4%	58.6%	40.2%	59.8%
28,981	LOGAN	15,905	8,363	7,353	189	1,010 R	52.6%	46.2%	53.2%	46.8%
109,206	LORAIN	42,656	15,906	24,393	2,357	8,487 D	37.3%	57.2%	39.5%	60.5%
347,709	LUCAS	132,979	45,853	74,155	12,971	28,302 D	34.5%	55.8%	38.2%	61.8%
20,253	MADISON	10,130	4,843	5,184	103	341 D	47.8%	51.2%	48.3%	51.7%
236,142	MAHONING	90,858	24,825	64,886	1,147	40,061 D	27.3%	71.4%	27.7%	72.3%
45,420	MARION	21,427	9,070	11,881	476	2,811 D	42.3%	55.4%	43.3%	56.7%
29,677	MEDINA	15,058	7,283	7,400	375	117 D	48.4%	49.1%	49.6%	50.4%
23,961	MEIGS	12,549	6,464	6,085		379 R	51.5%	48.5%	51.5%	48.5%
25,096	MERCER	13,204	3,602	7,217	2,385	3,615 D	27.3%	54.7%	33.3%	66.7%
51,301	MIAMI	25,286	11,343	12,754	1,189	1,411 D	44.9%	50.4%	47.1%	52.9%
18,426	MONROE	8,709	3,211	5,368	130	2,157 D	36.9%	61.6%	37.4%	62.6%
273,481	MONTGOMERY	127,778	44,742	76,430	6,606	31,688 D	35.0%	59.8%	36.9%	63.1%
13,583	MORGAN	7,801	4,630	3,093	78	1,537 R	59.4%	39.6%	60.0%	40.0%
14,489	MORROW	8,252	4,086	3,947	219	139 R	49.5%	47.8%	50.9%	49.1%
67,398	MUSKINGUM	32,573	15,454	16,265	854	811 D	47.4%	49.9%	48.7%	51.3%

OHIO

PRESIDENT 1936

1930 Census Population	County	Total Vote	Republican	Democratic	Other	Rep.-Dem. Plurality	Percentage Total Vote Rep.	Percentage Total Vote Dem.	Percentage Major Vote Rep.	Percentage Major Vote Dem.
14,961	NOBLE	8,319	4,384	3,865	70	519 R	52.7%	46.5%	53.1%	46.9%
24,109	OTTAWA	11,139	4,006	6,335	798	2,329 D	36.0%	56.9%	38.7%	61.3%
15,301	PAULDING	8,251	3,853	4,179	219	326 D	46.7%	50.6%	48.0%	52.0%
31,445	PERRY	15,785	6,826	8,508	451	1,682 D	43.2%	53.9%	44.5%	55.5%
27,238	PICKAWAY	12,763	4,920	7,813	30	2,893 D	38.5%	61.2%	38.6%	61.4%
13,876	PIKE	8,244	2,953	5,287	4	2,334 D	35.8%	64.1%	35.8%	64.2%
42,682	PORTAGE	22,463	8,035	13,798	630	5,763 D	35.8%	61.4%	36.8%	63.2%
22,455	PREBLE	12,290	5,593	6,366	331	773 D	45.5%	51.8%	46.8%	53.2%
25,074	PUTNAM	12,517	4,151	5,786	2,580	1,635 D	33.2%	46.2%	41.8%	58.2%
65,902	RICHLAND	32,758	11,220	20,070	1,468	8,850 D	34.3%	61.3%	35.9%	64.1%
45,181	ROSS	22,441	9,817	12,503	121	2,686 D	43.7%	55.7%	44.0%	56.0%
39,731	SANDUSKY	20,265	8,692	9,171	2,402	479 D	42.9%	45.3%	48.7%	51.3%
81,221	SCIOTO	40,380	17,860	22,243	277	4,383 D	44.2%	55.1%	44.5%	55.5%
47,941	SENECA	22,259	9,953	8,982	3,324	971 R	44.7%	40.4%	52.6%	47.4%
24,924	SHELBY	13,307	4,482	7,110	1,715	2,628 D	33.7%	53.4%	38.7%	61.3%
221,784	STARK	96,612	34,693	57,931	3,988	23,238 D	35.9%	60.0%	37.5%	62.5%
344,131	SUMMIT	133,696	38,991	91,836	2,869	52,845 D	29.2%	68.7%	29.8%	70.2%
123,063	TRUMBULL	50,329	16,887	32,384	1,058	15,497 D	33.6%	64.3%	34.3%	65.7%
68,193	TUSCARAWAS	32,965	10,317	21,991	657	11,674 D	31.3%	66.7%	31.9%	68.1%
19,192	UNION	10,950	5,673	5,157	120	516 R	51.8%	47.1%	52.4%	47.6%
26,273	VAN WERT	14,733	6,275	7,744	714	1,469 D	42.6%	52.6%	44.8%	55.2%
10,287	VINTON	5,974	3,056	2,902	16	154 R	51.2%	48.6%	51.3%	48.7%
27,348	WARREN	14,707	7,359	7,209	139	150 R	50.0%	49.0%	50.5%	49.5%
42,437	WASHINGTON	21,354	10,826	10,203	325	623 R	50.7%	47.8%	51.5%	48.5%
47,024	WAYNE	23,423	10,331	12,666	426	2,335 D	44.1%	54.1%	44.9%	55.1%
24,316	WILLIAMS	13,302	7,050	5,628	624	1,422 R	53.0%	42.3%	55.6%	44.4%
50,320	WOOD	24,778	11,716	11,255	1,807	461 R	47.3%	45.4%	51.0%	49.0%
19,036	WYANDOT	10,286	4,260	5,597	429	1,337 D	41.4%	54.4%	43.2%	56.8%
6,646,697	TOTAL	3,012,660	1,127,855	1,747,140	137,665	619,285 D	37.4%	58.0%	39.2%	60.8%

OHIO

PRESIDENT 1932

1930 Census Population	County	Total Vote	Republican	Democratic	Other	Rep.-Dem. Plurality	Percentage Total Vote Rep.	Total Vote Dem.	Major Vote Rep.	Major Vote Dem.
20,381	ADAMS	10,931	4,857	5,909	165	1,052 D	44.4%	54.1%	45.1%	54.9%
69,419	ALLEN	31,930	14,678	16,676	576	1,998 D	46.0%	52.2%	46.8%	53.2%
26,867	ASHLAND	14,086	6,549	7,302	235	753 D	46.5%	51.8%	47.3%	52.7%
68,361	ASHTABULA	28,282	15,644	11,386	1,252	4,258 R	55.3%	40.3%	57.9%	42.1%
44,175	ATHENS	19,343	9,897	8,915	531	982 R	51.2%	46.1%	52.6%	47.4%
28,034	AUGLAIZE	13,210	5,039	8,036	135	2,997 D	38.1%	60.8%	38.5%	61.5%
94,719	BELMONT	36,885	15,029	20,291	1,565	5,262 D	40.7%	55.0%	42.6%	57.4%
20,148	BROWN	10,662	3,930	6,601	131	2,671 D	36.9%	61.9%	37.3%	62.7%
114,084	BUTLER	44,008	19,673	22,516	1,819	2,843 D	44.7%	51.2%	46.6%	53.4%
16,057	CARROLL	7,510	4,487	2,802	221	1,685 R	59.7%	37.3%	61.6%	38.4%
24,103	CHAMPAIGN	12,712	6,191	6,396	125	205 D	48.7%	50.3%	49.2%	50.8%
90,936	CLARK	36,952	19,028	17,314	610	1,714 R	51.5%	46.9%	52.4%	47.6%
29,786	CLERMONT	16,667	7,684	8,662	321	978 D	46.1%	52.0%	47.0%	53.0%
21,547	CLINTON	11,368	5,953	5,252	163	701 R	52.4%	46.2%	53.1%	46.9%
86,484	COLUMBIANA	35,430	19,707	14,284	1,439	5,423 R	55.6%	40.3%	58.0%	42.0%
28,976	COSHOCTON	14,555	6,040	8,188	327	2,148 D	41.5%	56.3%	42.5%	57.5%
35,345	CRAWFORD	17,517	6,538	10,593	386	4,055 D	37.3%	60.5%	38.2%	61.8%
1,201,455	CUYAHOGA	370,578	166,337	185,731	18,510	19,394 D	44.9%	50.1%	47.2%	52.8%
38,009	DARKE	19,889	8,284	11,122	483	2,838 D	41.7%	55.9%	42.7%	57.3%
22,714	DEFIANCE	10,595	3,871	6,532	192	2,661 D	36.5%	61.7%	37.2%	62.8%
26,016	DELAWARE	13,300	6,833	6,196	271	637 R	51.4%	46.6%	52.4%	47.6%
42,133	ERIE	18,843	7,666	10,765	412	3,099 D	40.7%	57.1%	41.6%	58.4%
44,010	FAIRFIELD	18,704	8,050	10,410	244	2,360 D	43.0%	55.7%	43.6%	56.4%
20,755	FAYETTE	9,508	4,254	5,157	97	903 D	44.7%	54.2%	45.2%	54.8%
361,055	FRANKLIN	130,160	67,957	58,539	3,664	9,418 R	52.2%	45.0%	53.7%	46.3%
23,477	FULTON	9,344	4,487	4,673	184	186 D	48.0%	50.0%	49.0%	51.0%
23,050	GALLIA	10,002	5,646	4,190	166	1,456 R	56.4%	41.9%	57.4%	42.6%
15,414	GEAUGA	6,454	3,836	2,396	222	1,440 R	59.4%	37.1%	61.6%	38.4%
33,259	GREENE	15,481	8,455	6,600	426	1,855 R	54.6%	42.6%	56.2%	43.8%
41,486	GUERNSEY	18,106	8,750	9,026	330	276 D	48.3%	49.9%	49.2%	50.8%
589,356	HAMILTON	249,076	118,804	123,109	7,163	4,305 D	47.7%	49.4%	49.1%	50.9%
40,404	HANCOCK	19,061	9,260	9,370	431	110 D	48.6%	49.2%	49.7%	50.3%
27,635	HARDIN	16,084	7,215	8,717	152	1,502 D	44.9%	54.2%	45.3%	54.7%
18,844	HARRISON	8,439	4,759	3,512	168	1,247 R	56.4%	41.6%	57.5%	42.5%
22,524	HENRY	10,188	3,067	6,987	134	3,920 D	30.1%	68.6%	30.5%	69.5%
25,416	HIGHLAND	14,137	6,924	7,079	134	155 D	49.0%	50.1%	49.4%	50.6%
20,407	HOCKING	9,348	3,811	5,287	250	1,476 D	40.8%	56.6%	41.9%	58.1%
16,726	HOLMES	6,180	1,953	4,096	131	2,143 D	31.6%	66.3%	32.3%	67.7%
33,700	HURON	17,701	8,702	8,795	204	93 D	49.2%	49.7%	49.7%	50.3%
25,040	JACKSON	12,590	6,932	5,543	115	1,389 R	55.1%	44.0%	55.6%	44.4%
88,307	JEFFERSON	31,544	14,179	16,066	1,299	1,887 D	44.9%	50.9%	46.9%	53.1%
29,338	KNOX	15,486	8,272	7,008	206	1,264 R	53.4%	45.3%	54.1%	45.9%
41,674	LAKE	19,196	11,792	6,801	603	4,991 R	61.4%	35.4%	63.4%	36.6%
44,541	LAWRENCE	16,915	8,598	8,157	160	441 R	50.8%	48.2%	51.3%	48.7%
59,962	LICKING	27,815	13,355	13,904	556	549 D	48.0%	50.0%	49.0%	51.0%
28,981	LOGAN	14,352	7,469	6,678	205	791 R	52.0%	46.5%	52.8%	47.2%
109,206	LORAIN	40,971	20,897	18,753	1,321	2,144 R	51.0%	45.8%	52.7%	47.3%
347,709	LUCAS	117,060	47,796	64,902	4,362	17,106 D	40.8%	55.4%	42.4%	57.6%
20,253	MADISON	9,426	4,631	4,722	73	91 D	49.1%	50.1%	49.5%	50.5%
236,142	MAHONING	75,861	39,713	33,139	3,009	6,574 R	52.3%	43.7%	54.5%	45.5%
45,420	MARION	19,429	8,569	10,354	506	1,785 D	44.1%	53.3%	45.3%	54.7%
29,677	MEDINA	14,074	7,753	5,841	480	1,912 R	55.1%	41.5%	57.0%	43.0%
23,961	MEIGS	11,244	5,964	5,105	175	859 R	53.0%	45.4%	53.9%	46.1%
25,096	MERCER	11,929	3,314	8,462	153	5,148 D	27.8%	70.9%	28.1%	71.9%
51,301	MIAMI	23,402	12,157	10,677	568	1,480 R	51.9%	45.6%	53.2%	46.8%
18,426	MONROE	8,146	2,767	5,263	116	2,496 D	34.0%	64.6%	34.5%	65.5%
273,481	MONTGOMERY	105,717	49,267	51,270	5,180	2,003 D	46.6%	48.5%	49.0%	51.0%
13,583	MORGAN	7,282	3,957	3,107	218	850 R	54.3%	42.7%	56.0%	44.0%
14,489	MORROW	7,806	3,811	3,849	146	38 D	48.8%	49.3%	49.8%	50.2%
67,398	MUSKINGUM	30,285	16,366	13,378	541	2,988 R	54.0%	44.2%	55.0%	45.0%

OHIO

PRESIDENT 1932

1930 Census Population	County	Total Vote	Republican	Democratic	Other	Rep.-Dem. Plurality	Total Vote Rep.	Total Vote Dem.	Major Vote Rep.	Major Vote Dem.
14,961	NOBLE	8,020	3,950	3,966	104	16 D	49.3%	49.5%	49.9%	50.1%
24,109	OTTAWA	10,532	3,600	6,817	115	3,217 D	34.2%	64.7%	34.6%	65.4%
15,301	PAULDING	7,485	3,201	4,165	119	964 D	42.8%	55.6%	43.5%	56.5%
31,445	PERRY	14,643	7,225	6,714	704	511 R	49.3%	45.9%	51.8%	48.2%
27,238	PICKAWAY	10,907	4,395	6,414	98	2,019 D	40.3%	58.8%	40.7%	59.3%
13,876	PIKE	7,908	2,743	5,107	58	2,364 D	34.7%	64.6%	34.9%	65.1%
42,682	PORTAGE	19,981	9,586	9,662	733	76 D	48.0%	48.4%	49.8%	50.2%
22,455	PREBLE	11,625	5,205	6,221	199	1,016 D	44.8%	53.5%	45.6%	54.4%
25,074	PUTNAM	11,879	3,646	8,078	155	4,432 D	30.7%	68.0%	31.1%	68.9%
65,902	RICHLAND	28,249	12,531	15,225	493	2,694 D	44.4%	53.9%	45.1%	54.9%
45,181	ROSS	20,227	9,575	10,542	110	967 D	47.3%	52.1%	47.6%	52.4%
39,731	SANDUSKY	19,490	8,915	10,299	276	1,384 D	45.7%	52.8%	46.4%	53.6%
81,221	SCIOTO	33,590	17,225	15,817	548	1,408 R	51.3%	47.1%	52.1%	47.9%
47,941	SENECA	21,284	9,007	11,894	383	2,887 D	42.3%	55.9%	43.1%	56.9%
24,924	SHELBY	12,741	4,281	8,299	161	4,018 D	33.6%	65.1%	34.0%	66.0%
221,784	STARK	79,654	40,672	35,757	3,225	4,915 R	51.1%	44.9%	53.2%	46.8%
344,131	SUMMIT	105,911	47,691	53,965	4,255	6,274 D	45.0%	51.0%	46.9%	53.1%
123,063	TRUMBULL	42,913	23,029	17,871	2,013	5,158 R	53.7%	41.6%	56.3%	43.7%
68,193	TUSCARAWAS	29,905	12,369	16,648	888	4,279 D	41.4%	55.7%	42.6%	57.4%
19,192	UNION	9,969	4,912	4,943	114	31 D	49.3%	49.6%	49.8%	50.2%
26,273	VAN WERT	14,078	5,918	7,977	183	2,059 D	42.0%	56.7%	42.6%	57.4%
10,287	VINTON	5,419	2,715	2,655	49	60 R	50.1%	49.0%	50.6%	49.4%
27,348	WARREN	13,165	7,421	5,547	197	1,874 R	56.4%	42.1%	57.2%	42.8%
42,437	WASHINGTON	19,876	9,352	10,208	316	856 D	47.1%	51.4%	47.8%	52.2%
47,024	WAYNE	22,097	10,787	10,870	440	83 D	48.8%	49.2%	49.8%	50.2%
24,316	WILLIAMS	12,597	5,459	6,860	278	1,401 D	43.3%	54.5%	44.3%	55.7%
50,320	WOOD	22,318	10,566	11,332	420	766 D	47.3%	50.8%	48.3%	51.7%
19,036	WYANDOT	9,509	3,939	5,451	119	1,512 D	41.4%	57.3%	41.9%	58.1%
6,646,697	TOTAL	2,609,728	1,227,319	1,301,695	80,714	74,376 D	47.0%	49.9%	48.5%	51.5%

OHIO

PRESIDENT 1928

1920 Census Population	County	Total Vote	Republican	Democratic	Other	Rep.-Dem. Plurality	Percentage Total Vote Rep.	Total Vote Dem.	Major Vote Rep.	Major Vote Dem.
22,403	ADAMS	8,685	5,665	3,000	20	2,665 R	65.2%	34.5%	65.4%	34.6%
68,223	ALLEN	30,337	20,693	9,462	182	11,231 R	68.2%	31.2%	68.6%	31.4%
24,627	ASHLAND	12,097	8,745	3,256	96	5,489 R	72.3%	26.9%	72.9%	27.1%
65,545	ASHTABULA	25,118	18,870	5,951	297	12,919 R	75.1%	23.7%	76.0%	24.0%
50,430	ATHENS	15,855	11,101	4,546	208	6,555 R	70.0%	28.7%	70.9%	29.1%
29,527	AUGLAIZE	12,798	7,794	4,954	50	2,840 R	60.9%	38.7%	61.1%	38.9%
93,193	BELMONT	34,468	20,969	12,807	692	8,162 R	60.8%	37.2%	62.1%	37.9%
22,621	BROWN	9,155	5,681	3,422	52	2,259 R	62.1%	37.4%	62.4%	37.6%
87,025	BUTLER	45,042	29,124	15,663	255	13,461 R	64.7%	34.8%	65.0%	35.0%
15,942	CARROLL	6,937	5,572	1,321	44	4,251 R	80.3%	19.0%	80.8%	19.2%
25,071	CHAMPAIGN	11,006	7,651	3,296	59	4,355 R	69.5%	29.9%	69.9%	30.1%
80,728	CLARK	37,183	26,666	10,316	201	16,350 R	71.7%	27.7%	72.1%	27.9%
28,291	CLERMONT	13,983	9,732	4,194	57	5,538 R	69.6%	30.0%	69.9%	30.1%
23,036	CLINTON	9,797	7,150	2,603	44	4,547 R	73.0%	26.6%	73.3%	26.7%
83,131	COLUMBIANA	34,158	26,405	7,461	292	18,944 R	77.3%	21.8%	78.0%	22.0%
29,595	COSHOCTON	12,970	9,154	3,745	71	5,409 R	70.6%	28.9%	71.0%	29.0%
36,054	CRAWFORD	16,793	11,235	5,472	86	5,763 R	66.9%	32.6%	67.2%	32.8%
943,495	CUYAHOGA	364,108	194,508	166,188	3,412	28,320 R	53.4%	45.6%	53.9%	46.1%
42,911	DARKE	17,734	11,765	5,822	147	5,943 R	66.3%	32.8%	66.9%	33.1%
24,549	DEFIANCE	9,776	6,289	3,487		2,802 R	64.3%	35.7%	64.3%	35.7%
26,013	DELAWARE	11,880	8,049	3,720	111	4,329 R	67.8%	31.3%	68.4%	31.6%
39,789	ERIE	17,996	10,380	7,570	46	2,810 R	57.7%	42.1%	57.8%	42.2%
40,484	FAIRFIELD	17,788	12,072	5,619	97	6,453 R	67.9%	31.6%	68.2%	31.8%
21,518	FAYETTE	8,050	5,251	2,752	47	2,499 R	65.2%	34.2%	65.6%	34.4%
283,951	FRANKLIN	139,712	92,019	47,084	609	44,935 R	65.9%	33.7%	66.2%	33.8%
23,445	FULTON	8,253	6,416	1,788	49	4,628 R	77.7%	21.7%	78.2%	21.8%
23,311	GALLIA	7,509	5,513	1,916	80	3,597 R	73.4%	25.5%	74.2%	25.8%
15,036	GEAUGA	5,378	4,161	1,180	37	2,981 R	77.4%	21.9%	77.9%	22.1%
31,221	GREENE	13,528	10,030	3,385	113	6,645 R	74.1%	25.0%	74.8%	25.2%
45,352	GUERNSEY	15,080	11,174	3,709	197	7,465 R	74.1%	24.6%	75.1%	24.9%
493,678	HAMILTON	258,692	147,534	110,151	1,007	37,383 R	57.0%	42.6%	57.3%	42.7%
38,394	HANCOCK	17,410	13,151	4,158	101	8,993 R	75.5%	23.9%	76.0%	24.0%
29,167	HARDIN	13,517	8,137	5,306	74	2,831 R	60.2%	39.3%	60.5%	39.5%
19,625	HARRISON	7,676	6,095	1,516	65	4,579 R	79.4%	19.7%	80.1%	19.9%
23,362	HENRY	9,057	5,370	3,647	40	1,723 R	59.3%	40.3%	59.6%	40.4%
27,610	HIGHLAND	12,221	8,325	3,836	60	4,489 R	68.1%	31.4%	68.5%	31.5%
23,291	HOCKING	8,093	5,497	2,502	94	2,995 R	67.9%	30.9%	68.7%	31.3%
16,965	HOLMES	5,127	3,457	1,631	39	1,826 R	67.4%	31.8%	67.9%	32.1%
32,424	HURON	15,930	10,702	5,157	71	5,545 R	67.2%	32.4%	67.5%	32.5%
27,342	JACKSON	9,985	7,129	2,775	81	4,354 R	71.4%	27.8%	72.0%	28.0%
77,580	JEFFERSON	28,161	19,175	8,711	275	10,464 R	68.1%	30.9%	68.8%	31.2%
29,580	KNOX	13,724	10,028	3,601	95	6,427 R	73.1%	26.2%	73.6%	26.4%
28,667	LAKE	15,926	11,823	4,024	79	7,799 R	74.2%	25.3%	74.6%	25.4%
39,540	LAWRENCE	13,885	10,346	3,470	69	6,876 R	74.5%	25.0%	74.9%	25.1%
56,426	LICKING	26,517	19,130	7,244	143	11,886 R	72.1%	27.3%	72.5%	27.5%
30,104	LOGAN	12,531	9,602	2,858	71	6,744 R	76.6%	22.8%	77.1%	22.9%
90,612	LORAIN	38,205	24,386	13,607	212	10,779 R	63.8%	35.6%	64.2%	35.8%
275,721	LUCAS	124,081	78,435	44,977	669	33,458 R	63.2%	36.2%	63.6%	36.4%
19,662	MADISON	8,105	5,522	2,527	56	2,995 R	68.1%	31.2%	68.6%	31.4%
186,310	MAHONING	75,748	48,341	26,928	479	21,413 R	63.8%	35.5%	64.2%	35.8%
42,004	MARION	19,060	13,398	5,468	194	7,930 R	70.3%	28.7%	71.0%	29.0%
26,067	MEDINA	11,950	9,510	2,357	83	7,153 R	79.6%	19.7%	80.1%	19.9%
26,189	MEIGS	9,314	6,580	2,661	73	3,919 R	70.6%	28.6%	71.2%	28.8%
26,872	MERCER	11,326	5,129	6,155	42	1,026 D	45.3%	54.3%	45.5%	54.5%
48,428	MIAMI	22,066	16,063	5,867	136	10,196 R	72.8%	26.6%	73.2%	26.8%
20,660	MONROE	7,059	4,287	2,729	43	1,558 R	60.7%	38.7%	61.1%	38.9%
209,532	MONTGOMERY	110,461	71,279	38,517	665	32,762 R	64.5%	34.9%	64.9%	35.1%
14,555	MORGAN	5,805	4,359	1,397	49	2,962 R	75.1%	24.1%	75.7%	24.3%
15,570	MORROW	6,699	4,801	1,818	80	2,983 R	71.7%	27.1%	72.5%	27.5%
57,980	MUSKINGUM	28,798	22,120	6,507	171	15,613 R	76.8%	22.6%	77.3%	22.7%

OHIO

PRESIDENT 1928

1920 Census Population	County	Total Vote	Republican	Democratic	Other	Rep.-Dem. Plurality	Percentage Total Vote Rep.	Total Vote Dem.	Major Vote Rep.	Major Vote Dem.
17,849	NOBLE	6,715	4,462	2,190	63	2,272 R	66.4%	32.6%	67.1%	32.9%
22,193	OTTAWA	9,229	5,772	3,435	22	2,337 R	62.5%	37.2%	62.7%	37.3%
18,736	PAULDING	6,624	4,093	2,473	58	1,620 R	61.8%	37.3%	62.3%	37.7%
36,098	PERRY	13,279	8,551	4,653	75	3,898 R	64.4%	35.0%	64.8%	35.2%
25,788	PICKAWAY	9,806	5,871	3,894	41	1,977 R	59.9%	39.7%	60.1%	39.9%
14,151	PIKE	5,955	3,246	2,709		537 R	54.5%	45.5%	54.5%	45.5%
36,269	PORTAGE	16,948	12,086	4,756	106	7,330 R	71.3%	28.1%	71.8%	28.2%
23,238	PREBLE	10,263	6,693	3,513	57	3,180 R	65.2%	34.2%	65.6%	34.4%
27,751	PUTNAM	11,254	5,537	5,667	50	130 D	49.2%	50.4%	49.4%	50.6%
55,178	RICHLAND	25,909	18,468	7,295	146	11,173 R	71.3%	28.2%	71.7%	28.3%
41,556	ROSS	17,308	11,179	6,062	67	5,117 R	64.6%	35.0%	64.8%	35.2%
37,109	SANDUSKY	18,119	12,200	5,834	85	6,366 R	67.3%	32.2%	67.6%	32.4%
62,850	SCIOTO	28,530	20,997	7,425	108	13,572 R	73.6%	26.0%	73.9%	26.1%
43,176	SENECA	21,587	13,369	8,136	82	5,233 R	61.9%	37.7%	62.2%	37.8%
25,923	SHELBY	11,460	5,975	5,448	37	527 R	52.1%	47.5%	52.3%	47.7%
177,218	STARK	84,075	59,564	23,840	671	35,724 R	70.8%	28.4%	71.4%	28.6%
286,065	SUMMIT	110,785	78,504	31,506	775	46,998 R	70.9%	28.4%	71.4%	28.6%
83,920	TRUMBULL	39,194	29,710	9,110	374	20,600 R	75.8%	23.2%	76.5%	23.5%
63,578	TUSCARAWAS	27,568	20,494	6,805	269	13,689 R	74.3%	24.7%	75.1%	24.9%
20,918	UNION	8,331	5,876	2,386	69	3,490 R	70.5%	28.6%	71.1%	28.9%
28,210	VAN WERT	12,696	7,540	5,089	67	2,451 R	59.4%	40.1%	59.7%	40.3%
12,075	VINTON	4,408	2,810	1,559	39	1,251 R	63.7%	35.4%	64.3%	35.7%
25,716	WARREN	11,219	8,708	2,455	56	6,253 R	77.6%	21.9%	78.0%	22.0%
43,049	WASHINGTON	17,447	12,767	4,582	98	8,185 R	73.2%	26.3%	73.6%	26.4%
41,346	WAYNE	19,024	14,192	4,825	7	9,367 R	74.6%	25.4%	74.6%	25.4%
24,627	WILLIAMS	11,332	8,138	3,136	58	5,002 R	71.8%	27.7%	72.2%	27.8%
44,892	WOOD	20,126	15,409	4,612	105	10,797 R	76.6%	22.9%	77.0%	23.0%
19,481	WYANDOT	8,852	5,790	3,024	38	2,766 R	65.4%	34.2%	65.7%	34.3%
5,759,394	TOTAL	2,508,346	1,627,546	864,210	16,590	763,336 R	64.9%	34.5%	65.3%	34.7%

OHIO

PRESIDENT 1924

1920 Census Population	County	Total Vote	Republican	Democratic	Progressive	Other	Plurality	Percentage Total Vote Rep.	Dem.	Prog.
22,403	ADAMS	8,226	4,315	3,762	149		553 R	52.5%	45.7%	1.8%
68,223	ALLEN	25,437	15,711	7,378	2,283	65	8,333 R	61.8%	29.0%	9.0%
24,627	ASHLAND	10,966	5,777	4,377	802	10	1,400 R	52.7%	39.9%	7.3%
65,545	ASHTABULA	21,337	14,767	2,135	4,370	65	10,397 R	69.2%	10.0%	20.5%
50,430	ATHENS	14,943	8,695	2,669	3,501	78	5,194 R	58.2%	17.9%	23.4%
29,527	AUGLAIZE	10,618	5,507	3,952	1,143	16	1,555 R	51.9%	37.2%	10.8%
93,193	BELMONT	30,035	16,378	8,074	5,386	197	8,304 R	54.5%	26.9%	17.9%
22,621	BROWN	8,399	3,616	4,120	660	3	504 D	43.1%	49.1%	7.9%
87,025	BUTLER	34,398	19,349	11,612	3,339	98	7,737 R	56.3%	33.8%	9.7%
15,942	CARROLL	6,173	4,369	1,430	364	10	2,939 R	70.8%	23.2%	5.9%
25,071	CHAMPAIGN	10,245	6,181	3,575	478	11	2,606 R	60.3%	34.9%	4.7%
80,728	CLARK	30,615	20,340	8,415	1,816	44	11,925 R	66.4%	27.5%	5.9%
28,291	CLERMONT	12,445	6,867	4,544	1,019	15	2,323 R	55.2%	36.5%	8.2%
23,036	CLINTON	8,876	5,954	2,496	421	5	3,458 R	67.1%	28.1%	4.7%
83,131	COLUMBIANA	29,272	20,483	4,685	4,036	68	15,798 R	70.0%	16.0%	13.8%
29,595	COSHOCTON	11,729	5,837	4,415	1,456	21	1,422 R	49.8%	37.6%	12.4%
36,054	CRAWFORD	14,440	5,896	4,384	4,140	20	1,512 R	40.8%	30.4%	28.7%
943,495	CUYAHOGA	264,066	130,169	24,000	109,287	610	20,882 R	49.3%	9.1%	41.4%
42,911	DARKE	17,320	9,166	7,315	811	28	1,851 R	52.9%	42.2%	4.7%
24,549	DEFIANCE	9,213	4,841	3,227	1,134	11	1,614 R	52.5%	35.0%	12.3%
26,013	DELAWARE	11,142	6,731	3,537	866	8	3,194 R	60.4%	31.7%	7.8%
39,789	ERIE	14,151	7,689	2,968	3,462	32	4,227 R	54.3%	21.0%	24.5%
40,484	FAIRFIELD	15,393	8,281	5,890	1,200	22	2,391 R	53.8%	38.3%	7.8%
21,518	FAYETTE	7,536	4,542	2,696	293	5	1,846 R	60.3%	35.8%	3.9%
283,951	FRANKLIN	107,295	61,891	26,505	18,743	156	35,386 R	57.7%	24.7%	17.5%
23,445	FULTON	7,118	4,951	1,333	832	2	3,618 R	69.6%	18.7%	11.7%
23,311	GALLIA	7,066	4,325	2,284	453	4	2,041 R	61.2%	32.3%	6.4%
15,036	GEAUGA	4,662	3,375	635	642	10	2,733 R	72.4%	13.6%	13.8%
31,221	GREENE	11,523	8,410	2,471	628	14	5,939 R	73.0%	21.4%	5.4%
45,352	GUERNSEY	15,106	8,997	3,604	2,455	50	5,393 R	59.6%	23.9%	16.3%
493,678	HAMILTON	191,029	115,950	34,916	39,768	395	76,182 R	60.7%	18.3%	20.8%
38,394	HANCOCK	16,074	9,167	5,111	1,764	32	4,056 R	57.0%	31.8%	11.0%
29,167	HARDIN	13,254	7,112	5,523	613	6	1,589 R	53.7%	41.7%	4.6%
19,625	HARRISON	7,434	4,904	1,999	520	11	2,905 R	66.0%	26.9%	7.0%
23,362	HENRY	8,470	3,855	2,922	1,693		933 R	45.5%	34.5%	20.0%
27,610	HIGHLAND	11,976	6,845	4,583	535	13	2,262 R	57.2%	38.3%	4.5%
23,291	HOCKING	8,098	4,086	2,854	1,136	22	1,232 R	50.5%	35.2%	14.0%
16,965	HOLMES	4,768	1,824	2,539	400	5	715 D	38.3%	53.3%	8.4%
32,424	HURON	13,425	8,340	2,871	2,186	28	5,469 R	62.1%	21.4%	16.3%
27,342	JACKSON	9,727	5,977	2,848	869	33	3,129 R	61.4%	29.3%	8.9%
77,580	JEFFERSON	21,963	14,929	3,840	3,097	97	11,089 R	68.0%	17.5%	14.1%
29,580	KNOX	13,133	7,519	4,721	892	1	2,798 R	57.3%	35.9%	6.8%
28,667	LAKE	10,927	7,727	974	2,208	18	5,519 R	70.7%	8.9%	20.2%
39,540	LAWRENCE	10,648	6,798	2,729	1,098	23	4,069 R	63.8%	25.6%	10.3%
56,426	LICKING	23,788	13,914	7,428	2,418	28	6,486 R	58.5%	31.2%	10.2%
30,104	LOGAN	11,774	7,186	3,176	1,393	19	4,010 R	61.0%	27.0%	11.8%
90,612	LORAIN	27,774	17,062	3,965	6,680	67	10,382 R	61.4%	14.3%	24.1%
275,721	LUCAS	96,902	53,670	11,948	31,039	245	22,631 R	55.4%	12.3%	32.0%
19,662	MADISON	7,792	4,829	2,685	278		2,144 R	62.0%	34.5%	3.6%
186,310	MAHONING	55,264	37,647	9,335	8,102	180	28,312 R	68.1%	16.9%	14.7%
42,004	MARION	16,901	9,161	5,234	2,475	31	3,927 R	54.2%	31.0%	14.6%
26,067	MEDINA	9,971	6,756	1,844	1,351	20	4,912 R	67.8%	18.5%	13.5%
26,189	MEIGS	8,492	4,864	1,944	1,648	36	2,920 R	57.3%	22.9%	19.4%
26,872	MERCER	10,434	4,215	5,135	1,071	13	920 D	40.4%	49.2%	10.3%
48,428	MIAMI	18,901	11,851	5,296	1,726	28	6,555 R	62.7%	28.0%	9.1%
20,660	MONROE	6,589	2,674	3,742	165	8	1,068 D	40.6%	56.8%	2.5%
209,532	MONTGOMERY	81,210	50,845	21,860	8,312	193	28,985 R	62.6%	26.9%	10.2%
14,555	MORGAN	5,830	3,553	2,072	199	6	1,481 R	60.9%	35.5%	3.4%
15,570	MORROW	6,604	3,790	2,379	435		1,411 R	57.4%	36.0%	6.6%
57,980	MUSKINGUM	23,697	15,571	6,709	1,377	40	8,862 R	65.7%	28.3%	5.8%

OHIO

PRESIDENT 1924

1920 Census Population	County	Total Vote	Republican	Democratic	Progressive	Other	Plurality	Percentage Total Vote Rep.	Dem.	Prog.
17,849	NOBLE	7,048	4,284	2,485	272	7	1,799 R	60.8%	35.3%	3.9%
22,193	OTTAWA	7,991	4,137	2,571	1,274	9	1,566 R	51.8%	32.2%	15.9%
18,736	PAULDING	6,312	3,648	2,242	414	8	1,406 R	57.8%	35.5%	6.6%
36,098	PERRY	13,065	7,592	3,702	1,718	53	3,890 R	58.1%	28.3%	13.1%
25,788	PICKAWAY	9,009	4,166	4,539	293	11	373 D	46.2%	50.4%	3.3%
14,151	PIKE	5,856	2,569	3,185	100	2	616 D	43.9%	54.4%	1.7%
36,269	PORTAGE	13,749	8,583	2,994	2,131	41	5,589 R	62.4%	21.8%	15.5%
23,238	PREBLE	10,001	5,676	4,033	282	10	1,643 R	56.8%	40.3%	2.8%
27,751	PUTNAM	10,465	4,377	4,795	1,283	10	418 D	41.8%	45.8%	12.3%
55,178	RICHLAND	21,645	12,013	6,703	2,905	24	5,310 R	55.5%	31.0%	13.4%
41,556	ROSS	15,653	8,431	6,028	1,178	16	2,403 R	53.9%	38.5%	7.5%
37,109	SANDUSKY	15,408	9,381	4,388	1,626	13	4,993 R	60.9%	28.5%	10.6%
62,850	SCIOTO	19,401	12,189	5,532	1,643	37	6,657 R	62.8%	28.5%	8.5%
43,176	SENECA	18,091	9,641	6,290	2,119	41	3,351 R	53.3%	34.8%	11.7%
25,923	SHELBY	9,816	4,359	4,840	606	11	481 D	44.4%	49.3%	6.2%
177,218	STARK	63,562	40,858	12,544	9,960	200	28,314 R	64.3%	19.7%	15.7%
286,065	SUMMIT	82,371	53,774	17,533	10,855	209	36,241 R	65.3%	21.3%	13.2%
83,920	TRUMBULL	30,049	22,341	4,007	3,628	73	18,334 R	74.3%	13.3%	12.1%
63,578	TUSCARAWAS	23,825	13,573	5,566	4,602	84	8,007 R	57.0%	23.4%	19.3%
20,918	UNION	8,378	5,256	2,571	540	11	2,685 R	62.7%	30.7%	6.4%
28,210	VAN WERT	11,678	6,206	4,318	1,138	16	1,888 R	53.1%	37.0%	9.7%
12,075	VINTON	4,326	2,244	1,838	232	12	406 R	51.9%	42.5%	5.4%
25,716	WARREN	9,749	6,729	2,406	609	5	4,323 R	69.0%	24.7%	6.2%
43,049	WASHINGTON	15,239	8,704	5,727	780	28	2,977 R	57.1%	37.6%	5.1%
41,346	WAYNE	16,594	8,928	6,023	1,624	19	2,905 R	53.8%	36.3%	9.8%
24,627	WILLIAMS	10,285	5,802	2,795	1,671	17	3,007 R	56.4%	27.2%	16.2%
44,892	WOOD	16,325	10,665	3,291	2,347	22	7,374 R	65.3%	20.2%	14.4%
19,481	WYANDOT	7,811	3,973	3,271	561	6	702 R	50.9%	41.9%	7.2%
5,759,394	TOTAL	2,016,296	1,176,130	477,887	358,008	4,271	698,243 R	58.3%	23.7%	17.8%

OHIO

PRESIDENT 1920

1920 Census Population	County	Total Vote	Republican	Democratic	Other	Rep.-Dem. Plurality	Percentage Total Vote Rep.	Percentage Total Vote Dem.	Percentage Major Vote Rep.	Percentage Major Vote Dem.
22,403	ADAMS	9,199	4,974	4,194	31	780 R	54.1%	45.6%	54.3%	45.7%
68,223	ALLEN	26,082	13,978	11,658	446	2,320 R	53.6%	44.7%	54.5%	45.5%
24,627	ASHLAND	11,757	5,951	5,705	101	246 R	50.6%	48.5%	51.1%	48.9%
65,545	ASHTABULA	20,229	14,099	5,413	717	8,686 R	69.7%	26.8%	72.3%	27.7%
50,430	ATHENS	17,900	11,016	6,523	361	4,493 R	61.5%	36.4%	62.8%	37.2%
29,527	AUGLAIZE	11,752	6,752	4,792	208	1,960 R	57.5%	40.8%	58.5%	41.5%
93,193	BELMONT	29,201	14,761	13,347	1,093	1,414 R	50.5%	45.7%	52.5%	47.5%
22,621	BROWN	9,370	4,009	5,317	44	1,308 D	42.8%	56.7%	43.0%	57.0%
87,025	BUTLER	33,396	14,998	16,437	1,961	1,439 D	44.9%	49.2%	47.7%	52.3%
15,942	CARROLL	6,258	4,392	1,755	111	2,637 R	70.2%	28.0%	71.4%	28.6%
25,071	CHAMPAIGN	12,128	7,285	4,775	68	2,510 R	60.1%	39.4%	60.4%	39.6%
80,728	CLARK	34,540	19,869	14,097	574	5,772 R	57.5%	40.8%	58.5%	41.5%
28,291	CLERMONT	13,210	6,857	6,245	108	612 R	51.9%	47.3%	52.3%	47.7%
23,036	CLINTON	10,588	6,947	3,598	43	3,349 R	65.6%	34.0%	65.9%	34.1%
83,131	COLUMBIANA	28,023	16,846	9,774	1,403	7,072 R	60.1%	34.9%	63.3%	36.7%
29,595	COSHOCTON	12,051	6,154	5,617	280	537 R	51.1%	46.6%	52.3%	47.7%
36,054	CRAWFORD	15,829	7,082	8,467	280	1,385 D	44.7%	53.5%	45.5%	54.5%
943,495	CUYAHOGA	231,279	148,857	70,518	11,904	78,339 R	64.4%	30.5%	67.9%	32.1%
42,911	DARKE	18,162	9,552	8,459	151	1,093 R	52.6%	46.6%	53.0%	47.0%
24,549	DEFIANCE	9,890	5,987	3,723	180	2,264 R	60.5%	37.6%	61.7%	38.3%
26,013	DELAWARE	13,004	7,700	5,241	63	2,459 R	59.2%	40.3%	59.5%	40.5%
39,789	ERIE	14,039	8,755	4,831	453	3,924 R	62.4%	34.4%	64.4%	35.6%
40,484	FAIRFIELD	16,298	7,572	8,610	116	1,038 D	46.5%	52.8%	46.8%	53.2%
21,518	FAYETTE	9,301	5,446	3,812	43	1,634 R	58.6%	41.0%	58.8%	41.2%
283,951	FRANKLIN	110,064	59,691	48,452	1,921	11,239 R	54.2%	44.0%	55.2%	44.8%
23,445	FULTON	8,271	6,111	2,049	111	4,062 R	73.9%	24.8%	74.9%	25.1%
23,311	GALLIA	7,994	5,388	2,562	44	2,826 R	67.4%	32.0%	67.8%	32.2%
15,036	GEAUGA	4,853	3,722	1,081	50	2,641 R	76.7%	22.3%	77.5%	22.5%
31,221	GREENE	12,788	8,600	4,016	172	4,584 R	67.3%	31.4%	68.2%	31.8%
45,352	GUERNSEY	16,122	8,764	6,888	470	1,876 R	54.4%	42.7%	56.0%	44.0%
493,678	HAMILTON	196,966	112,590	77,598	6,778	34,992 R	57.2%	39.4%	59.2%	40.8%
38,394	HANCOCK	16,390	9,746	6,386	258	3,360 R	59.5%	39.0%	60.4%	39.6%
29,167	HARDIN	14,003	8,071	5,817	115	2,254 R	57.6%	41.5%	58.1%	41.9%
19,625	HARRISON	7,584	5,053	2,473	58	2,580 R	66.6%	32.6%	67.1%	32.9%
23,362	HENRY	8,681	5,738	2,829	114	2,909 R	66.1%	32.6%	67.0%	33.0%
27,610	HIGHLAND	13,267	7,570	5,654	43	1,916 R	57.1%	42.6%	57.2%	42.8%
23,291	HOCKING	8,527	4,335	4,082	110	253 R	50.8%	47.9%	51.5%	48.5%
16,965	HOLMES	5,325	2,065	3,211	49	1,146 D	38.8%	60.3%	39.1%	60.9%
32,424	HURON	13,915	9,348	4,398	169	4,950 R	67.2%	31.6%	68.0%	32.0%
27,342	JACKSON	10,929	5,949	4,878	102	1,071 R	54.4%	44.6%	54.9%	45.1%
77,580	JEFFERSON	21,816	13,038	8,064	714	4,974 R	59.8%	37.0%	61.8%	38.2%
29,580	KNOX	14,610	8,178	6,361	71	1,817 R	56.0%	43.5%	56.2%	43.8%
28,667	LAKE	10,323	7,465	2,711	147	4,754 R	72.3%	26.3%	73.4%	26.6%
39,540	LAWRENCE	11,702	7,616	3,955	131	3,661 R	65.1%	33.8%	65.8%	34.2%
56,426	LICKING	22,981	11,924	10,679	378	1,245 R	51.9%	46.5%	52.8%	47.2%
30,104	LOGAN	13,481	8,521	4,904	56	3,617 R	63.2%	36.4%	63.5%	36.5%
90,612	LORAIN	27,529	18,125	8,640	764	9,485 R	65.8%	31.4%	67.7%	32.3%
275,721	LUCAS	88,769	52,449	30,452	5,868	21,997 R	59.1%	34.3%	63.3%	36.7%
19,662	MADISON	9,185	5,397	3,769	19	1,628 R	58.8%	41.0%	58.9%	41.1%
186,310	MAHONING	46,570	29,736	14,941	1,893	14,795 R	63.9%	32.1%	66.6%	33.4%
42,004	MARION	19,541	11,320	8,065	156	3,255 R	57.9%	41.3%	58.4%	41.6%
26,067	MEDINA	10,122	6,846	3,120	156	3,726 R	67.6%	30.8%	68.7%	31.3%
26,189	MEIGS	10,324	6,541	3,606	177	2,935 R	63.4%	34.9%	64.5%	35.5%
26,872	MERCER	10,140	5,692	4,404	44	1,288 R	56.1%	43.4%	56.4%	43.6%
48,428	MIAMI	21,770	13,122	8,076	572	5,046 R	60.3%	37.1%	61.9%	38.1%
20,660	MONROE	6,736	2,825	3,861	50	1,036 D	41.9%	57.3%	42.3%	57.7%
209,532	MONTGOMERY	89,975	46,493	38,433	5,049	8,060 R	51.7%	42.7%	54.7%	45.3%
14,555	MORGAN	6,422	4,127	2,157	138	1,970 R	64.3%	33.6%	65.7%	34.3%
15,570	MORROW	7,378	4,484	2,858	36	1,626 R	60.8%	38.7%	61.1%	38.9%
57,980	MUSKINGUM	23,671	13,862	9,437	372	4,425 R	58.6%	39.9%	59.5%	40.5%

OHIO

PRESIDENT 1920

1920 Census Population	County	Total Vote	Republican	Democratic	Other	Rep.-Dem. Plurality	Percentage Total Vote Rep.	Total Vote Dem.	Major Vote Rep.	Major Vote Dem.
17,849	NOBLE	7,106	4,197	2,909		1,288 R	59.1%	40.9%	59.1%	40.9%
22,193	OTTAWA	7,299	4,336	2,867	96	1,469 R	59.4%	39.3%	60.2%	39.8%
18,736	PAULDING	7,366	4,549	2,739	78	1,810 R	61.8%	37.2%	62.4%	37.6%
36,098	PERRY	14,018	7,685	5,917	416	1,768 R	54.8%	42.2%	56.5%	43.5%
25,788	PICKAWAY	10,939	5,273	5,645	21	372 D	48.2%	51.6%	48.3%	51.7%
14,151	PIKE	5,904	3,075	2,799	30	276 R	52.1%	47.4%	52.3%	47.7%
36,269	PORTAGE	13,953	8,231	5,405	317	2,826 R	59.0%	38.7%	60.4%	39.6%
23,238	PREBLE	11,231	6,258	4,933	40	1,325 R	55.7%	43.9%	55.9%	44.1%
27,751	PUTNAM	9,899	5,157	4,673	69	484 R	52.1%	47.2%	52.5%	47.5%
55,178	RICHLAND	20,727	10,940	9,349	438	1,591 R	52.8%	45.1%	53.9%	46.1%
41,556	ROSS	16,526	9,330	7,063	133	2,267 R	56.5%	42.7%	56.9%	43.1%
37,109	SANDUSKY	14,461	8,933	5,295	233	3,638 R	61.8%	36.6%	62.8%	37.2%
62,850	SCIOTO	20,135	11,871	7,682	582	4,189 R	59.0%	38.2%	60.7%	39.3%
43,176	SENECA	18,500	10,064	8,175	261	1,889 R	54.4%	44.2%	55.2%	44.8%
25,923	SHELBY	11,176	5,452	5,642	82	190 D	48.8%	50.5%	49.1%	50.9%
177,218	STARK	59,608	37,483	18,437	3,688	19,046 R	62.9%	30.9%	67.0%	33.0%
286,065	SUMMIT	73,363	43,721	27,857	1,785	15,864 R	59.6%	38.0%	61.1%	38.9%
83,920	TRUMBULL	25,259	17,343	6,815	1,101	10,528 R	68.7%	27.0%	71.8%	28.2%
63,578	TUSCARAWAS	22,919	11,908	10,167	844	1,741 R	52.0%	44.4%	53.9%	46.1%
20,918	UNION	9,865	6,544	3,286	35	3,258 R	66.3%	33.3%	66.6%	33.4%
28,210	VAN WERT	12,493	7,495	4,899	99	2,596 R	60.0%	39.2%	60.5%	39.5%
12,075	VINTON	4,734	2,559	2,124	51	435 R	54.1%	44.9%	54.6%	45.4%
25,716	WARREN	11,491	7,464	3,956	71	3,508 R	65.0%	34.4%	65.4%	34.6%
43,049	WASHINGTON	15,944	9,279	6,286	379	2,993 R	58.2%	39.4%	59.6%	40.4%
41,346	WAYNE	16,890	8,932	7,751	207	1,181 R	52.9%	45.9%	53.5%	46.5%
24,627	WILLIAMS	11,336	7,000	4,183	153	2,817 R	61.8%	36.9%	62.6%	37.4%
44,892	WOOD	17,272	12,042	4,965	265	7,077 R	69.7%	28.7%	70.8%	29.2%
19,481	WYANDOT	9,029	4,560	4,443	26	117 R	50.5%	49.2%	50.6%	49.4%
5,759,394	TOTAL	2,021,653	1,182,022	780,037	59,594	401,985 R	58.5%	38.6%	60.2%	39.8%

OHIO

ELECTION NOTES

1956

1952

1948 Other vote was Wallace (Progressive)

1944

1940

1936 Other vote was 132,212 Lemke (Union); 5,251 Browder (Communist); 167 Thomas (Socialist); 28 Aiken (Socialist Labor); 7 scattered write-in. The statewide total in the other vote column includes the Socialist, Socialist Labor and scattered write-in votes which were not available by county.

1932 Other vote was 64,094 Thomas (Socialist); 7,421 Upshaw (Prohibition); 7,231 Foster (Communist); 1,968 Reynolds (Socialist Labor).

1928 Other vote was 8,683 Thomas (Socialist); 3,556 Varney (Prohibition); 2,836 Foster (Communist); 1,515 Reynolds (Socialist Labor).

1924 A special four-column table which gives the LaFollette (Progressive) vote is used to detail this election. Other vote was 3,025 Johns (Socialist Labor); 1,246 Wallace (Commonwealth Land).

1920 Other vote was 57,147 Debs (Socialist); 2,153 Macauley (Single Tax); 294 Watkins (Prohibition).

OKLAHOMA

POPULAR VOTE FOR PRESIDENT 1920 TO 1956

Year	Total Vote	Republican Vote	Republican Candidate	Democratic Vote	Democratic Candidate	Other Vote	Plurality	Total Vote Rep.	Total Vote Dem.	Major Vote Rep.	Major Vote Dem.
1956	859,350	473,769	Eisenhower, Dwight D.	385,581	Stevenson, Adlai E.		88,188 R	55.1%	44.9%	55.1%	44.9%
1952	948,984	518,045	Eisenhower, Dwight D.	430,939	Stevenson, Adlai E.		87,106 R	54.6%	45.4%	54.6%	45.4%
1948	721,599	268,817	Dewey, Thomas E.	452,782	Truman, Harry S.		183,965 D	37.3%	62.7%	37.3%	62.7%
1944	722,636	319,424	Dewey, Thomas E.	401,549	Roosevelt, Franklin D.	1,663	82,125 D	44.2%	55.6%	44.3%	55.7%
1940	826,212	348,872	Willkie, Wendell	474,313	Roosevelt, Franklin D.	3,027	125,441 D	42.2%	57.4%	42.4%	57.6%
1936	749,740	245,122	Landon, Alfred M.	501,069	Roosevelt, Franklin D.	3,549	255,947 D	32.7%	66.8%	32.8%	67.2%
1932	704,633	188,165	Hoover, Herbert C.	516,468	Roosevelt, Franklin D.		328,303 D	26.7%	73.3%	26.7%	73.3%
1928	618,427	394,046	Hoover, Herbert C.	219,174	Smith, Alfred E.	5,207	174,872 R	63.7%	35.4%	64.3%	35.7%
1924	527,828	225,756	Coolidge, Calvin	255,798	Davis, John W.	46,274	30,042 D	42.8%	48.5%	46.9%	53.1%
1920	485,678	243,840	Harding, Warren G.	216,122	Cox, James M.	25,716	27,718 R	50.2%	44.5%	53.0%	47.0%

ELECTORAL COLLEGE VOTE 1920 TO 1956

Year	Total	Republican	Democratic	Other
1956	8	8	—	—
1952	8	8	—	—
1948	10	—	10	—
1944	10	—	10	—
1940	11	—	11	—
1936	11	—	11	—
1932	11	—	11	—
1928	10	10	—	—
1924	10	—	10	—
1920	10	10	—	—

OKLAHOMA

OTTAWA
DELAWARE
ADAIR
SEQUOYAH
LE FLORE
McCURTAIN
CHEROKEE
CRAIG
MAYES
HASKELL
LATIMER
PUSHMATAHA
NOWATA
ROGERS
WAGONER
MUSKOGEE
McINTOSH
PITTSBURG
CHOCTAW
WASHINGTON
TULSA
OKMULGEE
ATOKA
OSAGE
CREEK
OKFUSKEE
HUGHES
COAL
BRYAN
PAWNEE
SEMINOLE
PONTOTOC
JOHNSTON
MAR-SHALL
KAY
NOBLE
PAYNE
LINCOLN
POTTA-WATOMIE
GARVIN
MURRAY
CARTER
LOVE
LOGAN
OKLAHOMA
CLEVELAND
McCLAIN
GRANT
GARFIELD
KINGFISHER
CANADIAN
GRADY
STEPHENS
JEFFERSON
ALFALFA
MAJOR
BLAINE
CADDO
COMANCHE
COTTON
WOODS
DEWEY
CUSTER
WASHITA
KIOWA
TILLMAN
WOODWARD
JACKSON
HARPER
ELLIS
ROGER MILLS
BECKHAM
GREER
HARMON
BEAVER
TEXAS
CIMARRON

OKLAHOMA

PRESIDENT 1956

1950 Census Population	County	Total Vote	Republican	Democratic	Other	Rep.-Dem. Plurality	Percentage Total Vote Rep.	Total Vote Dem.	Major Vote Rep.	Major Vote Dem.
14,918	ADAIR	5,570	3,152	2,418		734 R	56.6%	43.4%	56.6%	43.4%
10,699	ALFALFA	4,622	3,251	1,371		1,880 R	70.3%	29.7%	70.3%	29.7%
14,269	ATOKA	4,155	1,731	2,424		693 D	41.7%	58.3%	41.7%	58.3%
7,411	BEAVER	2,992	2,046	946		1,100 R	68.4%	31.6%	68.4%	31.6%
21,627	BECKHAM	6,755	3,194	3,561		367 D	47.3%	52.7%	47.3%	52.7%
15,049	BLAINE	5,699	3,855	1,844		2,011 R	67.6%	32.4%	67.6%	32.4%
28,999	BRYAN	8,668	2,939	5,729		2,790 D	33.9%	66.1%	33.9%	66.1%
34,913	CADDO	11,215	5,331	5,884		553 D	47.5%	52.5%	47.5%	52.5%
25,644	CANADIAN	9,598	5,702	3,896		1,806 R	59.4%	40.6%	59.4%	40.6%
36,455	CARTER	15,315	5,974	9,341		3,367 D	39.0%	61.0%	39.0%	61.0%
18,989	CHEROKEE	6,268	3,277	2,991		286 R	52.3%	47.7%	52.3%	47.7%
20,405	CHOCTAW	5,675	2,206	3,469		1,263 D	38.9%	61.1%	38.9%	61.1%
4,589	CIMARRON	1,865	1,053	812		241 R	56.5%	43.5%	56.5%	43.5%
41,443	CLEVELAND	13,753	7,766	5,987		1,779 R	56.5%	43.5%	56.5%	43.5%
8,056	COAL	2,516	920	1,596		676 D	36.6%	63.4%	36.6%	63.4%
55,165	COMANCHE	16,288	7,532	8,756		1,224 D	46.2%	53.8%	46.2%	53.8%
10,180	COTTON	3,287	1,398	1,889		491 D	42.5%	57.5%	42.5%	57.5%
18,263	CRAIG	6,649	3,543	3,106		437 R	53.3%	46.7%	53.3%	46.7%
43,143	CREEK	15,397	8,295	7,102		1,193 R	53.9%	46.1%	53.9%	46.1%
21,097	CUSTER	7,208	4,182	3,026		1,156 R	58.0%	42.0%	58.0%	42.0%
14,734	DELAWARE	5,757	3,078	2,679		399 R	53.5%	46.5%	53.5%	46.5%
8,789	DEWEY	3,344	1,896	1,448		448 R	56.7%	43.3%	56.7%	43.3%
7,326	ELLIS	2,836	1,916	920		996 R	67.6%	32.4%	67.6%	32.4%
52,820	GARFIELD	22,117	15,348	6,769		8,579 R	69.4%	30.6%	69.4%	30.6%
29,500	GARVIN	10,301	3,850	6,451		2,601 D	37.4%	62.6%	37.4%	62.6%
34,872	GRADY	11,964	5,191	6,773		1,582 D	43.4%	56.6%	43.4%	56.6%
10,461	GRANT	4,741	2,788	1,953		835 R	58.8%	41.2%	58.8%	41.2%
11,749	GREER	3,406	1,499	1,907		408 D	44.0%	56.0%	44.0%	56.0%
8,079	HARMON	2,580	837	1,743		906 D	32.4%	67.6%	32.4%	67.6%
5,977	HARPER	2,332	1,596	736		860 R	68.4%	31.6%	68.4%	31.6%
13,313	HASKELL	4,139	1,758	2,381		623 D	42.5%	57.5%	42.5%	57.5%
20,664	HUGHES	7,061	2,783	4,278		1,495 D	39.4%	60.6%	39.4%	60.6%
20,082	JACKSON	6,778	2,343	4,435		2,092 D	34.6%	65.4%	34.6%	65.4%
11,122	JEFFERSON	3,725	1,186	2,539		1,353 D	31.8%	68.2%	31.8%	68.2%
10,608	JOHNSTON	3,389	1,157	2,232		1,075 D	34.1%	65.9%	34.1%	65.9%
48,892	KAY	22,908	14,837	8,071		6,766 R	64.8%	35.2%	64.8%	35.2%
12,860	KINGFISHER	5,603	3,935	1,668		2,267 R	70.2%	29.8%	70.2%	29.8%
18,926	KIOWA	6,084	2,713	3,371		658 D	44.6%	55.4%	44.6%	55.4%
9,690	LATIMER	3,381	1,387	1,994		607 D	41.0%	59.0%	41.0%	59.0%
35,276	LE FLORE	9,586	4,310	5,276		966 D	45.0%	55.0%	45.0%	55.0%
22,102	LINCOLN	8,902	4,993	3,909		1,084 R	56.1%	43.9%	56.1%	43.9%
22,170	LOGAN	8,201	5,326	2,875		2,451 R	64.9%	35.1%	64.9%	35.1%
7,721	LOVE	2,487	731	1,756		1,025 D	29.4%	70.6%	29.4%	70.6%
14,681	MCCLAIN	5,062	2,081	2,981		900 D	41.1%	58.9%	41.1%	58.9%
31,588	MCCURTAIN	7,468	2,707	4,761		2,054 D	36.2%	63.8%	36.2%	63.8%
17,829	MCINTOSH	4,877	2,149	2,728		579 D	44.1%	55.9%	44.1%	55.9%
10,279	MAJOR	3,777	2,826	951		1,875 R	74.8%	25.2%	74.8%	25.2%
8,177	MARSHALL	3,251	1,151	2,100		949 D	35.4%	64.6%	35.4%	64.6%
19,743	MAYES	8,437	4,677	3,760		917 R	55.4%	44.6%	55.4%	44.6%
10,775	MURRAY	4,291	1,809	2,482		673 D	42.2%	57.8%	42.2%	57.8%
65,573	MUSKOGEE	21,470	11,057	10,413		644 R	51.5%	48.5%	51.5%	48.5%
12,156	NOBLE	5,553	3,536	2,017		1,519 R	63.7%	36.3%	63.7%	36.3%
12,734	NOWATA	5,436	3,168	2,268		900 R	58.3%	41.7%	58.3%	41.7%
16,948	OKFUSKEE	4,630	2,299	2,331		32 D	49.7%	50.3%	49.7%	50.3%
325,352	OKLAHOMA	142,907	85,395	57,512		27,883 R	59.8%	40.2%	59.8%	40.2%
44,561	OKMULGEE	14,329	6,703	7,626		923 D	46.8%	53.2%	46.8%	53.2%
33,071	OSAGE	13,235	7,296	5,939		1,357 R	55.1%	44.9%	55.1%	44.9%
32,218	OTTAWA	12,451	6,730	5,721		1,009 R	54.1%	45.9%	54.1%	45.9%
13,616	PAWNEE	5,654	3,390	2,264		1,126 R	60.0%	40.0%	60.0%	40.0%
46,430	PAYNE	15,701	9,381	6,320		3,061 R	59.7%	40.3%	59.7%	40.3%

OKLAHOMA

PRESIDENT 1956

1950 Census Population	County	Total Vote	Republican	Democratic	Other	Rep.-Dem. Plurality	Percentage Total Vote Rep.	Total Vote Dem.	Major Vote Rep.	Major Vote Dem.
41,031	PITTSBURG	13,621	5,239	8,382		3,143 D	38.5%	61.5%	38.5%	61.5%
30,875	PONTOTOC	10,764	4,814	5,950		1,136 D	44.7%	55.3%	44.7%	55.3%
43,517	POTTAWATOMIE	17,391	8,496	8,895		399 D	48.9%	51.1%	48.9%	51.1%
12,001	PUSHMATAHA	3,772	1,499	2,273		774 D	39.7%	60.3%	39.7%	60.3%
7,395	ROGER MILLS	2,439	1,072	1,367		295 D	44.0%	56.0%	44.0%	56.0%
19,532	ROGERS	7,672	4,487	3,185		1,302 R	58.5%	41.5%	58.5%	41.5%
40,672	SEMINOLE	11,127	5,230	5,897		667 D	47.0%	53.0%	47.0%	53.0%
19,773	SEQUOYAH	6,890	3,330	3,560		230 D	48.3%	51.7%	48.3%	51.7%
34,071	STEPHENS	13,848	6,324	7,524		1,200 D	45.7%	54.3%	45.7%	54.3%
14,235	TEXAS	5,206	3,320	1,886		1,434 R	63.8%	36.2%	63.8%	36.2%
17,598	TILLMAN	5,176	1,810	3,366		1,556 D	35.0%	65.0%	35.0%	65.0%
251,686	TULSA	127,024	83,219	43,805		39,414 R	65.5%	34.5%	65.5%	34.5%
16,741	WAGONER	6,081	3,537	2,544		993 R	58.2%	41.8%	58.2%	41.8%
32,880	WASHINGTON	18,017	12,488	5,529		6,959 R	69.3%	30.7%	69.3%	30.7%
17,657	WASHITA	5,743	2,552	3,191		639 D	44.4%	55.6%	44.4%	55.6%
14,526	WOODS	5,910	3,787	2,123		1,664 R	64.1%	35.9%	64.1%	35.9%
14,383	WOODWARD	5,023	3,405	1,618		1,787 R	67.8%	32.2%	67.8%	32.2%
2,233,351	TOTAL	859,350	473,769	385,581		88,188 R	55.1%	44.9%	55.1%	44.9%

OKLAHOMA

PRESIDENT 1952

1950 Census Population	County	Total Vote	Republican	Democratic	Other	Rep.-Dem. Plurality	Percentage Total Vote Rep.	Total Vote Dem.	Major Vote Rep.	Major Vote Dem.
14,918	ADAIR	5,762	3,037	2,725		312 R	52.7%	47.3%	52.7%	47.3%
10,699	ALFALFA	5,273	4,155	1,118		3,037 R	78.8%	21.2%	78.8%	21.2%
14,269	ATOKA	4,658	2,004	2,654		650 D	43.0%	57.0%	43.0%	57.0%
7,411	BEAVER	3,358	2,539	819		1,720 R	75.6%	24.4%	75.6%	24.4%
21,627	BECKHAM	8,476	4,504	3,972		532 R	53.1%	46.9%	53.1%	46.9%
15,049	BLAINE	6,677	4,851	1,826		3,025 R	72.7%	27.3%	72.7%	27.3%
28,999	BRYAN	10,079	3,340	6,739		3,399 D	33.1%	66.9%	33.1%	66.9%
34,913	CADDO	12,987	6,834	6,153		681 R	52.6%	47.4%	52.6%	47.4%
25,644	CANADIAN	11,492	7,289	4,203		3,086 R	63.4%	36.6%	63.4%	36.6%
36,455	CARTER	16,250	5,974	10,276		4,302 D	36.8%	63.2%	36.8%	63.2%
18,989	CHEROKEE	6,560	3,326	3,234		92 R	50.7%	49.3%	50.7%	49.3%
20,405	CHOCTAW	6,511	2,251	4,260		2,009 D	34.6%	65.4%	34.6%	65.4%
4,589	CIMARRON	2,143	1,438	705		733 R	67.1%	32.9%	67.1%	32.9%
41,443	CLEVELAND	14,339	8,149	6,190		1,959 R	56.8%	43.2%	56.8%	43.2%
8,056	COAL	2,861	1,106	1,755		649 D	38.7%	61.3%	38.7%	61.3%
55,165	COMANCHE	17,785	8,756	9,029		273 D	49.2%	50.8%	49.2%	50.8%
10,180	COTTON	4,014	1,897	2,117		220 D	47.3%	52.7%	47.3%	52.7%
18,263	CRAIG	6,965	3,830	3,135		695 R	55.0%	45.0%	55.0%	45.0%
43,143	CREEK	18,075	9,257	8,818		439 R	51.2%	48.8%	51.2%	48.8%
21,097	CUSTER	8,893	5,667	3,226		2,441 R	63.7%	36.3%	63.7%	36.3%
14,734	DELAWARE	6,085	3,399	2,686		713 R	55.9%	44.1%	55.9%	44.1%
8,789	DEWEY	3,864	2,583	1,281		1,302 R	66.8%	33.2%	66.8%	33.2%
7,326	ELLIS	3,300	2,583	717		1,866 R	78.3%	21.7%	78.3%	21.7%
52,820	GARFIELD	24,636	17,589	7,047		10,542 R	71.4%	28.6%	71.4%	28.6%
29,500	GARVIN	11,246	4,402	6,844		2,442 D	39.1%	60.9%	39.1%	60.9%
34,872	GRADY	14,058	6,348	7,710		1,362 D	45.2%	54.8%	45.2%	54.8%
10,461	GRANT	5,517	3,996	1,521		2,475 R	72.4%	27.6%	72.4%	27.6%
11,749	GREER	4,468	2,147	2,321		174 D	48.1%	51.9%	48.1%	51.9%
8,079	HARMON	2,961	1,057	1,904		847 D	35.7%	64.3%	35.7%	64.3%
5,977	HARPER	2,793	2,057	736		1,321 R	73.6%	26.4%	73.6%	26.4%
13,313	HASKELL	4,491	1,872	2,619		747 D	41.7%	58.3%	41.7%	58.3%
20,664	HUGHES	7,651	3,012	4,639		1,627 D	39.4%	60.6%	39.4%	60.6%
20,082	JACKSON	7,548	2,627	4,921		2,294 D	34.8%	65.2%	34.8%	65.2%
11,122	JEFFERSON	4,256	1,384	2,872		1,488 D	32.5%	67.5%	32.5%	67.5%
10,608	JOHNSTON	3,844	1,349	2,495		1,146 D	35.1%	64.9%	35.1%	64.9%
48,892	KAY	24,842	16,460	8,382		8,078 R	66.3%	33.7%	66.3%	33.7%
12,860	KINGFISHER	6,332	4,873	1,459		3,414 R	77.0%	23.0%	77.0%	23.0%
18,926	KIOWA	7,589	4,100	3,489		611 R	54.0%	46.0%	54.0%	46.0%
9,690	LATIMER	3,951	1,668	2,283		615 D	42.2%	57.8%	42.2%	57.8%
35,276	LE FLORE	10,980	4,631	6,349		1,718 D	42.2%	57.8%	42.2%	57.8%
22,102	LINCOLN	9,849	5,778	4,071		1,707 R	58.7%	41.3%	58.7%	41.3%
22,170	LOGAN	9,616	6,172	3,444		2,728 R	64.2%	35.8%	64.2%	35.8%
7,721	LOVE	2,778	806	1,972		1,166 D	29.0%	71.0%	29.0%	71.0%
14,681	MCCLAIN	5,527	2,326	3,201		875 D	42.1%	57.9%	42.1%	57.9%
31,588	MCCURTAIN	8,541	2,748	5,793		3,045 D	32.2%	67.8%	32.2%	67.8%
17,829	MCINTOSH	5,302	2,295	3,007		712 D	43.3%	56.7%	43.3%	56.7%
10,279	MAJOR	4,340	3,495	845		2,650 R	80.5%	19.5%	80.5%	19.5%
8,177	MARSHALL	3,492	1,204	2,288		1,084 D	34.5%	65.5%	34.5%	65.5%
19,743	MAYES	8,541	4,704	3,837		867 R	55.1%	44.9%	55.1%	44.9%
10,775	MURRAY	4,753	1,885	2,868		983 D	39.7%	60.3%	39.7%	60.3%
65,573	MUSKOGEE	24,850	11,810	13,040		1,230 D	47.5%	52.5%	47.5%	52.5%
12,156	NOBLE	6,225	4,422	1,803		2,619 R	71.0%	29.0%	71.0%	29.0%
12,734	NOWATA	5,883	3,226	2,657		569 R	54.8%	45.2%	54.8%	45.2%
16,948	OKFUSKEE	5,244	2,469	2,775		306 D	47.1%	52.9%	47.1%	52.9%
325,352	OKLAHOMA	165,691	95,492	70,199		25,293 R	57.6%	42.4%	57.6%	42.4%
44,561	OKMULGEE	16,832	6,717	10,115		3,398 D	39.9%	60.1%	39.9%	60.1%
33,071	OSAGE	14,445	7,731	6,714		1,017 R	53.5%	46.5%	53.5%	46.5%
32,218	OTTAWA	13,903	7,211	6,692		519 R	51.9%	48.1%	51.9%	48.1%
13,616	PAWNEE	6,249	3,975	2,274		1,701 R	63.6%	36.4%	63.6%	36.4%
46,430	PAYNE	17,095	10,605	6,490		4,115 R	62.0%	38.0%	62.0%	38.0%

OKLAHOMA

PRESIDENT 1952

1950 Census Population	County	Total Vote	Republican	Democratic	Other	Rep.-Dem. Plurality	Percentage Total Vote Rep.	Percentage Total Vote Dem.	Percentage Major Vote Rep.	Percentage Major Vote Dem.
41,031	PITTSBURG	15,455	5,909	9,546		3,637 D	38.2%	61.8%	38.2%	61.8%
30,875	PONTOTOC	12,597	5,389	7,208		1,819 D	42.8%	57.2%	42.8%	57.2%
43,517	POTTAWATOMIE	19,554	10,099	9,455		644 R	51.6%	48.4%	51.6%	48.4%
12,001	PUSHMATAHA	4,218	1,640	2,578		938 D	38.9%	61.1%	38.9%	61.1%
7,395	ROGER MILLS	3,146	1,667	1,479		188 R	53.0%	47.0%	53.0%	47.0%
19,532	ROGERS	8,703	4,873	3,830		1,043 R	56.0%	44.0%	56.0%	44.0%
40,672	SEMINOLE	13,744	6,668	7,076		408 D	48.5%	51.5%	48.5%	51.5%
19,773	SEQUOYAH	7,360	3,288	4,072		784 D	44.7%	55.3%	44.7%	55.3%
34,071	STEPHENS	14,490	6,461	8,029		1,568 D	44.6%	55.4%	44.6%	55.4%
14,235	TEXAS	6,111	4,196	1,915		2,281 R	68.7%	31.3%	68.7%	31.3%
17,598	TILLMAN	6,296	2,657	3,639		982 D	42.2%	57.8%	42.2%	57.8%
251,686	TULSA	120,590	73,862	46,728		27,134 R	61.3%	38.7%	61.3%	38.7%
16,741	WAGONER	6,287	3,321	2,966		355 R	52.8%	47.2%	52.8%	47.2%
32,880	WASHINGTON	17,572	11,334	6,238		5,096 R	64.5%	35.5%	64.5%	35.5%
17,657	WASHITA	7,091	3,914	3,177		737 R	55.2%	44.8%	55.2%	44.8%
14,526	WOODS	6,891	4,892	1,999		2,893 R	71.0%	29.0%	71.0%	29.0%
14,383	WOODWARD	6,153	4,463	1,690		2,773 R	72.5%	27.5%	72.5%	27.5%
2,233,351	TOTAL	948,984	518,045	430,939		87,106 R	54.6%	45.4%	54.6%	45.4%

OKLAHOMA

PRESIDENT 1948

1940 Census Population	County	Total Vote	Republican	Democratic	Other	Rep.-Dem. Plurality	Total Vote Rep.	Total Vote Dem.	Major Vote Rep.	Major Vote Dem.
15,755	ADAIR	5,474	2,407	3,067		660 D	44.0%	56.0%	44.0%	56.0%
14,129	ALFALFA	4,603	2,765	1,838		927 R	60.1%	39.9%	60.1%	39.9%
18,702	ATOKA	4,137	1,033	3,104		2,071 D	25.0%	75.0%	25.0%	75.0%
8,648	BEAVER	3,016	1,420	1,596		176 D	47.1%	52.9%	47.1%	52.9%
22,169	BECKHAM	5,854	1,310	4,544		3,234 D	22.4%	77.6%	22.4%	77.6%
18,543	BLAINE	5,430	2,835	2,595		240 R	52.2%	47.8%	52.2%	47.8%
38,138	BRYAN	9,114	1,366	7,748		6,382 D	15.0%	85.0%	15.0%	85.0%
41,567	CADDO	11,903	3,793	8,110		4,317 D	31.9%	68.1%	31.9%	68.1%
27,329	CANADIAN	9,297	3,729	5,568		1,839 D	40.1%	59.9%	40.1%	59.9%
43,292	CARTER	11,621	2,147	9,474		7,327 D	18.5%	81.5%	18.5%	81.5%
21,030	CHEROKEE	7,034	2,785	4,249		1,464 D	39.6%	60.4%	39.6%	60.4%
28,358	CHOCTAW	5,786	1,036	4,750		3,714 D	17.9%	82.1%	17.9%	82.1%
3,654	CIMARRON	1,544	650	894		244 D	42.1%	57.9%	42.1%	57.9%
27,728	CLEVELAND	10,227	3,671	6,556		2,885 D	35.9%	64.1%	35.9%	64.1%
12,811	COAL	2,588	464	2,124		1,660 D	17.9%	82.1%	17.9%	82.1%
38,988	COMANCHE	10,742	2,787	7,955		5,168 D	25.9%	74.1%	25.9%	74.1%
12,884	COTTON	3,351	738	2,613		1,875 D	22.0%	78.0%	22.0%	78.0%
21,083	CRAIG	6,989	2,807	4,182		1,375 D	40.2%	59.8%	40.2%	59.8%
55,503	CREEK	15,730	6,532	9,198		2,666 D	41.5%	58.5%	41.5%	58.5%
23,068	CUSTER	7,186	2,568	4,618		2,050 D	35.7%	64.3%	35.7%	64.3%
18,592	DELAWARE	5,500	2,343	3,157		814 D	42.6%	57.4%	42.6%	57.4%
11,981	DEWEY	3,543	1,494	2,049		555 D	42.2%	57.8%	42.2%	57.8%
8,466	ELLIS	2,942	1,522	1,420		102 R	51.7%	48.3%	51.7%	48.3%
45,484	GARFIELD	18,569	10,352	8,217		2,135 R	55.7%	44.3%	55.7%	44.3%
31,150	GARVIN	8,460	1,681	6,779		5,098 D	19.9%	80.1%	19.9%	80.1%
41,116	GRADY	11,018	2,882	8,136		5,254 D	26.2%	73.8%	26.2%	73.8%
13,128	GRANT	4,597	2,471	2,126		345 R	53.8%	46.2%	53.8%	46.2%
14,550	GREER	3,757	713	3,044		2,331 D	19.0%	81.0%	19.0%	81.0%
10,019	HARMON	2,606	266	2,340		2,074 D	10.2%	89.8%	10.2%	89.8%
6,454	HARPER	2,502	1,221	1,281		60 D	48.8%	51.2%	48.8%	51.2%
17,324	HASKELL	4,596	1,390	3,206		1,816 D	30.2%	69.8%	30.2%	69.8%
29,189	HUGHES	7,168	1,676	5,492		3,816 D	23.4%	76.6%	23.4%	76.6%
22,708	JACKSON	6,373	923	5,450		4,527 D	14.5%	85.5%	14.5%	85.5%
15,107	JEFFERSON	3,882	556	3,326		2,770 D	14.3%	85.7%	14.3%	85.7%
15,960	JOHNSTON	3,520	584	2,936		2,352 D	16.6%	83.4%	16.6%	83.4%
47,084	KAY	19,101	8,982	10,119		1,137 D	47.0%	53.0%	47.0%	53.0%
15,617	KINGFISHER	5,419	2,931	2,488		443 R	54.1%	45.9%	54.1%	45.9%
22,817	KIOWA	5,793	1,530	4,263		2,733 D	26.4%	73.6%	26.4%	73.6%
12,380	LATIMER	3,455	919	2,536		1,617 D	26.6%	73.4%	26.6%	73.4%
45,866	LE FLORE	9,607	2,821	6,786		3,965 D	29.4%	70.6%	29.4%	70.6%
29,529	LINCOLN	8,811	3,898	4,913		1,015 D	44.2%	55.8%	44.2%	55.8%
25,245	LOGAN	7,926	3,817	4,109		292 D	48.2%	51.8%	48.2%	51.8%
11,433	LOVE	2,440	249	2,191		1,942 D	10.2%	89.8%	10.2%	89.8%
19,205	MCCLAIN	4,359	908	3,451		2,543 D	20.8%	79.2%	20.8%	79.2%
41,318	MCCURTAIN	7,314	1,091	6,223		5,132 D	14.9%	85.1%	14.9%	85.1%
24,097	MCINTOSH	5,116	1,442	3,674		2,232 D	28.2%	71.8%	28.2%	71.8%
11,946	MAJOR	3,694	2,467	1,227		1,240 R	66.8%	33.2%	66.8%	33.2%
12,384	MARSHALL	2,924	469	2,455		1,986 D	16.0%	84.0%	16.0%	84.0%
21,668	MAYES	7,055	2,854	4,201		1,347 D	40.5%	59.5%	40.5%	59.5%
13,841	MURRAY	3,852	798	3,054		2,256 D	20.7%	79.3%	20.7%	79.3%
65,914	MUSKOGEE	20,452	6,592	13,860		7,268 D	32.2%	67.8%	32.2%	67.8%
14,826	NOBLE	5,200	2,430	2,770		340 D	46.7%	53.3%	46.7%	53.3%
15,774	NOWATA	4,807	2,119	2,688		569 D	44.1%	55.9%	44.1%	55.9%
26,279	OKFUSKEE	4,959	1,624	3,335		1,711 D	32.7%	67.3%	32.7%	67.3%
244,159	OKLAHOMA	100,115	40,161	59,954		19,793 D	40.1%	59.9%	40.1%	59.9%
50,101	OKMULGEE	14,835	4,368	10,467		6,099 D	29.4%	70.6%	29.4%	70.6%
41,502	OSAGE	11,107	3,951	7,156		3,205 D	35.6%	64.4%	35.6%	64.4%
35,849	OTTAWA	11,547	4,304	7,243		2,939 D	37.3%	62.7%	37.3%	62.7%
17,395	PAWNEE	5,372	2,651	2,721		70 D	49.3%	50.7%	49.3%	50.7%
36,057	PAYNE	13,189	5,799	7,390		1,591 D	44.0%	56.0%	44.0%	56.0%

OKLAHOMA

PRESIDENT 1948

1940 Census Population	County	Total Vote	Republican	Democratic	Other	Rep.-Dem. Plurality	Percentage: Total Vote Rep.	Total Vote Dem.	Major Vote Rep.	Major Vote Dem.
48,985	PITTSBURG	12,469	2,893	9,576		6,683 D	23.2%	76.8%	23.2%	76.8%
39,792	PONTOTOC	10,039	2,289	7,750		5,461 D	22.8%	77.2%	22.8%	77.2%
54,377	POTTAWATOMIE	14,980	4,760	10,220		5,460 D	31.8%	68.2%	31.8%	68.2%
19,466	PUSHMATAHA	3,766	789	2,977		2,188 D	21.0%	79.0%	21.0%	79.0%
10,736	ROGER MILLS	2,685	509	2,176		1,667 D	19.0%	81.0%	19.0%	81.0%
21,078	ROGERS	7,046	2,849	4,197		1,348 D	40.4%	59.6%	40.4%	59.6%
61,201	SEMINOLE	11,545	3,423	8,122		4,699 D	29.6%	70.4%	29.6%	70.4%
23,138	SEQUOYAH	6,526	2,077	4,449		2,372 D	31.8%	68.2%	31.8%	68.2%
31,090	STEPHENS	8,611	1,909	6,702		4,793 D	22.2%	77.8%	22.2%	77.8%
9,896	TEXAS	4,369	1,676	2,693		1,017 D	38.4%	61.6%	38.4%	61.6%
20,754	TILLMAN	5,129	1,058	4,071		3,013 D	20.6%	79.4%	20.6%	79.4%
193,363	TULSA	81,440	42,892	38,548		4,344 R	52.7%	47.3%	52.7%	47.3%
21,642	WAGONER	6,055	2,666	3,389		723 D	44.0%	56.0%	44.0%	56.0%
30,559	WASHINGTON	11,544	6,036	5,508		528 R	52.3%	47.7%	52.3%	47.7%
22,279	WASHITA	5,963	1,637	4,326		2,689 D	27.5%	72.5%	27.5%	72.5%
14,915	WOODS	5,753	2,871	2,882		11 D	49.9%	50.1%	49.9%	50.1%
16,270	WOODWARD	4,571	2,391	2,180		211 R	52.3%	47.7%	52.3%	47.7%
2,336,434	TOTAL	721,599	268,817	452,782		183,965 D	37.3%	62.7%	37.3%	62.7%

OKLAHOMA

PRESIDENT 1944

1940 Census Population	County	Total Vote	Republican	Democratic	Other	Rep.-Dem. Plurality	Percentage			
							Total Vote		Major Vote	
							Rep.	Dem.	Rep.	Dem.
15,755	ADAIR	5,564	2,792	2,760	12	32 R	50.2%	49.6%	50.3%	49.7%
14,129	ALFALFA	5,182	3,434	1,716	32	1,718 R	66.3%	33.1%	66.7%	33.3%
18,702	ATOKA	3,693	1,515	2,172	6	657 D	41.0%	58.8%	41.1%	58.9%
8,648	BEAVER	3,295	1,913	1,355	27	558 R	58.1%	41.1%	58.5%	41.5%
22,169	BECKHAM	5,657	2,034	3,608	15	1,574 D	36.0%	63.8%	36.1%	63.9%
18,543	BLAINE	5,591	3,480	2,097	14	1,383 R	62.2%	37.5%	62.4%	37.6%
38,138	BRYAN	8,874	1,677	7,180	17	5,503 D	18.9%	80.9%	18.9%	81.1%
41,567	CADDO	12,403	5,529	6,850	24	1,321 D	44.6%	55.2%	44.7%	55.3%
27,329	CANADIAN	9,492	4,674	4,800	18	126 D	49.2%	50.6%	49.3%	50.7%
43,292	CARTER	11,654	2,446	9,184	24	6,738 D	21.0%	78.8%	21.0%	79.0%
21,030	CHEROKEE	6,763	3,336	3,415	12	79 D	49.3%	50.5%	49.4%	50.6%
28,358	CHOCTAW	5,775	1,404	4,358	13	2,954 D	24.3%	75.5%	24.4%	75.6%
3,654	CIMARRON	1,579	822	746	11	76 R	52.1%	47.2%	52.4%	47.6%
27,728	CLEVELAND	8,903	3,642	5,240	21	1,598 D	40.9%	58.9%	41.0%	59.0%
12,811	COAL	2,724	760	1,959	5	1,199 D	27.9%	71.9%	28.0%	72.0%
38,988	COMANCHE	11,479	4,109	7,342	28	3,233 D	35.8%	64.0%	35.9%	64.1%
12,884	COTTON	3,994	1,266	2,711	17	1,445 D	31.7%	67.9%	31.8%	68.2%
21,083	CRAIG	6,485	3,111	3,363	11	252 D	48.0%	51.9%	48.1%	51.9%
55,503	CREEK	15,932	7,549	8,342	41	793 D	47.4%	52.4%	47.5%	52.5%
23,068	CUSTER	7,302	3,349	3,928	25	579 D	45.9%	53.8%	46.0%	54.0%
18,592	DELAWARE	5,126	2,660	2,373	93	287 R	51.9%	46.3%	52.9%	47.1%
11,981	DEWEY	3,987	2,166	1,808	13	358 R	54.3%	45.3%	54.5%	45.5%
8,466	ELLIS	3,051	1,939	1,104	8	835 R	63.6%	36.2%	63.7%	36.3%
45,484	GARFIELD	19,155	11,211	7,879	65	3,332 R	58.5%	41.1%	58.7%	41.3%
31,150	GARVIN	7,421	2,086	5,328	7	3,242 D	28.1%	71.8%	28.1%	71.9%
41,116	GRADY	11,778	4,069	7,689	20	3,620 D	34.5%	65.3%	34.6%	65.4%
13,128	GRANT	5,079	3,021	2,045	13	976 R	59.5%	40.3%	59.6%	40.4%
14,550	GREER	4,064	1,075	2,984	5	1,909 D	26.5%	73.4%	26.5%	73.5%
10,019	HARMON	2,446	503	1,933	10	1,430 D	20.6%	79.0%	20.6%	79.4%
6,454	HARPER	2,473	1,394	1,056	23	338 R	56.4%	42.7%	56.9%	43.1%
17,324	HASKELL	5,041	2,102	2,924	15	822 D	41.7%	58.0%	41.8%	58.2%
29,189	HUGHES	7,506	2,484	5,009	13	2,525 D	33.1%	66.7%	33.2%	66.8%
22,708	JACKSON	6,192	1,313	4,866	13	3,553 D	21.2%	78.6%	21.2%	78.8%
15,107	JEFFERSON	3,937	974	2,948	15	1,974 D	24.7%	74.9%	24.8%	75.2%
15,960	JOHNSTON	3,278	925	2,339	14	1,414 D	28.2%	71.4%	28.3%	71.7%
47,084	KAY	18,242	9,498	8,656	88	842 R	52.1%	47.5%	52.3%	47.7%
15,617	KINGFISHER	5,609	3,417	2,175	17	1,242 R	60.9%	38.8%	61.1%	38.9%
22,817	KIOWA	6,280	2,081	4,175	24	2,094 D	33.1%	66.5%	33.3%	66.7%
12,380	LATIMER	3,255	1,296	1,948	11	652 D	39.8%	59.8%	40.0%	60.0%
45,866	LE FLORE	9,349	3,667	5,660	22	1,993 D	39.2%	60.5%	39.3%	60.7%
29,529	LINCOLN	8,739	4,801	3,910	28	891 R	54.9%	44.7%	55.1%	44.9%
25,245	LOGAN	8,417	4,586	3,795	36	791 R	54.5%	45.1%	54.7%	45.3%
11,433	LOVE	2,405	446	1,955	4	1,509 D	18.5%	81.3%	18.6%	81.4%
19,205	MCCLAIN	4,801	1,492	3,301	8	1,809 D	31.1%	68.8%	31.1%	68.9%
41,318	MCCURTAIN	6,751	1,419	5,322	10	3,903 D	21.0%	78.8%	21.1%	78.9%
24,097	MCINTOSH	5,771	2,569	3,190	12	621 D	44.5%	55.3%	44.6%	55.4%
11,946	MAJOR	4,005	3,019	965	21	2,054 R	75.4%	24.1%	75.8%	24.2%
12,384	MARSHALL	3,024	752	2,261	11	1,509 D	24.9%	74.8%	25.0%	75.0%
21,668	MAYES	7,671	3,822	3,830	19	8 D	49.8%	49.9%	49.9%	50.1%
13,841	MURRAY	3,616	1,005	2,602	9	1,597 D	27.8%	72.0%	27.9%	72.1%
65,914	MUSKOGEE	19,990	8,280	11,679	31	3,399 D	41.4%	58.4%	41.5%	58.5%
14,826	NOBLE	5,373	3,060	2,300	13	760 R	57.0%	42.8%	57.1%	42.9%
15,774	NOWATA	5,326	2,730	2,581	15	149 R	51.3%	48.5%	51.4%	48.6%
26,279	OKFUSKEE	5,477	2,177	3,291	9	1,114 D	39.7%	60.1%	39.8%	60.2%
244,159	OKLAHOMA	100,392	42,464	57,812	116	15,348 D	42.3%	57.6%	42.3%	57.7%
50,101	OKMULGEE	15,192	5,430	9,737	25	4,307 D	35.7%	64.1%	35.8%	64.2%
41,502	OSAGE	12,410	5,557	6,846	7	1,289 D	44.8%	55.2%	44.8%	55.2%
35,849	OTTAWA	10,945	5,056	5,876	13	820 D	46.2%	53.7%	46.2%	53.8%
17,395	PAWNEE	5,786	3,310	2,460	16	850 R	57.2%	42.5%	57.4%	42.6%
36,057	PAYNE	11,702	6,048	5,624	30	424 R	51.7%	48.1%	51.8%	48.2%

OKLAHOMA

PRESIDENT 1944

1940 Census Population	County	Total Vote	Republican	Democratic	Other	Rep.-Dem. Plurality	Percentage Total Vote Rep.	Percentage Total Vote Dem.	Percentage Major Vote Rep.	Percentage Major Vote Dem.
48,985	PITTSBURG	12,626	4,068	8,535	23	4,467 D	32.2%	67.6%	32.3%	67.7%
39,792	PONTOTOC	9,533	2,960	6,552	21	3,592 D	31.1%	68.7%	31.1%	68.9%
54,377	POTTAWATOMIE	15,659	6,486	9,130	43	2,644 D	41.4%	58.3%	41.5%	58.5%
19,466	PUSHMATAHA	4,040	1,181	2,848	11	1,667 D	29.2%	70.5%	29.3%	70.7%
10,736	ROGER MILLS	3,176	1,148	2,015	13	867 D	36.1%	63.4%	36.3%	63.7%
21,078	ROGERS	6,956	3,739	3,209	8	530 R	53.8%	46.1%	53.8%	46.2%
61,201	SEMINOLE	11,692	4,560	7,116	16	2,556 D	39.0%	60.9%	39.1%	60.9%
23,138	SEQUOYAH	6,472	2,893	3,571	8	678 D	44.7%	55.2%	44.8%	55.2%
31,090	STEPHENS	8,974	2,766	6,189	19	3,423 D	30.8%	69.0%	30.9%	69.1%
9,896	TEXAS	3,870	1,731	2,119	20	388 D	44.7%	54.8%	45.0%	55.0%
20,754	TILLMAN	5,410	1,496	3,902	12	2,406 D	27.7%	72.1%	27.7%	72.3%
193,363	TULSA	76,188	42,663	33,436	89	9,227 R	56.0%	43.9%	56.1%	43.9%
21,642	WAGONER	5,848	3,467	2,373	8	1,094 R	59.3%	40.6%	59.4%	40.6%
30,559	WASHINGTON	11,641	6,533	5,090	18	1,443 R	56.1%	43.7%	56.2%	43.8%
22,279	WASHITA	6,248	2,706	3,524	18	818 D	43.3%	56.4%	43.4%	56.6%
14,915	WOODS	5,675	3,226	2,426	23	800 R	56.8%	42.7%	57.1%	42.9%
16,270	WOODWARD	5,225	3,055	2,152	18	903 R	58.5%	41.2%	58.7%	41.3%
2,336,434	TOTAL	722,636	319,424	401,549	1,663	82,125 D	44.2%	55.6%	44.3%	55.7%

OKLAHOMA

PRESIDENT 1940

1940 Census Population	County	Total Vote	Republican	Democratic	Other	Rep.-Dem. Plurality	Percentage Total Vote Rep.	Percentage Total Vote Dem.	Percentage Major Vote Rep.	Percentage Major Vote Dem.
15,755	ADAIR	6,484	3,275	3,203	6	72 R	50.5%	49.4%	50.6%	49.4%
14,129	ALFALFA	6,455	3,675	2,720	60	955 R	56.9%	42.1%	57.5%	42.5%
18,702	ATOKA	5,832	2,218	3,601	13	1,383 D	38.0%	61.7%	38.1%	61.9%
8,648	BEAVER	4,282	2,219	2,034	29	185 R	51.8%	47.5%	52.2%	47.8%
22,169	BECKHAM	6,783	2,148	4,598	37	2,450 D	31.7%	67.8%	31.8%	68.2%
18,543	BLAINE	7,216	4,080	3,095	41	985 R	56.5%	42.9%	56.9%	43.1%
38,138	BRYAN	11,310	2,190	9,095	25	6,905 D	19.4%	80.4%	19.4%	80.6%
41,567	CADDO	14,645	6,304	8,280	61	1,976 D	43.0%	56.5%	43.2%	56.8%
27,329	CANADIAN	10,237	4,699	5,506	32	807 D	45.9%	53.8%	46.0%	54.0%
43,292	CARTER	13,746	3,270	10,441	35	7,171 D	23.8%	76.0%	23.8%	76.2%
21,030	CHEROKEE	8,098	4,128	3,952	18	176 R	51.0%	48.8%	51.1%	48.9%
28,358	CHOCTAW	7,561	2,365	5,177	19	2,812 D	31.3%	68.5%	31.4%	68.6%
3,654	CIMARRON	1,853	841	989	23	148 D	45.4%	53.4%	46.0%	54.0%
27,728	CLEVELAND	9,650	3,660	5,933	57	2,273 D	37.9%	61.5%	38.2%	61.8%
12,811	COAL	3,535	1,148	2,377	10	1,229 D	32.5%	67.2%	32.6%	67.4%
38,988	COMANCHE	10,535	3,703	6,796	36	3,093 D	35.1%	64.5%	35.3%	64.7%
12,884	COTTON	4,760	1,616	3,121	23	1,505 D	33.9%	65.6%	34.1%	65.9%
21,083	CRAIG	7,917	3,582	4,316	19	734 D	45.2%	54.5%	45.4%	54.6%
55,503	CREEK	20,495	9,468	10,976	51	1,508 D	46.2%	53.6%	46.3%	53.7%
23,068	CUSTER	8,071	3,419	4,612	40	1,193 D	42.4%	57.1%	42.6%	57.4%
18,592	DELAWARE	6,739	3,305	3,417	17	112 D	49.0%	50.7%	49.2%	50.8%
11,981	DEWEY	5,038	2,613	2,391	34	222 R	51.9%	47.5%	52.2%	47.8%
8,466	ELLIS	3,836	2,162	1,657	17	505 R	56.4%	43.2%	56.6%	43.4%
45,484	GARFIELD	20,502	10,792	9,544	166	1,248 R	52.6%	46.6%	53.1%	46.9%
31,150	GARVIN	9,999	2,958	7,001	40	4,043 D	29.6%	70.0%	29.7%	70.3%
41,116	GRADY	12,417	4,299	8,075	43	3,776 D	34.6%	65.0%	34.7%	65.3%
13,128	GRANT	6,402	3,394	2,970	38	424 R	53.0%	46.4%	53.3%	46.7%
14,550	GREER	4,740	1,195	3,524	21	2,329 D	25.2%	74.3%	25.3%	74.7%
10,019	HARMON	3,041	731	2,292	18	1,561 D	24.0%	75.4%	24.2%	75.8%
6,454	HARPER	3,073	1,616	1,419	38	197 R	52.6%	46.2%	53.2%	46.8%
17,324	HASKELL	6,566	2,661	3,896	9	1,235 D	40.5%	59.3%	40.6%	59.4%
29,189	HUGHES	9,194	3,168	6,005	21	2,837 D	34.5%	65.3%	34.5%	65.5%
22,708	JACKSON	6,408	1,540	4,832	36	3,292 D	24.0%	75.4%	24.2%	75.8%
15,107	JEFFERSON	5,060	1,226	3,814	20	2,588 D	24.2%	75.4%	24.3%	75.7%
15,960	JOHNSTON	4,329	1,362	2,955	12	1,593 D	31.5%	68.3%	31.5%	68.5%
47,084	KAY	20,884	10,003	10,725	156	722 D	47.9%	51.4%	48.3%	51.7%
15,617	KINGFISHER	6,608	3,718	2,865	25	853 R	56.3%	43.4%	56.5%	43.5%
22,817	KIOWA	7,252	2,539	4,679	34	2,140 D	35.0%	64.5%	35.2%	64.8%
12,380	LATIMER	4,766	1,600	3,138	28	1,538 D	33.6%	65.8%	33.8%	66.2%
45,866	LE FLORE	13,087	4,664	8,379	44	3,715 D	35.6%	64.0%	35.8%	64.2%
29,529	LINCOLN	11,574	6,269	5,271	34	998 R	54.2%	45.5%	54.3%	45.7%
25,245	LOGAN	10,225	5,427	4,752	46	675 R	53.1%	46.5%	53.3%	46.7%
11,433	LOVE	3,183	687	2,485	11	1,798 D	21.6%	78.1%	21.7%	78.3%
19,205	MCCLAIN	5,641	1,862	3,768	11	1,906 D	33.0%	66.8%	33.1%	66.9%
41,318	MCCURTAIN	9,248	2,225	6,994	29	4,769 D	24.1%	75.6%	24.1%	75.9%
24,097	MCINTOSH	7,275	3,487	3,771	17	284 D	47.9%	51.8%	48.0%	52.0%
11,946	MAJOR	4,891	3,453	1,404	34	2,049 R	70.6%	28.7%	71.1%	28.9%
12,384	MARSHALL	3,770	1,032	2,723	15	1,691 D	27.4%	72.2%	27.5%	72.5%
21,668	MAYES	7,709	3,631	4,057	21	426 D	47.1%	52.6%	47.2%	52.8%
13,841	MURRAY	4,381	1,238	3,126	17	1,888 D	28.3%	71.4%	28.4%	71.6%
65,914	MUSKOGEE	22,551	9,585	12,917	49	3,332 D	42.5%	57.3%	42.6%	57.4%
14,826	NOBLE	6,674	3,441	3,226	7	215 R	51.6%	48.3%	51.6%	48.4%
15,774	NOWATA	7,060	3,406	3,615	39	209 D	48.2%	51.2%	48.5%	51.5%
26,279	OKFUSKEE	7,599	3,001	4,574	24	1,573 D	39.5%	60.2%	39.6%	60.4%
244,159	OKLAHOMA	89,617	35,639	53,649	329	18,010 D	39.8%	59.9%	39.9%	60.1%
50,101	OKMULGEE	17,796	6,696	11,016	84	4,320 D	37.6%	61.9%	37.8%	62.2%
41,502	OSAGE	15,481	6,419	9,019	43	2,600 D	41.5%	58.3%	41.6%	58.4%
35,849	OTTAWA	13,646	5,738	7,873	35	2,135 D	42.0%	57.7%	42.2%	57.8%
17,395	PAWNEE	7,464	3,991	3,435	38	556 R	53.5%	46.0%	53.7%	46.3%
36,057	PAYNE	14,539	6,772	7,704	63	932 D	46.6%	53.0%	46.8%	53.2%

OKLAHOMA

PRESIDENT 1940

1940 Census Population	County	Total Vote	Republican	Democratic	Other	Rep.-Dem. Plurality	Percentage Total Vote Rep.	Percentage Total Vote Dem.	Percentage Major Vote Rep.	Percentage Major Vote Dem.
48,985	PITTSBURG	14,676	4,484	10,169	23	5,685 D	30.6%	69.3%	30.6%	69.4%
39,792	PONTOTOC	12,794	3,449	9,310	35	5,861 D	27.0%	72.8%	27.0%	73.0%
54,377	POTTAWATOMIE	18,912	6,776	12,058	78	5,282 D	35.8%	63.8%	36.0%	64.0%
19,466	PUSHMATAHA	5,670	1,709	3,952	9	2,243 D	30.1%	69.7%	30.2%	69.8%
10,736	ROGER MILLS	4,106	1,504	2,580	22	1,076 D	36.6%	62.8%	36.8%	63.2%
21,078	ROGERS	8,139	4,086	4,028	25	58 R	50.2%	49.5%	50.4%	49.6%
61,201	SEMINOLE	18,083	6,880	11,167	36	4,287 D	38.0%	61.8%	38.1%	61.9%
23,138	SEQUOYAH	8,281	3,803	4,469	9	666 D	45.9%	54.0%	46.0%	54.0%
31,090	STEPHENS	9,172	2,989	6,149	34	3,160 D	32.6%	67.0%	32.7%	67.3%
9,896	TEXAS	4,777	1,918	2,831	28	913 D	40.2%	59.3%	40.4%	59.6%
20,754	TILLMAN	6,508	1,564	4,920	24	3,356 D	24.0%	75.6%	24.1%	75.9%
193,363	TULSA	73,575	40,342	33,098	135	7,244 R	54.8%	45.0%	54.9%	45.1%
21,642	WAGONER	7,618	4,647	2,946	25	1,701 R	61.0%	38.7%	61.2%	38.8%
30,559	WASHINGTON	13,676	7,347	6,289	40	1,058 R	53.7%	46.0%	53.9%	46.1%
22,279	WASHITA	7,245	2,978	4,256	11	1,278 D	41.1%	58.7%	41.2%	58.8%
14,915	WOODS	7,007	3,440	3,506	61	66 D	49.1%	50.0%	49.5%	50.5%
16,270	WOODWARD	6,243	3,403	2,806	34	597 R	54.5%	44.9%	54.8%	45.2%
2,336,434	TOTAL	826,212	348,872	474,313	3,027	125,441 D	42.2%	57.4%	42.4%	57.6%

OKLAHOMA

PRESIDENT 1936

1930 Census Population	County	Total Vote	Republican	Democratic	Other	Rep.-Dem. Plurality	Percentage Total Vote Rep.	Total Vote Dem.	Major Vote Rep.	Major Vote Dem.
14,756	ADAIR	5,972	2,699	3,257	16	558 D	45.2%	54.5%	45.3%	54.7%
15,228	ALFALFA	6,026	2,573	3,398	55	825 D	42.7%	56.4%	43.1%	56.9%
14,533	ATOKA	4,323	1,141	3,173	9	2,032 D	26.4%	73.4%	26.4%	73.6%
11,452	BEAVER	3,863	1,340	2,502	21	1,162 D	34.7%	64.8%	34.9%	65.1%
28,991	BECKHAM	6,780	1,352	5,372	56	4,020 D	19.9%	79.2%	20.1%	79.9%
20,452	BLAINE	7,196	2,877	4,242	77	1,365 D	40.0%	58.9%	40.4%	59.6%
32,277	BRYAN	9,488	1,362	8,106	20	6,744 D	14.4%	85.4%	14.4%	85.6%
50,779	CADDO	14,669	5,205	9,358	106	4,153 D	35.5%	63.8%	35.7%	64.3%
28,115	CANADIAN	9,508	3,325	6,135	48	2,810 D	35.0%	64.5%	35.1%	64.9%
41,419	CARTER	11,669	2,247	9,387	35	7,140 D	19.3%	80.4%	19.3%	80.7%
17,470	CHEROKEE	6,904	2,917	3,966	21	1,049 D	42.3%	57.4%	42.4%	57.6%
24,142	CHOCTAW	5,910	1,269	4,624	17	3,355 D	21.5%	78.2%	21.5%	78.5%
5,408	CIMARRON	1,910	555	1,342	13	787 D	29.1%	70.3%	29.3%	70.7%
24,948	CLEVELAND	9,022	2,643	6,304	75	3,661 D	29.3%	69.9%	29.5%	70.5%
11,521	COAL	3,160	603	2,550	7	1,947 D	19.1%	80.7%	19.1%	80.9%
34,317	COMANCHE	10,140	3,039	7,026	75	3,987 D	30.0%	69.3%	30.2%	69.8%
15,442	COTTON	5,040	1,181	3,842	17	2,661 D	23.4%	76.2%	23.5%	76.5%
18,052	CRAIG	7,354	2,964	4,377	13	1,413 D	40.3%	59.5%	40.4%	59.6%
64,115	CREEK	19,903	7,257	12,540	106	5,283 D	36.5%	63.0%	36.7%	63.3%
27,517	CUSTER	7,525	2,386	5,093	46	2,707 D	31.7%	67.7%	31.9%	68.1%
15,370	DELAWARE	6,045	2,632	3,398	15	766 D	43.5%	56.2%	43.6%	56.4%
13,250	DEWEY	4,863	1,846	2,980	37	1,134 D	38.0%	61.3%	38.3%	61.7%
10,541	ELLIS	3,847	1,324	2,493	30	1,169 D	34.4%	64.8%	34.7%	65.3%
45,588	GARFIELD	18,723	7,457	11,142	124	3,685 D	39.8%	59.5%	40.1%	59.9%
31,401	GARVIN	8,034	1,700	6,276	58	4,576 D	21.2%	78.1%	21.3%	78.7%
47,638	GRADY	12,099	3,013	9,025	61	6,012 D	24.9%	74.6%	25.0%	75.0%
14,150	GRANT	6,294	2,307	3,955	32	1,648 D	36.7%	62.8%	36.8%	63.2%
20,282	GREER	4,522	766	3,745	11	2,979 D	16.9%	82.8%	17.0%	83.0%
13,834	HARMON	2,912	331	2,570	11	2,239 D	11.4%	88.3%	11.4%	88.6%
7,761	HARPER	2,911	1,068	1,836	7	768 D	36.7%	63.1%	36.8%	63.2%
16,216	HASKELL	6,144	2,182	3,961	1	1,779 D	35.5%	64.5%	35.5%	64.5%
30,334	HUGHES	8,030	2,032	5,990	8	3,958 D	25.3%	74.6%	25.3%	74.7%
28,910	JACKSON	6,571	1,095	5,435	41	4,340 D	16.7%	82.7%	16.8%	83.2%
17,392	JEFFERSON	4,773	1,032	3,719	22	2,687 D	21.6%	77.9%	21.7%	78.3%
13,082	JOHNSTON	3,865	743	3,099	23	2,356 D	19.2%	80.2%	19.3%	80.7%
50,186	KAY	18,649	6,671	11,846	132	5,175 D	35.8%	63.5%	36.0%	64.0%
15,960	KINGFISHER	6,652	2,539	4,081	32	1,542 D	38.2%	61.3%	38.4%	61.6%
29,630	KIOWA	7,361	1,684	5,624	53	3,940 D	22.9%	76.4%	23.0%	77.0%
11,184	LATIMER	4,286	1,344	2,923	19	1,579 D	31.4%	68.2%	31.5%	68.5%
42,896	LE FLORE	11,969	3,894	8,061	14	4,167 D	32.5%	67.3%	32.6%	67.4%
33,738	LINCOLN	11,407	5,452	5,903	52	451 D	47.8%	51.7%	48.0%	52.0%
27,761	LOGAN	10,095	4,609	5,425	61	816 D	45.7%	53.7%	45.9%	54.1%
9,639	LOVE	2,687	440	2,227	20	1,787 D	16.4%	82.9%	16.5%	83.5%
21,575	MCCLAIN	5,300	1,191	4,092	17	2,901 D	22.5%	77.2%	22.5%	77.5%
34,759	MCCURTAIN	6,221	1,119	5,089	13	3,970 D	18.0%	81.8%	18.0%	82.0%
24,924	MCINTOSH	6,384	2,470	3,898	16	1,428 D	38.7%	61.1%	38.8%	61.2%
12,206	MAJOR	4,204	2,230	1,929	45	301 R	53.0%	45.9%	53.6%	46.4%
11,026	MARSHALL	3,278	415	2,840	23	2,425 D	12.7%	86.6%	12.7%	87.3%
17,883	MAYES	6,623	2,690	3,920	13	1,230 D	40.6%	59.2%	40.7%	59.3%
12,410	MURRAY	4,027	823	3,181	23	2,358 D	20.4%	79.0%	20.6%	79.4%
66,424	MUSKOGEE	19,829	6,452	13,344	33	6,892 D	32.5%	67.3%	32.6%	67.4%
15,139	NOBLE	6,375	2,461	3,901	13	1,440 D	38.6%	61.2%	38.7%	61.3%
13,611	NOWATA	6,084	2,552	3,512	20	960 D	41.9%	57.7%	42.1%	57.9%
29,016	OKFUSKEE	7,052	2,162	4,843	47	2,681 D	30.7%	68.7%	30.9%	69.1%
221,738	OKLAHOMA	75,631	24,312	50,946	373	26,634 D	32.1%	67.4%	32.3%	67.7%
56,558	OKMULGEE	17,093	4,975	12,061	57	7,086 D	29.1%	70.6%	29.2%	70.8%
47,334	OSAGE	15,056	4,917	10,090	49	5,173 D	32.7%	67.0%	32.8%	67.2%
38,542	OTTAWA	12,412	4,697	7,658	57	2,961 D	37.8%	61.7%	38.0%	62.0%
19,882	PAWNEE	7,064	2,961	4,031	72	1,070 D	41.9%	57.1%	42.3%	57.7%
36,905	PAYNE	12,921	4,783	8,081	57	3,298 D	37.0%	62.5%	37.2%	62.8%

OKLAHOMA

PRESIDENT 1936

1930 Census Population	County	Total Vote	Republican	Democratic	Other	Rep.-Dem. Plurality	Percentage Total Vote Rep.	Percentage Total Vote Dem.	Percentage Major Vote Rep.	Percentage Major Vote Dem.
50,778	PITTSBURG	13,668	3,651	9,974	43	6,323 D	26.7%	73.0%	26.8%	73.2%
32,469	PONTOTOC	10,136	2,015	8,079	42	6,064 D	19.9%	79.7%	20.0%	80.0%
66,572	POTTAWATOMIE	16,968	4,703	12,187	78	7,484 D	27.7%	71.8%	27.8%	72.2%
14,744	PUSHMATAHA	4,505	1,097	3,389	19	2,292 D	24.4%	75.2%	24.5%	75.5%
14,164	ROGER MILLS	4,429	989	3,383	57	2,394 D	22.3%	76.4%	22.6%	77.4%
18,956	ROGERS	7,451	3,119	4,290	42	1,171 D	41.9%	57.6%	42.1%	57.9%
79,621	SEMINOLE	15,768	4,001	11,695	72	7,694 D	25.4%	74.2%	25.5%	74.5%
19,505	SEQUOYAH	6,890	2,609	4,281		1,672 D	37.9%	62.1%	37.9%	62.1%
33,069	STEPHENS	8,071	1,636	6,390	45	4,754 D	20.3%	79.2%	20.4%	79.6%
14,100	TEXAS	4,471	1,223	3,229	19	2,006 D	27.4%	72.2%	27.5%	72.5%
24,390	TILLMAN	6,410	1,126	5,268	16	4,142 D	17.6%	82.2%	17.6%	82.4%
187,574	TULSA	70,343	28,759	41,256	328	12,497 D	40.9%	58.6%	41.1%	58.9%
22,428	WAGONER	5,117	2,119	2,977	21	858 D	41.4%	58.2%	41.6%	58.4%
27,777	WASHINGTON	11,429	5,201	6,202	26	1,001 D	45.5%	54.3%	45.6%	54.4%
29,435	WASHITA	7,029	1,792	5,205	32	3,413 D	25.5%	74.1%	25.6%	74.4%
17,005	WOODS	6,569	2,346	4,179	44	1,833 D	35.7%	63.6%	36.0%	64.0%
15,844	WOODWARD	5,831	2,430	3,361	40	931 D	41.7%	57.6%	42.0%	58.0%
2,396,040	TOTAL	749,740	245,122	501,069	3,549	255,947 D	32.7%	66.8%	32.8%	67.2%

OKLAHOMA

PRESIDENT 1932

1930 Census Population	County	Total Vote	Republican	Democratic	Other	Rep.-Dem. Plurality	Percentage Total Vote Rep.	Total Vote Dem.	Major Vote Rep.	Major Vote Dem.
14,756	ADAIR	5,753	1,941	3,812		1,871 D	33.7%	66.3%	33.7%	66.3%
15,228	ALFALFA	5,679	2,037	3,642		1,605 D	35.9%	64.1%	35.9%	64.1%
14,533	ATOKA	4,240	562	3,678		3,116 D	13.3%	86.7%	13.3%	86.7%
11,452	BEAVER	3,911	1,358	2,553		1,195 D	34.7%	65.3%	34.7%	65.3%
28,991	BECKHAM	6,871	892	5,979		5,087 D	13.0%	87.0%	13.0%	87.0%
20,452	BLAINE	6,447	1,728	4,719		2,991 D	26.8%	73.2%	26.8%	73.2%
32,277	BRYAN	8,506	825	7,681		6,856 D	9.7%	90.3%	9.7%	90.3%
50,779	CADDO	13,973	2,972	11,001		8,029 D	21.3%	78.7%	21.3%	78.7%
28,115	CANADIAN	9,316	2,549	6,767		4,218 D	27.4%	72.6%	27.4%	72.6%
41,419	CARTER	11,366	1,733	9,633		7,900 D	15.2%	84.8%	15.2%	84.8%
17,470	CHEROKEE	6,908	2,275	4,633		2,358 D	32.9%	67.1%	32.9%	67.1%
24,142	CHOCTAW	5,948	1,040	4,908		3,868 D	17.5%	82.5%	17.5%	82.5%
5,408	CIMARRON	2,466	571	1,895		1,324 D	23.2%	76.8%	23.2%	76.8%
24,948	CLEVELAND	7,837	1,868	5,969		4,101 D	23.8%	76.2%	23.8%	76.2%
11,521	COAL	3,088	300	2,788		2,488 D	9.7%	90.3%	9.7%	90.3%
34,317	COMANCHE	9,632	2,046	7,586		5,540 D	21.2%	78.8%	21.2%	78.8%
15,442	COTTON	5,184	758	4,426		3,668 D	14.6%	85.4%	14.6%	85.4%
18,052	CRAIG	6,985	2,124	4,861		2,737 D	30.4%	69.6%	30.4%	69.6%
64,115	CREEK	19,749	6,786	12,963		6,177 D	34.4%	65.6%	34.4%	65.6%
27,517	CUSTER	8,257	1,684	6,573		4,889 D	20.4%	79.6%	20.4%	79.6%
15,370	DELAWARE	5,153	1,469	3,684		2,215 D	28.5%	71.5%	28.5%	71.5%
13,250	DEWEY	4,906	1,051	3,855		2,804 D	21.4%	78.6%	21.4%	78.6%
10,541	ELLIS	3,884	1,089	2,795		1,706 D	28.0%	72.0%	28.0%	72.0%
45,588	GARFIELD	17,610	6,837	10,773		3,936 D	38.8%	61.2%	38.8%	61.2%
31,401	GARVIN	8,868	1,034	7,834		6,800 D	11.7%	88.3%	11.7%	88.3%
47,638	GRADY	11,281	2,034	9,247		7,213 D	18.0%	82.0%	18.0%	82.0%
14,150	GRANT	6,334	1,902	4,432		2,530 D	30.0%	70.0%	30.0%	70.0%
20,282	GREER	4,658	418	4,240		3,822 D	9.0%	91.0%	9.0%	91.0%
13,834	HARMON	3,231	189	3,042		2,853 D	5.8%	94.2%	5.8%	94.2%
7,761	HARPER	2,922	783	2,139		1,356 D	26.8%	73.2%	26.8%	73.2%
16,216	HASKELL	5,796	1,439	4,357		2,918 D	24.8%	75.2%	24.8%	75.2%
30,334	HUGHES	7,599	1,114	6,485		5,371 D	14.7%	85.3%	14.7%	85.3%
28,910	JACKSON	6,362	603	5,759		5,156 D	9.5%	90.5%	9.5%	90.5%
17,392	JEFFERSON	4,051	485	3,566		3,081 D	12.0%	88.0%	12.0%	88.0%
13,082	JOHNSTON	3,606	329	3,277		2,948 D	9.1%	90.9%	9.1%	90.9%
50,186	KAY	18,725	5,884	12,841		6,957 D	31.4%	68.6%	31.4%	68.6%
15,960	KINGFISHER	6,089	2,103	3,986		1,883 D	34.5%	65.5%	34.5%	65.5%
29,630	KIOWA	6,170	966	5,204		4,238 D	15.7%	84.3%	15.7%	84.3%
11,184	LATIMER	3,847	728	3,119		2,391 D	18.9%	81.1%	18.9%	81.1%
42,896	LE FLORE	11,043	2,363	8,680		6,317 D	21.4%	78.6%	21.4%	78.6%
33,738	LINCOLN	11,146	3,505	7,641		4,136 D	31.4%	68.6%	31.4%	68.6%
27,761	LOGAN	9,732	3,959	5,773		1,814 D	40.7%	59.3%	40.7%	59.3%
9,639	LOVE	2,613	187	2,426		2,239 D	7.2%	92.8%	7.2%	92.8%
21,575	MCCLAIN	5,905	818	5,087		4,269 D	13.9%	86.1%	13.9%	86.1%
34,759	MCCURTAIN	6,473	587	5,886		5,299 D	9.1%	90.9%	9.1%	90.9%
24,924	MCINTOSH	5,610	1,077	4,533		3,456 D	19.2%	80.8%	19.2%	80.8%
12,206	MAJOR	3,899	1,374	2,525		1,151 D	35.2%	64.8%	35.2%	64.8%
11,026	MARSHALL	3,555	319	3,236		2,917 D	9.0%	91.0%	9.0%	91.0%
17,883	MAYES	6,040	1,596	4,444		2,848 D	26.4%	73.6%	26.4%	73.6%
12,410	MURRAY	3,618	532	3,086		2,554 D	14.7%	85.3%	14.7%	85.3%
66,424	MUSKOGEE	17,972	5,351	12,621		7,270 D	29.8%	70.2%	29.8%	70.2%
15,139	NOBLE	6,049	1,635	4,414		2,779 D	27.0%	73.0%	27.0%	73.0%
13,611	NOWATA	5,673	1,900	3,773		1,873 D	33.5%	66.5%	33.5%	66.5%
29,016	OKFUSKEE	6,541	1,415	5,126		3,711 D	21.6%	78.4%	21.6%	78.4%
221,738	OKLAHOMA	62,368	21,238	41,130		19,892 D	34.1%	65.9%	34.1%	65.9%
56,558	OKMULGEE	16,049	4,762	11,287		6,525 D	29.7%	70.3%	29.7%	70.3%
47,334	OSAGE	15,608	4,775	10,833		6,058 D	30.6%	69.4%	30.6%	69.4%
38,542	OTTAWA	11,385	3,210	8,175		4,965 D	28.2%	71.8%	28.2%	71.8%
19,882	PAWNEE	7,280	2,280	5,000		2,720 D	31.3%	68.7%	31.3%	68.7%
36,905	PAYNE	11,693	3,874	7,819		3,945 D	33.1%	66.9%	33.1%	66.9%

OKLAHOMA

PRESIDENT 1932

1930 Census Population	County	Total Vote	Republican	Democratic	Other	Rep.-Dem. Plurality	Percentage Total Vote Rep.	Total Vote Dem.	Major Vote Rep.	Major Vote Dem.
50,778	PITTSBURG	12,932	2,396	10,536		8,140 D	18.5%	81.5%	18.5%	81.5%
32,469	PONTOTOC	8,434	1,207	7,227		6,020 D	14.3%	85.7%	14.3%	85.7%
66,572	POTTAWATOMIE	16,076	4,063	12,013		7,950 D	25.3%	74.7%	25.3%	74.7%
14,744	PUSHMATAHA	3,909	490	3,419		2,929 D	12.5%	87.5%	12.5%	87.5%
14,164	ROGER MILLS	4,159	511	3,648		3,137 D	12.3%	87.7%	12.3%	87.7%
18,956	ROGERS	7,226	1,879	5,347		3,468 D	26.0%	74.0%	26.0%	74.0%
79,621	SEMINOLE	15,502	3,348	12,154		8,806 D	21.6%	78.4%	21.6%	78.4%
19,505	SEQUOYAH	6,537	1,833	4,704		2,871 D	28.0%	72.0%	28.0%	72.0%
33,069	STEPHENS	8,718	1,012	7,706		6,694 D	11.6%	88.4%	11.6%	88.4%
14,100	TEXAS	5,405	1,372	4,033		2,661 D	25.4%	74.6%	25.4%	74.6%
24,390	TILLMAN	5,483	523	4,960		4,437 D	9.5%	90.5%	9.5%	90.5%
187,574	TULSA	60,871	25,541	35,330		9,789 D	42.0%	58.0%	42.0%	58.0%
22,428	WAGONER	5,520	1,505	4,015		2,510 D	27.3%	72.7%	27.3%	72.7%
27,777	WASHINGTON	11,576	4,713	6,863		2,150 D	40.7%	59.3%	40.7%	59.3%
29,435	WASHITA	6,936	887	6,049		5,162 D	12.8%	87.2%	12.8%	87.2%
17,005	WOODS	6,287	2,008	4,279		2,271 D	31.9%	68.1%	31.9%	68.1%
15,844	WOODWARD	5,602	1,614	3,988		2,374 D	28.8%	71.2%	28.8%	71.2%
2,396,040	TOTAL	704,633	188,165	516,468		328,303 D	26.7%	73.3%	26.7%	73.3%

OKLAHOMA

PRESIDENT 1928

1920 Census Population	County	Total Vote	Republican	Democratic	Other	Rep.-Dem. Plurality	Percentage Total Vote Rep.	Total Vote Dem.	Major Vote Rep.	Major Vote Dem.
13,703	ADAIR	4,831	2,867	1,944	20	923 R	59.3%	40.2%	59.6%	40.4%
16,253	ALFALFA	5,417	4,224	1,086	107	3,138 R	78.0%	20.0%	79.5%	20.5%
20,862	ATOKA	3,661	1,572	2,056	33	484 D	42.9%	56.2%	43.3%	56.7%
14,048	BEAVER	3,524	2,596	887	41	1,709 R	73.7%	25.2%	74.5%	25.5%
18,989	BECKHAM	6,110	3,810	2,201	99	1,609 R	62.4%	36.0%	63.4%	36.6%
15,875	BLAINE	5,032	3,413	1,543	76	1,870 R	67.8%	30.7%	68.9%	31.1%
40,700	BRYAN	6,950	3,014	3,885	51	871 D	43.4%	55.9%	43.7%	56.3%
34,207	CADDO	11,378	7,313	3,885	180	3,428 R	64.3%	34.1%	65.3%	34.7%
22,288	CANADIAN	7,875	5,011	2,786	78	2,225 R	63.6%	35.4%	64.3%	35.7%
40,247	CARTER	11,716	6,538	5,086	92	1,452 R	55.8%	43.4%	56.2%	43.8%
19,872	CHEROKEE	5,438	2,963	2,446	29	517 R	54.5%	45.0%	54.8%	45.2%
32,144	CHOCTAW	5,152	2,541	2,581	30	40 D	49.3%	50.1%	49.6%	50.4%
3,436	CIMARRON	1,725	1,139	566	20	573 R	66.0%	32.8%	66.8%	33.2%
19,389	CLEVELAND	6,093	3,738	2,291	64	1,447 R	61.3%	37.6%	62.0%	38.0%
18,406	COAL	2,996	1,283	1,681	32	398 D	42.8%	56.1%	43.3%	56.7%
26,629	COMANCHE	8,117	5,069	2,956	92	2,113 R	62.4%	36.4%	63.2%	36.8%
16,679	COTTON	4,048	2,419	1,605	24	814 R	59.8%	39.6%	60.1%	39.9%
19,160	CRAIG	6,444	3,511	2,897	36	614 R	54.5%	45.0%	54.8%	45.2%
62,480	CREEK	18,042	12,254	5,693	95	6,561 R	67.9%	31.6%	68.3%	31.7%
18,736	CUSTER	6,674	4,576	1,995	103	2,581 R	68.6%	29.9%	69.6%	30.4%
13,868	DELAWARE	4,360	2,603	1,706	51	897 R	59.7%	39.1%	60.4%	39.6%
12,434	DEWEY	3,804	2,486	1,175	143	1,311 R	65.4%	30.9%	67.9%	32.1%
11,673	ELLIS	3,110	1,953	1,122	35	831 R	62.8%	36.1%	63.5%	36.5%
37,500	GARFIELD	16,392	12,748	3,503	141	9,245 R	77.8%	21.4%	78.4%	21.6%
32,445	GARVIN	7,001	3,321	3,589	91	268 D	47.4%	51.3%	48.1%	51.9%
33,943	GRADY	10,109	6,332	3,667	110	2,665 R	62.6%	36.3%	63.3%	36.7%
16,072	GRANT	5,883	4,371	1,449	63	2,922 R	74.3%	24.6%	75.1%	24.9%
15,836	GREER	3,935	2,262	1,645	28	617 R	57.5%	41.8%	57.9%	42.1%
11,261	HARMON	2,517	1,431	1,060	26	371 R	56.9%	42.1%	57.4%	42.6%
7,623	HARPER	2,775	1,844	872	59	972 R	66.5%	31.4%	67.9%	32.1%
19,397	HASKELL	4,782	2,580	2,172	30	408 R	54.0%	45.4%	54.3%	45.7%
26,045	HUGHES	7,135	3,937	3,169	29	768 R	55.2%	44.4%	55.4%	44.6%
22,141	JACKSON	5,960	3,440	2,493	27	947 R	57.7%	41.8%	58.0%	42.0%
17,664	JEFFERSON	4,185	2,251	1,916	18	335 R	53.8%	45.8%	54.0%	46.0%
20,125	JOHNSTON	3,096	1,294	1,766	36	472 D	41.8%	57.0%	42.3%	57.7%
34,907	KAY	18,161	13,829	4,196	136	9,633 R	76.1%	23.1%	76.7%	23.3%
15,671	KINGFISHER	5,882	4,063	1,780	39	2,283 R	69.1%	30.3%	69.5%	30.5%
23,094	KIOWA	6,478	4,116	2,270	92	1,846 R	63.5%	35.0%	64.5%	35.5%
13,866	LATIMER	2,989	1,368	1,583	38	215 D	45.8%	53.0%	46.4%	53.6%
42,765	LE FLORE	9,847	5,168	4,622	57	546 R	52.5%	46.9%	52.8%	47.2%
33,406	LINCOLN	8,649	6,118	2,405	126	3,713 R	70.7%	27.8%	71.8%	28.2%
27,550	LOGAN	8,632	6,277	2,251	104	4,026 R	72.7%	26.1%	73.6%	26.4%
12,433	LOVE	2,111	843	1,268		425 D	39.9%	60.1%	39.9%	60.1%
19,326	MCCLAIN	4,356	2,399	1,913	44	486 R	55.1%	43.9%	55.6%	44.4%
37,905	MCCURTAIN	4,813	1,915	2,877	21	962 D	39.8%	59.8%	40.0%	60.0%
26,404	MCINTOSH	4,821	2,742	2,044	35	698 R	56.9%	42.4%	57.3%	42.7%
12,426	MAJOR	3,672	2,891	674	107	2,217 R	78.7%	18.4%	81.1%	18.9%
14,674	MARSHALL	2,501	1,063	1,358	80	295 D	42.5%	54.3%	43.9%	56.1%
16,829	MAYES	5,214	3,004	2,161	49	843 R	57.6%	41.4%	58.2%	41.8%
13,115	MURRAY	3,165	1,631	1,498	36	133 R	51.5%	47.3%	52.1%	47.9%
61,710	MUSKOGEE	16,369	9,972	6,343	54	3,629 R	60.9%	38.8%	61.1%	38.9%
13,560	NOBLE	5,448	3,607	1,777	64	1,830 R	66.2%	32.6%	67.0%	33.0%
15,899	NOWATA	4,712	2,930	1,763	19	1,167 R	62.2%	37.4%	62.4%	37.6%
25,051	OKFUSKEE	6,201	3,612	2,513	76	1,099 R	58.2%	40.5%	59.0%	41.0%
116,307	OKLAHOMA	52,953	36,608	16,073	272	20,535 R	69.1%	30.4%	69.5%	30.5%
55,072	OKMULGEE	15,056	9,149	5,834	73	3,315 R	60.8%	38.7%	61.1%	38.9%
36,536	OSAGE	15,632	10,555	5,010	67	5,545 R	67.5%	32.0%	67.8%	32.2%
41,108	OTTAWA	12,720	8,144	4,488	88	3,656 R	64.0%	35.3%	64.5%	35.5%
19,126	PAWNEE	6,523	4,489	1,949	85	2,540 R	68.8%	29.9%	69.7%	30.3%
30,180	PAYNE	10,893	7,864	2,904	125	4,960 R	72.2%	26.7%	73.0%	27.0%

OKLAHOMA

PRESIDENT 1928

1920 Census Population	County	Total Vote	Republican	Democratic	Other	Rep.-Dem. Plurality	Percentage Total Vote Rep.	Total Vote Dem.	Major Vote Rep.	Major Vote Dem.
52,570	PITTSBURG	11,942	5,875	5,960	107	85 D	49.2%	49.9%	49.6%	50.4%
30,949	PONTOTOC	6,597	3,356	3,203	38	153 R	50.9%	48.6%	51.2%	48.8%
46,028	POTTAWATOMIE	12,364	8,478	3,797	89	4,681 R	68.6%	30.7%	69.1%	30.9%
17,514	PUSHMATAHA	3,056	1,616	1,384	56	232 R	52.9%	45.3%	53.9%	46.1%
10,638	ROGER MILLS	3,067	1,948	986	133	962 R	63.5%	32.1%	66.4%	33.6%
17,605	ROGERS	5,665	3,477	2,147	41	1,330 R	61.4%	37.9%	61.8%	38.2%
23,808	SEMINOLE	12,495	8,072	4,423		3,649 R	64.6%	35.4%	64.6%	35.4%
26,786	SEQUOYAH	5,988	3,296	2,692		604 R	55.0%	45.0%	55.0%	45.0%
24,692	STEPHENS	8,279	5,192	2,982	105	2,210 R	62.7%	36.0%	63.5%	36.5%
13,975	TEXAS	4,179	2,890	1,240	49	1,650 R	69.2%	29.7%	70.0%	30.0%
22,433	TILLMAN	5,497	3,331	2,141	25	1,190 R	60.6%	38.9%	60.9%	39.1%
109,023	TULSA	54,998	38,769	16,062	167	22,707 R	70.5%	29.2%	70.7%	29.3%
21,371	WAGONER	4,497	2,726	1,745	26	981 R	60.6%	38.8%	61.0%	39.0%
27,002	WASHINGTON	9,877	7,258	2,563	56	4,695 R	73.5%	25.9%	73.9%	26.1%
22,237	WASHITA	5,645	3,572	2,024	49	1,548 R	63.3%	35.9%	63.8%	36.2%
15,939	WOODS	5,600	3,941	1,550	109	2,391 R	70.4%	27.7%	71.8%	28.2%
14,663	WOODWARD	4,616	3,188	1,347	81	1,841 R	69.1%	29.2%	70.3%	29.7%
2,028,283	TOTAL	618,427	394,046	219,174	5,207	174,872 R	63.7%	35.4%	64.3%	35.7%

OKLAHOMA

PRESIDENT 1924

1920 Census Population	County	Total Vote	Republican	Democratic	Other	Rep.-Dem. Plurality	Percentage: Total Vote Rep.	Percentage: Total Vote Dem.	Percentage: Major Vote Rep.	Percentage: Major Vote Dem.
13,703	ADAIR	4,488	2,317	1,942	229	375 R	51.6%	43.3%	54.4%	45.6%
16,253	ALFALFA	5,181	2,967	1,558	656	1,409 R	57.3%	30.1%	65.6%	34.4%
20,862	ATOKA	4,059	1,130	2,204	725	1,074 D	27.8%	54.3%	33.9%	66.1%
14,048	BEAVER	3,167	1,565	1,195	407	370 R	49.4%	37.7%	56.7%	43.3%
18,989	BECKHAM	4,387	1,357	2,496	534	1,139 D	30.9%	56.9%	35.2%	64.8%
15,875	BLAINE	4,647	2,255	1,488	904	767 R	48.5%	32.0%	60.2%	39.8%
40,700	BRYAN	7,072	1,780	4,593	699	2,813 D	25.2%	64.9%	27.9%	72.1%
34,207	CADDO	9,530	4,388	4,211	931	177 R	46.0%	44.2%	51.0%	49.0%
22,288	CANADIAN	7,397	3,070	3,065	1,262	5 R	41.5%	41.4%	50.0%	50.0%
40,247	CARTER	10,862	3,164	7,134	564	3,970 D	29.1%	65.7%	30.7%	69.3%
19,872	CHEROKEE	5,261	2,622	2,454	185	168 R	49.8%	46.6%	51.7%	48.3%
32,144	CHOCTAW	5,278	2,013	2,528	737	515 D	38.1%	47.9%	44.3%	55.7%
3,436	CIMARRON	1,422	586	672	164	86 D	41.2%	47.3%	46.6%	53.4%
19,389	CLEVELAND	5,008	1,672	2,841	495	1,169 D	33.4%	56.7%	37.0%	63.0%
18,406	COAL	3,179	800	1,772	607	972 D	25.2%	55.7%	31.1%	68.9%
26,629	COMANCHE	7,448	3,084	3,523	841	439 D	41.4%	47.3%	46.7%	53.3%
16,679	COTTON	3,705	1,581	1,825	299	244 D	42.7%	49.3%	46.4%	53.6%
19,160	CRAIG	5,786	2,519	3,096	171	577 D	43.5%	53.5%	44.9%	55.1%
62,480	CREEK	17,714	8,894	7,969	851	925 R	50.2%	45.0%	52.7%	47.3%
18,736	CUSTER	5,629	2,409	2,473	747	64 D	42.8%	43.9%	49.3%	50.7%
13,868	DELAWARE	3,555	1,563	1,729	263	166 D	44.0%	48.6%	47.5%	52.5%
12,434	DEWEY	3,464	1,539	1,126	799	413 R	44.4%	32.5%	57.7%	42.3%
11,673	ELLIS	3,078	1,499	879	700	620 R	48.7%	28.6%	63.0%	37.0%
37,500	GARFIELD	13,369	7,524	3,791	2,054	3,733 R	56.3%	28.4%	66.5%	33.5%
32,445	GARVIN	6,933	1,863	4,758	312	2,895 D	26.9%	68.6%	28.1%	71.9%
33,943	GRADY	8,586	2,640	5,091	855	2,451 D	30.7%	59.3%	34.1%	65.9%
16,072	GRANT	5,412	2,800	1,990	622	810 R	51.7%	36.8%	58.5%	41.5%
15,836	GREER	2,826	551	1,982	293	1,431 D	19.5%	70.1%	21.8%	78.2%
11,261	HARMON	1,456	339	1,049	68	710 D	23.3%	72.0%	24.4%	75.6%
7,623	HARPER	2,415	1,226	824	365	402 R	50.8%	34.1%	59.8%	40.2%
19,397	HASKELL	4,816	1,935	2,480	401	545 D	40.2%	51.5%	43.8%	56.2%
26,045	HUGHES	6,200	1,994	3,996	210	2,002 D	32.2%	64.5%	33.3%	66.7%
22,141	JACKSON	3,804	941	2,342	521	1,401 D	24.7%	61.6%	28.7%	71.3%
17,664	JEFFERSON	3,763	1,108	2,441	214	1,333 D	29.4%	64.9%	31.2%	68.8%
20,125	JOHNSTON	3,621	923	2,122	576	1,199 D	25.5%	58.6%	30.3%	69.7%
34,907	KAY	14,448	7,392	6,049	1,007	1,343 R	51.2%	41.9%	55.0%	45.0%
15,671	KINGFISHER	5,095	2,834	1,644	617	1,190 R	55.6%	32.3%	63.3%	36.7%
23,094	KIOWA	4,854	1,688	2,635	531	947 D	34.8%	54.3%	39.0%	61.0%
13,866	LATIMER	2,702	971	1,457	274	486 D	35.9%	53.9%	40.0%	60.0%
42,765	LE FLORE	8,247	3,326	4,069	852	743 D	40.3%	49.3%	45.0%	55.0%
33,406	LINCOLN	8,242	4,220	3,283	739	937 R	51.2%	39.8%	56.2%	43.8%
27,550	LOGAN	7,562	4,445	2,366	751	2,079 R	58.8%	31.3%	65.3%	34.7%
12,433	LOVE	2,728	479	1,713	536	1,234 D	17.6%	62.8%	21.9%	78.1%
19,326	MCCLAIN	4,011	1,233	2,519	259	1,286 D	30.7%	62.8%	32.9%	67.1%
37,905	MCCURTAIN	5,185	1,669	3,279	237	1,610 D	32.2%	63.2%	33.7%	66.3%
26,404	MCINTOSH	4,495	1,675	2,723	97	1,048 D	37.3%	60.6%	38.1%	61.9%
12,426	MAJOR	3,044	1,781	649	614	1,132 R	58.5%	21.3%	73.3%	26.7%
14,674	MARSHALL	3,346	866	1,935	545	1,069 D	25.9%	57.8%	30.9%	69.1%
16,829	MAYES	4,888	2,317	2,246	325	71 R	47.4%	45.9%	50.8%	49.2%
13,115	MURRAY	3,015	784	2,083	148	1,299 D	26.0%	69.1%	27.3%	72.7%
61,710	MUSKOGEE	13,697	6,158	6,895	644	737 D	45.0%	50.3%	47.2%	52.8%
13,560	NOBLE	5,240	2,680	1,927	633	753 R	51.1%	36.8%	58.2%	41.8%
15,899	NOWATA	4,500	2,296	2,049	155	247 R	51.0%	45.5%	52.8%	47.2%
25,051	OKFUSKEE	4,349	1,431	2,654	264	1,223 D	32.9%	61.0%	35.0%	65.0%
116,307	OKLAHOMA	43,085	17,504	21,708	3,873	4,204 D	40.6%	50.4%	44.6%	55.4%
55,072	OKMULGEE	12,838	6,015	5,927	896	88 R	46.9%	46.2%	50.4%	49.6%
36,536	OSAGE	14,202	6,363	7,070	769	707 D	44.8%	49.8%	47.4%	52.6%
41,108	OTTAWA	10,377	5,197	4,522	658	675 R	50.1%	43.6%	53.5%	46.5%
19,126	PAWNEE	6,021	3,093	2,376	552	717 R	51.4%	39.5%	56.6%	43.4%
30,180	PAYNE	9,933	4,817	4,342	774	475 R	48.5%	43.7%	52.6%	47.4%

OKLAHOMA

PRESIDENT 1924

1920 Census Population	County	Total Vote	Republican	Democratic	Other	Rep.-Dem. Plurality	Percentage Total Vote Rep.	Percentage Total Vote Dem.	Percentage Major Vote Rep.	Percentage Major Vote Dem.
52,570	PITTSBURG	10,765	3,554	6,062	1,149	2,508 D	33.0%	56.3%	37.0%	63.0%
30,949	PONTOTOC	6,620	1,859	4,268	493	2,409 D	28.1%	64.5%	30.3%	69.7%
46,028	POTTAWATOMIE	10,407	4,040	5,072	1,295	1,032 D	38.8%	48.7%	44.3%	55.7%
17,514	PUSHMATAHA	3,006	1,084	1,647	275	563 D	36.1%	54.8%	39.7%	60.3%
10,638	ROGER MILLS	2,783	946	1,318	519	372 D	34.0%	47.4%	41.8%	58.2%
17,605	ROGERS	5,345	2,207	2,901	237	694 D	41.3%	54.3%	43.2%	56.8%
23,808	SEMINOLE	5,808	2,326	3,007	475	681 D	40.0%	51.8%	43.6%	56.4%
26,786	SEQUOYAH	6,374	2,875	3,429	70	554 D	45.1%	53.8%	45.6%	54.4%
24,692	STEPHENS	7,534	2,377	4,745	412	2,368 D	31.6%	63.0%	33.4%	66.6%
13,975	TEXAS	3,962	1,745	1,812	405	67 D	44.0%	45.7%	49.1%	50.9%
22,433	TILLMAN	4,163	1,326	2,653	184	1,327 D	31.9%	63.7%	33.3%	66.7%
109,023	TULSA	35,179	19,537	14,377	1,265	5,160 R	55.5%	40.9%	57.6%	42.4%
21,371	WAGONER	3,903	1,646	1,985	272	339 D	42.2%	50.9%	45.3%	54.7%
27,002	WASHINGTON	8,300	4,579	3,487	234	1,092 R	55.2%	42.0%	56.8%	43.2%
22,237	WASHITA	4,054	1,357	2,325	372	968 D	33.5%	57.4%	36.9%	63.1%
15,939	WOODS	4,988	2,615	1,533	840	1,082 R	52.4%	30.7%	63.0%	37.0%
14,663	WOODWARD	4,015	1,831	1,418	766	413 R	45.6%	35.3%	56.4%	43.6%
2,028,283	TOTAL	527,828	225,756	255,798	46,274	30,042 D	42.8%	48.5%	46.9%	53.1%

OKLAHOMA

PRESIDENT 1920

1920 Census Population	County	Total Vote	Republican	Democratic	Other	Rep.-Dem. Plurality	Percentage Total Vote Rep.	Percentage Total Vote Dem.	Percentage Major Vote Rep.	Percentage Major Vote Dem.
13,703	ADAIR	3,761	2,181	1,559	21	622 R	58.0%	41.5%	58.3%	41.7%
16,253	ALFALFA	4,717	3,005	1,350	362	1,655 R	63.7%	28.6%	69.0%	31.0%
20,862	ATOKA	4,818	2,081	2,100	637	19 D	43.2%	43.6%	49.8%	50.2%
14,048	BEAVER	3,289	1,973	1,076	240	897 R	60.0%	32.7%	64.7%	35.3%
18,989	BECKHAM	4,745	1,755	2,347	643	592 D	37.0%	49.5%	42.8%	57.2%
15,875	BLAINE	4,520	2,786	1,296	438	1,490 R	61.6%	28.7%	68.3%	31.7%
40,700	BRYAN	8,053	3,127	4,502	424	1,375 D	38.8%	55.9%	41.0%	59.0%
34,207	CADDO	9,071	4,823	3,594	654	1,229 R	53.2%	39.6%	57.3%	42.7%
22,288	CANADIAN	7,444	3,881	3,268	295	613 R	52.1%	43.9%	54.3%	45.7%
40,247	CARTER	10,133	3,561	5,997	575	2,436 D	35.1%	59.2%	37.3%	62.7%
19,872	CHEROKEE	4,469	2,524	1,859	86	665 R	56.5%	41.6%	57.6%	42.4%
32,144	CHOCTAW	4,908	2,094	2,531	283	437 D	42.7%	51.6%	45.3%	54.7%
3,436	CIMARRON	1,178	630	465	83	165 R	53.5%	39.5%	57.5%	42.5%
19,389	CLEVELAND	4,985	2,283	2,397	305	114 D	45.8%	48.1%	48.8%	51.2%
18,406	COAL	3,997	1,744	1,768	485	24 D	43.6%	44.2%	49.7%	50.3%
26,629	COMANCHE	6,775	3,332	3,037	406	295 R	49.2%	44.8%	52.3%	47.7%
16,679	COTTON	4,252	1,820	2,260	172	440 D	42.8%	53.2%	44.6%	55.4%
19,160	CRAIG	6,081	3,094	2,903	84	191 R	50.9%	47.7%	51.6%	48.4%
62,480	CREEK	13,974	7,948	5,408	618	2,540 R	56.9%	38.7%	59.5%	40.5%
18,736	CUSTER	5,838	3,224	2,271	343	953 R	55.2%	38.9%	58.7%	41.3%
13,868	DELAWARE	3,480	2,059	1,282	139	777 R	59.2%	36.8%	61.6%	38.4%
12,434	DEWEY	3,358	1,738	995	625	743 R	51.8%	29.6%	63.6%	36.4%
11,673	ELLIS	3,012	1,786	845	381	941 R	59.3%	28.1%	67.9%	32.1%
37,500	GARFIELD	10,858	6,611	3,671	576	2,940 R	60.9%	33.8%	64.3%	35.7%
32,445	GARVIN	7,289	2,922	4,093	274	1,171 D	40.1%	56.2%	41.7%	58.3%
33,943	GRADY	8,158	3,403	4,277	478	874 D	41.7%	52.4%	44.3%	55.7%
16,072	GRANT	5,299	3,210	1,883	206	1,327 R	60.6%	35.5%	63.0%	37.0%
15,836	GREER	3,093	1,013	1,854	226	841 D	32.8%	59.9%	35.3%	64.7%
11,261	HARMON	1,881	643	1,123	115	480 D	34.2%	59.7%	36.4%	63.6%
7,623	HARPER	2,339	1,404	753	182	651 R	60.0%	32.2%	65.1%	34.9%
19,397	HASKELL	5,075	2,673	2,201	201	472 R	52.7%	43.4%	54.8%	45.2%
26,045	HUGHES	6,686	3,049	3,487	150	438 D	45.6%	52.2%	46.6%	53.4%
22,141	JACKSON	4,456	1,345	2,694	417	1,349 D	30.2%	60.5%	33.3%	66.7%
17,664	JEFFERSON	4,403	1,733	2,289	381	556 D	39.4%	52.0%	43.1%	56.9%
20,125	JOHNSTON	4,459	1,950	2,117	392	167 D	43.7%	47.5%	47.9%	52.1%
34,907	KAY	10,736	5,959	4,546	231	1,413 R	55.5%	42.3%	56.7%	43.3%
15,671	KINGFISHER	5,213	3,220	1,744	249	1,476 R	61.8%	33.5%	64.9%	35.1%
23,094	KIOWA	5,610	2,649	2,518	443	131 R	47.2%	44.9%	51.3%	48.7%
13,866	LATIMER	2,941	1,410	1,200	331	210 R	47.9%	40.8%	54.0%	46.0%
42,765	LE FLORE	9,084	4,934	3,764	386	1,170 R	54.3%	41.4%	56.7%	43.3%
33,406	LINCOLN	8,881	5,261	2,980	640	2,281 R	59.2%	33.6%	63.8%	36.2%
27,550	LOGAN	7,109	4,618	2,209	282	2,409 R	65.0%	31.1%	67.6%	32.4%
12,433	LOVE	2,525	711	1,662	152	951 D	28.2%	65.8%	30.0%	70.0%
19,326	MCCLAIN	4,298	1,733	2,315	250	582 D	40.3%	53.9%	42.8%	57.2%
37,905	MCCURTAIN	4,887	1,966	2,603	318	637 D	40.2%	53.3%	43.0%	57.0%
26,404	MCINTOSH	5,259	2,358	2,642	259	284 D	44.8%	50.2%	47.2%	52.8%
12,426	MAJOR	3,201	1,921	784	496	1,137 R	60.0%	24.5%	71.0%	29.0%
14,674	MARSHALL	3,345	1,487	1,589	269	102 D	44.5%	47.5%	48.3%	51.7%
16,829	MAYES	4,597	2,447	1,987	163	460 R	53.2%	43.2%	55.2%	44.8%
13,115	MURRAY	3,227	1,362	1,744	121	382 D	42.2%	54.0%	43.9%	56.1%
61,710	MUSKOGEE	11,664	5,187	6,378	99	1,191 D	44.5%	54.7%	44.9%	55.1%
13,560	NOBLE	4,133	2,467	1,515	151	952 R	59.7%	36.7%	62.0%	38.0%
15,899	NOWATA	4,451	2,679	1,697	75	982 R	60.2%	38.1%	61.2%	38.8%
25,051	OKFUSKEE	3,652	1,760	1,650	242	110 R	48.2%	45.2%	51.6%	48.4%
116,307	OKLAHOMA	34,359	15,350	17,820	1,189	2,470 D	44.7%	51.9%	46.3%	53.7%
55,072	OKMULGEE	10,455	5,367	4,495	593	872 R	51.3%	43.0%	54.4%	45.6%
36,536	OSAGE	8,622	4,567	3,801	254	766 R	53.0%	44.1%	54.6%	45.4%
41,108	OTTAWA	9,616	5,270	3,974	372	1,296 R	54.8%	41.3%	57.0%	43.0%
19,126	PAWNEE	5,303	2,976	1,955	372	1,021 R	56.1%	36.9%	60.4%	39.6%
30,180	PAYNE	8,370	4,583	3,238	549	1,345 R	54.8%	38.7%	58.6%	41.4%

OKLAHOMA

PRESIDENT 1920

1920 Census Population	County	Total Vote	Republican	Democratic	Other	Rep.-Dem. Plurality	Percentage Total Vote Rep.	Percentage Total Vote Dem.	Percentage Major Vote Rep.	Percentage Major Vote Dem.
52,570	PITTSBURG	11,387	5,371	5,361	655	10 R	47.2%	47.1%	50.0%	50.0%
30,949	PONTOTOC	6,376	2,370	3,800	206	1,430 D	37.2%	59.6%	38.4%	61.6%
46,028	POTTAWATOMIE	11,260	5,355	5,310	595	45 R	47.6%	47.2%	50.2%	49.8%
17,514	PUSHMATAHA	3,496	1,864	1,365	267	499 R	53.3%	39.0%	57.7%	42.3%
10,638	ROGER MILLS	2,552	1,193	931	428	262 R	46.7%	36.5%	56.2%	43.8%
17,605	ROGERS	5,519	2,844	2,459	216	385 R	51.5%	44.6%	53.6%	46.4%
23,808	SEMINOLE	5,569	3,382	1,869	318	1,513 R	60.7%	33.6%	64.4%	35.6%
26,786	SEQUOYAH	5,813	3,195	2,505	113	690 R	55.0%	43.1%	56.1%	43.9%
24,692	STEPHENS	5,197	2,035	2,816	346	781 D	39.2%	54.2%	42.0%	58.0%
13,975	TEXAS	3,295	1,762	1,398	135	364 R	53.5%	42.4%	55.8%	44.2%
22,433	TILLMAN	4,338	1,539	2,649	150	1,110 D	35.5%	61.1%	36.7%	63.3%
109,023	TULSA	24,999	14,357	10,025	617	4,332 R	57.4%	40.1%	58.9%	41.1%
21,371	WAGONER	2,965	1,432	1,375	158	57 R	48.3%	46.4%	51.0%	49.0%
27,002	WASHINGTON	7,099	4,105	2,805	189	1,300 R	57.8%	39.5%	59.4%	40.6%
22,237	WASHITA	4,515	2,070	2,125	320	55 D	45.8%	47.1%	49.3%	50.7%
15,939	WOODS	4,687	2,827	1,530	330	1,297 R	60.3%	32.6%	64.9%	35.1%
14,663	WOODWARD	4,219	2,492	1,437	290	1,055 R	59.1%	34.1%	63.4%	36.6%
2,028,283	TOTAL	485,678	243,840	216,122	25,716	27,718 R	50.2%	44.5%	53.0%	47.0%

OKLAHOMA

ELECTION NOTES

1956

1952

1948

1944 Other vote was Watson (Prohibition).

1940 Other vote was Babson (Prohibition).

1936 Other vote was 2,221 Thomas (Socialist); 1,328 Colvin (Prohibition).

1932

1928 Other vote was 3,924 Thomas (Socialist); 1,283 Webb (Farmer-Labor).

1924 Other vote was 46,274 LaFollette (41,142 Farmer-Labor and 5,132 Socialist). This combined ticket ran second in Love county.

1920 Other vote was Debs (Socialist). Sources vary in their county-by-county figures for this election. Frequently data on the Senatorial vote for 1920 have been used in place of the Presidential vote. In this compilation, county figures for each elector have been inspected and adjusted to produce the most reasonable construction of each county's vote for President.

OREGON

POPULAR VOTE FOR PRESIDENT 1920 TO 1956

Year	Total Vote	Republican Vote	Republican Candidate	Democratic Vote	Democratic Candidate	Other Vote	Plurality	Percentage Total Vote Rep.	Percentage Total Vote Dem.	Percentage Major Vote Rep.	Percentage Major Vote Dem.
1956	736,132	406,393	Eisenhower, Dwight D.	329,204	Stevenson, Adlai E.	535	77,189 R	55.2%	44.7%	55.2%	44.8%
1952	695,059	420,815	Eisenhower, Dwight D.	270,579	Stevenson, Adlai E.	3,665	150,236 R	60.5%	38.9%	60.9%	39.1%
1948	524,080	260,904	Dewey, Thomas E.	243,147	Truman, Harry S.	20,029	17,757 R	49.8%	46.4%	51.8%	48.2%
1944	480,147	225,365	Dewey, Thomas E.	248,635	Roosevelt, Franklin D.	6,147	23,270 D	46.9%	51.8%	47.5%	52.5%
1940	481,240	219,555	Willkie, Wendell	258,415	Roosevelt, Franklin D.	3,270	38,860 D	45.6%	53.7%	45.9%	54.1%
1936	414,021	122,706	Landon, Alfred M.	266,733	Roosevelt, Franklin D.	24,582	144,027 D	29.6%	64.4%	31.5%	68.5%
1932	368,751	136,019	Hoover, Herbert C.	213,871	Roosevelt, Franklin D.	18,861	77,852 D	36.9%	58.0%	38.9%	61.1%
1928	319,942	205,341	Hoover, Herbert C.	109,223	Smith, Alfred E.	5,378	96,118 R	64.2%	34.1%	65.3%	34.7%
1924 **	279,488	142,579	Coolidge, Calvin	67,589	Davis, John W.	69,320	74,176 R	51.0%	24.2%	67.8%	32.2%
1920	238,522	143,592	Harding, Warren G.	80,019	Cox, James M.	14,911	63,573 R	60.2%	33.5%	64.2%	35.8%

In 1924 other vote was 68,403 Progressive and 917 Socialist Labor.

ELECTORAL COLLEGE VOTE 1920 TO 1956

Year	Total	Republican	Democratic	Other
1956	6	6	—	—
1952	6	6	—	—
1948	6	6	—	—
1944	6	—	6	—
1940	5	—	5	—
1936	5	—	5	—
1932	5	—	5	—
1928	5	5	—	—
1924	5	5	—	—
1920	5	5	—	—

OREGON

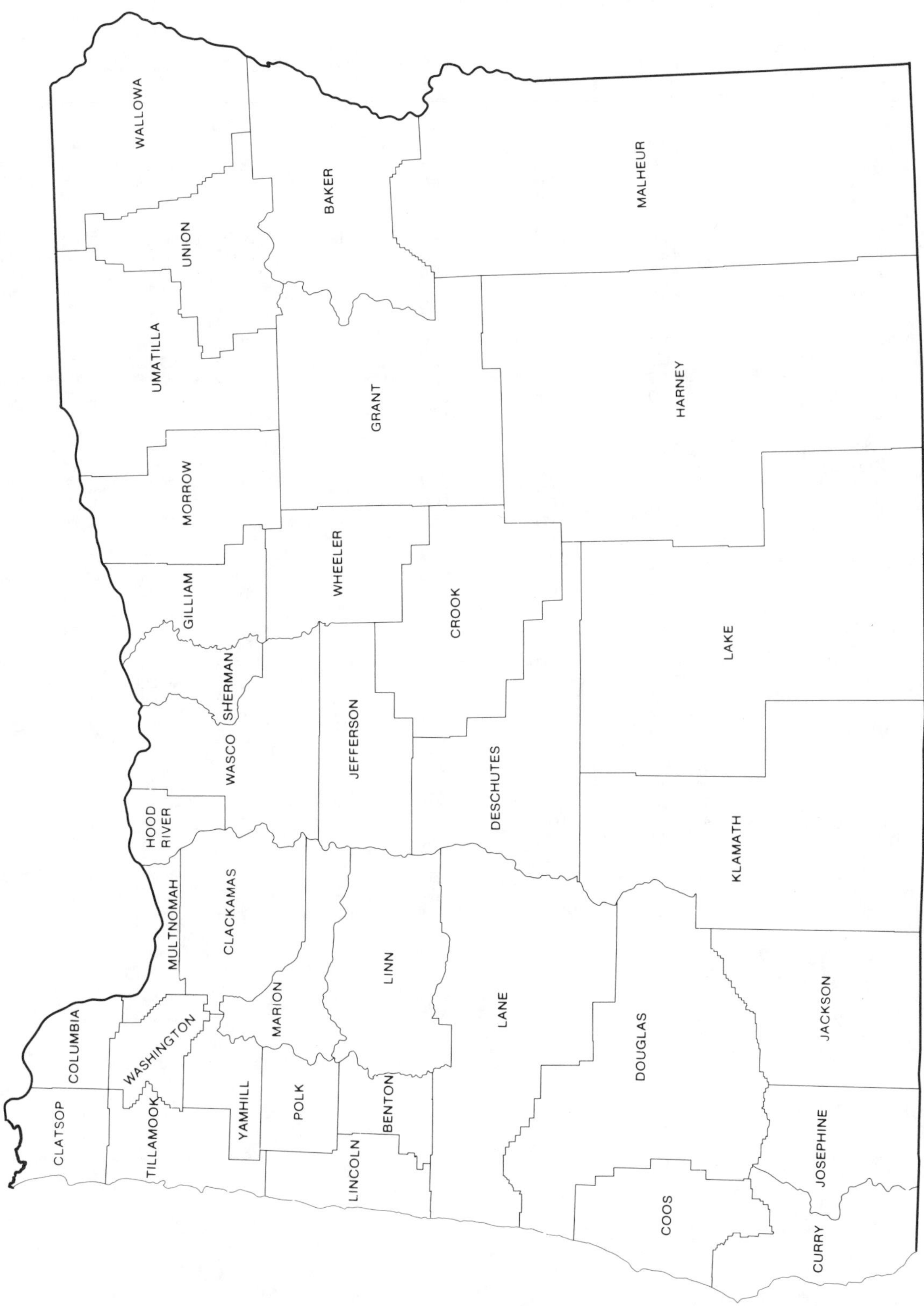
WALLOWA
BAKER
MALHEUR
UNION
UMATILLA
GRANT
HARNEY
MORROW
WHEELER
GILLIAM
CROOK
LAKE
SHERMAN
WASCO
JEFFERSON
DESCHUTES
HOOD RIVER
KLAMATH
MULTNOMAH
CLACKAMAS
LINN
LANE
MARION
COLUMBIA
WASHINGTON
DOUGLAS
JACKSON
CLATSOP
TILLAMOOK
YAMHILL
POLK
BENTON
LINCOLN
JOSEPHINE
COOS
CURRY

OREGON

PRESIDENT 1956

1950 Census Population	County	Total Vote	Republican	Democratic	Other	Rep.-Dem. Plurality	Percentage Total Vote Rep.	Percentage Total Vote Dem.	Percentage Major Vote Rep.	Percentage Major Vote Dem.
16,175	BAKER	7,146	3,706	3,431	9	275 R	51.9%	48.0%	51.9%	48.1%
31,570	BENTON	13,230	9,016	4,214		4,802 R	68.1%	31.9%	68.1%	31.9%
86,716	CLACKAMAS	45,784	25,314	20,416	54	4,898 R	55.3%	44.6%	55.4%	44.6%
30,776	CLATSOP	13,013	6,616	6,372	25	244 R	50.8%	49.0%	50.9%	49.1%
22,967	COLUMBIA	9,867	4,275	5,592		1,317 D	43.3%	56.7%	43.3%	56.7%
42,265	COOS	20,394	9,201	11,183	10	1,982 D	45.1%	54.8%	45.1%	54.9%
8,991	CROOK	3,684	1,879	1,805		74 R	51.0%	49.0%	51.0%	49.0%
6,048	CURRY	4,306	2,306	1,996	4	310 R	53.6%	46.4%	53.6%	46.4%
21,812	DESCHUTES	9,508	5,399	4,102	7	1,297 R	56.8%	43.1%	56.8%	43.2%
54,549	DOUGLAS	25,662	13,837	11,825		2,012 R	53.9%	46.1%	53.9%	46.1%
2,817	GILLIAM	1,331	793	538		255 R	59.6%	40.4%	59.6%	40.4%
8,329	GRANT	3,085	1,822	1,261	2	561 R	59.1%	40.9%	59.1%	40.9%
6,113	HARNEY	2,727	1,512	1,212	3	300 R	55.4%	44.4%	55.5%	44.5%
12,740	HOOD RIVER	5,599	3,149	2,445	5	704 R	56.2%	43.7%	56.3%	43.7%
58,510	JACKSON	29,948	17,201	12,733	14	4,468 R	57.4%	42.5%	57.5%	42.5%
5,536	JEFFERSON	2,476	1,356	1,117	3	239 R	54.8%	45.1%	54.8%	45.2%
26,542	JOSEPHINE	12,841	7,967	4,863	11	3,104 R	62.0%	37.9%	62.1%	37.9%
42,150	KLAMATH	18,175	9,740	8,434	1	1,306 R	53.6%	46.4%	53.6%	46.4%
6,649	LAKE	2,914	1,623	1,289	2	334 R	55.7%	44.2%	55.7%	44.3%
125,776	LANE	62,878	35,264	27,534	80	7,730 R	56.1%	43.8%	56.2%	43.8%
21,308	LINCOLN	9,979	5,346	4,624	9	722 R	53.6%	46.3%	53.6%	46.4%
54,317	LINN	22,622	12,469	10,153		2,316 R	55.1%	44.9%	55.1%	44.9%
23,223	MALHEUR	8,140	4,981	3,151	8	1,830 R	61.2%	38.7%	61.3%	38.7%
101,401	MARION	45,192	28,990	16,170	32	12,820 R	64.1%	35.8%	64.2%	35.8%
4,783	MORROW	1,985	1,092	893		199 R	55.0%	45.0%	55.0%	45.0%
471,537	MULTNOMAH	245,769	129,658	115,896	215	13,762 R	52.8%	47.2%	52.8%	47.2%
26,317	POLK	10,459	6,404	4,047	8	2,357 R	61.2%	38.7%	61.3%	38.7%
2,271	SHERMAN	1,091	671	420		251 R	61.5%	38.5%	61.5%	38.5%
18,606	TILLAMOOK	7,999	4,306	3,684	9	622 R	53.8%	46.1%	53.9%	46.1%
41,703	UMATILLA	17,339	9,654	7,678	7	1,976 R	55.7%	44.3%	55.7%	44.3%
17,962	UNION	8,140	3,749	4,389	2	640 D	46.1%	53.9%	46.1%	53.9%
7,264	WALLOWA	3,328	1,604	1,723	1	119 D	48.2%	51.8%	48.2%	51.8%
15,552	WASCO	8,497	4,332	4,165		167 R	51.0%	49.0%	51.0%	49.0%
61,269	WASHINGTON	36,028	22,001	14,027		7,974 R	61.1%	38.9%	61.1%	38.9%
3,313	WHEELER	1,174	605	569		36 R	51.5%	48.5%	51.5%	48.5%
33,484	YAMHILL	13,822	8,555	5,253	14	3,302 R	61.9%	38.0%	62.0%	38.0%
1,521,341	TOTAL	736,132	406,393	329,204	535	77,189 R	55.2%	44.7%	55.2%	44.8%

OREGON

PRESIDENT 1952

1950 Census Population	County	Total Vote	Republican	Democratic	Other	Rep.-Dem. Plurality	Percentage Total Vote Rep.	Total Vote Dem.	Major Vote Rep.	Major Vote Dem.
16,175	BAKER	6,838	4,253	2,562	23	1,691 R	62.2%	37.5%	62.4%	37.6%
31,570	BENTON	12,262	9,229	2,966	67	6,263 R	75.3%	24.2%	75.7%	24.3%
86,716	CLACKAMAS	40,620	24,174	16,219	227	7,955 R	59.5%	39.9%	59.8%	40.2%
30,776	CLATSOP	13,511	7,569	5,814	128	1,755 R	56.0%	43.0%	56.6%	43.4%
22,967	COLUMBIA	9,834	4,666	5,096	72	430 D	47.4%	51.8%	47.8%	52.2%
42,265	COOS	18,389	10,122	8,118	149	2,004 R	55.0%	44.1%	55.5%	44.5%
8,991	CROOK	3,681	2,124	1,490	67	634 R	57.7%	40.5%	58.8%	41.2%
6,048	CURRY	3,179	2,147	1,005	27	1,142 R	67.5%	31.6%	68.1%	31.9%
21,812	DESCHUTES	8,986	5,776	3,174	36	2,602 R	64.3%	35.3%	64.5%	35.5%
54,549	DOUGLAS	22,009	14,109	7,837	63	6,272 R	64.1%	35.6%	64.3%	35.7%
2,817	GILLIAM	1,329	911	415	3	496 R	68.5%	31.2%	68.7%	31.3%
8,329	GRANT	3,148	1,941	1,190	17	751 R	61.7%	37.8%	62.0%	38.0%
6,113	HARNEY	2,366	1,378	983	5	395 R	58.2%	41.5%	58.4%	41.6%
12,740	HOOD RIVER	5,267	3,310	1,930	27	1,380 R	62.8%	36.6%	63.2%	36.8%
58,510	JACKSON	27,060	18,279	8,674	107	9,605 R	67.5%	32.1%	67.8%	32.2%
5,536	JEFFERSON	2,217	1,488	723	6	765 R	67.1%	32.6%	67.3%	32.7%
26,542	JOSEPHINE	11,655	8,200	3,353	102	4,847 R	70.4%	28.8%	71.0%	29.0%
42,150	KLAMATH	17,989	11,517	6,407	65	5,110 R	64.0%	35.6%	64.3%	35.7%
6,649	LAKE	2,943	1,727	1,205	11	522 R	58.7%	40.9%	58.9%	41.1%
125,776	LANE	55,919	35,693	19,960	266	15,733 R	63.8%	35.7%	64.1%	35.9%
21,308	LINCOLN	9,252	5,559	3,632	61	1,927 R	60.1%	39.3%	60.5%	39.5%
54,317	LINN	21,959	13,761	8,058	140	5,703 R	62.7%	36.7%	63.1%	36.9%
23,223	MALHEUR	7,685	5,414	2,245	26	3,169 R	70.4%	29.2%	70.7%	29.3%
101,401	MARION	42,448	29,887	12,337	224	17,550 R	70.4%	29.1%	70.8%	29.2%
4,783	MORROW	2,045	1,254	786	5	468 R	61.3%	38.4%	61.5%	38.5%
471,537	MULTNOMAH	241,059	132,602	107,118	1,339	25,484 R	55.0%	44.4%	55.3%	44.7%
26,317	POLK	9,869	6,850	2,983	36	3,867 R	69.4%	30.2%	69.7%	30.3%
2,271	SHERMAN	1,107	747	355	5	392 R	67.5%	32.1%	67.8%	32.2%
18,606	TILLAMOOK	8,362	4,931	3,401	30	1,530 R	59.0%	40.7%	59.2%	40.8%
41,703	UMATILLA	17,667	10,529	7,098	40	3,431 R	59.6%	40.2%	59.7%	40.3%
17,962	UNION	7,663	4,114	3,526	23	588 R	53.7%	46.0%	53.8%	46.2%
7,264	WALLOWA	3,183	1,891	1,271	21	620 R	59.4%	39.9%	59.8%	40.2%
15,552	WASCO	6,914	4,362	2,517	35	1,845 R	63.1%	36.4%	63.4%	36.6%
61,269	WASHINGTON	31,584	20,250	11,191	143	9,059 R	64.1%	35.4%	64.4%	35.6%
3,313	WHEELER	1,188	719	468	1	251 R	60.5%	39.4%	60.6%	39.4%
33,484	YAMHILL	13,872	9,332	4,472	68	4,860 R	67.3%	32.2%	67.6%	32.4%
1,521,341	TOTAL	695,059	420,815	270,579	3,665	150,236 R	60.5%	38.9%	60.9%	39.1%

OREGON

PRESIDENT 1948

1940 Census Population	County	Total Vote	Republican	Democratic	Other	Rep.-Dem. Plurality	Percentage Total Vote Rep.	Percentage Total Vote Dem.	Percentage Major Vote Rep.	Percentage Major Vote Dem.
18,297	BAKER	6,040	2,841	3,035	164	194 D	47.0%	50.2%	48.3%	51.7%
18,629	BENTON	10,329	6,839	3,135	355	3,704 R	66.2%	30.4%	68.6%	31.4%
57,130	CLACKAMAS	30,083	14,431	14,263	1,389	168 R	48.0%	47.4%	50.3%	49.7%
24,697	CLATSOP	11,313	5,076	5,574	663	498 D	44.9%	49.3%	47.7%	52.3%
20,971	COLUMBIA	8,251	3,049	4,768	434	1,719 D	37.0%	57.8%	39.0%	61.0%
32,466	COOS	11,562	5,536	5,453	573	83 R	47.9%	47.2%	50.4%	49.6%
5,533	CROOK	2,141	960	1,149	32	189 D	44.8%	53.7%	45.5%	54.5%
4,301	CURRY	1,879	1,112	677	90	435 R	59.2%	36.0%	62.2%	37.8%
18,631	DESCHUTES	7,163	3,463	3,499	201	36 D	48.3%	48.8%	49.7%	50.3%
25,728	DOUGLAS	13,612	7,671	5,500	441	2,171 R	56.4%	40.4%	58.2%	41.8%
2,844	GILLIAM	1,184	623	544	17	79 R	52.6%	45.9%	53.4%	46.6%
6,380	GRANT	2,293	1,090	1,156	47	66 D	47.5%	50.4%	48.5%	51.5%
5,374	HARNEY	1,624	784	802	38	18 D	48.3%	49.4%	49.4%	50.6%
11,580	HOOD RIVER	4,042	2,134	1,761	147	373 R	52.8%	43.6%	54.8%	45.2%
36,213	JACKSON	19,072	11,226	7,342	504	3,884 R	58.9%	38.5%	60.5%	39.5%
2,042	JEFFERSON	1,227	622	559	46	63 R	50.7%	45.6%	52.7%	47.3%
16,301	JOSEPHINE	8,588	5,004	3,290	294	1,714 R	58.3%	38.3%	60.3%	39.7%
40,497	KLAMATH	14,898	7,072	7,520	306	448 D	47.5%	50.5%	48.5%	51.5%
6,293	LAKE	2,254	1,083	1,104	67	21 D	48.0%	49.0%	49.5%	50.5%
69,096	LANE	37,709	20,843	15,606	1,260	5,237 R	55.3%	41.4%	57.2%	42.8%
14,549	LINCOLN	7,656	3,587	3,720	349	133 D	46.9%	48.6%	49.1%	50.9%
30,485	LINN	15,755	7,936	7,260	559	676 R	50.4%	46.1%	52.2%	47.8%
19,767	MALHEUR	5,898	3,265	2,499	134	766 R	55.4%	42.4%	56.6%	43.4%
75,246	MARION	33,171	18,997	13,183	991	5,814 R	57.3%	39.7%	59.0%	41.0%
4,337	MORROW	1,622	751	838	33	87 D	46.3%	51.7%	47.3%	52.7%
355,099	MULTNOMAH	189,028	86,519	93,703	8,806	7,184 D	45.8%	49.6%	48.0%	52.0%
19,989	POLK	8,012	4,328	3,451	233	877 R	54.0%	43.1%	55.6%	44.4%
2,321	SHERMAN	1,000	532	454	14	78 R	53.2%	45.4%	54.0%	46.0%
12,263	TILLAMOOK	6,286	2,952	3,128	206	176 D	47.0%	49.8%	48.6%	51.4%
26,030	UMATILLA	11,761	5,726	5,891	144	165 D	48.7%	50.1%	49.3%	50.7%
17,399	UNION	6,698	2,668	3,808	222	1,140 D	39.8%	56.9%	41.2%	58.8%
7,623	WALLOWA	2,675	1,196	1,408	71	212 D	44.7%	52.6%	45.9%	54.1%
13,069	WASCO	5,296	2,740	2,438	118	302 R	51.7%	46.0%	52.9%	47.1%
39,194	WASHINGTON	21,589	11,455	9,424	710	2,031 R	53.1%	43.7%	54.9%	45.1%
2,974	WHEELER	841	414	411	16	3 R	49.2%	48.9%	50.2%	49.8%
26,336	YAMHILL	11,528	6,379	4,794	355	1,585 R	55.3%	41.6%	57.1%	42.9%
1,089,684	TOTAL	524,080	260,904	243,147	20,029	17,757 R	49.8%	46.4%	51.8%	48.2%

OREGON

PRESIDENT 1944

1940 Census Population	County	Total Vote	Republican	Democratic	Other	Rep.-Dem. Plurality	Percentage Total Vote Rep.	Total Vote Dem.	Major Vote Rep.	Major Vote Dem.
18,297	BAKER	5,641	2,494	3,116	31	622 D	44.2%	55.2%	44.5%	55.5%
18,629	BENTON	8,141	5,242	2,830	69	2,412 R	64.4%	34.8%	64.9%	35.1%
57,130	CLACKAMAS	26,987	12,492	14,060	435	1,568 D	46.3%	52.1%	47.0%	53.0%
24,697	CLATSOP	10,031	3,921	6,038	72	2,117 D	39.1%	60.2%	39.4%	60.6%
20,971	COLUMBIA	8,049	2,696	5,213	140	2,517 D	33.5%	64.8%	34.1%	65.9%
32,466	COOS	11,225	4,609	6,476	140	1,867 D	41.1%	57.7%	41.6%	58.4%
5,533	CROOK	2,105	932	1,145	28	213 D	44.3%	54.4%	44.9%	55.1%
4,301	CURRY	1,527	827	678	22	149 R	54.2%	44.4%	55.0%	45.0%
18,631	DESCHUTES	6,426	2,547	3,807	72	1,260 D	39.6%	59.2%	40.1%	59.9%
25,728	DOUGLAS	10,840	6,134	4,563	143	1,571 R	56.6%	42.1%	57.3%	42.7%
2,844	GILLIAM	1,060	492	567	1	75 D	46.4%	53.5%	46.5%	53.5%
6,380	GRANT	2,203	1,006	1,072	125	66 D	45.7%	48.7%	48.4%	51.6%
5,374	HARNEY	1,794	787	997	10	210 D	43.9%	55.6%	44.1%	55.9%
11,580	HOOD RIVER	4,012	2,008	1,960	44	48 R	50.0%	48.9%	50.6%	49.4%
36,213	JACKSON	15,426	8,598	6,668	160	1,930 R	55.7%	43.2%	56.3%	43.7%
2,042	JEFFERSON	723	419	297	7	122 R	58.0%	41.1%	58.5%	41.5%
16,301	JOSEPHINE	7,355	4,010	3,214	131	796 R	54.5%	43.7%	55.5%	44.5%
40,497	KLAMATH	12,717	5,969	6,656	92	687 D	46.9%	52.3%	47.3%	52.7%
6,293	LAKE	2,169	1,008	1,147	14	139 D	46.5%	52.9%	46.8%	53.2%
69,096	LANE	32,397	17,690	14,375	332	3,315 R	54.6%	44.4%	55.2%	44.8%
14,549	LINCOLN	5,813	2,801	2,947	65	146 D	48.2%	50.7%	48.7%	51.3%
30,485	LINN	13,493	6,877	6,480	136	397 R	51.0%	48.0%	51.5%	48.5%
19,767	MALHEUR	5,078	2,797	2,234	47	563 R	55.1%	44.0%	55.6%	44.4%
75,246	MARION	28,601	16,176	11,907	518	4,269 R	56.6%	41.6%	57.6%	42.4%
4,337	MORROW	1,596	747	836	13	89 D	46.8%	52.4%	47.2%	52.8%
355,099	MULTNOMAH	186,218	78,279	105,516	2,423	27,237 D	42.0%	56.7%	42.6%	57.4%
19,989	POLK	7,340	3,904	3,318	118	586 R	53.2%	45.2%	54.1%	45.9%
2,321	SHERMAN	996	475	518	3	43 D	47.7%	52.0%	47.8%	52.2%
12,263	TILLAMOOK	5,186	2,477	2,634	75	157 D	47.8%	50.8%	48.5%	51.5%
26,030	UMATILLA	10,391	5,379	4,967	45	412 R	51.8%	47.8%	52.0%	48.0%
17,399	UNION	6,424	2,413	3,951	60	1,538 D	37.6%	61.5%	37.9%	62.1%
7,623	WALLOWA	2,721	1,152	1,544	25	392 D	42.3%	56.7%	42.7%	57.3%
13,069	WASCO	4,786	2,429	2,313	44	116 R	50.8%	48.3%	51.2%	48.8%
39,194	WASHINGTON	18,677	9,362	9,110	205	252 R	50.1%	48.8%	50.7%	49.3%
2,974	WHEELER	962	544	414	4	130 R	56.5%	43.0%	56.8%	43.2%
26,336	YAMHILL	11,037	5,672	5,067	298	605 R	51.4%	45.9%	52.8%	47.2%
1,089,684	TOTAL	480,147	225,365	248,635	6,147	23,270 D	46.9%	51.8%	47.5%	52.5%

OREGON

PRESIDENT 1940

1940 Census Population	County	Total Vote	Republican	Democratic	Other	Rep.-Dem. Plurality	Percentage Total Vote Rep.	Total Vote Dem.	Major Vote Rep.	Major Vote Dem.
18,297	BAKER	7,493	3,101	4,353	39	1,252 D	41.4%	58.1%	41.6%	58.4%
18,629	BENTON	8,079	5,089	2,942	48	2,147 R	63.0%	36.4%	63.4%	36.6%
57,130	CLACKAMAS	25,153	11,416	13,547	190	2,131 D	45.4%	53.9%	45.7%	54.3%
24,697	CLATSOP	10,514	3,758	6,686	70	2,928 D	35.7%	63.6%	36.0%	64.0%
20,971	COLUMBIA	8,774	2,959	5,758	57	2,799 D	33.7%	65.6%	33.9%	66.1%
32,466	COOS	12,988	5,034	7,853	101	2,819 D	38.8%	60.5%	39.1%	60.9%
5,533	CROOK	2,398	942	1,439	17	497 D	39.3%	60.0%	39.6%	60.4%
4,301	CURRY	1,991	941	1,033	17	92 D	47.3%	51.9%	47.7%	52.3%
18,631	DESCHUTES	7,453	2,603	4,775	75	2,172 D	34.9%	64.1%	35.3%	64.7%
25,728	DOUGLAS	10,770	5,991	4,707	72	1,284 R	55.6%	43.7%	56.0%	44.0%
2,844	GILLIAM	1,307	518	785	4	267 D	39.6%	60.1%	39.8%	60.2%
6,380	GRANT	2,695	1,103	1,582	10	479 D	40.9%	58.7%	41.1%	58.9%
5,374	HARNEY	2,136	912	1,214	10	302 D	42.7%	56.8%	42.9%	57.1%
11,580	HOOD RIVER	4,689	2,305	2,367	17	62 D	49.2%	50.5%	49.3%	50.7%
36,213	JACKSON	15,339	8,507	6,754	78	1,753 R	55.5%	44.0%	55.7%	44.3%
2,042	JEFFERSON	896	423	467	6	44 D	47.2%	52.1%	47.5%	52.5%
16,301	JOSEPHINE	6,932	3,964	2,888	80	1,076 R	57.2%	41.7%	57.9%	42.1%
40,497	KLAMATH	15,610	6,169	9,345	96	3,176 D	39.5%	59.9%	39.8%	60.2%
6,293	LAKE	2,544	1,121	1,414	9	293 D	44.1%	55.6%	44.2%	55.8%
69,096	LANE	31,890	15,349	16,286	255	937 D	48.1%	51.1%	48.5%	51.5%
14,549	LINCOLN	6,565	2,962	3,510	93	548 D	45.1%	53.5%	45.8%	54.2%
30,485	LINN	12,959	6,523	6,360	76	163 R	50.3%	49.1%	50.6%	49.4%
19,767	MALHEUR	5,929	2,929	2,958	42	29 D	49.4%	49.9%	49.8%	50.2%
75,246	MARION	31,227	16,940	14,031	256	2,909 R	54.2%	44.9%	54.7%	45.3%
4,337	MORROW	1,749	758	979	12	221 D	43.3%	56.0%	43.6%	56.4%
355,099	MULTNOMAH	172,313	73,612	97,595	1,106	23,983 D	42.7%	56.6%	43.0%	57.0%
19,989	POLK	8,348	4,211	4,077	60	134 R	50.4%	48.8%	50.8%	49.2%
2,321	SHERMAN	1,248	575	670	3	95 D	46.1%	53.7%	46.2%	53.8%
12,263	TILLAMOOK	5,338	2,516	2,786	36	270 D	47.1%	52.2%	47.5%	52.5%
26,030	UMATILLA	10,160	5,193	4,935	32	258 R	51.1%	48.6%	51.3%	48.7%
17,399	UNION	7,196	2,642	4,500	54	1,858 D	36.7%	62.5%	37.0%	63.0%
7,623	WALLOWA	3,311	1,319	1,974	18	655 D	39.8%	59.6%	40.1%	59.9%
13,069	WASCO	5,576	2,553	3,001	22	448 D	45.8%	53.8%	46.0%	54.0%
39,194	WASHINGTON	17,103	8,367	8,626	110	259 D	48.9%	50.4%	49.2%	50.8%
2,974	WHEELER	1,360	705	652	3	53 R	51.8%	47.9%	52.0%	48.0%
26,336	YAMHILL	11,207	5,545	5,566	96	21 D	49.5%	49.7%	49.9%	50.1%
1,089,684	TOTAL	481,240	219,555	258,415	3,270	38,860 D	45.6%	53.7%	45.9%	54.1%

OREGON

PRESIDENT 1936

1930 Census Population	County	Total Vote	Republican	Democratic	Other	Rep.-Dem. Plurality	Percentage Total Vote Rep.	Percentage Total Vote Dem.	Percentage Major Vote Rep.	Percentage Major Vote Dem.
16,754	BAKER	7,151	1,768	4,991	392	3,223 D	24.7%	69.8%	26.2%	73.8%
16,555	BENTON	7,423	3,390	3,547	486	157 D	45.7%	47.8%	48.9%	51.1%
46,205	CLACKAMAS	21,303	5,830	14,203	1,270	8,373 D	27.4%	66.7%	29.1%	70.9%
21,124	CLATSOP	8,832	2,261	6,267	304	4,006 D	25.6%	71.0%	26.5%	73.5%
20,047	COLUMBIA	7,801	1,815	5,587	399	3,772 D	23.3%	71.6%	24.5%	75.5%
28,373	COOS	10,630	2,576	7,167	887	4,591 D	24.2%	67.4%	26.4%	73.6%
3,336	CROOK	1,752	589	1,086	77	497 D	33.6%	62.0%	35.2%	64.8%
3,257	CURRY	1,680	497	913	270	416 D	29.6%	54.3%	35.2%	64.8%
14,749	DESCHUTES	5,884	1,299	4,278	307	2,979 D	22.1%	72.7%	23.3%	76.7%
21,965	DOUGLAS	10,110	4,254	4,893	963	639 D	42.1%	48.4%	46.5%	53.5%
3,467	GILLIAM	1,411	362	983	66	621 D	25.7%	69.7%	26.9%	73.1%
5,940	GRANT	2,489	697	1,436	356	739 D	28.0%	57.7%	32.7%	67.3%
5,920	HARNEY	1,940	546	1,262	132	716 D	28.1%	65.1%	30.2%	69.8%
8,938	HOOD RIVER	4,195	1,249	2,759	187	1,510 D	29.8%	65.8%	31.2%	68.8%
32,918	JACKSON	13,914	4,866	7,520	1,528	2,654 D	35.0%	54.0%	39.3%	60.7%
2,291	JEFFERSON	803	253	514	36	261 D	31.5%	64.0%	33.0%	67.0%
11,498	JOSEPHINE	5,955	1,992	2,840	1,123	848 D	33.5%	47.7%	41.2%	58.8%
32,407	KLAMATH	12,222	3,225	8,562	435	5,337 D	26.4%	70.1%	27.4%	72.6%
4,833	LAKE	2,253	725	1,274	254	549 D	32.2%	56.5%	36.3%	63.7%
54,493	LANE	24,215	8,309	13,926	1,980	5,617 D	34.3%	57.5%	37.4%	62.6%
9,903	LINCOLN	5,042	1,585	3,024	433	1,439 D	31.4%	60.0%	34.4%	65.6%
24,700	LINN	11,211	4,110	5,856	1,245	1,746 D	36.7%	52.2%	41.2%	58.8%
11,269	MALHEUR	4,410	1,385	2,630	395	1,245 D	31.4%	59.6%	34.5%	65.5%
60,541	MARION	26,071	8,595	15,536	1,940	6,941 D	33.0%	59.6%	35.6%	64.4%
4,941	MORROW	1,874	518	1,181	175	663 D	27.6%	63.0%	30.5%	69.5%
338,241	MULTNOMAH	152,319	41,405	106,561	4,353	65,156 D	27.2%	70.0%	28.0%	72.0%
16,858	POLK	6,498	2,246	3,694	558	1,448 D	34.6%	56.8%	37.8%	62.2%
2,978	SHERMAN	1,213	337	823	53	486 D	27.8%	67.8%	29.1%	70.9%
11,824	TILLAMOOK	4,583	1,380	2,781	422	1,401 D	30.1%	60.7%	33.2%	66.8%
24,399	UMATILLA	9,411	2,943	5,753	715	2,810 D	31.3%	61.1%	33.8%	66.2%
17,492	UNION	6,712	1,517	4,643	552	3,126 D	22.6%	69.2%	24.6%	75.4%
7,814	WALLOWA	3,132	811	2,000	321	1,189 D	25.9%	63.9%	28.9%	71.1%
12,646	WASCO	5,184	1,278	3,573	333	2,295 D	24.7%	68.9%	26.3%	73.7%
30,275	WASHINGTON	13,612	4,148	8,641	823	4,493 D	30.5%	63.5%	32.4%	67.6%
2,799	WHEELER	1,190	502	663	25	161 D	42.2%	55.7%	43.1%	56.9%
22,036	YAMHILL	9,596	3,443	5,366	787	1,923 D	35.9%	55.9%	39.1%	60.9%
953,786	TOTAL	414,021	122,706	266,733	24,582	144,027 D	29.6%	64.4%	31.5%	68.5%

OREGON

PRESIDENT 1932

1930 Census Population	County	Total Vote	Republican	Democratic	Other	Rep.-Dem. Plurality	Percentage Total Vote Rep.	Percentage Total Vote Dem.	Percentage Major Vote Rep.	Percentage Major Vote Dem.
16,754	BAKER	6,674	2,097	4,420	157	2,323 D	31.4%	66.2%	32.2%	67.8%
16,555	BENTON	7,431	4,068	3,121	242	947 R	54.7%	42.0%	56.6%	43.4%
46,205	CLACKAMAS	18,608	5,964	11,575	1,069	5,611 D	32.1%	62.2%	34.0%	66.0%
21,124	CLATSOP	7,457	2,570	4,473	414	1,903 D	34.5%	60.0%	36.5%	63.5%
20,047	COLUMBIA	5,937	1,975	3,643	319	1,668 D	33.3%	61.4%	35.2%	64.8%
28,373	COOS	9,296	3,299	5,504	493	2,205 D	35.5%	59.2%	37.5%	62.5%
3,336	CROOK	1,656	626	990	40	364 D	37.8%	59.8%	38.7%	61.3%
3,257	CURRY	1,428	395	971	62	576 D	27.7%	68.0%	28.9%	71.1%
14,749	DESCHUTES	5,055	1,697	2,962	396	1,265 D	33.6%	58.6%	36.4%	63.6%
21,965	DOUGLAS	9,054	4,046	4,638	370	592 D	44.7%	51.2%	46.6%	53.4%
3,467	GILLIAM	1,343	470	854	19	384 D	35.0%	63.6%	35.5%	64.5%
5,940	GRANT	2,325	733	1,496	96	763 D	31.5%	64.3%	32.9%	67.1%
5,920	HARNEY	2,067	687	1,276	104	589 D	33.2%	61.7%	35.0%	65.0%
8,938	HOOD RIVER	3,256	1,387	1,685	184	298 D	42.6%	51.8%	45.1%	54.9%
32,918	JACKSON	13,639	5,459	7,519	661	2,060 D	40.0%	55.1%	42.1%	57.9%
2,291	JEFFERSON	766	253	477	36	224 D	33.0%	62.3%	34.7%	65.3%
11,498	JOSEPHINE	5,195	1,757	3,060	378	1,303 D	33.8%	58.9%	36.5%	63.5%
32,407	KLAMATH	10,755	3,483	6,772	500	3,289 D	32.4%	63.0%	34.0%	66.0%
4,833	LAKE	2,084	839	1,199	46	360 D	40.3%	57.5%	41.2%	58.8%
54,493	LANE	24,137	10,547	11,073	2,517	526 D	43.7%	45.9%	48.8%	51.2%
9,903	LINCOLN	3,994	1,415	2,376	203	961 D	35.4%	59.5%	37.3%	62.7%
24,700	LINN	10,031	4,106	5,366	559	1,260 D	40.9%	53.5%	43.3%	56.7%
11,269	MALHEUR	3,754	1,589	2,025	140	436 D	42.3%	53.9%	44.0%	56.0%
60,541	MARION	22,118	8,633	12,572	913	3,939 D	39.0%	56.8%	40.7%	59.3%
4,941	MORROW	1,601	579	929	93	350 D	36.2%	58.0%	38.4%	61.6%
338,241	MULTNOMAH	132,743	47,201	78,898	6,644	31,697 D	35.6%	59.4%	37.4%	62.6%
16,858	POLK	6,514	2,548	3,705	261	1,157 D	39.1%	56.9%	40.7%	59.3%
2,978	SHERMAN	1,112	423	665	24	242 D	38.0%	59.8%	38.9%	61.1%
11,824	TILLAMOOK	4,740	1,722	2,726	292	1,004 D	36.3%	57.5%	38.7%	61.3%
24,399	UMATILLA	8,877	2,930	5,631	316	2,701 D	33.0%	63.4%	34.2%	65.8%
17,492	UNION	6,350	1,705	4,450	195	2,745 D	26.9%	70.1%	27.7%	72.3%
7,814	WALLOWA	2,652	772	1,790	90	1,018 D	29.1%	67.5%	30.1%	69.9%
12,646	WASCO	4,664	1,740	2,776	148	1,036 D	37.3%	59.5%	38.5%	61.5%
30,275	WASHINGTON	11,554	4,201	6,824	529	2,623 D	36.4%	59.1%	38.1%	61.9%
2,799	WHEELER	1,165	519	632	14	113 D	44.5%	54.2%	45.1%	54.9%
22,036	YAMHILL	8,719	3,584	4,798	337	1,214 D	41.1%	55.0%	42.8%	57.2%
953,786	TOTAL	368,751	136,019	213,871	18,861	77,852 D	36.9%	58.0%	38.9%	61.1%

OREGON

PRESIDENT 1928

1920 Census Population	County	Total Vote	Republican	Democratic	Other	Rep.-Dem. Plurality	Percentage Total Vote Rep.	Total Vote Dem.	Major Vote Rep.	Major Vote Dem.
17,929	BAKER	5,679	3,721	1,861	97	1,860 R	65.5%	32.8%	66.7%	33.3%
13,744	BENTON	6,095	4,605	1,412	78	3,193 R	75.6%	23.2%	76.5%	23.5%
37,698	CLACKAMAS	15,486	9,216	5,918	352	3,298 R	59.5%	38.2%	60.9%	39.1%
23,030	CLATSOP	6,454	4,087	2,208	159	1,879 R	63.3%	34.2%	64.9%	35.1%
13,960	COLUMBIA	5,396	3,519	1,775	102	1,744 R	65.2%	32.9%	66.5%	33.5%
22,257	COOS	8,126	4,929	3,040	157	1,889 R	60.7%	37.4%	61.9%	38.1%
3,424	CROOK	1,382	877	487	18	390 R	63.5%	35.2%	64.3%	35.7%
3,025	CURRY	1,173	694	453	26	241 R	59.2%	38.6%	60.5%	39.5%
9,622	DESCHUTES	4,628	2,815	1,702	111	1,113 R	60.8%	36.8%	62.3%	37.7%
21,332	DOUGLAS	7,954	5,609	2,191	154	3,418 R	70.5%	27.5%	71.9%	28.1%
3,960	GILLIAM	1,408	880	515	13	365 R	62.5%	36.6%	63.1%	36.9%
5,496	GRANT	1,906	1,411	469	26	942 R	74.0%	24.6%	75.1%	24.9%
3,992	HARNEY	1,571	952	600	19	352 R	60.6%	38.2%	61.3%	38.7%
8,315	HOOD RIVER	2,769	1,806	905	58	901 R	65.2%	32.7%	66.6%	33.4%
20,405	JACKSON	10,676	8,053	2,463	160	5,590 R	75.4%	23.1%	76.6%	23.4%
3,211	JEFFERSON	811	481	308	22	173 R	59.3%	38.0%	61.0%	39.0%
7,655	JOSEPHINE	3,681	2,625	959	97	1,666 R	71.3%	26.1%	73.2%	26.8%
11,413	KLAMATH	7,267	4,453	2,721	93	1,732 R	61.3%	37.4%	62.1%	37.9%
3,991	LAKE	1,594	1,014	549	31	465 R	63.6%	34.4%	64.9%	35.1%
36,166	LANE	18,205	13,647	4,213	345	9,434 R	75.0%	23.1%	76.4%	23.6%
6,084	LINCOLN	3,663	2,100	1,464	99	636 R	57.3%	40.0%	58.9%	41.1%
24,550	LINN	8,691	5,877	2,645	169	3,232 R	67.6%	30.4%	69.0%	31.0%
10,907	MALHEUR	3,213	2,164	1,016	33	1,148 R	67.4%	31.6%	68.1%	31.9%
47,187	MARION	18,971	11,754	6,998	219	4,756 R	62.0%	36.9%	62.7%	37.3%
5,617	MORROW	1,685	1,093	543	49	550 R	64.9%	32.2%	66.8%	33.2%
275,898	MULTNOMAH	122,859	75,731	45,177	1,951	30,554 R	61.6%	36.8%	62.6%	37.4%
14,181	POLK	5,034	3,244	1,724	66	1,520 R	64.4%	34.2%	65.3%	34.7%
3,826	SHERMAN	1,144	759	375	10	384 R	66.3%	32.8%	66.9%	33.1%
8,810	TILLAMOOK	3,850	2,570	1,204	76	1,366 R	66.8%	31.3%	68.1%	31.9%
25,946	UMATILLA	7,780	5,277	2,390	113	2,887 R	67.8%	30.7%	68.8%	31.2%
16,636	UNION	5,444	3,219	2,154	71	1,065 R	59.1%	39.6%	59.9%	40.1%
9,778	WALLOWA	2,332	1,326	935	71	391 R	56.9%	40.1%	58.6%	41.4%
13,648	WASCO	4,513	2,746	1,699	68	1,047 R	60.8%	37.6%	61.8%	38.2%
26,376	WASHINGTON	9,879	6,162	3,544	173	2,618 R	62.4%	35.9%	63.5%	36.5%
2,791	WHEELER	902	677	224	1	453 R	75.1%	24.8%	75.1%	24.9%
20,529	YAMHILL	7,721	5,248	2,382	91	2,866 R	68.0%	30.9%	68.8%	31.2%
783,389	TOTAL	319,942	205,341	109,223	5,378	96,118 R	64.2%	34.1%	65.3%	34.7%

OREGON

PRESIDENT 1924

1920 Census Population	County	Total Vote	Republican	Democratic	Progressive	Other	Plurality	Percentage Total Vote Rep.	Dem.	Prog.
17,929	BAKER	6,172	2,803	2,004	1,356	9	799 R	45.4%	32.5%	22.0%
13,744	BENTON	5,631	3,417	1,579	623	12	1,838 R	60.7%	28.0%	11.1%
37,698	CLACKAMAS	13,548	5,864	3,099	4,508	77	1,356 R	43.3%	22.9%	33.3%
23,030	CLATSOP	5,881	3,313	1,373	1,158	37	1,940 R	56.3%	23.3%	19.7%
13,960	COLUMBIA	4,418	2,483	1,015	896	24	1,468 R	56.2%	23.0%	20.3%
22,257	COOS	8,070	3,905	1,757	2,359	49	1,546 R	48.4%	21.8%	29.2%
3,424	CROOK	1,429	725	434	266	4	291 R	50.7%	30.4%	18.6%
3,025	CURRY	1,214	664	224	317	9	347 R	54.7%	18.5%	26.1%
9,622	DESCHUTES	4,378	2,321	1,015	1,013	29	1,306 R	53.0%	23.2%	23.1%
21,332	DOUGLAS	7,849	4,219	1,666	1,943	21	2,276 R	53.8%	21.2%	24.8%
3,960	GILLIAM	1,470	738	521	207	4	217 R	50.2%	35.4%	14.1%
5,496	GRANT	1,979	1,126	459	380	14	667 R	56.9%	23.2%	19.2%
3,992	HARNEY	1,581	851	436	285	9	415 R	53.8%	27.6%	18.0%
8,315	HOOD RIVER	2,506	1,214	683	600	9	531 R	48.4%	27.3%	23.9%
20,405	JACKSON	9,141	4,868	1,840	2,408	25	2,460 R	53.3%	20.1%	26.3%
3,211	JEFFERSON	959	374	242	334	9	40 R	39.0%	25.2%	34.8%
7,655	JOSEPHINE	3,257	1,756	650	835	16	921 R	53.9%	20.0%	25.6%
11,413	KLAMATH	5,189	2,775	680	1,715	19	1,060 R	53.5%	13.1%	33.1%
3,991	LAKE	1,520	917	304	295	4	613 R	60.3%	20.0%	19.4%
36,166	LANE	14,275	8,551	3,255	2,416	53	5,296 R	59.9%	22.8%	16.9%
6,084	LINCOLN	2,544	1,328	641	552	23	687 R	52.2%	25.2%	21.7%
24,550	LINN	8,355	4,141	2,618	1,575	21	1,523 R	49.6%	31.3%	18.9%
10,907	MALHEUR	3,217	1,671	828	710	8	843 R	51.9%	25.7%	22.1%
47,187	MARION	16,016	8,351	3,996	3,631	38	4,355 R	52.1%	25.0%	22.7%
5,617	MORROW	1,858	991	397	462	8	529 R	53.3%	21.4%	24.9%
275,898	MULTNOMAH	97,764	48,866	21,733	26,932	233	21,934 R	50.0%	22.2%	27.5%
14,181	POLK	5,223	2,755	1,621	831	16	1,134 R	52.7%	31.0%	15.9%
3,826	SHERMAN	1,352	756	367	229		389 R	55.9%	27.1%	16.9%
8,810	TILLAMOOK	3,719	2,201	795	700	23	1,406 R	59.2%	21.4%	18.8%
25,946	UMATILLA	8,620	3,854	3,052	1,693	21	802 R	44.7%	35.4%	19.6%
16,636	UNION	5,663	2,428	1,816	1,398	21	612 R	42.9%	32.1%	24.7%
9,778	WALLOWA	2,707	1,253	973	471	10	280 R	46.3%	35.9%	17.4%
13,648	WASCO	4,681	2,409	1,185	1,069	18	1,224 R	51.5%	25.3%	22.8%
26,376	WASHINGTON	9,141	4,203	2,103	2,809	26	1,394 R	46.0%	23.0%	30.7%
2,791	WHEELER	1,001	685	213	103		472 R	68.4%	21.3%	10.3%
20,529	YAMHILL	7,160	3,803	2,015	1,324	18	1,788 R	53.1%	28.1%	18.5%
783,389	TOTAL	279,488	142,579	67,589	68,403	917	74,176 R	51.0%	24.2%	24.5%

OREGON

PRESIDENT 1920

1920 Census Population	County	Total Vote	Republican	Democratic	Other	Rep.-Dem. Plurality	Percentage Total Vote Rep.	Total Vote Dem.	Major Vote Rep.	Major Vote Dem.
17,929	BAKER	5,961	3,495	2,171	295	1,324 R	58.6%	36.4%	61.7%	38.3%
13,744	BENTON	5,663	3,752	1,719	192	2,033 R	66.3%	30.4%	68.6%	31.4%
37,698	CLACKAMAS	11,639	6,928	3,740	971	3,188 R	59.5%	32.1%	64.9%	35.1%
23,030	CLATSOP	5,697	3,498	1,687	512	1,811 R	61.4%	29.6%	67.5%	32.5%
13,960	COLUMBIA	3,262	2,007	970	285	1,037 R	61.5%	29.7%	67.4%	32.6%
22,257	COOS	6,205	3,272	2,297	636	975 R	52.7%	37.0%	58.8%	41.2%
3,424	CROOK	1,473	872	528	73	344 R	59.2%	35.8%	62.3%	37.7%
3,025	CURRY	984	599	280	105	319 R	60.9%	28.5%	68.1%	31.9%
9,622	DESCHUTES	3,040	1,649	1,072	319	577 R	54.2%	35.3%	60.6%	39.4%
21,332	DOUGLAS	7,315	4,402	2,428	485	1,974 R	60.2%	33.2%	64.5%	35.5%
3,960	GILLIAM	1,355	821	498	36	323 R	60.6%	36.8%	62.2%	37.8%
5,496	GRANT	1,910	1,310	497	103	813 R	68.6%	26.0%	72.5%	27.5%
3,992	HARNEY	1,622	1,026	479	117	547 R	63.3%	29.5%	68.2%	31.8%
8,315	HOOD RIVER	2,417	1,449	761	207	688 R	60.0%	31.5%	65.6%	34.4%
20,405	JACKSON	7,326	4,382	2,503	441	1,879 R	59.8%	34.2%	63.6%	36.4%
3,211	JEFFERSON	1,012	623	300	89	323 R	61.6%	29.6%	67.5%	32.5%
7,655	JOSEPHINE	2,581	1,606	819	156	787 R	62.2%	31.7%	66.2%	33.8%
11,413	KLAMATH	3,907	2,742	901	264	1,841 R	70.2%	23.1%	75.3%	24.7%
3,991	LAKE	1,576	1,136	358	82	778 R	72.1%	22.7%	76.0%	24.0%
36,166	LANE	12,447	7,714	3,986	747	3,728 R	62.0%	32.0%	65.9%	34.1%
6,084	LINCOLN	2,080	1,229	669	182	560 R	59.1%	32.2%	64.8%	35.2%
24,550	LINN	8,355	4,693	3,177	485	1,516 R	56.2%	38.0%	59.6%	40.4%
10,907	MALHEUR	3,620	2,352	1,075	193	1,277 R	65.0%	29.7%	68.6%	31.4%
47,187	MARION	13,298	8,798	3,831	669	4,967 R	66.2%	28.8%	69.7%	30.3%
5,617	MORROW	1,725	1,186	451	88	735 R	68.8%	26.1%	72.4%	27.6%
275,898	MULTNOMAH	77,174	44,806	27,607	4,761	17,199 R	58.1%	35.8%	61.9%	38.1%
14,181	POLK	4,594	2,709	1,653	232	1,056 R	59.0%	36.0%	62.1%	37.9%
3,826	SHERMAN	1,362	893	423	46	470 R	65.6%	31.1%	67.9%	32.1%
8,810	TILLAMOOK	2,737	1,664	828	245	836 R	60.8%	30.3%	66.8%	33.2%
25,946	UMATILLA	8,580	4,979	3,255	346	1,724 R	58.0%	37.9%	60.5%	39.5%
16,636	UNION	5,020	2,844	1,899	277	945 R	56.7%	37.8%	60.0%	40.0%
9,778	WALLOWA	2,674	1,612	896	166	716 R	60.3%	33.5%	64.3%	35.7%
13,648	WASCO	4,334	2,698	1,434	202	1,264 R	62.3%	33.1%	65.3%	34.7%
26,376	WASHINGTON	7,641	4,947	2,262	432	2,685 R	64.7%	29.6%	68.6%	31.4%
2,791	WHEELER	1,041	797	212	32	585 R	76.6%	20.4%	79.0%	21.0%
20,529	YAMHILL	6,895	4,102	2,353	440	1,749 R	59.5%	34.1%	63.5%	36.5%
783,389	TOTAL	238,522	143,592	80,019	14,911	63,573 R	60.2%	33.5%	64.2%	35.8%

OREGON

ELECTION NOTES

1956 Other vote was scattered write-in.

1952 Other vote was Hallinan (Progressive).

1948 Other vote was 14,978 Wallace (Progressive); 5,051 Thomas (Socialist).

1944 Other vote was 3,785 Thomas (Socialist); 2,362 Watson (Prohibition).

1940 Other vote was 2,487 Aiken (Socialist Labor); 398 Thomas (Socialist); 191 Browder (Communist); 154 Babson (Prohibition); 40 scattered write-in.

1936 Other vote was 21,831 Lemke (Union); 2,143 Thomas (Socialist); 500 Aiken (Socialist Labor); 104 Browder (Communist); 4 Colvin (Prohibition).

1932 Other vote was 15,450 Thomas (Socialist); 1,730 Reynolds (Socialist Labor); 1,681 Foster (Communist).

1928 Other vote was 2,720 Thomas (Socialist); 1,564 Reynolds (Socialist Labor); 1,094 Foster (Communist).

1924 A special four-column table which gives the LaFollette (Progressive) vote is used to detail this election. Other vote was Johns (Socialist Labor).

1920 Other vote was 9,801 Debs (Socialist); 3,595 Watkins (Prohibition); 1,515 Cox (Socialist Labor).

PENNSYLVANIA

POPULAR VOTE FOR PRESIDENT 1920 TO 1956

Year	Total Vote	Republican		Democratic		Other Vote	Plurality	Percentage			
								Total Vote		Major Vote	
		Vote	Candidate	Vote	Candidate			Rep.	Dem.	Rep.	Dem.
1956	4,576,503	2,585,252	Eisenhower, Dwight D.	1,981,769	Stevenson, Adlai E.	9,482	603,483 R	56.5%	43.3%	56.6%	43.4%
1952	4,580,969	2,415,789	Eisenhower, Dwight D.	2,146,269	Stevenson, Adlai E.	18,911	269,520 R	52.7%	46.9%	53.0%	47.0%
1948	3,735,348	1,902,197	Dewey, Thomas E.	1,752,426	Truman, Harry S.	80,725	149,771 R	50.9%	46.9%	52.0%	48.0%
1944	3,794,793	1,835,054	Dewey, Thomas E.	1,940,479	Roosevelt, Franklin D.	19,260	105,425 D	48.4%	51.1%	48.6%	51.4%
1940	4,078,714	1,889,848	Willkie, Wendell	2,171,035	Roosevelt, Franklin D.	17,831	281,187 D	46.3%	53.2%	46.5%	53.5%
1936	4,138,105	1,690,300	Landon, Alfred M.	2,353,788	Roosevelt, Franklin D.	94,017	663,488 D	40.8%	56.9%	41.8%	58.2%
1932	2,859,021	1,453,540	Hoover, Herbert C.	1,295,948	Roosevelt, Franklin D.	109,533	157,592 R	50.8%	45.3%	52.9%	47.1%
1928	3,150,612	2,055,382	Hoover, Herbert C.	1,067,586	Smith, Alfred E.	27,644	987,796 R	65.2%	33.9%	65.8%	34.2%
1924 **	2,144,850	1,401,481	Coolidge, Calvin	409,192	Davis, John W.	334,177	992,289 R	65.3%	19.1%	77.4%	22.6%
1920	1,851,248	1,218,215	Harding, Warren G.	503,202	Cox, James M.	129,831	715,013 R	65.8%	27.2%	70.8%	29.2%

In 1924 other vote was 307,567 Progressive; 13,035 American; 9,779 Prohibition; 2,735 Communist; 634 Socialist Labor; 296 Commonwealth Land and 131 scattered.

ELECTORAL COLLEGE VOTE 1920 TO 1956

Year	Total	Republican	Democratic	Other
1956	32	32	—	—
1952	32	32	—	—
1948	35	35	—	—
1944	35	—	35	—
1940	36	—	36	—
1936	36	—	36	—
1932	36	36	—	—
1928	38	38	—	—
1924	38	38	—	—
1920	38	38	—	—

PENNSYLVANIA

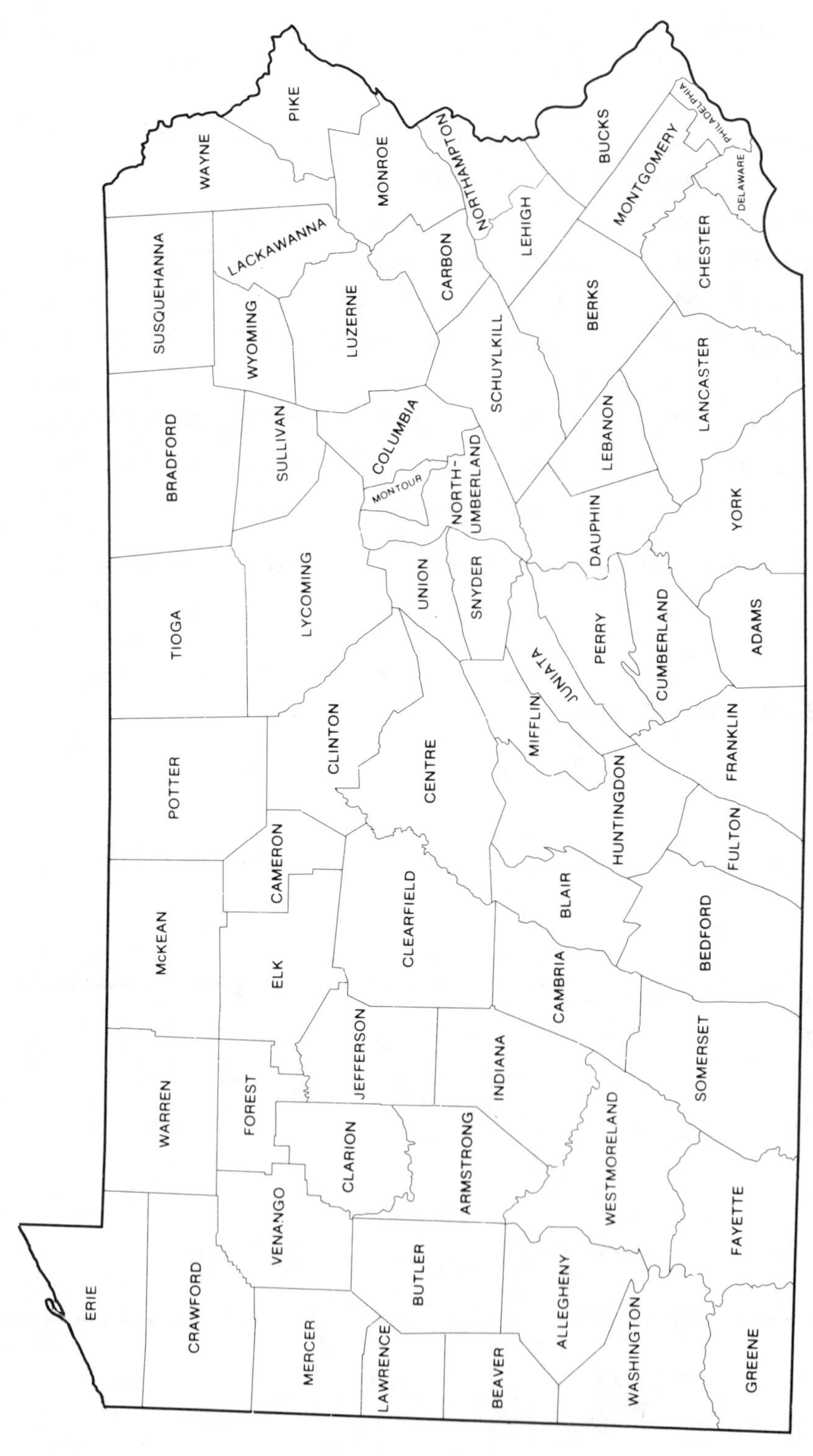

PENNSYLVANIA

PRESIDENT 1956

1950 Census Population	County	Total Vote	Republican	Democratic	Other	Rep.-Dem. Plurality	Percentage Total Vote Rep.	Total Vote Dem.	Major Vote Rep.	Major Vote Dem.
44,197	ADAMS	18,531	12,250	6,281		5,969 R	66.1%	33.9%	66.1%	33.9%
1,515,237	ALLEGHENY	702,030	384,939	315,989	1,102	68,950 R	54.8%	45.0%	54.9%	45.1%
80,842	ARMSTRONG	32,760	20,055	12,671	34	7,384 R	61.2%	38.7%	61.3%	38.7%
175,192	BEAVER	74,715	38,263	36,373	79	1,890 R	51.2%	48.7%	51.3%	48.7%
40,775	BEDFORD	17,474	11,423	6,038	13	5,385 R	65.4%	34.6%	65.4%	34.6%
255,740	BERKS	99,927	57,258	42,349	320	14,909 R	57.3%	42.4%	57.5%	42.5%
139,514	BLAIR	51,191	33,623	17,503	65	16,120 R	65.7%	34.2%	65.8%	34.2%
51,722	BRADFORD	20,931	15,399	5,502	30	9,897 R	73.6%	26.3%	73.7%	26.3%
144,620	BUCKS	98,583	59,862	38,541	180	21,321 R	60.7%	39.1%	60.8%	39.2%
97,320	BUTLER	39,989	26,238	13,672	79	12,566 R	65.6%	34.2%	65.7%	34.3%
209,541	CAMBRIA	88,249	46,373	41,753	123	4,620 R	52.5%	47.3%	52.6%	47.4%
7,023	CAMERON	3,304	2,462	841	1	1,621 R	74.5%	25.5%	74.5%	25.5%
57,558	CARBON	22,961	13,150	9,722	89	3,428 R	57.3%	42.3%	57.5%	42.5%
65,922	CENTRE	22,940	15,412	7,483	45	7,929 R	67.2%	32.6%	67.3%	32.7%
159,141	CHESTER	67,232	47,225	19,957	50	27,268 R	70.2%	29.7%	70.3%	29.7%
38,344	CLARION	15,011	10,048	4,955	8	5,093 R	66.9%	33.0%	67.0%	33.0%
85,957	CLEARFIELD	30,460	17,519	12,852	89	4,667 R	57.5%	42.2%	57.7%	42.3%
36,532	CLINTON	13,678	8,250	5,411	17	2,839 R	60.3%	39.6%	60.4%	39.6%
53,460	COLUMBIA	22,421	13,382	9,024	15	4,358 R	59.7%	40.2%	59.7%	40.3%
78,948	CRAWFORD	28,337	18,887	9,346	104	9,541 R	66.7%	33.0%	66.9%	33.1%
94,457	CUMBERLAND	43,272	29,468	13,651	153	15,817 R	68.1%	31.5%	68.3%	31.7%
197,784	DAUPHIN	90,943	61,342	29,226	375	32,116 R	67.5%	32.1%	67.7%	32.3%
414,234	DELAWARE	226,210	143,663	82,024	523	61,639 R	63.5%	36.3%	63.7%	36.3%
34,503	ELK	14,468	8,947	5,498	23	3,449 R	61.8%	38.0%	61.9%	38.1%
219,388	ERIE	88,555	54,430	33,802	323	20,628 R	61.5%	38.2%	61.7%	38.3%
189,899	FAYETTE	66,375	27,857	38,312	206	10,455 D	42.0%	57.7%	42.1%	57.9%
4,944	FOREST	2,158	1,535	622	1	913 R	71.1%	28.8%	71.2%	28.8%
75,927	FRANKLIN	30,193	19,121	11,060	12	8,061 R	63.3%	36.6%	63.4%	36.6%
10,387	FULTON	4,195	2,370	1,819	6	551 R	56.5%	43.4%	56.6%	43.4%
45,394	GREENE	17,403	7,562	9,827	14	2,265 D	43.5%	56.5%	43.5%	56.5%
40,872	HUNTINGDON	14,333	9,698	4,618	17	5,080 R	67.7%	32.2%	67.7%	32.3%
77,106	INDIANA	29,861	18,593	11,268		7,325 R	62.3%	37.7%	62.3%	37.7%
49,147	JEFFERSON	19,697	13,051	6,627	19	6,424 R	66.3%	33.6%	66.3%	33.7%
15,243	JUNIATA	7,044	4,258	2,779	7	1,479 R	60.4%	39.5%	60.5%	39.5%
257,396	LACKAWANNA	120,206	64,386	55,741	79	8,645 R	53.6%	46.4%	53.6%	46.4%
234,717	LANCASTER	95,801	69,026	26,538	237	42,488 R	72.1%	27.7%	72.2%	27.8%
105,120	LAWRENCE	45,025	25,037	19,923	65	5,114 R	55.6%	44.2%	55.7%	44.3%
81,683	LEBANON	33,003	22,556	10,406	41	12,150 R	68.3%	31.5%	68.4%	31.6%
198,207	LEHIGH	79,882	50,564	29,067	251	21,497 R	63.3%	36.4%	63.5%	36.5%
392,241	LUZERNE	158,820	92,458	65,155	1,207	27,303 R	58.2%	41.0%	58.7%	41.3%
101,249	LYCOMING	40,540	27,030	13,490	20	13,540 R	66.7%	33.3%	66.7%	33.3%
56,607	MCKEAN	19,950	14,725	5,152	73	9,573 R	73.8%	25.8%	74.1%	25.9%
111,954	MERCER	48,674	28,785	19,769	120	9,016 R	59.1%	40.6%	59.3%	40.7%
43,691	MIFFLIN	13,725	8,638	5,078	9	3,560 R	62.9%	37.0%	63.0%	37.0%
33,773	MONROE	15,679	10,081	5,506	92	4,575 R	64.3%	35.1%	64.7%	35.3%
353,068	MONTGOMERY	192,583	133,270	59,095	218	74,175 R	69.2%	30.7%	69.3%	30.7%
16,001	MONTOUR	6,051	3,976	2,072	3	1,904 R	65.7%	34.2%	65.7%	34.3%
185,243	NORTHAMPTON	77,697	43,375	33,749	573	9,626 R	55.8%	43.4%	56.2%	43.8%
117,115	NORTHUMBERLAND	45,765	28,583	17,141	41	11,442 R	62.5%	37.5%	62.5%	37.5%
24,782	PERRY	11,112	7,511	3,576	25	3,935 R	67.6%	32.2%	67.7%	32.3%
2,071,605	PHILADELPHIA	892,321	383,414	507,289	1,618	123,875 D	43.0%	56.9%	43.0%	57.0%
8,425	PIKE	5,383	4,160	1,219	4	2,941 R	77.3%	22.6%	77.3%	22.7%
16,810	POTTER	7,460	5,181	2,257	22	2,924 R	69.5%	30.3%	69.7%	30.3%
200,577	SCHUYLKILL	83,406	51,670	31,645	91	20,025 R	61.9%	37.9%	62.0%	38.0%
22,912	SNYDER	9,064	7,102	1,959	3	5,143 R	78.4%	21.6%	78.4%	21.6%
81,813	SOMERSET	33,748	20,568	13,163	17	7,405 R	60.9%	39.0%	61.0%	39.0%
6,745	SULLIVAN	3,297	2,007	1,286	4	721 R	60.9%	39.0%	60.9%	39.1%
31,970	SUSQUEHANNA	15,055	10,752	4,293	10	6,459 R	71.4%	28.5%	71.5%	28.5%
35,474	TIOGA	14,113	10,827	3,280	6	7,547 R	76.7%	23.2%	76.7%	23.3%
23,150	UNION	8,478	6,620	1,844	14	4,776 R	78.1%	21.8%	78.2%	21.8%

PENNSYLVANIA

PRESIDENT 1956

1950 Census Population	County	Total Vote	Republican	Democratic	Other	Rep.-Dem. Plurality	Percentage Total Vote Rep.	Percentage Total Vote Dem.	Percentage Major Vote Rep.	Percentage Major Vote Dem.
65,328	VENANGO	22,715	17,107	5,594	14	11,513 R	75.3%	24.6%	75.4%	24.6%
42,698	WARREN	16,651	12,145	4,463	43	7,682 R	72.9%	26.8%	73.1%	26.9%
209,628	WASHINGTON	87,615	39,465	48,052	98	8,587 D	45.0%	54.8%	45.1%	54.9%
28,478	WAYNE	12,768	9,658	3,092	18	6,566 R	75.6%	24.2%	75.7%	24.3%
313,179	WESTMORELAND	139,388	66,580	72,616	192	6,036 D	47.8%	52.1%	47.8%	52.2%
16,766	WYOMING	8,029	5,906	2,120	3	3,786 R	73.6%	26.4%	73.6%	26.4%
202,737	YORK	87,068	48,176	38,743	149	9,433 R	55.3%	44.5%	55.4%	44.6%
10,498,012	TOTAL	4,576,503	2,585,252	1,981,769	9,482	603,483 R	56.5%	43.3%	56.6%	43.4%

PENNSYLVANIA

PRESIDENT 1952

1950 Census Population	County	Total Vote	Republican	Democratic	Other	Rep.-Dem. Plurality	Percentage Total Vote Rep.	Total Vote Dem.	Major Vote Rep.	Major Vote Dem.
44,197	ADAMS	16,737	11,016	5,691	30	5,325 R	65.8%	34.0%	65.9%	34.1%
1,515,237	ALLEGHENY	733,072	359,224	370,945	2,903	11,721 D	49.0%	50.6%	49.2%	50.8%
80,842	ARMSTRONG	30,329	16,955	13,221	153	3,734 R	55.9%	43.6%	56.2%	43.8%
175,192	BEAVER	70,170	31,700	38,136	334	6,436 D	45.2%	54.3%	45.4%	54.6%
40,775	BEDFORD	14,734	9,419	5,255	60	4,164 R	63.9%	35.7%	64.2%	35.8%
255,740	BERKS	98,668	51,720	45,874	1,074	5,846 R	52.4%	46.5%	53.0%	47.0%
139,514	BLAIR	49,070	32,113	16,851	106	15,262 R	65.4%	34.3%	65.6%	34.4%
51,722	BRADFORD	20,908	15,894	4,959	55	10,935 R	76.0%	23.7%	76.2%	23.8%
144,620	BUCKS	65,329	40,753	24,301	275	16,452 R	62.4%	37.2%	62.6%	37.4%
97,320	BUTLER	40,723	25,243	15,295	185	9,948 R	62.0%	37.6%	62.3%	37.7%
209,541	CAMBRIA	90,250	39,294	50,774	182	11,480 D	43.5%	56.3%	43.6%	56.4%
7,023	CAMERON	3,341	2,307	1,020	14	1,287 R	69.1%	30.5%	69.3%	30.7%
57,558	CARBON	22,988	12,283	10,571	134	1,712 R	53.4%	46.0%	53.7%	46.3%
65,922	CENTRE	22,168	14,700	7,391	77	7,309 R	66.3%	33.3%	66.5%	33.5%
159,141	CHESTER	61,615	39,961	21,490	164	18,471 R	64.9%	34.9%	65.0%	35.0%
38,344	CLARION	14,649	9,340	5,212	97	4,128 R	63.8%	35.6%	64.2%	35.8%
85,957	CLEARFIELD	29,577	16,045	13,376	156	2,669 R	54.2%	45.2%	54.5%	45.5%
36,532	CLINTON	13,938	8,125	5,758	55	2,367 R	58.3%	41.3%	58.5%	41.5%
53,460	COLUMBIA	22,554	13,008	9,467	79	3,541 R	57.7%	42.0%	57.9%	42.1%
78,948	CRAWFORD	29,134	19,079	9,874	181	9,205 R	65.5%	33.9%	65.9%	34.1%
94,457	CUMBERLAND	39,155	26,302	12,762	91	13,540 R	67.2%	32.6%	67.3%	32.7%
197,784	DAUPHIN	89,656	58,385	30,985	286	27,400 R	65.1%	34.6%	65.3%	34.7%
414,234	DELAWARE	210,748	129,743	80,316	689	49,427 R	61.6%	38.1%	61.8%	38.2%
34,503	ELK	14,195	7,702	6,448	45	1,254 R	54.3%	45.4%	54.4%	45.6%
219,388	ERIE	85,846	48,836	36,619	391	12,217 R	56.9%	42.7%	57.1%	42.9%
189,899	FAYETTE	71,745	27,348	43,921	476	16,573 D	38.1%	61.2%	38.4%	61.6%
4,944	FOREST	2,161	1,511	627	23	884 R	69.9%	29.0%	70.7%	29.3%
75,927	FRANKLIN	25,416	16,474	8,868	74	7,606 R	64.8%	34.9%	65.0%	35.0%
10,387	FULTON	3,859	2,127	1,718	14	409 R	55.1%	44.5%	55.3%	44.7%
45,394	GREENE	17,119	6,964	10,125	30	3,161 D	40.7%	59.1%	40.8%	59.2%
40,872	HUNTINGDON	13,962	9,580	4,318	64	5,262 R	68.6%	30.9%	68.9%	31.1%
77,106	INDIANA	28,440	16,673	11,620	147	5,053 R	58.6%	40.9%	58.9%	41.1%
49,147	JEFFERSON	18,314	11,833	6,365	116	5,468 R	64.6%	34.8%	65.0%	35.0%
15,243	JUNIATA	6,589	3,863	2,705	21	1,158 R	58.6%	41.1%	58.8%	41.2%
257,396	LACKAWANNA	126,717	61,644	64,926	147	3,282 D	48.6%	51.2%	48.7%	51.3%
234,717	LANCASTER	92,721	64,193	28,146	382	36,047 R	69.2%	30.4%	69.5%	30.5%
105,120	LAWRENCE	44,738	23,319	21,164	255	2,155 R	52.1%	47.3%	52.4%	47.6%
81,683	LEBANON	32,472	20,726	11,611	135	9,115 R	63.8%	35.8%	64.1%	35.9%
198,207	LEHIGH	78,479	45,143	33,033	303	12,110 R	57.5%	42.1%	57.7%	42.3%
392,241	LUZERNE	162,261	88,967	72,579	715	16,388 R	54.8%	44.7%	55.1%	44.9%
101,249	LYCOMING	41,807	25,753	15,870	184	9,883 R	61.6%	38.0%	61.9%	38.1%
56,607	MCKEAN	20,776	15,256	5,373	147	9,883 R	73.4%	25.9%	74.0%	26.0%
111,954	MERCER	47,537	26,424	20,770	343	5,654 R	55.6%	43.7%	56.0%	44.0%
43,691	MIFFLIN	14,556	8,620	5,889	47	2,731 R	59.2%	40.5%	59.4%	40.6%
33,773	MONROE	15,304	9,502	5,760	42	3,742 R	62.1%	37.6%	62.3%	37.7%
353,068	MONTGOMERY	173,973	115,899	57,701	373	58,198 R	66.6%	33.2%	66.8%	33.2%
16,001	MONTOUR	5,996	3,725	2,264	7	1,461 R	62.1%	37.8%	62.2%	37.8%
185,243	NORTHAMPTON	76,738	39,131	36,993	614	2,138 R	51.0%	48.2%	51.4%	48.6%
117,115	NORTHUMBERLAND	46,769	28,861	17,789	119	11,072 R	61.7%	38.0%	61.9%	38.1%
24,782	PERRY	9,792	6,733	3,042	17	3,691 R	68.8%	31.1%	68.9%	31.1%
2,071,605	PHILADELPHIA	958,547	396,874	557,352	4,321	160,478 D	41.4%	58.1%	41.6%	58.4%
8,425	PIKE	5,204	3,810	1,383	11	2,427 R	73.2%	26.6%	73.4%	26.6%
16,810	POTTER	7,129	5,117	1,974	38	3,143 R	71.8%	27.7%	72.2%	27.8%
200,577	SCHUYLKILL	86,610	51,437	34,987	186	16,450 R	59.4%	40.4%	59.5%	40.5%
22,912	SNYDER	8,545	6,836	1,686	23	5,150 R	80.0%	19.7%	80.2%	19.8%
81,813	SOMERSET	31,820	18,589	13,167	64	5,422 R	58.4%	41.4%	58.5%	41.5%
6,745	SULLIVAN	3,253	2,011	1,239	3	772 R	61.8%	38.1%	61.9%	38.1%
31,970	SUSQUEHANNA	14,234	10,529	3,653	52	6,876 R	74.0%	25.7%	74.2%	25.8%
35,474	TIOGA	14,244	11,203	3,006	35	8,197 R	78.7%	21.1%	78.8%	21.2%
23,150	UNION	8,181	6,558	1,610	13	4,948 R	80.2%	19.7%	80.3%	19.7%

PENNSYLVANIA

PRESIDENT 1952

1950 Census Population	County	Total Vote	Republican	Democratic	Other	Rep.-Dem. Plurality	Percentage Total Vote Rep.	Percentage Total Vote Dem.	Percentage Major Vote Rep.	Percentage Major Vote Dem.
65,328	VENANGO	23,566	17,006	6,356	204	10,650 R	72.2%	27.0%	72.8%	27.2%
42,698	WARREN	16,150	11,555	4,442	153	7,113 R	71.5%	27.5%	72.2%	27.8%
209,628	WASHINGTON	92,036	36,041	55,725	270	19,684 D	39.2%	60.5%	39.3%	60.7%
28,478	WAYNE	12,187	9,623	2,530	34	7,093 R	79.0%	20.8%	79.2%	20.8%
313,179	WESTMORELAND	139,494	58,923	80,068	503	21,145 D	42.2%	57.4%	42.4%	57.6%
16,766	WYOMING	7,623	5,772	1,815	36	3,957 R	75.7%	23.8%	76.1%	23.9%
202,737	YORK	84,351	44,489	39,508	354	4,981 R	52.7%	46.8%	53.0%	47.0%
10,498,012	TOTAL	4,580,969	2,415,789	2,146,269	18,911	269,520 R	52.7%	46.9%	53.0%	47.0%

PENNSYLVANIA

PRESIDENT 1948

1940 Census Population	County	Total Vote	Republican	Democratic	Other	Rep.-Dem. Plurality	Percentage Total Vote Rep.	Total Vote Dem.	Major Vote Rep.	Major Vote Dem.
39,435	ADAMS	13,509	7,988	5,409	112	2,579 R	59.1%	40.0%	59.6%	40.4%
1,411,539	ALLEGHENY	594,506	253,272	326,303	14,931	73,031 D	42.6%	54.9%	43.7%	56.3%
81,087	ARMSTRONG	21,912	11,712	9,900	300	1,812 R	53.5%	45.2%	54.2%	45.8%
156,754	BEAVER	50,936	22,324	26,629	1,983	4,305 D	43.8%	52.3%	45.6%	54.4%
40,809	BEDFORD	9,879	6,028	3,851		2,177 R	61.0%	39.0%	61.0%	39.0%
241,884	BERKS	81,726	35,608	43,075	3,043	7,467 D	43.6%	52.7%	45.3%	54.7%
140,358	BLAIR	36,886	22,382	14,050	454	8,332 R	60.7%	38.1%	61.4%	38.6%
50,615	BRADFORD	16,367	11,783	4,421	163	7,362 R	72.0%	27.0%	72.7%	27.3%
107,715	BUCKS	47,084	29,411	16,655	1,018	12,756 R	62.5%	35.4%	63.8%	36.2%
87,590	BUTLER	27,724	17,449	9,818	457	7,631 R	62.9%	35.4%	64.0%	36.0%
213,459	CAMBRIA	70,422	27,725	41,533	1,164	13,808 D	39.4%	59.0%	40.0%	60.0%
6,852	CAMERON	2,465	1,596	858	11	738 R	64.7%	34.8%	65.0%	35.0%
61,735	CARBON	19,578	9,744	9,438	396	306 R	49.8%	48.2%	50.8%	49.2%
52,608	CENTRE	16,931	10,416	6,515		3,901 R	61.5%	38.5%	61.5%	38.5%
135,626	CHESTER	44,478	29,258	14,670	550	14,588 R	65.8%	33.0%	66.6%	33.4%
38,410	CLARION	11,850	6,866	4,984		1,882 R	57.9%	42.1%	57.9%	42.1%
92,094	CLEARFIELD	23,644	11,810	11,347	487	463 R	49.9%	48.0%	51.0%	49.0%
34,557	CLINTON	10,631	5,618	5,013		605 R	52.8%	47.2%	52.8%	47.2%
51,413	COLUMBIA	18,784	9,417	9,367		50 R	50.1%	49.9%	50.1%	49.9%
71,644	CRAWFORD	23,335	14,161	9,174		4,987 R	60.7%	39.3%	60.7%	39.3%
74,806	CUMBERLAND	29,695	18,028	11,421	246	6,607 R	60.7%	38.5%	61.2%	38.8%
177,410	DAUPHIN	75,386	46,861	27,729	796	19,132 R	62.2%	36.8%	62.8%	37.2%
310,756	DELAWARE	153,315	93,412	57,156	2,747	36,256 R	60.9%	37.3%	62.0%	38.0%
34,443	ELK	10,511	5,148	5,363		215 D	49.0%	51.0%	49.0%	51.0%
180,889	ERIE	63,245	33,806	28,159	1,280	5,647 R	53.5%	44.5%	54.6%	45.4%
200,999	FAYETTE	56,367	20,401	34,971	995	14,570 D	36.2%	62.0%	36.8%	63.2%
5,791	FOREST	1,941	1,209	687	45	522 R	62.3%	35.4%	63.8%	36.2%
69,378	FRANKLIN	19,664	12,151	7,352	161	4,799 R	61.8%	37.4%	62.3%	37.7%
10,673	FULTON	3,475	1,760	1,684	31	76 R	50.6%	48.5%	51.1%	48.9%
44,671	GREENE	12,934	4,717	8,015	202	3,298 D	36.5%	62.0%	37.0%	63.0%
41,836	HUNTINGDON	10,247	6,943	3,304		3,639 R	67.8%	32.2%	67.8%	32.2%
79,854	INDIANA	21,183	12,640	8,543		4,097 R	59.7%	40.3%	59.7%	40.3%
54,090	JEFFERSON	15,295	9,395	5,632	268	3,763 R	61.4%	36.8%	62.5%	37.5%
15,373	JUNIATA	5,459	3,121	2,299	39	822 R	57.2%	42.1%	57.6%	42.4%
301,243	LACKAWANNA	111,749	46,283	64,495	971	18,212 D	41.4%	57.7%	41.8%	58.2%
212,504	LANCASTER	68,499	46,306	21,308	885	24,998 R	67.6%	31.1%	68.5%	31.5%
96,877	LAWRENCE	32,599	17,186	14,632	781	2,554 R	52.7%	44.9%	54.0%	46.0%
72,641	LEBANON	25,241	15,553	9,418	270	6,135 R	61.6%	37.3%	62.3%	37.7%
177,533	LEHIGH	60,022	32,202	26,826	994	5,376 R	53.7%	44.7%	54.6%	45.4%
441,518	LUZERNE	135,611	71,674	61,869	2,068	9,805 R	52.9%	45.6%	53.7%	46.3%
93,633	LYCOMING	33,436	19,118	13,692	626	5,426 R	57.2%	40.9%	58.3%	41.7%
56,673	MCKEAN	15,272	10,218	4,785	269	5,433 R	66.9%	31.3%	68.1%	31.9%
101,039	MERCER	35,886	18,916	16,108	862	2,808 R	52.7%	44.9%	54.0%	46.0%
42,993	MIFFLIN	10,523	5,666	4,762	95	904 R	53.8%	45.3%	54.3%	45.7%
29,802	MONROE	12,587	6,674	5,913		761 R	53.0%	47.0%	53.0%	47.0%
289,247	MONTGOMERY	128,626	85,576	41,112	1,938	44,464 R	66.5%	32.0%	67.5%	32.5%
15,466	MONTOUR	4,670	2,690	1,964	16	726 R	57.6%	42.1%	57.8%	42.2%
168,959	NORTHAMPTON	61,504	27,030	33,209	1,265	6,179 D	43.9%	54.0%	44.9%	55.1%
126,887	NORTHUMBERLAND	40,485	23,535	16,478	472	7,057 R	58.1%	40.7%	58.8%	41.2%
23,213	PERRY	8,040	5,444	2,596		2,848 R	67.7%	32.3%	67.7%	32.3%
1,931,334	PHILADELPHIA	885,297	425,962	432,699	26,636	6,737 D	48.1%	48.9%	49.6%	50.4%
7,452	PIKE	4,101	2,893	1,208		1,685 R	70.5%	29.5%	70.5%	29.5%
18,201	POTTER	5,401	3,672	1,729		1,943 R	68.0%	32.0%	68.0%	32.0%
228,331	SCHUYLKILL	73,492	44,176	28,194	1,122	15,982 R	60.1%	38.4%	61.0%	39.0%
20,208	SNYDER	6,671	5,181	1,490		3,691 R	77.7%	22.3%	77.7%	22.3%
84,957	SOMERSET	22,978	13,910	8,727	341	5,183 R	60.5%	38.0%	61.4%	38.6%
7,504	SULLIVAN	2,862	1,752	1,084	26	668 R	61.2%	37.9%	61.8%	38.2%
33,893	SUSQUEHANNA	11,716	7,945	3,621	150	4,324 R	67.8%	30.9%	68.7%	31.3%
35,004	TIOGA	13,002	10,016	2,986		7,030 R	77.0%	23.0%	77.0%	23.0%
20,247	UNION	6,587	5,058	1,442	87	3,616 R	76.8%	21.9%	77.8%	22.2%

PENNSYLVANIA

PRESIDENT 1948

1940 Census Population	County	Total Vote	Republican	Democratic	Other	Rep.-Dem. Plurality	Percentage Total Vote Rep.	Percentage Total Vote Dem.	Percentage Major Vote Rep.	Percentage Major Vote Dem.
63,958	VENANGO	17,536	11,920	5,144	472	6,776 R	68.0%	29.3%	69.9%	30.1%
42,789	WARREN	12,814	8,378	4,103	333	4,275 R	65.4%	32.0%	67.1%	32.9%
210,852	WASHINGTON	75,166	26,860	46,327	1,979	19,467 D	35.7%	61.6%	36.7%	63.3%
29,934	WAYNE	9,992	7,708	2,284		5,424 R	77.1%	22.9%	77.1%	22.9%
303,411	WESTMORELAND	106,814	41,709	61,901	3,204	20,192 D	39.0%	58.0%	40.3%	59.7%
16,702	WYOMING	6,127	4,332	1,674	121	2,658 R	70.7%	27.3%	72.1%	27.9%
178,022	YORK	68,678	32,494	33,321	2,863	827 D	47.3%	48.5%	49.4%	50.6%
9,900,180	TOTAL	3,735,348	1,902,197	1,752,426	80,725	149,771 R	50.9%	46.9%	52.0%	48.0%

PENNSYLVANIA

PRESIDENT 1944

							Percentage			
							Total Vote		Major Vote	
1940 Census Population	County	Total Vote	Republican	Democratic	Other	Rep.-Dem. Plurality	Rep.	Dem.	Rep.	Dem.
39,435	ADAMS	14,735	8,787	5,881	67	2,906 R	59.6%	39.9%	59.9%	40.1%
1,411,539	ALLEGHENY	614,301	261,218	350,690	2,393	89,472 D	42.5%	57.1%	42.7%	57.3%
81,087	ARMSTRONG	23,984	13,656	10,202	126	3,454 R	56.9%	42.5%	57.2%	42.8%
156,754	BEAVER	56,658	23,555	32,743	360	9,188 D	41.6%	57.8%	41.8%	58.2%
40,809	BEDFORD	13,946	8,703	5,175	68	3,528 R	62.4%	37.1%	62.7%	37.3%
241,884	BERKS	81,410	35,274	43,889	2,247	8,615 D	43.3%	53.9%	44.6%	55.4%
140,358	BLAIR	43,106	24,925	18,003	178	6,922 R	57.8%	41.8%	58.1%	41.9%
50,615	BRADFORD	19,137	13,472	5,523	142	7,949 R	70.4%	28.9%	70.9%	29.1%
107,715	BUCKS	43,727	25,634	17,823	270	7,811 R	58.6%	40.8%	59.0%	41.0%
87,590	BUTLER	31,944	19,341	12,377	226	6,964 R	60.5%	38.7%	61.0%	39.0%
213,459	CAMBRIA	68,143	28,203	39,676	264	11,473 D	41.4%	58.2%	41.5%	58.5%
6,852	CAMERON	2,853	1,729	1,115	9	614 R	60.6%	39.1%	60.8%	39.2%
61,735	CARBON	20,970	9,837	11,060	73	1,223 D	46.9%	52.7%	47.1%	52.9%
52,608	CENTRE	18,242	10,048	8,064	130	1,984 R	55.1%	44.2%	55.5%	44.5%
135,626	CHESTER	45,411	26,655	18,548	208	8,107 R	58.7%	40.8%	59.0%	41.0%
38,410	CLARION	13,460	8,098	5,263	99	2,835 R	60.2%	39.1%	60.6%	39.4%
92,094	CLEARFIELD	27,836	13,986	13,617	233	369 R	50.2%	48.9%	50.7%	49.3%
34,557	CLINTON	11,675	5,915	5,703	57	212 R	50.7%	48.8%	50.9%	49.1%
51,413	COLUMBIA	19,053	9,336	9,647	70	311 D	49.0%	50.6%	49.2%	50.8%
71,644	CRAWFORD	24,591	15,205	9,216	170	5,989 R	61.8%	37.5%	62.3%	37.7%
74,806	CUMBERLAND	29,984	17,782	12,068	134	5,714 R	59.3%	40.2%	59.6%	40.4%
177,410	DAUPHIN	75,742	44,725	30,684	333	14,041 R	59.0%	40.5%	59.3%	40.7%
310,756	DELAWARE	143,309	78,533	64,021	755	14,512 R	54.8%	44.7%	55.1%	44.9%
34,443	ELK	11,809	5,645	6,097	67	452 D	47.8%	51.6%	48.1%	51.9%
180,889	ERIE	68,578	35,247	32,912	419	2,335 R	51.4%	48.0%	51.7%	48.3%
200,999	FAYETTE	57,489	21,945	35,093	451	13,148 D	38.2%	61.0%	38.5%	61.5%
5,791	FOREST	2,038	1,344	673	21	671 R	65.9%	33.0%	66.6%	33.4%
69,378	FRANKLIN	22,250	13,380	8,807	63	4,573 R	60.1%	39.6%	60.3%	39.7%
10,673	FULTON	3,857	2,084	1,758	15	326 R	54.0%	45.6%	54.2%	45.8%
44,671	GREENE	14,192	5,747	8,392	53	2,645 D	40.5%	59.1%	40.6%	59.4%
41,836	HUNTINGDON	12,320	8,106	4,131	83	3,975 R	65.8%	33.5%	66.2%	33.8%
79,854	INDIANA	23,426	14,388	8,863	175	5,525 R	61.4%	37.8%	61.9%	38.1%
54,090	JEFFERSON	17,547	10,970	6,425	152	4,545 R	62.5%	36.6%	63.1%	36.9%
15,373	JUNIATA	6,193	3,512	2,666	15	846 R	56.7%	43.0%	56.8%	43.2%
301,243	LACKAWANNA	106,578	47,261	59,190	127	11,929 D	44.3%	55.5%	44.4%	55.6%
212,504	LANCASTER	72,673	44,888	27,353	432	17,535 R	61.8%	37.6%	62.1%	37.9%
96,877	LAWRENCE	36,620	18,886	17,331	403	1,555 R	51.6%	47.3%	52.1%	47.9%
72,641	LEBANON	27,153	15,206	11,818	129	3,388 R	56.0%	43.5%	56.3%	43.7%
177,533	LEHIGH	61,033	31,584	29,134	315	2,450 R	51.7%	47.7%	52.0%	48.0%
441,518	LUZERNE	142,199	67,984	73,674	541	5,690 D	47.8%	51.8%	48.0%	52.0%
93,633	LYCOMING	35,741	19,886	15,658	197	4,228 R	55.6%	43.8%	55.9%	44.1%
56,673	MCKEAN	18,601	11,988	6,492	121	5,496 R	64.4%	34.9%	64.9%	35.1%
101,039	MERCER	36,407	19,606	16,589	212	3,017 R	53.9%	45.6%	54.2%	45.8%
42,993	MIFFLIN	11,952	6,205	5,693	54	512 R	51.9%	47.6%	52.2%	47.8%
29,802	MONROE	11,729	6,202	5,490	37	712 R	52.9%	46.8%	53.0%	47.0%
289,247	MONTGOMERY	126,827	78,260	47,815	752	30,445 R	61.7%	37.7%	62.1%	37.9%
15,466	MONTOUR	4,947	2,727	2,212	8	515 R	55.1%	44.7%	55.2%	44.8%
168,959	NORTHAMPTON	59,519	26,643	32,584	292	5,941 D	44.8%	54.7%	45.0%	55.0%
126,887	NORTHUMBERLAND	42,450	21,995	20,333	122	1,662 R	51.8%	47.9%	52.0%	48.0%
23,213	PERRY	9,030	5,722	3,265	43	2,457 R	63.4%	36.2%	63.7%	36.3%
1,931,334	PHILADELPHIA	845,630	346,380	496,367	2,883	149,987 D	41.0%	58.7%	41.1%	58.9%
7,452	PIKE	4,101	2,674	1,408	19	1,266 R	65.2%	34.3%	65.5%	34.5%
18,201	POTTER	6,404	4,474	1,894	36	2,580 R	69.9%	29.6%	70.3%	29.7%
228,331	SCHUYLKILL	76,744	40,671	35,852	221	4,819 R	53.0%	46.7%	53.1%	46.9%
20,208	SNYDER	7,514	5,696	1,795	23	3,901 R	75.8%	23.9%	76.0%	24.0%
84,957	SOMERSET	26,405	16,039	10,287	79	5,752 R	60.7%	39.0%	60.9%	39.1%
7,504	SULLIVAN	3,195	1,858	1,329	8	529 R	58.2%	41.6%	58.3%	41.7%
33,893	SUSQUEHANNA	13,080	8,819	4,212	49	4,607 R	67.4%	32.2%	67.7%	32.3%
35,004	TIOGA	13,708	10,381	3,248	79	7,133 R	75.7%	23.7%	76.2%	23.8%
20,247	UNION	7,330	5,585	1,704	41	3,881 R	76.2%	23.2%	76.6%	23.4%

PENNSYLVANIA

PRESIDENT 1944

1940 Census Population	County	Total Vote	Republican	Democratic	Other	Rep.-Dem. Plurality	Percentage: Total Vote Rep.	Total Vote Dem.	Major Vote Rep.	Major Vote Dem.
63,958	VENANGO	21,646	14,916	6,426	304	8,490 R	68.9%	29.7%	69.9%	30.1%
42,789	WARREN	13,853	9,276	4,440	137	4,836 R	67.0%	32.1%	67.6%	32.4%
210,852	WASHINGTON	74,030	27,615	46,023	392	18,408 D	37.3%	62.2%	37.5%	62.5%
29,934	WAYNE	11,074	8,242	2,793	39	5,449 R	74.4%	25.2%	74.7%	25.3%
303,411	WESTMORELAND	104,964	43,202	61,057	705	17,855 D	41.2%	58.2%	41.4%	58.6%
16,702	WYOMING	6,582	4,581	1,982	19	2,599 R	69.6%	30.1%	69.8%	30.2%
178,022	YORK	71,158	32,617	38,226	315	5,609 D	45.8%	53.7%	46.0%	54.0%
9,900,180	TOTAL	3,794,793	1,835,054	1,940,479	19,260	105,425 D	48.4%	51.1%	48.6%	51.4%

PENNSYLVANIA

PRESIDENT 1940

1940 Census Population	County	Total Vote	Republican	Democratic	Other	Rep.-Dem. Plurality	Percentage Total Vote Rep.	Total Vote Dem.	Major Vote Rep.	Major Vote Dem.
39,435	ADAMS	15,983	8,609	7,354	20	1,255 R	53.9%	46.0%	53.9%	46.1%
1,411,539	ALLEGHENY	634,060	263,285	367,926	2,849	104,641 D	41.5%	58.0%	41.7%	58.3%
81,087	ARMSTRONG	26,728	14,524	12,144	60	2,380 R	54.3%	45.4%	54.5%	45.5%
156,754	BEAVER	58,172	24,324	33,609	239	9,285 D	41.8%	57.8%	42.0%	58.0%
40,809	BEDFORD	16,301	8,864	7,388	49	1,476 R	54.4%	45.3%	54.5%	45.5%
241,884	BERKS	86,934	32,111	53,301	1,522	21,190 D	36.9%	61.3%	37.6%	62.4%
140,358	BLAIR	48,318	26,639	21,573	106	5,066 R	55.1%	44.6%	55.3%	44.7%
50,615	BRADFORD	21,480	14,826	6,605	49	8,221 R	69.0%	30.7%	69.2%	30.8%
107,715	BUCKS	45,967	25,169	20,586	212	4,583 R	54.8%	44.8%	55.0%	45.0%
87,590	BUTLER	33,421	19,450	13,875	96	5,575 R	58.2%	41.5%	58.4%	41.6%
213,459	CAMBRIA	73,393	30,306	42,894	193	12,588 D	41.3%	58.4%	41.4%	58.6%
6,852	CAMERON	3,251	1,793	1,450	8	343 R	55.2%	44.6%	55.3%	44.7%
61,735	CARBON	23,446	10,618	12,777	51	2,159 D	45.3%	54.5%	45.4%	54.6%
52,608	CENTRE	20,602	10,665	9,869	68	796 R	51.8%	47.9%	51.9%	48.1%
135,626	CHESTER	50,869	28,222	22,473	174	5,749 R	55.5%	44.2%	55.7%	44.3%
38,410	CLARION	15,633	9,035	6,564	34	2,471 R	57.8%	42.0%	57.9%	42.1%
92,094	CLEARFIELD	33,260	15,407	17,705	148	2,298 D	46.3%	53.2%	46.5%	53.5%
34,557	CLINTON	13,732	6,291	7,419	22	1,128 D	45.8%	54.0%	45.9%	54.1%
51,413	COLUMBIA	22,062	9,518	12,523	21	3,005 D	43.1%	56.8%	43.2%	56.8%
71,644	CRAWFORD	26,203	15,891	10,197	115	5,694 R	60.6%	38.9%	60.9%	39.1%
74,806	CUMBERLAND	31,116	15,297	15,758	61	461 D	49.2%	50.6%	49.3%	50.7%
177,410	DAUPHIN	80,975	42,394	38,305	276	4,089 R	52.4%	47.3%	52.5%	47.5%
310,756	DELAWARE	140,917	80,158	60,225	534	19,933 R	56.9%	42.7%	57.1%	42.9%
34,443	ELK	13,900	6,949	6,920	31	29 R	50.0%	49.8%	50.1%	49.9%
180,889	ERIE	68,698	36,608	31,735	355	4,873 R	53.3%	46.2%	53.6%	46.4%
200,999	FAYETTE	66,114	23,908	41,960	246	18,052 D	36.2%	63.5%	36.3%	63.7%
5,791	FOREST	2,736	1,811	919	6	892 R	66.2%	33.6%	66.3%	33.7%
69,378	FRANKLIN	25,836	13,084	12,713	39	371 R	50.6%	49.2%	50.7%	49.3%
10,673	FULTON	4,095	2,108	1,982	5	126 R	51.5%	48.4%	51.5%	48.5%
44,671	GREENE	16,974	6,726	10,214	34	3,488 D	39.6%	60.2%	39.7%	60.3%
41,836	HUNTINGDON	14,830	9,141	5,631	58	3,510 R	61.6%	38.0%	61.9%	38.1%
79,854	INDIANA	27,650	15,547	12,035	68	3,512 R	56.2%	43.5%	56.4%	43.6%
54,090	JEFFERSON	20,687	12,081	8,559	47	3,522 R	58.4%	41.4%	58.5%	41.5%
15,373	JUNIATA	7,093	3,507	3,579	7	72 D	49.4%	50.5%	49.5%	50.5%
301,243	LACKAWANNA	126,685	54,931	71,343	411	16,412 D	43.4%	56.3%	43.5%	56.5%
212,504	LANCASTER	77,394	44,939	32,210	245	12,729 R	58.1%	41.6%	58.2%	41.8%
96,877	LAWRENCE	38,342	19,361	18,814	167	547 R	50.5%	49.1%	50.7%	49.3%
72,641	LEBANON	26,837	13,449	13,315	73	134 R	50.1%	49.6%	50.3%	49.7%
177,533	LEHIGH	62,947	29,584	33,007	356	3,423 D	47.0%	52.4%	47.3%	52.7%
441,518	LUZERNE	181,884	79,685	101,577	622	21,892 D	43.8%	55.8%	44.0%	56.0%
93,633	LYCOMING	39,877	21,423	18,363	91	3,060 R	53.7%	46.0%	53.8%	46.2%
56,673	MCKEAN	21,928	14,822	6,991	115	7,831 R	67.6%	31.9%	68.0%	32.0%
101,039	MERCER	38,201	21,058	16,968	175	4,090 R	55.1%	44.4%	55.4%	44.6%
42,993	MIFFLIN	13,369	6,352	6,993	24	641 D	47.5%	52.3%	47.6%	52.4%
29,802	MONROE	12,687	6,001	6,670	16	669 D	47.3%	52.6%	47.4%	52.6%
289,247	MONTGOMERY	123,062	73,250	49,409	403	23,841 R	59.5%	40.1%	59.7%	40.3%
15,466	MONTOUR	5,807	2,723	3,080	4	357 D	46.9%	53.0%	46.9%	53.1%
168,959	NORTHAMPTON	58,955	25,385	33,304	266	7,919 D	43.1%	56.5%	43.3%	56.7%
126,887	NORTHUMBERLAND	49,363	22,914	26,315	134	3,401 D	46.4%	53.3%	46.5%	53.5%
23,213	PERRY	10,489	5,877	4,601	11	1,276 R	56.0%	43.9%	56.1%	43.9%
1,931,334	PHILADELPHIA	891,486	354,878	532,149	4,459	177,271 D	39.8%	59.7%	40.0%	60.0%
7,452	PIKE	4,426	2,596	1,818	12	778 R	58.7%	41.1%	58.8%	41.2%
18,201	POTTER	7,963	5,205	2,731	27	2,474 R	65.4%	34.3%	65.6%	34.4%
228,331	SCHUYLKILL	92,475	43,505	48,739	231	5,234 D	47.0%	52.7%	47.2%	52.8%
20,208	SNYDER	8,214	5,722	2,478	14	3,244 R	69.7%	30.2%	69.8%	30.2%
84,957	SOMERSET	31,506	17,369	14,085	52	3,284 R	55.1%	44.7%	55.2%	44.8%
7,504	SULLIVAN	3,692	2,059	1,626	7	433 R	55.8%	44.0%	55.9%	44.1%
33,893	SUSQUEHANNA	14,938	9,520	5,383	35	4,137 R	63.7%	36.0%	63.9%	36.1%
35,004	TIOGA	16,119	11,645	4,434	40	7,211 R	72.2%	27.5%	72.4%	27.6%
20,247	UNION	7,854	5,612	2,220	22	3,392 R	71.5%	28.3%	71.7%	28.3%

PENNSYLVANIA

PRESIDENT 1940

1940 Census Population	County	Total Vote	Republican	Democratic	Other	Rep.-Dem. Plurality	Percentage Total Vote Rep.	Percentage Total Vote Dem.	Percentage Major Vote Rep.	Percentage Major Vote Dem.
63,958	VENANGO	24,639	17,728	6,873	38	10,855 R	72.0%	27.9%	72.1%	27.9%
42,789	WARREN	16,938	11,016	5,825	97	5,191 R	65.0%	34.4%	65.4%	34.6%
210,852	WASHINGTON	80,140	29,026	50,829	285	21,803 D	36.2%	63.4%	36.3%	63.7%
29,934	WAYNE	12,693	9,203	3,460	30	5,743 R	72.5%	27.3%	72.7%	27.3%
303,411	WESTMORELAND	107,787	42,643	64,567	577	21,924 D	39.6%	59.9%	39.8%	60.2%
16,702	WYOMING	7,837	5,273	2,548	16	2,725 R	67.3%	32.5%	67.4%	32.6%
178,022	YORK	69,917	30,228	39,543	146	9,315 D	43.2%	56.6%	43.3%	56.7%
9,900,180	TOTAL	4,078,714	1,889,848	2,171,035	17,831	281,187 D	46.3%	53.2%	46.5%	53.5%

PENNSYLVANIA

PRESIDENT 1936

1930 Census Population	County	Total Vote	Republican	Democratic	Other	Rep.-Dem. Plurality	Percentage Total Vote Rep.	Total Vote Dem.	Major Vote Rep.	Major Vote Dem.
37,128	ADAMS	17,410	8,313	8,336	761	23 D	47.7%	47.9%	49.9%	50.1%
1,374,410	ALLEGHENY	562,176	176,224	366,593	19,359	190,369 D	31.3%	65.2%	32.5%	67.5%
79,298	ARMSTRONG	30,434	14,198	15,955	281	1,757 D	46.7%	52.4%	47.1%	52.9%
149,062	BEAVER	58,312	20,223	37,205	884	16,982 D	34.7%	63.8%	35.2%	64.8%
37,309	BEDFORD	18,182	9,014	8,937	231	77 R	49.6%	49.2%	50.2%	49.8%
231,717	BERKS	88,327	26,699	56,907	4,721	30,208 D	30.2%	64.4%	31.9%	68.1%
139,840	BLAIR	52,597	24,711	27,038	848	2,327 D	47.0%	51.4%	47.8%	52.2%
49,039	BRADFORD	24,936	16,643	8,078	215	8,565 R	66.7%	32.4%	67.3%	32.7%
96,727	BUCKS	48,895	23,860	24,159	876	299 D	48.8%	49.4%	49.7%	50.3%
80,480	BUTLER	33,309	16,772	16,008	529	764 R	50.4%	48.1%	51.2%	48.8%
203,146	CAMBRIA	72,304	24,378	46,687	1,239	22,309 D	33.7%	64.6%	34.3%	65.7%
5,307	CAMERON	3,385	1,801	1,538	46	263 R	53.2%	45.4%	53.9%	46.1%
63,380	CARBON	25,811	11,298	14,179	334	2,881 D	43.8%	54.9%	44.3%	55.7%
46,294	CENTRE	21,814	9,869	11,734	211	1,865 D	45.2%	53.8%	45.7%	54.3%
126,629	CHESTER	56,629	29,340	26,676	613	2,664 R	51.8%	47.1%	52.4%	47.6%
34,531	CLARION	17,189	8,477	8,412	300	65 R	49.3%	48.9%	50.2%	49.8%
86,727	CLEARFIELD	36,050	14,531	20,799	720	6,268 D	40.3%	57.7%	41.1%	58.9%
32,319	CLINTON	14,969	6,479	8,351	139	1,872 D	43.3%	55.8%	43.7%	56.3%
48,803	COLUMBIA	24,108	9,674	14,141	293	4,467 D	40.1%	58.7%	40.6%	59.4%
62,980	CRAWFORD	28,189	14,463	12,788	938	1,675 R	51.3%	45.4%	53.1%	46.9%
68,236	CUMBERLAND	34,021	14,912	18,850	259	3,938 D	43.8%	55.4%	44.2%	55.8%
165,231	DAUPHIN	83,500	39,598	43,256	646	3,658 D	47.4%	51.8%	47.8%	52.2%
280,264	DELAWARE	143,013	74,899	65,117	2,997	9,782 R	52.4%	45.5%	53.5%	46.5%
33,431	ELK	15,631	5,489	9,035	1,107	3,546 D	35.1%	57.8%	37.8%	62.2%
175,277	ERIE	65,345	25,607	33,042	6,696	7,435 D	39.2%	50.6%	43.7%	56.3%
198,542	FAYETTE	71,144	21,984	48,291	869	26,307 D	30.9%	67.9%	31.3%	68.7%
5,180	FOREST	2,953	1,757	1,157	39	600 R	59.5%	39.2%	60.3%	39.7%
65,010	FRANKLIN	29,413	13,616	15,632	165	2,016 D	46.3%	53.1%	46.6%	53.4%
9,231	FULTON	4,531	2,085	2,431	15	346 D	46.0%	53.7%	46.2%	53.8%
41,767	GREENE	18,474	6,359	12,006	109	5,647 D	34.4%	65.0%	34.6%	65.4%
39,021	HUNTINGDON	17,392	9,815	7,429	148	2,386 R	56.4%	42.7%	56.9%	43.1%
75,395	INDIANA	32,177	16,530	15,353	294	1,177 R	51.4%	47.7%	51.8%	48.2%
52,114	JEFFERSON	23,306	11,943	11,080	283	863 R	51.2%	47.5%	51.9%	48.1%
14,325	JUNIATA	7,407	3,576	3,782	49	206 D	48.3%	51.1%	48.6%	51.4%
310,397	LACKAWANNA	133,801	51,186	80,585	2,030	29,399 D	38.3%	60.2%	38.8%	61.2%
196,882	LANCASTER	82,273	42,272	38,454	1,547	3,818 R	51.4%	46.7%	52.4%	47.6%
97,258	LAWRENCE	38,090	15,458	21,994	638	6,536 D	40.6%	57.7%	41.3%	58.7%
67,103	LEBANON	27,476	13,213	13,800	463	587 D	48.1%	50.2%	48.9%	51.1%
172,893	LEHIGH	62,621	25,841	35,325	1,455	9,484 D	41.3%	56.4%	42.2%	57.8%
445,109	LUZERNE	188,479	81,672	104,809	1,998	23,137 D	43.3%	55.6%	43.8%	56.2%
93,421	LYCOMING	38,280	18,315	19,376	589	1,061 D	47.8%	50.6%	48.6%	51.4%
55,167	MCKEAN	22,181	11,837	9,733	611	2,104 R	53.4%	43.9%	54.9%	45.1%
99,246	MERCER	40,311	18,493	20,879	939	2,386 D	45.9%	51.8%	47.0%	53.0%
40,335	MIFFLIN	16,525	6,867	9,581	77	2,714 D	41.6%	58.0%	41.7%	58.3%
28,286	MONROE	14,079	5,778	8,212	89	2,434 D	41.0%	58.3%	41.3%	58.7%
265,804	MONTGOMERY	126,506	66,442	57,870	2,194	8,572 R	52.5%	45.7%	53.4%	46.6%
14,517	MONTOUR	5,914	2,350	3,534	30	1,184 D	39.7%	59.8%	39.9%	60.1%
169,304	NORTHAMPTON	61,136	22,827	36,871	1,438	14,044 D	37.3%	60.3%	38.2%	61.8%
128,504	NORTHUMBERLAND	54,318	21,758	31,849	711	10,091 D	40.1%	58.6%	40.6%	59.4%
21,744	PERRY	11,600	5,759	5,780	61	21 D	49.6%	49.8%	49.9%	50.1%
1,950,961	PHILADELPHIA	892,750	329,881	539,757	23,112	209,876 D	37.0%	60.5%	37.9%	62.1%
7,483	PIKE	4,741	2,304	2,396	41	92 D	48.6%	50.5%	49.0%	51.0%
17,489	POTTER	8,926	5,172	3,553	201	1,619 R	57.9%	39.8%	59.3%	40.7%
235,505	SCHUYLKILL	100,921	44,353	55,183	1,385	10,830 D	43.9%	54.7%	44.6%	55.4%
18,836	SNYDER	8,598	5,550	2,999	49	2,551 R	64.5%	34.9%	64.9%	35.1%
80,764	SOMERSET	33,741	17,375	16,184	182	1,191 R	51.5%	48.0%	51.8%	48.2%
7,499	SULLIVAN	3,922	2,121	1,740	61	381 R	54.1%	44.4%	54.9%	45.1%
33,806	SUSQUEHANNA	16,534	9,745	6,520	269	3,225 R	58.9%	39.4%	59.9%	40.1%
31,871	TIOGA	18,108	12,567	5,442	99	7,125 R	69.4%	30.1%	69.8%	30.2%
17,468	UNION	8,602	5,589	2,946	67	2,643 R	65.0%	34.2%	65.5%	34.5%

PENNSYLVANIA

PRESIDENT 1936

1930 Census Population	County	Total Vote	Republican	Democratic	Other	Rep.-Dem. Plurality	Percentage Total Vote Rep.	Percentage Total Vote Dem.	Percentage Major Vote Rep.	Percentage Major Vote Dem.
63,226	VENANGO	27,563	17,676	9,212	675	8,464 R	64.1%	33.4%	65.7%	34.3%
41,453	WARREN	18,767	9,440	8,495	832	945 R	50.3%	45.3%	52.6%	47.4%
204,802	WASHINGTON	77,168	23,342	52,878	948	29,536 D	30.2%	68.5%	30.6%	69.4%
28,420	WAYNE	14,380	9,347	4,864	169	4,483 R	65.0%	33.8%	65.8%	34.2%
294,995	WESTMORELAND	111,937	36,079	73,574	2,284	37,495 D	32.2%	65.7%	32.9%	67.1%
15,517	WYOMING	8,687	5,321	3,269	97	2,052 R	61.3%	37.6%	61.9%	38.1%
167,135	YORK	75,837	29,233	45,142	1,462	15,909 D	38.5%	59.5%	39.3%	60.7%
9,631,350	TOTAL	4,138,105	1,690,300	2,353,788	94,017	663,488 D	40.8%	56.9%	41.8%	58.2%

PENNSYLVANIA

PRESIDENT 1932

1930 Census Population	County	Total Vote	Republican	Democratic	Other	Rep.-Dem. Plurality	Percentage Total Vote Rep.	Total Vote Dem.	Major Vote Rep.	Major Vote Dem.
37,128	ADAMS	13,494	6,084	7,185	225	1,101 D	45.1%	53.2%	45.9%	54.1%
1,374,410	ALLEGHENY	359,003	152,326	189,839	16,838	37,513 D	42.4%	52.9%	44.5%	55.5%
79,298	ARMSTRONG	20,890	10,884	9,230	776	1,654 R	52.1%	44.2%	54.1%	45.9%
149,062	BEAVER	41,260	19,751	19,805	1,704	54 D	47.9%	48.0%	49.9%	50.1%
37,309	BEDFORD	12,152	6,597	5,075	480	1,522 R	54.3%	41.8%	56.5%	43.5%
231,717	BERKS	73,023	27,073	29,763	16,187	2,690 D	37.1%	40.8%	47.6%	52.4%
139,840	BLAIR	34,334	19,553	13,709	1,072	5,844 R	56.9%	39.9%	58.8%	41.2%
49,039	BRADFORD	18,188	11,521	5,970	697	5,551 R	63.3%	32.8%	65.9%	34.1%
96,727	BUCKS	37,807	22,331	14,135	1,341	8,196 R	59.1%	37.4%	61.2%	38.8%
80,480	BUTLER	21,075	11,543	8,717	815	2,826 R	54.8%	41.4%	57.0%	43.0%
203,146	CAMBRIA	51,145	21,351	28,197	1,597	6,846 D	41.7%	55.1%	43.1%	56.9%
5,307	CAMERON	2,236	1,438	748	50	690 R	64.3%	33.5%	65.8%	34.2%
63,380	CARBON	20,441	9,918	9,874	649	44 R	48.5%	48.3%	50.1%	49.9%
46,294	CENTRE	15,726	8,264	7,053	409	1,211 R	52.5%	44.8%	54.0%	46.0%
126,629	CHESTER	42,517	29,425	12,040	1,052	17,385 R	69.2%	28.3%	71.0%	29.0%
34,531	CLARION	13,011	5,991	6,651	369	660 D	46.0%	51.1%	47.4%	52.6%
86,727	CLEARFIELD	22,597	10,500	11,209	888	709 D	46.5%	49.6%	48.4%	51.6%
32,319	CLINTON	8,894	4,851	3,741	302	1,110 R	54.5%	42.1%	56.5%	43.5%
48,803	COLUMBIA	19,787	8,791	10,640	356	1,849 D	44.4%	53.8%	45.2%	54.8%
62,980	CRAWFORD	21,111	10,918	9,382	811	1,536 R	51.7%	44.4%	53.8%	46.2%
68,236	CUMBERLAND	25,751	13,098	12,086	567	1,012 R	50.9%	46.9%	52.0%	48.0%
165,231	DAUPHIN	60,152	36,278	22,412	1,462	13,866 R	60.3%	37.3%	61.8%	38.2%
280,264	DELAWARE	110,409	75,291	32,413	2,705	42,878 R	68.2%	29.4%	69.9%	30.1%
33,431	ELK	12,497	5,797	6,461	239	664 D	46.4%	51.7%	47.3%	52.7%
175,277	ERIE	40,442	18,371	19,592	2,479	1,221 D	45.4%	48.4%	48.4%	51.6%
198,542	FAYETTE	45,106	15,903	27,662	1,541	11,759 D	35.3%	61.3%	36.5%	63.5%
5,180	FOREST	1,721	1,090	569	62	521 R	63.3%	33.1%	65.7%	34.3%
65,010	FRANKLIN	20,757	10,992	9,338	427	1,654 R	53.0%	45.0%	54.1%	45.9%
9,231	FULTON	3,371	1,410	1,921	40	511 D	41.8%	57.0%	42.3%	57.7%
41,767	GREENE	14,393	4,808	9,322	263	4,514 D	33.4%	64.8%	34.0%	66.0%
39,021	HUNTINGDON	11,103	7,371	3,426	306	3,945 R	66.4%	30.9%	68.3%	31.7%
75,395	INDIANA	22,235	12,727	8,606	902	4,121 R	57.2%	38.7%	59.7%	40.3%
52,114	JEFFERSON	15,713	8,246	6,570	897	1,676 R	52.5%	41.8%	55.7%	44.3%
14,325	JUNIATA	5,681	2,752	2,805	124	53 D	48.4%	49.4%	49.5%	50.5%
310,397	LACKAWANNA	76,560	34,632	40,793	1,135	6,161 D	45.2%	53.3%	45.9%	54.1%
196,882	LANCASTER	61,019	34,502	24,406	2,111	10,096 R	56.5%	40.0%	58.6%	41.4%
97,258	LAWRENCE	23,709	13,064	9,390	1,255	3,674 R	55.1%	39.6%	58.2%	41.8%
67,103	LEBANON	17,784	10,487	5,924	1,373	4,563 R	59.0%	33.3%	63.9%	36.1%
172,893	LEHIGH	45,093	21,169	21,939	1,985	770 D	46.9%	48.7%	49.1%	50.9%
445,109	LUZERNE	115,928	52,672	60,975	2,281	8,303 D	45.4%	52.6%	46.3%	53.7%
93,421	LYCOMING	29,250	16,212	11,499	1,539	4,713 R	55.4%	39.3%	58.5%	41.5%
55,167	MCKEAN	15,335	9,970	4,661	704	5,309 R	65.0%	30.4%	68.1%	31.9%
99,246	MERCER	26,258	14,057	10,961	1,240	3,096 R	53.5%	41.7%	56.2%	43.8%
40,335	MIFFLIN	9,372	5,525	3,654	193	1,871 R	59.0%	39.0%	60.2%	39.8%
28,286	MONROE	11,199	4,659	6,357	183	1,698 D	41.6%	56.8%	42.3%	57.7%
265,804	MONTGOMERY	100,961	64,619	32,971	3,371	31,648 R	64.0%	32.7%	66.2%	33.8%
14,517	MONTOUR	4,880	2,159	2,677	44	518 D	44.2%	54.9%	44.6%	55.4%
169,304	NORTHAMPTON	46,133	20,779	24,009	1,345	3,230 D	45.0%	52.0%	46.4%	53.6%
128,504	NORTHUMBERLAND	42,464	17,982	23,114	1,368	5,132 D	42.3%	54.4%	43.8%	56.2%
21,744	PERRY	8,269	4,402	3,733	134	669 R	53.2%	45.1%	54.1%	45.9%
1,950,961	PHILADELPHIA	607,014	331,092	260,276	15,646	70,816 R	54.5%	42.9%	56.0%	44.0%
7,483	PIKE	3,558	1,649	1,844	65	195 D	46.3%	51.8%	47.2%	52.8%
17,489	POTTER	6,573	3,847	2,271	455	1,576 R	58.5%	34.6%	62.9%	37.1%
235,505	SCHUYLKILL	69,305	32,492	35,023	1,790	2,531 D	46.9%	50.5%	48.1%	51.9%
18,836	SNYDER	5,766	3,423	2,176	167	1,247 R	59.4%	37.7%	61.1%	38.9%
80,764	SOMERSET	20,249	11,857	7,919	473	3,938 R	58.6%	39.1%	60.0%	40.0%
7,499	SULLIVAN	3,115	1,457	1,602	56	145 D	46.8%	51.4%	47.6%	52.4%
33,806	SUSQUEHANNA	12,295	6,884	5,171	240	1,713 R	56.0%	42.1%	57.1%	42.9%
31,871	TIOGA	12,778	9,583	3,004	191	6,579 R	75.0%	23.5%	76.1%	23.9%
17,468	UNION	5,734	3,534	1,948	252	1,586 R	61.6%	34.0%	64.5%	35.5%

PENNSYLVANIA

PRESIDENT 1932

1930 Census Population	County	Total Vote	Republican	Democratic	Other	Rep.-Dem. Plurality	Percentage Total Vote Rep.	Percentage Total Vote Dem.	Percentage Major Vote Rep.	Percentage Major Vote Dem.
63,226	VENANGO	19,088	12,230	6,174	684	6,056 R	64.1%	32.3%	66.5%	33.5%
41,453	WARREN	13,753	7,872	5,254	627	2,618 R	57.2%	38.2%	60.0%	40.0%
204,802	WASHINGTON	52,536	21,447	28,934	2,155	7,487 D	40.8%	55.1%	42.6%	57.4%
28,420	WAYNE	10,111	6,215	3,666	230	2,549 R	61.5%	36.3%	62.9%	37.1%
294,995	WESTMORELAND	80,651	30,426	45,436	4,789	15,010 D	37.7%	56.3%	40.1%	59.9%
15,517	WYOMING	6,841	3,968	2,728	145	1,240 R	58.0%	39.9%	59.3%	40.7%
167,135	YORK	57,365	25,430	29,313	2,622	3,883 D	44.3%	51.1%	46.5%	53.5%
9,631,350	TOTAL	2,859,021	1,453,540	1,295,948	109,533	157,592 R	50.8%	45.3%	52.9%	47.1%

PENNSYLVANIA

PRESIDENT 1928

1920 Census Population	County	Total Vote	Republican	Democratic	Other	Rep.-Dem. Plurality	Percentage Total Vote Rep.	Total Vote Dem.	Major Vote Rep.	Major Vote Dem.
34,583	ADAMS	14,349	9,656	4,635	58	5,021 R	67.3%	32.3%	67.6%	32.4%
1,185,808	ALLEGHENY	379,209	215,626	160,733	2,850	54,893 R	56.9%	42.4%	57.3%	42.7%
75,568	ARMSTRONG	22,636	17,625	4,824	187	12,801 R	77.9%	21.3%	78.5%	21.5%
111,621	BEAVER	40,217	27,949	11,868	400	16,081 R	69.5%	29.5%	70.2%	29.8%
38,277	BEDFORD	11,767	9,602	1,966	199	7,636 R	81.6%	16.7%	83.0%	17.0%
200,854	BERKS	73,514	47,073	18,960	7,481	28,113 R	64.0%	25.8%	71.3%	28.7%
128,334	BLAIR	46,726	34,356	12,104	266	22,252 R	73.5%	25.9%	73.9%	26.1%
53,166	BRADFORD	21,609	17,251	4,281	77	12,970 R	79.8%	19.8%	80.1%	19.9%
82,476	BUCKS	37,168	28,421	8,446	301	19,975 R	76.5%	22.7%	77.1%	22.9%
77,270	BUTLER	26,327	19,880	6,283	164	13,597 R	75.5%	23.9%	76.0%	24.0%
197,839	CAMBRIA	56,945	29,494	27,024	427	2,470 R	51.8%	47.5%	52.2%	47.8%
6,297	CAMERON	2,071	1,564	501	6	1,063 R	75.5%	24.2%	75.7%	24.3%
62,565	CARBON	23,155	15,047	8,010	98	7,037 R	65.0%	34.6%	65.3%	34.7%
44,304	CENTRE	15,557	12,005	3,431	121	8,574 R	77.2%	22.1%	77.8%	22.2%
115,120	CHESTER	44,558	36,659	7,689	210	28,970 R	82.3%	17.3%	82.7%	17.3%
36,170	CLARION	13,038	9,183	3,746	109	5,437 R	70.4%	28.7%	71.0%	29.0%
103,236	CLEARFIELD	24,859	16,719	7,870	270	8,849 R	67.3%	31.7%	68.0%	32.0%
33,555	CLINTON	11,029	8,120	2,849	60	5,271 R	73.6%	25.8%	74.0%	26.0%
48,349	COLUMBIA	19,781	14,362	5,304	115	9,058 R	72.6%	26.8%	73.0%	27.0%
60,667	CRAWFORD	23,989	17,072	6,718	199	10,354 R	71.2%	28.0%	71.8%	28.2%
58,578	CUMBERLAND	24,551	19,170	5,189	192	13,981 R	78.1%	21.1%	78.7%	21.3%
153,116	DAUPHIN	58,617	49,108	9,115	394	39,993 R	83.8%	15.6%	84.3%	15.7%
173,084	DELAWARE	112,941	83,092	29,378	471	53,714 R	73.6%	26.0%	73.9%	26.1%
34,981	ELK	13,009	5,234	7,705	70	2,471 D	40.2%	59.2%	40.5%	59.5%
153,536	ERIE	50,097	30,542	19,278	277	11,264 R	61.0%	38.5%	61.3%	38.7%
188,104	FAYETTE	47,183	27,693	19,063	427	8,630 R	58.7%	40.4%	59.2%	40.8%
7,477	FOREST	2,018	1,707	289	22	1,418 R	84.6%	14.3%	85.5%	14.5%
62,275	FRANKLIN	19,518	16,345	3,027	146	13,318 R	83.7%	15.5%	84.4%	15.6%
9,617	FULTON	3,261	2,179	1,054	28	1,125 R	66.8%	32.3%	67.4%	32.6%
30,804	GREENE	12,299	6,910	5,293	96	1,617 R	56.2%	43.0%	56.6%	43.4%
39,848	HUNTINGDON	11,502	9,920	1,470	112	8,450 R	86.2%	12.8%	87.1%	12.9%
80,910	INDIANA	21,768	16,706	4,810	252	11,896 R	76.7%	22.1%	77.6%	22.4%
62,104	JEFFERSON	17,731	13,233	4,325	173	8,908 R	74.6%	24.4%	75.4%	24.6%
14,464	JUNIATA	5,361	4,396	919	46	3,477 R	82.0%	17.1%	82.7%	17.3%
286,311	LACKAWANNA	99,269	46,510	52,665	94	6,155 D	46.9%	53.1%	46.9%	53.1%
173,797	LANCASTER	68,192	55,530	12,146	516	43,384 R	81.4%	17.8%	82.1%	17.9%
85,545	LAWRENCE	26,702	20,012	6,417	273	13,595 R	74.9%	24.0%	75.7%	24.3%
63,152	LEBANON	20,464	16,841	3,278	345	13,563 R	82.3%	16.0%	83.7%	16.3%
148,101	LEHIGH	54,188	40,291	13,463	434	26,828 R	74.4%	24.8%	75.0%	25.0%
390,991	LUZERNE	141,411	67,872	73,319	220	5,447 D	48.0%	51.8%	48.1%	51.9%
83,100	LYCOMING	36,137	28,720	7,132	285	21,588 R	79.5%	19.7%	80.1%	19.9%
48,934	MCKEAN	19,066	14,012	4,964	90	9,048 R	73.5%	26.0%	73.8%	26.2%
93,788	MERCER	31,083	22,599	8,204	280	14,395 R	72.7%	26.4%	73.4%	26.6%
31,439	MIFFLIN	10,270	8,932	1,270	68	7,662 R	87.0%	12.4%	87.6%	12.4%
24,295	MONROE	10,762	7,469	3,266	27	4,203 R	69.4%	30.3%	69.6%	30.4%
199,310	MONTGOMERY	100,408	76,680	23,026	702	53,654 R	76.4%	22.9%	76.9%	23.1%
14,080	MONTOUR	5,150	3,692	1,445	13	2,247 R	71.7%	28.1%	71.9%	28.1%
153,506	NORTHAMPTON	52,575	37,403	14,768	404	22,635 R	71.1%	28.1%	71.7%	28.3%
122,079	NORTHUMBERLAND	50,490	30,949	19,249	292	11,700 R	61.3%	38.1%	61.7%	38.3%
22,875	PERRY	8,330	6,469	1,807	54	4,662 R	77.7%	21.7%	78.2%	21.8%
1,823,779	PHILADELPHIA	700,596	420,320	276,573	3,703	143,747 R	60.0%	39.5%	60.3%	39.7%
6,818	PIKE	3,395	2,354	1,024	17	1,330 R	69.3%	30.2%	69.7%	30.3%
21,089	POTTER	7,111	5,653	1,416	42	4,237 R	79.5%	19.9%	80.0%	20.0%
217,754	SCHUYLKILL	86,768	46,033	40,424	311	5,609 R	53.1%	46.6%	53.2%	46.8%
17,129	SNYDER	6,527	5,693	805	29	4,888 R	87.2%	12.3%	87.6%	12.4%
82,112	SOMERSET	21,057	16,404	4,489	164	11,915 R	77.9%	21.3%	78.5%	21.5%
9,520	SULLIVAN	3,162	2,044	1,101	17	943 R	64.6%	34.8%	65.0%	35.0%
34,763	SUSQUEHANNA	13,861	9,445	4,353	63	5,092 R	68.1%	31.4%	68.5%	31.5%
37,118	TIOGA	13,498	11,774	1,688	36	10,086 R	87.2%	12.5%	87.5%	12.5%
15,850	UNION	6,527	5,708	765	54	4,943 R	87.5%	11.7%	88.2%	11.8%

PENNSYLVANIA

PRESIDENT 1928

1920 Census Population	County	Total Vote	Republican	Democratic	Other	Rep.-Dem. Plurality	Percentage Total Vote Rep.	Percentage Total Vote Dem.	Percentage Major Vote Rep.	Percentage Major Vote Dem.
59,184	VENANGO	22,089	17,450	4,531	108	12,919 R	79.0%	20.5%	79.4%	20.6%
40,024	WARREN	15,056	12,077	2,835	144	9,242 R	80.2%	18.8%	81.0%	19.0%
188,992	WASHINGTON	48,893	31,099	17,149	645	13,950 R	63.6%	35.1%	64.5%	35.5%
27,435	WAYNE	11,783	8,576	3,148	59	5,428 R	72.8%	26.7%	73.1%	26.9%
273,568	WESTMORELAND	83,643	51,760	30,587	1,296	21,173 R	61.9%	36.6%	62.9%	37.1%
14,101	WYOMING	6,260	5,321	906	33	4,415 R	85.0%	14.5%	85.5%	14.5%
144,521	YORK	57,529	45,791	11,216	522	34,575 R	79.6%	19.5%	80.3%	19.7%
8,720,017	TOTAL	3,150,612	2,055,382	1,067,586	27,644	987,796 R	65.2%	33.9%	65.8%	34.2%

PENNSYLVANIA

PRESIDENT 1924

1920 Census Population	County	Total Vote	Republican	Democratic	Other	Rep.-Dem. Plurality	Percentage Total Vote Rep.	Total Vote Dem.	Major Vote Rep.	Major Vote Dem.
34,583	ADAMS	10,918	5,778	4,840	300	938 R	52.9%	44.3%	54.4%	45.6%
1,185,808	ALLEGHENY	253,013	149,296	21,984	81,733	127,312 R	59.0%	8.7%	87.2%	12.8%
75,568	ARMSTRONG	17,439	11,192	2,931	3,316	8,261 R	64.2%	16.8%	79.2%	20.8%
111,621	BEAVER	26,141	16,768	3,220	6,153	13,548 R	64.1%	12.3%	83.9%	16.1%
38,277	BEDFORD	9,971	6,154	2,315	1,502	3,839 R	61.7%	23.2%	72.7%	27.3%
200,854	BERKS	54,893	28,186	17,220	9,487	10,966 R	51.3%	31.4%	62.1%	37.9%
128,334	BLAIR	30,808	20,313	4,244	6,251	16,069 R	65.9%	13.8%	82.7%	17.3%
53,166	BRADFORD	15,784	11,620	2,307	1,857	9,313 R	73.6%	14.6%	83.4%	16.6%
82,476	BUCKS	26,108	17,460	6,582	2,066	10,878 R	66.9%	25.2%	72.6%	27.4%
77,270	BUTLER	18,880	13,113	3,462	2,305	9,651 R	69.5%	18.3%	79.1%	20.9%
197,839	CAMBRIA	47,764	24,728	13,563	9,473	11,165 R	51.8%	28.4%	64.6%	35.4%
6,297	CAMERON	1,770	1,366	260	144	1,106 R	77.2%	14.7%	84.0%	16.0%
62,565	CARBON	18,427	10,236	5,150	3,041	5,086 R	55.5%	27.9%	66.5%	33.5%
44,304	CENTRE	13,062	7,723	4,443	896	3,280 R	59.1%	34.0%	63.5%	36.5%
115,120	CHESTER	29,480	22,333	5,946	1,201	16,387 R	75.8%	20.2%	79.0%	21.0%
36,170	CLARION	10,698	5,913	3,642	1,143	2,271 R	55.3%	34.0%	61.9%	38.1%
103,236	CLEARFIELD	22,787	13,745	5,027	4,015	8,718 R	60.3%	22.1%	73.2%	26.8%
33,555	CLINTON	9,391	5,129	1,939	2,323	3,190 R	54.6%	20.6%	72.6%	27.4%
48,349	COLUMBIA	15,469	7,336	7,390	743	54 D	47.4%	47.8%	49.8%	50.2%
60,667	CRAWFORD	17,305	10,918	2,969	3,418	7,949 R	63.1%	17.2%	78.6%	21.4%
58,578	CUMBERLAND	19,160	10,196	7,643	1,321	2,553 R	53.2%	39.9%	57.2%	42.8%
153,116	DAUPHIN	40,916	27,838	9,004	4,074	18,834 R	68.0%	22.0%	75.6%	24.4%
173,084	DELAWARE	51,345	41,998	6,368	2,979	35,630 R	81.8%	12.4%	86.8%	13.2%
34,981	ELK	9,352	6,626	1,370	1,356	5,256 R	70.9%	14.6%	82.9%	17.1%
153,536	ERIE	31,784	19,480	3,502	8,802	15,978 R	61.3%	11.0%	84.8%	15.2%
188,104	FAYETTE	35,587	19,064	8,855	7,668	10,209 R	53.6%	24.9%	68.3%	31.7%
7,477	FOREST	1,587	1,130	280	177	850 R	71.2%	17.6%	80.1%	19.9%
62,275	FRANKLIN	16,645	9,791	5,770	1,084	4,021 R	58.8%	34.7%	62.9%	37.1%
9,617	FULTON	2,435	1,160	1,207	68	47 D	47.6%	49.6%	49.0%	51.0%
30,804	GREENE	10,976	4,590	5,874	512	1,284 D	41.8%	53.5%	43.9%	56.1%
39,848	HUNTINGDON	8,875	6,567	1,488	820	5,079 R	74.0%	16.8%	81.5%	18.5%
80,910	INDIANA	18,277	12,748	2,067	3,462	10,681 R	69.7%	11.3%	86.0%	14.0%
62,104	JEFFERSON	16,450	10,673	2,664	3,113	8,009 R	64.9%	16.2%	80.0%	20.0%
14,464	JUNIATA	3,792	2,177	1,420	195	757 R	57.4%	37.4%	60.5%	39.5%
286,311	LACKAWANNA	62,401	37,708	16,859	7,834	20,849 R	60.4%	27.0%	69.1%	30.9%
173,797	LANCASTER	58,034	42,787	12,091	3,156	30,696 R	73.7%	20.8%	78.0%	22.0%
85,545	LAWRENCE	19,406	12,533	1,880	4,993	10,653 R	64.6%	9.7%	87.0%	13.0%
63,152	LEBANON	12,783	9,494	2,464	825	7,030 R	74.3%	19.3%	79.4%	20.6%
148,101	LEHIGH	35,284	20,826	10,415	4,043	10,411 R	59.0%	29.5%	66.7%	33.3%
390,991	LUZERNE	87,396	46,475	20,472	20,449	26,003 R	53.2%	23.4%	69.4%	30.6%
83,100	LYCOMING	23,916	14,039	6,857	3,020	7,182 R	58.7%	28.7%	67.2%	32.8%
48,934	MCKEAN	13,149	9,072	2,376	1,701	6,696 R	69.0%	18.1%	79.2%	20.8%
93,788	MERCER	22,420	14,639	3,688	4,093	10,951 R	65.3%	16.4%	79.9%	20.1%
31,439	MIFFLIN	7,143	4,780	1,999	364	2,781 R	66.9%	28.0%	70.5%	29.5%
24,295	MONROE	7,819	3,462	3,901	456	439 D	44.3%	49.9%	47.0%	53.0%
199,310	MONTGOMERY	60,154	45,407	11,094	3,653	34,313 R	75.5%	18.4%	80.4%	19.6%
14,080	MONTOUR	4,476	2,499	1,799	178	700 R	55.8%	40.2%	58.1%	41.9%
153,506	NORTHAMPTON	35,022	20,459	11,459	3,104	9,000 R	58.4%	32.7%	64.1%	35.9%
122,079	NORTHUMBERLAND	31,177	17,516	7,571	6,090	9,945 R	56.2%	24.3%	69.8%	30.2%
22,875	PERRY	7,276	4,185	2,710	381	1,475 R	57.5%	37.2%	60.7%	39.3%
1,823,779	PHILADELPHIA	447,022	347,457	54,213	45,352	293,244 R	77.7%	12.1%	86.5%	13.5%
6,818	PIKE	2,917	1,581	993	343	588 R	54.2%	34.0%	61.4%	38.6%
21,089	POTTER	6,241	4,087	1,161	993	2,926 R	65.5%	18.6%	77.9%	22.1%
217,754	SCHUYLKILL	53,656	34,578	10,111	8,967	24,467 R	64.4%	18.8%	77.4%	22.6%
17,129	SNYDER	4,243	3,055	970	218	2,085 R	72.0%	22.9%	75.9%	24.1%
82,112	SOMERSET	17,032	12,389	2,315	2,328	10,074 R	72.7%	13.6%	84.3%	15.7%
9,520	SULLIVAN	2,791	1,668	913	210	755 R	59.8%	32.7%	64.6%	35.4%
34,763	SUSQUEHANNA	10,784	7,266	2,208	1,310	5,058 R	67.4%	20.5%	76.7%	23.3%
37,118	TIOGA	10,406	8,452	1,271	683	7,181 R	81.2%	12.2%	86.9%	13.1%
15,850	UNION	5,178	3,707	1,209	262	2,498 R	71.6%	23.3%	75.4%	24.6%

PENNSYLVANIA

PRESIDENT 1924

1920 Census Population	County	Total Vote	Republican	Democratic	Other	Rep.-Dem. Plurality	Percentage Total Vote Rep.	Percentage Total Vote Dem.	Percentage Major Vote Rep.	Percentage Major Vote Dem.
59,184	VENANGO	14,592	10,841	1,886	1,865	8,955 R	74.3%	12.9%	85.2%	14.8%
40,024	WARREN	11,986	8,502	2,161	1,323	6,341 R	70.9%	18.0%	79.7%	20.3%
188,992	WASHINGTON	36,797	22,315	6,706	7,776	15,609 R	60.6%	18.2%	76.9%	23.1%
27,435	WAYNE	7,655	5,578	1,477	600	4,101 R	72.9%	19.3%	79.1%	20.9%
273,568	WESTMORELAND	62,514	34,522	10,223	17,769	24,299 R	55.2%	16.4%	77.2%	22.8%
14,101	WYOMING	4,721	3,213	1,194	314	2,019 R	68.1%	25.3%	72.9%	27.1%
144,521	YORK	41,039	23,044	15,600	2,395	7,444 R	56.2%	38.0%	59.6%	40.4%
8,720,017	TOTAL	2,144,850	1,401,481	409,192	334,177	992,289 R	65.3%	19.1%	77.4%	22.6%

PENNSYLVANIA

PRESIDENT 1920

1920 Census Population	County	Total Vote	Republican	Democratic	Other	Rep.-Dem. Plurality	Percentage: Total Vote Rep.	Percentage: Total Vote Dem.	Percentage: Major Vote Rep.	Percentage: Major Vote Dem.
34,583	ADAMS	9,349	5,323	3,852	174	1,471 R	56.9%	41.2%	58.0%	42.0%
1,185,808	ALLEGHENY	200,702	138,908	40,278	21,516	98,630 R	69.2%	20.1%	77.5%	22.5%
75,568	ARMSTRONG	12,992	8,995	3,262	735	5,733 R	69.2%	25.1%	73.4%	26.6%
111,621	BEAVER	18,586	11,691	4,771	2,124	6,920 R	62.9%	25.7%	71.0%	29.0%
38,277	BEDFORD	9,405	5,800	2,594	1,011	3,206 R	61.7%	27.6%	69.1%	30.9%
200,854	BERKS	46,591	22,221	18,361	6,009	3,860 R	47.7%	39.4%	54.8%	45.2%
128,334	BLAIR	26,392	15,035	5,668	5,689	9,367 R	57.0%	21.5%	72.6%	27.4%
53,166	BRADFORD	15,900	11,947	2,825	1,128	9,122 R	75.1%	17.8%	80.9%	19.1%
82,476	BUCKS	21,681	14,130	6,867	684	7,263 R	65.2%	31.7%	67.3%	32.7%
77,270	BUTLER	15,653	10,467	3,829	1,357	6,638 R	66.9%	24.5%	73.2%	26.8%
197,839	CAMBRIA	30,712	19,629	6,961	4,122	12,668 R	63.9%	22.7%	73.8%	26.2%
6,297	CAMERON	2,004	1,364	497	143	867 R	68.1%	24.8%	73.3%	26.7%
62,565	CARBON	13,345	7,900	5,030	415	2,870 R	59.2%	37.7%	61.1%	38.9%
44,304	CENTRE	12,372	7,615	4,142	615	3,473 R	61.6%	33.5%	64.8%	35.2%
115,120	CHESTER	26,060	18,129	7,004	927	11,125 R	69.6%	26.9%	72.1%	27.9%
36,170	CLARION	8,662	4,615	3,487	560	1,128 R	53.3%	40.3%	57.0%	43.0%
103,236	CLEARFIELD	18,393	9,615	5,987	2,791	3,628 R	52.3%	32.6%	61.6%	38.4%
33,555	CLINTON	7,884	4,303	2,976	605	1,327 R	54.6%	37.7%	59.1%	40.9%
48,349	COLUMBIA	13,665	6,238	6,965	462	727 D	45.6%	51.0%	47.2%	52.8%
60,667	CRAWFORD	16,098	10,032	4,175	1,891	5,857 R	62.3%	25.9%	70.6%	29.4%
58,578	CUMBERLAND	15,674	8,579	6,455	640	2,124 R	54.7%	41.2%	57.1%	42.9%
153,116	DAUPHIN	39,923	26,094	11,990	1,839	14,104 R	65.4%	30.0%	68.5%	31.5%
173,084	DELAWARE	45,293	34,126	9,602	1,565	24,524 R	75.3%	21.2%	78.0%	22.0%
34,981	ELK	7,963	5,267	2,093	603	3,174 R	66.1%	26.3%	71.6%	28.4%
153,536	ERIE	30,569	19,465	6,311	4,793	13,154 R	63.7%	20.6%	75.5%	24.5%
188,104	FAYETTE	35,611	20,186	13,358	2,067	6,828 R	56.7%	37.5%	60.2%	39.8%
7,477	FOREST	1,762	993	389	380	604 R	56.4%	22.1%	71.9%	28.1%
62,275	FRANKLIN	13,857	8,376	5,020	461	3,356 R	60.4%	36.2%	62.5%	37.5%
9,617	FULTON	2,574	1,292	1,231	51	61 R	50.2%	47.8%	51.2%	48.8%
30,804	GREENE	10,028	4,253	5,592	183	1,339 D	42.4%	55.8%	43.2%	56.8%
39,848	HUNTINGDON	7,724	5,232	1,784	708	3,448 R	67.7%	23.1%	74.6%	25.4%
80,910	INDIANA	11,993	8,616	1,936	1,441	6,680 R	71.8%	16.1%	81.7%	18.3%
62,104	JEFFERSON	11,950	7,970	3,060	920	4,910 R	66.7%	25.6%	72.3%	27.7%
14,464	JUNIATA	3,628	2,112	1,443	73	669 R	58.2%	39.8%	59.4%	40.6%
286,311	LACKAWANNA	67,040	40,593	24,581	1,866	16,012 R	60.6%	36.7%	62.3%	37.7%
173,797	LANCASTER	40,542	29,549	9,521	1,472	20,028 R	72.9%	23.5%	75.6%	24.4%
85,545	LAWRENCE	14,676	9,448	2,720	2,508	6,728 R	64.4%	18.5%	77.6%	22.4%
63,152	LEBANON	12,401	8,778	3,016	607	5,762 R	70.8%	24.3%	74.4%	25.6%
148,101	LEHIGH	30,310	18,032	10,863	1,415	7,169 R	59.5%	35.8%	62.4%	37.6%
390,991	LUZERNE	75,575	49,419	23,473	2,683	25,946 R	65.4%	31.1%	67.8%	32.2%
83,100	LYCOMING	18,635	10,570	5,853	2,212	4,717 R	56.7%	31.4%	64.4%	35.6%
48,934	MCKEAN	11,406	7,830	2,505	1,071	5,325 R	68.6%	22.0%	75.8%	24.2%
93,788	MERCER	19,199	11,575	4,823	2,801	6,752 R	60.3%	25.1%	70.6%	29.4%
31,439	MIFFLIN	6,571	3,872	2,400	299	1,472 R	58.9%	36.5%	61.7%	38.3%
24,295	MONROE	6,828	3,278	3,396	154	118 D	48.0%	49.7%	49.1%	50.9%
199,310	MONTGOMERY	45,855	31,963	12,239	1,653	19,724 R	69.7%	26.7%	72.3%	27.7%
14,080	MONTOUR	4,271	2,296	1,872	103	424 R	53.8%	43.8%	55.1%	44.9%
153,506	NORTHAMPTON	24,204	14,227	9,086	891	5,141 R	58.8%	37.5%	61.0%	39.0%
122,079	NORTHUMBERLAND	29,581	17,288	9,854	2,439	7,434 R	58.4%	33.3%	63.7%	36.3%
22,875	PERRY	6,245	3,787	2,314	144	1,473 R	60.6%	37.1%	62.1%	37.9%
1,823,779	PHILADELPHIA	418,662	307,825	90,151	20,686	217,674 R	73.5%	21.5%	77.3%	22.7%
6,818	PIKE	2,272	1,319	880	73	439 R	58.1%	38.7%	60.0%	40.0%
21,089	POTTER	5,750	4,036	1,106	608	2,930 R	70.2%	19.2%	78.5%	21.5%
217,754	SCHUYLKILL	50,887	30,259	18,746	1,882	11,513 R	59.5%	36.8%	61.7%	38.3%
17,129	SNYDER	3,810	2,751	964	95	1,787 R	72.2%	25.3%	74.1%	25.9%
82,112	SOMERSET	16,404	12,436	2,912	1,056	9,524 R	75.8%	17.8%	81.0%	19.0%
9,520	SULLIVAN	2,814	1,620	1,061	133	559 R	57.6%	37.7%	60.4%	39.6%
34,763	SUSQUEHANNA	9,896	6,572	2,905	419	3,667 R	66.4%	29.4%	69.3%	30.7%
37,118	TIOGA	11,669	9,718	1,258	693	8,460 R	83.3%	10.8%	88.5%	11.5%
15,850	UNION	4,630	3,305	1,155	170	2,150 R	71.4%	24.9%	74.1%	25.9%

PENNSYLVANIA

PRESIDENT 1920

1920 Census Population	County	Total Vote	Republican	Democratic	Other	Rep.-Dem. Plurality	Percentage Total Vote Rep.	Total Vote Dem.	Major Vote Rep.	Major Vote Dem.
59,184	VENANGO	11,746	7,718	2,669	1,359	5,049 R	65.7%	22.7%	74.3%	25.7%
40,024	WARREN	11,974	7,791	2,180	2,003	5,611 R	65.1%	18.2%	78.1%	21.9%
188,992	WASHINGTON	29,625	18,514	8,827	2,284	9,687 R	62.5%	29.8%	67.7%	32.3%
27,435	WAYNE	7,060	5,164	1,589	307	3,575 R	73.1%	22.5%	76.5%	23.5%
273,568	WESTMORELAND	45,349	27,077	12,845	5,427	14,232 R	59.7%	28.3%	67.8%	32.2%
14,101	WYOMING	4,687	3,208	1,247	232	1,961 R	68.4%	26.6%	72.0%	28.0%
144,521	YORK	35,679	19,879	14,396	1,404	5,483 R	55.7%	40.3%	58.0%	42.0%
8,720,017	TOTAL	1,851,248	1,218,215	503,202	129,831	715,013 R	65.8%	27.2%	70.8%	29.2%

PENNSYLVANIA

ELECTION NOTES

1956 Other vote was 7,447 Hass (Socialist Labor); 2,035 Dobbs (Socialist Workers).

1952 Other vote was 8,951 Hamblen (Prohibition); 4,222 Hallinan (Progressive); 2,698 Hoopes (Socialist); 1,508 Dobbs (Socialist Workers); 1,377 Hass (Socialist Labor); 155 scattered write-in.

1948 Other vote was 55,161 Wallace (Progressive); 11,325 Thomas (Socialist); 10,538 Watson (Prohibition); 2,133 Dobbs (Socialist Workers); 1,461 Teichert (Socialist Labor); 107 scattered write-in.

1944 Other vote was 11,721 Thomas (Socialist); 5,750 Watson (Prohibition); 1,789 Teichert (Socialist Labor).

1940 Other vote was 10,967 Thomas (Socialist); 4,519 Browder (Communist); 1,518 Aiken (Socialist Labor); 827 scattered write-in. The statewide total in the other vote column includes the write-in votes which were not available by county.

1936 Other vote was 67,467 Lemke (Union); 14,375 Thomas (Socialist); 6,691 Colvin (Prohibition); 4,060 Browder (Communist); 1,424 Aiken (Socialist Labor).

1932 Other vote was 91,119 Thomas (Socialist); 11,319 Upshaw (Prohibition); 5,658 Foster (Communist); 725 Cox (Jobless); 659 Reynolds (Socialist Labor); 53 scattered write-in. The statewide total in the other vote column includes the write-in votes which were not available by county.

1928 Other vote was 18,647 Thomas (Socialist); 4,726 Foster (2,687 Labor and 2,039 Workers); 3,875 Varney (Prohibition); 382 Reynolds (Socialist Labor); 14 scattered write-in.

1924 Other vote was 307,567 LaFollette (214,126 Labor and 93,441 Socialist); 13,035 Nations (American); 9,779 Faris (Prohibition); 2,735 Foster (Communist); 634 Johns (Socialist Labor); 296 Wallace (Commonwealth Land); 131 scattered write-in. The statewide total in the other vote column includes the write-in votes which were not available by county. The LaFollette combined ticket ran second in Allegheny, Beaver, Blair, Crawford, Erie, Indiana, Lawrence, Washington and Westmoreland counties.

1920 Other vote was 70,021 Debs (Socialist); 42,612 Watkins (Prohibition); 15,642 Christensen (Farmer-Labor); 803 Macauley (Single Tax); 753 Cox (Socialist Labor).

RHODE ISLAND

POPULAR VOTE FOR PRESIDENT 1920 TO 1956

Year	Total Vote	Republican Vote	Republican Candidate	Democratic Vote	Democratic Candidate	Other Vote	Plurality	Percentage Total Vote Rep.	Percentage Total Vote Dem.	Percentage Major Vote Rep.	Percentage Major Vote Dem.
1956	387,609	225,819	Eisenhower, Dwight D.	161,790	Stevenson, Adlai E.		64,029 R	58.3%	41.7%	58.3%	41.7%
1952	414,498	210,935	Eisenhower, Dwight D.	203,293	Stevenson, Adlai E.	270	7,642 R	50.9%	49.0%	50.9%	49.1%
1948	327,702	135,787	Dewey, Thomas E.	188,736	Truman, Harry S.	3,179	52,949 D	41.4%	57.6%	41.8%	58.2%
1944	299,276	123,487	Dewey, Thomas E.	175,356	Roosevelt, Franklin D.	433	51,869 D	41.3%	58.6%	41.3%	58.7%
1940	321,152	138,654	Willkie, Wendell	182,181	Roosevelt, Franklin D.	317	43,527 D	43.2%	56.7%	43.2%	56.8%
1936	310,278	125,031	Landon, Alfred M.	164,338	Roosevelt, Franklin D.	20,909	39,307 D	40.3%	53.0%	43.2%	56.8%
1932	266,170	115,266	Hoover, Herbert C.	146,604	Roosevelt, Franklin D.	4,300	31,338 D	43.3%	55.1%	44.0%	56.0%
1928	237,194	117,522	Hoover, Herbert C.	118,973	Smith, Alfred E.	699	1,451 D	49.5%	50.2%	49.7%	50.3%
1924	210,115	125,286	Coolidge, Calvin	76,606	Davis, John W.	8,223	48,680 R	59.6%	36.5%	62.1%	37.9%
1920	167,981	107,463	Harding, Warren G.	55,062	Cox, James M.	5,456	52,401 R	64.0%	32.8%	66.1%	33.9%

ELECTORAL COLLEGE VOTE 1920 TO 1956

Year	Total	Republican	Democratic	Other
1956	4	4	—	—
1952	4	4	—	—
1948	4	—	4	—
1944	4	—	4	—
1940	4	—	4	—
1936	4	—	4	—
1932	4	—	4	—
1928	5	—	5	—
1924	5	5	—	—
1920	5	5	—	—

RHODE ISLAND

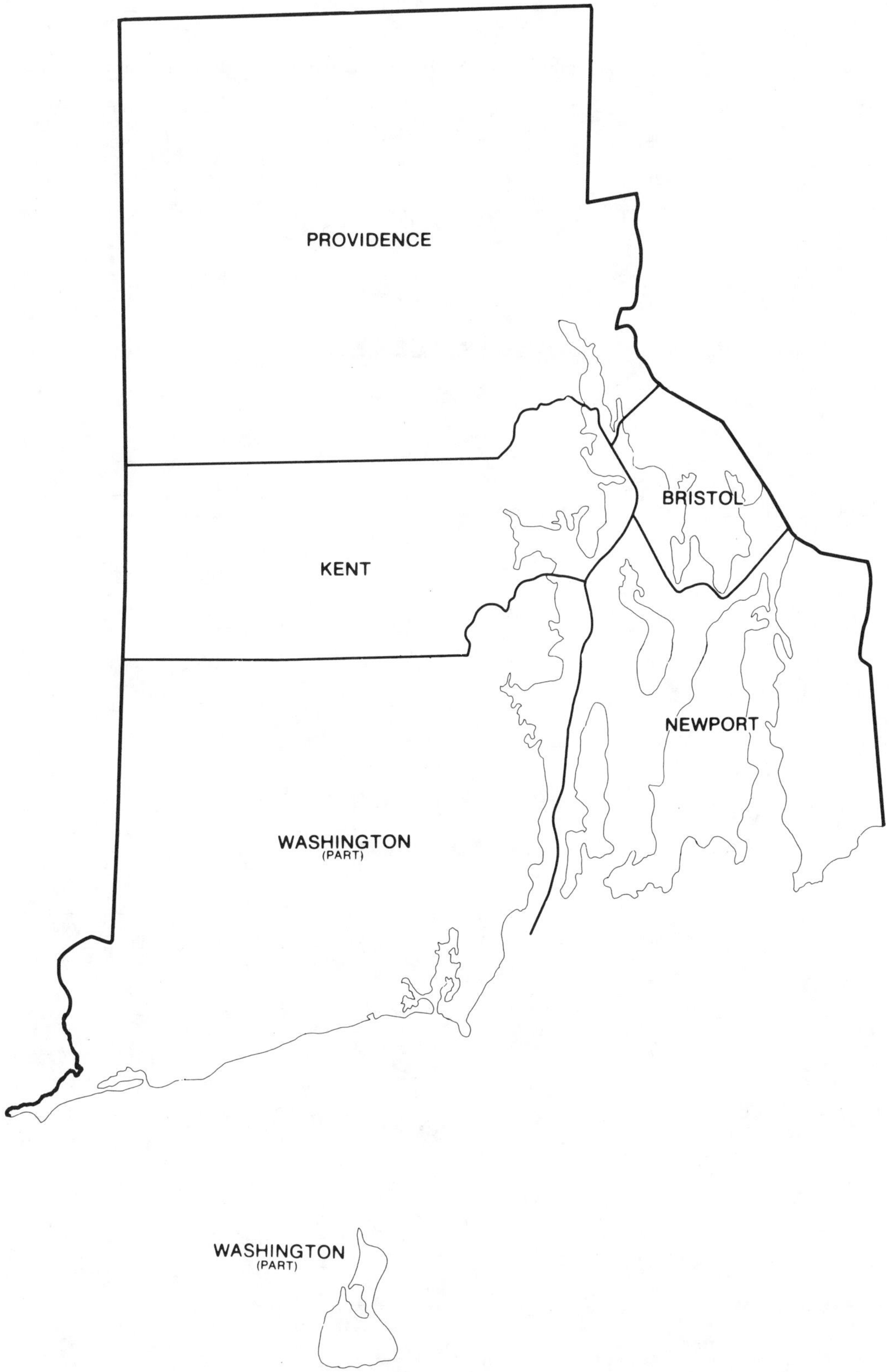
PROVIDENCE
KENT
BRISTOL
NEWPORT
WASHINGTON
(PART)
WASHINGTON
(PART)

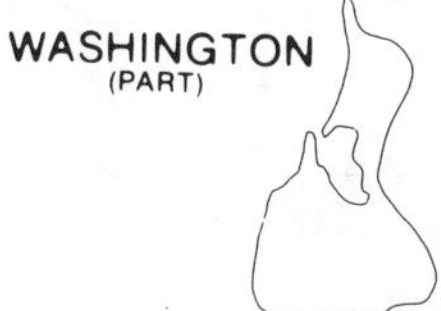

RHODE ISLAND

PRESIDENT 1956

1950 Census Population	County	Total Vote	Republican	Democratic	Other	Rep.-Dem. Plurality	Percentage Total Vote Rep.	Percentage Total Vote Dem.	Percentage Major Vote Rep.	Percentage Major Vote Dem.
29,079	BRISTOL	16,818	10,070	6,748		3,322 R	59.9%	40.1%	59.9%	40.1%
77,763	KENT	47,846	31,548	16,298		15,250 R	65.9%	34.1%	65.9%	34.1%
61,539	NEWPORT	25,496	16,063	9,433		6,630 R	63.0%	37.0%	63.0%	37.0%
574,973	PROVIDENCE	275,721	153,860	121,861		31,999 R	55.8%	44.2%	55.8%	44.2%
48,542	WASHINGTON	21,728	14,278	7,450		6,828 R	65.7%	34.3%	65.7%	34.3%
791,896	TOTAL	387,609	225,819	161,790		64,029 R	58.3%	41.7%	58.3%	41.7%

RHODE ISLAND

PRESIDENT 1952

1950 Census Population	County	Total Vote	Republican	Democratic	Other	Rep.-Dem. Plurality	Percentage Total Vote Rep.	Percentage Total Vote Dem.	Percentage Major Vote Rep.	Percentage Major Vote Dem.
29,079	BRISTOL	16,789	8,468	8,313	8	155 R	50.4%	49.5%	50.5%	49.5%
77,763	KENT	45,593	27,745	17,824	24	9,921 R	60.9%	39.1%	60.9%	39.1%
61,539	NEWPORT	26,262	15,136	11,116	10	4,020 R	57.6%	42.3%	57.7%	42.3%
574,973	PROVIDENCE	304,008	146,197	157,592	219	11,395 D	48.1%	51.8%	48.1%	51.9%
48,542	WASHINGTON	21,846	13,389	8,448	9	4,941 R	61.3%	38.7%	61.3%	38.7%
791,896	TOTAL	414,498	210,935	203,293	270	7,642 R	50.9%	49.0%	50.9%	49.1%

RHODE ISLAND

PRESIDENT 1948

1940 Census Population	County	Total Vote	Republican	Democratic	Other	Rep.-Dem. Plurality	Percentage Total Vote Rep.	Percentage Total Vote Dem.	Percentage Major Vote Rep.	Percentage Major Vote Dem.
25,548	BRISTOL	12,982	5,343	7,562	77	2,219 D	41.2%	58.2%	41.4%	58.6%
58,311	KENT	31,785	16,299	15,287	199	1,012 R	51.3%	48.1%	51.6%	48.4%
46,696	NEWPORT	20,146	10,756	9,254	136	1,502 R	53.4%	45.9%	53.8%	46.2%
550,298	PROVIDENCE	245,748	93,867	149,254	2,627	55,387 D	38.2%	60.7%	38.6%	61.4%
32,493	WASHINGTON	17,041	9,522	7,379	140	2,143 R	55.9%	43.3%	56.3%	43.7%
713,346	TOTAL	327,702	135,787	188,736	3,179	52,949 D	41.4%	57.6%	41.8%	58.2%

RHODE ISLAND

PRESIDENT 1944

1940 Census Population	County	Total Vote	Republican	Democratic	Other	Rep.-Dem. Plurality	Percentage Total Vote Rep.	Total Vote Dem.	Major Vote Rep.	Major Vote Dem.
25,548	BRISTOL	11,222	4,919	6,287	16	1,368 D	43.8%	56.0%	43.9%	56.1%
58,311	KENT	27,826	13,710	14,059	57	349 D	49.3%	50.5%	49.4%	50.6%
46,696	NEWPORT	20,831	9,435	11,375	21	1,940 D	45.3%	54.6%	45.3%	54.7%
550,298	PROVIDENCE	224,727	87,190	137,216	321	50,026 D	38.8%	61.1%	38.9%	61.1%
32,493	WASHINGTON	14,670	8,233	6,419	18	1,814 R	56.1%	43.8%	56.2%	43.8%
713,346	TOTAL	299,276	123,487	175,356	433	51,869 D	41.3%	58.6%	41.3%	58.7%

RHODE ISLAND

PRESIDENT 1940

1940 Census Population	County	Total Vote	Republican	Democratic	Other	Rep.-Dem. Plurality	Percentage Total Vote Rep.	Total Vote Dem.	Major Vote Rep.	Major Vote Dem.
25,548	BRISTOL	11,284	5,314	5,967	3	653 D	47.1%	52.9%	47.1%	52.9%
58,311	KENT	29,151	14,790	14,333	28	457 R	50.7%	49.2%	50.8%	49.2%
46,696	NEWPORT	20,541	9,882	10,645	14	763 D	48.1%	51.8%	48.1%	51.9%
550,298	PROVIDENCE	244,925	99,435	145,235	255	45,800 D	40.6%	59.3%	40.6%	59.4%
32,493	WASHINGTON	15,251	9,233	6,001	17	3,232 R	60.5%	39.3%	60.6%	39.4%
713,346	TOTAL	321,152	138,654	182,181	317	43,527 D	43.2%	56.7%	43.2%	56.8%

RHODE ISLAND

PRESIDENT 1936

1930 Census Population	County	Total Vote	Republican	Democratic	Other	Rep.-Dem. Plurality	Percentage Total Vote Rep.	Total Vote Dem.	Major Vote Rep.	Major Vote Dem.
25,089	BRISTOL	10,662	4,867	5,327	468	460 D	45.6%	50.0%	47.7%	52.3%
51,390	KENT	28,019	13,550	13,238	1,231	312 R	48.4%	47.2%	50.6%	49.4%
41,668	NEWPORT	19,361	9,358	9,499	504	141 D	48.3%	49.1%	49.6%	50.4%
540,016	PROVIDENCE	238,080	88,492	131,218	18,370	42,726 D	37.2%	55.1%	40.3%	59.7%
29,334	WASHINGTON	14,156	8,764	5,056	336	3,708 R	61.9%	35.7%	63.4%	36.6%
687,497	TOTAL	310,278	125,031	164,338	20,909	39,307 D	40.3%	53.0%	43.2%	56.8%

RHODE ISLAND

PRESIDENT 1932

1930 Census Population	County	Total Vote	Republican	Democratic	Other	Rep.-Dem. Plurality	Percentage Total Vote Rep.	Total Vote Dem.	Major Vote Rep.	Major Vote Dem.
25,089	BRISTOL	8,703	3,833	4,775	95	942 D	44.0%	54.9%	44.5%	55.5%
51,390	KENT	21,780	11,096	10,398	286	698 R	50.9%	47.7%	51.6%	48.4%
41,668	NEWPORT	16,636	8,633	7,838	165	795 R	51.9%	47.1%	52.4%	47.6%
540,016	PROVIDENCE	206,544	84,397	118,546	3,601	34,149 D	40.9%	57.4%	41.6%	58.4%
29,334	WASHINGTON	12,507	7,307	5,047	153	2,260 R	58.4%	40.4%	59.1%	40.9%
687,497	TOTAL	266,170	115,266	146,604	4,300	31,338 D	43.3%	55.1%	44.0%	56.0%

RHODE ISLAND

PRESIDENT 1928

1920 Census Population	County	Total Vote	Republican	Democratic	Other	Rep.-Dem. Plurality	Percentage Total Vote Rep.	Total Vote Dem.	Major Vote Rep.	Major Vote Dem.
23,113	BRISTOL	7,873	3,780	4,080	13	300 D	48.0%	51.8%	48.1%	51.9%
38,269	KENT	19,005	11,487	7,460	58	4,027 R	60.4%	39.3%	60.6%	39.4%
42,893	NEWPORT	15,359	8,578	6,748	33	1,830 R	55.8%	43.9%	56.0%	44.0%
475,190	PROVIDENCE	183,637	85,884	97,185	568	11,301 D	46.8%	52.9%	46.9%	53.1%
24,932	WASHINGTON	11,320	7,793	3,500	27	4,293 R	68.8%	30.9%	69.0%	31.0%
604,397	TOTAL	237,194	117,522	118,973	699	1,451 D	49.5%	50.2%	49.7%	50.3%

RHODE ISLAND

PRESIDENT 1924

1920 Census Population	County	Total Vote	Republican	Democratic	Other	Rep.-Dem. Plurality	Percentage Total Vote Rep.	Total Vote Dem.	Major Vote Rep.	Major Vote Dem.
23,113	BRISTOL	6,729	4,076	2,500	153	1,576 R	60.6%	37.2%	62.0%	38.0%
38,269	KENT	16,860	11,100	5,429	331	5,671 R	65.8%	32.2%	67.2%	32.8%
42,893	NEWPORT	14,289	9,608	3,975	706	5,633 R	67.2%	27.8%	70.7%	29.3%
475,190	PROVIDENCE	161,550	92,464	62,336	6,750	30,128 R	57.2%	38.6%	59.7%	40.3%
24,932	WASHINGTON	10,687	8,038	2,366	283	5,672 R	75.2%	22.1%	77.3%	22.7%
604,397	TOTAL	210,115	125,286	76,606	8,223	48,680 R	59.6%	36.5%	62.1%	37.9%

RHODE ISLAND

PRESIDENT 1920

1920 Census Population	County	Total Vote	Republican	Democratic	Other	Rep.-Dem. Plurality	Percentage Total Vote Rep.	Percentage Total Vote Dem.	Percentage Major Vote Rep.	Percentage Major Vote Dem.
23,113	BRISTOL	5,366	3,692	1,569	105	2,123 R	68.8%	29.2%	70.2%	29.8%
38,269	KENT	12,110	8,474	3,394	242	5,080 R	70.0%	28.0%	71.4%	28.6%
42,893	NEWPORT	12,146	9,319	2,228	599	7,091 R	76.7%	18.3%	80.7%	19.3%
475,190	PROVIDENCE	129,791	79,558	45,859	4,374	33,699 R	61.3%	35.3%	63.4%	36.6%
24,932	WASHINGTON	8,568	6,420	2,012	136	4,408 R	74.9%	23.5%	76.1%	23.9%
604,397	TOTAL	167,981	107,463	55,062	5,456	52,401 R	64.0%	32.8%	66.1%	33.9%

RHODE ISLAND

ELECTION NOTES

1956

1952 Other vote was 187 Hallinan (Progressive); 83 Hass (Socialist Labor).

1948 Other vote was 2,619 Wallace (Progressive); 429 Thomas (Socialist); 131 Teichert (Socialist Labor).

1944 Other vote was Watson (Prohibition).

1940 Other vote was 243 Browder (Communist); 74 Babson (Prohibition).

1936 Other vote was 19,569 Lemke (Union); 929 Aiken (Socialist Labor); 411 Browder (Communist).

1932 Other vote was 3,138 Thomas (Socialist); 546 Foster (Communist); 433 Reynolds (Socialist Labor); 183 Upshaw (Prohibition).

1928 Other vote was 416 Reynolds (Socialist Labor); 283 Foster (Communist).

1924 Other vote was 7,628 LaFollette (Progressive); 289 Foster (Communist); 268 Johns (Socialist Labor); 38 Wallace (Commonwealth Land).

1920 Other vote was 4,351 Debs (Socialist); 510 Watkins (Prohibition); 495 Cox (Socialist Labor); 100 Macauley (Single Tax).

SOUTH CAROLINA

POPULAR VOTE FOR PRESIDENT 1920 TO 1956

		Republican		Democratic				Percentage			
								Total Vote		Major Vote	
Year	Total Vote	Vote	Candidate	Vote	Candidate	Other Vote	Plurality	Rep.	Dem.	Rep.	Dem.
1956 **	300,583	75,700	Eisenhower, Dwight D.	136,372	Stevenson, Adlai E.	88,511	47,863 D	25.2%	45.4%	35.7%	64.3%
1952	341,087	168,082	Eisenhower, Dwight D.	173,004	Stevenson, Adlai E.	1	4,922 D	49.3%	50.7%	49.3%	50.7%
1948 **	142,571	5,386	Dewey, Thomas E.	34,423	Truman, Harry S.	102,762	68,184 SR	3.8%	24.1%	13.5%	86.5%
1944 **	103,382	4,617	Dewey, Thomas E.	90,601	Roosevelt, Franklin D.	8,164	82,802 D	4.5%	87.6%	4.8%	95.2%
1940	99,830	4,360	Willkie, Wendell	95,470	Roosevelt, Franklin D.		91,110 D	4.4%	95.6%	4.4%	95.6%
1936	115,437	1,646	Landon, Alfred M.	113,791	Roosevelt, Franklin D.		112,145 D	1.4%	98.6%	1.4%	98.6%
1932	104,407	1,978	Hoover, Herbert C.	102,347	Roosevelt, Franklin D.	82	100,369 D	1.9%	98.0%	1.9%	98.1%
1928	68,605	5,858	Hoover, Herbert C.	62,700	Smith, Alfred E.	47	56,842 D	8.5%	91.4%	8.5%	91.5%
1924	50,755	1,123	Coolidge, Calvin	49,008	Davis, John W.	624	47,885 D	2.2%	96.6%	2.2%	97.8%
1920	66,808	2,610	Harding, Warren G.	64,170	Cox, James M.	28	61,560 D	3.9%	96.1%	3.9%	96.1%

In 1956 other vote was 88,509 Independent (Uncommitted States Rights) and 2 scattered. In 1948 other vote was 102,607 States Rights; 154 Progressive and 1 Socialist. In 1944 other vote was 7,799 Southern Democratic and 365 Prohibition.

ELECTORAL COLLEGE VOTE 1920 TO 1956

Year	Total	Republican	Democratic	Other
1956	8	—	8	—
1952	8	—	8	—
1948	8	—	—	8 SR
1944	8	—	8	—
1940	8	—	8	—
1936	8	—	8	—
1932	8	—	8	—
1928	9	—	9	—
1924	9	—	9	—
1920	9	—	9	—

SOUTH CAROLINA

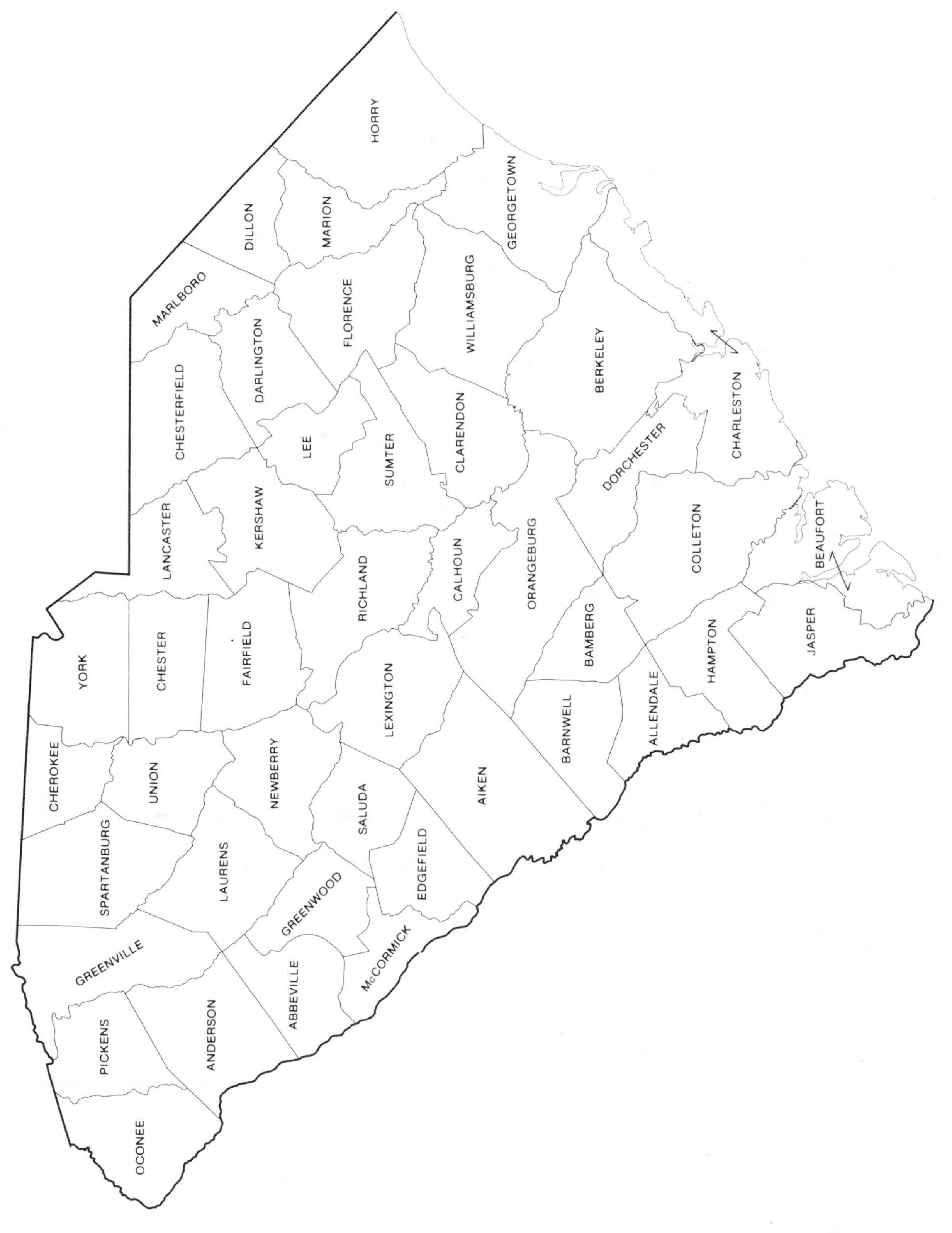

SOUTH CAROLINA

PRESIDENT 1956

1950 Census Population	County	Total Vote	Republican	Democratic	Independent	Other	Plurality	Percentage Total Vote Rep.	Dem.	Ind.
22,456	ABBEVILLE	3,581	339	2,985	257		2,646 D	9.5%	83.4%	7.2%
53,137	AIKEN	12,296	6,195	4,280	1,821		1,915 R	50.4%	34.8%	14.8%
11,773	ALLENDALE	1,317	262	380	675		295 I	19.9%	28.9%	51.3%
90,664	ANDERSON	14,771	2,186	11,344	1,241		9,158 D	14.8%	76.8%	8.4%
17,533	BAMBERG	1,874	326	430	1,118		688 I	17.4%	22.9%	59.7%
17,266	BARNWELL	3,009	520	1,914	575		1,339 D	17.3%	63.6%	19.1%
26,993	BEAUFORT	2,777	1,051	710	1,016		35 R	37.8%	25.6%	36.6%
30,251	BERKELEY	3,736	1,055	902	1,779		724 I	28.2%	24.1%	47.6%
14,753	CALHOUN	1,180	146	341	693		352 I	12.4%	28.9%	58.7%
164,856	CHARLESTON	25,073	7,487	4,028	13,558		6,071 I	29.9%	16.1%	54.1%
34,992	CHEROKEE	4,902	907	3,687	308		2,780 D	18.5%	75.2%	6.3%
32,597	CHESTER	4,699	1,007	2,951	741		1,944 D	21.4%	62.8%	15.8%
36,236	CHESTERFIELD	4,988	795	3,559	634		2,764 D	15.9%	71.4%	12.7%
32,215	CLARENDON	2,672	224	661	1,787		1,126 I	8.4%	24.7%	66.9%
28,242	COLLETON	4,048	635	1,463	1,948	2	485 I	15.7%	36.1%	48.1%
50,016	DARLINGTON	7,108	1,597	2,908	2,603		305 D	22.5%	40.9%	36.6%
30,930	DILLON	2,984	313	1,879	792		1,087 D	10.5%	63.0%	26.5%
22,601	DORCHESTER	3,217	504	862	1,851		989 I	15.7%	26.8%	57.5%
16,591	EDGEFIELD	2,042	516	525	1,001		476 I	25.3%	25.7%	49.0%
21,780	FAIRFIELD	2,648	519	961	1,168		207 I	19.6%	36.3%	44.1%
79,710	FLORENCE	9,765	1,855	3,463	4,447		984 I	19.0%	35.5%	45.5%
31,762	GEORGETOWN	4,361	1,057	1,020	2,284		1,227 I	24.2%	23.4%	52.4%
168,152	GREENVILLE	27,193	10,752	11,819	4,622		1,067 D	39.5%	43.5%	17.0%
41,628	GREENWOOD	6,753	1,120	4,386	1,247		3,139 D	16.6%	64.9%	18.5%
18,027	HAMPTON	2,056	359	564	1,133		569 I	17.5%	27.4%	55.1%
59,820	HORRY	8,171	1,092	4,835	2,244		2,591 D	13.4%	59.2%	27.5%
10,995	JASPER	1,271	403	210	658		255 I	31.7%	16.5%	51.8%
32,287	KERSHAW	5,389	1,518	1,875	1,996		121 I	28.2%	34.8%	37.0%
37,071	LANCASTER	6,637	1,610	4,398	629		2,788 D	24.3%	66.3%	9.5%
46,974	LAURENS	6,648	1,377	3,726	1,545		2,181 D	20.7%	56.0%	23.2%
23,173	LEE	2,465	250	943	1,272		329 I	10.1%	38.3%	51.6%
44,279	LEXINGTON	5,737	1,188	2,094	2,455		361 I	20.7%	36.5%	42.8%
9,577	MCCORMICK	869	102	485	282		203 D	11.7%	55.8%	32.5%
33,110	MARION	3,160	417	1,390	1,353		37 D	13.2%	44.0%	42.8%
31,766	MARLBORO	2,798	507	1,769	522		1,247 D	18.1%	63.2%	18.7%
31,771	NEWBERRY	5,130	1,061	2,671	1,398		1,273 D	20.7%	52.1%	27.3%
39,050	OCONEE	4,797	911	3,510	376		2,599 D	19.0%	73.2%	7.8%
68,726	ORANGEBURG	6,921	1,467	2,511	2,943		432 I	21.2%	36.3%	42.5%
40,058	PICKENS	4,278	1,747	1,847	684		100 D	40.8%	43.2%	16.0%
142,565	RICHLAND	22,384	6,714	6,154	9,516		2,802 I	30.0%	27.5%	42.5%
15,924	SALUDA	2,286	341	1,080	865		215 D	14.9%	47.2%	37.8%
150,349	SPARTANBURG	25,583	6,822	16,637	2,124		9,815 D	26.7%	65.0%	8.3%
57,634	SUMTER	6,034	1,356	937	3,741		2,385 I	22.5%	15.5%	62.0%
31,334	UNION	5,688	1,252	3,760	676		2,508 D	22.0%	66.1%	11.9%
43,807	WILLIAMSBURG	3,752	330	683	2,739		2,056 I	8.8%	18.2%	73.0%
71,596	YORK	11,535	3,508	6,835	1,192		3,327 D	30.4%	59.3%	10.3%
2,117,027	TOTAL	300,583	75,700	136,372	88,509	2	47,863 D	25.2%	45.4%	29.4%

SOUTH CAROLINA

PRESIDENT 1952

1950 Census Population	County	Total Vote	Republican	Democratic	Other	Rep.-Dem. Plurality	Percentage Total Vote Rep.	Percentage Total Vote Dem.	Percentage Major Vote Rep.	Percentage Major Vote Dem.
22,456	ABBEVILLE	3,746	970	2,776		1,806 D	25.9%	74.1%	25.9%	74.1%
53,137	AIKEN	8,628	4,282	4,346		64 D	49.6%	50.4%	49.6%	50.4%
11,773	ALLENDALE	1,191	751	440		311 R	63.1%	36.9%	63.1%	36.9%
90,664	ANDERSON	15,002	3,338	11,664		8,326 D	22.3%	77.7%	22.3%	77.7%
17,533	BAMBERG	2,157	1,407	750		657 R	65.2%	34.8%	65.2%	34.8%
17,266	BARNWELL	2,255	657	1,598		941 D	29.1%	70.9%	29.1%	70.9%
26,993	BEAUFORT	2,705	1,599	1,106		493 R	59.1%	40.9%	59.1%	40.9%
30,251	BERKELEY	4,190	2,482	1,708		774 R	59.2%	40.8%	59.2%	40.8%
14,753	CALHOUN	1,491	1,107	384		723 R	74.2%	25.8%	74.2%	25.8%
164,856	CHARLESTON	30,046	20,087	9,959		10,128 R	66.9%	33.1%	66.9%	33.1%
34,992	CHEROKEE	7,074	1,529	5,545		4,016 D	21.6%	78.4%	21.6%	78.4%
32,597	CHESTER	5,620	2,777	2,843		66 D	49.4%	50.6%	49.4%	50.6%
36,236	CHESTERFIELD	6,444	1,776	4,668		2,892 D	27.6%	72.4%	27.6%	72.4%
32,215	CLARENDON	3,026	2,073	953		1,120 R	68.5%	31.5%	68.5%	31.5%
28,242	COLLETON	4,665	2,760	1,905		855 R	59.2%	40.8%	59.2%	40.8%
50,016	DARLINGTON	9,181	3,463	5,718		2,255 D	37.7%	62.3%	37.7%	62.3%
30,930	DILLON	3,051	1,473	1,578		105 D	48.3%	51.7%	48.3%	51.7%
22,601	DORCHESTER	3,171	2,319	852		1,467 R	73.1%	26.9%	73.1%	26.9%
16,591	EDGEFIELD	2,418	1,665	753		912 R	68.9%	31.1%	68.9%	31.1%
21,780	FAIRFIELD	3,197	1,607	1,590		17 R	50.3%	49.7%	50.3%	49.7%
79,710	FLORENCE	10,576	5,236	5,340		104 D	49.5%	50.5%	49.5%	50.5%
31,762	GEORGETOWN	3,710	2,340	1,370		970 R	63.1%	36.9%	63.1%	36.9%
168,152	GREENVILLE	32,606	17,743	14,863		2,880 R	54.4%	45.6%	54.4%	45.6%
41,628	GREENWOOD	7,207	3,392	3,815		423 D	47.1%	52.9%	47.1%	52.9%
18,027	HAMPTON	2,420	1,633	787		846 R	67.5%	32.5%	67.5%	32.5%
59,820	HORRY	8,205	3,716	4,489		773 D	45.3%	54.7%	45.3%	54.7%
10,995	JASPER	1,436	800	636		164 R	55.7%	44.3%	55.7%	44.3%
32,287	KERSHAW	4,987	2,935	2,052		883 R	58.9%	41.1%	58.9%	41.1%
37,071	LANCASTER	8,069	3,080	4,989		1,909 D	38.2%	61.8%	38.2%	61.8%
46,974	LAURENS	7,097	3,400	3,697		297 D	47.9%	52.1%	47.9%	52.1%
23,173	LEE	2,596	1,669	927		742 R	64.3%	35.7%	64.3%	35.7%
44,279	LEXINGTON	7,531	4,018	3,513		505 R	53.4%	46.6%	53.4%	46.6%
9,577	MCCORMICK	1,202	577	624	1	47 D	48.0%	51.9%	48.0%	52.0%
33,110	MARION	3,923	2,313	1,610		703 R	59.0%	41.0%	59.0%	41.0%
31,766	MARLBORO	3,240	1,541	1,699		158 D	47.6%	52.4%	47.6%	52.4%
31,771	NEWBERRY	7,544	4,126	3,418		708 R	54.7%	45.3%	54.7%	45.3%
39,050	OCONEE	4,854	1,624	3,230		1,606 D	33.5%	66.5%	33.5%	66.5%
68,726	ORANGEBURG	7,524	4,695	2,829		1,866 R	62.4%	37.6%	62.4%	37.6%
40,058	PICKENS	5,961	3,096	2,865		231 R	51.9%	48.1%	51.9%	48.1%
142,565	RICHLAND	24,815	15,925	8,890		7,035 R	64.2%	35.8%	64.2%	35.8%
15,924	SALUDA	2,988	1,396	1,592		196 D	46.7%	53.3%	46.7%	53.3%
150,349	SPARTANBURG	31,911	10,028	21,883		11,855 D	31.4%	68.6%	31.4%	68.6%
57,634	SUMTER	6,740	4,726	2,014		2,712 R				
31,334	UNION	8,015	2,094	5,921		3,827 D	26.1%	73.9%	26.1%	73.9%
43,807	WILLIAMSBURG	3,896	2,576	1,320		1,256 R	66.1%	33.9%	66.1%	33.9%
71,596	YORK	12,776	5,281	7,495		2,214 D	41.3%	58.7%	41.3%	58.7%
2,117,027	TOTAL	341,087	168,082	173,004	1	4,922 D	49.3%	50.7%	49.3%	50.7%

SOUTH CAROLINA

PRESIDENT 1948

1940 Census Population	County	Total Vote	Republican	Democratic	States Rights	Other	Plurality	Percentage Total Vote Rep.	Dem.	St. Rgts.
22,931	ABBEVILLE	1,064	23	254	782	5	528 SR	2.2%	23.9%	73.5%
49,916	AIKEN	5,299	115	572	4,612		4,040 SR	2.2%	10.8%	87.0%
13,040	ALLENDALE	1,110	14	55	1,041		986 SR	1.3%	5.0%	93.8%
88,712	ANDERSON	4,028	105	2,581	1,342		1,239 D	2.6%	64.1%	33.3%
18,643	BAMBERG	1,873	34	124	1,714	1	1,590 SR	1.8%	6.6%	91.5%
20,138	BARNWELL	2,064	28	115	1,920	1	1,805 SR	1.4%	5.6%	93.0%
22,037	BEAUFORT	1,257	150	253	850	4	597 SR	11.9%	20.1%	67.6%
27,128	BERKELEY	1,919	58	323	1,534	4	1,211 SR	3.0%	16.8%	79.9%
16,229	CALHOUN	881	4	36	840	1	804 SR	0.5%	4.1%	95.3%
121,105	CHARLESTON	13,893	562	2,660	10,603	68	7,943 SR	4.0%	19.1%	76.3%
33,290	CHEROKEE	1,758	77	605	1,075	1	470 SR	4.4%	34.4%	61.1%
32,579	CHESTER	2,012	48	436	1,527	1	1,091 SR	2.4%	21.7%	75.9%
35,963	CHESTERFIELD	2,498	31	912	1,554	1	642 SR	1.2%	36.5%	62.2%
31,500	CLARENDON	1,590	16	107	1,467		1,360 SR	1.0%	6.7%	92.3%
26,268	COLLETON	2,599	39	223	2,337		2,114 SR	1.5%	8.6%	89.9%
45,198	DARLINGTON	2,760	104	726	1,930		1,204 SR	3.8%	26.3%	69.9%
29,625	DILLON	1,800	24	808	967	1	159 SR	1.3%	44.9%	53.7%
19,928	DORCHESTER	2,950	85	143	2,717	5	2,574 SR	2.9%	4.8%	92.1%
17,894	EDGEFIELD	1,830	6	27	1,797		1,770 SR	0.3%	1.5%	98.2%
24,187	FAIRFIELD	1,349	63	211	1,073	2	862 SR	4.7%	15.6%	79.5%
70,582	FLORENCE	5,110	192	1,189	3,729		2,540 SR	3.8%	23.3%	73.0%
26,352	GEORGETOWN	2,470	92	432	1,943	3	1,511 SR	3.7%	17.5%	78.7%
136,580	GREENVILLE	9,474	789	2,745	5,922	18	3,177 SR	8.3%	29.0%	62.5%
40,083	GREENWOOD	3,014	63	440	2,508	3	2,068 SR	2.1%	14.6%	83.2%
17,465	HAMPTON	1,622	10	81	1,530	1	1,449 SR	0.6%	5.0%	94.3%
51,951	HORRY	3,961	113	503	3,345		2,842 SR	2.9%	12.7%	84.4%
11,011	JASPER	887	31	141	715		574 SR	3.5%	15.9%	80.6%
32,913	KERSHAW	1,966	49	302	1,615		1,313 SR	2.5%	15.4%	82.1%
33,542	LANCASTER	2,534	30	855	1,649		794 SR	1.2%	33.7%	65.1%
44,185	LAURENS	2,629	69	513	2,047		1,534 SR	2.6%	19.5%	77.9%
24,908	LEE	1,333	36	142	1,155		1,013 SR	2.7%	10.7%	86.6%
35,994	LEXINGTON	2,861	58	566	2,237		1,671 SR	2.0%	19.8%	78.2%
10,367	MCCORMICK	743		30	713		683 SR		4.0%	96.0%
30,107	MARION	1,534	14	301	1,219		918 SR	0.9%	19.6%	79.5%
33,281	MARLBORO	1,479	41	354	1,083	1	729 SR	2.8%	23.9%	73.2%
33,577	NEWBERRY	3,161	47	349	2,758	7	2,409 SR	1.5%	11.0%	87.3%
36,512	OCONEE	1,957	135	666	1,155	1	489 SR	6.9%	34.0%	59.0%
63,707	ORANGEBURG	3,763	164	435	3,160	4	2,725 SR	4.4%	11.6%	84.0%
37,111	PICKENS	1,944	165	435	1,344		909 SR	8.5%	22.4%	69.1%
104,843	RICHLAND	9,193	670	2,419	6,096	8	3,677 SR	7.3%	26.3%	66.3%
17,192	SALUDA	1,914	15	187	1,712		1,525 SR	0.8%	9.8%	89.4%
127,733	SPARTANBURG	12,041	627	6,741	4,660	13	2,081 D	5.2%	56.0%	38.7%
52,463	SUMTER	3,477	154	605	2,718		2,113 SR	4.4%	17.4%	78.2%
31,360	UNION	3,419	46	1,283	2,090		807 SR	1.3%	37.5%	61.1%
41,011	WILLIAMSBURG	1,989	23	126	1,839	1	1,713 SR	1.2%	6.3%	92.5%
58,663	YORK	3,562	167	1,412	1,983		571 SR	4.7%	39.6%	55.7%
1,899,804	TOTAL	142,571	5,386	34,423	102,607	155	68,184 SR	3.8%	24.1%	72.0%

SOUTH CAROLINA

PRESIDENT 1944

1940 Census Population	County	Total Vote	Republican	Democratic	Other	Rep.-Dem. Plurality	Percentage Total Vote Rep.	Total Vote Dem.	Major Vote Rep.	Major Vote Dem.
22,931	ABBEVILLE	819	19	789	11	770 D	2.3%	96.3%	2.4%	97.6%
49,916	AIKEN	2,633	60	2,403	170	2,343 D	2.3%	91.3%	2.4%	97.6%
13,040	ALLENDALE	718	8	678	32	670 D	1.1%	94.4%	1.2%	98.8%
88,712	ANDERSON	2,978	89	2,687	202	2,598 D	3.0%	90.2%	3.2%	96.8%
18,643	BAMBERG	1,041	106	737	198	631 D	10.2%	70.8%	12.6%	87.4%
20,138	BARNWELL	1,506	8	1,482	16	1,474 D	0.5%	98.4%	0.5%	99.5%
22,037	BEAUFORT	797	108	594	95	486 D	13.6%	74.5%	15.4%	84.6%
27,128	BERKELEY	716	32	521	163	489 D	4.5%	72.8%	5.8%	94.2%
16,229	CALHOUN	686	1	602	83	601 D	0.1%	87.8%	0.2%	99.8%
121,105	CHARLESTON	8,581	1,184	6,260	1,137	5,076 D	13.8%	73.0%	15.9%	84.1%
33,290	CHEROKEE	1,721	68	1,620	33	1,552 D	4.0%	94.1%	4.0%	96.0%
32,579	CHESTER	1,625	89	1,441	95	1,352 D	5.5%	88.7%	5.8%	94.2%
35,963	CHESTERFIELD	3,262	15	3,222	25	3,207 D	0.5%	98.8%	0.5%	99.5%
31,500	CLARENDON	1,289	27	1,053	209	1,026 D	2.1%	81.7%	2.5%	97.5%
26,268	COLLETON	1,997	45	1,653	299	1,608 D	2.3%	82.8%	2.7%	97.3%
45,198	DARLINGTON	1,978	46	1,808	124	1,762 D	2.3%	91.4%	2.5%	97.5%
29,625	DILLON	1,004	27	864	113	837 D	2.7%	86.1%	3.0%	97.0%
19,928	DORCHESTER	1,676	65	1,181	430	1,116 D	3.9%	70.5%	5.2%	94.8%
17,894	EDGEFIELD	709	3	654	52	651 D	0.4%	92.2%	0.5%	99.5%
24,187	FAIRFIELD	863	21	798	44	777 D	2.4%	92.5%	2.6%	97.4%
70,582	FLORENCE	3,212	128	2,822	262	2,694 D	4.0%	87.9%	4.3%	95.7%
26,352	GEORGETOWN	1,408	52	1,197	159	1,145 D	3.7%	85.0%	4.2%	95.8%
136,580	GREENVILLE	8,094	711	7,107	276	6,396 D	8.8%	87.8%	9.1%	90.9%
40,083	GREENWOOD	2,686	71	2,381	234	2,310 D	2.6%	88.6%	2.9%	97.1%
17,465	HAMPTON	850	3	575	272	572 D	0.4%	67.6%	0.5%	99.5%
51,951	HORRY	2,728	137	2,403	188	2,266 D	5.0%	88.1%	5.4%	94.6%
11,011	JASPER	454	18	230	206	212 D	4.0%	50.7%	7.3%	92.7%
32,913	KERSHAW	1,971	21	1,872	78	1,851 D	1.1%	95.0%	1.1%	98.9%
33,542	LANCASTER	2,536	13	2,383	140	2,370 D	0.5%	94.0%	0.5%	99.5%
44,185	LAURENS	2,060	38	1,924	98	1,886 D	1.8%	93.4%	1.9%	98.1%
24,908	LEE	875	50	764	61	714 D	5.7%	87.3%	6.1%	93.9%
35,994	LEXINGTON	2,120	20	1,986	114	1,966 D	0.9%	93.7%	1.0%	99.0%
10,367	MCCORMICK	354	1	307	46	306 D	0.3%	86.7%	0.3%	99.7%
30,107	MARION	924	9	858	57	849 D	1.0%	92.9%	1.0%	99.0%
33,281	MARLBORO	979	34	874	71	840 D	3.5%	89.3%	3.7%	96.3%
33,577	NEWBERRY	2,343	70	1,940	333	1,870 D	3.0%	82.8%	3.5%	96.5%
36,512	OCONEE	1,498	106	1,316	76	1,210 D	7.1%	87.9%	7.5%	92.5%
63,707	ORANGEBURG	2,693	87	2,440	166	2,353 D	3.2%	90.6%	3.4%	96.6%
37,111	PICKENS	2,468	211	1,662	595	1,451 D	8.5%	67.3%	11.3%	88.7%
104,843	RICHLAND	7,077	140	6,590	347	6,450 D	2.0%	93.1%	2.1%	97.9%
17,192	SALUDA	1,080	14	924	142	910 D	1.3%	85.6%	1.5%	98.5%
127,733	SPARTANBURG	8,738	402	8,092	244	7,690 D	4.6%	92.6%	4.7%	95.3%
52,463	SUMTER	2,401	73	2,111	217	2,038 D	3.0%	87.9%	3.3%	96.7%
31,360	UNION	3,152	33	3,041	78	3,008 D	1.0%	96.5%	1.1%	98.9%
41,011	WILLIAMSBURG	1,291	27	1,118	146	1,091 D	2.1%	86.6%	2.4%	97.6%
58,663	YORK	2,791	127	2,637	27	2,510 D	4.6%	94.5%	4.6%	95.4%
1,899,804	TOTAL	103,382	4,617	90,601	8,164	85,984 D	4.5%	87.6%	4.8%	95.2%

SOUTH CAROLINA

PRESIDENT 1940

1940 Census Population	County	Total Vote	Republican	Democratic	Other	Rep.-Dem. Plurality	Percentage Total Vote Rep.	Total Vote Dem.	Major Vote Rep.	Major Vote Dem.
22,931	ABBEVILLE	1,039	32	1,007		975 D	3.1%	96.9%	3.1%	96.9%
49,916	AIKEN	2,861	89	2,772		2,683 D	3.1%	96.9%	3.1%	96.9%
13,040	ALLENDALE	935	30	905		875 D	3.2%	96.8%	3.2%	96.8%
88,712	ANDERSON	3,849	86	3,763		3,677 D	2.2%	97.8%	2.2%	97.8%
18,643	BAMBERG	917	13	904		891 D	1.4%	98.6%	1.4%	98.6%
20,138	BARNWELL	1,858	13	1,845		1,832 D	0.7%	99.3%	0.7%	99.3%
22,037	BEAUFORT	673	91	582		491 D	13.5%	86.5%	13.5%	86.5%
27,128	BERKELEY	581	91	490		399 D	15.7%	84.3%	15.7%	84.3%
16,229	CALHOUN	660	3	657		654 D	0.5%	99.5%	0.5%	99.5%
121,105	CHARLESTON	9,517	1,372	8,145		6,773 D	14.4%	85.6%	14.4%	85.6%
33,290	CHEROKEE	2,105	36	2,069		2,033 D	1.7%	98.3%	1.7%	98.3%
32,579	CHESTER	1,965	35	1,930		1,895 D	1.8%	98.2%	1.8%	98.2%
35,963	CHESTERFIELD	2,900	20	2,880		2,860 D	0.7%	99.3%	0.7%	99.3%
31,500	CLARENDON	1,208	54	1,154		1,100 D	4.5%	95.5%	4.5%	95.5%
26,268	COLLETON	1,262	65	1,197		1,132 D	5.2%	94.8%	5.2%	94.8%
45,198	DARLINGTON	1,455	60	1,395		1,335 D	4.1%	95.9%	4.1%	95.9%
29,625	DILLON	893	25	868		843 D	2.8%	97.2%	2.8%	97.2%
19,928	DORCHESTER	1,103	110	993		883 D	10.0%	90.0%	10.0%	90.0%
17,894	EDGEFIELD	1,074	9	1,065		1,056 D	0.8%	99.2%	0.8%	99.2%
24,187	FAIRFIELD	868	20	848		828 D	2.3%	97.7%	2.3%	97.7%
70,582	FLORENCE	2,692	95	2,597		2,502 D	3.5%	96.5%	3.5%	96.5%
26,352	GEORGETOWN	1,658	155	1,503		1,348 D	9.3%	90.7%	9.3%	90.7%
136,580	GREENVILLE	8,632	514	8,118		7,604 D	6.0%	94.0%	6.0%	94.0%
40,083	GREENWOOD	2,953	39	2,914		2,875 D	1.3%	98.7%	1.3%	98.7%
17,465	HAMPTON	1,222	24	1,198		1,174 D	2.0%	98.0%	2.0%	98.0%
51,951	HORRY	2,275	164	2,111		1,947 D	7.2%	92.8%	7.2%	92.8%
11,011	JASPER	459	41	418		377 D	8.9%	91.1%	8.9%	91.1%
32,913	KERSHAW	1,194	20	1,174		1,154 D	1.7%	98.3%	1.7%	98.3%
33,542	LANCASTER	3,219	14	3,205		3,191 D	0.4%	99.6%	0.4%	99.6%
44,185	LAURENS	2,737	40	2,697		2,657 D	1.5%	98.5%	1.5%	98.5%
24,908	LEE	845	20	825		805 D	2.4%	97.6%	2.4%	97.6%
35,994	LEXINGTON	1,513	17	1,496		1,479 D	1.1%	98.9%	1.1%	98.9%
10,367	MCCORMICK	430	11	419		408 D	2.6%	97.4%	2.6%	97.4%
30,107	MARION	734	18	716		698 D	2.5%	97.5%	2.5%	97.5%
33,281	MARLBORO	539	13	526		513 D	2.4%	97.6%	2.4%	97.6%
33,577	NEWBERRY	1,774	35	1,739		1,704 D	2.0%	98.0%	2.0%	98.0%
36,512	OCONEE	1,736	143	1,593		1,450 D	8.2%	91.8%	8.2%	91.8%
63,707	ORANGEBURG	2,412	56	2,356		2,300 D	2.3%	97.7%	2.3%	97.7%
37,111	PICKENS	2,198	76	2,122		2,046 D	3.5%	96.5%	3.5%	96.5%
104,843	RICHLAND	4,948	167	4,781		4,614 D	3.4%	96.6%	3.4%	96.6%
17,192	SALUDA	1,130	15	1,115		1,100 D	1.3%	98.7%	1.3%	98.7%
127,733	SPARTANBURG	9,367	248	9,119		8,871 D	2.6%	97.4%	2.6%	97.4%
52,463	SUMTER	—	—	—		—	—	—	—	—
31,360	UNION	3,691	29	3,662		3,633 D	0.8%	99.2%	0.8%	99.2%
41,011	WILLIAMSBURG	1,123	34	1,089		1,055 D	3.0%	97.0%	3.0%	97.0%
58,663	YORK	2,626	118	2,508		2,390 D	4.5%	95.5%	4.5%	95.5%
1,899,804	TOTAL	99,830	4,360	95,470		91,110 D	4.4%	95.6%	4.4%	95.6%

SOUTH CAROLINA

PRESIDENT 1936

1930 Census Population	County	Total Vote	Republican	Democratic	Other	Rep.-Dem. Plurality	Percentage Total Vote Rep.	Total Vote Dem.	Major Vote Rep.	Major Vote Dem.
23,323	ABBEVILLE	1,288	23	1,265		1,242 D	1.8%	98.2%	1.8%	98.2%
47,403	AIKEN	3,333	35	3,298		3,263 D	1.1%	98.9%	1.1%	98.9%
13,294	ALLENDALE	1,239	3	1,236		1,233 D	0.2%	99.8%	0.2%	99.8%
80,949	ANDERSON	4,051	26	4,025		3,999 D	0.6%	99.4%	0.6%	99.4%
19,410	BAMBERG	1,547	5	1,542		1,537 D	0.3%	99.7%	0.3%	99.7%
21,221	BARNWELL	2,159	2	2,157		2,155 D	0.1%	99.9%	0.1%	99.9%
21,815	BEAUFORT	544	43	501		458 D	7.9%	92.1%	7.9%	92.1%
22,236	BERKELEY	698	8	690		682 D	1.1%	98.9%	1.1%	98.9%
16,707	CALHOUN	822	1	821		820 D	0.1%	99.9%	0.1%	99.9%
101,050	CHARLESTON	8,432	417	8,015		7,598 D	4.9%	95.1%	4.9%	95.1%
32,201	CHEROKEE	2,303	23	2,280		2,257 D	1.0%	99.0%	1.0%	99.0%
31,803	CHESTER	2,166	11	2,155		2,144 D	0.5%	99.5%	0.5%	99.5%
34,334	CHESTERFIELD	3,210	18	3,192		3,174 D	0.6%	99.4%	0.6%	99.4%
30,036	CLARENDON	1,277	17	1,260		1,243 D	1.3%	98.7%	1.3%	98.7%
25,821	COLLETON	1,471	8	1,463		1,455 D	0.5%	99.5%	0.5%	99.5%
41,427	DARLINGTON	2,007	12	1,995		1,983 D	0.6%	99.4%	0.6%	99.4%
25,733	DILLON	1,109	5	1,104		1,099 D	0.5%	99.5%	0.5%	99.5%
18,956	DORCHESTER	917	28	889		861 D	3.1%	96.9%	3.1%	96.9%
19,326	EDGEFIELD	1,305	1	1,304		1,303 D	0.1%	99.9%	0.1%	99.9%
23,287	FAIRFIELD	1,018	13	1,005		992 D	1.3%	98.7%	1.3%	98.7%
61,027	FLORENCE	4,219	25	4,194		4,169 D	0.6%	99.4%	0.6%	99.4%
21,738	GEORGETOWN	1,334	61	1,273		1,212 D	4.6%	95.4%	4.6%	95.4%
117,009	GREENVILLE	8,402	92	8,310		8,218 D	1.1%	98.9%	1.1%	98.9%
36,078	GREENWOOD	3,083	19	3,064		3,045 D	0.6%	99.4%	0.6%	99.4%
17,243	HAMPTON	1,261	8	1,253		1,245 D	0.6%	99.4%	0.6%	99.4%
39,376	HORRY	2,927		2,927		2,927 D		100.0%		100.0%
9,988	JASPER	456	4	452		448 D	0.9%	99.1%	0.9%	99.1%
32,070	KERSHAW	1,420	20	1,400		1,380 D	1.4%	98.6%	1.4%	98.6%
27,980	LANCASTER	2,631		2,631		2,631 D		100.0%		100.0%
42,094	LAURENS	3,082	13	3,069		3,056 D	0.4%	99.6%	0.4%	99.6%
24,096	LEE	1,050	5	1,045		1,040 D	0.5%	99.5%	0.5%	99.5%
36,494	LEXINGTON	2,170	32	2,138		2,106 D	1.5%	98.5%	1.5%	98.5%
11,471	MCCORMICK	664	8	656		648 D	1.2%	98.8%	1.2%	98.8%
27,221	MARION	1,224	5	1,219		1,214 D	0.4%	99.6%	0.4%	99.6%
31,634	MARLBORO	995	7	988		981 D	0.7%	99.3%	0.7%	99.3%
34,681	NEWBERRY	2,624	9	2,615		2,606 D	0.3%	99.7%	0.3%	99.7%
33,368	OCONEE	2,110	53	2,057		2,004 D	2.5%	97.5%	2.5%	97.5%
63,864	ORANGEBURG	3,006	59	2,947		2,888 D	2.0%	98.0%	2.0%	98.0%
33,709	PICKENS	2,728	50	2,678		2,628 D	1.8%	98.2%	1.8%	98.2%
87,667	RICHLAND	6,880	152	6,728		6,576 D	2.2%	97.8%	2.2%	97.8%
18,148	SALUDA	1,334	10	1,324		1,314 D	0.7%	99.3%	0.7%	99.3%
116,323	SPARTANBURG	10,912	173	10,739		10,566 D	1.6%	98.4%	1.6%	98.4%
45,902	SUMTER	2,120	58	2,062		2,004 D	2.7%	97.3%	2.7%	97.3%
30,920	UNION	3,467	9	3,458		3,449 D	0.3%	99.7%	0.3%	99.7%
34,914	WILLIAMSBURG	1,290	6	1,284		1,278 D	0.5%	99.5%	0.5%	99.5%
53,418	YORK	3,152	69	3,083		3,014 D	2.2%	97.8%	2.2%	97.8%
1,738,765	TOTAL	115,437	1,646	113,791		112,145 D	1.4%	98.6%	1.4%	98.6%

SOUTH CAROLINA

PRESIDENT 1932

1930 Census Population	County	Total Vote	Republican	Democratic	Other	Rep.-Dem. Plurality	Percentage Total Vote Rep.	Total Vote Dem.	Major Vote Rep.	Major Vote Dem.
23,323	ABBEVILLE	1,194	9	1,184	1	1,175 D	0.8%	99.2%	0.8%	99.2%
47,403	AIKEN	3,393	47	3,346		3,299 D	1.4%	98.6%	1.4%	98.6%
13,294	ALLENDALE	1,118	10	1,108		1,098 D	0.9%	99.1%	0.9%	99.1%
80,949	ANDERSON	4,097	30	4,067		4,037 D	0.7%	99.3%	0.7%	99.3%
19,410	BAMBERG	1,613	15	1,598		1,583 D	0.9%	99.1%	0.9%	99.1%
21,221	BARNWELL	1,892	15	1,877		1,862 D	0.8%	99.2%	0.8%	99.2%
21,815	BEAUFORT	624	63	555	6	492 D	10.1%	88.9%	10.2%	89.8%
22,236	BERKELEY	963	22	941		919 D	2.3%	97.7%	2.3%	97.7%
16,707	CALHOUN	704	10	694		684 D	1.4%	98.6%	1.4%	98.6%
101,050	CHARLESTON	5,833	451	5,351	31	4,900 D	7.7%	91.7%	7.8%	92.2%
32,201	CHEROKEE	2,402	37	2,363	2	2,326 D	1.5%	98.4%	1.5%	98.5%
31,803	CHESTER	2,043	23	2,020		1,997 D	1.1%	98.9%	1.1%	98.9%
34,334	CHESTERFIELD	2,132	23	2,109		2,086 D	1.1%	98.9%	1.1%	98.9%
30,036	CLARENDON	987	25	962		937 D	2.5%	97.5%	2.5%	97.5%
25,821	COLLETON	1,914	5	1,908	1	1,903 D	0.3%	99.7%	0.3%	99.7%
41,427	DARLINGTON	1,441	31	1,409	1	1,378 D	2.2%	97.8%	2.2%	97.8%
25,733	DILLON	1,018	20	998		978 D	2.0%	98.0%	2.0%	98.0%
18,956	DORCHESTER	1,438	23	1,412	3	1,389 D	1.6%	98.2%	1.6%	98.4%
19,326	EDGEFIELD	1,326	10	1,316		1,306 D	0.8%	99.2%	0.8%	99.2%
23,287	FAIRFIELD	914	10	901	3	891 D	1.1%	98.6%	1.1%	98.9%
61,027	FLORENCE	3,226	29	3,195	2	3,166 D	0.9%	99.0%	0.9%	99.1%
21,738	GEORGETOWN	1,717	33	1,684		1,651 D	1.9%	98.1%	1.9%	98.1%
117,009	GREENVILLE	8,058	126	7,930	2	7,804 D	1.6%	98.4%	1.6%	98.4%
36,078	GREENWOOD	3,255	15	3,240		3,225 D	0.5%	99.5%	0.5%	99.5%
17,243	HAMPTON	1,800	18	1,782		1,764 D	1.0%	99.0%	1.0%	99.0%
39,376	HORRY	3,253	29	3,224		3,195 D	0.9%	99.1%	0.9%	99.1%
9,988	JASPER	410	11	399		388 D	2.7%	97.3%	2.7%	97.3%
32,070	KERSHAW	1,059	8	1,051		1,043 D	0.8%	99.2%	0.8%	99.2%
27,980	LANCASTER	3,108	5	3,103		3,098 D	0.2%	99.8%	0.2%	99.8%
42,094	LAURENS	2,767	13	2,750	4	2,737 D	0.5%	99.4%	0.5%	99.5%
24,096	LEE	752	10	742		732 D	1.3%	98.7%	1.3%	98.7%
36,494	LEXINGTON	147	5	141	1	136 D	3.4%	95.9%	3.4%	96.6%
11,471	MCCORMICK	535	5	530		525 D	0.9%	99.1%	0.9%	99.1%
27,221	MARION	960	12	948		936 D	1.3%	98.8%	1.3%	98.8%
31,634	MARLBORO	707	22	685		663 D	3.1%	96.9%	3.1%	96.9%
34,681	NEWBERRY	3,151	12	3,139		3,127 D	0.4%	99.6%	0.4%	99.6%
33,368	OCONEE	1,818	14	1,803	1	1,789 D	0.8%	99.2%	0.8%	99.2%
63,864	ORANGEBURG	2,757	111	2,643	3	2,532 D	4.0%	95.9%	4.0%	96.0%
33,709	PICKENS	2,742	57	2,685		2,628 D	2.1%	97.9%	2.1%	97.9%
87,667	RICHLAND	4,500	119	4,371	10	4,252 D	2.6%	97.1%	2.7%	97.3%
18,148	SALUDA	1,314	7	1,307		1,300 D	0.5%	99.5%	0.5%	99.5%
116,323	SPARTANBURG	9,444	227	9,216	1	8,989 D	2.4%	97.6%	2.4%	97.6%
45,902	SUMTER	1,876	59	1,809	8	1,750 D	3.1%	96.4%	3.2%	96.8%
30,920	UNION	3,147	14	3,131	2	3,117 D	0.4%	99.5%	0.4%	99.6%
34,914	WILLIAMSBURG	1,253	9	1,244		1,235 D	0.7%	99.3%	0.7%	99.3%
53,418	YORK	3,605	129	3,476		3,347 D	3.6%	96.4%	3.6%	96.4%
1,738,765	TOTAL	104,407	1,978	102,347	82	100,369 D	1.9%	98.0%	1.9%	98.1%

SOUTH CAROLINA

PRESIDENT 1928

1920 Census Population	County	Total Vote	Republican	Democratic	Other	Rep.-Dem. Plurality	Percentage Total Vote Rep.	Total Vote Dem.	Major Vote Rep.	Major Vote Dem.
27,139	ABBEVILLE	1,085	65	1,020		955 D	6.0%	94.0%	6.0%	94.0%
45,574	AIKEN	1,553	242	1,308	3	1,066 D	15.6%	84.2%	15.6%	84.4%
16,098	ALLENDALE	840	24	816		792 D	2.9%	97.1%	2.9%	97.1%
76,349	ANDERSON	1,841	61	1,780		1,719 D	3.3%	96.7%	3.3%	96.7%
20,962	BAMBERG	783	4	779		775 D	0.5%	99.5%	0.5%	99.5%
23,081	BARNWELL	1,062	34	1,028		994 D	3.2%	96.8%	3.2%	96.8%
22,269	BEAUFORT	541	124	414	3	290 D	22.9%	76.5%	23.0%	77.0%
22,558	BERKELEY	318	42	276		234 D	13.2%	86.8%	13.2%	86.8%
18,384	CALHOUN	584	7	577		570 D	1.2%	98.8%	1.2%	98.8%
108,450	CHARLESTON	6,075	1,759	4,298	18	2,539 D	29.0%	70.7%	29.0%	71.0%
27,570	CHEROKEE	1,477	89	1,388		1,299 D	6.0%	94.0%	6.0%	94.0%
33,389	CHESTER	1,323	36	1,285	2	1,249 D	2.7%	97.1%	2.7%	97.3%
31,969	CHESTERFIELD	1,385	23	1,362		1,339 D	1.7%	98.3%	1.7%	98.3%
34,878	CLARENDON	772	10	762		752 D	1.3%	98.7%	1.3%	98.7%
29,897	COLLETON	1,145	22	1,122	1	1,100 D	1.9%	98.0%	1.9%	98.1%
39,126	DARLINGTON	1,183	48	1,135		1,087 D	4.1%	95.9%	4.1%	95.9%
25,278	DILLON	579	21	558		537 D	3.6%	96.4%	3.6%	96.4%
19,459	DORCHESTER	1,149	44	1,105		1,061 D	3.8%	96.2%	3.8%	96.2%
23,928	EDGEFIELD	1,205	4	1,201		1,197 D	0.3%	99.7%	0.3%	99.7%
27,159	FAIRFIELD	875	94	781		687 D	10.7%	89.3%	10.7%	89.3%
50,406	FLORENCE	1,765	93	1,672		1,579 D	5.3%	94.7%	5.3%	94.7%
21,716	GEORGETOWN	660	74	586		512 D	11.2%	88.8%	11.2%	88.8%
88,498	GREENVILLE	4,664	546	4,116	2	3,570 D	11.7%	88.3%	11.7%	88.3%
35,791	GREENWOOD	2,959	38	2,921		2,883 D	1.3%	98.7%	1.3%	98.7%
19,550	HAMPTON	1,117	19	1,098		1,079 D	1.7%	98.3%	1.7%	98.3%
32,077	HORRY	1,251	27	1,224		1,197 D	2.2%	97.8%	2.2%	97.8%
9,868	JASPER	107	5	102		97 D	4.7%	95.3%	4.7%	95.3%
29,398	KERSHAW	1,288	14	1,274		1,260 D	1.1%	98.9%	1.1%	98.9%
28,628	LANCASTER	1,444	8	1,436		1,428 D	0.6%	99.4%	0.6%	99.4%
42,560	LAURENS	2,037	44	1,989	4	1,945 D	2.2%	97.6%	2.2%	97.8%
26,827	LEE	599	6	593		587 D	1.0%	99.0%	1.0%	99.0%
35,676	LEXINGTON	1,289	61	1,228		1,167 D	4.7%	95.3%	4.7%	95.3%
16,444	MCCORMICK	636	20	615	1	595 D	3.1%	96.7%	3.1%	96.9%
23,721	MARION	733	51	682		631 D	7.0%	93.0%	7.0%	93.0%
33,180	MARLBORO	756	27	729		702 D	3.6%	96.4%	3.6%	96.4%
35,552	NEWBERRY	2,094	12	2,077	5	2,065 D	0.6%	99.2%	0.6%	99.4%
30,117	OCONEE	1,335	70	1,263	2	1,193 D	5.2%	94.6%	5.3%	94.7%
64,907	ORANGEBURG	1,637	92	1,545		1,453 D	5.6%	94.4%	5.6%	94.4%
28,329	PICKENS	1,302	192	1,110		918 D	14.7%	85.3%	14.7%	85.3%
78,122	RICHLAND	3,602	444	3,158		2,714 D	12.3%	87.7%	12.3%	87.7%
22,088	SALUDA	801	5	796		791 D	0.6%	99.4%	0.6%	99.4%
94,265	SPARTANBURG	4,620	760	3,859	1	3,099 D	16.5%	83.5%	16.5%	83.5%
43,040	SUMTER	1,376	174	1,202		1,028 D	12.6%	87.4%	12.6%	87.4%
30,372	UNION	2,535	74	2,460	1	2,386 D	2.9%	97.0%	2.9%	97.1%
38,539	WILLIAMSBURG	847	22	825		803 D	2.6%	97.4%	2.6%	97.4%
50,536	YORK	1,376	227	1,145	4	918 D	16.5%	83.2%	16.5%	83.5%
1,683,724	TOTAL	68,605	5,858	62,700	47	56,842 D	8.5%	91.4%	8.5%	91.5%

SOUTH CAROLINA

PRESIDENT 1924

1920 Census Population	County	Total Vote	Republican	Democratic	Other	Rep.-Dem. Plurality	Percentage Total Vote Rep.	Percentage Total Vote Dem.	Percentage Major Vote Rep.	Percentage Major Vote Dem.
27,139	ABBEVILLE	737	19	681	37	662 D	2.6%	92.4%	2.7%	97.3%
45,574	AIKEN	1,509	16	1,488	5	1,472 D	1.1%	98.6%	1.1%	98.9%
16,098	ALLENDALE	464	14	450		436 D	3.0%	97.0%	3.0%	97.0%
76,349	ANDERSON	1,467	9	1,455	3	1,446 D	0.6%	99.2%	0.6%	99.4%
20,962	BAMBERG	729	7	708	14	701 D	1.0%	97.1%	1.0%	99.0%
23,081	BARNWELL	872	23	847	2	824 D	2.6%	97.1%	2.6%	97.4%
22,269	BEAUFORT	438	64	365	9	301 D	14.6%	83.3%	14.9%	85.1%
22,558	BERKELEY	527	26	501		475 D	4.9%	95.1%	4.9%	95.1%
18,384	CALHOUN	599	5	593	1	588 D	0.8%	99.0%	0.8%	99.2%
108,450	CHARLESTON	3,023	361	2,554	108	2,193 D	11.9%	84.5%	12.4%	87.6%
27,570	CHEROKEE	1,216	24	1,186	6	1,162 D	2.0%	97.5%	2.0%	98.0%
33,389	CHESTER	868	12	850	6	838 D	1.4%	97.9%	1.4%	98.6%
31,969	CHESTERFIELD	1,551	11	1,539	1	1,528 D	0.7%	99.2%	0.7%	99.3%
34,878	CLARENDON	636	20	615	1	595 D	3.1%	96.7%	3.1%	96.9%
29,897	COLLETON	813	11	800	2	789 D	1.4%	98.4%	1.4%	98.6%
39,126	DARLINGTON	966	3	956	7	953 D	0.3%	99.0%	0.3%	99.7%
25,278	DILLON	601	3	598		595 D	0.5%	99.5%	0.5%	99.5%
19,459	DORCHESTER	717	20	697		677 D	2.8%	97.2%	2.8%	97.2%
23,928	EDGEFIELD	915		915		915 D		100.0%		100.0%
27,159	FAIRFIELD	644	11	631	2	620 D	1.7%	98.0%	1.7%	98.3%
50,406	FLORENCE	1,301	32	1,217	52	1,185 D	2.5%	93.5%	2.6%	97.4%
21,716	GEORGETOWN	160	24	134	2	110 D	15.0%	83.8%	15.2%	84.8%
88,498	GREENVILLE	3,829	59	3,728	42	3,669 D	1.5%	97.4%	1.6%	98.4%
35,791	GREENWOOD	1,834	15	1,815	4	1,800 D	0.8%	99.0%	0.8%	99.2%
19,550	HAMPTON	737	3	730	4	727 D	0.4%	99.1%	0.4%	99.6%
32,077	HORRY	1,350	1	1,346	3	1,345 D	0.1%	99.7%	0.1%	99.9%
9,868	JASPER	128		89	39	89 D		69.5%		100.0%
29,398	KERSHAW	734	1	733		732 D	0.1%	99.9%	0.1%	99.9%
28,628	LANCASTER	1,363	8	1,355		1,347 D	0.6%	99.4%	0.6%	99.4%
42,560	LAURENS	2,115	6	2,105	4	2,099 D	0.3%	99.5%	0.3%	99.7%
26,827	LEE	—	—	—	—	—	—	—	—	—
35,676	LEXINGTON	1,404	7	1,395	2	1,388 D	0.5%	99.4%	0.5%	99.5%
16,444	MCCORMICK	551	15	520	16	505 D	2.7%	94.4%	2.8%	97.2%
23,721	MARION	618	2	616		614 D	0.3%	99.7%	0.3%	99.7%
33,180	MARLBORO	716		716		716 D		100.0%		100.0%
35,552	NEWBERRY	1,817	13	1,802	2	1,789 D	0.7%	99.2%	0.7%	99.3%
30,117	OCONEE	1,027	5	989	33	984 D	0.5%	96.3%	0.5%	99.5%
64,907	ORANGEBURG	1,807	67	1,727	13	1,660 D	3.7%	95.6%	3.7%	96.3%
28,329	PICKENS	1,082	35	1,044	3	1,009 D	3.2%	96.5%	3.2%	96.8%
78,122	RICHLAND	2,531	88	2,369	74	2,281 D	3.5%	93.6%	3.6%	96.4%
22,088	SALUDA	1,099	3	1,094	2	1,091 D	0.3%	99.5%	0.3%	99.7%
94,265	SPARTANBURG	—	—	—	—	—	—	—	—	—
43,040	SUMTER	1,216	18	1,136	62	1,118 D	1.5%	93.4%	1.6%	98.4%
30,372	UNION	1,896	27	1,862	7	1,835 D	1.4%	98.2%	1.4%	98.6%
38,539	WILLIAMSBURG	676	4	672		668 D	0.6%	99.4%	0.6%	99.4%
50,536	YORK	1,472	31	1,385	56	1,354 D	2.1%	94.1%	2.2%	97.8%
1,683,724	TOTAL	50,755	1,123	49,008	624	47,885 D	2.2%	96.6%	2.2%	97.8%

SOUTH CAROLINA

PRESIDENT 1920

1920 Census Population	County	Total Vote	Republican	Democratic	Other	Rep.-Dem. Plurality	Percentage: Total Vote Rep.	Total Vote Dem.	Major Vote Rep.	Major Vote Dem.
27,139	ABBEVILLE	881	13	868		855 D	1.5%	98.5%	1.5%	98.5%
45,574	AIKEN	1,713	64	1,649		1,585 D	3.7%	96.3%	3.7%	96.3%
16,098	ALLENDALE	451	11	440		429 D	2.4%	97.6%	2.4%	97.6%
76,349	ANDERSON	2,522	33	2,489		2,456 D	1.3%	98.7%	1.3%	98.7%
20,962	BAMBERG	688		688		688 D		100.0%		100.0%
23,081	BARNWELL	746	25	721		696 D	3.4%	96.6%	3.4%	96.6%
22,269	BEAUFORT	414	149	265		116 D	36.0%	64.0%	36.0%	64.0%
22,558	BERKELEY	572	24	548		524 D	4.2%	95.8%	4.2%	95.8%
18,384	CALHOUN	672	41	631		590 D	6.1%	93.9%	6.1%	93.9%
108,450	CHARLESTON	3,302	373	2,929		2,556 D	11.3%	88.7%	11.3%	88.7%
27,570	CHEROKEE	1,819	48	1,771		1,723 D	2.6%	97.4%	2.6%	97.4%
33,389	CHESTER	1,259	22	1,237		1,215 D	1.7%	98.3%	1.7%	98.3%
31,969	CHESTERFIELD	2,080	14	2,066		2,052 D	0.7%	99.3%	0.7%	99.3%
34,878	CLARENDON	902		902		902 D		100.0%		100.0%
29,897	COLLETON	1,005	15	990		975 D	1.5%	98.5%	1.5%	98.5%
39,126	DARLINGTON	1,280	18	1,262		1,244 D	1.4%	98.6%	1.4%	98.6%
25,278	DILLON	1,008	5	1,003		998 D	0.5%	99.5%	0.5%	99.5%
19,459	DORCHESTER	932	58	874		816 D	6.2%	93.8%	6.2%	93.8%
23,928	EDGEFIELD	976		976		976 D		100.0%		100.0%
27,159	FAIRFIELD	752	15	737		722 D	2.0%	98.0%	2.0%	98.0%
50,406	FLORENCE	1,842	79	1,763		1,684 D	4.3%	95.7%	4.3%	95.7%
21,716	GEORGETOWN	283	38	245		207 D	13.4%	86.6%	13.4%	86.6%
88,498	GREENVILLE	4,553	144	4,409		4,265 D	3.2%	96.8%	3.2%	96.8%
35,791	GREENWOOD	1,583	15	1,568		1,553 D	0.9%	99.1%	0.9%	99.1%
19,550	HAMPTON	623		623		623 D		100.0%		100.0%
32,077	HORRY	1,758	49	1,709		1,660 D	2.8%	97.2%	2.8%	97.2%
9,868	JASPER	219		219		219 D		100.0%		100.0%
29,398	KERSHAW	1,198	42	1,156		1,114 D	3.5%	96.5%	3.5%	96.5%
28,628	LANCASTER	1,643	10	1,633		1,623 D	0.6%	99.4%	0.6%	99.4%
42,560	LAURENS	2,298	35	2,263		2,228 D	1.5%	98.5%	1.5%	98.5%
26,827	LEE	752	18	734		716 D	2.4%	97.6%	2.4%	97.6%
35,676	LEXINGTON	1,872	59	1,813		1,754 D	3.2%	96.8%	3.2%	96.8%
16,444	MCCORMICK	557		557		557 D		100.0%		100.0%
23,721	MARION	809	1	808		807 D	0.1%	99.9%	0.1%	99.9%
33,180	MARLBORO	965	5	960		955 D	0.5%	99.5%	0.5%	99.5%
35,552	NEWBERRY	2,048	33	2,015		1,982 D	1.6%	98.4%	1.6%	98.4%
30,117	OCONEE	1,319	70	1,249		1,179 D	5.3%	94.7%	5.3%	94.7%
64,907	ORANGEBURG	2,810	284	2,526		2,242 D	10.1%	89.9%	10.1%	89.9%
28,329	PICKENS	1,018	63	955		892 D	6.2%	93.8%	6.2%	93.8%
78,122	RICHLAND	2,729	295	2,434		2,139 D	10.8%	89.2%	10.8%	89.2%
22,088	SALUDA	1,114	3	1,111		1,108 D	0.3%	99.7%	0.3%	99.7%
94,265	SPARTANBURG	4,766	182	4,584		4,402 D	3.8%	96.2%	3.8%	96.2%
43,040	SUMTER	1,344	194	1,150		956 D	14.4%	85.6%	14.4%	85.6%
30,372	UNION	2,178	16	2,162		2,146 D	0.7%	99.3%	0.7%	99.3%
38,539	WILLIAMSBURG	907	12	895		883 D	1.3%	98.7%	1.3%	98.7%
50,536	YORK	1,618	35	1,583		1,548 D	2.2%	97.8%	2.2%	97.8%
1,683,724	TOTAL	66,808	2,610	64,170	28	61,560 D	3.9%	96.1%	3.9%	96.1%

SOUTH CAROLINA

ELECTION NOTES

1956 A special four-column table which gives the Independent elector ticket vote is used to detail this election. Other vote was scattered write-in. The Independent ticket of electors was a States Rights group which was uncommitted to any Presidential candidate.

1952 Other vote was Hamblen (Prohibition write-in). Republican figures include 158,289 Independent and 9,793 Republican votes.

1948 A special four-column table which gives the Thurmond (States Rights) vote is used to detail this election. Other vote was 154 Wallace (Progressive); 1 Thomas (Socialist).

1944 Other vote was 7,799 Uncommitted Southern Democratic elector ticket; 365 Watson (Prohibition). Republican figures include 4,554 Republican and 63 Tolbert elector ticket votes. It should be noted that the plurality in the county-by-county table (85,984 D) is the Republican-Democratic plurality which differs from the three party plurality (82,802 D) on the state summary page.

1940 No returns were canvassed for Sumter county. The Republican figures include 2,496 Jeffersonian Democratic; 1,727 Republican and 137 Tolbert elector ticket votes.

1936 Republican figures include 953 Tolbert elector ticket and 693 Hambright elector ticket votes.

1932 Other vote was Thomas (Socialist).

1928 Other vote was Thomas (Socialist). Republican figures include 3,188 Republican and 2,670 Anti-Smith votes.

1924 Other vote was 623 LaFollette (Progressive); 1 scattered write-in. No returns were canvassed for Lee and Spartanburg counties.

1920 Other vote was Debs (Socialist). The statewide total in the other vote column is the Socialist vote which was not available by county. Republican figures include 2,244 Republican and 366 Insurgent Republican votes.

SOUTH DAKOTA

POPULAR VOTE FOR PRESIDENT 1920 TO 1956

		Republican		Democratic				Percentage			
								Total Vote		Major Vote	
Year	Total Vote	Vote	Candidate	Vote	Candidate	Other Vote	Plurality	Rep.	Dem.	Rep.	Dem.
1956	293,857	171,569	Eisenhower, Dwight D.	122,288	Stevenson, Adlai E.		49,281 R	58.4%	41.6%	58.4%	41.6%
1952	294,283	203,857	Eisenhower, Dwight D.	90,426	Stevenson, Adlai E.		113,431 R	69.3%	30.7%	69.3%	30.7%
1948	250,105	129,651	Dewey, Thomas E.	117,653	Truman, Harry S.	2,801	11,998 R	51.8%	47.0%	52.4%	47.6%
1944	232,076	135,365	Dewey, Thomas E.	96,711	Roosevelt, Franklin D.		38,654 R	58.3%	41.7%	58.3%	41.7%
1940	308,427	177,065	Willkie, Wendell	131,362	Roosevelt, Franklin D.		45,703 R	57.4%	42.6%	57.4%	42.6%
1936	296,452	125,977	Landon, Alfred M.	160,137	Roosevelt, Franklin D.	10,338	34,160 D	42.5%	54.0%	44.0%	56.0%
1932	288,438	99,212	Hoover, Herbert C.	183,515	Roosevelt, Franklin D.	5,711	84,303 D	34.4%	63.6%	35.1%	64.9%
1928	261,857	157,603	Hoover, Herbert C.	102,660	Smith, Alfred E.	1,594	54,943 R	60.2%	39.2%	60.6%	39.4%
1924 **	203,868	101,299	Coolidge, Calvin	27,214	Davis, John W.	75,355	25,944 R	49.7%	13.3%	78.8%	21.2%
1920 **	182,237	110,692	Harding, Warren G.	35,938	Cox, James M.	35,607	74,754 R	60.7%	19.7%	75.5%	24.5%

In 1924 other vote was Progressive. In 1920 other vote was 34,707 Farmer-Labor and 900 Prohibition.

ELECTORAL COLLEGE VOTE 1920 TO 1956

Year	Total	Republican	Democratic	Other
1956	4	4	—	—
1952	4	4	—	—
1948	4	4	—	—
1944	4	4	—	—
1940	4	4	—	—
1936	4	—	4	—
1932	4	—	4	—
1928	5	5	—	—
1924	5	5	—	—
1920	5	5	—	—

SOUTH DAKOTA

SOUTH DAKOTA

PRESIDENT 1956

1950 Census Population	County	Total Vote	Republican	Democratic	Other	Rep.-Dem. Plurality	Percentage Total Vote Rep.	Total Vote Dem.	Major Vote Rep.	Major Vote Dem.
	ARMSTRONG	—	—	—		—	—	—	—	—
5,020	AURORA	2,429	1,055	1,374		319 D	43.4%	56.6%	43.4%	56.6%
21,082	BEADLE	9,830	5,216	4,614		602 R	53.1%	46.9%	53.1%	46.9%
3,396	BENNETT	1,431	746	685		61 R	52.1%	47.9%	52.1%	47.9%
9,440	BON HOMME	4,840	2,696	2,144		552 R	55.7%	44.3%	55.7%	44.3%
17,851	BROOKINGS	7,913	5,293	2,620		2,673 R	66.9%	33.1%	66.9%	33.1%
32,617	BROWN	15,377	8,193	7,184		1,009 R	53.3%	46.7%	53.3%	46.7%
6,076	BRULE	3,211	1,317	1,894		577 D	41.0%	59.0%	41.0%	59.0%
1,615	BUFFALO	632	314	318		4 D	49.7%	50.3%	49.7%	50.3%
8,161	BUTTE	3,259	2,231	1,028		1,203 R	68.5%	31.5%	68.5%	31.5%
4,046	CAMPBELL	1,557	1,268	289		979 R	81.4%	18.6%	81.4%	18.6%
15,558	CHARLES MIX	5,319	2,202	3,117		915 D	41.4%	58.6%	41.4%	58.6%
8,369	CLARK	3,694	2,173	1,521		652 R	58.8%	41.2%	58.8%	41.2%
10,993	CLAY	4,560	2,632	1,928		704 R	57.7%	42.3%	57.7%	42.3%
18,944	CODINGTON	8,922	5,150	3,772		1,378 R	57.7%	42.3%	57.7%	42.3%
6,168	CORSON	2,506	1,394	1,112		282 R	55.6%	44.4%	55.6%	44.4%
5,517	CUSTER	2,367	1,514	853		661 R	64.0%	36.0%	64.0%	36.0%
16,522	DAVISON	7,865	4,056	3,809		247 R	51.6%	48.4%	51.6%	48.4%
12,294	DAY	5,623	2,652	2,971		319 D	47.2%	52.8%	47.2%	52.8%
7,689	DEUEL	3,061	1,698	1,363		335 R	55.5%	44.5%	55.5%	44.5%
4,968	DEWEY	2,109	1,197	912		285 R	56.8%	43.2%	56.8%	43.2%
5,636	DOUGLAS	2,526	1,713	813		900 R	67.8%	32.2%	67.8%	32.2%
7,275	EDMUNDS	3,265	1,685	1,580		105 R	51.6%	48.4%	51.6%	48.4%
10,439	FALL RIVER	3,527	2,377	1,150		1,227 R	67.4%	32.6%	67.4%	32.6%
4,752	FAULK	2,415	1,260	1,155		105 R	52.2%	47.8%	52.2%	47.8%
10,233	GRANT	4,691	2,621	2,070		551 R	55.9%	44.1%	55.9%	44.1%
8,556	GREGORY	3,740	1,945	1,795		150 R	52.0%	48.0%	52.0%	48.0%
3,167	HAAKON	1,530	936	594		342 R	61.2%	38.8%	61.2%	38.8%
7,058	HAMLIN	3,377	2,083	1,294		789 R	61.7%	38.3%	61.7%	38.3%
7,149	HAND	3,257	1,804	1,453		351 R	55.4%	44.6%	55.4%	44.6%
4,896	HANSON	2,237	1,050	1,187		137 D	46.9%	53.1%	46.9%	53.1%
2,289	HARDING	1,026	650	376		274 R	63.4%	36.6%	63.4%	36.6%
8,111	HUGHES	4,610	2,923	1,687		1,236 R	63.4%	36.6%	63.4%	36.6%
11,423	HUTCHINSON	5,290	3,870	1,420		2,450 R	73.2%	26.8%	73.2%	26.8%
2,811	HYDE	1,352	755	597		158 R	55.8%	44.2%	55.8%	44.2%
1,768	JACKSON	898	490	408		82 R	54.6%	45.4%	54.6%	45.4%
4,476	JERAULD	2,180	1,175	1,005		170 R	53.9%	46.1%	53.9%	46.1%
2,281	JONES	1,072	601	471		130 R	56.1%	43.9%	56.1%	43.9%
9,962	KINGSBURY	4,518	2,933	1,585		1,348 R	64.9%	35.1%	64.9%	35.1%
11,792	LAKE	5,462	3,404	2,058		1,346 R	62.3%	37.7%	62.3%	37.7%
16,648	LAWRENCE	6,525	4,654	1,871		2,783 R	71.3%	28.7%	71.3%	28.7%
12,767	LINCOLN	5,670	3,529	2,141		1,388 R	62.2%	37.8%	62.2%	37.8%
4,572	LYMAN	2,024	1,151	873		278 R	56.9%	43.1%	56.9%	43.1%
8,828	MCCOOK	4,140	2,382	1,758		624 R	57.5%	42.5%	57.5%	42.5%
7,071	MCPHERSON	2,858	2,225	633		1,592 R	77.9%	22.1%	77.9%	22.1%
7,835	MARSHALL	3,274	1,639	1,635		4 R	50.1%	49.9%	50.1%	49.9%
11,516	MEADE	4,125	2,467	1,658		809 R	59.8%	40.2%	59.8%	40.2%
3,046	MELLETTE	1,163	643	520		123 R	55.3%	44.7%	55.3%	44.7%
6,268	MINER	2,973	1,456	1,517		61 D	49.0%	51.0%	49.0%	51.0%
70,910	MINNEHAHA	35,378	22,285	13,093		9,192 R	63.0%	37.0%	63.0%	37.0%
9,252	MOODY	3,973	2,133	1,840		293 R	53.7%	46.3%	53.7%	46.3%
34,053	PENNINGTON	16,287	10,955	5,332		5,623 R	67.3%	32.7%	67.3%	32.7%
6,776	PERKINS	2,934	1,743	1,191		552 R	59.4%	40.6%	59.4%	40.6%
1,688	POTTER	2,288	1,445	843		602 R	63.2%	36.8%	63.2%	36.8%
14,929	ROBERTS	6,100	2,854	3,246		392 D	46.8%	53.2%	46.8%	53.2%
5,142	SANBORN	2,629	1,327	1,302		25 R	50.5%	49.5%	50.5%	49.5%
5,669	SHANNON	1,731	782	949		167 D	45.2%	54.8%	45.2%	54.8%
12,204	SPINK	5,556	2,683	2,873		190 D	48.3%	51.7%	48.3%	51.7%
2,055	STANLEY	1,154	587	567		20 R	50.9%	49.1%	50.9%	49.1%
2,713	SULLY	1,220	726	494		232 R	59.5%	40.5%	59.5%	40.5%

SOUTH DAKOTA

PRESIDENT 1956

1950 Census Population	County	Total Vote	Republican	Democratic	Other	Rep.-Dem. Plurality	Percentage Total Vote Rep.	Total Vote Dem.	Major Vote Rep.	Major Vote Dem.
4,758	TODD	1,581	748	833		85 D	47.3%	52.7%	47.3%	52.7%
9,139	TRIPP	3,899	2,064	1,835		229 R	52.9%	47.1%	52.9%	47.1%
12,100	TURNER	5,778	4,096	1,682		2,414 R	70.9%	29.1%	70.9%	29.1%
10,792	UNION	4,979	2,636	2,343		293 R	52.9%	47.1%	52.9%	47.1%
7,648	WALWORTH	3,541	2,132	1,409		723 R	60.2%	39.8%	60.2%	39.8%
1,551	WASHABAUGH	450	265	185		80 R	58.9%	41.1%	58.9%	41.1%
	WASHINGTON	—	—	—		—	—	—	—	—
16,804	YANKTON	7,050	4,063	2,987		1,076 R	57.6%	42.4%	57.6%	42.4%
2,606	ZIEBACH	1,099	627	472		155 R	57.1%	42.9%	57.1%	42.9%
649,740	TOTAL	293,857	171,569	122,288		49,281 R	58.4%	41.6%	58.4%	41.6%

SOUTH DAKOTA

PRESIDENT 1952

1950 Census Population	County	Total Vote	Republican	Democratic	Other	Rep.-Dem. Plurality	Percentage Total Vote Rep.	Total Vote Dem.	Major Vote Rep.	Major Vote Dem.
52	ARMSTRONG	11	6	5		1 R	54.5%	45.5%	54.5%	45.5%
5,020	AURORA	2,455	1,458	997		461 R	59.4%	40.6%	59.4%	40.6%
21,082	BEADLE	9,930	6,487	3,443		3,044 R	65.3%	34.7%	65.3%	34.7%
3,396	BENNETT	1,389	873	516		357 R	62.9%	37.1%	62.9%	37.1%
9,440	BON HOMME	4,815	3,157	1,658		1,499 R	65.6%	34.4%	65.6%	34.4%
17,851	BROOKINGS	7,849	5,988	1,861		4,127 R	76.3%	23.7%	76.3%	23.7%
32,617	BROWN	15,721	9,581	6,140		3,441 R	60.9%	39.1%	60.9%	39.1%
6,076	BRULE	2,970	1,578	1,392		186 R	53.1%	46.9%	53.1%	46.9%
1,615	BUFFALO	672	413	259		154 R	61.5%	38.5%	61.5%	38.5%
8,161	BUTTE	3,526	2,689	837		1,852 R	76.3%	23.7%	76.3%	23.7%
4,046	CAMPBELL	1,704	1,536	168		1,368 R	90.1%	9.9%	90.1%	9.9%
15,558	CHARLES MIX	6,106	3,316	2,790		526 R	54.3%	45.7%	54.3%	45.7%
8,369	CLARK	3,768	2,692	1,076		1,616 R	71.4%	28.6%	71.4%	28.6%
10,993	CLAY	4,714	3,302	1,412		1,890 R	70.0%	30.0%	70.0%	30.0%
18,944	CODINGTON	8,724	5,750	2,974		2,776 R	65.9%	34.1%	65.9%	34.1%
6,168	CORSON	2,546	1,757	789		968 R	69.0%	31.0%	69.0%	31.0%
5,517	CUSTER	2,377	1,725	652		1,073 R	72.6%	27.4%	72.6%	27.4%
16,522	DAVISON	8,001	4,774	3,227		1,547 R	59.7%	40.3%	59.7%	40.3%
12,294	DAY	5,999	3,648	2,351		1,297 R	60.8%	39.2%	60.8%	39.2%
7,689	DEUEL	3,158	2,279	879		1,400 R	72.2%	27.8%	72.2%	27.8%
4,916	DEWEY	1,961	1,301	660		641 R	66.3%	33.7%	66.3%	33.7%
5,636	DOUGLAS	2,631	2,103	528		1,575 R	79.9%	20.1%	79.9%	20.1%
7,275	EDMUNDS	3,191	2,178	1,013		1,165 R	68.3%	31.7%	68.3%	31.7%
10,439	FALL RIVER	3,871	2,863	1,008		1,855 R	74.0%	26.0%	74.0%	26.0%
4,752	FAULK	2,357	1,619	738		881 R	68.7%	31.3%	68.7%	31.3%
10,233	GRANT	4,734	3,234	1,500		1,734 R	68.3%	31.7%	68.3%	31.7%
8,556	GREGORY	3,835	2,463	1,372		1,091 R	64.2%	35.8%	64.2%	35.8%
3,167	HAAKON	1,572	1,176	396		780 R	74.8%	25.2%	74.8%	25.2%
7,058	HAMLIN	3,345	2,391	954		1,437 R	71.5%	28.5%	71.5%	28.5%
7,149	HAND	3,199	2,262	937		1,325 R	70.7%	29.3%	70.7%	29.3%
4,896	HANSON	2,093	1,320	773		547 R	63.1%	36.9%	63.1%	36.9%
2,289	HARDING	1,103	809	294		515 R	73.3%	26.7%	73.3%	26.7%
8,111	HUGHES	3,865	2,932	933		1,999 R	75.9%	24.1%	75.9%	24.1%
11,423	HUTCHINSON	5,197	4,322	875		3,447 R	83.2%	16.8%	83.2%	16.8%
2,811	HYDE	1,444	1,051	393		658 R	72.8%	27.2%	72.8%	27.2%
1,768	JACKSON	861	607	254		353 R	70.5%	29.5%	70.5%	29.5%
4,476	JERAULD	2,197	1,520	677		843 R	69.2%	30.8%	69.2%	30.8%
2,281	JONES	1,062	739	323		416 R	69.6%	30.4%	69.6%	30.4%
9,962	KINGSBURY	4,732	3,703	1,029		2,674 R	78.3%	21.7%	78.3%	21.7%
11,792	LAKE	5,486	4,020	1,466		2,554 R	73.3%	26.7%	73.3%	26.7%
16,648	LAWRENCE	7,260	5,559	1,701		3,858 R	76.6%	23.4%	76.6%	23.4%
12,767	LINCOLN	5,599	4,387	1,212		3,175 R	78.4%	21.6%	78.4%	21.6%
4,572	LYMAN	2,227	1,561	666		895 R	70.1%	29.9%	70.1%	29.9%
8,828	MCCOOK	4,118	2,991	1,127		1,864 R	72.6%	27.4%	72.6%	27.4%
7,071	MCPHERSON	3,351	2,915	436		2,479 R	87.0%	13.0%	87.0%	13.0%
7,835	MARSHALL	3,383	2,248	1,135		1,113 R	66.4%	33.6%	66.4%	33.6%
11,516	MEADE	4,443	3,109	1,334		1,775 R	70.0%	30.0%	70.0%	30.0%
3,046	MELLETTE	1,134	787	347		440 R	69.4%	30.6%	69.4%	30.6%
6,268	MINER	2,993	1,964	1,029		935 R	65.6%	34.4%	65.6%	34.4%
70,910	MINNEHAHA	32,949	23,559	9,390		14,169 R	71.5%	28.5%	71.5%	28.5%
9,252	MOODY	3,817	2,728	1,089		1,639 R	71.5%	28.5%	71.5%	28.5%
34,053	PENNINGTON	15,499	11,029	4,470		6,559 R	71.2%	28.8%	71.2%	28.8%
6,776	PERKINS	3,009	2,160	849		1,311 R	71.8%	28.2%	71.8%	28.2%
1,688	POTTER	2,204	1,625	579		1,046 R	73.7%	26.3%	73.7%	26.3%
14,929	ROBERTS	6,090	3,566	2,524		1,042 R	58.6%	41.4%	58.6%	41.4%
5,142	SANBORN	2,666	1,761	905		856 R	66.1%	33.9%	66.1%	33.9%
5,669	SHANNON	1,731	957	774		183 R	55.3%	44.7%	55.3%	44.7%
12,204	SPINK	5,676	3,693	1,983		1,710 R	65.1%	34.9%	65.1%	34.9%
2,055	STANLEY	984	695	289		406 R	70.6%	29.4%	70.6%	29.4%
2,713	SULLY	1,212	860	352		508 R	71.0%	29.0%	71.0%	29.0%

SOUTH DAKOTA

PRESIDENT 1952

1950 Census Population	County	Total Vote	Republican	Democratic	Other	Rep.-Dem. Plurality	Percentage Total Vote Rep.	Percentage Total Vote Dem.	Percentage Major Vote Rep.	Percentage Major Vote Dem.
4,758	TODD	1,636	1,025	611		414 R	62.7%	37.3%	62.7%	37.3%
9,139	TRIPP	4,235	2,790	1,445		1,345 R	65.9%	34.1%	65.9%	34.1%
12,100	TURNER	5,588	4,604	984		3,620 R	82.4%	17.6%	82.4%	17.6%
10,792	UNION	5,038	3,393	1,645		1,748 R	67.3%	32.7%	67.3%	32.7%
7,648	WALWORTH	3,631	2,369	1,262		1,107 R	65.2%	34.8%	65.2%	34.8%
1,551	WASHABAUGH	466	319	147		172 R	68.5%	31.5%	68.5%	31.5%
	WASHINGTON	—	—	—		—	—	—	—	—
16,804	YANKTON	7,022	4,802	2,220		2,582 R	68.4%	31.6%	68.4%	31.6%
2,606	ZIEBACH	1,151	779	372		407 R	67.7%	32.3%	67.7%	32.3%
649,740	TOTAL	294,283	203,857	90,426		113,431 R	69.3%	30.7%	69.3%	30.7%

SOUTH DAKOTA

PRESIDENT 1948

1940 Census Population	County	Total Vote	Republican	Democratic	Other	Rep.-Dem. Plurality	Percentage: Total Vote Rep.	Percentage: Total Vote Dem.	Percentage: Major Vote Rep.	Percentage: Major Vote Dem.
42	ARMSTRONG	7	1	6		5 D	14.3%	85.7%	14.3%	85.7%
5,387	AURORA	2,347	1,056	1,275	16	219 D	45.0%	54.3%	45.3%	54.7%
19,648	BEADLE	8,111	3,662	4,372	77	710 D	45.1%	53.9%	45.6%	54.4%
3,983	BENNETT	1,252	477	758	17	281 D	38.1%	60.5%	38.6%	61.4%
10,241	BON HOMME	4,408	2,283	2,077	48	206 R	51.8%	47.1%	52.4%	47.6%
16,560	BROOKINGS	6,926	3,975	2,907	44	1,068 R	57.4%	42.0%	57.8%	42.2%
29,676	BROWN	12,972	5,632	7,148	192	1,516 D	43.4%	55.1%	44.1%	55.9%
6,195	BRULE	2,744	1,056	1,646	42	590 D	38.5%	60.0%	39.1%	60.9%
1,853	BUFFALO	652	313	334	5	21 D	48.0%	51.2%	48.4%	51.6%
8,004	BUTTE	2,842	1,726	1,065	51	661 R	60.7%	37.5%	61.8%	38.2%
5,033	CAMPBELL	1,945	1,518	410	17	1,108 R	78.0%	21.1%	78.7%	21.3%
13,449	CHARLES MIX	4,935	1,800	3,086	49	1,286 D	36.5%	62.5%	36.8%	63.2%
8,955	CLARK	3,212	1,625	1,559	28	66 R	50.6%	48.5%	51.0%	49.0%
9,592	CLAY	4,361	2,228	2,080	53	148 R	51.1%	47.7%	51.7%	48.3%
17,014	CODINGTON	7,441	3,349	4,042	50	693 D	45.0%	54.3%	45.3%	54.7%
6,755	CORSON	2,325	1,154	1,154	17		49.6%	49.6%	50.0%	50.0%
6,023	CUSTER	2,148	1,217	917	14	300 R	56.7%	42.7%	57.0%	43.0%
15,336	DAVISON	7,128	2,996	4,064	68	1,068 D	42.0%	57.0%	42.4%	57.6%
13,565	DAY	5,681	2,438	3,146	97	708 D	42.9%	55.4%	43.7%	56.3%
8,450	DEUEL	2,719	1,357	1,324	38	33 R	49.9%	48.7%	50.6%	49.4%
5,709	DEWEY	1,606	864	727	15	137 R	53.8%	45.3%	54.3%	45.7%
6,348	DOUGLAS	2,042	1,301	736	5	565 R	63.7%	36.0%	63.9%	36.1%
7,814	EDMUNDS	2,765	1,493	1,253	19	240 R	54.0%	45.3%	54.4%	45.6%
8,089	FALL RIVER	3,411	2,037	1,348	26	689 R	59.7%	39.5%	60.2%	39.8%
5,168	FAULK	2,047	1,054	971	22	83 R	51.5%	47.4%	52.0%	48.0%
10,552	GRANT	4,060	1,972	2,052	36	80 D	48.6%	50.5%	49.0%	51.0%
9,554	GREGORY	3,562	1,723	1,793	46	70 D	48.4%	50.3%	49.0%	51.0%
3,515	HAAKON	1,300	753	519	28	234 R	57.9%	39.9%	59.2%	40.8%
7,562	HAMLIN	2,979	1,608	1,326	45	282 R	54.0%	44.5%	54.8%	45.2%
7,166	HAND	2,778	1,402	1,367	9	35 R	50.5%	49.2%	50.6%	49.4%
5,400	HANSON	1,828	860	953	15	93 D	47.0%	52.1%	47.4%	52.6%
3,010	HARDING	1,040	529	479	32	50 R	50.9%	46.1%	52.5%	47.5%
6,624	HUGHES	2,831	1,739	1,080	12	659 R	61.4%	38.1%	61.7%	38.3%
12,668	HUTCHINSON	4,151	2,906	1,209	36	1,697 R	70.0%	29.1%	70.6%	29.4%
3,113	HYDE	1,379	817	553	9	264 R	59.2%	40.1%	59.6%	40.4%
1,955	JACKSON	766	432	321	13	111 R	56.4%	41.9%	57.4%	42.6%
4,752	JERAULD	1,987	1,085	876	26	209 R	54.6%	44.1%	55.3%	44.7%
2,509	JONES	948	522	414	12	108 R	55.1%	43.7%	55.8%	44.2%
10,831	KINGSBURY	3,728	2,332	1,338	58	994 R	62.6%	35.9%	63.5%	36.5%
12,412	LAKE	4,982	2,837	2,093	52	744 R	56.9%	42.0%	57.5%	42.5%
19,093	LAWRENCE	6,045	3,778	2,209	58	1,569 R	62.5%	36.5%	63.1%	36.9%
13,171	LINCOLN	4,656	2,771	1,826	59	945 R	59.5%	39.2%	60.3%	39.7%
5,045	LYMAN	1,912	993	904	15	89 R	51.9%	47.3%	52.3%	47.7%
9,793	MCCOOK	3,471	2,064	1,387	20	677 R	59.5%	40.0%	59.8%	40.2%
8,353	MCPHERSON	2,668	2,034	611	23	1,423 R	76.2%	22.9%	76.9%	23.1%
8,880	MARSHALL	3,198	1,419	1,710	69	291 D	44.4%	53.5%	45.3%	54.7%
9,735	MEADE	3,769	2,053	1,681	35	372 R	54.5%	44.6%	55.0%	45.0%
4,107	MELLETTE	977	482	482	13		49.3%	49.3%	50.0%	50.0%
6,836	MINER	2,587	1,188	1,373	26	185 D	45.9%	53.1%	46.4%	53.6%
57,697	MINNEHAHA	26,125	14,047	11,770	308	2,277 R	53.8%	45.1%	54.4%	45.6%
9,341	MOODY	3,369	1,691	1,630	48	61 R	50.2%	48.4%	50.9%	49.1%
23,799	PENNINGTON	11,413	6,392	4,929	92	1,463 R	56.0%	43.2%	56.5%	43.5%
6,585	PERKINS	2,587	1,424	1,096	67	328 R	55.0%	42.4%	56.5%	43.5%
4,614	POTTER	2,101	1,044	1,039	18	5 R	49.7%	49.5%	50.1%	49.9%
15,887	ROBERTS	5,652	2,211	3,277	164	1,066 D	39.1%	58.0%	40.3%	59.7%
5,754	SANBORN	2,061	990	1,046	25	56 D	48.0%	50.8%	48.6%	51.4%
7,155	SHANNON	1,454	641	803	10	162 D	44.1%	55.2%	44.4%	55.6%
12,527	SPINK	5,067	2,310	2,702	55	392 D	45.6%	53.3%	46.1%	53.9%
1,959	STANLEY	887	522	359	6	163 R	58.9%	40.5%	59.3%	40.7%
2,668	SULLY	992	579	405	8	174 R	58.4%	40.8%	58.8%	41.2%

SOUTH DAKOTA

PRESIDENT 1948

1940 Census Population	County	Total Vote	Republican	Democratic	Other	Rep.-Dem. Plurality	Percentage Total Vote Rep.	Total Vote Dem.	Major Vote Rep.	Major Vote Dem.
5,714	TODD	1,438	625	796	17	171 D	43.5%	55.4%	44.0%	56.0%
9,937	TRIPP	3,818	1,845	1,918	55	73 D	48.3%	50.2%	49.0%	51.0%
13,270	TURNER	4,600	3,048	1,514	38	1,534 R	66.3%	32.9%	66.8%	33.2%
11,675	UNION	4,465	2,205	2,237	23	32 D	49.4%	50.1%	49.6%	50.4%
7,274	WALWORTH	3,155	1,607	1,513	35	94 R	50.9%	48.0%	51.5%	48.5%
1,980	WASHABAUGH	419	192	223	4	31 D	45.8%	53.2%	46.3%	53.7%
	WASHINGTON	—	—	—	—	—	—	—	—	—
16,725	YANKTON	5,893	2,904	2,932	57	28 D	49.3%	49.8%	49.8%	50.2%
2,875	ZIEBACH	980	463	503	14	40 D	47.2%	51.3%	47.9%	52.1%
642,961	TOTAL	250,105	129,651	117,653	2,801	11,998 R	51.8%	47.0%	52.4%	47.6%

SOUTH DAKOTA

PRESIDENT 1944

1940 Census Population	County	Total Vote	Republican	Democratic	Other	Rep.-Dem. Plurality	Percentage Total Vote Rep.	Total Vote Dem.	Major Vote Rep.	Major Vote Dem.
42	ARMSTRONG	4		4		4 D		100.0%		100.0%
5,387	AURORA	2,174	1,163	1,011		152 R	53.5%	46.5%	53.5%	46.5%
19,648	BEADLE	7,452	3,610	3,842		232 D	48.4%	51.6%	48.4%	51.6%
3,983	BENNETT	1,060	494	566		72 D	46.6%	53.4%	46.6%	53.4%
10,241	BON HOMME	4,534	2,553	1,981		572 R	56.3%	43.7%	56.3%	43.7%
16,560	BROOKINGS	6,209	4,136	2,073		2,063 R	66.6%	33.4%	66.6%	33.4%
29,676	BROWN	11,963	5,611	6,352		741 D	46.9%	53.1%	46.9%	53.1%
6,195	BRULE	2,414	1,002	1,412		410 D	41.5%	58.5%	41.5%	58.5%
1,853	BUFFALO	574	324	250		74 R	56.4%	43.6%	56.4%	43.6%
8,004	BUTTE	2,752	1,824	928		896 R	66.3%	33.7%	66.3%	33.7%
5,033	CAMPBELL	1,255	1,047	208		839 R	83.4%	16.6%	83.4%	16.6%
13,449	CHARLES MIX	4,872	2,171	2,701		530 D	44.6%	55.4%	44.6%	55.4%
8,955	CLARK	3,145	1,936	1,209		727 R	61.6%	38.4%	61.6%	38.4%
9,592	CLAY	3,766	1,970	1,796		174 R	52.3%	47.7%	52.3%	47.7%
17,014	CODINGTON	6,468	3,348	3,120		228 R	51.8%	48.2%	51.8%	48.2%
6,755	CORSON	1,794	1,008	786		222 R	56.2%	43.8%	56.2%	43.8%
6,023	CUSTER	2,000	1,288	712		576 R	64.4%	35.6%	64.4%	35.6%
15,336	DAVISON	6,151	2,929	3,222		293 D	47.6%	52.4%	47.6%	52.4%
13,565	DAY	5,080	2,593	2,487		106 R	51.0%	49.0%	51.0%	49.0%
8,450	DEUEL	3,090	1,910	1,180		730 R	61.8%	38.2%	61.8%	38.2%
5,709	DEWEY	1,424	913	511		402 R	64.1%	35.9%	64.1%	35.9%
6,348	DOUGLAS	2,202	1,483	719		764 R	67.3%	32.7%	67.3%	32.7%
7,814	EDMUNDS	2,723	1,762	961		801 R	64.7%	35.3%	64.7%	35.3%
8,089	FALL RIVER	3,060	1,938	1,122		816 R	63.3%	36.7%	63.3%	36.7%
5,168	FAULK	1,986	1,090	896		194 R	54.9%	45.1%	54.9%	45.1%
10,552	GRANT	3,753	2,278	1,475		803 R	60.7%	39.3%	60.7%	39.3%
9,554	GREGORY	3,680	2,067	1,613		454 R	56.2%	43.8%	56.2%	43.8%
3,515	HAAKON	1,019	638	381		257 R	62.6%	37.4%	62.6%	37.4%
7,562	HAMLIN	2,831	1,811	1,020		791 R	64.0%	36.0%	64.0%	36.0%
7,166	HAND	2,704	1,558	1,146		412 R	57.6%	42.4%	57.6%	42.4%
5,400	HANSON	1,934	1,070	864		206 R	55.3%	44.7%	55.3%	44.7%
3,010	HARDING	1,045	552	493		59 R	52.8%	47.2%	52.8%	47.2%
6,624	HUGHES	2,614	1,676	938		738 R	64.1%	35.9%	64.1%	35.9%
12,668	HUTCHINSON	4,498	3,799	699		3,100 R	84.5%	15.5%	84.5%	15.5%
3,113	HYDE	1,296	842	454		388 R	65.0%	35.0%	65.0%	35.0%
1,955	JACKSON	553	340	213		127 R	61.5%	38.5%	61.5%	38.5%
4,752	JERAULD	1,948	1,217	731		486 R	62.5%	37.5%	62.5%	37.5%
2,509	JONES	729	465	264		201 R	63.8%	36.2%	63.8%	36.2%
10,831	KINGSBURY	3,697	2,541	1,156		1,385 R	68.7%	31.3%	68.7%	31.3%
12,412	LAKE	4,499	2,956	1,543		1,413 R	65.7%	34.3%	65.7%	34.3%
19,093	LAWRENCE	5,394	3,528	1,866		1,662 R	65.4%	34.6%	65.4%	34.6%
13,171	LINCOLN	4,923	3,298	1,625		1,673 R	67.0%	33.0%	67.0%	33.0%
5,045	LYMAN	1,497	867	630		237 R	57.9%	42.1%	57.9%	42.1%
9,793	MCCOOK	3,679	2,516	1,163		1,353 R	68.4%	31.6%	68.4%	31.6%
8,353	MCPHERSON	2,700	2,290	410		1,880 R	84.8%	15.2%	84.8%	15.2%
8,880	MARSHALL	2,874	1,511	1,363		148 R	52.6%	47.4%	52.6%	47.4%
9,735	MEADE	3,076	1,912	1,164		748 R	62.2%	37.8%	62.2%	37.8%
4,107	MELLETTE	954	544	410		134 R	57.0%	43.0%	57.0%	43.0%
6,836	MINER	2,634	1,544	1,090		454 R	58.6%	41.4%	58.6%	41.4%
57,697	MINNEHAHA	24,136	13,920	10,216		3,704 R	57.7%	42.3%	57.7%	42.3%
9,341	MOODY	3,500	2,080	1,420		660 R	59.4%	40.6%	59.4%	40.6%
23,799	PENNINGTON	8,763	5,246	3,517		1,729 R	59.9%	40.1%	59.9%	40.1%
6,585	PERKINS	2,320	1,325	995		330 R	57.1%	42.9%	57.1%	42.9%
4,614	POTTER	1,718	1,001	717		284 R	58.3%	41.7%	58.3%	41.7%
15,887	ROBERTS	5,745	2,721	3,024		303 D	47.4%	52.6%	47.4%	52.6%
5,754	SANBORN	2,210	1,212	998		214 R	54.8%	45.2%	54.8%	45.2%
7,155	SHANNON	1,042	562	480		82 R	53.9%	46.1%	53.9%	46.1%
12,527	SPINK	4,650	2,365	2,285		80 R	50.9%	49.1%	50.9%	49.1%
1,959	STANLEY	618	384	234		150 R	62.1%	37.9%	62.1%	37.9%
2,668	SULLY	912	612	300		312 R	67.1%	32.9%	67.1%	32.9%

SOUTH DAKOTA

PRESIDENT 1944

1940 Census Population	County	Total Vote	Republican	Democratic	Other	Rep.-Dem. Plurality	Percentage Total Vote Rep.	Percentage Total Vote Dem.	Percentage Major Vote Rep.	Percentage Major Vote Dem.
5,714	TODD	1,420	737	683		54 R	51.9%	48.1%	51.9%	48.1%
9,937	TRIPP	3,551	1,911	1,640		271 R	53.8%	46.2%	53.8%	46.2%
13,270	TURNER	4,853	3,549	1,304		2,245 R	73.1%	26.9%	73.1%	26.9%
11,675	UNION	4,558	2,501	2,057		444 R	54.9%	45.1%	54.9%	45.1%
7,274	WALWORTH	2,755	1,533	1,222		311 R	55.6%	44.4%	55.6%	44.4%
1,980	WASHABAUGH	285	139	146		7 D	48.8%	51.2%	48.8%	51.2%
	WASHINGTON	—	—	—		—	—	—	—	—
16,725	YANKTON	5,672	3,313	2,359		954 R	58.4%	41.6%	58.4%	41.6%
2,875	ZIEBACH	685	331	354		23 D	48.3%	51.7%	48.3%	51.7%
642,961	TOTAL	232,076	135,365	96,711		38,654 R	58.3%	41.7%	58.3%	41.7%

SOUTH DAKOTA

PRESIDENT 1940

1940 Census Population	County	Total Vote	Republican	Democratic	Other	Rep.-Dem. Plurality	Percentage Total Vote Rep.	Total Vote Dem.	Major Vote Rep.	Major Vote Dem.
42	ARMSTRONG	—	—	—		—	—	—	—	—
5,387	AURORA	2,793	1,408	1,385		23 R	50.4%	49.6%	50.4%	49.6%
19,648	BEADLE	9,609	4,356	5,253		897 D	45.3%	54.7%	45.3%	54.7%
3,983	BENNETT	1,775	915	860		55 R	51.5%	48.5%	51.5%	48.5%
10,241	BON HOMME	5,509	3,046	2,463		583 R	55.3%	44.7%	55.3%	44.7%
16,560	BROOKINGS	7,687	5,016	2,671		2,345 R	65.3%	34.7%	65.3%	34.7%
29,676	BROWN	14,646	6,598	8,048		1,450 D	45.0%	55.0%	45.0%	55.0%
6,195	BRULE	3,187	1,352	1,835		483 D	42.4%	57.6%	42.4%	57.6%
1,853	BUFFALO	886	491	395		96 R	55.4%	44.6%	55.4%	44.6%
8,004	BUTTE	3,548	2,164	1,384		780 R	61.0%	39.0%	61.0%	39.0%
5,033	CAMPBELL	2,149	1,733	416		1,317 R	80.6%	19.4%	80.6%	19.4%
13,449	CHARLES MIX	6,296	2,993	3,303		310 D	47.5%	52.5%	47.5%	52.5%
8,955	CLARK	4,246	2,622	1,624		998 R	61.8%	38.2%	61.8%	38.2%
9,592	CLAY	4,729	2,463	2,266		197 R	52.1%	47.9%	52.1%	47.9%
17,014	CODINGTON	8,025	4,320	3,705		615 R	53.8%	46.2%	53.8%	46.2%
6,755	CORSON	3,037	1,709	1,328		381 R	56.3%	43.7%	56.3%	43.7%
6,023	CUSTER	2,947	1,796	1,151		645 R	60.9%	39.1%	60.9%	39.1%
15,336	DAVISON	7,889	3,659	4,230		571 D	46.4%	53.6%	46.4%	53.6%
13,565	DAY	6,574	3,277	3,297		20 D	49.8%	50.2%	49.8%	50.2%
8,450	DEUEL	3,470	2,304	1,166		1,138 R	66.4%	33.6%	66.4%	33.6%
5,709	DEWEY	2,477	1,396	1,081		315 R	56.4%	43.6%	56.4%	43.6%
6,348	DOUGLAS	3,017	1,977	1,040		937 R	65.5%	34.5%	65.5%	34.5%
7,814	EDMUNDS	3,784	2,341	1,443		898 R	61.9%	38.1%	61.9%	38.1%
8,089	FALL RIVER	3,825	2,420	1,405		1,015 R	63.3%	36.7%	63.3%	36.7%
5,168	FAULK	2,630	1,431	1,199		232 R	54.4%	45.6%	54.4%	45.6%
10,552	GRANT	5,020	2,981	2,039		942 R	59.4%	40.6%	59.4%	40.6%
9,554	GREGORY	4,513	2,478	2,035		443 R	54.9%	45.1%	54.9%	45.1%
3,515	HAAKON	1,836	1,129	707		422 R	61.5%	38.5%	61.5%	38.5%
7,562	HAMLIN	3,561	2,279	1,282		997 R	64.0%	36.0%	64.0%	36.0%
7,166	HAND	3,610	2,002	1,608		394 R	55.5%	44.5%	55.5%	44.5%
5,400	HANSON	2,624	1,408	1,216		192 R	53.7%	46.3%	53.7%	46.3%
3,010	HARDING	1,425	755	670		85 R	53.0%	47.0%	53.0%	47.0%
6,624	HUGHES	3,344	1,982	1,362		620 R	59.3%	40.7%	59.3%	40.7%
12,668	HUTCHINSON	6,154	5,051	1,103		3,948 R	82.1%	17.9%	82.1%	17.9%
3,113	HYDE	1,688	1,018	670		348 R	60.3%	39.7%	60.3%	39.7%
1,955	JACKSON	1,055	620	435		185 R	58.8%	41.2%	58.8%	41.2%
4,752	JERAULD	2,495	1,576	919		657 R	63.2%	36.8%	63.2%	36.8%
2,509	JONES	1,340	832	508		324 R	62.1%	37.9%	62.1%	37.9%
10,831	KINGSBURY	5,054	3,551	1,503		2,048 R	70.3%	29.7%	70.3%	29.7%
12,412	LAKE	6,068	4,179	1,889		2,290 R	68.9%	31.1%	68.9%	31.1%
19,093	LAWRENCE	8,803	5,288	3,515		1,773 R	60.1%	39.9%	60.1%	39.9%
13,171	LINCOLN	6,129	4,081	2,048		2,033 R	66.6%	33.4%	66.6%	33.4%
5,045	LYMAN	2,514	1,409	1,105		304 R	56.0%	44.0%	56.0%	44.0%
9,793	MCCOOK	5,006	3,310	1,696		1,614 R	66.1%	33.9%	66.1%	33.9%
8,353	MCPHERSON	3,665	2,839	826		2,013 R	77.5%	22.5%	77.5%	22.5%
8,880	MARSHALL	3,961	1,989	1,972		17 R	50.2%	49.8%	50.2%	49.8%
9,735	MEADE	4,491	2,560	1,931		629 R	57.0%	43.0%	57.0%	43.0%
4,107	MELLETTE	1,895	990	905		85 R	52.2%	47.8%	52.2%	47.8%
6,836	MINER	3,460	2,095	1,365		730 R	60.5%	39.5%	60.5%	39.5%
57,697	MINNEHAHA	28,923	16,664	12,259		4,405 R	57.6%	42.4%	57.6%	42.4%
9,341	MOODY	4,569	2,749	1,820		929 R	60.2%	39.8%	60.2%	39.8%
23,799	PENNINGTON	11,481	6,603	4,878		1,725 R	57.5%	42.5%	57.5%	42.5%
6,585	PERKINS	3,098	1,777	1,321		456 R	57.4%	42.6%	57.4%	42.6%
4,614	POTTER	2,332	1,278	1,054		224 R	54.8%	45.2%	54.8%	45.2%
15,887	ROBERTS	7,254	3,504	3,750		246 D	48.3%	51.7%	48.3%	51.7%
5,754	SANBORN	3,130	1,732	1,398		334 R	55.3%	44.7%	55.3%	44.7%
5,366	SHANNON	1,885	1,094	791		303 R	58.0%	42.0%	58.0%	42.0%
12,527	SPINK	6,109	2,975	3,134		159 D	48.7%	51.3%	48.7%	51.3%
1,959	STANLEY	1,220	679	541		138 R	55.7%	44.3%	55.7%	44.3%
2,668	SULLY	1,298	840	458		382 R	64.7%	35.3%	64.7%	35.3%

SOUTH DAKOTA

PRESIDENT 1940

1940 Census Population	County	Total Vote	Republican	Democratic	Other	Rep.-Dem. Plurality	Percentage Total Vote Rep.	Total Vote Dem.	Major Vote Rep.	Major Vote Dem.
5,714	TODD	2,483	1,245	1,238		7 R	50.1%	49.9%	50.1%	49.9%
9,937	TRIPP	4,581	2,492	2,089		403 R	54.4%	45.6%	54.4%	45.6%
13,270	TURNER	6,418	4,644	1,774		2,870 R	72.4%	27.6%	72.4%	27.6%
11,675	UNION	5,724	3,116	2,608		508 R	54.4%	45.6%	54.4%	45.6%
7,274	WALWORTH	3,486	1,921	1,565		356 R	55.1%	44.9%	55.1%	44.9%
1,980	WASHABAUGH	732	358	374		16 D	48.9%	51.1%	48.9%	51.1%
1,789	WASHINGTON	637	335	302		33 R	52.6%	47.4%	52.6%	47.4%
16,725	YANKTON	7,243	4,179	3,064		1,115 R	57.7%	42.3%	57.7%	42.3%
2,875	ZIEBACH	1,378	691	687		4 R	50.1%	49.9%	50.1%	49.9%
642,961	TOTAL	308,427	177,065	131,362		45,703 R	57.4%	42.6%	57.4%	42.6%

SOUTH DAKOTA

PRESIDENT 1936

1930 Census Population	County	Total Vote	Republican	Democratic	Other	Rep.-Dem. Plurality	Percentage Total Vote Rep.	Total Vote Dem.	Major Vote Rep.	Major Vote Dem.
80	ARMSTRONG	—	—	—	—	—	—	—	—	—
7,139	AURORA	2,963	1,082	1,801	80	719 D	36.5%	60.8%	37.5%	62.5%
22,917	BEADLE	9,011	2,965	5,843	203	2,878 D	32.9%	64.8%	33.7%	66.3%
4,590	BENNETT	1,349	530	807	12	277 D	39.3%	59.8%	39.6%	60.4%
11,737	BON HOMME	5,299	2,236	2,959	104	723 D	42.2%	55.8%	43.0%	57.0%
16,847	BROOKINGS	7,302	3,899	3,161	242	738 R	53.4%	43.3%	55.2%	44.8%
31,458	BROWN	13,993	4,505	9,177	311	4,672 D	32.2%	65.6%	32.9%	67.1%
7,416	BRULE	3,317	982	2,274	61	1,292 D	29.6%	68.6%	30.2%	69.8%
1,931	BUFFALO	795	368	410	17	42 D	46.3%	51.6%	47.3%	52.7%
8,589	BUTTE	3,145	1,525	1,519	101	6 R	48.5%	48.3%	50.1%	49.9%
5,629	CAMPBELL	2,027	1,236	736	55	500 R	61.0%	36.3%	62.7%	37.3%
16,703	CHARLES MIX	6,912	2,209	4,628	75	2,419 D	32.0%	67.0%	32.3%	67.7%
11,022	CLARK	4,087	1,883	2,036	168	153 D	46.1%	49.8%	48.0%	52.0%
10,088	CLAY	5,035	1,692	3,070	273	1,378 D	33.6%	61.0%	35.5%	64.5%
17,457	CODINGTON	7,620	3,005	4,256	359	1,251 D	39.4%	55.9%	41.4%	58.6%
9,535	CORSON	3,295	1,408	1,781	106	373 D	42.7%	54.1%	44.2%	55.8%
5,353	CUSTER	2,912	1,365	1,519	28	154 D	46.9%	52.2%	47.3%	52.7%
16,821	DAVISON	7,805	2,510	4,983	312	2,473 D	32.2%	63.8%	33.5%	66.5%
14,606	DAY	5,729	2,113	3,335	281	1,222 D	36.9%	58.2%	38.8%	61.2%
8,732	DEUEL	3,153	1,595	1,440	118	155 R	50.6%	45.7%	52.6%	47.4%
6,476	DEWEY	2,287	1,012	1,216	59	204 D	44.3%	53.2%	45.4%	54.6%
7,236	DOUGLAS	3,169	1,418	1,680	71	262 D	44.7%	53.0%	45.8%	54.2%
8,712	EDMUNDS	3,888	1,818	2,030	40	212 D	46.8%	52.2%	47.2%	52.8%
8,741	FALL RIVER	3,982	1,876	1,927	179	51 D	47.1%	48.4%	49.3%	50.7%
6,895	FAULK	2,555	1,111	1,404	40	293 D	43.5%	55.0%	44.2%	55.8%
10,729	GRANT	4,059	1,847	2,101	111	254 D	45.5%	51.8%	46.8%	53.2%
11,420	GREGORY	4,545	1,868	2,603	74	735 D	41.1%	57.3%	41.8%	58.2%
4,679	HAAKON	1,956	933	948	75	15 D	47.7%	48.5%	49.6%	50.4%
8,299	HAMLIN	3,554	1,857	1,622	75	235 R	52.3%	45.6%	53.4%	46.6%
9,485	HAND	3,237	1,289	1,721	227	432 D	39.8%	53.2%	42.8%	57.2%
6,131	HANSON	2,708	1,090	1,530	88	440 D	40.3%	56.5%	41.6%	58.4%
3,589	HARDING	1,382	524	819	39	295 D	37.9%	59.3%	39.0%	61.0%
7,009	HUGHES	3,312	1,547	1,662	103	115 D	46.7%	50.2%	48.2%	51.8%
13,904	HUTCHINSON	5,801	2,804	2,500	497	304 R	48.3%	43.1%	52.9%	47.1%
3,690	HYDE	1,514	795	683	36	112 R	52.5%	45.1%	53.8%	46.2%
2,636	JACKSON	1,104	481	593	30	112 D	43.6%	53.7%	44.8%	55.2%
5,816	JERAULD	2,504	1,075	1,343	86	268 D	42.9%	53.6%	44.5%	55.5%
3,177	JONES	1,264	608	620	36	12 D	48.1%	49.1%	49.5%	50.5%
12,805	KINGSBURY	5,076	2,813	2,037	226	776 R	55.4%	40.1%	58.0%	42.0%
12,379	LAKE	6,009	3,182	2,520	307	662 R	53.0%	41.9%	55.8%	44.2%
13,920	LAWRENCE	8,852	4,974	3,809	69	1,165 R	56.2%	43.0%	56.6%	43.4%
13,918	LINCOLN	6,026	2,918	2,541	567	377 R	48.4%	42.2%	53.5%	46.5%
6,335	LYMAN	2,440	1,090	1,321	29	231 D	44.7%	54.1%	45.2%	54.8%
10,316	MCCOOK	4,851	2,117	2,536	198	419 D	43.6%	52.3%	45.5%	54.5%
8,774	MCPHERSON	3,505	1,921	1,556	28	365 R	54.8%	44.4%	55.2%	44.8%
9,540	MARSHALL	3,387	1,105	2,220	62	1,115 D	32.6%	65.5%	33.2%	66.8%
11,482	MEADE	4,616	2,064	2,304	248	240 D	44.7%	49.9%	47.3%	52.7%
5,293	MELLETTE	1,527	711	808	8	97 D	46.6%	52.9%	46.8%	53.2%
8,376	MINER	3,552	1,377	2,051	124	674 D	38.8%	57.7%	40.2%	59.8%
50,872	MINNEHAHA	26,508	12,418	13,174	916	756 D	46.8%	49.7%	48.5%	51.5%
9,603	MOODY	4,560	1,992	2,366	202	374 D	43.7%	51.9%	45.7%	54.3%
20,079	PENNINGTON	10,428	4,442	5,557	429	1,115 D	42.6%	53.3%	44.4%	55.6%
8,717	PERKINS	3,425	1,408	1,940	77	532 D	41.1%	56.6%	42.1%	57.9%
5,762	POTTER	2,306	914	1,338	54	424 D	39.6%	58.0%	40.6%	59.4%
15,782	ROBERTS	5,951	1,934	3,820	197	1,886 D	32.5%	64.2%	33.6%	66.4%
7,326	SANBORN	3,204	1,174	1,919	111	745 D	36.6%	59.9%	38.0%	62.0%
4,058	SHANNON	1,336	667	634	35	33 R	49.9%	47.5%	51.3%	48.7%
15,304	SPINK	5,871	2,078	3,569	224	1,491 D	35.4%	60.8%	36.8%	63.2%
2,381	STANLEY	1,176	495	629	52	134 D	42.1%	53.5%	44.0%	56.0%
3,852	SULLY	1,138	667	437	34	230 R	58.6%	38.4%	60.4%	39.6%

SOUTH DAKOTA

PRESIDENT 1936

1930 Census Population	County	Total Vote	Republican	Democratic	Other	Rep.-Dem. Plurality	Percentage Total Vote Rep.	Percentage Total Vote Dem.	Percentage Major Vote Rep.	Percentage Major Vote Dem.
5,898	TODD	1,966	624	1,318	24	694 D	31.7%	67.0%	32.1%	67.9%
12,712	TRIPP	4,485	1,693	2,708	84	1,015 D	37.7%	60.4%	38.5%	61.5%
14,891	TURNER	6,526	3,214	2,923	389	291 R	49.2%	44.8%	52.4%	47.6%
11,480	UNION	5,785	1,845	3,520	420	1,675 D	31.9%	60.8%	34.4%	65.6%
8,791	WALWORTH	3,666	1,420	2,212	34	792 D	38.7%	60.3%	39.1%	60.9%
2,474	WASHABAUGH	561	238	313	10	75 D	42.4%	55.8%	43.2%	56.8%
1,827	WASHINGTON	392	158	234		76 D	40.3%	59.7%	40.3%	59.7%
16,589	YANKTON	7,438	2,702	4,349	387	1,647 D	36.3%	58.5%	38.3%	61.7%
4,039	ZIEBACH	1,319	561	737	21	176 D	42.5%	55.9%	43.2%	56.8%
692,849	TOTAL	296,452	125,977	160,137	10,338	34,160 D	42.5%	54.0%	44.0%	56.0%

SOUTH DAKOTA

PRESIDENT 1932

1930 Census Population	County	Total Vote	Republican	Democratic	Other	Rep.-Dem. Plurality	Percentage: Total Vote Rep.	Percentage: Total Vote Dem.	Percentage: Major Vote Rep.	Percentage: Major Vote Dem.
80	ARMSTRONG	17		17		17 D		100.0%		100.0%
7,139	AURORA	3,219	860	2,304	55	1,444 D	26.7%	71.6%	27.2%	72.8%
22,917	BEADLE	9,346	2,995	6,246	105	3,251 D	32.0%	66.8%	32.4%	67.6%
4,590	BENNETT	1,908	453	1,410	45	957 D	23.7%	73.9%	24.3%	75.7%
11,737	BON HOMME	4,886	1,354	3,504	28	2,150 D	27.7%	71.7%	27.9%	72.1%
16,847	BROOKINGS	6,599	3,231	3,247	121	16 D	49.0%	49.2%	49.9%	50.1%
31,458	BROWN	13,601	4,639	8,669	293	4,030 D	34.1%	63.7%	34.9%	65.1%
7,416	BRULE	3,315	797	2,465	53	1,668 D	24.0%	74.4%	24.4%	75.6%
1,931	BUFFALO	911	270	634	7	364 D	29.6%	69.6%	29.9%	70.1%
8,589	BUTTE	3,337	1,594	1,684	59	90 D	47.8%	50.5%	48.6%	51.4%
5,629	CAMPBELL	1,904	770	1,116	18	346 D	40.4%	58.6%	40.8%	59.2%
16,703	CHARLES MIX	6,846	1,397	5,399	50	4,002 D	20.4%	78.9%	20.6%	79.4%
11,022	CLARK	4,300	1,572	2,649	79	1,077 D	36.6%	61.6%	37.2%	62.8%
10,088	CLAY	4,624	1,514	3,040	70	1,526 D	32.7%	65.7%	33.2%	66.8%
17,457	CODINGTON	7,396	2,538	4,806	52	2,268 D	34.3%	65.0%	34.6%	65.4%
9,535	CORSON	3,484	946	2,403	135	1,457 D	27.2%	69.0%	28.2%	71.8%
5,353	CUSTER	2,568	977	1,548	43	571 D	38.0%	60.3%	38.7%	61.3%
16,821	DAVISON	7,480	2,147	5,233	100	3,086 D	28.7%	70.0%	29.1%	70.9%
14,606	DAY	6,191	1,983	3,910	298	1,927 D	32.0%	63.2%	33.7%	66.3%
8,732	DEUEL	2,812	1,131	1,658	23	527 D	40.2%	59.0%	40.6%	59.4%
6,476	DEWEY	2,327	710	1,591	26	881 D	30.5%	68.4%	30.9%	69.1%
7,236	DOUGLAS	3,066	1,045	2,005	16	960 D	34.1%	65.4%	34.3%	65.7%
8,712	EDMUNDS	3,836	1,183	2,588	65	1,405 D	30.8%	67.5%	31.4%	68.6%
8,741	FALL RIVER	4,029	1,351	2,603	75	1,252 D	33.5%	64.6%	34.2%	65.8%
6,895	FAULK	2,930	1,141	1,743	46	602 D	38.9%	59.5%	39.6%	60.4%
10,729	GRANT	4,472	1,515	2,887	70	1,372 D	33.9%	64.6%	34.4%	65.6%
11,420	GREGORY	4,472	1,169	3,278	25	2,109 D	26.1%	73.3%	26.3%	73.7%
4,679	HAAKON	2,234	797	1,245	192	448 D	35.7%	55.7%	39.0%	61.0%
8,299	HAMLIN	3,230	1,267	1,920	43	653 D	39.2%	59.4%	39.8%	60.2%
9,485	HAND	4,105	1,394	2,658	53	1,264 D	34.0%	64.8%	34.4%	65.6%
6,131	HANSON	2,650	845	1,783	22	938 D	31.9%	67.3%	32.2%	67.8%
3,589	HARDING	1,444	625	715	104	90 D	43.3%	49.5%	46.6%	53.4%
7,009	HUGHES	3,270	1,374	1,852	44	478 D	42.0%	56.6%	42.6%	57.4%
13,904	HUTCHINSON	5,192	1,504	3,630	58	2,126 D	29.0%	69.9%	29.3%	70.7%
3,690	HYDE	1,596	678	895	23	217 D	42.5%	56.1%	43.1%	56.9%
2,636	JACKSON	1,344	499	812	33	313 D	37.1%	60.4%	38.1%	61.9%
5,816	JERAULD	2,673	836	1,773	64	937 D	31.3%	66.3%	32.0%	68.0%
3,177	JONES	1,455	472	929	54	457 D	32.4%	63.8%	33.7%	66.3%
12,805	KINGSBURY	5,033	2,135	2,808	90	673 D	42.4%	55.8%	43.2%	56.8%
12,379	LAKE	5,407	2,222	3,090	95	868 D	41.1%	57.1%	41.8%	58.2%
13,920	LAWRENCE	6,868	3,708	3,106	54	602 R	54.0%	45.2%	54.4%	45.6%
13,918	LINCOLN	5,560	2,160	3,300	100	1,140 D	38.8%	59.4%	39.6%	60.4%
6,335	LYMAN	2,730	811	1,879	40	1,068 D	29.7%	68.8%	30.1%	69.9%
10,316	MCCOOK	4,422	1,436	2,884	102	1,448 D	32.5%	65.2%	33.2%	66.8%
8,774	MCPHERSON	3,302	606	2,650	46	2,044 D	18.4%	80.3%	18.6%	81.4%
9,540	MARSHALL	3,446	935	2,137	374	1,202 D	27.1%	62.0%	30.4%	69.6%
11,482	MEADE	4,608	1,735	2,687	186	952 D	37.7%	58.3%	39.2%	60.8%
5,293	MELLETTE	2,255	657	1,583	15	926 D	29.1%	70.2%	29.3%	70.7%
8,376	MINER	3,416	976	2,332	108	1,356 D	28.6%	68.3%	29.5%	70.5%
50,872	MINNEHAHA	23,273	10,288	12,646	339	2,358 D	44.2%	54.3%	44.9%	55.1%
9,603	MOODY	3,906	1,289	2,547	70	1,258 D	33.0%	65.2%	33.6%	66.4%
20,079	PENNINGTON	8,875	3,638	5,178	59	1,540 D	41.0%	58.3%	41.3%	58.7%
8,717	PERKINS	3,438	1,406	1,852	180	446 D	40.9%	53.9%	43.2%	56.8%
5,762	POTTER	2,350	660	1,668	22	1,008 D	28.1%	71.0%	28.4%	71.6%
15,782	ROBERTS	6,368	1,381	4,440	547	3,059 D	21.7%	69.7%	23.7%	76.3%
7,326	SANBORN	3,281	860	2,398	23	1,538 D	26.2%	73.1%	26.4%	73.6%
4,058	SHANNON	1,262	463	798	1	335 D	36.7%	63.2%	36.7%	63.3%
15,304	SPINK	6,635	2,433	4,046	156	1,613 D	36.7%	61.0%	37.6%	62.4%
2,381	STANLEY	1,336	553	757	26	204 D	41.4%	56.7%	42.2%	57.8%
3,852	SULLY	1,569	559	961	49	402 D	35.6%	61.2%	36.8%	63.2%

SOUTH DAKOTA

PRESIDENT 1932

1930 Census Population	County	Total Vote	Republican	Democratic	Other	Rep.-Dem. Plurality	Percentage Total Vote Rep.	Percentage Total Vote Dem.	Percentage Major Vote Rep.	Percentage Major Vote Dem.
5,898	TODD	2,034	533	1,485	16	952 D	26.2%	73.0%	26.4%	73.6%
12,712	TRIPP	4,846	1,147	3,647	52	2,500 D	23.7%	75.3%	23.9%	76.1%
14,891	TURNER	5,405	2,172	3,170	63	998 D	40.2%	58.6%	40.7%	59.3%
11,480	UNION	4,957	1,381	3,530	46	2,149 D	27.9%	71.2%	28.1%	71.9%
8,791	WALWORTH	3,320	1,049	2,221	50	1,172 D	31.6%	66.9%	32.1%	67.9%
2474	WASHABAUGH	761	134	612	15	478 D	17.6%	80.4%	18.0%	82.0%
1827	WASHINGTON	503	157	342	4	185 D	31.2%	68.0%	31.5%	68.5%
16,589	YANKTON	6,730	1,693	4,930	107	3,237 D	25.2%	73.3%	25.6%	74.4%
4,039	ZIEBACH	1,473	462	982	29	520 D	31.4%	66.7%	32.0%	68.0%
692,849	TOTAL	288,438	99,212	183,515	5,711	84,303 D	34.4%	63.6%	35.1%	64.9%

SOUTH DAKOTA

PRESIDENT 1928

1920 Census Population	County	Total Vote	Republican	Democratic	Other	Rep.-Dem. Plurality	Percentage: Total Vote Rep.	Percentage: Total Vote Dem.	Percentage: Major Vote Rep.	Percentage: Major Vote Dem.
	ARMSTRONG	7		7		7 D		100.0%		100.0%
7,246	AURORA	3,001	1,552	1,426	23	126 R	51.7%	47.5%	52.1%	47.9%
19,273	BEADLE	8,293	5,094	3,168	31	1,926 R	61.4%	38.2%	61.7%	38.3%
1,924	BENNETT	1,317	766	544	7	222 R	58.2%	41.3%	58.5%	41.5%
11,940	BON HOMME	4,441	2,262	2,166	13	96 R	50.9%	48.8%	51.1%	48.9%
16,119	BROOKINGS	6,547	4,586	1,915	46	2,671 R	70.0%	29.3%	70.5%	29.5%
29,509	BROWN	12,522	7,266	5,065	191	2,201 R	58.0%	40.4%	58.9%	41.1%
7,141	BRULE	3,080	1,431	1,599	50	168 D	46.5%	51.9%	47.2%	52.8%
1,715	BUFFALO	794	405	387	2	18 R	51.0%	48.7%	51.1%	48.9%
6,819	BUTTE	2,866	1,988	840	38	1,148 R	69.4%	29.3%	70.3%	29.7%
5,305	CAMPBELL	1,947	1,346	588	13	758 R	69.1%	30.2%	69.6%	30.4%
16,256	CHARLES MIX	6,140	3,087	3,039	14	48 R	50.3%	49.5%	50.4%	49.6%
11,136	CLARK	4,071	2,665	1,370	36	1,295 R	65.5%	33.7%	66.0%	34.0%
9,654	CLAY	4,057	2,573	1,474	10	1,099 R	63.4%	36.3%	63.6%	36.4%
16,549	CODINGTON	7,087	3,762	3,299	26	463 R	53.1%	46.6%	53.3%	46.7%
7,249	CORSON	3,245	1,847	1,374	24	473 R	56.9%	42.3%	57.3%	42.7%
3,907	CUSTER	2,190	1,464	715	11	749 R	66.8%	32.6%	67.2%	32.8%
14,139	DAVISON	6,571	3,821	2,729	21	1,092 R	58.1%	41.5%	58.3%	41.7%
15,194	DAY	5,865	3,180	2,642	43	538 R	54.2%	45.0%	54.6%	45.4%
8,759	DEUEL	2,902	1,869	999	34	870 R	64.4%	34.4%	65.2%	34.8%
4,802	DEWEY	2,293	1,293	996	4	297 R	56.4%	43.4%	56.5%	43.5%
6,993	DOUGLAS	2,838	1,949	879	10	1,070 R	68.7%	31.0%	68.9%	31.1%
8,336	EDMUNDS	3,355	1,743	1,597	15	146 R	52.0%	47.6%	52.2%	47.8%
6,985	FALL RIVER	3,489	2,216	1,258	15	958 R	63.5%	36.1%	63.8%	36.2%
6,442	FAULK	3,053	1,907	1,135	11	772 R	62.5%	37.2%	62.7%	37.3%
10,880	GRANT	4,216	2,508	1,656	52	852 R	59.5%	39.3%	60.2%	39.8%
12,700	GREGORY	4,287	2,274	2,001	12	273 R	53.0%	46.7%	53.2%	46.8%
4,596	HAAKON	1,951	1,255	663	33	592 R	64.3%	34.0%	65.4%	34.6%
8,054	HAMLIN	3,100	1,959	1,088	53	871 R	63.2%	35.1%	64.3%	35.7%
8,778	HAND	3,841	2,430	1,397	14	1,033 R	63.3%	36.4%	63.5%	36.5%
6,202	HANSON	2,711	1,576	1,129	6	447 R	58.1%	41.6%	58.3%	41.7%
3,953	HARDING	1,418	1,032	368	18	664 R	72.8%	26.0%	73.7%	26.3%
5,711	HUGHES	3,106	1,912	1,171	23	741 R	61.6%	37.7%	62.0%	38.0%
13,475	HUTCHINSON	4,077	2,145	1,898	34	247 R	52.6%	46.6%	53.1%	46.9%
3,315	HYDE	1,580	961	608	11	353 R	60.8%	38.5%	61.2%	38.8%
2,472	JACKSON	1,124	704	417	3	287 R	62.6%	37.1%	62.8%	37.2%
6,338	JERAULD	2,420	1,517	875	28	642 R	62.7%	36.2%	63.4%	36.6%
3,004	JONES	1,290	857	422	11	435 R	66.4%	32.7%	67.0%	33.0%
12,802	KINGSBURY	4,868	3,499	1,352	17	2,147 R	71.9%	27.8%	72.1%	27.9%
12,257	LAKE	4,807	3,048	1,744	15	1,304 R	63.4%	36.3%	63.6%	36.4%
13,029	LAWRENCE	5,947	4,141	1,785	21	2,356 R	69.6%	30.0%	69.9%	30.1%
13,893	LINCOLN	4,850	3,463	1,364	23	2,099 R	71.4%	28.1%	71.7%	28.3%
6,591	LYMAN	2,718	1,488	1,222	8	266 R	54.7%	45.0%	54.9%	45.1%
9,990	MCCOOK	4,005	2,234	1,758	13	476 R	55.8%	43.9%	56.0%	44.0%
7,705	MCPHERSON	2,711	1,234	1,468	9	234 D	45.5%	54.1%	45.7%	54.3%
9,596	MARSHALL	3,252	1,858	1,315	79	543 R	57.1%	40.4%	58.6%	41.4%
9,367	MEADE	4,308	2,845	1,441	22	1,404 R	66.0%	33.4%	66.4%	33.6%
3,850	MELLETTE	1,881	943	927	11	16 R	50.1%	49.3%	50.4%	49.6%
8,560	MINER	3,352	1,990	1,341	21	649 R	59.4%	40.0%	59.7%	40.3%
42,490	MINNEHAHA	20,608	13,741	6,805	62	6,936 R	66.7%	33.0%	66.9%	33.1%
9,742	MOODY	3,535	2,108	1,416	11	692 R	59.6%	40.1%	59.8%	40.2%
12,720	PENNINGTON	6,936	4,645	2,266	25	2,379 R	67.0%	32.7%	67.2%	32.8%
7,993	PERKINS	3,299	2,262	1,010	27	1,252 R	68.6%	30.6%	69.1%	30.9%
4,382	POTTER	2,350	1,240	1,100	10	140 R	52.8%	46.8%	53.0%	47.0%
16,514	ROBERTS	5,625	2,966	2,619	40	347 R	52.7%	46.6%	53.1%	46.9%
7,877	SANBORN	2,914	1,576	1,321	17	255 R	54.1%	45.3%	54.4%	45.6%
2,003	SHANNON	1,075	469	601	5	132 D	43.6%	55.9%	43.8%	56.2%
15,768	SPINK	6,352	3,868	2,451	33	1,417 R	60.9%	38.6%	61.2%	38.8%
2,908	STANLEY	1,184	739	437	8	302 R	62.4%	36.9%	62.8%	37.2%
2,831	SULLY	1,417	999	415	3	584 R	70.5%	29.3%	70.7%	29.3%

SOUTH DAKOTA

PRESIDENT 1928

1920 Census Population	County	Total Vote	Republican	Democratic	Other	Rep.-Dem. Plurality	Percentage Total Vote Rep.	Total Vote Dem.	Major Vote Rep.	Major Vote Dem.
2,784	TODD	1,629	789	831	9	42 D	48.4%	51.0%	48.7%	51.3%
11,970	TRIPP	4,519	2,396	2,099	24	297 R	53.0%	46.4%	53.3%	46.7%
14,871	TURNER	4,759	3,362	1,380	17	1,982 R	70.6%	29.0%	70.9%	29.1%
11,099	UNION	4,540	2,415	2,106	19	309 R	53.2%	46.4%	53.4%	46.6%
8,447	WALWORTH	3,092	1,854	1,216	22	638 R	60.0%	39.3%	60.4%	39.6%
1,166	WASHABAUGH	580	294	282	4	12 R	50.7%	48.6%	51.0%	49.0%
1,521	WASHINGTON	433	205	228		23 D	47.3%	52.7%	47.3%	52.7%
15,233	YANKTON	5,839	2,971	2,841	27	130 R	50.9%	48.7%	51.1%	48.9%
3,718	ZIEBACH	1,380	759	615	6	144 R	55.0%	44.6%	55.2%	44.8%
636,547	TOTAL	261,857	157,603	102,660	1,594	54,943 R	60.2%	39.2%	60.6%	39.4%

SOUTH DAKOTA

PRESIDENT 1924

1920 Census Population	County	Total Vote	Republican	Democratic	Progressive	Other	Plurality	Percentage Total Vote Rep.	Dem.	Prog.
	ARMSTRONG	—	—	—	—		—	—	—	—
7,246	AURORA	2,663	967	665	1,031		64 P	36.3%	25.0%	38.7%
19,273	BEADLE	6,494	3,466	851	2,177		1,289 R	53.4%	13.1%	33.5%
1,924	BENNETT	778	444	102	232		212 R	57.1%	13.1%	29.8%
11,940	BON HOMME	3,398	1,420	860	1,118		302 R	41.8%	25.3%	32.9%
16,119	BROOKINGS	4,516	2,740	361	1,415		1,325 R	60.7%	8.0%	31.3%
29,509	BROWN	9,705	4,708	1,010	3,987		721 R	48.5%	10.4%	41.1%
7,141	BRULE	2,856	1,060	650	1,146		86 P	37.1%	22.8%	40.1%
1,715	BUFFALO	744	309	225	210		84 R	41.5%	30.2%	28.2%
6,819	BUTTE	2,157	1,199	277	681		518 R	55.6%	12.8%	31.6%
5,305	CAMPBELL	1,175	641	46	488		153 R	54.6%	3.9%	41.5%
16,256	CHARLES MIX	5,382	1,680	1,306	2,396		716 P	31.2%	24.3%	44.5%
11,136	CLARK	2,962	1,684	325	953		731 R	56.9%	11.0%	32.2%
9,654	CLAY	3,345	1,415	492	1,438		23 P	42.3%	14.7%	43.0%
16,549	CODINGTON	4,500	1,862	627	2,011		149 P	41.4%	13.9%	44.7%
7,249	CORSON	2,414	1,364	140	910		454 R	56.5%	5.8%	37.7%
3,907	CUSTER	1,561	833	236	492		341 R	53.4%	15.1%	31.5%
14,139	DAVISON	5,417	2,801	578	2,038		763 R	51.7%	10.7%	37.6%
15,194	DAY	3,975	2,193	308	1,474		719 R	55.2%	7.7%	37.1%
8,759	DEUEL	2,258	1,362	168	728		634 R	60.3%	7.4%	32.2%
4,802	DEWEY	1,802	956	222	624		332 R	53.1%	12.3%	34.6%
6,993	DOUGLAS	2,239	1,125	317	797		328 R	50.2%	14.2%	35.6%
8,336	EDMUNDS	2,461	1,043	277	1,141		98 P	42.4%	11.3%	46.4%
6,985	FALL RIVER	2,670	1,392	342	936		456 R	52.1%	12.8%	35.1%
6,442	FAULK	1,983	1,112	277	594		518 R	56.1%	14.0%	30.0%
10,880	GRANT	2,920	1,227	202	1,491		264 P	42.0%	6.9%	51.1%
12,700	GREGORY	3,683	1,643	818	1,222		421 R	44.6%	22.2%	33.2%
4,596	HAAKON	1,598	797	319	482		315 R	49.9%	20.0%	30.2%
8,054	HAMLIN	2,184	1,144	207	833		311 R	52.4%	9.5%	38.1%
8,778	HAND	3,198	1,727	690	781		946 R	54.0%	21.6%	24.4%
6,202	HANSON	2,004	811	299	894		83 P	40.5%	14.9%	44.6%
3,953	HARDING	1,131	702	107	322		380 R	62.1%	9.5%	28.5%
5,711	HUGHES	2,368	1,260	325	783		477 R	53.2%	13.7%	33.1%
13,475	HUTCHINSON	3,623	893	180	2,550		1,657 P	24.6%	5.0%	70.4%
3,315	HYDE	1,324	669	257	398		271 R	50.5%	19.4%	30.1%
2,472	JACKSON	1,024	583	194	247		336 R	56.9%	18.9%	24.1%
6,338	JERAULD	1,993	1,054	228	711		343 R	52.9%	11.4%	35.7%
3,004	JONES	1,320	732	141	447		285 R	55.5%	10.7%	33.9%
12,802	KINGSBURY	3,415	2,242	333	840		1,402 R	65.7%	9.8%	24.6%
12,257	LAKE	4,163	1,888	297	1,978		90 P	45.4%	7.1%	47.5%
13,029	LAWRENCE	4,580	3,255	649	676		2,579 R	71.1%	14.2%	14.8%
13,893	LINCOLN	4,166	1,825	265	2,076		251 P	43.8%	6.4%	49.8%
6,591	LYMAN	2,395	1,061	387	947		114 R	44.3%	16.2%	39.5%
9,990	MCCOOK	3,090	1,368	457	1,265		103 R	44.3%	14.8%	40.9%
7,705	MCPHERSON	2,889	833	94	1,962		1,129 P	28.8%	3.3%	67.9%
9,596	MARSHALL	2,466	1,271	190	1,005		266 R	51.5%	7.7%	40.8%
9,367	MEADE	3,493	2,006	786	701		1,220 R	57.4%	22.5%	20.1%
3,850	MELLETTE	1,608	642	604	362		38 R	39.9%	37.6%	22.5%
8,560	MINER	2,791	995	308	1,488		493 P	35.7%	11.0%	53.3%
42,490	MINNEHAHA	15,773	8,822	1,524	5,427		3,395 R	55.9%	9.7%	34.4%
9,742	MOODY	2,833	1,181	234	1,418		237 P	41.7%	8.3%	50.1%
12,720	PENNINGTON	5,035	3,201	854	980		2,221 R	63.6%	17.0%	19.5%
7,993	PERKINS	2,400	1,421	277	702		719 R	59.2%	11.5%	29.2%
4,382	POTTER	1,797	1,075	283	439		636 R	59.8%	15.7%	24.4%
16,514	ROBERTS	4,255	1,744	215	2,296		552 P	41.0%	5.1%	54.0%
7,877	SANBORN	2,501	1,184	327	990		194 R	47.3%	13.1%	39.6%
2,003	SHANNON	1,116	992	76	48		916 R	88.9%	6.8%	4.3%
15,768	SPINK	4,520	2,613	595	1,312		1,301 R	57.8%	13.2%	29.0%
2,908	STANLEY	1,212	531	249	432		99 R	43.8%	20.5%	35.6%
2,831	SULLY	940	555	138	247		308 R	59.0%	14.7%	26.3%

SOUTH DAKOTA

PRESIDENT 1924

1920 Census Population	County	Total Vote	Republican	Democratic	Progressive	Other	Plurality	Percentage Total Vote Rep.	Dem.	Prog.
2,784	TODD	1,249	837	237	175		600 R	67.0%	19.0%	14.0%
11,970	TRIPP	3,880	1,647	932	1,301		346 R	42.4%	24.0%	33.5%
14,871	TURNER	3,719	1,708	285	1,726		18 P	45.9%	7.7%	46.4%
11,099	UNION	3,697	1,665	877	1,155		510 R	45.0%	23.7%	31.2%
8,447	WALWORTH	2,340	1,033	114	1,193		160 P	44.1%	4.9%	51.0%
1,166	WASHABAUGH	425	246	121	58		125 R	57.9%	28.5%	13.6%
1,521	WASHINGTON	316	277	31	8		246 R	87.7%	9.8%	2.5%
15,233	YANKTON	3,781	1,504	693	1,584		80 P	39.8%	18.3%	41.9%
3,718	ZIEBACH	1,198	659	153	386		273 R	55.0%	12.8%	32.2%
636,547	TOTAL	203,868	101,299	27,214	75,355		25,944 R	49.7%	13.3%	37.0%

SOUTH DAKOTA

PRESIDENT 1920

1920 Census Population	County	Total Vote	Republican	Democratic	Other	Rep.-Dem. Plurality	Percentage			
							Total Vote		Major Vote	
							Rep.	Dem.	Rep.	Dem.
	ARMSTRONG	—	—	—	—	—	—	—	—	—
7,246	AURORA	2,041	1,004	445	592	559 R	49.2%	21.8%	69.3%	30.7%
19,273	BEADLE	5,044	2,852	925	1,267	1,927 R	56.5%	18.3%	75.5%	24.5%
1,924	BENNETT	452	220	199	33	21 R	48.7%	44.0%	52.5%	47.5%
11,940	BON HOMME	3,517	1,872	960	685	912 R	53.2%	27.3%	66.1%	33.9%
16,119	BROOKINGS	3,996	2,743	564	689	2,179 R	68.6%	14.1%	82.9%	17.1%
29,509	BROWN	9,871	5,581	1,364	2,926	4,217 R	56.5%	13.8%	80.4%	19.6%
7,141	BRULE	2,030	1,036	671	323	365 R	51.0%	33.1%	60.7%	39.3%
1,715	BUFFALO	335	200	101	34	99 R	59.7%	30.1%	66.4%	33.6%
6,819	BUTTE	3,159	1,722	672	765	1,050 R	54.5%	21.3%	71.9%	28.1%
5,305	CAMPBELL	1,583	1,128	67	388	1,061 R	71.3%	4.2%	94.4%	5.6%
16,256	CHARLES MIX	4,028	2,021	1,305	702	716 R	50.2%	32.4%	60.8%	39.2%
11,136	CLARK	2,910	1,753	437	720	1,316 R	60.2%	15.0%	80.0%	20.0%
9,654	CLAY	3,046	1,885	907	254	978 R	61.9%	29.8%	67.5%	32.5%
16,549	CODINGTON	4,522	2,706	867	949	1,839 R	59.8%	19.2%	75.7%	24.3%
7,249	CORSON	2,378	1,448	484	446	964 R	60.9%	20.4%	74.9%	25.1%
3,907	CUSTER	1,289	784	383	122	401 R	60.8%	29.7%	67.2%	32.8%
14,139	DAVISON	4,810	2,605	1,105	1,100	1,500 R	54.2%	23.0%	70.2%	29.8%
15,194	DAY	4,579	2,739	436	1,404	2,303 R	59.8%	9.5%	86.3%	13.7%
8,759	DEUEL	2,243	1,569	159	515	1,410 R	70.0%	7.1%	90.8%	9.2%
4,802	DEWEY	1,390	880	335	175	545 R	63.3%	24.1%	72.4%	27.6%
6,993	DOUGLAS	1,964	1,247	386	331	861 R	63.5%	19.7%	76.4%	23.6%
8,336	EDMUNDS	2,462	1,486	283	693	1,203 R	60.4%	11.5%	84.0%	16.0%
6,985	FALL RIVER	2,026	1,236	680	110	556 R	61.0%	33.6%	64.5%	35.5%
6,442	FAULK	2,047	1,341	346	360	995 R	65.5%	16.9%	79.5%	20.5%
10,880	GRANT	3,022	1,813	350	859	1,463 R	60.0%	11.6%	83.8%	16.2%
12,700	GREGORY	3,182	1,833	744	605	1,089 R	57.6%	23.4%	71.1%	28.9%
4,596	HAAKON	1,436	713	393	330	320 R	49.7%	27.4%	64.5%	35.5%
8,054	HAMLIN	2,076	1,322	337	417	985 R	63.7%	16.2%	79.7%	20.3%
8,778	HAND	2,474	1,511	655	308	856 R	61.1%	26.5%	69.8%	30.2%
6,202	HANSON	1,930	1,001	418	511	583 R	51.9%	21.7%	70.5%	29.5%
3,953	HARDING	1,109	648	213	248	435 R	58.4%	19.2%	75.3%	24.7%
5,711	HUGHES	1,922	1,313	433	176	880 R	68.3%	22.5%	75.2%	24.8%
13,475	HUTCHINSON	3,662	1,873	243	1,546	1,630 R	51.1%	6.6%	88.5%	11.5%
3,315	HYDE	1,036	710	233	93	477 R	68.5%	22.5%	75.3%	24.7%
2,472	JACKSON	843	595	206	42	389 R	70.6%	24.4%	74.3%	25.7%
6,338	JERAULD	1,820	1,038	357	425	681 R	57.0%	19.6%	74.4%	25.6%
3,004	JONES	977	609	255	113	354 R	62.3%	26.1%	70.5%	29.5%
12,802	KINGSBURY	3,271	2,344	481	446	1,863 R	71.7%	14.7%	83.0%	17.0%
12,257	LAKE	3,334	2,333	398	603	1,935 R	70.0%	11.9%	85.4%	14.6%
13,029	LAWRENCE	4,359	2,986	1,201	172	1,785 R	68.5%	27.6%	71.3%	28.7%
13,893	LINCOLN	3,794	2,790	441	563	2,349 R	73.5%	11.6%	86.4%	13.6%
6,591	LYMAN	1,761	1,050	463	248	587 R	59.6%	26.3%	69.4%	30.6%
9,990	MCCOOK	3,080	1,864	565	651	1,299 R	60.5%	18.3%	76.7%	23.3%
7,705	MCPHERSON	2,016	1,470	112	434	1,358 R	72.9%	5.6%	92.9%	7.1%
9,596	MARSHALL	2,782	1,557	266	959	1,291 R	56.0%	9.6%	85.4%	14.6%
9,367	MEADE	3,245	1,894	894	457	1,000 R	58.4%	27.6%	67.9%	32.1%
3,850	MELLETTE	839	533	261	45	272 R	63.5%	31.1%	67.1%	32.9%
8,560	MINER	2,556	1,450	651	455	799 R	56.7%	25.5%	69.0%	31.0%
42,490	MINNEHAHA	13,127	8,290	2,534	2,303	5,756 R	63.2%	19.3%	76.6%	23.4%
9,742	MOODY	2,623	1,667	371	585	1,296 R	63.6%	14.1%	81.8%	18.2%
12,720	PENNINGTON	3,998	2,568	1,205	225	1,363 R	64.2%	30.1%	68.1%	31.9%
7,993	PERKINS	2,195	1,326	417	452	909 R	60.4%	19.0%	76.1%	23.9%
4,382	POTTER	1,484	1,073	255	156	818 R	72.3%	17.2%	80.8%	19.2%
16,514	ROBERTS	4,695	2,335	447	1,913	1,888 R	49.7%	9.5%	83.9%	16.1%
7,877	SANBORN	2,255	1,125	517	613	608 R	49.9%	22.9%	68.5%	31.5%
2,003	SHANNON	—	—	—	—	—	—	—	—	—
15,768	SPINK	4,491	2,923	785	783	2,138 R	65.1%	17.5%	78.8%	21.2%
2,908	STANLEY	1,053	598	394	61	204 R	56.8%	37.4%	60.3%	39.7%
2,831	SULLY	861	542	147	172	395 R	63.0%	17.1%	78.7%	21.3%

SOUTH DAKOTA

PRESIDENT 1920

1920 Census Population	County	Total Vote	Republican	Democratic	Other	Rep.-Dem. Plurality	Percentage Total Vote Rep.	Percentage Total Vote Dem.	Percentage Major Vote Rep.	Percentage Major Vote Dem.
2,784	TODD	—	—	—	—	—	—	—	—	—
11,970	TRIPP	3,066	1,819	968	279	851 R	59.3%	31.6%	65.3%	34.7%
14,871	TURNER	3,999	2,703	604	692	2,099 R	67.6%	15.1%	81.7%	18.3%
11,099	UNION	2,935	1,942	841	152	1,101 R	66.2%	28.7%	69.8%	30.2%
8,447	WALWORTH	2,298	1,411	478	409	933 R	61.4%	20.8%	74.7%	25.3%
1,166	WASHABAUGH	—	—	—	—	—	—	—	—	—
1,521	WASHINGTON	—	—	—	—	—	—	—	—	—
15,233	YANKTON	4,134	2,555	1,147	432	1,408 R	61.8%	27.7%	69.0%	31.0%
3,718	ZIEBACH	775	507	177	91	330 R	65.4%	22.8%	74.1%	25.9%
636,547	TOTAL	182,237	110,692	35,938	35,607	74,754 R	60.7%	19.7%	75.5%	24.5%

SOUTH DAKOTA

In early elections, the votes from a number of unorganized counties were reported with the returns from adjacent counties. Armstrong reported with Ziebach county; Shannon reported with Fall River county; Washabaugh reported with Jackson county; Washington reported with Pennington county and Todd reported with Tripp county. In 1943 Washington county merged with Shannon county. In 1954 Armstrong county merged with Dewey county.

ELECTION NOTES

1956

1952

1948 Other vote was Wallace (Progressive).

1944

1940

1936 Other vote was Lemke (Union).

1932 Other vote was 3,333 Harvey (Liberty); 1,551 Thomas (Socialist); 463 Upshaw (Prohibition); 364 Foster (Communist).

1928 Other vote was 927 Webb (Farmer-Labor); 443 Thomas (Socialist); 224 Foster (Communist).

1924 A special four-column table which gives the LaFollette (Progressive) vote is used to detail this election.

1920 Other vote was 34,707 Christensen (Farmer-Labor); 900 Watkins (Prohibition). Farmer-Labor candidates ran second in a number of counties.

TENNESSEE

POPULAR VOTE FOR PRESIDENT 1920 TO 1956

								Percentage			
		Republican		Democratic				Total Vote		Major Vote	
Year	Total Vote	Vote	Candidate	Vote	Candidate	Other Vote	Plurality	Rep.	Dem.	Rep.	Dem.
1956	939,404	462,288	Eisenhower, Dwight D.	456,507	Stevenson, Adlai E.	20,609	5,781 R	49.2%	48.6%	50.3%	49.7%
1952	892,553	446,147	Eisenhower, Dwight D.	443,710	Stevenson, Adlai E.	2,696	2,437 R	50.0%	49.7%	50.1%	49.9%
1948	550,283	202,914	Dewey, Thomas E.	270,402	Truman, Harry S.	76,967	67,488 D	36.9%	49.1%	42.9%	57.1%
1944	510,692	200,311	Dewey, Thomas E.	308,707	Roosevelt, Franklin D.	1,674	108,396 D	39.2%	60.4%	39.4%	60.6%
1940	522,823	169,153	Willkie, Wendell	351,601	Roosevelt, Franklin D.	2,069	182,448 D	32.4%	67.3%	32.5%	67.5%
1936	477,086	147,055	Landon, Alfred M.	328,083	Roosevelt, Franklin D.	1,948	181,028 D	30.8%	68.8%	30.9%	69.1%
1932	390,273	126,752	Hoover, Herbert C.	259,473	Roosevelt, Franklin D.	4,048	132,721 D	32.5%	66.5%	32.8%	67.2%
1928	353,192	195,388	Hoover, Herbert C.	157,143	Smith, Alfred E.	661	38,245 R	55.3%	44.5%	55.4%	44.6%
1924	301,030	130,831	Coolidge, Calvin	159,339	Davis, John W.	10,860	28,508 D	43.5%	52.9%	45.1%	54.9%
1920	428,036	219,229	Harding, Warren G.	206,558	Cox, James M.	2,249	12,671 R	51.2%	48.3%	51.5%	48.5%

ELECTORAL COLLEGE VOTE 1920 TO 1956

Year	Total	Republican	Democratic	Other
1956	11	11	—	—
1952	11	11	—	—
1948 **	12	—	11	1 SR
1944	12	—	12	—
1940	11	—	11	—
1936	11	—	11	—
1932	11	—	11	—
1928	12	12	—	—
1924	12	—	12	—
1920	12	12	—	—

In 1948 one of the twelve Democratic electors voted in the Electoral College for the States Rights candidates rather than for the national Democratic candidates.

TENNESSEE

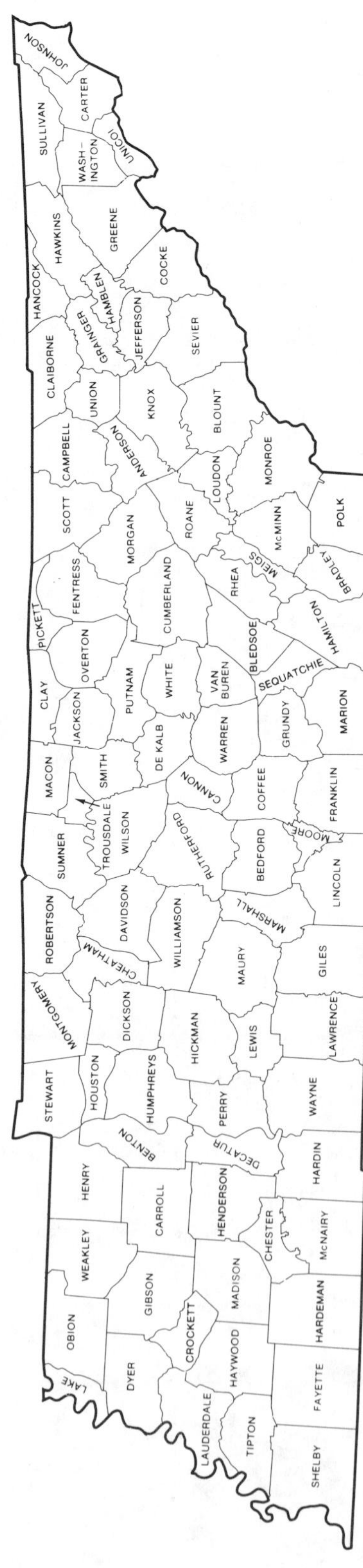
JOHNSON
SULLIVAN
CARTER
UNICOI
WASH-INGTON
HAWKINS
GREENE
HANCOCK
HAMBLEN
COCKE
GRAINGER
JEFFERSON
SEVIER
CLAIBORNE
UNION
KNOX
BLOUNT
CAMPBELL
ANDERSON
LOUDON
MONROE
SCOTT
MORGAN
ROANE
McMINN
POLK
MEIGS
BRADLEY
FENTRESS
CUMBERLAND
RHEA
PICKETT
OVERTON
HAMILTON
BLEDSOE
CLAY
PUTNAM
WHITE
VAN BUREN
SEQUATCHIE
JACKSON
GRUNDY
MARION
DE KALB
WARREN
MACON
SMITH
CANNON
COFFEE
FRANKLIN
TROUSDALE
WILSON
RUTHERFORD
MOORE
SUMNER
BEDFORD
LINCOLN
ROBERTSON
DAVIDSON
WILLIAMSON
MARSHALL
CHEATHAM
MAURY
GILES
MONTGOMERY
DICKSON
HICKMAN
LEWIS
LAWRENCE
STEWART
HOUSTON
HUMPHREYS
PERRY
WAYNE
BENTON
DECATUR
HARDIN
HENRY
CARROLL
HENDERSON
CHESTER
McNAIRY
WEAKLEY
GIBSON
MADISON
HARDEMAN
OBION
CROCKETT
HAYWOOD
LAKE
DYER
FAYETTE
LAUDERDALE
TIPTON
SHELBY

TENNESSEE

PRESIDENT 1956

1950 Census Population	County	Total Vote	Republican	Democratic	Other	Rep.-Dem. Plurality	Percentage: Total Vote Rep.	Percentage: Total Vote Dem.	Percentage: Major Vote Rep.	Percentage: Major Vote Dem.
59,407	ANDERSON	21,121	11,071	9,368	682	1,703 R	52.4%	44.4%	54.2%	45.8%
23,627	BEDFORD	6,825	2,258	4,517	50	2,259 D	33.1%	66.2%	33.3%	66.7%
11,495	BENTON	3,531	1,279	2,231	21	952 D	36.2%	63.2%	36.4%	63.6%
8,561	BLEDSOE	2,526	1,429	1,079	18	350 R	56.6%	42.7%	57.0%	43.0%
54,691	BLOUNT	17,867	12,667	5,076	124	7,591 R	70.9%	28.4%	71.4%	28.6%
32,338	BRADLEY	9,611	6,247	3,225	139	3,022 R	65.0%	33.6%	66.0%	34.0%
34,369	CAMPBELL	7,819	5,065	2,628	126	2,437 R	64.8%	33.6%	65.8%	34.2%
9,174	CANNON	2,475	919	1,547	9	628 D	37.1%	62.5%	37.3%	62.7%
26,553	CARROLL	7,590	4,235	3,232	123	1,003 R	55.8%	42.6%	56.7%	43.3%
42,432	CARTER	14,236	11,218	2,933	85	8,285 R	78.8%	20.6%	79.3%	20.7%
9,167	CHEATHAM	2,811	498	2,297	16	1,799 D	17.7%	81.7%	17.8%	82.2%
11,149	CHESTER	2,989	1,460	1,495	34	35 D	48.8%	50.0%	49.4%	50.6%
24,788	CLAIBORNE	5,428	3,377	1,973	78	1,404 R	62.2%	36.3%	63.1%	36.9%
8,701	CLAY	1,867	902	948	17	46 D	48.3%	50.8%	48.8%	51.2%
22,991	COCKE	6,715	5,526	1,121	68	4,405 R	82.3%	16.7%	83.1%	16.9%
23,049	COFFEE	7,369	2,389	4,930	50	2,541 D	32.4%	66.9%	32.6%	67.4%
16,624	CROCKETT	3,107	1,026	1,964	117	938 D	33.0%	63.2%	34.3%	65.7%
18,877	CUMBERLAND	5,161	3,200	1,925	36	1,275 R	62.0%	37.3%	62.4%	37.6%
321,758	DAVIDSON	94,874	37,077	56,822	975	19,745 D	39.1%	59.9%	39.5%	60.5%
9,442	DECATUR	3,101	1,512	1,554	35	42 D	48.8%	50.1%	49.3%	50.7%
11,680	DE KALB	3,693	1,690	1,982	21	292 D	45.8%	53.7%	46.0%	54.0%
18,805	DICKSON	5,114	1,247	3,799	68	2,552 D	24.4%	74.3%	24.7%	75.3%
33,473	DYER	7,407	2,682	4,524	201	1,842 D	36.2%	61.1%	37.2%	62.8%
27,535	FAYETTE	1,968	358	639	971	281 D	18.2%	32.5%	35.9%	64.1%
14,917	FENTRESS	3,212	2,233	934	45	1,299 R	69.5%	29.1%	70.5%	29.5%
25,431	FRANKLIN	6,595	1,727	4,791	77	3,064 D	26.2%	72.6%	26.5%	73.5%
48,132	GIBSON	11,713	3,481	7,884	348	4,403 D	29.7%	67.3%	30.6%	69.4%
26,961	GILES	6,186	1,401	4,750	35	3,349 D	22.6%	76.8%	22.8%	77.2%
13,086	GRAINGER	3,449	2,497	913	39	1,584 R	72.4%	26.5%	73.2%	26.8%
41,048	GREENE	11,402	7,396	3,949	57	3,447 R	64.9%	34.6%	65.2%	34.8%
12,558	GRUNDY	3,024	918	2,076	30	1,158 D	30.4%	68.7%	30.7%	69.3%
23,976	HAMBLEN	8,275	5,608	2,592	75	3,016 R	67.8%	31.3%	68.4%	31.6%
208,255	HAMILTON	64,830	34,429	28,287	2,114	6,142 R	53.1%	43.6%	54.9%	45.1%
9,116	HANCOCK	2,328	1,939	350	39	1,589 R	83.3%	15.0%	84.7%	15.3%
23,311	HARDEMAN	3,353	818	1,754	781	936 D	24.4%	52.3%	31.8%	68.2%
16,908	HARDIN	4,680	2,898	1,734	48	1,164 R	61.9%	37.1%	62.6%	37.4%
30,494	HAWKINS	10,164	6,916	3,180	68	3,736 R	68.0%	31.3%	68.5%	31.5%
26,212	HAYWOOD	3,028	516	2,217	295	1,701 D	17.0%	73.2%	18.9%	81.1%
17,173	HENDERSON	4,923	3,294	1,613	16	1,681 R	66.9%	32.8%	67.1%	32.9%
23,828	HENRY	8,068	2,337	5,625	106	3,288 D	29.0%	69.7%	29.4%	70.6%
13,353	HICKMAN	3,496	1,040	2,439	17	1,399 D	29.7%	69.8%	29.9%	70.1%
5,318	HOUSTON	1,385	340	1,033	12	693 D	24.5%	74.6%	24.8%	75.2%
11,030	HUMPHREYS	3,566	713	2,841	12	2,128 D	20.0%	79.7%	20.1%	79.9%
12,348	JACKSON	2,659	881	1,743	35	862 D	33.1%	65.6%	33.6%	66.4%
19,667	JEFFERSON	6,273	4,870	1,338	65	3,532 R	77.6%	21.3%	78.4%	21.6%
12,278	JOHNSON	4,220	3,690	503	27	3,187 R	87.4%	11.9%	88.0%	12.0%
223,007	KNOX	76,831	46,167	29,768	896	16,399 R	60.1%	38.7%	60.8%	39.2%
11,655	LAKE	2,246	512	1,673	61	1,161 D	22.8%	74.5%	23.4%	76.6%
25,047	LAUDERDALE	5,540	1,049	4,383	108	3,334 D	18.9%	79.1%	19.3%	80.7%
28,818	LAWRENCE	8,880	4,588	4,227	65	361 R	51.7%	47.6%	52.0%	48.0%
6,078	LEWIS	1,854	522	1,321	11	799 D	28.2%	71.3%	28.3%	71.7%
25,624	LINCOLN	5,692	1,207	4,434	51	3,227 D	21.2%	77.9%	21.4%	78.6%
23,182	LOUDON	7,524	4,583	2,844	97	1,739 R	60.9%	37.8%	61.7%	38.3%
32,024	MCMINN	10,153	6,075	3,950	128	2,125 R	59.8%	38.9%	60.6%	39.4%
20,390	MCNAIRY	5,838	3,349	2,403	86	946 R	57.4%	41.2%	58.2%	41.8%
13,599	MACON	3,296	2,207	1,069	20	1,138 R	67.0%	32.4%	67.4%	32.6%
60,128	MADISON	16,037	6,642	8,540	855	1,898 D	41.4%	53.3%	43.7%	56.3%
20,520	MARION	5,798	2,925	2,781	92	144 R	50.4%	48.0%	51.3%	48.7%
17,768	MARSHALL	5,745	1,527	4,100	118	2,573 D	26.6%	71.4%	27.1%	72.9%
40,368	MAURY	9,706	2,853	6,662	191	3,809 D	29.4%	68.6%	30.0%	70.0%

TENNESSEE

PRESIDENT 1956

1950 Census Population	County	Total Vote	Republican	Democratic	Other	Rep.-Dem. Plurality	Percentage Total Vote Rep.	Percentage Total Vote Dem.	Percentage Major Vote Rep.	Percentage Major Vote Dem.
6,080	MEIGS	1,631	847	759	25	88 R	51.9%	46.5%	52.7%	47.3%
24,513	MONROE	8,576	4,998	3,511	67	1,487 R	58.3%	40.9%	58.7%	41.3%
44,186	MONTGOMERY	10,934	2,778	8,034	122	5,256 D	25.4%	73.5%	25.7%	74.3%
3,948	MOORE	1,167	270	893	4	623 D	23.1%	76.5%	23.2%	76.8%
15,727	MORGAN	3,823	2,402	1,379	42	1,023 R	62.8%	36.1%	63.5%	36.5%
29,056	OBION	7,637	2,349	5,185	103	2,836 D	30.8%	67.9%	31.2%	68.8%
17,566	OVERTON	3,923	1,508	2,385	30	877 D	38.4%	60.8%	38.7%	61.3%
6,462	PERRY	1,760	694	1,052	14	358 D	39.4%	59.8%	39.7%	60.3%
5,093	PICKETT	1,556	985	560	11	425 R	63.3%	36.0%	63.8%	36.2%
14,074	POLK	3,669	2,136	1,533		603 R	58.2%	41.8%	58.2%	41.8%
29,869	PUTNAM	8,004	3,492	4,481	31	989 D	43.6%	56.0%	43.8%	56.2%
16,041	RHEA	4,517	2,516	1,930	71	586 R	55.7%	42.7%	56.6%	43.4%
31,665	ROANE	10,818	6,147	4,531	140	1,616 R	56.8%	41.9%	57.6%	42.4%
27,024	ROBERTSON	6,526	1,517	4,961	48	3,444 D	23.2%	76.0%	23.4%	76.6%
40,696	RUTHERFORD	9,306	2,713	6,494	99	3,781 D	29.2%	69.8%	29.5%	70.5%
17,362	SCOTT	4,149	3,282	842	25	2,440 R	79.1%	20.3%	79.6%	20.4%
5,685	SEQUATCHIE	1,556	683	859	14	176 D	43.9%	55.2%	44.3%	55.7%
23,375	SEVIER	8,038	6,950	1,043	45	5,907 R	86.5%	13.0%	87.0%	13.0%
482,393	SHELBY	135,025	65,690	62,051	7,284	3,639 R	48.7%	46.0%	51.4%	48.6%
14,098	SMITH	4,229	1,267	2,949	13	1,682 D	30.0%	69.7%	30.1%	69.9%
9,175	STEWART	2,696	560	2,120	16	1,560 D	20.8%	78.6%	20.9%	79.1%
95,063	SULLIVAN	33,506	18,903	14,106	497	4,797 R	56.4%	42.1%	57.3%	42.7%
33,533	SUMNER	9,527	2,123	7,368	36	5,245 D	22.3%	77.3%	22.4%	77.6%
29,782	TIPTON	6,045	983	4,828	234	3,845 D	16.3%	79.9%	16.9%	83.1%
5,520	TROUSDALE	1,247	209	1,032	6	823 D	16.8%	82.8%	16.8%	83.2%
15,886	UNICOI	5,119	3,978	1,111	30	2,867 R	77.7%	21.7%	78.2%	21.8%
8,670	UNION	2,703	2,154	535	14	1,619 R	79.7%	19.8%	80.1%	19.9%
3,985	VAN BUREN	991	381	602	8	221 D	38.4%	60.7%	38.8%	61.2%
22,271	WARREN	5,998	1,954	4,014	30	2,060 D	32.6%	66.9%	32.7%	67.3%
59,971	WASHINGTON	18,912	13,471	5,314	127	8,157 R	71.2%	28.1%	71.7%	28.3%
13,864	WAYNE	3,618	2,557	1,045	16	1,512 R	70.7%	28.9%	71.0%	29.0%
27,962	WEAKLEY	7,510	2,720	4,717	73	1,997 D	36.2%	62.8%	36.6%	63.4%
16,204	WHITE	3,759	1,346	2,378	35	1,032 D	35.8%	63.3%	36.1%	63.9%
24,307	WILLIAMSON	6,211	1,979	4,174	58	2,195 D	31.9%	67.2%	32.2%	67.8%
26,318	WILSON	7,544	2,266	5,221	57	2,955 D	30.0%	69.2%	30.3%	69.7%
3,291,718	TOTAL	939,404	462,288	456,507	20,609	5,781 R	49.2%	48.6%	50.3%	49.7%

TENNESSEE

PRESIDENT 1952

1950 Census Population	County	Total Vote	Republican	Democratic	Other	Rep.-Dem. Plurality	Percentage: Total Vote Rep.	Percentage: Total Vote Dem.	Percentage: Major Vote Rep.	Percentage: Major Vote Dem.
59,407	ANDERSON	19,466	10,489	8,939	38	1,550 R	53.9%	45.9%	54.0%	46.0%
23,627	BEDFORD	6,973	2,611	4,362		1,751 D	37.4%	62.6%	37.4%	62.6%
11,495	BENTON	3,772	1,304	2,452	16	1,148 D	34.6%	65.0%	34.7%	65.3%
8,561	BLEDSOE	2,417	1,229	1,158	30	71 R	50.8%	47.9%	51.5%	48.5%
54,691	BLOUNT	16,913	11,708	5,163	42	6,545 R	69.2%	30.5%	69.4%	30.6%
32,338	BRADLEY	7,269	4,606	2,646	17	1,960 R	63.4%	36.4%	63.5%	36.5%
34,369	CAMPBELL	6,943	4,557	2,346	40	2,211 R	65.6%	33.8%	66.0%	34.0%
9,174	CANNON	2,449	930	1,491	28	561 D	38.0%	60.9%	38.4%	61.6%
26,553	CARROLL	6,626	3,741	2,841	44	900 R	56.5%	42.9%	56.8%	43.2%
42,432	CARTER	11,844	9,019	2,707	118	6,312 R	76.1%	22.9%	76.9%	23.1%
9,167	CHEATHAM	2,776	536	2,222	18	1,686 D	19.3%	80.0%	19.4%	80.6%
11,149	CHESTER	3,158	1,674	1,484		190 R	53.0%	47.0%	53.0%	47.0%
24,788	CLAIBORNE	5,403	3,221	2,182		1,039 R	59.6%	40.4%	59.6%	40.4%
8,701	CLAY	1,821	842	968	11	126 D	46.2%	53.2%	46.5%	53.5%
22,991	COCKE	6,935	5,688	1,247		4,441 R	82.0%	18.0%	82.0%	18.0%
23,049	COFFEE	5,665	2,110	3,537	18	1,427 D	37.2%	62.4%	37.4%	62.6%
16,624	CROCKETT	3,509	1,343	2,155	11	812 D	38.3%	61.4%	38.4%	61.6%
18,877	CUMBERLAND	5,341	3,282	2,059		1,223 R	61.4%	38.6%	61.4%	38.6%
321,758	DAVIDSON	87,630	35,916	51,562	152	15,646 D	41.0%	58.8%	41.1%	58.9%
9,442	DECATUR	3,100	1,406	1,681	13	275 D	45.4%	54.2%	45.5%	54.5%
11,680	DE KALB	3,763	1,814	1,949		135 D	48.2%	51.8%	48.2%	51.8%
18,805	DICKSON	5,611	1,415	4,196		2,781 D	25.2%	74.8%	25.2%	74.8%
33,473	DYER	7,823	3,231	4,531	61	1,300 D	41.3%	57.9%	41.6%	58.4%
27,535	FAYETTE	2,202	1,029	1,173		144 D	46.7%	53.3%	46.7%	53.3%
14,917	FENTRESS	3,077	2,143	934		1,209 R	69.6%	30.4%	69.6%	30.4%
25,431	FRANKLIN	6,834	2,015	4,786	33	2,771 D	29.5%	70.0%	29.6%	70.4%
48,132	GIBSON	10,491	3,766	6,687	38	2,921 D	35.9%	63.7%	36.0%	64.0%
26,961	GILES	6,347	1,649	4,640	58	2,991 D	26.0%	73.1%	26.2%	73.8%
13,086	GRAINGER	3,972	3,030	937	5	2,093 R	76.3%	23.6%	76.4%	23.6%
41,048	GREENE	10,563	6,864	3,656	43	3,208 R	65.0%	34.6%	65.2%	34.8%
12,558	GRUNDY	3,302	709	2,583	10	1,874 D	21.5%	78.2%	21.5%	78.5%
23,976	HAMBLEN	7,488	5,031	2,395	62	2,636 R	67.2%	32.0%	67.7%	32.3%
208,255	HAMILTON	53,830	29,681	23,832	317	5,849 R	55.1%	44.3%	55.5%	44.5%
9,116	HANCOCK	2,302	1,830	458	14	1,372 R	79.5%	19.9%	80.0%	20.0%
23,311	HARDEMAN	4,029	1,256	2,747	26	1,491 D	31.2%	68.2%	31.4%	68.6%
16,908	HARDIN	4,148	2,459	1,677	12	782 R	59.3%	40.4%	59.5%	40.5%
30,494	HAWKINS	7,765	5,295	2,404	66	2,891 R	68.2%	31.0%	68.8%	31.2%
26,212	HAYWOOD	3,381	940	2,432	9	1,492 D	27.8%	71.9%	27.9%	72.1%
17,173	HENDERSON	4,918	3,317	1,601		1,716 R	67.4%	32.6%	67.4%	32.6%
23,828	HENRY	8,132	2,421	5,677	34	3,256 D	29.8%	69.8%	29.9%	70.1%
13,353	HICKMAN	3,679	1,044	2,625	10	1,581 D	28.4%	71.4%	28.5%	71.5%
5,318	HOUSTON	1,694	465	1,229		764 D	27.4%	72.6%	27.4%	72.6%
11,030	HUMPHREYS	3,569	898	2,670	1	1,772 D	25.2%	74.8%	25.2%	74.8%
12,348	JACKSON	2,827	1,138	1,686	3	548 D	40.3%	59.6%	40.3%	59.7%
19,667	JEFFERSON	5,860	4,622	1,228	10	3,394 R	78.9%	21.0%	79.0%	21.0%
12,278	JOHNSON	4,096	3,590	506		3,084 R	87.6%	12.4%	87.6%	12.4%
223,007	KNOX	71,178	44,358	26,681	139	17,677 R	62.3%	37.5%	62.4%	37.6%
11,655	LAKE	1,975	487	1,475	13	988 D	24.7%	74.7%	24.8%	75.2%
25,047	LAUDERDALE	5,730	1,390	4,340		2,950 D	24.3%	75.7%	24.3%	75.7%
28,818	LAWRENCE	8,931	4,561	4,299	71	262 R	51.1%	48.1%	51.5%	48.5%
6,078	LEWIS	1,859	540	1,308	11	768 D	29.0%	70.4%	29.2%	70.8%
25,624	LINCOLN	6,177	1,654	4,510	13	2,856 D	26.8%	73.0%	26.8%	73.2%
23,182	LOUDON	6,481	4,311	2,138	32	2,173 R	66.5%	33.0%	66.8%	33.2%
32,024	MCMINN	9,261	5,778	3,440	43	2,338 R	62.4%	37.1%	62.7%	37.3%
20,390	MCNAIRY	6,124	3,426	2,698		728 R	55.9%	44.1%	55.9%	44.1%
13,599	MACON	3,760	2,602	1,158		1,444 R	69.2%	30.8%	69.2%	30.8%
60,128	MADISON	15,919	7,243	8,623	53	1,380 D	45.5%	54.2%	45.7%	54.3%
20,520	MARION	5,190	2,227	2,938	25	711 D	42.9%	56.6%	43.1%	56.9%
17,768	MARSHALL	5,362	1,525	3,837		2,312 D	28.4%	71.6%	28.4%	71.6%
40,368	MAURY	10,959	3,582	7,377		3,795 D	32.7%	67.3%	32.7%	67.3%

TENNESSEE

PRESIDENT 1952

1950 Census Population	County	Total Vote	Republican	Democratic	Other	Rep.-Dem. Plurality	Percentage Total Vote Rep.	Total Vote Dem.	Major Vote Rep.	Major Vote Dem.
6,080	MEIGS	1,625	850	754	21	96 R	52.3%	46.4%	53.0%	47.0%
24,513	MONROE	8,313	4,581	3,693	39	888 R	55.1%	44.4%	55.4%	44.6%
44,186	MONTGOMERY	8,395	2,573	5,759	63	3,186 D	30.6%	68.6%	30.9%	69.1%
3,948	MOORE	1,180	354	826		472 D	30.0%	70.0%	30.0%	70.0%
15,727	MORGAN	4,057	2,565	1,492		1,073 R	63.2%	36.8%	63.2%	36.8%
29,056	OBION	7,345	2,682	4,623	40	1,941 D	36.5%	62.9%	36.7%	63.3%
17,566	OVERTON	3,681	1,453	2,209	19	756 D	39.5%	60.0%	39.7%	60.3%
6,462	PERRY	1,954	762	1,192		430 D	39.0%	61.0%	39.0%	61.0%
5,093	PICKETT	1,550	1,003	547		456 R	64.7%	35.3%	64.7%	35.3%
14,074	POLK	4,104	2,283	1,821		462 R	55.6%	44.4%	55.6%	44.4%
29,869	PUTNAM	7,279	3,183	4,096		913 D	43.7%	56.3%	43.7%	56.3%
16,041	RHEA	4,627	2,520	2,090	17	430 R	54.5%	45.2%	54.7%	45.3%
31,665	ROANE	9,285	5,583	3,702		1,881 R	60.1%	39.9%	60.1%	39.9%
27,024	ROBERTSON	6,897	1,834	5,063		3,229 D	26.6%	73.4%	26.6%	73.4%
40,696	RUTHERFORD	10,061	3,196	6,793	72	3,597 D	31.8%	67.5%	32.0%	68.0%
17,362	SCOTT	4,435	3,274	1,161		2,113 R	73.8%	26.2%	73.8%	26.2%
5,685	SEQUATCHIE	1,424	535	882	7	347 D	37.6%	61.9%	37.8%	62.2%
23,375	SEVIER	8,310	7,244	1,066		6,178 R	87.2%	12.8%	87.2%	12.8%
482,393	SHELBY	137,099	65,170	71,779	150	6,609 D	47.5%	52.4%	47.6%	52.4%
14,098	SMITH	4,058	1,412	2,622	24	1,210 D	34.8%	64.6%	35.0%	65.0%
9,175	STEWART	2,812	641	2,170	1	1,529 D	22.8%	77.2%	22.8%	77.2%
95,063	SULLIVAN	27,563	15,596	11,849	118	3,747 R	56.6%	43.0%	56.8%	43.2%
33,533	SUMNER	7,958	2,233	5,674	51	3,441 D	28.1%	71.3%	28.2%	71.8%
29,782	TIPTON	6,716	1,312	5,351	53	4,039 D	19.5%	79.7%	19.7%	80.3%
5,520	TROUSDALE	1,497	261	1,236		975 D	17.4%	82.6%	17.4%	82.6%
15,886	UNICOI	4,616	3,453	1,163		2,290 R	74.8%	25.2%	74.8%	25.2%
8,670	UNION	2,754	2,087	667		1,420 R	75.8%	24.2%	75.8%	24.2%
3,985	VAN BUREN	1,088	393	674	21	281 D	36.1%	61.9%	36.8%	63.2%
22,271	WARREN	5,513	1,912	3,568	33	1,656 D	34.7%	64.7%	34.9%	65.1%
59,971	WASHINGTON	17,347	12,023	5,245	79	6,778 R	69.3%	30.2%	69.6%	30.4%
13,864	WAYNE	3,451	2,439	1,008	4	1,431 R	70.7%	29.2%	70.8%	29.2%
27,962	WEAKLEY	7,275	3,043	4,198	34	1,155 D	41.8%	57.7%	42.0%	58.0%
16,204	WHITE	3,714	1,374	2,319	21	945 D	37.0%	62.4%	37.2%	62.8%
24,307	WILLIAMSON	6,432	2,326	4,085	21	1,759 D	36.2%	63.5%	36.3%	63.7%
26,318	WILSON	7,519	2,449	5,070		2,621 D	32.6%	67.4%	32.6%	67.4%
3,291,718	TOTAL	892,553	446,147	443,710	2,696	2,437 R	50.0%	49.7%	50.1%	49.9%

TENNESSEE

PRESIDENT 1948

1940 Census Population	County	Total Vote	Republican	Democratic	Other	Rep.-Dem. Plurality	Percentage Total Vote Rep.	Percentage Total Vote Dem.	Percentage Major Vote Rep.	Percentage Major Vote Dem.
26,504	ANDERSON	11,837	5,372	5,915	550	543 D	45.4%	50.0%	47.6%	52.4%
23,151	BEDFORD	4,301	771	2,393	1,137	1,622 D	17.9%	55.6%	24.4%	75.6%
11,976	BENTON	2,788	908	1,757	123	849 D	32.6%	63.0%	34.1%	65.9%
8,358	BLEDSOE	2,248	1,103	1,092	53	11 R	49.1%	48.6%	50.3%	49.7%
41,116	BLOUNT	9,543	6,152	3,141	250	3,011 R	64.5%	32.9%	66.2%	33.8%
28,498	BRADLEY	5,152	2,942	2,036	174	906 R	57.1%	39.5%	59.1%	40.9%
31,131	CAMPBELL	5,320	2,922	2,267	131	655 R	54.9%	42.6%	56.3%	43.7%
9,880	CANNON	2,127	558	1,408	161	850 D	26.2%	66.2%	28.4%	71.6%
25,978	CARROLL	6,173	2,651	2,818	704	167 D	42.9%	45.7%	48.5%	51.5%
35,127	CARTER	6,968	4,943	1,809	216	3,134 R	70.9%	26.0%	73.2%	26.8%
9,928	CHEATHAM	3,083	193	2,731	159	2,538 D	6.3%	88.6%	6.6%	93.4%
11,124	CHESTER	1,940	766	980	194	214 D	39.5%	50.5%	43.9%	56.1%
24,657	CLAIBORNE	4,686	2,507	2,068	111	439 R	53.5%	44.1%	54.8%	45.2%
10,904	CLAY	1,901	703	1,146	52	443 D	37.0%	60.3%	38.0%	62.0%
24,083	COCKE	4,614	3,576	939	99	2,637 R	77.5%	20.4%	79.2%	20.8%
18,959	COFFEE	3,601	599	2,041	961	1,442 D	16.6%	56.7%	22.7%	77.3%
17,330	CROCKETT	2,640	601	1,415	624	814 D	22.8%	53.6%	29.8%	70.2%
15,592	CUMBERLAND	3,721	1,988	1,607	126	381 R	53.4%	43.2%	55.3%	44.7%
257,267	DAVIDSON	37,643	8,410	20,877	8,356	12,467 D	22.3%	55.5%	28.7%	71.3%
10,261	DECATUR	3,020	1,291	1,565	164	274 D	42.7%	51.8%	45.2%	54.8%
14,588	DE KALB	4,412	1,751	2,412	249	661 D	39.7%	54.7%	42.1%	57.9%
19,718	DICKSON	3,145	485	2,337	323	1,852 D	15.4%	74.3%	17.2%	82.8%
34,920	DYER	5,364	989	3,503	872	2,514 D	18.4%	65.3%	22.0%	78.0%
30,322	FAYETTE	1,785	66	226	1,493	160 D	3.7%	12.7%	22.6%	77.4%
14,262	FENTRESS	2,634	1,587	962	85	625 R	60.3%	36.5%	62.3%	37.7%
23,892	FRANKLIN	4,461	589	2,948	924	2,359 D	13.2%	66.1%	16.7%	83.3%
44,835	GIBSON	5,971	1,137	3,917	917	2,780 D	19.0%	65.6%	22.5%	77.5%
29,240	GILES	4,872	717	3,676	479	2,959 D	14.7%	75.5%	16.3%	83.7%
14,356	GRAINGER	2,542	1,824	644	74	1,180 R	71.8%	25.3%	73.9%	26.1%
39,405	GREENE	7,875	4,375	3,282	218	1,093 R	55.6%	41.7%	57.1%	42.9%
11,552	GRUNDY	2,575	431	2,009	135	1,578 D	16.7%	78.0%	17.7%	82.3%
18,611	HAMBLEN	3,933	2,116	1,552	265	564 R	53.8%	39.5%	57.7%	42.3%
180,478	HAMILTON	30,189	10,434	16,968	2,787	6,534 D	34.6%	56.2%	38.1%	61.9%
11,231	HANCOCK	2,065	1,598	416	51	1,182 R	77.4%	20.1%	79.3%	20.7%
23,590	HARDEMAN	3,300	317	1,609	1,374	1,292 D	9.6%	48.8%	16.5%	83.5%
17,806	HARDIN	3,277	1,779	1,270	228	509 R	54.3%	38.8%	58.3%	41.7%
28,523	HAWKINS	5,819	3,637	2,019	163	1,618 R	62.5%	34.7%	64.3%	35.7%
27,699	HAYWOOD	2,129	148	1,050	931	902 D	7.0%	49.3%	12.4%	87.6%
19,220	HENDERSON	3,643	2,278	1,155	210	1,123 R	62.5%	31.7%	66.4%	33.6%
25,877	HENRY	4,276	604	3,292	380	2,688 D	14.1%	77.0%	15.5%	84.5%
14,873	HICKMAN	2,878	478	2,140	260	1,662 D	16.6%	74.4%	18.3%	81.7%
6,432	HOUSTON	1,455	202	1,159	94	957 D	13.9%	79.7%	14.8%	85.2%
12,421	HUMPHREYS	2,240	355	1,327	558	972 D	15.8%	59.2%	21.1%	78.9%
15,082	JACKSON	2,187	536	1,502	149	966 D	24.5%	68.7%	26.3%	73.7%
18,621	JEFFERSON	4,019	2,979	900	140	2,079 R	74.1%	22.4%	76.8%	23.2%
12,998	JOHNSON	2,908	2,413	433	62	1,980 R	83.0%	14.9%	84.8%	15.2%
178,468	KNOX	39,196	21,074	15,946	2,176	5,128 R	53.8%	40.7%	56.9%	43.1%
11,235	LAKE	1,502	179	833	490	654 D	11.9%	55.5%	17.7%	82.3%
24,461	LAUDERDALE	3,879	298	2,556	1,025	2,258 D	7.7%	65.9%	10.4%	89.6%
28,726	LAWRENCE	9,084	3,837	4,854	393	1,017 D	42.2%	53.4%	44.1%	55.9%
5,849	LEWIS	1,636	381	1,148	107	767 D	23.3%	70.2%	24.9%	75.1%
27,214	LINCOLN	4,088	361	2,969	758	2,608 D	8.8%	72.6%	10.8%	89.2%
19,838	LOUDON	4,515	2,605	1,673	237	932 R	57.7%	37.1%	60.9%	39.1%
30,781	MCMINN	7,662	4,432	3,016	214	1,416 R	57.8%	39.4%	59.5%	40.5%
20,424	MCNAIRY	4,969	2,390	2,267	312	123 R	48.1%	45.6%	51.3%	48.7%
14,904	MACON	2,510	1,708	738	64	970 R	68.0%	29.4%	69.8%	30.2%
54,115	MADISON	8,997	1,681	4,722	2,594	3,041 D	18.7%	52.5%	26.3%	73.7%
19,140	MARION	4,467	1,738	2,554	175	816 D	38.9%	57.2%	40.5%	59.5%
16,030	MARSHALL	4,295	517	3,059	719	2,542 D	12.0%	71.2%	14.5%	85.5%
40,357	MAURY	5,635	895	2,906	1,834	2,011 D	15.9%	51.6%	23.5%	76.5%

TENNESSEE

PRESIDENT 1948

1940 Census Population	County	Total Vote	Republican	Democratic	Other	Rep.-Dem. Plurality	Percentage Total Vote Rep.	Total Vote Dem.	Major Vote Rep.	Major Vote Dem.
6,393	MEIGS	1,590	748	788	54	40 D	47.0%	49.6%	48.7%	51.3%
24,275	MONROE	7,546	3,905	3,553	88	352 R	51.7%	47.1%	52.4%	47.6%
33,346	MONTGOMERY	4,505	646	3,310	549	2,664 D	14.3%	73.5%	16.3%	83.7%
4,093	MOORE	831	102	523	206	421 D	12.3%	62.9%	16.3%	83.7%
15,242	MORGAN	3,085	1,570	1,500	15	70 R	50.9%	48.6%	51.1%	48.9%
30,978	OBION	4,617	642	3,490	485	2,848 D	13.9%	75.6%	15.5%	84.5%
18,883	OVERTON	2,905	917	1,835	153	918 D	31.6%	63.2%	33.3%	66.7%
7,535	PERRY	1,748	459	1,196	93	737 D	26.3%	68.4%	27.7%	72.3%
6,213	PICKETT	1,437	849	566	22	283 R	59.1%	39.4%	60.0%	40.0%
15,473	POLK	2,990	1,529	1,412	49	117 R	51.1%	47.2%	52.0%	48.0%
26,250	PUTNAM	5,564	1,879	3,134	551	1,255 D	33.8%	56.3%	37.5%	62.5%
16,353	RHEA	4,151	2,077	1,897	177	180 R	50.0%	45.7%	52.3%	47.7%
27,795	ROANE	5,781	3,236	2,306	239	930 R	56.0%	39.9%	58.4%	41.6%
29,046	ROBERTSON	3,946	376	3,044	526	2,668 D	9.5%	77.1%	11.0%	89.0%
33,604	RUTHERFORD	6,078	854	4,151	1,073	3,297 D	14.1%	68.3%	17.1%	82.9%
15,966	SCOTT	3,024	2,016	972	36	1,044 R	66.7%	32.1%	67.5%	32.5%
5,038	SEQUATCHIE	1,373	420	907	46	487 D	30.6%	66.1%	31.7%	68.3%
23,291	SEVIER	6,003	5,049	840	114	4,209 R	84.1%	14.0%	85.7%	14.3%
358,250	SHELBY	65,176	14,566	23,854	26,756	9,288 D	22.3%	36.6%	37.9%	62.1%
16,148	SMITH	2,828	773	1,764	291	991 D	27.3%	62.4%	30.5%	69.5%
13,549	STEWART	2,411	331	1,962	118	1,631 D	13.7%	81.4%	14.4%	85.6%
69,085	SULLIVAN	15,120	6,984	7,626	510	642 D	46.2%	50.4%	47.8%	52.2%
32,719	SUMNER	5,006	793	3,688	525	2,895 D	15.8%	73.7%	17.7%	82.3%
28,036	TIPTON	4,681	209	3,066	1,406	2,857 D	4.5%	65.5%	6.4%	93.6%
6,113	TROUSDALE	1,229	104	1,014	111	910 D	8.5%	82.5%	9.3%	90.7%
14,128	UNICOI	2,861	1,927	844	90	1,083 R	67.4%	29.5%	69.5%	30.5%
9,030	UNION	2,156	1,603	513	40	1,090 R	74.4%	23.8%	75.8%	24.2%
4,090	VAN BUREN	978	298	636	44	338 D	30.5%	65.0%	31.9%	68.1%
19,764	WARREN	4,464	807	2,969	688	2,162 D	18.1%	66.5%	21.4%	78.6%
51,631	WASHINGTON	11,559	7,056	4,023	480	3,033 R	61.0%	34.8%	63.7%	36.3%
13,638	WAYNE	2,862	1,957	820	85	1,137 R	68.4%	28.7%	70.5%	29.5%
29,498	WEAKLEY	4,841	1,310	3,099	432	1,789 D	27.1%	64.0%	29.7%	70.3%
15,983	WHITE	2,682	635	1,719	328	1,084 D	23.7%	64.1%	27.0%	73.0%
25,220	WILLIAMSON	3,861	556	2,294	1,011	1,738 D	14.4%	59.4%	19.5%	80.5%
25,267	WILSON	4,699	854	3,133	712	2,279 D	18.2%	66.7%	21.4%	78.6%
2,915,841	TOTAL	550,283	202,914	270,402	76,967	67,488 D	36.9%	49.1%	42.9%	57.1%

TENNESSEE

PRESIDENT 1944

1940 Census Population	County	Total Vote	Republican	Democratic	Other	Rep.-Dem. Plurality	Percentage Total Vote Rep.	Percentage Total Vote Dem.	Percentage Major Vote Rep.	Percentage Major Vote Dem.
26,504	ANDERSON	6,920	3,424	3,476	20	52 D	49.5%	50.2%	49.6%	50.4%
23,151	BEDFORD	3,407	733	2,651	23	1,918 D	21.5%	77.8%	21.7%	78.3%
11,976	BENTON	3,124	1,195	1,901	28	706 D	38.3%	60.9%	38.6%	61.4%
8,358	BLEDSOE	1,982	1,187	795		392 R	59.9%	40.1%	59.9%	40.1%
41,116	BLOUNT	9,067	6,193	2,836	38	3,357 R	68.3%	31.3%	68.6%	31.4%
28,498	BRADLEY	3,951	2,616	1,312	23	1,304 R	66.2%	33.2%	66.6%	33.4%
31,131	CAMPBELL	5,270	3,244	2,008	18	1,236 R	61.6%	38.1%	61.8%	38.2%
9,880	CANNON	1,630	627	1,002	1	375 D	38.5%	61.5%	38.5%	61.5%
25,978	CARROLL	5,088	2,996	2,077	15	919 R	58.9%	40.8%	59.1%	40.9%
35,127	CARTER	6,556	4,873	1,662	21	3,211 R	74.3%	25.4%	74.6%	25.4%
9,928	CHEATHAM	1,616	216	1,398	2	1,182 D	13.4%	86.5%	13.4%	86.6%
11,124	CHESTER	2,091	931	1,156	4	225 D	44.5%	55.3%	44.6%	55.4%
24,657	CLAIBORNE	4,098	2,426	1,649	23	777 R	59.2%	40.2%	59.5%	40.5%
10,904	CLAY	1,404	650	754		104 D	46.3%	53.7%	46.3%	53.7%
24,083	COCKE	4,548	3,554	989	5	2,565 R	78.1%	21.7%	78.2%	21.8%
18,959	COFFEE	3,274	568	2,703	3	2,135 D	17.3%	82.6%	17.4%	82.6%
17,330	CROCKETT	2,212	782	1,421	9	639 D	35.4%	64.2%	35.5%	64.5%
15,592	CUMBERLAND	2,980	1,786	1,174	20	612 R	59.9%	39.4%	60.3%	39.7%
257,267	DAVIDSON	36,760	10,174	26,493	93	16,319 D	27.7%	72.1%	27.7%	72.3%
10,261	DECATUR	2,763	1,235	1,515	13	280 D	44.7%	54.8%	44.9%	55.1%
14,588	DE KALB	4,502	2,161	2,341		180 D	48.0%	52.0%	48.0%	52.0%
19,718	DICKSON	2,990	600	2,379	11	1,779 D	20.1%	79.6%	20.1%	79.9%
34,920	DYER	4,576	1,190	3,368	18	2,178 D	26.0%	73.6%	26.1%	73.9%
30,322	FAYETTE	1,591	172	1,417	2	1,245 D	10.8%	89.1%	10.8%	89.2%
14,262	FENTRESS	2,376	1,696	657	23	1,039 R	71.4%	27.7%	72.1%	27.9%
23,892	FRANKLIN	4,573	600	3,958	15	3,358 D	13.1%	86.6%	13.2%	86.8%
44,835	GIBSON	6,212	1,568	4,632	12	3,064 D	25.2%	74.6%	25.3%	74.7%
29,240	GILES	5,000	751	4,249		3,498 D	15.0%	85.0%	15.0%	85.0%
14,356	GRAINGER	2,550	1,938	605	7	1,333 R	76.0%	23.7%	76.2%	23.8%
39,405	GREENE	7,665	4,922	2,726	17	2,196 R	64.2%	35.6%	64.4%	35.6%
11,552	GRUNDY	1,887	406	1,462	19	1,056 D	21.5%	77.5%	21.7%	78.3%
18,611	HAMBLEN	3,724	2,001	1,723		278 R	53.7%	46.3%	53.7%	46.3%
180,478	HAMILTON	28,173	10,379	17,527	267	7,148 D	36.8%	62.2%	37.2%	62.8%
11,231	HANCOCK	2,364	1,929	431	4	1,498 R	81.6%	18.2%	81.7%	18.3%
23,590	HARDEMAN	2,400	444	1,949	7	1,505 D	18.5%	81.2%	18.6%	81.4%
17,806	HARDIN	3,500	2,124	1,358	18	766 R	60.7%	38.8%	61.0%	39.0%
28,523	HAWKINS	5,458	3,692	1,756	10	1,936 R	67.6%	32.2%	67.8%	32.2%
27,699	HAYWOOD	2,734	208	2,525	1	2,317 D	7.6%	92.4%	7.6%	92.4%
19,220	HENDERSON	3,579	2,570	1,009		1,561 R	71.8%	28.2%	71.8%	28.2%
25,877	HENRY	3,831	702	3,111	18	2,409 D	18.3%	81.2%	18.4%	81.6%
14,873	HICKMAN	2,846	618	2,223	5	1,605 D	21.7%	78.1%	21.8%	78.2%
6,432	HOUSTON	1,224	248	976		728 D	20.3%	79.7%	20.3%	79.7%
12,421	HUMPHREYS	1,701	367	1,327	7	960 D	21.6%	78.0%	21.7%	78.3%
15,082	JACKSON	2,114	695	1,407	12	712 D	32.9%	66.6%	33.1%	66.9%
18,621	JEFFERSON	4,143	3,159	966	18	2,193 R	76.2%	23.3%	76.6%	23.4%
12,998	JOHNSON	3,158	2,699	450	9	2,249 R	85.5%	14.2%	85.7%	14.3%
178,468	KNOX	39,452	20,742	18,482	228	2,260 R	52.6%	46.8%	52.9%	47.1%
11,235	LAKE	1,590	150	1,440		1,290 D	9.4%	90.6%	9.4%	90.6%
24,461	LAUDERDALE	4,117	381	3,732	4	3,351 D	9.3%	90.6%	9.3%	90.7%
28,726	LAWRENCE	9,021	4,359	4,662		303 D	48.3%	51.7%	48.3%	51.7%
5,849	LEWIS	1,207	252	955		703 D	20.9%	79.1%	20.9%	79.1%
27,214	LINCOLN	4,316	573	3,735	8	3,162 D	13.3%	86.5%	13.3%	86.7%
19,838	LOUDON	4,787	3,147	1,632	8	1,515 R	65.7%	34.1%	65.9%	34.1%
30,781	MCMINN	7,526	3,091	4,435		1,344 D	41.1%	58.9%	41.1%	58.9%
20,424	MCNAIRY	4,409	2,697	1,712		985 R	61.2%	38.8%	61.2%	38.8%
14,904	MACON	3,045	2,322	701	22	1,621 R	76.3%	23.0%	76.8%	23.2%
54,115	MADISON	7,517	1,793	5,706	18	3,913 D	23.9%	75.9%	23.9%	76.1%
19,140	MARION	4,533	1,761	2,666	106	905 D	38.8%	58.8%	39.8%	60.2%
16,030	MARSHALL	4,315	500	3,812	3	3,312 D	11.6%	88.3%	11.6%	88.4%
40,357	MAURY	5,579	747	4,814	18	4,067 D	13.4%	86.3%	13.4%	86.6%

TENNESSEE

PRESIDENT 1944

1940 Census Population	County	Total Vote	Republican	Democratic	Other	Rep.-Dem. Plurality	Percentage Total Vote Rep.	Total Vote Dem.	Major Vote Rep.	Major Vote Dem.
6,393	MEIGS	1,259	532	727		195 D	42.3%	57.7%	42.3%	57.7%
24,275	MONROE	6,819	3,424	3,385	10	39 R	50.2%	49.6%	50.3%	49.7%
33,346	MONTGOMERY	3,686	702	2,971	13	2,269 D	19.0%	80.6%	19.1%	80.9%
4,093	MOORE	885	143	742		599 D	16.2%	83.8%	16.2%	83.8%
15,242	MORGAN	2,600	1,399	1,201		198 R	53.8%	46.2%	53.8%	46.2%
30,978	OBION	4,298	615	3,670	13	3,055 D	14.3%	85.4%	14.4%	85.6%
18,883	OVERTON	2,389	935	1,449	5	514 D	39.1%	60.7%	39.2%	60.8%
7,535	PERRY	1,158	387	771		384 D	33.4%	66.6%	33.4%	66.6%
6,213	PICKETT	1,198	761	416	21	345 R	63.5%	34.7%	64.7%	35.3%
15,473	POLK	5,226	378	4,842	6	4,464 D	7.2%	92.7%	7.2%	92.8%
26,250	PUTNAM	4,558	1,770	2,788		1,018 D	38.8%	61.2%	38.8%	61.2%
16,353	RHEA	3,461	1,880	1,581		299 R	54.3%	45.7%	54.3%	45.7%
27,795	ROANE	4,699	2,711	1,971	17	740 R	57.7%	41.9%	57.9%	42.1%
29,046	ROBERTSON	3,708	622	3,074	12	2,452 D	16.8%	82.9%	16.8%	83.2%
33,604	RUTHERFORD	5,638	879	4,730	29	3,851 D	15.6%	83.9%	15.7%	84.3%
15,966	SCOTT	2,832	1,971	850	11	1,121 R	69.6%	30.0%	69.9%	30.1%
5,038	SEQUATCHIE	1,268	417	851		434 D	32.9%	67.1%	32.9%	67.1%
23,291	SEVIER	5,651	4,930	711	10	4,219 R	87.2%	12.6%	87.4%	12.6%
358,250	SHELBY	59,544	10,839	48,625	80	37,786 D	18.2%	81.7%	18.2%	81.8%
16,148	SMITH	3,006	887	2,107	12	1,220 D	29.5%	70.1%	29.6%	70.4%
13,549	STEWART	2,251	335	1,916		1,581 D	14.9%	85.1%	14.9%	85.1%
69,085	SULLIVAN	11,544	5,223	6,290	31	1,067 D	45.2%	54.5%	45.4%	54.6%
32,719	SUMNER	5,076	990	4,076	10	3,086 D	19.5%	80.3%	19.5%	80.5%
28,036	TIPTON	4,360	310	4,046	4	3,736 D	7.1%	92.8%	7.1%	92.9%
6,113	TROUSDALE	1,304	131	1,170	3	1,039 D	10.0%	89.7%	10.1%	89.9%
14,128	UNICOI	2,771	1,992	779		1,213 R	71.9%	28.1%	71.9%	28.1%
9,030	UNION	2,398	1,768	627	3	1,141 R	73.7%	26.1%	73.8%	26.2%
4,090	VAN BUREN	820	291	526	3	235 D	35.5%	64.1%	35.6%	64.4%
19,764	WARREN	3,429	848	2,560	21	1,712 D	24.7%	74.7%	24.9%	75.1%
51,631	WASHINGTON	10,602	6,485	4,060	57	2,425 R	61.2%	38.3%	61.5%	38.5%
13,638	WAYNE	2,820	2,185	630	5	1,555 R	77.5%	22.3%	77.6%	22.4%
29,498	WEAKLEY	5,039	1,595	3,434	10	1,839 D	31.7%	68.1%	31.7%	68.3%
15,983	WHITE	2,011	668	1,339	4	671 D	33.2%	66.6%	33.3%	66.7%
25,220	WILLIAMSON	3,268	602	2,656	10	2,054 D	18.4%	81.3%	18.5%	81.5%
25,267	WILSON	4,090	942	3,148		2,206 D	23.0%	77.0%	23.0%	77.0%
2,915,841	TOTAL	510,692	200,311	308,707	1,674	108,396 D	39.2%	60.4%	39.4%	60.6%

TENNESSEE

PRESIDENT 1940

1940 Census Population	County	Total Vote	Republican	Democratic	Other	Rep.-Dem. Plurality	Percentage			
							Total Vote		Major Vote	
							Rep.	Dem.	Rep.	Dem.
26,504	ANDERSON	4,091	1,852	2,218	21	366 D	45.3%	54.2%	45.5%	54.5%
23,151	BEDFORD	3,074	555	2,499	20	1,944 D	18.1%	81.3%	18.2%	81.8%
11,976	BENTON	2,877	858	1,996	23	1,138 D	29.8%	69.4%	30.1%	69.9%
8,358	BLEDSOE	2,844	1,317	1,527		210 D	46.3%	53.7%	46.3%	53.7%
41,116	BLOUNT	7,720	4,312	3,363	45	949 R	55.9%	43.6%	56.2%	43.8%
28,498	BRADLEY	4,615	2,617	1,976	22	641 R	56.7%	42.8%	57.0%	43.0%
31,131	CAMPBELL	5,512	2,799	2,688	25	111 R	50.8%	48.8%	51.0%	49.0%
9,880	CANNON	2,358	638	1,699	21	1,061 D	27.1%	72.1%	27.3%	72.7%
25,978	CARROLL	5,642	2,782	2,830	30	48 D	49.3%	50.2%	49.6%	50.4%
35,127	CARTER	6,480	4,238	2,171	71	2,067 R	65.4%	33.5%	66.1%	33.9%
9,928	CHEATHAM	2,266	331	1,932	3	1,601 D	14.6%	85.3%	14.6%	85.4%
11,124	CHESTER	2,552	1,015	1,537		522 D	39.8%	60.2%	39.8%	60.2%
24,657	CLAIBORNE	5,764	2,879	2,792	93	87 R	49.9%	48.4%	50.8%	49.2%
10,904	CLAY	1,825	537	1,288		751 D	29.4%	70.6%	29.4%	70.6%
24,083	COCKE	4,673	3,521	1,098	54	2,423 R	75.3%	23.5%	76.2%	23.8%
18,959	COFFEE	2,712	424	2,277	11	1,853 D	15.6%	84.0%	15.7%	84.3%
17,330	CROCKETT	2,790	733	2,048	9	1,315 D	26.3%	73.4%	26.4%	73.6%
15,592	CUMBERLAND	2,965	1,492	1,443	30	49 R	50.3%	48.7%	50.8%	49.2%
257,267	DAVIDSON	36,352	8,763	27,589		18,826 D	24.1%	75.9%	24.1%	75.9%
10,261	DECATUR	3,117	1,275	1,832	10	557 D	40.9%	58.8%	41.0%	59.0%
14,588	DE KALB	4,871	2,041	2,830		789 D	41.9%	58.1%	41.9%	58.1%
19,718	DICKSON	3,319	527	2,784	8	2,257 D	15.9%	83.9%	15.9%	84.1%
34,920	DYER	4,380	961	3,374	45	2,413 D	21.9%	77.0%	22.2%	77.8%
30,322	FAYETTE	1,906	78	1,826	2	1,748 D	4.1%	95.8%	4.1%	95.9%
14,262	FENTRESS	2,317	1,365	919	33	446 R	58.9%	39.7%	59.8%	40.2%
23,892	FRANKLIN	4,893	569	4,312	12	3,743 D	11.6%	88.1%	11.7%	88.3%
44,835	GIBSON	6,356	1,233	5,103	20	3,870 D	19.4%	80.3%	19.5%	80.5%
29,240	GILES	4,501	692	3,796	13	3,104 D	15.4%	84.3%	15.4%	84.6%
14,356	GRAINGER	2,557	1,688	842	27	846 R	66.0%	32.9%	66.7%	33.3%
39,405	GREENE	9,135	4,587	4,406	142	181 R	50.2%	48.2%	51.0%	49.0%
11,552	GRUNDY	2,056	298	1,749	9	1,451 D	14.5%	85.1%	14.6%	85.4%
18,611	HAMBLEN	3,877	1,794	2,055	28	261 D	46.3%	53.0%	46.6%	53.4%
180,478	HAMILTON	26,922	9,771	17,083	68	7,312 D	36.3%	63.5%	36.4%	63.6%
11,231	HANCOCK	2,701	1,673	1,014	14	659 R	61.9%	37.5%	62.3%	37.7%
23,590	HARDEMAN	2,875	319	2,549	7	2,230 D	11.1%	88.7%	11.1%	88.9%
17,806	HARDIN	4,247	2,264	1,957	26	307 R	53.3%	46.1%	53.6%	46.4%
28,523	HAWKINS	5,458	3,314	2,108	36	1,206 R	60.7%	38.6%	61.1%	38.9%
27,699	HAYWOOD	3,598	128	3,466	4	3,338 D	3.6%	96.3%	3.6%	96.4%
19,220	HENDERSON	4,222	2,653	1,560	9	1,093 R	62.8%	36.9%	63.0%	37.0%
25,877	HENRY	3,886	563	3,307	16	2,744 D	14.5%	85.1%	14.5%	85.5%
14,873	HICKMAN	3,434	644	2,776	14	2,132 D	18.8%	80.8%	18.8%	81.2%
6,432	HOUSTON	1,331	229	1,093	9	864 D	17.2%	82.1%	17.3%	82.7%
12,421	HUMPHREYS	2,097	377	1,717	3	1,340 D	18.0%	81.9%	18.0%	82.0%
15,082	JACKSON	2,660	605	2,046	9	1,441 D	22.7%	76.9%	22.8%	77.2%
18,621	JEFFERSON	3,004	1,921	1,062	21	859 R	63.9%	35.4%	64.4%	35.6%
12,998	JOHNSON	2,971	2,502	469		2,033 R	84.2%	15.8%	84.2%	15.8%
178,468	KNOX	34,304	13,877	20,226	201	6,349 D	40.5%	59.0%	40.7%	59.3%
11,235	LAKE	3,187	213	2,962	12	2,749 D	6.7%	92.9%	6.7%	93.3%
24,461	LAUDERDALE	6,603	317	6,279	7	5,962 D	4.8%	95.1%	4.8%	95.2%
28,726	LAWRENCE	5,836	1,877	3,936	23	2,059 D	32.2%	67.4%	32.3%	67.7%
5,849	LEWIS	1,716	368	1,343	5	975 D	21.4%	78.3%	21.5%	78.5%
27,214	LINCOLN	4,315	521	3,781	13	3,260 D	12.1%	87.6%	12.1%	87.9%
19,838	LOUDON	4,317	2,226	2,068	23	158 R	51.6%	47.9%	51.8%	48.2%
30,781	MCMINN	9,121	3,901	5,192	28	1,291 D	42.8%	56.9%	42.9%	57.1%
20,424	MCNAIRY	5,034	2,550	2,484		66 R	50.7%	49.3%	50.7%	49.3%
14,904	MACON	2,445	1,730	711	4	1,019 R	70.8%	29.1%	70.9%	29.1%
54,115	MADISON	7,448	1,271	6,154	23	4,883 D	17.1%	82.6%	17.1%	82.9%
19,140	MARION	5,435	2,158	3,242	35	1,084 D	39.7%	59.7%	40.0%	60.0%
16,030	MARSHALL	3,523	389	3,132	2	2,743 D	11.0%	88.9%	11.0%	89.0%
40,357	MAURY	5,186	634	4,529	23	3,895 D	12.2%	87.3%	12.3%	87.7%

TENNESSEE

PRESIDENT 1940

1940 Census Population	County	Total Vote	Republican	Democratic	Other	Rep.-Dem. Plurality	Percentage Total Vote Rep.	Percentage Total Vote Dem.	Percentage Major Vote Rep.	Percentage Major Vote Dem.
6,393	MEIGS	1,462	573	889		316 D	39.2%	60.8%	39.2%	60.8%
24,275	MONROE	7,416	3,253	4,121	42	868 D	43.9%	55.6%	44.1%	55.9%
33,346	MONTGOMERY	3,990	819	3,158	13	2,339 D	20.5%	79.1%	20.6%	79.4%
4,093	MOORE	982	106	869	7	763 D	10.8%	88.5%	10.9%	89.1%
15,242	MORGAN	3,231	1,448	1,783		335 D	44.8%	55.2%	44.8%	55.2%
30,978	OBION	4,914	536	4,360	18	3,824 D	10.9%	88.7%	10.9%	89.1%
18,883	OVERTON	2,733	988	1,718	27	730 D	36.2%	62.9%	36.5%	63.5%
7,535	PERRY	1,403	332	1,068	3	736 D	23.7%	76.1%	23.7%	76.3%
6,213	PICKETT	1,492	830	652	10	178 R	55.6%	43.7%	56.0%	44.0%
15,473	POLK	4,173	562	3,611		3,049 D	13.5%	86.5%	13.5%	86.5%
26,250	PUTNAM	4,544	1,576	2,963	5	1,387 D	34.7%	65.2%	34.7%	65.3%
16,353	RHEA	4,336	1,956	2,364	16	408 D	45.1%	54.5%	45.3%	54.7%
27,795	ROANE	4,650	2,245	2,384	21	139 D	48.3%	51.3%	48.5%	51.5%
29,046	ROBERTSON	3,767	490	3,258	19	2,768 D	13.0%	86.5%	13.1%	86.9%
33,604	RUTHERFORD	5,009	782	4,207	20	3,425 D	15.6%	84.0%	15.7%	84.3%
15,966	SCOTT	3,649	2,187	1,448	14	739 R	59.9%	39.7%	60.2%	39.8%
5,038	SEQUATCHIE	1,408	401	1,003	4	602 D	28.5%	71.2%	28.6%	71.4%
23,291	SEVIER	5,750	4,569	1,181		3,388 R	79.5%	20.5%	79.5%	20.5%
358,250	SHELBY	65,074	7,312	57,664	98	50,352 D	11.2%	88.6%	11.3%	88.7%
16,148	SMITH	2,906	648	2,244	14	1,596 D	22.3%	77.2%	22.4%	77.6%
13,549	STEWART	3,088	374	2,699	15	2,325 D	12.1%	87.4%	12.2%	87.8%
69,085	SULLIVAN	11,421	4,153	7,234	34	3,081 D	36.4%	63.3%	36.5%	63.5%
32,719	SUMNER	4,447	834	3,591	22	2,757 D	18.8%	80.8%	18.8%	81.2%
28,036	TIPTON	6,113	288	5,815	10	5,527 D	4.7%	95.1%	4.7%	95.3%
6,113	TROUSDALE	1,025	94	929	2	835 D	9.2%	90.6%	9.2%	90.8%
14,128	UNICOI	2,881	1,863	985	33	878 R	64.7%	34.2%	65.4%	34.6%
9,030	UNION	1,824	1,143	673	8	470 R	62.7%	36.9%	62.9%	37.1%
4,090	VAN BUREN	1,053	318	732	3	414 D	30.2%	69.5%	30.3%	69.7%
19,764	WARREN	2,887	546	2,323	18	1,777 D	18.9%	80.5%	19.0%	81.0%
51,631	WASHINGTON	8,327	4,719	3,565	43	1,154 R	56.7%	42.8%	57.0%	43.0%
13,638	WAYNE	3,592	2,486	1,100	6	1,386 R	69.2%	30.6%	69.3%	30.7%
29,498	WEAKLEY	4,648	1,139	3,474	35	2,335 D	24.5%	74.7%	24.7%	75.3%
15,983	WHITE	2,928	657	2,256	15	1,599 D	22.4%	77.0%	22.6%	77.4%
25,220	WILLIAMSON	3,746	505	3,215	26	2,710 D	13.5%	85.8%	13.6%	86.4%
25,267	WILSON	3,681	655	3,020	6	2,365 D	17.8%	82.0%	17.8%	82.2%
2,915,841	TOTAL	522,823	169,153	351,601	2,069	182,448 D	32.4%	67.3%	32.5%	67.5%

TENNESSEE

PRESIDENT 1936

1930 Census Population	County	Total Vote	Republican	Democratic	Other	Rep.-Dem. Plurality	Percentage Total Vote Rep.	Percentage Total Vote Dem.	Percentage Major Vote Rep.	Percentage Major Vote Dem.
19,722	ANDERSON	4,213	1,805	2,348	60	543 D	42.8%	55.7%	43.5%	56.5%
21,077	BEDFORD	2,961	514	2,428	19	1,914 D	17.4%	82.0%	17.5%	82.5%
11,237	BENTON	2,429	661	1,762	6	1,101 D	27.2%	72.5%	27.3%	72.7%
7,128	BLEDSOE	2,419	1,178	1,218	23	40 D	48.7%	50.4%	49.2%	50.8%
33,989	BLOUNT	7,199	4,119	3,056	24	1,063 R	57.2%	42.5%	57.4%	42.6%
22,870	BRADLEY	5,376	2,561	2,806	9	245 D	47.6%	52.2%	47.7%	52.3%
26,827	CAMPBELL	5,522	2,814	2,703	5	111 R	51.0%	48.9%	51.0%	49.0%
8,935	CANNON	1,670	498	1,166	6	668 D	29.8%	69.8%	29.9%	70.1%
26,132	CARROLL	5,323	2,282	2,989	52	707 D	42.9%	56.2%	43.3%	56.7%
29,223	CARTER	6,722	4,858	1,837	27	3,021 R	72.3%	27.3%	72.6%	27.4%
9,025	CHEATHAM	1,543	183	1,352	8	1,169 D	11.9%	87.6%	11.9%	88.1%
10,603	CHESTER	1,744	565	1,172	7	607 D	32.4%	67.2%	32.5%	67.5%
24,313	CLAIBORNE	5,450	2,400	3,036	14	636 D	44.0%	55.7%	44.2%	55.8%
9,577	CLAY	1,059	378	661	20	283 D	35.7%	62.4%	36.4%	63.6%
21,775	COCKE	4,954	3,731	1,217	6	2,514 R	75.3%	24.6%	75.4%	24.6%
16,801	COFFEE	2,570	408	2,148	14	1,740 D	15.9%	83.6%	16.0%	84.0%
17,359	CROCKETT	2,450	525	1,921	4	1,396 D	21.4%	78.4%	21.5%	78.5%
11,440	CUMBERLAND	2,849	1,409	1,426	14	17 D	49.5%	50.1%	49.7%	50.3%
222,854	DAVIDSON	30,158	4,467	25,530	161	21,063 D	14.8%	84.7%	14.9%	85.1%
10,106	DECATUR	2,421	919	1,502		583 D	38.0%	62.0%	38.0%	62.0%
14,213	DE KALB	5,105	2,140	2,947	18	807 D	41.9%	57.7%	42.1%	57.9%
18,491	DICKSON	2,437	402	2,022	13	1,620 D	16.5%	83.0%	16.6%	83.4%
31,405	DYER	3,999	557	3,355	87	2,798 D	13.9%	83.9%	14.2%	85.8%
28,891	FAYETTE	1,793	29	1,764		1,735 D	1.6%	98.4%	1.6%	98.4%
11,036	FENTRESS	2,111	1,299	743	69	556 R	61.5%	35.2%	63.6%	36.4%
21,796	FRANKLIN	4,066	519	3,534	13	3,015 D	12.8%	86.9%	12.8%	87.2%
46,528	GIBSON	5,730	958	4,744	28	3,786 D	16.7%	82.8%	16.8%	83.2%
28,016	GILES	4,378	600	3,760	18	3,160 D	13.7%	85.9%	13.8%	86.2%
12,737	GRAINGER	2,916	1,754	1,153	9	601 R	60.2%	39.5%	60.3%	39.7%
35,119	GREENE	9,057	4,313	4,708	36	395 D	47.6%	52.0%	47.8%	52.2%
9,717	GRUNDY	1,730	238	1,488	4	1,250 D	13.8%	86.0%	13.8%	86.2%
16,616	HAMBLEN	4,699	2,261	2,438		177 D	48.1%	51.9%	48.1%	51.9%
159,497	HAMILTON	23,589	6,917	16,568	104	9,651 D	29.3%	70.2%	29.5%	70.5%
9,673	HANCOCK	2,633	1,673	960		713 R	63.5%	36.5%	63.5%	36.5%
22,193	HARDEMAN	2,029	157	1,869	3	1,712 D	7.7%	92.1%	7.7%	92.3%
16,213	HARDIN	2,895	1,348	1,538	9	190 D	46.6%	53.1%	46.7%	53.3%
24,117	HAWKINS	5,589	3,300	2,278	11	1,022 R	59.0%	40.8%	59.2%	40.8%
26,063	HAYWOOD	1,756	29	1,725	2	1,696 D	1.7%	98.2%	1.7%	98.3%
17,655	HENDERSON	2,753	1,380	1,307	66	73 R	50.1%	47.5%	51.4%	48.6%
26,432	HENRY	3,718	470	3,223	25	2,753 D	12.6%	86.7%	12.7%	87.3%
13,613	HICKMAN	2,165	353	1,804	8	1,451 D	16.3%	83.3%	16.4%	83.6%
5,555	HOUSTON	1,006	193	813		620 D	19.2%	80.8%	19.2%	80.8%
12,039	HUMPHREYS	1,579	297	1,279	3	982 D	18.8%	81.0%	18.8%	81.2%
13,589	JACKSON	2,128	422	1,702	4	1,280 D	19.8%	80.0%	19.9%	80.1%
17,914	JEFFERSON	3,448	2,356	1,079	13	1,277 R	68.3%	31.3%	68.6%	31.4%
12,209	JOHNSON	3,415	2,882	533		2,349 R	84.4%	15.6%	84.4%	15.6%
155,902	KNOX	32,120	12,183	19,837	100	7,654 D	37.9%	61.8%	38.0%	62.0%
10,486	LAKE	3,720	113	3,604	3	3,491 D	3.0%	96.9%	3.0%	97.0%
23,406	LAUDERDALE	3,755	203	3,540	12	3,337 D	5.4%	94.3%	5.4%	94.6%
26,776	LAWRENCE	8,164	3,342	4,773	49	1,431 D	40.9%	58.5%	41.2%	58.8%
5,258	LEWIS	1,399	331	1,068		737 D	23.7%	76.3%	23.7%	76.3%
25,422	LINCOLN	3,888	430	3,451	7	3,021 D	11.1%	88.8%	11.1%	88.9%
17,805	LOUDON	4,507	2,343	2,146	18	197 R	52.0%	47.6%	52.2%	47.8%
29,019	MCMINN	8,432	4,310	4,077	45	233 R	51.1%	48.4%	51.4%	48.6%
19,901	MCNAIRY	3,403	1,613	1,742	48	129 D	47.4%	51.2%	48.1%	51.9%
13,872	MACON	2,290	1,402	876	12	526 R	61.2%	38.3%	61.5%	38.5%
51,059	MADISON	7,350	1,223	6,095	32	4,872 D	16.6%	82.9%	16.7%	83.3%
17,549	MARION	4,434	1,770	2,664		894 D	39.9%	60.1%	39.9%	60.1%
15,574	MARSHALL	2,739	300	2,431	8	2,131 D	11.0%	88.8%	11.0%	89.0%
34,016	MAURY	4,325	497	3,809	19	3,312 D	11.5%	88.1%	11.5%	88.5%

TENNESSEE

PRESIDENT 1936

1930 Census Population	County	Total Vote	Republican	Democratic	Other	Rep.-Dem. Plurality	Percentage Total Vote Rep.	Total Vote Dem.	Major Vote Rep.	Major Vote Dem.
6,127	MEIGS	1,747	740	994	13	254 D	42.4%	56.9%	42.7%	57.3%
21,377	MONROE	7,599	3,493	4,106		613 D	46.0%	54.0%	46.0%	54.0%
30,882	MONTGOMERY	4,180	838	3,314	28	2,476 D	20.0%	79.3%	20.2%	79.8%
4,037	MOORE	825	101	719	5	618 D	12.2%	87.2%	12.3%	87.7%
13,603	MORGAN	2,525	1,225	1,291	9	66 D	48.5%	51.1%	48.7%	51.3%
29,086	OBION	4,145	417	3,728		3,311 D	10.1%	89.9%	10.1%	89.9%
18,079	OVERTON	2,556	942	1,608	6	666 D	36.9%	62.9%	36.9%	63.1%
7,147	PERRY	1,111	210	896	5	686 D	18.9%	80.6%	19.0%	81.0%
5,615	PICKETT	1,120	651	454	15	197 R	58.1%	40.5%	58.9%	41.1%
15,686	POLK	4,062	1,755	2,283	24	528 D	43.2%	56.2%	43.5%	56.5%
23,759	PUTNAM	3,832	1,207	2,619	6	1,412 D	31.5%	68.3%	31.5%	68.5%
13,871	RHEA	4,201	1,964	2,199	38	235 D	46.8%	52.3%	47.2%	52.8%
24,477	ROANE	5,235	2,757	2,467	11	290 R	52.7%	47.1%	52.8%	47.2%
28,191	ROBERTSON	3,056	388	2,629	39	2,241 D	12.7%	86.0%	12.9%	87.1%
32,286	RUTHERFORD	4,710	580	4,101	29	3,521 D	12.3%	87.1%	12.4%	87.6%
14,080	SCOTT	2,847	2,012	827	8	1,185 R	70.7%	29.0%	70.9%	29.1%
4,047	SEQUATCHIE	1,198	353	840	5	487 D	29.5%	70.1%	29.6%	70.4%
20,480	SEVIER	5,308	4,126	1,144	38	2,982 R	77.7%	21.6%	78.3%	21.7%
306,482	SHELBY	63,698	2,113	61,504	81	59,391 D	3.3%	96.6%	3.3%	96.7%
15,473	SMITH	2,726	626	2,092	8	1,466 D	23.0%	76.7%	23.0%	77.0%
13,278	STEWART	2,028	303	1,718	7	1,415 D	14.9%	84.7%	15.0%	85.0%
51,087	SULLIVAN	9,795	3,492	6,269	34	2,777 D	35.7%	64.0%	35.8%	64.2%
28,622	SUMNER	3,666	517	3,146	3	2,629 D	14.1%	85.8%	14.1%	85.9%
27,498	TIPTON	4,799	116	4,683		4,567 D	2.4%	97.6%	2.4%	97.6%
5,629	TROUSDALE	839	72	765	2	693 D	8.6%	91.2%	8.6%	91.4%
12,678	UNICOI	2,756	1,850	879	27	971 R	67.1%	31.9%	67.8%	32.2%
11,371	UNION	2,759	1,785	963	11	822 R	64.7%	34.9%	65.0%	35.0%
3,516	VAN BUREN	941	251	690		439 D	26.7%	73.3%	26.7%	73.3%
20,209	WARREN	2,870	553	2,304	13	1,751 D	19.3%	80.3%	19.4%	80.6%
45,805	WASHINGTON	9,294	4,788	4,448	58	340 R	51.5%	47.9%	51.8%	48.2%
12,134	WAYNE	2,041	1,304	733	4	571 R	63.9%	35.9%	64.0%	36.0%
29,262	WEAKLEY	4,212	928	3,254	30	2,326 D	22.0%	77.3%	22.2%	77.8%
15,543	WHITE	1,414	591	814	9	223 D	41.8%	57.6%	42.1%	57.9%
22,845	WILLIAMSON	3,059	286	2,769	4	2,483 D	9.3%	90.5%	9.4%	90.6%
23,929	WILSON	3,650	539	3,108	3	2,569 D	14.8%	85.2%	14.8%	85.2%
2,616,556	TOTAL	477,086	147,055	328,083	1,948	181,028 D	30.8%	68.8%	30.9%	69.1%

TENNESSEE

PRESIDENT 1932

1930 Census Population	County	Total Vote	Republican	Democratic	Other	Rep.-Dem. Plurality	Percentage Total Vote Rep.	Percentage Total Vote Dem.	Percentage Major Vote Rep.	Percentage Major Vote Dem.
19,722	ANDERSON	2,697	1,605	1,081	11	524 R	59.5%	40.1%	59.8%	40.2%
21,077	BEDFORD	2,898	630	2,264	4	1,634 D	21.7%	78.1%	21.8%	78.2%
11,237	BENTON	2,021	455	1,540	26	1,085 D	22.5%	76.2%	22.8%	77.2%
7,128	BLEDSOE	1,994	960	1,034		74 D	48.1%	51.9%	48.1%	51.9%
33,989	BLOUNT	4,867	3,275	1,515	77	1,760 R	67.3%	31.1%	68.4%	31.6%
22,870	BRADLEY	2,902	1,570	1,295	37	275 R	54.1%	44.6%	54.8%	45.2%
26,827	CAMPBELL	4,609	2,735	1,834	40	901 R	59.3%	39.8%	59.9%	40.1%
8,935	CANNON	1,575	360	1,207	8	847 D	22.9%	76.6%	23.0%	77.0%
26,132	CARROLL	5,156	2,505	2,603	48	98 D	48.6%	50.5%	49.0%	51.0%
29,223	CARTER	6,629	5,055	1,574		3,481 R	76.3%	23.7%	76.3%	23.7%
9,025	CHEATHAM	1,562	180	1,370	12	1,190 D	11.5%	87.7%	11.6%	88.4%
10,603	CHESTER	1,357	356	985	16	629 D	26.2%	72.6%	26.5%	73.5%
24,313	CLAIBORNE	5,265	1,725	3,518	22	1,793 D	32.8%	66.8%	32.9%	67.1%
9,577	CLAY	1,196	361	819	16	458 D	30.2%	68.5%	30.6%	69.4%
21,775	COCKE	3,915	2,324	1,557	34	767 R	59.4%	39.8%	59.9%	40.1%
16,801	COFFEE	2,400	430	1,950	20	1,520 D	17.9%	81.3%	18.1%	81.9%
17,359	CROCKETT	2,467	513	1,934	20	1,421 D	20.8%	78.4%	21.0%	79.0%
11,440	CUMBERLAND	1,964	957	996	11	39 D	48.7%	50.7%	49.0%	51.0%
222,854	DAVIDSON	28,666	7,004	21,233	429	14,229 D	24.4%	74.1%	24.8%	75.2%
10,106	DECATUR	1,643	601	1,020	22	419 D	36.6%	62.1%	37.1%	62.9%
14,213	DE KALB	3,853	1,530	2,323		793 D	39.7%	60.3%	39.7%	60.3%
18,491	DICKSON	2,380	369	2,007	4	1,638 D	15.5%	84.3%	15.5%	84.5%
31,405	DYER	4,222	389	3,805	28	3,416 D	9.2%	90.1%	9.3%	90.7%
28,891	FAYETTE	1,346	42	1,287	17	1,245 D	3.1%	95.6%	3.2%	96.8%
11,036	FENTRESS	2,456	1,383	961	112	422 R	56.3%	39.1%	59.0%	41.0%
21,796	FRANKLIN	3,417	360	3,029	28	2,669 D	10.5%	88.6%	10.6%	89.4%
46,528	GIBSON	4,705	704	3,972	29	3,268 D	15.0%	84.4%	15.1%	84.9%
28,016	GILES	3,417	619	2,773	25	2,154 D	18.1%	81.2%	18.2%	81.8%
12,737	GRAINGER	2,353	1,325	995	33	330 R	56.3%	42.3%	57.1%	42.9%
35,119	GREENE	7,532	3,223	4,264	45	1,041 D	42.8%	56.6%	43.0%	57.0%
9,717	GRUNDY	1,191	198	978	15	780 D	16.6%	82.1%	16.8%	83.2%
16,616	HAMBLEN	3,522	1,458	2,032	32	574 D	41.4%	57.7%	41.8%	58.2%
159,497	HAMILTON	18,937	7,090	11,469	378	4,379 D	37.4%	60.6%	38.2%	61.8%
9,673	HANCOCK	1,640	1,089	551		538 R	66.4%	33.6%	66.4%	33.6%
22,193	HARDEMAN	2,680	281	2,377	22	2,096 D	10.5%	88.7%	10.6%	89.4%
16,213	HARDIN	1,851	1,036	806	9	230 R	56.0%	43.5%	56.2%	43.8%
24,117	HAWKINS	5,302	2,890	2,391	21	499 R	54.5%	45.1%	54.7%	45.3%
26,063	HAYWOOD	1,882	77	1,788	17	1,711 D	4.1%	95.0%	4.1%	95.9%
17,655	HENDERSON	2,029	1,058	958	13	100 R	52.1%	47.2%	52.5%	47.5%
26,432	HENRY	3,255	340	2,867	48	2,527 D	10.4%	88.1%	10.6%	89.4%
13,613	HICKMAN	2,205	385	1,812	8	1,427 D	17.5%	82.2%	17.5%	82.5%
5,555	HOUSTON	867	112	750	5	638 D	12.9%	86.5%	13.0%	87.0%
12,039	HUMPHREYS	1,703	231	1,455	17	1,224 D	13.6%	85.4%	13.7%	86.3%
13,589	JACKSON	1,986	256	1,726	4	1,470 D	12.9%	86.9%	12.9%	87.1%
17,914	JEFFERSON	3,317	2,275	975	67	1,300 R	68.6%	29.4%	70.0%	30.0%
12,209	JOHNSON	2,840	2,400	425	15	1,975 R	84.5%	15.0%	85.0%	15.0%
155,902	KNOX	20,927	9,774	10,755	398	981 D	46.7%	51.4%	47.6%	52.4%
10,486	LAKE	1,902	78	1,824		1,746 D	4.1%	95.9%	4.1%	95.9%
23,406	LAUDERDALE	2,350	174	2,137	39	1,963 D	7.4%	90.9%	7.5%	92.5%
26,776	LAWRENCE	4,948	1,684	3,240	24	1,556 D	34.0%	65.5%	34.2%	65.8%
5,258	LEWIS	936	137	799		662 D	14.6%	85.4%	14.6%	85.4%
25,422	LINCOLN	3,429	288	3,095	46	2,807 D	8.4%	90.3%	8.5%	91.5%
17,805	LOUDON	3,503	1,817	1,629	57	188 R	51.9%	46.5%	52.7%	47.3%
29,019	MCMINN	5,495	2,790	2,630	75	160 R	50.8%	47.9%	51.5%	48.5%
19,901	MCNAIRY	3,323	1,350	1,961	12	611 D	40.6%	59.0%	40.8%	59.2%
13,872	MACON	2,018	1,123	885	10	238 R	55.6%	43.9%	55.9%	44.1%
51,059	MADISON	6,029	1,124	4,813	92	3,689 D	18.6%	79.8%	18.9%	81.1%
17,549	MARION	3,618	1,406	2,212		806 D	38.9%	61.1%	38.9%	61.1%
15,574	MARSHALL	2,470	283	2,167	20	1,884 D	11.5%	87.7%	11.6%	88.4%
34,016	MAURY	3,952	535	3,392	25	2,857 D	13.5%	85.8%	13.6%	86.4%

TENNESSEE

PRESIDENT 1932

1930 Census Population	County	Total Vote	Republican	Democratic	Other	Rep.-Dem. Plurality	Percentage Total Vote Rep.	Percentage Total Vote Dem.	Percentage Major Vote Rep.	Percentage Major Vote Dem.
6,127	MEIGS	1,408	564	840	4	276 D	40.1%	59.7%	40.2%	59.8%
21,377	MONROE	4,478	1,504	2,954	20	1,450 D	33.6%	66.0%	33.7%	66.3%
30,882	MONTGOMERY	3,546	799	2,747		1,948 D	22.5%	77.5%	22.5%	77.5%
4,037	MOORE	996	65	923	8	858 D	6.5%	92.7%	6.6%	93.4%
13,603	MORGAN	2,185	1,184	983	18	201 R	54.2%	45.0%	54.6%	45.4%
29,086	OBION	3,569	334	3,183	52	2,849 D	9.4%	89.2%	9.5%	90.5%
18,079	OVERTON	2,905	661	2,231	13	1,570 D	22.8%	76.8%	22.9%	77.1%
7,147	PERRY	893	182	705	6	523 D	20.4%	78.9%	20.5%	79.5%
5,615	PICKETT	1,416	681	712	23	31 D	48.1%	50.3%	48.9%	51.1%
15,686	POLK	4,182	1,642	2,540		898 D	39.3%	60.7%	39.3%	60.7%
23,759	PUTNAM	4,214	1,281	2,911	22	1,630 D	30.4%	69.1%	30.6%	69.4%
13,871	RHEA	3,046	1,448	1,560	38	112 D	47.5%	51.2%	48.1%	51.9%
24,477	ROANE	3,709	2,036	1,625	48	411 R	54.9%	43.8%	55.6%	44.4%
28,191	ROBERTSON	3,034	252	2,752	30	2,500 D	8.3%	90.7%	8.4%	91.6%
32,286	RUTHERFORD	4,550	606	3,924	20	3,318 D	13.3%	86.2%	13.4%	86.6%
14,080	SCOTT	2,940	1,890	1,025	25	865 R	64.3%	34.9%	64.8%	35.2%
4,047	SEQUATCHIE	1,076	289	777	10	488 D	26.9%	72.2%	27.1%	72.9%
20,480	SEVIER	3,993	3,075	887	31	2,188 R	77.0%	22.2%	77.6%	22.4%
306,482	SHELBY	45,209	6,332	38,320	557	31,988 D	14.0%	84.8%	14.2%	85.8%
15,473	SMITH	2,668	595	2,057	16	1,462 D	22.3%	77.1%	22.4%	77.6%
13,278	STEWART	1,744	184	1,548	12	1,364 D	10.6%	88.8%	10.6%	89.4%
51,087	SULLIVAN	8,442	2,999	5,322	121	2,323 D	35.5%	63.0%	36.0%	64.0%
28,622	SUMNER	4,303	382	3,893	28	3,511 D	8.9%	90.5%	8.9%	91.1%
27,498	TIPTON	3,069	154	2,892	23	2,738 D	5.0%	94.2%	5.1%	94.9%
5,629	TROUSDALE	900	64	835	1	771 D	7.1%	92.8%	7.1%	92.9%
12,678	UNICOI	2,566	1,716	850		866 R	66.9%	33.1%	66.9%	33.1%
11,371	UNION	1,983	1,169	802	12	367 R	59.0%	40.4%	59.3%	40.7%
3,516	VAN BUREN	833	196	613	24	417 D	23.5%	73.6%	24.2%	75.8%
20,209	WARREN	2,765	410	2,325	30	1,915 D	14.8%	84.1%	15.0%	85.0%
45,805	WASHINGTON	7,138	3,691	3,345	102	346 R	51.7%	46.9%	52.5%	47.5%
12,134	WAYNE	1,639	1,082	543	14	539 R	66.0%	33.1%	66.6%	33.4%
29,262	WEAKLEY	4,577	783	3,777	17	2,994 D	17.1%	82.5%	17.2%	82.8%
15,543	WHITE	2,341	390	1,938	13	1,548 D	16.7%	82.8%	16.8%	83.2%
22,845	WILLIAMSON	3,087	261	2,777	49	2,516 D	8.5%	90.0%	8.6%	91.4%
23,929	WILSON	3,298	567	2,713	18	2,146 D	17.2%	82.3%	17.3%	82.7%
2,616,556	TOTAL	390,273	126,752	259,473	4,048	132,721 D	32.5%	66.5%	32.8%	67.2%

TENNESSEE

PRESIDENT 1928

1920 Census Population	County	Total Vote	Republican	Democratic	Other	Rep.-Dem. Plurality	Percentage Total Vote Rep.	Total Vote Dem.	Major Vote Rep.	Major Vote Dem.
18,298	ANDERSON	2,843	2,306	537		1,769 R	81.1%	18.9%	81.1%	18.9%
21,737	BEDFORD	2,937	1,405	1,532		127 D	47.8%	52.2%	47.8%	52.2%
12,046	BENTON	2,203	949	1,241	13	292 D	43.1%	56.3%	43.3%	56.7%
7,218	BLEDSOE	1,499	899	600		299 R	60.0%	40.0%	60.0%	40.0%
28,800	BLOUNT	4,855	4,135	715	5	3,420 R	85.2%	14.7%	85.3%	14.7%
18,652	BRADLEY	3,770	2,854	913	3	1,941 R	75.7%	24.2%	75.8%	24.2%
28,265	CAMPBELL	3,597	3,007	585	5	2,422 R	83.6%	16.3%	83.7%	16.3%
10,241	CANNON	1,210	588	622		34 D	48.6%	51.4%	48.6%	51.4%
24,361	CARROLL	4,751	2,987	1,743	21	1,244 R	62.9%	36.7%	63.2%	36.8%
21,488	CARTER	5,460	4,934	512	14	4,422 R	90.4%	9.4%	90.6%	9.4%
10,039	CHEATHAM	1,403	488	913	2	425 D	34.8%	65.1%	34.8%	65.2%
9,669	CHESTER	1,323	588	735		147 D	44.4%	55.6%	44.4%	55.6%
23,286	CLAIBORNE	3,790	2,565	1,225		1,340 R	67.7%	32.3%	67.7%	32.3%
9,193	CLAY	1,134	556	576	2	20 D	49.0%	50.8%	49.1%	50.9%
20,782	COCKE	3,634	2,909	722	3	2,187 R	80.0%	19.9%	80.1%	19.9%
17,344	COFFEE	2,311	1,126	1,175	10	49 D	48.7%	50.8%	48.9%	51.1%
17,438	CROCKETT	1,459	710	749		39 D	48.7%	51.3%	48.7%	51.3%
10,094	CUMBERLAND	1,695	1,188	507		681 R	70.1%	29.9%	70.1%	29.9%
167,815	DAVIDSON	28,839	15,359	13,453	27	1,906 R	53.3%	46.6%	53.3%	46.7%
10,198	DECATUR	1,560	748	812		64 D	47.9%	52.1%	47.9%	52.1%
15,370	DE KALB	3,951	2,261	1,690		571 R	57.2%	42.8%	57.2%	42.8%
19,342	DICKSON	2,319	891	1,428		537 D	38.4%	61.6%	38.4%	61.6%
29,983	DYER	3,503	842	2,661		1,819 D	24.0%	76.0%	24.0%	76.0%
31,499	FAYETTE	1,222	122	1,100		978 D	10.0%	90.0%	10.0%	90.0%
10,435	FENTRESS	1,792	1,399	375	18	1,024 R	78.1%	20.9%	78.9%	21.1%
20,641	FRANKLIN	2,632	928	1,698	6	770 D	35.3%	64.5%	35.3%	64.7%
43,388	GIBSON	4,291	1,372	2,911	8	1,539 D	32.0%	67.8%	32.0%	68.0%
30,948	GILES	3,693	1,032	2,661		1,629 D	27.9%	72.1%	27.9%	72.1%
13,369	GRAINGER	1,942	1,464	466	12	998 R	75.4%	24.0%	75.9%	24.1%
32,824	GREENE	5,896	3,599	2,297		1,302 R	61.0%	39.0%	61.0%	39.0%
9,753	GRUNDY	992	380	608	4	228 D	38.3%	61.3%	38.5%	61.5%
15,056	HAMBLEN	3,172	1,902	1,270		632 R	60.0%	40.0%	60.0%	40.0%
115,954	HAMILTON	20,537	13,244	7,190	103	6,054 R	64.5%	35.0%	64.8%	35.2%
10,454	HANCOCK	1,255	1,039	216		823 R	82.8%	17.2%	82.8%	17.2%
22,278	HARDEMAN	1,960	491	1,459	10	968 D	25.1%	74.4%	25.2%	74.8%
17,291	HARDIN	2,301	1,585	709	7	876 R	68.9%	30.8%	69.1%	30.9%
22,918	HAWKINS	4,165	2,969	1,190	6	1,779 R	71.3%	28.6%	71.4%	28.6%
25,386	HAYWOOD	2,202	178	2,024		1,846 D	8.1%	91.9%	8.1%	91.9%
18,436	HENDERSON	2,752	2,005	714	33	1,291 R	72.9%	25.9%	73.7%	26.3%
27,151	HENRY	3,713	1,041	2,667	5	1,626 D	28.0%	71.8%	28.1%	71.9%
16,216	HICKMAN	1,550	511	1,039		528 D	33.0%	67.0%	33.0%	67.0%
6,212	HOUSTON	632	374	258		116 R	59.2%	40.8%	59.2%	40.8%
13,482	HUMPHREYS	1,218	441	771	6	330 D	36.2%	63.3%	36.4%	63.6%
14,955	JACKSON	1,464	617	832	15	215 D	42.1%	56.8%	42.6%	57.4%
17,677	JEFFERSON	3,019	2,582	437		2,145 R	85.5%	14.5%	85.5%	14.5%
12,230	JOHNSON	3,261	3,057	196	8	2,861 R	93.7%	6.0%	94.0%	6.0%
112,926	KNOX	20,438	14,627	5,767	44	8,860 R	71.6%	28.2%	71.7%	28.3%
9,075	LAKE	1,126	166	960		794 D	14.7%	85.3%	14.7%	85.3%
21,494	LAUDERDALE	3,228	430	2,798		2,368 D	13.3%	86.7%	13.3%	86.7%
23,593	LAWRENCE	6,373	3,581	2,780	12	801 R	56.2%	43.6%	56.3%	43.7%
5,707	LEWIS	683	269	414		145 D	39.4%	60.6%	39.4%	60.6%
25,786	LINCOLN	3,127	743	2,377	7	1,634 D	23.8%	76.0%	23.8%	76.2%
16,275	LOUDON	2,719	2,128	590	1	1,538 R	78.3%	21.7%	78.3%	21.7%
25,133	MCMINN	6,481	4,440	2,025	16	2,415 R	68.5%	31.2%	68.7%	31.3%
18,350	MCNAIRY	3,535	2,326	1,209		1,117 R	65.8%	34.2%	65.8%	34.2%
14,922	MACON	2,356	1,937	419		1,518 R	82.2%	17.8%	82.2%	17.8%
43,824	MADISON	5,471	1,894	3,577		1,683 D	34.6%	65.4%	34.6%	65.4%
17,402	MARION	2,820	1,659	1,161		498 R	58.8%	41.2%	58.8%	41.2%
17,375	MARSHALL	2,319	735	1,584		849 D	31.7%	68.3%	31.7%	68.3%
35,403	MAURY	5,014	1,362	3,652		2,290 D	27.2%	72.8%	27.2%	72.8%

TENNESSEE

PRESIDENT 1928

1920 Census Population	County	Total Vote	Republican	Democratic	Other	Rep.-Dem. Plurality	Percentage Total Vote Rep.	Total Vote Dem.	Major Vote Rep.	Major Vote Dem.
6,077	MEIGS	1,311	722	589		133 R	55.1%	44.9%	55.1%	44.9%
22,060	MONROE	5,343	3,312	2,031		1,281 R	62.0%	38.0%	62.0%	38.0%
32,265	MONTGOMERY	3,616	1,748	1,868		120 D	48.3%	51.7%	48.3%	51.7%
4,491	MOORE	571	133	431	7	298 D	23.3%	75.5%	23.6%	76.4%
13,285	MORGAN	1,933	1,487	446		1,041 R	76.9%	23.1%	76.9%	23.1%
28,393	OBION	3,281	789	2,492		1,703 D	24.0%	76.0%	24.0%	76.0%
17,617	OVERTON	2,307	1,195	1,105	7	90 R	51.8%	47.9%	52.0%	48.0%
7,765	PERRY	982	360	622		262 D	36.7%	63.3%	36.7%	63.3%
5,205	PICKETT	1,135	745	383	7	362 R	65.6%	33.7%	66.0%	34.0%
14,243	POLK	2,784	1,760	1,012	12	748 R	63.2%	36.4%	63.5%	36.5%
22,231	PUTNAM	3,757	1,612	2,145		533 D	42.9%	57.1%	42.9%	57.1%
13,812	RHEA	2,434	1,588	846		742 R	65.2%	34.8%	65.2%	34.8%
24,624	ROANE	3,754	2,971	761	22	2,210 R	79.1%	20.3%	79.6%	20.4%
25,621	ROBERTSON	2,402	848	1,543	11	695 D	35.3%	64.2%	35.5%	64.5%
33,059	RUTHERFORD	3,544	1,429	2,115		686 D	40.3%	59.7%	40.3%	59.7%
13,411	SCOTT	2,948	2,700	244	4	2,456 R	91.6%	8.3%	91.7%	8.3%
3,632	SEQUATCHIE	681	298	383		85 D	43.8%	56.2%	43.8%	56.2%
22,384	SEVIER	4,185	3,874	308	3	3,566 R	92.6%	7.4%	92.6%	7.4%
223,216	SHELBY	30,101	11,969	18,040	92	6,071 D	39.8%	59.9%	39.9%	60.1%
17,134	SMITH	2,606	1,150	1,446	10	296 D	44.1%	55.5%	44.3%	55.7%
14,664	STEWART	1,660	403	1,257		854 D	24.3%	75.7%	24.3%	75.7%
36,259	SULLIVAN	7,367	4,151	3,216		935 R	56.3%	43.7%	56.3%	43.7%
27,708	SUMNER	3,589	1,045	2,541	3	1,496 D	29.1%	70.8%	29.1%	70.9%
30,258	TIPTON	2,329	425	1,889	15	1,464 D	18.2%	81.1%	18.4%	81.6%
5,996	TROUSDALE	787	179	607	1	428 D	22.7%	77.1%	22.8%	77.2%
10,120	UNICOI	2,427	2,044	376	7	1,668 R	84.2%	15.5%	84.5%	15.5%
11,615	UNION	2,192	1,826	360	6	1,466 R	83.3%	16.4%	83.5%	16.5%
2,624	VAN BUREN	517	257	260		3 D	49.7%	50.3%	49.7%	50.3%
17,306	WARREN	2,045	923	1,112	10	189 D	45.1%	54.4%	45.4%	54.6%
34,052	WASHINGTON	6,434	4,889	1,545		3,344 R	76.0%	24.0%	76.0%	24.0%
12,877	WAYNE	2,149	1,756	382	11	1,374 R	81.7%	17.8%	82.1%	17.9%
31,053	WEAKLEY	3,853	1,358	2,495		1,137 D	35.2%	64.8%	35.2%	64.8%
15,701	WHITE	1,798	776	1,022		246 D	43.2%	56.8%	43.2%	56.8%
23,409	WILLIAMSON	2,295	693	1,595	7	902 D	30.2%	69.5%	30.3%	69.7%
26,241	WILSON	2,678	1,049	1,629		580 D	39.2%	60.8%	39.2%	60.8%
2,337,885	TOTAL	353,192	195,388	157,143	661	38,245 R	55.3%	44.5%	55.4%	44.6%

TENNESSEE

PRESIDENT 1924

1920 Census Population	County	Total Vote	Republican	Democratic	Other	Rep.-Dem. Plurality	Percentage Total Vote Rep.	Total Vote Dem.	Major Vote Rep.	Major Vote Dem.
18,298	ANDERSON	2,152	1,487	550	115	937 R	69.1%	25.6%	73.0%	27.0%
21,737	BEDFORD	2,784	925	1,799	60	874 D	33.2%	64.6%	34.0%	66.0%
12,046	BENTON	1,856	708	1,109	39	401 D	38.1%	59.8%	39.0%	61.0%
7,218	BLEDSOE	1,179	686	483	10	203 R	58.2%	41.0%	58.7%	41.3%
28,800	BLOUNT	3,813	2,754	999	60	1,755 R	72.2%	26.2%	73.4%	26.6%
18,652	BRADLEY	2,829	1,780	1,011	38	769 R	62.9%	35.7%	63.8%	36.2%
28,265	CAMPBELL	3,551	2,620	648	283	1,972 R	73.8%	18.2%	80.2%	19.8%
10,241	CANNON	878	285	581	12	296 D	32.5%	66.2%	32.9%	67.1%
24,361	CARROLL	4,208	2,178	1,925	105	253 R	51.8%	45.7%	53.1%	46.9%
21,488	CARTER	4,250	3,665	557	28	3,108 R	86.2%	13.1%	86.8%	13.2%
10,039	CHEATHAM	1,069	181	868	20	687 D	16.9%	81.2%	17.3%	82.7%
9,669	CHESTER	1,267	485	768	14	283 D	38.3%	60.6%	38.7%	61.3%
23,286	CLAIBORNE	2,960	1,775	1,091	94	684 R	60.0%	36.9%	61.9%	38.1%
9,193	CLAY	1,167	483	673	11	190 D	41.4%	57.7%	41.8%	58.2%
20,782	COCKE	3,518	2,564	936	18	1,628 R	72.9%	26.6%	73.3%	26.7%
17,344	COFFEE	2,236	485	1,692	59	1,207 D	21.7%	75.7%	22.3%	77.7%
17,438	CROCKETT	1,775	587	1,168	20	581 D	33.1%	65.8%	33.4%	66.6%
10,094	CUMBERLAND	1,517	886	540	91	346 R	58.4%	35.6%	62.1%	37.9%
167,815	DAVIDSON	17,270	4,511	11,386	1,373	6,875 D	26.1%	65.9%	28.4%	71.6%
10,198	DECATUR	1,696	799	877	20	78 D	47.1%	51.7%	47.7%	52.3%
15,370	DE KALB	3,257	1,406	1,829	22	423 D	43.2%	56.2%	43.5%	56.5%
19,342	DICKSON	2,270	516	1,648	106	1,132 D	22.7%	72.6%	23.8%	76.2%
29,983	DYER	2,835	477	2,348	10	1,871 D	16.8%	82.8%	16.9%	83.1%
31,499	FAYETTE	1,273	65	1,181	27	1,116 D	5.1%	92.8%	5.2%	94.8%
10,435	FENTRESS	1,706	1,197	420	89	777 R	70.2%	24.6%	74.0%	26.0%
20,641	FRANKLIN	2,840	707	2,075	58	1,368 D	24.9%	73.1%	25.4%	74.6%
43,388	GIBSON	4,372	1,046	3,277	49	2,231 D	23.9%	75.0%	24.2%	75.8%
30,948	GILES	3,261	677	2,509	75	1,832 D	20.8%	76.9%	21.2%	78.8%
13,369	GRAINGER	2,148	1,463	664	21	799 R	68.1%	30.9%	68.8%	31.2%
32,824	GREENE	5,932	3,295	2,605	32	690 R	55.5%	43.9%	55.8%	44.2%
9,753	GRUNDY	764	173	394	197	221 D	22.6%	51.6%	30.5%	69.5%
15,056	HAMBLEN	2,715	1,342	1,316	57	26 R	49.4%	48.5%	50.5%	49.5%
115,954	HAMILTON	16,780	8,421	7,511	848	910 R	50.2%	44.8%	52.9%	47.1%
10,454	HANCOCK	1,340	1,028	305	7	723 R	76.7%	22.8%	77.1%	22.9%
22,278	HARDEMAN	1,904	253	1,595	56	1,342 D	13.3%	83.8%	13.7%	86.3%
17,291	HARDIN	1,805	1,175	625	5	550 R	65.1%	34.6%	65.3%	34.7%
22,918	HAWKINS	4,389	2,632	1,705	52	927 R	60.0%	38.8%	60.7%	39.3%
25,386	HAYWOOD	1,947	60	1,872	15	1,812 D	3.1%	96.1%	3.1%	96.9%
18,436	HENDERSON	2,677	1,616	1,009	52	607 R	60.4%	37.7%	61.6%	38.4%
27,151	HENRY	3,193	562	2,478	153	1,916 D	17.6%	77.6%	18.5%	81.5%
16,216	HICKMAN	1,258	315	922	21	607 D	25.0%	73.3%	25.5%	74.5%
6,212	HOUSTON	585	95	449	41	354 D	16.2%	76.8%	17.5%	82.5%
13,482	HUMPHREYS	1,258	216	1,005	37	789 D	17.2%	79.9%	17.7%	82.3%
14,955	JACKSON	1,469	363	1,089	17	726 D	24.7%	74.1%	25.0%	75.0%
17,677	JEFFERSON	3,451	2,701	716	34	1,985 R	78.3%	20.7%	79.0%	21.0%
12,230	JOHNSON	3,064	2,798	255	11	2,543 R	91.3%	8.3%	91.6%	8.4%
112,926	KNOX	19,003	10,713	6,952	1,338	3,761 R	56.4%	36.6%	60.6%	39.4%
9,075	LAKE	912	87	817	8	730 D	9.5%	89.6%	9.6%	90.4%
21,494	LAUDERDALE	1,868	242	1,596	30	1,354 D	13.0%	85.4%	13.2%	86.8%
23,593	LAWRENCE	4,689	2,379	2,237	73	142 R	50.7%	47.7%	51.5%	48.5%
5,707	LEWIS	525	191	307	27	116 D	36.4%	58.5%	38.4%	61.6%
25,786	LINCOLN	2,753	357	2,360	36	2,003 D	13.0%	85.7%	13.1%	86.9%
16,275	LOUDON	2,306	1,537	706	63	831 R	66.7%	30.6%	68.5%	31.5%
25,133	MCMINN	4,502	2,652	1,615	235	1,037 R	58.9%	35.9%	62.2%	37.8%
18,350	MCNAIRY	2,776	1,625	1,125	26	500 R	58.5%	40.5%	59.1%	40.9%
14,922	MACON	2,537	1,808	709	20	1,099 R	71.3%	27.9%	71.8%	28.2%
43,824	MADISON	4,931	1,110	3,422	399	2,312 D	22.5%	69.4%	24.5%	75.5%
17,402	MARION	2,241	1,076	1,055	110	21 R	48.0%	47.1%	50.5%	49.5%
17,375	MARSHALL	2,085	349	1,696	40	1,347 D	16.7%	81.3%	17.1%	82.9%
35,403	MAURY	3,944	844	3,000	100	2,156 D	21.4%	76.1%	22.0%	78.0%

TENNESSEE

PRESIDENT 1924

1920 Census Population	County	Total Vote	Republican	Democratic	Other	Rep.-Dem. Plurality	Percentage Total Vote Rep.	Total Vote Dem.	Major Vote Rep.	Major Vote Dem.
6,077	MEIGS	1,243	656	572	15	84 R	52.8%	46.0%	53.4%	46.6%
22,060	MONROE	4,743	2,487	2,238	18	249 R	52.4%	47.2%	52.6%	47.4%
32,265	MONTGOMERY	2,967	943	1,967	57	1,024 D	31.8%	66.3%	32.4%	67.6%
4,491	MOORE	537	41	492	4	451 D	7.6%	91.6%	7.7%	92.3%
13,285	MORGAN	1,769	1,105	416	248	689 R	62.5%	23.5%	72.6%	27.4%
28,393	OBION	3,778	484	3,233	61	2,749 D	12.8%	85.6%	13.0%	87.0%
17,617	OVERTON	2,489	904	1,536	49	632 D	36.3%	61.7%	37.0%	63.0%
7,765	PERRY	772	268	498	6	230 D	34.7%	64.5%	35.0%	65.0%
5,205	PICKETT	1,331	672	649	10	23 R	50.5%	48.8%	50.9%	49.1%
14,243	POLK	2,456	1,246	1,160	50	86 R	50.7%	47.2%	51.8%	48.2%
22,231	PUTNAM	4,018	1,489	2,474	55	985 D	37.1%	61.6%	37.6%	62.4%
13,812	RHEA	2,412	1,165	1,176	71	11 D	48.3%	48.8%	49.8%	50.2%
24,624	ROANE	2,638	1,680	812	146	868 R	63.7%	30.8%	67.4%	32.6%
25,621	ROBERTSON	1,946	229	1,668	49	1,439 D	11.8%	85.7%	12.1%	87.9%
33,059	RUTHERFORD	2,849	680	2,137	32	1,457 D	23.9%	75.0%	24.1%	75.9%
13,411	SCOTT	2,073	1,611	274	188	1,337 R	77.7%	13.2%	85.5%	14.5%
3,632	SEQUATCHIE	626	247	374	5	127 D	39.5%	59.7%	39.8%	60.2%
22,384	SEVIER	4,016	3,534	462	20	3,072 R	88.0%	11.5%	88.4%	11.6%
223,216	SHELBY	23,066	7,369	13,695	2,002	6,326 D	31.9%	59.4%	35.0%	65.0%
17,134	SMITH	2,449	695	1,723	31	1,028 D	28.4%	70.4%	28.7%	71.3%
14,664	STEWART	1,658	264	1,369	25	1,105 D	15.9%	82.6%	16.2%	83.8%
36,259	SULLIVAN	5,652	2,247	3,338	67	1,091 D	39.8%	59.1%	40.2%	59.8%
27,708	SUMNER	3,149	432	2,655	62	2,223 D	13.7%	84.3%	14.0%	86.0%
30,258	TIPTON	2,177	217	1,914	46	1,697 D	10.0%	87.9%	10.2%	89.8%
5,996	TROUSDALE	837	139	694	4	555 D	16.6%	82.9%	16.7%	83.3%
10,120	UNICOI	1,901	1,379	384	138	995 R	72.5%	20.2%	78.2%	21.8%
11,615	UNION	1,965	1,540	368	57	1,172 R	78.4%	18.7%	80.7%	19.3%
2,624	VAN BUREN	483	123	357	3	234 D	25.5%	73.9%	25.6%	74.4%
17,306	WARREN	1,874	490	1,356	28	866 D	26.1%	72.4%	26.5%	73.5%
34,052	WASHINGTON	5,179	3,258	1,842	79	1,416 R	62.9%	35.6%	63.9%	36.1%
12,877	WAYNE	1,859	1,395	452	12	943 R	75.0%	24.3%	75.5%	24.5%
31,053	WEAKLEY	4,327	1,153	3,150	24	1,997 D	26.6%	72.8%	26.8%	73.2%
15,701	WHITE	1,679	453	1,175	51	722 D	27.0%	70.0%	27.8%	72.2%
23,409	WILLIAMSON	1,917	243	1,626	48	1,383 D	12.7%	84.8%	13.0%	87.0%
26,241	WILSON	2,655	580	2,043	32	1,463 D	21.8%	76.9%	22.1%	77.9%
2,337,885	TOTAL	301,030	130,831	159,339	10,860	28,508 D	43.5%	52.9%	45.1%	54.9%

TENNESSEE

PRESIDENT 1920

1920 Census Population	County	Total Vote	Republican	Democratic	Other	Rep.-Dem. Plurality	Percentage Total Vote Rep.	Total Vote Dem.	Major Vote Rep.	Major Vote Dem.
18,298	ANDERSON	3,894	3,127	748	19	2,379 R	80.3%	19.2%	80.7%	19.3%
21,737	BEDFORD	4,238	2,056	2,182		126 D	48.5%	51.5%	48.5%	51.5%
12,046	BENTON	3,438	1,514	1,914	10	400 D	44.0%	55.7%	44.2%	55.8%
7,218	BLEDSOE	1,680	1,198	482		716 R	71.3%	28.7%	71.3%	28.7%
28,800	BLOUNT	7,094	5,540	1,550	4	3,990 R	78.1%	21.8%	78.1%	21.9%
18,652	BRADLEY	3,349	2,255	1,058	36	1,197 R	67.3%	31.6%	68.1%	31.9%
28,265	CAMPBELL	4,018	3,368	650		2,718 R	83.8%	16.2%	83.8%	16.2%
10,241	CANNON	1,457	687	770		83 D	47.2%	52.8%	47.2%	52.8%
24,361	CARROLL	7,956	4,741	3,215		1,526 R	59.6%	40.4%	59.6%	40.4%
21,488	CARTER	6,733	6,059	674		5,385 R	90.0%	10.0%	90.0%	10.0%
10,039	CHEATHAM	1,791	569	1,219	3	650 D	31.8%	68.1%	31.8%	68.2%
9,669	CHESTER	2,229	1,088	1,105	36	17 D	48.8%	49.6%	49.6%	50.4%
23,286	CLAIBORNE	3,848	2,612	1,236		1,376 R	67.9%	32.1%	67.9%	32.1%
9,193	CLAY	1,827	1,044	772	11	272 R	57.1%	42.3%	57.5%	42.5%
20,782	COCKE	4,255	3,294	929	32	2,365 R	77.4%	21.8%	78.0%	22.0%
17,344	COFFEE	2,925	882	2,043		1,161 D	30.2%	69.8%	30.2%	69.8%
17,438	CROCKETT	4,578	2,326	2,252		74 R	50.8%	49.2%	50.8%	49.2%
10,094	CUMBERLAND	2,042	1,485	557		928 R	72.7%	27.3%	72.7%	27.3%
167,815	DAVIDSON	20,346	6,811	13,354	181	6,543 D	33.5%	65.6%	33.8%	66.2%
10,198	DECATUR	2,780	1,608	1,149	23	459 R	57.8%	41.3%	58.3%	41.7%
15,370	DE KALB	4,555	2,572	1,983		589 R	56.5%	43.5%	56.5%	43.5%
19,342	DICKSON	3,617	1,472	2,145		673 D	40.7%	59.3%	40.7%	59.3%
29,983	DYER	4,417	1,166	3,181	70	2,015 D	26.4%	72.0%	26.8%	73.2%
31,499	FAYETTE	2,640	346	2,294		1,948 D	13.1%	86.9%	13.1%	86.9%
10,435	FENTRESS	2,523	1,808	694	21	1,114 R	71.7%	27.5%	72.3%	27.7%
20,641	FRANKLIN	5,064	1,558	3,504	2	1,946 D	30.8%	69.2%	30.8%	69.2%
43,388	GIBSON	9,170	3,209	5,942	19	2,733 D	35.0%	64.8%	35.1%	64.9%
30,948	GILES	5,359	2,224	3,129	6	905 D	41.5%	58.4%	41.5%	58.5%
13,369	GRAINGER	3,054	2,158	895	1	1,263 R	70.7%	29.3%	70.7%	29.3%
32,824	GREENE	8,606	5,677	2,924	5	2,753 R	66.0%	34.0%	66.0%	34.0%
9,753	GRUNDY	1,355	447	745	163	298 D	33.0%	55.0%	37.5%	62.5%
15,056	HAMBLEN	2,928	1,571	1,301	56	270 R	53.7%	44.4%	54.7%	45.3%
115,954	HAMILTON	21,037	10,793	9,910	334	883 R	51.3%	47.1%	52.1%	47.9%
10,454	HANCOCK	2,124	1,740	384		1,356 R	81.9%	18.1%	81.9%	18.1%
22,278	HARDEMAN	3,190	895	2,272	23	1,377 D	28.1%	71.2%	28.3%	71.7%
17,291	HARDIN	4,487	3,077	1,398	12	1,679 R	68.6%	31.2%	68.8%	31.2%
22,918	HAWKINS	4,070	2,650	1,381	39	1,269 R	65.1%	33.9%	65.7%	34.3%
25,386	HAYWOOD	2,176	101	2,068	7	1,967 D	4.6%	95.0%	4.7%	95.3%
18,436	HENDERSON	4,346	3,112	1,217	17	1,895 R	71.6%	28.0%	71.9%	28.1%
27,151	HENRY	6,633	1,957	4,613	63	2,656 D	29.5%	69.5%	29.8%	70.2%
16,216	HICKMAN	2,847	1,470	1,362	15	108 R	51.6%	47.8%	51.9%	48.1%
6,212	HOUSTON	1,193	385	790	18	405 D	32.3%	66.2%	32.8%	67.2%
13,482	HUMPHREYS	2,231	674	1,534	23	860 D	30.2%	68.8%	30.5%	69.5%
14,955	JACKSON	2,284	1,187	1,097		90 R	52.0%	48.0%	52.0%	48.0%
17,677	JEFFERSON	4,392	3,583	741	68	2,842 R	81.6%	16.9%	82.9%	17.1%
12,230	JOHNSON	3,918	3,627	291		3,336 R	92.6%	7.4%	92.6%	7.4%
112,926	KNOX	18,931	12,005	6,801	125	5,204 R	63.4%	35.9%	63.8%	36.2%
9,075	LAKE	1,552	352	1,192	8	840 D	22.7%	76.8%	22.8%	77.2%
21,494	LAUDERDALE	3,503	1,190	2,313		1,123 D	34.0%	66.0%	34.0%	66.0%
23,593	LAWRENCE	6,453	3,843	2,610		1,233 R	59.6%	40.4%	59.6%	40.4%
5,707	LEWIS	853	446	403	4	43 R	52.3%	47.2%	52.5%	47.5%
25,786	LINCOLN	3,560	1,091	2,463	6	1,372 D	30.6%	69.2%	30.7%	69.3%
16,275	LOUDON	2,575	1,872	686	17	1,186 R	72.7%	26.6%	73.2%	26.8%
25,133	MCMINN	4,471	2,800	1,636	35	1,164 R	62.6%	36.6%	63.1%	36.9%
18,350	MCNAIRY	5,075	3,212	1,863		1,349 R	63.3%	36.7%	63.3%	36.7%
14,922	MACON	4,276	3,208	1,066	2	2,142 R	75.0%	24.9%	75.1%	24.9%
43,824	MADISON	7,945	2,665	5,280		2,615 D	33.5%	66.5%	33.5%	66.5%
17,402	MARION	4,580	2,662	1,874	44	788 R	58.1%	40.9%	58.7%	41.3%
17,375	MARSHALL	2,596	753	1,828	15	1,075 D	29.0%	70.4%	29.2%	70.8%
35,403	MAURY	4,113	1,379	2,693	41	1,314 D	33.5%	65.5%	33.9%	66.1%

TENNESSEE

PRESIDENT 1920

1920 Census Population	County	Total Vote	Republican	Democratic	Other	Rep.-Dem. Plurality	Percentage Total Vote Rep.	Total Vote Dem.	Major Vote Rep.	Major Vote Dem.
6,077	MEIGS	1,627	915	712		203 R	56.2%	43.8%	56.2%	43.8%
22,060	MONROE	4,420	2,575	1,845		730 R	58.3%	41.7%	58.3%	41.7%
32,265	MONTGOMERY	4,384	1,780	2,564	40	784 D	40.6%	58.5%	41.0%	59.0%
4,491	MOORE	587	90	497		407 D	15.3%	84.7%	15.3%	84.7%
13,285	MORGAN	3,072	2,248	816	8	1,432 R	73.2%	26.6%	73.4%	26.6%
28,393	OBION	5,874	1,307	4,547	20	3,240 D	22.3%	77.4%	22.3%	77.7%
17,617	OVERTON	3,735	1,939	1,779	17	160 R	51.9%	47.6%	52.2%	47.8%
7,765	PERRY	1,439	747	692		55 R	51.9%	48.1%	51.9%	48.1%
5,205	PICKETT	1,503	896	607		289 R	59.6%	40.4%	59.6%	40.4%
14,243	POLK	1,811	1,018	775	18	243 R	56.2%	42.8%	56.8%	43.2%
22,231	PUTNAM	5,728	2,732	2,996		264 D	47.7%	52.3%	47.7%	52.3%
13,812	RHEA	2,413	1,341	1,051	21	290 R	55.6%	43.6%	56.1%	43.9%
24,624	ROANE	2,812	1,974	838		1,136 R	70.2%	29.8%	70.2%	29.8%
25,621	ROBERTSON	4,248	1,191	3,046	11	1,855 D	28.0%	71.7%	28.1%	71.9%
33,059	RUTHERFORD	5,287	1,881	3,406		1,525 D	35.6%	64.4%	35.6%	64.4%
13,411	SCOTT	2,802	2,537	221	44	2,316 R	90.5%	7.9%	92.0%	8.0%
3,632	SEQUATCHIE	1,057	509	545	3	36 D	48.2%	51.6%	48.3%	51.7%
22,384	SEVIER	6,417	6,006	404	7	5,602 R	93.6%	6.3%	93.7%	6.3%
223,216	SHELBY	24,843	8,597	15,986	260	7,389 D	34.6%	64.3%	35.0%	65.0%
17,134	SMITH	5,131	1,981	3,150		1,169 D	38.6%	61.4%	38.6%	61.4%
14,664	STEWART	3,244	849	2,366	29	1,517 D	26.2%	72.9%	26.4%	73.6%
36,259	SULLIVAN	7,920	3,593	4,327		734 D	45.4%	54.6%	45.4%	54.6%
27,708	SUMNER	4,963	1,268	3,674	21	2,406 D	25.5%	74.0%	25.7%	74.3%
30,258	TIPTON	3,776	906	2,816	54	1,910 D	24.0%	74.6%	24.3%	75.7%
5,996	TROUSDALE	1,530	574	955	1	381 D	37.5%	62.4%	37.5%	62.5%
10,120	UNICOI	3,135	2,584	547	4	2,037 R	82.4%	17.4%	82.5%	17.5%
11,615	UNION	3,032	2,607	423	2	2,184 R	86.0%	14.0%	86.0%	14.0%
2,624	VAN BUREN	582	223	351	8	128 D	38.3%	60.3%	38.9%	61.1%
17,306	WARREN	3,012	1,010	1,986	16	976 D	33.5%	65.9%	33.7%	66.3%
34,052	WASHINGTON	7,122	4,858	2,260	4	2,598 R	68.2%	31.7%	68.2%	31.8%
12,877	WAYNE	3,284	2,617	654	13	1,963 R	79.7%	19.9%	80.0%	20.0%
31,053	WEAKLEY	7,166	2,741	4,395	30	1,654 D	38.3%	61.3%	38.4%	61.6%
15,701	WHITE	3,657	1,456	2,201		745 D	39.8%	60.2%	39.8%	60.2%
23,409	WILLIAMSON	2,950	946	2,004		1,058 D	32.1%	67.9%	32.1%	67.9%
26,241	WILSON	4,296	1,532	2,760	4	1,228 D	35.7%	64.2%	35.7%	64.3%
2,337,885	TOTAL	428,036	219,229	206,558	2,249	12,671 R	51.2%	48.3%	51.5%	48.5%

TENNESSEE

ELECTION NOTE

1956 Other vote was 19,820 Andrews (States Rights); 789 Holtwick (Prohibition). States Rights candidates carried Fayette county.

1952 Other vote was 1,432 Hamblen (Prohibition); 885 Hallinan (Progressive); 379 MacArthur (Christian Nationalist).

1948 Other vote was 73,815 Thurmond (States Rights); 1,864 Wallace (Progressive); 1,288 Thomas (Socialist). States Rights candidates carried Fayette and Shelby counties and ran second in Bedford, Coffee, Crockett, Franklin, Hardeman, Haywood, Humphreys, Lake, Lauderdale, Lincoln, Madison, Marshall, Maury, Moore, Robertson, Rutherford, Tipton and Williamson counties.

1944 Other vote was 882 Watson (Prohibition); 792 Thomas (Socialist).

1940 Other vote was 1,606 Babson (Prohibition); 463 Thomas (Socialist).

1936 Other vote was 692 Thomas (Socialist); 634 Colvin (Prohibition); 326 Browder (Communist); 296 Lemke (Union).

1932 Other vote was 1,998 Upshaw (Prohibition); 1,796 Thomas (Socialist); 254 Foster (Communist).

1928 Other vote was 567 Thomas (Socialist); 94 Foster (Communist).

1924 Other vote was 10,666 LaFollette (Progressive); 100 Nations (American); 94 Faris (Prohibition). Progressive candidates ran second in Grundy county.

1920 Other vote was Debs (Socialist).

TEXAS

POPULAR VOTE FOR PRESIDENT 1920 TO 1956

Year	Total Vote	Republican		Democratic		Other Vote	Plurality	Percentage			
								Total Vote		Major Vote	
		Vote	Candidate	Vote	Candidate			Rep.	Dem.	Rep.	Dem.
1956	1,955,168	1,080,619	Eisenhower, Dwight D.	859,958	Stevenson, Adlai E.	14,591	220,661 R	55.3%	44.0%	55.7%	44.3%
1952	2,075,946	1,102,878	Eisenhower, Dwight D.	969,228	Stevenson, Adlai E.	3,840	133,650 R	53.1%	46.7%	53.2%	46.8%
1948	1,249,577	303,467	Dewey, Thomas E.	824,235	Truman, Harry S.	121,875	520,768 D	24.3%	66.0%	26.9%	73.1%
1944	1,150,334	191,423	Dewey, Thomas E.	821,605	Roosevelt, Franklin D.	137,306	630,182 D	16.6%	71.4%	18.9%	81.1%
1940	1,124,437	212,692	Willkie, Wendell	909,974	Roosevelt, Franklin D.	1,771	697,282 D	18.9%	80.9%	18.9%	81.1%
1936	849,701	104,661	Landon, Alfred M.	739,952	Roosevelt, Franklin D.	5,088	635,291 D	12.3%	87.1%	12.4%	87.6%
1932	874,382	98,218	Hoover, Herbert C.	771,109	Roosevelt, Franklin D.	5,055	672,891 D	11.2%	88.2%	11.3%	88.7%
1928	717,733	372,324	Hoover, Herbert C.	344,542	Smith, Alfred E.	867	27,782 R	51.9%	48.0%	51.9%	48.1%
1924	657,054	130,794	Coolidge, Calvin	483,381	Davis, John W.	42,879	352,587 D	19.9%	73.6%	21.3%	78.7%
1920	486,109	114,658	Harding, Warren G.	287,920	Cox, James M.	83,531	173,262 D	23.6%	59.2%	28.5%	71.5%

ELECTORAL COLLEGE VOTE 1920 TO 1956

Year	Total	Republican	Democratic	Other
1956	24	24	—	—
1952	24	24	—	—
1948	23	—	23	—
1944	23	—	23	—
1940	23	—	23	—
1936	23	—	23	—
1932	23	—	23	—
1928	20	20	—	—
1924	20	—	20	—
1920	20	—	20	—

TEXAS

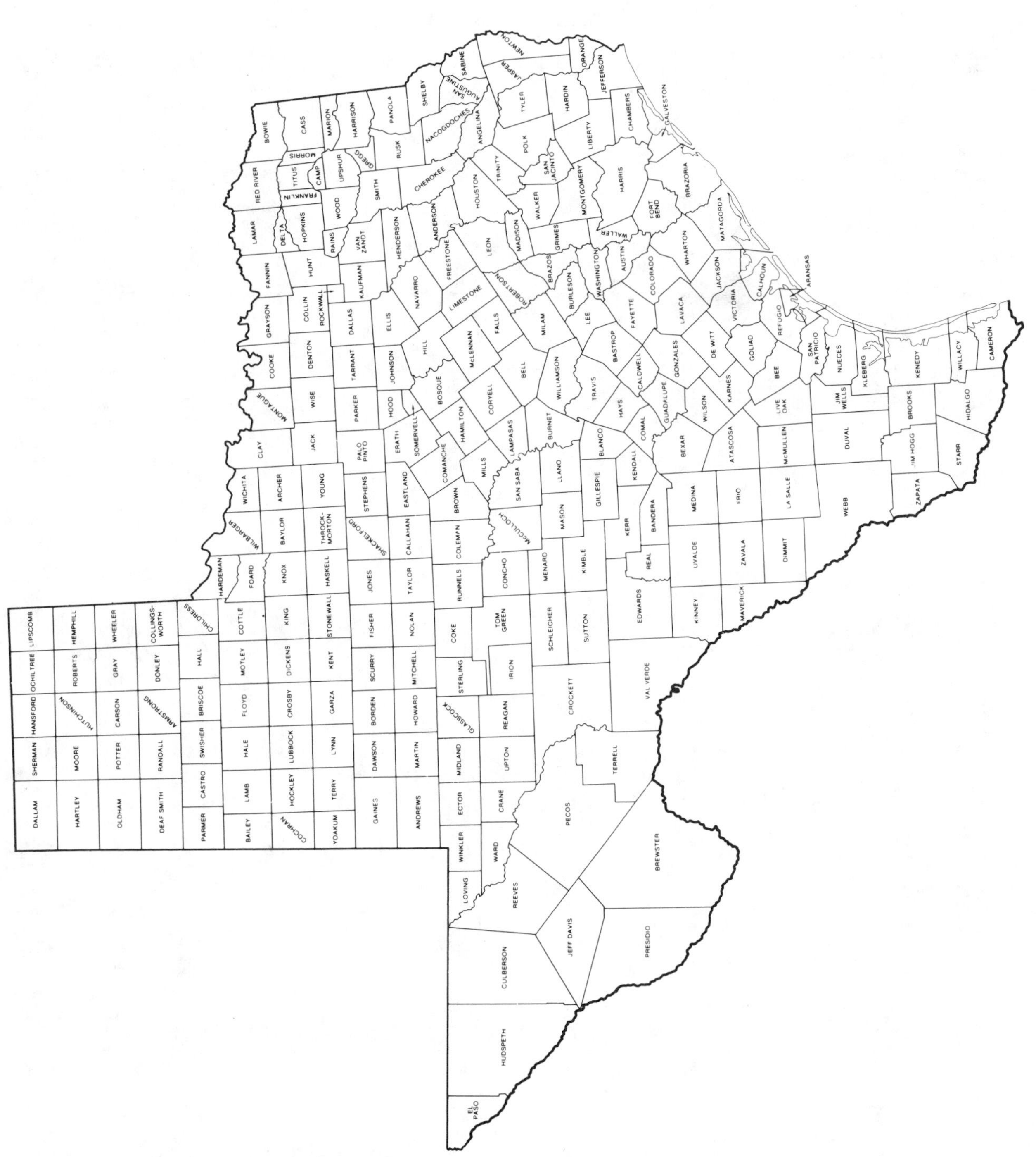
NEWTON
ORANGE
SABINE
JASPER
JEFFERSON
SAN AUGUSTINE
SHELBY
PANOLA
HARRISON
MARION
CASS
BOWIE
TYLER
HARDIN
CHAMBERS
GALVESTON
NACOGDOCHES
ANGELINA
POLK
LIBERTY
MORRIS
GREGG
RUSK
RED RIVER
TITUS
CAMP
UPSHUR
SMITH
CHEROKEE
TRINITY
SAN JACINTO
HARRIS
BRAZORIA
FRANKLIN
WOOD
HOUSTON
WALKER
MONTGOMERY
FORT BEND
LAMAR
DELTA
HOPKINS
RAINS
VAN ZANDT
HENDERSON
ANDERSON
LEON
MADISON
GRIMES
WALLER
WHARTON
MATAGORDA
FANNIN
HUNT
KAUFMAN
FREESTONE
ROBERTSON
BRAZOS
WASHINGTON
AUSTIN
COLORADO
JACKSON
CALHOUN
ARANSAS
GRAYSON
COLLIN
ROCKWALL
DALLAS
ELLIS
NAVARRO
LIMESTONE
BURLESON
LEE
FAYETTE
LAVACA
VICTORIA
REFUGIO
COOKE
DENTON
TARRANT
JOHNSON
HILL
McLENNAN
FALLS
MILAM
BASTROP
DE WITT
GOLIAD
SAN PATRICIO
NUECES
KLEBERG
KENEDY
WILLACY
CAMERON
MONTAGUE
WISE
PARKER
HOOD
BOSQUE
CORYELL
BELL
WILLIAMSON
TRAVIS
CALDWELL
GONZALES
KARNES
BEE
LIVE OAK
JIM WELLS
BROOKS
HIDALGO
CLAY
JACK
PALO PINTO
ERATH
SOMERVELL
HAMILTON
LAMPASAS
BURNET
HAYS
GUADALUPE
WILSON
ATASCOSA
McMULLEN
DUVAL
JIM HOGG
STARR
WICHITA
ARCHER
YOUNG
STEPHENS
EASTLAND
COMANCHE
MILLS
SAN SABA
LLANO
BLANCO
COMAL
KENDALL
BEXAR
MEDINA
FRIO
LA SALLE
WEBB
ZAPATA
WILBARGER
BAYLOR
THROCK-MORTON
SHACKELFORD
CALLAHAN
BROWN
McCULLOCH
MASON
GILLESPIE
KERR
BANDERA
UVALDE
ZAVALA
DIMMIT
HARDEMAN
FOARD
KNOX
HASKELL
JONES
TAYLOR
COLEMAN
CONCHO
MENARD
KIMBLE
REAL
EDWARDS
KINNEY
MAVERICK
LIPSCOMB
HEMPHILL
WHEELER
COLLINGS-WORTH
CHILDRESS
COTTLE
KING
STONEWALL
FISHER
NOLAN
RUNNELS
COKE
TOM GREEN
SCHLEICHER
SUTTON
OCHILTREE
ROBERTS
GRAY
DONLEY
HALL
MOTLEY
DICKENS
KENT
SCURRY
MITCHELL
STERLING
IRION
CROCKETT
VAL VERDE
HANSFORD
HUTCHINSON
CARSON
ARMSTRONG
BRISCOE
FLOYD
CROSBY
GARZA
BORDEN
HOWARD
GLASSCOCK
REAGAN
SHERMAN
MOORE
POTTER
RANDALL
SWISHER
HALE
LUBBOCK
LYNN
DAWSON
MARTIN
MIDLAND
UPTON
TERRELL
DALLAM
HARTLEY
OLDHAM
DEAF SMITH
CASTRO
LAMB
HOCKLEY
TERRY
GAINES
ANDREWS
ECTOR
CRANE
PECOS
PARMER
BAILEY
COCHRAN
YOAKUM
WINKLER
WARD
BREWSTER
LOVING
REEVES
JEFF DAVIS
PRESIDIO
CULBERSON
HUDSPETH
EL PASO

TEXAS

PRESIDENT 1956

1950 Census Population	County	Total Vote	Republican	Democratic	Other	Rep.-Dem. Plurality	Percentage: Total Vote Rep.	Total Vote Dem.	Major Vote Rep.	Major Vote Dem.
31,875	ANDERSON	6,914	4,181	2,710	23	1,471 R	60.5%	39.2%	60.7%	39.3%
5,002	ANDREWS	2,113	1,131	968	14	163 R	53.5%	45.8%	53.9%	46.1%
36,032	ANGELINA	10,096	5,274	4,781	41	493 R	52.2%	47.4%	52.5%	47.5%
4,252	ARANSAS	1,189	757	425	7	332 R	63.7%	35.7%	64.0%	36.0%
6,816	ARCHER	1,899	825	1,067	7	242 D	43.4%	56.2%	43.6%	56.4%
2,215	ARMSTRONG	798	372	422	4	50 D	46.6%	52.9%	46.9%	53.1%
20,048	ATASCOSA	3,307	1,804	1,492	11	312 R	54.6%	45.1%	54.7%	45.3%
14,663	AUSTIN	3,726	2,501	1,215	10	1,286 R	67.1%	32.6%	67.3%	32.7%
7,592	BAILEY	2,151	871	1,274	6	403 D	40.5%	59.2%	40.6%	59.4%
4,410	BANDERA	1,424	1,083	336	5	747 R	76.1%	23.6%	76.3%	23.7%
19,622	BASTROP	4,045	1,531	2,504	10	973 D	37.8%	61.9%	37.9%	62.1%
6,875	BAYLOR	1,766	715	1,047	4	332 D	40.5%	59.3%	40.6%	59.4%
18,174	BEE	4,345	2,401	1,929	15	472 R	55.3%	44.4%	55.5%	44.5%
73,824	BELL	13,932	4,285	9,603	44	5,318 D	30.8%	68.9%	30.9%	69.1%
500,460	BEXAR	113,331	65,901	46,790	640	19,111 R	58.1%	41.3%	58.5%	41.5%
3,780	BLANCO	1,418	796	615	7	181 R	56.1%	43.4%	56.4%	43.6%
1,106	BORDEN	368	127	240	1	113 D	34.5%	65.2%	34.6%	65.4%
11,836	BOSQUE	3,331	1,654	1,670	7	16 D	49.7%	50.1%	49.8%	50.2%
61,966	BOWIE	14,602	6,823	7,675	104	852 D	46.7%	52.6%	47.1%	52.9%
46,549	BRAZORIA	16,881	9,536	7,137	208	2,399 R	56.5%	42.3%	57.2%	42.8%
38,390	BRAZOS	8,436	4,942	3,463	31	1,479 R	58.6%	41.1%	58.8%	41.2%
7,309	BREWSTER	1,324	837	479	8	358 R	63.2%	36.2%	63.6%	36.4%
3,528	BRISCOE	1,008	357	648	3	291 D	35.4%	64.3%	35.5%	64.5%
9,195	BROOKS	1,920	802	1,108	10	306 D	41.8%	57.7%	42.0%	58.0%
28,607	BROWN	6,880	3,664	3,195	21	469 R	53.3%	46.4%	53.4%	46.6%
13,000	BURLESON	2,915	1,173	1,726	16	553 D	40.2%	59.2%	40.5%	59.5%
10,356	BURNET	2,590	1,163	1,422	5	259 D	44.9%	54.9%	45.0%	55.0%
19,350	CALDWELL	4,265	1,747	2,513	5	766 D	41.0%	58.9%	41.0%	59.0%
9,222	CALHOUN	2,992	1,912	1,067	13	845 R	63.9%	35.7%	64.2%	35.8%
9,087	CALLAHAN	2,353	1,140	1,199	14	59 D	48.4%	51.0%	48.7%	51.3%
125,170	CAMERON	21,022	11,952	8,829	241	3,123 R	56.9%	42.0%	57.5%	42.5%
8,740	CAMP	2,029	958	1,053	18	95 D	47.2%	51.9%	47.6%	52.4%
6,852	CARSON	2,044	1,061	976	7	85 R	51.9%	47.7%	52.1%	47.9%
26,732	CASS	5,409	2,970	2,395	44	575 R	54.9%	44.3%	55.4%	44.6%
5,417	CASTRO	2,006	697	1,305	4	608 D	34.7%	65.1%	34.8%	65.2%
7,871	CHAMBERS	2,393	1,520	860	13	660 R	63.5%	35.9%	63.9%	36.1%
38,694	CHEROKEE	6,961	4,022	2,912	27	1,110 R	57.8%	41.8%	58.0%	42.0%
12,123	CHILDRESS	2,780	1,268	1,503	9	235 D	45.6%	54.1%	45.8%	54.2%
9,896	CLAY	2,808	990	1,813	5	823 D	35.3%	64.6%	35.3%	64.7%
5,928	COCHRAN	1,523	599	923	1	324 D	39.3%	60.6%	39.4%	60.6%
4,045	COKE	1,245	549	690	6	141 D	44.1%	55.4%	44.3%	55.7%
15,503	COLEMAN	3,841	2,247	1,577	17	670 R	58.5%	41.1%	58.8%	41.2%
41,692	COLLIN	9,137	3,823	5,280	34	1,457 D	41.8%	57.8%	42.0%	58.0%
9,139	COLLINGSWORTH	2,055	815	1,229	11	414 D	39.7%	59.8%	39.9%	60.1%
17,576	COLORADO	4,367	2,691	1,648	28	1,043 R	61.6%	37.7%	62.0%	38.0%
16,357	COMAL	4,557	3,397	1,140	20	2,257 R	74.5%	25.0%	74.9%	25.1%
15,516	COMANCHE	3,878	1,900	1,962	16	62 D	49.0%	50.6%	49.2%	50.8%
5,078	CONCHO	1,142	574	567	1	7 R	50.3%	49.6%	50.3%	49.7%
22,146	COOKE	6,473	4,164	2,272	37	1,892 R	64.3%	35.1%	64.7%	35.3%
16,284	CORYELL	3,883	1,509	2,372	2	863 D	38.9%	61.1%	38.9%	61.1%
6,099	COTTLE	1,469	329	1,138	2	809 D	22.4%	77.5%	22.4%	77.6%
3,965	CRANE	1,348	626	707	15	81 D	46.4%	52.4%	47.0%	53.0%
3,981	CROCKETT	1,009	702	305	2	397 R	69.6%	30.2%	69.7%	30.3%
9,582	CROSBY	2,514	704	1,804	6	1,100 D	28.0%	71.8%	28.1%	71.9%
1,825	CULBERSON	596	324	269	3	55 R	54.4%	45.1%	54.6%	45.4%
7,640	DALLAM	2,103	1,018	1,074	11	56 D	48.4%	51.1%	48.7%	51.3%
614,799	DALLAS	192,695	125,361	65,472	1,862	59,889 R	65.1%	34.0%	65.7%	34.3%
19,113	DAWSON	3,670	1,615	2,049	6	434 D	44.0%	55.8%	44.1%	55.9%
9,111	DEAF SMITH	3,055	1,685	1,361	9	324 R	55.2%	44.5%	55.3%	44.7%
8,964	DELTA	1,877	605	1,262	10	657 D	32.2%	67.2%	32.4%	67.6%

TEXAS

PRESIDENT 1956

1950 Census Population	County	Total Vote	Republican	Democratic	Other	Rep.-Dem. Plurality	Percentage Total Vote Rep.	Percentage Total Vote Dem.	Percentage Major Vote Rep.	Percentage Major Vote Dem.
41,365	DENTON	10,346	5,350	4,972	24	378 R	51.7%	48.1%	51.8%	48.2%
22,973	DE WITT	4,849	3,401	1,435	13	1,966 R	70.1%	29.6%	70.3%	29.7%
7,177	DICKENS	1,808	565	1,243		678 D	31.3%	68.8%	31.3%	68.8%
10,654	DIMMIT	1,139	705	427	7	278 R	61.9%	37.5%	62.3%	37.7%
6,216	DONLEY	1,731	826	903	2	77 D	47.7%	52.2%	47.8%	52.2%
15,643	DUVAL	4,575	1,459	3,110	6	1,651 D	31.9%	68.0%	31.9%	68.1%
23,942	EASTLAND	6,108	3,580	2,512	16	1,068 R	58.6%	41.1%	58.8%	41.2%
42,102	ECTOR	14,108	8,805	5,109	194	3,696 R	62.4%	36.2%	63.3%	36.7%
2,908	EDWARDS	669	533	133	3	400 R	79.7%	19.9%	80.0%	20.0%
45,645	ELLIS	8,820	3,585	5,211	24	1,626 D	40.6%	59.1%	40.8%	59.2%
194,968	EL PASO	33,882	18,532	15,157	193	3,375 R	54.7%	44.7%	55.0%	45.0%
18,434	ERATH	5,171	2,775	2,377	19	398 R	53.7%	46.0%	53.9%	46.1%
26,724	FALLS	4,507	1,819	2,674	14	855 D	40.4%	59.3%	40.5%	59.5%
31,253	FANNIN	6,420	1,910	4,504	6	2,594 D	29.8%	70.2%	29.8%	70.2%
24,176	FAYETTE	5,904	3,574	2,282	48	1,292 R	60.5%	38.7%	61.0%	39.0%
11,023	FISHER	2,343	673	1,664	6	991 D	28.7%	71.0%	28.8%	71.2%
10,535	FLOYD	3,221	1,445	1,767	9	322 D	44.9%	54.9%	45.0%	55.0%
4,216	FOARD	932	243	687	2	444 D	26.1%	73.7%	26.1%	73.9%
31,056	FORT BEND	6,316	3,779	2,464	73	1,315 R	59.8%	39.0%	60.5%	39.5%
6,257	FRANKLIN	1,641	556	1,082	3	526 D	33.9%	65.9%	33.9%	66.1%
15,696	FREESTONE	3,455	1,627	1,813	15	186 D	47.1%	52.5%	47.3%	52.7%
10,357	FRIO	1,721	825	886	10	61 D	47.9%	51.5%	48.2%	51.8%
8,909	GAINES	2,779	1,244	1,527	8	283 D	44.8%	54.9%	44.9%	55.1%
113,066	GALVESTON	33,506	17,567	15,603	336	1,964 R	52.4%	46.6%	53.0%	47.0%
6,281	GARZA	1,415	628	786	1	158 D	44.4%	55.5%	44.4%	55.6%
10,520	GILLESPIE	3,315	3,070	240	5	2,830 R	92.6%	7.2%	92.7%	7.3%
1,089	GLASSCOCK	398	224	174		50 R	56.3%	43.7%	56.3%	43.7%
6,219	GOLIAD	1,247	902	338	7	564 R	72.3%	27.1%	72.7%	27.3%
21,164	GONZALES	4,037	1,767	2,260	10	493 D	43.8%	56.0%	43.9%	56.1%
24,728	GRAY	8,153	5,047	3,034	72	2,013 R	61.9%	37.2%	62.5%	37.5%
70,467	GRAYSON	16,330	7,402	8,876	52	1,474 D	45.3%	54.4%	45.5%	54.5%
61,258	GREGG	14,519	9,440	4,881	198	4,559 R	65.0%	33.6%	65.9%	34.1%
15,135	GRIMES	2,374	1,281	1,079	14	202 R	54.0%	45.5%	54.3%	45.7%
25,392	GUADALUPE	6,425	4,296	2,099	30	2,197 R	66.9%	32.7%	67.2%	32.8%
28,211	HALE	7,663	3,804	3,848	11	44 D	49.6%	50.2%	49.7%	50.3%
10,930	HALL	2,179	687	1,487	5	800 D	31.5%	68.2%	31.6%	68.4%
10,660	HAMILTON	2,843	1,709	1,124	10	585 R	60.1%	39.5%	60.3%	39.7%
4,202	HANSFORD	1,465	919	545	1	374 R	62.7%	37.2%	62.8%	37.2%
10,212	HARDEMAN	2,409	1,119	1,281	9	162 D	46.5%	53.2%	46.6%	53.4%
19,535	HARDIN	4,520	2,130	2,371	19	241 D	47.1%	52.5%	47.3%	52.7%
806,701	HARRIS	254,549	155,555	93,961	5,033	61,594 R	61.1%	36.9%	62.3%	37.7%
47,745	HARRISON	7,795	5,048	2,668	79	2,380 R	64.8%	34.2%	65.4%	34.6%
1,913	HARTLEY	803	353	448	2	95 D	44.0%	55.8%	44.1%	55.9%
13,736	HASKELL	3,341	993	2,340	8	1,347 D	29.7%	70.0%	29.8%	70.2%
17,840	HAYS	3,904	1,873	2,017	14	144 D	48.0%	51.7%	48.1%	51.9%
4,123	HEMPHILL	1,022	620	401	1	219 R	60.7%	39.2%	60.7%	39.3%
23,405	HENDERSON	5,569	2,479	3,065	25	586 D	44.5%	55.0%	44.7%	55.3%
160,446	HIDALGO	23,327	13,270	9,804	253	3,466 R	56.9%	42.0%	57.5%	42.5%
31,282	HILL	6,707	2,487	4,199	21	1,712 D	37.1%	62.6%	37.2%	62.8%
20,407	HOCKLEY	5,186	2,001	3,175	10	1,174 D	38.6%	61.2%	38.7%	61.3%
5,287	HOOD	1,852	751	1,095	6	344 D	40.6%	59.1%	40.7%	59.3%
23,490	HOPKINS	5,347	2,206	3,118	23	912 D	41.3%	58.3%	41.4%	58.6%
22,825	HOUSTON	3,958	1,941	1,998	19	57 D	49.0%	50.5%	49.3%	50.7%
26,722	HOWARD	7,571	3,051	4,506	14	1,455 D	40.3%	59.5%	40.4%	59.6%
4,298	HUDSPETH	692	316	368	8	52 D	45.7%	53.2%	46.2%	53.8%
42,731	HUNT	8,592	4,508	4,051	33	457 R	52.5%	47.1%	52.7%	47.3%
31,580	HUTCHINSON	9,336	5,110	4,184	42	926 R	54.7%	44.8%	55.0%	45.0%
1,590	IRION	432	252	178	2	74 R	58.3%	41.2%	58.6%	41.4%
7,755	JACK	2,347	1,327	997	23	330 R	56.5%	42.5%	57.1%	42.9%
12,916	JACKSON	3,852	2,259	1,571	22	688 R	58.6%	40.8%	59.0%	41.0%

TEXAS

PRESIDENT 1956

1950 Census Population	County	Total Vote	Republican	Democratic	Other	Rep.-Dem. Plurality	Percentage Total Vote Rep.	Total Vote Dem.	Major Vote Rep.	Major Vote Dem.
20,049	JASPER	4,308	2,430	1,856	22	574 R	56.4%	43.1%	56.7%	43.3%
2,090	JEFF DAVIS	407	239	165	3	74 R	58.7%	40.5%	59.2%	40.8%
195,083	JEFFERSON	55,429	30,102	25,057	270	5,045 R	54.3%	45.2%	54.6%	45.4%
5,389	JIM HOGG	906	282	617	7	335 D	31.1%	68.1%	31.4%	68.6%
27,991	JIM WELLS	6,122	3,348	2,752	22	596 R	54.7%	45.0%	54.9%	45.1%
31,390	JOHNSON	7,340	3,750	3,560	30	190 R	51.1%	48.5%	51.3%	48.7%
22,147	JONES	4,677	2,073	2,594	10	521 D	44.3%	55.5%	44.4%	55.6%
17,139	KARNES	3,417	1,764	1,636	17	128 R	51.6%	47.9%	51.9%	48.1%
31,170	KAUFMAN	5,750	2,816	2,902	32	86 D	49.0%	50.5%	49.2%	50.8%
5,423	KENDALL	1,873	1,519	341	13	1,178 R	81.1%	18.2%	81.7%	18.3%
632	KENEDY	135	125	10		115 R	92.6%	7.4%	92.6%	7.4%
2,249	KENT	755	234	519	2	285 D	31.0%	68.7%	31.1%	68.9%
14,022	KERR	4,594	3,555	1,025	14	2,530 R	77.4%	22.3%	77.6%	22.4%
4,619	KIMBLE	1,307	821	484	2	337 R	62.8%	37.0%	62.9%	37.1%
870	KING	224	46	177	1	131 D	20.5%	79.0%	20.6%	79.4%
2,668	KINNEY	660	368	289	3	79 R	55.8%	43.8%	56.0%	44.0%
21,991	KLEBERG	4,572	2,121	2,436	15	315 D	46.4%	53.3%	46.5%	53.5%
10,082	KNOX	2,100	835	1,262	3	427 D	39.8%	60.1%	39.8%	60.2%
43,033	LAMAR	8,381	4,154	4,202	25	48 D	49.6%	50.1%	49.7%	50.3%
20,015	LAMB	5,177	1,840	3,325	12	1,485 D	35.5%	64.2%	35.6%	64.4%
9,929	LAMPASAS	2,447	1,308	1,134	5	174 R	53.5%	46.3%	53.6%	46.4%
7,485	LA SALLE	1,024	449	574	1	125 D	43.8%	56.1%	43.9%	56.1%
22,159	LAVACA	4,941	2,509	2,412	20	97 R	50.8%	48.8%	51.0%	49.0%
10,144	LEE	2,274	1,200	1,061	13	139 R	52.8%	46.7%	53.1%	46.9%
12,024	LEON	2,346	1,079	1,260	7	181 D	46.0%	53.7%	46.1%	53.9%
26,729	LIBERTY	6,503	4,129	2,318	56	1,811 R	63.5%	35.6%	64.0%	36.0%
25,251	LIMESTONE	5,171	2,097	3,067	7	970 D	40.6%	59.3%	40.6%	59.4%
3,658	LIPSCOMB	1,154	806	345	3	461 R	69.8%	29.9%	70.0%	30.0%
9,054	LIVE OAK	1,639	1,077	521	41	556 R	65.7%	31.8%	67.4%	32.6%
5,377	LLANO	1,709	672	1,034	3	362 D	39.3%	60.5%	39.4%	60.6%
227	LOVING	91	55	36		19 R	60.4%	39.6%	60.4%	39.6%
101,048	LUBBOCK	26,576	13,970	12,540	66	1,430 R	52.6%	47.2%	52.7%	47.3%
11,030	LYNN	2,667	861	1,800	6	939 D	32.3%	67.5%	32.4%	67.6%
11,701	MCCULLOCH	2,455	1,292	1,158	5	134 R	52.6%	47.2%	52.7%	47.3%
130,194	MCLENNAN	31,853	15,561	16,181	111	620 D	48.9%	50.8%	49.0%	51.0%
1,187	MCMULLEN	413	226	185	2	41 R	54.7%	44.8%	55.0%	45.0%
7,996	MADISON	1,458	733	713	12	20 R	50.3%	48.9%	50.7%	49.3%
10,172	MARION	1,848	1,126	709	13	417 R	60.9%	38.4%	61.4%	38.6%
5,541	MARTIN	1,227	318	903	6	585 D	25.9%	73.6%	26.0%	74.0%
4,945	MASON	1,390	885	504	1	381 R	63.7%	36.3%	63.7%	36.3%
21,559	MATAGORDA	5,909	3,927	1,904	78	2,023 R	66.5%	32.2%	67.3%	32.7%
12,292	MAVERICK	1,560	721	820	19	99 D	46.2%	52.6%	46.8%	53.2%
17,013	MEDINA	4,201	2,668	1,516	17	1,152 R	63.5%	36.1%	63.8%	36.2%
4,175	MENARD	932	614	318		296 R	65.9%	34.1%	65.9%	34.1%
25,785	MIDLAND	11,841	8,287	3,468	86	4,819 R	70.0%	29.3%	70.5%	29.5%
23,585	MILAM	5,466	2,486	2,969	11	483 D	45.5%	54.3%	45.6%	54.4%
5,999	MILLS	1,648	912	735	1	177 R	55.3%	44.6%	55.4%	44.6%
14,357	MITCHELL	2,982	1,091	1,891		800 D	36.6%	63.4%	36.6%	63.4%
17,070	MONTAGUE	4,372	2,003	2,358	11	355 D	45.8%	53.9%	45.9%	54.1%
24,504	MONTGOMERY	5,974	3,360	2,572	42	788 R	56.2%	43.1%	56.6%	43.4%
13,349	MOORE	4,049	1,820	2,219	10	399 D	44.9%	54.8%	45.1%	54.9%
9,433	MORRIS	3,075	1,463	1,592	20	129 D	47.6%	51.8%	47.9%	52.1%
3,963	MOTLEY	926	411	511	4	100 D	44.4%	55.2%	44.6%	55.4%
30,326	NACOGDOCHES	6,165	3,285	2,855	25	430 R	53.3%	46.3%	53.5%	46.5%
39,916	NAVARRO	7,931	3,193	4,723	15	1,530 D	40.3%	59.6%	40.3%	59.7%
10,832	NEWTON	2,076	1,030	1,037	9	7 D	49.6%	50.0%	49.8%	50.2%
19,808	NOLAN	4,780	2,232	2,535	13	303 D	46.7%	53.0%	46.8%	53.2%
165,471	NUECES	40,059	19,985	19,912	162	73 R	49.9%	49.7%	50.1%	49.9%
6,024	OCHILTREE	1,740	1,209	512	19	697 R	69.5%	29.4%	70.2%	29.8%
1,672	OLDHAM	578	284	294		10 D	49.1%	50.9%	49.1%	50.9%

TEXAS

PRESIDENT 1956

1950 Census Population	County	Total Vote	Republican	Democratic	Other	Rep.-Dem. Plurality	Percentage Total Vote Rep.	Total Vote Dem.	Major Vote Rep.	Major Vote Dem.
40,567	ORANGE	11,462	5,501	5,910	51	409 D	48.0%	51.6%	48.2%	51.8%
17,154	PALO PINTO	5,199	2,818	2,369	12	449 R	54.2%	45.6%	54.3%	45.7%
19,250	PANOLA	4,836	2,538	2,225	73	313 R	52.5%	46.0%	53.3%	46.7%
21,528	PARKER	6,588	3,390	3,165	33	225 R	51.5%	48.0%	51.7%	48.3%
5,787	PARMER	2,404	1,028	1,362	14	334 D	42.8%	56.7%	43.0%	57.0%
9,939	PECOS	2,367	1,425	931	11	494 R	60.2%	39.3%	60.5%	39.5%
16,194	POLK	3,144	1,663	1,465	16	198 R	52.9%	46.6%	53.2%	46.8%
73,366	POTTER	20,712	11,943	8,720	49	3,223 R	57.7%	42.1%	57.8%	42.2%
7,354	PRESIDIO	1,019	494	517	8	23 D	48.5%	50.7%	48.9%	51.1%
4,266	RAINS	952	427	524	1	97 D	44.9%	55.0%	44.9%	55.1%
13,774	RANDALL	7,400	4,609	2,774	17	1,835 R	62.3%	37.5%	62.4%	37.6%
3,127	REAGAN	1,054	669	384	1	285 R	63.5%	36.4%	63.5%	36.5%
2,479	REAL	541	350	191		159 R	64.7%	35.3%	64.7%	35.3%
21,851	RED RIVER	4,534	1,956	2,567	11	611 D	43.1%	56.6%	43.2%	56.8%
11,745	REEVES	2,856	1,492	1,356	8	136 R	52.2%	47.5%	52.4%	47.6%
10,113	REFUGIO	2,552	1,355	1,188	9	167 R	53.1%	46.6%	53.3%	46.7%
1,031	ROBERTS	399	279	118	2	161 R	69.9%	29.6%	70.3%	29.7%
19,908	ROBERTSON	3,508	1,285	2,212	11	927 D	36.6%	63.1%	36.7%	63.3%
6,156	ROCKWALL	1,583	657	920	6	263 D	41.5%	58.1%	41.7%	58.3%
16,771	RUNNELS	3,863	2,416	1,442	5	974 R	62.5%	37.3%	62.6%	37.4%
42,348	RUSK	8,573	5,140	3,381	52	1,759 R	60.0%	39.4%	60.3%	39.7%
8,568	SABINE	1,715	801	913	1	112 D	46.7%	53.2%	46.7%	53.3%
8,837	SAN AUGUSTINE	1,997	900	1,086	11	186 D	45.1%	54.4%	45.3%	54.7%
7,172	SAN JACINTO	1,329	565	755	9	190 D	42.5%	56.8%	42.8%	57.2%
35,842	SAN PATRICIO	7,052	3,302	3,728	22	426 D	46.8%	52.9%	47.0%	53.0%
8,666	SAN SABA	2,222	797	1,419	6	622 D	35.9%	63.9%	36.0%	64.0%
2,852	SCHLEICHER	811	471	336	4	135 R	58.1%	41.4%	58.4%	41.6%
22,779	SCURRY	4,949	2,250	2,691	8	441 D	45.5%	54.4%	45.5%	54.5%
5,001	SHACKELFORD	1,409	849	555	5	294 R	60.3%	39.4%	60.5%	39.5%
23,479	SHELBY	5,440	1,988	3,403	49	1,415 D	36.5%	62.6%	36.9%	63.1%
2,443	SHERMAN	869	481	383	5	98 R	55.4%	44.1%	55.7%	44.3%
74,701	SMITH	18,792	12,255	6,468	69	5,787 R	65.2%	34.4%	65.5%	34.5%
2,542	SOMERVELL	781	467	309	5	158 R	59.8%	39.6%	60.2%	39.8%
13,948	STARR	3,274	547	2,727		2,180 D	16.7%	83.3%	16.7%	83.3%
10,597	STEPHENS	2,971	1,832	1,126	13	706 R	61.7%	37.9%	61.9%	38.1%
1,282	STERLING	373	223	150		73 R	59.8%	40.2%	59.8%	40.2%
3,679	STONEWALL	1,138	306	829	3	523 D	26.9%	72.8%	27.0%	73.0%
3,746	SUTTON	838	546	290	2	256 R	65.2%	34.6%	65.3%	34.7%
8,249	SWISHER	2,684	876	1,802	6	926 D	32.6%	67.1%	32.7%	67.3%
361,253	TARRANT	111,197	66,329	43,922	946	22,407 R	59.6%	39.5%	60.2%	39.8%
63,370	TAYLOR	16,699	9,488	7,177	34	2,311 R	56.8%	43.0%	56.9%	43.1%
3,189	TERRELL	569	350	217	2	133 R	61.5%	38.1%	61.7%	38.3%
13,107	TERRY	3,526	1,473	2,050	3	577 D	41.8%	58.1%	41.8%	58.2%
3,618	THROCKMORTON	1,127	466	656	5	190 D	41.3%	58.2%	41.5%	58.5%
17,302	TITUS	4,305	1,971	2,301	33	330 D	45.8%	53.4%	46.1%	53.9%
58,929	TOM GREEN	14,033	9,070	4,923	40	4,147 R	64.6%	35.1%	64.8%	35.2%
160,980	TRAVIS	43,631	23,551	19,982	98	3,569 R	54.0%	45.8%	54.1%	45.9%
10,040	TRINITY	1,967	865	1,091	11	226 D	44.0%	55.5%	44.2%	55.8%
11,292	TYLER	2,541	1,734	797	10	937 R	68.2%	31.4%	68.5%	31.5%
20,822	UPSHUR	4,764	2,737	1,995	32	742 R	57.5%	41.9%	57.8%	42.2%
5,307	UPTON	1,840	999	834	7	165 R	54.3%	45.3%	54.5%	45.5%
16,015	UVALDE	3,463	2,449	994	20	1,455 R	70.7%	28.7%	71.1%	28.9%
16,635	VAL VERDE	3,267	1,660	1,598	9	62 R	50.8%	48.9%	51.0%	49.0%
22,593	VAN ZANDT	5,070	2,142	2,919	9	777 D	42.2%	57.6%	42.3%	57.7%
31,241	VICTORIA	8,904	5,596	3,280	28	2,316 R	62.8%	36.8%	63.0%	37.0%
20,163	WALKER	3,326	1,991	1,287	48	704 R	59.9%	38.7%	60.7%	39.3%
11,961	WALLER	2,397	1,426	929	42	497 R	59.5%	38.8%	60.6%	39.4%
13,346	WARD	3,432	1,772	1,638	22	134 R	51.6%	47.7%	52.0%	48.0%
20,542	WASHINGTON	3,923	2,975	933	15	2,042 R	75.8%	23.8%	76.1%	23.9%
56,141	WEBB	8,587	2,744	5,827	16	3,083 D	32.0%	67.9%	32.0%	68.0%

TEXAS

PRESIDENT 1956

1950 Census Population	County	Total Vote	Republican	Democratic	Other	Rep.-Dem. Plurality	Percentage Total Vote Rep.	Percentage Total Vote Dem.	Percentage Major Vote Rep.	Percentage Major Vote Dem.
36,077	WHARTON	8,203	4,714	3,439	50	1,275 R	57.5%	41.9%	57.8%	42.2%
10,317	WHEELER	2,443	1,178	1,252	13	74 D	48.2%	51.2%	48.5%	51.5%
98,493	WICHITA	24,948	12,181	12,726	41	545 D	48.8%	51.0%	48.9%	51.1%
20,552	WILBARGER	4,587	2,230	2,347	10	117 D	48.6%	51.2%	48.7%	51.3%
20,920	WILLACY	2,948	1,656	1,261	31	395 R	56.2%	42.8%	56.8%	43.2%
38,853	WILLIAMSON	7,367	2,947	4,402	18	1,455 D	40.0%	59.8%	40.1%	59.9%
14,672	WILSON	3,678	1,519	2,149	10	630 D	41.3%	58.4%	41.4%	58.6%
10,064	WINKLER	2,777	1,471	1,287	19	184 R	53.0%	46.3%	53.3%	46.7%
16,141	WISE	4,524	2,058	2,443	23	385 D	45.5%	54.0%	45.7%	54.3%
21,308	WOOD	4,722	2,508	2,199	15	309 R	53.1%	46.6%	53.3%	46.7%
4,339	YOAKUM	1,915	923	989	3	66 D	48.2%	51.6%	48.3%	51.7%
16,810	YOUNG	4,130	2,083	2,028	19	55 R	50.4%	49.1%	50.7%	49.3%
4,405	ZAPATA	1,524	637	886	1	249 D	41.8%	58.1%	41.8%	58.2%
11,201	ZAVALA	1,427	896	528	3	368 R	62.8%	37.0%	62.9%	37.1%
7,711,194	TOTAL	1,955,168	1,080,619	859,958	14,591	220,661 R	55.3%	44.0%	55.7%	44.3%

TEXAS

PRESIDENT 1952

1950 Census Population	County	Total Vote	Republican	Democratic	Other	Rep.-Dem. Plurality	Percentage: Total Vote Rep.	Total Vote Dem.	Major Vote Rep.	Major Vote Dem.
31,875	ANDERSON	8,109	4,637	3,462	10	1,175 R	57.2%	42.7%	57.3%	42.7%
5,002	ANDREWS	1,729	805	920	4	115 D	46.6%	53.2%	46.7%	53.3%
36,032	ANGELINA	10,942	4,705	6,224	13	1,519 D	43.0%	56.9%	43.1%	56.9%
4,252	ARANSAS	1,325	818	503	4	315 R	61.7%	38.0%	61.9%	38.1%
6,816	ARCHER	2,212	937	1,272	3	335 D	42.4%	57.5%	42.4%	57.6%
2,215	ARMSTRONG	996	562	425	9	137 R	56.4%	42.7%	56.9%	43.1%
20,048	ATASCOSA	4,281	2,147	2,124	10	23 R	50.2%	49.6%	50.3%	49.7%
14,663	AUSTIN	4,413	2,964	1,445	4	1,519 R	67.2%	32.7%	67.2%	32.8%
7,592	BAILEY	2,162	1,118	1,039	5	79 R	51.7%	48.1%	51.8%	48.2%
4,410	BANDERA	1,710	1,350	358	2	992 R	78.9%	20.9%	79.0%	21.0%
19,622	BASTROP	4,694	1,540	3,148	6	1,608 D	32.8%	67.1%	32.8%	67.2%
6,875	BAYLOR	2,024	879	1,142	3	263 D	43.4%	56.4%	43.5%	56.5%
18,174	BEE	4,126	2,536	1,583	7	953 R	61.5%	38.4%	61.6%	38.4%
73,824	BELL	14,358	4,862	9,484	12	4,622 D	33.9%	66.1%	33.9%	66.1%
500,460	BEXAR	116,136	65,391	50,260	485	15,131 R	56.3%	43.3%	56.5%	43.5%
3,780	BLANCO	1,618	919	697	2	222 R	56.8%	43.1%	56.9%	43.1%
1,106	BORDEN	392	182	210		28 D	46.4%	53.6%	46.4%	53.6%
11,836	BOSQUE	3,929	1,982	1,940	7	42 R	50.4%	49.4%	50.5%	49.5%
61,966	BOWIE	16,954	6,501	10,437	16	3,936 D	38.3%	61.6%	38.4%	61.6%
46,549	BRAZORIA	16,761	8,360	8,386	15	26 D	49.9%	50.0%	49.9%	50.1%
38,390	BRAZOS	8,896	4,681	4,213	2	468 R	52.6%	47.4%	52.6%	47.4%
7,309	BREWSTER	1,705	1,096	609		487 R	64.3%	35.7%	64.3%	35.7%
3,528	BRISCOE	1,203	692	508	3	184 R	57.5%	42.2%	57.7%	42.3%
9,195	BROOKS	2,387	809	1,577	1	768 D	33.9%	66.1%	33.9%	66.1%
28,607	BROWN	8,424	4,635	3,778	11	857 R	55.0%	44.8%	55.1%	44.9%
13,000	BURLESON	3,410	1,052	2,347	11	1,295 D	30.9%	68.8%	31.0%	69.0%
10,356	BURNET	2,703	1,270	1,431	2	161 D	47.0%	52.9%	47.0%	53.0%
19,350	CALDWELL	4,941	2,052	2,887	2	835 D	41.5%	58.4%	41.5%	58.5%
9,222	CALHOUN	2,222	1,406	813	3	593 R	63.3%	36.6%	63.4%	36.6%
9,087	CALLAHAN	2,938	1,431	1,502	5	71 D	48.7%	51.1%	48.8%	51.2%
125,170	CAMERON	21,602	14,018	7,559	25	6,459 R	64.9%	35.0%	65.0%	35.0%
8,740	CAMP	2,487	951	1,535	1	584 D	38.2%	61.7%	38.3%	61.7%
6,852	CARSON	2,552	1,471	1,071	10	400 R	57.6%	42.0%	57.9%	42.1%
26,732	CASS	5,665	2,502	3,160	3	658 D	44.2%	55.8%	44.2%	55.8%
5,417	CASTRO	1,996	1,169	825	2	344 R	58.6%	41.3%	58.6%	41.4%
7,871	CHAMBERS	2,617	1,497	1,116	4	381 R	57.2%	42.6%	57.3%	42.7%
38,694	CHEROKEE	7,707	3,825	3,868	14	43 D	49.6%	50.2%	49.7%	50.3%
12,123	CHILDRESS	3,771	1,890	1,879	2	11 R	50.1%	49.8%	50.1%	49.9%
9,896	CLAY	3,316	1,272	2,044		772 D	38.4%	61.6%	38.4%	61.6%
5,928	COCHRAN	1,693	780	906	7	126 D	46.1%	53.5%	46.3%	53.7%
4,045	COKE	1,317	576	736	5	160 D	43.7%	55.9%	43.9%	56.1%
15,503	COLEMAN	4,387	2,555	1,824	8	731 R	58.2%	41.6%	58.3%	41.7%
41,692	COLLIN	9,950	4,037	5,906	7	1,869 D	40.6%	59.4%	40.6%	59.4%
9,139	COLLINGSWORTH	2,657	1,334	1,321	2	13 R	50.2%	49.7%	50.2%	49.8%
17,576	COLORADO	5,290	3,237	2,043	10	1,194 R	61.2%	38.6%	61.3%	38.7%
16,357	COMAL	4,606	3,350	1,252	4	2,098 R	72.7%	27.2%	72.8%	27.2%
15,516	COMANCHE	4,596	2,411	2,181	4	230 R	52.5%	47.5%	52.5%	47.5%
5,078	CONCHO	1,516	808	708		100 R	53.3%	46.7%	53.3%	46.7%
22,146	COOKE	7,050	4,385	2,657	8	1,728 R	62.2%	37.7%	62.3%	37.7%
16,284	CORYELL	4,092	1,658	2,432	2	774 D	40.5%	59.4%	40.5%	59.5%
6,099	COTTLE	1,862	494	1,368		874 D	26.5%	73.5%	26.5%	73.5%
3,965	CRANE	1,488	621	857	10	236 D	41.7%	57.6%	42.0%	58.0%
3,981	CROCKETT	960	654	306		348 R	68.1%	31.9%	68.1%	31.9%
9,582	CROSBY	2,603	1,053	1,550		497 D	40.5%	59.5%	40.5%	59.5%
1,825	CULBERSON	583	331	252		79 R	56.8%	43.2%	56.8%	43.2%
7,640	DALLAM	2,673	1,464	1,197	12	267 R	54.8%	44.8%	55.0%	45.0%
614,799	DALLAS	188,462	118,218	69,394	850	48,824 R	62.7%	36.8%	63.0%	37.0%
19,113	DAWSON	4,481	2,388	2,093		295 R	53.3%	46.7%	53.3%	46.7%
9,111	DEAF SMITH	3,483	2,468	1,006	9	1,462 R	70.9%	28.9%	71.0%	29.0%
8,964	DELTA	2,295	707	1,585	3	878 D	30.8%	69.1%	30.8%	69.2%

TEXAS

PRESIDENT 1952

1950 Census Population	County	Total Vote	Republican	Democratic	Other	Rep.-Dem. Plurality	Percentage Total Vote Rep.	Percentage Total Vote Dem.	Percentage Major Vote Rep.	Percentage Major Vote Dem.
41,365	DENTON	11,137	5,840	5,289	8	551 R	52.4%	47.5%	52.5%	47.5%
22,973	DE WITT	6,018	4,075	1,934	9	2,141 R	67.7%	32.1%	67.8%	32.2%
7,177	DICKENS	2,035	782	1,249	4	467 D	38.4%	61.4%	38.5%	61.5%
10,654	DIMMIT	1,460	954	503	3	451 R	65.3%	34.5%	65.5%	34.5%
6,216	DONLEY	2,056	1,150	900	6	250 R	55.9%	43.8%	56.1%	43.9%
15,643	DUVAL	3,989	672	3,316	1	2,644 D	16.8%	83.1%	16.9%	83.1%
23,942	EASTLAND	7,906	4,518	3,370	18	1,148 R	57.1%	42.6%	57.3%	42.7%
42,102	ECTOR	13,537	8,259	5,270	8	2,989 R	61.0%	38.9%	61.0%	39.0%
2,908	EDWARDS	798	586	210	2	376 R	73.4%	26.3%	73.6%	26.4%
45,645	ELLIS	10,482	4,183	6,275	24	2,092 D	39.9%	59.9%	40.0%	60.0%
194,968	EL PASO	34,647	20,005	14,595	47	5,410 R	57.7%	42.1%	57.8%	42.2%
18,434	ERATH	5,915	3,249	2,664	2	585 R	54.9%	45.0%	54.9%	45.1%
26,724	FALLS	5,257	1,962	3,287	8	1,325 D	37.3%	62.5%	37.4%	62.6%
31,253	FANNIN	7,465	2,099	5,363	3	3,264 D	28.1%	71.8%	28.1%	71.9%
24,176	FAYETTE	6,800	4,240	2,557	3	1,683 R	62.4%	37.6%	62.4%	37.6%
11,023	FISHER	2,359	952	1,405	2	453 D	40.4%	59.6%	40.4%	59.6%
10,535	FLOYD	3,534	2,066	1,463	5	603 R	58.5%	41.4%	58.5%	41.5%
4,216	FOARD	1,256	418	830	8	412 D	33.3%	66.1%	33.5%	66.5%
31,056	FORT BEND	7,226	3,974	3,241	11	733 R	55.0%	44.9%	55.1%	44.9%
6,257	FRANKLIN	1,923	564	1,358	1	794 D	29.3%	70.6%	29.3%	70.7%
15,696	FREESTONE	4,611	1,707	2,902	2	1,195 D	37.0%	62.9%	37.0%	63.0%
10,357	FRIO	2,001	1,011	983	7	28 R	50.5%	49.1%	50.7%	49.3%
8,909	GAINES	2,905	1,350	1,540	15	190 D	46.5%	53.0%	46.7%	53.3%
113,066	GALVESTON	34,920	15,715	19,058	147	3,343 D	45.0%	54.6%	45.2%	54.8%
6,281	GARZA	1,541	742	797	2	55 D	48.2%	51.7%	48.2%	51.8%
10,520	GILLESPIE	3,995	3,687	300	8	3,387 R	92.3%	7.5%	92.5%	7.5%
1,089	GLASSCOCK	432	235	197		38 R	54.4%	45.6%	54.4%	45.6%
6,219	GOLIAD	1,518	1,065	452	1	613 R	70.2%	29.8%	70.2%	29.8%
21,164	GONZALES	4,815	2,249	2,563	3	314 D	46.7%	53.2%	46.7%	53.3%
24,728	GRAY	8,857	5,467	3,367	23	2,100 R	61.7%	38.0%	61.9%	38.1%
70,467	GRAYSON	18,194	7,736	10,435	23	2,699 D	42.5%	57.4%	42.6%	57.4%
61,258	GREGG	18,794	10,583	7,969	242	2,614 R	56.3%	42.4%	57.0%	43.0%
15,135	GRIMES	2,920	1,557	1,362	1	195 R	53.3%	46.6%	53.3%	46.7%
25,392	GUADALUPE	6,740	4,396	2,330	14	2,066 R	65.2%	34.6%	65.4%	34.6%
28,211	HALE	8,226	4,858	3,351	17	1,507 R	59.1%	40.7%	59.2%	40.8%
10,930	HALL	2,999	1,253	1,744	2	491 D	41.8%	58.2%	41.8%	58.2%
10,660	HAMILTON	3,448	2,130	1,313	5	817 R	61.8%	38.1%	61.9%	38.1%
4,202	HANSFORD	1,692	1,234	456	2	778 R	72.9%	27.0%	73.0%	27.0%
10,212	HARDEMAN	2,821	1,571	1,242	8	329 R	55.7%	44.0%	55.8%	44.2%
19,535	HARDIN	5,082	1,653	3,423	6	1,770 D	32.5%	67.4%	32.6%	67.4%
806,701	HARRIS	254,497	146,665	107,604	228	39,061 R	57.6%	42.3%	57.7%	42.3%
47,745	HARRISON	9,229	4,708	4,516	5	192 R	51.0%	48.9%	51.0%	49.0%
1,913	HARTLEY	874	468	402	4	66 R	53.5%	46.0%	53.8%	46.2%
13,736	HASKELL	3,777	1,290	2,481	6	1,191 D	34.2%	65.7%	34.2%	65.8%
17,840	HAYS	4,208	2,135	2,070	3	65 R	50.7%	49.2%	50.8%	49.2%
4,123	HEMPHILL	1,482	892	590		302 R	60.2%	39.8%	60.2%	39.8%
23,405	HENDERSON	6,974	2,534	4,439	1	1,905 D	36.3%	63.7%	36.3%	63.7%
160,446	HIDALGO	24,602	15,303	9,251	48	6,052 R	62.2%	37.6%	62.3%	37.7%
31,282	HILL	7,747	3,242	4,504	1	1,262 D	41.8%	58.1%	41.9%	58.1%
20,407	HOCKLEY	5,620	2,651	2,962	7	311 D	47.2%	52.7%	47.2%	52.8%
5,287	HOOD	2,136	780	1,356		576 D	36.5%	63.5%	36.5%	63.5%
23,490	HOPKINS	6,218	2,460	3,750	8	1,290 D	39.6%	60.3%	39.6%	60.4%
22,825	HOUSTON	5,126	2,222	2,900	4	678 D	43.3%	56.6%	43.4%	56.6%
26,722	HOWARD	8,202	3,412	4,779	11	1,367 D	41.6%	58.3%	41.7%	58.3%
4,298	HUDSPETH	622	355	262	5	93 R	57.1%	42.1%	57.5%	42.5%
42,731	HUNT	10,581	5,614	4,953	14	661 R	53.1%	46.8%	53.1%	46.9%
31,580	HUTCHINSON	10,465	5,369	5,083	13	286 R	51.3%	48.6%	51.4%	48.6%
1,590	IRION	550	268	282		14 D	48.7%	51.3%	48.7%	51.3%
7,755	JACK	2,539	1,406	1,130	3	276 R	55.4%	44.5%	55.4%	44.6%
12,916	JACKSON	3,698	2,113	1,584	1	529 R	57.1%	42.8%	57.2%	42.8%

TEXAS

PRESIDENT 1952

1950 Census Population	County	Total Vote	Republican	Democratic	Other	Rep.-Dem. Plurality	Percentage Total Vote Rep.	Percentage Total Vote Dem.	Percentage Major Vote Rep.	Percentage Major Vote Dem.
20,049	JASPER	4,543	1,946	2,595	2	649 D	42.8%	57.1%	42.9%	57.1%
2,090	JEFF DAVIS	489	306	183		123 R	62.6%	37.4%	62.6%	37.4%
195,083	JEFFERSON	54,795	25,363	29,384	48	4,021 D	46.3%	53.6%	46.3%	53.7%
5,389	JIM HOGG	1,362	309	1,053		744 D	22.7%	77.3%	22.7%	77.3%
27,991	JIM WELLS	7,339	3,592	3,745	2	153 D	48.9%	51.0%	49.0%	51.0%
31,390	JOHNSON	8,485	3,985	4,496	4	511 D	47.0%	53.0%	47.0%	53.0%
22,147	JONES	5,633	2,941	2,680	12	261 R	52.2%	47.6%	52.3%	47.7%
17,139	KARNES	4,260	2,374	1,884	2	490 R	55.7%	44.2%	55.8%	44.2%
31,170	KAUFMAN	6,729	2,964	3,762	3	798 D	44.0%	55.9%	44.1%	55.9%
5,423	KENDALL	2,164	1,786	370	8	1,416 R	82.5%	17.1%	82.8%	17.2%
632	KENEDY	122	108	14		94 R	88.5%	11.5%	88.5%	11.5%
2,249	KENT	786	259	526	1	267 D	33.0%	66.9%	33.0%	67.0%
14,022	KERR	5,029	3,683	1,337	9	2,346 R	73.2%	26.6%	73.4%	26.6%
4,619	KIMBLE	1,605	1,077	525	3	552 R	67.1%	32.7%	67.2%	32.8%
870	KING	255	66	189		123 D	25.9%	74.1%	25.9%	74.1%
2,668	KINNEY	690	384	306		78 R	55.7%	44.3%	55.7%	44.3%
21,991	KLEBERG	5,231	2,037	3,193	1	1,156 D	38.9%	61.0%	38.9%	61.1%
10,082	KNOX	2,590	1,033	1,556	1	523 D	39.9%	60.1%	39.9%	60.1%
43,033	LAMAR	9,453	3,929	5,524		1,595 D	41.6%	58.4%	41.6%	58.4%
20,015	LAMB	5,672	2,913	2,748	11	165 R	51.4%	48.4%	51.5%	48.5%
9,929	LAMPASAS	2,677	1,478	1,199		279 R	55.2%	44.8%	55.2%	44.8%
7,485	LA SALLE	1,382	565	816	1	251 D	40.9%	59.0%	40.9%	59.1%
22,159	LAVACA	6,361	3,599	2,750	12	849 R	56.6%	43.2%	56.7%	43.3%
10,144	LEE	2,707	1,316	1,389	2	73 D	48.6%	51.3%	48.7%	51.3%
12,024	LEON	3,114	1,266	1,842	6	576 D	40.7%	59.2%	40.7%	59.3%
26,729	LIBERTY	7,746	4,106	3,632	8	474 R	53.0%	46.9%	53.1%	46.9%
25,251	LIMESTONE	6,627	2,485	4,132	10	1,647 D	37.5%	62.4%	37.6%	62.4%
3,658	LIPSCOMB	1,379	1,174	204	1	970 R	85.1%	14.8%	85.2%	14.8%
9,054	LIVE OAK	2,026	1,443	573	10	870 R	71.2%	28.3%	71.6%	28.4%
5,377	LLANO	1,944	840	1,102	2	262 D	43.2%	56.7%	43.3%	56.7%
227	LOVING	95	71	24		47 R	74.7%	25.3%	74.7%	25.3%
101,048	LUBBOCK	27,845	16,137	11,650	58	4,487 R	58.0%	41.8%	58.1%	41.9%
11,030	LYNN	3,121	1,351	1,762	8	411 D	43.3%	56.5%	43.4%	56.6%
11,701	MCCULLOCH	3,420	1,788	1,623	9	165 R	52.3%	47.5%	52.4%	47.6%
130,194	MCLENNAN	32,278	14,974	17,251	53	2,277 D	46.4%	53.4%	46.5%	53.5%
1,187	MCMULLEN	447	290	156	1	134 R	64.9%	34.9%	65.0%	35.0%
7,996	MADISON	1,844	692	1,152		460 D	37.5%	62.5%	37.5%	62.5%
10,172	MARION	1,849	877	970	2	93 D	47.4%	52.5%	47.5%	52.5%
5,541	MARTIN	1,516	562	952	2	390 D	37.1%	62.8%	37.1%	62.9%
4,945	MASON	1,678	1,069	606	3	463 R	63.7%	36.1%	63.8%	36.2%
21,559	MATAGORDA	6,224	4,122	2,101	1	2,021 R	66.2%	33.8%	66.2%	33.8%
12,292	MAVERICK	1,802	839	962	1	123 D	46.6%	53.4%	46.6%	53.4%
17,013	MEDINA	5,044	3,204	1,840		1,364 R	63.5%	36.5%	63.5%	36.5%
4,175	MENARD	1,242	843	399		444 R	67.9%	32.1%	67.9%	32.1%
25,785	MIDLAND	11,200	7,956	3,244		4,712 R	71.0%	29.0%	71.0%	29.0%
23,585	MILAM	5,778	2,539	3,227	12	688 D	43.9%	55.8%	44.0%	56.0%
5,999	MILLS	1,966	1,089	875	2	214 R	55.4%	44.5%	55.4%	44.6%
14,357	MITCHELL	3,460	1,417	2,031	12	614 D	41.0%	58.7%	41.1%	58.9%
17,070	MONTAGUE	5,383	2,367	3,012	4	645 D	44.0%	56.0%	44.0%	56.0%
24,504	MONTGOMERY	6,410	2,969	3,432	9	463 D	46.3%	53.5%	46.4%	53.6%
13,349	MOORE	4,035	1,909	2,114	12	205 D	47.3%	52.4%	47.5%	52.5%
9,433	MORRIS	2,613	890	1,722	1	832 D	34.1%	65.9%	34.1%	65.9%
3,963	MOTLEY	1,190	675	513	2	162 R	56.7%	43.1%	56.8%	43.2%
30,326	NACOGDOCHES	6,447	2,891	3,556		665 D	44.8%	55.2%	44.8%	55.2%
39,916	NAVARRO	12,345	3,592	8,745	8	5,153 D	29.1%	70.8%	29.1%	70.9%
10,832	NEWTON	2,548	917	1,630	1	713 D	36.0%	64.0%	36.0%	64.0%
19,808	NOLAN	6,043	2,907	3,123	13	216 D	48.1%	51.7%	48.2%	51.8%
165,471	NUECES	39,359	19,124	20,156	79	1,032 D	48.6%	51.2%	48.7%	51.3%
6,024	OCHILTREE	2,183	1,755	426	2	1,329 R	80.4%	19.5%	80.5%	19.5%
1,672	OLDHAM	624	341	280	3	61 R	54.6%	44.9%	54.9%	45.1%

TEXAS

PRESIDENT 1952

1950 Census Population	County	Total Vote	Republican	Democratic	Other	Rep.-Dem. Plurality	Percentage Total Vote Rep.	Percentage Total Vote Dem.	Percentage Major Vote Rep.	Percentage Major Vote Dem.
40,567	ORANGE	10,913	4,491	6,403	19	1,912 D	41.2%	58.7%	41.2%	58.8%
17,154	PALO PINTO	5,917	3,029	2,876	12	153 R	51.2%	48.6%	51.3%	48.7%
19,250	PANOLA	4,982	2,080	2,897	5	817 D	41.8%	58.1%	41.8%	58.2%
21,528	PARKER	6,976	3,523	3,434	19	89 R	50.5%	49.2%	50.6%	49.4%
5,787	PARMER	2,166	1,503	663		840 R	69.4%	30.6%	69.4%	30.6%
9,939	PECOS	2,650	1,573	1,076	1	497 R	59.4%	40.6%	59.4%	40.6%
16,194	POLK	3,694	1,454	2,238	2	784 D	39.4%	60.6%	39.4%	60.6%
73,366	POTTER	24,232	14,931	9,259	42	5,672 R	61.6%	38.2%	61.7%	38.3%
7,354	PRESIDIO	1,391	770	621		149 R	55.4%	44.6%	55.4%	44.6%
4,266	RAINS	1,088	500	588		88 D	46.0%	54.0%	46.0%	54.0%
13,774	RANDALL	6,214	4,305	1,905	4	2,400 R	69.3%	30.7%	69.3%	30.7%
3,127	REAGAN	994	533	460	1	73 R	53.6%	46.3%	53.7%	46.3%
2,479	REAL	753	450	303		147 R	59.8%	40.2%	59.8%	40.2%
21,851	RED RIVER	5,450	1,964	3,484	2	1,520 D	36.0%	63.9%	36.0%	64.0%
11,745	REEVES	3,118	1,727	1,385	6	342 R	55.4%	44.4%	55.5%	44.5%
10,113	REFUGIO	2,832	1,427	1,401	4	26 R	50.4%	49.5%	50.5%	49.5%
1,031	ROBERTS	470	379	91		288 R	80.6%	19.4%	80.6%	19.4%
19,908	ROBERTSON	4,007	1,378	2,626	3	1,248 D	34.4%	65.5%	34.4%	65.6%
6,156	ROCKWALL	1,785	602	1,175	8	573 D	33.7%	65.8%	33.9%	66.1%
16,771	RUNNELS	4,480	2,622	1,853	5	769 R	58.5%	41.4%	58.6%	41.4%
42,348	RUSK	11,340	5,634	5,694	12	60 D	49.7%	50.2%	49.7%	50.3%
8,568	SABINE	2,302	729	1,573		844 D	31.7%	68.3%	31.7%	68.3%
8,837	SAN AUGUSTINE	2,089	730	1,359		629 D	34.9%	65.1%	34.9%	65.1%
7,172	SAN JACINTO	1,541	494	1,043	4	549 D	32.1%	67.7%	32.1%	67.9%
35,842	SAN PATRICIO	6,540	3,220	3,315	5	95 D	49.2%	50.7%	49.3%	50.7%
8,666	SAN SABA	2,653	900	1,752	1	852 D	33.9%	66.0%	33.9%	66.1%
2,852	SCHLEICHER	1,049	628	421		207 R	59.9%	40.1%	59.9%	40.1%
22,779	SCURRY	5,100	2,620	2,480		140 R	51.4%	48.6%	51.4%	48.6%
5,001	SHACKELFORD	1,837	1,057	776	4	281 R	57.5%	42.2%	57.7%	42.3%
23,479	SHELBY	6,047	1,792	4,249	6	2,457 D	29.6%	70.3%	29.7%	70.3%
2,443	SHERMAN	988	669	317	2	352 R	67.7%	32.1%	67.8%	32.2%
74,701	SMITH	19,410	10,947	8,450	13	2,497 R	56.4%	43.5%	56.4%	43.6%
2,542	SOMERVELL	953	494	450	9	44 R	51.8%	47.2%	52.3%	47.7%
13,948	STARR	3,675	620	3,055		2,435 D	16.9%	83.1%	16.9%	83.1%
10,597	STEPHENS	3,747	2,272	1,471	4	801 R	60.6%	39.3%	60.7%	39.3%
1,282	STERLING	435	277	158		119 R	63.7%	36.3%	63.7%	36.3%
3,679	STONEWALL	1,157	319	836	2	517 D	27.6%	72.3%	27.6%	72.4%
3,746	SUTTON	932	581	351		230 R	62.3%	37.7%	62.3%	37.7%
8,249	SWISHER	2,922	1,843	1,074	5	769 R	63.1%	36.8%	63.2%	36.8%
361,253	TARRANT	109,842	63,680	45,968	194	17,712 R	58.0%	41.8%	58.1%	41.9%
63,370	TAYLOR	18,251	10,260	7,936	55	2,324 R	56.2%	43.5%	56.4%	43.6%
3,189	TERRELL	722	426	295	1	131 R	59.0%	40.9%	59.1%	40.9%
13,107	TERRY	3,931	1,823	2,105	3	282 D	46.4%	53.5%	46.4%	53.6%
3,618	THROCKMORTON	1,314	586	728		142 D	44.6%	55.4%	44.6%	55.4%
17,302	TITUS	5,031	1,887	3,142	2	1,255 D	37.5%	62.5%	37.5%	62.5%
58,929	TOM GREEN	15,519	9,698	5,797	24	3,901 R	62.5%	37.4%	62.6%	37.4%
160,980	TRAVIS	40,051	20,850	19,155	46	1,695 R	52.1%	47.8%	52.1%	47.9%
10,040	TRINITY	2,683	958	1,725		767 D	35.7%	64.3%	35.7%	64.3%
11,292	TYLER	2,770	1,466	1,304		162 R	52.9%	47.1%	52.9%	47.1%
20,822	UPSHUR	5,437	2,391	3,040	6	649 D	44.0%	55.9%	44.0%	56.0%
5,307	UPTON	1,793	940	850	3	90 R	52.4%	47.4%	52.5%	47.5%
16,015	UVALDE	4,044	2,805	1,230	9	1,575 R	69.4%	30.4%	69.5%	30.5%
16,635	VAL VERDE	3,373	1,725	1,647	1	78 R	51.1%	48.8%	51.2%	48.8%
22,593	VAN ZANDT	6,203	2,279	3,911	13	1,632 D	36.7%	63.1%	36.8%	63.2%
31,241	VICTORIA	7,438	4,306	3,128	4	1,178 R	57.9%	42.1%	57.9%	42.1%
20,163	WALKER	3,976	1,897	2,078	1	181 D	47.7%	52.3%	47.7%	52.3%
11,961	WALLER	2,753	1,487	1,264	2	223 R	54.0%	45.9%	54.1%	45.9%
13,346	WARD	3,836	1,994	1,840	2	154 R	52.0%	48.0%	52.0%	48.0%
20,542	WASHINGTON	4,876	3,519	1,354	3	2,165 R	72.2%	27.8%	72.2%	27.8%
56,141	WEBB	8,996	2,784	6,208	4	3,424 D	30.9%	69.0%	31.0%	69.0%

TEXAS

PRESIDENT 1952

1950 Census Population	County	Total Vote	Republican	Democratic	Other	Rep.-Dem. Plurality	Percentage Total Vote Rep.	Percentage Total Vote Dem.	Percentage Major Vote Rep.	Percentage Major Vote Dem.
36,077	WHARTON	9,259	5,232	4,022	5	1,210 R	56.5%	43.4%	56.5%	43.5%
10,317	WHEELER	3,202	1,645	1,551	6	94 R	51.4%	48.4%	51.5%	48.5%
98,493	WICHITA	25,731	12,197	13,505	29	1,308 D	47.4%	52.5%	47.5%	52.5%
20,552	WILBARGER	5,666	3,019	2,646	1	373 R	53.3%	46.7%	53.3%	46.7%
20,920	WILLACY	3,574	2,244	1,324	6	920 R	62.8%	37.0%	62.9%	37.1%
38,853	WILLIAMSON	8,663	3,646	5,010	7	1,364 D	42.1%	57.8%	42.1%	57.9%
14,672	WILSON	4,015	1,823	2,187	5	364 D	45.4%	54.5%	45.5%	54.5%
10,064	WINKLER	3,064	1,550	1,508	6	42 R	50.6%	49.2%	50.7%	49.3%
16,141	WISE	5,434	2,309	3,121	4	812 D	42.5%	57.4%	42.5%	57.5%
21,308	WOOD	5,780	2,748	3,026	6	278 D	47.5%	52.4%	47.6%	52.4%
4,339	YOAKUM	1,733	858	873	2	15 D	49.5%	50.4%	49.6%	50.4%
16,810	YOUNG	5,192	2,649	2,536	7	113 R	51.0%	48.8%	51.1%	48.9%
4,405	ZAPATA	1,143	526	616	1	90 D	46.0%	53.9%	46.1%	53.9%
11,201	ZAVALA	1,723	1,043	677	3	366 R	60.5%	39.3%	60.6%	39.4%
7,711,194	TOTAL	2,075,946	1,102,878	969,228	3,840	133,650 R	53.1%	46.7%	53.2%	46.8%

TEXAS

PRESIDENT 1948

1940 Census Population	County	Total Vote	Republican	Democratic	Other	Rep.-Dem. Plurality	Percentage Total Vote Rep.	Total Vote Dem.	Major Vote Rep.	Major Vote Dem.
37,092	ANDERSON	5,198	1,199	3,242	757	2,043 D	23.1%	62.4%	27.0%	73.0%
1,277	ANDREWS	957	101	816	40	715 D	10.6%	85.3%	11.0%	89.0%
32,201	ANGELINA	6,339	1,000	4,377	962	3,377 D	15.8%	69.0%	18.6%	81.4%
3,469	ARANSAS	685	235	418	32	183 D	34.3%	61.0%	36.0%	64.0%
7,599	ARCHER	1,855	191	1,599	65	1,408 D	10.3%	86.2%	10.7%	89.3%
2,495	ARMSTRONG	816	97	686	33	589 D	11.9%	84.1%	12.4%	87.6%
19,275	ATASCOSA	2,732	704	1,895	133	1,191 D	25.8%	69.4%	27.1%	72.9%
17,384	AUSTIN	2,865	1,260	1,252	353	8 R	44.0%	43.7%	50.2%	49.8%
6,318	BAILEY	1,452	234	1,115	103	881 D	16.1%	76.8%	17.3%	82.7%
4,234	BANDERA	1,132	570	445	117	125 R	50.4%	39.3%	56.2%	43.8%
21,610	BASTROP	3,237	443	2,518	276	2,075 D	13.7%	77.8%	15.0%	85.0%
7,755	BAYLOR	1,676	101	1,522	53	1,421 D	6.0%	90.8%	6.2%	93.8%
16,481	BEE	2,374	801	1,441	132	640 D	33.7%	60.7%	35.7%	64.3%
44,863	BELL	9,113	1,069	7,548	496	6,479 D	11.7%	82.8%	12.4%	87.6%
338,176	BEXAR	66,279	26,202	35,970	4,107	9,768 D	39.5%	54.3%	42.1%	57.9%
4,264	BLANCO	1,569	497	1,003	69	506 D	31.7%	63.9%	33.1%	66.9%
1,396	BORDEN	233	18	203	12	185 D	7.7%	87.1%	8.1%	91.9%
15,761	BOSQUE	2,956	501	2,303	152	1,802 D	16.9%	77.9%	17.9%	82.1%
50,208	BOWIE	10,343	1,161	7,028	2,154	5,867 D	11.2%	67.9%	14.2%	85.8%
27,069	BRAZORIA	8,363	2,133	4,783	1,447	2,650 D	25.5%	57.2%	30.8%	69.2%
26,977	BRAZOS	5,530	1,533	3,459	538	1,926 D	27.7%	62.5%	30.7%	69.3%
6,478	BREWSTER	1,341	312	940	89	628 D	23.3%	70.1%	24.9%	75.1%
4,056	BRISCOE	807	83	692	32	609 D	10.3%	85.7%	10.7%	89.3%
6,362	BROOKS	1,282	217	1,029	36	812 D	16.9%	80.3%	17.4%	82.6%
25,924	BROWN	6,481	1,071	5,059	351	3,988 D	16.5%	78.1%	17.5%	82.5%
18,334	BURLESON	2,434	240	2,051	143	1,811 D	9.9%	84.3%	10.5%	89.5%
10,771	BURNET	2,324	287	1,955	82	1,668 D	12.3%	84.1%	12.8%	87.2%
24,893	CALDWELL	3,616	623	2,792	201	2,169 D	17.2%	77.2%	18.2%	81.8%
5,911	CALHOUN	1,030	346	589	95	243 D	33.6%	57.2%	37.0%	63.0%
11,568	CALLAHAN	2,211	258	1,844	109	1,586 D	11.7%	83.4%	12.3%	87.7%
83,202	CAMERON	11,859	4,689	6,778	392	2,089 D	39.5%	57.2%	40.9%	59.1%
10,285	CAMP	1,488	180	923	385	743 D	12.1%	62.0%	16.3%	83.7%
6,624	CARSON	1,754	413	1,301	40	888 D	23.5%	74.2%	24.1%	75.9%
33,496	CASS	3,899	457	2,540	902	2,083 D	11.7%	65.1%	15.2%	84.8%
4,631	CASTRO	1,374	189	1,158	27	969 D	13.8%	84.3%	14.0%	86.0%
7,511	CHAMBERS	1,392	302	787	303	485 D	21.7%	56.5%	27.7%	72.3%
43,970	CHEROKEE	4,806	1,154	3,079	573	1,925 D	24.0%	64.1%	27.3%	72.7%
12,149	CHILDRESS	2,801	273	2,415	113	2,142 D	9.7%	86.2%	10.2%	89.8%
12,524	CLAY	2,583	332	2,131	120	1,799 D	12.9%	82.5%	13.5%	86.5%
3,735	COCHRAN	1,186	119	971	96	852 D	10.0%	81.9%	10.9%	89.1%
4,590	COKE	1,008	65	909	34	844 D	6.4%	90.2%	6.7%	93.3%
20,571	COLEMAN	3,429	545	2,695	189	2,150 D	15.9%	78.6%	16.8%	83.2%
47,190	COLLIN	7,250	1,155	5,516	579	4,361 D	15.9%	76.1%	17.3%	82.7%
10,331	COLLINGSWORTH	2,089	198	1,779	112	1,581 D	9.5%	85.2%	10.0%	90.0%
17,812	COLORADO	3,155	900	1,316	939	416 D	28.5%	41.7%	40.6%	59.4%
12,321	COMAL	3,074	1,752	1,212	110	540 R	57.0%	39.4%	59.1%	40.9%
19,245	COMANCHE	3,505	408	2,915	182	2,507 D	11.6%	83.2%	12.3%	87.7%
6,192	CONCHO	1,346	174	1,156	16	982 D	12.9%	85.9%	13.1%	86.9%
24,909	COOKE	5,026	1,194	3,241	591	2,047 D	23.8%	64.5%	26.9%	73.1%
20,226	CORYELL	2,761	310	2,350	101	2,040 D	11.2%	85.1%	11.7%	88.3%
7,079	COTTLE	1,453	102	1,318	33	1,216 D	7.0%	90.7%	7.2%	92.8%
2,841	CRANE	921	70	812	39	742 D	7.6%	88.2%	7.9%	92.1%
2,809	CROCKETT	545	127	400	18	273 D	23.3%	73.4%	24.1%	75.9%
10,046	CROSBY	2,069	168	1,731	170	1,563 D	8.1%	83.7%	8.8%	91.2%
1,653	CULBERSON	306	38	244	24	206 D	12.4%	79.7%	13.5%	86.5%
6,494	DALLAM	1,943	399	1,504	40	1,105 D	20.5%	77.4%	21.0%	79.0%
398,564	DALLAS	94,344	35,664	47,464	11,216	11,800 D	37.8%	50.3%	42.9%	57.1%
15,367	DAWSON	3,141	393	2,605	143	2,212 D	12.5%	82.9%	13.1%	86.9%
6,056	DEAF SMITH	2,089	535	1,496	58	961 D	25.6%	71.6%	26.3%	73.7%
12,858	DELTA	1,900	146	1,594	160	1,448 D	7.7%	83.9%	8.4%	91.6%

TEXAS

PRESIDENT 1948

1940 Census Population	County	Total Vote	Republican	Democratic	Other	Rep.-Dem. Plurality	Percentage Total Vote Rep.	Percentage Total Vote Dem.	Percentage Major Vote Rep.	Percentage Major Vote Dem.
33,658	DENTON	6,953	1,531	4,549	873	3,018 D	22.0%	65.4%	25.2%	74.8%
24,935	DE WITT	3,647	1,612	1,808	227	196 D	44.2%	49.6%	47.1%	52.9%
7,847	DICKENS	1,700	115	1,492	93	1,377 D	6.8%	87.8%	7.2%	92.8%
8,542	DIMMIT	1,318	384	863	71	479 D	29.1%	65.5%	30.8%	69.2%
7,487	DONLEY	1,692	241	1,372	79	1,131 D	14.2%	81.1%	14.9%	85.1%
20,565	DUVAL	3,679	117	3,551	11	3,434 D	3.2%	96.5%	3.2%	96.8%
30,345	EASTLAND	6,665	1,177	5,121	367	3,944 D	17.7%	76.8%	18.7%	81.3%
15,051	ECTOR	5,694	1,145	4,305	244	3,160 D	20.1%	75.6%	21.0%	79.0%
2,933	EDWARDS	539	185	329	25	144 D	34.3%	61.0%	36.0%	64.0%
47,733	ELLIS	7,665	1,055	5,792	818	4,737 D	13.8%	75.6%	15.4%	84.6%
131,067	EL PASO	21,448	5,544	15,341	563	9,797 D	25.8%	71.5%	26.5%	73.5%
20,760	ERATH	4,002	598	3,172	232	2,574 D	14.9%	79.3%	15.9%	84.1%
35,984	FALLS	4,218	546	3,385	287	2,839 D	12.9%	80.3%	13.9%	86.1%
41,064	FANNIN	7,065	553	6,132	380	5,579 D	7.8%	86.8%	8.3%	91.7%
29,246	FAYETTE	5,298	1,737	3,106	455	1,369 D	32.8%	58.6%	35.9%	64.1%
12,932	FISHER	2,285	149	2,063	73	1,914 D	6.5%	90.3%	6.7%	93.3%
10,659	FLOYD	2,653	344	2,174	135	1,830 D	13.0%	81.9%	13.7%	86.3%
5,237	FOARD	876	90	751	35	661 D	10.3%	85.7%	10.7%	89.3%
32,963	FORT BEND	3,613	1,016	2,058	539	1,042 D	28.1%	57.0%	33.1%	66.9%
8,378	FRANKLIN	1,527	146	1,236	145	1,090 D	9.6%	80.9%	10.6%	89.4%
21,138	FREESTONE	3,230	460	2,265	505	1,805 D	14.2%	70.1%	16.9%	83.1%
9,207	FRIO	1,341	345	898	98	553 D	25.7%	67.0%	27.8%	72.2%
8,136	GAINES	1,794	207	1,465	122	1,258 D	11.5%	81.7%	12.4%	87.6%
81,173	GALVESTON	18,792	4,857	12,491	1,444	7,634 D	25.8%	66.5%	28.0%	72.0%
5,678	GARZA	1,110	176	861	73	685 D	15.9%	77.6%	17.0%	83.0%
10,670	GILLESPIE	3,413	2,741	593	79	2,148 R	80.3%	17.4%	82.2%	17.8%
1,193	GLASSCOCK	278	69	188	21	119 D	24.8%	67.6%	26.8%	73.2%
8,798	GOLIAD	1,035	450	454	131	4 D	43.5%	43.9%	49.8%	50.2%
26,075	GONZALES	3,599	666	2,612	321	1,946 D	18.5%	72.6%	20.3%	79.7%
23,911	GRAY	5,696	1,594	3,699	403	2,105 D	28.0%	64.9%	30.1%	69.9%
69,499	GRAYSON	14,148	2,174	10,991	983	8,817 D	15.4%	77.7%	16.5%	83.5%
58,027	GREGG	10,565	2,477	5,104	2,984	2,627 D	23.4%	48.3%	32.7%	67.3%
21,960	GRIMES	1,720	336	901	483	565 D	19.5%	52.4%	27.2%	72.8%
25,596	GUADALUPE	4,908	2,502	2,119	287	383 R	51.0%	43.2%	54.1%	45.9%
18,813	HALE	5,310	1,013	3,995	302	2,982 D	19.1%	75.2%	20.2%	79.8%
12,117	HALL	2,376	174	2,122	80	1,948 D	7.3%	89.3%	7.6%	92.4%
13,303	HAMILTON	2,339	478	1,725	136	1,247 D	20.4%	73.7%	21.7%	78.3%
2,783	HANSFORD	1,128	206	895	27	689 D	18.3%	79.3%	18.7%	81.3%
11,073	HARDEMAN	1,976	226	1,654	96	1,428 D	11.4%	83.7%	12.0%	88.0%
15,875	HARDIN	3,043	196	2,233	614	2,037 D	6.4%	73.4%	8.1%	91.9%
528,961	HARRIS	122,617	43,117	58,488	21,012	15,371 D	35.2%	47.7%	42.4%	57.6%
50,900	HARRISON	5,588	946	2,504	2,138	1,558 D	16.9%	44.8%	27.4%	72.6%
1,873	HARTLEY	567	83	477	7	394 D	14.6%	84.1%	14.8%	85.2%
14,905	HASKELL	2,999	181	2,735	83	2,554 D	6.0%	91.2%	6.2%	93.8%
15,349	HAYS	2,987	555	2,239	193	1,684 D	18.6%	75.0%	19.9%	80.1%
4,170	HEMPHILL	1,178	201	930	47	729 D	17.1%	78.9%	17.8%	82.2%
31,822	HENDERSON	4,413	540	3,669	204	3,129 D	12.2%	83.1%	12.8%	87.2%
106,059	HIDALGO	16,018	6,220	9,526	272	3,306 D	38.8%	59.5%	39.5%	60.5%
38,355	HILL	5,395	657	4,362	376	3,705 D	12.2%	80.9%	13.1%	86.9%
12,693	HOCKLEY	3,631	346	3,071	214	2,725 D	9.5%	84.6%	10.1%	89.9%
6,674	HOOD	1,504	169	1,273	62	1,104 D	11.2%	84.6%	11.7%	88.3%
30,274	HOPKINS	4,667	479	3,885	303	3,406 D	10.3%	83.2%	11.0%	89.0%
31,137	HOUSTON	3,104	532	2,014	558	1,482 D	17.1%	64.9%	20.9%	79.1%
20,990	HOWARD	5,052	561	4,179	312	3,618 D	11.1%	82.7%	11.8%	88.2%
3,149	HUDSPETH	498	49	437	12	388 D	9.8%	87.8%	10.1%	89.9%
48,793	HUNT	7,067	1,195	5,082	790	3,887 D	16.9%	71.9%	19.0%	81.0%
19,069	HUTCHINSON	6,009	1,382	4,527	100	3,145 D	23.0%	75.3%	23.4%	76.6%
1,963	IRION	440	63	366	11	303 D	14.3%	83.2%	14.7%	85.3%
10,206	JACK	1,817	265	1,426	126	1,161 D	14.6%	78.5%	15.7%	84.3%
11,720	JACKSON	1,972	488	1,343	141	855 D	24.7%	68.1%	26.7%	73.3%

TEXAS

PRESIDENT 1948

1940 Census Population	County	Total Vote	Republican	Democratic	Other	Rep.-Dem. Plurality	Total Vote Rep.	Total Vote Dem.	Major Vote Rep.	Major Vote Dem.
17,491	JASPER	2,527	284	1,777	466	1,493 D	11.2%	70.3%	13.8%	86.2%
2,375	JEFF DAVIS	402	75	309	18	234 D	18.7%	76.9%	19.5%	80.5%
145,329	JEFFERSON	33,514	5,749	22,475	5,290	16,726 D	17.2%	67.1%	20.4%	79.6%
5,449	JIM HOGG	829	73	725	31	652 D	8.8%	87.5%	9.1%	90.9%
20,239	JIM WELLS	5,299	1,402	3,781	116	2,379 D	26.5%	71.4%	27.0%	73.0%
30,384	JOHNSON	5,202	707	4,042	453	3,335 D	13.6%	77.7%	14.9%	85.1%
23,378	JONES	4,177	432	3,599	146	3,167 D	10.3%	86.2%	10.7%	89.3%
19,248	KARNES	2,971	592	2,198	181	1,606 D	19.9%	74.0%	21.2%	78.8%
38,308	KAUFMAN	4,890	764	3,479	647	2,715 D	15.6%	71.1%	18.0%	82.0%
5,080	KENDALL	1,789	1,207	511	71	696 R	67.5%	28.6%	70.3%	29.7%
700	KENEDY	81	31	45	5	14 D	38.3%	55.6%	40.8%	59.2%
3,413	KENT	534	33	479	22	446 D	6.2%	89.7%	6.4%	93.6%
11,650	KERR	3,204	1,520	1,505	179	15 R	47.4%	47.0%	50.2%	49.8%
5,064	KIMBLE	1,250	303	851	96	548 D	24.2%	68.1%	26.3%	73.7%
1,066	KING	241	6	231	4	225 D	2.5%	95.9%	2.5%	97.5%
4,533	KINNEY	575	175	370	30	195 D	30.4%	64.3%	32.1%	67.9%
13,344	KLEBERG	2,873	697	2,083	93	1,386 D	24.3%	72.5%	25.1%	74.9%
10,090	KNOX	2,008	157	1,792	59	1,635 D	7.8%	89.2%	8.1%	91.9%
50,425	LAMAR	8,365	1,018	6,306	1,041	5,288 D	12.2%	75.4%	13.9%	86.1%
17,606	LAMB	3,947	475	3,286	186	2,811 D	12.0%	83.3%	12.6%	87.4%
9,167	LAMPASAS	1,807	276	1,459	72	1,183 D	15.3%	80.7%	15.9%	84.1%
8,003	LA SALLE	913	135	719	59	584 D	14.8%	78.8%	15.8%	84.2%
25,485	LAVACA	4,511	1,165	3,046	300	1,881 D	25.8%	67.5%	27.7%	72.3%
12,751	LEE	2,122	465	1,540	117	1,075 D	21.9%	72.6%	23.2%	76.8%
17,733	LEON	1,690	184	1,231	275	1,047 D	10.9%	72.8%	13.0%	87.0%
24,541	LIBERTY	3,917	735	2,199	983	1,464 D	18.8%	56.1%	25.1%	74.9%
33,781	LIMESTONE	4,532	688	3,289	555	2,601 D	15.2%	72.6%	17.3%	82.7%
3,764	LIPSCOMB	1,049	354	668	27	314 D	33.7%	63.7%	34.6%	65.4%
9,799	LIVE OAK	1,567	479	945	143	466 D	30.6%	60.3%	33.6%	66.4%
5,996	LLANO	1,680	253	1,384	43	1,131 D	15.1%	82.4%	15.5%	84.5%
285	LOVING	95	29	62	4	33 D	30.5%	65.3%	31.9%	68.1%
51,782	LUBBOCK	15,207	2,837	11,114	1,256	8,277 D	18.7%	73.1%	20.3%	79.7%
11,931	LYNN	2,529	224	2,179	126	1,955 D	8.9%	86.2%	9.3%	90.7%
13,208	MCCULLOCH	2,644	393	2,166	85	1,773 D	14.9%	81.9%	15.4%	84.6%
101,898	MCLENNAN	20,157	3,088	16,034	1,035	12,946 D	15.3%	79.5%	16.1%	83.9%
1,374	MCMULLEN	302	61	222	19	161 D	20.2%	73.5%	21.6%	78.4%
12,029	MADISON	1,134	134	801	199	667 D	11.8%	70.6%	14.3%	85.7%
11,457	MARION	1,082	200	703	179	503 D	18.5%	65.0%	22.1%	77.9%
5,556	MARTIN	1,077	77	945	55	868 D	7.1%	87.7%	7.5%	92.5%
5,378	MASON	1,356	498	836	22	338 D	36.7%	61.7%	37.3%	62.7%
20,066	MATAGORDA	3,299	1,016	1,628	655	612 D	30.8%	49.3%	38.4%	61.6%
10,071	MAVERICK	994	270	695	29	425 D	27.2%	69.9%	28.0%	72.0%
16,106	MEDINA	3,520	1,492	1,875	153	383 D	42.4%	53.3%	44.3%	55.7%
4,521	MENARD	996	283	663	50	380 D	28.4%	66.6%	29.9%	70.1%
11,721	MIDLAND	3,818	1,410	2,032	376	622 D	36.9%	53.2%	41.0%	59.0%
33,120	MILAM	4,292	646	3,261	385	2,615 D	15.1%	76.0%	16.5%	83.5%
7,951	MILLS	1,418	205	1,135	78	930 D	14.5%	80.0%	15.3%	84.7%
12,477	MITCHELL	2,484	230	2,181	73	1,951 D	9.3%	87.8%	9.5%	90.5%
20,442	MONTAGUE	3,557	475	2,872	210	2,397 D	13.4%	80.7%	14.2%	85.8%
23,055	MONTGOMERY	3,338	544	1,795	999	1,251 D	16.3%	53.8%	23.3%	76.7%
4,461	MOORE	2,101	323	1,748	30	1,425 D	15.4%	83.2%	15.6%	84.4%
9,810	MORRIS	1,556	143	1,164	249	1,021 D	9.2%	74.8%	10.9%	89.1%
4,994	MOTLEY	901	75	774	52	699 D	8.3%	85.9%	8.8%	91.2%
35,392	NACOGDOCHES	4,534	833	3,195	506	2,362 D	18.4%	70.5%	20.7%	79.3%
51,308	NAVARRO	6,494	1,188	4,679	627	3,491 D	18.3%	72.1%	20.2%	79.8%
13,700	NEWTON	1,399	110	957	332	847 D	7.9%	68.4%	10.3%	89.7%
17,309	NOLAN	4,069	552	3,408	109	2,856 D	13.6%	83.8%	13.9%	86.1%
92,661	NUECES	21,783	5,577	15,240	966	9,663 D	25.6%	70.0%	26.8%	73.2%
4,213	OCHILTREE	1,403	344	1,025	34	681 D	24.5%	73.1%	25.1%	74.9%
1,385	OLDHAM	458	100	339	19	239 D	21.8%	74.0%	22.8%	77.2%

TEXAS

PRESIDENT 1948

1940 Census Population	County	Total Vote	Republican	Democratic	Other	Rep.-Dem. Plurality	Percentage Total Vote Rep.	Total Vote Dem.	Major Vote Rep.	Major Vote Dem.
17,382	ORANGE	6,813	987	4,957	869	3,970 D	14.5%	72.8%	16.6%	83.4%
18,456	PALO PINTO	5,045	977	3,736	332	2,759 D	19.4%	74.1%	20.7%	79.3%
22,513	PANOLA	2,818	256	1,751	811	1,495 D	9.1%	62.1%	12.8%	87.2%
20,482	PARKER	4,080	806	3,061	213	2,255 D	19.8%	75.0%	20.8%	79.2%
5,890	PARMER	1,421	280	1,091	50	811 D	19.7%	76.8%	20.4%	79.6%
8,185	PECOS	1,801	317	1,430	54	1,113 D	17.6%	79.4%	18.1%	81.9%
20,635	POLK	2,270	317	1,422	531	1,105 D	14.0%	62.6%	18.2%	81.8%
54,265	POTTER	14,222	4,110	9,622	490	5,512 D	28.9%	67.7%	29.9%	70.1%
10,925	PRESIDIO	1,153	212	907	34	695 D	18.4%	78.7%	18.9%	81.1%
7,334	RAINS	944	111	739	94	628 D	11.8%	78.3%	13.1%	86.9%
7,185	RANDALL	2,772	722	1,936	114	1,214 D	26.0%	69.8%	27.2%	72.8%
1,997	REAGAN	579	112	444	23	332 D	19.3%	76.7%	20.1%	79.9%
2,420	REAL	616	156	446	14	290 D	25.3%	72.4%	25.9%	74.1%
29,769	RED RIVER	3,957	323	2,987	647	2,664 D	8.2%	75.5%	9.8%	90.2%
8,006	REEVES	1,789	309	1,383	97	1,074 D	17.3%	77.3%	18.3%	81.7%
10,383	REFUGIO	2,199	489	1,637	73	1,148 D	22.2%	74.4%	23.0%	77.0%
1,289	ROBERTS	418	76	317	25	241 D	18.2%	75.8%	19.3%	80.7%
25,710	ROBERTSON	2,897	246	2,147	504	1,901 D	8.5%	74.1%	10.3%	89.7%
7,051	ROCKWALL	1,252	117	947	188	830 D	9.3%	75.6%	11.0%	89.0%
18,903	RUNNELS	3,615	526	2,954	135	2,428 D	14.6%	81.7%	15.1%	84.9%
51,023	RUSK	7,375	1,294	4,322	1,759	3,028 D	17.5%	58.6%	23.0%	77.0%
10,896	SABINE	1,432	104	1,078	250	974 D	7.3%	75.3%	8.8%	91.2%
12,471	SAN AUGUSTINE	1,265	137	858	270	721 D	10.8%	67.8%	13.8%	86.2%
9,056	SAN JACINTO	774	106	509	159	403 D	13.7%	65.8%	17.2%	82.8%
28,871	SAN PATRICIO	3,823	963	2,649	211	1,686 D	25.2%	69.3%	26.7%	73.3%
11,012	SAN SABA	2,303	184	2,050	69	1,866 D	8.0%	89.0%	8.2%	91.8%
3,083	SCHLEICHER	645	107	495	43	388 D	16.6%	76.7%	17.8%	82.2%
11,545	SCURRY	2,308	201	2,040	67	1,839 D	8.7%	88.4%	9.0%	91.0%
6,211	SHACKELFORD	1,146	211	892	43	681 D	18.4%	77.8%	19.1%	80.9%
29,235	SHELBY	4,036	307	3,051	678	2,744 D	7.6%	75.6%	9.1%	90.9%
2,026	SHERMAN	592	98	479	15	381 D	16.6%	80.9%	17.0%	83.0%
69,090	SMITH	11,309	3,181	6,473	1,655	3,292 D	28.1%	57.2%	33.0%	67.0%
3,071	SOMERVELL	583	91	446	46	355 D	15.6%	76.5%	16.9%	83.1%
13,312	STARR	2,188	179	1,996	13	1,817 D	8.2%	91.2%	8.2%	91.8%
12,356	STEPHENS	2,890	572	2,132	186	1,560 D	19.8%	73.8%	21.2%	78.8%
1,404	STERLING	268	17	244	7	227 D	6.3%	91.0%	6.5%	93.5%
5,589	STONEWALL	1,064	65	968	31	903 D	6.1%	91.0%	6.3%	93.7%
3,977	SUTTON	622	131	433	58	302 D	21.1%	69.6%	23.2%	76.8%
6,528	SWISHER	2,042	307	1,670	65	1,363 D	15.0%	81.8%	15.5%	84.5%
225,521	TARRANT	60,739	17,157	36,325	7,257	19,168 D	28.2%	59.8%	32.1%	67.9%
44,147	TAYLOR	10,373	1,658	8,184	531	6,526 D	16.0%	78.9%	16.8%	83.2%
2,952	TERRELL	265	78	171	16	93 D	29.4%	64.5%	31.3%	68.7%
11,160	TERRY	2,685	236	2,283	166	2,047 D	8.8%	85.0%	9.4%	90.6%
4,275	THROCKMORTON	1,120	63	1,026	31	963 D	5.6%	91.6%	5.8%	94.2%
19,228	TITUS	3,055	379	2,339	337	1,960 D	12.4%	76.6%	13.9%	86.1%
39,302	TOM GREEN	9,116	1,822	6,777	517	4,955 D	20.0%	74.3%	21.2%	78.8%
111,053	TRAVIS	27,207	5,994	19,598	1,615	13,604 D	22.0%	72.0%	23.4%	76.6%
13,705	TRINITY	1,315	150	905	260	755 D	11.4%	68.8%	14.2%	85.8%
11,948	TYLER	1,551	177	895	479	718 D	11.4%	57.7%	16.5%	83.5%
26,178	UPSHUR	3,165	555	2,118	492	1,563 D	17.5%	66.9%	20.8%	79.2%
4,297	UPTON	1,024	155	811	58	656 D	15.1%	79.2%	16.0%	84.0%
13,246	UVALDE	2,545	866	1,550	129	684 D	34.0%	60.9%	35.8%	64.2%
15,453	VAL VERDE	1,978	672	1,242	64	570 D	34.0%	62.8%	35.1%	64.9%
31,155	VAN ZANDT	4,350	578	3,264	508	2,686 D	13.3%	75.0%	15.0%	85.0%
23,741	VICTORIA	4,042	1,262	2,435	345	1,173 D	31.2%	60.2%	34.1%	65.9%
19,868	WALKER	2,564	570	1,439	555	869 D	22.2%	56.1%	28.4%	71.6%
10,280	WALLER	1,634	448	812	374	364 D	27.4%	49.7%	35.6%	64.4%
9,575	WARD	2,658	414	2,119	125	1,705 D	15.6%	79.7%	16.3%	83.7%
25,387	WASHINGTON	3,742	1,904	1,647	191	257 R	50.9%	44.0%	53.6%	46.4%
45,916	WEBB	5,695	1,004	4,595	96	3,591 D	17.6%	80.7%	17.9%	82.1%

TEXAS

PRESIDENT 1948

1940 Census Population	County	Total Vote	Republican	Democratic	Other	Rep.-Dem. Plurality	Percentage Total Vote Rep.	Percentage Total Vote Dem.	Percentage Major Vote Rep.	Percentage Major Vote Dem.
36,158	WHARTON	4,685	1,354	2,811	520	1,457 D	28.9%	60.0%	32.5%	67.5%
12,411	WHEELER	2,460	370	2,010	80	1,640 D	15.0%	81.7%	15.5%	84.5%
73,604	WICHITA	15,866	2,887	12,235	744	9,348 D	18.2%	77.1%	19.1%	80.9%
20,474	WILBARGER	3,800	529	2,963	308	2,434 D	13.9%	78.0%	15.1%	84.9%
13,230	WILLACY	1,924	676	1,139	109	463 D	35.1%	59.2%	37.2%	62.8%
41,698	WILLIAMSON	7,026	1,094	5,638	294	4,544 D	15.6%	80.2%	16.3%	83.7%
17,066	WILSON	3,020	593	2,313	114	1,720 D	19.6%	76.6%	20.4%	79.6%
6,141	WINKLER	1,983	296	1,588	99	1,292 D	14.9%	80.1%	15.7%	84.3%
19,074	WISE	3,778	448	3,064	266	2,616 D	11.9%	81.1%	12.8%	87.2%
24,360	WOOD	3,885	629	2,590	666	1,961 D	16.2%	66.7%	19.5%	80.5%
5,354	YOAKUM	1,020	119	861	40	742 D	11.7%	84.4%	12.1%	87.9%
19,004	YOUNG	3,898	516	3,175	207	2,659 D	13.2%	81.5%	14.0%	86.0%
3,916	ZAPATA	1,047	414	632	1	218 D	39.5%	60.4%	39.6%	60.4%
11,603	ZAVALA	986	306	618	62	312 D	31.0%	62.7%	33.1%	66.9%
6,414,824	TOTAL	1,249,577	303,467	824,235	121,875	520,768 D	24.3%	66.0%	26.9%	73.1%

TEXAS

PRESIDENT 1944

1940 Census Population	County	Total Vote	Republican	Democratic	Other	Rep.-Dem. Plurality	Percentage Total Vote Rep.	Total Vote Dem.	Major Vote Rep.	Major Vote Dem.
37,092	ANDERSON	5,474	467	4,342	665	3,875 D	8.5%	79.3%	9.7%	90.3%
1,277	ANDREWS	404	48	329	27	281 D	11.9%	81.4%	12.7%	87.3%
32,201	ANGELINA	5,898	1,001	4,387	510	3,386 D	17.0%	74.4%	18.6%	81.4%
3,469	ARANSAS	621	150	456	15	306 D	24.2%	73.4%	24.8%	75.2%
7,599	ARCHER	2,097	194	1,674	229	1,480 D	9.3%	79.8%	10.4%	89.6%
2,495	ARMSTRONG	800	132	623	45	491 D	16.5%	77.9%	17.5%	82.5%
19,275	ATASCOSA	2,646	685	1,757	204	1,072 D	25.9%	66.4%	28.1%	71.9%
17,384	AUSTIN	3,184	619	1,316	1,249	697 D	19.4%	41.3%	32.0%	68.0%
6,318	BAILEY	1,458	358	943	157	585 D	24.6%	64.7%	27.5%	72.5%
4,234	BANDERA	1,258	634	532	92	102 R	50.4%	42.3%	54.4%	45.6%
21,610	BASTROP	3,289	385	2,604	300	2,219 D	11.7%	79.2%	12.9%	87.1%
7,755	BAYLOR	1,789	102	1,568	119	1,466 D	5.7%	87.6%	6.1%	93.9%
16,481	BEE	2,411	848	1,306	257	458 D	35.2%	54.2%	39.4%	60.6%
44,863	BELL	8,955	763	6,960	1,232	6,197 D	8.5%	77.7%	9.9%	90.1%
338,176	BEXAR	60,427	23,588	35,024	1,815	11,436 D	39.0%	58.0%	40.2%	59.8%
4,264	BLANCO	1,512	533	846	133	313 D	35.3%	56.0%	38.7%	61.3%
1,396	BORDEN	308	34	237	37	203 D	11.0%	76.9%	12.5%	87.5%
15,761	BOSQUE	3,335	504	2,502	329	1,998 D	15.1%	75.0%	16.8%	83.2%
50,208	BOWIE	8,902	790	7,045	1,067	6,255 D	8.9%	79.1%	10.1%	89.9%
27,069	BRAZORIA	7,691	850	5,543	1,298	4,693 D	11.1%	72.1%	13.3%	86.7%
26,977	BRAZOS	4,375	464	3,358	553	2,894 D	10.6%	76.8%	12.1%	87.9%
6,478	BREWSTER	1,186	237	864	85	627 D	20.0%	72.8%	21.5%	78.5%
4,056	BRISCOE	828	80	615	133	535 D	9.7%	74.3%	11.5%	88.5%
6,362	BROOKS	635	142	403	90	261 D	22.4%	63.5%	26.1%	73.9%
25,924	BROWN	3,544	430	2,426	688	1,996 D	12.1%	68.5%	15.1%	84.9%
18,334	BURLESON	2,407	158	1,992	257	1,834 D	6.6%	82.8%	7.3%	92.7%
10,771	BURNET	2,112	228	1,697	187	1,469 D	10.8%	80.4%	11.8%	88.2%
24,893	CALDWELL	3,888	704	2,916	268	2,212 D	18.1%	75.0%	19.4%	80.6%
5,911	CALHOUN	1,073	158	732	183	574 D	14.7%	68.2%	17.8%	82.2%
11,568	CALLAHAN	2,463	224	1,962	277	1,738 D	9.1%	79.7%	10.2%	89.8%
83,202	CAMERON	11,846	5,309	5,998	539	689 D	44.8%	50.6%	47.0%	53.0%
10,285	CAMP	1,368	180	977	211	797 D	13.2%	71.4%	15.6%	84.4%
6,624	CARSON	1,763	446	1,216	101	770 D	25.3%	69.0%	26.8%	73.2%
33,496	CASS	3,742	541	2,866	335	2,325 D	14.5%	76.6%	15.9%	84.1%
4,631	CASTRO	1,203	222	838	143	616 D	18.5%	69.7%	20.9%	79.1%
7,511	CHAMBERS	1,329	179	1,038	112	859 D	13.5%	78.1%	14.7%	85.3%
43,970	CHEROKEE	5,146	598	3,918	630	3,320 D	11.6%	76.1%	13.2%	86.8%
12,149	CHILDRESS	2,797	299	2,295	203	1,996 D	10.7%	82.1%	11.5%	88.5%
12,524	CLAY	2,980	311	2,307	362	1,996 D	10.4%	77.4%	11.9%	88.1%
3,735	COCHRAN	1,000	123	716	161	593 D	12.3%	71.6%	14.7%	85.3%
4,590	COKE	959	65	824	70	759 D	6.8%	85.9%	7.3%	92.7%
20,571	COLEMAN	3,704	498	2,887	319	2,389 D	13.4%	77.9%	14.7%	85.3%
47,190	COLLIN	8,344	974	6,574	796	5,600 D	11.7%	78.8%	12.9%	87.1%
10,331	COLLINGSWORTH	2,162	261	1,725	176	1,464 D	12.1%	79.8%	13.1%	86.9%
17,812	COLORADO	3,098	638	1,517	943	879 D	20.6%	49.0%	29.6%	70.4%
12,321	COMAL	2,989	2,021	787	181	1,234 R	67.6%	26.3%	72.0%	28.0%
19,245	COMANCHE	3,787	356	2,941	490	2,585 D	9.4%	77.7%	10.8%	89.2%
6,192	CONCHO	1,364	151	1,090	123	939 D	11.1%	79.9%	12.2%	87.8%
24,909	COOKE	4,938	919	3,270	749	2,351 D	18.6%	66.2%	21.9%	78.1%
20,226	CORYELL	3,159	413	2,518	228	2,105 D	13.1%	79.7%	14.1%	85.9%
7,079	COTTLE	2,776	130	2,551	95	2,421 D	4.7%	91.9%	4.8%	95.2%
2,841	CRANE	639	58	552	29	494 D	9.1%	86.4%	9.5%	90.5%
2,809	CROCKETT	492	112	323	57	211 D	22.8%	65.7%	25.7%	74.3%
10,046	CROSBY	2,127	201	1,691	235	1,490 D	9.4%	79.5%	10.6%	89.4%
1,653	CULBERSON	251	17	200	34	183 D	6.8%	79.7%	7.8%	92.2%
6,494	DALLAM	1,610	323	1,118	169	795 D	20.1%	69.4%	22.4%	77.6%
398,564	DALLAS	94,036	21,099	60,909	12,028	39,810 D	22.4%	64.8%	25.7%	74.3%
15,367	DAWSON	2,872	472	2,149	251	1,677 D	16.4%	74.8%	18.0%	82.0%
6,056	DEAF SMITH	1,805	508	1,117	180	609 D	28.1%	61.9%	31.3%	68.7%
12,858	DELTA	1,987	133	1,706	148	1,573 D	6.7%	85.9%	7.2%	92.8%

TEXAS

PRESIDENT 1944

1940 Census Population	County	Total Vote	Republican	Democratic	Other	Rep.-Dem. Plurality	Percentage Total Vote Rep.	Total Vote Dem.	Major Vote Rep.	Major Vote Dem.
33,658	DENTON	7,110	771	5,584	755	4,813 D	10.8%	78.5%	12.1%	87.9%
24,935	DE WITT	4,187	1,879	1,884	424	5 D	44.9%	45.0%	49.9%	50.1%
7,847	DICKENS	1,879	141	1,617	121	1,476 D	7.5%	86.1%	8.0%	92.0%
8,542	DIMMIT	977	328	554	95	226 D	33.6%	56.7%	37.2%	62.8%
7,487	DONLEY	1,562	280	1,170	112	890 D	17.9%	74.9%	19.3%	80.7%
20,565	DUVAL	3,518	136	3,353	29	3,217 D	3.9%	95.3%	3.9%	96.1%
30,345	EASTLAND	6,072	643	4,607	822	3,964 D	10.6%	75.9%	12.2%	87.8%
15,051	ECTOR	3,091	432	2,265	394	1,833 D	14.0%	73.3%	16.0%	84.0%
2,933	EDWARDS	586	187	348	51	161 D	31.9%	59.4%	35.0%	65.0%
47,733	ELLIS	8,304	666	7,065	573	6,399 D	8.0%	85.1%	8.6%	91.4%
131,067	EL PASO	15,718	2,072	11,426	2,220	9,354 D	13.2%	72.7%	15.4%	84.6%
20,760	ERATH	4,171	411	3,330	430	2,919 D	9.9%	79.8%	11.0%	89.0%
35,984	FALLS	4,219	377	3,191	651	2,814 D	8.9%	75.6%	10.6%	89.4%
41,064	FANNIN	7,163	677	5,984	502	5,307 D	9.5%	83.5%	10.2%	89.8%
29,246	FAYETTE	6,030	1,611	3,156	1,263	1,545 D	26.7%	52.3%	33.8%	66.2%
12,932	FISHER	2,332	154	2,041	137	1,887 D	6.6%	87.5%	7.0%	93.0%
10,659	FLOYD	2,448	370	1,756	322	1,386 D	15.1%	71.7%	17.4%	82.6%
5,237	FOARD	1,080	84	925	71	841 D	7.8%	85.6%	8.3%	91.7%
32,963	FORT BEND	3,980	442	2,781	757	2,339 D	11.1%	69.9%	13.7%	86.3%
8,378	FRANKLIN	1,601	147	1,336	118	1,189 D	9.2%	83.4%	9.9%	90.1%
21,138	FREESTONE	3,022	277	2,427	318	2,150 D	9.2%	80.3%	10.2%	89.8%
9,207	FRIO	1,369	293	951	125	658 D	21.4%	69.5%	23.6%	76.4%
8,136	GAINES	1,471	173	1,173	125	1,000 D	11.8%	79.7%	12.9%	87.1%
81,173	GALVESTON	15,074	1,542	11,748	1,784	10,206 D	10.2%	77.9%	11.6%	88.4%
5,678	GARZA	1,159	144	842	173	698 D	12.4%	72.6%	14.6%	85.4%
10,670	GILLESPIE	3,573	2,950	333	290	2,617 R	82.6%	9.3%	89.9%	10.1%
1,193	GLASSCOCK	269	34	185	50	151 D	12.6%	68.8%	15.5%	84.5%
8,798	GOLIAD	1,348	609	641	98	32 D	45.2%	47.6%	48.7%	51.3%
26,075	GONZALES	3,987	841	2,804	342	1,963 D	21.1%	70.3%	23.1%	76.9%
23,911	GRAY	4,989	1,739	3,067	183	1,328 D	34.9%	61.5%	36.2%	63.8%
69,499	GRAYSON	14,070	1,372	11,636	1,062	10,264 D	9.8%	82.7%	10.5%	89.5%
58,027	GREGG	9,077	1,412	6,401	1,264	4,989 D	15.6%	70.5%	18.1%	81.9%
21,960	GRIMES	1,970	137	1,559	274	1,422 D	7.0%	79.1%	8.1%	91.9%
25,596	GUADALUPE	4,343	2,556	1,583	204	973 R	58.9%	36.4%	61.8%	38.2%
18,813	HALE	4,379	712	3,066	601	2,354 D	16.3%	70.0%	18.8%	81.2%
12,117	HALL	2,108	164	1,812	132	1,648 D	7.8%	86.0%	8.3%	91.7%
13,303	HAMILTON	2,499	344	1,790	365	1,446 D	13.8%	71.6%	16.1%	83.9%
2,783	HANSFORD	842	203	590	49	387 D	24.1%	70.1%	25.6%	74.4%
11,073	HARDEMAN	2,173	223	1,756	194	1,533 D	10.3%	80.8%	11.3%	88.7%
15,875	HARDIN	3,126	243	2,632	251	2,389 D	7.8%	84.2%	8.5%	91.5%
528,961	HARRIS	104,119	11,843	71,077	21,199	59,234 D	11.4%	68.3%	14.3%	85.7%
50,900	HARRISON	5,009	619	3,588	802	2,969 D	12.4%	71.6%	14.7%	85.3%
1,873	HARTLEY	520	26	484	10	458 D	5.0%	93.1%	5.1%	94.9%
14,905	HASKELL	3,083	261	2,573	249	2,312 D	8.5%	83.5%	9.2%	90.8%
15,349	HAYS	2,428	495	1,690	243	1,195 D	20.4%	69.6%	22.7%	77.3%
4,170	HEMPHILL	1,143	274	792	77	518 D	24.0%	69.3%	25.7%	74.3%
31,822	HENDERSON	4,220	427	3,219	574	2,792 D	10.1%	76.3%	11.7%	88.3%
106,059	HIDALGO	12,234	4,080	7,250	904	3,170 D	33.3%	59.3%	36.0%	64.0%
38,355	HILL	5,984	516	4,876	592	4,360 D	8.6%	81.5%	9.6%	90.4%
12,693	HOCKLEY	3,367	319	2,641	407	2,322 D	9.5%	78.4%	10.8%	89.2%
6,674	HOOD	1,472	146	1,203	123	1,057 D	9.9%	81.7%	10.8%	89.2%
30,274	HOPKINS	4,876	533	3,981	362	3,448 D	10.9%	81.6%	11.8%	88.2%
31,137	HOUSTON	3,146	233	2,329	584	2,096 D	7.4%	74.0%	9.1%	90.9%
20,990	HOWARD	4,334	334	3,588	412	3,254 D	7.7%	82.8%	8.5%	91.5%
3,149	HUDSPETH	396	35	333	28	298 D	8.8%	84.1%	9.5%	90.5%
48,793	HUNT	8,037	714	6,200	1,123	5,486 D	8.9%	77.1%	10.3%	89.7%
19,069	HUTCHINSON	3,826	864	2,760	202	1,896 D	22.6%	72.1%	23.8%	76.2%
1,963	IRION	453	54	363	36	309 D	11.9%	80.1%	12.9%	87.1%
10,206	JACK	1,964	217	1,484	263	1,267 D	11.0%	75.6%	12.8%	87.2%
11,720	JACKSON	2,296	344	1,708	244	1,364 D	15.0%	74.4%	16.8%	83.2%

TEXAS

PRESIDENT 1944

1940 Census Population	County	Total Vote	Republican	Democratic	Other	Rep.-Dem. Plurality	Percentage Total Vote Rep.	Percentage Total Vote Dem.	Percentage Major Vote Rep.	Percentage Major Vote Dem.
17,491	JASPER	2,427	341	1,850	236	1,509 D	14.1%	76.2%	15.6%	84.4%
2,375	JEFF DAVIS	417	51	331	35	280 D	12.2%	79.4%	13.4%	86.6%
145,329	JEFFERSON	29,080	4,525	22,066	2,489	17,541 D	15.6%	75.9%	17.0%	83.0%
5,449	JIM HOGG	713	77	620	16	543 D	10.8%	87.0%	11.0%	89.0%
20,239	JIM WELLS	3,191	1,113	1,908	170	795 D	34.9%	59.8%	36.8%	63.2%
30,384	JOHNSON	5,896	546	4,757	593	4,211 D	9.3%	80.7%	10.3%	89.7%
23,378	JONES	4,117	361	3,417	339	3,056 D	8.8%	83.0%	9.6%	90.4%
19,248	KARNES	2,856	692	1,920	244	1,228 D	24.2%	67.2%	26.5%	73.5%
38,308	KAUFMAN	5,136	430	4,251	455	3,821 D	8.4%	82.8%	9.2%	90.8%
5,080	KENDALL	1,762	1,337	309	116	1,028 R	75.9%	17.5%	81.2%	18.8%
700	KENEDY	82	60	16	6	44 R	73.2%	19.5%	78.9%	21.1%
3,413	KENT	658	31	572	55	541 D	4.7%	86.9%	5.1%	94.9%
11,650	KERR	2,943	1,358	1,377	208	19 D	46.1%	46.8%	49.7%	50.3%
5,064	KIMBLE	1,247	225	880	142	655 D	18.0%	70.6%	20.4%	79.6%
1,066	KING	256	13	228	15	215 D	5.1%	89.1%	5.4%	94.6%
4,533	KINNEY	602	200	401	1	201 D	33.2%	66.6%	33.3%	66.7%
13,344	KLEBERG	1,957	421	1,473	63	1,052 D	21.5%	75.3%	22.2%	77.8%
10,090	KNOX	2,142	156	1,785	201	1,629 D	7.3%	83.3%	8.0%	92.0%
50,425	LAMAR	7,747	725	6,283	739	5,558 D	9.4%	81.1%	10.3%	89.7%
17,606	LAMB	3,444	616	2,407	421	1,791 D	17.9%	69.9%	20.4%	79.6%
9,167	LAMPASAS	2,066	212	1,693	161	1,481 D	10.3%	81.9%	11.1%	88.9%
8,003	LA SALLE	860	127	692	41	565 D	14.8%	80.5%	15.5%	84.5%
25,485	LAVACA	4,955	960	3,406	589	2,446 D	19.4%	68.7%	22.0%	78.0%
12,751	LEE	2,196	771	953	472	182 D	35.1%	43.4%	44.7%	55.3%
17,733	LEON	1,898	140	1,569	189	1,429 D	7.4%	82.7%	8.2%	91.8%
24,541	LIBERTY	3,455	336	2,561	558	2,225 D	9.7%	74.1%	11.6%	88.4%
33,781	LIMESTONE	5,058	239	4,299	520	4,060 D	4.7%	85.0%	5.3%	94.7%
3,764	LIPSCOMB	1,032	396	551	85	155 D	38.4%	53.4%	41.8%	58.2%
9,799	LIVE OAK	1,405	548	642	215	94 D	39.0%	45.7%	46.1%	53.9%
5,996	LLANO	1,538	198	1,199	141	1,001 D	12.9%	78.0%	14.2%	85.8%
285	LOVING	84	18	60	6	42 D	21.4%	71.4%	23.1%	76.9%
51,782	LUBBOCK	10,856	1,169	7,654	2,033	6,485 D	10.8%	70.5%	13.2%	86.8%
11,931	LYNN	2,493	263	1,968	262	1,705 D	10.5%	78.9%	11.8%	88.2%
13,208	MCCULLOCH	2,804	463	2,088	253	1,625 D	16.5%	74.5%	18.1%	81.9%
101,898	MCLENNAN	18,631	1,668	15,336	1,627	13,668 D	9.0%	82.3%	9.8%	90.2%
1,374	MCMULLEN	375	106	223	46	117 D	28.3%	59.5%	32.2%	67.8%
12,029	MADISON	1,307	65	1,115	127	1,050 D	5.0%	85.3%	5.5%	94.5%
11,457	MARION	1,381	219	1,057	105	838 D	15.9%	76.5%	17.2%	82.8%
5,556	MARTIN	986	131	758	97	627 D	13.3%	76.9%	14.7%	85.3%
5,378	MASON	1,496	420	822	254	402 D	28.1%	54.9%	33.8%	66.2%
20,066	MATAGORDA	3,067	412	1,854	801	1,442 D	13.4%	60.4%	18.2%	81.8%
10,071	MAVERICK	1,122	302	787	33	485 D	26.9%	70.1%	27.7%	72.3%
16,106	MEDINA	3,389	1,607	1,469	313	138 R	47.4%	43.3%	52.2%	47.8%
4,521	MENARD	1,122	96	776	250	680 D	8.6%	69.2%	11.0%	89.0%
11,721	MIDLAND	2,929	302	1,688	939	1,386 D	10.3%	57.6%	15.2%	84.8%
33,120	MILAM	4,974	623	3,537	814	2,914 D	12.5%	71.1%	15.0%	85.0%
7,951	MILLS	1,817	172	1,428	217	1,256 D	9.5%	78.6%	10.8%	89.3%
12,477	MITCHELL	2,573	218	2,215	140	1,997 D	8.5%	86.1%	9.0%	91.0%
20,442	MONTAGUE	3,710	429	2,900	381	2,471 D	11.6%	78.2%	12.9%	87.1%
23,055	MONTGOMERY	3,620	219	2,902	499	2,683 D	6.0%	80.2%	7.0%	93.0%
4,461	MOORE	1,394	313	999	82	686 D	22.5%	71.7%	23.9%	76.1%
9,810	MORRIS	1,476	122	1,269	85	1,147 D	8.3%	86.0%	8.8%	91.2%
4,994	MOTLEY	935	107	744	84	637 D	11.4%	79.6%	12.6%	87.4%
35,392	NACOGDOCHES	4,182	319	3,226	637	2,907 D	7.6%	77.1%	9.0%	91.0%
51,308	NAVARRO	7,401	449	6,298	654	5,849 D	6.1%	85.1%	6.7%	93.3%
13,700	NEWTON	1,224	187	910	127	723 D	15.3%	74.3%	17.0%	83.0%
17,309	NOLAN	3,747	322	3,071	354	2,749 D	8.6%	82.0%	9.5%	90.5%
92,661	NUECES	15,773	3,819	11,091	863	7,272 D	24.2%	70.3%	25.6%	74.4%
4,213	OCHILTREE	1,309	307	863	139	556 D	23.5%	65.9%	26.2%	73.8%
1,385	OLDHAM	409	93	277	39	184 D	22.7%	67.7%	25.1%	74.9%

TEXAS

PRESIDENT 1944

1940 Census Population	County	Total Vote	Republican	Democratic	Other	Rep.-Dem. Plurality	Percentage Total Vote Rep.	Percentage Total Vote Dem.	Percentage Major Vote Rep.	Percentage Major Vote Dem.
17,382	ORANGE	5,840	910	4,500	430	3,590 D	15.6%	77.1%	16.8%	83.2%
18,456	PALO PINTO	4,126	416	3,291	419	2,875 D	10.1%	79.8%	11.2%	88.8%
22,513	PANOLA	2,502	221	2,106	175	1,885 D	8.8%	84.2%	9.5%	90.5%
20,482	PARKER	4,555	559	3,503	493	2,944 D	12.3%	76.9%	13.8%	86.2%
5,890	PARMER	1,384	415	810	159	395 D	30.0%	58.5%	33.9%	66.1%
8,185	PECOS	1,653	305	1,226	122	921 D	18.5%	74.2%	19.9%	80.1%
20,635	POLK	2,254	154	1,817	283	1,663 D	6.8%	80.6%	7.8%	92.2%
54,265	POTTER	10,084	2,759	6,519	806	3,760 D	27.4%	64.6%	29.7%	70.3%
10,925	PRESIDIO	1,024	211	648	165	437 D	20.6%	63.3%	24.6%	75.4%
7,334	RAINS	916	137	628	151	491 D	15.0%	68.6%	17.9%	82.1%
7,185	RANDALL	2,115	409	1,439	267	1,030 D	19.3%	68.0%	22.1%	77.9%
1,997	REAGAN	520	53	426	41	373 D	10.2%	81.9%	11.1%	88.9%
2,420	REAL	549	163	326	60	163 D	29.7%	59.4%	33.3%	66.7%
29,769	RED RIVER	3,823	466	2,991	366	2,525 D	12.2%	78.2%	13.5%	86.5%
8,006	REEVES	1,510	201	1,157	152	956 D	13.3%	76.6%	14.8%	85.2%
10,383	REFUGIO	1,468	376	991	101	615 D	25.6%	67.5%	27.5%	72.5%
1,289	ROBERTS	418	89	289	40	200 D	21.3%	69.1%	23.5%	76.5%
25,710	ROBERTSON	3,042	126	2,681	235	2,555 D	4.1%	88.1%	4.5%	95.5%
7,051	ROCKWALL	1,358	98	1,153	107	1,055 D	7.2%	84.9%	7.8%	92.2%
18,903	RUNNELS	3,787	685	2,657	445	1,972 D	18.1%	70.2%	20.5%	79.5%
51,023	RUSK	6,844	637	5,232	975	4,595 D	9.3%	76.4%	10.9%	89.1%
10,896	SABINE	1,449	203	1,169	77	966 D	14.0%	80.7%	14.8%	85.2%
12,471	SAN AUGUSTINE	1,278	102	1,176		1,074 D	8.0%	92.0%	8.0%	92.0%
9,056	SAN JACINTO	720	53	522	145	469 D	7.4%	72.5%	9.2%	90.8%
28,871	SAN PATRICIO	3,841	878	2,712	251	1,834 D	22.9%	70.6%	24.5%	75.5%
11,012	SAN SABA	2,393	177	2,109	107	1,932 D	7.4%	88.1%	7.7%	92.3%
3,083	SCHLEICHER	695	84	520	91	436 D	12.1%	74.8%	13.9%	86.1%
11,545	SCURRY	2,176	285	1,761	130	1,476 D	13.1%	80.9%	13.9%	86.1%
6,211	SHACKELFORD	1,339	135	1,007	197	872 D	10.1%	75.2%	11.8%	88.2%
29,235	SHELBY	3,564	428	2,927	209	2,499 D	12.0%	82.1%	12.8%	87.2%
2,026	SHERMAN	584	97	454	33	357 D	16.6%	77.7%	17.6%	82.4%
69,090	SMITH	9,538	936	6,671	1,931	5,735 D	9.8%	69.9%	12.3%	87.7%
3,071	SOMERVELL	621	87	406	128	319 D	14.0%	65.4%	17.6%	82.4%
13,312	STARR	1,395	68	1,312	15	1,244 D	4.9%	94.1%	4.9%	95.1%
12,356	STEPHENS	2,804	217	2,104	483	1,887 D	7.7%	75.0%	9.3%	90.7%
1,404	STERLING	358	18	330	10	312 D	5.0%	92.2%	5.2%	94.8%
5,589	STONEWALL	1,080	89	902	89	813 D	8.2%	83.5%	9.0%	91.0%
3,977	SUTTON	636	118	449	69	331 D	18.6%	70.6%	20.8%	79.2%
6,528	SWISHER	1,819	331	1,275	213	944 D	18.2%	70.1%	20.6%	79.4%
225,521	TARRANT	51,065	4,113	36,791	10,161	32,678 D	8.1%	72.0%	10.1%	89.9%
44,147	TAYLOR	9,742	602	7,975	1,165	7,373 D	6.2%	81.9%	7.0%	93.0%
2,952	TERRELL	504	156	329	19	173 D	31.0%	65.3%	32.2%	67.8%
11,160	TERRY	2,780	273	2,304	203	2,031 D	9.8%	82.9%	10.6%	89.4%
4,275	THROCKMORTON	1,184	76	970	138	894 D	6.4%	81.9%	7.3%	92.7%
19,228	TITUS	3,107	265	2,612	230	2,347 D	8.5%	84.1%	9.2%	90.8%
39,302	TOM GREEN	8,306	1,125	6,272	909	5,147 D	13.5%	75.5%	15.2%	84.8%
111,053	TRAVIS	19,230	2,324	14,384	2,522	12,060 D	12.1%	74.8%	13.9%	86.1%
13,705	TRINITY	1,548	127	1,132	289	1,005 D	8.2%	73.1%	10.1%	89.9%
11,948	TYLER	1,421	219	1,037	165	818 D	15.4%	73.0%	17.4%	82.6%
26,178	UPSHUR	3,369	446	2,369	554	1,923 D	13.2%	70.3%	15.8%	84.2%
4,297	UPTON	915	105	742	68	637 D	11.5%	81.1%	12.4%	87.6%
13,246	UVALDE	2,356	856	1,322	178	466 D	36.3%	56.1%	39.3%	60.7%
15,453	VAL VERDE	1,985	676	1,210	99	534 D	34.1%	61.0%	35.8%	64.2%
31,155	VAN ZANDT	4,205	503	3,139	563	2,636 D	12.0%	74.6%	13.8%	86.2%
23,741	VICTORIA	3,684	936	2,331	417	1,395 D	25.4%	63.3%	28.7%	71.3%
19,868	WALKER	2,037	145	1,638	254	1,493 D	7.1%	80.4%	8.1%	91.9%
10,280	WALLER	1,436	190	1,007	239	817 D	13.2%	70.1%	15.9%	84.1%
9,575	WARD	1,819	268	1,448	103	1,180 D	14.7%	79.6%	15.6%	84.4%
25,387	WASHINGTON	4,025	534	1,387	2,104	853 D	13.3%	34.5%	27.8%	72.2%
45,916	WEBB	5,571	776	4,742	53	3,966 D	13.9%	85.1%	14.1%	85.9%

TEXAS

PRESIDENT 1944

1940 Census Population	County	Total Vote	Republican	Democratic	Other	Rep.-Dem. Plurality	Percentage Total Vote Rep.	Percentage Total Vote Dem.	Percentage Major Vote Rep.	Percentage Major Vote Dem.
36,158	WHARTON	5,042	529	3,754	759	3,225 D	10.5%	74.5%	12.4%	87.6%
12,411	WHEELER	2,615	511	1,869	235	1,358 D	19.5%	71.5%	21.5%	78.5%
73,604	WICHITA	14,616	1,597	11,392	1,627	9,795 D	10.9%	77.9%	12.3%	87.7%
20,474	WILBARGER	4,419	517	3,382	520	2,865 D	11.7%	76.5%	13.3%	86.7%
13,230	WILLACY	1,737	754	846	137	92 D	43.4%	48.7%	47.1%	52.9%
41,698	WILLIAMSON	7,431	1,239	5,284	908	4,045 D	16.7%	71.1%	19.0%	81.0%
17,066	WILSON	3,533	676	2,666	191	1,990 D	19.1%	75.5%	20.2%	79.8%
6,141	WINKLER	1,193	120	1,004	69	884 D	10.1%	84.2%	10.7%	89.3%
19,074	WISE	3,979	444	3,114	421	2,670 D	11.2%	78.3%	12.5%	87.5%
24,360	WOOD	4,041	485	3,045	511	2,560 D	12.0%	75.4%	13.7%	86.3%
5,354	YOAKUM	839	106	646	87	540 D	12.6%	77.0%	14.1%	85.9%
19,004	YOUNG	4,114	327	3,183	604	2,856 D	7.9%	77.4%	9.3%	90.7%
3,916	ZAPATA	547	43	501	3	458 D	7.9%	91.6%	7.9%	92.1%
11,603	ZAVALA	1,129	342	696	91	354 D	30.3%	61.6%	32.9%	67.1%
6,414,824	TOTAL	1,150,334	191,423	821,605	137,306	630,182 D	16.6%	71.4%	18.9%	81.1%

TEXAS

PRESIDENT 1940

1940 Census Population	County	Total Vote	Republican	Democratic	Other	Rep.-Dem. Plurality	Percentage Total Vote Rep.	Total Vote Dem.	Major Vote Rep.	Major Vote Dem.
37,092	ANDERSON	5,976	688	5,281	7	4,593 D	11.5%	88.4%	11.5%	88.5%
1,277	ANDREWS	466	26	440		414 D	5.6%	94.4%	5.6%	94.4%
32,201	ANGELINA	6,572	572	5,993	7	5,421 D	8.7%	91.2%	8.7%	91.3%
3,469	ARANSAS	677	141	536		395 D	20.8%	79.2%	20.8%	79.2%
7,599	ARCHER	2,181	276	1,904	1	1,628 D	12.7%	87.3%	12.7%	87.3%
2,495	ARMSTRONG	974	82	891	1	809 D	8.4%	91.5%	8.4%	91.6%
19,275	ATASCOSA	2,344	418	1,922	4	1,504 D	17.8%	82.0%	17.9%	82.1%
17,384	AUSTIN	2,807	1,400	1,404	3	4 D	49.9%	50.0%	49.9%	50.1%
6,318	BAILEY	1,397	330	1,066	1	736 D	23.6%	76.3%	23.6%	76.4%
4,234	BANDERA	1,317	432	881	4	449 D	32.8%	66.9%	32.9%	67.1%
21,610	BASTROP	2,996	502	2,492	2	1,990 D	16.8%	83.2%	16.8%	83.2%
7,755	BAYLOR	1,807	139	1,667	1	1,528 D	7.7%	92.3%	7.7%	92.3%
16,481	BEE	2,707	948	1,759		811 D	35.0%	65.0%	35.0%	65.0%
44,863	BELL	8,468	1,050	7,418		6,368 D	12.4%	87.6%	12.4%	87.6%
338,176	BEXAR	56,696	18,270	38,214	212	19,944 D	32.2%	67.4%	32.3%	67.7%
4,264	BLANCO	1,567	520	1,042	5	522 D	33.2%	66.5%	33.3%	66.7%
1,396	BORDEN	419	44	375		331 D	10.5%	89.5%	10.5%	89.5%
15,761	BOSQUE	3,680	595	3,083	2	2,488 D	16.2%	83.8%	16.2%	83.8%
50,208	BOWIE	8,049	1,107	6,937	5	5,830 D	13.8%	86.2%	13.8%	86.2%
27,069	BRAZORIA	4,585	799	3,781	5	2,982 D	17.4%	82.5%	17.4%	82.6%
26,977	BRAZOS	4,777	617	4,151	9	3,534 D	12.9%	86.9%	12.9%	87.1%
6,478	BREWSTER	1,248	245	1,001	2	756 D	19.6%	80.2%	19.7%	80.3%
4,056	BRISCOE	1,066	154	910	2	756 D	14.4%	85.4%	14.5%	85.5%
6,362	BROOKS	875	201	670	4	469 D	23.0%	76.6%	23.1%	76.9%
25,924	BROWN	5,195	663	4,523	9	3,860 D	12.8%	87.1%	12.8%	87.2%
18,334	BURLESON	2,321	319	1,999	3	1,680 D	13.7%	86.1%	13.8%	86.2%
10,771	BURNET	2,412	233	2,177	2	1,944 D	9.7%	90.3%	9.7%	90.3%
24,893	CALDWELL	4,159	659	3,499	1	2,840 D	15.8%	84.1%	15.8%	84.2%
5,911	CALHOUN	1,088	152	935	1	783 D	14.0%	85.9%	14.0%	86.0%
11,568	CALLAHAN	2,623	309	2,310	4	2,001 D	11.8%	88.1%	11.8%	88.2%
83,202	CAMERON	9,433	3,370	6,035	28	2,665 D	35.7%	64.0%	35.8%	64.2%
10,285	CAMP	1,545	200	1,343	2	1,143 D	12.9%	86.9%	13.0%	87.0%
6,624	CARSON	2,000	362	1,636	2	1,274 D	18.1%	81.8%	18.1%	81.9%
33,496	CASS	3,580	454	3,126		2,672 D	12.7%	87.3%	12.7%	87.3%
4,631	CASTRO	1,226	224	1,000	2	776 D	18.3%	81.6%	18.3%	81.7%
7,511	CHAMBERS	1,500	219	1,279	2	1,060 D	14.6%	85.3%	14.6%	85.4%
43,970	CHEROKEE	6,104	801	5,293	10	4,492 D	13.1%	86.7%	13.1%	86.9%
12,149	CHILDRESS	3,067	335	2,729	3	2,394 D	10.9%	89.0%	10.9%	89.1%
12,524	CLAY	2,790	427	2,357	6	1,930 D	15.3%	84.5%	15.3%	84.7%
3,735	COCHRAN	891	122	765	4	643 D	13.7%	85.9%	13.8%	86.2%
4,590	COKE	1,066	94	967	5	873 D	8.8%	90.7%	8.9%	91.1%
20,571	COLEMAN	3,723	454	3,257	12	2,803 D	12.2%	87.5%	12.2%	87.8%
47,190	COLLIN	8,412	1,028	7,373	11	6,345 D	12.2%	87.6%	12.2%	87.8%
10,331	COLLINGSWORTH	2,346	307	2,034	5	1,727 D	13.1%	86.7%	13.1%	86.9%
17,812	COLORADO	2,844	1,166	1,674	4	508 D	41.0%	58.9%	41.1%	58.9%
12,321	COMAL	2,706	1,852	851	3	1,001 R	68.4%	31.4%	68.5%	31.5%
19,245	COMANCHE	3,837	610	3,226	1	2,616 D	15.9%	84.1%	15.9%	84.1%
6,192	CONCHO	1,500	189	1,310	1	1,121 D	12.6%	87.3%	12.6%	87.4%
24,909	COOKE	5,853	1,358	4,483	12	3,125 D	23.2%	76.6%	23.2%	76.8%
20,226	CORYELL	3,705	549	3,155	1	2,606 D	14.8%	85.2%	14.8%	85.2%
7,079	COTTLE	1,743	237	1,506		1,269 D	13.6%	86.4%	13.6%	86.4%
2,841	CRANE	884	68	815	1	747 D	7.7%	92.2%	7.7%	92.3%
2,809	CROCKETT	552	132	420		288 D	23.9%	76.1%	23.9%	76.1%
10,046	CROSBY	2,002	276	1,720	6	1,444 D	13.8%	85.9%	13.8%	86.2%
1,653	CULBERSON	349	45	303	1	258 D	12.9%	86.8%	12.9%	87.1%
6,494	DALLAM	1,974	427	1,539	8	1,112 D	21.6%	78.0%	21.7%	78.3%
398,564	DALLAS	66,136	16,574	49,431	131	32,857 D	25.1%	74.7%	25.1%	74.9%
15,367	DAWSON	3,174	361	2,808	5	2,447 D	11.4%	88.5%	11.4%	88.6%
6,056	DEAF SMITH	1,647	423	1,219	5	796 D	25.7%	74.0%	25.8%	74.2%
12,858	DELTA	2,404	190	2,214		2,024 D	7.9%	92.1%	7.9%	92.1%

TEXAS

PRESIDENT 1940

1940 Census Population	County	Total Vote	Republican	Democratic	Other	Rep.-Dem. Plurality	Percentage Total Vote Rep.	Percentage Total Vote Dem.	Percentage Major Vote Rep.	Percentage Major Vote Dem.
33,658	DENTON	7,292	899	6,386	7	5,487 D	12.3%	87.6%	12.3%	87.7%
24,935	DE WITT	3,791	1,735	2,056		321 D	45.8%	54.2%	45.8%	54.2%
7,847	DICKENS	1,979	246	1,728	5	1,482 D	12.4%	87.3%	12.5%	87.5%
8,542	DIMMIT	1,079	340	736	3	396 D	31.5%	68.2%	31.6%	68.4%
7,487	DONLEY	1,843	213	1,619	11	1,406 D	11.6%	87.8%	11.6%	88.4%
20,565	DUVAL	3,384	151	3,232	1	3,081 D	4.5%	95.5%	4.5%	95.5%
30,345	EASTLAND	6,887	1,063	5,818	6	4,755 D	15.4%	84.5%	15.4%	84.6%
15,051	ECTOR	3,239	451	2,783	5	2,332 D	13.9%	85.9%	13.9%	86.1%
2,933	EDWARDS	740	175	565		390 D	23.6%	76.4%	23.6%	76.4%
47,733	ELLIS	8,578	692	7,881	5	7,189 D	8.1%	91.9%	8.1%	91.9%
131,067	EL PASO	16,165	3,764	12,374	27	8,610 D	23.3%	76.5%	23.3%	76.7%
20,760	ERATH	4,123	646	3,459	18	2,813 D	15.7%	83.9%	15.7%	84.3%
35,984	FALLS	4,908	958	3,949	1	2,991 D	19.5%	80.5%	19.5%	80.5%
41,064	FANNIN	8,276	792	7,478	6	6,686 D	9.6%	90.4%	9.6%	90.4%
29,246	FAYETTE	5,052	2,441	2,606	5	165 D	48.3%	51.6%	48.4%	51.6%
12,932	FISHER	2,467	199	2,260	8	2,061 D	8.1%	91.6%	8.1%	91.9%
10,659	FLOYD	2,371	484	1,880	7	1,396 D	20.4%	79.3%	20.5%	79.5%
5,237	FOARD	1,139	142	997		855 D	12.5%	87.5%	12.5%	87.5%
32,963	FORT BEND	3,849	748	3,101		2,353 D	19.4%	80.6%	19.4%	80.6%
8,378	FRANKLIN	1,806	183	1,621	2	1,438 D	10.1%	89.8%	10.1%	89.9%
21,138	FREESTONE	4,000	481	3,514	5	3,033 D	12.0%	87.9%	12.0%	88.0%
9,207	FRIO	1,252	236	1,012	4	776 D	18.8%	80.8%	18.9%	81.1%
8,136	GAINES	1,709	197	1,509	3	1,312 D	11.5%	88.3%	11.5%	88.5%
81,173	GALVESTON	13,632	2,443	11,161	28	8,718 D	17.9%	81.9%	18.0%	82.0%
5,678	GARZA	1,278	198	1,073	7	875 D	15.5%	84.0%	15.6%	84.4%
10,670	GILLESPIE	3,704	3,213	487	4	2,726 R	86.7%	13.1%	86.8%	13.2%
1,193	GLASSCOCK	311	41	268	2	227 D	13.2%	86.2%	13.3%	86.7%
8,798	GOLIAD	1,453	580	868	5	288 D	39.9%	59.7%	40.1%	59.9%
26,075	GONZALES	3,732	722	3,008	2	2,286 D	19.3%	80.6%	19.4%	80.6%
23,911	GRAY	5,540	1,217	4,315	8	3,098 D	22.0%	77.9%	22.0%	78.0%
69,499	GRAYSON	13,884	1,340	12,530	14	11,190 D	9.7%	90.2%	9.7%	90.3%
58,027	GREGG	10,990	1,584	9,391	15	7,807 D	14.4%	85.5%	14.4%	85.6%
21,960	GRIMES	3,199	298	2,899	2	2,601 D	9.3%	90.6%	9.3%	90.7%
25,596	GUADALUPE	4,661	2,473	2,182	6	291 R	53.1%	46.8%	53.1%	46.9%
18,813	HALE	4,323	906	3,405	12	2,499 D	21.0%	78.8%	21.0%	79.0%
12,117	HALL	2,445	219	2,221	5	2,002 D	9.0%	90.8%	9.0%	91.0%
13,303	HAMILTON	2,922	655	2,263	4	1,608 D	22.4%	77.4%	22.4%	77.6%
2,783	HANSFORD	880	150	725	5	575 D	17.0%	82.4%	17.1%	82.9%
11,073	HARDEMAN	2,815	362	2,453		2,091 D	12.9%	87.1%	12.9%	87.1%
15,875	HARDIN	3,225	226	2,997	2	2,771 D	7.0%	92.9%	7.0%	93.0%
528,961	HARRIS	94,453	20,797	73,520	136	52,723 D	22.0%	77.8%	22.1%	77.9%
50,900	HARRISON	5,196	681	4,515		3,834 D	13.1%	86.9%	13.1%	86.9%
1,873	HARTLEY	655	110	545		435 D	16.8%	83.2%	16.8%	83.2%
14,905	HASKELL	3,350	405	2,941	4	2,536 D	12.1%	87.8%	12.1%	87.9%
15,349	HAYS	2,828	453	2,371	4	1,918 D	16.0%	83.8%	16.0%	84.0%
4,170	HEMPHILL	1,038	170	868		698 D	16.4%	83.6%	16.4%	83.6%
31,822	HENDERSON	4,914	803	4,111		3,308 D	16.3%	83.7%	16.3%	83.7%
106,059	HIDALGO	12,285	4,787	7,471	27	2,684 D	39.0%	60.8%	39.1%	60.9%
38,355	HILL	6,629	627	6,002		5,375 D	9.5%	90.5%	9.5%	90.5%
12,693	HOCKLEY	2,649	261	2,382	6	2,121 D	9.9%	89.9%	9.9%	90.1%
6,674	HOOD	1,485	166	1,318	1	1,152 D	11.2%	88.8%	11.2%	88.8%
30,274	HOPKINS	5,511	551	4,955	5	4,404 D	10.0%	89.9%	10.0%	90.0%
31,137	HOUSTON	4,056	474	3,579	3	3,105 D	11.7%	88.2%	11.7%	88.3%
20,990	HOWARD	4,703	367	4,329	7	3,962 D	7.8%	92.0%	7.8%	92.2%
3,149	HUDSPETH	481	54	426	1	372 D	11.2%	88.6%	11.3%	88.8%
48,793	HUNT	9,044	877	8,156	11	7,279 D	9.7%	90.2%	9.7%	90.3%
19,069	HUTCHINSON	4,129	1,101	3,019	9	1,918 D	26.7%	73.1%	26.7%	73.3%
1,963	IRION	637	74	560	3	486 D	11.6%	87.9%	11.7%	88.3%
10,206	JACK	2,352	305	2,046	1	1,741 D	13.0%	87.0%	13.0%	87.0%
11,720	JACKSON	1,804	296	1,506	2	1,210 D	16.4%	83.5%	16.4%	83.6%

TEXAS

PRESIDENT 1940

1940 Census Population	County	Total Vote	Republican	Democratic	Other	Rep.-Dem. Plurality	Percentage Total Vote Rep.	Percentage Total Vote Dem.	Percentage Major Vote Rep.	Percentage Major Vote Dem.
17,491	JASPER	2,456	220	2,236		2,016 D	9.0%	91.0%	9.0%	91.0%
2,375	JEFF DAVIS	424	50	374		324 D	11.8%	88.2%	11.8%	88.2%
145,329	JEFFERSON	24,591	4,860	19,694	37	14,834 D	19.8%	80.1%	19.8%	80.2%
5,449	JIM HOGG	910	100	810		710 D	11.0%	89.0%	11.0%	89.0%
20,239	JIM WELLS	3,026	914	2,105	7	1,191 D	30.2%	69.6%	30.3%	69.7%
30,384	JOHNSON	6,183	649	5,532	2	4,883 D	10.5%	89.5%	10.5%	89.5%
23,378	JONES	4,094	401	3,688	5	3,287 D	9.8%	90.1%	9.8%	90.2%
19,248	KARNES	2,642	631	2,010	1	1,379 D	23.9%	76.1%	23.9%	76.1%
38,308	KAUFMAN	5,751	516	5,232	3	4,716 D	9.0%	91.0%	9.0%	91.0%
5,080	KENDALL	1,744	1,321	421	2	900 R	75.7%	24.1%	75.8%	24.2%
700	KENEDY	106	68	38		30 R	64.2%	35.8%	64.2%	35.8%
3,413	KENT	792	79	712	1	633 D	10.0%	89.9%	10.0%	90.0%
11,650	KERR	2,756	1,112	1,634	10	522 D	40.3%	59.3%	40.5%	59.5%
5,064	KIMBLE	1,336	219	1,117		898 D	16.4%	83.6%	16.4%	83.6%
1,066	KING	289	23	266		243 D	8.0%	92.0%	8.0%	92.0%
4,533	KINNEY	577	156	418	3	262 D	27.0%	72.4%	27.2%	72.8%
13,344	KLEBERG	2,064	429	1,631	4	1,202 D	20.8%	79.0%	20.8%	79.2%
10,090	KNOX	1,952	253	1,699		1,446 D	13.0%	87.0%	13.0%	87.0%
50,425	LAMAR	8,805	761	8,038	6	7,277 D	8.6%	91.3%	8.6%	91.4%
17,606	LAMB	3,783	513	3,259	11	2,746 D	13.6%	86.1%	13.6%	86.4%
9,167	LAMPASAS	2,251	244	2,006	1	1,762 D	10.8%	89.1%	10.8%	89.2%
8,003	LA SALLE	818	112	706		594 D	13.7%	86.3%	13.7%	86.3%
25,485	LAVACA	3,836	1,412	2,419	5	1,007 D	36.8%	63.1%	36.9%	63.1%
12,751	LEE	2,106	1,150	954	2	196 R	54.6%	45.3%	54.7%	45.3%
17,733	LEON	2,601	252	2,349		2,097 D	9.7%	90.3%	9.7%	90.3%
24,541	LIBERTY	3,966	497	3,458	11	2,961 D	12.5%	87.2%	12.6%	87.4%
33,781	LIMESTONE	5,345	559	4,784	2	4,225 D	10.5%	89.5%	10.5%	89.5%
3,764	LIPSCOMB	1,231	445	774	12	329 D	36.1%	62.9%	36.5%	63.5%
9,799	LIVE OAK	1,390	499	888	3	389 D	35.9%	63.9%	36.0%	64.0%
5,996	LLANO	1,727	238	1,484	5	1,246 D	13.8%	85.9%	13.8%	86.2%
285	LOVING	119	21	98		77 D	17.6%	82.4%	17.6%	82.4%
51,782	LUBBOCK	9,413	1,283	8,113	17	6,830 D	13.6%	86.2%	13.7%	86.3%
11,931	LYNN	2,878	255	2,618	5	2,363 D	8.9%	91.0%	8.9%	91.1%
13,208	MCCULLOCH	2,816	443	2,373		1,930 D	15.7%	84.3%	15.7%	84.3%
101,898	MCLENNAN	18,165	2,178	15,952	35	13,774 D	12.0%	87.8%	12.0%	88.0%
1,374	MCMULLEN	413	77	336		259 D	18.6%	81.4%	18.6%	81.4%
12,029	MADISON	1,561	127	1,434		1,307 D	8.1%	91.9%	8.1%	91.9%
11,457	MARION	1,420	167	1,253		1,086 D	11.8%	88.2%	11.8%	88.2%
5,556	MARTIN	1,181	136	1,044	1	908 D	11.5%	88.4%	11.5%	88.5%
5,378	MASON	1,702	634	1,065	3	431 D	37.3%	62.6%	37.3%	62.7%
20,066	MATAGORDA	2,813	651	2,156	6	1,505 D	23.1%	76.6%	23.2%	76.8%
10,071	MAVERICK	1,045	166	875	4	709 D	15.9%	83.7%	15.9%	84.1%
16,106	MEDINA	3,229	1,480	1,749		269 D	45.8%	54.2%	45.8%	54.2%
4,521	MENARD	1,400	246	1,153	1	907 D	17.6%	82.4%	17.6%	82.4%
11,721	MIDLAND	2,570	646	1,921	3	1,275 D	25.1%	74.7%	25.2%	74.8%
33,120	MILAM	5,209	1,110	4,083	16	2,973 D	21.3%	78.4%	21.4%	78.6%
7,951	MILLS	1,946	287	1,658	1	1,371 D	14.7%	85.2%	14.8%	85.2%
12,477	MITCHELL	2,657	251	2,401	5	2,150 D	9.4%	90.4%	9.5%	90.5%
20,442	MONTAGUE	3,888	530	3,352	6	2,822 D	13.6%	86.2%	13.7%	86.3%
23,055	MONTGOMERY	3,755	408	3,347		2,939 D	10.9%	89.1%	10.9%	89.1%
4,461	MOORE	1,189	224	959	6	735 D	18.8%	80.7%	18.9%	81.1%
9,810	MORRIS	1,834	82	1,752		1,670 D	4.5%	95.5%	4.5%	95.5%
4,994	MOTLEY	1,007	100	907		807 D	9.9%	90.1%	9.9%	90.1%
35,392	NACOGDOCHES	5,432	440	4,988	4	4,548 D	8.1%	91.8%	8.1%	91.9%
51,308	NAVARRO	8,415	721	7,683	11	6,962 D	8.6%	91.3%	8.6%	91.4%
13,700	NEWTON	2,116	174	1,940	2	1,766 D	8.2%	91.7%	8.2%	91.8%
17,309	NOLAN	3,794	471	3,314	9	2,843 D	12.4%	87.3%	12.4%	87.6%
92,661	NUECES	12,842	3,065	9,740	37	6,675 D	23.9%	75.8%	23.9%	76.1%
4,213	OCHILTREE	1,507	294	1,213		919 D	19.5%	80.5%	19.5%	80.5%
1,385	OLDHAM	499	82	416	1	334 D	16.4%	83.4%	16.5%	83.5%

TEXAS

PRESIDENT 1940

1940 Census Population	County	Total Vote	Republican	Democratic	Other	Rep.-Dem. Plurality	Percentage Total Vote Rep.	Total Vote Dem.	Major Vote Rep.	Major Vote Dem.
17,382	ORANGE	3,376	358	3,011	7	2,653 D	10.6%	89.2%	10.6%	89.4%
18,456	PALO PINTO	3,090	510	2,571	9	2,061 D	16.5%	83.2%	16.6%	83.4%
22,513	PANOLA	3,052	179	2,871	2	2,692 D	5.9%	94.1%	5.9%	94.1%
20,482	PARKER	4,253	558	3,687	8	3,129 D	13.1%	86.7%	13.1%	86.9%
5,890	PARMER	1,435	370	1,062	3	692 D	25.8%	74.0%	25.8%	74.2%
8,185	PECOS	1,925	332	1,583	10	1,251 D	17.2%	82.2%	17.3%	82.7%
20,635	POLK	2,922	280	2,642		2,362 D	9.6%	90.4%	9.6%	90.4%
54,265	POTTER	9,514	2,285	7,203	26	4,918 D	24.0%	75.7%	24.1%	75.9%
10,925	PRESIDIO	1,084	163	917	4	754 D	15.0%	84.6%	15.1%	84.9%
7,334	RAINS	1,333	251	1,080	2	829 D	18.8%	81.0%	18.9%	81.1%
7,185	RANDALL	2,162	382	1,779	1	1,397 D	17.7%	82.3%	17.7%	82.3%
1,997	REAGAN	609	88	520	1	432 D	14.4%	85.4%	14.5%	85.5%
2,420	REAL	579	126	453		327 D	21.8%	78.2%	21.8%	78.2%
29,769	RED RIVER	4,458	555	3,899	4	3,344 D	12.4%	87.5%	12.5%	87.5%
8,006	REEVES	1,554	247	1,305	2	1,058 D	15.9%	84.0%	15.9%	84.1%
10,383	REFUGIO	1,952	458	1,487	7	1,029 D	23.5%	76.2%	23.5%	76.5%
1,289	ROBERTS	466	55	408	3	353 D	11.8%	87.6%	11.9%	88.1%
25,710	ROBERTSON	3,366	175	3,191		3,016 D	5.2%	94.8%	5.2%	94.8%
7,051	ROCKWALL	1,605	95	1,510		1,415 D	5.9%	94.1%	5.9%	94.1%
18,903	RUNNELS	3,929	835	3,088	6	2,253 D	21.3%	78.6%	21.3%	78.7%
51,023	RUSK	8,613	704	7,901	8	7,197 D	8.2%	91.7%	8.2%	91.8%
10,896	SABINE	1,785	157	1,626	2	1,469 D	8.8%	91.1%	8.8%	91.2%
12,471	SAN AUGUSTINE	1,444	119	1,325		1,206 D	8.2%	91.8%	8.2%	91.8%
9,056	SAN JACINTO	884	119	764	1	645 D	13.5%	86.4%	13.5%	86.5%
28,871	SAN PATRICIO	3,963	980	2,963	20	1,983 D	24.7%	74.8%	24.9%	75.1%
11,012	SAN SABA	2,528	221	2,304	3	2,083 D	8.7%	91.1%	8.8%	91.2%
3,083	SCHLEICHER	718	117	601		484 D	16.3%	83.7%	16.3%	83.7%
11,545	SCURRY	2,583	280	2,303		2,023 D	10.8%	89.2%	10.8%	89.2%
6,211	SHACKELFORD	1,753	229	1,521	3	1,292 D	13.1%	86.8%	13.1%	86.9%
29,235	SHELBY	5,070	349	4,720	1	4,371 D	6.9%	93.1%	6.9%	93.1%
2,026	SHERMAN	613	82	528	3	446 D	13.4%	86.1%	13.4%	86.6%
69,090	SMITH	10,975	1,557	9,410	8	7,853 D	14.2%	85.7%	14.2%	85.8%
3,071	SOMERVELL	670	138	532		394 D	20.6%	79.4%	20.6%	79.4%
13,312	STARR	1,268	68	1,200		1,132 D	5.4%	94.6%	5.4%	94.6%
12,356	STEPHENS	3,223	471	2,750	2	2,279 D	14.6%	85.3%	14.6%	85.4%
1,404	STERLING	441	16	425		409 D	3.6%	96.4%	3.6%	96.4%
5,589	STONEWALL	1,328	156	1,172		1,016 D	11.7%	88.3%	11.7%	88.3%
3,977	SUTTON	657	84	571	2	487 D	12.8%	86.9%	12.8%	87.2%
6,528	SWISHER	1,733	298	1,432	3	1,134 D	17.2%	82.6%	17.2%	82.8%
225,521	TARRANT	43,589	7,474	36,062	53	28,588 D	17.1%	82.7%	17.2%	82.8%
44,147	TAYLOR	8,850	983	7,852	15	6,869 D	11.1%	88.7%	11.1%	88.9%
2,952	TERRELL	550	133	417		284 D	24.2%	75.8%	24.2%	75.8%
11,160	TERRY	2,261	145	2,116		1,971 D	6.4%	93.6%	6.4%	93.6%
4,275	THROCKMORTON	1,133	138	995		857 D	12.2%	87.8%	12.2%	87.8%
19,228	TITUS	3,941	255	3,686		3,431 D	6.5%	93.5%	6.5%	93.5%
39,302	TOM GREEN	7,497	1,049	6,433	15	5,384 D	14.0%	85.8%	14.0%	86.0%
111,053	TRAVIS	20,503	3,128	17,300	75	14,172 D	15.3%	84.4%	15.3%	84.7%
13,705	TRINITY	2,069	274	1,791	4	1,517 D	13.2%	86.6%	13.3%	86.7%
11,948	TYLER	1,556	228	1,326	2	1,098 D	14.7%	85.2%	14.7%	85.3%
26,178	UPSHUR	3,998	518	3,480		2,962 D	13.0%	87.0%	13.0%	87.0%
4,297	UPTON	1,432	370	1,062		692 D	25.8%	74.2%	25.8%	74.2%
13,246	UVALDE	2,433	556	1,871	6	1,315 D	22.9%	76.9%	22.9%	77.1%
15,453	VAL VERDE	2,247	616	1,628	3	1,012 D	27.4%	72.5%	27.5%	72.5%
31,155	VAN ZANDT	5,715	721	4,975	19	4,254 D	12.6%	87.1%	12.7%	87.3%
23,741	VICTORIA	3,451	956	2,493	2	1,537 D	27.7%	72.2%	27.7%	72.3%
19,868	WALKER	2,376	218	2,158		1,940 D	9.2%	90.8%	9.2%	90.8%
10,280	WALLER	1,366	300	1,065	1	765 D	22.0%	78.0%	22.0%	78.0%
9,575	WARD	2,227	281	1,931	15	1,650 D	12.6%	86.7%	12.7%	87.3%
25,387	WASHINGTON	3,317	1,868	1,449		419 R	56.3%	43.7%	56.3%	43.7%
45,916	WEBB	4,926	775	4,147	4	3,372 D	15.7%	84.2%	15.7%	84.3%

TEXAS

PRESIDENT 1940

1940 Census Population	County	Total Vote	Republican	Democratic	Other	Rep.-Dem. Plurality	Percentage Total Vote Rep.	Percentage Total Vote Dem.	Percentage Major Vote Rep.	Percentage Major Vote Dem.
36,158	WHARTON	4,740	760	3,976	4	3,216 D	16.0%	83.9%	16.0%	84.0%
12,411	WHEELER	3,124	517	2,600	7	2,083 D	16.5%	83.2%	16.6%	83.4%
73,604	WICHITA	13,887	2,206	11,672	9	9,466 D	15.9%	84.0%	15.9%	84.1%
20,474	WILBARGER	3,952	697	3,249	6	2,552 D	17.6%	82.2%	17.7%	82.3%
13,230	WILLACY	1,920	740	1,173	7	433 D	38.5%	61.1%	38.7%	61.3%
41,698	WILLIAMSON	7,671	1,714	5,944	13	4,230 D	22.3%	77.5%	22.4%	77.6%
17,066	WILSON	3,359	605	2,750	4	2,145 D	18.0%	81.9%	18.0%	82.0%
6,141	WINKLER	1,512	172	1,340		1,168 D	11.4%	88.6%	11.4%	88.6%
19,074	WISE	4,251	498	3,751	2	3,253 D	11.7%	88.2%	11.7%	88.3%
24,360	WOOD	4,249	585	3,659	5	3,074 D	13.8%	86.1%	13.8%	86.2%
5,354	YOAKUM	1,019	134	885		751 D	13.2%	86.8%	13.2%	86.8%
19,004	YOUNG	4,195	478	3,712	5	3,234 D	11.4%	88.5%	11.4%	88.6%
3,916	ZAPATA	1,279	495	784		289 D	38.7%	61.3%	38.7%	61.3%
11,603	ZAVALA	998	259	739		480 D	26.0%	74.0%	26.0%	74.0%
6,414,824	TOTAL	1,124,437	212,692	909,974	1,771	697,282 D	18.9%	80.9%	18.9%	81.1%

TEXAS

PRESIDENT 1936

1930 Census Population	County	Total Vote	Republican	Democratic	Other	Rep.-Dem. Plurality	Percentage: Total Vote		Percentage: Major Vote	
							Rep.	Dem.	Rep.	Dem.
34,643	ANDERSON	4,040	289	3,749	2	3,460 D	7.2%	92.8%	7.2%	92.8%
736	ANDREWS	306	18	287	1	269 D	5.9%	93.8%	5.9%	94.1%
27,803	ANGELINA	4,290	342	3,943	5	3,601 D	8.0%	91.9%	8.0%	92.0%
2,219	ARANSAS	277	60	206	11	146 D	21.7%	74.4%	22.6%	77.4%
9,684	ARCHER	1,822	146	1,672	4	1,526 D	8.0%	91.8%	8.0%	92.0%
3,329	ARMSTRONG	933	33	897	3	864 D	3.5%	96.1%	3.5%	96.5%
15,654	ATASCOSA	2,350	285	2,041	24	1,756 D	12.1%	86.9%	12.3%	87.7%
18,860	AUSTIN	1,929	290	1,635	4	1,345 D	15.0%	84.8%	15.1%	84.9%
5,186	BAILEY	993	191	788	14	597 D	19.2%	79.4%	19.5%	80.5%
3,784	BANDERA	1,171	431	720	20	289 D	36.8%	61.5%	37.4%	62.6%
23,888	BASTROP	2,602	198	2,395	9	2,197 D	7.6%	92.0%	7.6%	92.4%
7,418	BAYLOR	1,642	100	1,541	1	1,441 D	6.1%	93.8%	6.1%	93.9%
15,721	BEE	2,082	603	1,462	17	859 D	29.0%	70.2%	29.2%	70.8%
50,030	BELL	6,621	475	6,119	27	5,644 D	7.2%	92.4%	7.2%	92.8%
292,533	BEXAR	48,982	12,951	35,781	250	22,830 D	26.4%	73.0%	26.6%	73.4%
3,842	BLANCO	1,372	313	1,056	3	743 D	22.8%	77.0%	22.9%	77.1%
1,505	BORDEN	248	26	220	2	194 D	10.5%	88.7%	10.6%	89.4%
15,750	BOSQUE	2,638	350	2,283	5	1,933 D	13.3%	86.5%	13.3%	86.7%
48,563	BOWIE	5,521	472	5,030	19	4,558 D	8.5%	91.1%	8.6%	91.4%
23,054	BRAZORIA	2,785	462	2,284	39	1,822 D	16.6%	82.0%	16.8%	83.2%
21,835	BRAZOS	2,659	45	2,610	4	2,565 D	1.7%	98.2%	1.7%	98.3%
6,624	BREWSTER	981	151	828	2	677 D	15.4%	84.4%	15.4%	84.6%
5,590	BRISCOE	913	64	849		785 D	7.0%	93.0%	7.0%	93.0%
5,901	BROOKS	483	117	365	1	248 D	24.2%	75.6%	24.3%	75.7%
26,382	BROWN	4,458	448	3,971	39	3,523 D	10.0%	89.1%	10.1%	89.9%
19,848	BURLESON	1,601	135	1,466		1,331 D	8.4%	91.6%	8.4%	91.6%
10,355	BURNET	1,696	111	1,583	2	1,472 D	6.5%	93.3%	6.6%	93.4%
31,397	CALDWELL	3,291	247	3,019	25	2,772 D	7.5%	91.7%	7.6%	92.4%
5,385	CALHOUN	781	92	685	4	593 D	11.8%	87.7%	11.8%	88.2%
12,785	CALLAHAN	1,991	245	1,739	7	1,494 D	12.3%	87.3%	12.3%	87.7%
77,540	CAMERON	8,206	2,160	5,887	159	3,727 D	26.3%	71.7%	26.8%	73.2%
10,063	CAMP	1,017	78	939		861 D	7.7%	92.3%	7.7%	92.3%
7,745	CARSON	1,728	147	1,568	13	1,421 D	8.5%	90.7%	8.6%	91.4%
30,030	CASS	2,630	169	2,461		2,292 D	6.4%	93.6%	6.4%	93.6%
4,720	CASTRO	1,025	65	950	10	885 D	6.3%	92.7%	6.4%	93.6%
5,710	CHAMBERS	1,121	134	984	3	850 D	12.0%	87.8%	12.0%	88.0%
43,180	CHEROKEE	4,218	302	3,908	8	3,606 D	7.2%	92.7%	7.2%	92.8%
16,044	CHILDRESS	2,307	209	2,076	22	1,867 D	9.1%	90.0%	9.1%	90.9%
14,545	CLAY	2,380	196	2,168	16	1,972 D	8.2%	91.1%	8.3%	91.7%
1,963	COCHRAN	749	58	683	8	625 D	7.7%	91.2%	7.8%	92.2%
5,253	COKE	966	68	888	10	820 D	7.0%	91.9%	7.1%	92.9%
23,669	COLEMAN	3,177	269	2,900	8	2,631 D	8.5%	91.3%	8.5%	91.5%
46,180	COLLIN	6,210	531	5,669	10	5,138 D	8.6%	91.3%	8.6%	91.4%
14,461	COLLINGSWORTH	2,172	158	2,012	2	1,854 D	7.3%	92.6%	7.3%	92.7%
19,129	COLORADO	1,815	372	1,435	8	1,063 D	20.5%	79.1%	20.6%	79.4%
11,984	COMAL	2,171	554	1,611	6	1,057 D	25.5%	74.2%	25.6%	74.4%
18,430	COMANCHE	3,005	355	2,587	63	2,232 D	11.8%	86.1%	12.1%	87.9%
7,645	CONCHO	1,165	76	1,089		1,013 D	6.5%	93.5%	6.5%	93.5%
24,136	COOKE	4,392	686	3,686	20	3,000 D	15.6%	83.9%	15.7%	84.3%
19,999	CORYELL	2,223	150	2,064	9	1,914 D	6.7%	92.8%	6.8%	93.2%
9,395	COTTLE	1,359	86	1,265	8	1,179 D	6.3%	93.1%	6.4%	93.6%
2,221	CRANE	647	25	622		597 D	3.9%	96.1%	3.9%	96.1%
2,590	CROCKETT	308	75	231	2	156 D	24.4%	75.0%	24.5%	75.5%
11,023	CROSBY	1,867	153	1,711	3	1,558 D	8.2%	91.6%	8.2%	91.8%
1,228	CULBERSON	262	23	239		216 D	8.8%	91.2%	8.8%	91.2%
7,830	DALLAM	1,727	220	1,436	71	1,216 D	12.7%	83.1%	13.3%	86.7%
325,691	DALLAS	49,657	7,204	42,153	300	34,949 D	14.5%	84.9%	14.6%	85.4%
13,573	DAWSON	1,992	156	1,829	7	1,673 D	7.8%	91.8%	7.9%	92.1%
5,979	DEAF SMITH	1,387	142	1,236	9	1,094 D	10.2%	89.1%	10.3%	89.7%
13,138	DELTA	1,549	82	1,466	1	1,384 D	5.3%	94.6%	5.3%	94.7%

TEXAS

PRESIDENT 1936

1930 Census Population	County	Total Vote	Republican	Democratic	Other	Rep.-Dem. Plurality	Percentage Total Vote Rep.	Percentage Total Vote Dem.	Percentage Major Vote Rep.	Percentage Major Vote Dem.
32,822	DENTON	5,523	476	5,021	26	4,545 D	8.6%	90.9%	8.7%	91.3%
27,441	DE WITT	2,602	616	1,977	9	1,361 D	23.7%	76.0%	23.8%	76.2%
8,601	DICKENS	1,561	115	1,445	1	1,330 D	7.4%	92.6%	7.4%	92.6%
8,828	DIMMIT	1,021	296	704	21	408 D	29.0%	69.0%	29.6%	70.4%
10,262	DONLEY	1,664	133	1,513	18	1,380 D	8.0%	90.9%	8.1%	91.9%
12,191	DUVAL	3,068	163	2,901	4	2,738 D	5.3%	94.6%	5.3%	94.7%
34,156	EASTLAND	5,418	724	4,659	35	3,935 D	13.4%	86.0%	13.4%	86.6%
3,958	ECTOR	908	81	816	11	735 D	8.9%	89.9%	9.0%	91.0%
2,764	EDWARDS	514	157	354	3	197 D	30.5%	68.9%	30.7%	69.3%
53,936	ELLIS	5,975	319	5,644	12	5,325 D	5.3%	94.5%	5.3%	94.7%
131,597	EL PASO	13,809	1,773	11,920	116	10,147 D	12.8%	86.3%	12.9%	87.1%
20,804	ERATH	2,995	290	2,694	11	2,404 D	9.7%	89.9%	9.7%	90.3%
38,771	FALLS	3,556	140	3,411	5	3,271 D	3.9%	95.9%	3.9%	96.1%
41,163	FANNIN	5,617	368	5,242	7	4,874 D	6.6%	93.3%	6.6%	93.4%
30,708	FAYETTE	3,420	595	2,820	5	2,225 D	17.4%	82.5%	17.4%	82.6%
13,563	FISHER	2,229	155	2,068	6	1,913 D	7.0%	92.8%	7.0%	93.0%
12,409	FLOYD	2,095	217	1,863	15	1,646 D	10.4%	88.9%	10.4%	89.6%
6,315	FOARD	1,005	74	928	3	854 D	7.4%	92.3%	7.4%	92.6%
29,718	FORT BEND	2,775	176	2,588	11	2,412 D	6.3%	93.3%	6.4%	93.6%
8,494	FRANKLIN	1,017	90	925	2	835 D	8.8%	91.0%	8.9%	91.1%
22,589	FREESTONE	2,069	134	1,929	6	1,795 D	6.5%	93.2%	6.5%	93.5%
9,411	FRIO	1,219	193	1,019	7	826 D	15.8%	83.6%	15.9%	84.1%
2,800	GAINES	726	42	680	4	638 D	5.8%	93.7%	5.8%	94.2%
64,401	GALVESTON	11,106	1,666	9,370	70	7,704 D	15.0%	84.4%	15.1%	84.9%
5,586	GARZA	942	132	807	3	675 D	14.0%	85.7%	14.1%	85.9%
11,020	GILLESPIE	2,514	1,421	1,016	77	405 R	56.5%	40.4%	58.3%	41.7%
1,263	GLASSCOCK	283	29	252	2	223 D	10.2%	89.0%	10.3%	89.7%
10,093	GOLIAD	1,511	323	1,184	4	861 D	21.4%	78.4%	21.4%	78.6%
28,337	GONZALES	3,033	352	2,674	7	2,322 D	11.6%	88.2%	11.6%	88.4%
22,090	GRAY	4,839	464	4,347	28	3,883 D	9.6%	89.8%	9.6%	90.4%
65,843	GRAYSON	11,597	947	10,627	23	9,680 D	8.2%	91.6%	8.2%	91.8%
15,778	GREGG	7,121	621	6,489	11	5,868 D	8.7%	91.1%	8.7%	91.3%
22,642	GRIMES	1,989	136	1,851	2	1,715 D	6.8%	93.1%	6.8%	93.2%
28,925	GUADALUPE	4,237	1,266	2,962	9	1,696 D	29.9%	69.9%	29.9%	70.1%
20,189	HALE	3,582	451	3,109	22	2,658 D	12.6%	86.8%	12.7%	87.3%
16,966	HALL	2,346	126	2,195	25	2,069 D	5.4%	93.6%	5.4%	94.6%
13,523	HAMILTON	2,132	202	1,929	1	1,727 D	9.5%	90.5%	9.5%	90.5%
3,548	HANSFORD	921	74	826	21	752 D	8.0%	89.7%	8.2%	91.8%
14,532	HARDEMAN	2,208	207	1,991	10	1,784 D	9.4%	90.2%	9.4%	90.6%
13,936	HARDIN	2,470	119	2,351		2,232 D	4.8%	95.2%	4.8%	95.2%
359,328	HARRIS	67,533	8,083	59,205	245	51,122 D	12.0%	87.7%	12.0%	88.0%
48,937	HARRISON	3,708	302	3,400	6	3,098 D	8.1%	91.7%	8.2%	91.8%
2,185	HARTLEY	600	40	560		520 D	6.7%	93.3%	6.7%	93.3%
16,669	HASKELL	2,872	156	2,713	3	2,557 D	5.4%	94.5%	5.4%	94.6%
14,915	HAYS	2,259	286	1,964	9	1,678 D	12.7%	86.9%	12.7%	87.3%
4,637	HEMPHILL	1,134	121	1,008	5	887 D	10.7%	88.9%	10.7%	89.3%
30,583	HENDERSON	3,525	260	3,259	6	2,999 D	7.4%	92.5%	7.4%	92.6%
77,004	HIDALGO	10,053	2,962	6,782	309	3,820 D	29.5%	67.5%	30.4%	69.6%
43,036	HILL	4,980	265	4,710	5	4,445 D	5.3%	94.6%	5.3%	94.7%
9,298	HOCKLEY	1,833	90	1,731	12	1,641 D	4.9%	94.4%	4.9%	95.1%
6,779	HOOD	1,094	102	988	4	886 D	9.3%	90.3%	9.4%	90.6%
29,410	HOPKINS	3,018	261	2,753	4	2,492 D	8.6%	91.2%	8.7%	91.3%
30,017	HOUSTON	2,559	99	2,458	2	2,359 D	3.9%	96.1%	3.9%	96.1%
22,888	HOWARD	3,332	230	3,094	8	2,864 D	6.9%	92.9%	6.9%	93.1%
3,728	HUDSPETH	388	24	363	1	339 D	6.2%	93.6%	6.2%	93.8%
49,016	HUNT	6,147	335	5,801	11	5,466 D	5.4%	94.4%	5.5%	94.5%
14,848	HUTCHINSON	2,873	390	2,478	5	2,088 D	13.6%	86.3%	13.6%	86.4%
2,049	IRION	530	49	476	5	427 D	9.2%	89.8%	9.3%	90.7%
9,046	JACK	1,306	183	1,113	10	930 D	14.0%	85.2%	14.1%	85.9%
10,980	JACKSON	1,128	171	952	5	781 D	15.2%	84.4%	15.2%	84.8%

TEXAS

PRESIDENT 1936

1930 Census Population	County	Total Vote	Republican	Democratic	Other	Rep.-Dem. Plurality	Percentage Total Vote Rep.	Percentage Total Vote Dem.	Percentage Major Vote Rep.	Percentage Major Vote Dem.
17,064	JASPER	1,612	109	1,500	3	1,391 D	6.8%	93.1%	6.8%	93.2%
1,800	JEFF DAVIS	325	33	291	1	258 D	10.2%	89.5%	10.2%	89.8%
133,391	JEFFERSON	20,808	2,544	18,187	77	15,643 D	12.2%	87.4%	12.3%	87.7%
4,919	JIM HOGG	760	48	712		664 D	6.3%	93.7%	6.3%	93.7%
13,456	JIM WELLS	2,038	338	1,691	9	1,353 D	16.6%	83.0%	16.7%	83.3%
33,317	JOHNSON	4,647	337	4,281	29	3,944 D	7.3%	92.1%	7.3%	92.7%
24,233	JONES	3,703	305	3,396	2	3,091 D	8.2%	91.7%	8.2%	91.8%
23,316	KARNES	2,447	371	2,067	9	1,696 D	15.2%	84.5%	15.2%	84.8%
40,905	KAUFMAN	4,175	229	3,943	3	3,714 D	5.5%	94.4%	5.5%	94.5%
4,970	KENDALL	1,104	693	405	6	288 R	62.8%	36.7%	63.1%	36.9%
701	KENEDY	126	30	96		66 D	23.8%	76.2%	23.8%	76.2%
3,851	KENT	564	31	533		502 D	5.5%	94.5%	5.5%	94.5%
10,151	KERR	2,589	994	1,586	9	592 D	38.4%	61.3%	38.5%	61.5%
4,119	KIMBLE	833	151	681	1	530 D	18.1%	81.8%	18.1%	81.9%
1,193	KING	224	13	211		198 D	5.8%	94.2%	5.8%	94.2%
3,980	KINNEY	532	175	357		182 D	32.9%	67.1%	32.9%	67.1%
12,451	KLEBERG	1,708	156	1,488	64	1,332 D	9.1%	87.1%	9.5%	90.5%
11,368	KNOX	2,000	171	1,823	6	1,652 D	8.6%	91.2%	8.6%	91.4%
48,529	LAMAR	5,939	308	5,621	10	5,313 D	5.2%	94.6%	5.2%	94.8%
17,452	LAMB	2,630	300	2,320	10	2,020 D	11.4%	88.2%	11.5%	88.5%
8,677	LAMPASAS	1,599	134	1,462	3	1,328 D	8.4%	91.4%	8.4%	91.6%
8,228	LA SALLE	778	74	704		630 D	9.5%	90.5%	9.5%	90.5%
27,550	LAVACA	2,620	403	2,204	13	1,801 D	15.4%	84.1%	15.5%	84.5%
13,390	LEE	1,427	271	1,155	1	884 D	19.0%	80.9%	19.0%	81.0%
19,898	LEON	1,846	97	1,748	1	1,651 D	5.3%	94.7%	5.3%	94.7%
19,868	LIBERTY	3,068	244	2,813	11	2,569 D	8.0%	91.7%	8.0%	92.0%
39,497	LIMESTONE	4,058	196	3,857	5	3,661 D	4.8%	95.0%	4.8%	95.2%
4,512	LIPSCOMB	1,253	273	973	7	700 D	21.8%	77.7%	21.9%	78.1%
8,956	LIVE OAK	1,145	231	874	40	643 D	20.2%	76.3%	20.9%	79.1%
5,538	LLANO	1,409	107	1,302		1,195 D	7.6%	92.4%	7.6%	92.4%
195	LOVING	163	21	118	24	97 D	12.9%	72.4%	15.1%	84.9%
39,104	LUBBOCK	7,063	622	6,425	16	5,803 D	8.8%	91.0%	8.8%	91.2%
12,372	LYNN	2,158	169	1,983	6	1,814 D	7.8%	91.9%	7.9%	92.1%
13,883	MCCULLOCH	2,111	323	1,772	16	1,449 D	15.3%	83.9%	15.4%	84.6%
98,682	MCLENNAN	13,759	1,116	12,489	154	11,373 D	8.1%	90.8%	8.2%	91.8%
1,351	MCMULLEN	302	37	265		228 D	12.3%	87.7%	12.3%	87.7%
12,227	MADISON	1,172	45	1,127		1,082 D	3.8%	96.2%	3.8%	96.2%
10,371	MARION	1,048	129	919		790 D	12.3%	87.7%	12.3%	87.7%
5,785	MARTIN	854	70	775	9	705 D	8.2%	90.7%	8.3%	91.7%
5,511	MASON	1,147	359	787	1	428 D	31.3%	68.6%	31.3%	68.7%
17,678	MATAGORDA	2,164	459	1,700	5	1,241 D	21.2%	78.6%	21.3%	78.7%
6,120	MAVERICK	1,096	166	890	40	724 D	15.1%	81.2%	15.7%	84.3%
13,989	MEDINA	3,031	969	2,050	12	1,081 D	32.0%	67.6%	32.1%	67.9%
4,447	MENARD	853	115	734	4	619 D	13.5%	86.0%	13.5%	86.5%
8,005	MIDLAND	1,428	190	1,229	9	1,039 D	13.3%	86.1%	13.4%	86.6%
37,915	MILAM	4,383	288	4,077	18	3,789 D	6.6%	93.0%	6.6%	93.4%
8,293	MILLS	1,170	165	1,005		840 D	14.1%	85.9%	14.1%	85.9%
14,183	MITCHELL	2,231	192	2,035	4	1,843 D	8.6%	91.2%	8.6%	91.4%
19,159	MONTAGUE	3,128	324	2,789	15	2,465 D	10.4%	89.2%	10.4%	89.6%
14,588	MONTGOMERY	2,638	186	2,443	9	2,257 D	7.1%	92.6%	7.1%	92.9%
1,555	MOORE	631	47	583	1	536 D	7.4%	92.4%	7.5%	92.5%
10,028	MORRIS	1,272	52	1,220		1,168 D	4.1%	95.9%	4.1%	95.9%
6,812	MOTLEY	933	64	867	2	803 D	6.9%	92.9%	6.9%	93.1%
30,290	NACOGDOCHES	4,289	209	4,075	5	3,866 D	4.9%	95.0%	4.9%	95.1%
60,507	NAVARRO	6,120	293	5,815	12	5,522 D	4.8%	95.0%	4.8%	95.2%
12,524	NEWTON	1,206	93	1,111	2	1,018 D	7.7%	92.1%	7.7%	92.3%
19,323	NOLAN	3,196	268	2,913	15	2,645 D	8.4%	91.1%	8.4%	91.6%
51,779	NUECES	7,940	1,234	6,597	109	5,363 D	15.5%	83.1%	15.8%	84.2%
5,224	OCHILTREE	1,262	109	1,111	42	1,002 D	8.6%	88.0%	8.9%	91.1%
1,404	OLDHAM	462	20	437	5	417 D	4.3%	94.6%	4.4%	95.6%

TEXAS

PRESIDENT 1936

1930 Census Population	County	Total Vote	Republican	Democratic	Other	Rep.-Dem. Plurality	Percentage Total Vote Rep.	Percentage Total Vote Dem.	Percentage Major Vote Rep.	Percentage Major Vote Dem.
15,149	ORANGE	2,479	190	2,281	8	2,091 D	7.7%	92.0%	7.7%	92.3%
17,576	PALO PINTO	3,123	371	2,738	14	2,367 D	11.9%	87.7%	11.9%	88.1%
24,063	PANOLA	2,543	95	2,425	23	2,330 D	3.7%	95.4%	3.8%	96.2%
18,759	PARKER	2,896	375	2,493	28	2,118 D	12.9%	86.1%	13.1%	86.9%
5,869	PARMER	1,078	135	936	7	801 D	12.5%	86.8%	12.6%	87.4%
7,812	PECOS	1,498	167	1,330	1	1,163 D	11.1%	88.8%	11.2%	88.8%
17,555	POLK	1,760	141	1,618	1	1,477 D	8.0%	91.9%	8.0%	92.0%
46,080	POTTER	7,643	1,018	6,496	129	5,478 D	13.3%	85.0%	13.5%	86.5%
10,154	PRESIDIO	1,049	106	938	5	832 D	10.1%	89.4%	10.2%	89.8%
7,114	RAINS	741	63	676	2	613 D	8.5%	91.2%	8.5%	91.5%
7,071	RANDALL	1,804	142	1,656	6	1,514 D	7.9%	91.8%	7.9%	92.1%
3,028	REAGAN	543	66	477		411 D	12.2%	87.8%	12.2%	87.8%
2,197	REAL	265	55	210		155 D	20.8%	79.2%	20.8%	79.2%
30,923	RED RIVER	2,887	199	2,685	3	2,486 D	6.9%	93.0%	6.9%	93.1%
6,407	REEVES	1,230	100	1,127	3	1,027 D	8.1%	91.6%	8.1%	91.9%
7,691	REFUGIO	1,305	242	1,058	5	816 D	18.5%	81.1%	18.6%	81.4%
1,457	ROBERTS	453	27	426		399 D	6.0%	94.0%	6.0%	94.0%
27,240	ROBERTSON	2,721	86	2,633	2	2,547 D	3.2%	96.8%	3.2%	96.8%
7,658	ROCKWALL	1,195	26	1,168	1	1,142 D	2.2%	97.7%	2.2%	97.8%
21,821	RUNNELS	3,317	313	2,985	19	2,672 D	9.4%	90.0%	9.5%	90.5%
32,484	RUSK	6,548	433	6,107	8	5,674 D	6.6%	93.3%	6.6%	93.4%
11,998	SABINE	1,326	108	1,216	2	1,108 D	8.1%	91.7%	8.2%	91.8%
12,471	SAN AUGUSTINE	1,118	64	1,054		990 D	5.7%	94.3%	5.7%	94.3%
9,711	SAN JACINTO	631	67	564		497 D	10.6%	89.4%	10.6%	89.4%
23,836	SAN PATRICIO	2,725	482	2,213	30	1,731 D	17.7%	81.2%	17.9%	82.1%
10,273	SAN SABA	1,654	147	1,505	2	1,358 D	8.9%	91.0%	8.9%	91.1%
3,166	SCHLEICHER	548	78	469	1	391 D	14.2%	85.6%	14.3%	85.7%
12,188	SCURRY	1,912	162	1,746	4	1,584 D	8.5%	91.3%	8.5%	91.5%
6,695	SHACKELFORD	1,305	152	1,153		1,001 D	11.6%	88.4%	11.6%	88.4%
28,627	SHELBY	3,312	136	3,167	9	3,031 D	4.1%	95.6%	4.1%	95.9%
2,314	SHERMAN	602	34	568		534 D	5.6%	94.4%	5.6%	94.4%
53,123	SMITH	7,788	660	7,116	12	6,456 D	8.5%	91.4%	8.5%	91.5%
3,016	SOMERVELL	378	57	317	4	260 D	15.1%	83.9%	15.2%	84.8%
11,409	STARR	2,618	320	2,289	9	1,969 D	12.2%	87.4%	12.3%	87.7%
16,560	STEPHENS	3,080	681	2,380	19	1,699 D	22.1%	77.3%	22.2%	77.8%
1,431	STERLING	398	14	384		370 D	3.5%	96.5%	3.5%	96.5%
5,667	STONEWALL	1,061	59	1,001	1	942 D	5.6%	94.3%	5.6%	94.4%
2,807	SUTTON	462	64	398		334 D	13.9%	86.1%	13.9%	86.1%
7,343	SWISHER	1,597	140	1,453	4	1,313 D	8.8%	91.0%	8.8%	91.2%
197,553	TARRANT	33,762	3,781	29,791	190	26,010 D	11.2%	88.2%	11.3%	88.7%
41,023	TAYLOR	6,898	678	6,169	51	5,491 D	9.8%	89.4%	9.9%	90.1%
2,660	TERRELL	408	84	324		240 D	20.6%	79.4%	20.6%	79.4%
8,883	TERRY	1,719	87	1,619	13	1,532 D	5.1%	94.2%	5.1%	94.9%
5,253	THROCKMORTON	1,083	132	949	2	817 D	12.2%	87.6%	12.2%	87.8%
16,003	TITUS	1,952	77	1,872	3	1,795 D	3.9%	95.9%	4.0%	96.0%
36,033	TOM GREEN	5,499	627	4,803	69	4,176 D	11.4%	87.3%	11.5%	88.5%
77,777	TRAVIS	13,425	1,154	12,092	179	10,938 D	8.6%	90.1%	8.7%	91.3%
13,637	TRINITY	1,348	151	1,196	1	1,045 D	11.2%	88.7%	11.2%	88.8%
11,448	TYLER	1,192	116	1,076		960 D	9.7%	90.3%	9.7%	90.3%
22,297	UPSHUR	2,567	321	2,243	3	1,922 D	12.5%	87.4%	12.5%	87.5%
5,968	UPTON	813	81	728	4	647 D	10.0%	89.5%	10.0%	90.0%
12,945	UVALDE	2,098	354	1,743	1	1,389 D	16.9%	83.1%	16.9%	83.1%
14,924	VAL VERDE	1,771	504	1,262	5	758 D	28.5%	71.3%	28.5%	71.5%
32,315	VAN ZANDT	3,531	245	3,257	29	3,012 D	6.9%	92.2%	7.0%	93.0%
20,048	VICTORIA	2,435	352	2,081	2	1,729 D	14.5%	85.5%	14.5%	85.5%
18,528	WALKER	1,786	69	1,715	2	1,646 D	3.9%	96.0%	3.9%	96.1%
10,014	WALLER	1,002	111	889	2	778 D	11.1%	88.7%	11.1%	88.9%
4,599	WARD	1,213	98	1,113	2	1,015 D	8.1%	91.8%	8.1%	91.9%
25,394	WASHINGTON	2,173	176	1,993	4	1,817 D	8.1%	91.7%	8.1%	91.9%
42,128	WEBB	4,290	696	3,594		2,898 D	16.2%	83.8%	16.2%	83.8%

TEXAS

PRESIDENT 1936

1930 Census Population	County	Total Vote	Republican	Democratic	Other	Rep.-Dem. Plurality	Percentage Total Vote Rep.	Percentage Total Vote Dem.	Percentage Major Vote Rep.	Percentage Major Vote Dem.
29,681	WHARTON	3,355	307	3,034	14	2,727 D	9.2%	90.4%	9.2%	90.8%
15,555	WHEELER	2,704	277	2,415	12	2,138 D	10.2%	89.3%	10.3%	89.7%
74,416	WICHITA	10,788	1,327	9,428	33	8,101 D	12.3%	87.4%	12.3%	87.7%
24,579	WILBARGER	3,613	316	3,279	18	2,963 D	8.7%	90.8%	8.8%	91.2%
10,499	WILLACY	1,399	376	1,002	21	626 D	26.9%	71.6%	27.3%	72.7%
44,146	WILLIAMSON	5,383	375	4,995	13	4,620 D	7.0%	92.8%	7.0%	93.0%
17,606	WILSON	2,864	286	2,573	5	2,287 D	10.0%	89.8%	10.0%	90.0%
6,784	WINKLER	975	63	903	9	840 D	6.5%	92.6%	6.5%	93.5%
19,178	WISE	3,090	348	2,737	5	2,389 D	11.3%	88.6%	11.3%	88.7%
24,183	WOOD	2,950	192	2,751	7	2,559 D	6.5%	93.3%	6.5%	93.5%
1,263	YOAKUM	245	13	227	5	214 D	5.3%	92.7%	5.4%	94.6%
20,128	YOUNG	3,381	304	3,065	12	2,761 D	9.0%	90.7%	9.0%	91.0%
2,867	ZAPATA	316	34	282		248 D	10.8%	89.2%	10.8%	89.2%
10,349	ZAVALA	1,002	209	788	5	579 D	20.9%	78.6%	21.0%	79.0%
5,824,715	TOTAL	849,701	104,661	739,952	5,088	635,291 D	12.3%	87.1%	12.4%	87.6%

TEXAS

PRESIDENT 1932

1930 Census Population	County	Total Vote	Republican	Democratic	Other	Rep.-Dem. Plurality	Percentage Total Vote Rep.	Percentage Total Vote Dem.	Percentage Major Vote Rep.	Percentage Major Vote Dem.
34,643	ANDERSON	4,627	259	4,354	14	4,095 D	5.6%	94.1%	5.6%	94.4%
736	ANDREWS	193	6	186	1	180 D	3.1%	96.4%	3.1%	96.9%
27,803	ANGELINA	5,253	287	4,962	4	4,675 D	5.5%	94.5%	5.5%	94.5%
2,219	ARANSAS	308	39	268	1	229 D	12.7%	87.0%	12.7%	87.3%
9,684	ARCHER	1,654	97	1,555	2	1,458 D	5.9%	94.0%	5.9%	94.1%
3,329	ARMSTRONG	877	63	813	1	750 D	7.2%	92.7%	7.2%	92.8%
15,654	ATASCOSA	2,307	192	2,101	14	1,909 D	8.3%	91.1%	8.4%	91.6%
18,860	AUSTIN	2,955	142	2,806	7	2,664 D	4.8%	95.0%	4.8%	95.2%
5,186	BAILEY	958	104	851	3	747 D	10.9%	88.8%	10.9%	89.1%
3,784	BANDERA	1,249	359	883	7	524 D	28.7%	70.7%	28.9%	71.1%
23,888	BASTROP	3,259	180	3,077	2	2,897 D	5.5%	94.4%	5.5%	94.5%
7,418	BAYLOR	1,493	55	1,437	1	1,382 D	3.7%	96.2%	3.7%	96.3%
15,721	BEE	2,724	534	2,180	10	1,646 D	19.6%	80.0%	19.7%	80.3%
50,030	BELL	8,354	724	7,607	23	6,883 D	8.7%	91.1%	8.7%	91.3%
292,533	BEXAR	45,594	7,466	37,765	363	30,299 D	16.4%	82.8%	16.5%	83.5%
3,842	BLANCO	1,367	127	1,233	7	1,106 D	9.3%	90.2%	9.3%	90.7%
1,505	BORDEN	249	7	242		235 D	2.8%	97.2%	2.8%	97.2%
15,750	BOSQUE	3,489	272	3,214	3	2,942 D	7.8%	92.1%	7.8%	92.2%
48,563	BOWIE	5,829	541	5,269	19	4,728 D	9.3%	90.4%	9.3%	90.7%
23,054	BRAZORIA	3,576	617	2,948	11	2,331 D	17.3%	82.4%	17.3%	82.7%
21,835	BRAZOS	2,801	195	2,588	18	2,393 D	7.0%	92.4%	7.0%	93.0%
6,624	BREWSTER	1,010	130	875	5	745 D	12.9%	86.6%	12.9%	87.1%
5,590	BRISCOE	1,023	42	977	4	935 D	4.1%	95.5%	4.1%	95.9%
5,901	BROOKS	697	86	608	3	522 D	12.3%	87.2%	12.4%	87.6%
26,382	BROWN	4,375	330	4,024	21	3,694 D	7.5%	92.0%	7.6%	92.4%
19,848	BURLESON	2,545	119	2,423	3	2,304 D	4.7%	95.2%	4.7%	95.3%
10,355	BURNET	2,050	144	1,904	2	1,760 D	7.0%	92.9%	7.0%	93.0%
31,397	CALDWELL	3,610	291	3,317	2	3,026 D	8.1%	91.9%	8.1%	91.9%
5,385	CALHOUN	944	100	834	10	734 D	10.6%	88.3%	10.7%	89.3%
12,785	CALLAHAN	2,285	152	2,133		1,981 D	6.7%	93.3%	6.7%	93.3%
77,540	CAMERON	8,985	1,785	7,146	54	5,361 D	19.9%	79.5%	20.0%	80.0%
10,063	CAMP	1,491	73	1,416	2	1,343 D	4.9%	95.0%	4.9%	95.1%
7,745	CARSON	1,603	212	1,391		1,179 D	13.2%	86.8%	13.2%	86.8%
30,030	CASS	3,359	224	3,135		2,911 D	6.7%	93.3%	6.7%	93.3%
4,720	CASTRO	1,023	66	949	8	883 D	6.5%	92.8%	6.5%	93.5%
5,710	CHAMBERS	939	91	843	5	752 D	9.7%	89.8%	9.7%	90.3%
43,180	CHEROKEE	4,368	233	4,125	10	3,892 D	5.3%	94.4%	5.3%	94.7%
16,044	CHILDRESS	2,238	153	2,072	13	1,919 D	6.8%	92.6%	6.9%	93.1%
14,545	CLAY	2,523	151	2,365	7	2,214 D	6.0%	93.7%	6.0%	94.0%
1,963	COCHRAN	388	31	345	12	314 D	8.0%	88.9%	8.2%	91.8%
5,253	COKE	1,047	57	983	7	926 D	5.4%	93.9%	5.5%	94.5%
23,669	COLEMAN	3,128	235	2,881	12	2,646 D	7.5%	92.1%	7.5%	92.5%
46,180	COLLIN	6,698	589	6,059	50	5,470 D	8.8%	90.5%	8.9%	91.1%
14,461	COLLINGSWORTH	1,879	115	1,753	11	1,638 D	6.1%	93.3%	6.2%	93.8%
19,129	COLORADO	3,069	331	2,715	23	2,384 D	10.8%	88.5%	10.9%	89.1%
11,984	COMAL	2,402	176	2,211	15	2,035 D	7.3%	92.0%	7.4%	92.6%
18,430	COMANCHE	3,339	192	3,134	13	2,942 D	5.8%	93.9%	5.8%	94.2%
7,645	CONCHO	1,174	44	1,126	4	1,082 D	3.7%	95.9%	3.8%	96.2%
24,136	COOKE	4,265	470	3,775	20	3,305 D	11.0%	88.5%	11.1%	88.9%
19,999	CORYELL	3,541	191	3,347	3	3,156 D	5.4%	94.5%	5.4%	94.6%
9,395	COTTLE	1,234	38	1,196		1,158 D	3.1%	96.9%	3.1%	96.9%
2,221	CRANE	454	37	416	1	379 D	8.1%	91.6%	8.2%	91.8%
2,590	CROCKETT	497	168	329		161 D	33.8%	66.2%	33.8%	66.2%
11,023	CROSBY	1,698	108	1,590		1,482 D	6.4%	93.6%	6.4%	93.6%
1,228	CULBERSON	304	18	285	1	267 D	5.9%	93.8%	5.9%	94.1%
7,830	DALLAM	2,300	341	1,935	24	1,594 D	14.8%	84.1%	15.0%	85.0%
325,691	DALLAS	46,653	8,919	37,363	371	28,444 D	19.1%	80.1%	19.3%	80.7%
13,573	DAWSON	1,813	153	1,659	1	1,506 D	8.4%	91.5%	8.4%	91.6%
5,979	DEAF SMITH	1,505	198	1,307		1,109 D	13.2%	86.8%	13.2%	86.8%
13,138	DELTA	2,101	87	2,013	1	1,926 D	4.1%	95.8%	4.1%	95.9%

TEXAS

PRESIDENT 1932

1930 Census Population	County	Total Vote	Republican	Democratic	Other	Rep.-Dem. Plurality	Percentage Total Vote Rep.	Total Vote Dem.	Major Vote Rep.	Major Vote Dem.
32,822	DENTON	5,677	520	5,115	42	4,595 D	9.2%	90.1%	9.2%	90.8%
27,441	DE WITT	3,521	309	3,206	6	2,897 D	8.8%	91.1%	8.8%	91.2%
8,601	DICKENS	1,562	63	1,491	8	1,428 D	4.0%	95.5%	4.1%	95.9%
8,828	DIMMIT	1,090	241	843	6	602 D	22.1%	77.3%	22.2%	77.8%
10,262	DONLEY	1,773	141	1,626	6	1,485 D	8.0%	91.7%	8.0%	92.0%
12,191	DUVAL	1,596	30	1,566		1,536 D	1.9%	98.1%	1.9%	98.1%
34,156	EASTLAND	5,556	598	4,958		4,360 D	10.8%	89.2%	10.8%	89.2%
3,958	ECTOR	595	37	530	28	493 D	6.2%	89.1%	6.5%	93.5%
2,764	EDWARDS	804	224	575	5	351 D	27.9%	71.5%	28.0%	72.0%
53,936	ELLIS	7,604	527	7,033	44	6,506 D	6.9%	92.5%	7.0%	93.0%
131,597	EL PASO	14,392	2,841	11,336	215	8,495 D	19.7%	78.8%	20.0%	80.0%
20,804	ERATH	3,629	284	3,319	26	3,035 D	7.8%	91.5%	7.9%	92.1%
38,771	FALLS	4,084	181	3,896	7	3,715 D	4.4%	95.4%	4.4%	95.6%
41,163	FANNIN	5,815	460	5,338	17	4,878 D	7.9%	91.8%	7.9%	92.1%
30,708	FAYETTE	5,233	245	4,985	3	4,740 D	4.7%	95.3%	4.7%	95.3%
13,563	FISHER	1,506	105	1,395	6	1,290 D	7.0%	92.6%	7.0%	93.0%
12,409	FLOYD	2,126	145	1,976	5	1,831 D	6.8%	92.9%	6.8%	93.2%
6,315	FOARD	948	53	882	13	829 D	5.6%	93.0%	5.7%	94.3%
29,718	FORT BEND	3,265	148	3,109	8	2,961 D	4.5%	95.2%	4.5%	95.5%
8,494	FRANKLIN	1,362	56	1,305	1	1,249 D	4.1%	95.8%	4.1%	95.9%
22,589	FREESTONE	2,656	170	2,481	5	2,311 D	6.4%	93.4%	6.4%	93.6%
9,411	FRIO	1,140	142	998		856 D	12.5%	87.5%	12.5%	87.5%
2,800	GAINES	562	44	510	8	466 D	7.8%	90.7%	7.9%	92.1%
64,401	GALVESTON	12,582	2,011	10,491	80	8,480 D	16.0%	83.4%	16.1%	83.9%
5,586	GARZA	904	87	812	5	725 D	9.6%	89.8%	9.7%	90.3%
11,020	GILLESPIE	3,317	662	2,642	13	1,980 D	20.0%	79.7%	20.0%	80.0%
1,263	GLASSCOCK	254	42	212		170 D	16.5%	83.5%	16.5%	83.5%
10,093	GOLIAD	1,718	170	1,542	6	1,372 D	9.9%	89.8%	9.9%	90.1%
28,337	GONZALES	3,728	337	3,384	7	3,047 D	9.0%	90.8%	9.1%	90.9%
22,090	GRAY	3,975	505	3,446	24	2,941 D	12.7%	86.7%	12.8%	87.2%
65,843	GRAYSON	10,992	1,317	9,631	44	8,314 D	12.0%	87.6%	12.0%	88.0%
15,778	GREGG	5,565	341	5,204	20	4,863 D	6.1%	93.5%	6.1%	93.9%
22,642	GRIMES	2,223	153	2,065	5	1,912 D	6.9%	92.9%	6.9%	93.1%
28,925	GUADALUPE	4,451	691	3,751	9	3,060 D	15.5%	84.3%	15.6%	84.4%
20,189	HALE	3,437	369	3,029	39	2,660 D	10.7%	88.1%	10.9%	89.1%
16,966	HALL	2,218	91	2,114	13	2,023 D	4.1%	95.3%	4.1%	95.9%
13,523	HAMILTON	2,642	164	2,474	4	2,310 D	6.2%	93.6%	6.2%	93.8%
3,548	HANSFORD	901	67	803	31	736 D	7.4%	89.1%	7.7%	92.3%
14,532	HARDEMAN	2,135	145	1,985	5	1,840 D	6.8%	93.0%	6.8%	93.2%
13,936	HARDIN	2,944	161	2,783		2,622 D	5.5%	94.5%	5.5%	94.5%
359,328	HARRIS	55,970	8,604	46,886	480	38,282 D	15.4%	83.8%	15.5%	84.5%
48,937	HARRISON	4,604	528	4,057	19	3,529 D	11.5%	88.1%	11.5%	88.5%
2,185	HARTLEY	660	74	586		512 D	11.2%	88.8%	11.2%	88.8%
16,669	HASKELL	2,500	154	2,330	16	2,176 D	6.2%	93.2%	6.2%	93.8%
14,915	HAYS	2,050	220	1,822	8	1,602 D	10.7%	88.9%	10.8%	89.2%
4,637	HEMPHILL	1,052	133	918	1	785 D	12.6%	87.3%	12.7%	87.3%
30,583	HENDERSON	3,760	219	3,522	19	3,303 D	5.8%	93.7%	5.9%	94.1%
77,004	HIDALGO	12,784	2,969	9,695	120	6,726 D	23.2%	75.8%	23.4%	76.6%
43,036	HILL	5,662	360	5,297	5	4,937 D	6.4%	93.6%	6.4%	93.6%
9,298	HOCKLEY	1,623	76	1,513	34	1,437 D	4.7%	93.2%	4.8%	95.2%
6,779	HOOD	1,230	106	1,119	5	1,013 D	8.6%	91.0%	8.7%	91.3%
29,410	HOPKINS	5,159	261	4,891	7	4,630 D	5.1%	94.8%	5.1%	94.9%
30,017	HOUSTON	3,255	165	3,087	3	2,922 D	5.1%	94.8%	5.1%	94.9%
22,888	HOWARD	2,895	149	2,733	13	2,584 D	5.1%	94.4%	5.2%	94.8%
3,728	HUDSPETH	373	31	341	1	310 D	8.3%	91.4%	8.3%	91.7%
49,016	HUNT	7,340	465	6,856	19	6,391 D	6.3%	93.4%	6.4%	93.6%
14,848	HUTCHINSON	2,508	505	1,976	27	1,471 D	20.1%	78.8%	20.4%	79.6%
2,049	IRION	456	47	398	11	351 D	10.3%	87.3%	10.6%	89.4%
9,046	JACK	1,634	189	1,429	16	1,240 D	11.6%	87.5%	11.7%	88.3%
10,980	JACKSON	1,214	182	1,030	2	848 D	15.0%	84.8%	15.0%	85.0%

TEXAS

PRESIDENT 1932

1930 Census Population	County	Total Vote	Republican	Democratic	Other	Rep.-Dem. Plurality	Percentage Total Vote Rep.	Percentage Total Vote Dem.	Percentage Major Vote Rep.	Percentage Major Vote Dem.
17,064	JASPER	2,084	93	1,990	1	1,897 D	4.5%	95.5%	4.5%	95.5%
1,800	JEFF DAVIS	302	46	252	4	206 D	15.2%	83.4%	15.4%	84.6%
133,391	JEFFERSON	20,865	3,584	17,129	152	13,545 D	17.2%	82.1%	17.3%	82.7%
4,919	JIM HOGG	479	51	428		377 D	10.6%	89.4%	10.6%	89.4%
13,456	JIM WELLS	1,621	162	1,449	10	1,287 D	10.0%	89.4%	10.1%	89.9%
33,317	JOHNSON	5,405	530	4,858	17	4,328 D	9.8%	89.9%	9.8%	90.2%
24,233	JONES	3,188	224	2,934	30	2,710 D	7.0%	92.0%	7.1%	92.9%
23,316	KARNES	2,650	186	2,458	6	2,272 D	7.0%	92.8%	7.0%	93.0%
40,905	KAUFMAN	4,389	268	4,116	5	3,848 D	6.1%	93.8%	6.1%	93.9%
4,970	KENDALL	1,609	416	1,185	8	769 D	25.9%	73.6%	26.0%	74.0%
701	KENEDY	129	5	123	1	118 D	3.9%	95.3%	3.9%	96.1%
3,851	KENT	587	23	561	3	538 D	3.9%	95.6%	3.9%	96.1%
10,151	KERR	2,804	623	2,165	16	1,542 D	22.2%	77.2%	22.3%	77.7%
4,119	KIMBLE	1,014	121	890	3	769 D	11.9%	87.8%	12.0%	88.0%
1,193	KING	228	4	224		220 D	1.8%	98.2%	1.8%	98.2%
3,980	KINNEY	768	89	678	1	589 D	11.6%	88.3%	11.6%	88.4%
12,451	KLEBERG	1,950	198	1,727	25	1,529 D	10.2%	88.6%	10.3%	89.7%
11,368	KNOX	1,706	102	1,600	4	1,498 D	6.0%	93.8%	6.0%	94.0%
48,529	LAMAR	6,307	375	5,911	21	5,536 D	5.9%	93.7%	6.0%	94.0%
17,452	LAMB	3,288	271	2,978	39	2,707 D	8.2%	90.6%	8.3%	91.7%
8,677	LAMPASAS	1,944	120	1,824		1,704 D	6.2%	93.8%	6.2%	93.8%
8,228	LA SALLE	905	92	810	3	718 D	10.2%	89.5%	10.2%	89.8%
27,550	LAVACA	4,613	224	4,378	11	4,154 D	4.9%	94.9%	4.9%	95.1%
13,390	LEE	1,941	110	1,831		1,721 D	5.7%	94.3%	5.7%	94.3%
19,898	LEON	2,076	108	1,958	10	1,850 D	5.2%	94.3%	5.2%	94.8%
19,868	LIBERTY	2,796	247	2,527	22	2,280 D	8.8%	90.4%	8.9%	91.1%
39,497	LIMESTONE	4,635	215	4,416	4	4,201 D	4.6%	95.3%	4.6%	95.4%
4,512	LIPSCOMB	1,271	349	865	57	516 D	27.5%	68.1%	28.7%	71.3%
8,956	LIVE OAK	1,192	114	1,070	8	956 D	9.6%	89.8%	9.6%	90.4%
5,538	LLANO	1,337	108	1,229		1,121 D	8.1%	91.9%	8.1%	91.9%
195	LOVING	215	27	187	1	160 D	12.6%	87.0%	12.6%	87.4%
39,104	LUBBOCK	5,953	590	5,330	33	4,740 D	9.9%	89.5%	10.0%	90.0%
12,372	LYNN	2,048	110	1,930	8	1,820 D	5.4%	94.2%	5.4%	94.6%
13,883	MCCULLOCH	2,277	265	2,006	6	1,741 D	11.6%	88.1%	11.7%	88.3%
98,682	MCLENNAN	13,185	1,108	11,972	105	10,864 D	8.4%	90.8%	8.5%	91.5%
1,351	MCMULLEN	270	12	258		246 D	4.4%	95.6%	4.4%	95.6%
12,227	MADISON	1,364	20	1,344		1,324 D	1.5%	98.5%	1.5%	98.5%
10,371	MARION	951	84	861	6	777 D	8.8%	90.5%	8.9%	91.1%
5,785	MARTIN	744	44	694	6	650 D	5.9%	93.3%	6.0%	94.0%
5,511	MASON	1,141	309	828	4	519 D	27.1%	72.6%	27.2%	72.8%
17,678	MATAGORDA	2,461	408	2,039	14	1,631 D	16.6%	82.9%	16.7%	83.3%
6,120	MAVERICK	1,056	199	847	10	648 D	18.8%	80.2%	19.0%	81.0%
13,989	MEDINA	3,036	515	2,516	5	2,001 D	17.0%	82.9%	17.0%	83.0%
4,447	MENARD	1,053	150	901	2	751 D	14.2%	85.6%	14.3%	85.7%
8,005	MIDLAND	1,402	136	1,245	21	1,109 D	9.7%	88.8%	9.8%	90.2%
37,915	MILAM	4,963	264	4,676	23	4,412 D	5.3%	94.2%	5.3%	94.7%
8,293	MILLS	1,567	133	1,434		1,301 D	8.5%	91.5%	8.5%	91.5%
14,183	MITCHELL	1,640	148	1,490	2	1,342 D	9.0%	90.9%	9.0%	91.0%
19,159	MONTAGUE	3,381	262	3,090	29	2,828 D	7.7%	91.4%	7.8%	92.2%
14,588	MONTGOMERY	2,099	126	1,971	2	1,845 D	6.0%	93.9%	6.0%	94.0%
1,555	MOORE	607	56	549	2	493 D	9.2%	90.4%	9.3%	90.7%
10,028	MORRIS	1,291	38	1,253		1,215 D	2.9%	97.1%	2.9%	97.1%
6,812	MOTLEY	936	34	900	2	866 D	3.6%	96.2%	3.6%	96.4%
30,290	NACOGDOCHES	3,726	117	3,603	6	3,486 D	3.1%	96.7%	3.1%	96.9%
60,507	NAVARRO	6,915	512	6,392	11	5,880 D	7.4%	92.4%	7.4%	92.6%
12,524	NEWTON	1,635	46	1,586	3	1,540 D	2.8%	97.0%	2.8%	97.2%
19,323	NOLAN	2,675	219	2,453	3	2,234 D	8.2%	91.7%	8.2%	91.8%
51,779	NUECES	7,662	967	6,659	36	5,692 D	12.6%	86.9%	12.7%	87.3%
5,224	OCHILTREE	1,291	183	1,097	11	914 D	14.2%	85.0%	14.3%	85.7%
1,404	OLDHAM	493	61	432		371 D	12.4%	87.6%	12.4%	87.6%

TEXAS

PRESIDENT 1932

1930 Census Population	County	Total Vote	Republican	Democratic	Other	Rep.-Dem. Plurality	Percentage Total Vote Rep.	Total Vote Dem.	Major Vote Rep.	Major Vote Dem.
15,149	ORANGE	3,078	244	2,830	4	2,586 D	7.9%	91.9%	7.9%	92.1%
17,576	PALO PINTO	3,128	392	2,722	14	2,330 D	12.5%	87.0%	12.6%	87.4%
24,063	PANOLA	2,709	50	2,630	29	2,580 D	1.8%	97.1%	1.9%	98.1%
18,759	PARKER	3,482	372	3,074	36	2,702 D	10.7%	88.3%	10.8%	89.2%
5,869	PARMER	1,319	148	1,154	17	1,006 D	11.2%	87.5%	11.4%	88.6%
7,812	PECOS	1,448	180	1,261	7	1,081 D	12.4%	87.1%	12.5%	87.5%
17,555	POLK	2,229	110	2,117	2	2,007 D	4.9%	95.0%	4.9%	95.1%
46,080	POTTER	7,643	1,233	6,366	44	5,133 D	16.1%	83.3%	16.2%	83.8%
10,154	PRESIDIO	977	112	863	2	751 D	11.5%	88.3%	11.5%	88.5%
7,114	RAINS	985	41	937	7	896 D	4.2%	95.1%	4.2%	95.8%
7,071	RANDALL	1,638	231	1,394	13	1,163 D	14.1%	85.1%	14.2%	85.8%
3,028	REAGAN	808	124	681	3	557 D	15.3%	84.3%	15.4%	84.6%
2,197	REAL	424	89	335		246 D	21.0%	79.0%	21.0%	79.0%
30,923	RED RIVER	3,333	145	3,181	7	3,036 D	4.4%	95.4%	4.4%	95.6%
6,407	REEVES	1,211	122	1,085	4	963 D	10.1%	89.6%	10.1%	89.9%
7,691	REFUGIO	1,394	172	1,201	21	1,029 D	12.3%	86.2%	12.5%	87.5%
1,457	ROBERTS	491	36	451	4	415 D	7.3%	91.9%	7.4%	92.6%
27,240	ROBERTSON	2,544	148	2,396		2,248 D	5.8%	94.2%	5.8%	94.2%
7,658	ROCKWALL	1,299	62	1,237		1,175 D	4.8%	95.2%	4.8%	95.2%
21,821	RUNNELS	3,220	235	2,975	10	2,740 D	7.3%	92.4%	7.3%	92.7%
32,484	RUSK	5,566	483	5,074	9	4,591 D	8.7%	91.2%	8.7%	91.3%
11,998	SABINE	1,849	57	1,789	3	1,732 D	3.1%	96.8%	3.1%	96.9%
12,471	SAN AUGUSTINE	1,821	19	1,802		1,783 D	1.0%	99.0%	1.0%	99.0%
9,711	SAN JACINTO	848	16	828	4	812 D	1.9%	97.6%	1.9%	98.1%
23,836	SAN PATRICIO	2,566	407	2,142	17	1,735 D	15.9%	83.5%	16.0%	84.0%
10,273	SAN SABA	2,028	122	1,904	2	1,782 D	6.0%	93.9%	6.0%	94.0%
3,166	SCHLEICHER	592	76	516		440 D	12.8%	87.2%	12.8%	87.2%
12,188	SCURRY	1,711	105	1,604	2	1,499 D	6.1%	93.7%	6.1%	93.9%
6,695	SHACKELFORD	1,438	117	1,316	5	1,199 D	8.1%	91.5%	8.2%	91.8%
28,627	SHELBY	3,734	120	3,594	20	3,474 D	3.2%	96.3%	3.2%	96.8%
2,314	SHERMAN	609	91	515	3	424 D	14.9%	84.6%	15.0%	85.0%
53,123	SMITH	8,201	750	7,424	27	6,674 D	9.1%	90.5%	9.2%	90.8%
3,016	SOMERVELL	624	43	561	20	518 D	6.9%	89.9%	7.1%	92.9%
11,409	STARR	786	32	754		722 D	4.1%	95.9%	4.1%	95.9%
16,560	STEPHENS	2,969	256	2,684	29	2,428 D	8.6%	90.4%	8.7%	91.3%
1,431	STERLING	367	13	354		341 D	3.5%	96.5%	3.5%	96.5%
5,667	STONEWALL	1,026	50	976		926 D	4.9%	95.1%	4.9%	95.1%
2,807	SUTTON	485	113	372		259 D	23.3%	76.7%	23.3%	76.7%
7,343	SWISHER	1,631	166	1,448	17	1,282 D	10.2%	88.8%	10.3%	89.7%
197,553	TARRANT	33,513	5,251	27,836	426	22,585 D	15.7%	83.1%	15.9%	84.1%
41,023	TAYLOR	5,885	639	5,235	11	4,596 D	10.9%	89.0%	10.9%	89.1%
2,660	TERRELL	613	133	479	1	346 D	21.7%	78.1%	21.7%	78.3%
8,883	TERRY	1,543	87	1,448	8	1,361 D	5.6%	93.8%	5.7%	94.3%
5,253	THROCKMORTON	1,029	95	932	2	837 D	9.2%	90.6%	9.3%	90.7%
16,003	TITUS	2,602	75	2,523	4	2,448 D	2.9%	97.0%	2.9%	97.1%
36,033	TOM GREEN	5,714	739	4,957	18	4,218 D	12.9%	86.8%	13.0%	87.0%
77,777	TRAVIS	13,376	1,532	11,718	126	10,186 D	11.5%	87.6%	11.6%	88.4%
13,637	TRINITY	1,582	65	1,514	3	1,449 D	4.1%	95.7%	4.1%	95.9%
11,448	TYLER	1,495	44	1,450	1	1,406 D	2.9%	97.0%	2.9%	97.1%
22,297	UPSHUR	3,040	129	2,900	11	2,771 D	4.2%	95.4%	4.3%	95.7%
5,968	UPTON	1,110	92	1,012	6	920 D	8.3%	91.2%	8.3%	91.7%
12,945	UVALDE	2,186	422	1,759	5	1,337 D	19.3%	80.5%	19.3%	80.7%
14,924	VAL VERDE	1,835	421	1,412	2	991 D	22.9%	76.9%	23.0%	77.0%
32,315	VAN ZANDT	4,428	190	4,203	35	4,013 D	4.3%	94.9%	4.3%	95.7%
20,048	VICTORIA	2,972	190	2,777	5	2,587 D	6.4%	93.4%	6.4%	93.6%
18,528	WALKER	1,903	83	1,811	9	1,728 D	4.4%	95.2%	4.4%	95.6%
10,014	WALLER	1,283	89	1,192	2	1,103 D	6.9%	92.9%	6.9%	93.1%
4,599	WARD	755	70	678	7	608 D	9.3%	89.8%	9.4%	90.6%
25,394	WASHINGTON	3,545	99	3,443	3	3,344 D	2.8%	97.1%	2.8%	97.2%
42,128	WEBB	4,969	657	4,299	13	3,642 D	13.2%	86.5%	13.3%	86.7%

TEXAS

PRESIDENT 1932

1930 Census Population	County	Total Vote	Republican	Democratic	Other	Rep.-Dem. Plurality	Percentage Total Vote Rep.	Percentage Total Vote Dem.	Percentage Major Vote Rep.	Percentage Major Vote Dem.
29,681	WHARTON	3,792	405	3,357	30	2,952 D	10.7%	88.5%	10.8%	89.2%
15,555	WHEELER	2,445	165	2,263	17	2,098 D	6.7%	92.6%	6.8%	93.2%
74,416	WICHITA	10,413	1,479	8,889	45	7,410 D	14.2%	85.4%	14.3%	85.7%
24,579	WILBARGER	3,609	199	3,397	13	3,198 D	5.5%	94.1%	5.5%	94.5%
10,499	WILLACY	1,302	259	1,042	1	783 D	19.9%	80.0%	19.9%	80.1%
44,146	WILLIAMSON	7,214	418	6,783	13	6,365 D	5.8%	94.0%	5.8%	94.2%
17,606	WILSON	2,612	174	2,435	3	2,261 D	6.7%	93.2%	6.7%	93.3%
6,784	WINKLER	728	78	642	8	564 D	10.7%	88.2%	10.8%	89.2%
19,178	WISE	2,980	286	2,681	13	2,395 D	9.6%	90.0%	9.6%	90.4%
24,183	WOOD	3,516	189	3,308	19	3,119 D	5.4%	94.1%	5.4%	94.6%
1,263	YOAKUM	257	11	245	1	234 D	4.3%	95.3%	4.3%	95.7%
20,128	YOUNG	3,482	320	3,156	6	2,836 D	9.2%	90.6%	9.2%	90.8%
2,867	ZAPATA	295	24	271		247 D	8.1%	91.9%	8.1%	91.9%
10,349	ZAVALA	953	166	783	4	617 D	17.4%	82.2%	17.5%	82.5%
5,824,715	TOTAL	874,382	98,218	771,109	5,055	672,891 D	11.2%	88.2%	11.3%	88.7%

TEXAS

PRESIDENT 1928

1920 Census Population	County	Total Vote	Republican	Democratic	Other	Rep.-Dem. Plurality	Percentage Total Vote Rep.	Percentage Total Vote Dem.	Percentage Major Vote Rep.	Percentage Major Vote Dem.
34,318	ANDERSON	3,561	1,814	1,747		67 R	50.9%	49.1%	50.9%	49.1%
350	ANDREWS	91	66	25		41 R	72.5%	27.5%	72.5%	27.5%
22,287	ANGELINA	3,514	1,209	2,305		1,096 D	34.4%	65.6%	34.4%	65.6%
2,064	ARANSAS	313	161	152		9 R	51.4%	48.6%	51.4%	48.6%
5,254	ARCHER	1,664	799	865		66 D	48.0%	52.0%	48.0%	52.0%
2,816	ARMSTRONG	690	316	373	1	57 D	45.8%	54.1%	45.9%	54.1%
12,702	ATASCOSA	1,570	888	682		206 R	56.6%	43.4%	56.6%	43.4%
18,874	AUSTIN	2,597	466	2,129	2	1,663 D	17.9%	82.0%	18.0%	82.0%
517	BAILEY	552	410	142		268 R	74.3%	25.7%	74.3%	25.7%
4,001	BANDERA	1,256	936	317	3	619 R	74.5%	25.2%	74.7%	25.3%
26,649	BASTROP	2,384	850	1,534		684 D	35.7%	64.3%	35.7%	64.3%
7,027	BAYLOR	1,275	491	784		293 D	38.5%	61.5%	38.5%	61.5%
12,137	BEE	2,236	1,189	1,043	4	146 R	53.2%	46.6%	53.3%	46.7%
46,412	BELL	6,452	3,366	3,079	7	287 R	52.2%	47.7%	52.2%	47.8%
202,096	BEXAR	33,160	16,477	16,626	57	149 D	49.7%	50.1%	49.8%	50.2%
4,063	BLANCO	1,155	615	539	1	76 R	53.2%	46.7%	53.3%	46.7%
965	BORDEN	171	98	73		25 R	57.3%	42.7%	57.3%	42.7%
18,032	BOSQUE	2,765	1,526	1,235	4	291 R	55.2%	44.7%	55.3%	44.7%
39,472	BOWIE	5,227	2,225	3,002		777 D	42.6%	57.4%	42.6%	57.4%
20,614	BRAZORIA	2,674	1,588	1,086		502 R	59.4%	40.6%	59.4%	40.6%
21,975	BRAZOS	2,221	738	1,480	3	742 D	33.2%	66.6%	33.3%	66.7%
4,822	BREWSTER	684	406	273	5	133 R	59.4%	39.9%	59.8%	40.2%
2,948	BRISCOE	641	301	336	4	35 D	47.0%	52.4%	47.3%	52.7%
4,560	BROOKS	492	160	332		172 D	32.5%	67.5%	32.5%	67.5%
21,682	BROWN	4,029	2,033	1,992	4	41 R	50.5%	49.4%	50.5%	49.5%
16,855	BURLESON	1,897	339	1,558		1,219 D	17.9%	82.1%	17.9%	82.1%
9,499	BURNET	1,404	936	467	1	469 R	66.7%	33.3%	66.7%	33.3%
25,160	CALDWELL	2,400	1,189	1,211		22 D	49.5%	50.5%	49.5%	50.5%
4,700	CALHOUN	711	333	375	3	42 D	46.8%	52.7%	47.0%	53.0%
11,844	CALLAHAN	1,919	979	940		39 R	51.0%	49.0%	51.0%	49.0%
36,662	CAMERON	6,757	3,544	3,202	11	342 R	52.4%	47.4%	52.5%	47.5%
11,103	CAMP	1,134	494	640		146 D	43.6%	56.4%	43.6%	56.4%
3,078	CARSON	1,484	891	592	1	299 R	60.0%	39.9%	60.1%	39.9%
30,041	CASS	3,021	1,323	1,698		375 D	43.8%	56.2%	43.8%	56.2%
1,948	CASTRO	703	319	384		65 D	45.4%	54.6%	45.4%	54.6%
4,162	CHAMBERS	498	256	242		14 R	51.4%	48.6%	51.4%	48.6%
37,633	CHEROKEE	3,871	1,933	1,938		5 D	49.9%	50.1%	49.9%	50.1%
10,933	CHILDRESS	2,164	1,438	726		712 R	66.5%	33.5%	66.5%	33.5%
16,864	CLAY	2,487	1,327	1,160		167 R	53.4%	46.6%	53.4%	46.6%
67	COCHRAN	306	197	109		88 R	64.4%	35.6%	64.4%	35.6%
4,557	COKE	656	450	206		244 R	68.6%	31.4%	68.6%	31.4%
18,805	COLEMAN	3,104	1,645	1,459		186 R	53.0%	47.0%	53.0%	47.0%
49,609	COLLIN	6,876	3,476	3,377	23	99 R	50.6%	49.1%	50.7%	49.3%
9,154	COLLINGSWORTH	1,787	1,179	608		571 R	66.0%	34.0%	66.0%	34.0%
19,013	COLORADO	2,682	891	1,787	4	896 D	33.2%	66.6%	33.3%	66.7%
8,824	COMAL	2,403	508	1,893	2	1,385 D	21.1%	78.8%	21.2%	78.8%
25,748	COMANCHE	2,794	1,483	1,311		172 R	53.1%	46.9%	53.1%	46.9%
5,847	CONCHO	875	446	426	3	20 R	51.0%	48.7%	51.1%	48.9%
25,667	COOKE	4,190	2,262	1,924	4	338 R	54.0%	45.9%	54.0%	46.0%
20,601	CORYELL	2,430	1,123	1,306	1	183 D	46.2%	53.7%	46.2%	53.8%
6,901	COTTLE	924	473	451		22 R	51.2%	48.8%	51.2%	48.8%
37	CRANE	286	127	159		32 D	44.4%	55.6%	44.4%	55.6%
1,500	CROCKETT	355	291	64		227 R	82.0%	18.0%	82.0%	18.0%
6,084	CROSBY	1,732	1,004	728		276 R	58.0%	42.0%	58.0%	42.0%
912	CULBERSON	157	72	85		13 D	45.9%	54.1%	45.9%	54.1%
4,528	DALLAM	1,166	618	539	9	79 R	53.0%	46.2%	53.4%	46.6%
210,551	DALLAS	44,787	27,272	17,437	78	9,835 R	60.9%	38.9%	61.0%	39.0%
4,309	DAWSON	1,875	1,448	427		1,021 R	77.2%	22.8%	77.2%	22.8%
3,747	DEAF SMITH	981	570	411		159 R	58.1%	41.9%	58.1%	41.9%
15,887	DELTA	1,713	753	958	2	205 D	44.0%	55.9%	44.0%	56.0%

TEXAS

PRESIDENT 1928

1920 Census Population	County	Total Vote	Republican	Democratic	Other	Rep.-Dem. Plurality	Total Vote Rep.	Total Vote Dem.	Major Vote Rep.	Major Vote Dem.
35,355	DENTON	4,986	2,587	2,384	15	203 R	51.9%	47.8%	52.0%	48.0%
27,971	DE WITT	2,741	1,142	1,594	5	452 D	41.7%	58.2%	41.7%	58.3%
5,876	DICKENS	1,156	741	415		326 R	64.1%	35.9%	64.1%	35.9%
5,296	DIMMIT	884	626	258		368 R	70.8%	29.2%	70.8%	29.2%
8,035	DONLEY	1,585	1,092	491	2	601 R	68.9%	31.0%	69.0%	31.0%
8,251	DUVAL	1,679	434	1,245		811 D	25.8%	74.2%	25.8%	74.2%
58,505	EASTLAND	5,734	3,233	2,501		732 R	56.4%	43.6%	56.4%	43.6%
760	ECTOR	319	168	151		17 R	52.7%	47.3%	52.7%	47.3%
2,283	EDWARDS	609	546	59	4	487 R	89.7%	9.7%	90.2%	9.8%
55,700	ELLIS	7,981	3,569	4,399	13	830 D	44.7%	55.1%	44.8%	55.2%
101,877	EL PASO	12,164	6,050	6,114		64 D	49.7%	50.3%	49.7%	50.3%
28,385	ERATH	3,377	1,923	1,372	82	551 R	56.9%	40.6%	58.4%	41.6%
36,217	FALLS	3,368	877	2,484	7	1,607 D	26.0%	73.8%	26.1%	73.9%
48,186	FANNIN	4,651	2,122	2,525	4	403 D	45.6%	54.3%	45.7%	54.3%
29,965	FAYETTE	4,341	689	3,647	5	2,958 D	15.9%	84.0%	15.9%	84.1%
11,009	FISHER	2,096	1,259	837		422 R	60.1%	39.9%	60.1%	39.9%
9,758	FLOYD	1,842	1,176	666		510 R	63.8%	36.2%	63.8%	36.2%
4,747	FOARD	905	430	466	9	36 D	47.5%	51.5%	48.0%	52.0%
22,931	FORT BEND	2,357	631	1,724	2	1,093 D	26.8%	73.1%	26.8%	73.2%
9,304	FRANKLIN	1,099	386	713		327 D	35.1%	64.9%	35.1%	64.9%
23,264	FREESTONE	2,499	1,178	1,318	3	140 D	47.1%	52.7%	47.2%	52.8%
9,296	FRIO	932	673	258	1	415 R	72.2%	27.7%	72.3%	27.7%
1,018	GAINES	452	312	140		172 R	69.0%	31.0%	69.0%	31.0%
53,150	GALVESTON	10,372	4,401	5,951	20	1,550 D	42.4%	57.4%	42.5%	57.5%
4,253	GARZA	1,079	794	285		509 R	73.6%	26.4%	73.6%	26.4%
10,015	GILLESPIE	2,625	1,447	1,174	4	273 R	55.1%	44.7%	55.2%	44.8%
555	GLASSCOCK	158	124	34		90 R	78.5%	21.5%	78.5%	21.5%
9,348	GOLIAD	1,024	554	468	2	86 R	54.1%	45.7%	54.2%	45.8%
28,438	GONZALES	2,431	1,112	1,319		207 D	45.7%	54.3%	45.7%	54.3%
4,663	GRAY	2,863	1,871	986	6	885 R	65.4%	34.4%	65.5%	34.5%
74,165	GRAYSON	10,892	6,277	4,600	15	1,677 R	57.6%	42.2%	57.7%	42.3%
16,767	GREGG	1,644	646	996	2	350 D	39.3%	60.6%	39.3%	60.7%
23,101	GRIMES	1,876	701	1,175		474 D	37.4%	62.6%	37.4%	62.6%
27,719	GUADALUPE	3,318	1,442	1,872	4	430 D	43.5%	56.4%	43.5%	56.5%
10,104	HALE	3,248	2,143	1,098	7	1,045 R	66.0%	33.8%	66.1%	33.9%
11,137	HALL	1,902	1,409	493		916 R	74.1%	25.9%	74.1%	25.9%
14,676	HAMILTON	1,916	927	989		62 D	48.4%	51.6%	48.4%	51.6%
1,354	HANSFORD	737	417	319	1	98 R	56.6%	43.3%	56.7%	43.3%
12,487	HARDEMAN	2,243	1,333	910		423 R	59.4%	40.6%	59.4%	40.6%
15,983	HARDIN	1,983	951	1,032		81 D	48.0%	52.0%	48.0%	52.0%
186,667	HARRIS	48,810	27,188	21,536	86	5,652 R	55.7%	44.1%	55.8%	44.2%
43,565	HARRISON	3,804	1,776	2,023	5	247 D	46.7%	53.2%	46.7%	53.3%
1,109	HARTLEY	342	179	163		16 R	52.3%	47.7%	52.3%	47.7%
14,193	HASKELL	2,974	1,430	1,532	12	102 D	48.1%	51.5%	48.3%	51.7%
15,920	HAYS	1,708	1,088	620		468 R	63.7%	36.3%	63.7%	36.3%
4,280	HEMPHILL	806	489	317		172 R	60.7%	39.3%	60.7%	39.3%
28,327	HENDERSON	2,854	1,128	1,726		598 D	39.5%	60.5%	39.5%	60.5%
38,110	HIDALGO	8,335	4,285	4,034	16	251 R	51.4%	48.4%	51.5%	48.5%
43,332	HILL	4,859	2,446	2,413		33 R	50.3%	49.7%	50.3%	49.7%
137	HOCKLEY	1,009	765	235	9	530 R	75.8%	23.3%	76.5%	23.5%
8,759	HOOD	1,121	640	479	2	161 R	57.1%	42.7%	57.2%	42.8%
34,791	HOPKINS	3,617	1,767	1,845	5	78 D	48.9%	51.0%	48.9%	51.1%
28,601	HOUSTON	2,099	763	1,336		573 D	36.4%	63.6%	36.4%	63.6%
6,962	HOWARD	1,480	812	665	3	147 R	54.9%	44.9%	55.0%	45.0%
962	HUDSPETH	240	123	117		6 R	51.2%	48.8%	51.2%	48.8%
50,350	HUNT	6,519	3,009	3,510		501 D	46.2%	53.8%	46.2%	53.8%
721	HUTCHINSON	1,845	1,115	730		385 R	60.4%	39.6%	60.4%	39.6%
1,610	IRION	378	259	119		140 R	68.5%	31.5%	68.5%	31.5%
9,863	JACK	1,521	1,068	450	3	618 R	70.2%	29.6%	70.4%	29.6%
11,244	JACKSON	1,046	572	473	1	99 R	54.7%	45.2%	54.7%	45.3%

TEXAS

PRESIDENT 1928

1920 Census Population	County	Total Vote	Republican	Democratic	Other	Rep.-Dem. Plurality	Percentage Total Vote Rep.	Percentage Total Vote Dem.	Percentage Major Vote Rep.	Percentage Major Vote Dem.
15,569	JASPER	1,511	611	898	2	287 D	40.4%	59.4%	40.5%	59.5%
1,445	JEFF DAVIS	270	157	112	1	45 R	58.1%	41.5%	58.4%	41.6%
73,120	JEFFERSON	16,231	9,209	7,006	16	2,203 R	56.7%	43.2%	56.8%	43.2%
1,914	JIM HOGG	372	109	263		154 D	29.3%	70.7%	29.3%	70.7%
6,587	JIM WELLS	1,173	423	747	3	324 D	36.1%	63.7%	36.2%	63.8%
37,286	JOHNSON	5,166	3,181	1,981	4	1,200 R	61.6%	38.3%	61.6%	38.4%
22,323	JONES	3,566	1,995	1,563	8	432 R	55.9%	43.8%	56.1%	43.9%
19,049	KARNES	1,907	855	1,052		197 D	44.8%	55.2%	44.8%	55.2%
41,276	KAUFMAN	4,375	1,718	2,657		939 D	39.3%	60.7%	39.3%	60.7%
4,779	KENDALL	1,042	663	377	2	286 R	63.6%	36.2%	63.7%	36.3%
1,033	KENEDY	130	12	118		106 D	9.2%	90.8%	9.2%	90.8%
3,335	KENT	526	363	163		200 R	69.0%	31.0%	69.0%	31.0%
5,842	KERR	2,147	1,575	570	2	1,005 R	73.4%	26.5%	73.4%	26.6%
3,581	KIMBLE	821	660	157	4	503 R	80.4%	19.1%	80.8%	19.2%
655	KING	130	85	45		40 R	65.4%	34.6%	65.4%	34.6%
3,746	KINNEY	382	182	200		18 D	47.6%	52.4%	47.6%	52.4%
7,837	KLEBERG	1,446	751	695		56 R	51.9%	48.1%	51.9%	48.1%
9,240	KNOX	1,781	992	784	5	208 R	55.7%	44.0%	55.9%	44.1%
55,742	LAMAR	5,058	2,887	2,163	8	724 R	57.1%	42.8%	57.2%	42.8%
1,175	LAMB	1,706	1,266	440		826 R	74.2%	25.8%	74.2%	25.8%
8,800	LAMPASAS	1,476	899	567	10	332 R	60.9%	38.4%	61.3%	38.7%
4,821	LA SALLE	806	327	479		152 D	40.6%	59.4%	40.6%	59.4%
28,964	LAVACA	3,753	911	2,842		1,931 D	24.3%	75.7%	24.3%	75.7%
14,014	LEE	1,625	449	1,176		727 D	27.6%	72.4%	27.6%	72.4%
18,286	LEON	1,407	543	862	2	319 D	38.6%	61.3%	38.6%	61.4%
14,637	LIBERTY	1,995	1,070	918	7	152 R	53.6%	46.0%	53.8%	46.2%
33,283	LIMESTONE	4,250	1,642	2,608		966 D	38.6%	61.4%	38.6%	61.4%
3,684	LIPSCOMB	1,119	776	331	12	445 R	69.3%	29.6%	70.1%	29.9%
4,171	LIVE OAK	867	484	383		101 R	55.8%	44.2%	55.8%	44.2%
5,360	LLANO	953	439	514		75 D	46.1%	53.9%	46.1%	53.9%
82	LOVING	16	6	10		4 D	37.5%	62.5%	37.5%	62.5%
11,096	LUBBOCK	5,065	3,079	1,979	7	1,100 R	60.8%	39.1%	60.9%	39.1%
4,751	LYNN	2,029	1,268	754	7	514 R	62.5%	37.2%	62.7%	37.3%
11,020	MCCULLOCH	2,035	1,294	741		553 R	63.6%	36.4%	63.6%	36.4%
82,921	MCLENNAN	11,087	5,744	5,330	13	414 R	51.8%	48.1%	51.9%	48.1%
952	MCMULLEN	192	96	94	2	2 R	50.0%	49.0%	50.5%	49.5%
11,956	MADISON	816	364	452		88 D	44.6%	55.4%	44.6%	55.4%
10,886	MARION	1,083	443	640		197 D	40.9%	59.1%	40.9%	59.1%
1,146	MARTIN	543	330	213		117 R	60.8%	39.2%	60.8%	39.2%
4,824	MASON	1,053	807	244	2	563 R	76.6%	23.2%	76.8%	23.2%
16,589	MATAGORDA	2,029	1,194	829	6	365 R	58.8%	40.9%	59.0%	41.0%
7,418	MAVERICK	491	311	180		131 R	63.3%	36.7%	63.3%	36.7%
11,679	MEDINA	2,648	1,243	1,400	5	157 D	46.9%	52.9%	47.0%	53.0%
3,162	MENARD	823	589	234		355 R	71.6%	28.4%	71.6%	28.4%
2,449	MIDLAND	700	347	350	3	3 D	49.6%	50.0%	49.8%	50.2%
38,104	MILAM	4,116	1,270	2,842	4	1,572 D	30.9%	69.0%	30.9%	69.1%
9,019	MILLS	1,216	774	442		332 R	63.7%	36.3%	63.7%	36.3%
7,527	MITCHELL	1,845	1,099	746		353 R	59.6%	40.4%	59.6%	40.4%
22,200	MONTAGUE	2,971	1,519	1,452		67 R	51.1%	48.9%	51.1%	48.9%
17,334	MONTGOMERY	1,519	613	905	1	292 D	40.4%	59.6%	40.4%	59.6%
571	MOORE	211	87	124		37 D	41.2%	58.8%	41.2%	58.8%
10,289	MORRIS	1,067	287	780		493 D	26.9%	73.1%	26.9%	73.1%
4,107	MOTLEY	799	450	349		101 R	56.3%	43.7%	56.3%	43.7%
28,457	NACOGDOCHES	2,703	822	1,879	2	1,057 D	30.4%	69.5%	30.4%	69.6%
50,624	NAVARRO	6,989	3,341	3,648		307 D	47.8%	52.2%	47.8%	52.2%
12,196	NEWTON	962	397	564	1	167 D	41.3%	58.6%	41.3%	58.7%
10,868	NOLAN	2,510	1,475	1,035		440 R	58.8%	41.2%	58.8%	41.2%
22,807	NUECES	5,469	2,481	2,985	3	504 D	45.4%	54.6%	45.4%	54.6%
2,331	OCHILTREE	826	556	270		286 R	67.3%	32.7%	67.3%	32.7%
709	OLDHAM	329	172	157		15 R	52.3%	47.7%	52.3%	47.7%

TEXAS

PRESIDENT 1928

1920 Census Population	County	Total Vote	Republican	Democratic	Other	Rep.-Dem. Plurality	Percentage			
							Total Vote		Major Vote	
							Rep.	Dem.	Rep.	Dem.
15,379	ORANGE	2,166	919	1,247		328 D	42.4%	57.6%	42.4%	57.6%
23,431	PALO PINTO	3,162	2,001	1,161		840 R	63.3%	36.7%	63.3%	36.7%
21,755	PANOLA	1,735	420	1,312	3	892 D	24.2%	75.6%	24.2%	75.8%
23,382	PARKER	3,288	2,178	1,110		1,068 R	66.2%	33.8%	66.2%	33.8%
1,699	PARMER	943	620	315	8	305 R	65.7%	33.4%	66.3%	33.7%
3,857	PECOS	1,092	524	562	6	38 D	48.0%	51.5%	48.3%	51.7%
16,784	POLK	1,506	508	994	4	486 D	33.7%	66.0%	33.8%	66.2%
16,710	POTTER	6,264	3,627	2,637		990 R	57.9%	42.1%	57.9%	42.1%
12,202	PRESIDIO	569	254	315		61 D	44.6%	55.4%	44.6%	55.4%
8,099	RAINS	751	202	544	5	342 D	26.9%	72.4%	27.1%	72.9%
3,675	RANDALL	1,392	733	659		74 R	52.7%	47.3%	52.7%	47.3%
377	REAGAN	616	387	229		158 R	62.8%	37.2%	62.8%	37.2%
1,461	REAL	577	479	98		381 R	83.0%	17.0%	83.0%	17.0%
35,829	RED RIVER	2,838	1,172	1,666		494 D	41.3%	58.7%	41.3%	58.7%
4,457	REEVES	738	344	394		50 D	46.6%	53.4%	46.6%	53.4%
4,050	REFUGIO	1,054	383	671		288 D	36.3%	63.7%	36.3%	63.7%
1,469	ROBERTS	347	243	104		139 R	70.0%	30.0%	70.0%	30.0%
27,933	ROBERTSON	2,239	751	1,487	1	736 D	33.5%	66.4%	33.6%	66.4%
8,591	ROCKWALL	1,139	289	850		561 D	25.4%	74.6%	25.4%	74.6%
17,074	RUNNELS	3,148	1,645	1,494	9	151 R	52.3%	47.5%	52.4%	47.6%
31,689	RUSK	2,765	1,033	1,732		699 D	37.4%	62.6%	37.4%	62.6%
12,299	SABINE	1,226	419	807		388 D	34.2%	65.8%	34.2%	65.8%
13,737	SAN AUGUSTINE	1,288	467	821		354 D	36.3%	63.7%	36.3%	63.7%
9,867	SAN JACINTO	800	296	503	1	207 D	37.0%	62.9%	37.0%	63.0%
11,386	SAN PATRICIO	1,967	1,388	579		809 R	70.6%	29.4%	70.6%	29.4%
10,045	SAN SABA	1,434	682	752		70 D	47.6%	52.4%	47.6%	52.4%
1,851	SCHLEICHER	364	227	137		90 R	62.4%	37.6%	62.4%	37.6%
9,003	SCURRY	2,061	1,597	462	2	1,135 R	77.5%	22.4%	77.6%	22.4%
4,960	SHACKELFORD	1,092	558	533	1	25 R	51.1%	48.8%	51.1%	48.9%
27,464	SHELBY	2,648	676	1,961	11	1,285 D	25.5%	74.1%	25.6%	74.4%
1,473	SHERMAN	385	248	137		111 R	64.4%	35.6%	64.4%	35.6%
46,769	SMITH	5,836	3,493	2,343		1,150 R	59.9%	40.1%	59.9%	40.1%
3,563	SOMERVELL	377	241	136		105 R	63.9%	36.1%	63.9%	36.1%
11,089	STARR	815	79	736		657 D	9.7%	90.3%	9.7%	90.3%
15,403	STEPHENS	2,952	1,789	1,163		626 R	60.6%	39.4%	60.6%	39.4%
1,053	STERLING	289	122	167		45 D	42.2%	57.8%	42.2%	57.8%
4,086	STONEWALL	942	442	500		58 D	46.9%	53.1%	46.9%	53.1%
1,598	SUTTON	382	290	92		198 R	75.9%	24.1%	75.9%	24.1%
4,388	SWISHER	1,261	887	374		513 R	70.3%	29.7%	70.3%	29.7%
152,800	TARRANT	29,689	20,481	9,208		11,273 R	69.0%	31.0%	69.0%	31.0%
24,081	TAYLOR	5,950	4,050	1,891	9	2,159 R	68.1%	31.8%	68.2%	31.8%
1,595	TERRELL	451	364	85	2	279 R	80.7%	18.8%	81.1%	18.9%
2,236	TERRY	1,029	622	407		215 R	60.4%	39.6%	60.4%	39.6%
3,589	THROCKMORTON	1,007	703	304		399 R	69.8%	30.2%	69.8%	30.2%
18,128	TITUS	1,618	469	1,149		680 D	29.0%	71.0%	29.0%	71.0%
15,210	TOM GREEN	4,148	2,618	1,528	2	1,090 R	63.1%	36.8%	63.1%	36.9%
57,616	TRAVIS	9,351	4,847	4,487	17	360 R	51.8%	48.0%	51.9%	48.1%
13,623	TRINITY	1,142	456	686		230 D	39.9%	60.1%	39.9%	60.1%
10,415	TYLER	965	298	666	1	368 D	30.9%	69.0%	30.9%	69.1%
22,472	UPSHUR	2,210	649	1,553	8	904 D	29.4%	70.3%	29.5%	70.5%
253	UPTON	459	270	189		81 R	58.8%	41.2%	58.8%	41.2%
10,769	UVALDE	1,971	1,224	747		477 R	62.1%	37.9%	62.1%	37.9%
12,706	VAL VERDE	1,474	854	620		234 R	57.9%	42.1%	57.9%	42.1%
30,784	VAN ZANDT	3,312	1,502	1,789	21	287 D	45.4%	54.0%	45.6%	54.4%
18,271	VICTORIA	2,373	663	1,710		1,047 D	27.9%	72.1%	27.9%	72.1%
18,556	WALKER	1,235	488	747		259 D	39.5%	60.5%	39.5%	60.5%
10,292	WALLER	881	376	504	1	128 D	42.7%	57.2%	42.7%	57.3%
2,615	WARD	472	216	256		40 D	45.8%	54.2%	45.8%	54.2%
26,624	WASHINGTON	2,766	275	2,491		2,216 D	9.9%	90.1%	9.9%	90.1%
29,152	WEBB	2,385	767	1,615	3	848 D	32.2%	67.7%	32.2%	67.8%

TEXAS

PRESIDENT 1928

1920 Census Population	County	Total Vote	Republican	Democratic	Other	Rep.-Dem. Plurality	Percentage Total Vote Rep.	Total Vote Dem.	Major Vote Rep.	Major Vote Dem.
24,288	WHARTON	2,696	1,151	1,545		394 D	42.7%	57.3%	42.7%	57.3%
7,397	WHEELER	1,794	1,038	750	6	288 R	57.9%	41.8%	58.1%	41.9%
72,911	WICHITA	12,079	7,226	4,853		2,373 R	59.8%	40.2%	59.8%	40.2%
15,112	WILBARGER	3,040	1,590	1,447	3	143 R	52.3%	47.6%	52.4%	47.6%
	WILLACY	785	389	396		7 D	49.6%	50.4%	49.6%	50.4%
42,934	WILLIAMSON	5,531	1,833	3,689	9	1,856 D	33.1%	66.7%	33.2%	66.8%
17,289	WILSON	2,121	622	1,499		877 D	29.3%	70.7%	29.3%	70.7%
81	WINKLER	472	162	310		148 D	34.3%	65.7%	34.3%	65.7%
23,363	WISE	3,234	2,141	1,093		1,048 R	66.2%	33.8%	66.2%	33.8%
27,707	WOOD	2,806	1,161	1,645		484 D	41.4%	58.6%	41.4%	58.6%
504	YOAKUM	152	86	66		20 R	56.6%	43.4%	56.6%	43.4%
13,379	YOUNG	3,101	1,826	1,275		551 R	58.9%	41.1%	58.9%	41.1%
2,929	ZAPATA	315	19	296		277 D	6.0%	94.0%	6.0%	94.0%
3,108	ZAVALA	800	571	229		342 R	71.4%	28.6%	71.4%	28.6%
4,663,228	TOTAL	717,733	372,324	344,542	867	27,782 R	51.9%	48.0%	51.9%	48.1%

TEXAS

PRESIDENT 1924

1920 Census Population	County	Total Vote	Republican	Democratic	Other	Rep.-Dem. Plurality	Percentage Total Vote Rep.	Total Vote Dem.	Major Vote Rep.	Major Vote Dem.
34,318	ANDERSON	1,191	562	374	255	188 R	47.2%	31.4%	60.0%	40.0%
350	ANDREWS	71	7	60	4	53 D	9.9%	84.5%	10.4%	89.6%
22,287	ANGELINA	4,419	333	3,914	172	3,581 D	7.5%	88.6%	7.8%	92.2%
2,064	ARANSAS	278	75	195	8	120 D	27.0%	70.1%	27.8%	72.2%
5,254	ARCHER	1,117	146	883	88	737 D	13.1%	79.1%	14.2%	85.8%
2,816	ARMSTRONG	556	106	426	24	320 D	19.1%	76.6%	19.9%	80.1%
12,702	ATASCOSA	1,389	303	869	217	566 D	21.8%	62.6%	25.9%	74.1%
18,874	AUSTIN	3,627	457	2,601	569	2,144 D	12.6%	71.7%	14.9%	85.1%
517	BAILEY	250	63	166	21	103 D	25.2%	66.4%	27.5%	72.5%
4,001	BANDERA	924	442	425	57	17 R	47.8%	46.0%	51.0%	49.0%
26,649	BASTROP	3,452	494	2,711	247	2,217 D	14.3%	78.5%	15.4%	84.6%
7,027	BAYLOR	1,163	135	1,012	16	877 D	11.6%	87.0%	11.8%	88.2%
12,137	BEE	2,077	944	987	146	43 D	45.5%	47.5%	48.9%	51.1%
46,412	BELL	9,457	1,632	7,273	552	5,641 D	17.3%	76.9%	18.3%	81.7%
202,096	BEXAR	24,699	9,898	10,838	3,963	940 D	40.1%	43.9%	47.7%	52.3%
4,063	BLANCO	1,078	317	586	175	269 D	29.4%	54.4%	35.1%	64.9%
965	BORDEN	96	10	86		76 D	10.4%	89.6%	10.4%	89.6%
18,032	BOSQUE	3,017	403	2,534	80	2,131 D	13.4%	84.0%	13.7%	86.3%
39,472	BOWIE	4,464	740	3,455	269	2,715 D	16.6%	77.4%	17.6%	82.4%
20,614	BRAZORIA	2,994	1,114	1,761	119	647 D	37.2%	58.8%	38.7%	61.3%
21,975	BRAZOS	2,444	255	2,128	61	1,873 D	10.4%	87.1%	10.7%	89.3%
4,822	BREWSTER	500	113	366	21	253 D	22.6%	73.2%	23.6%	76.4%
2,948	BRISCOE	476	53	397	26	344 D	11.1%	83.4%	11.8%	88.2%
4,560	BROOKS	268	59	205	4	146 D	22.0%	76.5%	22.3%	77.7%
21,682	BROWN	3,963	396	3,467	100	3,071 D	10.0%	87.5%	10.3%	89.7%
16,855	BURLESON	2,744	224	2,496	24	2,272 D	8.2%	91.0%	8.2%	91.8%
9,499	BURNET	2,060	277	1,725	58	1,448 D	13.4%	83.7%	13.8%	86.2%
25,160	CALDWELL	2,797	399	2,194	204	1,795 D	14.3%	78.4%	15.4%	84.6%
4,700	CALHOUN	902	181	686	35	505 D	20.1%	76.1%	20.9%	79.1%
11,844	CALLAHAN	1,946	244	1,614	88	1,370 D	12.5%	82.9%	13.1%	86.9%
36,662	CAMERON	3,667	1,266	2,225	176	959 D	34.5%	60.7%	36.3%	63.7%
11,103	CAMP	1,416	187	1,186	43	999 D	13.2%	83.8%	13.6%	86.4%
3,078	CARSON	952	306	611	35	305 D	32.1%	64.2%	33.4%	66.6%
30,041	CASS	3,211	997	2,125	89	1,128 D	31.0%	66.2%	31.9%	68.1%
1,948	CASTRO	369	68	219	82	151 D	18.4%	59.3%	23.7%	76.3%
4,162	CHAMBERS	565	239	315	11	76 D	42.3%	55.8%	43.1%	56.9%
37,633	CHEROKEE	5,099	666	4,343	90	3,677 D	13.1%	85.2%	13.3%	86.7%
10,933	CHILDRESS	1,366	178	1,117	71	939 D	13.0%	81.8%	13.7%	86.3%
16,864	CLAY	1,833	318	1,402	113	1,084 D	17.3%	76.5%	18.5%	81.5%
67	COCHRAN	72	9	59	4	50 D	12.5%	81.9%	13.2%	86.8%
4,557	COKE	766	80	673	13	593 D	10.4%	87.9%	10.6%	89.4%
18,805	COLEMAN	3,341	502	2,763	76	2,261 D	15.0%	82.7%	15.4%	84.6%
49,609	COLLIN	9,365	1,981	7,215	169	5,234 D	21.2%	77.0%	21.5%	78.5%
9,154	COLLINGSWORTH	988	234	731	23	497 D	23.7%	74.0%	24.2%	75.8%
19,013	COLORADO	3,162	681	2,105	376	1,424 D	21.5%	66.6%	24.4%	75.6%
8,824	COMAL	2,465	312	330	1,823	18 D	12.7%	13.4%	48.6%	51.4%
25,748	COMANCHE	846	456	276	114	180 R	53.9%	32.6%	62.3%	37.7%
5,847	CONCHO	781	90	668	23	578 D	11.5%	85.5%	11.9%	88.1%
25,667	COOKE	4,086	525	3,170	391	2,645 D	12.8%	77.6%	14.2%	85.8%
20,601	CORYELL	3,389	429	2,890	70	2,461 D	12.7%	85.3%	12.9%	87.1%
6,901	COTTLE	658	59	580	19	521 D	9.0%	88.1%	9.2%	90.8%
37	CRANE	—	—	—	—	—	—	—	—	—
1,500	CROCKETT	182	112	69	1	43 R	61.5%	37.9%	61.9%	38.1%
6,084	CROSBY	1,554	278	1,242	34	964 D	17.9%	79.9%	18.3%	81.7%
912	CULBERSON	117	15	93	9	78 D	12.8%	79.5%	13.9%	86.1%
4,528	DALLAM	1,045	254	506	285	252 D	24.3%	48.4%	33.4%	66.6%
210,551	DALLAS	39,837	8,618	30,207	1,012	21,589 D	21.6%	75.8%	22.2%	77.8%
4,309	DAWSON	1,299	185	1,079	35	894 D	14.2%	83.1%	14.6%	85.4%
3,747	DEAF SMITH	763	192	538	33	346 D	25.2%	70.5%	26.3%	73.7%
15,887	DELTA	2,716	479	2,186	51	1,707 D	17.6%	80.5%	18.0%	82.0%

TEXAS

PRESIDENT 1924

1920 Census Population	County	Total Vote	Republican	Democratic	Other	Rep.-Dem. Plurality	Percentage Total Vote Rep.	Total Vote Dem.	Major Vote Rep.	Major Vote Dem.
35,355	DENTON	5,805	712	4,708	385	3,996 D	12.3%	81.1%	13.1%	86.9%
27,971	DE WITT	3,791	868	2,131	792	1,263 D	22.9%	56.2%	28.9%	71.1%
5,876	DICKENS	1,020	161	849	10	688 D	15.8%	83.2%	15.9%	84.1%
5,296	DIMMIT	493	180	289	24	109 D	36.5%	58.6%	38.4%	61.6%
8,035	DONLEY	1,234	273	893	68	620 D	22.1%	72.4%	23.4%	76.6%
8,251	DUVAL	1,057	89	947	21	858 D	8.4%	89.6%	8.6%	91.4%
58,505	EASTLAND	5,682	972	4,548	162	3,576 D	17.1%	80.0%	17.6%	82.4%
760	ECTOR	155	12	138	5	126 D	7.7%	89.0%	8.0%	92.0%
2,283	EDWARDS	564	346	204	14	142 R	61.3%	36.2%	62.9%	37.1%
55,700	ELLIS	9,040	1,220	7,678	142	6,458 D	13.5%	84.9%	13.7%	86.3%
101,877	EL PASO	—	—	—	—	—	—	—	—	—
28,385	ERATH	3,954	406	3,396	152	2,990 D	10.3%	85.9%	10.7%	89.3%
36,217	FALLS	3,456	448	2,817	191	2,369 D	13.0%	81.5%	13.7%	86.3%
48,186	FANNIN	6,462	653	5,596	213	4,943 D	10.1%	86.6%	10.4%	89.6%
29,965	FAYETTE	6,455	1,450	3,851	1,154	2,401 D	22.5%	59.7%	27.4%	72.6%
11,009	FISHER	2,013	302	1,653	58	1,351 D	15.0%	82.1%	15.4%	84.6%
9,758	FLOYD	1,392	166	1,197	29	1,031 D	11.9%	86.0%	12.2%	87.8%
4,747	FOARD	715	95	585	35	490 D	13.3%	81.8%	14.0%	86.0%
22,931	FORT BEND	2,250	356	1,690	204	1,334 D	15.8%	75.1%	17.4%	82.6%
9,304	FRANKLIN	1,336	118	1,157	61	1,039 D	8.8%	86.6%	9.3%	90.7%
23,264	FREESTONE	3,172	608	2,484	80	1,876 D	19.2%	78.3%	19.7%	80.3%
9,296	FRIO	808	158	637	13	479 D	19.6%	78.8%	19.9%	80.1%
1,018	GAINES	441	37	342	62	305 D	8.4%	77.6%	9.8%	90.2%
53,150	GALVESTON	7,619	1,912	5,068	639	3,156 D	25.1%	66.5%	27.4%	72.6%
4,253	GARZA	944	331	588	25	257 D	35.1%	62.3%	36.0%	64.0%
10,015	GILLESPIE	2,702	768	352	1,582	416 R	28.4%	13.0%	68.6%	31.4%
555	GLASSCOCK	109	14	89	6	75 D	12.8%	81.7%	13.6%	86.4%
9,348	GOLIAD	1,333	438	733	162	295 D	32.9%	55.0%	37.4%	62.6%
28,438	GONZALES	3,290	463	2,499	328	2,036 D	14.1%	76.0%	15.6%	84.4%
4,663	GRAY	1,189	581	608		27 D	48.9%	51.1%	48.9%	51.1%
74,165	GRAYSON	10,335	1,973	7,413	949	5,440 D	19.1%	71.7%	21.0%	79.0%
16,767	GREGG	1,671	177	1,286	208	1,109 D	10.6%	77.0%	12.1%	87.9%
23,101	GRIMES	2,345	177	2,136	32	1,959 D	7.5%	91.1%	7.7%	92.3%
27,719	GUADALUPE	4,089	1,657	831	1,601	826 R	40.5%	20.3%	66.6%	33.4%
10,104	HALE	2,041	507	1,446	88	939 D	24.8%	70.8%	26.0%	74.0%
11,137	HALL	1,353	229	1,060	64	831 D	16.9%	78.3%	17.8%	82.2%
14,676	HAMILTON	2,327	202	2,035	90	1,833 D	8.7%	87.5%	9.0%	91.0%
1,354	HANSFORD	363	76	263	24	187 D	20.9%	72.5%	22.4%	77.6%
12,487	HARDEMAN	1,408	256	1,099	53	843 D	18.2%	78.1%	18.9%	81.1%
15,983	HARDIN	2,278	645	1,516	117	871 D	28.3%	66.5%	29.8%	70.2%
186,667	HARRIS	32,479	8,953	20,648	2,878	11,695 D	27.6%	63.6%	30.2%	69.8%
43,565	HARRISON	3,262	463	2,573	226	2,110 D	14.2%	78.9%	15.3%	84.7%
1,109	HARTLEY	243	61	156	26	95 D	25.1%	64.2%	28.1%	71.9%
14,193	HASKELL	2,606	428	2,050	128	1,622 D	16.4%	78.7%	17.3%	82.7%
15,920	HAYS	2,089	394	1,616	79	1,222 D	18.9%	77.4%	19.6%	80.4%
4,280	HEMPHILL	643	167	405	71	238 D	26.0%	63.0%	29.2%	70.8%
28,327	HENDERSON	4,304	405	3,819	80	3,414 D	9.4%	88.7%	9.6%	90.4%
38,110	HIDALGO	4,872	996	3,662	214	2,666 D	20.4%	75.2%	21.4%	78.6%
43,332	HILL	6,688	807	5,778	103	4,971 D	12.1%	86.4%	12.3%	87.7%
137	HOCKLEY	94	20	69	5	49 D	21.3%	73.4%	22.5%	77.5%
8,759	HOOD	1,256	122	1,074	60	952 D	9.7%	85.5%	10.2%	89.8%
34,791	HOPKINS	4,834	557	4,156	121	3,599 D	11.5%	86.0%	11.8%	88.2%
28,601	HOUSTON	3,784	457	3,289	38	2,832 D	12.1%	86.9%	12.2%	87.8%
6,962	HOWARD	1,447	186	1,100	161	914 D	12.9%	76.0%	14.5%	85.5%
962	HUDSPETH	142	34	84	24	50 D	23.9%	59.2%	28.8%	71.2%
50,350	HUNT	7,810	836	6,828	146	5,992 D	10.7%	87.4%	10.9%	89.1%
721	HUTCHINSON	234	69	159	6	90 D	29.5%	67.9%	30.3%	69.7%
1,610	IRION	288	73	205	10	132 D	25.3%	71.2%	26.3%	73.7%
9,863	JACK	1,470	290	1,154	26	864 D	19.7%	78.5%	20.1%	79.9%
11,244	JACKSON	1,169	354	758	57	404 D	30.3%	64.8%	31.8%	68.2%

TEXAS

PRESIDENT 1924

1920 Census Population	County	Total Vote	Republican	Democratic	Other	Rep.-Dem. Plurality	Percentage Total Vote Rep.	Percentage Total Vote Dem.	Percentage Major Vote Rep.	Percentage Major Vote Dem.
15,569	JASPER	1,719	176	1,526	17	1,350 D	10.2%	88.8%	10.3%	89.7%
1,445	JEFF DAVIS	184	49	117	18	68 D	26.6%	63.6%	29.5%	70.5%
73,120	JEFFERSON	10,756	4,348	5,925	483	1,577 D	40.4%	55.1%	42.3%	57.7%
1,914	JIM HOGG	158	19	139		120 D	12.0%	88.0%	12.0%	88.0%
6,587	JIM WELLS	992	213	654	125	441 D	21.5%	65.9%	24.6%	75.4%
37,286	JOHNSON	5,761	851	4,600	310	3,749 D	14.8%	79.8%	15.6%	84.4%
22,323	JONES	3,677	566	3,010	101	2,444 D	15.4%	81.9%	15.8%	84.2%
19,049	KARNES	2,496	531	1,727	238	1,196 D	21.3%	69.2%	23.5%	76.5%
41,276	KAUFMAN	6,531	884	5,573	74	4,689 D	13.5%	85.3%	13.7%	86.3%
4,779	KENDALL	1,232	689	136	407	553 R	55.9%	11.0%	83.5%	16.5%
1,033	KENEDY	75	7	67	1	60 D	9.3%	89.3%	9.5%	90.5%
3,335	KENT	474	80	386	8	306 D	16.9%	81.4%	17.2%	82.8%
5,842	KERR	1,809	892	735	182	157 R	49.3%	40.6%	54.8%	45.2%
3,581	KIMBLE	707	223	465	19	242 D	31.5%	65.8%	32.4%	67.6%
655	KING	87	4	83		79 D	4.6%	95.4%	4.6%	95.4%
3,746	KINNEY	315	158	144	13	14 R	50.2%	45.7%	52.3%	47.7%
7,837	KLEBERG	1,155	226	721	208	495 D	19.6%	62.4%	23.9%	76.1%
9,240	KNOX	1,935	455	1,399	81	944 D	23.5%	72.3%	24.5%	75.5%
55,742	LAMAR	5,979	596	5,224	159	4,628 D	10.0%	87.4%	10.2%	89.8%
1,175	LAMB	507	121	356	30	235 D	23.9%	70.2%	25.4%	74.6%
8,800	LAMPASAS	1,846	228	1,596	22	1,368 D	12.4%	86.5%	12.5%	87.5%
4,821	LA SALLE	541	73	458	10	385 D	13.5%	84.7%	13.7%	86.3%
28,964	LAVACA	5,271	746	3,290	1,235	2,544 D	14.2%	62.4%	18.5%	81.5%
14,014	LEE	2,284	271	1,561	452	1,290 D	11.9%	68.3%	14.8%	85.2%
18,286	LEON	2,394	311	2,004	79	1,693 D	13.0%	83.7%	13.4%	86.6%
14,637	LIBERTY	2,189	639	1,506	44	867 D	29.2%	68.8%	29.8%	70.2%
33,283	LIMESTONE	5,434	523	4,868	43	4,345 D	9.6%	89.6%	9.7%	90.3%
3,684	LIPSCOMB	949	405	430	114	25 D	42.7%	45.3%	48.5%	51.5%
4,171	LIVE OAK	1,012	323	596	93	273 D	31.9%	58.9%	35.1%	64.9%
5,360	LLANO	1,077	88	928	61	840 D	8.2%	86.2%	8.7%	91.3%
82	LOVING	14	2	12		10 D	14.3%	85.7%	14.3%	85.7%
11,096	LUBBOCK	2,343	411	1,740	192	1,329 D	17.5%	74.3%	19.1%	80.9%
4,751	LYNN	1,501	313	1,131	57	818 D	20.9%	75.3%	21.7%	78.3%
11,020	MCCULLOCH	1,844	495	1,327	22	832 D	26.8%	72.0%	27.2%	72.8%
82,921	MCLENNAN	10,721	2,384	7,882	455	5,498 D	22.2%	73.5%	23.2%	76.8%
952	MCMULLEN	223	111	109	3	2 R	49.8%	48.9%	50.5%	49.5%
11,956	MADISON	1,743	146	1,592	5	1,446 D	8.4%	91.3%	8.4%	91.6%
10,886	MARION	1,051	347	620	84	273 D	33.0%	59.0%	35.9%	64.1%
1,146	MARTIN	426	92	327	7	235 D	21.6%	76.8%	22.0%	78.0%
4,824	MASON	718	171	384	163	213 D	23.8%	53.5%	30.8%	69.2%
16,589	MATAGORDA	2,374	893	1,353	128	460 D	37.6%	57.0%	39.8%	60.2%
7,418	MAVERICK	491	261	199	31	62 R	53.2%	40.5%	56.7%	43.3%
11,679	MEDINA	2,279	816	986	477	170 D	35.8%	43.3%	45.3%	54.7%
3,162	MENARD	578	247	304	27	57 D	42.7%	52.6%	44.8%	55.2%
2,449	MIDLAND	447	44	399	4	355 D	9.8%	89.3%	9.9%	90.1%
38,104	MILAM	6,334	930	5,087	317	4,157 D	14.7%	80.3%	15.5%	84.5%
9,019	MILLS	1,515	175	1,289	51	1,114 D	11.6%	85.1%	12.0%	88.0%
7,527	MITCHELL	1,446	169	1,242	35	1,073 D	11.7%	85.9%	12.0%	88.0%
22,200	MONTAGUE	3,269	586	2,236	447	1,650 D	17.9%	68.4%	20.8%	79.2%
17,334	MONTGOMERY	1,689	166	1,500	23	1,334 D	9.8%	88.8%	10.0%	90.0%
571	MOORE	92	9	82	1	73 D	9.8%	89.1%	9.9%	90.1%
10,289	MORRIS	—	—	—	—	—	—	—	—	—
4,107	MOTLEY	525	62	453	10	391 D	11.8%	86.3%	12.0%	88.0%
28,457	NACOGDOCHES	3,669	204	3,418	47	3,214 D	5.6%	93.2%	5.6%	94.4%
50,624	NAVARRO	7,482	996	6,409	77	5,413 D	13.3%	85.7%	13.5%	86.5%
12,196	NEWTON	948	145	782	21	637 D	15.3%	82.5%	15.6%	84.4%
10,868	NOLAN	1,840	337	1,421	82	1,084 D	18.3%	77.2%	19.2%	80.8%
22,807	NUECES	—	—	—	—	—	—	—	—	—
2,331	OCHILTREE	562	155	352	55	197 D	27.6%	62.6%	30.6%	69.4%
709	OLDHAM	272	71	187	14	116 D	26.1%	68.8%	27.5%	72.5%

TEXAS

PRESIDENT 1924

1920 Census Population	County	Total Vote	Republican	Democratic	Other	Rep.-Dem. Plurality	Percentage Total Vote Rep.	Total Vote Dem.	Major Vote Rep.	Major Vote Dem.
15,379	ORANGE	1,933	509	1,385	39	876 D	26.3%	71.7%	26.9%	73.1%
23,431	PALO PINTO	2,631	473	1,926	232	1,453 D	18.0%	73.2%	19.7%	80.3%
21,755	PANOLA	2,233	119	2,088	26	1,969 D	5.3%	93.5%	5.4%	94.6%
23,382	PARKER	2,979	438	2,391	150	1,953 D	14.7%	80.3%	15.5%	84.5%
1,699	PARMER	341	91	214	36	123 D	26.7%	62.8%	29.8%	70.2%
3,857	PECOS	662	192	440	30	248 D	29.0%	66.5%	30.4%	69.6%
16,784	POLK	2,142	272	1,839	31	1,567 D	12.7%	85.9%	12.9%	87.1%
16,710	POTTER	3,811	831	2,394	586	1,563 D	21.8%	62.8%	25.8%	74.2%
12,202	PRESIDIO	348	68	267	13	199 D	19.5%	76.7%	20.3%	79.7%
8,099	RAINS	1,098	151	899	48	748 D	13.8%	81.9%	14.4%	85.6%
3,675	RANDALL	845	154	627	64	473 D	18.2%	74.2%	19.7%	80.3%
377	REAGAN	144	31	111	2	80 D	21.5%	77.1%	21.8%	78.2%
1,461	REAL	498	300	188	10	112 R	60.2%	37.8%	61.5%	38.5%
35,829	RED RIVER	3,543	311	3,183	49	2,872 D	8.8%	89.8%	8.9%	91.1%
4,457	REEVES	512	96	387	29	291 D	18.8%	75.6%	19.9%	80.1%
4,050	REFUGIO	934	256	585	93	329 D	27.4%	62.6%	30.4%	69.6%
1,469	ROBERTS	347	104	241	2	137 D	30.0%	69.5%	30.1%	69.9%
27,933	ROBERTSON	2,261	226	1,971	64	1,745 D	10.0%	87.2%	10.3%	89.7%
8,591	ROCKWALL	1,471	93	1,371	7	1,278 D	6.3%	93.2%	6.4%	93.6%
17,074	RUNNELS	3,162	458	2,564	140	2,106 D	14.5%	81.1%	15.2%	84.8%
31,689	RUSK	3,815	651	3,097	67	2,446 D	17.1%	81.2%	17.4%	82.6%
12,299	SABINE	1,218	61	1,150	7	1,089 D	5.0%	94.4%	5.0%	95.0%
13,737	SAN AUGUSTINE	1,553	78	1,475		1,397 D	5.0%	95.0%	5.0%	95.0%
9,867	SAN JACINTO	700	104	585	11	481 D	14.9%	83.6%	15.1%	84.9%
11,386	SAN PATRICIO	2,163	987	1,097	79	110 D	45.6%	50.7%	47.4%	52.6%
10,045	SAN SABA	2,017	187	1,814	16	1,627 D	9.3%	89.9%	9.3%	90.7%
1,851	SCHLEICHER	365	118	246	1	128 D	32.3%	67.4%	32.4%	67.6%
9,003	SCURRY	1,610	269	1,292	49	1,023 D	16.7%	80.2%	17.2%	82.8%
4,960	SHACKELFORD	1,456	727	729		2 D	49.9%	50.1%	49.9%	50.1%
27,464	SHELBY	3,698	160	3,408	130	3,248 D	4.3%	92.2%	4.5%	95.5%
1,473	SHERMAN	300	87	188	25	101 D	29.0%	62.7%	31.6%	68.4%
46,769	SMITH	5,723	1,079	4,473	171	3,394 D	18.9%	78.2%	19.4%	80.6%
3,563	SOMERVELL	469	42	403	24	361 D	9.0%	85.9%	9.4%	90.6%
11,089	STARR	779	23	756		733 D	3.0%	97.0%	3.0%	97.0%
15,403	STEPHENS	2,661	372	2,184	105	1,812 D	14.0%	82.1%	14.6%	85.4%
1,053	STERLING	269	25	243	1	218 D	9.3%	90.3%	9.3%	90.7%
4,086	STONEWALL	1,067	171	778	118	607 D	16.0%	72.9%	18.0%	82.0%
1,598	SUTTON	269	124	143	2	19 D	46.1%	53.2%	46.4%	53.6%
4,388	SWISHER	819	212	573	34	361 D	25.9%	70.0%	27.0%	73.0%
152,800	TARRANT	22,151	5,859	13,673	2,619	7,814 D	26.5%	61.7%	30.0%	70.0%
24,081	TAYLOR	3,660	441	3,157	62	2,716 D	12.0%	86.3%	12.3%	87.7%
1,595	TERRELL	316	122	109	85	13 R	38.6%	34.5%	52.8%	47.2%
2,236	TERRY	1,001	160	823	18	663 D	16.0%	82.2%	16.3%	83.7%
3,589	THROCKMORTON	719	174	539	6	365 D	24.2%	75.0%	24.4%	75.6%
18,128	TITUS	1,589		1,589		1,589 D		100.0%		100.0%
15,210	TOM GREEN	2,794	554	2,116	124	1,562 D	19.8%	75.7%	20.7%	79.3%
57,616	TRAVIS	9,827	1,909	7,573	345	5,664 D	19.4%	77.1%	20.1%	79.9%
13,623	TRINITY	1,692	146	1,504	42	1,358 D	8.6%	88.9%	8.8%	91.2%
10,415	TYLER	1,044	90	929	25	839 D	8.6%	89.0%	8.8%	91.2%
22,472	UPSHUR	2,911	258	2,611	42	2,353 D	8.9%	89.7%	9.0%	91.0%
253	UPTON	40	4	35	1	31 D	10.0%	87.5%	10.3%	89.7%
10,769	UVALDE	1,715	351	1,312	52	961 D	20.5%	76.5%	21.1%	78.9%
12,706	VAL VERDE	998	457	434	107	23 R	45.8%	43.5%	51.3%	48.7%
30,784	VAN ZANDT	3,957		3,957		3,957 D		100.0%		100.0%
18,271	VICTORIA	2,418	459	1,653	306	1,194 D	19.0%	68.4%	21.7%	78.3%
18,556	WALKER	1,996	201	1,792	3	1,591 D	10.1%	89.8%	10.1%	89.9%
10,292	WALLER	1,461	203	1,239	19	1,036 D	13.9%	84.8%	14.1%	85.9%
2,615	WARD	274	42	206	26	164 D	15.3%	75.2%	16.9%	83.1%
26,624	WASHINGTON	4,137	496	3,568	73	3,072 D	12.0%	86.2%	12.2%	87.8%
29,152	WEBB	1,794	429	1,313	52	884 D	23.9%	73.2%	24.6%	75.4%

TEXAS

PRESIDENT 1924

1920 Census Population	County	Total Vote	Republican	Democratic	Other	Rep.-Dem. Plurality	Percentage Total Vote Rep.	Percentage Total Vote Dem.	Percentage Major Vote Rep.	Percentage Major Vote Dem.
24,288	WHARTON	2,989	858	2,020	111	1,162 D	28.7%	67.6%	29.8%	70.2%
7,397	WHEELER	1,151	197	908	46	711 D	17.1%	78.9%	17.8%	82.2%
72,911	WICHITA	8,481	2,189	5,831	461	3,642 D	25.8%	68.8%	27.3%	72.7%
15,112	WILBARGER	1,578	269	1,222	87	953 D	17.0%	77.4%	18.0%	82.0%
	WILLACY	434	110	307	17	197 D	25.3%	70.7%	26.4%	73.6%
42,934	WILLIAMSON	7,578	934	6,324	320	5,390 D	12.3%	83.5%	12.9%	87.1%
17,289	WILSON	2,454	495	1,633	326	1,138 D	20.2%	66.5%	23.3%	76.7%
81	WINKLER	16	1	15		14 D	6.3%	93.8%	6.3%	93.8%
23,363	WISE	3,641	532	2,958	151	2,426 D	14.6%	81.2%	15.2%	84.8%
27,707	WOOD	3,280	342	2,806	132	2,464 D	10.4%	85.5%	10.9%	89.1%
504	YOAKUM	112	9	95	8	86 D	8.0%	84.8%	8.7%	91.3%
13,379	YOUNG	2,373	322	2,000	51	1,678 D	13.6%	84.3%	13.9%	86.1%
2,929	ZAPATA	498	197	300	1	103 D	39.6%	60.2%	39.6%	60.4%
3,108	ZAVALA	453	95	326	32	231 D	21.0%	72.0%	22.6%	77.4%
4,663,228	TOTAL	657,054	130,794	483,381	42,879	352,587 D	19.9%	73.6%	21.3%	78.7%

TEXAS

PRESIDENT 1920

1920 Census Population	County	Total Vote	Republican	Democratic	Other	Rep.-Dem. Plurality	Percentage Total Vote Rep.	Percentage Total Vote Dem.	Percentage Major Vote Rep.	Percentage Major Vote Dem.
34,318	ANDERSON	3,926	323	2,355	1,248	2,032 D	8.2%	60.0%	12.1%	87.9%
350	ANDREWS	83	9	74		65 D	10.8%	89.2%	10.8%	89.2%
22,287	ANGELINA	2,672	205	1,661	806	1,456 D	7.7%	62.2%	11.0%	89.0%
2,064	ARANSAS	202	49	146	7	97 D	24.3%	72.3%	25.1%	74.9%
5,254	ARCHER	641	169	449	23	280 D	26.4%	70.0%	27.3%	72.7%
2,816	ARMSTRONG	506	87	405	14	318 D	17.2%	80.0%	17.7%	82.3%
12,702	ATASCOSA	766	185	531	50	346 D	24.2%	69.3%	25.8%	74.2%
18,874	AUSTIN	2,892	568	538	1,786	30 R	19.6%	18.6%	51.4%	48.6%
517	BAILEY	—	—	—	—	—	—	—	—	—
4,001	BANDERA	611	249	311	51	62 D	40.8%	50.9%	44.5%	55.5%
26,649	BASTROP	2,166	484	1,088	594	604 D	22.3%	50.2%	30.8%	69.2%
7,027	BAYLOR	859	139	632	88	493 D	16.2%	73.6%	18.0%	82.0%
12,137	BEE	923	283	545	95	262 D	30.7%	59.0%	34.2%	65.8%
46,412	BELL	6,081	483	3,595	2,003	3,112 D	7.9%	59.1%	11.8%	88.2%
202,096	BEXAR	17,047	8,898	6,926	1,223	1,972 R	52.2%	40.6%	56.2%	43.8%
4,063	BLANCO	1,708	378	426	904	48 D	22.1%	24.9%	47.0%	53.0%
965	BORDEN	105	4	89	12	85 D	3.8%	84.8%	4.3%	95.7%
18,032	BOSQUE	2,544	567	1,556	421	989 D	22.3%	61.2%	26.7%	73.3%
39,472	BOWIE	3,851	1,032	2,396	423	1,364 D	26.8%	62.2%	30.1%	69.9%
20,614	BRAZORIA	2,605	1,235	1,184	186	51 R	47.4%	45.5%	51.1%	48.9%
21,975	BRAZOS	2,172	277	1,281	614	1,004 D	12.8%	59.0%	17.8%	82.2%
4,822	BREWSTER	347	125	210	12	85 D	36.0%	60.5%	37.3%	62.7%
2,948	BRISCOE	332	39	262	31	223 D	11.7%	78.9%	13.0%	87.0%
4,560	BROOKS	164	37	127		90 D	22.6%	77.4%	22.6%	77.4%
21,682	BROWN	2,436	397	1,708	331	1,311 D	16.3%	70.1%	18.9%	81.1%
16,855	BURLESON	1,988	142	981	865	839 D	7.1%	49.3%	12.6%	87.4%
9,499	BURNET	1,270	241	795	234	554 D	19.0%	62.6%	23.3%	76.7%
25,160	CALDWELL	2,067	269	1,240	558	971 D	13.0%	60.0%	17.8%	82.2%
4,700	CALHOUN	561	95	363	103	268 D	16.9%	64.7%	20.7%	79.3%
11,844	CALLAHAN	1,204	213	804	187	591 D	17.7%	66.8%	20.9%	79.1%
36,662	CAMERON	1,846	909	920	17	11 D	49.2%	49.8%	49.7%	50.3%
11,103	CAMP	1,321	156	661	504	505 D	11.8%	50.0%	19.1%	80.9%
3,078	CARSON	647	208	428	11	220 D	32.1%	66.2%	32.7%	67.3%
30,041	CASS	3,397	1,446	1,563	388	117 D	42.6%	46.0%	48.1%	51.9%
1,948	CASTRO	275	111	158	6	47 D	40.4%	57.5%	41.3%	58.7%
4,162	CHAMBERS	563	278	240	45	38 R	49.4%	42.6%	53.7%	46.3%
37,633	CHEROKEE	3,572	478	2,233	861	1,755 D	13.4%	62.5%	17.6%	82.4%
10,933	CHILDRESS	1,441	163	1,206	72	1,043 D	11.3%	83.7%	11.9%	88.1%
16,864	CLAY	1,821	446	1,324	51	878 D	24.5%	72.7%	25.2%	74.8%
67	COCHRAN	—	—	—	—	—	—	—	—	—
4,557	COKE	564	58	444	62	386 D	10.3%	78.7%	11.6%	88.4%
18,805	COLEMAN	2,214	355	1,445	414	1,090 D	16.0%	65.3%	19.7%	80.3%
49,609	COLLIN	5,778	1,338	4,045	395	2,707 D	23.2%	70.0%	24.9%	75.1%
9,154	COLLINGSWORTH	1,007	307	640	60	333 D	30.5%	63.6%	32.4%	67.6%
19,013	COLORADO	2,475	477	765	1,233	288 D	19.3%	30.9%	38.4%	61.6%
8,824	COMAL	1,820	765	181	874	584 R	42.0%	9.9%	80.9%	19.1%
25,748	COMANCHE	2,860	930	1,633	297	703 D	32.5%	57.1%	36.3%	63.7%
5,847	CONCHO	675	151	405	119	254 D	22.4%	60.0%	27.2%	72.8%
25,667	COOKE	3,388	1,003	2,170	215	1,167 D	29.6%	64.0%	31.6%	68.4%
20,601	CORYELL	2,722	444	1,542	736	1,098 D	16.3%	56.6%	22.4%	77.6%
6,901	COTTLE	664	121	472	71	351 D	18.2%	71.1%	20.4%	79.6%
37	CRANE	—	—	—	—	—	—	—	—	—
1,500	CROCKETT	171	80	89	2	9 D	46.8%	52.0%	47.3%	52.7%
6,084	CROSBY	782	146	572	64	426 D	18.7%	73.1%	20.3%	79.7%
912	CULBERSON	47	6	40	1	34 D	12.8%	85.1%	13.0%	87.0%
4,528	DALLAM	736	195	478	63	283 D	26.5%	64.9%	29.0%	71.0%
210,551	DALLAS	21,349	4,986	14,390	1,973	9,404 D	23.4%	67.4%	25.7%	74.3%
4,309	DAWSON	419	75	296	48	221 D	17.9%	70.6%	20.2%	79.8%
3,747	DEAF SMITH	666	205	459	2	254 D	30.8%	68.9%	30.9%	69.1%
15,887	DELTA	1,499	316	1,081	102	765 D	21.1%	72.1%	22.6%	77.4%

TEXAS

PRESIDENT 1920

1920 Census Population	County	Total Vote	Republican	Democratic	Other	Rep.-Dem. Plurality	Percentage Total Vote Rep.	Percentage Total Vote Dem.	Percentage Major Vote Rep.	Percentage Major Vote Dem.
35,355	DENTON	2,600	900	1,257	443	357 D	34.6%	48.3%	41.7%	58.3%
27,971	DE WITT	3,309	1,277	971	1,061	306 R	38.6%	29.3%	56.8%	43.2%
5,876	DICKENS	579	109	433	37	324 D	18.8%	74.8%	20.1%	79.9%
5,296	DIMMIT	343	108	231	4	123 D	31.5%	67.3%	31.9%	68.1%
8,035	DONLEY	1,001	206	766	29	560 D	20.6%	76.5%	21.2%	78.8%
8,251	DUVAL	480	86	387	7	301 D	17.9%	80.6%	18.2%	81.8%
58,505	EASTLAND	4,069	941	2,942	186	2,001 D	23.1%	72.3%	24.2%	75.8%
760	ECTOR	125	23	100	2	77 D	18.4%	80.0%	18.7%	81.3%
2,283	EDWARDS	529	297	201	31	96 R	56.1%	38.0%	59.6%	40.4%
55,700	ELLIS	5,857	819	4,081	957	3,262 D	14.0%	69.7%	16.7%	83.3%
101,877	EL PASO	8,286	4,070	4,143	73	73 D	49.1%	50.0%	49.6%	50.4%
28,385	ERATH	2,743	358	1,914	471	1,556 D	13.1%	69.8%	15.8%	84.2%
36,217	FALLS	3,883	585	1,878	1,420	1,293 D	15.1%	48.4%	23.8%	76.2%
48,186	FANNIN	5,182	1,103	3,461	618	2,358 D	21.3%	66.8%	24.2%	75.8%
29,965	FAYETTE	4,525	1,099	932	2,494	167 R	24.3%	20.6%	54.1%	45.9%
11,009	FISHER	994	152	743	99	591 D	15.3%	74.7%	17.0%	83.0%
9,758	FLOYD	1,066	167	841	58	674 D	15.7%	78.9%	16.6%	83.4%
4,747	FOARD	1,017	101	491	425	390 D	9.9%	48.3%	17.1%	82.9%
22,931	FORT BEND	541		27	514	27 D		5.0%		100.0%
9,304	FRANKLIN	—	—	—	—	—	—	—	—	—
23,264	FREESTONE	2,752	378	1,463	911	1,085 D	13.7%	53.2%	20.5%	79.5%
9,296	FRIO	532	102	421	9	319 D	19.2%	79.1%	19.5%	80.5%
1,018	GAINES	143	9	134		125 D	6.3%	93.7%	6.3%	93.7%
53,150	GALVESTON	5,372	1,628	2,933	811	1,305 D	30.3%	54.6%	35.7%	64.3%
4,253	GARZA	473	28	392	53	364 D	5.9%	82.9%	6.7%	93.3%
10,015	GILLESPIE	2,104	1,270	137	697	1,133 R	60.4%	6.5%	90.3%	9.7%
555	GLASSCOCK	117	25	91	1	66 D	21.4%	77.8%	21.6%	78.4%
9,348	GOLIAD	2,163	1,513	448	202	1,065 R	69.9%	20.7%	77.2%	22.8%
28,438	GONZALES	2,484	748	1,299	437	551 D	30.1%	52.3%	36.5%	63.5%
4,663	GRAY	811	251	529	31	278 D	30.9%	65.2%	32.2%	67.8%
74,165	GRAYSON	7,945	2,125	5,241	579	3,116 D	26.7%	66.0%	28.8%	71.2%
16,767	GREGG	1,522	257	1,050	215	793 D	16.9%	69.0%	19.7%	80.3%
23,101	GRIMES	1,449	214	1,027	208	813 D	14.8%	70.9%	17.2%	82.8%
27,719	GUADALUPE	3,245	1,839	560	846	1,279 R	56.7%	17.3%	76.7%	23.3%
10,104	HALE	1,679	352	1,279	48	927 D	21.0%	76.2%	21.6%	78.4%
11,137	HALL	1,204	194	922	88	728 D	16.1%	76.6%	17.4%	82.6%
14,676	HAMILTON	1,672	422	1,075	175	653 D	25.2%	64.3%	28.2%	71.8%
1,354	HANSFORD	184	54	124	6	70 D	29.3%	67.4%	30.3%	69.7%
12,487	HARDEMAN	1,325	253	967	105	714 D	19.1%	73.0%	20.7%	79.3%
15,983	HARDIN	1,376	202	999	175	797 D	14.7%	72.6%	16.8%	83.2%
186,667	HARRIS	28,837	7,735	14,808	6,294	7,073 D	26.8%	51.4%	34.3%	65.7%
43,565	HARRISON	3,181	377	2,134	670	1,757 D	11.9%	67.1%	15.0%	85.0%
1,109	HARTLEY	234	81	144	9	63 D	34.6%	61.5%	36.0%	64.0%
14,193	HASKELL	1,637	254	1,127	256	873 D	15.5%	68.8%	18.4%	81.6%
15,920	HAYS	1,656	242	1,075	339	833 D	14.6%	64.9%	18.4%	81.6%
4,280	HEMPHILL	678	253	417	8	164 D	37.3%	61.5%	37.8%	62.2%
28,327	HENDERSON	2,889	538	1,684	667	1,146 D	18.6%	58.3%	24.2%	75.8%
38,110	HIDALGO	3,559	1,108	2,409	42	1,301 D	31.1%	67.7%	31.5%	68.5%
43,332	HILL	5,155	1,022	3,254	879	2,232 D	19.8%	63.1%	23.9%	76.1%
137	HOCKLEY	—	—	—	—	—	—	—	—	—
8,759	HOOD	1,020	175	697	148	522 D	17.2%	68.3%	20.1%	79.9%
34,791	HOPKINS	3,694	837	2,548	309	1,711 D	22.7%	69.0%	24.7%	75.3%
28,601	HOUSTON	2,981	385	1,475	1,121	1,090 D	12.9%	49.5%	20.7%	79.3%
6,962	HOWARD	907	107	703	97	596 D	11.8%	77.5%	13.2%	86.8%
962	HUDSPETH	135	37	97	1	60 D	27.4%	71.9%	27.6%	72.4%
50,350	HUNT	5,788	880	4,397	511	3,517 D	15.2%	76.0%	16.7%	83.3%
721	HUTCHINSON	247	106	135	6	29 D	42.9%	54.7%	44.0%	56.0%
1,610	IRION	224	45	148	31	103 D	20.1%	66.1%	23.3%	76.7%
9,863	JACK	881	253	566	62	313 D	28.7%	64.2%	30.9%	69.1%
11,244	JACKSON	1,055	355	562	138	207 D	33.6%	53.3%	38.7%	61.3%

TEXAS

PRESIDENT 1920

1920 Census Population	County	Total Vote	Republican	Democratic	Other	Rep.-Dem. Plurality	Percentage Total Vote Rep.	Total Vote Dem.	Major Vote Rep.	Major Vote Dem.
15,569	JASPER	1,095	62	793	240	731 D	5.7%	72.4%	7.3%	92.7%
1,445	JEFF DAVIS	132	41	91		50 D	31.1%	68.9%	31.1%	68.9%
73,120	JEFFERSON	6,450	1,110	4,246	1,094	3,136 D	17.2%	65.8%	20.7%	79.3%
1,914	JIM HOGG	93	23	70		47 D	24.7%	75.3%	24.7%	75.3%
6,587	JIM WELLS	524	169	304	51	135 D	32.3%	58.0%	35.7%	64.3%
37,286	JOHNSON	4,224	661	3,041	522	2,380 D	15.6%	72.0%	17.9%	82.1%
22,323	JONES	2,282	270	1,792	220	1,522 D	11.8%	78.5%	13.1%	86.9%
19,049	KARNES	1,548	484	642	422	158 D	31.3%	41.5%	43.0%	57.0%
41,276	KAUFMAN	4,462	573	3,070	819	2,497 D	12.8%	68.8%	15.7%	84.3%
4,779	KENDALL	1,159	846	142	171	704 R	73.0%	12.3%	85.6%	14.4%
1,033	KENEDY	—	—	—	—	—	—	—	—	—
3,335	KENT	283	45	214	24	169 D	15.9%	75.6%	17.4%	82.6%
5,842	KERR	1,149	464	612	73	148 D	40.4%	53.3%	43.1%	56.9%
3,581	KIMBLE	491	150	299	42	149 D	30.5%	60.9%	33.4%	66.6%
655	KING	160		157	3	157 D		98.1%		100.0%
3,746	KINNEY	247	137	98	12	39 R	55.5%	39.7%	58.3%	41.7%
7,837	KLEBERG	673	172	455	46	283 D	25.6%	67.6%	27.4%	72.6%
9,240	KNOX	1,030	159	773	98	614 D	15.4%	75.0%	17.1%	82.9%
55,742	LAMAR	5,006	639	3,765	602	3,126 D	12.8%	75.2%	14.5%	85.5%
1,175	LAMB	419	136	264	19	128 D	32.5%	63.0%	34.0%	66.0%
8,800	LAMPASAS	1,348	227	778	343	551 D	16.8%	57.7%	22.6%	77.4%
4,821	LA SALLE	314	53	252	9	199 D	16.9%	80.3%	17.4%	82.6%
28,964	LAVACA	3,194	100	1,249	1,845	1,149 D	3.1%	39.1%	7.4%	92.6%
14,014	LEE	2,219	325	712	1,182	387 D	14.6%	32.1%	31.3%	68.7%
18,286	LEON	2,079	220	1,124	735	904 D	10.6%	54.1%	16.4%	83.6%
14,637	LIBERTY	—	—	—	—	—	—	—	—	—
33,283	LIMESTONE	3,390	408	2,165	817	1,757 D	12.0%	63.9%	15.9%	84.1%
3,684	LIPSCOMB	821	425	350	46	75 R	51.8%	42.6%	54.8%	45.2%
4,171	LIVE OAK	496	161	234	101	73 D	32.5%	47.2%	40.8%	59.2%
5,360	LLANO	1,092	184	665	243	481 D	16.8%	60.9%	21.7%	78.3%
82	LOVING	—	—	—	—	—	—	—	—	—
11,096	LUBBOCK	1,452	204	1,180	68	976 D	14.0%	81.3%	14.7%	85.3%
4,751	LYNN	682	76	538	68	462 D	11.1%	78.9%	12.4%	87.6%
11,020	MCCULLOCH	1,102	210	786	106	576 D	19.1%	71.3%	21.1%	78.9%
82,921	MCLENNAN	7,809	1,655	4,975	1,179	3,320 D	21.2%	63.7%	25.0%	75.0%
952	MCMULLEN	106	33	72	1	39 D	31.1%	67.9%	31.4%	68.6%
11,956	MADISON	1,126	63	650	413	587 D	5.6%	57.7%	8.8%	91.2%
10,886	MARION	1,130	392	430	308	38 D	34.7%	38.1%	47.7%	52.3%
1,146	MARTIN	175	33	136	6	103 D	18.9%	77.7%	19.5%	80.5%
4,824	MASON	673	269	304	100	35 D	40.0%	45.2%	46.9%	53.1%
16,589	MATAGORDA	2,094	918	992	184	74 D	43.8%	47.4%	48.1%	51.9%
7,418	MAVERICK	475	296	173	6	123 R	62.3%	36.4%	63.1%	36.9%
11,679	MEDINA	1,689	772	519	398	253 R	45.7%	30.7%	59.8%	40.2%
3,162	MENARD	426	203	197	26	6 R	47.7%	46.2%	50.7%	49.3%
2,449	MIDLAND	341	68	271	2	203 D	19.9%	79.5%	20.1%	79.9%
38,104	MILAM	4,828	371	2,598	1,859	2,227 D	7.7%	53.8%	12.5%	87.5%
9,019	MILLS	1,181	247	669	265	422 D	20.9%	56.6%	27.0%	73.0%
7,527	MITCHELL	850	89	694	67	605 D	10.5%	81.6%	11.4%	88.6%
22,200	MONTAGUE	1,395	474	714	207	240 D	34.0%	51.2%	39.9%	60.1%
17,334	MONTGOMERY	1,450	203	935	312	732 D	14.0%	64.5%	17.8%	82.2%
571	MOORE	115	13	101	1	88 D	11.3%	87.8%	11.4%	88.6%
10,289	MORRIS	908	164	669	75	505 D	18.1%	73.7%	19.7%	80.3%
4,107	MOTLEY	391	40	345	6	305 D	10.2%	88.2%	10.4%	89.6%
28,457	NACOGDOCHES	2,727	238	1,794	695	1,556 D	8.7%	65.8%	11.7%	88.3%
50,624	NAVARRO	5,172	821	3,328	1,023	2,507 D	15.9%	64.3%	19.8%	80.2%
12,196	NEWTON	668	58	420	190	362 D	8.7%	62.9%	12.1%	87.9%
10,868	NOLAN	1,154	175	923	56	748 D	15.2%	80.0%	15.9%	84.1%
22,807	NUECES	1,778	385	1,246	147	861 D	21.7%	70.1%	23.6%	76.4%
2,331	OCHILTREE	416	135	281		146 D	32.5%	67.5%	32.5%	67.5%
709	OLDHAM	192	52	139	1	87 D	27.1%	72.4%	27.2%	72.8%

TEXAS

PRESIDENT 1920

1920 Census Population	County	Total Vote	Republican	Democratic	Other	Rep.-Dem. Plurality	Percentage Total Vote Rep.	Total Vote Dem.	Major Vote Rep.	Major Vote Dem.
15,379	ORANGE	1,295	121	1,055	119	934 D	9.3%	81.5%	10.3%	89.7%
23,431	PALO PINTO	2,172	342	1,645	185	1,303 D	15.7%	75.7%	17.2%	82.8%
21,755	PANOLA	1,659	268	1,086	305	818 D	16.2%	65.5%	19.8%	80.2%
23,382	PARKER	2,369	488	1,765	116	1,277 D	20.6%	74.5%	21.7%	78.3%
1,699	PARMER	341	140	189	12	49 D	41.1%	55.4%	42.6%	57.4%
3,857	PECOS	814	394	386	34	8 R	48.4%	47.4%	50.5%	49.5%
16,784	POLK	1,285	255	810	220	555 D	19.8%	63.0%	23.9%	76.1%
16,710	POTTER	1,771	358	1,374	39	1,016 D	20.2%	77.6%	20.7%	79.3%
12,202	PRESIDIO	366	122	238	6	116 D	33.3%	65.0%	33.9%	66.1%
8,099	RAINS	769	189	462	118	273 D	24.6%	60.1%	29.0%	71.0%
3,675	RANDALL	551	183	360	8	177 D	33.2%	65.3%	33.7%	66.3%
377	REAGAN	49		49		49 D		100.0%		100.0%
1,461	REAL	310	111	177	22	66 D	35.8%	57.1%	38.5%	61.5%
35,829	RED RIVER	3,538	799	2,263	476	1,464 D	22.6%	64.0%	26.1%	73.9%
4,457	REEVES	550	91	457	2	366 D	16.5%	83.1%	16.6%	83.4%
4,050	REFUGIO	645	360	227	58	133 R	55.8%	35.2%	61.3%	38.7%
1,469	ROBERTS	239	60	173	6	113 D	25.1%	72.4%	25.8%	74.2%
27,933	ROBERTSON	2,515	225	1,634	656	1,409 D	8.9%	65.0%	12.1%	87.9%
8,591	ROCKWALL	994	104	873	17	769 D	10.5%	87.8%	10.6%	89.4%
17,074	RUNNELS	1,855	332	1,197	326	865 D	17.9%	64.5%	21.7%	78.3%
31,689	RUSK	2,843	745	1,535	563	790 D	26.2%	54.0%	32.7%	67.3%
12,299	SABINE	985	61	637	287	576 D	6.2%	64.7%	8.7%	91.3%
13,737	SAN AUGUSTINE	1,544	121	658	765	537 D	7.8%	42.6%	15.5%	84.5%
9,867	SAN JACINTO	691	7	320	364	313 D	1.0%	46.3%	2.1%	97.9%
11,386	SAN PATRICIO	955	308	620	27	312 D	32.3%	64.9%	33.2%	66.8%
10,045	SAN SABA	1,476	180	874	422	694 D	12.2%	59.2%	17.1%	82.9%
1,851	SCHLEICHER	304	81	211	12	130 D	26.6%	69.4%	27.7%	72.3%
9,003	SCURRY	1,006	151	801	54	650 D	15.0%	79.6%	15.9%	84.1%
4,960	SHACKELFORD	527	116	342	69	226 D	22.0%	64.9%	25.3%	74.7%
27,464	SHELBY	2,336	150	1,700	486	1,550 D	6.4%	72.8%	8.1%	91.9%
1,473	SHERMAN	247	77	170		93 D	31.2%	68.8%	31.2%	68.8%
46,769	SMITH	4,673	707	2,965	1,001	2,258 D	15.1%	63.4%	19.3%	80.7%
3,563	SOMERVELL	374	92	198	84	106 D	24.6%	52.9%	31.7%	68.3%
11,089	STARR	510	92	418		326 D	18.0%	82.0%	18.0%	82.0%
15,403	STEPHENS	845	141	643	61	502 D	16.7%	76.1%	18.0%	82.0%
1,053	STERLING	186	17	152	17	135 D	9.1%	81.7%	10.1%	89.9%
4,086	STONEWALL	547	134	356	57	222 D	24.5%	65.1%	27.3%	72.7%
1,598	SUTTON	305	104	190	11	86 D	34.1%	62.3%	35.4%	64.6%
4,388	SWISHER	601	148	443	10	295 D	24.6%	73.7%	25.0%	75.0%
152,800	TARRANT	17,108	3,486	12,431	1,191	8,945 D	20.4%	72.7%	21.9%	78.1%
24,081	TAYLOR	2,438	300	1,932	206	1,632 D	12.3%	79.2%	13.4%	86.6%
1,595	TERRELL	268	95	155	18	60 D	35.4%	57.8%	38.0%	62.0%
2,236	TERRY	355	39	270	46	231 D	11.0%	76.1%	12.6%	87.4%
3,589	THROCKMORTON	498	72	399	27	327 D	14.5%	80.1%	15.3%	84.7%
18,128	TITUS	1,795	508	1,094	193	586 D	28.3%	60.9%	31.7%	68.3%
15,210	TOM GREEN	1,650	256	1,264	130	1,008 D	15.5%	76.6%	16.8%	83.2%
57,616	TRAVIS	5,905	1,204	3,541	1,160	2,337 D	20.4%	60.0%	25.4%	74.6%
13,623	TRINITY	1,128	125	643	360	518 D	11.1%	57.0%	16.3%	83.7%
10,415	TYLER	1,393	115	1,066	212	951 D	8.3%	76.5%	9.7%	90.3%
22,472	UPSHUR	2,330	616	1,222	492	606 D	26.4%	52.4%	33.5%	66.5%
253	UPTON	71	25	46		21 D	35.2%	64.8%	35.2%	64.8%
10,769	UVALDE	1,021	237	743	41	506 D	23.2%	72.8%	24.2%	75.8%
12,706	VAL VERDE	718	296	418	4	122 D	41.2%	58.2%	41.5%	58.5%
30,784	VAN ZANDT	3,206	728	1,958	520	1,230 D	22.7%	61.1%	27.1%	72.9%
18,271	VICTORIA	1,879	782	686	411	96 R	41.6%	36.5%	53.3%	46.7%
18,556	WALKER	1,723	404	788	531	384 D	23.4%	45.7%	33.9%	66.1%
10,292	WALLER	1,250	167	674	409	507 D	13.4%	53.9%	19.9%	80.1%
2,615	WARD	265	79	181	5	102 D	29.8%	68.3%	30.4%	69.6%
26,624	WASHINGTON	3,220	684	796	1,740	112 D	21.2%	24.7%	46.2%	53.8%
29,152	WEBB	1,117	468	633	16	165 D	41.9%	56.7%	42.5%	57.5%

TEXAS

PRESIDENT 1920

1920 Census Population	County	Total Vote	Republican	Democratic	Other	Rep.-Dem. Plurality	Percentage Total Vote Rep.	Total Vote Dem.	Major Vote Rep.	Major Vote Dem.
24,288	WHARTON	2,363	852	836	675	16 R	36.1%	35.4%	50.5%	49.5%
7,397	WHEELER	752	198	516	38	318 D	26.3%	68.6%	27.7%	72.3%
72,911	WICHITA	5,410	1,487	3,812	111	2,325 D	27.5%	70.5%	28.1%	71.9%
15,112	WILBARGER	1,542	335	1,118	89	783 D	21.7%	72.5%	23.1%	76.9%
	WILLACY	62	9	53		44 D	14.5%	85.5%	14.5%	85.5%
42,934	WILLIAMSON	5,051	819	2,677	1,555	1,858 D	16.2%	53.0%	23.4%	76.6%
17,289	WILSON	1,779	820	753	206	67 R	46.1%	42.3%	52.1%	47.9%
81	WINKLER	19	2	17		15 D	10.5%	89.5%	10.5%	89.5%
23,363	WISE	2,725	579	2,031	115	1,452 D	21.2%	74.5%	22.2%	77.8%
27,707	WOOD	3,160	798	1,643	719	845 D	25.3%	52.0%	32.7%	67.3%
504	YOAKUM	81		79	2	79 D		97.5%		100.0%
13,379	YOUNG	1,470	209	1,214	47	1,005 D	14.2%	82.6%	14.7%	85.3%
2,929	ZAPATA	162	98	50	14	48 R	60.5%	30.9%	66.2%	33.8%
3,108	ZAVALA	381	101	264	16	163 D	26.5%	69.3%	27.7%	72.3%
4,663,228	TOTAL	486,109	114,658	287,920	83,531	173,262 D	23.6%	59.2%	28.5%	71.5%

TEXAS

In 1921 most of Willacy county was renamed Kenedy and a new Willacy county was organized from parts of Cameron, Hidalgo and Kenedy counties. The following unorganized counties became fully organized counties with the same name: Hockley in 1921; Cochran in 1924; Crane in 1927 and Loving in 1931. In earlier elections, state canvass reports omit all or part of the vote in some counties. Where possible, unofficial figures have been used to complete the state records.

ELECTION NOTES

1956 Other vote was Andrews (States Rights).

1952 Other vote was 1,983 Hamblen (Prohibition); 1,563 MacArthur (833 Christian Nationalist and 730 Constitution); 294 Hallinan (Progressive).

1948 Other vote was 113,920 Thurmond (States Rights); 3,918 Wallace (Progressive); 3,115 Watson (Prohibition); 922 Thomas (Socialist). States Rights candidates ran second in a number of counties. Data from the files of the American Institute of Public Opinion have been used to supplement the incomplete state canvassed returns.

1944 Other vote was 135,444 Texas Regulars elector ticket; 1,018 Watson (Prohibition); 594 Thomas (Socialist); 250 Smith (America First). Texas Regulars carried Washington county and ran second in others.

1940 Other vote was 928 Babson (Prohibition); 628 Thomas (Socialist); 215 Browder (Communist). Data from Edgar Eugene Robinson's studies have been used to supplement the incomplete state canvassed returns.

1936 Other vote was 3,187 Lemke (Union); 1,122 Thomas (Socialist); 522 Colvin (Prohibition); 257 Browder (Communist). The statewide total in the other vote column includes the 522 Prohibition votes which were not available by county.

1932 Other vote was 4,414 Thomas (Socialist); 243 Harvey (Liberty); 207 Foster (Communist); 157 Jacksonian elector ticket; 34 scattered write-in. The statewide total in the other vote column includes the Jacksonian and write-in votes which were not available by county.

1928 Other vote was 658 Thomas (Socialist); 209 Foster (Communist).

1924 Other vote was LaFollette (Progressive). Progressive candidates carried Comal and Gillespie counties and ran second in Austin, Castro, Dallam, Gaines, Gregg, Guadalupe, Kendall, Lavaca and Lee counties. No votes were canvassed for El Paso, Nueces or Morris counties.

1920 Other vote was 48,098 Ferguson (American); 27,309 Black-and-Tan Republican elector ticket; 8,124 Debs (Socialist). In several counties the state canvass report was unclear; in these counties where possible, the interpretation developed in Edgar Eugene Robinson's studies have been used.

UTAH

POPULAR VOTE FOR PRESIDENT 1920 TO 1956

Year	Total Vote	Republican Vote	Republican Candidate	Democratic Vote	Democratic Candidate	Other Vote	Plurality	Percentage Total Vote Rep.	Total Vote Dem.	Major Vote Rep.	Major Vote Dem.
1956	333,995	215,631	Eisenhower, Dwight D.	118,364	Stevenson, Adlai E.		97,267 R	64.6%	35.4%	64.6%	35.4%
1952	329,554	194,190	Eisenhower, Dwight D.	135,364	Stevenson, Adlai E.		58,826 R	58.9%	41.1%	58.9%	41.1%
1948	276,306	124,402	Dewey, Thomas E.	149,151	Truman, Harry S.	2,753	24,749 D	45.0%	54.0%	45.5%	54.5%
1944	248,319	97,891	Dewey, Thomas E.	150,088	Roosevelt, Franklin D.	340	52,197 D	39.4%	60.4%	39.5%	60.5%
1940	247,819	93,151	Willkie, Wendell	154,277	Roosevelt, Franklin D.	391	61,126 D	37.6%	62.3%	37.6%	62.4%
1936	216,679	64,555	Landon, Alfred M.	150,248	Roosevelt, Franklin D.	1,876	85,693 D	29.8%	69.3%	30.1%	69.9%
1932	206,578	84,795	Hoover, Herbert C.	116,750	Roosevelt, Franklin D.	5,033	31,955 D	41.0%	56.5%	42.1%	57.9%
1928	176,603	94,618	Hoover, Herbert C.	80,985	Smith, Alfred E.	1,000	13,633 R	53.6%	45.9%	53.9%	46.1%
1924 **	156,990	77,327	Coolidge, Calvin	47,001	Davis, John W.	32,662	30,326 R	49.3%	29.9%	62.2%	37.8%
1920	145,828	81,555	Harding, Warren G.	56,639	Cox, James M.	7,634	24,916 R	55.9%	38.8%	59.0%	41.0%

In 1924 other vote was Progressive.

ELECTORAL COLLEGE VOTE 1920 TO 1956

Year	Total	Republican	Democratic	Other
1956	4	4	—	—
1952	4	4	—	—
1948	4	—	4	—
1944	4	—	4	—
1940	4	—	4	—
1936	4	—	4	—
1932	4	—	4	—
1928	4	4	—	—
1924	4	4	—	—
1920	4	4	—	—

UTAH

CACHE
RICH
BOX ELDER
WEBER
MORGAN
DAVIS
SUMMIT
DAGGETT
SALT LAKE
TOOELE
WASATCH
DUCHESNE
UINTAH
UTAH
JUAB
CARBON
SANPETE
MILLARD
EMERY
GRAND
SEVIER
BEAVER
PIUTE
WAYNE
IRON
GARFIELD
SAN JUAN
WASHINGTON
KANE

UTAH

PRESIDENT 1956

1950 Census Population	County	Total Vote	Republican	Democratic	Other	Rep.-Dem. Plurality	Percentage Total Vote Rep.	Percentage Total Vote Dem.	Percentage Major Vote Rep.	Percentage Major Vote Dem.
4,856	BEAVER	2,220	1,190	1,030		160 R	53.6%	46.4%	53.6%	46.4%
19,734	BOX ELDER	8,493	5,804	2,689		3,115 R	68.3%	31.7%	68.3%	31.7%
33,536	CACHE	14,020	10,349	3,671		6,678 R	73.8%	26.2%	73.8%	26.2%
24,901	CARBON	8,967	4,507	4,460		47 R	50.3%	49.7%	50.3%	49.7%
364	DAGGETT	192	102	90		12 R	53.1%	46.9%	53.1%	46.9%
30,867	DAVIS	18,172	12,122	6,050		6,072 R	66.7%	33.3%	66.7%	33.3%
8,134	DUCHESNE	2,730	1,856	874		982 R	68.0%	32.0%	68.0%	32.0%
6,304	EMERY	2,622	1,679	943		736 R	64.0%	36.0%	64.0%	36.0%
4,151	GARFIELD	1,468	1,115	353		762 R	76.0%	24.0%	76.0%	24.0%
1,903	GRAND	1,372	1,044	328		716 R	76.1%	23.9%	76.1%	23.9%
9,642	IRON	4,632	3,321	1,311		2,010 R	71.7%	28.3%	71.7%	28.3%
5,981	JUAB	2,537	1,512	1,025		487 R	59.6%	40.4%	59.6%	40.4%
2,299	KANE	1,041	939	102		837 R	90.2%	9.8%	90.2%	9.8%
9,387	MILLARD	3,860	2,667	1,193		1,474 R	69.1%	30.9%	69.1%	30.9%
2,519	MORGAN	1,343	905	438		467 R	67.4%	32.6%	67.4%	32.6%
1,911	PIUTE	728	548	180		368 R	75.3%	24.7%	75.3%	24.7%
1,673	RICH	814	561	253		308 R	68.9%	31.1%	68.9%	31.1%
274,895	SALT LAKE	148,217	95,179	53,038		42,141 R	64.2%	35.8%	64.2%	35.8%
5,315	SAN JUAN	1,544	1,119	425		694 R	72.5%	27.5%	72.5%	27.5%
13,891	SANPETE	5,661	3,883	1,778		2,105 R	68.6%	31.4%	68.6%	31.4%
12,072	SEVIER	4,878	3,646	1,232		2,414 R	74.7%	25.3%	74.7%	25.3%
6,745	SUMMIT	2,911	2,031	880		1,151 R	69.8%	30.2%	69.8%	30.2%
14,636	TOOELE	6,073	3,390	2,683		707 R	55.8%	44.2%	55.8%	44.2%
10,300	UINTAH	3,660	2,840	820		2,020 R	77.6%	22.4%	77.6%	22.4%
81,912	UTAH	38,118	25,371	12,747		12,624 R	66.6%	33.4%	66.6%	33.4%
5,574	WASATCH	2,602	1,738	864		874 R	66.8%	33.2%	66.8%	33.2%
9,836	WASHINGTON	4,049	3,172	877		2,295 R	78.3%	21.7%	78.3%	21.7%
2,205	WAYNE	782	499	283		216 R	63.8%	36.2%	63.8%	36.2%
83,319	WEBER	40,289	22,542	17,747		4,795 R	56.0%	44.0%	56.0%	44.0%
688,862	TOTAL	333,995	215,631	118,364		97,267 R	64.6%	35.4%	64.6%	35.4%

UTAH

PRESIDENT 1952

1950 Census Population	County	Total Vote	Republican	Democratic	Other	Rep.-Dem. Plurality	Percentage Total Vote Rep.	Percentage Total Vote Dem.	Percentage Major Vote Rep.	Percentage Major Vote Dem.
4,856	BEAVER	2,315	1,277	1,038		239 R	55.2%	44.8%	55.2%	44.8%
19,734	BOX ELDER	8,834	5,850	2,984		2,866 R	66.2%	33.8%	66.2%	33.8%
33,536	CACHE	14,409	10,167	4,242		5,925 R	70.6%	29.4%	70.6%	29.4%
24,901	CARBON	9,560	3,770	5,790		2,020 D	39.4%	60.6%	39.4%	60.6%
364	DAGGETT	176	90	86		4 R	51.1%	48.9%	51.1%	48.9%
30,867	DAVIS	15,027	9,067	5,960		3,107 R	60.3%	39.7%	60.3%	39.7%
8,134	DUCHESNE	3,211	1,969	1,242		727 R	61.3%	38.7%	61.3%	38.7%
6,304	EMERY	2,733	1,552	1,181		371 R	56.8%	43.2%	56.8%	43.2%
4,151	GARFIELD	1,542	1,065	477		588 R	69.1%	30.9%	69.1%	30.9%
1,903	GRAND	934	675	259		416 R	72.3%	27.7%	72.3%	27.7%
9,642	IRON	4,771	3,175	1,596		1,579 R	66.5%	33.5%	66.5%	33.5%
5,981	JUAB	2,914	1,711	1,203		508 R	58.7%	41.3%	58.7%	41.3%
2,299	KANE	1,107	943	164		779 R	85.2%	14.8%	85.2%	14.8%
9,387	MILLARD	4,293	2,994	1,299		1,695 R	69.7%	30.3%	69.7%	30.3%
2,519	MORGAN	1,329	862	467		395 R	64.9%	35.1%	64.9%	35.1%
1,911	PIUTE	738	531	207		324 R	72.0%	28.0%	72.0%	28.0%
1,673	RICH	820	569	251		318 R	69.4%	30.6%	69.4%	30.6%
274,895	SALT LAKE	143,646	84,176	59,470		24,706 R	58.6%	41.4%	58.6%	41.4%
5,315	SAN JUAN	1,297	876	421		455 R	67.5%	32.5%	67.5%	32.5%
13,891	SANPETE	6,367	4,146	2,221		1,925 R	65.1%	34.9%	65.1%	34.9%
12,072	SEVIER	5,441	3,996	1,445		2,551 R	73.4%	26.6%	73.4%	26.6%
6,745	SUMMIT	3,218	1,955	1,263		692 R	60.8%	39.2%	60.8%	39.2%
14,636	TOOELE	6,730	3,209	3,521		312 D	47.7%	52.3%	47.7%	52.3%
10,300	UINTAH	3,942	2,806	1,136		1,670 R	71.2%	28.8%	71.2%	28.8%
81,912	UTAH	36,240	20,913	15,327		5,586 R	57.7%	42.3%	57.7%	42.3%
5,574	WASATCH	2,645	1,677	968		709 R	63.4%	36.6%	63.4%	36.6%
9,836	WASHINGTON	4,017	2,941	1,076		1,865 R	73.2%	26.8%	73.2%	26.8%
2,205	WAYNE	811	536	275		261 R	66.1%	33.9%	66.1%	33.9%
83,319	WEBER	40,487	20,692	19,795		897 R	51.1%	48.9%	51.1%	48.9%
688,862	TOTAL	329,554	194,190	135,364		58,826 R	58.9%	41.1%	58.9%	41.1%

UTAH

PRESIDENT 1948

1940 Census Population	County	Total Vote	Republican	Democratic	Other	Rep.-Dem. Plurality	Percentage Total Vote Rep.	Percentage Total Vote Dem.	Percentage Major Vote Rep.	Percentage Major Vote Dem.
5,014	BEAVER	2,264	1,057	1,190	17	133 D	46.7%	52.6%	47.0%	53.0%
18,832	BOX ELDER	7,475	3,790	3,667	18	123 R	50.7%	49.1%	50.8%	49.2%
29,797	CACHE	12,946	6,514	6,383	49	131 R	50.3%	49.3%	50.5%	49.5%
18,459	CARBON	9,360	2,704	6,397	259	3,693 D	28.9%	68.3%	29.7%	70.3%
564	DAGGETT	165	69	95	1	26 D	41.8%	57.6%	42.1%	57.9%
15,784	DAVIS	10,936	4,718	6,147	71	1,429 D	43.1%	56.2%	43.4%	56.6%
8,958	DUCHESNE	2,870	1,266	1,588	16	322 D	44.1%	55.3%	44.4%	55.6%
7,072	EMERY	2,673	1,147	1,511	15	364 D	42.9%	56.5%	43.2%	56.8%
5,253	GARFIELD	1,567	924	642	1	282 R	59.0%	41.0%	59.0%	41.0%
2,070	GRAND	827	418	400	9	18 R	50.5%	48.4%	51.1%	48.9%
8,331	IRON	3,911	2,289	1,596	26	693 R	58.5%	40.8%	58.9%	41.1%
7,392	JUAB	2,912	1,396	1,501	15	105 D	47.9%	51.5%	48.2%	51.8%
2,561	KANE	989	769	220		549 R	77.8%	22.2%	77.8%	22.2%
9,613	MILLARD	4,029	2,184	1,817	28	367 R	54.2%	45.1%	54.6%	45.4%
2,611	MORGAN	1,265	587	670	8	83 D	46.4%	53.0%	46.7%	53.3%
2,203	PIUTE	763	440	315	8	125 R	57.7%	41.3%	58.3%	41.7%
2,028	RICH	766	399	366	1	33 R	52.1%	47.8%	52.2%	47.8%
211,623	SALT LAKE	116,917	52,479	62,957	1,481	10,478 D	44.9%	53.8%	45.5%	54.5%
4,712	SAN JUAN	983	558	418	7	140 R	56.8%	42.5%	57.2%	42.8%
16,063	SANPETE	6,413	3,336	3,041	36	295 R	52.0%	47.4%	52.3%	47.7%
12,112	SEVIER	4,750	2,791	1,943	16	848 R	58.8%	40.9%	59.0%	41.0%
8,714	SUMMIT	3,206	1,617	1,556	33	61 R	50.4%	48.5%	51.0%	49.0%
9,133	TOOELE	4,884	2,036	2,798	50	762 D	41.7%	57.3%	42.1%	57.9%
9,898	UINTAH	3,153	1,513	1,622	18	109 D	48.0%	51.4%	48.3%	51.7%
57,382	UTAH	29,886	13,395	16,191	300	2,796 D	44.8%	54.2%	45.3%	54.7%
5,754	WASATCH	2,389	1,165	1,219	5	54 D	48.8%	51.0%	48.9%	51.1%
9,269	WASHINGTON	3,617	2,029	1,580	8	449 R	56.1%	43.7%	56.2%	43.8%
2,394	WAYNE	831	367	460	4	93 D	44.2%	55.4%	44.4%	55.6%
56,714	WEBER	33,559	12,445	20,861	253	8,416 D	37.1%	62.2%	37.4%	62.6%
550,310	TOTAL	276,306	124,402	149,151	2,753	24,749 D	45.0%	54.0%	45.5%	54.5%

UTAH

PRESIDENT 1944

1940 Census Population	County	Total Vote	Republican	Democratic	Other	Rep.-Dem. Plurality	Percentage			
							Total Vote		Major Vote	
							Rep.	Dem.	Rep.	Dem.
5,014	BEAVER	2,088	958	1,128	2	170 D	45.9%	54.0%	45.9%	54.1%
18,832	BOX ELDER	7,201	3,058	4,138	5	1,080 D	42.5%	57.5%	42.5%	57.5%
29,797	CACHE	11,948	4,938	6,998	12	2,060 D	41.3%	58.6%	41.4%	58.6%
18,459	CARBON	7,696	2,318	5,364	14	3,046 D	30.1%	69.7%	30.2%	69.8%
564	DAGGETT	173	75	98		23 D	43.4%	56.6%	43.4%	56.6%
15,784	DAVIS	8,851	3,663	5,179	9	1,516 D	41.4%	58.5%	41.4%	58.6%
8,958	DUCHESNE	2,769	1,140	1,629		489 D	41.2%	58.8%	41.2%	58.8%
7,072	EMERY	2,402	974	1,427	1	453 D	40.5%	59.4%	40.6%	59.4%
5,253	GARFIELD	1,402	842	559	1	283 R	60.1%	39.9%	60.1%	39.9%
2,070	GRAND	813	428	380	5	48 R	52.6%	46.7%	53.0%	47.0%
8,331	IRON	3,621	1,930	1,677	14	253 R	53.3%	46.3%	53.5%	46.5%
7,392	JUAB	2,680	1,192	1,483	5	291 D	44.5%	55.3%	44.6%	55.4%
2,561	KANE	906	662	244		418 R	73.1%	26.9%	73.1%	26.9%
9,613	MILLARD	3,803	1,889	1,909	5	20 D	49.7%	50.2%	49.7%	50.3%
2,611	MORGAN	1,206	535	671		136 D	44.4%	55.6%	44.4%	55.6%
2,203	PIUTE	727	381	346		35 R	52.4%	47.6%	52.4%	47.6%
2,028	RICH	789	394	395		1 D	49.9%	50.1%	49.9%	50.1%
211,623	SALT LAKE	105,598	39,327	66,114	157	26,787 D	37.2%	62.6%	37.3%	62.7%
4,712	SAN JUAN	881	513	367	1	146 R	58.2%	41.7%	58.3%	41.7%
16,063	SANPETE	6,267	3,196	3,071		125 R	51.0%	49.0%	51.0%	49.0%
12,112	SEVIER	4,445	2,345	2,095	5	250 R	52.8%	47.1%	52.8%	47.2%
8,714	SUMMIT	3,242	1,479	1,761	2	282 D	45.6%	54.3%	45.6%	54.4%
9,133	TOOELE	4,559	1,753	2,802	4	1,049 D	38.5%	61.5%	38.5%	61.5%
9,898	UINTAH	3,000	1,479	1,519	2	40 D	49.3%	50.6%	49.3%	50.7%
57,382	UTAH	25,713	9,946	15,722	45	5,776 D	38.7%	61.1%	38.7%	61.3%
5,754	WASATCH	2,309	1,058	1,249	2	191 D	45.8%	54.1%	45.9%	54.1%
9,269	WASHINGTON	3,270	1,575	1,694	1	119 D	48.2%	51.8%	48.2%	51.8%
2,394	WAYNE	755	325	430		105 D	43.0%	57.0%	43.0%	57.0%
56,714	WEBER	29,205	9,518	19,639	48	10,121 D	32.6%	67.2%	32.6%	67.4%
550,310	TOTAL	248,319	97,891	150,088	340	52,197 D	39.4%	60.4%	39.5%	60.5%

. UTAH

PRESIDENT 1940

1940 Census Population	County	Total Vote	Republican	Democratic	Other	Rep.-Dem. Plurality	Percentage Total Vote Rep.	Percentage Total Vote Dem.	Percentage Major Vote Rep.	Percentage Major Vote Dem.
5,014	BEAVER	2,405	1,101	1,303	1	202 D	45.8%	54.2%	45.8%	54.2%
18,832	BOX ELDER	7,986	3,248	4,736	2	1,488 D	40.7%	59.3%	40.7%	59.3%
29,797	CACHE	13,058	5,184	7,867	7	2,683 D	39.7%	60.2%	39.7%	60.3%
18,459	CARBON	7,456	2,242	5,180	34	2,938 D	30.1%	69.5%	30.2%	69.8%
564	DAGGETT	256	96	160		64 D	37.5%	62.5%	37.5%	62.5%
15,784	DAVIS	6,707	2,836	3,865	6	1,029 D	42.3%	57.6%	42.3%	57.7%
8,958	DUCHESNE	3,308	1,322	1,982	4	660 D	40.0%	59.9%	40.0%	60.0%
7,072	EMERY	2,919	1,006	1,901	12	895 D	34.5%	65.1%	34.6%	65.4%
5,253	GARFIELD	1,844	1,030	814		216 R	55.9%	44.1%	55.9%	44.1%
2,070	GRAND	881	432	446	3	14 D	49.0%	50.6%	49.2%	50.8%
8,331	IRON	3,998	2,060	1,915	23	145 R	51.5%	47.9%	51.8%	48.2%
7,392	JUAB	3,553	1,412	2,136	5	724 D	39.7%	60.1%	39.8%	60.2%
2,561	KANE	1,014	675	339		336 R	66.6%	33.4%	66.6%	33.4%
9,613	MILLARD	4,255	1,943	2,302	10	359 D	45.7%	54.1%	45.8%	54.2%
2,611	MORGAN	1,274	575	699		124 D	45.1%	54.9%	45.1%	54.9%
2,203	PIUTE	910	442	466	2	24 D	48.6%	51.2%	48.7%	51.3%
2,028	RICH	922	447	475		28 D	48.5%	51.5%	48.5%	51.5%
211,623	SALT LAKE	102,926	35,427	67,318	181	31,891 D	34.4%	65.4%	34.5%	65.5%
4,712	SAN JUAN	1,047	528	515	4	13 R	50.4%	49.2%	50.6%	49.4%
16,063	SANPETE	7,250	3,722	3,524	4	198 R	51.3%	48.6%	51.4%	48.6%
12,112	SEVIER	5,228	2,703	2,521	4	182 R	51.7%	48.2%	51.7%	48.3%
8,714	SUMMIT	3,948	1,730	2,215	3	485 D	43.8%	56.1%	43.9%	56.1%
9,133	TOOELE	4,108	1,476	2,625	7	1,149 D	35.9%	63.9%	36.0%	64.0%
9,898	UINTAH	3,399	1,624	1,773	2	149 D	47.8%	52.2%	47.8%	52.2%
57,382	UTAH	23,956	8,740	15,168	48	6,428 D	36.5%	63.3%	36.6%	63.4%
5,754	WASATCH	2,702	1,199	1,502	1	303 D	44.4%	55.6%	44.4%	55.6%
9,269	WASHINGTON	3,621	1,625	1,993	3	368 D	44.9%	55.0%	44.9%	55.1%
2,394	WAYNE	881	380	500	1	120 D	43.1%	56.8%	43.2%	56.8%
56,714	WEBER	26,007	7,946	18,037	24	10,091 D	30.6%	69.4%	30.6%	69.4%
550,310	TOTAL	247,819	93,151	154,277	391	61,126 D	37.6%	62.3%	37.6%	62.4%

UTAH

PRESIDENT 1936

1930 Census Population	County	Total Vote	Republican	Democratic	Other	Rep.-Dem. Plurality	Percentage Total Vote Rep.	Total Vote Dem.	Major Vote Rep.	Major Vote Dem.
5,136	BEAVER	2,261	913	1,337	11	424 D	40.4%	59.1%	40.6%	59.4%
17,810	BOX ELDER	7,231	2,180	5,001	50	2,821 D	30.1%	69.2%	30.4%	69.6%
27,424	CACHE	11,957	3,258	8,606	93	5,348 D	27.2%	72.0%	27.5%	72.5%
17,798	CARBON	6,510	1,348	5,040	122	3,692 D	20.7%	77.4%	21.1%	78.9%
411	DAGGETT	208	78	128	2	50 D	37.5%	61.5%	37.9%	62.1%
14,021	DAVIS	5,782	1,841	3,920	21	2,079 D	31.8%	67.8%	32.0%	68.0%
8,263	DUCHESNE	3,085	1,070	1,970	45	900 D	34.7%	63.9%	35.2%	64.8%
7,042	EMERY	2,869	938	1,909	22	971 D	32.7%	66.5%	32.9%	67.1%
4,642	GARFIELD	1,772	842	928	2	86 D	47.5%	52.4%	47.6%	52.4%
1,813	GRAND	809	272	521	16	249 D	33.6%	64.4%	34.3%	65.7%
7,227	IRON	3,289	1,396	1,844	49	448 D	42.4%	56.1%	43.1%	56.9%
8,605	JUAB	3,377	1,027	2,319	31	1,292 D	30.4%	68.7%	30.7%	69.3%
2,235	KANE	918	519	395	4	124 R	56.5%	43.0%	56.8%	43.2%
9,945	MILLARD	3,833	1,466	2,313	54	847 D	38.2%	60.3%	38.8%	61.2%
2,536	MORGAN	1,228	483	739	6	256 D	39.3%	60.2%	39.5%	60.5%
1,956	PIUTE	951	339	611	1	272 D	35.6%	64.2%	35.7%	64.3%
1,873	RICH	880	388	488	4	100 D	44.1%	55.5%	44.3%	55.7%
194,102	SALT LAKE	86,929	23,819	62,386	724	38,567 D	27.4%	71.8%	27.6%	72.4%
3,496	SAN JUAN	961	432	520	9	88 D	45.0%	54.1%	45.4%	54.6%
16,022	SANPETE	6,748	2,738	3,959	51	1,221 D	40.6%	58.7%	40.9%	59.1%
11,199	SEVIER	4,767	1,899	2,816	52	917 D	39.8%	59.1%	40.3%	59.7%
9,527	SUMMIT	3,784	1,422	2,344	18	922 D	37.6%	61.9%	37.8%	62.2%
9,413	TOOELE	3,399	1,029	2,361	9	1,332 D	30.3%	69.5%	30.4%	69.6%
9,035	UINTAH	3,258	1,193	1,986	79	793 D	36.6%	61.0%	37.5%	62.5%
49,021	UTAH	20,695	6,173	14,387	135	8,214 D	29.8%	69.5%	30.0%	70.0%
5,636	WASATCH	2,334	1,029	1,299	6	270 D	44.1%	55.7%	44.2%	55.8%
7,420	WASHINGTON	3,164	1,145	2,005	14	860 D	36.2%	63.4%	36.3%	63.7%
2,067	WAYNE	854	329	522	3	193 D	38.5%	61.1%	38.7%	61.3%
52,172	WEBER	22,826	4,989	17,594	243	12,605 D	21.9%	77.1%	22.1%	77.9%
507,847	TOTAL	216,679	64,555	150,248	1,876	85,693 D	29.8%	69.3%	30.1%	69.9%

UTAH

PRESIDENT 1932

1930 Census Population	County	Total Vote	Republican	Democratic	Other	Rep.-Dem. Plurality	Percentage Total Vote Rep.	Percentage Total Vote Dem.	Percentage Major Vote Rep.	Percentage Major Vote Dem.
5,136	BEAVER	2,201	969	1,218	14	249 D	44.0%	55.3%	44.3%	55.7%
17,810	BOX ELDER	6,827	3,048	3,695	84	647 D	44.6%	54.1%	45.2%	54.8%
27,424	CACHE	11,444	4,829	6,522	93	1,693 D	42.2%	57.0%	42.5%	57.5%
17,798	CARBON	6,120	1,655	4,239	226	2,584 D	27.0%	69.3%	28.1%	71.9%
411	DAGGETT	170	90	79	1	11 R	52.9%	46.5%	53.3%	46.7%
14,021	DAVIS	5,618	2,562	3,006	50	444 D	45.6%	53.5%	46.0%	54.0%
8,263	DUCHESNE	3,072	1,333	1,590	149	257 D	43.4%	51.8%	45.6%	54.4%
7,042	EMERY	2,848	1,112	1,613	123	501 D	39.0%	56.6%	40.8%	59.2%
4,642	GARFIELD	1,644	1,125	493	26	632 R	68.4%	30.0%	69.5%	30.5%
1,813	GRAND	805	278	506	21	228 D	34.5%	62.9%	35.5%	64.5%
7,227	IRON	3,163	1,599	1,358	206	241 R	50.6%	42.9%	54.1%	45.9%
8,605	JUAB	3,245	1,220	1,969	56	749 D	37.6%	60.7%	38.3%	61.7%
2,235	KANE	860	618	229	13	389 R	71.9%	26.6%	73.0%	27.0%
9,945	MILLARD	3,855	1,916	1,881	58	35 R	49.7%	48.8%	50.5%	49.5%
2,536	MORGAN	1,175	568	602	5	34 D	48.3%	51.2%	48.5%	51.5%
1,956	PIUTE	854	433	403	18	30 R	50.7%	47.2%	51.8%	48.2%
1,873	RICH	867	398	469		71 D	45.9%	54.1%	45.9%	54.1%
194,102	SALT LAKE	82,292	32,224	48,012	2,056	15,788 D	39.2%	58.3%	40.2%	59.8%
3,496	SAN JUAN	940	460	459	21	1 R	48.9%	48.8%	50.1%	49.9%
16,022	SANPETE	6,833	3,147	3,600	86	453 D	46.1%	52.7%	46.6%	53.4%
11,199	SEVIER	4,593	2,225	2,303	65	78 D	48.4%	50.1%	49.1%	50.9%
9,527	SUMMIT	3,536	1,434	2,028	74	594 D	40.6%	57.4%	41.4%	58.6%
9,413	TOOELE	3,323	1,407	1,865	51	458 D	42.3%	56.1%	43.0%	57.0%
9,035	UINTAH	3,190	1,355	1,778	57	423 D	42.5%	55.7%	43.2%	56.8%
49,021	UTAH	20,536	7,953	12,140	443	4,187 D	38.7%	59.1%	39.6%	60.4%
5,636	WASATCH	2,163	1,042	1,103	18	61 D	48.2%	51.0%	48.6%	51.4%
7,420	WASHINGTON	3,047	1,378	1,648	21	270 D	45.2%	54.1%	45.5%	54.5%
2,067	WAYNE	808	398	401	9	3 D	49.3%	49.6%	49.8%	50.2%
52,172	WEBER	20,549	8,019	11,541	989	3,522 D	39.0%	56.2%	41.0%	59.0%
507,847	TOTAL	206,578	84,795	116,750	5,033	31,955 D	41.0%	56.5%	42.1%	57.9%

UTAH

PRESIDENT 1928

1920 Census Population	County	Total Vote	Republican	Democratic	Other	Rep.-Dem. Plurality	Percentage Total Vote Rep.	Percentage Total Vote Dem.	Percentage Major Vote Rep.	Percentage Major Vote Dem.
5,139	BEAVER	2,090	1,149	936	5	213 R	55.0%	44.8%	55.1%	44.9%
18,788	BOX ELDER	5,825	3,317	2,488	20	829 R	56.9%	42.7%	57.1%	42.9%
26,992	CACHE	10,071	5,297	4,748	26	549 R	52.6%	47.1%	52.7%	47.3%
15,489	CARBON	5,188	2,184	2,954	50	770 D	42.1%	56.9%	42.5%	57.5%
400	DAGGETT	138	107	31		76 R	77.5%	22.5%	77.5%	22.5%
11,450	DAVIS	4,818	2,508	2,296	14	212 R	52.1%	47.7%	52.2%	47.8%
9,093	DUCHESNE	2,497	1,585	899	13	686 R	63.5%	36.0%	63.8%	36.2%
7,411	EMERY	2,308	1,317	965	26	352 R	57.1%	41.8%	57.7%	42.3%
4,768	GARFIELD	1,354	1,024	325	5	699 R	75.6%	24.0%	75.9%	24.1%
1,808	GRAND	660	347	310	3	37 R	52.6%	47.0%	52.8%	47.2%
5,787	IRON	2,528	1,823	682	23	1,141 R	72.1%	27.0%	72.8%	27.2%
9,871	JUAB	3,279	1,557	1,714	8	157 D	47.5%	52.3%	47.6%	52.4%
2,054	KANE	708	566	141	1	425 R	79.9%	19.9%	80.1%	19.9%
9,659	MILLARD	3,720	2,263	1,440	17	823 R	60.8%	38.7%	61.1%	38.9%
2,542	MORGAN	968	513	454	1	59 R	53.0%	46.9%	53.1%	46.9%
2,770	PIUTE	676	434	237	5	197 R	64.2%	35.1%	64.7%	35.3%
1,890	RICH	694	470	224		246 R	67.7%	32.3%	67.7%	32.3%
159,282	SALT LAKE	68,940	34,393	34,127	420	266 R	49.9%	49.5%	50.2%	49.8%
3,379	SAN JUAN	685	449	231	5	218 R	65.5%	33.7%	66.0%	34.0%
17,505	SANPETE	6,195	3,694	2,482	19	1,212 R	59.6%	40.1%	59.8%	40.2%
11,281	SEVIER	3,840	2,424	1,399	17	1,025 R	63.1%	36.4%	63.4%	36.6%
7,862	SUMMIT	3,032	1,748	1,260	24	488 R	57.7%	41.6%	58.1%	41.9%
7,965	TOOELE	3,148	1,707	1,421	20	286 R	54.2%	45.1%	54.6%	45.4%
8,470	UINTAH	2,483	1,589	880	14	709 R	64.0%	35.4%	64.4%	35.6%
40,792	UTAH	16,807	8,771	7,955	81	816 R	52.2%	47.3%	52.4%	47.6%
4,625	WASATCH	2,317	1,340	973	4	367 R	57.8%	42.0%	57.9%	42.1%
6,764	WASHINGTON	2,547	1,686	857	4	829 R	66.2%	33.6%	66.3%	33.7%
2,097	WAYNE	619	422	195	2	227 R	68.2%	31.5%	68.4%	31.6%
43,463	WEBER	18,468	9,934	8,361	173	1,573 R	53.8%	45.3%	54.3%	45.7%
449,396	TOTAL	176,603	94,618	80,985	1,000	13,633 R	53.6%	45.9%	53.9%	46.1%

UTAH

PRESIDENT 1924

1920 Census Population	County	Total Vote	Republican	Democratic	Progressive	Other	Plurality	Percentage Total Vote Rep.	Dem.	Prog.
5,139	BEAVER	1,854	989	578	287		411 R	53.3%	31.2%	15.5%
18,788	BOX ELDER	5,493	3,086	1,841	566		1,245 R	56.2%	33.5%	10.3%
26,992	CACHE	9,562	4,973	3,915	674		1,058 R	52.0%	40.9%	7.0%
15,489	CARBON	4,996	1,878	1,528	1,590		288 R	37.6%	30.6%	31.8%
400	DAGGETT	131	97	26	8		71 R	74.0%	19.8%	6.1%
11,450	DAVIS	4,080	2,265	1,507	308		758 R	55.5%	36.9%	7.5%
9,093	DUCHESNE	2,217	1,277	731	209		546 R	57.6%	33.0%	9.4%
7,411	EMERY	2,278	979	916	383		63 R	43.0%	40.2%	16.8%
4,768	GARFIELD	1,183	823	308	52		515 R	69.6%	26.0%	4.4%
1,808	GRAND	580	278	243	59		35 R	47.9%	41.9%	10.2%
5,787	IRON	2,150	1,429	485	236		944 R	66.5%	22.6%	11.0%
9,871	JUAB	3,041	1,325	1,241	475		84 R	43.6%	40.8%	15.6%
2,054	KANE	642	515	117	10		398 R	80.2%	18.2%	1.6%
9,659	MILLARD	3,439	1,917	1,025	497		892 R	55.7%	29.8%	14.5%
2,542	MORGAN	891	482	360	49		122 R	54.1%	40.4%	5.5%
2,770	PIUTE	648	398	208	42		190 R	61.4%	32.1%	6.5%
1,890	RICH	645	403	211	31		192 R	62.5%	32.7%	4.8%
159,282	SALT LAKE	58,602	27,215	14,853	16,534		10,681 R	46.4%	25.3%	28.2%
3,379	SAN JUAN	668	380	232	56		148 R	56.9%	34.7%	8.4%
17,505	SANPETE	5,983	3,374	2,228	381		1,146 R	56.4%	37.2%	6.4%
11,281	SEVIER	3,740	2,111	1,201	428		910 R	56.4%	32.1%	11.4%
7,862	SUMMIT	2,794	1,597	825	372		772 R	57.2%	29.5%	13.3%
7,965	TOOELE	2,468	1,295	674	499		621 R	52.5%	27.3%	20.2%
8,470	UINTAH	2,128	1,296	716	116		580 R	60.9%	33.6%	5.5%
40,792	UTAH	15,010	6,946	5,226	2,838		1,720 R	46.3%	34.8%	18.9%
4,625	WASATCH	2,109	1,105	727	277		378 R	52.4%	34.5%	13.1%
6,764	WASHINGTON	2,149	1,181	868	100		313 R	55.0%	40.4%	4.7%
2,097	WAYNE	578	331	241	6		90 R	57.3%	41.7%	1.0%
43,463	WEBER	16,931	7,382	3,970	5,579		1,803 R	43.6%	23.4%	33.0%
449,396	TOTAL	156,990	77,327	47,001	32,662		30,326 R	49.3%	29.9%	20.8%

UTAH

PRESIDENT 1920

1920 Census Population	County	Total Vote	Republican	Democratic	Other	Rep.-Dem. Plurality	Percentage Total Vote Rep.	Total Vote Dem.	Major Vote Rep.	Major Vote Dem.
5,139	BEAVER	1,837	1,056	741	40	315 R	57.5%	40.3%	58.8%	41.2%
18,788	BOX ELDER	5,812	3,421	2,330	61	1,091 R	58.9%	40.1%	59.5%	40.5%
26,992	CACHE	9,397	5,063	4,239	95	824 R	53.9%	45.1%	54.4%	45.6%
15,489	CARBON	3,560	1,675	1,559	326	116 R	47.1%	43.8%	51.8%	48.2%
400	DAGGETT	128	94	32	2	62 R	73.4%	25.0%	74.6%	25.4%
11,450	DAVIS	4,122	2,463	1,632	27	831 R	59.8%	39.6%	60.1%	39.9%
9,093	DUCHESNE	2,466	1,523	822	121	701 R	61.8%	33.3%	64.9%	35.1%
7,411	EMERY	2,398	1,285	1,029	84	256 R	53.6%	42.9%	55.5%	44.5%
4,768	GARFIELD	1,431	1,023	393	15	630 R	71.5%	27.5%	72.2%	27.8%
1,808	GRAND	598	306	278	14	28 R	51.2%	46.5%	52.4%	47.6%
5,787	IRON	2,010	1,399	561	50	838 R	69.6%	27.9%	71.4%	28.6%
9,871	JUAB	3,185	1,692	1,308	185	384 R	53.1%	41.1%	56.4%	43.6%
2,054	KANE	690	501	186	3	315 R	72.6%	27.0%	72.9%	27.1%
9,659	MILLARD	3,515	2,199	1,167	149	1,032 R	62.6%	33.2%	65.3%	34.7%
2,542	MORGAN	945	544	397	4	147 R	57.6%	42.0%	57.8%	42.2%
2,770	PIUTE	843	538	283	22	255 R	63.8%	33.6%	65.5%	34.5%
1,890	RICH	671	449	222		227 R	66.9%	33.1%	66.9%	33.1%
159,282	SALT LAKE	50,873	27,841	19,249	3,783	8,592 R	54.7%	37.8%	59.1%	40.9%
3,379	SAN JUAN	807	523	260	24	263 R	64.8%	32.2%	66.8%	33.2%
17,505	SANPETE	6,219	3,741	2,406	72	1,335 R	60.2%	38.7%	60.9%	39.1%
11,281	SEVIER	3,988	2,506	1,425	57	1,081 R	62.8%	35.7%	63.7%	36.3%
7,862	SUMMIT	2,514	1,503	874	137	629 R	59.8%	34.8%	63.2%	36.8%
7,965	TOOELE	2,470	1,387	916	167	471 R	56.2%	37.1%	60.2%	39.8%
8,470	UINTAH	2,239	1,354	817	68	537 R	60.5%	36.5%	62.4%	37.6%
40,792	UTAH	14,532	7,752	6,377	403	1,375 R	53.3%	43.9%	54.9%	45.1%
4,625	WASATCH	1,738	1,061	665	12	396 R	61.0%	38.3%	61.5%	38.5%
6,764	WASHINGTON	2,156	1,138	1,008	10	130 R	52.8%	46.8%	53.0%	47.0%
2,097	WAYNE	639	396	224	19	172 R	62.0%	35.1%	63.9%	36.1%
43,463	WEBER	14,045	7,122	5,239	1,684	1,883 R	50.7%	37.3%	57.6%	42.4%
449,396	TOTAL	145,828	81,555	56,639	7,634	24,916 R	55.9%	38.8%	59.0%	41.0%

UTAH

ELECTION NOTES

1956

1952

1948 Other vote was 2,679 Wallace (Progressive); 74 Dobbs (Socialist Workers).

1944 Other vote was Thomas (Socialist).

1940 Other vote was 200 Thomas (Socialist); 191 Browder (Communist).

1936 Other vote was 1,121 Lemke (Union); 432 Thomas (Socialist); 280 Browder (Communist); 43 Colvin (Prohibition).

1932 Other vote was 4,087 Thomas (Socialist); 946 Foster (Communist).

1928 Other vote was 954 Thomas (Socialist); 46 Foster (Communist).

1924 A special four-column table which gives the LaFollette (Progressive) vote is used to detail this election.

1920 Other vote was 4,475 Christensen (Farmer-Labor); 3,159 Debs (Socialist).

VERMONT

POPULAR VOTE FOR PRESIDENT 1920 TO 1956

Year	Total Vote	Republican Vote	Republican Candidate	Democratic Vote	Democratic Candidate	Other Vote	Plurality	Percentage Total Vote Rep.	Percentage Total Vote Dem.	Percentage Major Vote Rep.	Percentage Major Vote Dem.
1956	152,978	110,390	Eisenhower, Dwight D.	42,549	Stevenson, Adlai E.	39	67,841 R	72.2%	27.8%	72.2%	27.8%
1952	153,557	109,717	Eisenhower, Dwight D.	43,355	Stevenson, Adlai E.	485	66,362 R	71.5%	28.2%	71.7%	28.3%
1948	123,382	75,926	Dewey, Thomas E.	45,557	Truman, Harry S.	1,899	30,369 R	61.5%	36.9%	62.5%	37.5%
1944	125,361	71,527	Dewey, Thomas E.	53,820	Roosevelt, Franklin D.	14	17,707 R	57.1%	42.9%	57.1%	42.9%
1940	143,062	78,371	Willkie, Wendell	64,269	Roosevelt, Franklin D.	422	14,102 R	54.8%	44.9%	54.9%	45.1%
1936	143,689	81,023	Landon, Alfred M.	62,124	Roosevelt, Franklin D.	542	18,899 R	56.4%	43.2%	56.6%	43.4%
1932	136,980	78,984	Hoover, Herbert C.	56,266	Roosevelt, Franklin D.	1,730	22,718 R	57.7%	41.1%	58.4%	41.6%
1928	135,191	90,404	Hoover, Herbert C.	44,440	Smith, Alfred E.	347	45,964 R	66.9%	32.9%	67.0%	33.0%
1924	102,917	80,498	Coolidge, Calvin	16,124	Davis, John W.	6,295	64,374 R	78.2%	15.7%	83.3%	16.7%
1920	89,961	68,212	Harding, Warren G.	20,919	Cox, James M.	830	47,293 R	75.8%	23.3%	76.5%	23.5%

ELECTORAL COLLEGE VOTE 1920 TO 1956

Year	Total	Republican	Democratic	Other
1956	3	3	—	—
1952	3	3	—	—
1948	3	3	—	—
1944	3	3	—	—
1940	3	3	—	—
1936	3	3	—	—
1932	3	3	—	—
1928	4	4	—	—
1924	4	4	—	—
1920	4	4	—	—

VERMONT

GRAND ISLE
FRANKLIN
ORLEANS
ESSEX
LAMOILLE
CHITTENDEN
CALEDONIA
WASHINGTON
ADDISON
ORANGE
RUTLAND
WINDSOR
BENNINGTON
WINDHAM

VERMONT

PRESIDENT 1956

1950 Census Population	County	Total Vote	Republican	Democratic	Other	Rep.-Dem. Plurality	Percentage Total Vote Rep.	Percentage Total Vote Dem.	Percentage Major Vote Rep.	Percentage Major Vote Dem.
19,442	ADDISON	7,658	5,990	1,668		4,322 R	78.2%	21.8%	78.2%	21.8%
24,115	BENNINGTON	11,157	8,434	2,719	4	5,715 R	75.6%	24.4%	75.6%	24.4%
24,049	CALEDONIA	9,304	7,560	1,744		5,816 R	81.3%	18.7%	81.3%	18.7%
62,570	CHITTENDEN	24,582	14,108	10,474		3,634 R	57.4%	42.6%	57.4%	42.6%
6,257	ESSEX	2,434	1,714	719	1	995 R	70.4%	29.5%	70.4%	29.6%
29,894	FRANKLIN	11,965	7,125	4,840		2,285 R	59.5%	40.5%	59.5%	40.5%
3,406	GRAND ISLE	1,582	978	604		374 R	61.8%	38.2%	61.8%	38.2%
11,388	LAMOILLE	4,142	3,464	678		2,786 R	83.6%	16.4%	83.6%	16.4%
17,027	ORANGE	6,690	5,616	1,072	2	4,544 R	83.9%	16.0%	84.0%	16.0%
21,190	ORLEANS	7,396	5,344	2,052		3,292 R	72.3%	27.7%	72.3%	27.7%
45,905	RUTLAND	19,735	14,570	5,165		9,405 R	73.8%	26.2%	73.8%	26.2%
42,870	WASHINGTON	15,876	11,351	4,520	5	6,831 R	71.5%	28.5%	71.5%	28.5%
28,749	WINDHAM	12,475	9,979	2,474	22	7,505 R	80.0%	19.8%	80.1%	19.9%
40,885	WINDSOR	17,982	14,157	3,820	5	10,337 R	78.7%	21.2%	78.8%	21.2%
377,747	TOTAL	152,978	110,390	42,549	39	67,841 R	72.2%	27.8%	72.2%	27.8%

VERMONT

PRESIDENT 1952

1950 Census Population	County	Total Vote	Republican	Democratic	Other	Rep.-Dem. Plurality	Percentage Total Vote Rep.	Percentage Total Vote Dem.	Percentage Major Vote Rep.	Percentage Major Vote Dem.
19,442	ADDISON	7,748	6,057	1,667	24	4,390 R	78.2%	21.5%	78.4%	21.6%
24,115	BENNINGTON	11,437	8,385	3,018	34	5,367 R	73.3%	26.4%	73.5%	26.5%
24,049	CALEDONIA	9,423	7,595	1,807	21	5,788 R	80.6%	19.2%	80.8%	19.2%
62,570	CHITTENDEN	23,385	13,533	9,746	106	3,787 R	57.9%	41.7%	58.1%	41.9%
6,257	ESSEX	2,306	1,592	705	9	887 R	69.0%	30.6%	69.3%	30.7%
29,894	FRANKLIN	12,018	6,949	5,018	51	1,931 R	57.8%	41.8%	58.1%	41.9%
3,406	GRAND ISLE	1,650	976	665	9	311 R	59.2%	40.3%	59.5%	40.5%
11,388	LAMOILLE	4,160	3,516	633	11	2,883 R	84.5%	15.2%	84.7%	15.3%
17,027	ORANGE	6,719	5,610	1,082	27	4,528 R	83.5%	16.1%	83.8%	16.2%
21,190	ORLEANS	7,858	5,830	2,003	25	3,827 R	74.2%	25.5%	74.4%	25.6%
45,905	RUTLAND	19,986	13,980	5,970	36	8,010 R	69.9%	29.9%	70.1%	29.9%
42,870	WASHINGTON	16,503	11,979	4,460	64	7,519 R	72.6%	27.0%	72.9%	27.1%
28,749	WINDHAM	12,595	9,774	2,790	31	6,984 R	77.6%	22.2%	77.8%	22.2%
40,885	WINDSOR	17,769	13,941	3,791	37	10,150 R	78.5%	21.3%	78.6%	21.4%
377,747	TOTAL	153,557	109,717	43,355	485	66,362 R	71.5%	28.2%	71.7%	28.3%

VERMONT

PRESIDENT 1948

1940 Census Population	County	Total Vote	Republican	Democratic	Other	Rep.-Dem. Plurality	Percentage Total Vote Rep.	Total Vote Dem.	Major Vote Rep.	Major Vote Dem.
17,944	ADDISON	5,869	4,148	1,615	106	2,533 R	70.7%	27.5%	72.0%	28.0%
22,286	BENNINGTON	9,374	5,840	3,340	194	2,500 R	62.3%	35.6%	63.6%	36.4%
24,320	CALEDONIA	8,542	5,873	2,585	84	3,288 R	68.8%	30.3%	69.4%	30.6%
52,098	CHITTENDEN	17,739	8,509	8,903	327	394 D	48.0%	50.2%	48.9%	51.1%
6,490	ESSEX	1,946	1,055	881	10	174 R	54.2%	45.3%	54.5%	45.5%
29,601	FRANKLIN	10,444	4,897	5,455	92	558 D	46.9%	52.2%	47.3%	52.7%
3,802	GRAND ISLE	1,563	724	822	17	98 D	46.3%	52.6%	46.8%	53.2%
11,028	LAMOILLE	3,181	2,344	816	21	1,528 R	73.7%	25.7%	74.2%	25.8%
17,048	ORANGE	5,276	4,061	1,139	76	2,922 R	77.0%	21.6%	78.1%	21.9%
21,718	ORLEANS	6,004	3,775	2,204	25	1,571 R	62.9%	36.7%	63.1%	36.9%
45,638	RUTLAND	16,853	10,206	6,452	195	3,754 R	60.6%	38.3%	61.3%	38.7%
41,546	WASHINGTON	12,883	7,720	4,839	324	2,881 R	59.9%	37.6%	61.5%	38.5%
27,850	WINDHAM	10,140	7,148	2,770	222	4,378 R	70.5%	27.3%	72.1%	27.9%
37,862	WINDSOR	13,568	9,626	3,736	206	5,890 R	70.9%	27.5%	72.0%	28.0%
359,231	TOTAL	123,382	75,926	45,557	1,899	30,369 R	61.5%	36.9%	62.5%	37.5%

VERMONT

PRESIDENT 1944

1940 Census Population	County	Total Vote	Republican	Democratic	Other	Rep.-Dem. Plurality	Percentage Total Vote Rep.	Total Vote Dem.	Major Vote Rep.	Major Vote Dem.
17,944	ADDISON	6,184	4,097	2,079	8	2,018 R	66.3%	33.6%	66.3%	33.7%
22,286	BENNINGTON	8,961	5,252	3,709		1,543 R	58.6%	41.4%	58.6%	41.4%
24,320	CALEDONIA	7,890	5,086	2,804		2,282 R	64.5%	35.5%	64.5%	35.5%
52,098	CHITTENDEN	18,301	7,513	10,788		3,275 D	41.1%	58.9%	41.1%	58.9%
6,490	ESSEX	2,190	1,064	1,126		62 D	48.6%	51.4%	48.6%	51.4%
29,601	FRANKLIN	10,411	4,374	6,036	1	1,662 D	42.0%	58.0%	42.0%	58.0%
3,802	GRAND ISLE	1,468	667	801		134 D	45.4%	54.6%	45.4%	54.6%
11,028	LAMOILLE	3,243	2,212	1,031		1,181 R	68.2%	31.8%	68.2%	31.8%
17,048	ORANGE	5,581	4,117	1,464		2,653 R	73.8%	26.2%	73.8%	26.2%
21,718	ORLEANS	6,458	3,801	2,657		1,144 R	58.9%	41.1%	58.9%	41.1%
45,638	RUTLAND	16,655	9,544	7,111		2,433 R	57.3%	42.7%	57.3%	42.7%
41,546	WASHINGTON	12,911	7,162	5,749		1,413 R	55.5%	44.5%	55.5%	44.5%
27,850	WINDHAM	10,089	6,708	3,376	5	3,332 R	66.5%	33.5%	66.5%	33.5%
37,862	WINDSOR	15,019	9,930	5,089		4,841 R	66.1%	33.9%	66.1%	33.9%
359,231	Total	125,361	71,527	53,820	14	17,707 R	57.1%	42.9%	57.1%	42.9%

VERMONT

PRESIDENT 1940

1940 Census Population	County	Total Vote	Republican	Democratic	Other	Rep.-Dem. Plurality	Percentage Total Vote Rep.	Total Vote Dem.	Major Vote Rep.	Major Vote Dem.
17,944	ADDISON	7,118	4,500	2,593	25	1,907 R	63.2%	36.4%	63.4%	36.6%
22,286	BENNINGTON	10,180	5,845	4,308	27	1,537 R	57.4%	42.3%	57.6%	42.4%
24,320	CALEDONIA	9,260	5,793	3,444	23	2,349 R	62.6%	37.2%	62.7%	37.3%
52,098	CHITTENDEN	19,061	7,926	11,069	66	3,143 D	41.6%	58.1%	41.7%	58.3%
6,490	ESSEX	2,907	1,365	1,531	11	166 D	47.0%	52.7%	47.1%	52.9%
29,601	FRANKLIN	12,760	5,258	7,439	63	2,181 D	41.2%	58.3%	41.4%	58.6%
3,802	GRAND ISLE	1,719	716	998	5	282 D	41.7%	58.1%	41.8%	58.2%
11,028	LAMOILLE	4,034	2,566	1,463	5	1,103 R	63.6%	36.3%	63.7%	36.3%
17,048	ORANGE	6,579	4,527	2,029	23	2,498 R	68.8%	30.8%	69.1%	30.9%
21,718	ORLEANS	7,789	4,480	3,294	15	1,186 R	57.5%	42.3%	57.6%	42.4%
45,638	RUTLAND	19,681	10,829	8,798	54	2,031 R	55.0%	44.7%	55.2%	44.8%
41,546	WASHINGTON	16,203	8,426	7,727	50	699 R	52.0%	47.7%	52.2%	47.8%
27,850	WINDHAM	11,159	7,031	4,101	27	2,930 R	63.0%	36.8%	63.2%	36.8%
37,862	WINDSOR	14,612	9,109	5,475	28	3,634 R	62.3%	37.5%	62.5%	37.5%
359,231	TOTAL	143,062	78,371	64,269	422	14,102 R	54.8%	44.9%	54.9%	45.1%

VERMONT

PRESIDENT 1936

1930 Census Population	County	Total Vote	Republican	Democratic	Other	Rep.-Dem. Plurality	Percentage Total Vote Rep.	Total Vote Dem.	Major Vote Rep.	Major Vote Dem.
17,952	ADDISON	7,831	5,161	2,646	24	2,515 R	65.9%	33.8%	66.1%	33.9%
21,655	BENNINGTON	9,834	5,515	4,166	153	1,349 R	56.1%	42.4%	57.0%	43.0%
27,253	CALEDONIA	9,423	6,054	3,342	27	2,712 R	64.2%	35.5%	64.4%	35.6%
47,471	CHITTENDEN	18,775	7,757	10,962	56	3,205 D	41.3%	58.4%	41.4%	58.6%
7,067	ESSEX	2,680	1,474	1,203	3	271 R	55.0%	44.9%	55.1%	44.9%
29,975	FRANKLIN	12,360	5,507	6,817	36	1,310 D	44.6%	55.2%	44.7%	55.3%
3,944	GRAND ISLE	1,568	712	852	4	140 D	45.4%	54.3%	45.5%	54.5%
10,947	LAMOILLE	4,137	2,846	1,279	12	1,567 R	68.8%	30.9%	69.0%	31.0%
16,694	ORANGE	6,763	4,956	1,796	11	3,160 R	73.3%	26.6%	73.4%	26.6%
23,036	ORLEANS	7,720	5,038	2,662	20	2,376 R	65.3%	34.5%	65.4%	34.6%
48,453	RUTLAND	20,391	10,794	9,543	54	1,251 R	52.9%	46.8%	53.1%	46.9%
41,733	WASHINGTON	16,490	8,351	8,073	66	278 R	50.6%	49.0%	50.8%	49.2%
26,015	WINDHAM	11,095	7,369	3,699	27	3,670 R	66.4%	33.3%	66.6%	33.4%
37,416	WINDSOR	14,622	9,489	5,084	49	4,405 R	64.9%	34.8%	65.1%	34.9%
359,611	TOTAL	143,689	81,023	62,124	542	18,899 R	56.4%	43.2%	56.6%	43.4%

VERMONT

PRESIDENT 1932

1930 Census Population	County	Total Vote	Republican	Democratic	Other	Rep.-Dem. Plurality	Percentage Total Vote Rep.	Total Vote Dem.	Major Vote Rep.	Major Vote Dem.
17,952	ADDISON	8,428	5,295	3,031	102	2,264 R	62.8%	36.0%	63.6%	36.4%
21,655	BENNINGTON	9,416	5,250	3,964	202	1,286 R	55.8%	42.1%	57.0%	43.0%
27,253	CALEDONIA	9,741	6,066	3,621	54	2,445 R	62.3%	37.2%	62.6%	37.4%
47,471	CHITTENDEN	16,435	7,208	9,104	123	1,896 D	43.9%	55.4%	44.2%	55.8%
7,067	ESSEX	2,980	1,567	1,397	16	170 R	52.6%	46.9%	52.9%	47.1%
29,975	FRANKLIN	11,286	4,999	6,179	108	1,180 D	44.3%	54.7%	44.7%	55.3%
3,944	GRAND ISLE	1,477	649	811	17	162 D	43.9%	54.9%	44.5%	55.5%
10,947	LAMOILLE	3,729	2,599	1,096	34	1,503 R	69.7%	29.4%	70.3%	29.7%
16,694	ORANGE	6,212	4,305	1,830	77	2,475 R	69.3%	29.5%	70.2%	29.8%
23,036	ORLEANS	7,729	5,132	2,530	67	2,602 R	66.4%	32.7%	67.0%	33.0%
48,453	RUTLAND	19,951	10,821	8,924	206	1,897 R	54.2%	44.7%	54.8%	45.2%
41,733	WASHINGTON	14,540	8,393	5,777	370	2,616 R	57.7%	39.7%	59.2%	40.8%
26,015	WINDHAM	11,129	7,347	3,659	123	3,688 R	66.0%	32.9%	66.8%	33.2%
37,416	WINDSOR	13,927	9,353	4,343	231	5,010 R	67.2%	31.2%	68.3%	31.7%
359,611	TOTAL	136,980	78,984	56,266	1,730	22,718 R	57.7%	41.1%	58.4%	41.6%

VERMONT

PRESIDENT 1928

1920 Census Population	County	Total Vote	Republican	Democratic	Other	Rep.-Dem. Plurality	Percentage Total Vote Rep.	Total Vote Dem.	Major Vote Rep.	Major Vote Dem.
18,666	ADDISON	7,278	5,247	2,003	28	3,244 R	72.1%	27.5%	72.4%	27.6%
21,577	BENNINGTON	9,630	6,114	3,498	18	2,616 R	63.5%	36.3%	63.6%	36.4%
25,762	CALEDONIA	8,474	6,616	1,832	26	4,784 R	78.1%	21.6%	78.3%	21.7%
43,708	CHITTENDEN	17,235	8,156	9,052	27	896 D	47.3%	52.5%	47.4%	52.6%
7,364	ESSEX	2,514	1,703	805	6	898 R	67.7%	32.0%	67.9%	32.1%
30,026	FRANKLIN	11,548	6,031	5,477	40	554 R	52.2%	47.4%	52.4%	47.6%
3,784	GRAND ISLE	1,642	830	801	11	29 R	50.5%	48.8%	50.9%	49.1%
11,858	LAMOILLE	3,854	3,262	576	16	2,686 R	84.6%	14.9%	85.0%	15.0%
17,279	ORANGE	6,167	5,223	914	30	4,309 R	84.7%	14.8%	85.1%	14.9%
23,913	ORLEANS	6,895	5,561	1,320	14	4,241 R	80.7%	19.1%	80.8%	19.2%
46,213	RUTLAND	21,262	12,621	8,609	32	4,012 R	59.4%	40.5%	59.4%	40.6%
38,921	WASHINGTON	14,353	9,891	4,408	54	5,483 R	68.9%	30.7%	69.2%	30.8%
26,373	WINDHAM	10,824	8,410	2,398	16	6,012 R	77.7%	22.2%	77.8%	22.2%
36,984	WINDSOR	13,515	10,739	2,747	29	7,992 R	79.5%	20.3%	79.6%	20.4%
352,428	TOTAL	135,191	90,404	44,440	347	45,964 R	66.9%	32.9%	67.0%	33.0%

VERMONT

PRESIDENT 1924

1920 Census Population	County	Total Vote	Republican	Democratic	Other	Rep.-Dem. Plurality	Percentage Total Vote Rep.	Percentage Total Vote Dem.	Percentage Major Vote Rep.	Percentage Major Vote Dem.
18,666	ADDISON	5,619	4,927	557	135	4,370 R	87.7%	9.9%	89.8%	10.2%
21,577	BENNINGTON	7,325	5,341	1,466	518	3,875 R	72.9%	20.0%	78.5%	21.5%
25,762	CALEDONIA	7,422	6,205	929	288	5,276 R	83.6%	12.5%	87.0%	13.0%
43,708	CHITTENDEN	11,286	8,008	2,658	620	5,350 R	71.0%	23.6%	75.1%	24.9%
7,364	ESSEX	2,187	1,391	576	220	815 R	63.6%	26.3%	70.7%	29.3%
30,026	FRANKLIN	6,847	4,594	1,649	604	2,945 R	67.1%	24.1%	73.6%	26.4%
3,784	GRAND ISLE	1,320	861	343	116	518 R	65.2%	26.0%	71.5%	28.5%
11,858	LAMOILLE	2,876	2,480	305	91	2,175 R	86.2%	10.6%	89.0%	11.0%
17,279	ORANGE	5,621	4,657	724	240	3,933 R	82.9%	12.9%	86.5%	13.5%
23,913	ORLEANS	5,877	5,006	619	252	4,387 R	85.2%	10.5%	89.0%	11.0%
46,213	RUTLAND	14,320	10,642	2,477	1,201	8,165 R	74.3%	17.3%	81.1%	18.9%
38,921	WASHINGTON	11,474	8,525	1,715	1,234	6,810 R	74.3%	14.9%	83.3%	16.7%
26,373	WINDHAM	9,183	7,638	1,091	454	6,547 R	83.2%	11.9%	87.5%	12.5%
36,984	WINDSOR	11,560	10,223	1,015	322	9,208 R	88.4%	8.8%	91.0%	9.0%
352,428	TOTAL	102,917	80,498	16,124	6,295	64,374 R	78.2%	15.7%	83.3%	16.7%

VERMONT

PRESIDENT 1920

1920 Census Population	County	Total Vote	Republican	Democratic	Other	Rep.-Dem. Plurality	Percentage Total Vote Rep.	Percentage Total Vote Dem.	Percentage Major Vote Rep.	Percentage Major Vote Dem.
18,666	ADDISON	5,077	4,515	503	59	4,012 R	88.9%	9.9%	90.0%	10.0%
21,577	BENNINGTON	5,841	4,172	1,615	54	2,557 R	71.4%	27.6%	72.1%	27.9%
25,762	CALEDONIA	7,300	5,537	1,694	69	3,843 R	75.8%	23.2%	76.6%	23.4%
43,708	CHITTENDEN	10,865	7,215	3,564	86	3,651 R	66.4%	32.8%	66.9%	33.1%
7,364	ESSEX	1,804	1,243	552	9	691 R	68.9%	30.6%	69.2%	30.8%
30,026	FRANKLIN	7,298	4,869	2,342	87	2,527 R	66.7%	32.1%	67.5%	32.5%
3,784	GRAND ISLE	1,296	928	354	14	574 R	71.6%	27.3%	72.4%	27.6%
11,858	LAMOILLE	2,816	2,311	458	47	1,853 R	82.1%	16.3%	83.5%	16.5%
17,279	ORANGE	4,704	3,713	938	53	2,775 R	78.9%	19.9%	79.8%	20.2%
23,913	ORLEANS	5,177	4,400	738	39	3,662 R	85.0%	14.3%	85.6%	14.4%
46,213	RUTLAND	12,229	8,940	3,192	97	5,748 R	73.1%	26.1%	73.7%	26.3%
38,921	WASHINGTON	8,471	6,418	1,953	100	4,465 R	75.8%	23.1%	76.7%	23.3%
26,373	WINDHAM	6,908	5,551	1,302	55	4,249 R	80.4%	18.8%	81.0%	19.0%
36,984	WINDSOR	10,175	8,400	1,714	61	6,686 R	82.6%	16.8%	83.1%	16.9%
352,428	TOTAL	89,961	68,212	20,919	830	47,293 R	75.8%	23.3%	76.5%	23.5%

VERMONT

ELECTION NOTE

1956 Other vote was scattered write-in.

1952 Other vote was 282 Hallinan (Progressive); 185 Hoopes (Socialist); 18 scattered write-in.

1948 Other vote was 1,279 Wallace (Progressive); 585 Thomas (Socialist); 35 scattered write-in.

1944 Other vote was scattered write-in.

1940 Other vote was 411 Browder (Communist); 11 scattered write-in.

1936 Other Vote was 405 Browder (Communist); 137 scattered write-in.

1932 Other vote was 1,533 Thomas (Socialist); 195 Foster (Communist); 2 scattered write-in.

1928 Other vote was 338 Varney (Prohibition); 9 scattered write-in.

1924 Other vote was 5,964 LaFollette (Progressive); 326 Faris (Prohibition); 5 scattered write-in.

1920 Other vote was 774 Watkins (Prohibition); 56 scattered write-in.

VIRGINIA

POPULAR VOTE FOR PRESIDENT 1920 TO 1956

Year	Total Vote	Republican		Democratic		Other Vote	Plurality	Percentage			
								Total Vote		Major Vote	
		Vote	Candidate	Vote	Candidate			Rep.	Dem.	Rep.	Dem.
1956	697,978	386,459	Eisenhower, Dwight D.	267,760	Stevenson, Adlai E.	43,759	118,699 R	55.4%	38.4%	59.1%	40.9%
1952	619,689	349,037	Eisenhower, Dwight D.	268,677	Stevenson, Adlai E.	1,975	80,360 R	56.3%	43.4%	56.5%	43.5%
1948	419,256	172,070	Dewey, Thomas E.	200,786	Truman, Harry S.	46,400	28,716 D	41.0%	47.9%	46.1%	53.9%
1944	388,485	145,243	Dewey, Thomas E.	242,276	Roosevelt, Franklin D.	966	97,033 D	37.4%	62.4%	37.5%	62.5%
1940	346,608	109,363	Willkie, Wendell	235,961	Roosevelt, Franklin D.	1,284	126,598 D	31.6%	68.1%	31.7%	68.3%
1936	334,590	98,336	Landon, Alfred M.	234,980	Roosevelt, Franklin D.	1,274	136,644 D	29.4%	70.2%	29.5%	70.5%
1932	297,942	89,637	Hoover, Herbert C.	203,979	Roosevelt, Franklin D.	4,326	114,342 D	30.1%	68.5%	30.5%	69.5%
1928	305,364	164,609	Hoover, Herbert C.	140,146	Smith, Alfred E.	609	24,463 R	53.9%	45.9%	54.0%	46.0%
1924	223,603	73,328	Coolidge, Calvin	139,717	Davis, John W.	10,558	66,389 D	32.8%	62.5%	34.4%	65.6%
1920	231,000	87,456	Harding, Warren G.	141,670	Cox, James M.	1,874	54,214 D	37.9%	61.3%	38.2%	61.8%

ELECTORAL COLLEGE VOTE 1920 TO 1956

Year	Total	Republican	Democratic	Other
1956	12	12	—	—
1952	12	12	—	—
1948	11	—	11	—
1944	11	—	11	—
1940	11	—	11	—
1936	11	—	11	—
1932	11	—	11	—
1928	12	12	—	—
1924	12	—	12	—
1920	12	—	12	—

VIRGINIA

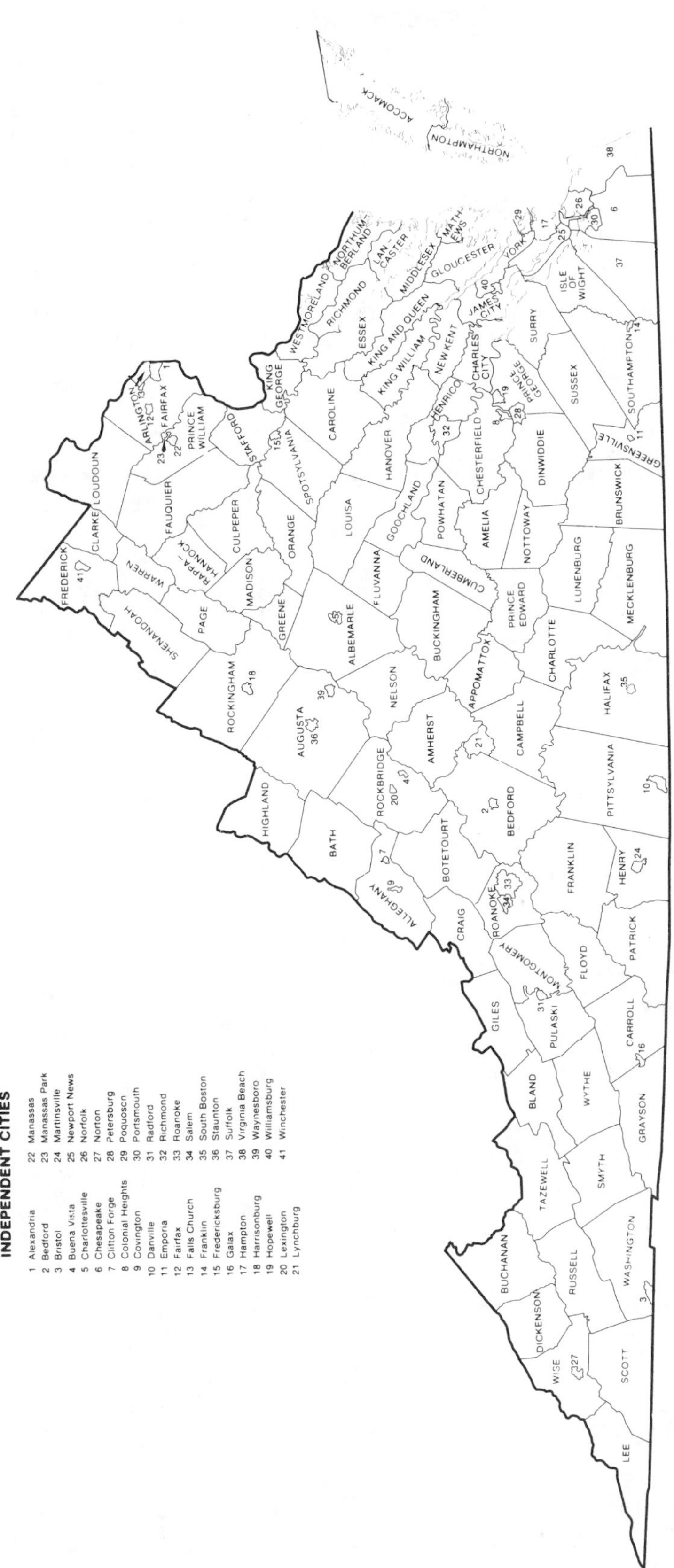
INDEPENDENT CITIES
1 Alexandria
2 Bedford
3 Bristol
4 Buena Vista
5 Charlottesville
6 Chesapeake
7 Clifton Forge
8 Colonial Heights
9 Covington
10 Danville
11 Emporia
12 Fairfax
13 Falls Church
14 Franklin
15 Fredericksburg
16 Galax
17 Hampton
18 Harrisonburg
19 Hopewell
20 Lexington
21 Lynchburg
22 Manassas
23 Manassas Park
24 Martinsville
25 Newport News
26 Norfolk
27 Norton
28 Petersburg
29 Poquoson
30 Portsmouth
31 Radford
32 Richmond
33 Roanoke
34 Salem
35 South Boston
36 Staunton
37 Suffolk
38 Virginia Beach
39 Waynesboro
40 Williamsburg
41 Winchester
ACCOMACK
NORTHAMPTON
NORTHUM-BERLAND
WESTMORELAND
LAN-CASTER
RICHMOND
MATH-EWS
MIDDLESEX
GLOUCESTER
ESSEX
KING AND QUEEN
KING WILLIAM
NEW KENT
JAMES CITY
YORK
CHARLES CITY
ISLE OF WIGHT
SURRY
SUSSEX
SOUTHAMPTON
PRINCE GEORGE
HENRICO
KING GEORGE
CAROLINE
ARLINGTON
FAIRFAX
PRINCE WILLIAM
STAFFORD
SPOTSYLVANIA
HANOVER
CHESTERFIELD
DINWIDDIE
GREENSVILLE
LOUDOUN
FAUQUIER
CULPEPER
ORANGE
LOUISA
GOOCHLAND
POWHATAN
AMELIA
NOTTOWAY
BRUNSWICK
CLARKE
FREDERICK
WARREN
RAPPA-HANNOCK
MADISON
FLUVANNA
CUMBERLAND
LUNENBURG
MECKLENBURG
SHENANDOAH
PAGE
GREENE
ALBEMARLE
BUCKINGHAM
PRINCE EDWARD
CHARLOTTE
ROCKINGHAM
AUGUSTA
NELSON
APPOMATTOX
HALIFAX
AMHERST
CAMPBELL
PITTSYLVANIA
HIGHLAND
ROCKBRIDGE
BEDFORD
BATH
BOTETOURT
FRANKLIN
HENRY
ALLEGHANY
ROANOKE
CRAIG
MONTGOMERY
FLOYD
PATRICK
GILES
PULASKI
CARROLL
BLAND
WYTHE
GRAYSON
TAZEWELL
SMYTH
BUCHANAN
RUSSELL
WASHINGTON
DICKENSON
WISE
SCOTT
LEE

VIRGINIA

PRESIDENT 1956

1950 Census Population	County	Total Vote	Republican	Democratic	Other	Rep.-Dem. Plurality	Percentage Total Vote Rep.	Percentage Total Vote Dem.	Percentage Major Vote Rep.	Percentage Major Vote Dem.
33,832	ACCOMACK	5,204	2,823	2,213	168	610 R	54.2%	42.5%	56.1%	43.9%
26,662	ALBEMARLE	4,386	2,508	1,412	466	1,096 R	57.2%	32.2%	64.0%	36.0%
23,139	ALLEGHANY	2,054	1,135	822	97	313 R	55.3%	40.0%	58.0%	42.0%
7,908	AMELIA	1,728	745	403	580	342 R	43.1%	23.3%	64.9%	35.1%
20,332	AMHERST	3,590	1,529	1,933	128	404 D	42.6%	53.8%	44.2%	55.8%
8,764	APPOMATTOX	2,086	853	1,079	154	226 D	40.9%	51.7%	44.2%	55.8%
135,449	ARLINGTON	39,725	21,868	16,674	1,183	5,194 R	55.0%	42.0%	56.7%	43.3%
34,154	AUGUSTA	5,092	3,466	1,484	142	1,982 R	68.1%	29.1%	70.0%	30.0%
6,296	BATH	1,264	739	479	46	260 R	58.5%	37.9%	60.7%	39.3%
29,627	BEDFORD COUNTY	6,046	3,148	2,649	249	499 R	52.1%	43.8%	54.3%	45.7%
6,436	BLAND	1,947	1,113	813	21	300 R	57.2%	41.8%	57.8%	42.2%
15,766	BOTETOURT	3,758	2,280	1,377	101	903 R	60.7%	36.6%	62.3%	37.7%
20,136	BRUNSWICK	3,160	799	1,357	1,004	558 D	25.3%	42.9%	37.1%	62.9%
35,748	BUCHANAN	6,831	3,191	3,616	24	425 D	46.7%	52.9%	46.9%	53.1%
12,288	BUCKINGHAM	1,721	751	648	322	103 R	43.6%	37.7%	53.7%	46.3%
28,877	CAMPBELL	5,916	2,827	2,674	415	153 R	47.8%	45.2%	51.4%	48.6%
12,471	CAROLINE	1,969	907	853	209	54 R	46.1%	43.3%	51.5%	48.5%
26,695	CARROLL	5,828	4,060	1,739	29	2,321 R	69.7%	29.8%	70.0%	30.0%
4,676	CHARLES CITY	917	661	174	82	487 R	72.1%	19.0%	79.2%	20.8%
14,057	CHARLOTTE	2,839	791	1,431	617	640 D	27.9%	50.4%	35.6%	64.4%
40,400	CHESTERFIELD	10,894	5,787	3,306	1,801	2,481 R	53.1%	30.3%	63.6%	36.4%
7,074	CLARKE	1,605	785	725	95	60 R	48.9%	45.2%	52.0%	48.0%
3,452	CRAIG	993	485	501	7	16 D	48.8%	50.5%	49.2%	50.8%
13,242	CULPEPER	2,661	1,502	966	193	536 R	56.4%	36.3%	60.9%	39.1%
7,252	CUMBERLAND	1,319	566	331	422	235 R	42.9%	25.1%	63.1%	36.9%
23,393	DICKENSON	7,153	3,444	3,695	14	251 D	48.1%	51.7%	48.2%	51.8%
18,839	DINWIDDIE	2,628	807	1,282	539	475 D	30.7%	48.8%	38.6%	61.4%
6,530	ESSEX	1,076	597	328	151	269 R	55.5%	30.5%	64.5%	35.5%
98,557	FAIRFAX COUNTY	37,267	20,761	15,633	873	5,128 R	55.7%	41.9%	57.0%	43.0%
21,248	FAUQUIER	3,802	2,112	1,567	123	545 R	55.5%	41.2%	57.4%	42.6%
11,351	FLOYD	2,796	1,970	799	27	1,171 R	70.5%	28.6%	71.1%	28.9%
7,121	FLUVANNA	1,363	734	417	212	317 R	53.9%	30.6%	63.8%	36.2%
24,560	FRANKLIN COUNTY	4,354	2,125	2,142	87	17 D	48.8%	49.2%	49.8%	50.2%
17,537	FREDERICK	3,360	1,882	1,405	73	477 R	56.0%	41.8%	57.3%	42.7%
18,956	GILES	4,379	2,270	2,016	93	254 R	51.8%	46.0%	53.0%	47.0%
10,343	GLOUCESTER	2,276	1,319	723	234	596 R	58.0%	31.8%	64.6%	35.4%
8,934	GOOCHLAND	1,493	748	508	237	240 R	50.1%	34.0%	59.6%	40.4%
21,379	GRAYSON	6,496	4,039	2,426	31	1,613 R	62.2%	37.3%	62.5%	37.5%
4,745	GREENE	849	539	246	64	293 R	63.5%	29.0%	68.7%	31.3%
16,319	GREENSVILLE	2,490	724	994	772	270 D	29.1%	39.9%	42.1%	57.9%
41,442	HALIFAX	5,799	1,782	2,470	1,547	688 D	30.7%	42.6%	41.9%	58.1%
21,985	HANOVER	4,202	2,272	1,109	821	1,163 R	54.1%	26.4%	67.2%	32.8%
57,340	HENRICO	21,101	12,702	5,032	3,367	7,670 R	60.2%	23.8%	71.6%	28.4%
31,219	HENRY	5,102	2,436	2,582	84	146 D	47.7%	50.6%	48.5%	51.5%
4,069	HIGHLAND	1,091	633	432	26	201 R	58.0%	39.6%	59.4%	40.6%
14,906	ISLE OF WIGHT	2,757	1,298	1,324	135	26 D	47.1%	48.0%	49.5%	50.5%
6,317	JAMES CITY	1,164	728	312	124	416 R	62.5%	26.8%	70.0%	30.0%
6,299	KING AND QUEEN	906	495	289	122	206 R	54.6%	31.9%	63.1%	36.9%
6,710	KING GEORGE	1,267	655	563	49	92 R	51.7%	44.4%	53.8%	46.2%
7,589	KING WILLIAM	1,427	887	357	183	530 R	62.2%	25.0%	71.3%	28.7%
8,640	LANCASTER	1,953	1,380	373	200	1,007 R	76.9%	20.8%	78.7%	21.3%
36,106	LEE	8,304	4,548	3,714	42	834 R	53.7%	43.8%	55.0%	45.0%
21,147	LOUDOUN	4,660	2,489	1,960	211	529 R	50.5%	39.7%	55.9%	44.1%
12,826	LOUISA	2,429	1,152	795	482	357 R	44.4%	30.6%	59.2%	40.8%
14,116	LUNENBURG	2,339	580	1,111	648	531 D	32.2%	61.6%	34.3%	65.7%
8,273	MADISON	1,495	850	533	112	317 R	56.1%	35.2%	61.5%	38.5%
7,148	MATHEWS	1,556	1,018	406	132	612 R	43.2%	17.2%	71.5%	28.5%
33,497	MECKLENBURG	4,434	1,498	2,004	932	506 D	40.6%	54.4%	42.8%	57.2%
6,715	MIDDLESEX	1,243	721	338	184	383 R	61.5%	28.8%	68.1%	31.9%
29,780	MONTGOMERY	6,559	4,598	1,848	113	2,750 R	70.5%	28.3%	71.3%	28.7%

VIRGINIA

PRESIDENT 1956

1950 Census Population	County	Total Vote	Republican	Democratic	Other	Rep.-Dem. Plurality	Total Vote Rep.	Total Vote Dem.	Major Vote Rep.	Major Vote Dem.
25,238	NANSEMOND	4,360	1,753	2,492	115	739 D	39.5%	56.2%	41.3%	58.7%
14,042	NELSON	2,054	764	1,215	75	451 D	35.2%	56.0%	38.6%	61.4%
3,995	NEW KENT	880	510	178	192	332 R	66.3%	23.1%	74.1%	25.9%
99,937	NORFOLK COUNTY	10,920	4,558	6,026	336	1,468 D	42.0%	55.5%	43.1%	56.9%
17,300	NORTHAMPTON	2,477	1,264	1,132	81	132 R	47.2%	42.3%	52.8%	47.2%
10,012	NORTHUMBERLAND	1,900	1,191	428	281	763 R	46.1%	16.6%	73.6%	26.4%
15,479	NOTTOWAY	3,329	1,124	1,242	963	118 D	41.1%	45.4%	47.5%	52.5%
12,755	ORANGE	2,510	1,344	794	372	550 R	61.4%	36.3%	62.9%	37.1%
15,152	PAGE	3,781	2,372	1,358	51	1,014 R	62.9%	36.0%	63.6%	36.4%
15,642	PATRICK	3,062	1,345	1,677	40	332 D	35.3%	44.0%	44.5%	55.5%
66,096	PITTSYLVANIA	7,794	2,870	4,136	788	1,266 D	39.2%	56.4%	41.0%	59.0%
5,556	POWHATAN	1,348	729	297	322	432 R	27.8%	11.3%	71.1%	28.9%
15,398	PRINCE EDWARD	2,965	932	437	1,596	495 R	61.0%	28.6%	68.1%	31.9%
19,679	PRINCE GEORGE	1,490	689	642	159	47 R	44.0%	41.0%	51.8%	48.2%
22,612	PRINCE WILLIAM	3,970	2,023	1,851	96	172 R	51.3%	47.0%	52.2%	47.8%
42,277	PRINCESS ANNE	9,253	4,675	4,342	236	333 R	51.5%	47.8%	51.8%	48.2%
27,758	PULASKI	5,578	3,517	1,994	67	1,523 R	63.4%	35.9%	63.8%	36.2%
6,112	RAPPAHANNOCK	1,075	514	523	38	9 D	45.8%	46.6%	49.6%	50.4%
6,189	RICHMOND COUNTY	1,121	761	274	86	487 R	55.1%	19.9%	73.5%	26.5%
41,486	ROANOKE COUNTY	10,753	7,509	2,899	345	4,610 R	71.4%	27.6%	72.1%	27.9%
23,359	ROCKBRIDGE	3,418	2,273	1,039	106	1,234 R	66.7%	30.5%	68.6%	31.4%
35,079	ROCKINGHAM	6,027	4,324	1,605	98	2,719 R	72.5%	26.9%	72.9%	27.1%
26,818	RUSSELL	7,224	3,550	3,641	33	91 D	49.1%	50.3%	49.4%	50.6%
27,640	SCOTT	8,754	5,116	3,595	43	1,521 R	58.2%	40.9%	58.7%	41.3%
21,169	SHENANDOAH	6,019	4,164	1,769	86	2,395 R	69.5%	29.5%	70.2%	29.8%
30,187	SMYTH	7,204	4,771	2,374	59	2,397 R	63.9%	31.8%	66.8%	33.2%
26,522	SOUTHAMPTON	3,655	1,290	2,039	326	749 D	37.0%	58.5%	38.8%	61.2%
11,920	SPOTSYLVANIA	2,395	1,244	993	158	251 R	53.0%	42.3%	55.6%	44.4%
11,902	STAFFORD	2,652	1,563	978	111	585 R	55.7%	34.8%	61.5%	38.5%
6,220	SURRY	1,307	425	616	266	191 D	30.3%	43.9%	40.8%	59.2%
12,785	SUSSEX	1,997	785	851	361	66 D	45.7%	49.6%	48.0%	52.0%
47,512	TAZEWELL	7,535	3,960	3,495	80	465 R	52.6%	46.4%	53.1%	46.9%
14,801	WARREN	3,405	2,003	1,322	80	681 R	59.3%	39.1%	60.2%	39.8%
37,536	WASHINGTON	8,250	4,651	3,547	52	1,104 R	55.6%	42.4%	56.7%	43.3%
10,148	WESTMORELAND	1,897	1,033	695	169	338 R	57.9%	38.9%	59.8%	40.2%
56,336	WISE	10,495	4,871	5,567	57	696 D	46.4%	53.0%	46.7%	53.3%
23,327	WYTHE	5,307	3,484	1,766	57	1,718 R	65.1%	33.0%	66.4%	33.6%
11,750	YORK	2,927	1,759	1,064	104	695 R	62.3%	37.7%	62.3%	37.7%
	City									
61,787	ALEXANDRIA	16,449	8,633	7,451	365	1,182 R	52.5%	45.3%	53.7%	46.3%
15,954	BRISTOL	3,457	1,794	1,645	18	149 R	51.9%	47.6%	52.2%	47.8%
5,214	BUENA VISTA	897	545	326	26	219 R	60.8%	36.3%	62.6%	37.4%
25,969	CHARLOTTESVILLE	6,023	3,746	1,783	494	1,963 R	62.2%	29.6%	67.8%	32.2%
5,795	CLIFTON FORGE	1,830	1,125	633	72	492 R	61.5%	34.6%	64.0%	36.0%
6,077	COLONIAL HEIGHTS	2,172	1,037	956	179	81 R	47.7%	44.0%	52.0%	48.0%
	COVINGTON	2,909	1,639	1,189	81	450 R	56.3%	40.9%	58.0%	42.0%
35,066	DANVILLE	7,726	4,561	2,409	756	2,152 R	59.0%	31.2%	65.4%	34.6%
7,535	FALLS CHURCH	2,752	1,462	1,233	57	229 R	53.1%	44.8%	54.2%	45.8%
12,158	FREDERICKSBURG	2,775	1,672	934	169	738 R	60.3%	33.7%	64.2%	35.8%
	GALAX	1,114	761	346	7	415 R	68.3%	31.1%	68.7%	31.3%
5,966	HAMPTON	12,983	7,432	5,108	443	2,324 R	57.2%	39.3%	59.3%	40.7%
10,810	HARRISONBURG	2,893	2,265	571	57	1,694 R	78.3%	19.7%	79.9%	20.1%
10,219	HOPEWELL	3,539	1,908	1,388	243	520 R	53.9%	39.2%	57.9%	42.1%
47,727	LYNCHBURG	10,502	6,806	3,362	334	3,444 R	64.8%	32.0%	66.9%	33.1%
17,251	MARTINSVILLE	3,561	2,125	1,368	68	757 R	59.7%	38.4%	60.8%	39.2%
42,358	NEWPORT NEWS	7,095	3,779	3,069	247	710 R	53.3%	43.3%	55.2%	44.8%
213,513	NORFOLK CITY	34,525	18,650	14,571	1,304	4,079 R	54.0%	42.2%	56.1%	43.9%
	NORTON	1,241	684	552	5	132 R	55.1%	44.5%	55.3%	44.7%
35,054	PETERSBURG	5,449	3,166	1,882	401	1,284 R	58.1%	34.5%	62.7%	37.3%

VIRGINIA

PRESIDENT 1956

1950 Census Population	City	Total Vote	Republican	Democratic	Other	Rep.-Dem. Plurality	Percentage Total Vote Rep.	Percentage Total Vote Dem.	Percentage Major Vote Rep.	Percentage Major Vote Dem.
80,039	PORTSMOUTH	11,436	5,390	5,683	363	293 D	47.1%	49.7%	48.7%	51.3%
9,026	RADFORD	3,058	1,910	1,118	30	792 R	62.5%	36.6%	63.1%	36.9%
230,310	RICHMOND CITY	44,291	27,367	10,758	6,166	16,609 R	61.8%	24.3%	71.8%	28.2%
91,921	ROANOKE CITY	24,082	16,708	6,751	623	9,957 R	69.4%	28.0%	71.2%	28.8%
10,434	SOUTH NORFOLK	3,609	1,521	1,871	217	350 D	42.1%	51.8%	44.8%	55.2%
19,927	STAUNTON	3,881	2,908	843	130	2,065 R	74.9%	21.7%	77.5%	22.5%
12,339	SUFFOLK	2,812	1,617	1,103	92	514 R	57.5%	39.2%	59.4%	40.6%
	VIRGINIA BEACH	2,543	1,355	1,111	77	244 R	53.3%	43.7%	54.9%	45.1%
39,875	WARWICK	8,640	4,872	3,406	362	1,466 R	56.4%	39.4%	58.9%	41.1%
12,357	WAYNESBORO	2,886	2,049	748	89	1,301 R	71.0%	25.9%	73.3%	26.7%
6,735	WILLIAMSBURG	1,238	775	362	101	413 R	62.6%	29.2%	68.2%	31.8%
13,841	WINCHESTER	3,419	2,375	945	99	1,430 R	69.5%	27.6%	71.5%	28.5%
3,318,680	TOTAL	697,978	386,459	267,760	43,759	118,699 R	55.4%	38.4%	59.1%	40.9%

VIRGINIA

PRESIDENT 1952

1950 Census Population	County	Total Vote	Republican	Democratic	Other	Rep.-Dem. Plurality	Percentage Total Vote Rep.	Total Vote Dem.	Major Vote Rep.	Major Vote Dem.
33,832	ACCOMACK	4,864	2,626	2,220	18	406 R	54.0%	45.6%	54.2%	45.8%
26,662	ALBEMARLE	4,183	2,523	1,642	18	881 R	60.3%	39.3%	60.6%	39.4%
23,139	ALLEGHANY	4,849	2,564	2,274	11	290 R	52.9%	46.9%	53.0%	47.0%
7,908	AMELIA	1,551	832	703	16	129 R	53.6%	45.3%	54.2%	45.8%
20,332	AMHERST	3,500	1,407	2,078	15	671 D	40.2%	59.4%	40.4%	59.6%
8,764	APPOMATTOX	1,891	929	957	5	28 D	49.1%	50.6%	49.3%	50.7%
135,449	ARLINGTON	36,380	22,158	14,032	190	8,126 R	60.9%	38.6%	61.2%	38.8%
34,154	AUGUSTA	4,879	3,414	1,453	12	1,961 R	70.0%	29.8%	70.1%	29.9%
6,296	BATH	1,221	765	451	5	314 R	62.7%	36.9%	62.9%	37.1%
29,627	BEDFORD COUNTY	5,353	2,916	2,426	11	490 R	54.5%	45.3%	54.6%	45.4%
6,436	BLAND	1,748	1,000	743	5	257 R	57.2%	42.5%	57.4%	42.6%
15,766	BOTETOURT	3,286	2,021	1,264	1	757 R	61.5%	38.5%	61.5%	38.5%
20,136	BRUNSWICK	2,747	1,098	1,635	14	537 D	40.0%	59.5%	40.2%	59.8%
35,748	BUCHANAN	6,029	2,330	3,613	86	1,283 D	38.6%	59.9%	39.2%	60.8%
12,288	BUCKINGHAM	1,741	811	919	11	108 D	46.6%	52.8%	46.9%	53.1%
28,877	CAMPBELL	5,178	2,447	2,713	18	266 D	47.3%	52.4%	47.4%	52.6%
12,471	CAROLINE	1,825	858	954	13	96 D	47.0%	52.3%	47.4%	52.6%
26,695	CARROLL	5,495	3,774	1,711	10	2,063 R	68.7%	31.1%	68.8%	31.2%
4,676	CHARLES CITY	850	342	492	16	150 D	40.2%	57.9%	41.0%	59.0%
14,057	CHARLOTTE	2,596	949	1,630	17	681 D	36.6%	62.8%	36.8%	63.2%
40,400	CHESTERFIELD	8,046	4,482	3,546	18	936 R	55.7%	44.1%	55.8%	44.2%
7,074	CLARKE	1,530	809	716	5	93 R	52.9%	46.8%	53.0%	47.0%
3,452	CRAIG	915	425	490		65 D	46.4%	53.6%	46.4%	53.6%
13,242	CULPEPER	2,498	1,507	987	4	520 R	60.3%	39.5%	60.4%	39.6%
7,252	CUMBERLAND	1,277	695	574	8	121 R	54.4%	44.9%	54.8%	45.2%
23,393	DICKENSON	6,144	2,913	3,210	21	297 D	47.4%	52.2%	47.6%	52.4%
18,839	DINWIDDIE	2,472	983	1,462	27	479 D	39.8%	59.1%	40.2%	59.8%
6,530	ESSEX	1,163	610	545	8	65 R	52.5%	46.9%	52.8%	47.2%
98,557	FAIRFAX COUNTY	21,379	13,020	8,329	30	4,691 R	60.9%	39.0%	61.0%	39.0%
21,248	FAUQUIER	3,675	2,068	1,597	10	471 R	56.3%	43.5%	56.4%	43.6%
11,351	FLOYD	2,268	1,626	619	23	1,007 R	71.7%	27.3%	72.4%	27.6%
7,121	FLUVANNA	1,254	724	519	11	205 R	57.7%	41.4%	58.2%	41.8%
24,560	FRANKLIN COUNTY	4,026	1,976	2,012	38	36 D	49.1%	50.0%	49.5%	50.5%
17,537	FREDERICK	3,134	1,803	1,326	5	477 R	57.5%	42.3%	57.6%	42.4%
18,956	GILES	3,655	1,935	1,717	3	218 R	52.9%	47.0%	53.0%	47.0%
10,343	GLOUCESTER	2,046	1,073	961	12	112 R	52.4%	47.0%	52.8%	47.2%
8,934	GOOCHLAND	1,548	714	820	14	106 D	46.1%	53.0%	46.5%	53.5%
21,379	GRAYSON	7,201	4,449	2,734	18	1,715 R	61.8%	38.0%	61.9%	38.1%
4,745	GREENE	792	537	250	5	287 R	67.8%	31.6%	68.2%	31.8%
16,319	GREENSVILLE	2,273	988	1,259	26	271 D	43.5%	55.4%	44.0%	56.0%
41,442	HALIFAX	5,587	2,274	3,296	17	1,022 D	40.7%	59.0%	40.8%	59.2%
21,985	HANOVER	3,777	2,257	1,518	2	739 R	59.8%	40.2%	59.8%	40.2%
57,340	HENRICO	16,035	10,682	5,339	14	5,343 R	66.6%	33.3%	66.7%	33.3%
31,219	HENRY	4,220	1,871	2,323	26	452 D	44.3%	55.0%	44.6%	55.4%
4,069	HIGHLAND	1,118	696	419	3	277 R	62.3%	37.5%	62.4%	37.6%
14,906	ISLE OF WIGHT	2,237	996	1,227	14	231 D	44.5%	54.9%	44.8%	55.2%
6,317	JAMES CITY	875	527	346	2	181 R	60.2%	39.5%	60.4%	39.6%
6,299	KING AND QUEEN	810	415	387	8	28 R	51.2%	47.8%	51.7%	48.3%
6,710	KING GEORGE	1,090	577	503	10	74 R	52.9%	46.1%	53.4%	46.6%
7,589	KING WILLIAM	1,272	730	533	9	197 R	57.4%	41.9%	57.8%	42.2%
8,640	LANCASTER	1,997	1,228	753	16	475 R	61.2%	37.5%	62.0%	38.0%
36,106	LEE	8,891	4,622	4,242	27	380 R	52.1%	47.8%	52.1%	47.9%
21,147	LOUDOUN	4,630	2,540	2,075	15	465 R	54.9%	44.8%	55.0%	45.0%
12,826	LOUISA	2,172	1,135	1,025	12	110 R	52.4%	47.3%	52.5%	47.5%
14,116	LUNENBURG	2,373	837	1,528	8	691 D	35.3%	64.4%	35.4%	64.6%
8,273	MADISON	1,558	1,012	540	6	472 R	65.0%	34.7%	65.2%	34.8%
7,148	MATHEWS	1,489	951	533	5	418 R	62.5%	35.0%	64.1%	35.9%
33,497	MECKLENBURG	4,454	1,891	2,525	38	634 D	42.7%	57.1%	42.8%	57.2%
6,715	MIDDLESEX	1,221	705	507	9	198 R	57.7%	41.5%	58.2%	41.8%
29,780	MONTGOMERY	5,491	3,881	1,600	10	2,281 R	70.7%	29.1%	70.8%	29.2%

VIRGINIA

PRESIDENT 1952

1950 Census Population	County	Total Vote	Republican	Democratic	Other	Rep.-Dem. Plurality	Percentage: Total Vote Rep.	Total Vote Dem.	Major Vote Rep.	Major Vote Dem.
25,238	NANSEMOND	3,553	1,168	2,360	25	1,192 D	33.0%	66.8%	33.1%	66.9%
14,042	NELSON	1,970	740	1,222	8	482 D	37.6%	62.1%	37.7%	62.3%
3,995	NEW KENT	862	455	400	7	55 R	52.5%	46.1%	53.2%	46.8%
99,937	NORFOLK COUNTY	12,392	5,614	6,766	12	1,152 D	45.3%	54.6%	45.3%	54.7%
17,300	NORTHAMPTON	2,608	1,307	1,289	12	18 R	50.3%	49.6%	50.3%	49.7%
10,012	NORTHUMBERLAND	1,806	1,230	573	3	657 R	67.7%	31.5%	68.2%	31.8%
15,479	NOTTOWAY	2,850	1,454	1,381	15	73 R	51.1%	48.5%	51.3%	48.7%
12,755	ORANGE	2,453	1,525	916	12	609 R	62.2%	37.4%	62.5%	37.5%
15,152	PAGE	4,101	2,649	1,441	11	1,208 R	64.7%	35.2%	64.8%	35.2%
15,642	PATRICK	2,872	1,314	1,554	4	240 D	45.3%	53.6%	45.8%	54.2%
66,096	PITTSYLVANIA	6,900	2,893	3,976	31	1,083 D	42.1%	57.8%	42.1%	57.9%
5,556	POWHATAN	1,063	558	498	7	60 R	52.6%	46.9%	52.8%	47.2%
15,398	PRINCE EDWARD	2,290	1,359	926	5	433 R	59.1%	40.3%	59.5%	40.5%
19,679	PRINCE GEORGE	1,166	541	612	13	71 D	46.4%	52.5%	46.9%	53.1%
22,612	PRINCE WILLIAM	3,295	1,619	1,653	23	34 D	49.4%	50.4%	49.5%	50.5%
42,277	PRINCESS ANNE	6,230	3,180	3,037	13	143 R	51.1%	48.8%	51.2%	48.8%
27,758	PULASKI	4,538	2,815	1,715	8	1,100 R	62.1%	37.8%	62.1%	37.9%
6,112	RAPPAHANNOCK	1,139	619	518	2	101 R	54.3%	45.5%	54.4%	45.6%
6,189	RICHMOND COUNTY	1,055	727	326	2	401 R	67.8%	30.4%	69.0%	31.0%
41,486	ROANOKE COUNTY	8,726	6,017	2,689	20	3,328 R	69.0%	30.8%	69.1%	30.9%
23,359	ROCKBRIDGE	3,138	2,068	1,059	11	1,009 R	65.9%	33.8%	66.1%	33.9%
35,079	ROCKINGHAM	5,950	4,350	1,591	9	2,759 R	73.0%	26.7%	73.2%	26.8%
26,818	RUSSELL	6,206	2,937	3,253	16	316 D	47.4%	52.6%	47.4%	52.6%
27,640	SCOTT	7,693	4,703	2,990		1,713 R	61.1%	38.8%	61.1%	38.9%
21,169	SHENANDOAH	6,024	4,284	1,734	6	2,550 R	71.0%	28.7%	71.2%	28.8%
30,187	SMYTH	5,685	3,694	1,972	19	1,722 R	65.1%	34.7%	65.2%	34.8%
26,522	SOUTHAMPTON	3,177	1,166	2,000	11	834 D	36.5%	62.6%	36.8%	63.2%
11,920	SPOTSYLVANIA	2,397	1,174	1,194	29	20 D	49.2%	50.1%	49.6%	50.4%
11,902	STAFFORD	2,504	1,411	1,077	16	334 R	56.3%	42.9%	56.7%	43.3%
6,220	SURRY	1,006	414	572	20	158 D	41.7%	57.6%	42.0%	58.0%
12,785	SUSSEX	1,851	888	956	7	68 D	47.4%	51.0%	48.2%	51.8%
47,512	TAZEWELL	5,789	3,232	2,527	30	705 R	56.0%	43.8%	56.1%	43.9%
14,801	WARREN	3,261	1,888	1,362	11	526 R	57.9%	41.8%	58.1%	41.9%
37,536	WASHINGTON	6,599	3,810	2,778	11	1,032 R	57.8%	42.1%	57.8%	42.2%
10,148	WESTMORELAND	1,877	1,117	754	6	363 R	59.1%	39.9%	59.7%	40.3%
56,336	WISE	8,660	3,911	4,729	20	818 D	45.2%	54.7%	45.3%	54.7%
23,327	WYTHE	5,246	3,580	1,654	12	1,926 R	68.1%	31.5%	68.4%	31.6%
11,750	YORK	2,642	1,335	1,287	20	48 R	50.9%	49.1%	50.9%	49.1%
	City									
61,787	ALEXANDRIA	15,072	8,579	6,471	22	2,108 R	56.9%	42.9%	57.0%	43.0%
15,954	BRISTOL	3,009	1,574	1,432	3	142 R	52.3%	47.6%	52.4%	47.6%
5,214	BUENA VISTA	906	513	392	1	121 R	56.6%	43.3%	56.7%	43.3%
25,969	CHARLOTTESVILLE	5,474	3,292	2,174	8	1,118 R	60.1%	39.7%	60.2%	39.8%
5,795	CLIFTON FORGE	1,751	936	811	4	125 R	53.5%	46.3%	53.6%	46.4%
6,077	COLONIAL HEIGHTS	1,732	896	835	1	61 R	51.7%	48.2%	51.8%	48.2%
35,066	DANVILLE	8,146	4,765	3,323	58	1,442 R	58.5%	40.8%	58.9%	41.1%
7,535	FALLS CHURCH	2,317	1,386	930	1	456 R	59.8%	40.1%	59.8%	40.2%
12,158	FREDERICKSBURG	2,510	1,536	970	4	566 R	61.2%	38.6%	61.3%	38.7%
5,966	HAMPTON	10,481	5,505	4,946	30	559 R	52.5%	47.2%	52.7%	47.3%
10,810	HARRISONBURG	2,876	2,238	635	3	1,603 R	77.8%	22.1%	77.9%	22.1%
10,219	HOPEWELL	3,308	1,640	1,657	11	17 D	49.6%	50.1%	49.7%	50.3%
47,727	LYNCHBURG	10,949	7,090	3,848	11	3,242 R	64.8%	35.1%	64.8%	35.2%
17,251	MARTINSVILLE	3,174	1,772	1,391	11	381 R	55.8%	43.8%	56.0%	44.0%
42,358	NEWPORT NEWS	6,843	2,769	4,051	23	1,282 D	40.5%	59.2%	40.6%	59.4%
213,513	NORFOLK CITY	26,074	14,166	11,862	46	2,304 R	54.3%	45.5%	54.4%	45.6%
35,054	PETERSBURG	5,179	2,822	2,342	15	480 R	54.5%	45.2%	54.6%	45.4%
80,039	PORTSMOUTH	9,855	3,621	6,188	46	2,567 D	36.7%	62.8%	36.9%	63.1%
9,026	RADFORD	2,638	1,523	1,108	7	415 R	57.7%	42.0%	57.9%	42.1%
230,310	RICHMOND CITY	48,610	29,300	19,235	75	10,065 R	60.3%	39.6%	60.4%	39.6%

VIRGINIA

PRESIDENT 1952

1950 Census Population	City	Total Vote	Republican	Democratic	Other	Rep.-Dem. Plurality	Percentage Total Vote Rep.	Percentage Total Vote Dem.	Percentage Major Vote Rep.	Percentage Major Vote Dem.
91,921	ROANOKE CITY	23,747	15,673	8,042	32	7,631 R	66.0%	33.9%	66.1%	33.9%
10,434	SOUTH NORFOLK	2,897	1,098	1,782	17	684 D	37.9%	61.5%	38.1%	61.9%
19,927	STAUNTON	3,528	2,578	945	5	1,633 R	73.1%	26.8%	73.2%	26.8%
12,339	SUFFOLK	2,837	1,622	1,209	6	413 R	57.2%	42.6%	57.3%	42.7%
	VIRGINIA BEACH	2,191	1,310	881		429 R	59.8%	40.2%	59.8%	40.2%
39,875	WARWICK	6,124	3,307	2,806	11	501 R	54.0%	45.8%	54.1%	45.9%
12,357	WAYNESBORO	2,413	1,680	730	3	950 R	69.6%	30.3%	69.7%	30.3%
6,735	WILLIAMSBURG	1,283	797	483	3	314 R	62.1%	37.6%	62.3%	37.7%
13,841	WINCHESTER	3,432	2,375	1,055	2	1,320 R	69.2%	30.7%	69.2%	30.8%
33,186,680	TOTAL	619,689	349,037	268,677	1,975	80,360 R	56.3%	43.4%	56.5%	43.5%

VIRGINIA

PRESIDENT 1948

1940 Census Population	County	Total Vote	Republican	Democratic	Other	Rep.-Dem. Plurality	Percentage			
							Total Vote		Major Vote	
							Rep.	Dem.	Rep.	Dem.
33,030	ACCOMACK	3,104	1,088	1,669	347	581 D	35.1%	53.8%	39.5%	60.5%
24,652	ALBEMARLE	2,443	984	1,178	281	194 D	40.3%	48.2%	45.5%	54.5%
22,688	ALLEGHANY	3,850	1,425	2,253	172	828 D	37.0%	58.5%	38.7%	61.3%
8,495	AMELIA	1,058	372	443	243	71 D	35.2%	41.9%	45.6%	54.4%
20,273	AMHERST	2,466	460	1,481	525	1,021 D	18.7%	60.1%	23.7%	76.3%
9,020	APPOMATTOX	1,666	238	1,182	246	944 D	14.3%	70.9%	16.8%	83.2%
57,040	ARLINGTON	20,111	10,774	7,798	1,539	2,976 R	53.6%	38.8%	58.0%	42.0%
42,772	AUGUSTA	3,454	1,690	1,355	409	335 R	48.9%	39.2%	55.5%	44.5%
7,191	BATH	938	488	375	75	113 R	52.0%	40.0%	56.5%	43.5%
29,687	BEDFORD COUNTY	3,609	1,084	1,556	969	472 D	30.0%	43.1%	41.1%	58.9%
6,731	BLAND	1,628	822	738	68	84 R	50.5%	45.3%	52.7%	47.3%
16,447	BOTETOURT	2,631	1,363	1,026	242	337 R	51.8%	39.0%	57.1%	42.9%
19,575	BRUNSWICK	2,202	229	1,067	906	838 D	10.4%	48.5%	17.7%	82.3%
31,477	BUCHANAN	5,325	2,085	3,174	66	1,089 D	39.2%	59.6%	39.6%	60.4%
13,398	BUCKINGHAM	1,267	354	728	185	374 D	27.9%	57.5%	32.7%	67.3%
26,048	CAMPBELL	2,876	668	1,554	654	886 D	23.2%	54.0%	30.1%	69.9%
13,945	CAROLINE	1,312	397	731	184	334 D	30.3%	55.7%	35.2%	64.8%
25,904	CARROLL	3,737	2,456	1,196	85	1,260 R	65.7%	32.0%	67.3%	32.7%
4,275	CHARLES CITY	497	167	258	72	91 D	33.6%	51.9%	39.3%	60.7%
15,861	CHARLOTTE	1,667	285	964	418	679 D	17.1%	57.8%	22.8%	77.2%
31,183	CHESTERFIELD	4,730	1,428	2,600	702	1,172 D	30.2%	55.0%	35.5%	64.5%
7,159	CLARKE	1,158	384	482	292	98 D	33.2%	41.6%	44.3%	55.7%
3,769	CRAIG	796	317	456	23	139 D	39.8%	57.3%	41.0%	59.0%
13,365	CULPEPER	1,699	682	804	213	122 D	40.1%	47.3%	45.9%	54.1%
7,505	CUMBERLAND	813	219	424	170	205 D	26.9%	52.2%	34.1%	65.9%
21,266	DICKENSON	5,172	2,197	2,945	30	748 D	42.5%	56.9%	42.7%	57.3%
18,166	DINWIDDIE	1,500	261	961	278	700 D	17.4%	64.1%	21.4%	78.6%
32,283	ELIZABETH CITY COUNTY	4,788	1,617	2,744	427	1,127 D	33.8%	57.3%	37.1%	62.9%
7,006	ESSEX	651	221	329	101	108 D	33.9%	50.5%	40.2%	59.8%
40,929	FAIRFAX COUNTY	9,489	4,930	3,719	840	1,211 R	52.0%	39.2%	57.0%	43.0%
21,039	FAUQUIER	2,667	1,102	1,291	274	189 D	41.3%	48.4%	46.1%	53.9%
11,967	FLOYD	1,745	1,266	434	45	832 R	72.6%	24.9%	74.5%	25.5%
7,088	FLUVANNA	852	319	447	86	128 D	37.4%	52.5%	41.6%	58.4%
25,864	FRANKLIN COUNTY	2,813	1,100	1,343	370	243 D	39.1%	47.7%	45.0%	55.0%
14,008	FREDERICK	2,404	921	1,244	239	323 D	38.3%	51.7%	42.5%	57.5%
14,635	GILES	3,115	1,448	1,529	138	81 D	46.5%	49.1%	48.6%	51.4%
9,548	GLOUCESTER	1,274	434	719	121	285 D	34.1%	56.4%	37.6%	62.4%
8,454	GOOCHLAND	1,140	292	683	165	391 D	25.6%	59.9%	29.9%	70.1%
21,916	GRAYSON	6,568	3,669	2,741	158	928 R	55.9%	41.7%	57.2%	42.8%
5,218	GREENE	714	420	261	33	159 R	58.8%	36.6%	61.7%	38.3%
14,866	GREENSVILLE	1,427	301	710	416	409 D	21.1%	49.8%	29.8%	70.2%
41,271	HALIFAX	3,870	521	1,323	2,026	802 D	13.5%	34.2%	28.3%	71.7%
18,500	HANOVER	2,202	838	1,048	316	210 D	38.1%	47.6%	44.4%	55.6%
41,960	HENRICO	4,970	2,092	2,321	557	229 D	42.1%	46.7%	47.4%	52.6%
26,481	HENRY	2,537	730	1,318	489	588 D	28.8%	52.0%	35.6%	64.4%
4,875	HIGHLAND	1,090	579	423	88	156 R	53.1%	38.8%	57.8%	42.2%
13,381	ISLE OF WIGHT	1,591	442	1,064	85	622 D	27.8%	66.9%	29.3%	70.7%
4,907	JAMES CITY	445	177	198	70	21 D	39.8%	44.5%	47.2%	52.8%
6,954	KING AND QUEEN	547	171	293	83	122 D	31.3%	53.6%	36.9%	63.1%
5,431	KING GEORGE	720	316	248	156	68 R	43.9%	34.4%	56.0%	44.0%
7,855	KING WILLIAM	971	348	476	147	128 D	35.8%	49.0%	42.2%	57.8%
8,786	LANCASTER	1,174	459	560	155	101 D	39.1%	47.7%	45.0%	55.0%
39,296	LEE	8,466	4,297	4,069	100	228 R	50.8%	48.1%	51.4%	48.6%
20,291	LOUDOUN	3,245	1,430	1,545	270	115 D	44.1%	47.6%	48.1%	51.9%
13,665	LOUISA	1,691	701	782	208	81 D	41.5%	46.2%	47.3%	52.7%
13,844	LUNENBURG	1,718	251	1,126	341	875 D	14.6%	65.5%	18.2%	81.8%
8,465	MADISON	1,188	662	428	98	234 R	55.7%	36.0%	60.7%	39.3%
7,149	MATHEWS	1,031	490	458	83	32 R	47.5%	44.4%	51.7%	48.3%
31,933	MECKLENBURG	3,053	513	2,117	423	1,604 D	16.8%	69.3%	19.5%	80.5%
6,673	MIDDLESEX	879	271	457	151	186 D	30.8%	52.0%	37.2%	62.8%

VIRGINIA

PRESIDENT 1948

1940 Census Population	County	Total Vote	Republican	Democratic	Other	Rep.-Dem. Plurality	Percentage: Total Vote Rep.	Percentage: Total Vote Dem.	Percentage: Major Vote Rep.	Percentage: Major Vote Dem.
21,206	MONTGOMERY	3,473	2,070	1,126	277	944 R	59.6%	32.4%	64.8%	35.2%
22,771	NANSEMOND	2,773	413	2,115	245	1,702 D	14.9%	76.3%	16.3%	83.7%
16,241	NELSON	1,741	371	1,204	166	833 D	21.3%	69.2%	23.6%	76.4%
4,092	NEW KENT	514	140	277	97	137 D	27.2%	53.9%	33.6%	66.4%
35,828	NORFOLK COUNTY	7,089	1,830	4,696	563	2,866 D	25.8%	66.2%	28.0%	72.0%
17,597	NORTHAMPTON	1,758	525	997	236	472 D	29.9%	56.7%	34.5%	65.5%
10,463	NORTHUMBERLAND	1,146	535	429	182	106 R	46.7%	37.4%	55.5%	44.5%
15,556	NOTTOWAY	1,963	486	1,004	473	518 D	24.8%	51.1%	32.6%	67.4%
12,649	ORANGE	1,852	726	856	270	130 D	39.2%	46.2%	45.9%	54.1%
14,863	PAGE	4,055	2,236	1,611	208	625 R	55.1%	39.7%	58.1%	41.9%
16,613	PATRICK	1,840	648	760	432	112 D	35.2%	41.3%	46.0%	54.0%
61,697	PITTSYLVANIA	5,666	1,164	3,149	1,353	1,985 D	20.5%	55.6%	27.0%	73.0%
5,671	POWHATAN	663	238	338	87	100 D	35.9%	51.0%	41.3%	58.7%
14,922	PRINCE EDWARD	1,718	459	740	519	281 D	26.7%	43.1%	38.3%	61.7%
12,226	PRINCE GEORGE	1,210	317	745	148	428 D	26.2%	61.6%	29.8%	70.2%
17,738	PRINCE WILLIAM	2,083	760	1,162	161	402 D	36.5%	55.8%	39.5%	60.5%
19,984	PRINCESS ANNE	3,715	1,329	2,008	378	679 D	35.8%	54.1%	39.8%	60.2%
22,767	PULASKI	3,452	1,691	1,412	349	279 R	49.0%	40.9%	54.5%	45.5%
7,208	RAPPAHANNOCK	1,034	311	617	106	306 D	30.1%	59.7%	33.5%	66.5%
6,634	RICHMOND COUNTY	615	296	240	79	56 R	48.1%	39.0%	55.2%	44.8%
42,897	ROANOKE COUNTY	7,455	3,988	2,876	591	1,112 R	53.5%	38.6%	58.1%	41.9%
22,384	ROCKBRIDGE	2,284	1,062	994	228	68 R	46.5%	43.5%	51.7%	48.3%
31,289	ROCKINGHAM	5,182	3,219	1,680	283	1,539 R	62.1%	32.4%	65.7%	34.3%
26,627	RUSSELL	5,243	2,447	2,689	107	242 D	46.7%	51.3%	47.6%	52.4%
26,989	SCOTT	6,272	3,520	2,676	76	844 R	56.1%	42.7%	56.8%	43.2%
20,898	SHENANDOAH	5,180	3,349	1,603	228	1,746 R	64.7%	30.9%	67.6%	32.4%
28,861	SMYTH	4,822	2,897	1,750	175	1,147 R	60.1%	36.3%	62.3%	37.7%
26,442	SOUTHAMPTON	2,100	339	1,462	299	1,123 D	16.1%	69.6%	18.8%	81.2%
9,905	SPOTSYLVANIA	1,510	517	818	175	301 D	34.2%	54.2%	38.7%	61.3%
9,548	STAFFORD	1,579	732	708	139	24 R	46.4%	44.8%	50.8%	49.2%
6,193	SURRY	774	134	460	180	326 D	17.3%	59.4%	22.6%	77.4%
12,485	SUSSEX	1,220	244	614	362	370 D	20.0%	50.3%	28.4%	71.6%
41,607	TAZEWELL	4,706	2,278	2,258	170	20 R	48.4%	48.0%	50.2%	49.8%
11,352	WARREN	2,483	1,016	1,291	176	275 D	40.9%	52.0%	44.0%	56.0%
9,248	WARWICK	3,165	1,014	1,822	329	808 D	32.0%	57.6%	35.8%	64.2%
38,197	WASHINGTON	5,693	2,972	2,510	211	462 R	52.2%	44.1%	54.2%	45.8%
9,512	WESTMORELAND	1,276	568	503	205	65 R	44.5%	39.4%	53.0%	47.0%
52,458	WISE	7,845	2,836	4,862	147	2,026 D	36.2%	62.0%	36.8%	63.2%
22,721	WYTHE	3,336	2,077	976	283	1,101 R	62.3%	29.3%	68.0%	32.0%
8,857	YORK	1,376	418	826	132	408 D	30.4%	60.0%	33.6%	66.4%
	City									
33,523	ALEXANDRIA	8,707	3,903	3,917	887	14 D	44.8%	45.0%	49.9%	50.1%
9,768	BRISTOL	2,462	879	1,451	132	572 D	35.7%	58.9%	37.7%	62.3%
4,335	BUENA VISTA	563	234	297	32	63 D	41.6%	52.8%	44.1%	55.9%
19,400	CHARLOTTESVILLE	3,367	1,419	1,527	421	108 D	42.1%	45.4%	48.2%	51.8%
6,461	CLIFTON FORGE	1,405	451	818	136	367 D	32.1%	58.2%	35.5%	64.5%
32,749	DANVILLE	5,448	1,579	2,334	1,535	755 D	29.0%	42.8%	40.4%	59.6%
10,066	FREDERICKSBURG	1,931	810	816	305	6 D	41.9%	42.3%	49.8%	50.2%
5,898	HAMPTON	1,235	371	727	137	356 D	30.0%	58.9%	33.8%	66.2%
8,768	HARRISONBURG	2,352	1,377	751	224	626 R	58.5%	31.9%	64.7%	35.3%
8,679	HOPEWELL	1,981	570	1,242	169	672 D	28.8%	62.7%	31.5%	68.5%
44,541	LYNCHBURG	6,747	2,373	2,480	1,894	107 D	35.2%	36.8%	48.9%	51.1%
10,080	MARTINSVILLE	2,061	642	814	605	172 D	31.1%	39.5%	44.1%	55.9%
37,067	NEWPORT NEWS	5,239	1,453	3,420	366	1,967 D	27.7%	65.3%	29.8%	70.2%
144,332	NORFOLK CITY	18,460	7,556	9,370	1,534	1,814 D	40.9%	50.8%	44.6%	55.4%
30,631	PETERSBURG	3,831	1,189	2,019	623	830 D	31.0%	52.7%	37.1%	62.9%

VIRGINIA

PRESIDENT 1948

1940 Census Population	City	Total Vote	Republican	Democratic	Other	Rep.-Dem. Plurality	Percentage Total Vote Rep.	Total Vote Dem.	Major Vote Rep.	Major Vote Dem.
50,745	PORTSMOUTH	7,381	2,056	4,612	713	2,556 D	27.9%	62.5%	30.8%	69.2%
6,990	RADFORD	1,765	850	826	89	24 R	48.2%	46.8%	50.7%	49.3%
193,042	RICHMOND CITY	35,301	14,549	16,466	4,286	1,917 D	41.2%	46.6%	46.9%	53.1%
69,287	ROANOKE CITY	13,200	6,542	5,343	1,315	1,199 R	49.6%	40.5%	55.0%	45.0%
8,038	SOUTH NORFOLK	1,283	347	857	79	510 D	27.0%	66.8%	28.8%	71.2%
13,337	STAUNTON	2,673	1,323	914	436	409 R	49.5%	34.2%	59.1%	40.9%
11,343	SUFFOLK	2,070	741	1,030	299	289 D	35.8%	49.8%	41.8%	58.2%
	WAYNESBORO	1,794	833	839	122	6 D	46.4%	46.8%	49.8%	50.2%
3,942	WILLIAMSBURG	849	334	312	203	22 R	39.3%	36.7%	51.7%	48.3%
12,095	WINCHESTER	2,546	1,272	894	380	378 R	50.0%	35.1%	58.7%	41.3%
2,677,773	TOTAL	419,256	172,070	200,786	46,400	28,716 D	41.0%	47.9%	46.1%	53.9%

VIRGINIA

PRESIDENT 1944

1940 Census Population	County	Total Vote	Republican	Democratic	Other	Rep.-Dem. Plurality	Percentage Total Vote Rep.	Percentage Total Vote Dem.	Percentage Major Vote Rep.	Percentage Major Vote Dem.
33,030	ACCOMACK	2,795	1,045	1,747	3	702 D	37.4%	62.5%	37.4%	62.6%
24,652	ALBEMARLE	2,701	964	1,725	12	761 D	35.7%	63.9%	35.8%	64.2%
22,688	ALLEGHANY	3,300	1,308	1,985	7	677 D	39.6%	60.2%	39.7%	60.3%
8,495	AMELIA	851	295	553	3	258 D	34.7%	65.0%	34.8%	65.2%
20,273	AMHERST	3,039	442	2,585	12	2,143 D	14.5%	85.1%	14.6%	85.4%
9,020	APPOMATTOX	1,385	270	1,109	6	839 D	19.5%	80.1%	19.6%	80.4%
57,040	ARLINGTON	15,499	8,317	7,122	60	1,195 R	53.7%	46.0%	53.9%	46.1%
42,772	AUGUSTA	5,247	2,319	2,913	15	594 D	44.2%	55.5%	44.3%	55.7%
7,191	BATH	1,089	504	581	4	77 D	46.3%	53.4%	46.5%	53.5%
29,687	BEDFORD COUNTY	3,608	1,068	2,534	6	1,466 D	29.6%	70.2%	29.7%	70.3%
6,731	BLAND	1,506	744	762		18 D	49.4%	50.6%	49.4%	50.6%
16,447	BOTETOURT	2,562	1,272	1,275	15	3 D	49.6%	49.8%	49.9%	50.1%
19,575	BRUNSWICK	1,447	208	1,239		1,031 D	14.4%	85.6%	14.4%	85.6%
31,477	BUCHANAN	4,805	1,971	2,826	8	855 D	41.0%	58.8%	41.1%	58.9%
13,398	BUCKINGHAM	1,012	286	723	3	437 D	28.3%	71.4%	28.3%	71.7%
26,048	CAMPBELL	2,633	634	1,995	4	1,361 D	24.1%	75.8%	24.1%	75.9%
13,945	CAROLINE	1,391	383	1,004	4	621 D	27.5%	72.2%	27.6%	72.4%
25,904	CARROLL	3,729	2,352	1,375	2	977 R	63.1%	36.9%	63.1%	36.9%
4,275	CHARLES CITY	465	139	326		187 D	29.9%	70.1%	29.9%	70.1%
15,861	CHARLOTTE	1,830	356	1,473	1	1,117 D	19.5%	80.5%	19.5%	80.5%
31,183	CHESTERFIELD	3,772	901	2,860	11	1,959 D	23.9%	75.8%	24.0%	76.0%
7,159	CLARKE	1,236	415	816	5	401 D	33.6%	66.0%	33.7%	66.3%
3,769	CRAIG	892	327	564	1	237 D	36.7%	63.2%	36.7%	63.3%
13,365	CULPEPER	1,773	750	1,022	1	272 D	42.3%	57.6%	42.3%	57.7%
7,505	CUMBERLAND	685	218	463	4	245 D	31.8%	67.6%	32.0%	68.0%
21,266	DICKENSON	4,554	1,762	2,786	6	1,024 D	38.7%	61.2%	38.7%	61.3%
18,166	DINWIDDIE	1,377	279	1,096	2	817 D	20.3%	79.6%	20.3%	79.7%
32,283	ELIZABETH CITY COUNTY	3,704	1,128	2,563	13	1,435 D	30.5%	69.2%	30.6%	69.4%
7,006	ESSEX	689	179	508	2	329 D	26.0%	73.7%	26.1%	73.9%
40,929	FAIRFAX COUNTY	7,662	4,046	3,582	34	464 R	52.8%	46.8%	53.0%	47.0%
21,039	FAUQUIER	3,204	1,089	2,110	5	1,021 D	34.0%	65.9%	34.0%	66.0%
11,967	FLOYD	2,062	1,424	630	8	794 R	69.1%	30.6%	69.3%	30.7%
7,088	FLUVANNA	870	291	577	2	286 D	33.4%	66.3%	33.5%	66.5%
25,864	FRANKLIN COUNTY	3,224	1,206	2,002	16	796 D	37.4%	62.1%	37.6%	62.4%
14,008	FREDERICK	2,156	938	1,213	5	275 D	43.5%	56.3%	43.6%	56.4%
14,635	GILES	2,910	1,203	1,703	4	500 D	41.3%	58.5%	41.4%	58.6%
9,548	GLOUCESTER	1,349	410	934	5	524 D	30.4%	69.2%	30.5%	69.5%
8,454	GOOCHLAND	925	230	691	4	461 D	24.9%	74.7%	25.0%	75.0%
21,916	GRAYSON	5,914	3,298	2,607	9	691 R	55.8%	44.1%	55.9%	44.1%
5,218	GREENE	676	393	282	1	111 R	58.1%	41.7%	58.2%	41.8%
14,866	GREENSVILLE	1,237	279	954	4	675 D	22.6%	77.1%	22.6%	77.4%
41,271	HALIFAX	3,870	512	3,351	7	2,839 D	13.2%	86.6%	13.3%	86.7%
18,500	HANOVER	2,051	575	1,471	5	896 D	28.0%	71.7%	28.1%	71.9%
41,960	HENRICO	4,331	1,263	3,056	12	1,793 D	29.2%	70.6%	29.2%	70.8%
26,481	HENRY	2,270	727	1,538	5	811 D	32.0%	67.8%	32.1%	67.9%
4,875	HIGHLAND	1,176	641	535		106 R	54.5%	45.5%	54.5%	45.5%
13,381	ISLE OF WIGHT	1,608	430	1,178		748 D	26.7%	73.3%	26.7%	73.3%
4,907	JAMES CITY	478	161	317		156 D	33.7%	66.3%	33.7%	66.3%
6,954	KING AND QUEEN	529	166	363		197 D	31.4%	68.6%	31.4%	68.6%
5,431	KING GEORGE	690	340	348	2	8 D	49.3%	50.4%	49.4%	50.6%
7,855	KING WILLIAM	998	280	718		438 D	28.1%	71.9%	28.1%	71.9%
8,786	LANCASTER	1,061	390	666	5	276 D	36.8%	62.8%	36.9%	63.1%
39,296	LEE	8,399	3,921	4,470	8	549 D	46.7%	53.2%	46.7%	53.3%
20,291	LOUDOUN	3,294	1,485	1,802	7	317 D	45.1%	54.7%	45.2%	54.8%
13,665	LOUISA	1,572	634	930	8	296 D	40.3%	59.2%	40.5%	59.5%
13,844	LUNENBURG	1,393	184	1,205	4	1,021 D	13.2%	86.5%	13.2%	86.8%
8,465	MADISON	1,428	811	616	1	195 R	56.8%	43.1%	56.8%	43.2%
7,149	MATHEWS	1,107	491	615	1	124 D	44.4%	55.6%	44.4%	55.6%
31,933	MECKLENBURG	2,991	430	2,561		2,131 D	14.4%	85.6%	14.4%	85.6%
6,673	MIDDLESEX	816	186	627	3	441 D	22.8%	76.8%	22.9%	77.1%

VIRGINIA

PRESIDENT 1944

1940 Census Population	County	Total Vote	Republican	Democratic	Other	Rep.-Dem. Plurality	Percentage Total Vote Rep.	Percentage Total Vote Dem.	Percentage Major Vote Rep.	Percentage Major Vote Dem.
21,206	MONTGOMERY	3,607	1,936	1,652	19	284 R	53.7%	45.8%	54.0%	46.0%
22,771	NANSEMOND	1,749	351	1,398		1,047 D	20.1%	79.9%	20.1%	79.9%
16,241	NELSON	1,819	427	1,390	2	963 D	23.5%	76.4%	23.5%	76.5%
4,092	NEW KENT	487	158	329		171 D	32.4%	67.6%	32.4%	67.6%
35,828	NORFOLK COUNTY	7,011	1,527	5,467	17	3,940 D	21.8%	78.0%	21.8%	78.2%
17,597	NORTHAMPTON	1,493	381	1,108	4	727 D	25.5%	74.2%	25.6%	74.4%
10,463	NORTHUMBERLAND	1,221	525	695	1	170 D	43.0%	56.9%	43.0%	57.0%
15,556	NOTTOWAY	1,930	472	1,453	5	981 D	24.5%	75.3%	24.5%	75.5%
12,649	ORANGE	1,896	694	1,199	3	505 D	36.6%	63.2%	36.7%	63.3%
14,863	PAGE	4,234	2,574	1,653	7	921 R	60.8%	39.0%	60.9%	39.1%
16,613	PATRICK	2,096	706	1,383	7	677 D	33.7%	66.0%	33.8%	66.2%
61,697	PITTSYLVANIA	4,724	1,224	3,492	8	2,268 D	25.9%	73.9%	26.0%	74.0%
5,671	POWHATAN	694	230	461	3	231 D	33.1%	66.4%	33.3%	66.7%
14,922	PRINCE EDWARD	1,492	425	1,063	4	638 D	28.5%	71.2%	28.6%	71.4%
12,226	PRINCE GEORGE	1,098	301	796	1	495 D	27.4%	72.5%	27.4%	72.6%
17,738	PRINCE WILLIAM	2,108	763	1,340	5	577 D	36.2%	63.6%	36.3%	63.7%
19,984	PRINCESS ANNE	2,953	993	1,959	1	966 D	33.6%	66.3%	33.6%	66.4%
22,767	PULASKI	3,458	1,302	2,155	1	853 D	37.7%	62.3%	37.7%	62.3%
7,208	RAPPAHANNOCK	797	297	497	3	200 D	37.3%	62.4%	37.4%	62.6%
6,634	RICHMOND COUNTY	701	336	364	1	28 D	47.9%	51.9%	48.0%	52.0%
42,897	ROANOKE COUNTY	6,536	3,146	3,380	10	234 D	48.1%	51.7%	48.2%	51.8%
22,384	ROCKBRIDGE	2,608	961	1,638	9	677 D	36.8%	62.8%	37.0%	63.0%
31,289	ROCKINGHAM	5,839	3,714	2,104	21	1,610 R	63.6%	36.0%	63.8%	36.2%
26,627	RUSSELL	5,350	2,385	2,945	20	560 D	44.6%	55.0%	44.7%	55.3%
26,989	SCOTT	5,983	3,089	2,888	6	201 R	51.6%	48.3%	51.7%	48.3%
20,898	SHENANDOAH	5,485	3,517	1,962	6	1,555 R	64.1%	35.8%	64.2%	35.8%
28,861	SMYTH	4,999	2,726	2,266	7	460 R	54.5%	45.3%	54.6%	45.4%
26,442	SOUTHAMPTON	1,895	284	1,599	12	1,315 D	15.0%	84.4%	15.1%	84.9%
9,905	SPOTSYLVANIA	1,251	504	744	3	240 D	40.3%	59.5%	40.4%	59.6%
9,548	STAFFORD	1,418	714	698	6	16 R	50.4%	49.2%	50.6%	49.4%
6,193	SURRY	726	123	602	1	479 D	16.9%	82.9%	17.0%	83.0%
12,485	SUSSEX	980	201	773	6	572 D	20.5%	78.9%	20.6%	79.4%
41,607	TAZEWELL	5,128	2,271	2,832	25	561 D	44.3%	55.2%	44.5%	55.5%
11,352	WARREN	1,798	761	1,034	3	273 D	42.3%	57.5%	42.4%	57.6%
9,248	WARWICK	2,661	807	1,849	5	1,042 D	30.3%	69.5%	30.4%	69.6%
38,197	WASHINGTON	5,664	2,792	2,849	23	57 D	49.3%	50.3%	49.5%	50.5%
9,512	WESTMORELAND	1,344	532	808	4	276 D	39.6%	60.1%	39.7%	60.3%
52,458	WISE	6,420	1,817	4,588	15	2,771 D	28.3%	71.5%	28.4%	71.6%
22,721	WYTHE	3,287	1,822	1,465		357 R	55.4%	44.6%	55.4%	44.6%
8,857	YORK	1,096	318	760	18	442 D	29.0%	69.3%	29.5%	70.5%
	City									
33,523	ALEXANDRIA	7,823	3,405	4,391	27	986 D	43.5%	56.1%	43.7%	56.3%
9,768	BRISTOL	2,198	628	1,561	9	933 D	28.6%	71.0%	28.7%	71.3%
4,335	BUENA VISTA	582	179	402	1	223 D	30.8%	69.1%	30.8%	69.2%
19,400	CHARLOTTESVILLE	3,255	1,055	2,188	12	1,133 D	32.4%	67.2%	32.5%	67.5%
6,461	CLIFTON FORGE	1,502	415	1,082	5	667 D	27.6%	72.0%	27.7%	72.3%
32,749	DANVILLE	4,366	1,231	3,121	14	1,890 D	28.2%	71.5%	28.3%	71.7%
10,066	FREDERICKSBURG	1,793	698	1,092	3	394 D	38.9%	60.9%	39.0%	61.0%
5,898	HAMPTON	1,287	297	987	3	690 D	23.1%	76.7%	23.1%	76.9%
8,768	HARRISONBURG	2,602	1,302	1,292	8	10 R	50.0%	49.7%	50.2%	49.8%
8,679	HOPEWELL	1,657	368	1,284	5	916 D	22.2%	77.5%	22.3%	77.7%
44,541	LYNCHBURG	6,713	2,396	4,302	15	1,906 D	35.7%	64.1%	35.8%	64.2%
10,080	MARTINSVILLE	1,553	458	1,093	2	635 D	29.5%	70.4%	29.5%	70.5%
37,067	NEWPORT NEWS	5,309	1,237	4,051	21	2,814 D	23.3%	76.3%	23.4%	76.6%
144,332	NORFOLK CITY	16,996	4,958	12,010	28	7,052 D	29.2%	70.7%	29.2%	70.8%
30,631	PETERSBURG	2,981	719	2,256	6	1,537 D	24.1%	75.7%	24.2%	75.8%

VIRGINIA

PRESIDENT 1944

1940 Census Population	City	Total Vote	Republican	Democratic	Other	Rep.-Dem. Plurality	Percentage Total Vote Rep.	Percentage Total Vote Dem.	Percentage Major Vote Rep.	Percentage Major Vote Dem.
50,745	PORTSMOUTH	6,877	1,129	5,735	13	4,606 D	16.4%	83.4%	16.4%	83.6%
6,990	RADFORD	1,423	597	824	2	227 D	42.0%	57.9%	42.0%	58.0%
193,042	RICHMOND CITY	31,387	8,737	22,584	66	13,847 D	27.8%	72.0%	27.9%	72.1%
69,287	ROANOKE CITY	12,451	5,095	7,322	34	2,227 D	40.9%	58.8%	41.0%	59.0%
8,038	SOUTH NORFOLK	1,168	241	924	3	683 D	20.6%	79.1%	20.7%	79.3%
13,337	STAUNTON	2,012	847	1,159	6	312 D	42.1%	57.6%	42.2%	57.8%
11,343	SUFFOLK	1,914	569	1,342	3	773 D	29.7%	70.1%	29.8%	70.2%
3,942	WILLIAMSBURG	671	211	454	6	243 D	31.4%	67.7%	31.7%	68.3%
12,095	WINCHESTER	2,102	1,095	1,000	7	95 R	52.1%	47.6%	52.3%	47.7%
2,677,773	TOTAL	388,485	145,243	242,276	966	97,033 D	37.4%	62.4%	37.5%	62.5%

VIRGINIA

PRESIDENT 1940

1940 Census Population	County	Total Vote	Republican	Democratic	Other	Rep.-Dem. Plurality	Percentage			
							Total Vote		Major Vote	
							Rep.	Dem.	Rep.	Dem.
33,030	ACCOMACK	2,366	882	1,476	8	594 D	37.3%	62.4%	37.4%	62.6%
24,652	ALBEMARLE	2,458	804	1,648	6	844 D	32.7%	67.0%	32.8%	67.2%
22,688	ALLEGHANY	3,329	1,164	2,153	12	989 D	35.0%	64.7%	35.1%	64.9%
8,495	AMELIA	831	267	562	2	295 D	32.1%	67.6%	32.2%	67.8%
20,273	AMHERST	2,347	292	2,048	7	1,756 D	12.4%	87.3%	12.5%	87.5%
9,020	APPOMATTOX	1,363	215	1,144	4	929 D	15.8%	83.9%	15.8%	84.2%
57,040	ARLINGTON	9,862	4,365	5,440	57	1,075 D	44.3%	55.2%	44.5%	55.5%
42,772	AUGUSTA	4,564	1,768	2,774	22	1,006 D	38.7%	60.8%	38.9%	61.1%
7,191	BATH	1,163	527	630	6	103 D	45.3%	54.2%	45.5%	54.5%
29,687	BEDFORD COUNTY	3,340	791	2,535	14	1,744 D	23.7%	75.9%	23.8%	76.2%
6,731	BLAND	1,449	693	753	3	60 D	47.8%	52.0%	47.9%	52.1%
16,447	BOTETOURT	2,422	1,085	1,329	8	244 D	44.8%	54.9%	44.9%	55.1%
19,575	BRUNSWICK	1,456	164	1,288	4	1,124 D	11.3%	88.5%	11.3%	88.7%
31,477	BUCHANAN	3,848	1,291	2,554	3	1,263 D	33.5%	66.4%	33.6%	66.4%
13,398	BUCKINGHAM	1,123	289	829	5	540 D	25.7%	73.8%	25.8%	74.2%
26,048	CAMPBELL	2,819	456	2,358	5	1,902 D	16.2%	83.6%	16.2%	83.8%
13,945	CAROLINE	1,447	305	1,136	6	831 D	21.1%	78.5%	21.2%	78.8%
25,904	CARROLL	3,386	1,835	1,546	5	289 R	54.2%	45.7%	54.3%	45.7%
4,275	CHARLES CITY	330	92	238		146 D	27.9%	72.1%	27.9%	72.1%
15,861	CHARLOTTE	1,721	251	1,467	3	1,216 D	14.6%	85.2%	14.6%	85.4%
31,183	CHESTERFIELD	4,261	879	3,354	28	2,475 D	20.6%	78.7%	20.8%	79.2%
7,159	CLARKE	1,380	333	1,043	4	710 D	24.1%	75.6%	24.2%	75.8%
3,769	CRAIG	957	299	656	2	357 D	31.2%	68.5%	31.3%	68.7%
13,365	CULPEPER	1,794	579	1,208	7	629 D	32.3%	67.3%	32.4%	67.6%
7,505	CUMBERLAND	559	157	396	6	239 D	28.1%	70.8%	28.4%	71.6%
21,266	DICKENSON	4,343	1,785	2,551	7	766 D	41.1%	58.7%	41.2%	58.8%
18,166	DINWIDDIE	1,400	264	1,129	7	865 D	18.9%	80.6%	19.0%	81.0%
32,283	ELIZABETH CITY COUNTY	3,000	652	2,337	11	1,685 D	21.7%	77.9%	21.8%	78.2%
7,006	ESSEX	693	145	547	1	402 D	20.9%	78.9%	21.0%	79.0%
40,929	FAIRFAX COUNTY	5,660	2,371	3,263	26	892 D	41.9%	57.7%	42.1%	57.9%
21,039	FAUQUIER	2,637	756	1,874	7	1,118 D	28.7%	71.1%	28.7%	71.3%
11,967	FLOYD	2,214	1,482	729	3	753 R	66.9%	32.9%	67.0%	33.0%
7,088	FLUVANNA	821	241	579	1	338 D	29.4%	70.5%	29.4%	70.6%
25,864	FRANKLIN COUNTY	2,968	925	2,037	6	1,112 D	31.2%	68.6%	31.2%	68.8%
14,008	FREDERICK	2,406	773	1,631	2	858 D	32.1%	67.8%	32.2%	67.8%
14,635	GILES	2,744	1,024	1,716	4	692 D	37.3%	62.5%	37.4%	62.6%
9,548	GLOUCESTER	1,180	241	937	2	696 D	20.4%	79.4%	20.5%	79.5%
8,454	GOOCHLAND	1,004	180	820	4	640 D	17.9%	81.7%	18.0%	82.0%
21,916	GRAYSON	5,526	2,806	2,703	17	103 R	50.8%	48.9%	50.9%	49.1%
5,218	GREENE	645	282	363		81 D	43.7%	56.3%	43.7%	56.3%
14,866	GREENSVILLE	999	152	843	4	691 D	15.2%	84.4%	15.3%	84.7%
41,271	HALIFAX	3,826	373	3,441	12	3,068 D	9.7%	89.9%	9.8%	90.2%
18,500	HANOVER	1,719	364	1,347	8	983 D	21.2%	78.4%	21.3%	78.7%
41,960	HENRICO	6,027	2,005	3,993	29	1,988 D	33.3%	66.3%	33.4%	66.6%
26,481	HENRY	2,280	474	1,795	11	1,321 D	20.8%	78.7%	20.9%	79.1%
4,875	HIGHLAND	1,182	628	549	5	79 R	53.1%	46.4%	53.4%	46.6%
13,381	ISLE OF WIGHT	1,346	208	1,138		930 D	15.5%	84.5%	15.5%	84.5%
4,907	JAMES CITY	454	146	306	2	160 D	32.2%	67.4%	32.3%	67.7%
6,954	KING AND QUEEN	490	124	365	1	241 D	25.3%	74.5%	25.4%	74.6%
5,431	KING GEORGE	683	167	515	1	348 D	24.5%	75.4%	24.5%	75.5%
7,855	KING WILLIAM	932	235	697		462 D	25.2%	74.8%	25.2%	74.8%
8,786	LANCASTER	1,036	317	711	8	394 D	30.7%	68.8%	30.8%	69.2%
39,296	LEE	6,809	2,623	4,180	6	1,557 D	38.5%	61.3%	38.6%	61.4%
20,291	LOUDOUN	3,231	1,061	2,156	14	1,095 D	32.8%	66.7%	33.0%	67.0%
13,665	LOUISA	1,482	573	896	13	323 D	39.0%	60.9%	39.0%	61.0%
13,844	LUNENBURG	1,359	144	1,213	2	1,069 D	10.6%	89.1%	10.6%	89.4%
8,465	MADISON	1,342	646	692	4	46 D	48.1%	51.5%	48.3%	51.7%
7,149	MATHEWS	947	349	592	6	243 D	37.0%	62.7%	37.1%	62.9%
31,933	MECKLENBURG	2,713	308	2,402	3	2,094 D	11.4%	88.6%	11.4%	88.6%
6,673	MIDDLESEX	713	125	586	2	461 D	17.2%	80.5%	17.6%	82.4%

VIRGINIA

PRESIDENT 1940

1940 Census Population	County	Total Vote	Republican	Democratic	Other	Rep.-Dem. Plurality	Percentage: Total Vote Rep.	Percentage: Total Vote Dem.	Percentage: Major Vote Rep.	Percentage: Major Vote Dem.
21,206	MONTGOMERY	4,075	1,890	2,168	17	278 D	46.5%	53.4%	46.6%	53.4%
22,771	NANSEMOND	1,538	129	1,408	1	1,279 D	8.4%	91.6%	8.4%	91.6%
16,241	NELSON	1,626	330	1,291	5	961 D	20.4%	79.6%	20.4%	79.6%
4,092	NEW KENT	419	133	286		153 D	31.5%	67.8%	31.7%	68.3%
35,828	NORFOLK COUNTY	4,475	639	3,821	15	3,182 D	14.3%	85.6%	14.3%	85.7%
17,597	NORTHAMPTON	1,228	359	866	3	507 D	29.2%	70.5%	29.3%	70.7%
10,463	NORTHUMBERLAND	1,102	386	712	4	326 D	34.8%	64.2%	35.2%	64.8%
15,556	NOTTOWAY	1,674	373	1,290	11	917 D	22.3%	77.0%	22.4%	77.6%
12,649	ORANGE	1,759	464	1,283	12	819 D	26.4%	73.0%	26.6%	73.4%
14,863	PAGE	3,237	1,630	1,596	11	34 R	50.4%	49.4%	50.5%	49.5%
16,613	PATRICK	1,999	514	1,479	6	965 D	25.6%	73.6%	25.8%	74.2%
61,697	PITTSYLVANIA	4,455	728	3,710	17	2,982 D	16.4%	83.6%	16.4%	83.6%
5,671	POWHATAN	669	157	510	2	353 D	23.1%	75.1%	23.5%	76.5%
14,922	PRINCE EDWARD	1,435	313	1,110	12	797 D	21.9%	77.8%	22.0%	78.0%
12,226	PRINCE GEORGE	925	156	766	3	610 D	16.9%	82.8%	16.9%	83.1%
17,738	PRINCE WILLIAM	1,940	500	1,435	5	935 D	25.8%	73.9%	25.8%	74.2%
19,984	PRINCESS ANNE	2,137	445	1,689	3	1,244 D	20.8%	78.9%	20.9%	79.1%
22,767	PULASKI	3,255	1,023	2,226	6	1,203 D	31.5%	68.5%	31.5%	68.5%
7,208	RAPPAHANNOCK	816	225	588	3	363 D	27.4%	71.5%	27.7%	72.3%
6,634	RICHMOND COUNTY	741	257	475	9	218 D	33.0%	61.0%	35.1%	64.9%
42,897	ROANOKE COUNTY	5,888	2,302	3,539	47	1,237 D	39.3%	60.4%	39.4%	60.6%
22,384	ROCKBRIDGE	2,535	902	1,618	15	716 D	35.1%	62.9%	35.8%	64.2%
31,289	ROCKINGHAM	5,544	2,922	2,569	53	353 R	53.1%	46.7%	53.2%	46.8%
26,627	RUSSELL	5,200	2,080	3,109	11	1,029 D	40.0%	59.8%	40.1%	59.9%
26,989	SCOTT	5,464	2,982	2,474	8	508 R	54.5%	45.2%	54.7%	45.3%
20,898	SHENANDOAH	5,991	3,527	2,450	14	1,077 R	58.9%	40.9%	59.0%	41.0%
28,861	SMYTH	4,570	2,134	2,420	16	286 D	46.7%	53.0%	46.9%	53.1%
26,442	SOUTHAMPTON	1,733	213	1,508	12	1,295 D	12.3%	87.4%	12.4%	87.6%
9,905	SPOTSYLVANIA	1,154	365	785	4	420 D	31.7%	68.1%	31.7%	68.3%
9,548	STAFFORD	1,269	463	803	3	340 D	36.6%	63.4%	36.6%	63.4%
6,193	SURRY	778	120	658		538 D	15.4%	84.4%	15.4%	84.6%
12,485	SUSSEX	903	164	737	2	573 D	18.0%	81.1%	18.2%	81.8%
41,607	TAZEWELL	5,472	2,356	3,108	8	752 D	43.1%	56.8%	43.1%	56.9%
11,352	WARREN	1,833	491	1,338	4	847 D	26.4%	71.8%	26.8%	73.2%
9,248	WARWICK	1,373	305	1,065	3	760 D	22.2%	77.7%	22.3%	77.7%
38,197	WASHINGTON	5,976	2,697	3,245	34	548 D	45.4%	54.6%	45.4%	54.6%
9,512	WESTMORELAND	1,203	357	845	1	488 D	29.4%	69.6%	29.7%	70.3%
52,458	WISE	5,998	1,448	4,538	12	3,090 D	24.1%	75.6%	24.2%	75.8%
22,721	WYTHE	3,215	1,507	1,695	13	188 D	46.8%	52.7%	47.1%	52.9%
8,857	YORK	980	177	787	16	610 D	18.4%	81.6%	18.4%	81.6%
	City									
33,523	ALEXANDRIA	5,831	1,802	4,004	25	2,202 D	30.9%	68.7%	31.0%	69.0%
9,768	BRISTOL	1,904	423	1,465	16	1,042 D	22.2%	76.9%	22.4%	77.6%
4,335	BUENA VISTA	395	113	280	2	167 D	28.6%	70.9%	28.8%	71.2%
19,400	CHARLOTTESVILLE	2,515	743	1,759	13	1,016 D	29.5%	69.9%	29.7%	70.3%
6,461	CLIFTON FORGE	1,543	353	1,179	11	826 D	22.9%	76.4%	23.0%	77.0%
32,749	DANVILLE	4,141	787	3,324	30	2,537 D	19.0%	80.3%	19.1%	80.9%
10,066	FREDERICKSBURG	1,565	522	1,037	6	515 D	33.4%	66.3%	33.5%	66.5%
5,898	HAMPTON	1,194	215	975	4	760 D	18.0%	81.7%	18.1%	81.9%
8,768	HARRISONBURG	2,481	1,000	1,462	19	462 D	40.3%	58.9%	40.6%	59.4%
8,679	HOPEWELL	1,290	308	981	1	673 D	23.9%	76.0%	23.9%	76.1%
44,541	LYNCHBURG	6,631	1,966	4,656	9	2,690 D	29.6%	70.2%	29.7%	70.3%
10,080	MARTINSVILLE	1,254	269	980	5	711 D	21.5%	78.1%	21.5%	78.5%
37,067	NEWPORT NEWS	4,799	863	3,907	29	3,044 D	18.0%	81.4%	18.1%	81.9%
144,332	NORFOLK CITY	14,304	3,485	10,783	36	7,298 D	24.4%	75.4%	24.4%	75.6%
30,631	PETERSBURG	2,815	604	2,193	18	1,589 D	21.5%	77.9%	21.6%	78.4%

VIRGINIA

PRESIDENT 1940

1940 Census Population	City	Total Vote	Republican	Democratic	Other	Rep.-Dem. Plurality	Percentage Total Vote Rep.	Percentage Total Vote Dem.	Percentage Major Vote Rep.	Percentage Major Vote Dem.
50,745	PORTSMOUTH	5,753	675	5,053	25	4,378 D	11.7%	87.8%	11.8%	88.2%
6,990	RADFORD	1,216	417	793	6	376 D	34.3%	65.2%	34.5%	65.5%
193,042	RICHMOND CITY	25,439	6,031	19,332	76	13,301 D	23.7%	76.0%	23.8%	76.2%
69,287	ROANOKE CITY	10,542	3,553	6,942	47	3,389 D	33.7%	65.9%	33.9%	66.1%
8,038	SOUTH NORFOLK	1,076	156	920		764 D	14.5%	85.5%	14.5%	85.5%
13,337	STAUNTON	1,744	687	1,042	15	355 D	39.4%	59.7%	39.7%	60.3%
11,343	SUFFOLK	1,598	383	1,215		832 D	24.0%	76.0%	24.0%	76.0%
3,942	WILLIAMSBURG	541	168	367	6	199 D	31.1%	67.8%	31.4%	68.6%
12,095	WINCHESTER	2,067	945	1,114	8	169 D	45.7%	53.9%	45.9%	54.1%
2,677,773	TOTAL	346,608	109,363	235,961	1,284	126,598 D	31.6%	68.1%	31.7%	68.3%

VIRGINIA

PRESIDENT 1936

1930 Census Population	County	Total Vote	Republican	Democratic	Other	Rep.-Dem. Plurality	Percentage Total Vote Rep.	Percentage Total Vote Dem.	Percentage Major Vote Rep.	Percentage Major Vote Dem.
35,854	ACCOMACK	2,259	670	1,583	6	913 D	29.7%	70.1%	29.7%	70.3%
26,981	ALBEMARLE	2,467	635	1,825	7	1,190 D	25.7%	74.0%	25.8%	74.2%
20,188	ALLEGHANY	3,345	1,319	2,013	13	694 D	39.4%	60.2%	39.6%	60.4%
8,979	AMELIA	997	239	753	5	514 D	24.0%	75.5%	24.1%	75.9%
19,020	AMHERST	1,976	236	1,734	6	1,498 D	11.9%	87.8%	12.0%	88.0%
8,402	APPOMATTOX	1,587	204	1,375	8	1,171 D	12.9%	86.6%	12.9%	87.1%
26,615	ARLINGTON	7,835	2,825	4,971	39	2,146 D	36.1%	63.4%	36.2%	63.8%
38,163	AUGUSTA	4,571	1,668	2,872	31	1,204 D	36.5%	62.8%	36.7%	63.3%
8,137	BATH	1,130	514	614	2	100 D	45.5%	54.3%	45.6%	54.4%
29,091	BEDFORD COUNTY	2,906	619	2,276	11	1,657 D	21.3%	78.3%	21.4%	78.6%
6,031	BLAND	1,425	642	778	5	136 D	45.1%	54.6%	45.2%	54.8%
15,457	BOTETOURT	2,901	1,343	1,544	14	201 D	46.3%	53.2%	46.5%	53.5%
20,486	BRUNSWICK	1,365	60	1,303	2	1,243 D	4.4%	95.5%	4.4%	95.6%
16,740	BUCHANAN	2,699	808	1,886	5	1,078 D	29.9%	69.9%	30.0%	70.0%
13,315	BUCKINGHAM	1,220	273	945	2	672 D	22.4%	77.5%	22.4%	77.6%
22,885	CAMPBELL	2,363	370	1,987	6	1,617 D	15.7%	84.1%	15.7%	84.3%
15,263	CAROLINE	1,367	258	1,104	5	846 D	18.9%	80.8%	18.9%	81.1%
22,141	CARROLL	5,368	3,245	2,122	1	1,123 R	60.5%	39.5%	60.5%	39.5%
4,881	CHARLES CITY	312	79	233		154 D	25.3%	74.7%	25.3%	74.7%
16,061	CHARLOTTE	1,922	190	1,727	5	1,537 D	9.9%	89.9%	9.9%	90.1%
26,049	CHESTERFIELD	3,173	621	2,522	30	1,901 D	19.6%	79.5%	19.8%	80.2%
7,167	CLARKE	1,141	198	940	3	742 D	17.4%	82.4%	17.4%	82.6%
3,562	CRAIG	1,049	395	653	1	258 D	37.7%	62.2%	37.7%	62.3%
13,306	CULPEPER	1,824	551	1,266	7	715 D	30.2%	69.4%	30.3%	69.7%
7,535	CUMBERLAND	616	136	476	4	340 D	22.1%	77.3%	22.2%	77.8%
16,163	DICKENSON	3,830	1,146	2,683	1	1,537 D	29.9%	70.1%	29.9%	70.1%
18,492	DINWIDDIE	1,475	127	1,343	5	1,216 D	8.6%	91.1%	8.6%	91.4%
19,835	ELIZABETH CITY COUNTY	2,540	597	1,925	18	1,328 D	23.5%	75.8%	23.7%	76.3%
6,976	ESSEX	645	116	527	2	411 D	18.0%	81.7%	18.0%	82.0%
25,264	FAIRFAX COUNTY	4,527	1,584	2,913	30	1,329 D	35.0%	64.3%	35.2%	64.8%
21,071	FAUQUIER	2,672	629	2,037	6	1,408 D	23.5%	76.2%	23.6%	76.4%
11,698	FLOYD	2,273	1,566	699	8	867 R	68.9%	30.8%	69.1%	30.9%
7,466	FLUVANNA	808	217	586	5	369 D	26.9%	72.5%	27.0%	73.0%
24,337	FRANKLIN COUNTY	3,272	975	2,285	12	1,310 D	29.8%	69.8%	29.9%	70.1%
13,167	FREDERICK	2,058	665	1,386	7	721 D	32.3%	67.3%	32.4%	67.6%
12,804	GILES	2,596	1,047	1,547	2	500 D	40.3%	59.6%	40.4%	59.6%
11,019	GLOUCESTER	1,297	281	1,012	4	731 D	21.7%	78.0%	21.7%	78.3%
7,953	GOOCHLAND	870	228	638	4	410 D	26.2%	73.3%	26.3%	73.7%
20,017	GRAYSON	6,352	3,343	3,005	4	338 R	52.6%	47.3%	52.7%	47.3%
5,980	GREENE	663	321	341	1	20 D	48.4%	51.4%	48.5%	51.5%
13,388	GREENSVILLE	884		884		884 D		100.0%		100.0%
41,283	HALIFAX	4,642	302	4,331	9	4,029 D	6.5%	93.3%	6.5%	93.5%
17,009	HANOVER	1,736	327	1,397	12	1,070 D	18.8%	80.5%	19.0%	81.0%
30,310	HENRICO	4,919	1,285	3,610	24	2,325 D	26.1%	73.4%	26.3%	73.7%
20,088	HENRY	2,252	458	1,790	4	1,332 D	20.3%	79.5%	20.4%	79.6%
4,525	HIGHLAND	1,040	522	515	3	7 R	50.2%	49.5%	50.3%	49.7%
13,409	ISLE OF WIGHT	1,235	207	1,025	3	818 D	16.8%	83.0%	16.8%	83.2%
3,879	JAMES CITY	372	70	302		232 D	18.8%	81.2%	18.8%	81.2%
7,618	KING AND QUEEN	497	124	372	1	248 D	24.9%	74.8%	25.0%	75.0%
5,297	KING GEORGE	766	295	469	2	174 D	38.5%	61.2%	38.6%	61.4%
7,929	KING WILLIAM	910	211	696	3	485 D	23.2%	76.5%	23.3%	76.7%
8,896	LANCASTER	1,014	322	689	3	367 D	31.4%	67.3%	31.8%	68.2%
30,419	LEE	6,199	2,066	4,120	13	2,054 D	33.4%	66.5%	33.4%	66.6%
19,852	LOUDOUN	3,162	867	2,287	8	1,420 D	27.4%	72.2%	27.5%	72.5%
14,309	LOUISA	1,598	486	1,100	12	614 D	30.6%	69.3%	30.6%	69.4%
14,058	LUNENBURG	1,370	77	1,291	2	1,214 D	5.6%	94.3%	5.6%	94.4%
8,952	MADISON	1,467	662	804	1	142 D	45.0%	54.7%	45.2%	54.8%
7,884	MATHEWS	1,079	452	622	5	170 D	42.0%	57.8%	42.1%	57.9%
32,622	MECKLENBURG	2,934	202	2,730	2	2,528 D	6.9%	93.0%	6.9%	93.1%
7,273	MIDDLESEX	781	123	653	5	530 D	15.3%	81.1%	15.9%	84.1%

VIRGINIA

PRESIDENT 1936

1930 Census Population	County	Total Vote	Republican	Democratic	Other	Rep.-Dem. Plurality	Percentage Total Vote Rep.	Percentage Total Vote Dem.	Percentage Major Vote Rep.	Percentage Major Vote Dem.
19,605	MONTGOMERY	3,713	1,852	1,832	29	20 R	50.2%	49.7%	50.3%	49.7%
22,530	NANSEMOND	1,654	175	1,478	1	1,303 D	10.6%	89.4%	10.6%	89.4%
16,345	NELSON	1,577	370	1,204	3	834 D	23.5%	76.5%	23.5%	76.5%
4,300	NEW KENT	427	120	307		187 D	27.9%	71.4%	28.1%	71.9%
30,082	NORFOLK COUNTY	4,406	652	3,734	20	3,082 D	14.9%	85.1%	14.9%	85.1%
18,565	NORTHAMPTON	1,255	277	975	3	698 D	22.1%	77.9%	22.1%	77.9%
11,081	NORTHUMBERLAND	878	260	618		358 D	29.2%	69.5%	29.6%	70.4%
14,866	NOTTOWAY	1,568	260	1,297	11	1,037 D	16.6%	82.9%	16.7%	83.3%
12,070	ORANGE	1,636	402	1,227	7	825 D	24.6%	75.0%	24.7%	75.3%
14,852	PAGE	3,447	1,551	1,888	8	337 D	45.0%	54.8%	45.1%	54.9%
15,787	PATRICK	2,320	726	1,588	6	862 D	31.3%	68.5%	31.4%	68.6%
61,424	PITTSYLVANIA	4,255	556	3,694	5	3,138 D	13.1%	86.9%	13.1%	86.9%
6,143	POWHATAN	596	158	438		280 D	26.3%	73.0%	26.5%	73.5%
14,520	PRINCE EDWARD	1,410	253	1,153	4	900 D	18.0%	81.8%	18.0%	82.0%
10,311	PRINCE GEORGE	844	128	713	3	585 D	15.1%	84.1%	15.2%	84.8%
13,951	PRINCE WILLIAM	1,982	457	1,512	13	1,055 D	23.2%	76.6%	23.2%	76.8%
16,282	PRINCESS ANNE	2,368	436	1,925	7	1,489 D	18.4%	81.4%	18.5%	81.5%
20,566	PULASKI	3,521	1,180	2,337	4	1,157 D	33.5%	66.4%	33.6%	66.4%
7,717	RAPPAHANNOCK	928	241	686	1	445 D	26.0%	74.0%	26.0%	74.0%
6,878	RICHMOND COUNTY	668	217	451		234 D	31.0%	64.5%	32.5%	67.5%
35,289	ROANOKE COUNTY	5,558	2,105	3,422	31	1,317 D	38.0%	61.8%	38.1%	61.9%
20,902	ROCKBRIDGE	2,516	868	1,635	13	767 D	34.1%	64.2%	34.7%	65.3%
29,709	ROCKINGHAM	5,794	2,834	2,916	44	82 D	49.1%	50.6%	49.3%	50.7%
25,957	RUSSELL	4,760	1,599	3,143	18	1,544 D	33.7%	66.3%	33.7%	66.3%
24,181	SCOTT	4,168	2,046	2,122		76 D	48.9%	50.7%	49.1%	50.9%
20,655	SHENANDOAH	6,028	3,152	2,861	15	291 R	52.3%	47.4%	52.4%	47.6%
25,125	SMYTH	4,421	2,067	2,337	17	270 D	46.9%	53.0%	46.9%	53.1%
26,870	SOUTHAMPTON	1,826	148	1,673	5	1,525 D	8.1%	91.6%	8.1%	91.9%
10,056	SPOTSYLVANIA	1,294	453	836	5	383 D	35.1%	64.7%	35.1%	64.9%
8,050	STAFFORD	1,250	596	651	3	55 D	47.7%	52.1%	47.8%	52.2%
7,096	SURRY	804	87	715	2	628 D	10.8%	89.2%	10.8%	89.2%
12,100	SUSSEX	1,006	126	880		754 D	12.3%	85.6%	12.5%	87.5%
32,477	TAZEWELL	4,995	1,981	2,992	22	1,011 D	39.8%	60.1%	39.8%	60.2%
8,340	WARREN	1,604	426	1,174	4	748 D	26.4%	72.8%	26.6%	73.4%
8,829	WARWICK	1,075	200	870	5	670 D	18.7%	81.3%	18.7%	81.3%
33,850	WASHINGTON	4,654	2,047	2,595	12	548 D	44.1%	55.9%	44.1%	55.9%
8,497	WESTMORELAND	1,167	296	871		575 D	25.1%	73.8%	25.4%	74.6%
51,167	WISE	7,470	2,057	5,399	14	3,342 D	27.6%	72.3%	27.6%	72.4%
20,704	WYTHE	4,878	2,781	2,089	8	692 R	56.7%	42.6%	57.1%	42.9%
7,615	YORK	988	228	729	31	501 D	23.8%	76.2%	23.8%	76.2%
	City									
24,149	ALEXANDRIA	4,650	1,225	3,381	44	2,156 D	26.3%	72.7%	26.6%	73.4%
8,840	BRISTOL	1,682	311	1,364	7	1,053 D	18.5%	81.1%	18.6%	81.4%
4,002	BUENA VISTA	540	177	363		186 D	32.8%	67.2%	32.8%	67.2%
15,245	CHARLOTTESVILLE	1,742	335	1,393	14	1,058 D	19.2%	80.0%	19.4%	80.6%
6,839	CLIFTON FORGE	1,550	343	1,199	8	856 D	22.1%	77.4%	22.2%	77.8%
22,247	DANVILLE	3,845	549	3,266	30	2,717 D	14.3%	84.9%	14.4%	85.6%
6,819	FREDERICKSBURG	1,357	411	944	2	533 D	30.3%	69.6%	30.3%	69.7%
6,382	HAMPTON	1,162	190	971	1	781 D	16.4%	83.6%	16.4%	83.6%
7,232	HARRISONBURG	2,297	894	1,390	13	496 D	38.9%	60.5%	39.1%	60.9%
11,327	HOPEWELL	1,651	332	1,309	10	977 D	20.1%	79.3%	20.2%	79.8%
40,661	LYNCHBURG	5,092	1,373	3,697	22	2,324 D	27.0%	72.6%	27.1%	72.9%
7,705	MARTINSVILLE	1,208	255	949	4	694 D	21.1%	78.6%	21.2%	78.8%
34,417	NEWPORT NEWS	4,962	919	4,021	22	3,102 D	18.5%	81.0%	18.6%	81.4%
129,710	NORFOLK CITY	13,849	3,229	10,561	59	7,332 D	23.3%	76.3%	23.4%	76.6%
28,564	PETERSBURG	2,651	444	2,192	15	1,748 D	16.7%	82.7%	16.8%	83.2%

VIRGINIA

PRESIDENT 1936

1930 Census Population	City	Total Vote	Republican	Democratic	Other	Rep.-Dem. Plurality	Percentage Total Vote Rep.	Percentage Total Vote Dem.	Percentage Major Vote Rep.	Percentage Major Vote Dem.
45,704	PORTSMOUTH	6,509	861	5,617	31	4,756 D	13.2%	86.3%	13.3%	86.7%
6,227	RADFORD	1,078	421	650	7	229 D	39.1%	60.3%	39.3%	60.7%
182,929	RICHMOND CITY	23,348	4,478	18,784	86	14,306 D	19.2%	80.5%	19.3%	80.7%
69,206	ROANOKE CITY	10,504	3,363	7,087	54	3,724 D	32.0%	67.5%	32.2%	67.8%
7,857	SOUTH NORFOLK	1,002	172	823	7	651 D	17.2%	82.1%	17.3%	82.7%
11,990	STAUNTON	1,668	568	1,091	9	523 D	34.1%	65.4%	34.2%	65.8%
10,271	SUFFOLK	1,641	281	1,360		1,079 D	17.1%	82.9%	17.1%	82.9%
3,778	WILLIAMSBURG	489	96	389	4	293 D	19.6%	79.6%	19.8%	80.2%
10,855	WINCHESTER	1,851	743	1,096	12	353 D	40.1%	59.2%	40.4%	59.6%
2,421,851	TOTAL	334,590	98,336	234,980	1,274	136,644 D	29.4%	70.2%	29.5%	70.5%

VIRGINIA

PRESIDENT 1932

1930 Census Population	County	Total Vote	Republican	Democratic	Other	Rep.-Dem. Plurality	Percentage Total Vote Rep.	Percentage Total Vote Dem.	Percentage Major Vote Rep.	Percentage Major Vote Dem.
35,854	ACCOMACK	3,007	527	2,458	22	1,931 D	17.5%	81.7%	17.7%	82.3%
26,981	ALBEMARLE	2,491	508	1,949	34	1,441 D	20.4%	78.2%	20.7%	79.3%
20,188	ALLEGHANY	2,417	1,095	1,293	29	198 D	45.3%	53.5%	45.9%	54.1%
8,979	AMELIA	854	142	701	11	559 D	16.6%	82.1%	16.8%	83.2%
19,020	AMHERST	1,980	195	1,764	21	1,569 D	9.8%	89.1%	10.0%	90.0%
8,402	APPOMATTOX	1,337	204	1,123	10	919 D	15.3%	84.0%	15.4%	84.6%
26,615	ARLINGTON	6,234	2,806	3,285	143	479 D	45.0%	52.7%	46.1%	53.9%
38,163	AUGUSTA	4,237	1,541	2,606	90	1,065 D	36.4%	61.5%	37.2%	62.8%
8,137	BATH	992	384	594	14	210 D	38.7%	59.9%	39.3%	60.7%
29,091	BEDFORD COUNTY	2,831	469	2,321	41	1,852 D	16.6%	82.0%	16.8%	83.2%
6,031	BLAND	1,356	556	783	17	227 D	41.0%	57.7%	41.5%	58.5%
15,457	BOTETOURT	3,058	1,209	1,808	41	599 D	39.5%	59.1%	40.1%	59.9%
20,486	BRUNSWICK	1,424	52	1,361	11	1,309 D	3.7%	95.6%	3.7%	96.3%
16,740	BUCHANAN	2,103	727	1,372	4	645 D	34.6%	65.2%	34.6%	65.4%
13,315	BUCKINGHAM	1,090	204	870	16	666 D	18.7%	79.8%	19.0%	81.0%
22,885	CAMPBELL	2,021	301	1,692	28	1,391 D	14.9%	83.7%	15.1%	84.9%
15,263	CAROLINE	1,364	270	1,076	18	806 D	19.8%	78.9%	20.1%	79.9%
22,141	CARROLL	3,026	1,461	1,537	28	76 D	48.3%	50.8%	48.7%	51.3%
4,881	CHARLES CITY	335	85	245	5	160 D	25.4%	73.1%	25.8%	74.2%
16,061	CHARLOTTE	1,477	169	1,300	8	1,131 D	11.4%	88.0%	11.5%	88.5%
26,049	CHESTERFIELD	2,698	726	1,886	86	1,160 D	26.9%	69.9%	27.8%	72.2%
7,167	CLARKE	973	124	841	8	717 D	12.7%	86.4%	12.8%	87.2%
3,562	CRAIG	966	302	649	15	347 D	31.3%	67.2%	31.8%	68.2%
13,306	CULPEPER	1,782	417	1,349	16	932 D	23.4%	75.7%	23.6%	76.4%
7,535	CUMBERLAND	608	84	511	13	427 D	13.8%	84.0%	14.1%	85.9%
16,163	DICKENSON	3,878	1,228	2,635	15	1,407 D	31.7%	67.9%	31.8%	68.2%
18,492	DINWIDDIE	1,140	104	1,028	8	924 D	9.1%	90.2%	9.2%	90.8%
19,835	ELIZABETH CITY COUNTY	1,959	700	1,226	33	526 D	35.7%	62.6%	36.3%	63.7%
6,976	ESSEX	524	101	420	3	319 D	19.3%	80.2%	19.4%	80.6%
25,264	FAIRFAX COUNTY	4,154	1,368	2,714	72	1,346 D	32.9%	65.3%	33.5%	66.5%
21,071	FAUQUIER	2,396	379	1,999	18	1,620 D	15.8%	83.4%	15.9%	84.1%
11,698	FLOYD	1,752	1,051	699	2	352 R	60.0%	39.9%	60.1%	39.9%
7,466	FLUVANNA	768	176	579	13	403 D	22.9%	75.4%	23.3%	76.7%
24,337	FRANKLIN COUNTY	3,077	812	2,245	20	1,433 D	26.4%	73.0%	26.6%	73.4%
13,167	FREDERICK	2,016	456	1,536	24	1,080 D	22.6%	76.2%	22.9%	77.1%
12,804	GILES	2,802	1,016	1,754	32	738 D	36.3%	62.6%	36.7%	63.3%
11,019	GLOUCESTER	1,211	280	916	15	636 D	23.1%	75.6%	23.4%	76.6%
7,953	GOOCHLAND	810	166	629	15	463 D	20.5%	77.7%	20.9%	79.1%
20,017	GRAYSON	3,958	1,624	2,306	28	682 D	41.0%	58.3%	41.3%	58.7%
5,980	GREENE	652	258	394		136 D	39.6%	60.4%	39.6%	60.4%
13,388	GREENSVILLE	811	112	692	7	580 D	13.8%	85.3%	13.9%	86.1%
41,283	HALIFAX	3,901	275	3,583	43	3,308 D	7.0%	91.8%	7.1%	92.9%
17,009	HANOVER	1,332	238	1,073	21	835 D	17.9%	80.6%	18.2%	81.8%
30,310	HENRICO	3,875	1,291	2,458	126	1,167 D	33.3%	63.4%	34.4%	65.6%
20,088	HENRY	1,503	342	1,146	15	804 D	22.8%	76.2%	23.0%	77.0%
4,525	HIGHLAND	838	355	464	19	109 D	42.4%	55.4%	43.3%	56.7%
13,409	ISLE OF WIGHT	1,275	284	982	9	698 D	22.3%	77.0%	22.4%	77.6%
3,879	JAMES CITY	425	116	302	7	186 D	27.3%	71.1%	27.8%	72.2%
7,618	KING AND QUEEN	535	154	368	13	214 D	28.8%	68.8%	29.5%	70.5%
5,297	KING GEORGE	682	203	475	4	272 D	29.8%	69.6%	29.9%	70.1%
7,929	KING WILLIAM	804	177	612	15	435 D	22.0%	76.1%	22.4%	77.6%
8,896	LANCASTER	927	272	639	16	367 D	28.7%	67.3%	29.9%	70.1%
30,419	LEE	4,915	1,985	2,892	38	907 D	40.4%	58.9%	40.7%	59.3%
19,852	LOUDOUN	3,071	600	2,440	31	1,840 D	19.5%	79.3%	19.7%	80.3%
14,309	LOUISA	1,281	366	879	36	513 D	29.1%	69.8%	29.4%	70.6%
14,058	LUNENBURG	1,247	92	1,141	14	1,049 D	7.4%	91.9%	7.5%	92.5%
8,952	MADISON	1,380	522	849	9	327 D	37.7%	61.3%	38.1%	61.9%
7,884	MATHEWS	1,154	488	652	14	164 D	42.3%	56.5%	42.8%	57.2%
32,622	MECKLENBURG	2,478	275	2,188	15	1,913 D	11.1%	88.1%	11.2%	88.8%
7,273	MIDDLESEX	742	127	595	20	468 D	15.9%	74.4%	17.6%	82.4%

VIRGINIA

PRESIDENT 1932

1930 Census Population	County	Total Vote	Republican	Democratic	Other	Rep.-Dem. Plurality	Percentage Total Vote Rep.	Total Vote Dem.	Major Vote Rep.	Major Vote Dem.
19,605	MONTGOMERY	3,405	1,522	1,805	78	283 D	45.7%	54.1%	45.7%	54.3%
22,530	NANSEMOND	1,466	196	1,264	6	1,068 D	13.4%	86.3%	13.4%	86.6%
16,345	NELSON	1,702	238	1,457	7	1,219 D	14.0%	85.7%	14.0%	86.0%
4,300	NEW KENT	406	115	286	5	171 D	27.6%	68.8%	28.7%	71.3%
30,082	NORFOLK COUNTY	4,059	1,072	2,926	61	1,854 D	26.8%	73.0%	26.8%	73.2%
18,565	NORTHAMPTON	1,577	298	1,264	15	966 D	19.0%	80.5%	19.1%	80.9%
11,081	NORTHUMBERLAND	884	245	630	9	385 D	26.6%	68.4%	28.0%	72.0%
14,866	NOTTOWAY	1,671	277	1,348	46	1,071 D	17.0%	82.7%	17.0%	83.0%
12,070	ORANGE	1,567	309	1,253	5	944 D	19.2%	77.9%	19.8%	80.2%
14,852	PAGE	3,158	1,261	1,851	46	590 D	40.2%	59.0%	40.5%	59.5%
15,787	PATRICK	1,853	486	1,342	25	856 D	25.7%	71.1%	26.6%	73.4%
61,424	PITTSYLVANIA	3,840	656	3,124	60	2,468 D	17.3%	82.3%	17.4%	82.6%
6,143	POWHATAN	555	108	433	14	325 D	18.9%	75.7%	20.0%	80.0%
14,520	PRINCE EDWARD	1,197	196	970	31	774 D	16.7%	82.7%	16.8%	83.2%
10,311	PRINCE GEORGE	719	115	597	7	482 D	15.7%	81.7%	16.2%	83.8%
13,951	PRINCE WILLIAM	1,907	386	1,499	22	1,113 D	20.1%	78.2%	20.5%	79.5%
16,282	PRINCESS ANNE	1,902	432	1,451	19	1,019 D	22.6%	75.8%	22.9%	77.1%
20,566	PULASKI	3,454	1,109	2,314	31	1,205 D	32.3%	67.5%	32.4%	67.6%
7,717	RAPPAHANNOCK	720	124	590	6	466 D	17.2%	81.9%	17.4%	82.6%
6,878	RICHMOND COUNTY	659	192	461	6	269 D	27.1%	65.1%	29.4%	70.6%
35,289	ROANOKE COUNTY	4,268	1,704	2,509	55	805 D	40.0%	58.9%	40.4%	59.6%
20,902	ROCKBRIDGE	2,619	811	1,764	44	953 D	29.6%	64.4%	31.5%	68.5%
29,709	ROCKINGHAM	5,107	2,194	2,750	163	556 D	44.3%	55.5%	44.4%	55.6%
25,957	RUSSELL	4,671	1,386	3,274	11	1,888 D	29.5%	69.8%	29.7%	70.3%
24,181	SCOTT	3,841	1,673	2,137	31	464 D	43.1%	55.1%	43.9%	56.1%
20,655	SHENANDOAH	5,217	2,514	2,635	68	121 D	48.2%	50.5%	48.8%	51.2%
25,125	SMYTH	4,196	1,843	2,287	66	444 D	44.4%	55.1%	44.6%	55.4%
26,870	SOUTHAMPTON	1,557	182	1,357	18	1,175 D	11.7%	87.2%	11.8%	88.2%
10,056	SPOTSYLVANIA	1,147	346	784	17	438 D	30.5%	69.0%	30.6%	69.4%
8,050	STAFFORD	1,191	454	731	6	277 D	38.0%	61.2%	38.3%	61.7%
7,096	SURRY	736	73	653	10	580 D	9.9%	88.1%	10.1%	89.9%
12,100	SUSSEX	825	122	688	15	566 D	14.3%	80.6%	15.1%	84.9%
32,477	TAZEWELL	4,762	2,005	2,713	44	708 D	42.4%	57.4%	42.5%	57.5%
8,340	WARREN	1,472	367	1,096	9	729 D	24.0%	71.5%	25.1%	74.9%
8,829	WARWICK	900	242	645	13	403 D	27.2%	72.4%	27.3%	72.7%
33,850	WASHINGTON	4,627	1,774	2,784	69	1,010 D	38.9%	61.0%	38.9%	61.1%
8,497	WESTMORELAND	857	212	641	4	429 D	23.1%	70.0%	24.9%	75.1%
51,167	WISE	7,744	2,405	5,276	63	2,871 D	31.2%	68.4%	31.3%	68.7%
20,704	WYTHE	3,484	1,589	1,866	29	277 D	45.5%	53.4%	46.0%	54.0%
7,615	YORK	804	309	457	38	148 D	40.3%	59.7%	40.3%	59.7%
	City									
24,149	ALEXANDRIA	4,184	1,199	2,941	44	1,742 D	28.7%	70.3%	29.0%	71.0%
8,840	BRISTOL	1,583	307	1,252	24	945 D	19.4%	79.1%	19.7%	80.3%
4,002	BUENA VISTA	438	154	258	26	104 D	35.2%	58.9%	37.4%	62.6%
15,245	CHARLOTTESVILLE	1,704	409	1,287	8	878 D	24.0%	75.5%	24.1%	75.9%
6,839	CLIFTON FORGE	1,271	328	917	26	589 D	25.8%	72.1%	26.3%	73.7%
22,247	DANVILLE	3,084	740	2,264	80	1,524 D	24.0%	73.4%	24.6%	75.4%
6,819	FREDERICKSBURG	1,191	366	812	13	446 D	30.7%	68.2%	31.1%	68.9%
6,382	HAMPTON	1,084	294	772	18	478 D	27.1%	71.2%	27.6%	72.4%
7,232	HARRISONBURG	1,692	665	995	32	330 D	39.3%	58.8%	40.1%	59.9%
11,327	HOPEWELL	1,320	342	957	21	615 D	25.9%	72.5%	26.3%	73.7%
40,661	LYNCHBURG	4,936	1,200	3,656	80	2,456 D	24.3%	74.1%	24.7%	75.3%
7,705	MARTINSVILLE	958	212	739	7	527 D	22.1%	77.1%	22.3%	77.7%
34,417	NEWPORT NEWS	4,304	1,515	2,703	86	1,188 D	35.2%	62.8%	35.9%	64.1%
129,710	NORFOLK CITY	13,467	4,403	8,814	250	4,411 D	32.7%	65.4%	33.3%	66.7%
28,564	PETERSBURG	2,440	490	1,920	30	1,430 D	20.1%	78.7%	20.3%	79.7%

VIRGINIA

PRESIDENT 1932

1930 Census Population	City	Total Vote	Republican	Democratic	Other	Rep.-Dem. Plurality	Percentage Total Vote Rep.	Percentage Total Vote Dem.	Percentage Major Vote Rep.	Percentage Major Vote Dem.
45,704	PORTSMOUTH	5,294	1,840	3,344	110	1,504 D	34.8%	63.2%	35.5%	64.5%
6,227	RADFORD	909	341	542	26	201 D	37.5%	59.6%	38.6%	61.4%
182,929	RICHMOND CITY	20,681	5,602	14,631	448	9,029 D	27.1%	70.7%	27.7%	72.3%
69,206	ROANOKE CITY	9,540	3,195	6,215	130	3,020 D	33.5%	65.1%	34.0%	66.0%
7,857	SOUTH NORFOLK	945	329	597	19	268 D	34.8%	63.2%	35.5%	64.5%
11,990	STAUNTON	1,555	551	988	16	437 D	35.4%	63.5%	35.8%	64.2%
10,271	SUFFOLK	1,287	265	1,013	9	748 D	20.6%	78.7%	20.7%	79.3%
3,778	WILLIAMSBURG	505	99	387	19	288 D	19.6%	76.6%	20.4%	79.6%
10,855	WINCHESTER	1,910	698	1,179	33	481 D	36.5%	61.7%	37.2%	62.8%
2,421,851	TOTAL	297,942	89,637	203,979	4,326	114,342 D	30.1%	68.5%	30.5%	69.5%

VIRGINIA

PRESIDENT 1928

1920 Census Population	County	Total Vote	Republican	Democratic	Other	Rep.-Dem. Plurality	Total Vote Rep.	Total Vote Dem.	Major Vote Rep.	Major Vote Dem.
34,795	ACCOMACK	3,195	1,367	1,826	2	459 D	42.8%	57.2%	42.8%	57.2%
26,005	ALBEMARLE	2,419	846	1,571	2	725 D	35.0%	64.9%	35.0%	65.0%
15,332	ALLEGHANY	2,264	1,642	622		1,020 R	72.5%	27.5%	72.5%	27.5%
9,800	AMELIA	776	277	498	1	221 D	35.7%	64.2%	35.7%	64.3%
19,771	AMHERST	1,900	447	1,442	11	995 D	23.5%	75.9%	23.7%	76.3%
9,255	APPOMATTOX	1,334	446	885	3	439 D	33.4%	66.3%	33.5%	66.5%
16,040	ARLINGTON	5,744	4,274	1,444	26	2,830 R	74.4%	25.1%	74.7%	25.3%
34,671	AUGUSTA	4,198	2,679	1,507	12	1,172 R	63.8%	35.9%	64.0%	36.0%
6,389	BATH	1,144	731	409	4	322 R	63.9%	35.8%	64.1%	35.9%
30,669	BEDFORD COUNTY	2,562	1,118	1,436	8	318 D	43.6%	56.0%	43.8%	56.2%
5,593	BLAND	1,402	826	575	1	251 R	58.9%	41.0%	59.0%	41.0%
16,557	BOTETOURT	2,778	1,575	1,200	3	375 R	56.7%	43.2%	56.8%	43.2%
21,025	BRUNSWICK	1,168	245	922	1	677 D	21.0%	78.9%	21.0%	79.0%
15,441	BUCHANAN	2,707	1,333	1,365	9	32 D	49.2%	50.4%	49.4%	50.6%
14,885	BUCKINGHAM	1,178	579	599		20 D	49.2%	50.8%	49.2%	50.8%
26,716	CAMPBELL	1,776	801	967	8	166 D	45.1%	54.4%	45.3%	54.7%
15,954	CAROLINE	1,280	638	639	3	1 D	49.8%	49.9%	50.0%	50.0%
21,283	CARROLL	3,589	2,459	1,117	13	1,342 R	68.5%	31.1%	68.8%	31.2%
4,793	CHARLES CITY	312	207	105		102 R	66.3%	33.7%	66.3%	33.7%
17,540	CHARLOTTE	1,516	403	1,112	1	709 D	26.6%	73.4%	26.6%	73.4%
20,496	CHESTERFIELD	2,414	1,325	1,082	7	243 R	54.9%	44.8%	55.0%	45.0%
7,165	CLARKE	989	248	740	1	492 D	25.1%	74.8%	25.1%	74.9%
4,100	CRAIG	942	451	489	2	38 D	47.9%	51.9%	48.0%	52.0%
13,292	CULPEPER	1,590	753	836	1	83 D	47.4%	52.6%	47.4%	52.6%
9,111	CUMBERLAND	659	213	442	4	229 D	32.3%	67.1%	32.5%	67.5%
13,542	DICKENSON	3,754	1,868	1,879	7	11 D	49.8%	50.1%	49.9%	50.1%
17,949	DINWIDDIE	1,280	332	945	3	613 D	25.9%	73.8%	26.0%	74.0%
19,111	ELIZABETH CITY COUNTY	1,942	1,122	807	13	315 R	57.8%	41.6%	58.2%	41.8%
8,542	ESSEX	516	195	321		126 D	37.8%	62.2%	37.8%	62.2%
21,943	FAIRFAX COUNTY	3,743	2,507	1,229	7	1,278 R	67.0%	32.8%	67.1%	32.9%
21,869	FAUQUIER	2,506	972	1,531	3	559 D	38.8%	61.1%	38.8%	61.2%
13,115	FLOYD	1,915	1,481	433	1	1,048 R	77.3%	22.6%	77.4%	22.6%
8,547	FLUVANNA	778	327	447	4	120 D	42.0%	57.5%	42.2%	57.8%
26,283	FRANKLIN COUNTY	3,394	1,529	1,861	4	332 D	45.1%	54.8%	45.1%	54.9%
12,461	FREDERICK	2,151	1,006	1,140	5	134 D	46.8%	53.0%	46.9%	53.1%
11,901	GILES	2,614	1,313	1,293	8	20 R	50.2%	49.5%	50.4%	49.6%
11,894	GLOUCESTER	1,201	614	587		27 R	51.1%	48.9%	51.1%	48.9%
8,863	GOOCHLAND	754	318	431	5	113 D	42.2%	57.2%	42.5%	57.5%
19,816	GRAYSON	4,454	2,728	1,713	13	1,015 R	61.2%	38.5%	61.4%	38.6%
6,369	GREENE	683	423	259	1	164 R	61.9%	37.9%	62.0%	38.0%
11,606	GREENSVILLE	839	318	519	2	201 D	37.9%	61.9%	38.0%	62.0%
41,374	HALIFAX	3,845	1,091	2,742	12	1,651 D	28.4%	71.3%	28.5%	71.5%
18,088	HANOVER	1,423	592	831		239 D	41.6%	58.4%	41.6%	58.4%
18,972	HENRICO	3,261	1,887	1,349	25	538 R	57.9%	41.4%	58.3%	41.7%
20,238	HENRY	2,409	1,139	1,267	3	128 D	47.3%	52.6%	47.3%	52.7%
4,931	HIGHLAND	999	623	371	5	252 R	62.4%	37.1%	62.7%	37.3%
14,433	ISLE OF WIGHT	1,086	555	531		24 R	51.1%	48.9%	51.1%	48.9%
3,676	JAMES CITY	407	204	201	2	3 R	50.1%	49.4%	50.4%	49.6%
9,161	KING AND QUEEN	603	319	280	4	39 R	52.9%	46.4%	53.3%	46.7%
5,762	KING GEORGE	724	413	309	2	104 R	57.0%	42.7%	57.2%	42.8%
8,739	KING WILLIAM	764	329	431	4	102 D	43.1%	56.4%	43.3%	56.7%
9,757	LANCASTER	835	520	315		205 R	61.5%	37.2%	62.3%	37.7%
25,293	LEE	5,731	3,337	2,383	11	954 R	58.3%	41.6%	58.3%	41.7%
20,577	LOUDOUN	3,244	1,325	1,915	4	590 D	40.9%	59.1%	40.9%	59.1%
17,089	LOUISA	1,507	772	734	1	38 R	51.3%	48.7%	51.3%	48.7%
15,260	LUNENBURG	1,513	314	1,199		885 D	20.7%	79.1%	20.8%	79.2%
9,595	MADISON	1,355	772	580	3	192 R	57.1%	42.9%	57.1%	42.9%
8,447	MATHEWS	1,287	855	431	1	424 R	66.4%	33.5%	66.5%	33.5%
31,208	MECKLENBURG	2,537	784	1,752	1	968 D	30.9%	69.0%	30.9%	69.1%
8,157	MIDDLESEX	717	318	397	2	79 D	44.0%	55.0%	44.5%	55.5%

VIRGINIA

PRESIDENT 1928

1920 Census Population	County	Total Vote	Republican	Democratic	Other	Rep.-Dem. Plurality	Percentage Total Vote Rep.	Percentage Total Vote Dem.	Percentage Major Vote Rep.	Percentage Major Vote Dem.
18,595	MONTGOMERY	2,835	1,861	967	7	894 R	65.8%	34.2%	65.8%	34.2%
20,199	NANSEMOND	1,387	649	737	1	88 D	46.8%	53.1%	46.8%	53.2%
17,277	NELSON	1,835	618	1,216	1	598 D	33.7%	66.2%	33.7%	66.3%
4,541	NEW KENT	397	217	178	2	39 R	54.9%	45.1%	54.9%	45.1%
49,634	NORFOLK COUNTY	3,349	1,922	1,418	9	504 R	57.5%	42.4%	57.5%	42.5%
17,852	NORTHAMPTON	1,623	688	935		247 D	42.3%	57.5%	42.4%	57.6%
11,518	NORTHUMBERLAND	1,032	744	286	2	458 R	72.2%	27.7%	72.2%	27.8%
14,161	NOTTOWAY	1,654	667	986	1	319 D	40.4%	59.6%	40.4%	59.6%
13,320	ORANGE	1,578	732	846		114 D	46.4%	53.6%	46.4%	53.6%
14,770	PAGE	2,605	1,580	1,025		555 R	60.5%	39.3%	60.7%	39.3%
16,850	PATRICK	2,080	1,191	883	6	308 R	57.2%	42.4%	57.4%	42.6%
56,493	PITTSYLVANIA	4,293	2,598	1,688	7	910 R	60.6%	39.4%	60.6%	39.4%
6,552	POWHATAN	476	189	287		98 D	39.3%	59.7%	39.7%	60.3%
14,767	PRINCE EDWARD	1,198	494	699	5	205 D	41.3%	58.5%	41.4%	58.6%
12,915	PRINCE GEORGE	665	235	428	2	193 D	35.3%	64.4%	35.4%	64.6%
13,660	PRINCE WILLIAM	1,643	817	826		9 D	49.7%	50.3%	49.7%	50.3%
13,626	PRINCESS ANNE	1,883	1,040	841	2	199 R	55.3%	44.7%	55.3%	44.7%
17,111	PULASKI	3,819	1,998	1,821		177 R	52.3%	47.7%	52.3%	47.7%
8,070	RAPPAHANNOCK	842	329	513		184 D	39.1%	60.9%	39.1%	60.9%
7,434	RICHMOND COUNTY	759	467	292		175 R	61.4%	38.4%	61.5%	38.5%
22,395	ROANOKE COUNTY	3,961	2,675	1,284	2	1,391 R	67.4%	32.4%	67.6%	32.4%
20,626	ROCKBRIDGE	2,524	1,206	1,311	7	105 D	47.8%	51.9%	47.9%	52.1%
30,047	ROCKINGHAM	5,231	3,822	1,402	7	2,420 R	73.1%	26.8%	73.2%	26.8%
26,786	RUSSELL	4,520	2,006	2,511	3	505 D	44.4%	55.5%	44.4%	55.6%
24,776	SCOTT	5,275	2,916	2,355	4	561 R	55.1%	44.5%	55.3%	44.7%
20,808	SHENANDOAH	5,029	3,420	1,589	20	1,831 R	68.1%	31.6%	68.3%	31.7%
22,125	SMYTH	4,700	2,751	1,937	12	814 R	58.7%	41.3%	58.7%	41.3%
27,555	SOUTHAMPTON	1,493	648	844	1	196 D	43.4%	56.5%	43.4%	56.6%
10,571	SPOTSYLVANIA	1,094	654	439	1	215 R	59.7%	40.1%	59.8%	40.2%
8,104	STAFFORD	1,240	797	441	2	356 R	64.3%	35.6%	64.4%	35.6%
9,305	SURRY	700	157	541	2	384 D	22.5%	77.5%	22.5%	77.5%
12,834	SUSSEX	932	385	547		162 D	40.7%	57.8%	41.3%	58.7%
27,840	TAZEWELL	5,065	3,072	1,979	14	1,093 R	60.8%	39.2%	60.8%	39.2%
8,852	WARREN	1,276	564	710	2	146 D	43.7%	55.0%	44.3%	55.7%
11,417	WARWICK	765	465	298	2	167 R	60.9%	39.1%	60.9%	39.1%
32,376	WASHINGTON	6,132	3,449	2,666	17	783 R	56.4%	43.6%	56.4%	43.6%
10,240	WESTMORELAND	947	554	393		161 R	57.8%	41.0%	58.5%	41.5%
46,500	WISE	9,075	4,504	4,559	12	55 D	49.7%	50.3%	49.7%	50.3%
20,217	WYTHE	4,060	2,540	1,516	4	1,024 R	62.6%	37.4%	62.6%	37.4%
8,046	YORK	837	642	194	1	448 R	76.8%	23.2%	76.8%	23.2%
	City									
18,060	ALEXANDRIA	2,926	1,617	1,307	2	310 R	55.3%	44.7%	55.3%	44.7%
6,729	BRISTOL	1,556	630	922	4	292 D	40.5%	59.3%	40.6%	59.4%
3,911	BUENA VISTA	440	267	172	1	95 R	60.7%	39.1%	60.8%	39.2%
10,688	CHARLOTTESVILLE	1,703	708	992	3	284 D	41.6%	58.3%	41.6%	58.4%
6,164	CLIFTON FORGE	1,372	781	591		190 R	56.9%	43.1%	56.9%	43.1%
21,539	DANVILLE	3,561	2,360	1,196	5	1,164 R	66.3%	33.6%	66.4%	33.6%
5,882	FREDERICKSBURG	1,293	697	594	2	103 R	53.9%	45.9%	54.0%	46.0%
6,138	HAMPTON	1,160	544	615	1	71 D	46.9%	53.0%	46.9%	53.1%
5,875	HARRISONBURG	1,655	1,037	616	2	421 R	62.7%	37.2%	62.7%	37.3%
1,397	HOPEWELL	988	505	482	1	23 R	51.1%	48.8%	51.2%	48.8%
30,070	LYNCHBURG	4,717	2,730	1,987		743 R	57.9%	42.1%	57.9%	42.1%
35,596	NEWPORT NEWS	5,083	3,118	1,951	14	1,167 R	61.3%	38.4%	61.5%	38.5%
115,777	NORFOLK CITY	14,309	8,392	5,888	29	2,504 R	58.6%	41.1%	58.8%	41.2%
31,012	PETERSBURG	2,290	909	1,379	2	470 D	39.7%	60.2%	39.7%	60.3%
54,387	PORTSMOUTH	6,090	3,474	2,587	29	887 R	57.0%	42.5%	57.3%	42.7%

VIRGINIA

PRESIDENT 1928

1920 Census Population	City	Total Vote	Republican	Democratic	Other	Rep.-Dem. Plurality	Percentage Total Vote Rep.	Percentage Total Vote Dem.	Percentage Major Vote Rep.	Percentage Major Vote Dem.
4,627	RADFORD	899	524	373	2	151 R	58.3%	41.5%	58.4%	41.6%
171,667	RICHMOND CITY	21,029	10,767	10,213	49	554 R	51.2%	48.6%	51.3%	48.7%
50,842	ROANOKE CITY	10,501	6,471	4,018	12	2,453 R	61.6%	38.3%	61.7%	38.3%
7,724	SOUTH NORFOLK	1,023	865	158		707 R	84.6%	15.4%	84.6%	15.4%
10,623	STAUNTON	1,765	1,026	733	6	293 R	58.1%	41.5%	58.3%	41.7%
9,123	SUFFOLK	1,212	573	637	2	64 D	47.3%	52.6%	47.4%	52.6%
2,462	WILLIAMSBURG	408	98	310		212 D	24.0%	76.0%	24.0%	76.0%
6,883	WINCHESTER	1,968	1,168	794	6	374 R	59.3%	40.3%	59.5%	40.5%
2,309,187	TOTAL	305,364	164,609	140,146	609	24,463 R	53.9%	45.9%	54.0%	46.0%

VIRGINIA

PRESIDENT 1924

1920 Census Population	County	Total Vote	Republican	Democratic	Other	Rep.-Dem. Plurality	Total Vote Rep.	Total Vote Dem.	Major Vote Rep.	Major Vote Dem.
34,795	ACCOMACK	2,429	307	2,087	35	1,780 D	12.6%	85.9%	12.8%	87.2%
26,005	ALBEMARLE	1,802	366	1,383	53	1,017 D	20.3%	76.7%	20.9%	79.1%
15,332	ALLEGHANY	1,631	856	589	186	267 R	52.5%	36.1%	59.2%	40.8%
9,800	AMELIA	540	153	372	15	219 D	28.3%	68.9%	29.1%	70.9%
19,771	AMHERST	1,327	129	1,092	106	963 D	9.7%	82.3%	10.6%	89.4%
9,255	APPOMATTOX	1,073	101	952	20	851 D	9.4%	88.7%	9.6%	90.4%
16,040	ARLINGTON	2,921	1,307	1,209	405	98 R	44.7%	41.4%	51.9%	48.1%
34,671	AUGUSTA	3,265	1,265	1,920	80	655 D	38.7%	58.8%	39.7%	60.3%
6,389	BATH	835	407	404	24	3 R	48.7%	48.4%	50.2%	49.8%
30,669	BEDFORD COUNTY	2,274	432	1,811	31	1,379 D	19.0%	79.6%	19.3%	80.7%
5,593	BLAND	1,219	609	604	6	5 R	50.0%	49.5%	50.2%	49.8%
16,557	BOTETOURT	2,754	1,264	1,427	63	163 D	45.9%	51.8%	47.0%	53.0%
21,025	BRUNSWICK	982	65	887	30	822 D	6.6%	90.3%	6.8%	93.2%
15,441	BUCHANAN	1,966	1,080	870	16	210 R	54.9%	44.3%	55.4%	44.6%
14,885	BUCKINGHAM	851	213	623	15	410 D	25.0%	73.2%	25.5%	74.5%
26,716	CAMPBELL	1,983	372	1,468	143	1,096 D	18.8%	74.0%	20.2%	79.8%
15,954	CAROLINE	1,083	223	840	20	617 D	20.6%	77.6%	21.0%	79.0%
21,283	CARROLL	3,016	1,743	1,257	16	486 R	57.8%	41.7%	58.1%	41.9%
4,793	CHARLES CITY	232	82	141	9	59 D	35.3%	60.8%	36.8%	63.2%
17,540	CHARLOTTE	1,244	154	1,006	84	852 D	12.4%	80.9%	13.3%	86.7%
20,496	CHESTERFIELD	1,324	282	967	75	685 D	21.3%	73.0%	22.6%	77.4%
7,165	CLARKE	779	76	687	16	611 D	9.8%	88.2%	10.0%	90.0%
4,100	CRAIG	833	300	512	21	212 D	36.0%	61.5%	36.9%	63.1%
13,292	CULPEPER	1,108	190	876	42	686 D	17.1%	79.1%	17.8%	82.2%
9,111	CUMBERLAND	487	61	398	28	337 D	12.5%	81.7%	13.3%	86.7%
13,542	DICKENSON	3,047	1,294	1,618	135	324 D	42.5%	53.1%	44.4%	55.6%
17,949	DINWIDDIE	830	122	685	23	563 D	14.7%	82.5%	15.1%	84.9%
19,111	ELIZABETH CITY COUNTY	1,104	312	698	94	386 D	28.3%	63.2%	30.9%	69.1%
8,542	ESSEX	384	60	315	9	255 D	15.6%	82.0%	16.0%	84.0%
21,943	FAIRFAX COUNTY	2,550	765	1,586	199	821 D	30.0%	62.2%	32.5%	67.5%
21,869	FAUQUIER	1,713	345	1,277	91	932 D	20.1%	74.5%	21.3%	78.7%
13,115	FLOYD	1,513	984	515	14	469 R	65.0%	34.0%	65.6%	34.4%
8,547	FLUVANNA	617	136	452	29	316 D	22.0%	73.3%	23.1%	76.9%
26,283	FRANKLIN COUNTY	2,993	1,077	1,902	14	825 D	36.0%	63.5%	36.2%	63.8%
12,461	FREDERICK	1,827	484	1,314	29	830 D	26.5%	71.9%	26.9%	73.1%
11,901	GILES	2,230	852	1,319	59	467 D	38.2%	59.1%	39.2%	60.8%
11,894	GLOUCESTER	730	109	616	5	507 D	14.9%	84.4%	15.0%	85.0%
8,863	GOOCHLAND	598	164	394	40	230 D	27.4%	65.9%	29.4%	70.6%
19,816	GRAYSON	3,076	1,442	1,611	23	169 D	46.9%	52.4%	47.2%	52.8%
6,369	GREENE	535	240	285	10	45 D	44.9%	53.3%	45.7%	54.3%
11,606	GREENSVILLE	573	132	417	24	285 D	23.0%	72.8%	24.0%	76.0%
41,374	HALIFAX	2,665	374	2,245	46	1,871 D	14.0%	84.2%	14.3%	85.7%
18,088	HANOVER	905	135	732	38	597 D	14.9%	80.9%	15.6%	84.4%
18,972	HENRICO	1,605	416	1,052	137	636 D	25.9%	65.5%	28.3%	71.7%
20,238	HENRY	1,697	565	1,097	35	532 D	33.3%	64.6%	34.0%	66.0%
4,931	HIGHLAND	972	454	508	10	54 D	46.7%	52.3%	47.2%	52.8%
14,433	ISLE OF WIGHT	827	190	631	6	441 D	23.0%	76.3%	23.1%	76.9%
3,676	JAMES CITY	240	54	173	13	119 D	22.5%	72.1%	23.8%	76.2%
9,161	KING AND QUEEN	452	134	314	4	180 D	29.6%	69.5%	29.9%	70.1%
5,762	KING GEORGE	503	206	280	17	74 D	41.0%	55.7%	42.4%	57.6%
8,739	KING WILLIAM	533	148	372	13	224 D	27.8%	69.8%	28.5%	71.5%
9,757	LANCASTER	668	90	564	14	474 D	11.7%	73.4%	13.8%	86.2%
25,293	LEE	4,946	2,456	2,376	114	80 R	49.9%	48.3%	50.8%	49.2%
20,577	LOUDOUN	2,031	152	1,794	85	1,642 D	7.6%	89.6%	7.8%	92.2%
17,089	LOUISA	1,046	282	707	57	425 D	23.3%	58.5%	28.5%	71.5%
15,260	LUNENBURG	1,036	130	686	220	556 D	15.3%	80.6%	15.9%	84.1%
9,595	MADISON	971	347	589	35	242 D	36.7%	62.3%	37.1%	62.9%
8,447	MATHEWS	883	195	678	10	483 D	21.8%	75.8%	22.3%	77.7%
31,208	MECKLENBURG	1,956	286	1,649	21	1,363 D	14.7%	84.9%	14.8%	85.2%
8,157	MIDDLESEX	523	78	438	7	360 D	13.5%	75.6%	15.1%	84.9%

VIRGINIA

PRESIDENT 1924

1920 Census Population	County	Total Vote	Republican	Democratic	Other	Rep.-Dem. Plurality	Percentage Total Vote Rep.	Total Vote Dem.	Major Vote Rep.	Major Vote Dem.
18,595	MONTGOMERY	2,169	964	1,142	63	178 D	44.9%	53.2%	45.8%	54.2%
20,199	NANSEMOND	652	99	539	14	440 D	15.2%	82.5%	15.5%	84.5%
17,277	NELSON	1,431	350	1,042	39	692 D	24.9%	74.1%	25.1%	74.9%
4,541	NEW KENT	279	86	178	15	92 D	28.5%	58.9%	32.6%	67.4%
49,634	NORFOLK COUNTY	1,369	289	1,000	80	711 D	22.2%	77.0%	22.4%	77.6%
17,852	NORTHAMPTON	1,159	180	941	38	761 D	15.9%	83.2%	16.1%	83.9%
11,518	NORTHUMBERLAND	729	130	589	10	459 D	15.1%	68.6%	18.1%	81.9%
14,161	NOTTOWAY	1,161	181	840	140	659 D	16.9%	78.2%	17.7%	82.3%
13,320	ORANGE	1,068	181	834	53	653 D	15.4%	71.2%	17.8%	82.2%
14,770	PAGE	2,057	885	1,015	157	130 D	46.3%	53.1%	46.6%	53.4%
16,850	PATRICK	1,932	783	1,138	11	355 D	38.5%	55.9%	40.8%	59.2%
56,493	PITTSYLVANIA	3,556	880	2,563	113	1,683 D	25.5%	74.2%	25.6%	74.4%
6,552	POWHATAN	368	110	247	11	137 D	30.1%	67.5%	30.8%	69.2%
14,767	PRINCE EDWARD	863	140	714	9	574 D	16.2%	82.4%	16.4%	83.6%
12,915	PRINCE GEORGE	381	90	279	12	189 D	22.5%	69.8%	24.4%	75.6%
13,660	PRINCE WILLIAM	1,170	269	847	54	578 D	22.2%	70.1%	24.1%	75.9%
13,626	PRINCESS ANNE	858	137	690	31	553 D	14.9%	75.0%	16.6%	83.4%
17,111	PULASKI	3,282	1,422	1,767	93	345 D	44.3%	55.0%	44.6%	55.4%
8,070	RAPPAHANNOCK	505	89	395	21	306 D	18.2%	80.6%	18.4%	81.6%
7,434	RICHMOND COUNTY	471	125	340	6	215 D	21.5%	58.4%	26.9%	73.1%
22,395	ROANOKE COUNTY	1,890	695	1,078	117	383 D	38.0%	58.9%	39.2%	60.8%
20,626	ROCKBRIDGE	2,132	680	1,394	58	714 D	31.1%	63.8%	32.8%	67.2%
30,047	ROCKINGHAM	4,133	1,982	2,041	110	59 D	48.4%	49.8%	49.3%	50.7%
26,786	RUSSELL	4,478	1,848	2,554	76	706 D	41.3%	57.1%	42.0%	58.0%
24,776	SCOTT	4,912	2,666	2,177	69	489 R	53.5%	43.7%	55.0%	45.0%
20,808	SHENANDOAH	4,537	2,214	2,186	137	28 R	49.9%	49.3%	50.3%	49.7%
22,125	SMYTH	4,172	2,232	1,907	33	325 R	52.9%	45.2%	53.9%	46.1%
27,555	SOUTHAMPTON	1,404	203	1,119	82	916 D	15.0%	82.6%	15.4%	84.6%
10,571	SPOTSYLVANIA	736	255	448	33	193 D	34.0%	59.8%	36.3%	63.7%
8,104	STAFFORD	929	433	450	46	17 D	46.8%	48.6%	49.0%	51.0%
9,305	SURRY	502	72	388	42	316 D	15.4%	82.9%	15.7%	84.3%
12,834	SUSSEX	747	132	607	8	475 D	13.0%	59.7%	17.9%	82.1%
27,840	TAZEWELL	5,477	2,631	2,568	278	63 R	50.2%	49.0%	50.6%	49.4%
8,852	WARREN	888	150	699	39	549 D	16.0%	74.4%	17.7%	82.3%
11,417	WARWICK	323	58	248	17	190 D	18.1%	77.5%	19.0%	81.0%
32,376	WASHINGTON	6,021	2,848	3,083	90	235 D	47.9%	51.9%	48.0%	52.0%
10,240	WESTMORELAND	655	157	484	14	327 D	11.3%	34.9%	24.5%	75.5%
46,500	WISE	8,224	3,322	4,157	745	835 D	44.1%	55.2%	44.4%	55.6%
20,217	WYTHE	3,946	1,996	1,899	51	97 R	51.0%	48.6%	51.2%	48.8%
8,046	YORK	395	75	305	15	230 D	19.7%	80.3%	19.7%	80.3%
	City									
18,060	ALEXANDRIA	1,960	556	1,136	268	580 D	28.4%	58.0%	32.9%	67.1%
6,729	BRISTOL	1,506	440	1,036	30	596 D	29.2%	68.8%	29.8%	70.2%
3,911	BUENA VISTA	392	149	235	8	86 D	38.0%	59.9%	38.8%	61.2%
10,688	CHARLOTTESVILLE	1,160	218	831	111	613 D	18.8%	71.6%	20.8%	79.2%
6,164	CLIFTON FORGE	953	225	447	281	222 D	23.6%	46.9%	33.5%	66.5%
21,539	DANVILLE	2,241	473	1,577	191	1,104 D	21.1%	70.4%	23.1%	76.9%
5,882	FREDERICKSBURG	809	223	558	28	335 D	27.6%	69.0%	28.6%	71.4%
6,138	HAMPTON	615	129	471	15	342 D	21.0%	76.6%	21.5%	78.5%
5,875	HARRISONBURG	1,270	631	624	15	7 R	49.7%	49.1%	50.3%	49.7%
1,397	HOPEWELL	491	206	277	8	71 D	42.0%	56.4%	42.7%	57.3%
30,070	LYNCHBURG	2,816	602	2,086	128	1,484 D	21.4%	74.1%	22.4%	77.6%
35,596	NEWPORT NEWS	2,783	917	1,574	292	657 D	33.0%	56.6%	36.8%	63.2%
115,777	NORFOLK CITY	7,924	2,447	5,061	416	2,614 D	30.9%	63.9%	32.6%	67.4%
31,012	PETERSBURG	1,595	228	1,331	36	1,103 D	14.3%	83.4%	14.6%	85.4%
54,387	PORTSMOUTH	3,433	624	2,206	603	1,582 D	18.2%	64.3%	22.0%	78.0%

VIRGINIA

PRESIDENT 1924

1920 Census Population	City	Total Vote	Republican	Democratic	Other	Rep.-Dem. Plurality	Percentage Total Vote Rep.	Percentage Total Vote Dem.	Percentage Major Vote Rep.	Percentage Major Vote Dem.
4,627	RADFORD	807	314	394	99	80 D	38.9%	48.8%	44.4%	55.6%
171,667	RICHMOND CITY	13,421	2,600	9,904	917	7,304 D	19.4%	73.8%	20.8%	79.2%
50,842	ROANOKE CITY	6,435	1,747	3,930	758	2,183 D	27.1%	61.1%	30.8%	69.2%
7,724	SOUTH NORFOLK	439	134	281	24	147 D	30.5%	64.0%	32.3%	67.7%
10,623	STAUNTON	1,609	549	1,022	38	473 D	34.1%	63.5%	34.9%	65.1%
9,123	SUFFOLK	760	179	557	24	378 D	23.6%	73.3%	24.3%	75.7%
2,462	WILLIAMSBURG	228	31	196	1	165 D	13.6%	86.0%	13.7%	86.3%
6,883	WINCHESTER	1,258	420	820	18	400 D	33.4%	65.2%	33.9%	66.1%
2,309,187	TOTAL	223,603	73,328	139,717	10,558	66,389 D	32.8%	62.5%	34.4%	65.6%

VIRGINIA

PRESIDENT 1920

1920 Census Population	County	Total Vote	Republican	Democratic	Other	Rep.-Dem. Plurality	Percentage Total Vote Rep.	Total Vote Dem.	Major Vote Rep.	Major Vote Dem.
34,795	ACCOMACK	2,480	409	2,026	45	1,617 D	16.5%	81.7%	16.8%	83.2%
26,005	ALBEMARLE	2,128	541	1,587		1,046 D	25.4%	74.6%	25.4%	74.6%
15,332	ALLEGHANY	1,417	736	663	18	73 R	51.9%	46.8%	52.6%	47.4%
9,800	AMELIA	574	179	389	6	210 D	31.2%	67.8%	31.5%	68.5%
19,771	AMHERST	1,270	168	1,094	8	926 D	13.2%	86.1%	13.3%	86.7%
9,255	APPOMATTOX	1,032	190	837	5	647 D	18.4%	81.1%	18.5%	81.5%
16,040	ARLINGTON	1,870	997	835	38	162 R	53.3%	44.7%	54.4%	45.6%
34,671	AUGUSTA	3,879	1,707	2,106	66	399 D	44.0%	54.3%	44.8%	55.2%
6,389	BATH	710	362	343	5	19 R	51.0%	48.3%	51.3%	48.7%
30,669	BEDFORD COUNTY	2,381	583	1,774	24	1,191 D	24.5%	74.5%	24.7%	75.3%
5,593	BLAND	881	478	403		75 R	54.3%	45.7%	54.3%	45.7%
16,557	BOTETOURT	2,574	1,240	1,331	3	91 D	48.2%	51.7%	48.2%	51.8%
21,025	BRUNSWICK	995	125	866	4	741 D	12.6%	87.0%	12.6%	87.4%
15,441	BUCHANAN	1,755	1,078	675	2	403 R	61.4%	38.5%	61.5%	38.5%
14,885	BUCKINGHAM	1,062	311	749	2	438 D	29.3%	70.5%	29.3%	70.7%
26,716	CAMPBELL	1,738	375	1,341	22	966 D	21.6%	77.2%	21.9%	78.1%
15,954	CAROLINE	984	308	665	11	357 D	31.3%	67.6%	31.7%	68.3%
21,283	CARROLL	3,791	2,520	1,265	6	1,255 R	66.5%	33.4%	66.6%	33.4%
4,793	CHARLES CITY	202	82	119	1	37 D	40.6%	58.9%	40.8%	59.2%
17,540	CHARLOTTE	1,634	364	1,266	4	902 D	22.3%	77.5%	22.3%	77.7%
20,496	CHESTERFIELD	1,279	302	964	13	662 D	23.6%	75.4%	23.9%	76.1%
7,165	CLARKE	976	154	774	48	620 D	15.8%	79.3%	16.6%	83.4%
4,100	CRAIG	699	315	381	3	66 D	45.1%	54.5%	45.3%	54.7%
13,292	CULPEPER	1,306	330	973	3	643 D	25.3%	74.5%	25.3%	74.7%
9,111	CUMBERLAND	531	114	413	4	299 D	21.5%	77.8%	21.6%	78.4%
13,542	DICKENSON	1,990	1,067	903	20	164 R	53.6%	45.4%	54.2%	45.8%
17,949	DINWIDDIE	824	186	636	2	450 D	22.6%	77.2%	22.6%	77.4%
19,111	ELIZABETH CITY COUNTY	1,148	439	675	34	236 D	38.2%	58.8%	39.4%	60.6%
8,542	ESSEX	420	101	319		218 D	24.0%	76.0%	24.0%	76.0%
21,943	FAIRFAX COUNTY	2,617	987	1,598	32	611 D	37.7%	61.1%	38.2%	61.8%
21,869	FAUQUIER	1,941	568	1,365	8	797 D	29.3%	70.3%	29.4%	70.6%
13,115	FLOYD	1,865	1,355	497	13	858 R	72.7%	26.6%	73.2%	26.8%
8,547	FLUVANNA	717	146	562	9	416 D	20.4%	78.4%	20.6%	79.4%
26,283	FRANKLIN COUNTY	3,151	1,381	1,765	5	384 D	43.8%	56.0%	43.9%	56.1%
12,461	FREDERICK	2,236	875	1,337	24	462 D	39.1%	59.8%	39.6%	60.4%
11,901	GILES	1,987	877	1,104	6	227 D	44.1%	55.6%	44.3%	55.7%
11,894	GLOUCESTER	969	283	677	9	394 D	29.2%	69.9%	29.5%	70.5%
8,863	GOOCHLAND	602	212	384	6	172 D	35.2%	63.8%	35.6%	64.4%
19,816	GRAYSON	3,934	2,153	1,781		372 R	54.7%	45.3%	54.7%	45.3%
6,369	GREENE	724	414	306	4	108 R	57.2%	42.3%	57.5%	42.5%
11,606	GREENSVILLE	538	111	424	3	313 D	20.6%	78.8%	20.7%	79.3%
41,374	HALIFAX	2,697	586	2,103	8	1,517 D	21.7%	78.0%	21.8%	78.2%
18,088	HANOVER	1,133	224	903	6	679 D	19.8%	79.7%	19.9%	80.1%
18,972	HENRICO	1,453	338	1,078	37	740 D	23.3%	74.2%	23.9%	76.1%
20,238	HENRY	1,585	698	871	16	173 D	44.0%	55.0%	44.5%	55.5%
4,931	HIGHLAND	857	474	379	4	95 R	55.3%	44.2%	55.6%	44.4%
14,433	ISLE OF WIGHT	1,005	245	759	1	514 D	24.4%	75.5%	24.4%	75.6%
3,676	JAMES CITY	271	61	207	3	146 D	22.5%	76.4%	22.8%	77.2%
9,161	KING AND QUEEN	528	181	347		166 D	34.3%	65.7%	34.3%	65.7%
5,762	KING GEORGE	503	253	249	1	4 R	50.3%	49.5%	50.4%	49.6%
8,739	KING WILLIAM	535	176	353	6	177 D	32.9%	66.0%	33.3%	66.7%
9,757	LANCASTER	546	138	404	4	266 D	25.1%	73.6%	25.5%	74.5%
25,293	LEE	3,761	2,162	1,592	7	570 R	57.2%	42.1%	57.6%	42.4%
20,577	LOUDOUN	2,506	757	1,720	29	963 D	30.5%	69.2%	30.6%	69.4%
17,089	LOUISA	1,003	312	684	7	372 D	31.0%	68.0%	31.3%	68.7%
15,260	LUNENBURG	1,036	208	818	10	610 D	20.1%	78.9%	20.3%	79.7%
9,595	MADISON	941	431	499	11	68 D	45.6%	52.7%	46.3%	53.7%
8,447	MATHEWS	856	216	624	16	408 D	25.5%	73.7%	25.7%	74.3%
31,208	MECKLENBURG	1,890	264	1,619	7	1,355 D	14.0%	85.9%	14.0%	86.0%
8,157	MIDDLESEX	609	170	438	1	268 D	26.7%	68.9%	28.0%	72.0%

VIRGINIA

PRESIDENT 1920

1920 Census Population	County	Total Vote	Republican	Democratic	Other	Rep.-Dem. Plurality	Percentage Total Vote Rep.	Percentage Total Vote Dem.	Percentage Major Vote Rep.	Percentage Major Vote Dem.
18,595	MONTGOMERY	2,157	1,160	969	28	191 R	54.4%	45.5%	54.5%	45.5%
20,199	NANSEMOND	933	243	690		447 D	26.0%	74.0%	26.0%	74.0%
17,277	NELSON	1,367	392	973	2	581 D	28.7%	71.3%	28.7%	71.3%
4,541	NEW KENT	299	109	190		81 D	35.6%	62.1%	36.5%	63.5%
57,358	NORFOLK COUNTY	2,672	813	1,824	35	1,011 D	30.8%	69.0%	30.8%	69.2%
17,852	NORTHAMPTON	1,178	217	954	7	737 D	18.4%	81.1%	18.5%	81.5%
11,518	NORTHUMBERLAND	763	221	536	6	315 D	29.2%	70.8%	29.2%	70.8%
14,161	NOTTOWAY	975	154	821		667 D	15.8%	84.1%	15.8%	84.2%
13,320	ORANGE	977	258	718	1	460 D	26.2%	72.8%	26.4%	73.6%
14,770	PAGE	1,982	1,126	846	10	280 R	57.0%	42.8%	57.1%	42.9%
16,850	PATRICK	2,387	1,230	1,154	3	76 R	51.2%	48.0%	51.6%	48.4%
56,493	PITTSYLVANIA	3,896	1,162	2,715	19	1,553 D	29.9%	70.0%	30.0%	70.0%
6,552	POWHATAN	406	140	263	3	123 D	34.6%	64.9%	34.7%	65.3%
14,767	PRINCE EDWARD	965	189	774	2	585 D	19.5%	80.0%	19.6%	80.4%
12,915	PRINCE GEORGE	506	127	375	4	248 D	25.2%	74.4%	25.3%	74.7%
13,660	PRINCE WILLIAM	1,182	393	786	3	393 D	33.1%	66.3%	33.3%	66.7%
13,626	PRINCESS ANNE	717	105	610	2	505 D	14.5%	84.5%	14.7%	85.3%
17,111	PULASKI	3,531	1,710	1,814	7	104 D	48.5%	51.4%	48.5%	51.5%
8,070	RAPPAHANNOCK	630	210	418	2	208 D	33.4%	66.6%	33.4%	66.6%
7,434	RICHMOND COUNTY	527	206	321		115 D	36.3%	56.5%	39.1%	60.9%
22,395	ROANOKE COUNTY	2,282	955	1,286	41	331 D	42.4%	57.1%	42.6%	57.4%
20,626	ROCKBRIDGE	2,432	1,054	1,365	13	311 D	42.6%	55.2%	43.6%	56.4%
30,047	ROCKINGHAM	4,588	2,464	2,068	56	396 R	54.3%	45.6%	54.4%	45.6%
26,786	RUSSELL	3,481	1,772	1,704	5	68 R	50.9%	48.9%	51.0%	49.0%
24,776	SCOTT	4,127	2,449	1,671	7	778 R	59.1%	40.3%	59.4%	40.6%
20,808	SHENANDOAH	4,787	2,683	2,077	27	606 R	56.2%	43.5%	56.4%	43.6%
22,125	SMYTH	3,414	1,883	1,516	15	367 R	55.1%	44.4%	55.4%	44.6%
27,555	SOUTHAMPTON	1,582	250	1,314	18	1,064 D	15.8%	83.3%	16.0%	84.0%
10,571	SPOTSYLVANIA	834	380	440	14	60 D	46.2%	53.5%	46.3%	53.7%
8,104	STAFFORD	1,060	599	459	2	140 R	56.5%	43.3%	56.6%	43.4%
9,305	SURRY	492	92	397	3	305 D	18.7%	80.7%	18.8%	81.2%
12,834	SUSSEX	717	166	548	3	382 D	23.0%	75.8%	23.2%	76.8%
27,840	TAZEWELL	4,187	2,408	1,770	9	638 R	57.3%	42.2%	57.6%	42.4%
8,852	WARREN	1,034	293	720	21	427 D	28.6%	70.2%	28.9%	71.1%
11,417	WARWICK	267	109	152	6	43 D	41.6%	58.0%	41.8%	58.2%
32,376	WASHINGTON	4,935	2,672	2,251	12	421 R	54.3%	45.7%	54.3%	45.7%
10,240	WESTMORELAND	530	133	396	1	263 D	23.8%	70.8%	25.1%	74.9%
46,500	WISE	5,853	3,236	2,587	30	649 R	55.4%	44.3%	55.6%	44.4%
20,217	WYTHE	3,582	2,104	1,465	13	639 R	58.9%	41.0%	59.0%	41.0%
8,046	YORK	377	92	281	4	189 D	24.7%	75.3%	24.7%	75.3%
	City									
18,060	ALEXANDRIA	2,379	921	1,417	41	496 D	38.7%	59.6%	39.4%	60.6%
6,729	BRISTOL	1,134	344	784	6	440 D	30.3%	69.1%	30.5%	69.5%
3,911	BUENA VISTA	417	154	262	1	108 D	36.9%	62.8%	37.0%	63.0%
10,688	CHARLOTTESVILLE	1,407	351	1,041	15	690 D	24.9%	74.0%	25.2%	74.8%
6,164	CLIFTON FORGE	1,033	274	727	32	453 D	26.5%	70.4%	27.4%	72.6%
21,539	DANVILLE	2,476	551	1,888	37	1,337 D	22.3%	76.3%	22.6%	77.4%
5,882	FREDERICKSBURG	893	299	581	13	282 D	33.5%	65.1%	34.0%	66.0%
6,138	HAMPTON	767	152	601	14	449 D	19.8%	78.4%	20.2%	79.8%
5,875	HARRISONBURG	1,307	704	594	9	110 R	53.9%	45.4%	54.2%	45.8%
1,397	HOPEWELL	139	41	97	1	56 D	29.5%	69.8%	29.7%	70.3%
30,070	LYNCHBURG	2,731	609	2,096	26	1,487 D	22.3%	76.7%	22.5%	77.5%
35,596	NEWPORT NEWS	3,203	1,450	1,703	50	253 D	45.3%	53.2%	46.0%	54.0%
115,777	NORFOLK CITY	8,417	2,386	5,953	78	3,567 D	28.3%	70.7%	28.6%	71.4%
31,012	PETERSBURG	2,566	485	2,072	9	1,587 D	18.9%	80.7%	19.0%	81.0%
54,387	PORTSMOUTH	4,348	1,061	3,228	59	2,167 D	24.4%	74.2%	24.7%	75.3%

VIRGINIA

PRESIDENT 1920

1920 Census Population	City	Total Vote	Republican	Democratic	Other	Rep.-Dem. Plurality	Percentage Total Vote Rep.	Percentage Total Vote Dem.	Percentage Major Vote Rep.	Percentage Major Vote Dem.
4,627	RADFORD	660	245	402	13	157 D	37.1%	60.9%	37.9%	62.1%
171,667	RICHMOND CITY	19,595	4,515	14,878	202	10,363 D	23.0%	75.9%	23.3%	76.7%
50,842	ROANOKE CITY	7,144	2,329	4,715	100	2,386 D	32.6%	66.0%	33.1%	66.9%
10,623	STAUNTON	1,645	705	931	9	226 D	42.9%	56.6%	43.1%	56.9%
9,123	SUFFOLK	1,074	302	761	11	459 D	28.1%	70.9%	28.4%	71.6%
2,462	WILLIAMSBURG	228	62	166		104 D	27.2%	72.8%	27.2%	72.8%
6,883	WINCHESTER	1,300	540	736	24	196 D	41.5%	56.6%	42.3%	57.7%
2,309,187	TOTAL	231,000	87,456	141,670	1,874	54,214 D	37.9%	61.3%	38.2%	61.8%

VIRGINIA

Under Virginia's local government system a number of urban areas are organized as cities independent of county authority. The number of these independent cities is subject to change and their boundaries alter from year to year. There were 22 independent cities voting in the 1920 election; 23 voting in the elections of 1924 and 1928; 24 voting in the elections of 1932, 1936, 1940 and 1944; 25 voting in the 1948 election; 29 voting in the 1952 election and 32 voting in the 1956 election. Only the cities and counties that voted in each Presidential election are carried in the tables. In 1921 South Norfolk city became independent from Norfolk county. In 1929 Martinsville city became independent from Henry county. In 1948 Waynesboro city became independent from Augusta county. In 1951 Colonial Heights city became independent from Chesterfield, Falls Chruch city became independent from Farifax county, Virginia Beach city became independent from Princess Anne county and Warwick city and county became the independent city of Warwick. In 1953 Covington city became independent from Alleghany county, Galax city was organized independent from parts of Carroll and Grayson counties and Norton city became independent from Wise county. Changes in the county population and population figures for the cities which became independent between decennial censuses is not available.

ELECTION NOTES

1956 Other vote was 42,964 Andrews (States Rights); 444 Hoopes (Socialist); 351 Hass (Socialist Labor). States Rights candidates carried Prince Edward county and ran second in others.

1952 Other vote was 1,160 Hass (Socialist Labor); 504 Hoopes (Socialist); 311 Hallinan (Progressive).

1948 Other vote was 43,393 Thurmond (States Rights); 2,047 Wallace (Progressive); 726 Thomas (Socialist); 234 Teichert (Socialist Labor). States Rights candidates carried Halifax county and ran second in others.

1944 Other vote was 459 Watson (Prohibition); 417 Thomas (Socialist); 90 Teichert (Socialist Labor).

1940 Other vote was 882 Babson (Prohibition); 282 Thomas (Socialist); 72 Browder (Communist); 48 Aiken (Socialist Labor).

1936 Other vote was 594 Colvin (Prohibition); 313 Thomas (Socialist); 233 Lemke (Union); 98 Browder (Communist); 36 Aiken (Socialist Labor).

1932 Other vote was 2,382 Thomas (Socialist); 1,843 Upshaw (Prohibition); 86 Foster (Communist); 15 Cox (Jobless).

1928 Other vote was 249 Thomas (Socialist); 181 Reynolds (Socialist Labor); 179 Foster (Communist).

1924 Other vote was 10,369 LaFollette (Progressive); 189 Johns (Socialist Labor).

1920 Other vote was 826 Watkins (Prohibition); 808 Debs (Socialist); 240 Christensen (Farmer-Labor).

WASHINGTON

POPULAR VOTE FOR PRESIDENT 1920 TO 1956

Year	Total Vote	Republican Vote	Republican Candidate	Democratic Vote	Democratic Candidate	Other Vote	Plurality	Percentage Total Vote Rep.	Percentage Total Vote Dem.	Percentage Major Vote Rep.	Percentage Major Vote Dem.
1956	1,150,889	620,430	Eisenhower, Dwight D.	523,002	Stevenson, Adlai E.	7,457	97,428 R	53.9%	45.4%	54.3%	45.7%
1952	1,102,708	599,107	Eisenhower, Dwight D.	492,845	Stevenson, Adlai E.	10,756	106,262 R	54.3%	44.7%	54.9%	45.1%
1948	905,058	386,314	Dewey, Thomas E.	476,165	Truman, Harry S.	42,579	89,851 D	42.7%	52.6%	44.8%	55.2%
1944	856,328	361,689	Dewey, Thomas E.	486,774	Roosevelt, Franklin D.	7,865	125,085 D	42.2%	56.8%	42.6%	57.4%
1940	793,833	322,123	Willkie, Wendell	462,145	Roosevelt, Franklin D.	9,565	140,022 D	40.6%	58.2%	41.1%	58.9%
1936	692,338	206,892	Landon, Alfred M.	459,579	Roosevelt, Franklin D.	25,867	252,687 D	29.9%	66.4%	31.0%	69.0%
1932	614,814	208,645	Hoover, Herbert C.	353,260	Roosevelt, Franklin D.	52,909	144,615 D	33.9%	57.5%	37.1%	62.9%
1928	500,840	335,844	Hoover, Herbert C.	156,772	Smith, Alfred E.	8,224	179,072 R	67.1%	31.3%	68.2%	31.8%
1924 **	421,549	220,224	Coolidge, Calvin	42,842	Davis, John W.	158,483	69,497 R	52.2%	10.2%	83.7%	16.3%
1920 **	398,715	223,137	Harding, Warren G.	84,298	Cox, James M.	91,280	138,839 R	56.0%	21.1%	72.6%	27.4%

In 1924 other vote was 150,727 Progressive; 5,991 American; 1,004 Socialist Labor and 761 Communist. In 1920 other vote was 77,246 Farmer-Labor; 8,913 Socialist; 3,800 Prohibition and 1,321 Socialist Labor.

ELECTORAL COLLEGE VOTE 1920 TO 1956

Year	Total	Republican	Democratic	Other
1956	9	9	—	—
1952	9	9	—	—
1948	8	—	8	—
1944	8	—	8	—
1940	8	—	8	—
1936	8	—	8	—
1932	8	—	8	—
1928	7	7	—	—
1924	7	7	—	—
1920	7	7	—	—

WASHINGTON

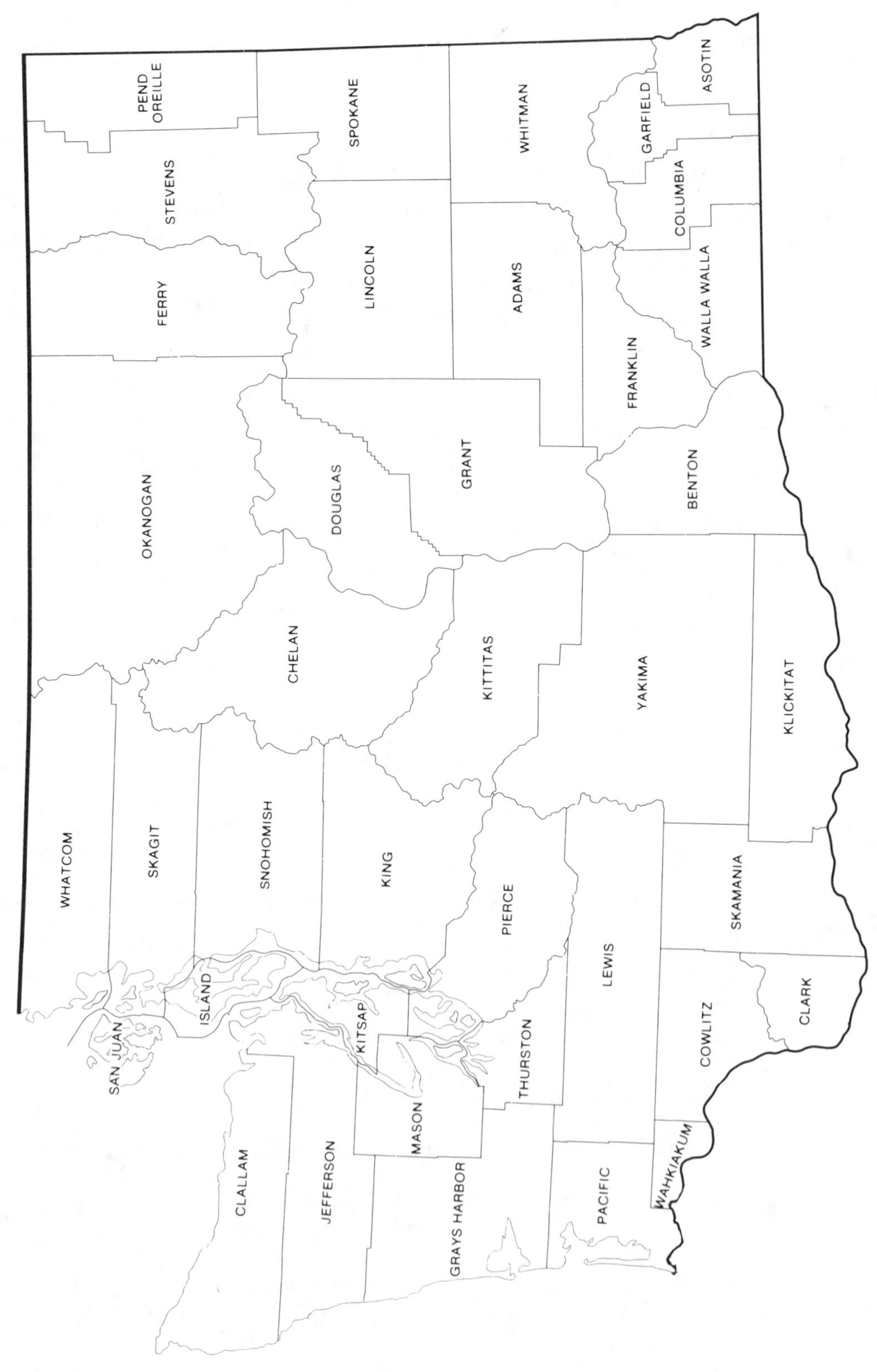
PEND OREILLE
SPOKANE
WHITMAN
ASOTIN
GARFIELD
STEVENS
COLUMBIA
LINCOLN
ADAMS
WALLA WALLA
FERRY
FRANKLIN
OKANOGAN
DOUGLAS
GRANT
BENTON
CHELAN
KITTITAS
YAKIMA
KLICKITAT
WHATCOM
SKAGIT
SNOHOMISH
KING
PIERCE
LEWIS
SKAMANIA
ISLAND
SAN JUAN
KITSAP
THURSTON
COWLITZ
CLARK
MASON
WAHKIAKUM
CLALLAM
JEFFERSON
GRAYS HARBOR
PACIFIC

WASHINGTON

PRESIDENT 1956

1950 Census Population	County	Total Vote	Republican	Democratic	Other	Rep.-Dem. Plurality	Percentage Total Vote Rep.	Total Vote Dem.	Major Vote Rep.	Major Vote Dem.
6,584	ADAMS	3,944	2,267	1,673	4	594 R	57.5%	42.4%	57.5%	42.5%
10,878	ASOTIN	5,200	2,608	2,586	6	22 R	50.2%	49.7%	50.2%	49.8%
51,370	BENTON	25,571	13,807	11,760	4	2,047 R	54.0%	46.0%	54.0%	46.0%
39,301	CHELAN	18,122	10,405	7,600	117	2,805 R	57.4%	41.9%	57.8%	42.2%
26,396	CLALLAM	12,500	6,852	5,632	16	1,220 R	54.8%	45.1%	54.9%	45.1%
85,307	CLARK	39,046	19,330	19,665	51	335 D	49.5%	50.4%	49.6%	50.4%
4,860	COLUMBIA	2,162	1,423	739		684 R	65.8%	34.2%	65.8%	34.2%
53,369	COWLITZ	24,410	11,912	12,448	50	536 D	48.8%	51.0%	48.9%	51.1%
10,817	DOUGLAS	5,645	2,602	3,034	9	432 D	46.1%	53.7%	46.2%	53.8%
4,096	FERRY	1,493	662	830	1	168 D	44.3%	55.6%	44.4%	55.6%
13,563	FRANKLIN	8,090	3,763	4,322	5	559 D	46.5%	53.4%	46.5%	53.5%
3,204	GARFIELD	1,606	966	639	1	327 R	60.1%	39.8%	60.2%	39.8%
24,346	GRANT	13,549	6,603	6,938	8	335 D	48.7%	51.2%	48.8%	51.2%
53,644	GRAYS HARBOR	24,514	11,599	12,858	57	1,259 D	47.3%	52.5%	47.4%	52.6%
11,079	ISLAND	5,222	3,196	2,009	17	1,187 R	61.2%	38.5%	61.4%	38.6%
11,618	JEFFERSON	4,057	2,300	1,750	7	550 R	56.7%	43.1%	56.8%	43.2%
732,992	KING	386,223	213,504	167,443	5,276	46,061 R	55.3%	43.4%	56.0%	44.0%
75,724	KITSAP	37,685	17,986	19,641	58	1,655 D	47.7%	52.1%	47.8%	52.2%
22,235	KITTITAS	8,830	5,097	3,726	7	1,371 R	57.7%	42.2%	57.8%	42.2%
12,049	KLICKITAT	5,379	2,794	2,577	8	217 R	51.9%	47.9%	52.0%	48.0%
43,755	LEWIS	19,688	11,949	7,714	25	4,235 R	60.7%	39.2%	60.8%	39.2%
10,970	LINCOLN	5,390	3,114	2,273	3	841 R	57.8%	42.2%	57.8%	42.2%
15,022	MASON	7,886	4,026	3,840	20	186 R	51.1%	48.7%	51.2%	48.8%
29,131	OKANOGAN	10,754	5,448	5,298	8	150 R	50.7%	49.3%	50.7%	49.3%
16,558	PACIFIC	7,635	3,799	3,824	12	25 D	49.8%	50.1%	49.8%	50.2%
7,413	PEND OREILLE	3,031	1,488	1,540	3	52 D	49.1%	50.8%	49.1%	50.9%
275,876	PIERCE	115,544	57,078	57,728	738	650 D	49.4%	50.0%	49.7%	50.3%
3,245	SAN JUAN	1,693	1,105	584	4	521 R	65.3%	34.5%	65.4%	34.6%
43,273	SKAGIT	21,440	12,149	9,243	48	2,906 R	56.7%	43.1%	56.8%	43.2%
4,788	SKAMANIA	2,209	1,014	1,193	2	179 D	45.9%	54.0%	45.9%	54.1%
111,580	SNOHOMISH	62,327	30,052	31,950	325	1,898 D	48.2%	51.3%	48.5%	51.5%
221,561	SPOKANE	109,287	60,335	48,833	119	11,502 R	55.2%	44.7%	55.3%	44.7%
18,580	STEVENS	8,322	4,499	3,808	15	691 R	54.1%	45.8%	54.2%	45.8%
44,884	THURSTON	24,009	14,093	9,897	19	4,196 R	58.7%	41.2%	58.7%	41.3%
3,835	WAHKIAKUM	1,767	808	953	6	145 D	45.7%	53.9%	45.9%	54.1%
40,135	WALLA WALLA	17,910	11,827	6,076	7	5,751 R	66.0%	33.9%	66.1%	33.9%
66,733	WHATCOM	32,191	17,414	14,533	244	2,881 R	54.1%	45.1%	54.5%	45.5%
32,469	WHITMAN	13,434	8,572	4,854	8	3,718 R	63.8%	36.1%	63.8%	36.2%
135,723	YAKIMA	53,124	31,984	20,991	149	10,993 R	60.2%	39.5%	60.4%	39.6%
2,378,963	TOTAL	1,150,889	620,430	523,002	7,457	97,428 R	53.9%	45.4%	54.3%	45.7%

WASHINGTON

PRESIDENT 1952

1950 Census Population	County	Total Vote	Republican	Democratic	Other	Rep.-Dem. Plurality	Percentage Total Vote Rep.	Total Vote Dem.	Major Vote Rep.	Major Vote Dem.
6,584	ADAMS	3,290	2,181	1,104	5	1,077 R	66.3%	33.6%	66.4%	33.6%
10,878	ASOTIN	4,894	2,722	2,160	12	562 R	55.6%	44.1%	55.8%	44.2%
51,370	BENTON	23,364	13,412	9,889	63	3,523 R	57.4%	42.3%	57.6%	42.4%
39,301	CHELAN	18,084	11,164	6,867	53	4,297 R	61.7%	38.0%	61.9%	38.1%
26,396	CLALLAM	11,938	6,442	5,390	106	1,052 R	54.0%	45.1%	54.4%	45.6%
85,307	CLARK	37,328	18,973	18,153	202	820 R	50.8%	48.6%	51.1%	48.9%
4,860	COLUMBIA	2,283	1,511	765	7	746 R	66.2%	33.5%	66.4%	33.6%
53,369	COWLITZ	23,746	12,366	11,242	138	1,124 R	52.1%	47.3%	52.4%	47.6%
10,817	DOUGLAS	5,329	2,954	2,361	14	593 R	55.4%	44.3%	55.6%	44.4%
4,096	FERRY	1,450	687	754	9	67 D	47.4%	52.0%	47.7%	52.3%
13,563	FRANKLIN	6,107	3,291	2,798	18	493 R	53.9%	45.8%	54.0%	46.0%
3,204	GARFIELD	1,733	1,157	559	17	598 R	66.8%	32.3%	67.4%	32.6%
24,346	GRANT	8,915	4,512	4,381	22	131 R	50.6%	49.1%	50.7%	49.3%
53,644	GRAYS HARBOR	24,683	12,168	12,317	198	149 D	49.3%	49.9%	49.7%	50.3%
11,079	ISLAND	4,703	2,901	1,772	30	1,129 R	61.7%	37.7%	62.1%	37.9%
11,618	JEFFERSON	4,305	2,355	1,933	17	422 R	54.7%	44.9%	54.9%	45.1%
732,992	KING	371,771	200,507	165,583	5,681	34,924 R	53.9%	44.5%	54.8%	45.2%
75,724	KITSAP	37,596	16,876	20,531	189	3,655 D	44.9%	54.6%	45.1%	54.9%
22,235	KITTITAS	9,174	5,201	3,937	36	1,264 R	56.7%	42.9%	56.9%	43.1%
12,049	KLICKITAT	5,011	2,845	2,140	26	705 R	56.8%	42.7%	57.1%	42.9%
43,755	LEWIS	19,571	12,287	7,115	169	5,172 R	62.8%	36.4%	63.3%	36.7%
10,970	LINCOLN	5,405	3,422	1,974	9	1,448 R	63.3%	36.5%	63.4%	36.6%
15,022	MASON	7,700	3,827	3,830	43	3 D	49.7%	49.7%	50.0%	50.0%
29,131	OKANOGAN	10,950	6,085	4,817	48	1,268 R	55.6%	44.0%	55.8%	44.2%
16,558	PACIFIC	7,663	3,846	3,778	39	68 R	50.2%	49.3%	50.4%	49.6%
7,413	PEND OREILLE	2,962	1,566	1,380	16	186 R	52.9%	46.6%	53.2%	46.8%
275,876	PIERCE	113,811	56,515	56,132	1,164	383 R	49.7%	49.3%	50.2%	49.8%
3,245	SAN JUAN	1,766	1,133	619	14	514 R	64.2%	35.1%	64.7%	35.3%
43,273	SKAGIT	19,952	11,446	8,321	185	3,125 R	57.4%	41.7%	57.9%	42.1%
4,788	SKAMANIA	2,050	1,072	978		94 R	52.3%	47.7%	52.3%	47.7%
111,580	SNOHOMISH	55,801	26,749	28,518	534	1,769 D	47.9%	51.1%	48.4%	51.6%
221,561	SPOKANE	103,236	56,958	45,827	451	11,131 R	55.2%	44.4%	55.4%	44.6%
18,580	STEVENS	7,885	4,458	3,355	72	1,103 R	56.5%	42.5%	57.1%	42.9%
44,884	THURSTON	23,840	13,904	9,764	172	4,140 R	58.3%	41.0%	58.7%	41.3%
3,835	WAHKIAKUM	1,760	815	928	17	113 D	46.3%	52.7%	46.8%	53.2%
40,135	WALLA WALLA	17,817	11,987	5,738	92	6,249 R	67.3%	32.2%	67.6%	32.4%
66,733	WHATCOM	30,828	17,590	12,877	361	4,713 R	57.1%	41.8%	57.7%	42.3%
32,469	WHITMAN	13,560	8,905	4,611	44	4,294 R	65.7%	34.0%	65.9%	34.1%
135,723	YAKIMA	50,447	32,317	17,647	483	14,670 R	64.1%	35.0%	64.7%	35.3%
2,378,963	TOTAL	1,102,708	599,107	492,845	10,756	106,262 R	54.3%	44.7%	54.9%	45.1%

WASHINGTON

PRESIDENT 1948

1940 Census Population	County	Total Vote	Republican	Democratic	Other	Rep.-Dem. Plurality	Percentage: Total Vote Rep.	Total Vote Dem.	Major Vote Rep.	Major Vote Dem.
6,209	ADAMS	2,683	1,394	1,267	22	127 R	52.0%	47.2%	52.4%	47.6%
8,365	ASOTIN	3,583	1,384	2,054	145	670 D	38.6%	57.3%	40.3%	59.7%
12,053	BENTON	14,467	5,852	8,458	157	2,606 D	40.5%	58.5%	40.9%	59.1%
34,412	CHELAN	15,351	7,392	7,702	257	310 D	48.2%	50.2%	49.0%	51.0%
21,848	CLALLAM	10,097	4,178	5,412	507	1,234 D	41.4%	53.6%	43.6%	56.4%
49,852	CLARK	30,132	11,546	17,154	1,432	5,608 D	38.3%	56.9%	40.2%	59.8%
5,549	COLUMBIA	2,112	1,062	1,015	35	47 R	50.3%	48.1%	51.1%	48.9%
40,155	COWLITZ	18,902	7,098	11,075	729	3,977 D	37.6%	58.6%	39.1%	60.9%
8,651	DOUGLAS	4,033	1,703	2,251	79	548 D	42.2%	55.8%	43.1%	56.9%
4,701	FERRY	1,340	473	824	43	351 D	35.3%	61.5%	36.5%	63.5%
6,307	FRANKLIN	4,130	1,541	2,525	64	984 D	37.3%	61.1%	37.9%	62.1%
3,383	GARFIELD	1,531	749	747	35	2 R	48.9%	48.8%	50.1%	49.9%
14,668	GRANT	6,277	2,081	4,067	129	1,986 D	33.2%	64.8%	33.8%	66.2%
53,166	GRAYS HARBOR	23,215	8,357	13,660	1,198	5,303 D	36.0%	58.8%	38.0%	62.0%
6,098	ISLAND	3,680	1,805	1,694	181	111 R	49.0%	46.0%	51.6%	48.4%
8,918	JEFFERSON	3,676	1,610	1,911	155	301 D	43.8%	52.0%	45.7%	54.3%
504,980	KING	291,635	131,039	143,295	17,301	12,256 D	44.9%	49.1%	47.8%	52.2%
44,387	KITSAP	30,678	9,869	19,538	1,271	9,669 D	32.2%	63.7%	33.6%	66.4%
20,230	KITTITAS	8,348	3,446	4,588	314	1,142 D	41.3%	55.0%	42.9%	57.1%
11,357	KLICKITAT	4,252	1,951	2,206	95	255 D	45.9%	51.9%	46.9%	53.1%
41,393	LEWIS	17,953	9,047	8,394	512	653 R	50.4%	46.8%	51.9%	48.1%
11,361	LINCOLN	4,924	2,348	2,518	58	170 D	47.7%	51.1%	48.3%	51.7%
11,603	MASON	6,501	2,524	3,613	364	1,089 D	38.8%	55.6%	41.1%	58.9%
24,546	OKANOGAN	9,935	4,083	5,644	208	1,561 D	41.1%	56.8%	42.0%	58.0%
15,928	PACIFIC	7,052	2,749	3,902	401	1,153 D	39.0%	55.3%	41.3%	58.7%
7,156	PEND OREILLE	2,567	1,009	1,465	93	456 D	39.3%	57.1%	40.8%	59.2%
182,081	PIERCE	90,786	34,396	50,674	5,716	16,278 D	37.9%	55.8%	40.4%	59.6%
3,157	SAN JUAN	1,575	881	636	58	245 R	55.9%	40.4%	58.1%	41.9%
37,650	SKAGIT	18,192	8,176	9,080	936	904 D	44.9%	49.9%	47.4%	52.6%
4,633	SKAMANIA	1,842	707	1,067	68	360 D	38.4%	57.9%	39.9%	60.1%
88,754	SNOHOMISH	46,260	17,018	25,924	3,318	8,906 D	36.8%	56.0%	39.6%	60.4%
164,652	SPOKANE	88,988	37,086	49,649	2,253	12,563 D	41.7%	55.8%	42.8%	57.2%
19,275	STEVENS	7,434	2,977	4,205	252	1,228 D	40.0%	56.6%	41.5%	58.5%
37,285	THURSTON	20,804	9,511	10,461	832	950 D	45.7%	50.3%	47.6%	52.4%
4,286	WAHKIAKUM	1,597	622	877	98	255 D	38.9%	54.9%	41.5%	58.5%
30,547	WALLA WALLA	15,378	7,993	7,102	283	891 R	52.0%	46.2%	53.0%	47.0%
60,355	WHATCOM	28,451	12,850	13,736	1,865	886 D	45.2%	48.3%	48.3%	51.7%
27,221	WHITMAN	12,740	6,411	6,015	314	396 R	50.3%	47.2%	51.6%	48.4%
99,019	YAKIMA	41,957	21,396	19,760	801	1,636 R	51.0%	47.1%	52.0%	48.0%
1,736,191	TOTAL	905,058	386,314	476,165	42,579	89,851 D	42.7%	52.6%	44.8%	55.2%

WASHINGTON

PRESIDENT 1944

1940 Census Population	County	Total Vote	Republican	Democratic	Other	Rep.-Dem. Plurality	Percentage Total Vote Rep.	Percentage Total Vote Dem.	Percentage Major Vote Rep.	Percentage Major Vote Dem.
6,209	ADAMS	2,740	1,666	1,062	12	604 R	60.8%	38.8%	61.1%	38.9%
8,365	ASOTIN	3,270	1,367	1,888	15	521 D	41.8%	57.7%	42.0%	58.0%
12,053	BENTON	8,172	3,905	4,233	34	328 D	47.8%	51.8%	48.0%	52.0%
34,412	CHELAN	13,713	7,081	6,557	75	524 R	51.6%	47.8%	51.9%	48.1%
21,848	CLALLAM	9,051	3,551	5,441	59	1,890 D	39.2%	60.1%	39.5%	60.5%
49,852	CLARK	31,549	12,312	18,861	376	6,549 D	39.0%	59.8%	39.5%	60.5%
5,549	COLUMBIA	2,270	1,211	1,039	20	172 R	53.3%	45.8%	53.8%	46.2%
40,155	COWLITZ	16,799	6,157	10,485	157	4,328 D	36.7%	62.4%	37.0%	63.0%
8,651	DOUGLAS	3,665	1,809	1,832	24	23 D	49.4%	50.0%	49.7%	50.3%
4,701	FERRY	1,315	518	792	5	274 D	39.4%	60.2%	39.5%	60.5%
6,307	FRANKLIN	3,371	1,381	1,974	16	593 D	41.0%	58.6%	41.2%	58.8%
3,383	GARFIELD	1,612	925	677	10	248 R	57.4%	42.0%	57.7%	42.3%
14,668	GRANT	3,902	1,530	2,354	18	824 D	39.2%	60.3%	39.4%	60.6%
53,166	GRAYS HARBOR	21,767	7,834	13,803	130	5,969 D	36.0%	63.4%	36.2%	63.8%
6,098	ISLAND	3,187	1,487	1,662	38	175 D	46.7%	52.1%	47.2%	52.8%
8,918	JEFFERSON	3,262	1,415	1,829	18	414 D	43.4%	56.1%	43.6%	56.4%
504,980	KING	286,604	118,719	165,308	2,577	46,589 D	41.4%	57.7%	41.8%	58.2%
44,387	KITSAP	35,491	11,224	24,016	251	12,792 D	31.6%	67.7%	31.9%	68.1%
20,230	KITTITAS	7,686	3,423	4,227	36	804 D	44.5%	55.0%	44.7%	55.3%
11,357	KLICKITAT	4,127	1,980	2,089	58	109 D	48.0%	50.6%	48.7%	51.3%
41,393	LEWIS	16,726	8,896	7,706	124	1,190 R	53.2%	46.1%	53.6%	46.4%
11,361	LINCOLN	5,066	2,723	2,328	15	395 R	53.8%	46.0%	53.9%	46.1%
11,603	MASON	5,397	1,976	3,379	42	1,403 D	36.6%	62.6%	36.9%	63.1%
24,546	OKANOGAN	8,764	4,084	4,642	38	558 D	46.6%	53.0%	46.8%	53.2%
15,928	PACIFIC	6,176	2,419	3,745	12	1,326 D	39.2%	60.6%	39.2%	60.8%
7,156	PEND OREILLE	2,452	1,052	1,385	15	333 D	42.9%	56.5%	43.2%	56.8%
182,081	PIERCE	86,370	31,626	53,269	1,475	21,643 D	36.6%	61.7%	37.3%	62.7%
3,157	SAN JUAN	1,354	703	644	7	59 R	51.9%	47.6%	52.2%	47.8%
37,650	SKAGIT	17,332	7,805	9,409	118	1,604 D	45.0%	54.3%	45.3%	54.7%
4,633	SKAMANIA	1,647	668	968	11	300 D	40.6%	58.8%	40.8%	59.2%
88,754	SNOHOMISH	43,130	15,182	27,345	603	12,163 D	35.2%	63.4%	35.7%	64.3%
164,652	SPOKANE	82,306	36,359	45,491	456	9,132 D	44.2%	55.3%	44.4%	55.6%
19,275	STEVENS	7,165	3,151	3,951	63	800 D	44.0%	55.1%	44.4%	55.6%
37,285	THURSTON	17,766	7,900	9,708	158	1,808 D	44.5%	54.6%	44.9%	55.1%
4,286	WAHKIAKUM	1,545	532	1,003	10	471 D	34.4%	64.9%	34.7%	65.3%
30,547	WALLA WALLA	13,235	7,364	5,793	78	1,571 R	55.6%	43.8%	56.0%	44.0%
60,355	WHATCOM	28,098	12,890	14,787	421	1,897 D	45.9%	52.6%	46.6%	53.4%
27,221	WHITMAN	11,490	6,000	5,449	41	551 R	52.2%	47.4%	52.4%	47.6%
99,019	YAKIMA	36,756	20,864	15,643	249	5,221 R	56.8%	42.6%	57.2%	42.8%
1,736,191	TOTAL	856,328	361,689	486,774	7,865	125,085 D	42.2%	56.8%	42.6%	57.4%

WASHINGTON

PRESIDENT 1940

1940 Census Population	County	Total Vote	Republican	Democratic	Other	Rep.-Dem. Plurality	Percentage Total Vote Rep.	Percentage Total Vote Dem.	Percentage Major Vote Rep.	Percentage Major Vote Dem.
6,209	ADAMS	2,918	1,508	1,397	13	111 R	51.7%	47.9%	51.9%	48.1%
8,365	ASOTIN	3,611	1,483	2,107	21	624 D	41.1%	58.3%	41.3%	58.7%
12,053	BENTON	5,139	2,670	2,414	55	256 R	52.0%	47.0%	52.5%	47.5%
34,412	CHELAN	15,273	8,019	7,181	73	838 R	52.5%	47.0%	52.8%	47.2%
21,848	CLALLAM	9,631	3,555	5,966	110	2,411 D	36.9%	61.9%	37.3%	62.7%
49,852	CLARK	21,925	8,776	12,931	218	4,155 D	40.0%	59.0%	40.4%	59.6%
5,549	COLUMBIA	2,685	1,461	1,218	6	243 R	54.4%	45.4%	54.5%	45.5%
40,155	COWLITZ	17,714	6,078	11,420	216	5,342 D	34.3%	64.5%	34.7%	65.3%
8,651	DOUGLAS	3,971	1,959	1,972	40	13 D	49.3%	49.7%	49.8%	50.2%
4,701	FERRY	1,849	590	1,247	12	657 D	31.9%	67.4%	32.1%	67.9%
6,307	FRANKLIN	2,983	1,084	1,868	31	784 D	36.3%	62.6%	36.7%	63.3%
3,383	GARFIELD	1,727	1,003	714	10	289 R	58.1%	41.3%	58.4%	41.6%
14,668	GRANT	5,601	1,487	4,097	17	2,610 D	26.5%	73.1%	26.6%	73.4%
53,166	GRAYS HARBOR	23,487	8,369	14,861	257	6,492 D	35.6%	63.3%	36.0%	64.0%
6,098	ISLAND	3,057	1,371	1,626	60	255 D	44.8%	53.2%	45.7%	54.3%
8,918	JEFFERSON	3,655	1,540	2,083	32	543 D	42.1%	57.0%	42.5%	57.5%
504,980	KING	241,803	95,504	143,134	3,165	47,630 D	39.5%	59.2%	40.0%	60.0%
44,387	KITSAP	19,596	5,525	13,861	210	8,336 D	28.2%	70.7%	28.5%	71.5%
20,230	KITTITAS	8,660	3,401	5,203	56	1,802 D	39.3%	60.1%	39.5%	60.5%
11,357	KLICKITAT	4,794	2,139	2,627	28	488 D	44.6%	54.8%	44.9%	55.1%
41,393	LEWIS	18,726	9,228	9,280	218	52 D	49.3%	49.6%	49.9%	50.1%
11,361	LINCOLN	5,552	2,627	2,896	29	269 D	47.3%	52.2%	47.6%	52.4%
11,603	MASON	5,346	1,775	3,465	106	1,690 D	33.2%	64.8%	33.9%	66.1%
24,546	OKANOGAN	9,655	4,244	5,362	49	1,118 D	44.0%	55.5%	44.2%	55.8%
15,928	PACIFIC	7,145	2,704	4,393	48	1,689 D	37.8%	61.5%	38.1%	61.9%
7,156	PEND OREILLE	3,097	1,268	1,812	17	544 D	40.9%	58.5%	41.2%	58.8%
182,081	PIERCE	80,311	27,188	51,670	1,453	24,482 D	33.9%	64.3%	34.5%	65.5%
3,157	SAN JUAN	1,675	808	860	7	52 D	48.2%	51.3%	48.4%	51.6%
37,650	SKAGIT	17,970	7,985	9,796	189	1,811 D	44.4%	54.5%	44.9%	55.1%
4,633	SKAMANIA	2,079	765	1,292	22	527 D	36.8%	62.1%	37.2%	62.8%
88,754	SNOHOMISH	40,585	13,638	26,185	762	12,547 D	33.6%	64.5%	34.2%	65.8%
164,652	SPOKANE	78,793	33,228	44,852	713	11,624 D	42.2%	56.9%	42.6%	57.4%
19,275	STEVENS	8,208	3,238	4,904	66	1,666 D	39.4%	59.7%	39.8%	60.2%
37,285	THURSTON	18,573	7,275	11,092	206	3,817 D	39.2%	59.7%	39.6%	60.4%
4,286	WAHKIAKUM	1,825	642	1,164	19	522 D	35.2%	63.8%	35.5%	64.5%
30,547	WALLA WALLA	13,821	7,883	5,875	63	2,008 R	57.0%	42.5%	57.3%	42.7%
60,355	WHATCOM	28,834	13,351	14,877	606	1,526 D	46.3%	51.6%	47.3%	52.7%
27,221	WHITMAN	12,799	6,356	6,351	92	5 R	49.7%	49.6%	50.0%	50.0%
99,019	YAKIMA	38,760	20,398	18,092	270	2,306 R	52.6%	46.7%	53.0%	47.0%
1,736,191	TOTAL	793,833	322,123	462,145	9,565	140,022 D	40.6%	58.2%	41.1%	58.9%

WASHINGTON

PRESIDENT 1936

1930 Census Population	County	Total Vote	Republican	Democratic	Other	Rep.-Dem. Plurality	Percentage Total Vote Rep.	Total Vote Dem.	Major Vote Rep.	Major Vote Dem.
7,719	ADAMS	2,661	657	1,944	60	1,287 D	24.7%	73.1%	25.3%	74.7%
8,136	ASOTIN	3,443	916	2,261	266	1,345 D	26.6%	65.7%	28.8%	71.2%
10,952	BENTON	4,527	1,610	2,402	515	792 D	35.6%	53.1%	40.1%	59.9%
31,634	CHELAN	13,486	4,975	8,030	481	3,055 D	36.9%	59.5%	38.3%	61.7%
20,449	CLALLAM	8,418	2,404	5,586	428	3,182 D	28.6%	66.4%	30.1%	69.9%
40,316	CLARK	18,554	4,868	12,714	972	7,846 D	26.2%	68.5%	27.7%	72.3%
5,325	COLUMBIA	2,412	807	1,391	214	584 D	33.5%	57.7%	36.7%	63.3%
31,906	COWLITZ	14,292	3,617	10,147	528	6,530 D	25.3%	71.0%	26.3%	73.7%
7,561	DOUGLAS	3,445	1,025	2,290	130	1,265 D	29.8%	66.5%	30.9%	69.1%
4,292	FERRY	1,516	320	1,130	66	810 D	21.1%	74.5%	22.1%	77.9%
6,137	FRANKLIN	2,594	622	1,784	188	1,162 D	24.0%	68.8%	25.9%	74.1%
3,662	GARFIELD	1,679	652	983	44	331 D	38.8%	58.5%	39.9%	60.1%
5,666	GRANT	5,328	694	4,560	74	3,866 D	13.0%	85.6%	13.2%	86.8%
59,982	GRAYS HARBOR	21,622	5,053	15,851	718	10,798 D	23.4%	73.3%	24.2%	75.8%
5,369	ISLAND	2,813	921	1,687	205	766 D	32.7%	60.0%	35.3%	64.7%
8,346	JEFFERSON	3,425	1,063	2,279	83	1,216 D	31.0%	66.5%	31.8%	68.2%
463,517	KING	210,045	66,544	138,597	4,904	72,053 D	31.7%	66.0%	32.4%	67.6%
30,776	KITSAP	16,347	3,440	12,414	493	8,974 D	21.0%	75.9%	21.7%	78.3%
18,154	KITTITAS	7,218	1,941	5,044	233	3,103 D	26.9%	69.9%	27.8%	72.2%
9,825	KLICKITAT	3,898	1,190	2,545	163	1,355 D	30.5%	65.3%	31.9%	68.1%
40,034	LEWIS	16,705	5,885	9,619	1,201	3,734 D	35.2%	57.6%	38.0%	62.0%
11,876	LINCOLN	5,069	1,325	3,627	117	2,302 D	26.1%	71.6%	26.8%	73.2%
10,060	MASON	4,398	1,015	3,087	296	2,072 D	23.1%	70.2%	24.7%	75.3%
18,519	OKANOGAN	8,667	2,367	5,622	678	3,255 D	27.3%	64.9%	29.6%	70.4%
14,970	PACIFIC	6,447	1,732	4,395	320	2,663 D	26.9%	68.2%	28.3%	71.7%
7,155	PEND OREILLE	2,875	813	1,903	159	1,090 D	28.3%	66.2%	29.9%	70.1%
163,842	PIERCE	69,891	18,331	48,988	2,572	30,657 D	26.2%	70.1%	27.2%	72.8%
3,097	SAN JUAN	1,595	690	775	130	85 D	43.3%	48.6%	47.1%	52.9%
35,142	SKAGIT	15,615	5,222	9,639	754	4,417 D	33.4%	61.7%	35.1%	64.9%
2,891	SKAMANIA	2,310	406	1,863	41	1,457 D	17.6%	80.6%	17.9%	82.1%
78,861	SNOHOMISH	35,569	8,882	25,081	1,606	16,199 D	25.0%	70.5%	26.2%	73.8%
150,477	SPOKANE	70,125	19,951	48,117	2,057	28,166 D	28.5%	68.6%	29.3%	70.7%
18,550	STEVENS	6,935	1,981	4,536	418	2,555 D	28.6%	65.4%	30.4%	69.6%
31,351	THURSTON	15,775	4,425	10,647	703	6,222 D	28.1%	67.5%	29.4%	70.6%
3,862	WAHKIAKUM	1,583	419	1,098	66	679 D	26.5%	69.4%	27.6%	72.4%
28,441	WALLA WALLA	11,670	4,584	6,562	524	1,978 D	39.3%	56.2%	41.1%	58.9%
59,128	WHATCOM	25,756	9,035	15,428	1,293	6,393 D	35.1%	59.9%	36.9%	63.1%
28,014	WHITMAN	11,973	3,955	7,753	265	3,798 D	33.0%	64.8%	33.8%	66.2%
77,402	YAKIMA	31,657	12,555	17,200	1,902	4,645 D	39.7%	54.3%	42.2%	57.8%
1,563,396	TOTAL	692,338	206,892	459,579	25,867	252,687 D	29.9%	66.4%	31.0%	69.0%

WASHINGTON

PRESIDENT 1932

1930 Census Population	County	Total Vote	Republican	Democratic	Other	Rep.-Dem. Plurality	Percentage Total Vote Rep.	Percentage Total Vote Dem.	Percentage Major Vote Rep.	Percentage Major Vote Dem.
7,719	ADAMS	2,430	867	1,504	59	637 D	35.7%	61.9%	36.6%	63.4%
8,136	ASOTIN	3,052	960	1,994	98	1,034 D	31.5%	65.3%	32.5%	67.5%
10,952	BENTON	4,597	1,694	2,633	270	939 D	36.9%	57.3%	39.1%	60.9%
31,634	CHELAN	13,859	5,584	7,316	959	1,732 D	40.3%	52.8%	43.3%	56.7%
20,449	CLALLAM	7,537	1,870	3,954	1,713	2,084 D	24.8%	52.5%	32.1%	67.9%
40,316	CLARK	15,160	4,901	9,104	1,155	4,203 D	32.3%	60.1%	35.0%	65.0%
5,325	COLUMBIA	2,298	714	1,491	93	777 D	31.1%	64.9%	32.4%	67.6%
31,906	COWLITZ	11,113	3,767	5,443	1,903	1,676 D	33.9%	49.0%	40.9%	59.1%
7,561	DOUGLAS	3,362	1,179	1,941	242	762 D	35.1%	57.7%	37.8%	62.2%
4,292	FERRY	1,445	322	1,035	88	713 D	22.3%	71.6%	23.7%	76.3%
6,137	FRANKLIN	2,473	838	1,540	95	702 D	33.9%	62.3%	35.2%	64.8%
3,662	GARFIELD	1,506	669	818	19	149 D	44.4%	54.3%	45.0%	55.0%
5,666	GRANT	2,410	840	1,376	194	536 D	34.9%	57.1%	37.9%	62.1%
59,982	GRAYS HARBOR	18,436	5,141	10,310	2,985	5,169 D	27.9%	55.9%	33.3%	66.7%
5,369	ISLAND	2,662	803	1,517	342	714 D	30.2%	57.0%	34.6%	65.4%
8,346	JEFFERSON	3,267	952	1,994	321	1,042 D	29.1%	61.0%	32.3%	67.7%
463,517	KING	184,031	63,346	108,738	11,947	45,392 D	34.4%	59.1%	36.8%	63.2%
30,776	KITSAP	14,173	3,465	10,002	706	6,537 D	24.4%	70.6%	25.7%	74.3%
18,154	KITTITAS	6,684	1,963	4,266	455	2,303 D	29.4%	63.8%	31.5%	68.5%
9,825	KLICKITAT	3,643	1,335	2,155	153	820 D	36.6%	59.2%	38.3%	61.7%
40,034	LEWIS	15,594	4,647	8,454	2,493	3,807 D	29.8%	54.2%	35.5%	64.5%
11,876	LINCOLN	4,595	1,748	2,725	122	977 D	38.0%	59.3%	39.1%	60.9%
10,060	MASON	3,902	995	2,181	726	1,186 D	25.5%	55.9%	31.3%	68.7%
18,519	OKANOGAN	6,947	2,277	3,969	701	1,692 D	32.8%	57.1%	36.5%	63.5%
14,970	PACIFIC	5,588	1,737	3,099	752	1,362 D	31.1%	55.5%	35.9%	64.1%
7,155	PEND OREILLE	2,761	855	1,772	134	917 D	31.0%	64.2%	32.5%	67.5%
163,842	PIERCE	65,327	19,006	38,451	7,870	19,445 D	29.1%	58.9%	33.1%	66.9%
3,097	SAN JUAN	1,501	607	786	108	179 D	40.4%	52.4%	43.6%	56.4%
35,142	SKAGIT	13,888	4,246	8,395	1,247	4,149 D	30.6%	60.4%	33.6%	66.4%
2,891	SKAMANIA	1,462	444	934	84	490 D	30.4%	63.9%	32.2%	67.8%
78,861	SNOHOMISH	30,963	9,310	18,352	3,301	9,042 D	30.1%	59.3%	33.7%	66.3%
150,477	SPOKANE	65,125	24,848	36,953	3,324	12,105 D	38.2%	56.7%	40.2%	59.8%
18,550	STEVENS	6,994	2,247	4,262	485	2,015 D	32.1%	60.9%	34.5%	65.5%
31,351	THURSTON	13,722	4,241	6,308	3,173	2,067 D	30.9%	46.0%	40.2%	59.8%
3,862	WAHKIAKUM	1,364	442	730	192	288 D	32.4%	53.5%	37.7%	62.3%
28,441	WALLA WALLA	10,575	4,653	5,578	344	925 D	44.0%	52.7%	45.5%	54.5%
59,128	WHATCOM	22,511	9,254	11,355	1,902	2,101 D	41.1%	50.4%	44.9%	55.1%
28,014	WHITMAN	11,011	4,727	5,945	339	1,218 D	42.9%	54.0%	44.3%	55.7%
77,402	YAKIMA	26,846	11,151	13,880	1,815	2,729 D	41.5%	51.7%	44.5%	55.5%
1,563,396	TOTAL	614,814	208,645	353,260	52,909	144,615 D	33.9%	57.5%	37.1%	62.9%

WASHINGTON

PRESIDENT 1928

1920 Census Population	County	Total Vote	Republican	Democratic	Other	Rep.-Dem. Plurality	Percentage Total Vote Rep.	Percentage Total Vote Dem.	Percentage Major Vote Rep.	Percentage Major Vote Dem.
9,623	ADAMS	2,299	1,473	807	19	666 R	64.1%	35.1%	64.6%	35.4%
6,539	ASOTIN	2,612	1,812	776	24	1,036 R	69.4%	29.7%	70.0%	30.0%
10,903	BENTON	3,789	2,650	1,080	59	1,570 R	69.9%	28.5%	71.0%	29.0%
20,906	CHELAN	9,954	7,672	2,239	43	5,433 R	77.1%	22.5%	77.4%	22.6%
11,368	CLALLAM	5,065	3,319	1,705	41	1,614 R	65.5%	33.7%	66.1%	33.9%
32,805	CLARK	12,442	7,786	4,467	189	3,319 R	62.6%	35.9%	63.5%	36.5%
6,093	COLUMBIA	2,041	1,328	689	24	639 R	65.1%	33.8%	65.8%	34.2%
11,791	COWLITZ	8,554	5,882	2,581	91	3,301 R	68.8%	30.2%	69.5%	30.5%
9,392	DOUGLAS	2,653	1,760	862	31	898 R	66.3%	32.5%	67.1%	32.9%
5,143	FERRY	1,399	640	732	27	92 D	45.7%	52.3%	46.6%	53.4%
5,877	FRANKLIN	2,161	1,339	799	23	540 R	62.0%	37.0%	62.6%	37.4%
3,875	GARFIELD	1,422	1,004	412	6	592 R	70.6%	29.0%	70.9%	29.1%
7,771	GRANT	2,067	1,407	641	19	766 R	68.1%	31.0%	68.7%	31.3%
44,745	GRAYS HARBOR	16,286	10,798	5,258	230	5,540 R	66.3%	32.3%	67.3%	32.7%
5,489	ISLAND	2,087	1,487	556	44	931 R	71.3%	26.6%	72.8%	27.2%
6,557	JEFFERSON	2,306	1,472	810	24	662 R	63.8%	35.1%	64.5%	35.5%
389,273	KING	146,678	96,263	46,604	3,811	49,659 R	65.6%	31.8%	67.4%	32.6%
33,162	KITSAP	10,392	6,544	3,668	180	2,876 R	63.0%	35.3%	64.1%	35.9%
17,737	KITTITAS	5,392	3,207	2,136	49	1,071 R	59.5%	39.6%	60.0%	40.0%
9,268	KLICKITAT	2,959	1,936	975	48	961 R	65.4%	33.0%	66.5%	33.5%
36,840	LEWIS	13,010	9,253	3,591	166	5,662 R	71.1%	27.6%	72.0%	28.0%
15,141	LINCOLN	4,559	2,718	1,807	34	911 R	59.6%	39.6%	60.1%	39.9%
4,919	MASON	2,772	1,745	992	35	753 R	63.0%	35.8%	63.8%	36.2%
17,094	OKANOGAN	5,003	3,245	1,722	36	1,523 R	64.9%	34.4%	65.3%	34.7%
14,891	PACIFIC	4,817	3,247	1,523	47	1,724 R	67.4%	31.6%	68.1%	31.9%
6,363	PEND OREILLE	2,024	1,206	793	25	413 R	59.6%	39.2%	60.3%	39.7%
144,127	PIERCE	54,146	35,748	17,402	996	18,346 R	66.0%	32.1%	67.3%	32.7%
3,605	SAN JUAN	1,220	814	400	6	414 R	66.7%	32.8%	67.1%	32.9%
33,373	SKAGIT	11,329	8,336	2,848	145	5,488 R	73.6%	25.1%	74.5%	25.5%
2,357	SKAMANIA	1,127	631	473	23	158 R	56.0%	42.0%	57.2%	42.8%
67,690	SNOHOMISH	24,507	16,516	7,419	572	9,097 R	67.4%	30.3%	69.0%	31.0%
141,289	SPOKANE	54,758	35,858	18,527	373	17,331 R	65.5%	33.8%	65.9%	34.1%
21,605	STEVENS	6,048	3,813	2,147	88	1,666 R	63.0%	35.5%	64.0%	36.0%
22,366	THURSTON	10,351	7,203	3,013	135	4,190 R	69.6%	29.1%	70.5%	29.5%
3,472	WAHKIAKUM	975	578	382	15	196 R	59.3%	39.2%	60.2%	39.8%
27,539	WALLA WALLA	9,666	6,774	2,859	33	3,915 R	70.1%	29.6%	70.3%	29.7%
50,600	WHATCOM	19,021	14,621	4,100	300	10,521 R	76.9%	21.6%	78.1%	21.9%
31,323	WHITMAN	10,101	7,065	2,969	67	4,096 R	69.9%	29.4%	70.4%	29.6%
63,710	YAKIMA	22,848	16,694	6,008	146	10,686 R	73.1%	26.3%	73.5%	26.5%
1,356,621	TOTAL	500,840	335,844	156,772	8,224	179,072 R	67.1%	31.3%	68.2%	31.8%

WASHINGTON

PRESIDENT 1924

1920 Census Population	County	Total Vote	Republican	Democratic	Progressive	Other	Plurality	Percentage Total Vote Rep.	Dem.	Prog.
9,623	ADAMS	2,026	760	228	1,036	2	276 P	37.5%	11.3%	51.1%
6,539	ASOTIN	2,352	1,094	508	728	22	366 R	46.5%	21.6%	31.0%
10,903	BENTON	3,997	1,812	437	1,711	37	101 R	45.3%	10.9%	42.8%
20,906	CHELAN	8,177	4,543	995	2,584	55	1,959 R	55.6%	12.2%	31.6%
11,368	CLALLAM	4,089	2,129	283	1,639	38	490 R	52.1%	6.9%	40.1%
32,805	CLARK	10,954	5,215	2,004	3,573	162	1,642 R	47.6%	18.3%	32.6%
6,093	COLUMBIA	2,153	1,122	522	492	17	600 R	52.1%	24.2%	22.9%
11,791	COWLITZ	5,882	3,274	927	1,609	72	1,665 R	55.7%	15.8%	27.4%
9,392	DOUGLAS	2,536	1,070	398	1,053	15	17 R	42.2%	15.7%	41.5%
5,143	FERRY	1,470	507	349	605	9	98 P	34.5%	23.7%	41.2%
5,877	FRANKLIN	2,276	709	237	1,301	29	592 P	31.2%	10.4%	57.2%
3,875	GARFIELD	1,341	875	324	140	2	551 R	65.2%	24.2%	10.4%
7,771	GRANT	1,989	813	332	823	21	10 P	40.9%	16.7%	41.4%
44,745	GRAYS HARBOR	13,751	8,273	1,239	4,079	160	4,194 R	60.2%	9.0%	29.7%
5,489	ISLAND	1,799	832	114	830	23	2 R	46.2%	6.3%	46.1%
6,557	JEFFERSON	1,763	913	143	692	15	221 R	51.8%	8.1%	39.3%
389,273	KING	112,940	60,438	7,404	41,146	3,952	19,292 R	53.5%	6.6%	36.4%
33,162	KITSAP	8,750	3,954	490	4,215	91	261 P	45.2%	5.6%	48.2%
17,737	KITTITAS	4,998	2,360	455	2,112	71	248 R	47.2%	9.1%	42.3%
9,268	KLICKITAT	2,811	1,482	518	790	21	692 R	52.7%	18.4%	28.1%
36,840	LEWIS	12,007	6,973	1,544	3,392	98	3,581 R	58.1%	12.9%	28.3%
15,141	LINCOLN	4,424	2,042	743	1,629	10	413 R	46.2%	16.8%	36.8%
4,919	MASON	1,840	902	179	741	18	161 R	49.0%	9.7%	40.3%
17,094	OKANOGAN	5,021	2,531	721	1,735	34	796 R	50.4%	14.4%	34.6%
14,891	PACIFIC	4,138	2,672	501	930	35	1,742 R	64.6%	12.1%	22.5%
6,363	PEND OREILLE	2,008	1,025	231	749	3	276 R	51.0%	11.5%	37.3%
144,127	PIERCE	44,818	21,376	4,232	18,467	743	2,909 R	47.7%	9.4%	41.2%
3,605	SAN JUAN	1,116	744	86	284	2	460 R	66.7%	7.7%	25.4%
33,373	SKAGIT	10,576	5,071	699	4,714	92	357 R	47.9%	6.6%	44.6%
2,357	SKAMANIA	1,022	533	207	275	7	258 R	52.2%	20.3%	26.9%
67,690	SNOHOMISH	21,473	10,484	1,548	8,929	512	1,555 R	48.8%	7.2%	41.6%
141,289	SPOKANE	47,473	23,403	6,036	17,824	210	5,579 R	49.3%	12.7%	37.5%
21,605	STEVENS	5,944	2,909	685	2,273	77	636 R	48.9%	11.5%	38.2%
22,366	THURSTON	8,871	5,125	943	2,710	93	2,415 R	57.8%	10.6%	30.5%
3,472	WAHKIAKUM	820	496	89	228	7	268 R	60.5%	10.9%	27.8%
27,539	WALLA WALLA	9,290	5,465	1,662	2,125	38	3,340 R	58.8%	17.9%	22.9%
50,600	WHATCOM	16,110	9,214	927	5,812	157	3,402 R	57.2%	5.8%	36.1%
31,323	WHITMAN	9,516	4,960	1,745	2,787	24	2,173 R	52.1%	18.3%	29.3%
63,710	YAKIMA	19,028	12,124	2,157	3,965	782	8,159 R	63.7%	11.3%	20.8%
1,356,621	TOTAL	421,549	220,224	42,842	150,727	7,756	69,497 R	52.2%	10.2%	35.8%

WASHINGTON

PRESIDENT 1920

1920 Census Population	County	Total Vote	Republican	Democratic	Other	Rep.-Dem. Plurality	Percentage Total Vote Rep.	Percentage Total Vote Dem.	Percentage Major Vote Rep.	Percentage Major Vote Dem.
9,623	ADAMS	2,271	1,525	515	231	1,010 R	67.2%	22.7%	74.8%	25.2%
6,539	ASOTIN	1,866	1,210	497	159	713 R	64.8%	26.6%	70.9%	29.1%
10,903	BENTON	3,847	2,001	975	871	1,026 R	52.0%	25.3%	67.2%	32.8%
20,906	CHELAN	6,635	3,885	1,540	1,210	2,345 R	58.6%	23.2%	71.6%	28.4%
11,368	CLALLAM	3,302	1,775	489	1,038	1,286 R	53.8%	14.8%	78.4%	21.6%
32,805	CLARK	9,295	4,852	2,941	1,502	1,911 R	52.2%	31.6%	62.3%	37.7%
6,093	COLUMBIA	2,144	1,376	662	106	714 R	64.2%	30.9%	67.5%	32.5%
11,791	COWLITZ	3,687	2,267	801	619	1,466 R	61.5%	21.7%	73.9%	26.1%
9,392	DOUGLAS	2,743	1,587	918	238	669 R	57.9%	33.5%	63.4%	36.6%
5,143	FERRY	1,359	592	505	262	87 R	43.6%	37.2%	54.0%	46.0%
5,877	FRANKLIN	1,887	839	571	477	268 R	44.5%	30.3%	59.5%	40.5%
3,875	GARFIELD	1,316	869	370	77	499 R	66.0%	28.1%	70.1%	29.9%
7,771	GRANT	2,366	1,378	684	304	694 R	58.2%	28.9%	66.8%	33.2%
44,745	GRAYS HARBOR	11,622	5,920	3,378	2,324	2,542 R	50.9%	29.1%	63.7%	36.3%
5,489	ISLAND	1,725	883	285	557	598 R	51.2%	16.5%	75.6%	24.4%
6,557	JEFFERSON	1,832	1,128	322	382	806 R	61.6%	17.6%	77.8%	22.2%
389,273	KING	107,124	58,584	17,369	31,171	41,215 R	54.7%	16.2%	77.1%	22.9%
33,162	KITSAP	10,098	4,989	1,350	3,759	3,639 R	49.4%	13.4%	78.7%	21.3%
17,737	KITTITAS	5,202	2,837	1,119	1,246	1,718 R	54.5%	21.5%	71.7%	28.3%
9,268	KLICKITAT	2,777	1,649	745	383	904 R	59.4%	26.8%	68.9%	31.1%
36,840	LEWIS	11,285	6,160	2,212	2,913	3,948 R	54.6%	19.6%	73.6%	26.4%
15,141	LINCOLN	4,671	3,038	1,395	238	1,643 R	65.0%	29.9%	68.5%	31.5%
4,919	MASON	1,779	997	383	399	614 R	56.0%	21.5%	72.2%	27.8%
17,094	OKANOGAN	5,064	2,784	1,260	1,020	1,524 R	55.0%	24.9%	68.8%	31.2%
14,891	PACIFIC	3,976	2,607	874	495	1,733 R	65.6%	22.0%	74.9%	25.1%
6,363	PEND OREILLE	1,987	1,079	651	257	428 R	54.3%	32.8%	62.4%	37.6%
144,127	PIERCE	42,491	22,048	8,259	12,184	13,789 R	51.9%	19.4%	72.7%	27.3%
3,605	SAN JUAN	1,250	833	196	221	637 R	66.6%	15.7%	81.0%	19.0%
33,373	SKAGIT	10,306	5,320	1,840	3,146	3,480 R	51.6%	17.9%	74.3%	25.7%
2,357	SKAMANIA	776	409	247	120	162 R	52.7%	31.8%	62.3%	37.7%
67,690	SNOHOMISH	20,567	10,793	3,056	6,718	7,737 R	52.5%	14.9%	77.9%	22.1%
141,289	SPOKANE	43,301	26,219	13,412	3,670	12,807 R	60.6%	31.0%	66.2%	33.8%
21,605	STEVENS	5,894	3,282	1,452	1,160	1,830 R	55.7%	24.6%	69.3%	30.7%
22,366	THURSTON	7,388	3,899	1,367	2,122	2,532 R	52.8%	18.5%	74.0%	26.0%
3,472	WAHKIAKUM	857	494	164	199	330 R	57.6%	19.1%	75.1%	24.9%
27,539	WALLA WALLA	8,812	5,957	2,338	517	3,619 R	67.6%	26.5%	71.8%	28.2%
50,600	WHATCOM	15,920	9,157	2,288	4,475	6,869 R	57.5%	14.4%	80.0%	20.0%
31,323	WHITMAN	9,809	6,344	2,806	659	3,538 R	64.7%	28.6%	69.3%	30.7%
63,710	YAKIMA	19,484	11,571	4,062	3,851	7,509 R	59.4%	20.8%	74.0%	26.0%
1,356,621	TOTAL	398,715	223,137	84,298	91,280	138,839 R	56.0%	21.1%	72.6%	27.4%

WASHINGTON

ELECTION NOTES

1956 Other vote was Hass (Socialist Labor).

1952 Other vote was 7,290 MacArthur (Christian Nationalist); 2,460 Hallinan (Progressive); 633 Hass (Socialist Labor); 254 Hoopes (Socialist); 119 Dobbs (Socialist Workers).

1948 Other vote was 31,692 Wallace (Progressive); 6,117 Watson (Prohibition); 3,534 Thomas (Socialist); 1,133 Teichert (Socialist Labor); 103 Dobbs (Socialist Workers).

1944 Other vote was 3,824 Thomas (Socialist); 2,396 Watson (Prohibition); 1,645 Teichert (Socialist Labor).

1940 Other vote was 4,586 Thomas (Socialist); 2,626 Browder (Communist); 1,686 Babson (Prohibition); 667 Aiken (Socialist Labor).

1936 Other vote was 17,463 Lemke (Union); 3,496 Thomas (Socialist); 1,907 Browder (Communist); 1,598 Dudley (Christian); 1,041 Colvin (Prohibition); 362 Aiken (Socialist Labor).

1932 Other vote was 30,308 Harvey (Liberty); 17,080 Thomas (Socialist); 2,972 Foster (Communist); 1,540 Upshaw (Prohibition); 1,009 Reynolds (Socialist Labor).

1928 Other vote was 4,068 Reynolds (Socialist Labor); 2,615 Thomas (Socialist); 1,541 Foster (Communist).

1924 A special four-column table which gives the LaFollette (Progressive) vote is used to detail this election. Other vote was 5,991 Nations (American); 1,004 Johns (Socialist Labor); 761 Foster (Communist).

1920 Other vote was 77,246 Christensen (Farmer-Labor); 8,913 Debs (Socialist); 3,800 Watkins (Prohibition); 1,321 Cox (Socialist Labor). Farmer-Labor candidates ran second in several counties.

WEST VIRGINIA

POPULAR VOTE FOR PRESIDENT 1920 TO 1956

Year	Total Vote	Republican		Democratic		Other Vote	Plurality	Percentage			
								Total Vote		Major Vote	
		Vote	Candidate	Vote	Candidate			Rep.	Dem.	Rep.	Dem.
1956	830,831	449,297	Eisenhower, Dwight D.	381,534	Stevenson, Adlai E.		67,763 R	54.1%	45.9%	54.1%	45.9%
1952	873,548	419,970	Eisenhower, Dwight D.	453,578	Stevenson, Adlai E.		33,608 D	48.1%	51.9%	48.1%	51.9%
1948	748,750	316,251	Dewey, Thomas E.	429,188	Truman, Harry S.	3,311	112,937 D	42.2%	57.3%	42.4%	57.6%
1944	715,596	322,819	Dewey, Thomas E.	392,777	Roosevelt, Franklin D.		69,958 D	45.1%	54.9%	45.1%	54.9%
1940	868,076	372,414	Willkie, Wendeil	495,662	Roosevelt, Franklin D.		123,248 D	42.9%	57.1%	42.9%	57.1%
1936	829,945	325,358	Landon, Alfred M.	502,582	Roosevelt, Franklin D.	2,005	177,224 D	39.2%	60.6%	39.3%	60.7%
1932	743,774	330,731	Hoover, Herbert C.	405,124	Roosevelt, Franklin D.	7,919	74,393 D	44.5%	54.5%	44.9%	55.1%
1928	642,752	375,551	Hoover, Herbert C.	263,784	Smith, Alfred E.	3,417	111,767 R	58.4%	41.0%	58.7%	41.3%
1924	583,662	288,635	Coolidge, Calvin	257,232	Davis, John W.	37,795	31,403 R	49.5%	44.1%	52.9%	47.1%
1920	509,936	282,007	Harding, Warren G.	220,785	Cox, James M.	7,144	61,222 R	55.3%	43.3%	56.1%	43.9%

ELECTORAL COLLEGE VOTE 1920 TO 1956

Year	Total	Republican	Democratic	Other
1956	8	8	—	—
1952	8	—	8	—
1948	8	—	8	—
1944	8	—	8	—
1940	8	—	8	—
1936	8	—	8	—
1932	8	—	8	—
1928	8	8	—	—
1924	8	8	—	—
1920	8	8	—	—

WEST VIRGINIA

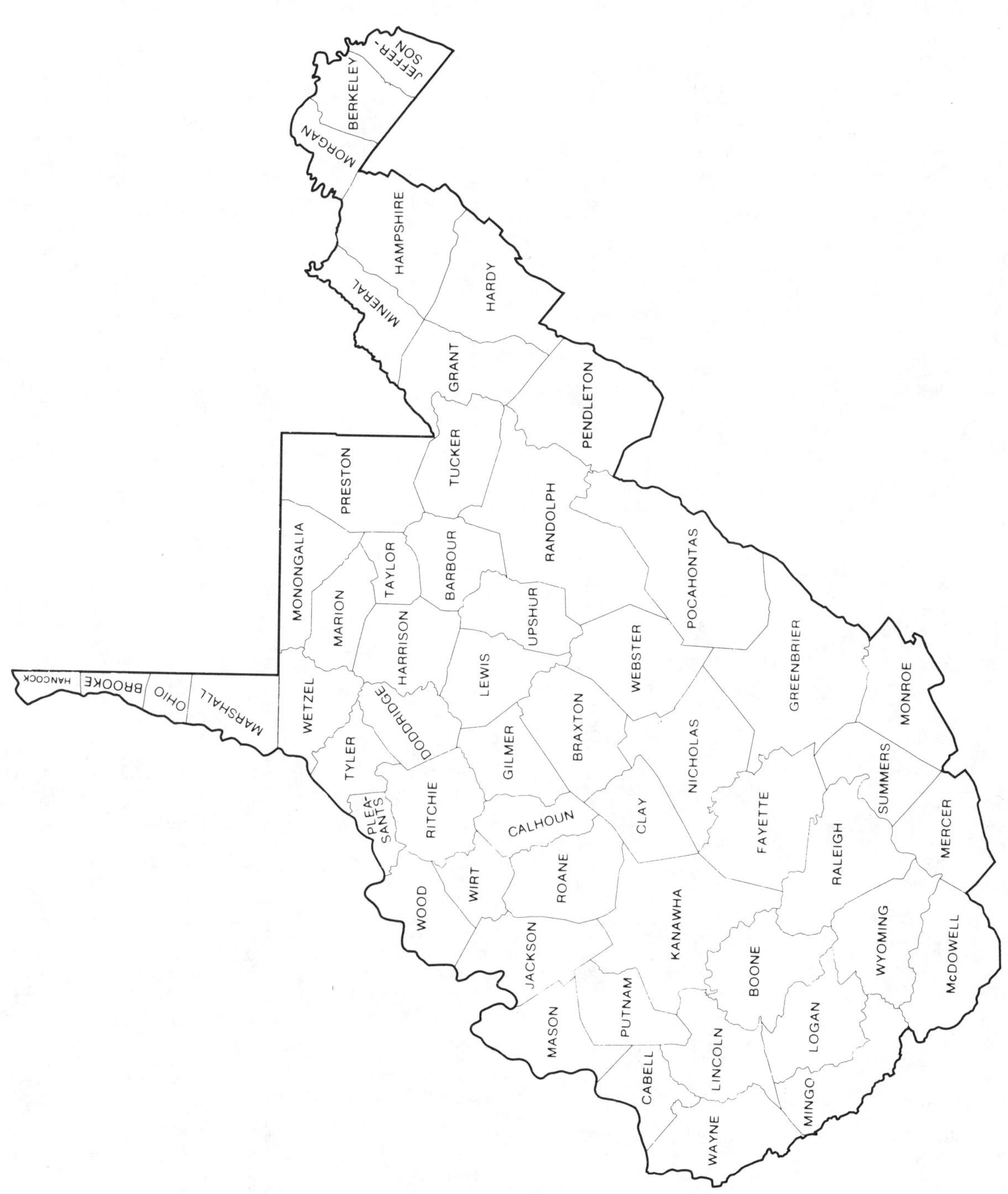

WEST VIRGINIA

PRESIDENT 1956

1950 Census Population	County	Total Vote	Republican	Democratic	Other	Rep.-Dem. Plurality	Percentage Total Vote Rep.	Percentage Total Vote Dem.	Percentage Major Vote Rep.	Percentage Major Vote Dem.
19,745	BARBOUR	8,167	4,460	3,707		753 R	54.6%	45.4%	54.6%	45.4%
30,359	BERKELEY	14,720	9,071	5,649		3,422 R	61.6%	38.4%	61.6%	38.4%
33,173	BOONE	12,322	5,196	7,126		1,930 D	42.2%	57.8%	42.2%	57.8%
18,082	BRAXTON	7,354	3,441	3,913		472 D	46.8%	53.2%	46.8%	53.2%
26,904	BROOKE	13,016	5,944	7,072		1,128 D	45.7%	54.3%	45.7%	54.3%
108,035	CABELL	47,290	28,882	18,408		10,474 R	61.1%	38.9%	61.1%	38.9%
10,259	CALHOUN	4,022	2,094	1,928		166 R	52.1%	47.9%	52.1%	47.9%
14,961	CLAY	5,448	2,820	2,628		192 R	51.8%	48.2%	51.8%	48.2%
9,026	DODDRIDGE	3,529	2,594	935		1,659 R	73.5%	26.5%	73.5%	26.5%
82,443	FAYETTE	26,504	10,218	16,286		6,068 D	38.6%	61.4%	38.6%	61.4%
9,746	GILMER	3,790	1,774	2,016		242 D	46.8%	53.2%	46.8%	53.2%
8,756	GRANT	4,042	3,408	634		2,774 R	84.3%	15.7%	84.3%	15.7%
39,295	GREENBRIER	14,501	7,684	6,817		867 R	53.0%	47.0%	53.0%	47.0%
12,577	HAMPSHIRE	5,032	2,676	2,356		320 R	53.2%	46.8%	53.2%	46.8%
34,388	HANCOCK	18,274	8,750	9,524		774 D	47.9%	52.1%	47.9%	52.1%
10,032	HARDY	4,461	2,202	2,259		57 D	49.4%	50.6%	49.4%	50.6%
85,296	HARRISON	39,401	21,860	17,541		4,319 R	55.5%	44.5%	55.5%	44.5%
15,299	JACKSON	7,580	4,984	2,596		2,388 R	65.8%	34.2%	65.8%	34.2%
17,184	JEFFERSON	6,733	3,380	3,353		27 R	50.2%	49.8%	50.2%	49.8%
239,629	KANAWHA	108,886	58,597	50,289		8,308 R	53.8%	46.2%	53.8%	46.2%
21,074	LEWIS	9,397	6,203	3,194		3,009 R	66.0%	34.0%	66.0%	34.0%
22,466	LINCOLN	9,926	4,954	4,972		18 D	49.9%	50.1%	49.9%	50.1%
77,391	LOGAN	25,382	10,588	14,794		4,206 D	41.7%	58.3%	41.7%	58.3%
98,887	MCDOWELL	28,003	11,138	16,865		5,727 D	39.8%	60.2%	39.8%	60.2%
71,521	MARION	32,304	16,112	16,192		80 D	49.9%	50.1%	49.9%	50.1%
36,893	MARSHALL	17,686	10,223	7,463		2,760 R	57.8%	42.2%	57.8%	42.2%
23,537	MASON	10,075	6,306	3,769		2,537 R	62.6%	37.4%	62.6%	37.4%
75,013	MERCER	27,884	14,648	13,236		1,412 R	52.5%	47.5%	52.5%	47.5%
22,333	MINERAL	10,000	6,412	3,588		2,824 R	64.1%	35.9%	64.1%	35.9%
47,409	MINGO	17,930	7,916	10,014		2,098 D	44.1%	55.9%	44.1%	55.9%
60,797	MONONGALIA	25,062	14,046	11,016		3,030 R	56.0%	44.0%	56.0%	44.0%
13,123	MONROE	6,301	3,529	2,772		757 R	56.0%	44.0%	56.0%	44.0%
8,276	MORGAN	4,050	2,946	1,104		1,842 R	72.7%	27.3%	72.7%	27.3%
27,696	NICHOLAS	10,143	5,263	4,880		383 R	51.9%	48.1%	51.9%	48.1%
71,672	OHIO	35,356	22,165	13,191		8,974 R	62.7%	37.3%	62.7%	37.3%
9,313	PENDLETON	3,958	1,959	1,999		40 D	49.5%	50.5%	49.5%	50.5%
6,369	PLEASANTS	3,725	2,144	1,581		563 R	57.6%	42.4%	57.6%	42.4%
12,480	POCAHONTAS	5,470	2,937	2,533		404 R	53.7%	46.3%	53.7%	46.3%
31,399	PRESTON	11,318	7,953	3,365		4,588 R	70.3%	29.7%	70.3%	29.7%
21,021	PUTNAM	10,314	5,560	4,754		806 R	53.9%	46.1%	53.9%	46.1%
96,273	RALEIGH	32,582	16,318	16,264		54 R	50.1%	49.9%	50.1%	49.9%
30,558	RANDOLPH	11,145	5,448	5,697		249 D	48.9%	51.1%	48.9%	51.1%
12,535	RITCHIE	5,611	4,140	1,471		2,669 R	73.8%	26.2%	73.8%	26.2%
18,408	ROANE	7,854	4,701	3,153		1,548 R	59.9%	40.1%	59.9%	40.1%
19,183	SUMMERS	7,577	3,712	3,865		153 D	49.0%	51.0%	49.0%	51.0%
18,422	TAYLOR	7,822	4,743	3,079		1,664 R	60.6%	39.4%	60.6%	39.4%
10,600	TUCKER	4,455	2,326	2,129		197 R	52.2%	47.8%	52.2%	47.8%
10,535	TYLER	4,989	3,671	1,318		2,353 R	73.6%	26.4%	73.6%	26.4%
19,242	UPSHUR	7,788	5,707	2,081		3,626 R	73.3%	26.7%	73.3%	26.7%
38,696	WAYNE	16,084	8,429	7,655		774 R	52.4%	47.6%	52.4%	47.6%
17,888	WEBSTER	5,529	2,457	3,072		615 D	44.4%	55.6%	44.4%	55.6%
20,154	WETZEL	8,833	5,024	3,809		1,215 R	56.9%	43.1%	56.9%	43.1%
5,119	WIRT	2,628	1,444	1,184		260 R	54.9%	45.1%	54.9%	45.1%
66,540	WOOD	34,416	21,096	13,320		7,776 R	61.3%	38.7%	61.3%	38.7%
37,540	WYOMING	14,162	7,044	7,118		74 D	49.7%	50.3%	49.7%	50.3%
2,005,552	TOTAL	830,831	449,297	381,534		67,763 R	54.1%	45.9%	54.1%	45.9%

WEST VIRGINIA

PRESIDENT 1952

1950 Census Population	County	Total Vote	Republican	Democratic	Other	Rep.-Dem. Plurality	Percentage Total Vote Rep.	Percentage Total Vote Dem.	Percentage Major Vote Rep.	Percentage Major Vote Dem.
19,745	BARBOUR	8,993	4,504	4,489		15 R	50.1%	49.9%	50.1%	49.9%
30,359	BERKELEY	15,260	8,149	7,111		1,038 R	53.4%	46.6%	53.4%	46.6%
33,173	BOONE	12,309	4,100	8,209		4,109 D	33.3%	66.7%	33.3%	66.7%
18,082	BRAXTON	7,641	3,382	4,259		877 D	44.3%	55.7%	44.3%	55.7%
26,904	BROOKE	12,664	5,073	7,591		2,518 D	40.1%	59.9%	40.1%	59.9%
108,035	CABELL	49,640	27,461	22,179		5,282 R	55.3%	44.7%	55.3%	44.7%
10,259	CALHOUN	4,239	2,101	2,138		37 D	49.6%	50.4%	49.6%	50.4%
14,961	CLAY	5,348	2,534	2,814		280 D	47.4%	52.6%	47.4%	52.6%
9,026	DODDRIDGE	3,781	2,741	1,040		1,701 R	72.5%	27.5%	72.5%	27.5%
82,443	FAYETTE	31,497	9,190	22,307		13,117 D	29.2%	70.8%	29.2%	70.8%
9,746	GILMER	4,104	1,813	2,291		478 D	44.2%	55.8%	44.2%	55.8%
8,756	GRANT	3,956	3,282	674		2,608 R	83.0%	17.0%	83.0%	17.0%
39,295	GREENBRIER	15,460	7,374	8,086		712 D	47.7%	52.3%	47.7%	52.3%
12,577	HAMPSHIRE	4,564	2,173	2,391		218 D	47.6%	52.4%	47.6%	52.4%
34,388	HANCOCK	16,292	6,520	9,772		3,252 D	40.0%	60.0%	40.0%	60.0%
10,032	HARDY	4,448	2,037	2,411		374 D	45.8%	54.2%	45.8%	54.2%
85,296	HARRISON	41,720	21,193	20,527		666 R	50.8%	49.2%	50.8%	49.2%
15,299	JACKSON	7,442	4,845	2,597		2,248 R	65.1%	34.9%	65.1%	34.9%
17,184	JEFFERSON	7,170	3,134	4,036		902 D	43.7%	56.3%	43.7%	56.3%
239,629	KANAWHA	111,401	56,861	54,540		2,321 R	51.0%	49.0%	51.0%	49.0%
21,074	LEWIS	9,534	6,254	3,280		2,974 R	65.6%	34.4%	65.6%	34.4%
22,466	LINCOLN	9,883	4,784	5,099		315 D	48.4%	51.6%	48.4%	51.6%
77,391	LOGAN	28,450	9,148	19,302		10,154 D	32.2%	67.8%	32.2%	67.8%
98,887	MCDOWELL	35,320	10,663	24,657		13,994 D	30.2%	69.8%	30.2%	69.8%
71,521	MARION	34,869	14,979	19,890		4,911 D	43.0%	57.0%	43.0%	57.0%
36,893	MARSHALL	17,960	9,271	8,689		582 R	51.6%	48.4%	51.6%	48.4%
23,537	MASON	9,926	6,102	3,824		2,278 R	61.5%	38.5%	61.5%	38.5%
75,013	MERCER	30,961	14,267	16,694		2,427 D	46.1%	53.9%	46.1%	53.9%
22,333	MINERAL	10,143	5,598	4,545		1,053 R	55.2%	44.8%	55.2%	44.8%
47,409	MINGO	19,708	6,852	12,856		6,004 D	34.8%	65.2%	34.8%	65.2%
60,797	MONONGALIA	26,263	13,111	13,152		41 D	49.9%	50.1%	49.9%	50.1%
13,123	MONROE	6,303	3,447	2,856		591 R	54.7%	45.3%	54.7%	45.3%
8,276	MORGAN	3,813	2,699	1,114		1,585 R	70.8%	29.2%	70.8%	29.2%
27,696	NICHOLAS	10,001	4,386	5,615		1,229 D	43.9%	56.1%	43.9%	56.1%
71,672	OHIO	37,121	20,575	16,546		4,029 R	55.4%	44.6%	55.4%	44.6%
9,313	PENDLETON	3,850	1,859	1,991		132 D	48.3%	51.7%	48.3%	51.7%
6,369	PLEASANTS	3,532	1,900	1,632		268 R	53.8%	46.2%	53.8%	46.2%
12,480	POCAHONTAS	5,584	2,841	2,743		98 R	50.9%	49.1%	50.9%	49.1%
31,399	PRESTON	12,337	8,059	4,278		3,781 R	65.3%	34.7%	65.3%	34.7%
21,021	PUTNAM	9,746	4,944	4,802		142 R	50.7%	49.3%	50.7%	49.3%
96,273	RALEIGH	36,709	14,005	22,704		8,699 D	38.2%	61.8%	38.2%	61.8%
30,558	RANDOLPH	12,428	5,452	6,976		1,524 D	43.9%	56.1%	43.9%	56.1%
12,535	RITCHIE	5,903	4,238	1,665		2,573 R	71.8%	28.2%	71.8%	28.2%
18,408	ROANE	8,525	4,922	3,603		1,319 R	57.7%	42.3%	57.7%	42.3%
19,183	SUMMERS	7,959	3,496	4,463		967 D	43.9%	56.1%	43.9%	56.1%
18,422	TAYLOR	8,463	4,711	3,752		959 R	55.7%	44.3%	55.7%	44.3%
10,600	TUCKER	4,812	2,235	2,577		342 D	46.4%	53.6%	46.4%	53.6%
10,535	TYLER	5,011	3,488	1,523		1,965 R	69.6%	30.4%	69.6%	30.4%
19,242	UPSHUR	8,172	5,938	2,234		3,704 R	72.7%	27.3%	72.7%	27.3%
38,696	WAYNE	15,738	7,059	8,679		1,620 D	44.9%	55.1%	44.9%	55.1%
17,888	WEBSTER	5,996	2,229	3,767		1,538 D	37.2%	62.8%	37.2%	62.8%
20,154	WETZEL	8,851	4,476	4,375		101 R	50.6%	49.4%	50.6%	49.4%
5,119	WIRT	2,524	1,474	1,050		424 R	58.4%	41.6%	58.4%	41.6%
66,540	WOOD	34,071	19,917	14,154		5,763 R	58.5%	41.5%	58.5%	41.5%
37,540	WYOMING	15,153	6,124	9,029		2,905 D	40.4%	59.6%	40.4%	59.6%
2,005,552	TOTAL	873,548	419,970	453,578		33,608 D	48.1%	51.9%	48.1%	51.9%

WEST VIRGINIA

PRESIDENT 1948

1940 Census Population	County	Total Vote	Republican	Democratic	Other	Rep.-Dem. Plurality	Percentage Total Vote Rep.	Total Vote Dem.	Major Vote Rep.	Major Vote Dem.
19,869	BARBOUR	8,100	3,834	4,238	28	404 D	47.3%	52.3%	47.5%	52.5%
29,016	BERKELEY	12,873	6,042	6,797	34	755 D	46.9%	52.8%	47.1%	52.9%
28,556	BOONE	9,697	2,909	6,769	19	3,860 D	30.0%	69.8%	30.1%	69.9%
21,658	BRAXTON	7,158	2,864	4,287	7	1,423 D	40.0%	59.9%	40.1%	59.9%
25,513	BROOKE	10,512	3,718	6,680	114	2,962 D	35.4%	63.5%	35.8%	64.2%
97,459	CABELL	42,410	18,599	23,680	131	5,081 D	43.9%	55.8%	44.0%	56.0%
12,455	CALHOUN	3,681	1,549	2,126	6	577 D	42.1%	57.8%	42.1%	57.9%
15,206	CLAY	5,352	2,366	2,978	8	612 D	44.2%	55.6%	44.3%	55.7%
10,923	DODDRIDGE	3,599	2,433	1,166		1,267 R	67.6%	32.4%	67.6%	32.4%
80,628	FAYETTE	29,278	7,451	21,707	120	14,256 D	25.4%	74.1%	25.6%	74.4%
12,046	GILMER	3,776	1,421	2,355		934 D	37.6%	62.4%	37.6%	62.4%
8,805	GRANT	3,484	2,816	664	4	2,152 R	80.8%	19.1%	80.9%	19.1%
38,520	GREENBRIER	12,562	4,935	7,598	29	2,663 D	39.3%	60.5%	39.4%	60.6%
12,974	HAMPSHIRE	3,718	1,351	2,357	10	1,006 D	36.3%	63.4%	36.4%	63.6%
31,572	HANCOCK	12,973	4,561	8,242	170	3,681 D	35.2%	63.5%	35.6%	64.4%
10,813	HARDY	3,878	1,433	2,435	10	1,002 D	37.0%	62.8%	37.0%	63.0%
82,911	HARRISON	35,757	14,534	21,109	114	6,575 D	40.6%	59.0%	40.8%	59.2%
16,598	JACKSON	6,923	4,277	2,639	7	1,638 R	61.8%	38.1%	61.8%	38.2%
16,762	JEFFERSON	6,009	2,199	3,797	13	1,598 D	36.6%	63.2%	36.7%	63.3%
195,619	KANAWHA	94,695	41,144	53,213	338	12,069 D	43.4%	56.2%	43.6%	56.4%
22,271	LEWIS	8,341	4,829	3,477	35	1,352 R	57.9%	41.7%	58.1%	41.9%
22,886	LINCOLN	8,514	4,065	4,433	16	368 D	47.7%	52.1%	47.8%	52.2%
67,768	LOGAN	23,559	7,362	16,121	76	8,759 D	31.2%	68.4%	31.4%	68.6%
94,354	MCDOWELL	31,472	9,687	21,545	240	11,858 D	30.8%	68.5%	31.0%	69.0%
68,683	MARION	31,357	11,201	19,866	290	8,665 D	35.7%	63.4%	36.1%	63.9%
40,189	MARSHALL	15,122	6,986	7,989	147	1,003 D	46.2%	52.8%	46.7%	53.3%
22,270	MASON	9,491	5,453	4,038		1,415 R	57.5%	42.5%	57.5%	42.5%
68,289	MERCER	25,348	10,065	15,201	82	5,136 D	39.7%	60.0%	39.8%	60.2%
22,215	MINERAL	8,996	4,382	4,586	28	204 D	48.7%	51.0%	48.9%	51.1%
40,802	MINGO	15,292	4,896	10,362	34	5,466 D	32.0%	67.8%	32.1%	67.9%
51,252	MONONGALIA	21,683	9,329	12,138	216	2,809 D	43.0%	56.0%	43.5%	56.5%
13,577	MONROE	5,588	2,956	2,632		324 R	52.9%	47.1%	52.9%	47.1%
8,743	MORGAN	3,267	2,159	1,104	4	1,055 R	66.1%	33.8%	66.2%	33.8%
24,070	NICHOLAS	8,432	3,391	5,018	23	1,627 D	40.2%	59.5%	40.3%	59.7%
73,115	OHIO	33,147	15,757	16,995	395	1,238 D	47.5%	51.3%	48.1%	51.9%
10,884	PENDLETON	3,543	1,592	1,944	7	352 D	44.9%	54.9%	45.0%	55.0%
6,692	PLEASANTS	3,099	1,548	1,536	15	12 R	50.0%	49.6%	50.2%	49.8%
13,906	POCAHONTAS	5,132	2,373	2,754	5	381 D	46.2%	53.7%	46.3%	53.7%
30,416	PRESTON	9,596	6,020	3,527	49	2,493 R	62.7%	36.8%	63.1%	36.9%
19,511	PUTNAM	8,164	3,722	4,426	16	704 D	45.6%	54.2%	45.7%	54.3%
86,687	RALEIGH	30,259	10,414	19,697	148	9,283 D	34.4%	65.1%	34.6%	65.4%
30,259	RANDOLPH	10,412	3,802	6,586	24	2,784 D	36.5%	63.3%	36.6%	63.4%
15,389	RITCHIE	5,345	3,619	1,712	14	1,907 R	67.7%	32.0%	67.9%	32.1%
20,787	ROANE	7,908	4,213	3,684	11	529 R	53.3%	46.6%	53.3%	46.7%
20,409	SUMMERS	7,412	2,782	4,630		1,848 D	37.5%	62.5%	37.5%	62.5%
19,919	TAYLOR	7,871	3,948	3,888	35	60 R	50.2%	49.4%	50.4%	49.6%
13,173	TUCKER	4,693	2,102	2,557	34	455 D	44.8%	54.5%	45.1%	54.9%
12,559	TYLER	4,753	3,160	1,579	14	1,581 R	66.5%	33.2%	66.7%	33.3%
18,360	UPSHUR	7,419	5,068	2,323	28	2,745 R	68.3%	31.3%	68.6%	31.4%
35,566	WAYNE	12,031	4,394	7,618	19	3,224 D	36.5%	63.3%	36.6%	63.4%
18,080	WEBSTER	5,267	1,527	3,726	14	2,199 D	29.0%	70.7%	29.1%	70.9%
22,342	WETZEL	7,829	3,326	4,477	26	1,151 D	42.5%	57.2%	42.6%	57.4%
6,475	WIRT	2,532	1,291	1,233	8	58 R	51.0%	48.7%	51.1%	48.9%
62,399	WOOD	28,493	14,198	14,224	71	26 D	49.8%	49.9%	50.0%	50.0%
29,774	WYOMING	10,948	4,198	6,725	25	2,527 D	38.3%	61.4%	38.4%	61.6%
1,901,974	TOTAL	748,750	316,251	429,188	3,311	112,937 D	42.2%	57.3%	42.4%	57.6%

WEST VIRGINIA

PRESIDENT 1944

1940 Census Population	County	Total Vote	Republican	Democratic	Other	Rep.-Dem. Plurality	Percentage Total Vote Rep.	Total Vote Dem.	Major Vote Rep.	Major Vote Dem.
19,869	BARBOUR	7,711	3,993	3,718		275 R	51.8%	48.2%	51.8%	48.2%
29,016	BERKELEY	11,970	6,151	5,819		332 R	51.4%	48.6%	51.4%	48.6%
28,556	BOONE	9,815	3,449	6,366		2,917 D	35.1%	64.9%	35.1%	64.9%
21,658	BRAXTON	7,336	3,023	4,313		1,290 D	41.2%	58.8%	41.2%	58.8%
25,513	BROOKE	9,314	3,588	5,726		2,138 D	38.5%	61.5%	38.5%	61.5%
97,459	CABELL	42,881	19,861	23,020		3,159 D	46.3%	53.7%	46.3%	53.7%
12,455	CALHOUN	3,941	1,687	2,254		567 D	42.8%	57.2%	42.8%	57.2%
15,206	CLAY	4,509	2,114	2,395		281 D	46.9%	53.1%	46.9%	53.1%
10,923	DODDRIDGE	3,611	2,611	1,000		1,611 R	72.3%	27.7%	72.3%	27.7%
80,628	FAYETTE	25,461	7,932	17,529		9,597 D	31.2%	68.8%	31.2%	68.8%
12,046	GILMER	4,160	1,651	2,509		858 D	39.7%	60.3%	39.7%	60.3%
8,805	GRANT	3,566	2,996	570		2,426 R	84.0%	16.0%	84.0%	16.0%
38,520	GREENBRIER	12,021	4,790	7,231		2,441 D	39.8%	60.2%	39.8%	60.2%
12,974	HAMPSHIRE	4,123	1,638	2,485		847 D	39.7%	60.3%	39.7%	60.3%
31,572	HANCOCK	11,619	4,285	7,334		3,049 D	36.9%	63.1%	36.9%	63.1%
10,813	HARDY	3,600	1,489	2,111		622 D	41.4%	58.6%	41.4%	58.6%
82,911	HARRISON	32,436	14,408	18,028		3,620 D	44.4%	55.6%	44.4%	55.6%
16,598	JACKSON	6,887	4,486	2,401		2,085 R	65.1%	34.9%	65.1%	34.9%
16,762	JEFFERSON	5,870	2,103	3,767		1,664 D	35.8%	64.2%	35.8%	64.2%
195,619	KANAWHA	83,888	36,488	47,400		10,912 D	43.5%	56.5%	43.5%	56.5%
22,271	LEWIS	8,334	4,984	3,350		1,634 R	59.8%	40.2%	59.8%	40.2%
22,886	LINCOLN	7,829	4,175	3,654		521 R	53.3%	46.7%	53.3%	46.7%
67,768	LOGAN	22,692	8,000	14,692		6,692 D	35.3%	64.7%	35.3%	64.7%
94,354	MCDOWELL	30,323	11,023	19,300		8,277 D	36.4%	63.6%	36.4%	63.6%
68,683	MARION	29,224	11,584	17,640		6,056 D	39.6%	60.4%	39.6%	60.4%
40,189	MARSHALL	14,974	7,800	7,174		626 R	52.1%	47.9%	52.1%	47.9%
22,270	MASON	9,271	5,609	3,662		1,947 R	60.5%	39.5%	60.5%	39.5%
68,289	MERCER	24,895	10,034	14,861		4,827 D	40.3%	59.7%	40.3%	59.7%
22,215	MINERAL	8,624	4,635	3,989		646 R	53.7%	46.3%	53.7%	46.3%
40,802	MINGO	14,261	4,711	9,550		4,839 D	33.0%	67.0%	33.0%	67.0%
51,252	MONONGALIA	20,076	9,647	10,429		782 D	48.1%	51.9%	48.1%	51.9%
13,577	MONROE	5,745	3,130	2,615		515 R	54.5%	45.5%	54.5%	45.5%
8,743	MORGAN	3,198	2,303	895		1,408 R	72.0%	28.0%	72.0%	28.0%
24,070	NICHOLAS	7,564	3,259	4,305		1,046 D	43.1%	56.9%	43.1%	56.9%
73,115	OHIO	33,610	16,165	17,445		1,280 D	48.1%	51.9%	48.1%	51.9%
10,884	PENDLETON	4,015	1,838	2,177		339 D	45.8%	54.2%	45.8%	54.2%
6,692	PLEASANTS	3,129	1,622	1,507		115 R	51.8%	48.2%	51.8%	48.2%
13,906	POCAHONTAS	5,237	2,340	2,897		557 D	44.7%	55.3%	44.7%	55.3%
30,416	PRESTON	9,782	6,785	2,997		3,788 R	69.4%	30.6%	69.4%	30.6%
19,511	PUTNAM	7,943	4,025	3,918		107 R	50.7%	49.3%	50.7%	49.3%
86,687	RALEIGH	28,311	10,323	17,988		7,665 D	36.5%	63.5%	36.5%	63.5%
30,259	RANDOLPH	9,980	3,681	6,299		2,618 D	36.9%	63.1%	36.9%	63.1%
15,389	RITCHIE	5,613	3,963	1,650		2,313 R	70.6%	29.4%	70.6%	29.4%
20,787	ROANE	8,437	4,650	3,787		863 R	55.1%	44.9%	55.1%	44.9%
20,409	SUMMERS	7,366	2,967	4,399		1,432 D	40.3%	59.7%	40.3%	59.7%
19,919	TAYLOR	7,543	3,890	3,653		237 R	51.6%	48.4%	51.6%	48.4%
13,173	TUCKER	4,893	2,220	2,673		453 D	45.4%	54.6%	45.4%	54.6%
12,559	TYLER	4,857	3,429	1,428		2,001 R	70.6%	29.4%	70.6%	29.4%
18,360	UPSHUR	7,358	5,332	2,026		3,306 R	72.5%	27.5%	72.5%	27.5%
35,566	WAYNE	11,143	4,516	6,627		2,111 D	40.5%	59.5%	40.5%	59.5%
18,080	WEBSTER	4,880	1,595	3,285		1,690 D	32.7%	67.3%	32.7%	67.3%
22,342	WETZEL	7,939	3,604	4,335		731 D	45.4%	54.6%	45.4%	54.6%
6,475	WIRT	2,588	1,418	1,170		248 R	54.8%	45.2%	54.8%	45.2%
62,399	WOOD	28,242	14,566	13,676		890 R	51.6%	48.4%	51.6%	48.4%
29,774	WYOMING	11,001	4,253	6,748		2,495 D	38.7%	61.3%	38.7%	61.3%
1,901,974	TOTAL	715,596	322,819	392,777		69,958 D	45.1%	54.9%	45.1%	54.9%

WEST VIRGINIA

PRESIDENT 1940

1940 Census Population	County	Total Vote	Republican	Democratic	Other	Rep.-Dem. Plurality	Percentage Total Vote Rep.	Total Vote Dem.	Major Vote Rep.	Major Vote Dem.
19,869	BARBOUR	9,601	4,576	5,025		449 D	47.7%	52.3%	47.7%	52.3%
29,016	BERKELEY	15,220	6,562	8,658		2,096 D	43.1%	56.9%	43.1%	56.9%
28,556	BOONE	12,032	4,128	7,904		3,776 D	34.3%	65.7%	34.3%	65.7%
21,658	BRAXTON	9,765	4,056	5,709		1,653 D	41.5%	58.5%	41.5%	58.5%
25,513	BROOKE	10,420	4,004	6,416		2,412 D	38.4%	61.6%	38.4%	61.6%
97,459	CABELL	49,152	21,027	28,125		7,098 D	42.8%	57.2%	42.8%	57.2%
12,455	CALHOUN	4,763	1,891	2,872		981 D	39.7%	60.3%	39.7%	60.3%
15,206	CLAY	6,366	2,881	3,485		604 D	45.3%	54.7%	45.3%	54.7%
10,923	DODDRIDGE	4,788	3,293	1,495		1,798 R	68.8%	31.2%	68.8%	31.2%
80,628	FAYETTE	32,563	10,307	22,256		11,949 D	31.7%	68.3%	31.7%	68.3%
12,046	GILMER	5,343	2,067	3,276		1,209 D	38.7%	61.3%	38.7%	61.3%
8,805	GRANT	4,052	3,195	857		2,338 R	78.8%	21.2%	78.8%	21.2%
38,520	GREENBRIER	16,615	6,451	10,164		3,713 D	38.8%	61.2%	38.8%	61.2%
12,974	HAMPSHIRE	5,028	1,751	3,277		1,526 D	34.8%	65.2%	34.8%	65.2%
31,572	HANCOCK	13,512	4,997	8,515		3,518 D	37.0%	63.0%	37.0%	63.0%
10,813	HARDY	4,364	1,674	2,690		1,016 D	38.4%	61.6%	38.4%	61.6%
82,911	HARRISON	39,657	17,087	22,570		5,483 D	43.1%	56.9%	43.1%	56.9%
16,598	JACKSON	8,403	5,104	3,299		1,805 R	60.7%	39.3%	60.7%	39.3%
16,762	JEFFERSON	7,629	2,332	5,297		2,965 D	30.6%	69.4%	30.6%	69.4%
195,619	KANAWHA	98,045	40,113	57,932		17,819 D	40.9%	59.1%	40.9%	59.1%
22,271	LEWIS	10,501	5,935	4,566		1,369 R	56.5%	43.5%	56.5%	43.5%
22,886	LINCOLN	10,046	4,818	5,228		410 D	48.0%	52.0%	48.0%	52.0%
67,768	LOGAN	26,870	9,860	17,010		7,150 D	36.7%	63.3%	36.7%	63.3%
94,354	MCDOWELL	38,355	13,906	24,449		10,543 D	36.3%	63.7%	36.3%	63.7%
68,683	MARION	34,384	13,349	21,035		7,686 D	38.8%	61.2%	38.8%	61.2%
40,189	MARSHALL	18,224	9,324	8,900		424 R	51.2%	48.8%	51.2%	48.8%
22,270	MASON	10,760	6,239	4,521		1,718 R	58.0%	42.0%	58.0%	42.0%
68,289	MERCER	29,558	11,395	18,163		6,768 D	38.6%	61.4%	38.6%	61.4%
22,215	MINERAL	10,328	5,133	5,195		62 D	49.7%	50.3%	49.7%	50.3%
40,802	MINGO	17,395	5,776	11,619		5,843 D	33.2%	66.8%	33.2%	66.8%
51,252	MONONGALIA	23,307	10,367	12,940		2,573 D	44.5%	55.5%	44.5%	55.5%
13,577	MONROE	6,686	3,403	3,283		120 R	50.9%	49.1%	50.9%	49.1%
8,743	MORGAN	3,849	2,563	1,286		1,277 R	66.6%	33.4%	66.6%	33.4%
24,070	NICHOLAS	9,611	4,299	5,312		1,013 D	44.7%	55.3%	44.7%	55.3%
73,115	OHIO	39,786	18,073	21,713		3,640 D	45.4%	54.6%	45.4%	54.6%
10,884	PENDLETON	4,687	1,977	2,710		733 D	42.2%	57.8%	42.2%	57.8%
6,692	PLEASANTS	3,675	1,896	1,779		117 R	51.6%	48.4%	51.6%	48.4%
13,906	POCAHONTAS	6,490	2,886	3,604		718 D	44.5%	55.5%	44.5%	55.5%
30,416	PRESTON	12,943	8,213	4,730		3,483 R	63.5%	36.5%	63.5%	36.5%
19,511	PUTNAM	9,156	4,268	4,888		620 D	46.6%	53.4%	46.6%	53.4%
86,687	RALEIGH	34,857	11,752	23,105		11,353 D	33.7%	66.3%	33.7%	66.3%
30,259	RANDOLPH	12,661	4,196	8,465		4,269 D	33.1%	66.9%	33.1%	66.9%
15,389	RITCHIE	7,421	4,982	2,439		2,543 R	67.1%	32.9%	67.1%	32.9%
20,787	ROANE	10,475	5,317	5,158		159 R	50.8%	49.2%	50.8%	49.2%
20,409	SUMMERS	9,085	3,644	5,441		1,797 D	40.1%	59.9%	40.1%	59.9%
19,919	TAYLOR	9,809	4,841	4,968		127 D	49.4%	50.6%	49.4%	50.6%
13,173	TUCKER	5,986	2,654	3,332		678 D	44.3%	55.7%	44.3%	55.7%
12,559	TYLER	6,380	4,354	2,026		2,328 R	68.2%	31.8%	68.2%	31.8%
18,360	UPSHUR	8,948	6,086	2,862		3,224 R	68.0%	32.0%	68.0%	32.0%
35,566	WAYNE	15,327	5,701	9,626		3,925 D	37.2%	62.8%	37.2%	62.8%
18,080	WEBSTER	6,646	2,067	4,579		2,512 D	31.1%	68.9%	31.1%	68.9%
22,342	WETZEL	10,033	4,443	5,590		1,147 D	44.3%	55.7%	44.3%	55.7%
6,475	WIRT	3,372	1,818	1,554		264 R	53.9%	46.1%	53.9%	46.1%
62,399	WOOD	30,967	15,005	15,962		957 D	48.5%	51.5%	48.5%	51.5%
29,774	WYOMING	12,180	4,378	7,802		3,424 D	35.9%	64.1%	35.9%	64.1%
1,901,974	TOTAL	868,076	372,414	495,662		123,248 D	42.9%	57.1%	42.9%	57.1%

WEST VIRGINIA

PRESIDENT 1936

1930 Census Population	County	Total Vote	Republican	Democratic	Other	Rep.-Dem. Plurality	Percentage Total Vote Rep.	Total Vote Dem.	Major Vote Rep.	Major Vote Dem.
18,628	BARBOUR	9,198	3,875	5,284	39	1,409 D	42.1%	57.4%	42.3%	57.7%
28,030	BERKELEY	14,960	6,585	8,336	39	1,751 D	44.0%	55.7%	44.1%	55.9%
24,586	BOONE	11,174	3,477	7,697		4,220 D	31.1%	68.9%	31.1%	68.9%
22,579	BRAXTON	9,392	3,709	5,667	16	1,958 D	39.5%	60.3%	39.6%	60.4%
24,663	BROOKE	9,495	3,485	5,955	55	2,470 D	36.7%	62.7%	36.9%	63.1%
90,786	CABELL	46,409	19,003	27,319	87	8,316 D	40.9%	58.9%	41.0%	59.0%
10,866	CALHOUN	5,115	1,733	3,369	13	1,636 D	33.9%	65.9%	34.0%	66.0%
13,125	CLAY	5,905	2,513	3,387	5	874 D	42.6%	57.4%	42.6%	57.4%
10,488	DODDRIDGE	4,744	3,023	1,716	5	1,307 R	63.7%	36.2%	63.8%	36.2%
72,050	FAYETTE	32,886	8,942	23,864	80	14,922 D	27.2%	72.6%	27.3%	72.7%
10,641	GILMER	5,291	1,858	3,433		1,575 D	35.1%	64.9%	35.1%	64.9%
8,441	GRANT	3,923	2,923	995	5	1,928 R	74.5%	25.4%	74.6%	25.4%
35,878	GREENBRIER	16,672	5,881	10,738	53	4,857 D	35.3%	64.4%	35.4%	64.6%
11,836	HAMPSHIRE	5,325	1,512	3,792	21	2,280 D	28.4%	71.2%	28.5%	71.5%
28,511	HANCOCK	11,771	3,957	7,756	58	3,799 D	33.6%	65.9%	33.8%	66.2%
9,816	HARDY	4,542	1,581	2,956	5	1,375 D	34.8%	65.1%	34.8%	65.2%
78,567	HARRISON	38,678	14,180	24,361	137	10,181 D	36.7%	63.0%	36.8%	63.2%
16,124	JACKSON	8,172	4,711	3,453	8	1,258 R	57.6%	42.3%	57.7%	42.3%
15,780	JEFFERSON	7,501	2,040	5,443	18	3,403 D	27.2%	72.6%	27.3%	72.7%
157,667	KANAWHA	86,301	35,387	50,801	113	15,414 D	41.0%	58.9%	41.1%	58.9%
21,794	LEWIS	11,084	5,499	5,531	54	32 D	49.6%	49.9%	49.9%	50.1%
19,156	LINCOLN	9,752	4,382	5,370		988 D	44.9%	55.1%	44.9%	55.1%
58,534	LOGAN	25,542	7,069	18,424	49	11,355 D	27.7%	72.1%	27.7%	72.3%
90,479	MCDOWELL	35,481	9,975	25,471	35	15,496 D	28.1%	71.8%	28.1%	71.9%
66,655	MARION	32,443	11,403	20,859	181	9,456 D	35.1%	64.3%	35.3%	64.7%
39,831	MARSHALL	17,241	7,967	9,198	76	1,231 D	46.2%	53.3%	46.4%	53.6%
20,788	MASON	10,782	5,894	4,852	36	1,042 R	54.7%	45.0%	54.8%	45.2%
61,323	MERCER	29,183	10,762	18,391	30	7,629 D	36.9%	63.0%	36.9%	63.1%
20,084	MINERAL	9,859	4,486	5,333	40	847 D	45.5%	54.1%	45.7%	54.3%
38,319	MINGO	17,064	5,771	11,278	15	5,507 D	33.8%	66.1%	33.8%	66.2%
50,083	MONONGALIA	22,582	8,811	13,677	94	4,866 D	39.0%	60.6%	39.2%	60.8%
11,949	MONROE	6,695	3,268	3,413	14	145 D	48.8%	51.0%	48.9%	51.1%
8,406	MORGAN	4,184	2,555	1,620	9	935 R	61.1%	38.7%	61.2%	38.8%
20,686	NICHOLAS	9,906	3,964	5,872	70	1,908 D	40.0%	59.3%	40.3%	59.7%
72,077	OHIO	36,758	13,743	22,899	116	9,156 D	37.4%	62.3%	37.5%	62.5%
9,660	PENDLETON	4,450	1,800	2,637	13	837 D	40.4%	59.3%	40.6%	59.4%
6,545	PLEASANTS	3,735	1,820	1,907	8	87 D	48.7%	51.1%	48.8%	51.2%
14,555	POCAHONTAS	6,978	2,850	4,118	10	1,268 D	40.8%	59.0%	40.9%	59.1%
29,043	PRESTON	12,997	7,553	5,410	34	2,143 R	58.1%	41.6%	58.3%	41.7%
16,737	PUTNAM	8,720	3,938	4,756	26	818 D	45.2%	54.5%	45.3%	54.7%
68,072	RALEIGH	31,885	9,001	22,840	44	13,839 D	28.2%	71.6%	28.3%	71.7%
25,049	RANDOLPH	11,842	3,711	8,109	22	4,398 D	31.3%	68.5%	31.4%	68.6%
15,594	RITCHIE	7,486	4,639	2,825	22	1,814 R	62.0%	37.7%	62.2%	37.8%
19,478	ROANE	10,341	5,282	5,047	12	235 R	51.1%	48.8%	51.1%	48.9%
20,468	SUMMERS	9,311	3,521	5,779	11	2,258 D	37.8%	62.1%	37.9%	62.1%
19,114	TAYLOR	9,898	4,061	5,795	42	1,734 D	41.0%	58.5%	41.2%	58.8%
13,374	TUCKER	6,169	2,335	3,801	33	1,466 D	37.9%	61.6%	38.1%	61.9%
12,785	TYLER	6,559	4,031	2,509	19	1,522 R	61.5%	38.3%	61.6%	38.4%
17,944	UPSHUR	8,934	5,745	3,163	26	2,582 R	64.3%	35.4%	64.5%	35.5%
31,206	WAYNE	14,588	5,603	8,954	31	3,351 D	38.4%	61.4%	38.5%	61.5%
14,216	WEBSTER	6,618	1,987	4,613	18	2,626 D	30.0%	69.7%	30.1%	69.9%
22,334	WETZEL	10,262	3,770	6,463	29	2,693 D	36.7%	63.0%	36.8%	63.2%
6,358	WIRT	3,413	1,612	1,783	18	171 D	47.2%	52.2%	47.5%	52.5%
56,521	WOOD	29,414	12,574	16,829	11	4,255 D	42.7%	57.2%	42.8%	57.2%
20,926	WYOMING	10,335	3,601	6,734		3,133 D	34.8%	65.2%	34.8%	65.2%
1,729,205	TOTAL	829,945	325,358	502,582	2,005	177,224 D	39.2%	60.6%	39.3%	60.7%

WEST VIRGINIA

PRESIDENT 1932

1930 Census Population	County	Total Vote	Republican	Democratic	Other	Rep.-Dem. Plurality	Percentage Total Vote Rep.	Percentage Total Vote Dem.	Percentage Major Vote Rep.	Percentage Major Vote Dem.
18,628	BARBOUR	8,022	3,652	4,228	142	576 D	45.5%	52.7%	46.3%	53.7%
28,030	BERKELEY	13,527	6,370	7,009	148	639 D	47.1%	51.8%	47.6%	52.4%
24,586	BOONE	9,593	3,555	5,973	65	2,418 D	37.1%	62.3%	37.3%	62.7%
22,579	BRAXTON	9,661	3,560	6,043	58	2,483 D	36.8%	62.6%	37.1%	62.9%
24,663	BROOKE	9,206	4,010	4,919	277	909 D	43.6%	53.4%	44.9%	55.1%
90,786	CABELL	41,950	17,999	23,498	453	5,499 D	42.9%	56.0%	43.4%	56.6%
10,866	CALHOUN	4,724	1,564	3,139	21	1,575 D	33.1%	66.4%	33.3%	66.7%
13,125	CLAY	5,499	2,443	3,038	18	595 D	44.4%	55.2%	44.6%	55.4%
10,488	DODDRIDGE	4,723	2,780	1,943		837 R	58.9%	41.1%	58.9%	41.1%
72,050	FAYETTE	29,509	12,170	17,127	212	4,957 D	41.2%	58.0%	41.5%	58.5%
10,641	GILMER	5,078	1,530	3,511	37	1,981 D	30.1%	69.1%	30.4%	69.6%
8,441	GRANT	3,433	2,477	920	36	1,557 R	72.2%	26.8%	72.9%	27.1%
35,878	GREENBRIER	14,684	5,111	9,467	106	4,356 D	34.8%	64.5%	35.1%	64.9%
11,836	HAMPSHIRE	4,988	1,258	3,681	49	2,423 D	25.2%	73.8%	25.5%	74.5%
28,511	HANCOCK	9,220	4,328	4,603	289	275 D	46.9%	49.9%	48.5%	51.5%
9,816	HARDY	4,116	1,267	2,824	25	1,557 D	30.8%	68.6%	31.0%	69.0%
78,567	HARRISON	33,354	14,641	18,081	632	3,440 D	43.9%	54.2%	44.7%	55.3%
16,124	JACKSON	8,215	4,084	4,131		47 D	49.7%	50.3%	49.7%	50.3%
15,780	JEFFERSON	7,119	1,734	5,350	35	3,616 D	24.4%	75.2%	24.5%	75.5%
157,667	KANAWHA	74,821	35,455	38,617	749	3,162 D	47.4%	51.6%	47.9%	52.1%
21,794	LEWIS	10,381	4,704	5,546	131	842 D	45.3%	53.4%	45.9%	54.1%
19,156	LINCOLN	8,757	3,881	4,876		995 D	44.3%	55.7%	44.3%	55.7%
58,534	LOGAN	23,283	10,683	12,529	71	1,846 D	45.9%	53.8%	46.0%	54.0%
90,479	MCDOWELL	28,514	16,069	12,365	80	3,704 R	56.4%	43.4%	56.5%	43.5%
66,655	MARION	29,464	12,638	15,975	851	3,337 D	42.9%	54.2%	44.2%	55.8%
39,831	MARSHALL	15,647	7,416	7,994	237	578 D	47.4%	51.1%	48.1%	51.9%
20,788	MASON	9,758	4,655	5,027	76	372 D	47.7%	51.5%	48.1%	51.9%
61,323	MERCER	27,093	11,088	15,900	105	4,812 D	40.9%	58.7%	41.1%	58.9%
20,084	MINERAL	8,869	4,519	4,098	252	421 R	51.0%	46.2%	52.4%	47.6%
38,319	MINGO	16,501	7,801	8,657	43	856 D	47.3%	52.5%	47.4%	52.6%
50,083	MONONGALIA	19,221	8,417	10,319	485	1,902 D	43.8%	53.7%	44.9%	55.1%
11,949	MONROE	6,247	2,978	3,267	2	289 D	47.7%	52.3%	47.7%	52.3%
8,406	MORGAN	3,483	2,082	1,358	43	724 R	59.8%	39.0%	60.5%	39.5%
20,686	NICHOLAS	9,097	3,684	5,327	86	1,643 D	40.5%	58.6%	40.9%	59.1%
72,077	OHIO	35,020	15,836	18,652	532	2,816 D	45.2%	53.3%	45.9%	54.1%
9,660	PENDLETON	4,047	1,502	2,530	15	1,028 D	37.1%	62.5%	37.3%	62.7%
6,545	PLEASANTS	3,525	1,580	1,921	24	341 D	44.8%	54.5%	45.1%	54.9%
14,555	POCAHONTAS	6,195	2,623	3,531	41	908 D	42.3%	57.0%	42.6%	57.4%
29,043	PRESTON	11,346	6,359	4,872	115	1,487 R	56.0%	42.9%	56.6%	43.4%
16,737	PUTNAM	7,590	3,411	4,098	81	687 D	44.9%	54.0%	45.4%	54.6%
68,072	RALEIGH	27,078	11,441	15,456	181	4,015 D	42.3%	57.1%	42.5%	57.5%
25,049	RANDOLPH	10,923	3,418	7,397	108	3,979 D	31.3%	67.7%	31.6%	68.4%
15,594	RITCHIE	7,317	4,055	3,179	83	876 R	55.4%	43.4%	56.1%	43.9%
19,478	ROANE	9,455	4,361	5,094		733 D	46.1%	53.9%	46.1%	53.9%
20,468	SUMMERS	9,010	3,220	5,724	66	2,504 D	35.7%	63.5%	36.0%	64.0%
19,114	TAYLOR	8,285	3,856	4,293	136	437 D	46.5%	51.8%	47.3%	52.7%
13,374	TUCKER	5,550	2,204	3,244	102	1,040 D	39.7%	58.5%	40.5%	59.5%
12,785	TYLER	6,390	3,734	2,582	74	1,152 R	58.4%	40.4%	59.1%	40.9%
17,944	UPSHUR	8,292	5,077	3,147	68	1,930 R	61.2%	38.0%	61.7%	38.3%
31,206	WAYNE	13,420	4,682	8,648	90	3,966 D	34.9%	64.4%	35.1%	64.9%
14,216	WEBSTER	5,475	1,781	3,664	30	1,883 D	32.5%	66.9%	32.7%	67.3%
22,334	WETZEL	9,547	3,351	6,118	78	2,767 D	35.1%	64.1%	35.4%	64.6%
6,358	WIRT	3,476	1,486	1,944	46	458 D	42.8%	55.9%	43.3%	56.7%
56,521	WOOD	25,673	12,144	13,294	235	1,150 D	47.3%	51.8%	47.7%	52.3%
20,926	WYOMING	8,403	4,007	4,396		389 D	47.7%	52.3%	47.7%	52.3%
1,729,205	TOTAL	743,774	330,731	405,124	7,919	74,393 D	44.5%	54.5%	44.9%	55.1%

WEST VIRGINIA

PRESIDENT 1928

1920 Census Population	County	Total Vote	Republican	Democratic	Other	Rep.-Dem. Plurality	Percentage Total Vote Rep.	Percentage Total Vote Dem.	Percentage Major Vote Rep.	Percentage Major Vote Dem.
18,028	BARBOUR	7,514	4,023	3,491		532 R	53.5%	46.5%	53.5%	46.5%
24,554	BERKELEY	12,059	8,477	3,540	42	4,937 R	70.3%	29.4%	70.5%	29.5%
15,319	BOONE	8,835	4,000	4,805	30	805 D	45.3%	54.4%	45.4%	54.6%
23,973	BRAXTON	8,651	4,028	4,582	41	554 D	46.6%	53.0%	46.8%	53.2%
16,527	BROOKE	7,744	5,277	2,419	48	2,858 R	68.1%	31.2%	68.6%	31.4%
65,746	CABELL	36,583	21,091	15,340	152	5,751 R	57.7%	41.9%	57.9%	42.1%
10,268	CALHOUN	3,942	1,745	2,179	18	434 D	44.3%	55.3%	44.5%	55.5%
11,486	CLAY	4,494	2,551	1,929	14	622 R	56.8%	42.9%	56.9%	43.1%
11,976	DODDRIDGE	4,121	2,919	1,202		1,717 R	70.8%	29.2%	70.8%	29.2%
60,377	FAYETTE	25,416	12,961	12,351	104	610 R	51.0%	48.6%	51.2%	48.8%
10,668	GILMER	4,044	1,705	2,313	26	608 D	42.2%	57.2%	42.4%	57.6%
8,993	GRANT	3,197	2,648	542	7	2,106 R	82.8%	17.0%	83.0%	17.0%
26,242	GREENBRIER	12,624	6,423	6,141	60	282 R	50.9%	48.6%	51.1%	48.9%
11,713	HAMPSHIRE	3,926	1,779	2,132	15	353 D	45.3%	54.3%	45.5%	54.5%
19,975	HANCOCK	7,374	5,461	1,884	29	3,577 R	74.1%	25.5%	74.3%	25.7%
9,601	HARDY	3,582	1,611	1,965	6	354 D	45.0%	54.9%	45.1%	54.9%
74,793	HARRISON	30,331	17,502	12,483	346	5,019 R	57.7%	41.2%	58.4%	41.6%
18,658	JACKSON	6,602	4,150	2,452		1,698 R	62.9%	37.1%	62.9%	37.1%
15,729	JEFFERSON	6,384	3,050	3,312	22	262 D	47.8%	51.9%	47.9%	52.1%
119,650	KANAWHA	61,535	35,788	25,563	184	10,225 R	58.2%	41.5%	58.3%	41.7%
20,455	LEWIS	9,221	5,290	3,825	106	1,465 R	57.4%	41.5%	58.0%	42.0%
19,378	LINCOLN	7,239	3,823	3,416		407 R	52.8%	47.2%	52.8%	47.2%
41,006	LOGAN	21,389	11,404	9,944	41	1,460 R	53.3%	46.5%	53.4%	46.6%
68,571	MCDOWELL	23,135	14,810	8,294	31	6,516 R	64.0%	35.9%	64.1%	35.9%
54,571	MARION	26,663	16,088	10,133	442	5,955 R	60.3%	38.0%	61.4%	38.6%
33,681	MARSHALL	14,112	9,204	4,785	123	4,419 R	65.2%	33.9%	65.8%	34.2%
21,459	MASON	7,992	5,125	2,814	53	2,311 R	64.1%	35.2%	64.6%	35.4%
49,558	MERCER	23,210	12,887	10,273	50	2,614 R	55.5%	44.3%	55.6%	44.4%
19,849	MINERAL	8,212	5,860	2,310	42	3,550 R	71.4%	28.1%	71.7%	28.3%
26,364	MINGO	13,732	6,904	6,801	27	103 R	50.3%	49.5%	50.4%	49.6%
33,618	MONONGALIA	17,734	11,364	6,182	188	5,182 R	64.1%	34.9%	64.8%	35.2%
13,141	MONROE	5,388	3,025	2,346	17	679 R	56.1%	43.5%	56.3%	43.7%
8,357	MORGAN	3,308	2,539	758	11	1,781 R	76.8%	22.9%	77.0%	23.0%
20,717	NICHOLAS	7,481	3,917	3,495	69	422 R	52.4%	46.7%	52.8%	47.2%
62,892	OHIO	33,415	20,064	13,132	219	6,932 R	60.0%	39.3%	60.4%	39.6%
9,652	PENDLETON	3,631	1,710	1,921		211 D	47.1%	52.9%	47.1%	52.9%
7,379	PLEASANTS	3,032	1,821	1,210	1	611 R	60.1%	39.9%	60.1%	39.9%
15,002	POCAHONTAS	5,654	3,141	2,487	26	654 R	55.6%	44.0%	55.8%	44.2%
27,996	PRESTON	10,216	7,783	2,355	78	5,428 R	76.2%	23.1%	76.8%	23.2%
17,531	PUTNAM	5,793	3,346	2,406	41	940 R	57.8%	41.5%	58.2%	41.8%
42,482	RALEIGH	21,947	11,581	10,366		1,215 R	52.8%	47.2%	52.8%	47.2%
26,804	RANDOLPH	9,597	4,436	5,085	76	649 D	46.2%	53.0%	46.6%	53.4%
16,506	RITCHIE	5,959	4,195	1,711	53	2,484 R	70.4%	28.7%	71.0%	29.0%
20,129	ROANE	7,511	4,472	3,007	32	1,465 R	59.5%	40.0%	59.8%	40.2%
19,092	SUMMERS	7,832	4,063	3,752	17	311 R	51.9%	47.9%	52.0%	48.0%
18,742	TAYLOR	7,705	5,101	2,548	56	2,553 R	66.2%	33.1%	66.7%	33.3%
16,791	TUCKER	4,872	2,525	2,263	84	262 R	51.8%	46.4%	52.7%	47.3%
14,186	TYLER	5,533	3,881	1,591	61	2,290 R	70.1%	28.8%	70.9%	29.1%
17,851	UPSHUR	7,017	5,277	1,683	57	3,594 R	75.2%	24.0%	75.8%	24.2%
26,012	WAYNE	10,849	5,630	5,177	42	453 R	51.9%	47.7%	52.1%	47.9%
11,562	WEBSTER	4,252	1,936	2,306	10	370 D	45.5%	54.2%	45.6%	54.4%
23,069	WETZEL	8,539	4,428	4,052	59	376 R	51.9%	47.5%	52.2%	47.8%
7,536	WIRT	2,869	1,561	1,272	36	289 R	54.4%	44.3%	55.1%	44.9%
42,306	WOOD	21,721	15,184	6,412	125	8,772 R	69.9%	29.5%	70.3%	29.7%
15,180	WYOMING	7,034	3,987	3,047		940 R	56.7%	43.3%	56.7%	43.3%
1,463,701	TOTAL	642,752	375,551	263,784	3,417	111,767 R	58.4%	41.0%	58.7%	41.3%

WEST VIRGINIA

PRESIDENT 1924

1920 Census Population	County	Total Vote	Republican	Democratic	Other	Rep.-Dem. Plurality	Percentage Total Vote Rep.	Total Vote Dem.	Major Vote Rep.	Major Vote Dem.
18,028	BARBOUR	7,371	3,347	3,188	836	159 R	45.4%	43.3%	51.2%	48.8%
24,554	BERKELEY	10,205	5,427	4,366	412	1,061 R	53.2%	42.8%	55.4%	44.6%
15,319	BOONE	7,284	3,010	3,326	948	316 D	41.3%	45.7%	47.5%	52.5%
23,973	BRAXTON	9,490	4,192	5,168	130	976 D	44.2%	54.5%	44.8%	55.2%
16,527	BROOKE	6,501	3,858	2,037	606	1,821 R	59.3%	31.3%	65.4%	34.6%
65,746	CABELL	32,969	15,581	16,211	1,177	630 D	47.3%	49.2%	49.0%	51.0%
10,268	CALHOUN	3,633	1,399	2,231	3	832 D	38.5%	61.4%	38.5%	61.5%
11,486	CLAY	3,920	1,843	2,037	40	194 D	47.0%	52.0%	47.5%	52.5%
11,976	DODDRIDGE	4,419	2,777	1,594	48	1,183 R	62.8%	36.1%	63.5%	36.5%
60,377	FAYETTE	22,558	10,555	9,563	2,440	992 R	46.8%	42.4%	52.5%	47.5%
10,668	GILMER	4,350	1,570	2,750	30	1,180 D	36.1%	63.2%	36.3%	63.7%
8,993	GRANT	3,105	2,344	658	103	1,686 R	75.5%	21.2%	78.1%	21.9%
26,242	GREENBRIER	11,288	4,768	6,048	472	1,280 D	42.2%	53.6%	44.1%	55.9%
11,713	HAMPSHIRE	4,204	1,172	2,993	39	1,821 D	27.9%	71.2%	28.1%	71.9%
19,975	HANCOCK	5,321	3,775	1,187	359	2,588 R	70.9%	22.3%	76.1%	23.9%
9,601	HARDY	3,750	1,272	2,442	36	1,170 D	33.9%	65.1%	34.2%	65.8%
74,793	HARRISON	30,710	15,165	13,470	2,075	1,695 R	49.4%	43.9%	53.0%	47.0%
18,658	JACKSON	6,734	3,739	2,936	59	803 R	55.5%	43.6%	56.0%	44.0%
15,729	JEFFERSON	6,433	1,870	4,368	195	2,498 D	29.1%	67.9%	30.0%	70.0%
119,650	KANAWHA	52,951	26,018	22,726	4,207	3,292 R	49.1%	42.9%	53.4%	46.6%
20,455	LEWIS	9,470	4,839	4,410	221	429 R	51.1%	46.6%	52.3%	47.7%
19,378	LINCOLN	6,690	3,164	3,355	171	191 D	47.3%	50.1%	48.5%	51.5%
41,006	LOGAN	15,051	7,062	7,377	612	315 D	46.9%	49.0%	48.9%	51.1%
68,571	MCDOWELL	19,732	12,422	5,561	1,749	6,861 R	63.0%	28.2%	69.1%	30.9%
54,571	MARION	24,066	12,167	9,386	2,513	2,781 R	50.6%	39.0%	56.5%	43.5%
33,681	MARSHALL	13,342	7,413	4,710	1,219	2,703 R	55.6%	35.3%	61.1%	38.9%
21,459	MASON	8,090	4,225	3,308	557	917 R	52.2%	40.9%	56.1%	43.9%
49,558	MERCER	21,370	9,159	10,058	2,153	899 D	42.9%	47.1%	47.7%	52.3%
19,849	MINERAL	7,157	3,551	2,860	746	691 R	49.6%	40.0%	55.4%	44.6%
26,364	MINGO	11,070	4,656	5,313	1,101	657 D	42.1%	48.0%	46.7%	53.3%
33,618	MONONGALIA	14,110	6,994	4,977	2,139	2,017 R	49.6%	35.3%	58.4%	41.6%
13,141	MONROE	5,430	2,713	2,686	31	27 R	50.0%	49.5%	50.3%	49.7%
8,357	MORGAN	2,984	1,883	919	182	964 R	63.1%	30.8%	67.2%	32.8%
20,717	NICHOLAS	7,434	3,347	3,956	131	609 D	45.0%	53.2%	45.8%	54.2%
62,892	OHIO	26,626	14,402	8,753	3,471	5,649 R	54.1%	32.9%	62.2%	37.8%
9,652	PENDLETON	3,508	1,462	2,037	9	575 D	41.7%	58.1%	41.8%	58.2%
7,379	PLEASANTS	3,323	1,619	1,675	29	56 D	48.7%	50.4%	49.1%	50.9%
15,002	POCAHONTAS	5,661	2,782	2,777	102	5 R	49.1%	49.1%	50.0%	50.0%
27,996	PRESTON	9,375	6,396	2,445	534	3,951 R	68.2%	26.1%	72.3%	27.7%
17,531	PUTNAM	6,123	2,862	2,946	315	84 D	46.7%	48.1%	49.3%	50.7%
42,482	RALEIGH	17,486	8,643	7,776	1,067	867 R	49.4%	44.5%	52.6%	47.4%
26,804	RANDOLPH	9,637	3,526	5,314	797	1,788 D	36.6%	55.1%	39.9%	60.1%
16,506	RITCHIE	6,632	4,152	2,403	77	1,749 R	62.6%	36.2%	63.3%	36.7%
20,129	ROANE	7,601	4,097	3,504		593 R	53.9%	46.1%	53.9%	46.1%
19,092	SUMMERS	7,524	3,124	3,998	402	874 D	41.5%	53.1%	43.9%	56.1%
18,742	TAYLOR	6,890	3,683	2,499	708	1,184 R	53.5%	36.3%	59.6%	40.4%
16,791	TUCKER	4,992	2,277	2,127	588	150 R	45.6%	42.6%	51.7%	48.3%
14,186	TYLER	5,672	3,425	2,137	110	1,288 R	60.4%	37.7%	61.6%	38.4%
17,851	UPSHUR	7,019	4,930	1,952	137	2,978 R	70.2%	27.8%	71.6%	28.4%
26,012	WAYNE	10,247	3,999	5,870	378	1,871 D	39.0%	57.3%	40.5%	59.5%
11,562	WEBSTER	4,180	1,617	2,523	40	906 D	38.7%	60.4%	39.1%	60.9%
23,069	WETZEL	8,732	3,458	4,998	276	1,540 D	39.6%	57.2%	40.9%	59.1%
7,536	WIRT	3,104	1,491	1,587	26	96 D	48.0%	51.1%	48.4%	51.6%
42,306	WOOD	20,055	10,086	9,378	591	708 R	50.3%	46.8%	51.8%	48.2%
15,180	WYOMING	6,083	3,327	2,358	398	969 R	54.7%	38.8%	58.5%	41.5%
1,463,701	TOTAL	583,662	288,635	257,232	37,795	31,403 R	49.5%	44.1%	52.9%	47.1%

WEST VIRGINIA

PRESIDENT 1920

1920 Census Population	County	Total Vote	Republican	Democratic	Other	Rep.-Dem. Plurality	Percentage Total Vote Rep.	Total Vote Dem.	Major Vote Rep.	Major Vote Dem.
18,028	BARBOUR	6,651	3,763	2,777	111	986 R	56.6%	41.8%	57.5%	42.5%
24,554	BERKELEY	9,748	5,259	4,399	90	860 R	53.9%	45.1%	54.5%	45.5%
15,319	BOONE	5,315	2,674	2,529	112	145 R	50.3%	47.6%	51.4%	48.6%
23,973	BRAXTON	8,563	4,274	4,269	20	5 R	49.9%	49.9%	50.0%	50.0%
16,527	BROOKE	5,335	3,060	2,129	146	931 R	57.4%	39.9%	59.0%	41.0%
65,746	CABELL	26,283	13,170	12,845	268	325 R	50.1%	48.9%	50.6%	49.4%
10,268	CALHOUN	3,447	1,671	1,773	3	102 D	48.5%	51.4%	48.5%	51.5%
11,486	CLAY	3,514	1,981	1,533		448 R	56.4%	43.6%	56.4%	43.6%
11,976	DODDRIDGE	4,297	3,135	1,137	25	1,998 R	73.0%	26.5%	73.4%	26.6%
60,377	FAYETTE	19,934	10,561	9,003	370	1,558 R	53.0%	45.2%	54.0%	46.0%
10,668	GILMER	3,510	1,635	1,854	21	219 D	46.6%	52.8%	46.9%	53.1%
8,993	GRANT	2,942	2,417	492	33	1,925 R	82.2%	16.7%	83.1%	16.9%
26,242	GREENBRIER	9,899	4,850	4,994	55	144 D	49.0%	50.4%	49.3%	50.7%
11,713	HAMPSHIRE	3,467	1,214	2,221	32	1,007 D	35.0%	64.1%	35.3%	64.7%
19,975	HANCOCK	4,364	2,768	1,435	161	1,333 R	63.4%	32.9%	65.9%	34.1%
9,601	HARDY	3,375	1,354	2,014	7	660 D	40.1%	59.7%	40.2%	59.8%
74,793	HARRISON	24,759	13,784	10,206	769	3,578 R	55.7%	41.2%	57.5%	42.5%
18,658	JACKSON	7,181	4,330	2,831	20	1,499 R	60.3%	39.4%	60.5%	39.5%
15,729	JEFFERSON	6,147	2,168	3,944	35	1,776 D	35.3%	64.2%	35.5%	64.5%
119,650	KANAWHA	43,769	23,781	19,284	704	4,497 R	54.3%	44.1%	55.2%	44.8%
20,455	LEWIS	8,082	4,618	3,310	154	1,308 R	57.1%	41.0%	58.2%	41.8%
19,378	LINCOLN	6,008	3,339	2,649	20	690 R	55.6%	44.1%	55.8%	44.2%
41,006	LOGAN	9,936	4,304	5,588	44	1,284 D	43.3%	56.2%	43.5%	56.5%
68,571	MCDOWELL	17,282	12,198	5,068	16	7,130 R	70.6%	29.3%	70.6%	29.4%
54,571	MARION	20,811	11,494	8,734	583	2,760 R	55.2%	42.0%	56.8%	43.2%
33,681	MARSHALL	12,380	7,208	4,814	358	2,394 R	58.2%	38.9%	60.0%	40.0%
21,459	MASON	8,203	4,912	3,177	114	1,735 R	59.9%	38.7%	60.7%	39.3%
49,558	MERCER	16,650	8,613	7,981	56	632 R	51.7%	47.9%	51.9%	48.1%
19,849	MINERAL	6,297	3,646	2,516	135	1,130 R	57.9%	40.0%	59.2%	40.8%
26,364	MINGO	8,906	3,972	4,934		962 D	44.6%	55.4%	44.6%	55.4%
33,618	MONONGALIA	10,584	6,773	3,442	369	3,331 R	64.0%	32.5%	66.3%	33.7%
13,141	MONROE	5,532	3,001	2,519	12	482 R	54.2%	45.5%	54.4%	45.6%
8,357	MORGAN	2,542	1,817	712	13	1,105 R	71.5%	28.0%	71.8%	28.2%
20,717	NICHOLAS	7,305	3,691	3,564	50	127 R	50.5%	48.8%	50.9%	49.1%
62,892	OHIO	26,842	15,735	10,278	829	5,457 R	58.6%	38.3%	60.5%	39.5%
9,652	PENDLETON	3,399	1,581	1,814	4	233 D	46.5%	53.4%	46.6%	53.4%
7,379	PLEASANTS	3,123	1,657	1,440	26	217 R	53.1%	46.1%	53.5%	46.5%
15,002	POCAHONTAS	5,421	2,836	2,540	45	296 R	52.3%	46.9%	52.8%	47.2%
27,996	PRESTON	9,004	6,729	2,150	125	4,579 R	74.7%	23.9%	75.8%	24.2%
17,531	PUTNAM	5,915	3,223	2,578	114	645 R	54.5%	43.6%	55.6%	44.4%
42,482	RALEIGH	13,646	7,668	5,916	62	1,752 R	56.2%	43.4%	56.4%	43.6%
26,804	RANDOLPH	9,018	4,158	4,676	184	518 D	46.1%	51.9%	47.1%	52.9%
16,506	RITCHIE	6,495	4,377	2,050	68	2,327 R	67.4%	31.6%	68.1%	31.9%
20,129	ROANE	7,324	4,232	3,082	10	1,150 R	57.8%	42.1%	57.9%	42.1%
19,092	SUMMERS	7,187	3,611	3,552	24	59 R	50.2%	49.4%	50.4%	49.6%
18,742	TAYLOR	6,080	3,649	2,311	120	1,338 R	60.0%	38.0%	61.2%	38.8%
16,791	TUCKER	4,688	2,498	1,966	224	532 R	53.3%	41.9%	56.0%	44.0%
14,186	TYLER	5,509	3,654	1,762	93	1,892 R	66.3%	32.0%	67.5%	32.5%
17,851	UPSHUR	6,396	4,936	1,418	42	3,518 R	77.2%	22.2%	77.7%	22.3%
26,012	WAYNE	8,244	3,754	4,490		736 D	45.5%	54.5%	45.5%	54.5%
11,562	WEBSTER	3,509	1,562	1,942	5	380 D	44.5%	55.3%	44.6%	55.4%
23,069	WETZEL	7,804	3,619	4,103	82	484 D	46.4%	52.6%	46.9%	53.1%
7,536	WIRT	3,061	1,680	1,376	5	304 R	54.9%	45.0%	55.0%	45.0%
42,306	WOOD	19,478	10,463	8,839	176	1,624 R	53.7%	45.4%	54.2%	45.8%
15,180	WYOMING	4,775	2,950	1,825		1,125 R	61.8%	38.2%	61.8%	38.2%
1,463,701	TOTAL	509,936	282,007	220,785	7,144	61,222 R	55.3%	43.3%	56.1%	43.9%

WEST VIRGINIA

ELECTION NOTES

1956

1952

1948 Other vote was Wallace (Progressive).

1944

1940

1936 Other vote was 1,173 Colvin (Prohibition); 832 Thomas (Socialist).

1932 Other vote was 5,133 Thomas (Socialist); 2,342 Upshaw (Prohibition); 444 Foster (Communist).

1928 Other vote was 1,703 Varney (Prohibition); 1,313 Thomas (Socialist); 401 Foster (Communist).

1924 Other vote was 36,723 LaFollette (21,820 Farmer-Labor and 14,903 Socialist); 1,072 Nations (American).

1920 Other vote was 5,618 Debs (Socialist); 1,526 Watkins (Prohibition).

WISCONSIN

POPULAR VOTE FOR PRESIDENT 1920 TO 1956

Year	Total Vote	Republican		Democratic		Other Vote	Plurality	Percentage			
								Total Vote		Major Vote	
		Vote	Candidate	Vote	Candidate			Rep.	Dem.	Rep.	Dem.
1956	1,550,558	954,844	Eisenhower, Dwight D.	586,768	Stevenson, Adlai E.	8,946	368,076 R	61.6%	37.8%	61.9%	38.1%
1952	1,607,370	979,744	Eisenhower, Dwight D.	622,175	Stevenson, Adlai E.	5,451	357,569 R	61.0%	38.7%	61.2%	38.8%
1948	1,276,800	590,959	Dewey, Thomas E.	647,310	Truman, Harry S.	38,531	56,351 D	46.3%	50.7%	47.7%	52.3%
1944	1,339,152	674,532	Dewey, Thomas E.	650,413	Roosevelt, Franklin D.	14,207	24,119 R	50.4%	48.6%	50.9%	49.1%
1940	1,405,522	679,206	Willkie, Wendell	704,821	Roosevelt, Franklin D.	21,495	25,615 D	48.3%	50.1%	49.1%	50.9%
1936	1,258,560	380,828	Landon, Alfred M.	802,984	Roosevelt, Franklin D.	74,748	422,156 D	30.3%	63.8%	32.2%	67.8%
1932	1,114,814	347,741	Hoover, Herbert C.	707,410	Roosevelt, Franklin D.	59,663	359,669 D	31.2%	63.5%	33.0%	67.0%
1928	1,016,831	544,205	Hoover, Herbert C.	450,259	Smith, Alfred E.	22,367	93,946 R	53.5%	44.3%	54.7%	45.3%
1924 **	840,827	311,614	Coolidge, Calvin	68,115	Davis, John W.	461,098	142,064 P	37.1%	8.1%	82.1%	17.9%
1920	701,281	498,576	Harding, Warren G.	113,422	Cox, James M.	89,283	385,154 R	71.1%	16.2%	81.5%	18.5%

In 1924 other vote was 453,678 Progressive; 3,773 Communist; 2,918 Prohibition; 458 Socialist Labor and 271 Commonwealth Land.

ELECTORAL COLLEGE VOTE 1920 TO 1956

Year	Total	Republican	Democratic	Other
1956	12	12	—	—
1952	12	12	—	—
1948	12	—	12	—
1944	12	12	—	—
1940	12	—	12	—
1936	12	—	12	—
1932	12	—	12	—
1928	13	13	—	—
1924	13	—	—	13 PROGRESSIVE
1920	13	13	—	—

WISCONSIN

DOUGLAS
BAYFIELD
IRON
ASHLAND
VILAS
BURNETT
WASHBURN
SAWYER
FLORENCE
PRICE
ONEIDA
FOREST
POLK
BARRON
RUSK
LINCOLN
LANGLADE
MARINETTE
TAYLOR
ST. CROIX
DUNN
CHIPPEWA
MENOM-
INEE
OCONTO
MARATHON
PIERCE
EAU CLAIRE
CLARK
SHAWANO
DOOR
PEPIN
BUFFALO
TREMPEALEAU
JACKSON
WOOD
PORTAGE
WAUPACA
OUTAGAMIE
BROWN
KEWAUNEE
WAUSHARA
WINNE-
BAGO
CALUMET
MANITOWOC
LA
CROSSE
MONROE
ADAMS
JUNEAU
MARQUETTE
GREEN
LAKE
FOND DU LAC
SHEBOY-
GAN
VERNON
RICHLAND
SAUK
COLUMBIA
DODGE
WASHING-
TON
OZAUKEE
CRAWFORD
GRANT
IOWA
DANE
JEFFERSON
WAUSHARA
MILWAUKEE
LAFAYETTE
GREEN
ROCK
WALWORTH
RACINE
KENOSHA

WISCONSIN

PRESIDENT 1956

1950 Census Population	County	Total Vote	Republican	Democratic	Other	Rep.-Dem. Plurality	Percentage Total Vote Rep.	Percentage Total Vote Dem.	Percentage Major Vote Rep.	Percentage Major Vote Dem.
7,906	ADAMS	3,117	1,854	1,244	19	610 R	59.5%	39.9%	59.8%	40.2%
19,461	ASHLAND	7,819	4,121	3,677	21	444 R	52.7%	47.0%	52.8%	47.2%
34,703	BARRON	14,126	8,634	5,419	73	3,215 R	61.1%	38.4%	61.4%	38.6%
13,760	BAYFIELD	5,806	3,096	2,691	19	405 R	53.3%	46.3%	53.5%	46.5%
98,314	BROWN	46,808	32,878	13,642	288	19,236 R	70.2%	29.1%	70.7%	29.3%
14,719	BUFFALO	5,661	3,387	2,266	8	1,121 R	59.8%	40.0%	59.9%	40.1%
10,236	BURNETT	4,198	2,198	1,986	14	212 R	52.4%	47.3%	52.5%	47.5%
18,840	CALUMET	8,308	6,166	2,099	43	4,067 R	74.2%	25.3%	74.6%	25.4%
42,839	CHIPPEWA	16,461	9,781	6,617	63	3,164 R	59.4%	40.2%	59.6%	40.4%
32,459	CLARK	12,754	7,941	4,765	48	3,176 R	62.3%	37.4%	62.5%	37.5%
34,023	COLUMBIA	15,330	10,120	5,158	52	4,962 R	66.0%	33.6%	66.2%	33.8%
17,652	CRAWFORD	6,681	4,123	2,522	36	1,601 R	61.7%	37.7%	62.0%	38.0%
169,357	DANE	76,213	38,955	36,891	367	2,064 R	51.1%	48.4%	51.4%	48.6%
57,611	DODGE	24,366	17,569	6,704	93	10,865 R	72.1%	27.5%	72.4%	27.6%
20,870	DOOR	8,622	6,722	1,859	41	4,863 R	78.0%	21.6%	78.3%	21.7%
46,715	DOUGLAS	20,502	9,183	11,276	43	2,093 D	44.8%	55.0%	44.9%	55.1%
27,341	DUNN	10,604	6,401	4,189	14	2,212 R	60.4%	39.5%	60.4%	39.6%
54,187	EAU CLAIRE	22,439	13,122	9,276	41	3,846 R	58.5%	41.3%	58.6%	41.4%
3,756	FLORENCE	1,731	1,003	723	5	280 R	57.9%	41.8%	58.1%	41.9%
67,829	FOND DU LAC	29,666	21,496	7,940	230	13,556 R	72.5%	26.8%	73.0%	27.0%
9,437	FOREST	3,575	2,039	1,527	9	512 R	57.0%	42.7%	57.2%	42.8%
41,460	GRANT	16,958	11,648	5,208	102	6,440 R	68.7%	30.7%	69.1%	30.9%
24,172	GREEN	10,779	7,114	3,614	51	3,500 R	66.0%	33.5%	66.3%	33.7%
14,749	GREEN LAKE	7,113	5,441	1,643	29	3,798 R	76.5%	23.1%	76.8%	23.2%
19,610	IOWA	8,417	5,201	3,176	40	2,025 R	61.8%	37.7%	62.1%	37.9%
8,714	IRON	4,176	1,930	2,226	20	296 D	46.2%	53.3%	46.4%	53.6%
16,073	JACKSON	6,378	3,614	2,755	9	859 R	56.7%	43.2%	56.7%	43.3%
43,069	JEFFERSON	19,931	13,357	6,452	122	6,905 R	67.0%	32.4%	67.4%	32.6%
18,930	JUNEAU	7,598	5,135	2,428	35	2,707 R	67.6%	32.0%	67.9%	32.1%
75,238	KENOSHA	38,796	21,367	17,094	335	4,273 R	55.1%	44.1%	55.6%	44.4%
17,366	KEWAUNEE	7,509	5,106	2,364	39	2,742 R	68.0%	31.5%	68.4%	31.6%
67,587	LA CROSSE	29,622	18,264	11,258	100	7,006 R	61.7%	38.0%	61.9%	38.1%
18,137	LAFAYETTE	7,978	4,733	3,212	33	1,521 R	59.3%	40.3%	59.6%	40.4%
21,975	LANGLADE	7,841	5,004	2,804	33	2,200 R	63.8%	35.8%	64.1%	35.9%
22,235	LINCOLN	9,343	6,329	2,880	134	3,449 R	67.7%	30.8%	68.7%	31.3%
67,159	MANITOWOC	29,199	18,078	10,800	321	7,278 R	61.9%	37.0%	62.6%	37.4%
80,337	MARATHON	38,051	22,586	15,301	164	7,285 R	59.4%	40.2%	59.6%	40.4%
35,748	MARINETTE	14,060	8,874	5,113	73	3,761 R	63.1%	36.4%	63.4%	36.6%
8,839	MARQUETTE	3,785	2,796	975	14	1,821 R	73.9%	25.8%	74.1%	25.9%
871,047	MILWAUKEE	407,318	227,253	177,286	2,779	49,967 R	55.8%	43.5%	56.2%	43.8%
31,378	MONROE	11,811	7,460	4,311	40	3,149 R	63.2%	36.5%	63.4%	36.6%
26,238	OCONTO	10,525	6,836	3,632	57	3,204 R	65.0%	34.5%	65.3%	34.7%
20,648	ONEIDA	9,648	6,261	3,328	59	2,933 R	64.9%	34.5%	65.3%	34.7%
81,722	OUTAGAMIE	34,077	26,090	7,725	262	18,365 R	76.6%	22.7%	77.2%	22.8%
23,361	OZAUKEE	14,086	9,808	4,139	139	5,669 R	69.6%	29.4%	70.3%	29.7%
7,462	PEPIN	3,015	1,975	1,040		935 R	65.5%	34.5%	65.5%	34.5%
21,448	PIERCE	9,458	5,782	3,644	32	2,138 R	61.1%	38.5%	61.3%	38.7%
24,944	POLK	10,906	5,894	4,985	27	909 R	54.0%	45.7%	54.2%	45.8%
34,858	PORTAGE	15,386	8,320	7,010	56	1,310 R	54.1%	45.6%	54.3%	45.7%
16,344	PRICE	6,848	4,028	2,778	42	1,250 R	58.8%	40.6%	59.2%	40.8%
109,585	RACINE	54,919	31,968	22,646	305	9,322 R	58.2%	41.2%	58.5%	41.5%
19,245	RICHLAND	7,874	5,062	2,783	29	2,279 R	64.3%	35.3%	64.5%	35.5%
92,778	ROCK	42,987	28,980	13,834	173	15,146 R	67.4%	32.2%	67.7%	32.3%
16,790	RUSK	6,395	3,433	2,929	33	504 R	53.7%	45.8%	54.0%	46.0%
25,905	ST. CROIX	12,484	6,956	5,499	29	1,457 R	55.7%	44.0%	55.8%	44.2%
38,120	SAUK	16,016	10,644	5,292	80	5,352 R	66.5%	33.0%	66.8%	33.2%
10,323	SAWYER	4,374	2,823	1,520	31	1,303 R	64.5%	34.8%	65.0%	35.0%
35,249	SHAWANO	13,122	9,388	3,675	59	5,713 R	71.5%	28.0%	71.9%	28.1%
80,631	SHEBOYGAN	36,852	22,077	14,540	235	7,537 R	59.9%	39.5%	60.3%	39.7%
18,456	TAYLOR	6,654	3,843	2,759	52	1,084 R	57.8%	41.5%	58.2%	41.8%

WISCONSIN

PRESIDENT 1956

1950 Census Population	County	Total Vote	Republican	Democratic	Other	Rep.-Dem. Plurality	Percentage Total Vote Rep.	Total Vote Dem.	Major Vote Rep.	Major Vote Dem.
23,730	TREMPEALEAU	10,094	5,476	4,602	16	874 R	54.3%	45.6%	54.3%	45.7%
27,906	VERNON	11,140	6,200	4,923	17	1,277 R	55.7%	44.2%	55.7%	44.3%
9,363	VILAS	4,972	3,683	1,267	22	2,416 R	74.1%	25.5%	74.4%	25.6%
41,584	WALWORTH	21,790	16,696	4,922	172	11,774 R	76.6%	22.6%	77.2%	22.8%
11,665	WASHBURN	4,752	2,798	1,935	19	863 R	58.9%	40.7%	59.1%	40.9%
33,902	WASHINGTON	16,683	12,167	4,447	69	7,720 R	72.9%	26.7%	73.2%	26.8%
85,901	WAUKESHA	51,084	35,212	15,496	376	19,716 R	68.9%	30.3%	69.4%	30.6%
35,056	WAUPACA	15,003	11,798	3,133	72	8,665 R	78.6%	20.9%	79.0%	21.0%
13,920	WAUSHARA	6,127	4,717	1,387	23	3,330 R	77.0%	22.6%	77.3%	22.7%
91,103	WINNEBAGO	40,254	28,759	11,115	380	17,644 R	71.4%	27.6%	72.1%	27.9%
50,500	WOOD	21,583	15,091	6,412	80	8,679 R	69.9%	29.7%	70.2%	29.8%
3,434,575	TOTAL	1,550,558	954,844	586,768	8,946	368,076 R	61.6%	37.8%	61.9%	38.1%

WISCONSIN

PRESIDENT 1952

1950 Census Population	County	Total Vote	Republican	Democratic	Other	Rep.-Dem. Plurality	Percentage Total Vote Rep.	Total Vote Dem.	Major Vote Rep.	Major Vote Dem.
7,906	ADAMS	3,457	2,259	1,180	18	1,079 R	65.3%	34.1%	65.7%	34.3%
19,461	ASHLAND	8,320	4,451	3,828	41	623 R	53.5%	46.0%	53.8%	46.2%
34,703	BARRON	14,981	10,013	4,902	66	5,111 R	66.8%	32.7%	67.1%	32.9%
13,760	BAYFIELD	6,107	3,419	2,616	72	803 R	56.0%	42.8%	56.7%	43.3%
98,314	BROWN	44,836	30,400	14,342	94	16,058 R	67.8%	32.0%	67.9%	32.1%
14,719	BUFFALO	6,232	4,233	1,988	11	2,245 R	67.9%	31.9%	68.0%	32.0%
10,236	BURNETT	4,440	2,683	1,741	16	942 R	60.4%	39.2%	60.6%	39.4%
18,840	CALUMET	8,615	6,640	1,970	5	4,670 R	77.1%	22.9%	77.1%	22.9%
42,839	CHIPPEWA	17,854	11,429	6,380	45	5,049 R	64.0%	35.7%	64.2%	35.8%
32,459	CLARK	13,116	9,406	3,652	58	5,754 R	71.7%	27.8%	72.0%	28.0%
34,023	COLUMBIA	16,425	11,133	5,272	20	5,861 R	67.8%	32.1%	67.9%	32.1%
17,652	CRAWFORD	7,588	5,323	2,256	9	3,067 R	70.2%	29.7%	70.2%	29.8%
169,357	DANE	76,927	38,724	37,987	216	737 R	50.3%	49.4%	50.5%	49.5%
57,611	DODGE	26,336	19,298	7,001	37	12,297 R	73.3%	26.6%	73.4%	26.6%
20,870	DOOR	9,430	7,621	1,790	19	5,831 R	80.8%	19.0%	81.0%	19.0%
46,715	DOUGLAS	21,313	9,677	11,538	98	1,861 D	45.4%	54.1%	45.6%	54.4%
27,341	DUNN	11,094	7,475	3,593	26	3,882 R	67.4%	32.4%	67.5%	32.5%
54,187	EAU CLAIRE	23,658	14,069	9,554	35	4,515 R	59.5%	40.4%	59.6%	40.4%
3,756	FLORENCE	1,963	1,147	809	7	338 R	58.4%	41.2%	58.6%	41.4%
67,829	FOND DU LAC	30,625	22,794	7,724	107	15,070 R	74.4%	25.2%	74.7%	25.3%
9,437	FOREST	3,793	1,990	1,791	12	199 R	52.5%	47.2%	52.6%	47.4%
41,460	GRANT	18,556	14,327	4,197	32	10,130 R	77.2%	22.6%	77.3%	22.7%
24,172	GREEN	11,281	7,949	3,326	6	4,623 R	70.5%	29.5%	70.5%	29.5%
14,749	GREEN LAKE	7,717	6,117	1,590	10	4,527 R	79.3%	20.6%	79.4%	20.6%
19,610	IOWA	8,952	6,211	2,722	19	3,489 R	69.4%	30.4%	69.5%	30.5%
8,714	IRON	4,416	1,733	2,662	21	929 D	39.2%	60.3%	39.4%	60.6%
16,073	JACKSON	7,071	4,235	2,819	17	1,416 R	59.9%	39.9%	60.0%	40.0%
43,069	JEFFERSON	20,743	13,884	6,827	32	7,057 R	66.9%	32.9%	67.0%	33.0%
18,930	JUNEAU	8,164	5,978	2,163	23	3,815 R	73.2%	26.5%	73.4%	26.6%
75,238	KENOSHA	38,827	18,917	19,768	142	851 D	48.7%	50.9%	48.9%	51.1%
17,366	KEWAUNEE	8,482	6,482	1,972	28	4,510 R	76.4%	23.2%	76.7%	23.3%
67,587	LA CROSSE	31,132	19,271	11,808	53	7,463 R	61.9%	37.9%	62.0%	38.0%
18,137	LAFAYETTE	8,653	5,731	2,905	17	2,826 R	66.2%	33.6%	66.4%	33.6%
21,975	LANGLADE	9,269	5,841	3,371	57	2,470 R	63.0%	36.4%	63.4%	36.6%
22,235	LINCOLN	10,007	6,877	3,092	38	3,785 R	68.7%	30.9%	69.0%	31.0%
67,159	MANITOWOC	30,901	18,950	11,879	72	7,071 R	61.3%	38.4%	61.5%	38.5%
80,337	MARATHON	35,373	20,702	14,541	130	6,161 R	58.5%	41.1%	58.7%	41.3%
35,748	MARINETTE	15,087	9,313	5,727	47	3,586 R	61.7%	38.0%	61.9%	38.1%
8,839	MARQUETTE	4,218	3,379	835	4	2,544 R	80.1%	19.8%	80.2%	19.8%
871,047	MILWAUKEE	426,006	219,477	204,474	2,055	15,003 R	51.5%	48.0%	51.8%	48.2%
31,378	MONROE	12,495	8,744	3,717	34	5,027 R	70.0%	29.7%	70.2%	29.8%
26,238	OCONTO	11,220	7,807	3,382	31	4,425 R	69.6%	30.1%	69.8%	30.2%
20,648	ONEIDA	10,062	6,224	3,808	30	2,416 R	61.9%	37.8%	62.0%	38.0%
81,722	OUTAGAMIE	36,020	26,603	9,373	44	17,230 R	73.9%	26.0%	73.9%	26.1%
23,361	OZAUKEE	12,939	8,665	4,241	33	4,424 R	67.0%	32.8%	67.1%	32.9%
7,462	PEPIN	3,255	2,348	896	11	1,452 R	72.1%	27.5%	72.4%	27.6%
21,448	PIERCE	10,021	6,763	3,241	17	3,522 R	67.5%	32.3%	67.6%	32.4%
24,944	POLK	11,282	6,966	4,274	42	2,692 R	61.7%	37.9%	62.0%	38.0%
34,858	PORTAGE	16,087	8,499	7,537	51	962 R	52.8%	46.9%	53.0%	47.0%
16,344	PRICE	7,491	4,376	3,048	67	1,328 R	58.4%	40.7%	58.9%	41.1%
109,585	RACINE	56,049	30,628	25,241	180	5,387 R	54.6%	45.0%	54.8%	45.2%
19,245	RICHLAND	8,875	6,605	2,260	10	4,345 R	74.4%	25.5%	74.5%	25.5%
92,778	ROCK	43,065	27,837	15,183	45	12,654 R	64.6%	35.3%	64.7%	35.3%
16,790	RUSK	6,964	4,134	2,777	53	1,357 R	59.4%	39.9%	59.8%	40.2%
25,905	ST. CROIX	12,726	7,607	5,094	25	2,513 R	59.8%	40.0%	59.9%	40.1%
38,120	SAUK	17,666	12,347	5,267	52	7,080 R	69.9%	29.8%	70.1%	29.9%
10,323	SAWYER	4,694	3,146	1,527	21	1,619 R	67.0%	32.5%	67.3%	32.7%
35,249	SHAWANO	14,501	11,131	3,334	36	7,797 R	76.8%	23.0%	77.0%	23.0%
80,631	SHEBOYGAN	37,432	22,084	15,136	212	6,948 R	59.0%	40.4%	59.3%	40.7%
18,456	TAYLOR	7,710	4,892	2,768	50	2,124 R	63.5%	35.9%	63.9%	36.1%

WISCONSIN

PRESIDENT 1952

1950 Census Population	County	Total Vote	Republican	Democratic	Other	Rep.-Dem. Plurality	Percentage Total Vote Rep.	Total Vote Dem.	Major Vote Rep.	Major Vote Dem.
23,730	TREMPEALEAU	10,548	6,501	4,021	26	2,480 R	61.6%	38.1%	61.8%	38.2%
27,906	VERNON	11,663	7,619	4,032	12	3,587 R	65.3%	34.6%	65.4%	34.6%
9,363	VILAS	5,204	3,687	1,497	20	2,190 R	70.8%	28.8%	71.1%	28.9%
41,584	WALWORTH	22,372	16,906	5,417	49	11,489 R	75.6%	24.2%	75.7%	24.3%
11,665	WASHBURN	5,237	3,184	2,039	14	1,145 R	60.8%	38.9%	61.0%	39.0%
33,902	WASHINGTON	17,100	12,626	4,440	34	8,186 R	73.8%	26.0%	74.0%	26.0%
85,901	WAUKESHA	46,111	30,238	15,756	117	14,482 R	65.6%	34.2%	65.7%	34.3%
35,056	WAUPACA	16,826	13,693	3,105	28	10,588 R	81.4%	18.5%	81.5%	18.5%
13,920	WAUSHARA	6,713	5,447	1,242	24	4,205 R	81.1%	18.5%	81.4%	18.6%
91,103	WINNEBAGO	41,328	28,172	13,016	140	15,156 R	68.2%	31.5%	68.4%	31.6%
50,500	WOOD	21,749	14,707	6,914	128	7,793 R	67.6%	31.8%	68.0%	32.0%
3,434,575	TOTAL	1,607,370	979,744	622,175	5,451	357,569 R	61.0%	38.7%	61.2%	38.8%

WISCONSIN

PRESIDENT 1948

1940 Census Population	County	Total Vote	Republican	Democratic	Other	Rep.-Dem. Plurality	Percentage Total Vote Rep.	Total Vote Dem.	Major Vote Rep.	Major Vote Dem.
8,449	ADAMS	2,761	1,259	1,419	83	160 D	45.6%	51.4%	47.0%	53.0%
21,801	ASHLAND	7,509	3,135	4,110	264	975 D	41.7%	54.7%	43.3%	56.7%
34,289	BARRON	12,016	5,516	6,148	352	632 D	45.9%	51.2%	47.3%	52.7%
15,827	BAYFIELD	5,835	2,338	3,081	416	743 D	40.1%	52.8%	43.1%	56.9%
83,109	BROWN	36,558	17,729	18,449	380	720 D	48.5%	50.5%	49.0%	51.0%
16,090	BUFFALO	4,993	2,350	2,563	80	213 D	47.1%	51.3%	47.8%	52.2%
11,382	BURNETT	3,899	1,590	2,177	132	587 D	40.8%	55.8%	42.2%	57.8%
17,618	CALUMET	6,909	4,185	2,662	62	1,523 R	60.6%	38.5%	61.1%	38.9%
40,703	CHIPPEWA	14,102	6,146	7,702	254	1,556 D	43.6%	54.6%	44.4%	55.6%
33,972	CLARK	11,175	5,885	4,840	450	1,045 R	52.7%	43.3%	54.9%	45.1%
32,517	COLUMBIA	12,169	6,406	5,615	148	791 R	52.6%	46.1%	53.3%	46.7%
18,328	CRAWFORD	7,185	3,465	3,639	81	174 D	48.2%	50.6%	48.8%	51.2%
130,660	DANE	60,664	22,934	35,486	2,244	12,552 D	37.8%	58.5%	39.3%	60.7%
54,280	DODGE	19,288	10,831	8,212	245	2,619 R	56.2%	42.6%	56.9%	43.1%
19,095	DOOR	7,459	4,911	2,440	108	2,471 R	65.8%	32.7%	66.8%	33.2%
47,119	DOUGLAS	19,248	6,252	12,278	718	6,026 D	32.5%	63.8%	33.7%	66.3%
27,375	DUNN	9,382	4,319	4,894	169	575 D	46.0%	52.2%	46.9%	53.1%
46,999	EAU CLAIRE	18,042	7,825	9,971	246	2,146 D	43.4%	55.3%	44.0%	56.0%
4,177	FLORENCE	1,758	756	885	117	129 D	43.0%	50.3%	46.1%	53.9%
62,353	FOND DU LAC	23,083	13,760	8,904	419	4,856 R	59.6%	38.6%	60.7%	39.3%
11,805	FOREST	3,563	1,251	2,208	104	957 D	35.1%	62.0%	36.2%	63.8%
40,639	GRANT	15,089	8,299	6,575	215	1,724 R	55.0%	43.6%	55.8%	44.2%
23,146	GREEN	8,398	4,403	3,881	114	522 R	52.4%	46.2%	53.2%	46.8%
14,092	GREEN LAKE	5,729	3,939	1,722	68	2,217 R	68.8%	30.1%	69.6%	30.4%
20,595	IOWA	7,794	3,745	3,917	132	172 D	48.0%	50.3%	48.9%	51.1%
10,049	IRON	4,209	1,281	2,665	263	1,384 D	30.4%	63.3%	32.5%	67.5%
16,599	JACKSON	5,563	2,553	2,921	89	368 D	45.9%	52.5%	46.6%	53.4%
38,868	JEFFERSON	15,728	8,244	7,256	228	988 R	52.4%	46.1%	53.2%	46.8%
18,708	JUNEAU	6,809	3,793	2,889	127	904 R	55.7%	42.4%	56.8%	43.2%
63,505	KENOSHA	32,109	12,780	17,987	1,342	5,207 D	39.8%	56.0%	41.5%	58.5%
16,680	KEWAUNEE	6,478	3,646	2,746	86	900 R	56.3%	42.4%	57.0%	43.0%
59,653	LA CROSSE	23,260	10,525	12,345	390	1,820 D	45.2%	53.1%	46.0%	54.0%
18,695	LAFAYETTE	7,104	3,288	3,740	76	452 D	46.3%	52.6%	46.8%	53.2%
23,227	LANGLADE	8,081	3,441	4,346	294	905 D	42.6%	53.8%	44.2%	55.8%
22,536	LINCOLN	7,894	4,339	3,368	187	971 R	55.0%	42.7%	56.3%	43.7%
61,617	MANITOWOC	24,863	10,947	13,401	515	2,454 D	44.0%	53.9%	45.0%	55.0%
75,915	MARATHON	28,079	11,494	15,898	687	4,404 D	40.9%	56.6%	42.0%	58.0%
36,225	MARINETTE	12,565	5,869	6,468	228	599 D	46.7%	51.5%	47.6%	52.4%
9,097	MARQUETTE	3,166	2,033	1,095	38	938 R	64.2%	34.6%	65.0%	35.0%
766,885	MILWAUKEE	342,910	138,672	187,637	16,601	48,965 D	40.4%	54.7%	42.5%	57.5%
30,080	MONROE	10,490	5,347	4,970	173	377 R	51.0%	47.4%	51.8%	48.2%
27,075	OCONTO	9,247	4,865	4,269	113	596 R	52.6%	46.2%	53.3%	46.7%
18,938	ONEIDA	8,015	3,729	4,081	205	352 D	46.5%	50.9%	47.7%	52.3%
70,032	OUTAGAMIE	27,672	16,161	11,233	278	4,928 R	58.4%	40.6%	59.0%	41.0%
18,985	OZAUKEE	9,208	4,866	4,159	183	707 R	52.8%	45.2%	53.9%	46.1%
7,897	PEPIN	2,764	1,333	1,381	50	48 D	48.2%	50.0%	49.1%	50.9%
21,471	PIERCE	8,306	3,753	4,395	158	642 D	45.2%	52.9%	46.1%	53.9%
26,197	POLK	9,572	3,974	5,330	268	1,356 D	41.5%	55.7%	42.7%	57.3%
35,800	PORTAGE	13,791	5,424	8,154	213	2,730 D	39.3%	59.1%	39.9%	60.1%
18,467	PRICE	6,785	2,952	3,373	460	421 D	43.5%	49.7%	46.7%	53.3%
94,047	RACINE	43,797	19,029	23,266	1,502	4,237 D	43.4%	53.1%	45.0%	55.0%
20,381	RICHLAND	6,906	3,836	2,990	80	846 R	55.5%	43.3%	56.2%	43.8%
80,173	ROCK	33,692	17,068	16,150	474	918 R	50.7%	47.9%	51.4%	48.6%
17,737	RUSK	6,239	2,623	3,401	215	778 D	42.0%	54.5%	43.5%	56.5%
24,842	ST. CROIX	10,701	4,326	6,173	202	1,847 D	40.4%	57.7%	41.2%	58.8%
33,700	SAUK	13,307	7,140	5,831	336	1,309 R	53.7%	43.8%	55.0%	45.0%
11,540	SAWYER	4,559	2,257	2,177	125	80 R	49.5%	47.8%	50.9%	49.1%
35,378	SHAWANO	10,659	6,286	4,192	181	2,094 R	59.0%	39.3%	60.0%	40.0%
76,221	SHEBOYGAN	28,942	12,459	15,339	1,144	2,880 D	43.0%	53.0%	44.8%	55.2%
20,105	TAYLOR	6,124	2,579	3,184	361	605 D	42.1%	52.0%	44.8%	55.2%

WISCONSIN

PRESIDENT 1948

1940 Census Population	County	Total Vote	Republican	Democratic	Other	Rep.-Dem. Plurality	Percentage Total Vote Rep.	Percentage Total Vote Dem.	Percentage Major Vote Rep.	Percentage Major Vote Dem.
24,381	TREMPEALEAU	8,463	3,650	4,711	102	1,061 D	43.1%	55.7%	43.7%	56.3%
29,940	VERNON	9,470	4,139	5,226	105	1,087 D	43.7%	55.2%	44.2%	55.8%
8,894	VILAS	4,571	2,665	1,688	218	977 R	58.3%	36.9%	61.2%	38.8%
33,103	WALWORTH	16,151	10,509	5,377	265	5,132 R	65.1%	33.3%	66.2%	33.8%
12,496	WASHBURN	4,925	2,059	2,708	158	649 D	41.8%	55.0%	43.2%	56.8%
28,430	WASHINGTON	11,565	6,876	4,495	194	2,381 R	59.5%	38.9%	60.5%	39.5%
62,744	WAUKESHA	31,950	17,324	13,952	674	3,372 R	54.2%	43.7%	55.4%	44.6%
34,614	WAUPACA	12,982	8,764	4,020	198	4,744 R	67.5%	31.0%	68.6%	31.4%
14,268	WAUSHARA	5,164	3,594	1,430	140	2,164 R	69.6%	27.7%	71.5%	28.5%
80,507	WINNEBAGO	31,110	17,165	13,116	829	4,049 R	55.2%	42.2%	56.7%	43.3%
44,465	WOOD	16,247	8,073	7,999	175	74 R	49.7%	49.2%	50.2%	49.8%
3,137,587	TOTAL	1,276,800	590,959	647,310	38,531	56,351 D	46.3%	50.7%	47.7%	52.3%

WISCONSIN

PRESIDENT 1944

1940 Census Population	County	Total Vote	Republican	Democratic	Other	Rep.-Dem. Plurality	Percentage Total Vote Rep.	Percentage Total Vote Dem.	Percentage Major Vote Rep.	Percentage Major Vote Dem.
8,449	ADAMS	3,072	1,579	1,478	15	101 R	51.4%	48.1%	51.7%	48.3%
21,801	ASHLAND	7,839	3,183	4,609	47	1,426 D	40.6%	58.8%	40.8%	59.2%
34,289	BARRON	12,823	7,137	5,585	101	1,552 R	55.7%	43.6%	56.1%	43.9%
15,827	BAYFIELD	5,890	2,475	3,362	53	887 D	42.0%	57.1%	42.4%	57.6%
83,109	BROWN	35,426	17,762	17,576	88	186 R	50.1%	49.6%	50.3%	49.7%
16,090	BUFFALO	5,406	3,416	1,948	42	1,468 R	63.2%	36.0%	63.7%	36.3%
11,382	BURNETT	4,019	2,119	1,868	32	251 R	52.7%	46.5%	53.1%	46.9%
17,618	CALUMET	7,626	5,611	1,966	49	3,645 R	73.6%	25.8%	74.1%	25.9%
40,703	CHIPPEWA	14,351	7,691	6,567	93	1,124 R	53.6%	45.8%	53.9%	46.1%
33,972	CLARK	12,657	7,948	4,612	97	3,336 R	62.8%	36.4%	63.3%	36.7%
32,517	COLUMBIA	13,924	7,867	5,997	60	1,870 R	56.5%	43.1%	56.7%	43.3%
18,328	CRAWFORD	7,351	4,199	3,130	22	1,069 R	57.1%	42.6%	57.3%	42.7%
130,660	DANE	60,651	23,021	37,076	554	14,055 D	38.0%	61.1%	38.3%	61.7%
54,280	DODGE	21,883	14,102	7,667	114	6,435 R	64.4%	35.0%	64.8%	35.2%
19,095	DOOR	8,305	5,668	2,599	38	3,069 R	68.2%	31.3%	68.6%	31.4%
47,119	DOUGLAS	20,263	7,132	12,985	146	5,853 D	35.2%	64.1%	35.5%	64.5%
27,375	DUNN	9,905	5,980	3,853	72	2,127 R	60.4%	38.9%	60.8%	39.2%
46,999	EAU CLAIRE	18,520	9,470	8,962	88	508 R	51.1%	48.4%	51.4%	48.6%
4,177	FLORENCE	1,678	765	897	16	132 D	45.6%	53.5%	46.0%	54.0%
62,353	FOND DU LAC	26,306	16,785	9,378	143	7,407 R	63.8%	35.6%	64.2%	35.8%
11,805	FOREST	3,840	1,391	2,436	13	1,045 D	36.2%	63.4%	36.3%	63.7%
40,639	GRANT	16,345	10,226	6,091	28	4,135 R	62.6%	37.3%	62.7%	37.3%
23,146	GREEN	9,699	5,556	4,101	42	1,455 R	57.3%	42.3%	57.5%	42.5%
14,092	GREEN LAKE	6,784	4,571	2,190	23	2,381 R	67.4%	32.3%	67.6%	32.4%
20,595	IOWA	8,228	4,608	3,585	35	1,023 R	56.0%	43.6%	56.2%	43.8%
10,049	IRON	4,268	1,345	2,894	29	1,549 D	31.5%	67.8%	31.7%	68.3%
16,599	JACKSON	6,256	3,182	3,040	34	142 R	50.9%	48.6%	51.1%	48.9%
38,868	JEFFERSON	17,317	10,245	6,988	84	3,257 R	59.2%	40.4%	59.4%	40.6%
18,708	JUNEAU	7,637	4,733	2,857	47	1,876 R	62.0%	37.4%	62.4%	37.6%
63,505	KENOSHA	31,121	12,436	18,325	360	5,889 D	40.0%	58.9%	40.4%	59.6%
16,680	KEWAUNEE	6,780	4,153	2,611	16	1,542 R	61.3%	38.5%	61.4%	38.6%
59,653	LA CROSSE	25,103	12,784	12,247	72	537 R	50.9%	48.8%	51.1%	48.9%
18,695	LAFAYETTE	8,147	4,421	3,696	30	725 R	54.3%	45.4%	54.5%	45.5%
23,227	LANGLADE	8,369	4,036	4,310	23	274 D	48.2%	51.5%	48.4%	51.6%
22,536	LINCOLN	8,598	5,564	2,938	96	2,626 R	64.7%	34.2%	65.4%	34.6%
61,617	MANITOWOC	26,247	14,047	11,949	251	2,098 R	53.5%	45.5%	54.0%	46.0%
75,915	MARATHON	29,477	15,782	13,192	503	2,590 R	53.5%	44.8%	54.5%	45.5%
36,225	MARINETTE	13,712	7,159	6,483	70	676 R	52.2%	47.3%	52.5%	47.5%
9,097	MARQUETTE	3,883	2,853	1,016	14	1,837 R	73.5%	26.2%	73.7%	26.3%
766,885	MILWAUKEE	354,830	142,448	205,282	7,100	62,834 D	40.1%	57.9%	41.0%	59.0%
30,080	MONROE	11,354	7,277	4,013	64	3,264 R	64.1%	35.3%	64.5%	35.5%
27,075	OCONTO	10,322	5,923	4,348	51	1,575 R	57.4%	42.1%	57.7%	42.3%
18,938	ONEIDA	7,383	3,253	4,076	54	823 D	44.1%	55.2%	44.4%	55.6%
70,032	OUTAGAMIE	28,389	18,294	9,955	140	8,339 R	64.4%	35.1%	64.8%	35.2%
18,985	OZAUKEE	9,323	5,655	3,579	89	2,076 R	60.7%	38.4%	61.2%	38.8%
7,897	PEPIN	2,959	1,902	1,029	28	873 R	64.3%	34.8%	64.9%	35.1%
21,471	PIERCE	8,233	5,137	3,033	63	2,104 R	62.4%	36.8%	62.9%	37.1%
26,197	POLK	9,945	5,329	4,489	127	840 R	53.6%	45.1%	54.3%	45.7%
35,800	PORTAGE	14,125	5,405	8,678	42	3,273 D	38.3%	61.4%	38.4%	61.6%
18,467	PRICE	6,819	3,258	3,515	46	257 D	47.8%	51.5%	48.1%	51.9%
94,047	RACINE	44,325	18,220	25,697	408	7,477 D	41.1%	58.0%	41.5%	58.5%
20,381	RICHLAND	8,226	5,088	3,109	29	1,979 R	61.9%	37.8%	62.1%	37.9%
80,173	ROCK	35,376	18,477	16,766	133	1,711 R	52.2%	47.4%	52.4%	47.6%
17,737	RUSK	6,388	3,092	3,238	58	146 D	48.4%	50.7%	48.8%	51.2%
24,842	ST. CROIX	10,678	5,660	4,930	88	730 R	53.0%	46.2%	53.4%	46.6%
33,700	SAUK	15,546	9,751	5,690	105	4,061 R	62.7%	36.6%	63.2%	36.8%
11,540	SAWYER	4,400	2,421	1,947	32	474 R	55.0%	44.3%	55.4%	44.6%
35,378	SHAWANO	12,811	8,732	4,015	64	4,717 R	68.2%	31.3%	68.5%	31.5%
76,221	SHEBOYGAN	30,938	15,291	15,062	585	229 R	49.4%	48.7%	50.4%	49.6%
20,105	TAYLOR	6,621	3,194	3,215	212	21 D	48.2%	48.6%	49.8%	50.2%

WISCONSIN

PRESIDENT 1944

1940 Census Population	County	Total Vote	Republican	Democratic	Other	Rep.-Dem. Plurality	Percentage Total Vote Rep.	Percentage Total Vote Dem.	Percentage Major Vote Rep.	Percentage Major Vote Dem.
24,381	TREMPEALEAU	9,242	4,719	4,496	27	223 R	51.1%	48.6%	51.2%	48.8%
29,940	VERNON	11,121	5,676	5,409	36	267 R	51.0%	48.6%	51.2%	48.8%
8,894	VILAS	4,132	2,021	2,079	32	58 D	48.9%	50.3%	49.3%	50.7%
33,103	WALWORTH	16,683	10,901	5,696	86	5,205 R	65.3%	34.1%	65.7%	34.3%
12,496	WASHBURN	4,533	2,441	2,059	33	382 R	53.8%	45.4%	54.2%	45.8%
28,430	WASHINGTON	12,847	8,921	3,840	86	5,081 R	69.4%	29.9%	69.9%	30.1%
62,744	WAUKESHA	31,326	17,995	13,038	293	4,957 R	57.4%	41.6%	58.0%	42.0%
34,614	WAUPACA	15,442	11,495	3,879	68	7,616 R	74.4%	25.1%	74.8%	25.2%
14,268	WAUSHARA	6,189	4,675	1,485	29	3,190 R	75.5%	24.0%	75.9%	24.1%
80,507	WINNEBAGO	32,420	19,310	12,841	269	6,469 R	59.6%	39.6%	60.1%	39.9%
44,465	WOOD	16,520	9,569	6,861	90	2,708 R	57.9%	41.5%	58.2%	41.8%
3,137,587	TOTAL	1,339,152	674,532	650,413	14,207	24,119 R	50.4%	48.6%	50.9%	49.1%

WISCONSIN

PRESIDENT 1940

1940 Census Population	County	Total Vote	Republican	Democratic	Other	Rep.-Dem. Plurality	Percentage Total Vote Rep.	Total Vote Dem.	Major Vote Rep.	Major Vote Dem.
8,449	ADAMS	3,730	1,818	1,883	29	65 D	48.7%	50.5%	49.1%	50.9%
21,801	ASHLAND	9,309	3,592	5,586	131	1,994 D	38.6%	60.0%	39.1%	60.9%
34,289	BARRON	14,227	7,806	6,183	238	1,623 R	54.9%	43.5%	55.8%	44.2%
15,827	BAYFIELD	7,342	2,829	4,387	126	1,558 D	38.5%	59.8%	39.2%	60.8%
83,109	BROWN	36,040	16,379	19,526	135	3,147 D	45.4%	54.2%	45.6%	54.4%
16,090	BUFFALO	6,675	4,056	2,516	103	1,540 R	60.8%	37.7%	61.7%	38.3%
11,382	BURNETT	5,105	2,510	2,513	82	3 D	49.2%	49.2%	50.0%	50.0%
17,618	CALUMET	7,725	5,327	2,324	74	3,003 R	69.0%	30.1%	69.6%	30.4%
40,703	CHIPPEWA	16,171	8,781	7,250	140	1,531 R	54.3%	44.8%	54.8%	45.2%
33,972	CLARK	14,420	9,501	4,683	236	4,818 R	65.9%	32.5%	67.0%	33.0%
32,517	COLUMBIA	15,387	8,260	7,021	106	1,239 R	53.7%	45.6%	54.1%	45.9%
18,328	CRAWFORD	8,293	4,667	3,595	31	1,072 R	56.3%	43.3%	56.5%	43.5%
130,660	DANE	62,787	21,845	40,331	611	18,486 D	34.8%	64.2%	35.1%	64.9%
54,280	DODGE	23,859	14,651	8,948	260	5,703 R	61.4%	37.5%	62.1%	37.9%
19,095	DOOR	8,260	5,461	2,750	49	2,711 R	66.1%	33.3%	66.5%	33.5%
47,119	DOUGLAS	23,515	7,695	15,548	272	7,853 D	32.7%	66.1%	33.1%	66.9%
27,375	DUNN	11,639	6,968	4,545	126	2,423 R	59.9%	39.0%	60.5%	39.5%
46,999	EAU CLAIRE	19,832	9,595	10,129	108	534 D	48.4%	51.1%	48.6%	51.4%
4,177	FLORENCE	2,011	1,008	980	23	28 R	50.1%	48.7%	50.7%	49.3%
62,353	FOND DU LAC	27,342	16,804	10,323	215	6,481 R	61.5%	37.8%	61.9%	38.1%
11,805	FOREST	4,639	1,672	2,951	16	1,279 D	36.0%	63.6%	36.2%	63.8%
40,639	GRANT	18,759	11,143	7,458	158	3,685 R	59.4%	39.8%	59.9%	40.1%
23,146	GREEN	10,364	5,711	4,565	88	1,146 R	55.1%	44.0%	55.6%	44.4%
14,092	GREEN LAKE	7,314	4,919	2,357	38	2,562 R	67.3%	32.2%	67.6%	32.4%
20,595	IOWA	9,140	4,978	4,025	137	953 R	54.5%	44.0%	55.3%	44.7%
10,049	IRON	5,269	1,672	3,525	72	1,853 D	31.7%	66.9%	32.2%	67.8%
16,599	JACKSON	7,780	3,741	3,975	64	234 D	48.1%	51.1%	48.5%	51.5%
38,868	JEFFERSON	18,169	10,178	7,842	149	2,336 R	56.0%	43.2%	56.5%	43.5%
18,708	JUNEAU	8,706	5,268	3,354	84	1,914 R	60.5%	38.5%	61.1%	38.9%
63,505	KENOSHA	29,777	12,182	17,174	421	4,992 D	40.9%	57.7%	41.5%	58.5%
16,680	KEWAUNEE	7,272	3,862	3,389	21	473 R	53.1%	46.6%	53.3%	46.7%
59,653	LA CROSSE	26,924	13,711	13,079	134	632 R	50.9%	48.6%	51.2%	48.8%
18,695	LAFAYETTE	9,419	5,059	4,315	45	744 R	53.7%	45.8%	54.0%	46.0%
23,227	LANGLADE	9,814	4,523	5,190	101	667 D	46.1%	52.9%	46.6%	53.4%
22,536	LINCOLN	9,984	5,812	3,951	221	1,861 R	58.2%	39.6%	59.5%	40.5%
61,617	MANITOWOC	26,126	12,616	13,142	368	526 D	48.3%	50.3%	49.0%	51.0%
75,915	MARATHON	29,469	15,264	13,724	481	1,540 R	51.8%	46.6%	52.7%	47.3%
36,225	MARINETTE	15,483	7,688	7,703	92	15 D	49.7%	49.8%	50.0%	50.0%
9,097	MARQUETTE	4,312	3,086	1,195	31	1,891 R	71.6%	27.7%	72.1%	27.9%
766,885	MILWAUKEE	351,197	131,120	209,861	10,216	78,741 D	37.3%	59.8%	38.5%	61.5%
30,080	MONROE	12,863	8,042	4,673	148	3,369 R	62.5%	36.3%	63.2%	36.8%
27,075	OCONTO	11,577	6,238	5,273	66	965 R	53.9%	45.5%	54.2%	45.8%
18,938	ONEIDA	9,146	3,694	5,375	77	1,681 D	40.4%	58.8%	40.7%	59.3%
70,032	OUTAGAMIE	30,067	17,733	12,168	166	5,565 R	59.0%	40.5%	59.3%	40.7%
18,985	OZAUKEE	8,723	4,913	3,662	148	1,251 R	56.3%	42.0%	57.3%	42.7%
7,897	PEPIN	3,522	2,272	1,194	56	1,078 R	64.5%	33.9%	65.6%	34.4%
21,471	PIERCE	9,999	6,624	3,259	116	3,365 R	66.2%	32.6%	67.0%	33.0%
26,197	POLK	11,248	6,031	4,979	238	1,052 R	53.6%	44.3%	54.8%	45.2%
35,800	PORTAGE	15,912	5,670	10,148	94	4,478 D	35.6%	63.8%	35.8%	64.2%
18,467	PRICE	8,093	3,879	4,042	172	163 D	47.9%	49.9%	49.0%	51.0%
94,047	RACINE	42,978	18,753	23,532	693	4,779 D	43.6%	54.8%	44.3%	55.7%
20,381	RICHLAND	9,139	5,527	3,524	88	2,003 R	60.5%	38.6%	61.1%	38.9%
80,173	ROCK	37,898	20,141	17,543	214	2,598 R	53.1%	46.3%	53.4%	46.6%
17,737	RUSK	7,160	3,484	3,578	98	94 D	48.7%	50.0%	49.3%	50.7%
24,842	ST. CROIX	11,876	6,857	4,898	121	1,959 R	57.7%	41.2%	58.3%	41.7%
33,700	SAUK	15,707	9,363	6,106	238	3,257 R	59.6%	38.9%	60.5%	39.5%
11,540	SAWYER	5,233	2,745	2,439	49	306 R	52.5%	46.6%	53.0%	47.0%
35,378	SHAWANO	11,774	6,377	5,241	156	1,136 R	54.2%	44.5%	54.9%	45.1%
76,221	SHEBOYGAN	31,747	15,305	15,800	642	495 D	48.2%	49.8%	49.2%	50.8%
20,105	TAYLOR	7,678	3,668	3,771	239	103 D	47.8%	49.1%	49.3%	50.7%

WISCONSIN

PRESIDENT 1940

1940 Census Population	County	Total Vote	Republican	Democratic	Other	Rep.-Dem. Plurality	Percentage Total Vote Rep.	Percentage Total Vote Dem.	Percentage Major Vote Rep.	Percentage Major Vote Dem.
24,381	TREMPEALEAU	10,579	5,319	5,175	85	144 R	50.3%	48.9%	50.7%	49.3%
29,940	VERNON	12,492	6,614	5,776	102	838 R	52.9%	46.2%	53.4%	46.6%
8,894	VILAS	4,798	2,251	2,470	77	219 D	46.9%	51.5%	47.7%	52.3%
33,103	WALWORTH	17,154	11,594	5,449	111	6,145 R	67.6%	31.8%	68.0%	32.0%
12,496	WASHBURN	5,762	2,805	2,901	56	96 D	48.7%	50.3%	49.2%	50.8%
28,430	WASHINGTON	13,380	8,501	4,683	196	3,818 R	63.5%	35.0%	64.5%	35.5%
62,744	WAUKESHA	29,943	16,726	12,859	358	3,867 R	55.9%	42.9%	56.5%	43.5%
34,614	WAUPACA	15,866	11,099	4,616	151	6,483 R	70.0%	29.1%	70.6%	29.4%
14,268	WAUSHARA	6,685	4,872	1,747	66	3,125 R	72.9%	26.1%	73.6%	26.4%
80,507	WINNEBAGO	34,535	18,697	15,570	268	3,127 R	54.1%	45.1%	54.6%	45.4%
44,465	WOOD	18,402	9,654	8,574	174	1,080 R	52.5%	46.6%	53.0%	47.0%
3,137,587	TOTAL	1,405,522	679,206	704,821	21,495	25,615 D	48.3%	50.1%	49.1%	50.9%

WISCONSIN

PRESIDENT 1936

1930 Census Population	County	Total Vote	Republican	Democratic	Other	Rep.-Dem. Plurality	Percentage: Total Vote		Percentage: Major Vote	
							Rep.	Dem.	Rep.	Dem.
8,003	ADAMS	3,579	1,191	2,289	99	1,098 D	33.3%	64.0%	34.2%	65.8%
21,054	ASHLAND	8,681	2,439	5,904	338	3,465 D	28.1%	68.0%	29.2%	70.8%
34,301	BARRON	13,355	5,067	7,419	869	2,352 D	37.9%	55.6%	40.6%	59.4%
15,006	BAYFIELD	6,663	2,071	4,366	226	2,295 D	31.1%	65.5%	32.2%	67.8%
70,249	BROWN	31,077	8,433	21,417	1,227	12,984 D	27.1%	68.9%	28.3%	71.7%
15,330	BUFFALO	6,194	2,481	3,434	279	953 D	40.1%	55.4%	41.9%	58.1%
10,233	BURNETT	4,460	1,422	2,801	237	1,379 D	31.9%	62.8%	33.7%	66.3%
16,848	CALUMET	7,113	1,972	4,694	447	2,722 D	27.7%	66.0%	29.6%	70.4%
37,342	CHIPPEWA	14,796	5,760	7,854	1,182	2,094 D	38.9%	53.1%	42.3%	57.7%
34,165	CLARK	13,132	5,196	6,931	1,005	1,735 D	39.6%	52.8%	42.8%	57.2%
30,503	COLUMBIA	15,054	5,607	8,936	511	3,329 D	37.2%	59.4%	38.6%	61.4%
16,781	CRAWFORD	7,956	2,857	4,377	722	1,520 D	35.9%	55.0%	39.5%	60.5%
112,737	DANE	52,908	15,233	35,856	1,819	20,623 D	28.8%	67.8%	29.8%	70.2%
52,092	DODGE	22,599	6,829	14,782	988	7,953 D	30.2%	65.4%	31.6%	68.4%
18,182	DOOR	7,664	3,146	3,952	566	806 D	41.0%	51.6%	44.3%	55.7%
46,583	DOUGLAS	22,163	5,079	16,684	400	11,605 D	22.9%	75.3%	23.3%	76.7%
27,037	DUNN	10,975	4,570	5,619	786	1,049 D	41.6%	51.2%	44.9%	55.1%
41,087	EAU CLAIRE	17,260	6,802	10,065	393	3,263 D	39.4%	58.3%	40.3%	59.7%
3,768	FLORENCE	1,932	800	1,037	95	237 D	41.4%	53.7%	43.5%	56.5%
59,883	FOND DU LAC	25,931	9,179	14,821	1,931	5,642 D	35.4%	57.2%	38.2%	61.8%
11,118	FOREST	4,535	1,334	3,092	109	1,758 D	29.4%	68.2%	30.1%	69.9%
38,469	GRANT	17,503	7,196	9,170	1,137	1,974 D	41.1%	52.4%	44.0%	56.0%
21,870	GREEN	9,859	3,700	5,941	218	2,241 D	37.5%	60.3%	38.4%	61.6%
13,913	GREEN LAKE	6,877	2,926	3,840	111	914 D	42.5%	55.8%	43.2%	56.8%
20,039	IOWA	9,094	3,623	4,988	483	1,365 D	39.8%	54.8%	42.1%	57.9%
9,933	IRON	4,341	902	3,319	120	2,417 D	20.8%	76.5%	21.4%	78.6%
16,468	JACKSON	6,979	2,235	4,537	207	2,302 D	32.0%	65.0%	33.0%	67.0%
36,785	JEFFERSON	17,324	5,599	11,144	581	5,545 D	32.3%	64.3%	33.4%	66.6%
17,264	JUNEAU	8,152	3,084	4,544	524	1,460 D	37.8%	55.7%	40.4%	59.6%
63,277	KENOSHA	27,245	7,268	18,137	1,840	10,869 D	26.7%	66.6%	28.6%	71.4%
16,037	KEWAUNEE	6,717	1,527	4,971	219	3,444 D	22.7%	74.0%	23.5%	76.5%
54,455	LA CROSSE	22,840	7,558	14,455	827	6,897 D	33.1%	63.3%	34.3%	65.7%
18,649	LAFAYETTE	9,247	3,801	4,976	470	1,175 D	41.1%	53.8%	43.3%	56.7%
21,544	LANGLADE	8,684	2,635	5,837	212	3,202 D	30.3%	67.2%	31.1%	68.9%
21,072	LINCOLN	9,222	3,120	5,520	582	2,400 D	33.8%	59.9%	36.1%	63.9%
58,674	MANITOWOC	24,026	5,094	15,539	3,393	10,445 D	21.2%	64.7%	24.7%	75.3%
70,629	MARATHON	27,076	7,328	17,898	1,850	10,570 D	27.1%	66.1%	29.0%	71.0%
33,530	MARINETTE	14,272	4,938	8,884	450	3,946 D	34.6%	62.2%	35.7%	64.3%
9,388	MARQUETTE	3,917	1,957	1,812	148	145 R	50.0%	46.3%	51.9%	48.1%
725,263	MILWAUKEE	296,958	54,811	221,512	20,635	166,701 D	18.5%	74.6%	19.8%	80.2%
28,739	MONROE	12,008	4,695	6,491	822	1,796 D	39.1%	54.1%	42.0%	58.0%
26,386	OCONTO	11,034	3,774	6,729	531	2,955 D	34.2%	61.0%	35.9%	64.1%
15,899	ONEIDA	8,056	2,294	5,208	554	2,914 D	28.5%	64.6%	30.6%	69.4%
62,790	OUTAGAMIE	27,364	9,485	16,163	1,716	6,678 D	34.7%	59.1%	37.0%	63.0%
17,394	OZAUKEE	7,918	1,785	5,594	539	3,809 D	22.5%	70.6%	24.2%	75.8%
7,450	PEPIN	3,446	1,466	1,785	195	319 D	42.5%	51.8%	45.1%	54.9%
21,043	PIERCE	9,216	3,935	4,061	1,220	126 D	42.7%	44.1%	49.2%	50.8%
26,567	POLK	10,499	3,596	5,618	1,285	2,022 D	34.3%	53.5%	39.0%	61.0%
33,827	PORTAGE	14,844	3,969	10,576	299	6,607 D	26.7%	71.2%	27.3%	72.7%
17,284	PRICE	7,652	2,215	5,098	339	2,883 D	28.9%	66.6%	30.3%	69.7%
90,217	RACINE	37,771	10,850	24,474	2,447	13,624 D	28.7%	64.8%	30.7%	69.3%
19,525	RICHLAND	8,686	4,245	4,080	361	165 R	48.9%	47.0%	51.0%	49.0%
74,206	ROCK	33,729	14,693	17,991	1,045	3,298 D	43.6%	53.3%	45.0%	55.0%
16,081	RUSK	6,780	2,453	3,877	450	1,424 D	36.2%	57.2%	38.8%	61.2%
25,455	ST. CROIX	11,218	4,316	4,679	2,223	363 D	38.5%	41.7%	48.0%	52.0%
32,030	SAUK	14,812	5,626	8,355	831	2,729 D	38.0%	56.4%	40.2%	59.8%
8,878	SAWYER	4,733	1,726	2,834	173	1,108 D	36.5%	59.9%	37.9%	62.1%
33,516	SHAWANO	12,925	3,679	8,865	381	5,186 D	28.5%	68.6%	29.3%	70.7%
71,235	SHEBOYGAN	28,063	8,865	17,415	1,783	8,550 D	31.6%	62.1%	33.7%	66.3%
17,685	TAYLOR	6,989	1,758	4,721	510	2,963 D	25.2%	67.5%	27.1%	72.9%

WISCONSIN

PRESIDENT 1936

1930 Census Population	County	Total Vote	Republican	Democratic	Other	Rep.-Dem. Plurality	Percentage Total Vote Rep.	Percentage Total Vote Dem.	Percentage Major Vote Rep.	Percentage Major Vote Dem.
23,910	TREMPEALEAU	9,832	3,339	5,929	564	2,590 D	34.0%	60.3%	36.0%	64.0%
28,537	VERNON	11,357	4,811	6,044	502	1,233 D	42.4%	53.2%	44.3%	55.7%
7,294	VILAS	4,145	1,298	2,559	288	1,261 D	31.3%	61.7%	33.7%	66.3%
31,058	WALWORTH	16,066	8,462	7,093	511	1,369 R	52.7%	44.1%	54.4%	45.6%
11,103	WASHBURN	5,215	1,650	3,220	345	1,570 D	31.6%	61.7%	33.9%	66.1%
26,551	WASHINGTON	12,092	3,589	7,129	1,374	3,540 D	29.7%	59.0%	33.5%	66.5%
52,358	WAUKESHA	25,194	8,921	14,982	1,291	6,061 D	35.4%	59.5%	37.3%	62.7%
33,513	WAUPACA	14,561	6,680	6,920	961	240 D	45.9%	47.5%	49.1%	50.9%
14,427	WAUSHARA	6,421	3,302	2,636	483	666 R	51.4%	41.1%	55.6%	44.4%
76,622	WINNEBAGO	31,621	11,679	18,522	1,420	6,843 D	36.9%	58.6%	38.7%	61.3%
37,865	WOOD	15,953	4,902	9,982	1,069	5,080 D	30.7%	62.6%	32.9%	67.1%
2,939,006	TOTAL	1,258,560	380,828	802,984	74,748	422,156 D	30.3%	63.8%	32.2%	67.8%

WISCONSIN

PRESIDENT 1932

1930 Census Population	County	Total Vote	Republican	Democratic	Other	Rep.-Dem. Plurality	Percentage: Total Vote Rep.	Total Vote Dem.	Major Vote Rep.	Major Vote Dem.
8,003	ADAMS	2,949	777	2,120	52	1,343 D	26.3%	71.9%	26.8%	73.2%
21,054	ASHLAND	8,328	2,646	5,405	277	2,759 D	31.8%	64.9%	32.9%	67.1%
34,301	BARRON	11,701	3,852	7,413	436	3,561 D	32.9%	63.4%	34.2%	65.8%
15,006	BAYFIELD	5,335	2,035	2,981	319	946 D	38.1%	55.9%	40.6%	59.4%
70,249	BROWN	27,634	7,150	19,990	494	12,840 D	25.9%	72.3%	26.3%	73.7%
15,330	BUFFALO	5,028	1,711	3,252	65	1,541 D	34.0%	64.7%	34.5%	65.5%
10,233	BURNETT	3,833	1,281	2,437	115	1,156 D	33.4%	63.6%	34.5%	65.5%
16,848	CALUMET	6,785	1,213	5,485	87	4,272 D	17.9%	80.8%	18.1%	81.9%
37,342	CHIPPEWA	13,421	4,792	8,445	184	3,653 D	35.7%	62.9%	36.2%	63.8%
34,165	CLARK	11,999	3,132	8,372	495	5,240 D	26.1%	69.8%	27.2%	72.8%
30,503	COLUMBIA	13,641	4,970	8,455	216	3,485 D	36.4%	62.0%	37.0%	63.0%
16,781	CRAWFORD	6,768	1,943	4,754	71	2,811 D	28.7%	70.2%	29.0%	71.0%
112,737	DANE	47,823	19,083	26,841	1,899	7,758 D	39.9%	56.1%	41.6%	58.4%
52,092	DODGE	21,148	4,936	15,874	338	10,938 D	23.3%	75.1%	23.7%	76.3%
18,182	DOOR	6,734	2,488	4,149	97	1,661 D	36.9%	61.6%	37.5%	62.5%
46,583	DOUGLAS	18,949	7,888	9,715	1,346	1,827 D	41.6%	51.3%	44.8%	55.2%
27,037	DUNN	9,108	3,898	4,936	274	1,038 D	42.8%	54.2%	44.1%	55.9%
41,087	EAU CLAIRE	15,350	7,487	7,565	298	78 D	48.8%	49.3%	49.7%	50.3%
3,768	FLORENCE	1,744	714	965	65	251 D	40.9%	55.3%	42.5%	57.5%
59,883	FOND DU LAC	25,004	8,436	16,143	425	7,707 D	33.7%	64.6%	34.3%	65.7%
11,118	FOREST	3,413	768	2,595	50	1,827 D	22.5%	76.0%	22.8%	77.2%
38,469	GRANT	15,919	5,986	9,701	232	3,715 D	37.6%	60.9%	38.2%	61.8%
21,870	GREEN	8,758	3,190	5,406	162	2,216 D	36.4%	61.7%	37.1%	62.9%
13,913	GREEN LAKE	6,683	2,179	4,446	58	2,267 D	32.6%	66.5%	32.9%	67.1%
20,039	IOWA	7,856	3,113	4,621	122	1,508 D	39.6%	58.8%	40.3%	59.7%
9,933	IRON	3,523	891	2,338	294	1,447 D	25.3%	66.4%	27.6%	72.4%
16,468	JACKSON	5,919	1,983	3,813	123	1,830 D	33.5%	64.4%	34.2%	65.8%
36,785	JEFFERSON	16,448	5,062	11,230	156	6,168 D	30.8%	68.3%	31.1%	68.9%
17,264	JUNEAU	6,870	2,018	4,723	129	2,705 D	29.4%	68.7%	29.9%	70.1%
63,277	KENOSHA	23,903	7,307	14,373	2,223	7,066 D	30.6%	60.1%	33.7%	66.3%
16,037	KEWAUNEE	6,122	879	5,200	43	4,321 D	14.4%	84.9%	14.5%	85.5%
54,455	LA CROSSE	20,811	7,686	12,919	206	5,233 D	36.9%	62.1%	37.3%	62.7%
18,649	LAFAYETTE	8,213	3,246	4,886	81	1,640 D	39.5%	59.5%	39.9%	60.1%
21,544	LANGLADE	8,849	2,340	6,332	177	3,992 D	26.4%	71.6%	27.0%	73.0%
21,072	LINCOLN	8,272	2,958	5,093	221	2,135 D	35.8%	61.6%	36.7%	63.3%
58,674	MANITOWOC	20,805	4,573	15,696	536	11,123 D	22.0%	75.4%	22.6%	77.4%
70,629	MARATHON	24,601	6,210	17,744	647	11,534 D	25.2%	72.1%	25.9%	74.1%
33,530	MARINETTE	12,185	5,249	6,508	428	1,259 D	43.1%	53.4%	44.6%	55.4%
9,388	MARQUETTE	3,922	1,365	2,504	53	1,139 D	34.8%	63.8%	35.3%	64.7%
725,263	MILWAUKEE	259,388	54,693	170,202	34,493	115,509 D	21.1%	65.6%	24.3%	75.7%
28,739	MONROE	9,954	3,022	6,757	175	3,735 D	30.4%	67.9%	30.9%	69.1%
26,386	OCONTO	9,465	2,915	6,440	110	3,525 D	30.8%	68.0%	31.2%	68.8%
15,899	ONEIDA	6,913	1,992	4,542	379	2,550 D	28.8%	65.7%	30.5%	69.5%
62,790	OUTAGAMIE	25,118	8,517	16,186	415	7,669 D	33.9%	64.4%	34.5%	65.5%
17,394	OZAUKEE	7,160	1,182	5,770	208	4,588 D	16.5%	80.6%	17.0%	83.0%
7,450	PEPIN	3,125	1,152	1,931	42	779 D	36.9%	61.8%	37.4%	62.6%
21,043	PIERCE	7,980	3,537	4,115	328	578 D	44.3%	51.6%	46.2%	53.8%
26,567	POLK	9,232	3,425	5,421	386	1,996 D	37.1%	58.7%	38.7%	61.3%
33,827	PORTAGE	12,820	3,434	9,195	191	5,761 D	26.8%	71.7%	27.2%	72.8%
17,284	PRICE	6,459	2,023	4,114	322	2,091 D	31.3%	63.7%	33.0%	67.0%
90,217	RACINE	33,097	10,754	19,960	2,383	9,206 D	32.5%	60.3%	35.0%	65.0%
19,525	RICHLAND	7,435	3,256	4,027	152	771 D	43.8%	54.2%	44.7%	55.3%
74,206	ROCK	30,008	16,825	12,612	571	4,213 R	56.1%	42.0%	57.2%	42.8%
16,081	RUSK	5,410	1,942	3,194	274	1,252 D	35.9%	59.0%	37.8%	62.2%
25,455	ST. CROIX	10,698	4,059	6,374	265	2,315 D	37.9%	59.6%	38.9%	61.1%
32,030	SAUK	12,867	5,063	7,638	166	2,575 D	39.3%	59.4%	39.9%	60.1%
8,878	SAWYER	3,700	1,179	2,381	140	1,202 D	31.9%	64.4%	33.1%	66.9%
33,516	SHAWANO	10,367	2,450	7,593	324	5,143 D	23.6%	73.2%	24.4%	75.6%
71,235	SHEBOYGAN	26,661	7,454	18,029	1,178	10,575 D	28.0%	67.6%	29.3%	70.7%
17,685	TAYLOR	5,947	1,107	4,219	621	3,112 D	18.6%	70.9%	20.8%	79.2%

WISCONSIN

PRESIDENT 1932

1930 Census Population	County	Total Vote	Republican	Democratic	Other	Rep.-Dem. Plurality	Percentage Total Vote Rep.	Percentage Total Vote Dem.	Percentage Major Vote Rep.	Percentage Major Vote Dem.
23,910	TREMPEALEAU	8,759	2,874	5,786	99	2,912 D	32.8%	66.1%	33.2%	66.8%
28,537	VERNON	9,057	2,979	5,939	139	2,960 D	32.9%	65.6%	33.4%	66.6%
7,294	VILAS	3,319	1,138	2,036	145	898 D	34.3%	61.3%	35.9%	64.1%
31,058	WALWORTH	14,852	7,858	6,790	204	1,068 R	52.9%	45.7%	53.6%	46.4%
11,103	WASHBURN	4,328	1,501	2,619	208	1,118 D	34.7%	60.5%	36.4%	63.6%
26,551	WASHINGTON	10,985	2,209	8,570	206	6,361 D	20.1%	78.0%	20.5%	79.5%
52,358	WAUKESHA	22,609	8,538	13,487	584	4,949 D	37.8%	59.7%	38.8%	61.2%
33,513	WAUPACA	13,536	5,082	8,179	275	3,097 D	37.5%	60.4%	38.3%	61.7%
14,427	WAUSHARA	5,738	2,541	3,073	124	532 D	44.3%	53.6%	45.3%	54.7%
76,622	WINNEBAGO	27,852	11,505	15,591	756	4,086 D	41.3%	56.0%	42.5%	57.5%
37,865	WOOD	13,621	4,100	9,215	306	5,115 D	30.1%	67.7%	30.8%	69.2%
2,939,006	TOTAL	1,114,814	347,741	707,410	59,663	359,669 D	31.2%	63.5%	33.0%	67.0%

WISCONSIN

PRESIDENT 1928

1920 Census Population	County	Total Vote	Republican	Democratic	Other	Rep.-Dem. Plurality	Percentage Total Vote Rep.	Total Vote Dem.	Major Vote Rep.	Major Vote Dem.
9,287	ADAMS	2,580	1,624	914	42	710 R	62.9%	35.4%	64.0%	36.0%
24,538	ASHLAND	7,372	3,639	3,570	163	69 R	49.4%	48.4%	50.5%	49.5%
34,281	BARRON	11,746	8,455	3,185	106	5,270 R	72.0%	27.1%	72.6%	27.4%
17,201	BAYFIELD	5,171	3,279	1,709	183	1,570 R	63.4%	33.0%	65.7%	34.3%
61,889	BROWN	26,004	9,371	16,465	168	7,094 D	36.0%	63.3%	36.3%	63.7%
15,615	BUFFALO	4,892	3,027	1,836	29	1,191 R	61.9%	37.5%	62.2%	37.8%
10,735	BURNETT	3,670	2,742	880	48	1,862 R	74.7%	24.0%	75.7%	24.3%
17,228	CALUMET	6,323	2,405	3,871	47	1,466 D	38.0%	61.2%	38.3%	61.7%
36,482	CHIPPEWA	13,561	7,514	5,985	62	1,529 R	55.4%	44.1%	55.7%	44.3%
35,120	CLARK	11,121	6,948	3,938	235	3,010 R	62.5%	35.4%	63.8%	36.2%
30,468	COLUMBIA	12,545	7,615	4,819	111	2,796 R	60.7%	38.4%	61.2%	38.8%
16,772	CRAWFORD	6,745	3,452	3,238	55	214 R	51.2%	48.0%	51.6%	48.4%
89,432	DANE	43,170	23,680	19,126	364	4,554 R	54.9%	44.3%	55.3%	44.7%
49,742	DODGE	19,434	9,660	9,536	238	124 R	49.7%	49.1%	50.3%	49.7%
19,073	DOOR	6,134	3,636	2,456	42	1,180 R	59.3%	40.0%	59.7%	40.3%
49,771	DOUGLAS	18,432	11,280	6,762	390	4,518 R	61.2%	36.7%	62.5%	37.5%
26,970	DUNN	9,274	7,096	2,045	133	5,051 R	76.5%	22.1%	77.6%	22.4%
35,771	EAU CLAIRE	14,555	10,079	4,385	91	5,694 R	69.2%	30.1%	69.7%	30.3%
3,602	FLORENCE	1,545	993	540	12	453 R	64.3%	35.0%	64.8%	35.2%
56,119	FOND DU LAC	24,517	12,593	11,719	205	874 R	51.4%	47.8%	51.8%	48.2%
9,850	FOREST	3,631	1,918	1,677	36	241 R	52.8%	46.2%	53.4%	46.6%
39,044	GRANT	16,794	10,052	6,630	112	3,422 R	59.9%	39.5%	60.3%	39.7%
21,568	GREEN	8,027	5,152	2,812	63	2,340 R	64.2%	35.0%	64.7%	35.3%
14,875	GREEN LAKE	5,716	3,038	2,622	56	416 R	53.1%	45.9%	53.7%	46.3%
21,504	IOWA	8,669	5,484	3,129	56	2,355 R	63.3%	36.1%	63.7%	36.3%
10,261	IRON	3,132	1,274	1,724	134	450 D	40.7%	55.0%	42.5%	57.5%
17,746	JACKSON	5,791	4,353	1,364	74	2,989 R	75.2%	23.6%	76.1%	23.9%
35,022	JEFFERSON	15,033	8,612	6,305	116	2,307 R	57.3%	41.9%	57.7%	42.3%
19,209	JUNEAU	6,541	3,777	2,708	56	1,069 R	57.7%	41.4%	58.2%	41.8%
51,284	KENOSHA	22,363	11,330	10,638	395	692 R	50.7%	47.6%	51.6%	48.4%
16,091	KEWAUNEE	5,569	1,556	3,988	25	2,432 D	27.9%	71.6%	28.1%	71.9%
44,355	LA CROSSE	20,295	11,321	8,877	97	2,444 R	55.8%	43.7%	56.1%	43.9%
20,002	LAFAYETTE	8,771	5,134	3,585	52	1,549 R	58.5%	40.9%	58.9%	41.1%
21,471	LANGLADE	7,879	3,715	4,078	86	363 D	47.2%	51.8%	47.7%	52.3%
21,084	LINCOLN	7,180	4,025	3,091	64	934 R	56.1%	43.1%	56.6%	43.4%
51,644	MANITOWOC	18,032	7,519	10,292	221	2,773 D	41.7%	57.1%	42.2%	57.8%
65,259	MARATHON	21,091	10,127	10,675	289	548 D	48.0%	50.6%	48.7%	51.3%
34,361	MARINETTE	11,424	6,516	4,781	127	1,735 R	57.0%	41.9%	57.7%	42.3%
10,443	MARQUETTE	3,903	2,554	1,313	36	1,241 R	65.4%	33.6%	66.0%	34.0%
539,449	MILWAUKEE	206,237	82,025	110,668	13,544	28,643 D	39.8%	53.7%	42.6%	57.4%
28,666	MONROE	9,759	5,936	3,709	114	2,227 R	60.8%	38.0%	61.5%	38.5%
27,104	OCONTO	8,979	4,661	4,253	65	408 R	51.9%	47.4%	52.3%	47.7%
13,996	ONEIDA	5,707	3,100	2,504	103	596 R	54.3%	43.9%	55.3%	44.7%
55,113	OUTAGAMIE	24,964	12,378	12,474	112	96 D	49.6%	50.0%	49.8%	50.2%
16,335	OZAUKEE	6,292	2,338	3,864	90	1,526 D	37.2%	61.4%	37.7%	62.3%
7,481	PEPIN	3,140	1,839	1,276	25	563 R	58.6%	40.6%	59.0%	41.0%
21,663	PIERCE	9,595	6,491	3,017	87	3,474 R	67.6%	31.4%	68.3%	31.7%
26,870	POLK	9,190	6,905	2,177	108	4,728 R	75.1%	23.7%	76.0%	24.0%
33,649	PORTAGE	11,995	5,161	6,764	70	1,603 D	43.0%	56.4%	43.3%	56.7%
18,517	PRICE	5,542	3,210	2,223	109	987 R	57.9%	40.1%	59.1%	40.9%
78,961	RACINE	30,806	17,423	13,021	362	4,402 R	56.6%	42.3%	57.2%	42.8%
19,823	RICHLAND	8,022	5,685	2,262	75	3,423 R	70.9%	28.2%	71.5%	28.5%
66,150	ROCK	30,384	21,497	8,726	161	12,771 R	70.8%	28.7%	71.1%	28.9%
16,403	RUSK	5,539	3,524	1,925	90	1,599 R	63.6%	34.8%	64.7%	35.3%
26,106	ST. CROIX	11,026	6,855	4,083	88	2,772 R	62.2%	37.0%	62.7%	37.3%
32,548	SAUK	12,729	7,496	5,151	82	2,345 R	58.9%	40.5%	59.3%	40.7%
8,243	SAWYER	3,063	1,882	1,129	52	753 R	61.4%	36.9%	62.5%	37.5%
33,975	SHAWANO	9,065	5,198	3,779	88	1,419 R	57.3%	41.7%	57.9%	42.1%
59,913	SHEBOYGAN	24,701	12,640	11,439	622	1,201 R	51.2%	46.3%	52.5%	47.5%
18,045	TAYLOR	4,849	2,648	2,095	106	553 R	54.6%	43.2%	55.8%	44.2%

WISCONSIN

PRESIDENT 1928

1920 Census Population	County	Total Vote	Republican	Democratic	Other	Rep.-Dem. Plurality	Percentage Total Vote Rep.	Percentage Total Vote Dem.	Percentage Major Vote Rep.	Percentage Major Vote Dem.
24,506	TREMPEALEAU	8,613	5,596	2,963	54	2,633 R	65.0%	34.4%	65.4%	34.6%
29,252	VERNON	9,254	6,596	2,559	99	4,037 R	71.3%	27.7%	72.0%	28.0%
5,649	VILAS	2,753	1,609	1,083	61	526 R	58.4%	39.3%	59.8%	40.2%
29,327	WALWORTH	14,196	9,846	4,253	97	5,593 R	69.4%	30.0%	69.8%	30.2%
11,377	WASHBURN	4,138	2,898	1,192	48	1,706 R	70.0%	28.8%	70.9%	29.1%
25,713	WASHINGTON	10,122	4,163	5,827	132	1,664 D	41.1%	57.6%	41.7%	58.3%
42,612	WAUKESHA	20,311	12,218	7,846	247	4,372 R	60.2%	38.6%	60.9%	39.1%
34,200	WAUPACA	12,345	8,928	3,307	110	5,621 R	72.3%	26.8%	73.0%	27.0%
16,712	WAUSHARA	5,394	4,068	1,260	66	2,808 R	75.4%	23.4%	76.4%	23.6%
63,897	WINNEBAGO	26,501	16,191	9,995	315	6,196 R	61.1%	37.7%	61.8%	38.2%
34,643	WOOD	12,988	6,655	6,167	166	488 R	51.2%	47.5%	51.9%	48.1%
2,632,067	TOTAL	1,016,831	544,205	450,259	22,367	93,946 R	53.5%	44.3%	54.7%	45.3%

WISCONSIN

PRESIDENT 1924

1920 Census Population	County	Total Vote	Republican	Democratic	Progressive	Other	Plurality	Percentage Total Vote Rep.	Dem.	Prog.
9,287	ADAMS	2,687	779	173	1,724	11	945 P	29.0%	6.4%	64.2%
24,538	ASHLAND	7,004	2,272	449	4,204	79	1,932 P	32.4%	6.4%	60.0%
34,281	BARRON	9,180	2,703	377	6,010	90	3,307 P	29.4%	4.1%	65.5%
17,201	BAYFIELD	4,600	1,675	205	2,601	119	926 P	36.4%	4.5%	56.5%
61,889	BROWN	20,080	7,611	2,328	10,024	117	2,413 P	37.9%	11.6%	49.9%
15,615	BUFFALO	4,006	1,324	176	2,474	32	1,150 P	33.1%	4.4%	61.8%
10,735	BURNETT	3,158	958	76	2,088	36	1,130 P	30.3%	2.4%	66.1%
17,228	CALUMET	5,046	938	569	3,503	36	2,565 P	18.6%	11.3%	69.4%
36,482	CHIPPEWA	12,308	5,135	560	6,517	96	1,382 P	41.7%	4.5%	52.9%
35,120	CLARK	10,010	3,130	552	6,208	120	3,078 P	31.3%	5.5%	62.0%
30,468	COLUMBIA	11,690	4,724	907	5,968	91	1,244 P	40.4%	7.8%	51.1%
16,772	CRAWFORD	5,658	1,687	936	2,977	58	1,290 P	29.8%	16.5%	52.6%
89,432	DANE	39,208	12,280	2,081	24,595	252	12,315 P	31.3%	5.3%	62.7%
49,742	DODGE	16,971	5,167	2,019	9,610	175	4,443 P	30.4%	11.9%	56.6%
19,073	DOOR	4,904	1,891	235	2,715	63	824 P	38.6%	4.8%	55.4%
49,771	DOUGLAS	15,039	5,887	638	8,255	259	2,368 P	39.1%	4.2%	54.9%
26,970	DUNN	7,916	3,177	284	4,385	70	1,208 P	40.1%	3.6%	55.4%
35,771	EAU CLAIRE	11,083	5,149	629	5,222	83	73 P	46.5%	5.7%	47.1%
3,602	FLORENCE	1,183	594	49	523	17	71 R	50.2%	4.1%	44.2%
56,119	FOND DU LAC	20,460	8,516	2,222	9,576	146	1,060 P	41.6%	10.9%	46.8%
9,850	FOREST	2,710	1,104	299	1,259	48	155 P	40.7%	11.0%	46.5%
39,044	GRANT	14,169	5,714	1,518	6,825	112	1,111 P	40.3%	10.7%	48.2%
21,568	GREEN	8,331	2,922	423	4,885	101	1,963 P	35.1%	5.1%	58.6%
14,875	GREEN LAKE	5,309	1,988	1,090	2,187	44	199 P	37.4%	20.5%	41.2%
21,504	IOWA	8,213	3,291	689	4,133	100	842 P	40.1%	8.4%	50.3%
10,261	IRON	2,634	1,058	84	1,400	92	342 P	40.2%	3.2%	53.2%
17,746	JACKSON	5,155	1,662	255	3,167	71	1,505 P	32.2%	4.9%	61.4%
35,022	JEFFERSON	13,611	4,250	1,374	7,885	102	3,635 P	31.2%	10.1%	57.9%
19,209	JUNEAU	6,164	1,917	403	3,785	59	1,868 P	31.1%	6.5%	61.4%
51,284	KENOSHA	18,649	10,341	1,517	6,695	96	3,646 R	55.5%	8.1%	35.9%
16,091	KEWAUNEE	4,260	1,018	395	2,804	43	1,786 P	23.9%	9.3%	65.8%
44,355	LA CROSSE	17,647	5,733	1,252	10,543	119	4,810 P	32.5%	7.1%	59.7%
20,002	LAFAYETTE	7,699	2,671	1,265	3,681	82	1,010 P	34.7%	16.4%	47.8%
21,471	LANGLADE	7,149	2,572	926	3,578	73	1,006 P	36.0%	13.0%	50.0%
21,084	LINCOLN	6,918	1,857	503	4,465	93	2,608 P	26.8%	7.3%	64.5%
51,644	MANITOWOC	16,345	4,828	1,599	9,814	104	4,986 P	29.5%	9.8%	60.0%
65,259	MARATHON	19,088	5,577	1,109	12,193	209	6,616 P	29.2%	5.8%	63.9%
34,361	MARINETTE	8,981	4,911	571	3,411	88	1,500 R	54.7%	6.4%	38.0%
10,443	MARQUETTE	3,556	1,109	587	1,820	40	711 P	31.2%	16.5%	51.2%
539,449	MILWAUKEE	148,029	50,730	14,510	81,697	1,092	30,967 P	34.3%	9.8%	55.2%
28,666	MONROE	9,965	2,661	428	6,747	129	4,086 P	26.7%	4.3%	67.7%
27,104	OCONTO	7,735	2,562	602	4,506	65	1,944 P	33.1%	7.8%	58.3%
13,996	ONEIDA	5,350	1,769	324	3,196	61	1,427 P	33.1%	6.1%	59.7%
55,113	OUTAGAMIE	18,160	6,426	1,255	10,357	122	3,931 P	35.4%	6.9%	57.0%
16,335	OZAUKEE	4,900	1,015	592	3,264	29	2,249 P	20.7%	12.1%	66.6%
7,481	PEPIN	2,194	1,226	206	737	25	489 R	55.9%	9.4%	33.6%
21,663	PIERCE	6,805	2,788	298	3,661	58	873 P	41.0%	4.4%	53.8%
26,870	POLK	7,434	2,793	317	4,251	73	1,458 P	37.6%	4.3%	57.2%
33,649	PORTAGE	10,280	2,854	2,010	5,347	69	2,493 P	27.8%	19.6%	52.0%
18,517	PRICE	5,346	1,754	323	3,151	118	1,397 P	32.8%	6.0%	58.9%
78,961	RACINE	25,969	13,040	1,463	11,298	168	1,742 R	50.2%	5.6%	43.5%
19,823	RICHLAND	6,338	2,669	898	2,660	111	9 R	42.1%	14.2%	42.0%
66,150	ROCK	24,320	14,815	1,453	7,923	129	6,892 R	60.9%	6.0%	32.6%
16,403	RUSK	4,940	1,932	272	2,677	59	745 P	39.1%	5.5%	54.2%
26,106	ST. CROIX	9,073	3,600	718	4,693	62	1,093 P	39.7%	7.9%	51.7%
32,548	SAUK	11,052	3,935	555	6,400	162	2,465 P	35.6%	5.0%	57.9%
8,243	SAWYER	2,638	990	135	1,487	26	497 P	37.5%	5.1%	56.4%
33,975	SHAWANO	8,965	2,063	471	6,337	94	4,274 P	23.0%	5.3%	70.7%
59,913	SHEBOYGAN	20,181	6,974	1,350	11,714	143	4,740 P	34.6%	6.7%	58.0%
18,045	TAYLOR	4,710	1,389	185	3,079	57	1,690 P	29.5%	3.9%	65.4%

WISCONSIN

PRESIDENT 1924

1920 Census Population	County	Total Vote	Republican	Democratic	Progressive	Other	Plurality	Percentage Total Vote Rep.	Dem.	Prog.
24,506	TREMPEALEAU	6,664	2,083	373	4,148	60	2,065 P	31.3%	5.6%	62.2%
29,252	VERNON	8,779	2,670	406	5,599	104	2,929 P	30.4%	4.6%	63.8%
5,649	VILAS	2,073	873	119	1,038	43	165 P	42.1%	5.7%	50.1%
29,327	WALWORTH	13,080	7,484	1,162	4,335	99	3,149 R	57.2%	8.9%	33.1%
11,377	WASHBURN	3,655	1,422	158	2,043	32	621 P	38.9%	4.3%	55.9%
25,713	WASHINGTON	8,131	1,987	980	5,081	83	3,094 P	24.4%	12.1%	62.5%
42,612	WAUKESHA	15,459	7,026	1,965	6,348	120	678 R	45.4%	12.7%	41.1%
34,200	WAUPACA	10,781	3,654	665	6,395	67	2,741 P	33.9%	6.2%	59.3%
16,712	WAUSHARA	4,522	1,602	249	2,606	65	1,004 P	35.4%	5.5%	57.6%
63,897	WINNEBAGO	23,078	11,239	1,801	9,891	147	1,348 R	48.7%	7.8%	42.9%
34,643	WOOD	11,442	3,469	548	7,303	122	3,834 P	30.3%	4.8%	63.8%
2,632,067	TOTAL	840,827	311,614	68,115	453,678	7,420	142,064 P	37.1%	8.1%	54.0%

WISCONSIN

PRESIDENT 1920

1920 Census Population	County	Total Vote	Republican	Democratic	Other	Rep.-Dem. Plurality	Percentage Total Vote Rep.	Total Vote Dem.	Major Vote Rep.	Major Vote Dem.
9,287	ADAMS	2,007	1,528	392	87	1,136 R	76.1%	19.5%	79.6%	20.4%
24,538	ASHLAND	5,646	4,005	1,081	560	2,924 R	70.9%	19.1%	78.7%	21.3%
34,281	BARRON	8,176	6,887	742	547	6,145 R	84.2%	9.1%	90.3%	9.7%
17,201	BAYFIELD	3,458	2,536	589	333	1,947 R	73.3%	17.0%	81.2%	18.8%
61,889	BROWN	14,345	8,845	3,877	1,623	4,968 R	61.7%	27.0%	69.5%	30.5%
15,615	BUFFALO	3,609	3,082	299	228	2,783 R	85.4%	8.3%	91.2%	8.8%
10,735	BURNETT	2,545	2,025	187	333	1,838 R	79.6%	7.3%	91.5%	8.5%
17,228	CALUMET	4,766	3,730	586	450	3,144 R	78.3%	12.3%	86.4%	13.6%
36,482	CHIPPEWA	8,175	6,750	1,103	322	5,647 R	82.6%	13.5%	86.0%	14.0%
35,120	CLARK	7,833	6,246	745	842	5,501 R	79.7%	9.5%	89.3%	10.7%
30,468	COLUMBIA	8,882	7,394	1,201	287	6,193 R	83.2%	13.5%	86.0%	14.0%
16,772	CRAWFORD	4,846	3,600	1,112	134	2,488 R	74.3%	22.9%	76.4%	23.6%
89,432	DANE	29,488	22,842	4,879	1,767	17,963 R	77.5%	16.5%	82.4%	17.6%
49,742	DODGE	14,658	11,354	2,293	1,011	9,061 R	77.5%	15.6%	83.2%	16.8%
19,073	DOOR	4,321	3,817	385	119	3,432 R	88.3%	8.9%	90.8%	9.2%
49,771	DOUGLAS	10,736	7,250	2,111	1,375	5,139 R	67.5%	19.7%	77.4%	22.6%
26,970	DUNN	6,370	5,596	491	283	5,105 R	87.8%	7.7%	91.9%	8.1%
35,771	EAU CLAIRE	9,625	7,856	1,193	576	6,663 R	81.6%	12.4%	86.8%	13.2%
3,602	FLORENCE	1,050	912	98	40	814 R	86.9%	9.3%	90.3%	9.7%
56,119	FOND DU LAC	16,819	12,543	3,409	867	9,134 R	74.6%	20.3%	78.6%	21.4%
9,850	FOREST	1,902	1,429	379	94	1,050 R	75.1%	19.9%	79.0%	21.0%
39,044	GRANT	11,911	9,638	1,971	302	7,667 R	80.9%	16.5%	83.0%	17.0%
21,568	GREEN	6,455	5,466	633	356	4,833 R	84.7%	9.8%	89.6%	10.4%
14,875	GREEN LAKE	4,580	3,457	890	233	2,567 R	75.5%	19.4%	79.5%	20.5%
21,504	IOWA	6,667	5,428	942	297	4,486 R	81.4%	14.1%	85.2%	14.8%
10,261	IRON	2,206	1,714	268	224	1,446 R	77.7%	12.1%	86.5%	13.5%
17,746	JACKSON	4,250	3,652	410	188	3,242 R	85.9%	9.6%	89.9%	10.1%
35,022	JEFFERSON	11,029	8,865	1,844	320	7,021 R	80.4%	16.7%	82.8%	17.2%
19,209	JUNEAU	5,399	4,385	774	240	3,611 R	81.2%	14.3%	85.0%	15.0%
51,284	KENOSHA	12,584	9,791	1,724	1,069	8,067 R	77.8%	13.7%	85.0%	15.0%
16,091	KEWAUNEE	3,326	2,622	598	106	2,024 R	78.8%	18.0%	81.4%	18.6%
44,355	LA CROSSE	13,611	10,067	2,588	956	7,479 R	74.0%	19.0%	79.5%	20.5%
20,002	LAFAYETTE	6,429	4,893	1,357	179	3,536 R	76.1%	21.1%	78.3%	21.7%
21,471	LANGLADE	5,913	4,059	1,619	235	2,440 R	68.6%	27.4%	71.5%	28.5%
21,084	LINCOLN	5,149	3,713	838	598	2,875 R	72.1%	16.3%	81.6%	18.4%
51,644	MANITOWOC	13,579	8,378	2,018	3,183	6,360 R	61.7%	14.9%	80.6%	19.4%
65,259	MARATHON	17,329	11,356	2,133	3,840	9,223 R	65.5%	12.3%	84.2%	15.8%
34,361	MARINETTE	8,124	6,138	1,314	672	4,824 R	75.6%	16.2%	82.4%	17.6%
10,443	MARQUETTE	3,196	2,436	687	73	1,749 R	76.2%	21.5%	78.0%	22.0%
539,449	MILWAUKEE	142,311	73,410	25,464	43,437	47,946 R	51.6%	17.9%	74.2%	25.8%
28,666	MONROE	8,146	6,784	978	384	5,806 R	83.3%	12.0%	87.4%	12.6%
27,104	OCONTO	6,058	4,735	1,030	293	3,705 R	78.2%	17.0%	82.1%	17.9%
13,996	ONEIDA	3,733	2,424	833	476	1,591 R	64.9%	22.3%	74.4%	25.6%
55,113	OUTAGAMIE	14,915	11,140	3,121	654	8,019 R	74.7%	20.9%	78.1%	21.9%
16,335	OZAUKEE	4,660	3,523	835	302	2,688 R	75.6%	17.9%	80.8%	19.2%
7,481	PEPIN	2,140	1,817	265	58	1,552 R	84.9%	12.4%	87.3%	12.7%
21,663	PIERCE	5,375	4,441	644	290	3,797 R	82.6%	12.0%	87.3%	12.7%
26,870	POLK	5,960	4,796	752	412	4,044 R	80.5%	12.6%	86.4%	13.6%
33,649	PORTAGE	8,452	5,527	2,656	269	2,871 R	65.4%	31.4%	67.5%	32.5%
18,517	PRICE	4,028	2,990	551	487	2,439 R	74.2%	13.7%	84.4%	15.6%
78,961	RACINE	20,021	14,406	3,650	1,965	10,756 R	72.0%	18.2%	79.8%	20.2%
19,823	RICHLAND	5,040	3,862	917	261	2,945 R	76.6%	18.2%	80.8%	19.2%
66,150	ROCK	19,337	16,152	2,447	738	13,705 R	83.5%	12.7%	86.8%	13.2%
16,403	RUSK	3,362	2,609	441	312	2,168 R	77.6%	13.1%	85.5%	14.5%
26,106	ST. CROIX	7,637	5,601	1,638	398	3,963 R	73.3%	21.4%	77.4%	22.6%
32,548	SAUK	9,522	8,074	946	502	7,128 R	84.8%	9.9%	89.5%	10.5%
8,243	SAWYER	2,104	1,668	302	134	1,366 R	79.3%	14.4%	84.7%	15.3%
33,975	SHAWANO	7,925	5,836	525	1,564	5,311 R	73.6%	6.6%	91.7%	8.3%
59,913	SHEBOYGAN	17,396	11,994	1,895	3,507	10,099 R	68.9%	10.9%	86.4%	13.6%
18,045	TAYLOR	3,724	2,707	282	735	2,425 R	72.7%	7.6%	90.6%	9.4%

WISCONSIN

PRESIDENT 1920

1920 Census Population	County	Total Vote	Republican	Democratic	Other	Rep.-Dem. Plurality	Percentage Total Vote Rep.	Percentage Total Vote Dem.	Percentage Major Vote Rep.	Percentage Major Vote Dem.
24,506	TREMPEALEAU	5,636	4,748	718	170	4,030 R	84.2%	12.7%	86.9%	13.1%
29,252	VERNON	6,621	5,694	629	298	5,065 R	86.0%	9.5%	90.1%	9.9%
5,649	VILAS	1,367	903	255	209	648 R	66.1%	18.7%	78.0%	22.0%
29,327	WALWORTH	10,458	8,437	1,631	390	6,806 R	80.7%	15.6%	83.8%	16.2%
11,377	WASHBURN	2,585	2,023	352	210	1,671 R	78.3%	13.6%	85.2%	14.8%
25,713	WASHINGTON	7,748	5,949	1,328	471	4,621 R	76.8%	17.1%	81.8%	18.2%
42,612	WAUKESHA	12,097	8,665	2,759	673	5,906 R	71.6%	22.8%	75.8%	24.2%
34,200	WAUPACA	9,997	8,302	888	807	7,414 R	83.0%	8.9%	90.3%	9.7%
16,712	WAUSHARA	4,903	4,176	482	245	3,694 R	85.2%	9.8%	89.7%	10.3%
63,897	WINNEBAGO	17,308	12,035	3,397	1,876	8,638 R	69.5%	19.6%	78.0%	22.0%
34,643	WOOD	9,721	6,863	1,051	1,807	5,812 R	70.6%	10.8%	86.7%	13.3%
2,632,067	TOTAL	701,281	498,576	113,422	89,283	385,154 R	71.1%	16.2%	81.5%	18.5%

WISCONSIN

ELECTION NOTE

1956 Other vote was 6,918 Andrews (States Rights); 754 Hoopes (Socialist); 710 Hass (Socialist Labor); 564 Dobbs (Socialist Workers).

1952 Other vote was 2,174 Hallinan (Progressive); 1,350 Dobbs (Socialist Workers); 1,157 Hoopes (Socialist); 770 Hass (Socialist Labor).

1948 Other vote was 25,282 Wallace (Progressive); 12,547 Thomas (Socialist); 399 Teichert (Socialist Labor); 303 Dobbs (Socialist Workers).

1944 Other vote was 13,205 Thomas (Socialist); 1,002 Teichert (Socialist Labor).

1940 Other vote was 15,071 Thomas (Socialist); 2,394 Browder (Communist); 2,148 Babson (Prohibition); 1,882 Aiken (Socialist Labor).

1936 Other vote was 60,297 Lemke (Union); 10,626 Thomas (Socialist); 2,197 Browder (Communist); 1,071 Colvin (Prohibition); 557 Aiken (Socialist Labor).

1932 Other vote was 53,379 Thomas (Socialist); 3,105 Foster (Communist); 2,672 Upshaw (Prohibition); 494 Reynolds (Socialist Labor); 13 scattered write-in.

1928 Other vote was 18,213 Thomas (Socialist); 2,245 Varney (Prohibition); 1,528 Foster (Communist); 381 Reynolds (Socialist Labor).

1924 A special four-column table which gives the LaFollette (Progressive) vote is used to detail this election. Other vote was 3,773 Foster (Communist); 2,918 Faris (Prohibition); 458 Johns (Socialist Labor); 271 Wallace (Commonwealth Land).

1920 Other vote was 80,635 Debs (Socialist); 8,648 Watkins (Prohibition). Socialist candidates ran second in several counties.

WYOMING

POPULAR VOTE FOR PRESIDENT 1920 TO 1956

Year	Total Vote	Republican Vote	Republican Candidate	Democratic Vote	Democratic Candidate	Other Vote	Plurality	Percentage Total Vote Rep.	Percentage Total Vote Dem.	Percentage Major Vote Rep.	Percentage Major Vote Dem.
1956	124,127	74,573	Eisenhower, Dwight D.	49,554	Stevenson, Adlai E.		25,019 R	60.1%	39.9%	60.1%	39.9%
1952	129,253	81,049	Eisenhower, Dwight D.	47,934	Stevenson, Adlai E.	270	33,115 R	62.7%	37.1%	62.8%	37.2%
1948	101,425	47,947	Dewey, Thomas E.	52,354	Truman, Harry S.	1,124	4,407 D	47.3%	51.6%	47.8%	52.2%
1944	101,340	51,921	Dewey, Thomas E.	49,419	Roosevelt, Franklin D.		2,502 R	51.2%	48.8%	51.2%	48.8%
1940	112,240	52,633	Willkie, Wendell	59,287	Roosevelt, Franklin D.	320	6,654 D	46.9%	52.8%	47.0%	53.0%
1936	103,382	38,739	Landon, Alfred M.	62,624	Roosevelt, Franklin D.	2,019	23,885 D	37.5%	60.6%	38.2%	61.8%
1932	96,962	39,583	Hoover, Herbert C.	54,370	Roosevelt, Franklin D.	3,009	14,787 D	40.8%	56.1%	42.1%	57.9%
1928	82,835	52,748	Hoover, Herbert C.	29,299	Smith, Alfred E.	788	23,449 R	63.7%	35.4%	64.3%	35.7%
1924 **	79,900	41,858	Coolidge, Calvin	12,868	Davis, John W.	25,174	16,684 R	52.4%	16.1%	76.5%	23.5%
1920	56,253	35,091	Harding, Warren G.	17,429	Cox, James M.	3,733	17,662 R	62.4%	31.0%	66.8%	33.2%

In 1924 other vote was Progressive.

ELECTORAL COLLEGE VOTE 1920 TO 1956

Year	Total	Republican	Democratic	Other
1956	3	3	—	—
1952	3	3	—	—
1948	3	—	3	—
1944	3	3	—	—
1940	3	—	3	—
1936	3	—	3	—
1932	3	—	3	—
1928	3	3	—	—
1924	3	3	—	—
1920	3	3	—	—

WYOMING

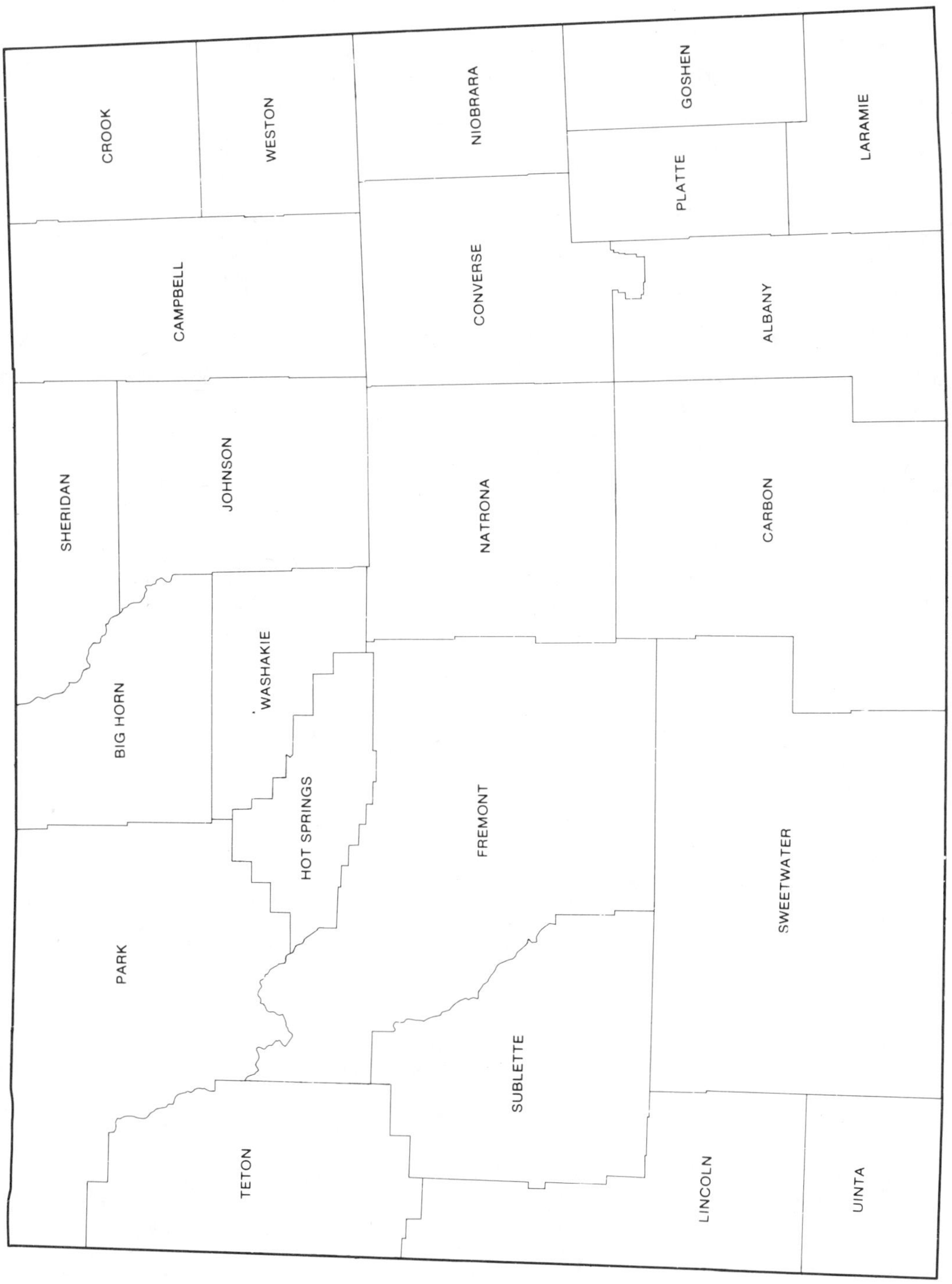
CROOK
WESTON
NIOBRARA
GOSHEN
LARAMIE
PLATTE
CAMPBELL
CONVERSE
ALBANY
SHERIDAN
JOHNSON
NATRONA
CARBON
WASHAKIE
BIG HORN
HOT SPRINGS
FREMONT
SWEETWATER
PARK
SUBLETTE
TETON
LINCOLN
UINTA

WYOMING

PRESIDENT 1956

1950 Census Population	County	Total Vote	Republican	Democratic	Other	Rep.-Dem. Plurality	Percentage Total Vote Rep.	Total Vote Dem.	Major Vote Rep.	Major Vote Dem.
19,055	ALBANY	7,722	4,315	3,407		908 R	55.9%	44.1%	55.9%	44.1%
13,176	BIG HORN	5,182	3,369	1,813		1,556 R	65.0%	35.0%	65.0%	35.0%
4,839	CAMPBELL	2,129	1,473	656		817 R	69.2%	30.8%	69.2%	30.8%
15,742	CARBON	6,554	3,336	3,218		118 R	50.9%	49.1%	50.9%	49.1%
5,933	CONVERSE	2,606	1,855	751		1,104 R	71.2%	28.8%	71.2%	28.8%
4,738	CROOK	1,565	1,139	426		713 R	72.8%	27.2%	72.8%	27.2%
19,580	FREEMONT	7,456	4,887	2,569		2,318 R	65.5%	34.5%	65.5%	34.5%
12,634	GOSHEN	4,955	2,825	2,130		695 R	57.0%	43.0%	57.0%	43.0%
5,250	HOT SPRINGS	2,640	1,663	977		686 R	63.0%	37.0%	63.0%	37.0%
4,707	JOHNSON	2,420	1,842	578		1,264 R	76.1%	23.9%	76.1%	23.9%
47,662	LARAMIE	19,653	10,581	9,072		1,509 R	53.8%	46.2%	53.8%	46.2%
9,023	LINCOLN	3,827	2,264	1,563		701 R	59.2%	40.8%	59.2%	40.8%
31,437	NATRONA	17,258	10,796	6,462		4,334 R	62.6%	37.4%	62.6%	37.4%
4,701	NIOBRARA	1,766	1,248	518		730 R	70.7%	29.3%	70.7%	29.3%
15,182	PARK	6,357	4,397	1,960		2,437 R	69.2%	30.8%	69.2%	30.8%
7,925	PLATTE	3,347	1,848	1,499		349 R	55.2%	44.8%	55.2%	44.8%
20,185	SHERIDAN	8,750	5,546	3,204		2,342 R	63.4%	36.6%	63.4%	36.6%
2,481	SUBLETTE	1,252	901	351		550 R	72.0%	28.0%	72.0%	28.0%
22,017	SWEETWATER	8,102	3,355	4,747		1,392 D	41.4%	58.6%	41.4%	58.6%
2,593	TETON	1,401	1,089	312		777 R	77.7%	22.3%	77.7%	22.3%
7,331	UINTA	3,063	1,742	1,321		421 R	56.9%	43.1%	56.9%	43.1%
7,252	WASHAKIE	3,254	2,265	989		1,276 R	69.6%	30.4%	69.6%	30.4%
6,733	WESTON	2,868	1,837	1,031		806 R	64.1%	35.9%	64.1%	35.9%
290,529	TOTAL	124,127	74,573	49,554		25,019 R	60.1%	39.9%	60.1%	39.9%

WYOMING

PRESIDENT 1952

1950 Census Population	County	Total Vote	Republican	Democratic	Other	Rep.-Dem. Plurality	Percentage Total Vote Rep.	Total Vote Dem.	Major Vote Rep.	Major Vote Dem.
19,055	ALBANY	7,652	4,560	3,082	10	1,478 R	59.6%	40.3%	59.7%	40.3%
13,176	BIG HORN	5,620	3,859	1,755	6	2,104 R	68.7%	31.2%	68.7%	31.3%
4,839	CAMPBELL	2,494	1,823	666	5	1,157 R	73.1%	26.7%	73.2%	26.8%
15,742	CARBON	6,661	3,403	3,242	16	161 R	51.1%	48.7%	51.2%	48.8%
5,933	CONVERSE	2,916	2,056	850	10	1,206 R	70.5%	29.1%	70.8%	29.2%
4,738	CROOK	2,173	1,734	423	16	1,311 R	79.8%	19.5%	80.4%	19.6%
19,580	FREEMONT	8,063	5,881	2,161	21	3,720 R	72.9%	26.8%	73.1%	26.9%
12,634	GOSHEN	5,058	3,396	1,648	14	1,748 R	67.1%	32.6%	67.3%	32.7%
5,250	HOT SPRINGS	2,432	1,573	856	3	717 R	64.7%	35.2%	64.8%	35.2%
4,707	JOHNSON	2,524	1,980	543	1	1,437 R	78.4%	21.5%	78.5%	21.5%
47,662	LARAMIE	19,051	10,785	8,187	79	2,598 R	56.6%	43.0%	56.8%	43.2%
9,023	LINCOLN	4,030	2,321	1,709		612 R	57.6%	42.4%	57.6%	42.4%
31,437	NATRONA	16,695	10,663	6,021	11	4,642 R	63.9%	36.1%	63.9%	36.1%
4,701	NIOBRARA	2,259	1,652	588	19	1,064 R	73.1%	26.0%	73.8%	26.3%
15,182	PARK	7,175	5,067	2,084	24	2,983 R	70.6%	29.0%	70.9%	29.1%
7,925	PLATTE	3,524	2,148	1,364	12	784 R	61.0%	38.7%	61.2%	38.8%
20,185	SHERIDAN	9,655	6,522	3,124	9	3,398 R	67.6%	32.4%	67.6%	32.4%
2,481	SUBLETTE	1,359	1,013	344	2	669 R	74.5%	25.3%	74.6%	25.4%
22,017	SWEETWATER	9,374	3,567	5,807		2,240 D	38.1%	61.9%	38.1%	61.9%
2,593	TETON	1,483	1,166	317		849 R	78.6%	21.4%	78.6%	21.4%
7,331	UINTA	3,248	1,801	1,444	3	357 R	55.4%	44.5%	55.5%	44.5%
7,252	WASHAKIE	3,033	2,148	880	5	1,268 R	70.8%	29.0%	70.9%	29.1%
6,733	WESTON	2,774	1,931	839	4	1,092 R	69.6%	30.2%	69.7%	30.3%
290,529	TOTAL	129,253	81,049	47,934	270	33,115 R	62.7%	37.1%	62.8%	37.2%

WYOMING

PRESIDENT 1948

1940 Census Population	County	Total Vote	Republican	Democratic	Other	Rep.-Dem. Plurality	Percentage Total Vote Rep.	Percentage Total Vote Dem.	Percentage Major Vote Rep.	Percentage Major Vote Dem.
13,946	ALBANY	6,045	2,858	3,141	46	283 D	47.3%	52.0%	47.6%	52.4%
12,911	BIG HORN	4,823	2,429	2,370	24	59 R	50.4%	49.1%	50.6%	49.4%
6,048	CAMPBELL	2,071	1,201	856	14	345 R	58.0%	41.3%	58.4%	41.6%
12,644	CARBON	5,813	2,319	3,439	55	1,120 D	39.9%	59.2%	40.3%	59.7%
6,631	CONVERSE	2,338	1,327	996	15	331 R	56.8%	42.6%	57.1%	42.9%
5,463	CROOK	1,892	1,166	712	14	454 R	61.6%	37.6%	62.1%	37.9%
16,095	FREEMONT	6,400	3,357	3,019	24	338 R	52.5%	47.2%	52.7%	47.3%
12,207	GOSHEN	3,909	2,029	1,843	37	186 R	51.9%	47.1%	52.4%	47.6%
4,607	HOT SPRINGS	1,764	791	928	45	137 D	44.8%	52.6%	46.0%	54.0%
4,980	JOHNSON	2,045	1,351	682	12	669 R	66.1%	33.3%	66.5%	33.5%
33,651	LARAMIE	14,524	6,200	8,226	98	2,026 D	42.7%	56.6%	43.0%	57.0%
10,286	LINCOLN	3,738	1,730	1,925	83	195 D	46.3%	51.5%	47.3%	52.7%
23,858	NATRONA	11,608	5,341	6,183	84	842 D	46.0%	53.3%	46.3%	53.7%
5,988	NIOBRARA	1,745	975	753	17	222 R	55.9%	43.2%	56.4%	43.6%
10,976	PARK	5,145	2,655	2,461	29	194 R	51.6%	47.8%	51.9%	48.1%
8,013	PLATTE	2,853	1,366	1,465	22	99 D	47.9%	51.3%	48.3%	51.7%
19,255	SHERIDAN	7,601	3,698	3,852	51	154 D	48.7%	50.7%	49.0%	51.0%
2,778	SUBLETTE	1,126	622	496	8	126 R	55.2%	44.0%	55.6%	44.4%
19,407	SWEETWATER	8,085	2,538	5,146	401	2,608 D	31.4%	63.6%	33.0%	67.0%
2,543	TETON	1,289	719	556	14	163 R	55.8%	43.1%	56.4%	43.6%
7,223	UINTA	2,898	1,239	1,632	27	393 D	42.8%	56.3%	43.2%	56.8%
5,858	WASHAKIE	1,925	1,074	851		223 R	55.8%	44.2%	55.8%	44.2%
4,958	WESTON	1,788	962	822	4	140 R	53.8%	46.0%	53.9%	46.1%
250,742	TOTAL	101,425	47,947	52,354	1,124	4,407 D	47.3%	51.6%	47.8%	52.2%

WYOMING

PRESIDENT 1944

1940 Census Population	County	Total Vote	Republican	Democratic	Other	Rep.-Dem. Plurality	Percentage Total Vote Rep.	Total Vote Dem.	Major Vote Rep.	Major Vote Dem.
13,946	ALBANY	6,199	2,970	3,229		259 D	47.9%	52.1%	47.9%	52.1%
12,911	BIG HORN	4,973	2,659	2,314		345 R	53.5%	46.5%	53.5%	46.5%
6,048	CAMPBELL	2,408	1,514	894		620 R	62.9%	37.1%	62.9%	37.1%
12,644	CARBON	5,681	2,698	2,983		285 D	47.5%	52.5%	47.5%	52.5%
6,631	CONVERSE	2,580	1,601	979		622 R	62.1%	37.9%	62.1%	37.9%
5,463	CROOK	1,934	1,244	690		554 R	64.3%	35.7%	64.3%	35.7%
16,095	FREEMONT	5,370	3,193	2,177		1,016 R	59.5%	40.5%	59.5%	40.5%
12,207	GOSHEN	4,188	2,674	1,514		1,160 R	63.8%	36.2%	63.8%	36.2%
4,607	HOT SPRINGS	1,846	877	969		92 D	47.5%	52.5%	47.5%	52.5%
4,980	JOHNSON	2,140	1,384	756		628 R	64.7%	35.3%	64.7%	35.3%
33,651	LARAMIE	14,868	7,326	7,542		216 D	49.3%	50.7%	49.3%	50.7%
10,286	LINCOLN	3,789	1,649	2,140		491 D	43.5%	56.5%	43.5%	56.5%
23,858	NATRONA	10,086	5,196	4,890		306 R	51.5%	48.5%	51.5%	48.5%
5,988	NIOBRARA	2,138	1,312	826		486 R	61.4%	38.6%	61.4%	38.6%
10,976	PARK	4,828	2,571	2,257		314 R	53.3%	46.7%	53.3%	46.7%
8,013	PLATTE	3,320	1,776	1,544		232 R	53.5%	46.5%	53.5%	46.5%
19,255	SHERIDAN	7,664	3,802	3,862		60 D	49.6%	50.4%	49.6%	50.4%
2,778	SUBLETTE	1,153	683	470		213 R	59.2%	40.8%	59.2%	40.8%
19,407	SWEETWATER	8,222	2,623	5,599		2,976 D	31.9%	68.1%	31.9%	68.1%
2,543	TETON	1,136	637	499		138 R	56.1%	43.9%	56.1%	43.9%
7,223	UINTA	3,059	1,305	1,754		449 D	42.7%	57.3%	42.7%	57.3%
5,858	WASHAKIE	1,907	1,130	777		353 R	59.3%	40.7%	59.3%	40.7%
4,958	WESTON	1,851	1,097	754		343 R	59.3%	40.7%	59.3%	40.7%
250,742	TOTAL	101,340	51,921	49,419		2,502 R	51.2%	48.8%	51.2%	48.8%

WYOMING

PRESIDENT 1940

1940 Census Population	County	Total Vote	Republican	Democratic	Other	Rep.-Dem. Plurality	Percentage Total Vote Rep.	Total Vote Dem.	Major Vote Rep.	Major Vote Dem.
13,946	ALBANY	6,804	2,756	4,018	30	1,262 D	40.5%	59.1%	40.7%	59.3%
12,911	BIG HORN	5,475	2,859	2,594	22	265 R	52.2%	47.4%	52.4%	47.6%
6,048	CAMPBELL	2,675	1,540	1,128	7	412 R	57.6%	42.2%	57.7%	42.3%
12,644	CARBON	6,320	2,882	3,429	9	547 D	45.6%	54.3%	45.7%	54.3%
6,631	CONVERSE	3,286	1,889	1,395	2	494 R	57.5%	42.5%	57.5%	42.5%
5,463	CROOK	2,233	1,359	869	5	490 R	60.9%	38.9%	61.0%	39.0%
16,095	FREEMONT	6,453	3,788	2,644	21	1,144 R	58.7%	41.0%	58.9%	41.1%
12,207	GOSHEN	4,858	2,861	1,982	15	879 R	58.9%	40.8%	59.1%	40.9%
4,607	HOT SPRINGS	2,194	913	1,266	15	353 D	41.6%	57.7%	41.9%	58.1%
4,980	JOHNSON	2,247	1,460	781	6	679 R	65.0%	34.8%	65.1%	34.9%
33,651	LARAMIE	13,820	5,955	7,808	57	1,853 D	43.1%	56.5%	43.3%	56.7%
10,286	LINCOLN	4,605	1,765	2,839	1	1,074 D	38.3%	61.7%	38.3%	61.7%
23,858	NATRONA	11,949	5,555	6,373	21	818 D	46.5%	53.3%	46.6%	53.4%
5,988	NIOBRARA	2,632	1,427	1,200	5	227 R	54.2%	45.6%	54.3%	45.7%
10,976	PARK	5,282	2,512	2,747	23	235 D	47.6%	52.0%	47.8%	52.2%
8,013	PLATTE	3,622	1,758	1,849	15	91 D	48.5%	51.0%	48.7%	51.3%
19,255	SHERIDAN	8,268	3,814	4,439	15	625 D	46.1%	53.7%	46.2%	53.8%
2,778	SUBLETTE	1,402	771	627	4	144 R	55.0%	44.7%	55.2%	44.8%
19,407	SWEETWATER	9,094	2,439	6,637	18	4,198 D	26.8%	73.0%	26.9%	73.1%
2,543	TETON	1,353	623	728	2	105 D	46.0%	53.8%	46.1%	53.9%
7,223	UINTA	3,351	1,335	2,007	9	672 D	39.8%	59.9%	39.9%	60.1%
5,858	WASHAKIE	2,033	1,080	942	11	138 R	53.1%	46.3%	53.4%	46.6%
4,958	WESTON	2,284	1,292	985	7	307 R	56.6%	43.1%	56.7%	43.3%
250,742	TOTAL	112,240	52,633	59,287	320	6,654 D	46.9%	52.8%	47.0%	53.0%

WYOMING

PRESIDENT 1936

1930 Census Population	County	Total Vote	Republican	Democratic	Other	Rep.-Dem. Plurality	Percentage Total Vote Rep.	Percentage Total Vote Dem.	Percentage Major Vote Rep.	Percentage Major Vote Dem.
12,041	ALBANY	5,539	1,777	3,685	77	1,908 D	32.1%	66.5%	32.5%	67.5%
11,222	BIG HORN	5,236	1,996	3,156	84	1,160 D	38.1%	60.3%	38.7%	61.3%
6,720	CAMPBELL	2,784	1,322	1,435	27	113 D	47.5%	51.5%	48.0%	52.0%
11,391	CARBON	5,373	2,041	3,257	75	1,216 D	38.0%	60.6%	38.5%	61.5%
7,145	CONVERSE	3,251	1,556	1,639	56	83 D	47.9%	50.4%	48.7%	51.3%
5,333	CROOK	2,350	1,218	1,088	44	130 R	51.8%	46.3%	52.8%	47.2%
10,490	FREEMONT	5,533	2,357	3,050	126	693 D	42.6%	55.1%	43.6%	56.4%
11,754	GOSHEN	4,751	2,047	2,639	65	592 D	43.1%	55.5%	43.7%	56.3%
5,476	HOT SPRINGS	2,319	796	1,419	104	623 D	34.3%	61.2%	35.9%	64.1%
4,816	JOHNSON	2,333	1,266	949	118	317 R	54.3%	40.7%	57.2%	42.8%
26,845	LARAMIE	12,140	4,356	7,594	190	3,238 D	35.9%	62.6%	36.5%	63.5%
10,894	LINCOLN	4,160	1,376	2,747	37	1,371 D	33.1%	66.0%	33.4%	66.6%
24,272	NATRONA	11,907	3,810	7,819	278	4,009 D	32.0%	65.7%	32.8%	67.2%
4,723	NIOBRARA	2,245	1,086	1,124	35	38 D	48.4%	50.1%	49.1%	50.9%
8,207	PARK	4,315	1,618	2,594	103	976 D	37.5%	60.1%	38.4%	61.6%
9,695	PLATTE	3,406	1,546	1,730	130	184 D	45.4%	50.8%	47.2%	52.8%
16,875	SHERIDAN	7,680	2,726	4,731	223	2,005 D	35.5%	61.6%	36.6%	63.4%
1,944	SUBLETTE	1,338	638	667	33	29 D	47.7%	49.9%	48.9%	51.1%
18,165	SWEETWATER	8,097	1,797	6,232	68	4,435 D	22.2%	77.0%	22.4%	77.6%
2,003	TETON	1,352	501	795	56	294 D	37.1%	58.8%	38.7%	61.3%
6,572	UINTA	3,015	1,015	1,972	28	957 D	33.7%	65.4%	34.0%	66.0%
4,109	WASHAKIE	1,963	810	1,109	44	299 D	41.3%	56.5%	42.2%	57.8%
4,673	WESTON	2,295	1,084	1,193	18	109 D	47.2%	52.0%	47.6%	52.4%
223,565	TOTAL	103,382	38,739	62,624	2,019	23,885 D	37.5%	60.6%	38.2%	61.8%

WYOMING

PRESIDENT 1932

1930 Census Population	County	Total Vote	Republican	Democratic	Other	Rep.-Dem. Plurality	Percentage Total Vote Rep.	Total Vote Dem.	Major Vote Rep.	Major Vote Dem.
12,041	ALBANY	5,289	2,281	2,665	343	384 D	43.1%	50.4%	46.1%	53.9%
11,222	BIG HORN	4,563	2,334	2,155	74	179 R	51.2%	47.2%	52.0%	48.0%
6,720	CAMPBELL	2,980	1,161	1,728	91	567 D	39.0%	58.0%	40.2%	59.8%
11,391	CARBON	5,073	2,088	2,836	149	748 D	41.2%	55.9%	42.4%	57.6%
7,145	CONVERSE	3,477	1,569	1,860	48	291 D	45.1%	53.5%	45.8%	54.2%
5,333	CROOK	2,413	1,062	1,317	34	255 D	44.0%	54.6%	44.6%	55.4%
10,490	FREEMONT	4,374	1,696	2,612	66	916 D	38.8%	59.7%	39.4%	60.6%
11,754	GOSHEN	4,590	1,954	2,545	91	591 D	42.6%	55.4%	43.4%	56.6%
5,476	HOT SPRINGS	2,353	742	1,466	145	724 D	31.5%	62.3%	33.6%	66.4%
4,816	JOHNSON	2,340	1,101	1,171	68	70 D	47.1%	50.0%	48.5%	51.5%
26,845	LARAMIE	10,938	5,116	5,435	387	319 D	46.8%	49.7%	48.5%	51.5%
10,894	LINCOLN	4,006	1,673	2,275	58	602 D	41.8%	56.8%	42.4%	57.6%
24,272	NATRONA	11,533	4,368	6,777	388	2,409 D	37.9%	58.8%	39.2%	60.8%
4,723	NIOBRARA	2,185	908	1,237	40	329 D	41.6%	56.6%	42.3%	57.7%
8,207	PARK	3,757	1,600	2,043	114	443 D	42.6%	54.4%	43.9%	56.1%
9,695	PLATTE	3,624	1,430	1,893	301	463 D	39.5%	52.2%	43.0%	57.0%
16,875	SHERIDAN	7,142	2,738	4,260	144	1,522 D	38.3%	59.6%	39.1%	60.9%
1,944	SUBLETTE	1,172	512	633	27	121 D	43.7%	54.0%	44.7%	55.3%
18,165	SWEETWATER	6,983	2,043	4,637	303	2,594 D	29.3%	66.4%	30.6%	69.4%
2,003	TETON	1,115	406	699	10	293 D	36.4%	62.7%	36.7%	63.3%
6,572	UINTA	2,958	1,250	1,658	50	408 D	42.3%	56.1%	43.0%	57.0%
4,109	WASHAKIE	1,751	711	1,009	31	298 D	40.6%	57.6%	41.3%	58.7%
4,673	WESTON	2,346	840	1,459	47	619 D	35.8%	62.2%	36.5%	63.5%
223,565	TOTAL	96,962	39,583	54,370	3,009	14,787 D	40.8%	56.1%	42.1%	57.9%

WYOMING

PRESIDENT 1928

1920 Census Population	County	Total Vote	Republican	Democratic	Other	Rep.-Dem. Plurality	Percentage Total Vote Rep.	Total Vote Dem.	Major Vote Rep.	Major Vote Dem.
9,283	ALBANY	4,586	2,941	1,618	27	1,323 R	64.1%	35.3%	64.5%	35.5%
12,105	BIG HORN	3,596	2,646	933	17	1,713 R	73.6%	25.9%	73.9%	26.1%
5,233	CAMPBELL	2,297	1,528	744	25	784 R	66.5%	32.4%	67.3%	32.7%
9,525	CARBON	4,655	3,019	1,609	27	1,410 R	64.9%	34.6%	65.2%	34.8%
7,871	CONVERSE	2,893	2,040	845	8	1,195 R	70.5%	29.2%	70.7%	29.3%
5,524	CROOK	2,053	1,466	582	5	884 R	71.4%	28.3%	71.6%	28.4%
11,820	FREEMONT	3,738	2,267	1,449	22	818 R	60.6%	38.8%	61.0%	39.0%
8,064	GOSHEN	3,298	2,483	777	38	1,706 R	75.3%	23.6%	76.2%	23.8%
5,164	HOT SPRINGS	2,205	1,220	940	45	280 R	55.3%	42.6%	56.5%	43.5%
4,617	JOHNSON	1,977	1,369	590	18	779 R	69.2%	29.8%	69.9%	30.1%
20,699	LARAMIE	8,973	5,862	3,029	82	2,833 R	65.3%	33.8%	65.9%	34.1%
12,487	LINCOLN	3,919	2,217	1,687	15	530 R	56.6%	43.0%	56.8%	43.2%
14,635	NATRONA	11,023	7,141	3,818	64	3,323 R	64.8%	34.6%	65.2%	34.8%
6,321	NIOBRARA	1,919	1,424	469	26	955 R	74.2%	24.4%	75.2%	24.8%
7,298	PARK	3,260	2,175	1,062	23	1,113 R	66.7%	32.6%	67.2%	32.8%
7,421	PLATTE	3,256	2,206	932	118	1,274 R	67.8%	28.6%	70.3%	29.7%
18,182	SHERIDAN	6,250	3,616	2,563	71	1,053 R	57.9%	41.0%	58.5%	41.5%
	SUBLETTE	895	573	316	6	257 R	64.0%	35.3%	64.5%	35.5%
13,640	SWEETWATER	5,599	2,528	2,974	97	446 D	45.2%	53.1%	45.9%	54.1%
	TETON	770	495	270	5	225 R	64.3%	35.1%	64.7%	35.3%
6,611	UINTA	2,468	1,439	1,012	17	427 R	58.3%	41.0%	58.7%	41.3%
3,106	WASHAKIE	1,366	966	392	8	574 R	70.7%	28.7%	71.1%	28.9%
4,631	WESTON	1,839	1,127	688	24	439 R	61.3%	37.4%	62.1%	37.9%
194,402	TOTAL	82,835	52,748	29,299	788	23,449 R	63.7%	35.4%	64.3%	35.7%

WYOMING

PRESIDENT 1924

1920 Census Population	County	Total Vote	Republican	Democratic	Progressive	Other	Plurality	Percentage Total Vote Rep.	Dem.	Prog.
9,283	ALBANY	4,535	2,164	743	1,628		536 R	47.7%	16.4%	35.9%
12,105	BIG HORN	3,715	2,023	459	1,233		790 R	54.5%	12.4%	33.2%
5,233	CAMPBELL	2,141	1,121	577	443		544 R	52.4%	27.0%	20.7%
9,525	CARBON	4,395	2,398	733	1,264		1,134 R	54.6%	16.7%	28.8%
7,871	CONVERSE	3,007	1,758	524	725		1,033 R	58.5%	17.4%	24.1%
5,524	CROOK	1,795	978	468	349		510 R	54.5%	26.1%	19.4%
11,820	FREEMONT	3,839	1,986	561	1,292		694 R	51.7%	14.6%	33.7%
8,064	GOSHEN	2,855	1,603	464	788		815 R	56.1%	16.3%	27.6%
5,164	HOT SPRINGS	2,211	1,011	231	969		42 R	45.7%	10.4%	43.8%
4,617	JOHNSON	1,891	1,097	501	293		596 R	58.0%	26.5%	15.5%
20,699	LARAMIE	7,442	3,944	1,120	2,378		1,566 R	53.0%	15.0%	32.0%
12,487	LINCOLN	3,094	1,493	576	1,025		468 R	48.3%	18.6%	33.1%
14,635	NATRONA	13,755	8,267	1,631	3,857		4,410 R	60.1%	11.9%	28.0%
6,321	NIOBRARA	1,693	820	202	671		149 R	48.4%	11.9%	39.6%
7,298	PARK	2,897	1,607	530	760		847 R	55.5%	18.3%	26.2%
7,421	PLATTE	2,791	1,383	436	972		411 R	49.6%	15.6%	34.8%
18,182	SHERIDAN	5,917	2,530	1,115	2,272		258 R	42.8%	18.8%	38.4%
	SUBLETTE	846	570	183	93		387 R	67.4%	21.6%	11.0%
13,640	SWEETWATER	5,026	2,119	688	2,219		100 P	42.2%	13.7%	44.2%
	TETON	626	342	173	111		169 R	54.6%	27.6%	17.7%
6,611	UINTA	2,474	1,126	427	921		205 R	45.5%	17.3%	37.2%
3,106	WASHAKIE	1,204	724	209	271		453 R	60.1%	17.4%	22.5%
4,631	WESTON	1,751	794	317	640		154 R	45.3%	18.1%	36.6%
194,402	TOTAL	79,900	41,858	12,868	25,174		16,684 R	52.4%	16.1%	31.5%

WYOMING

PRESIDENT 1920

1920 Census Population	County	Total Vote	Republican	Democratic	Other	Rep.-Dem. Plurality	Percentage Total Vote Rep.	Percentage Total Vote Dem.	Percentage Major Vote Rep.	Percentage Major Vote Dem.
9,283	ALBANY	2,990	1,769	1,145	76	624 R	59.2%	38.3%	60.7%	39.3%
12,105	BIG HORN	3,278	2,157	1,082	39	1,075 R	65.8%	33.0%	66.6%	33.4%
5,233	CAMPBELL	1,540	1,027	493	20	534 R	66.7%	32.0%	67.6%	32.4%
9,525	CARBON	3,085	1,871	1,039	175	832 R	60.6%	33.7%	64.3%	35.7%
7,871	CONVERSE	2,249	1,561	679	9	882 R	69.4%	30.2%	69.7%	30.3%
5,524	CROOK	1,389	934	451	4	483 R	67.2%	32.5%	67.4%	32.6%
11,820	FREEMONT	3,245	2,194	994	57	1,200 R	67.6%	30.6%	68.8%	31.2%
8,064	GOSHEN	2,057	1,496	552	9	944 R	72.7%	26.8%	73.0%	27.0%
5,164	HOT SPRINGS	1,876	1,212	529	135	683 R	64.6%	28.2%	69.6%	30.4%
4,617	JOHNSON	1,733	1,202	525	6	677 R	69.4%	30.3%	69.6%	30.4%
20,699	LARAMIE	5,430	3,399	1,810	221	1,589 R	62.6%	33.3%	65.3%	34.7%
12,487	LINCOLN	3,346	2,043	1,154	149	889 R	61.1%	34.5%	63.9%	36.1%
14,635	NATRONA	4,467	2,957	1,153	357	1,804 R	66.2%	25.8%	71.9%	28.1%
6,321	NIOBRARA	1,318	969	345	4	624 R	73.5%	26.2%	73.7%	26.3%
7,298	PARK	2,311	1,630	666	15	964 R	70.5%	28.8%	71.0%	29.0%
7,421	PLATTE	2,139	1,405	694	40	711 R	65.7%	32.4%	66.9%	33.1%
18,182	SHERIDAN	4,377	2,645	1,192	540	1,453 R	60.4%	27.2%	68.9%	31.1%
	SUBLETTE	—	—	—	—	—	—	—	—	—
13,640	SWEETWATER	3,221	1,744	1,216	261	528 R	54.1%	37.8%	58.9%	41.1%
	TETON	—	—	—	—	—	—	—	—	—
6,611	UINTA	2,139	1,194	914	31	280 R	55.8%	42.7%	56.6%	43.4%
3,106	WASHAKIE	947	609	333	5	276 R	64.3%	35.2%	64.6%	35.4%
4,631	WESTON	1,563	1,073	463	27	610 R	68.7%	29.6%	69.9%	30.1%
194,402	TOTAL	56,253	35,091	17,429	3,733	17,662 R	62.4%	31.0%	66.8%	33.2%

WYOMING

The total of the population column for each census includes persons living in Yellowstone National Park and not under jurisdiction of any county. In 1923 Sublette county was organized from parts of Fremont and Lincoln counties; Teton county was organized from part of Lincoln county. Population data for the years between the 1920 and 1930 Census are not available.

ELECTION NOTES

1956

1952 Other vote was 194 Hamblen (Prohibition); 40 Hoopes (Socialist); 36 Hass (Socialist Labor).

1948 Other vote was 931 Wallace (Progressive); 137 Thomas (Socialist); 56 Teichert (Socialist Labor).

1944

1940 Other vote was 172 Babson (Prohibition); 148 Thomas (Socialist).

1936 Other vote was 1,653 Lemke (Union); 200 Thomas (Socialist); 91 Browder (Communist); 75 Colvin (Prohibition).

1932 Other vote was 2,829 Thomas (Socialist); 180 Foster (Communist).

1928 Other vote was Thomas (Socialist).

1924 A special four-column table which gives the LaFollette (Progressive) vote is used to detail this election.

1920 Other vote was 2,180 Christensen (Farmer-Labor); 1,288 Debs (Socialist); 265 Watkins (Prohibition). The statewide total in the other vote column includes the Socialist and Prohibition votes which were not available by county.

1956 PRESIDENTIAL PRIMARIES

In 1956 seventeen states, the District of Columbia and the Territory of Alaska held Presidential primaries. In some states balloting was for delegate slates pledged to a specific Presidential candidate or unpledged; in others, electors indicated a personal preference as to their party's nominee.

The state-by-state Republican and Democratic tables, included at the end of this section, detail in chronological order the vote for major candidates in each party. An asterisk in the table indicates write-in votes for a candidate not on the ballot.

Republican candidates on the ballot or who received write-in votes were S. C. Arnold, John W. Bricker, John B. Chapple, Lar Daly, Dwight D. Eisenhower, Christian A. Herter and William F. Knowland.

Democratic candidates on the ballot or who received write-in votes were Averell Harriman, Estes Kefauver, John F. Kennedy, Frank J. Lausche, John W. McCormack and Adlai E. Stevenson

CALIFORNIA JUNE 5

Republican 1,354,764 Eisenhower slate.

Democratic 1,139,964 Stevenson slate; 680,722 Kefauver slate.

FLORIDA MAY 29

Republican 39,690 Eisenhower slate; 3,457 Knowland slate.

Democratic 230,285 Stevenson slate; 216,549 Kefauver slate.

ILLINOIS APRIL 10

Republican 781,710 Eisenhower; 33,534 Knowland; 8,364 Daly; 91 scattered write-in.

Democratic 717,742 Stevenson; 34,092 Kefauver (write-in); 1,640 scattered write-in.

INDIANA MAY 8

Republican 351,903 Eisenhower; 13,320 Daly.

Democratic 242,842 Kefauver.

MARYLAND MAY 7

Republican 66,904 Eisenhower; 3,131 Unpledged delegates.

Democratic 112,768 Kefauver; 58,366 Unpledged delegates.

MASSACHUSETTS APRIL 24

Republican No candidate names appeared on the ballot and all votes were write-in as follows: 51,951 Eisenhower; 550 Herter; 316 Nixon; 250 Knowland; 1,572 scattered write-in.

Democratic No candidate names appeared on the ballot and all votes were write-in as follows: 26,128 McCormack; 19,024 Stevenson; 4,547 Kefauver; 949 Kennedy; 394 Harriman; 253 Lausche; 3,229 scattered write-in.

1956 PRESIDENTIAL PRIMARIES

MINNESOTA MARCH 20

Republican 198,111 Eisenhower slate; 3,209 Knowland slate; 51 scattered write-in.

Democratic 245,885 Kefauver slate; 186,723 Stevenson slate; 48 scattered write-in.

MONTANA JUNE 5

Republican 32,732 S. C. Arnold (stand-in for Eisenhower); 5,447 Daly.

Democratic 77,228 Kefauver.

NEBRASKA MAY 15

Republican 102,576 Eisenhower; 230 scattered write-in.

Democratic 55,265 Kefauver; 3,556 scattered write-in.

NEW HAMPSHIRE MARCH 13

Republican 56,464 Eisenhower; 600 scattered write-in.

Democratic 21,701 Kefauver; 3,945 scattered write-in.

NEW JERSEY APRIL 17

Republican 357,066 Eisenhower; 23 scattered write-in.

Democratic 117,056 Kefauver; 5,230 scattered write-in.

OHIO MAY 8

Republican 478,453 Bricker delegate slate.

Democratic 276,670 Lausche delegate slate.

OREGON MAY 18

Republican 231,418 Eisenhower.

Democratic No candidate names appeared on the ballot and all votes were write-in as follows: 98,131 Stevenson; 62,987 Kefauver; 1,887 Harriman.

PENNSYLVANIA APRIL 24

Republican 951,932 Eisenhower; 43,508 Knowland; 976 scattered write-in.

Democratic 642,172 Stevenson; 36,552 Kefauver (write-in); 7,482 scattered write-in.

SOUTH DAKOTA JUNE 5

Republican 59,374 Unpledged delegate slate (unofficially pledged to Eisenhower).

Democratic 30,940 Kefauver delegate slate.

1956 PRESIDENTIAL PRIMARIES

WEST VIRGINIA MAY 8

Republican 111,883 Unpledged delegates at-large.

Democratic 112,832 Unpledged delegates at-large.

WISCONSIN APRIL 3

Republican 437,089 Eisenhower slate; 18,743 Chapple slate.

Democratic 330,665 Kefauver.

DISTRICT OF COLUMBIA MAY 1

Republican 18,101 Eisenhower.

Democratic 17,306 Stevenson; 8,837 Kefauver.

ALASKA TERRITORY APRIL 24

Republican 8,291 Eisenhower; 488 Knowland.

Democratic 7,123 Stevenson; 4,536 Kefauver.

1956 REPUBLICAN PREFERENCE PRIMARIES

Date		State	Total Vote	Eisenhower	Bricker	Knowland	Unpledged	Other
March	13	New Hampshire	57,064	56,464	—	—	—	600
	20	Minnesota	201,371	198,111	—	3,209	—	51
April	3	Wisconsin	455,832	437,089	—	—	—	18,743
	10	Illinois	823,699	781,710	—	33,534	—	8,455
	17	New Jersey	357,089	357,066	—	—	—	23
	24	Alaska Territory	8,779	8,291	—	488	—	—
	24	Massachusetts	54,639	51,951 *	—	250 *	—	2,438
	24	Pennsylvania	996,416	951,932	—	43,508	—	976
May	1	District of Columbia	18,101	18,101	—	—	—	—
	7	Maryland	70,035	66,904	—	—	3,131	—
	8	Indiana	365,223	351,903	—	—	—	13,320
	8	Ohio	478,453	—	478,453	—	—	—
	8	West Virginia	111,883	—	—	—	111,883	—
	15	Nebraska	102,806	102,576	—	—	—	230
	18	Oregon	231,418	231,418	—	—	—	—
	29	Florida	43,147	39,690	—	3,457	—	—
June	5	California	1,354,764	1,354,764	—	—	—	—
	5	Montana	38,179	—	—	—	—	38,179
	5	South Dakota	59,374	—	—	—	59,374	—
		Total	5,828,272	5,007,970	478,453	84,446	174,388	83,015
				85.9%	8.2%	1.4%	3.0%	1.4%

An asterisk (*) indicates write-in. In addition to scattered votes, "other" includes 32,732 Arnold (stand-in candidate for Eisenhower in Montana); 27,131 Daly; 18,743 Chapple.

1956 DEMOCRATIC PREFERENCE PRIMARIES

Date		State	Total Vote	Stevenson	Kefauver	Lausche	Unpledged	Other
March	13	New Hampshire	25,646	—	21,701	—	—	3,945
	20	Minnesota	432,656	186,723	245,885	—	—	48
April	3	Wisconsin	330,665	—	330,665	—	—	—
	10	Illinois	753,474	717,742	34,092 *	—	—	1,640
	17	New Jersey	122,286	—	117,056	—	—	5,230
	24	Alaska Territory	11,659	7,123	4,536	—	—	—
	24	Massachusetts	54,524	19,024	4,547	253 *	—	30,700
	24	Pennsylvania	686,206	642,172	36,552 *	—	—	7,482
May	1	District of Columbia	26,143	17,306	8,837	—	—	—
	7	Maryland	171,134	—	112,768	—	58,366	—
	8	Indiana	242,842	—	242,842	—	—	—
	8	Ohio	276,670	—	—	276,670	—	—
	8	West Virginia	112,832	—	—	—	112,832	—
	15	Nebraska	58,821	—	55,265	—	—	3,556
	18	Oregon	163,005	98,131 *	62,987 *	—	—	1,887
	29	Florida	446,834	230,285	216,549	—	—	—
June	5	California	1,820,686	1,139,964	680,722	—	—	—
	5	Montana	77,228	—	77,228	—	—	—
	5	South Dakota	30,940	—	30,940	—	—	—
		Total	5,844,251	3,058,470	2,283,172	276,923	171,198	54,488
				52.3%	39.1%	4.7%	2.9%	0.9%

An asterisk (*) indicates write-in. In addition to scattered votes, "other" includes 26,126 McCormack; 2,281 Harriman; 949 Kennedy.

1952 PRESIDENTIAL PRIMARIES

In 1952 fifteen states and the District of Columbia held Presidential primaries though there was no Republican balloting in Florida, Maryland or the District of Columbia. In some states balloting was for delegate slates pledged to a specific Presidential candidate or unpledged; in others, electors indicated a personal preference as to their party's nominee.

The state-by-state Republican and Democratic tables, included at the end of this section, detail in chronological order the vote for major candidates in each party. As asterisk in the table indicates write-in votes for a candidate not on the ballot.

Republican candidates on the ballot or who received write-in votes were Riley Bender, Dwight D. Eisenhower, Kenny, Douglas MacArthur, Wayne L. Morse, Ritter, Slettendahl, Harold E. Stassen, Stearns, Robert A. Taft, Earl Warren and Thomas H. Werdel.

Democratic candidates on the ballot or who received write-in votes were Charles Broughton, Edmund G. Brown, Sr., Robert J. Bulkley, Compton, William O. Douglas, Dwight D. Eisenhower, James A. Farley, Fox, Averell Harriman, Hubert H. Humphrey, Robert S. Kerr, Estes Kefauver, Douglas MacArthur, Richard B. Russell, Shaw, Adlai E. Stevenson, Robert A. Taft, and Harry S. Truman.

CALIFORNIA JUNE 3

Republican 1,029,495 Warren slate; 521,110 Werdel slate.

Democratic 1,155,839 Kefauver slate; 485,578 Brown slate.

FLORIDA MAY 6

Republican No primary held.

Democratic 367,980 Russell; 285,358 Kefauver; 11,331 Compton; 9,965 Shaw.

ILLINOIS APRIL 8

Republican 935,867 Taft; 155,041 Stassen; 147,518 Eisenhower (write-in); 22,321 Bender; 7,504 MacArthur (write-in); 2,841 Warren; 1,229 Other.

Democratic 526,301 Kefauver; 54,336 Stevenson; 9,024 Truman; 6,655 Eisenhower (write-in); 3,798 Other.

MARYLAND MAY 5

Republican No primary held

Democratic 137,885 Kefauver; 46,361 Unpledged delegates.

MASSACHUSETTS APRIL 29

Republican No candidate names appeared on the ballot and all votes were write-in as follows: 254,898 Eisenhower; 110,188 Taft.

Democratic No candidate names appeared on the ballot and all votes were write-in as follows: 29,287 Kefauver; 16,007 Eisenhower; 7,256 Truman.

MINNESOTA MARCH 18

Republican 129,706 Stassen; 108,692 Eisenhower (write-in); 24,093 Taft (write-in); 5,365 Warren (write-in); 1,369 MacArthur (write-in); 22,712 Slettendahl; 386 Other.

Democratic 102,527 Humphrey; 20,182 Kefauver (write-in); 3,634 Truman (write-in); 1,753 Eisenhower (write-in).

1952 PRESIDENTIAL PRIMARIES

NEBRASKA APRIL 1

Republican 79,357 Taft (write-in); 66,078 Eisenhower (write-in); 53,238 Stassen; 7,478 MacArthur (write-in); 1,872 Warren (write-in); 10,411 Kenny; 767 Other.

Democratic 64,531 Kefauver; 42,467 Kerr.

NEW HAMPSHIRE MARCH 11

Republican 46,661 Eisenhower; 35,838 Taft; 6,574 Stassen; 3,227 MacArthur; 230 Other.

Democratic 19,800 Kefauver; 15,927 Truman; 40 Stevenson (write-in); 228 Other.

NEW JERSEY APRIL 15

Republican 390,591 Eisenhower; 228,916 Taft; 23,559 Stassen.

Democratic 154,964 Kefauver.

OHIO MAY 6

Republican 663,791 Taft at-large delegates slate; 178,739 Stassen at-large delegates slate.

Democratic 305,992 Kefauver at-large delegates slate; 184,880 Bulkley at-large delegates slate.

OREGON MAY 16

Republican 172,486 Eisenhower; 44,034 Warren; 18,603 MacArthur; 18,009 Taft (write-in); 7,105 Morse; 6,610 Stassen; 350 Other.

Democratic 142,440 Kefauver; 29,532 Douglas; 20,353 Stevenson; 4,690 Eisenhower (write-in).

PENNSYLVANIA APRIL 22

Republican 863,785 Eisenhower; 178,629 Taft (write-in); 120,305 Stassen; 6,028 MacArthur (write-in); 3,158 Warren; 1,388 Other.

Democratic No candidate names appeared on the ballot and all votes were write-in as follows: 93,160 Kefauver; 28,660 Eisenhower; 26,504 Truman; 8,311 Taft; 3,745 Harriman; 3,678 Stevenson; 1,691 Russell; 9,026 scattered write-in.

SOUTH DAKOTA JUNE 3

Republican 64,695 Taft; 63,879 Eisenhower.

Democratic 22,812 Kefauver; 11,741 Unpledged.

WEST VIRGINIA MAY 13

Republican 139,812 Taft; 38,251 Stassen.

Democratic 191,471 Unpledged at-large delegates.

WISCONSIN APRIL 1

Republican 315,541 Taft; 262,271 Warren; 169,679 Stassen; 26,208 Ritter; 2,925 Stearns.

Democratic 207,520 Kefauver; 18,322 Fox; 15,683 Broughton.

1952 PRESIDENTIAL PRIMARIES

DISTRICT OF COLUMBIA JUNE 17

Republican No primary held.

Democratic 14,075 Harriman; 3,377 Kefauver; 1,329 scattered write-in.

1952 REPUBLICAN PREFERENCE PRIMARIES

Date		State	Total Vote	Taft	Eisenhower	Warren	Stassen	Werdel	Other
March	11	New Hampshire	92,530	35,838	46,661	—	6,574	—	3,457
	18	Minnesota	292,323	24,093 *	108,692 *	5,365 *	129,706	—	24,467
April	1	Nebraska	219,201	79,357 *	66,078 *	1,872 *	53,238	—	18,656
	1	Wisconsin	776,624	315,541	—	262,271	169,679	—	29,133
	8	Illinois	1,272,321	935,867	147,518 *	2,841	155,041	—	31,054
	15	New Jersey	643,066	228,916	390,591	—	23,559	—	—
	22	Pennsylvania	1,173,293	178,629 *	863,785	3,158	120,305	—	7,416
	29	Massachusetts	365,086	110,188 *	254,898 *	—	—	—	—
May	5	Maryland	No primary held	—	—	—	—	—	—
	6	Florida	No primary held	—	—	—	—	—	—
	6	Ohio	842,530	663,791	—	—	178,739	—	—
	13	West Virginia	178,063	139,812	—	—	38,251	—	—
	16	Oregon	267,197	18,009 *	172,486	44,034	6,610	—	26,058
June	3	California	1,550,605	—	—	1,029,495	—	521,110	—
	3	South Dakota	128,574	64,695	63,879	—	—	—	—
	17	District of Columbia	No primary held	—	—	—	—	—	—
		Total	7,801,413	2,794,736	2,114,588	1,349,036	881,702	521,110	140,241
				35.8%	27.1%	17.3%	11.3%	6.7%	1.8%

An asterisk (*) indicates write-in. In addition to scattered votes, "other" includes 44,209 MacArthur; 26,208 Ritter; 22,712 Slettendahl; 22,321 Bender; 10,411 Kenny; 7,105 Morse; 2,952 Stearns.

1952 DEMOCRATIC PREFERENCE PRIMARIES

Date		State	Total Vote	Kefauver	Brown	Russell	Humphrey	Stevenson	Unpledged	Other
March	11	New Hampshire	35,995	19,800	—	—	—	40 *	—	16,155
	18	Minnesota	128,096	20,182 *	—	—	102,527	—	—	5,387
April	1	Nebraska	106,998	64,531	—	—	—	—	—	42,467
	1	Wisconsin	241,525	207,520	—	—	—	—	—	34,005
	8	Illinois	600,114	526,301	—	—	—	54,336	—	19,477
	15	New Jersey	154,964	154,964	—	—	—	—	—	—
	22	Pennsylvania	174,775	93,160 *	—	1,691 *	—	3,678 *	—	76,246
	29	Massachusetts	52,550	29,287 *	—	—	—	—	—	23,263
May	5	Maryland	184,246	137,885	—	—	—	—	46,361	—
	6	Florida	674,634	285,358	—	367,980	—	—	—	21,296
	6	Ohio	490,872	305,992	—	—	—	—	—	184,880
	13	West Virginia	191,471	—	—	—	—	—	191,471	—
	16	Oregon	197,015	142,440	—	—	—	20,353	—	34,222
June	3	California	1,641,417	1,155,839	485,578	—	—	—	—	—
	3	South Dakota	34,553	22,812	—	—	—	—	11,741	—
	17	District of Columbia	18,781	3,377	—	—	—	—	—	15,404
		Total	4,928,006	3,169,448	485,578	369,671	102,527	78,407	249,573	472,802
				64.3%	9.9%	7.5%	2.1%	1.6%	5.1%	9.6%

An asterisk (*) indicates write-in. In addition to scattered votes, "other" includes 184,880 Bulkley; 62,345 Truman; 57,765 Eisenhower (write-in); 42,467 Kerr; 29,532 Douglas; 18,322 Fox; 15,683 Broughton; 11,331 Compton; 9,965 Shaw; 151 MacArthur (write-in) and 77 Farley.

1948 PRESIDENTIAL PRIMARIES

In 1948 fourteen states held Presidential primaries though there was no Republican balloting in Alabama and Florida. In some states balloting was for delegate slates pledged to a specific Presidential candidate or unpledged; in others, electors indicated a personal preference as to their party's nominee.

The state-by-state Republican and Democratic tables, included at the end of this section, detail in chronological order the vote for major candidates in each party. An asterisk in the table indicates write-in votes for a candidate not on the ballot.

Republican candidates on the ballot or who received write-in votes were Riley A. Bender, Byer, Thomas E. Dewey, Alfred E. Driscoll, Dwight D. Eisenhower, Douglas MacArthur, Edward Martin, Joseph W. Martin, Harold E. Stassen, Robert A. Taft, Harry S. Truman, Arthur Vandenberg, Vander Pyl, Henry A. Wallace, and Earl Warren.

Democratic candidates on the ballot or who received write-in votes were Dwight D. Eisenhower, Scott Lucas, Douglas MacArthur, Harold E. Stassen, Harry S. Truman and Henry A. Wallace.

ALABAMA MAY 4

Republican No primary held.

Democratic 161,629 Unpledged delegates at large.

CALIFORNIA JUNE 1

Republican 769,520 Warren.

Democratic 811,920 Truman.

FLORIDA MAY 4

Republican No primary held.

Democratic 92,169 Unpledged delegate slate.

ILLINOIS APRIL 13

Republican 324,029 Bender; 6,672 MacArthur; 1,572 Stassen; 953 Dewey; 705 Taft; 475 scattered write-in.

Democratic 16,299 Truman; 1,709 Eisenhower (write-in); 427 Lucas; 1.513 Other.

MASSACHUSETTS APRIL 27

Republican 72,191 Unpledged delegates at large.

Democratic 51,207 Unpledged delegates at large (favorable to Truman).

NEBRASKA APRIL 13

Republican 80,979 Stassen; 64,242 Dewey; 21,608 Taft; 9,590 Vandenberg; 6,893 MacArthur; 1,761 Warren; 910 Joseph W. Martin; 24 Other.

Democratic 67,672 Truman; 894 Other.

NEW HAMPSHIRE MARCH 9

Republican 28,854 Unpledged delegates at large.

Democratic 4,409 Unpledged delegates at large (favorable to Truman).

1948 PRESIDENTIAL PRIMARIES

NEW JERSEY APRIL 20

Republican No candidate names appeared on the ballot and all votes were write-in as follows: 3,714 Dewey; 3,123 Stassen; 718 MacArthur; 516 Vandenberg; 495 Taft; 288 Eisenhower; 64 Joseph W. Martin; 44 Driscoll; 14 Warren.

Democratic No candidate names appeared on the ballot and all votes were write-in as follows: 1,100 Truman; 87 Wallace; 2 scattered write-in.

OHIO MAY 4

Republican 426,767 Unpledged delegates at large (most favorable to Taft).

Democratic 271,146 Unpledged delegates at large.

OREGON MAY 21

Republican 117,554 Dewey; 107,946 Stassen; 1,474 Other.

Democratic 112,962 Truman; 7,436 Other.

PENNSYLVANIA APRIL 27

Republican 81,242 Stassen (write-in); 76,988 Dewey (write-in); 45,072 Edward Martin; 18,254 MacArthur (write-in); 15,166 Taft (write-in); 8,818 Vandenberg; 4,907 Truman (write-in); 4,726 Eisenhower (write-in); 1,452 Wallace (write-in); 1,537 scattered write-in.

Democratic 328,891 Truman; 4,502 Eisenhower (write-in); 4,329 Wallace (write-in); 1,301 Stassen (write-in); 1,220 MacArthur (write-in); 2,409 scattered write-in.

SOUTH DAKOTA JUNE 1

Republican 45,463 Unpledged slate headed by Hitchcock.

Democratic 11,193 Truman slate; 8,016 Unpledged slate.

WEST VIRGINIA MAY 11

Republican 110,775 Stassen; 15,675 Byer; 6,735 Vander Pyl.

Democratic 157,102 Unpledged delegates at large.

WISCONSIN APRIL 6

Republican 64,076 Stassen; 55,302 MacArthur; 40,943 Dewey; 2,429 Other.

Democratic 25,415 Truman; 4,906 Other.

1948 REPUBLICAN PREFERENCE PRIMARIES

Date		State	Total Vote	Warren	Stassen	Bender	Dewey	MacArthur	Unpledged	Other
March	9	New Hampshire	28,854	—	—	—	—	—	28,854	—
April	6	Wisconsin	162,750	—	64,076	—	40,943	55,302	—	2,429
	13	Illinois	334,406	—	1,572	324,029	953	6,672	—	1,180
	13	Nebraska	186,007	1,761	80,979	—	64,242	6,893	—	32,132
	20	New Jersey	8,976	14 *	3,123 *	—	3,714 *	718 *	—	1,407
	27	Massachusetts	72,191	—	—	—	—	—	72,191	—
	27	Pennsylvania	258,162	—	81,242 *	—	76,988 *	18,254 *	—	81,678
May	4	Alabama	No primary held	—	—	—	—	—	—	—
	4	Florida	No primary held	—	—	—	—	—	—	—
	4	Ohio	426,767	—	—	—	—	—	426,767	—
	11	West Virginia	133,185	—	110,775	—	—	—	—	22,410
	21	Oregon	226,974	—	107,946	—	117,554	—	—	1,474
June	1	California	769,520	769,520	—	—	—	—	—	—
	1	South Dakota	45,463	—	—	—	—	—	45,463	—
		Total	2,653,255	771,295	449,713	324,029	304,394	87,839	573,275	142,710
				29.1%	16.9%	12.2%	11.5%	3.3%	21.6%	5.4%

An asterisk (*) indicates write-in. In addition to scattered votes, "other" includes 45,072 Edward Martin; 37,974 Taft; 18,924 Vandenberg; 15,675 Byer; 6,735 Vander Pyl; 5,041 Eisenhower; 4,907 Truman (write-in); 1,452 Wallace (write-in); 974 Joseph W. Martin; 44 Driscoll.

1948 DEMOCRATIC PREFERENCE PRIMARIES

Date		State	Total Vote	Truman	Unpledged	Other
March	9	New Hampshire	4,409	—	4,409	—
April	6	Wisconsin	30,321	25,415	—	4,906
	13	Illinois	19,948	16,299	—	3,649
	13	Nebraska	68,566	67,672	—	894
	20	New Jersey	1,189	1,100 *	—	89
	27	Massachusetts	51,207	—	51,207	—
	27	Pennsylvania	342,652	328,891	—	13,761
May	4	Alabama	161,629	—	161,629	—
	4	Florida	92,169	—	92,169	—
	4	Ohio	271,146	—	271,146	—
	11	West Virginia	157,102	—	157,102	—
	21	Oregon	120,398	112,962	—	7,436
June	1	California	811,920	811,920	—	—
	1	South Dakota	19,209	11,193	8,016	—
		Total	2,151,865	1,375,452	745,678	30,735
				63.9%	34.7%	1.4%

An asterisk (*) indicates write-in. In addition to scattered votes, "other" includes 4,416 Wallace (write-in); 6,211 Eisenhower (write-in); 1,301 Stassen (write-in); 1,220 MacArthur (write-in); 427 Lucas.

1944 PRESIDENTIAL PRIMARIES

In 1944 fifteen states held Presidential primaries though there was no Republican balloting in Alabama or Florida and no Democratic balloting in Maryland. In some states balloting was for delegate slates pledged to a specific Presidential candidate or unpledged; in others, electors indicated a personal preference as to their party's nominee.

The state-by-state Republican and Democratic tables, included at the end of this section, detail in chronological order the vote for major candidates in each party. An asterisk in the table indicates write-in votes for a candidate not on the ballot.

Republican candidates on the ballot or who received write-in votes were Riley A. Bender, John W. Bricker, Thomas E. Dewey, Everett M. Dirksen, Douglas MacArthur, Edward Martin, Franklin D. Roosevelt, Harold E. Stassen, Earl Warren and Wendell Willkie.

Democratic candidates on the ballot or who received write-in votes were Claude R. Linger and Franklin D. Roosevelt.

ALABAMA MAY 2

Republican No primary held.

Democratic 116,922 Unpledged delegates at large (favored Roosevelt).

CALIFORNIA MAY 16

Republican 594,439 Warren.

Democratic 770,222 Roosevelt.

FLORIDA MAY 2

Republican No primary held.

Democratic 118,518 Unpledged delegates at large.

ILLINOIS APRIL 11

Republican 550,354 MacArthur; 37,575 Bender; 9,192 Dewey (write-in); 581 Dirksen (write-in); 148 Bricker (write-in); 111 Stassen (write-in); 107 Willkie (write-in).

Democratic 47,561 Roosevelt; 343 Other.

MARYLAND MAY 1

Republican 17,600 Unpledged slate; 4,701 Willkie slate.

Democratic No primary held.

MASSACHUSETTS APRIL 25

Republican 53,511 Unpledged delegates at large.

Democratic 57,299 Unpledged delegates at large.

NEBRASKA APRIL 11

Republican 51,800 Stassen; 18,418 Dewey; 8,249 Willkie; 432 Other.

Democratic 37,405 Roosevelt; 319 Other.

1944 PRESIDENTIAL PRIMARIES

NEW HAMPSHIRE MARCH 14

Republican 16,723 Unpledged delegates at large.

Democratic 6,772 Unpledged delegates at large (all favored Roosevelt).

NEW JERSEY MAY 16

Republican 17,393 Dewey; 618 Willkie; 203 Bricker; 129 MacArthur; 106 Stassen; 1,720 Other.

Democratic 16,884 Roosevelt; 60 Other.

OHIO MAY 9

Republican 360,139 Unpledged delegate-at-large slate headed by John W. Bricker.

Democratic 164,915 Unpledged delegate-at-large slate headed by Joseph T. Ferguson.

OREGON MAY 19

Republican No candidate names appeared on the ballot and all votes were write-in as follows: 50,001 Dewey; 6,061 Stassen; 3,333 Willkie; 3,018 Bricker; 191 MacArthur; 1,340 scattered write-in.

Democratic 79,833 Roosevelt; 1,057 Other.

PENNSYLVANIA APRIL 25

Republican 146,706 Dewey (write-in); 9,032 MacArthur (write-in); 3,650 Willkie (write-in); 2,936 Bricker (write-in); 2,406 Martin; 1,502 Stassen (write-in); 8,815 scattered write-in.

Democratic 322,469 Roosevelt; 961 Other.

SOUTH DAKOTA MAY 2

Republican 33,497 Stassen slate headed by Charles A. Christopherson; 22,135 Dewey slate headed by Joe H. Bottum.

Democratic 7,414 Unpledged slate headed by Fred Hildebrandt (favored Roosevelt); 6,727 Unpledged slate headed by Powell (favored Roosevelt).

WEST VIRGINIA MAY 9

Republican 91,602 Unpledged delegates at large.

Democratic 59,282 Linger.

WISCONSIN APRIL 5

Republican 102,421 MacArthur; 21,036 Dewey; 7,928 Stassen; 6,439 Willkie; 3,307 Other.

Democratic 49,632 Roosevelt; 3,014 Other.

1944 REPUBLICAN PREFERENCE PRIMARIES

Date		State	Total Vote	MacArthur	Warren	Dewey	Stassen	Unpledged	Other
March	14	New Hampshire	16,723	—	—	—	—	16,723	—
April	5	Wisconsin	141,131	102,421	—	21,036	7,928	—	9,746
	11	Illinois	598,068	550,354	—	9,192 *	111 *	—	38,411
	11	Nebraska	78,899	—	—	18,418	51,800	—	8,681
	25	Massachusetts	53,511	—	—	—	—	53,511	—
	25	Pennsylvania	175,047	9,032 *	—	146,706 *	1,502 *	—	17,807
May	1	Maryland	22,301	—	—	—	—	17,600	4,701
	2	Alabama	No primary held	—	—	—	—	—	—
	2	Florida	No primary held	—	—	—	—	—	—
	2	South Dakota	55,632	—	—	22,135	33,497	—	—
	9	Ohio	360,139	—	—	—	—	360,139	—
	9	West Virginia	91,602	—	—	—	—	91,602	—
	16	California	594,439	—	594,439	—	—	—	—
	16	New Jersey	20,169	129 *	—	17,393 *	106 *	—	4
	19	Oregon	63,944	191 *	—	50,001 *	6,061 *	—	7,691
		Total	2,271,605	662,127	594,439	284,881	101,005	539,575	89,578
				29.1%	26.2%	12.5%	4.4%	23.8%	3.9%

An asterisk (*) indicates write-in. In addition to scattered, "other" includes 37,575 Bender; 27,097 Willkie; 10,535 Roosevelt (write-in); 6,305 Bricker; 2,406 Martin; 581 Dirksen.

1944 DEMOCRATIC PREFERENCE PRIMARIES

Date		State	Total Vote	Roosevelt	Unpledged	Other
March	14	New Hampshire	6,772	—	6,772	—
April	5	Wisconsin	52,646	49,632	—	3,014
	11	Illinois	47,904	47,561	—	343
	11	Nebraska	37,724	37,405	—	319
	25	Massachusetts	57,299	—	57,299	—
	25	Pennsylvania	323,430	322,469	—	961
May	1	Maryland	No primary held	—	—	—
	2	Alabama	116,922	—	116,922	—
	2	Florida	118,518	—	118,518	—
	2	South Dakota	14,141	—	14,141	—
	9	Ohio	164,915	—	164,915	—
	9	West Virginia	59,282	—	—	59,282
	16	California	770,222	770,222	—	—
	16	New Jersey	16,944	16,884	—	60
	19	Oregon	80,890	79,833	—	1,057
		Total	1,867,609	1,324,006	478,567	65,036
				70.9%	25.6%	3.5%

In addition to scattered votes, "other" includes 59,282 Linger.

1940 PRESIDENTIAL PRIMARIES

In 1940 fourteen states held Presidential primaries though there was no Republican balloting in Alabama and no Democratic balloting in Maryland. In some states balloting was for delegate slates pledged to a specific Presidential candidate or unpledged; in others, electors indicated a personal preference as to their party's nominee.

The state-by-state Republican and Democratic tables, included at the end of this section, detail in chronological order the vote for major candidates in each party. An asterisk in the table indicates write-in votes for a candidate not on the ballot.

Republican candidates on the ballot or who received write-in votes were John W. Bricker, R. N. Davis, Thomas E. Dewey, Herbert C. Hoover, Arthur H. James, Charles L. McNary, Franklin D. Roosevelt, Robert A. Taft, Arthur Vandenberg and Wendell Willkie.

Democratic candidates on the ballot or who received write-in votes were H. C. Allen, John N. Garner and Franklin D. Roosevelt.

ALABAMA MAY 7

Republican No primary held.

Democratic 196,508 Unpledged delegate slate headed by William B. Bankhead.

CALIFORNIA MAY 7

Republican 538,112 Unpledged delegate slate headed by Jerrold L. Seawell.

Democratic 723,782 Roosevelt slate; 114,594 Garner slate; 90,718 Unpledged delegate slate headed by Willis Allen; 48,337 Unpledged delegate slate headed by Ellis E. Patterson.

ILLINOIS APRIL 9

Republican 977,225 Dewey; 552 scattered write-in.

Democratic 1,176,531 Roosevelt; 190,801 Garner; 35 scattered write-in.

MARYLAND MAY 6

Republican 54,802 Dewey.

Democratic No primary held.

MASSACHUSETTS APRIL 30

Republican 98,975 Unpledged delegates at large.

Democratic 76,919 Unpledged delegates at large (most delegates favored James A. Farley).

NEBRASKA APRIL 9

Republican 102,915 Dewey; 71,798 Vandenberg.

Democratic 111,902 Roosevelt.

NEW HAMPSHIRE MARCH 12

Republican 34,616 Unpledged delegates at large.

Democratic 10,501 Unpledged delegates at large (favorable to Roosevelt).

1940 PRESIDENTIAL PRIMARIES

NEW JERSEY MAY 21

Republican 340,734 Dewey; 20,143 Willkie (write-in); 595 Taft (write-in); 168 Vandenberg (write-in); 1,202 scattered write-in.

Democratic No candidate names appeared on the ballot; Roosevelt received 34,278 write-in votes.

OHIO MAY 14

Republican 510,025 Taft; 2,059 Dewey (write-in); 188 Bricker (write-in); 83 Vandenberg (write-in); 53 Willkie (write-in); 69 scattered write-in.

Democratic 283,952 Unpledged delegate slate headed by Charles Sawyer.

OREGON MAY 17

Republican 133,488 McNary; 5,190 Dewey; 254 Taft (write-in); 237 Willkie (write-in); 36 Vandenberg (write-in).

Democratic 109,913 Roosevelt; 15,584 Garner; 601 Other.

PENNSYLVANIA APRIL 23

Republican 52,661 Dewey; 8,172 James; 5,213 Taft; 2,384 Vandenberg; 1,082 Hoover, 707 Willkie; 8,757 Other.

Democratic 724,657 Roosevelt.

SOUTH DAKOTA MAY 5

Republican 52,566 Unpledged delegate slate.

Democratic 27,636 Unpledged delegate slate.

WEST VIRGINIA MAY 14

Republican 106,123 Davis.

Democratic 102,729 Allen.

WISCONSIN APRIL 2

Republican 70,168 Dewey; 26,182 Vandenberg; 341 Taft.

Democratic 322,991 Roosevelt; 105,662 Garner.

1940 REPUBLICAN PREFERENCE PRIMARIES

Date	State	Total Vote	Dewey	Taft	McNary	Davis	Vandenberg	Unpledged	Other
March 12	New Hampshire	34,616	—	—	—	—	—	34,616	—
April 2	Wisconsin	96,691	70,168	341	—	—	26,182	—	—
9	Illinois	977,777	977,225	—	—	—	—	—	552
9	Nebraska	174,713	102,915	—	—	—	71,798	—	—
23	Pennsylvania	78,976	52,661	5,213	—	—	2,384	—	18,718
30	Massachusetts	98,975	—	—	—	—	—	98,975	—
May 5	South Dakota	52,566	—	—	—	—	—	52,566	—
6	Maryland	54,802	54,802	—	—	—	—	—	—
7	Alabama	No primary held	—	—	—	—	—	—	—
7	California	538,112	—	—	—	—	—	538,112	—
14	Ohio	512,477	2,059*	510,025	—	—	83*	—	310
14	West Virginia	106,123	—	—	—	106,123	—	—	—
17	Oregon	139,205	5,190	254*	133,488	—	36*	—	237
21	New Jersey	362,842	340,734	595*	—	—	168*	—	21,345
	Total	3,227,875	1,605,754	516,428	133,488	106,123	100,651	724,269	41,162
			49.7%	16.0%	4.1%	3.3%	3.1%	22.4%	1.3%

An asterisk (*) indicates write-in. In addition to scattered votes, "other" includes 21,140 Willkie; 9,496 Roosevelt (write-in); 8,172 James; 1,082 Hoover; 188 Bricker.

1940 DEMOCRATIC PREFERENCE PRIMARIES

Date		State	Total Vote	Roosevelt	Garner	Unpledged	Other
March	12	New Hampshire	10,501	—	—	10,501	—
April	2	Wisconsin	428,653	322,991	105,662	—	—
	9	Illinois	1,367,367	1,176,531	190,801	—	35
	9	Nebraska	111,902	111,902	—	—	—
	23	Pennsylvania	724,657	724,657	—	—	—
	30	Massachusetts	76,919	—	—	76,919	—
May	5	South Dakota	27,636	—	—	27,636	—
	6	Maryland	No primary held	—	—	—	—
	7	Alabama	196,508	—	—	196,508	—
	7	California	977,431	723,782	114,594	139,055	—
	14	Ohio	283,952	—	—	283,952	—
	14	West Virginia	102,729	—	—	—	102,729
	17	Oregon	126,098	109,913	15,584	—	601
	21	New Jersey	34,278	34,278*	—	—	—
		Total	4,468,631	3,204,054	426,641	734,571	103,365
				71.7%	9.5%	16.4%	2.3%

An asterisk (*) indicates write-in. In addition to scattered votes, "other" includes 102,729 Allen.

1936 PRESIDENTIAL PRIMARIES

In 1936 fourteen states held Presidential primaries though there was no Republican balloting in Florida or Maryland. In some states balloting was for delegate slates pledged to a specific Presidential candidate or unpledged; in others, electors indicated a personal preference as to their party's nominee.

The state-by-state Republican and Democratic tables, included at the end of this section, detail in chronological order the vote for major candidates in each party. An asterisk in the table indicates write-in votes for a candidate not on the ballot.

Republican candidates on the ballot or who received write-in votes were William E. Borah, Leo J. Chassee, Stephen A. Day, Warren E. Green, Herbert C. Hoover, Frank Knox, Alfred M. Landon and Earl Warren.

Democratic candidates on the ballot or who received write-in votes were Henry Breckinridge, Charles E. Coughlin, Joseph A. Coutremarsh, John N. Garner, John S. McGroarty, Franklin D. Roosevelt, Upton Sinclair and Alfred E. Smith.

CALIFORNIA MAY 5

Republican 350,917 Warren; 260,170 Landon.

Democratic 790,235 Roosevelt; 106,068 Sinclair; 61,391 McGroarty.

FLORIDA JUNE 6

Republican No primary held.

Democratic 242,906 Roosevelt; 27,982 Coutremarsh.

ILLINOIS APRIL 14

Republican 491,575 Knox; 419,220 Borah; 3,775 Landon; 205 scattered write-in.

Democratic 1,416,411 Roosevelt; 411 scattered write-in.

MARYLAND MAY 4

Republican No primary held.

Democratic 100,269 Roosevelt; 18,150 Breckinridge; 1,739 Unpledged delegates.

MASSACHUSETTS APRIL 28

Republican No candidate names appeared on the ballot and all votes were write-in as follows: 76,862 Landon; 7,276 Hoover; 4,259 Borah; 1,987 Knox; 5,032 scattered write-in.

Democratic No candidate names appeared on the ballot and all votes were write-in as follows: 51,924 Roosevelt; 2,928 Smith; 2,854 Coughlin; 2,774 scattered write-in.

NEBRASKA APRIL 14

Republican 70,240 Borah; 23,117 Landon; 973 Other.

Democratic 139,743 Roosevelt.

NEW HAMPSHIRE MARCH 10

Republican 32,992 Unpledged delegates at large (favorable to Knox).

Democratic 15,752 Unpledged delegates at large (favorable to Roosevelt).

1936 PRESIDENTIAL PRIMARIES

NEW JERSEY MAY 19

Republican 347,142 Landon; 91,052 Borah.

Democratic 49,956 Breckinridge; 11,676 Roosevelt (write-in).

OHIO MAY 12

Republican 155,732 Day; 11,015 Landon.

Democratic 514,366 Roosevelt; 32,950 Breckinridge.

OREGON MAY 15

Republican 91,949 Borah; 4,467 Landon; 5,557 Other.

Democratic 88,305 Roosevelt; 208 Other.

PENNSYLVANIA APRIL 28

Republican 459,982 Borah.

Democratic 720,309 Roosevelt; 35,351 Breckinridge.

SOUTH DAKOTA MAY 5

Republican 44,518 Unpledged delegate slate headed by Warren E. Green (favorable to Landon); 44,261 Borah delegate slate.

Democratic 48,262 Roosevelt slate.

WEST VIRGINIA MAY 12

Republican 105,855 Borah; 18,986 Chassee.

Democratic 288,799 Roosevelt; 8,162 Coutremarsh.

WISCONSIN APRIL 7

Republican 187,334 Borah; 3,360 Landon.

Democratic 401,773 Roosevelt; 108 Garner; 46 Smith.

1936 REPUBLICAN PREFERENCE PRIMARIES

Date		State	Total Vote	Borah	Landon	Knox	Warren	Day	Other
March	10	New Hampshire	32,992	—	—	—	—	—	32,992
April	7	Wisconsin	190,694	187,334	3,360	—	—	—	—
	14	Illinois	914,775	419,220	3,775	491,575	—	—	205
	14	Nebraska	94,330	70,240	23,117	—	—	—	973
	28	Massachusetts	95,416	4,259*	76,862*	1,987*	—	—	12,308
	28	Pennsylvania	459,982	459,982	—	—	—	—	—
May	4	Maryland	No primary held	—	—	—	—	—	—
	5	Califronia	611,087	—	260,170	—	350,917	—	—
	5	South Dakota	88,779	44,261	—	—	—	—	44,518
	12	Ohio	166,747	—	11,015	—	—	155,732	—
	12	West Virginia	124,841	105,855	—	—	—	—	18,986
	15	Oregon	101,973	91,949	4,467	—	—	—	5,557
	19	New Jersey	438,194	91,052	347,142	—	—	—	—
June	6	Florida	No primary held	—	—	—	—	—	—
		Total	3,319,810	1,474,152	729,908	493,562	350,917	155,732	115,539
				44.4%	22.0%	14.9%	10.6%	4.7%	3.5%

An asterisk (*) indicates write-in. In addition to scattered votes, "other" includes 77,510 Unpledged; 7,276 Hoover; 18,986 Chassee.

1936 DEMOCRATIC PREFERENCE PRIMARIES

Date		State	Total Vote	Roosevelt	Breckinridge	Sinclair	Other
March	10	New Hampshire	15,752	—	—	—	15,752
April	7	Wisconsin	401,927	401,773	—	—	154
	14	Illinois	1,416,822	1,416,411	—	—	411
	14	Nebraska	139,743	139,743	—	—	—
	28	Massachusetts	60,480	51,924*	—	—	8,556
	28	Pennsylvania	755,660	720,309	35,351	—	—
May	4	Maryland	120,158	100,269	18,150	—	1,739
	5	Califronia	957,694	790,235	—	106,068	61,391
	5	South Dakota	48,262	48,262	—	—	—
	12	Ohio	547,316	514,366	32,950	—	—
	12	West Virginia	296,961	288,799	—	—	8,162
	15	Oregon	88,513	88,305	—	—	208
	19	New Jersey	61,632	11,676*	49,956	—	—
June	6	Florida	270,888	242,906	—	—	27,982
		Total	5,181,808	4,814,978	136,407	106,068	124,355
				92.9%	2.6%	2.0%	2.4%

An asterisk (*) indicates write-in. In addition to scattered votes, "other" includes 61,391 McGroarty; 36,144 Coutremarsh; 17,491 Unpledged; 2,974 Smith; 2,854 Coughlin; 108 Garner.

1932 PRESIDENTIAL PRIMARIES

In 1932 seventeen states held Presidential primaries though there was no Republican voting in Alabama, Georgia or Florida and no Democratic voting in Maryland. In some states balloting was for delegate slates pledged to a specific Presidential candidate or unpledged; in others, electors indicated a personal preference as to their party's nominee.

The state-by-state Republican and Democratic tables, included at the end of this section, detail in chronological order the vote for major candidates in each party. An asterisk in the table indicates write-in votes for a candidate not on the ballot.

Republican candidates on the ballot or who received write-in votes were Jacob S. Coxey, Charles G. Dawes, Joseph I. France, Herbert C. Hoover and George W. Norris.

Democratic candidates on the ballot or who received write-in votes were Newton D. Baker, Leo J. Chassee, John N. Garner, Howard, James H. Lewis, William H. Murray, Franklin D. Roosevelt, Alfred E. Smith and George White.

ALABAMA MAY 3

Republican No primary held.

Democratic 134,781 Unpledged delegates (favorable to Roosevelt).

CALIFORNIA MAY 3

Republican 657,420 Hoover.

Democratic 222,385 Garner; 175,008 Roosevelt; 141,517 Smith.

FLORIDA JUNE 7

Republican No primary held.

Democratic 203,372 Roosevelt; 24,847 Murray; 3,645 Chassee.

GEORGIA MARCH 23

Republican No primary held.

Democratic 51,498 Roosevelt; 5,541 Howard.

ILLINOIS APRIL 13

Republican 345,498 France; 4,368 Hoover; 129 Dawes.

Democratic 590,130 Lewis; 1,084 Roosevelt (write-in); 266 Smith (write-in); 72 scattered write-in.

MARYLAND MAY 2

Republican 27,324 Hoover; 17,008 France; 1,236 Unpledged delegates.

Democratic No primary held.

MASSACHUSETTS APRIL 26

Republican 57,534 Unpledged delegates at large (favorable to Hoover).

Democratic 153,465 Smith slate; 56,454 Roosevelt slate.

1932 PRESIDENTIAL PRIMARIES

NEBRASKA APRIL 12

Republican 40,481 France; 13,934 Hoover.

Democratic 91,393 Roosevelt; 27,359 Garner; 25,214 Murray.

NEW HAMPSHIRE MARCH 8

Republican 22,903 Unpledged delegates at large (favorable to Hoover).

Democratic 15,401 Unpledged delegates at large (favorable to Roosevelt).

NEW JERSEY MAY 17

Republican 141,330 France; 10,116 Hoover.

Democratic 5,234 Smith; 3,219 Roosevelt.

NORTH DAKOTA MARCH 15

Republican 36,000 France; 25,000 Coxey (unofficial estimates).

Democratic 52,000 Roosevelt; 32,000 Murray (unofficial estimates).

OHIO MAY 10

Republican 75,844 Coxey; 44,853 France; 8,154 Hoover.

Democratic 112,512 Murray; 1,999 Roosevelt (write-in); 951 Smith (write-in); 834 White; 289 Baker; 72 Garner (write-in).

OREGON MAY 20

Republican 72,681 France; 32,599 Hoover.

Democratic 48,554 Roosevelt; 11,993 Murray; 1,214 Other.

PENNSYLVANIA APRIL 26

Republican 352,092 France; 20,662 Hoover; 6,126 Other.

Democratic 133,002 Roosevelt; 101,227 Smith; 563 Other.

SOUTH DAKOTA MAY 3

Republican 64,464 Unpledged delegate slate headed by Johnson (favorable to Hoover); 35,133 Unpledged delegate slate headed by Bogue.

Democratic 35,370 Roosevelt.

WEST VIRGINIA MAY 10

Republican 88,005 France.

Democratic 219,671 Roosevelt; 19,826 Murray; 3,727 Chassee.

1932 PRESIDENTIAL PRIMARIES

WISCONSIN APRIL 5

Republican 139,514 Norris; 6,588 Hoover.

Democratic 241,742 Roosevelt; 3,502 Smith (write-in).

1932 REPUBLICAN PREFERENCE PRIMARIES

Date		State	Total Vote	France	Hoover	Coxey	Unpledged	Other
March	8	New Hampshire	22,903	—	—	—	22,903	—
	15	North Dakota	61,000	36,000	—	25,000	—	—
	23	Georgia	No primary held	—	—	—	—	—
April	5	Wisconsin	146,102	—	6,588	—	—	139,514
	12	Nebraska	54,415	40,481	13,934	—	—	—
	13	Illinois	349,995	345,498	4,368	—	—	129
	26	Massachusetts	57,534	—	—	—	57,534	—
	26	Pennsylvania	378,880	352,092	20,662	—	—	6,126
May	2	Maryland	45,568	17,008	27,324	—	1,236	—
	3	Alabama	No primary held	—	—	—	—	—
	3	Califronia	657,420	—	657,420	—	—	—
	3	South Dakota	99,597	—	—	—	99,597	—
	10	Ohio	128,851	44,853	8,154	75,844	—	—
	10	West Virginia	88,005	88,005	—	—	—	—
	17	New Jersey	151,446	141,330	10,116	—	—	—
	20	Oregon	105,280	72,681	32,599	—	—	—
June	7	Florida	No primary held	—	—	—	—	—
		Total	2,346,996	1,137,948	781,165	100,844	181,270	145,769
				48.5%	33.3%	4.3%	7.7%	6.2%

In addition to scattered votes, "other" includes 139,514 Norris; 129 Dawes.

1932 DEMOCRATIC PREFERENCE PRIMARIES

Date		State	Total Vote	Roosevelt	Lewis	Smith	Garner	Murray	Unpledged	Other
March	8	New Hampshire	15,401	—	—	—	—	—	15,401	—
	15	North Dakota	84,000	52,000	—	—	—	32,000	—	—
	23	Georgia	57,039	51,498	—	—	—	—	—	5,541
April	5	Wisconsin	245,244	241,742	—	3,502 *	—	—	—	—
	12	Nebraska	143,966	91,393	—	—	27,359	25,214	—	—
	13	Illinois	591,552	1,084 *	590,130	266 *	—	—	—	72
	26	Massachusetts	209,919	56,454	—	153,465	—	—	—	—
	26	Pennsylvania	234,792	133,002	—	101,227	—	—	—	563
May	2	Maryland	No primary held	—	—	—	—	—	—	—
	3	Alabama	134,781	—	—	—	—	—	134,781	—
	3	Califronia	538,910	175,008	—	141,517	222,385	—	—	—
	3	South Dakota	35,370	35,370	—	—	—	—	—	—
	10	Ohio	116,657	1,999 *	—	951 *	72 *	112,512	—	1,123
	10	West Virginia	243,224	219,671	—	—	—	19,826	—	3,727
	17	New Jersey	8,453	3,219	—	5,234	—	—	—	—
	20	Oregon	61,761	48,554	—	—	—	11,993	—	1,214
June	7	Florida	231,864	203,372	—	—	—	24,847	—	3,645
		Total	2,952,933	1,314,366	590,130	406,162	249,816	226,392	150,182	15,885
				44.5%	20.0%	13.8%	8.5%	7.7%	5.1%	0.5%

An asterisk (*) indicates write-in). In addition to scattered votes, "other" includes 7,372 Chassee; 5,541 Howard; 834 White; 289 Baker.

1928 PRESIDENTIAL PRIMARIES

In 1928 eighteen states held Presidential primaries though there was no Republican voting in Alabama or Florida and No Democratic voting in Maryland. No data is available for the Republican or Democratic primary in Pennsylvania. In some states balloting was for delegate slates pledged to a specific Presidential candidate or unpledged; in others, electors indicated a personal preference as to their party's nominee.

The state-by-state Republican and Democratic tables, included at the end of this section, detail in chronological order the vote for major candidates in each party. An asterisk in the table indicates write-in votes for a candidate not on the ballot.

Republican candidates on the ballot or who received write-in votes were Calvin Coolidge, Charles G. Dawes, Alvan Fuller, Guy D. Goff, Herbert C. Hoover, Frank O. Lowden, George W. Norris, Robert G. Ross, James E. Watson and Frank B. Willis.

Democratic candidates on the ballot or who received write-in votes were Victor Donahey, Gilbert M. Hitchcock, William G. McAdoo, Poling, Atlee Pomerene, James A. Reed, Alfred E. Smith, Thomas Walsh, Evans Woollen and Workman.

ALABAMA MAY 8

Republican No primary held.

Democratic 138,957 Unpledged delegates at large.

CALIFORNIA MAY 1

Republican 567,219 Hoover.

Democratic 134,471 Smith; 60,004 Reed; 46,770 Walsh; 7,263 Poling.

FLORIDA JUNE 5

Republican No primary held.

Democratic 108,167 Unpledged delegates at large.

ILLINOIS APRIL 10

Republican 1,172,278 Lowden; 4,368 Hoover (write-in); 2,420 Coolidge (write-in); 756 Dawes (write-in); 946 scattered write-in.

Democratic 44,212 Smith; 3,786 Reed; 213 McAdoo.

INDIANA MAY 7

Republican 228,795 Watson; 203,279 Hoover.

Democratic 146,934 Woollen.

MARYLAND MAY 7

Republican 27,128 Hoover; 5,426 Unpledged delegates.

Democratic No primary held.

1928 PRESIDENTIAL PRIMARIES

MASSACHUSETTS APRIL 28

Republican 100,279 Hoover (write-in); 7,767 Coolidge (write-in); 1,686 Fuller; 1,040 Lowden (write-in); 6,950 Other.

Democratic 38,081 Smith; 254 Walsh; 478 Other.

NEBRASKA APRIL 10

Republican 96,726 Norris; 6,815 Hoover; 711 Lowden; 679 Dawes; 452 Coolidge.

Democratic 51,019 Hitchcock; 4,755 Smith.

NEW HAMPSHIRE MARCH 13

Republican 25,603 Unpledged delegates at large (favorable to Hoover).

Democratic 9,716 Unpledged delegates at large (favorable to Smith).

NEW JERSEY MAY 15

Republican 382,907 Hoover.

Democratic No candidate names appeared on the ballot; Smith received 28,506 write-in votes.

NORTH DAKOTA MARCH 20

Republican 95,857 Lowden.

Democratic 10,822 Smith.

OHIO APRIL 24

Republican 217,430 Hoover; 84,461 Willis; 8,280 Ross; 4,311 Dawes; 3,676 Lowden; 910 Other.

Democratic 42,365 Smith; 13,957 Pomerene; 7,935 Donahey.

OREGON MAY 18

Republican 101,129 Hoover; 1,322 Lowden.

Democratic 17,444 Smith; 11,272 Walsh; 6,360 Reed; 881 Workman.

PENNSYLVANIA APRIL 24

Republican No data available.

Democratic No data available.

MICHIGAN APRIL 2

Republican 282,809 Hoover; 5,349 Lowden; 1,666 Coolidge.

Democratic 77,276 Smith; 1,034 Walsh; 324 Reed.

1928 PRESIDENTIAL PRIMARIES

SOUTH DAKOTA MAY 22

Republican 34,264 Unpledged delegates at large (favorable to Lowden).

Democratic 6,221 Unpledged delegates at large (favorable to Smith).

WEST VIRGINIA MAY 29

Republican 128,429 Goff; 109,303 Hoover.

Democratic 81,739 Smith; 75,796 Reed; 5,789 Workman.

WISCONSIN APRIL 3

Republican 162,822 Norris; 17,659 Hoover; 3,302 Lowden; 680 Coolidge, 505 Dawes; 1,894 Other.

Democratic 61,097 Reed; 19,781 Smith; 541 Walsh.

1928 REPUBLICAN PREFERENCE PRIMARIES

Date		State	Total Vote	Hoover	Lowden	Norris	Watson	Goff	Unpledged	Other
March	13	New Hampshire	25,603	—	—	—	—	—	25,603	—
	20	North Dakota	95,857	—	95,857	—	—	—	—	—
April	2	Michigan	289,824	282,809	5,349	—	—	—	—	1,666
	3	Wisconsin	186,862	17,659	3,302	162,822	—	—	—	3,079
	10	Illinois	1,180,768	4,368 *	1,172,278	—	—	—	—	4,122
	10	Nebraska	105,383	6,815	711	96,726	—	—	—	1,131
	24	Ohio	319,068	217,430	3,676	—	—	—	—	97,962
	24	Pennsylvania	No data available	—	—	—	—	—	—	—
	28	Massachusetts	117,722	100,279 *	1,040 *	—	—	—	—	16,403
May	1	California	567,219	567,219	—	—	—	—	—	—
	7	Indiana	432,074	203,279	—	—	228,795	—	—	—
	7	Maryland	32,554	27,128	—	—	—	—	5,426	—
	8	Alabama	No primary held	—	—	—	—	—	—	—
	15	New Jersey	382,907	382,907	—	—	—	—	—	—
	18	Oregon	102,451	101,129	1,322	—	—	—	—	—
	22	South Dakota	34,264	—	—	—	—	—	34,264	—
	29	West Virginia	237,732	109,303	—	—	—	128,429	—	—
June	5	Florida	No primary held	—	—	—	—	—	—	—
		Total	4,110,288	2,020,325	1,283,535	259,548	228,795	128,429	65,293	124,363
				49.2%	31.2%	6.3%	5.6%	3.1%	1.6%	3.0%

An asterisk (*) indicates write-in. In addition to scattered votes, "other" includes 84,461 Willis; 12,985 Coolidge; 8,280 Ross; 6,251 Dawes; 1,686 Fuller.

1928 DEMOCRATIC PREFERENCE PRIMARIES

Date		State	Total Vote	Smith	Reed	Woollen	Unpledged	Other
March	13	New Hampshire	9,716	—	—	—	9,716	—
	20	North Dakota	10,822	10,822	—	—	—	—
April	2	Michigan	78,634	77,276	324	—	—	1,034
	3	Wisconsin	81,419	19,781	61,097	—	—	541
	10	Illinois	48,211	44,212	3,786	—	—	213
	10	Nebraska	55,774	4,755	—	—	—	51,019
	24	Ohio	64,257	42,365	—	—	—	21,892
	24	Pennsylvania	No data available	—	—	—	—	—
	28	Massachusetts	38,813	38,081	—	—	—	732
May	1	California	248,508	134,471	60,004	—	—	54,033
	7	Indiana	146,934	—	—	146,934	—	—
	7	Maryland	No primary held	—	—	—	—	—
	8	Alabama	138,957	—	—	—	138,957	—
	15	New Jersey	28,506	28,506 *	—	—	—	—
	18	Oregon	35,957	17,444	6,360	—	—	12,153
	22	South Dakota	6,221	—	—	—	6,221	—
	29	West Virginia	163,324	81,739	75,796	—	—	5,789
June	5	Florida	108,167	—	—	—	108,167	—
		Total	1,264,220	499,452	207,367	146,934	263,061	147,406
				39.5%	16.4%	11.6%	20.8%	11.7%

An asterisk (*) indicates write-in. In addition to scattered votes, "other" includes 59,871 Walsh; 51,019 Hitchcock; 13,957 Pomerene; 7,935 Donahey; 7,263 Poling; 6,670 Workman; 213 McAdoo.

1924 PRESIDENTIAL PRIMARIES

In 1924 seventeen states held Presidential primaries though no Democratic primary was held in Indiana, Maryland or West Virginia. In some states balloting was for delegate slates pledged to a specific Presidential candidate or unpledged; in others, electors indicated a personal preference as to their party's nominee.

The state-by-state Republican and Democratic tables, included at the end of this section, detail in chronological order the vote for major candidates in each party. As asterisk in the table indicates write-in votes for a candidate not on the ballot.

Republican candidates on the ballot or who received write-in votes were Calvin Coolidge, Hiram Johnson and Robert M. LaFollette.

Democratic candidates on the ballot or who received write-in votes were James M. Cox, Woodbridge N. Ferris, Henry Ford, William G. McAdoo, George S. Silzer and Alfred E. Smith.

CALIFORNIA MAY 6

Republican 310,618 Coolidge; 261,566 Johnson.

Democratic 110,235 McAdoo; 18,586 Unpledged delegates.

ILLINOIS APRIL 8

Republican 533,193 Coolidge; 385,590 Johnson; 278 LaFollette (write-in); 21 scattered write-in.

Democratic 180,544 McAdoo; 235 Smith (write-in); 1,724 scattered write-in.

INDIANA MAY 6

Republican 330,045 Coolidge; 62,603 Johnson.

Democratic No primary held.

MARYLAND MAY 5

Republican 19,657 Coolidge; 1,326 Unpledged delegates; 3 Johnson (write-in).

Democratic No primary held.

MASSACHUSETTS APRIL 29

Republican 84,840 Coolidge.

Democratic 30,341 Unpledged delegates at large.

MICHIGAN APRIL 7

Republican 236,191 Coolidge; 103,739 Johnson; 11,312 others.

Democratic 48,567 Ford; 42,028 Ferris; 435 scattered write-in.

MONTANA MAY 28

Republican 19,200 Coolidge.

Democratic 10,058 McAdoo.

1924 PRESIDENTIAL PRIMARIES

NEBRASKA APRIL 8

Republican 79,676 Coolidge; 45,032 Johnson; 627 scattered write-in.

Democratic No candidate names appeared on the ballot and all votes were write-in as follows: 9,342 McAdoo; 700 Smith; 6,268 scattered write-in.

NEW HAMPSHIRE MARCH 11

Republican 17,170 Coolidge.

Democratic 6,687 Unpledged delegates.

NEW JERSEY APRIL 22

Republican 111,739 Coolidge; 13,626 Johnson.

Democratic 35,601 Silzer; 721 Smith (write-in); 69 McAdoo (write-in); 38 scattered write-in.

NORTH DAKOTA MARCH 18

Republican 52,815 Coolidge; 40,252 LaFollette; 32,363 Johnson.

Democratic 11,273 McAdoo.

OHIO APRIL 29

Republican 173,613 Coolidge; 27,578 Johnson.

Democratic 74,183 Cox; 29,267 McAdoo.

OREGON MAY 16

Republican 99,187 Coolidge; 30,042 Johnson.

Democratic 33,664 McAdoo.

PENNSYLVANIA APRIL 22

Republican No candidate names appeared on the ballot and all votes were write-in as follows: 117,262 Coolidge; 4,345 Johnson; 1,224 LaFollette; 10,523 Other.

Democratic No candidate names appeared on the ballot and all votes were write-in as follows: 10,376 McAdoo; 9,029 Smith; 4,341 scattered write-in.

SOUTH DAKOTA MARCH 25

Republican 40,935 Johnson; 39,791 Coolidge.

Democratic 6,983 McAdoo slate; 2,040 Unpledged delegate slate.

WEST VIRGINIA MAY 27

Republican 162,042 Coolidge.

Democratic No primary held.

1924 PRESIDENTIAL PRIMARIES

WISCONSIN APRIL 1

Republican No candidate names appeared on the ballot and all votes were write-in as follows: 40,738 LaFollette; 23,324 Coolidge; 411 Johnson; 688 scattered write-in.

Democratic 54,922 McAdoo; 5,774 Smith; 19,827 scattered write-in.

1924 REPUBLICAN PREFERENCE PRIMARIES

Date		State	Total Vote	Coolidge	Johnson	LaFollette	Other
March	11	New Hampshire	17,170	17,170	—	—	—
	18	North Dakota	125,430	52,815	32,363	40,252	—
	25	South Dakota	80,726	39,791	40,935	—	—
April	1	Wisconsin	65,161	23,324 *	411 *	40,738 *	688
	7	Michigan	351,242	236,191	103,739	—	11,312
	8	Illinois	919,082	533,193	385,590	278 *	21
	8	Nebraska	125,335	79,676	45,032	—	627
	22	New Jersey	125,365	111,739	13,626	—	—
	22	Pennsylvania	133,354	117,262 *	4,345 *	1,224 *	10,523
	29	Massachusetts	84,840	84,840	—	—	—
	29	Ohio	201,191	173,613	27,578	—	—
May	5	Maryland	20,986	19,657	3 *	—	1,326
	6	California	572,184	310,618	261,566	—	—
	6	Indiana	392,648	330,045	62,603	—	—
	16	Oregon	129,229	99,187	30,042	—	—
	27	West Virginia	162,042	162,042	—	—	—
	28	Montana	19,200	19,200	—	—	—
		Total	3,525,185	2,410,363	1,007,833	82,492	24,497
				68.4%	28.6%	2.3%	0.7%

An asterisk (*) indicates write-in. In addition to scattered votes, "other" includes 1,326 for Unpledged delegates.

1924 DEMOCRATIC PREFERENCE PRIMARIES

Date		State	Total Vote	McAdoo	Cox	Ford	Ferris	Silzer	Smith	Unpledged	Other
March	11	New Hampshire	6,687	—	—	—	—	—	—	6,687	—
	18	North Dakota	11,273	11,273	—	—	—	—	—	—	—
	25	South Dakota	9,023	6,983	—	—	—	—	—	2,040	—
April	1	Wisconsin	80,523	54,922	—	—	—	—	5,774	—	19,827
	7	Michigan	91,030	—	—	48,567	42,028	—	—	—	435
	8	Illinois	182,503	180,544	—	—	—	—	235 *	—	1,724
	8	Nebraska	16,310	9,342 *	—	—	—	—	700 *	—	6,268
	22	New Jersey	36,429	69 *	—	—	—	35,601	721 *	—	38
	22	Pennsylvania	23,746	10,376 *	—	—	—	—	9,029 *	—	4,341
	29	Massachusetts	30,341	—	—	—	—	—	—	30,341	—
	29	Ohio	103,450	29,267	74,183	—	—	—	—	—	—
May	5	Maryland	No primary held	—	—	—	—	—	—	—	—
	6	California	128,821	110,235	—	—	—	—	—	18,586	—
	6	Indiana	No primary held	—	—	—	—	—	—	—	—
	16	Oregon	33,664	33,664	—	—	—	—	—	—	—
	27	West Virginia	No primary held	—	—	—	—	—	—	—	—
	28	Montana	10,058	10,058	—	—	—	—	—	—	—
		Total	763,858	456,733	74,183	48,567	42,028	35,601	16,459	57,654	32,633
				59.8%	9.7%	6.4%	5.5%	4.7%	2.2%	7.5%	4.3%

An asterisk (*) indicates write-in.

1920 PRESIDENTIAL PRIMARIES

In 1920 twenty states held Presidential primaries though there was no Democratic voting in Indiana, Maryland, North Carolina or West Virginia. In some states balloting was for delegate slates pledged to a specific Presidential candidate or unpledged; in others, electors indicated a personal preference as to their party's nominee.

The state-by-state Republican and Democratic tables, included at the end of this section, detail in chronological order the vote for major candidates in each party. An asterisk in the table indicates write-in votes for a candidate not on the ballot.

Republican candidates on the ballot or who received write-in votes were Warren G. Harding, Herbert C. Hoover, Hiram Johnson, Frank O. Lowden, John J. Pershing, Robert G. Ross, Edward R. Wood and Leonard Wood.

Democratic candidates on the ballot or who received write-in votes were James M. Cox, Edward I. Edwards, Gilbert M. Hitchcock, William G. McAdoo, A. Mitchell Palmer and Robert G. Ross.

CALIFORNIA MAY 4

Republican 369,853 Johnson; 209,009 Hoover.

Democratic 23,831 Unpledged delegates.

ILLINOIS APRIL 13

Republican 236,802 Lowden; 156,719 Leonard Wood; 64,201 Johnson; 3,401 Hoover (write-in); 2,674 Other.

Democratic No candidate names appeared on the ballot and all votes were write-in as follows: 6,933 Edwards; 3,838 McAdoo; 266 Cox; 10,418 scattered write-in.

INDIANA MAY 4

Republican 85,708 Leonard Wood; 79,840 Johnson; 39,627 Lowden; 20,782 Harding.

Democratic No primary held.

MARYLAND MAY 3

Republican 15,900 Leonard Wood; 8,059 Johnson.

Democratic No primary held.

MASSACHUSETTS APRIL 27

Republican 93,356 Unpledged delegates.

Democratic 21,226 Unpledged delegates.

MICHIGAN APRIL 5

Republican 156,939 Johnson; 112,568 Leonard Wood; 62,418 Lowden; 52,503 Hoover; 24,729 Other.

Democratic 18,665 McAdoo; 16,642 Edwards; 11,187 Palmer; 42,000 Other.

MONTANA APRIL 23

Republican 21,034 Johnson; 6,804 Leonard Wood; 6,503 Lowden; 5,076 Hoover; 723 Harding.

Democratic No candidates names appeared on the ballot and all 2,994 votes were scattered write-in.

1920 PRESIDENTIAL PRIMARIES

NEBRASKA APRIL 20

Republican 63,161 Johnson; 42,385 Leonard Wood; 27,669 Pershing; 1,698 Ross; 1,734 Other.

Democratic 37,452 Gilbert M. Hitchcock; 13,179 Ross; 5,051 Other.

NEW HAMPSHIRE MARCH 9

Republican 8,591 Leonard Wood slate of at-large delegates; 5,604 Unpledged slate of at-large delegates; 2,000 Johnson slate of at-large delegates.

Democratic 7,103 Unpledged at-large delegates (favoring Hoover).

NEW JERSEY APRIL 27

Republican 52,909 Leonard Wood; 51,685 Johnson; 900 Hoover.

Democratic 4,163 Edwards; 180 McAdoo (write-in); 213 scattered write-in.

NEW YORK APRIL 6

Republican 199,149 Unpledged delegates at-large.

Democratic 113,300 Unpledged delegates at-large.

NORTH CAROLINA JUNE 5

Republican 15,375 Johnson; 5,603 Leonard Wood.

Democratic No primary held.

NORTH DAKOTA MARCH 16

Republican 30,573 Johnson; 987 Leonard Wood (write-in); 265 Lowden (write-in).

Democratic No candidate names appeared on the ballot and all votes were write-in as follows: 49 McAdoo; 340 scattered write-in.

OHIO APRIL 27

Republican 123,257 Harding; 108,565 Leonard Wood; 16,783 Johnson (write-in); 10,467 Hoover (write-in).

Democratic 85,838 Cox; 292 McAdoo (write-in); 1,647 scattered write-in.

OREGON MAY 21

Republican 46,163 Johnson; 43,770 Leonard Wood; 15,581 Lowden; 14,557 Hoover.

Democratic 24,951 McAdoo; 361 scattered write-in.

PENNSYLVANIA MAY 18

Republican 257,841 Edward R. Wood; 10,869 Johnson (write-in); 3,878 Leonard Wood (write-in); 2,825 Hoover (write-in); 4,059 scattered write-in.

Democratic 80,356 Palmer; 26,875 McAdoo; 674 Edwards (write-in); 1,132 scattered write-in.

1920 PRESIDENTIAL PRIMARIES

SOUTH DAKOTA MARCH 23

Republican 31,265 Leonard Wood; 26,981 Lowden; 26,301 Johnson; 1,144 Other.

Democratic No candidate names appeared on the ballot and all 6,612 votes were scattered write-in.

VERMONT MAY 18

Republican 3,451 Leonard Wood; 564 Hoover (write-in); 402 Johnson (write-in); 29 Lowden (write-in); 777 scattered write-in.

Democratic No candidate names appeared on the ballot and all votes were write-in as follows: 137 McAdoo; 58 Edwards; 14 Cox; 227 scattered write-in.

WEST VIRGINIA MAY 25

Republican 27,255 Leonard Wood; 33,849 Other (most were cast for West Virginia Senator Howard Sutherland).

Democratic No primary held.

WISCONSIN APRIL 6

Republican No candidate names appeared on the ballot and all votes were write-in as follows: 4,505 Leonard Wood; 3,910 Hoover; 2,413 Johnson; 921 Lowden; 18,350 scattered write-in.

Democratic No candidate names appeared on the ballot and all votes were write-in as follows: 76 Cox; 3,391 scattered write-in.

1920 REPUBLICAN PREFERENCE PRIMARIES

Date		State	Total Vote	Johnson	Leonard Wood	Lowden	Hoover	Edward Wood	Harding	Unpledged	Other
March	9	New Hampshire	16,195	2,000	8,591	—	—	—	—	5,604	—
	16	North Dakota	31,825	30,573	987 *	265 *	—	—	—	—	—
	23	South Dakota	85,691	26,301	31,265	26,981	—	—	—	—	1,144
April	5	Michigan	409,157	156,939	112,568	62,418	52,503	—	—	—	24,729
	6	New York	199,149	—	—	—	—	—	—	199,149	—
	6	Wisconsin	30,099	2,413 *	4,505 *	921 *	3,910 *	—	—	—	18,350
	13	Illinois	463,797	64,201	156,719	236,802	3,401 *	—	—	—	2,674
	20	Nebraska	136,647	63,161	42,385	—	—	—	—	—	31,101
	23	Montana	40,140	21,034	6,804	6,503	5,076	—	723	—	—
	27	Massachusetts	93,356	—	—	—	—	—	—	93,356	—
	27	New Jersey	105,494	51,685	52,909	—	900	—	—	—	—
	27	Ohio	259,072	16,783 *	108,565	—	10,467 *	—	123,257	—	—
May	3	Maryland	23,959	8,059	15,900	—	—	—	—	—	—
	4	California	578,862	369,853	—	—	209,009	—	—	—	—
	4	Indiana	225,957	79,840	85,708	39,627	—	—	20,782	—	—
	18	Pennsylvania	279,472	10,869 *	3,878 *	—	2,825 *	257,841	—	—	4,059
	18	Vermont	5,223	402 *	3,451	29 *	564 *	—	—	—	777
	21	Oregon	120,071	46,163	43,770	15,581	14,557	—	—	—	—
	25	West Virginia	61,104	—	27,255	—	—	—	—	—	33,849
June	5	North Carolina	20,978	15,375	5,603	—	—	—	—	—	—
		Total	3,186,248	965,651	710,863	389,127	303,212	257,841	144,762	298,109	116,683
				30.3%	22.3%	12.2%	9.5%	8.1%	4.5%	9.4%	3.7%

An asterisk (*) indicates write-in. In addition to scattered votes, "other" includes 27,669 Pershing; 1,698 Ross.

1920 DEMOCRATIC PREFERENCE PRIMARIES

Date		State	Total Vote	Palmer	Cox	McAdoo	Hitchcock	Edwards	Unpledged	Other
March	9	New Hampshire	7,103	—	—	—	—	—	7,103	—
	16	North Dakota	389	—	—	49 *	—	—	—	340
	23	South Dakota	6,612	—	—	—	—	—	—	6,612
April	5	Michigan	88,494	11,187	—	18,665	—	16,642	—	42,000
	6	New York	113,300	—	—	—	—	—	113,300	—
	6	Wisconsin	3,467	—	76 *	—	—	—	—	3,391
	13	Illinois	21,455	—	266 *	3,838 *	—	6,933 *	—	10,418
	20	Nebraska	55,682	—	—	—	37,452	—	—	18,230
	23	Montana	2,994	—	—	—	—	—	—	2,994
	27	Massachusetts	21,226	—	—	—	—	—	21,226	—
	27	New Jersey	4,556	—	—	180 *	—	4,163	—	213
	27	Ohio	87,777	—	85,838	292 *	—	—	—	1,647
May	3	Maryland	No primary held	—	—	—	—	—	—	—
	4	California	23,831	—	—	—	—	—	23,831	—
	4	Indiana	No primary held	—	—	—	—	—	—	—
	18	Pennsylvania	109,037	80,356	—	26,875	—	674 *	—	1,132
	18	Vermont	436	—	14 *	137 *	—	58 *	—	227
	21	Oregon	25,312	—	—	24,951	—	—	—	361
	25	West Virginia	No primary held	—	—	—	—	—	—	—
June	5	North Carolina	No primary held	—	—	—	—	—	—	—
		Total	571,671	91,543	86,194	74,987	37,452	28,470	165,460	87,565
				16.0%	15.1%	13.1%	6.6%	5.0%	28.9%	15.3%

An asterisk (*) indicates write-in. In addition to scattered votes, "other" includes 13,179 Ross.